# EDITORIAL BOARD

**ROBERT C. CLARK**
DIRECTING EDITOR
Distinguished Service Professor and Austin Wakeman Scott
Professor of Law and Former Dean of the Law School
Harvard University

**DANIEL A. FARBER**
Sho Sato Professor of Law and Director, Environmental Law Program
University of California at Berkeley

**HEATHER K. GERKEN**
J. Skelly Wright Professor of Law
Yale University

**SAMUEL ISSACHAROFF**
Bonnie and Richard Reiss Professor of Constitutional Law
New York University

**HERMA HILL KAY**
Barbara Nachtrieb Armstrong Professor of Law and
Former Dean of the School of Law
University of California at Berkeley

**HAROLD HONGJU KOH**
Sterling Professor of International Law and
Former Dean of the Law School
Yale University

**SAUL LEVMORE**
William B. Graham Distinguished Service Professor of Law and
Former Dean of the Law School
University of Chicago

**THOMAS W. MERRILL**
Charles Evans Hughes Professor of Law
Columbia University

**ROBERT L. RABIN**
A. Calder Mackay Professor of Law
Stanford University

**CAROL M. ROSE**
Gordon Bradford Tweedy Professor Emeritus of Law and Organization and
Professional Lecturer in Law
Yale University
Lohse Chair in Water and Natural Resources
University of Arizona

UNIVERSITY CASEBOOK SERIES®

# FUNDAMENTALS OF MODERN PROPERTY LAW

**SEVENTH EDITION**

EDWARD H. RABIN
Professor of Law, Emeritus
University of California at Davis

ROBERTA ROSENTHAL KWALL
Raymond P. Niro Professor of Law
DePaul University College of Law

JEFFREY L. KWALL
Kathleen and Bernard Beazley Professor of Law
Loyola University Chicago School of Law

CRAIG ANTHONY (TONY) ARNOLD
Boehl Chair in Property and Land Use
University of Louisville Brandeis School of Law

FOUNDATION PRESS

The publisher is not engaged in rendering legal or other professional advice, and this publication is not a substitute for the advice of an attorney. If you require legal or other expert advice, you should seek the services of a competent attorney or other professional.

*University Casebook Series* is a trademark registered in the U.S. Patent and Trademark Office.

© 1974, 1982, 1992, 2000, 2006 FOUNDATION PRESS
© 2011 By THOMSON REUTERS/FOUNDATION PRESS
© 2017 LEG, Inc. d/b/a West Academic
    444 Cedar Street, Suite 700
    St. Paul, MN 55101
    1-877-888-1330

Printed in the United States of America

**ISBN:** 978-1-60930-326-6

*To Jane*
EHR

*To Shanna, Rachel, Nisa & Andrew*
RRK & JLK

*To Mom and Dad*
CAA

# PREFACE

Property law has something for everyone. For the traditionalist, it oozes with tradition. For the reformer, it cries out for reform. For all of us, it embodies the often unexpressed assumptions on which our society rests.

The seventh edition of *Fundamentals of Modern Property Law* retains the highly successful problem method that has long characterized this landmark casebook: students take on the role of the lawyer in fact-rich hypothetical problems (Assignments) with multiple legal issues. Each Assignment builds students' lawyering skills of analysis and problem solving, as they master the fundamental principles and doctrines of property law. In addition, many Assignments are ideal for instructor-designed simulations of other professional skills, such as client interviewing and counseling, negotiation, oral advocacy, drafting, and objective and persuasive writing.

The seventh edition tracks contemporary trends and changes in property law. It continues the book's emphasis on emerging issues of environmental sustainability with Assignments on Zoning and Land Use Regulation, Water Rights and the Public Trust, and Environmentally Sensitive Lands. These Assignments reflect the "greening" of property law and the relevance of these issues to students. They also facilitate exploration of core property concepts: rule-of-capture, first-in-time priority, appurtenancy, tort damages versus government regulation, negative externalities, cumulative harms, expectations-based rights, the morality of property, the relative roles of legislative bodies and courts in changing property law, and the mix of public and private characteristics of property.

The seventh edition replaces the former Assignment on Mortgages with a new Assignment covering Mortgages and Foreclosures. Core concepts are described more thoroughly and set in the context of contemporary real-estate finance as impacted by the recent subprime mortgage/foreclosure crisis. A new Problem and cases require students to grapple with the tensions between protections for homeowners and borrowers in foreclosure, and efficient foreclosure procedures for lenders and investors.

This seventh edition perpetuates our emphasis on two other dimensions of property law. First, a comprehensive introduction to Intellectual Property law is provided. The novel legal problems raised by advances in technology and the growth of the Internet demand that students receive early exposure to the burgeoning law of intangible property. Therefore, three Assignments dealing with Intellectual Property appear at the end of the casebook. Instructors may choose to assign them at any point in the course.

This edition also continues to emphasize a planning perspective. The first-year law curriculum tends to focus on controversies and may mislead students into thinking that lawyers spend all of their time resolving controversies. In fact, the majority of lawyers concentrate on planning to avoid controversies. Thus, law students should be sensitized to that perspective from the beginning of law school. For example, rather than focusing only on how a dispute between a landlord and a tenant will be resolved, it is important to consider how the underlying lease might have been drafted to avoid the dispute. This planning perspective is explored in many contexts throughout the seventh edition.

Like the prior six editions, this seventh edition is divided into Assignments. An average Assignment should take between one and three hours of class time, depending on the desired depth of treatment. The subjects covered are fundamental to the work of the modern practicing attorney. Subjects of mainly historical interest have been de-emphasized.

Most of the cases and other material have been liberally abridged. Major deletions are indicated by an ellipsis. Many of the original footnotes in the cases have been deleted and those that remain are numbered consecutively, rather than preserving the original numbering from the case. Editorial additions are designated as such.

We owe gratitude to many individuals. Professor R. Kwall expresses her appreciation to her research assistants Molly Dugan Bloem, Rabiya Bilfaqi, Sara Cruse, and Angela Oldham. Professor J. Kwall thanks his research assistants Jennifer Radis and Elizabeth Abramson, and Loyola University Chicago School of Law for research support. Professor Arnold thanks his research assistants Daniel Graham, Dominic Stine, and Christopher Ahlers, and both the University of Louisville Brandeis School of Law and the UCLA School of Law for research support.

Let us now begin our study.

EDWARD H. RABIN
Davis, California

ROBERTA ROSENTHAL KWALL
Chicago, Illinois

JEFFREY L. KWALL
Chicago, Illinois

CRAIG ANTHONY (TONY) ARNOLD
Louisville, Kentucky

January, 2017

# SCOPE OF BOOK: OVERVIEW

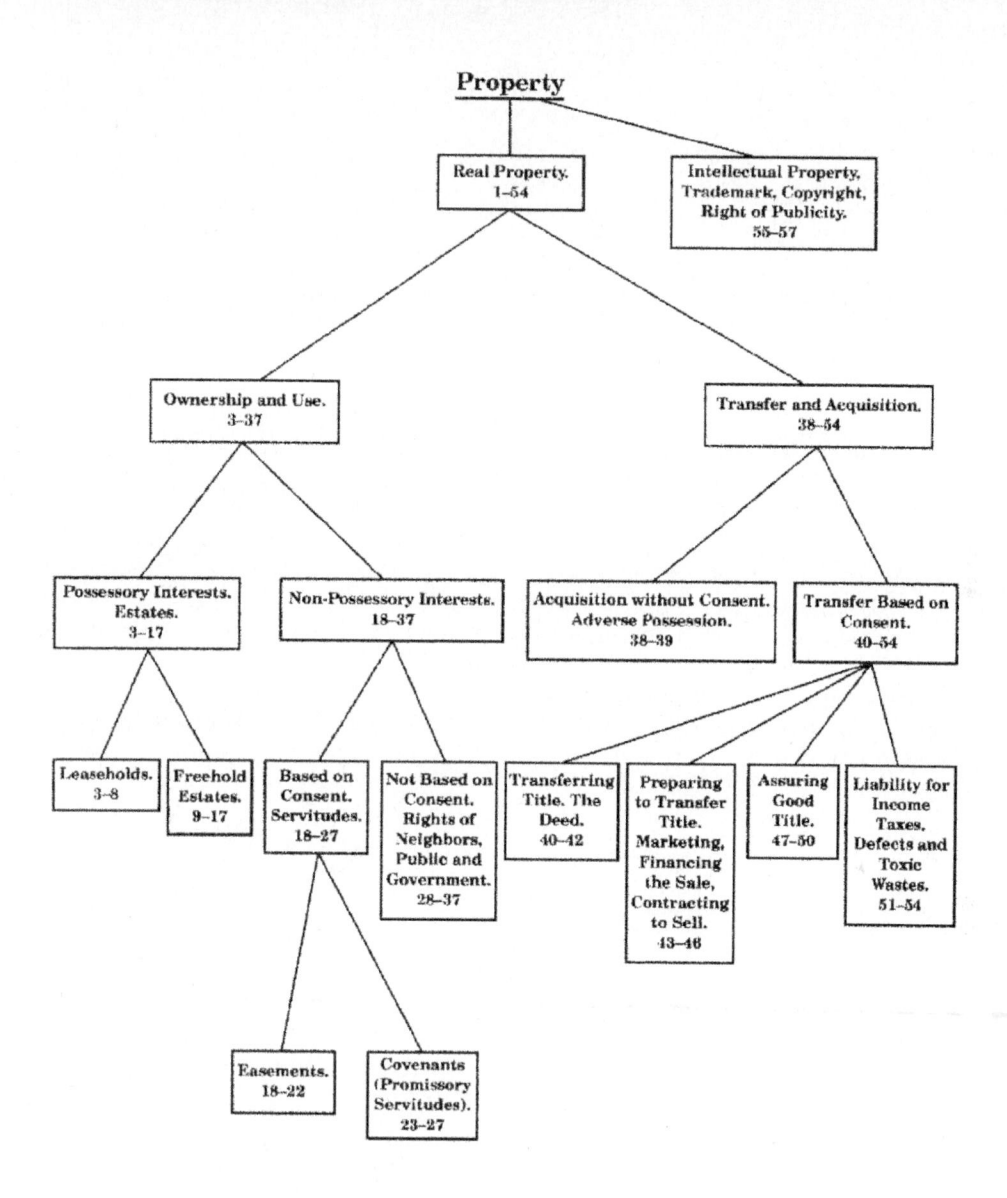

```
                                Property
                                   |
                ┌──────────────────┴──────────────────┐
         Real Property.                    Intellectual Property.
            1-54                           Trademark, Copyright,
                                            Right of Publicity.
                                                 55-57
              │
    ┌─────────┴─────────┐
Ownership and Use.          Transfer and Acquisition.
     3-37                            38-54
```

- Ownership and Use. 3-37
  - Possessory Interests. Estates. 3-17
    - Leaseholds. 3-8
    - Freehold Estates. 9-17
  - Non-Possessory Interests. 18-37
    - Based on Consent. Servitudes. 18-27
      - Easements. 18-22
      - Covenants (Promissory Servitudes). 23-27
    - Not Based on Consent. Rights of Neighbors, Public and Government. 28-37

- Transfer and Acquisition. 38-54
  - Acquisition without Consent. Adverse Possession. 38-39
  - Transfer Based on Consent. 40-54
    - Transferring Title. The Deed. 40-42
    - Preparing to Transfer Title. Marketing, Financing the Sale, Contracting to Sell. 43-46
    - Assuring Good Title. 47-50
    - Liability for Income Taxes, Defects and Toxic Wastes. 51-54

Number references are to Assignments.

vii

# ACKNOWLEDGMENTS

Craig Anthony (Tony) Arnold, "Fair and Healthy Land Use: Environmental Justice and Planning" (American Planning Association, 2007), excerpts reprinted with permission of Craig Anthony (Tony) Arnold.

Eric T. Freyfogle, "The Owning and Taking of Environmentally Sensitive Lands," 43 UCLA Law Review 77 (1995), excerpts reprinted with permission of Eric T. Freyfogle.

J.B. Ruhl, "Making Nuisance Ecological," 58 Case Western Reserve Law Review 753 (2008), excerpts reprinted with permission of J.B. Ruhl.

Mark Squillace, "From 'Navigable Waters' to 'Constitutional Waters': The Future of Federal Wetlands Regulation," 40 University of Michigan Journal of Law Reform 799 (2007), reprinted with permission of Mark Squillace and the University of Michigan Journal of Law Reform.

# SUMMARY OF CONTENTS

PREFACE..................................................................................................V
SCOPE OF BOOK: OVERVIEW................................................................ VII
ACKNOWLEDGMENTS............................................................................. IX
TABLE OF CASES.................................................................................XXIX

## I. INTRODUCTION

**Assignment 1. The Right to Exclude Others from Private Property**..........................................................................................1

**Assignment 2. The Right to Exclude Others from Semi-Private Property: Free Speech Rights Versus Property Rights**..............25

## II. NON-FREEHOLD ESTATES

    A.    Scope of Duties and Rights During the Lease Term............43

**Assignment 3. Landlord-Tenant: The Right of Exclusive Physical Possession**...........................................................................43
a.    Lease or License?..................................................................43
b.    Interference with Actual Physical Possession and Quiet Enjoyment ............................................................................52

**Assignment 4. Implied Landlord's Duties and Implied Conditions to Tenant's Obligations**...................................................63

**Assignment 5. Landlord's Tort Liability for Personal Injuries**........93

    B.    Scope of Duties and Rights upon Termination of Lease ...................................................................................117

**Assignment 6. Landlord's Motives in Selecting or Removing Tenants**.......................................................................................117

**Assignment 7. Assignments and Subleases**.........................................143
a.    Distinctions Between Assignments and Subleases .............143
b.    Tenant's Right to Assign or Sublease ..................................159

**Assignment 8. Tenant's Breach: Landlord's Remedies**.....................169

## III. FREEHOLD ESTATES

    A.    Non-Concurrent Estates ......................................................191

**Assignment 9. Introduction to Present and Future Estates: Terminology**..............................................................................191

**Assignment 10. Introduction to the Common Law Rule Against Perpetuities** ...............................................................................217

Assignment 11. Modern Perpetuities Developments ........................ 239

Assignment 12. Life Estates and Associated Future Interests: The Doctrine of Waste ........................................................................ 261

Assignment 13. Restraints on Alienation ............................................... 281

      B.    Concurrent Estates ..................................................................... 303

Assignment 14. Concurrent Estates: Creation ...................................... 303

Assignment 15. Concurrent Estates: Administration ........................ 323

Assignment 16. Joint Tenancies: Termination (Severance) ............ 337

Assignment 17. Marital Property ............................................................. 349

## IV. NON-POSSESSORY INTERESTS (SERVITUDES)

      A.    Easements ..................................................................................... 373

Assignment 18. Express Easements: Classification and Manner of Creation ........................................................................................... 373

Assignment 19. Express Easements: Interpretation and Extent .... 401

Assignment 20. Express Easements: Succession ................................ 423

Assignment 21. Express Easements: Termination and Extinguishment .............................................................................. 445

Assignment 22. Non-Express Easements ............................................... 475

      B.    Covenants Running with the Land (Promissory Servitudes) ................................................................................. 497

Assignment 23. Creation and Validity .................................................... 497

Assignment 24–25. Enforcement and Running of Covenants .......... 523

Assignment 26. Defenses to the Enforcement of Covenants ........... 567

Assignment 27. Common Interest Communities ................................. 587

      C.    Rights of Neighbors ................................................................... 607

Assignment 28. Nuisance ............................................................................ 607

      D.    Government Authority, Public Uses, and Private Rights ............................................................................................ 637

Assignment 29. Governmental Power to Take Property: The Public Use Requirement ............................................................. 637

**Assignment 30. Zoning and Land Use Regulation** ............................ 665

**Assignment 31–32. Takings: Physical, Regulatory and Exactions** ................................................................................. 697
a. Overview ........................................................................... 697
b. Physical Takings ............................................................... 700
c. Regulatory Takings ........................................................... 714
d. Development Exactions .................................................... 757

**Assignment 33. Exclusion, Discrimination, Equal Protection and Due Process** .................................................................. 773

**Assignment 34. Religious Land Uses** ....................................... 809

**Assignment 35–36. Water Rights and the Public Trust Doctrine** ............................................................................... 835
a. Groundwater Rights ......................................................... 853
b. The Public Trust Doctrine ................................................ 868

**Assignment 37. Environmentally Sensitive Lands** ................... 891

## V. TRANSFER OF INTERESTS IN REAL PROPERTY

### A. Transfer Without Written Instruments ............................ 929

**Assignment 38–39. Adverse Possession** ................................... 929

### B. Transfer with Written Instruments ................................. 979

**Assignment 40. The Requirement of a Written Instrument** ...... 979
a. Informal Documents of Conveyance (Deeds) .................... 979
b. Contracts for the Sale of Real Estate ............................... 990

**Assignment 41. Deed Descriptions** ........................................ 1011

**Assignment 42. Deed Must Be Delivered** .............................. 1033

**Assignment 43. Real Estate Brokers** ..................................... 1053

**Assignment 44. Contracting for Marketable Title** ................. 1073

**Assignment 45. Remedies for Breach of Marketing Contract** ... 1091
a. Damages .......................................................................... 1091
b. Specific Performance ....................................................... 1106

**Assignment 46. Introduction to Mortgages and Foreclosures** ... 1119

**Assignment 47. Covenants of Title** ........................................ 1169

**Assignment 48–49. Recording Statutes** ................................. 1193

**Assignment 50. Title Insurance** ............................................ 1235

Assignment 51. Introduction to Income Tax Issues Affecting
   Home Buyers and Sellers .................................................................1267

Assignment 52. The Time Between the Contract and Deed: The
   Doctrine of Equitable Conversion ..................................................1281

Assignment 53. After the Closing: Implied Warranty of Fitness
   and the Duty to Disclose ..................................................................1305

Assignment 54. Liability for Toxic Wastes ..........................................1335

## VI. INTRODUCTION TO INTELLECTUAL PROPERTY LAW

Assignment 55. Trademark Law ............................................................1359

Assignment 56. Copyright Law ..............................................................1405

Assignment 57. The Right of Publicity .................................................1439

Index ..............................................................................................................1465

# TABLE OF CONTENTS

Preface .................................................................................................................. V
Scope of Book: Overview ................................................................................... VII
Acknowledgments ................................................................................................ IX
Table of Cases ................................................................................................. XXIX

## I. INTRODUCTION

**Assignment 1. The Right to Exclude Others from Private Property** ........................................................................................................ 1
    1. Introduction ................................................................................................ 1
    2. Principal Problem ...................................................................................... 2
    3. Materials for Solution of Principal Problem ........................................... 3
        Jacque v. Steenberg Homes, Inc. ............................................................. 3
        Notes ......................................................................................................... 11
        Intel Corporation v. Hamidi ................................................................... 13
        Notes ......................................................................................................... 22

**Assignment 2. The Right to Exclude Others from Semi-Private Property: Free Speech Rights vs. Property Rights** ..................... 25
    1. Introduction .............................................................................................. 25
    2. Principal Problem .................................................................................... 25
    3. Materials for Solution of Principal Problem ......................................... 26
        State of New Jersey v. Shack ................................................................. 26
        Notes ......................................................................................................... 32
        New Jersey Coalition Against War in the Middle East v. J.M.B. Realty Corporation .............................................................................. 33
        Notes ......................................................................................................... 40

## II. NON-FREEHOLD ESTATES

    A. Scope of Duties and Rights During the Lease Term ............ 43

**Assignment 3. Landlord-Tenant: The Right of Exclusive Physical Possession** ..................................................................................... 43
a. Lease or License? ........................................................................................... 43
    1. Principal Problem .................................................................................... 43
    2. Materials for Solution of Principal Problem ......................................... 44
        Beckett v. City of Paris Dry Goods Co. ................................................ 44
        Wenner and City of Phoenix v. Dayton-Hudson Corporation ........ 47
        Notes ......................................................................................................... 51
b. Interference with Actual Physical Possession and Quiet Enjoyment ...................................................................................................... 52
    1. Interference at the Commencement of the Lease Term ..................... 52
    2. Interference During the Lease Term .................................................... 53
    3. Principal Problem .................................................................................... 54
    4. Materials for Solution of Principal Problem ......................................... 55
        Smith v. McEnany ................................................................................... 55

Echo Consulting Services, Inc. v. North Conway Bank ................56
Notes .............................................................................................61

**Assignment 4. Implied Landlord's Duties and Implied Conditions to Tenant's Obligations ........................................................63**
1. Introduction ..............................................................................63
2. Principal Problem .....................................................................65
3. Materials for Solution of Principal Problem ..........................65
   Marini v. Ireland ......................................................................65
   Knight v. Hallsthammar ..........................................................69
   Wade v. Jobe .............................................................................77
   Davidow v. Inwood North Professional Group .....................81
   Notes .........................................................................................84
4. Types of Common Law Tenancies ..........................................89

**Assignment 5. Landlord's Tort Liability for Personal Injuries ........93**
1. Introduction ..............................................................................93
2. Principal Problem .....................................................................94
3. Materials for Solution of Principal Problem ..........................95
   Asper v. Haffley ........................................................................95
   Merrill v. Jansma .....................................................................98
   Peterson v. Superior Court of Riverside County .................102
   Trentacost v. Brussel .............................................................109
   Notes .......................................................................................114

    B.   Scope of Duties and Rights upon Termination of Lease ......................................................................................117

**Assignment 6. Landlord's Motives in Selecting or Removing Tenants ............................................................................117**
1. Introduction ............................................................................117
2. Principal Problem ...................................................................119
3. Materials for Solution of Principal Problem ........................119
   Kramarsky v. Stahl Management ..........................................119
   Marina Point, Ltd. v. Stephen Wolfson ...............................121
   United States v. Starrett City Associates .............................129
   Notes .......................................................................................137

**Assignment 7. Assignments and Subleases ....................................143**
  a.   Distinctions Between Assignments and Subleases .............143
1. Introduction ............................................................................143
2. Principal Problem ...................................................................144
3. Materials for Solution of Principal Problem ........................145
   A.D. Juilliard & Co. v. American Woolen Co. ....................145
   Abernathy v. Adous ................................................................150
   Notes .......................................................................................156
  b.   Tenant's Right to Assign or Sublease .................................159
1. Introduction ............................................................................159
2. Principal Problem ...................................................................160

3. Materials for Solution of Principal Problem ............................... 160
    Newman v. Hinky Dinky Omaha-Lincoln, Inc. ........................ 160
    United States v. Epstein ............................................................ 164
    Notes ............................................................................................ 166

**Assignment 8. Tenant's Breach: Landlord's Remedies ...................... 169**
1. Introduction ................................................................................. 169
2. Principal Problem ....................................................................... 170
3. Materials for Solution of Principal Problem ............................... 171
    Reid v. Mutual of Omaha Insurance Co. .................................. 171
    Isbey v. Crews ........................................................................... 181
    Ruud v. Larson ........................................................................... 184
    Notes ............................................................................................ 188

### III.   FREEHOLD ESTATES

  A.  **Non-Concurrent Estates** ................................................................. 191

**Assignment 9. Introduction to Present and Future Estates: Terminology ........................................................................................ 191**
1. Introduction ................................................................................. 191
2. The Fee Simple Absolute ............................................................ 195
3. Defeasible Fees ........................................................................... 197
4. Life Estates and Their Associated Future Interests ................... 200
5. Distinguishing Between Equitable and Legal Estates ................ 208
6. Modern Trends Regarding Future Interests ............................... 209
7. Review Outline ............................................................................ 210
8. Problem Set ................................................................................. 212
9. Sample Statute of Descent and Distribution .............................. 213

**Assignment 10. Introduction to the Common Law Rule Against Perpetuities ....................................................................................... 217**
1. Introduction ................................................................................. 217
2. Principal Problem ....................................................................... 218
3. Materials for Solution of Principal Problem ............................... 219
4. Problem Sets ............................................................................... 232

**Assignment 11. Modern Perpetuities Developments ......................... 239**
1. Introduction ................................................................................. 239
2. Principal Problem ....................................................................... 239
3. Materials for Solution of Principal Problem ............................... 239
    Abrams v. Templeton ................................................................ 243
    Notes ............................................................................................ 247
    Symphony Space, Inc. v. Pergola Properties, Inc. .................... 247
    Notes ............................................................................................ 258

**Assignment 12. Life Estates and Associated Future Interests: The Doctrine of Waste ..................................................................... 261**
1. Introduction ................................................................................. 261
2. Principal Problem ....................................................................... 262

## TABLE OF CONTENTS

  3. Materials for Solution of Principal Problem ........................263
   Melms v. Pabst Brewing Co. ............................................263
   Anne Barnett Zauner v. Leonie Sullivan Brewer ...............267
   McIntyre v. Scarbrough.....................................................275
   Notes .................................................................................278

### Assignment 13. Restraints on Alienation ...........................................281
  1. Introduction......................................................................281
  2. Principal Problem ............................................................282
  3. Materials for Solution of Principal Problem ........................283
   RTS Landfill, Inc. v. Appalachian Waste Systems, LLC.............283
   Ferrero Construction Company v. Dennis Rourke
     Corporation................................................................286
   Urquhart v. Teller ............................................................295
   Notes .................................................................................299

  **B.** **Concurrent Estates** ..................................................................303

### Assignment 14. Concurrent Estates: Creation ....................................303
  1. Introduction......................................................................303
  2. Principal Problem ............................................................308
  3. Materials for Solution of Principal Problem ........................308
   Adamson v. Adamson........................................................308
   Margarite v. Ewald ............................................................312
   Kurpiel v. Kurpiel ..............................................................316
   S.S. Weems v. Frost National Bank of San Antonio...............317
   Notes .................................................................................318

### Assignment 15. Concurrent Estates: Administration........................323
  1. Introduction......................................................................323
  2. Principal Problem ............................................................323
  3. Materials for Solution of Principal Problem ........................324
   Gillmor v. Gillmor ............................................................324
   Barrow v. Barrow .............................................................327
   Notes .................................................................................333

### Assignment 16. Joint Tenancies: Termination (Severance) ............337
  1. Introduction......................................................................337
  2. Principal Problem ............................................................337
  3. Materials for Solution of Principal Problem ........................337
   Harms v. Sprague .............................................................337
   Hutchinson National Bank v. Brown..................................342
   Minonk State Bank v. Grassman........................................344
   Notes .................................................................................347

### Assignment 17. Marital Property .........................................................349
  1. Introduction......................................................................349
  2. Community Property Jurisdictions...................................350
  3. Common Law Property Jurisdictions ...............................351
  4. Principal Problem ............................................................354

5.　Materials for Solution of Principal Problem on Human
　　　　Capital ............................................................................................355
　　　　O'Brien v. O'Brien ..........................................................................355
　　　　Simmons v. Simmons ......................................................................360
　　　　Notes ................................................................................................370

## IV.　NON-POSSESSORY INTERESTS (SERVITUDES)

A.　Easements ....................................................................................373

### Assignment 18. Express Easements: Classification and Manner of Creation ............................................................................373
　　1.　Introduction ....................................................................................373
　　2.　Principal Problem ..........................................................................380
　　3.　Materials for Solution of Principal Problem ...................................381
　　　　Northwest Realty Co. v. Jacobs ......................................................381
　　　　Greaves v. McGee ..........................................................................386
　　　　Hurst v. Baker ................................................................................390
　　　　Notes ................................................................................................395

### Assignment 19. Express Easements: Interpretation and Extent ....401
　　1.　Introduction ....................................................................................401
　　2.　Principal Problem ..........................................................................408
　　3.　Materials for Solution of Principal Problem ...................................409
　　　　Brown v. Voss ..................................................................................409
　　　　Note ..................................................................................................412
　　　　M.P.M. Builders, LLC v. Dwyer ......................................................413
　　　　Notes ................................................................................................417
　　　　Hayes v. Aquia Marina, Inc. ...........................................................418
　　　　Notes ................................................................................................421

### Assignment 20. Express Easements: Succession ............................423
　　1.　Introduction ....................................................................................423
　　2.　Succession of Appurtenant Easements ..........................................424
　　3.　Succession of Easements In Gross ................................................427
　　4.　Principal Problem ..........................................................................429
　　5.　Materials for Solution of Principal Problem ...................................430
　　　　Nelson v. Johnson ..........................................................................430
　　　　Burcky v. Knowles ..........................................................................432
　　　　Crane v. Crane ................................................................................436
　　　　O'Donovan v. McIntosh v. Huggins ................................................437
　　　　Notes ................................................................................................441

### Assignment 21. Express Easements: Termination and Extinguishment ......................................................................445
　　1.　Introduction ....................................................................................445
　　2.　Principal Problem ..........................................................................453
　　3.　Materials for Solution of Principal Problem ...................................454
　　　　Wetmore v. The Ladies of Loretto, Wheaton ..................................454
　　　　Notes ................................................................................................459

　　　　Pavlik v. Consolidation Coal Co. ....................................................459
　　　　Notes ...........................................................................................463
　　　　Mueller v. Hoblyn..........................................................................463
　　　　Notes ...........................................................................................473

**Assignment 22. Non-Express Easements ................................................475**
　　1.　Introduction..................................................................................475
　　2.　Principal Problem ........................................................................483
　　3.　Materials for Solution of Principal Problem ..............................484
　　　　Hillside Development Company v. Fields ...................................484
　　　　Ward v. Slavecek..........................................................................489
　　　　Epstein Family Partnership Levitz Furniture Corp. v. Kmart
　　　　　　Corp. .....................................................................................491
　　　　Notes ...........................................................................................494

　　B.　**Covenants Running with the Land (Promissory**
　　　　**Servitudes)** ..............................................................................497

**Assignment 23. Creation and Validity .....................................................497**
　　1.　Introduction..................................................................................497
　　2.　Terminology.................................................................................497
　　3.　Principal Problem ........................................................................500
　　4.　Materials for Solution of Principal Problem ..............................501
　　　　Natore A. Nahrstedt v. Lakeside Village Condominium
　　　　　　Association ...........................................................................501
　　　　Hill v. Community of Damien .....................................................509
　　　　Franklin v. Spadafora ..................................................................516
　　　　Notes ...........................................................................................520

**Assignment 24-25. Enforcement and Running of Covenants..........523**
　　1.　Introduction..................................................................................523
　　2.　Principal Problem ........................................................................535
　　3.　Materials for Solution of Principal Problem ..............................536
　　　　Runyon v. Warren and Claire Paley Midgett Realty ...................536
　　　　Davidson Bros., Inc. v. D. Katz & Sons, Inc. ..............................548
　　　　Eagle Enterprises, Inc. v. Gross...................................................561
　　　　Notes ...........................................................................................564

**Assignment 26. Defenses to the Enforcement of Covenants ...........567**
　　1.　Introduction..................................................................................567
　　2.　Principal Problem ........................................................................568
　　3.　Materials for Solution of Principal Problem ..............................568
　　　　Chevy Chase Village v. Jaggers ...................................................568
　　　　City of Bowie, Maryland v. MIE Properties, Inc. .......................575
　　　　Orange and Rockland Utilities, Inc. v. Philwold Estates, Inc.....579
　　　　Notes ...........................................................................................583

**Assignment 27. Common Interest Communities ...............................587**
　　1.　Introduction..................................................................................587
　　2.　Principal Problem ........................................................................588

3. Materials for Solution of Principal Problem...............................589
   Westmoreland Association, Inc. v. West Cutter Estates, Ltd. ....589
   Evergreen Highlands Ass'n v. West...........................................593
   Majestic View Condo. Ass'n, Inc. v. Bolotin ...............................600
   Raintree of Albemarle Homeowners Ass'n, Inc. v. Jones ...........603
   Notes ..............................................................................................605

C. Rights of Neighbors .................................................................607

Assignment 28. Nuisance.................................................................607
1. Introduction.................................................................................607
2. Principal Problem........................................................................609
3. Materials for Solution of Principal Problem...............................610
   Excerpts from Rabin, Nuisance Law: Rethinking
      Fundamental Assumptions......................................................610
   Boomer v. Atlantic Cement Co. ....................................................613
   Spur Industries, Inc. v. Del E. Webb Development Co................620
   Prah v. Maretti...............................................................................629
   Notes ..............................................................................................634

D. Government Authority, Public Uses, and Private
   Rights.........................................................................................637

Assignment 29. Governmental Power to Take Property: The
   Public Use Requirement.............................................................637
1. Introduction.................................................................................637
2. Principal Problem........................................................................637
3. Materials for Solution of Principal Problem...............................638
   Hawaii Housing Authority v. Midkiff...........................................638
   County of Wayne v. Hathcock ......................................................642
   Kelo v. City of New London .........................................................648
   Notes ..............................................................................................658

Assignment 30. Zoning and Land Use Regulation ............................665
1. Introduction.................................................................................665
2. Types of Land Use Regulation ....................................................668
3. Principal Problem........................................................................672
4. Materials for Solution of Principal Problem...............................674
   Village of Euclid v. Ambler Realty Co. ........................................674
   Notes ..............................................................................................678
   Western Land Equities, Inc. v. City of Logan .............................680
   Maryland Reclamation Associates, Inc. v. Harford County ........685
   Notes ..............................................................................................690
   Van Sicklen v. Browne..................................................................691
   Notes ..............................................................................................693

Assignment 31–32. Takings: Physical, Regulatory and
   Exactions ....................................................................................697
a. Overview......................................................................................697

b.  Physical Takings ................................................................. 700
    1.  Principal Problem ......................................................... 700
    2.  Materials for Solution of Principal Problem ................. 700
        Loretto v. Teleprompter Manhattan CATV Corp. ....... 700
        Yee v. City of Escondido. ............................................. 707
        Notes ............................................................................. 713
c.  Regulatory Takings............................................................. 714
    1.  Introduction................................................................... 714
    2.  Principal Problem ......................................................... 714
    3.  Materials for Solution of Principal Problem ................. 715
        Pennsylvania Coal Co. v. Mahon .................................. 715
        Penn Central Transportation Co. v. City of New York ....... 719
        Lucas v. South Carolina Coastal Council ..................... 730
        Palazzolo v. Rhode Island ............................................. 738
        Tahoe-Sierra Preservation Council, Inc. v. Tahoe Regional
            Planning Agency...................................................... 744
        Notes ............................................................................. 753
d.  Development Exactions ..................................................... 757
    1.  Introduction................................................................... 757
    2.  Principal Problem ......................................................... 757
    3.  Materials for Solution of Principal Problem ................. 758
        Florence Dolan v. City of Tigard .................................. 758
        Notes ............................................................................. 769

## Assignment 33. Exclusion, Discrimination, Equal Protection and Due Process ................................................................. 773
1.  Introduction........................................................................... 773
2.  Principal Problem .................................................................. 777
3.  Materials for Solution of Principal Problem ......................... 778
    Village of Arlington Heights v. Metropolitan Housing
        Development Corp........................................................ 778
    City of Cleburne, Texas v. Cleburne Living Center, Inc. ...... 786
    Bay Area Addiction Research and Treatment, Inc. v. City of
        Antioch. ........................................................................ 791
    Notes ..................................................................................... 798

## Assignment 34. Religious Land Uses ....................................... 809
1.  Introduction........................................................................... 809
2.  Principal Problem .................................................................. 817
3.  Materials for Solution of Principal Problem ......................... 819
    Messiah Baptist Church v. County of Jefferson, State of
        Colorado ....................................................................... 819
    Civil Liberties for Urban Believers v. City of Chicago ......... 825
    Notes ..................................................................................... 832

## Assignment 35–36. Water Rights and the Public Trust Doctrine ................................................................................ 835
1.  Introduction........................................................................... 835
2.  Principal Problem .................................................................. 850

| | | |
|---|---|---|
| 3. | Materials for Solution of Principal Problem | 853 |
| | a. Groundwater Rights | 853 |
| | State v. Michels Pipeline Construction, Inc. | 853 |
| | Sipriano v. Great Spring Waters of America, Inc. | 859 |
| | Notes | 865 |
| | b. The Public Trust Doctrine | 868 |
| | National Audubon Society v. Superior Court | 868 |
| | In the Matter of the Water Use Permit Applications (the Waiahole Ditch case) | 876 |
| | Notes | 888 |

**Assignment 37. Environmentally Sensitive Lands** ............................ 891
1. Introduction ............................................................................................. 891
2. Principal Problem .................................................................................. 900
3. Materials for Solution of Principal Problem .................................... 900
   Just v. Marinette County ........................................................................ 900
   Palazzolo v. State of Rhode Island ....................................................... 908
   Notes ........................................................................................................... 925

## V. TRANSFER OF INTERESTS IN REAL PROPERTY

A. Transfer Without Written Instruments ............................................. 929

**Assignment 38–39. Adverse Possession** ................................................. 929
1. Introduction ............................................................................................. 929
2. A Sample Statute ..................................................................................... 932
   Notes ........................................................................................................... 934
3. Principal Problem A: Possession That is Hostile, Adverse or Under a Claim of Right .......................................................................... 936
4. Materials for Solution of Principal Problem A ................................. 937
   Tioga Coal Co. v. Supermarkets General Corp. .................................. 937
   Halpern v. The Lacy Investment Corp. ................................................ 941
   ITT Rayonier, Inc. v. Bell ........................................................................ 943
   Notes ........................................................................................................... 946
5. Principal Problem B: Possession That Is Exclusive, Open, Notorious, Actual and Continuous ...................................................... 948
6. Materials for Solution of Principal Problem B ................................. 950
   ITT Rayonier, Inc. v. Bell ........................................................................ 950
   Marengo Cave Co. v. Ross ....................................................................... 951
   Notes ........................................................................................................... 958
   Howard v. Kunto ...................................................................................... 960
   Ray v. Beacon Hudson Mountain Corp. ............................................... 964
   Notes ........................................................................................................... 968
7. Acquisition of Non-Possessory Interests in Land Through Adverse Use ............................................................................................. 973
8. Agreed Boundaries ................................................................................. 976

B. Transfer with Written Instruments .......................................... 979

**Assignment 40. The Requirement of a Written Instrument** ........... 979
  a.  Informal Documents of Conveyance (Deeds)................................ 979
      1.  Introduction.............................................................................. 979
      2.  Principal Problem .................................................................... 979
      3.  Materials for Solution of Principal Problem ............................ 980
          In re O'Neil's Will............................................................... 981
          Bowlin v. Keifer................................................................. 982
          Harris v. Strawbridge ........................................................ 984
          Notes .................................................................................. 988
  b.  Contracts for the Sale of Real Estate ....................................... 990
      1.  Introduction.............................................................................. 990
      2.  Principal Problem .................................................................... 991
      3.  Materials for Solution of Principal Problem ............................ 992
          Walker v. Ireton ................................................................. 992
          Nessralla v. Peck ............................................................... 999
          Gulden v. Sloan ............................................................... 1001
          Notes ................................................................................ 1008

**Assignment 41. Deed Descriptions**............................................... 1011
      1.  Introduction............................................................................ 1011
          Producers Lumber & Supply Co. v. Olney Bldg. Co. .......... 1011
          Note.................................................................................. 1015
      2.  Methods of Describing Land.................................................. 1015
          Asotin County Port District v. Clarkston Community Corp. ..... 1016
          Powell v. Schultz ............................................................. 1019
          Note.................................................................................. 1020
          Grand Lodge of Georgia v. City of Thomasville ............... 1020
          Note.................................................................................. 1021
          Ramsey v. Arizona Title Ins. & Trust Co. ......................... 1028
          Note.................................................................................. 1031
      3.  Review Problem ..................................................................... 1031

**Assignment 42. Deed Must Be Delivered** ..................................... 1033
      1.  Introduction............................................................................ 1033
      2.  Principal Problem A: Delivery Without Escrow ..................... 1034
      3.  Materials for Solution of Principal Problem A ...................... 1035
          Williams v. Cole .............................................................. 1035
          Kresser v. Peterson .......................................................... 1039
          Lenhart v. Desmond......................................................... 1040
          Notes ................................................................................ 1043
      4.  Principal Problem B: "Death Escrows" ................................. 1044
      5.  Materials for Solution of Principal Problem B ...................... 1044
          Ignacio Vasquez v. Brigido Vasquez ............................... 1044
          Rosengrant v. Rosengrant ................................................ 1048
          Notes ................................................................................ 1051

**Assignment 43. Real Estate Brokers**............................................. 1053
      1.  Introduction............................................................................ 1053

    2. Principal Problem ...................................................................... 1057
    3. Materials for Solution of Principal Problem .............................. 1058
        Ellsworth Dobbs, Inc. v. Johnson v. Iarussi .............................. 1058
        Easton v. Strassburger ................................................................ 1066
        Notes ............................................................................................ 1071

### Assignment 44. Contracting for Marketable Title .......................... 1073
    1. Introduction .................................................................................. 1073
    2. Principal Problem ...................................................................... 1075
    3. Materials for Solution of Principal Problem .............................. 1076
        Laba v. Carey .............................................................................. 1076
        Madhavan v. Sucher .................................................................. 1081
        Voorheesville Rod and Gun Club v. E. W. Tompkins
            Company ................................................................................ 1083
        Nelson v. Anderson .................................................................... 1086
        Notes ............................................................................................ 1089

### Assignment 45. Remedies for Breach of Marketing Contract ....... 1091
a. Damages ............................................................................................ 1091
    1. Introduction .................................................................................. 1091
    2. Principal Problem: Liquidated Damages for Buyer's
       Default .......................................................................................... 1092
    3. Materials for the Solution of Principal Problem ........................ 1093
        Covington v. Robinson .............................................................. 1093
        Colonial at Lynnfield, Inc. v. Sloan ............................................ 1096
        Strouse v. Starbuck .................................................................... 1101
        Notes ............................................................................................ 1105
b. Specific Performance ........................................................................ 1106
    1. Introduction .................................................................................. 1106
    2. Principal Problem: Seller's Default ............................................ 1106
    3. Materials for Solution of Principal Problem .............................. 1107
        Giannini v. First National Bank of Des Plaines ........................ 1107
        Hilton v. Nelsen .......................................................................... 1112
        Notes ............................................................................................ 1117

### Assignment 46. Introduction to Mortgages and Foreclosures ..... 1119
    1. Introduction .................................................................................. 1119
    2. Principal Problem ...................................................................... 1136
    3. Materials for Solution of Principal Problem .............................. 1138
        Debrunner v. Deutsche Bank National Trust Company .......... 1138
        JPMorgan Chase Bank, N.A. v. Erlandson ................................ 1143
        Eaton v. Federal National Mortgage Association .................... 1150
        Good v. Wells Fargo Bank, N.A. ................................................ 1160
        Notes ............................................................................................ 1167

### Assignment 47. Covenants of Title ................................................... 1169
    1. Introduction .................................................................................. 1169
        Questions .................................................................................... 1175
    2. Principal Problem ...................................................................... 1175

3.　Materials for Solution of Principal Problem .............................. 1176
　　　　　Holmes Development, LLC v. Cook ...................................... 1176
　　　　　St. Paul Title Insurance Corp. v. Owen ..................................... 1182
　　　　　Notes .......................................................................................... 1186
　　　　　Babb v. Weemer ........................................................................ 1187
　　　　　Notes .......................................................................................... 1191

**Assignment 48–49. Recording Statutes** ................................................. **1193**
　　　1.　Principal Problem ....................................................................... 1193
　　　2.　The Basic Rules ........................................................................... 1193
　　　3.　Principal Cases: Problems of Notice ....................................... 1208
　　　　　Jefferson County v. Mosley ..................................................... 1208
　　　　　Notes .......................................................................................... 1214
　　　　　Martinique Realty Corp. v. Hull ............................................... 1216
　　　　　Gates Rubber Co. v. Ulman ..................................................... 1221
　　　　　Notes .......................................................................................... 1228
　　　　　Sabo v. Horvath ........................................................................ 1228
　　　　　Notes .......................................................................................... 1232
　　　4.　Review Question on Recording Problems ............................... 1234

**Assignment 50. Title Insurance** ............................................................. **1235**
　　　1.　Introduction ................................................................................. 1235
　　　2.　Principal Problem ....................................................................... 1238
　　　3.　Materials for Solution of Principal Problem .............................. 1239
　　　　　Lick Mill Creek Apartments v. Chicago Title Ins. Co. ............. 1256
　　　　　Notes .......................................................................................... 1263
　　　　　Holmes v. Alabama Title Company ......................................... 1263
　　　　　Note ............................................................................................ 1266

**Assignment 51. Introduction to Income Tax Issues Affecting
Home Buyers and Sellers** ......................................................................... **1267**
　　　1.　Introduction ................................................................................. 1267
　　　2.　Principal Problem ....................................................................... 1272
　　　3.　Materials for Solution of Principal Problem .............................. 1273
　　　　　Excerpts from IRS Publication 530—Tax Information for
　　　　　　　Homeowners ....................................................................... 1273
　　　　　Excerpts from IRS Publication 936—Home Mortgage Interest
　　　　　　　Deduction ............................................................................ 1274
　　　　　Excerpts from IRS Publication 523—Selling Your Home ......... 1276
　　　　　Notes .......................................................................................... 1278

**Assignment 52. The Time Between the Contract and Deed: The
Doctrine of Equitable Conversion** ......................................................... **1281**
　　　1.　Introduction ................................................................................. 1281
　　　2.　Principal Problem ....................................................................... 1283
　　　3.　Materials for Solution of Principal Problem .............................. 1284
　　　　　DiDonato v. Reliance Standard Life Ins. Co. ........................... 1284
　　　　　Skelly Oil Co. v. Ashmore ......................................................... 1286
　　　　　Lucenti v. Cayuga Apartments, Inc. ......................................... 1293
　　　　　Notes .......................................................................................... 1297

**Assignment 53. After the Closing: Implied Warranty of Fitness and the Duty to Disclose** .................................................................. 1305
    1.   Introduction .................................................................................. 1305
    2.   Principal Problem ........................................................................ 1310
    3.   Materials for Solution of Principal Problem ............................. 1311
          Lempke v. Dagenais ................................................................... 1311
          Reed v. King ............................................................................... 1318
          Frickel v. Sunnyside Enterprises, Inc. ...................................... 1321
          Notes ............................................................................................ 1331

**Assignment 54. Liability for Toxic Wastes** ........................................ 1335
    1.   Introduction .................................................................................. 1335
    2.   Principal Problem ........................................................................ 1338
    3.   Materials for Solution of Principal Problem ............................. 1339
          United States v. Monsanto Co. .................................................. 1339
          Notes ............................................................................................ 1346

## VI.   INTRODUCTION TO INTELLECTUAL PROPERTY LAW

**Assignment 55. Trademark Law** ......................................................... 1359
    1.   Introduction to Intellectual Property Law ................................ 1359
    2.   Introduction to Trademark Law ................................................. 1363
    3.   Principal Problem ........................................................................ 1370
    4.   Materials for Solution of Principal Problem ............................. 1371
          Jordache Enterprises, Inc. v. Levi Strauss & Co. ..................... 1371
          Packman v. Chicago Tribune Co. and Front Page News,
                Inc. ........................................................................................ 1380
          Silverman v. CBS, Inc. ............................................................... 1392
          Notes ............................................................................................ 1396

**Assignment 56. Copyright Law** ........................................................... 1405
    1.   Introduction .................................................................................. 1405
    2.   Principal Problem ........................................................................ 1411
    3.   Materials for Solution of Principal Problem ............................. 1412
          Feist Publications, Inc. v. Rural Telephone Service Co. ......... 1412
          Community for Creative Non-Violence v. Reid ....................... 1418
          Religious Technology Center v. Lerma .................................... 1424
          Notes ............................................................................................ 1434

**Assignment 57. The Right of Publicity** .............................................. 1439
    1.   Introduction .................................................................................. 1439
    2.   Principal Problem ........................................................................ 1439
    3.   Materials for Solution of Principal Problem ............................. 1441
          Feist Publications, Inc. v. Rural Telephone Service Co. ......... 1441
          National Basketball Ass'n & NBA Properties, Inc. v.
                Motorola, Inc. ...................................................................... 1441
          State ex rel. Elvis Presley Intern. Memorial Foundation v.
                Crowell ................................................................................. 1448

White v. Samsung Electronics America, Inc. ..............................1456
Notes ...................................................................................................1460

INDEX ........................................................................................................1465

# TABLE OF CASES

The principal cases are in bold type.

200 Eighth Avenue Restaurant Corp. v. Daytona Holding Corp., 167
1266 Apartment Corp. v. New Horizon Deli, Inc., 118
A & A Weston, Inc. v. 39 Main, 143
A & N Cleaners & Launderers, Inc., United States v., 1349
A. Perin Dev. Co., LLC v. Ty-Par Realty, Inc., 405
A.B. v. Hous. Auth. of S. Bend, 139
**A.D. Juilliard & Co. v. American Woolen Co.**, 145
Aaron v. Boston Redev. Auth., 970
Abbott v. Pearson, 385
Abercrombie & Fitch Co. v. Hunting World, Inc., 1375
**Abernathy v. Adous**, 150
**Abrams v. Templeton**, 243
Academy of Motion Picture Arts and Sciences v. Creative House Promotions Inc., 1400
Academy Spires, Inc. v. Brown, 78
Acme Realty Co. v. Schinasi, 1080
Adams v. Buffalo Forge Co., 441
**Adamson v. Adamson**, 308
Adjudication of the Existing Rights to the Use of All the Water Within the Missouri River Drainage Area, In re, 840
Adkins v. Edwards, 327, 329, 330
Adult Group Properties, Ltd. v. Imler, 515
Agard, In re, 1151
Agere Syst., Inc. v. Advanced Envtl. Tech. Corp., 1336
Agins v. Tiburon, 753, 762
Agricultural Labor Relations Board v. Superior Court, 32
AIMCO Props., LLC v. Dziewisz, 117, 118
AIU Ins. Co. v. Superior Court, 1263
AKG Real Estate, LLC v. Kosterman, 405, 418, 445, 584
Albertson's, Inc. v. Young, 41
Alexander's v. Arnold Constable Corp., 552
Algermissen v. Sutin, 947
Allen v. Allen, 334
Allen v. Harkness Stone Co., Inc., 170
Alley v. Rodgers, 1095
Allied Chemical Corp., United States v., 1261
Allinder v. Bessemer C.I. & L. Co., 1186
Alpert, In re Estate of, 341

Amalgamated Food Employees Union Local 590 v. Logan Valley Plaza, Inc., 27
Amann v. Faidy, 346
Amarillo, City of v. Ware, 617
American Geophysical Union v. Texaco, Inc., 1428
American National Bank & Trust Co. v. McGinnis, 341
Amundson v. Severson, 1289
Anderson v. Mauk, 1051
Anderson v. Owens-Corning Fiberglas Corp., 108
Anderson v. Steinway & Sons, 1299
Anderson v. Yaworski, 1282
Andrus v. Allard, 705, 749
Andy Warhol Enters., Inc. v. Time Inc., 1377
Angelos v. First Interstate Bank, 174
Anheuser-Busch, Inc. v. L. & L. Wings, Inc., 1400
Animas Valley Sand & Gravel, Inc. v. Board of County Comm'rs, 754
**Anne Barnett Zauner v. Leonie Sullivan Brewer**, 267
Anzalone v. Pan-Am Equities, 115
Apollo Stereo Music Co. v. Kling, 52
Apple Computer, Inc. v. Microsoft Corp., 1435
Archibald v. New York Cent. & Hudson Riv. R. R. Co., 968
Arcidi v. Town of Rye, 402
Arena v. Hegyhaty, 1299
Argyelan v. Haviland, 608
Arizona State Tax Comm. v. Staggs Realty Corp., 51
Arkansas Game and Fish Commission v. United States, 714
Arkansas v. McIlroy, 845
**Arlington Heights, Village of v. Metropolitan Housing Development Corp.**, 778
Armour v. Marino, 470
Armstrong v. Cione, 104
Armstrong v. United States, 722, 739, 750, 762
Armstrong v. Wilson, 794
Aronsohn v. Mandara, 1312, 1314
Arthur v. Starrett City Assocs., 130
Ashauer, State ex rel. v. Hostetter, 319
**Asotin County Port District v. Clarkston Community Corp.**, 1016
**Asper v. Haffley**, 95
Assembly of God v. Sangster, 343

Associated Home Builders of the Greater Eastbay, Inc. v. City of Livermore, 804
Atchison v. City of Englewood, 291
Atlantic Research Corp., United States v., 1336, 1352
Atlantic Richfield Co. v. Arco Globus Int'l Co., Inc., 1369
Austell v. Swann, 276
Avco Community Developers, Inc. v. South Coast Regional Comm'n, 682, 690
B & R Oil Co., Inc. v. Ray's Mobile Homes, Inc., 159, 161, 162
B.W.S. Invs. v. Mid-Am Rests., Inc., 86
**Babb v. Weemer**, 1187
Baeth v. Hoisveen, 844
Bakeman v. Talbot, 583
Baker v. Selden, 1418
Baldridge v. Centgraf, 995
Baley & Selover v. All Am. Van & Storage, 59
Ball v. Foreman, 393
Ballard v. Roth, 693
Bamford v. Upper Republican Natural Res. Dist., 844
Bandlow v. Thieme, 264
Bangerter v. Orem City Corporation, 807
Bank of N.Y. v. Bailey, 1152
Barash v. Pennsylvania Terminal Real Estate Corp., 57
Barcamerica Int'l USA v. Tyfield Importers, Inc., 1403
Barela v. Superior Court of Orange County, 118
Barnard v. Brown, 1082
Barnard v. Cohen, 6
Barnes v. Boardman, 1153
Barnes v. Mac Brown & Co. Inc., 1317
**Barrow v. Barrow**, 327, 329
Barry v. Covich, 1000
Bartels v. Bartels, 371
Bartholomew v. Marshall, 317
Basch v. Tidewater etc. Co., 1225, 1226
Baseball Pub. Co. v. Bruton, 52
Bassett v. Harrison, 406
Bath & Body Works Brand Mgmt., Inc. v. Summit Entm't, LLC, 1400
Batick v. Seymour, 273
Bauby v. Krasow, 543
Bauer v. Waste Mgmt. of Connecticut, Inc., 688, 689
**Bay Area Addiction Research and Treatment, Inc. v. City of Antioch.**, 791
Bayer v. United Drug Co., 1398
Beach Lateral Water Users Ass'n v. Harrison, 404

Beacham v. Lake Zurich Property Owners Ass'n, 837
Beal v. Eastern Air Devices, Inc., 52
Beams v. Werth, 1024
Becker v. IRM Corp., 102, 103, 104, 105, 108
**Beckett v. City of Paris Dry Goods Co.**, 44, 49
Beckwith v. Rossi, 440
Beebe v. Swerda, 469
Belle Terre, Village of v. Boraas, 773, 781
Belotti v. Bickhardt, 967
Bender v. Bender, 370
Bender, Matter of v. Board of Regents, 358
Berberian v. Avery, 911
Berg v. Stromme, 1323, 1326
Berkeley, City of v. Superior Court, 870, 871
Berlier v. George, 1300
Berman & Sons, Inc. v. Jefferson, 72
Berman v. Parker, 640, 650, 652
Berman v. Watergate West, Inc., 1312
Beutler v. Maynard, 967
Biggs v. Steinway & Sons, 1299
Biltmore Village, Inc. v. Royal, Biltmore Village, 232
Bird v. Bird, 330
Blackett v. Olanoff, 59
Blackman, United States v., 379
Blackwell v. Atkinson, 1190
Blair v. Board of Adjustment of Borough of Hatboro, 693
Blakeley v. Gorin, 584
Block v. Hirsh, 641, 747
Blood v. Edgar's, Inc., 1159
Board of County Comm'rs v. Park County Sportsmen's Ranch, LLP, 866
Board of Education v. Miles, 232
Bocchini v. Gorn Management Co., 85
Boerne, City of v. Flores, 811, 826
Bollinger v. McMinn, 1014
Bonczkowski v. Kucharski, 341
Booma v. Bigelow-Sanford Carpet Co., 1157
**Boomer v. Atlantic Cement Co.**, 613, 626
Boone v. Kingsbury, 873
Bortolotti v. Hayden, 299
Boss Barbara, Inc. v. Newbill, 162
Bostwick v. Beach, 1295
Boudreau v. Coleman, 477
Boudreau v. General Electric Co., 97
Boulevard Plaza Corp. v. Campbell, 1114
Bourbeau v. The Jonathan Woodner Co., 141

**Bowie, Maryland, City of v. MIE Properties, Inc.**, 575
Bowles v. United States, 894
**Bowlin v. Keifer**, 982
Box L Corp. v. Teton County, 401, 423
Boyd v. Carter, 118
Boyer v. Dennis, 446
Boyles v. Hausmann, 597, 599
Brady v. Slater, 189
Braitman, 111, 113
Brand v. Prince, 966, 967
Branson School Dist. v. Romer, 848
Brant v. Hargrove, 341
Brashier v. Burkett, 387
Braunfeld v. Brown, 822, 823
Brede v. Koop, 947
Bredeson v. Nickolay, 1116
Brenner v. Sukenik, 314
Brewer v. Erwin, 86
Brewer v. Marshall, 549, 551
Bridge Publications, Inc. v. Vien, 1432
Bridge v. Wellington, 988
Bristol-Myers Squibb Co. v. McNeil-P.P.C., Inc., 1378
Brock v. Dole, 264, 265
Brock v. Watts Realty Co., Inc., 114, 115
Brookfield Communications v. West Coast Entertainment Corp., 1397
Brown v. Hot, Sexy & Safer Prod., Inc., 815
Brown v. Independent Baptist Church of Woburn, 230
Brown v. Manter, 988
Brown v. McAnally, 412
Brown v. National Bank, 394
Brown v. Superior Court, 108
**Brown v. Voss**, 405, **409**
Bruken Realty Corp., 250, 251, 253, 254, 255
Bryant v. Blevins, 976, 977
Buchanan Marine Inc. v. McCormack Sand Co., 21
Buchanan v. Cassell, 962
Buckeye Community Hope Found. v. City of Cuyahoga Falls, 799, 801
Buckley v. Patterson, 1116
Buettner v. Nostdahl, 1003
Buffalo Academy of the Sacred Heart v. Boehm Bros., Inc., 1233
Buffalo Seminary v. McCarthy, 251, 252, 254, 256
Buick v. Highland Meadow Estates at Castle Peak Ranch, Inc., 596
Building Monitoring Systems, Inc. v. Paxton, 189
Burack v. Tollig, 1296
**Burcky v. Knowles**, 423, 424, 428, **432**
Burke v. Backus, 1146

Burkhart v. Lillehaug, 415
Burney v. Housing Auth., 132
Burns Manufacturing Co. v. Boehm, 492
Burns v. McCormick, 1009
Burrow-Giles Lithographic Co. v. Sarony, 1414
Bush v. Bourland, 151
Bush v. Gaffney, 1014
Bushby v. Washington County Conservation Bd., 848
Busteed v. Cambridge Savings Bank, 987
Butler v. Butler, 315
Butler v. Lee, 477
Butler, Commonwealth v., 315
Byron v. Gerring Industries, Inc., 187
C.F. Seabrook Co. v. Beck, 80
Caban v. Mohammed, 350
Cain v. Powers, 510
Calder v. Bull, 654
Caldwell v. Gurley Refining Co., 1338
Califano v. Webster, 350
Califano v. Westcott, 350
California Fish Co., People v., 872
California Lettuce Growers v. Union Sugar Co., 163
Camelback Del Este Homeowners Ass'n v. Warner, 585
Campbell v. Acuff-Rose Music, Inc., 1427, 1429, 1432
Canton v. Commissioner of the Mass. Highway Dep't, 1157
Cantwell v. Connecticut, 822
Caplan v. Palace Realty Co., N.J., 1218
Cappaert v. United States, 845
Cappiello v. Cappiello, 359
Carlie v. Morgan, 89
Carneal v. Kendig, 553
Carner v. Shapiro, 60
Carolene Prods. Co., United States v., 794
Carpenter's Estate, In re, 348
Carpentieri v. Gayle, 118
Carrsow-Franklin, In re, 1168
Carson v. Here's Johnny Portable Toilets, Inc., 1451, 1462
Carson, Executrix v. Ellis, 343
Carter v. County of Hanover, 479, 494
Carter's Estate, In re, 318
Casco Marina Development, L.L.C. v. District of Columbia Redevelopment Land Agency, 167
Case v. Kadota Fig Ass'n of Producers, Cal.App., 49
Castle Associates v. Schwartz, 470, 471, 472
Castle Hills First Baptist Church v. City of Castle Hills, 815
Castle Rock v. Gonzales, 657

Caughlin Ranch Homeowners Association v. Caughlin Club, 597, 599
Caullett v. Stanley Stilwell & Sons, Inc., 553, 557
Causby, United States v., 618, 703, 707, 723, 747
Centaur Communications v. A/S/M Communications, 1377
Centel Cable Television Co. of Ohio v. Cook, 404
Centex Homes Corp. v. Boag, 1110
Central Eureka Mining Co., United States v., 723
Central Hudson Gas & Elec. Corp. v. Public Serv. Comm'n, 1402, 1459
Chalifoux v. New Caney Indep. Sch. Dist., 815
Chalk v. United States Dist. Court, 796
Champlin's Realty Assocs., L.P. v. Tillson, 914
Chancey v. Georgia Power Company, 942
Change of Appropriation Water Rights, Matter of Application for, 841
Chaplin v. Sanders, 944, 945, 946, 959
Charles v. Verhagen, 813
Cherberg v. Peoples Nat. Bank of Washington, 59
Cherry v. Cherry, 304
**Chevy Chase Village v. Jaggers**, **568**, 577
Chevy Chase Village v. Mont. Co., 573
Chicago Title Ins. Co. v. Kumar, 1260, 1262
Chicago, B. & Q. R. Co. v. Chicago, 642, 697, 722
Christian Gospel Church v. San Francisco, 694
Chun Quan Yee Hop, Estate of, 241
Church of Lukumi Babalu Aye, Inc. v. City of Hialeah, 814, 829
Cincinnati v. Vester, 654
Citibrook II, LLC v. Morgan's Foods of Missouri, Inc., 301
Citizens for Preservation of Waterman Lake v. Davis, 911, 912
Citizens to Preserve Overton Park v. Volpe, 784
City Mill Co., Ltd. v. Honolulu Sewer & Water Comm'n, 882
**Civil Liberties for Urban Believers v. City of Chicago**, **825**
Claremont Terrace Homeowners' Assn. v. United States, 1225, 1226, 1227

Clawans v. Ordway B. & L. Ass'n, 1220
Claxton v. Atlantic Richfield Co., 115
Clay v. Landreth, 1299
Clearview Coal Co., Commonwealth v., 716
**Cleburne, Texas, City of v. Cleburne Living Center, Inc.**, **786**, 816
Clem v. Valentine, 571
Clickner v. Magothy River Ass'n, 975
Clifton, City of v. Passaic Valley Water Comm'n, 848
Cline v. American Aggregates Corp., 849
Coffin v. Left Hand Ditch Co., 839
Coggan v. Coggan, 327, 329, 331
Cohen v. Kosdon, 1109
Colberg, Inc. v. State of California ex rel. Dept Pub. Wks., 870
Colby v. McLaughlin, 553
Cole v. Lake Co., 435
Coles Trading Co. v. Spiegel, Inc., 153
Collier, In re, 1208
**Colonial at Lynnfield, Inc. v. Sloan, 1096**
Columbia Casualty Co. v. Sodini, 343
Commander Oil Corp. v. Barlo Equipment Corp., 1338
Commerce Bancorp, Inc. v. BankAtlantic, 1400
Commerce Oil Refining Corp. v. Miner, 911
Commonwealth Electric Co. v. MacCardell, 1208
Commonwealth Realty v. Bowers, 292
**Community for Creative Non-Violence v. Reid**, **1418**, 1419
Computer Assoc. Int'l, Inc. v. Altai, Inc., 1444
Conaster v. Johnson, 845
Conner v. Conner, 358
Conner v. How, 1148
Connors v. Annino, 1157
Constructors Ass'n of W. Pa. v. Kreps, 133
Contracts Funding & Mortgage Exchange v. Maynes, Utah, 681, 683
Converse v. Fong, 1117
Coomes v. Aero Theatre & Shopping Center, 553
Cooper Indus., Inc. v. Aviall Servs., Inc., 1335
Cooper v. Jevne, 1067
Cornerstone Bible Church v. City of Hastings, 815, 816
Corporation of Presiding Bishop of Church of Jesus Christ of Latter-

Day Saints v. City of Porterville, 821
Corrigan Co. Mechanical Contractors, Inc. v. Fleischer, 1102
Cosmopolitan Homes, Inc. v. Weller, 1312
Costco Companies, Inc. v. Gallant, 41
Cottonwood Christian Ctr. v. Cypress Redevelopment Agency, 813
Coughlin v. Anderson, 402
Country World Casinos v. Tommyknocker Casino, 1187
Courtney v. Courtney, 370
Courtright, Matter of Estate of v. Robertson, 1043
Covertech Fabricating, Inc. v. TVM Bldg. Prods., 1369
**Covington v. Robinson**, 1093
Cox, In re, 122, 126
Crabbe v. Veve Associates, 467
Craft, United States v., 304
Craig v. Boren, 350
**Crane v. Crane**, 427, 428, 429, **436**
Crawford v. Crawford, 942
Creekside Apartments v. Poteat, 89
Creque v. Texaco Antilles, Ltd., 299
Crescent Tool Co. v. Kilborn & Bishop Co., 1398
Cronan v. Castle Gas Co., Inc., 278
Crowley v. Adams, 1154
Cummings v. Dosam, Inc., 538
Cushman Virginia Corporation v. Barnes, 419, 420
Cutter v. Wilkinson, 813
Cuyahoga Falls, City of v. Buckeye Community Hope Foundation, 801
D.A.D., Inc. v. Moring, 341
Dagley, Commonwealth v., 1159
Daily Mines Co. v. Control Mines, Inc., 1030
Dallas Cowboys Cheerleaders, Inc. v. Pussycat Cinema, Ltd., 1374
Damascus Community Church v. Clackamas County, 834
Daniel v. Daniel, 370
Danpar Associates v. Somersville Mills Sales Room, Inc., 159
Das v. WMC Mortg. Corp., 1142
**Davidow v. Inwood North Professional Group**, 81
**Davidson Bros., Inc. v. D. Katz & Sons, Inc.**, 548
Davis v. Mitchell, 1453
Dawn Donut Co., Inc. v. Hart's Food Stores, Inc., 1403
De Peyster v. Michael, 250
**Debrunner v. Deutsche Bank National Trust Company**, 1138
Deck v. Missouri, 657
Dedham Water Co. v. Cumberland Farms Dairy, Inc., 1342
Deegan v. Deegan, 317

DeHaven v. Hall, 406
DeKay v. U.S. Fish & Wildlife Service, 840
Delgado v. Heritage Life Ins. Co., 1259
Dellar v. Samuel Goldwyn, Inc., 1410
Dennis Rourke Corp. v. Ferrero Constr. Co., 287
Department of Transportation v. Humphries, 1200
Deslauriers v. Senesac, 345, 346
Devins v. Borough of Bogota, 970
Di Leo v. Pecksto Holding Corp., 967
Di Pasco v. Prosser, 488
Diana Shooting Club v. Lamoreaux, 7
Dickhut v. Norton, 189
**DiDonato v. Reliance Standard Life Ins. Co.**, 1284
Dill v. Excel Packing Company, 628
Dimura v. Williams, 939
Dixon v. Salvation Army, 1297
Doe v. Beach House Dev. Co., 115
Doe v. Dominion Bank of Washington, N.A., 114, 115
Doe v. TCI Cablevision, 1463
Doenz v. Garber, 472
Doherty v. Allman, 264
Dolan v. City of Tigard, 7
Donahue Schriber Realty Group, Inc. v. Nu Creation Outreach, 41
Donchez v. Coors Brewing Co., 1399
Doo v. Packwood, 553, 559
Door Sys., Inc. v. Pro-Line Door Sys., Inc., 1384
Douglaston Civic Assn., Matter of v. Galvin, 590
Downing House Realty v. Hampe, 446
Drees Co., Inc. v. Thompson, 401
Dress Shirt Sales, Inc. v. Hotel Martinique Assocs., 165
Duane Reade v. IG Second Generation Partners, L.P., 167
Duffield v. Duffield, 345
Duffy v. Dwyer, 1206
Duncan v. Peterson, 976
Dundalk Holding Co. v. Easter, 574
Dunham v. Ware Savings Bank, 517
Dunn v. Winans, 998
Dutcher v. Owens, 1109
Dyett v. Pendleton, 85
Dyker Meadow Land & Improvement Co. v. Cook, 1085
E & J, Inc. v. Redevelopment Agency of Woonsocket, 908
**Eagle Enterprises, Inc. v. Gross**, 540, **561**
East Bay Asian Local Dev. Corp. v. State, 816
East Haven Associates Inc. v. Gurian, 61, 85

## Table of Cases

East River Steamship Corp. v. Transamerica Delaval, Inc., 1332
East St. Johns Shingle Co. v. City of Portland, 628
**Easton v. Strassburger**, 1056, **1066**
Eastside Exhibition Corp. v. 210 E. 86th St. Corp., 85
Eastwood Lands, Inc. v. United States Steel Corp., 1265
Eastwood v. Superior Court, 1457
**Eaton v. Federal National Mortgage Association**, 1150
**Echo Consulting Services, Inc. v. North Conway Bank**, 56
Edgar v. Hunt, 297, 298
Edison Bros. Stores, Inc. v. Cosmair, Inc., 1375, 1376, 1378
Edmonds, City of v. Williams, 469
Edwards Aquifer Auth. v. Day, 866
Edwards v. Friborg, 1291
Edwards v. Fry, 995
El Cerrito, Inc. v. Ryndak, 963
Eldridge v. Cowell, 870
Eli Lilly & Co. v. Natural Answers, Inc., 1384
Elkus v. Elkus, 1460
Elliott v. Lachance, 1313
Ellis v. Ellis, 1103
Ellis v. Morris, 1311, 1318, 1332
**Ellsworth Dobbs, Inc. v. Johnson v. Iarussi**, 1055, 1056, **1058**
Elsinore Christian Ctr. v. City of Lake Elsinore, 813
**Elvis Presley Intern. Memorial Foundation, State ex rel. v. Crowell**, 1448
Employment Division, Department of Human Resources of Oregon v. Smith, 810, 829
Encyclopaedia Britannica Educational Corp. v. Crooks, 1431
Engle v. Clark, 627
**Epstein Family Partnership Levitz Furniture Corp. v. Kmart Corp.**, 491
Epstein, United States v., 164
Erie R. Co. v. Tompkins, 1445
Espenschied v. Mallick, 86
Etheridge v. Etheridge, 334
Ettore v. Philco Television Broadcasting Corp., 1450
ETW Corp. v. Jireh Publishing, Inc., 1463
**Euclid, Village of v. Ambler Realty Co.**, 633, **674**, 723, 747, 762, 765, 773, 781, 820, 831
**Evergreen Highlands Ass'n v. West**, 593
Ewing v. Tanner, 942
Executive Sandwich Shoppe, Inc. v. Carr Realty Corp., 168

F & L Center Co. v. Cunningham Drug Stores, Inc., 159
Fair Housing Congress v. Weber, 138
Fair Housing in Huntington Comm. v. Town of Huntington, 806
Farris Constr. Co. v. 3032 Briarcliff Rd. Associates, 477
Fashion Valley Mall, LLC v. National Labor Relations Bd., 40
Fassitt v. Seip, 327
Faubion v. Elder, 963, 964
Fay v. Cheney, 1154
FCC v. Florida Power Corp., 710, 712
Federal National Mortgage Ass'n v. Elliott, 343
Feinberg Bros. Agency, Inc. v. Berted Realty Co., Inc., 1072
**Feist Publications, Inc. v. Rural Telephone Service Co.**, 1405, 1412, 1425, 1441, 1443, 1459
Feld v. Kantrowitz, 1217, 1220
Feldman v. Lisansky, 1295
Fellmer v. Gruber, 1300
Feltner, Jr. v. Columbia Pictures Television, Inc., 1437
Fenno v. Sayre, 1212
Fenster v. Hyken, 974
Ferguson Ranch, Inc. v. Murray, 473
Ferguson v. Ferguson, 947
Ferguson v. Keene, 908
Ferguson v. Rochford, 271
Ferguson v. Village of Hamburg, 618
Fernandez v. Vazquez, 163
Ferrari S.p.A. Esercizio Fabbriche Automobili E Corse v. McBurnie Coachcraft Inc., 1403
**Ferrero Construction Company v. Dennis Rourke Corporation**, **286**
Financial Information, Inc. v. Moody's Investors Service, Inc., 1445
First Covenant Church of Seattle v. City of Seattle, 816
First English Evangelical Lutheran Church of Glendale v. County of Los Angeles, 746
First National Pictures Distributing Corp. v. Seawell, 184
Fischer, Matter of, 256
Fish Const. Co. v. Moselle Coach Works, Inc., 86
Fisher v. Allen, 349
Fisher v. Comer Plantation, Inc., 1053
Fitchie v. Brown, 292
Fitzpatrick v. Mer. Safe, Etc. Co., 287
Flemings v. Contributory Retirement Appeal Bd., 1156
Fletcher v. Peck, 784
**Florence Dolan v. City of Tigard**, **758**

# TABLE OF CASES

Florida Rock Indus. v. United States, 894
Flying Diamond Oil Corp. v. Newton Sheep Co., 525, 539
Flying Dog Brewery, LLLP v. Mich. Liquor Control Comm'n, 1402
Flynn v. AK Peters, Ltd., 1399
Fogerty v. Fantasy, Inc., 1405
Forbes v. Volk, Wyo., 1041
Ford v. Ja-Sin, Del.Super., 97
Forderhause v. Cherokee Water Co., 289
Fordyce Lumber Company v. Wallace, 983
Forseth v. Village of Sussex, 831
Forstmann v. Joray Holding Co., 615
Four Seas Inv. Corp. v. International Hotel Tenants' Ass'n, 86
Fowler v. Borough of Westville, 139
Frances T. v. Village Green Owners Association, 116
Franco-American Charolaise, Ltd. v. Oklahoma Water Resources Bd., 837, 842
**Franklin v. Spadafora, 516**
Freedom Baptist Church v. Township of Middletown, 813
Frey v. Wubbena, 346
**Frickel v. Sunnyside Enterprises, Inc., 1321**
Friedenberg v. New York Dep't of Envtl Conservation, 894
Friends of Endangered Species, Inc. v. Jantzen, 666
Frontiero v. Richardson, 350, 787
Fruth Farms, Ltd. v. Village of Holgate, 403, 404
Ft. Smith, City of v. Western Hide & Fur Co., 628
Fulton v. Fulton, 333
Funk v. Funk, 162
Gagne v. Hartmeier, 152, 155
Gallagher v. Bell, 534
Gardner v. Simpson, Fin., 86
Garrett v. City of Escondido, 138, 139
Gaskill v. Robbins, 1460
**Gates Rubber Co. v. Ulman, 1221**
General Healthcare, Ltd. v. Qashat, 1402
General Motors Corp. v. Lanard Toys, Inc., 1400
General Motors Corp., United States v., 704
George v. Veach, 1315
Geren v. Deutsche Bank National, 1141
Germany v. Murdock, 426
Germon v. BAC Home Loans Servicing, L.P., 1142
Gerry v. Johnston, 52
Ghen v. Rich, 865

**Giannini v. First National Bank of Des Plaines, 1107**
Gibson v. LaClair, 61
Gibson v. United States, 845
Gignilliat v. Gignilliat, Savitz & Bettis, L.L.P., 1461
Gillen-Crow Pharmacies, Inc. v. Mandzak, 553
Gilles v. Sprout, 1300
Gillis v. Bonelli-Adams Co., 1289
**Gillmor v. Gillmor, 324**
Gilpin v. Jacob Ellis Realties, 560
Gimbel Brothers, Inc. v. Brook Shopping Centers, Inc., 258
Giordano v. Miller, 167
Glass v. Goeckel, 846, 847
Glass v. Hulbert, 1000
Glenn v. Poole, 421
Glines v. Auger, 435
Glow Industries, Inc. v. Jennifer Lopez, Coty, Inc., 1397
Goldberg v. Charlie's Chevrolet, Inc., 1102
Goldblatt v. Town of Hempstead, 706, 723
Golden Gateway Center v. Golden Gateway Tenants Ass'n, 40
Golden v. Planning Board of Town of Ramapo, 804
Golden, Matter of v. Planning Bd., 1085
Goldstein v. California, 1414
Goldstein v. Pataki, 661
Gomes v. Countrywide Home Loans, Inc., 1142
Gomillion v. Lightfoot, 783
**Good v. Wells Fargo Bank, N.A., 1160**
Goodwin v. Johnson, 415
Gordon Investment Co. v. Jones, 159
Gordon v. Anderson, 1000
Gordon v. Hoy, 425
Gordonsville, Town of v. Zinn, 837
Gorieb v. Fox, 749
Gottdiener v. Mailhot, 59
Gould v. Board of Education, 257
Grady v. Schmitz, 544
Graham v. Bryant, 276
Graham v. Graham, 363
Grand Bissell Towers, Inc. v. Joan Gagnon, Enter., Inc., 1103
**Grand Lodge of Georgia v. City of Thomasville, 1020**
Granite Properties Ltd. Partnership v. Manns, 477
Granquist v. McKean, 1004
Grayson v. Huntington, 848
Greater Providence Chamber of Commerce v. Rhode Island, 914
**Greaves v. McGee, 386**
Green Party of New Jersey v. Hartz Mountain Industries, 41

## Table of Cases

Green v. Horn, 968
Green v. Superior Court, 71, 85, 106, 107, 112
Greenberg, People ex rel. v. Reid, 358
Greenman v. Yuba Power Products, Inc., 76, 103, 105
Griffin High School v. Illinois High School Athletic Assoc., 831
Griffin v. Reynolds, 1185
Grigsby, Estate of, 348
Grimm v. Grimm, 277
Griswold v. Connecticut, 28
Groswird v. Hayne Investments, Inc., 1299
Grosz v. City of Miami Beach, Fla., 822, 824
Grotrian, Helfferich, Schulz, Th. Steinweg Nachf. v. Steinway & Sons, 1374
Grubb v. Guilford Ass'n, 573
Grygiel v. Monches Fish & Game Club, Inc., 405
Guillette v. Daly Dry Wall, Inc., 1233
Guinn v. United States, 783
Guiseppi v. Walling, 136
**Gulden v. Sloan, 1001**
Guskin v. Guskin, 1460
Guthrie v. Hardy, 401
Haalelea v. Montgomery, 884
Hadacheck v. Sebastian, 724
Haelan Laboratories, Inc. v. Topps Chewing Gum, Inc., 1451
Hagen v. Anderson, 1109
Hagen v. Dahmer, 1461
Hague v. Wells Fargo Bank, N.A., 1141
Hall v. American Oil Co., 553
Hall v. City of Santa Barbara, 709
Hall v. Hamilton, 343, 344
Hall v. Warren, 78
Hall v. Weeks, 1095
Hall v. Wood, 608
Halle v. Newbold, 571
**Halpern v. The Lacy Investment Corp., 941**
Haman for Kootenai County, State ex rel. v. Fox, 975
Hamilton v. Hopkins, 1056
Hamilton v. Traub, 1008
Hannah v. Kenny, 942
Hansen v. Davis, 448, 449
Hardin v. Wolf, 340
Harkins & Co. v. Lewis, 959
Harloff v. City of Sarasota, 838
**Harms v. Sprague, 337,** 341
Harper & Row, Publishers, Inc. v. Nation Enterprises, 1413, 1414, 1415, 1425, 1429, 1430, 1432
Harris v. Brooks, 838
Harris v. Perl, 1065
**Harris v. Strawbridge, 984**
Harris v. Town of Lincoln, 908

Harrison v. State Highways and Transp. Com'n, 467
Hartman v. Duke, 1453
Hartog v. Siegler, 334
Hatlestad v. Mut. Trust Life Ins. Co., 1145
Haugan v. Haugan, 371
**Hawaii Housing Authority v. Midkiff, 638,** 651
Hawaii, County of v. Sotomura, 879
Hawaiian Commercial & Sugar Co. v. Wailuku Sugar Co., 886
Hawaii-Pacific Apparel Group, Inc. v. Cleveland Browns Football Co. LLC, 1403
Hawkes v. Kehoe, 1282
Hawkins v. Hawkins, 19
Hawley v. McCabe, 1212
**Hayes v. Aquia Marina, Inc., 418,** 466
Hayes v. Midland Credit Co., 1145
Hayes v. Waverly & Passaic R.R., 553
Heard v. Stratford I Ltd. P'ship, 140
Heartz v. City of Concord, 405
Heatter v. Lucas, 314
Hecht v. Meller, 1297
Heerdt v. Brand, 1295
Heffron v. Int'l Soc'y for Krishna Consciousness, Inc., 825
Heflin v. Phillips, 1184, 1185
Hein v. Lee, Wyo., 1043
Heinzman v. Howard, 1300
Heiselt v. Heiselt, 326
Hendrickson v. Freericks, 162
Hendrickson v. Minneapolis Federal Savings & Loan Association, 347, 348
Hennessey v. Pyne, 912
Hercules Powder Co. v. Continental Can Co., 553, 558, 559
Hernandez v. Hernandez, 333
Herren v. Pettengill, 415
Hess v. Chase Manhattan Bank, 1353
Heuer v. Rubin, 559
Hidden Harbour Estates, Inc. v. Norman, 601, 602
Hiddleston v. Nebraska Jewish Education Society, 232
High Plains A & M, LLC v. Southeastern Colorado Water Conservancy Dist., 841
Hild v. Avland Development Co., 1110
Hilder v. St. Peter, 78
**Hill v. Community of Damien, 509**
Hills Development Co. v. Bernards Township in Somerset County (Mount Laurel III), 802
**Hillside Development Company v. Fields, 484**
Hilton v. Hallmark Cards, 1463

**Hilton v. Nelsen**, 1112
Hinds v. Henry, 1061
Hinman v. Barnes, 393
Hinrichs v. Whitburn, 815
Hinson v. Delis, 78, 80
Hirsch v. S.C. Johnson & Son, 1462
HM Holdings, Inc. v. Rankin, 1263
Hocking v. Title Ins. & Trust Co., 1260, 1261
Hodge v. Sloan, 553
Hoenig v. Lubetkin, 270
Hoffman v. Capital Cities/ABC, Inc., 1463
Holbrook v. Carter, 325
Hollander v. Central Metal & Supply Co., 288
Hollywood Lumber Co. v. Love, 1189
**Holmes Development, LLC v. Cook, 1176**
**Holmes v. Alabama Title Company, 1263**
Holmes' Estate, In re, 314
Holt v. Holt, 420
Holt v. Winpisinger, 1423
Holy Properties Limited, L.P. v. Kenneth Cole Productions, Inc., 170, 188
Homa-Goff Interiors, Inc. v. Cowden, 162
Hood v. Neil, 407
Hoover v. Crane, 837, 838
Hoover v. Wright, Mo., 1291
Horne v. U.S. Dept. of Agriculture, 23, 698
House v. Thornton, 1323
Housing Auth. of the City of Bayonne v. Mims, 118
Houston Bellaire, Ltd. v. TCP LB Portfolio I, L.P., 494
**Howard v. Kunto, 960**
Howe v. Wilder, 1154
Hoyt v. American Traders, Inc., 304
Hudson County Water Co. v. McCarter, 844
Hudspeth v. Eastern Oregon Land Co., 526
Hughes v. Washington, 849
Hummelman v. Mounts, 988
Hurd v. Hodge, 521
**Hurst v. Baker, 390**
**Hutchinson National Bank v. Brown, 342**
Hydro Resources Corp. v. Gray, 866
Hydro-Manufacturing, Inc. v. Kayser-Roth Corp., 912
Hynson v. Jeffries, 278
I.E. Associates v. Safeco Title Ins. Co., 1142
I.H.T. Corp. v. Saffir Publishing Corp., 1394
Iafrate v. Ramsden, 912

**Ignacio Vasquez v. Brigido Vasquez, 1044**
Il Giardino, LLC v. Belle Haven Land Co., 405
Illinois Central Railroad Company v. Illinois, 846, 871, 878
Illinois Public Aid Com. v. Stille, 340
Imperial Colliery Co. v. Fout, 118
Impink v. Bank of America, 1141
Innovative Health Systems, Inc. v. City of White Plains, 793, 794, 795, 806
Insurance Rating Bd. v. Commissioner of Ins., 1157
**Intel Corporation v. Hamidi, 13**
International Bancorp, LLC v. Societe des Bains de Mer et du Cercle des Estrangers a Monaco, 1400
International News Service v. Associated Press, 1441, 1445
Irving Inv. Corp. v. Gordon, 559
Irwin v. Phillips, 839
**Isbey v. Crews, 181**
Islamic Center v. City of Starkville, 814
**ITT Rayonier, Inc. v. Bell**, 943, 945, **950**
J. E. D. Associates, Inc. v. Atkinson, 763
Jaber v. Miller, 152, 155
Jack Spring, Inc. v. Little, 189
Jackson v. Lacey, 339
Jackson v. Mort. Elec. Registration Sys., Inc., 1145
Jackson v. O'Connell, 339
Jackson v. Williams, 512
Jackvony v. Poncelet, 467
Jaimes v. Lucas Metropolitan Housing Auth., 133, 134
James v. Valtierra, 781
Jancik v. Department of Housing and Urban Development, 140
Janik v. Janik, 334
Jarrell v. Hartman, 72
Javins v. First National Realty Corp., 78, 79
**Jefferson County v. Mosley, 1208**
Jefferson Davis Parish School Board v. Fontenot, 974
Jefferson v. Hackney, 783
Jenkins v. St. Tammany Parish Police Jury, 694
Jenkins v. State Dep't of Water Resources, 841
Jennison v. Walker, 414
John C. Cutler Ass'n v. DeJay Stores, Inc., 174
Johnson v. Howe, 1148
Johnson v. Keith, 519, 520
Johnson v. McIntosh, 929, 931
Johnson v. Muntz, 340

## Table of Cases

Johnson v. North American Life & Casualty Co., 1111
Johnson v. Shaw, 553
Johnson v. Transportation Agency, 133
Jones v. Adams, 849
Jones v. Andy Griffith Products, Inc., 182
Jones v. Innkeepers, Inc., 151
Jones v. Linder, 998
Jones v. Marable, 1453
Jooss v. Fey, 317
**Jordache Enterprises, Inc. v. Levi Strauss & Co., 1371**, 1400
Jordan v. Talbot, 14
Joseph Brothers Co. v. F.W. Woolworth Co., 143
**JPMorgan Chase Bank, N.A. v. Erlandson, 1143**
**Just v. Marinette County**, 633, 847, **900**
Kagan, In re, 317
Kahn v. Shevin, 350
Kaiser Aetna v. United States, 7, 703, 704, 710, 762, 768
Kallman v. Radioshack Corp., 189
Kamada v. RX Group Limited, 187
Kano Invs., L.L.C. v. Kojis Constr., L.L.C., 159
Karner v. Roy White Flowers, Inc., 585
**Kelo v. City of New London, 648**
Kend v. Crestwood Realty Co., 1299
Kendall v. Ernest Pestana, Inc., 159, 162, 163, 164, 167
Kendall-Jackson Winery, Ltd. v. E. & J Gallo Winery, 1397
Kennedy Park Homes Ass'n v. City of Lackawanna, 133, 781, 783
Kenney v. Medlin Const. & Realty Co., 1318
Kenworthy v. Tullis, 988
Kerrick v. Schoenberg, 553
Kesseler v. Bowditch, 414
Keyes v. Guy Bailey Homes, Inc., 1315
Keystone Bituminous Coal Assn. v. DeBenedictis, 746, 749
King v. Lang, 423, 427
King v. Oahu Railway & Land Co., 879
King-Seeley Thermos Co. v. Aladdin Industries, Inc., 1398
Kink v. Combs, 9
Kirk v. Bray, 276
Klatzl's Estate, Matter of, 317
Kline v. Burns, 60
Kling v. Ghilarducci, 340, 341
Klos v. Gockel, 1323, 1324, 1327, 1328
Knapp v. Eagle Prop. Mgmt. Corp., 141

Knapp v. Simmons, 87
Knight v. Connecticut Dep't of Pub. Health, 815
**Knight v. Hallsthammar, 69**
Knight v. Knight, 319
Knight v. Madison, 407
Kolbe v. JP Morgan Chase Bank, N.A., 1141
Kolouch v. Kramer, 470, 471
Kootenai Envt'l. Alliance v. Panhandle Yacht Club, 847
KP Permanent Make-Up, Inc. vs. Lasting Impression I, Inc., 1398
Krafick v. Krafick, 362
**Kramarsky v. Stahl Management, 119**
Kramer v. Baltimore, 693
Kregos v. Associated Press, 1426
Kreitz v. Behrensmeyer, 346
**Kresser v. Peterson, 1039**
Kroninger v. Anast, 1299
Kubby v. Hammond, 626
Kubo v. Agricultural Labor Relations Board, 32
**Kurpiel v. Kurpiel, 316**
Kutanovski v. Kutanovski, 358
Kynerd v. Hulen, 385
La Paz, County of v. Yakima Compost Co., 52
**Laba v. Carey, 1076**, 1078
LaFollette, State ex rel. v. Reuter, 903
Lague, Inc. v. Royea, 451
Laguna Royale Owners Ass'n v. Darger, 519
Lake Michigan Fed. v. U.S. Army Corps of Engineers, 847
Lakeland Property Owners Association v. Larson, 596
Lakewood, Ohio Congregation of Jehovah's Witnesses, Inc. v. City of Lakewood, Ohio, 823, 824
Lamson & Co. v. Abrams, 1153
Lane v. Vitek Real Estate Indus. Group, 1142
Lane v. Wilson, 783
LaSara Grain v. First National Bank of Mercedes, 1312
Lawler v. Byrne, 340
Lawrence v. La Jolla Beach & Tennis Club, Inc., 115
Lawrence v. Town of Concord, 959
Lax v. 29 Woodmere Blvd. Owners, Inc., 140
Lazy Dog Ranch v. Telluray Ranch Corp., 402, 406
LeBaron v. Crismon, 1030
Legal Tender Cases, 731
Leishman v. White, 56
LeMay v. Anderson, 423
Lemmon v. Hardy, 841
Lemon v. Kurtzman, 825

## TABLE OF CASES

**Lempke v. Dagenais, 1311**
**Lenhart v. Desmond, 1040**
Lerman v. Levine, 333
Les Ballets Trockadero de Monte Carlo, Inc. v. Trevino, 1369
Lesman v. Lesman, 359
Lewey v. H.C. Frick Coke Co., 955
Lewis v. Young, 405, 415
Li v. Yellow Cab Co., 1069
Libman v. Levenson, 1282, 1289, 1291
**Lick Mill Creek Apartments v. Chicago Title Ins. Co., 1256**
Life Teen, Inc. v. Yavapai County, 813
Lightcap v. Bradley, 340
Lightner Mining Co. v. Lane, 957
Lincoln Trust Co. v. Williams Bldg. Corp., 1085
Lindsey v. Normet, 781
Lingle v. Chevron USA, Inc., 698, 754
Lingsch v. Savage, 1067, 1319
Little Blue Natural Resources Dist. v. Lower Platte North Natural Resources Dist., 837
Lois Sportswear, U.S.A., Inc. v. Levi Strauss & Co., 1374, 1375, 1377
Long v. Keller, 1301
**Loretto v. Teleprompter Manhattan CATV Corp., 700,** 709, 732, 739, 747
Losson v. Blodgett, 46
Loveladies Harbor, Inc. v. United States, 894, 927
Lowe v. Morrison, 304
Lucas v. Forty-Fourth General Assembly of Colorado, 789
Lucas v. Rawl Family Ltd. Partnership, 608
**Lucas v. South Carolina Coastal Council, 608, 730, 738, 911, 912,** 927
**Lucenti v. Cayuga Apartments, Inc., 1293**
Lundberg v. Nw. Nat'l Bank of Minneapolis, 1148
Lunsford v. Deutsche Bank Trust Co. Americas as, Tr., 1163
Lux v. Haggin, 837
Lynch v. Andrew, 1101
Lyng v. Northwest Indian Cemetery Protective Ass'n, 822
Lyondell Chem. Co., In re, 1335
M.M. Newcomer Co. v. Newcomer's New Store, 1454
**M.P.M. Builders, LLC v. Dwyer,** 405, **413**
MacDonald v. Perry, 627
Machin v. Royale Green Condominium Association, 116
Mackintosh v. Stewart, 1185

MacMeekin v. Low Income Hous. Inst., Inc., 416
Madhani v. Cooper, 114, 115
**Madhavan v. Sucher, 1081**
Mafetone v. Forest Manor Homes, 1079
Maggio v. Pruzansky, 959
Maher v. City of New Orleans, 726
Mahoney v. Tingley, 1105
Majauskas v. Majauskas, 360
**Majestic View Condo. Ass'n, Inc. v. Bolotin, 600**
Manhattan Apartments, Inc. v. Simeon, 1055
Mann-Hoff v. Boyer, 491
Mannillo v. Gorski, 959
Manning v. Smith, 988
Mansur v. Eubanks, 97
Marathon Oil Co. v. Rone, 146
Marcus Cable Associates v. Krohn, 401, 404, 422
Marcus v. Rowley, 1430, 1431, 1432
**Marengo Cave Co. v. Ross, 951**
**Margarite v. Ewald, 312**
**Marina Point, Ltd. v. Stephen Wolfson, 121**
Marina Point, Ltd. v. Wolfson, 117, 119
**Marini v. Ireland,** 31, **65,** 78
Marks v. Whitney, 847
Marlenee v. Brown, 1226
Marsh v. Alabama, 27, 35, 37
MAR-SON, Inc. v. Terwaho Enterprises, Inc., 185
Martin Luther King Center for Social Change, Inc. v. American Heritage Products, Inc., 1454
Martin, State ex rel. v. Juneau, 903
Martinez v. Woodmar IV Condominiums Homeowners Association, Inc., 116
**Martinique Realty Corp. v. Hull, 1216**
Maryland Commission on Human Relations v. Greenbelt Homes, Inc., 520
**Maryland Reclamation Associates, Inc. v. Harford County, 685**
Marynick v. Bockelmann, 170
Mason v. Hoyle, 837
Mason v. U.E.S.S. Leasing Corp., 115
Massachusetts Board of Retirement v. Murgia, 788
Massey v. Prothero, Utah, 325
Matcha v. Mattox on Behalf of People, 975
Matthews v. Bay Head Improvement Ass'n, 847
Maxtone-Graham v. Burtchaell, 1430
Mayor and Council of Forsyth v. Hooks, 942

## Table of Cases

Mazdabrook Commons Homeowners' Ass'n v. Khan, 40
Mazer v. Stein, 1405
MCA, Inc. v. Wilson, 1428
McAllister v. Schettler, 1117
McBryde Sugar Co. v. Robinson, 849, 880
McCann v. Chasm Power Co., 615
McCann v. R.W Dunteman Co., 447
McClain v. Holder, 318
McClellan v. Tottenhoff, 101
McDonald's Corp. v. McBagel's, Inc., 1375
McFadden v. Sein, 404
McGinnis v. Royster, 782
McGlashan v. Spade Rockledge Terrace Condo Dev. Corp., 608
McGregor-Doniger Inc. v. Drizzle Inc., 1375
McIntosh, In re, 264
**McIntyre v. Scarbrough, 275**
McKenrick v. Savings Bank, 571
McKnight v. Basilides, 333
McNeil v. Attaway, 1030
McPike v. Heaton, 1189
McWilliams v. Bragg, 6
Meadows v. Brich, 1036
Mease v. Fox, 78, 85
Mechanics' Foundry v. Ryall, 16
Mehdizadeh v. Mincer, 974
Mellinger v. Ticor Title Insurance Co., 1090
**Melms v. Pabst Brewing Co., 263**
Melodies, Inc. v. Mirabile, 52
Memmott v. Bosh, Utah, 325
Memphis Development Foundation v. Factors, Etc., Inc., 1454
Mendelson v. McCabe, 16
Menzer v. Elkhart Lake, 904
Mercantile-Safe Deposit & Trust Co. v. Mayor & City Council of Baltimore, 578
Merchants National Bank v. Olson, 341
Mercury Machine Importing Corp. v. City of, New York, 257
Meresse v. Stelma, 597, 599
**Merrill v. Jansma, 98**
Merritt v. Parker, 837
MERSCORP, Inc. v. Romaine, 1151
Mertens v. Berendsen, 1259
Meskell v. Meskell, 1000
Messer v. Leveson, 424
**Messiah Baptist Church v. County of Jefferson, State of Colorado, 819**
Metromedia, Inc. v. City of Pasadena, 693
Metropolitan Housing Development Corp. v. Village of Arlington Heights, 806
Metropolitan Housing Development Corp. v. Village of Arlington Heights (Arlington Heights II), 805, 806
Metropolitan Opera Ass'n v. Wagner-Nichols Recorder Corp., 1445
Metzger v. Hochrein, 632
Michaels v. Brookchester, Inc., 112
**Michels Pipeline Construction, Inc., State v., 853**
Michigan Citizens for Water Conservation v. Nestle Waters North America Inc., 837
Middletown Trust Co. v. Gaffey, 270
Midler v. Ford Motor Co., 1462
Midrash Sephardi, Inc. v. Town of Surfside, 813, 832, 833
Miller v. City of New York, 52
Miller v. Clary, 562
Miller v. Cundiff, 93
Miller v. Kirkpatrick, 406
Miller v. McCamish, 1003
Miller v. Rau, 967
Miller v. Reed, 815, 830
Miller v. Schoene, 724
Miller v. Whitworth, 115
Milliken v. Jacono, 1071, 1333
Ministers Benefit Board v. Meriden Trust Co., 270
**Minonk State Bank v. Grassman, 344**
Misco Industries, Inc. v. Board of Sedgwick County Comm'rs, 343
Mississippi Band of Choctaw Indians v. Holyfield, 1422
Missouri Pacific R. Co. v. Nebraska, 640
Missouri State Oil Co. v. Fuse, 488
Mitchell v. Castellaw, 489
Mobil Oil Corp. v. Pegasus Petroleum Corp., 1374
Mobil Oil Credit Corp. v. DST Realty, Inc., 87
Moeller v. Lien, 1141
Monge v. Maya Magazines, Inc., 1410
Monger v. Lutterloh, 183
Monnot v. Murphy, 968
**Monsanto Co., United States v., 1336, 1339**
Monterey v. Del Monte Dunes, Ltd., 699, 757, 927
Montgomery County v. Glenmont Hills Assocs., 141
Montgomery v. Columbia Knoll Condo. Council, 421
Moore v. Carlson, 1147
Moore v. Davis, 1031
Moore v. Dick, 1154, 1155
Moore v. Regents of the University of California, 23, 1464
Moorman Manufacturing Co. v. National Tank Co., 1316

Moorman v. Tower Mgt. Co., 87
Morgan Lake Co. v. New York, New Haven & Hartford R.R. Co., 562, 563
Morris v. Bacon, 1153
Morris v. Flores, 1105
Morrison v. Piper, 254, 256
Moseley v. Bishop, 525
Motel 6, Inc. v. Pfile, 491
Motschenbacher v. R.J. Reynolds Tobacco Co., 1462
Moxley v. Laramie Builders, Inc., 1314, 1315
Moylan v. Dykes, 423
MTA v. Bruken Realty Corp., 257
**Mueller v. Hoblyn, 463**
Muench v. Public Service Comm., 903
Mugler v. Kansas, 731
Muller v. Killam, 1047
Murphy v. Mercantile-Safe Deposit & Trust Co., 292
Murphy v. New Milford Zoning Comm'n, 833
Murphy v. Smallridge, 118
Musgrove v. Cordova Coal, Land & Improvement Co., 1183
Mushroom Makers, Inc. v. R.G. Barry Corp., 1374
Myer v. Myer, 371
Myers v. Bartholomew, 947
Mygatt v. Coe, 562
Myrick v. James, 440
National Ass'n of Home Builders v. Babbitt, 666
**National Audubon Society v. Superior Court**, 848, **868**
**National Basketball Ass'n & NBA Properties, Inc. v. Motorola, Inc.**, 1441
National Lead Co. v. Kanawha Block Co., 411
National Properties Corp. v. Polk County, 426, 427
National Union Bank at Dover v. Segur, 552
**Natore A. Nahrstedt v. Lakeside Village Condominium Association, 501**
Natural Prods. Co. v. Dolese & Shepard Co., 553
Navajo Circle, Inc. v. Development Concepts Corp., 1332
Neal & Co. v. United States, 165
Nectow v. Cambridge, 679, 723, 781
**Nelson v. Anderson, 1086**
**Nelson v. Johnson**, 423, 424, **430**
Nelson v. Parker, 397
Neponsit Property Owners' Ass'n v. Emigrant Indus. Sav. Bank, 539, 562, 563, 564, 591
Neptune City v. Avon-By-the-Sea, 847

**Nessralla v. Peck, 999**
Nevells v. Carter, 959
New Era Publications v. Carol Publishing Group, 1429, 1430
**New Jersey Coalition Against War in the Middle East v. J.M.B. Realty Corporation, 33**
**New Jersey, State of v. Shack, 26**
New Mexico, United States v., 845
New Orleans v. Dukes, 520
New York, City of v. Wilson & Co., 968
New York, State of v. Shore Realty Corp., 1338, 1346
Newby v. Alto Riviera Apartments, 127
**Newman v. Hinky Dinky Omaha-Lincoln, Inc.**, 159, **160**
Newton v. McKay, 986
Niagara Mohawk Power Corp. v. Chevron USA, Inc., 1336
Nichols v. City of Evansdale, 479
Nicholson v. 300 Broadway Realty Corp., 540, 562, 563, 564
NLRB v. Amax Coal Co., 1421
Nogarr, People v., 341
Nollan v. California Coastal Comm'n, 741, 758, 761
North Carolina, State of v. Hudson, 837
North Miami, City of v. Berger, 1354
Northeastern Pharmaceutical & Chemical Co., Inc., United States v., 1346
Northern Indiana Public Service Co. v. W.J. & M.S. Vesey, 617
**Northwest Realty Co. v. Jacobs, 381**
Norton v. Burleaud, 1312, 1314, 1318
Norville v. Carr-Gottstein Foods Co., 166
Norwest Bank Hastings Nat'l Ass'n v. Franzmeier, 1147
Nutter v. Stockton, 278
**O'Brien v. O'Brien, 355**
O'Connor v. Village Green Owners Ass'n, 521
**O'Donovan v. McIntosh v. Huggins, 437**
O'Mara v. Town of Wappinger, 1206
O'Neil v. Picillo, 1336
**O'Neil's Will, In re, 981**
O'Neill v. Williams, 441
Obergefell v. Hodges, 140, 304, 372
Old Port Cove Holdings, Inc. v. Old Port Cove Condominium Ass'n One, Inc., 299
Old Town Development Company v. Langford, 99
Oliver v. Hewitt, 553
Olsen v. Country Club Sports, Inc., 177

## Table of Cases

Olwell v. Clark, Utah, 325
Oney v. West Buena Vista Land Co., 421
Open Door Alcoholism Program, Inc. v. Board of Adjustment, 515
Oracle Am., Inc. v. Google Inc., 1410
**Orange and Rockland Utilities, Inc. v. Philwold Estates, Inc., 579**
Oregon v. Hay, 847
Orr v. Orr, 350
Osborne v. Talbot, 573
Otero v. New York City Housing Auth., 132
Overheiser v. Lackey, 316
Owens v. Holzheid, 492
Owl Drug Co., In re, 50
Owsley v. Robinson, 406
**Packman v. Chicago Tribune Co. and Front Page News, Inc., 1380**
Padayachi v. IndyMac Bank, 1142
**Palazzolo v. Rhode Island**, 608, **738**, 754, **908**
Pallas v. Black, 1117
Palm Beach Isles Assoc. v. United States, 845
Palmer v. Thompson, 782
Palmore v. Sidoti, 789
Pamerqua Realty Corp., 1086
Pandol & Sons v. Agricultural Labor Relations Board, 32
Pantry, Inc. v. Mosley, 166
Papadopoulos v. Target Corp., 1158
Pappenheim v. Metropolitan El. Ry. Co., 617
Paradise, United States v., 133, 134
Parameswaran, In re, 304
Parent Ass'n of Andrew Jackson High School v. Ambach, 134, 136
Partridge v. Berliner, 340, 341
Pasquince v. Brighton Arms Apartments, 141
Patsy's Italian Rest., Inc. v. Banas, 1403
Patterson v. Sharek, 407
**Pavlik v. Consolidation Coal Co., 459**
Payne v. Clark, 1285
Payne v. Palisades Interstate Park Commission, 256
Payton v. Abbott Labs, 1158
Payton v. New York, 657
Pearl Brewing Co. v. McNaboe, 1008
Pedro v. January, 274
Peele v. Wilson Co. Bd. of Educ., 290
Peeples v. Port of Bellingham, 945
Pendergrass v. Fagan, 117
**Penn Central Transportation Co. v. City of New York**, 702, **719**, 731, 732, 738, 747

Pennsylvania Bank & Trust Co. v. Thompson, 314
**Pennsylvania Coal Co. v. Mahon**, 711, **715**, 723, 724, 728, 731, 739
People's Trust & Savings Bank v. Haas, 339
Perdue v. Gargano, 1163
Perfect Fit Indus., Inc. v. Acme Quilting Co., Inc., 1400
Perkins v. Langdon, 183
Peters v. Narick, 350
**Peterson v. Superior Court of Riverside County, 102**
Pettus v. Keeling, 421
Phelps Dodge Corp. v. Arizona Dep't of Water Resources, 840
Philadelphia Elec. Co. v. Hercules, Inc., 912
Philadelphia Steel Abrasive Co. v. Louis J. Gedicke Sons, 493
Philbin v. Carr, 954
Phillips Petroleum Co. v. Mississippi, 846
Phillips v. Bacon, 1301
Phoenix, City of v. Johnson, 626
Picardi v. Zimmiond, 403, 404, 406
Pierson v. Post, 865
Pinewood Estates of Michigan v. Barnegat Township Leveling Board, 709
Pioneer Mill Co., Inc. v. Dow, 947
Pioneer Trust & Savings Bank v. Mount Prospect, 764
Pirone v. MacMillan, Inc., 1461
Pittsburgh Cellular Telephone Co. v. Board of Supervisors, 694
Plaza Dev. Co. v. W. Cooper Enters., LLC, 158
Plyler v. Doe, 787
Plymouth Coal Co. v. Pennsylvania, 716
Pokorny v. Salas, 423
Polaroid Corp. v. Polarad Elecs. Corp., 1374
Poletown Neighborhood Council v. Detroit, 643, 659
Polisiuk v. Mayers, 1295
Pollard v. Saxe & Yolles Dev. Co., 76
Pollock v. Morelli, 60
Popov v. Hayashi, 865
Port of Longview v. Int'l Raw Materials, Ltd., 118
Posadas de Puerto Rico Assoc. v. Tourism Company of Puerto Rico, 1402
Post v. Campau, 1082
Potter v. Garrett, 332
Potts v. Garionis, 1052
Powell v. Dayton, S. & G.R.R. Co., 1282
**Powell v. Schultz, 1019**
Powers v. Wilkinson, 1159

TABLE OF CASES     xliii

**Prah v. Maretti., 629**
Preciado v. Wilde, 947
Presbytery of Southeast Iowa v. Harris, 232
Price v. Eastham, 404
Price v. Hal Roach Studios, Inc., 1454
Price, United States v., 1346
Procter v. Foxmeyer Drug Co., 298
**Producers Lumber & Supply Co. v. Olney Bldg. Co., 1011**
Producers Oil Co. v. Gore, 289
Pro-Football, Inc. v. Harjo, 1399
Progress Development Corp. v. Mitchell, 783
Properties, LP v. Barr, 405
Providence, City of v. Comstock, 914
Prudential Stewart Realty v. Sonnenfeldt, 1056
PruneYard Shopping Center v. Robins, 704, 766, 768
Public Access Shoreline Hawai'i v. Hawai'i County Planning Comm'n, 847
Publicker Chemical Corp. v. Belcher Oil Co., 170
Pugh v. Holmes, 86, 96, 97
Pumpelly v. Green Bay Company, 703, 710
Purdy v. Zaver, 493
Pure Oil Co. v. Kindall, 394
Pyle v. Gilbert, 837, 849
Quadro Stations Inc. v. Gilley, 553, 558, 559
Quinn v. Quinn, 1001
Ragland v. Kelner, 1045, 1047
Ragona v. Di Maggio, 479
**Raintree of Albemarle Homeowners Ass'n, Inc. v. Jones, 603**
Raleigh Assoc. v. Henry, 1079
Ramapo Mfg. Co. v. Mapes, 967
**Ramsey v. Arizona Title Ins. & Trust Co., 1028**
Rands, United States v., 845
Raney v. Tompkins, 553
Rankin v. FPL Energy, LLC, 609
Ransom v. Bebernitz, 241
Rapanos v. United States, 894
Rappaport v. Nichols, 111
**Ray v. Beacon Hudson Mountain Corp., 964**
Recalde v. Bae Cleaners, Inc., 138
Redarowicz v. Ohlendorf, 1312, 1313
Reddy Communications, Inc. v. Environmental Action Foundation, 1402
Redevelopment Agency of Chula Vista v. Rados Bros., 653
Reed v. Elmore, 546
**Reed v. King**, 1071, **1318**
Reed v. Reed, 350
Regan v. Lanze, 1085

Regents v. Bakke, 134
Reichert v. Pure Oil Co., 1115
**Reid v. Mutual of Omaha Insurance Co., 78, 171**
**Religious Technology Center v. Lerma, 1424, 1429**
Renee Cleaners Inc. v. Good Deal Supermarkets of N.J., 552
Rennert v. Shirk, 956
Reno v. Matley, 525
Reste Realty Corp. v. Cooper, 31, 59, 60, 66
Reuter v. Department of Natural Resources, 903
Rhodes v. Palmetto Pathway Homes, Inc., 512
Rice v. Six Flags Over Georgia, LLC, 115
Rich v. Schwab, 118
Richards Asphalt Co. v. Bunge Corp., 467
Richards v. Powercraft Homes, Inc., 1315, 1317
Richmond, City of v. United States, 783
Riddle v. Harmon, 346, 348
Ridge Chevrolet-Oldsmobile, Inc. v. Scarano, 1117
Ridgeway v. Ridgeway, 367
Rindge Co. v. Los Angeles, 641
Ring v. Mpath Interactive, Inc., 168
River Park v. City of Highland Park, 831, 832
Rivera v. Selfon Home Repairs and Improvements Co., 96, 97
Riverside Bayview Homes, Inc., United States v., 666, 894
Riverton Community Assn. v. Myers, 592
Rizzo v. Landmark Realty Corp., 1296
Roaring Fork Club, L.P. v. St. Jude's Co., 415, 416, 417
Roberts v. Roberts, Utah, 325
Robins v. PruneYard Shopping Ctr., 41
Robinson v. Ariyoshi, 880
Robinson v. Grossman, 1071
Robinson v. Jiffy Executive Limousine Co., 492
Roby v. Newton, 277
Rockafellor v. Gray, 1186
Rock-Koshkonong Lake District v. State Department of Natural Resources, 927
Rodgers v. Wright, 1369
Roe, Matter of, 257
Rogers v. Hall, 182
Rogers v. State Roads Comm., 570, 572
Roscoe-Gill v. Newman, 1105
Rosenberg v. Rosenberg, 366

## Table of Cases

**Rosengrant v. Rosengrant**, 1043, 1048
Ross v. Ponemon, 298
Routledge v. Routledge, 187
Rowe v. Great Atlantic & Pacific Tea Co., Inc., 159
Rowe v. Town of North Hampton, 907
Rowell v. Gulf, M. & O. R.R., 389
**RTS Landfill, Inc. v. Appalachian Waste Systems, LLC**, 283
Ruby Co., United States v., 970
Rudman v. Cowles Communications, 258
Rudolph v. First Southern Federal Sav. & Loan Assoc., 1332
Runyon v. Paley, 526, 542
**Runyon v. Warren and Claire Paley Midgett Realty**, 536
**Ruud v. Larson**, 184
Ryan v. Volpone Stamp Co., 1461
Ryan v. Ward, 292
S.P. Growers Ass'n v. Rodriguez, 118
**S.S. Weems v. Frost National Bank of San Antonio**, 317
**Sabo v. Horvath**, 1228
Saelzler v. Advanced Group 400, 116
Salinger v. Random House, Inc., 1430
Salvation Army v. Department of Community Affairs, 815
Sam Andrews' Sons v. Agricultural Labor Relations Board, 32
San Antonio Independent School District v. Rodriguez, 781, 798
San Antonio, City of v. El Dorado Amusement Co., 754
San Carlos Apache Tribe v. Superior Court, 847
Sanborn, In re, 879
Sanders v. Lutz, 423
Sandy Island Corp. v. Ragsdale, 437
Santa Teresa Citizen Action Group v. City of San Jose, 848
Sargent v. Ross, 97
Savings Bank v. Raphael, 420
Scanlon, People v., 360
Scanvec Amiable Ltd. v. Chang, 1369
Schad v. Borough of Mount Ephraim, 821, 822
Schadewald v. Brule, 412
Scheftel's, Matter of, 1297
Scherman v. Stern, 559
Schlagel v. Lombardi, 939
Schmid, State v., 33, 36, 40
Schmutzer v. Smith, 421
Schnakenberg v. Gibraltar Savings and Loan Ass'n, 1220
Schneider v. Mobile County, 389
Schneiker v. Gordon, 175
School Board of Nassau County v. Arline, 796
Schumacher v. Truman, 1226

Schwinn Bicycle Co. v. Ross Bicycles, Inc., 1400
Scott v. Staggs, 327
Scott v. Strickland, 1313
Scott, United States v., 513, 514
Scully v. Fitzgerald, 114
Seesholts v. Beers, 327, 329
Seidner, Inc. v. Ralston Purina Co., 911
Sellers v. Greer, 1108
Severns v. Union Pac. R.R., 232
Shack, State v., 1359
Shalimar Dev., Inc. v. FDIC, 1055
Shantee Point, Inc., In re Appeals of, 403
Sheets v. Dillon, 538
Sheffield v. Hogg, 987
Sheldon v. Metro-Goldwyn Pictures Corp., 1408, 1414
Shell Oil Co. v. Revere, 520
Shelley v. Kraemer, 506
Sherbert v. Verner, 810, 822, 824, 825
Sherrill v. Connor, 267
Shively v. Bowlby, 844, 882, 913
Shively v. Shively, 1460
Shokal v. Dunn, 841
Shroyer v. Shroyer, 1036, 1037
Sierad v. Lilly, 59
Sigmund v. Starwood Urban Retail VI, LLC, 115
Sikora v. Wenzel, 114
Silacci v. Abramson, 974
Siller v. Hartz Mountain Associates, 521
**Silverman v. CBS, Inc.**, 1392
**Simmons v. Simmons**, 360
Simon v. Solomon, 86
Simons, People v., 305
Simpson v. Kistler Investment Co., 397
Singleterry v. City of Albuquerque, 513
**Sipriano v. Great Spring Waters of America, Inc.**, 859
Sisk v. Caswell, 1190
Skally v. Shute, 56
Skansi v. Novak, 945
**Skelly Oil Co. v. Ashmore**, 1286, 1300
Skvarla v. Park, 447
Sloan v. Sarah Rhodes, LLC, 401, 403
Slocum v. Leffler, 1299
Smerchek v. Hamilton, 299
Smith v. Dixon, 1095
Smith v. Fair Employment & Hous. Comm'n, 140
Smith v. Farmers' State Bank, 1111
Smith v. Furbish, 434
Smith v. Hardware Dealers Mut. Fire Ins. Co., 1300

Smith v. Huston, 401
Smith v. Lagow Const. & Dev. Co., 114, 115
**Smith v. McEnany, 55**, 58
Smith v. Minich, 277
Smith v. Muellner, 446, 449
Smith v. Town of Clarkton, 133
Smith v. Whitener, 154
Smyczynski v. Goeseke, 1055
Smyles v. Hastings, 472
Snell's Estate, Matter of, 316
Snortland v. Larson, 159
Snyder v. ICI Explosives USA, Inc., 1103
Society of Jesus of New England v. Boston Landmarks Comm'n, 816
Soderberg v. Holt, 1186
Soens v. City of Racine, 904
Solid Waste Agency of Northern Cook County v. U.S. Army Corps of Engineers, 894
Solomon v. Solomon, 1460
Sommer v. Kridel, 175
Sony Corp. of America v. Universal City Studios, Inc., 1432
Soufal v. Griffith, 1147
South Shore Bank v. Stewart Title Guar. Co., 1262
Southern Burlington County N.A.A.C.P. v. Mount Laurel Township (Mount Laurel I), 801
Southern Burlington County N.A.A.C.P. v. Mount Laurel Township (Mount Laurel II), 801
Southern Cal. Hous. Rights Ctr. v. Krug, 138
Southwest Florida Water Management Dist. v. Charlotte County, 838
Speedee Mart, Inc. v. Stovall, 179
Spence v. Wells Fargo Bank, N.A., 1142
Sperling v. Title Guar. & Trust Co., 1079
Spherex, Inc. v. Alexander Grant & Co., 1313
Spiegel v. Ferraro, 470, 471, 472
**Spur Industries, Inc. v. Del E. Webb Development Co., 620**
St. James Village, Inc. v. Cunningham, 405
St. Johns Water Management District, 770
**St. Paul Title Insurance Corp. v. Owen, 1182**
St. Paul, City of v. St. Anthony Flats Ltd. P'ship, 1148
Stackhouse v. Cook, 1008
Stagman v. Kyhos, 421
Standard Oil Co. v. Dye, 1287
Stanton v. Stanton, 350

Stark v. American National Bank of, Beaumont, 146
Starkey Point Prop. Owners' Assn. v. Wilson, 593
**Starrett City Associates, United States v., 129**, 130
State Commission for Human Rights v. Kennelly, 121
State Dep't of Ecology v. Grimes, 840
State Dep't of Parks v. Idaho Dept. of Water Admin., 840
State Farm Fire & Cas. Co. v. Morgan, 278
State Farm Mut. Auto. Ins. Co. v. Campbell, 12
Steil v. Smith, 401, 403
Stein v. Chase Home Fin., LLC, 1145
Stephano v. News Group Publications, Inc., 1461
Stephenson v. Warner, 78
Stevens v. Rockport Granite Co., 629
Stoiber v. Honeychuck, 86
Stokely v. Conner, 330
Stokes Seeds Ltd. v. Geo. W. Park Seed Co., Inc., 1433
Stop the Beach Renourishment, Inc. v. Florida Dept. of Envtl. Prot., 850, 899
Stover v. Milam, 403
Stranahan v. Fred Meyer, Inc., 40
Stratford v. Lattimer, 387
Stratton Claimants v. Morris Claimants, 1453
Stratton v. Mt. Hermon Boys' School, 837
Strickley v. Highland Boy Gold Mining Co., 650
Stricklin v. Meadows, 423
**Strouse v. Starbuck, 1101**
Sts. Constantine & Helen Greek Orthodox Church, Inc. v. City of New Berlin, 833
Subafilms, Ltd. v. MGM-Pathe Communications Co., 1410
Summers v. Summers, 345
Sun Oil Co. v. Trent Auto Wash, Inc., 553
Sunday Canyon Property Owners Association v. Annett, 598, 600
Sundowner, Inc. v. King, 633
Suntrust Bank v. Houghton Mifflin Co., 1436
Superior Form Builders, Inc. v. Chase Taxidermy Supply Co., 1433, 1434
Superior Glass Co. v. First Bristol County Nat'l Bank, 1001
Support Ministries for Persons with AIDS, Inc. v. Village of Waterford, 514
Svoboda v. Johnson, 974

## Table of Cases

Swanner v. Anchorage Equal Rights Comm'n, 140
Sweezey v. Neel, 405
Sycamore Realty Company v. People's Counsel of Baltimore County, 685, 686
Sylvia Landfield Trust v. City of Los Angeles, 85
**Symphony Space, Inc. v. Pergola Properties, Inc.**, 243, **247**
Szajna v. General Motors Corp., 1317
Taco Cabana International, Inc. v. Two Pesos, Inc., 1403
**Tahoe-Sierra Preservation Council, Inc. v. Tahoe Regional Planning Agency**, 744, 804
Tamburello v. Monahan, 1155
Tan v. Arnel Management Co., 115
Taylor v. Gibbs, 182
Taylor v. Rancho Santa Barbara, 117
TCPIP Holding Co., Inc. v. Haar Communications, Inc., 1400
Tenafly Eruv Ass'n v. Borough of Tenafly, 815
Tennessee Coal, Iron & R. Co. v. Gardner, 1212
Tennessee Envt'l Council v. Bright Par 3 Assoc., LP, 408
Tenn-Tex Properties v. Brownell-Electro, Inc., 61
Terlinde v. Neely, 1314
Territory v. Liliuokalani, 884
Texas Co. v. Harker, 572, 577
Texas Dep't of Hous. & Cmty. Affairs v. Inclusive Cmtys. Project, Inc., 140, 806
The Daniel Ball, 844
Thomas v. Anchorage Equal Rights Commission, 140, 814, 815
Thomas v. Review Bd. of the Ind. Employment Sec. Div., 824
Thomason v. Abbott, 983
Thompson v. E.I.G. Palace Mall, 479
Thompson v. Gould, 1282
Thompson v. Poirier, 59
Thompson v. Schlittenhart, 950
Thomson, Estate of v. Wade, 397
Thornburg v. Port of Portland, 757
Thornton, State ex rel. v. Hay, 975
Thread and Gage Co., Inc. v. Kucinski, 1110
Three Sixty Five Club v. Shostak, 1226
Thrifty-Tel, Inc. v. Bezenek, 14
Thurston Enterprises, Inc. v. Baldi, 406
Tiller v. Hinton, 426, 427, 429
Tindall v. Yeats, 339, 340
**Tioga Coal Co. v. Supermarkets General Corp.**, **937**
Todd v. Stewart, 327

Topanga Ass'n for a Scenic Community v. County of Los Angeles, 694
Tosh v. Witts, 492
Townsend v. Townsend, 1453
Trade-Mark Cases, 1367, 1414
Traficante v. Pope, 545
Transportation Co. v. Chicago, 731
Traynor's Will, In re, 316
**Trentacost v. Brussel**, 97, **109**
Tristram's Landing Inc. v. Wait, 1072
Trustees of Schools of Tp. No. 1 v. Batdorf, 232
Tuccillo v. Geisha NYC, LLC, 1400
Tucker v. Marcus, 6
Tucker v. Pulaski Federal Savings & Loan Association, 300
Tulare Irrigation Dist. v. Lindsay-Strathmore Irrigation Dist., 842
Tulare Lake Basin Water Storage Dist. v. United States, 844
Turner v. Glenn, 546
Turner v. Rust, 983
Turner v. United Cerebral Palsy Ass'n, 513
Turrentine v. Thompson, 982
Twin County Recycling Corp. v. Yevoli, 694
Two Pesos, Inc. v. Taco Cabana, Inc., 1375
Tyus v. Resta, 1330
U.S. Bank Nat'l Ass'n v. Ibanez, 1153
U.S. EPA, Sustainable Reuse of Brownfields: Resources for Communities, EPA, 1356
Uhlaender v. Henricksen, 1451, 1462
Ulan v. Vend-A-Coin, 52
Union Sq. Park Community Coalition, Inc. v. New York City Dept. of Parks & Recreation, 52
United Bhd. of Carpenters v. NLRB, 40
United Public Workers v. Mitchell, 28
United States National Bank of Oregon v. Homeland, Inc., 187
United Steelworkers v. Weber, 133, 134
**Urquhart v. Teller**, **295**
Uston v. Resorts International Hotel, Inc., 32
Utah Oil Refining Co. v. Leigh, 325
Vaerst v. Tanzman, 104
Van Antwerp v. Horan, 339, 340
**Van Sicklen v. Browne**, **691**
Van Sloun v. Agans Bros., 159
Van Valkenburgh v. Lutz, 967, 968
Vandeleigh Indus., LLC v. Storage Partners of Kirkwood, LLC, 449
Vandergrift v. Buckley, 327, 329, 330
Vandiver v. Hardin County Bd. of Educ., 815
Varner v. Rice, 983

Vasichek v. Thorsen, 1004
Veal, In re, 1142
Veitch v. Woodward Iron Co., 1213
Vezey v. Green, 972
Video Views, Inc. v. Studio 21 Ltd., 1433
Village Gate Homeowners Ass'n v. Hales, 604
Villas at Parkside Partners v. City of Farmers Branch, 138
Virgin Enterprises, Ltd. v. Nawab, 1400
Vlachos v. Witherow, 938
**Voorheesville Rod and Gun Club v. E. W. Tompkins Company, 1083**, 1084
Vought v. Stucker Mesa Domestic Pipeline Co., 840
**Wade v. Jobe, 77**
Waggoner v. Edwards, 146
Wainwright Sec.'s, Inc. v. Wall St. Transcript Corp., 1409
Waits v. Frito-Lay Inc., 1462
Walcek v. United States, 754
Walker v. Boozer, 406
**Walker v. Ireton**, 990, **992**
Walling v. Przybylo, 934
Walls, In re, 304
Wally v. Lehr, 315
Walnut Valley State Bank v. Stovall, 344
Walsh v. Young, 58
Walt Disney Co. v. Powell, 1433
Waltimyer v. Smith, 973
Walton County v. Stop the Beach Renourishment, Inc., 755, 849
Walton v. Piqua State Bank, 343
**Ward v. Slavecek, 489**
Warmack v. Merchants Nat'l Bk., Ft. Smith, 162
Warner Bros., Inc. v. American Broadcasting Cos., 1374
Warner Valley Stock Co. v. Lynch, 840
Warren v. Hoch, 1295
Warren, Town of v. Thornton-Whitehouse, 914
Warstler v. Cibrian, 1105
Warth v. Seldin, 782
Washington Metro. Area Transit Auth. v. Georgetown Univ., 401
Washington v. Davis, 782, 783, 784
Wasserburger v. Coffee, 842
Wastvedt v. State, 185
Water Pik, Inc. v. Med-Systems, Inc., 1399
**Water Use Permit Applications, In the Matter of, 848, 876**
Watkins v. Wyatt, 1453
Watson v. Wolff-Goldman Realty Co., 274

**Wayne, County of v. Hathcock, 642**, 653
Webb v. Mullins, 988
Webb's Fabulous Pharmacies, Inc. v. Beckwith, 736
Weber v. Texas Co., 289, 294
Weida v. Ferry, 912
Weinberg v. Brother, 1154
Weinstein v. Griffin, 183
Welbon v. Webster, 1148
Welborn v. Henry, 319
Welk v. GMAC Mortg., LLC, 1145
Wellenkamp v. Bank of America, 300
Welsch v. Goswick, 515
Wengler v. Druggists Mutual Ins. Co., 350
**Wenner and City of Phoenix v. Dayton-Hudson Corporation, 47**
West v. Evergreen Highlands Ass'n, 596
Westbrook v. Wright, 495
Westchester, Matter of County of v. P. & M. Materials Corp., 1296
Western & Southern Life Ins. Co. v. State Bd. of Equalization, 641
**Western Land Equities, Inc. v. City of Logan, 680**
**Westmoreland Association, Inc. v. West Cutter Estates, Ltd., 589**
**Wetmore v. The Ladies of Loretto, Wheaton**, 411, **454**
Whalen v. Union Bag & Paper Co., 614, 615
Whelan Associates v. Jaslow Dental Laboratory, 1425
White Egret Condominium v. Franklin, 601
White v. Pulaski Electr. Syst., 970
**White v. Samsung Electronics America, Inc., 1456**
White v. U.S. Dep't of Hous. & Dev., 138
Whitley v. Irwin, 1300
Wicklund, State v., 40
Wiener v. Southcoast Childcare Ctrs., Inc., 115
Wildenstein & Co. v. Wallis, 251, 252, 254, 300
Wilkinson v. Wilkinson, 264
Willard v. First Church of Christ, Scientist, Pacifica, 397
**Williams v. Cole, 1035**
Williams v. Lubbering, 31
Williams, In re, 1206
Williamson County Regional Planning Comm'n v. Hamilton Bank, 699
Willow River Power Co., United States v., 845
Windemere Homeowners Association, Inc. v. McCue, 598

Windward Partners v. Delos Santos, 118
Winters v. United States, 845
Wisconsin P. & L. Co. v. Public Service Comm., 904
Wisconsin v. Yoder, 823, 825
Witter v. Taggart, 1233
Wolcott v. Winchester, 1153, 1154
Wolfe v. Hatheway, 269
Wolski v. DeLuca, 445
Wood v. Nelson, 951
Wood v. North Salt Lake, 682
Wood v. Picillo, 912
Wood v. Wood, 359
Woods v. Bivens, 947
World Exhibit Corp. v. City Bank Farmers Trust Co., 1295
Wright v. Brady, 189
Wright v. Conner, 277
Wright v. Warner Books, Inc., 1428
Wygant v. Jackson Bd. of Educ., 133
Wynton W., Commonwealth v., 1157
Wyoming Hereford Ranch v. Hammond Packing Co., 841
Wysocki v. Kugel, 968
Yakavonis v. Tilton, 333
**Yee v. City of Escondido**, **707**, 709, 747
Yick Wo v. Hopkins, 783
Young v. Newbro, 951
Yunghans v. O'Toole, 1043
Zacchini v. Scripps-Howard Broadcasting Co., 1452, 1462
Zettlemoyer v. Transcontinental Gas Pipeline Corp., 403
Zimring, State v., 879
Zito v. Gerken, 597
Zobmondo Entm't, LLC v. Falls Media, LLC, 1397
Zomisky v. Zamiska, 313, 315

UNIVERSITY CASEBOOK SERIES®

# FUNDAMENTALS OF MODERN PROPERTY LAW

**SEVENTH EDITION**

# I. INTRODUCTION

## ASSIGNMENT 1

# THE RIGHT TO EXCLUDE OTHERS FROM PRIVATE PROPERTY

### 1. INTRODUCTION

Every human society has a property system. Such a system controls the acquisition, use and distribution of valued resources. These resources may take the form of real property, tangible personal property, intangible personal property such as corporate stock, and intellectual property such as patents, trademarks or trade secrets. Often, in casual speech, we refer to a particular object as property. "Get off my property!" "This is the property that I want to sell." In law, however, the institution of property refers not to the thing that is owned, but to the legal relations among people with respect to a particular item of wealth. The proverbial single person on an island has no property in a legal sense. Only when others arrive can we meaningfully talk about property in the land or things on the island.

Many types of property systems exist. Communal or tribal systems have been used in many non-western societies. Other societies place most forms of wealth in governmental hands, as in a communist country. The United States emphasizes private ownership, although of course many resources are owned by various governments. In this course, we concentrate on the private property system.

Although our private property system is of ancient origin, modern scholars do not agree on its essential characteristics. In an earlier era, theorists tended to emphasize the unitary nature of ownership. One either owned something or did not own anything. The owner had the right to use or dispose of the thing owned, with relatively little regard for the rights of others. One who owned something owned almost all of the rights connected to that thing, and one who did not own it had almost no rights with respect to it. Currently, most theorists think of ownership of property as a "bundle of rights" or figuratively, a "bundle of sticks." One might have a right to use a thing, but not to sell, bequeath or otherwise transfer it. Alternatively, one might have a right to use or transfer land, but not to build on or otherwise develop it. Under this theory, the bundle of rights can be disaggregated into distinct rights or sticks. According to this view, it is misleading to talk of ownership of any object; one can only talk of owning a number of distinct rights with respect to that object.

Other theories of property abound. Professor Singer, for example, objects to the traditional focus on the owner's rights, which leads to a blurring or obliteration of the obligations or duties associated with ownership.[1] Professor Mossoff argues that the original conception of property or ownership as a unitary concept rather than a "bundle of rights" still has much to recommend it.[2] He contends that the owner's right to exclude others from the thing owned is "essential to the concept of property, but it is not the only characteristic, nor is it the most fundamental. Other elements of property—acquisition, use, and disposal—are necessary for a *sufficient* description of this concept."[3] In contrast, Professor Merrill takes the position that the owner's right to exclude others is the *sin qua non* of property. "Give someone the right to exclude others from a valued resource, i.e., a resource that is scarce relative to the human demand for it, and you give them property. Deny someone the exclusion right and they do not have property."[4] Professor Arnold, like Professor Mossoff, also objects to the "bundle of rights" metaphor.[5] According to Arnold, the bundle of rights metaphor wrongly directs attention away from the characteristics of the thing owned (whether tangible or intangible). It obscures the duty of stewardship of earth's natural resources, as well as having other disadvantages. Arnold prefers the metaphor of a "web of interests" to that of the "bundle of sticks."

The theories summarized in the previous paragraph represent only a sample of modern thinking on the nature of property. As you proceed through the course, consider how these theories and others to which you will be exposed suggest answers to the questions posed.

All theories of property recognize that the right to exclude others is an important attribute of property. Yet this right, like most rights, is not absolute. In the Principal Problem that follows, consider when and how the right to exclude admits of exceptions.

## 2. Principal Problem

Amanda owns a women's fashion accessories boutique on a fashionable street. Next door, Carl owns a similar store for men. Due to the vagaries of parking availability, Amanda frequently parks her expensive car in front of Carl's store. Just as frequently, Carl parks his car in front of Amanda's store. When there are no customers in his store,

---

[1] See Jane B. Baron, Review Essay, The Expressive Transparency of Property, 102 Colum. L. Rev. 208 (2002) discussing Joseph William Singer, The Edges of the Field: Lessons on the Obligations of Ownership (2000), and Joseph William Singer, Entitlement: The Paradoxes of Property (2000).

[2] Adam Mossoff, What Is Property? Putting the Pieces Back Together, 45 Ariz. L. Rev. 371 (2003).

[3] Id. at 376.

[4] Thomas W. Merrill, Property and the Right to Exclude, 77 Neb. L. Rev. 730 (1998).

[5] Craig Anthony (Tony) Arnold, The Reconstitution of Property: Property as a Web of Interests, 26 Harv. Env. L. Rev. 281 (2002).

Carl often stands in front of the store to get some fresh air and a change of scenery. When Carl's car is parked in front of his store, he usually leans on it when he is standing outside. When Amanda's car is parked in front of Carl's store, Carl also leans on that car. Carl has never scratched or otherwise damaged Amanda's car, and there is no reason to believe that he will do so in the future. Amanda is proud of her car, and resents Carl's use of her car as a support. She has politely asked Carl not to lean on her car, but he has ignored her requests and told her repeatedly to "chill out." The more he asks her to "chill out", the more heated she gets. She feels that Carl's conduct is disrespectful of her and of her rights as the owner of her car. Finally, exasperated beyond endurance by Carl's indifference to her wishes, she comes to you for advice.

After some discussion with Amanda, you determine that she is not interested in damages from Carl. She only wants a court order (an injunction) that will make him "stand on his own two feet and stay off my property." You, of course, are unwilling to commence legal proceedings unless you believe there is a reasonable chance of success.

Before reading the materials that follow, articulate your reaction to Amanda's complaint. After studying the remaining materials in this Assignment, state your conclusions concerning Amanda's cause of action.

## 3. Materials for Solution of Principal Problem

### Jacque v. Steenberg Homes, Inc.

Supreme Court of Wisconsin, 1997.
563 N.W.2d 154.

■ BABLITCH, J.

Steenberg Homes had a mobile home to deliver. Unfortunately for Harvey and Lois Jacque (the Jacques), the easiest route of delivery was across their land. Despite adamant protests by the Jacques, Steenberg plowed a path through the Jacques' snow-covered field and via that path, delivered the mobile home. Consequently, the Jacques sued Steenberg Homes for intentional trespass. At trial, Steenberg Homes conceded the intentional trespass, but argued that no compensatory damages had been proved, and that punitive damages could not be awarded without compensatory damages. Although the jury awarded the Jacques $1 in nominal damages and $100,000 in punitive damages, the circuit court set aside the jury's award of $100,000. The court of appeals affirmed, reluctantly concluding that it could not reinstate the punitive damages because it was bound by precedent establishing that an award of nominal damages will not sustain a punitive damage award. We conclude that when nominal damages are awarded for an intentional trespass to land, punitive damages may, in the discretion of the jury, be awarded. We further conclude that the $100,000 awarded by the jury is not excessive.

Accordingly, we reverse and remand for reinstatement of the punitive damage award.

I.

Plaintiffs, Lois and Harvey Jacque, are an elderly couple, now retired from farming, who own roughly 170 acres near Wilke's Lake in the town of Schleswig. The defendant, Steenberg Homes, Inc. (Steenberg), is in the business of selling mobile homes. In the fall of 1993, a neighbor of the Jacques purchased a mobile home from Steenberg. Delivery of the mobile home was included in the sales price.

Steenberg determined that the easiest route to deliver the mobile home was across the Jacques' land. Steenberg preferred transporting the home across the Jacques' land because the only alternative was a private road which was covered in up to seven feet of snow and contained a sharp curve which would require sets of "rollers" to be used when maneuvering the home around the curve.

Steenberg asked the Jacques on several separate occasions whether it could move the home across the Jacques' farm field. The Jacques refused. The Jacques were sensitive about allowing others on their land because they had lost property valued at over $10,000 to other neighbors in an adverse possession action in the mid-1980s. Despite repeated refusals from the Jacques, Steenberg decided to sell the mobile home, which was to be used as a summer cottage, and delivered it on February 15, 1994.

On the morning of delivery, Mr. Jacque observed the mobile home parked on the corner of the town road adjacent to his property. He decided to find out where the movers planned to take the home. The movers, who were Steenberg employees, showed Mr. Jacque the path they planned to take with the mobile home to reach the neighbor's lot. The path cut across the Jacques' land. Mr. Jacque informed the movers that it was the Jacques' land they were planning to cross and that Steenberg did not have permission to cross their land. He told them that Steenberg had been refused permission to cross the Jacques' land.

One of Steenberg's employees called the assistant manager, who then came out to the Jacques' home. In the meantime, the Jacques called and asked some of their neighbors and the town chairman to come over immediately. Once everyone was present, the Jacques showed the assistant manager an aerial map and plat book of the township to prove their ownership of the land, and reiterated their demand that the home not be moved across their land.

At that point, the assistant manager asked Mr. Jacque how much money it would take to get permission. Mr. Jacque responded that it was not a question of money; the Jacques just did not want Steenberg to cross their land. Mr. Jacque testified that he told Steenberg to "Follow the road, that is what the road is for." Steenberg employees left the meeting without permission to cross the land.

At trial, one of Steenberg's employees testified that, upon coming out of the Jacques' home, the assistant manager stated: "I don't give a _____ what Mr. Jacque said, just get the home in there any way you can." The other Steenberg employee confirmed this testimony and further testified that the assistant manager told him to park the company truck in such a way that no one could get down the town road to see the route the employees were taking with the home. The assistant manager denied giving these instructions, and Steenberg argued that the road was blocked for safety reasons.

The employees, after beginning down the private road, ultimately used a "bobcat" to cut a path through the Jacques' snow-covered field and hauled the home across the Jacques' land to the neighbor's lot. One employee testified that upon returning to the office and informing the assistant manager that they had gone across the field, the assistant manager reacted by giggling and laughing. The other employee confirmed this testimony. The assistant manager disputed this testimony.

When a neighbor informed the Jacques that Steenberg had, in fact, moved the mobile home across the Jacques' land, Mr. Jacque called the Manitowoc County Sheriff's Department. After interviewing the parties and observing the scene, an officer from the sheriff's department issued a $30 citation to Steenberg's assistant manager.

The Jacques commenced an intentional tort action in Manitowoc County Circuit Court, Judge Allan J. Deehr presiding, seeking compensatory and punitive damages from Steenberg. The case was tried before a jury. At the completion of the Jacques' case, Steenberg moved for a directed verdict. For purposes of the motion, Steenberg admitted to an intentional trespass to land, but asked the circuit court to find that the Jacques were not entitled to compensatory damages or punitive damages based on insufficiency of the evidence. The circuit court denied Steenberg's motion and the questions of punitive and compensatory damages were submitted to the jury. The jury awarded the Jacques $1 nominal damages and $100,000 punitive damages. Steenberg filed post-verdict motions claiming that the punitive damage award must be set aside because Wisconsin law did not allow a punitive damage award unless the jury also awarded compensatory damages. Alternatively, Steenberg asked the circuit court to remit the punitive damage award. The circuit court granted Steenberg's motion to set aside the award. Consequently, it did not reach Steenberg's motion for remittitur.

This case presents three issues: (1) whether an award of nominal damages for intentional trespass to land may support a punitive damage award and, if so; (2) whether the law should apply to Steenberg or should only be applied prospectively and, if we apply the law to Steenberg; (3) whether the $100,000 in punitive damages awarded by the jury is excessive. . . .

## II.

Steenberg argues that, as a matter of law, punitive damages could not be awarded by the jury because punitive damages must be supported by an award of compensatory damages and here the jury awarded only nominal and punitive damages. The Jacques contend that the rationale supporting the compensatory damage award requirement is inapposite when the wrongful act is an intentional trespass to land. We agree with the Jacques.

Our analysis begins with a statement of the rule and the rationale supporting the rule. First, we consider the individual and societal interests implicated when an intentional trespass to land occurs. Then, we analyze the rationale supporting the rule in light of these interests.

The general rule was stated in Barnard v. Cohen, 165 Wis. 417, 162 N.W. 480 (1917), where the question presented was: "In an action for libel, can there be a recovery of punitory damages if only nominal compensatory damages are found?" With the bare assertion that authority and better reason supported its conclusion, the Barnard court said no. Barnard continues to state the general rule of punitive damages in Wisconsin. See Tucker v. Marcus, 142 Wis. 2d 425, 438–40, 418 N.W.2d 818 (1988). The rationale for the compensatory damage requirement is that if the individual cannot show actual harm, he or she has but a nominal interest, hence, society has little interest in having the unlawful, but otherwise harmless, conduct deterred, therefore, punitive damages are inappropriate.

However, whether nominal damages can support a punitive damage award in the case of an intentional trespass to land has never been squarely addressed by this court. Nonetheless, Wisconsin law is not without reference to this situation. In 1854, the court established punitive damages, allowing the assessment of "damages as a punishment to the defendant for the purpose of making an example." McWilliams v. Bragg, 3 Wis. 424, 425 (1854). The McWilliams court related the facts and an illustrative tale from the English case of Merest v. Harvey, 128 Eng. Rep. 761 (C.P. 1814), to explain the rationale underlying punitive damages.

In *Merest*, a landowner was shooting birds in his field when he was approached by the local magistrate who wanted to hunt with him. Although the landowner refused, the magistrate proceeded to hunt. When the landowner continued to object, the magistrate threatened to have him jailed and dared him to file suit. Although little actual harm had been caused, the English court upheld damages of 500 pounds, explaining "in a case where a man disregards every principle which actuates the conduct of gentlemen, what is to restrain him except large damages?" McWilliams, 3 Wis. 424 at 428.

To explain the need for punitive damages, even where actual harm is slight, *McWilliams* related the hypothetical tale from *Merest* of an intentional trespasser:

> Suppose a gentleman has a paved walk in his paddock, before his window, and that a man intrudes and walks up and down before the window of his house, and looks in while the owner is at dinner, is the trespasser permitted to say "here is a halfpenny for you which is the full extent of the mischief I have done." Would that be a compensation? I cannot say that it would be....

McWilliams, 3 Wis. at 380–81. Thus, in the case establishing punitive damages in this state, this court recognized that in certain situations of trespass, the actual harm is not in the damage done to the land, which may be minimal, but in the loss of the individual's right to exclude others from his or her property and, the court implied that this right may be punished by a large damage award despite the lack of measurable harm.

Steenberg contends that the rule established in Barnard prohibits a punitive damage award, as a matter of law, unless the plaintiff also receives compensatory damages. Because the Jacques did not receive a compensatory damage award, Steenberg contends that the punitive damage award must be set aside. The Jacques argue that the rationale for not allowing nominal damages to support a punitive damage award is inapposite when the wrongful act involved is an intentional trespass to land. The Jacques argue that both the individual and society have significant interests in deterring intentional trespass to land, regardless of the lack of measurable harm that results. We agree with the Jacques. An examination of the individual interests invaded by an intentional trespass to land, and society's interests in preventing intentional trespass to land, leads us to the conclusion that the Barnard rule should not apply when the tort supporting the award is intentional trespass to land.

We turn first to the individual landowner's interest in protecting his or her land from trespass. The United States Supreme Court has recognized that the private landowner's right to exclude others from his or her land is "one of the most essential sticks in the bundle of rights that are commonly characterized as property." Dolan v. City of Tigard, 512 U.S. 374, 384, 129 L. Ed. 2d 304, 114 S. Ct. 2309 (1994); (quoting Kaiser Aetna v. United States, 444 U.S. 164, 176, 62 L. Ed. 2d 332, 100 S. Ct. 383 (1979)). This court has long recognized "every person['s] constitutional right to the exclusive enjoyment of his own property for any purpose which does not invade the rights of another person." Diana Shooting Club v. Lamoreaux, 114 Wis. 44, 59, 89 N.W. 880 (1902) (holding that the victim of an intentional trespass should have been allowed to take judgment for nominal damages and costs). Thus, both this court and the Supreme Court recognize the individual's legal right to exclude others from private property.

Yet a right is hollow if the legal system provides insufficient means to protect it. Felix Cohen offers the following analysis summarizing the relationship between the individual and the state regarding property rights:

That is property to which the following label can be attached:

To the world:

> Keep off X unless you have my permission, which I may grant or withhold.

Signed: Private Citizen

Endorsed: The state

Felix S. Cohen, Dialogue on Private Property, IX Rutgers Law Review 357, 374 (1954). Harvey and Lois Jacque have the right to tell Steenberg Homes and any other trespasser, "No, you cannot cross our land." But that right has no practical meaning unless protected by the State. And, as this court recognized as early as 1854, a "halfpenny" award does not constitute state protection.

The nature of the nominal damage award in an intentional trespass to land case further supports an exception to Barnard. Because a legal right is involved, the law recognizes that actual harm occurs in every trespass. The action for intentional trespass to land is directed at vindication of the legal right. W. Page Keeton, Prosser and Keeton on Torts, sec. 13 (5th ed. 1984). The law infers some damage from every direct entry upon the land of another. Id. The law recognizes actual harm in every trespass to land whether or not compensatory damages are awarded. Id. Thus, in the case of intentional trespass to land, the nominal damage award represents the recognition that, although immeasurable in mere dollars, actual harm has occurred.

The potential for harm resulting from intentional trespass also supports an exception to Barnard. A series of intentional trespasses, as the Jacques had the misfortune to discover in an unrelated action, can threaten the individual's very ownership of the land. The conduct of an intentional trespasser, if repeated, might ripen into prescription or adverse possession and, as a consequence, the individual landowner can lose his or her property rights to the trespasser.

In sum, the individual has a strong interest in excluding trespassers from his or her land. Although only nominal damages were awarded to the Jacques, Steenberg's intentional trespass caused actual harm. We turn next to society's interest in protecting private property from the intentional trespasser.

Society has an interest in punishing and deterring intentional trespassers beyond that of protecting the interests of the individual landowner. Society has an interest in preserving the integrity of the legal system. Private landowners should feel confident that wrongdoers who trespass upon their land will be appropriately punished. When landowners have confidence in the legal system, they are less likely to resort to "self-help" remedies. In *McWilliams*, the court recognized the importance of "preventing the practice of dueling, [by permitting] juries to punish insult by exemplary damages." McWilliams, 3 Wis. at 381. Although dueling is rarely a modern form of self-help, one can easily imagine a frustrated landowner taking the law into his or her own hands when faced with a brazen trespasser, like Steenberg, who refuses to heed no trespass warnings.

People expect wrongdoers to be appropriately punished. Punitive damages have the effect of bringing to punishment types of conduct that, though oppressive and hurtful to the individual, almost invariably go unpunished by the public prosecutor. Kink v. Combs, 28 Wis. 2d 65, 135 N.W.2d 789 (1965). The $30 forfeiture was certainly not an appropriate punishment for Steenberg's egregious trespass in the eyes of the Jacques. It was more akin to *Merest's* "halfpenny." If punitive damages are not allowed in a situation like this, what punishment will prohibit the intentional trespass to land? Moreover, what is to stop Steenberg Homes from concluding, in the future, that delivering its mobile homes via an intentional trespass and paying the resulting Class B forfeiture, is not more profitable than obeying the law? Steenberg Homes plowed a path across the Jacques' land and dragged the mobile home across that path, in the face of the Jacques' adamant refusal. A $30 forfeiture and a $1 nominal damage award are unlikely to restrain Steenberg Homes from similar conduct in the future. An appropriate punitive damage award probably will.

In sum, as the court of appeals noted, the Barnard rule sends the wrong message to Steenberg Homes and any others who contemplate trespassing on the land of another. It implicitly tells them that they are free to go where they please, regardless of the landowner's wishes. As long as they cause no compensable harm, the only deterrent intentional trespassers face is the nominal damage award of $1, the modern equivalent of *Merest's* halfpenny, and the possibility of a Class B forfeiture under Wis. Stat. sec. 943.13. We conclude that both the private landowner and society have much more than a nominal interest in excluding others from private land. Intentional trespass to land causes actual harm to the individual, regardless of whether that harm can be measured in mere dollars. Consequently, the Barnard rationale will not support a refusal to allow punitive damages when the tort involved is an intentional trespass to land. Accordingly, assuming that the other requirements for punitive damages have been met, we hold that nominal damages may support a punitive damage award in an action for intentional trespass to land. . . .

## IV.

Finally, we consider whether the jury's $100,000 punitive damage award to the Jacques is excessive. In this case, the circuit court, finding that the issue was moot, rejected Steenberg's motion for remittitur without review. Because we conclude that the nominal damages awarded to the Jacques support the jury's punitive damage award, and because we conclude that our holding today applies to Steenberg, the issue is not moot. Therefore, we review the $100,000 award to determine whether it is clearly excessive. We conclude that it is not.

The Supreme Court has recently clarified the three factors a court must consider when determining whether a punitive damage award violates the Due Process Clause: (1) the degree of reprehensibility of the conduct; (2) the disparity between the harm or potential harm suffered by the plaintiff and the punitive damage award; and (3) the difference between this remedy and the civil or criminal penalties authorized or imposed in comparable cases. Gore, 116 S. Ct. at 1598–99, 1603.

We turn first to the reprehensibility factor. The most important indicium of the reasonableness of a punitive damage award is the degree of reprehensibility of the defendant's conduct. Punitive damages should reflect the egregiousness of the offense. Id. at 1599. In other words, some wrongs are more blameworthy than others and the punishment should fit the crime. In this case, the "crime" was Steenberg's brazen, intentional trespass on the Jacques' land.

Steenberg's intentional trespass reveals an indifference and a reckless disregard for the law, and for the rights of others. At trial, Steenberg took an arrogant stance, arguing essentially that yes, we intentionally trespassed on the Jacques' land, but we cannot be punished for that trespass because the law protects us. We reject that position. We are further troubled by Steenberg's utter disregard for the rights of the Jacques. Despite numerous unambiguous refusals by the Jacques to allow Steenberg access to their land, Steenberg delivered the mobile home across the Jacques' land.

Furthermore, . . . Steenberg Homes acted deviously. After the conversation in the Jacques' kitchen, the Jacques, their neighbors, and the town chairman were satisfied that the matter was resolved, and Steenberg would not trespass on the Jacques' land. Nevertheless, the Steenberg employees testified that as they walked out of the Jacques' home, the assistant manager told them to use any means to deliver the mobile home. This conduct is reprehensible. We conclude that the degree of reprehensibility of Steenberg's conduct supports the imposition of a substantial punitive award. . . .

Our concern for deterrence is guided by our recognition of the nature of Steenberg's business. Steenberg sells and delivers mobile homes. It is, therefore, likely that they will again be faced with what was, apparently for them, a dilemma. Should they trespass and pay the forfeiture, which in this case was $30? Or, should they take the more costly course and obey the law? Today we alleviate the uncertainty for Steenberg Homes. We feel certain that the $100,000 will serve to encourage the latter course by removing the profit from the intentional trespass.

Punitive damages, by removing the profit from illegal activity, can help to deter such conduct. In order to effectively do this, punitive damages must be in excess of the profit created by the misconduct so that the defendant recognizes a loss. It can hardly be said that the $30 forfeiture paid by Steenberg significantly affected its profit for delivery of the mobile home. One hundred thousand dollars will.

Finally, a substantial punitive damage award serves to assure that tort claims involving egregious conduct will be prosecuted. By allowing punitive damages, the self interest of the plaintiff might lead to prosecution of a claim that might not otherwise be pursued. A $100,000 punitive damage award will not only give potential trespassers reason to pause before trespassing, it will also give aggrieved landowners reason to pursue a trespass action. . . .

The punitive award neither shocks our conscience, nor takes our breath away. On the contrary, it is the brazen conduct of Steenberg Homes that we find shocking, not the $100,000 punitive damages award.

In conclusion, we hold that when nominal damages are awarded for an intentional trespass to land, punitive damages may, in the discretion of the jury, be awarded. Our decision today shall apply to Steenberg Homes. Finally, we hold that the $100,000 punitive damages awarded by the jury is not excessive.

## NOTES

1. *Why protect private property?* Jeremy Bentham (1748–1832) was an English philosopher and legal theorist. He founded the theory of utilitarianism under which legal and social institutions are to be judged by their contribution to human welfare, rather than by their logical consistency or ancient pedigree. Professor Michelman wrote the following regarding Bentham's view of property:

> Property, according to Bentham, is most aptly regarded as the collection of rules which are presently accepted as governing the exploitation and enjoyment of resources. So regarded, property becomes a "basis of expectations" founded on existing rules; that is to say, property is the institutionally established understanding that extant rules governing the relationships among men with respect to resources will continue in existence. The justification—Bentham regards it as a practical necessity—for adherence to such an understanding is that only through such adherence can we hope for a minimally acceptable level of productivity. The human motivations which result in production are, he believes, such that they will not operate in the absence of secure expectations about future enjoyment of product.[6]

---

[6] Michelman, *Property, Utility and Fairness: Comments on the Ethical Foundations of "Just Compensation" Law*, 80 Harv. L. Rev. 1165, 1211 (1967).

What does this excerpt suggest is the chief justification of private property?

2. *Another view.* Contrast with Bentham's view of property, that of Rousseau. "The first man who, having fenced off a plot of land, thought of saying 'This is mine' and found people simple enough to believe him was the real founder of civil society. How many crimes, wars, murders, how many miseries and horrors might the human race have been spared by the one who, upon pulling up the stakes or filling in the ditch, had shouted to his fellow men, 'Beware of listening to this imposter; you are lost, if you forget that the fruits of the earth belong to all and that the earth belongs to no one.'"[7]

3. *Is private property beneficial to the public, or does it merely benefit private interests?* The court stated that society has an interest in punishing and deterring intentional trespassers. Apart from society's interest in seeing that all legal rules are followed, what is society's interest in the protection of private property? Assuming that society has an interest in the protection of private property, when does society's interest conflict with the protection of private property? Apparently it was much less expensive for Steenberg Homes to trespass than to move the mobile home over the road. How can we justify a rule that requires unnecessary expenditure of valuable time and money over one that would have allowed Steenberg to trespass and then pay damages to the Jacques? Should the law not seek to prevent the waste of resources rather than require such a waste? Is this a case where the immediate short term effect of the rule against trespassing is wasteful, but the long term effect is beneficial?

4. *Some trespasses permitted.* "[T]he Second Restatement of Torts contains more than twenty sections—exceptions to the law of trespass—enumerating 'privileged' entries on land over the owner's objection. These include: entry by a remainderman to view waste or make repairs; entry to abate a private nuisance; entry by a former licensee to remove his possessions; entry by a traveler on a public highway that has become impassable to enter neighboring land to continue his journey; and entry because of private necessity [e.g., docking a boat at a private pier during a storm]."[8] Why has the common law made "exceptions" to the rule permitting a private landowner to exclude others?

5. *Punitive damages.* In State Farm Mut. Auto. Ins. Co. v. Campbell, 538 U.S. 408 (2003), the Court opined that "in practice, few awards exceeding a single-digit ratio between punitive and compensatory damages, to a significant degree, will satisfy due process." Id. at 425. It did concede, however, that "ratios greater than those we have previously upheld may comport with due process where a particularly egregious act has resulted in only a small amount of economic damages." Id. (quotation marks and

---

[7] Jean-Jacques Rousseau (1712–1778) *as quoted in* David Denby, Great Books 282 (1996).

[8] Curtis Berger, *Pruneyard Revisited: Political Activity on Private Lands*, 66 N.Y.U. L Rev. 633, 667 (1991).

citations omitted). Presumably, the punitive damages awarded in *Steenberg* would have to be upheld, if at all, under this latter standard.

## Intel Corporation v. Hamidi
### Supreme Court of California, 2003.
### 30 Cal.4th 1342.

■ WERDEGAR, J.

[H]amidi, a former Intel engineer, together with others, formed an organization named Former and Current Employees of Intel (FACE-Intel) to disseminate information and views critical of Intel's employment and personnel policies and practices. FACE-Intel maintained a Web site (which identified Hamidi as Webmaster and as the organization's spokesperson) containing such material. In addition, over a 21-month period Hamidi, on behalf of FACE-Intel, sent six mass e-mails to employee addresses on Intel's electronic mail system. The messages criticized Intel's employment practices, warned employees of the dangers those practices posed to their careers, suggested employees consider moving to other companies, solicited employees' participation in FACE-Intel, and urged employees to inform themselves further by visiting FACE-Intel's Web site. The messages stated that recipients could, by notifying the sender of their wishes, be removed from FACE-Intel's mailing list; Hamidi did not subsequently send messages to anyone who requested removal.

Each message was sent to thousands of addresses (as many as 35,000 according to FACE-Intel's Web site), though some messages were blocked by Intel before reaching employees. Intel's attempt to block internal transmission of the messages succeeded only in part; Hamidi later admitted he evaded blocking efforts by using different sending computers. When Intel, in March 1998, demanded in writing that Hamidi and FACE-Intel stop sending e-mails to Intel's computer system, Hamidi asserted the organization had a right to communicate with willing Intel employees; he sent a new mass mailing in September 1998.

The summary judgment record contains no evidence Hamidi breached Intel's computer security in order to obtain the recipient addresses for his messages; indeed, internal Intel memoranda show the company's management concluded no security breach had occurred. Hamidi stated he created the recipient address list using an Intel directory on a floppy disk anonymously sent to him. Nor is there any evidence that the receipt or internal distribution of Hamidi's electronic messages damaged Intel's computer system or slowed or impaired its functioning. Intel did present uncontradicted evidence, however, that many employee recipients asked a company official to stop the messages and that staff time was consumed in attempts to block further messages from FACE-Intel. According to the FACE-Intel Web site, moreover, the messages had prompted discussions between "[e]xcited and nervous managers" and the company's human resources department.

Intel sued Hamidi and FACE-Intel, pleading a cause of action for trespass to chattels and seeking an injunction against further e-mail messages. The trial court granted Intel's motion for summary judgment, permanently enjoining Hamidi, FACE-Intel, and their agents "from sending unsolicited e-mail to addresses on Intel's computer systems." Hamidi appealed.

The Court of Appeal, with one justice dissenting, affirmed the grant of injunctive relief. The majority took the view that the use of or intermeddling with another's personal property is actionable as a trespass to chattels without proof of any actual injury to the personal property; even if Intel could not show any damages resulting from Hamidi's sending of messages, "it showed he was disrupting its business by using its property and therefore is entitled to injunctive relief based on a theory of trespass to chattels." The dissenting justice warned that the majority's application of the trespass to chattels tort to "unsolicited electronic mail that causes no harm to the private computer system that receives it" would "expand the tort of trespass to chattel in untold ways and to unanticipated circumstances."

Discussion

[U]nder California law, trespass to chattels "lies where an intentional interference with the possession of personal property *has proximately caused injury.*" (*Thrifty-Tel, Inc. v. Bezenek* (1996) 46 Cal.App.4th 1559, 1566, italics added.) In cases of interference with possession of personal property not amounting to conversion, "the owner has a cause of action for trespass or case, *and may recover only the actual damages suffered by reason of the impairment of the property or the loss of its use.*" (*Zaslow v. Kroenert, supra,* 29 Cal.2d at p. 551, italics added; accord, *Jordan v. Talbot* (1961) 55 Cal.2d 597, 610). In modern American law generally, "[t]respass remains as an occasional remedy for minor interferences, *resulting in some damage,* but not sufficiently serious or sufficiently important to amount to the greater tort" of conversion. (Prosser & Keeton, Torts, *supra,* § 15, p. 90, italics added.)

The Restatement, too, makes clear that some actual injury must have occurred in order for a trespass to chattels to be actionable. Under section 218 of the Restatement Second of Torts, dispossession alone, without further damages, is actionable (see *id.,* par. (a) & com. d, pp. 420–421), but other forms of interference require some additional harm to the personal property or the possessor's interests in it. (*Id.,* pars. (b)–(d).) "The interest of a possessor of a chattel in its inviolability, unlike the similar interest of a possessor of land, is not given legal protection by an action for nominal damages for harmless intermeddlings with the chattel. In order that an actor who interferes with another's chattel may be liable, his conduct must affect some other and more important interest of the possessor. *Therefore, one who intentionally intermeddles with another's chattel is subject to liability only if his intermeddling is harmful to the possessor's materially valuable interest in the physical condition, quality, or value of the chattel, or if the possessor is deprived of the use of the chattel for a substantial time, or some other legally protected interest of the possessor is affected as stated in Clause (c).* Sufficient legal protection of the possessor's interest in the mere inviolability of his chattel is afforded by his privilege to use reasonable force to protect his possession against even harmless interference." (*Id.*, com. e, pp. 421–422, italics added.)

The Court of Appeal (quoting 7 Speiser et al., American Law of Torts (1990) Trespass, § 23:23, p. 667) referred to "a number of very early cases [showing that] any unlawful interference, however slight, with the enjoyment by another of his personal property, is a trespass." But while a harmless use or touching of personal property may be a technical trespass (see Rest.2d Torts, § 217), an interference (not amounting to dispossession) is not *actionable*, under modern California and broader American law, without a showing of harm. As already discussed, this is the rule embodied in the Restatement (Rest.2d Torts, § 218) and adopted by California law.

In this respect, as Prosser explains, modern day trespass to chattels differs both from the original English writ and from the action for trespass to land: "Another departure from the original rule of the old writ of trespass concerns the necessity of some actual damage to the chattel before the action can be maintained. Where the defendant merely interferes without doing any harm-as where, for example, he merely lays hands upon the plaintiff's horse, or sits in his car-there has been a division of opinion among the writers, and a surprising dearth of authority. *By analogy to trespass to land there might be a technical tort in such a case.... Such scanty authority as there is, however, has considered that the dignitary interest in the inviolability of chattels, unlike that as to land, is not sufficiently important to require any greater defense than the privilege of using reasonable force when necessary to protect them. Accordingly it has been held that nominal damages will not be awarded, and that in the absence of any actual damage the action will not lie.*" (Prosser & Keeton, Torts, *supra*, § 14, p. 87, italics added.)

Intel suggests that the requirement of actual harm does not apply here because it sought only injunctive relief, as protection from future injuries. But as Justice Kolkey, dissenting below, observed, "[t]he fact the relief sought is injunctive does not excuse a showing of injury, whether actual or threatened." Indeed, in order to obtain injunctive relief the plaintiff must ordinarily show that the defendant's wrongful acts threaten to cause *irreparable* injuries, ones that cannot be adequately compensated in damages. 5 Witkin, Cal. Procedure (4th ed. 1997) Pleading, § 782, p. 239. Even in an action for trespass to real property, in which damage to the property is not an element of the cause of action, "the extraordinary remedy of injunction" cannot be invoked without showing the likelihood of irreparable harm. *Mechanics' Foundry v. Ryall* (1888) 75 Cal. 601, 603; see *Mendelson v. McCabe* (1904) 144 Cal. 230, 232–233. A fortiori, to issue an injunction without a showing of likely irreparable injury in an action for trespass to chattels, in which injury to the personal property or the possessor's interest in it *is* an element of the action, would make little legal sense.

The dispositive issue in this case, therefore, is whether the undisputed facts demonstrate Hamidi's actions caused or threatened to cause damage to Intel's computer system, or injury to its rights in that personal property, such as to entitle Intel to judgment as a matter of law. . . .

Relying on a line of decisions, most from federal district courts, applying the tort of trespass to chattels to various types of unwanted electronic contact between computers, Intel contends that, while its computers were not damaged by receiving Hamidi's messages, its interest in the "physical condition, quality or value" (Rest.2d Torts, § 218, com. e, p. 422) of the computers was harmed. We disagree. The cited line of decisions does not persuade us that the mere sending of electronic communications that assertedly cause injury only because of their contents constitutes an actionable trespass to a computer system through which the messages are transmitted. Rather, the decisions finding electronic contact to be a trespass to computer systems have generally involved some actual or threatened interference with the computers' functioning.

In *Thrifty-Tel, Inc. v. Bezenek, supra,* 46 Cal.App.4th at pages 1566–1567 (*Thrifty-Tel*), the California Court of Appeal held that evidence of automated searching of a telephone carrier's system for authorization codes supported a cause of action for trespass to chattels. The defendant's automated dialing program "overburdened the [plaintiff's] system, denying some subscribers access to phone lines" (*id.* at p. 1564), showing the requisite injury.

Following *Thrifty-Tel*, a series of federal district court decisions held that sending UCE through an ISP's equipment may constitute trespass to the ISP's computer system. The lead case [is] *CompuServe Inc. v. Cyber Promotions, Inc., supra,* 962 F. Supp. 1015, 1021–1023 (*CompuServe*). . . .

In each of these spamming cases, the plaintiff showed, or was prepared to show, some interference with the efficient functioning of its computer system. In *CompuServe*, the plaintiff ISP's mail equipment monitor stated that mass UCE mailings, especially from nonexistent addresses such as those used by the defendant, placed "a tremendous burden" on the ISP's equipment, using "disk space and drain[ing] the processing power," making those resources unavailable to serve subscribers. . . .

In the decisions so far reviewed, the defendant's use of the plaintiff's computer system was held sufficient to support an action for trespass when it actually did, or threatened to, interfere with the intended functioning of the system, as by significantly reducing its available memory and processing power. In *Ticketmaster, supra*, 2000 WL 1887522, the one case where no such effect, actual or threatened, had been demonstrated, the court found insufficient evidence of harm to support a trespass action. These decisions do not persuade us to Intel's position here, for Intel has demonstrated neither any appreciable effect on the operation of its computer system from Hamidi's messages, nor any likelihood that Hamidi's actions will be replicated by others if found not to constitute a trespass....

We next consider whether California common law should be *extended* to cover, as a trespass to chattels, an otherwise harmless electronic communication whose contents are objectionable. We decline to so expand California law. Intel, of course, was not the recipient of Hamidi's messages, but rather the owner and possessor of computer servers used to relay the messages, and it bases this tort action on that ownership and possession. The property rule proposed is a rigid one, under which the sender of an electronic message would be strictly liable to the owner of equipment through which the communication passes-here, Intel-for any consequential injury flowing from the *contents* of the communication. The arguments of amici curiae and academic writers on this topic, discussed below, leave us highly doubtful whether creation of such a rigid property rule would be wise.

Writing on behalf of several industry groups appearing as amici curiae, Professor Richard A. Epstein of the University of Chicago urges us to excuse the required showing of injury to personal property in cases of unauthorized electronic contact between computers, "extending the rules of trespass to real property to all interactive Web sites and servers." The court is thus urged to recognize, for owners of a particular species of personal property, computer servers, the same interest in inviolability as is generally accorded a possessor of land. In effect, Professor Epstein suggests that a company's server should be its castle, upon which any unauthorized intrusion, however harmless, is a trespass.

Epstein's argument derives, in part, from the familiar metaphor of the Internet as a physical space, reflected in much of the language that has been used to describe it: "cyberspace," "the information superhighway," e-mail "addresses," and the like. Of course, the Internet is also frequently called simply the "Net," a term, Hamidi points out, "evoking a fisherman's chattel." A major component of the Internet is the World Wide "Web," a descriptive term suggesting neither personal nor real property, and "cyberspace" itself has come to be known by the oxymoronic phrase "virtual reality," which would suggest that any real property "located" in "cyberspace" must be "virtually real" property. Metaphor is a two-edged sword....

The plain fact is that computers, even those making up the Internet, are-like such older communications equipment as telephones and fax machines-personal property, not realty. Professor Epstein observes that "[a]lthough servers may be moved in real space, they cannot be moved in cyberspace," because an Internet server must, to be useful, be accessible at a known address. But the same is true of the telephone: to be useful for incoming communication, the telephone must remain constantly linked to the same number (or, when the number is changed, the system must include some forwarding or notification capability, a qualification that also applies to computer addresses). Does this suggest that an unwelcome message delivered through a telephone or fax machine should be viewed as a trespass to a type of real property? We think not: As already discussed, the contents of a telephone communication may cause a variety of injuries and may be the basis for a variety of tort actions (e.g., defamation, intentional infliction of emotional distress, invasion of privacy), but the injuries are not to an interest in property, much less real property, and the appropriate tort is not trespass.

[Reversed]

■ BROWN, J., Dissenting.

Candidate A finds the vehicles that candidate B has provided for his campaign workers, and A spray paints the water soluble message, "Fight corruption, vote for A" on the bumpers. The majority's reasoning would find that notwithstanding the time it takes the workers to remove the paint and the expense they incur in altering the bumpers to prevent further unwanted messages, candidate B does not deserve an injunction unless the paint is so heavy that it reduces the cars' gas mileage or otherwise depreciates the cars' market value. Furthermore, candidate B has an obligation to permit the paint's display, because the cars are driven by workers and not B personally, because B allows his workers to use the cars to pick up their lunch or retrieve their children from school, or because the bumpers display B's own slogans. I disagree....

*The Trial Court Correctly Issued the Injunction*

Intel had the right to exclude the unwanted speaker from its property, which Hamidi does not dispute; he does not argue that he has a right to force unwanted messages on Intel. The instant case thus turns on the question of whether Intel deserves a remedy for the continuing violation of its rights. I believe it does, and as numerous cases have demonstrated, an injunction to prevent a trespass to chattels is an appropriate means of enforcement.

The majority does not find that Hamidi has an affirmative right to have Intel transmit his messages, but denies Intel any remedy. Admittedly, the case would be easier if precise statutory provisions supported relief, but in the rapidly changing world of technology, in which even technologically savvy providers like America Online and CompuServe are one step behind spammers, the Legislature will likely remain three or four steps behind. In any event, the absence of a statutory remedy does not privilege Hamidi's interference with Intel's property. Nor are content-based speech torts adequate for violations of property rights unrelated to the speech's content. In any event, the possibility of another avenue for relief does not preclude an injunction for trespass to chattels.

The majority denies relief on the theory that Intel has failed to establish the requisite actual injury. As discussed, *post*, however, the injunction was properly granted because the rule requiring actual injury pertains to damages, not equitable relief, and thus courts considering comparable intrusions have provided injunctive relief without a showing of actual injury. Furthermore, there was actual injury as (1) Intel suffered economic loss; (2) it is sufficient for the injury to impair the chattel's utility to the owner rather than the chattel's market value; and (3) even in the absence of any injury to the owner's utility, it is nevertheless a trespass where one party expropriates for his own use the resources paid for by another.

*Harmless Trespasses to Chattels May Be Prevented*

Defendant Hamidi used Intel's server in violation of the latter's demand to stop. This unlawful use of Intel's system interfered with the use of the system by Intel employees. This misconduct creates a cause of action. "[I]t is a trespass to damage goods or destroy them, *to make an unpermitted use of them*, or to move them from one place to another." (Prosser & Keeton on Torts (5th ed. 1984) Trespass to Chattels, § 14, p. 85, italics added.) "[T]he unlawful taking away of another's personal property, the seizure of property upon a wrongful execution, and *the appropriation of another's property to one's own use, even for a temporary purpose*, constitute trespasses, although a mere removal of property without injuring it is not a trespass *when done by one acting rightfully*." (7 Speiser et al., American Law of Torts (1990) Trespass, § 23:23, p. 667, italics added (*Speiser*).)

Regardless of whether property is real or personal, it is beyond dispute that an individual has the right to have his personal property free from interference. There is some division among authorities regarding the available remedy, particularly whether a harmless trespass supports a claim for nominal damages. The North Carolina Court of Appeal has found there is no damage requirement for a trespass to chattel. (See *Hawkins v. Hawkins* (1991) 101 N.C.App. 529). "A trespass to goods is actionable *per se* without any proof of actual damage. Any unauthorized touching or moving of an object is actionable at the suit of the possessor of it, even though no harm ensues." (Salmond & Heuston, The Law of Torts (21st ed. 1996) Trespass to Goods, § 6.2, p. 95.) Several authorities consider a harmless trespass to goods actionable per se only if it is intentional. The Restatement Second of Torts, section 218, which is less inclined to favor liability, likewise forbids unauthorized use and recognizes the inviolability of personal property. However, the Restatement permits the owner to *prevent the injury* beforehand, or *receive compensation* afterward, but not to *profit from the trespass* through the remedy of damages unrelated to actual harm, which could result in a windfall. "The interest of a possessor of a chattel in its inviolability, unlike the similar interest of a possessor of land, is not given legal protection *by an action for nominal damages* for harmless intermeddlings with the chattel. . . . Sufficient legal protection of the possessor's interest in the mere *inviolability of his chattel* is afforded by his *privilege to use reasonable force* to protect his possession against *even harmless interference*." (Rest.2d Torts, § 218, com. e, pp. 421–422, italics added.) Accordingly, the protection of land and chattels may differ on the question of nominal damages unrelated to actual injury. The authorities agree, however, that (1) the chattel is inviolable, (2) the trespassee need not tolerate even harmless interference, and (3) the possessor may use reasonable force to prevent it. Both California law and the Restatement authorize reasonable force regardless of whether the property in question is real or personal. (Civ. Code, § 51; Rest.2d Torts, § 77.)

The law's special respect for land ownership supports liability for damages even without actual harm. (Speiser, *supra*, § 23:1, p. 592.) By contrast, one who suffers interference with a chattel may *prevent* the interference before or during the fact, *or recover actual damages* (corresponding to the harm suffered), but at least according to the Restatement, may not recover damages in excess of those suffered. But the Restatement expressly refutes defendant's assertion that only real property is inviolable. From the modest distinction holding that only victims of a trespass to land may profit in the form of damages exceeding actual harm, defendant offers the position that only trespasses to land may be *prevented*. The law is to the contrary; numerous cases have authorized injunctive relief to safeguard the inviolability of personal property. . . .

In 1996, the Appellate Division of the New York Supreme Court considered the claim of plaintiff Tillman, who sought to enjoin the unwanted delivery of a newspaper onto his property. (*Tillman, supra*, 648 N.Y.S.2d 630.) He offered no specific critique of the newspaper's content, observing only " '[t]here is no reason that we have to clean up [defendant's] mess.' " *Id.* at p. 632. Citing *Rowan, Martin,* and *Lloyd,* the court rejected the defendants' argument "that there is nothing a homeowner can do to stop the dumping on his or her property of pamphlets or newspapers, no matter how offensive they might be," and instead upheld Tillman's right to prevent the mail's delivery, regardless of whether his objection was due to the quantity (volume) or quality (content) of the messages. (*Tillman,* at p. 636.) In authorizing injunctive relief, the *Tillman* court found no need to quantify the actual damage created by the delivery; it merely noted that the homeowner should not be forced either "to allow such unwanted newspapers to accumulate, or to expend the time and energy necessary to gather and to dispose of them." (*Ibid.*) Subsequent courts have extended this policy to the delivery of e-mail as well. . . .

To the majority, Hamidi's ability to outwit Intel's cyber defenses justifies denial of Intel's claim to exclusive use of its property. Under this reasoning, it is not right but might that determines the extent of a party's possessory interest. Although the world often works this way, the legal system should not. . . .

*The unlawful use of another's property is a trespass, regardless of its effect on the property's utility to the owner*

Finally, even if Hamidi's interference did not affect the server's utility to Intel, it would still amount to a trespass. Intel has poured millions of dollars into a resource that Hamidi has now appropriated for his own use. As noted above, "the appropriation of another's property to one's own use, even for a temporary purpose, constitute[s] [a] trespass." (Speiser, *supra*, § 23:23, p. 667, fn. omitted.) The use by one party of property whose costs have been paid by another amounts to an unlawful taking of those resources-even if there is no unjust enrichment by the trespassing party.

In *Buchanan Marine Inc. v. McCormack Sand Co.* (E.D.N.Y. 1990) 743 F. Supp. 139 (*Buchanan*), the plaintiff built and maintained mooring buoys for use by its own tugboats. The defendants' barges used the buoy over the plaintiff's objection. (*Id.* at pp. 140–141.) The federal district court found such unlawful use could constitute a trespass to chattels (if the facts were proved), and thus denied the defendants' motion for summary judgment. "[D]efendants' meddling with [the buoy] is either a trespass to a chattel or perhaps a conversion for which [the plaintiff] may seek relief in the form of damages and an injunction." (*Id.* at pp. 141–142.) There was an allegation of damage (to the plaintiff's barge, not the buoy itself), which could support a claim for damages, but this was not a prerequisite for injunctive relief. Even if the defendants did not injure the buoys in any way, they still had no right to expropriate the plaintiff's property for their own advantage. . . .

The principles of both personal liberty and social utility should counsel us to usher the common law of property into the digital age.

■ MOSK, J., Dissenting.

[T]he law of trespass to chattels has not universally been limited to physical damage. I believe it is entirely consistent to apply that legal theory to these circumstances-that is, when a proprietary computer system is being used contrary to its owner's purposes and expressed desires, and self-help has been ineffective. Intel correctly expects protection from an intruder who misuses its proprietary system, its nonpublic directories, and its supposedly controlled connection to the Internet to achieve his bulk mailing objectives-incidentally, without even having to pay postage. . . .

The Restatement Second of Torts explains that a trespass to a chattel occurs if "the chattel is impaired as to its *condition, quality, or value*" or if "harm is caused to some . . . thing in which the possessor has a legally protected interest." (Rest.2d Torts, § 218, subds. (b) & (d), p. 420, italics added.) As to this tort, a current prominent treatise on the law of torts explains that "[t]he defendant may interfere with the chattel by interfering with the plaintiff's access or use" and observes that the tort has been applied so as "to protect computer systems from electronic invasions by way of unsolicited email or the like." (1 Dobbs, The Law of Torts (2001) § 60, pp. 122–123.) Moreover, "[t]he harm necessary to trigger liability for trespass to chattels can be . . . harm to something other than the chattel itself." (*Id.*, pp. 124–125.) The Restatement points out that, unlike a possessor of land, a possessor of a chattel is not given legal protection from harmless invasion, but the "actor" may be liable if the conduct affects "some other and more important *interest* of the possessor." (Rest.2d Torts, § 218, com. e, p. 421, italics added.)

The Restatement explains that the rationale for requiring harm for trespass to a chattel but not for trespass to land is the availability and effectiveness of self-help in the case of trespass to a chattel. "Sufficient legal protection of the possessor's interest in the mere inviolability of his chattel is afforded by his privilege to use reasonable force to protect his possession against even harmless interference." (Rest.2d Torts, § 218, com. e, p. 422.) Obviously, "force" is not available to prevent electronic trespasses. As shown by Intel's inability to prevent Hamidi's intrusions, self-help is not an adequate alternative to injunctive relief. . . .

As discussed above, I believe that existing legal principles are adequate to support Intel's request for injunctive relief. But even if the injunction in this case amounts to an extension of the traditional tort of trespass to chattels, this is one of those cases in which, as Justice Cardozo suggested, "[t]he creative element in the judicial process finds its opportunity and power" in the development of the law. (Cardozo, Nature of the Judicial Process (1921) p. 165.)[9]

## NOTES

1. *Reasonable force.* The majority opinion in *Hamidi* quotes the Restatement's view that "Sufficient legal protection of the possessor's interest in the mere inviolability of his chattel is afforded by his privilege to use reasonable force to protect his possession against even harmless interference." Suppose Amanda in the Principal Problem attempted to pull or push Carl off her car and Carl resisted. Apparently the Restatement is recommending such a tactic in preference to the granting of an injunction. Do you agree with the Restatement's position?

2. *Judicial disagreement.* The trial judge, two out of the three Court of Appeal judges, and three out of the seven California Supreme Court judges would have granted the injunction to Intel. Thus, six judges would have granted the injunction and only five would have denied it. Of course the four judge majority on the Supreme Court has the final say. The point here is that

---

[9] "It is revolting to have no better reason for a rule of law than that so it was laid down in the time of Henry IV." (Holmes, *The Path of the Law* (1897) 10 Harv. L. Rev. 457, 469.)

this was a very difficult case and strong arguments could be and were made on both sides.

3. *Real property versus personal property.* In *Hamidi,* the court recognized a distinction between the protection given real property and the lesser protection given personal property. What justification, if any, did the majority give for the distinction? Do you agree that a distinction should be made? In terms of requiring governments to compensate property owners when governments physically take private property, the U.S. Supreme Court has stated (nearly unanimously) that personal property rights do not deserve less protection than real property rights.[10] In the Principal Problem, if Carl had stood on Amanda's front steps *Steenberg* suggests that she could have obtained an injunction to stop his actions, even if he caused her no monetary damage. Indeed, *Steenberg* also suggests that she could have been awarded substantial damages. Does this suggest that if he leaned against her car she should also be able to get an injunction preventing him from doing so, as well as substantial damages?

4. *Why, why, why?* "The reason of the law is the life of the law, for tho' a man can tell the law, yet if he know not the reason thereof, he shall soon forget his superficial knowledge, but when he findeth the right reason of the law and so bringeth it to his nature that he comprehendeth it as his own, this will not only serve him for the understanding of that particular case but of many others." Coke's Commentary on Littleton's Tenures f. 183b (1628). To what extent do the reasons, expressed and unexpressed, behind the decisions in the two major cases help us solve the Principal Problem?

5. *Dignitary interest.* The majority opinion in *Hamidi* quotes Prosser & Keeton which refers to the "dignitary interest" of the owner in the "inviolability of chattels." One function of property is to protect or express the personhood or individuality of its owner. In an important article, Professor Radin explores this concept and argues that a distinction should be made between fungible property, like money, and property having a more direct connection to the person. This latter type of property she originally called personal property, but later preferred to call constitutive property.[11] Can the difference in result and attitude between *Steenberg* and *Hamidi* be explained by the differences in types of property or owners? Where on this continuum does Amanda's car fall? What does this suggest about how the Principal Problem should be decided?

6. *Intangible property.* Should the owners of intangible property such as copyrights, trademarks, patents and trade secrets also have a right to exclude? Can you think of any policies which would conflict with such a right in the context of intangible property?

7. *Body parts.* In Moore v. Regents of the University of California,[12] the Supreme Court of California grappled with an action by a patient against a doctor, a university and others based on the defendants' patenting of a cell

---

[10] Horne v. U.S. Dept. of Agriculture, 576 U.S. ___, 135 S.Ct. 2419 (2015).
[11] See Margaret Jane Radin, Property and Personhood, 34 Stan. L. Rev. 957 (1982); Margaret Jane Radin, Reinterpreting Property 2 (1993).
[12] 51 Cal.3d 120, 793 P.2d 479 (Cal. 1990), *cert. denied,* 499 U.S. 936 (1991).

line from the plaintiff's white blood cells. The court held that although the plaintiff had a cause of action for breach of fiduciary duty and lack of informed consent, he could not maintain an action for conversion.[13] In so holding, the court essentially rejected the argument of an ownership interest in extracorporeal body parts. Does an individual have a property interest in her body parts? Should the extracorporeal nature of the cells in *Moore* be determinative?

---

[13] "Conversion" has been defined as "the act of appropriating the property of another to one's own benefit, or to the benefit of a third person." *Black's Law Dictionary* (10th ed. 2014), *available at* Westlaw BLACKS.

# ASSIGNMENT 2

# THE RIGHT TO EXCLUDE OTHERS FROM SEMI-PRIVATE PROPERTY: FREE SPEECH RIGHTS VS. PROPERTY RIGHTS

## 1. INTRODUCTION

Assignment 1 explored the right to exclude others from truly private property. This Assignment considers how that same right applies to semi-private property such as shopping malls, unfenced parking lots serving adjacent office buildings, and migrant labor camps. Here, Professor Arnold's insight that the nature of the object subject to property rights defines and modifies these rights becomes important.[1]

Property rights, like most other rights, are not absolute. When they conflict with other rights (such as those involving expressive activity), one of these rights must be modified. This Assignment explores which right must be modified and how the modification is made.

## 2. PRINCIPAL PROBLEM

Your client, Dr. Land, is a medical doctor who often performs abortions. Recently a group of anti-abortion activists began distributing leaflets in front of the main entrance to her office. The leaflets refer to abortion as "murder," and in highly charged language urge Land's patients not to have abortions. Many of her patients are upset by the contents of the leaflets. However, those distributing the leaflets have been polite and have not obstructed the entrance to Land's office. Land's office is on the ground floor of one of the buildings in an office complex and has an entrance that opens directly onto a walkway that connects to the parking lot. The complex consists of six buildings, each of which is two stories high. It contains medical offices as well as general commercial offices. Land has asked the owners of the complex to expel the "pro-life" protesters. The owners are willing to do this if you will furnish them with an opinion that the "pro-life" people have no right to remain on the premises. Before formulating your opinion, consider the following materials.

---

[1] Craig Anthony (Tony) Arnold, The Reconstitution of Property: Property as a Web of Interests, 26 Harv. Env. L. Rev. 281, 296 (2002).

## 3. MATERIALS FOR SOLUTION OF PRINCIPAL PROBLEM

### State of New Jersey v. Shack
Supreme Court of New Jersey, 1971.
58 N.J. 297, 277 A.2d 369.

■ WEINTRAUB, C.J.

Defendants entered upon private property to aid migrant farmworkers employed and housed there. Having refused to depart upon the demand of the owner, defendants were charged with violating N.J.S.A. 2A:170–31 which provides that "[a]ny person who trespasses on any lands . . . after being forbidden so to trespass by the owner . . . is a disorderly person and shall be punished by a fine of not more than $50." Defendants were convicted in the Municipal Court of Deerfield Township and again on appeal in the County Court of Cumberland County on a trial *de novo*. R. 3:23–8(a). We certified their further appeal before argument in the Appellate Division.

Before us, no one seeks to sustain these convictions. The complaints were prosecuted in the Municipal Court and in the County Court by counsel engaged by the complaining landowner, Tedesco. However Tedesco did not respond to this appeal, and the county prosecutor, while defending abstractly the constitutionality of the trespass statute, expressly disclaimed any position as to whether the statute reached the activity of these defendants.

Complainant, Tedesco, a farmer, employs migrant workers for his seasonal needs. As part of their compensation, these workers are housed at a camp on his property.

Defendant Tejeras is a field worker for the Farm Workers Division of the Southwest Citizens Organization for Poverty Elimination, known by the acronym SCOPE, a nonprofit corporation funded by the Office of Economic Opportunity pursuant to an act of Congress, 42 U.S.C.A. §§ 2861–2864. The role of SCOPE includes providing for the "health services of the migrant farm worker."

Defendant Shack is a staff attorney with the Farm Workers Division of Camden Regional Legal Services, Inc., known as "CRLS," also a nonprofit corporation funded by the Office of Economic Opportunity pursuant to an act of Congress, 42 U.S.C.A. § 2809(a)(3). The mission of CRLS includes legal advice and representation for these workers.

Differences had developed between Tedesco and these defendants prior to the events which led to the trespass charges now before us. Hence when defendant Tejeras wanted to go upon Tedesco's farm to find a migrant worker who needed medical aid for the removal of 28 sutures, he called upon defendant Shack for his help with respect to the legalities involved. Shack, too, had a mission to perform on Tedesco's farm; he wanted to discuss a legal problem with another migrant worker there employed and housed. Defendants arranged to go to the farm together. Shack carried literature to inform the migrant farmworkers of the assistance available to them under federal statutes, but no mention seems to have been made of that literature when Shack was later confronted by Tedesco.

Defendants entered upon Tedesco's property and as they neared the camp site where the farmworkers were housed, they were confronted by Tedesco who inquired of their purpose. Tejeras and Shack stated their missions. In response, Tedesco offered to find the injured worker, and as to the worker who needed legal advice, Tedesco also offered to locate the man but insisted that the consultation would have to take place in Tedesco's office and in his presence. Defendants declined, saying they had the right to see the men in the privacy of their living quarters and without Tedesco's supervision. Tedesco thereupon summoned a State Trooper who, however, refused to remove defendants except upon Tedesco's written complaint. Tedesco then executed the formal complaints charging violations of the trespass statute.

I

The constitutionality of the trespass statute, as applied here, is challenged on several scores.

It is urged that the First Amendment rights of the defendants and of the migrant farmworkers were thereby offended. Reliance is placed on Marsh v. Alabama, 326 U.S. 501, 66 S.Ct. 276, 90 L.Ed. 265 (1946), where it was held that free speech was assured by the First Amendment in a company-owned town which was open to the public generally and was indistinguishable from any other town except for the fact that the title to the property was vested in a private corporation. Hence a Jehovah's Witness who distributed literature on a sidewalk within the town could not be held as a trespasser. Later, on the strength of that case, it was held that there was a First Amendment right to picket peacefully in a privately owned shopping center which was found to be the functional equivalent of the business district of the company-owned town in *Marsh*. Amalgamated Food Employees Union Local 590 v. Logan Valley Plaza, Inc., 391 U.S. 308, 88 S.Ct. 1601, 20 L.Ed.2d 603 (1968). Those cases rest upon the fact that the property was in fact opened to the general public. There may be some migrant camps with the attributes of the company town in *Marsh* and of course they would come within its holding. But there is nothing of that character in the case before us, and hence there would have to be an extension of *Marsh* to embrace the immediate situation.

Defendants also maintain that the application of the trespass statute to them is barred by the Supremacy Clause of the United States Constitution, Art. VI, cl. 2, and this on the premise that the application of the trespass statute would defeat the purpose of the federal statutes, under which SCOPE and CRLS are funded, to reach and aid the migrant farmworker. The brief of the United States, *amicus curiae,* supports that approach. Here defendants rely upon cases construing the National Labor Relations Act, 29 U.S.C.A. § 151 et seq., and holding that an employer may in some circumstances be guilty of an unfair labor practice in violation of that statute if the employer denies union organizers an opportunity to communicate with his employees at some suitable place upon the employer's premises. The brief of New Jersey State Office of Legal Services, *amicus curiae,* asserts the workers' Sixth Amendment right to counsel in criminal matters is involved and suggests also that a right to counsel in civil matters is a "penumbra" right emanating from the whole Bill of Rights under the thinking of Griswold v. Connecticut, 381 U.S. 479, 85 S.Ct. 1678, 14 L.Ed.2d 510 (1965), or is a privilege of national citizenship protected by the privileges and immunities clause of the Fourteenth Amendment, or is a right "retained by the people" under the Ninth Amendment, citing a dictum in United Public Workers v. Mitchell, 330 U.S. 75, 94, 67 S.Ct. 556, 91 L.Ed. 754, 770 (1947).

These constitutional claims are not established by any definitive holding. We think it unnecessary to explore their validity. The reason is that we are satisfied that under our State law the ownership of real property does not include the right to bar access to governmental services available to migrant workers and hence there was no trespass within the meaning of the penal statute. The policy considerations which underlie that conclusion may be much the same as those which would be weighed with respect to one or more of the constitutional challenges, but a decision in nonconstitutional terms is more satisfactory, because the interests of migrant workers are more expansively served in that way than they would be if they had no more freedom than these constitutional concepts could be found to mandate if indeed they apply at all.

## II

Property rights serve human values. They are recognized to that end, and are limited by it. Title to real property cannot include dominion over the destiny of persons the owner permits to come upon the premises. Their well-being must remain the paramount concern of a system of law. Indeed the needs of the occupants may be so imperative and their strength so weak, that the law will deny the occupants the power to contract away what is deemed essential to their health, welfare, or dignity.

Here we are concerned with a highly disadvantaged segment of our society. We are told that every year farmworkers and their families numbering more than one million leave their home areas to fill the seasonal demand for farm labor in the United States. The Migratory Farm Labor Problem in the United States (1969 Report of Subcommittee on Migratory Labor of the United States Senate Committee on Labor and Public Welfare), p. 1. The migrant farmworkers come to New Jersey in substantial numbers. . . .

The migrant farmworkers are a community within but apart from the local scene. They are rootless and isolated. Although the need for their labors is evident, they are unorganized and without economic or political power. It is their plight alone that summoned government to their aid. In response, Congress provided under Title III–B of the Economic Opportunity Act of 1964 (42 U.S.C.A. § 2701 et seq.) for "assistance for migrant and other seasonally employed farmworkers and their families." Section 2861 states "the purpose of this part is to assist migrant and seasonal farmworkers and their families to improve their living conditions and develop skills necessary for a productive and self-sufficient life in an increasingly complex and technological society." Section 2862(b)(1) provides for funding of programs "to meet the immediate needs of migrant and seasonal farmworkers and their families, such as day care for children, education, health services, improved housing and sanitation (including the provision and maintenance of emergency and temporary housing and sanitation facilities), legal advice and representation, and consumer training and counseling." As we have said, SCOPE is engaged in a program funded under this section, and CRLS also pursues the objectives of this section, although, we gather, it is funded under § 2809(a)(3), which is not limited in its concern to the migrant and other seasonally employed farmworkers and seeks "to further the cause of justice among persons living in poverty by mobilizing the assistance of lawyers and legal institutions and by providing legal advice, legal representation, counseling, education, and other appropriate services."

These ends would not be gained if the intended beneficiaries could be insulated from efforts to reach them. It is in this framework that we must decide whether the camp operator's rights in his lands may stand between the migrant workers and those who would aid them. The key to that aid is communication. Since the migrant workers are outside the mainstream of the communities in which they are housed and are unaware of their rights and opportunities and of the services available to them, they can be reached only by positive efforts tailored to that end. The Report of the Governor's Task Force on Migrant Farm Labor (1968) noted that "One of the major problems related to seasonal farm labor is the lack of adequate direct information with regard to the availability of public services," and that "there is a dire need to provide the workers with basic educational and informational material in a language and style that can be readily understood by the migrant" (pp. 101–102). The report stressed the problem of access and deplored the notion that property rights may stand as a barrier, saying "In our judgment, 'no trespass' signs represent the last dying remnants of paternalistic behavior" (p. 63).

A man's right in his real property of course is not absolute. It was a maxim of the common law that one should so use his property as not to injure the rights of others. Broom, Legal Maxims (10th ed. Kersley 1939), p. 238; 39 Words and Phrases, "Sic Utere Tuo ut Alienum Non Laedas," p. 335. Although hardly a precise solvent of actual controversies, the maxim does express the inevitable proposition that rights are relative and there must be an accommodation when they meet. Hence it has long been true that necessity, private or public, may justify entry upon the lands of another. For a catalogue of such situations, see Prosser, Torts (3d ed. 1964), § 24, pp. 127–129; 6A American Law of Property (A.J. Casner ed. 1954) § 28.10, p. 31; 52 Am.Jur., "Trespass," §§ 40–41, pp. 867–869. See also Restatement, Second, Torts (1965) §§ 197–211.

The subject is not static. As pointed out in 5 Powell, Real Property (Rohan 1970) § 745, pp. 493–494, while society will protect the owner in his permissible interests in land, yet

> [S]uch an owner must expect to find the absoluteness of his property rights curtailed by the organs of society, for the promotion of the best interests of others for whom these organs also operate as protective agencies. The necessity for such curtailments is greater in a modern industrialized and urbanized society than it was in the relatively simple American society of fifty, 100, or 200 years ago. The current balance between individualism and dominance of the social interest depends not only upon political and social ideologies, but also upon the physical and social facts of the time and place under discussion.

Professor Powell added in § 746, pp. 494–496:

> As one looks back along the historic road traversed by the law of land in England and in America, one sees a change from the viewpoint that he who owns may do as he pleases with what he owns, to a position which hesitatingly embodies an ingredient of stewardship; which grudgingly, but steadily, broadens the recognized scope of social interests in the utilization of things. . . .
>
> To one seeing history through the glasses of religion, these changes may seem to evidence increasing embodiments of the golden rule. To one thinking in terms of political and economic ideologies, they are likely to be labeled evidences of "social enlightenment," or of "creeping socialism" or even of "communistic infiltration," according to the individual's assumed definitions and retained or acquired prejudices. With slight attention to words or labels, time marches on toward new adjustments between individualism and the social interests.
>
> This process involves not only the accommodation between the right of the owner and the interests of the general public in his use of his property, but involves also an accommodation between the right of the owner and the right of individuals who are parties with him in consensual transactions relating to use of the property. Accordingly substantial alterations have been made as between a landlord and his

tenant. See Reste Realty Corp. v. Cooper, 53 N.J. 444, 451–453, 251 A.2d 268 (1969); Marini v. Ireland, 56 N.J. 130, 141–143, 265 A.2d 526 (1970).

The argument in this case understandably included the question whether the migrant worker should be deemed to be a tenant and thus entitled to the tenant's right to receive visitors, Williams v. Lubbering, 73 N.J.L. 317, 319–320, 63 A. 90 (Sup.Ct.1906), or whether his residence on the employer's property should be deemed to be merely incidental and in aid of his employment, and hence to involve no possessory interest in the realty. . . .

We see no profit in trying to decide upon a conventional category and then forcing the present subject into it. That approach would be artificial and distorting. The quest is for a fair adjustment of the competing needs of the parties, in the light of the realities of the relationship between the migrant worker and the operator of the housing facility.

Thus approaching the case, we find it unthinkable that the farmer-employer can assert a right to isolate the migrant worker in any respect significant for the worker's well-being. The farmer, of course, is entitled to pursue his farming activities without interference, and this defendants readily concede. But we see no legitimate need for a right in the farmer to deny the worker the opportunity for aid available from federal, State, or local services, or from recognized charitable groups seeking to assist him. Hence representatives of these agencies and organizations may enter upon the premises to seek out the worker at his living quarters. So, too, the migrant worker must be allowed to receive visitors there of his own choice, so long as there is no behavior hurtful to others, and members of the press may not be denied reasonable access to workers who do not object to seeing them.

It is not our purpose to open the employer's premises to the general public if in fact the employer himself has not done so. We do not say, for example, that solicitors or peddlers of all kinds may enter on their own; we may assume for the present that the employer may regulate their entry or bar them, at least if the employer's purpose is not to gain a commercial advantage for himself or if the regulation does not deprive the migrant worker of practical access to things he needs.

And we are mindful of the employer's interest in his own and in his employees' security. Hence he may reasonably require a visitor to identify himself, and also to state his general purpose if the migrant worker has not already informed him that the visitor is expected. But the employer may not deny the worker his privacy or interfere with his opportunity to live with dignity and to enjoy associations customary among our citizens. These rights are too fundamental to be denied on the basis of an interest in real property and too fragile to be left to the unequal bargaining strength of the parties.

It follows that defendants here invaded no possessory right of the farmer-employer. Their conduct was therefore beyond the reach of the trespass statute. The judgments are accordingly reversed and the matters remanded to the County with directions to enter judgments of acquittal.

## NOTES

1. *Blackstone's legacy.* "[T]he right of meum and tuum, or property, in lands once being established, it follows, as a necessary consequence, that this right must be exclusive; that is, that the owner may retain to himself the sole use and occupation of his soil: every entry, therefore, thereon without the owner's leave, and especially if contrary to his express order, is a trespass or transgression." 3 Blackstone's Commentaries 209 (1765). Was Blackstone followed in *Shack*? If not, why not?

2. *Source of authority.* What case, statute, constitutional provision, or rule of law did the New Jersey Supreme Court rely on in *Shack*?

In a subsequent decision, Uston v. Resorts International Hotel, Inc.,[2] the New Jersey Supreme Court again qualified a property owner's right to exclude by holding that "[p]roperty owners have no legitimate interest in unreasonably excluding particular members of the public when they open their premises for public use."[3] *Uston* involved a casino's exclusion of a patron based on his "card counting" method of playing blackjack. New Jersey is one of the few states to have judicially adopted this rule of law, although the legislatures of some other states have enacted statutes which are hospitable to this trend.[4]

3. *Precedential value.* The complainant, Tedesco, did not appear at the appeal before the New Jersey Supreme Court. The defendants, however, were represented by the Camden Regional Legal Services, Inc., and were also supported in amicus briefs filed by the Attorney General of New Jersey, the New Jersey State Office of Legal Services, and the United States Attorney. Why did the court not merely enter a default judgment without an opinion? How would you respond to the contention that the decision is entitled to very little weight because the court heard only one side of the case?

4. *Access to farm labor camps.* In Agricultural Labor Relations Board v. Superior Court,[5] the California Supreme Court upheld, by a 4–3 vote, the right of union organizers to enter farm labor camps pursuant to rules promulgated by the ALRB. The appeal was dismissed by the United States Supreme Court for want of a substantial federal question. In so doing, was the Supreme Court impliedly approving of *Shack*?

---

[2] 89 N.J. 163, 445 A.2d 370 (1982).

[3] Id. at 173, 445 A.2d at 375.

[4] Comment, *Patron's Right of Access to Premises Generally Open to the Public*, 1983 U. Ill. L. Rev. 533, 543–45, 551–52 (1983). For a valuable article considering the right to exclude in the context of racial discrimination see Joseph W. Singer, *No Right to Exclude: Public Accommodations and Private Property*, 90 Nw. U. L. Rev. 1283 (1996).

[5] 16 Cal.3d 392, 128 Cal.Rptr. 183, 546 P.2d 687 (1976), *appeal dismissed for want of a substantial federal question sub nom.* Kubo v. Agricultural Labor Relations Board, 429 U.S. 802 (1976), and Pandol & Sons v. Agricultural Labor Relations Board, 429 U.S. 802 (1976). However, reasonable time, place and manner restrictions will be enforced. Sam Andrews' Sons v. Agricultural Labor Relations Board, 47 Cal.3d 157, 763 P.2d 881 (1988).

## New Jersey Coalition Against War in the Middle East v. J.M.B. Realty Corporation

Supreme Court of New Jersey, 1994.
138 N.J. 326, 650 A.2d 757.

■ WILENTZ, C.J.

The question in this case is whether the defendant regional and community shopping centers must permit leafletting on societal issues. We hold that they must, subject to reasonable conditions set by them. Our ruling is limited to leafletting at such centers, and it applies nowhere else. It is based on our citizens' right of free speech embodied in our State Constitution. N.J. Const. art. I, PP 6, 18. It follows the course we set in our decision in State v. Schmid, 84 N.J. 535 (1980).

In *Schmid* we ruled that our State Constitution conferred on our citizens an affirmative right of free speech that was protected not only from governmental restraint—the extent of First Amendment protection—but from the restraint of private property owners as well. We noted that those state constitutional protections are "available against unreasonably restrictive or oppressive conduct on the part of private entities that have otherwise assumed a constitutional obligation not to abridge the individual exercise of such freedoms because of the public use of their property." Id. at 560. And we set forth the standard to determine what public use will give rise to that constitutional obligation. The standard takes into account the normal use of the property, the extent and nature of the public's invitation to use it, and the purpose of the expressional activity in relation to both its private and public use. This "multi-faceted" standard determines whether private property owners "may be required to permit, subject to suitable restrictions, the reasonable exercise by individuals of the constitutional freedoms of speech and assembly." Id. at 563. That is to say, they determine whether, taken together, the normal uses of the property, the extent of the public's invitation, and the purpose of free speech in relation to the property's use result in a suitability for free speech on the property that on balance, is sufficiently compelling to warrant limiting the private property owner's right to exclude it; a suitability so compelling as to be constitutionally required.

Applying *Schmid*, we find the existence of the constitutional obligation to allow free speech at these regional and community shopping centers clear. Although the ultimate purpose of these shopping centers is commercial, their normal use is all-embracing, almost without limit, projecting a community image, serving as their own communities, encompassing practically all aspects of a downtown business district, including expressive uses and community events. We know of no private property that more closely resembles public property. The public's invitation to use the property—the second factor of the standard—is correspondingly broad, its all-inclusive scope suggested by the very few restrictions on the invitation that are claimed, but not advertised, by defendants. For the ordinary citizen it is not just an invitation to shop, but to do whatever one would do downtown, including doing very little of anything.

As for the third factor of the standard—the relationship between the purposes of the expressional activity and the use of the property—the free speech sought to be exercised, plaintiff's leafletting, is wholly consonant with the use of these properties. Conversely, the right sought is no more discordant with defendants' uses of their property than is the leafletting that has been exercised for centuries within downtown business districts discordant with their use. Furthermore, it is just as consonant with the centers' use as other uses permitted there. Indeed, four of these centers actually permitted plaintiff's leafletting (although it took place in only two of those).

We therefore find the existence of a constitutional obligation to permit the leafletting plaintiff seeks at these regional and community shopping centers; we find that the balance of factors clearly predominates in favor of that obligation; its denial in this case is unreasonably restrictive and oppressive of free speech: were it extended to all regional and community shopping centers, it would block a channel of free speech that could reach hundreds of thousands of people, carrying societal messages that are at its very core. The true dimensions of that denial of this constitutional obligation are apparent only when it is understood that the former channel to these people through the downtown business districts has been severely diminished, and that this channel is its practical substitute.

We hold that *Schmid* requires that the free speech sought by the plaintiff—the non-commercial leafletting and its normal accompanying speech (without megaphone, soapbox, speeches, or demonstrations)—be permitted by defendants subject to such reasonable rules and regulations as may be imposed by them. This free speech can be, and we have no doubt will be, carefully controlled by these centers. There will be no pursuit or harassment of shoppers. Given this limited free speech right—leafletting, given the centers' broad power to regulate it, and given experience elsewhere, we are confident that it is consonant with the commercial purposes of the centers and the varied purposes of their shoppers and non-shoppers.

We recognize the concerns of the defendants, including their concern that they will be hurt. Those concerns bear on the extent and exercise of the constitutional right and we have addressed them in this opinion. We recognize the depth and legitimacy of those concerns even apart from their constitutional relevance. Defendants have expended enormous efforts and funds in bringing about the success of these centers. We hope they recognize the legitimacy of the constitutional concern that in the process of creating new downtown business districts, they will have seriously diminished the value of free speech if it can be shut off at their centers. Their commercial success has been striking but with that success goes a constitutional responsibility.

Without doubt, despite the fact that the speech permitted—leafletting—is the least obtrusive and the easiest to regulate, and despite the centers' broad power to regulate, some people will not like it, any more perhaps than they liked free speech at the downtown business districts. Dislike for free speech, however, has never been the determinant of its protection or its benefit. We live with it, we permit it, as we have for more than two hundred years. It is free speech, it is constitutionally protected; it is part of this State, and so are these centers. . . .

## II

Before reaching our discussion of the law, we must first examine the background against which this question is raised. We know its most important outline. Regional and community shopping centers significantly compete with and have in fact significantly displaced downtown business districts as the gathering point of citizens, both here in New Jersey and across America. . . .

## III

We shall briefly summarize the lengthy history of the law of free speech that underlies this case. The relevant historical starting point is Marsh v. Alabama, 326 U.S. 501, 66 S. Ct. 276, 90 L. Ed. 265 (1946). In *Marsh*, the United States Supreme Court held that the First Amendment's guarantee of free speech was violated when the private owners of a company town prevented distribution of literature in its downtown business district. Finding that the company town had all the attributes of a municipality, the Court held that the private owner's action was "state action" for constitutional free speech purposes. In a democracy, the Court recognized, citizens "must make decisions which affect the welfare of community and nation. To act as good citizens they must be informed. In order to enable them to be properly informed their information must be uncensored." Id. at 508, 66 S. Ct. at 280, 90 L. Ed. at 270. The paramount right of the citizens to be informed overrode the rights of the property owners in the constitutional balance. Id. at 509, 66 S. Ct. at 280, 90 L. Ed. at 270.

The question whether citizens may exercise a right of free speech at privately-owned shopping centers without permission of the owners has been litigated extensively. . . . From these cases we learn that the Federal Constitution does not prevent private owners from prohibiting free speech leafletting at their shopping centers because the owners' conduct does not amount to "state action"; that practically every state, when its constitutional free speech provisions have been asserted, has ruled the same way, again on the basis of a legal conclusion that state action was required. We are not out-of-step, however, every state that has found certain of its constitutional free-speech-related provisions effective regardless of "state action" has ruled that shopping center owners cannot prohibit that free speech. There have been four such rulings: California (general free speech provision), Massachusetts (free and equal election provision), Oregon (initiative and referendum provision), and Washington (initiative provision). Put differently, no state with a constitutional free-speech-related provision unencumbered by any "state action" requirement has allowed shopping centers to prohibit that speech on their premises. Colorado is apparently the only state that found its constitutional "state action" requirement satisfied in the shopping center context, and ruled on that ground that the owners' denial was unconstitutional and required that leafletting be permitted.

## IV

In New Jersey, we have once before discussed the application of our State constitutional right of free speech to private conduct. In State v. Schmid, 84 N.J. 535 (1980), appeal dismissed sub nom. Princeton University v. Schmid, 455 U.S. 100, 102 S. Ct. 867, 70 L. Ed. 2d 855 (1982), we held that the right conferred by the State Constitution was secure not only from State interference but—under certain conditions—from the interference of an owner of private property even when exercised on that private property. Id. at 559. Specifically, we held that Schmid, though lacking permission from Princeton University, had the right to enter the campus, distribute leaflets, and sell political materials. We ruled that the right of free speech could be exercised on the campus subject to the University's reasonable regulations. . . .

We reaffirm our holding in *Schmid*. The test to determine the existence of the constitutional obligation is multi-faceted; the outcome depends on a consideration of all three factors of the standard and ultimately on a balancing between the protections to be accorded the rights of private property owners and the free speech rights of individuals to leaflet on their property. . . .

We decide this case not only on the basis of the three-pronged test in *Schmid*, but also by the general balancing of expressional rights and private property rights. Schmid, supra, 84 N.J. at 560–62. The standard and its elements are specifically designed with that balancing in mind. A more general analysis of the balance provides a further test of the correctness of our determination.

The essence of the balance is fairly described by Justice Handler in *Schmid*:

> Private property does not "lose its private character merely because the public is generally invited to use it for designated purposes." Nevertheless, as private property becomes, on a sliding scale, committed either more or less to public use and enjoyment, there is actuated, in effect, a counterbalancing between expressional and property rights. Or, as stated in *Marsh*, "the more an owner, for his advantage, opens up his

property for use by the public in general, the more do his rights become circumscribed by the statutory and constitutional rights of those who use it." Marsh v. Alabama, 326 U.S. 501, 506, 66 S. Ct. 276, 278, 90 L. Ed. 265, 268 (1946).

There is no doubt about the outcome of this balance. On one side, the weight of the private property owners' interest in controlling and limiting activities on their property has greatly diminished in view of the uses permitted and invited on that property. The private property owners in this case, the operators of regional and community malls, have intentionally transformed their property into a public square or market, a public gathering place, a downtown business district, a community; they have told this public in every way possible that the property is theirs, to come to, to visit, to do what they please, and hopefully to shop and spend; they have done so in many ways, but mostly through the practically unlimited permitted public uses found and encouraged on their property. The sliding scale cannot slide any farther in the direction of public use and diminished private property interests.

On the other side of the balance, the weight of plaintiff's free speech interest is the most substantial in our constitutional scheme. Those interests involve speech that is central to the purpose of our right of free speech. At these centers, free speech, such as leafletting, can be exercised without discernible interference with the owners' profits or the shoppers' and non-shoppers' enjoyment. The weight of the free speech interest is thus composed of a constant and a variable: the constant is the quality of free speech, here free speech that is the most important to society; the variable is its potential interference with this diminished private property interest of the owner. Given the limited free speech right sought, leafletting accompanied only by that speech normally associated with and necessary for leafletting, and subject to the owners' broad power to regulate, that interference, if any, will be negligible. . . .

Like many constitutional determinations, our decision today applies a constitutional provision written many years ago to a society changed in ways that could not have been foreseen. One of those changes is relatively modern: the vastly increased capability to achieve mass communication, primarily, for the moment at least, to do so through television. This emergence of television as the preeminent medium for mass communication provides no justification to deny plaintiff this constitutional right. Most fundamentally, the general right of free speech through one means has never depended on a lack of any other means; radio never diminished the right of free speech at downtown business districts. . . .

If constitutional provisions of this magnitude should be interpreted in light of a changed society, and we believe they should, the most important change is the emergence of these centers as the competitors of the downtown business district and to a great extent as the successors to the downtown business district. The significance of the historical path of free speech is unmistakable and compelling: the parks, the squares, and the streets, traditionally the home of free speech, were succeeded by the downtown business districts, often including those areas, the downtown business districts where that free speech followed. Those districts have now been substantially displaced by these centers. If our State constitutional right of free speech has any substance, it must continue to follow that historic path. It cannot stop at the downtown business district that has become less and less effective as a public forum. It cannot be silenced "as the traditional realm of grassroots political activity withers away." Curtis J. Berger, Pruneyard Revisited: Political Activity on Private Lands, 66 N.Y.U. L. Rev. 633, 661 (1991).

We look back and we look ahead in an effort to determine what a constitutional provision means. If free speech is to mean anything in the future, it must be exercised at these centers. Our constitutional right encompasses more than leafletting and associated speech on sidewalks located in empty downtown business districts. It means communicating with the people in the new commercial and social centers; if the people have left for the shopping centers, our constitutional right includes the right to go there too, to follow them, and to talk to them.

We do not believe that those who adopted a constitutional provision granting a right of free speech wanted it to diminish in importance as society changed, to be dependent on the unrelated accidents of economic transformation, or to be silenced because of a new way of doing business. . . .

## VI

Our holding today applies to all regional shopping centers. That holding is based on their essential nature. The mammoth size of these regional centers, the proliferation of uses, the all-embracing quality of the implied invitation, and the compatibility of free speech with those uses: the inevitable presence and coexistence of all of those factors more than satisfy the three elements of the *Schmid* standard. Furthermore, these regional shopping centers are, in all significant respects, the functional equivalent of a downtown business district, a fact that provides further support for our holding. These are the essential places for the preservation of the free speech that nourishes society and was found in downtown business districts when they flourished.

As for the manner of speech, our ruling is confined to leafletting and associated free speech: the speech that normally and necessarily accompanies leafletting. Plaintiff has sought no more. It does not include bullhorns, megaphones, or even a soapbox; it does not include placards, pickets, parades, and demonstrations; it does not include anything other than normal speech and then only such as is necessary to the effectiveness of the leafletting. The free speech associated with leafletting, handbilling, and pamphleteering, as commonly understood, is only that which is needed to attract the attention of passersby—in a normal voice—to the cause and to the fact that leaflets are available, without pressure, harassment, following, pestering, of any kind. Additionally, the sale of literature and the solicitation of funds on the spot (as distinguished from appeals found in the leaflets themselves) are not covered by the protection. In that connection, we are in accord with the reasoning of decisions in other jurisdictions. . . .

These are the basic limits on the manner of exercising the kind of free speech that has been sought in this case. They are not intended at all to foreclose the owners from adopting time, place, and manner rules and regulations that impose further and greater limits—nor are they intended to prevent the owners from granting greater rights.

There is concern, understandable concern, about the possibility of confrontation, disturbance, and even violence—concerns not just for business, but for the safety and security of people at the premises. Freedom of speech has always had this potential, controversy being part of its nature. Defendants' fears are not fanciful, but this is hardly a novel problem. This country, and its cities, and more to the point, its downtown business districts, have successfully dealt with it and lived with it for centuries.

We do not believe our opinion will result in any harm to these centers, to their businesses, nor any less enjoyment for those who visit, shoppers and non-shoppers. The free speech we have permitted—leafletting only, no speeches, no parades, no demonstrations—is the least intrusive form of free speech and the easiest to control. The experience elsewhere proves the ability of those centers to absorb such speech without harm. The rare instances of disturbance resulted from circumstances most unlikely to occur here. Obviously, we cannot guarantee that disturbances will not occur as a result of our decision. Indeed, we could not guarantee freedom from such disturbances even in the absence of a right to leaflet. However, the slim possibility of disruption is the price we all pay as citizens of this state; the danger that some will abuse their rights is a necessary result of our constitutional commitment to free speech.

The centers' power to impose regulations concerning the time, place, and manner of exercising the right of free speech is extremely broad. We assume that in most cases malls can limit the time of leafletting to specific days, and a specific number of days. Certainly no individual or group will be entitled to be present any more often than is necessary to convey the message. . . .

. . .

■ GARIBALDI, J., Dissenting.

Today the Court holds that the New Jersey Constitution requires that owners of privately-owned-and-operated shopping malls who invite the public onto their property for commercial purposes must allow the public free access to that property to engage in unrestricted expressional activities, including, through the distribution of leaflets and petitions to shoppers, the promotion of various political or social views. To reach that conclusion, the majority distorts the test announced in State v. Schmid, 84 N.J. 535, 563 (1980); dismisses completely the rights of private-property owners to regulate and control the use of their own property; disregards the trial court's findings of fact, developed after an extensive eleven-day trial; and instead relies primarily on old theories that the United States Supreme Court and most other state courts long ago discarded.

Under the majority's rudderless standard, whether property is owned privately or publicly is irrelevant; whether the message is discordant with the private property's use and purpose likewise makes no difference; and whether less-convenient but equally accessible and effective means of distribution exist is of no moment. So long as the private property, here a shopping mall, offers an opportunity for many people to congregate, the private-property owners must grant those people free access for expressional activity, regardless of the message or of its disruptive effect. Although the Court duly notes that such access will be subject to reasonable restrictions of time, place, and manner, its opinion reveals that the restrictions will be minimal and will present more problems and lawsuits than they will solve. . . .

## NOTES

1. *State courts are divided.* As illustrated by the *New Jersey Coalition* case, the U.S. Constitution does not compel the states to permit free speech activities in privately owned shopping centers. But it does allow the states to compel such shopping centers to permit free speech activities. In effect, the states are free to determine the boundaries of free speech rights and private property rights. The expansion of one right necessarily results in the contraction of the other.

*New Jersey Coalition* represents the minority view. Most courts that have ruled on the question have held that state constitutions protect free speech from governmental actions (state actions), but not from the actions of private parties such as the owners of shopping centers or apartment houses.[6] The following states—California, Colorado, Florida, Massachusetts, New Jersey, Washington, and possibly Delaware—recognize some right of expressive activity in shopping centers. At least twenty-one states have rejected the assertion of such a right.[7] Many of the decisions depend on the precise wording and legislative history of the state constitution. Assuming

---

[6] See, e.g., United Bhd. of Carpenters v. NLRB, 540 F.3d 957 (9th Cir. 2008) (shopping center); Fashion Valley Mall, LLC v. National Labor Relations Bd. 42 Cal.4th 850 (2007) (shopping center); Mazdabrook Commons Homeowners' Ass'n v. Khan, 210 N.J. 482 (2012) (window and door of condo); Golden Gateway Center v. Golden Gateway Tenants Ass'n, 26 Cal.4th 1013 (2001) (hallways of apartment house); Stranahan v. Fred Meyer, Inc., 331 Or. 38 (2000) (shopping center); State v. Wicklund, 589 N.W.2d 793 (Minn. 1999) (shopping center). See Jennifer Niles Coffin, The United Mall of America: Free Speech, State Constitutions, and the Growing Fortress of Private Property, 33 Univ. of Mich. J. of Law Reform 615 (2000).

[7] See James M. Hirschhorn & Jeffrey H. Newman, Managing "Free Speech" at the Mall, 21 ACREL News, No. 1, p. 11 (May 2003).

that the wording and legislative history of the governing state constitution doesn't mandate a particular result, which result would you prefer and why?

2. *Large shopping centers, free speech; small centers, no free speech?* In the *New Jersey Coalition* case, the court seemed to suggest that although reasonable free speech activities had to be permitted in large shopping centers, they probably had no legal protection in small shopping centers. California has taken a similar position.[8] Is the distinction valid? Suppose that large shopping centers barred all community events? How should this affect the rights of free speech advocates? Should the protection of freedom of assembly afforded to labor unions be stifled in shopping centers?

3. *Time, place and manner regulations.* California and New Jersey allow the manager of a shopping center to impose reasonable time, place and manner restrictions on expressive activity within the center. How restrictive can these be? A California case allowed regulations prohibiting petition gatherers from operating during the 34 busiest days of the year, or on more than five days within any thirty day period.[9] On the other hand, a New Jersey case held invalid a mall owner's attempt to restrict to one day a year any one organization's expressive activity at the mall, and also rejected a requirement that that organization provide a $1,000,000 insurance policy protecting the mall owner from liability arising out of the expressive activity.[10]

4. *Free Access to Clinic Entrances (FACE) statute.* It is a federal offense, punishable by fine or imprisonment, to interfere by force or threat of force or by physical obstruction of access to a clinic providing reproductive health services. 18 U.S.C. § 248.

5. *From a real place to cyberspace: free speech and the Internet.* Scholars have described the Internet as "a place where people meet to communicate, where businesses meet consumers and sell their products, and where investments in web site development and presence are electronic versions of property."[11] Is cyberspace akin to real property? If so, should the same free speech standards and analysis apply to both real property and cyberspace? Or should the nature of the Internet as an unprecedented medium of global communication trigger greater free speech protection?

---

[8] Compare Robins v. PruneYard Shopping Ctr., 23 Cal.3d 899 (1979), aff'd 447 U.S. 74 (1980) (regional center), with Albertson's, Inc. v. Young, 107 Cal.App.4th 106 (2003) (neighborhood center) See also Donahue Schriber Realty Group, Inc. v. Nu Creation Outreach, 232 Cal.App.4th 1171 (2014).

[9] Costco Companies, Inc. v. Gallant, 96 Cal.App.4th 740 (2002).

[10] Green Party of New Jersey v. Hartz Mountain Industries, 164 N.J. 127 (2000).

[11] Ronnie Cohen & Janine S. Hiller, Towards a Theory of Cyberplace: A Proposal for a New Legal Framework, 10 Rich. J.L. & Tech. 2, ¶ 57 (2003).

## II. NON-FREEHOLD ESTATES

### A. SCOPE OF DUTIES AND RIGHTS DURING THE LEASE TERM

### ASSIGNMENT 3

# LANDLORD-TENANT: THE RIGHT OF EXCLUSIVE PHYSICAL POSSESSION

A leasehold estate is a possessory interest that normally gives the tenant the right to exclusive possession. In Assignment 1, we explored the boundaries of a landowner's right to exclusive physical possession of owned property. In this Assignment we explore the boundaries of a tenant's right to exclusive physical possession of leased property. This Assignment is divided into two parts. Part a. examines the difference between a lease and a license. Part b. examines the tenant's rights to possession and quiet enjoyment under a lease.

### a. LEASE OR LICENSE?

A lease is a possessory interest in land. A license merely authorizes the licensee to use land in the possession of another. The license arises from the consent of the owner of the possessory interest. Since different rules govern licenses and leases, it is often necessary to distinguish between them. Here, as in so many areas of the law, legal reasoning is often circular. Sometimes courts find that because a lease has been created, the tenant has a right to exclusive possession. At other times courts find that because the tenant has a right to exclusive possession, a lease has been created. One should resist the temptation to approach such questions from too high a level of abstraction. The practical context in which the question of lease or license is raised must never be overlooked. A court will be reluctant to find that a particular arrangement is a license if this will create an injustice or thwart an important public policy. In fact, one may question whether any controversy should ever be decided merely by classifying the interest involved as a lease or a license.

#### 1. PRINCIPAL PROBLEM

The City of Los Angeles ("the City") owns a sports stadium and the surrounding property. The Los Angeles Football Association ("LAFA") owns the local professional football team. Twenty years ago, the City entered into an agreement with LAFA that allows LAFA to use the stadium to host all of its home football games in return for a specified percentage of its profits to be paid to the City. As part of the deal, the City agreed to maintain 12,000 parking spots for football fan parking, but LAFA allowed the City to have discretion over the location and specifications of this parking lot so long as the City meets LAFA's needs. The agreement refers to the City and LAFA as "lessor" and "lessee" respectively, but it lacks a legal description of the real property at issue. The agreement grants LAFA "exclusive control" over the stadium on specified dates to conduct football games, but it reserves control over concessions, security, and parking to the City. In addition, the agreement prohibits LAFA from assigning its obligations under the agreement to a third party.

The City wants to develop the stadium and the surrounding property into a multi-purpose sports complex, so it has issued a building permit to a local developer to build an office complex on part of the parking lot. Also, the City is trying to negotiate for other sports teams to use the stadium as their home field. Upon learning of these plans, LAFA sued the City for a violation of the terms of its lease. In response, the City argued that its agreement with LAFA is a license, not a lease, and that the City can revoke the license at will. After considering the following materials, discuss who should prevail.

## 2. Materials for Solution of Principal Problem

### Beckett v. City of Paris Dry Goods Co.
Supreme Court of California, 1939.
14 Cal.2d 633, 96 P.2d 122.

■ EDMONDS, J.

In this case, the court is called upon to determine whether a contract made by the parties is a lease or only a license to occupy certain property. The plaintiff recovered damages for unlawful eviction, but the trial judge refused to allow certain amounts claimed and each of the parties has appealed from the judgment.

The defendant agreed in writing with the plaintiff, who is an optometrist, that the latter might, for a period of three years, conduct a first-class optical department in its large store. The space to be occupied at any time was to be designated by the defendant, which was to supply all light, heat, water, telephone and elevator service. Dr. Beckett agreed to furnish equipment, fixtures and show-cases conforming in style and finish with those used in the store, and to pay it twenty per cent of his total monthly sales as consideration for the right to do business upon the conditions stated. It was further stipulated that all money taken in by Dr. Beckett should be deposited with the cashier of the City of Paris at the end of each day, and that the latter would later render a statement to him showing the balance of his account after deduction of amounts chargeable to him for rental, advertising, and uncollectible bills.

By the terms of the contract Dr. Beckett was required to purchase merchandise in his own name and upon his own credit, and he agreed to provide liability insurance indemnifying the store against liability arising because of his negligence or that of his employees. Other provisions are that he "cannot assign this lease or any interest therein" without the written consent of the dry goods company and that "on the last day of the term created hereby", he will "forthwith quietly and peaceably surrender and yield up unto the . . . [department store] any occupied premises."

Following the execution of this agreement, Dr. Beckett took possession of several rooms designated by the City of Paris and occupied them for more than two years. The store then notified him that it was canceling the agreement because of asserted violation of the provision requiring the deposit of receipts with its cashier, and it requested that he vacate on the evening of December 7th. This date was later postponed for three weeks, but immediately thereafter all of the plaintiff's instruments and merchandise were taken out of his rooms and he was excluded therefrom.

The department store contends that its agreement gave Dr. Beckett only a license to use the premises, and that the contract could, therefore, be terminated for just cause at any time. In support of its position, the defendant points out that no definite space was set apart for Dr. Beckett to occupy, and that it was given control of his business in matters of advertising policy and the keeping of accounts. By the terms of the contract, Dr. Beckett also agreed to discharge any employee who should "become objectionable" to the store. Under these circumstances, says the City of Paris, it is obvious that the parties intended the optical department to be an integral part of the store which Dr. Beckett had only a license to manage and operate; hence it had the right to terminate that license at any time and to exclude him from the premises.

A lease is both a contract and a conveyance; under such an agreement there are rights and obligations based upon the relationship of landlord and tenant as well as upon the contractual promises. It is well recognized that no particular legal terminology is required in the making of a lease, but it is essential that the instrument show an intention to establish the relationship of landlord and tenant.

Although Dr. Beckett agreed to conduct his business in accordance with the policy of the store, to do his billing through the company's office, to discharge employees who were objectionable to the company, and to cooperate in other matters, there are other provisions in the agreement which definitely point to an intention that the relationship between them should be that of lessor and lessee. For example, the agreement provides that "the designated space shall be delivered to second party in good, tenantable condition", and that Dr. Beckett shall have "the sole and exclusive right to conduct the optical department." It also bound Dr. Beckett, in terms common to leases, "to pay as a monthly rental a sum equivalent to twenty per cent (20%) of the total monthly sales of said department." Also, not only do the parties use the term "lease" in their agreement but the provision which forbids assignment without the consent of the department store is not applicable to a license, which is "a personal, revocable and unassignable permission to do one or more acts on the land of another without possessing any interest therein."

Moreover, throughout the whole instrument, rights are given and language is used which definitely indicates that a lease was intended. The phrases "good, tenantable condition", "cannot assign this lease", "space demised", and "monthly rental" are the terminology of a lease. The use of these words is not conclusive of intention but strongly indicates that the parties contemplated such a relationship. Nor does the retention by the store of a certain amount of control over the management of the optical department, or the requirement that Dr. Beckett adhere to the rules and regulations governing its operations, negative this intention.

A lease must include a definite description of the property leased and an agreement for rental to be paid at particular times during a specified term. (Losson v. Blodgett, 1 Cal.App. (2d) 13 [36 Pac. (2d) 147]). Yet, where one goes into possession of premises under a contract containing an ambiguous or uncertain description of property to be occupied and pays the stipulated rent, it will be enforced as a lease if the parties acted upon it as relating to particular premises.

When the litigants made their contract, they stated only that "the space to be occupied by said [optical] department at any time" was to be designated by the City of Paris, and "shall be delivered to . . . [Dr. Beckett] in good tenantable condition." This provision is not inconsistent with the requirements of a lease and in cases which have arisen under facts strikingly similar to those in the present controversy it has been held that an agreement under which an owner of real property allows another to conduct his own separate business in a stall or section of a store or lot creates the relationship of landlord and tenant rather than licensor and licensee.

Both parties agree that if the agreement is a lease, violations of the requirement for all money received to be turned in at the end of each day are not sufficient to justify a forfeiture of it. This is the correct construction of their contract and the plaintiff is, therefore, entitled to recover upon his cause of action for eviction.

Passing to a consideration of the points presented by Dr. Beckett upon his appeal from the judgment, he first challenges the conclusion of the trial judge concerning the amount of his actual damages. It is undisputed that during the year immediately preceding his eviction, his average monthly earnings were $259.61. As he was evicted three months before the expiration of his lease, he is entitled to the sum of $778.83 for loss of profits instead of $666 allowed as actual damages. Also, the defendant does not deny that Dr. Beckett expended $35 for the removal of his furniture and equipment. This sum is recoverable by him. . . .

The judgment is therefore modified by adding the sum of $147.83 to the amount of $666 for which damages were awarded and as so modified the judgment is affirmed, the appellant Lawrence G. Beckett to recover costs on appeal.

## Wenner and City of Phoenix v. Dayton-Hudson Corporation
Court of Appeals of Arizona, 1979.
123 Ariz. 203, 598 P.2d 1022.

■ DONOFRIO, ACTING PRESIDING JUDGE.

This is an appeal by defendants/appellants, City of Phoenix, from an adverse decision by the Superior Court of Maricopa County holding that the income received by plaintiff/appellee from certain agreements with retailers was not taxable under the Phoenix City Code § 14–2(a)(12).

The pertinent undisputed facts can be stated as follows: Appellee operates department stores within the city limits of Phoenix under the trade name "Diamonds." As part of its business operations, appellee enters into agreements with other retailers to maintain certain departments within its stores. Some of these departments for example include: the beauty salon, the shoe department, the fur salon and the furniture department.

The agreement entered into grants the retailer the exclusive right to operate a particular type of department within appellee's store, and the retailer is allowed to conduct only that type of business within the store. In consideration of appellee furnishing certain services, the retailer pays appellee a percentage of his gross receipts with a minimum monthly payment designated. The agreements are for a definite term and are automatically renewed absent any notice of termination, but the appellee may terminate the agreement at any time the retailer is in default.

The income derived by appellee from these agreements was assessed a one (1) percent privilege tax by appellant City of Phoenix through Paul Wenner, the City Treasurer, under the provisions of § 14–2(a)(12). Appellee paid the assessed tax under protest and was granted a hearing by appellants. Appellant Wenner found that the tax was proper and upheld the tax as assessed. After exhausting the administrative remedies provided, appellee brought an action in the Superior Court challenging the tax. The trial court granted appellee's motion for summary judgment and entered judgment in favor of appellee for $20,364.22 plus interest and costs. This appeal followed.

Section 14–2 of the Phoenix City Code provides in part as follows:

There is hereby levied upon persons on account of their business activities within the City and shall be collected by the collector for the purpose of raising revenue to be used in defraying the necessary expenses of the City, privilege taxes to the extent hereinafter provided, to be measured by the gross sales or gross income of persons, whether derived from residents of the City or not, or whether derived from within the City or from without, and all of said gross sales or gross income shall be used to measure the tax with exceptions as set forth in Subsections (b) and (d) of this Section, and in Section 14–40 and Section 14–41 of the Phoenix City Code in accordance with the following schedule:

(a) An amount equal to one percent of the gross proceeds of sale or gross income from the business upon every person engaging or continuing within the City in the following businesses:

. . .

(12) *Leasing or renting for a consideration the use or occupancy of real property,* including any improvements, rights or interest in such property to the person in actual possession or occupation of the leased premises. (Emphasis supplied.)

Appellants contend that the agreement between appellee and the retailer is a lease and not a license. They argue that if one looks beyond the words used in the agreement calling it a license and views the provisions of the agreement as a whole, the legal effect is a lease and not a license. In support of this argument appellants cite several cases. We shall hereinafter discuss these authorities.

Section 5 of the agreement in question sets forth a declaration of the parties' intent that the agreement is a license. Though this clause is persuasive, it is not controlling upon us, and we must determine if the whole agreement is in accord with this intent and only creates a license agreement.

Section 5. *Licensee engaged in an independent business*

. . .

(d) *This agreement shall be construed as a mere license* by Licensor to Licensee to operate said concession in said store of licensor. *It shall not be construed as a lease, sublease or rental agreement.* It is understood and agreed that licensee has no interest whatsoever in the real property upon which the concession is operated and no right to exclusive possession of any portion of licensor's store building. (Emphasis supplied.)

Under the agreement appellee was obligated to furnish the licensee/retailer an agreeable amount of space in its store, but such space was not specifically delineated within the agreement. In fact, the space may be changed from time to time at appellee's direction. The agreement provides that the retailer is not granted any interest whatsoever in the real property upon which the department is operated or exclusive possession of any particular portion of appellee's building. The licensee-retailer only has access to appellee's store when said store is open to the public, and may only conduct business at such times as it is open.

Appellee requires licensee to use appellee's trademark and its trade name in conducting its business. Thus, licensee receives the benefit of being able to do business under the respected and generally known name of appellee. Further, appellee provides licensee with:

> regular lighting, electrical, air-conditioning, elevator and escalator service . . . , deposit and change cashier service, . . . charge account service . . . , sales books . . . , wrapping supplies, one (1) telephone, . . . telephone service, . . . janitor service . . . , hot and cold water and heating. . . . [Section 7(a)].

For the right to use appellee's name and trademark and for the services provided licensee agrees to reimburse appellee a percentage of the sales it experiences by doing business in appellee's store.

We find every indication that the parties have intended to create a licensor-licensee relationship in the instant agreement. Bearing this in mind we shall now look at the authorities cited by appellants.

Appellants cite *Beckett v. City of Paris Dry Goods Co.*, 14 Cal.2d 633, 96 P.2d 122 (1939), for the proposition that the agreement contained in that cause is nearly identical to the one in question here and that the California courts construed that agreement to be a lease instead of a license. Appellants seem to rely heavily on the particular statement concerning the non-assignability provision of the agreement in the *City of Paris* case to hold that it was a lease. Appellants try to convince this Court that the California Supreme Court based its decision that the agreement was a lease solely on the presence of a non-assignability clause in the agreement.

We do not agree with appellants' argument as it concerns the *City of Paris* case as we can distinguish it from the present set of facts. From a reading of *City of Paris*, and the case of *Case v. Kadota Fig Ass'n of Producers*, Cal.App., 207 P.2d 86 (1949), and subsequent Supreme Court opinion, 35 Cal.2d 596, 220 P.2d 912 (1950), we find that the California court was persuaded most heavily by factors other than the non-assignability clause of that agreement. In *Kadota Fig*, supra, the California appellate court stated that the agreement in *City of Paris* "was held to be a lease mostly because the use of terminology like '*this lease*,' '*good, tenantable condition*,' '*space demised*' showed that this was the relation (sic) which the parties intended." 207 P.2d at 96 (Emphasis supplied.)

The provisions of the agreement before us in the instant appeal do not contain such characteristic terminology of a lease. We do not find, as was present in *City of Paris,* anything in the instant cause that shows the intention to create a landlord/tenant relationship, or the giving of exclusive possession or an interest in the property over and above a personal right of operation as against appellee.

The non-assignment clause contained within the instant agreement, upon close examination, is not the routine non-assignment clause of a lease, but a correct statement of the law putting a licensee on notice of his inability to assign this agreement, and that if he attempts an assignment he will be in breach of his contract. We include the clause for a better understanding of its content:

Section 19. Assignment

This agreement is personal to the licensee, and licensee may not assign this agreement or any right thereunder nor give any security interest therein or in any rights thereunder nor may this agreement be assigned by operation of law. Any assignment of this agreement or rights thereunder by licensee or by operation of law or the giving of any security interest therein shall at licensor's option constitute a breach of this agreement and be void.

The *Kadota Fig* case further gives support to our holding that the agreement is a license when it notes that "the rule of revocability of a license at pleasure is not without modifications and exceptions." This language is in compliance with the Restatement of Property § 519, comment b. (1944) which reads:

The fact that a license is terminable at the will of the licensor does not necessarily mean that the licensor can terminate it without incurring liability for doing so. It means only that the interest in land which the license constitutes has disappeared. The licensor may be bound by contract not to so exercise his will as to terminate the license, and when so bound will be liable in damages for breach of his contract. Restatement of Property § 519, comment b. (1944) [See also other comments of § 519.]

Next, appellants cite the case of *In re Owl Drug Co.,* 12 F.Supp. 439 (Nevada District Court 1935), in support of their argument. However, we must again distinguish this case from the instant appeal. The *Owl Drug Co.* case agreement again has language and provisions throughout it showing an intent of the parties to create a lease. The terms "lessor" and "lessee" are used throughout the agreement, and the phrase "rent for the premises" is used to describe the money paid each month for the use of the area. The *Owl Drug Co.* court found the following clause to be most significant in finding the agreement to be a lease:

and the abatement of the use of said building or the premises herein leased by reason of any breach of any of said rules or regulations by said lessee, his agents, servants or employees shall not terminate or in any way affect the obligations of the lessee hereunder. 12 F.Supp. at 443.

The *Owl* court further said in explanation of this clause:

> In other words, upon the abatement of the use of the building or of the portion leased, brought on by any act of the lessee, he is not released from any of the obligations under the lease. 12 F.Supp. at 443.

The agreement before this Court does not contain such a provision. Once the agreement has been terminated for a breach, licensee is liable only for accrued debts and contract damages, not for lost rent as it would be if the agreement was a lease.

We also note that the agreement in the *Owl Drug Co.* case contained a clause which would not allow the "lease" to be assigned or transferred, or any part of the premises be sublet without the written consent of the lessor. Further, the agreement provided that the terms, covenants and conditions of the "lease" are made to "enure" to the benefit of the "lessee," his "executors" or "administrators," and any of his "successors" or "assigns" who have become such by consent of the "lessor." These all being terms and conditions of a lease and not a license the *Owl* and *Paris* agreements are distinguishable from our instant agreement.

The agreement used by appellee is carefully drawn, perhaps with the above-cited cases in mind, and has created what the parties intended, a license, and nothing more. From the foregoing we can only conclude that as a matter of law the agreement between appellee and its merchant retailers does not rise to the level of a leasehold interest, but is a mere license.

Appellants, at oral argument before this Court, contended that the City Ordinance § 14–2(a)(12) is broad enough to tax even a license agreement. With this contention we disagree.

The Arizona Supreme Court has stated many times that revenue statutes should be construed liberally in favor of the taxpayer and strictly against the State. In *Arizona State Tax Comm. v. Staggs Realty Corp.*, 85 Ariz. 294, 297, 337 P.2d 281, 283 (1959), the Supreme Court stated that, "it is especially important in tax cases to begin with the words of the operative statute. We have repeatedly said that such words will be read to gain their fair meaning, but not to gather new objects of taxation by strained construction or implication."

Judgment affirmed.

## NOTES

1. *Restatement's position.* Restatement (Second) of Property: Landlord & Tenant § 1.1, illus. 1 (1977) provides that the fact that a tenant can be shifted from one location to another within a building does not prevent the

arrangement from creating a landlord-tenant relationship. The Restatement also states: "The relationship between landlord and tenant may endure for any fixed period of time." Restatement (Second) of Property: Landlord & Tenant § 1.4.

2. *Significance of nomenclature.* How significant should it be that in *Beckett* the parties called their agreement a "lease," whereas in *Wenner* the parties called their agreement a "license"? It has been stated that a court is not bound by a "misdescription" made by the parties in their contract.[1]

Presumably, in *Wenner,* if the parties had consistently called their contract a "lease," the court would have found that a lease had been created and would have upheld the tax. Why would the parties ever call their contract a lease if this would result in additional taxes? Apart from taxation, would there be any practical consequences to calling the agreement a lease? Should the words "lease" and "license" have the same meaning in every context?

3. *Careful drafting.* To what extent can the parties control whether their relationship will be treated as a lease or a license by careful drafting of their agreement? What problems exist when the parties have conflicting goals with respect to their legal relationship?

4. *Consequences of terminating a license.* "The fact that a license is terminable at the will of the licensor does not necessarily mean that the licensor can terminate it without incurring liability for doing so." Restatement of Property § 519 cmt. b. (1944). Such a situation is likely to occur when the licensor has simultaneously assumed contractual duties that will be breached by the revocation of the license, or the licensee has made valuable improvements to the land in reasonable reliance on the license.[2] A license agreement that does not refer to revocability or does not designate a specified duration may be terminated by the licensor at any time without cause.

## b. Interference with Actual Physical Possession and Quiet Enjoyment

### 1. Interference at the Commencement of the Lease Term

All states agree that by the mere act of signing the lease the landlord impliedly promises that she is granting the right to physical possession of the leased premises. This is an aspect of the landlord's *covenant of quiet*

---

[1] See, e.g., Union Sq. Park Community Coalition, Inc. v. New York City Dept. of Parks & Recreation, 22 N.Y.3d 648 (N.Y. 2014); Baseball Pub. Co. v. Bruton, 302 Mass. 54, 56, 18 N.E.2d 362, 364 (1938); Beal v. Eastern Air Devices, Inc., 9 Mass.App.Ct. 910, 403 N.E.2d 438 (1980); Miller v. City of New York, 15 N.Y.2d 34, 203 N.E.2d 478, 255 N.Y.S.2d 78 (1964).

[2] See, e.g., County of La Paz v. Yakima Compost Co., 224 Ariz. 590 (Ariz. Ct. App. 2010); Apollo Stereo Music Co. v. Kling, 528 P.2d 976, 978 (Colo. App. 1974); Gerry v. Johnston, 85 Idaho 226, 231, 378 P.2d 198, 201–02 (1963); Melodies, Inc. v. Mirabile, 4 Misc. 2d 1062, 1063, 163 N.Y.S.2d 131, 133–34 (City Ct. 1957), modified on other grounds, 179 N.Y.S.2d 991 (App. Div. 1958); cf. Ulan v. Vend-A-Coin, 27 Ariz. App. 713, 716, 558 P.2d 741, 744 (Ct. App. 1976).

*enjoyment* implied in all leases. Most states go further and hold that the landlord is obligated to furnish actual physical possession to the tenant. A few states follow the rule (sometimes called the "American" rule) that it is up to the tenant to deal with any trespasser or holdover tenant (*i.e.*, the prior tenant who refuses to vacate the leased premises), and that the landlord's implied grant of the legal right to possession does not include a promise to deliver actual possession. Courts adopting the majority rule argue that their position most accords with the expectations of the parties, or at least of the tenant, when the lease was signed.[3] Courts supporting the minority view argue that the landlord should not be held responsible for the acts of independent wrongdoers. They also argue that since the landlord is not usually responsible for the acts of trespassers during the lease term itself, she should not be responsible for the acts of trespassers before the term begins. Cannot the two situations be distinguished? Is it possible clearly to articulate why one rule is better than the other? In this context what do we mean by "better"?

Restatement (Second) of Property: Landlord & Tenant § 6.2 (1977) adopts, in general, the majority rule with respect to a holdover tenant or other person improperly in possession on the date the tenant is entitled to possession. Both the Uniform Land Transactions Act § 2–307 (1975) and the Uniform Residential Landlord Tenant Act § 2.103 (2015) also appear to follow the majority rule.[4]

All courts following the majority rule hold that the tenant is excused from paying rent for the period during which she is unable to obtain actual physical possession of the premises. However, when the incoming tenant is denied the right to actual exclusive physical possession of the property by a holdover tenant the issue of the incoming tenant's right to terminate the lease must be addressed. Restatement (Second) of Property: Landlord & Tenant § 6.2 (1977) states that the incoming tenant may not terminate if the landlord removes the holdover within a "reasonable" period of time.

## 2. INTERFERENCE DURING THE LEASE TERM

Sometimes the tenant's right to exclusive physical possession is obstructed during the lease term itself. If, during the term, the tenant's possession is disturbed by a wrongdoer acting independently of the landlord, the tenant has no cause of action against the landlord in the absence of the landlord's negligence. On the other hand, where tenant's possession is disturbed by someone with paramount title the tenant has a good cause of action against the landlord for damages arising from the

---

[3] See generally, Weissenberger, The Landlord's Duty to Deliver Possession: The Overlooked Reform, 46 Univ. of Cincinnati L.Rev. 937 (1977).

[4] See generally Sullivan, *Forgotten Lessons from the Common Law, The Uniform Residential Landlord and Tenant Act, and the Holdover Tenant*, 84 Wash. U. L. Rev. 1287, 1315–16 (2006) (discussing the implementation of the URLTA and its shortcomings with respect to the holdover tenant).

breach of the landlord's covenant of quiet enjoyment. One with paramount title has a right of possession superior to that of the tenant (*e.g.*, a mortgagee of the landlord who forecloses on the property). Why should the tenant be able to have a claim against the landlord when the possession is disturbed by one with paramount title but not when possession is disturbed by a wrongdoer acting independently of the landlord?

There is yet another type of situation that can result in a disruption of the tenant's quiet enjoyment. What should be the appropriate response when the landlord herself (or someone for whom the landlord is responsible) physically dispossesses the tenant from part of the leased premises? Should rent during the period of this actual partial eviction be entirely abated? Should it matter whether partial eviction was made absent intent by, or under an honest mistake of, the landlord? Should all of the rent be abated only if the partial dispossession was substantial? Should the tenant be confined simply to an action for damages and for recovery of the disputed area, without any rent abatement? Can one distinguish a judgment awarding "damages," and one ordering a reduction in rent?

### Does Tenant Have a Claim Against Landlord?

| Time of Interference | Possession Disturbed by | | |
|---|---|---|---|
| | Landlord | Wrongdoer | One with Paramount Title |
| Commencement of term | Yes | Yes (majority) | Yes |
| During term | Yes | No | Yes |

## 3. PRINCIPAL PROBLEM

Leo leased a building to Theresa that Theresa used as a restaurant. Leo also owned adjacent property that he leased to Tri-State Auto Parks as a parking lot. Shortly after Theresa started her restaurant she began using a strip of the land leased to Tri-State for the storage of garbage. This strip, approximately 5 feet by 48 feet, was adjacent to Theresa's building. Tri-State did not object to this practice and later erected four iron posts marking the strip. Several years later the municipal Health Department informed Theresa that she could not continue the unenclosed storage of garbage on the strip because of the odor and fire danger. Theresa unsuccessfully negotiated with Tri-State for additional space, and then, with the approval of Leo, began construction of an extension of her building that enclosed the strip. One week after the work began, Tri-State's attorney sent a letter to Theresa protesting the encroachment and demanding that the work be stopped. Theresa, however, was on a three month vacation on a remote island in the South Pacific and could not be reached. The building was completed six weeks later. Tri-State stopped paying the rent, which was $3,000 per month, and Leo is suing for the rent. After reviewing the following materials, discuss the rights of the parties.

## 4. MATERIALS FOR SOLUTION OF PRINCIPAL PROBLEM

### Smith v. McEnany
Supreme Judicial Court of Massachusetts, 1897.
170 Mass. 26, 48 N.E. 781.

■ HOLMES, J.

This is an action upon a lease for rent and for breach of a covenant to repair. The defense is an eviction. The land is a lot in the city of Boston, the part concerned being covered by a shed which was used by the defendant to store wagons. The eviction relied on was the building of a permanent brick wall for a building on adjoining land belonging to the plaintiff's husband, which encroached 9 inches, by the plaintiff's admission, or, as his witness testified, from measurements, 13 1/2 inches, or, as the defendant said, 2 feet, for 34 feet along the back of the shed. The wall was built with the plaintiff's assent, and with knowledge that it encroached on the demised premises. The judge ruled that the defendant had a right to treat this as an eviction determining the lease. The plaintiff asked to have the ruling so qualified as to make the question depend upon whether the wall made the premises "uninhabitable for the purpose for which they were hired, materially changing the character and beneficial enjoyment thereof." This was refused, and the plaintiff excepted.

The refusal was right. It is settled in this state, in accordance with the law of England, that a wrongful eviction of the tenant by the landlord from a part of the premises suspends the rent under the lease. The main reason which is given for the decisions is that the enjoyment of the whole consideration is the foundation of the debt and the condition of the covenant, and that the obligation to pay cannot be apportioned. It also is said that the landlord shall not apportion his own wrong, following an expression in some of the older English books. But this does not so much explain the rule as suggest the limitation that there may be an apportionment when the eviction is by title paramount or when the lessor's entry is rightful.

It leaves open the question why the landlord may not show that his wrong extended only to a part of the premises. No doubt the question equally may be asked why the lease is construed to exclude apportionment, and it may be that this is partly due to the traditional doctrine that the rent issues out of the land, and that the whole rent is charged on every part of the land. Gilbert, Rents, 178, 179, gives this as one ground why the lessor shall not discharge any part from the burden and continue to charge the rest, coupled with considerations partly of a feudal nature. But the same view naturally would be taken if the question arose now for the first time. The land is hired as one whole. If by his own fault the landlord withdraws a part of it he cannot recover either on the lease or outside of it for the occupation of the residue.

It follows from the nature of the reason for the decisions which we have stated that, when the tenant proves a wrongful deforcement by the landlord from an appreciable part of the premises, no inquiry is open as to the greater or less importance of the parcel from which the tenant is deforced. Outside the rule de minimis, the degree of interference with the use and enjoyment of the premises is important only in the case of acts not physically excluding the tenant, but alleged to have an equally serious practical effect, just as the intent is important only in the case of acts not necessarily amounting to an entry and deforcement of the tenant. Skally v. Shute, 132 Mass. 367. The inquiry is for the purpose of settling whether the landlord's acts had the alleged effect; that is, whether the tenant is evicted from any portion of the land. If that is admitted, the rent is suspended because, by the terms of the instrument as construed, the tenant has made it an absolute condition that he should have the whole of the demised premises, at least as against willful interference on the landlord's part.

We must repeat that we do not understand any question, except the one which we have dealt with, to be before us. An eviction like the present does not necessarily end the lease (Leishman v. White, 1 Allen, 489, 490), or other obligations of the tenant under it, such as the covenant to repair.

Exceptions overruled.

## Echo Consulting Services, Inc. v. North Conway Bank

Supreme Court of New Hampshire, 1995.
140 N.H. 566, 669 A.2d 227.

■ BROCK, CHIEF JUSTICE.

The plaintiff, Echo Consulting Services, Inc. (Echo), sued its landlord, North Conway Bank (the bank), claiming constructive eviction, partial actual eviction, breach of an implied covenant of quiet enjoyment, and breach of the lease. Echo appeals the decision of the Superior Court (Fitzgerald, J.) denying all of Echo's claims after a bench trial. We affirm in part, reverse in part, and remand.

Pursuant to a written lease dated March 15, 1986, Echo leased premises on the downstairs floor of a building in Conway, together with "common right of access" thereto. When the bank purchased the building from Echo's prior landlord, it assumed the lease and became Echo's landlord.

The bank undertook a series of renovations to make the building suitable for a branch banking business on the main, street-level floor.

These renovations, occurring on and off through 1987, created noise, dirt, and occasional interruptions of electric service. The construction work also made the rear parking lot inaccessible. During most of 1987, therefore, many of Echo's employees used the street-level parking lot in front of the building; they gained access to Echo's downstairs office by first using the main, street-level access to the building and then walking downstairs. On October 13, the bank changed the locks on the main floor access door for security reasons, and Echo's employees were no longer able to get in or out of the building through that door after regular business hours. At that point, Echo's only means of access after hours was through the rear door, and Echo presented testimony that even that access was obstructed and difficult at times. The parties disagree as to the extent of these interferences, and as to the damage that they caused to Echo's permissible uses of its leasehold.

On appeal, Echo argues that the trial court erred by: (1) confusing the legal standards for constructive eviction and partial actual eviction; (2) finding that locking the street-level access doors did not constitute a partial actual eviction; (3) ruling that there was no constructive eviction; and (4) applying the wrong legal standard to determine the quiet enjoyment issue.

This case involves a commercial, as distinguished from a residential, lease. Since we have not addressed in the commercial context all of the issues raised here, we will draw some insight from residential lease cases, even though the applicable law may be more protective in the residential context.

In any lease, along with the tenant's possessory interest, the law implies a covenant of quiet enjoyment, which obligates the landlord to refrain from interferences with the tenant's possession during the tenancy. See generally 2 R. Powell, Powell on Real Property ¶¶ 231[2], 232[1] (1994). There are several ways in which a landlord might breach that covenant, each giving rise to a different claim by the tenant. The landlord's actual physical dispossession of the tenant from the leased premises constitutes an actual eviction, either total or partial, as well as a breach of the covenant. Id. ¶ 231[2]. "Interferences by the landlord that fall short of a physical exclusion but that nevertheless substantially interfere with the tenant's enjoyment of the premises, causing the tenant to vacate, are actionable by the tenant as 'constructive' evictions." Id. ¶ 232[1], at 16B–27. The landlord's general breach of the covenant of quiet enjoyment, even if not "substantial" enough to constitute a constructive eviction, nevertheless entitles the tenant to damages. Id. ¶ 232[1], at 16B–32 to 16B–33. We turn now to addressing each of Echo's claims separately.

I. Partial Actual Eviction

A partial actual eviction occurs when the landlord deprives the tenant of physical possession of some portion of the leased property, including denial of access to the leased premises. See Barash v.

Pennsylvania Terminal Real Estate Corp., 26 N.Y.2d 77, 308 N.Y.S.2d 649, 256 N.E.2d 707, 709 (N.Y.1970); Restatement (Second) of Property § 6.1 reporter's note 2, at 236 (1976); 2 Powell, supra ¶ 231[2][b], at 16B–24. A landlord cannot apportion a tenant's rights under a lease. See Barash, 26 N.Y.2d 77, 308 N.Y.S.2d 649, 256 N.E.2d 707 at 710; Smith v. McEnany, 170 Mass. 26, 48 N.E. 781 (1897). Thus, the bank cannot apportion Echo's rights to choose which door to enter if the lease gives Echo a right to two different doors for access.

Echo, however, was not physically deprived of any portion of the property leased to it, nor of any appurtenant rights given to it under the lease. For its claim of partial actual eviction, Echo relies on the following language in the lease: "approximately 1,890 square feet of floor area, together with common right of access thereto, a common use of the parking lot." Echo argues that this language gives it a right of access through the main, street-level door, since that door is the only door that was actually used in common by both the bank and Echo. We disagree.

A lease is a form of contract that is construed in accordance with the standard rules of contract interpretation. When construing disputed provisions in a lease, we must analyze the entire document to determine the meaning intended by the parties. Language used by the parties to the agreement should be given its standard meaning as understood by reasonable people. In the absence of ambiguity, the intent of the parties to a lease is to be determined from the plain meaning of the language used. "The meaning of a contract is ultimately a matter of law for this court to decide, including the determination whether a contract term is ambiguous." Walsh v. Young, 139 N.H. 693, 695, 660 A.2d 1139, 1141 (1995) (quotation omitted).

The word "common" in Echo's lease modifies the phrase "right of access." Thus it plainly means only that the tenant's right to access is not an exclusive right; it is in "common" with the landlord's. The lease is not ambiguous; it cannot reasonably be construed to afford Echo the right in "common" to use the street-level door simply because that is the door which the bank chose actually to use. We interpret the trial court's finding that "Echo employees had access to their offices through at least one door at all times" to be a determination that such access was reasonable. That is all that is required under the language of this lease.

The trial court apparently applied the standard for constructive eviction in ruling on the actual eviction claim. Even though this was error, we affirm its decision on this issue because it reached the correct result and there are valid alternative grounds to reach that result. Since Echo was not physically deprived of any portion of the premises to which it had a right under the lease, the partial actual eviction claim was properly denied.

## II. Constructive Eviction

A constructive eviction is similar to a partial actual eviction except that no actual physical deprivation takes place. A constructive eviction occurs when the landlord so deprives the tenant of the beneficial use or enjoyment of the property that the action is tantamount to depriving the tenant of physical possession. Barash, 26 N.Y.2d 77, 308 N.Y.S.2d 649, 256 N.E.2d at 710; Restatement (Second) of Property, supra; 2 Powell, supra ¶ 232[1], at 16B–27.

The bank argues that a constructive eviction claim will not lie unless the landlord intends that its actions (1) render the premises unfit for occupancy or (2) permanently interfere with the tenant's beneficial use or enjoyment of the premises. We disagree.

It is well established that "the landlord's conduct, and not his intentions, is controlling." Blackett v. Olanoff, 371 Mass. 714, 358 N.E.2d 817, 819 (1977); cf. Restatement (Second) of Property § 6.1 (1976 & Supp.1995) (not mentioning any requirement that the landlord intend to evict the tenant). The bank mistakenly relies on one prior case to support its view that intent is required for a constructive eviction. See Thompson v. Poirier, 120 N.H. 584, 420 A.2d 297 (1980). Although Thompson contains allegations of intentional conduct on the landlord's part, intent was not a necessary element of our decision, and the prevailing view is to the contrary. For example, even though no intent was or could have been found, courts have found a constructive eviction where a nuisance outside the leased premises—such as excessive noise from neighboring tenants—was attributable to, though not affirmatively undertaken by, the landlord. See, e.g., Blackett, 358 N.E.2d at 819; Gottdiener v. Mailhot, 179 N.J.Super. 286, 431 A.2d 851, 854 (1981).

The focus of the inquiry in a constructive eviction case is not on intent but on the extent of the interference, i.e., whether, in the factual circumstances of the case, the interference is substantial enough that it is tantamount to depriving the tenant of physical possession. See, e.g., Baley & Selover v. All Am. Van & Storage, 97 Nev. 370, 632 P.2d 723, 724 (1981); Reste Realty Corp. v. Cooper, 53 N.J. 444, 251 A.2d 268, 274–75 (1969); see also 2 Powell, supra ¶ 232[1], at 16B–27; Restatement (Second) of Property, supra. The law regarding this substantiality requirement has moved over the years "in the direction of an increase in the landlord's responsibilities." 2 Powell, supra ¶ 232[1], at 16B–27. Even without any affirmative activity on the landlord's part, courts have found a constructive eviction where the landlord fails to perform a lease covenant, fails to perform statutory obligations, or fails to perform a duty that is implied from the circumstances. Sierad v. Lilly, 204 Cal.App.2d 770, 22 Cal.Rptr. 580, 583 (1962) (deprivation of use of parking space impliedly included in the lease); Cherberg v. Peoples Nat. Bank of Washington, 88 Wash.2d 595, 564 P.2d 1137, 1142 (1977) (landlord's failure to repair outside wall rendering it unsafe); see 2 Powell, supra ¶ 232[1], at 16B–29 to 16B–30.

As we held in connection with the partial actual eviction claim, the lease here did not grant Echo a right to use the particular door of its choosing. The lease provision was satisfied since, as the trial court found, Echo employees had access to their offices through at least one door at all times. Likewise, the trial court found "the interruptions and noise [from construction activities] were intermittent and temporary and did not substantially interfere or deprive Echo of the use of the premises."

### III. The Covenant of Quiet Enjoyment

A breach of the covenant of quiet enjoyment occurs when the landlord substantially interferes with the tenant's beneficial use or enjoyment of the premises. 2 Powell, supra ¶ 232[1], at 16B–27. Even if not substantial enough to rise to the level of a constructive eviction, see Reste, 251 A.2d at 274–75, such interference may constitute a breach of the covenant of quiet enjoyment entitling the tenant to damages. Carner v. Shapiro, 106 So.2d 87, 89 (Fla.Dist.Ct.App.1958); see Restatement (Second) of Property § 5 (changes in the physical condition of the premises which make them unsuitable for the use contemplated by the parties), § 6 (conduct by the landlord, or by a third party under the landlord's control, which interferes with the tenant's permissible use of the premises); 2 Powell, supra ¶ 232[1], at 16B–27.

The trial court concluded that quiet enjoyment only protects a tenant's possession against repossession by the landlord or one claiming title superior to the landlord. Although our prior cases have not addressed any other basis for a claim that the covenant of quiet enjoyment has been breached, they have not rejected such a claim either. We do not believe such a view of the covenant of quiet enjoyment constitutes good law today; many other courts have extended the covenant beyond mere denial of actual possession. Pollock v. Morelli, 245 Pa.Super. 388, 369 A.2d 458, 461 n. 1 (1976); see Restatement (Second) of Property §§ 5–6; 2 Powell, supra ¶ 232[1], at 16B–29.

When reasons of public policy dictate, "[c]ourts have a duty to reappraise old doctrines in the light of the facts and values of contemporary life—particularly old common law doctrines which the courts themselves created and developed." Kline v. Burns, 111 N.H. 87, 91, 276 A.2d 248, 251 (1971) (quotation omitted). Our society has evolved considerably since the tenurial system of property law was created by the courts. The complexities, interconnectedness, and sheer density of modern society create many more ways in which a landlord or his agents may potentially interfere with a tenant's use and enjoyment of leased premises. Even without rising to the level of a constructive eviction and requiring the tenant to vacate the premises, such interferences may deprive the tenant of expectations under the lease and reduce the value of the lease, requiring in fairness an award of compensatory damages. Moreover, under modern business conditions, there is "no reason why a lessee, after establishing itself on the leased premises, should be forced to await eviction by the lessor or surrender the premises, often at great loss, before claiming a breach of the covenant for interference with the use and possession of the premises" that is not substantial enough to rise to the level of a total eviction. Tenn-Tex Properties v. Brownell-Electro, Inc., 778 S.W.2d 423, 428 (Tenn.1989) (quotation omitted). Likewise, the landlord's greater level of knowledge of and control over the leased premises and the surrounding property militates in favor of a more modern view of the covenant of quiet enjoyment than the trial court adopted.

Since the trial court understandably, but erroneously, believed the implied covenant of quiet enjoyment protected only Echo's possession of the property, the court did not consider Echo's claim that the bank's construction activities breached the covenant by depriving Echo of the beneficial use of the premises. There was conflicting testimony as to whether such a breach occurred, and, if so, the damages caused thereby. These are questions of fact for the trial court to determine in the first instance. See Gibson v. LaClair, 135 N.H. 129, 133, 600 A.2d 455, 458 (1991). Accordingly, we reverse the trial court's conclusion on this issue and remand the quiet enjoyment claim for further proceedings consistent with this opinion.

We note, however, that our holding as to the definition of a covenant of quiet enjoyment effects a change in the common law in New Hampshire, and that others might have relied on the view of the covenant that our older cases had set forth. We decline, therefore, to make this change retroactive. Instead, for anyone who is not a party to the instant action, we will only apply this new interpretation prospectively.

Affirmed in part; reversed in part; remanded.

## NOTES

1. *Partial actual eviction.* Restatement (Second) of Property: Landlord & Tenant § 6.1 (1977) provides that the tenant can argue constructive eviction without even vacating the premises. It also rejects the majority rule providing for total abatement of rent on actual partial eviction by landlord, and instead relies on the normal legal and equitable remedies for breach of contract. See Reporter's Note to § 6.1, para. 6. Some jurisdictions, such as New York, continue to recognize partial eviction, so that the tenant must only vacate the part of the leased premises that is unusable for its intended purpose for constructive eviction to be applicable. See East Haven Associates Inc. v. Gurian, 64 Misc. 2d 276 (N.Y. Civ. Ct. 1970). Between the approaches in *Smith* and the Restatement, which rule is "better" and why? What does "better" mean in this context? Is it possible to reconcile these rules by focusing on whether the landlord's encroachment was deliberate or by mistake? How does the Principal Problem compare to *Smith* in this regard?

*Echo* concludes, in the context of discussing constructive eviction, that the landlord's intent is not an element of the cause of action. Do you agree? Does the Principal Problem involve a constructive eviction? The next Assignment also addresses constructive eviction.

2. *Covenant of quiet enjoyment.* Do you agree with *Echo's* holding that a breach of the doctrine of quiet enjoyment can occur even though the tenant is not constructively evicted? How should courts determine compensation for such a breach? Does *Echo* or the Principal Problem present a stronger case for breach of the covenant of quiet enjoyment?

3. *Residential vs. commercial.* The Principal Problem and the two Principal Cases all involve commercial property. Would it make sense to distinguish commercial property from residential property?

# ASSIGNMENT 4

# IMPLIED LANDLORD'S DUTIES AND IMPLIED CONDITIONS TO TENANT'S OBLIGATIONS

## 1. INTRODUCTION

In this Assignment we explore two major questions. (1) What landlord covenants, duties and promises are implied under different circumstances? (2) When a landlord breaches an express or implied covenant, what are the tenant's remedies?

*Implied Duties*

As we learned from the previous Assignment, the landlord has the duty (1) to provide the tenant with the legal right to possession, (2) not to interfere with the tenant's physical possession, and (3) in most jurisdictions, to make possession actually available to the tenant. Similarly, all courts would agree that the landlord has the duty to comply with express covenants made in the lease. In addition, a landlord may have a duty to perform acts that she did not expressly promise to perform. When the landlord fails to do something that she did not expressly promise to do, at least three questions must be considered. First, did the landlord impliedly promise to do the thing in question? Second, does the landlord's failure to perform the implied promise justify the tenant's termination of the lease? Third, if the tenant does not wish to, or cannot, terminate the lease, what other remedies does the tenant have?

In this Assignment, we try to determine what landlord duties should be implied. If a landlord shows a residence to a prospective tenant and the residence contains the usual plumbing and electrical outlets, is she impliedly representing that these items are in good working order? If, after the tenant moves in, he learns that the sink does not work and that no electricity can be obtained from the outlets, he would surely have good cause to complain. By giving the tenant a cause of action in such a case, the law is simply protecting the reasonable expectations of the parties.

Is the landlord also impliedly promising that if, through no fault of the tenant, the sink or other appliances break during the term, the landlord will fix them? Here no doubt custom and usage will play an important role. What is customary at that time and place for that kind of rental property? Perhaps a more fundamental question asks, what are the factors that shape a particular custom? One of the most important factors is who, tenant or landlord, is better able to make the repair efficiently? Most landlords would be reluctant to have a short-term tenant enter into a contract for major repairs. On the other hand, a tenant is normally expected to change burned out light bulbs in a residence because it is efficient and less expensive to have the tenant rather than the landlord change the bulbs. What other factors are likely to influence the custom of apportioning certain maintenance and repair duties between the landlord and the tenant?

Until the early 1960s, the general rule was that the landlord of residential or other premises made no implied covenants concerning the quality of the premises rented. Thereafter courts and legislatures overwhelmingly rejected this position. Today the law in the vast majority of jurisdictions is that there is an implied warranty of habitability in most residential leases. However, not all leases are short-term residential leases. Leases may involve industrial, agricultural, or commercial property. They may be short-term or long-term. They may involve unimproved or improved property. It seems unlikely that the covenants implied in one type of lease would necessarily be implied in another type of lease. Currently, a warranty of fitness is sometimes implied in non-residential leased premises.

*Tenant Remedies for Breach of Landlord's Covenants*

Once a court finds that a landlord has breached an implied duty in a particular situation, it is necessary to consider whether the tenant should be allowed to rescind the lease or to exercise other remedies. The tenant's duty to perform his covenants is not always conditioned on the landlord's performance of every one of her covenants. A minor breach by the landlord does not justify the tenant's refusal to pay the rent or termination of the lease. Often the tenant's sole remedy for the landlord's breach of a minor covenant is to sue the landlord for damages. In other words, the tenant's duty of performance is not conditional or dependent on the landlord's performance of minor covenants. On the other hand, if the landlord wrongfully evicts the tenant from the premises, the tenant is justified in terminating the lease. In this case, the tenant's obligations under the lease are conditional or dependent on the landlord's performing her implied promise not to interfere with the tenant's possession.

If a landlord breaches a duty (either one that is expressly contained in the lease or one that is determined to be implied), the tenant can obtain a monetary judgment against the landlord, compensating the tenant for damages caused by the landlord's breach. This compensation is subject to the usual limitations on the extent of contract damages. Often, however, a tenant would like to use other, or additional, remedies. For example, a tenant may claim that the landlord's breach justifies a complete termination of the lease. Or a tenant may claim that landlord's breach justifies a tenant in not paying ("withholding") rent temporarily, and then paying only a reduced ("abated") rent, the amount to be determined by a court. In other cases, the tenant may want to repair the item that the landlord expressly or impliedly promised to repair and then deduct the cost of the repair from the rent.

## 2. PRINCIPAL PROBLEM

The meat packing district in the city of Centreville has an old warehouse that was recently converted into studio lofts for working artists. Each 1,000 square foot loft contains a huge open area with two enclosed toilets. There is no kitchen per se, but each loft also comes equipped with a microwave and small refrigerator (but no stove or conventional oven). The intent behind the conversion was to afford artist-occupants a space to work on their art in their respective lofts, as well as a common area to display and sell their art to the public. Thus, the complex also contains a large common area that was intended to be used as an open-area market where the artists could sell their wares to the public. Many artists choose to fix their lofts up in a manner that enables them to stay overnight from time to time so they can work on their artwork anytime they choose. In the summer of 2009, sculptor Nesa Browne rented one of these lofts for a two year term. When a representative from the loft management company (the landlord) showed Nesa the loft, he told her that one of the two toilets was not operational but that he would repair it soon. Nesa was pleasantly surprised by the low monthly rent for the loft of $600 per month.

After she moved in, Nesa discovered that the loft lacked hot water. When she complained to the landlord, he replied by saying that unless she was some sort of idiot, she must have realized that such a cheap rental surely would be missing something critical like hot water. Furthermore, the open area market has become virtually unusable due to severe flooding from recent rainstorms. This is anticipated to be a long-term problem because the land designated for the market was apparently pitched incorrectly from the outset of the development's construction. Nonetheless, Nesa wants to stay in the loft because she really enjoys the community of artists who are her neighbors. Also, it is a good location for soliciting business because it is right by the train station and the major highway. She comes to you for advice and asks you: 1. whether an implied warranty of habitability has been breached with respect to the toilet, the hot water, and the market; and 2. if so, what remedies she can expect to obtain.

## 3. MATERIALS FOR SOLUTION OF PRINCIPAL PROBLEM

### Marini v. Ireland
Supreme Court of New Jersey, 1970.
56 N.J. 130, 265 A.2d 526.

■ HANEMAN J.

It becomes necessary to consider the merits of defendant's equitable defense that the failure of the landlord to repair the toilet constituted a breach of the covenant of habitability or quiet enjoyment and gave rise to defendant's entitlement to self-help, permitting her to repair the toilet and offset the cost thereof against her rent.

We are here concerned with the lease of premises for residential purposes. The lease provides:

> WITNESSETH, that the said party of the first part hath let, and by these presents doth grant, demise and to farm let unto the said party of the second part, all that contains 4 rooms and bath, apartment situated in the city and county of camden [sic.], state [sic.] of New Jersey, known and designated as 503-B Rand Street. . . .
>
> . . . nor use or permit any part thereof to be used for any other purpose than dwelling. . . .

As the lease contains no express covenant to repair, we are obliged to determine whether there arises an implied covenant, however categorized, which would require the landlord to make repairs.

A lease was originally considered a conveyance of an interest in real estate. Thus, the duties and obligations of the parties, implied as well as express, were dealt with according to the law of property and not of the law of contracts.

The guidelines employed to construe contracts have been modernly applied to the construction of leases. 3 Thompson on Real Property 377 (1959).

. . .

In Reste Realty Corporation v. Cooper, 53 N.J. 444 (1969), this Court said at p. 452, 251 A.2d 268, at p. 272:

> Moreover, an awareness by legislatures of the inequality of bargaining power between landlord and tenant in many cases, and the need for tenant protection, has produced remedial tenement house and multiple dwelling statutes. See e.g. N.J.S.A. 55:13A–1 et seq., and the regulations thereunder. It has come to be recognized that ordinarily the lessee does not have as much knowledge of the condition of the premises as the lessor. Building code requirements and violations are known or made known to the lessor, not the lessee. He is in a better position to know of latent defects, structural and otherwise, in a building which might go unnoticed by a lessee who rarely has sufficient knowledge or expertise to see or to discover them. A prospective lessee, such as a small businessman, cannot be expected to know if the plumbing or wiring systems are adequate or conform to local codes. Nor should he be expected to hire experts to advise him. Ordinarily all this information should be considered readily available to the lessor who in turn can inform the prospective lessee. These factors have produced persuasive arguments for reevaluation of the *caveat emptor*

doctrine and, for imposition of an implied warranty that the premises are suitable for the leased purposes and conform to local codes and zoning laws.

A covenant in a lease can arise only by necessary implication from specific language of the lease or because it is indispensable to carry into effect the purpose of the lease. In determining, under contract law, what covenants are implied, the object which the parties had in view and intended to be accomplished, is of primary importance. The subject matter and circumstances of the letting give at least as clear a clue to the natural intentions of the parties as do the written words. It is of course not the province of the court to make a new contract or to supply any material stipulations or conditions which contravene the agreements of the parties. Terms are to be implied not because they are just or reasonable, but rather for the reason that the parties must have intended them and have only failed to express them ... or because they are necessary to give business efficacy to the contract as written, or to give the contract the effect which the parties, as fair and reasonable men, presumably would have agreed on if, having in mind the possibility of the situation which has arisen, they contracted expressly in reference thereto.

So here, the lease expressly described the leased premises as "4 rooms and bath, apartment" and restricted the use thereof for one purpose—"dwelling." Patently, "the effect which the parties, as fair and reasonable men, presumably would have agreed on," was that the premises were habitable and fit for living. The very object of the letting was to furnish the defendant with quarters suitable for living purposes. This is what the landlord at least impliedly (if not expressly) represented he had available and what the tenant was seeking. In a modern setting, the landlord should, in residential letting, be held to an implied covenant against latent defects, which is another manner of saying, habitability and livability fitness.

It is a mere matter of semantics whether we designate this covenant one "to repair" or "of habitability and livability fitness." Actually it is a covenant that at the inception of the lease, there are no latent defects in facilities vital to the use of the premises for residential purposes because of faulty original construction or deterioration from age or normal usage. And further it is a covenant that these facilities will remain in usable condition during the entire term of the lease. In performance of this covenant the landlord is required to maintain those facilities in a condition which renders the property livable.

It is eminently fair and just to charge a landlord with the duty of warranting that a building or part thereof rented for residential purposes is fit for that purpose at the inception of the term and will remain so during the entire term. Of course, ancillary to such understanding it must be implied that he has further agreed to repair damage to vital facilities caused by ordinary wear and tear during said term. Where damage has been caused maliciously or by abnormal or unusual use, the tenant is conversely liable for repair. The nature of vital facilities and the extent and type of maintenance and repair required is limited and governed by the type of property rented and the amount of rent reserved. Failure to so maintain the property would constitute a constructive eviction.

It becomes necessary to consider the respective rights and duties which accompany such an implied covenant. We must recognize that historically, the landlord's covenant to alter or repair premises and the tenant's covenant to pay rent were generally regarded as independent covenants. The landlord's failure to perform did not entitle the tenant to make the repair and offset the cost thereof against future rent. It only gave rise to a separate cause of action for breach of covenant.

This result also eventuated from the application of the law of real estate rather than of contract. The concept of mutually dependent promises was not originally applied to the ascertainment of whether covenants in leases were dependent or independent. However, presently we recognize that covenants are dependent or independent according to the intention of the parties and the good sense of the case.

Our courts have on a case by case basis held various lease covenants and covenants to pay rent as dependent and under the guise of a constructive eviction have considered breach of the former as giving the right to the tenant to remove from the premises and terminate his obligation to pay rent.

It is of little comfort to a tenant in these days of housing shortage to accord him the right, upon a constructive eviction, to vacate the premises and end his obligation to pay rent. Rather he should be accorded the alternative remedy of terminating the cause of the constructive eviction where as here the cause is the failure to make reasonable repairs. This latter course of action is accompanied by the right to offset the cost of such repairs as are reasonable in the light of the value of the leasehold against the rent. His pursuit of the latter form of relief should of course be circumscribed by the aforementioned conditions.

If, therefore, a landlord fails to make repairs and replacements of vital facilities necessary to maintain the premises in a livable condition for a period of time adequate to accomplish such repair and replacements, the tenant may cause the same to be done and deduct the cost thereof from future rents. The tenant's recourse to such self-help must be preceded by timely and adequate notice to the landlord of the faulty condition in order to accord him the opportunity to make the necessary replacement or repair. If the tenant is unable to give such notice after a reasonable attempt, he may nonetheless proceed to repair or replace. This does not mean that the tenant is relieved from the payment of rent so long as the landlord fails to repair. The tenant has only the alternative remedies of making the repairs or removing from the premises upon such a constructive eviction.

We realize that the foregoing may increase the trials and appeals in landlord and tenant dispossess cases and thus increase the burden of the judiciary. By way of warning, however, it should be noted that the foregoing does not constitute an invitation to obstruct the recovery of possession by a landlord legitimately entitled thereto. It is therefore suggested that if the trial of the matter is delayed the defendant may be required to deposit the full amount of unpaid rent in order to protect the landlord if he prevails. Also, an application for a stay of an order of removal on appeal should be critically analyzed and not automatically granted.

Reversed and remanded for trial in accordance with the above.

## Knight v. Hallsthammar
Supreme Court of California, 1981.
29 Cal.3d 46, 171 Cal.Rptr. 707, 623 P.2d 268.

■ BIRD, CHIEF JUSTICE.

This court must decide whether a residential tenant may be held to have impliedly waived a landlord's breach of implied warranty of habitability by (1) continuing to live in premises despite knowledge of the defects or (2) failing to allow a landlord a reasonable time to repair before withholding rent.

### I.

On May 18, 1977, plaintiff landlords became owners of a 30-unit apartment building at 1305 Ocean Front Walk in Venice, California. They had bought the property from a Norman Baker and his parents.

On May 19th, Western Investment Properties, Inc. (hereinafter W.I.P.), which had been hired by plaintiffs to manage the property, sent a letter to the tenants indicating there would be a substantial increase in the rent. On May 26th Clara Breit, as representative of the "1305 Ocean Front Walk Tenants Association," sent a letter to W.I.P. stating that the tenants would withhold all future rent payments because of both the state of disrepair of the apartment building and the new rent increases. Neither W.I.P. nor plaintiffs responded to this letter.

When confronted in late May by tenants and the news media, an employee of W.I.P. allegedly indicated that the only repairs that would be made were to the vacant apartments and any common areas. No repairs were contemplated as to the occupied units until they became vacant. In early June, the tenants were served with three-day notices to pay the new rent or face eviction. These consolidated unlawful detainer actions by plaintiffs followed.

At the trial below, evidence was introduced by the tenants that plaintiffs had breached their implied warranty of habitability. The tenants complained of wall cracks, peeling paint, water leaks, heating and electrical fixture problems, broken or inoperable windows, rodents and cockroaches, and the lack of sufficient heat in the apartments. All of these conditions existed before plaintiffs acquired ownership. The defendants had personally complained to the manager about the conditions of their apartments before service of the three-day notices and before plaintiffs' ownership. Some complaints had also been lodged with Norman Baker. Only a portion of the complaints had resulted in corrections.

Plaintiff James E. Knight testified that he had first inspected some of the units during escrow in April, and, in August, had made a detailed itemization of needed improvements. Knight also testified that he had made plans for major renovation of the common areas and exterior, and in June W.I.P. had coordinated bids for renovation of the common areas. Since assuming ownership, Knight had made a few improvements to the common areas. Knight went on to testify that in early June he hired a pest control company to spray the apartments, and that he retained the company on a monthly service basis. When he received a complaint about the elevator shaft, he took care of it and hired an elevator maintenance service to make monthly checks.

In August, Knight had heard some complaints about the lack of heating and about the fact that tenant Breit did not have a heater. He had the manager install a steam radiator in Breit's apartment in September. The central heating was not turned on at all during the summer.

Knight testified that the tenants had not paid him any rent, and that the reasonable value of the premises was that which was stated in the 30-day notices for rent increases which had been served on the tenants in May.

Lawrence Young, a health officer for Los Angeles County, testified that he had inspected a few of the apartments during five visits between June 2d and August 5th. During that period Young noted seven violations which were abated upon his orders. He testified that the violations did not render the building uninhabitable (condemnable) under health department standards. That definition refers to a lack of any water, hot or cold, and to extensive sewage leakage or structurally unsound conditions.

The jury was unable to reach a verdict with respect to three tenants but returned a verdict in favor of plaintiffs against four tenants. These appeals followed, based upon defendants' claim that the trial court erroneously gave certain instructions requested by plaintiffs while refusing to give other instructions requested by defendants.

II.

First, this court must address the issue of a residential tenant who continues to live in uninhabitable premises after learning of the defects and whether this fact waives the landlord's breach of the implied warranty of habitability recognized by this court in Green v. Superior Court (1974) 10 Cal.3d 616, 111 Cal.Rptr. 704, 517 P.2d 1168.

In *Green,* a landlord commenced an unlawful detainer action seeking possession of leased premises and back rent. The tenant admitted nonpayment of rent but defended on the ground that the landlord had failed to maintain the premises in a habitable condition. This court held that there is in California a common law implied warranty of habitability in residential leases, and that under this warranty a landlord "covenants that premises he leases for living quarters will be maintained in a habitable state for the duration of the lease." (Id., at p. 637, 111 Cal.Rptr. 704, 517 P.2d 1168.) Further, a tenant may raise a landlord's breach of the implied warranty of habitability as a defense in an unlawful detainer proceeding. (Id., at pp. 622–629, 631–637, 111 Cal.Rptr. 704, 517 P.2d 1168.) Recognizing that at least one other court had held that such a warranty generally could not be waived by any provision in the lease or rental agreement, this court in *Green* stated that "public policy requires that landlords generally not be permitted to use their superior bargaining power to negate the warranty of habitability rule." (Id., at p. 625, fn. 9, 111 Cal.Rptr. 704, 517 P.2d 1168.) "[T]he severe shortage of low and moderate cost housing has left tenants with little bargaining power.... [E]ven when defects are apparent the low income tenant frequently has no realistic alternative but to accept such housing with the expectation that the landlord will make the necessary repairs." (Id., at p. 625, 111 Cal.Rptr. 704, 517 P.2d 1168.)

The declaration in *Green* of an implied warranty of habitability and of a public policy which generally prohibits waiver of that warranty is consistent with California's statutory pattern of landlord-tenant relations. Provisions of the Civil Code "are to be liberally construed with a view to effect its objects and to promote justice." (Civ.Code, § 4.) Further, "[a]ll contracts which have for their object, directly or indirectly, to exempt anyone from responsibility for ... violation of law, whether willful or negligent, are against the policy of the law." (Id., § 1668.) The Legislature has declared that "[t]he lessor of a building intended for the occupation of human beings must, in the absence of an agreement to the contrary, put it into a condition fit for such occupation, and repair all subsequent dilapidations thereof, which render it untenantable...." (Id., § 1941.)

Section 1942 of the same code provides a remedy by which a tenant may deduct rent payments needed to cure conditions which the landlord should have corrected. This statutory remedy is available only twice in any 12-month period and is not available unless the tenant has satisfied certain procedural prerequisites. However, the Legislature has recently made clear that "[t]he remedy provided by [section 1942] is in addition to any other remedy provided by this chapter, the rental agreement, or other applicable statutory or common law." (Id. § 1942, subd. (d), added by Stats.1979, ch. 307, § 3.)

The Legislature has further provided that "[a]ny agreement by a lessee of a dwelling waiving or modifying his rights under Section 1941 or 1942 shall be void as contrary to public policy with respect to any condition which renders the premises untenantable." (Civ.Code, § 1942.1).

In the present case, the trial court instructed the jury that a tenant may not defend an unlawful detainer action upon the basis of a landlord's breach of the implied warranty of habitability unless "[t]he defective condition was unknown to the tenant at the time of the occupancy of his or her apartment." However, the fact that a tenant was or was not aware of specific defects is not determinative of the duty of a landlord to maintain premises which are habitable. The same reasons which imply the existence of the warranty of habitability—the inequality of bargaining power, the shortage of housing, and the impracticability of imposing upon tenants a duty of inspection—also compel the conclusion that a tenant's lack of knowledge of defects is not a prerequisite to the landlord's breach of the warranty. Therefore, the trial court erred in giving this instruction.

Next, this court must decide whether the trial court erred when it instructed the jury that a breach of the implied warranty of habitability would be a defense to the unlawful detainer action *only if* plaintiff landlords had been allowed "a reasonable time to correct the defect while the tenant remained in possession." As pointed out by the Supreme Judicial Court of Massachusetts, "[t]he landlord's lack of fault and reasonable efforts to repair do not prolong the duty to pay full rent." (Berman & Sons, Inc. v. Jefferson (1979) 379 Mass. 196, 396 N.E.2d 981, 983; see also Jarrell v. Hartman (1977) 48 Ill.App.3d 985, 6 Ill.Dec. 812, 814, 363 N.E.2d 626, 628.) Also, it is significant that section 1941 of the California Civil Code speaks of a lessor's duty to put a building into a condition fit for occupation *and* to repair all later defects which make the premises uninhabitable. At least in a situation where, as here, a landlord has notice of alleged uninhabitable conditions not caused by the tenants themselves, a landlord's breach of the implied warranty of habitability exists whether or not he has had a "reasonable" time to repair. Otherwise, the mutual dependence of a landlord's obligation to maintain habitable premises, and of a tenant's duty to pay rent, would make no sense. (See Green v. Superior Court, supra, at pp. 634, 635, 111 Cal.Rptr. 704, 517 P.2d 1168.) Accordingly, the trial court erred in instructing that the tenants could not succeed in their defense unless the landlords had been allowed a "reasonable" time to repair.

### III.

Under Green v. Superior Court, supra, a residential tenant may not be deemed to have exempted a landlord from the implied warranty of habitability by continuing to live in uninhabitable premises, and breach of the warranty does not and should not depend upon a tenant's lack of knowledge of the conditions which make the premises uninhabitable.

Further, in an unlawful detainer action, a tenant's defense that a landlord has breached an implied warranty of habitability should not depend on whether the landlord has had a "reasonable" time to repair, because the issue is whether the premises are in fact inhabitable.

The trial court's erroneous instructions to the jury and failure to set forth properly the standards of habitability were likely to mislead the jury, and therefore the judgment is reversed.

■ CLARK, JUSTICE, dissenting.

In these consolidated unlawful detainer actions, the jury after a 15-day trial in September and October 1977 returned a verdict against appellants Maria Hallsthammar, Clara Breit, and Cecelia DeCaprio. The jury was unable to reach agreement as to three other tenants. Pursuant to the jury verdicts, the judgments awarded plaintiffs possession of appellants' apartments and $625 against Hallsthammar and Breit and $575 against DeCaprio. The sums represent five months rent. . . .

The following facts should be emphasized. Plaintiffs purchased a 30-unit apartment building on Ocean Front Walk in Venice, California, on 18 May 1977. They retained the resident manager who had been there 30 years. The following day a letter was sent to each tenant announcing substantial rent increases beginning 1 July.[1] The letter also stated the new owners would immediately undertake extensive refurbishment of the common areas in the buildings. Moreover, tenants were advised to inform the manager of problems and were provided with alternative phone numbers in case the manager was unavailable or emergencies arose.[2]

On 26 May, appellant Breit, as a representative of the tenants association, sent a letter notifying plaintiffs that further rental payments were being withheld because of the existing disrepairs and new rent increases. There was no response to the letter. Some tenants picketed the premises, seeking to dissuade prospective tenants from renting. Incidents of vandalism and harassment of owners were reported.

The evidence as to the apartments of the three appellants reveals an open space existed under the front door of Breit's apartment permitting air and dirt to blow in. The light in the bathroom burned out often necessitating replacement. The refrigerator-freezer door could come off its hinges, and cracks were reported in a window. The living room electrical outlet voltage was insufficient to operate all of the household appliances. Although Breit had problems with cockroaches, there was no evidence as to how often or how many. After she complained there was no heater, the resident manager installed a radiator for her.

DeCaprio did not testify as to the condition of her apartment. However, the record indicates she reported broken window and plumbing

---

[1] Rents for ocean view apartments were apparently doubled.
[2] Only one call was received. Appellant DeCaprio notified the owners of a broken window and leaky pipe. They were repaired.

problems sometime in early June. They were repaired. There also had been cockroaches in her apartment but again the evidence did not disclose how often or how many.

The radiator in Hallsthammer's apartment never functioned properly during her rental period; only two of the seven spokes would heat up. And although the leak in her sink was fixed in late June, there were many cracks in the walls and ceilings, and paint peeling near a window. The kitchen light switch was defective. As a result, Hallsthammer had to unscrew the lightbulb to turn off the light. She told the resident manager about these problems many times but did not telephone the owners. Unlike the other two apartments, there were no cockroaches reported.

There was evidence the building's hallways were inadequately lighted and dirty, some carpeting was old and frayed, the lobby area was often dirty and the elevator sometimes failed to stop at floor level. The central heating was turned off in early summer before plaintiffs purchased the building and remained off through the summer and until trial of the instant case in mid-October.

The owners sought bids for renovation after taking possession. They painted the front entrance and some of the hallway French doors and windows. New carpeting was placed in the elevator, hallways and landings. Repairs were made to hallways and back stairway. The owners contracted with a pest control company in June for monthly and on-call service and on 19 June the company sprayed for cockroaches. They also employed an elevator maintenance firm for monthly servicing. They refurbished vacant apartments by repainting, recarpeting the living areas, placing new vinyls on kitchen and bathroom floors, and in about five apartments, converting the bathtub to shower-tub combination. During the rent strike, plaintiffs paid utilities and received from the prior owners a grace period on trust deed payments.

A county health department officer inspected the building on 2 June and 4 times thereafter. He found 7 violations and ordered plaintiffs to abate; plaintiffs complied. The health officer testified the offenses were minor in nature and did not render the premises uninhabitable under health department condemnation standards, to wit when a building or portion of it is totally unfit for human habitation with no fresh water, hot or cold, extensive sewage leakage, or structurally unsound conditions.

Appellants do not claim the evidence establishes the defense of uninhabitability as a matter of law or that the evidence is insufficient to support the verdict. Rather, they challenge certain instructions given.

Appellants claim that the implied warranty of habitability may not be waived and that the trial court erred in instructing the jury that in order to defend an unlawful detainer action on the ground of breach of implied warranty, it must appear the tenant did not have knowledge of the condition at the time of occupancy.

In a free market community, the primary determinant of agreed rent is the physical condition of the premises. The lessor is ordinarily aware of rent charged for comparable properties in nearby locations. The tenant chooses his apartment in light of rent demanded for comparable premises, aware of other apartments offering more or fewer advantages. The relationship between physical condition of the premises and rentals is illustrated by the facts of this case. So long as the rents remained low, the tenants paid the rent notwithstanding the physical conditions assertedly rendering the premises uninhabitable.

Should the tenant be permitted to conclude his bargain aware of the shortcomings of the premises, then later require the lessor to provide improved property at the earlier agreed rental?

Only the most compelling circumstances should prevent the tenant and landlord from freely agreeing the premises shall be leased in whatever condition for commensurate rent, both aware that better premises would call for higher rent. For example, in some of the mild weather areas, tenants may be willing to forego heating facilities in view of the low rent charged. Similarly, willing parties should not be prevented from agreeing the tenant will undertake improving the premises for commensurate rent.

Civil Code section 1941 setting forth landlord duty to place premises in habitable condition provides the duty is imposed "in the absence of an agreement to the contrary."

*Green* effectively recognized the implied warranty may be waived in appropriate situations. First, in defining the warranty we repeatedly spoke in terms of maintaining the leased premises, duty to maintain habitable premises or duty to repair rather than a duty to construct new improvements. E.g., (10 Cal.3d at pp. 623, 625, 637, 111 Cal.Rptr. 704, 517 P.2d 1168.) Similarly, the court spoke of the legitimate expectation of the tenant that the premises will be fit for habitation during the duration of the lease term. (10 Cal.3d at p. 627, 111 Cal.Rptr. 704, 517 P.2d 1168.) No such expectation exists when the tenant is aware of a defective physical condition upon leasing and the landlord has not indicated he would repair or improve.

Second, much of the reasoning in *Green* reflects that in appropriate circumstances the implied warranty may be waived. Thus, in *Green* we analogized to the implied warranty of fitness and merchantability in the sale of goods. (10 Cal.3d at p. 626, 111 Cal.Rptr. 704, 517 P.2d 1168.) In such sale, the circumstances may negate or exclude the implied warranties. (Com.Code, § 2316; 2 Witkin, Summary of Cal.Law (8th ed. 1973) pp. 1146–1147.) Again, what are the expectations of the parties?

Third, the new common law rules adopted in *Green* may in some cases create waiver. We held in *Green* that breach of the implied warranty of habitability creates a defense in unlawful detainer actions on the theory that the breach was directly related to the rent due and thus to the right of possession—the issue litigated in the summary unlawful detainer proceedings. (10 Cal.3d at p. 635, 111 Cal.Rptr. 704, 517 P.2d 1168.) We also recognized that when the tenant establishes breach of the implied warranty, the landlord remains entitled to the fair rental value of the defective premises and unless paid may reacquire possession. (10 Cal.3d at pp. 638–639, 111 Cal.Rptr. 704, 517 P.2d 1168.) When the contracted rent is equal to or less than fair rental value, the *Green* rule itself creates a waiver of the implied warranty.

It is true that in *Green,* footnote 9, we stated that public policy requires that the implied warranty "generally could not be waived by any provision in the lease or rental agreement." (10 Cal.3d at p. 625, 111 Cal.Rptr. 704, 517 P.2d 1168.) However, the statement refers to general contractual waivers and should not be read to prohibit specific waivers of conditions existing at the time the lease is executed. Otherwise a tenant, fully aware of the defects and having no expectation of landlord repair, could enter a lease at low rent and later refuse payment. The implied covenant should not permit inequitable conduct.

Accordingly, when a tenant is aware of the defect at the time the lease is entered and it is apparent the landlord will not repair, the tenant may not defend an unlawful detainer action on the ground the defect is a breach of implied warranty of habitability. There was no error in instructing the jury that in order to defend on that ground a tenant must establish he was unaware of the defect at the time the lease was entered.

The trial court also instructed that in order to establish the defense of breach of implied warranty the tenant must notify the landlord of the alleged defect within a reasonable time after he discovered it, or should have discovered it.

When a tenant, aware the premises are not habitable, continues to pay the agreed rent without complaint, he reflects that he did not contemplate repairs by the landlord, that in light of the rent charged he is willing to bear the defects, or that he does not consider the claimed defects sufficiently important to render the premises uninhabitable.

In any event, it would be inequitable to permit the tenant to continue occupying the premises for months or perhaps years paying rent without complaint and then seek to recover that rent on the basis of breach of the implied warranty. (Cal.U.Com.Code, § 2607, subd. (3); Greenman v. Yuba Power Products, Inc. (1963) 59 Cal.2d 57, 61, 27 Cal.Rptr. 697, 377 P.2d 897.) In addition, in many cases the cost of repair would be minor whereas the impairment of use would be substantial. Clearly, it would be inequitable to permit the tenant to remain on the premises paying rent without complaint and then recover substantial rent on the basis of breach of implied warranty.

In Pollard v. Saxe & Yolles Dev. Co. (1974) 12 Cal.3d 374, 380, 115 Cal.Rptr. 648, 525 P.2d 88, concluding a warranty of quality exists for sales of new buildings, we imposed the notice requirement. "The requirement of notice of breach is based on a sound commercial rule designed to allow the defendant opportunity for repairing the defective item, reducing damages, avoiding defective products in the future, and negotiating settlements. The notice requirement also protects against stale claims." By analogy and for the same reasons, we conclude there was no error in recognizing the duty in tenants to give notice of the asserted breach within a reasonable time.

The judgment should be affirmed.

## Wade v. Jobe
Supreme Court of Utah, 1991.
818 P.2d 1006.

■ DURHAM, JUSTICE.

In June 1988, defendant Lynda Jobe (the tenant) rented a house in Ogden, Utah, from plaintiff Clyde Wade (the landlord). Jobe had three young children. Shortly after she took occupancy, the tenant discovered numerous defects in the dwelling, and within a few days, she had no hot water. Investigation revealed that the flame of the water heater had been extinguished by accumulated sewage and water in the basement which also produced a foul odor throughout the house. The tenant notified the landlord, who came to the premises a number of times, each time pumping the sewage and water from the basement onto the sidewalk and relighting the water heater. These and other problems persisted from July through October 1988.

In November 1988, the tenant notified the landlord that she would withhold rent until the sewage problem was solved permanently. The situation did not improve, and an inspection by the Ogden City Inspection Division (the division) in December 1988 revealed that the premises were unsafe for human occupancy due to the lack of a sewer connection and other problems. Within a few weeks, the division made another inspection, finding numerous code violations which were a substantial hazard to the health and safety of the occupants. The division issued a notice that the property would be condemned if the violations were not remedied.

After the tenant moved out of the house, the landlord brought suit in the second circuit court to recover the unpaid rent. The tenant filed a counterclaim, seeking an offset against rent owed because of the uninhabitable condition.

At trial, the landlord was awarded judgment of unpaid rent of $770, the full rent due under the parties' original agreement. The tenant was denied any offsets, and her counterclaim was dismissed. This appeal followed.

## WARRANTY OF HABITABILITY

In recent years, this court has conformed the common law in this state to contemporary conditions by rejecting the strict application of traditional property law to residential leases, recognizing that it is often more appropriate to apply contract law. See Reid v. Mutual of Omaha Ins. Co., 776 P.2d 896, 902 n. 3 (Utah 1989); Williams v. Melby, 699 P.2d at 726–27; Hall v. Warren, 632 P.2d at 850. Similarly, we have expanded landlord liability in tort. See Williams; Hall; Stephenson v. Warner, 581 P.2d 567 (Utah 1978) (landlord must use ordinary care to ensure leased premises are reasonably safe). Consistent with prevailing trends in consumer law, products liability law, and the law of torts, we reject the rule of caveat emptor and recognize the common law implied warranty of habitability in residential[3] leases.

The determination of whether a dwelling is habitable depends on the individual facts of each case. To guide the trial court in determining whether there is a breach of the warranty of habitability, we describe some general standards that the landlord is required to satisfy. We note initially that the warranty of habitability does not require the landlord to maintain the premises in perfect condition at all times, nor does it preclude minor housing code violations or other defects. Moreover, the landlord will not be liable for defects caused by the tenant. See Javins v. First National Realty Corp., 428 F.2d 1071, 1082 n. 62 (1970); Hinson v. Delis, 26 Cal.App.3d 62, 102 Cal.Rptr. 661 (1972); Marini v. Ireland, 56 N.J. 130, 265 A.2d 526 (1970). Further, the landlord must have a reasonable time to repair material defects before a breach can be established.

As a general rule, the warranty of habitability requires that the landlord maintain "bare living requirements," see Academy Spires, Inc. v. Brown, 111 N.J.Super. 477, 268 A.2d 556, 559 (1970), and that the premises are fit for human occupation. See Mease v. Fox, 200 N.W.2d 791 (Iowa 1972); Hilder v. St. Peter, 144 Vt. 150, 478 A.2d 202, 208 (1984). Failure to supply heat or hot water, for example, breaches the warranty. A breach is not shown, however, by evidence of minor deficiencies such as the malfunction of venetian blinds, minor water leaks or wall cracks, or a need for paint. See Academy Spires, Inc. v. Brown, 268 A.2d at 559.

Substantial compliance with building and housing code standards will generally serve as evidence of the fulfillment of a landlord's duty to provide habitable premises. Evidence of violations involving health or safety, by contrast, will often sustain a tenant's claim for relief. See Green v. Superior Court, 517 P.2d at 1182–83. At the same time, just because the housing code provides a basis for implication of the warranty, a code violation is not necessary to establish a breach so long as the claimed defect has an impact on the health or safety of the tenant. Hilder v. St. Peter, 478 A.2d at 209.

---

[3] We do not decide whether the warranty is implied in commercial leases.

In the instant case, in support of her claim that the premises were not in habitable condition, the tenant presented two city housing inspection reports detailing numerous code violations which were, in the words of the trial judge, "a substantial hazard to the health and safety of the occupants." Those violations included the presence of raw sewage on the sidewalks and stagnant water in the basement, creating a foul odor. At trial, the tenant testified that she had repeatedly informed the landlord of the problem with the sewer connection and the resulting lack of hot water, but the landlord never did any more than temporarily alleviate the problem. The landlord did not controvert the evidence of substantial problems. At trial, the court granted judgment for the landlord, concluding that Utah law did not recognize an implied warranty of habitability for residential rental premises. As discussed above, we have now recognized the warranty. We therefore remand this case to the trial court to determine whether the landlord has breached the implied warranty of habitability as defined in this opinion. If the trial court finds a breach of the warranty of habitability, it must then determine damages.

A.  Remedies

Under traditional property law, a lessee's covenant to pay rent was viewed as independent of any covenants on the part of the landlord. Even when a lessor expressly covenanted to make repairs, the lessor's breach did not justify the lessee's withholding rent. Under the prevailing contemporary view of the residential lease as a contractual transaction, however, see Javins, 428 F.2d at 1075, the tenant's obligation to pay rent is conditioned upon the landlord's fulfilling his part of the bargain. The payment of rent by the tenant and the landlord's duty to provide habitable premises are, as a result, dependent covenants.

Once the landlord has breached his duty to provide habitable conditions, there are at least two ways the tenant can treat the duty to pay rent. The tenant may continue to pay rent to the landlord or withhold the rent.[4] If the tenant continues to pay full rent to the landlord during the period of uninhabitability, the tenant can bring an affirmative action to establish the breach and receive a reimbursement for excess rents paid. Rent withholding, on the other hand, deprives the landlord of the rent due during the default, thereby motivating the landlord to repair the premises. See 2 R. Powell, The Law of Real Property ¶ 228[6][d], at 16A–51 (1990).[5]

---

[4] In addition, some jurisdictions recognize rent application, also known as "repair and deduct," allowing the tenant to use the rent money to repair the premises. Because this remedy has not been relied on or sought in the instant case, we do not at this time make a ruling on its availability in Utah.

[5] The majority of jurisdictions that permit rent withholding allow the tenant to retain the funds subject to the discretionary power of the court to order the deposit of the rent into escrow. See 2 R. Powell, The Law of Real Property ¶ 228[6][d], at 16A–54 (1990). Like the court in Javins, we think this type of escrow account would provide a useful protective procedure in the right circumstances. See Javins, 428 F.2d at 1083 n. 67.

Some jurisdictions have taken the position that the tenant is entitled to an abatement only against the withheld rent in a rent collection case, holding that damages for the uninhabitable conditions existing prior to the tenant's withholding must be recovered in a separate action. See C.F. Seabrook Co. v. Beck, 174 N.J.Super. 577, 417 A.2d 89 (1980). We reject this reasoning; it is more in keeping with the policy behind our adoption of the warranty of habitability to provide for retroactive abatement of the rent during the period of the landlord's default whether or not the tenant withholds rent.[6]

B. Damages

In general, courts have applied contract remedies when a breach of the warranty of habitability has been shown. One available remedy, therefore, is damages. Special damages may be recovered when, as a foreseeable result of the landlord's breach, the tenant suffers personal injury, property damage, relocation expenses, or other similar injuries. General damages recoverable in the form of rent abatement or reimbursement to the tenant are more difficult to calculate.

Several different measures for determining the amount of rent abatement to which a tenant is entitled have been used by the courts. The first of these is the fair rental value of the premises as warranted less their fair rental value in the unrepaired condition. Under this approach, the contract rent may be considered as evidence of the value of the premises as warranted. Another measure is the contract rent less the fair rental value of the premises in the unrepaired condition. Methodological difficulties inherent in both of these measures, combined with the practical difficulties of producing evidence on fair market value,[7] however, limit the efficacy of those measures for dealing with residential leases. For this reason, a number of courts have adopted what is called the "percentage diminution" (or percentage reduction in use) approach which places more discretion with the trier of fact.

Under the percentage diminution approach, the tenant's recovery reflects the percentage by which the tenant's use and enjoyment of the premises has been reduced by the uninhabitable conditions. See generally Annotation, Measure of Damages for Landlord's Breach of Implied Warranty of Habitability, 1 A.L.R.4th 1182 (1980). In applying this approach, the trial court must carefully review the materiality of the particular defects and the length of time such defects have existed. See Academy Spires, Inc. v. Brown, 268 A.2d at 562. It is true that the percentage diminution approach requires the trier of fact to exercise broad discretion and some subjective judgment to determine the degree

---

[6] Before the tenant may receive a rent abatement, she must put the landlord in breach by giving her actual or constructive notice of the defects and a reasonable time in which to make repairs. See Hinson v. Delis, 26 Cal.App.3d 62, 102 Cal.Rptr. 661 (1972).

[7] Under either approach, at least one market value is almost certain to require expert testimony. The production of such testimony will increase the cost, in time and money, of the typical case.

to which the defective conditions have diminished the habitability of the premises. It should be noted, however, that despite their theoretical appeal, the other approaches are not objectively precise either.[8] Furthermore, they involve the use of an expert witness's subjective opinion of the "worth" of habitable and uninhabitable premises.

As the foregoing discussion demonstrates, the determination of appropriate damages in cases of a breach of the warranty of habitability will often be a difficult task. None of the approaches described above is inherently illegitimate, but we think that the percentage diminution approach has a practical advantage in that it will generally obviate the need for expert testimony and reduce the cost and complexity of enforcing the warranty of habitability. We acknowledge the limitation of the method but conclude that it is as sound in its result as any other and more workable in practice. We will have to depend on development of the rule in specific cases to determine whether it will be universally applicable.

CONCLUSION

We remand this case to the trial court to determine whether the landlord breached the implied warranty of habitability as defined in this opinion. If the trial court determines that he was not in breach, the landlord will be entitled to payment for all the past due rent. If the trial court determines that his breach of the warranty of habitability totally excused the tenant's rent obligation (i.e., rendered the premises virtually uninhabitable), the landlord's action to recover rent due will fail. If the trial court determines that the landlord's breach partially excused the tenant's rent obligation, the tenant will be entitled to a percentage rent abatement for the period during which the house was uninhabitable.

## Davidow v. Inwood North Professional Group

Supreme Court of Texas, 1988.
747 S.W.2d 373.

■ SPEARS, JUSTICE.

This case presents the question of whether there is an implied warranty by a commercial landlord that the leased premises are suitable for their intended commercial purpose. Respondent Inwood North Professional Group—Phase I sued petitioner Dr. Joseph Davidow for unpaid rent on medical office space leased by Dr. Davidow. The jury

---

[8] For a detailed critique of the assumptions and limitations of all three measures of damage described in this opinion, see Smith, Tenant Remedies for Breach of Habitability: Tort Dimensions of a Contract Concept, 35 Kan.L.Rev. 505, 518 (1987). Later in the article, the author argues, "Habitability should be separated into two distinct actions, one a tort action the other contract, based upon whether the duty to repair the defect is waivable." Id. At 547. Nonwaivable duties (regarding risks to health and safety) "certainly [are] not contractual in nature because [their] existence does not stem from the parties' bargain in fact. . . . Tenant actions based on nonwaivable housing defects should sound in tort and be remedied solely under tort principles." Id.

found that Inwood materially breached the lease agreement and that the defects rendered the office space unsuitable for use as a medical office. The trial court rendered judgment that Inwood take nothing and that Dr. Davidow recover damages for lost time and relocation expenses. The court of appeals reversed the trial court judgment and rendered judgment that Inwood recover unpaid rents for the remainder of the lease period and that Dr. Davidow take nothing. . . .

Dr. Davidow entered into a five-year lease agreement with Inwood for medical office space. The lease required Dr. Davidow to pay Inwood $793.26 per month as rent. The lease also required Inwood to provide air conditioning, electricity, hot water, janitor and maintenance services, light fixtures, and security services. Shortly after moving into the office space, Dr. Davidow began experiencing problems with the building. The air conditioning did not work properly, often causing temperatures inside the office to rise above eighty-five degrees. The roof leaked whenever it rained, resulting in stained tiles and rotting, mildewed carpet. Patients were directed away from certain areas during rain so that they would not be dripped upon in the waiting room. Pests and rodents often infested the office. The hallways remained dark because hallway lights were unreplaced for months. Cleaning and maintenance were not provided. The parking lot was constantly filled with trash. Hot water was not provided, and on one occasion Dr. Davidow went without electricity for several days because Inwood failed to pay the electric bill. Several burglaries and various acts of vandalism occurred. Dr. Davidow finally moved out of the premises and discontinued rent payments approximately fourteen months before the lease expired.

Inwood sued Dr. Davidow for the unpaid rent and costs of restoration. Dr. Davidow answered by general denial and the affirmative defenses of material breach of the lease agreement, a void lease, and breach of an implied warranty that the premises were suitable for use as a medical office. The jury found that Inwood materially breached the lease, that Inwood warranted to Dr. Davidow that the lease space was suitable for a medical office, and that the lease space was not suitable for a medical office. . . .

With one justice dissenting, the court of appeals reversed the trial court judgment and rendered judgment in favor of Inwood for unpaid rent. The court of appeals held that because Inwood's covenant to maintain and repair the premises was independent of Dr. Davidow's covenant to pay rent, Inwood's breach of its covenant did not justify Dr. Davidow's refusal to pay rent. The court of appeals also held that the implied warranty of habitability does not extend to commercial leaseholds and that Dr. Davidow's pleadings did not support an award of affirmative relief.

Inwood contends that the defense of material breach of the covenant to repair is insufficient as a matter of law to defeat a landlord's claim for unpaid rent. In Texas, the courts have held that the landlord's covenant to repair the premises and the tenant's covenant to pay rent are independent covenants.... Thus, a tenant is still under a duty to pay rent even though his landlord has breached his covenant to make repairs.

This theory of independent covenants in leases was established in early property law prior to the development of the concept of mutually dependent covenants in contract law. At common law, the lease was traditionally regarded as a conveyance of an interest in land, subject to the doctrine of *caveat emptor*. The landlord was required only to deliver the right of possession to the tenant; the tenant, in return, was required to pay rent to the landlord. Once the landlord delivered the right of possession, his part of the agreement was completed. The tenant's duty to pay rent continued as long as he retained possession, even if the buildings on the leasehold were destroyed or became uninhabitable. The landlord's breach of a lease covenant did not relieve the tenant of his duty to pay rent for the remainder of the term because the tenant still retained everything he was entitled to under the lease—the right of possession. All lease covenants were therefore considered independent.

When a commercial tenant such as Dr. Davidow leases office space, many of the same considerations are involved. A significant number of commentators have recognized the similarities between residential and commercial tenants and concluded that residential warranties should be expanded to cover commercial property. *See, e.g.,* Chused, *Contemporary Dilemmas of the Javins Defense: A Note on the Need for Procedural Reform in Landlord-Tenant Law,* 67 Geo.L.J. 1385, 1389 (1979); Greenfield & Margolies, *An Implied Warranty of Fitness in Nonresidential Leases,* 45 Albany L.Rev. 855 (1981); Levinson & Silver, *Do Commercial Property Tenants Possess Warranties of Habitability?,* 14 Real Estate L.J. 59 (1985).

It cannot be assumed that a commercial tenant is more knowledgeable about the quality of the structure than a residential tenant. A businessman cannot be expected to possess the expertise necessary to adequately inspect and repair the premises, and many commercial tenants lack the financial resources to hire inspectors and repairmen to assure the suitability of the premises. Additionally, because commercial tenants often enter into short-term leases, the tenants have limited economic incentive to make any extensive repairs to their premises. Levinson & Silver, *supra,* at 68. Consequently, commercial tenants generally rely on their landlords' greater abilities to inspect and repair the premises.

In light of the many similarities between residential and commercial tenants and the modern trend towards increased consumer protection, a number of courts have indicated a willingness to apply residential property warranties to commercial tenancy situations.

There is no valid reason to imply a warranty of habitability in residential leases and not in commercial leases. Although minor distinctions can be drawn between residential and commercial tenants, those differences do not justify limiting the warranty to residential leaseholds. Therefore, we hold there is an implied warranty of suitability by the landlord in a commercial lease that the premises are suitable for their intended commercial purpose. This warranty means that at the inception of the lease there are no latent defects in the facilities that are vital to the use of the premises for their intended commercial purpose and that these essential facilities will remain in a suitable condition. If, however, the parties to a lease expressly agree that the tenant will repair certain defects, then the provisions of the lease will control.

We recognized in *Kamarath* that the primary objective underlying a residential leasing arrangement is "to furnish [the tenant] with quarters suitable for living purposes." *Kamarath,* 568 S.W.2d at 661. The same objective is present in a commercial setting. A commercial tenant desires to lease premises suitable for their intended commercial use. A commercial landlord impliedly represents that the premises are in fact suitable for that use and will remain in a suitable condition. The tenant's obligation to pay rent and the landlord's implied warranty of suitability are therefore mutually dependent.

The existence of a breach of the implied warranty of suitability in commercial leases is usually a fact question to be determined from the particular circumstances of each case. Among the factors to be considered when determining whether there has been a breach of this warranty are: the nature of the defect; its effect on the tenant's use of the premises; the length of time the defect persisted; the age of the structure; the amount of the rent; the area in which the premises are located; whether the tenant waived the defects; and whether the defect resulted from any unusual or abnormal use by the tenant.

The jury found that Inwood leased the space to Dr. Davidow for use as a medical office and that Inwood knew of the intended use. The evidence and jury findings further indicate that Dr. Davidow was unable to use the space for the intended purpose because acts and omissions by Inwood rendered the space unsuitable for use as a medical office. The jury findings establish that Inwood breached the implied warranty of suitability. Dr. Davidow was therefore justified in abandoning the premises and discontinuing his rent payments.

For the reasons stated, the part of the court of appeals judgment awarding Inwood damages for unpaid rent and attorney's fees is reversed and judgment is here rendered that Inwood take nothing. . . .

### NOTES

1. *Constructive eviction.* Traditionally, if the landlord breached any of her covenants the tenant's sole remedy was to sue for damages caused by the breach. The tenant could not recover damages by reducing or withholding all or some of the rent. If the tenant did attempt to recover damages by withholding all or some of the rent, the landlord could use a summary dispossess action to evict the tenant. This harsh doctrine was mitigated only

slightly by the tenant's right to rely on the doctrine of constructive eviction in appropriate cases.[9]

The doctrine of constructive eviction provides that sometimes the acts or omissions of the landlord may have the effect of evicting the tenant, although the landlord does not physically prevent the tenant from occupying the premises. For example, the landlord's failure to provide heat or water may make it impossible for the tenant to remain on the premises, although there is no actual entry on the premises. Similarly, the landlord's failure to control the unreasonable noise created by a neighboring tenant, when the landlord has the legal right to do so, is an omission that may result in the constructive eviction of the tenant.[10] If a court finds that a tenant has been constructively evicted, the lease is terminated and the tenant owes no rent for the period following the termination.

The constructive eviction doctrine is usually interpreted to mean that the tenant claiming constructive eviction must leave the premises within a reasonable time after the landlord's objectionable act or omission. The theory is that the tenant cannot simultaneously claim to be evicted and yet stay on the premises.[11] This is an unrealistic position in cases where the tenant has no other place to go.[12] Moreover, if the tenant does vacate the premises, and a jury later finds that there was no landlord misconduct amounting to constructive eviction, the tenant may find himself in the position of having to pay rent on both the vacated premises and the new premises. Because of these drawbacks, the doctrine of constructive eviction is not used frequently. Tenants usually prefer to rely on the doctrine of implied warranty of habitability or fitness.

2. *Measure of damages.* In cases like *Davidow* or *Marini*, where the landlord's performance falls below the tenant's reasonable expectations, the measure of damages should be the difference between the value of what was impliedly promised, and the value of what was delivered.[13] But a case like *Knight* raises some perplexing issues. Before the rent increases, the tenants in *Knight* were getting what they expected: poor accommodations in return

---

[9] In some states, such as Louisiana, constructive eviction from one's leasehold can also give rise to a plaintiff's loss of use claim. See Solstice Oil & Gas I LLC v. OBES Inc., 2015 U.S. Dist. LEXIS 61936, *28 (E.D. La. May 12, 2015).

[10] Bocchini v. Gorn Management Co., 69 Md.App. 1, 515 A.2d 1179 (1986); Dyett v. Pendleton, 8 Cow. 727 (N.Y.1826) (first case recognizing constructive eviction doctrine). But see Eastside Exhibition Corp. v. 210 E. 86th St. Corp., 18 N.Y.3d 617, 619 (N.Y. 2012) ("we see no need to apply a rule, derived from feudal concepts, that any intrusion—no matter how small—on the demised premises must result in full rent abatement" in regard to the constructive eviction doctrine first applied in Dyett).

[11] A minority of jurisdictions, like Connecticut and New York, recognize partial constructive eviction absent the tenant vacating the entire premises. The tenant only needs to vacate the portion of the premises that is uninhabitable due to the landlord's failure. See Premier Entm't Servs., LLC v. Gesualdi, 2014 Conn. Super. LEXIS 2622 (Conn. Super. Ct. Nov. 6, 2014). See also East Haven Associates Inc. v. Gurian, 64 Misc. 2d 276 (N.Y. Civ. Ct. 1970).

[12] See Sylvia Landfield Trust v. City of Los Angeles, 729 F.3d 1189, 1192 (9th Cir. Cal. 2013) (affirming that constructive eviction gives little help to the typical low income tenant because the tenant must vacate the premises).

[13] See, e.g., Green v. Superior Court of City and County of San Francisco, 10 Cal.3d 616, 638, 111 Cal.Rptr. 704, 719, 517 P.2d 1168, 1183 (1974); Mease v. Fox, 200 N.W.2d 791, 797 (Iowa 1972).

for cheap rents. If the normal measure of contract damages were used, the tenants could receive no damages since there would be no difference between the value of what they in fact were promised and the value of what they actually got. Realistically speaking, the landlord in *Knight* did not breach a *contractual* promise, since he provided no less than what he expressly or impliedly promised.

The landlord's duty that was breached in *Knight* was not based on contract, but on a duty that was imposed in law, either by statute or by the common law. Consequently, theories of damages other than contractual theories would have to be used. Some courts have measured the damages by the difference between the value of what should have been provided and the value of what was actually provided. This could result in the tenant occupying premises that conformed with the agreement of the parties, and yet the landlord owing the tenant more than the tenant had promised to pay in rent. Do you see how this could happen? Is there anything "wrong" or "absurd" about such a situation?[14]

*Wade* and other courts have adopted the "percentage reduction in rent" method of measuring damages.[15] Under this method the rent is reduced by the percentage that the enjoyment of the premises has been reduced as a result of the landlord's breach. *Wade* criticizes the other methods of calculating damages on the ground that they "involve the use of an expert witness's subjective opinion of the 'worth' of habitable and uninhabitable premises." Do you agree? Would the percentage reduction approach be useful in the Principal Problem? Finally, very few courts have permitted damages for mental or emotional distress caused by the landlord's breach of a duty.[16]

3. *Non-residential leases.* In *Davidow* the court extended an "implied warranty of suitability" to a commercial lease. The majority of states, however, do not imply such a warranty in commercial situations.[17] Most

---

[14] See Rabin, *The Revolution in Residential Landlord Tenant Law: Causes and Consequences,* 69 Cornell L.Rev. 517, 525 (1984). See also footnote 8 in *Wade* (advocating that non-waivable housing defects should not be adjudicated under contract law but instead should be remedied under tort law). Compare Brooks v. Quinn & Quinn, 2010 U.S. Dist. LEXIS 14206 (D. Del. Feb. 19, 2010) (when a lease is silent as to the imposition of a contractual duty to repair to be placed on the tenant, the court defers to the landlord's statutory duty of care).

[15] See, e.g., Pugh v. Holmes, 486 Pa. 272, 405 A.2d 897 (1979). See also, Restatement (Second) of Property: Landlord & Tenant § 11.1 (1976).

[16] Stoiber v. Honeychuck, 101 Cal.App.3d 903, 162 Cal.Rptr. 194 (1980); Simon v. Solomon, 385 Mass. 91, 431 N.E.2d 556 (1982); Brewer v. Erwin, 287 Or. 435, 600 P.2d 398 (1979). See generally, Smith, *Tenant Remedies for Breach of Habitability: Tort Dimensions of a Contract Concept,* 35 U.Kan.L.Rev. 505 (1987). See also Gardner v. Simpson Fin., 963 F. Supp. 2d 72 (D. Mass. 2013) (jury initially granted damages for emotional distress caused by a landlord's breach of duty, but court subsequently granted the landlord's motion for a new trial or remittitur as to the tenants' emotional distress damages due to an absence of medical or psychiatric evidence supporting tenants' emotional damages).

[17] See, e.g., Espenschied v. Mallick, 633 A.2d 388, 394 (D.C. 1993); B.W.S. Invs. v. Mid-Am Rests., Inc., 459 N.W.2d 759, 763 (N.D. 1990). In California there is a divide amongst appellate courts regarding an implied warranty in commercial leases. Cf. Four Seas Inv. Corp. v. International Hotel Tenants' Ass'n, 81 Cal. App. 3d 604, 613, 146 Cal. Rptr. 531, 535 (Ct. App. 1978) (recognizing the potential application of an implied warranty in small commercial settings) with Fish Const. Co. v. Moselle Coach Works, Inc., 148 Cal. App. 3d 654, 658, 196 Cal. Rptr. 174, 176 (Ct. App. 1983) (stating that the implied warranty is "not applicable to unlawful detainer actions involving commercial tenancies"). The latter case appears to reflect the more commonly followed approach. In Missouri, courts may find that an implied covenant to repair

8. *Leases and State Consumer Sales Practices Acts.* In *Wade*, the tenant also sought damages and declaratory relief under the Utah Consumer Sales Practices Act. In a part of the opinion not reprinted in the casebook, two of the justices of the state Supreme Court concluded that the renting of residential housing is a consumer transaction within the meaning of the state consumer protection statute (the other members of the court did not join in that part of the opinion because they felt the tenant would receive adequate relief on her implied warranty of habitability counterclaim). In so concluding, they relied on the language of the statute stating that it applies to "goods, services, or other property both tangible and intangible."[29] This view also has support in other jurisdictions.[30] However, subsequent to *Wade*, Utah enacted a more specific statute, the Utah Fit Premises Act,[31] which provides specific remedies to residential tenants whose rental units become uninhabitable due to violations of health and safety standards. In light of this statute, the Supreme Court of Utah concluded that the dictum in *Wade* regarding the applicability of the state Consumer Sales Practices Act should not be relied upon in cases where plaintiffs are seeking damages for uninhabitable premises.[32] Should residential leases be within the scope of state consumer sales practices acts? What about commercial leases?

## 4. TYPES OF COMMON LAW TENANCIES

In *Knight*, the new landlords bought the complex in May, 1977 and announced rent increases effective in July. How could the lessors have done this if the lessees had a lease in effect? Although the court does not specify, the lessees probably were occupying the premises under a monthly periodic tenancy as opposed to a tenancy for years. At common law there were three kinds of non-freehold estates: the tenancy for years, the periodic tenancy and the tenancy at will. A fourth category, the "tenancy at sufferance" is not really an estate at all, but rather is a convenient way to classify a certain kind of possession. The Statute of Frauds in most jurisdictions mandates that a lease for more than one year must be in writing to be valid.

The form of tenancy is primarily important with respect to the issue of the duration of the tenancy, particularly its date of termination. The tenancy for years terminates automatically at the end of the designated term; the periodic tenancy can only be terminated at the end of the period involved, after proper notice is given; the tenancy at will requires no advance notice for termination; and the tenancy at sufferance traditionally can be terminated without notice, or, at the landlord's election, such a tenant can be required to complete another term. Now you can see why the lessors in *Knight* were able to raise the rent so soon

---

[29] Utah Code Ann. § 13–11–3(2).

[30] See, e.g., Creekside Apartments v. Poteat, 116 N.C.App. 26, 36 446 S.E.2d 826, 832 (1994) (landlord's failure to maintain leased premises in habitable condition and subsequent demand for rent constitutes an unfair and deceptive trade practice).

[31] Utah Code Ann. §§ 57–22–1 to–6 (2015).

[32] Carlie v. Morgan, 922 P.2d 1, 5 (Utah 1996).

after taking possession. Courts frequently attempt to answer the question of whether a tenancy has terminated by classifying the tenancy. Here is a brief overview and the types of common law tenancies and their attributes.

*The Tenancy for Years*

*Definition and Characteristics.* A tenancy that is for any fixed or computable period of time has traditionally been called a tenancy for years. When the beginning and ending times of a lease are on designated calendar dates, the lease is for a fixed period. A lease for a computable period, on the other hand, contains a formula for determining the starting date and the ending date. A tenancy for years requires certainty of duration. The death of either the landlord or the tenant does not terminate a tenancy for years.

*Creation.* A tenancy for years is created by express agreement between landlord and tenant.

*Termination.* The tenancy for years terminates automatically at the end of the period specified in the agreement. Neither party need give notice of termination.

*Periodic Tenancy*

*Definition and Characteristics.* A periodic tenancy continues for successive periods until terminated. It is automatically renewed at the end of each period until terminated. The death of either the landlord or tenant does not affect the duration of a periodic tenancy. Typical periodic tenancies are week to week, month to month, and year to year.

*Creation.* A periodic tenancy may be created by express agreement. More typically, it is inferred from the facts. For instance, a periodic tenancy results when the tenant takes possession with no duration specified but with the reservation or payment of periodic rent. It also results when a lease attempting to create a tenancy for years is invalid because of failure to comply with the controlling Statute of Frauds. Originally this situation resulted in a tenancy at will, but under modern statutes a periodic tenancy is usually created, provided that the transaction calls for periodic rent payments.

*Termination.* To terminate a periodic tenancy, notice is required, thus giving the parties limited certainty as to the duration of the tenancy. At common law, a year to year tenancy required notice of six months prior to the end of the period. For other periodic tenancies notice equal to the length of the period was required. Furthermore, the notice had to terminate the tenancy as of the end of the term. Statutes in many states have shortened the required period of notice for year to year tenancies. The Second Restatement of Property recommends a month's notice for all periodic tenancies of a month or more, with the exception of property leased for agricultural purposes.[33]

---

[33] Restatement (Second) of Property: Landlord & Tenant § 1.5 cmt. f (1977).

## Tenancy at Will

*Definition and Characteristics.* The tenancy at will is a fragile device, resting on the uncertain foundation of the continuing agreement of both parties. It has no designated period of duration other than the will of both parties.

*Creation.* A tenancy at will may be created by express agreement. However, it is usually inferred from the circumstances. For instance, a letting for an undefined period with no reservation (i.e., stipulation for) or payment of periodic rent will create a tenancy at will.

*Termination.* A tenancy at will terminates, as might be expected, at the will of either party. It also terminates on the death of either party, or when the landlord conveys the property or the tenant attempts to assign his interest. At common law, no particular notice was needed to terminate the tenancy at will. However, modern statutes require notice of intent to terminate.

## Tenancy (or Occupancy) at Sufferance

A tenancy at sufferance results when a tenant originally in rightful possession under a valid lease "holds over" (remains in possession) after his lease expires. The tenant at sufferance falls just short of being a trespasser. His right to possession is based on the landlord's laches or neglect. At common law, the landlord could bring an action to evict the holdover tenant or could consent to his possession, normally by accepting rent, and treat the holdover as an election to extend the lease for another term or period. This harsh rule was justified by the theory that strong sanctions are needed against holdovers. It has been modified by statute in many states. The Second Restatement of Property modifies the rule to provide that the landlord may not unilaterally hold the tenant to another term where equitable considerations justify giving the tenant an extension of time to vacate.[34] A few states also have statutes which require the landlord to provide the tenant at sufferance with notice before terminating the tenancy or instituting an ouster action.[35] When a landlord accepts continued rent payments from a holdover tenant, a growing number of jurisdictions imply the creation of a month-to-month period tenancy, rather than a full lease extension.[36]

---

[34] Restatement (Second) of Property: Landlord & Tenant § 14.4 (1977).

[35] See, e.g., Ky.Rev.Stat.Ann § 383.195 (2015) (one month's written notice to terminate); Mo.Ann.Stat. § 441.060 (West 2015) (one month's written notice); N.Y.Real Prop.Law § 228 (McKinney 2015) (at least thirty days written notice to terminate or maintain an action to recover possession).

[36] See, e.g., Ariz. Rev. Stat. Ann § 33–342 (2015); N.Y. Real Prop. § 232–c (2015).

## ASSIGNMENT 5

# LANDLORD'S TORT LIABILITY FOR PERSONAL INJURIES

## 1. INTRODUCTION

This Assignment deals with the landlord's liability for personal injuries suffered by either the tenant or other persons on the leased premises.[1] In recent years, the landlord's tort liability for personal injuries has grown enormously. During the early 1970's, the general rule was that the landlord was not liable for personal injuries caused by defects in the premises unless the particular circumstances at issue fit within one of the well-defined exceptions to this rule. In contrast, today the general rule is that the landlord is liable for such injuries.[2] The introductory part of this Assignment discusses the various exceptions to the prior law of non-liability, while the remainder explores the parameters of the landlord's current liability for personal injuries.

The law as it existed in 1965 was summarized in the Restatement (Second) of Torts, sections 355 and 356:

*Section 355. Conditions Arising After Lessor Transfers Possession: General Rule.*

Except as stated in sections 357 and 360–62, a lessor of land is not subject to liability to his lessee or others upon the land with the consent of the lessee or sublessee for physical harm caused by any dangerous condition which comes into existence after the lessee has taken possession.

*Section 356. Conditions Existing When Lessor Transfers Possession: General Rule.*

Except as stated in sections 357–62, a lessor of land is not liable to his lessee or to others on the land for physical harm caused by any dangerous condition, whether natural or artificial, which existed when the lessee took possession.

The exceptions specified in sections 357–362 are rather limited. Under section 357, the landlord was liable if he contracted to make certain repairs, failed to make the repairs, although he could have made them if he had used reasonable care, and the plaintiff was injured because of this failure. Under section 358, the landlord was liable if he knew or should have known of a dangerous condition that the lessee did

---

[1] The rules discussed in this Assignment also apply to physical injury to property.

[2] But see Miller v. Cundiff, 245 S.W.3d 786 (Ky. Ct. App. 2007) (departing from the current trend by holding that landlords are not liable for compensatory damages for personal injuries in tort).

not know or have reason to know of, failed to warn the lessee, and the lessee or those on the land with the lessee's consent were injured by this condition. Section 359 provides for landlord liability in certain cases involving premises open to the public such as theaters. Under sections 360 and 361, a landlord was responsible for injuries suffered as a result of defects in that part of the premises over which he retained control, if the landlord failed to exercise reasonable care to keep that part of the premises safe. An example would be an injury suffered because of a defective elevator used by several tenants in an apartment house, when the landlord failed to use reasonable care to maintain the elevator. No liability ensues under this exception, however, unless the lessor could have discovered the condition through exercising reasonable care and unless the lessor could have corrected the situation.

From the above summary, it can be seen that the occasions on which the landlord was liable for personal injury were strictly limited. The exceptions to the general rule of non-liability were based essentially on negligence. The plaintiff generally had to prove the lessor's knowledge or notice of the defect, and that he had a reasonable opportunity to repair the premises. Thus, before a landlord could be held liable, it was always necessary to show that he had failed to use reasonable care to avoid the injury that occurred. Moreover, when the defect causing the injury was on the leased premises itself, rather than in an area used by other tenants, the landlord had no duty to make any repairs, in the absence of a contract to do so. Even when the landlord contracted to make repairs, failed to do so and an injury resulted, the landlord was not liable unless the tenant showed that the failure to repair was attributable to the landlord's negligence.

In sum, according to the law as it existed in the early 1970's, the landlord had no duty to repair obvious ("patent") defects that existed at the time the lease was first entered into. Nor did he have a duty to repair nonobvious ("latent") defects so long as he disclosed them to the lessee. Similarly, the landlord usually had no duty to repair defects that arose during the course of the lease. Consequently, he was not liable if such defects resulted in personal injury to the tenant or to others.

As indicated above, the law in this area has changed substantially in recent years. Now, lessors are generally liable for personal injuries suffered on the leased premises. The Principal Problem and the accompanying materials explore the contours of this liability.

## 2. PRINCIPAL PROBLEM

The Winston family has run a successful import-export business for nearly fifty years. They have accumulated substantial wealth from their business. They remain active in the business and it is still thriving. Fifteen years ago, they developed a three acre tract of land with a high-rise office building and rented out the space to numerous local companies. Seven years ago, they decided to put a gym and swimming pool in the building so that the employees of its tenants could exercise during their work day. The Winstons hired a reputable company to install the swimming pool and diving board and they had access to the area during the construction process.

One of their tenants was a diet center called Rapid Weight Loss Center ("Rapid"). Rapid had a ten year lease with the Winstons. Arthur Jenkins was one of Rapid's employees. Arthur was about thirty pounds overweight and was told by Rapid's management that he had to lose weight to keep his job. Arthur decided to start exercising more frequently. One day, as he was about to dive off the diving board into the pool, the board fell off its stand, hurling a startled Arthur against the side of the pool. Arthur sustained three broken ribs, a broken leg, a broken arm, plus a mild concussion.

An investigation subsequent to Arthur's accident revealed that the board fell off the stand because the screws holding the board to the stand rusted after several years of use because they were not made of stainless steel. The Winstons had someone inspect the screws visually every year, but the only way the Winstons could have known about the rusted screws would have been to have someone unscrew the screws and examine them. The Winstons were aware of the remote possibility that the screws could rust, but they never considered having the screws removed and examined due to the relative infrequency with which this type of occurrence happens. Removing the screws would have been expensive and inconvenient. Moreover, the screws had always passed a visual inspection.

Arthur comes to you for advice. He wants to sue Rapid, the company that installed the pool and the diving board, and the Winstons for damages as a result of his accident. Unfortunately, the company that installed the pool is out of business, and Rapid is judgment proof. As a practical matter, therefore, the Winstons are the only potential defendants. Before advising Arthur as to the scope of the Winstons' liability, consider the following materials.

3. MATERIALS FOR SOLUTION OF PRINCIPAL PROBLEM

## Asper v. Haffley
Superior Court of Pennsylvania, 1983.
312 Pa.Super. 424, 458 A.2d 1364.

■ PRICE, JUDGE.

In September of 1976, Joni Marie Asper died of smoke inhalation in a fire which occurred in the apartment which her father, John Asper, rented from appellee, Ronald Wayne Haffley. As a result of her death, the administratrix of Joni's estate instituted proceedings against Mr. Haffley. In August of 1980, appellee's motion for summary judgment was granted and this appeal followed.

Mr. Haffley purchased the premises on which the fire occurred in 1972. Prior to May of 1976, appellee used the front portion of the one story building as an office in connection with his insurance business. The rear portion was used as his own residence. Appellee eventually ceased to reside on the premises and made certain alterations to the structure in anticipation of renting the rear portion of the building. The wall which separated the office from the residence was changed to eliminate two doorways which had connected the living area to the office area. Additionally, appellee installed storm windows on the inside of the windows in the living area. These storm windows could not be opened except by breaking the window panes.

In May of 1976, appellee leased the living area to John Asper, who then occupied the apartment with his four daughters, one of whom was Joni Marie Asper. In the early morning of September 8, 1976, the fire occurred in which Joni, the only person then present, perished. At the time of the fire Joni was apparently in her bedroom and would have been unable to use the exit to the outside because of the location of the fire blocking that means of escape. Evidence of bruises, abrasions and cuts on Joni's hands and arms would permit an inference that she had made an unsuccessful attempt to break through the storm window in her bedroom to escape the fire.

In granting summary judgment to Mr. Haffley, the court below determined that under general principles limiting the scope of landlord liability, appellant had not alleged sufficient facts on which appellee could be held liable on a theory of negligence. [W]e find that appellant is entitled to present her negligence claim at trial for determination by the factfinder.

We [disagree with the finding of] the court below that appellant did not allege sufficient facts on which appellee could be held liable on a theory of negligence. As this court noted in *Rivera v. Selfon Home Repairs and Improvements Co.,* 294 Pa. Superior Ct. 41, 439 A.2d 739 (1982), our Supreme Court in 1979 adopted an implied warranty of habitability in residential leases. *Pugh v. Holmes,* 486 Pa. 272, 405 A.2d 897 (1979).

In the instant case, the facts alleged and reasonable inferences therefrom were sufficient, if proved, to support a finding that a dangerous condition (the sealed windows and lack of alternative exit) existed with respect to the premises leased, that the landlord was aware of the dangerous condition and failed to exercise reasonable care to correct the condition, and that the existence of the condition was in violation of an implied warranty of habitability.

As we stated in *Rivera, supra,* this is precisely the subject of the Restatement of Property (Second) § 17.6, comment a, b, c (1977), representing the modern weight of authority in this area:

Landlord Under Legal Duty to Repair Dangerous Condition

A landlord is subject to liability for physical harm caused to the tenant or his subtenant by a dangerous condition existing before or arising after the tenant has taken possession, if he has failed to exercise reasonable care to repair the condition and the existence of the condition is in violation of

(1) an implied warranty of habitability; or

(2) a duty created by statute or administrative regulation.

*Rivera, supra* 294 Pa. Superior Ct. at 47, 439 A.2d at 742. *Cf. Ford v. Ja-Sin,* Del.Super., 420 A.2d 184, 187 n. 4 (1980) (holding that a tenant's guest could recover for her personal injuries against the landlord upon a showing of simple negligence under the Delaware Landlord-Tenant Code, 25 Del.C. § 5101 *et seq.,* consistent with Restatement of Property (Second) § 17.6 (1977)); *Sargent v. Ross,* 113 N.H. 388, 308 A.2d 528 (1973) (landlords, as well as other members of society subject to reasonable duty of care, conclusion springing naturally from court's prior decision adopting implied warranty of habitability and abolishing caveat emptor).

We hold, in accord with our decision in *Rivera, supra,* and under the authority of *Pugh, supra,* and the Restatement of Property (Second) § 17.6 (1977), that the question of appellee's liability on a theory of negligence is a matter for determination by the factfinder.

Therefore, the order is reversed and the case remanded for trial consistent with this opinion.

■ WIEAND, JUDGE, concurring:

I agree with the majority that the alleged negligence of the appellee landlord was an issue for determination by the fact finder. However, I am unable to agree that in order to recover the appellant must prove, in addition to negligence, the landlord's breach of an implied warranty of habitability. A breach of a landlord's obligation to provide safe and habitable premises gives rise, in my opinion, to potential liability under two alternative and separate theories: breach of an implied warranty of habitability and/or conventional negligence. See: *Trentacost v. Brussel,* 82 N.J. 214, 231, 412 A.2d 436, 445 (1980); *Water Use Permit Applications, In the Matter of* 380 Mass. 162, 402 N.E.2d at 1050 n. 9. The injured tenant may recover damages for breach of an implied warranty of habitability for all injuries sustained, whether to his person or to his property, if they have been caused by the landlord's breach. See and compare: *Boudreau v. General Electric Co.,* 2 Haw.App. 10, 17, 625 P.2d 384, 390 (1981); *Mansur v. Eubanks,* 401 So.2d 1328 (Fla.1981); *Trentacost v. Brussel, supra* 82 N.J. at 227, 412 A.2d at 443; 13 Pa.C.S. § 2715(b)(2).[3] The injured tenant may also proceed under general

---

[3] 13 Pa.C.S. § 2715(b)(2) provides:

(b) Consequential damages.—Consequential damages resulting from the breach of the seller include:

principles of tort law, without proving a breach of the implied warranty of habitability, and can recover damages for injuries proximately caused by the landlord's failure to exercise reasonable care to make the premises safe. See and compare: *Water Use Permit Applications, In the Matter of* 380 Mass. 162, 402 N.E.2d at 1049; *Pagelsdorf v. Safeco Insurance Company of America, supra* 91 Wis.2d at 743, 284 N.W.2d at 61; *Stephenson v. Warner, supra* 581 P.2d at 568; *Dwyer v. Skyline Apartments, Inc., supra.*

## Merrill v. Jansma
Supreme Court of Wyoming, 2004.
86 P.3d 270.

■ KITE, J.

FACTS

The facts, viewed in the light most favorable to the party opposing the summary judgment motion, are that on February 19, 2000, Ms. Merrill injured her right shoulder when she fell as she was ascending the front steps leading to the porch and front door of the mobile home her daughter, Sherri Pritchard, rented from Ms. Jansma. The step became loose during the time Ms. Pritchard rented the home. Prior to the fall, Ms. Pritchard attempted to repair the step by securing it with nails. When that failed, she informed the manager of the property that the step was loose. The manager suggested Ms. Pritchard try using screws to secure the step. Ms. Pritchard told the manager she did not have a screw gun. The manager had one and said she would screw the step into place. Subsequently, and without Ms. Pritchard's knowledge, the manager attempted to repair the step. Apparently, that effort was unsuccessful and Ms. Merrill fell when the step separated from the porch as she stepped on it.

Ms. Merrill filed a negligence claim against Ms. Jansma as the owner of the property alleging she knew or reasonably should have known the step was dangerous and failed to exercise reasonable care to alleviate the danger. She further alleged Ms. Jansma owed a duty of care to her as a visitor to the rental property. She sought damages for the injuries she sustained in the fall from the step, including medical expenses, lost earnings and damages for emotional distress and pain and suffering. Ms. Jansma answered the complaint and then filed a motion for summary judgment, claiming she owed no legal duty to Ms. Merrill. The district court granted Ms. Jansma's motion for summary judgment, holding that, as a matter of law, she had no legal duty to Ms. Merrill under either the Residential Rental Property Act or the common law as set forth in § 362 of the Restatement.

---

(1) . . .

(2) injury to person or property proximately resulting from any breach of warranty.

## DISCUSSION

### Residential Rental Property Act

In its summary judgment order, the district court held Ms. Jansma owed no duty to Ms. Merrill under the Residential Rental Property Act, Wyo. Stat. Ann. § 1–21–1201, et seq. (2001) because Ms. Merrill failed to give Ms. Jansma written notice of the loose step as required by the act. Ms. Merrill contends this holding is incorrect in two respects. First, she cites § 1–21–1202(a) of the act, which states: "[e]ach owner and his agent renting or leasing a residential rental unit shall maintain that unit in a safe and sanitary condition fit for human habitation." Ms. Merrill asserts that, by the enactment of this provision, the legislature abrogated the common law rule of landlord immunity and imposed a broad affirmative duty upon landlords and their agents to maintain rental properties in a reasonably safe condition. She claims Ms. Jansma breached this duty by failing to maintain, or have her manager maintain, the steps leading up to Ms. Pritchard's home.

Citing the rule that legislative abrogation or modification of the common law will not be presumed absent explicit, unambiguous language demonstrating that intent, Ms. Jansma argues the Residential Rental Property Act does not abrogate the common law rule of landlord immunity. Ms. Jansma asserts the act does not explicitly repeal the common law and, when read as a whole, does not support the conclusion that the legislature intended to impose a general duty requiring a landlord to maintain rental premises, including steps, on a single-dwelling unit. Rather, she contends, it is clear the legislature intended only to set out minimum health and safety requirements.

a. Historical Development

[T]he principle of tort immunity for the landlord developed . . . as part and parcel of the concept that a lease is primarily a conveyance of real estate. The landlord was not liable to the tenant or third persons for personal injury or personal property damage caused by a defect present at the transfer of possession or by defects arising during the term of the leasehold. Old Town Development Company v. Langford, 349 N.E.2d 744, 753–54 (Ind. App.1976).

With the transition from a mostly rural to a more urban society, however, the rule of landlord immunity gave way slightly to some judicially recognized exceptions.... Five exceptions to the rule of landlord immunity emerged. A landlord could be held liable in tort for (1) defects in premises leased for admission of the public; (2) a breach of a covenant to repair; (3) negligent repairs; (4) defects in "common areas" under the landlord's control; and more recently (5) defects constituting a violation of a provision of the applicable building or housing code.

Despite, or perhaps in part because of the exceptions, there was by the 1960s increasing "discontent with the appearance of unfairness in the landlord's general immunity from tort liability, and with the artificiality and increasing complexity of the various exceptions to this seemingly archaic rule of nonliability." W.L. Prosser & W.P. Keeton, Prosser & Keeton on Torts, 446 (5th ed.1984). As a result, some courts began to re-examine landlord tenant law.

In addition to the courts that rejected the common law in favor of recognition of an implied warranty of habitability, other courts cast aside landlord immunity on the basis of general negligence principles. . . .

Altogether, over forty states have discarded the common law rule of landlord immunity and recognize a duty in some form, either through legislation, judicial declaration, or both. Among the states with legislation addressing the landlord-tenant relationship, the statutory language varies considerably.

Landlord-tenant law has evolved considerably from the days when the common law rule was established. Today, the vast majority of states recognize that a landlord has a duty to maintain rental property in a safe, habitable condition. With this overview in mind, we turn to a discussion of the law in Wyoming.

b. The Law in Wyoming

Despite the overwhelming movement in other states to replace the rule of landlord immunity, Wyoming up to now has continued to apply the common law rule—absent a contractual provision to repair, a landlord generally owes no duty to a tenant or a tenant's guests for dangerous or defective conditions of the premises.

[D]uring the 1997 legislative session, a bill addressing landlord-tenant relations was introduced and assigned to committee where it was defeated without reaching the floor of either chamber. Two years later, during the 1999 legislative session, it was modified, reintroduced, amended, and passed into law as the Wyoming Residential Rental Property Act, § 1–21–1201, et seq.

[W]e turn to the question before us—the effect, if any, of Wyoming's landlord-tenant statute on the common law rule of landlord immunity. [W]e note first the absence of explicit language stating that the act is intended to abrogate, preserve, or modify the general common-law rule of landlord immunity. The act does not contain a statement of purpose nor does it reference in any manner the common law rule of landlord immunity. It likewise makes no reference to personal injury claims arising from unsafe conditions on rental premises.

The act does, however, clearly and expressly impose a duty on landlords not previously recognized in Wyoming law. Section 1–21–1202(a) requires landlords to maintain rental units in a safe, sanitary and habitable condition. Section 1–21–1203(a)(i) prohibits landlords from renting premises that are not reasonably safe, sanitary and fit for human occupancy. Ms. Merrill asserts the imposition of the duty is itself sufficient evidence of legislative intent and that an express statement of intent to abrogate the common law is unnecessary—no duty existed before, a duty clearly exists now, therefore, the act abrogated, or at least modified, the common-law rule of landlord immunity.

In contrast, Ms. Jansma contends the language is insufficient to change the common law of immunity. She argues the act must contain explicit language stating that the common law is abrogated, repealed or modified in order for this court to conclude the legislature intended to change the common law.

It is well-established that legislative intent to repeal the common law will not be inferred absent clear language evidencing that intent. However, effectuation of such repeal does not require the use of some particular word or words. It requires instead plain, unambiguous language making it clear that is what was intended.

The need for change in the common law pertaining to landlord-tenant relations has been recognized in most other states. This Court likewise acknowledged that change was warranted but declined to act judicially, believing it was a matter for the legislature. Our legislature subsequently acted with the adoption of the Residential Rental Property Act. It acted with plain language that leaves no room for disputable inference. The language of the act does not require us to presume the legislature intended to modify the common law. Nor does it suggest a change in the common law by doubtful implication or by unclear, ambiguous language. Rather, the language of the act clearly states that landlords have a duty not previously recognized in Wyoming.

We hold that the Residential Rental Property Act imposed a duty on landlords to provide and maintain premises in a safe and sanitary condition fit for human habitation. We further hold that this legislatively created duty establishes a new standard of conduct for purposes of personal injuries occurring on rental property. As we said in McClellan v. Tottenhoff, 666 P.2d 408, 413 (Wyo.1983), the duty of exercising care to protect another person may exist either at common law or be imposed by statute, and where legislation is silent as to whether it establishes a new standard of conduct for purposes of a tort action, it is up to the judiciary to decide whether it has that effect. Here, the statute imposed the duty, and we conclude that it likewise establishes a new standard of conduct in cases involving personal injuries occurring on rental property—a standard of reasonable care under all of the circumstances.

CONCLUSION

With the enactment of the Residential Rental Property Act, Wyoming joined the majority of other states by modifying the rule of landlord immunity and imposing a duty on owners of rental property to maintain them in a safe, sanitary and habitable condition. The imposition of that legislatively created duty gives rise to a new standard of care applicable in cases involving personal injuries occurring on rental property, i.e. reasonable care under the circumstances. Upon establishing that a breach of this standard proximately caused injury, the injured party is entitled to prove any damages recoverable in a personal injury claim. The remedies provided for in the act are limited to cases where corrective action is sought by a tenant in the form of an order requiring the landlord to make repairs, refund or excuse rental payments or allow the tenant to be excused from the lease.

Reversed and remanded for further proceedings.

## Peterson v. Superior Court of Riverside County
Supreme Court of California, 1995.
10 Cal.4th 1185.

■ GEORGE, J.

In Becker v. IRM Corp., 38 Cal.3d 454 (1985) (hereafter *Becker*), this court concluded that under California's products liability doctrine (which provides generally that manufacturers, retailers, and others in the marketing chain of a product are strictly liable in tort for personal injuries caused by a defective product), a residential landlord may be held strictly liable for an injury to its tenant caused by a defect in a leased dwelling. We granted review in the present case to decide whether *Becker* was wrongly decided and should be overruled, or, if *Becker* is not overruled, whether the principles underlying that decision apply outside the landlord-tenant context and warrant the imposition of strict products liability upon the proprietor of a hotel for an injury to its guest caused by a defect in the hotel premises.

In an amended complaint filed March 19, 1990 (the last amended complaint), plaintiff Nadine L. Peterson alleged that, while a guest at the Palm Springs Marquis Hotel, she slipped and fell in the bathtub while taking a shower, sustaining serious head injuries. Plaintiff alleged that the bottom surface of the bathtub was "extremely slick and slippery" and that the bathtub had no "safety measures" such as "anti-skid surfaces, grab rails, rubber mats, or the like." Plaintiff named as defendants, among others, the owners of the hotel, Banque Paribas and Palm Springs Marquis, Inc., the operator of the hotel, Harbaugh Hotel Management Corporation, and the manufacturer of the bathtub, the Kohler Company. In addition to a cause of action for negligence, plaintiff brought a cause of action for "strict liability in tort," asserting the bathtub was a "defective product" because the bathtub "was so smooth, slippery, and slick as to have provided no friction or slip resistance whatsoever. . . ."

During discovery proceedings, the Kohler Company entered into a settlement with plaintiff for the sum of $600,000. The superior court found that this settlement was entered into in good faith.

Prior to trial, defendants Banque Paribas and Harbaugh Hotel Management Corporation (hereinafter defendants) filed a motion in limine[4] to preclude plaintiff "from introducing any evidence or making any reference that strict liability applies to this case" on the ground that the "Becker v. IRM rationale does not apply to the present case. . . ." [The trial court granted the motion.]

[T]he Court of Appeal issued an opinion holding that a peremptory writ of mandate should be issued directing the trial court, among other things, to permit plaintiff to proceed on her strict liability theory, and concluding that *Becker* applied to hotel proprietors. Upon petition by defendants, we again granted review to decide whether *Becker* should be overruled and, alternatively, whether under that decision the proprietor of a hotel is strictly liable in tort for injuries to guests caused by defects in the premises.

## II

The sole issue in the case before us is whether the trial court erred in granting defendants' in limine motion to preclude plaintiff from arguing that, pursuant to our decision in *Becker*, the proprietor of a hotel is strictly liable under the doctrine of products liability for injuries to hotel guests caused by defects in the premises. For the reasons that follow, we conclude, upon reconsideration, that the decision in *Becker* constitutes an unwarranted extension of the doctrine of products liability and should be overruled. As we explain, the circumstance that landlords and hotel proprietors lease residential dwellings and rent hotel rooms to the public does not bring them within the class of persons who properly may be held strictly liable under the doctrine of products liability.

The plaintiff in *Becker* was injured when he fell against a shower door in the apartment he rented from the defendant. The door, which was made of untempered glass, broke and severely lacerated the plaintiff's arm. The only visible difference between shower doors with tempered glass and those with untempered glass in the apartment complex in question was a "very small mark in the corner of each piece of glass." (*Becker, supra,* 38 Cal.3d at p.458.) The apartment was part of a 36-unit complex built more than 10 years before it was acquired by the defendant.

Relying upon the rule announced in Greenman v. Yuba Power Products, Inc., 59 Cal.2d 57 (1963) and its progeny, which imposed strict liability for personal injury caused by a defective product placed into the stream of commerce, this court observed that "a lease for a dwelling contains an implied warranty of habitability" and concluded that, in renting a dwelling, a landlord makes an "implied assurance of safety." (*Becker, supra,* 38 Cal.3d at p.462, 465.) Accordingly, this court held "that a landlord engaged in the business of leasing dwellings is strictly liable in tort for injuries resulting from a latent defect in the premises when

---

[4] Editor's note. A motion in limine is filed before trial begins to exclude certain evidence from the trial.

the defect existed at the time the premises were let to the tenant. [Fn. omitted.]" (*id.* at p.464.)

The decision in *Becker* has received a chilly reception. The Court of Appeal in Vaerst v. Tanzman, 222 Cal.App.3d 1535 (1990) held that *Becker* did not apply if the tenant was injured by a patent defect in leased premises (an allegedly defectively designed handrail on a stairway) or if the landlord leased only his own family residence on a temporary basis. Concluding that "*Becker* must be limited to its facts" (*id.* at p.1541), the Court of Appeal stated in a footnote: "We note that *Becker* represents a minority view to which Chief Justice Lucas and Justice Mosk vigorously dissented. The overwhelming weight of outside authority consistently holds that the imposition of strict liability upon the landlord for latent defects in premises is unjustified in the absence of a showing that the landlord had notice or knowledge of the defect because the landlord is not an insurer of the property. [Citations.]" (*id.* at p.1541, fn.2.)

The only other state, of which we are aware, to discuss the holding in *Becker* imposing strict liability upon landlords, adopted the contrary rule. Armstrong v. Cione, 738 P.2d 79, 84 (1987). The Armstrong case involved circumstances nearly identical to those in *Becker*; a tenant was injured by the breaking of a shower door made with untempered glass. The Supreme Court of Hawaii, citing with approval the dissent in *Becker*, held that strict products liability did not apply to the landlord. Many commentators have [also] criticized the decision in *Becker*. [Citations omitted].

The decision in *Becker*, judicially engrafting products liability principles onto the law governing landlord liability and holding landlords strictly liable for injuries caused by defects in leased premises, represents a minority view that does not appear to be gaining acceptance. . . .

In addition to discussing strict liability, the decision in *Becker*, as previously noted, considered the plaintiff's cause of action for negligence: "[A] landlord in caring for his property must act toward his tenant as a reasonable person under all of the circumstances including the likelihood of injury, the probable seriousness of injury, the burden of reducing or avoiding the risk, and his degree of control over the risk-creating defect. [Citations.]" (*Becker, supra*, 38 Cal.3d 454, 468.) The decision in *Becker* further held that a landlord has a duty to inspect rental premises "to determine whether they meet bare living standards, including whether they are safe," both when purchasing the rental property and when leasing the premises to a tenant. (*Ibid.*) This court distinguished those cases in which injuries were caused by defects that "developed after purchase of the building by the defendant and while the apartment was in possession of the tenant," observing that "[t]he duty to inspect should charge the defendant only with those matters which would have been disclosed by a reasonable inspection." (*Id.* at p.469.)

In the portion of the opinion addressing the products liability doctrine, however, the decision in *Becker* went far beyond holding landlords liable for injuries caused by their own fault, and imposed liability for injuries caused by defects that the landlord had not created, that would not have been disclosed by a reasonable inspection, and of which the landlord had no knowledge. As noted above, *Becker* applied principles of products liability and held "that a landlord engaged in the business of leasing dwellings is strictly liable in tort for injuries resulting from a latent defect in the premises when the defect existed at the time the premises were let to the tenant. [Fn. omitted.]" (*Becker, supra,* 38 Cal.3d 454, 464.)

The effect of imposing upon landlords liability without fault is to compel them to insure the safety of their tenants in situations in which injury is caused by a defect of which the landlord neither knew nor should have known. As noted above, every other jurisdiction that has considered this issue expressly has rejected the approach followed by *Becker*.

Justifying its significant and unprecedented expansion of a landlord's liability for injuries to tenants by applying the law of products liability to the relationship between landlord and tenant, *Becker* reasoned that an apartment itself should be considered a "product" that a landlord places into the stream of commerce. *Becker*'s reasoning in reaching that conclusion, however, is flawed in several respects.

As noted in *Becker*, this court held in Greenman v. Yuba Power Products, Inc., *supra,* 59 Cal.2d 57, 62, that "[a] manufacturer is strictly liable in tort when an article he places on the market, knowing that it is to be used without inspection for defects, proves to have a defect that causes injury to a human being." In Vandermark v. Ford Motor Co., *supra,* 61 Cal.2d 256, 262–263, we held that a retailer of manufactured goods also is strictly liable in tort: "Retailers like manufacturers are engaged in the business of distributing goods to the public. They are an integral part of the overall producing and marketing enterprise that should bear the cost of injuries resulting from defective products. [Citation.] In some cases the retailer may be the only member of that enterprise reasonably available to the injured plaintiff. In other cases the retailer himself may play a substantial part in insuring that the product is safe or may be in a position to exert pressure on the manufacturer to that end; the retailer's strict liability thus serves as an added incentive to safety. Strict liability on the manufacturer and retailer alike affords maximum protection to the injured plaintiff and works no injustice to the defendants, for they can adjust the costs of such protection between them in the course of their continuing business relationship."

Most of the preceding reasons for imposing strict liability upon a retailer of a defective product do not apply to landlords or hotel proprietors who rent residential premises. A landlord or hotel owner, unlike a retailer, often cannot exert pressure upon the manufacturer to make the product safe and cannot share with the manufacturer the costs of insuring the safety of the tenant, because a landlord or hotel owner generally has no "continuing business relationship" with the manufacturer of the defective product.

In the present case, for example, plaintiff's products liability claim is premised upon the assertion that the bathtub in her hotel room was defective because its surface was too slippery. But a hotel owner is not a part of the chain of distribution of a bathtub that is installed in a hotel room. In such circumstances, the bathtub left the stream of commerce when [it was] purchased and installed in the premises. The mere circumstance that it was contemplated customers would use the product in question or be benefitted by [it] does not transform the owners of the business into the equivalent of retailers of the products.

We need not, and do not, decide whether different considerations would apply in the event the landlord or hotel owner had participated in the construction of the building. But in such circumstances strict liability would attach, if at all, based upon the landlord's status as a builder who is engaged in the business of constructing (i.e. manufacturing) rental properties.

The record before us in the present case does not disclose whether defendants constructed the hotel. Plaintiff did not argue in the courts below, or in the briefs filed in this court, that strict liability applies because defendants had constructed the hotel. Accordingly, neither the trial court nor the Court of Appeal ruled upon this issue. Thus, we express no opinion regarding whether, or under what circumstances, strict liability might be imposed upon a landlord or hotel proprietor who participated in the construction of the building or otherwise created the defective product that caused the injury. On remand, plaintiff may seek leave from the superior court to raise such issues.

[Regarding] a landlord or hotel owner who purchases an apartment building or hotel, defects in such a structure may have been created by the builder, a subcontractor, a manufacturer of building supplies or fixtures, a previous owner of the building, or a previous tenant of the apartment or guest of the hotel. Because the landlord or hotel owner generally has no continuing business relationship, or other ready channel of communication, with any of these persons or entities, only in rare cases would the imposition of strict liability upon the landlord or hotel owner create an impetus to manufacture safer products.

As to [a] second justification for the imposition of strict liability—an implied representation of safety—this court in *Becker* held that a tenant renting a dwelling has an expectation of safety similar to that of a consumer purchasing a new product, even if the building is not new. This conclusion was based upon the implied warranty of habitability contained in a residential lease, recognized in Green v. Superior Court, 10 Cal.3d 616 (1974)—a warranty that the court in *Becker* viewed as constituting an "implied assurance of safety made by the landlord." (*Becker, supra*, 38 Cal.3d at p.465.) The conclusion reached in *Becker*,

[T]he conclusion we reach by no means absolves hotel proprietors or landlords of all potential responsibility for such injuries; on the contrary, hotel proprietors and landlords still may be held liable under general tort principles for injuries resulting from defects in their premises if they have breached the applicable standard of care. Neither is the injured tenant or guest deprived of any strict products liability cause of action that may lie against the manufacturer, distributor, or retailer of a defective product that causes the injury. In the present case, for example, plaintiff named as a defendant the manufacturer of the bathtub and has entered into a settlement with the manufacturer for the sum of $600,000. Upon remand, plaintiff may proceed against the remaining defendants on her cause of action for negligence.

## Trentacost v. Brussel
Supreme Court of New Jersey, 1980.
82 N.J. 214, 412 A.2d 436.

■ PASHMAN, J.

Once again this Court is asked to examine the contours of the relationship between residential landlords and their tenants. Specifically, the question is whether a landlord who provides inadequate security for common areas of rental premises may be liable for failing to prevent a criminal assault upon a tenant. The trial court entered judgment for the tenant upon a jury's award of damages. The Appellate Division affirmed. 164 N.J.Super. 9, 395 A.2d 540 (App.Div.1978). We granted defendant's petition for certification, 81 N.J. 48, 404 A.2d 1148 (1979), to consider whether the landlord was obligated to secure the entrance to the common areas of plaintiff's building. We now affirm.

*Facts*

On the afternoon of December 21, 1973, plaintiff, Florence Trentacost, returned to her apartment at 273 Monroe Street, Passaic, New Jersey, from an afternoon of shopping. After she had entered her building and reached the top of a flight of stairs leading to her apartment, someone grabbed her ankles from behind and dragged her down the stairs. Her attacker, who remains unknown, left her bleeding in the ground floor hallway but returned almost immediately to steal her purse. Conscious yet unable to speak, she lay helpless for several minutes until a tenant leaving the building noticed her. Another neighbor then called the police, who took plaintiff to a nearby hospital.

Mrs. Trentacost was hospitalized for 15 days. Her injuries included a dislocated right shoulder, fractures of the left shoulder, left ankle and jaw, lacerations about the mouth and broken teeth. She wore casts on her arms and leg for about a month and a half, and at the time of trial in late 1976 still suffered from pain and loss of mobility.

At the time of the attack, plaintiff was 61 years old and a widow. She had rented her four-room apartment for more than ten years from defendant, Dr. Nathan T. Brussel. The building consisted of eight dwelling units located over street level stores with access provided by front and rear entrances. A padlock secured the back entrance, but there was no lock on the front door, which both plaintiff and apparently her assailant had used to enter the premises.

There was considerable evidence at trial regarding criminal and other suspicious activity in the vicinity of plaintiff's residence. A Passaic city detective testified that in the three years preceding the incident, the police had investigated from 75 to 100 crimes in the neighborhood, mostly burglaries and street muggings. Another policeman stated that "civil disturbances" had occurred in the area between 1969 and 1971. Two months before she was attacked, Mrs. Trentacost had herself reported to defendant an attempt to break into the building's cellar. At other times she had notified the landlord of the presence of unauthorized persons in the hallways. Plaintiff claimed the defendant had promised to install a lock on the front door, but he denied ever discussing the subject prior to the assault on plaintiff.

At the close of evidence, the trial court granted plaintiff's motion to strike the defense of contributory negligence. The judge instructed the jury in part as follows:

> A landlord owes to his tenants the duty of exercising reasonable care to guard against foreseeable dangers arising from the use of premises in connection with those portions which remain within the landlord's control.... The relationship between a landlord and his tenant does not impose upon the landlord the duty to protect a tenant from the crime of third persons. Only upon proper proof that the landlord unreasonably enhanced the risk of the criminal activity by failing to take reasonable measures to safeguard the tenants from foreseeable criminal conduct and a showing of suitable notice of existing defects to the landlord can a tenant recover damages from his landlord.

After the jury returned a verdict for plaintiff of $3,000, the trial court denied defendant's motion for judgment notwithstanding the verdict. R. 4:40–2. When defendant refused to consent to an *additur* of $15,000,[5] the court granted plaintiff's motion for a new trial as to damages. A second jury found damages in the sum of $25,000. Defendant then appealed.

[T]he Appellate Division affirmed.

*Liability for Foreseeable Criminal Conduct*

As the Appellate Division correctly recognized, *Braitman* supplies the focal point of controversy regarding the landlord's duty. In that case the tenants had suffered property loss resulting from theft because of a defective "dead bolt" lock on the apartment door. We held that "upon a

---

[5] Editor's note: An "additur" enables a court to increase an inadequate jury verdict with the consent of the defendant as a condition to denying a motion for a new trial.

logical extension of the principles of our own case law," a landlord could be held liable for creating an "unreasonably enhanced" risk of loss resulting from foreseeable criminal conduct. As in *Braitman,* here the landlord was confronted with the existence of a high level of crime in the neighborhood. Yet he failed to install a lock on the front door leading in to the building's lobby. By failing to do anything to arrest or even reduce the risk of criminal harm to his tenants, the landlord effectively and unreasonably enhanced that risk. See *Braitman,* 68 N.J. at 381–382, 346 A.2d 76.

We reiterate that our holding in *Braitman* lies well within traditional principles of negligence law. "Negligence is tested by whether the reasonably prudent person at the time and place should recognize and foresee an unreasonable risk or likelihood of harm or danger to others." *Rappaport v. Nichols,* 31 N.J. 188, 201, 156 A.2d 1, 8 (1959). If the reasonably prudent person would foresee danger resulting from another's voluntary, criminal acts, the fact that another's actions are beyond defendant's control does not preclude liability. Foreseeability of harm, not the fact of another's intervention, is the crucial factor in determining "whether a *duty* exists to take measures to guard against [criminal activity]." *Goldberg,* 38 N.J. at 583, 186 A.2d at 293.

Application of these principles in *Braitman* led to the imposition of liability for a landlord's failure to provide adequate security against foreseeable criminal conduct. See *Braitman,* 68 N.J. at 378–381, 346 A.2d 76. They also support affirmance of plaintiff's judgment in the present case. There was ample evidence that criminal activity affecting the Monroe Street building was reasonably foreseeable. More than one witness testified to the high incidence of crime in the neighborhood. Plaintiff's own, unchallenged testimony related an attempted theft within the building. Against this background, the jury could readily view the absence of a lock on the front entrance—an area outside an individual tenant's control—as exemplifying a callous disregard for the residents' safety in violation of ordinary standards of care. Since there was sufficient evidence for concluding that the mugging was a foreseeable result of the landlord's negligence, the jury's finding of liability was warranted.

*Theories of Landlord Liability*

Although we need go no further to affirm the judgment for the tenant, we choose not to ignore the alternative theories of landlord liability discussed in *Braitman.* A majority of that Court found that a violation of an administrative regulation governing the condition of multiple dwellings was independent evidence of negligence, 68 N.J. at 385–386, 346 A.2d 76, while two members considered that breach to establish negligence conclusively, *id.* at 389, 346 A.2d 76 (Clifford and Schreiber, JJ., concurring). Three members raised the possibility of imposing liability for unsafe premises based on the landlord's implied warranty of habitability. *Id.* at 387–388, 346 A.2d 76 (separate views of

Hughes, C.J., Sullivan and Pashman, JJ.). There was also mention of liability based on a covenant implied in fact to furnish adequate security. *Id.* at 389, 346 A.2d 76 (Clifford and Schreiber, JJ., concurring).

Over four years have passed since we decided *Braitman.* During this period the need for judicial guidance regarding landlord liability has grown. Although we need not reconcile the alternative theories of *Braitman* to resolve this case, we nevertheless take this opportunity to clarify the scope of a residential landlord's duty to his tenant.

This Court has long recognized that traditional principles of property law, when applied in the context of a residential lease, have "lagged behind changes in dwelling habits and economic realities." *Michaels v. Brookchester, Inc.,* 26 N.J. 379, 382, 140 A.2d 199, 201 (1958). Leases acquired the character of conveyances of real property when their primary function was to govern the relationship between landowners and farmers. Unlike the original, medieval tenant, the modern apartment dweller rents not for profit but for shelter.

It is undisputed that maintaining minimum conditions of habitability including security is beyond an individual tenant's control. Where the task involves the common areas of a multiple-dwelling building, tenants' efforts are entirely precluded. Nor in this highly mobile society should tenants be required to invest substantial sums in improvements that might outlast their tenancy. The landlord, however, can spread the cost of maintenance over an extended period of time among all residents enjoying its benefits.

Recognizing the landlord's "greater opportunity, incentive and capacity . . . to inspect and maintain," *Green v. Superior Ct.,* 10 Cal.3d at 627, 517 P.2d at 1175, 111 Cal.Rptr. at 711, as well as the tenant's lack of bargaining power, this Court has endeavored to give effect to the legitimate expectations which characterize the modern residential tenancy. Since our decision in *Marini v. Ireland,* we have imposed upon the landlord an implied warranty of habitability which arises from his economic and social relationship with his tenants. The scope of this warranty extends to all "facilities vital to the use of the premises for residential purposes."

Among the "facilities vital to the use of the premises" are the provisions for the tenant's security. Unfortunately, crime against person and property is an inescapable fact of modern life. Its presence threatens the suburban enclave as well as the inner city. Tenants universally expect some effective means of excluding intruders from multiple dwellings; without a minimum of security, their well-being is as precarious as if they had no heat or sanitation. Recognizing that a safer and more secure apartment is truly more livable, landlords frequently offer superior protective measures as an inducement for entering into premium lease agreements. Under modern living conditions, an apartment is clearly not habitable unless it provides a reasonable measure of security from the risk of criminal intrusion.

In *Braitman* we considered but declined to resolve whether the implied warranty is "flexible enough to encompass appropriate security devices." 68 N.J. at 388, 346 A.2d at 87 (separate opinion of Hughes, C.J., Sullivan and Pashman, JJ.). We now conclude that it is and therefore hold that the landlord's implied warranty of habitability obliges him to furnish reasonable safeguards to protect tenants from foreseeable criminal activity on the premises.

The "premises" which the landlord must secure necessarily encompass the common areas of multiple dwellings. There is no doubt that the rent charged by a landlord includes a portion for maintaining such areas. We consider the provision of some measure of security in these areas to be "vital to the use of the premises."

Examining the facts of this case, we find that defendant breached his implied warranty by failing to secure in any way the front entrance of the building. The absence of even a simple slip lock—the most elementary of safeguards—permitted the halls and stairwells to become virtually public ways, completely accessible to the criminal element. Defendant did nothing to protect against the threat of crime which seriously impaired the quality of residential life in his building. Since the landlord's implied undertaking to provide adequate security exists independently of his knowledge of any risks, there is no need to prove notice of such a defective and unsafe condition to establish the landlord's contractual duty. It is enough that defendant did not take measures which were in fact reasonable for maintaining a habitable residence.

By failing to provide adequate security, the landlord has impaired the habitability of the tenant's apartment. He has therefore breached his implied warranty of habitability and is liable to the tenant for the injuries attributable to that breach.

*Conclusion*

Although he is not an insurer of his tenants' safety, a landlord is definitely no mere bystander. Accordingly, the expense involved in making a dwelling secure and habitable does not diminish the landlord's responsibility.

Our analysis has led to the conclusion that a landlord has a legal duty to take reasonable security measures for tenant protection on the premises. His obligation to provide safe and habitable premises gives rise to potential liability on alternative grounds of conventional negligence and the implied warranty of habitability. Together these theories will serve to protect the otherwise precarious position of the individual tenant in a manner consistent with modern conceptions of public policy.

For the foregoing reasons, the judgment of the Appellate Division is affirmed.

■ CLIFFORD, J., Dissenting in part.

I take this opportunity to register disagreement with the notion that liability can be imposed on the defendant landlord on the theory of implied warranty of habitability. Emphasizing the growing presence of crime in society the Court declares today that "the landlord's implied warranty of habitability obliges him to furnish reasonable safeguards to protect tenants from foreseeable criminal activity on the premises", *ante* at 218; and that "[s]ince [this] undertaking exists independently of [the landlord's] knowledge of any risks, there is no need to prove notice of a defective and unsafe condition." *Ante* at 218.

The harsh realities of modern life are all too well-known. I share the majority's concern with them. But novel application of the implied warranty of habitability to the baleful conditions reflected in those realities is unwarranted and ill-advised. In practical effect this exercise predicates what amounts to absolute liability solely upon the relationship between the landlord and tenant and upon loose notions of foreseeability. In my view the existence of a duty here should not be grounded simply on a special relationship between the parties but rather should arise from the particular circumstances of the case, including foreseeability. Clearly the inquiry must involve a fair balancing of the relative interests of the parties, the nature of the risk, and the public interest in the proposed solution. *Goldberg, supra,* 38 N.J. at 583, 186 A.2d 291. This process has been well served in the past through the application of traditional negligence principles. I perceive no compelling reason for departing from that practice.

## NOTES

1. *Impact of* Trentacost. What are the advantages and disadvantages from Arthur's standpoint of the rationale in *Trentacost*?

2. *Lessor's liability for injuries resulting from third-party criminal activity: effect of prior crimes.* For a time, the property law concept that a lease is essentially a sale of property protected landlords from liability for injuries inflicted on tenants by criminal attack, just as the same concept protected them from liability for injuries inflicted by defective premises. What policies support the traditional rule against extending liability to landlords for third-party criminal activity? Although some of the language in *Trentacost* comes close to suggesting a strict liability theory, most courts that have held the lessor liable in a situation involving third-party criminal activity have done so on a pure negligence theory rather than one of strict liability.[6] Some states require landlords to have an increased awareness as to the criminal activity taking place on the leased premises for a court to

---

[6] See, e.g., Ashraf v. Haleluk, 2012 N.J. Super. Unpub. LEXIS 2070 (App.Div. Aug. 31, 2012); Scully v. Fitzgerald, 179 N.J. 114, 843 A.2d 1110 (2004); Madhani v. Cooper, 106 Cal.App.4th 412, 130 Cal.Rptr.2d 778 (2003); Smith v. Lagow Const. & Dev. Co., 2002 S.D. 37, 642 N.W.2d 187 (2002); Sikora v. Wenzel, 88 Ohio St.3d 493, 727 N.E.2d 1277 (2000);.Doe v. Dominion Bank of Washington, N.A., 963 F.2d 1552 (D.C.Cir.1992);Brock v. Watts Realty Co., Inc., 582 So.2d 438 (Ala.1991).

recognize a landlord's duty to protect against an intervening criminal act. Therefore, besides situations in which (1) the landlord has created an environment conducive to criminal activity; or (2) an express or implied contract to offer the tenant reasonable protection has been found, courts may impose liability if the landlord has superior knowledge of the likelihood of criminal attack and fails to disclose that knowledge to the tenant.[7]

Should the landlord-tenant relationship in and of itself be considered sufficiently contractual to impose liability on the landlord for third-party criminal activity? Do you think that such liability should be extended to commercial as well as residential settings? Should the implied warranty of habitability require landlords to take affirmative measures to protect tenants against criminal attacks?

Virtually all courts willing to impose liability on landlords for criminal attack require that the criminal act be foreseeable.[8] Foreseeability is a somewhat nebulous concept, but it has been determined to be something more than the mere possibility that a crime will be committed. Suppose the evidence at trial reveals that the lessor was aware of prior crimes in the area of his building, but that the nature of these crimes differed from the crime which caused the injury to a particular plaintiff. Should the prior crimes that occurred have to be similar or identical to the crime in question in order for a tenant to recover from the landlord for injuries sustained as a result of third-party criminal activity?

3. *Exculpatory clauses.* Should a lessor be allowed to waive his liability for personal injuries to a tenant or someone on the premises with the tenant's permission through an exculpatory clause in the lease? Should

---

[7] See Means v. Kanawha Pizza, LLC, 2011 W. Va. LEXIS 185, *8 (W. Va. May 16, 2011) (a duty will be imposed if a landlord's affirmative actions or omissions have unreasonably created or increased the risk of injury to the tenant from the criminal activity of a third party); Sigmund v. Starwood Urban Retail VI, LLC, 617 F.3d 512 (D.C. Cir. 2010) (listing facts warranting heightened standard of foreseeability imposed on the landlord); Madhani v. Cooper, 106 Cal.App.4th 412, 130 Cal.Rptr.2d 778 (2003) ("Landlord owed a duty of care to protect tenant from foreseeable future assaults of co-tenant when landlord learned that co-tenant had engaged in repeated acts of assault and battery against tenant such that it was foreseeable that violent outbursts would eventually result in serious injury."); Smith v. Lagow Construction & Developing Co., 2002 S.D. 37, 642 N.W.2d 187 (2002) ("Although a landlord owes no general duty to tenants to protect them from crime, such a duty arises when a landlord's affirmative acts or omissions create a foreseeably high risk to the tenant."); Anzalone v. Pan-Am Equities, 271 A.D.2d 307, 706 N.Y.S.2d 409 (2000) ("A landlord's duty to protect against criminal intruders arises only when ambient crime has demonstrably infiltrated the premises, or when the landlord is otherwise on notice as to the serious risk of such infiltration."); Miller v. Whitworth, 455 S.E.2d 821, 827 (W.Va.1995) ("a duty will be imposed if a landlord's affirmative actions or omissions have unreasonably created or increased the risk of injury to the tenant from the criminal activity of a third party"). See also Shannon Kelly, South Dakota Supreme Court Opens the Door to Landlord Liability for Criminal Attacks Committed By Third Parties on the Premises: Smith v. Lagow Construction & Developing Company, 48 S.D. L. Rev. 365 (2003).

[8] Lawrence v. La Jolla Beach & Tennis Club, Inc., 231 Cal. App. 4th 11 (Cal. App. 4th Dist. 2014); Tan v. Arnel Management Co., 170 Cal. App. 4th 1087, 1088 (Cal. App. 2d Dist. 2009); Wiener v. Southcoast Childcare Ctrs., Inc., 12 Cal.Rptr.3d 615, 32 Cal.4th 1138 (2004); Claxton v. Atlantic Richfield Co., 133 Cal.Rptr.2d 425, 108 Cal.App.4th 327 (2003); Mason v. U.E.S.S. Leasing Corp., 756 N.E.2d 58, 730 N.Y.S.2d 770 (2001); Rice v. Six Flags Over Georgia, LLC, 572 S.E.2d 322 (Ga.App. 2002); Doe v. Beach House Dev. Co., 737 N.E.2d 141 (Ohio App.2000); Doe v. Dominion Bank of Washington, N.A., 963 F.2d 1552, 1560 (D.C.Cir.1992);Brock v. Watts Realty Co., Inc., 582 So.2d 438, 440 (Ala.1991).

the issue of waiver be made to depend upon whether the court is enforcing liability for personal injuries based on an implied warranty of habitability theory?

4. *Condominium associations.* There have been several cases involving condominium association liability for personal injuries sustained by either the condominium unit owners or their tenants, guests, invitees, and customers. A condominium can be defined as real estate "in which individuals possess their own units in fee and own an undivided interest in the common areas in proportion to their share in the ownership of the entire project."[9] Although most condominiums are residential, they may be commercial or industrial as well. Generally the regulation and administration of a condominium's affairs are handled by a Board of Directors of the condominium association (the Association Board). It is the job of the Association Board to assess and collect sufficient money to maintain and repair the common facilities of the condominium.

In Machin v. Royale Green Condominium Association,[10] a wrongful death action by a father for the drowning of his infant son, the court reversed a summary judgment in favor of the defendant condominium association based on evidence of the association's negligence in that the gate to the pool did not self-close or have a spring lock, and therefore was in violation of a county code. Courts also have held that a condominium association should be held to the same standard of care as a landlord regarding injuries sustained by residents resulting from third-party criminal activity.[11]

5. *Causation.* In Saelzler v. Advanced Group 400, 107 Cal.Rptr.2d 617, 23 P.3d 1143, 25 Cal.4th 763 (2001), a sharply divided California Supreme Court found that the plaintiff's proof of causation was inadequate because she could not prove that the presence of security guards, as well as the taking of other security precautions, would have prevented the attack. The court found that the plaintiff failed to show that the defendants' alleged breach of duty actually caused her injuries because the plaintiff could not prove the identity of her assailants and thus, was unable to show that her assailants were unauthorized to enter the premises. This decision militates against innocent persons assaulted on premises where landowners breach their duties to take meaningful steps to secure the premises. Should the burden of causation be shifted from the victims to the landowners who breach their duty to provide security measures?[12]

---

[9] Blackburn & Melia, Ohio Condominium Law Reform: A Comparative Critique, 29 Case W.Res.L.Rev. 145, 147 (1978).

[10] 507 So.2d 646 (Dist.Ct.App.Fla.1987).

[11] See, e.g., Martinez v. Woodmar IV Condominiums Homeowners Association, Inc., 189 Ariz. 206, 941 P.2d 218 (Ariz. 1997); Frances T. v. Village Green Owners Association, 42 Cal.3d 490, 229 Cal.Rptr. 456, 723 P.2d 573 (1986).

[12] See Julie Davies, Undercutting Premises Liability: Reflections On The Use And Abuse Of Causation Doctrine, 40 San Diego L. Rev. 971 (2003); Dennis Yokoyama, The Law Of Causation In Actions Involving Third-Party Assaults When The Landowner Negligently Fails To Hire Security Guards: A Critical Examination Of Saelzler v. Advanced Group 400, 40 Cal. W. L. Rev. 79 (2003).

## B. Scope of Duties and Rights upon Termination of Lease

## Assignment 6

# Landlord's Motives in Selecting or Removing Tenants

### 1. Introduction

Under the common law a landlord had complete freedom in selecting or rejecting tenants. The landlord had a legal right to be bigoted or unreasonable. Similarly, at the end of a tenancy the landlord could refuse to renew the tenancy for arbitrary reasons. Under the Fair Housing Act ("FHA", Title VIII of the Civil Rights Act of 1968, as amended) it is now unlawful to discriminate in the sale or rental of most housing on the grounds of "race, color, religion, sex, familial status, or national origin." 42 U.S.C. § 3604(b). It is also unlawful to discriminate because of a tenant's physical or mental handicap. 42 U.S.C.§ 3604(f). Discrimination in the sale or rental of housing may also be barred under state law.[1]

Certain residential landlords are exempt from the Fair Housing Act. For example, a landlord is exempt if she is offering to lease a unit in a building of four units or less, one unit of which she occupies.[2]

Landlords are not only restricted in selecting tenants at the beginning of a lease, but their ability to remove tenants at the end of the lease may also be limited. In some states, leases are presumed to expire after the initial lease term unless the parties specifically agree to a new contract.[3] In these jurisdictions, landlords retain the discretion to remove an unwanted tenant at the end of the lease term. Elsewhere, leases are presumed to renew automatically, and these jurisdictions often impose a "good cause requirement" pursuant to which the landlord must have a statutorily acceptable reason for discontinuing the lease.[4] When state

---

[1] See, e.g., Marina Point, Ltd. v. Wolfson, 30 Cal.3d 721, 180 Cal.Rptr. 496, 640 P.2d 115 (1982) (prohibiting discrimination against children) reprinted below. But see Taylor v. Rancho Santa Barbara, 206 F.3d 932 (9th Cir. 2000) (upholding state law permitting owners of mobile home park to restrict residence based on age).

[2] 42 U.S.C. § 3603(b)(2). The act covers all dwellings unless specifically exempted. 42 U.S.C. § 3603(a)(2).

[3] See, e.g., Or. Rev. Stat. § 90.100(17) (2015); Wyo. Stat. § 34–2–129 (2015); Pendergrass v. Fagan, 218 Or. App. 533, 537, 180 P.3d 110, 113 (Ct. App. 2008).

[4] See, e.g., N.H. Rev. Stat. Ann. § 540:2(II) (2015); See also JP Morgan Chase Bank v. Grimes, 2015 N.H. LEXIS 30, *1 (N.H. Apr. 7, 2015) (a landlord who desired to market, sell and/or convey the property in a vacant condition satisfied the good cause requirement for purposes of terminating a tenancy); AIMCO Props., LLC v. Dziewisz, 152 N.H. 587, 591, 883

law sanctions the automatic renewal of leases or provides for rent stabilized apartments,[5] landlords face greater difficulties in removing tenants and eviction claims are common.

Most states prohibit "retaliatory evictions."[6] These restrictions prevent landlords from evicting a tenant for reporting a violation to authorities or taking other actions relating to their tenancy.[7] Certain types of retaliation raise challenging questions of statutory interpretation and public policy. For example, several courts have held that tenants should be protected from retaliation for their legal acts that are not directly related to their rights as tenants.[8] It has also been held that a tenant who leaves the premises because of a threat of retaliatory eviction is entitled to damages.[9] Public policy is mindful of potential hardships arbitrary evictions could pose to residential tenants, but should commercial tenants also be protected by the same policy? Courts are divided on this issue.[10]

This Assignment explores the limits on the landlord's right to exercise discretion in choosing tenants. It does not examine retaliatory eviction.

---

A.2d 310, 313 (2005). "Good cause" is often narrowly defined, and the non-renewal is commonly limited to situations of either a serious or repeated breach by the tenant. See *AIMCO Props., LLC*, 152 N.H. at 591, 883 A.2d at 313; Carroll, The International Trend Toward Requiring Good Cause for Tenant Eviction: Dangerous Portents for the United States?, 38 Seton Hall L. Rev. 427 (2008).

[5] In order to ensure affordable housing, some municipalities have rent stabilization ordinances. Leases of rent stabilized apartments are automatically renewed and generally can be terminated only when landlords seek to remove the property from the rental market for use as a primary residence for themselves or a member of their immediate family. See, e.g., N.Y. Comp. Codes R. & Regs. tit. 9, § 2524.4(a) (2015).

[6] See, e.g., Md. Real Prop. Code Ann. § 8–208.1 (2015); N.C. Gen. Stat. § 42–37.1 (2014); Vt. Stat. Ann. tit. 9 § 4465 (2015). See generally Annotation, Retaliatory Eviction for Reporting Landlord's Violation of the Law, 23 A.L.R.5th 140 (1995).

[7] Tenants prevailed in the following retaliatory eviction cases: Boyd v. Carter, 227 Cal. App. 4th Supp. 1 (Cal. Super. Ct. 2014) (landlord cannot retaliate for tenant complaint of violation of implied warranty of habitability); Carpentieri v. Gayle, No. HDSP151240, 2009 WL 1067555 (Conn. Super. Ct. April 16, 2009) (determining that tenant's reports to town authority of housing code violations supported a finding of retaliatory eviction); Housing Auth. of the City of Bayonne v. Mims, 396 N.J. Super. 195, 933 A.2d 613 (Super. Ct. App. Div. 2007) (determining that tenant's complaints regarding the condition of premises supported a finding of retaliatory eviction).

[8] Barela v. Superior Court of Orange County, 30 Cal. 3d 244, 636 P.2d 582 (1981) (landlord cannot retaliate for tenant complaint concerning criminal acts of landlord); Windward Partners v. Delos Santos, 59 Haw. 104, 577 P.2d 326 (1978) (landlord cannot retaliate against tenants who participate in zoning hearing); S.P. Growers Ass'n v. Rodriguez, 17 Cal. 3d 719, 552 P.2d 721 (1976) (landlord cannot retaliate when tenant sued landlord in labor dispute). But see Imperial Colliery Co. v. Fout, 179 W. Va. 776, 373 S.E.2d 489 (1988) (tenants' involvement in labor strike is not incidental to tenancy and thus could not be the basis for a retaliation claim).

[9] See, e.g., Lang Pham v. Corbett, 2015 Wash. App. LEXIS 1076 (Wash. Ct. App. May 26, 2015); Rich v. Schwab, 75 Cal. Rptr. 2d 170 (Ct. App. 1998); Murphy v. Smallridge, 196 W. Va. 35, 468 S.E.2d 167 (1996).

[10] Compare Port of Longview v. Int'l Raw Materials, Ltd., 96 Wash. App. 431, 979 P.2d 917 (Ct. App. 1999) (applying the doctrine of retaliatory eviction to commercial tenants); with 1266 Apartment Corp. v. New Horizon Deli, Inc., 368 N.J. Super. 456, 847 A.2d 9 (Super. Ct. App. Div. 2004) (refraining from applying the doctrine to commercial tenants).

## 2. PRINCIPAL PROBLEM

Linda Leach has recently acquired a 50 unit residential apartment house. She announces that all new leases, either with existing tenants or new tenants, will be executed only with tenants who can demonstrate that their monthly income exceeds three times the monthly rent (the "three-times-rent" requirement). In addition she intends to require a showing that the income used to meet the three-times-rent requirement is earned income as opposed to income from investments, welfare payments, spousal support payments or other unearned income (the "earned income" requirement). Your client, Tamela Harris, is currently a tenant in the apartment house. Most of her income comes from a combination of spousal support and public assistance payments. Her total monthly income is less than three times the monthly rent.

You will argue that Leach's new requirements are invalid for two reasons. First, you believe that both requirements are unreasonable and therefore invalid on their face. Second, you believe that you can show that the two requirements effectively discriminate against women and racial minorities. Statistically, more women than men receive public assistance, spousal support or child support. Consequently, the earned income requirement will tend to prevent women from becoming or remaining tenants. Moreover, racial minorities and women on average tend to have substantially lower incomes than men. Consequently, they will have more difficulty than non-minority men in meeting the three-times-rent requirement.

Assume that your jurisdiction has a statute similar to the Unruh Act quoted in footnote 11 of Marina Point, Ltd. v. Wolfson, reprinted below. Consider whether Leach's actions would violate such a statute. Consider also whether Leach's actions should be treated as a violation of the federal Fair Housing Act, quoted in the Introduction to this Assignment.

Leach will undoubtedly attempt to defend her requirements on the ground that they are legitimate business decisions not motivated by racial or gender prejudice. Before deciding to accept Harris's case, consider the material below.

## 3. MATERIALS FOR SOLUTION OF PRINCIPAL PROBLEM

### Kramarsky v. Stahl Management
Supreme Court of New York, Special Term, 1977.
92 Misc.2d 1030, 401 N.Y.S.2d 943.

■ GREENFIELD, JUSTICE.

This is an application brought on by Order to Show Cause, pursuant to § 297, Subdivision 6 of the Executive Law for an order enjoining respondents from selling, renting, leasing, or otherwise disposing of Apartment 9J at 225 West 106th Street to anyone other than petitioner until final determination of a complaint against respondent Stahl Management now pending before the State Division of Human Rights.

The application is based upon a complaint of discrimination by one Judith Pierce, a black divorced woman, who contends that Stahl Management unlawfully discriminated against her by refusing to rent an apartment because of her race, sex and marital status. In support of that contention, she points to the willingness of the respondent to rent an apartment to a later white applicant.

Respondent denies any illegal discrimination insisting that Ms. Pierce was not turned down because she was black, female or divorced, but for other reasons. In support of this contention, he demonstrates that 30% of his apartments have been rented to blacks, including the last two for which there were both black and white applicants and that 60% of the apartments have been rented to unmarried persons. The reason for her rejection, the landlord contends, is that her application indicated that in the eyes of the landlord she would be an undesirable tenant.

The application form is a one page sheet in which Ms. Pierce indicated that she was employed as general counsel to the New York City Commission on Human Rights, that she had earned a salary of $28,000 plus a year and that she had previously been employed with the Legal Services Corporation. Under the space for Repairs and Remarks she had written in "Painting-New Rulings". Mr. Stahl, the individual who operated the respondent, candidly admits that the information on the application indicated that "she would be a source of trouble to me as a tenant." Rather than a lawyer attuned to her legal rights, he would have preferred, all other things being equal, a person who was likely to be less informed and more passive.

The Human Rights Law (Executive Law, Article 15) provides in § 296, Subdivision 5:

(a) It shall be an unlawful discriminatory practice for the owner, lessee, sub-lessee, assignee, or managing agent of, or other person having the right to sell, rent or lease a housing accommodation, constructed or to be constructed, or any agent or employee thereof:

(1) To refuse to sell, rent, lease or otherwise to deny to or withhold from any person or group of persons such a housing accommodation because of the race, creed, color, national origin, sex, or disability or marital status of such person or persons.

(2) To discriminate against any person because of his race, creed, color, national origin, sex, or disability or marital status in the terms, conditions or privileges of the sale, rental or lease of any such housing accommodation or in the furnishing of facilities or services in connection therewith.

Absent a supervening statutory proscription, a landlord is free to do what he wishes with his property, and to rent or not to rent to any given person at his whim. The only restraints which the law has imposed upon free exercise of his discretion is that he may not use race, creed, color, national origin, sex or marital status as criteria. So, regrettable though it may be, a landlord can employ other criteria to determine the acceptability of his tenants-occupational, physical or otherwise. He may decide not to rent to singers because they are too noisy, or not to rent to bald-headed men because he has been told they give wild parties. He can bar his premises to the lowest strata of society, should he choose, or to the highest, if that be his personal desire.

Thus, this court concludes that there is nothing illegal in a landlord discriminating against lawyers as a group, or trying to keep out of his building intelligent persons, aware of their rights, who may give him trouble in the future. A landlord has a "right to be selective and to reject a prospective tenant because of his or her failure to meet standards of acceptability other than those which concern themselves with one's race or color or standards which are otherwise proscribed by statute." State Commission for Human Rights v. Kennelly, 30 A.D.2d 310, 312, 291 N.Y.S.2d 686, 689.

Although the courts, in the interest of justice, will endeavor to facilitate to the fullest the legislative intent and public policy underlying antidiscrimination legislation, the facts and circumstances of this case do not warrant injunctive relief. The court is not persuaded that there is a reasonable likelihood that the charge of discrimination can be sustained. Accordingly, the application is denied and the temporary restraining order vacated.

## Marina Point, Ltd. v. Stephen Wolfson

Supreme Court of California, 1982.
30 Cal.3d 721, 180 Cal.Rptr. 496, 640 P.2d 115.

■ TOBRINER, JUSTICE.

In this case we must determine whether, under California law, an owner of an apartment complex may lawfully refuse to rent any of its apartments to a family solely because the family includes a minor child. In the landlord's action to eject the family, the municipal court, found, inter alia, that "[c]hildren are rowdier, noisier, more mischievous and more boisterous than adults," and upheld the landlord's policy of excluding all families with minor children. The tenants now appeal from the judgment in favor of the landlord, contending that the exclusionary policy violates their statutory rights under the Unruh Civil Rights Act (Civ.Code, § 51 et seq.) and the California Fair Housing Law (Health & Saf.Code, § 35700 et seq., now Gov.Code, § 12955) and, in addition, impermissibly infringes upon their state and federal constitutional rights of familial privacy (U.S. Const., 9th & 14th Amends., Cal. Const., art. I, § 1) and equal protection of the law. (U.S. Const., 14th Amend.; Cal. Const., art. I, § 7.)

For the reasons discussed below, we have concluded that the landlord's broad, class-based exclusionary practice violates the Unruh Civil Rights Act (hereafter Unruh Act or act); in light of this conclusion, we have no occasion in this case to address any of the tenants' more sweeping and far-reaching constitutional contentions. As we shall explain, the municipal court, in finding the challenged practice compatible with the Unruh Act, proceeded from the erroneous premise that under that act "[n]ot every class . . . is protected from exclusion," but rather that "[i]t is only such class . . . that is protected as is set forth in the [s]tatutes or who come under the [s]tatutes by judicial determination." Finding that "[t]here is no decision to include children, parents with children, or families with children, as a protected class by the wording of the [s]tatutes themselves or by judicial determination," the court concluded that the challenged practice fell outside the scope of the act.

As we shall point out, the municipal court's approach conflicts with the interpretation of the Unruh Act unanimously adopted by this court a decade ago in *In re Cox* (1970) 3 Cal.3d 205, 90 Cal.Rptr. 24, 474 P.2d 992. In *Cox,* after reviewing the origin, legislative evolution and prior judicial decisions construing the Unruh Act and its predecessors, our court concluded that the "identification of particular bases of discrimination-color, race, religion, ancestry and national origin-[in the current version of the act] . . . *is illustrative rather than restrictive.*" (Italics added.) (3 Cal.3d at p. 216, 90 Cal.Rptr. 24, 474 P.2d 992.) Although we recognized that in recent years the act had been invoked most often "by persons alleging discrimination on racial grounds," we emphasized that the act's "language and its history compel the conclusion that the Legislature intended to prohibit *all* arbitrary discrimination by business establishments." (Italics added.) (*Id.*) Thus, contrary to the municipal court's conclusion, the fact that the landlord's exclusionary policy in this case discriminated against children and families with children, rather than a specific racial or religious group or some other classification specifically involved in a prior judicial decision, does not place the exclusionary practice beyond the reach of the Unruh Act.

The landlord maintains, however, that even if the municipal court did err in its analysis of the Unruh Act, we should nevertheless affirm the trial court judgment on the grounds that the exclusionary policy at issue is "reasonable," not "arbitrary," and hence not violative of the Unruh Act. Relying, inter alia, upon the court's finding that "[c]hildren are rowdier, noisier, more mischievous and more boisterous than adults," the landlord claims that it may seek to achieve its legitimate interest in a quiet and peaceful residential atmosphere by excluding *all* minors from its housing accommodations, thus providing its adult tenants with a "child free" environment.

As we shall explain, however, the landlord's argument overlooks the individual nature of the statutory right of equal access to business establishments that is afforded "all persons" by the Unruh Act. Derived from the early common law right of equal access to the services of innkeepers or common carriers, the Unruh Act prohibits business establishments from withholding their services or goods from a broad class of individuals in order to "cleanse" their operations from the alleged characteristics of the members of an excluded class.

As our prior decisions teach, the Unruh Act preserves the traditional broad authority of owners and proprietors of business establishments to adopt reasonable rules regulating the conduct of patrons or tenants; it imposes no inhibitions on an owner's right to exclude any individual who violates such rules. Under the act, however, an individual who has committed no such misconduct cannot be excluded solely because he falls within a class of persons whom the owner believes is more likely to engage in misconduct than some other group. Whether the exclusionary policy rests on the alleged undesirable propensities of those of a particular race, nationality, occupation, political affiliation, or age, in this context the Unruh Act protects individuals from such arbitrary discrimination.

Accordingly, we conclude that the judgment in favor of the landlord should be reversed.

The Facts and Proceedings Below.

Plaintiff Marina Point, Ltd. (hereafter landlord or Marina Point) is a privately owned apartment complex, which, at the time of trial, consisted of 846 separate apartment units. The apartment complex, located in Marina del Rey, an unincorporated area in the County of Los Angeles, stands on land owned, and leased by the county to Marina Point. The master lease between the county and Marina Point specifically forbids Marina Point from discriminating on the basis of race, religion or national ancestry, but contains no provision with respect to other forms of discrimination.

In January 1974, defendants Stephen and Lois Wolfson signed a one-year lease for an apartment in the Marina Point complex with occupancy to begin on February 1 of that year. Although the printed form lease that the Wolfsons then signed contained a clause which provided that no minors under the age of 18 could reside in the leased premises without the landlord's written permission, Marina Point acknowledges that at that time it followed a policy of renting its apartments to families with children as well as to families without children.

In October 1974, Marina Point altered its rental policy with the objective of ultimately excluding all children from the apartment complex. At that time, well over 60 families with children lived in apartments in the complex, and Marina Point decided that while it would allow the children already there to remain, it would not rent any apartments to new families with children or with pregnant women.

In February 1975, the Wolfsons renewed their lease for a one-year period; the form lease again contained the same clause with respect to children as had appeared in the initial lease. In September 1975, Lois Wolfson gave birth to a son, Adam, who thereafter resided with his parents in the family apartment in Marina Point. In February 1976, the Wolfsons renewed their lease for another year; although the lease again contained the identical clause as to written consent for children, the Wolfsons apparently did not specifically inform the landlord of Adam's presence, and the lease made no reference to him.

In the fall of 1976, the landlord's manager learned that the Wolfsons had a child living in the apartment; shortly thereafter, the landlord informed them that their lease, due to expire on January 31, 1977, would not be renewed, and that the sole reason for such nonrenewal was Adam's presence on the premises.

After some negotiation between the parties, Marina Point agreed to a three-month extension of the Wolfsons' lease; the new lease agreement, which again contained the same provision as to children, specified that the premises would be occupied by the Wolfsons and their son. Thereafter, upon the Wolfsons' request, the landlord agreed to an additional one-month extension of the lease to May 31, 1977.

When the Wolfsons failed to vacate the premises on May 31, the landlord commenced the present unlawful detainer action in municipal court. In their answer, the Wolfsons maintained that the landlord's policy of discriminating against families with children violated both statutory constitutional [sic] prescriptions, and, as such, did not provide a lawful basis for their eviction. The landlord acknowledges that if its exclusion of the Wolfsons does in fact contravene statutory or constitutional strictures, such illegality would indeed provide a valid defense to the unlawful detainer action.

At trial, the landlord conceded that its nonrenewal of the Wolfsons' lease rested solely on its current general policy of refusing to rent any of its apartments to families with children, but the landlord denied that this policy violated any statutory or constitutional principle. In defense of its exclusionary policy, the landlord's apartment manager testified that the decision to bar families with children rested in part on a number of past instances in which young tenants had engaged in annoying or potentially dangerous activities, ranging from acts of arson to roller skating and batting practice in the hallways to the attempted solicitation of snacks from the landlord's office staff.

The manager did not indicate, however, what proportion of the tenant children engaged in such activities or what steps, short of the blanket exclusionary policy, the landlord had implemented to deal with the problem, such as promulgating general rules as to permissible and impermissible conduct or excluding from the complex those families whose children repeatedly committed disruptive or destructive acts. Moreover, the landlord introduced no evidence that the Wolfsons' child had ever engaged in any such activity and, indeed, two of the Wolfsons' immediate neighbors testified that Adam's presence was not annoying to them at all.

As an additional explanation for the exclusionary policy, the apartment manager testified that the Marina Point complex had no special facilities for children, such as playground equipment, and no suitable area for children to play. The manager conceded, however, that the facilities of the complex had remained unaltered since the landlord had implemented its "no children" policy. In addition, the evidence revealed that, even at the time of trial, seven children were still living in apartments in the Marina Point complex.

Finally, the landlord presented testimony of two expert witnesses who had been in the real estate business for many years. These witnesses testified that in their opinion children, as a class, generally cause more wear and tear on property than adults do, and that as a consequence, landlords who rent to families with children generally have higher maintenance costs than landlords who exclude children. The witnesses presented no statistical data in support of their conclusion, but simply testified on the basis of their general experience. . . .

At the conclusion of the trial, the municipal court ruled in favor of Marina Point, rejecting the Wolfsons' contention that the landlord's policy of excluding all families with children violated their statutory or constitutional rights. The court's formal findings of fact contain findings, inter alia, that the landlord's "exclusion of children . . . proceeds from a reasonable economic motive to promote a quiet and peaceful environment free from noise and damage caused by children." . . .

Contrary to the municipal court's conclusion, the antidiscrimination provisions of the Unruh Act are not confined only to a limited category of "protected classes" but rather protect "all persons" from any arbitrary discrimination by a business establishment.

In evaluating the legality of the challenged exclusionary policy in this case, we must recognize at the outset that in California, unlike many other jurisdictions, the Legislature has sharply circumscribed an apartment owner's traditional discretion to accept and reject tenants on the basis of the landlord's own likes or dislikes. California has brought such landlords within the embrace of the broad statutory provisions of the Unruh Act, Civil Code section 51.[11] Emanating from and modeled upon traditional "public accommodations" legislation, the Unruh Act expanded the reach of such statutes from common carriers and places of

---

[11] Section 51 presently provides: "All persons within the jurisdiction of this state are free and equal, and no matter what their sex, race, color, religion, ancestry or national origin are entitled to the full and equal accommodations, advantages, facilities, privileges or services in all business establishments of every kind whatsoever.

"This section shall not be construed to confer any right or privilege on a person which is conditioned or limited by law or which is applicable alike to persons of every sex, color, race, religion, ancestry or national origin." [The statute currently also prohibits discrimination based on disability.—Eds.]

public accommodation and recreation, e.g., railroads, hotels, restaurants, theaters and the like, to include "all business establishments of every kind whatsoever." . . .

The municipal court properly recognized that Marina Point, as a "business establishment," was generally subject to the Unruh Act. It concluded, however, that the act provided no protection to the Wolfsons because it found that the subjects, i.e., "victims," of the discriminatory practice in this case, described variously as "children" or "families with children," did not fall within what the court believed to be a limited set of "protected classes" shielded from discriminatory treatment by the act. As already noted, the court, in elaborating upon its understanding of the Unruh Act, stated in this regard: "Not every class is protected. It is only such class or person that is protected as is set forth in the Statutes or who come under the Statutes by judicial determination." Because discrimination against children or against families with children was not in explicit terms proscribed by the language of section 51 or by any prior judicial decision, the court determined that any such discrimination was beyond the scope of the act.

The municipal court's interpretation of the act directly conflicts with this court's interpretation of the Unruh Act a decade ago in *In re Cox, supra,* 3 Cal.3d 205, 90 Cal.Rptr. 24, 474 P.2d 992. In *Cox,* an individual who claimed that he had been excluded from a shopping center because a friend with whom he was talking "wore long hair and dressed in an unconventional manner" (3 Cal.3d at p. 210, 90 Cal.Rptr. 24, 474 P.2d 992), asserted that such exclusion was barred by the Unruh Act. Relying upon the fact that the act, by its terms, expressly referred only to discrimination on the basis of "race, color, religion, ancestry or national origin," the city argued in response that the act's proscriptions were limited to discrimination which was based on the specifically enumerated forbidden criteria, and did not encompass the alleged discrimination against "hippies" or their associates.

After reviewing the common law origin, the legislative history and the past judicial interpretations of the act and its statutory predecessors, our court unanimously concluded in *Cox* that the "identification of particular bases of discrimination-color, race, religion, ancestry, and national origin-*is illustrative rather than restrictive.* [Citation.] Although the legislation has been invoked primarily by persons alleging discrimination on racial grounds, its language and its history compel the conclusion that the Legislature intended to prohibit *all arbitrary discrimination by business establishments.*" (Italics added.) (3 Cal.3d at p. 216, 90 Cal.Rptr. 24, 474 P.2d 992.) . . .

Moreover, subsequent to our decision in *Cox,* the Legislature effectively confirmed our interpretation of the act as barring all forms of arbitrary discrimination. In 1974, the Legislature amended section 51, reenacting the prior provisions of the statute and adding "sex" to the specifically enumerated bases of discrimination listed in the Unruh Act.

In sending the bill to the Governor for his signature, the Chairman of the Select Committee on Housing and Urban Affairs explained: "The purpose of the bill is to bring it to the attention of the legal profession that the Unruh Act provides a remedy for arbitrary discrimination against women (or men) in public accommodations which are business enterprises. This bill does not bring such discrimination under the Unruh Act because that Act has been interpreted as making *all* arbitrary discrimination illegal, on whatever basis. The listing of possible bases of discrimination has no legal effect, but is merely illustrative." (Original emphasis.) The chairman attached to his letter a copy of a legislative counsel opinion, discussing our decision in *Cox* and confirming the chairman's view of the legislation.

It is a well-established principle of statutory construction that when the Legislature amends a statute without altering portions of the provision that have previously been judicially construed, the Legislature is presumed to have been aware of and to have acquiesced in the previous judicial construction. Accordingly, reenacted portions of the statute are given the same construction they received before the amendment.

In light of the legislative history noted above, this principle of construction particularly applies to the instant case for here we need not simply presume that the Legislature knew of this court's interpretation of section 51 in *Cox* at the time of the 1974 amendment; the legislative documents establish beyond question that the Legislature was well aware of *Cox*'s construction of section 51. . . .

The landlord's blanket exclusion of all families with minor children is not permissible under the Unruh Act even if children "as a class" are "noisier, rowdier, more mischievous and more boisterous" than adults.

The landlord maintains, however, that even if the municipal court erred in concluding that the Unruh Act did not apply because children or families with children were not a "protected class" under the act, the judgment in its favor should nonetheless be affirmed. It asserts that the trial court's findings of fact demonstrate that its policy of excluding all families with children from its apartment complex is "reasonable" and not "arbitrary" and, as such, is not barred by the Unruh Act. . . .

As our decisions . . . teach, although entrepreneurs unquestionably possess broad authority to protect their enterprises from improper and disruptive behavior, under the Unruh Act entrepreneurs must generally exercise this legitimate interest directly by excluding those persons who are in fact disruptive. Entrepreneurs cannot pursue a broad status-based exclusionary policy that operates to deprive innocent individuals of the services of the business enterprise to which section 51 grants "all persons" access.[12] . . .

---

[12] Although the case of *Newby v. Alto Riviera Apartments* (1976) 60 Cal.App.3d 288, 131 Cal.Rptr. 547, involved a landlord's threatened eviction of a tenant on the basis of the tenant's own conduct and thus is clearly distinguishable from the instant matter, some language in the *Newby* opinion does conflict with the above analysis of the Unruh Act and must be disapproved.

Conclusion.

A society that sanctions wholesale discrimination against its children in obtaining housing engages in suspect activity. Even the most primitive society fosters the protection of its young; such a society would hardly discriminate against children in their need for shelter. Yet here the landlord would single out children as a class for exclusion from shelter although such discrimination against racial minorities or religious groups would be unquestionably illegal. Indeed, under the Unruh Act we have condemned *any* arbitrary discrimination against any class.

The argument is launched that children clearly may be excluded from certain kinds of housing, such as housing for the aged, housing for special classes or purposes, and therefore that the instant exclusion is justified. But we do not here adjudge such special purpose housing. We have before us a mammoth apartment complex consisting of 846 separate apartments which proposes to engage in wholesale discrimination against children. To permit such discrimination is to approve of widespread, and potentially universal, exclusion of children from housing. Neither statute nor interpretation of statute, however, sanctions the sacrifice of the well-being of children on the alter of a landlord's profit, or possibly some tenants' convenience.

The judgment is reversed.

■ RICHARDSON, JUSTICE, Dissenting.

I respectfully dissent.

This case illustrates a truism: the answer to a legal question frequently depends upon how the question is phrased. If the issue before us is, as framed by the majority (*ante,* p. 510 of 180 Cal.Rptr., p. 129 of 640 P.2d) should we approve "wholesale discrimination against children," or the "universal exclusion of children from housing" or sanction "the sacrifice of the well-being of children on the altar of a landlord's profit, or possibly some tenants' convenience," the answer is a thundering "no." We'll choose children over a landlord's profit and greed every time. If, however, the question is put a little differently, and we inquire—do our middle aged or older citizens, having worked long and hard, having raised their own children, having paid both their taxes and their dues to society retain a right to spend their remaining years in a relatively quiet,

---

In *Newby,* the court stated: "Action by a landlord which does not restrict the right of a tenant to insure habitable living premises, and does not discriminate on the basis of race, sex, color, religion, ancestry, or national origin, is not actionable under the [Unruh Act] if it proceeds from a motive of rational self-interest, i.e., if it is rationally related to the facilities provided." (*Id.* at p. 302, 131 Cal.Rptr. 547.)

This statement is surely over broad since an entrepreneur may pursue many discriminatory practices "from a motive of rational self-interest," e.g., economic gain, which would unquestionably violate the Unruh Act. For example, an entrepreneur may find it economically advantageous to exclude all homosexuals, or alternatively all nonhomosexuals, from his restaurant or hotel, but such a "rational" economic motive would not, of course, validate the practice. (See *Stoumen v. Reilly, supra,* 37 Cal.2d 713, 234 P.2d 969.)

peaceful and tranquil environment of their own choice? The answer to such a question is, why not? There are two conflicting social policies present in this case, and a just society including its law courts should try to accommodate and serve them both.

## United States v. Starrett City Associates
United States Court of Appeals, Second Circuit, 1988.
840 F.2d 1096.

■ MINER, CIRCUIT JUDGE:

The United States Attorney General, on behalf of the United States ("the government"), commenced this action under Title VIII of the Civil Rights Act of 1968 ("Fair Housing Act" or "the Act") against defendants-appellants Starrett City Associates, Starrett City, Inc. and Delmar Management Company (collectively, "Starrett") in the United States District Court for the Eastern District of New York (Neaher, J.). The government maintained that Starrett's practices of renting apartments in its Brooklyn housing complex solely on the basis of applicants' race or national origin, and of making apartments unavailable to black and hispanic applicants that are then made available to white applicants, violate section 804(a), (b), (c) and (d) of the Act, 42 U.S.C. § 3604(a)–(d) (1982).

The parties made cross-motions for summary judgment based on extensive documentary submissions. The district court granted summary judgment in favor of the government and permanently enjoined appellants from discriminating on the basis of race in the rental of apartments. Starrett appeals from this judgment.

Background

Appellants constructed, own and operate "Starrett City," the largest housing development in the nation, consisting of 46 high-rise buildings containing 5,881 apartments in Brooklyn, New York. The complex's rental office opened in December 1973. Starrett has made capital contributions of $19,091,000 to the project, the New York State Housing Finance Agency has made $362,720,000 in mortgage loans, and the U.S. Department of Housing and Urban Development subsidizes Starrett's monthly mortgage interest payments. The United Housing Foundation abandoned a project to build a development of cooperative apartments at the Starrett City site in 1971. Starrett proposed to construct rental units on the site on the condition that the New York City Board of Estimate approve a transfer to Starrett of the city real estate tax abatement granted to the original project. The transfer created "substantial community opposition" because "the neighborhood surrounding the project and past experience with subsidized housing" created fear that "the conversion to rental apartments would result in Starrett City's becoming an overwhelmingly minority development." *United States v. Starrett City Assocs.*, 660 F.Supp. 668, 670 (E.D.N.Y.1987). The transfer was approved, however, "upon the assurance of Starrett City's developer that it was intended to create a racially integrated community." *Id.*

Starrett has sought to maintain a racial distribution by apartment of 64% white, 22% black and 8% hispanic at Starrett City. Starrett claims that these racial quotas are necessary to prevent the loss of white tenants, which would transform Starrett City into a predominantly minority complex. Starrett points to the difficulty it has had in attracting an integrated applicant pool from the time Starrett City opened, despite extensive advertising and promotional efforts. Because of these purported difficulties, Starrett adopted a tenanting procedure to promote and maintain the desired racial balance. This procedure has resulted in relatively stable percentages of whites and minorities living at Starrett City between 1975 and the present.

The tenanting procedure requires completion of a preliminary information card stating, *inter alia,* the applicant's race or national origin, family composition, income and employment. The rental office at Starrett City receives and reviews these applications. Those that are found preliminarily eligible, based on family composition, income, employment and size of apartment sought, are placed in "the active file," in which separate records by race are maintained for apartment sizes and income levels. Applicants are told in an acknowledgment letter that no apartments are presently available, but that their applications have been placed in the active file and that they will be notified when a unit becomes available for them. When an apartment becomes available, applicants are selected from the active file for final processing, creating a processed applicant pool. As vacancies arise, applicants of a race or national origin similar to that of the departing tenants are selected from the pool and offered apartments.

In December 1979, a group of black applicants brought an action against Starrett in the United States District Court for the Eastern District of New York. The district court certified the plaintiff class in June 1983. *Arthur v. Starrett City Assocs.,* 98 F.R.D. 500 (E.D.N.Y.1983). Plaintiffs alleged that Starrett's tenanting procedures violated federal and state law by discriminating against them on the basis of race. The parties stipulated to a settlement in May 1984, and a consent decree was entered subsequently, *see Arthur v. Starrett City Assocs.,* slip op. at 1 (E.D.N.Y. April 2, 1985). The decree provided that Starrett would, depending on apartment availability, make an additional 35 units available each year for a five-year period to black and minority applicants.

The government commenced the present action against Starrett in June 1984, "to place before the [c]ourt the issue joined but left expressly unresolved" in the *Arthur* consent decree: the "legality of defendants' policy and practice of limiting the number of apartments available to minorities in order to maintain a prescribed degree of racial balance." *United States v. Starrett City Assocs.,* 605 F.Supp. 262, 263

(E.D.N.Y.1985). The complaint alleged that Starrett, through its tenanting policies, discriminated in violation of the Fair Housing Act.

Starrett maintained that the tenanting procedures "were adopted at the behest of the [s]tate solely to achieve and maintain integration and were not motivated by racial animus." 660 F.Supp. at 673. To support their position, appellants submitted the written testimony of three housing experts. They described the "white flight" and "tipping" phenomena, in which white residents migrate out of a community as the community becomes poor and the minority population increases, resulting in the transition to a predominantly minority community. Acknowledging that "'the tipping point for a particular housing development, depending as it does on numerous factors and the uncertainties of human behavior, is difficult to predict with precision,'" one expert stated that the point at which tipping occurs has been estimated at from 1% to 60% minority population, but that the consensus ranged between 10% and 20%. Another expert, who had prepared a report in 1980 on integration at Starrett City for the New York State Division of Housing and Community Renewal, estimated the complex's tipping point at approximately 40% black on a population basis. A third expert, who had been involved in integrated housing ventures since the 1950's, found that a 2:1 white-minority ratio produced successful integration.

The court, however, accepted the government's contention that Starrett's practices of making apartments unavailable for blacks, while reserving them for whites, and conditioning rental to minorities based on a "tipping formula" derived only from race or national origin are clear violations of the Fair Housing Act. The district court found that apartment opportunities for blacks and hispanics were far fewer "than would be expected if race and national origin were not taken into account," while opportunities for whites were substantially greater than what their application rates projected. Minority applicants waited up to ten times longer than the average white applicant before they were offered an apartment.

The court concluded that Starrett's obligation was "simply and solely to comply with the Fair Housing Act" by treating "black and other minority applicants . . . on the same basis as whites in seeking available housing at Starrett City." *Id.* The court noted that Starrett did not dispute any of the operative facts alleged to show violations of the Fair Housing Act. Accordingly, Judge Neaher granted summary judgment for the government, enjoining Starrett from discriminating against applicants on the basis of race and "[r]equiring [them] to adopt written, objective, uniform, nondiscriminatory tenant selection standards and procedures" subject to the court's approval. *Id.* at 679. The court retained jurisdiction over the parties for three years.

On appeal, Starrett presses arguments similar to those it made before the district court. We affirm the district court's judgment.

Discussion

Title VIII of the Civil Rights Act of 1968 ("Fair Housing Act" or "the Act"), 42 U.S.C. §§ 3601–3631 (1982), was enacted pursuant to Congress' thirteenth amendment powers, "to provide, within constitutional limitations, for fair housing throughout the United States." 42 U.S.C. § 3601. Section 3604 of the statute prohibits discrimination because of race, color or national origin in the sale or rental of housing by, *inter alia:* (1) refusing to rent or make available any dwelling, *id.* § 3604(a); (2) offering discriminatory "terms, conditions or privileges" of rental, *id.* § 3604(b); (3) making, printing or publishing "any notice, statement, or advertisement . . . that indicates any preference, limitation, or discrimination based on race, color . . . or national origin," *id.* § 3604(c); and (4) representing to any person "that any dwelling is not available for . . . rental when such dwelling is in fact so available," *id.* § 3604(d).

Housing practices unlawful under Title VIII include not only those motivated by a racially discriminatory purpose, but also those that disproportionately affect minorities.

Starrett's allocation of public housing facilities on the basis of racial quotas, by denying an applicant access to a unit otherwise available solely because of race, produces a "discriminatory effect . . . [that] could hardly be clearer," *Burney v. Housing Auth.*, 551 F.Supp. 746, 770 (W.D.Pa.1982). Appellants do not contend that the plain language of section 3604 does not proscribe their practices. Rather, they claim to be "clothed with governmental authority" and thus obligated, under *Otero v. New York City Housing Auth.*, 484 F.2d 1122 (2d Cir.1973), to effectuate the purpose of the Fair Housing Act by affirmatively promoting integration and preventing "the reghettoization of a model integrated community." We need not decide whether Starrett is a state actor, however. Even if Starrett were a state actor with such a duty, the racial quotas and related practices employed at Starrett City to maintain integration violate the antidiscrimination provisions of the Act.

Both Starrett and the government cite to the legislative history of the Fair Housing Act in support of their positions. This history consists solely of statements from the floor of Congress. *See Hunter,* 459 F.2d at 210 n. 4. These statements reveal "that at the time that Title VIII was enacted, Congress believed that strict adherence to the anti-discrimination provisions of the [A]ct" would eliminate "racially discriminatory housing practices [and] ultimately would result in residential integration." *Burney,* 551 F.Supp. at 769; *see* Rubinowitz & Trosman, *Affirmative Action and the American Dream: Implementing Fair Housing Policies in Federal Homeownership Programs,* 74 Nw.U.L.Rev. 491, 538 n. 178 (1979). Thus, Congress saw the antidiscrimination policy as the means to effect the antisegregation-integration policy. *See* 551 F.Supp. at 769. While quotas promote Title VIII's integration policy, they contravene its antidiscrimination policy, bringing the dual goals of the Act into conflict. The legislative history provides no further guidance for resolving this conflict.

We therefore look to analogous provisions of federal law enacted to prohibit segregation and discrimination as guides in determining to what extent racial criteria may be used to maintain integration. Both the thirteenth amendment, pursuant to which Title VIII was enacted, and the fourteenth amendment empower Congress to act in eradicating racial discrimination, *Constructors Ass'n of W. Pa. v. Kreps,* 573 F.2d 811, 816 n. 12 (3d Cir.1978), and both the fourteenth amendment and Title VIII are informed by the congressional goal of eradicating racial discrimination through the principle of antidiscrimination, *see Kennedy Park Homes Ass'n v. City of Lackawanna,* 318 F.Supp. 669, 694 (W.D.N.Y.), *aff'd,* 436 F.2d 108 (2d Cir.1970), *cert. denied,* 401 U.S. 1010, 91 S.Ct. 1256, 28 L.Ed.2d 546 (1971) (stating that each of these provisions "proscribes discriminatory conduct because of race or color"). Further, the parallel between the antidiscrimination objectives of Title VIII and Title VII of the Civil Rights Act of 1964, 42 U.S.C. §§ 2000e–2000e–17 (1982), has been recognized. *See, e.g., Smith v. Town of Clarkton,* 682 F.2d 1055, 1065 (4th Cir.1982). Thus, the Supreme Court's analysis of what constitutes permissible race-conscious affirmative action under provisions of federal law with goals similar to those of Title VIII provides a framework for examining the affirmative use of racial quotas under the Fair Housing Act.

Although any racial classification is presumptively discriminatory, a race-conscious affirmative action plan does not necessarily violate federal constitutional or statutory provisions, *see, e.g., United States v. Paradise,* 107 S.Ct. 1053, 1064 (1987) (plurality opinion) (fourteenth amendment); *United Steelworkers v. Weber,* 443 U.S. 193, 208, 99 S.Ct. 2721, 2729 (1979) (Title VII). However, a race-conscious plan cannot be "ageless in [its] reach into the past, and timeless in [its] ability to affect the future." *Wygant v. Jackson Bd. of Educ.,* 476 U.S. 267, 106 S.Ct. 1842, 1848 (1986) (plurality opinion). A plan employing racial distinctions must be temporary in nature with a defined goal as its termination point. *See, e.g., Johnson v. Transportation Agency,* 107 S.Ct. 1442, 1456 (1987); *see also Jaimes v. Lucas Metropolitan Housing Auth.,* 833 F.2d 1203, 1208 (6th Cir.1987) (stating that affirmative integration plan for public housing authority "should end upon the [district] court's finding that its goal has been accomplished"). Moreover, we observe that societal discrimination alone seems "insufficient and over expansive" as the basis for adopting so-called "benign" practices with discriminatory effects "that work against innocent people," *Wygant,* 106 S.Ct. at 1848, in the drastic and burdensome way that rigid racial quotas do. Furthermore, the use of quotas generally should be based on some history of racial discrimination or imbalance within the entity seeking to employ them. Finally, measures designed to increase or ensure minority participation, such as "access" quotas have generally been upheld, *see, e.g., Johnson,* 107 S.Ct.

at 1456–57; *Paradise,* 107 S.Ct. at 1070–71; *Weber,* 443 U.S. at 208, 99 S.Ct. at 2729. However, programs designed to maintain integration by limiting minority participation, such as ceiling quotas, are of doubtful validity, *see Jaimes,* 833 F.2d at 1207 (invalidating public housing authority integration plan to the extent it acts as strict racial quota), because they "single out those least well represented in the political process to bear the brunt of a benign program," *Fullilove,* 448 U.S. at 519, 100 S.Ct. at 2796 (Marshall, J., concurring) (quoting *Regents v. Bakke,* 438 U.S. 265, 361, 98 S.Ct. 2733, 2784 (1978) (Brennan, J., concurring in part and dissenting in part)).

Starrett's use of ceiling quotas to maintain integration at Starrett City lacks each of these characteristics. First, Starrett City's practices have only the goal of integration maintenance. The quotas already have been in effect for ten years. Appellants predict that their race-conscious tenanting practices must continue for at least fifteen more years, but fail to explain adequately how that approximation was reached. In any event, these practices are far from temporary. Since the goal of integration maintenance is purportedly threatened by the potential for "white flight" on a continuing basis, no definite termination date for Starrett's quotas is perceivable. Second, appellants do not assert, and there is no evidence to show, the existence of prior racial discrimination or discriminatory imbalance adversely affecting whites within Starrett City or appellants' other complexes. On the contrary, Starrett City was initiated as an integrated complex, and Starrett's avowed purpose for employing race-based tenanting practices is to maintain that initial integration. Finally, Starrett's quotas do not provide minorities with access to Starrett City, but rather act as a ceiling to their access. Thus, the impact of appellants' practices falls squarely on minorities, for whom Title VIII was intended to open up housing opportunities. Starrett claims that its use of quotas serves to keep the numbers of minorities entering Starrett City low enough to avoid setting off a wave of "white flight." Although the "white flight" phenomenon may be a factor "take[n] into account in the integration equation," *Parent Ass'n of Andrew Jackson High School v. Ambach,* 598 F.2d 705, 720 (2d Cir.1979), it cannot serve to justify attempts to maintain integration at Starrett City through inflexible racial quotas that are neither temporary in nature nor used to remedy past racial discrimination or imbalance within the complex.

Appellants' reliance on *Otero* is misplaced. In *Otero* the New York City Housing Authority ("NYCHA") relocated over 1800 families in the Lower East Side of Manhattan to make way for the construction of new apartment buildings. Pursuant to its regulations, NYCHA offered the former site occupants first priority of returning to any housing built within the urban renewal area. However, because the response by the largely minority former site residents seeking to return was nearly seven times greater than expected, NYCHA declined to follow its regulation in order to avoid creating a "pocket ghetto" that would "tip" an integrated community towards a predominantly minority community. It instead rented up half of these apartments to non-former site occupants, 88% of whom were white.

In a suit brought by former site occupants who were denied the promised priority, the district court held as a matter of law that "affirmative action to achieve racially balanced communities was not permitted where it would result in depriving minority groups" of public housing, and thus granted summary judgment in favor of plaintiffs. This court reversed the grant of summary judgment, stating that public housing authorities had a federal constitutional and statutory duty "to fulfill, as much as possible, the goal of open, integrated residential housing patterns and to prevent the increase of segregation, in ghettos," but we recognized that "the effect in some instances might be to prevent some members of a racial minority from residing in publicly assisted housing in a particular location." *Id.* at 1133–34.

*Otero* does not, however, control in this case. The challenge in *Otero* did not involve procedures for the long-term maintenance of specified levels of integration, but rather, the rental of 171 of 360 new apartments to non-former site occupants, predominantly white, although former site residents, largely minority, sought those apartments and were entitled to priority under NYCHA's own regulation. The *Otero* court did not delineate the statutory or constitutional limits on permissible means of integration, but held only that NYCHA's rent-up practice could not be declared invalid as a matter of law under those limits. In fact, the court in *Otero* observed that the use of race-conscious tenanting practices might allow landlords "to engage in social engineering, subject only to general undefined control through judicial supervision" and could "constitute a form of unlawful racial discrimination." *Id.* at 1136.

It is particularly important to note that the NYCHA action challenged in *Otero* only applied to a single event-the initial rent up of the new complexes-and determined tenancy in the first instance alone. NYCHA sought only to prevent the immediate creation of a "pocket ghetto" in the Lower East Side, which had experienced a steady loss of white population, that would tip the precarious racial balance there, resulting in increased white flight and inevitable "non-white ghettoization of the community." *Id.* at 1124. Further, the suspension of NYCHA's regulation did not operate as a strict racial quota, because the former site residents entitled to a rental priority were approximately 40% white. As a one-time measure in response to the special circumstances of the Lower East Side in the early 1970's, the action challenged in *Otero* had an impact on non-whites as a group far less burdensome or discriminatory than Starrett City's continuing practices.

Conclusion

We do not intend to imply that race is always an inappropriate consideration under Title VIII in efforts to promote integrated housing. We hold only that Title VIII does not allow appellants to use rigid racial quotas of indefinite duration to maintain a fixed level of integration at Starrett City by restricting minority access to scarce and desirable rental accommodations otherwise available to them. We therefore affirm the judgment of the district court.

■ JON O. NEWMAN, CIRCUIT JUDGE, dissenting:

In my view, the defendants are entitled to prevail simply on the statutory issue to which the Government has limited its lawsuit. Though the terms of the statute literally encompass the defendants' actions, the statute was never intended to apply to such actions. This statute was intended to bar perpetuation of segregation. To apply it to bar maintenance of integration is precisely contrary to the congressional policy "to provide, within constitutional limitations, for fair housing throughout the United States." 42 U.S.C. § 3601.

We have been wisely cautioned by Learned Hand that "[t]here is no surer way to misread a document than to read it literally." *Guiseppi v. Walling,* 144 F.2d 608, 624 (2d Cir.1944) (concurring opinion), *aff'd sub nom. Gemsco, Inc. v. Walling,* 324 U.S. 244, 65 S.Ct. 605 (1945).

Title VIII bars discriminatory housing practices in order to end segregated housing. Starrett City is not promoting segregated housing. On the contrary, it is maintaining integrated housing. It is surely not within the spirit of the Fair Housing Act to enlist the Act to bar integrated housing.

Acknowledging the significance of the ruling in *Otero,* the Court distinguishes it essentially on the ground that *Otero* involved a policy of limited duration, applicable only to the period in which those displaced from the site were applying for housing in the new project, whereas Starrett City seeks to pursue a long-term policy of maintaining integration. I see nothing in the text or legislative history of Title VIII that supports such a distinction. If, as the Court holds, Title VIII bars Starrett City's race-conscious rental policy, even though adopted to promote and maintain integration, then it would bar such policies whether adopted on a short-term or a long-term basis. Since the Act makes no distinction among the durations of rental policies alleged to violate its terms, *Otero's* upholding of a race-conscious rental policy adopted to promote integration cannot be ignored simply because the policy was of limited duration.[13]

---

[13] The Court, drawing a parallel between Title VIII and Title VII, which bars discrimination in employment, 42 U.S.C. § 2000e (1982), supports its view of Title VIII with Supreme Court decisions approving only limited use of race-conscious remedies under statutory and constitutional standards in the employment context. Though Titles VIII and VII share a common objective of combatting discrimination, their differing contexts preclude the assumption that the law of affirmative action developed for employment is readily applicable to housing. The Title VII cases have not been concerned with a "tipping point" beyond which a work force might become segregated. Yet that is a demonstrated fact of life in the context of housing. *Cf. Parent Ass'n of Andrew Jackson High School v. Ambach,* 598 F.2d 705, 718–20 (2d Cir.1979) (recognizing validity of a "tipping point" concern in the public school context in the course of framing a remedial desegregation decree). The statutory issue arising under Title VIII should be decided on the basis of what practices Congress was proscribing when it enacted this

Whether integration of private housing complexes should be maintained through the use of race-conscious rental policies that deny minorities an equal opportunity to rent is a highly controversial issue of social policy. There is a substantial argument against imposing any artificial burdens on minorities in their quest for housing. On the other hand, there is a substantial argument against forcing an integrated housing complex to become segregated, even if current conditions make integration feasible only by means of imposing some extra delay on minority applicants for housing. Officials of the Department of Justice are entitled to urge the former policy. Respected civil rights advocates like the noted psychologist, Dr. Kenneth Clark, are entitled to urge the latter policy, as he has done in an affidavit filed in this suit. That policy choice should be left to the individual decisions of private property owners unless and until Congress or the New York legislature decides for the Nation or for New York that it prefers to outlaw maintenance of integration. I do not believe Congress made that decision in 1968, and it is a substantial question whether it would make such a decision today. Until Congress acts, we should not lend our authority to the result this lawsuit will surely bring about. In the words of Dr. Clark:

> [I]t would be a tragedy of the highest magnitude if this litigation were to lead to the destruction of one of the model integrated communities in the United States.

Because the Fair Housing Act does not require this tragedy to occur, I respectfully dissent.

## NOTES

1. *Occupation and other reputational criteria.* The result in *Kramarsky* was overruled in 1986 by an amendment to the New York City Human Rights Law.[14] This amendment expressly prohibits discrimination based on occupation.[15] However, most jurisdictions do not apparently have this type of tenant protection in place.[16]

2. *Adults-only policies.* Although the landlord in *Marina* may have had a reasonable economic motive in attempting to exclude children, families with children are now protected by both the Fair Housing Act and state statutes prohibiting discrimination based on familial status.[17] Accordingly, landlords can no longer have formal written policies refusing acceptance of tenants with minor children, verbally discourage these families from

---

provision. Whether the constitutional standards for affirmative action differ between the employment and housing contexts need not be considered since the Government has explicitly declined in this litigation to advance any claim of unconstitutional action.

[14] New York, N.Y., Local Law No. 59 (Nov. 25, 1986), codified at New York, N.Y., Admin. Code § 8–102(18) and 8–107(5)(n).

[15] N.Y. City Admin. Code § 8–107(5)(n) (2015).

[16] See, e.g., Conn. Gen. Stat. § 46a–64c(a) (2014); Va. Code Ann. § 36–96.3(A) (2015). But see Del. Code Ann. tit. 25, § 5116(a) (2015) (specifying "occupation").

[17] 42 U.S.C. § 3604(a) (2015); see also Cal. Gov't Code § 12955(a)(2015) (amended in 1992 to include familial status); 5 M.R.S. § 4581 (2015). The Virginia statute is rare in specifying "elderliness" as a protected class. See Va. Code Ann. § 36–96.3(A)(1) (2015).

applying, or otherwise "steer" these families to other properties.[18] Nor may landlords apply stereotypical views on financial stability and reliability to justify discriminating against, for example, an unmarried mother with children.[19] Age restrictive policies are still permissible, however, if the apartment building or complex qualifies as "housing for older persons."[20]

In Fair Housing Congress v. Weber, 993 F.Supp. 1286 (C.D.Cal.1997), the landlord had a rule as follows: "Children will not be allowed to play or run around inside the building area at any time because of disturbance to other tenants or damage to building property." The court held that this rule violated the Fair Housing Act, 42 U.S.C. 3604, which prohibits discrimination on the basis of familial status, and therefore prohibits discrimination against families with children. *Query*, if the word "persons" were substituted for the word "children," would the rule be valid?

3. *Apartheid.* Professor Kushner, a highly respected scholar in the fair housing field, has called the *Starrett* case "the most significant endorsement of apartheid in America since *Plessy v. Ferguson,* which upheld the institution of racial segregation."[21] Do you agree?

The issue of impermissible racial discrimination is also presented in recent attempts by municipalities to enforce ordinances requiring landlords to screen based on citizenship or eligible immigration status.[22] These ordinances "sanction landlords who rent to unauthorized immigrants and may also require that all prospective tenants have their immigration status verified prior to entering into a residential lease."[23] Might such ordinances encourage masked racial discrimination by landlords? Are there any legitimate business justifications for landlords to discriminate based on citizenship status, or is such discrimination arbitrary? Moreover, in complying with these ordinances, would landlords be violating the tenants' constitutional rights? One court found that there was little evidence to support the city's claim that illegal aliens were in fact the cause of urban blight, thereby suggesting that the ordinance's justification itself was based

---

[18] Fair Hous. Ctr. of Southwest Mich. v. Hunt, 2012 U.S. Dist. LEXIS 190419 (W.D. Mich. Mar. 29, 2012); S. Cal. Hous. Rights Ctr. v. Krug, 564 F. Supp. 2d 1138 (C.D. Cal. 2007).

[19] White v. U.S. Dep't of Hous. & Dev., 475 F.3d 898 (7th Cir. 2007).

[20] 42 U.S.C. § 3607(b); 5 M.R.S. § 4581 (2015); Del. Code Ann. tit. 25, § 5116(d) (2015); Tex. Prop. Code Ann. § 301.043 (2015).

[21] James Kushner, *The Fair Housing Amendments Act of 1988: The Second Generation of Fair Housing,* 42 Vand.L.Rev. 1049, 1118 (1989).

[22] See, e.g., Villas at Parkside Partners v. City of Farmers Branch, 577 F. Supp. 2d 858 (N.D. Tex. 2008); Garrett v. City of Escondido, 465 F. Supp. 2d 1043 (S.D. Cal. 2006). Federal statutes and most state statutes do not expressly prohibit discrimination based on citizenship status, but instead only on the basis of race, color, or national origin. See, e.g., Fair Housing Act, 42 U.S.C. § 3604; Cal. Gov't Code § 12955; Va. Code Ann. § 36–96.3. The New Jersey statute is unusual in that it prohibits discrimination based on both national origin and nationality. See N.J. Stat. Ann. § 10:5–12(g)(1) (2015). In addition, New York City is unique in specifying a ban on discrimination based on "alienage" or "citizenship status." N.Y. City Admin. Code § 8–107(5)(a)(1). See also Recalde v. Bae Cleaners, Inc., 20 Misc. 3d 827 (N.Y. Sup. Ct. 2008) (tenant was granted a preliminary injunction to continue to occupy rent controlled apartment where landlord based termination of lease on questionable immigration status). Recently, California has also prohibited landlords from inquiring as to their prospective tenants' immigration and citizenship status. Calif. Civil Code § 1940.3.

[23] Oliveri, Between a Rock and a Hard Place: Landlords, Latinos, Anti-Illegal Immigrant Ordinances, and Housing Discrimination, 62 Vand. L. Rev. 55, 57 (2009).

on impermissible stereotypes and prejudices.[24] Citizenship or immigration status-based discrimination continues to attract the attention of commentators.[25]

4. *Fair Housing Amendments Act of 1988*. The 1988 Amendments (P.L. 100–430) significantly increased the scope and effectiveness of tenant protections and remedies.[26] It protects the disabled and families with children from discrimination. It allows the imposition of large punitive damages and in general provides an improved enforcement framework.[27] Attorney's fees are permitted under the Fair Housing Act.

The Fair Housing Act broadly defines a handicap as a "physical or mental impairment which substantially limits one or more of such person's major life activities."[28] However, it explicitly excludes current illicit drug users.[29]

Some have argued that despite the 1988 amendments, discrimination continues to be a major problem.[30] What more can be done to eliminate discrimination in housing?[31]

---

[24] *Garrett*, 465 F. Supp. 2d at 1053–54.

[25] See, e.g., Villazor, Rediscovering Oyama v. California: At the Intersection of Property, Race, and Citizenship, 87 Wash. U. L. Rev. 979 (2012); Bartolomeo, Immigration and the Constitutionality of Local Self Help: Escondido's Undocumented Immigrant Rental Ban, 17 S. Cal. Rev. L. & Soc. Just. 855 (2008); Bono, Don't You Be My Neighbor: Restrictive Housing Ordinances as the New Jim Crow, 3 Mod. Am. 29 (2007); Campbell, Local Illegal Immigration Relief Act Ordinances: A Legal, Policy, and Litigation Analysis, 84 Denv. U.L. Rev. 1041 (2007); Motomura, Immigration Outside the Law, 108 Colum. L. Rev. 2037 (2008); O'Byrne, Municipal Overreaching: Federal Preemption as It Applies to Town Ordinances Outlawing the Rental of Housing to Undocumented Aliens, 14 Tex. Hisp. J.L. & Pol'y 69 (2008).

[26] See Johnson, The Last Plank: Rethinking Public and Private Power to Advance Fair Housing, 13 U. Pa. J. Const. L. 1191 (2011); Kushner, supra, n. 22; Leland Ware, *New Weapons for an Old Battle: The Enforcement Provisions of the 1988 Amendments to the Fair Housing Act*, 7 Admin. L.J. Am. U. 59 (1993); Keith Aoki, *Fair Housing Amendments Act of 1988*, 24 Harv. C.R.-C.L. L. Rev. 249 (1989).

[27] See Timothy Moran, *Punitive Damages in Fair Housing Litigation: Ending Unwise Restrictions on a Necessary Remedy*, 36 Harv. C.R.-C.L. L. Rev. 279 (2001) (recommending an overhaul of the liability standards for punitive damages in fair housing cases).

[28] 42 U.S.C. sec. 3602(h).

[29] Id. Although the phrase "current illicit drug user" is not defined in the statute, courts have applied it in a manner consistent with the Americans with Disabilities Act and the Rehabilitation Act so as to exclude those who have been in recovery for only a short time. See, e.g., A.B. v. Hous. Auth. of S. Bend, 498 Fed. Appx. 620, 621 (7th Cir. Ind. 2012); Fowler v. Borough of Westville, 97 F. Supp.2d 602 (D.N.J. 2000). In *Fowler*, however, the court determined that a recovering drug abuser could be considered handicapped even though the abuser took cocaine four months after the complaint was filed; handicapped status was measured at the time the allegedly discriminatory housing acts occurred.

[30] John Nelson, *The Perpetuation of Segregation: The Senior Housing Exemption in the 1988 Amendments to the Fair Housing Act*, 26 T. Jefferson L. Rev. 103 (2003) (arguing that the exception allowing senior housing to exclude children operates to deny minorities equal housing opportunities); Wendell Pritchett, *Where Shall We Live? Class and the Limitations of Fair Housing Law*, 35 Urb. Law. 399 (2003) (calling for a more nuanced understanding of the relationship between housing discrimination and racial segregation); Erin Ziaja, *Do Independent and Assisted Living Communities Violate the Fair Housing Amendments Act and the Americans with Disabilities Act?*, 9 Elder L.J. 313 (2001) (recommending class action suits to enforce the elderly's civil rights).

[31] See, e.g., Schwemm, Overcoming Structural Barriers to Integrated Housing: A Back-to-the-Future Reflection on the Fair Housing Act's "Affirmatively Further" Mandate, 100 Ky. L.J. 125 (2011–2012) (discussing the Fair Housing Act's goal of residential integration and recently implemented pro-integration initiatives); Victor Goode and Conrad Johnson, *Emotional*

5. *Discriminatory intent versus discriminatory impact.* The court in *Starrett* followed most courts in holding that "Housing practices unlawful under Title VIII [The Fair Housing Act] include not only those motivated by a racially discriminatory purpose, but also those that disproportionately affect minorities." 840 F.2d at 1100. In Tex. Dep't of Hous. & Cmty. Affairs v. Inclusive Cmtys. Project, Inc.,[32] the Supreme Court reaffirmed that the FHA not only allows claims arising from intentional discrimination, but also disparate impact claims involving practices that have a discriminatory effect. Under this view, tenants can prove a violation of the act without offering evidence concerning the intent of the landlord. To what extent does this view make it easy for Harris, in the Principal Problem, to win? If a landlord raised rents, and this had a disparate impact on women, minorities and the disabled, would this constitute a violation of the act?[33]

It has been held that under certain circumstances a landlord's inquiries concerning the race of a prospective tenant could constitute a violation of the Fair Housing Act, even if no direct proof of discriminatory intent existed.[34]

6. *Discrimination based on marital status.* The FHA prohibits discrimination based on "familial status" which relates to the presence of children. Several states prohibit discrimination based on marital status. Is a landlord prohibited from discriminating against unmarried couples if this lifestyle is contrary to the landlord's religious convictions? Several courts have held that statutes prohibiting discrimination against unmarried couples do not violate a landlord's right to free exercise of religion.[35]

With respect to same-sex couples, even before the Supreme Court ruling in Obergefell v. Hodges legalizing gay marriage,[36] some statutes prohibited landlords from discriminating not only based upon marital status, but also

---

*Harm in Housing Discrimination Cases: A New Look at a Lingering Problem*, 30 Fordham Urb. L.J. 1143 (2003) (examining the potential for awarding damages based on emotional harm); David Thomas, *Fixing Up Fair Housing Laws: Are We Ready For Reform?*, 53 S.C. L. Rev. 7 (2001) (advocating resort to servitude reform and corrective state legislation authorizing an open property easement pursuant to which someone holding an interest in real property is prohibited from engaging in racial discrimination in the sale or rental of that interest); Terry Gentle, Jr., *Rethinking Conciliation Under the Fair Housing Act*, 67 Tenn. L. Rev. 425 (2000) (advocating more formal forms of dispute resolution).

[32] 135 S. Ct. 2507 (U.S. 2015).

[33] See generally, Douglas Kmiec, *Discriminatory Intent vs. Discriminatory Effect or Impact*, 2 Zoning & Plan. Deskbook § 7:28 (2d ed.) (2004); John Theuman, Annotation, *Evidence of Discriminatory Effect Alone as Sufficient to Prove, or to Establish Prima Facie Case of, Violation of Fair Housing Act*, 100 A.L.R. Fed. 97 (1990).

[34] Jancik v. Department of Housing and Urban Development, 44 F.3d 553 (7th Cir.1995).

[35] See, e.g., Lax v. 29 Woodmere Blvd. Owners, Inc., 812 F. Supp. 2d 228 (E.D.N.Y. 2011); Thomas v. Anchorage Equal Rights Commission, 102 P.3d 937 (Alaska 2004); Smith v. Fair Employment & Hous. Comm'n, 12 Cal. 4th 1143, 913 P.2d 909 (1996); Swanner v. Anchorage Equal Rights Comm'n, 874 P.2d 274 (Alaska 1994). But see Heard v. Stratford I Ltd. P'ship, 811 N.Y.S.2d 841 (App. Div. 2006) (affirming prior New York case law that prohibits landlords from discriminating against individuals because they are unmarried, but allows discrimination against individuals who wish to live with a non-spouse). See also Miller, Annotation, Landlord's Refusal to Rent to Unmarried Couple as Protected by Landlord's Religious Beliefs, 10 A.L.R.6th 513 (2008) (providing background and analysis of the various approaches that courts have taken on this issue).

[36] 135 S. Ct. 1039 (2015).

based on civil union status, domestic partnership status, gender identity or expression.[37]

7. *Discrimination based on source of income.* Landlords may have an economic motive to differentiate between sources of income. For example, landlords may believe that investment income or child support is less reliable than steady employment income. Some state statutes or local ordinances now expressly prohibit discrimination based on source of income.[38] Thus, the landlord in the Principal Problem may not be allowed to enforce that part of her "new requirements policy."

Federal housing assistance regulations suggest that participation in housing assistance programs is voluntary, and therefore, landlords are not required to accept housing subsidies such as "Section 8 vouchers" created through the 1998 Quality Housing and Work Responsibility Act and its predecessors.[39] However, if state or local regulations prohibit discrimination based on source of income, and define "source of income" as including Section 8 vouchers,[40] would participation in the program in effect be mandatory for landlords? Courts have generally held that landlords cannot use source of income as a factor to screen out housing subsidy recipients.[41] That said, landlords may rely on legitimate, non-discriminatory grounds such as an applicant's rental or credit history to refuse to rent to voucher holders.[42] Moreover, if a landlord, for non-discriminatory reasons, charges a rent that exceeds the amount a voucher holder can pay, the landlord is not required to lower the stipulated rent payment.[43]

---

[37] See, e.g., N.J. Stat. Ann. § 10:5–12(g)(1).

[38] See, e.g., Cal. Gov't Code § 12955(a); Conn. Gen. Stat. § 46a–64c(a)(2); N.J. Stat. Ann. § 10:5–12(g)(1).

[39] See Knapp v. Eagle Prop. Mgmt. Corp., 54 F.3d 1272, 1280 (7th Cir. 1995); Section 8 Housing Assistance Payment Programs, 49 Fed Reg. 12215, 12221 (Mar. 29, 1984). For a succinct history of federal housing assistance programs, see Montgomery County v. Glenmont Hills Assocs., 402 Md. 250, 278–79, 936 A.2d 325, 342 (2007).

[40] Montgomery County, Maryland has enacted regulations that appear to require landlord participation in housing assistance programs. See Montgomery County Code, ch. 27, § 27–6,–12 (2009). Section 27–6 of the Montgomery County Code defines source of income as inclusive of "any government or private assistance, grant, or loan program." Section 27–12 prohibits housing discrimination on the basis of source of income.

[41] See, e.g., *Montgomery County*, 936 A.2d at 325; Bourbeau v. The Jonathan Woodner Co., 549 F. Supp. 2d 78 (D.D.C. 2008).

[42] *Bourbeau*, 549 F. Supp. 2d at 87; Pasquince v. Brighton Arms Apartments, 378 N.J. Super. 588, 876 A.2d 834 (Super. Ct. App. Div. 2005).

[43] *Bourbeau*, 549 F. Supp. 2d at 87.

## ASSIGNMENT 7

# ASSIGNMENTS AND SUBLEASES

### a. DISTINCTIONS BETWEEN ASSIGNMENTS AND SUBLEASES

#### 1. INTRODUCTION

It is often necessary to distinguish between assignments and subleases. An assignment is a transfer of all of the tenant's rights under the lease to the transferee. Under a sublease, the original tenant transfers less than all of her rights to the transferee.

EXAMPLE 1: Tenant, "T", enters into a ten year lease with Landlord "L", providing for rental payments of $10,000 per month. There is no clause in the lease prohibiting assignments or subleases. After one year, T transfers all of his interest under the lease in the balance of the term to E for the sum of $40,000. E is to pay the rent directly to L. There has been an assignment and not a sublease.

EXAMPLE 2: Same as Example 1, except that T transfers only three years of the remaining nine year term to E, and E pays his rent to T, not L. A sublease has been created because T transferred less than all of his rights to E.

In some cases it is more difficult to classify a transfer as an assignment or a sublease.

EXAMPLE 3: Same as Example 1, except that T transfers one-half of the demised premises for the balance of the term to E. Is this an assignment of one-half the premises or a sublease? Most courts treat this as a partial assignment.[1]

EXAMPLE 4: Same as Example 1, except that T transfers all but one day of the balance of the term to E. This is a sublease, not an assignment.[2]

EXAMPLE 5: Same as Example 1, except that payment of the rent is to be made to T, and T reserves the right to reenter should the rent not be paid. Authorities are split as to whether this is an assignment or a sublease.[3]

---

[1] 2 Restatement (Second) of Property (Landlord & Tenant) § 15.1, Reporter's Note 8 (1977).

[2] Joseph Brothers Co. v. F.W. Woolworth Co., 844 F.2d 369 (6th Cir.1988).

[3] 2 Restatement (Second) of Property (Landlord & Tenant) § 15.1, Reporter's Note 8 (1977). The Restatement takes the position that this is a sublease, but probably the majority of jurisdictions follow the traditional rule and treat this as an assignment. But see A & A Weston, Inc. v. 39 Main, 11 Mass.L.Rptr. 696 (2000) (endorsing the Restatement's view that any reversionary interest is a sublease).

EXAMPLE 6: Same as Example 1, except that payment of the rent is to be made to T, and this rent is higher than the rent that T must pay to L under the head lease. Most courts treat this as an assignment although there is some contrary authority.[4]

Although a court may believe it necessary to resolve the abstract issue of whether a particular arrangement is an assignment or a sublease, no court is ever directly faced with this question. Instead, a court is faced with a more concrete problem: Should the injured party collect damages or receive some other form of relief from the other party? Do not lose sight of the real question faced by the court in these cases and the practical effect on the parties.

## 2. Principal Problem

Terry leases an apartment from Larry for $800 per month under a two year lease. Six months later, Terry and Alyssa execute an agreement that provides in pertinent part as follows:

Sublease, December 10, 20__.

Terry hereby subleases apartment 12B in 300 Oak Ave., Dixon, Anystate, to Alyssa for the balance of the term of Terry's lease with Larry. In consideration therefore, Alyssa agrees to pay Terry the sum of $900 per month rent.

Six months pass, during which Alyssa regularly mails $900 per month to Terry, who has moved to a distant city. One day Larry informs Alyssa that Terry has not paid three month's back rent and that since Alyssa is Terry's assignee, she must pay the overdue $2,400. Alyssa attempts to contact Terry and learns that Terry's telephone has been disconnected and that he has left for parts unknown. Alyssa does not believe that she should have to pay twice. She has already paid her rent to Terry and she does not understand why she should have to pay rent for the same period to Larry. Alyssa is so disgusted with Larry's demand for rent that she wants to move out immediately, regardless of whether she must pay the $2,400. Larry, however, claims that as an assignee of the lease, Alyssa is obligated to stay for the balance of the term, or at least pay damages if she terminates the lease before the end of the term. Alyssa comes to you for advice. Before you render advice, consider the following material.

---

[4] 2 Powell on Real Property § 17.04[2] (2014).

## 3. MATERIALS FOR SOLUTION OF PRINCIPAL PROBLEM

## A.D. Juilliard & Co. v. American Woolen Co.
Supreme Court of Rhode Island.
69 R.I. 215, 32 A.2d 800 (1943).

■ CAPOTOSTO, JUSTICE.

This is an action in assumpsit to recover installments of rent and taxes in the total amount of $2,935.83, allegedly due for the period between September, 1940, and March, 1941, under a lease of certain premises in the city of Providence. A justice of the superior court, sitting without a jury, rendered a decision for the defendant. The case is before us on plaintiff's exception to this decision and also on certain other exceptions to rulings in the case.

On May 12, 1893, the Atlantic Mills leased certain premises in the city of Providence to the Riverside Worsted Mills for the term ending September 1, 1955. In this lease the specific covenant which the plaintiff asserts the defendant has assumed is to pay rent and certain other charges as therein set forth. This lease contains no restrictions whatever against assignment, nor does it provide that, upon an assignment of the lease, the assignee should assume and be bound for the entire unexpired term by the covenant just mentioned. The plaintiff succeeded to the rights of the lessor in this lease on December 4, 1936.

On April 15, 1899, the lessee, Riverside Worsted Mills, assigned the lease to the American Woolen Company, a New Jersey corporation, which in turn assigned it, on February 15, 1916, to the defendant American Woolen Company, a Massachusetts corporation. Four assignments of the lessee's interests occurred between 1916 and the bringing of this suit on April 14, 1941. The names of the successive assignees and the dates of such assignments are as follows: National & Providence Worsted Mills, a subsidiary of the defendant, December 22, 1931; American Woolen Company, the present defendant, December 26, 1934; Textile Realty Company, also a subsidiary of the defendant, June 1, 1939; and Reo Realty Company, November 21, 1939. The defendant admits that it was virtually the lessee until the lease was assigned to the Reo Realty Company, but denies that in this assignment it retained any beneficial interest in or control of the lease or premises covered thereby. In not one of these assignments did the assignee agree to assume the obligation to pay rent for the unexpired term of the lease.

The plaintiff's first contention raises a question of law, which appears not to have been heretofore considered by this court, so far as we have been able to ascertain. Broadly stated, this contention is that the assignee of a lease of real property, as here, is liable for the payment of the stipulated rent for the entire unexpired term, notwithstanding that the assignee did not agree to assume such obligation and assigned the lease before the expiration of the term.

This contention is contrary to the overwhelming weight of authority both in England and this country. Excepting certain decisions by the Texas civil court of appeals, which we will presently consider, the courts in this country have consistently held that, in the absence of the assumption by the assignee of the obligations of the lease, the liability of such assignee to the lessor rests in privity of estate which is terminated by a new assignment of the lease made by the assignee. This firmly established principle of law is subject to an exception which we will consider later in this opinion in connection with plaintiff's third main contention.

The plaintiff urges that as this court is "unfettered by prior decisions" on the subject, it should reject the "archaic doctrine" which has been "blindly followed" by most of the American courts since 1797, and adopt the "progressive rule" of the Texas court. In support of this progressive rule, so-called, the plaintiff cites three decisions by the Texas court of civil appeals of three different districts: Waggoner v. Edwards, Tex.Civ.App., 83 S.W.2d 386; Marathon Oil Co. v. Rone, Tex.Civ.App., 83 S.W.2d 1028; Stark v. American National Bank of Beaumont, Tex.Civ.App., 100 S.W.2d 208.

In the Waggoner case, upon which the plaintiff most strongly relies, it was held that notwithstanding "the absence of an express agreement on the part of an assignee of the unexpired term of a lease of real property to assume and pay the rentals contracted to be paid by the original lessee . . . the assignee under such circumstances becomes primarily liable for the debt, and the original lessee only secondarily liable. The lessee having enjoyed and exercised his right to dispose of such leasehold estate, the assignee is held to take the estate subject to all the terms and conditions expressed in the original lease contract, and is bound to the original lessor for the performance of the obligations which were imposed upon his assignor, or, in other words, he simply stands in the shoes of the original lessee." 68 S.W.2d 655, 662. The Marathon Oil Co. and Stark cases are to the same effect.

But at page 212 of 100 S.W.2d of its opinion on motion for rehearing in the Stark case, which is the latest of the three Texas cases cited to us by the plaintiff, the court frankly says that it decided that case as it did "solely because the holding follows the present rule of decision in this state", although it was "firmly convinced that the rule is not sound and that it is contrary to the holdings of the vast majority of other jurisdictions." The court there urges the supreme court of that state to promulgate a rule of decision "in keeping with the great weight of authority and which it is believed is more consistent with the principles of justice." It then gives its reasons for suggesting such a change. In view of the cogency of these reasons against the Texas rule, we think that a somewhat extensive quotation from that opinion is justified here.

At page 213 of 100 S.W.2d of the opinion under consideration the court says that the effect of the Texas rule is to "place an assignee in complete privity of contract with the original lessor as a matter of law by reason of the assignment alone, without any stipulation or agreement on his part to become so bound. . . . When a property owner leases his property to another and confers upon such lessee the rights to assign to whomsoever he pleases, he impliedly relies upon his lessee for the performance of the covenants of the lease. In addition to that he has the personal obligation of each assignee so long as he keeps the estate and also the right at all times to repossess his property for a breach of covenant. And while the lessee, when he assigns, may impose upon his assignee the obligations of the original lease contract, that matter should be left to the contract of the parties. It should not be read into an assignment as a mere legal implication."

Apparently the Texas rule has never been squarely considered by the supreme court of that state, for no decision of that court to that effect has been cited to us by either party in this case, nor have we been able to find one in our own investigation.

The plaintiff here further argues that the majority rule under consideration, which makes an assignee who does not expressly assume to pay the rent stipulated in the original lease liable only for such rent as accrues while privity of estate exists, may not operate unfairly in cases of short term leases, but that in long term leases, as in the instant case, it results in "an artificially induced lack of mutuality", which "should not commend itself to a court which is not bound by the precedent of its own decisions." In the Stark case, the court, at page 213 of 100 S.W.2d of that opinion, takes a contrary view and says that the Texas rule, which makes an assignee liable by mere legal implication in the circumstances above stated "is unnecessarily harsh and unjust and may, in its operation, tend to hamper the assignment of long term leases." But, whatever may be the practical result under either rule, the plain answer to the plaintiff's argument on this point is that the lessor has it within his power to protect himself against any detriment to him by incorporating adequate provisions in the lease concerning assignments thereof. If he chooses to execute a lease without adequately protecting his rights as lessor thereunder, he cannot thereafter complain if, by force of law, he is deprived of a benefit that he might otherwise have secured for himself.

After careful examination and consideration of the majority rule and of the Texas rule, our conclusion is that the former of these rules is not the blind following of an old English doctrine, as the plaintiff would like to have us believe, but that it is the embodiment of the considered judgment of American courts whose opinions should not be cast aside by mere summary characterization. In our opinion, the majority rule, which, in the absence of any restrictions in the lease governing its assignment, has the effect of leaving the matter of the assumption by an assignee of future rentals for the unexpired term of the lease to the contract between him and his assignor, is the sounder rule. We therefore cannot agree with the plaintiff's first contention. . . .

Plaintiff's [next] contention is that the assignment of the lease from the Textile Realty Company, which was admittedly a subsidiary of the defendant, to the Reo Realty Company was "colorable" and therefore did not terminate defendant's liability, even though it had not assumed the obligations of the lease.

The law on this point is also well settled. As early as 1780, in Eaton v. Jaques, Douglas 455, at page 460, Lord Mansfield said: "In leases, the lessee being a party to the original contract, continues always liable, notwithstanding any assignment; the assignee is only liable in respect of his possession of the thing. He bears the burden while he enjoys the benefit, and no longer...." Unless fraudulent or colorable, a new assignment of the lease terminates the assignee's liability to the lessor for rent subsequently accruing. See authorities hereinbefore cited by us in discussing plaintiff's first main contention. If such assignee, by a new assignment, fairly relinquishes not only possession of the leased premises but also all benefits therefrom, it is immaterial that the new assignee may be financially irresponsible, or that he gave no consideration, or even that he received a bonus as an inducement to accept the assignment of the lease.

The case is different, however, where such assignee makes an assignment which, though proper in form, leaves him as a matter of fact in possession of the leased premises or in receipt of benefits therefrom. In such case the assignment is colorable and will not terminate his liability to the lessor for rent, while he, in reality, continues in possession of the premises covered by the lease or enjoys any benefits from the use of such property.

The plaintiff here contends that the assignment by the Textile Realty Company to the Reo Realty Company was colorable. The defendant admits that it created the Textile Realty Company to serve as a medium for the sale of certain properties that it considered either useless or unprofitable, but it vigorously denies that the assignment to the Reo Realty Company was not in good faith.

Among the properties that the defendant desired to sell and which it transferred to the Textile Realty Company for that purpose were the lease under consideration and some vacant land with a railroad siding, which vacant land it had been unable to sell in the open market. In July, 1939, one Aaron J. Oster, who was in the scrap metal business, became interested in those properties and bought them the following November for $630.30, taking title thereto in the name of the Reo Realty Company, a corporation controlled by him and in which the defendant, according to the record before us, had no interest whatever. Oster, who testified that he purchased the property for "the sole reason of using it and making money with it", then tried to secure from the plaintiff a reduction of the rent payable under the lease but was unsuccessful. There is evidence that the Reo Realty Company paid one installment of rent and expended some money in repairs. We have thus summarized our understanding of the evidence because it is impossible to refer specifically in this opinion to the large amount of correspondence, memoranda and agreements which bear upon this aspect of the case.

The plaintiff claims that the transaction between the defendant, through the Textile Realty Company, and Oster, through the Reo Realty Company, was nothing more than a scheme by the former's officials "to procure a rent reduction and in effect a new lease." It draws this conclusion mainly from the fact that the Reo Realty Company was a new corporation without known assets and that it paid so small a sum for an assignment of the lease and a deed of the vacant land.

The trial justice found that the transaction under consideration was in good faith; that on or about November 29, 1939, the Reo Realty Company "entered into exclusive control and possession of the leased premises", and that since that date "neither the American Woolen Company, the defendant, nor the Textile Realty Company has exercised any control over the leased premises; nor have they or either of them, had possession of such premises." We have found no competent evidence in contradiction of these findings of the trial justice. Unless resort is had to speculation or unwarranted suspicion, there is nothing to show, as the plaintiff states in its brief, that the transaction "envisaged", in the event that Oster failed to obtain a reduction of the rent, "the collapse of the dummy, Reo Realty Company, and the leaving of the property in the same status as if that company had never been formed and no assignment had been attempted." A fair consideration of the record before us shows that each of the parties in interest was assisted by able counsel and dealt with each other at arm's length in effecting a business transaction, which each party considered beneficial to itself.

Granting, as the plaintiff argues, that the amount paid by Oster for the leasehold and the vacant land was relatively small, yet according to the authorities hereinbefore cited on the point under consideration, this fact was not enough to render the assignment from the Textile Realty Company to the Reo Realty Company colorable, so as to continue the liability, to the plaintiff, of the defendant as an assignee of the lease in constructive possession of the premises. In the absence of collusion, and we find none in the circumstances of this case, the defendant, which was not bound contractually to the contrary, could sell or dispose of its property on such terms as it chose in order to relieve itself of the burden resulting from the possession of property that had become useless or unprofitable, so long as it relinquished all benefits therefrom. For the reasons stated, the trial justice was not in error in finding that the assignment of the lease to the Reo Realty Company terminated defendant's liability for rent under the lease.

The plaintiff's exceptions are all overruled, and the case is remitted to the superior court for the entry of judgment on the decision.

## Abernathy v. Adous
Court of Appeals of Arkansas, 2004.
85 Ark.App. 242.

■ BAKER, J.

This appeal is brought from an order declaring appellee Abdulazize Adous the assignee of a commercial-lease contract and further declaring that equity should intervene to avoid forfeiture of the lease contract. We reverse and remand.

The property that is the subject of the lease is a service station/convenience store in West Memphis. When the lease was executed in 1992, appellants, the owners of the property, agreed to build the service station for the original lessee, appellee Griffith Petroleum, Inc. (GPI). Appellants financed the construction through Fidelity National Bank. The lease was for a ten-year term, to begin upon completion of construction, with six consecutive five-year options to renew. The monthly lease payment for the first ten years was to be the amount that appellants owed to Fidelity National Bank ($3,412.60), plus the additional sum of $583.33 per month, for a total of $3,995.93. GPI agreed to write two checks each month, one directly to Fidelity National for $3,412.60 and the other to appellants for $583.33. Among the provisions of the lease were that the lessee would be in default upon failure to pay rent in a timely manner or upon becoming insolvent. The lease contained no prohibition against subleasing or assignment.

GPI began operating the service station as a lessee on or about August 1992. On November 15, 1996, it executed a document titled "Sublease Agreement" with Maref Quran whereby Quran would operate the facility for an initial term of five years and eight months with six consecutive five-year options. Quran's lease payment for the initial term was to be "the exact amount that William G. Abernathy and Anne Abernathy (the record title holders to the real property) are responsible for paying their lender who has the long-term financing on the leased premises, plus the additional sum of Five Hundred Eighty Three and 33/100 Dollars ($583.33) per month." Quran was to make the rental payments to GPI, who would then remit the payments to Fidelity and appellants. On July 14, 1997, appellee Abdulazize Adous was added as a subtenant of the site under a document styled "Addendum to Sublease Agreement." Eventually, he became the sole subtenant.

After executing his sublease, Adous made monthly lease payments to GPI, who in turn made payments to Fidelity National and appellants. There is no evidence that appellants knew of the sublease. However, Adous's operation of the business apparently continued without controversy until January 2001, when GPI failed to pay rent to appellants. Appellants filed an unlawful-detainer action against GPI as lessee and Adous as sublessee, seeking to recover possession of the property.[5] On March 15, 2001, GPI and Adous (apparently doing business as Coastal C-Mart) paid $11,985.99 into the court registry, representing three months' rent for January through March 2001. Shortly thereafter, appellants nonsuited their action, and the court clerk distributed the $11,985.99, plus interest, to them.

In April 2001, GPI again failed to pay the rent it owed. Adous tendered the rent directly to appellants, but it was refused. On May 1, 2001, Adous sued appellants and GPI for specific performance, seeking an order directing appellants to accept all rental payments made by him or, alternatively, directing GPI to accept the payments and then remit them to appellants and/or Fidelity National. Adous pled $3,995.33 into the court registry, representing one month's rent, a practice he would continue each month while awaiting trial.

On June 8, 2001, appellants notified GPI that they were terminating the 1992 lease for nonpayment of rent. Later, when they discovered that GPI had become insolvent, they sent a supplemental notice to GPI and Adous, terminating the lease on that ground. Despite the fact that appellants demanded surrender of the premises in their notices of termination, Adous remained on the property.

A trial was held in circuit court on June 26, 2002, with the trial judge sitting as finder of fact. Appellants argued that Adous's rights as a subtenant were derived from GPI's rights as the original lessee, and thus, when GPI breached the 1992 lease by failing to pay rent and by becoming insolvent, Adous's right of occupancy, being derivative, was terminated. Adous agreed that a sublessee's rights are generally derivative of the original lessee's, but he argued that, for various equitable reasons, appellants should not be permitted to declare a forfeiture of the sublease in this case.

On August 5, 2002, the trial judge issued a letter ruling in which he declared Adous a "bona fide assignee" of the 1992 lease and "entitled to enjoy the status of lessee, under assignment for the said original lease." The court also determined that forfeiture of Adous's lease would be inequitable. Appellants now argue on appeal that these findings were erroneous because: 1) Adous was a sublessee rather than an assignee; 2) as a sublessee, Adous was required to surrender possession of the premises upon breach by the original lessee, GPI; 3) forfeiture of the sublease was not inequitable. We agree with each of these arguments.

[T]here is an important distinction between a sublessee and an assignee for purposes of this case. A sublessee's right to possession terminates when the original landlord declares a forfeiture of the original lease. See *Bush v. Bourland*, 206 Ark. 275, 174 S.W.2d 936 (1943); 49 Am.Jur.2d *Landlord & Tenant* § 1185 (2d ed.1995). An assignee, however, acquires privity of estate with the original landlord, see *Jones*

---

[5] Appellants' naming of Adous as a sublessee is the first indication in the record that appellants were aware of the existence of the sublease.

*v. Innkeepers, Inc.*, 12 Ark.App. 364, 676 S.W.2d 761 (1984), and enters into a landlord-tenant relationship with the original landlord. *See* 52 C.J.S. *Landlord & Tenant* § 50 (2003). The assignee's estate continues if he meets his obligations under the assignment, *e.g.*, to pay rent. *Id.* at § 53.

At common law, the distinction between a sublease and an assignment depended upon whether the original lessee transferred his estate for the entire remainder of the lease term, in which case it would be an assignment, or for less than the entire term, in which case it would be a sublease. *See Gagne v. Hartmeier*, 271 Ark. 845, 611 S.W.2d 194 (Ark.App.1981). However, Arkansas has rejected that approach and has adopted the rule that the intention of the parties is to govern in determining whether an instrument is an assignment or a sublease, although the duration of the primary term, as compared with the duration of the transfer, may be considered in arriving at that intention. *Id.; Jaber v. Miller*, 219 Ark. 59, 239 S.W.2d 760 (1951). Our review of the evidence leads us to the conclusion that the parties clearly intended Adous to be a sublessee.

The most telling indicator of Adous's and GPI's intention in this case is that they have consistently referred to their arrangement as a sublease. The characterization that the parties give to their relationship is a significant factor to be considered in determining whether they intended to create a sublease or an assignment. *See Jaber v. Miller, supra*. The instruments of transfer in this case are entitled "subleases." Further, in their pleadings and at trial, the parties exclusively referred to GPI's transfer to Adous as a sublease rather than an assignment. Until the trial court declared Adous an assignee, the parties had never contemplated him being anything other than a sublessee. Thus, as in *Jaber*, the parties' intention should govern.

Another factor indicating that the parties intended to create a sublease is Adous's payment of rent to GPI rather than to appellants or Fidelity National. This is consistent with the rule that, in a sublease, the relationship between the original lessee and the sublessee is that of landlord and tenant, and the sublessee incurs no liability directly to the original lessor for payment of rent. 49 Am.Jur.2d *Landlord & Tenant* §§ 1179, 1184 (1995).

A third indicator that the arrangement was a sublease is found in the possibility of repossession by GPI. The Sublease Agreement provides:

> In the event that Lessor [GPI] elects to repossess the premises without terminating the sublease, then Lessee shall be liable for and shall pay to Lessor all rent and other indebtedness accrued to the date of such repossession. . . .

Such a right to reenter and repossess indicates that GPI has not relinquished its right to the leasehold, as it would have done in the case of an assignment. *See generally* 52 C.J.S. *Landlord & Tenant* § 55 (2003); *Coles Trading Co. v. Spiegel, Inc.,* 187 F.2d 984 (9th Cir.1951).

Admittedly, there are some parts of the arrangement between Adous and GPI that are consistent with an assignment. The amount of Adous's rent was exactly the amount of the rent to be paid under the original lease; Adous agreed to observe the terms of the original lease; and the property was transferred to Adous for what appears to be the remainder of the original lease term. However, these factors simply do not override the undisputed fact that the parties very clearly intended a sublease. Both they and their attorneys have consistently considered this arrangement to be a sublease. Our polestar is the intention of the parties. *Jaber, supra.* Because the evidence points so strongly to the conclusion that the parties intended Adous to be a sublessee rather than an assignee, we hold that the trial court clearly erred in finding that Adous was an assignee.

Finally, we reach the issue of whether the maxim that equity abhors a forfeiture should be applied in this case. The trial court determined that forfeiture would not be equitable because Adous had shown his ability to perform under the lease; the original lease contained no prohibition against subletting; Adous was operating an ongoing business on the site; and appellants would not be prejudiced by Adous's continued occupation of the site. However, the trial court applied these considerations after finding that Adous was an assignee. We have now determined that Adous was a sublessee. We therefore, in our *de novo* review, re-examine the equitable considerations in light of Adous's status as a sublessee.

Certainly, forfeitures are not favorites of the law. However, because Adous is a sublessee, he has no privity of estate nor a landlord-tenant relationship with appellants. 49 Am.Jur.2d *Landlord & Tenant* § 1184 (2d ed.1995). To allow equity to intervene to prevent forfeiture of the sublease in this situation would create a relationship between appellants and Adous that appellants never desired, that none of the parties ever contemplated, and that, in fact, has never existed. Further, as a sublessee, Adous's fate with regard to the property must rise and fall with that of the original lessee, GPI. *See Bush v. Bourland, supra.* Adous considered himself a sublessee and, by virtue of agreeing to the terms of the original lease, was surely aware of its provisions; he must have understood that his status depended upon the continued performance of the original lease by GPI. Therefore, this is not a situation in which Adous was caught unaware. Finally, appellants' decision to terminate the lease was based not only upon GPI's failure to pay rent, but upon GPI's insolvency. While Adous may have proved an able substitute to meet GPI's rent obligation, he could not restore GPI to solvency. Equity should not deprive appellants of their ability to terminate a lease on that ground.

Based on the foregoing, we hold that equity should not intervene to prohibit forfeiture of the sublease in this case. We therefore reverse and remand the trial court's decree with directions to enter an order consistent with this opinion.

■ ROBBINS, J., dissenting.

Whether Adous is characterized as a sublessee or an assignee is a distinction without a difference. Either characterization would permit the trial court to apply equitable considerations to avoid forfeiture of the sublease.

The absence of privity between Adous and appellants has no bearing on whether equity may intervene to enjoin a forfeiture. In *Smith v. Whitener,* 42 Ark.App. 225, 856 S.W.2d 328 (1993), this court held that privity of parties was not required in order for a plaintiff to assert the equitable remedy of unjust enrichment. Further, the cases from other jurisdictions cited by the majority do not prohibit the intervention of equity on behalf of a sublessee; rather, they decline to invoke equity under the particular facts of those cases.

Our inquiry in the case at bar should simply be whether the trial court's decision to apply equity was clearly erroneous. I do not believe that it was. A court of equity, even in the absence of special circumstances of fraud, accident, or mistake, may relieve against a forfeiture incurred by the breach of a covenant to pay rent, on the payment or tender of all arrears of rent and interest by a defaulting lessee. The grounds upon which a court of equity proceeds in this connection are: that the rent is the object of the parties, and the forfeiture only an incident intended to secure its payment; that the measure of damages is fixed and certain; and that when the principal and interest are paid, the compensation is complete. Further, the doctrine of equity is not for forfeiture, and the most vital question in determining whether a court of equity will grant relief against a penalty or forfeiture is said to be the ability and willingness of the party in default subsequently to perform the condition or make compensation for his failure of performance. Although these cases involved the application of equity between the original lessor and lessee, under the particular facts of the case at bar, I believe this distinction makes no difference.

This was a long-term commercial lease in which appellants as lessors did not see fit to prohibit either an assignment or a sublease. Thus, they surely could not be surprised that a sublease was executed, nor could Adous be charged with notice that a sublease would be looked upon by appellants with disfavor. Further, before the controversy arose in this case, Adous had apparently operated the gas station and convenience store for over three years without incident and without prejudice to appellants. After the controversy arose, he proved his continuing ability to operate at the site and pay rent in a timely manner. Thus, appellants have received exactly what they sought-a lease of the facility over a long period of time with timely payment of rent. The inequity in this case lies in the fact that Adous, who has agreed to uphold the terms of the original lease and has paid rent in a regular fashion, must now forfeit the business he has operated simply because GPI, who after 1997 was acting as a mere conduit, became unable to pay rent. This is the type of forfeiture that equity should prevent, and I believe the trial court was correct in attempting to do so. I therefore respectfully dissent.

■ ROAF, J., dissenting.

While I agree with and also join Judge Robbins' dissent, I would not reach the issue of whether the trial court could apply equitable considerations to the forfeiture of a sublease, because I would affirm the trial court's finding that Adous was an assignee of the lease between the Abernathys and Griffen Petroleum, Inc. (GPI).

The majority has found that the three factors indicating the arrangement is a sublease overrode the three factors which suggest that it is an assignment, placing great emphasis on the parties' characterization of the instrument as a sublease. The other two factors favoring a sublease are the fact that Adous paid rent to GPI rather than directly to the Abernathys, and a clause in the agreement giving GPI the right of reentry and possession of the premises. However, this right of reentry was available *only in the event of a default* by Adous, *and only pursuant to a judgment or writ issued in an appropriate legal proceeding.* In *Jaber v. Miller,* 219 Ark. 59, 239 S.W.2d 760 (1951), the supreme court expressly rejected the appellee's argument that reserved rights of reentry rendered an agreement a sublease, in reversing the trial court's ruling that the document in question was a sublease rather than an assignment. This court also reversed the trial court's characterization of an instrument as a sublease despite the appellee's retention of the right of reentry for nonpayment of rent and other rights, noting that "none of the rights retained by appellant rise to the dignity of a reversionary estate." *Gagne v. Hartmeier,* 271 Ark. 845, 611 S.W.2d 194 (Ark.App.1981). These two cases are relied upon by the majority to a great extent, however; they suggest that the nature of the rights transferred is key to the determination of the parties' intent, and in both cases the instrument in question was found to be an assignment despite factors indicating the contrary.

In this instance, the factors favoring assignment are equally as compelling or even stronger. First, the amount of Adous's rent was exactly the amount of the rent to be paid under the original lease. Had the amounts been different, that would have indicated a sublease. 52 C.J.S. *Landlord & Tenant* § 43 (2003). Second, the Second Addendum to the Sublease contains the following provision:

> COMPLIANCE WITH ORIGINAL LEASE: New Lessees shall perform and observe the terms and conditions to be performed on the part of [GPI] in the original Lease Agreement pertaining to this property between [GPI] and . . . Abernathy. Additionally, New Lessees agree to indemnify [GPI] against any and all claims, damages, costs, and expenses in respect to New Lessees

nonperformance or nonobservance of any terms or conditions contained in the original Lease Agreement.

Incorporation of the original lease into the transferring instrument indicates an assignment. *Gagne v. Hartmeier, supra.* Thirdly, GPI transferred the lease to Adous for the entire remainder of the original lease term. The original primary term of the lease was ten years, to begin upon completion of construction. According to William Abernathy, construction was completed in August 1992. Thus, when the first subtenancy agreement was executed in November 1996, there was approximately five years and nine months remaining in the original term, plus options. The agreement between GPI and Adous was for five years and eight months *plus options*.

In sum, GPI transferred all of its rights of any significance in the lease, including options to renew, to Adous. Adous faithfully performed in a timely manner for a number of years, until he was compelled to file suit for specific performance in May 2001 because the Abernathys refused to accept rent tendered directly by him. As in *Gagne, supra,* there was no reversionary estate remaining to GPI. I cannot say that the trial court's characterization of this contractual arrangement as an assignment despite the parties' labeling it as a sublease was clearly erroneous.

### NOTES

1. *Privity of contract and privity of estate. Juilliard* shows that there are two theories on which a landlord can attempt to enforce promises in the lease against assignees or sublessees. The first of these theories is a contract theory. If a sublessee or assignee expressly assumes the obligations of the head lease, she is contractually bound to perform.

> EXAMPLE 1: L leases to T. In the lease T promises to turn off the lights by 10 p.m. T assigns the lease to B, and B expressly assumes the duties of the head lease. B is contractually bound to turn off the lights by 10 p.m.

The express assumption of the duties by the assignee or sublessee does not, however, relieve the original lessee of her contractual obligation to perform. In the above example, if B does not turn off the lights by 10 p.m., L can sue T (as well as B) for any damages suffered as a result of the breach.

The second theory on which a landlord can attempt to enforce promises in the lease against subsequent transferees is an estate theory. The estate theory provides that a covenant that touches and concerns the premises will pass to an assignee of the lease even if the assignee does not consent to be bound by the covenant. However, these covenants are not binding on sublessees (in contrast to assignees). The covenant is binding on the assignee of the lessee because the assignee has a direct relation to the lessor. In contrast, the covenant is not binding on the sublessee because the sublessee is insulated from the lessor by the lessee. Thus, the assignee is said to have "privity of estate" with the lessor while the sublessee does not.

EXAMPLE 2: L leases to T. In the lease T promises to provide steam generated on the leased premises to the adjoining premises of L. T *assigns* to B. B does not expressly assume the term of the head lease, and thus is not contractually bound. However, B is bound on an estate theory, since her status as assignee of T's lease moves her into privity of estate with L.

EXAMPLE 3: L leases to T. In the lease T promises to provide steam generated on the leased premises to the adjoining premises of L. T *subleases* to B. B does not expressly assume the terms of the head lease, and is thus not contractually bound. B is not bound on an estate theory either. Sublessees are not in privity of estate with the landlord. Therefore, L cannot get damages from B if B does not provide steam. However, if neither T nor B provides steam, L may terminate the lease, thereby evicting both T and B. Moreover, L may be able to enforce certain equitable remedies against B (see note 3).

A person who was once in privity of estate with the landlord is not bound on the estate theory after assigning her interest. Therefore, in Example 2, L could not enforce the promise against T on an *estate* theory *after the assignment*. (Recall from the earlier discussion that T would be bound, even after the assignment, on a *contract* theory.) In this context, then, privity of estate can be thought of like a football. The football starts in the hands of the original lessee. If an assignment is made the football is lateraled to the assignee. Subleases do not count as laterals. Enforcement on an estate theory is only possible when a player has the ball. Enforcement against sublessees on an estate theory is not possible, because a sublessee never gets the ball. Enforcement under the estate theory against one who assigned to someone else is not possible because the ball has been lateraled to another player. Note that the reason for the holding in *Julliard* is now fairly clear. The landlord (at that time Atlantic Mills) leased the premises to Riverside. (Riverside is now carrying the privity of estate football). Riverside *assigned* (lateraled) to American Woolen, and American Woolen did not expressly assume the duties of the lease. American Woolen, for all practical purposes, held the property until assigning (lateraling) to Reo Realty. Enforcement against American Woolen on a contract theory is not possible because American Woolen did not expressly assume the terms of the lease. Enforcement on a privity of estate theory is also impossible. Although American Woolen was once in privity of estate (carrying the football), it assigned (lateraled) to Reo Realty. Therefore enforcement on a privity of estate theory is only possible against Reo Realty (because Reo Realty now has the ball). Hence the court's holding that American Woolen is not liable for rent.

All of this is more authoritatively, but less colorfully, explained in Restatement (Second) of Property (Landlord & Tenant) § 16.1 (1977).

2. *Touch and concern.* If the transfer from the original tenant to the transferee is an "assignment," the transferee is traditionally considered to be bound by every promise contained in the lease that "touches and concerns"

the transferred interest. Rent is always considered to touch and concern the leased premises. Other covenants, however, might be deemed "collateral" to the lease and therefore may not be binding on the transferee. See Assignment 25–26 for further discussion of "touch and concern."

3. *Privity of estate not required in equity.* If a sublessee of the original tenant has not expressly assumed the obligations of the original lease, the sublessee is not liable for monetary damages for failing to comply with these obligations. The sublessee is not liable because no privity of estate exists between the original landlord and the sublessee. However, the original lessor may be able to enforce some of these covenants by using equitable remedies. Historically, equity courts did not require privity of estate between the landlord and a transferee of the original tenant. See Assignment 25–26.

4. *Principal Problem revisited.* If we assume that Terry cannot be found, where do the equities lie? Both Alyssa and Larry chose to deal with Terry. If Alyssa is forced to pay Larry $2,400 this is unfair to her. If she need not pay the $2,400, Larry loses $2,400 that is owed to him and the "rule" that an assignee of a lease must pay the rent and perform the other covenants will be ignored.

5. *Why distinguish between assignments and subleases?* It has been suggested that the distinction between assignments and subleases is unwarranted and that subleases should be treated the same as assignments.[6] Surely in some instances the distinction seems absurd. Why should major legal consequences revolve around whether a transfer by a lessee is for the entire remaining term or for the entire remaining term minus one day? On the other hand, would it not be unjust to impose all of the obligations of the original lease on a subtenant who takes possession under a sublease that runs for one year when the original lease is for thirty years? Should it be possible to resolve disputes between the lessor and the transferee of the original lessee without reference to the concepts of assignment and sublease? What policies should shape the rules in this area? Does the existing emphasis on the supposed differences between assignments and subleases distract us from more relevant questions? Note that this approach is reflected in one of the dissenting opinions in Abernathy.

6. *Substance over form.* In the Principal Problem the transaction was called a sublease, whereas in *Juilliard* it was called an assignment. Does it make any difference what the parties call their transaction?[7] Note that this issue is raised in Abernathy.

7. *Avoiding litigation through proper planning and drafting.* The *Juilliard* court stated, "[L]essor has it within his power to protect himself against any detriment to him by incorporating adequate provisions in the lease concerning assignments thereof. If he chooses to execute a lease without adequately protecting his rights as lessor thereunder, he cannot

---

[6] Curtis, *Assignments and Subleases: An Archaic Distinction,* 17 Pacific Law J. 1247 (1986); Jaccard, *The Scope of Liability Between Landlord and Subtenant,* 16 Colum.J. of Law and Social Problems 365 (1981).

[7] See Plaza Dev. Co. v. W. Cooper Enters., LLC, 12 N.E.3d 506 (Ohio Ct. App., Franklin County 2014) (implying that whether the parties refer to an agreement as a sublease or an assignment can impact the determination of which of the two exists).

thereafter complain if, by force of law, he is deprived of a benefit that he might otherwise have secured for himself." What should the lessor have done at the planning stage to avoid this litigation? What might Alyssa have done at the planning stage to avoid the controversy that arose in the Principal Problem? See Samuels, Drafters Beware: Do Not Get Trapped By Silence In a Lease, 25 Probate & Property 32 (July/Aug. 2011).

## b. TENANT'S RIGHT TO ASSIGN OR SUBLEASE

### 1. INTRODUCTION

In the absence of a lease provision restricting the tenant's right to assign or sublet, the tenant may assign or sublet without the landlord's permission.[8] This follows from the general rule that the law favors the free alienability of estates in land. Lease provisions restricting the tenant's right to assign or sublet are strictly construed. Thus a provision against assignments does not affect subleases, and a provision against subleases does not affect assignments.[9]

Leases often prohibit assignments or subleases without the landlord's consent.[10] Traditionally the landlord had the right to withhold consent arbitrarily.[11] In recent years however, most courts have interpreted such a provision to mean that the landlord cannot withhold her consent arbitrarily.[12] The Restatement takes the position that the landlord cannot unreasonably withhold her consent to an assignment or a sublease "unless a freely negotiated provision in the lease gives the landlord an absolute right to withhold consent."[13] Such a formulation leaves many questions to be decided. What is an "unreasonable" withholding of consent? When is a provision in a lease "freely negotiated"? Should a lease provision that simply states that "tenant shall not assign this lease," be treated differently from a lease provision that states that "tenant shall not assign this lease without the prior written consent of the landlord"? Can a printed provision in a residential lease form ever be considered as freely negotiated? Freedom of contract

---

[8] See Rowe v. Great Atlantic & Pacific Tea Co., Inc., 46 N.Y.2d 62, 412 N.Y.S.2d 827, 385 N.E.2d 566 (1978). But see Kano Invs., L.L.C. v. Kojis Constr., L.L.C., 113 So. 3d 1113 (La.App. 3 Cir. 2013) (finding that when a lease specifically requires the tenant to obtain permission from the landlord to assign or sublet, and the tenant fails to obtain written consent to an assignment of the lease, the tenant violates the lease agreement).

[9] See Gordon Investment Co. v. Jones, 123 Colo. 253, 227 P.2d 336 (1951).

[10] See James C. McLoughlin, Annot., When Lessor May Withhold Consent Under Unqualified Provision in Lease Prohibiting Assignment or Subletting of Leased Premises Without Lessor's Consent, 21 A.L.R.4th 188 (1983, as supplemented).

[11] See, e.g., Snortland v. Larson, 364 N.W.2d 67 (N.D.1985) (applying Minnesota law); F & L Center Co. v. Cunningham Drug Stores, Inc., 19 Ohio App.3d 72, 482 N.E.2d 1296 (1984); B & R Oil Co., Inc. v. Ray's Mobile Homes, Inc., 139 Vt. 122, 422 A.2d 1267 (1980); Danpar Associates v. Somersville Mills Sales Room, Inc., 182 Conn. 444, 438 A.2d 708 (1980).

[12] See, No Frills Supermarkets v. Brookside Omaha, Ltd. P'ship, 2011 Neb. App. LEXIS 85 (Neb. Ct. App. July 5, 2011); Van Sloun v. Agans Bros., 778 N.W.2d 174 (Iowa 2010); Kendall v. Ernest Pestana, Inc., 40 Cal.3d 488, 220 Cal.Rptr. 818, 709 P.2d 837 (1985); Newman v. Hinky Dinky Omaha-Lincoln, Inc., 229 Neb. 382, 427 N.W.2d 50 (1988), (reprinted in this Assignment).

[13] 2 Restatement (Second) of Property (Landlord & Tenant) § 15.2(2) (1977).

surely is an important policy that should be given due weight. What are the countervailing policies against enforcing the landlord's negotiated right to withhold consent to an assignment or a subletting? Are those policies as strong when applied to a two year lease as they are when they are applied to a fifty year lease? Some of these questions may be relevant to the following Principal Problem.

## 2. Principal Problem

Tanya, a first year medical student, signs a lease for an apartment for $600 per month, the lease to be for a term of two years. The lease contains the following provision:

> Tenant shall not assign or sublease the demised premises.

After a few months, Tanya decides to take another apartment. She advertises in the local newspaper and finds Hal, who is willing to take over the old apartment. The agreement between Tanya and Hal is that Hal will sublease the apartment from Tanya for a term of one year and pay rent to Tanya of $800 per month. Hal is the owner of a large gasoline station and has an excellent credit record. However, Hal has tattoos all over his body and several pierced body parts. In general, Hal projects a somewhat unconventional image. When Hal and Tanya ask for Luke Landlord's written permission for the proposed arrangement, Luke refuses. First, he claims that "people like Hal make poor tenants, cheapen the appearance of the premises, are usually poor housekeepers, throw wild parties, are objectionable to other tenants, and often default in their rent payments." When Hal points out that he makes an excellent steady income, Luke is not persuaded to change his mind. In addition, Luke objects that Tanya stands to make $200 per month on the deal. If anyone is to receive $800 per month it should be Luke, not Tanya, Luke claims. Luke does offer to release Tanya from her lease without any liability, but Tanya refuses and comes to you for legal advice.

Assume that no controlling authority exists in your jurisdiction, and that you must render advice based on reason and precedents taken from other jurisdictions.

## 3. Materials for Solution of Principal Problem

### Newman v. Hinky Dinky Omaha-Lincoln, Inc.
Supreme Court of Nebraska, 1988.
229 Neb. 382, 427 N.W.2d 50.

■ SHANAHAN, JUSTICE.

This is a forcible entry and detainer action which resulted in a judgment of restitution of real estate to the plaintiff-lessor, Raquel H. Newman. Hinky Dinky Omaha-Lincoln, Inc. (Hinky Dinky), the occupant and sublessee, appeals, thereby presenting to this court a question of first impression, namely: In the absence of an express lease provision specifically permitting a lessor to withhold consent to an assignment of the lease or subletting, must a lessor have a commercially reasonable objection to the assignment or subletting, when the lease allows assignment or subletting only with the lessor's consent?

Newman is the owner of real estate located in Lincoln, Nebraska. On July 1, 1977, Newman entered into a written lease of the premises with American Community Stores Corporation (ACS), a Texas corporation. The lease refers to Newman as the "Landlord" and ACS as the "Tenant," and calls for payment of fixed rent, with additional rent based on the tenant's gross receipts. ACS operated a chain of Hinky Dinky supermarkets in Nebraska. Section 10.1 of the lease provides: "Tenant may not assign or transfer this Lease voluntarily or by operation of law or sublet the Leased Premises or any portion thereof without the written consent of Landlord first had and obtained."

ACS ceased all operations of its Hinky Dinky grocery store chain on February 16, 1985. Before that date, ACS asked Newman's consent for a proposed lease assignment to Nash Finch Company, and a subsequent sublease by Nash Finch to the appellant, Hinky Dinky. Although brief negotiations ensued concerning ACS' arrangement for the prospective lease assignment and sublease, Newman did not consent to the proposal. Later in February, ACS' lease assignment to Nash Finch and the sublease to Hinky Dinky were executed without Newman's consent.

On March 1, 1985, Newman notified ACS, Nash Finch, and Hinky Dinky, which then occupied the premises, that ACS was in default under the lease as the result of the assignment and subletting without Newman's consent, and on March 4, Newman served a "Notice to Vacate Premises" upon those entities. Newman accepted rental payments from Nash Finch during negotiations to resolve the conflict concerning the propriety and efficacy of the assignment and sublease. When negotiations reached impasse, on August 14, Newman served a "Notice to Quit" on the occupant, Hinky Dinky, and filed a petition for restitution of the premises on August 22, 1985. Whether Newman's acceptance of rent payments constituted a waiver was a matter of dispute by the parties.

After a hearing on Newman's motion for summary judgment, the district court ruled that there was no genuine issue of material fact whether Newman, as lessor, properly withheld consent to the assignment and sublease because, as a matter of law, a landlord may withhold consent for any reason. Citing *B & R Oil Company v. Ray's Mobile Homes*, 139 Vt. 122, 422 A.2d 1267 (1980), the district court stated that "the landlord may withhold consent for whatever reason the landlord deems proper.... There is not a genuine issue of fact as to this point." However, the court found that a factual issue existed on the question whether Newman had waived her rights under the lease by accepting rent payments, knowing that, without Newman's consent, ACS had assigned the lease to Nash Finch, which sublet to Hinky Dinky. Consequently, after granting summary judgment to Newman on the issue of the lessor's consent, the court proceeded to try the question of waiver. After trial, the district court held that Newman's acceptance of rent payments was not a waiver under the lease, and then granted Newman a judgment for restitution of the premises.

Hinky Dinky argues that the district court erred in (1) granting Newman a partial summary judgment by holding that a lessor may withhold consent to an assignment for any reason, and (2) finding that Newman's acceptance of rent after the alleged breach of lease had occurred was not a waiver.

Partial summary judgment for Newman is correct only if, as a matter of law, Newman was entitled to withhold consent to an assignment and sublease for any reason, that is, Newman had an absolute right to withhold consent. However, if Newman could withhold consent only on the basis of a reasonable objection, a factual issue concerning reasonableness precluded a summary judgment on the lessor's right to withhold consent to the assignment and sublease in the case at hand.

Hinky Dinky does not contend that Newman's consent to an assignment or sublease was unnecessary, but suggests that a lessor cannot unreasonably withhold consent. On the other hand, Newman suggests that, according to the language of the lease, a lessor has an absolute right to withhold consent to a lease assignment or subletting, however unreasonable or arbitrary the lessor's refusal might be. . . .

Newman relies on *B & R Oil Company v. Ray's Mobile Homes,* 139 Vt. 122, 422 A.2d 1267 (1980), in which the Vermont Supreme Court, construing lease language identical to the consent requirement in Newman's lease, embraced a rule recognizing a lessor's right to arbitrarily withhold consent to an assignment of a lease.

Another line of authority, however, recognizes that, where a lease contains an approval clause, such as a provision stating that the lease cannot be assigned without the lessor's prior consent, a lessor may withhold consent only when the lessor has a good faith reasonable objection to assignment of the lease, even in the absence of a lease provision stating that the lessor's consent will not be unreasonably withheld. See, *Kendall v. Ernest Pestana, Inc.,* 40 Cal.3d 488, 709 P.2d 837, 220 Cal.Rptr. 818 (1985); *Boss Barbara, Inc. v. Newbill,* 97 N.M. 239, 638 P.2d 1084 (1982); *Funk v. Funk,* 102 Idaho 521, 633 P.2d 586 (1981); *Hendrickson v. Freericks,* 620 P.2d 205 (Alaska 1980); *Warmack v. Merchants Nat'l Bk., Ft. Smith,* 272 Ark. 166, 612 S.W.2d 733 (1981); *Homa-Goff Interiors, Inc. v. Cowden,* 350 So.2d 1035 (Ala.1977). Many courts which adhere to the foregoing rule of reasonableness have accepted the general principle recited in Restatement (Second) of Property § 15.2(2) at 100 (1977):

> A restraint on alienation without the consent of the landlord of the tenant's interest in the leased property is valid, but the

landlord's consent to an alienation by the tenant cannot be withheld unreasonably, unless a freely negotiated provision in the lease gives the landlord an absolute right to withhold consent.

For example, see *Kendall v. Ernest Pestana, Inc., supra.* As the California Supreme Court observed in *Kendall:*

> [W]here a contract confers on one party a discretionary power affecting the rights of the other, a duty is imposed to exercise that discretion in good faith and in accordance with fair dealing. [Citations omitted.] Here the lessor retains the discretionary power to approve or disapprove an assignee proposed by the other party to the contract; this discretionary power should therefore be exercised in accordance with commercially reasonable standards. Where a lessee is entitled to sublet under common law, but has agreed to limit that right by first acquiring the consent of the landlord, we believe the lessee has a right to expect that consent will not be unreasonably withheld. [Citation omitted.]

40 Cal.3d at 500, 709 P.2d at 845, 220 Cal.Rptr. at 826 (quoting *Cal. Lettuce Growers v. Union Sugar Co.,* 45 Cal.2d 474, 289 P.2d 785 (1955), and *Fernandez v. Vazquez,* 397 So.2d 1171 (Fla.App.1981)).

Factors to be considered in determining whether a lessor has acted with good faith and reasonably in withholding consent to an assignment of a commercial lease or subletting include: financial responsibility of the proposed assignee or sublessee; the assignee's or sublessee's suitability for the particular property; legality of the proposed use; need for alteration of the premises; and the nature of the occupancy. See *Kendall v. Ernest Pestana, Inc., supra.* Pertinent to an assignee's or sublessee's financial responsibility under the lease may be past revenue received by the assignee or sublessee and, insofar as demonstrable or ascertainable, prospective receipts in relation to rent based on gross receipts from the business conducted or to be conducted on the leased premises. The foregoing factors are neither exhaustive nor components in an arithmetical formula for reasonableness. None of the factors is weighted so that more or less weight is attributable or assigned to any particular factor utilized in evaluating a lessor's good faith or reasonableness in withholding consent to a commercial lease assignment or subletting. Additional factors may be educed in future situations involving a lessor's withholding consent in cases similar to that now reviewed by this court. . . .

We believe that the rule of reasonableness, expressed in *Kendall v. Ernest Pestana, Inc.,* 40 Cal.3d 488, 709 P.2d 837, 220 Cal.Rptr. 818 (1985), is the correct rule and, therefore, hold that where a commercial lease does not expressly permit a lessor to withhold consent to an assignment or subletting and contains an approval clause, such as a provision that there can be no assignment of the lease or subletting without the lessor's prior consent, a lessor may withhold consent only when the lessor has a good faith and reasonable objection to assignment of the lease or subletting, even in the absence of a lease provision that the lessor's consent will not be unreasonably withheld. In the case before us, the lease does not expressly permit or authorize Newman to withhold consent to an assignment of the lease or subletting. In the absence of an express provision of such nature, that is, a lessor's right to withhold consent, the provisions of the lease in question require that the lessor act in good faith and reasonably in withholding consent to an assignment or subletting. Whether Newman acted in good faith and reasonably in withholding consent to the assignment and sublease is a question of material fact. See *Chadd v. Midwest Franchise Corp., supra.*

Although the court's opinion in *Kendall v. Ernest Pestana, Inc., supra,* and Restatement (Second) of Property § 15.2(2) (1977) contain expressions of a policy against a restraint on alienation, our decision today is limited to the issue raised by the parties, namely, the question of a lessor's good faith and reasonableness in withholding consent to an assignment of the lease or subletting, when the commercial lease in question does not contain an express provision specifically permitting a lessor's withholding consent. We leave for another day and another case the question whether an express lease provision permitting a lessor to withhold consent amounts to a restraint on alienation, in contravention of public policy in Nebraska.

By concluding that Newman could withhold consent for any reason regarding assignment and subletting, the district court erred in granting Newman a summary judgment on the question concerning the lessor's withheld consent. Unless and until it is determined that Newman's withholding consent to the proposed assignment and sublease was in good faith and reasonable, it is unnecessary to determine whether Newman waived a right to declare a default under the lease in question. Consequently, adjudication of the waiver question is premature. The judgments of the district court are reversed. This matter is remanded for further proceedings.

## United States v. Epstein
United States District Court, S.D. New York, 1998.
27 F.Supp.2d 404.

■ CHIN, D.J.

In this case, the United States (the "Government") seeks to evict defendants from a building formerly used as a residence by the Deputy Consul General of the Islamic Republic of Iran ("Iran"). After diplomatic and consular relations with Iran were severed in 1980, the Office of Foreign Missions ("OFM") of the United States Department of State took possession of the building pursuant to the Foreign Missions Act, 22 U.S.C. § 4301 et seq. OFM leased the building to defendant Jeffrey E.

Epstein in 1992. Epstein sublet the building to defendant Ivan S. Fisher in 1996, purportedly without the Government's consent. Fisher, in turn, sublet a portion of the building to several subtenants.

In 1996, the Government purported to terminate Epstein's lease and brought this action to eject Epstein and Fisher from the building. The Government later amended its complaint to assert a claim for ejectment against the subtenants as well. The Government also sought to recover back rent from Epstein and Fisher.

[An] issue to be decided on this motion is whether OFM was entitled to refuse Epstein's proposed sublet to Fisher arbitrarily, or whether it breached a duty of good faith and fair dealing implicit in the lease agreement by unreasonably refusing to grant such consent in writing. Resolution of this issue turns on whether federal contract law or New York landlord-tenant law applies.

Generally, under New York law, where a lease requires a tenant to obtain the prior written consent of the landlord to sublet or assign leased premises, a landlord may refuse consent arbitrarily, unless the lease contains a clause specifically stating that the landlord may not unreasonably withhold such consent. See Dress Shirt Sales, Inc. v. Hotel Martinique Assocs., 12 N.Y.2d 339, 239 N.Y.S.2d 660, 662, 190 N.E.2d 10 (Ct.App.1963). The Assignment and Sublet Clause in the lease between OFM and Epstein required Epstein to obtain prior written consent of OFM to a proposed sublet, but it contained no provision prohibiting OFM from unreasonably withholding such written consent.

The Government, relying on New York landlord-tenant law, asserts that it was entitled to withhold its consent to Epstein's proposed sublet to Fisher for any reason, or for no reason at all. Epstein and Fisher, however, disagree. They contend that, because the Government is a party to the lease, interpretation of the lease is governed by principles of federal common law, not New York State law. Pursuant to federal common law of contracts, Epstein and Fisher continue, the lease between OFM and Epstein contains an implied covenant of good faith and fair dealing, citing Neal & Co. v. United States, 36 Fed. Cl. 600 (1996), aff'd, 121 F.3d 683 (Fed.Cir.1997). The requirement of good faith and fair dealing, they argue, prohibits OFM from withholding consent unreasonably. OFM's refusal to consent to Epstein's proposed sublet of the Premises to Fisher, they contend, was motivated by its desire to enter into a lease with Galinas at a higher rent beginning February 1, 1997. Such conduct was unreasonable, they argue, and, therefore, OFM breached the implied covenant of good faith and fair dealing in the lease.

. . .

[A]s between general federal contract principles and specific state landlord-tenant law, the latter should be applied. Land is unique. It is logical, therefore, that a landlord should have virtually complete say in who occupies its property. It makes sense for the law to permit a landlord to unreasonably withhold consent to a proposed sublet unless the parties specifically bargain otherwise. See Alex M. Johnson, Jr., Correctly Interpreting Long-Term Leases Pursuant to Modern Contract Law: Toward a Theory of Relational Leases, 74 Va. L.Rev. 751, 758 (1988) (discussing the majority view that absent contractual agreement to the contrary landlords are permitted to unreasonably withhold consent to a sublet or assignment, and noting that the rule stems from the "paramount importance of the lessor's ability to control the selection of his tenants so as to protect the value of his reversionary interest" in the leasehold).

I therefore adopt the relevant rule of New York landlord-tenant law for purposes of deciding the remaining issue in this dispute, and hold that, consistent with New York law, OFM was entitled to arbitrarily withhold its consent to Epstein's request to sublet the Premises to Fisher. Even assuming OFM had a hidden agenda in refusing Epstein's request to sublet to Fisher, specifically, that it preferred to enter into a new lease with Galinas at a higher rental price, it was entitled to withhold its consent to a sublet for a good reason, a bad reason, or no reason at all. There existed no implied covenant of good faith and fair dealing in its lease with Epstein requiring OFM to act reasonably in deciding whether to approve Epstein's proposed sublet, and, therefore, OFM cannot be held liable for a breach thereof. Thus, I need not reach the issue of whether OFM in fact unreasonably withheld consent. And, as Fisher was occupying the Premises pursuant to an illegal sublet, OFM was within its rights to terminate Epstein's lease.

## NOTES

1. *Term and type of lease.* Hinky Dinky involved a lease of commercial premises with a term that probably exceeded ten years. *Epstein* involved a shorter term commercial lease. The lease in the Principal Problem is a residential lease for a term of only two years. Should these differences be considered material?

2. *The sounds of silence.* The lease in *Hinky Dinky* prohibited assignments or subleases "without the written consent of Landlord first had and obtained." This also was the case in *Epstein*. The lease in the Principal Problem simply prohibited assignments or subleases. There was no reference to the consent of the landlord. Is this a significant difference?

3. *Greed.* In the Principal Problem, Luke wanted to get the benefit of the $800 rent rather than permitting Tanya to get this benefit. Is such a desire "unreasonable"? If not, should landlords be able to withhold consent to an assignment or a sublease for the sole reason that if the lease is terminated they will be able to relet for a higher amount? It has been held that this is not a valid reason.[14]

---

[14] See, e.g., Pantry, Inc. v. Mosley, 126 So. 3d 152, 153 (Ala. 2013) (finding it unreasonable for the landlord to withhold consent to an assignment of a lease to extract higher rent than contracted for in the lease); Norville v. Carr-Gottstein Foods Co., 84 P.3d 996, 1001

4. *Arbitrariness.* Suppose the lease specifically states that the landlord shall be able to withhold consent "arbitrarily, for any reason or for no reason." Should such a clause be given effect? Can you add to the factors bearing on reasonableness that are listed in *Hinky Dinky*?

5. *Courtesy.* Suppose a tenant makes an assignment of the lease without obtaining the landlord's consent, although the lease requires such consent. Suppose also that the new tenant could not have reasonably been rejected by the landlord. Could the landlord terminate the lease on the ground that consent was never obtained? Should it make a difference whether the original tenant at least requested the consent of the landlord?

6. *Legislative developments.* The *Hinky-Dinky* opinion adopted the reasoning of Kendall v. Ernest Pestana, Inc., 40 Cal.3d 488, 220 Cal.Rptr. 818, 709 P.2d 837 (1985). The California legislature responded to *Kendall* by passing Cal.Civ.Code §§ 1995.010–1995.270 (2015).[15] The California statute follows *Kendall* by providing that if the lease requires the landlord's consent for a transfer, but provides no standard for giving or withholding consent, the restriction on transfer shall be construed to include an implied standard that the landlord's consent may not be unreasonably withheld. However it also provides that a "restriction on transfer of a tenant's interest in a lease may absolutely prohibit transfer." Is this latter aspect of the California statute sensible? Why might the California legislature have taken this position?

In Alaska, a landlord's consent may be withheld only upon grounds that are statutorily specified. These "reasonable" grounds for rejecting prospective tenants include: insufficient credit standing or financial responsibility; number of persons in household; number of persons under the age of 18 in household; unwillingness of prospective occupant to assume same terms of existing lease; proposed maintenance of pets; proposed commercial activity; or written information from previous landlord setting out abuses of other premises.[16] Do you think this is a better way of measuring reasonableness? Should the landlord be permitted to exercise more discretion than this statute permits?

7. *Financial viability of assignee/sublessee.* In 200 Eighth Avenue Restaurant Corp. v. Daytona Holding Corp., 740 N.Y.S.2d 330, 331, 293 A.D.2d 353 (2002), the court held that the landlord's refusal to consent to an assignment was reasonable when the proposed assignee did not provide adequate financial information in a timely manner to enable the landlord to

---

(Alaska 2004) (concluding it is not reasonable for a landlord to withhold consent to a sublease to obtain a higher rent than the rent for which the landlord originally contracted); Casco Marina Development, L.L.C. v. District of Columbia Redevelopment Land Agency, 834 A.2d 77, 84 (D.C. 2003) (observing that a landlord cannot withhold consent to a sublease to get a better bargain); Giordano v. Miller, 733 N.Y.S.2d 94, 288 A.D.2d 181, 182 (2001) (holding that landlord's refusal to give consent was unreasonable where the landlord demanded a fee as a condition precedent to granting consent for the proposed assignment); Duane Reade v. IG Second Generation Partners, L.P., 708 N.Y.S.2d 273, 276, 184 Misc.2d 674, 677 (2000) (holding that landlord's refusal to consent to a sublease was unreasonable because the landlord sought to obtain a significantly higher rent from another tenant).

[15] Delaware § 5508 similarly requires a landlord's consent to not be withheld unreasonably absent any contrary writing within the rental agreement. 25 Del.C. § 5508 (2015).

[16] See AK ST § 34.03.060 (2015).

ascertain if the assignee would be financially responsible. Similarly in Executive Sandwich Shoppe, Inc. v. Carr Realty Corp., 749 A.2d 724, 736 (D.C. 2000), the court held that the landlord's withholding of consent was reasonable because the proposed assignee's financial disclosures showed irregularities and because the proposed assignee insisted on taking an action specifically prohibited under the lease. By contrast, the court in Ring v. Mpath Interactive, Inc., 302 F.Supp. 2d 301 (S.D.N.Y. 2004) determined it was unreasonable for a commercial landlord to withhold consent based on an unsubstantiated belief that the proposed assignee would be a financial risk. The court then held that a landlord's reasonable refusal must be based on objective factors, such as the assignee's financial status and the proposed use of the new occupancy.

# ASSIGNMENT 8

# TENANT'S BREACH: LANDLORD'S REMEDIES

## 1. INTRODUCTION

The traditional rules of law in this area are evolving and are becoming more consonant with modern ideas. The introductory paragraphs in this Assignment summarize very briefly the traditional rules while the major cases treat the modern modifications of these rules.

The primary issue with which we are concerned in this Assignment is as follows: if a tenant unjustifiably abandons the leased premises can the landlord do nothing, wait for the end of the term, and then sue for the unpaid rent, or must he promptly attempt to mitigate damages by making a bona fide effort to find a new tenant? The question of the landlord's right to damages from a defaulting tenant is closely related to the tenant's right to assign or sublease the premises, the topic that we considered in the last Assignment.

Under the traditional view, a landlord who attempted to mitigate by re-entering and re-leasing might find that he had destroyed all his rights to a recovery against the tenant. The doctrine of "surrender" treated a landlord who re-entered the premises without properly preserving his rights as having "accepted" the tenant's "offer" to surrender the premises and, therefore, having waived any right to additional damages. Since the landlord's possession was inconsistent with the continuation of the lease, the lease came to an end, along with any right of the landlord under the lease. Of course, the doctrine of surrender tended to discourage landlords from mitigating damages, at least where the original tenant was solvent and could be expected to satisfy a judgment against him.

In response to the surrender doctrine, many leases contain a provision permitting the landlord to relet the premises "for the tenant's account" upon the tenant's abandonment. Such provisions, even if effective, can have serious drawbacks. For example, a few states require the lessor to wait until the end of the term before suing, while others allow the lessor to sue for the rent as it becomes due. Both of these approaches, however, are inconvenient for the landlord since he is forced either to wait a long while to collect his rent or to bring multiple suits over a long period of time. In addition, sometimes provisions permitting the lessor to relet for the tenant's account are strictly construed and are treated as an acceptance of the tenant's offer to surrender the premises. The hostility shown by many courts to the landlord's right to relet for the tenant's account has led to re-entry provisions in leases which contain several hundred words of fine print.

The Restatement (Second) of Property (Landlord & Tenant) § 12.1, Comment i (1977) opposes requiring landlords to mitigate damages:

> A tenant who abandons leased property is not entitled to insist on action by the landlord to mitigate the damages, absent an agreement otherwise. Abandonment of property is an invitation to vandalism, and the law should not encourage such conduct by putting a duty of mitigation of damages on the landlord.

Although there are still jurisdictions that adhere to the traditional view disfavoring mitigation,[1] the trend now seems to be that lessors are required to mitigate their damages upon a tenant's default.[2] All states agree, however, that a defaulting tenant may offset the amount he owes the landlord by any amounts collected by the landlord as rent from third parties during the term of the lease. The courts will not permit the landlord to collect the full rent from the defaulting tenant and also collect rent from another party because this would result in a windfall to the landlord.

The cases in this Assignment reflect the modern trend requiring mitigation. Many questions remain for the courts to resolve in applying the mitigation requirement.

## 2. PRINCIPAL PROBLEM

Your client, Jack Lesser, owns a downtown office building (the "Jackson Building"). Three years ago, he leased part of the ground floor to A.B. Drugger, a local pharmacist, for a five year period. The lease contained the following pertinent clauses: 1) Lessor shall not lease other space in Jackson Building to other retail drugstores; 2) The designated premises shall be used for no other purpose and shall not be otherwise occupied except upon and with the written consent of the Lessor; and 3) Lessee shall not sublet any part of the premises nor assign this lease or any interest in it without the prior written consent of Lessor. Lessor's consent thereto shall not be withheld unreasonably.

Six months ago, while the lease still had about two and a half years left, Lesser received the following letter, with the keys to the premises enclosed:

---

[1] See, e.g., Allen v. Harkness Stone Co., Inc., 271 Ga.App. 397 (2004) (holding that the commercial landlord has no duty to mitigate if the tenant abandons the leased premises provided the landlord refuses to accept the tenant's offer of surrender and the lease remains in force); Publicker Chemical Corp. v. Belcher Oil Co., 792 F.2d 482, 487 (5th Cir.1986) (applying Louisiana law); Holy Properties Limited, L.P. v. Kenneth Cole Productions, Inc., 661 N.E.2d 694 (Ct. App. N.Y. 1995) Marynick v. Bockelmann, 773 S.W.2d 665, 673 (Tex.App.1989), reversed on other grounds, 788 S.W.2d 569 (Tex.1990).

[2] See Stephanie G. Flynn, *Duty to Mitigate Damages Upon a Tenant's Abandonment*, 34 Real Prop. Prob. & Tr. J. 721 (2000) (discussing the history and application of the duty to mitigate); Edwin Smith, Jr., Comment, *Extending the Contractual Duty to Mitigate Damages to Landlords When a Tenant Abandons the Lease*, 42 Baylor L.Rev. 553, 558 (1990) (noting that twenty-eight states have adopted the duty to mitigate, at least in the context of residential leases).

Dear Jack:

As you know, business has been terrible at my present location. I have decided to relocate a few blocks away in the old Haley Building, and enclose the keys to my present premises. By the way, I have a friend who might be interested in leasing this space for a hair salon.

Sincerely,

A.B. Drugger

Mr. Lesser responded with the following letter:

Dear A.B.:

I have received your keys. Please be advised that I consider the lease fully binding and will hold you legally responsible for all your obligations thereunder.

Very truly yours,

Jack Lesser

Lesser never followed up on Drugger's friend as a possible substitute tenant. In the next few months, however, Lesser did attempt to relet the abandoned premises by making it known among his acquaintances that he was looking for a new tenant. Unfortunately, Lesser had little luck. He rented the premises for a few weeks to a local political organization which used it as temporary headquarters for an election campaign. Lesser has also used a part of the premises for the storage of some old office equipment he owned. He has placed a "for rent" sign in the window but this has elicited little response. Lesser has taken no other action to rent the premises. He was able, however, to rent another vacant space on the ground floor of the Jackson Building to National Drugs, Inc., a cut-rate drug outfit. National was not interested in the premises originally rented to Drugger since they were too small.

Lesser now comes to you for advice. Before advising him, consider the following materials.

### 3. MATERIALS FOR SOLUTION OF PRINCIPAL PROBLEM

**Reid v. Mutual of Omaha Insurance Co.**
Supreme Court of Utah, 1989.
776 P.2d 896.

■ ZIMMERMAN, JUSTICE:

Mutual of Omaha ("Mutual") appeals from a judgment in a nonjury trial finding it liable to Mervin and Ethna Reid ("the Reids") for breach of a lease for office space. Mutual contends that the trial court erred in rejecting its claim that the Reids had constructively evicted Mutual and that it also erred in calculating the damages due the Reids. We affirm the judgment of liability for breach of the lease but reverse in part on the determination of damages.

In September of 1980, Mutual, as tenant, and the Reids, as landlord, entered a five-year lease agreement for office space at a monthly rate of $1,100. The lease term was to end in October of 1985. Mutual took possession of the premises, which it used to conduct an insurance sales business. Soon afterward, another tenant moved into adjoining space in the building. The other tenant, Intermountain Marketing ("Intermountain"), operated a door-to-door cookware sales business and used its office space to train its large sales force. Mutual made numerous complaints to the Reids that Intermountain's personnel were excessively noisy, occupied all of Mutual's parking spaces, and otherwise interfered with Mutual's business. Mutual felt that the Reids did not respond adequately to the frequent complaints and, in February of 1982, gave notice and vacated the premises. In April of 1982, the Reids filed suit, claiming that Mutual had breached the lease and was liable for the monthly rental for the three and a half years remaining on the five-year term. Mutual counterclaimed, contending that it had been constructively evicted by the Reids' failure to control the activities of Intermountain. While the litigation was proceeding, the Reids remodeled the premises at issue and leased them to Intermountain for the remainder of the five-year term at a rate comparable to what Mutual had been paying. However, in November of 1982, Intermountain vacated and declared bankruptcy; from that point through the date of trial, the premises were left vacant.

A bench trial was held in July of 1983. After hearing extensive evidence, the court found against Mutual on its counterclaim for constructive eviction, concluding that the noisy conditions were not sufficiently disruptive to amount to a constructive eviction. The court found that Mutual had breached the lease agreement and awarded the Reids damages under the terms of the agreement. These consisted of the total of the unpaid rents, including both those that had accrued through the date of trial and those that would accrue from the date of trial through the end of the lease term in 1985, less rents actually received from Intermountain during the time it occupied the Mutual premises, plus the costs of reletting and attorney fees.

Before this Court, Mutual attacks the trial court's failure to find for it on the constructive eviction counterclaim. In the event that challenge fails, Mutual contends that the trial court erred in calculating the damages due from Mutual to the Reids.

[In this part of the opinion, the court rejected Mutual's constructive eviction argument and affirmed Mutual's breach of the lease by abandoning the premises and failing to pay rent after February of 1982.]

Mutual next argues that even if the trial court properly rejected its constructive eviction claim and found it to have breached the lease, the Reids were entitled only to damages for nonpayment of rents measured by those rents that came due between the date of Mutual's last payment and the date of the reletting to Intermountain. Mutual contends that the trial court erred when it included in the measure of damages the unpaid rents that accrued after this reletting.

In support of this argument, Mutual relies upon the common law doctrine of "surrender and acceptance." Under that doctrine, when a tenant surrenders the premises to a landlord before a lease term expires and the landlord accepts that surrender, the tenant is no longer in privity of estate with the landlord and therefore has no obligation to pay any rents accruing after the date of the acceptance. Phrased in contract law parlance, the lease is treated as having been rescinded or terminated by mutual agreement. Mutual contends that this common law doctrine was applicable under the terms of the lease agreement. It then argues that the Reids' actions in remodeling the premises and reletting them to Intermountain amounted to an acceptance of surrender that relieved Mutual of its obligation to pay further rents. At common law, the critical issue in applying the doctrine of surrender and acceptance is determining whether the landlord intended to accept the surrender. This intention may be express or implied. The lease agreement between the Reids and Mutual deals specifically with the question of how the functional equivalent of an intent to accept a surrender, denominated an "election by Landlord to terminate this Lease," would be manifested. Paragraph 19 of the lease agreement states in part:

> If Tenant shall make default in the payment of the rent reserved ... or if the leased premises ... shall be abandoned or vacated ... then Landlord, in addition to any other rights or remedies it may have, shall have the immediate right of re-entry.... *No such re-entry or taking possession of the premises by Landlord shall be construed as an election by Landlord to terminate this Lease unless the termination thereof be decreed by a court of competent jurisdiction or stated specifically by the Landlord in writing addressed to Tenant.* (Emphasis added.)

It is undisputed that the Reids did not elect to terminate the lease (or in common law terminology, accept the surrender) by means of a writing addressed to Mutual. But Mutual argues that the language referring to a termination of the lease "decreed by a court" should be read to mean that a termination has occurred if a court, applying the common law rules for determining the landlord's intentions from its actions, concludes that there has been an acceptance of a surrender. Mutual then argues that the trial court erred when it failed to decree that the Reids' conduct constituted an acceptance of surrender that terminated the lease. At common law, a tenant raising the affirmative defense of surrender and acceptance has the burden of proving the landlord's intent to accept the surrender. And the determination of the landlord's intention is a question of fact. Here, then, when the trial court found that the Reids' actions amounted to a reentry and "reletting without termination," it effectively determined that Mutual had not met its burden of proof on the factual question of intent. Therefore, on appeal Mutual has the burden of marshalling the supporting evidence and then demonstrating that the trial court's finding on this point lacks adequate record support under the "clearly erroneous" standard. We conclude that Mutual has not met that burden. Our previous cases have held that conduct such as the Reids'—reentering, remodeling, and reletting the premises—is relevant to, but not conclusive evidence of, an intent to accept the surrendered premises and terminate the lease.[3] *See John C. Cutler Ass'n v. DeJay Stores, Inc.,* 3 Utah 2d at 111–12, 279 P.2d at 702–03. We affirm the trial court's finding that the Reids' conduct was a reletting without termination.

Mutual next contends that even if it was liable for some rents accruing after the premises had been relet, the trial court erred in fixing the amount.

Mutual's challenge relates to that portion of the award dealing with rents that were to accrue between the date of trial and the end of the original lease term. Mutual contends that the judgment entered fails to ensure that the Reids would mitigate their damages by reletting the premises.

We are thus faced with the question of whether Utah law imposes a duty upon landlords to mitigate their damages by reletting premises after a tenant has wrongfully vacated and defaulted on the covenant to pay rent. There is no controlling statute, and our research has revealed no case in which we have directly addressed the question. However, the concept of landlords mitigating their damages by reletting has been mentioned in several cases where the doctrine of surrender and acceptance was at issue.[4] In those cases, the Court spoke favorably of, at a minimum, allowing landlords to mitigate by reletting without the risk

---

[3] As we explain in the latter part of this opinion, lessors in the Reids' position have what effectively amounts to an obligation to mitigate damages by seeking to relet the premises. That duty to mitigate, which reflects general principles of contract law, was not expressly considered in our older cases in which reletting was viewed as relevant, although not conclusive, evidence of the acceptance of surrender. Our ruling today requires a reevaluation of those cases. Because we now hold that there is a duty to relet, it follows that it would be unfair and inappropriate to treat such reletting alone as sufficient evidence to show that the landlord intended to accept a surrender of the premises and free the tenant from all obligation for future rents. *See* Humbach, *The Common-Law Conception of Leasing: Mitigating Habitability, and Dependence of Covenants,* 60 Wash.U.L.Q. 1213, 1240–56 (1983) [hereinafter Humbach, 60 Wash.U.L.Q.]. . . .

[M]odern landlord-tenant relationships, while steeped in the tradition of ancient property law, have taken on substantive characteristics so similar to commercial transactions that certain of the legal principles developed in the law of contracts in the context of commercial transactions are now appropriately applied to leases, regardless of whether use is made of labels derived from the law of property conveyance or of contract. Our concern with substance rather than form is reflected in the law we apply in the present case with respect to the manner in which a lease may be terminated and to the requirement that a nonbreaching party must act reasonably to mitigate damages. Whether these rules are labeled as deriving from property law or contract law is of little concern.

[4] The concept of mitigation of damages is grounded in traditional contract law principles and is known as the doctrine of "avoidable consequences." Under this doctrine, a party injured by a breach of contract may not recover damages that he or she, with reasonable effort, could have avoided. *See Angelos v. First Interstate Bank,* 671 P.2d 772, 777 (Utah 1983); Restatement (Second) of Contract § 350 (1981); 5A Corbin, *Corbin on Contracts* § 1039 (1964).

that such mitigation efforts would be treated as an acceptance of surrender. [citations omitted]

In looking to the law of other jurisdictions, we find a split of authority on the question. In states following what has been described as the traditional rule, landlords are not required to mitigate by reletting. See Restatement (Second) of Property § 12.1(3) (1977). A number of states have recently reconsidered the traditional view and, following what has been termed a trend rule, have imposed by statute or judicial decision some obligation to relet. *See, e.g., Schneiker v. Gordon,* 732 P.2d 603 (Colo.1987); *Sommer v. Kridel,* 74 N.J. 446, 378 A.2d 767 (1977). These two competing rules reflect an evolution in the underlying doctrinal approach that has begun to have an impact on many issues of landlord-tenant law. As commentators have noted, the traditional rule imposing no duty to mitigate has its roots in ancient property law concepts under which leaseholds are considered estates in land. The trend rule reflects the more modern view that leases are essentially commercial transactions, contractual in nature. *See Kwall, Retained Jurisdiction in Damage Actions Based on Anticipatory Breach: A Missing Link in Landlord-Tenant Law,* 37 Case W.Res.L.Rev. 273, 274 (1986).

A number of justifications have been advanced in support of the traditional rule. One is that forcing a landlord to mitigate is unfair when the conduct constituting mitigation might be viewed as evidence of an acceptance of a surrender, a result not actually in accordance with the landlord's intentions. Another justification is equitable in nature: it is unfair to allow the breaching tenant to force on the innocent landlord an affirmative duty to seek out new tenants and perhaps let the premises to tenants not entirely suitable in the landlord's subjective view. A final ground offered for retaining the traditional rule is simply that it is of long standing and in conformance with underlying property law notions. *See generally* 21 A.L.R.3d at 548–49.

The first of these justifications for the traditional rule can be easily obviated. As already noted, there is no reason to permit mitigating conduct to be used as indicia of an intent to accept a surrender. As for the second, there is some validity to the concern that the breaching party should not be able to force its landlord to seek other tenants on pain of losing bargained-for rents. However, we think this point is outweighed by the policy arguments in favor of the modern rule, and we think any unfairness to the landlord can largely be eliminated by careful application of a rule requiring reasonable mitigation efforts only.

As for the final justification offered for the traditional rule, it is true that that rule reflects ancient property law concepts; however, those concepts themselves are no longer consonant with most modern landlord-tenant relationships. First, the ancient law of leaseholds was developed in the context of leases of agricultural land. Those leases generally ran from growing season to growing season. If a tenant vacated after planting time had passed, it was unrealistic to expect the landlord to find a new tenant interested in leasing land that was essentially useless for the remainder of the term. Therefore, a rule requiring mitigation by reletting would have been highly artificial in the practical context of most landlord-tenant relationships. But today, agricultural leases constitute only a minor part of the modern leasing market. Growing seasons are irrelevant to the leasing of residential premises and commercial buildings. Second, the traditional rule also stems from the ancient concept that a leasehold is a complete conveyance of a real property interest such that the tenant becomes, for a defined term of years, the owner of the property and the landlord simply has no present ownership interest in the property during the lease term. It would be logically inconsistent with this concept of a lease to impose upon the landlord, who has no interest in the property during the lease term, the obligation to relet the property for the remainder of that term. Today, leases are generally viewed as commercial transactions in which the landlord retains the estate but permits its use by another on specified conditions; leases are seldom seen as complete conveyances of the underlying property for a specified term. Our unlawful detainer statutes *sub silentio* recognize this changed view of a landlord's retained interest in the property when they authorize a landlord to evict a breaching tenant and reenter and relet the premises in very short order. *See* Utah Code Ann. §§ 78–36–8.5, 78–36–12, 78–36–12.6 (1987).

In sum, the principal justifications given to support the traditional rule are to a large extent anachronistic. In contrast, we find persuasive the reasons advanced in support of the trend rule requiring the landlord to take steps to mitigate its losses. For example, the economies of both the state and the nation benefit from a rule that encourages the reletting of premises, which returns them to productive use, rather than permitting a landlord to let them sit idle while it seeks rents from the breaching tenant.

In addition, the trend rule is more in keeping with the current policy disfavoring contractual penalties. Damages recoverable under a liquidated damages provision in a contract will generally be limited to an amount that represents a reasonable estimation, made at the time the contract was drafted, of what would be necessary to compensate the nonbreaching party for losses caused by the breach. This policy is based on the view that any liquidated damages provision not so limited results in the imposition of a penalty on the breaching party that is not permitted.... Similarly, allowing a landlord to leave property idle when it could be profitably leased and force an absent tenant to pay rent for that idled property permits the landlord to recover more damages than it may reasonably require to be compensated for the tenant's breach. This is analogous to imposing a disfavored penalty upon the tenant.

Finally, the trend rule is more in line with the policy favoring mitigation that we have adopted in other areas of the law. For example, mitigation is generally required when damages are sought in tort cases, as well as in contract cases.

In light of these considerations, we conclude that a mitigation requirement is generally appropriate in the context of modern landlord-tenant transactions, and we join those courts now following the trend rule described above. We hold that a landlord who seeks to hold a breaching tenant liable for unpaid rents has an obligation to take commercially reasonable steps to mitigate its losses, which ordinarily means that the landlord must seek to relet the premises.

Certain aspects of our holding require some elaboration. Because a landlord may occasionally bring an action for unpaid rents and other amounts due before the lease term expires, as happened here, it is appropriate that we spell out how the mitigation obligation is to be handled, both as to past due and future accruing rents. If the trial of the landlord's action occurs after the end of the lease agreement, the landlord then has the burden of proving both the amount of damages and the fact that it took appropriate mitigation efforts. Assuming the landlord carries this burden, a judgment and damage award on the whole cause arising out of the breach can then be rendered. However, if the trial occurs before the end of the lease term, a judgment cannot be entered for rents that have not yet accrued; any damage award must be limited to taking account only of rents that have accrued as of the trial date. To recover for later accruing rents, the landlord must bring a supplemental proceeding or proceedings in which it can prove that additional rents have accrued and that reasonable efforts to mitigate those losses have been taken.

Another point warranting clarification is the affirmative nature of the mitigation obligation. Some courts imposing a mitigation requirement do not require landlords to show active efforts to relet; instead, the landlord can carry its proof-of-mitigation burden simply by showing that it was passively receptive to opportunities to relet the premises. We conclude that this minimal showing does not serve the policies that underlie the adoption of a mitigation requirement. We prefer to follow those courts that have required that the landlord take positive steps reasonably calculated to effect a reletting of the premises. [citations omitted] Only by following such a course can we ensure that serious efforts are made to redeploy the rental property in a productive fashion by those who are best able to accomplish that end and who are also best able to prove that required mitigation efforts have been carried out.

A further word about the standard by which a landlord's efforts to mitigate are to be measured: the standard is one of objective commercial reasonableness. *See Olsen v. Country Club Sports, Inc.,* 110 Idaho at 794, 718 P.2d at 1232. A landlord is obligated to take such steps as would be expected of a reasonable landlord letting out a similar property in the same market conditions. Obviously, the objective commercial reasonableness of mitigation efforts is a fact question that depends heavily on the particularities of the property and the relevant market at the pertinent point in time.

Since we have imposed on the landlord an affirmative obligation to seek a new tenant, it is appropriate that costs reasonably incurred in readying the property and in reletting or attempting to relet be added to the amount recoverable from the breaching tenant. . . . Such costs may include not only expenses incurred in seeking new tenants, but also costs of repairs or alterations of the premises reasonably necessary to successfully relet them. *See Illinois Landlords' Duty,* 34 DePaul L.Rev. at 1059. As in the present case, it is not uncommon for property, particularly commercial property, to be modified to meet the needs of a new tenant. So long as the expenses incurred in the process of reletting, or attempting to relet the property are commercially reasonable, they should be borne by the breaching tenant. *See Illinois Landlords' Duty,* 34 DePaul L.Rev. at 1058–61.

Finally, our ruling that damage awards must take into account only those rents that have actually accrued as of the time of trial deserves explanation. If the trial is held after the lease term has expired, it is a relatively simple matter to assess the landlord's recoverable losses by taking into account the degree to which the landlord has fulfilled its duty to mitigate. However, when the term has not expired by the time of trial, it is impossible to evaluate the adequacy of the mitigation efforts the landlord will have to make in the future with respect to rents that have not yet come due, and it is equally impossible to determine whether those efforts will be successful in reducing losses from future accruing rents. Some means must be devised to permit recovery of actual losses occasioned by future accruing rents while ensuring that the landlord fulfills its duty to mitigate losses.

Commentators have described three basic approaches to this problem of accounting for rental obligations accruing after the date of trial. They are the multiple-cause-of-action rule, the anticipatory-breach doctrine, and the retained-jurisdiction concept. We conclude that only one of these approaches, that of retained jurisdiction, adequately accommodates the values we judge to be important in fashioning a remedy.

The first of these approaches to the problem is labeled the multiple-cause-of-action approach. Under it, the landlord can recover only those rents that have accrued through the time of trial. Once a judgment is entered, the case is closed and the court's jurisdiction over the parties and subject matter ends. To recover additional rents that may accrue after trial, the landlord must initiate a new suit.[5] *See* Kwall, 37 Case W.Res.L.Rev. at 274–75.

---

[5] The commentators also note a variant of this approach, which may be termed a single-recovery rule, under which the landlord is limited to a single remedy for all obligations under the lease agreement. The landlord must elect between waiting to bring suit after the term has ended or bringing suit earlier and effectively forfeiting later accruing rents. *See* Kwall, *Retained*

We find this approach unsatisfactory since it requires a landlord to either forego expected periodic rental payments and bring suit for a lump sum at the end of the lease term or undertake the expenses and difficulties of bringing several separate claims over the length of the term. With either choice, the landlord risks having the tenant leave the court's geographical jurisdiction.

A number of courts have sought to avoid the problems of the multiple-cause-of-action approach by following one of the two other approaches. The first is to apply to leases the contract doctrine of anticipatory breach. *See generally* Restatement (Second) of Contracts §§ 250–57 (1981); A. Corbin, *Corbin on Contracts* § 959 (1964). Under this approach, the landlord can bring suit prior to the expiration of the lease term and obtain a recovery that includes not only already accrued rents, but also an amount that represents the present value of the amount by which the total of the future rents due under the lease exceeds the fair market rental value of the premises over the same period. *See Speedee Mart, Inc. v. Stovall*, 664 S.W.2d 174, 177 (Tex.Ct.App.1983). This permits an immediate resolution of the damage issue without placing the landlord at risk of not being able to successfully prosecute further actions against the tenant for the future accruing rents.

We conclude that the anticipatory-breach approach does not go far enough in avoiding the problem of speculative damages. It requires a trial court to award what amounts to speculative damages because the damages are to be based on projections as to the future fair market rental value of the premises throughout the term of the lease, which may be for years. Such projections also will inevitably be imperfect in accounting for the landlord's real success at reletting the premises.[6] Thus, this approach sacrifices too much to uncertainty for both the landlord and the tenant in the interest of achieving a quick resolution. We conclude that such a trade-off is unnecessary in light of the availability of a better approach.

The third approach, and the one we adopt, is that of retained jurisdiction. This approach, like the multiple-course-of-action approach, allows the landlord to obtain a judgment soon after the tenant's breach; but rather than requiring the institution of an entirely new suit (or suits) to collect future rents, it permits the court to retain jurisdiction over the parties and the subject matter and enter new damage awards as additional rents accrue. *See* Kwall, 37 Case W.Res.L.Rev. at 328–38. And, unlike the anticipatory-breach approach, this approach does not depend on speculative projections of future events that may lead to under or

---

*Jurisdiction in Damage Actions Based on Anticipatory Breach: A Missing Link in Landlord-Tenant Law*, 37 Case W.Res.L.Rev. 273, 330 (1986); *Humbach*, 60 Wash.U.L.Q. at 1251. We reject this variant for much the same reasons we find the multiple-cause-of-action approach to be unsatisfactory.

6. Some courts following the anticipatory-breach approach have dealt with the concern over awarding speculative damages by arbitrarily limiting the landlord's recovery to rents accruing in a period shorter than the lease term, a period for which damages can be projected with some certainty. *See* Kwall, 37 Case W.Res.L.Rev. at 285–89; 2 Powell, *The Law of Real Property* ¶ 249[1], at 17–65. We find this stunted recovery rule also to be unsatisfactory.

overestimation of a landlord's losses. Damage awards will be based on past events only and will take into account the landlord's mitigation efforts. This approach, therefore, should provide an incentive to the landlord to see that its mitigation duty is fulfilled, lest it be denied some of the damages it would otherwise be entitled to.

The retained jurisdiction approach should be implemented as follows: When a landlord's action for breach of a lease is tried before the expiration of the lease term and the finder of fact determines that the tenant has breached the lease, the amount awarded should represent only those rents that have come due as of the time of trial. This judgment will be immediately enforceable. Rents accruing after the trial, on the other hand, may be recovered through what will amount to rather brief supplemental proceedings. To provide this remedy, the trial court should retain jurisdiction of the underlying action.[7] After additional unpaid rents have accrued, the landlord may return to the court, without the risks and burdens that attend the filing of a new action, for a simple determination of additional losses suffered through the date of the supplemental proceedings and whether the landlord has fulfilled its ongoing duty to mitigate. Under the law-of-the-case doctrine, the initial determination of the tenant's liability would govern in any supplemental proceedings.

As Professor Kwall has observed, the concept of retained jurisdiction has been used effectively in other areas of the law where a fair resolution of the matter requires that a mechanism be available for accommodating future developments. Examples include divorce adjudications, probate matters, providing for specific enforcement of certain long-term contracts other than realty leases, and workers' compensation matters. Kwall, 37 Case W.Res.L.Rev. at 291–328. It should be equally effective in the lease context and is well worth the minimal additional burden it may impose on the parties. *See* Kwall, 37 Case W.Res.L.Rev. at 328–38.

Applying the retained-jurisdiction approach to the present case requires a vacation of part of the judgment and a remand for further proceedings. The trial court found that the Reids had mitigated their damages through the time of trial. We have affirmed that finding and therefore affirm the judgment to the extent that it is based on rents that accrued through the date of trial. The second part of the court's order, however, apparently awarded the Reids damages for rents that accrued after the trial, without imposing on the Reids a continuing affirmative duty to mitigate these subsequently accruing losses. Therefore, that portion of the judgment must be reversed. However, since the trial court continues to have jurisdiction over the case insofar as it relates to rents accruing after trial, the Reids are free to return to the court and reduce to judgment additional damages they may have incurred as a result of

---

[7] Because the entire claim of the landlord against the tenant as it had accrued through the time of trial would be adjudicated in the initial judgment, it would be final for purposes of appeal.

rents accruing over the remainder of the now-expired term or additional costs they incurred as a result of their efforts to mitigate. Of course, the Reids must prove at such a proceeding that they have fulfilled their ongoing duty to mitigate.

## Isbey v. Crews
Court of Appeals of North Carolina, 1981.
55 N.C.App. 47, 284 S.E.2d 534.

This is a civil action wherein plaintiffs, lessors, seek to recover from the defendants, lessees, $2,867.33 because of the latter's alleged breach of a rental agreement.

Plaintiffs moved for summary judgment. The record discloses the following uncontroverted facts:

Plaintiffs and defendants entered into a lease on 14 September 1976 by which the plaintiffs agreed to lease to defendants certain premises located in Asheville. The lease was for a renewable term of five years and was for a rental sum of $172,040, "said rental due and payable in . . . equal monthly installments of . . . ($2867.33) . . . , payable in advance on the first day possession of said premises is delivered to [defendants] and on the same day of each month thereafter during the term of this lease. . . ." The lease also contained the following relevant provisions:

1. The leased premises shall be used and occupied by Lessee as and only for physicians' offices and for a dialysis unit and for no other purposes whatsoever without Lessor's written consent . . .

. . .

4. The Lessee shall not assign this lease or sublet the premises or any part thereof, or use the same or any part thereof, or permit the same, or any part thereof, to be used for any other purpose than as above stipulated, or make any alterations therein, or additions thereto, without the written consent of the Lessor . . .

From the time defendants moved into the building and including 15 August 1980, the defendants made all of the rental payments provided for in the lease. After operating a dialysis facility at the premises leased by plaintiffs, the defendants moved out on 22 May 1980 and acquired other premises. After the defendants vacated the premises, they sought plaintiffs' permission to sublet the property to a company which sells and distributes medical supplies. Plaintiffs refused to permit the defendants to sublet the premises. Plaintiffs thereupon brought this action to recover from defendants the sum of $2,867.33 (plus interest) which the defendants allegedly were required to pay under the lease as rent due on 17 September 1980. From summary judgment awarding plaintiffs $2,867.33 plus interest, defendants appealed.

■ HEDRICK, JUDGE.

Defendants assign as error the court's entry of summary judgment. Summary judgment is properly entered if there is no genuine issue of material fact, but a motion for summary judgment must be denied if there is such an issue of fact. An issue of fact is material, for the purpose of determining whether a motion for summary judgment should be denied, if the facts as alleged would constitute a legal defense or would affect the result of the action or would prevent the party against whom it is resolved from prevailing in the action. In the present case, defendants argue that there were two issues of material fact which should have precluded summary judgment.

Defendants first argue that there was an issue of material fact as to whether plaintiffs unreasonably refused to consent to the sublease proposed by defendants. Defendants contend this issue is material because an unreasonable refusal would constitute a material breach, by plaintiffs, of the lease agreement and would thereby entitle defendants to terminate the lease and their obligations to pay rent thereunder. Defendants would have us read into the lease agreement an obligation on the part of the lessor not to *unreasonably* withhold consent to a subtenant proposed by the lessee.

A tenant for an estate for years, however, may be *absolutely* barred from transferring his term by either assignment or sublease if there is an express covenant in the lease forbidding assignments and subletting. J. Webster, *Real Estate Law in North Carolina* § 70 (1971); *Rogers v. Hall*, 227 N.C. 363, 42 S.E.2d 347 (1947). A fortiori, a tenant may be subjected to a lesser restraint than an absolute prohibition on alienation, to wit, an express covenant which allows the tenant to transfer his term if he receives the lessor's consent, but which bars the tenant from such a transfer if the lessor reasonably or unreasonably withholds his consent. The lease in the present case contains such an express restraint, forbidding the lessee from alienating the premises "without the written consent of the lessor;" nowhere did the lease state that such consent would not be unreasonably withheld. If it had, the lessor's withholding of consent could not be based on arbitrary considerations of personal taste, sensibility, or convenience, however honest the judgment. *Jones v. Andy Griffith Products, Inc.*, 35 N.C.App. 170, 241 S.E.2d 140, *disc. rev. denied*, 295 N.C. 90, 244 S.E.2d 258 (1978). The lessor plaintiffs in the present case, however, did not relinquish their rights to exert their own subjective criteria in deciding who could or could not be subtenants. A court does not insert terms into a contract when the parties elected to omit such terms, *Taylor v. Gibbs*, 268 N.C. 363, 150 S.E.2d 506 (1966), and we will not here insert a requirement that the lessor not unreasonably withhold his consent.

We hold, therefore, that the record discloses that the defendants breached their agreement with plaintiffs when they refused to make the rental payment which fell due on 17 September 1980, and plaintiffs are entitled as a matter of law to recover damages for such breach.

Defendants argue there is a genuine issue of material fact as to the amount of damages plaintiffs are entitled to recover for any breach. This argument presents the question of how damages are to be computed when a tenant abandons the leased premises and fails to pay rent therefor, in breach of the lease, and the lease agreement contemplates, as here, that the premises will be occupied by a specific type of tenant and will be put exclusively to a specific kind of use. In computing breach of contract damages,

> the general rule is that a party who is injured by breach of contract is entitled to compensation for the injury sustained and is entitled to be placed, as near as this can be done in money, in the same position he would have occupied if the contract had been performed. Stated generally, the measure of damages for the breach of a contract is the amount which would have been received if the contract had been performed as made, which means the value of the contract, including the profits and advantages which are its direct results and fruits.

*Perkins v. Langdon*, 237 N.C. 159, 169–70, 74 S.E.2d 634, 643 (1953). This formulation is especially relevant in the present case insofar as it takes account of the possibly peculiar value to plaintiffs of having the *defendants* perform their obligations under the lease agreement.

With respect to the question of mitigation of damages, the law in North Carolina is that the nonbreaching party to a lease contract has a duty to mitigate his damages upon breach of such contract. *Weinstein v. Griffin*, 241 N.C. 161, 84 S.E.2d 549 (1954); *Monger v. Lutterloh*, 195 N.C. 274, 142 S.E. 12 (1928); J. Webster, *Real Estate Law in North Carolina* § 225 (1971). Hence, when the tenant abandons the leased premises and fails to pay rent, the landlord can recover only those damages which he could not with reasonable diligence avoid by reletting the premises.... If the landlord fails to use such reasonable diligence, his recovery as against the tenant will be limited to the difference between what he would have received had the lease agreement been performed, and the fair market value of what he could have received had he used reasonable diligence to mitigate.... If the landlord does mitigate by reletting, his recovery will consist of what he would have received had the lease been performed, less the net value of what he did receive from reletting during the relevant contract period.... These rules can take account of the peculiar advantages the lessor contracted for under the lease, and any quantifiable disadvantages which the lessor may suffer from having as his tenant someone other than the lessee with whom he contracted; hence, even if held to a duty to mitigate, the lessor may be made whole.

While the nonbreaching party is under duty to use reasonable diligence to minimize the loss occasioned by the injuring party's breach of contract, the burden is on the breaching party to prove that the nonbreaching party failed to exercise reasonable diligence to minimize the loss. *First National Pictures Distributing Corp. v. Seawell,* 205 N.C. 359, 171 S.E. 354 (1933). In the present case the plaintiffs supported their motion for summary judgment with evidentiary matter which disclosed that there was no genuine issue with respect to the defendants' breach and to the amount of damages suffered by plaintiffs because of such breach. The defendants, on the other hand, offered in opposition to the motion for summary judgment no evidence with respect to plaintiffs' failure to exercise reasonable diligence to mitigate their loss. In the affidavit filed in opposition to the motion for summary judgment the defendants merely stated

> [t]he space in question has remained vacant since we moved out on May 22, 1980 and as far as I have been able to determine no one, particularly Dr. Isbey or Mr. Morris, has made any effort to rent the space since the termination of our lease on September 17, 1980.

This statement is nothing more than the conclusion of the affiant. The record is devoid of any evidence that the plaintiffs failed to exercise reasonable diligence to relet the premises after the defendants breached the contract. We hold the record discloses no genuine issue of material fact as to defendants' breach or as to the amount of loss suffered by plaintiffs as a result of such breach.

Affirmed.

## Ruud v. Larson

Supreme Court of North Dakota, 1986.
392 N.W.2d 62.

■ GIERKE, JUSTICE.

Raymond and Yvonne Larson [Larson] appeal from a district court judgment awarding damages to Arthur and Ruby Ruud [Ruud] for Larson's breach of a real estate lease. We affirm.

In 1966, Ruud executed a ten-year lease to Raymond Larson, Obed Oas, and Judith Oas on a parcel of property on Main Avenue in Fargo. Larson constructed and operated a car wash and gasoline sales outlet on the property. In 1976, Ruud leased the property to Larson for another ten-year term. Larson failed to make timely rental payments for January and February 1982 and failed to pay the 1981 property taxes as required by the lease. Ruud commenced this action in March 1982.

Ruud's action against Larson for breach of the lease was tried to the court. The trial court found that Larson had breached the lease by failing to pay real estate taxes for 1981, 1982, 1983, 1984, and the first six months of 1985; failing to make rental payments totalling $24,500; failing to provide liability insurance; and failing to keep the property in good repair. The court also specifically found that Ruud had made diligent, good faith efforts to sublease the property and thereby mitigate damages. The trial court awarded damages for the breach and ordered Larson to pay Ruud's attorney's fees, as provided under the terms of the lease.

The sole issue raised by Larson on appeal is whether the trial court's finding that Ruud made a good faith effort to mitigate damages is clearly erroneous.

We have previously held that a landlord generally has a duty to mitigate the damages which arise out of his tenant's default. *MAR-SON, Inc. v. Terwaho Enterprises, Inc.*, 259 N.W.2d 289, 291 (N.D.1977). Once the tenant defaults, the landlord has a duty to make a good faith effort, expending reasonable effort and diligence, to relet the property. *MAR-SON, supra*, 259 N.W.2d at 292. The burden is upon the tenant to establish a lack of good faith by the landlord; in the absence of such a showing, it will be presumed that the landlord acted in good faith. *MAR-SON, supra*, 259 N.W.2d at 293. The determination whether the landlord has made a good faith effort to mitigate damages is a finding of fact which will be set aside on appeal only if it is clearly erroneous. *MAR-SON, supra*, 259 N.W.2d at 292. A finding of fact is clearly erroneous when, although there may be some evidence to support it, the reviewing court on the entire evidence is left with a definite and firm conviction that a mistake has been made. *Wastvedt v. State*, 371 N.W.2d 330, 334 (N.D.1985).

Prior to trial, counsel for Ruud and Larson agreed to withhold further proceedings in this action because Larson's corporation, Mid-State Oil Company, had filed for bankruptcy.[8] On July 16, 1982, the bankruptcy court approved the sale of substantially all of Mid-State's assets to Charles Luna. According to testimony by Ruud's counsel, Larson thereafter proposed a possible sublease of the Main Avenue property to Luna, with Larson agreeing to pay the tax arrearages due under the lease.

Larson's counsel drafted and forwarded to Ruud a proposed sublease. Ruud's counsel, dissatisfied with certain language in the proposed sublease, redrafted it and sent a signed copy to Larson's counsel.[9] Although the sublease did not mention back taxes, the cover letter to counsel reiterated that the sublease was contingent upon Larson's agreement to pay the tax arrearages. Larson did not sign the sublease, but instead responded by making three alternative counter-proposals, offering to purchase the land from Ruud or to sell the building

---

[8] Matters were significantly complicated at this point because Mid-State was claiming an interest in the leased premises and the building thereon.

[9] The rejection of Larson's proposed sublease by Ruud's counsel was unrelated to the agreement to pay tax arrearages. The sublease prepared by Larson's counsel ran from Mid-State to Luna, and stated that the original 1976 lease to Larson had been assigned to Mid-State. Because Ruud consistently claimed that Mid-State had no interest in the property, the sublease was rejected and redrafted by Ruud's counsel to reflect Ruud's understanding of the agreement reached by the parties.

to Ruud. The counter-proposals were rejected, and the property was never subleased to Luna.

Larson contends that Ruud refused to sublease the property to Luna unless Larson agreed to pay the back taxes and attorney's fees, and that, as a matter of law, a landlord may not condition his consent to a sublease upon payment of all arrearages under the lease. Ruud concedes for the purposes of this case that in mitigating damages a landlord cannot make approval of a sublease contingent upon payment of all arrearages, but he claims that this principle has no application to this case.

The Luna sublease agreement was negotiated by counsel for the parties. As part of that agreement, Larson *agreed* to pay tax arrearages and attorney's fees as required by the lease. This is not, therefore, a case in which the tenant has located and presented a sublessee, and the landlord has refused to agree to the sublease until all arrearages are paid. Rather, there were negotiations between counsel for the parties, and an agreement was reached which would provide a new tenant to assume Larson's responsibility under the lease.

The record does not indicate that Larson ever expressly requested that Ruud consent to a sublease to Luna without requiring payment of the arrearages. Upon receiving the executed sublease agreement from Ruud, Larson did not request that he be released from his agreement to pay the arrearages. He refused to sign the agreement, and instead made a written counter-proposal offering to purchase the land from Ruud or to sell the building thereon to Ruud.

The trial court specifically found that Ruud made a good faith effort to arrange a sublease of the property to Luna, but that Larson decided not to proceed with this sublease. Having reviewed the record, we conclude that this finding is not clearly erroneous.

When the Luna sublease could not be arranged, Larson made other attempts to sublease the property through a Fargo realtor. Because Ruud had been threatened by Mid-State's bankruptcy counsel with a contempt citation if Ruud interfered with the property, Ruud made no attempt to sublease the property until the bankruptcy court ruled in November 1983 that Mid-State had no interest in the property. Immediately after the bankruptcy court's ruling, Ruud took possession of the property and completed necessary repairs and cleaning. Ruud made diligent attempts to rent the property, including over 140 contacts with approximately 50 prospective tenants. Ruud received no written offers to lease the property.

Larson contends that Ruud's failure to hire a real estate agent and seeking an increased rent when attempting to relet the property established a lack of good faith.

Although failure to hire a real estate agent may be a factor to consider in determining whether a landlord has made a good faith effort to relet the premises, it does not, as a matter of law, bar the landlord's claim. *See Kamada v. RX Group Limited,* 639 S.W.2d 146, 149 (Mo.Ct.App.1982). The record establishes that Larson employed a real estate agent who was unsuccessful in reletting the property, and Larson has presented no evidence to show that Ruud's use of a real estate agent would have resulted in a reletting of the property. *See Kamada, supra.* The record documents the extensive efforts of Ruud in attempting to secure a new tenant.

Larson contends that Ruud's attempt to secure a higher rental establishes lack of good faith. The record indicates that Ruud sought to relet the property at $1,200 per month, whereas the 1976 lease between Ruud and Larson required $700 monthly payments. Although attempting to relet at a higher monthly rent is a factor which may be considered in determining whether the landlord has made a good faith effort to relet the premises, it does not, as a matter of law, bar the landlord's claim. *See United States National Bank of Oregon v. Homeland, Inc.,* 291 Or. 374, 383, 631 P.2d 761, 766 (1981).

Larson's own witness, an experienced commercial realtor in Fargo, testified that $1,200 was a reasonable rental for the property at that time. Furthermore, Larson, in attempting to relet the property, was also seeking $1,200 per month. Larson presented no evidence which would indicate that $1,200 per month was not a fair rental value for the property, nor did Larson present evidence that any offers to lease at a lesser amount were received or rejected by Ruud.

The trial court made the following finding of fact:

> The Ruuds, after regaining possession and doing some repair, advertised the property in the local newspaper and used a well maintained sign in an effort to rent the property. These attempts produced over 140 contacts and 50 or more potential tenants. The Ruuds were capable of renting the building on their own behalf. The Ruuds' efforts to lease the premises to another tenant were all vigorous, substantial and in good faith.

The party challenging a finding of fact on appeal bears the burden of demonstrating that the finding is clearly erroneous. *Routledge v. Routledge,* 377 N.W.2d 542, 546 (N.D.1985); *Byron v. Gerring Industries, Inc.,* 328 N.W.2d 819, 821 (N.D.1982). We have thoroughly reviewed the record and we are not left with a definite and firm conviction that a mistake has been made; therefore, the trial court's findings are not clearly erroneous.

The judgment is affirmed.

■ LEVINE, JUSTICE, dissenting.

Ruud does not take issue with the principle that in mitigating damages, a landlord may not make approval of a sublease contingent upon payment of all arrearages. With this proposition, I agree. Building upon this premise, the majority concludes that if, however, in negotiations, the tenant agrees to pay these arrearages and then reneges, the landlord may make approval of a sublease contingent upon payment of all arrearages. With this proposition, I disagree. I cannot discern a reason for the distinction drawn, and therefore I dissent.

Apparently, there is some sort of estoppel theory underlying the majority's rationale—that a tenant, having agreed, and then disagreed, to undertake payment of arrearages to facilitate a sublease agreement, is estopped from expecting the fruition of that sublease, absent payment of arrearages, even though the landlord has no legal right to demand such payment as a condition precedent in the first place.

It is not the tenant's good faith that we are evaluating here—it is the landlord's good faith in mitigating damages. Because the tenant produced a willing, able and suitable subtenant, I believe that the landlord acted neither reasonably nor in good faith when he rejected the offer to sublease. It must be remembered that under the sublease Larson remained liable for all obligations as tenant under the lease, and under the lease Larson was responsible for arrearages and attorney's fees. Thus no special agreement was necessary to hold Larson responsible for obligations he owed under the lease.

I therefore respectfully dissent.

## NOTES

1. *A bird in the hand.* Why, even in a no duty to mitigate jurisdiction,[10] might a prudent lessor wish to act immediately to relet the premises after a tenant's breach?

2. *Burden of proof.* Reid places the burden of proof regarding mitigation on the nonbreaching landlord, whereas *Isbey* and *Ruud* place it on the breaching tenant. Which view do you think is preferable?

3. *Proper drafting.* How might an abandonment clause in a lease be worded to minimize the likelihood of litigation after the tenant's breach?

4. *Waiver.* Should the duty to mitigate be waivable? Should it matter whether the property at issue is residential or commercial? For that matter, should there be a distinction in the application of the mitigation requirement generally as between commercial and residential properties?

5. *Rerenting for longer periods.* In *Ruud,* the court held that the lessor's asking for a higher rent upon rerenting did not undermine the reasonableness of his mitigation efforts. What if the lessor seeks a new lease for a term longer than the original lease? Should such action terminate the original lease and the defaulting tenant's liability?

6. *Musical chairs.* Suppose a lessor owns two properties and the tenant of one property moves into the property abandoned by the defaulting tenant. Should the lessor be able to recover from the defaulting tenant the

---

[10] Note that New York follows the rule that the landlord has no duty to mitigate. Holy Properties v. Kenneth Cole Productions, 87 N.Y.2d 130 (1995).

rent owed on the property vacated by the tenant who moved into the abandoned property?

7. *Affirmative measures.* Does *Isbey* actually require the landlord to take affirmative measures to mitigate her damages?

8. *The essence of reasonableness. Ruud* illustrates the application of the reasonableness requirement. Understandably, it is a very subjective concept.[11] In determining whether a lessor who owns several properties has made reasonable efforts to mitigate his damages, should he be required to give preference to the abandoned premises in showing his properties to prospective tenants? If not, how would he satisfy the mitigation requirement for the abandoned premises?

9. *Assignments/subleases and mitigation.* In *Isbey*, the court observed that the landlord did not have to consent to the proffered subtenant. Is this a sensible view? *Ruud* suggests that it would come out differently on this issue. How does the mitigation requirement operate in light of the holding in *Isbey*?

10. *Lessor's reletting at increased rent.* If the lessor relets the vacated premises at an increased rent, should he be entitled to keep this additional amount, or should he have to credit it against any amounts owed to him by the abandoning tenant?

11. *Summary possession.* The summary possession remedy is available by statute in every state and is an important component of landlords' remedies generally. These statutes allow a landlord to bring a civil action for possession of the leased premises. Most jurisdictions also allow the landlord to join a claim for rent due. Typically, a landlord can bring a summary possession action against a tenant who is wrongfully occupying the premises or who has not paid the rent. Many courts have held, however, that tenants being sued for summary possession can interpose affirmative defenses such as breach of the implied warranty of habitability[12] or retaliatory eviction.[13]

12. *The Principal Problem.* In the Principal Problem, did Drugger surrender the premises? If so, did Lesser accept the surrender? Assuming that Lesser has a duty to mitigate his damages, has he used "reasonable diligence" to relet the premises abandoned by Drugger? What is the effect of the clause in the lease which provides that the premises should not be used for any other purpose without the written consent of the lessor?

---

[11] See, e.g., Kallman v. Radioshack Corp., 315 F.3d 731, 741 (7th Cir. 2002) ("[W]e do not find that attempts by a landlord to maximize the amount of rent collected from a new tenant per se indicate unreasonable efforts to mitigate damages, but in this case, given the poor condition of the property, delay in engaging a broker, and other restrictive terms of the lease, it was not clear error for the district court to find the efforts unreasonable here.").

[12] Recall that Marini v. Ireland, reprinted in Assignment 4, was an action for summary possession. *See also* Jack Spring, Inc. v. Little, 280 N.E.2d 208 (Ill. 1972).

[13] *See, e.g.,* Brady v. Slater, 2004 WL 1946142 (Utah App. Sept. 2, 2004); Building Monitoring Systems, Inc. v. Paxton, 905 P.2d 1215 (Utah 1995); Wright v. Brady, 889 P.2d 105 (Ct. App. Idaho 1995); Dickhut v. Norton, 173 N.W.2d 297 (Wis. 1970).

## III. FREEHOLD ESTATES

### A. NON-CONCURRENT ESTATES

### ASSIGNMENT 9

# INTRODUCTION TO PRESENT AND FUTURE ESTATES: TERMINOLOGY

### 1. INTRODUCTION

Many people may have rights, privileges or immunities with respect to a parcel of land. Suppose O is what is commonly called the "owner" of Blackacre. O, as lessor, might lease Blackacre to T, as tenant. T then has certain very substantial rights in Blackacre, particularly the right to possession. Since O has transferred certain of his rights to T by virtue of the lease, it is accurate to say that O and T both own certain rights in Blackacre. Indeed, in many cases T's rights may be far more valuable than O's rights.

> EXAMPLE 1 (Tenant with rights more valuable than landlord's): O leases Blackacre to T under a 99 year lease, the rent to be $1 per year. T's interest is far more valuable than O's interest. Here, the conventional observation that O "owns" Blackacre and that T "only leases" Blackacre is quite misleading. It would be more accurate to say that O has certain rights in Blackacre, that T has certain other rights, and that T's rights are far more valuable and substantial than O's rights. Or to state the matter in more technical language, O owns a reversion in fee simple in Blackacre, and T owns an estate for years. O's reversion in fee simple follows T's estate for years.

In Example 1, T has a present estate in Blackacre. A present estate in Blackacre is an interest in Blackacre which carries with it a present right to exclusive possession.

There are numerous kinds of interests in land that are not estates in land.

> EXAMPLE 2 (Interests which are not estates in land): O, the "owner" of Blackacre, grants an easement to E to use a road crossing Blackacre. O also mortgages Blackacre to M, a lending institution, for $100,000. E has the rights of an easement holder, and M the rights of a mortgagee. Neither E nor M owns an estate in Blackacre.

A right-of-way easement holder has no right to the exclusive possession of any portion of Blackacre although he may enter upon Blackacre in the course of exercising his right of way. Therefore, the easement holder does not own an "estate" in Blackacre. Technically, he owns what is called an "incorporeal hereditament." Similarly, a mortgagee in most jurisdictions does not have a present estate in Blackacre because she does not presently have the right to exclusive possession of Blackacre. It is the right to exclusive possession that lets us say that the tenant under a one year lease of a single apartment in an apartment building has an estate in land. By contrast, the mortgagee of the entire building, who has an interest many times more valuable and permanent than that of the tenant, does not have an estate in land.

Estates are classified into present and future estates. Since future estates are commonly called "future interests", we shall adopt that terminology here. A future interest is an interest in land which (1) may become possessory, but which is not now possessory, and (2) is "a segment of ownership measured in terms of duration." Restatement, Property § 153 (1936). What is a "segment of ownership measured in terms of duration"?

In our system of jurisprudence, land has four dimensions, three of which are spatial and the fourth is temporal. The spatial dimensions are: length, width, and height. The temporal dimension is, of course, time. Each of these dimensions can be divided and sold or otherwise conveyed separately.

> EXAMPLE 3 (Spatial division): O owns Blackacre, consisting of forty acres of land. If he grants twenty acres of it to A, O has divided Blackacre by length and/or width. If O grants A the space between 20 feet and 100 feet above ground level over all of Blackacre, O has divided Blackacre by height.

> EXAMPLE 4 (Temporal division): O owns Blackacre. O grants A "a life estate for the duration of A's life" in all of Blackacre. O has divided Blackacre by time. A's interest is a present estate, called a "life estate"; O's interest is a future estate, called a "reversion."

In Examples 3 and 4, after O's grant to A, it would no longer be accurate to say that O "owns" Blackacre. Rather, O owns part of Blackacre and A owns another part. The Restatement correctly points out that certain interests that may become possessory in the future are not future interests because they are not "segments of ownership measured in terms of duration." For example, if a mortgagor defaults in her obligations under the mortgage, the mortgagee may foreclose the mortgage and ultimately gain possession of Blackacre. In most states, however, the mortgagee's interest is not a future estate because it is not a segment of ownership measured in terms of duration.

We are concerned with the legal problems arising from the division of Blackacre into segments of time. What are the segments of time into which Blackacre can be divided? What are they called? How are these interests created? What are their characteristics or incidents? What rights, privileges, or immunities does the owner of such interests have? What are the legal rights and duties existing between the owners of these various interests? Although most of the discussion of present and future estates contained in this Assignment focuses on transfers of interests in land, many of the concepts we will be examining also are applicable to transfers of other forms of property, particularly beneficial interests in trusts.

Prior Assignments in this casebook have explored certain estates in land: the estate for years (also known as the tenancy for years), the estate from year to year (periodic tenancy), and the estates (tenancies) at will or at sufferance. Collectively, these are known as the non-freehold estates. We now turn to the category of estates known as freehold estates.

To understand fully the concept of a freehold estate, it is important to recall the traditional beginning of the feudal system of land tenures in England. In the year 1066, William the Conqueror conquered England. He rewarded some 1,500 of his Norman followers by granting tenancies of large tracts of lands to them. The happy recipients did not thereby become the "owners" of the land in question. They were viewed as "tenants" who held "of the King" as a reward for their past efforts, and during their good behavior. In return for the land he received, each tenant swore homage and fealty to the king, and to render certain payments and services. The conveyance of the land was for a temporary period initially, usually the life of the recipient. Upon the death of the life tenant the land would revert back to the king. The conveyance of the land can be thought of as a kind of pension for faithful service, not as a grant of ownership of the land. The estates created by these conveyances came to be known as freehold interests or estates. Although these conveyances originally were between the king and his principal followers, known as tenants in chief, the latter soon repeated the process by "subinfeudating" to new tenants. Thus the structure of feudal landholdings in England resembled a pyramid, with the king at the top, followed by his tenants in chief, who were tenants to the king but who also were landlords to various smaller tenants.

Under the feudal system it was essential that someone be "seised" of a parcel of land at all times. The person seised of the parcel was responsible for the feudal payments and services, and if seisin was suspended the lord would lose the value of these benefits. Seisin can be thought of as possession of a freehold estate. One consequence of the feudal emphasis on seisin was that land was transferred by a ceremony known as feoffment with livery of seisin. The transferor and the transferee went on the land and there, in a public ceremony, seisin, symbolized by a twig, a clod of earth, or the keys to the manor house, was transferred.

Studying estates in land is much like studying a foreign language in that it requires one to learn a new vocabulary. The following chart outlines the freehold estates in land which are the focus of this Assignment. In many instances, the owner of any present estate may elect to transfer a present interest to another party, but retain a future interest in the property for himself, or to transfer the future interest to another third-party grantee. Thus, with the exception of the fee simple absolute, all present estates have associated future interests which can be retained by the grantor or conveyed to a third-party grantee.

### FREEHOLD ESTATES IN REAL PROPERTY

| Present Estate | Future Interest Retained By Grantor | Future Interest Created in 3rd Party Grantee |
|---|---|---|
| 1. Fee Simple Absolute | None | None |
| 2. Fee Simple Defeasible | | |
|    a. Fee Simple Determinable | Possibility of Reverter | Executory Interest Note: Remainders never can follow any fee simple |

Language hints: "while", "during", "until", "for so long as" suggest a fee simple determinable.

| | | |
|---|---|---|
|    b. Fee Simple Subject to Condition Subsequent | Power of Termination | Executory Interest |

Language hints: "provided, however", "but if", "on condition that", "if, however" all suggest a fee simple subject to a condition subsequent.

| | | |
|---|---|---|
| 3. Life Estate | Reversion | Remainder |

| Present Estate | Future Interest Retained By Grantor | Future Interest Created in 3rd Party Grantee |
|---|---|---|
| 4. Defeasible Life Estate (Can be either a determinable life estate or a life estate subject to a condition subsequent: see language hints under fee simple defeasible to make this determination.) | Reversion, Power of Termination[1] | Remainder, Executory Interest |

The purpose of this Assignment is to enable you to become comfortable with the terminology necessary for an understanding of the legal issues associated with the division of property into segments of time. We shall postpone the more difficult theoretical applications of this general topic until subsequent Assignments. Let us begin our study of estates in land with "the highest estate known to the common law": the fee simple absolute.

## 2. THE FEE SIMPLE ABSOLUTE

As indicated by the chart, one who owns land in fee simple absolute does not share it with the holder of another freehold interest. When Blackacre is held in fee simple absolute, ownership in terms of time is undivided. No other person currently owns any segment of Blackacre's time.

If A had a life estate in Blackacre and B owned all the other possible estates in Blackacre, A and B could join together and convey a fee simple absolute to C. An analogy may help here. If A owns one third, and B owns two thirds of Blackacre, together A and B can convey all of Blackacre. Similarly, if A owns a life estate and B owns the remainder, together they can convey "all," i.e., a fee simple absolute in Blackacre.

The holder of a fee simple absolute does not necessarily have absolute dominion over Blackacre. Zoning and related laws may prohibit her from conducting many activities on her land. She may be obliged to pay taxes on her land, not to conduct a nuisance on it, and to adhere to other obligations and restrictions on ownership. When one says that A

---

[1] According to the Restatement, the owner of a fee simple absolute who conveys a lesser estate such as a determinable life estate keeps only a reversion, rather than both a reversion and a possibility of reverter. See Restatement of Property § 23 illustrations 3, 5, 6 & 7 (1936). Inconsistently, if the owner of a fee simple absolute grants a lesser estate subject to a condition subsequent, the grantor retains a power of termination in addition to her reversion. See Restatement of Property §§ 24 illustration 3, 155 comment c (1936).

owns Blackacre in fee simple absolute, one is merely saying that A does not share ownership of Blackacre, in terms of the time dimension, with anyone else.

In modern times, the fee simple absolute has become the most common form of estate. Therefore, a conveyance of "Blackacre to A" is presumed to be a conveyance to A in fee simple absolute. This was not always the case. Because the original grants by William the Conqueror were intended to be only for the life of the recipient, an inheritable estate was the exception rather than the rule. A grant "to A" was assumed to be merely for A's life rather than to create an inheritable estate. From this historical setting grew the rule that "words of inheritance" had to be used for the effective creation of a fee simple. The phrase "to A *and his heirs*" had to be used if A was to get a fee simple. Today, few, if any, states follow this ancient requirement. Nevertheless, many instruments of conveyance still grant Blackacre "to A and his heirs", thus paying harmless tribute to the ancient doctrine.

Suppose an individual conveyed Blackacre to "A and his heirs." As noted above, this conveyance gave a fee simple absolute to A. What did the conveyance give to A's heirs?[2] A conveyance to "A and his heirs" did not give anything directly to A's heirs. Instead, the words "and his heirs" were used to emphasize the fact that A was receiving an inheritable estate, which he could transfer completely to another party during his lifetime or which he could devise or let pass by intestacy at his death. A's heirs would inherit the property only if A did not dispose of it in one of these two ways.

The phrase to "A and his heirs" meant that A's heirs *might* be able to inherit the property because A has received an inheritable estate by virtue of the original conveyance. That phrase did not mean that A's heirs necessarily would inherit, since A might otherwise dispose of it. In the confusing terminology of the day, it was said that the phrase was "one of limitation, and not one of purchase." The word "limitation" referred to those words in a conveyance that described the nature of the interest conveyed or created. In this case, the phrase "and his heirs" are words of limitation because they describe the inheritable characteristic of A's estate. "Purchase", as used here in its archaic sense, meant any type of conveyance from the first taker, other than by inheritance. A's heirs were not considered purchasers because A's heirs were not receiving anything directly under the terms of the original conveyance, but would only receive the property by inheriting it from the first taker, A, in the event A had not otherwise disposed of it.

---

[2] An individual's heirs are those parties entitled to inherit an individual's property according to the statute governing intestate succession of a particular state. See the Illinois statute of descent and distribution reprinted at the end of this Assignment for an example.

## 3. DEFEASIBLE FEES

We have just seen that the fee simple absolute is an inheritable estate, and as such, its duration essentially is infinite.[3] A defeasible fee has the potential for infinite duration, but unlike a fee simple absolute, it may be subject to an early termination if certain prescribed events take place. There are essentially two categories of defeasible fees: the fee simple determinable and the fee simple subject to a condition subsequent.[4]

*The fee simple determinable.* A fee simple determinable is created when a conveyance creates a fee simple but also contains a limitation providing that the fee shall expire upon the occurrence of a stated event.

> EXAMPLE 5 (Fee simple determinable with possibility of reverter): O grants Blackacre "to the Karo School District, *for so long as* Blackacre is used as the site of a school." This limitation is enforceable. If the Karo School District uses the property for any purpose other than a school, the property will *automatically revert* to O. The school district has a *fee simple determinable*.

Any combination of words that clearly indicates that a fee will *automatically* terminate upon a specified occurrence creates a fee simple determinable in the grantee. Certain words indicate an automatic termination of the determinable fee. Thus, if the conveyance contained in a deed or will uses language such as "for so long as," "while," "during," or "until," to specify the occurrence that will terminate the fee, the creation of a fee simple determinable generally is presumed.

> EXAMPLE 6 (Fee simple determinable subject to executory limitation): O grants Blackacre "to the Karo School District *while* Blackacre is used as the site of a school, and when it is not, to X and her heirs." Again, the school district has a *fee simple determinable*. The school district's interest may also be described as a *fee simple subject to an executory limitation*. (For now, the rule against perpetuities is ignored.)

The primary difference between Examples 5 and 6 lies in where the property will go upon the termination of the school district's fee simple determinable. In Example 5, the property will automatically revert back

---

[3] Of course, if the owner of a fee simple absolute does not convey the fee to another party during his lifetime and dies without a will and without any heirs who are qualified to take his property under the state statute of descent and distribution, the fee simple absolute will come to an end and escheat to the state. See the Illinois statute of descent and distribution reprinted at the end of this Assignment. This scenario, however, is extremely remote in the vast majority of instances since most people have at least one relative who would qualify as an heir under the relevant state law. Note the broad range of relatives qualified to take under the Illinois statute.

[4] Most commentators add a third category, the fee simple subject to an executory limitation or interest. When a defeasible fee is followed by a future interest that is created in someone other than the grantor, the defeasible fee is labeled a fee simple subject to an executory limitation. Because both the fee simple determinable and the fee simple subject to a condition subsequent can be followed by an executory interest, we have subsumed this third category of defeasible fees within the other two. See the chart of Freehold Estates in Real Property on page 194.

to O, the grantor. The future interest label given to O's interest is a *possibility of reverter*. A possibility of reverter is created when a grantor transfers an estate of the same duration as his original estate, but attaches to the grant a special limitation which, when and if it occurs, will operate automatically to return the property to the grantor.[5] In Example 5, O owned Blackacre in fee simple absolute. Since Blackacre might always be used for school purposes, it is proper to call the estate transferred to the school district a fee.[6] Nevertheless, a possibility of reverter in O is created by the attachment of the special limitation requiring that the property be used for school purposes only.

In Example 6, Blackacre is to pass automatically to X, rather than to O, in the event Blackacre no longer is used as the site of a school. X has a future interest in Blackacre known as an *executory interest*. An executory interest is created when a conveyance provides that, upon the termination of the determinable fee, the property is to pass automatically to someone other than the original grantor.

If the language of the grant does not expressly provide for an automatic termination of the fee, courts will not find a determinable fee.

> EXAMPLE 7 (Fee simple absolute): O grants Blackacre "to A to be used for cemetery purposes." A has a fee simple absolute, not a fee simple determinable. O has no right to Blackacre if A uses Blackacre for other than cemetery purposes. However, the language may be sufficient to create a covenant that O could enforce by an injunction or damages. Covenants will be studied later in this book.

*The fee simple subject to a condition subsequent.* A fee simple subject to a condition subsequent is created when, after creating a fee simple, a limitation provides that a conveyor or his successor in interest *shall have the power to terminate* the fee simple upon the occurrence of a stated event.

> EXAMPLE 8 (Fee simple subject to a condition subsequent): O grants Blackacre "to the Karo County School District, but if school operations are ever permanently suspended on Blackacre, then grantor or his successor in interest shall have the power to enter and terminate the interest of the school district." The school district has a *fee simple subject to a condition subsequent*.

Unlike the determinable fee, the fee simple subject to a condition subsequent does not terminate automatically upon the occurrence of the stipulated event. Instead, the fee will be terminated only when the

---

[5] See generally Restatement of Property § 154(3) (1936); Bergin & Haskell, Preface to Estates in Land and Future Interests 58 (2nd ed. 1984).

[6] If the interest created is not of potentially infinite duration, but instead terminates after a number of years, an estate for years rather than a defeasible fee is created. Thus, if O grants Blackacre "to A until 10 years from today," A has an estate for years.

grantor exercises his reserved right to re-enter the property. The future interest label given to the interest reserved by the grantor in this situation is a *power of termination* or a *right of entry*. Thus, when a grantor conveys a fee simple subject to a condition subsequent and provides that upon the occurrence of a stated event the grantor has the power to terminate the estate so conveyed, the grantor has retained a power of termination.[7]

Functionally, little difference exists between a possibility of reverter and a power of termination because the owner of either kind of a defeasible fee generally will not voluntarily relinquish ownership of the property in question. As a practical matter, therefore, the holder of both the possibility of reverter and the power of termination will have to take affirmative steps to oust the defeasible fee owner from the property. Some states have recognized this reality by abolishing the distinction between possibilities of reverter and powers of termination.[8] Unfortunately, it remains necessary in many jurisdictions to differentiate the two. Decisional or statutory law in a particular state may subject the two interests to different rules. For instance, a sizeable minority of American jurisdictions follow the common law rule that powers of termination cannot be transferred through a conveyance executed during the transferor's lifetime (i.e., through an *inter vivos* conveyance).[9] Possibilities of reverter, on the other hand, may pass *inter vivos* in the great majority of jurisdictions.[10] In a small number of jurisdictions, any effort to convey a power of termination destroys it. The blame for these anomalies is attributable to the legal profession, which through inertia and indifference has permitted them to persist.

Suppose a particular conveyance does not expressly provide for re-entry, but nevertheless contains language stating that the fee will terminate upon a specified event. How do we know whether the grantor intended to create a determinable fee subject to an automatic termination or a fee that is subject to a condition subsequent? Recall that certain buzzwords have developed over time that indicate the creation of a determinable fee. The same is true with respect to the fee simple subject to a condition subsequent. If the deed or conveyance contains language such as "but if," "on condition that," "provided, however," or "if, however," courts generally presume that the grantor intended to create a fee simple subject to a condition subsequent.[11]

---

[7] See Restatement of Property §§ 24 comment b, 45, 155 (1936).

[8] See Cal.Civ.Code § 885.020; Ky.Rev.Stat.Ann. § 381.218. Both California and Kentucky now treat possibilities of reverter as powers of termination.

[9] 3 Powell on Real Property 21.02[3](b) (2005) (listing about twenty jurisdictions that follow the old common law rule either by statute or decisional law). See also Restatement of Property § 160 comment c (1936). Powell notes, however, that the modern trend and majority rule is to permit the *inter vivos* transfer of the power of termination.

[10] See 3 Powell on Real Property 21.02[2](a) (2005).

[11] See generally Restatement of Property § 45 comment m (1936); 1 American Law of Property 2.6 (1952).

EXAMPLE 9 (Fee simple subject to a condition subsequent with a power of termination): O owns Blackacre in fee simple absolute and transfers it "to Trinity Church *on the condition that* Blackacre shall be used for church purposes only." Absent other facts suggesting a contrary intent, Trinity Church has a *fee simple subject to a condition subsequent* and O has a *power of termination* or *right of entry*.

A fee simple subject to a condition subsequent can be followed by an executory interest rather than a power of termination. This occurs when the grant states that the property is to be transferred to someone other than the original grantor upon the occurrence of the stipulated condition. Such a fee is referred to as a *fee simple subject to an executory limitation*.

EXAMPLE 10 (Fee simple subject to an executory limitation): O grants Blackacre "to A, *but if* Blackacre ceases to be used for church purposes, then to B." The Restatement of Property calls the condition subsequent attaching to A's interest an *executory limitation*.[12] A's interest is a *fee simple subject to an executory limitation*. B has an *executory interest*. (The rule against perpetuities is ignored for now.)

## 4. LIFE ESTATES AND THEIR ASSOCIATED FUTURE INTERESTS

A life estate is created when a grantor transfers to another party an estate that terminates at the death of the transferee. Such a life estate generally is not an inheritable estate.

EXAMPLE 11 (Life estate): O, owner of Blackacre in fee simple absolute, grants Blackacre "to A for life." A has a *life estate* in Blackacre and his interest in the property terminates at his death. A cannot devise Blackacre to someone else. If A dies without a will, A's heirs cannot inherit the property.

Occasionally, someone receives a life estate *pur autre vie,* an estate for the life of another.

EXAMPLE 12 (Life estate *pur autre vie*): O, owner of Blackacre in fee simple absolute, grants Blackacre to "A for the life of B." A has an estate for the life of B; B has nothing. On A's death during B's life, A's interest passes to his heirs or devisees in most American jurisdictions.

Some conveyances are drafted so that a life estate can be terminated in ways in addition to the death of the life tenant. Such life estates are called *defeasible life estates* and operate very similarly to the defeasible fees discussed earlier. Thus, a particular defeasible life estate can be categorized as either a determinable life estate or a life estate subject to a condition subsequent. The various buzzwords identified in the prior

---

[12] See Restatement of Property § 25 (1936).

section on defeasible fees are useful in determining the particular type of defeasible life estate contained in a conveyance.

> EXAMPLE 13 (Determinable life estate): O, owner of Blackacre in fee simple absolute, grants Blackacre to "A for life *or until* she goes to law school." The use of the language "or until" is indicative of a determinable life estate. Thus, A has a determinable life estate which will terminate either when she dies or goes to law school.

> EXAMPLE 14 (Life estate subject to a condition subsequent): O, owner of Blackacre in fee simple absolute, grants Blackacre to "A for life, *on the condition that* she never goes to law school." Here, the language suggests that A has a life estate subject to a condition subsequent. The result is similar to Example 13, since A's life estate will terminate either at her death or when she goes to law school.

When a life estate is created, a future interest in the property can be retained in the original grantor, or granted to another transferee under the terms of the conveyance. In all of the prior examples, O owned Blackacre in fee simple absolute and transferred a life estate to A. Thus, O transferred an estate whose duration was conceptually shorter than his original estate. Whenever a grantor transfers an estate whose duration is conceptually shorter than his original estate, and fails to designate another party as the next taker of the estate, the grantor is deemed to have retained a future interest in the property called a *reversion*.[13]

> EXAMPLE 15 (Estate for years with a reversion): O owns a life estate in Blackacre and grants to A "an estate in Blackacre for a two year term." O transferred to A an *estate for years,* which is regarded as conceptually shorter in duration than O's original life estate. Therefore, O has retained a *reversion* in Blackacre.

The owner of property can designate another transferee as the next taker of the estate following the termination of the life estate. The future interest possessed by such a subsequent transferee can be either an *executory interest* or a *remainder*. You have already been introduced to the concept of an executory interest in the discussion of defeasible fees. Recall that an executory interest is any future interest following a defeasible fee granted to someone other than the original grantor. In the context of such grants, no distinction was made between remainders and executory interests because, for reasons that are entirely historical, remainders never can follow an estate in fee simple, even one that is defeasible.[14] Since both remainders and executory interests can follow defeasible life estates, however, it is necessary to distinguish between these types of future interests.

---

[13] See generally Restatement of Property § 154(1) comment a (1936).
[14] See id. at § 156 comment d.

To be a remainder, a future interest must satisfy two requirements. First, it must be a future interest created in someone other than the original grantor. Second, if it ever becomes a present estate, it must do so upon, but not before, the natural expiration of all of the previous estates of limited duration which were created at the same time as the remainder interest.[15] The death of the life tenant *always* is regarded as a natural expiration of the life tenant's estate. Thus, the future interest created in someone other than the grantor following a regular, as opposed to a defeasible, life estate, always will be classified as a remainder rather than an executory interest.

EXAMPLE 16 (Life estate with remainder): O, owner of Blackacre in fee simple absolute, grants it "to A for life, then to B." A has a life estate in Blackacre, which is a present possessory interest. B's future interest in Blackacre is a *remainder*. The two requirements discussed above are satisfied. First, B is not the original grantor. Second, B's future interest will become a present possessory estate upon, but not before, the natural expiration of A's life estate. As soon as A dies, B's remainder interest will become a present estate. A's death results in the natural expiration of A's life estate, which is an estate of limited duration and prior to that of B's future interest. Finally, the original conveyance simultaneously created A's life estate and B's remainder interest.

EXAMPLE 17 (Life estate with remainder for life and reversion): O, owner of Blackacre in fee simple absolute, grants it "to A for life, then to B for life." A has a present possessory life estate in Blackacre. B has a *remainder for life* in Blackacre. In this example, unlike Examples 15 and 16, O has retained a reversion in Blackacre. Although O conveyed two life estates in Blackacre, both estates are conceptually shorter in duration than O's fee simple absolute.

Remainder interests can be classified into the following four categories: (1) absolutely vested remainders; (2) vested remainders subject to defeasance; (3) contingent remainders; and (4) vested remainders subject to open. An understanding of each of these categories is essential for mastering the law of future interests.

*Absolutely vested remainders.* In addition to the two requirements for a remainder discussed above, absolutely vested remainders must meet two further requirements. First, there must be no conditions precedent to the remainder's becoming a present possessory interest other than the *natural expiration* of the prior possessory estates. Second, it must always be "theoretically" possible to determine those parties who

---

[15] Id. at § 156.

will get possession of the remainder should the prior possessory estates end.[16]

> EXAMPLE 18 (Vested remainder in fee simple): O grants Blackacre to "A for life, then to B." B has a remainder in fee simple absolute which is vested from the moment of its creation. First, it is not subject to any conditions other than the termination of A's life estate by A's death, which is the natural expiration of A's life estate. Second, we theoretically know the identity of those individuals who will get possession of Blackacre whenever A's life estate ends. B, or his heirs, devisees, or assignees have an absolute right to Blackacre upon the termination of A's life estate. Even if B dies before A, B's successors will take Blackacre. O, having transferred his entire fee simple absolute, has nothing left.

> EXAMPLE 19 (Vested life estate remainder): O, owner of Blackacre in fee simple absolute, grants it to "A for life, remainder to B for life." B's life estate remainder is absolutely vested despite the fact that should B predecease A, B will not enjoy the possession of Blackacre. B's life estate is not subject to any conditions other than that inherent in all life estates: that it can be enjoyed in possession only while the life tenant is alive. O retains a reversion, despite the fact that the limitation does not expressly refer to it.

The concept of a *natural expiration* is one which can be difficult to understand. We have seen that the death of the individual possessing a life estate constitutes the natural expiration of the life estate. But there are other types of natural expirations. In general, the same buzzwords which are regarded as creating a fee simple determinable also are indicative of an estate which is thought to expire naturally. (Note that the concept of natural expiration focuses on the prior (present) estate, not on the remainder person.)

> EXAMPLE 20 (Vested remainder in fee simple): O, owner of Blackacre in fee simple absolute, grants it to "A for life *or until* she goes to law school, then to B." A has a determinable life estate which will terminate either upon her death or if she goes to law school. The "or until" language, which is indicative of a determinable life estate, also suggests that A's estate will naturally expire in the event she goes to law school. Thus, B is regarded as having a *vested remainder in fee simple*. O, having transferred his entire fee simple absolute, is left with nothing.

*Vested Remainders Subject to Defeasance Compared With Contingent Remainders.* The difficulty of distinguishing between vested

---

[16] Bergin & Haskell, Preface to Estates in Land and Future Interests 66–67 (2nd ed. 1984). See generally Restatement of Property § 157(a) comments f & i (1936); 1 American Law of Property § 4.33 (1952).

remainders subject to defeasance (complete divestment) and contingent remainders is legendary. One helpful formula is as follows: "A remainder is vested in A, when, throughout its continuance, A, or A and his heirs, have the right to the immediate possession, whenever and however the preceding freehold estates may determine. A remainder is contingent if, in order for it to come into possession, the fulfillment of some condition precedent other than the determination of the preceding freehold estates is necessary." Gray, The Rule Against Perpetuities 101 (4th ed. 1942).

Often, the difference between a vested remainder subject to defeasance and a contingent remainder rests merely on the form of expression, rather than the substance of the condition. Language suggestive of a condition subsequent, such as "but if" and "provided, however," generally operates to create a vested remainder subject to defeasance, rather than a contingent remainder.

> EXAMPLE 21 (Vested remainder subject to defeasance): O, owner of Blackacre in fee simple absolute, grants it "to A for life, remainder to Joan, *but should* Joan die before A, the remainder is to go to X." The remainder to Joan is *vested subject to defeasance* by Joan's death before A. X has an executory interest.

In contrast, if the language used is more suggestive of a condition precedent (other than the natural expiration of any prior estates created simultaneously with the remainder), the remainder is regarded as contingent, rather than vested.

> EXAMPLE 22 (Contingent remainder): O, owner of Blackacre in fee simple absolute, grants it "to A for life, remainder to the then oldest daughter of A who survives him." A has three daughters at the time of the conveyance. The remainder to A's oldest daughter is a *contingent remainder* since nothing is given, even tentatively, to a daughter who does not survive him. The only gift is to the oldest daughter of A who survives A. Survival is a condition precedent in this case.

Some general rules for distinguishing between conditions subsequent and conditions precedent have been summarized as follows:

> When conditional language in a transfer ... follows language that, taken alone, would be said to create a vested remainder, the condition so created is a condition subsequent. If, however, the conditional language appears before the language creating the remainder, or the conditional language seems to be a part of the description of the remainderman, the condition created thereby is a condition precedent.

Bergin & Haskell, Preface to Estates in Land and Future Interests 72 (3rd ed. 1989).

> EXAMPLE 23 (Alternative contingent remainders): O, owner of Blackacre in fee simple absolute, grants it "to A for life, then if

B is a student at A's death, to B; otherwise to C." Here, B and C have *alternate contingent remainders*. B's remainder is subject to the condition precedent of being a student. C's remainder is subject to the condition precedent of B *not* being a student. Note that if C's interest becomes one that is possessory, it will be upon the natural expiration of A's life estate, and therefore qualifies generally as a remainder.

EXAMPLE 24 (Contingent remainder for life and vested remainder): O, owner of Blackacre in fee simple absolute, grants it "to A for life; then, if B graduates from law school before A's death, to B for life; then to D." B has a contingent remainder for life because it is subject to the condition precedent of B graduating from law school before A's death. D's remainder is vested because it will take effect at the natural expiration of either A's or B's life estate (again, the death of the life tenant being considered a natural expiration of the life estate).

A remainder to unborn or unascertained people always is contingent. This rule has particular relevance when dealing with remainders to the "heirs" or "issue" of persons either alive or not yet born.

EXAMPLE 25 (Contingent remainder to heirs of a living person): O grants Blackacre to "A for life, remainder to the heirs of B." B is alive at the time of the grant. B's "heirs" cannot be ascertained until his death. Before B's death he merely has heirs apparent or presumptive.[17] Therefore, the remainder to B's heirs is contingent.

EXAMPLE 26 (Contingent remainder to unborn persons): O devises Blackacre to "A for life, remainder to A's children." If A does not have any children at the time of the devise, the remainder is contingent.

*Vested Remainders Subject to Open: Class Gifts.* A remainder to a class such as children, grandchildren, or siblings raises special problems. If a remainder is vested in a class, but additional people may later qualify for membership in that class, for most purposes the remainder is considered to be *vested subject to open* (vested subject to partial divestment) to allow additional members to join.

EXAMPLE 27 (Vested remainder subject to open): A transfers Blackacre "to B for life, remainder to the children of B." B has a child, C. C has a *vested remainder subject to open* to let in other children born to B.[18]

---

[17] "An *heir presumptive* is a person who will inherit if the potential intestate dies immediately, but who may be excluded if another more closely related heir is born. An *heir apparent* is certain to inherit unless he or she dies first or is excluded by a valid will." Bryan A. Garner, A Dictionary of Modern Legal Usage 401 (2nd ed. 1995).

[18] Restatement of Property § 157, illustration 2 (1936).

At this point, you may be wondering (justifiably so) why it is important to determine whether a remainder is absolutely vested, vested subject to defeasance, contingent, or vested subject to open. Let us assure you that these distinctions are critical from the standpoint of applying the Rule Against Perpetuities, which is explored in Assignments 10 and 11. They are also important in other contexts that will not be explored in this course, but may be explored in more advanced courses dealing with wills, trusts and estate planning. For now, however, we must ask you to be patient, and to accept our word that real-world consequences do, in fact, turn on the distinctions we have been exploring.

*Executory Interests.* Earlier in this discussion it was noted that both remainders and executory interests can follow defeasible life estates. It was also noted that only executory interests can follow defeasible fees. We shall see shortly that executory interests also can follow vested remainders subject to complete defeasance. How then can the remainder be distinguished from the executory interest?

At the outset, note that both remainders and executory interests are future interests created in someone other than the original grantor. Executory interests, however, differ from remainders in that they do not await the natural expiration of all prior estates. Instead, executory interests "rudely" cut-short or divest either a vested present or future estate created in another transferee, or a present estate in the original grantor or his successors.[19] Once again, language generally is the key to determining whether a particular estate is thought to expire naturally (in which case the subsequent future interest would be classified as a remainder) or whether a particular estate is regarded as being abruptly truncated or divested by an executory interest.

EXAMPLE 28 (Shifting executory interest): O, owner of Blackacre in fee simple absolute, grants it "to A for life, then to B; *but if* B registers for law school, to C and his heirs." Here, A has a present possessory life estate and B has a vested remainder subject to complete defeasance. C has an executory interest. The "but if" language suggests that C's interest will never become possessory without divesting, or cutting short, B's vested estate. Note that if B registers for law school while A is alive, C's executory interest will divest a future estate in B. If, however, B registers for law school after A's death, C's executory interest will divest a present, possessory estate in B. C's executory interest is called a "shifting" executory interest, which is one that truncates the vested estate of another transferee, which was created at the same time as the executory interest.

EXAMPLE 29 (Determinable fee subject to an executory interest): O, owner of Blackacre in fee simple absolute, grants it

---

[19] See generally Restatement of Property §§ 25, 158 (1936); 1 American Law of Property § 4.53 (1952).

"to A and her heirs *while* the United Nations maintains its headquarters in New York, then to B and her heirs."[20] Here, A has a determinable fee subject to an executory interest.[21] Although the "while" language is indicative of a natural expiration, B cannot have a remainder because a remainder cannot follow a fee simple. Therefore, B has an executory interest. O has nothing, as he gave his entire fee simple absolute away.

EXAMPLE 30 (Vested remainder): O, owner of Blackacre in fee simple absolute, grants it "to A for life or *for so long as* she does not go to law school, then to B." A has a determinable life estate which will expire naturally either at her death or if she goes to law school. B has a vested remainder, rather than an executory interest, because the "for so long as" language suggests that when B takes Blackacre, it will be upon the natural expiration of A's estate. O has nothing, as he gave away his entire fee simple absolute.

EXAMPLE 31 (Shifting executory interest): O, owner of Blackacre in fee simple absolute, grants it "to A for life, *but should* she go to law school, then to B." Here, A has a defeasible life estate subject to an executory interest. B has a shifting executory interest because the "but should" language indicates an abrupt truncation of A's estate rather than a natural expiration. In this case, O has retained a reversion because O would get the property back in the event A dies without ever going to law school. Note that if B's executory interest ever becomes a present, possessory estate, it will not only divest A's life estate, but also O's reversion.

EXAMPLE 32 (Springing executory interest): O, owner of Blackacre in fee simple absolute, grants it "to A for life, and five months after A's death, to B." In this case, the property will revert back to O for five months after A's death. B has an executory interest. When B's estate becomes one that is presently possessory, it will divest or truncate a present estate in the original grantor (or his successors, if he is no longer alive). B's executory interest is called a "springing" executory interest, which is one that, upon vesting, "springs" from the original grantor or his heirs rather than from a simultaneously created estate in someone other than the grantor.

---

[20] Note that the executory interest in B and her heirs violates the common law rule against perpetuities and thus would be void in those jurisdictions that retain that rule.

[21] See Restatement of Property § 47 (1936).

## 5. DISTINGUISHING BETWEEN EQUITABLE AND LEGAL ESTATES

The various estates catalogued in the preceding discussion can arise in the context of either legal interests or equitable interests. The Restatement of Property § 6 (1936) defines a legal interest as one that "has its origin in the principles, standards and rules developed by courts of laws as distinguished from courts of chancery." An equitable interest is one that has its "origins in the principles, standards and rules developed by courts of chancery." These definitions are not very helpful because they assume familiarity with the differences between the ancient courts of law and chancery as they existed centuries ago. For a complete understanding of this subject, one must turn to the history books. At the risk of oversimplification, however, some basic questions arising in the context of a modern real property practice can be answered without resorting to history.

Generally, the holder of the formal legal title owns a legal interest, whereas the holder of the beneficial interest in the land owns an equitable interest. In most cases, legal and beneficial ownership is in the same individual and there is no need to distinguish between the two forms of ownership. Where one person has an enforceable beneficial interest in a particular item of property while another person holds formal legal title, however, both kinds of interests exist. Such instances usually arise because one person holds property in trust for the other. The trust may be express or implied, may rest on the volition of the parties, or may be imposed by operation of law irrespective of the will of both parties.

> EXAMPLE 33 (Legal vs. equitable interests): A grants property to T to hold in trust for A during A's life and to distribute the property to A's children on A's death. T has a legal interest in the property, and A has a present equitable interest in the property. Essentially, T holds the legal title to the property for the benefit of A. A's children have a future legal and equitable interest in the property.

In modern times, most future interests take the form of beneficial interests in trusts. A person may place property in trust for someone else for a variety of reasons, including a concern that the beneficial owner may not have the ability or maturity to manage the trust assets independently. Thus, control over the property is vested in the legal owner, the trustee, who manages the trust property for the benefit of the beneficial owner.

Equitable future interests in land or personalty rarely cause the inconvenience that legal interests do. Legal future interests in land tend to make it difficult to use the land in an efficient manner, and to lock land uses into the rigid scheme of a long dead transferor. In contrast, a trustee, either by the express terms of the creating instrument or otherwise, usually may sell the assets comprising the trust (be they land or personalty) and reinvest the proceeds elsewhere.

In England, almost all *legal* future interests in land are prohibited. In the United States, some states have sought to limit the inconvenience caused by stale powers of termination or possibilities of reverter by providing by statute that such interests may last only a limited period of time.

## 6. MODERN TRENDS REGARDING FUTURE INTERESTS

Many modern scholars have deplored the unnecessary distinctions and archaic complexity of the common law system of estates.[22] In addition, many states have legislatively reduced the need to distinguish between certain types of future interests. For example, California has abolished the distinction between remainders and executory interests, calling both interests remainders.[23] It has also abolished the distinction between possibilities of reverter and powers of termination, treating the former as the latter.[24] Consequently, "Fees simple determinable and possibilities of reverter are abolished."[25] Executory interests that "terminate a fee simple estate in real property" are to be treated as powers of termination.[26] Thus, under California law, determinable fees and possibilities of reverter no longer exist, and a limitation that would have created these interests is to be deemed as creating a fee subject to a condition subsequent and a power of termination.[27] Almost all executory interests are to be treated as either remainders or powers of termination.[28] Other states have also abolished some of the old distinctions among the estates.[29]

It seems likely that the trend toward the simplification of the law of estates will continue, and that someday law students will no longer have the dubious pleasure of immersion in this arcane and partly archaic area of the law.[30]

---

[22] See, e.g., T.P. Gallanis, The Future of Future Interests, 60 Wash. & Lee L. Rev. 513 (2003); Lawrence W. Waggoner, Reformulating the Structure of Estates: A Proposal for Legislative Action, 85 Harv. L. Rev. 729 (1972).

[23] Cal. Civil Code §§ 769, 778.

[24] Cal. Civil Code §§ 885.010(1), 885.020.

[25] Cal. Civil Code § 885.020.

[26] Cal. Civil Code § 885.010(a)(2).

[27] Cal. Civil Code § 885.020.

[28] Cal. Civil Code §§ 769, 778, 885.010(a)(2).

[29] See, e.g., Ky. Rev. Stat. Ann. § 381.218 (eliminating distinctions between types of defeasible fees); N.Y. Est., Powers & Trusts L. § 6–3.2 (treating executory interests as remainders).

[30] See T.P. Gallanis, The Future of Future Interests, 60 Wash. & Lee L. Rev. 513 (2003) (proposing a comprehensive statute simplifying and reforming the law of present and future interests).

7. REVIEW OUTLINE

## FREEHOLD ESTATES IN LAND: A SIMPLIFIED SUMMARY

I. Fee simple (present interest)
   (a) Absolute
   (b) Defeasible
       1. Future interest in grantor (reversionary interest)
           a. Automatic transfer
               (1) present interest: fee simple determinable
               (2) future interest: possibility of reverter
               (3) language: until; so long as; etc.
           b. Transfer depends on action of future interest holder
               (1) present interest: fee simple subject to condition subsequent
               (2) future interest: power of termination, right of entry
               (3) language: on condition that; but if
       2. Future interest in someone other than grantor
           a. Present interest: fee simple subject to executory limitation
           b. Future interest: executory interest
           c. Language: until . . . then to; but if . . . then to

II. Life estate (present interest)
   (a) Present interest: life estate
   (b) Future interest
       1. In grantor: reversion
       2. In one other than grantor: remainder
           a. Vested Remainder
               (1) absolutely vested ("A for life, then to B.")
               (2) vested subject to open (" . . . then to A's children," A having at least one child.)
               (3) vested subject to divestment (vested subject to condition subsequent) (" . . . then to B, but if . . . then to C".) B's remainder is vested subject to divestment. C has an executory interest since C cuts short B's interest.

        b. Contingent Remainder
            (1) subject to condition precedent ("... then to B if the [described event] occurs")
            (2) in favor of unascertained person
                (a) heirs, issue etc. of a living person
                (b) then oldest child, etc.
    3. In one other than grantor: executory interests
        a. Cuts short the life estate.
        b. Example: "To A for life ... but if ... then to X." X has an executory interest.
III. Future interests retained by the grantor or the estate of the testator (reversionary interests)
    (a) Possibility of reverters and powers of termination: usually follow a fee
    (b) Reversions: follow a life estate or non-freehold tenancy (for years, periodic, tenancy at will, or tenancy at sufferance)
IV. Future interests in favor of one who is not the grantor
    (a) Must be either a remainder or an executory interest
        1. Remainders
            a. Never follow a fee
            b. Follows natural termination of a life estate
        2. Executory interests
            a. A future interest that follows a fee and is not created in favor of a grantor is always an executory interest
            b. A future interest that is not a reversionary interest and that cuts short a previous interest is an executory interest.
                (1) Example: To A for life, then to B, but if B dies before A, then to C. C has an executory interest since it cuts short B's remainder.
V. Distinguishing vested remainders subject to divestment from contingent remainders
    (a) A vested remainder subject to divestment can also be called a vested remainder subject to a condition subsequent. A contingent remainder can also be called a remainder subject to a condition precedent. Thus, whether a remainder is vested subject to divestment or is contingent depends on whether the condition is subsequent or precedent.

1. Whether a condition is precedent or subsequent depends on the form of the language used, rather than the substance of the condition.

    a. Examples

        (1) "To A for life, remainder to A's surviving children" creates a contingent remainder in A's children because the condition of survival precedes the gift to the children.

        (2) "To A for life, remainder to A's children who survive her." This also creates a contingent remainder. Although the word "survive" follows the word "children," there is a single gift to children who survive A—the remainder is not first given and then taken away.

        (3) "To A for life, remainder to A's children, B, C, and D, but if any such child fails to survive A, such child's share shall be given to his or her issue." Here the remainder is first given, and then taken away if a child fails to survive A. Thus, the condition of survival is a condition subsequent and B, C, and D have vested remainders subject to divestment (also called defeasance). Their issue have executory interests because the gifts to the issue cut short the gift to the ancestor.

        (4) "To A for life, then to B's heirs."

            (a) If B is alive when the gift is made, the remainder is a contingent remainder.

            (b) If B is dead when the gift is made, the remainder might be a vested remainder or a contingent remainder, depending on how the court construes the phrase "B's heirs."

                i) If B's heirs are picked at B's death or at the time of the grant, the remainder is vested.

                ii) If B's heirs are picked at the death of A (as if B died a moment after A), the remainder is contingent.

8. PROBLEM SET

Identify the state of the title created by each of the following conveyances. Any interest conveyed is a fee simple absolute unless otherwise indicated.

Exale: O to A for life, then to B.

A has a present, possessory life estate. B has a vested remainder.

Problems:

1. O to A for life, but if A remarries, then to B.
2. O to A for life, then to B and her heirs, but if B ever remarries, then to C and her heirs.
3. O to A for life for so long as A does not smoke marijuana on the premises.
4. O to A for life; but if marijuana is smoked on the premises, then to B.
5. O to A; but if marijuana is smoked on the premises, then to B.
6. O to A for life, remainder to those children of A who live to age 21. Make the following assumptions as to the state of affairs at the time of the transfer:
    a. A is alive but does not have any children.
    b. A is alive and has a 14-year-old child.
    c. A is alive and has a 21-year-old child.

## 9. SAMPLE STATUTE OF DESCENT AND DISTRIBUTION

### ILLINOIS COMPILED STATUTES

755 ILCS 5/2–1, Probate.

#### RULES OF DESCENT AND DISTRIBUTION

§ 5/2–1. Rules of descent and distribution. The intestate real and personal estate of a resident decedent and the intestate real estate in this State of a nonresident decedent, after all just claims against his estate are fully paid, descends and shall be distributed as follows:

(a) If there is a surviving spouse and also a descendant of the decedent: ½ of the entire estate to the surviving spouse and ½ to the decedent's descendants per stirpes.

(b) If there is no surviving spouse but a descendant of the decedent: the entire estate to the decedent's descendants per stirpes.

(c) If there is a surviving spouse but no descendant of the decedent: the entire estate to the surviving spouse.

(d) If there is no surviving spouse or descendant but a parent, brother, sister or descendant of a brother or sister of the decedent: the entire estate to the parents, brothers and sisters of the decedent in equal parts, allowing to the surviving parent if one is dead a double portion and to the descendants of a deceased brother or sister per stirpes the portion which the deceased brother or sister would have taken if living.[31]

(e) If there is no surviving spouse, descendant, parent, brother, sister or descendant of a brother or sister of the decedent but a grandparent or descendant of a grandparent of the decedent: (1) ½ of the entire estate to the decedent's maternal grandparents in equal parts or to the survivor of them, or if there is none surviving, to their descendants per stirpes, and (2) ½ of the entire estate to the decedent's paternal grandparents in equal parts or to the survivor of them, or if there is none surviving, to their descendants per stirpes. If there is no surviving paternal grandparent or descendant of a paternal grandparent, but a maternal grandparent or descendant of a maternal grandparent of the decedent: the entire estate to the decedent's maternal grandparents in equal parts or to the survivor of them, or if there is none surviving, to their descendants per stirpes. If there is no surviving maternal grandparent or descendant of a maternal grandparent, but a paternal grandparent or descendant of a paternal grandparent of the decedent: the entire estate to the decedent's paternal grandparents in equal parts or to the survivor of them, or if there is none surviving, to their descendants per stirpes.

(f) If there is no surviving spouse, descendant, parent, brother, sister, descendant of a brother or sister or grandparent or descendant of a grandparent of the decedent: (1) ½ of the entire estate to the decedent's maternal great-grandparents in equal parts or to the survivor of them, or if there is none surviving, to their descendants per stirpes, and (2) ½ of the entire estate to the decedent's paternal great-grandparents in equal parts or to the survivor of them, or if there is none surviving, to their descendants per stirpes. If there is no surviving paternal great-grandparent or descendant of a paternal great-grandparent, but a maternal great-grandparent or descendant of a maternal great-grandparent of the decedent: the entire estate to the decedent's maternal great-grandparents in equal parts or to the survivor of them, or if there is none surviving, to their descendants per stirpes. If there is no surviving maternal great-grandparent or descendant of a maternal great-grandparent, but a paternal great-grandparent or descendant of a paternal great-grandparent of the decedent: the entire estate to the decedent's paternal great-grandparents in equal parts or to the survivor of them, or if there is none surviving, to their descendants per stirpes.

(g) If there is no surviving spouse, descendant, parent, brother, sister, descendant of a brother or sister, grandparent, descendant of a grandparent, great-grandparent or descendant of a great-grandparent of the decedent: the entire estate in equal parts to the nearest kindred of

---

[31] Editor's note: However, Illinois allows the courts to reduce a parent's intestate share of a child's estate if that parent willfully neglected, deserted or failed to support the deceased child. See 755 ILCS § 5/6.5, Parent Neglecting Child.

the decedent in equal degree (computing by the rules of the civil law) and without representation.

(h) If there is no surviving spouse and no known kindred of the decedent: the real estate escheats to the county in which it is located; the personal estate physically located within this State and the personal estate physically located or held outside this State which is the subject of ancillary administration of an estate being administered within this State escheats to the county of which the decedent was a resident, or, if the decedent was not a resident of this State, to the county in which it is located; all other personal property of the decedent of every class and character, wherever situate, or the proceeds thereof, shall escheat to this State and be delivered to the Director of Financial Institutions of the State pursuant to the Uniform Disposition of Unclaimed Property Act.

# ASSIGNMENT 10

# INTRODUCTION TO THE COMMON LAW RULE AGAINST PERPETUITIES

## 1. INTRODUCTION

The origin of the rule against perpetuities can be traced to 1682 when the celebrated Duke of Norfolk's case was decided.[1] In the opinion, Lord Nottingham identified the basic underlying criteria for judging when a limitation imposed on the ability to transfer an ownership interest in property is invalid. "I will tell you where I will stop [upholding limitations]: I will stop wherever any visible inconvenience doth appear." Thus, the court declared that an interest that unduly interfered with the free alienability of land for too long a time (a "perpetuity") would be held void. The opinion reaffirms the overriding interest of society in the wise use of land, as against the uncontrolled will of the original conveyor. In a remarkable series of cases stretching over the next 150 years, the English courts gradually defined the concept of "inconvenience."

Although the origin of the rule can be traced to the Duke of Norfolk's case, the need for the rule arose in 1535. In that fateful year, the Statute of Uses was passed. Although originally merely a revenue measure designed to curb the avoidance of feudal incidents (the taxes of the day), the Statute of Uses had the side effect of revolutionizing the system of conveyancing. It made possible the creation of important new types of future interests called *executory interests*. (Before 1535, the common law recognized only remainders, reversions, possibilities of reverter, and powers of termination.) Ultimately, certain types of executory interests were to prove too "inconvenient". This provided the impetus for developing the rule against perpetuities, which was intended to limit inconvenient interests.

In 1886, an American law professor, John Chipman Gray, wrote the classic treatment of the subject. J. Gray, The Rule Against Perpetuities. Gray's statement of the rule soon became *the* rule both in the United States and England. In fact, in some states Gray's formulation of the rule was passed as a statute. Gray's treatise went through four editions, the last of which appeared in 1942. In 1938, another American law professor, W. Barton Leach, prepared a lucid and readable summary of the rule,

---

[1] 3 Ch.Cas. 1, 22 Eng.Rep. 931 (Ch. 1682).

especially suitable for law students.[2] Largely as a result of Leach's work, the movement for reform of the rule gained strength.

After extensive and sometimes acrimonious debate, the American Law Institute adopted a far reaching modification of the rule in 1983.[3] More recently, the National Conference of Commissioners on Uniform State Laws approved the Uniform Statutory Rule Against Perpetuities, which surpassed even the Restatement in the degree to which the common law rule was modified.[4] In addition, many states now preclude the rule from applying under various circumstances, and nearly all states have modified the rule to some extent. This reform movement is given a fuller treatment in Assignment 11.

The rule against perpetuities bears the imprint of an amazing variety of legal institutions and personalities. King, Parliament, King's Bench, treatise and law review authors, American courts, legislatures and institutes all have played significant roles in the development of the rule. Were it not for the complexity and subtlety of the doctrine of estates, the rule would not have been necessary at all.

The rule against perpetuities can be violated only by the following future interests: executory interests, contingent remainders, and vested remainders subject to open. The reasons for this limited application are entirely historical. Executory interests received legal recognition several hundred years after remainders and reversionary interests. Thus, it is not surprising that the legal rules governing executory interests differ from those governing the older interests. Similarly, remainders are governed by rules somewhat different from reversions, possibilities of reverter and powers of termination, all of which received recognition at a far earlier date than remainders. Thus, reversions, possibilities of reverter, and powers of termination are completely unaffected by the rule against perpetuities. The next oldest form of future interests, remainders, are subject to the rule to some extent. Finally, the newest form of future interests, executory interests, are most affected by the rule against perpetuities. These young upstarts, deriving from a statute scarcely four hundred years old, are not given the same deference that is due the more mature interests. In light of the disparate impact of the rule against perpetuities, it now should be apparent why the appropriate classification of a particular future interest is critical.

## 2. PRINCIPAL PROBLEM

Testatrix, Maedel Sellers, died survived by two children, Johny Ray Sellers and Edna Ray Walker. Edna has three children: Toby, Eddie and Bobbie, who were all born before the death of testatrix. Johny has one

---

[2] Leach, Perpetuities in a Nutshell, 51 Harv.L.Rev. 638 (1938). See also Leach, Perpetuities: The Nutshell Revisited, 78 Harv.L.Rev. 973 (1965).

[3] See Restatement (Second) of Property §§ 1.1–1.6 (Donative Transfers) (1983).

[4] See Uniform Statutory Rule Against Perpetuities, Unif. Prob. Code §§ 2–901 to 2–906.

child, Chad, who was born after the death of testatrix. The third and fourth paragraphs of the will provide as follows:

III. I give, devise and bequeath all the rest and residue of my said property and estate, real, personal or mixed, community or separate, wherever situated, of which I may die seized and possessed, to my daughter, Edna Ray Sellers Walker, and my son, Johny Ray Sellers for life, if they both survive me, to have and to hold said residue of my estate as joint tenants during their joint lives; provided, however, if only one of my said children survive me, or if both survive me but one later dies then I give and devise to my surviving child an estate for life in one-half of said residue and to the living issue of my deceased child an estate for life in the other one-half of said residue. *Upon the death of the last survivor of my son and daughter or upon my death if neither my son nor my daughter survives me, I give, devise and bequeath all the rest and residue of my estate to the issue of my daughter, Edna Ray Sellers Walker, and my son, Johny Ray Sellers, as joint tenants during the respective lives of said issue and the life of the survivor, or, if only one of such issue survives me, then I give and devise such property and estate to such survivor for life.* (Emphasis added.)

IV. Upon the death of the last surviving life tenant heretofore provided for in paragraph THIRD of this Will, I give, devise and bequeath the remainder of my said property and estate in fee simple title to the persons who would be entitled to inherit said property in accordance with the laws of descent and distribution of the State of Texas, if I had died intestate immediately after the death of the last surviving life tenant heretofore provided for in paragraph THIRD of this Will.

You are the attorney for the executor. The various parties and their attorneys have different opinions concerning the meaning and validity of the above quoted paragraphs. It will be necessary to bring an action to have the court determine the effect of these clauses. As a necessary part of this action, you must prepare a memorandum of law setting forth the various possible methods of dealing with the limitation in question, and recommending the one method that, in your opinion, is best.

Before preparing your memorandum, consider the following materials.

## 3. Materials for Solution of Principal Problem

According to the classic treatment of the subject, the rule against perpetuities in its common law form provides as follows: "*No interest is good unless it must vest, if at all, not later than twenty-one years after some life in being at the creation of the interest.*" Gray, The Rule Against Perpetuities § 201 (4th ed. 1942). Although this statement undoubtedly is incomprehensible at this point, the following discussion should clarify the rule by elaborating upon each of its salient aspects.

*Identification of the Measuring Life*

The identification of the measuring life is one of the most problematic aspects of the rule against perpetuities. The rule requires that an interest must vest not later than twenty-one years after some life in being at the creation of the interest. It is easiest to think of a measuring life as one that will "save" the limitation. The proper question, therefore, is as follows: Is there any life in existence at the creation of the interest of which it can be said for a certainty that the interest will vest within 21 years after the end of that life? In general, try to identify a measuring life by looking to persons named in the limitation. If one qualifies to save the limitation, look no further. If none of the persons named in the limitation qualify to save the limitation, try relatives of the persons named.

> EXAMPLE 1 ("Good" executory interest): O grants Blackacre "to B, but should liquor be sold on the premises *during the life of B*, then over to C." B has a fee simple subject to a condition subsequent, and C has an executory interest. C's interest is subject to the rule, but in this case it will not violate it. C's interest is good since it will vest in possession, if at all, within B's life, and B was alive (i.e., was a "life in being") when the grant was made.
>
> EXAMPLE 2: A dies leaving a will under which he devises Blackacre to "B for life, then to B's children jointly for their lives, then to those of B's grandchildren, equally, who are alive at the death of the survivor of all of B's children." B is alive at the death of A, and has some children but no grandchildren.
>
>> a. ("Good" vested remainder): B's children have vested remainders for life, subject to open. On B's death, they become absolutely vested remainders for life. These interests are subject to the rule, but do not violate it because B can be a measuring life. All of the interests of B's children will vest within 21 years after B's death. In fact, they will vest in possession no later than B's death.
>>
>> b. (Void contingent remainders): B's grandchildren have contingent remainders, which also are subject to the rule. Here, the devise to the grandchildren will not satisfy the rule because there is no one who can act as a measuring life to save the disposition to B's grandchildren. There is no one alive *at the time the interests are created* (which, in this case, would be the death of A) of whom it can be said with certainty that the interest to B's grandchildren will vest within 21 years of the end of such life. B may have more children after A's death and those afterborn children may

survive B and all of his existing children. In such a case, the gift to B's grandchildren will not necessarily vest within the period of the rule. Suppose B has three children at the time the interests are created and subsequently has another child called C. One year later, B and all of his children, except for C, are killed in a plane crash. C grows up and, twenty-five years later, has two children of his own. C's children will only be eligible to take their interests upon C's death, and under this scenario, their interests will vest later than allowed by the rule.

c. ("Good" contingent remainders): If B were dead when A died, the interest to B's grandchildren would be good. B obviously cannot have any more children and thus all of B's present children can serve as measuring lives. The disposition to B's grandchildren will vest in possession at the death of the last survivor of B's children, all of whom were lives in being at the creation of the interest.

d. ("Good" reversion in A's estate): If B died without ever having had children, the remainders to B's children and grandchildren would be ineffective. Ownership of Blackacre would return to A's estate, since whatever A did not effectively devise returns to A's estate. There it will be distributed under the residuary clause[5] of A's will, or (if there is no effective residuary clause) by intestacy. Since reversionary interests are not subject to the rule against perpetuities, this reversionary interest is unaffected by the rule.

EXAMPLE 3 ("Good" contingent remainders): O grants Blackacre "to A for life, then to B's grandchildren who reach the age of 21." Assume B is dead at the time the interest is created. At this time, B has children, but no grandchildren. B's grandchildren have contingent remainders, which are subject to the rule, but which do not violate it in this example. Here, B's children qualify as "saving" or measuring lives although they are not named in the disposition. Why? Because the interest to B's grandchildren will vest in possession not later than 21 years after the death of B's living children, none of whom can be born after the limitation, and thus are lives in being.

EXAMPLE 4 ("Good" executory interests): A grant of property "to my descendants alive at the death of the survivor of X, Y, and Z" is good under the rule even if X, Y, and Z take nothing under the grant. They are measuring lives although they are not beneficiaries under the grant. The lives used as measuring lives,

---

[5] The "residuary clause" in a will disposes of all the testator's property that remains after satisfying all debts and all the specific bequests and devises in the testator's will.

however, cannot be so numerous as to make it impractical to keep track of them.

For purposes of the rule, a "life in being" includes the life of one conceived but not yet born, assuming the fetus is born alive. Assume, in Example 3, that B was dead but his wife was pregnant when A died. The disposition to B's grandchildren would be good in this case because a fetus which is born alive qualifies as a life in being. The rule inalterably presumes that no one will conceive a child after his or her death, but this presumption is at odds with current reproductive technology, including the availability and use of frozen human eggs, sperm, or embryos far in the future. Yet this change in available reproductive technology has occurred roughly at the same time that most states have modified or abolished the rule, which has meant that few if any courts have had to address the conflicts between a legal fiction and the medical reality. Posthumous conception has had more relevance with regard to who qualifies as an heir, beneficiary, or interest-holder, but it has received considerable academic interest regarding the rule against perpetuities.[6]

An interest that must vest, if at all, within twenty-one years after its creation is good, despite the fact that it is unrelated to lives in being. Thus, a grant of property "to B fifteen years from today if the gravel pit is still in operation" is good.

*The Meaning of "Vest"*

The meaning of "vest" is another of the more difficult concepts relating to the rule. The word "vest" as used with respect to the rule against perpetuities does not have precisely the same meaning that it has in other contexts. In other contexts, a vested interest is one not subject to a condition precedent. Yet, as explained below, a possibility of reverter clearly is subject to a condition precedent but still is treated as vested for purposes of the rule.

The rule against perpetuities is a rule against future interests that remain "unvested" for too long a time. To put the thought in traditional terminology, it is a rule against "remoteness of vesting". *It is not a rule against trusts or future interests that last too long.*

EXAMPLE 5 ("Good" joint life estate): Same limitation and facts as in Example 2. The life estate in B's children is good although it may last for longer than the period of the rule. B may have additional children (i.e., lives not in being at the creation of the interests), and these afterborn children may live more than 21 years longer than any lives in being at the creation of the interests. Thus, their joint life estate may extend for a period beyond the period of the rule, but will still be good, because it

---

[6] See, e.g., Greenfield, Dad Was Born a Thousand Years Ago? An Examination of Post-Mortem Conception and Inheritance with a Focus on the Rule Against Perpetuities, 8 Minn. J.L. Sci. & Tech. 277 (2007); Hoffman & Morriss, Birth After Death: Perpetuities and the New Reproductive Technologies, 38 Ga. L. Rev. 575 (2004).

must vest in possession no later than the death of B, a life in being at the creation of the interests.

We have seen that reversions, powers of termination, and possibilities of reverter are not subject to the rule. Under the arcane logic of the rule, these three interests vest as soon as they are created. Therefore, they never violate the rule, and are unaffected by it.

EXAMPLE 6 (Possibility of reverter always "good"): A grants Blackacre to "B, so long as liquor is not sold on the property." B has a fee simple determinable and A has a valid possibility of reverter in Blackacre that will become possessory if liquor is ever sold on the premises. Although A's interest is subject to a condition precedent for a period that may exceed the period of the rule, A's interest is good because possibilities of reverter are considered "vested" at their creation.

The meaning of "vest" as it pertains to executory interests also is relatively easy to apply. For purposes of the rule, an executory interest vests either when (1) it becomes possessory, or (2) it is not subject to a condition, and it must become possessory at the end of a precisely computable period of time.[7]

EXAMPLE 7 (Void executory interest): A grants Blackacre to "B so long as the United Nations Headquarters remain in New York, and if they move, then to C." Since C's executory interest is not certain to vest in possession within the period of the rule, and since it does not vest in interest within a precisely computable period of time, C's interest is void under the rule.

In contrast, the meaning of "vest" as applied to remainders is an extremely challenging concept. Remainders are considered vested for purposes of the rule if they vest either *in possession* or *in interest*.[8] A remainder vests in possession when it becomes a possessory or present interest.

EXAMPLE 8 ("Good" contingent remainder; reversion always "good"): A grants Blackacre "to B for life, then jointly to those of B's children who survive B." At the time of the grant, B is alive and has two children. Initially, B has a present, possessory life estate, B's children have a contingent remainder, and A has a reversion. B's interest is good because it vests in possession immediately. The contingent (non-vested) remainder in B's children is good because it must vest in possession no later than the end of B's life, which is a life in being at the creation of the

---

[7] Restatement of Property, § 370, comment h (1944). Accord, 6 American Law of Property § 24.20 (Casner ed. 1952); Restatement (Second) of Property, § 1.4, comment b (Donative Transfers) (1983); 3 Simes & Smith, Future Interests § 1236 (2d ed. 1956). Contra, Gray, The Rule Against Perpetuities § 201 n. 3 (4th ed. 1942). Gray apparently takes the position that executory interests vest only when they become presently possessory.

[8] The rule relating to when class gifts vest in interest is discussed later in this Assignment.

interest. The reversion in A is good because reversions are never bad under the rule.

The concept of vesting *in interest* can best be understood by considering the four basic types of remainders separately: (1) absolutely vested; (2) vested subject to defeasance; (3) contingent; and (4) vested subject to open.

*Absolutely Vested Remainders.* Remainders are good under the rule if, at the time of their creation, they must become absolutely vested within the period of the rule.

EXAMPLE 9 (Absolutely vested remainder always "good"): A grants Greenacre "to B for life, then to B's oldest child for life, then to C." At the time of the grant, B has no children. All of the interests are good. The contingent remainder in B's oldest child will vest in possession, if at all, no later than the end of B's life, a life in being at the creation of the interest. The remainder in C is not certain to vest in *possession* within the period of the rule, since possession is postponed until the death of B's oldest child, who is not a life in being. However, C's remainder is still good because it became absolutely vested *in interest* at the moment of its creation, since it was not subject to any condition other than the natural expiration of the preceding life estates.

*Vested Remainders Subject to Defeasance and Contingent Remainders.* Remainders that must become vested subject to defeasance within the period of the rule are good, whereas remainders that may remain contingent for a time exceeding the period of the rule are bad.

EXAMPLE 10 ("Good" vested remainder subject to defeasance): O grants Blackacre "to A for life, remainder to A's daughter Shanna, but should Shanna ever attend law school, the remainder is to go to X." At the time of the grant, A is alive, and has a daughter, Shanna. Shanna's interest is good under the rule because it is vested subject to defeasance from the moment of its creation. X's executory interest is good since it will vest in possession, if at all, during Shanna's life.

EXAMPLE 11 ("Good" and "bad" contingent remainders): In his will, O devises his home "to A for life, then to A's widow for life, and then to the children of A who are then living." Assume that at the time the interest is created (i.e., when O dies), A is married to a woman named Cecilia, and that A has no children. Here, A has a present, possessory life estate which is vested from the moment of its creation and thus is good under the rule. A's widow has a contingent remainder, because, until A dies, we do not know with certainty the identity of his widow (he may divorce Cecilia or she may die before A and A may marry someone else). Still, the widow's contingent remainder is good under the rule because it is certain to vest in possession and interest at the death of A, a life in being at the creation of the interest. A's children also have contingent remainders, because their interests are subject to the condition precedent of surviving A's widow (recall the *then living* language of the devise). Their contingent remainder is bad under the rule because it is not certain to vest within 21 years after the death of a life in being. Both A's widow and his children all may be born after O's death, and could outlive A by more than 21 years. Therefore, no measuring lives exist to "save" the gift. This particular scenario is called the "unborn widow" hypothetical.[9]

EXAMPLE 12 (Valid contingent remainder): A devises Redacre "to B for life, then to B's children for their joint lives, then to the person who is President of the United States when B dies." At the time of the devise, B is alive, but has no children. The devise to the President is good. It was not vested at its creation (i.e., at A's death) since until B dies it is not possible to point to any person and identify him or her as the recipient of the remainder. Therefore, the interest is a contingent remainder due to the unascertainability of the taker. But the remainder interest will vest *in interest* no later than the death of B, a life in being at the creation of the interest. The fact that the remainderman will not necessarily take possession within the period of the rule is immaterial since the remainder is certain to vest in interest at the end of B's life, and thus is certain to vest within the period of the rule. Note that if the described President is dead at the death of the survivor of B's children, Redacre will pass to that President's estate, to be distributed to her heirs or devisees.

*Vested Remainders Subject to Open: Class Gifts.* With class gifts, the gift is considered vested for purposes of the rule against perpetuities only when the exact share of each individual class member is vested.

EXAMPLE 13 (Valid vested remainder subject to open): O grants Blackacre "to A for life, remainder to the children of B." Assume B has two children at the time of the grant. The children have a vested remainder subject to open to admit afterborn members of the class. Such a remainder is not considered vested for purposes of the Rule. Nevertheless, this particular remainder is good since it will vest by becoming possessory at the end of A's life, a life in being. Note that B also can be used as a measuring life.

The rules regarding class gifts can get confusing, but two important points must be remembered. *First*, if the interest of even one potential member of the class can violate the rule, the entire class gift is invalid. This has come to be known as the "all or nothing" rule. *Second*, to

---

[9] In some states, statutes exist which state that A's widow is presumed to be a person alive at O's death. Cal.Prob. Code § 21231 (2015); 765 ILCS 305/4(c)(1)(C) (2015); N.Y.Est.Powers & Trusts Law § 9–1.3(c) (2015).

determine if a rule against perpetuities violation exists, it is necessary to determine who qualifies for membership in the class. It is only after membership is determined that the interest of each member can be analyzed from the standpoint of whether it violates the rule (remember *all* the class interests must vest within the period of the rule).

*The Rule of Convenience.* To determine membership in a particular class, the class is deemed to close when the following two events have occurred: 1) someone qualifies for distribution; *and* 2) the gift is available for distribution. Both requirements must be satisfied. Once a class is closed, no afterborn members will be eligible to share in the gift, although members who are already in being at the time the class is closed but who have not met certain conditions required under the grant will be eligible to participate once they have satisfied the stipulated conditions. This rule, governing when a class closes, is known as the "rule of convenience", since it does not permit the class to remain open longer than convenient. Unfortunately, the rule of convenience, which encourages a relatively early closing of a class, can be highly inconvenient to those excluded from the class.

EXAMPLE 14 (Valid class gift): A to "B for life, remainder to B's grandchildren." At the time of the grant, B is alive and has one grandchild, C. C has a vested remainder subject to open. C's precise share in the remainder depends on whether B will have additional grandchildren before he dies. For purposes of the rule against perpetuities, C's remainder is not vested at the time of the conveyance, since the precise share C will receive will not be known until B's death. Here, the class will close at B's death, since that is the time the gift will be available for distribution and we know that someone, C, will be qualified to take the gift at that time (although there may be other takers if B has additional grandchildren subsequent to the grant and before B's death). Therefore, the class gift to B's grandchildren is good. Grandchildren born after B's death will be barred from taking because of the rule of convenience. It would be too inconvenient to delay distribution until the death of all of B's children so as to provide for any possible grandchildren born after B's death.

EXAMPLE 15 (Valid class gift): O devises property "to A for life, remainder to B's children." Assume that at O's death, A and B are alive, and B has two children. B's children have vested remainders subject to open. Here, the class will close when A dies, at which time all of B's living children (and the estates of those who predeceased A) will be eligible to share in the gift. A child of B conceived after A's death would take nothing since it would be too "inconvenient" to keep the class open until B dies. The class gift is valid because the interests of all members of the class will vest in possession at A's death, and A was a life in being at the creation of the interest. B can also be used as a measuring life.

EXAMPLE 16 (Void class gift): A grants Greenacre "to the children of my brother B, whether now or hereafter born, for their lives, jointly, and at the death of the last survivor of said children, to B's grandchildren equally." Assume B is alive at the time of the grant and has two children, C1 and C2, and two grandchildren, GC1 and GC2. The gift to the children of B is good since it must vest within the lifetime of B, a life in being. The remainder in GC1 and GC2 is vested subject to open to let other grandchildren join the class. The remainder in the grandchildren violates the rule. The class will not close until the death of the last survivor of B's children. This last survivor may not be either C1 or C2, but an afterborn child (remember that B is alive at the time of the grant and thus can have more children). This afterborn child may outlive all lives in existence at the creation of the interest and have children of his own (afterborn grandchildren of B who, were it not for the rule against perpetuities, would be entitled to share in the remainder). Thus, the precise share going to GC1 and GC2 may remain uncertain for a period exceeding the period of the rule. Recall that the gift to *all* class members must be valid under the rule; otherwise the gift to none of them is valid. Under the scenario outlined here, no measuring life could save the gift to the afterborn children of an afterborn child of B, and thus the entire class gift must fail. The "all or nothing" rule strikes again. Query, would the answer change if B were dead at the time of the grant?

EXAMPLE 17 (Void class gift): O grants Blackacre "to A for life, remainder to such of B's children who reach the age of 30." Assume B is alive at the time of the grant and has a child who is 30. The class gift to B's children is invalid. The class will not close until A's death. During A's life, B can have another child born after the grant, and two years after the birth of this child everyone else except for this afterborn child could die. Under this scenario, the interest of the afterborn child will not vest within 21 years after any life in being. Again, because the interest of one potential member of the class is bad under the rule, the entire class gift is bad.

Note that if B is *dead* at the time of the grant, the entire class gift is valid. If B is dead, B cannot have any more children and the children living at the time of the grant can be their own lives in being (i.e., even if some of these children are under the age of 9 when the interest is created, they all can serve as their own measuring lives). Their interest will vest, if at all, within their own lives.

EXAMPLE 18 (Valid class gift): Testator ("T") bequeaths his residuary estate[10] to those of his brothers and sisters who reach the age of 25. Assume T has a brother who is 25 at the time of T's death, and that T's parents are alive. There are no other siblings. The class gift is valid. Here, the class closes immediately upon T's death, because the gift is available for distribution and someone is qualified to take. The only members of the class are those who are alive at T's death, all of whom are lives in being at the creation of the interest. Note that this gift would be valid regardless of whether T's parents are alive or dead at the time of T's death. Because the class closes immediately on T's death, the possibility of afterborn brothers or sisters of T does not change the result. This example differs from Example 17 because here there is no intervening life estate. Thus the class closes as soon as the class gift is created (i.e., at T's death). Consequently, the class closes at once, and all members of the class are lives in being. In contrast, in Example 17, some members of the class might be born after the instrument speaks.

Note that the gift in this example would be *invalid* if the oldest of T's siblings at T's death is only 19, *unless* T's parents are dead. Why? Because the class will not close for another 6 years, during which time T's parents could have another child. Everyone else in the world except for this afterborn child could die, and the interest of such child then would vest after all lives in being plus 21 years. The possibility that the interest will vest beyond the period of the rule with respect to one member of the class renders the entire class gift invalid.

EXAMPLE 19 (Valid class gift): T bequeaths $100,000 to A's children. Assume that A is alive but has no children at T's death. Here, the gift is available for distribution but no one is entitled to take. Although standard class closing principles would suggest that the class will close upon the birth of A's first child, an exception to the class closing doctrine maintains that the class will remain open in this instance until A's death. Upon the birth of A's first child, that child probably would receive the entire amount, subject to partial divestment by later siblings.[11] In this example, A's unborn children have an executory interest which is valid under the rule. A is alive at the time the interest is created, and thus can serve as a measuring life.

---

[10] The "residuary estate" is all the testator's property that remains after satisfying all debts and all the specific bequests and devises in the testator's will.

[11] See generally Bergin & Haskell, Preface To Estates In Land And Future Interests 142–143 (2nd ed. 1984). The authors note that probably a bond would be required to secure the oldest child's obligation to repay. Little authority exists with respect to this type of situation.

Under the traditional common law rule, it must be mathematically certain *when the interest is created* that the interest will vest within the period of the rule. If there is any possibility, *no matter how remote,* that the interest might not vest within the period of the rule, the interest is void. In determining what is a "possibility", the common law went to the brink of logic. It assumed that (1) any person, regardless of age or medical facts, was capable of reproduction, (2) one of mature years might marry an infant, and (3) events that normally transpire in a few months might take more than 21 years.

Recall Example 11 (the "unborn widow" hypothetical): Cecilia will not necessarily be A's widow. Cecilia may predecease or divorce A, A may remarry someone (Widow 2) not alive at the creation of the interest, and Widow 2 may outlive by more than 21 years all lives in being at the creation of the interest.

> EXAMPLE 20 (Void contingent remainder): A devises property in trust to T with the trust to terminate and the trust property to be distributed to A's issue then living "five years after the date upon which an order distributing the trust property to the trustee is made by the court having jurisdiction over the probation of this will." The contingent remainder of the trust property is bad because the will might not be probated within the period of the rule, and thus the interests of the beneficiaries might not vest in time.[12]

An interest does not necessarily have to vest to be valid under the rule. What is important for purposes of the rule is that it must vest, *if at all,* within the period of the rule.

> EXAMPLE 21 (Valid contingent remainder): A grants Redacre "to B for life, then to B's children living at B's death and if none are then living, then to C." B has no children. There is no assurance that the contingent remainder to B's children will *ever* vest. Similarly, there is no assurance that C's alternate contingent remainder will ever vest. Nevertheless, both interests are good since they will vest "if at all" no later than the end of B's life, and B is a life in being.

*Effect of an Invalid Interest*

What happens when an interest is found to be "bad" under the rule? In most cases, the bad part of the limitation is simply struck out and the rest of the limitation is given effect.[13]

---

[12] Statutes in some jurisdictions provide that when the vesting of an interest is contingent upon the probate of an estate, it is presumed that such interest will vest within the period of the rule. See 765 ILCS 305/4(c)(1)(B) (2009); N.Y.Est.Powers & Trusts Law § 9–1.3(d) (2009); Restatement of Property § 374, comment f (1944).

[13] Under the doctrine of "infectious invalidity", if the court decides that the testator would have preferred to have the entire limitation struck, rather than merely the invalid part, this may be done.

EXAMPLE 22 (Void executory interest): A grants Blackacre "to B, but should liquor ever be sold on the premises, then over to C." B has a fee simple subject to an executory limitation, and C has an executory interest. C's executory interest is bad under the rule since there is no assurance that C's interest will become possessory within 21 years after the life of any person living when the grant was made. If the void limitation to C is struck out, we are left simply with a limitation to B. Thus, after giving effect to the rule against perpetuities, B receives a fee simple absolute in Blackacre.

EXAMPLE 23 (Void executory interest): A grants Blackacre "to B, for so long as liquor is not sold on the premises, but if it should be, then Blackacre shall become C's property." As explained in the previous example, C's executory interest is void. In contrast to the prior example, however, B in this case is left with a fee simple determinable rather than a fee simple absolute. Also, because of the invalidity of the gift to C, A retains a possibility of reverter (recall that a possibility of reverter is not subject to the rule against perpetuities).

EXAMPLE 24 (Void contingent remainder): A devises Blackacre "to B for life, then to B's children jointly for their lives, then to those of B's grandchildren, equally, who are alive at the death of the survivor of all of B's children." Assume that the residuary clause of A's will grants the residue of A's estate to X and that B is alive at the death of A. As discussed earlier in connection with Example 2, the devise to B's grandchildren is bad under the rule. Since the devise to B's grandchildren is bad, we are left with a valid limitation to B for life, followed by a valid limitation to B's children for life. After the death of the survivor of all of B's children there is a reversion to A. A, however, by the residuary clause of his will, has granted all property not otherwise disposed of to X. Since A's reversion has been devised to X, our ultimate conclusion after giving effect to the rule against perpetuities is that following the life estates, X has a reversion in fee simple absolute.[14]

*Time When Interests Are Created*

As the previous examples illustrate, an interest created by a will is "created" when the testator dies. An interest created by a deed is created when the deed is delivered. An important exception to these two simple rules is that if the deed is revocable the interest is deemed created when the deed becomes irrevocable.

---

[14] Cf. Brown v. Independent Baptist Church of Woburn, 325 Mass. 645, 91 N.E.2d 922 (1950). Some courts might disagree with Brown and might hold that X has an invalid executory interest. The failure of the executory interest would result in Blackacre passing by intestacy. See Simes, Is the Rule Against Perpetuities Doomed?, 52 Mich.L.Rev. 179, 179–180 n. 4 (1953).

EXAMPLE 25 (Valid contingent remainder): A grants property "to T in trust for the benefit of X for life, then to X's children who reach 25." A, the grantor, retains the power to revoke the trust at any time. Assume that X is alive at the time of the grant, but predeceases A, who dies without having revoked the trust. The contingent remainder to X's children is good since their interest is deemed created at the time the trust became irrevocable—when A died. At that time, X's children could be treated as measuring lives since their interests would vest, if at all, within their own lives. Had there been no power of revocation, the contingent remainder to X's children would have been bad because it would have been deemed created when the trust was established, and X at that time could have had afterborn children whose interests would not necessarily have vested, if at all, within the period of the rule.

*Limiting Powers of Termination and Possibilities of Reverter: A Comparative Approach*

As discussed earlier in this Assignment, the rule against perpetuities does not apply to possibilities of reverter and powers of termination. Thus, under the common law the use of land could be tied up forever through the use of these reversionary interests. The common law's failure to set a limitation on the lifespan of these future interests has resulted in the perpetuation of numerous restrictions on land use serving little or no justifiable purpose.

State legislatures have attempted to respond to this problem by enacting various measures designed to curtail the perpetual viability of these reversionary interests. For example, some states limit the length of time during which a power of termination or possibility of reverter can last. Typical durations are 30 or 40 years.[15] A number of states also have statutes, often called Marketable Title Acts, which require the holders of possibilities of reverter and powers of termination to rerecord notice of their intent to preserve their interest in the property. A typical statute requires the holder of the interest to rerecord every 30 years.[16] Such a statute extinguishes many interests because holders of the interests are either unaware of the statute, or view their interests as not being valuable enough to merit a trip down to the county recording office.[17] Many states allow the statutory measures discussed above to apply

---

[15] See, e.g., 765 ILCS 330/4 (2009) (40-year limitation).

[16] See, e.g., Cal.Civ.Code § 885.030 (2009).

[17] Other measures designed to limit the enforceability of stale possibilities of reverter and powers of termination include statutes such as Cal.Civ.Code § 885.040(b)(1) (2009) which extinguish such interests if they are "of no actual and substantial benefit to the holder of the power". See also Minn.Stat.Ann. § 500.20 (2009); N.Y.Real Prop.Act & Proc.Law § 1951 (2009). Another scheme limits enforcement by providing that if the condition is broken after a certain number of years, the holder of the interest only would be able to seek injunctive relief, rather than compelling a reversion of the property. See, e.g., Fla.Stat.Ann. § 689.18(7) (2009). Many of these statutes have express exemptions, such as California's exemption of conservation interests. See Cal.Civ.Code §§ 815, 816, 880.240, 885.015 (2009).

retroactively, that is to interests created before the legislation,[18] but some states apply them only prospectively.[19]

In this Assignment, we have examined the more important aspects of the rule against perpetuities. The treatment has been far from complete. For example, certain specialized rules relating to powers of appointment, class gifts, and charitable dispositions have not been explored at all. You should be aware that you merely have been introduced to the rule against perpetuities in its common law form. Although some additional material is offered in the next Assignment, a complete treatment must be left to more specialized courses such as those in Future Interests or Estate Planning.

## 4. PROBLEM SETS

We suggest using the following four steps in analyzing any rule against perpetuities problem:

1. Identify and classify the interests in question.

2. Determine the time of vesting of these interests.

3. Determine the validity of these interests under the rule against perpetuities.

4. If the rule is violated, determine who receives the invalid interest.

*Problem Set A*

The following problem set with answers will enable you to test your basic understanding of the material presented in this chapter.

1. O to A for life, then to B.

   Answer: A has a life estate vested in possession. B has a vested remainder. O has not retained any interest. All interests are good since all interests are vested.

2. O to A for life, then to B if he reaches the age of 25. Assume B is a newborn infant.

   Answer: A has a life estate vested in possession. B has a contingent remainder since his reaching 25 is a condition precedent to its vesting. O has a reversion, in case B's remainder never vests. All interests are good. A's interest is vested. B's

---

[18] For example, the Illinois, Iowa, and Nebraska statutes have been construed to apply retroactively. See Trustees of Schools of Tp. No. 1 v. Batdorf, 130 N.E.2d 111 (Ill. 1955); Presbytery of Southeast Iowa v. Harris, 226 N.W.2d 232 (Iowa 1975); Hiddleston v. Nebraska Jewish Education Society, 186 N.W.2d 904 (Neb. 1971). See also Severns v. Union Pac. R.R., 125 Cal. Rptr.2d 100 (Cal.App. 2002) (statute is constitutional notwithstanding its application to existing interests).

[19] See, e.g., Board of Education v. Miles, 207 N.E.2d 181 (N.Y. 1965) (holding retroactive application of a 30-year rerecording statute unconstitutional); Biltmore Village, Inc. v. Royal Biltmore Village, 71 So.2d 727 (Fla.1954) (holding Florida statute unconstitutional as applied to existing interests).

interest will vest, if at all, within B's life. O's reversion is good since reversions are always treated as vested.

3. O to A for life, then to B if he reaches the age of 150. Assume B is a newborn infant.

   Answer: A has a life estate vested in possession. B has a contingent remainder since his reaching 150 is a condition precedent to its vesting. O has a reversion, in case B's remainder never vests. All interests are good. A's life estate and O's reversion vest immediately. B's contingent remainder is good because it will vest, if at all, within B's life. B can be used as his own measuring life. For purposes of applying the rule against perpetuities, it does not matter that the remainder may *never* vest in possession. All that matters is that if the interest does vest, it will vest within a life in being plus 21 years.

4. O to A for life, remainder to B's children.

   a. Assume that when the deed is delivered that A is alive and B is living and has no children.

   Answer: A has a life estate vested in possession. B's unborn children have contingent remainders (they are unascertained persons). O has a reversion. All interests are good. The interests of O and A vest immediately. The contingent remainder in B's unborn children is good because B can be a measuring life. All of his children's contingent remainders will vest in interest on B's death if A is then alive. If A is then dead, their interest will vest in possession as well as interest on B's death. Note that A cannot be a measuring life that will save the interest of B's children since if none of B's children are born when A dies, the class will not close on A's death and B may have his first child more than 21 years after A's death.

   b. Assume that when the deed is delivered, B is living and has one daughter.

   Answer: A has a life estate vested in possession. B's daughter has a vested remainder subject to open to admit afterborn members of the class. O has retained no interest. The remainder in B's children is good. B can be a measuring life and the class must close on B's death. Note that A can also be a measuring life since the rule of convenience requires that the class closes on A's death because there is a daughter entitled to distribution, regardless of whether the daughter is still alive at A's death.

   c. Assume that when the deed is delivered, B is dead leaving a daughter and a son.

   Answer: A has a life estate vested in possession. B's son and daughter have indefeasibly vested remainders. The interests in

B's son and daughter are good. The rule does not invalidate totally vested interests.

d. Assume that when the deed is delivered, A is dead and B is dead leaving a daughter, a son, and a wife who is pregnant.

Answer: A has a life estate in possession which never took effect. The remainder in B's daughter and son is now the possessory interest, and the fetus has an executory interest. There is no perpetuities problem. The class will close immediately upon the creation of the interest. B's son and daughter will each get ⅓ now, and if the fetus is born alive, it will also get ⅓. If the fetus is not born alive, B's son and daughter will each get ½. It might also be possible to argue that B's son and daughter should get ½ now, subject to divestment if the fetus is born alive. Note that neither A nor B can be a measuring life for the unborn child because they were not alive when the interest was created. Nevertheless, the interest of the fetus is good since it will vest, if at all, within its own life (or within nine months).

5. O to A for life, remainder to B's heirs.

a. Assume B is alive when the interest is created.

Answer: A has a life estate vested in possession. B's heirs have a contingent remainder because the heirs of a living person are unascertainable. O has a reversion that will become possessory in the unlikely event that B dies without heirs. All interests are good. The interests of A and O vest immediately. O's interest is treated as vested because all reversionary interests are vested, even if they are subject to conditions. With respect to B's heirs, B is the measuring life. Their interest will vest on B's death.

b. Assume B is dead when the interest is created.

Answer: A has a life estate vested in possession. B's heirs have a vested remainder. All interests are good since all the interests are vested. B's heirs were determined at B's death.

6. O to A for life, remainder to such of B's children as attain the age of 21.

a. Assume that when the deed is delivered, A is alive and B is living and has no children.

Answer: A has a life estate vested in possession. B's unborn children have contingent remainders since there is no ascertainable person in being who fits the description of the grantee. Also there is a condition precedent of reaching 21. O has a reversion. The remainder to B's children is good because B is a life in being and the remainders will vest within 21 years of B's death.

b. Assume B is living and has a daughter under 21.

Answer: The classification of all the interests is the same as in 6.a. The daughter's interest still is a contingent remainder since she has not yet attained the age of 21. There is no perpetuities problem because B can act as the measuring life to validate the interest in B's children.

c. Assume B is living and has a daughter over 21.

Answer: A has a life estate vested in possession. B's daughter has a vested remainder subject to open to admit afterborn members of the class. B's unborn children (and those children who are living but not yet 21) have contingent remainders. The remainder in B's children is good since B can still act as the measuring life. Note that if the daughter is 21 at A's death, the class would close immediately on A's death (*i.e.*, when the gift is available for distribution and someone is qualified to take the gift). In this situation, upon A's death the maximum number of participants and the minimum share of the daughter are fixed (all *living* children and fetuses will have an opportunity to share if they attain the age of 21).

7. O to A for life, then to such of B's children as reach the age of 22.

a. Assume B is alive and has a child who is 12.

Answer: A has a life estate vested in possession. B's 12 year old child, as well as all of B's unborn children, have contingent remainders. O has a reversion. The contingent remainder in B's children is void because there is no measuring life. The remainder in B's 12 year old child might never vest, since that child might die before age 22. B could have an afterborn child whose interest would vest beyond a life in being plus 21 years.

b. Assume B is dead leaving a child who is 12 and a wife who is pregnant.

Answer: A has a life estate vested in possession. B's 12 year old child and the fetus have contingent remainders. O has a reversion. There is no perpetuities problem since the child and the fetus can be their own measuring lives because their interests must vest or fail within their own lifetimes. The difference between 7.b. and 7.a. is that here, B is dead and cannot have any more children after the interest is created.

8. O to A for life, then to such of B's children as attain the age of 40.

a. Assume that at the time the deed is delivered, B is a male, has a son and a daughter, both over 40, and another son who is 18. B is 80 years old and has retired to a monastery to live out his life. Also assume that A is alive when the interest is created.

Answer: A has a life estate vested in possession. B's two older children have vested remainders subject to open. The 18 year old has a contingent remainder (and other contingent remainders exist in B's unborn children). There is a perpetuities problem because during A's lifetime, there is a possibility of B renouncing his vows and having more children because the class will stay open until A's death. The interests of these afterborn children may not vest within the period of the rule. Recall that for purposes of the rule against perpetuities, everyone alive is assumed to be capable of procreation, regardless of age. The fact that B has several children over 40 does not save the remainder. Although their minimum share will be known at B's death, their maximum share might not be known until 40 years after B's death. For a class gift to be good, the precise number of its members must be certain within the period of the rule. Since the interest in B's children is bad, O has a reversion following A's life estate.

b. Assume that A is dead when the deed is delivered.

Answer: A has a life estate in possession that never took effect. The remainder in B's two oldest children is now the possessory interest. The 18 year old has an executory interest. There is no perpetuities problem now since the class will close automatically upon the creation of the interest because B's two oldest children are entitled to take their ⅓ shares immediately. If B's youngest child subsequently reaches the age of 40, he will be entitled to his ⅓ share later. If the youngest child never reaches 40, B's older children will get ½ each. The maximum number of participants (3) is fixed upon the creation of the interest. The minimum number of participants will be known within the lives of B's children alive at the creation of their interest. Afterborn children will not participate in the gift. It might also be possible to argue that B's two older children should get ½ now, subject to divestment if the 18 year old subsequently reaches 40.

*Problem Set B*

Before attempting the Principal Problem at the beginning of this Assignment, consider the following dispositions.

1. By deed, O grants Blackacre to A for life, then to B for life, then to B's children who survive him.

2. By deed, O grants Blackacre to the Northwest Coal Company for so long as the property is used for mining purposes; if the property ceases to be used for mining purposes, then to A.

3. T bequeaths certain stock certificates "to my widow for life, and on her death, to such of my children as reach age 25; however, if any of my children die before reaching age 25 leaving children, then such children shall take the share that their parent would have taken had

that parent lived to age 25." Does the age of T's children make any difference?

# ASSIGNMENT 11
# MODERN PERPETUITIES DEVELOPMENTS

## 1. INTRODUCTION

The rule against perpetuities is clearly on the decline. Only one jurisdiction—Alabama—retains the common law rule against perpetuities in its classic form. Seven states have abolished the rule entirely.[1] Most states have relaxed the rule by statute or judicial decision. The most widely adopted modification is the Uniform Statutory Rule Against Perpetuities (USRAP). Twenty-seven jurisdictions have adopted USRAP.[2] In this Assignment, we will concentrate on USRAP because so many states have adopted it.

## 2. PRINCIPAL PROBLEM

Assume that your state is considering the adoption of USRAP. You have been asked by the local bar association to study USRAP, summarize some of its principal provisions, and evaluate their desirability. To focus your thinking, consider how the Principal Problem in Assignment 10 would be treated under USRAP.

## 3. MATERIALS FOR SOLUTION OF PRINCIPAL PROBLEM

*The Ninety Year "Wait and See" Period*

Section 1(a) of USRAP provides in pertinent part as follows:

A nonvested property interest is invalid unless:

(1) when the interest is created, it is certain to vest or terminate no later than 21 years after the death of an individual then alive; or

(2) the interest either vests or terminates within 90 years after its creation.

Paragraph (1) is simply a restatement of the common law rule against perpetuities. Paragraph (2), however, provides that an interest that would be invalid under the common law rule against perpetuities will nevertheless be valid if it in fact "vests or terminates within 90 years

---

[1] Idaho, Kentucky, New Jersey, Pennsylvania, Rhode Island, South Dakota and Wisconsin.

[2] Alaska, Arizona, Arkansas, California, Colorado, Connecticut, District of Columbia, Florida, Georgia, Hawaii, Indiana, Kansas, Massachusetts, Michigan, Minnesota, Montana, Nebraska, Nevada, New Mexico, North Carolina, North Dakota, Oregon, South Carolina, Tennessee, Utah, Virginia and West Virginia. In addition, New Jersey and South Dakota adopted USRAP before then abolishing RAP altogether.

after its creation." Thus, under USRAP, an interest is valid if it either is good under the common law rule, or it in fact vests or terminates within ninety years after its creation. Consequently, an interest cannot be invalidated earlier than ninety years after its creation. In effect, most interests that would be invalidated under the common law will be valid under the ninety year rule.

> EXAMPLE 1: George grants property in trust to Tina for the benefit of Alice for life, then to Alice's children for their lives, then the principal is to be distributed to Alice's grandchildren. At the time of the grant, Alice is alive but has no children or grandchildren. Under the common law rule against perpetuities, the interest of Alice's grandchildren would be void, and George would retain a reversion following the death of Alice and Alice's children. Under USRAP, a court considering the validity of the limitation would do nothing for ninety years. If all of Alice's children died within the ninety year period following the creation of the interest in Alice's grandchildren (the time of delivery of the grant), the interest of Alice's grandchildren would be valid. The court "waits and sees" whether the interest of Alice's grandchildren vests in interest or possession within the ninety year period. Under the traditional common law approach, a court would have invalidated the interest of the grandchildren as soon as it was presented with the question—normally long before the end of the ninety year period.

Because most interests that are void under the traditional rule would in fact vest within the ninety year period, USRAP has the effect of making the common law rule immaterial in most instances. Some states adopted a wait-and-see approach before the passage of USRAP.[3] The wait-and-see period under these statutes was much shorter than the ninety year period provided for in USRAP. A highly respected scholar has argued that the effect of USRAP is, as a practical matter, to abolish the rule against perpetuities.[4]

> If the Uniform Statute is enacted, no interest created thereafter can be declared in violation of the Rule against Perpetuities for 90 years after the date of its creation. All interests are valid for this period. At the end of 90 years, a court will take down the old books on the Rule against Perpetuities, determine what then existing contingent interests did not satisfy the common law Rule ... and, as to any such interests, reform them to vest at

---

[3] See, e.g., Alaska, Iowa, Kentucky, Minnesota, Nevada, New Mexico, Ohio, Pennsylvania, Rhode Island, South Carolina, South Dakota, Vermont, Virginia and Washington.

[4] See Jesse Dukeminier, *The Uniform Statutory Rule Against Perpetuities: Ninety Years in Limbo,* 34 UCLA L. Rev. 1023 (1987)

once.... Can the Rule against Perpetuities really survive 90 years in desuetude?[5]

Professor Dukeminier argues that it cannot. If, following the adoption of USRAP, there can be no litigation involving the rule against perpetuities for ninety years, is it likely that anyone will try to apply the rule after the ninety year period elapses? Do we really have, in USRAP, a *de facto* covert repeal of the rule, as to interests created after USRAP is adopted? If so, why not simply repeal the rule outright and avoid the pretense that USRAP simply modifies the rule?

*Reformation of Invalid Interests*

Section 3 of USRAP provides:

Upon the petition of an interested person, a court shall reform a disposition in the manner that most closely approximates the transferor's manifested plan of distribution and is within the 90 years allowed [by USRAP] if:

(1) a nonvested property interest or a power of appointment becomes invalid under Section 1 (statutory rule against perpetuities) [or]

(2) a class gift is not but might become invalid ... and the time has arrived when the share of any class member is to take effect in possession or enjoyment....

The power of a court to "reform" or rewrite a disposition has been recognized by some, but not all courts, even in the absence of an enabling statute.[6] Of course it is not always easy to ascertain the testator's "manifested plan of distribution" and to rewrite the will accordingly. The process is sometimes referred to as one of "equitable approximation" or as applying the doctrine of *cy pres*.[7] Traditionally, however, the courts did not have the power of equitable approximation, and upon finding an interest to be invalid, that interest was struck from the will (or other dispositive instrument). Hence, the invalid interest would return to the testator to pass under his or her residuary clause, or if this were not possible, pass as intestate property.[8]

The difference between the traditional equitable approximation approach and that adopted by USRAP is illustrated by Example 2.

EXAMPLE 2: Tom devises real property to Annette for life, then to Annette's children for their lives, and upon the death of the survivor of Annette's children, the remainder shall pass to the

---

[5] *Id.* at 1025–26.

[6] See, e.g., Estate of Chun Quan Yee Hop, 469 P.2d 183 (Haw. 1970); cf. Ransom v. Bebernitz, 782 A.2d 1155 (Vt. 2001) (discussing statutory authority to reform a will that violates the rule against perpetuities).

[7] From the French phrase meaning "as near as (possible)."

[8] Intestate property is property of a decedent that is not disposed of by will or other estate planning instrument. It is distributed to the decedent's heirs pursuant to the applicable state statute of intestacy.

descendants of Annette's children, per stirpes.[9] At the time of the devise, Annette is alive and has two children, Bill and Carol, ages 30 and 35. The devise to the descendants of Annette's children violates the common law rule against perpetuities because Annette might have a third child, and that child might survive the first two (and Annette) for more than twenty-one years. Thus, the ultimate takers might not be ascertained within the period of the rule.

Under the doctrine of equitable approximation, followed in some states, a court would attempt to reform the devise so that it would be valid, regardless of what actually happens in the years following the devise. For example, a court might rewrite the will so that upon the death of Bill and Carol the remainder would pass to the grandchildren of Annette or their descendants, per stirpes. Under this rewritten limitation, the remainder would vest in the grandchildren of Annette or their descendants no later than the end of lives in being (Bill and Carol) when the interest was created.

Under USRAP, the court would wait until there were no living children of Annette, thus arriving at the time "when the share of any class member is to take effect in possession or enjoyment...." If that time occurs within the ninety year period, or immediately following the death of Bill and Carol, there would be no need to reform the devise since the limitation would be valid. If, however, a third child of Annette, Don, lived more than twenty-one years after Bill, Carol, and Annette, and died after the ninety year period, a court would try to reform the original instrument. For example, it might order that the remainder vest only in those grandchildren of Annette who were alive at the end of the ninety year period, or to the descendants of the deceased grandchildren of Annette who were living at the end of the ninety year period.

Example 2 illustrates that reformation is necessary far less often under USRAP than it would be under the more conventional equitable approximation doctrine. However, on those occasions when reformation would be necessary under USRAP, it might be quite difficult to reform the instrument in accordance with the testator's wishes, because of the long period of time that would pass from the creation of the instrument to the time of reformation. Under USRAP the ultimate provisions of the

---

[9] "Per stirpes" literally means "by (family) stocks." That is, each branch of the family is treated equally, rather than each individual. Thus if a gift is to the issue (i.e. descendants) of A, per stirpes, and A dies leaving a daughter who survives her who has two children, and a son who predeceased A, leaving three children, the daughter would receive half the gift, and the children of A's son would each receive one-third of the son's half. Thus the son's branch or stock of the family would receive an amount equal to that given to the daughter's branch, although the daughter would receive three times more than any one of the son's children, and the daughter's children would receive nothing.

instrument as reformed might not be known for a very long time. Whether the advantages outweigh the disadvantages of the USRAP scheme of "reformation" or "equitable approximation" is a question that is open to debate.

*Non-Donative Transactions Under USRAP*

Section 4 of USRAP provides that the rule against perpetuities does not apply to a nonvested property interest "arising out of a non-donative transfer. . . ." Under the common law rule against perpetuities, an option to purchase land would be treated as void if it purported to be effective for longer than the period of the rule. Often there are no lives in being that are pertinent to the option. Thus, the maximum allowable period for such an option would be simply twenty-one years.[10] Thus an option to purchase land, exercisable by a corporation, that purported to be good for forty years would be treated as entirely void. Does such a result embody sound public policy or represent an unwise and unfair "trap for the unwary"?

The common law rule that options are subject to the rule against perpetuities is subject to exceptions. For example, as explained more fully in *Symphony Space*, reprinted below, an option to purchase held by a lessee for the term of the lease may be valid even if it can be exercised for a period longer than the period of the rule.

Reprinted below are two cases that are *not* governed by USRAP. They illustrate some of the ways that modern courts deal with the common law rule and with some of the ameliorative doctrines and statutes that modify it. These cases, by way of contrast, may help you evaluate the impact of USRAP.

## Abrams v. Templeton
Court of Appeals of South Carolina, 1995.
320 S.C. 325, 465 S.E.2d 117.

■ HEARN, J.

This case involves the construction of a 1914 will which violates the rule against perpetuities. Pursuant to *S.C. Code Ann. § 27–6–60(B)* (1991), the trial judge inserted a savings clause into a provision of the will to prevent a forfeiture. We affirm as modified.

The testator, Mary Ann Taylor Ramage, executed her will in 1914 and died in 1915. She was survived by her husband Frank, a son Albert, and various grandchildren. The testator's daughter, Alma Templeton, predeceased her, but left five surviving children: Frank, Bob, Charlie, Grace and Anna. In her will, the testator devised approximately one hundred and thirty acres of land to Alma's children (the Templeton side).

---

[10] Symphony Space v. Pergola Properties, 669 N.E.2d 799 (N.Y. 1996) (reprinted below).

The testator further devised a one hundred and sixty acre tract of land, the subject of this action:

> to my husband Frank Ramage during the term of his natural life and at his death ... to my son Albert Ramage ... to have, hold, and enjoy the same during his the said Albert Ramage's natural life, and at his death to his children to hold and enjoy during the term of their natural life and at their death their several interests to be divided among their children.

The trial judge determined the clause violated the rule against perpetuities which provides:

> No interest is good unless it must vest, if at all, no later than twenty-one years after some life in being at the creation of the interest. Simes, Law of Future Interests, (2d ed. 1966) § 127 at 265.[11]

The trial judge found the provision of the testator's will which created a gift over to her great-grandchildren ("at their death their several interests to be divided among their children") was non-vested for the purposes of the rule against perpetuities. The gift over to the great-grandchildren was a class gift. See *61 Am. Jur. 2d Perpetuities, etc., § 33* at 41 ("While gifts to a class, where the class is open until some future time, are technically vested, if there are members of the class in being at the time of making the gift, from the standpoint of the perpetuity rule the gifts are on the same footing as purely contingent gifts, and are not regarded as vested until the final membership of the class is determined ... "). Because the class could continue to expand during the lifetime of the testator's grandchildren, for purposes of the rule against perpetuities, it is considered nonvested because it remained "open" after the gift was made.

S.C. Code Ann. § 27–6–60(B)(1991) provides:

> If a nonvested property interest or a power of appointment was created before July 1, 1987, and is determined in a judicial proceeding, commenced on or after July 1, 1987, to violate this State's rule against perpetuities as that rule existed before July 1, 1987, a court upon the petition of an interested person shall reform the disposition by inserting a savings clause that preserves most closely the transferor's plan of distribution and that brings that plan within the limits of the rule against perpetuities applicable when the nonvested property interest or power of appointment was created.

Both parties concede that the gift over to the testator's great-grandchildren violates the rule. Therefore, section 27–6–60(B) directs the trial judge to "reform the disposition by inserting a savings clause that

---

[11] In 1987, South Carolina enacted the Uniform Rule Against Perpetuities (*S.C. Code Ann. § 27–6–10* et seq.) which supersedes the common law rule.

preserves most closely a transferor's plan of distribution and that brings that plan within the limits of the rule against perpetuities...."[12]

The trial judge found that the testator's intended plan of distribution was to equally benefit each "side" of her family: Alma's descendants (the Templeton branch) and Albert's descendants (the Ramage branch). We agree.

Each branch of the family received approximately the same acreage and divided the personal property equally with the exception of a watch and chain. A common sense reading of the provision dealing with the one hundred and sixty acre tract shows the testator intended to create successive life estates in her son and his children with the remainder over to their children. Clearly, the testator wanted this tract to stay with the Ramage branch of the family and not to include the Templeton branch which received other real and personal property.

In an attempt to bring the provision of the will within the limits of the perpetuities rule and to preserve the testator's intent, the trial judge inserted a savings clause as follows:

> I will, devise and bequeath to my son Albert Ramage all that certain tract of land situate in the county and state aforesaid, containing about one hundred sixty acres more or less ... to have, hold, and enjoy the same during his the said Albert Ramage's natural life, and at his death to his children *who are alive at the time of my death* to hold and enjoy during the term of their natural life and at their death their several interests to be divided among their children.

As a result, the "measuring life" for the purposes of the perpetuities rule becomes the testator's grandchildren, all of whom were alive at the time of the testator's death and whose children, the testator's great-grandchildren, would have to be born during the lives of these grandchildren.

Albert had nine children (the testator's grandchildren). Five of these children survived Albert and had children, while the remaining four of his children died childless. The trial judge ordered, in accordance with the testator's presumed intent, the shares of the grandchildren who died without children to augment the share of those who had children. Therefore, he ordered that the entire interest in the one hundred sixty acre tract should pass one-fifth to each set of children of the five grandchildren who died with children.

---

[12] South Carolina's version of the Uniform Statutory Rule Against Perpetuities (S.C. Code Ann. §§ 27–6–10 et seq. (1991)) provides that a nonvested interest violates the statutory rule against perpetuities if it fails to satisfy either the common law rule against perpetuities time period or the statutory 90-year wait-and-see time period. If a nonvested interest fails to satisfy either test, section 27–6–60(B) requires that a court reform the disposition. Thus, the statutory rule against perpetuities "effectively allows three bites of the apple to a nonvested interest...."

Appellants, the testator's heirs-at-law in the Templeton branch, contend the gift over to the great-grandchildren was void as violative of the rule against perpetuities. Therefore, since the testator's grandchildren had only life estates in the property, at their deaths the remainder reverted back to the testator to pass to her heirs-at-law. We disagree.

To void the gift over to the great-grandchildren would be to invoke the drastic result *S.C. Code Ann. § 27–6–60(B)* sought to prevent. The South Carolina General Assembly adopted this statutory provision to avoid the remorseless application of the common law rule. The law abhors a forfeiture. The law abhors intestacy and will indulge every presumption in favor of the validity of the will. Clearly, the statute mandates the courts attempt to reconstruct the will so as to save the gift rather than declare it void.

Appellants contend that if the entire gift is not void, they are entitled to at least their intestacy portion of the interest of the grandchildren who died childless. The law is clear that the ultimate fee in every tract of land must rest somewhere. Title to real estate cannot be held in abeyance; it must be vested somewhere. Therefore, appellants argue, because the testator's grandchildren had only life estates in the subject property, the testator must have retained the ultimate reversion subject to divestment if great-grandchildren were born to each of Albert's children. Since four of the testator's grandchildren died without children, and there was no residuary clause or alternative disposition of the interests of those who died childless, their four-ninths interests must revert back to the testator, and, therefore, pass by intestate succession to the testator's heirs-at-law.

We agree with appellants to the extent that the trial judge's savings clause, while it cures the perpetuities rule violation, leaves the four-ninths interest of the childless grandchildren "floating." However, we agree with the trial judge's finding that the testator intended to benefit both "sides" of her family equally and wanted all interest in the subject property to remain with Albert's descendants. Therefore, to effect the trial judge's order to augment the interests of the testator's great-grandchildren on Albert's side with the shares of those grandchildren who died childless, we modify the will to state:

> I will, devise and bequeath to my son Albert Ramage all that certain tract of land situate in the county and state aforesaid, containing about one hundred sixty acres more or less ... to have, hold, and enjoy the same during his the said Albert Ramage's natural life, and at his death to his children *who are alive at the time of my death* to hold and enjoy during the term of their natural life and at their death their several interests to be divided among their children, *or if any of Albert Ramage's children die childless, his or her interest in default be divided among those who have children.*

This reconstruction of the testator's will no longer violates the rule against perpetuities and clearly effectuates the intent of the testator.

## NOTES

1. *Rewriting the will.* The statute permitted a revision of the will to cure a perpetuities problem. Yet the court appeared to rewrite the will to cure not only a perpetuities problem, but also the failure to provide for the case where a grandchild died without issue. Was that proper?

2. *Older wills.* The statute provided, in effect, that wills written before July 1, 1987 are to be governed by the classic rule against perpetuities, while wills written after this date are governed by South Carolina's version of USRAP. Does this make sense? Does a testator writing a will in 1986 that violates the common law rule rely on the fact that her disposition is invalid? If she does not rely on that fact, who does?

3. *Principal Problem.* How would the court that decided Abrams v. Templeton have solved the Principal Problem?

## Symphony Space, Inc. v. Pergola Properties, Inc.
Court of Appeals of New York, 1996.
88 N.Y.2d 466, 669 N.E.2d 799.

■ KAYE, CHIEF JUDGE:

This case presents the novel question whether options to purchase commercial property are exempt from the prohibition against remote vesting embodied in New York's Rule against Perpetuities (EPTL 9–1.1[b]). Because an exception for commercial options finds no support in our law, we decline to exempt all commercial option agreements from the statutory Rule against Perpetuities.

Here, we agree with the trial court and Appellate Division that the option defendants seek to enforce violates the statutory prohibition against remote vesting and is therefore unenforceable.

Facts

The subject of this proceeding is a two-story building situated on the Broadway block between 94th and 95th Streets on Manhattan's Upper West Side. In 1978, Broadwest Realty Corporation owned this building, which housed a theater and commercial space. Broadwest had been unable to secure a permanent tenant for the theater—approximately 58% of the total square footage of the building's floor space. Broadwest also owned two adjacent properties, Pomander Walk (a residential complex) and the Healy Building (a commercial building). Broadwest had been operating its properties at a net loss.

Plaintiff Symphony Space, Inc., a not-for-profit entity devoted to the arts, had previously rented the theater for several one-night engagements. In 1978, Symphony and Broadwest engaged in a transaction whereby Broadwest sold the entire building to Symphony for the below-market price of $10,010 and leased back the income-producing commercial property, excluding the theater, for $1 per year. Broadwest maintained liability for the existing $243,000 mortgage on the property as well as certain maintenance obligations. As a condition of the sale, Symphony, for consideration of $10, also granted Broadwest an option to repurchase the entire building. Notably, the transaction did not involve Pomander Walk or the Healy Building.

The purpose of this arrangement was to enable Symphony, as a not-for-profit corporation, to seek a property tax exemption for the entire building—which constituted a single tax parcel—predicated on its use of the theater. The sale-and-leaseback would thereby reduce Broadwest's real estate taxes by $30,000 per year, while permitting Broadwest to retain the rental income from the leased commercial space in the building, which the trial court found produced $140,000 annually. The arrangement also furthered Broadwest's goal of selling all the properties, by allowing Broadwest to postpone any sale until property values in the area increased and until the commercial leases expired. Symphony, in turn, would have use of the theater at minimal cost, once it received a tax exemption.

Thus, on December 1, 1978, Symphony and Broadwest—both sides represented by counsel—executed a contract for sale of the property from Broadwest to Symphony for the purchase price of $10,010. The contract specified that $10 was to be paid at the closing and $10,000 was to be paid by means of a purchase-money mortgage.

The parties also signed several separate documents, each dated December 31, 1978:

(1) a deed for the property from Broadwest to Symphony;

(2) a lease from Symphony to Broadwest of the entire building except the theater for rent of $1 per year and for the term January 1, 1979 to May 31, 2003, unless terminated earlier;

(3) a 25-year, $10,000 mortgage and mortgage note from Symphony as mortgagor to Broadwest as mortgagee, with full payment due on December 31, 2003; and

(4) an option agreement by which Broadwest obtained from Symphony the exclusive right to repurchase all of the property, including the theater.

It is the option agreement that is at the heart of the present dispute. Section 3 of that agreement provides that Broadwest may exercise its option to purchase the property during any of the following "Exercise Periods":

(a) at any time after July 1, 1979, so long as the Notice of Election specifies that the Closing is to occur during any of the calendar years 1987, 1993, 1998 and 2003;

(b) at any time following the maturity of the indebtedness evidenced by the Note and secured by the Mortgage, whether by acceleration or otherwise;

(c) during the ninety days immediately following any termination of the Lease by the lessor thereof other than for nonpayment of rent or any termination of the Lease by the lessee thereof . . . ;

(d) during the ninety days immediately following the thirtieth day after Broadwest shall have sent Symphony a notice specifying a default by Symphony of any of its covenants or obligations under the Mortgage. . . . Section 1 states that "Broadwest may exercise its option at any time during any Exercise Period." That section further specifies that the notice of election must be sent at least 180 days prior to the closing date if the option is exercised pursuant to section 3(a) and at least 90 days prior to the closing date if exercised pursuant to any other subdivision.

The following purchase prices of the property, contingent upon the closing date, are set forth in section 4: $15,000 if the closing date is on or before December 31, 1987; $20,000 if on or before December 31, 1993; $24,000 if on or before December 31, 1998; and $28,000 if on or before December 31, 2003. Importantly, the option agreement specifies in section 5 that "Broadwest's right to exercise the option granted hereby is . . . unconditional and shall not be in any way affected or impaired by Broadwest's performance or nonperformance, actual or asserted, of any obligation to be performed under the Lease or any other agreement or instrument by or between Broadwest and Symphony," other than that Broadwest was required to pay Symphony any unpaid rent on the closing date. Finally, section 6 established that the option constituted "a covenant running with the land, inuring to the benefit of heirs, successors and assigns of Broadwest."

Symphony ultimately obtained a tax exemption for the theater. In the summer of 1981, Broadwest sold and assigned its interest under the lease, option agreement, mortgage and mortgage note, as well as its ownership interest in the contiguous Pomander Walk and Healy Building, to defendants' nominee for $4.8 million. The nominee contemporaneously transferred its rights under these agreements to defendants Pergola Properties, Inc., Bradford N. Swett, Casandium Limited and Darenth Consultants as tenants in common.

Subsequently, defendants initiated a cooperative conversion of Pomander Walk, which was designated a landmark in 1982, and the value of the properties increased substantially. An August 1988 appraisal of the entire blockfront, including the Healy Building and the unused air and other development rights available from Pomander Walk, valued the property at $27 million assuming the enforceability of the option. By contrast, the value of the leasehold interest plus the Healy

Building without the option were appraised at $5.5 million. Due to Symphony's alleged default on the mortgage note, defendant Swett served Symphony with notice in January 1985 that it was exercising the option on behalf of all defendants. The notice set a closing date of May 6, 1985. Symphony, however, disputed both that it was in default and Swett's authority to exercise the option for all of the defendants. According to Symphony, moreover, it then discovered that the option agreement was possibly invalid. Consequently, in March 1985, Symphony initiated this declaratory judgment action against defendants, arguing that the option agreement violated the New York statutory prohibition against remote vesting and clogged its equity of redemption under the mortgage. . . .

Thereafter, the parties cross-moved for summary judgment in the instant declaratory judgment proceeding. The trial court granted Symphony's motion while denying that of defendants. In particular, the court concluded that the Rule against Perpetuities applied to the commercial option contained in the parties' agreement, that the option violated the Rule and that Symphony was entitled to exercise its equitable right to redeem the mortgage. The trial court also dismissed defendants' counterclaim for rescission of the agreements underlying the transaction based on the parties' mutual mistake. In a comprehensive writing by Justice Ellerin, the Appellate Division likewise determined that the commercial option was unenforceable under the Rule against Perpetuities and that rescission was inappropriate. The Appellate Division certified the following question to us: "Was the order of the Supreme Court, as affirmed by this Court, properly made?" We conclude that it was and now affirm.

Statutory Background

The Rule against Perpetuities evolved from judicial efforts during the 17th century to limit control of title to real property by the dead hand of landowners reaching into future generations. Underlying both early and modern rules restricting future dispositions of property is the principle that it is socially undesirable for property to be inalienable for an unreasonable period of time. These rules thus seek "to ensure the productive use and development of property by its current beneficial owners by simplifying ownership, facilitating exchange and freeing property from unknown or embarrassing impediments to alienability" (MTA v. Bruken Realty Corp., 67 N.Y.2d 156, 161, citing De Peyster v. Michael, 6 N.Y. 467, 494).

The traditional statement of the common law Rule against Perpetuities was set forth by Professor John Chipman Gray: "No interest is good unless it must vest, if at all, not later than twenty-one years after some life in being at the creation of the interest" (Gray, The Rule Against Perpetuities s 201 at 191 [4th ed.1942]).

In New York, the rules regarding suspension of the power of alienation and remoteness in vesting—the Rule against Perpetuities—

have been statutory since 1830. Prior to 1958, the perpetuities period was two lives in being plus actual periods of minority (see, former RPL § 42). Widely criticized as unduly complex and restrictive, the statutory period was revised in 1958 and 1960, restoring the common law period of lives in being plus 21 years (see, L 1958, ch 153; L 1960, ch 448).

Formerly, the rule against remote vesting in New York was narrower than the common law rule, encompassing only particular interests (see, former RPL §§ 46, 50; Buffalo Seminary v. McCarthy, 86 A.D.2d 435, 440, affd 58 N.Y.2d 867). A further 1965 amendment enacted a broad prohibition against remote vesting (see, L 1965, ch 670, s 1). This amendment was intended to make clear that the American common law rule of perpetuities was now fully in force in New York (see, 1965 N.Y. Legis Ann, at 206–207).

New York's current statutory Rule against Perpetuities is found in EPTL 9–1.1. Subdivision (a) sets forth the suspension of alienation rule and deems void any estate in which the conveying instrument suspends the absolute power of alienation for longer than lives in being at the creation of the estate plus 21 years (see, EPTL 9–1.1[a][2]). The prohibition against remote vesting is contained in subdivision (b), which states that "[n]o estate in property shall be valid unless it must vest, if at all, not later than twenty-one years after one or more lives in being at the creation of the estate and any period of gestation involved" (EPTL 9–1.1[b]). This Court has described subdivision (b) as "a rigid formula that invalidates any interest that may not vest within the prescribed time period" and has "capricious consequences" (Wildenstein & Co. v. Wallis, 79 N.Y.2d 641, 647–648). Indeed, these rules are predicated upon the public policy of the State and constitute non-waivable, legal prohibitions (see, MTA v. Bruken Realty Corp., 67 N.Y.2d at 161).

In addition to these statutory formulas, New York also retains the more flexible common law rule against unreasonable restraints on alienation. Unlike the statutory Rule against Perpetuities, which is measured exclusively by the passage of time, the common law rule evaluates the reasonableness of the restraint based on its duration, purpose and designated method for fixing the purchase price. (See, Wildenstein & Co v. Wallis, 79 N.Y.2d at 648; MTA v. Bruken Realty Corp, 67 N.Y.2d at 161–162, supra).

Against this background, we consider the option agreement at issue.

Validity of the Option Agreement

Defendants proffer three grounds for upholding the option: that the statutory prohibition against remote vesting does not apply to commercial options; that the option here cannot be exercised beyond the statutory period; and that this Court should adopt the "wait and see" approach to the Rule against Perpetuities. We consider each in turn.

Under the common law, options to purchase land are subject to the rule against remote vesting (see, Simes, Handbook of the Law of Future

Interests s 132 [2d ed 1966]; Simes and Smith, The Law of Future Interests s 1244 [2d ed]; Leach, Perpetuities In a Nutshell, 51 Harv L Rev 638, 660; see also, London & South Western Ry. Co v. Gomm, 20 Ch D. 562). Such options are specifically enforceable and give the option holder a contingent, equitable interest in the land (Dukeminier, A Modern Guide to Perpetuities, 74 Calif L Rev 1867, 1908; Leach, Perpetuities In Perspective: Ending the Rule's Reign of Terror, 65 Harv L Rev 721, 736–737). This creates a disincentive for the landowner to develop the property and hinders its alienability, thereby defeating the policy objectives underlying the Rule against Perpetuities (see, Dukeminier, A Modern Guide to Perpetuities, 74 Calif L Rev at 1908; 5A Powell, Real Property, P 771[1]).

Typically, however, options to purchase are part of a commercial transaction. For this reason, subjecting them to the Rule against Perpetuities has been deemed "a step of doubtful wisdom" (Leach, Perpetuities in Perspective: Ending the Rule's Reign of Terror, 65 Harv L Rev at 737; see also, Dukeminier, A Modern Guide to Perpetuities, 74 Calif L Rev at 1908; Note, Options and the Rule Against Perpetuities, 13 U Fla L Rev 214, 214–215). As one vocal critic, Professor W. Barton Leach, has explained,

> [T]he Rule grew up as a limitation on family dispositions; and the period of lives in being plus twenty-one years is adapted to these gift transactions. The pressures which created the Rule do not exist with reference to arms-length contractual transactions, and neither lives in being nor twenty-one years are periods which are relevant to business men and their affairs (Leach, Perpetuities: New Absurdity, Judicial and Statutory Correctives, 73 Harvard L Rev 1318, 1321–1322).

Professor Leach, however, went on to acknowledge that, under common law, "due to an overemphasis on concepts derived from the nineteenth century, we are stuck with the application of the Rule to options to purchase," urging that "this should not be extended to other commercial transactions" (id., at 1322; see also, Simes and Smith, The Law of Future Interests, at s 1244). It is now settled in New York that, generally, EPTL 9–1.1(b) applies to options. In Buffalo Seminary v. McCarthy (86 A.D.2d 435, supra), the Court held that an unlimited option in gross to purchase real property was void under the statutory rule against remote vesting, and we affirmed the Appellate Division decision on the opinion of then-Justice Hancock (58 N.Y.2d 867). Since then, we have reiterated that options in real estate are subject to the statutory rule (see, e.g., Wildenstein & Co v. Wallis, 79 N.Y.2d at 648, supra).

Although the particular option at issue in Buffalo Seminary was part of a private transaction between neighboring landowners, the reasoning employed in that case establishes that EPTL 9–1.1(b) applies equally to commercial purchase options. In reaching its conclusion in Buffalo

Seminary, the Court explained that, prior to 1965, New York's narrow statutory rule against remote vesting did not encompass options (86 A.D.2d at 443). A review of the history of the broad provision enacted in 1965, however, established that the Legislature specifically intended to incorporate the American common law rules governing perpetuities into the New York statute (id., at 441–442). Because the common law rule against remote vesting encompasses purchase options that might vest beyond the permissible period, the Court concluded that EPTL 9–1.1(b) necessarily encompasses such options (id., at 443). Inasmuch as the common law prohibition against remote vesting applies to both commercial and noncommercial options, it likewise follows that the Legislature intended EPTL 9–1.1(b) to apply to commercial purchase options as well. Consequently, creation of a general exception to EPTL 9–1.1(b) for all purchase options that are commercial in nature, as advocated by defendants, would remove an entire class of contingent future interests that the Legislature intended the statute to cover. While defendants offer compelling policy reasons—echoing those voiced by Professor Leach—for refusing to apply the traditional rule against remote vesting to these commercial option contracts, such statutory reformation would require legislative action similar to that undertaken by numerous other state lawmakers (see, e.g., Cal Prob Code s 21225 [Deering 1995]; Fla Stat ch 689.225; Ill Ann Stat ch 765, para 305/4 [Smith-Hurd 1996]).

Our decision in MTA v. Bruken Realty Corp. (67 N.Y.2d 156) is not to the contrary. In Bruken, we held that EPTL 9–1.1(b) did not apply to a preemptive right in a "commercial and governmental transaction" that lasted beyond the statutory perpetuities period. In doing so, we explained that, unlike options, preemptive rights (or rights of first refusal) only marginally affect transferability:

> An option grants to the holder the power to compel the owner of property to sell it whether the owner is willing to part with ownership or not. A preemptive right, or right of first refusal, does not give its holder the power to compel an unwilling owner to sell; it merely requires the owner, when and if he decides to sell, to offer the property first to the party holding the preemptive right so that he may meet a third-party offer or buy the property at some other price set by a previously stipulated method (id., at 163).

Enforcement of the preemptive right in the context of the governmental and commercial transaction, moreover, actually encouraged the use and development of the land, outweighing any minor impediment to alienability (id., at 165–166).

Bruken merely recognized that the Legislature did not intend EPTL 9–1.1(b) to apply to those contingent future interests in real property that encourage the holder to develop the property by insuring an opportunity to benefit from the improvements and to recapture any investment (see

MTA v. Bruken Realty Corp, 67 N.Y.2d at 165; Morrison v. Piper, 77 N.Y.2d at 170, supra). In these limited circumstances, enforcement would promote the purposes underlying the rule.

Bruken, then, did not create a sweeping exception to EPTL 9–1.1(b) for commercial purchase options. Indeed, we have since emphasized that options to purchase are to be treated differently than preemptive rights, underscoring that preemptive rights impede alienability only minimally whereas purchase options vest substantial control over the transferability of property in the option holder (see, Wildenstein & Co v. Wallis, 79 N.Y.2d at 648, supra; Morrison v. Piper, 77 N.Y.2d at 169–170, supra). We have also clarified that even preemptive rights are ordinarily subject to the statutory rule against remote vesting (see, Morrison v. Piper, 77 N.Y.2d 165, supra). Only where the right arises in a governmental or commercial agreement is the minor restraint on transferability created by the preemptive right offset by the holder's incentive to improve the property.

Here, the option agreement creates precisely the sort of control over future disposition of the property that we have previously associated with purchase options and that the common law rule against remote vesting—and thus EPTL 9–1.1(b)—seeks to prevent. As the Appellate Division explained, the option grants its holder absolute power to purchase the property at the holder's whim and at a token price set far below market value. This Sword of Damocles necessarily discourages the property owner from investing in improvements to the property. Furthermore, the option's existence significantly impedes the owner's ability to sell the property to a third party, as a practical matter rendering it inalienable.

That defendants, the holder of this option, are also the lessees of a portion of the premises does not lead to a different conclusion here. Generally, an option to purchase land that originates in one of the lease provisions, is not exercisable after lease expiration, and is incapable of separation from the lease, is valid even though the holder's interest may vest beyond the perpetuities period (see Berg, Long-Term Options and the Rule Against Perpetuities, 37 Calif L Rev at 21; Leach, Perpetuities: New Absurdity, Judicial and Statutory Correctives, 73 Harv L Rev at 1320; Simes and Smith, The Law of Future Interests, s 1244). Such options—known as options "appendant" or "appurtenant" to leases—encourage the possessory holder to invest in maintaining and developing the property by guaranteeing the option holder the ultimate benefit of any such investment. Options appurtenant thus further the policy objectives underlying the rule against remote vesting and are not contemplated by EPTL 9–1.1(b) (see, MTA v. Bruken Realty Corp, 67 N.Y.2d at 165, supra; see also, Buffalo Seminary v. McCarthy, 86 A.D.2d at 441 n5, supra).

To be sure, the option here arose within a larger transaction that included a lease. Nevertheless, not all of the property subject to the purchase option here is even occupied by defendants. The option encompasses the entire building—both the commercial space and the theater—yet defendants are leasing only the commercial space. With regard to the theater space, a disincentive exists for Symphony to improve the property, since it will eventually be claimed by the option holder at the predetermined purchase price. Furthermore, the option is not contained in the lease itself, but in a separate agreement. Indeed, section 5 of the option agreement specifies that the right to exercise the option is wholly independent from the lease, stating that it "shall not be in any way affected or impaired by performance or nonperformance, actual or asserted, of any obligation to be performed under the Lease or any other agreement." The duration of the option, moreover, exceeds the term of the lease. Consequently, defendants could compel Symphony to sell them the property even after they have ceased possession as lessee. Put simply, the option here cannot qualify as an option appurtenant and significantly deters development of the property. If the option is exercisable beyond the statutory perpetuities period, refusing to enforce it would thus further the purpose and rationale underlying the statutory prohibition against remote vesting.

Defendants alternatively claim that section 3(a) of the agreement does not permit exercise of the option after expiration of the statutory perpetuities period. According to defendants, only the possible closing dates fall outside the permissible time frame.

Where, as here, the parties to a transaction are corporations and no measuring lives are stated in the instruments, the perpetuities period is simply 21 years (see, MTA v. Bruken Realty Corp, 67 N.Y.2d at 161, supra). Section 1 of the parties' agreement allows the option holder to exercise the option "at any time during any Exercise Period" set forth in section 3. Section 3(a), moreover, expressly provides that the option may be exercised "at any time after July 1, 1979," so long as the closing date is scheduled during 1987, 1993, 1998 or 2003.

Even factoring in the requisite notice, then, the option could potentially be exercised as late as July 2003—more than 24 years after its creation in December 1978. Defendants' contention that section 3(a) does not permit exercise of the option beyond the 21-year period is thus contradicted by the plain language of the instrument.

Nor can EPTL 9–1.3—the "saving statute"—be invoked to shorten the duration of the exercise period under section 3(a) of the agreement. That statute mandates that, "[u]nless a contrary intention appears," certain rules of construction govern with respect to any matter affecting the rule against perpetuities (EPTL 9–1.3[a]). The specified canons of construction include that "[i]t shall be presumed that the creator intended the estate to be valid" (EPTL 9–1.3[b]) and "[w]here the duration or vesting of an estate is contingent upon * * * the occurrence of any specified contingency, it shall be presumed that the creator of such estate intended such contingency to occur, if at all, within twenty-one years from the effective date of the instrument creating such estate" (EPTL 9–1.3[d]).

By presuming that the creator intended the estate to be valid, the statute seeks to avoid annulling dispositions due to inadvertent violations of the Rule against Perpetuities. The provisions of EPTL 9–1.3, however, are merely rules of construction. While the statute obligates reviewing courts, where possible, to avoid constructions that frustrate the parties' intended purposes (see, Morrison v. Piper, 77 N.Y.2d 165, 173–174), it does not authorize courts to rewrite instruments that unequivocally allow interests to vest outside the perpetuities period (compare, EPTL 9–1.2 [reducing age contingency to 21 years, where interest is invalid because contingent on a person reaching an age in excess of 21 years]).

Indeed, by their terms, the rules of construction in EPTL 9–1.3 apply only if "a contrary intention" does not appear in the instrument. Thus, as the Practice Commentary explains, "[t]he court cannot validate an unambiguous disposition on the basis of the grantor's probable intent, but where construction is needed, [subparagraph b] will be useful in helping to establish the creator's intent" (Turano, Practice Commentary, McKinney's Cons Laws of NY, Book 17B, EPTL 9–1.3, at 543).

For example, where a deed contains contradictory phrases, one of which is valid under the Rule (see, Morrison v. Piper, 77 N.Y.2d 165, 173–174), or where one of two possible interpretations of a term in an agreement would comply with the Rule (see, Payne v. Palisades Interstate Park Commission, 204 A.D.2d 787), the court will adopt the construction validating the disposition (see also, Restatement of Property s 375 [1944]). By contrast, an option containing no limitation in duration demonstrates the parties' intent that it last indefinitely, and EPTL 9–1.3 does not permit "an extensive rewriting of the option agreement * * * so as to make it conform to the permissible period" (see, Buffalo Seminary v. McCarthy, 86 A.D.2d at 447, supra). The unambiguous language of the agreement here expresses the parties' intent that the option be exercisable "at any time" during a 24-year period pursuant to section 3(a). The section thus does not permit a construction that the parties intended the option to last only 21 years.

Given the contrary intention manifested in the instrument itself, the saving statute is simply inapplicable. . . .

Defendants next urge that we adopt the "wait and see" approach to the Rule against Perpetuities: an interest is valid if it actually vests during the perpetuities period, irrespective of what might have happened (see, Dukeminier, A Modern Guide to Perpetuities, 74 Calif L Rev 1867, 1880). The option here would survive under the "wait and see" approach since it was exercised by 1987, well within the 21-year limitation.

This Court, however, has long refused to "wait and see" whether a perpetuities violation in fact occurs. As explained in Matter of Fischer

(307 N.Y. 149, 157), "[i]t is settled beyond dispute that in determining whether a will has illegally suspended the power of alienation, the courts will look to what might have happened under the terms of the will rather than to what has actually happened since the death of the testator" (see also, Matter of Roe, 281 N.Y. 541, 547–548).

The very language of EPTL 9–1.1, moreover, precludes us from determining the validity of an interest based upon what actually occurs during the perpetuities period. Under the statutory rule against remote vesting, an interest is invalid "unless it must vest, if at all, not later than twenty-one years after one or more lives in being" (EPTL 9–1.1[b]). That is, an interest is void from the outset if it may vest too remotely (see, Turano, Practice Commentary, McKinney's Cons Laws of NY, Book 17B, EPTL 9–1.1, at 481; see, also, MTA v. Bruken Realty Corp, 67 N.Y.2d at 163, supra ["(t)he validity of the provision must be judged by the circumstances existing at the time of the grant"]). Because the option here could have vested after expiration of the 21-year perpetuities period, it offends the rule. We note that the desirability of the "wait and see" doctrine has been widely debated (see, 5A Powell, Real Property, PP 827F[1][3]; see also, Waggoner, Perpetuities Reform, 81 Mich. L Rev 1718 [describing "wait and see" as "[t]he most controversial of the reform methods"]). Its incorporation into EPTL 9–1.1, in any event, must be accomplished by the Legislature, not the courts.

We therefore conclude that the option agreement is invalid under EPTL 9–1.1(b). In light of this conclusion, we need not decide whether the option violated Symphony's equitable right to redeem the mortgage.

Remedy

As a final matter, defendants argue that, if the option fails, the contract of sale conveying the property from Broadwest to Symphony should be rescinded due to the mutual mistake of the parties. We conclude that rescission is inappropriate and therefore do not pass upon whether Broadwest's claim for rescission was properly assigned to defendant Pergola.

A contract entered into under mutual mistake of fact is generally subject to rescission (see, Gould v. Board of Education, 81 N.Y.2d 446, 453). CPLR 3005 provides that when relief against mistake is sought, it shall not be denied merely because the mistake is one of law rather than fact. Relying on this provision, defendants maintain that neither Symphony nor Broadwest realized that the option violated the Rule against Perpetuities at the time they entered into the agreement and that both parties intended the option to be enforceable.

CPLR 3005, however, does not equate all mistakes of law with mistakes of fact (see, Mercury Machine Importing Corp. v. City of New York, 3 N.Y.2d 418, 427). Rather, the provision "removes technical objections in instances where recoveries can otherwise be justified by analogy with mistakes of fact" (id.). Indeed, this Court has held that the predecessor statute did not mandate the court to grant relief where taxes had been paid on the assumption that a taxing statute subsequently found to be unconstitutional was valid (id.). Likewise, CPLR 3005 "does not permit a mere misreading of the law by any party to cancel an agreement" (Siegel, Practice Commentary, McKinney's Cons Laws of NY, Book 7B, CPLR 3005, at 621).

Here, the parties' mistake amounts to nothing more than a misunderstanding as to the applicable law, and CPLR 3005 does not direct undoing of the transaction (cf., Gimbel Brothers, Inc. v. Brook Shopping Centers, Inc., 118 A.D.2d 532 [lack of diligence in determining legal obligations under contract did not entitle party to restitution on the ground that it acted under a mistake of law]).

The remedy of rescission, moreover, lies in equity and is a matter of discretion (Rudman v. Cowles Communications, 30 N.Y.2d 1, 13). Defendants' plea that the unenforceability of the option is contrary to the intent of the original parties ignores that the effect of the Rule against Perpetuities—which is a statutory prohibition, not a rule of construction—is always to defeat the intent of parties who create a remotely vesting interest. As explained by the Appellate Division, there is "an irreconcilable conflict in applying a remedy which is designed to void a transaction because it fails to carry out the parties' true intent to a transaction in which the mistake made by the parties was the application of the Rule against Perpetuities, the purpose of which is to defeat the intent of the parties" (214 A.D.2d 66, 80).

The Rule against Perpetuities reflects the public policy of the State. Granting the relief requested by defendants would thus be contrary to public policy, since it would lead to the same result as enforcing the option and tend to compel performance of contracts violative of the Rule. Similarly, damages are not recoverable where options to acquire real property violate the Rule against Perpetuities, since that would amount to giving effect to the option (see, 5A Powell, Real Property, P 771[3]).

Accordingly, the order of the Appellate Division should be affirmed, with costs, and the certified question answered in the affirmative. Order affirmed, with costs, and certified question answered in the affirmative.

## NOTES

1. *The cost of ignorance.* According to the court, the value of the entire blockfront was $27 million if the option was enforceable. If it was not enforceable the properties were worth $5.5 million. The original sale in 1978 could easily have been structured so as to avoid violating the rule against perpetuities, but apparently nobody considered the possible application of the rule when the sale was being considered. Similarly, the defendants who purchased the option and associated rights from Broadwest in 1981 for $4.8 million also never considered the possible relevance of the rule. Do these facts reflect more badly on the rule as it applies to option agreements or on the lawyers who apparently overlooked a key issue?

2. *Can a lawyer be too smart for her client's good?* The court's decision, by destroying the original seller's option to repurchase, effectively gave property worth many millions of dollars to the original buyer, a nonprofit institution (Symphony). Symphony paid only $10,010 for this property, of which only $10 was paid in cash. Thus Symphony received a windfall of many millions of dollars and the defendants incurred an equivalent loss. The court rejected various theories that might have avoided this harsh result.

For example, the court recognized that an option contained in a lease is not governed by the rule against perpetuities, provided certain conditions are satisfied. What conditions were not satisfied to come under this rule? Similarly, the court recognized that some jurisdictions would hold the option to be good because it was in fact exercised within the period of the rule, but it declined to follow these other jurisdictions. The court also acknowledged that most authorities believed the rule against perpetuities should not be applied to land purchase options, but the court believed that it had no power to follow these authorities. Moreover, the argument that the entire transaction should be rescinded because it was based on a mutual mistake was also rejected by the court. Was the court simply applying basic principles when it ruled against the defendant in all of these matters? Perhaps the court lacked sympathy for the defendant's plight because the option originated in a tax-avoidance scheme that was just a little too cute. If this latter factor in fact influenced the court, should it have? Was not the plaintiff a party to and a beneficiary of the tax avoidance scheme just as much as were defendants' predecessors?

3. *Growth versus stultification of the law.* The New York Court of Appeals seemed to believe that when the legislature adopted the common law rule against perpetuities this made it inappropriate for the court to use the common law method of adaptation to modify the rule as changing times and philosophies required. Do you agree with the court's approach? If the court's approach is correct, does this suggest that legislative codifications of common law rules are to be avoided?

4. *The rest of the story.* Following the court's decision, Symphony Space sold the airspace above its theater to a developer for several million dollars. The developer built a seventeen floor apartment house over the theater.[13]

---

[13] See David W. Dunlap, Filling the Space Atop Symphony Space, N.Y. Times, July 18, 1999, § 11, at 1.

## ASSIGNMENT 12

# LIFE ESTATES AND ASSOCIATED FUTURE INTERESTS: THE DOCTRINE OF WASTE

### 1. INTRODUCTION

*Principal and Income.* When the ownership of property is divided into present and future interests, it is necessary to adopt a framework for determining the rights and liabilities of the owner of the present interest (the life tenant) and the owner of the future interest (the remainderman). Such a framework insures that all receipts and expenditures are properly accounted for. In general, the life tenant is entitled to receipts constituting ordinary and recurring items of income earned by the property such as rents, interest and dividends. In contrast, the life tenant typically is not entitled to any portion of the principal such as proceeds from the sale of the property. In terms of expenditures, the life tenant is responsible for ordinary maintenance expenditures but not for major permanent improvements.

Today, questions of principal and income are governed largely by statute. The original Uniform Principal and Income Act (1931) was revised in 1962. The Act was revised again in 1997 and 2008. More than forty states and the District of Columbia have adopted the 1997 Act.

*Waste.* A life tenant may wish to exploit the property in various ways that may infringe on the rights of the remainderman. For example, can the life tenant remove and sell part of the property by cutting the timber, extracting the oil and gas, mining the coal, or removing the soil? Can the life tenant demolish an old structure that is economically obsolete and build a new structure? What duties does the life tenant have? Can he neglect the maintenance of the property and permit it to become overgrown with weeds? If the roof leaks, must he replace it at his own expense even if the remainderman ultimately will receive most of the benefit?

There are two basic categories of waste: permissive and commissive. Permissive waste occurs when the life tenant fails to preserve and protect the property by exercising the ordinary care of a prudent person. In other words, the life tenant has the duty to maintain the property in a reasonable manner by making all repairs necessary to preserve the value of the estate for the remainderman. This duty includes the payment of all normal maintenance expenses such as taxes and interest on the mortgage. The life tenant is not required, however, to spend more than he receives from the property.

Commissive waste occurs when the life tenant damages the property in such a way that the property's value is permanently reduced. Nevertheless, if certain acts can be justified as a reasonable exercise of the life tenant's right of enjoyment, they will not be considered commissive waste, even if these acts do in fact reduce the value of the remainderman's future interest. In general, however, drastic changes in the method of operation that may diminish the remainderman's interest cannot be instituted without the remainderman's consent. Thus, a new mine or lumber operation cannot be opened, but an old one can be continued.

As you might expect, it is sometimes difficult to determine whether certain activities on the part of the life tenant constitute waste. Consider the following problem.

## 2. Principal Problem

In 1985, Ward Seagram died and left his home, Highland House, and all its contents to his wife June for life, and upon her death, to his son, Ward, Jr., by a previous marriage. Highland House is a large home—four stories and over 20 rooms—and is filled with antiques. In 2000, the home was valued at over $2,000,000.

In 2000, June began spending nine months each year in Florida, returning to Highland House for the summer months. The cold winters at Highland House aggravated several of June's chronic health problems. She continued to pay the taxes and insurance and tried to rent the home out for the winter months. After several unsuccessful attempts to rent the home, June simply boarded up the house and padlocked the doors when she left for Florida. Despite her attempts to secure the house, it was burglarized several times. June's lack of attention to the house has begun to show. The landscaping has deteriorated and the house requires major repair and restoration. Ward, Jr. visited the property several times over the last ten years. He attempted to clean up the grounds a few times and fixed a couple of holes in the roof.

Six months ago, June received an offer to buy Highland House and all its contents for $850,000. June would like to sell the house, but Ward Jr. refused to grant permission to sell the property. Two weeks after the aborted sale, a fire damaged the house.

Ward Jr. has retained you to help him in this matter. He would like to know if he can sue June for damages to the property, or at least get the property transferred to him so he can try to salvage his inheritance.

## 3. Materials for Solution of Principal Problem

### Melms v. Pabst Brewing Co.
Supreme Court of Wisconsin, 1899.
104 Wis. 7, 79 N.W. 738.

■ WINSLOW, J.

This is an action for waste, brought by reversioners against the defendant, which is the owner of an estate for the life of another in a quarter of an acre of land in the city of Milwaukee. The waste claimed is the destruction of a dwelling house upon the land, and the grading of the same down to the level of the street. It clearly appears by the evidence that after the purchase of this land by the brewing company the general character of real estate upon Virginia street about the homestead rapidly changed, so that soon after the year 1890 it became wholly undesirable and unprofitable as residence property. Factories and railway tracks increased in the vicinity, and the balance of the property was built up with brewing buildings, until the quarter of an acre homestead in question became an isolated lot and building, standing from 20 to 30 feet above the level of the street, the balance of the property having been graded down in order to fit it for business purposes. The evidence shows without material dispute that, owing to these circumstances, the residence, which was at one time a handsome and desirable one, became of no practical value, and would not rent for enough to pay taxes and insurance thereon; whereas, if the property were cut down to the level of the street, so that it was capable of being used as business property, it would again be useful, and its value would be largely enhanced. Under these circumstances, and prior to the judgment in the former action, the defendant removed the building, and graded down the property to about the level of the street, and these are the acts which it is claimed constitute waste. The action was tried before the court without a jury, and the court found, in addition to the facts above stated, that the removal of the building and grading down of the earth was done by the defendant in 1891 and 1892, believing itself to be the owner in fee simple of the property, and that by said acts the estate of the plaintiffs in the property was substantially increased, and that the plaintiffs have been in no way injured thereby. Upon these findings the complaint was dismissed, and the plaintiffs appeal.

Our statutes recognize waste, and provide a remedy by action, and the recovery of double damages therefor (Rev.St.1898, § 3170 et seq.); but they do not define it. It may be either voluntary or permissive, and may be of houses, gardens, orchards, lands, or woods (Id. § 3171); but, in order to ascertain whether a given act constitutes waste or not, recourse must be had to the common law as expounded by the text-books and decisions. In the present case a large dwelling house, expensive when constructed, has been destroyed, and the ground has been graded down, by the owner of the life estate, in order to make the property serve business purposes. That these acts would constitute waste under ordinary circumstances cannot be doubted. It is not necessary to delve deeply into the Year Books, or philosophize extensively as to the meaning of early judicial utterances, in order to arrive at this conclusion. The following definition of "waste" was approved by this court in Bandlow v. Thieme, 53 Wis. 57, 9 N.W. 920: "It may be defined to be any act or omission of duty by a tenant of land which does a lasting injury to the freehold, tends to the permanent loss of the owner of the fee, or to destroy or lessen the value of the inheritance, or to destroy the identity of the property, or impair the evidence of title." In the same case it was also said: "The damage being to the inheritance, and the heir of the reversioner having the right of action to recover it, imply that the injury must be of a lasting and permanent character." And in Brock v. Dole, 66 Wis. 142, 28 N.W. 334, it was also said that "any material change in the nature and character of the buildings made by the tenant is waste, although the value of the property should be enhanced by the alteration." These recent judicial utterances in this court settle the general rules which govern waste without difficulty, and it may be said, also, that these rules are in accord with the general current of the authorities elsewhere. But, while they are correct as general expressions of the law upon the subject, and were properly applicable to the cases under consideration, it must be remembered that they are general rules only, and, like most general propositions, are not to be accepted without limitation or reserve under any and all circumstances. Thus the ancient English rule which prevented the tenant from converting a meadow into arable land was early softened down, and the doctrine of meliorating waste was adopted, which, without changing the legal definition of waste, still allowed the tenant to change the course of husbandry upon the estate if such change be for the betterment of the estate. Bewes, Waste, p. 134, and cases cited. Again, and in accordance with this same principle, the rule that any change in a building upon the premises constitutes waste has been greatly modified, even in England; and it is now well settled that, while such change may constitute technical waste, still it will not be enjoined in equity when it clearly appears that the change will be, in effect, a meliorating change, which rather improves the inheritance than injures it. Doherty v. Allman, 3 App.Cas. 709; In re McIntosh, 61 Law J.Q.B. 164. Following the same general line of reasoning, it was early held in the United States that, while the English doctrine as to waste was a part of our common law, still that the cutting of timber in order to clear up wild land and fit it for cultivation, if consonant with the rules of good husbandry, was not waste, although such acts would clearly have been waste in England. Tied. Real Prop. (Eng.Ed.) § 74; Rice, Mod. Law Real Prop. §§ 160, 161; Wilkinson v. Wilkinson, 59 Wis. 557, 18 N.W. 527. These familiar examples of departure from ancient rules will serve to show that, while definitions have remained much the same, the law upon the subject of waste is not an unchanging and unchangeable code, which was crystallized for all time in the days of feudal tenures, but that it is subject to such reasonable modifications as may be demanded by the growth of civilization and varying conditions. And so it is now laid down that the same act may be waste in one part of the country while in another it is a legitimate use of the land, and that the usages and customs of each community enter largely into the settlement of the question. Tied. Real Prop. (Eng.Ed.) § 73. This is entirely consistent with, and in fact springs from, the central idea upon which the disability of waste is now, and always has been, founded, namely, the preservation of the property for the benefit of the owner of the future estate without permanent injury to it. This element will be found in all the definitions of waste, namely, that it must be an act resulting in permanent injury to the inheritance or future estate. It has been frequently said that this injury may consist either in diminishing the value of the inheritance, or increasing its burdens, or in destroying the identity of the property, or impairing the evidence of title. The last element of injury so enumerated, while a cogent and persuasive one in former times, has lost most, if not all, of its force, at the present time. It was important when titles were not registered, and descriptions of land were frequently dependent upon natural monuments, or the uses to which the land was put; but since the universal adoption of accurate surveys, and the establishment of the system of recording conveyances, there can be few acts which will impair any evidence of title. Doherty v. Allman, supra; Bewes, Waste, pp. 129, 130, et seq. But the principle that the reversioner or remainder-man is ordinarily entitled to receive the identical estate, or, in other words, that the identity of the property is not to be destroyed, still remains, and it has been said that changes in the nature of buildings, though enhancing the value of the property, will constitute waste if they change the identity of the estate. Brock v. Dole, supra. This principle was enforced in the last-named case, where it was held that a tenant from year to year of a room in a frame building would be enjoined from constructing a chimney in the building against the objection of his landlord. The importance of this rule to the landlord or owner of the future estate cannot be denied. Especially is it valuable and essential to the protection of a landlord who rents his premises for a short time. He has fitted his premises for certain uses. He leases them for such uses, and he is entitled to receive them back at the end of the term still fitted for those uses; and he may well say that he does not choose to have a different property returned to him from that which he leased, even if, upon the taking of testimony, it might be found of greater value by reason of the change. Many cases will be found sustaining this rule; and that it is a wholesome rule of law, operating to prevent lawless acts on the part of tenants, cannot be doubted, nor is it intended to depart therefrom in this decision. The case now before us, however, bears little likeness to such a case, and contains elements so radically different from those present in Brock v. Dole that we cannot regard that case as controlling this one.

There are no contract relations in the present case. The defendants are the grantees of a life estate, and their rights may continue for a number of years. The evidence shows that the property became valueless for the purpose of residence property as the result of the growth and development of a great city. Business and manufacturing interests advanced and surrounded the once elegant mansion, until it stood isolated and alone, standing upon just enough ground to support it, and surrounded by factories and railway tracks, absolutely undesirable as a residence, and incapable of any use as business property. Here was a complete change of conditions, not produced by the tenant, but resulting from causes which none could control. Can it be reasonably or logically said that this entire change of condition is to be completely ignored, and the ironclad rule applied that the tenant can make no change in the uses of the property because he will destroy its identity? Must the tenant stand by, and preserve the useless dwelling house, so that he may at some future time turn it over to the reversioner, equally useless? Certainly, all the analogies are to the contrary. As we have before seen, the cutting of timber, which in England was considered waste, has become in this country an act which may be waste or not, according to the surrounding conditions and the rules of good husbandry; and the same rule applies to the change of a meadow to arable land. The changes of conditions which justify these departures from early inflexible rules are no more marked nor complete than is the change of conditions which destroys the value of residence property as such, and renders it only useful for business purposes. Suppose the house in question had been so situated that it could have been remodeled into business property; would any court of equity have enjoined such remodeling under the circumstances here shown, or ought any court to render a judgment for damages for such an act? Clearly, we think not. Again, suppose an orchard to have become permanently unproductive through disease or death of the trees, and the land to have become far more valuable, by reason of new conditions, as a vegetable garden or wheat field, is the life tenant to be compelled to preserve or renew the useless orchard, and forego the advantages to be derived from a different use? Or suppose a farm to have become absolutely unprofitable by reason of change of market conditions as a grain farm, but very valuable as a tobacco plantation, would it be waste for the life tenant to change the use accordingly, and remodel a now useless barn or granary into a tobacco shed? All these questions naturally suggest their own answer, and it is certainly difficult to see why, if change of conditions is so potent in the case of timber, orchards, or kind of crops, it should be of no effect in the case of buildings similarly affected. It is certainly true that a case involving so complete a change of situation as regards buildings has been rarely, if ever, presented to the courts, yet we are not without authorities approaching very nearly to the case before us. Thus, in the case of Doherty v. Allman, before cited, a court of equity refused an injunction preventing a tenant for a long term from changing storehouses into dwelling houses, on the ground that by change of conditions the demand for storehouses had ceased, and the property had become worthless, whereas it might be productive when fitted for dwelling houses. Again, in the case of Sherrill v. Connor, 107 N.C. 630, 12 S.E. 588, which was an action for permissive waste against a tenant in dower, who had permitted large barns and outbuildings upon a plantation to fall into decay, it was held that, as these buildings had been built before the Civil War to accommodate the operation of the plantation by slaves, it was not necessarily waste to tear them down, or allow them to remain unrepaired, after the war, when the conditions had completely changed by reason of the emancipation, and the changed methods of use resulting therefrom; and that it became a question for the jury whether a prudent owner of the fee, if in possession, would have suffered the unsuitable barns and buildings to have fallen into decay, rather than incur the cost of repair. This last case is very persuasive and well reasoned, and it well states the principle which we think is equally applicable to the case before us. In the absence of any contract, express or implied, to use the property for a specified purpose, or to return it in the same condition in which it was received, a radical and permanent change of surrounding conditions, such as is presented in the case before us, must always be an important, and sometimes a controlling, consideration upon the question whether a physical change in the use of the buildings constitutes waste. In the present case this consideration was regarded by the trial court as controlling, and we are satisfied that this is the right view. This case is not to be construed as justifying a tenant in making substantial changes in the leasehold property, or the buildings thereon, to suit his own whim or convenience, because, perchance, he may be able to show that the change is in some degree beneficial. Under all ordinary circumstances the landlord or reversioner, even in the absence of any contract, is entitled to receive the property at the close of the tenancy substantially in the condition in which it was when the tenant received it; but when, as here, there has occurred a complete and permanent change of surrounding conditions, which has deprived the property of its value and usefulness as previously used, the question whether a life tenant, not bound by contract to restore the property in the same condition in which he received it, has been guilty of waste in making changes necessary to make the property useful, is a question of fact for the jury under proper instructions, or for the court, where, as in the present case, the question is tried by the court. Judgment affirmed.

### Anne Barnett Zauner v. Leonie Sullivan Brewer

Supreme Court of Connecticut, 1991.
220 Conn. 176, 596 A.2d 388.

■ GLASS, ASSOCIATE JUSTICE.

In this will construction case, the plaintiff, Anne Barnett Zauner, challenges the judgment of the Superior Court in favor of the defendant, Leonie Sullivan (Walker) Brewer, following the granting of the defendant's motion for summary judgment. Because we conclude that genuine issues of material fact exist as to the intended meaning of a disputed provision of the will of the testatrix, Virginia R. Ward, and as to whether the defendant had committed waste actionable by the plaintiff under General Statutes § 52–563[1] and subject to immediate relief in damages, we reverse.

The plaintiff was the wife and is the sole devisee of the testatrix' now deceased only son, John S. Barnett. The defendant was the wife of the testatrix' physician and friend, Eddie Brewer. The focus of the present dispute is a will executed by the testatrix in July, 1967 which provided in article three for the disposition of a thirty-three acre parcel of property known as "Beaver Dam" (property). The property at that time consisted of a newly constructed house and recently landscaped grounds, as well as a clear and swimmable man-made pond complete with a boat house and dock for recreational purposes. Article three provided: "I devise to my friend, LEONIE SULLIVAN WALKER [BREWER], for and during the term of her natural life my residence real estate [the property] in the town of Salisbury, and, at her death, or if she surrenders the premises prior thereto, the remainder interest therein to my son, JOHN S. BARNETT."

Upon the testatrix' death in October, 1967, the defendant, in accordance with article three of the testatrix' will, entered into possession of the property and made her home there. The defendant resided on the property until September, 1988, when she purchased and began to occupy a home elsewhere and leased the property to a third party. To date, a third party remains in possession of the property pursuant to a lease executed by the defendant.

After learning of the defendant's leasing of the property, the plaintiff commenced this action in the Superior Court alleging that, under article three of the testatrix' will, such leasing constituted a "surrender" of "the premises" that entitled the plaintiff to immediate possession of and title to the property in fee simple. The plaintiff further alleged that by permitting the buildings and grounds of the property to become out of repair, the defendant had committed "waste" within the meaning of § 52–563 that had greatly diminished the value of the property. In addition to possession and title, the plaintiff sought relief in the form of money damages and "such other and appropriate equitable relief as the court may deem appropriate."

Upon completion of discovery, the defendant moved for summary judgment pursuant to Practice Book § 384 on the grounds that: (1) because the phrase "surrenders the premises" in the testatrix' will unambiguously meant the "yielding up of an estate for life or years to

---

[1] "[General Statutes] Sec. 52–563. LIABILITY FOR WASTE BY TENANT FOR LIFE OR YEARS. Any person who, having no greater interest in real property than an estate for years, or for life, created by the act of the parties and not by the act of the law, commits waste upon the premises, beyond what tenants for years or life created by operation of law may do, shall be liable to the party injured in an action on this section, unless he was expressly authorized, by the contract under which the interest is created, to do the acts complained of."

him who has an immediate estate in reversion or remainder"; Black's Law Dictionary (5th Ed.); she had not, as a matter of law, effected a "surrender" of "the premises" by leasing the property to a third party; and (2) the plaintiff could not maintain a claim of waste under § 52–563 because she had failed to allege that the defendant's waste had substantially and permanently damaged the property, and, alternatively, § 52–563 did not authorize relief in the form of damages for waste before the termination of the defendant's tenancy. After hearing the parties and considering the evidence proffered in support of their respective claims, the court rendered summary judgment in favor of the defendant. The plaintiff then appealed to the Appellate Court, and we transferred the appeal to this court in accordance with Practice Book § 4023.

On appeal, the plaintiff argues that the trial court improperly determined that no genuine issue of material fact existed as to whether: (1) the defendant's leasing of the property constituted a "surrender" of "the premises" within the intended meaning of that phrase in the testatrix' will; and (2) the defendant committed waste actionable by the plaintiff and subject to immediate relief in damages under § 52–563. We agree.

The plaintiff first claims that the trial court improperly determined that no genuine issue of material fact existed as to whether the defendant's leasing of the property constituted a "surrender" of "the premises" within the intended meaning of article three of the testatrix' will. According to the plaintiff, the phrase "surrenders the premises" was an ambiguous expression of testamentary intent that required the trial court to consider extrinsic evidence in order to determine whether the testatrix intended that a leasing of the property constitute a surrender of the premises. The defendant counters that the testatrix' use of the word "surrender" in the will unambiguously evinced her intent that a surrender of the premises mean a "surrender" as defined in the law of estates: "A yielding up of an estate for life or years to him who has an immediate estate in reversion or remainder. . . ." Black's Law Dictionary (5th Ed.). Consequently, the defendant maintains that, as a matter of law, she did not surrender the premises when she leased the property to a third party. We agree with the plaintiff.

In construing a will, the "meaning of language used cannot be determined by an arbitrary rule of legal definition, but depends in each case on the peculiar provisions and character of the special will in question, which must to a large extent be its own interpreter." Wolfe v. Hatheway, 81 Conn. 181, 185, 70 A. 645 (1908). The proper contextual examination of a word carrying a technical legal meaning, for example, may indicate that the testatrix used the word in a nontechnical or otherwise more restricted sense. In such instances, the expressed intent of the testatrix must be effectuated by construing the particular word accordingly. Moreover, testamentary language "susceptible of different meanings is to be given that meaning which will most nearly effectuate the [testatrix'] intention." Middletown Trust Co. v. Gaffey, 96 Conn. 61, 67, 112 A. 689 (1921). "This requires the court, at times, to resort to extrinsic facts as an aid in explaining any language whose meaning the [testatrix] has left uncertain." Ministers Benefit Board v. Meriden Trust Co., 139 Conn. 435, 444, 94 A.2d 917 (1953).

An examination of the word "surrender" in its context in article three of the testatrix' will discloses that she employed the word as a transitive verb, followed by the object "the premises." Although the "usual and appropriate meaning" of the word premises in the law of estates denotes an interest or estate, the word "is used in common parlance to signify land, with its appurtenances" and the "buildings thereon." Black's Law Dictionary (5th Ed.); see Webster's Ninth New Collegiate Dictionary. The susceptibility of the word premises to "a duplicity of meaning"; Cornell v. Cornell, supra, 382, 334 A.2d 888; creates an ambiguity as to the precise act that the testatrix intended to amount to a surrender of the premises when she used those words in her will. This ambiguity is further compounded by the susceptibility of the word surrender to a similar duplicity of meaning. Specifically, the technical meaning of the word surrender in the law of estates, "as referring to the transfer of an estate, has been somewhat obscured by its frequent use in an untechnical sense, as referring to the relinquishment or yielding up, not of an estate, but of the physical possession of the premises. . . ." 4 H. Tiffany, Real Property § 960.

In view of these ambiguities, we conclude that the intended meaning of the entire phrase "surrenders the premises" in article three of the testatrix' will is not discernible from the language of the will alone. The issue of the legal effect of the defendant's act of leasing the property, therefore, cannot be resolved without resort to "extrinsic evidence as an aid in removing the doubt and in finding the [testatrix'] true intention from the language through which [she] expressed [herself]." Hoenig v. Lubetkin, 137 Conn. 516, 519, 79 A.2d 278 (1951). The trial court should not have summarily adjudicated that issue.

The plaintiff next argues that the trial court improperly determined that no genuine issue of material fact existed as to whether the defendant committed waste actionable by the plaintiff and subject to immediate relief in damages under § 52–563. The defendant responds with two alternative contentions. First, she contends that the plaintiff's claim of waste was not actionable under § 52–563 because the plaintiff failed to allege or produce evidence demonstrating that the defendant's waste had caused "permanent and substantial" injury to the property. Second, the defendant contends that § 52–563 authorizes only equitable relief, and not relief in damages, before the termination of her life tenancy. We consider the defendant's alternative contentions in turn.

Section 52–563 provides: "Any person who, having no greater interest in real property than an estate for years, or for life, created by the act of the parties and not by the act of the law, commits waste upon the premises, beyond what tenants for years or life created by operation of law may do, shall be liable to the party injured in an action on this section, unless he was expressly authorized, by the contract under which the interest is created, to do the acts complained of." With respect to the defendant's contention that the plaintiff's claim of waste was not actionable under § 52–563 in the absence of substantial or permanent injury to the property, the plaintiff directs our attention to the following evidence that she submitted in opposition to the defendant's motion for summary judgment: building inspector William Conrad's affidavit asserting that the defendant had neglected to make a number of "ordinary repairs" necessary "to preserve the property"; the defendant's deposition testimony acknowledging her failure to maintain particular areas of the property and certain of the structures thereon and photographs depicting the property in its original condition in approximately 1969 and its comparatively deteriorated condition in approximately 1989. The plaintiff asserts that this evidence raised a genuine and material factual issue as to whether the defendant committed waste by failing to make ordinary repairs to the property, thus entitling her to bring an action against the defendant under § 52–563.

The defendant concedes that the plaintiff's evidence disclosed that "some ordinary repairs were needed to preserve the property and keep it in a reasonable state of repair." In addition, the defendant acknowledges that she was "responsible" for making such repairs. The defendant nonetheless contends that the evidence was insufficient to preclude summary judgment because it did not show that her failure to make ordinary repairs had resulted in permanent and substantial injury to the property. Although the defendant does not attempt to ground this contention upon the language of § 52–563, an endorsement of her position would require that we construe the word injured in the statute to require permanent and substantial injury, in the absence of which, as the defendant asserts, a claim of waste does not "rise to the level of an actionable claim" under the statute. Because such a construction of § 52–563 to a large extent would absolve the defendant of her acknowledged duty to make ordinary repairs, we reject it.

A life tenant is bound to keep the land and the structures comprising the estate " 'in as good repair as they were when he took them, not excepting ordinary or natural wear and tear. . . .' " Ferguson v. Rochford, 84 Conn. 202, 205, 79 A. 177 (1911). The obligation to make ordinary repairs is twofold. The tenant not only has the duty to make the ordinary repairs required to remedy a presently existing condition of substantial disrepair that may have injured the property substantially or permanently, but also has the duty to make any ordinary repairs necessary to prevent the property from progressively declining to the point where its deterioration, and the resultant injury to the inheritance, is substantial or permanent.[2]

Like a tenant who fails to repair a presently existing condition of substantial disrepair, a tenant who fails to make preventive ordinary repairs "commits waste" of the permissive variety within the meaning of § 52–563. Id., at 204–205, 79 A. 177; see 4 G. Thompson, supra, § 1853, p. 400 ("[p]ermissive waste, as the name implies, consists in the mere neglect or omission to do what will prevent injury"). If, as the defendant urges, a claim of waste were not actionable under the statute until permissive waste produced substantial and permanent injury to the property, a tenant effectively would be relieved of the preventive aspect of the duty to make ordinary repairs because no right of action would exist to enforce that duty. Because it would have been irrational for the legislature to mismatch the scope of a life tenant's duty to make ordinary repairs and the scope of the right to enforce that duty, thereby rendering the tenant less than fully accountable for inaction that unquestionably constitutes "waste" under § 52–563, we conclude that the legislature intended that such duty and such right be correlative in scope. The party to whom the life tenant owes the duty to make ordinary repairs is therefore actionably "injured" within the meaning of § 52–563 if the tenant "commits waste" by failing fully to discharge either aspect of that duty. The relief furnished to redress permissive waste proved to have been committed necessarily will reflect the degree of injury to the property occasioned by such waste.

[W]e conclude that the plaintiff established a sufficient factual predicate from which it could be determined, as a matter of law, that a genuine and material factual dispute existed as to whether the defendant had committed permissive waste by neglecting to perform preservative acts comprehended within both aspects of her duty to make ordinary repairs. The declarations in the affidavit by Conrad indicated that the defendant had not made preventive ordinary repairs in that the front posts supporting the boat dock were "splitting and must be replaced," the mortar on a retaining wall had "cracked" and the wall had "moved," and "the wall coverings throughout the house [had] begun to come off the walls." With respect to the defendant's failure to remedy presently existing conditions of substantial disrepair, Conrad asserted that "the support for the boat house [had] been seriously damaged and it appeared

---

[2] The drafters of the Restatement illustrate the dual aspects of a tenant's duty "to preserve the land and structures in a reasonable state of repair" as follows: "A, owning Blackacre in fee simple absolute, transfers Blackacre 'to B for life.' At the time of the transfer, a house is located on Blackacre. I. B. permits the exterior wood of this house to go without repainting until the boards are exposed to weather. The repainting of this exterior woodwork is necessary to prevent a progressive weathering of the structure. Such repainting is within the duty 'to preserve the land and structures in a reasonable state of repair.' II. B permits the interior woodwork to go without repainting and the walls to go without repapering for a period of fifteen years. These omissions amount to substantial deterioration of the structure. Repainting and repapering the interior of such house is within the duty 'to preserve the land and structures in a reasonable state of repair.'" 1 Restatement, Property § 139, comment (c), illustration 3.

to be sinking at one corner," and further, "the pond . . . [had] grown in on all sides and is essentially unusable."

The defendant similarly acknowledged in her deposition testimony that she had ceased efforts to control the vegetation that had begun growing in the swimming area when it "got the better of [her]," and that while the island in the center of the pond had experienced "tremendous growth" during her tenancy, she had taken no action to control that growth since 1983. Notwithstanding the affidavit submitted by the defendant wherein real estate broker and appraiser Robinson Leach, Jr., contrarily alleged that his inspection of the property revealed "nothing other than 'normal wear and tear,'" this evidence can hardly be characterized as excluding "any real doubt as to the existence of any genuine issue of material fact" concerning the defendant's commission of permissive waste. Batick v. Seymour, 186 Conn. 632, 637, 443 A.2d 471 (1982). The court, therefore, should not have rendered summary judgment for the defendant on the plaintiff's claim that the defendant had committed permissive waste under § 52–563.

With respect to the defendant's alternative contention that § 52–563 authorizes only equitable relief and not relief in money damages for waste before the termination of her life tenancy, we initially note that even if we were to agree with her, we nevertheless would conclude that summary judgment on the plaintiff's claim of waste was improper. The plaintiff's prayer for relief not only included a request for money damages, but also a request for "such other and appropriate equitable relief as the court may deem appropriate." Because § 52–563, as the defendant concedes, clearly authorizes immediate equitable relief for the commission of permissive waste, summary judgment should not have been rendered on the ground that no relief presently was available to the plaintiff even if she were to have proved her claim of waste. We nonetheless address the issue of whether § 52–563 authorizes relief in the form of damages before the termination of a life tenancy because it is likely to arise on remand.

In support of her claim that a life tenant is not "liable" under § 52–563 to pay damages for waste before the termination of the tenancy, the defendant principally relies upon an American Law Reports annotation reporting a number of cases from other jurisdictions so limiting a contingent remainderman's right to collect damages for waste. See annot., 56 A.L.R.3d 677, 681. The jurisdictions noted in the annotation relieve a life tenant from legal liability to a contingent remainderman on various grounds, each tied to the uncertainty that the future interest ever will become possessory.[3]

---

[3] As the drafters of the annotation note, however, many jurisdictions afford contingent remaindermen a legal remedy that reflects the tenuous nature of their interests. The Oregon Supreme Court, for example, has adopted a rule that "if the contingency is fairly certain, and, therefore, the likelihood of damage to the remainderman is high," the contingent remainderman is "entitled to a determination of the amount of damages and to an impounding of the

The comparative certainty of possession attendant to ownership of an indefeasibly vested future interest in fee simple absolute, the type of interest owned by the plaintiff, entitles the owner thereof to the maximum protection available both in equity and at law. See 2 Restatement, Property § 187, comment (a). It has been said that such an owner "may secure compensatory damages for injuries sustained. . . . He may enjoin threatened acts of waste, or secure a mandatory injunction to compel the performance of a duty by the life tenant with respect to the care of the premises." L. Simes & A. Smith, supra, § 1654(c).

While we have not previously considered whether a life tenant likewise is "liable" under § 52–563 to pay damages for any injury to the inheritance caused by permissive waste, we see no principled reason why the immediacy of an indefeasibly vested future interest owner's remedy in damages should turn upon the variety of waste committed by the tenant. The variety of waste committed does not diminish the certainty of such an owner's future possession of the wasted property, nor does the inaction that constitutes permissive waste necessarily produce less damage to the inheritance than an act of voluntary waste, which, under Hamden v. Rice, supra, gives rise to an immediate right of action for damages under § 52–563 irrespective of whether the life tenant remains in possession. Furthermore, the possibility that the tenant may choose to repair the damage caused by permissive waste before the termination of the tenancy does not, as the defendant claims, justify the suspension of such an owner's ability to obtain relief in damages under § 52–563 until such termination. Voluntary waste does not consist solely of acts irrevocably destructive, but includes acts subject to reparation at the tenant's election such as the unjustified removal of "anything which has been fixed, or in any manner fastened, to the house," such as "doors, floors, or wainscot." 2 Z. Swift, Digest of the Laws of the State of Connecticut p. 517; see C. Smith & R. Boyer, supra, pp. 238–39. Because the prospect of possible restoration does not prevent an indefeasibly vested future interest owner from obtaining immediate relief in damages "to the extent of the injury" to the inheritance caused by an act of voluntary waste; Hamden v. Rice, supra; that prospect should not bar the owner from obtaining similarly immediate relief for any injury caused by the inaction of permissive waste.

Having discerned no sound basis for distinguishing between the remedies immediately available to the owner of an indefeasibly vested future interest in fee simple absolute insofar as voluntary and permissive waste are concerned, we conclude that the available remedies should be coextensive. A life tenant, therefore, may be "liable" under § 52–563 to pay damages to such an owner for either voluntary or permissive waste before the termination of the tenancy. Consequently, the trial court should not have rendered summary judgment in the defendant's favor on

---

proceeds. . . ." Pedro v. January, 261 Or. 582, 596–98, 494 P.2d 868 (1972), following Watson v. Wolff-Goldman Realty Co., 95 Ark. 18, 24–25, 128 S.W. 581 (1910).

the ground that § 52–563 does not authorize immediate relief in damages even if the plaintiff were to have proved that the defendant had committed permissive waste. Both equitable and legal relief, in the court's discretion, presently are available to the plaintiff under § 52–563.

The judgment is reversed and the case is remanded for further proceedings according to law.

### McIntyre v. Scarbrough
Supreme Court of Georgia, 1996.
266 Ga. 824, 471 S.E.2d 199.

■ THOMPSON, JUSTICE.

In October 1988, plaintiffs Russell and Sally Scarbrough purchased from defendant Dillie McIntyre a 16.59 acre tract of land by warranty deed, with reservation of a life estate in Ms. McIntyre in 1.2 acres which included a mobile home, porch, and shed. The reservation provided: "[L]ife estate is for [McIntyre's] natural life and during her occupancy of this tract as a personal residence. As to this tract, [McIntyre] shall be responsible for maintenance and upkeep of the property and all improvements thereon and for payment of ad valorem taxes."

In 1994, the plaintiffs brought a petition to establish title and to terminate the life estate, and subsequently moved for summary judgment, asserting that: (1) the defendant ceased occupying the tract as a personal residence in violation of the warranty deed, and (2) committed waste by failing to maintain the property and improvements thereon. After initially denying summary judgment to the plaintiffs, the trial court reversed its ruling on motion for reconsideration. Because the evidence conclusively established that the life tenant failed to exercise ordinary care for the preservation of the property, we agree with the trial court that she forfeited her interest to the remaindermen and that they are entitled to immediate possession.

The evidence on summary judgment showed the following: The Scarbroughs both averred by affidavit that they had not seen Ms. McIntyre on the property since 1990; that there was no water or gas service to the mobile home, nor a mailbox on the property; and that the structure is in a state of dilapidation. Ms. Scarbrough further averred that ad valorem property taxes had accrued on the McIntyre property since 1990, and that she (Ms. Scarbrough) was forced to pay the arrearage to avoid injury to her remainder interest. The Scarbroughs also offered the affidavit of a fire marshall who opined that the mobile home appeared to have been vacant for some time; that it was in a general state of decay and disrepair; and that it posed fire and health hazards and was unfit for habitation.

In response, Ms. McIntyre offered her own affidavit in which she stated that she is now 90 years of age, that she had been recently unable to occupy her residence due to health problems, and that she was in the process of renovating her home to make it fit for habitation. A July 29, 1994 sheriff's entry of service form shows that Ms. McIntyre could not be located and served because she was residing in a convalescent home outside the court's jurisdiction.

Ms. McIntyre also offered the affidavit of her grandson who averred that she had been confined away from home for medical reasons, that she had always expressed her intention of returning to the home and occupying it for the remainder of her life, that she had never removed any of her personal belongings during the time she was away, and that he completed certain repairs to the mobile home making it fit for habitation.

The trial court found that the warranty deed required Ms. McIntyre to occupy the tract as a personal residence as a condition of her life estate, concluding that "occupy" meant to "to dwell in" according to Webster's New Universal Unabridged Dictionary. Relying on the affidavits of record, the court found as a matter of law that Ms. McIntyre failed to occupy the property. However, the court's definition of occupancy was too narrow.

"Occupy" is more expansively defined in Black's Law Dictionary, p. 1231 (Rev. 4th ed.1968) as "to hold possession of; to hold or keep for use; to possess." Because one may occupy a residence by holding it or keeping it for use, the court erred in imposing a requirement that permanent physical presence was necessary to fulfill the occupancy requirement of the warranty deed. Evidence that Ms. McIntyre had never removed any of her personal belongings during the time she had been away for medical reasons, as well as her stated ongoing intent to occupy the residence until her death, raises a question of fact as to whether she continued to occupy the residence while residing elsewhere for medical recuperation.

The trial court, however, correctly determined that the plaintiffs were entitled to judgment as a matter of law under plaintiffs' alternative theory of recovery, that the life estate was extinguished under the doctrine of waste.

A life tenant is entitled to the full use and enjoyment of the property if in such use he or she exercises the ordinary care of a prudent person for its preservation and protection and commits no acts which would permanently injure the remainder interest. OCGA § 44–6–83; Graham v. Bryant, 211 Ga. 856, 89 S.E.2d 640 (1955). The unrebutted evidence shows that Ms. McIntyre had failed to pay ad valorem property taxes on the 1.2 acre tract for the years 1991 through 1993, or on the improvements for the years 1992 through 1994. In Austell v. Swann, 74 Ga. 278, 281 (1885), this Court stated that "a neglect to pay the burdens imposed by law upon the property during the term would be a want of such ordinary care as a prudent person should exercise for its protection and preservation, and would tend to divest the title to the fee by exposing it, or a portion of it, to sale, to raise the taxes levied on it." See also Kirk v. Bray, 181 Ga. 814, 831, 184 S.E. 733, 742 (1935) (a remainderman has a right to cause forfeiture for waste for non-payment of taxes). In Smith v. Minich, 215 Ga. 386, 110 S.E.2d 649 (1959), this Court found the non-payment of taxes as one element in a forfeiture proceeding. In the present case, not only was the defendant obligated by law to maintain taxes on her portion of the property, but she also specifically agreed to pay ad valorem taxes as a condition of the warranty deed. Although the question of waste is generally one for a jury, see Wright v. Conner, 200 Ga. 413, 37 S.E.2d 353 (1946), the undisputed facts show that the defendant failed to exercise ordinary care for the preservation of the property, and to comply with a condition of the warranty deed, resulting in forfeiture of the life estate as a matter of law.

Judgment affirmed.

■ BENHAM, CHIEF JUSTICE, dissenting.

I agree fully with the first division of the majority opinion, and I believe the evidence submitted on motion for summary judgment would, in a trial, support a verdict for the Scarbroughs. I do not believe, however, that they are entitled to judgment as a matter of law, so I must dissent from the majority opinion's affirmance of the trial court grant of summary judgment on the issue of waste.

As the majority opinion correctly notes, the question of waste is generally one for a jury. Wright v. Conner, 200 Ga. 413, 37 S.E.2d 353 (1946). That is especially so in a case such as the present one where there is evidence presented in defense of the life estate to the effect that any damage to the estate has been unintentional and due to the circumstances of the holder of the life estate rather than from disregard of the estate. Wright adopts from Roby v. Newton, 121 Ga. 679, 683, 49 S.E. 694 (1905), the analysis of the statute now codified as OCGA § 44-6-83. In Roby, this court noted that, as forfeitures are not favored, the statute must be strictly construed, as a criminal statute must be. The court went on to construe the statute as requiring a concurrence of permissive (lack of due care) and voluntary (active) waste, and held that the waste which would authorize forfeiture must be committed "in such a manner as to indicate an utter disregard of the rights of those who are thereafter to take."

In the present case, there is evidence that Ms. McIntyre has made some efforts, through the agency of her son, to reverse the deterioration of the property and that she has been ill and unable to care for the property adequately, although she has always intended to return to it. That evidence, if believed, does not show the wilful behavior required to warrant a forfeiture. The evidence offered in favor of forfeiture does not demand, as a matter of law, a finding of wilfulness. As this court noted in Grimm v. Grimm, 153 Ga. 655, 113 S.E. 91 (1922), "if the life tenant from poverty or inability to keep the premises from falling into decay, allowed them to get in such condition, such conduct would be merely permissive, and would not be voluntary...."

"The question of intent . . . fits the pattern of those issues of material fact which are not appropriate issues for summary judgment but are decided by the trier of fact." State Farm Fire & Cas. Co. v. Morgan, 258 Ga. 276, 368 S.E.2d 509 (1988). The question of whether Ms. McIntyre's conduct with regard to the life estate she holds has been so egregiously wasteful as to warrant forfeiture of her interest in the property should be submitted to a jury. I must, therefore, dissent to the affirmance of the trial court's grant of summary judgment on that issue.

## NOTES

1. *Careful drafting.* Could the controversy in the *Zauner* case have been avoided if more care had been taken when drafting the will of Virginia Ward (the "testatrix")? Could the controversy in the *McIntyre* case have been avoided if more care had been taken in drafting the reservation of McIntyre's life estate in the deed used to convey the land to Scarbrough?

2. *Life tenant's right to sell property.* Should a life tenant ever have the authority to sell the property? Some jurisdictions have statutes which permit the owner of any present interest in real property to apply to a court for an order directing the sale of such property whenever such sale is "expedient."[4] What does the term "expedient" mean in this context? In England, the life tenant always has the power to sell the property and to substitute the proceeds for the original real estate. Should a similar system be adopted in this country?

3. *Creation of a life estate without impeachment of waste.* Suppose the instrument creating the life tenancy provides that the life tenant is not accountable to anyone for waste. Should such a provision be upheld?

4. *Open mine doctrine.* The "open mine" doctrine is an important exception to the common law prohibition of waste. This doctrine provides that a life tenant may continue to exploit any natural resource on the property as long as that exploitation began before the life tenancy.[5] Additionally, the life tenant is entitled to keep all proceeds of the operation for herself. However, if the operation is the result of a lease that was granted prior to creation of the life tenancy, the tenant may not unilaterally renew that lease upon its expiration.[6]

The right to proceeds under the open mine doctrine can be superseded by statute. For example, in Hynson v. Jeffries,[7] the court decided that Mrs. Hynson, the owner of a life interest in producing oil and gas wells, could not claim all royalties from producing oil wells under the open mine doctrine. Although the wells had been producing before the creation of her life interest,

---

[4] See, e.g., Mass.Gen.L. ch. 183 § 49 (2003); Me.Rev.Stat. 33 § 153 (2008); N.H.Rev.Laws § 477:39 (2009); New York Real Prop. Actions & Proc. §§ 1602, 1604 (2008); R.I.Gen.Laws 34–4–7 (2008). The statutes in Massachusetts, New Hampshire, and New York allow both present and future interest holders to petition for a sale of the property.

[5] See Hynson v. Jeffries, 697 So.2d 792 (Miss. App. 1997).

[6] See Nutter v. Stockton, 626 P.2d 861 (Okla.1981). However, a lease renewal under the open mine doctrine might be permitted if the grantor intended this possibility. Cronan v. Castle Gas Co., Inc., 512 A. 2d 1 (Pa. Super. 1986).

[7] 697 So.2d 792 (Miss. App. 1997).

the will that created her interest did not specify that royalties would constitute income. The ambiguity in the will was resolved through application of the Uniform Principal and Income Act.

Under the Act, Mrs. Hynson's life interest—a right to receive royalty on mineral interests—was subject to a provision that provided 27½% of all royalties should go to the principal to reimburse the remainderman for the depletion of his future interest.

5. *Remedies.* What should be the appropriate remedy when a remainderman sues a life tenant for waste? Should the remedy depend on whether the remainderman's interest is contingent or vested? Must a remainderman bring an action for waste as soon as he becomes aware of the life tenant's activity, or would it be justifiable for the remainderman to wait to sue until the life tenant's death? Should the answer depend on whether the action involves commissive or permissive waste?

6. *Future generations and the waste of natural resources.* The responsibility of the present generation to protect future generations' use and enjoyment of resources and the environment can be analogized to the life tenant's responsibilities to protect the remainder interest(s). Future generations have increasingly been characterized by scholars as beneficiaries of a trust in natural resources and the environment.[8] The trust concept has been criticized for lacking a legally cognizable creator (settlor), a well-defined purpose, and adequate restraints on present generations' management of the planet for future generations.[9]

> A more accurate analogy may be that present generations are life tenants of the earth's resources and future generations hold remainder interests. However, the doctrine of waste historically disfavored environmental preservation of land and resources, instead encouraging development and exploitative use.[10] Property law may be evolving, though, to characterize present consumption as morally and legally wasteful.[11] The doctrine of usufruct and the doctrine of waste, taken together, would prohibit current users of land and natural resources from destroying or impairing their essential character or long-term productivity.[12] Who should enforce the rights of future generations? One approach is built on the increasingly

---

[8] See Weiss, The Planetary Trust: Conservation and Intergenerational Equity, 11 Ecology L.Q. 495 (1984) (arguing that the present generation holds a global natural and cultural heritage in trust for future generations and owes them fiduciary duties of conservation); Wood, Advancing the Sovereign Trust of Government to Safeguard the Environment for Present and Future Generations (Part I): Ecological Realism and the Need for a Paradigm Shift, 39 Envtl. L. 43 (2009) (urging a new paradigm of a "Nature's Trust" in which the government is the trustee, owing both present and future generations fiduciary duties to conserve the environment and natural resources).

[9] Gaba, We Do Not Hold the Earth in Trust, 33 Envtl. L. Rep. 10325 (2003).

[10] Sprankling, The Antiwilderness Bias in American Property Law, 63 U. Chi. L. Rev. 519 (1996).

[11] Guth, Law for an Ecological Age, 9 Vt. J. Envtl. L. 431 (2008).

[12] Frischmann, Some Thoughts on Shortsightedness and Intergenerational Equity, 36 Loy. U. Chi. L.J. 457 (2005).

influential concept of ecosystem services. Nature's ecological systems—watersheds, wetlands, forests, coastal dunes, savannas, and many others—provide critical services on which humans and our economy depend, such as climate regulation, flood and erosion control, filtration of water pollutants, pollination, and food production. One estimate by economists and scientists puts the total value of ecosystem services at $33 trillion per year, greater than the combined gross domestic product of all the nations in the world.[13] One way to protect this "natural capital" for future generations from degradation and over-consumption by the present generation is to incorporate the concept of ecosystem services into common law property doctrines.[14] Based on your study of the doctrine of waste in this Assignment, what opportunities or obstacles do you see for using the doctrine in this way?

---

[13] Costanza et al., The Value of the World's Ecosystem Services and Natural Capital, 387 Nature 253 (1997).

[14] Ruhl, Lant, and Kraft, The Law and Policy of Ecosystem Services (2007).

# ASSIGNMENT 13

# RESTRAINTS ON ALIENATION

1. INTRODUCTION

Proposition 1: The owner of property should be free to sell, give, or devise, all or any part of it to anyone, without legal hindrance.

Proposition 2: One who accepts property with a commitment not to sell, give, or devise all or any part of it to certain people or to all people, for a limited or unlimited time, should honor that commitment, and the law should enforce it.

Either of the above propositions, taken alone, might seem to be a self-evident truth. Yet the clash between them is apparent. Obviously, neither statement can be taken literally. The first statement is contradicted by the fact that a husband (or wife) cannot give or devise all of his (or her) wealth to someone other than the surviving spouse, thus leaving the surviving spouse destitute. All states have some spousal protection from disinheritance. Similarly, in most jurisdictions a landowner cannot subdivide his or her land without obtaining government approval concerning the size and shape of lots, provision of roads and utilities, and many other matters. The second statement is contradicted by the fact that a grantee can ignore a limitation that violates the rule against perpetuities or is otherwise against public policy.

Section 3.4 of the Restatement Third, Property (Servitudes) provides that a "servitude that imposes a direct restraint on alienation ... is invalid" if unreasonable. "Reasonableness is determined by weighing the utility of the restraint against the injurious consequences of enforcing the restraint." Direct restraints "include absolute prohibitions on some transfers, prohibitions on transfer without the consent of another, options to purchase land, and rights of first refusal."[1]

Section 3.5 of the Restatement Third, Property (Servitudes) deals with indirect restraints. These are valid unless they lack a rational basis. Indirect restraints include transfer fees payable by the grantor to another and use restrictions that may affect the value of property.[2] The Third Restatement's rules governing direct and indirect restraints require lawyers and judges to exercise judgment in determining the validity of these restraints.[3] The materials that follow ask you to do the same.

---

[1] Section 3.4, cmt. b.
[2] Id.
[3] In contrast, the Restatement Second, Property (Donative Transactions) §§ 4.1–4.3 (1983) promulgates more precise and rigid rules.

## 2. PRINCIPAL PROBLEM

The Tenmile Condominiums, located in the town of Highland Park, are operated by the Tenmile Condominium Association, which is a corporation composed of all condominium owners. All sixty condominiums are identical in their physical layout, each containing two bedrooms, a living room/dining room combination, kitchen, and two bathrooms. All sixty units are subject to the covenants, conditions, and restrictions contained in the condominium declaration. The declaration creates the following "right of preemption" in the Board of Managers of the condominium, defined as a first right to purchase, at the market value, any other unit offered for sale:

> In the event an owner of a unit desires to sell such unit and receives a bona fide offer for such sale, the unit shall be offered to the Board of Managers, who shall have a first right either to purchase such offered unit at the market price, or to produce a purchaser who will purchase the unit at the market price. Notice of such bona fide offer shall be given to the Board of Managers. The Board of Managers shall have thirty days from the date of notification to exercise this right of first refusal, and if not exercised, the sale may be made to the third party offeror.

All of the terms, covenants and conditions contained in the declaration are "deemed to run with the land" and are binding on all condominium unit owners and "their grantees, successors, heirs, executors, administrators, devisees or assigns."

Slope Investment Corporation owned unit 211 of the Tenmile Condominiums. Slope entered into a contract with Dolores and Donald Burgett for the sale of unit 211. Delores and Donald were newcomers to Highland Park and were accustomed to much higher prices for real estate in their former place of residence. Thus, they immediately agreed to pay Slope its requested price of $400,000, believing they were getting a great deal. All previous sales of Tenmile Condominiums ranged from $300,000 to $350,000. Meanwhile, Slope notified the Board of Managers of the terms of the proposed sale of its unit.

Before the prescribed thirty day period had elapsed, the Cambridge Company, a condominium unit owner and general partnership formed to purchase and rent real estate, notified the Board of Managers of its desire to purchase an available unit. The Board of Managers exercised its right of first refusal within the thirty day period and offered Slope $300,000 for unit 211. Slope nevertheless proceeded to convey the unit to the Burgetts.

The Board of Managers and Cambridge have instituted an action against Slope and the Burgetts, requesting that the conveyance of unit 211 to the Burgetts be set aside. The Burgetts are somewhat upset by the fact that they feel they overpaid for their condominium, but still want to retain the unit. They have hired you as their attorney and want you to develop a defense strategy and to evaluate their chances for success. Consider the following materials before advising your client.

## 3. MATERIALS FOR SOLUTION OF PRINCIPAL PROBLEM

### RTS Landfill, Inc. v. Appalachian Waste Systems, LLC

Court of Appeals of Georgia, 2004.
267 Ga.App. 56, 598 S.E.2d 798.

■ MIKELL, J.

Pursuant to an asset purchase agreement executed on December 31, 1996, RTS Landfill, Inc. ("RTS"), formerly known as Sanifill of Georgia, Inc. ("Sanifill"), sold one of its operating divisions, Starr Sanitation ("Starr"), a solid waste collection, hauling, recycling, and transfer station business, to Appalachian Waste Systems, LLC, ("Appalachian"), a company wholly owned and formed by Gerald S. Proctor and Sheryl D. Proctor, who were then employed by RTS's parent company, to complete the acquisition. The asset purchase agreement granted RTS a preemptive right of first refusal.... This appeal concerns the enforceability of those provisions. Specifically, RTS appeals from a series of orders declaring the provisions unenforceable and granting injunctive relief to Appalachian. For the reasons set forth below, we affirm the ruling that the preemptive right was unenforceable....

The second clause in dispute, entitled "Seller's Right of First Refusal and Repurchase Option," provides in pertinent part as follows:

> Purchaser and the Owners [(Appalachian and the Proctors)] hereby grant Seller [(RTS)] . . . a right of first refusal and the option to purchase any or all of the Purchase Assets and any or all of the membership interests in Purchaser, in the event that Purchaser receives and desires to accept any bona fide offer from a third party (an "Offer").... Seller's right pursuant to this Section 1.3 shall entitle Seller to purchase the assets at a price equal to the Offer *less* $500,000. Upon receipt of any such Offer, Purchaser shall provide written notice to Seller, which shall identify the third party offeror and attach a copy of such Offer. Receipt of such notice shall activate Seller's option. Upon receipt, Seller shall have thirty (30) days thereafter to notify Purchaser of its intent to purchase the subject assets or interests pursuant to the same general terms of the third party Offer and at the price stated herein. The closing shall occur no later than thirty (30) days thereafter.

Invoking the above-cited clause, Appalachian notified RTS on December 3, 2002, that it had received an offer from Advanced Disposal Services North Georgia LLC ("Advanced"), to purchase a 20 percent membership interest in Appalachian for $2.5 million. RTS claimed that the notice did not contain sufficient information to permit RTS to evaluate the offer and determine whether to exercise its right of first refusal. . . .

RTS first argues that the trial court erred in ruling, as a matter of law, that the right of first refusal constituted an unlawful restraint on alienation under *Shiver v. Benton.* In *Shiver,* the Supreme Court stated that the method of setting the price is critical to deciding whether a right of first refusal, which is more accurately termed a preemptive right, is a direct restraint on alienation.

> If the holder of the preemption right is merely entitled to meet the offer of an open market purchaser, there is little clog on alienability. But if he has a right to purchase at a fixed price, or at a reduced price from that offered in the market, it is likely to involve a sacrifice by the owner in order to alienate the property. Hence, it becomes a far more serious interference with alienability.

The Court held that the right of first refusal under consideration was not a restraint on alienation, reasoning that because it was "not tied to . . . some method of pricing which may not reflect true market value, but is conditioned upon meeting a sale price which the seller is willing to accept, the Agreement encourages the development of the property to its fullest potential."

*Shiver* concerned an interest in real property. The interest at issue in the present case, a membership interest in a limited liability company, is deemed personal property under Georgia law. No Georgia case addresses restraints against the alienability of such an interest, but it appears that restraints on alienation of personal property are disfavored. "It is the policy of the law to encourage free alienability of property, and attempts to remove either land or chattels from circulation in trade are discouraged not only by the rule against perpetuities, . . . but by the rule against unreasonable restraints on alienation."

RTS argues that *Shiver* does not stand for the proposition that restraints on alienation are unlawful if they permit the holder of the right to purchase the property at a discount. Rather, RTS contends, the court must determine whether the discount is reasonable under the circumstances. In support of its argument, RTS relies on *Colby v. Colby*, in which the Vermont Supreme Court upheld a repurchase option at a fixed price of $500 for property with a market value of $90,000. But in that case, the original price for the property was nominal, and the option price restored the original nominal consideration as well as repaid the option holders for sums spent on improvements by themselves and their ancestors. In addition, the property transfer was intended for the enjoyment of the descendants. The case is inapposite in the context of this arms-length commercial transaction.

However, other jurisdictions apply similar factors in deciding whether a preemptive right is reasonable. In New York, for example the "reasonableness of . . . preemptive first refusal rights . . . depend[ ] upon their duration, price and purpose." Similarly, the Supreme Judicial Court of Maine considers "1) the purpose for which the restraint is imposed; 2) the duration of the restraint; and 3) the method of determining the price." That court held that because the preemptive right of first refusal at issue was limited by a fixed price and endured forever, it violated the rule against perpetuities.

The Maine court relied in part on *Hartnett v. Jones*. In *Shiver*, our Supreme Court cited *Hartnett*, as well as *Robroy Land Co. v. Prather*, for the proposition that a preemptive right which is unlimited in duration does not violate the rule against perpetuities as long as the pricing method is based upon matching the offer of a third party. Instead, *Shiver* held that the right must be enforced within a reasonable time. RTS argues that its preemptive right should be reformed to require performance within a reasonable time. Based on its pricing method, however, we cannot agree.

We resolve the issue in the case at bar in light of *Shiver* and complementary foreign authorities. *Shiver* held that a preemptive right conditioned upon meeting a price that is acceptable to the property owner is not a restraint on alienation. In this case, we are faced with the converse of that proposition. Our question is whether a preemptive right which sets a price less than what is offered by a third party is void per se as a restraint on alienation. We believe that *Shiver* does not call for an inflexible rule. Based on the guidance provided by foreign authorities, we conclude that, in determining the validity of a preemptive right, a court must take into consideration its duration, price, and the purpose for which it was imposed. Applying these factors to the case at bar, we hold that the preemptive right granted to RTS fails the first two prongs of this test because it is unlimited in duration and sets a price of $500,000 less than what a third party might offer. As for the third prong, the trial court found as a fact that no legitimate business reason existed for the $500,000 discount. Testimony at the hearing reflected that no witness for RTS was aware of the rationale behind the discount. Moreover, RTS moved to quash Appalachian's subpoena for the individual who had personal knowledge of the transaction, and he did not testify at the hearing. According to Proctor's testimony, the individual was his boss, Miller Matthews. Matthews had advised Proctor to consider purchasing Starr and had informed Proctor that his job was in jeopardy. Proctor further testified that the $800,000 purchase price accurately represented the value of Starr; that it was a "fair deal" for both the Proctors and RTS; and that although the Proctors would have preferred to exclude the right of first refusal, they understood that it was a condition of RTS performing the transaction. This evidence supports the trial court's finding as to the third prong of the test. Therefore, the court did not err in determining that the preemptive right of first refusal was unenforceable. . . .

## Ferrero Construction Company v. Dennis Rourke Corporation

Court of Appeals of Maryland, 1988.
311 Md. 560, 536 A.2d 1137.

■ ELDRIDGE, JUDGE.

The principal question in this case is whether the Rule Against Perpetuities applies to a right of first refusal to purchase an interest in property.

The pertinent facts are as follows. On April 27, 1981, the plaintiff Dennis Rourke Corp. and the defendant Ferrero Construction Co. entered into a contract for the purchase of two lots on Mercy Court in Montgomery County, Maryland. This contract contained the following clause:

> In consideration of this contract, the Seller [Ferrero] agrees to extend to the Purchaser [Rourke] a first right of refusal on the future sale of any of the seven lots remaining on Mercy Court.

Rourke never recorded this contract. Settlement under the contract apparently occurred in May 1981.

On March 12, 1984, Ferrero notified Rourke by mail of a third party offer to purchase Lot 27, one of the remaining lots on Mercy Court. The letter contained the terms of the third party's offer and afforded Rourke the opportunity "to submit a contract" by March 21, 1984, for it "to be considered." Rourke immediately stated that it was exercising its right of first refusal and requested that Ferrero provide a copy of the third party's offer so that Rourke could prepare a contract with identical terms and conditions. On March 21, 1984, Rourke received a copy of the third party's offer. The next day, Rourke submitted a contract that in its essential terms conformed to the third party's offer. Subsequently, Rourke stated that it was prepared to settle on April 24, 1984. Ferrero responded that it had decided to reject both offers and that it would not appear at settlement. Ferrero in fact did not appear at the settlement and, on April 26, 1984, returned both offers, unsigned.

Rourke brought this action for specific performance in the Circuit Court for Montgomery County. In the first count of its amended complaint, Rourke claimed that it was entitled to a conveyance of Lot 27 by virtue of its exercise of the right of first refusal. In the second count, Rourke alleged that, independent of the exercise of the right of first refusal, Ferrero and Rourke had agreed upon a contract for the purchase and sale of Lot 27.

At trial, after the conclusion of Rourke's case, the trial court granted Ferrero's motion for judgment on count one, ruling that Rourke's right of first refusal violated the Rule Against Perpetuities and was, consequently, void. As to the second count, after the presentation of all of the evidence, the trial court held that Ferrero's letter of March 12, 1984, constituted an offer and that Rourke accepted the offer by stating its intent to exercise the right of first refusal. Nevertheless, the court ruled that Ferrero's offer was premised on the parties' mistaken belief that the right of first refusal was valid. Consequently, the court concluded that the parties had not formed a contract, as both had proceeded under a mutual mistake of law.

The Court of Special Appeals reversed on the ground that the Rule Against Perpetuities was inapplicable and that the right of first refusal was valid. *Dennis Rourke Corp. v. Ferrero Constr. Co.*, 64 Md.App. 694, 498 A.2d 689 (1985). . . .

## I.

Subject to a few statutory exceptions, the common law Rule Against Perpetuities remains in effect in Maryland. Maryland Code (1974), §§ 11–102 to –103 of the Estates and Trusts Article. *See also* Code (1974), § 4–409 of the Estates and Trusts Article. In *Fitzpatrick v. Mer. Safe, Etc. Co.*, 220 Md. 534, 541, 155 A.2d 702, 705 (1959), this Court adopted Professor Gray's formulation of the Rule Against Perpetuities: " '[n]o interest is good unless it must vest, if at all, not later than twenty-one years after some life in being at the creation of the interest.' " Gray, *The Rule Against Perpetuities*, § 201 (4th ed. 1942). The *Fitzpatrick* Court described the Rule Against Perpetuities as follows (220 Md. at 541, 155 A.2d 702):

> It is a rule of law, not one of construction, and it applies to legal and equitable estates of both realty and personalty. It is not a rule that invalidates interests which last too long, but interests which vest too remotely; in other words, the Rule is not concerned with the duration of estates, but the time of their vesting.

The vast majority of courts and commentators have held that rights of first refusal, which are more commonly known as "preemptive rights," are interests in property and not merely contract rights. 5A *Powell on Real Property*, ¶ 771[2] (1987). This is so because, if the property owner attempts to sell to someone other than the owner of the right of first refusal ("the preemptioner"), the latter may have a court of equity enter a decree of specific performance ordering that the property be conveyed to him. 5A *Powell on Real Property, supra,* ¶ 711[1], n. 9. Thus, the preemptioner acquires an equitable interest, which will vest only when the property owner decides to sell. *See* Note, *Real Property Pre-emptive Right or Right of Refusal Violative of The Rule Against Perpetuities?*, 40 Mo.L.Rev. 389, 391–392 (1975) (a right of first refusal "is in the nature of a springing executory interest").

As rights of first refusal are interests in property, the great majority of American jurisdictions have applied the Rule Against Perpetuities to such rights.

In addition, the Restatement has adopted the majority position. IV Restatement of Property § 413 comment e (1944). *See also* 5A *Powell on Real Property, supra,* ¶ 771[2] ("Options to purchase or to repurchase land, unconnected with a lease, commonly denominated options in gross, have generally been held bad under the common law rule against perpetuities, when not restricted in duration so as to comply with the permissible period under that rule").

In light of this widespread acceptance of the majority view, we should hesitate before attempting to fashion an exception to the Rule Against Perpetuities for rights of first refusal. In this area of property law, vested rights and settled expectations are at stake. A departure from settled law might introduce doubt as to the value of vested rights. Moreover, the contours of an exception for rights of first refusal might prove difficult to define. Consequently, the policies favoring certainty and stability strongly support our following the majority of courts and applying the Rule Against Perpetuities to rights of first refusal.

A right of first refusal is a type of option. IV Restatement of Property, *supra,* § 413 comment b (rights of first refusal are "analogous to options on a condition precedent"). Again, the majority rule, in England as well as in this country, is that the Rule Against Perpetuities generally applies to options. IV Restatement of Property, *supra,* § 393. In the area of options, courts in the 300 years since the High Court of Chancery decided the *Duke of Norfolk's Case,* 3 Ch.Cas. 1, 22 Eng.Rep. 931 (1681), have developed three exceptions to the Rule Against Perpetuities. The Rule does not apply to a lessee's option to renew a lease, *Bridges v. Hitchcock,* 5 Br.P.C. 6, 2 Eng.Rep. 498 (1715); IV Restatement of Property, *supra,* § 395(b). It does not apply to a lessee's option to purchase all or part of the leased premises, IV Restatement of Property, *supra,* § 395(a); *Hollander v. Central Metal & Supply Co.,* 109 Md. 131, 71 A. 442 (1908). And it is inapplicable to a usufructuary's option to extend the scope of an easement or profit, IV Restatement of Property, *supra,* §§ 393 comment j, 399. *See generally,* 5A *Powell on Real Property, supra,* ¶ 771[2]. All options may violate the Rule Against Perpetuities. Nevertheless, courts have justified these three narrow exceptions because these three types of options yield social benefits that offset the consequences of that violation. *Ibid.*

In urging us to exempt rights of first refusal from the Rule Against Perpetuities, Rourke would have us undertake such a balancing process. Again, however, it is significant that a majority of courts have struck the balance against creating the exception Rourke seeks.

We recognize that a minority of courts have held the Rule Against Perpetuities inapplicable to certain rights of first refusal. Most of the cases adopting the minority position involve unique interests in land, rather than the traditional fee estate involved in this case. For example, *Weber v. Texas Co.*, 83 F.2d 807 (5th Cir.), *cert. denied*, 299 U.S. 561, 57 S.Ct. 23, 81 L.Ed. 413 (1936), *Producers Oil Co. v. Gore*, 610 P.2d 772 (Okla.1980), and *Forderhause v. Cherokee Water Co.*, 623 S.W.2d 435 (Tex.Civ.App.1981), *rev'd on other grounds*, 641 S.W.2d 522 (Tex.1982), all involve rights of first refusal in connection with oil, gas, and mineral leases. As the Supreme Court of Oklahoma stated in the *Producers Oil* case (610 P.2d at 774):

> Mineral leases and their accompanying operating agreements have built in duration. Oil and gas production cannot last indefinitely and rights are always terminable.... [T]he provision for preemptive rights ... can last only as long as the agreement and the lease itself continu[e].

The Court of Special Appeals in the present case and other courts adopting the minority view reach their conclusion by assuming that the sole policy underlying the Rule Against Perpetuities is the elimination of restraints on alienation. Thus, in effect, the minority view postulates that an interest should not be subject to the Rule unless the interest constitutes a restraint on alienation. The minority view then distinguishes rights of first refusal from ordinary options. As stated in VI *American Law of Property, supra*, § 26.64, at 507:

> An option creates in the optionee a power to compel the owner of property to sell it at a stipulated price whether or not he be willing to part with ownership. A pre-emption does not give to the pre-emptioner the power to compel an unwilling owner to sell; it merely requires the owner, when and if he decides to sell, to offer the property first to the person entitled to the pre-emption, at the stipulated price. Upon receiving such an offer, the pre-emptioner may elect whether he will buy. If he decides not to buy, then the owner of the property may sell to anyone.

Based on this distinction, the minority view contends that, unlike ordinary options, at least some rights of first refusal do not restrain alienation; consequently, the minority view concludes that such rights of first refusal should not be subject to the Rule Against Perpetuities.

Even assuming the validity of the distinction between rights of first refusal and other options, the minority view errs in assuming that an interest should not be subject to the Rule unless the interest constitutes a restraint on alienation. In making this assumption, courts adopting the minority view confuse the Rule Against Perpetuities with the rule against unreasonable restraints on alienation. Admittedly, both rules belong to "a family of related rules that regulate the devolution of wealth from generation to generation." R. Lynn, *The Modern Rule Against Perpetuities* 9 (1966). These two rules are nonetheless distinct. The Rule Against Perpetuities prevents property interests from vesting remotely. The rule against restraints on alienation, on the other hand, prevents grantors from unreasonably depriving grantees of the power to alienate their estates.

The policies underlying these two rules are likewise not identical. Obviously, the rule against restraints on alienation serves to facilitate the alienability of property. Similarly, one of the purposes of the Rule Against Perpetuities is to facilitate the alienability of property. *See Commonwealth Realty v. Bowers, supra,* 261 Md. at 297, 274 A.2d 353; *Hollander v. Central Metal & Supply Co., supra,* 109 Md. at 159, 71 A. 442. Contrary to the minority view, however, the Rule Against Perpetuities is not simply a rule against restraints on alienation. L. Simes, *supra,* § 120, at 253. Instead, the Rule Against Perpetuities is concerned with restrictions that render title uncertain. *See* 2 H. Tiffany, *The Law of Real Property,* § 392 (3d ed. 1939). Without the Rule Against Perpetuities, it would be possible at some distant point for a remotely vesting future interest to divest the current owner's estate. Because of this threat of divestment, the owner might be deterred from making the most effective use of the property, even if he never has any desire to alienate his estate. Thus, by voiding certain remotely vesting future interests, the Rule Against Perpetuities eliminates this deterrent both for owners who wish to alienate their estates and for owners who have no intention of ever doing so. *See* 2 H. Tiffany, *The Law of Real Property, supra,* § 392. Consequently, from the standpoint of the Rule Against Perpetuities, it is irrelevant whether a particular future interest imposes a light burden, a heavy burden, or no burden at all upon the alienability of property.

Even if the minority view were correct that an interest should not be subject to the Rule Against Perpetuities unless that interest constitutes a restraint on alienation, we would disagree that rights of first refusal should not be subject to the Rule. In our opinion, rights of first refusal do restrain the alienability of property. In this respect, however, it is necessary first to distinguish among the various types of rights of first refusal.

Some rights of first refusal permit the right's owner to purchase property at a fixed price if the property owner, his heirs, or assigns should ever desire to sell. Plainly a right of first refusal at a fixed price inhibits alienability. Often, with the passage of time, the fixed price will bear no relationship to the property's actual market value. *See, e.g., Peele v. Wilson Co. Bd. of Educ.,* 56 N.C.App. 555, 289 S.E.2d 890, *petition denied,* 306 N.C. 386, 294 S.E.2d 210 (1982) (property owner had received bid at $4,300, while right of first refusal would have permitted heirs to pay only $50). Because the owner must often offer the property to the preemptioner at an artificially low price, the owner is deterred from selling the property or from increasing its value by making improvements. Consequently, even the minority view acknowledges that the Rule Against Perpetuities should apply to rights of first refusal at a fixed price. VI *American Law of Property, supra,* § 26.67, at 510.

A second type of right of first refusal permits the preemptioner to purchase the property at "market value" if the owner, his heirs or assigns should ever desire to sell. Some authorities would find the Rule Against Perpetuities inapplicable to such a right. *Metropolitan Transp. Auth. v. Bruken Realty Corp., supra,* 67 N.Y.2d 156, 492 N.E.2d 379, 501 N.Y.S.2d 306; VI *American Law of Property, supra,* § 26.67, at 511. Nevertheless, a right of first refusal to purchase at market value also effects a substantial restraint on alienability. A potential purchaser's offer might, in the preemptioner's opinion, exceed market value. The preemptioner could then contend that he need pay only some lesser amount. Fearing that a determination of the parties' rights would have to await the uncertain outcome of litigation, a prospective purchaser might be deterred from ever making an initial offer. 40 A.L.R.3d 920, 927 (1970).

The third type of right of first refusal permits the preemptioner to purchase the property at a price equal to any bona fide offer that the owner, his heirs or assigns desire to accept. In this situation, however, many prospective purchasers, recognizing that a matching offer from the preemptioner will defeat their bids, simply will not bid on the property. This in turn will depress the property's value and discourage the owner from attempting to sell. Moreover, even a right of first refusal tied to a bona fide offer may constitute an unreasonable restraint on alienation if the right is of unlimited duration. *See* Restatement of Property, *supra,* § 406 comment i.[4] Similarly, if, as in this case, the right of first refusal is unrecorded, the task of ascertaining and locating the holder of the preemptive right at some remote point in the future might also become so difficult that the right of first refusal could constitute an unreasonable restraint on alienation. *Atchison v. City of Englewood,* 170 Colo. 295, 307–308, 463 P.2d 297, 303 (1969). Thus, contrary to the minority view, we conclude that rights of first refusal restrain alienation.

It remains to assess the validity of Rourke's right of first refusal under the Rule Against Perpetuities.

We first observe that Rourke's right of first refusal was not limited to a term of years but was of unlimited duration. *Compare Westpark, Inc. v. Seaton Land Co., supra,* 225 Md. 433, 171 A.2d 736. Moreover, in this case, the right was conveyed between two corporations, which theoretically have a perpetual existence. Thus, under the conveyance as drafted, the right of first refusal might vest well beyond the period of

---

[4] The Court of Special Appeals concluded that Rourke's right of first refusal did not constitute an unreasonable restraint on alienation under IV Restatement of Property, *supra,* § 406. Section 406, the general rule on unreasonable restraints on alienation, expressly states that its provisions are subject to IV Restatement of Property, *supra,* § 413. Section 413 provides that a right of first refusal is not an unreasonable restraint on alienation "unless it violates the rule against perpetuities." Thus, § 413 and not § 406 contains the final word as to the reasonableness of rights of first refusal. Nevertheless, the Court of Special Appeals did not assess Rourke's right of first refusal under § 413.

some life in being plus twenty-one years that is prescribed in the Rule.[5] Consequently, the circuit court correctly held that the right of first refusal in this case violated the Rule Against Perpetuities and, therefore, was unenforceable.

[In Part II. of the opinion, the court held that Ferrero's correspondence to Rourke regarding the third party's offer did not constitute an offer to Rourke, independent of the right of first refusal.]

Judgment reversed, and case remanded.

■ COLE, JUDGE, dissenting.

Because the policies underlying the Rule Against Perpetuities are not furthered by its application in this case and because the right of first refusal in this case is not violative of the Rule Against Unreasonable Restraints on Alienation, I respectfully dissent.

The most commonly recognized definition of the Rule Against Perpetuities, which we have previously adopted, was set forth by Professor Gray: "No interest is good unless it must vest, if at all, not later than twenty-one years after some life in being at the creation of the interest." J. Gray, *The Rule Against Perpetuities* § 201 (4th ed. 1942); *see also Commonwealth Realty Corp. v. Bowers,* 261 Md. 285, 296, 274 A.2d 353, 358 (1971). The Rule Against Perpetuities, judicially created in *Duke of Norfolk's Case,* 3 Ch.Cas. 1, 22 Eng.Rep. 931 (1681), has survived several centuries notwithstanding that it often frustrates and annoys both lawyers and their clients. This frustration occurs because the rule voids all contingent interests in property that do not vest within the time period provided by the rule. Therefore, when the rule is applied, it purposefully thwarts the express intent of the testator, settlor, donor, or contracting parties by destroying the contingent property right created. *Murphy v. Mercantile-Safe Deposit & Trust Co.,* 236 Md. 282, 290, 203 A.2d 889, 893 (1964). Recognizing this problem this Court should hesitate to invalidate interests in property, especially those that have evolved from a bargained-for exchange, for no better reason than that the Rule Against Perpetuities dictates such a result. Accordingly, I decline to endorse the majority approach which mechanically applies the rule. Instead, I believe the Court should apply the rule only when necessary to preserve its underlying policies.

The underlying policies of the Rule Against Perpetuities are to "preserve the freedom of alienation, and to prevent restrictions on the circulation of property." *Ryan v. Ward,* 192 Md. 342, 348, 64 A.2d 258, 260 (1949). In other words, if a remotely vesting property interest hinders a property's alienability, marketability, or development, the interest should be subject to the Rule Against Perpetuities.

---

[5] Corporations such as Rourke and Ferrero cannot be used as measuring lives for purposes of the Rule Against Perpetuities. Fitchie v. Brown, 211 U.S. 321, 334, 29 S.Ct. 106, 110, 53 L.Ed. 202 (1908); L. Simes & A. Smith, *supra,* § 1223, at 108.

In determining if the Rule applies, it is important to distinguish rights of first refusal from options, and to recognize that different types of rights of first refusal exist. The majority suggests that a right of first refusal is a type of option. An option, however, gives the holder the immediate right to tender the purchase price and force the owner to sell. A right of first refusal, on the other hand, does not give the holder the power to require the owner to sell at any time, but instead only requires the owner to offer the property to the holder once the owner has decided to sell. In addition, the operative document creating a right of first refusal normally dictates whether the holder will exercise the right at a fixed price or a price which reflects true market value. While a fixed price will normally have a negative impact on the alienability of the land, a price reflecting true market value will not.

In this case, the right of first refusal could be exercised only if Rourke agreed to match an acceptable third party offer for the land. As this price should reflect true market value, the alienability and marketability of land is unaffected. Accordingly, although the right may not vest within the time constraints of the Rule Against Perpetuities, there is no need to void the right because such action does not further the policies of the Rule.

The majority argues that the policies underlying the Rule Against Perpetuities are furthered by voiding this right of first refusal. It asserts that although one of the purposes of the Rule Against Perpetuities is to facilitate the alienability of property, the Rule is also concerned with any restrictions that render title uncertain and unmarketable. However, the majority fails to distinguish between these two concerns and does not provide any evidence as to how this right of first refusal renders Ferrero's title uncertain or unmarketable.

The majority states that the great majority of American jurisdictions have applied the Rule Against Perpetuities to rights of first refusal. I believe that several of the cases cited to support this position are distinguishable. In particular, no less than eight of the cases cited involve rights to purchase at a *fixed price*. As previously stated, when the price is fixed, the alienability of the land is clearly affected. However, when the price to be paid is the market value of the land, alienability is no longer affected. Since this case arises from a granting clause which mandates that the selling price shall be equivalent to an acceptable offer from a third party, cases where the selling price is fixed are inapposite.

There is substantial authority supporting the proposition that the Rule Against Perpetuities should not apply to void rights of first refusal. The leading case in this area is *Weber v. Texas Co., supra*, where the lessee attempted to exercise his preemptive right to purchase the lessor's reserved royalty interest in an oil and gas lease. The lessee's right extended to his heirs and assigns and lasted as long as oil or gas could be produced on the subject land. The lessor refused to honor the lessee's preemptive right and argued that the preemptive right violated the Rule

Against Perpetuities. The Fifth Circuit Court of Appeals rejected the lessor's argument and provided the following analysis:

> The rule against perpetuities springs from considerations of public policy. The underlying reason for and purpose of the rule is to avoid fettering real property with future interests dependent upon contingencies unduly remote which isolate the property and exclude it from commerce and development for long periods of time, thus working an indirect restraint upon alienation, which is regarded at common law as a public evil.
>
> The option under consideration is within neither the purpose of nor the reason for the rule. This is not an exclusive option to the lessee to buy at a fixed price which may be exercised at some remote time beyond the limit of the rule against perpetuities, meanwhile forestalling alienation. The option simply gives the lessee the prior right to take the lessor's royalty interest at the same price the lessor could secure from another purchaser whenever the lessor desires to sell. It amounts to no more than a continuing and preferred right to buy at the market price whenever the lessor desires to sell. This does not restrain free alienation by the lessor. He may sell at any time, but must afford the lessee the prior right to buy. The lessee cannot prevent a sale. His sole right is to accept or reject as a preferred purchaser when the lessor is ready to sell. The option is therefore not objectionable as a perpetuity.

*Weber*, 83 F.2d at 808 (citations omitted).

Several courts have recently adopted the approach set forth in *Weber*. I similarly find the rationale in *Weber* to be persuasive. A right of first refusal is impotent to put property outside the stream of commerce. The holder of a right of first refusal cannot force the owner to sell the property. Nor can the holder prevent a sale once the owner has decided to sell. The holder of the right is limited to either accepting or rejecting the offer when the owner desires to sell. Moreover, because the right of first refusal in this case is not to be exercised at a fixed price, but is instead based on a price the owner is willing to accept from a third party, the right does not discourage the owner from placing improvements on the property, and the owner is assured of getting the fair market value for his land and added improvements.

Ferrero argues, and the majority agrees, that the outstanding right of first refusal "could discourage prospective developer purchasers from spending time and money for architectural and engineering services, to arrange financing and to negotiate a complicated real estate sales contract, knowing that preemption is possible." The majority concludes that the right restrains the alienability of the land. I disagree.

Prospective buyers always face the risk that their investigatory efforts will be wasted due to unavoidable market forces. A prospective developer might study the property and then conclude that a purchase would not be wise. The prospective buyer might also make an offer that the owner finds too low. Finally, another buyer may come along and offer a higher price. Thus, the risk of investigatory costs being wasted is present in every property acquisition. To the extent that a right of first refusal heightens this risk, I find it to be *de minimis.*

In sum, I believe that a right of first refusal does not hinder the alienability, marketability, or development of property and therefore conclude that the rule against perpetuities should not apply. I therefore dissent.

### Urquhart v. Teller
Supreme Court of Montana, 1998.
288 Mont. 497, 958 P.2d 714.

■ JUSTICE W. WILLIAM LEAPHART.

Appellants Robert and Evelyn Urquhart (the Urquharts) appeal from the April 2, 1997 opinion and order of the Twenty-First Judicial District Court, Ravalli County, granting partial summary judgment in favor of Respondents Otto Teller (Teller) and The Cinnabar Foundation (Cinnabar) on the Urquharts' claim to enforce an option to purchase. We affirm.

The parties raise the following issue: Did the District Court err in holding that the Urquharts may not exercise the preemptive right of first refusal contained in the Contract for Deed?

Factual and Procedural Background

Teller and his late wife, Elena Teller, were the owners of 280 acres of land in Ravalli County, Montana. In May 1971, the Tellers entered into an agreement with the Urquharts to sell approximately 270 acres, reserving 10 acres to the Tellers (Contract for Deed). The parties executed the agreement and deposited an unrestricted Warranty Deed in escrow.

The Contract for Deed contained the following provision:

IT IS SPECIFICALLY AGREED by and between the parties hereto that should Sellers choose to dispose of said ten acre tract, Buyers shall have the option to purchase said tract for the sum of $10,000.00, and in addition thereto the sum of $2000.00 in the event there is added to the house on said premises a bedroom and bath. PROVIDED, HOWEVER, that this option shall be non-assignable unless coupled with the assignment of this contract and the sale of the said premises and this option as a unit, and shall absolutely expire unless said option be exercised by Buyers within six months of written notice by Sellers that the property is to be disposed of. On death of Sellers, Buyers shall have the right to exercise said option, but the time for payment thereof shall be extended to six months after notice is given hereunder by the personal representatives or heirs of Sellers. Death of Buyers, however, shall not terminate this option. . . .

Teller states that he intended to grant the Urquharts a temporary option during the term of the Contract for Deed to ensure that the property would not be divided should he or his wife die before the Contract for Deed was paid off. The Urquharts claim that Teller intended to grant them an option exercisable upon sale of the property or upon the death of the Tellers and that Teller was told by his attorney that the option would continue in full force after the Contract for Deed was paid off.

On January 17, 1979, the Urquharts paid off the Contract for Deed, and the unrestricted Warranty Deed was released from escrow and recorded. After paying off the Contract for Deed, the Urquharts built a home, machine shed, hay barn, and another house on the property. In 1982, the Urquharts conveyed all of their remaining interest in the 270 acres to the Urquhart Revocable Living Trust. The Urquhart Revocable Living Trust conveyed the property to Spring Creek Investments, a partnership. In the contract for sale with Spring Creek Investments, the Urquharts, as trustees of the Urquhart Revocable Living Trust, purported to assign the option, but agreed to exercise it on Spring Creek's behalf if it were deemed non-assignable.

In the fall of 1993, Teller conveyed his 10-acre parcel to Cinnabar, a non-profit corporation dedicated to the conservation and protection of Montana's lands and waters, as a charitable gift. The value of the 10-acres plus improvements had increased to between $375,000 and $400,000. On August 23, 1994, the Urquharts, individually and as trustees of the Urquhart Revocable Living Trust, filed suit in the District Court seeking to enforce the option.

All parties filed motions and cross-motions for summary judgment. On March 31, 1997, the District Court entered its opinion and order granting partial summary judgment for Teller and Cinnabar on the Urquharts' claim to specifically enforce the option. The District Court held that the option, which it characterized as a preemptive right of first refusal, was limited to the duration of the Contract for Deed, constituted an unreasonable restraint on alienation, and violated the Rule against Perpetuities. The court also found that, considering the fair market value of the property, it would be inequitable to enforce the terms of the right of first refusal.

Discussion

As noted by the District Court, the "option" provision is actually a preemptive right of first refusal, triggered only upon Teller's choosing to sell or transfer the 10-acre parcel or upon his death. The Urquharts argue that the right of first refusal was triggered when Teller transferred the property to Cinnabar and that the District Court erred in refusing to grant the Urquharts' request for specific performance. The District Court held that the right of first refusal was enforceable only during the period of the Contract for Deed, was an unreasonable restraint on alienation, and violated the Rule against Perpetuities. The court also held that granting the Urquharts specific performance would be inequitable. We agree that the right of first refusal is an unreasonable restraint on alienation. Because we determine that the right of first refusal is void, we need not reach the issues of its possible duration or of the equities of specific performance.

Under Montana law, a condition restraining alienation, when repugnant to the interest created, is void. Section 70–1–405, MCA. This Court discussed the reasonableness of a restraint on alienation in Edgar v. Hunt (1985), 218 Mont. 30, 706 P.2d 120. In that case, the Hunts sold real property to Omer and Alma Edgar. Edgar, 706 P.2d at 121. The parties agreed that the Hunts would have the first option to purchase the property for $7,000 on written notice from the Edgars of their intention to sell. Edgar, 706 P.2d at 121. After the death of her husband, Alma Edgar filed a quiet title action, seeking to invalidate the option agreement. Edgar, 706 P.2d at 121. The district court granted summary judgment for Edgar, holding that there was no consideration to support the option and that it was an unreasonable restraint on alienation. Edgar, 706 P.2d at 121.

This Court set forth the factors to be considered in determining whether a restraint is void under § 70–1–405, MCA: The type of price set is important. If the price is fixed and greatly disproportionate to the market value of the property, this supports a finding of unreasonableness. Secondly, the intent of the parties contracting for the preemptive right is a factor. If, from the circumstances, it appears that the particular restraint, or the price set thereby, is primarily for the purpose of restraining the alienability of the property, it will weigh heavily against the validity of the restraint. On the other hand, if the circumstances suggest that the restraint was freely entered into by mutual consent as a normal incident of an equal bargaining relationship in order to promote the original transfer of the property, the scales will tip back towards the reasonableness of the restraint. [Citations omitted.] Edgar, 706 P.2d at 122. The Edgar Court remanded to the district court to consider the option provision in light of these factors.

In this case, the price set in the 1971 right of first refusal is fixed at $10,000 (or $12,000 in the event a house was erected on the property). Some 23 years later, the market value of the 10-acre parcel and improvements thereon had increased to between $370,000 and $400,000. Obviously, at nearly 35 times greater, the market value is grossly disproportionate to the option price. Other courts considering the issue have found much smaller variances in option and market price to be unreasonable. For example, a New Jersey court found that a $10,000 fixed option to purchase property valued at $40,000 was an unreasonable restraint. Ross v. Ponemon (N.J. Super. 1970), 109 N.J. Super. 363, 263 A.2d 195. A Texas court held an option price of $79,955 to be unreasonable where the property value had risen to $550,000. Procter v. Foxmeyer Drug Co. (Tex.App.1994), 884 S.W.2d 853.

In determining the reasonableness of a restraint, we also consider whether the restraint was entered into by mutual consent as a normal incident of an equal bargaining relationship or whether the parties intended for it to restrain the alienation of the property. If the person imposing the restraint has some interest in land which he is seeking to protect by the enforcement of the restraint and if the enforcement of the restraint accomplishes a worthwhile purpose, the restraint is more likely to be reasonable. Edgar, 706 P.2d at 122 (citing Restatement of Property: Perpetuities and other Social Restrictions (1994) [hereinafter "Restatement of Property"] § 406 cmt. i).

In this case, the evidence does not suggest that the Urquharts intended for the right of first refusal to restrain Teller from transferring his ten acres, but rather that the Urquharts sought to ensure they would be able to buy the acreage adjoining their own if they so desired. However, since the parties entered the agreement, the Urquharts have conveyed their entire interest in the property, and the property is now in the hands of several different owners. Thus, the Urquharts' legitimate purpose of obtaining ownership to neighboring property can no longer be served by enforcing the option. Enforcing the right of first refusal at this point would simply restrain Teller from transferring the property or give the Urquharts the bargain purchase of the century.

The Restatement's reasonableness factors also include whether the restraint is limited in duration, allows a substantial variety of types of transfers, or is limited as to the number of persons to whom transfer is prohibited. Restatement of Property § 406. The Urquharts' right of first refusal states, in part:

> On death of Sellers, Buyers shall have the right to exercise said option, but the time for payment thereof shall be extended to six months after notice is given hereunder by the personal representatives or heirs of Sellers. Death of Buyers, however, shall not terminate this option. . . .

Thus, the right of first refusal affects the alienability of the property in all types of transfers to all transferees.

Further, the District Court found that the right was of potential perpetual duration and therefore violated the Rule against Perpetuities. The District Court concluded that, under the language of the right, if the personal representatives or heirs of Sellers failed to give Buyer notice of Seller's death, the six-month period would never be triggered and the right would go on in perpetuity. However, in interpreting similar option language, other courts have held that when death triggers the buyer's right, the representatives or heirs of the seller are required to give the buyer notice within a reasonable time of death. See, e.g., Smerchek v. Hamilton (Kan.App.1980), 4 Kan. App. 2d 346, 606 P.2d 491. The Rule against Perpetuities should not be applied when it is possible to give an instrument a construction which leads to its validity. Therefore, we adopt the interpretation of the right of first refusal that does not violate the rule and determine that the right of first refusal imposed an obligation on Teller's heirs or representatives to give the Urquharts notice of death within a reasonable time. However, that the restraint could be interpreted as existing in perpetuity further supports our holding that it is an unreasonable restraint on alienation.

Under the Restatement of Property, a restraint that tends to increase the value of the property or that is imposed on property that is not otherwise marketable is more reasonable. Restatement of Property § 406. In this case, the right of first refusal fixes the price of the property, property that has appreciated in value to almost $400,000, at $10,000. Obviously, such a restraint decreases, rather than increases, the value of the property. Further, the property's market value and location in the Bitterroot Valley suggest that without the fixed price restraint, the property would be highly marketable.

We determine that the right of first refusal is an unreasonable restraint on alienation. The District Court correctly concluded that, under § 70–1–405, MCA, the right is repugnant to Teller's interest and therefore void.

## NOTES

1. *Law in flux.* Judge Cole's observation in his *Ferrero Construction* dissent that there is growing authority to not apply RAP to rights of first refusal (and even options to purchase) has become more true over time. See Creque v. Texaco Antilles, Ltd., 2001 WL 292539 (Terr. V.I. 2001); Bortolotti v. Hayden, 866 N.E.2d 882 (Mass. 2007); Old Port Cove Holdings, Inc. v. Old Port Cove Condominium Ass'n One, Inc., 986 So.2d 1279 (Fla. 2008). Recall from Assignment 11 that RAP is in rapid decline or obsolescence in most jurisdictions. What are the effects of these changes?

2. *Public policies and preemptive rights.* What are the underlying policies justifying the preemptive right at issue in the Principal Problem? Are there any policies that militate against the enforcement of such rights of first refusal? Should the policies on either side influence whether the rule against perpetuities should be applied to the preemptive right?

3. *Transfers of leaseholds.* One aspect of restraints on alienation that we have already examined is the question whether the landlord has the right to prevent the tenant from subletting or assigning. See Assignment 3.

4. *Due-on-sale clauses.* Many mortgages contain "due-on-sale" clauses. These clauses provide, in effect, that if the mortgagor sells the property, the entire debt secured by the mortgage would become due. It was sometimes held that such clauses were unenforceable as unreasonable

restraints on alienation.[6] In 1982, however, Congress passed a statute that, subject to certain exceptions, made due-on-sale clauses enforceable.[7]

5. *Personal property*. Both the rule against perpetuities and the rule against restraints on alienation apply to personal property, including the beneficial interests in trusts of real or personal property.

In Wildenstein & Co. v. Wallis, 79 N.Y.2d 641, 595 N.E.2d 828 (1992), the court was confronted with a preemptive right to buy artwork of world famous French Impressionist painters. Hal Wallis, a film producer whose credits included "Casablanca," was an avid collector of such works. His wife transferred two of these paintings to swindlers who sold them to Wildenstein & Co., a dealer in fine art. Wallis recovered them pursuant to a settlement agreement that gave Wildenstein a right of first refusal covering 15 named paintings. The agreement had no specified time limit. When Wildenstein sought to enforce the agreement against Wallis's heir, the heir argued that the agreement was void because it violated both the rule against perpetuities and the rule against restraints on alienation. The New York Court of Appeals upheld the agreement. With respect to the rule against perpetuities, the court held that the preemptive rights "serve significant commercial interests by facilitating broader marketing of world-renowned art treasures while posing, at the most, only a minimal limitation on the alienability of the works. . . ." 79 N.Y.2d at 651. With respect to the rule against unreasonable restraints on alienation, the court opined that "It ill behooves a court to substitute its sense of unreasonableness for the parties' arm's length agreement [settling] . . . an essentially commercial dispute. . . ." 79 N.Y.2d at 652.

The court seemed to be saying that preemptive rights in commercial transactions should not be governed by the rules against perpetuities or against unreasonable restraints on alienation, at least where the preemptive right was commercially reasonable. Yet only a few years later, the court applied the rule against perpetuities to an option to purchase real estate in a commercial context. See Symphony Space, Inc. v. Pergola Properties, Inc., reprinted in Assignment 11. Can you explain why the court distinguished between commercial options and commercial preemptive rights?

6. *Restraints on use compared with restraints on alienation*. Restraints on use are common. One example is a condition that the conveyed property be used only for residential purposes. Such a use restraint is an indirect partial restraint on alienation since a buyer who wants to use the property for non-residential purposes would be reluctant to purchase the property. Nevertheless, such restraints on use are not usually considered restraints on alienation. See Restatement Third, Property (Servitudes) § 3.5, comment d (2000). However, a restrictive covenant that limited use of property specifically to a Kentucky Fried Chicken restaurant "forever" was

---

[6] See, e.g., Tucker v. Pulaski Federal Savings & Loan Association, 252 Ark. 849, 481 S.W.2d 725 (1972); Wellenkamp v. Bank of America, 21 Cal.3d 943, 148 Cal.Rptr. 379, 582 P.2d 970 (1978).

[7] Garn-St. Germain Depository Institution Act of 1982, § 341, 12 U.S.C. § 1701j–3.

invalid. Citibrook II, LLC v. Morgan's Foods of Missouri, Inc., 239 S.W.3d 631 (Mo. Ct. App. 2007).

## B. Concurrent Estates

## Assignment 14

# Concurrent Estates: Creation

## 1. Introduction

When two or more people own the same interest in the same property at the same time they are said to own a concurrent estate. As the following discussion illustrates, there are several forms of concurrent estates.

*Forms of Concurrent Estates*

*Tenancy in Common.* Grantor grants Merrywood "to Alyssa and Ben." This creates a tenancy in common, which is the form favored by the law. Tenants in common have an undivided interest in the property. This means that neither tenant can exclude the other from any portion of the property. However, there is no requirement that this undivided interest be equal.

EXAMPLE 1: Oliver conveys Greenacre "to Cassie and Darren as tenants in common, Cassie to take a 75% interest, Darren to take a 25% interest." Cassie seeks to exclude Darren from part of the property. Result: Cassie may not exclude Darren from any part of the property, even though Cassie owns a greater interest.

EXAMPLE 2: Cassie and Darren sell the property conveyed to them in Example 1 for $10,000. Result: Cassie will receive $7,500 and Darren will receive $2,500.

In the absence of an intent to convey unequal interests to tenants in common, it is presumed that the interests are equal.

EXAMPLE 3: Olga conveys Blackacre "to Elizabeth and Franklin." Elizabeth and Franklin are tenants in common, each with an undivided 50% interest in Blackacre.

*Joint Tenancy.* Grantor grants Greenwood "to Gary and Helen as joint tenants, and not tenants in common." A joint tenancy has been created. The principal difference between a joint tenancy and a tenancy in common is that each joint tenant has a right of survivorship. Tenants in common do not have this right. Under a right of survivorship, the remaining joint tenant or tenants take the share of the property that the dead joint tenant had, as if the property had originally come directly from the grantor. Under a tenancy in common, that share would pass to the heirs or devisees of the deceased tenant. Unlike tenants in common, joint tenants always possess an equal undivided interest in the property.

*Tenancy by the Entirety.* Grantor grants Oakwood "to Hector and Wendy, husband and wife, as tenants by the entirety." Tenancies by the entirety can exist only between husband and wife. Most American jurisdictions maintain some form of tenancies by the entirety. Tenancies by the entirety resemble joint tenancies because both give a right of survivorship to all tenants. Also, as in the case of joint tenants, tenants by the entirety have an equal interest in the property. However, tenancies by the entirety differ in important respects from joint tenancies. The modern rule is that creditors of an individual spouse may not reach any property that the debtor spouse holds as a tenant by the entirety.[1] The rationale is that such a rule is necessary to protect the non-debtor spouse. Joint tenants do not enjoy this protection from creditors. Also, a joint tenancy can be converted into a tenancy in common by the unilateral act of one of the tenants. Tenancies by the entirety cannot be converted into tenancies in common by the act of just one tenant. The unilateral termination of joint tenancies will be dealt with in Assignment 16. Perhaps the most archaic feature of a tenancy by the entirety as it existed under common law was the husband's right to use the rents and profits of the property for his own purposes. Husband and wife were considered "entire" or "one"—and the husband was "entirely the one." Today, all states treat the spouses' rights in entirety property equally.

Additionally, even prior to the Supreme Court's decision in *Obergefell v. Hodges* legalizing gay marriage,[2] states were increasingly affording gay and lesbian couples the same property rights as heterosexual couples. Some states even explicitly codified the right to hold a tenancy by the entirety for parties to a civil union.[3] It will be interesting to see what developments occur post *Obergefell*.

*Community Property.* Grantor grants Elmwood to "Henry and Wendy, husband and wife, as community property." Ten states—Arizona, California, Idaho, Louisiana, Nevada, New Mexico, Texas, Washington, and, in part, Alaska and Wisconsin (as well as Puerto Rico and some Native American Territories)—are governed by the community property

---

[1] In some jurisdictions, however, creditors of a debtor spouse can reach property held in a tenancy by the entirety, subject to a right of survivorship in the other spouse. See, e.g., Hoyt v. American Traders, Inc., 301 Or. 599, 725 P.2d 336, 338 n. 1 (1986); In re Parameswaran, 50 B.R. 780, 783 (S.D.N.Y.1985); Cherry v. Cherry, 168 N.J.Super. 386, 391, 403 A.2d 45, 47 (1979). Cf. Lowe v. Morrison, 289 Ark. 459, 711 S.W.2d 833, 834 (1986) (creditor of debtor spouse can obtain a lien against the debtor's interest in the land but such claim can only be perfected on the death of the non-debtor spouse); In re Walls, 45 B.R. 145, 146 (Bkrtcy.Tenn.1984) ("A judgment creditor may levy on the survivorship interest of a tenant by the entirety, but the creditor succeeds to the estate only in the event his debtor outlives the other tenant by the entirety."). Additionally, the federal government can reach property held in a tenancy by the entirety to satisfy a tax obligation of the debtor spouse. United States v. Craft, 535 U.S. 274 (2002) (holding that a debtor's tenancy by the entirety interest represented a sufficient separate property interest in land on which to attach a federal tax lien because the right of unilateral alienation was the only property right in the "bundle of rights" not held by the debtor).

[2] 135 S. Ct. 2584 (2015).

[3] See, e.g., Colo. Rev. Stat. Ann. § 14–15–107(5)(a)(2015); Hawaii Rev. Stat. Ann. § 572–1.7(a)(2016); 750 Ill. Comp. Stat. Ann. § 75/20 (2016); Vt. Stat. Ann. tit. 15, §§ 1204(a), 1204(e)(1); N.J. Stat. Ann. § 37:1–32(a).

system. Community property exists only between husband and wife. It is usually derived from the earnings of either spouse while married. In community property jurisdictions at least half the community property must go to the surviving spouse upon the other spouse's death. In California, for example, section 682.1 of the state code provides for the possibility of community property with the right of survivorship, with the community property thus functioning similarly to a joint tenancy. Under the statute, the community property of a husband and wife will pass to the surviving spouse without administration and can be severed according to the same procedures as in a joint tenancy. The transfer instrument, however, must clearly indicate that the parties intend a right of survivorship for their community property.[4] The community property system is discussed in more detail in Assignments 17–18.

*Partitioning Concurrent Estates*

As discussed above, co-tenants (tenants under any of the concurrent estates listed above) have an undivided interest in the property. No tenant may exclude any other tenant from any part of the property. However, in certain circumstances this undivided interest may be divided. This division is called a partition. Partitioning may occur in two ways.

*Voluntary Partitioning.* If all co-tenants agree to divide a piece of property, such a division is permissible. The tenants may agree either to a division in kind or a division by sale. A division in kind of the property physically divides the property into pieces, and each co-tenant takes possession of a piece. A division by sale occurs when the property is sold, and each co-tenant takes a share of the proceeds. It has been said that the grantor may forbid partitioning of the estate, voluntary or otherwise, when the grant is made.[5] However, cases on this point are rare, and such a provision may constitute an unreasonable restraint on alienation.

*Partition by Judicial Proceeding.* In addition to voluntary partitions, a joint tenant or tenant in common has the right to demand partition in most jurisdictions. Tenants by the entirety and holders of community property do not have the right to demand partition. Other co-tenants may defend against this right by showing that the co-tenant demanding partition has agreed not to exercise this right. Like voluntary partitioning, judicial partitioning may result in two kinds of division:

> *Division in Kind.* This division preserves the physical estate and gives each co-tenant a possessory interest in part of the estate. Originally this was the only kind of partitioning allowed. Courts still refer to it as the preferred method, although practical considerations usually demand division by sale, and not division in kind. If the court is able to divide the estate into nearly, but not exactly, equal portions, the court may demand that the

---

[4] People v. Simons, 66 Cal. Rptr. 3d 571, 579 (Cal. Ct. App. 2007).
[5] 7-50 Powell on Real Property § 50.07 (2009).

benefitted co-tenant pay a sum of money to the other co-tenant to make up the difference. This sum is called an owelty.

*Division by Sale.* In most instances a property's value rests largely on one improvement, such as a house. In this case, division in kind is not possible, and the property will be ordered sold. The proceeds are split according to the interest that each co-tenant held. The court may direct either a public or private sale of the property. If the price is inadequate, the court will order a second sale. Mixed divisions—physical splitting of part of the property and sale of the remainder—are also possible.

*Creation of Concurrent Estates*

*The Four Unities for Joint Tenancy.* Any of the concurrent estates listed above can be created by grant deed. The common law had one quirk, now rejected by most courts, with which you should be familiar. If Jim was the owner of Elmwood, and granted it "to Jim and Kelsey as joint tenants," the rather formalistic common law held that a tenancy in common rather than a joint tenancy was created. This was based on the common law requirement that *four unities* must be present to form a joint tenancy.

*Unity of Time.* All tenants must take their interest at the same time.

*Unity of Title.* All tenants must take their interest from the same source, either the same deed, will, or intestate.

*Unity of Interest.* All tenants must have an equal and identical interest in the property.

*Unity of Possession.* All tenants must have a possessory interest in the whole.

The conveyance from Jim to "Jim and Kelsey as joint tenants" was said to violate the unity of time since Jim's interest had formed before Kelsey had any interest in the property. The failure of any one of these unities created a tenancy in common. Tenancies by the entirety also require the four unities, plus a unity of person. This unity of person could be achieved only through marriage.

This requirement of unity of time was routinely circumvented by the use of a straw person[6]. In the above example, Jim would convey to a straw person, and the straw person would convey to Jim and Kelsey as joint tenants. Occasionally someone unfamiliar with this quaint bit of foolery neglected to use a straw person and the intent to create a joint tenancy was defeated. Fortunately such cases are becoming rarer as courts or legislatures abolish the straw person requirement. Although some courts still purport to abide by the unities requirements, the unities are not a meaningful vehicle for analysis. When a court finds that the four unities

---

[6] A "straw man" has been defined as "a third party used in some transactions as a temporary transferee to allow the principal parties to accomplish something that is otherwise impermissible." *Black's Law Dictionary* (10th ed. 2014), *available at* Westlaw BLACKS.

are satisfied, it is usually merely stating its conclusion that a joint tenancy exists.

*Distinguishing Forms of Concurrent Estates.* At early common law an ambiguous grant was construed as a joint tenancy, not as a tenancy in common. However, in modern American jurisdictions this presumption is reversed, usually by statute. One reason to favor the tenancy in common is that it would be capricious to give all of the property to the surviving joint tenant and leave the decedent joint tenant's heirs with no interest. This result may seem less harsh when the concurrent tenants are husband and wife. Courts seem more inclined to find a joint tenancy between husband and wife, than to find one between unmarried persons.

There is another reason why joint tenancies are disfavored. Any joint tenant can convert his interest into a tenancy in common by conveying it to a third party. This can be done without the knowledge, or even over the protests of the other co-tenant.

EXAMPLE 4: Linda and Michael are joint tenants of Gumwood. Linda conveys all her interest to Nisa. Michael and Nisa are now tenants in common.

EXAMPLE 5: Olga, Peter, and Richard are joint tenants of Rockwood. Olga conveys her interest to Sandra. Sandra now has a tenancy in common consisting of an undivided one-third interest in Rockwood. Peter and Richard now have a joint tenancy between themselves in an undivided two-thirds interest in Rockwood. If Sandra dies her one-third interest will go to Sandra's heirs or devisees. If Peter dies his interest will go to Richard.

Example 4 illustrates the more usual case. By permitting one joint tenant to destroy ("sever") the joint tenancy at will a premium is put on careful planning and drafting of conveyances. Do you see why?

Although both joint tenants have a right of survivorship, the values of these rights may be unequal under certain circumstances. For example, if one joint tenant is 90 years old and the other is 20 years old, the value of the younger joint tenant's interest in the property will be much greater. If they contributed equally to the acquisition of the property, the inequality of values may be unfair. However, either tenant has the right to sever her interest at will. What effect does the right to sever have on the value of these interests?

*The Importance of Careful Planning and Proper Drafting.* Since joint tenancies and tenancies by the entirety include the right of survivorship, but tenancies in common do not, the drafter of any conveyance, whether will, trust, or deed, must make the kind of estate intended indisputably clear. When creating a joint tenancy, it is customary to dispose of the property "as joint tenants with right of survivorship and not as tenants in common." A conveyance to "Thomas and Vera" without further designation is sufficient in most states to create a tenancy in common, although one "to Thomas and Vera, as tenants in common" is preferable. As the following cases show, litigation is likely when the drafter of the conveyance does not make the intent clear. As you read the following materials, consider how litigation might have been avoided by careful planning and proper drafting of the conveyances.

## 2. PRINCIPAL PROBLEM

Jack was a long time friend of the family. He died leaving his farm, Pollenacre, "to Bart and Rose Lee, and their son Ron Lee, jointly." Bart and Rose were married at the time the will was probated. Ron was a minor and still living with Bart and Rose. Twenty-five years later Ron died, leaving all his interest in the property to his friend, Josephine. Josephine has filed suit seeking a declaration that she has a ½ interest in Pollenacre. Alternatively, she claims a ⅓ share. Bart and Rose have been served with the complaint and summons. They come to you and insist that Josephine has no interest in Pollenacre. Before drafting an answer to the complaint, consider the following materials. Assume that you are in a jurisdiction that recognizes tenancies by the entirety.

## 3. MATERIALS FOR SOLUTION OF PRINCIPAL PROBLEM

### Adamson v. Adamson
Supreme Court of Oregon, 1975.
273 Or. 382, 541 P.2d 460.

■ BRYSON, JUSTICE.

This is a suit to determine the equitable interest in a land sale contract between plaintiff, a named purchaser, and defendant-intervenor who obtained the interest of a named co-purchaser. The trial court decreed that plaintiff owned two-thirds and defendant-intervenor owned one-third of the equitable interest and ordered an accounting and sale of the parties' interest. The court also awarded attorney fees to plaintiff. Defendant-intervenor appeals.

This suit is essentially a family dispute wherein the parties seek judicial interpretation of events pertaining to the equitable interest of the parties in a fourplex apartment in Portland, Oregon. Plaintiff Margaret Adamson married Brian Adamson the only child of Joel and Inez Adamson,[7] in April of 1964. Thereafter, plaintiff and Brian, who were then living with Inez Adamson, Brian's mother, began searching for their own house in which to reside.

Brian located a fourplex for sale which he desired to purchase. He approached both of his parents to discuss the feasibility of purchasing the

---

[7] Prior to trial Inez Adamson, a defendant, transferred her interest to her former husband, Joel Adamson, defendant-intervenor. Inez and Joel had been separated approximately eight years and were divorced in December, 1973, all prior to the time of trial. Inez T. Adamson and Nita H. Hunt, vendor, are not parties to this appeal.

fourplex. After some discussion Brian, as sole purchaser, signed an earnest money agreement with the seller, Hunt. At the closing of the transaction and execution of the sales contract, Inez advanced the down payment of $5,000. A sales contract was prepared by the realtor at Brian's direction, which read in part:

> THIS CONTRACT, made this *20th* day of *May,* 1965, between *Alden G. Hunt and Nita M. Hunt (husband and wife)* hereinafter called the seller, and *Brian J. Adamson and Margaret Adamson (husband and wife) and Inez T. Adamson,* hereinafter called the buyer.
>
>> WITNESSETH, That in consideration for the stipulations herein contained and the payments to be made as hereinafter specified, the seller hereby agrees to sell to the buyer and the buyer agrees to purchase from the seller the following described real estate. . . . (Description of property omitted).
>
> /s/ Brian J. Adamson     (seal)    /s/ Alden G. Hunt     (seal)
>
> /s/ Margaret A. Adamson   (seal)    /s/ Nita M. Hunt      (seal)
>
>                                                     /s/ Inez T. Adamson    (seal)

Stated in chronological order, certain exhibits were received affecting the real property involved herein:

1. May 20, 1965: Execution of the contract to purchase by Margaret and Brian Adamson, husband and wife, and Inez Adamson;
2. April 14, 1972: Deed, Brian Adamson and plaintiff, Margaret Adamson, husband and wife, to Joel Adamson, Brian's father, of interest in fourplex;
3. June 12, 1972: Petition for divorce filed, Margaret Adamson v. Brian Adamson, praying that the plaintiff's and defendant's interests in the fourplex involved herein be set aside to petitioner as her sole property;
4. April 13, 1973: Divorce decree awarding petitioner, plaintiff herein, all right, title and interest of the parties in and to the fourplex;
5. October 9, 1973: This suit filed;
6. October 24, 1973: Deed, Inez T. Adamson to Joel, defendant-intervenor, of all of her interest in and to the fourplex.

Defendant first contends that, contrary to the executed land sale contract, plaintiff and Brian had no interest in the fourplex and the court erred in so finding. He argues that both plaintiff's and Brian's names were placed "on the contract as a kind of 'insurance' if something happened to" Inez, Brian's mother; that plaintiff and Brian "would receive one-half of Inez's interest if Inez died."

We have reviewed all of the testimony and exhibits and although it is conflicting, we conclude that the evidence adduced demonstrates that plaintiff and Brian had an equitable interest in the fourplex as set forth in the land sale contract dated May 20, 1965.

The defendant-intervenor also contends that the trial court erred in decreeing that the deed by plaintiff and Brian J. Adamson of April 14, 1972, to Joel Adamson conveying their interest in and to the fourplex real property was void and of no legal effect. He argues that the deed was given for an adequate consideration as stated in the deed, "$850.00" and other property or value.

Plaintiff contends that Brian and defendant-intervenor conspired together and through duress and coercion acted fraudulently in obtaining plaintiff's signature to said deed and in transferring the equitable interest of plaintiff and Brian in the fourplex to defendant-intervenor.

The trial court found:

> [I]t was evident to the parties as time went on when this final transaction happened here in April (deed by Brian and plaintiff to defendant-intervenor) that the marriage was on the rocks and everyone suddenly looks to their own when that happens, and Margaret here relied a great deal on her father-in-law and had a high respect and trust in him. She (plaintiff) was in a state of discomfort. She was overdue with the childbirth. . . .

The court further found that plaintiff had been "threatened," and "harassment" and "coercion" had been exerted against her.

The record shows that prior to the execution of the deed in question, defendant-intervenor became aware of two problems: (1) that his son, Brian, who had been unemployed, was having financial difficulty and was being pursued by creditors; (2) that Brian and plaintiff were having marital difficulty. Plaintiff had separated from Brian, and a divorce was imminent after plaintiff's pregnancy was terminated. It is also clear from the record that defendant-intervenor masterminded the execution of the deed in question; it was his idea. Both his son, Brian, and plaintiff relied upon and accepted his advice and trusted him. He testified:

> Q. Mr. Adamson, up until the time Margaret separated from her husband she always trusted you and relied on what you told her, didn't she?
>
> A. I believe she did, yes, sir.

Plaintiff testified to the same effect and that Brian followed his father's instructions. It is clear that a confidential relationship existed between plaintiff and her father-in-law.

... A confidential relationship exists between two persons when one has gained the confidence of the other and purports to act or advise with the other's interest in mind.

The evidence shows that defendant-intervenor prepared the deed of April 14, 1972, and he arranged for its execution at the bank. On the day in question, he went to plaintiff's home and drove plaintiff and Brian to the bank without any discussion of the document and had plaintiff execute the deed before a notary public, a bank employee. Plaintiff described what occurred as follows:

THE COURT: ... Were you aware that you transferred your interest or whatever your interest may be in the fourplex?

THE WITNESS: No.

...

THE COURT: What did you think you were signing on the day that your husband brought you down to the bank there?

THE WITNESS: He told me I was signing a correction—as I remember a correction to the paper I had signed earlier referring to the property sale of property on Burnside, and that is what I thought. ...

She further testified:

A. I had always trusted Mr. Adamson and him in our business dealings.

Q. When you were at the bank and you signed the deed why didn't you read it, Mrs. Adamson?

A. Because I didn't want it either in the first place. I was rather sick and I was leaning on the counter. I didn't read it. I just took their word for it.

Q. Did you have a chance to read it?

A. I probably could have read it, but I didn't.

Plaintiff filed her petition for divorce approximately two months after she had executed the deed of April 14, 1972. Her child was born May 5, 1972. As stated, it is abundantly clear that at the time defendant-intervenor secured the execution of the deed, both he and Brian were aware that a divorce was imminent. It is equally clear that the conveyance was made to hinder or delay plaintiff from recovering, in a divorce suit, Brian's interest in the fourplex, his only tangible asset. Defendant-intervenor attempted to explain the consideration of $850 by stating that it was sums that he had advanced to his son after his son's marriage to plaintiff for the payment of creditors, but the evidence would indicate such payments were in the form of a gift, not uncommon between parents and children during marriage difficulty.

In plaintiff's divorce suit against Brian Adamson (file was received as an exhibit in this suit), she prayed that she be "awarded as her sole and separate property all of the right, title and interest of the parties in and to" the fourplex involved herein. The divorce decree granted her this relief.

We conclude, as did the trial court, that the conveyance by deed of April 14, 1972, was obtained by fraud to hinder or prevent plaintiff's recovery of Brian's equitable interest in the fourplex, in the divorce suit, and is therefore set aside and held to be void.

The trial court reached the same conclusion on the facts as we have but decreed that "plaintiff is the owner of an undivided two-thirds (⅔) and defendant in intervention is the owner of an undivided one-third (⅓) of the equitable interest of the buyers in and to the following described real property under the terms" of the land sale contract.

Defendant-intervenor contends "(w)hatever interest Brian and Margaret may have had under the contract (if any) was taken by them as an entity, as tenants by the entirety. . . . They had at the most a one-half interest as tenants by the entirety, and Inez Adamson held a one-half interest individually," which she conveyed to defendant-intervenor. We agree. The concept of tenancy by the entirety is that the husband and wife are but one person in the law.

> Estates by the entireties are creatures of the common law created by legal fiction and based wholly on the common law doctrine that the husband and wife are one, and, therefore, there is but one estate and, in contemplation of law, but the person owning the whole.

4A Powell on Real Property § 622 (1974) states, at page 688:

> Complications arise when the conveyance of land runs to H and W and a third named person, or to H and W plus a second couple, H and W. The historical unity of husband and wife is apparent in the tendency of courts to award each couple only a single share under such a conveyance.

We find that by virtue of the decree which dissolved the marriage of plaintiff and Brian and awarded plaintiff all of Brian's interest in the fourplex, plaintiff holds an undivided one-half equitable interest in the fourplex pursuant to the land sale contract. Defendant-intervenor, by virtue of the deed from Inez, holds the remaining undivided one-half equitable interest.

### Margarite v. Ewald
Superior Court of Pennsylvania, 1977.
252 Pa.Super. 244, 381 A.2d 480.

■ JACOBS, JUDGE.

We are asked on this appeal to review a determination by the common pleas court of Philadelphia County that the plaintiff-appellee has a one-sixth interest in property originally deeded to his mother and stepfather and another person. For the reasons hereinafter set forth, we reverse.

The real estate in question was conveyed by deed dated January 16, 1967, to "John Ewald and Mary B. Ewald his wife and Joseph Ewald[8] . . . *as tenants in common with right of survivorship.*" The appellee is the son of Mary B. Ewald by her first marriage. Mary B. Ewald died intestate on November 8, 1973, and left appellee and John Ewald, her second husband, as her sole heirs at law. John Ewald, appellee's stepfather, died thereafter on August 20, 1974, and bequeathed his entire estate to his brother George Ewald. The other grantee to the original deed, Joseph Ewald, is still living.

The appellee filed a petition for a declaratory judgment asking the court below to interpret the deed and decide whether appellee's mother, Mary B. Ewald, had acquired any interest which passed to appellee upon her death. The case was submitted on stipulated facts and, after oral argument, the lower court held that the deed created a tenancy in common in which each grantee owned a one-third interest. Thus, the court ruled that appellee owned a one-sixth interest in the property which represented his intestate share of his mother's estate. The court en banc affirmed this determination, and a timely appeal was taken to our Court.

The appellants contend that the deed created a tenancy by the entireties in which John Ewald and Mary B. Ewald, his wife, held a one-half interest and upon the death of Mary B. Ewald her spouse John Ewald became the sole owner of their entireties interest. We agree.

The terms used in the deed are patently contradictory. It is basic property law that "a right of survivorship" is not associated with a "tenancy in common." The deed therefore cites a legal impossibility. The lower court recognized these facts and based its holding, that a tenancy in common was created among the parties, on: 1) the statutory presumption that a conveyance or devise carries with it no right of survivorship unless clearly expressed; 2) the emerging legal recognition that a married woman may hold property in her own right without any legal disabilities formerly associated with the legal fiction of the unity of husband and wife; and 3) the public policy against restrictions on alienation of property.

The lower court was correct when it noted that since the passage of the Act of 1812 there is a presumption that a conveyance or devise to two or more persons, not husband or wife or trustees, carries with it no right of survivorship unless clearly expressed. Zomisky v. Zamiska, 449 Pa. 239, 241, 296 A.2d 722, 723 (1972). Thus, the law in our Commonwealth is that unless the terms of the agreement expressly or by necessary implication call for a joint tenancy a tenancy in common will be

---

[8] Editor's note: The opinion does not reveal Joseph Ewald's relationship to the other parties in the case.

presumed. Pennsylvania Bank & Trust Co. v. Thompson, 432 Pa. 262, 247 A.2d 771 (1968). However, it has also been said that when property, real or personal, is placed in the names of husband and wife without more, a tenancy by entireties is presumed to have been created, Holmes' Estate, 414 Pa. 403, 200 A.2d 745 (1964); Brenner v. Sukenik, 410 Pa. 324, 189 A.2d 246 (1963); Heatter v. Lucas, 367 Pa. 296, 80 A.2d 749 (1951); and in order to rebut that presumption there must be clear and convincing evidence to the contrary.

In the case at bar we are faced with a conveyance to three persons, two of whom are identified as husband and wife. The effect of the latter presumption referred to above thus becomes less certain. In Heatter v. Lucas, supra, however, our Supreme Court was faced with an analogous situation. In *Heatter,* a farm had been deeded to "Francis Lucas, a single man, and Joseph Lucas and Matilda Lucas, his wife," with the habendum clause[9] providing "to Have and to Hold the same unto and for the use of the said parties of the second part their heirs and assigns forever,. . . ." The court discussed the application of the presumption of a tenancy by entireties in such a conveyance and held that "a conveyance to three parties two of whom are husband and wife *but neither designated as such,* shall, *in the absence of any language in the conveyance disclosing a contrary intention,* be deemed a conveyance of one-third shares." Id. at 300, 80 A.2d at 752. The *Heatter* court went on to note, however, that the fact that the conveyance was to "Francis Lucas, a single man, *and* Joseph Lucas and Matilda Lucas, *his wife,*" sufficiently indicated an intent that the husband and wife take by the entireties. The terms of the conveyance in the case at bar expressly refer to John Ewald and Mary B. Ewald, *his wife.* We refuse to treat the words "his wife" as mere surplusage. They represent the classic form for the creation of a tenancy by entireties. Furthermore, the use of a double "and" in the granting clause indicates an intent that two units, one couple and one single person, take the property and that each acquire a half interest.[10] See Heatter v. Lucas, supra at 301, 80 A.2d at 752. Because of the express identification of the marital entity in the deed, and the use of the double "and", we believe that the parties must be taken to have considered and given significance to the marital status of two of the grantees. We therefore hold that, the interest of John Ewald and Mary B. Ewald were those of tenants by the

---

[9] The "habendum" clause in a deed describes the nature of the interest being granted. By contrast, the "granting" clause actually conveys the property interest.

[10] See Comment, Creation and Termination of Joint Tenancies in Pennsylvania, 80 Dick.L.Rev. 92, 99 n. 57 (1975): "(I)n a transfer to A, B, and C, a conveyance of one third shares will be presumed. The qualitative presumption arising out of the marital union is not strong enough to interfere with the quantitative interests apparent on the face of the instrument. However, a double 'and' in the granting clause, i.e. to A and B his wife and C, will indicate that two units, one couple and one single person, take the property and that each acquires a half interest."

entireties.[11] As such, upon the death of Mary B. Ewald, the entire interest vested in her husband.

A contrary conclusion is not warranted because of the use of the words "as tenants in common with right of survivorship." We believe that through the use of these terms the correct conclusion is that the one-half interest of the married couple, although held by the entireties as between themselves, was held in common in relation to the interest of Joseph Ewald.

Unlike the case of Wally v. Lehr, 2 Pa.D. & C.2d 722 (1954), we are not confronted with a conveyance to a husband and wife, and a third party "as joint tenants with a right of survivorship and not as tenants in common." In that case the interest between the married couple, who held their half interest by the entireties, was clearly that of a joint tenant with the third party. Nor does the case of Zomisky v. Zamiska, 449 Pa. 239, 296 A.2d 722, 723 (1972) warrant a different result. In that case the conveyance was to "Mike Zamiska and George Zamiska as joint tenants and as in common with the right of survivorship." The Supreme Court held that the use of the words "with right of survivorship" when used *in conjunction with* the term "joint tenants" removed any ambiguity and made it clear that the intention of the parties was to create a joint tenancy. Id. at 244, 296 A.2d 722, 724. That is not the case here. For, as we noted above, when the concept of a right of survivorship is considered in the context of a tenancy in common, the ambiguity is compounded not diminished.

In order to engraft the right of survivorship on a co-tenancy which might otherwise be a tenancy in common, the intent to do so must be expressed with sufficient clarity to overcome the statutory presumption that survivorship is not intended. We see no reason why the rule should be different where, as in this case, the interests in the land are held between a married couple who hold by the entireties and a third person. The intent to create a right of survivorship was not sufficiently expressed in the deed. A tenancy in common was thus created between the husband and wife and Joseph Ewald.

The declaratory judgment entered by the lower court is vacated and the record is remanded for the entry of a declaratory judgment in accordance with this opinion.

---

[11] The appellee argues that the presumption that a husband and wife take as tenants by the entireties, absent contrary language, violates the Equal Rights Amendment of the Pennsylvania Constitution, Art. I, § 28, which reads:

Equality of rights under the law shall not be denied or abridged in the Commonwealth of Pennsylvania because of the sex of the individual.

We find no merit in this contention. The purpose of this constitutional provision was to end *discriminatory* treatment on account of sex. Commonwealth v. Butler, 458 Pa. 289, 328 A.2d 851 (1974). There is nothing discriminatory in the application of the above rule. It is not a one-sided presumption as the type voided in Butler v. Butler, 464 Pa. 522, 347 A.2d 477 (1975). The effect of the rule varies according to the order of death within the marital unit. Had John Ewald died first the entire one-half interest would have been vested in Mary B. Ewald. There is simply no basis upon which to say that the rule deprives a woman of her right to own property.

## Kurpiel v. Kurpiel
Supreme Court, Special Term, Nassau County, Part I, 1966.
50 Misc.2d 604, 271 N.Y.S.2d 114.

■ MARIO PITTONI, JUSTICE.

The action is for the partition of real property in the Town of Huntington, Suffolk County. Plaintiff and defendant Jenny Kurpiel are husband and wife. Defendant Edward Kurpiel is their son. Prior to June 1, 1955, plaintiff was the sole owner of the property involved. On June 1, 1955, plaintiff conveyed the parcel by deed to "Joseph Kurpiel, Jenny Kurpiel and Edward Kurpiel all residing at 1481 Seamans Neck Road, Seaford, Nassau County, New York, jointly and not as tenants in common."

In addition to denying that the parties by this conveyance were joint tenants, defendants plead two defenses. The first is that plaintiff may not maintain the action because plaintiff has neither actual nor constructive possession of the property-defendant Jenny Kurpiel allegedly having been awarded exclusive possession of the premises by an order of the Family Court of the County of Suffolk on November 17, 1965. The second is that plaintiff and defendant Jenny Kurpiel are tenants by the entirety of an undivided one-half of the premises and as a tenant by the entirety, plaintiff may not maintain the action.

As to the first defense, the order of the Family Court dated November 17, 1965 merely directed plaintiff to "stay away from the petitioner (Jenny Kurpiel) and the family home at all times until further order of the court." The Family Court did not have jurisdiction to determine nor have before it the question of ownership or the right of possession and it made no attempt to pass upon that issue in its order. Second, even though defendants as co-tenants are in actual possession plaintiff, by reason of his record title, has a right to possession which entitles him to maintain a partition action.

The second defense is also without merit. The deed was prepared by an attorney. It expressly states that the named grantees were to take jointly. The authorities upon which the defendants rely (Overheiser v. Lackey, 207 N.Y. 229, 100 N.E. 738, Matter of Snell's Estate, 173 Misc. 282, 17 N.Y.S.2d 510, In re Traynor's Will, 34 Misc.2d 399, 226 N.Y.S.2d 304) are not applicable. In *Overheiser* a testator gave and devised "to my daughters Eliza Jane Marsh and Hester Marsh, jointly, the lot of ground" etc. and the Court noted that as the Will was not prepared by a lawyer familiar with the technical distinctions between different kinds of estates the word "jointly" was not used in a technical sense to express the intent of creating "a joint tenancy to negative the presumption established by our statute that a tenancy in common was intended" (207 N.Y. p. 237, 100 N.E. p. 740). Again, in *Snell,* supra, it was noted that the Will was prepared by a layman and therefore the use of the word "jointly" was insufficient to overcome the presumption that a tenancy in common was intended. Likewise, in *Traynor,* supra, the Will was prepared by a layman. Here, as stated at the outset, the deed was prepared by an attorney. In addition, defendants do not contend that the tenancy in common presumed by the statute (Sec. 66, Real Property Law) was created as to all the grantees, but rather that as to Joseph and Jenny Kurpiel a tenancy by the entirety was created of a one-half interest in property, with Edward Kurpiel the owner as joint tenant of the other one-half interest. Were the words "jointly and not as tenants in common" omitted from the deed, the conclusion that husband and wife held one half by the entirety and that their son was a tenant in common with them of the other half would be sound (Bartholomew v. Marshall, 257 App. Div. 1060, 13 N.Y.S.2d 568). The conveyance here however is similar to that discussed in Jooss v. Fey, 129 N.Y. 17, 29 N.E. 136. There, the habendum clause was to the grantees "as joint tenants and not as tenants in common" and the Court held those words clearly expressed the intent that the grantees held as joint tenants and not as tenants by the entirety. The mere fact that in place of the words "joint tenants" of the *Jooss* case, the word "jointly" is used in the subject deed does not make the intent of the grantor less clearly expressed. Moreover, even if the words were absent from the subject deed which show the intent of the grantor, a partition action would still lie (Deegan v. Deegan, 247 App.Div. 340, 287 N.Y.S. 230) because the husband and wife would only be the owners of a one half interest. However, I hold, upon the basis of the expressed intent in the deed and upon the legal authorities, that the grantees were joint tenants, with each having a present one third interest in the property. In re Kagan, 49 Misc.2d 445, 267 N.Y.S.2d 740, cited by defendants, is distinguishable for the words of the grant differ; the conveyance was from a third party to husband and wife creating a presumption of a tenancy by the entirety which is not present on a conveyance from a husband to himself and his wife (Matter of Klatzl's Estate, 216 N.Y. 83, 110 N.E. 181), and the deed, although prepared by an attorney, was according to Justice Conroy "poorly drafted."

Accordingly plaintiff's motions are granted. Cross motion is denied.

## S.S. Weems v. Frost National Bank of San Antonio

Court of Civil Appeals of Texas, 1957.
301 S.W.2d 714.

■ FRASER, JUSTICE.

This is an appeal from the decision of the trial court construing the will of Zuleika Weems Felder, who died March 27, 1953. In the will, testatrix named the Frost National Bank of San Antonio, Texas, as independent executor, and in order to more clearly present the facts, the [pertinent part of the] will in controversy is herein set forth:

> 3. I own a one-third of one-eighth interest in the gas and sulphur royalty on about five hundred (500) acres of land in

Wharton County, Texas, which was sold to the Texas-Gulf Sulphur Co.; I do devise and bequeath a one-half of my one-third interest unto my cousins M.A. Weems, Mrs. A.I. Craig, Z.E. Weems, and S.S. Weems, children of Dr. M.L. Weems, deceased, all of whom reside in Brazoria County, Texas, said one-half of my one-third interest to be held by them jointly. I do devise and bequeath unto my brother, W.G. Foote, of Los Angeles, Calif., the other one-half of my one-third interest in said Wharton County royalty. If my brother W.G. Foote should die before I do, then it is my will that the above mentioned cousins now residing in Brazoria County, Texas, have my entire one-third interest in said royalty.

Appellants have made vigorous representations that because of the wording in paragraph 3, wherein the will says "said one-half of my one-third interest to be held by them jointly" creates a class gift or joint tenancy. With this position we cannot agree. In view of the meaning of Article 2580 of the Texas Statutes, V.A.T.S. Probate Code, § 46, and the holding in McClain v. Holder, Tex. Civ. App., 279 S.W.2d 105 (n.r.e.), it is clear that the word "jointly" is not sufficient to create the right of survivorship in the absence of words of survival, and does not, of itself create a joint tenancy. The case of In re Carter's Estate, 1927, 203 Iowa 603, 213 N.W. 392, 394, and cases cited, illustrates the fact that a devise in a will "for their joint use and benefit" is actually a tenancy in common, and not a joint tenancy.

We therefore hold that the trial court was correct in his holding that the testatrix did not intend to, and in fact did not, create a class gift by the terms of paragraph 3 of her will.

Finding no error, the decision, therefore, of the trial court is accordingly affirmed.

## NOTES

1. *Application of cases to Principal Problem.*

    a. *Ewald, Adamson,* and *Kurpiel* all involve a conveyance to a husband and wife plus a third party. Yet, only two of the cases find that a tenancy by the entirety was created between the husband and wife. Can you fashion a rule out of these cases?

    b. In representing Bart and Rose, would you argue for or against the conclusion that a tenancy by the entirety was created between them? What facts from the Principal Problem would you argue most strongly to support this conclusion? How much weight do you give the various cases?

    c. *Kurpiel* finds a joint tenancy was created when the operative word is "jointly." *Weems* rejects this conclusion, at least absent "words of survival." Do you consider "not as tenants in common" words of survival?

d. If your tentative conclusion is to reconcile *Kurpiel* and *Weems* solely on the words used in the grant, consider the relationship of the parties. The grant in *Weems* was to four siblings, all apparently of adult age, and not residing together. In *Kurpiel* the grant was to a husband and wife and their son, all living at the same residence. Was the *Kurpiel* court predisposed towards finding a right of survivorship because the parties apparently formed a family unit? The same factor is present in the Principal Problem. How much difference should this make?

e. Will Josephine argue for or against the conclusion that "jointly" in the Principal Problem made Ron a joint tenant? What facts support her argument?

f. *Weems* is a Texas Court of Civil Appeals case. The Texas Court of Civil Appeals is an intermediate appellate court. *Kurpiel* is a trial court opinion, but is more recent. How do you assess the influence of each opinion?

2. *Tenants in common with a right of survivorship.* Not all courts agree with *Ewald's* assertion that a tenancy in common with a right of survivorship is "patently contradictory". In Knight v. Knight, 62 Tenn.App. 70, 458 S.W.2d 803 (1970), for example, the defendants owned land that was conveyed to them as tenants by the entirety. However, the court set aside the divorce decree that one defendant had obtained to dissolve a previous marriage. This annulled the marriage between the defendants, making a tenancy by the entirety between them impossible. Finding a clear intent by the parties to form a right of survivorship, the court held that the defendants were tenants in common with a right of survivorship. This right of survivorship, unlike the right of survivorship between joint tenants, is not unilaterally severable.

3. *Unmarried "husbands and wives."* When a tenancy by the entirety fails, because it turns out that the parties are not married, courts have created a dizzying array of interests. Along with the tenancy in common with right of survivorship found in Knight v. Knight, supra, courts have found both joint tenancies and tenancies in common. The tenancy that is found seems to turn both on the facts of the case and how strongly the jurisdiction favors tenancies in common. If the parties believed that they were married, as in *Knight*, courts seem more anxious to find a right of survivorship. But in a case such as State ex rel. Ashauer v. Hostetter, 344 Mo. 665, 127 S.W.2d 697 (1939), where the conveyor tried to form a tenancy by the entirety between his two daughters, courts generally will find a tenancy in common.[12] Divorce turns a tenancy by the entirety into a tenancy in common. In contrast, a divorce does not necessarily sever a joint tenancy because the survivorship right inherent in a joint tenancy does not stem from the marital relationship.

---

[12] But see Welborn v. Henry, 252 So.2d 779 (Miss.1971) (deed to deceased and niece as tenants by the entirety upheld as joint tenancy with a right of survivorship pursuant to terms of state statute).

4. *Statutes.* Some states have carried the disfavor of joint tenancies to the point of abolishing them. See for example Alaska Stat. § 34.15.130 (2009). Research of the law of concurrent estates in a particular jurisdiction should always begin with the codes. Most jurisdictions have statutes altering or codifying the common law.

5. *Murder.* Killing the victim to get the inheritance has long been a favorite topic of the authors of "whodunit" mysteries. But these books might just as easily have concentrated on the killing of joint tenants. The cases are in conflict as to whether the killer takes any portion of Blackacre after the killing of his fellow joint tenants. The modern trend is to allow the killer to take a one-half interest, or no interest, in the property.

6. *Spouses.* It appears that the presumption against joint tenancies, as it applies to joint tenancies between spouses, is the result of a historical accident rather than a conscious policy decision. In Bracton's time (he died in 1268), a concurrent estate was assumed to be a tenancy in common rather than a joint tenancy, in the absence of a specific provision. Thereafter, joint tenancies came to be preferred for several reasons connected with the feudal system of land tenures. Perhaps the most significant of these was based on the fact that on the death of a joint tenant the property passed to the survivor without the payment of certain feudal charges. With the demise of the feudal system of land tenures this reason for the preference for joint tenancies over tenancies in common disappeared. The American colonies and states recognized the anachronistic nature of the preference for joint tenancies and from an early date passed statutes reversing the preference so that now tenancies in common were to be preferred over joint tenancies. The earliest such statute was passed in 1643 in the Plymouth Colony.

A tenancy by the entirety was the preferred construction of a grant to a husband and wife. Most American courts held that the statutes preferring tenancies in common to joint tenancies did not apply to the tenancy by entireties that existed between husband and wife. This was justifiable on the ground that the statutes did not refer to such tenancies, but referred only to joint tenancies and tenancies in common. In 1839, however, an additional element complicated the question of the continued existence of tenancies by entireties. In that year, Mississippi became the first state to pass a Married Women's Property Act. In the next few decades most other states passed similar laws. In general, these laws gave married women the right to own and manage their own property. Few or none of them mentioned tenancies by entireties specifically. In many states it was held that such statutes abolished, by necessary implication, tenancies by entireties. These decisions were seen as beneficial to wives since they relieved wives of the archaic features of tenancies by entireties, especially the management of the property by the husband. But they also had the effect of abolishing the right of survivorship which was also an incident of the tenancy. A grant to a man and woman who were husband and wife would, in many jurisdictions, result in a tenancy in common since tenancies by entireties were construed to be abolished by the Married Women's Property Act, and thus the grant would be governed by the preexisting statutory presumption against joint tenancies. It therefore appears that the desirability of implying a right of survivorship in a concurrent estate between a husband and wife was never consciously and deliberately studied. An earlier commentator has suggested that such a right should be implied. See Hines, Real Property Joint Tenancies: Law, Fact and Fancy, 51 Iowa L.Rev. 582 (1966); Hines, Personal Property Joint Tenancies: More Law, Fact and Fancy, 54 Minn.L.Rev. 509 (1970).

> Property rules should be designed to assure realization of the intent of the ordinary property owner, not to protect against the rare eccentric. The co-ownership of today almost always involves a married couple. Reliable indicators show that when a husband and wife own property together they intend a survivorship arrangement in the overwhelming majority of cases. There is no good reason why the law should insist on a presumption against this intent. Therefore, it is recommended that the legislature declare survivorship to be the preferred construction in co-ownerships between spouses.

54 Minn.L.Rev. 509, at 550.

Professor Hines' analysis undoubtedly made good sense when it was made. Is it now possible, however, that changing social patterns have made his analysis misleading? With the startling recent increase in divorces and second or third marriages, it has now become common for a married person to have children by a previous marriage. In such cases, if the right of survivorship were lightly presumed, the children by a previous marriage of a deceased spouse might be unintentionally disinherited. Perhaps this is a case where an objectionable legal rule (the presumption against a right of survivorship even as between married people) has been made unobjectionable by subsequent social developments. Life, as it were, may have caught up with law. Of course, developments on this issue post *Obergefell* will undoubtedly arise.

# ASSIGNMENT 15

# CONCURRENT ESTATES: ADMINISTRATION

### 1. INTRODUCTION

Sometimes concurrent ownership of property can raise difficult issues regarding the respective liabilities and remedies of the co-tenants. For example, in what circumstances should one co-tenant's exclusive physical occupation of the property influence the determination of liability for expenses? How should profits be divided in this situation? The Principal Problem explores these and related issues.

### 2. PRINCIPAL PROBLEM

Kelley, Amber, and Danielle, three friends living in Chicago, decide to purchase an 18th century Victorian-style house in northern Wisconsin to open a bed and breakfast. They purchased the house as tenants in common, with each holding a one-third interest in the property. Unfortunately, before they can get the bed and breakfast up and running, Danielle's apartment burns down. Together, the friends decide that Danielle should move into the house they just purchased until she can save some money and find a new place in Chicago.

After moving into the house, Danielle decides that the slower pace of life in northern Wisconsin is exactly what she needed. Without telling Kelley and Amber, she opens a small massage therapy business in the house. To accommodate her new business, she hires a handyman to do some "minor" remodeling to the first floor. In the process of this remodeling, the handyman discovers major problems with the electrical system. Danielle hires an electrician to come in and update the electrical system, and she pays for these repairs herself.

All is well until Kelley and Amber write Danielle to see if she is ready to move out so they can move forward with their plans for a bed and breakfast. Danielle does not respond to their letter, so they decide to drive up to the house to see what is wrong. When they arrive, they find that Danielle is running a massage therapy business out of the house and they leave, both very angry with Danielle.

Kelley and Amber then write Danielle another letter demanding that she pay them rent for using the property exclusively over the past six months. Danielle responds in writing, refusing to pay rent, saying that it is "her house too" and that they had all agreed she could live there. Kelley and Amber retain you to file a claim against Danielle for "their fair share" of Danielle's use of the house. How would you assess their chances of recovering rents from Danielle?

## 3. MATERIALS FOR SOLUTION OF PRINCIPAL PROBLEM

### Gillmor v. Gillmor
Supreme Court of Utah, 1984.
694 P.2d 1037.

■ STEWART, JUSTICE:

The defendant Edward Leslie Gillmor appeals from a $29,760 judgment awarded to Florence Gillmor, a cotenant, because defendant obstructed her from exercising her right to occupy land in which she owned an undivided interest with the defendant and C. Frank Gillmor. The property is made up of several large parcels amounting to some 33,000 acres located in Summit, Tooele, and Salt Lake counties.

Two brothers, the parties' fathers, Frank and Edward Lincoln Gillmor, had owned the land and used it for their ranching business. Upon the death of Frank Gillmor, his one-half interest in the property passed in equal shares to his sons, the defendant and C. Frank Gillmor. Edward Lincoln Gillmor continued the ranching business, and for several years grazed cattle and sheep on portions of the common properties. Upon the death of Edward Lincoln Gillmor, his one-half interest passed to his daughter, the plaintiff Florence Gillmor, and she, C. Frank, and the defendant became tenants in common.

In May 1979, the plaintiff filed the instant suit for an accounting and damages for the defendant's exclusive use of the property since January 1, 1979. She also filed a separate suit for partition of the common properties.[1]

The trial was divided into two phases to determine first the damages from January 1, 1979, to May 31, 1980, and second the damages from June 1, 1980, to December 31, 1980. The trial court held that from January 1, 1979, to May 31, 1980, the defendant had grazed livestock on the common properties in such a manner as to constitute exclusive use of the properties and thereby exclude the plaintiff from grazing her livestock on those properties. The trial court awarded a $21,544.91 judgment for one-half the rental value of the properties in favor of Florence Gillmor and against defendant. Defendant did not appeal that decision.

In the second phase of the trial, the trial court found that "[b]etween June 1, 1980 and December 31, 1980, defendant Edward Gillmor continued to graze his sheep and cattle on the common properties in Salt Lake and Summit counties or to use said lands to produce feed for his cattle and sheep, and such use . . . was to the exclusion of the plaintiff."

---

[1] That suit was concluded by our affirmance of the trial court's decree of partition in *Gillmor v. Gillmor,* Utah, 657 P.2d 736 (1982).

On appeal, the defendant argues with respect to the second judgment (1) that "there is no evidence or finding on the issue of ouster," and (2) that even if there were an ouster, the damages are excessive.

The law is that a cotenant may sue for his share of rents and profits from common property if he has been ousted from possession of the common property. *Roberts v. Roberts,* Utah, 584 P.2d 378, 380 (1978). The defendant argues that the trial court did not find that the defendant ousted the plaintiff. The trial court did not specifically use that term in its findings of fact and conclusions of law, but it did find that the defendant had both exercised exclusive use and possession and had also excluded the plaintiff from use of the common properties.

Mere exclusive use of commonly held properties by one cotenant is not sufficient to establish an ouster. A tenant in common has the right to use and occupy the entire property held in cotenancy without liability to other cotenants. Each cotenant has the right to "free and unobstructed possession . . . without liability for rents for the use and occupation thereof." *Utah Oil Refining Co. v. Leigh,* 98 Utah 149, 155, 96 P.2d 1100, 1102 (1939).

> That one cotenant is not liable to his cotenant for rents for the occupancy of the common property is elemental. And this is true even though [the cotenant] uses it and derives income therefrom, as where he occupies . . . or farms a piece and takes the crops; or uses it for storage purposes; as long as he does not interfere with the cotenant's right to likewise occupy, use and enjoy.

98 Utah at 155, 96 P.2d at 1103 (citations omitted).

However, a cotenant who ousts another cotenant or acts in such a fashion as to necessarily exclude a fellow cotenant, violates the rights of that cotenant. To establish a right to share in the rents and profits from the common property, it must be established that a cotenant has used the property so as to "necessarily exclude his cotenant." *Utah Oil Refining Co.,* 98 Utah at 155, 96 P.2d at 1103.

Exclusive use means more than one cotenant using the entire property; it requires either an act of exclusion or use of such a nature that it necessarily prevents another cotenant from exercising his rights in the property.[2]

The defendant contends that the trial court erred in finding that the defendant had exercised exclusive possession and use of the common properties in such a manner as to exclude the plaintiff from using the land. We disagree. The plaintiff sought to graze livestock on the land to the extent of her interest, but was effectively prevented from doing so.

---

[2] It follows that the burden to establish ouster in a suit to recover rents and profits is less stringent than the burden to establish ouster in an adverse possession action. *Massey v. Prothero,* Utah, 664 P.2d 1176 (1983); *Olwell v. Clark,* Utah, 658 P.2d 585 (1982); *Memmott v. Bosh,* Utah, 520 P.2d 1342 (1974); *Holbrook v. Carter,* 19 Utah 2d 288, 431 P.2d 123 (1967).

She sent defendant a letter expressing her intent to graze her livestock on the properties in proportion to her ownership and requested that the defendant accommodate her plans by altering his operations accordingly. The defendant refused to respond and continued to graze the lands to their maximum capacity. He even acknowledged that additional grazing would have damaged the range land. The defendant asserts that at various times he or his attorney invited the plaintiff onto the lands, but he never indicated any intention to alter his operations so as to accommodate the plaintiff's use of the land. Had the plaintiff grazed her livestock on the common properties while defendant's livestock was also there, the land would have been overgrazed. Indeed, the defendant admitted that if the plaintiff had attempted to put additional sheep on the land, he would have sought an injunction to prevent damage to the land.

We hold that when a cotenant out of possession makes a clear, unequivocal demand to use land that is in the exclusive possession of another cotenant, and that cotenant refuses to accommodate the other tenant's right to use the land, the tenant out of possession has established a claim for relief. It is not necessary that the out of possession cotenant resort to force or to means that would damage the common property to establish a right to legal redress.

The defendant also argues that he is entitled to an offset for repairs made on the common property. Sometime after June 1, 1980, he repaired a range fence and a ditch on the common property. He asserts that the fence repairs directly benefited the plaintiff because she now owns land which borders the fence.

Where a cotenant in sole possession makes repairs or improvements to the common property without the consent of his fellow cotenants, he generally has no right of contribution. In Heiselt v. Heiselt, 10 Utah 2d 126, 131–32, 349 P.2d 175, 178–79 (1960) (quoting 14 Am.Jur. Cotenancy § 49 at 115 (1938)), we stated:

> While contrary doctrines have been enunciated and the question is conceded to be one of great difficulty, it appears to be generally agreed that a cotenant who has made improvements upon the common property without the assent of his cotenants is not ordinarily entitled to contribution and cannot, as a matter of right, charge them with the value or costs thereof or maintain any action that would result in a personal judgment against them.... Compensation for improvements is allowed, however, where the other cotenants have stood by and permitted him to proceed to his detriment.

A cotenant may, however, be required to contribute his pro rata share of expenses if the cotenant in possession acted in good faith, with the bona fide belief that he was the sole owner of the property, or when the repairs were essential to preserve or protect the common estate. Furthermore, where, as here, a cotenant out of possession seeks an

On appeal, the district court, in a simple three-line opinion, stated its affirmance was "on the authority of *Adkins v. Edwards,* 317 So.2d 770 (Fla. 2d DCA 1975). In so doing, we are in conflict with *Vandergrift v. Buckley,* 472 So.2d 1325 (Fla. 5th DCA 1985)." *Barrow,* 505 So.2d at 506.

To resolve the issue presented by the acknowledged conflict, we find it appropriate to review the applicable case law, beginning with our decision in *Coggan v. Coggan,* 239 So.2d 17 (Fla.1970). In *Coggan,* a former wife of a doctor brought an action against her former husband for partition of his office building and for an accounting of one-half the rental value. The building had been jointly owned by the parties until their divorce, at which time they became tenants in common. Nothing was stated in the decree or by agreement as to its use and possession, and the former husband continued in possession, paying the taxes, making necessary repairs, and exercising complete control over the property. On appeal, the district court recognized the common law rule that, when one tenant in common has exclusive possession of the lands and uses those lands for his own benefit but does not receive rents or profits therefrom, he is not liable or accountable to his cotenant not in possession unless he holds adversely or as a result of ouster or the equivalent thereof. *Coggan v. Coggan,* 230 So.2d 34, 36 (Fla. 2d DCA 1969), aff'd in part, quashed in part, 239 So.2d 17 (Fla.1970). In *Coggan,* the evidence at trial revealed that the doctor had always considered himself the sole owner of the property and believed his former wife had no rights therein; however, there was no evidence that he had ever expressed that attitude to her or that she was cognizant of his claim. The district court found that under these circumstances the husband's actions were the equivalent of an ouster and granted the former wife's claim for rents. 230 So.2d at 36. Upon review by this Court, we quashed that holding and stated:

> The possession of a tenant in common is presumed to be the possession of all cotenants until the one in possession brings home to the other the knowledge that he claims the exclusive right or title. . . .
>
> *There can be no holding adversely or ouster or its equivalent, by one cotenant unless such holding is manifested or communicated to the other.* Where a tenant out of possession claims an accounting of a tenant in possession, he must show that the tenant in possession is holding the exclusive possession of the property adversely or holding the exclusive possession as a result of ouster or the equivalent thereof. This possession must be attended with such circumstances as to evince a claim of the exclusive right or title by the tenant in possession imparted to the tenant out of possession.

239 So.2d at 19 (citations omitted; emphasis added).

The Fourth District Court of Appeal, in *Seesholts v. Beers,* 270 So.2d 434 (Fla. 4th DCA 1972), followed our *Coggan* decision in a situation involving a former marital home. That court refused to distinguish

*Coggan* on the basis that it involved commercial real property rather than a former marital residence. *Id.* at 436.

In *Adkins v. Edwards,* 317 So.2d 770 (Fla. 2d DCA 1975), the Second District Court of Appeal rejected the *Seesholts* decision and distinguished our *Coggan* decision, reasoning that the nature of the properties involved in *Coggan* was such that joint occupancy by the cotenants was not effectively precluded. The *Adkins* court held:

> In cases like this there frequently exists an aura of hostility and awkwardness not necessarily common to cotenancy of lands or other properties held for commercial purposes. While *neither of the parties contended that he or she was ousted from possession,* it is unrealistic to believe that parties who could not get along living together while they were married would be expected to enjoy common usage of the former marital home after their divorce.

*Id.* at 771 (emphasis added).

In *Vandergrift,* the former spouses held the former marital home as tenants in common. The former wife was in possession of the marital home and the former husband instituted the partition action. The former wife requested she be compensated for improvements and the former husband responded by making a claim for one-half the reasonable rental value of the home after the date of her remarriage. The trial judge granted the former husband's claim even though no demand for possession or a prior claim for rental value was made. The district court reversed, relying on *Coggan* and *Seesholts,* stating:

> Because there was no evidence here that the former wife claimed adversely to the former husband when she continued in possession of the former marital residence after she remarried or that she made it known to her former husband that she claimed exclusive right or title, there is no evidence of ouster.

472 So.2d at 1328.

The reasoning of the district court in *Adkins* is clearly contrary to the rule initially approved by this Court in 1875 in *Bird v. Bird,* 15 Fla. 424 (1875). In *Bird,* we held that when one cotenant has exclusive possession of lands owned as a tenant in common with another, and uses those lands for his own benefit and does not receive rents or profits therefrom, such cotenant is not liable or accountable to his cotenant out of possession unless such cotenant in exclusive possession holds adversely or as a result of ouster or the equivalent thereof. *Id.* at 442. We explained what ouster meant in *Stokely v. Conner,* 69 Fla. 412, 68 So. 452 (1915), where we stated that:

> a tenant in common, to show an ouster of his cotenant, must show acts of possession inconsistent with, and exclusive of, the rights of such cotenant, and such as would amount to an ouster between landlord and tenant, and knowledge on the part of his

cotenant of his claim of exclusive ownership. He has the right to assume that the possession of his cotenant is his possession, until informed to the contrary, either by express notice, or by acts and declarations that may be equivalent to notice. Exclusive possession by one tenant in common, and receipt of the rents and profits of the common land, for a great length of time, is not sufficient to create a legal presumption of the actual ouster of a cotenant.

*Id.* at 440–41, 68 So. at 459 (citation omitted). We stated in *Coggan* that "[t]here can be no holding adversely or ouster or its equivalent, by one cotenant unless such holding is manifested or communicated to the other." 239 So.2d at 19. In the instant case, as reflected by the trial judge's findings, there was no communication by the cotenant in possession to the cotenant out of possession that the former was holding the property exclusively and adversely to the latter. We reaffirm our decision in *Coggan*.

Under these facts, we first reaffirm the necessity for communication mandated by the common law rule. Accepting the district court's holding would result in significant changes not only in the law of partition, but also in the law of adverse possession, because it would start the time for adverse possession running with a former spouse's occupancy of the former marital home when he or she is a cotenant. We reject respondent's argument that we should overrule the common law principles of partition and make an exception with regard to the communication requirement for former spouses who hold former marital property as cotenants. To hold that the occupation by one cotenant of the former marital home presumptively ousts the other former spouse cotenant would only create additional legal problems for parties to dissolution proceedings.

Second, we find that there is an existing applicable exception which was not discussed in the majority opinions of *Adkins, Vandergrift,* and *Seesholts*. It also was not discussed in *Coggan* or *Bird* because it was not applicable. It is an established principle of law that when a cotenant in possession seeks contribution for amounts expended in the improvement or preservation of the property, his claim may be offset by the value of his or her use of the property which has exceeded his or her proportionate share of ownership. A general statement concerning this exception is contained in 51 A.L.R.2d 388 entitled "Accountability of cotenants for rents and profits or use and occupation." It states:

> Nevertheless where one owner has enjoyed the occupancy and in any way seeks the assistance of a court in obtaining contribution from others in respect of improvements or protective expenditures made, he is ordinarily charged, *by way of offset,* with the reasonable value of his occupancy in excess of his proportionate share, *even though he would not otherwise be liable;* and similar adjustments are commonly made in partition suits generally.

Annotation, 51 A.L.R.2d 388, 395 (1957) (emphasis added, footnote omitted).

We applied this exception in *Potter v. Garrett,* 52 So.2d 115 (Fla.1951), in a partition suit in which a cotenant in possession sought recovery from the cotenant out of possession of one-half the money she had paid toward the mortgage, taxes, and insurance on the property. In reversing the striking of the claim for offset by the tenant out of possession, we stated:

> We think appellee is entitled to reimbursement for one-half the money she paid on the principal and interest of the mortgage, for taxes and insurance and for other moneys she spent on essential improvements to preserve the property. The appellant is entitled to have credited against this amount one-half of such sum or sums as may be found to be a reasonable rental for the use of the property during the time it was occupied by appellee after the death of the last parent.

*Id.* at 116. This holding does not conflict with *Coggan* because *Coggan* involved an affirmative claim by a cotenant out of possession for one-half the rental of the property held by the cotenant in possession. There was no claim in *Coggan* by the cotenant in possession for contribution for the expenses incurred in the upkeep of the property and, hence, there was no offset to be considered. Nor was there any offset involved in *Bird.*

It is clear that, under this exception, Donna Barrow is entitled to claim the reasonable rental value solely as an offset against the claim of the cotenant, James Barrow, for the costs of maintaining the property. Here, Donna Barrow's claim for the rental value is limited to $2,591.00, the amount of James Barrow's claim, since the rental value exceeds his claim.

In conclusion, we hold: (1) the possession of a tenant in common is presumed to be the possession of all tenants until the one in possession communicates to the other the knowledge that he or she claims the exclusive right or title and there can be no holding adversely or ouster by the cotenant in possession unless the adverse holding is communicated to the other; (2) where one cotenant has exclusive possession of lands and uses the lands for his or her own benefit and does not receive rents or profits therefrom, such a cotenant is *not* liable or accountable to the cotenant out of possession unless he or she holds adversely or as a result of ouster or its equivalent; and (3) when a cotenant in possession seeks contribution for amounts expended in the improvement or preservation of the property, that claim may be offset by cotenants out of possession by the reasonable rental value of the use of the property by the cotenant in possession to the extent it has exceeded his or her proportionate share of ownership.

Finally, we note that animosity can exist between other family members or former business partners holding property as cotenants as can exist between former spouses. To avoid subsequent litigation between former spouses, we emphasize that it is in the best interests of all parties that property dispositions in matrimonial matters be concluded, if at all possible, in the dissolution proceedings, including a determination, if possible, of possession of any property held in a cotenancy.

Accordingly, we quash the decision of the district court and disapprove the reasoning in *Adkins*. To the extent that they preclude an offset for reasonable rental value, we also disapprove *Seeholts* and *Vandergrift*. We direct the Second District Court of Appeal to remand this cause to the trial court for further proceedings consistent with this opinion.

It is so ordered.

## NOTES

1. *Liability for rent.* Under the common law, a co-tenant who derived profits from the property did not have a duty to compensate the other co-tenants for any profits he received. This approach was modified by the Statute of Anne (1704), which is widely adopted in the United States. As interpreted, the statute requires a co-tenant who receives rent from a third party to account for it to the other co-tenants. Under the prevailing case law, a co-tenant, in the absence of ouster, need not account for the rental value of his *own* possession. A minority position in this country requires a co-tenant to account for both rent derived from a third party as well as the value of a co-tenant's own possession.[4]

2. *Importance of proper planning and drafting.* Would the result in *Barrow* have been different if the parties involved had drafted a property settlement agreement that specified whether either party would be entitled to exclusive possession and/or use of the property following the divorce? See Hernandez v. Hernandez, 645 So. 2d 171, 176 (Fla. Dist. Ct. App. 1994) (finding that the husband was "not entitled to an offset of one-half of the fair rental value for the period of the wife's exclusive possession" only after distinguishing *Barrow* on the basis of the presence of a "property settlement agreement which provided for exclusive use and occupancy subsequent to divorce.")

3. *Liability for profits.* Traditionally, absent an ouster, the law does not require a co-tenant to account for any benefits accruing from his personal use of the land as long as such use does not reduce the value of the land. Under this view, when a co-tenant merely consumes crops from the land or

---

[4] See, e.g., Lerman v. Levine, 14 Conn.App. 402, 541 A.2d 523 (1988) (applying the state statute mandating an accounting for use and occupancy absent ouster); McKnight v. Basilides, 19 Wash.2d 391, 143 P.2d 307 (1943). But see Yakavonis v. Tilton, 93 Wash.App. 304, 311–12, 968 P.2d 908, 912 (1998), which states that the Washington Supreme Court precedent, *McKnight* and Fulton v. Fulton, 57 Wash.2d 331, 357 P.2d 169 (1960), appear to conflict. The *Yakavonis* court chose to follow the more recent *Fulton* precedent and found that "both the Washington Supreme Court precedent and the attributes of real property ownership prevent the use of rental value to offset expenses where the occupying tenant's actions are not hostile to the nonoccupying cotenant's interests." *Yakavonis*, 93 Wash.App. at 312, 968 P.2d at 912.

obtains profits from crops personally harvested, no liability generally is found under the theory that one co-tenant has the right to reasonable enjoyment of the property. See 2 American Law of Property § 6.14 at 60–62 (1952). Some jurisdictions, however, require an accounting whenever one co-tenant takes profits or benefits in a greater proportion than his interest, even if no ouster has occurred.[5] In addition, when one co-tenant ousts his fellow co-tenants from possession, liability for profits generally will ensue.

4.  *Remedy for ouster.* A co-tenant who has been ousted can bring an action in ejectment demanding the right to joint possession with the defendant and an accounting of profits representing "the reasonable value of the use and occupation." 2 American Law of Property § 6.13 at 56 (1952). If an ousted co-tenant fails to bring such an action in ejectment, he risks losing title to the property to the ousting co-tenant through adverse possession. How should the courts determine when an ouster has occurred? Should the criteria differ when, as in the facts of the Principal Problem, the property at issue is not capable of being occupied or used jointly?

5.  *Liability for waste.* Should a co-tenant who takes action resulting in permanent damage to the property be liable to the other co-tenants in an action for waste? Are there any factors that distinguish this situation from one involving acts of waste committed by a life tenant or a tenant for years?

6.  *Liability for taxes, interest payments, and other carrying charges.* In general, a co-tenant who is not in sole possession of the property may request contribution from his co-tenants for payments of taxes, interest on mortgages, and other types of necessary carrying charges. If, however, the co-tenant who pays these expenses has been in the sole possession of the property, and the value of his use and occupation exceeds these payments, no action for contribution may be brought. See generally 2 American Law of Property § 6.17 at 75–76 (1952). Some cases imply that a co-tenant in sole possession of the property can get contribution for such expenses if they exceed the amount that he would be required to pay for rent, even if he is not otherwise liable for rental payments to his other co-tenants.[6] It is, however, difficult to find cases ordering an affirmative award for contribution in these circumstances, since the rental value of the premises generally exceeds the co-tenant's claim for expenses. A co-tenant who has ousted his fellow co-tenants may not seek contribution for these expenses, but may offset the amount of rent owed to his co-tenants by the amount of their share of these expenses.

7.  *Liability for repairs and improvements.* A co-tenant in sole possession who makes necessary repairs upon the property generally is not

---

[5] See, e.g., Etheridge v. Etheridge, 41 N.C. App. 44, 255 S.E.2d 729 (1979). In some jurisdictions, statutes exist that mandate this result. See, e.g., 765 Ill. Comp. Stat. 1005/4a (2010) (requiring an accounting when one co-tenant uses the profits or benefits from real estate in a greater proportion than his interest); 12 Vt. Stat. Ann. § 4251 (2015)(requiring an accounting when one joint tenant receives more than his just proportion of any estate or interest). Under this approach, it is immaterial whether an ouster exists since any co-tenant in possession of the property must share all profits in excess of his proportionate share.

[6] See, e.g., Allen v. Allen, 687 S.W.2d 660, 662 (Mo. Ct. App.1985); Janik v. Janik, 474 N.E.2d 1054, 1058 (Ind. Ct. App.1985); Hartog v. Siegler, 615 S.W.2d 632, 637 (Mo. Ct. App.1981).

entitled to seek contribution from his other co-tenants, absent an agreement to the contrary. In such instances, the occupying co-tenant's value of possession is regarded as the proper compensation. If co-tenants cannot agree on the propriety of repairs, or on any other matter involving the property, the appropriate remedy is partition (see Assignment 14 for a more complete discussion of partition). Nevertheless, the cases do reveal that in an action for rents and profits, and in the accounting component of a partition action, a co-tenant who has expended funds for reasonably necessary repairs will be credited with such expenditures. *Gillmor* is consistent with this approach in that the plaintiff there was seeking an accounting and damages for the defendant's exclusive use of the property and she had filed a separate suit for partition, in which she had prevailed.

With respect to improvements, however, a co-tenant can neither compel contribution from the other co-tenants nor receive credit for such expenses in an action for rents and profits. Nevertheless, the co-tenant who made the improvements generally will receive the full monetary value of any improvements in an action for partition. This can be accomplished, where possible, through a physical division of the property in which the part which has been improved is awarded to the co-tenant funding the improvements. Where such a physical division is not possible, the property will be sold, and the co-tenant paying for the improvements will receive an additional amount representing the increase in value due to the improvements. See generally 2 American Law of Property § 6.18 at 77–84 (1952).

What rationale underlies the difference in treatment regarding repairs and improvements? Why should a co-tenant who makes a necessary repair be able to receive credit for the repair in an action for rents and profits, but a co-tenant who improves the property is left to recover the value of such improvements only in connection with a partition action? How should a court determine whether a particular action taken by a co-tenant constitutes a repair or an improvement?

8. *Query.* Compare the following situations:

EXAMPLE 1: Alex is an occupying co-tenant, without ouster. The fair value of his occupancy is $10,000. Carrying charges on a mortgage encumbering the property are $8,000, and Alex pays this. Under the prevailing rule, Alex cannot get reimbursement from his co-tenant nor can his co-tenant charge Alex for the value of his occupancy.

EXAMPLE 2: Bonnie is an occupying co-tenant. Under an honest belief that she is the sole owner, she forbids her co-tenant from using the property. The fair value of Bonnie's occupancy is $10,000. Carrying charges on a mortgage encumbering the property are $8,000, and Bonnie pays this amount. Bonnie owes her co-tenant $1,000.

EXAMPLE 3: Clara is an occupying co-tenant, without ouster. The fair value of her occupancy is $10,000. There is no mortgage. Clara need not pay for her occupancy. Compare this situation with Example 1.

Are the results in these three examples consistent?

# ASSIGNMENT 16

# JOINT TENANCIES: TERMINATION (SEVERANCE)

## 1. INTRODUCTION

A joint tenancy may be unilaterally severed without notice to the other joint tenant. A joint tenancy is destroyed when there is an outright conveyance of one party's joint interest to a third party. In addition, certain unilateral actions by one joint tenant, short of an outright conveyance, are sufficient to sever the joint tenancy and its right of survivorship. As you read the following materials, consider where the line should be drawn between a conveyance that destroys the joint tenancy (regardless of intent to do so) and other unilateral activities on the part of a joint tenant.

## 2. PRINCIPAL PROBLEM

Raymond Johnson and Hazel Tenhet owned a parcel of land as joint tenants. Without Tenhet's knowledge, Johnson leased the property to defendant Boswell for a period of 10 years at an annual rental of $15,000. Johnson died three months after the execution of the lease. Tenhet brought suit to have the lease declared invalid.

Tenhet is arguing that Johnson's unilateral grant of the lease did not destroy her right of survivorship, and that the lease terminated on Johnson's death. The lower court has held that although Tenhet's right of survivorship was not destroyed, Tenhet must share the realty with Boswell for the term of the lease. Once the lease expires, Tenhet will own the property in fee simple absolute.

After considering the following materials, discuss how the appellate court should decide the case.

## 3. MATERIALS FOR SOLUTION OF PRINCIPAL PROBLEM

### Harms v. Sprague
Supreme Court of Illinois, 1984.
105 Ill.2d 215, 85 Ill.Dec. 331, 473 N.E.2d 930.

■ MORAN, JUSTICE.

Plaintiff, William H. Harms, filed a complaint to quiet title and for declaratory judgment in the circuit court of Greene County. Plaintiff had taken title to certain real estate with his brother John R. Harms, as a joint tenant, with full right of survivorship. The plaintiff named, as a defendant, Charles D. Sprague, the executor of the estate of John Harms and the devisee of all the real and personal property of John Harms. Also named as defendants were Carl T. and Mary E. Simmons, alleged mortgagees of the property in question. Defendant Sprague filed a counterclaim against plaintiff, challenging plaintiff's claim of ownership of the entire tract of property and asking the court to recognize his (Sprague's) interest as a tenant in common, subject to a mortgage lien. At issue was the effect the granting of a mortgage by John Harms had on the joint tenancy. Also at issue was whether the mortgage survived the death of John Harms as a lien against the property.

The trial court held that the mortgage given by John Harms to defendants Carl and Mary Simmons severed the joint tenancy. Further, the court found that the mortgage survived the death of John Harms as a lien against the undivided one-half interest in the property which passed to Sprague by and through the will of the deceased. The appellate court reversed, finding that the mortgage given by one joint tenant of his interest in the property does not sever the joint tenancy. Accordingly, the appellate court held that plaintiff, as the surviving joint tenant, owned the property in its entirety, unencumbered by the mortgage lien. Defendant Sprague filed a petition for leave to appeal in this court. Subsequently, defendants Carl and Mary Simmons petitioned this court to supplement Sprague's petition for leave to appeal. That motion was granted and the petition for leave to appeal was allowed.

Two issues are raised on appeal: (1) Is a joint tenancy severed when less than all of the joint tenants mortgage their interest in the property? and (2) Does such a mortgage survive the death of the mortgagor as a lien on the property?

A review of the stipulation of facts reveals the following. Plaintiff, William Harms, and his brother John Harms, took title to real estate located in Roodhouse, on June 26, 1973, as joint tenants. The warranty deed memorializing this transaction was recorded on June 29, 1973, in the office of the Greene County recorder of deeds.

Carl and Mary Simmons owned a lot and home in Roodhouse. Charles Sprague entered into an agreement with the Simmons whereby Sprague was to purchase their property for $25,000. Sprague tendered $18,000 in cash and signed a promissory note for the balance of $7,000. Because Sprague had no security for the $7,000, he asked his friend, John Harms, to co-sign the note and give a mortgage[1] on his interest in the joint tenancy property. Harms agreed, and on June 12, 1981, John Harms and Charles Sprague, jointly and severally, executed a promissory note for $7,000 payable to Carl and Mary Simmons. The note states that the principal sum of $7,000 was to be paid from the proceeds of the sale of John Harms' interest in the joint tenancy property, but in any event no later than six months from the date the note was signed. The note reflects

---

[1] Editor's note: A mortgage is an interest in property which the borrower gives to the lender as security for the repayment of the loan. If the borrower defaults, the mortgage enables the lender to claim the property ahead of the other creditors of the borrower.

that five monthly interest payments had been made, with the last payment recorded November 6, 1981. In addition, John Harms executed a mortgage, in favor of the Simmonses, on his undivided one-half interest in the joint tenancy property, to secure payment of the note. William Harms was unaware of the mortgage given by his brother.

John Harms moved from his joint tenancy property to the Simmons property which had been purchased by Charles Sprague. On December 10, 1981, John Harms died. By the terms of John Harms' will, Charles Sprague was the devisee of his entire estate. The mortgage given by John Harms to the Simmonses was recorded on December 29, 1981.

Prior to the appellate court decision in the instant case, no court of this State had directly addressed the principal question we are confronted with herein-the effect of a mortgage, executed by less than all of the joint tenants, on the joint tenancy. Nevertheless, there are numerous cases which have considered the severance issue in relation to other circumstances surrounding a joint tenancy. All have necessarily focused on the four unities which are fundamental to both the creation and the perpetuation of the joint tenancy. These are the unities of interest, title, time, and possession. (*Jackson v. O'Connell* (1961), 23 Ill.2d 52, 55, 177 N.E.2d 194; *Tindall v. Yeats* (1946), 392 Ill. 502, 507, 64 N.E.2d 903.) The voluntary or involuntary destruction of any of the unities by one of the joint tenants will sever the joint tenancy. *Van Antwerp v. Horan* (1945), 390 Ill. 449, 451, 61 N.E.2d 358.

In a series of cases, this court has considered the effect that judgment liens upon the interest of one joint tenant have on the stability of the joint tenancy. In *People's Trust & Savings Bank v. Haas* (1927), 328 Ill. 468, 160 N.E. 85, the court found that a judgment lien secured against one joint tenant did not serve to extinguish the joint tenancy. As such, the surviving joint tenant "succeeded to the title in fee to the whole of the land by operation of law." 328 Ill. 468, 471, 160 N.E. 85.

Citing to *Haas* for this general proposition, the court in *Van Antwerp v. Horan* (1945), 390 Ill. 449, 61 N.E.2d 358, extended the holding in *Haas* to the situation where a levy is made under execution upon the interest of the debtor joint tenant. The court found that the levy was "not such an act as can be said to have the effect of a divestiture of title . . . [so as to destroy the] identity of interest or of any other unity which must occur before . . . the estate of joint tenancy has been severed and destroyed." 390 Ill. 449, 455, 61 N.E.2d 358.

In yet another case involving the attachment of a judgment lien upon the interest of a joint tenant, *Jackson v. Lacey* (1951), 408 Ill. 530, 97 N.E.2d 839, the court held that the estate of joint tenancy had not been destroyed. As in *Van Antwerp*, the judgment creditor had levied on the interest of the joint tenant debtor. In addition, that interest was sold by the bailiff of the municipal court to the other joint tenant, who died intestate before the time of redemption expired. While the court recognized that a conveyance, even if involuntary, destroys the unity of title and severs the joint tenancy, it held that there would be no conveyance until the redemption period had expired without a redemption. As such, title was not as yet divested and the estate in joint tenancy was unaltered.

Clearly, this court adheres to the rule that a lien on a joint tenant's interest in property will not effectuate a severance of the joint tenancy, absent the conveyance by a deed following the expiration of a redemption period. (See *Johnson v. Muntz* (1936), 364 Ill. 482, 4 N.E.2d 826.) It follows, therefore, that if Illinois perceives a mortgage as merely a lien on the mortgagor's interest in property rather than a conveyance of title from mortgagor to mortgagee, the execution of a mortgage by a joint tenant, on his interest in the property, would not destroy the unity of title and sever the joint tenancy.

Early cases in Illinois, however, followed the title theory of mortgages. In 1900, this court recognized the common law precept that a mortgage was a conveyance of a legal estate vesting title to the property in the mortgagee. (*Lightcap v. Bradley* (1900), 186 Ill. 510, 519, 58 N.E. 221.) Consistent with this title theory of mortgages, therefore, there are many cases which state, in *dicta,* that a joint tenancy is severed by one of the joint tenants mortgaging his interest to a stranger. (*Lawler v. Byrne* (1911), 252 Ill. 194, 196, 96 N.E. 892; *Hardin v. Wolf* (1925), 318 Ill. 48, 59, 148 N.E. 868; *Partridge v. Berliner* (1927), 325 Ill. 253, 258–59, 156 N.E. 352; *Van Antwerp v. Horan* (1945), 390 Ill. 449, 453, 61 N.E.2d 358; *Tindall v. Yeats* (1946), 392 Ill. 502, 511, 64 N.E.2d 903; *Illinois Public Aid Com. v. Stille* (1958), 14 Ill.2d 344, 353, 153 N.E.2d 59 (personal property).) Yet even the early case of *Lightcap v. Bradley,* cited above, recognized that the title held by the mortgagee was for the limited purpose of protecting his interests. The court went on to say that "the mortgagor is the owner for every other purpose and against every other person. The title of the mortgagee is anomalous, and exists only between him and the mortgagor. . . ." *Lightcap v. Bradley* (1900), 186 Ill. 510, 522–23, 58 N.E. 221.

Because our cases had early recognized the unique and narrow character of the title that passed to a mortgagee under the common law title theory, it was not a drastic departure when this court expressly characterized the execution of a mortgage as a mere lien in *Kling v. Ghilarducci* (1954), 3 Ill.2d 454, 121 N.E.2d 752. In *Kling,* the court was confronted with the question of when a separation of title, necessary to create an easement by implication, had occurred. The court found that title to the property was not separated with the execution of a trust deed but rather only upon execution and delivery of a master's deed. The court stated:

> In some jurisdictions the execution of a mortgage is a severance, in others, the execution of a mortgage is not a severance. In Illinois the giving of a mortgage is not a separation of title, for the holder of the mortgage takes only a lien thereunder. After

foreclosure of a mortgage and until delivery of the master's deed under the foreclosure sale, purchaser acquires no title to the land either legal or equitable. Title to land sold under mortgage foreclosure remains in the mortgagor or his grantee until the expiration of the redemption period and conveyance by the master's deed.

3 Ill.2d 454, 460, 121 N.E.2d 752.

*Kling* and later cases rejecting the title theory do not involve the severance of joint tenancies. As such, they have not expressly disavowed the *dicta* of joint tenancy cases which have stated that the act of mortgaging by one joint tenant results in the severance of the joint tenancy. We find, however, that implicit in *Kling* and our more recent cases which follow the lien theory of mortgages is the conclusion that a joint tenancy is not severed when one joint tenant executes a mortgage on his interest in the property, since the unity of title has been preserved. As the appellate court in the instant case correctly observed: "If giving a mortgage creates only a lien, then a mortgage should have the same effect on a joint tenancy as a lien created in other ways." (119 Ill.App.3d 503, 507, 75 Ill.Dec. 155, 456 N.E.2d 976.) Other jurisdictions following the lien theory of mortgages have reached the same result. *People v. Nogarr* (1958), 164 Cal.App.2d 591, 330 P.2d 858; *D.A.D., Inc. v. Moring* (Fla.App.1969), 218 So.2d 451; *American National Bank & Trust Co. v. McGinnis* (Okla.1977), 571 P.2d 1198; *Brant v. Hargrove* (Ariz.Ct.App.1981), 129 Ariz. 475, 632 P.2d 978.

A joint tenancy has been defined as "a present estate in all the joint tenants, each being seized of the whole. . . ." (*Partridge v. Berliner* (1927), 325 Ill. 253, 257, 156 N.E. 352.) An inherent feature of the estate of joint tenancy is the right of survivorship, which is the right of the last survivor to take the whole of the estate. (*In re Estate of Alpert* (1983), 95 Ill.2d 377, 381, 69 Ill.Dec. 361, 447 N.E.2d 796; *Bonczkowski v. Kucharski* (1958), 13 Ill.2d 443, 451, 150 N.E. 144.) Because we find that a mortgage given by one joint tenant of his interest in the property does not sever the joint tenancy, we hold that the plaintiff's right of survivorship became operative upon the death of his brother. As such plaintiff is now the sole owner of the estate, in its entirety.

Further, we find that the mortgage executed by John Harms does not survive as a lien on plaintiff's property. A surviving joint tenant succeeds to the share of the deceased joint tenant by virtue of the conveyance which created the joint tenancy, not as the successor of the deceased. (*In re Estate of Alpert* (1983), 95 Ill.2d 377, 381, 69 Ill.Dec. 361, 447 N.E.2d 796.) The property right of the mortgaging joint tenant is extinguished at the moment of his death. While John Harms was alive, the mortgage existed as a lien on his interest in the joint tenancy. Upon his death, his interest ceased to exist and along with it the lien of the mortgage. (*Merchants National Bank v. Olson* (1975), 27 Ill.App.3d 432, 434, 325 N.E.2d 633.) Under the circumstances of this case, we would note that the mortgage given by John Harms to the Simmonses was only valid as between the original parties during the lifetime of John Harms since it was unrecorded. (Ill.Rev.Stat.1981, ch. 30, par. 29; 27 Ill.L. & Prac. *Mortgages* sec. 65 (1956).) In addition, recording the mortgage subsequent to the death of John Harms was a nullity. As we stated above, John Harms' property rights in the joint tenancy were extinguished when he died. Thus, he no longer had a property interest upon which the mortgage lien could attach.

Judgment affirmed.

## Hutchinson National Bank v. Brown
Court of Appeals of Kansas, 1988.
12 Kan.App.2d 673, 753 P.2d 1299.

■ RULON, JUDGE.

Plaintiff, Hutchinson National Bank and Trust Company, appeals from the declaratory judgment granted defendant, Ida Brown, by the Reno County District Court. The primary issue on appeal is whether a unilateral pledge of a certificate of deposit,[2] held in joint tenancy, severs any one of the four unities required for the continued existence of a joint tenancy. We find that the unity of interest is severed and reverse.

The essential facts are not disputed by the parties. The district court summarized the facts as follows:

> On May 22, 1981, Harry Brown purchased a $15,000 certificate of deposit at the Hutchinson National Bank. It was issued, at his request, in the names of Harry and his wife, Ida, as joint tenants. On May 21, 1984, the grandson of Harry, Dale Brown, applied for a loan of $15,000 at Hutchinson National Bank. Harry was with Dale. The Bank indicated that it would need some security for such a loan, and Harry agreed to pledge the certificate of deposit. Harry and Dale both signed the note and security agreement. Harry told Ida what he had done shortly afterwards. Harry died on January 19, 1985, and the Bank paid the interest on the certificate of deposit to Ida until this case was filed. On March 27, 1986, Dale Brown filed a petition in bankruptcy. On July 11, 1986, the Bank filed this suit, asking that it be allowed to apply the $15,000 certificate of deposit against the note of Dale Brown.

The district court concluded that (1) the pledge of the certificate of deposit in joint tenancy did not sever the joint tenancy; (2) Ida had no duty to inform the Bank that she did not consent to the pledge by Harry

---

[2] Editor's note: A certificate of deposit is an instrument issued by a bank or a financial institution in exchange for a deposit of funds for a specified period of time. As consideration for the deposit, the bank promises to pay the depositor a specified amount of interest expressed as a percentage of the deposit. A penalty is usually imposed on the depositor for early withdrawal of the deposit.

and was not estopped to contest the pledge; and (3) at Harry's death, the certificate of deposit passed, by operation of law, to Ida free and clear of any lien or security interest of the Hutchinson National Bank.

Judgment was entered for Ida.

It is well settled that the creation and continued existence of a joint tenancy requires the coexistence of four unities: time, title, interest, and possession.

A joint tenancy may be terminated (1) by mutual agreement of the parties; (2) by any conduct or course of dealing sufficient to indicate that all the parties have mutually treated their interests as belonging to them in common; or (3) by operation of law upon the destruction of any one or more of the necessary unities. *Carson, Executrix v. Ellis,* 186 Kan. 112, 115, 348 P.2d 807 (1960); *Federal National Mortgage Ass'n v. Elliott,* 1 Kan.App.2d 366, 370, 566 P.2d 21 (1977). The record in the present case does not indicate that (1) Harry and Ida mutually agreed to terminate the joint tenancy or (2) they mutually engaged in any conduct or course of dealing that would indicate they both treated their interest in the CD as belonging to them in common. The question, therefore, is whether the pledge destroyed one of the four required unities.

A pledge, by definition, "is a bailment of personal property as security for a debt . . . , the property being redeemable on specified terms and subject to sale in the event of default." *Columbia Casualty Co. v. Sodini,* 159 Kan. 478, 484, 156 P.2d 524 (1945). Our Supreme Court has held that a pledge constitutes a lien on the property pledged, *Walton v. Piqua State Bank,* 204 Kan. 741, 754, 466 P.2d 316 (1970), and that a mortgage creates a lien upon real property. *Misco Industries, Inc. v. Board of Sedgwick County Comm'rs,* 235 Kan. 958, 962, 685 P.2d 866 (1984).

In *Misco,* the court set forth the following definition of a lien:

A lien is a hold or claim which one has upon the property of another as security for a debt or charge, as a tie that binds the property to a debt or claim for its satisfaction, as a right to possess and retain property until a charge attaching to it is paid or discharged, as a charge imposed upon specific property by which it is made security for the performance of an act, and as being synonymous with a charge or encumbrance upon a thing. 235 Kan. at 962, 685 P.2d 866 (citing *Assembly of God v. Sangster,* 178 Kan. 678, 680, 290 P.2d 1057 [1955]).

In the present case, the Bank relies heavily upon *Hall v. Hamilton,* 233 Kan. 880, 667 P.2d 350 (1983). The issue in *Hall* was whether a joint tenancy in real estate was subject to involuntary partition. The court held that one joint tenant has the right to sever his or her joint interest. Partition is one approach a cotenant may pursue to sever the joint tenancy. The court further stated:

> It is undisputed that any joint tenant may sever his or her joint tenancy interest in real property by ... mortgaging the joint tenancy interest.... Once the joint tenancy interest is severed, a tenancy in common results.

233 Kan. at 885, 667 P.2d 350.

The Bank contends that the plain language in *Hall* requires Kansas courts to find that a pledge acts as a severance of the joint tenancy interest because there is no legal distinction in the operative effect of a mortgage or pledge (other than the type of property encumbered). We agree.

We have reviewed the cases relied upon by the district court and cited by counsel but do not find them dispositive of the narrow issue before us.

Here, the pledge by Harry was a formal act which severed the original unity of interest required for the continued existence of the joint tenancy. The lien represents a charge against the certificate of deposit to secure the repayment of the note. By virtue of Harry's unilateral pledge, Ida was deprived of her use and enjoyment of her undivided interest in the certificate of deposit.

The unilateral pledge severed the unity of interest, dissolved the joint tenancy as a matter of law, and created a tenancy in common. The severance of the joint tenancy gives rise to a rebuttable presumption of equal ownership. *Walnut Valley State Bank v. Stovall,* 223 Kan. 459, 462, 574 P.2d 1382 (1978). Ida retains a one-half interest in the certificate of deposit unless the presumption of equal ownership is rebutted upon remand. Because remand is required, we need not reach the other issues raised by the Bank.

Reversed and remanded.

## Minonk State Bank v. Grassman

Supreme Court of Illinois, 1983.
95 Ill.2d 392, 69 Ill.Dec. 387, 447 N.E.2d 822.

■ GOLDENHERSH, JUSTICE.

Minonk State Bank (hereinafter referred to as plaintiff), as administrator of the estate of Agnes Grassman, filed an action in the circuit court of Woodford County seeking a declaratory judgment that decedent was the owner of an undivided one-half interest in certain real estate and that Ida Grassman (hereinafter referred to as defendant) was a tenant in common with decedent in the ownership of the property, and not a joint tenant with right of survivorship. In two additional counts plaintiff sought partition of, and authority to sell (Ill.Rev.Stat.1977, ch. 110½, par. 20/4), the real estate. The circuit court entered judgment declaring that defendant, Ida Grassman, was the sole surviving joint tenant of the disputed property and dismissed the remainder of plaintiff's complaint as moot. The appellate court reversed and remanded and we granted defendant's petition for leave to appeal.

A detailed statement of the facts is contained in the appellate court opinion and we need only briefly review them. The record shows that by means of a conveyance dated August 22, 1938, the real estate here involved was conveyed to Gustav, Agnes, Ida and Frieda Grassman as joint tenants. Gustav and Frieda died, leaving decedent and defendant surviving. Defendant executed and recorded a deed which conveyed the land from herself as grantor to herself as grantee. The deed contains the following provision:

> (This deed is made for the purpose to dissolve any and all rights of the survivorship under a certain deed heretofore given by and between the above Grantor, Frieda Grassman and Agnes Grassman).

Decedent had no knowledge of this conveyance.

The circuit court concluded that *Duffield v. Duffield* (1915), 268 Ill. 29, 108 N.E. 673, and *Deslauriers v. Senesac* (1928), 331 Ill. 437, 163 N.E. 327, required it to hold that the purported conveyance did not effect the transfer of any interest in the land. It also held that the enactment of section 1b of "An Act to revise the law in relation to joint rights and obligations" (Ill.Rev.Stat.1977, ch. 76, par. 1b) affected only the creation, and not the termination, of joint tenancies. In reversing, the appellate court held that a joint tenant may unilaterally sever a joint tenancy, that the conveyance effectuated the termination of the joint tenancy, and that the decedent was a tenant in common with an undivided one-half interest in the real estate.

Defendant contends that the appellate court, and this court, are precluded from changing the common law rule that a joint tenant cannot destroy the right of survivorship by conveying property to herself. Specifically, defendant argues that section 1 of "An Act to revise the law in relation to the common law" (Ill.Rev.Stat.1977, ch. 28, par. 1) (the "reception statute") specifically precludes this court from changing the common law of England as it existed prior to the fourth year of James the First unless it is repealed by the General Assembly. Defendant argues that section 1b of "An Act to revise the law in relation to joint rights and obligations" (Ill.Rev.Stat.1977, ch. 76, par. 1b), the statute which effectively overruled this court's decision in *Deslauriers v. Senesac* (1928), 331 Ill. 437, 163 N.E. 327, and provided that a joint tenancy may be created notwithstanding the fact that the grantor is named as a grantee, applies only to the creation of joint tenancies and not to their termination. Citing *Summers v. Summers* (1968), 40 Ill.2d 338, 342, 239 N.E.2d 795, defendant argues that the statute, which is in derogation of the common law, must be strictly and narrowly construed, and that the statute should not be read to overrule that portion of *Deslauriers* which held that to be valid at common law a conveyance must have a separate grantor and grantee.

Plaintiff, citing *Amann v. Faidy* (1953), 415 Ill. 422, 114 N.E.2d 412, argues that the reception statute did not adopt "just those precedents which happened to have already been announced by English courts at the close of the sixteenth century, but rather a system of law whose outstanding characteristic is its adaptability and capacity for growth." (415 Ill. 422, 433, 114 N.E.2d 412.) Plaintiff contends that the reception statute was not designed to preclude judicial recognition of the realities of modern conveyancing and that, in any event, the General Assembly has itself changed certain requirements concerning conveyancing as it relates to joint tenancies "and has thereby recognized change in this area."

We agree with plaintiff that, as noted in *Amann,* it is necessary for the common law to keep pace with "the gradual changes of trade, commerce, arts, inventions and the exigencies and usages of the country." 415 Ill. 422, 434, 114 N.E.2d 412, quoting *Kreitz v. Behrensmeyer* (1894), 149 Ill. 496, 502, 36 N.E. 983.

The appellate court has reviewed the development of the law governing joint tenancies from the 13th century through our decision in *Deslauriers v. Senesac* (1928), 331 Ill. 437, 163 N.E. 327, the enactment of "An Act to revise the law in relation to joint rights and obligations" (Ill.Rev.Stat.1953, ch. 76, par. 1b), and our decision in *Frey v. Wubbena* (1962), 26 Ill.2d 62, 185 N.E.2d 850. (103 Ill.App.3d 1106, 1108–10, 59 Ill.Dec. 802, 432 N.E.2d 386.) The appellate court concluded, and we agree, that the rules applicable to the creation and severance of joint tenancies, in this situation, should be the same.

The common law requirement that there be a separate grantor and grantee was based on considerations concerning the manner in which land transfers were effectuated and recorded. The California Court of Appeals, in discussing whether a conveyance requires a separate grantor and grantee, noted:

> That two-to-transfer notion stems from the English common law feoffment ceremony with livery of seisin. [Citation.] ... It is apparent from the requirement of livery of seisin that one could not enfeoff oneself-that is, one could not be both grantor and grantee in a single transaction. Handing oneself a dirt clod is ungainly. Just as livery of seisin has become obsolete, so should ancient vestiges of that ceremony give way to modern conveyancing realities. (*Riddle v. Harmon* (1980), 102 Cal.App.3d 524, 528–29, 162 Cal.Rptr. 530, 533.)

In Illinois, the General Assembly has provided that livery of seisin is no longer necessary for the conveyance of real property and that a writing is sufficient to effectuate such a conveyance. (Ill.Rev.Stat.1977, ch. 30, par. 1.) Whatever problem a conveyance to oneself presented to the common law feoffment ceremony, such a conveyance presents no problem to our present system of conveyancing. We adopt the rationale of the appellate court and hold that defendant severed the joint tenancy by conveying the property to herself.

Finally, defendant argues that there is an important distinction between the creation and the severance of a joint tenancy. Defendant argues that the creation of a joint tenancy is "akin to a quasi contract or shared common venture" and that, because of the appellate court's holding, the parties to this "joint venture no longer are able to rely upon the relationship that led to them originally entering into the purchase of the property in question." We recognize that in certain situations, *e.g.,* where consideration is given for the creation of a joint tenancy or one of the joint tenants takes some irrevocable action in reliance upon the creation or existence of a joint tenancy, problems may arise if one tenant may unilaterally dissolve the joint tenancy. (See *Hendrickson v. Minneapolis Federal Savings & Loan Association* (1968), 281 Minn. 462, 466, 161 N.W.2d 688, 692; *cf.* 2 W. Blackstone, Commentaries *195.) Such a situation is not presented here; the record does not show that either party gave consideration for the creation of the joint tenancy or relied, to her detriment, on its continued existence.

For the reasons stated, the judgment of the appellate court is affirmed.

Judgment affirmed.

## NOTES

1. *Mortgages vs. leases.* How strong a precedent is *Harms* for Tenhet in the Principal Problem? Is there any way Boswell can mitigate the negative impact of this decision? Does *Harms* or *Hutchinson* reach a more desirable result? Should mortgages be treated the same as leases for purposes of determining whether they constitute a severance?

An exhaustive student comment notes that there is authority for the proposition that the joint tenancy is severed during the term of the lease, but is revived if upon termination of the lease, both joint tenants are still living. Another solution having support is that the joint tenancy continues notwithstanding the lease, but the surviving joint tenant's interest in the property is subject to the lease. This approach is called temporary or partial severance. See Sodergren, Consequences of a Lease to a Third Party Made by One Joint Tenant, 66 Cal. L. Rev. 69 (1978). In light of these diverse approaches, it would seem that a court should feel free to decide the matter on policy grounds. What policies should be relevant in this context?

2. *Survival of encumbrances.* How workable is the court's determination in *Harms* that the mortgage should not survive as a lien on the property following the death of the mortgagor? How could the mortgagee's interests be more effectively protected? Why is such protection desirable?

3. *Unilateral severance. Minonk* illustrates the prevailing view with respect to a joint tenant's unilateral severance of the tenancy through one

instrument.[3] What policies justify the court's decision in *Minonk*? Are there any countervailing considerations that the court failed to take into account?

4. *Judicial consistency.* It might seem that *Minonk* is not consistent in philosophy with *Harms*, even though both decisions are from the same court and were rendered in consecutive years. In *Harms*, the court strove to preserve the right of survivorship as against a claim of destruction based on the execution of the mortgage. In *Minonk*, the court found that the right of survivorship was destroyed despite the absence of any real conveyance. Is it possible to reconcile these cases?

*Minonk* suggests that Boswell should win in the Principal Problem since if a tenancy can be terminated by an illusory transfer it would seem that it should be terminated by a transfer of a leasehold. If you were representing Tenhet in the Principal Problem, how might you try to distinguish *Minonk*?

---

[3] Other cases adhering to the same position include In re Carpenter's Estate, 189 Cal.Rptr. 651, 140 Cal.App.3d 709 (1983); Estate of Grigsby, 184 Cal.Rptr. 886 (1982); Riddle v. Harmon, 162 Cal.Rptr. 530 (1980); Hendrickson v. Minneapolis Fed. Sav. & Loan Ass'n, 281 Minn. 462, 161 N.W.2d 688 (1968). California has enacted legislation making it possible for a joint tenant to effect a unilateral severance of the joint tenancy by simply executing a written declaration of severance. Cal. Civ. Code sec. 683.2(a)(2) (2015).

# ASSIGNMENT 17

# MARITAL PROPERTY

## 1. INTRODUCTION

At common law, a widow was entitled to "dower"—a life estate in one third of all real estate of which the husband was seised under an estate of inheritance during the marriage. In an era when most wealth was in the form of real estate, dower rights served moderately well in providing a modicum of economic security for a widow. With changing circumstances, however, the institution of dower became outmoded. Life estates in real property are of limited practical value. They can rarely be sold or mortgaged, and thus their existence makes it difficult to develop land profitably. More importantly, in most instances real estate is not the principal asset of the husband's estate. Therefore, dower rights in real estate are not extensive enough to provide economic security for most surviving widows.

Under the doctrine of "curtesy," the widower was given a life estate in all of his wife's land of which she was seised of an estate of inheritance during marriage, provided a child of the marriage was born alive. The touching scene often portrayed in old etchings of the husband anxiously listening at the door of the delivery room may have portrayed his anxiety over his estate of curtesy rather than any tender solicitude for mother and child. The husband's curtesy estate in all of the wife's land contrasted sharply, and unfairly, with the wife's dower estate in one-third of the husband's land.

In 1839, Mississippi became the first state to enact legislation establishing the right of married women to manage their own property. The background of the legislation is filled with irony. Two years earlier the Mississippi Court of Errors and Appeals had held that a certain married woman could manage her property and convey it to her daughter without her husband's consent.[1] She could do this because she was a member of the Chickasaw nation and under Chickasaw law a married woman had complete control of her own property. Thereafter the Mississippi legislature decided that white women should have, in effect, the same property rights as Chickasaw women. One of the many jarring notes in this seemingly happy story is that the "property" involved was an African-American slave.[2]

Today, the common law marital property system discussed above is no longer used by any state. In fact, any gender-based distinction in

---

[1] Fisher v. Allen, 3 Miss. (2 Howard) 611 (1837).

[2] The tangled background to the 1839 legislation is well told in Benson, Fisher v. Allen: The Southern Origins of the Married Women's Property Acts, 6 J. of Southern Legal History 97 (1998).

Thus, a spouse who does not work outside the home may have less economic power than the wage earner. The law may require one spouse to support the other, but it does not give the supported spouse a legal right to participate on an equal basis in major financial decisions. The joint checking or savings account is a convenience, not a legal obligation.

*Disposition of Property on Death of One Spouse During Marriage.* Almost all of the common law jurisdictions impose some restrictions on the power of one spouse to disinherit the other. Usually the surviving spouse is protected by statutes that give him or her the power to reject the share given by the will and to elect to take a specified share (usually one third) of the decedent's probate estate.[6] Such a minimum share is sometimes called a "non-barrable" or "forced" share. A spouse may try to avoid leaving the surviving spouse anything by dissipating the funds before death, or by placing them in trust, life insurance, or joint tenancy form, thus taking them out of the probate estate. Section 2–202 of the Uniform Probate Code offers protection from such a stratagem. It permits the surviving spouse to elect to take a share in many forms of wealth that are not technically within the probate estate, such as certain types of trust property and life insurance on the life of the deceased spouse.

No matter how well drawn, a statute that only gives the surviving spouse a non-barrable or "forced" share in the property of the deceased spouse does not entirely address the problem. If the spouse who works in the home dies first, he or she has no testamentary power over the property held in the name of the other spouse. This may work a serious injustice.

> EXAMPLE 2: H and W are married. H devotes his full time to the care of the home and of the children, thus permitting W to devote her undivided attention to a successful real estate business, established after the marriage with borrowed funds. Both H and W have children by former marriages. After many years of marriage H dies, and shortly thereafter W dies. H's will leaves all of "his" property to his children by a former marriage, and W's will leaves all of "her" property to her children by a former marriage. W's real estate business is worth $2,000,000. H has no property in his own name.
>
> RESULT: W's children receive $2,000,000; H's children receive nothing. Had W died first, H would have been entitled to his elective share of W's estate, which in turn would go to his children on his death.

---

[6] A probate estate is "a decedent's property subject to administration by a personal representative." Black's Law Dictionary 1396 (10th ed. 2014). The personal representative (executor or administrator) of the estate collects the decedent's assets, pays decedent's tax and other liabilities, and distributes the remainder of the estate to the beneficiaries. *Black's Law Dictionary* (10th ed. 2014), *available at* Westlaw BLACKS.

The above result should be contrasted with that in a community property state. There, W's children would receive $1,000,000 and H's children would receive the same, regardless of which spouse died first.

*Disposition of Property on Divorce.* In modern common law property jurisdictions, all of which have adopted "equitable distribution" systems, the courts divide the property owned by the spouses at the time of the divorce, based on the dictates of equity and fairness. The fact that the property was acquired by one spouse, or is in that spouse's name, is not controlling. Factors that the courts usually consider in deciding upon an "equitable" distribution of the marital property include: (1) the contribution of each spouse to the marriage and to the acquisition, preservation or appreciation of the marital assets, and (2) the needs of each spouse, considering the duration of the marriage, the health and circumstances of the parties, and the present and prospective earnings of each party. Of course, the different statutes vary considerably.

In assessing contributions to the marriage, the modern trend is for common law jurisdictions to consider the nonmonetary contributions of a spouse who does not work outside the home in determining spousal maintenance and property division.[7] Thus, the emphasis on the partnership aspects of marriage originally characteristic of the community property states now appears to be reflected, at least theoretically, in the property dispositions of the common law states. As the following discussion illustrates, however, the law in many of these states, as well as in the community property states, falls somewhat short of this ideal.

Discussion Question. As between community property and common law marital property systems, which is preferable?

*Effects of Disposition on Divorce.* Despite the existing legislative authorizations for considering the respective financial needs of the divorcing parties in property divisions, courts may be unwilling to employ need-based discretionary factors.[8] At times, courts address need through spousal maintenance (alimony). Spousal maintenance awards, however, are often insufficient and frequently difficult to collect.

*Marital Property Compared with Spousal Maintenance.* In general, state statutes appear to place more emphasis on property division as opposed to spousal maintenance in settling the financial matters of a divorcing couple.[9] This trend is probably desirable. Although spousal

---

[7] See generally Freed & Walker, Family Law in the Fifty States: An Overview, 21 Fam. L.Q. 417, 462 (1988).

[8] See Reynolds, The Relationship of Property Division and Alimony: The Division of Property to Address Need, 56 Fordham L. Rev. 827, 843 (1988).

[9] This trend is reflected in § 308 of the Uniform Marriage & Divorce Act, which directs the court to rely on a property division to provide for the support of a needy spouse rather than spousal maintenance when the property is sufficient. See also Reynolds, supra note 8, at 842–843.

maintenance generally is modifiable on a showing of changed circumstances, a distribution of marital property is a fixed, permanent arrangement. Thus, a distribution of marital property fosters a clean break between the former spouses, whereas spousal maintenance tends to perpetuate a relationship that neither party really wants. Of course, a distribution of marital property is only the better solution where a divorcing couple has acquired property to divide. Where the spouses have no real or personal property of value, or where the value of their assets is negligible, spousal maintenance is the only way to treat the parties equitably.

In many jurisdictions, spousal maintenance is limited in time and amount. Thus, an incentive exists for one spouse to seek to enhance his or her financial position by including "human capital" as marital property to which both spouses have a claim. The Principal Problem addresses this issue.

## 4. Principal Problem

Wanda and Harry Jones met while undergraduates at American University. Although Harry was a year ahead of her, Wanda took several classes with Harry and the two eventually fell in love. They were married two months after Harry's graduation.

After their honeymoon, Harry took an entry-level position with a prominent investment brokerage firm. His plan was to support Wanda while she finished school and to gain some first-hand knowledge of the business world before applying for admission to an M.B.A. program.

Wanda graduated the following year, and began her own career as an accountant. She thought about pursuing a master's degree, but she and Harry agreed that she would continue to work at her accounting job, which she enjoyed, while Harry attended Stanford Business School. Harry could not afford to go otherwise and his firm had promised him a highly coveted and well-paying position upon graduation. It was an opportunity Wanda knew they should not pass up.

As the months passed, the M.B.A. program seemed to change Harry. He became rude and condescending, always boasting about his own forecasted success and taking for granted the long hours Wanda spent at work and in maintaining their home. Nevertheless, Wanda continued to support her husband, anticipating the financial benefits to come and believing that once relieved of the stress of school, Harry would revert back to the kind, gentle man she had married.

Sadly, Wanda's hope was shattered, when three weeks after Harry's graduation, he served her with divorce papers. You are the family court judge presiding over the Jones' dissolution proceedings. They own a car

---

The Uniform Marriage & Divorce Act has been adopted as a general framework in several states including Arizona, Colorado, Illinois, Kentucky, Minnesota, Missouri, Montana, and Washington (note that Arizona and Washington also are community property states).

and some inexpensive furniture, but for the most part, all of their marital earnings have been used to pay educational and living expenses. How do you divide their "property" between them? Would your decision change if Wanda had obtained her bachelor's degree at the same time as Harry? If Harry had waited until five years after his graduation from business school to file for divorce? Ten years?

Consider the following materials before making your decision.

## 5. Materials for Solution of Principal Problem on Human Capital

### O'Brien v. O'Brien
Court of Appeals of New York, 1985.
489 N.E.2d 712.

■ SIMONS, JUDGE.

In this divorce action, the parties' only asset of any consequence is the husband's newly acquired license to practice medicine. The principal issue presented is whether that license, acquired during their marriage, is marital property subject to equitable distribution under Domestic Relations Law § 236(B)(5). Supreme Court held that it was and accordingly made a distributive award in defendant's favor.... On appeal to the Appellate Division, a majority of that court held that plaintiff's medical license is not marital property.... It modified the judgement and remitted the case to Supreme Court for further proceedings, specifically for a determination of maintenance and a rehabilitative award....

We now hold that plaintiff's medical license constitutes "marital property" within the meaning of Domestic Relations Law § 236(B)(1)(c) and that it is therefore subject to equitable distribution pursuant to subdivision 5 of that part....

I

Plaintiff and defendant married on April 3, 1971. At the time both were employed as teachers at the same private school. Defendant had a bachelor's degree and a temporary teaching certificate but required 18 months of postgraduate classes at an approximate cost of $3,000, excluding living expenses, to obtain permanent certification in New York. She claimed, and the trial court found, that she had relinquished the opportunity to obtain permanent certification while plaintiff pursued his education. At the time of the marriage, plaintiff had completed only three and one-half years of college but shortly afterward he returned to school at night to earn his bachelor's degree and to complete sufficient premedical courses to enter medical school. In September 1973 the parties moved to Guadalajara, Mexico, where plaintiff became a full-time medical student. While he pursued his studies defendant held several teaching and tutorial positions and contributed her earnings to their joint expenses. The parties returned to New York in December 1976 so that plaintiff could complete the last two semesters of medical school and internship training here. After they returned, defendant resumed her former teaching position and she remained in it at the time this action was commenced. Plaintiff was licensed to practice medicine in October 1980. He commenced this action for divorce two months later. At the time of trial, he was a resident in general surgery.

During the marriage both parties contributed to paying the living and educational expenses and they received additional help from both of their families. They disagreed on the amounts of their respective contributions but it is undisputed that in addition to performing household work and managing the family finances defendant was gainfully employed throughout the marriage, that she contributed all of her earnings to their living and educational expenses and that her financial contributions exceeded those of plaintiff. The trial court found that she had contributed 76% of the parties' income exclusive of a $10,000 student loan obtained by defendant. Finding that plaintiff's medical degree and license are marital property, the court received evidence of its value and ordered a distributive award to defendant.

Defendant presented expert testimony that the present value of plaintiff's medical license was $472,000. Her expert testified that he arrived at this figure by comparing the average income of a college graduate and that of a general surgeon between 1985, when plaintiff's residency would end, and 2012, when he would reach age 65. After considering Federal income taxes, an inflation rate of 10% and a real interest rate of 3% he capitalized the difference in average earnings and reduced the amount to present value. He also gave his opinion that the present value of defendant's contribution was $103,390. Plaintiff offered no expert testimony on the subject.

The court, after considering the life-style that plaintiff would enjoy from the enhanced earning potential his medical license would bring and defendant's contributions and efforts toward attainment of it, made a distributive award to her of $188,800, representing 40% of the value of the license, and ordered it paid in 11 annual installments of various amounts beginning November 1, 1982 and ending November 1, 1992. The court also directed plaintiff to maintain a life insurance policy on his life for defendant's benefit for the unpaid balance of the award....

On these cross appeals, defendant seeks reinstatement of the judgement of the trial court. Plaintiff contends that the Appellate Division correctly held that a professional license is not marital property....

## II

The Equitable Distribution Law contemplates only two classes of property: marital property and separate property (Domestic Relations

Law § 236[B][1][c], [d]). The former, which is subject to equitable distribution, is defined broadly as "all property acquired by either or both spouses during the marriage and before the execution of a separation agreement or the commencement of a matrimonial action, regardless of the form in which title is held" (Domestic Relations Law § 236[B][1][c] [emphasis added]; see § 236[B][5][b], [c]). Plaintiff does not contend that his license is excluded from distribution because it is separate property; rather, he claims that it is not property at all but represents a personal attainment in acquiring knowledge....

Section 236 provides that in making an equitable distribution of marital property, "the court shall consider: ... (6) any equitable claim to, interest in, or direct or indirect contribution made to the acquisition of such property by the party not having title, including joint efforts or expenditures and contributions and services as a spouse, parent, wage earner and homemaker, and to the career or career potential of the other party [and] ... (9) the impossibility or difficulty of evaluating any component asset or any interest in a business, corporation or profession" (Domestic Relations Law § 236[B][5][d][6], [9]). Where equitable distribution of marital property is appropriate but "the distribution of an interest in a business, corporation or profession would be contrary to law" the court shall make a distributive award in lieu of an actual distribution of the property (Domestic Relations Law § 236[B][5][e]). The words mean exactly what they say: that an interest in a profession or professional career potential is marital property which may be represented by direct or indirect contributions of the non-title-holding spouse, including financial contributions and nonfinancial contributions made by caring for the home and family....

Equitable distribution was based on the premise that a marriage is, among other things, an economic partnership to which both parties contribute as spouse, parent, wage earner or homemaker (id., at 130; see, Governor's Memorandum of Approval, 1980 McKinney's Session Laws of N.Y., at 1863). Consistent with this purpose, and implicit in the statutory scheme as a whole, is the view that upon dissolution of the marriage there should be a winding up of the parties' economic affairs and a severance of their economic ties by an equitable distribution of the marital assets. Thus, the concept of alimony, which often served as a means of lifetime support and dependence for one spouse upon the other long after the marriage was over, was replaced with the concept of maintenance which seeks to allow "the recipient spouse an opportunity to achieve [economic] independence" (Assembly Memorandum, 1980 N.Y.Legis.Ann., at 130).

The determination that a professional license is marital property is also consistent with the conceptual base upon which the statute rests. As this case demonstrates, few undertakings during a marriage better qualify as the type of joint effort that the statute's economic partnership theory is intended to address than contributions toward one spouse's acquisition of a professional license. Working spouses are often required to contribute substantial income as wage earners, sacrifice their own educational or career goals and opportunities for child rearing, perform the bulk of household duties and responsibilities and forego the acquisition of marital assets that could have been accumulated if the professional spouse had been employed rather than occupied with the study and training necessary to acquire a professional license. In this case, nearly all of the parties' nine-year marriage was devoted to the acquisition of plaintiff's medical license and defendant played a major role in that project. She worked continuously during the marriage and contributed all of her earnings to their joint effort, she sacrificed her own educational and career opportunities, and she traveled with plaintiff to Mexico for three and one-half years while he attended medical school there. The Legislature has decided, by its explicit reference in the statute to the contributions of one spouse to the other's profession or career (see, Domestic Relations Law § 236[B][5][d][6], [9]; [e]), that these contributions represent investments in the economic partnership of the marriage and that the product of the parties' joint efforts, the professional license, should be considered marital property....

Plaintiff's principal argument, adopted by the majority in the Appellate Division, is that a professional license is not marital property because it does not fit within the traditional view of property as something which has an exchange value on the open market and is capable of sale, assignment or transfer. The position does not withstand analysis for at least two reasons. First, as we have observed, it ignores the fact that whether a professional license constitutes marital property is to be judged by the language of the statute which created this new species of property previously unknown at common law or under prior statutes. Thus, whether the license fits within traditional property concepts is of no consequence. Second, it is an overstatement to assert that a professional license could not be considered property even outside the context of section 236(B). A professional license is a valuable property right, reflected in the money, effort and lost opportunity for employment expended in its acquisition, and also in the enhanced earning capacity it affords its holder, which may not be revoked without due process of law (see, Matter of Bender v. Board of Regents, 262 App.Div. 627, 631, 30 N.Y.S.2d 779; People ex rel. Greenberg v. Reid, 151 App.Div. 324, 326, 136 N.Y.S. 428). That a professional license has no market value is irrelevant. Obviously, a license may not be alienated as may other property and for that reason the working spouse's interest in it is limited. The Legislature has recognized that limitation, however, and has provided for an award in lieu of its actual distribution (see, Domestic Relations Law § 236[B][5][e]).

Plaintiff also contends that alternative remedies should be employed, such as an award of rehabilitative maintenance or reimbursement for direct financial contributions (see, e.g., Kutanovski v. Kutanovski, 109 A.D.2d 822, 824, 486 N.Y.S.2d 338; Conner v. Conner,

97 A.D.2d 88, 101, 468 N.Y.S.2d 482; supra; Lesman v. Lesman, 88 A.D.2d 153, 158–159, 452 N.Y.S.2d 935; supra). The statute does not expressly authorize retrospective maintenance or rehabilitative awards and we have no occasion to decide in this case whether the authority to do so may ever be implied from its provisions (but see, Cappiello v. Cappiello, 66 N.Y.2d 107, 495 N.Y.S.2d 318, 485 N.E.2d 983). It is sufficient to observe that normally a working spouse should not be restricted to that relief because to do so frustrates the purposes underlying the Equitable Distribution Law. Limiting a working spouse to a maintenance award, either general or rehabilitative, not only is contrary to the economic partnership concept underlying the statute but also retains the uncertain and inequitable economic ties of dependence that the Legislature sought to extinguish by equitable distribution. Maintenance is subject to termination upon the recipient's remarriage and a working spouse may never receive adequate consideration for his or her contribution and may even be penalized for the decision to remarry if that is the only method of compensating the contribution. As one court said so well, "[t]he function of equitable distribution is to recognize that when a marriage ends, each of the spouses, based on the totality of the contributions made to it, has a stake in and right to a share of the marital assets accumulated while it endured, not because that share is needed, but because those assets represent the capital product of what was essentially a partnership entity" (Wood v. Wood, 119 Misc.2d 1076, 1079, 465 N.Y.S.2d 475). The Legislature stated its intention to eliminate such inequities by providing that a supporting spouse's "direct or indirect contribution" be recognized, considered and rewarded (Domestic Relations Law § 236[B][5][d][6]).

Turning to the question of valuation, it has been suggested that even if a professional license is considered marital property, the working spouse is entitled only to reimbursement of his or her direct financial contributions (see, Note, Equitable Distribution of Degrees and Licenses: Two Theories Toward Compensating Spousal Contributions, 49 Brooklyn L.Rev. 301, 317–322). By parity of reasoning, a spouse's down payment on real estate or contribution to the purchase of securities would be limited to the money contributed, without any remuneration for any incremental value in the asset because of price appreciation. Such a result is completely at odds with the statute's requirement that the court give full consideration to both direct and indirect contributions "made to the acquisition of such marital property by the party not having title, including joint efforts or expenditures and contributions and services as a spouse, parent, wage earner and homemaker" (Domestic Relations Law 236[B][5][d][6]). If the license is marital property, then the working spouse is entitled to an equitable portion of it, not a return of funds advanced.

When other marital assets are of sufficient value to provide for the supporting spouse's equitable portion of the marital property, including his or her contributions to the acquisition of the professional license, however, the court retains the discretion to distribute these other marital assets or to make a distributive award in lieu of an actual distribution of the value of the professional spouse's license (see, Majauskas v. Majauskas, 61 N.Y.2d 481, 493, 474 N.Y.S.2d 699, 463 N.E.2d 15, supra).

■ MEYER, JUDGE (concurring).

I concur in Judge Simons' opinion but write separately to point up for consideration by the Legislature the potential for unfairness involved in distributive awards based upon a license of a professional still in training.

An equity court normally has power to "change its decrees where there has been a change of circumstances" (People v. Scanlon, 11 N.Y.2d 459, 462, 230 N.Y.S.2d 708, 184 N.E.2d 302, on second appeal 13 N.Y.2d 982, 244 N.Y.S.2d 781, 194 N.E.2d 689). The implication of Domestic Relations Law § 236(B)(9)(b), which deals with modification of an order or decree as to maintenance or child support, is, however, that a distributive award pursuant to section 236(B)(5)(e), once made, is not subject to change. Yet a professional in training who is not finally committed to a career choice when the distributive award is made may be locked into a particular kind of practice simply because the monetary obligations imposed by the distributive award made on the basis of the trial judge's conclusion (prophecy may be a better word) as to what the career choice will be leaves him or her no alternative. . . .

### Simmons v. Simmons
Supreme Court of Connecticut, 1998.
244 Conn. 158, 708 A.2d 949.

■ CALLAHAN, J.

[T]he trial court made the following findings of fact: The plaintiff and the defendant were married on September 23, 1983, in Fayetteville, North Carolina. At the time of their marriage, the plaintiff was twenty-three years of age and was a sergeant in the United States Army. The defendant was forty-three years of age and was working as a bartender. There are no children of the marriage. The defendant, however, had six children of her own prior to her marriage to the plaintiff.

During the course of the marriage, both the plaintiff and the defendant pursued their individual educational goals. The defendant obtained two associates degrees, one as a surgical technician and one in nursing, culminating in her becoming a registered nurse in 1991. The plaintiff received his undergraduate degree in 1990 and entered medical school. He completed medical school in 1994 and entered a surgical residency program at St. Raphael's Hospital in New Haven, causing the family to relocate to Connecticut from North Carolina. The defendant and the plaintiff both paid their own educational expenses and both were employed and jointly supporting the family unit until the plaintiff entered medical school, when he was prohibited from maintaining outside employment. The plaintiff received loans and grants to pay for medical school and to defray some of the household expenses. The defendant worked and supported the family while the plaintiff attended medical school. She provided financial and emotional support as well as her services as a homemaker. She did not, however, make any direct financial contribution toward the cost of the plaintiff's medical school education.

In the third year of his five year surgical residency, the plaintiff filed an action for dissolution of marriage. At trial, the defendant argued that the plaintiff's medical degree was property subject to equitable distribution pursuant to § 46b–81 upon dissolution of the marriage. She presented an expert witness, Steven Shapiro, an economist, who testified regarding the present value of the plaintiff's medical degree. Shapiro testified that the plaintiff's future earning potential, reduced to present value, was approximately $3.4 million as a plastic surgeon and $2.8 million as a general surgeon. He concluded that the average of the two, $3.1 million, represents the appropriate value to be assigned to the plaintiff's medical degree. The defendant claimed that the degree's present value should be equitably distributed between the parties and demanded in excess of $1.5 million as a property settlement. [T]he trial court concluded that the plaintiff's medical degree was not property subject to equitable distribution pursuant to § 46b–81. The court then issued an order dissolving the marriage, denying alimony to both parties and ordering distribution of the parties' debts and assets. The defendant appealed. . . .

The first issue raised by the defendant is whether the plaintiff's medical degree is property subject to equitable distribution pursuant to § 46b–81 upon dissolution of the marriage. This is a question of first impression for Connecticut. It is not, however, a new question nationwide. At least thirty-five states have addressed the issue and substantial ink has been expended by academicians and practitioners on this subject. It has been labeled with a number of appellations, the most common of which is the "working spouse/student spouse syndrome," apparently so called because it represents an unfortunate circumstance that too often arises in family courts. In its most basic form, it is typified by one spouse who works to provide primary support for the family unit while the other spouse obtains an education, meanwhile earning either nothing or substantially less than he or she otherwise might have earned. Typically, it is also characterized by a relatively short marriage and a working spouse who has made significant sacrifices, for example, forgoing or delaying educational or child rearing opportunities and the current enjoyment of income that could have been produced by the student spouse. The expectation that the future benefit of increased earning capacity would be the reward shared by both is dashed when the marriage disintegrates and one of the parties files an action for dissolution before the anticipated benefits are realized. The critical problem in these situations is that the couple usually has few, if any, assets to be distributed at the time of the dissolution of the marriage. The degree, with its potential for increased earning power, is, therefore, the only thing of real economic value to the parties.

The defendant argues that she fits within this paradigm and is entitled to share in the benefits of the plaintiff's medical degree by way of a distribution pursuant to § 46b–81 conferring on her an equitable portion of the value of the plaintiff's medical degree. In support of this argument, the defendant asserts that 46b–81 adopts an " 'all property,' equitable distribution scheme"; Krafick v. Krafick, 234 Conn. 783, 792, 663 A.2d 365 (1995); pursuant to which this court has given an expansive definition of property that necessarily includes an advanced degree obtained during the marriage. The crux of the defendant's argument rests upon selected language from our opinion in Krafick. The plaintiff counters that a medical degree cannot be distributed as property because it has no inherent value independent of the holder and does not fit within the statutory definition of property. We conclude that the plaintiff's medical degree is not property subject to distribution pursuant to § 46b–81. . . .

In Krafick, we were called upon to determine whether the term property in 46b–81, which is not defined by the statute or clarified by its legislative history, was broad enough to include vested, though unmatured, pension rights. To that end, we concluded that the legislature intended to adopt the commonly accepted legal definition of property as set forth in Black's Law Dictionary (6th Ed.1990) p. 1095, which "defines 'property' as the term 'commonly used to denote everything which is the subject of ownership, corporeal or incorporeal, tangible or intangible, visible or invisible, real or personal; everything that has an exchangeable value or which goes to make up wealth or estate. It extends to every species of valuable right and interest, and includes real and personal property, easements, franchises, and incorporeal hereditament.' " Krafick v. Krafick, supra. By adopting that definition, we acknowledged that the legislature intended the term to be broad in scope. While we do not retreat from the definition of property espoused in Krafick, we also recognize that it is not without limits. We conclude that the plaintiff's medical degree falls outside those limits.

Whether the interest of a party to a dissolution is subject to distribution pursuant to 46b–81, depends on whether that interest is: (1) a "presently existing property [interest]" or (2) a "mere expectancy." "[Section] 46b–81 applies only to presently existing property interests, not 'mere expectancies.' " Therefore, the former interest is subject to equitable distribution upon dissolution, while the latter is not. The prototypical nonproperty interest is an anticipated inheritance, which we consistently have deemed to be a mere expectancy that is precluded from equitable distribution under 46b–81. In Krafick, we stated that unlike a property interest, an "expectancy may never be realized.... The term expectancy describes the interest of a person who merely foresees that he might receive a future beneficence.... *[T]he defining characteristic of an expectancy is that its holder has no enforceable right to his beneficence.*" Krafick v. Krafick, supra, 234 Conn. at 797, 663 A.2d 365.

By contrast, a vested pension benefit is property within the meaning of 46b–81 and, thus, is subject to equitable distribution because it represents a presently existing, enforceable contract right. We reasoned that "vested pension benefits represent an employee's *right* to receive payment in the future, subject ordinarily to his or her living until the age of retirement. The fact that a *contractual right* is contingent upon future events does not degrade that right to an expectancy." Consequently, the defining characteristic of property for purposes of § 46b–81 is the present existence of the right and the ability to enforce that right.

The defendant first argues, by analogy, that a medical degree is substantially similar to pension benefits because both are a means to obtain deferred compensation. In both circumstances, she argues, the marital unit forgoes current income and invests those resources to acquire the benefit of future income....

The defendant's argument is unpersuasive because an advanced degree entails no presently existing, enforceable right to receive any particular income in the future. It represents nothing more than an opportunity for the degree holder, through his or her own efforts, in the absence of any contingency that might limit or frustrate those efforts, to earn income in the future.... Consequently, we conclude that an advanced degree is properly classified as an expectancy rather than a presently existing property interest. It is not, therefore, subject to equitable distribution upon dissolution pursuant to 46b–81.

The great weight of authority supports this conclusion.[10] The oft-cited rationale for concluding that a degree is not property subject to distribution is found in Graham v. Graham, 194 Colo. 429, 574 P.2d 75 (1978). There, the Colorado Supreme Court concluded that "[a]n educational degree ... is simply not encompassed even by the broad views of the concept of 'property.' It does not have an exchange value or any objective transferable value on an open market. It is personal to the holder. It terminates on death of the holder and is not inheritable. It cannot be assigned, sold, transferred, conveyed or pledged. An advanced degree is a cumulative product of many years of previous education, combined with diligence and hard work. It may not be acquired by mere expenditure of money. It is simply an intellectual achievement that may potentially assist in future acquisition of property. In our view, it has none of the attributes of property in the usual sense of the term."

---

[10] Thirty-five states have addressed this issue. Of them, thirty-four have declined to consider an educational degree marital property subject to equitable distribution. [Citations omitted.]

We agree that an advanced degree has no inherent value extrinsic to the recipient. Its only value rests in the possibility of the enhanced earning capacity that it might afford sometime in the future. The possibility of future earnings, however, represents a mere expectancy, not a present right. We previously have concluded that "[t]he terms 'estate' and 'property,' as used in the statute [§ 46b–81] connote presently existing interests. 'Property' entails 'interests that a person has already acquired in specific benefits.' " Rubin v. Rubin, supra, 204 Conn. at 230–31, 527 A.2d 1184. In Rubin, we declined to allow a property division in contemplation of an anticipated inheritance. We concluded that "the relevance of probable future income in determining the fair and equitable division of existing property . . . does not establish jurisdiction to make allowances from . . . property other than that held at the time."

The defendant reminds us that "the primary aim of property distribution is to recognize that marriage is, among other things, 'a shared enterprise or joint undertaking in the nature of a partnership to which both spouses contribute—directly and indirectly, financially and nonfinancially—the fruits of which are distributable at divorce.' " Krafick v. Krafick, supra, 234 Conn. at 795, 663 A.2d 365. She argues that the only way to effectuate this purpose in these circumstances is to conclude that the plaintiff's medical degree is marital property. We disagree.

There are other ways to compensate the defendant for her contribution to the plaintiff's degree without subjecting it to classification as property subject to equitable distribution. See B. Herring, supra, 19 J. Marshall L. Rev. 1 (analyzing variety of solutions adopted by courts). Furthermore, while we have acknowledged that the marital union is akin to a partnership, we have never held that it is an actual economic partnership. The parties to a marriage do not enter into the relationship with a set of ledgers and make yearly adjustments to their capital accounts. "Marriage is not a business arrangement, and this Court would be loathe to promote any more tallying of respective debits and credits than already occurs in the average household." Hoak v. Hoak, supra, 179 W. Va. at 514, 370 S.E.2d 473. Reducing the relationship, even when it has broken down, to such base terms serves only to degrade and undermine that relationship and the parties.

The second issue raised by the defendant is whether, if it is assumed that the plaintiff's degree is not property subject to distribution pursuant to § 46b–81, the trial court abused its discretion by failing to take proper account of the plaintiff's degree in structuring a property settlement and in denying her alimony. The following additional facts are relevant to this issue. When this case was decided by the trial court, the plaintiff was thirty-six years of age with an annual gross income of $45,660 from his residency position. The defendant was fifty-six years of age and employed part time as a registered nurse earning approximately $36,000 annually. She had earned approximately $67,000 in the previous year. The parties owned minimal assets, including their older automobiles, approximately

$5,800 in cash, some collectibles, including rare books and stamps, and other miscellaneous personalty. After concluding that neither party was solely responsible for the irretrievable breakdown, the trial court ordered the dissolution of the marriage; denied alimony to either party; allowed each party to retain the personal property currently in that party's possession; made the plaintiff solely responsible for a joint debt to the Internal Revenue Service, but otherwise made each party responsible for that party's own debts, which included the plaintiff's medical school loans amounting to approximately $40,000; ordered the plaintiff to pay the defendant $5,800, which was the total amount of cash in the joint accounts of the parties at the time of the parties' separation and which the plaintiff unilaterally had withdrawn; and ordered both parties to be responsible for their own attorneys' fees. . . .

We do, however, find merit in the defendant's second claim, that the trial court abused its discretion in failing to award her alimony. An award of alimony is governed by § 46b–82, which mandates that the court "shall consider the length of the marriage, the causes for the annulment, dissolution of the marriage or legal separation, the age, health, station, occupation, amount and sources of income, vocational skills, employability, estate and needs of each of the parties and the award, if any, which the court may make pursuant to section 46b–81. . . ." We continue mindful of the substantial deference that this court affords the decisions of the trial court in a dissolution case. We consider this case, however, to present one of those rare situations in which we must conclude that there was an abuse of that discretion.

The trial court, in its memorandum of decision, acknowledged the need to consider the plaintiff's medical degree in determining an award of alimony. Further, the court specifically referred to the statutory factors related to the earning capacity of both parties as well as other economic factors in making that determination. It went on, however, to conclude that "consideration of the statutory factors in this case [does] not justify the award of alimony to the defendant." In support of its conclusion, the court analyzed the facts, noting that "[t]he defendant provided no direct financial contributions to the plaintiff's attainment of his medical degree. He paid for his own education costs and incurred large medical school loans, of which approximately $40,000 remains outstanding. The defendant also did not forgo educational and career opportunities in order to support her husband. Much to her credit, she was able to further her education and attain her career goal of becoming a licensed nurse during the marriage. She is presently employed as a nurse and is able to financially support herself at a standard of living to which she was accustomed during marriage. . . . The economic condition in which a divorce decree leaves the parties is a paramount concern for the court in a dissolution proceeding. A severing of the marriage bond in this case will not result in just one party facing a rewarding professional future. Both parties will remain able to support themselves and able to pursue their chosen careers." We have [two] problems with respect to the trial court's analysis.

First, we find no reference to the age of the defendant. This court does not mandate that any one factor should be given greater weight than other factors, nor do we require that the court recite every factor in its memorandum of decision. We believe, however, that this particular omission is significant in light of the substantial age disparity between the parties. The defendant was fifty-six years of age at the time of trial, while the plaintiff was thirty-six years of age. Although the defendant may be able to continue to pursue her chosen career, she is significantly limited in the duration of that career because of her age. Moreover, she currently has no significant assets and she is not likely to accumulate any prior to her retirement. Any savings she might have garnered in anticipation of her retirement were necessarily consumed during the years of the plaintiff's medical education because she was the sole support of the family unit. It is not unlikely or unreasonable to believe that the plaintiff's medical degree was the defendant's retirement plan. . . .

[Secondly,] we are concerned by the trial court's reference to the defendant's ability to sustain herself at a level to which she had become accustomed during the marriage. While an absence of need may be a customary criterion for determining the propriety of an award of alimony, this is an atypical case. "Need is to be satisfied if it can be, but those cases and the authorities on which [this rule] rests are not to be read as necessarily limiting alimony by the dependent spouse's need." Rosenberg v. Rosenberg, 33 Mass. App. 903, 904, 595 N.E.2d 792 (1992). The only reason the defendant was accustomed to a standard of living commensurate with her salary alone is that she had become the sole support of the family unit in order to allow the plaintiff an opportunity to attain his medical degree. In view of the foregoing factors, we conclude that the trial court abused its discretion by not awarding the defendant some alimony, thereby depriving her of any opportunity for future support. . . .

In concluding that alimony is a proper means of sharing the future earning of a spouse's advanced degree, we are supported by the conclusions of courts interpreting statutes similar to ours. . . .

Sound public policy militates in favor of using an alimony award rather than a property settlement in these circumstances. To conclude that the plaintiff's medical degree is property and to distribute it to the defendant as such would, in effect, sentence the plaintiff to a life of involuntary servitude in order to achieve the financial value that has been attributed to his degree. The plaintiff may become disabled, die or fail his medical boards and be precluded from the practice of medicine. He may chose an alternative career either within medicine or in an unrelated field or a career as a medical missionary, earning only a subsistence income. An award of alimony will allow the court to consider these changes if and when they occur. . . .

Finally, we recognize that a nominal alimony award may often be appropriate when the present circumstances will not support a substantial award. Nominal awards, however, are all that are necessary to afford the court continuing jurisdiction to make appropriate modifications. We have stated that "because some alimony was awarded, [one dollar per year] with no preclusion of modification, if the circumstances warrant, a change in the award can be obtained at some future date." Ridgeway v. Ridgeway, 180 Conn. 533, 543, 429 A.2d 801 (1980). Concededly, in this case, no significant alimony appears to have been warranted at the time of trial. This was particularly true because, at the time of dissolution, the defendant's salary was roughly equal to that of the plaintiff and, with further effort, could have been increased significantly. The failure to award any alimony at the time of trial, however, permanently precluded the defendant from seeking alimony at a future date should those circumstances change.

[T]he judgment is reversed in part and the case is remanded to the trial court for further proceedings consistent with this opinion.

## SELECTED SECTIONS OF THE CALIFORNIA FAMILY CODE

§ 752. Separate property; interest of parties.

Except as otherwise provided by statute, neither husband nor wife has any interest in the separate property of the other.

§ 760. Community property defined.

Except as otherwise provided by statute, all property, real or personal, wherever situated, acquired by a married person during the marriage while domiciled in this state is community property.

§ 770. Separate property of married person.

(a) Separate property of a married person includes all of the following:

(1) All property owned by the person before marriage.

(2) All property acquired by the person after marriage by gift, bequest, devise, or descent.

(3) The rents, issues, and profits of the property described in this section.

(b) A married person may, without the consent of the person's spouse, convey the person's separate property.

§ 2550. Manner of division of community estate.

Except upon the written agreement of the parties, . . . the court shall . . . divide the community estate of the parties equally.

§ 2641. Community contributions to education or training.

(a) "Community contributions to education or training" as used in this section means payments made with community ... property for education or training or for the repayment of a loan incurred for education or training. ...

(b) Subject to the limitations provided in this section, upon dissolution of marriage or legal separation of the parties:

(1) The community shall be reimbursed for community contributions to education or training of a party that substantially enhances the earning capacity of the party. ...

(2) A loan incurred during marriage for the education or training of a party shall not be included among the liabilities of the community for the purpose of division pursuant to this division but shall be assigned for payment by the party.

(c) The reimbursement and assignment required by this section shall be reduced or modified to the extent circumstances render such a disposition unjust, including, but not limited to, any of the following:

(1) The community has substantially benefited from the education, training, or loan incurred for the education or training of the party. There is a rebuttable presumption. affecting the burden of proof, that the community has not substantially benefited from community contributions to the education or training made less than 10 years before the commencement of the proceeding, and that the community has substantially benefited from community contributions to the education or training made more than 10 years before the commencement of the proceeding.

(2) The education or training received by the party is offset by the education or training received by the other party for which community contributions have been made.

(3) The education or training enables the party receiving the education or training to engage in gainful employment that substantially reduces the need of the party for support that would otherwise be required.

(d) Reimbursement for community contributions and assignment of loans pursuant to this section is the exclusive remedy of the community or a party for the education or training and any resulting enhancement of the earning capacity of a party. However, nothing in this subdivision limits consideration of the effect of the education, training, or enhancement, or the amount reimbursed pursuant to this section, on the circumstances of the parties for the purpose of an order for support pursuant to Section 4320.

(e) This section is subject to an express written agreement of the parties to the contrary.

§ 4320. Determination of amount due for support; considerations.

In ordering spousal support under this part, the court shall consider all of the following circumstances:

(a) The extent to which the earning capacity of each party is sufficient to maintain the standard of living established during the marriage, taking into account all of the following:

(1) The marketable skills of the supported party; the job market for those skills; the time and expenses required for the supported party to acquire the appropriate education or training to develop those skills; and the possible need for retraining or education to acquire other, more marketable skills or employment.

(2) The extent to which the supported party's present or future earning capacity is impaired by periods of unemployment that were incurred during the marriage to permit the supported party to devote time to domestic duties.

(b) The extent to which the supported party contributed to the attainment of an education, training, a career position, or a license by the supporting party.

(c) The ability of the supporting party to pay spousal support, taking into account the supporting party's earning capacity, earned and unearned income, assets, and standard of living.

(d) The needs of each party based on the standard of living established during the marriage.

(e) The obligations and assets, including the separate property, of each party.

(f) The duration of the marriage.

(g) The ability of the supported party to engage in gainful employment without unduly interfering with the interests of dependent children in the custody of the party.

(h) The age and health of the parties.

(i) Documented evidence of any history of domestic violence. . . .

(j) The immediate and specific tax consequences to each party.

(k) The balance of the hardships to each party.

(*l*) The goal that the supported party shall be self-supporting within a reasonable period of time. Except in the case of a marriage of long duration as described in Section 4336, a "reasonable period of time" for purposes of this section generally shall be one-half the length of the marriage. However, nothing in this section is intended to limit the court's discretion to order support for a greater or lesser length of time, based on any of the other factors listed in this section, Section 4336, and the circumstances of the parties.

(m) The criminal conviction of an abusive spouse shall be considered in making a reduction or elimination of a spousal support award in accordance with Section 4325.

(n) Any other factors the court determines are just and equitable.

## NOTES

1. *Marital property.* Are professional degrees and licenses distinguishable from disability and retirement pensions with respect to whether they should constitute marital property subject to division upon divorce? In what ways? Should vested benefits and unvested benefits be treated differently with respect to whether they should constitute marital property subject to division upon divorce? Why?[11] What should be the operative policies in deciding whether all of these non-traditional types of property interests should constitute marital property? Most law review articles take the position that human capital, including professional degrees, should be treated as property upon the dissolution of the marriage.[12] Yet, as indicated in *Simmons*, most courts have rejected this position. One can only speculate on the reason for this divergence.

2. *Methods of distribution.* The materials following the Principal Problem demonstrate some different approaches that have been employed to remedy the inequities present when one spouse works to support the other through school, and is handed a divorce decree on or shortly after the student spouse's graduation. In *O'Brien*, the highest court of New York opted to treat a spouse's medical license as marital property subject to equitable distribution. Its decision rested heavily on express statutory language requiring consideration of a spouse's contributions and services as a wage earner and homemaker "to the career or career potential of the other party." As noted above, however, this approach has been almost unanimously rejected by legislatures and courts alike. In fact, very recently O'Brien was statutorily reversed.The state statute now provides "The court shall not consider as marital property subject to distribution the value of a spouse's enhanced earning capacity arising from a license, degree, celebrity goodwill, or career enhancement. However, in arriving at an equitable division of marital property, the court shall consider the direct or indirect contributions to the development during marriage of the enhanced earning capacity of other other spouse."[13]

---

[11] Courts have found that unvested benefits are property subject to equitable distribution, and that as such, the unvested benefits should be considered during the division of property. See e.g., Daniel v. Daniel, 139 Ohio St. 3d 275, 11 N.E.3d 1119 (2014); Bender v. Bender, 258 Conn. 733, A.2d 197 (2001); Courtney v. Courtney 256 Ga. 97, 344 S.E.2d 421 (1986).

[12] See, e.g., Kelly, The Marital Partnership Pretense and Career Assets: The Ascendancy of Self Over the Marital Community, 81 B.U. L. Rev. 59 (2001); Keller, The Rhetoric of Marriage, Achievement, and Power: An Analysis of Judicial Opinions Considering the Treatment of Professional Degrees as Marital Property, 21 Ver. L. Rev. 408 (1996); Davis, Enhanced Earning Capacity/Human Capital: The Reluctance to Call It Property, 17 Women's Rts. L. Rep. 109 (1996).

[13] NY Legis 269 (2915) 2015 Sess. Law News of N.Y Ch. 269 (A.7645)(McKinney 2015).

Another way of addressing this situation is to award the working spouse reimbursement maintenance, or periodic payments designed to compensate for his or her contributions to the student spouse's education. What sort of contributions should be considered in fixing the award? In *Simmons*, the court addressed only financial contributions, implying that homemaking and child-rearing services should not to be considered in fixing an award of reimbursement maintenance. The California Family Code § 2641(a) takes the same approach. Should a reimbursement award include compensation for these services? Should the award take into consideration the income the family would have received had the student spouse worked instead of attending school? What about the educational or vocational opportunities the working spouse passed up to support the student spouse?[14]

Finally, some courts address this situation by increasing the working spouse's property settlement and/or maintenance award to reflect the increased future earning potential attributable to the student spouse's degree or license. In contrast, the *Simmons* court held that maintenance would be appropriate although need was not shown because the non-student spouse would be unable to support herself in the future due to her age.[15] Taking another approach, the California Family Code requires equal property division, but allows the enhanced earning capacity of the student spouse to be considered in fixing an award of spousal maintenance. Which alternative is best? Can you think of any other viable methods of compensation?

3. *Valuation problems.* Those few courts which have distributed the value of degrees and licenses on divorce have generally computed the difference between the lifetime earnings expectancy of a licensed person and that of an unlicensed person. Part of this difference is then awarded to the unlicensed spouse, after that amount is discounted to present value.[16] However, most courts are disinclined to treat a professional degree or license as marital property because of the many problems triggered by such valuation attempts. For example, should the institution which awarded the degree be considered in fixing its value? How does the degree holder's relative performance figure into the value of his or her degree? Will the degree holder live and work to age sixty-five? Will he or she become disabled? These and similar questions require speculation in which very few courts are willing to indulge, especially where these questions can be avoided by relying on alternative remedies, such as reimbursement and spousal maintenance.

---

[14] For cases that explore several approaches to these questions, see Myer v. Myer, 620 N.W.2d 382 (Wis. 2000), Haugan v. Haugan, 343 N.W.2d 796 (Wis.1984).

[15] Another Connecticut court declined to award alimony for contributions to a medical degree that had been earned more than twenty years before the divorce, because the value of the degree was reflected in the assets that the couple had acquired. Bartels v. Bartels, 858 A.2d 879 (Conn. App. 2004).

[16] The present value of a future payment is the amount of money that must be invested today in order for the investment plus interest earned thereon to equal the amount of the future payment by the time the future payment is to be made.

4. *Forced career paths.* Will treating a degree or license as marital property force the student spouse into an undesired career path? How might this concern be addressed?

5. *Professional degrees compared to licenses and other forms of human capital.* Should professional degrees be treated the same as licenses for purposes of distributing marital property on divorce? Should undergraduate degrees be treated the same as graduate degrees? Should training, experience or reputation acquired during the marriage but not represented by a degree or license be considered marital property?

6. *Same sex marriages and property rights.* In 2015, the United States Supreme Court substantially changed the definition of marriage in *Obergefell v. Hodges*.[17] In this case, the Court legalized same-sex marriage and rendered the Defense of Marriage Act (DOMA) unconstitutional. Prior to the Court's decision, 37 states had legalized same-sex marriage. Post *Obergefell*, the laws governing property division, which once applied only to heterosexual couples, now apply to all married couples. The parameters of this decision regarding property issues facing same-sex couples will likely be developed in future case law.

---

[17] 576 U.S. ___, 135 S.Ct. 2584 (2015).

# IV. NON-POSSESSORY INTERESTS (SERVITUDES)

## A. EASEMENTS

## ASSIGNMENT 18

# EXPRESS EASEMENTS: CLASSIFICATION AND MANNER OF CREATION

## 1. INTRODUCTION

*The Concept of Servitudes*

Interests in real property can be classified as either possessory or non-possessory. The owner of a possessory interest has a present or potential right to the possession of real property. In contrast, the owner of a non-possessory interest has certain rights in real property possessed by another person. Some of these non-possessory rights are called "servitudes."[1] The land owned or possessed by one party "serves" another party.

The law of servitudes has become increasingly important in recent years. Most new residential developments make extensive use of servitudes. Usually all of the houses in a subdivision of single family houses are subject to servitudes of various types. For example, each owner of a house in a subdivision may have the right, by virtue of an agreement, to prevent her neighbor from using his property for anything but residential purposes. Such a right in the land of her neighbor is one type of servitude, a "restrictive covenant" or "equitable servitude." All of the lot owners in the subdivision may be required, by virtue of an agreement, to make monthly or annual payments to be used for the maintenance of common facilities, such as tennis courts or bike paths, that are maintained by a homeowners' association. This type of servitude is called an "affirmative covenant." Within the subdivision, various utility companies are likely to have easements permitting them to lay pipes and wires across land owned and possessed by others. These, too, are a form of servitude denoted as an "affirmative easement."

Condominiums, whether residential or commercial, have a legal structure that depends on the law of servitudes. Each owner of a unit or

---

[1] Among the non-possessory rights that are not classified as "servitudes" are those rights protected by the law of private nuisance (Assignment 28).

apartment within the condominium promises to pay for the maintenance of the condominium and to regulate his conduct in accordance with the rules governing the condominium. Each owner of a condominium unit has rights against the other owners. Each owner is both benefited and burdened by servitudes.

The legal structure of the modern shopping center also extensively uses the law of servitudes. Regardless of whether the retail stores in the center lease or buy the land that they occupy, each store will require rights of access and parking throughout the center. By means of agreements concluded with the developer and others, each store will have specified rights to control the conduct of the other occupants of the center. These rights take the form of various types of servitudes.

Servitudes usually arise from formal agreements evidenced by written documents. The law governing servitudes is governed more by property concepts, however, than by contract law. In this regard, the obligation of a servitude usually "runs with the land." That is, the creator of the servitude usually is responsible for complying with the servitude only while he or she owns the land. A subsequent owner of the land (the successor to the creator of the servitude), is usually required to comply with the servitude despite the fact that she never expressly agreed to comply. Similarly, the benefit of a servitude often runs with the land benefited by the servitude. In many cases, the holder of an easement or other servitude can use it only while owning or possessing the land benefited by the easement, and the new owner of the land benefited can enforce the servitude even if there is no express assignment of the benefit to her.

Easements, real covenants and equitable servitudes are among the most important types of servitudes.[2] In recent years, many authorities have suggested that these three types of servitudes should largely lose their separate identity and be governed by the same terminology and rules of law.[3] In this casebook, however, we will examine easements before considering real covenants and equitable servitudes. The law of easements is relatively stable and simple. Thus, it is preferable to study easements before proceeding to the more complex and evolving rules governing covenants.

---

[2] Two other types of servitudes are profits and licenses. A profit is the right to take material such as soil or wood from the land of another. In general, the law governing profits corresponds to that governing easements. A license resembles an affirmative easement. The licensee has the right to enter on and use land possessed by another. For example, one may have the right to hunt on another's land, or one may purchase a license (a "ticket") to view a performance in a theater. However, a license is usually revocable at the will of the possessor of the land, whereas an easement is of a more permanent nature. See Restatement of Property § 519 (1944). Although the possessor of land may have the power to revoke the license, she may be liable for damages for a wrongful revocation.

[3] Restatement (Third) of Property (Servitudes), Introduction (2000).

*Easements*

The Restatement of Property § 450 (1944)[4] defines an easement as follows:

An easement is an interest in land in the possession of another which

(a) entitles the owner of such interest to a limited use or enjoyment of the land in which the interest exists;

(b) entitles him to protection as against third persons from interference in such use or enjoyment;

(c) is not subject to the will of the possessor of the land;

(d) is not a normal incident of the possession of any land possessed by the owner of the interest; and

(e) is capable of creation by conveyance.[5]

The land subject to the easement (i.e., burdened by the easement) is called the servient estate. The land benefited by the easement, if any, is called the dominant estate.

> EXAMPLE 1: *Dominant and servient estates.* Alice owns Blackacre and Ben owns Whiteacre. Alice grants Ben a right of way easement that permits Ben to use a road across Blackacre to get to Whiteacre. Whiteacre is the dominant estate; Blackacre is the servient estate. Blackacre is burdened by the easement; Whiteacre is benefited.

*Affirmative and Negative Easements*

Easements are classified as either affirmative or negative. The holder of an affirmative easement has the right to do things which, were it not for the easement, she would not be permitted to do.[6] The holder of a negative easement may, by virtue of the easement, prevent the possessor of the land burdened by the easement from performing acts upon the land that he would otherwise have a legal right to perform.[7]

> EXAMPLE 2: *Affirmative easement.* Carl owns Blackacre and Whiteacre. Carl grants Blackacre to Denise, reserving for Carl the right to use the road crossing Blackacre in order to have access to Whiteacre. Carl has reserved an affirmative easement.

> EXAMPLE 3: *Negative easement.* Ellie owns a house on Whiteacre and is afraid that Frank, who owns the adjoining

---

[4] The Restatement (Third) of Property (Servitudes) § 1.2 defines easement as follows: "An easement creates a nonpossessory right to enter and use land in the possession of another and obligates the possessor not to interfere with the uses authorized by the easement.... The burden of an easement... is always appurtenant. The benefit may be either appurtenant or in gross.... As used in this Restatement, the term "easement" includes an irrevocable license to enter and use land in the possession of another and excludes a negative easement." This definition is not inconsistent with the Restatement of Property § 450 (1944) definition.

[5] Requirement (e) does not appear in the Restatement (Third) of Property (Servitudes) § 1.2 (2000).

[6] Restatement (Third) of Property (Servitudes) § 1.2 cmt. a (2000).

[7] Restatement (Third) of Property (Servitudes) § 1.3(2) (2000).

parcel, Blackacre, will build a structure on Blackacre that will block the flow of light and air to Ellie's windows. Ellie pays $5,000 for an easement by which Frank agrees to build no structure on his property that will cut off the flow of light and air to Ellie's windows. Ellie has a negative easement in Blackacre, the servient estate. Ellie has the right to restrict Frank's use of the servient estate. Since Ellie only has the right to prevent Frank from using Frank's land in certain ways, and Ellie has no additional right under the easement to do anything on Frank's land, Ellie's easement is negative rather than affirmative.

Neither negative nor affirmative easements require any affirmative act by the owner of the servient estate. Under both types of easement the owner of the servient estate merely refrains from interfering with the rights of the easement holder. An affirmative easement is affirmative because it permits the holder of the easement to do something on the servient land that otherwise would not be allowed. A negative easement is negative because it prevents the possessor of the servient estate from doing something that otherwise would be allowed. A negative easement does not authorize an affirmative act on the servient land by the owner of the easement.

EXAMPLE 4: *Affirmative easement.* George has an easement to enter upon Heather's land. Heather has no affirmative duty to act. Heather's sole duty is to refrain from interfering with George's right of entry. George has an affirmative easement.

EXAMPLE 5: *Negative easement.* Isaac has an easement of light and air over Joan's land. Joan has no affirmative duty to act. Joan's sole duty is to refrain from interfering with Isaac's right to light and air. Isaac's easement is negative since the easement does not entitle Isaac to perform any act on Joan's land.

In early times, negative easements were limited to 1) easements protecting the flow of light or air in a defined channel, 2) lateral or subjacent support of a building on the land of the easement holder, and 3) easements protecting the flow of an artificial stream to the land of the holder of the easement. Today, negative easements (with the exception of conservation easements) are considered restrictive covenants.[8] We will examine restrictive covenants in Assignment 24.

*Appurtenant or In Gross*

Easements are classified as "appurtenant" or "in gross." These terms help to describe the people who may benefit from the easement. They do not describe the person or property burdened by the easement.

*Appurtenant.* All of the easements described in the previous examples are appurtenant easements, because they attach to and benefit

---

[8] Restatement (Third) of Property (Servitudes) § 1.3(3) (2000).

a particular parcel of land. That parcel is called the dominant estate. When the dominant estate is transferred, any easement appurtenant to it automatically passes with it. Similarly, an appurtenant easement cannot be conveyed without simultaneously transferring the dominant estate. Just as the tail must follow the dog, an appurtenant easement must follow the dominant estate.

The competent draftsperson who intends to create an appurtenant easement will expressly designate the easement as appurtenant to a described dominant estate. Unfortunately, in many cases the creating instrument does not describe the easement as either appurtenant or in gross. In such cases, the courts will determine the nature of the easement from the surrounding circumstances. If the recipient of the easement owned a nearby parcel of land that would benefit from the easement, it is presumed that an appurtenant easement was created unless there is strong evidence to the contrary. There are three reasons for this presumption of appurtenancy. First, since most easements are intended to be appurtenant, it is reasonable to assume that the questioned easement was also so intended, at least in the absence of contrary evidence. Second, since an appurtenant easement passes automatically with a grant of the dominant estate, a finding of appurtenancy tends to protect the grantee of that estate from the consequences of an inadvertent failure to include a separate grant of an easement with a grant of the fee. Third, any detriment to the servient estate is usually offset by a benefit to the dominant estate. This offset would not exist if the easement were in gross.

*In Gross.* Easements in gross do not attach to and benefit a particular parcel of land. They may be personal to the easement owner. English law does not recognize easements in gross.[9] Under American law, however, affirmative easements in gross are fairly common.

> EXAMPLE 6: *Affirmative easement in gross.* Kurt, the owner of Blackacre, grants an easement across Blackacre to a railroad company. The railroad company does not own any land in the area. Since the easement is not appurtenant to any parcel, it is an easement in gross.

*Conservation Easements*

Despite the common law's failure to recognize negative easements in gross and the tendency to treat servitudes restricting uses of property as covenants, all states and territories now have statutes authorizing the creation of conservation easements. A conservation easement is "a legal agreement between a landowner and a land trust or government agency that permanently limits uses of the land in order to protect its

---

[9] See Restatement (Third) of Property (Servitudes) § 1.5 Reporter's Notes (2000); Sturley, The "Land Obligation": An English Proposal for Reform, 55 S.Cal.L.Rev. 1417, 1428 (1982).

conservation values."[10] The Uniform Conservation Easement Act (UCEA) provides the following more detailed definition of conservation easement: "a nonpossessory interest of a holder in real property imposing limitations or affirmative obligations the purposes of which include retaining or protecting natural, scenic, or open-space use, protecting natural resources, maintaining or enhancing air or water quality, or preserving the historical, architectural, archaeological, or cultural aspects of property."[11] About half of the state statutes are patterned after the UCEA.[12]

Conservation easements are express in-gross negative easements: property interests in restricting the uses of servient estates. Conservation easements can also impose affirmative obligations on servient estate owners to achieve the easements' intended conservation purposes. These purposes might include removing invasive species, fencing the land and excluding others, maintaining historic structures in good repair, and allowing public access and periodic inspections. The typical conservation easement perpetually restricts the use and development of the land to those activities consistent with the easement's stated conservation purposes. The easement is recorded in the deed records so that all subsequent holders of property interests in the land are bound by it (i.e., it runs with the land). The landowner and his or her successors continue to own, use, possess, and transfer the servient estate, but are subject to the restrictions (and affirmative obligations) in the conservation easement.

Notwithstanding the general features of conservation easements, this area of law contains significant variation. For example, authorized holders of conservation easements include large national land trusts focused on ecological conservation goals, such as The Nature Conservancy,[13] state agencies seeking to preserve prime agricultural lands from development, such as the Kentucky Division of Conservation's Purchase of Agricultural Conservation Easements (PACE) program,[14] and local historic preservation organizations that hold conservation easements in historic structures and facades, such as the L'Enfant Trust in Washington, D.C.[15] State and territorial statutes vary regarding who may hold conservation easements, their permissible or mandatory

---

[10] Land Trust Alliance, Conserving Your Land Protects Communities, http://www.landtrustalliance.org/conserve/how-to-conserve-your-land-1/ (last visited July 27, 2010).

[11] Uniform Conservation Easement Act, 12 U.L.A. 170 § 1(1) (1996).

[12] Some states adopted conservation easement statutes prior to the UCEA's promulgation. See, e.g., Cal. Gov't Code § 6953 (2008) (enacted 1959); N.Y. Gen. Mun. Law § 247 (1999) (enacted 1960).

[13] For more information regarding The Nature Conservancy, see The Nature Conservancy, http://www.nature.org (last visited Mar. 29, 2010).

[14] See Kentucky Division of Conservation, Purchase of Agricultural Conservation Easements (PACE), http://conservation.ky.gov/Pages/PACE.aspx (last visited June 14, 2015).

[15] For more information regarding L'Enfant Trust, see L'Enfant Trust: Voluntary Preservation Through Conservation Easements, http://www.lenfant.org/ (last visited July 27, 2010).

length, and the purposes for which conservation easements may be created.[16] While conservation easements may be donated by private land owners, they also may be sold to qualified grantees or may even be imposed on land owners by government agencies as conditions of land-use or environmental regulatory permits (i.e., as exactions, discussed in Assignments 31–32). State legislation authorizing conservation easements fills a void left by the common law.[17]

The actual practice of conservation easement creation is driven in large part by federal tax policy that recognizes the public benefits of privately donated conservation easements. The Internal Revenue Code grants charitable tax deductions and estate tax benefits for donations of "qualified real property interests," including perpetual conservation easements, to "qualified organizations," which may be government agencies or certain charitable organizations.[18] The conservation easement must be perpetual and it must be exclusively for conservation purposes, which are defined as follows: 1) preservation of land for outdoor recreation or education; 2) protection of natural habitats for fish and wildlife; 3) preservation of open space; and 4) preservation of historic land and structures.[19]

The primary reason for according favorable tax treatment to conservation easements is that they achieve environmental conservation and historic/cultural preservation goals that could not be achieved solely by government regulation or government acquisitions of property.[20] However, critics suggest that these "private" conservation efforts supplant regulation.[21] While conservation easements are privately—and usually voluntarily—created restrictions on land use for conservation

---

[16] See, e.g., Ala. Code § 35–18–1(1) (2009) (including protection of silvicultural resources and paleontological conditions as appropriate conservation easement purposes); Ala. Code § 35–18–2(c) (limiting length of conservation easements to 30 years or life of the grantor); Kan. Stat. Ann. § 58–3811(d) (2008) (limiting length of conservation easements to life of the grantor); Miss. Code Ann. § 89–19–3(2)(b) (1999) (authorizing private and educational corporations to hold conservation easements); N.M. Stat. Ann. § 47–12–2(A) (2003) (precluding government agencies from holding conservation easements).

[17] But see United States v. Blackman, 270 Va. 68, 613 S.E.2d 442 (2005) (involving a rare case in which the Virginia Supreme Court recognized a conservation easement created prior to the enactment of state legislation).

[18] See generally Internal Revenue Code, 26 U.S.C. §§ 170(h), 501(c)(3). See also 26 C.F.R. § 1.170A–14 (2009).

[19] 26 C.F.R. § 1.170A–14(d). With the potential for landowners to claim highly inflated deductions for conservation easements, retain use and development rights that are incompatible with conservation, or create "shell" land trusts to facilitate land development by "holding" value-generating environmental amenities, both the I.R.S. and state agencies are giving conservation transactions increasing scrutiny. See, e.g., Lay, Conservation Easement Conundrums: Colorado and Other Western States Crack Down on Abusers, High Country News, Mar. 31, 2008.

[20] Cheever & McLaughlin, Why Environmental Lawyers Should Know (and Care) About Land Trusts and Their Private Land Conservation Transactions, 34 Envtl. L. Rep. 10223 (2004); Morrissette, Conservation Easements and the Public Good: Preserving the Environment on Private Lands, 41 Nat. Resources J. 373 (2001).

[21] Echeverria, Regulating versus Paying Land Owners to Protect the Environment, 26 J. Land Resources & Envtl. L. 1 (2005).

purposes, they have significant foundations in public policy and government support.

*Creation of Express Easements*

Sometimes an easement is created by operation of law, without the benefit of any written document or other express agreement. This type of easement is considered in Assignment 23. In most cases, however, easements are created by a written instrument. Usually the writing takes the form of either a "grant" of an easement to the grantee, or a "reservation" of an easement in favor of the grantor who conveys a fee or other interest to another.

> EXAMPLE 7: *Grant of easement.* Lisa, the owner of Blackacre, *grants* Matt a right of way easement across it. The grant is in the form usually used for the conveyance of a fee to real estate, except that an easement is conveyed rather than a fee. Matt now has a right of way easement across Blackacre, created by grant.
>
> EXAMPLE 8: *Reservation of easement.* Nina, the owner of Blackacre and Whiteacre, grants Whiteacre to Orin, *reserving* a right of way across Whiteacre in favor of Nina. Nina now has a right of way over Whiteacre, created by reservation.

Easements created by grant or reservation must comply with the usual formalities for the creation or transfer of an interest in real property. Ordinarily they must be in writing and signed by the grantor of the easement or of the estate from which the reservation is carved.

In creating an interest in real property, it is essential that the drafter clearly specify whether an easement or some other interest, such as a fee or leasehold, is being created. Moreover, as illustrated in the following material, the drafter should avoid transferring a fee to a grantee while simultaneously attempting to create an easement in a person other than the grantor or grantee.

Since similar formalities are required to grant an express easement and a fee, it is often unclear whether a fee or an easement was created. In construing the grant, the court attempts to give effect to the intention of the parties by carefully examining the words of the grant in the light of the circumstances existing when the grant was made. Consider, for example, the following problem.

## 2. PRINCIPAL PROBLEM

Al Fizzey owns a large parcel of farmland, the front end of which adjoins a public highway. After several years of farming, Al decides that his real calling is to become a lawyer. Not needing all of the acreage he had used for farming, Al decides to split his tract of land and to sell one of the parcels. Al decides to retain the back half of the master tract (Parcel B), where he had built his farmhouse, and to put the tract of land bordering the local highway (Parcel A) up for sale. Both tracts have access to the public highway system. However, a paved private road passes over the middle of Parcel A to Parcel B which is more convenient to use, and is a wider, safer road than the dirt road that leads from the public highway to the back parcel. For many years Al has utilized this private road to travel from the farmhouse to the highway.

After several months on the market, Al finally sells Parcel A to Barbara Trone. Al offers Parcel A for $400,000 but suggests that Barbara can buy the property for $390,000 if Barbara will agree to permit him use of the road that intersects Parcel A. Barbara accepts the $390,000 price with the condition pertaining to Al's use of the paved private road. Al drafts and delivers a deed to Parcel A that provides, in pertinent part, that "Al Fizzey, grantor, hereby conveys Parcel A to Barbara Trone, grantee, reserving and excepting, however, the road that intersects Parcel A and links Parcel B to the highway bordering Parcel A. Furthermore, grantee may erect fences bordering roadway but must refrain from erecting gates that will impede access to the abovementioned paved private road." Barbara pays the $390,000 and accepts and records the deed.

While in the process of constructing her house, Barbara discovers that there is coal under her property. Al hears of this and demands that he be compensated for any coal removed from under "his" road. Barbara refuses, claiming that Al is entitled to nothing.

Among other things, consider the following cases in evaluating Al's chances of recovering from Barbara for any coal removed from under the road.

If you were representing Al when the deed was drafted, what language would you have used in the deed to avoid this controversy? What if you were representing Barbara when the deed was drafted?

## 3. MATERIALS FOR SOLUTION OF PRINCIPAL PROBLEM

### Northwest Realty Co. v. Jacobs
Supreme Court of South Dakota, 1978.
273 N.W.2d 141.

■ ZASTROW, JUSTICE.

Northwest Realty Co. (plaintiff) sought an injunction requiring Ted and Olive Jacobs (defendants) to remove large amounts of fill dirt from the property in dispute. Defendants counter-claimed seeking a judgment quieting title to the property in them and enjoining the plaintiff from interfering with defendants' use and enjoyment of the property in question. From the judgment in favor of plaintiff, defendants appeal. We reverse.

The facts of this case were stipulated to between the parties and are essentially as follows. The Iowa Irrigation Ditch Company (Iowa Ditch) was incorporated in 1895. Its articles of incorporation provided as follows:

> This company is formed for the purpose of locating, constructing and maintaining dams, ditches and flumes for the purpose of conducting the waters of Rapid Creek out upon the land in Pennington County, South Dakota, for irrigation purposes, milling and domestic use.

Iowa Ditch then began to obtain quitclaim deeds along the course of the proposed irrigation ditch. The various deeds obtained range from unconditional fees to easements with "reverter to grantor" clauses. Several tracts of land which the ditch crossed had no conveyances of record to Iowa Ditch.

On April 26, 1898, Jacob A.C. Smith (Smith) executed and delivered a quitclaim deed to Iowa Ditch which is shown in the records of the register of deeds as follows:

KNOW ALL MEN BY THESE PRESENTS:

That *Jacob A.C. Smith* of the County of *Pennington* in the *State of South Dakota,* party of the first part, in consideration of the sum of *Fifty* Dollars in hand paid by *The Iowa Irrigation Ditch Company a Corporation with its principal office at Rapid City,* County of *Pennington* and *State of South Dakota,* party of the second part, the receipt whereof is hereby acknowledged, do hereby grant, remise, release and *quit-claim* unto the said party of the second part, *its successors* and assigns forever, *all his estate,* right, title, *interest, claim, property and demand, of, in and to the following real property,* situate in the County of Pennington, State of South Dakota, and described as follows:

> *A Strip of land not exceeding forty (40) feet in width following the course of the survey of the Iowa Irrigation Ditch Co. as shown by the recorded plat thereof across lot four (4) Section five, (5) in Township One (1) North of Range Eight (8) East B.H.M. to be used as a right of way for an Irrigation Ditch.*
>
> *It is hereby agreed as a further consideration for payment of this right of way, that the party of the second part will furnish water at the regular established price fixed by said second party, for the purpose of irrigating all the land owned by the party of the first part, as soon as the ditch contains water that can be used for this purpose, and the party of the second part also agrees to place a bridge over said ditch at such place as the party of the first part may demand.*

TO HAVE AND TO HOLD the same, together with all the hereditaments and appurtenances thereunto in anywise appertaining.

WITNESS my hand and seal this 26*th* day of *April* A.D. *1898.*

*Jacob A.C. Smith (SEAL)*[22]

The recorded plat referred to in the deed shows only the location of a single line of the proposed ditch.

Shares of stock were issued to the owners of each tract of land irrigated from the ditch. Tom Phillips, a successor in interest to Smith, held three shares in the Iowa Ditch Corporation. Those three shares were assigned by the only heir of Phillips to the defendants on January 1, 1977.

In the flood of June 9, 1972, the head gate of the ditch was destroyed and portions of the ditch itself were severely damaged. On January 4, 1973, the stockholders of Iowa Ditch, finding the expense of reconstructing the ditch prohibitive, voted to dissolve the corporation and deliver quitclaim deeds to the stockholders who owned property adjacent to the ditch which was subject to easements for the ditch.

On February 12, 1973, the directors of the corporation adopted a resolution to convey "the real property owned by the corporation" to Kenneth Shabina and four others. At a stockholders' meeting, a similar resolution was adopted. A quitclaim deed to the property in question was issued to Shabina, who in turn conveyed it to plaintiff.

The land on either side of the ditch which had been owned by Smith was eventually replatted as Lots 5 and 6 of Campbell Square Addition to the City of Rapid City. Defendants acquired Lot 6 on October 19, 1973, and Lot 5 on January 24, 1975.

After acquiring the lots, defendants filled a portion of the ditch; part of the former ditch is now a paved parking area used in defendant's automobile dealership. Plaintiff subsequently brought this action, claiming fee title to the ditch, to have defendants remove the fill from the ditch.

The issue to be determined in this appeal is whether the Smith-Iowa Ditch deed conveyed a fee title or only a right-of-way easement.

The quitclaim deed in question contains a clause granting all of Smith's interest in the strip of property, SDCL 43–25–10, 43–25–11, and a description of the property which restricts the grant to an easement for a right-of-way, SDCL 43–13–1. Because of the inconsistency of these clauses, it is necessary to use established rules of construction to aid in ascertaining the grantor's intention.

The paramount rule of construction is that the intention of the parties, and the grantor in particular, is to be ascertained by a fair consideration of the entire instrument and the language therein, without undue emphasis on any particular part or provision of the document.

Words are to be construed in context and a construction should be adopted which gives effect to all words. Each word and provision should

---

[22] The handwritten material is italicized.

be given that significance which is consistent with, and will effectuate the manifest intention of the parties.

Furthermore, a grant is to be construed in favor of the grantee, SDCL 43–4–16, 26 C.J.S. Deeds § 82e; 23 Am.Jur.2d Deeds § 165; 4 Tiffany on Real Property (3rd ed.) § 978; 2 Thompson 319; 3 Powell 407; and a fee simple title is presumed to be intended to pass by a grant of real property *unless it appears from the grant that a lesser estate was intended.* SDCL 43–25–15; 26 C.J.S. Deeds § 104c; 23 Am.Jur.2d Deeds § 165; 4 Tiffany on Real Property § 978. Where the term "right of way" is used in a deed it usually indicates that only an easement or a right of passage is being conveyed or reserved. In such a case the instrument should be construed as conveying an easement unless the instrument, considered as a whole, indicates that the parties intended the passage of fee title.

If, however, construction of the instrument as a whole leaves the intention of the parties in doubt, consideration must be given to the situation and circumstances of the parties at the time of the execution of the deed in order to determine what was within their contemplation at that time.

The resolution of the problem of determining whether a deed intended to convey a fee simple title or an easement involves the consideration of the following factors: (1) the amount of consideration; (2) the particularity of the description of the property conveyed; (3) the extent of the limitation upon the use of the property; (4) the type of interest which best serves the manifested purpose of the parties; (5) the peculiarities of wording used in the conveyance document; (6) to whom the property was assessed and who paid the taxes on the property; and (7) how the parties to the conveyance, or the heirs or assigns, have treated the property.

The record shows that Smith had acquired the entirety of Lot 4 consisting of 41 acres for $120 seven months prior to the grant in question. In comparison, it may appear that the consideration given is more than nominal and is evidence of an intent to grant an estate in fee to Iowa Ditch. However, the consideration is not inconsistent with a perpetual easement of an irregular irrigation ditch that divides the property by a meandering trench.

The degree of precision of the description of the strip of land is lacking and is much more indicative of a grant of easement than a fee. The plat of the survey for the irrigation ditch is simply a single line crossing several parcels of property. It does not indicate the width or final location of the proposed ditch.

The description in the deed indicates that it is not to exceed 40 feet along the course of the survey. The line on the survey is not designated as the center line, and, therefore, the actual ditch could be 40 feet on either side of that line. Easements do not require a definite statement of their width, dimensions, or exact location. The conveyance of fee title, however, requires a reasonable certainty of the boundaries.

The wording of the deed purports to grant the property to Iowa Ditch and "its successors and assigns forever." These words of inheritance and succession, although not required by statutes (SDCL 43–25–4, formerly C.L. 1887, § 3241), were considered at common law equally necessary to create either a fee simple title or a perpetual easement. 25 Am.Jur.2d, Easements § 100; 23 Am.Jur.2d, Deeds, § 38. The use of this phrase is of no assistance in determining the intent of the grantor.

The deed recites that Smith did "grant . . . all of his estate, right, title, interest, claim, property and demand, of, and to . . . a strip of land . . . across lot four . . . to be used as a right of way for an irrigation ditch." Although use of the terms "over and across," "across," or "over" when used alone in a deed does not imply an easement, Kynerd v. Hulen, 1925, (5 Cir.), 5 F.2d 160, when used in conjunction with a restriction of the use as a right-of-way, it is considered to be evidence that an easement was intended.

In considering the restrictions upon the use of the property conveyed, the deed quite clearly restricts the use to a right-of-way for irrigation purposes. In addition, it provides that part of the consideration of the grant is the providing of irrigation water for grantor's land "as soon as the ditch contains water." There seems to be little doubt that the grantor's intention was to restrict the use of the strip of land to that of an irrigation ditch and irrigation purposes.

The final factor to be considered is whether the rights granted will be best served by an easement or a fee estate for the manifested purpose of the parties. Certainly, a perpetual easement would provide Iowa Ditch with all the rights necessary for the construction and repair of an irrigation ditch. The indefiniteness of the location of the strip could allow the corporation to deviate from the course of the original construction as might be necessitated by future events. The latitude of an easement would appear to suit the requirements of Iowa Ditch more than the original construction area, which title would be restricted to if a fee simple were intended.

The indefinite but restricted width and meandering length of the grant suggests that any use other than that of an irrigation ditch is unlikely.

Consequently we hold that the Smith-Iowa Ditch deed only conveyed a right-of-way easement. The deed contained no specific measurement of the property conveyed. The granting of an easement was consistent with the needs of Iowa Ditch as is the language in the instrument and the use of the land. In addition, Iowa Ditch never paid the property taxes on the strip of land. These factors and the public policy discouraging separate ownership on narrow strips of land, Abbott v. Pearson, 1975, 257 Ark. 694, 520 S.W.2d 204, require reversal of the judgment of the trial court.

## Greaves v. McGee
Supreme Court of Alabama, 1986.
492 So.2d 307.

■ HOUSTON, JUSTICE.

This is a dispute over mineral rights. The appellees, Willard McGee, Rachel McGee, and McGee, Ltd., a limited partnership, filed a complaint for a declaratory judgment in the Circuit Court of Lamar County against Peyton Greaves and the Lamar County Commission, seeking to establish their ownership of the minerals underlying a public road which crosses their land. The appellant, Greaves, counterclaimed for a declaratory judgment to establish his right to the minerals in question. The case was tried before the court, which found for the appellees. Lamar County has not appealed. We affirm.

The trial court made the following findings of fact:

1. On May 25, 1926, W.C. York acquired title to the Northeast Quarter of the Northeast Quarter and the East One-Half of the Southeast Quarter of the Northeast Quarter of Section 24, Township 16 South, Range 16 West, Lamar County, Alabama, from J.G. Gault and wife by virtue of deed recorded in Deed Book 53, Page 56, in the records in the Office of the Judge of Probate of Lamar County, Alabama.

On September 18, 1928, W.C. York and wife executed an instrument in favor of Lamar County, Alabama, the same being attached hereto as Exhibit 'A.' [That deed is set out later in this opinion.]

The instrument referred to in the court's findings as Exhibit "A" reads, in pertinent part, as follows:

KNOW ALL MEN BY THESE PRESENTS, That for and in consideration of ONE DOLLAR ($1.00) in hand paid to the undersigned grantors W.C. York and wife by the Commissioner's Court of Lamar County, the receipt whereof is hereby acknowledged, and for the further consideration that Lamar County, through the Court of County Commissioners, shall locate and maintain a public highway of second grade along and through our land, we do hereby release, quitclaim and convey to the County of Lamar, a body corporate, for the use and purpose of maintaining a public highway, all of our right, title, interest and claim in and to the following strip of land twenty feet wide to be used for the purpose of constructing a road of second grade through the following described real estate, to-wit:

A right of way for public road twenty feet in width described as follows: S 1/2 of SE 1/4 of SE 1/4 of SE 1/4, Section 13, T. 16, R. 16, West. Also NE 1/4 of NE 1/4 and the East 15 acres of SE

1/4 of NE 1/4, Section 24, T. 16, R. 16 West. Also SW 1/4 of NW 1/4, Section 19, T. 16, R. 15 West.

Said strip of land so conveyed is intended to be a strip through any land that said road is now located on, or may hereafter be located on by Lamar County, its agents, officers or its engineer....

... TO HAVE AND TO HOLD unto Lamar County, a body corporate, forever, for the purpose of maintaining and operating a public road, or highway.

The Lamar County Commission executed an oil, gas and mineral lease in favor of Greaves which purports to cover the lands described in the instrument from W.C. York and wife in favor of Lamar County.

The dispositive issue in this case is whether the Yorks conveyed a fee simple interest in a strip of their land to Lamar County or simply a right of way across their land. If a fee simple interest was conveyed, then the judgment of the trial court would have to be reversed. The appellant would have the right to the minerals by virtue of his oil, gas, and mineral lease from Lamar County. If only a right of way was conveyed, then the judgment would have to be affirmed.

In *Brashier v. Burkett,* 350 So.2d 309 (Ala.1977), the Court stated:

It is a fundamental precept of property law that courts should construe instruments so as to give effect to the intent of the parties. Ala.Code, Tit. 47, §§ 17, 23 (1940); *Stratford v. Lattimer,* 255 Ala. 201, 50 So.2d 420 (1951). Yet, any court undertaking the dissection of such an instrument in order to ascertain the intent of the parties is faced with a task which, by its very nature, is plagued with the difficulties and uncertainties that necessarily accompany any probe into mental processes. Fortunately, however, the burden placed on the courts in scrutinizing deeds is facilitated by a body of judicially and legislatively created guidelines for the construction of deeds conveying property. Initially, the court should seek to ascertain the intention of the parties by looking to the entire instrument. Tit. 47, §§ 17, 23, Code of Alabama 1940; *Stratford v. Lattimer, supra.* The court should be careful to try to give meaning to every clause and provision of the instrument. Second, the court should look to the factual situation and the circumstances existing at the time the instrument was created. Finally, the court may look to the subsequent acts of the parties to determine the correct construction of the instrument.

For the following reasons, we hold that the Yorks conveyed only a right of way to Lamar County and that right of way was for the express purpose of constructing and maintaining a public road.

Looking to the language of the instrument as a whole, it appears that the subject of the conveyance is "a right of way for [a] public road twenty feet in width." The instrument is replete with references to the limited purpose of the conveyance (i.e., to allow for the construction and maintenance of a public road across the Yorks' land). We disagree with the appellant's contention that the reference in the granting clause to a "strip of land" clearly establishes that the Yorks intended to convey a fee. When the intent to convey an easement is manifest, the employment of terms that would otherwise describe corporeal property only will not suffice to defeat the purpose of the grant or render the instrument void as a grant of an easement. The term "land" may, and often does, when consistent with the manifest intent of the parties as gleaned from the instrument as a whole, comprehend an easement as distinguished from a fee in the soil.

Furthermore, the instrument recites that the "strip of land so conveyed [was] intended to be a strip through any [of the Yorks'] land that [the] road was [then] located on, or [might thereafter] be located on by Lamar County." An inference can be drawn from this language that the road in question was already under construction at the time of the conveyance and that the location for the remainder of the road to be constructed was to be discretionary with the county. The language, "may hereafter be located on by Lamar County" also gives rise to an inference that the road, once completed, was subject to future relocation anywhere on the York land at the discretion of the county.

The appellees argue that the uncertain description of the "strip of land" renders the instrument ineffective as a conveyance of a fee simple title as a matter of law. They further argue that such an uncertain description is indicative of the Yorks' intent to convey only a right of way.

The appellant insists that the instrument is effective as a conveyance of fee simple title, because the location of the strip is capable of ascertainment. He argues that it is where the road was located at that time or where it was eventually located and exists presently.

The trial court found that no evidence was presented at trial that the "strip of land" could be ascertained and determined to have a fixed and locatable boundary in and across the Yorks' land. It further found that the road had been moved and relocated on several occasions.

The "open" description contained in the instrument strongly implies that no conveyance of a fee was contemplated by the Yorks. Even assuming that the appellant had presented evidence at trial sufficiently establishing the road's location so that the instrument could possibly have been effective (at least as far as the description is concerned) to create a fee interest, it is not reasonable to infer that the Yorks would have intended such a result. Quite obviously, the Yorks were not certain at the time of the conveyance where the road would ultimately be located or relocated on their land. This kind of uncertainty is simply not consistent with an intent to convey a fee interest.

Looking to the subsequent actions of the parties, we find that Lamar County, in response to the appellees' request for admissions, admits that the York instrument conveyed to it only a right of way for the purpose of constructing and maintaining a public road. Judge Allen, Chairman of the Lamar County Commission, testified that the county had never claimed any interest in the minerals underlying the road.

The appellant relies principally upon *Schneider v. Mobile County,* 284 Ala. 304, 224 So.2d 657 (1969), and *Rowell v. Gulf, M. & O. R.R.,* 248 Ala. 463, 28 So.2d 209 (1946), in support of his argument that the York instrument conveyed a fee. However, these cases are distinguishable from the present case.

In *Schneider,* the granting clauses of the two deeds in question were identical except for the cash consideration. They recited that for the stated consideration the grantors "have GRANTED, BARGAINED, SOLD, and by these presents do hereby GRANT, BARGAIN, SELL, and CONVEY unto the said Mobile County, Alabama, its heirs and assigns, *the following described Real Estate* situated in the county of Mobile and State of Alabama, to wit. . . ." (Emphasis added.) The language quoted above was then followed in one of the questioned deeds by a description, which read in part as follows: "*A strip of land, to be used as right of way* for the Citronelle Road, 30 feet wide being 15 feet on each side of the following described line." The pertinent part of the description in the other deed read: "*A strip of land 50 feet wide, to be used as right of way* for the Citronelle Road, being 25 feet on each side of the following described line." (Emphasis added.)

*Rowell* also involved the construction of two deeds. The granting clauses of those deeds, except for the differences in the amount of cash consideration, were identical and recited that the grantors "for the further consideration of the benefits to accrue to us from the construction of a railroad *on the strip of land and in the station ground herein conveyed,* do grant, bargain, sell and convey unto the said Mobile & Ohio Railroad Company *for right of way and station grounds that certain tract of land* situated in Mobile County, Alabama, more particularly described as follows, to wit. . . ." (Emphasis added.) After the description of the land, the deeds recited: "The *station grounds and right of way herein conveyed and the tract of land herein described* being according to a map and survey signed by J.E. Buck, C.E." (Emphasis added.)

In both *Schneider* and *Rowell,* the deeds in question affirmatively showed that a conveyance of specifically described land was made, accompanied by a recitation of the use to which that land was to be put, and the Court held that a fee simple title was conveyed to the land described.

In the present case, the granting clause, in pertinent part, recites that "W.C. York and wife . . . for the further consideration that Lamar County . . . shall locate and maintain a public highway . . . through our land . . . do hereby release, quitclaim, and convey to the County of Lamar

... for the use and purpose of maintaining a public highway, all of our right, title, interest and claim in and to the following strip of land twenty feet wide to be used for the purpose of constructing a road." This language is followed by a description which reads: "a right of way for public road twenty feet in width." This description is then followed by a description of the land through which the road was to run. Thus the reference to the "strip of land twenty feet wide to be used for the purpose of constructing a road" in the last line of the granting clause is to "a right of way for public road twenty feet in width" as set out in the description clause. The reference to the "following described real estate" in the last line of the granting clause is to the land described in the description clause through which the right of way was to run. When the granting and description clauses are considered together, it can be seen that the "strip of land" referred to in the last line of the granting clause is characterized in the description clause as a right of way.

As heretofore indicated, we are of the opinion that the judgment of the trial court is due to be affirmed.

## Hurst v. Baker[23]

Supreme Court of Ohio, 1997.
1997 WL 215767.

■ STEPHENSON, PRESIDING JUDGE.

This is an appeal from a judgment entered by the Common Pleas Court of Gallia County, Ohio, upon a bench trial, finding in favor of Delores R. Baker, Debra M. Elliott and Douglas Elliott, defendants below and appellees herein, on their counterclaim to quiet title to property claimed by Steven P. Hurst and Ann Hurst, plaintiffs below and appellants herein.

This case involves a dispute over a roadway by contiguous property owners. Both the roadway, and the properties appurtenant thereto, were originally part of a much greater tract of land acquired by a common title holder more than eighty years ago. The record reveals the following facts germane to those lands as well as to the proceedings below.

Approximately ninety-four acres of real estate located in Walnut Township of Gallia County, Ohio (hereinafter referred to as "the master tract"), were conveyed to John and Effie Lowks in April of 1912. Shortly thereafter, Mr. and Mrs. Lowks split off a portion of the master tract and conveyed it to William A. Lowks. The deed for this property (hereinafter referred to as "the forty acre tract") provided in pertinent part:

---

[23] Editor's Note: As evidenced by its citation, Hurst v. Baker is an unreported Ohio case. Any unreported Ohio case decided before May 1, 2002 may only be considered "persuasive" authority. Therefore, although Hurst v. Baker represents the current state of the law in Ohio, it would not be deemed mandatory authority in an Ohio court. See the comments to rule 4 of the Ohio Supreme Court Rules for the Reporting of Opinions.

We J.W. Lowks and Effie Lowks . . . hereby Grant, Bargain, Sell and Convey to the said Wm. A. Lowks his heirs and assigns forever, [t]he following described premises to wit:—containing forty acres more or less, and being in Section No. 9. Also a road 20 ft. wide commencing at the comers of Aug Rott and W.A. Lowks land and running on a [s]traight line through said J.W. Lowks land to a locust tree near said J.W. Lowks [r]esidence said road passing to the right of said tree. Thence on a straight line to the public road[.] The said J.W. Lowks is to keep both sides of said road fenced and no gates allowed.[24]

William A. Lowks died intestate a little more than nine years after acquiring this property. An affidavit transferring the property to his heirs-at-law gave no specific description of the land. However, in 1933, those heirs sold the forty acre tract to Pearl and Willard Haynes and the deed affecting that conveyance gave substantially the same description of the property as the original deed from John and Effie Lowks. Mr. and Mrs. Haynes then sold the forty acre tract to Leonard and Florence Burton. This time, a different legal description was given for the land. The deed also provided that the grantees (Mr. and Mrs. Burton) would receive "an open roadway in common, twenty feet wide, extending westerly across the land formerly owned by Lowks, now owned by Baker, extending to the county road known as Lowks road." The description of the road as a "roadway in common" was thereafter continued in all further conveyances of the property up to, and including, the acquisition of the forty acre tract by appellants in 1981.

Appellees also acquired their property, through mesne conveyances, from the original master tract owned by John and Effie Lowks. In 1931, after splitting off the aforementioned forty acre tract to William A. Lowks, the remainder of the master tract was conveyed to Perry and Cora Lowks. The deed for this property (hereinafter referred to as "the fifty-four acre tract") gave substantially the same legal description as the deed conveying the master tract to John and Effie Lowks and then excepted therefrom the legal description of the forty acre tract and the road. An identical description was used eighteen years later when the property was conveyed to a Mr. Ernest Baker. However, when the Bakers sold this land in 1967, a new legal description was set out to define the fifty-four acre tract. The deed further provided that "a roadway 20 feet in width" running through the property was excepted from the conveyance. This sort of description was thereafter used in all instruments affecting title to the fifty-four acre tract up to, and including, the most recent transfer in 1994.

---

[24] While not entirely clear from the exhibits admitted into evidence below, it would seem that the forty acre tract conveyed to William A. Lowks was located in a back portion of the master tract and the only means of ingress/egress from that forty acre tract to a public thoroughfare was the road specified in that deed.

Appellants commenced the action below on April 7, 1995, asserting that they were the owners of the fee simple interest in the roadway specified in their chain of title to the forty acre tract. They sought to have that interest quieted against any claim of interest by the owners of the fifty-four acre tract. Appellees filed an answer denying that appellants owned a fee simple interest in the disputed roadway. It was asserted by appellees that the road through their property was "merely an easement . . . to be used in common" by the owners of both tracts.

On September 22, 1995, the matter came on for hearing as to which party owned the fee simple interest in the disputed roadway. Both sides stipulated to the admission of deeds in their respective chain(s) of title. The bench trial concluded with both parties stipulating that they, and their predecessors in title, had all made continual use of the road at issue herein.

A judgment was entered on October 13, 1995, determining that appellees were the fee simple owners of the roadway. The trial court conceded that, "[a]t first blush and upon initial reading," the transfer from John and Effie Lowks to William A. Lowks gives one "the impression that this road was given in fee." However, the court was concerned about language in the deed concerning "fencing and gates." It was reasoned that the authority of a grantor to erect fences and gates around a roadway was more consistent with the grant of an easement than a fee interest. The court also reasoned that a deed purporting to convey a "road" or "roadway" is usually construed as passing an easement rather than a fee interest in the absence of any indication of a contrary intent. Further, the court found it unlikely that John and Effie Lowks would convey a fee interest in the roadway through the remainder of their property to the back forty acre tract. Such action would have, effectively, cut the remaining fifty-four acres into two separate parcels. These factors, together with the aforementioned testimony of Mr. Barnes, led the court to conclude that the fee simple ownership of the roadway had passed to appellees down the chain of title to the fifty-four acre tract. Appellants were determined to have received only an easement from their forty acre tract, through the fifty-four acre tract, to the public road.

A second hearing was held on April 12, 1996, to determine the nature of the easement over the disputed roadway and the parties rights and responsibilities with respect to each other's interest(s). Both sides presented evidence and, on May 10, 1996, the trial court entered judgment finding that the easement was "non-exclusive" and could "be used in common" by both parties. Appellants were adjudged to have the responsibility for maintaining the roadway in good repair and appellees were instructed that they could not farm the fifty-four acre tract (i.e. the servient estate) in any manner which could interfere with ingress/egress to the back forty acre tract. A survey giving a precise location and metes and bounds description of the easement was later approved by the trial court. This appeal followed.

Appellants argue in their assignment of error that they are the owners of the fee simple interest in the disputed roadway and that the lower court erroneously adjudicated this issue in favor of appellees. This case turns on the language used in the deed conveying the roadway and the forty acre tract. It is well settled that the construction of a deed is a matter of law for the courts. Appellate courts typically apply a de novo standard of review to questions of law. We will therefore apply a de novo standard in reviewing the judgment entered below. This means that we afford no deference to the trial court's decision and will conduct our own independent review to determine whether the judgment was appropriate.

That being said, we now turn our attention to the merits of the assignment of error. Appellants argue that the lower court erroneously ruled in favor of appellees and that they are, in fact, the fee simple owners of the disputed roadway. We agree. The outcome of this case is governed by the original deed from John and Effie Lowks to William A. Lowks in 1912.

It is undisputed that this deed conveyed a fee simple interest in the forty acre tract to William A. Lowks. The question posited to us in the cause sub judice is whether the road specified in that same deed was also a fee simple grant. For the following reasons, we answer that question in the affirmative. Our analysis begins with the well settled principle that it is the intent of the parties to this instrument which will control its interpretation. See Ball v. Foreman (1881), 37 Ohio St. 132, 141–142. If that intention is clear from the language of the deed, then it will be given effect regardless of technical rules of construction. Hinman v. Barnes (1946), 146 Ohio St. 497, 508, 66 N.E.2d 911; also see 4 Tiffany, Real Property, supra at 89, § 477. We find that the language of this deed is sufficiently clear to determine that a fee interest to the disputed roadway was conveyed to William A. Lowks and continued in the chain of title to the forty acre tract down to appellants.

As noted above, there is no dispute that a fee interest was conveyed in the forty acres. The legal description to the property then goes on the state that a road was "also" included in the grant. The word "also" is generally defined to mean "in addition" or "likewise." American Heritage dictionary (2d Ed.1985) 97. It implies that the additional element following the use of this term "is equal in weight to what precedes it." In other words, with respect to the deed at issue herein, the road conveyed to William A. Lowks would be "equal in weight" to the grant of the forty acres which precedes it in the legal description. Given that the grant of such forty acres was in fee simple, it logically follows that the grant of the road was also in fee simple. Our conclusion is further buttressed by the fact that the grantors never once made use of any terms such as "easement" or "right-of-way" which would have clearly indicated that only a means of ingress/egress was being transferred. In the end, we simply are not persuaded that the clear grant of a "road" in this deed was meant to pass on any estate less than a fee simple interest in that road and we are certainly not convinced that the grant should be read as an easement when such a term is not used once in the instrument of conveyance.

This would seem to have been the initial conclusion of the trial court which ruled that, at first blush, the deed gave the impression that the "road was given in fee." The court was troubled, however, by language in the deed which required the grantor "to keep both sides of said road fenced and no gates allowed." It was ultimately concluded that this requirement lent support to appellee's position that only an easement was given. We disagree. The language regarding fences and gates in this deed is just as supportive of the grant being in fee as it is of an easement having been given. The requirement that the grantor maintain fences, and refrain from erecting gates, is in the deed simply to ensure that the grantee has unimpeded access back along the road to the forty acre tract. This would be of concern to the owner of that tract irrespective of whether he owned the road in fee or merely had an easement to use it.

The lower court also relied on certain rules of construction in reaching its conclusion that only an easement was granted in the deed. As discussed previously, however, technical rules of construction are not to be employed when the language of the deed is clear. We have already determined that the deed from John and Effie Lowks was unambiguous and, on its face, conveyed a fee interest in the road to William A. Lowks. Thus, there was no need to resort to these rules of construction. Even assuming arguendo that the grant was ambiguous, and those rules needed to be employed in the cause sub judice we would still find that they support a transfer of a fee interest rather than an easement.

It has long been the rule in Ohio that instruments such as deeds must be construed most strongly in favor of the grantee, and against the grantor, in order to derogate as little as possible from the extent of the grant. See Pure Oil Co. v. Kindall (1927), 116 Ohio St. 188, 202–203, 156 N.E. 119; Brown v. National Bank (1886), 44 Ohio St. 269, 273, 6 N.E. 648. This would require us to construe the subject deed as passing a fee simple interest in the roadway to William A. Lowks as this is the more expansive reading of the grant. A more restrictive construction of the deed (i.e. to pass only an easement rather than the fee itself) would be in derogation of the potential extent to which the grant could be interpreted.

Similarly, deeds must be construed as conveying the grantor's entire interest in the land described therein unless a clear limitation is placed. See 14 Powell, Real Property (1988) 81A–19, § 899[3]; also see 26 Corpus Juris Secundum (1956) 897, Deeds, § 104. A fee interest is obviously a greater estate than an easement. Thus, in the absence of a limitation by John and Effie Lowks as to the extent of the interest in the road being conveyed to William A. Lowks, we must presume that it was a fee simple grant rather than an easement as this would have been the entirety of their estate.

A more specific corollary to this rule applies in those instances where it must be determined if the transfer of a strip of land passed an easement or fee simple interest. In the absence of language relating to the use or purpose of the grant, or language limiting the estate conveyed, a transfer of a strip of land is generally construed as passing an estate in fee. See 23 American Jurisprudence 2d (1983) 254, Deeds, § 265. There is nothing in the deed from John and Effie Lowks which either limits the estate in the transferred road or restricts its use in such a way as to indicate that it was only passing an easement for ingress/egress. Here again, we are compelled to reach the conclusion that the entire fee interest in the road was passed to William A. Lowks.

We also do not share the trial court's concern that a fee interest in the road would effectively cut the fifty-four acre tract into two separate parcels. It was stipulated below that appellees and their predecessors in title have used the road "continually" through the years. "Indeed, the court even found that all parties had used the road" in common for a number of years "and that each of them had an 'easement'" for its use. This would certainly indicate that there is no problem for appellees to gain access from one portion of the fifty-four acre tract to the other portion. It would also appear from the legal descriptions in the deeds, as well as the maps introduced into evidence below, that the fifty-four acre fronts on "Lowks Road" and that this thoroughfare would provide additional access to appellees from one portion of their land to another. We agree with the trial court that it would have been unusual for John and Effie Lowks to divide up their land in this manner. However, there was no legal impediment to taking such action and we are not persuaded that the result is so bizarre or egregious as to rebut the clear language in the deed.

For all these reasons, we find that John and Effie Lowks conveyed a fee simple interest in the roadway to William A. Lowks. There is no indication that any of the grantee's successors in title ever subsequently conveyed that interest to the owners of the fifty-four acre tract. Thus, we conclude that the fee interest in the roadway stayed with the chain of title to the forty acre tract and was ultimately acquired by appellants in 1981. The trial court erred in its ruling that appellants had only an easement to use this road and that the fee interest therein belonged to appellees. Accordingly, the assignment of error is sustained.

The judgment of the trial court is reversed and this matter is remanded for preparation of an entry showing that appellants are the fee simple owners of the roadway heretofore defined below. A further hearing may also be held to determine the rights and responsibilities of appellees with respect to their easement over this roadway.

## NOTES

1. *The importance of proper drafting.* When the language in a grant is clear and unambiguous, the words of conveyance will usually be given effect

without further interpretation by the courts. However, while a clear, concise, and carefully planned grant is essential, the drafter should keep in mind rules of construction and public policy concerns that are used by the courts. Why should even a meticulous drafter consider such factors as public policy when drafting a grant? What if this drafter wanted to convey a fee simple title in a very narrow strip of land?

2. *Fee title presumed.* A basic rule of construction is that fee simple titles are presumed to have been conveyed unless the grant indicates that a transfer of a lesser estate was intended by the parties. Does this mean that a drafter wishing to convey a fee simple title need not be too concerned with the language used since a fee is presumed when the grant is unclear? In this regard, consider the results of *Northwest Realty* and *Greaves*.

3. *Grants construed in favor of the grantee.* Why do you suppose courts will construe an ambiguously drafted grant against the grantor and in favor of the grantee? Is this a fair result?

4. *Policy discouraging separate ownership of strips of land.* Despite the rules of construction discussed in Notes 2 and 3, *Greaves* and *Northwest Realty* concluded that an ambiguous instrument conveyed to the grantee an easement rather than a fee, thus holding in favor of the grantor. The last sentence in the *Northwest Realty* opinion mentions the policy that discourages separate ownership of strips of land that bisect property. The court invoked this policy to support a holding that preserved the unity of the grantor's parcel of land. In the Principal Problem, does this policy favor Al or Barb?

5. *Identifying drafting errors.* What were some of the major problems with the language of the grants used by the parties in each of the cases in this Assignment? What changes to the language would have resulted in a fee simple title conveyance in *Northwest Realty* and *Greaves*?

6. *"Many tons of rock."* Charles S. Whiting, Esq., of Rapid City, South Dakota, who represented Mr. Jacobs in Northwest Realty Co. v. Jacobs, was kind enough to provide the following information:

> The Defendant, Theodore C. Jacobs, had established an automobile garage and sales agency. Having acquired the land adjacent to the ditch and believing the ditch to have been abandoned and the land to have reverted to the owners of the adjacent property, had filled in the ditch with many tons of rock, broken concrete and earth, and had paved the area for use as a parking lot in connection with his garage business. If he had been forced to comply with the Judgment at the trial court, he not only would have lost the use of a large area which was vitally needed in connection with his business, but would also have been put to perhaps as much as $100,000 expenses in removing the material with which he had filled the ditch.

To what extent do you think that this factual background influenced the decision of the court? How would the factual background influence the court in the Principal Problem?

7. *Roads, strips and ways.* In *Greaves*, the court distinguishes Schneider v. Mobile County and Rowell v. Gulf, M. & O. R.R. Does the

language of the deed in the Principal Problem more closely resemble the language of *Greaves* or that of the cases that *Greaves* distinguishes?

8. *Reservations and exceptions.* An "exception" retains for the grantor a pre-existing interest in a described geographical part of the property or recognizes a previously existing property right in a third party. A "reservation" retains for the grantor a newly created property right.

EXAMPLE 1: *Exception.* Alice owns a fee interest in a hundred acre tract. No one else has any interest in this tract. Alice sells "all my hundred acres, retaining however a fee interest, forty feet wide, along the North boundary." Alice has "excepted" a strip forty feet wide from the grant. It is an "exception" because a specified geographic area has been retained, with the grantor, Alice, holding the same interest as she previously held.

EXAMPLE 2: *Recognition of easement by exception.* Ben owns a fee interest in a 100 acre tract. Carrie has a right of way easement over the tract. Ben sells the property to Dale "subject to Carrie's easement." Ben has excepted the easement from the grant. The exception excludes from the grant a pre-existing legal interest in Carrie, a third party. Ben has not created an easement by exception, but has merely recognized a previously existing interest in Carrie.

EXAMPLE 3: *Reservation of easement.* Ernest owns a fee interest in a 100 acre tract. No one else has any interest in this tract. Ernest sells to Fran "all my hundred acres, retaining an easement for a right of way, forty feet wide, along the North boundary." Ernest has "reserved" an easement. It is a "reservation" because the easement did not exist before the grant to Fran.

9. *Stranger-to-the-deed.* Although it is well established that a grantor may create a reservation or an exception for herself, the ability of a grantor to create such a right in a third person is not so clear. The traditional rule is that a deed with a reservation or exception by the grantor in favor of a third party does not create a valid interest in favor of that third party. See Estate of Thomson v. Wade, 69 N.Y.2d 570, 516 N.Y.S.2d 614, 509 N.E.2d 309 (1987). This is based on the common law rule that a reservation or exception in a deed cannot *create* rights in a third party (compare Example 2 above in which Ben is not creating an easement by exception but instead recognizing a previously existing interest in Carrie). Although this adherence to the "stranger-to-the-deed" rule may frustrate the intent of a grantor, many states uphold the rule on the grounds that the rule protects bona fide purchasers and avoids conflicts of ownership. Id., 69 N.Y.2d at 570, 516 N.Y.S.2d at 614, 509 N.E.2d at 309.

Several states have eliminated the "stranger-to-the-deed" rule on the ground that it frustrates the grantor's intent.[25] The following excerpt is an explanation of this line of reasoning.

---

[25] Nelson v. Parker, 687 N.E.2d 187 (Ind.1997); Simpson v. Kistler Investment Co., 713 P.2d 751 (Wyoming, 1986); Willard v. First Church of Christ, Scientist, Pacifica, 7 Cal.3d 473,

For more than one hundred years American courts have espoused the commendable theory that the intention of the grantor should be the controlling factor in interpreting deeds and that technicalities should not defeat the obvious intent of the grantor. Despite this purported liberal construction of deeds, many of these same courts have upheld, at least in name, the archaic common law rule that reservations to strangers are ineffective. This obvious inconsistency has at times led to highly undesirable results. Admittedly, the courts have been reluctant to apply the rule. Unfortunately, however, it has been the practice of many courts to avoid rather than abandon the rule. In an attempt to give effect to the intention of the grantor by circumventing technical rules of construction, the courts have resorted to technicalities as artificial as those they were seeking to avoid, and the resultant unpredictability is precisely what the common law rule sought to eliminate.

Today the common law rule has clearly outlived the reasons for its existence. Its abandonment is a significant step towards creating clarity and uniformity in conveyancing. Unfortunately, to date only three states have abandoned this obviously archaic and impractical rule; indeed its rejection is less than a trend. However, such abandonment is the only true solution to a problem area of the law that has become unnecessarily contrived.

Comment, Reservations in Favor of Strangers to the Title: California Abandons the Common Law Rule, 24 Hastings L.J., 469, 484–485 (1973).

EXAMPLE 4: *Exception*. Nick owns a fee interest in a hundred acre tract. No one else owns any interest in it. Nick conveys the tract to Olga, "however, Peter is to have a fee interest in a strip of land, forty feet wide, along the North boundary." Nick has attempted to make an exception in favor of Peter. It is an "exception" because it pertains to a pre-existing fee interest in a described geographical part of the property. Traditionally, an exception in favor of a third party is invalid.

EXAMPLE 5: *Reservation*. Rachel owns a fee interest in a hundred acre tract. No one else owns any interest in it. Rachel conveys the tract to Sam, "except that Tina is to have a right of way easement in a strip of land, forty feet wide, along the North boundary." Rachel has attempted to make a reservation in favor of Tina. It is a reservation because the easement did not exist before the grant to Sam. Traditionally, a reservation in favor of a third party is invalid.

Do you agree with the *Estate of Thomson* court that in the area of property law, "stability and adherence to precedent are generally more important than a better or even a 'correct' rule of law?"

---

475, 102 Cal.Rptr. 739, 741, 498 P.2d 987, 989 (1972). See also Restatement (Third) of Property (Servitudes) § 2.6(2) (2000).

10. *USLTA.* Section 2–204(b) of the Uniform Simplification of Land Transfers Act (1977) provides as follows:

> An exception or reservation of an interest in real estate may be made in favor of a person not a party to the conveyance or who has no other interest in the real estate.

Would you recommend that such a statute be adopted in your state?

# ASSIGNMENT 19

# EXPRESS EASEMENTS: INTERPRETATION AND EXTENT

## 1. INTRODUCTION

Once it is determined that an easement was in fact created, questions arise regarding the scope of the easement, and the rights and obligations of both the easement holder and the owner of the servient estate. Issues about scope include: 1) the length, width, and location of the easement; 2) the type(s) of uses authorized by the easement; 3) the anticipated frequency and intensity of uses of the easement; 4) whether the easement can be relocated by one of the parties; 5) whether the easement holder can use the easement to benefit property other than the original dominant estate; 6) the maintenance and repair rights and obligations of the parties; and 7) others' use of the easement, including use by the servient estate owner. The primary goal of the courts is to effectuate the parties' intent with respect to the purposes or uses for which the easement was created.

*Easement Language.* In determining the extent of these rights and obligations, the language of the granting instrument must be examined first. If this language is clear and unambiguous, it is given effect.[1] Where such factors as the width, length, and location of the easement are fixed by the granting instrument, a court may not consider any other factors, such as what is necessary and reasonable to the effective use of the easement, in interpreting the extent of the easement.[2] Thus a carefully drafted document greatly increases the likelihood that the intent of the parties will be effectuated and decreases the likelihood of expensive and disruptive litigation. However, a judicial finding that an easement's language is unambiguous does not mean that the parties—or even other judges—agree on the language's meaning.[3] Moreover, at least one

---

[1] Box L Corp. v. Teton County, 92 P.3d 811, 815 (Wyo. 2004).

[2] Sloan v. Sarah Rhodes, LLC, 560 S.E.2d 653, 655 (Ga. 2002); Guthrie v. Hardy, 28 P.3d 467, 475 (Mont. 2001).

[3] See, e.g., Steil v. Smith, 901 P.2d 395 (Wyo. 1995) (holding that a reasonable person would not think that the term "agricultural related purposes" would include big game hunting, despite the trial court's determination that it did and the easement holder's argument that the language could be read to include big game hunting); Drees Co., Inc. v. Thompson, 868 N.E.2d 32, 39–40 (Ind. App. 2007) (holding that terms like "ingress and egress," "non-exclusive," and "private roadway" were not ambiguous despite both trial court findings and easement holders' arguments to the contrary); Washington Metro. Area Transit Auth. v. Georgetown Univ., 347 F.3d 941, 945–48 (D.C. Cir. 2003) (analyzing two parties' conflicting claims to unambiguous easement language). Compare the opinions of the majority and the dissent in Marcus Cable Associates v. Krohn, 90 S.W.3d 697 (Tex. 2002), regarding whether cable-television lines constituted "an electric transmission or distribution line or system" in the plain and ordinary meaning of those words. But see Smith v. Huston, 251 S.W.3d 808, 823 (Tex. App. 2008) ("If an easement is susceptible to more than one reasonable interpretation, it is ambiguous.").

jurisdiction allows the consideration of extrinsic evidence to determine whether the language is ambiguous or unambiguous.[4] Thus, ambiguity or clarity may be in the eye of the beholder in some cases.

*Easement Language in Light of Surrounding Circumstances and Reasonable Expectations.* If the grant does not expressly and clearly set forth some aspect of the easement's scope, the court will look to the intentions and reasonable expectations of the parties.[5] Unless it can be shown that the parties intended otherwise, "the holder of an easement or profit is entitled to use the servient estate in a manner that is reasonably necessary for the convenient enjoyment of the servitude."[6] In determining the intent of the parties, courts should consider the language used by the grantor in the granting instrument in the light of the surrounding circumstances. In determining the intent of the parties concerning the scope of the easement, courts have considered the following factors among others:

(a) Whether the easement is granted or reserved (easements that are reserved are interpreted more restrictively since ambiguities in a deed are generally construed against the grantor).

(b) The amount of the consideration, if any, that the original beneficiary of the easement gave for the easement (the giving of substantial consideration suggests an interpretation that favors the beneficiary of the easement). Similarly, if the amount of consideration approximates what would have been paid for a fee (as opposed to an easement) this is a factor that may suggest that the parties intended to convey a fee, rather than an easement.

(c) The prior use of the land on which the easement is now located. If the land was used in a certain way before the easement was created, this may suggest that a continuation of that use was contemplated by the parties.

(d) The subsequent conduct of the parties. If immediately after the creation of the easement a certain use was tolerated or accepted, this implies that such a use was contemplated by the parties when the easement was created.

*Easement Length, Width, and Location.* When the instrument creating the easement fails to fix the length, width, and location of the easement, but merely establishes a right-of-way "over" a particular area, strip, or parcel of ground, the easement is generally construed to extend over only so much of that area as is reasonably necessary to effect the

---

[4] Lazy Dog Ranch v. Telluray Ranch Corp., 965 P.2d 1229, 1235–37 (Colo. 1998).

[5] Coughlin v. Anderson, 853 A.2d 460, 474 (Conn. 2004); Arcidi v. Town of Rye, 846 A.2d 535, 542 (N.H. 2004).

[6] Restatement (Third) of Property (Servitudes) § 4.10 (2000).

purpose of the easement. The easement does not necessarily encompass the entire area mentioned in the instrument.[7]

> EXAMPLE 1 (Determining location of easement): Al gives the Water Company the right to lay pipes across Blackacre. There is no mention of the depth. The pipes are laid four feet deep. After some time, Al decides to build homes on Blackacre and finds that the pipes must be lowered. Can the pipes be lowered, and if so, who must bear the expense of lowering the pipes? Although the grant does not set a specific location for the easement, both parties' acquiescence to the installation of the pipes at four feet, and the continued use of those pipes at four feet, fixed the location of the easement at four feet.[8] Under the majority rule, once the location of an easement is fixed, it cannot be moved without the consent of the owners of both the servient and dominant estates (absent a clause in the grant to the contrary). If Water Company consents, Al will be permitted to lower the pipes at Al's expense since Al gains the benefit of moving them.[9]

*Types, Frequency, and Intensity of Uses.* The general rule is that an easement owner's use of the easement for purposes that differ from or exceed the expressly authorized purposes of the easement is a trespass and is not allowed.[10] However, there is a distinction between new modes of uses and new or additional uses.[11] Courts may need to determine whether particular uses fall within the category or type of easement uses that the parties contemplated when creating the express easement. New uses may arise as conditions evolve, technology advances, or the easement holder's activities change. The servient estate owner may resist these new uses as being excessively burdensome or beyond what he or she agreed as an allowed use of his or her property. Depending on the jurisdiction and the facts of the case, courts may consider the express language of the easement instrument, the parties' reasonable expectations based on surrounding circumstances, or whether the new use appreciably increases the burden on the servient estate. These considerations reflect a tension between: a) adhering strictly to the parties' original easement language on the assumption that new uses can be added by mutual modification of the easement,[12] and b) assuming that the parties intended the easement's uses to reasonably evolve as conditions change, thus allowing beneficial uses similar in type and

---

[7] Stover v. Milam, 557 S.E.2d 390 (W. Va. 2001); Zettlemoyer v. Transcontinental Gas Pipeline Corp., 657 A.2d 920 (Pa. 1995).

[8] Stover v. Milam, 557 S.E.2d 390 (W. Va. 2001).

[9] In re Appeals of Shantee Point, Inc., 811 A.2d 1243, 1254 (Vt. 2002); Sloan v. Sarah Rhodes, LLC, 560 S.E.2d 653, 655 (Ga. 2002).

[10] Picardi v. Zimmiond, 693 N.W.2d 656, 664 (S.D. 2005).

[11] Fruth Farms, Ltd. v. Village of Holgate, 442 F. Supp.2d 470, 480–81 (N.D. Ohio 2006).

[12] See, e.g., Steil v. Smith, 901 P.2d 395 (Wyo. 1995) (holding that an easement for "agricultural purposes" does not include use for hunting).

overall burden on the servient estate.[13] For example, the Texas Supreme Court held that an easement for "an electric transmission or distribution line or system" could not be used for cable television lines.[14] By contrast, the Ohio Supreme Court held that an electric energy transmission and energy distribution easement could be used for cable television lines.[15]

Moreover, in the absence of express language to the contrary, the grantor and grantee of an easement are assumed to have contemplated a normal increase in the frequency and intensity of use of the easement over the years. Where the easement is appurtenant, this increased use must be the result of a normal development of the dominant estate.[16] Such increased use will be permitted as long as no unreasonable additional burden is placed upon the servient estate.[17] Note, though, that a change in the intensity of use is considered to be an easier case than a change in the type of use.[18] The line between the two is not always clear. For example, uses by guests and invitees may prompt a court to inquire into whether the easement is being used for new or additional purposes beyond those authorized in the easement's express terms or is being converted from an appurtenant easement to an in-gross easement.[19]

EXAMPLE 2 (Determining scope of easement): Alice owns lake front property. Alice grants Bob a right of way from Bob's property to the lake. Bob wants to use Alice's dock and boat launch ramp. Since the grant is not specific, the court must determine what the parties intended. If this cannot be done, the court must determine what is a reasonable and convenient use of the easement. If the party bringing the suit opposes the use of the dock and boat launch, he or she has the burden of proving that the use is unreasonable or unintended by the parties

EXAMPLE 3 (Increased use of easement): X allows Y to construct and maintain a sewer line under X's property, in exchange for which X is able to use the line for the benefit of X's property. X sells part of the property to each of three people, who start building dwellings and prepare to connect with the sewer. The sewer line is capable of serving all of them. Y brings an action to enjoin them from using the sewer. Y loses. The right to use the sewer line is an easement appurtenant to X's property. If the partitioning of the dominant estate was a normal and

---

[13] See, e.g., Beach Lateral Water Users Ass'n v. Harrison, 130 P.3d 1138 (Idaho 2006) (ditch easement for agricultural irrigation could be used for drainage because new use would impose no greater burden on servient estate).

[14] Marcus Cable Associates, L.P. v. Krohn, 90 S.W.3d 697 (Tex. 2002).

[15] Centel Cable Television Co. of Ohio v. Cook, 567 N.E.2d 1010 (Ohio 1991).

[16] Restatement (Third) of Property (Servitudes) § 4.10 (2000).

[17] Fruth Farms, Ltd. v. Village of Holgate, 442 F. Supp.2d 470, 479 (N.D. Ohio 2006).

[18] McFadden v. Sein, 88 P.3d 740, 743 (Idaho 2004); Price v. Eastham, 75 P.3d 1051, 1058–59 (Alaska 2003) (prescriptive easement).

[19] Fruth Farms, Ltd. v. Village of Holgate, 442 F. Supp.2d 470 (N.D. Ohio 2006); Picardi v. Zimmiond, 693 N.W.2d 656 (S.D. 2005).

foreseeable change in the use of the property, the owner of each part can use the easement, as long as no unreasonable additional burden is placed upon the servient estate.[20]

*Easement Relocation.* In the majority of jurisdictions in the United States, neither the owner of the dominant estate nor the owner of the servient estate may unilaterally relocate an easement once it has been fixed. A small number of jurisdictions follow a different rule. In these jurisdictions, the servient estate is permitted to relocate an easement, provided that the relocated easement affords the dominant estate benefits that are substantially similar to those that the dominant estate enjoyed under the original easement.[21] Although the drafters of the Restatement (Third) of Property (Servitudes) recognize the minority status of the latter rule, they have nonetheless chosen to adopt it.[22] Following promulgation of the Restatement's relocation rule, a number of courts have expressly rejected it.[23]

*Use for Non-Dominant Land.* The standard rule is that the owner of an appurtenant easement cannot use the easement, nor permit its use, for the service of land which was not part of the dominant estate at the time the easement was created. Such a use is considered a trespass.[24] Despite the seeming clarity and universality of this rule, one court allowed use of an easement for non-dominant land owned by the easement holder prior to the creation of the easement,[25] and another court held that there was no mis-use of an easement by third parties to cross the servient estate to get to the dominant estate in order to access a third (non-dominant) parcel for hunting.[26] The Connecticut Supreme Court applies the rule only when the rule's underlying purpose—to prevent increased burden to the servient estate—will be served and allows extensions of an easement's use to "enlargement[s] of the dominant estate" when there is no additional burden on the servient estate, but does not allow extension of the easement's benefits to third-party owners and users of non-dominant properties.[27]

---

[20] Restatement (Third) of Property (Servitudes) § 5.7(1) (2000); Backman & Thomas, A Practical Guide to Disputes Between Adjoining Landowners—Easements § 1.04[2] (2003).

[21] M.P.M. Builders, LLC v. Dwyer, 809 N.E.2d 1053, 1056–57 (Mass. 2004), reprinted infra; Lewis v. Young, 705 N.E.2d 649, 653–54 (N.Y. 1998).

[22] Restatement (Third) of Property (Servitudes) § 4.8 (2000).

[23] A. Perin Dev. Co., LLC v. Ty-Par Realty, Inc., 667 S.E.2d 324 (N.C. App. 2008); Sweezey v. Neel, 904 A.2d 1050 (Vt. 2006); AKG Real Estate, LLC v. Kosterman, 717 N.W.2d 835, 845 (Wis. 2006). See also St. James Village, Inc. v. Cunningham, 210 P.3d 190 (Nev. 2009) (adopting Restatement relocation rule but only when the easement instrument did not expressly fix the location of easement initially); NcNaughton Properties, LP v. Barr, 981 A.2d 222 (Pa. Super. 2009) (rejecting Restatement relocation rule for express easements but allowing its application to prescriptive easements).

[24] Il Giardino, LLC v. Belle Haven Land Co., 757 A.2d 1103, 1111, 1113 (Conn. 2000); Brown v. Voss, 715 P.2d 514 (Wash. 1986), reprinted infra.

[25] Heartz v. City of Concord, 808 A.2d 76 (N.H. 2002).

[26] Grygiel v. Monches Fish & Game Club, Inc., 770 N.W.2d 749 (Wis. App. 2009), petition for review granted, 775 N.W.2d 531 (Wis., Oct. 22, 2009).

[27] Il Giardino, LLC v. Belle Haven Land Co., 757 A.2d 1103, 1112–1113 (Conn. 2000).

EXAMPLE 4 (Limit on use of easement): Carl, owner of Blackacre, grants Donna, owner of Whiteacre, an access easement to use a road across Blackacre. Donna tells Ed, a good friend who owns an adjoining parcel of land, that Ed can also use the road. Carl objects. Carl is within his rights under the majority rule. Carl granted Donna an easement appurtenant to Whiteacre. It is to be enjoyed by the holder of the dominant estate and is not to be used to serve non-dominant land.[28]

*Maintenance and Repair.* In the absence of an express provision in the written instrument governing easement maintenance and repair obligations, the easement owner is assumed to have a duty to make those repairs necessary so as not to interfere with the servient owner's use and enjoyment of his property.[29] Similarly, the easement owner has the right to make such repairs and improvements as are required to accomplish the purpose of the easement, as long as she does not unreasonably increase the burden on the servient estate.[30] The owner of the servient estate has no such repair or maintenance obligations.

EXAMPLE 5 (Easement owner's duty to repair): Carl, owner of Blackacre and Whiteacre, sells Whiteacre to Donna for the purpose of drilling oil. Carl grants Donna an easement of ingress and egress over an access road that crosses Blackacre to the highway by which to transport the oil. In the process, Donna spills so much oil on the access road that Carl cannot safely drive on it. Donna must clean up the oil. The owner of an easement has a duty to use and maintain the easement in such a manner so as not to impose unreasonable additional burdens on the servient estate. When such a burden is imposed, it is the duty of the easement owner to make such repairs as will rectify the condition.[31]

*Servient Estate Owner's Duties and Non-Exclusivity of Easement.* The servient estate owner has a duty to refrain from interfering with the easement owner's enjoyment of her rights.[32] However, since the easement owner is not entitled to exclusive possession of the burdened portion of the servient estate, the servient owner can use his property in whatever manner he chooses, so long as he does not hinder the use and enjoyment of the easement.[33]

---

[28] Bassett v. Harrison, 807 A.2d 695, 704–05 (Md. 2002).

[29] Walker v. Boozer, 95 P.3d 69, 73–74 (Idaho 2004). See also DeHaven v. Hall, 753 N.W.2d 429 (S.D. 2008) (dominant estate owner ordered to repair and maintain easement roadway but not required to reimburse servient estate owner for its maintenance and improvement expenses).

[30] Lazy Dog Ranch v. Telluray Ranch Corp., 965 P.2d 1229, 1238 (Colo. 1998).

[31] Thurston Enterprises, Inc. v. Baldi, 519 A.2d 297, 302 (N.H. 1986).

[32] Walker v. Boozer, 95 P.3d 69, 74 (Idaho 2004).

[33] Miller v. Kirkpatrick, 833 A.2d 536, 544 (Md. 2003); Owsley v. Robinson, 65 P.3d 374, 377 (Wyo. 2003). For example, the servient estate owner may build structures and park cars in the easement provided that they do not impede the easement owner's ingress and egress. Picardi

EXAMPLE 6 (No right to exclusive possession): Carl, owner of Blackacre, grants Donna, owner of Whiteacre, an easement of ingress and egress across a road on Blackacre. Carl subsequently grants Ed, owner of Pinkacre, a similar easement over the same road. Donna is not entitled to exclusive possession of the easement. As long as Ed's use does not interfere with Donna's use, Donna cannot successfully object.[34]

EXAMPLE 7: Alf is the owner of an easement of right of way over Berta's land. Berta places a large pipe across the way, thus obstructing Alf's use of the way. Alf is entitled to damages. He can also get an injunction forcing Berta to remove the pipe if damages would be inadequate.[35]

*The Interpretation and Enforcement of Conservation Easements.* Issues of the scope, interpretation, and enforcement of conservation easements, which were introduced in Assignment 18, differ from those of affirmative easements. The most common question is whether the servient estate owner's use or intended use of his or her property violates the terms of the conservation easement, which imposes restrictions on the use and development of the servient estate. Many conservation easements are carefully and precisely drafted. The land trust or government agency usually wants to secure the conservation purposes it desires by thoroughly limiting potentially incompatible land uses or activities. In addition, scrutiny of conservation easement terms by the Internal Revenue Service and other government agencies for tax appraisal and deduction purposes motivates the parties to define carefully the permissible and impermissible uses (and even the servient estate owner's affirmative obligations, if applicable) and the land trust's inspection and enforcement rights. However, changes in ownership of the servient estate, new circumstances, heightened development pressures, and overstretched land trust staff or volunteers can create the potential that the servient estate owner is tempted to use or develop the land in ways that arguably violate the conservation easement. If the land trust or government agency is unable or unwilling to enforce the easement against the land owner, should the public—usually neighbors, environmentalists, or historic preservationists—have standing to do so?

In general, state statutes do not give members of the public standing to enforce conservation easements.[36] In an exceptional case, a Tennessee court held that members of the public had standing because the state statute gave standing to any conservation easement beneficiary and the

---

v. Zimmiond, 693 N.W.2d 656 (S.D. 2005); Patterson v. Sharek, 924 A.2d 1005 (D.C. Ct. App. 2007).

[34] Knight v. Madison, 634 N.W.2d 540, 543 (S.D. 2001) (implied easement).

[35] Hood v. Neil, 502 So.2d 749 (Ala.1987).

[36] Brown, A Time to Preserve: A Call for Formal Private-Party Rights in Perpetual Conservation Easements, 40 Ga. L. Rev. 85, 88–90 (2005).

public was a beneficiary of conservation easements under state law.[37] The Tennessee Legislature promptly responded by removing the language on which public standing was based.[38] Professor Carol Brown makes a strong case that members of the public should have a common-law property interest in standing to enforce conservation easements because of the inherent public and community benefits of these easements and the public benefits that grantors obtain when creating them.[39] Would your assessment of Professor Brown's proposal be influenced by a study finding violations of 43 conservation easements out of the 315 conservation easements in the San Francisco Bay area and the fact that land trusts monitored only 75 percent of their conservation easements for compliance, while government agencies holding conservation easements only monitored 30 percent of their easements?[40]

## 2. PRINCIPAL PROBLEM

Anna Vieja owns a large tract of rural land. The land is divided into a south lot, lot 1, and a north lot, lot 2. The highway, which runs along the southern border of lot 1, may only be reached from lot 2 by crossing lot 1. Anna occupies lot 2 year round. Anna sells lot 1 to Country Joe Lasso, a rancher, reserving for herself a right of way through lot 1 to the highway. The pertinent part of the granting instrument states:

> Grantor, Anna Vieja, hereby reserves to grantor a right of way over Lot 1. Grantor shall have and maintain an easement of ingress and egress appurtenant to Lot 2 by which owner of Lot 2, grantor, may access the highway. Such easement shall lie within and be limited to a strip of land running north and south the length of Lot 1, bordering the easternmost boundary of Lot 1, from Lot 2 to the highway, of a uniform width of 25 feet. Furthermore, grantor shall at all times have free and unrestricted access to the gate lying within the right of way on Lot 1 and separating Lot 1 from the highway.

A few years after Anna's sale of Lot 1 to Joe, Anna decides to subdivide Lot 2 into thirty residential lots, expecting to provide access to these lots by the easement across Lot 1. Moreover, she has purchased an additional lot, Lot 3, on which she plans to build a new residence for herself, to replace her old residence on Lot 2, which she will raze.

Joe objects both to having thirty new houses served by the easement and to having the easement serve Anna's new residence on Lot 3. Joe is

---

[37] Tennessee Envt'l Council v. Bright Par 3 Assoc., LP, 2004 WL 419720 (Tenn. App. 2004).

[38] Tenn. Code Ann. § 66-9-307 (amended 2005) (amendment applicable to conservation easements created after July 1, 2005).

[39] Brown, A Time to Preserve: A Call for Formal Private-Party Rights in Perpetual Conservation Easements, 40 Ga. L. Rev. 85 (2005).

[40] Morrissette, Conservation Easements and the Public Good: Preserving the Environment on Private Lands, 41 Nat. Resources J. 373, 391 (2001) (citing Bay Area Open Space Council, Ensuring the Promise of Conservation Easements (1999)).

also planning to build about thirty houses on Lot 1. His site planner has designed a plan that will require the easement to be located on the western boundary of Lot 1 (rather than the eastern boundary). It appears that Anna's lot would be equally well served whether the easement is on the eastern or western boundary of Lot 1. Joe is willing to pay all expenses associated with the relocating the easement. However Anna refuses to agree to the relocation unless Joe drops his objections to her plans. He would like to relocate the easement and still successfully object to Anna's plans. What advice would you give him?

## 3. Materials for Solution of Principal Problem

### Brown v. Voss
Supreme Court of Washington, 1986.
715 P.2d 514.

■ BRACHTENBACH, JUSTICE.

The question posed is to what extent, if any, the holder of a private road easement can traverse the servient estate to reach not only the original dominant estate, but a subsequently acquired parcel when those two combined parcels are used in such a way that there is no increase in the burden on the servient estate. The trial court denied the injunction sought by the owners of the servient estate. The Court of Appeals reversed. We reverse the Court of Appeals and reinstate the judgment of the trial court.

A portion of an exhibit depicts the involved parcels.

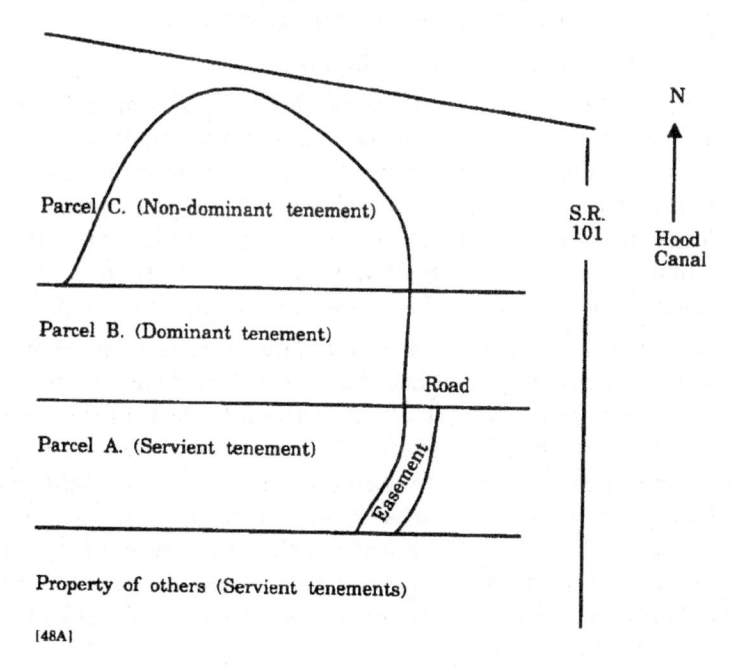

In 1952 the predecessors in title of parcel A granted to the predecessor owners of parcel B a private road easement across parcel A for "ingress to and egress from" parcel B. Defendants acquired parcel A in 1973. Plaintiffs bought parcel B on April 1, 1977 and parcel C on July 31, 1977, but from two different owners. Apparently, the previous owners of parcel C were not parties to the easement grant.

When plaintiffs acquired parcel B a single family dwelling was situated thereon. They intended to remove that residence and replace it with a single family dwelling which would straddle the boundary line common to parcels B and C.

Plaintiffs began clearing both parcels B and C and moving fill materials in November 1977. Defendants first sought to bar plaintiff's use of the easement in April 1979 by which time plaintiffs had spent more than $11,000 in developing their property for building.

Defendants placed logs, a concrete sump and a chain link fence within the easement. Plaintiffs sued for removal of the obstructions, an injunction against defendant's interference with their use of the easement, and damages. Defendants counterclaimed for damages and an injunction against plaintiffs using the easement other than for parcel B.

The trial court awarded each party $1 in damages. The award against the plaintiffs was for a slight inadvertent trespass outside the easement. . . .

The trial court denied defendant's request for an injunction and granted the plaintiffs the right to use the easement for access to parcels B and C "as long as plaintiffs [sic] properties (B and C) are developed and used solely for the purpose of a single family residence."

The Court of Appeals reversed, holding:

In sum, we hold that, in denying the Vosses' request for an injunction, the trial court's decision was based upon untenable grounds. We reverse and remand for entry of an order enjoining the use of the easement across Parcel A to gain access to a residence any part of which is located on parcel C, or to further the construction of any residence on parcels B or C if the construction activities would require entry onto parcel C.

The easement in this case was created by express grant. Accordingly, the extent of the right acquired is to be determined from the terms of the grant properly construed to give effect to the intention of the parties. By the express terms of the 1952 grant, the predecessor owners of parcel B acquired a private road easement across parcel A and the right to use the easement for ingress to and egress from Parcel B. Both plaintiffs and defendants agree that the 1952 grant created an easement appurtenant to parcel B as the dominant estate. Thus, plaintiffs, as owners of the dominant estate, acquired rights in the use of the easement for ingress to and egress from parcel B.

However, plaintiffs have no such easement rights in connection with their ownership of parcel C, which was not a part of the original dominant estate under the terms of the 1952 grant. As a general rule, an easement appurtenant to one parcel of land may not be extended by the owner of the dominant estate to other parcels owned by him, whether adjoining or distinct tracts, to which the easement is not appurtenant.

Plaintiffs, nonetheless, contend that extension of the use of the easement for the benefit of nondominant property does not constitute a misuse of the easement, where as here, there is no evidence of an increase in the burden on the servient statute. We do not agree. If an easement is appurtenant to a particular parcel of land, any extension thereof to other parcels is a misuse of the easement. *Wetmore v. Ladies of Loretto, Wheaton,* 73 Ill.App.2d 454 (1966). As noted by one court in a factually similar case, "[I]n this context this classic rule of property law is directed to the rights of the respective parties rather than the actual burden on the servitude." *National Lead Co. v. Kanawha Block Co.,* 288 F.Supp. 357 (1968). Under the express language of the 1952 grant, plaintiffs only have rights in the use of the easement for the benefit of parcel B. Although, as plaintiffs contend, their planned use of the easement to gain access to a single family residence located partially on parcel B and partially on parcel C is perhaps no more than technical misuse of the easement, we conclude that it is misuse nonetheless.

However, it does not follow from this conclusion alone that defendants are entitled to injunctive relief. Since the awards of $1 in damages were not appealed, only the denial of an injunction to defendants is in issue. Some fundamental principles applicable to a request for an injunction must be considered. (1) The proceeding is equitable and addressed to the sound discretion of the trial court. (2) The trial court is vested with a broad discretionary power to shape and fashion injunctive relief to fit the *particular facts, circumstances, and equities of the case before it.* Appellate courts give great weight to the trial court's exercise of that discretion. (3) One of the essential criteria for injunctive relief is actual and substantial injury sustained by the person seeking the injunction.

The trial court found as facts, upon substantial evidence, that plaintiffs have acted reasonably in the development of their property, that there is and was no damage to the defendants from plaintiffs' use of the easement, that there was no increase in the volume of travel on the easement, that there was no increase in the burden on the servient estate, that defendants sat by for more than a year while plaintiffs expended more than $11,000 on their project, and that defendants' counterclaim was an effort to gain "leverage" against plaintiffs' claim. In addition, the court found from the evidence that plaintiffs would suffer considerable hardship if the injunction were granted whereas no appreciable hardship or damages would flow to defendants from its denial. Finally, the court limited plaintiffs' use of the combined parcels solely to the same purpose for which the original parcel was used—*i.e.*, for a single family residence.

Based upon the equities of the case, as found by the trial court, we are persuaded that the trial court acted within its discretion. The Court of Appeals is reversed and the trial court is affirmed.

■ DORE, JUSTICE (dissenting).

The majority grants the privilege to extend the agreement to nondominant property on the basis that the trial court found no appreciable hardship or damage to the servient owners. However, as conceded by the majority, any extension of the use of an easement to benefit a nondominant estate constitutes a misuse of the easement. Misuse of an easement is a trespass. . . .

In addition, an injunction would not interfere with the Brown's right to use the easement as expressly granted, *i.e.*, for access to parcel B. An injunction would merely require the Browns to acquire access to parcel C if they want to build a home that straddles parcels B and C. One possibility would be to condemn a private way of necessity over their existing easement in an action under RCW 8.24.010. See *Brown v. McAnally,* 97 Wash.2d 360 (1982).

I would affirm the Court of Appeals decision as a correct application of the law of easements. If the Browns desire access to their landlocked parcel they have the benefit of the statutory procedure for condemnation of a private way of necessity.

## NOTE

*A trend toward excused misuse?* As noted in the Introduction, there are several examples of courts refusing to enjoin use of an easement for a nondominant parcel owned by the easement holder if there is no additional increase in burden to the servient estate. However, a Michigan court, expressly noting that *Brown v. Voss* is not the law in Michigan, held that servient estate owners were entitled to an injunction against use of an easement for a non-dominant parcel despite lack of evidence that the use of the easement would increase in any way.[41] Nonetheless, Lee Strang argues that *Brown v. Voss* represents a trend in U.S. property law to favor contract concepts and remedies over traditional property concepts and remedies.[42] Professor Strang urges a rule that would allow "courts to award damages when two conditions are met: (1) the dominant tenant's servicing of nondominant land does not pose an unreasonable burden on the servient estate; and (2) the cost to the dominant tenant of ceasing his servicing of

---

[41] Schadewald v. Brule, 570 N.W.2d 788 (Mich. App. 1997).

[42] Strang, Damages as the Appropriate Remedy for "Abuse" of an Easement: Moving Toward Consistency, Efficiency, and Fairness in Property Law, 15 Geo. Mason L. Rev. 933 (2008).

nondominant land is substantially greater than the benefit to the servient tenant."[43]

## M.P.M. Builders, LLC v. Dwyer
Supreme Judicial Court of Massachusetts, 2004.
809 N.E.2d 1053.

■ COWIN, J.

We are asked to decide whether the owner of a servient estate may change the location of an easement without the consent of the easement holder. We conclude that, subject to certain limitations, described below, the servient estate owner may do so.

1. *Facts.* The essential facts are not in dispute. The defendant, Leslie Dwyer, owns a parcel of land in Raynham abutting property owned by the plaintiff, M.P.M. Builders, L.L.C. (M.P.M.). Dwyer purchased his parcel in 1941, and, in the deed, he was also conveyed an easement, a "right of way along the cartway to Pine Street," across M.P.M.'s land. The cartway branches so that it provides Dwyer access to his property at three separate points. The deed describes the location of the easement and contains no language concerning its relocation.

In July, 2002, M.P.M. received municipal approval for a plan to subdivide and develop its property into seven house lots. Because Dwyer's easement cuts across and interferes with construction on three of M.P.M.'s planned lots, M.P.M. offered to construct two new access easements to Dwyer's property. The proposed easements would continue to provide unrestricted access from the public street (Pine Street) to Dwyer's parcel in the same general areas as the existing cartway. The relocation of the easement would allow unimpeded construction by M.P.M. on its three house lots. M.P.M. has agreed to clear and construct the new access ways, at its own expense, so "that they are as convenient [for the defendant] as the existing cartway." Dwyer objected to the proposed easement relocation, "preferring to maintain [his] right of way in the same place that it has been and has been used by [him] for the past 62 years."

2. *Procedural history.* M.P.M. sought a declaration that it has a right unilaterally to relocate Dwyer's easement. When M.P.M. moved for summary judgment, a Land Court judge found that there were no material issues of fact in dispute, denied M.P.M.'s motion for summary judgment, entered summary judgment against M.P.M., and dismissed the case.

The judge recognized that this case was "a clear example of an increasingly common situation where a dominant tenant is able to block development on the servient land because of the common-law rule which . . . may well be the result of unreflective repetition of a misapplied

---

[43] Id. at 933.

rationale." He noted that the rule conflicts with the "right of a servient tenant to use his land in any lawful manner that does not interfere with the purpose of the easement." Nevertheless, he concluded that under the "settled" common law, once the location of an easement has been fixed it cannot be changed except by agreement of the estate owners. The judge concluded that, unless this court decides "to dispel the uncertainty that now exists and adapt the common law to present-day circumstances," he was bound to apply the law currently in effect. We granted M.P.M.'s application for direct appellate review to decide whether our law should permit the owner of a servient estate to change the location of an easement without the easement holder's consent. . . .

3. *Discussion.* The parties disagree whether our common law permits the servient estate owner to relocate an easement without the easement holder's consent. Dwyer, citing language in our cases, contends that, once the location of an easement has been defined, it cannot be changed except by agreement of the parties. . . . M.P.M. claims that our common law permits the servient estate owner to relocate an easement as long as such relocation would not materially increase the cost of, or inconvenience to, the easement holder's use of the easement for its intended purpose. M.P.M. urges us to clarify the law by expressly adopting the modern rule proposed by the American Law Institute in the *Restatement (Third) of Property (Servitudes) § 4.8 (3)* (2000). This section provides that:

> Unless expressly denied by the terms of an easement, as defined in § 1.2, the owner of the servient estate is entitled to make reasonable changes in the location or dimensions of an easement, at the servient owner's expense, to permit normal use or development of the servient estate, but only if the changes do not (a) significantly lessen the utility of the easement, (b) increase the burdens on the owner of the easement in its use and enjoyment, or (c) frustrate the purpose for which the easement was created.

*Section 4.8 (3)* is a default rule, to apply only in the absence of an express prohibition against relocation in the instrument creating the easement and only to changes made by the servient, not the dominant, estate owner.[44] It "is designed to permit development of the servient estate to the extent it can be accomplished without unduly interfering with the legitimate interests of the easement holder." Id. at *comment f,* at 563. *Section 4.8 (3)* maximizes the over-all property utility by increasing the value of the servient estate without diminishing the value

---

[44] We previously have concluded that the dominant estate owner, that is, the easement holder, may not unilaterally relocate an easement. See *Kesseler v. Bowditch, 223 Mass. 265, 269–270, 111 N.E. 887 (1916); Jennison v. Walker, 77 Mass. 423, 11 Gray 423, 426 (1858).* According to the Restatement, many jurisdictions have erroneously expanded that sensible restriction into one that prevents the owner of the servient estate from relocating the easement without the consent of the easement holder. *Restatement (Third) of Property (Servitudes) § 4.8 (3) comment f,* at 563 (2000).

of the dominant estate; minimizes the cost associated with an easement by reducing the risk that the easement will prevent future beneficial development of the servient estate; and encourages the use of easements. See Id.; *Roaring Fork Club, L.P. v. St. Jude's Co.*, 36 P.3d 1229, 1236 (Colo. 2001). Regardless of what heretofore has been the common law, we conclude that § 4.8 (3) of the Restatement is a sensible development in the law and now adopt it as the law of the Commonwealth.

We are persuaded that § 4.8 (3) strikes an appropriate balance between the interests of the respective estate owners by permitting the servient owner to develop his land without unreasonably interfering with the easement holder's rights. The rule permits the servient owner to relocate the easement subject to the stated limitations as a "fair tradeoff for the vulnerability of the servient estate to increased use of the easement to accommodate changes in technology and development of the dominant estate." *Restatement (Third) of Property (Servitudes), supra at comment f*, at 563. Therefore, under § 4.8 (3), the owner of the servient estate is "able to make the fullest use of his or her property allowed by law, subject only to the requirement that he or she not damage other vested rights holders." *Roaring Fork Club, L.P. v. St. Jude's Co., supra* at 1237.

It is a long-established rule in the Commonwealth that the owner of real estate may make any and all beneficial uses of his property consistent with the easement. [T]he rights of the owner of the easement are protected notwithstanding changes made by the servient estate owner as long as the purpose for which the easement was originally granted is preserved. We conclude that § 4.8 (3) is consistent with these principles in its protection of the interests of the easement holder: a change may not significantly lessen the utility of the easement, increase the burden on the use and enjoyment by the owner of the easement, or frustrate the purpose for which the easement was created. The servient owner must bear the entire expense of the changes in the easement.

Dwyer urges us to reject the Restatement approach. He argues that adoption of § 4.8 (3) will devalue easements, create uncertainty in property interests, and lead to an increase in litigation over property rights.[45] Our adoption of § 4.8 (3) will neither devalue easements nor

---

[45] Dwyer correctly states that the majority of jurisdictions require mutual consent to change the location of an easement. See Restatement (Third) of Property (Servitudes), supra at comment f, at 563; Note, The Right of Owners of Servient Estates to Relocate Easements Unilaterally, 109 Harv. L. Rev. 1693, 1694 (1996). However, most of these decisions were issued prior to the publication of the Restatement (Third) of Property (Servitudes) (2000). Of the State appellate courts that have addressed the issue since § 4.8 (3) was drafted, four have adopted, or referred with approval to, the rule in some form. See Roaring Fork Club, L.P. v. St. Jude's Co., 36 P.3d 1229, 1236, 1238 (Colo. 2001) (adopting rule but requiring declaratory judgment prior to relocation); Lewis v. Young, 92 N.Y.2d 443, 452, 705 N.E.2d 649, 682 N.Y.S.2d 657 (1998) (adopting rule for easements not expressly defined in grant); Goodwin v. Johnson, 357 S.C. 49, 57–58, 591 S.E.2d 34 (Ct. App. 2003) (adopting Restatement position for easements by necessity); Burkhart v. Lillehaug, 2003 SD 62, 664 N.W.2d 41, 43–44 (S.D. 2003) (applying Restatement § 4.8 (3) to changes made to easement). We have found only two State appellate courts that have expressly rejected it. See Herren v. Pettengill, 273 Ga. 122, 124, 538 S.E.2d

place property interests in an uncertain status. An easement is by definition a limited, nonpossessory interest in realty. See *Restatement (Third) of Property (Servitudes) § 1.2* (2000) ("An easement creates a nonpossessory right to enter and use land in the possession of another and obligates the possessor not to interfere with the uses authorized by the easement"); 3 Powell, Real Property § 405 at 34–13 (P. Rohan ed. 1992) ("The requirement that the easement involve only a limited use or enjoyment of the servient tenement is a corollary of the nonpossessory character of the interest" [emphasis in original]). The owner of the servient estate is in possession of the estate burdened by the easement. An easement is created to serve a particular objective, not to grant the easement holder the power to veto other uses of the servient estate that do not interfere with that purpose.

The limitations embodied in *§ 4.8 (3)* ensure a relocated easement will continue to serve the purpose for which it was created. So long as the easement continues to serve its intended purpose, reasonably altering the location of the easement does not destroy the value of it. For the same reason, a relocated easement is not any less certain as a property interest. The only uncertainty generated by *§ 4.8 (3)* is in the easement's location. A rule that permits the easement holder to prevent any reasonable changes in the location of an easement would render an access easement virtually a possessory interest rather than what it is, merely a right of way. Finally, parties retain the freedom to contract for greater certainty as to the easement's location by incorporating consent requirements into their agreement.

"Clearly, the best course is for the [owners] to agree to alterations that would accommodate both parties' use of their respective properties to the fullest extent possible." *Roaring Fork Club, L.P. v. St. Jude's Co.,* supra at 1237. In some cases, the parties will be unable to reach a meeting of the minds on the location of an easement. In the absence of agreement between the owners of the dominant and servient estates concerning the relocation of an easement, the servient estate owner should seek a declaration from the court that the proposed changes meet the criteria in *§ 4.8 (3)*. Such an action gives the servient owner an opportunity to demonstrate that relocation comports with the Restatement requirements and the dominant owner an opportunity to demonstrate that the proposed alterations will cause damage. The servient owner may not resort to self-help remedies, see *Id. at 1237* (after failing to reach agreement with easement holder, servient owner went forward with construction), and, as M.P.M. did here, should obtain a declaratory judgment before making any alterations.

Although Dwyer may be correct that increased litigation could result as a consequence of adopting *§ 4.8 (3)*, we do not reject desirable developments in the law solely because such developments may result in

---

735 (2000); MacMeekin v. Low Income Hous. Inst., Inc., 111 Wn. App. 188, 207, 45 P.3d 570 (2002).

disputes spurring litigation. *Section 4.8 (3)* "imposes upon the easement holder the burden and risk of bringing suit against an unreasonable relocation," but this "far surpasses in utility and fairness the traditional rule that left the servient land owner remediless against an unreasonable easement holder." *Roaring Fork Club, L.P. v. St. Jude's Co., supra at 1237*, quoting, Note, Balancing the Equities: Is Missouri Adopting a Progressive Rule for Relocation of Easements?, *61 Mo. L. Rev. 1039, 1060 (1996)*. We trust that, over time, uncertainties will diminish and litigation will subside as easement holders realize that in some circumstances unilateral changes to an easement, paid for by the servient estate owner, will be enforced by courts. Dominant and servient estate owners will have an incentive to negotiate a result rather than having a court impose one on them.

We return to the facts of this case. The Land Court judge ruled correctly under existing law. But we conclude that *§ 4.8 (3)* of the Restatement best complies with present-day realities. The deed creating Dwyer's easement does not expressly prohibit relocation. Therefore, M.P.M. may relocate the easement at its own expense if the proposed change in location does not significantly lessen the utility of the easement, increase the burdens on Dwyer's use and enjoyment of the easement, or frustrate the purpose for which the easement was created. M.P.M. shall pay for all the costs of relocating the easement.

Because we cannot determine from the present record whether the proposed relocation of the easement meets the aforementioned criteria, we vacate the judgment and remand the case to the Land Court for further proceedings consistent with this opinion.

## NOTES

1. *Conflicting views.* Restatement 4.8 does not give the easement owner the right to relocate the easement, although it does give that right to the owner of the servient estate, subject to various conditions. Is there a justification for the asymmetry? Professor Orth thinks not.[46] He believes that more important than the question of asymmetry, is the objection that the Restatement position devalues easements "in comparison with other property rights characterized as possessory, thereby depriving the easement owner of one of the prime protections accorded private property—the ability to refuse to suffer the loss of property to a private person even if that person offers other property of equal value in exchange."[47]

As discussed in the Introduction, a number of courts have rejected the Restatement rule allowing unilateral relocation of the easement. According to the Supreme Court of Wisconsin:

These courts have rejected the position advanced by the Restatement as a threat to the certainty of property rights and real estate transactions, as a

---

[46] Orth, Relocating Easements: A Response to Professor French, 38 Real Prop. Prob. & Tr. J. 643 (2004).

[47] Id. at 653.

catalyst for increased litigation, and as a means for purchasers of servient estates to reap a windfall at the expense of owners of dominant estates. We agree that these reasons for rejecting the Restatement's position are more compelling than the economic inefficiencies that might result from bilateral monopolies and holdout easement owners.[48]

Do you agree with the Supreme Court of Wisconsin? In the Principal Problem, if Country Joe cannot unilaterally relocate the easement to the western boundary of Lot 1, what are his options? Does the majority rule impede the economic use of Country Joe's land? Or would the Restatement impede the economic use of Anna Vieja's land? Could the parties have anticipated the potential for relocation and drafted a provision in the original easement governing the circumstances under which a party could unilaterally relocate the easement? Or could they now bargain to a mutually beneficial outcome? If Country Joe is unable to relocate the easement, does it mean that Anna's use of the easement in its current location is preferable from the perspective of economic utility, equity, or the overall functioning of the property law system?

2. *Procedure.* Restatement 4.8 gives a right to relocate the easement, under certain conditions, without requiring prior court approval. *M.P.M. Builders* and several other courts have insisted on prior court approval. How does this affect the advice you would give to Country Joe in the Principal Problem?

## Hayes v. Aquia Marina, Inc.
Supreme Court of Virginia, 1992.
414 S.E.2d 820.

■ STEPHENSON, JUSTICE.

The principal issue in this appeal is whether an easement across the servient estates will be overburdened by the proposed expanded use of the dominant estate. Robert C. Hayes and others (collectively, Hayes) brought a chancery suit against Aquia Marina, Inc., Warren E. Gnegy, and Cynthia Gnegy (collectively, Gnegy). Hayes alleged, inter alia, that a proposed expansion of a marina located on Gnegy's land (the dominant estate or marina property) would overburden the easement across Hayes's lands (the servient estates). Hayes, therefore, sought to have the trial court enjoin the proposed expanded use of the dominant estate.

The cause was referred to a commissioner in chancery. The commissioner filed a report containing the following findings: (1) a perpetual easement exists across the servient estates for ingress to and egress from the dominant estate; (2) the easement is not limited solely for domestic use, but may be used commercially by the marina and its customers and by boat owners and their guests; (3) the proposed expansion of the marina from 84 to 280 boat slips is a reasonable use of the dominant estate; (4) the resulting increase in traffic over the

---

[48] AKG Real Estate, LLC v. Kosterman, 717 N.W.2d 835, 846 (Wis. 2006).

easement will not change the type, only the degree, of use and will not overburden the easement; and (5) paving the easement is reasonable and a proper means of maintenance.

By a final decree, entered March 5, 1991, the trial court overruled all of Hayes's exceptions to the commissioner's report and confirmed the report in all respects. Hayes appeals. We must view the evidence in the light most favorable to Gnegy, the prevailing party at trial. The marina property is a 2.58-acre tract situate on Aquia Creek in Stafford County. The easement is the sole means of land access to the marina property.

The litigants' predecessors in title entered into a written agreement, executed February 3, 1951, for "the establishment of a certain roadway or right of way beginning at the Northern terminus of State Highway No. 666, and terminating at the property division line between [the servient estates], and where [the dominant estate] adjoins the same on the North side thereof" and for "the continuation of said right of way." The agreement recited that "the State Department of Highways will be requested . . . to take over into the State Highway System the present roadway beginning at the North terminus of said State Highway No. 666, and leading through [the servient estates]." The roadway that was intended to be taken into the state highway system was "approximately something less than one-half mile in length." The "newly established private roadway" was "approximately 1,120 feet in length" and "fifteen feet wide along its entire distance." The agreement provided that the parties thereto "shall have an easement of right of way over the entire length [thereof]." The record indicates that the portion of the easement, beginning at the northern terminus of State Highway No. 666, became a part of the state highway system in 1962. The record also indicates that the "private roadway" is constructed of dirt and gravel.

By 1959, three residential buildings, a wooden pier, and 10 boat slips were located on the dominant estate. This small marina was operated commercially. Between 1961 and 1962, the current marina was constructed. This marina has been operated commercially for the general public from 1964 until the present. The marina consists of 84 boat slips, a public boat launch, and a gas dock

In September 1989, Stafford County granted Gnegy a permit to expand the marina by increasing the number of boat slips to 280. After the proposed expansion, the marina will continue to provide the same services it has provided since 1964. There has never been a "traffic problem" with the easement. An expert witness on emergency services testified that there never had been a problem with access to the marina property and none was anticipated if the proposed expansion occurred.

As a general rule, when an easement is created by grant or reservation and the instrument creating the easement does not limit the use to be made of it, the easement may be used for "any purpose to which the dominant estate may then, or in the future, reasonably be devoted." *Cushman Virginia Corporation v. Barnes*, 204 Va. 245 (1963). Stated differently, an easement created by a general grant or reservation, without words limiting it to any particular use of the dominant estate, is not affected by any reasonable change in the use of the dominant estate. *Savings Bank v. Raphael*, 201 Va. 718 (1960) (citing Ribble, 1 Minor on Real Property § 107, at 146 n. 2 (2d ed. 1928)). However, no use may be made of the easement which is different from that established at the time of its creation and which imposes an additional burden upon the servient estate. *Cushman Corporation*, 204 Va. at 253.

Hayes contends that, by using the phrase, "private roadway," in the easement agreement, the parties to the agreement intended to limit the use of the easement to domestic purposes, thereby prohibiting commercial uses. Gnegy contends, on the other hand, that the agreement created an easement for access without limitation. The commissioner and the trial court adopted Gnegy's contention. When the agreement is read as a whole, it is clear that the phrase, "private roadway," was used to distinguish that portion of the easement that would not become a part of the state highway system from that portion of the easement that could be taken into the system. Thus, the phrase is descriptive, not restrictive.

Consequently, we hold that the agreement creating the easement for access contains no terms of limitation upon the easement's use. Additionally, the record supports the conclusion that the operation of a marina is a use to which the dominant estate reasonably can be, and has been, devoted. Hayes further contends that the proposed expansion of the marina will impose an additional and unreasonable burden upon the easement. Having alleged that the proposed expansion will impose an additional burden upon the easement, Hayes has the burden of proving this allegation. *Holt v. Holt*, 174 Va. 120 (1939). A contention similar to the one advanced by Hayes was presented in *Cushman Corporation*, supra. In *Cushman Corporation*, as in the present case, the instruments creating the easement contain no language limiting the easement's use. 204 Va. at 253. When the easement was established, the dominant estate, a 126.67-acre tract, was used as a farm and contained two single-family dwellings with appurtenant servant and tenant houses. A controversy arose when the dominant owner proposed to subdivide the tract for residential and commercial uses. The trial court limited the easement to its original uses. We reversed the ruling, stating, inter alia:

> The fact that the dominant estate is divided and a portion or portions conveyed away does not, in and of itself, mean that an additional burden is imposed upon the servient estate. The result may be that the degree of burden is increased, but that is not sufficient to deny use of the right of way to an owner of a portion so conveyed. After weighing the evidence, both the commissioner and the trial court concluded that the proposed expansion would not unreasonably burden the easement. On appeal, a decree confirming a commissioner's report is presumed to be correct and will be affirmed unless plainly wrong.

In the present case, we cannot say that the trial court's conclusion is plainly wrong. Indeed, we think that it is supported by the evidence and by well-established principles of law. Here, as in *Cushman Corporation*, the proposed expansion will not, "in and of itself," impose an "additional burden" upon the easement, even though the "degree of burden" may be increased. Therefore, assuming, without deciding, that an expanded use of the dominant estate could be of such degree as to impose an additional and unreasonable burden upon an easement, such is not the situation in the present case.

Finally, Hayes contends that Gnegy does not have the right to pave the easement. Hayes acknowledges, and we agree, that the owner of a dominant estate has a duty to maintain an easement. *Pettus v. Keeling*, 232 Va. 483 (1987); *Oney v. West Buena Vista Land Co.*, 104 Va. 580 (1905). However, Hayes reasons that, because the owner of a dominant estate has a duty to maintain an easement, it follows that the owner does not have a right to improve the easement. We agree that there is a distinction between maintenance and improvement. See *Montgomery v. Columbia Knoll Condo. Council*, 231 Va. 437 (1986). However, we do not agree that the owner of a dominant estate does not have the right to make reasonable improvements to an easement.

Although we previously have not addressed the "improvement" issue, courts in other jurisdictions have held that the owner of a dominant estate has the right to make reasonable improvements to an easement, so long as the improvement does not unreasonably increase the burden upon the servient estate. See, e.g., *Stagman v. Kyhos*, 19 Mass.App.Ct. 590 (1985); *Glenn v. Poole*, 12 Mass.App.Ct. 292 (1981); *Schmutzer v. Smith*, 679 S.W.2d 453 (Tenn.App.1984). Such improvement may include paving a roadway. See, e.g., *Stagman*, supra; *Schmutzer*, supra. Ordinarily, the reasonableness of the improvement is a question of fact. We adopt these principles of law.

In the present case, the commissioner and the trial court found that the proposed paving of the roadway by Gnegy, under the existing facts and circumstances, is reasonable. We will affirm this finding; it is supported by the evidence and is not plainly wrong. Accordingly, the trial court's judgment will be affirmed.

## NOTES

1. *Prescriptive easements compared with express easements.* Sometimes an easement is created by adverse use (prescription) rather than by an express agreement. See generally Assignment 38–39, dealing with the doctrines of adverse possession and adverse use. In such a case, the permitted use is limited by the extent of the prior adverse use. Courts are more cautious about allowing a significant expansion of the permitted use

than they would be if the easement were based on an express grant or reservation.[49]

2. *Intensity, mode, and type of use.* As discussed in the Introduction, the general rule prohibiting new or additional types of uses and the general rule allowing reasonable increases in intensity of allowed uses create the need for courts to determine whether a different mode of use is: a) more like a reasonably anticipated increase in the burden of an expressly allowed use, or b) more like an entirely new use altogether. In *Hayes*, the court's analysis of the degree of increased burden imposed by more boat slips and traffic followed the court's determination that "private roadway" use could encompass both residential and commercial uses of the road. However, in determining that cable-television lines constituted a materially different—and therefore unauthorized—use of an electric transmission and distribution easement, the Texas Supreme Court articulated the following concern:

> The common law does allow some flexibility in determining an easement holder's rights. In particular, the manner, frequency, and intensity of an easement's use may change over time to accommodate technological development. But such changes must fall within the purposes for which the easement was created, as determined by the grant's terms.... [A]n express easement encompasses only those technological developments that further the particular purpose for which the easement was granted. Otherwise, easements would effectively become possessory, rather than nonpossessory, land interests.[50]

What does the court mean by easements becoming possessory land interests if easement uses were to follow technological development, instead of being constrained by the purposes originally articulated by the parties? Would cable television lines in an electric line easement pose some particular harm to the servient estate owner's property rights? Does this rule hold back technological change? Or do the users of new technology have other means for being able to use existing easements?

---

[49] Restatement (Third) of Property (Servitudes) § 4.8 cmt. e (2000).
[50] Marcus Cable Associates v. Krohn, 90 S.W.3d 697, 701–02 (Tex. 2002).

# ASSIGNMENT 20

# EXPRESS EASEMENTS: SUCCESSION

## 1. INTRODUCTION

When will successors to the original grantor and grantee of an easement be bound by the rights and obligations that arise upon its creation?

The first step in determining whether an easement may be transferred is to ascertain whether the easement is appurtenant or in gross. If the granting instrument designates the easement as either appurtenant or in gross, the words of the grant are given effect.[1] In many cases, the grant does not specify whether the easement is appurtenant or in gross. In such cases, the court will attempt to determine whether the parties intended the easement to be personal to the grantee and therefore non-transferrable.[2] In ascertaining the intention of the parties, the court will look to the language of the grant and to the circumstances surrounding the grant.[3] Courts may consider such circumstances as the type of rights conveyed by the easement and the relationship between the easement and other real property owned by the grantee.[4] In ascertaining the intent of the parties, there is a presumption that the parties intended the easement to be appurtenant.[5] Here again, litigation can generally be avoided if the granting instrument is clearly drafted at the outset.

> EXAMPLE 1 (Presumption of appurtenancy): Fred owns Blackacre and Whiteacre, two contiguous lots. Fred sells Whiteacre to Gert, reserving for himself an easement of ingress and egress across Whiteacre because Blackacre is landlocked. The reservation in the deed is "in favor of the owner of Blackacre, personally." The easement is appurtenant to Blackacre despite the use of the word "personally" because it is also to "the owner of Blackacre." When the granting instrument is ambiguous, there is a strong presumption of an appurtenant easement, which may only be overcome by significant evidence showing an intention to make an easement in gross. Although

---

[1] Burcky v. Knowles, 413 A.2d 585 (N.H. 1980), reprinted infra; Sanders v. Lutz, 109 N.M. 193 (1989); Pokorny v. Salas, 81 P.3d 171 (Wyo. 2003); Restatement (Third) of Property (Servitudes) § 4.1 (2000).

[2] King v. Lang, 42 P.3d 698 (Idaho 2002); Nelson v. Johnson, 679 P.2d 662 (Idaho 1984), reprinted infra.

[3] LeMay v. Anderson, 397 A.2d 984 (Me.1979); Box L Corp. v. Teton County, 92 P.3d 811 (Wyo. 2004).

[4] Moylan v. Dykes, 226 Cal.Rptr. 673 (1986).

[5] Nelson v. Johnson, 679 P.2d 662 (Idaho 1984), reprinted infra; Stricklin v. Meadows, 544 S.E.2d 87 (W.Va. 2001).

the instrument claims that the easement is "personal" (suggesting that it is not appurtenant), it also states that it is for the benefit of "the owner of Blackacre," suggesting that it is appurtenant. Because the granting instrument is ambiguous, the intention of the parties must be ascertained from the surrounding circumstances. The fact that Blackacre is landlocked suggests that the parties intended the easement to be appurtenant. There is no other evidence to overcome the presumption of an easement appurtenant.[6]

## 2. Succession of Appurtenant Easements

*Succession to Dominant Estate*

Absent an express provision in the deed stating otherwise, an appurtenant easement is presumed to be transferred with the dominant estate. Thus, one who succeeds to the possession of the dominant estate may enjoy the benefits of the easement. The benefit of the easement runs with the land unless the terms of the transfer or the terms of the creation of the easement preclude the benefit from running.[7] This is true whether the successor entered into possession pursuant to an express conveyance, adverse possession, or intestate transfer, and whether possession is rightful or wrongful.[8] The successor's rights and privileges are the same as those of his predecessors, subject to all qualifications and conditions on the easement.[9]

> EXAMPLE 2 (Presumption that benefit of appurtenant easement passes with grant of dominant estate): Fred, owner of Blackacre, grants Gert, owner of Whiteacre, an easement to use a driveway on Blackacre to get to Whiteacre. Gert sells Whiteacre to Helen. The deed is silent as to the easement. Helen can use the easement. The benefit of an appurtenant easement runs with the land even if the deed transferring the estate does not mention the easement. Fred granted Gert an appurtenant easement, which attaches to and benefits the dominant estate, Whiteacre. Appurtenant easements are presumed to pass with grants of the dominant estate unless expressly excluded from the conveyance or barred by the terms of the easement at creation.[10]

The rules regarding succession of an appurtenant easement depend upon whether the dominant or servient estate is transferred. In either case, the express words of the deed creating the easement are always

---

[6] Messer v. Leveson, 23 A.D.2d 834 (N.Y. App. Div. 1965).
[7] Burcky v. Knowles, 413 A.2d 585 (N.H. 1980), reprinted infra; Nelson v. Johnson, 679 P.2d 662 (Idaho 1984), reprinted infra.
[8] Restatement (Third) of Property (Servitudes) § 5.2 (2000).
[9] Id.
[10] Burcky v. Knowles, 413 A.2d 585 (N.H. 1980), reprinted infra.

given effect.[11] Ordinarily, the easement passes with the dominant estate. If the deed creating the easement precludes the easement from passing with the dominant estate, two scenarios may arise. If the terms of the original deed provide that the easement will be extinguished upon transfer of the dominant estate, such will be the case. If the terms of the original deed provide that, upon transfer of the dominant estate, the appurtenant easement will become an easement in gross for the benefit of the transferor, such will also be the case. If the deed creating the easement prohibits its transfer with the dominant estate but does not specify the consequences of a transfer of the dominant estate, either the easement is extinguished or the provision in the original deed preventing transfer of the easement is ineffective in which case the easement passes with the dominant estate.

> EXAMPLE 3 (Attempt to reserve benefit of appurtenant easement when transferring dominant estate): Fred, owner of Blackacre, grants Gert, owner of Whiteacre, an easement appurtenant to draw water from a well on Blackacre for the benefit of Whiteacre. Gert sells Whiteacre to Helen and expressly excludes the easement from the conveyance. Gert purchases Pinkacre, an adjoining parcel, and attempts to use the easement for the benefit of Pinkacre. Fred objects. Gert cannot use the easement for the benefit of non-dominant land. A provision in a deed transferring the dominant estate providing that the benefit of an appurtenant easement shall not pass to the grantee of the dominant estate can change an easement appurtenant into an easement in gross only if the terms of the creation of the easement permit such a change. Otherwise, the provision against transfer is ineffective or the easement is extinguished. In this example, because the provision against transfer is unconditional, the easement was probably extinguished.[12]

Suppose there is an attempt to transfer an appurtenant easement separately from the dominant estate? The attempt would not be effective, but would usually not extinguish the easement.[13] Suppose there is a transfer of the dominant estate, but the transferor attempts to retain the easement? Depending on circumstances the easement may pass with the dominant estate or be extinguished.[14]

*Succession to Servient Estate*

A transfer of the dominant estate raises the issue of the running of the benefit of the appurtenant easement. A transfer of the servient estate raises the issue of the running of the burden of the appurtenant

---

[11] Gordon v. Hoy, 211 Va. 539 (1971); Restatement (Third) of Property (Servitudes) § 4.1 cmt. d (2000).
[12] Restatement of Property § 487 cmt. b, illus. 1 (1944).
[13] Restatement (Third) of Property (Servitudes) § 5.6 illus. 1 (2000).
[14] Restatement of Property § 487 cmt. b (1944).

easement. If the servient estate is transferred, the burden of the easement runs with the land so as to be enforceable against the successors of the servient estate if the original parties intended that it run and if the successor to the servient estate had notice of the easement.[15] Parties almost always "intend" the burden of an easement to run. If no contrary intention is expressed in the granting instrument, courts presume the parties intended the burden to run. They view the easement as carved out of the servient estate, making it permanently less than it used to be.[16]

If the successor to the servient estate *purchases* the servient estate without notice of the easement, under most modern recording statutes the easement will be extinguished and the new owner of the servient estate will not be subject to the burden of the easement.[17] Notice of the existence of the easement may be either actual or constructive. If the easement is recorded, the successor has constructive notice of the easement, implied by law, whether or not the successor is actually aware of the easement.[18] Whenever an easement is recorded, if the parties intended the burden to run with the land, it will. If the easement was not recorded, the burden of the easement may still run with the land if the purchaser has notice of the easement. If the purchaser has knowledge of the easement, no matter how it was derived, he or she is subject to the burden of the easement. If the purchaser has knowledge of conditions on the land or elsewhere sufficient to make a reasonable person suspect that an easement exists, he or she is charged with such notice as would have been gleaned from making an inquiry. Any purchaser with knowledge or notice of the easement takes subject to the easement.[19] In most jurisdictions, a successor who is *not* a purchaser for value is subject to the easement regardless of whether the successor (who is not a purchaser) has notice of the easement.

> EXAMPLE 4 (Burden of easement runs if intent and notice requirements are satisfied): Isaac, owner of Blackacre, grants half of Blackacre to Jan, together with the right to use a road on the part retained by Isaac for access to a highway. Isaac subsequently sells the part of Blackacre he retained to Kate. Kate seeks to prevent Jan from using the road. The burden of the easement runs with the land if the original parties intended that it run, and if the purchaser of the servient estate has notice of the easement. If there is no evidence to the contrary, it is presumed that the original parties intended the burden of the

---

[15] Tiller v. Hinton, 19 Ohio St.3d 66 (1985); Backman & Thomas, A Practical Guide to Disputes Between Adjoining Landowners—Easements § 1.04[1], [3] (2003).

[16] Backman & Thomas, A Practical Guide to Disputes Between Adjoining Landowners—Easements § 1.04[3] (2003).

[17] Id.

[18] National Properties Corp. v. Polk County, 351 N.W.2d 509 (Iowa 1984).

[19] National Properties Corp. v. Polk County, 351 N.W.2d 509, 511 (Iowa 1984); Germany v. Murdock, 99 N.M. 679 (1983).

easement to run. If the deed to Jan was recorded, or if the nature and location of the easement put Kate on inquiry as to its existence, Kate had notice and is bound.[20]

## 3. SUCCESSION OF EASEMENTS IN GROSS

*The Position of the Restatement (Third) of Property (Servitudes)*

An easement in gross will not pass when the owner of the easement sells his or her land.[21] Instead, for the benefit of the easement in gross to pass to a successor of the grantee, the easement must be assigned. However, not all easements in gross are assignable. If the granting instrument contains an express provision as to the assignability of the easement, it will be given effect.[22] Otherwise, the court will make a presumption that the benefit of an easement in gross is assignable, unless it is found to be personal.[23] It would be personal if it appears from all of the circumstances that the parties did not intend it to be transferable.[24] Thus, under the Restatement view, all easements in gross are assignable unless the parties did not intend the easement to be assignable, or the assignability would offend some important public policy.[25]

*The Older View*

If the primary purpose of the easement is to gain economic benefit, the easement is deemed commercial in nature and there arises a rebuttable presumption that it is assignable.[26] Unless the terms of the creation or the terms of the transfer provide that the easement is non-assignable, or there is strong evidence to indicate that the parties intended the commercial easement to be non-assignable, the benefit of the easement passes through the assignment.[27]

If the primary purpose of the easement is to gain personal satisfaction, the easement is deemed non-commercial in nature and there arises a rebuttable presumption that it is not assignable.[28] This presumption may be overcome in most jurisdictions if there is sufficient evidence to suggest that the parties intended the easement to be assignable, although some jurisdictions find all non-commercial

---

[20] National Properties Corp. v. Polk County, 351 N.W.2d 509 (Iowa 1984); Tiller v. Hinton, 19 Ohio St.3d 66 (1985); Backman & Thomas, A Practical Guide to Disputes Between Adjoining Landowners—Easements § 1.04[1], [3] (2003).

[21] King v. Lang, 42 P.3d 698 (Idaho 2002); Crane v. Crane, 683 P.2d 1062 (Utah 1984), reprinted infra; Restatement (Third) of Property (Servitudes) § 5.8 cmt. b (2000).

[22] Restatement of Property §§ 4.1, 4.6 (2000); 2 American Law of Property § 8.82 (1952).

[23] Restatement (Third) of Property (Servitudes) § 4.6 (2000).

[24] Id.

[25] Restatement (Third) of Property (Servitudes) § 4.6 cmt. b (2000).

[26] Crane v. Crane, 683 P.2d 1062 (Utah 1984), reprinted infra; Restatement of Property § 489 cmts. b, c (1944); 2 American Law of Property §§ 8.80, 8.83 (1952).

[27] Restatement of Property § 489 cmt. b, § 490 cmt. a (1944).

[28] Crane v. Crane, 683 P.2d 1062 (Utah 1984), reprinted infra; Restatement of Property § 491 cmts. a, b (1944); 2 American Law of Property §§ 8.80, 8.83 (1952).

easements in gross non-assignable.[29] In determining the intent of the parties, the court will look to:

(a) the relationship between the grantor of the easement and the grantee (the more personal the relationship, the less likely the parties intended the easement to be assignable);[30]

(b) the degree to which assignability of the easement increases the burden on the servient estate either by increasing its use or decreasing its value (the greater the burden, the less likely the owner of the servient estate intended the easement to be assignable);[31]

(c) consideration paid for the easement (the purchase price should to some degree reflect the intention of the parties as to alienability; the greater the cost of the easement, the more likely the parties intended the grantee to be able to recoup some of those costs by selling the easement);[32] and

(d) the degree to which the use of the easement is temporary and personal (if the use is temporary and personal, the parties probably intended the easement to be used only by the grantee for the time designated, and so it is probably non-assignable).[33]

EXAMPLE 5 (Commercial easements in gross presumed alienable): Art grants to Barbara the right to take coal from Art's land. Barbara then sells this right to Charley. Art objects to Charley's taking of the coal. Art cannot prevent Charley from taking the coal. Easements in gross of a commercial character are presumed to be alienable. Absent evidence that the parties intended otherwise, Barbara has a right to sell the easement.[34]

EXAMPLE 6 (Noncommercial easements in gross presumed non-assignable): Otto grants to Ed, his closest friend, an easement to walk across his beach front property so that Ed can swim in the ocean. Ed owns no land in the vicinity. Ed is moving to another state and wishes to transfer the easement to his son. In all likelihood, Otto can prevent Ed's son from using the easement. The easement in gross is of a non-commercial nature, and under the older view is therefore presumed to be non-assignable. Even under the newer view, the close relationship between the grantor and grantee and the lack of consideration

---

[29] Crane v. Crane, 683 P.2d 1062 (Utah 1984) reprinted infra; Restatement of Property § 491 cmts. a, b (1944).

[30] Restatement of Property § 492 cmt. d (1944).

[31] Restatement of Property § 492 cmt. e (1944).

[32] Restatement of Property § 492 cmt. f (1944).

[33] Burcky v. Knowles, 413 A.2d 585 (N.H. 1980), reprinted infra.

[34] Crane v. Crane, 683 P.2d 1062 (Utah 1984), reprinted infra; Restatement of Property §§ 489, 490 (1944); 2 American Law of Property § 8.6 (1952).

paid for the easement suggest that the parties intended the easement to be personal to Ed, and thus non-assignable.[35]

To transfer an assignable easement in gross, there must be a valid assignment of the easement. The formal requirements for such an assignment are identical to those required for the transfer of an interest in land.[36]

Although by definition the benefit of an easement in gross does not attach to the land of the easement holder, the burden of an easement in gross does attach to the land of the servient estate. Therefore, if land subject to an easement in gross is assigned, the burden of the easement in gross runs with the land in the same way as would the burden of an appurtenant easement.[37] If the original parties intended the burden to run, and the successor to the servient estate has notice of the easement, the burden of the easement will pass with the servient estate so as to be binding on the successor to the servient estate.[38]

## 4. Principal Problem

Nelson Properties Inc., owned by Cyndi Carpenter, is a land development group specializing in upscale housing. Its most recent project was Clearwater Lake Estates, an expensive private community developed around a man-made lake. One attraction of the community was that, by purchasing a lot in the community, every homeowner would have access to Clearwater Lake. The lake is an artificial lake created by Nelson Properties and is owned by it.

Tom Goldigger, Dick Workalot, and Harry Ambishus, three upwardly mobile young bachelors who went to college with Cyndi, have a love of snorkeling. After meeting with her old friends, Cyndi convinced Tom, Dick, and Harry to buy three adjoining lots on the lake. All of the deeds were recorded. The deeds to all of the lots provide that:

> Grantee, and his immediate family only, shall enjoy unrestricted and free use of the lake so long as Grantee refrains from all behavior which may disturb the tranquil atmosphere of the community.

After three straight months of falling stock prices, Tom, Dick, and Harry were forced to sell their homes. Anita Perks, Ruth Latterclymer, and Dyan Dinero, each having a family with five actively swimming children, purchased the homes. The deeds to Anita, Ruth, and Dyan, which were all promptly recorded, provided in pertinent part that:

---

[35] Crane v. Crane, 683 P.2d 1062 (Utah 1984) reprinted infra; Restatement (Third) of Property (Servitudes) § 4.6 (2) (2000); 2 American Law of Property § 8.79 (1952).
[36] Restatement (Third) of Property (Servitudes) § 5.8(1) (2000).
[37] Restatement of Property § 455 cmt. a (1944).
[38] Tiller v. Hinton, 19 Ohio St.3d 66 (1985); Backman & Thomas, A Practical Guide to Disputes Between Adjoining Landowners—Easements § 1.04[1], [3] (2003).

Grantor hereby grants and conveys to Grantee the below described property, and Grantee takes subject to all easements and encumbrances burdening the said land.

It was January when Anita, Ruth, and Dyan moved into their new homes, so none of them attempted to use the lake. The following month, Nelson Properties sold the remaining unsold lots, including the lake, to Wannahatchi Properties, Inc.

When summer came, Anita, Ruth, and Dyan, and all fifteen of their children, followed the rest of the property owners into the refreshing waters of the lake. Dyan even dusted off her Jetski and took it out on the lake, although she did not see any other motor vehicles in use.

After one month of using the lake, Anita, Ruth, and Dyan were gruffly and rudely asked by Wannahatchi to stop using the lake. Wannahatchi claims that the deeds from Nelson Properties to Tom, Dick, and Harry created non-assignable easements to use the lake, and therefore Anita, Ruth and Dyan had no right to use it.

Feeling cheated and angry, Anita, Ruth, and Dyan come to you for help. They each want to continue using the lake in exactly the same way that they had in the past How would you advise them? In determining the rights of Anita, Ruth, and Dyan, consider the following materials.

## 5. MATERIALS FOR SOLUTION OF PRINCIPAL PROBLEM

### Nelson v. Johnson
Supreme Court of Idaho, 1984.
679 P.2d 662.

■ HUNTLEY, JUSTICE.

By this appeal we are asked to review the decision of the district court wherein it was determined that an easement in favor of the respondents, Lyle and Loa Nelson, exists. Because the findings of the district court are supported by substantial and competent evidence, we affirm.

In 1956, Robert and Marjorie Wake owned certain land in Cassia County. They carried on a dry farming operation on a portion of the land and the rest of the estate was used as a cattle ranch.

On December 28, 1956, the dry farm was sold to Jesse and Maud Hess. The contract of sale contained the following clause:

> It is hereby expressly agreed that the sellers hereby reserve and the purchasers agree to give, the right to the use of water in the Butler Springs located in the NW ¼ of the NE ¼ of said Section 15, for the watering of livestock owned by the sellers, together with an easement and right of way from the said springs Eastward across the NE ¼ of the NE ¼ of said Section 15, and

the N ½ of the N ½ of said Section 14, generally along the line near the bottom of Butler Spring Hollow.

In 1963, the Hesses sold the farm to Raymond and Wilma Johnson, the appellants herein. The terms of that contract provided that the Johnsons would have uninterrupted possession of the property, "excepting only that permissive use of the premises as is set forth in that certain contract dated the 20th [sic] day of December, 1956, between ROBERT C. WAKE and MARJORIE E. WAKE and the Vendors." The 1956 contract had not been recorded, nor had a deed between the Wakes and Hesses been executed as of 1963; however, the Johnsons had actual notice of the provisions of the Wake-Hess contract. A deed reflecting the terms of the 1956 contract was eventually executed and recorded in 1964.

The Wakes continued the use of the access road, [and] Butler Springs until they sold the home ranch and cattle operation in 1964. In the sale contract the Wakes expressly granted to the new owners, "their rights, to the water of Butler Springs . . . consisting of approximately 40 acres which the same was reserved by R.C. Wake and wife, in a Contract for Real Estate with Jean Hess dated December 26, [sic] 1956." In 1973, the property was purchased by the Nelsons, the respondents. A corrected warranty deed which included "[r]ight for stock water in Butler Springs located in the NW ¼, NE ¼ of Section 15 and easements on part of Section 15 and 14" was recorded in April of 1979.

The Johnsons have at all times since the purchase from the Hesses in 1964 been the owners of the farmland and Mr. Johnson testified that all owners of the ranch, previous to the Nelsons, had used the easements as a matter of right. Shortly after the Nelsons took possession of the ranch however, the Johnsons purported to grant permission to use the road and Butler Springs to the Nelsons, which "permission" was revoked by a letter sent the Nelsons in 1978. In 1979 the Johnsons placed locks on the gates across the access road.

The Nelsons filed a complaint in district court alleging that they had easement interests in the Butler Springs area. The court ruled for the Nelsons, holding that the easement reserved in the 1956 Wake-Hess contract was appurtenant to the ranch.

In construing an easement in a particular case, the instrument granting the easement is to be interpreted in connection with the intention of the parties, and the circumstances in existence at the time the easement was granted and utilized. The trial court in this case determined that the easement reserved in the 1956 Wake-Hess contract was appurtenant in nature, with a dominant estate in the cattle ranch and a servient estate in the farm, and that the easement had consequently passed with the dominant estate upon each transfer of title. The evidence fully supports that interpretation. The language of the reservation clause in the contract, as well as the established pattern of use of the Butler Springs area, indicate a clear intention by the parties that the easement be for the benefit of the cattle ranch. There is no showing that the parties intended it to be a mere personal right.

The definitions of "appurtenant" and "in gross" further make it clear that the easement is appurtenant. The primary distinction between an easement in gross and an easement appurtenant is that in the latter there is, and in the former there is not, a dominant estate to which the easement is attached. An easement in gross is merely a personal interest in the land of another; whereas an easement appurtenant is an interest which is annexed to the possession of the dominant tenement and passes with it. An appurtenant easement must bear some relation to the use of the dominant estate and is incapable of existence separate from it; any attempted severance from the dominant estate must fail. The easement in the Butler Springs area is a beneficial and useful adjunct of the cattle ranch, and it would be of little use apart from the operations of the ranch. Moreover, in case of doubt, the weight of authority holds that the easement should be presumed appurtenant. Accordingly, the decision of the trial court is affirmed as to the reserved easement.

## Burcky v. Knowles
Supreme Court of New Hampshire, 1980.
413 A.2d 585.

■ BOIS, JUSTICE.

This is a petition for declaratory judgment to determine easement rights over the defendants' land. The principal issue is whether a prior deed created an easement appurtenant or in gross. The Trial Court found an easement in gross, denied the plaintiffs the right to cross the defendants' land, and reserved and transferred the plaintiffs' exceptions. We reverse.

The defendants' predecessor in title purchased property located in North Hampton from Samuel Garland in 1934. Garland transferred the parcel by warranty deed with the following reservation:

> Reserving to the grantor the right to pass and repass over a strip of land fifteen (15) feet in width, lying adjacent to and northerly of said homestead lot of the grantee and extending from said Post Road to the rear of the lot hereby conveyed.

In 1953, Garland sold to the defendants' predecessor in title an additional lot which was located to the west of and contiguous to the defendants' original lot. Garland also transferred this parcel by warranty deed with the following reservation:

> Reserving to the grantor the right to pass and repass by foot, horse, and/or vehicle, over a strip of land fifteen (15) feet in width, lying adjacent to and northerly of said homestead lot of the grantee, and continuing the right of way reserved to the grantor (in the grantor's deed above referred to) between said

Post Road and the rear of the land surveyed to the grantee by said deed, on to the rear of the within granted parcel, so as to assure the grantor, his heirs and assigns of all necessary rights of ingress and egress for all purposes between said Post Road and his reserved pasture land which lies westerly and northwesterly of the within granted parcel.

The plaintiffs are successors in title to the remainder of Garland's land.

*The 1934 Deed*

The first stage of inquiry is to interpret the reservation clause in the 1934 deed. The initial thrust of inquiry of the court below was to determine whether the 1934 easement was appurtenant or in gross. The court appeared to rely heavily on the fact that the 1934 reservation clause did not contain words of inheritance, and concluded therefrom that it had to determine the intention of the parties in 1934, taking into consideration all the facts and surrounding circumstances at the time of the conveyance. After hearing all the evidence, the court found that Garland did not intend to create a permanent easement but an easement in gross, personal to himself and for the purpose of affording access to pastureland for his livestock. The court ruled that the plaintiffs had no legal claim to an easement across the defendants' land because the original easement did not run with the land.

The language in the 1934 deed reserves to the grantor nothing more or less than "the right to pass and repass over a strip of land fifteen (15) feet in length. . . ." We find this language in the context of the 1934 deed to constitute an appurtenant easement for the following reasons: (1) the language creates two distinct tenements in which a dominant estate is benefited by use of an easement on a servient estate; (2) the language is clear and unambiguous; and (3) no inference can be drawn from the absence of words of inheritance.

An appurtenant easement is a nonpossessory right to the use of another's land. It is an incorporeal right generally created for the purpose of benefiting the owner of the dominant estate (land to which the easement is attached) *as the possessor* of such estate; it runs with the land, is incapable of existence separate and apart from the dominant tenement, and is inheritable.

An easement in gross is also an incorporeal, nonpossessory right to the use of another's land, but it is a mere personal interest. It belongs to its owner independently of his ownership or possession of other land; it is generally not inheritable, and vests only in *the person* to whom it is granted.

The 1934 reservation clause presents a classic example of an appurtenant easement, where a grantor conveys a portion of his property to another, reserving in the deed the right to pass and repass across that property, (presumably) to benefit the agricultural utilization of the grantor's land. *See* 3 Powell, Real Property *supra* at 34–19 (1979). While the lower court may have been correct in concluding that the original easement was intended to afford Garland access to pastureland for his livestock, its focus was misdirected. The language used was not personal to Garland, and a reserved right in a conveyance which is not in its very nature a mere personal and temporary right will always be held an easement running with the land absent some controlling provision to the contrary. Furthermore, the general rule of construction favors appurtenant easements over easements in gross, and an easement is never presumed to be in gross or a mere personal right when it can be fairly construed to be appurtenant to some other estate.

The court below heard extrinsic evidence to determine the intention of the parties at the time of the 1934 conveyance. In only two cases is a court justified in placing itself in the situation of the parties at the time of the conveyance and taking into consideration all the facts and surrounding circumstances to determine their intentions: (1) where the extent and reasonable *use* of the easement is at issue; (2) where the language used is ambiguous.

In this case, it is the existence and not the reasonable use of an easement which is at issue; and the language used is plain and clear. While the language is general in nature, it is not ambiguous. The defendants even admit in their brief that "[t]he language of the 1934 deed was unambiguous." The grant of a general right to pass and repass entitles the dominant owner to use the right of way for any necessary or convenient purpose of passing pertaining to the ownership and occupancy of his land to which the right of way is appurtenant. Accordingly, we find that the court erred in going beyond the four corners of the 1934 deed.

The 1934 deed reserved the right to pass and repass across the grantee's property "to the grantor," and not "to the grantor, his heirs and assigns." The court below appeared to give substantial import to the absence of words of inheritance in this reservation clause in finding it necessary to look beyond the deed to ascertain the intent of the parties.

We have long held that the lack of words of inheritance in a deed, devise or trust has no legal effect, nor does it create an inference as to the intent of the parties. Words of inheritance originated with the introduction of the feudal law into England by William the Conqueror. The Anglo-Saxons as a people had been reduced to a state of vassalage under the kings and barons, and "the iron fetters of tenure" on land originally created as a means of national defense became a means for the feudal aristocracy "to gratify ancestral pride and maintain family splendor." *Smith v. Furbish,* 68 N.H. 123, 146–47 (1894).

> A feudal grant was ... made in consideration of the personal abilities of the feudatory, and his competency to render military service; and it was consequently confined to the life of the donee, unless there was an express provision that it should go to his

heir. Words of inheritance were never adapted to or suited for the land system of New Hampshire, and never became part of the law of this State. *Id.* at 147–48, 44 A. 398; *Cole v. Lake Co.,* 54 N.H 242 (1874).

We acknowledge that *Glines v. Auger,* 93 N.H. 340 (1945) may have clouded this issue by stating that the lack of words of inheritance "is not conclusive" of the parties' intent, and proceeding then to review the surrounding circumstances to determine their intent. However, we reaffirm earlier cases which hold that the absence of words of inheritance in an easement is not only "not conclusive" of the parties intent, but has no bearing on the parties intent.

Accordingly, we find that the easement reserved in the 1934 deed was appurtenant, and ran with the land.

*Subsequent Conveyances*

Having determined that the reservation clause in the 1934 deed was an appurtenant easement, our focus shifts to the 1953 deed.

The 1953 deed from Garland extended the original easement over a newly sold piece of property, and broadened the language of the easement over both tracts of property to include the right to pass "by foot horse and/or vehicle" over the grantee's land, to assure the grantor, "his heirs and assigns" of "all necessary rights of ingress and egress for all purposes" between the road and his land, *i.e.,* over both pieces of property. Although the original easement was extended across an additional piece of land, it was not broadened in scope because the words of inheritance added nothing, and the other additional language did not grant any use that would have been prohibited under the 1934 deed as a reasonable use in the service of the dominant tenement. Accordingly, we find the 1953 deed valid and sufficient to convey an appurtenant easement over both pieces of property as expressed therein.

Our final focus shifts to the effect of Garland's deed to his son Page, and two subsequent deeds of conveyance which failed to make reference to the easements in the 1953/1934 deeds. It is well established that once an easement has become appurtenant to a dominant estate, a conveyance of that estate carries with it the easement belonging to it, whether mentioned in the deed or not. Accordingly, the subsequent conveyances of Garland's land which failed to make reference to the easements in the prior deeds did not destroy the plaintiffs' rights in those easements.

The meaning and legal effect of a grant of right-of-way is a question of law reviewable by this court. We hold that the plaintiffs are entitled to easement rights contained in the 1934 and 1953 deeds to cross the land of the defendants'.

Reversed.

## Crane v. Crane
Supreme Court of Utah, 1984.
683 P.2d 1062.

■ OAKS, JUSTICE:

This is a suit by the twelve members of an unincorporated grazing association to establish the existence of an easement by prescription to drive their cattle across defendants' land in the spring and fall. The district court decreed the easement. We affirm.

Defendants own about 1,950 acres of land adjoining the Fishlake National Forest approximately ten miles east of Salina. Their property lies on either side of and includes Water Hollow Canyon. A dirt road follows this canyon in a northeasterly direction from Salina Creek and the highway for about three miles to the west boundary of defendants' property. It then crosses that property for about two miles to the boundary of the national forest. Since 1947, 30,000 acres in this area of the national forest—the Water Hollow C & H Allotment—has been designated for grazing 681 cattle. The twelve plaintiffs are the current holders of these 681 permits. Functioning as the Water Hollow Grazing Association, an unincorporated association, plaintiffs hire riders to move their cattle up Salina Canyon and Water Hollow Canyon to the allotment area in the spring and to bring them back in the fall. They cross defendants' property en route each way.

Plaintiffs claim an easement. Since the claimed easement is not appurtenant to any particular dominant estate (none of the plaintiffs own land adjoining defendants), it is an easement in gross. Legal requirements pertaining to the dominant and servient estates are therefore inapplicable.

Like other easements, an easement in gross can be acquired by prescription. An easement by prescription arises under our common law from a use of the servient estate that is "open, notorious, adverse, and continuous for a period of 20 years." . . .

Each of the plaintiffs acquired his cattle grazing permit from a predecessor who had been driving cattle across the trail or road since the association was formed in 1950. The legal issue is whether an easement in gross acquired by a predecessor could be transferred to a successor by purchase or descent.

According to the traditional general rule, an easement in gross is merely a personal interest in the real estate of another, and it cannot be transferred by assignment, inheritance, or otherwise. Under that general rule, none of these ten plaintiffs could prevail since none could have acquired the easement of a predecessor.

However, in the circumstances of this case, the general rule is either inapplicable or subject to an exception. An easement in gross that is not transferable is often referred to as "a noncommercial easement in gross."

In contrast, modern cases generally state that easements in gross are transferable when they are commercial in character. This idea apparently began with cases involving easements in gross for railroads, telephone, telegraph and electric power lines, pipelines, and ditches. Easements of that type have been held transferable almost without exception from early times. 3 R. Powell, *The Law of Real Property* ¶ 419 (1981). Apparently generalizing from these precedents, the *Restatement of Property* § 489 (1944) declares: "Easements in gross, if of a commercial character, are alienable property interests." Professor Powell affirms that this statement is "a true photograph of the net distillation of American law on the topic." 3 R. Powell, *The Law of Real Property* ¶ 419 (1981).

Another authority even refers to "a growing recognition" of the assignability of all easements in gross, except those intended to benefit only the first recipient. H.T. Tiffany, *The Law of Real Property* § 761 (3d ed. Supp. 1983 at 93).

For purposes of the issue in this case, we approve and apply the following definition: "An easement in gross is of a commercial character when the use authorized by it results primarily in economic benefit rather than personal satisfaction." *Sandy Island Corp. v. Ragsdale*, 143 S.E.2d at 807. The easement in this case involves a herd of cattle being driven to their summer range. The cattle are being raised for profit rather than for personal use. That falls within the definition of a commercial use. An easement in gross for this purpose is therefore transferable under the authorities cited above. . . .

The decree [of the Trial Court] appropriately limits the easement in gross to the nature and extent of the use by which it was acquired.

As modified by this opinion, the decree is affirmed.

### O'Donovan v. McIntosh v. Huggins
Supreme Judicial Court of Maine, 1999.
728 A.2d 681.

■ DANA, J.

Timothy P. O'Donovan and John A. McIntosh Jr. appeal from a partial summary judgment entered in the Superior Court in favor of Susan Huggins. O'Donovan and McIntosh argue that the court erred when it declared that an easement in gross held by McIntosh over Huggins's property was not assignable. We agree and vacate the judgment.

In 1987, McIntosh purchased real property at 184 Foreside Road in Falmouth. The property is adjacent to the Fish parcel[39] and separates the Fish parcel from Foreside Road. McIntosh also purchased an option on the Fish parcel and then optioned both 184 Foreside Road and his

---

[39] The Fish parcel is so named because the Fish family owned this land.

option on the Fish parcel to Casco Partners, Inc., which sought to construct a multiple lot subdivision on the Fish parcel. When Casco Partners did not proceed with the subdivision and McIntosh's option on the Fish parcel lapsed, McIntosh decided to sell 184 Foreside Road to Huggins and retain a right of way and an easement across it that would allow access to and the development of the Fish parcel.

On May 30, 1989, McIntosh conveyed the property to Huggins by warranty deed, reserving an easement for access to the Fish parcel. Concerning the easement, the deed stated:

> Excepting and reserving for the benefit of the Grantor and his heirs and assigns, a right of way and easement for access (50) feet in width to be used in common with the Grantee, her heirs and assigns, extending northerly from Foreside Road.... Said right of way and easement shall (1) be for the purpose of ingress and egress to and from the lot herein conveyed and other land adjacent to and behind the above described parcel, commonly known as the "Fish parcel" and (2) not be located any closer to the house now standing on the property than 27 feet. The assigns of the Grantor herein shall be limited to those building and/or occupying a subdivision located on the above—mentioned "Fish parcel." Also reserving the right to install utilities... over and under said right of way for the use and benefit of said other land. The foregoing right of way and easement shall also include the right of Grantor to enter on Grantee's land as is reasonably necessary to maintain, repair, and replace said utilities. The foregoing right of way and easement shall be subject to a duty owed by the Grantor to the Grantee, her heirs and assigns, to maintain, replace and repair the Grantee's property in the event of any disruption or damage caused to that property by the use of this right of way and easement. By acceptance of this deed the Grantor and Grantee agree to convey the right of way above mentioned to the Town of Falmouth in the event that it shall be accepted as a public way.

The deed also incorporated by reference an attached side agreement that would be "binding on subsequent owners" of the easement and in which Huggins agreed not to actively oppose any application for development permits for the Fish parcel. In April 1995, O'Donovan, the president of Black Bear Development, Inc., entered into a purchase and sale agreement with the owners of the Fish parcel. On January 1, 1996, O'Donovan entered into a purchase and sale agreement with McIntosh for the easement. Black Bear filed an application for subdivision approval with the Town of Falmouth Planning Board. In January 1996, the Board held the first in a series of open public meetings to address the application. The Board eventually suspended the application after a dispute arose regarding the transferability of the easement.

After the Board suspended the proposal, O'Donovan, in May 1997, filed a complaint against McIntosh and Huggins seeking, inter alia, a declaratory judgment pursuant to *14 M.R.S.A. §§ 5951–5963 (1980 & Supp. 1998)* concerning his right to purchase and sell the easement. McIntosh and O'Donovan filed a joint motion for a partial summary judgment, arguing that the easement may be transferred, conveyed, or otherwise assigned to O'Donovan. Huggins objected to the motion and filed a cross-motion for a summary judgment. The court granted Huggins's motion, concluding that the easement was not assignable. The court certified the judgment to allow O'Donovan and McIntosh to appeal pursuant to M.R. Civ. P. 54(b).

An easement is a right of use over the property of another. The law recognizes two different types of easements: an easement in gross and an easement appurtenant. An easement appurtenant is created to benefit the dominant tenement and runs with the land. To be appurtenant, however, the easement must also be attached to or related to a dominant estate of the grantor. Here, because McIntosh owned no dominant estate to which the easement could be appurtenant, the easement is in gross. Consequently, the question becomes whether the easement in gross is assignable. We hold that the easement is assignable because the parties clearly expressed that intent in the language of the deed.

Although we have categorically stated that an easement in gross is not assignable, we have also suggested that such an easement may be assignable in certain circumstances. Most important, we have never applied the rule—that an easement in gross is not assignable—to frustrate the parties' clear intent, as set forth in the deed, that the holder may assign the easement.

Our focus on the intent of the parties in this case is in accord with those courts that assess the parties' intent to determine the alienability of an easement in gross. Such an approach is consistent with those authorities that increasingly recognize and advocate the free alienability of easements in gross. See Restatement Of Property §§ 491, 492 (1944) (alienability of noncommercial easement determined by the manner and terms of its creation); 2 American Law Of Property § 8.82 (1952) ("There seems to be no reason to deny to parties who create easements in gross the privilege of making them alienable if they wish to do so."); 4 Richard R. Powell, Powell On Real Property § 34.16, at 34–218 (1998) (noting only barriers to alienability of easement in gross is finding of creator's manifest intent to bar alienation and courts' misplaced fear of "resultant surcharge" on the land); 3 Herbert Thorndike Tiffany, Tiffany On Real Property § 761 (Supp.1998) ("[T]here is a growing recognition of the assignability of all easements in gross except those demonstrably intended to benefit only the individual who is its first recipient.").

The conclusion that an easement in gross is assignable when the parties intend is consistent with our general policy favoring the free alienability of property. The alienability of an easement in gross promotes the free alienability of land, a general policy of property law. See Restatement of Property § 489 cmt. a (1944). The Restatement explains that "[t]his policy arises from a belief that the social interest is promoted by the greater utilization of the subject matter of property resulting from the freedom of alienation of interests in it." *Id.* In furtherance of this policy, we have adhered to the traditional rule of construction that whenever possible an easement is construed to be appurtenant to the land of the person for whose use the easement is created, thereby ensuring that the easement is alienable. Similarly, we have held that a profit a prendre—the right to take from the land something that is a product of the soil—is freely assignable even when that right is in gross. See *Beckwith v. Rossi,* 157 Me. 532 (1961). In addition, to give effect to the intent of the parties and promote alienability, we have abolished the technical requirement that the word "heirs" be used to preserve an interest of perpetual duration. See *O'Neill,* 527 A.2d at 324. It is consistent with the policy of promoting a high degree of alienability that we hold an easement in gross may be assignable.

Finally, we reject Huggins's argument that stare decisis compels us to hold that the easement in gross is not alienable despite the parties' contrary intent. Although we appreciate the need for uniformity and certainty produced by stare decisis, we have also recognized that "where the authorities supporting the prior rule have been drastically eroded, [and] . . . the suppositions on which it rested are disapproved in the better-considered recent cases and in authoritative scholarly writings, and . . . the holding of the [prior] case is counterproductive to its purposes, the situation is appropriate for legal change by the court's decision." *Myrick v. James,* 444 A.2d 987 (Me.1982). With respect to the nontransferability of an easement in gross, the primary argument proffered to support the rule is that alienability will unfairly burden the servient estate. The servient tenement holder, however, is protected because an easement holder may only use the easement in a manner consistent with the intent of the parties that created the easement.

Moreover, modern authority almost unanimously rejects the restrictive rule against alienability. See, e.g., Jon W. Bruce & James W. Ely Jr., The Law of Easements and Licenses in Land ¶ 9.03[3] (1995) ("[C]ommentators have unanimously supported judicial recognition that easements in gross may be transferred."). Because the reasons supporting the rule against alienability are no longer compelling and because modern authorities disapprove of the unduly restrictive nature of the rule, we conclude that the rule against alienability cannot used to frustrate the parties' intent that an easement be alienable.

The easement created by McIntosh and Huggins is alienable because the parties demonstrated their intent that the easement be alienable in the clear language of the deed. We construe the deed to give effect to the grantor's intent. Here, the deed created an easement "[e]xcepting and reserving the benefit of the Grantor and his heirs and assigns ..." and limited the assigns "to those building and/or occupying" the fish parcel. McIntosh and Huggins also agreed to convey the right of way to the Town of Falmouth if the Town accepted it as a public way. Moreover, the side agreement referenced in and attached to the deed bound the "subsequent owners" of the easement and prohibited Huggins from opposing development of the Fish parcel. As expressed by the clear language of the deed, McIntosh and Huggins intended that McIntosh would be free to assign the easement. The court, therefore, erred when it concluded that the easement was not assignable.

The Judgment is vacated. Remanded to the Superior Court for further proceedings consistent with this opinion.

■ WATHEN, C.J., with whom CLIFFORD, J., joins, dissenting.

I respectfully dissent. The intent of the parties is relevant in clarifying whether an easement is appurtenant or in gross. Once that is determined, however, there is no proposition of Maine decisional law more firmly settled than the principle that an easement in gross is personal and not assignable. See *O'Neill v. Williams*, 527 A.2d 322 (Me.1987) ("An easement in gross is a purely personal right, is not assignable, and terminates upon the death of the individual for whom it was created.").

Stare decisis embodies the "important social policy of continuity in law" and we have expressed our particular reluctance to abandon past precedent when to do so would "interfere with the valid reliance interests of litigants arising from contract rights, real property rights or rights to property by descent." See *Adams v. Buffalo Forge Co.*, 443 A.2d 932 (Me.1982). If there is a need for changing the law, it is better addressed by the Legislature. Our ruling necessarily acts on the past as well as the future and is capable of resurrecting long forgotten easements to dash the settled expectations of landowners and title examiners. I would affirm the judgment.

## NOTES

1. *Commercial or non-commercial. Crane* suggests that whether an easement in gross is assignable depends almost entirely upon whether it is deemed of a commercial or non-commercial nature. This represents the older view. Under the new Restatement, however, there should be no distinction between commercial and non-commercial easements in gross, with respect to assignability. Why has the law in this area changed? Is the newer view preferable? Or should courts continue to distinguish between commercial and non-commercial easements with respect to assignability?

2. *Does the benefit run with the land or with an estate in the land?* In the Principal Problem, assume that Anita, Ruth, and Dyan merely leased the lots from Tom, Dick, and Harry. Would their rights to use the lake as lessees be any different from their rights as owners?

3. *Does the benefit run with possession or only with rightful possession?* In *Crane*, the commercial easement in gross was a prescriptive easement, but it was still deemed transferable. In the Principal Problem, assume that Tom still owns his lot, but has not occupied it for two years. Further assume that Anita is occupying Tom's lot adversely, but she has yet to occupy the lot for the period of time needed to establish a prescriptive easement. As concerns Tom, Anita is still a trespasser, even if she is occupying the lot. Can Anita use the lake?

4. *Constructive notice.* In the Principal Problem, assume the deed from Harry to Dyan did not include the restriction in the deed from Nelson Properties to Harry which required the Grantee to refrain "from all behavior which may disturb the tranquil atmosphere of the community." Absent this provision in the deed from Harry to Dyan, does Dyan have any better chance of using her Jetski on the lake?

5. *Ambiguities and fatuities. Burcky* states that, when the language of a deed is unambiguous, no inferences may be made as to the intention of the parties. The language must control. In the Principal Problem, does the language of the deed, "Grantee, and his immediate family only," unambiguously denote an easement personal to Tom, Dick, and Harry?

6. *Severance of appurtenant easements. Nelson* states that, in an appurtenant easement, any attempted severance of the easement from the dominant estate must fail. Can you reconcile this with the rule that an appurtenant easement can be turned into an easement in gross if the instrument creating the easement permits?

7. *Non-transferable easements in gross versus transferable easements in gross.* In *Nelson,* since there was an express assignment of the easement why did it make a difference whether the easement was appurtenant or in gross?

8. *Free alienability of easements in gross.* In *O'Donovan,* when addressing the question of whether the easement was assignable, the court placed great emphasis on the intent of the parties and elected not to follow traditional rules which restrict the alienability of easements in gross. The court stated that its decision, to find that an easement in gross is assignable if the parties so intend, is consistent with a general policy favoring the free alienability of property. Can you see reasons to retain the traditional rules? Is this newer view preferable as the law grows to conform with the needs of our changing society?

9. *Divisibility of easements in gross. O'Donovan* involved the assignability of an easement in gross. A related issue is the divisibility of such an easement. Can the owner of an assignable easement in gross permit other parties as well as himself to use the easement? The new Restatement § 5.9 provides that "[t]ransferable benefits in gross may be divided unless contrary to the terms of the servitude, or unless the division unreasonably increases the burden on the servient estate." Thus a transferable easement

in gross is presumed to be divisible unless there are reasons to hold otherwise. This position is supported by substantial authority.[40]

---

[40] See Reporter's Note to § 5.9.

## ASSIGNMENT 21

# EXPRESS EASEMENTS: TERMINATION AND EXTINGUISHMENT

## 1. INTRODUCTION

*Express Terms and Impossibility.* An express easement can terminate in accordance with the terms of its creation, or through extinguishment as the result of subsequent events. If the easement is created to last a specified period of time, or to serve a particular purpose, it terminates upon the expiration of this period or when the purpose has been accomplished or can no longer be accomplished.

> EXAMPLE 1 (Time limit): Arlene grants Bill an easement of right of way across her land. The granting instrument states that the easement will terminate in ten years. Ten years pass. Bill can no longer cross the land over Arlene's protest. An easement may be limited in duration by the grant.

> EXAMPLE 2 (Loss of purpose of easement): Andy grants Bertha an easement across Blackacre for the stated purpose of getting to the highway. The highway is later abandoned. Bertha can no longer use the easement. The purpose of the easement is gone. There is no reason to burden the servient estate when the intended benefit to the dominant estate no longer exists.[1]

*Changed Conditions.* The Restatement (Third) of Servitudes § 7.18(2) (2002) "permits an easement to be terminated—where changed conditions exist—because the easement has become unreasonably burdensome upon the servient estate, obsolete, or economically wasteful."[2] The Wisconsin Supreme Court, however, has rejected this position, stating that "even at the risk of sanctioning unneighborly and economically unproductive behavior, this court must safeguard property rights."[3] The competing arguments about whether the doctrine of changed conditions should be used to terminate express easements are likely to be considered by many courts in coming years. It is difficult to predict how many jurisdictions will embrace the Restatement and how many will reject it.

---

[1] Compare Wolski v. DeLuca, 490 N.Y.S. 2d 869 (N.Y. App. Div., 1985) (where deed conveying the right of way indicated that one geographical boundary of the easement was an ice house parcel but did not specifically state that the purpose of the easement was to provide access to the ice house, the easement was not extinguished by the destruction of the ice house).

[2] AKG Real Estate, LLC v. Kosterman, 717 N.W.2d 835, 842 (Wis. 2006).

[3] Id. at 845.

*Release and Abandonment.* The easement owner himself can, through his actions, terminate his easement rights. An owner may terminate his easement by releasing it in a formal written instrument that meets the requirements necessary to create an easement.[4] Less formally, the easement holder can terminate his rights by "abandoning" the easement.[5] Abandonment results when the easement owner, intending to relinquish his easement rights, engages in sufficiently unequivocal conduct manifesting his intent. Failure to utilize the easement for its authorized use is evidence of an intent to abandon. Non-use alone, however, no matter how long continued, is seldom sufficient to extinguish an easement.[6] Abandonment is generally found in affirmative conduct on the part of the easement holder which is inconsistent with an intention to continue using the easement. Courts are more willing to find abandonment of an easement than of other interests in land, since extinguishment of easements clears up titles and encourages full use of the servient estate. However, intent to abandon is difficult to prove.[7]

EXAMPLE 3 (No abandonment): Alf, owner of Blackacre, has an easement giving him the right to take water from a spring on Whiteacre. Alf tells the owner of Whiteacre that he no longer wishes to use the easement and later writes him a letter stating that he is relinquishing all rights to take the water. Alf's right to take the water is not extinguished unless the letter meets the formal requirements for an effective release.

EXAMPLE 4 (Abandonment): Ariadne is the owner of Lot 1; Bart is the owner of adjacent Lot 2. Ariadne has an easement to cross Lot 2 in order to enter Lot 1 at the east side. Ariadne then constructs a building on Lot 1 which has its easterly wall running the entire length of the property line on the property line. After constructing the building, Ariadne tells Bart, "I guess I won't need that access route anymore." Three years later Ariadne tears the building down and wishes to use the easement across Bart's land. Ariadne may not use the easement. The building plus the words would probably be enough to show an abandonment.

---

[4] Restatement (Third) of Property (Servitudes) § 7.3 (2000).

[5] Restatement (Third) of Property (Servitudes) § 7.4 (2000).

[6] Restatement (Third) of Property (Servitudes) § 7.4 cmt. c (2000). But see Calif. Civil Code § 887.050 (failure to use easement for 20 years normally constitutes abandonment).

[7] Downing House Realty v. Hampe, 497 A.2d 862 (N.H. 1985) (nonuse of easement for over forty years due to the erection of a fence without an opening and the growth of two large trees did not result in an abandonment because the fence and trees could have been easily removed and thus were not permanent structures); Boyer v. Dennis, 742 N.W.2d 518 (S.D. 2007) (no intent to abandon right-of-way despite bolted access gate, encroaching foliage, and partial or temporary blockage by junk cars and wood piles, because the easement could still be used for pedestrian ingress and egress); Smith v. Muellner, 932 A.2d 382 (Conn. 2007) (allowing large chestnut tree and other vegetation to grow in easement was merely evidence of non-use, not intent to abandon).

EXAMPLE 5 (No abandonment): Andy has an easement of right of way across Brit's land. Andy does not use the easement for 30 years because he has been out of the country. When Andy returns he wishes to use the easement. Andy may use the easement. Andy must intentionally relinquish an easement, and nonuse is only evidence of this intention. Here, there is no persuasive evidence that Andy intended to abandon his rights.[8]

EXAMPLE 6 (Probably no abandonment): Alisa is the owner of Lot 1; Barbara is the owner of Lot 2. Alisa has an easement to cross Lot 2 in order to reach a paved road. Subsequently, a new road is built which abuts Lot 1. Alisa commences to use the new road on a regular basis. Ten years later she wishes to use the easement across Lot 2. Alisa can probably use the easement. Nonuse is only evidence of intent to abandon. Unless Barbara can show that Alisa's conduct constituted an intentional relinquishment or was unequivocally inconsistent with an intention to continue using the easement, Alisa can still use it.

EXAMPLE 7 (Probably an abandonment): Ellen has an easement of right of way to walk across Bob's land. Bob constructs a garage which abuts on the common property line where the easement originates. Ellen can open doors on both ends of the garage to use her easement. Over the years Ellen never uses the easement and also permits a tree to grow in front of the garage so that it is impossible to open the door by the property line to use the easement. After not using the easement for fifteen years she fells the tree and asserts her right to cross Bob's land. Bob protests. Bob will likely prevail. Ellen's permitting the tree to grow so as to preclude her use of the easement was an act inconsistent with an intent to use the easement. Such an act is considerably more probative of an intent to abandon than mere nonuse. However, Ellen has a potentially convincing argument that letting the tree grow was mere non-use, because she could always cut it down, as she did.

*Misuse and Overuse.* Finally, the easement owner can terminate his easement by improper exercise of his rights. Generally, misuse or overuse of an easement is not sufficient to extinguish it, although the servient owner can get an injunction to enjoin such excessive use.[9] However, when the court is unable to remedy the situation by limiting the use of the easement, and the alternatives are permitting misuse or no use at all, the court will generally find an extinguishment of the easement.

EXAMPLE 8 (Easement extinguished): Evelyn, owner of Blackacre, grants Jack, owner of Whiteacre (an adjoining parcel

---

[8] See Skvarla v. Park, 303 S.E.2d 354 (N.C. Ct. App. 1983) (easement was not extinguished by abandonment, despite nonuse for seventy years, where there was no evidence of unequivocal acts by easement owner indicating an intent to abandon).

[9] McCann v. R.W Dunteman Co., 609 N.E. 2d 1076 (Ill.App. 1993).

immediately to the north of Blackacre) an easement to cross a road on Blackacre which runs south to a public street. The road is linked to a road across Whiteacre which runs north to another public street. Jack subsequently dedicates the road on Whiteacre to the public. Public use of the road across Whiteacre leads to public use of the continuation of this road across Blackacre. It becomes apparent that this misuse of the road across Blackacre cannot be prevented without blocking off the connection between the two parts of the road, thereby extinguishing the easement. Evelyn sues to extinguish the easement. Evelyn wins. Jack caused the misuse when he dedicated the road across Whiteacre to the public. The misuse could not be prevented without extinguishing the easement.

*Lack of Notice.* Certain acts or conduct of the servient owner can serve to extinguish an easement burdening his land. As discussed in Assignment 20, under most modern recording statutes the burden of an express easement will not run if the successor in interest to the servient estate is a bona fide purchaser for value without notice of the easement. Thus, if the easement owner has not recorded his easement, the purchaser does not have actual knowledge of the easement, and if an inspection of the premises does not give notice of its existence, the servient owner can terminate the easement rights by selling his property to a bona fide purchaser without notice.

EXAMPLE 9 (Easement extinguished): Jim, owner of Blackacre, has an unrecorded easement giving him bathing privileges in a pond on Whiteacre, an adjoining parcel owned by Mindy. Mindy sells Whiteacre to Carol, and fails to tell her about Jim's easement for fear that Carol would refuse to buy if she knew of the easement. Since the easement is unrecorded and since Jim is on vacation when Carol purchases (thus not using his bathing privileges), Carol has no notice of Jim's rights. When Jim returns, he wishes to bathe in the pond and Carol protests. Carol prevails. Since Carol is a bona fide purchaser for value who bought Whiteacre without notice of the easement, she takes free and clear of Jim's interest, under modern recording statutes. Jim should have recorded his easement to protect his rights.

*Prescription.* The servient owner can also extinguish an easement by making adverse use of the burdened parcel for the same period of time necessary to acquire an easement by prescription.[10] Since the servient owner's use of the burdened portion of his estate is not necessarily adverse to the easement holder's rights, only conduct which is incompatible with the authorized right of use will start the prescriptive period running in favor of the servient owner.[11] The burden on the

---

[10] For a complete discussion of adverse use and prescriptive easements, see Assignment 38–39.

[11] Hansen v. Davis, 220 P.3d 911 (Alaska 2009).

servient owner of establishing sufficiently adverse acts is quite high. Courts tend to distinguish between temporary and easily removable improvements (not sufficient) and "permanent and expensive improvements that are difficult and damaging to remove" (sufficient).[12] In one case, a stone wall, a mature chestnut tree, and hedges that blocked the use of an easement for more than 30 years did not constitute adverse use against the easement owner because these obstructions could be removed.[13] The court observed that precedents treated stone walls, wire fences, wood fences, and vegetation blocking easement access as removable and therefore not adverse obstructions. By contrast, "substantial, permanent structures obstructing easement areas" included buildings, elevated structures spanning a gangway, and a six-foot high and eight-foot wide outdoor fireplace.[14] Note the bias in the court's assumption that ecologically valuable mature trees can easily be removed, whereas artificial structures like buildings and fireplaces cannot be moved or removed. Making it even harder for servient owners to establish adverse use of the easement, some jurisdictions do not allow the prescriptive period to begin to run until the easement owner attempts to use the easement.[15]

> EXAMPLE 10 (No extinguishment of easement): Mickie owns an easement of right of way across a road on Blackacre which is owned by Chuck. Due to a severe illness, Mickie does not use the easement for six years, during which time Chuck continuously uses the road. Upon her recovery, Mickie wishes to use the road again and Chuck protests. The statutory period for acquiring an easement by prescription is five years. Mickie can use the road. Chuck's use was not "adverse" because his conduct was not actionable by Mickie. The fact that Mickie has an easement to use the road does not mean that Chuck cannot also use it, as long as Chuck's use does not interfere with Mickie's easement.

> EXAMPLE 11 (Possible termination of easement by adverse use): Joan is the owner of an easement of right of way across Blackacre, which is owned by Gary. Gary builds a fence across the way that he keeps locked. Six years after the fence is erected, Joan brings an action to quiet title to her easement. The statutory period for acquiring an easement by prescription is five years. In the absence of other facts or circumstances, Joan may have lost her easement. Gary will argue that he has terminated this easement by adverse use for the statutory period.[16] However, a court might decide that structures like

---

[12] Hansen v. Davis, 220 P.3d 911, 917 (Alaska 2009).
[13] Smith v. Muellner, 932 A.2d 382 (Conn. 2007).
[14] Id. at 391–92.
[15] See, e.g., Mueller v. Hoblyn, reprinted infra; Vandeleigh Indus., LLC v. Storage Partners of Kirkwood, LLC, 901 A.2d 91, 105–06 (Del. 2006). But see Hansen v. Davis, 220 P.3d 911, 917 (Alaska 2009) (rejecting this rule).
[16] Restatement (Third) of the Law Property (Servitudes) § 7.7 illust. 1 (2000).

fences could be removed easily and thus do not constitute adverse use.

*Merger.* Under certain circumstances, conduct of both the easement owner and the owner of the servient estate together will work to extinguish an easement. One situation arises when the easement holder acquires ownership of the servient estate. When this occurs, the easement holder gains rights of use greater than those held pursuant to his easement. As a result, the lesser rights are swallowed up by the greater rights. This process is referred to as "merger". The very definition of an easement—a right in land in the possession of another—makes extinguishment under these circumstances appropriate.

EXAMPLE 12 (Termination by merger): Jimmy is the owner of Blackacre. Beth is the owner of Whiteacre, an adjoining parcel. Beth has an easement to draw water from a spring on Blackacre. Jimmy later sells Blackacre to Clara. Beth sells Whiteacre to Clara at the same time. Later Clara sells Blackacre to Dan and Whiteacre to Evie. Evie now wishes to get water from the spring on Blackacre. Dan can enjoin this use. The two estates merged at one time in Clara and thus the benefit and burden were in the same person. This extinguishes the easement because it makes no sense to have an easement in one's own land. Subsequent severance of the estates does not revive the old easement in most states.

EXAMPLE 13 (Suspension of easement for limited period): Alex, owner of Blackacre, has an easement of right of way across Whiteacre, an adjoining parcel owned by Boris. Boris subsequently conveys a life estate in Whiteacre to Alex, who possesses both parcels until his death. Alex's son, who takes over ownership of Blackacre upon his father's death, seeks to use the easement across Whiteacre. Boris objects. Alex's son can use the easement. The extinguishment of an easement, when caused by unity of ownership of the dominant and servient estates alone, extends only as far as this unity of ownership. Since the unity of ownership involved in this problem was limited to a life estate, the easement was merely suspended for the duration of the life estate.

*Estoppel.* Extinguishment by estoppel, like extinguishment through merger, requires actions on the part of both parties to an easement. Estoppel operates when the servient owner, reasonably relying on actions of the easement owner, engages in conduct inconsistent with the continuance of the easement. If the servient owner would suffer unreasonable harm by a restoration of the easement rights, the easement owner is estopped from asserting these rights and the easement is extinguished.

EXAMPLE 14 (Extinguishment by estoppel): Shanna, the owner of Blackacre, also owns an easement of right of way over

Whiteacre, owned by Bill. Although Shanna has no intention of abandoning her easement, she fails to use the way for five years. Bill, reasonably believing that Shanna intends to abandon the easement, begins to construct a building blocking the way. Shanna sees Bill working but says nothing until Bill builds half the building. She then asserts her right to use the way. Estoppel operates to extinguish Shanna's easement.[17]

*Third Party Actions.* Actions by third parties can extinguish easements through such devices as eminent domain, mortgage foreclosure, and tax sales. These devices can be used to terminate easements against the will of both the easement holder and the owner of the servient estate.

*Conservation Easements.* A current hot-bed of debate about easement termination or modification has arisen in the field of conservation easements. Most conservation easements are perpetual, in part due to their intended purposes and in part due to federal tax requirements to qualify for charitable tax deductions. Under what circumstances, if any, should conservation easements be modified or terminated? The issue is not merely academic.

Land trusts or government agencies may be willing to accommodate landowners' desire to use their conservation lands for purposes inconsistent with an easement. For example, a recent controversy involved proposed subdivision development on an encumbered historic plantation property in Maryland.[18] In addition, an attempt to terminate an agricultural, open space, and wildlife conservation easement on a Wyoming ranch occurred to allow coalbed methane development.[19] While a host of issues are raised by these cases, we address three in particular.

First, some have argued that perpetual conservation easements pose dangers to the property law system by binding future generations to inflexible and arguably inefficient conservation choices made by today's generations.[20] However, it has also been argued that conservation easements' perpetual constraints on certain land uses efficiently serve as

---

[17] See Mueller v. Hoblyn, reprinted below. A few jurisdictions may require reliance by the owner of the servient estate upon the easement owner's acts of abandonment as an element of abandonment generally. See Lague, Inc. v. Royea, 568 A.2d 357 (Vt. 1989) (discussing, but ultimately rejecting this position).

[18] McLaughlin, Amending Perpetual Conservation Easements: A Case Study of the Myrtle Grove Controversy, 40 U. Rich. L. Rev. 1031 (2006).

[19] McLaughlin & Weeks, *Hicks v. Dowd*, Conservation Easements, and the Charitable Trust Doctrine: Setting the Record Straight, 10 Wyo. L. Rev. 73 (2010); McLaughlin, Could Coalbed Methane Be the Death of Conservation Easements?, 29(5) Wyo. Lawyer 18 (Oct. 2006).

[20] Korngold, Solving the Contentious Issues of Private Conservation Easements: Promoting Flexibility for the Future and Engaging the Public Land Use Process, 2007 Utah L. Rev. 1039 (2007); Korngold, Resolving the Intergenerational Conflicts of Real Property Law: Preserving Free Markets and Personal Autonomy for Future Generations, 56 Am. U. L. Rev. 1525 (2007); Mahoney, The Illusion of Perpetuity and the Preservation of Privately Owned Lands, 44 Nat. Resources J. 573 (2004); Korngold, Privately Held Conservation Servitudes: A Policy Analysis in the Context of in Gross Real Covenants and Easements, 63 Tex. L. Rev. 433 (1984).

land owners' self-selected constraints on development temptations, create private ordering of property arrangements regarding conservation, and resolve temporal "tragedies of the commons."[21]

Second, the very purposes of conservation easements may require a certain degree of flexibility. A basic principle of the ecological sciences is that nature is dynamic, adapting and changing in often nonlinear and unpredictable ways.[22] Changing conditions may stimulate or force adaptations that vastly alter the conditions on which conservation easements are drafted, such as mass migrations of plant and animal species in response to climate change—a phenomenon called "climate surfing."[23] Thus, at a minimum, conservation easements must be drafted with enough specificity to achieve their conservation purposes and prevent harmful uses of the land but with enough flexibility to provide for "adaptive management" of the conservation land as conditions change.[24] Inflexible easements or unpredictable changes may require that some conservation easements be modified or terminated because they no longer can achieve the purposes for which they were created.

Third, the concern exists that easy modification or termination rules will allow landowners to claim the benefits of conservation easements only when they are convenient but then alter their constraints when land-use and development pressures become great. This potential undermines the public's interests in the conservation purposes for which the easements were granted (as well as raising potential tax implications that are not explored here). Professor Nancy McLaughlin has proposed that conservation easements be treated as charitable trusts that can be modified only by a court in a *cy pres* proceeding to ensure that the stated conservation purposes are served as much as possible or are truly no longer capable of being achieved.[25] Alternatively, Professor Carol Brown has proposed that the members of the public be granted standing to enforce conservation easement purposes through litigation.[26]

---

[21] Thompson, The Trouble with Time: Influencing the Conservation Choices of Future Generations, 44 Nat. Resources J. 601 (2004).

[22] See, e.g., Holling, Adaptive Environmental Assessment and Management (1978); Gunderson & Holling, Panarchy: Understanding Transformation in Human and Natural Systems (2001). See also Greene, Dynamic Conservation Easements: Facing the Problem of Perpetuity in Land Conservation, 28 Seattle U. L. Rev. 883 (2005).

[23] Olmsted, Climate Surfing: A Conceptual Guide to Drafting Conservation Easements in the Age of Global Warming, 23 St. John's J. Legal Comment. 765 (2008).

[24] Id.; Greene, Dynamic Conservation Easements: Facing the Problem of Perpetuity in Land Conservation, 28 Seattle U. L. Rev. 883 (2005).

[25] McLaughlin, Rethinking the Perpetual Nature of Conservation Easements, 29 Harv. Envtl. L. Rev. 421 (2005). See also Richardson, Conservation Easements as Charitable Trusts in Kansas: Striking the Appropriate Balance Among the Grantor's Intent, the Public's Interest, and the Need for Flexibility, 49 Washburn L.J. 175 (2009).

[26] Brown, A Time to Preserve: A Call for Formal Private-Party Rights in Perpetual Conservation Easements, 40 Ga. L. Rev. 85 (2005).

## 2. Principal Problem

```
+------------------------------------------+
|        +----------+----------+           |
|        | C's land | A's land |           |
|        +----------+----------+           |
|                                          |
|                                          |
|                B's land                  |
|                                          |
|                                          |
|   +--------------------------------------+
|   |              Road 1                  |
+---+--------------------------------------+
```

In the above diagram all of the land is cattle grazing land improved only with fences. C wants to drive cattle across B's land to Road 1, and offers to pay B $10,000 for an easement providing him with such a privilege. B thinks this is a good idea and asks you as his lawyer to explain the legal ramifications of such a proposal and to outline the key clauses in the document that will protect B's interest.

Review the foregoing materials and read the following cases in preparing to advise your client, B.

## 3. MATERIALS FOR SOLUTION OF PRINCIPAL PROBLEM

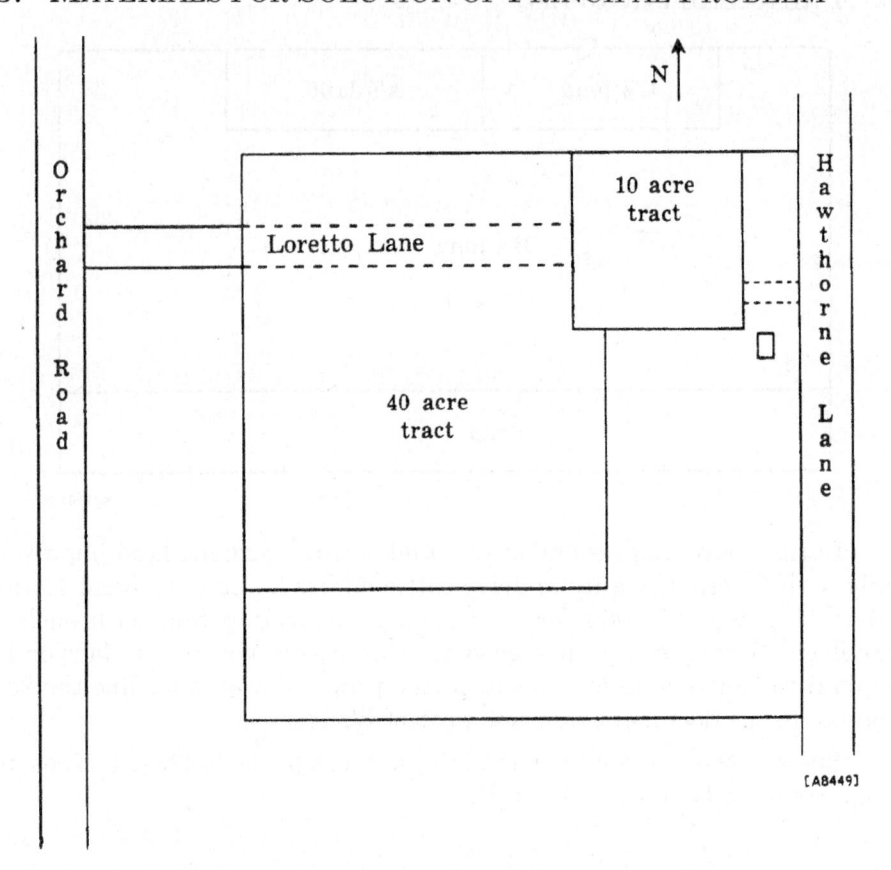

### Wetmore v. The Ladies of Loretto, Wheaton
Appellate Court of Illinois, 1966.
220 N.E. 2d 491.

■ DAVIS, JUSTICE.

This is an appeal from a judgment entered by the trial court in which the issues on both the complaint and counterclaim were found in favor of the plaintiff, Horace O. Wetmore, and against the defendant, The Ladies of Loretto, Wheaton, an Illinois not-for-profit corporation. The nature and extent of the right of the defendant to use a certain roadway is the critical issue involved in this litigation.

Since 1928, the plaintiff, and his family before him, owned a tract of land near Wheaton, consisting of approximately 80 acres. The principal access to this tract was by means of Hawthorne Lane, a roadway extending north from the easterly edge of the tract.

The plaintiff sold 10 acres of this tract to the defendant in 1946. These acres, located along the north edge of the larger tract, were carved out of its middle and were improved with a large mansion house, swimming pool, sunken gardens, and various out-buildings. The 10-acre parcel was landlocked, and the plaintiff granted to the defendant an express easement across the remainder of his tract to the east. This easement was over an existing driveway which ran in front of plaintiff's residence—to the east of the property sold to defendant—out to Hawthorne Lane, and then north, along Hawthorne Lane.

In 1957, representatives of the defendant approached the plaintiff, stating that it would like to open its own roadway west from its 10-acre tract, to Orchard Road. A portion of the land retained by the plaintiff, after his conveyance to the defendant, consisted of 40 acres west and south of the 10-acre tract that the defendant had purchased. The west line of this 40-acre tract was approximately 1400 feet east of Orchard Road—a public road. The plaintiff, however, also owned a strip of land 33 feet wide, extending westerly from the west line of this 40-acre tract to Orchard Road.

Presumably, plaintiff could have sold that 33 foot strip to defendant, together with a strip of land 33 feet wide extending easterly therefrom over the 40 acre tract to the 10 acre tract. This would have given defendant its own road. However, the plaintiff told the defendant that he was not interested in selling just a roadway to the west out of the 10-acre tract but said that he might sell the entire 40-acre tract, including the 33-foot strip extending to Orchard Road. The defendant advised the plaintiff that if it could purchase the 33-foot-strip of land, it would build a new road out to the west—which was in the opposite direction from plaintiff's residence and Hawthorne Lane.

At the time of the negotiations for the sale of the 40-acre tract, plaintiff attempted to get the defendant to give up its express easement appurtenant to the 10-acre tract—over the driveway in front of his house and over Hawthorne Lane. The defendant declined but said that as soon as its roadway to the west was built it would direct the bulk of its traffic over that road; and that, consequently, the driveway in front of the plaintiff's residence would receive less use. Apparently, this was satisfactory to the plaintiff, who prepared a memorandum dated October 28, 1957, in which he acknowledged that defendant wished to continue its easement on Hawthorne Lane and the driveway in front of his house. The 40-acre tract was then sold to defendant in 1957. No reference was made to any easement in the conveyance of the 40-acre tract.

The defendant built a road westerly to Orchard Road, which was called Loretto Lane. It ran through the 40-acre tract and across the 33-foot strip of land that the defendant purchased from the plaintiff. It was completed in June of 1960. Prior to that time, the relations between the plaintiff and the defendant had deteriorated. Throughout the 1950's the defendant conducted a kindergarten and music classes on the 10 acre tract and the plaintiff became quite upset by the extent of the attendant use of the driveway and Hawthorne Lane, which totaled 40 to 50 vehicles daily, as well as limited use by pedestrians. On rare occasions the defendant also had picnics, garden parties and other parties which would result in additional traffic over Hawthorne Lane and in front of plaintiff's residence. All of these activities, however, were conducted on the 10 acres.

After the conveyance of the 40-acre parcel of land to the defendant, the plaintiff continued in his efforts to obtain defendant's release of the easement in front of his house. As early as 1958, he threatened suit if the defendant would not give up its easement. After Loretto Lane was opened in June of 1960, the defendant made verbal requests and sent out maps and directions to those going to and from the convent, asking them to use Loretto Lane rather than Hawthorne Lane. Apparently, these efforts were quite successful in that the traffic over Hawthorne Lane, within a reasonable time after the construction of Loretto Lane, was reduced generally to about 5 cars per day.

The plaintiff, however, was not satisfied with the efforts of the defendant in this respect. He hired a deputy sheriff to turn back traffic going to the convent on Hawthorne Lane. This officer admonished such persons that they were trespassing on a private road. He also personally stopped vehicles on the Lane, told the drivers that they were trespassers, and directed them to turn around. Plaintiff also ejected pedestrians from the driveway in front of his house. At times his conduct was such that it obviously frightened the young people at the convent, as well as the Sisters. On one occasion, when the plaintiff came on defendant's property to object to the use of the Lane, one of the Sisters was compelled to call the sheriff to remove him. The plaintiff also installed a gate on the roadway that set off an alarm bell—both by the gate and in his house—when the gate was opened. There were numerous incidents and confrontations resulting from plaintiff's assertions that the defendant was without right to use or enjoy the easement previously expressly granted to it.

In 1962, the defendant began the construction of a House of Studies, part of which was on the original 10-acre tract purchased by the defendant and part on the 40 acre tract. The building was completed in August of 1963. It is one inseparable structure with the portion on the 10-acre tract being indivisible from the portion on the 40-acre tract. While this building is joined by a passageway to the chapel, it is, however, separate, distinct and apart from the other structures on the 10-acre tract.

The completion of the House of Studies building was the catalyst that gave rise to this suit. Plaintiff's complaint alleges that upon the completion of this building located partly on the 10 acre tract and partly on the 40-acre tract, the easement granted for the benefit of the 10-acre tract was extended by the defendant to the 40-acre tract; that the entire installation (all of the buildings) of defendant on the two tracts are operated as a composite unit and cannot be segregated as to that use pertaining to the 40 and that use pertaining to the 10-acre tracts; and that defendant's use of the easement previously granted therefore, should be enjoined by reason of its extension to the 40-acre tract.

The defendant's answer stated that upon the conveyance of the 40-acre tract to it in 1957, there was created an implied easement benefiting this tract over the route previously granted by the express easement. It also denied that the use to which the 40-acre tract was put justified enjoining the use of the express easement appurtenant to the 10-acre tract. Other issues were raised which we will discuss later.

The trial court found that there was no implied easement upon conveyance of the 40-acre tract to the defendant; that defendant's use of the 10 and 40 acre tracts cannot be segregated; and that the express easement appurtenant to the 10 acre tract was thus abandoned and suspended by operation of law. The trial court enjoined any further use of Hawthorne Lane by the defendant until such time as the defendant's installation on the 10 and the 40 acre tracts shall be so altered or changed as to permit the use of Hawthorne Lane for the benefit of the 10-acre tract only, and not for the benefit of the 40-acre tract.

The plaintiff obtained an injunction preventing the continued use of the express easement appurtenant to the 10-acre tract by reason of its use for the benefit of the nondominant 40-acre tract. The defendant contends that not every extension of the use of an easement to an additional tract is a misuse; and that it is only where the extension materially changes the burden on the servient estate, either as to the type of use or the amount, that there is a misuse.

We do not understand that to be the law. If an easement is appurtenant to one tract of land, any extension thereof to another tract of land is a misuse. . . .

Conceding, that when the defendant constructed the House of Studies principally on the 10 acre but partly on the 40-acre tract the use of the easement for the benefit of this building constituted a misuse, the court is still confronted with the question of whether the remedy of injunction sought by the plaintiff and granted by the trial court, was proper. In all of the cases cited by the plaintiff, it was held that either an injunction was proper or that the easement was extinguished if it was impossible to sever or distinguish between the authorized and unauthorized use of the servient tenement. The majority of these cases pertained to the construction of a single, inseparable building, partly on the dominant and partly on the non-dominant estate. The authorized and unauthorized use made of a roadway or easement for access to such building was quite understandably held to be indistinguishable.

Such is not the factual situation here. The House of Studies building, constructed partly on the 10-acre tract and partly on the 40-acre tract, is separate and distinct from the other buildings on the 10-acre tract. As to the use made of the chapel, mansion house, sunken gardens and other facilities on the 10-acre tract, access to these areas and the functions to take place thereon can be separated and distinguished from the functions to take place on the 40-acre tract relating to the House of Studies building. We find no factual justification for the finding that the entire installation of defendant on the 10 and 40 acre tracts cannot be segregated, or for the injunction prohibiting any use of Hawthorne Lane until such time as defendant's "Installation" be changed or altered.

Two other factors impress us in this respect. First, in the cases cited relative to extending the benefit of an easement to non-dominant lands, the owner of the dominant tract was responsible for the extension of the burden and the owner of the servient tenement had no connection or control over such an extension. The plaintiff here, however, was the one who conveyed the additional 40 acres to the defendant. He made this conveyance with full knowledge that the defendant intended to use the additional land for purposes other than as a roadway to the west, and that the defendant would not give up its existing easement benefiting the 10 acre tract. The plaintiff was not totally without command or control over the extension of the use of the easement.

Second, and most significant in this respect is the fact that prior to the construction of any facilities on the 40-acre tract or any use thereof, the vehicular traffic over the easement, solely for the benefit of the 10-acre tract, reached 40 to 50 cars per day, and there was also certain pedestrian use of the easement. On special occasions the traffic was greater. After the erection of the facilities on the 40-acre tract and after the construction of Loretto Lane over the 40-acre tract and the concerted efforts of defendant to direct traffic over this Lane rather than over Hawthorne Lane and the driveway in front of plaintiff's house, the traffic over Hawthorne Lane and the driveway was reduced to 4 to 5 cars per day. Yet, with knowledge of these facts, the plaintiff sought and invoked the equitable powers of the court to enjoin the defendant's limited use of such access way.

While the erection of the House of Studies building on part of the 40-acre tract results in a technical misuse of the easement granted appurtenant to the 10-acre tract, such trivial and inconsequential misuse neither justifies the issuance of an injunction restraining defendant's right to use the easement expressly granted, nor warrants the authorization granted to plaintiff to close Hawthorne Lane as a means of access to defendant's property. A court of chancery will not require the doing or prohibition of an act where the benefit to be obtained does not warrant the hardship imposed. Under the facts of this case, it would be unconscionable to enjoin the use of the easement granted to defendant in 1946.

As to the punitive damages claimed by defendant, such are not a favorite in the law. It is only where a wrongful act is accompanied by aggravating circumstances such as willfulness, wantonness, malice or oppression that such damages are recoverable. Defendant is entitled, however, in view of plaintiff's past conduct, to an injunction sought in its counterclaim, restraining the plaintiff and his agents from wrongful entries upon defendant's property and from interfering with defendant's proper use of the express easement.

The decree is reversed and the cause is remanded to the trial court with directions to enter a decree in conformance with the views expressed herein and to take such further and other steps as may be necessary to implement such views.

Reversed and remanded.

## NOTES

1. *Plaintiff's position.* What is the basis for plaintiff's argument that the right of way easement should be extinguished or that the use of the easement should be enjoined? On what well-established legal principles was plaintiff relying? Why did plaintiff lose?

2. *Rationale.* The court finds that total enjoyment of the easement should not be enjoined because authorized and unauthorized use can be separated and distinguished. How persuasive is the court's reasoning?

3. *Pivotal factors.* What major factors influenced the court's decision?

4. *Principal Problem.* Based on the outcome of this case, what provisions should be included in the instrument granting C the cattle driving privilege?

## Pavlik v. Consolidation Coal Co.

United States Court of Appeals, Sixth Circuit, 1972.
456 F.2d 378.

■ EDWARDS, CIRCUIT JUDGE.

This appeal concerns a dispute about the interpretation of the defeasance clause of an easement for a "pipeline for transportation of coal slurry." The easement had been granted by appellants' predecessors in title to the land affected, to the predecessors in title of the appellee. Jurisdiction is based on diversity of citizenship and, hence, Ohio law applies. The District Judge who heard this case on a record consisting entirely of stipulated facts held that the fact that the pipeline had not been used for over one year to transport coal slurry, but was being maintained in readiness to do so, did not serve to terminate the easement. We believe his construction of the contract was in error and we reverse.

The critical language of the easement is contained in the granting clause and in the defeasance clause:

### Granting Clause

IN CONSIDERATION of Ten and no/100 Dollars ($10.00), receipt of which is hereby acknowledged, the undersigned Fred S. Wellman, and Frances M. Wellman, husband and wife, hereinafter called grantor, hereby grants to Pittsburgh Consolidation Coal Company, a Pennsylvania corporation qualified in Ohio, the grantee, its successors and assigns, a thirty feet wide perpetual right of way, as set forth on plat attached hereto as Exhibit "A" and made a part hereof, over and through the grantor's lands in the Township of Mentor, County of Lake, State of Ohio, and described as follows: (Description omitted) . . . for the purposes and with the rights of constructing, maintaining, operating, altering, repairing, replacing and removing one pipe line for the transportation of coal slurry, with free ingress and egress over said lands for said purposes.

## Defeasance Clause

It is a condition of this deed that, if at any time said pipe line shall cease to be used for the purpose set forth herein for the period of one year, then all rights of the grantee obtained by this deed shall cease and determine, and the land across which said right of way goes shall be free and clear of the easement granted hereby, without further act or writing; provided, however, that, if requested, grantee agrees to execute a formal release of said easement.

The stipulated facts which appear relevant to decision of this case include the following:

In 1956 the easement just recited in part was signed by the predecessors in title of the parties to this suit. The consideration was $995, including $75 for attorney's fees.

In 1955 Pittsburgh Consolidation Coal had signed a contract with Cleveland Electric Illuminating Company to supply it with thousands of tons of coal per year through a coal slurry pipeline extending 103 miles and terminating at CEI's Eastlake, Ohio, plant. The pipeline was built at a total cost of $14,500,000 and was in successful operation from its construction date in 1957 until August of 1963.

On May 14, 1963, appellee Consolidation Coal and CEI entered into a supplemental agreement whereby the pipeline was to be placed in an inactive state. The contract called for Consolidation to receive $105,097 per month for the life of its original 15-year contract, without the delivery of any coal at all, but under the obligation to maintain the pipeline in a stand-by condition, ready to go into operation on notice "as soon as practicable." This contract recited that the deactivation resulted from reductions in rail freight rates occurring since the activation of the coal slurry pipeline.

As of the deactivation, at the request of Consolidation, the parties negotiated a supplemental agreement for continuation of the contract for another year with the same defeasance clause included therein. The net effect of each supplemental agreement (there were 15 of them) was to extend the defeasance clause from a new date. The last extension was for

30 days, until May 27, 1967, after which time no further extensions were granted.

As to the purposes for the extensions, the parties stipulated:

Since prior to June 15, 1964, Consolidation Coal Company and its predecessors have been negotiating with Albert Pavlik for an amendment of the Wellman Easement which would not contain any time limitation for lack of use and which would permit its use for all products, including solids, liquids, gases and mixtures thereof, and one of the reasons that the aforesaid extension agreements were executed was to preserve the status quo of the parties during the said negotiations.

After failure of negotiations and notice from the Pavliks that the easement had terminated, the Pavliks filed suit in state court seeking a declaration of rights under the contract.

Consolidation removed the case to the United States District Court and filed counterclaims. The sole issue appealed is whether or not the District Judge was correct in holding under the facts stated above that the easement was not terminated.

We believe that the District Judge's holding was in error. When the pipeline was deactivated, the defeasance clause should have been given its intended effect.

First, we feel that the language of the easement is not ambiguous. The plain language of the defeasance clause was, we believe, intended by the parties to refer to the operation of the pipeline for the transmission of coal slurry. When transmission of coal slurry ceased for a year, the defeasance clause became fully operative. We recognize, of course, that the granting clause twice employs the plural word "purposes" to refer to the rights of "constructing, maintaining, operating, altering, repairing, replacing and removing one pipeline for the transportation of coal slurry." But in terms of the defeasance clause read in conjunction with the granting clause, we believe that the easement only sets forth one purpose for the pipeline, namely, "for the transportation of coal slurry." When clear contract language itself reveals the intent of the parties, there is no need to turn to rules of construction.

Second, if interpretation of the intention of the parties might be held to be required as to the granting and defeasance clauses, we would look first at the other terms of the contract taken as a whole. The meager price Consolidation's predecessor had paid ($995) was appropriate for the contract's rigid pro-grantor terms.[27] Over and above the harshness of the defeasance clause, the grantor also has the right to use the property as he sees fit and if his proposed use would require removal of the pipeline,

---

[27] The parties stipulated that two weeks earlier the grantee had paid $30,000 for a somewhat longer easement over adjacent land, but on conditions, including the defeasance clause, much more favorable to the grantee. No appeal was taken from the portion of the judgment that held this easement to be still in effect.

he can demand that Consolidation remove and relocate it at any time. The pro-grantor provisions of the easement read as a whole support the interpretation above.

Third, (assuming interpretation outside the contract itself is called for) there were 15 occasions where Consolidation and Pavlik signed supplemental agreements after termination of the operation of the pipeline. These agreements were made at Consolidation's request and Consolidation paid small sums for them.

Actions of the parties reflecting their subsequent construction of a contract may be looked at in construing its purposes. Obviously, if Consolidation had felt that termination of transmission of coal slurry had no effect on its easement, it would have had no occasion to request the supplemental agreements to extend the defeasance clause.

It appears to us that these supplemental agreements properly read represented full recognition of the effectiveness of the defeasance clause by the parties themselves as of the termination of the transmission of coal slurry.

The judgment of the District Court is vacated and the case is remanded for further proceedings consistent with this opinion.

■ MCCREE, CIRCUIT JUDGE (dissenting).

I respectfully dissent. It is clear to me that the easement was granted for the purpose of "constructing, maintaining, operating, altering, repairing, replacing and removing" a pipeline for the transportation of coal slurry. It is equally clear that the pipeline is still maintained for the transportation of coal slurry and that there has been no cessation of that use. The construction which the majority gives the instrument selects one of the seven stated purposes of the easement, operating, as the only purpose.

I am also unpersuaded that the parties have given a contrary construction to the instrument by their subsequent conduct. In the first place, the extension agreements provided:

> ... if at any time said pipeline *shall* cease to be used for the purpose ... after [a stated date subsequent to the extension agreement], then all rights of the Grantee ... shall cease. (Emphasis added.)

The use of this language indicates that the parties did not agree that the pipeline *had* ceased to be used for the purpose set forth in the granting instrument. Of more significance, however, is the fact that the extension agreements were executed, as the majority opinion recites, "to preserve the status quo ... during negotiations," which concerned, in part, the transmission through the pipeline of products in addition to coal slurry. Further, evidence of settlement negotiations is inadmissible to prove facts material to the dispute which they concern.

Finally, I do not regard the amount of consideration paid for the easement in 1956 as relevant in ascertaining the parties' intent at that time. It appears that the land was completely idle and perhaps unsuited for any purpose other than as a right-of-way for a pipeline. Also, if the grantor should desire at any time to use the land, the grantee would be required to relocate the pipeline and right-of-way at his own expense. The value of an easement subject to relocation at the will of the grantor might be no more than the amount paid here. But that fact is not material to the issue before us.

I would affirm the judgment of Judge Lambros.

## NOTES

1. *Purpose of the grant.* As the dissent points out, the defeasance clause provides that the grantee's right would terminate if the pipeline were not used for the purpose for which it was granted for one year. The pipeline was granted for seven "purposes" and defendant has ceased to use it for only one of these enumerated purposes. Why does the court conclude that defendant's easement rights were extinguished?

2. *Conditional grants.* Conditional grants are generally said to be disfavored by courts. Why is the court in *Pavlik* willing to construe the ambiguous language of this deed so as to give effect to the condition placed on the grants?

3. *Careful drafting.* If you had represented the coal company when the original deed was drafted, how would you have written the key phrases of the defeasance clause?

4. *Possible protections.* Does this case give you any ideas as to possible ways in which B could protect himself against misuse by C in the Principal Problem?

### Mueller v. Hoblyn
Supreme Court of Wyoming, 1994.
887 P.2d 500.

■ TAYLOR, JUSTICE.

The right to use an easement is at issue in these consolidated appeals. The owners of the dominant estate filed an action against the owner of the servient estate to quiet title to the easement. The owners of the dominant estate claimed they had been denied use of the easement. The owner of the servient estate maintained the entire easement had been lost by adverse possession. Using a variety of procedural means, other present and former owners of dominant estates also became parties to this action. After a bench trial, the district court determined that only a small portion of the easement near a water well had been terminated by adverse possession. We affirm in part and reverse in part.

Facts

In 1963, Herbert J. Engleman and Glenys G. Engleman (Englemans) owned a single undivided tract of property in Laramie County, Wyoming. The western boundary of the property had access to Yellowstone Road, a highway north of the City of Cheyenne. On July 15, 1963, the Englemans conveyed a parcel of land within their tract to REB, Inc. (REB). The parcel of land REB purchased was located east of Yellowstone Road.

The Englemans also conveyed an easement to REB to provide access to Yellowstone Road. The easement gave REB the right to use a private road to travel across the parcel of land which the Englemans owned. The recorded instrument contained a legal description of the property owned by the Englemans and the property owned by REB, but it did not describe, with particularity, the location of the easement.

On April 21, 1969, the Englemans transferred title to their remaining parcel of land to Henry Dale Mueller and Jean Louise Mueller (Mueller). The conveyance expressly stated that Mueller took the property: "Subject to easements of record." At the time Mueller purchased this parcel of land, access to the REB property was customarily obtained by traveling down a dirt driveway which was located outside the fenced northern boundary of Mueller's property. . . .

On September 21, 1979, REB sold a parcel of the land the corporation had acquired from the Englemans to a predecessor-in-interest of George A. Refior and Nancy M. Refior (Refiors). The conveyance transferred all of REB's rights in that parcel of land, including a right to use the easement. The easement was described, with particularity, as including the northern twenty feet of the property Mueller had purchased from the Englemans.

On October 30, 1987, the Refiors conveyed their interests in the parcel of land by warranty deed to Lawrence R. Coffee (Coffee).

On February 27, 1981, REB sold another parcel of the land formerly owned by the Englemans to a predecessor-in-interest of Ralph Johnson (Johnson). This conveyance also transferred a right to use the easement described, with particularity, as including the northern twenty feet of Mueller's property.

On October 1, 1986, Johnson executed a contract for deed to convey his interests to Richard F. Hoblyn and Gary D. Hoblyn (collectively Hoblyn).

Coffee and Hoblyn both experienced difficulty using the existing dirt driveway to access their properties. Snow drifts sometimes blocked portions of the nearly mile-long driveway during the winter months. Finally, in 1990, Coffee had the land surveyed. The survey disclosed that, except for a small overlapping portion, the route of the dirt driveway did not correspond with the easement. Coffee and Hoblyn individually requested permission to use the easement from Mueller. Mueller refused. Mueller claimed that no one had ever used the easement and he was using the land burdened by the easement for agricultural crops and a water well.

On July 11, 1991, Hoblyn filed an action against Mueller in district court to quiet title to the easement. Mueller responded with a counterclaim against Hoblyn and a third-party complaint against Coffee and other landowners who allegedly had a right to use the easement in their chain of title. Johnson was granted permission to intervene in the action.

The district court found that in 1977, Mueller had drilled a water well within the easement boundaries. The district court concluded that by drilling the water well, Mueller terminated by adverse possession a two-hundred foot long portion of the easement despite the fact the well had never been used for irrigation purposes as Mueller had intended. All other claims for relief were denied. Multiple appeals were filed challenging the district court's decision.

Discussion

The incorporeal nature of an easement corresponds with the slight degree of control the easement holder has over the servient estate. Restatement of Property, *supra,* at § 450 cmt. c. The owner of the servient estate retains all rights to the property except as limited by the easement.

The fee or leasehold owner of the land to which an easement applies retains all the incidents of ownership in the land that do not contradict the particular rights of the easement holder. Thus if the easement holder has the right to cross over the land of another at a certain point, the owner of the underlying property ordinarily has the right to use the exact same part of the property in any way that does not prevent the easement holder from the actions which the easement grants.

The use of the servient estate is at the core of this dispute. Mueller admits that from 1963 to 1990, all parties believed that the location of the dirt driveway corresponded to the easement the Englemans granted REB. During this same time, however, Mueller maintains that his boundary fencing, agricultural use of the servient estate and drilling of a water well have prevented use of the easement. Under these circumstances, Mueller argues the district court erred in finding that the rights of the owners of the dominant estates to use only a portion of the easement had been terminated by adverse possession. Instead, Mueller asserts that the entire easement has been extinguished under one of several alternative theories.

Coffee and Hoblyn and their predecessors-in-interest admit that they have obtained access to their properties by traveling over the dirt driveway north of Mueller's property line. Coffee and Hoblyn maintain, however, that their rights to use the easement could not be terminated until they made a demand upon Mueller to use the land. Under these circumstances, Coffee and Hoblyn argue that the district court erred in finding that a portion of the easement had been terminated by adverse possession. Instead, Coffee and Hoblyn assert that they have the right to use the easement for a private road. Our review discloses that the right to use the easement has not been terminated by operation of law.

In 1963, the Englemans granted an easement to REB for access to their parcel of land by a private road. The Englemans' parcel of land became the servient estate, burdened by the easement. The REB property became the dominant estate, benefitted by the easement.

In 1969, when Mueller purchased the Englemans' property, he took with record notice of the existence of the easement, if not of the exact location. Presently, Wyoming law requires specific descriptions for easements recorded after May 20, 1981. Wyo. Stat. § 34–1–141(a) (1990). However, the easement granted by the Englemans is valid and enforceable under our prior law.

In 1979, when REB first sold a parcel of the land the corporation had acquired from the Englemans, REB effectively subdivided its holdings. Subdivision means that each of the parts of the dominant estate succeed to the privileges of use of the servient estate authorized by the easement. Restatement of Property, *supra*, § 488.

> The fact that the dominant estate is divided and a portion or portions conveyed away does not, in and of itself, mean that an additional burden is imposed upon the servient estate. The result may be that the *degree* of burden is increased, but that is not sufficient to deny use of the right of way to an owner of a portion so conveyed.

Hayes v. Aquia Marina, Inc., 243 Va. 255, 414 S.E.2d 820, 823 (1992).

The easement granted by the Englemans provided for unlimited use for ingress and egress. Subdivision, therefore, did not create an additional burden on the easement since the use remained the same. Restatement of Property, *supra*, § 488. We hold that while the degree of the burden was increased, the easement was not terminated when REB subdivided its parcel of land.

Easements may be terminated by abandonment. Abandonment occurs when one person relinquishes or surrenders rights or property to another. Abandonment of an easement requires an intentional relinquishment indicated by conduct which discloses the intention to surrender the right to use the land authorized by the easement.

There is no evidence of an intentional relinquishment by Coffee, Hoblyn or their predecessors-in-interest of their rights to use the easement. For example, there is no evidence the owners of the dominant estates ever constructed any permanent buildings or structures to obstruct the route of the easement onto their lands. Restatement of Property, *supra*, § 504 cmt. e. Nevertheless, Mueller maintains that use by the owners of the dominant estates of the dirt driveway from 1963 to 1990 should have terminated the easement. We disagree.

Abandonment requires more than simple nonuse of an easement, no matter how long the period of nonuse. Restatement of Property, *supra*, at § 504 cmt. d. In *Harrison v. State Highways and Transp. Com'n*, 732 S.W.2d 214, 221 (Mo.App.1987), the court found an easement to remove fill dirt for use in highway construction was not abandoned even though it had not been used in twenty-four years. "The question of abandonment is largely one of intention, and intention to abandon must be proved and it may be inferred only from strong and convincing evidence."

The court in *Richards Asphalt Co. v. Bunge Corp.*, 399 N.W.2d 188, 192–93 (Minn.App.1987), determined that an easement for a railroad spur was not abandoned despite nonuse for sixteen years. During this period, the owner of the dominant estate had obstructed the railroad tracks with four to seven feet of fill dirt to control periodic flooding. The court, however, found that placing the fill dirt and leaving it for sixteen years did not disclose a permanent intent to abandon the easement. "A claim of abandonment can be upheld only where nonuse is accompanied by affirmative and unequivocal acts indicative of an intent to abandon and is inconsistent with the continued existence of the easement."

Coffee, Hoblyn and their predecessors-in-interest did not attempt to make use of the entire easement across Mueller's property for twenty-seven years. However, the right to use the land was not relinquished by mere nonuse. *Richards Asphalt Co.*, 399 N.W.2d at 192–93; *Harrison*, 732 S.W.2d at 221. The mere nonuse of the easement did not disclose an affirmative and unequivocal intent to abandon the easement.

The use of an alternative access route from 1963 to 1990 also does not establish an intent to abandon the easement. In *Jackvony v. Poncelet*, 584 A.2d 1112, 1117 (R.I.1991), the owner of the dominant estate had two available routes to access his property. The court determined that despite the fact the alternative route was more convenient, the owner of the dominant estate retained the right to use and enjoy an easement giving him access to another route. *Id.* The court reiterated that abandonment would only be found when there is an expression of an intent to abandon the easement.

While Coffee and Hoblyn did make use of another means of access, the failure to use the easement does not mean the purpose of the easement ceased to exist. *Crabbe v. Veve Associates*, 150 Vt. 53, 1048 (1988). The easement holders retained the right to use the easement even if they used an alternative route. *Jackvony*, 584 A.2d at 1117. We hold that Coffee, Hoblyn and their predecessors-in-interest did not abandon the easement granted by the Englemans.

Detrimental reliance on the conduct of the owners of a dominant estate may also result in a termination of the easement. Restatement of Property, *supra*, at § 505 acknowledges that the owner of a servient estate may seek to terminate an easement by estoppel:

An easement is extinguished when action is taken by the owner of the servient tenement inconsistent with the continued existence of the easement, if

> (a) such action is taken in reasonable reliance upon conduct of the owner of the easement; and
>
> (b) the owner of the easement might reasonably have foreseen such reliance and the consequent action; and
>
> (c) the restoration of the privilege of use authorized by the easement would cause unreasonable harm to the owner of the servient tenement.

Mueller, however, failed to make any showing of conduct by Coffee, Hoblyn or their predecessors-in-interest that he reasonably relied upon to his detriment. We hold that the easement was not terminated by estoppel.

Finally, adverse possession for the statutory period of ten years may result in the termination of an easement. Wyo. Stat. § 1–3–103 (1988). To terminate an easement by adverse possession, the owner of the servient estate must take an action that would be permitted only if the easement did not exist.

> An easement is extinguished by a use of the servient tenement by the possessor of it which would be privileged if, and only if, the easement did not exist, provided
>
> (a) the use is adverse as to the owner of the easement and
>
> (b) the adverse use is, for the period of prescription, continuous and uninterrupted.

Restatement of Property, *supra,* at § 506.

This court has identified several elements which must be satisfied to establish adverse possession of land. The party claiming adverse possession must show actual, open, notorious, exclusive and hostile possession of another's property for ten years under a claim of right or color of title.

The elements of adverse possession of land are very similar to the elements necessary to establish adverse possession of an easement. There is, however, an analytical distinction between the two categories of adverse possession. The owner of the servient estate claiming adverse possession of an easement already has the right to possess and use the land so long as that use is not inconsistent with the easement. Therefore, the owner of a servient estate must prove the use of the servient estate made during the period of adverse possession is sufficiently hostile and inconsistent with the use permitted by the easement.

To extinguish an easement over (or use of) the servient tenements, the servient tenement owner must demonstrate a visible, notorious and continuous adverse and hostile use of said land which is inconsistent with the use made and rights held by the easement holder, not merely possession which is inconsistent with another's claim of title.

Just as the creation of an easement by prescription is not favored in the law, the termination of an easement by adverse possession is not favored. . . .

The district court ruled that Mueller's actions in drilling a water well on a portion of the easement terminated by adverse possession the rights held by Coffee and Hoblyn to use a two-hundred foot long portion of the easement. The district court also determined that Mueller had failed to establish his adverse possession of the remainder of the easement. The district court found that Mueller's actions in maintaining boundary fencing or making agricultural use of the land burdened by the easement were "not sufficient" to terminate the easement by adverse possession.

Mueller maintains the district court erred in ruling that only the portion of the easement around the water well was terminated by adverse possession. Mueller asserts that his use of the land was sufficiently hostile and notorious to terminate the entire easement by adverse possession. Mueller argues that as the owner of the servient estate, he has proven that his use of the land has been inconsistent with the use permitted by the easement.

Coffee and Hoblyn contend that no portion of the right to use the easement has been terminated by adverse possession. Coffee and Hoblyn assert that Mueller's actions prior to 1990 were not adverse to their interests because Mueller was permitted to make use of his land until the owners of the dominant estates requested to use the easement. Coffee and Hoblyn argue that Mueller's actions were nothing more than an exercise of his right as the landowner to use and develop his property. We agree that Mueller's actions in maintaining boundary fencing, growing various crops and drilling the water well did not terminate any portion of the easement by adverse possession.

Other courts have specifically addressed the rights of the owner of a servient estate to use land burdened by an unused easement. In *Beebe v. Swerda,* 58 Wash.App. 375, 793 P.2d 442, 443–44 (1990), the owner of a dominant estate demanded the right to use an easement for a private road. The owner of the servient estate claimed the previously unused easement had been terminated by adverse possession. The court found that despite the improvements the owner of the servient estate had made to the land, the easement was not terminated by adverse possession. "This right of the servient estate owner to the use of the property covered by the easement during periods when the easement is not being used means that the use of the area covered by the easement is not adverse to the owner of the dominant estate." The court affirmed a lower court order that required the owner of the servient estate to remove his improvements within thirty days of the time the dominant estate owner sought to use the easement. *Id. See also City of Edmonds v. Williams,* 54 Wash.App. 632, 774 P.2d 1241, 1244 (1989) (holding easement was not terminated by adverse possession when the owner of the servient estate constructed a fence across an unused easement).

In *Kolouch v. Kramer,* 120 Idaho 65, 813 P.2d 876, 877 (1991), the Supreme Court of Idaho considered whether the owner of the servient estate had terminated, by adverse possession, the right to use an easement for a private road. The owner of the servient estate had placed six trees down the center of the easement, constructed a fence inside the boundary of the easement, constructed a concrete irrigation diversion system on one end of the easement and placed several large boulders on the easement. The court determined that when an easement has never been used, the owner of the servient estate had a right to use the land "for any purpose not inconsistent with the purpose reserved in the easement." The court held that the owner of the servient estate had not made adverse or inconsistent use of the land prior to the time the owner of the dominant estate needed to use the easement.

*Kolouch* builds upon a rule first announced in *Castle Associates v. Schwartz,* 63 A.D.2d 481, 407 N.Y.S.2d 717 (1978). In *Castle Associates,* the court considered whether an unused easement created by a grant in 1903 had been terminated. Seventy-three years later, the owner of the dominant estate demanded the right to use the easement. The owner of the servient estate claimed his actions in fencing the land had terminated the easement by adverse possession. The court considered a variety of precedents and summarized:

> Where an easement has been created but no occasion has arisen for its use, the owner of the servient tenement may fence his land and such use will not be deemed adverse to the existence of the easement until such time as (1) the need for the right of way arises, (2) a demand is made by the owner of the dominant tenement that the easement be opened, and (3) the owner of the servient tenement refuses to do so.

*See also Armour v. Marino,* 527 N.Y.S.2d 632, 633 (1988) (holding unused easement created by a grant was not terminated by adverse possession despite obstructions by owners of servient estate which included fencing, trees and a garden).

The court in *Spiegel v. Ferraro,* 543 N.Y.S.2d 15, 17 (1989) recognized the limited nature of the exception to general principles of adverse possession contained in the holdings of *Castle Associates, Armour* and similar cases:

> The theory underlying the exception is that easements not definitively located and developed through use are not yet in functional existence and therefore the owner of the easement could not be expected to have notice of the adverse claim until either the easement is opened or the owner demands that it be opened. It is only at such point, therefore, that the use of the

easement by another is deemed to be adverse to the owner and the prescriptive period beings to run. . . .

We are persuaded that no portion of the easement granted by the Englemans was terminated by adverse possession. The easement has never been developed through use. Therefore, the period of adverse possession began in 1990 when Coffee and Hoblyn demanded the easement be opened and Mueller refused. At that time, Coffee and Hoblyn were first placed on notice that another was claiming actual, open, notorious, exclusive and hostile possession of their property under a claim or right or color of title.

Prior to 1990, Mueller's use of the land was simply "not inconsistent with the purpose reserved in the easement." *Kolouch,* 813 P.2d at 880. As the owner of the servient estate, Mueller maintained boundary fencing. An easement for a private road which has been "definitively and functionally in existence" may be terminated by adverse possession when access is obstructed for the prescriptive period. *Spiegel,* 541 N.E.2d at 17. However, the maintenance of a fence which obstructs an unused easement does not terminate the easement by adverse possession. *Castle Associates,* 407 N.Y.S.2d at 723.

Mueller also used the land for seasonal cultivation of agricultural crops. This use also was not inconsistent with rights held by the owners of the dominant estates. The owners of the dominant estates have the right to demand the easement be cleared when they are ready to use it.

Finally, Mueller drilled a water well within the boundaries of the easement. After the water well was completed, Mueller capped it. Mueller maintains he still intends to use the water well for crop irrigation at some point in the future. Drilling a water well, however, was not adverse to the continued existence of this previously unused easement.

From 1963 to 1990, the various landowners failed to develop and use the easement granted by the Englemans. Every landowner took with knowledge of the existence of the easement. However, no one took prudent precautions when purchasing their lands to develop and use the easement. As a result, numerous problems have developed which have pitted neighbor against neighbor in complex litigation. No matter how just the resolution under the law, everyone has suffered.

■ THOMAS, JUSTICE, dissenting.

I cannot agree with the decision in this case according to the majority opinion. I am satisfied the trial court and this court have placed this jurisdiction in the minority with respect to the acquisition of an easement right-of-way by adverse possession. Annotation, *Loss of Private Easement by Nonuser or Adverse Possession,* 25 A.L.R.2d 1265. 1329 (1952). In relying upon *Kolouch v. Kramer,* 120 Idaho 65, 813 P.2d 876 (Idaho 1991), the trial court and this court have rested upon unstable ground.

*Kolouch* expanded upon *Castle Associates v. Schwartz,* 63 A.D.2d 481, 407 N.Y.S.2d 717 (1978). The Idaho court and this court both ignored the severe limitation placed upon *Castle Associates* by the New York Court of Appeals in *Spiegel v. Ferraro,* 543 N.Y.S.2d 15, 17 (1989):

> A narrow exception to this general rule [an easement created by grant may be extinguished by adverse possession] has evolved with regard to the extinguishment of easements that have not been definitively located through use. In *Smyles v. Hastings,* 22 N.Y. 217, 224, we held that an easement that was not so definitively located through use and which lead to a "wild and unoccupied" parcel, was not extinguished by adverse possession because the owner of the easement had had no occasion to assert the right of way during part of the prescriptive period. Relying on *Smyles,* the Appellate Division has held that such "paper" easements may not be extinguished by adverse possession absent a demand by the owner that the easement be opened and a refusal by the party in adverse possession *(Castle Assocs. v. Schwartz,* 490, 407 N.Y.S.2d 717). In *Castle,* the court held that an easement created by grant as the result of a subdivision, but never located, was not extinguished by adverse possession because the owner of the easement had never demanded that the easement be opened.

Then, following the language quoted by the majority, the New York Court of Appeals reversed a holding by the Appellate Division that denied extinguishment of an easement and ruled the case did not fall within the *Castle* exception.

While the trial court found Mueller's conduct of fencing off and cultivating the easement was not sufficient to result in forfeiture of the easement by adverse possession, that conclusion is clearly contrary to the rule of adverse possession in vogue in Wyoming, articulated in *Doenz v. Garber,* 665 P.2d 932 (Wyo.1983). The clear implication of *Doenz* is that fencing plus cultivation results in gaining title in fee by adverse possession.

The product of the majority decision in this case is to adopt as the rule in Wyoming for extinguishment of an easement by adverse possession a very narrowly confined rule in New York as it apparently has been liberalized by the Idaho court. Consequently, the rule of adverse possession for acquiring fee title to land in Wyoming is disparate and quite different from the rule with respect to extinguishing an easement by adverse possession. I can find no logic or justifiable public policy in this departure.

In the instant case, the majority reversed that aspect of the trial court's decision which extinguished the easement for 100 feet on the east, west, and south of the well. The trial court's decision in that regard clearly is justified by the majority rule with respect to permanent structures in the claimed easement. I would affirm that part of the trial court's decision, but I would reverse the ruling that the balance of the claimed easement had not been extinguished by adverse possession. The other property owners are not without remedy in Wyoming *(Ferguson Ranch, Inc. v. Murray,* 811 P.2d 287 (Wyo.1991)), and holding that the entire easement has been extinguished avoids the anomaly of requiring an action for a private road to fill in the remaining 200 feet. Furthermore, extinguishment of the entire easement comports with the usual rule in Wyoming with respect to adverse possession.

## NOTES

1. *Adverse possession. Hoblyn* relies heavily on the original Restatement of Property. On most of the issues discussed in the case, the new Restatement (Third) of Property (Servitudes) is similar in substance to the original Restatement. However, on the issue of adverse possession, it is unclear whether the new Restatement is in accord with *Hoblyn*. Compare § 7.7, illus. 5 with § 4.9, illus. 1. If you were writing the new Restatement, would you follow the rule announced in *Hoblyn*, or would you follow the position of the dissent?

The Supreme Court of Wyoming found the easement was not extinguished, the dissenting judge believed it was extinguished, and the trial court had determined that only 200 feet of the easement was extinguished. How would you have decided the *Hoblyn* case if you had been one of the judges?

2. *Lessons for drafters.* In *Hoblyn*, the servient owner claimed that the easement was extinguished because (1) the dominant estate had been subdivided and therefore the easement would inevitably be over-used, (2) the easement had been abandoned, (3) the owners of the dominant estate were estopped from asserting the easement, and (4) the easement had been lost because of the adverse possession of the servient owner. The court rejected all of these arguments. What does this suggest concerning how you should advise B in the Principal Problem?

3. *Sauce for the goose.* In *Hoblyn*, the court writes, "Just as the creation of an easement by prescription is not favored by the law, the termination of an easement by adverse possession is not favored." What arguments can you make suggesting that the termination of an easement by adverse possession should be found more readily than the creation of an easement by prescription? Which position do you think is preferable?

4. *A statutory distinction.* Section 811 of the California Civil Code provides:

A servitude [i.e., an easement] is extinguished:

1. By the vesting of the right to the servitude and the right to the servient tenement in the same person;

2. By the destruction of the servient tenement;

3. By the performance of any act upon either tenement, by the owner of the servitude, or with his assent, which is incompatible with its nature or exercise; or,

4. When the servitude was acquired by enjoyment, by disuse thereof by the owner of the servitude for the period prescribed for acquiring title by enjoyment.

Paragraph 4, above, distinguishes between a servitude acquired "by enjoyment" (i.e., by adverse use) and one acquired by an express grant or reservation. Is that distinction justified?

5. *Principal Problem.* The preceding cases illustrate the importance of including clear and express provisions in a deed to deal with the question of when and under what conditions the easement granted will terminate. In preparing to advise B, in the Principal Problem, and in drafting the deed creating the easement, consider the following questions:

    a. What is your primary concern? How can you achieve it?

    b. What matters should the deed specifically deal with?

    c. What provisions do you feel are essential in protecting B's interests?

    d. What formalities would be required in your state for the effective creation of a valid easement?

    e. Would it better serve your client to grant an easement in gross or an easement appurtenant?

## ASSIGNMENT 22
# NON-EXPRESS EASEMENTS

## 1. INTRODUCTION

The normal method of creating an easement is by express grant or reservation in a written instrument. Rarely is the existence of an express easement an issue. However, in cases where there is no written instrument, the very existence of a non-express easement may be contested. Non-express easements can be thought of as informal easements and may arise through implication from prior use, implication from a map or boundary description showing streets or other areas of common use, necessity, or prescription.

Both implied easements and easements by necessity originate under circumstances in which land under common ownership is divided into separately owned parts by means of a conveyance. The intent to create an easement may be implied from the terms and circumstances surrounding such a conveyance. Furthermore, "[n]o particular verbal formula is required" to establish such intent.[1] Unfortunately, the implied easement doctrine may sometimes lead to the erroneous conclusion that the parties intended either the grantee or the grantor to have an easement in the parcel of land retained or the parcel conveyed.

Several factors may be considered in determining whether an easement should be implied, including:[2]

(1) The terms of the conveyance,

(2) The consideration paid,

(3) Whether the claim is made against a simultaneous conveyee,

(4) The extent of necessity of the easement,

(5) Whether reciprocal benefits result to the conveyor and the conveyee,

(6) The manner in which the land was used prior to its conveyance, and the subsequent actions taken by the parties involved,

(7) The extent to which the manner of prior use was or might have been known to the parties,

(8) The result that would best meet the reasonable expectations of land owners and purchasers, and arrive at results that are fair to all parties,

---

[1] Restatement (Third) of Property (Servitudes) § 2.2, cmt. d (2000).
[2] This non-exhaustive list of factors has been derived from the Restatement of Property § 476 and the Restatement (Third) of Property (Servitudes) §§ 2.2, 2.11–2.12 (2000).

(9) The ability of parties to act to avoid the confusion,

(10) Public policy considerations, such as the avoidance of economic waste and the promotion of full utilization of land,

(11) The size, shape, and location of the land in question, and

(12) Whether the claimant is the conveyor or the conveyee.[3]

The Restatement (Third) of Property § 212(d) (2000) and the weight of authority distinguishes easements by necessity from other implied easements. Accordingly, this book also maintains the distinction.

*Easements Implied from Prior Use*

To determine whether an implied easement exists, emphasis is placed on the use of the claimed dominant and servient parcels prior to severance of the common ownership.[4] The owner of a parcel of land cannot have a true easement over his own land. However, he can use part of his land for the benefit and service of another part, thereby giving rise to a "quasi-easement," a "quasi-servient estate" (the burdened portion of his property) and a "quasi-dominant estate" (the benefited portion).

> EXAMPLE 1 (Quasi-easement): Xavier, the owner of several adjoining lots, builds a sewer line running from a house on Lot 1 underneath the other lots. Xavier uses the sewer line for five years for the benefit of Lot 1. Xavier's utilization of the other lots for the benefit of Lot 1 can be seen as a quasi-easement. Lot 1 is then the quasi-dominant estate. The other lots form the quasi-servient estates.

When the common owner of the two parcels conveys the quasi-dominant estate, the grantee may claim an implied easement by grant in the quasi-servient estate under the proper circumstances. Similarly, if the parcel retained by the common owner is the quasi-dominant estate, he may be in a position to assert a claim to an easement implied by reservation in the lot conveyed. An easement is implied "if, at the time of the severance, the parties had reasonable grounds to expect that the conveyance would not terminate the right to continue the prior use."[5] In order to establish such "reasonable grounds," the quasi-easement must have been apparent, its use must have been continuous, and it must be important or reasonably necessary for the enjoyment of the claimed dominant estate. Since grants are generally construed against the grantor, courts often require a stricter adherence to the above requirements and a greater degree of necessity before implying an

---

[3] The majority of courts do not recognize the distinction between conveyor and conveyee claimants. Under Restatement (Third) of Property (Servitudes) § 2.12, reporter's notes (2000), easements are implied in favor of the grantor as readily as in favor of the grantee under the rules stated in this section. See also 4–34 Powell on Real Property § 34.08.

[4] See Restatement (Third) of Property (Servitudes) § 2.12 (2000).

[5] Id.

easement in favor of the grantor.[6] By contrast, the 2000 Restatement takes the position that the degree of necessity required to imply an easement in favor of the grantor is no greater than that needed to imply an easement in favor of the grantee.[7]

> EXAMPLE 2 (Easement appurtenant): Alyssa is the owner of Lot 1 and Lot 2, adjoining parcels. Alyssa runs a sewer line from a house on Lot 1 across Lot 2 to the main sewer line. Also, Alyssa uses a dirt road across Lot 1 for access to Lot 2 from a street adjacent to Lot 1. Alyssa then conveys Lot 1 to Barry. Can Barry use the sewer, and Alyssa the road?

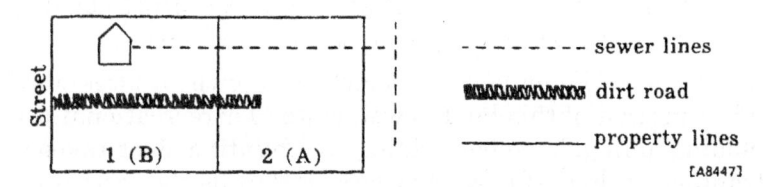

A court would probably find that Barry had an easement appurtenant to Lot 1 implied by grant to use the sewer line across Lot 2. Similarly, a court would probably find that Alyssa had an easement appurtenant to Lot 2 implied by reservation to use the road across Lot 1 for access to the street.[8]

The enumerated requirements for implication of easements emphasize that the basis for these easements is the intention of the parties. Thus, if the easement is apparent (i.e., discoverable upon careful inspection of the premises), if the use is continuous (as opposed to occasional or temporary), and if the easement is important for enjoyment of the claimed dominant estate, a court can reasonably find that the parties intended that the easement be created.[9]

> EXAMPLE 3 (Apparent, continuous, and necessary): Evan owns property upon which he erects two dwelling houses only a few feet apart. The roofs of both houses extend beyond the line of the side of the house, forming eaves twelve inches apart. Evan sells one of these houses to Franklin. According to the description in the deed, the land conveyed cuts off ten inches of the eaves and part of the porch of the house retained. Franklin brings suit to force Evan to remove the overhanging part of the eaves and

---

[6] See, e.g., Boudreau v. Coleman, 29 Mass.App.Ct. 621, 629, 564 N.E.2d 1, 5 (1990); Granite Properties Ltd. Partnership v. Manns, 117 Ill.2d 425, 439–440, 111 Ill.Dec. 593, 601, 512 N.E.2d 1230, 1238 (1987).

[7] See Restatement (Third) of Property (Servitudes) § 2.12, cmt. e (2000). At least one state, Georgia, refuses to recognize any easements implied by reservation. Farris Constr. Co. v. 3032 Briarcliff Rd. Associates, 247 Ga. 578, 277 S.E.2d 673 (1981).

[8] See generally, Restatement (Third) of Property (Servitudes) § 2.12, illus. 6 and cmt. g (2000).

[9] See, e.g., Butler v. Lee, 774 P.2d 1150 (Utah App.1989) (court found that parties intended that purchasers take title subject to easement although sales contract expressly disavowed any other agreements between the parties).

porch. Franklin loses. Use by Evan of the burdened parcel was apparent, continuous and reasonably necessary. Thus Evan has an easement in the lot conveyed.

EXAMPLE 4 (Apparent, continuous, and necessary): George, owner of two adjoining parcels, constructs a driveway between his two lots which he uses for both parcels. The entire driveway is reasonably necessary to gain access to each parcel comfortably. George sells one of these lots to Helen, who tries to use the entire driveway. Helen can probably use the driveway. The location of the driveway on both parcels makes the easement apparent to both parties. Use was continuous and is reasonably necessary for enjoyment of the lot conveyed.

EXAMPLE 5 (No implied easement): Jack owns a large plot of land. A portion of this land is well suited for recreational uses, including hiking, horseback riding, and hunting. Jack takes full advantage of this. After a few years, Jack sells the recreational portion of his land to Karen. Jack subsequently seeks to continue his use of the property conveyed for pleasure and recreation. Jack cannot continue his use of the property. He does not have an implied easement for pleasure and recreational purposes. Jack's use of the property was not apparent or necessary for the enjoyment of the claimed dominant estate.

The alleged purpose of the doctrine of implied easements is to give effect to the intentions of the parties. Thus, an easement will not be implied in the face of evidence proving that no such intent existed.

EXAMPLE 6 (No implied easement): Linda is the owner of Lots 1 and 2, and continuously uses a road on Lot 1 for access to Lot 2 from a street adjoining Lot 1. Although Lot 2 has other means of access to streets, the road across Lot 1 is the most convenient. Linda subsequently sells Lot 2 to Mike. Mike offers Linda $2,000 more if she will permit Mike to use the road across Lot 1. Linda refuses, stating that she does not want her property perpetually burdened by an easement. Mike subsequently seeks to use the road across Lot 1, claiming an implied easement. Mike loses. The prior negotiations between Linda and Mike clearly indicate that the parties did not intend for Mike to have an easement across Lot 1.

In determining the scope of an implied easement, a court cannot look to written language for guidance. The extent of use prior to severance is the major factor in making this determination. Courts will, however, generally permit additional use arising from foreseeable changes in the dominant estate, as long as no unreasonable additional burden is thereby placed on the servient estate. Other rights and obligations of the parties are determined in the same manner as in the case of express easements created pursuant to a written instrument silent on these matters.

EXAMPLE 7 (Implied easement): Natalie, the owner of a number of lots, places an electric line supplying electric services to a house on Lot 1 through the ceiling of the garage on adjacent Lot 2. The line terminates in a utility box located on a party wall between the lots. The electric wires run from the utility box to the house on Lot 1. Natalie sells Lot 1 to Paul and Lot 2 to Rich. For twenty years the electric line is maintained as originally installed, giving a service of 115 volts. Due to improvements on his property, Paul now needs 220 volts properly to serve his home. This would require rewiring. Rich refuses to permit Paul to enter his premises to make the necessary changes.

Paul can make the changes. Paul has an implied easement over Rich's property. Since the increase in electric requirements resulted from normal development of Paul's premises and since the increased burden on Rich's premises from the change would be insignificant, Paul can enlarge the use to meet his present requirements.[10]

Rules governing rights of successors and termination of implied easements are generally the same as those regulating express easements that do address these matters. However, the courts appear more inclined to terminate implied easements than express easements.[11] Since every implied easement is appurtenant, it is presumed to pass with grants of the dominant estate, except as prevented by the terms of the transfer or by the circumstances surrounding its creation.

*Easements by Necessity*

The easement by necessity is an important category of non-express easements. Easements by necessity are sometimes considered to be a subcategory of implied easements.[12] The easement by necessity derives its name from the fact that the existence of the easement is necessary for the reasonable use and enjoyment of the dominant parcel. The requirements for finding an easement by necessity are (1) an original unity of ownership of the claimed dominant and servient estates, and (2) the existence of the necessity at the time of severance. Courts will look to the distant past in search of the required unity of ownership. Unlike the general implied easements discussed in the preceding section, however, the use of the claimed dominant and servient parcels prior to severance of the common ownership is unimportant in establishing an easement by necessity. Typically, the element of necessity is more important for easements by necessity than for implied easements generally.

---

[10] See Ragona v. Di Maggio, 42 Misc.2d 1042, 249 N.Y.S.2d 705 (1964).

[11] See, e.g., Calif. Civil Code § 811(4) (unlike express easement, easement by prescription can be extinguished by "disuse" for five years).

[12] See, e.g., Nichols v. City of Evansdale, 687 N.W.2d 562, 568 (Iowa 2004); Thompson v. E.I.G. Palace Mall, 657 N.W.2d 300, 304 (2003); Carter v. County of Hanover, 255 Va. 160, 168, 496 S.E.2d 42 (1998). See also Restatement (Third) of Property (Servitudes) § 2.15, cmts. b and d (2000).

Easements by necessity may be justified by the public policy in favor of promoting the full utilization of land. However, most courts try to justify easements by necessity as giving effect to the intention of the parties. That is, one who conveys an interest must have intended to convey with it all rights necessary for the enjoyment of the interest conveyed, or must have intended to retain all rights necessary for the enjoyment of any interest retained. Such intent will be implied "unless the language or circumstances of the conveyance clearly indicate that the parties intended to deprive the property of those rights."[13] The strong public policy for easements by necessity will often lead courts to find an intent to create an easement by necessity "unless it affirmatively appears from the language or circumstances of the conveyance" that the parties intended a different result.[14]

> EXAMPLE 1 (Easement by necessity): Al owns two lots of which only one has access to a highway. Al conveys the parcel having no such access to Bonita. The deed to Bonita contains no language indicating an intention to create an easement of way in favor of Bonita. Bonita wishes to use a path across the lot retained by Al for access to the highway and Al objects. Bonita has an easement by necessity across the lot retained by Al.
>
> EXAMPLE 2 (Easement by necessity): Cassie is the owner of an apartment building. The various apartments in it are served by common halls and stairways. Cassie leases one of the apartments in the building to Daniel by a valid lease. Daniel's only means of access to and from his apartment is by use of these halls and stairways. An easement by necessity to use the common halls and stairways is implied and runs concurrently with the lease.
>
> EXAMPLE 3 (Easement by necessity): Ellen owns land which contains coal mines. Ellen conveys the coal to Frank, but retains title to the remaining land. The language of the conveyance in no way refers to easements of access necessary to enable Frank to mine the coal. Frank is entitled to an easement of access by necessity.

The most prevalent type of easement by necessity is a right of way that arises upon conveyance or retention of a landlocked parcel of land. When a person conveys property that has no means of access except over land retained by the grantor or in the possession of a stranger, the grantee's need for a right-of-way easement is deemed to be absolute. The same is true of the grantor's need if he retains an inaccessible parcel. When the necessity is absolute, courts have no trouble finding an easement. On the other hand, if the easement would merely be convenient, the claimant has very little hope of establishing easement

---

[13] Id.
[14] Restatement (Third) of Property (Servitudes) § 2.15, cmt. e (2000).

rights. The most difficult cases are where the degree of necessity is high or reasonable. While some courts insist upon absolute necessity, others are willing to relax this rule under the proper circumstances.

> EXAMPLE 4 (Meaning of "necessity"): Gary owned a parcel of land, part of which abutted a lake. Gary sold to Holly a portion of the land which abutted the lake but was otherwise surrounded by land retained by Gary. Although Holly could not reach her parcel by any overland route without crossing Gary's land, no right of way was mentioned in the deed. For several years, Holly used her parcel for summer camping purposes only and reached it by traveling on a public highway on the other side of the lake and then proceeded across the lake by boat. Subsequently, Holly decides to build a year-round residence on the parcel and transports all of the building materials to her parcel by boat. Before actually beginning construction she learns that the road on the other side of the lake sometimes becomes impassable during the winter because of snow and ice and that the lake itself occasionally freezes. Holly approaches Gary to acquire an express easement across his land, but Gary refuses to grant it. Can Holly claim an easement by necessity to cross Gary's land?

> Whether Holly will prevail depends largely on how broadly or narrowly the particular court construes the element of necessity. Clearly a right of way across Gary's land is not strictly or absolutely necessary for Holly to make some reasonable, albeit seasonal, use of his parcel. On the other hand, such a right of way is strictly necessary and not merely convenient for Holly to make full use of the parcel. Moreover, the use to which Holly seeks to put her land is probably reasonable under the circumstances and thus Holly satisfies a standard of reasonable necessity. The court additionally would consider whether the public policy favoring beneficial use of land would be satisfied without establishing an easement by necessity, whether a necessity existed at the time of the conveyance, and the presumed intent of the parties at the time of the conveyance.

Determining the scope or extent of easements by necessity presents few problems. Since the purpose of an easement by necessity is to promote the productive use of land, courts grant those rights that are reasonably essential to use of the land. The rights granted terminate as soon as this necessity disappears.[15]

> EXAMPLE 5 (Locating easement by necessity): Jenna conveys to Kyle a landlocked parcel of land, retaining an adjoining parcel that is adjacent to a highway. Kyle wishes to cross over the

---

[15] Jon W. Bruce & James W. Ely, Jr., The Law of Easements and Licenses in Land § 10.03[2] (1995).

parcel retained by Jenna in order to have access to the highway. Jenna admits that Kyle has this right, but the parties cannot agree as to where this access route should be. What factors will a court consider in locating Kyle's easement? A court will consider distance, injury to the person on whose estate the passage is granted, practicality, and benefit to the dominant parcel. The court will also look at prior conduct of the parties as evidence of their intent and of the necessity.

EXAMPLE 6 (Terminating easement by necessity): Laura, owner of Blackacre and Whiteacre, conveys Blackacre to Mike. The deed is silent as to any easement rights; but since Blackacre is landlocked, Mike uses a road across Whiteacre for access to the highway. Mike subsequently purchases Pinkacre, another adjoining parcel which is adjacent to a highway. Laura claims that Mike no longer has the right to use the road across Whiteacre. Laura is correct. The easement by necessity arose for the purpose of making utilization of Blackacre possible by affording it access to the highway. When Mike acquired Pinkacre, the necessity disappeared since Mike could now use his own land for access. Thus, the easement expired.

Problems concerning the scope or extent of easements by necessity may arise when there are changes in either the nature of the use of the easement or in the activity on the servient estate. In such cases, the necessity of using the easement must be balanced by considering either the additional burdens on the servient estate caused by an expanded use of the easement, or the burdens caused by restricting the use that can be made of the servient estate.

EXAMPLE 7 (Scope of easement by necessity): Nisa uses a footpath as an easement by necessity to reach her lot by crossing a lot retained by Olga, her grantor. Subsequently Nisa builds a dwelling on her lot and commences to use the easement via automobile. Olga objects, asserting that the easement is limited by the mode in which the dominant estate was used at the time the easement was created. Nisa wins. The scope of an easement by necessity is deemed to be coextensive with the present and future reasonable uses of the dominant estate. The new use will be permitted so long as it results from reasonable development of the dominant tenement without unduly burdening the servient tenement.

EXAMPLE 8 (Limits on easement by necessity): Penny has an easement by necessity to cross land retained by Ricky, her grantor, to reach her lot from a highway. For ten years Penny has crossed via a paved road two miles in length which provides a direct route between her lot and the highway. Now, because oil has been discovered on Ricky's land near the roads, Ricky decides to tear up the road and build a new, more circuitous one in a different location. Because the traveling time between her lot and the highway will be increased threefold, Penny files suit to enjoin Ricky from interfering with her easement. Ricky wins. Because the easement is one by necessity, Penny is entitled only to a reasonable way and not to one in a particular location. Moreover, requiring Ricky to leave the present way intact would interfere with his ability to develop the servient estate in a reasonable manner. Under the circumstances, the additional burden to Penny in traveling the longer route would not justify enjoining Ricky from developing his estate so long as he concomitantly provides Penny with an alternate reasonable way.

Most cases involving non-express easements center around the question of whether an easement was ever created. The Principal Problem raises this question.

## 2. Principal Problem

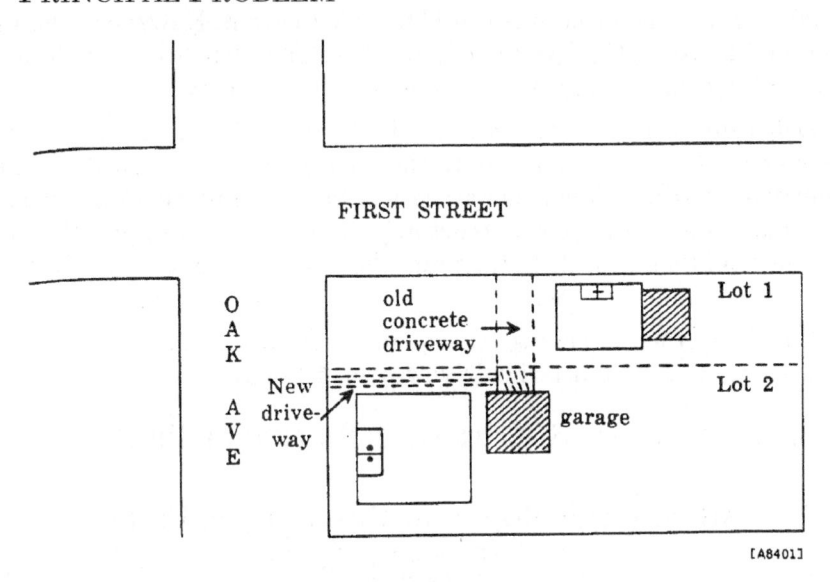

Al was the owner of Lots 1 and 2, which together form a rectangular tract of land at the southeast corner of First Street and Oak Avenue, extending sixty feet along the east side of Oak Avenue and ninety feet along the south side of First Street. Al built a garage on Lot 2, directly behind a dwelling house located thereon. The dwelling faced Oak Avenue, but the garage faced First Street and was connected to it by a concrete driveway constructed at the same time. While Al was the owner, he used the driveway on Lot 1 for access from First Street.

Al subsequently sold Lot 2, together with the house and garage, to Becky, retaining Lot 1. Although the deed was silent as to any easement rights, Becky used the driveway for access to the garage. After a few months, Becky decided to lay a cement strip next to an existing sidewalk along the north side of the dwelling. Together the strip and sidewalk, located entirely on Lot 2, constituted a driveway opening onto Oak Avenue. Although access to the garage by use of the new driveway was very difficult, Becky was able to manage. However, she continued to use the original driveway as well.

After three years, Al sold Lot 1 to Carl. Carl had inspected the premises and noticed the driveway, but the deed to Carl was silent as to any easement rights in favor of Lot 2.

Carl erected a home on Lot 1 and moved in. He became quite upset when he noticed Becky using the driveway and spoke to her about it. Becky, a peaceable woman, did not wish to start any trouble, so she agreed to pay Carl $15 per month for the use of the driveway on Lot 1.

This arrangement continued for about a year. Becky then decided to move. Becky sold Lot 2, including the house and garage, to Deb. Although the deed to Deb was silent as to any easement rights, Deb had inspected the premises, noticed the driveway (having driven over it herself to visit Becky), and assumed that she would be able to use it. However, when she attempted to use it, Carl protested, insisting that Deb either pay him $25 per month for use or stop "trespassing" on his property.

Deb refuses to pay the money. Unfortunately she is a miserable driver and thus can gain access to the garage over the driveway on her property only after a laborious process of backing and turning. Deb also fears that if Carl were to construct any building or wall upon the party line, she would not be able to turn into the garage from her own driveway at all.

Consider the following cases in evaluating Deb's chances of establishing a right to use the driveway over Lot 1.

## 3. MATERIALS FOR SOLUTION OF PRINCIPAL PROBLEM

### Hillside Development Company v. Fields

Missouri Court of Appeals, 1996.
928 S.W.2d 886.

■ LAURA DENVIR STITH, JUDGE.

Defendant-Appellant Roscoe Fields alleges that the trial court erred in rejecting his argument that he had an implied, or "visible" easement over the portion of the property of Plaintiff-Respondent Hillside Development Company on which sits a part of the driveway to Mr. Fields' home. We agree. The undisputed facts establish all of the elements for creation of a visible easement: the driveway constitutes an obvious and visible benefit to the residential lot, was constructed as a permanent means of access to and from the garage, was used for many years prior to the subdivision of the property as a means of access to the garage, and is reasonably necessary for the full beneficial use and enjoyment of the premises.

All of the property which now belongs to Mr. Fields and to Hillside once constituted a single piece of property owned by Carl Nelson. In 1967, Mr. Nelson constructed a house on the portion of the property now belonging to Mr. Fields. The only public road providing access to the house was located on the south side of the property. For reasons not disclosed by the record, however, the house was designed with a basement garage located on the north side of the house. Consequently, in order to reach the garage, the driveway openly and visibly circles around the front (east) side and part of the far (north) side of the house in order to reach the garage entrance at the northwest corner of the house.[16]

This arrangement, while perhaps not perfect, has provided access to the garage from the public road since the house was constructed. It cannot be mistaken for anything other than an artificial improvement intended to create a beneficial, useful and permanent means of vehicular access from the public road to the garage. It caused no difficulties during the period in which Mr. Nelson owned the property on which the house and driveway are located as well as approximately 30 acres of surrounding land. When Mr. Nelson died in the 1970s, however, he left all of the house, driveway and surrounding real estate to Shriners Hospital. In 1984, the hospital subdivided the property. It sold off most of the unimproved land to plaintiff Hillside, including all or nearly all of the land on which the driveway was located. It retained the portion of the land on which the house was located. In addition, the title documents expressly reserve an ingress-egress easement for the use of the retained residential lot and house. This express easement runs along the portion of the driveway leading from the road to the house. This prevents the land on which the house is located from being landlocked. For reasons lost to history, however, this easement did not fully correspond with the location of the driveway. Rather, it failed to include a curved portion of the driveway measuring approximately 20 yards by 12 yards and which runs in front of the house.

In 1987, the hospital sold the house and lot to Mr. Fields. Due to the prior sale to Hillside, the title to the property bought by Mr. Fields noted that the curved portion of the driveway (located just a few yards from the front of the house) was not included in the title to Mr. Fields' property nor included in the express ingress-egress easement.

At the time of closing, Mr. Fields had read the title report and was aware that Hillside had record title to the disputed portion of the driveway, and does not claim that Hillside told him that he had a right to use the driveway, but he did testify that the realtor had represented

---

[16] The arrangement may be explained by the fact that the house's septic tanks and lines are located at the rear, or west, side of the house, and would be damaged if a driveway were placed over them. The record does not reveal whether the tanks and lines were in place prior to the time the driveway was constructed.

to him before he bought the house that he had either ownership or a right to use the driveway due to adverse possession, as the driveway went with the house. Mr. Fields said he accepted the realtor's statements and did not believe there would be a problem regarding use of the driveway. In addition, the record reveals that when Hillside subdivided and sold some of the land it had purchased from the hospital, it specifically excepted from the lots sold the triangular area at the back of its property over which Mr. Fields' driveway runs.

In 1992, Hillside filed a lawsuit against Mr. Fields for trespass and ejectment. Mr. Fields counterclaimed seeking a declaratory judgment that he had an implied easement across the disputed portion of the driveway. The parties filed cross-motions for summary judgment. The trial court rejected the implied easement theory and denied Mr. Fields' summary judgment motion, entering judgment in favor of Hillside for ejectment and trespass. This appeal followed. . . .

The sole issue for resolution is whether Mr. Fields obtained an implied easement for use of the driveway to his home. Hillside claims that Mr. Fields is precluded from claiming an implied easement because he was aware prior to closing that the encroachment was documented of record in the title report and because he was also aware that the express ingress-egress easement did not extend across the disputed portion of the driveway.

We disagree with the legal conclusions Hillside draws from the evidence. Neither the lack of an express easement for the driveway nor the existence of an express ingress-egress easement negates the existence of an easement implied from pre-existing use, also referred to as a visible easement. To the contrary, it is only when the title to property does not contain the claimed easement that the question even arises whether an implied easement exists, for if the easement were in the title, then it would be an express easement, not an implied one.

Missouri courts have developed the following four-factor test for the establishment of a visible easement:

1. There must have been a unity of common ownership followed by a separation of title of the subject property into dominant and servient estates;

2. The purported easement must have been constructed, altered or artificially arranged by the common owner so as to constitute an open, obvious and visible benefit or advantage to the claimant's property and a burden to the servient portion of the premises;

3. The purported easement must have been used long enough before the separation of title and under such circumstances so as to show that the alteration or artificial arrangement was intended to be permanent; and

4. The purported easement must be reasonably necessary for the full beneficial use and enjoyment of the dominant estate.

There is no genuine issue of material fact that the first factor for establishment of a visible easement is satisfied. There was unity of ownership of the land in Carl Nelson and Shriners Hospital. This was followed by separation of the title into the property owned by Hillside and that retained by Shriners Hospital and later purchased by Mr. Fields.

Mr. Fields also satisfied the second factor of the test. The driveway was constructed by Mr. Nelson at the time the house was built and since that time has constituted an open, obvious and visible benefit to the advantage of Mr. Fields' property (which in this regard is considered the dominant estate), and a burden to the portion of the land owned by Hillside (which in this regard is considered the subservient estate).

The third requirement for establishment of a visible easement is also satisfied, for the house and driveway had been used for some 17 years prior to the separation of title through subdivision of the land by the hospital. Having been constructed of asphalt in a well-defined path from the public street and around the front of the house to the garage entrance to the north, the driveway clearly was meant to provide a permanent means of vehicular access to the garage. While Hillside says that Mr. Fields could not have relied on the easement as a means of access because it was not included in the title to the land, this misses the point. As noted above, an implied easement necessarily arises at the time of severance by the common owner and by definition does not appear of record. Thus, Mr. Fields' awareness of Hillside's ownership is entirely consistent with his assertion of an implied easement given the open and obvious nature of the driveway leading to the garage. This is particularly true in light of the explanation given by the real estate agent that the driveway went with the house and the principle that Hillside stands in the shoes of the common grantor, Mr. Nelson.

Hillside also contests whether the law permits a finding that Mr. Fields established the fourth factor, that the easement is "reasonably necessary for the full beneficial use and enjoyment of the dominant estate." Hillside argues that having access to the garage is a mere convenience and not reasonably necessary where, as here, the property owner has an alternative legal means of access to his property. It notes that Mr. Fields' property would not be landlocked without the easement, and that he could build a new driveway at the back of his property or build a new garage. It suggests the expense and difficulty involved in such a venture, and the fact that it would make the current garage and driveway of no beneficial use to the property, does not provide a basis on which to find that the easement is reasonably necessary to the beneficial use and enjoyment of the dominant estate.

In making these arguments, Hillside inappropriately draws from the law governing the establishment of easements by necessity. It is well established that an easement by necessity will not arise in the absence of proof of strict or absolute necessity for the easement. See, e.g., Restatement of Property § 476 (1944). Because Mr. Fields' property would not be landlocked without the easement, he concedes that he cannot show the strict necessity required to establish an easement by necessity.

The rules governing establishment of an easement by necessity are not the same as those governing establishment of a visible easement, however. As noted above, in order to establish the latter, one needs to show only reasonable, not absolute, necessity. Just what constitutes reasonable necessity has been extensively litigated in Missouri and elsewhere. It is true, as Hillside notes, that some cases have stated that "the tendency of the courts, as a general rule, is to discourage implied grants of easements, since the obvious result, especially in urban communities, is to fetter estates, retard buildings and improvements, and violate the policy of recording acts." Missouri State Oil Co. v. Fuse, 360 Mo. 1022, 232 S.W.2d 501, 506 (1950).

Other, often later, cases, however, have recognized competing public policy considerations with regard to implied easements, including the policy favoring utilization of land and the principle that courts should not presume that parties intended to render land unfit for occupancy. Causey, 398 S.W.2d at 197. In this regard, Causey held that parties are presumed to have "contracted with a view to the condition of the property as it actually was at the time of the transaction and that after sale neither party has a right, without the consent of the other, to change to the detriment of the other, a condition which openly and visibly exists." Id. The principle of estoppel also often supplies another theoretical underpinning for implied easements because the party resisting the easement is said to stand in the shoes of the owner who created the quasi-easement prior to a subdivision of the land. See Di Pasco v. Prosser, 364 Mo. 1193, 274 S.W.2d 279 (1954).

In any event, the doctrine of visible easements looks at whether the easement is necessary to the full enjoyment of the dominant estate. While without the easement Mr. Fields would not be landlocked, he would not be able to use the garage or much of that portion of the driveway which is located on his property.[17]

In similar situations, a number of prior Missouri cases have recognized that a garage specifically constructed for use by the dominant estate at a time prior to separation of title to the property is reasonably necessary for the full beneficial use and enjoyment of the premises. These cases hold that access to other parts of one's property is not the controlling factor under a claim of a visible easement where the property owner is denied the use and enjoyment of such a significant, valuable and beneficial portion of the premises.

---

[17] In fact, were Mr. Fields to build a new driveway at the rear of his property, as suggested by Hillside, he would damage or not be able to use the septic tank and lines.

Here, absent recognition of a visible easement, Mr. Fields would not have full enjoyment of his estate, for he could not utilize his garage in a reasonable manner. We thus find that use of the driveway to Mr. Fields' garage is reasonably necessary for his full beneficial use and enjoyment of the premises. For these reasons, we reverse the judgment entered in favor of Hillside for trespass and ejectment and remand for further proceedings in accordance with this opinion.

All concur.

## Ward v. Slavecek
### Court of Civil Appeals of Texas, 1971.
### 466 S.W.2d 91.

■ WILSON, JUSTICE.

Plaintiff-appellant states that this non-jury case was pleaded and tried as one of implied easement, and we will so consider it.

Plaintiff and defendants own adjacent lots, each fronting 50 feet on the west side of Wood Street in Cleburne, and extending westerly 163 feet to an alley. The title to both lots is [derived] from a common predecessor in title who built a driveway before 1919 centered approximately on the east-west division line between the two lots to serve as an approach to his garage. Plaintiff's predecessor in title purchased his lot from this common owner in 1925, and in 1928 defendant's predecessor acquired the other lot. The latter then constructed a garage on his lot and began to use the original driveway in common with his neighbor and with his consent. The driveway was so used in common until 1970 when defendants built a metal fence on their property which divided the driveway in such a manner that plaintiff alleges she cannot use it, and her garage is useless. Plaintiff asserts, as we construe her argument, that the evidence establishes an implied easement in her favor on and over the driveway as a matter of law.

[Among] the requirements for engrafting an easement by implication . . . is that the easement "must be necessary to the use of the dominant estate," the degree of necessity being "strict necessity". See Mitchell v. Castellaw, 151 Tex. 56, 246 S.W.2d 163 (1952).

WARD v. SLAVECEK
466 S.W.2d 91 (Tex.Civ.App.1971).

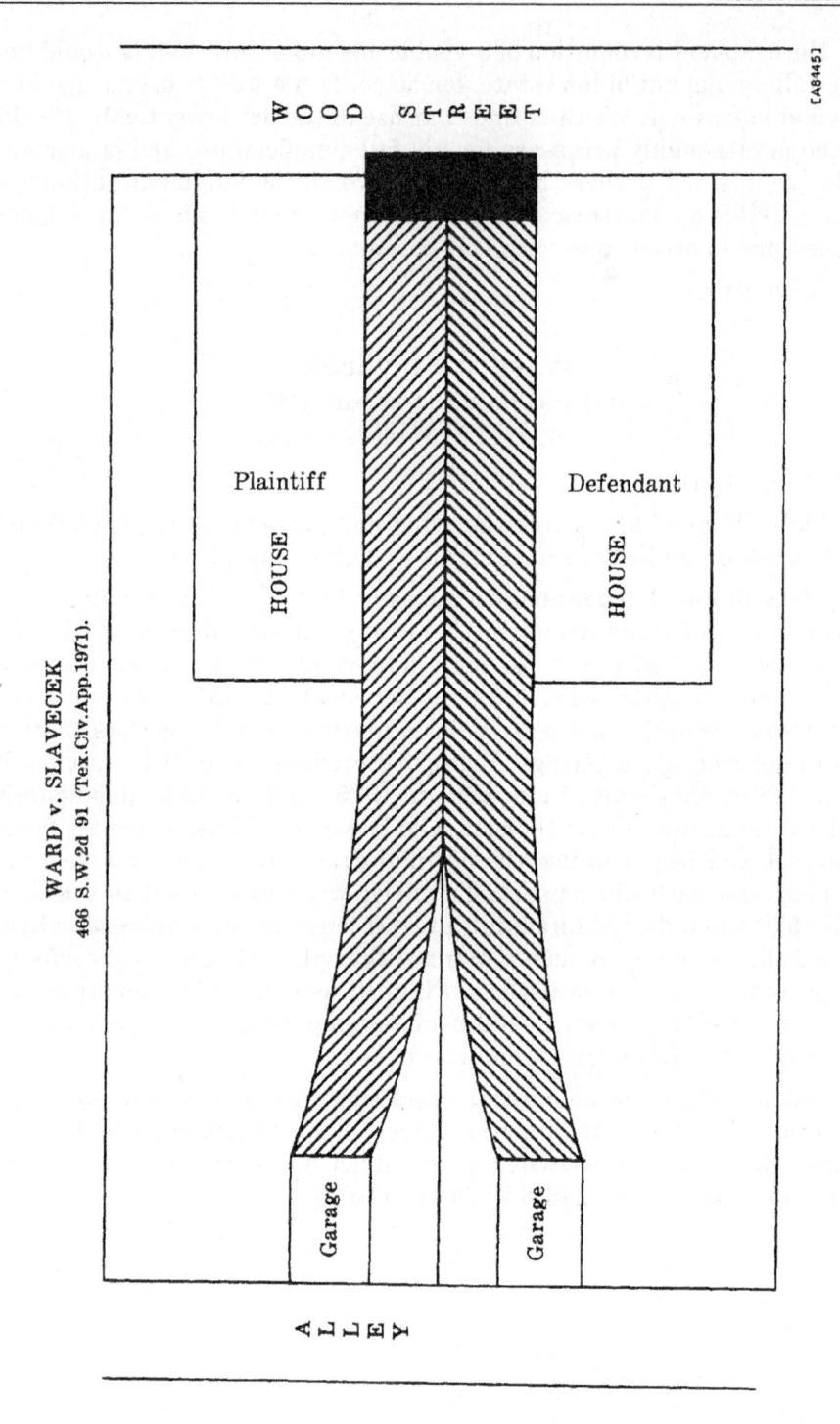

The trial court found that there is an open alley on the west end of plaintiff's lot, accessible to them. No point is presented attacking this finding; and there is adequate evidence that the alley could be used for access to the garage, and had been so used in the past. There is evidence of probative force that a clear space of 9–9.5 feet exists between the metal fence and plaintiff's house, providing sufficient clearance for automobiles to be driven from Wood Street to plaintiff's garage.

Under the express and implied findings as to necessity and the evidence supporting them, it may not be said that plaintiff has established an implied easement as a matter of law, and the record sustains the trial court's determination to the contrary. Appellant's points are overruled. The take-nothing judgment is affirmed.

## Epstein Family Partnership Levitz Furniture Corp. v. Kmart Corp.
United States Court of Appeals, Third Circuit, 1994.
13 F.3d 762.

■ HUTCHINSON, CIRCUIT JUDGE.

Appellant, Kmart Corporation ("Kmart"), appeals an order of the United States District Court for the Eastern District of Pennsylvania. Appellee, the Louis W. Epstein Family Partnership ("Epstein"), holds an easement over the Kmart property. The easement is dedicated to ingress and egress from Epstein's land-locked parcel. The district court's order enjoined Kmart from removing a sign on its property that had been erected and maintained by Epstein's tenant, Levitz Furniture Co. ("Levitz"). It held that Levitz had an implied easement or, in the alternative, an easement by estoppel, permitting the sign on the Kmart parcel.

Kmart contends that Levitz has not shown it has either an easement by implication or an easement by estoppel to maintain its sign on Kmart property.

[W]e note that Levitz erected [the sign] in 1963 just north of the easement area on the MacArthur Road frontage of what is now Kmart's property. Under the initial terms of a 1962 lease between the Epstein brothers and Levitz, however, Levitz covenanted that it would not, "without the consent of the Lessor in writing . . . [e]rect or install any exterior signs." App. at 131–32. While the district court found that Levitz initially erected the sign with the oral consent or permission of the lessor, Levitz apparently never complied with the lease by obtaining written consent. Epstein, 828 F.Supp. at 337, 341–42. The district court, nevertheless, held that Levitz had secured both an easement by implication in favor of the sign.

An easement by implication arises when the parties intended to create an easement but neglected to include or embody it in a written agreement. See Motel 6, Inc. v. Pfile, 718 F.2d 80, 84 n. 9 (3d Cir.1983) ("The law of implied easements . . . is ultimately justified in terms of the imputed intention of the parties to the conveyance."); Mann-Hoff v. Boyer, 413 Pa.Super. 1, 604 A.2d 703, 707 ("[A]n easement by implication can only be found 'where the intent of the parties is clearly demonstrated by the terms of the grant, the surroundings of the property and other res gestae of the transaction.'" (quoting Hann, 562 A.2d at 893)), alloc. denied, 531 Pa. 655, 613 A.2d 560 (1992). The proper test for determining when an implied easement exists is an issue of some debate in Pennsylvania. See Mann-Hoff, 604 A.2d at 706–07 (noting conflict).

Some courts have used the "traditional test," while others have used the Restatement of Property test and still others have employed a hybrid approach. See Mann-Hoff, 604 A.2d at 706. In Motel 6, we noted the divergent lines of authority and then elected to apply the traditional test set forth in Burns Manufacturing Co. v. Boehm, 467 Pa. 307, 356 A.2d 763 (1976), at that time the Pennsylvania Supreme Court's most recent pronouncement on the issue. Motel 6, 718 F.2d at 85. In Burns the court stated:

> [W]here an owner of land subjects part of it to an open, visible, permanent and continuous servitude or easement in favor of another part and then aliens either, the purchaser takes subject to the burden or the benefit as the case may be, and this irrespective of whether or not the easement constituted a necessary right of way.

Burns, 356 A.2d at 767 (quoting Tosh v. Witts, 381 Pa. 255, 113 A.2d 226, 228 (1955)).

Our conclusion in Motel 6 is somewhat undermined by the more recent decision of the Pennsylvania Superior Court in Mann-Hoff. Cf. Robinson v. Jiffy Executive Limousine Co., 4 F.3d 237 (3d Cir.1993) (reversing prediction of New Jersey state law as to liability for torts committed by independent contractors based upon intervening state appellate decisions rejecting our conclusion). In Mann-Hoff, the court quoted the Burns language we relied on in Motel 6 and then rejected it in favor of a more "elucidating" description of the state of Pennsylvania law as set forth in Owens v. Holzheid, 335 Pa.Super. 231, 484 A.2d 107, 116 (1984) (Montemuro, J., dissenting). Mann-Hoff, 604 A.2d at 706. Other Pennsylvania courts applying either the Restatement test or the traditional test have required an implied easement to be essential to beneficial enjoyment of the dominant property. The superior court in Mann-Hoff seems to have concluded that there is no clear authority in Pennsylvania on this point and that the Restatement approach and the traditional test must coexist. It then refused to select either of the competing approaches, concluding that a weakened notion of necessity was involved in both. The court thus held the easement did not have to be an "absolute necessity" for use of the dominant estate but rather simply "convenient or beneficial to the dominant estate."

Like the court in Mann-Hoff, we need not select between the competing tests. As mentioned supra, the tests are but a surrogate for determining the intention of the parties at the time of the severance of the estates. Moreover, a common theme of both tests is that the parties intended a permanent encumbrance on the servient estate. See Mann-

Hoff, 604 A.2d at 706 (discussing traditional test); id. at 708 (discussing Restatement test). We think the facts of this case indicate that the parties did not intend to create an easement in favor of Levitz because the circumstances surrounding the execution of the Declaration of Easements demonstrate the parties' apparent willingness to provide expressly for easements on other portions of the estate. In addition, the requirement that the use be permanent, which is necessary to an implied easement, is not present.

In 1975, when the Epsteins severed the estate, they expressly provided for an easement of ingress and egress in favor of Levitz but said nothing about the sign. When circumstances suggest that an agreement among parties would include mention of all intended grants, "it [is] not unreasonable to require that they insert a provision in the agreement of sale which would have reserved the same. The absence of such a reservation suggests most strongly that [the alleged right] was not intended to be retained." Purdy v. Zaver, 398 Pa.Super. 190, 580 A.2d 1127, 1133 (1990). While failure to make express provision for a right may not always indicate an intent to withhold it, we think the omission of a particular right from an express grant of others relating to the same property cuts strongly against any inference of an intent to make the unmentioned grant.

Moreover, we think the requirement of both tests that Levitz's use be "permanent" has not been met. In Pennsylvania, the proponent of the easement must show that its use indicates a permanent arrangement. See, e.g., Burns, 356 A.2d at 767; Mann-Hoff, 604 A.2d at 706–07. In Mann-Hoff, the court held that a grant of the use of a parking lot until the sale of the servient estate was not permanent. Mann-Hoff, 604 A.2d at 708. In the case of a right-of-way, Pennsylvania courts have presumed permanency from the nature of the use unless the surrounding circumstances dictate otherwise. See Burns, 356 A.2d at 767 n. 5; Philadelphia Steel Abrasive Co. v. Louis J. Gedicke Sons, 343 Pa. 524, 23 A.2d 490, 492 (1942). In Motel 6, we applied the presumption of permanence that attaches to a right of way to a sewer line and sewage treatment services. Motel 6, 718 F.2d at 86. We do not think, however, that a free-standing road sign possesses the inherent permanent characteristics of a right-of-way or a sewer line and sewage treatment services. Thus a presumption that a road sign was a permanent encumbrance on the servient estate is inappropriate.

The parties may still intend a permanent encumbrance, however, where the nature of the contested use or object does not raise any presumption of permanency. In that case, we may look to the interest of the owner/lessor to determine whether the parties intended to create a permanent encumbrance.

In determining whether Levitz's sign is intended to be a permanent encumbrance, we are mindful that permanency describes the nature of the object, not the nature of the user's interest in the object. Thus, a tenant may construct a permanent object, such as a road, although the tenant's right to use the land on which the road sits is limited by the duration of the lease.

In the instant case, however, Levitz was a leaseholder who had the ability to "[e]rect or install any exterior signs" only with the written permission of the lessor. App. at 131–32 (1962 Lease); id. at 153–54 (1967 Lease). When the parties severed the estate in 1975, the lease term was to end in 1982 with one option to renew for an additional fifteen years. Thus, at the time of severance, Levitz's right to maintain the sign under the lease could extend at most until 1997. At that time, the owner of the servient property could revoke the permission to erect signs on its property. At the time of severance, the most Levitz could hope for was a guarantee of seven more years with an option for fifteen more if it renewed the lease. When a lease terminates, tenants normally take signs with them; roads and sewers are left behind. Signs like that involved in this case are not permanent fixtures. Accordingly, we think the facts indicate that the owners did not intend to subject the servient estate to a permanent encumbrance for a sign in the location in which Levitz maintains it; rather, at best, we think they intended one that would terminate with the lease. Thus, we conclude that the evidence surrounding the severance of the estates in 1975 does not imply that an easement exists in favor of the Levitz sign on the theory Levitz has argued. . . .

Accordingly, we reject the district court's conclusion that Levitz holds an easement by estoppel or easement by implication over the Kmart parcel and direct the district court to modify the injunction accordingly.

## NOTES

1. *Degree of necessity.* The foregoing materials suggest at least four possibilities regarding the requisite degree of necessity for an implied easement. *Epstein* discards the necessity requirement altogether, while *Ward* endorses the "strict" necessity test.[18] In between these extremes is the Restatement of Property, which considers necessity as a single element in a balancing test, and the test of "reasonable" necessity adopted by the court in *Hillside*. In general, the necessity requirement for an easement implied from prior use requires a showing of need which, by definition, may be less than that required to establish an easement by necessity, but something more than simple convenience.[19] Which standard is the best? Should it matter whether the easement is being retained by the grantor or implied in favor of a grantee?

---

[18] However, the *Ward* case has limited application in Texas. Texas courts apply the "strict necessity" requirement to an implied reservation of an easement, but a "reasonable necessity" requirement to an implied grant of an easement. See Houston Bellaire, Ltd. v. TCP LB Portfolio I, L.P., 981 S.W.2d 916, 921 (Tex. App.—Houston [1st Dist.] 1998, no pet.)

[19] See, e.g., Carter v. County of Hanover, 255 Va. 160, 169, 496 S.E.2d 42, 46 (1998).

2. *Time of severance of common ownership.* The determination as to whether or not the requirements for an implied easement are met is to be determined at the time of the severance of the unity of ownership. In the Principal Problem, will this help Deb in persuading a court that she has an implied easement?

3. *Apparency.* In Westbrook v. Wright,[20] the court found an implied easement for a sewer line where a common owner sold the dominant estate first and the heirs of the common owner were the present owners of the servient estate. In discussing the apparency requirement, the court stated that the use must have been apparent at the time of the grant and that the easement was apparent because its existence was "indicated by signs which might be seen or known on a careful inspection by a person ordinarily conversant with the subject."[21] Is this sound reasoning?[22]

4. *Distinguishing precedent.* What arguments can be made to minimize the effects of *Ward* as authority against Deb in the Principal Problem?

5. *Principal Problem revisited.* Although courts look for the enumerated requirements of an implied easement to a certain extent, the factor of overriding importance in most implied easement cases is whether the facts of the case indicate that the original parties to the severance intended and assumed that an easement would be created. The four or five requirements generally listed by most courts are really factors that go to prove that this intention must have been present. In considering Deb's chances of establishing her rights to an implied easement in the driveway, consider the following questions:

 a. Can or should Becky's payment of a monthly rental to Carl, and her building of a second driveway be seen as an abandonment—an intentional relinquishment of her easement rights?

 b. Are the requirements for an implied easement satisfied in this case?

 c. What other factor of this problem could be used to help Deb?

 d. What are the policies against implied easements? What policies favor implied easements?

6. *Easements implied from a map or boundary reference.* In addition to the implied easements discussed in this Assignment, the new Restatement recognizes easements implied from a map or boundary reference.[23] Land may be conveyed with a description of the land that refers to a particular map. If the map shows certain use rights, such as a park, beach, or other area

---

[20] 477 S.W.2d 663 (Tex.Civ.App.1972).

[21] Id. at 666.

[22] Restatement (Third) of Property (Servitudes) § 2.12 (2000) provides that an easement based on prior use must be either apparent, known to the parties, or for underground utilities serving either parcel.

[23] See Restatement (Third) of Property (Servitudes) §§ 2.11, 2.13 (2000).

designated for some common use or benefit, the grantee takes the land with an implied easement that restricts the use of the land to the uses indicated on the map. For example, if the map shows that the land conveyed has a footpath access to a beach, the land has the benefit of an implied easement to use the footpath and the beach (assuming that the grantor has the power to create such an easement). Similarly, if the land is conveyed with reference to a road as a boundary, the grantee takes the land with the benefit of an implied easement allowing her access to the road (again, assuming that the grantor has the power to create such an easement). The rationale for allowing such implied easements is that it is assumed that the grantor who uses such descriptions intended to give the grantee the "use rights shown on the map, or in the street used as a boundary, and the grantee reasonably expects to receive them."[24]

---

[24] See Restatement (Third) of Property (Servitudes) §§ 2.13, cmt. a (2000).

## B. Covenants Running with the Land (Promissory Servitudes)

## ASSIGNMENT 23

# Creation and Validity

### 1. Introduction

Although the factual situations involving covenants are usually not complicated, the law in this area is an unspeakable quagmire. When the confused English law of real covenants and equitable servitudes was adopted by the fifty United States, each state added variations of its own. In 1940, the American Law Institute undertook to restate the law of covenants and this bred the naive hope that, out of the confusion, order would emerge. The Restatement, however, was so controversial in its resolution of these difficult issues that Judge Clark felt impelled to write an entire book exposing its "errors" in delightfully intemperate language.[1] The Restatement sections dealing with servitudes have been rewritten,[2] and, so far, they have been met with a kinder, gentler reception than did their predecessors.

Despite the discouraging doctrinal confusion, covenants are widely used. Historically, a covenant was a solemn written promise under seal. Today seals are rarely used, and the word "covenant" is a synonym for "promise." Virtually every subdivision, shopping center, planned unit development, homeowners association and condominium uses covenants as part of its legal framework. Any development having common areas, such as play areas, tennis courts, parking lots, swimming pools, private streets or landscaped grounds, collects maintenance fees from the individual homeowners. These homeowners make affirmative covenants to contribute money for the upkeep of these areas. In addition, the homeowners in a subdivision or condominium, and the retail merchants in a shopping center, usually make numerous negative covenants to protect the order, beauty and tranquility of the development.

### 2. Terminology

Servitudes may be defined as rights in land possessed by another (other than possessory interests or liens), in addition to those normally implied from the ownership of land. The right to be free from a nuisance maintained on my neighbor's land is not a servitude since it is a right normally implied from the ownership of land. A right of way across my neighbor's land is a servitude since it is a right in land possessed by

---

[1] Clark, Real Covenants and Other Interests Which "Run with Land" (2d ed. 1947).
[2] See Restatement (Third) of Property (Servitudes) (2000).

another that is not normally implied from the mere ownership of my own land.

In the previous Assignments, we explored one major type of servitude: easements. In the next few Assignments we explore the other major type of servitude: promissory servitudes. A promissory servitude usually originates in a promise or agreement to do or refrain from doing a specified act. Traditionally, promissory servitudes were divided into two types: (1) real covenants, or covenants running with the land, and (2) equitable servitudes. There is little current justification for this division, and the trend is to call both types of promissory servitudes simply "covenants" or "covenants running with the land." The new Restatement, for instance, eliminates any distinction and simply refers to this form of property interest as a covenant that runs with the land.[3] In this book, the phrases "covenants" or "covenants running with the land" will refer to all types of promissory servitudes.

*"Real Covenants" Compared with "Equitable Servitudes"*

Although there is little, if any, justification for distinguishing between "real covenants" and "equitable servitudes," courts often do so. Thus, we must understand the distinction even if we are unhappy with its continuing existence. "Real covenants" are covenants that the law courts (as opposed to the equity courts) recognized as running with the land. The English law courts were reluctant to give effect to too many kinds of real covenants. They therefore required that certain stringent conditions be met for a covenant to run "at law." In the famous equity court case of Tulk v. Moxhay,[4] the Court of Chancery held that a covenant that could not run "at law," might, under appropriate circumstances, run in equity.

Today, courts of equity and law are merged in almost all states. When we say that a certain covenant is enforceable at law (a "real covenant"), we mean that the breach of that covenant will give rise to a cause of action for damages, a legal remedy. When we say that a certain covenant is enforceable only in equity (an "equitable servitude"), we mean that it may be enforced by an equitable remedy, typically an injunction. The legal remedy of damages will not be available when a covenant is only enforceable in equity.

Sometimes an equitable servitude is called a "restrictive covenant" or a "negative covenant." These terms emphasize that most equitable servitudes restrict the use of the burdened land by prohibiting the owner from using the land in certain specified ways. In contrast, most real

---

[3] Restatement (Third) of Property (Servitudes) § 1.4 (2000).

[4] 2 Ph. 774, 41 Eng.Rep. 1143 (Ch. 1848). Although Tulk v. Moxhay is generally considered to have established the principle that certain covenants that could not run at law could run in equity, it appears that several earlier cases had established the same principle. See Natelson, Running with the Land in Montana, 51 Mont. L. Rev. 17, 30 n. 56 (1990).

covenants are affirmative in nature. Real covenants require the servient owner to take certain specified acts.

> EXAMPLE 1 (Affirmative vs. negative covenants): Alice effectively covenants that she will use the house that she is buying only for a single family residence, and that she will pay monthly dues to the Homeowners Association in amounts to be set by it from time to time. She also promises to abide by the rules and regulations reasonably promulgated by the Homeowners Association.
>
> The promise to use the property only as a single family residence will be interpreted as a negative covenant. Alice is not really promising to use the house as a residence, but rather promising that she will not use it for any other purpose. Leaving the house vacant would not normally be interpreted as a breach of the covenant. The promise to pay dues, a promise to perform an affirmative act, is an affirmative covenant. The promise to abide by the rules of the Homeowners Association is affirmative in form, but negative in substance. She is promising not to violate the rules. It can be seen that sometimes the nature of the covenant, affirmative or negative, is not entirely clear.

In many cases, a covenant may be enforced by both equitable and legal remedies. In such a case, the covenant is both a real covenant and an equitable servitude. Usually the plaintiff in such a case will seek an injunction and thus will be treating it as an equitable servitude. If the plaintiff also seeks damages for the defendant's breach of the covenant, the plaintiff is treating the covenant as both a real covenant and as an equitable servitude.

*Covenant Disputes Do Not Always Involve Issues of Succession*

In the next Assignment, we will be discussing covenants that "run with the land." Most promises or contracts, of course, do not run with the land. These types of covenants are sometimes described as covenants "in gross" because they benefit a person, rather than a particular parcel of land. If, by a binding contract, Bill agrees to sell Cathy 1000 widgets, this contract is usually personal, and does not run with the land owned by either Bill or Cathy. If Bill sells his land to Dave, Bill will still be responsible for selling the widgets and Dave will have no responsibility for the contract. Similarly if Cathy sells her land to Ellen, Cathy will still be entitled to enforce the contract and Ellen will have no rights under the contract. However, if the contract or covenant between Bill and Cathy "runs with the land" Dave may be obligated to sell the widgets and Ellen may be entitled to buy them. Moreover, in at least some cases, Bill and Cathy, the original covenantors, will be relieved of their obligations and rights when they transfer their lands to others.

If the dispute is between the original contracting parties, it is immaterial whether the promise is one that runs with the land.

EXAMPLE 2 (Contract question-running not at issue): Fran owns parcels 1 and 2. She sells parcel 1 to Gus, using a deed that provides that Fran will use parcel 2 only for residential purposes. The deed is silent concerning whether this covenant runs with the land. Thereafter Fran proposes to build a commercial structure on parcel 2. Gus objects. The facts raise only a contract question, not a property or "running" issue. It is immaterial whether the covenant runs with the land. Since Fran and Gus are the original contracting parties, the court need not decide whether the covenant runs.

As the next Assignment will show, the common law set limits on the kinds of covenants that could run with the land. By contrast, this Assignment explores the enforceability of covenants, on public policy grounds, even as between the original parties. Another aspect of the law involving the creation and validity of covenants deals with instances in which a covenant will be implied because there is no express written promise. This subject is treated in the Notes following the major cases.

## 3. Principal Problem

Sue purchased a newly constructed, single family house in a subdivision known as Bluehills from the developer of that subdivision. All of the two hundred houses in the subdivision are subject to a Declaration of Covenants, Conditions and Restrictions that was created and recorded before any lot in Bluehills was sold. Sue read the Declaration before she moved in. Paragraph 12 of the Declaration provides that all units within the subdivision "are to be owner-occupied (no rentals)." After Sue buys her house she lives in it for several years. Thereafter she finds a job in a distant part of the city and moves to a neighborhood closer to her job. She rents her house to John and Amy, a young couple who answered her "for rent" advertisement. Shortly thereafter, the POA sues to enjoin Sue from renting the unit to any person.

Sue seeks your advice. She feels that the rental prohibition is "not right" and should not be enforceable. The POA insists that Sue knew of the restriction when she bought the property (which is true) and therefore should not be permitted to complain of it now. Advise Sue after reading the following material.

## 4. MATERIALS FOR SOLUTION OF PRINCIPAL PROBLEM

### Natore A. Nahrstedt v. Lakeside Village Condominium Association

Supreme Court of California, 1994.
8 Cal.4th 361, 878 P.2d 1275, 33 Cal.Rptr.2d 63.

■ KENNARD, JUSTICE.

A homeowner in a 530-unit condominium complex sued to prevent the homeowners association from enforcing a restriction against keeping cats, dogs, and other animals in the condominium development. The owner asserted that the restriction, which was contained in the project's declaration recorded by the condominium project's developer, was "unreasonable" as applied to her because she kept her three cats indoors and because her cats were "noiseless" and "created no nuisance." Agreeing with the premise underlying the owner's complaint, the Court of Appeal concluded that the homeowners association could enforce the restriction only upon proof that plaintiff's cats would be likely to interfere with the right of other homeowners "to the peaceful and quiet enjoyment of their property."

[T]he narrow issue here is whether a pet restriction that is contained in the recorded declaration of a condominium complex is enforceable against the challenge of a homeowner. As we shall explain, the Legislature, in Civil Code section 1354, has required that courts enforce the covenants, conditions and restrictions contained in the recorded declaration of a common interest development "unless unreasonable."

Because a stable and predictable living environment is crucial to the success of condominiums and other common interest residential developments, and because recorded use restrictions are a primary means of ensuring this stability and predictability, the Legislature in section 1354 has afforded such restrictions a presumption of validity and has required of challengers that they demonstrate the restriction's "unreasonableness" by the deferential standard applicable to equitable servitudes. Under this standard established by the Legislature, enforcement of a restriction does not depend upon the conduct of a particular condominium owner. Rather, the restriction must be uniformly enforced in the condominium development to which it was intended to apply unless the plaintiff owner can show that the burdens it imposes on affected properties so substantially outweigh the benefits of the restriction that it should not be enforced against any owner. Here, the Court of Appeal did not apply this standard in deciding that plaintiff had stated a claim for declaratory relief. Accordingly, we reverse the judgment of the Court of Appeal and remand for further proceedings consistent with the views expressed in this opinion.

## I

Lakeside Village is a large condominium development in Culver City, Los Angeles County. It consists of 530 units spread throughout 12 separate 3-story buildings. The residents share common lobbies and hallways, in addition to laundry and trash facilities.

The Lakeside Village project is subject to certain covenants, conditions and restrictions (hereafter CC & R's) that were included in the developer's declaration recorded with the Los Angeles County Recorder on April 17, 1978, at the inception of the development project. Ownership of a unit includes membership in the project's homeowners association, the Lakeside Village Condominium Association (hereafter Association), the body that enforces the project's CC & R's, including the pet restriction, which provides in relevant part: "No animals (which shall mean dogs and cats), livestock, reptiles or poultry shall be kept in any unit."[5]

In January 1988, plaintiff Natore Nahrstedt purchased a Lakeside Village condominium and moved in with her three cats. When the Association learned of the cats' presence, it demanded their removal and assessed fines against Nahrstedt for each successive month that she remained in violation of the condominium project's pet restriction.

Nahrstedt then brought this lawsuit against the Association, its officers, and two of its employees, asking the trial court to invalidate the assessments, to enjoin future assessments, and to declare the pet restriction "unreasonable" as applied to indoor cats (such as hers) that are not allowed free run of the project's common areas. Nahrstedt also alleged she did not know of the pet restriction when she bought her condominium. The complaint incorporated by reference the grant deed, the declaration of CC & R's, and the condominium plan for the Lakeside Village condominium project.

The Association demurred to the complaint. In its supporting points and authorities, the Association argued that the pet restriction furthers the collective "health, happiness and peace of mind" of persons living in close proximity within the Lakeside Village condominium development, and therefore is reasonable as a matter of law. The trial court sustained the demurrer as to each cause of action and dismissed Nahrstedt's complaint. Nahrstedt appealed.

A divided Court of Appeal reversed the trial court's judgment of dismissal. In the majority's view, the complaint stated a claim for declaratory relief based on its allegations that Nahrstedt's three cats were kept inside her condominium unit and did not bother her neighbors. According to the majority, whether a condominium use restriction is "unreasonable," as that term is used in section 1354, hinges on the facts of a particular homeowner's case. Thus, the majority reasoned, Nahrstedt

---

[5] The CC & R's permit residents to keep "domestic fish and birds."

would be entitled to declaratory relief if application of the pet restriction in her case would not be reasonable. . . .

The dissenting justice took the view that enforcement of the Lakeside Village pet restriction against Nahrstedt should not depend on the "reasonableness" of the restriction as applied to Nahrstedt. To evaluate on a case-by-case basis the reasonableness of a recorded use restriction included in the declaration of a condominium project, the dissent said, would be at odds with the legislature's intent that such restrictions be regarded as presumptively reasonable and subject to enforcement under the rules governing equitable servitudes.

On the Association's petition, we granted review to decide when a condominium owner can prevent enforcement of a use restriction that the project's developer has included in the recorded declaration of CC & R's. To facilitate the reader's understanding of the function served by use restrictions in condominium developments and related real property ownership arrangements, we begin with a broad overview of the general principles governing common interest forms of real property ownership.

## II

Today, condominiums, cooperatives, and planned-unit developments with homeowners associations have become a widely accepted form of real property ownership. These ownership arrangements are known as "common interest" developments. The owner not only enjoys many of the traditional advantages associated with individual ownership of real property, but also acquires an interest in common with others in the amenities and facilities included in the project. It is this hybrid nature of property rights that largely accounts for the popularity of these new and innovative forms of ownership in the 20th century.

To divide a plot of land into interests severable by blocks or planes, the attorney for the land developer must prepare a declaration that must be recorded prior to the sale of any unit in the county where the land is located. The declaration, which is the operative document for the creation of any common interest development, is a collection of covenants, conditions and servitudes that govern the project. Typically, the declaration describes the real property and any structures on the property, delineates the common areas within the project as well as the individually held lots or units, and sets forth restrictions pertaining to the use of the property.

Use restrictions are an inherent part of any common interest development and are crucial to the stable, planned environment of any shared ownership arrangement. The viability of shared ownership of improved real property rests on the existence of extensive reciprocal servitudes, together with the ability of each co-owner to prevent the property's partition.

The restrictions on the use of property in any common interest development may limit activities conducted in the common areas as well as in the confines of the home itself. Commonly, use restrictions preclude alteration of building exteriors, limit the number of persons that can occupy each unit, and place limitations on—or prohibit altogether—the keeping of pets.

Restrictions on property use are not the only characteristic of common interest ownership. Ordinarily, such ownership also entails mandatory membership in an owners association, which, through an elected board of directors, is empowered to enforce any use restrictions contained in the project's declaration or master deed and to enact new rules governing the use and occupancy of property within the project.

Thus, subordination of individual property rights to the collective judgment of the owners association together with restrictions on the use of real property comprise the chief attributes of owning property in a common interest development. Notwithstanding the limitations on personal autonomy that are inherent in the concept of shared ownership of residential property, common interest developments have increased in popularity in recent years, in part because they generally provide a more affordable alternative to ownership of a single-family home.

In California, as we explained at the outset, our Legislature has made common interest development use restrictions contained in a project's recorded declaration "enforceable . . . unless unreasonable." (§ 1354, subd. (a), italics added.) In states lacking such legislative guidance, some courts have adopted a standard under which a common interest development's recorded use restrictions will be enforced so long as they are "reasonable." Although no one definition of the term "reasonable" has gained universal acceptance, most courts have applied what one commentator calls "equitable reasonableness," upholding only those restrictions that provide a reasonable means to further the collective "health, happiness and enjoyment of life" of owners of a common interest development.

### III

In California, common interest developments are subject to the provisions of the Davis-Stirling Common Interest Development Act (hereafter Davis-Stirling Act or Act). (§ 1350 et seq.) Pertinent here is the Act's provision for the enforcement of use restrictions contained in the project's recorded declaration. That provision, subdivision (a) of section 1354, states in relevant part: "The covenants and restrictions in the declaration shall be enforceable equitable servitudes, *unless unreasonable*, and shall inure to the benefit of and bind all owners of separate interests in the development." (Italics added.) To determine when a restrictive covenant included in the declaration of a common interest development cannot be enforced, we must construe section 1354. In doing so, our primary task is to ascertain legislative intent, giving the words of the statute their ordinary meaning. The words, however, must be read in context, considering the nature and purpose of the statutory enactment.

As we have mentioned in the preceding paragraph, section 1354 states that covenants and restrictions appearing in the recorded declaration of a common interest development are "enforceable equitable servitudes, unless unreasonable." The provision's express reference to "equitable servitudes" evidences the Legislature's intent that recorded use restrictions falling within section 1354 are to be treated as equitable servitudes. Thus, although under general rules governing equitable servitudes a subsequent purchaser of land subject to restrictions must have actual notice of the restrictions, actual notice is not required to enforce recorded use restrictions covered by section 1354 against a subsequent purchaser. Rather, the inclusion of covenants and restrictions in the declaration recorded with the county recorder provides sufficient notice to permit the enforcement of such recorded covenants and restrictions as equitable servitudes.

Under the law of equitable servitudes, courts may enforce a promise about the use of land even though the person who made the promise has transferred the land to another. The underlying idea is that a landowner's promise to refrain from particular conduct pertaining to land creates in the beneficiary of that promise "an equitable interest in the land of the promisor." The doctrine is useful chiefly to enforce uniform building restrictions under a general plan for an entire tract of land or for a subdivision.

In choosing equitable servitude law as the standard for enforcing CC & R's in common interest developments, the Legislature has manifested a preference in favor of their enforcement. The Legislature did, however, set a condition for the mandatory enforcement of a declaration's CC & R's: a covenant, condition or restriction is "enforceable ... *unless unreasonable.*" The Legislature's use of the phrase "unless unreasonable" in section 1354 was a marked change from the prior version of that statutory provision, which stated that "restrictions shall be enforceable equitable servitudes *where reasonable.*" Under settled principles of statutory construction, such a material alteration of a statute's phrasing signals the Legislature's intent to give an enactment a new meaning. Here, the change in statutory language, from "where reasonable" to "unless unreasonable," cloaked use restrictions contained in a condominium development's recorded declaration with a presumption of reasonableness by shifting the burden of proving otherwise to the party challenging the use restriction. How is that burden satisfied? To answer this question, we must examine the principles governing enforcement of equitable servitudes.

As noted earlier, equitable servitudes permit courts to enforce promises restricting land use when there is no privity of contract between the party seeking to enforce the promise and the party resisting enforcement. Like any promise given in exchange for consideration, an agreement to refrain from a particular use of land is subject to contract principles, under which courts try "to effectuate the legitimate desires of the covenanting parties." When landowners express the intention to limit land use, "that intention should be carried out."

Thus, when enforcing equitable servitudes, courts are generally disinclined to question the wisdom of agreed-to restrictions. This rule does not apply, however, when the restriction does not comport with public policy. Equity will not enforce any restrictive covenant that violates public policy. (See *Shelley v. Kraemer* (1948) 334 U.S. 1, 68 S.Ct. 836, 92 L.Ed. 1161 [racial restriction unenforceable]; s 53, subd. (b) [voiding property use restrictions based on "sex, race, color, religion, ancestry, national origin, or disability"].) Nor will courts enforce as equitable servitudes those restrictions that are arbitrary, that is, bearing no rational relationship to the protection, preservation, operation or purpose of the affected land.

An equitable servitude will be enforced unless it violates public policy; it bears no rational relationship to the protection, preservation, operation or purpose of the affected land; or it otherwise imposes burdens on the affected land that are so disproportionate to the restriction's beneficial effects that the restriction should not be enforced.

With these principles of equitable servitude law to guide us, we now turn to section 1354. As mentioned earlier, under subdivision (a) of section 1354 the use restrictions for a common interest development that are set forth in the recorded declaration are "enforceable equitable servitudes, unless unreasonable." In other words, such restrictions should be enforced unless they are wholly arbitrary, violate a fundamental public policy, or impose a burden on the use of affected land that far outweighs any benefit.

When courts accord a presumption of validity to all such recorded use restrictions and measure them against deferential standards of equitable servitude law, it discourages lawsuits by owners of individual units seeking personal exemptions from the restrictions. This also promotes stability and predictability in two ways. It provides substantial assurance to prospective condominium purchasers that they may rely with confidence on the promises embodied in the project's recorded CC & R's. And it protects all owners in the planned development from unanticipated increases in association fees to fund the defense of legal challenges to recorded restrictions.

Refusing to enforce the CC & R's contained in a recorded declaration, or enforcing them only after protracted litigation that would require justification of their application on a case-by-case basis, would impose great strain on the social fabric of the common interest development. It would frustrate owners who had purchased their units in reliance on the CC & R's. It would put the owners and the homeowners association in the difficult and divisive position of deciding whether particular CC & R's should be applied to a particular owner.

## IV

Here, the Court of Appeals failed to consider the rules governing equitable servitudes in holding that Nahrstedt's complaint challenging the Lakeside Village restriction against the keeping of cats in condominium units stated a cause of action for declaratory relief. Instead, the court concluded that factual allegations by Nahrstedt that her cats are kept inside her condominium unit and do not bother her neighbors were sufficient to have the trial court decide whether enforcement of the restriction against Nahrstedt would be reasonable.

As we have explained, courts will enforce an equitable servitude unless it violates a fundamental public policy, it bears no rational relationship to the protection, preservation, operation or purpose of the affected land, or its harmful effects on land use are otherwise so disproportionate to its benefits to affected homeowners that it should not be enforced. In determining whether a restriction is "unreasonable" under section 1354, and thus not enforceable, the focus is on the restriction's effect on the project as a whole, not on the individual homeowner.

## V

Under the holding we adopt today, the reasonableness or unreasonableness of a condominium use restriction that the Legislature has made subject to section 1354 is to be determined not by reference to facts that are specific to the objecting homeowner, but by reference to the common interest development as a whole. As we have explained, when, as here, a restriction is contained in the declaration of the common interest development and is recorded with the county recorder, the restriction is presumed to be reasonable and will be enforced uniformly against all residents of the common interest development unless the restriction is arbitrary, imposes burdens on the use of lands it affects that substantially outweigh the restriction's benefits to the development's residents, or violates a fundamental public policy.

Accordingly, here Nahrstedt could prevent enforcement of the Lakeside Village pet restriction by proving that the restriction is arbitrary, that it is substantially more burdensome than beneficial to the affected properties, or that it violates a fundamental public policy. Nahrstedt's complaint fails to adequately allege any of these three grounds of unreasonableness.

We conclude, as a matter of law, that the recorded pet restriction of the Lakeside Village condominium development prohibiting cats or dogs but allowing some other pets is not arbitrary, but is rationally related to health, sanitation and noise concerns legitimately held by residents of a high-density condominium project such as Lakeside Village, which includes 530 units in 12 separate 3-story buildings.

Nahrstedt's complaint alleges no facts that could possibly support a finding that the burden of the restriction on the affected property is so disproportionate to its benefit that the restriction is unreasonable and should not be enforced. Also, the complaint's allegations center on Nahrstedt and her cats (that she keeps them inside her condominium unit and that they do not bother her neighbors), without any reference to the effect on the condominium development as a whole, thus rendering the allegations legally insufficient to overcome section 1354's presumption of the restriction's validity.

■ ARABIAN, JUSTICE, dissenting.

I respectfully dissent. While technical merit may commend the majority's analysis, its application to the facts presented reflects a narrow, indeed chary, view of the law that eschews the human spirit in favor of arbitrary efficiency. In my view, the resolution of this case well illustrates the conventional wisdom, and fundamental truth, of the Spanish proverb, "It is better to be a mouse in a cat's mouth than a man in a lawyer's hands."

I find the provision known as the "pet restriction" contained in the covenants, conditions, and restrictions (CC & R's) governing the Lakeside Village project patently arbitrary and unreasonable within the meaning of Civil Code section 1354. Beyond dispute, human beings have long enjoyed an abiding and cherished association with their household animals. Given the substantial benefits derived from pet ownership, the undue burden on the use of property imposed on condominium owners who can maintain pets within the confines of their units without creating a nuisance or disturbing the quiet enjoyment of others substantially outweighs whatever meager utility the restriction may serve in the abstract. It certainly does not promote "health, happiness [or] peace of mind" commensurate with its tariff on the quality of life for those who value the companionship of animals. Worse, it contributes to the fraying of our social fabric.

While pet ownership may not be a fundamental right as such, unquestionably it is an integral aspect of our daily existence which cannot be lightly dismissed and should not suffer unwarranted intrusion into its circle of privacy.

Moreover, unlike most conduct controlled by CC & R's, the activity at issue here is strictly confined to the owner's interior space; it does not in any manner invade other units or the common areas. Owning a home of one's own has always epitomized the American dream. More than simply embodying the notion of having "one's castle," it represents the sense of freedom and self-determination emblematic of our national character. Granted, those who live in multi-unit developments cannot exercise this freedom to the same extent possible on a large estate. But owning pets that do not disturb the quiet enjoyment of others does not reasonably come within this compromise. Nevertheless, with no demonstrated or discernible benefit, the majority arbitrarily sacrifice the dream to the tyranny of the "commonality."

[T]he majority's failure to consider the real burden imposed by the pet restriction unfortunately belittles and trivializes the interest at stake here. Pet ownership substantially enhances the quality of life for those who desire it. When others are not only undisturbed by, but completely unaware of, the presence of pets being enjoyed by their neighbors, the balance of benefit and burden is rendered disproportionate and unreasonable, rebutting any presumption of validity. Their view, shorn of grace and guiding philosophy, is devoid of the humanity that must temper the interpretation and application of all laws, for in a civilized society that is the source of their authority. As judicial architects of the rules of life, we better serve when we construct halls of harmony rather than walls of wrath.

I would affirm the judgment of the Court of Appeal.

## Hill v. Community of Damien
Supreme Court of New Mexico, 1996.
121 N.M. 353, 911 P.2d 861.

■ FROST, JUSTICE.

Defendant-Appellant Community of Damien of Molokai (Community) appeals from the district court's ruling in favor of Plaintiffs-Appellees, enjoining the further use of the property at 716 Rio Arriba, S.E., Albuquerque, as a group home for individuals with AIDS.

Plaintiffs-Appellees argue that the group home violates a restrictive covenant. The Community contends that the group home is a permitted use under the covenant and, alternatively, that enforcing the restrictive covenant against the group home would violate the Federal Fair Housing Act, 42 U.S.C. §§ 3601–3631 (1988) [hereinafter FHA]. We note jurisdiction under SCRA 1986, 12–102(A)(1) (Repl.Pamp.1992), and reverse.

The underlying facts of this case are not in dispute. The Community is a private, nonprofit corporation which provides homes to people with AIDS as well as other terminal illnesses. In December 1992, the Community leased the residence at 716 Rio Arriba, S.E., Albuquerque, located in a planned subdivision called Four Hills Village, for use as a group home for four individuals with AIDS. The four residents who subsequently moved into the Community's group home were unrelated, and each required some degree of in-home nursing care.

Plaintiffs-Appellees, William Hill, III, Derek Head, Charlene Leamons, and Bernard Dueto (hereinafter Neighbors) live in Four Hills Village on the same dead-end street as the group home. Shortly after the group home opened, the Neighbors noticed an increase in traffic on Rio Arriba street, going to and from the group home. The Neighbors believed that the Community's use of its house as a group home for people with AIDS violated one of the restrictive covenants applicable to all the homes in the sixteenth installment of Four Hills Village. Installment sixteen encompasses the Community's group home and the Neighbors' houses. The applicable covenant provides in relevant part:

> No lot shall ever be used for any purpose other than *single family residence purposes*. No dwelling house located thereon shall ever be used for other than *single family residence purposes*, nor shall any outbuildings or structure located thereon be used in a manner other than incidental to such *family residence purposes*. The erection or maintenance or use of any building, or the use of any lot for other purposes, including, but not restricted to such examples as stores, shops, flats, duplex houses, apartment houses, rooming houses, tourist courts, schools, churches, hospitals, and filling stations is hereby expressly prohibited.

Reservations, Covenants and Restrictions, Four Hills Village (Sixteenth Installment) (filed in the Bernalillo County Clerk's Office, Apr. 5, 1973) (emphasis added). The Neighbors specifically argue that the term "single family residence" does not include group homes in which unrelated people live together.

On August 12, 1993, the Neighbors filed for an injunction to enforce the covenant and to prevent further use of the Community's house as a group home. The Community defended on the grounds that the covenant did not prohibit the group home and, in the alternative, that enforcement of the covenant would violate the FHA. The Community also counterclaimed to permanently enjoin enforcement of the covenant and to recover attorney's fees. After hearing evidence at two separate hearings, the trial court held that the restrictive covenant prevented the use of the Community's house as a group home for people with AIDS and issued a permanent injunction against the Community. The trial court entered specific findings that the Community's use of the home generated a significant number of vehicle trips up and down the street and that the increased traffic had detrimentally altered the character of the neighborhood.

The Community appealed the trial court's order, and we granted a stay of the permanent injunction pending this appeal. We now review the Community's claims regarding the proper interpretation of the restrictive covenant.

The issue before us is the applicability of the Four Hills restrictive covenant to the Community's group home. As this Court noted in *Cain v. Powers*, 100 N.M. 184, 186, 668 P.2d 300, 302 (1983), in determining whether to enforce a restrictive covenant, we are guided by certain general rules of construction. First, if the language is unclear or ambiguous, we will resolve the restrictive covenant in favor of the free enjoyment of the property and against restrictions. Second, we will not read restrictions on the use and enjoyment of the land into the covenant by implication. Third, we must interpret the covenant reasonably, but strictly, so as not to create an illogical, unnatural, or strained construction. Fourth, we must give words in the restrictive covenant their ordinary and intended meaning.

*Operating a Group Home Constitutes Residential Use*

At issue here is the proper interpretation of the restriction, "No lot shall ever be used for any purpose other than single family residence purposes." The trial court held that the Community's use of property as a group home for four, unrelated individuals with AIDS violated this restriction. In reaching its conclusion that the group home violated the residential use restriction, the trial court made two specific findings regarding the nature of the current use of the home. The court found that the "Community uses the house . . . as a non profit hostel for providing services to handicapped individuals" and that the "Community uses of the residence are much closer to the uses commonly associated with health care facilities, apartment houses, and rooming houses than uses which are commonly associated with single family residences." Thus the trial court apparently concluded that the property was being used for commercial purposes rather than residential purposes. However, we find that the trial court's conclusions are incorrect as a matter of law.

It is undisputed that the group home is designed to provide the four individuals who live in the house with a traditional family structure, setting, and atmosphere, and that the individuals who reside there use the home much as would any family with a disabled family member. The four residents share communal meals. They provide support for each other socially, emotionally, and financially. They also receive spiritual guidance together from religious leaders who visit them on Tuesday evenings.

To provide for their health care needs, the residents contract with a private nursing service for health-care workers. These health-care workers do not reside at the home, and they are not affiliated with the Community in any way. The number of hours of service provided by the health-care workers is determined by a case-management group assigned by the state pursuant to a state program. The in-home health services that the residents receive from the health-care workers are precisely the same services to which any disabled individual would be entitled regardless of whether he or she lived in a group home or alone in a private residence. The health-care workers do most of the cooking and cleaning. The residents do their own shopping unless they are physically unable to leave the home.

The Community's role in the group home is to provide oversight and administrative assistance. It organizes the health-care workers' schedules to ensure that a nurse is present twenty-four hours per day, and it provides oversight to ensure that the workers are doing their jobs properly. It also receives donations of food and furniture on behalf of the residents. The Community provides additional assistance for the residents at times when they are unable to perform tasks themselves. A Community worker remains at the house during the afternoon and evening but does not reside at the home. The Community, in turn, collects rent from the residents based on the amount of social security income the residents receive, and it enforces a policy of no drinking or drug use in the home.

The Community's activities in providing the group home for the residents do not render the home a nonresidential operation such as a hospice or boarding house. As the South Carolina Supreme Court noted when faced with a similar situation involving a group home for mentally impaired individuals:

> This Court finds persuasive the reasoning of other jurisdictions which have held that the incident necessities of operating a group home such as maintaining records, filing accounting reports, managing, supervising, and providing care for individuals in exchange for monetary compensation are collateral to the prime purpose and function of a family housekeeping unit. Hence, these activities do not, in and of themselves, change the character of a residence from private to commercial.

*Rhodes v. Palmetto Pathway Homes, Inc.*, 303 S.C. 308, 400 S.E.2d 484, 485–86 (1991). In *Jackson v. Williams*, 714 P.2d 1017, 1022 (Okla.1985), the Oklahoma Supreme Court similarly concluded:

> The essential purpose of the group home is to create a normal family atmosphere dissimilar from that found in traditional institutional care for the mentally handicapped. The operation of a group home is thus distinguishable from a use that is commercial—i.e., a boarding house that provides food and lodging only—or is institutional in character.

We agree with the conclusions reached by the South Carolina Supreme Court and other jurisdictions that the purpose of the group home is to provide the residents with a traditional family structure and atmosphere. Accordingly, we conclude as a matter of law that, given the undisputed facts regarding how the Community operates the group home and regarding the nature of the family life in the home, the home is used for residential purposes in compliance with the restrictive covenant.

*Residents of Group Home Meet Single Family Requirement*

The Neighbors also argue on appeal that the four, unrelated residents of the group home do not constitute a "single family" as required by the restrictive covenant. The Neighbors contend that the restrictive covenant should be interpreted such that the term "family" encompasses only individuals related by blood or by law. We disagree.

The word "family" is not defined in the restrictive covenant and nothing in the covenant suggests that it was the intent of the framers to limit the term to a discrete family unit comprised only of individuals related by blood or by law. Accordingly, the use of the term "family" in the covenant is ambiguous. As we noted above, we must resolve any ambiguity in the restrictive covenant in favor of the free enjoyment of the property. This rule of construction therefore militates in favor of a conclusion that the term "family" encompasses a broader group than just related individuals and against restricting the use of the property solely to a traditional nuclear family.

In addition, there are several other factors that lead us to define the term "family" as including unrelated individuals. First, the Albuquerque municipal zoning ordinance provides a definition of family that is at odds with the restrictive definition suggested by the Neighbors. The Albuquerque zoning ordinance includes within the definition of the term "family," "[a]ny group of not more than five [unrelated] persons living together in a dwelling." Albuquerque, N.M., Rev. Ordinances, art. XIV, s 7–14–5(B)(41) (1974 & Supp.1991).

The Neighbors argue that the zoning code definition is irrelevant to the scope of the covenant. They point to *Singleterry v. City of Albuquerque*, 96 N.M. 468, 470, 632 P.2d 345, 347 (1981), in which this Court stated, "It is well established that zoning ordinances cannot relieve private property from valid restrictive covenants if the ordinances are less restrictive." However, we agree with the Colorado Court of Appeals which noted, "While [the zoning] statute has no direct applicability to private covenants, it is some indication of the type of groups that might logically, as a matter of public policy, be included within the concept of a single family." *Turner v. United Cerebral Palsy Ass'n*, 772 P.2d 628, 630 (Colo.Ct.App.1988) (construing term "family" in covenant to include unrelated group home residents). In the present case, we are not using the zoning ordinances to relieve the Community of its obligations under the restrictive covenant. We are instead looking to the definition of family within the zoning ordinance as persuasive evidence for a proper interpretation of the ambiguous term in the covenant. The Albuquerque zoning ordinance would include the residents of the group home within its definition of family.

Second, there is a strong public policy in favor of including small group homes within the definition of the term "family." The federal government has expressed a clear policy in favor of removing barriers preventing individuals with physical and mental disabilities from living in group homes in residential settings and against restrictive definitions of "families" that serve to exclude congregate living arrangements for the disabled. The FHA squarely sets out this important public policy. As the court in *United States v. Scott*, 788 F.Supp. 1555, 1561 n. 5 (D.Kan.1992), stated, "The legislative history of the amended Fair Housing Act reflects the national policy of deinstitutionalizing disabled individuals and integrating them into the mainstream of society." The Scott court further noted that the Act "is intended to prohibit special restrictive covenants or other terms or conditions, or denials of service because of an individual's handicap and which . . . exclud[e], for example, congregate living arrangements for persons with handicaps." Id. at 1561 (alterations in original) (quoting H.R.Rep. No. 711, 100th Cong., 2d Sess. 23–24 (1988), reprinted in 1988 U.S.C.C.A.N. 2173, 2184–85). It "protects against efforts to restrict the ability of individuals with handicaps to live in communities." Id. This policy is applicable to the present case because the FHA's protections for handicapped people extend to individuals with AIDS. See *Support Ministries for Persons with AIDS, Inc. v. Village of Waterford*, 808 F.Supp. 120, 129 (N.D.N.Y.1992) ("The legislative history of the 1988 amendments to the FHA reveals that Congress intended to include among handicapped persons those who are HIV-positive...."). The Developmental Disabilities Assistance and Bill of Rights Act, 42 U.S.C. s 6000 (1988 & Supp. II 1990), and the Rehabilitation Act of 1973, 29 U.S.C. s 701 (1988 & Supp. IV 1992), also identify a national policy favoring persons with disabilities living independently in normal communities and opposing barriers to this goal. See *Scott*, 788 F.Supp. at 1561 n. 5.

In New Mexico, the Developmental Disabilities Act, NMSA 1978, s 28–16A–2 (Cum.Supp.1995), expresses a clear state policy in favor of integrating disabled individuals into communities. Although this act is directed at assisting individuals with developmental disabilities, such as autism or mental retardation, we find that this important state policy applies with equal force to individuals with any form of disability or handicap.

Furthermore, the state grant of zoning authority to municipalities, NMSA 1978, s 3–21–1(C) (Repl.Pamp.1995), expressly provides:

> All state-licensed or state-operated community residences for the mentally ill or developmentally disabled serving ten or fewer persons may be considered a residential use of property for purposes of zoning and may be permitted use in all districts in which residential uses are permitted generally, including particularly residential zones for single-family dwellings.

Although this section may not necessarily require that municipalities include community residences within single-family residential zones, it clearly indicates a preference for municipalities adopting this inclusionary approach.

Both the federal and state governments have expressed a strong policy encouraging locating group homes in single-family residential areas and treating them as if they constituted traditional families. This overwhelming public policy is extremely persuasive in directing us toward an expansive interpretation of the term "family." ...

Third, other jurisdictions have consistently held that restrictive covenants mandating single-family residences do not bar group homes in which the occupants live as a family unit. For example the Williams court noted, "When ... the restrictive covenant under consideration prohibits occupancy of more than one family unit but does not address itself to the composition of the family, a court is loathe to restrict a family unit to that composed of persons who are related, one to another, by consanguinity or affinity." *Williams*, 714 P.2d at 1023; see also *Welsch v. Goswick*, 130 Cal.App.3d 398, 181 Cal.Rptr. 703, 709–10 (1982) (noting that policy considerations mandate that covenant be interpreted to allow residential care facilities of six or fewer people); *Maull v. Community Living for the Handicapped, Inc.*, 813 S.W.2d 90, 92 (Mo.Ct.App.1991) ("[G]roup homes where the residents function in a family setting, interdependent on one another in carrying out the daily operation and routine of the residence meet the single family requirement of the covenant."), transfer denied, (Aug. 8, 1991); *Montana ex rel. Region II Child & Family Servs., Inc. v. District Court*, 187 Mont. 126, 609 P.2d 245, 248 (1980) (holding group home constituted family as required by covenant). But see *Adult Group Properties, Ltd. v. Imler*, 505 N.E.2d 459, 465–67 (Ind.Ct.App.1987) (questionable conclusion that the undefined term "family" in the covenant included only "father, mother and children, immediate blood relatives"), transfer denied, (Oct. 15, 1987).

Accordingly, we reject the Neighbors' claim that the term "family" in the restrictive covenants should be read to include only individuals related by blood or by law. We agree with the court in *Open Door Alcoholism Program, Inc. v. Board of Adjustment*, 200 N.J.Super. 191, 491 A.2d 17, 21 (App.Div.1985), which noted, "The controlling factor in considering whether a group of unrelated individuals living together as a single housekeeping unit constitutes a family . . . is whether the residents bear the generic character of a relatively permanent functioning family unit." As we already discussed above, the individuals living in the Community's group home do operate as a family unit. Much of the activities of the residents are communal in nature. More importantly, the residents provide moral support and guidance for each other and together create an environment that assists them in living with the disease that has afflicted them. We find that the Community's group home "exhibit[s] [the] kind of stability, permanency and functional lifestyle which is equivalent to that of the traditional family unit." Id. at 22. We therefore conclude that the Community's use of the property as a group home does not violate the Four Hills restrictive covenant.

*Findings Regarding Increased Traffic*

The Neighbors strenuously argue that the covenant should be interpreted to exclude the group home because the group home's operation has an adverse impact on the neighborhood. In support of this claim, the Neighbors point to the trial court's findings that "[t]he amount of vehicular traffic generated by [the] Community's use of the house . . . greatly exceeds what is expected in an average residential area" and that, as a result, "the character of [the] residential neighborhood relative to traffic and to parked vehicles has been significantly altered to the detriment of this residential neighborhood and its [sic] residents."

[I]f we had concluded that the group home did violate the restrictive covenant, the amount of traffic generated by the nonconforming use might then become relevant in evaluating the harm suffered by the other landowners and in determining the appropriate remedy. However, the amount of traffic generated by the group home simply does not affect the threshold question whether Community's use of the property as a group home violates the restrictive covenant requirement that the property not be used for any purpose other than single-family residence purposes. Accordingly, because the covenants do not regulate traffic or off-street parking, and because the amount of traffic generated by the group home is irrelevant to whether the home is used for single-family residential purposes, we conclude that the Neighbors' argument is without merit.

[The court also concluded that even if the residents of the group home did not constitute a family within the meaning of the restrictive covenant, applying the restriction under the facts of this case would violate the FHA.]

## Franklin v. Spadafora
Supreme Judicial Court of Massachusetts, Middlesex, 1983.
388 Mass. 764, 447 N.E.2d 1244.

■ NOLAN, JUSTICE.

The issue here is whether a trust by-law adopted by the defendants, trustees of the Melrose Towers Condominium Trust (trust), limiting to two the number of units in the Melrose Towers Condominium (condominium) which may be owned by any one person or entity, represents an unreasonable restraint on alienation or operates to deny the plaintiffs equal protection of the laws or due process of law. The case was submitted to a judge of the Superior Court on a statement of agreed facts. The judge entered a judgment declaring that the by-law was "valid and not unconstitutional." The plaintiffs appealed to the Appeals Court, and we transferred the case here on our own motion. We affirm.

The facts are as follows. On September 25, 1980, the trustees voted to amend the by-laws of the trust to restrict to two the number of condominium units which could be owned by any one person or entity. The amendment was duly recorded in the Registry of Deeds. In adopting the amendment, the trustees acted pursuant to the applicable by-law and with the written consent of condominium unit owners holding 80.45% of the beneficial interest under the trust.

On the date of the amendment, the plaintiff George J. Franklin, Jr., owned six units in the condominium complex.[6] On October 17, 1980, Franklin, as buyer, executed a purchase and sale agreement with the plaintiffs, Daniel and Florence A. Clarke, as sellers, for the purchase of a condominium unit owned by the Clarkes. As required by the Master Deed, the Clarkes then informed the trustees of the pending sale so that the trustees might exercise their right of first refusal. Thereafter, the

---

[6] No issue is presented concerning the effect of the amendment on Franklin's ownership of these units.

trustees notified the Clarkes that the sale was in violation of the by-law amendment. Franklin and the Clarkes then brought this action in the Superior Court for declaratory relief from the by-law amendment. After the action was filed, the Clarkes sold the unit to Franklin on April 16, 1981. In his judgment upholding the validity of the by-law amendment, the judge also declared that "the Clarke-Franklin deed . . . is null and void."

*Restraint on Alienation.*

Reasonable restraints on alienation may be enforced. *Dunham v. Ware Savings Bank,* 384 Mass. 63, 423 N.E.2d 998, and authorities cited. The following factors, if found, tend to support a conclusion that the restraint is reasonable: "1. the one imposing the restraint has some interest in land which he is seeking to protect by the enforcement of the restraint; 2. the restraint is limited in duration; 3. the enforcement of the restraint accomplishes a worthwhile purpose; 4. the type of conveyances prohibited are ones not likely to be employed to any substantial degree by the one restrained; 5. the number of persons to whom alienation is prohibited is small. . . ." Restatement of Property § 406 comment i (1944). None of these factors is determinative, nor is the list exhaustive. Each case must be examined in light of all the circumstances. However, we think that consideration of these factors in the context of the condominium housing arrangement, see G.L. c. 183A, is sufficient to demonstrate the reasonableness of the restraint here at issue. We consider the factors seriatim.

1. *Interest in the land.* In the context of condominium housing, we do not interpret this factor as requiring that those who seek to enforce the restriction possess an interest in the specific unit at issue so long as they possess an interest in the condominium complex where the unit is situated. There is no question here but that the trustees possess such an interest.

2. *Duration of restraint.* The plaintiffs did not argue before the trial judge that the restraint is unreasonable in duration nor do they make such an argument here. Therefore, we could treat the issue as waived. However, because our case law indicates that a restraint on alienation which may extend "for a period beyond that fixed by the rule against perpetuities is contrary to public policy and cannot be enforced," we take time to touch upon the issue of duration.

The amendment is not by its terms limited in duration. However, the trust by-laws may be amended at any time by the trustees, provided they have the written consent of unit owners "entitled to not less than fifty-one percent (51%) of the beneficial interest" under the trust. We think that this arrangement is a reasonable adjustment to the demands of condominium management and that the restraint at issue here, which is subject to the will of the majority in the manner described, is not unreasonable in duration. To the extent cases such as *Bowen v. Campbell, supra,* and *Roberts v. Jones, supra,* proclaim as absolute a rule of public policy measured by the period fixed by the rule against perpetuities, we decline to apply slavishly the rule to a form of property ownership little known at the time that these cases were decided. However, we caution that our decision is limited to the particular facts of this case. Our decision might well be different if, for instance, the by-laws could not be amended at any time or if the restraint at issue precluded all alienation of the property or allowed alienation only to an unreasonably small number of people.

3. *Worthwhile purpose.* The plaintiffs do not challenge the judge's finding that the "declared purpose" of the amendment was to encourage "maximum occupancy by resident owners." They do assert that there was no evidence to support the judge's further conclusions that "[i]mplicit in this purpose is the desire to impart a degree of continuity of residence, inhibit transiency and safeguard the value of investment" and that enforcement of rules and regulations against tenants is more difficult than with resident owners. To the extent that the by-law would promote owner occupancy, we cannot conclude on this record that such an objective is against public policy or in itself not worthwhile. Indeed, we agree with the trial judge that a "desire to impart a degree of continuity of residence, inhibit transiency and safeguard the value of investment" is implicit within the by-law amendment and its "declared purpose," and we think that such objectives are proper. Those who live in condominiums must be willing to give up a certain degree of personal choice in order to promote the welfare of the majority of the owners.

On this point, the plaintiffs also contend that the by-laws themselves belie the purpose of the amendment because the by-laws would not prohibit a person who owns two units from leasing either or both of them. However, the amendment may also be construed as a compromise between the desire of the majority of unit owners to maintain the residential character of the condominium and the right of a person owning one or two units to use his property as he desires. As so construed, the amendment is a reasonable means of achieving the majority's proper goal.

4. *Type of conveyance prohibited.* The conveyance prohibited by the amendment is not any sale of a unit but only sale of a unit to a person who already owns two. There is nothing in the record to indicate how often such sales have been proposed. However, noting that the amendment applies to all unit owners and not just the Clarkes, we can safely assume that an amendment passed with the consent of persons holding 80.45% of the beneficial interest under the trust is not one which would prohibit a conveyance likely to be employed by those persons. We note also that the plaintiffs have failed to produce any evidence which would show that even those persons, other than the plaintiffs, who did not consent to the amendment were constrained in any substantial way.

5. *Number of persons affected.* The amendment allows alienation of the property to all persons except those who already own two units.

Although the number of persons owning two units is not disclosed in the record, it is evident that this number is relatively small, if not minute, when compared to the number of persons to whom the Clarkes could properly sell their unit.

On the issue of reasonableness generally, the plaintiffs contend that the amendment is unreasonable because it has been applied against Franklin in an arbitrary and discriminatory manner. In so far as the amendment is a restraint on alienation, of course, it has not been applied against Franklin at all. Further, assuming arguendo that discrimination against the buyer is a factor in determining the reasonableness of a restraint on alienation, the plaintiffs have made no showing that the amendment has not been or would not be applied to void sales to others in a position similar to Franklin.

As evident from the discussion above, the record in this case is deficient in a number of areas where more information might have tended to support the plaintiffs' claim. However, even on the best of records, we think that the plaintiffs could not prevail on their claim that the amendment was unreasonably restrictive, given the small number of persons to whom transfer would be prohibited.

*The Constitutional Challenges.*

The plaintiffs here contend that the amendment has denied them equal protection of the laws and due process of law under the Fourteenth Amendment to the United States and arts. 1 and 10 of the Massachusetts Declaration of Rights. Specifically, they allege that Franklin has been "effectively denied his right to own property," and that both Franklin and the Clarkes have been denied "their constitutional rights to dispose of their property as they see fit."

The judge found that there was no State action sufficient to trigger the constitutional guarantees claimed. Because we conclude that the amendment did not deprive the plaintiffs of any constitutional rights, we may assume, without deciding, that the amendment represents State action. See *Johnson v. Keith,* 368 Mass. 316, 321–322, 331 N.E.2d 879 (1975) (condominium by-laws, because amendable and compliance required, resemble municipal by-laws more than private deed restrictions). But see *Laguna Royale Owners Ass'n v. Darger,* 119 Cal.App.3d 670, 683, 174 Cal.Rptr. 136 (1981) (expressing doubt whether actions of condominium association constituted "state action").

There can be no doubt that the Fourteenth Amendment to the United States Constitution and the analogous provisions of our State Constitution safeguard the rights of property owners to use and enjoy their property. However, the rights are not absolute; they may be made subject to reasonable regulations designed to promote general welfare.

In the present case, we are not concerned with an unqualified right of the plaintiffs to buy or sell property. Rather, we are concerned with their rights to buy and sell property within the condominium. As unit owners, they are by statute subject to the terms of the condominium's by-laws. G.L. c. 183A, § 4(3). Since the plaintiffs' decisions to purchase units within the condominium were no doubt voluntary, any restrictions imposed on the plaintiffs' right to buy or sell property within the condominium are, for this reason, essentially self-imposed. In addition, and as noted previously, G.L. c. 183A, §§ 8(*g*) & 11(*e*), contemplate that restrictions may be imposed on the uses that may be made of units. In these circumstances, we do not view the amendment as impinging on fundamental rights of the plaintiffs. See *White Egret Condominium, Inc., supra*. Therefore, the amendment's limitation to two of the number of units a person may own does not set up a classification scheme requiring "strict scrutiny." See *New Orleans v. Dukes*, 427 U.S. 297, 303, 96 S.Ct. 2513, 2516, 49 L.Ed.2d 511 (1976).

We have previously likened condominium trust by-laws to municipal by-laws. *Johnson v. Keith*, 368 Mass. 316, 322, 331 N.E.2d 879 (1975). We think that the test employed in determining the constitutional validity of municipal by-laws affecting economic relations is appropriate to the present inquiry, especially given our assumption that the amendment represents State action. Accordingly, we hold that, "[i]f a [by-law amendment] serves a legitimate purpose, and if the means the [condominium association] adopted are rationally related to the achievement of that purpose, the [amendment] will withstand constitutional challenge." *Shell Oil Co. v. Revere*, 383 Mass. 682, 421 N.E.2d 1181.

## NOTES

1.  *Differences and distinctions. Spadafora* and *Nahrstedt* involved an apartment house condominium, whereas the Principal Problem and *Hill* involve a property owner's association in which the individual residences are single family units. *Spadafora* involved a change in the rules after the plaintiffs bought the property, whereas the Principal Problem, *Nahrstedt* and *Hill* do not. *Spadafora* involved a partial restraint on leasing, by means of a partial restraint on sales, whereas the Principal Problem and *Hill* involve a total restraint on leasing. How significant are these differences? Is the restriction in *Nahrstedt* more arbitrary and unreasonable than the one in the Principal Problem?

2.  *Consenting to unreasonable covenants.* In a case involving a cooperative apartment house, the covenant prohibited anyone other than a "family member," as defined, from occupying the unit. A male friend of the female family member moved into the unit and the housing cooperative forced him to leave. The court held that this action did not violate a state civil rights statute prohibiting discrimination on the basis of marital status.[7] The court did not discuss other possible grounds for attacking the covenant. If a particular covenant is unreasonable, should a court be able to nullify it,

---

[7] See Maryland Commission on Human Relations v. Greenbelt Homes, Inc., 300 Md. 75, 475 A.2d 1192 (1984).

even if the covenant was drafted using clear language and was pointed out to the purchaser before she purchased the property? If there should be a reasonableness requirement, what should be its content? Should there be a presumption of validity? Should the results vary depending on the level of sophistication of the parties?

In *Spadafora*, the court likened condominium by-laws to municipal by-laws, for purposes of determining the standard of review. Aren't there significant differences? In Siller v. Hartz Mountain Associates,[8] the court analogized the board of directors of a condominium association to that of a corporation and adopted a "business judgment" test in reviewing a condominium's by-laws. Which test is preferable? Are there other alternatives?

3. *Racial restrictions.* At one time covenants prohibiting ownership or occupancy by certain racial or religious minorities were fairly common. Such covenants are clearly unconstitutional and unenforceable.[9]

4. *No children allowed.* California has held that a covenant against children in a condominium violates that state's civil rights act.[10] However, the Federal Fair Housing Act authorizes the exclusion of children from certain housing designed for "older persons," as defined in the statute.[11] Recall also Assignment 5, which addressed whether landlords can refuse to lease to people with children.

5. *The Federal Fair Housing Act.* In a part of the opinion not reprinted in the text, the court in *Hill* noted the application of the Federal Fair Housing Act (FHA) to cases involving discrimination against people with disabilities.[12] Section 3604(f)(1) of the FHA provides that it is unlawful "[t]o discriminate in the sale or rental, or to otherwise make unavailable or deny, a dwelling to any buyer or renter because of a handicap of . . . a person residing in or intending to reside in that dwelling after it is sold, rented, or made available." Moreover, § 3604(f)(3)(B) states: "For purposes of this subsection, discrimination includes . . . a refusal to make reasonable accommodations in rules, policies, practices, or services, when such accommodations may be necessary to afford such person equal opportunity to use and enjoy a dwelling. . . ." The *Hill* court observed that these provisions create three distinct claims for violations of § 3604(f) of the FHA: discriminatory intent, disparate impact, and reasonable accommodation. See also Assignments 5 and 33.

---

[8] 93 N.J. 370, 461 A.2d 568 (1983), cert. denied, 464 U.S. 961 (1983).

[9] See Hurd v. Hodge, 334 U.S. 24, 68 S.Ct. 847, 92 L.Ed. 1187 (1948).

[10] See O'Connor v. Village Green Owners Ass'n, 33 Cal.3d 790, 191 Cal.Rptr. 320, 662 P.2d 427 (1983).

[11] See 42 U.S.C. § 3607(b)(2)(C) (2005). The statutory requirements essentially provide that: (1) at least eighty percent of the occupied units are occupied by at least one person who is 55 years of age or older; (2) the housing facility or community publishes and adheres to policies and procedures that demonstrate the intent to provide housing for persons age fifty-five or older; and (3) the housing facility complies with HUD rules and regulations for verification of occupancy.

[12] See 42 U.S.C. §§ 3601 et seq.

# ASSIGNMENT 24–25

# ENFORCEMENT AND RUNNING OF COVENANTS

## 1. INTRODUCTION

The preceding Assignment examined the law governing the enforceability of a covenant between the original covenanting parties. This Assignment examines the law involving the "running" of a covenant which comes into play when one (or both) of the original covenanting parties transfers the property benefitted or burdened by the covenant. When a promise is made *by* a landowner, purchaser, or occupant, the question arises: Does the *burden* of the promise run with the land of the promisor? When a promise is made *to* a landowner, purchaser or occupant, the question is: Does the *benefit* of the promise run with the land of the promisee? If the covenant runs with the land of the covenantor, her land is deemed burdened by the covenant. If the covenant runs with the land of the covenantee, his land is deemed benefited by the covenant.

The running requirements are applied separately to the benefited and burdened sides. Thus, situations can result in which there is running on one side but not the other. Where such is the case, enforcement by, or against, an original party to the covenant may be possible, although enforcement by, or against, a successor is not.

In addition to the burden-benefit distinction, it is important to differentiate between covenants at law and equitable servitudes. Traditionally, courts have used the analysis for covenants at law when the plaintiff requested monetary relief. In contrast, courts invoked the rules for equitable servitudes when the plaintiff requested injunctive relief. Maintaining separate requirements for covenants at law and equitable servitudes no longer makes sense in a time when most courts have merged their legal and equitable divisions. Nevertheless, many cases in this area of property law continue to invoke this duality of analysis.

Historically, covenants would run only if they met certain running requirements: intent, notice, touch and concern, vertical privity, and horizontal privity. The running analysis differed for the burden and benefit sides. Moreover, the running analysis differed depending on whether the court was enforcing the covenant at law or in equity. In this casebook, an approach that calls for the application of these historical requirements is referred to as the "traditional" approach. The term "traditional" is used to distinguish this approach from more contemporary applications that modify and, in certain instances, abandon some of the historical requirements. As a general matter, the most difficult running requirements to apply have been touch and concern and horizontal privity. As will be discussed, the meaning of touch and concern has been hotly debated. Also, the horizontal privity requirement often prevented the enforcement of covenants at law. A trend is underway to simplify the law in this area, however, as courts are beginning to follow the lead of the new Restatement of Property and do away with both horizontal privity and touch and concern. The new Restatement also rejects the vertical privity doctrine. The following materials will explore both the traditional application of all of the running requirements and also explain the more recent approaches under the new Restatement.

i. *Intent*

The intent that is critical when analyzing whether a covenant runs is *the intent of the original contracting parties at the time they entered into the covenant.* When a promisee attempts to enforce a covenant against a successor of the promisor, the promisee must show that the original contracting parties intended the promise to run with the burdened land. Similarly, when a successor to the promisee attempts to enforce a covenant against the promisor, the promisee's successor must show that the original contracting parties intended the benefit of the promise to run with the benefited land. Ideally, this intent is evidenced by language contained in the original written promise to the effect that the parties intend for the burden of the promise to run with the land burdened, and for the benefit of the promise to run with the land benefited. The lack of such language, however, is not fatal. A court may infer an intent that the burden and/or benefit run from the nature of the promise and from the surrounding circumstances.

>EXAMPLE 1: (Intent that covenant run.) Ellen owns parcels 1 and 2. She conveys parcel 2 to Franklin. The conveyance provides that Franklin promises not to use parcel 2 as a toxic waste dump. Ellen then conveys parcel 1 to Gina, and Franklin conveys parcel 2 to Horace. A court may reasonably infer that Ellen and Franklin intended that both the benefit and burden of this covenant would run with parcels 1 and 2, so as to bind Horace for the benefit of Gina, despite the absence of words expressly so stating. A careful draftsperson, however, would have included language explicitly evidencing this intention.

ii. *Notice*

A covenant will not be binding on a bona fide purchaser for value of the burdened land if the purchaser did not have notice of it. Usually, a purchaser has notice of the covenant from the fact that the covenant has been recorded in the land records of the appropriate county, and could be discovered by a competent search of those records by an attorney or title company. Sometimes a purchaser has actual knowledge (as opposed to mere notice) of a covenant, because she has been directly informed of it.

In every case where the purchaser has knowledge of the covenant she also has notice of it. The reverse, however, is not true. A purchaser may have notice of a covenant because it is properly recorded, but may not have knowledge of it since she did not make a competent title search. To be binding on the purchaser, she must only have notice of the covenant before she purchases the land.

Although the requirement of notice derives from the English case of Tulk v. Moxhay,[1] it currently rests in large part on the recording statute of the governing state.[2] Thus, the governing statute must be closely examined before rendering a definitive opinion as to whether the relevant party had notice. In most states, a donee of the original promisor, in contrast to a bona fide purchaser, will be bound by the promise even without notice.

*iii. Touch and Concern*

*Conflicting views on the touch and concern requirement.* As a general matter, "touch and concern" requires that the covenant have some type of relationship with the land that is the subject of the covenant. Great controversies have surrounded the meaning, purpose, effect and desirability of the touch and concern requirement. As discussed below, the original Restatement avoided the use of the phrase "touch and concern" but nonetheless attempted to codify its meaning by requiring the covenant to affect the benefited land in a physical way. The new Restatement completely abandons the concept of touch and concern.[3] Traditionally, courts have applied the touch and concern requirement but have defined it somewhat differently. Many courts adhere to a popular formulation of touch and concern, originally espoused by Judge Clark in his book, Real Covenants and Other Interests Which "Run with the Land", 2d ed. (1947). His view was that " . . . if the promisee's (promisor's) legal relations in respect to [the] land are increased [decreased]—his legal interest as owner rendered more [less] valuable by the promise— the benefit [burden] of the covenant touches or concerns that land."[4] In essence, this test looks to whether the covenant's performance or nonperformance affects the land's use or value so as to be regarded as an integral part of the property.[5] A somewhat broader formulation of touch and concern asks whether the covenant is "logically connected" to the property at issue.[6] In general, the trend is away from requiring that the covenant touch and concern the land in a physical sense.[7] Those courts that apply touch and concern concentrate primarily on whether the

---

[1] 2 Phillips 774, 41 Eng.Rep. 1143 (Ch.1848).
[2] Recording statutes are examined in Assignment 48–49.
[3] See Restatement (Third) of Property (Servitudes) § 3.2 (2000).
[4] Reno v. Matley, 79 Nev. 49, 378 P.2d 256 (1963).
[5] See Flying Diamond Oil Corp. v. Newton Sheep Co., 776 P.2d 618, 624 (Utah 1989).
[6] See Moseley v. Bishop, 470 N.E.2d 773, 777 (1984).
[7] See Flying Diamond Oil Corp. v. Newton Sheep Co., 776 P.2d 618, 624 (Utah 1989).

covenant has some economic impact on the parties' ownership rights by either enhancing or decreasing the value of the land at issue.[8]

*The old Restatement's view of touch and concern: the burden.* Although the 1944 Restatement does not use the phrase "touch and concern", it does address the issue. Section 537 provides that the burden of a covenant runs at law only when it concerns the "physical use or enjoyment" of land:

> The successors in title to land respecting the use of which the owner has made a promise can be bound as promisors only if—
>
> (a) the performance of the promise will benefit the promisee or other beneficiary of the promise in the physical use or enjoyment of the land possessed by him, or
>
> (b) the consummation of the transaction of which the promise is a part will operate to benefit and is for the benefit of the promisor in the physical use or enjoyment of land possessed by him,
>
> and the burden on the land of the promisor bears a reasonable relation to the benefit received by the person benefited.

Section 537 thus provides that the burden of a covenant does not run *at law* unless the covenant benefits the land of either the promisee or the promisor in a physical way. (Note, however, that § 537 does not explicitly require the burden to be physical.) The fact that the burden of the covenant touches and concerns the land is not alone sufficient. In contrast, section 539, comment k of the 1944 Restatement provides that the burden may run *in equity* even if it does not affect the land to be benefited in a physical way. Thus, according to the old Restatement, the burden of a covenant against business competition may run in equity but not at law because there is no physical benefit to any land because of such a covenant.

*The old Restatement's view of touch and concern: the benefit.* Section 543 of the old Restatement of Property also states that the benefit of a covenant can run only if "the performance of the promise will constitute an advantage in a physical sense to the beneficiary in the use of his land, decrease the commercial competition in his use of it, or constitute a return to the beneficiary of the promise for a use of it by the promisor." This view has been largely discredited, however, and even courts applying the touch and concern requirement are inclined toward the view that the benefit does not have to be physical.[9]

*The new Restatement.* The new Restatement abandons the touch and concern requirement completely.[10] Comment b to section 3.2 of the

---

[8] See Runyon v. Paley, 331 N.C. 293, 300 (1992), reprinted in this Assignment.

[9] See Hudspeth v. Eastern Oregon Land Co., 247 Or. 372, 430 P.2d 353, 356–57 (1967).

[10] See Restatement (Third) of Property (Servitudes) § 3.2 (2000).

Restatement (Third) of Property (Servitudes) summarizes the reasons for abandoning the touch and concern requirement.

> As the need for the touch and concern doctrine has decreased, criticism of the doctrine has increased. Its vagueness, its obscurity, its intent-defeating character, and its growing redundancy have become increasingly apparent. Although courts still use the rhetoric of touch and concern, they increasingly determine the validity of servitudes on the basis of the rules stated in this Chapter. They look to the legitimacy and importance of the purposes to be served by the servitude in the particular context, the fairness of the arrangement, its impact on alienability and marketability of the property, its impact on competition, and the degree to which it interferes with the fundamental rights and expectations of property owners. In modern law there is no need to use the obsolete and confusing rhetoric of touch and concern to determine whether the parties were successful in creating an interest that runs with the land.[11]

Section 3.1 of the new Restatement provides that a covenant should be permitted to run (regardless of whether it touches and concerns the land) "unless it is illegal or unconstitutional or violates public policy." Examples of covenants that violate public policy include covenants that directly and unreasonably restrain alienation (section 3.4) or unreasonably restrain trade or competition (section 3.6).

*Toward a policy approach to the "touch and concern" issue.* It seems reasonably clear that the "touch and concern" requirement reflects a belief that certain types of covenants, if permitted to run, would usually do more harm than good, and thus should not be permitted to run. We offer the following as a supplement to the approach adopted by the new Restatement, described above.

In our view, the touch and concern requirement is simply a rough and misleading way of promoting an important, but largely unarticulated policy. The law is simply trying to prevent the running of those promises whose running is likely to prove "too inconvenient" either to society or to successors of the promisor. In deciding whether a promise is likely to be too inconvenient if it runs, one should weigh the advantages of permitting this type of promise to run against the disadvantages. In view of the swiftly changing social, economic and technological features of our society, it seems likely that what is "too inconvenient" at one time or place may be very convenient at another. Therefore, no rigid test will be satisfactory at all times and places.

Factors tending to make a covenant inconvenient or unreasonable include the following:

---

[11] Restatement (Third) of Property (Servitudes) § 3.2, cmt. b (2000).

    a. its duration is long or indefinite,

    b. the burden on the land of the promisor is greater than the benefit to the land of the promisee,

    c. the purposes of the covenant could be accomplished by means other than a covenant running with the land,

    d. the covenant serves only frivolous or whimsical purposes,

    e. the existence of the covenant makes it difficult to sell or use the property, and

    f. the promise can be performed by the original promisor as easily as it can be performed by the person in possession.[12]

To the extent that the opposite of these factors is true with respect to a particular covenant, courts should be more willing to effectuate the intent of the parties that it should run.

EXAMPLE 2: (*Facts and conclusion.*) Irene owns Blackacre and Jackson owns Whiteacre. Irene promises to give twenty piano lessons to Jackson for $400. Neither the benefit nor the burden runs with the land. If Irene sells Blackacre to Kelly, Kelly is not obliged to give piano lessons to Jackson. If Jackson sells Whiteacre to Larry, Larry cannot demand piano lessons from Irene or Kelly.

*Analysis.* The parties have not expressed an intent that the covenant run with the land, and it is not reasonable to infer such an intent. Moreover, even if the parties had expressed such an intent, and even if all successive owners of Blackacre and Whiteacre knew of the agreement, the covenant would not run. The traditional approach would explain this result by observing that the covenant did not "touch and concern" either Blackacre or Whiteacre, and only covenants that touch and concern the land will run.

EXAMPLE 3: (*Facts and conclusion.*) Marla owns Merrywood and Sadwood, an adjoining tract. Marla sells Sadwood to Dina by a deed that contains this language: "By accepting this deed, Dina hereby promises on behalf of herself and all successive owners and occupiers of Sadwood, that the premises will be used for residential purposes only. Said covenant is for the benefit of Marla and her assigns and is binding on Dina and her assigns and shall run with both Merrywood and Sadwood." If Dina thereafter sells to Tatjana, who has notice of the original promise before purchasing, Tatjana is bound by it even though

---

[12] With respect to item f, see generally, Stake, Toward an Economic Understanding of Touch and Concern, 1988 Duke L.J. 925. Professor Stake notes that the relevant question to ask is whether any inefficiency would be avoided by placing the benefit/burden with the successor instead of the promisee/promisor. If not, the covenant does not touch and concern the land.

she personally never promised anything. The burden of this covenant has run with the land. If Marla thereafter sells Merrywood to Paul, Paul can enforce the covenant against Dina if Dina is then the owner of Sadwood, or against Tatjana, if Tatjana is then the owner of Sadwood. In other words, the benefit of the covenant has run with Merrywood, and the burden has run with Sadwood.

*Analysis.* The parties have expressly indicated their intent to have the benefit and burden run with their respective parcels. The covenant touches and concerns both parcels. Moreover, since Tatjana had notice of the covenant before purchasing the property, Tatjana cannot claim that enforcement of the covenant is unfair as to her.

iv. *"Vertical" Privity*

*What is it?* "Vertical privity" refers to the relationship between the promisor and his successors, or to the relationship between the promisee and her successors. A grantee, heir or devisee of the promisee/promisor is a "successor" of the promisee/promisor and thus receives her interest in the land from the promisee. In these circumstances, vertical privity exists between the original promisee/promisor and her successor. In contrast, an adverse possessor (one who occupies the property without the permission of the record property owner), or one who takes her interest in the land by title paramount or superior to the promisee/promisor (*e.g.,* one who takes through a foreclosure proceeding) does not receive her interest from the original covenanting party and therefore is not a "successor." In these situations, no vertical privity exists between the original covenanting party and the subsequent occupier of the land. Under the traditional approach as exemplified in this context by the old Restatement, vertical privity is a necessary requirement to enforce both the benefit as well as the burden of a covenant at law. The type of vertical privity required differs, however, depending on whether enforcement of the benefit or the burden is at issue.

*The traditional view regarding the required relationship: running of the benefit.* According to the old Restatement, vertical privity is necessary to enforce the benefit of a promise at law. Therefore, one who obtains an interest by adverse possession or paramount title cannot enforce a promise.[13] However, with respect to the running of the benefit, it is not necessary that the successor succeed to the same interest as the promisee; succession to *any* interest that will benefit from the enforcement of the promise will do.[14] This type of relationship in which a successor to the original promisee has a lesser estate than the promisee is called "relaxed" vertical privity. To illustrate, a life tenant of the

---

[13] See Restatement of Property § 547 cmt. d (1944).
[14] See Restatement of Property § 547 cmts. c and e (1944).

original promisee has "relaxed" vertical privity with the promisee, and therefore the life tenant can enforce the promise even though the life tenant has an estate of lesser duration than the original promisee.

*The traditional view regarding the required relationship: running of the burden.* According to the old Restatement, for the burden of a covenant to run *at law,* the successor to the promisor must have succeeded to the *same* estate as that owned by original promisor.[15] For example, an assignee of a lessee is bound at law by the promises contained in the original lease (provided that the other requirements for the running of a burden are met) since the assignee succeeds to the same estate as the original lessee. This type of vertical privity often is called "strict" vertical privity. Compare "strict" vertical privity with the "relaxed" vertical privity required for the running of the benefit of a covenant.

Remember that vertical privity is a requirement only for enforcement of covenants at law. In effect, the burden of the covenant runs *at law* with the *estate* of the original promisor rather than with the *land* of the original promisor. In contrast, the burden of the covenant runs *in equity* with the *land* of the promisor rather than with the *estate* of the promisor[16] (this also is true regarding running of the benefit in equity). In equity, any person who acquires *any* possessory interest in the land of the promisor (or promisee) will be bound (benefited) by the promise. Thus when the promisee or her successor seeks equitable relief, the question of the defendant's vertical privity with the promisor is irrelevant. To illustrate, a sublessee (i.e., one who succeeds to an estate that is less than that of the original lessee) is not bound at law by the promises made in the original lease but can be enjoined from breaching any covenant contained in the lease (for purposes of such an action in equity, the covenant will be deemed an equitable servitude).

*The new Restatement and vertical privity.* Section 5.2 of the new Restatement rejects the concept of vertical privity and instead draws some distinctions between affirmative and negative covenants. Recall that affirmative covenants require the property owner to take certain specified actions. In contrast, negative covenants require the property owner merely to refrain from taking action. The new Restatement states that "except as otherwise provided by the terms of the servitude . . . an appurtenant benefit or burden runs to all subsequent owners and possessors of the benefited and burdened property, including a lessee, life tenant, adverse possessor, and persons who acquire title through a lien-foreclosure proceeding."[17] The Restatement adopts three exceptions to this general rule. First, one who holds a title superior to that of the

---

[15] See Restatement of Property § 535 (1944).
[16] See Restatement of Property § 539 cmt. i (1944).
[17] Restatement (Third) of Property (Servitudes) § 5.2 (2000).

original creator of the servitude cannot be burdened.[18] Second, with respect to affirmative covenants, persons who hold estates of lesser duration than those of the original covenanting parties generally are not subject to burdens and cannot obtain the benefits of such covenants, except in certain situations involving lessees[19] and life tenants.[20] Third, persons holding possession adversely generally cannot obtain the benefits of affirmative covenants, with the exception of covenants to repair, maintain and render services to the property.[21]

A few points about the new Restatement's position should be emphasized. First, the new Restatement provides that its rules are default rules that apply only when the parties to the original covenant fail to specify otherwise.[22] Second, the Restatement's position that all persons who hold estates of lesser duration than the original covenanting parties can neither obtain benefits nor be subject to the burdens of affirmative covenants, is qualified for lessees and life tenants. In other words, in certain instances lessees and life tenants can be subject to the burdens and can obtain the benefits of affirmative covenants. Third, this part of the Restatement does not govern the succession of benefits and burdens of lease covenants by assignees and sublessees of the original lessee. These lease covenant rules appear in Chapter 16 of the Second Restatement of Property (governing Landlord and Tenant law).[23]

Finally, although the new Restatement precludes persons holding adversely from obtaining the benefits of many affirmative covenants, it allows such persons to be subject to the burdens of covenants. Yet, the Restatement allows persons holding adversely to obtain the benefit of affirmative covenants to repair, maintain and render services to the property.[24] Moreover, the Restatement also draws a distinction between persons who hold possession adversely, and those who have acquired title by adverse possession. With respect to persons who have acquired title

---

[18] For example, generally an easement is lost by the foreclosure of a mortgage on the servient tenement when the mortgage was executed before the easement's creation.

[19] Section 5.3 specifies which affirmative covenant benefits and burdens run to lessees. It states that the benefits of affirmative covenants to repair, maintain or render services to the property run. It also states that affirmative covenant benefits that "can be enjoyed by the lessee without diminishing its value to the lessor and without materially increasing the burden of performance on the person obligated to perform the covenant" run. With respect to the burdens of affirmative covenants, those that "can more reasonably be performed by a person in possession than by the holder of a reversion in the burdened property run to the lessee."

[20] Section 5.4 provides that the benefits and burdens of affirmative covenants generally run to life tenants, except that "the life tenant's liability for performance of affirmative covenants is limited to the value of the life estate."

[21] See § 5.5 (also allowing the benefit of affirmative covenants to run to persons possessing the property adversely to the owner where the benefits "can be enjoyed by the person in possession without diminishing their value to the owner of the property and without materially increasing the burden of performance on the person obligated to perform the covenant").

[22] See § 5.2 cmt. a.

[23] See § 5.3 cmt. a.

[24] See § 5.5(1).

by adverse possession, all benefits and burdens will run to the same extent that they would run to persons who acquire title by other means.[25]

EXAMPLE 4: (*Vertical privity.*) Lessee under a sixty year lease makes two promises to his lessor: Lessee promises never to sell shoes on the premises, and to pay the real estate taxes. The lease provides that these promises are intended to run with the leased premises. Lessee *creates a life estate* of his interest in favor of Rachel. Rachel has notice of Lessee's promises. The agreement between Lessee and Rachel is silent concerning the promise not to sell shoes and the promise to pay the real estate taxes. What result if Rachel sells shoes on the property and fails to pay the real estate taxes?

*Result under the traditional view of vertical privity.* Lessor could enjoin Rachel from selling shoes on the premises. The fact that Rachel does not have the same interest as Lessee does not prevent Lessor from obtaining equitable relief from Rachel (recall that vertical privity is not a requirement in equity). Also, Lessor may obtain declaratory relief in equity requiring Rachel to pay the real estate taxes. However, Lessor would not be entitled to recover monetary damages from Rachel based on Rachel's prior sales of the shoes and also based on Rachel's failure to pay these taxes. The fact that Rachel is not in strict vertical privity with Lessee (because Rachel only has a life estate and therefore does not have exactly the same interest as Lessee) precludes Rachel from being held liable on the burdens of these covenants at law.[26]

*Result under the new Restatement.* Under § 5.2 of the new Restatement, the burden of the negative covenant not to sell shoes clearly passes to Rachel. Rachel presumably is liable both at law and in equity (although an injunction will not be issued if a judgment for damages is an adequate remedy). With respect to the covenant to pay the real estate taxes, § 5.2 must be read in conjunction with § 5.4 since Rachel is a life tenant and the covenant is affirmative. Section 5.4 provides that "except as otherwise provided by its terms, the benefits and burdens of an affirmative covenant created prior to creation of a life estate in

---

[25] See § 5.2 cmt. g.

[26] The old Restatement's different treatment of the vertical privity requirement at law and in equity, with respect to the running of the burden, may lead to results that are difficult to justify. For example, Lessor could enjoin the further sale of shoes, but could not obtain compensation for the damages caused by sales that have already occurred. Keep in mind as well that the covenant not to sell shoes is a negative covenant which typically is enforced in equity rather than at law.

The covenant to pay the real estate taxes is an affirmative covenant, which typically is enforced at law. Arguably, there is some justification for insulating from liability persons who take a lesser estate than the original promisor. This analysis suggests that the dividing line on the vertical privity question should be between affirmative and negative covenants, rather than between law and equity. The new Restatement moves somewhat in this direction.

the property to which the benefits or burdens are appurtenant run to the life tenant, subject to the proviso that the life tenant's liability for performance of affirmative covenants is limited to the value of the life estate." Thus, assuming payment of the real estate taxes does not exceed the value of Rachel's life estate, Rachel is liable for payment. Consistent with the negative covenant not to sell shoes, presumably this affirmative covenant can be enforced both at law and in equity.

v.  *"Horizontal" Privity*

*What is it?* The traditional view is that for the burden of a covenant to run at law, there must be a certain kind of relationship between the original contracting parties, in addition to the relationship they share stemming from the covenant itself. This required relation between the original contracting parties is known as "horizontal privity." There are many different views concerning the nature of the required relationship.

*The required relationship: the traditional view.* As noted above, "horizontal privity" refers to the relationship between the original promisor and promisee. There is no requirement of horizontal privity for the benefit of a covenant to run, either at law or in equity. In addition, there is no requirement of horizontal privity for the burden of a covenant to run in equity. In England, the required relationship for the burden of a covenant to run at law is the relationship of landlord and tenant. Thus, the burden cannot run at law in England if the relationship between the original covenanting parties consists of the transfer of a fee interest. Most United States courts endorse a less restrictive view of horizontal privity, however, and will find this requirement satisfied if the covenantor and the covenantee have the relationship of

> (a) landlord and tenant; or
>
> (b) easement holder and owner of servient estate; or
>
> (c) grantor and grantee (*i.e.*, a land transfer between the parties).

Significantly, the above list omits the simple relationship of neighboring landowners.

> EXAMPLE 5: (*No horizontal privity.*) Shanna and Tom are neighboring landowners. They agree in writing that neither party will use his or her land for commercial purposes and duly record their agreement. Shanna sells her parcel to Victor who promptly uses his property for commercial purposes, to the detriment of Tom. According to the old Restatement, Victor is not liable to pay damages to Tom.[27]

*The required relationship: the new Restatement.* Modern academic commentators are unanimous in disapproving of any horizontal privity

---

[27] See Restatement of Property § 534 cmt. a (1944).

requirement.[28] Following this trend, § 2.4 of the new Restatement specifically provides that "[n]o privity relationship between the parties is necessary to create a servitude." By statute, California has dispensed with the horizontal privity requirement[29] and other jurisdictions have done so by case law.[30] It seems likely that other states will eventually also abandon the doctrine.

*vi. Summary*

*The traditional view*: Under the traditional approach, a simple diagram illustrates the appropriate requirements for each running issue:

| At Law | | Equity | |
|---|---|---|---|
| Burden | Benefit | Burden | Benefit |
| Intent | Intent | Intent | Intent |
| Notice | | Notice | |
| Touch and Concern | Touch and Concern | Touch and Concern | Touch and Concern |
| Horizontal Privity | | | |
| Strict Vertical Privity | Relaxed Vertical Privity | | |

A comparison of the requirements for each category listed above allows for five concluding observations. *First*, intent for the covenant to run is required for every category. *Second*, touch and concern also is a universal requirement under the traditional formulation. *Third*, notice is a requirement only for enforcing the burden of a covenant, be it at law or in equity. This makes sense intuitively, because if courts are going to impose a burden of some sort upon a covenantor, there must be some insurance that the burdened party had the requisite degree of notice before purchasing the burdened property.

*Fourth*, in general terms, saying that two parties are in privity is another way of saying that they share the requisite relationship so that each party can enforce both the benefits and burdens respecting their properties against each other. There are three types of privity listed in the charts above. Horizontal privity, which pertains to the relationship between the two *original* parties to the covenant, is a requirement only for the running of a burden of a covenant at law. Vertical privity defines the relationship between *successors to each of the original covenanting parties*. Strict vertical privity is required to enforce the burden of a

---

[28] See, e.g., Browder, Running Covenants and Public Policy, 77 Mich.L.Rev. 12, 25 (1978); Berger, A Policy Analysis of Promises Respecting the Use of Land, 55 Minn.L.Rev. 167, 195 (1970); Note, Covenants Running with the Land: Viable Doctrine or Common Law Relic?, 7 Hofstra L.Rev. 139, 150 n. 70 (1978).

[29] Cal. Civ. Code § 1468 (2005).

[30] See, e.g., Gallagher v. Bell, 69 Md.App. 199, 217, 516 A.2d 1028 (Ct.App.Md. 1986).

covenant at law, whereas only relaxed vertical privity is required to enforce the benefit of a covenant at law. As these requirements suggest, it is by far more difficult to enforce the burden of a covenant at law than it is to enforce the benefit of a covenant at law under the traditional analysis. Again, this makes sense intuitively. If the law is going to impose a burden on a party, more safeguards arguably should be imposed than when enforcement of a benefit is at issue. This analysis also suggests that if the privity requirements are not met, either the original promisee or her successors may be entitled to enforce the benefit of a covenant, but the burden will not run to a successor of the promisor. In this situation, the plaintiff may have a legal right to enforce the benefit of the covenant, but will be unable to obtain monetary relief from the current owner of the burdened land.

*Fifth*, privity of any sort is only a requirement for enforcing covenants at law rather than equitable servitudes. Thus, a plaintiff in the situation described above who has a right to enforce the benefit of a covenant but who cannot sue a particular defendant at law because one of the privity requirements is missing can always attempt to enforce the covenant as an equitable servitude and thus side-step the privity requirements altogether. This strategy, if successful, will entitle the plaintiff to an injunction enforcing the terms of the covenant (but no money damages).

*The new Restatement view*: The analysis of whether a covenant runs with the land of a promisor or promisee is much simpler under the new Restatement, mainly because it makes no distinction between real covenants and equitable servitudes. Consistent with the traditional approach, intent and notice are still always required. The touch and concern requirement, however, does not exist under the new Restatement. That requirement is replaced by the requirement that covenants not be illegal, unconstitutional, or against public policy.

As for the privity requirements, the traditional concept of vertical privity is abandoned in favor of the approach that covenants run to all subsequent possessors of either the burdened or benefited land, with only three exceptions that make small distinctions between affirmative and negative covenants. Finally, no horizontal privity (relationship between the original parties) of any kind is necessary to find that a covenant runs with either the burdened or benefited property.

## 2. Principal Problem

George owned Blackacre and Ellen owned Whiteacre, an adjoining tract. Both properties were improved with vacation homes, but Blackacre had a working water well whereas Whiteacre's water was trucked in during the summer. Ellen approached George concerning Ellen's use of the well on Blackacre. After extensive negotiations the parties executed and recorded an agreement that contained the following provisions:

George shall make available to Ellen seasonably from May 1st to October 1st of each year, water not exceeding 500 gallons per day, and Ellen agrees to pay George the sum of two thousand dollars ($2,000.00) per year for said water. Both parties agree to use their respective properties only for one single family residence. The covenants herein contained shall run with the land.

For a few years both parties honored the agreement. Then George leased Blackacre to Lori for ninety-nine years. Ellen also sold her property to Nisa. The lease to Lori made no mention of the agreement between George and Ellen, and Lori never expressly agreed to abide by it. However, Lori did have actual knowledge of its terms before agreeing to lease Blackacre. Lori is refusing to sell the water to Nisa. She also is planning to subdivide Blackacre and build and sell several houses on the newly-created lots. Nisa has spent $60,000 in improving her property in reliance on George's agreement. Nisa sues Lori for damages that she will suffer if Lori proceeds with her plans, and "for such other further and different relief as to the court seems fair and appropriate." Analyze the probable outcome of Nisa's action based on the traditional view, the new Restatement, and the cases that follow.

3. MATERIALS FOR SOLUTION OF PRINCIPAL PROBLEM

### Runyon v. Warren and Claire Paley Midgett Realty
Supreme Court of North Carolina, 1992.
331 N.C. 293.

■ MEYER, JUSTICE.

This case involves a suit to enjoin defendants from constructing condominium units on their property adjacent to the Pamlico Sound on Ocracoke Island. Plaintiffs maintain that defendants' property is subject to restrictive covenants that prohibit the construction of condominiums. The sole question presented for our review is whether plaintiffs are entitled to enforce the restrictive covenants.

On 17 May 1937, Ruth Bragg Gaskins acquired a four-acre tract of land located in the Village of Ocracoke bounded on the west by the Pamlico Sound and on the east by Silver Lake. By various deeds, Mrs. Gaskins conveyed out several lots, which were later developed for residential use.

One and one-half acres of the sound-front property, part of which is at issue here, were conveyed by Mrs. Gaskins and her husband to plaintiffs Runyon on 1 May 1954. On 6 January 1960, the Runyons reconveyed the one and one-half acre tract, together with a second tract consisting of one-eighth of an acre, to Mrs. Gaskins. By separate deeds dated 8 January 1960, Mrs. Gaskins, then widowed, conveyed to the Runyons a lake-front lot and a fifteen-foot-wide strip of land that runs to the shore of Pamlico Sound from the roadway separating the lake-front and sound-front lots. This fifteen-foot strip was part of the one and one-half acre parcel that the Runyons had reconveyed to Mrs. Gaskins.

The next day, 9 January 1960, Mrs. Gaskins conveyed the remainder of the one and one-half acre parcel to Doward H. Brugh and his wife, Jacquelyn O. Brugh. Included in the deed of conveyance from Mrs. Gaskins to the Brughs was the following:

> BUT this land is being conveyed subject to certain restrictions as to the use thereof, running with said land by whomsoever owned, until removed as herein set out; said restrictions, which are expressly assented to by [the Brughs], in accepting this deed, are as follows:
>
> (1) Said lot shall be used for residential purposes and not for business, manufacturing, commercial or apartment house purposes; provided, however, this restriction shall not apply to churches or to the office of a professional man which is located in his residence, and
>
> (2) Not more than two residences and such outbuildings as are appurtenant thereto, shall be erected or allowed to remain on said lot. This restriction shall be in full force and effect until such time as adjacent or nearby properties are turned to commercial use, in which case the restrictions herein set out will no longer apply. The word "nearby" shall, for all intents and purposes, be construed to mean within 450 feet thereof.
>
> TO HAVE AND TO HOLD the aforesaid tract or parcel of land and all privileges and appurtenances thereunto belonging or in anywise thereunto appertaining, unto them, the [Brughs], as tenants by the entirety, their heirs and assigns, to their only use and behoof in fee simple absolute forever, [b]ut subject always to the restrictions as to use as hereinabove set out.

Prior to the conveyance of this land to the Brughs, Mrs. Gaskins had constructed a residential dwelling in which she lived on lake-front property across the road from the property conveyed to the Brughs. Mrs. Gaskins retained this land and continued to live on this property until her death in August 1961. Plaintiff Williams has since acquired the property retained by Mrs. Gaskins.

By mesne conveyances, defendant Warren D. Paley acquired the property conveyed by Mrs. Gaskins to the Brughs. Thereafter, defendant Warren Paley and his wife, defendant Claire Paley, entered into a partnership with defendant Midgett Realty and began constructing condominium units on the property.

Plaintiffs brought this suit, seeking to enjoin defendants from using the property in a manner that is inconsistent with the restrictive covenants included in the deed from Mrs. Gaskins to the Brughs. In their complaint, plaintiffs alleged that the restrictive covenants were placed on the property "for the benefit of [Mrs. Gaskins'] property and neighboring property owners, specifically including and intending to benefit the Runyons." Plaintiffs further alleged that the "restrictive covenants have not been removed and are enforceable by plaintiffs."

Defendants moved to dismiss the lawsuit, and plaintiffs thereafter moved for summary judgment. Following a hearing on both motions, the trial court granted defendants' motion to dismiss for failure to state a claim upon which relief could be granted and, pursuant to Rule 54(b), rendered a final judgment after having determined that there was no just reason for delay in any appeal of the matter. The Court of Appeals affirmed the trial court.

Having considered the evidence presented to the trial court, we conclude that plaintiff Williams presented sufficient evidence to show that the covenants at issue here are real covenants enforceable by her as an owner of property retained by Mrs. Gaskins, the covenantee. Accordingly, we reverse that part of the Court of Appeals' decision that affirmed the trial court's dismissal of plaintiff Williams' claim. However, we agree with the Court of Appeals that the covenants are not enforceable by the Runyons, and we therefore affirm that part of the Court of Appeals' decision that concerns the dismissal of the Runyons' claim.

It is well established that an owner of land in fee has a right to sell his land subject to any restrictions he may see fit to impose, provided that the restrictions are not contrary to public policy. Sheets v. Dillon, 221 N.C. 426, 431, 20 S.E.2d 344, 347 (1942). Such restrictions are often included as covenants in the deed conveying the property and may be classified as either personal covenants or real covenants that are said to run with the land. See 5 Richard R. Powell, Powell on Real Property ¶ 673 (1991) [hereinafter Powell on Real Property]. The significant distinction between these types of covenants is that a personal covenant creates a personal obligation or right enforceable at law only between the original covenanting parties, 5 Powell on Real Property ¶ 673[1], at 60–41, whereas a real covenant creates a servitude upon the land subject to the covenant ("the servient estate") for the benefit of another parcel of land ("the dominant estate"), Cummings v. Dosam, Inc., 273 N.C. 28, 32, 159 S.E.2d 513, 517 (1968). As such, a real covenant may be enforced at law or in equity by the owner of the dominant estate against the owner of the servient estate, whether the owners are the original covenanting parties or successors in interest.

I. *Real Covenants at Law*

A restrictive covenant is a real covenant that runs with the land of the dominant and servient estates only if (1) the subject of the covenant touches and concerns the land, (2) there is privity of estate between the party enforcing the covenant and the party against whom the covenant is being enforced, and (3) the original covenanting parties intended the benefits and the burdens of the covenant to run with the land.

A. *Touch and Concern*

As noted by several courts and commentators, the touch and concern requirement is not capable of being reduced to an absolute test or precise definition. See Neponsit Property Owners' Ass'n v. Emigrant Indus. Sav. Bank, 278 N.Y. 248, 256–58, 15 N.E.2d 793, 795–96, reh'g denied, 278 N.Y. 704, 16 N.E.2d 852 (1938); Charles E. Clark, Real Covenants and Other Interests Which "Run With Land" 96 (2d ed. 1947) [hereinafter Clark, Real Covenants]. Focusing on the nature of the burdens and benefits created by a covenant, the court must exercise its best judgment to determine whether the covenant is related to the covenanting parties' ownership interests in their land. Clark, Real Covenants 97.

For a covenant to touch and concern the land, it is not necessary that the covenant have a physical effect on the land. Flying Diamond Oil Corp. v. Newton Sheep Co., 776 P.2d 618, 624 (Utah 1989). It is sufficient that the covenant have some economic impact on the parties' ownership rights by, for example, enhancing the value of the dominant estate and decreasing the value of the servient estate. 7 George W. Thompson, Commentaries on the Modern Law of Real Property § 3155, at 84 (1962) [hereinafter Thompson on Real Property]. It is essential, however, that the covenant in some way affect the legal rights of the covenanting parties as landowners. Where the burdens and benefits created by the covenant are of such a nature that they may exist independently from the parties' ownership interests in land, the covenant does not touch and concern the land and will not run with the land.

Although not alone determinative of the issue, the nature of the restrictive covenants at issue in this case (building or use restrictions) is strong evidence that the covenants touch and concern the dominant and servient estates. As recognized by some courts, a restriction limiting the use of land clearly touches and concerns the estate burdened with the covenant because it restricts the owner's use and enjoyment of the property and thus affects the value of the property. A use restriction does not, however, always touch and concern the dominant estate. To meet the requirement that the covenant touch and concern the dominant estate, it must be shown that the covenant somehow affects the dominant estate by, for example, increasing the value of the dominant estate.

In the case at bar, plaintiffs have shown that the covenants sought to be enforced touch and concern not only the servient estate owned by defendants, but also the properties owned by plaintiffs. The properties owned by defendants, plaintiff Williams, and plaintiffs Runyon comprise only a portion of what was at one time a four-acre tract bounded on one side by the Pamlico Sound and on the other by Silver Lake. If able to enforce the covenants against defendants, plaintiffs would be able to restrict the use of defendants' property to uses that accord with the restrictive covenants. Considering the close proximity of the lands involved here and the relatively secluded nature of the area where the properties are located, we conclude that the right to restrict the use of defendants' property would affect plaintiffs' ownership interests in the property owned by them, and therefore the covenants touch and concern their lands.

B. *Privity of Estate*

In order to enforce a restrictive covenant as one running with the land at law, the party seeking to enforce the covenant must also show that he is in privity of estate with the party against whom he seeks to enforce the covenant. 5 Powell on Real Property ¶ 673[2]; 7 Thompson on Real Property § 3155, at 84. Although the origin of privity of estate is not certain, the privity requirement has been described as a substitute for privity of contract, which exists between the original covenanting parties and which is ordinarily required to enforce a contractual promise. 3 Tiffany Real Property § 851, at 451 n. 32. Thus, where the covenant is sought to be enforced by someone not a party to the covenant or against someone not a party to the covenant, the party seeking to enforce the covenant must show that he has a sufficient legal relationship with the party against whom enforcement is sought to be entitled to enforce the covenant.

For the enforcement at law of a covenant running with the land, most states require two types of privity: (1) privity of estate between the covenantor and covenantee at the time the covenant was created ("horizontal privity"), and (2) privity of estate between the covenanting parties and their successors in interest ("vertical privity"). William B. Stoebuck, Running Covenants: An Analytical Primer, 52 Wash.L.Rev. 861, 867 (1977) [hereinafter Stoebuck, 52 Wash.L.Rev. 861]. The majority of jurisdictions have held that horizontal privity exists when the original covenanting parties make their covenant in connection with the conveyance of an estate in land from one of the parties to the other. 7 Thompson on Real Property § 3155, at 85, and cases cited therein. A few courts, on the other hand, have dispensed with the showing of horizontal privity altogether, requiring only a showing of vertical privity. See, e.g., Nicholson v. 300 Broadway Realty Corp., 7 N.Y.2d 240, 164 N.E.2d 832, 196 N.Y.S.2d 945 (1959) (vertical privity sufficient); but see Eagle Enters. v. Gross, 39 N.Y.2d 505, 349 N.E.2d 816, 384 N.Y.S.2d 717 (1976) (referring to vertical privity as meeting horizontal privity requirement).

Vertical privity, which is ordinarily required to enforce a real covenant at law, requires a showing of succession in interest between the original covenanting parties and the current owners of the dominant and servient estates. As one scholar has noted:

> The most obvious implication of this principle [of vertical privity] is that the burden of a real covenant may be enforced against remote parties only when they have succeeded to the covenantor's *estate* in land. Such parties stand in privity of estate with the covenantor. Likewise, the benefit may be enforced by remote parties only when they have succeeded to

the covenantee's *estate*. They are in privity of estate with the covenantee.

Stoebuck, 52 Wash.L.Rev. 861, 876 (emphasis added).

We adhere to the rule that a party seeking to enforce a covenant as one running with the land at law must show the presence of both horizontal and vertical privity. In order to show horizontal privity, it is only necessary that a party seeking to enforce the covenant show that there was some "connection of interest" between the original covenanting parties, such as, here, the conveyance of an estate in land. Accord Restatement of Property § 534 (1944).

In the case sub judice, plaintiffs have shown the existence of horizontal privity. The record shows that the covenants at issue in this case were created in connection with the transfer of an estate in fee of property then owned by Mrs. Gaskins. By accepting the deed of conveyance, defendants' predecessors in title, the Brughs, covenanted to use the property for the purposes specified in the deed and thereby granted to Mrs. Gaskins a servitude in their property.

To review the sufficiency of vertical privity in this case, it is necessary to examine three distinct relationships: (1) the relationship between defendants and the Brughs as the covenantors; (2) the relationship between plaintiff Williams and the covenantee, Mrs. Gaskins; and (3) the relationship between plaintiffs Runyon and Mrs. Gaskins. The evidence before us shows that the Brughs conveyed all of their interest in the restricted property and that by mesne conveyances defendant Warren Paley succeeded to a fee simple estate in the property. Thus, he is in privity of estate with the covenantors. Any legal interests held by the other defendants were acquired by them from defendant Warren Paley. As successors to the interest held by defendant Warren Paley, they too are in privity of estate with the covenantors. Plaintiff Williams has also established a privity of estate between herself and the covenantee. Following the death of Mrs. Gaskins, the property retained by Mrs. Gaskins was conveyed by her heirs to her daughter, Eleanor Gaskins. Thereafter, Eleanor Gaskins conveyed to plaintiff Williams a fee simple absolute in that property. The mere fact that defendants and plaintiff Williams did not acquire the property directly from the original covenanting parties is of no moment. Regardless of the number of conveyances that transpired, defendants and plaintiff Williams have succeeded to the estates then held by the covenantor and covenantee, and thus they are in vertical privity with their successors in interest. Plaintiffs Runyon have not, however, made a sufficient showing of vertical privity. The Runyons have not succeeded in any interest in land held by Mrs. Gaskins at the time the covenant was created. The only interest in land held by the Runyons was acquired by them prior to the creation of the covenant. Therefore, they have not shown vertical privity of estate between themselves and the covenantee with respect to the property at issue in this case. Because the Runyons were not parties to the covenant and are not in privity with the original parties, they may not enforce the covenant as a real covenant running with the land at law.

C. *Intent of the Parties*

Defendants argue that plaintiff Williams is precluded from enforcing the restrictive covenants because the covenanting parties who created the restrictions intended that the restrictions be enforceable only by Mrs. Gaskins, the original covenantee. According to defendants, such a conclusion is necessitated where, as here, the instrument creating the covenants does not expressly state that persons other than the covenantee may enforce the covenants. We disagree.

Defendants correctly note that our law does not favor restrictions on the use of real property. It is generally stated that "[r]estrictions in a deed will be regarded as for the personal benefit of the grantor unless a contrary intention appears, and the burden of showing that they constitute covenants running with the land is upon the party claiming the benefit of the restriction." Stegall, 278 N.C. at 101, 178 S.E.2d at 828. This, however, does not mean that we will always regard a restriction as personal to the covenantee unless the restriction expressly states that persons other than the covenantee may enforce the covenant.

"Whether restrictions imposed upon land ... create a personal obligation or impose a servitude upon the land enforceable by subsequent purchasers [of the covenantee's property] is determined by the intention of the parties at the time the deed containing the restriction was delivered." Stegall, 278 N.C. at 100, 178 S.E.2d at 828; Reed, 246 N.C. at 224, 98 S.E.2d at 362. The question of the parties' intention is one that the court must decide by applying our well-established principles of contract construction.

Ordinarily, the parties' intent must be ascertained from the deed or other instrument creating the restriction. Stegall, 278 N.C. at 100, 178 S.E.2d at 828. However, when the language used in the instrument is ambiguous, the court, in determining the parties' intention, must look to the language of the instrument, the nature of the restriction, the situation of the parties, and the circumstances surrounding their transaction.

We conclude that the language of the deed creating the restrictions at issue here is ambiguous with regard to the intended enforcement of the restrictions. The deed from Mrs. Gaskins to the Brughs provided that the property conveyed was being made "subject to certain restrictions as to the use thereof, running with said land by whomsoever owned, until removed [due to a change of conditions in the surrounding properties] as herein set out." As noted by the dissent in the Court of Appeals, this provision unequivocally expresses the parties' intention that the burden of the restrictions runs with the land conveyed by the deed. Runyon v. Paley, 103 N.C.App. 208, 215, 405 S.E.2d 216, 220 (1991) (Greene, J., concurring in part and dissenting in part). In the habendum clause of the deed, the parties also included language providing that the estate granted shall be "*subject* always to the restrictions as to use as hereinabove set out." (Emphasis added.) We conclude that the language of the deed creating the restrictions is such that it can reasonably be interpreted to establish an intent on the part of the covenanting parties not only to bind successors to the covenantor's interest, but also to benefit the property retained by the covenantee.

Having determined that the instrument creating the restrictions at issue here is ambiguous as to the parties' intention that the benefit of the covenants runs with the land, we must determine whether plaintiff Williams has produced sufficient evidence to show that the covenanting parties intended that the covenants be enforceable by the covenantee's successors in interest. Defendants argue that plaintiff Williams has not met her burden because (1) the covenants do not expressly state that the benefit of the covenant was to run with any land retained by the covenantee; and (2) plaintiff Williams has not shown that the property was conveyed as part of a general plan of subdivision, development, and sales subject to uniform restrictions. While evidence of the foregoing would clearly establish the parties' intent to benefit the covenantee's successors, such evidence is not the only evidence that may be used to prove the parties' intent.

We find strong evidence in the record of this case to suggest that the covenanting parties intended the restrictive covenants to be real covenants, the benefit of which attached to the land retained by Mrs. Gaskins, the covenantee. The covenants at issue here are building and use restrictions that restrict the use of the burdened property to "two residences and such out-buildings as are appurtenant thereto" to be used for "residential purposes." The covenants expressly prohibit the use of the property for "business, manufacturing, commercial or apartment house purposes." The only exception provided by the covenants is that the latter restriction "shall not apply to churches or to the office of a professional man which is located in his residence." As noted by some courts, restrictions limiting the use of property to residential purposes have a significant impact on the value of neighboring land, and thus the very nature of such a restriction suggests that the parties intended that the restriction benefit land rather than the covenantee personally. See, e.g., Bauby v. Krasow, 107 Conn. 109, 115, 139 A. 508, 510 (1927) (concluding that only reasonable inference to be drawn from use restriction "is that its sole purpose was to protect the [covenantee's] homestead"); accord Elliston v. Reacher, 2 Ch. 374, aff'd, 2 Ch. 665 (1908). We need not decide whether the nature of a building or use restriction, in and of itself, is sufficient evidence of the parties' intent that the benefit run with the land, however.

In this case, the evidence also shows that the property now owned by defendants was once part of a larger, relatively secluded tract bounded by Silver Lake and the Pamlico Sound. Prior to conveying the property now owned by defendants, Mrs. Gaskins had erected on a portion of the tract a single-family residence in which she lived. At some point, her property was subdivided into several lots. Mrs. Gaskins conveyed several of these lots, on which residences were thereafter erected. Although none of these deeds of conveyance contained restrictions limiting the use of the property to residential purposes, it is reasonable to assume that Mrs. Gaskins, by later restricting the use of defendants' property, intended to preserve the residential character and value of the relatively secluded area. This evidence is further supported by the fact that Mrs. Gaskins retained land across the road from the property now owned by defendants and continued to reside in her dwelling located on the retained land. We believe that this evidence of the parties' situation and of the circumstances surrounding their transaction strongly supports a finding that the covenanting parties intended that the restrictive covenants inure to the benefit of Mrs. Gaskins' land and not merely to Mrs. Gaskins personally.

Moreover, we conclude that the language of the deed creating the restrictive covenants supports a finding that the parties intended the benefit of the covenants to attach to the real property retained by Mrs. Gaskins. The pertinent language of the deed provides that the property was conveyed subject to certain use restrictions "running with said land by whomsoever owned, until removed," and that the property is "subject always to the restrictions." As the Connecticut Appellate Court concluded after analyzing similar language in Grady v. Schmitz, 16 Conn.App. 292, 547 A.2d 563, cert. denied, 209 Conn. 822, 551 A.2d 755 (1988), we believe that this language suggests a broad, rather than a limited, scope of enforcement. That the deed expressly stated that the covenants were to run with the land and continue indefinitely, unless and until the surrounding property is "turned to commercial use," indicates that the parties intended the restrictive covenants to be enforceable by Mrs. Gaskins as the owner of the land retained by her or by her successors in interest to the retained land. See Grady, 16 Conn.App. at 297, 547 A.2d at 566.

Having reviewed the language of the deed creating the restrictive covenants, the nature of the covenants, and the evidence concerning the covenanting parties' situation and the circumstances surrounding their transaction, we conclude that plaintiff Williams presented ample evidence establishing that the parties intended that the restrictive covenants be enforceable by the owner of the property retained by Mrs. Gaskins and now owned by plaintiff Williams. Defendants did not offer any contrary evidence of the parties' intent but relied solely upon the theory that plaintiff Williams could not enforce the restrictions because the covenants did not expressly state the parties' intent and because plaintiff Williams had failed to show that the covenants were created as part of a common scheme of development. Based upon the uncontradicted evidence presented by plaintiff Williams, the trial court erred in concluding that plaintiff Williams, the successor in interest to the property retained by Mrs. Gaskins, was not entitled to enforce the restrictive covenants against defendants.

## II. *Equitable Servitudes*

With regard to plaintiffs Runyon, we must go further because, in certain circumstances, a party unable to enforce a restrictive covenant as a real covenant running with the land may nevertheless be able to enforce the covenant as an equitable servitude. Although damages for breach of a restrictive covenant are available only when the covenant is shown to run with the land at law, "performance of a covenant will be decreed in favor of persons claiming under the parties to the agreement or by virtue of their relationship thereto, notwithstanding the technical character and form of the covenant." 20 Am.Jur.2d Covenants, Conditions, and Restrictions § 26, at 596 (1965). To enforce a restriction in equity, it is immaterial that privity of estate is absent.

In this case, plaintiffs seek injunctive relief, which is available for the breach of an equitable servitude. Therefore, we now examine the question of whether plaintiffs Runyon, although unable to enforce the covenants [as covenants at law], may nevertheless enforce the covenants against defendants on the theory of equitable servitudes.

"Even though a promise is unenforceable as a covenant at law because of failure to meet one of the requirements, the promise may be enforced as an equitable servitude against the promisor or a subsequent taker who acquired the land with notice of the restrictions on it." Traficante v. Pope, 115 N.H. 356, 359, 341 A.2d 782, 784 (1975). In order to enforce a restrictive covenant on the theory of equitable servitude, it must be shown (1) that the covenant touches and concerns the land, and (2) that the original covenanting parties intended the covenant to bind the person against whom enforcement is sought and to benefit the person seeking to enforce the covenant. 5 Powell on Real Property ¶ 673[1], at 60-44.

### A. *Touch and Concern*

Whether a covenant is of such a *character* that it touches and concerns land is determined according to the same principles applicable to real covenants running at law. Plaintiffs Runyon have shown that the covenants at issue here meet the legal requirement that the covenants touch and concern defendants' property as well as the property owned by the Runyons. Because a covenant that touches and concerns the land at law will also touch and concern the land in equity, we need not further examine this requirement.

### B. *Intent of the Parties*

[W]e conclude that plaintiffs Runyon have failed to show that the original covenanting parties intended that they be permitted to enforce the covenants either in a personal capacity or as owners of any land they now own. The Runyons were not parties to the covenants, and neither they nor their property are mentioned, either explicitly or implicitly, as intended beneficiaries in the deed creating the covenants or in any other instrument in the public records pertaining to defendants' property. Although they own property closely situated to defendants', in an area which was primarily residential at the time the restrictive covenants were created, they did not acquire their property as part of a plan or scheme to develop the area as residential property. In fact, they acquired their property free of any restrictions as to the use of their property. Finally, the Runyons purchased their property prior to the creation of the restrictive covenants at issue here, and thus they cannot be said to be successors in interest to any property retained by the covenantee that was intended to be benefitted by the covenants.

III. *Notice*

It is well settled in our state that a restrictive covenant is not enforceable, either at law or in equity, against a subsequent purchaser of property burdened by the covenant unless notice of the covenant is contained in an instrument in his chain of title. N.C.G.S. § 47–18 provides:

> No . . . conveyance of land . . . shall be valid to pass any property interest as against . . . purchasers for a valuable consideration . . . but from the time of registration thereof in the county where the land lies. . . .

N.C.G.S. § 47–18(a) (1984). Unlike in many states, actual knowledge, no matter how full and formal, is not sufficient to bind a purchaser in our state without notice of the existence of a restrictive covenant. Turner v. Glenn, 220 N.C. 620, 625, 18 S.E.2d 197, 201 (1942).

> A purchaser is chargeable with notice of the existence of the restriction only if a proper search of the public records would have revealed it. . . . If the restrictive covenant is contained in a separate instrument or rests in parol and not in a deed in the chain of title and is not referred to in such deed a purchaser, under our registration law, has no constructive notice of it.

Id.

Notwithstanding the fact that the covenants at issue here were created in a properly recorded deed of conveyance from Mrs. Gaskins to defendants' predecessors, defendants contend that they are purchasers for value and that N.C.G.S. § 47–18 precludes enforcement of the restrictions against them. Relying on Reed v. Elmore, 246 N.C. 221, 98 S.E.2d 360, defendants argue that a restrictive covenant is not enforceable against a subsequent purchaser of the property unless the instruments in the chain of title *expressly* state "*both* an intention to bind succeeding grantees and an intention to permit enforcement by successors of the grantor or named beneficiaries."

While it would be advisable to include an express provision with respect to the rights of enforcement in the conveyance that creates them, we do not agree that such notice, as defendants demand, is required. An examination of our case law reveals that we have required the certainty of an express statement in the chain of title only with respect to the existence of a restrictive covenant. See Reed, 246 N.C. 221, 98 S.E.2d 360; Turner, 220 N.C. 620, 18 S.E.2d 197. " 'If the restrictive covenant is contained in a separate instrument or rests in parol and [is] not [referred to] in a deed in the chain of title,' " a subsequent purchaser will take the property free of restrictions. Reed, 246 N.C. at 230, 98 S.E.2d at 367 (quoting Turner, 220 N.C. at 625, 18 S.E.2d at 201). Where, however, the restriction is contained in the chain of title, we have not hesitated to enforce the restriction against a subsequent purchaser when the court may reasonably infer that the covenant was created for the benefit of the party seeking enforcement.

This is not to say that a restrictive covenant, the existence of which is clearly set forth in the chain of title, may be enforced by any person who is able to show by any means possible that the covenanting parties intended that he be permitted to enforce the covenant. For a restrictive covenant to be enforceable against a subsequent purchaser, there must be some evidence in the public records from which it reasonably may be inferred that the covenant was intended to benefit, either personally or as a landowner, the party seeking enforcement.

In this case, a proper search of the public records pertaining to defendants' property would have revealed not only the existence of the restrictive covenants, but also that prior to the conveyance the property was part of a larger tract owned by Mrs. Gaskins. Upon conveying the property to defendants' predecessors, Mrs. Gaskins did not part with all of her property but retained adjacent or nearby property that would be benefitted by the restrictive covenants. From this evidence, it reasonably may be inferred that the restrictive covenants were intended to benefit the property retained by Mrs. Gaskins. Therefore, plaintiff Williams, Mrs. Gaskins' successor in title, has shown that the public records provided sufficient notice to defendants to enable her to enforce the restrictive covenants against them.

The Runyons have not made a sufficient showing so as to charge defendants with notice of the existence of any restriction that may have inured or was intended to inure to their benefit. While the records in defendants' chain of title unambiguously provide notice of the restrictive covenants, they do not in any way suggest any right of enforcement in favor of the Runyons, either personally or as owners of any land.

For the reasons stated herein, we conclude that the restrictive covenants contained in the deed from Mrs. Gaskins to defendants' predecessors are not personal covenants that became unenforceable at Mrs. Gaskins' death but are real covenants appurtenant to the property retained by Mrs. Gaskins at the time of the conveyance to defendants' predecessors in interest. As a successor in interest to the property retained by Mrs. Gaskins, plaintiff Williams is therefore entitled to seek enforcement of the restrictive covenants against defendants. We therefore reverse that part of the Court of Appeals' decision that affirmed the trial court's dismissal of plaintiff Williams' claim and remand this case to that court for further proceedings not inconsistent with this opinion.

We further conclude that the Runyons have not proffered sufficient evidence to show that they have standing to enforce the restrictive covenants, either personally or as owners of any land intended to be benefitted by the restrictions. We therefore affirm that part of the Court of Appeals' decision that affirmed the trial court's dismissal of the Runyons' claim.

## Davidson Bros., Inc. v. D. Katz & Sons, Inc.
Supreme Court of New Jersey, 1990.
121 N.J. 196, 579 A.2d 288.

■ GARIBALDI, JUSTICE.

This case presents [the] issue . . . whether a restrictive covenant in a deed, providing that the property shall not be used as a supermarket or grocery store, is enforceable against the original covenantor's successor, a subsequent purchaser with actual notice of the covenant.

The facts are not in dispute. Prior to September 1980 plaintiff, Davidson Bros., Inc., along with Irisondra, Inc., a related corporation, owned certain premises located at 263–271 George Street and 30 Morris Street in New Brunswick (the "George Street" property). Plaintiff operated a supermarket on that property for approximately seven to eight months. The store operated at a loss allegedly because of competing business from plaintiff's other store, located two miles away (the "Elizabeth Street" property). Consequently, plaintiff and Irisondra conveyed, by separate deeds, the George Street property to defendant D. Katz & Sons, Inc., with a restrictive covenant not to operate a supermarket on the premises. Specifically, each deed contained the following covenant:

> The lands and premises described herein and conveyed hereby are conveyed subject to the restriction that said lands and premises shall not be used as and for a supermarket or grocery store of a supermarket type, however designated, for a period of forty (40) years from the date of this deed. This restriction shall be a covenant attached to and running with the lands.

The deeds were duly recorded in Middlesex County Clerk's office on September 10, 1980. According to plaintiff's complaint, its operation of both stores resulted in losses in both stores. Plaintiff alleges that after the closure of the George Street store, its Elizabeth Street store increased in sales by twenty percent and became profitable. Plaintiff held a leasehold interest in the Elizabeth Street property, which commenced in 1978 for a period of twenty years, plus two renewal terms of five years.

According to defendants New Brunswick Housing Authority (the "Authority") and City of New Brunswick (the "City"), the closure of the George Street store did not benefit the residents of downtown New Brunswick. Defendants allege that many of the residents who lived two blocks away from the George Street store in multi-family and senior-citizen housing units were forced to take public transportation and taxis to the Elizabeth Street store because there were no other markets in downtown New Brunswick, save for two high-priced convenience stores.

The residents requested the aid of the City and the Authority in attracting a new food retailer to this urban-renewal area. For six years, those efforts were unsuccessful. Finally, in 1986, an executive of C-Town, a division of a supermarket chain, approached representatives of New Brunswick about securing financial help from the City to build a supermarket.

Despite its actual notice of the covenant the Authority, on October 23, 1986, purchased the George Street property from Katz for $450,000, and agreed to lease from Katz at an annual net rent of $19,800.00, the adjacent land at 263–265 George Street for use as a parking lot. The Authority invited proposals for the lease of the property to use as a supermarket. C-Town was the only party to submit a proposal at a public auction. The proposal provided for an aggregate rent of one dollar per year during the five-year lease term with an agreement to make $10,000 in improvements to the exterior of the building and land. The Authority accepted the proposal in 1987. All the defendants in this case had actual notice of the restrictions contained in the deed and of plaintiff's intent to enforce the same. Not only were the deeds recorded but the contract of sale between Katz and the Housing Authority specifically referred to the restrictive covenant and the pending action.

Plaintiff filed this action in the Chancery Division against defendants D. Katz & Sons, Inc., the City of New Brunswick, and C-Town. The complaint requested a declaratory judgment that the noncompetition covenant was binding on all subsequent owners of the George Street property. That complaint was then amended to include defendant the New Brunswick Housing Authority.

Plaintiff moved for summary judgment, to which defendants responded by submitting three affidavits, one from Agnes Scott, President of the New Brunswick Home Tenants Council; one from Richard M. Keefe, Executive Director of the Housing and Urban Development Authority of New Brunswick; and one from Frank R. Nero, Director of the Department of Policy and Economic Development for New Brunswick, all alleging the need for a supermarket in the area of George Street.

The trial court denied plaintiff's motion and held, in an unreported opinion, that the covenant was unenforceable, relying on Brewer v. Marshall & Cheseman, 19 N.J.Eq. 537 (E. & A.1868). That case held that the burden of a covenant will not run with the land and therefore bind a successor unless the covenant "affects the physical use of the land itself." This view "effectively stifles any possibility of covenants relating to competition," 5 R. Powell & P. Rohan, Powell on Real Property § 675[3], 60–108 (rev. ed. 1989). (5 Powell). Although the Brewer decision was an old case, (1868), the trial court was satisfied that it was still controlling and found that the covenant was unenforceable because it did not "touch and concern" the land.

After the court denied plaintiff's motion for summary judgment, defendants moved for summary judgment, which was granted. Plaintiff appealed, and in an unreported opinion, the Appellate Division affirmed the trial court's judgment. For purposes of its decision the Appellate Division assumed that Brewer was not applicable, that noncompetitive covenants may run with the land in appropriate cases, that a leasehold interest in land is a sufficient interest to enforce a covenant, that two miles between the burdened and benefitted properties does not itself prevent a covenant from being enforced, and that the George Street store would impair the profitability of the Elizabeth Street store. Although the Appellate Division found "some merit" to plaintiff's argument that Brewer v. Marshall, supra, 19 N.J.Eq. 537, no longer represented the current law in New Jersey, the court held that the covenant was unenforceable against a subsequent grantee because the benefit did not "touch and concern" plaintiff's Elizabeth Street property. Specifically, the court reasoned that because the covenant restricted such a comparatively small portion of the market area, less than one-half an acre, and did not impair the use of the other 2,000 acres in the market circle from which the Elizabeth store draws its clientele, the covenant did not enhance the value of the retained estate, and therefore, as a matter of law, would not bind a subsequent purchaser. In contrast to the trial court's decision, the Appellate Division's rationale was premised on the failure of the benefit of the covenant to run, not of the burden.

We granted plaintiff's petition for certification.

Covenants regarding property uses have historical roots in the courts of both law and equity. The English common-law courts first dealt with the issue in Spencer's Case, 5 Co. 16a, 77 Eng.Rep. 72 (Q.B.1583). The court established two criteria for the enforcement of covenants against successors. First, the original covenanting parties must intend that the covenant run with the land. Second, the covenant must "touch and concern" the land. Id. at 16b, 77 Eng.Rep. at 74. The court explained the concept of "touch and concern" in this manner:

> But although the covenant be for him [an original party to the promise] and his assigns, yet if the thing to be done be merely collateral to the land, and doth not touch and concern the thing demised in any sort, there the assignee shall not be charged. As if the lessee covenants for him and his assignees to build a house upon the land of the lessor which is no parcel of the demise, or to pay any collateral sum to the lessor, or to a stranger, it shall

not bind the assignee, because it is merely collateral, and in no manner touches or concerns the thing that was demised, or that is assigned over, and therefore in such case the assignee of the thing demised cannot be charged with it, no more than any other stranger. [Ibid.]

The English common-law courts also developed additional requirements of horizontal privity, vertical privity, and that the covenant have "proper form," in order for the covenant to run with the land. C. Clark, Real Covenants and Other Interests Which Run With the Land 94, 95 (2d ed. 1947) (Real Covenants). Those technical requirements made it difficult, if not impossible, to protect property through the creation of real covenants. Commentary, "Real Covenants in Restraint of Trade—When Do They Run With the Land?," 20 Ala.L.Rev. 114, 115 (1967).

To mitigate and to eliminate many of the formalities and privity rules formulated by the common-law courts, the English chancery courts in Tulk v. Moxhay, 2 Phil. 774, 41 Eng.Rep. 1143 (Ch. 1848), created the doctrine of equitable servitudes. In Tulk, land was conveyed subject to an agreement that it would be kept open and maintained for park use. A subsequent grantee, with notice of the restriction, acquired the park. The court held that it would be unfair for the original covenantor to rid himself of the burden to maintain the park by simply selling the land. In enjoining the new owner from violating the agreement, the court stated:

> It is said that, the covenant being one which does not run with the land, this court cannot enforce it, but the question is, not whether the covenant runs with the land, but whether a party shall be permitted to use the land in a manner inconsistent with the contract entered into by his vendor, and with notice of which he purchased. Of course, the price would be affected by the covenant, and nothing could be more inequitable than that the original purchaser should be able to sell the property the next day for a greater price, in consideration of the assignee being allowed to escape from the liability which he had himself undertaken.

[Id. at 777–78, 41 Eng.Rep. 1144].

The court thus enforced the covenant on the basis that the successor had purchased the property with notice of the restriction. Adequate notice obliterated any express requirement of "touch and concern."

Our inquiry of New Jersey law on restrictive property use covenants commences with a re-examination of the rule set forth in Brewer v. Marshall & Cheseman, supra, 19 N.J.Eq. at 537, that a covenant will not run with the land unless it affects the physical use of the land. Hence, the burden side of a noncompetition covenant is personal to the covenantor and is, therefore, not enforceable against a purchaser. In Brewer v. Marshall & Cheseman, the court objected to all noncompetition covenants on the basis of public policy and refused to consider them in the context of the doctrine of equitable servitudes. Similarly, in National Union Bank at Dover v. Segur, 39 N.J.L. 173 (Sup.Ct.1877), the court held that only the benefit of a noncompetition covenant would run with the land, but the burden would be personal to the covenantor. Because the burden of a noncompetition covenant is deemed to be personal in these cases, enforcement would be possible only against the original covenantor. As soon as the covenantor sold the property, the burden would cease to exist.

Brewer and National Union Bank have been subsequently interpreted as embodying the "unnecessarily strict" position that "while the benefit of [a noncompetition covenant] will run with the land, the burden of the covenant is necessarily personal to the covenantor." 5 Powell, supra, § 675[3] at 60–109. This blanket prohibition of noncompetition covenants has been ignored in more recent decisions that have allowed the burden of a noncompetition covenant to run, see Renee Cleaners Inc. v. Good Deal Supermarkets of N.J., 89 N.J.Super. 186, 214 A.2d 437 (App.Div.1965) (enforcing at law covenant not to lease property for dry-cleaning business as against subsequent purchaser of land); Alexander's v. Arnold Constable Corp., 105 N.J.Super. 14, 28, 250 A.2d 792 (Ch.1969) (enforcing promise entered into by prior holders of land not to operate department store as against current landowner). Nonetheless, Brewer may still retain some vitality, as evidenced by the trial court's reliance on it in this case.

The per se prohibition that noncompetition covenants regarding the use of property do not run with the land is not supported by modern real-covenant law, and indeed, appears to have support only in the Restatement of Property section on the running of real covenants, § 537 comment f. 5 Powell, supra, at § 675 [3] at 60–109. Specifically, that approach is rejected in the Restatement's section on equitable servitudes, see Restatement of Property, § 539 comment k (1944).[31]

Commentators also consider the Brewer rule an anachronism and in need of change, as do we. 5 Powell, supra, ¶ 678 at 192. Accordingly, to the extent that Brewer holds that a noncompetition covenant will not run with the land, it is overruled.

Plaintiff also argues that the "touch and concern" test likewise should be eliminated in determining the enforceability of fully negotiated contracts, in favor of a simpler "reasonableness" standard that has been adopted in most jurisdictions. . . . New Jersey courts, however, continue to focus on the "touch and concern" requirement as the pivotal inquiry in ascertaining whether a covenant runs with the land. Under New Jersey

---

[31] Editor's Note: The new Restatement has abandoned this absolute stance against the running of covenants not to compete. It now takes the approach that all servitudes are valid unless they are illegal, unconstitutional, or violate public policy. Restatement (Third) of Property (Servitudes) § 3.1 (2000). Covenants not to compete are specifically addressed in § 3.6, which states that such a covenant is valid unless it is an "unreasonable restraint on trade or competition."

law, a covenant that "exercise[s] [a] direct influence on the occupation, use or enjoyment of the premises" satisfies the "touch and concern" rule. Caullett v. Stanley Stilwell & Sons, Inc., 67 N.J.Super. 111, 116, 170 A.2d 52 (App.Div.1961). The covenant must touch and concern both the burdened and the benefitted property in order to run with the land. Ibid.; Hayes v. Waverly & Passaic R.R., 51 N.J.Eq. 345, 27 A. 648 (Ch. 1893). Because the law frowns on the placing of restrictions on the freedom of alienation of land, New Jersey courts will enforce a covenant only if it produces a countervailing benefit to justify the burden. Restatement of Property § 543, comment c (1944); Reichman, supra, 55 S.Cal.L.Rev. at 1229.

Unlike New Jersey, which has continued to rely on the "touch and concern" requirement, most other jurisdictions have omitted "touch and concern" from their analysis and have focused instead on whether the covenant is reasonable. See, e.g., Doo v. Packwood, 265 Cal.App.2d 752, 71 Cal.Rptr. 477 (1968) (covenant not to sell groceries on property conveyed); Natural Prods. Co. v. Dolese & Shepard Co., 309 Ill. 230, 140 N.E. 840 (1923) (covenant not to sell stone on property conveyed); Coomes v. Aero Theatre & Shopping Center, 207 Md. 432, 114 A.2d 631 (1955) (covenant not to compete with shopping center); Raney v. Tompkins, 197 Md. 98, 78 A.2d 183 (1951) (covenant not to compete with gas station); Sun Oil Co. v. Trent Auto Wash, Inc., 379 Mich. 182, 150 N.W.2d 818 (1967) (covenant not to use retained land as gas station); Kerrick v. Schoenberg, 328 S.W.2d 595 (Mo.1959) (covenant not to use retained land for gasoline station); Hall v. American Oil Co., 504 S.W.2d 313 (Mo.Ct.App.1973) (covenant not to use land for gasoline station); Johnson v. Shaw, 101 N.H. 182, 137 A.2d 399 (1957) (covenant not to use land for gasoline stations or overnight cabins); Quadro Stations Inc. v. Gilley, 7 N.C.App. 227, 172 S.E.2d 237 (1970) (covenant not to use land for sale of petroleum products); Gillen-Crow Pharmacies, Inc. v. Mandzak, 5 Ohio St.2d 201, 215 N.E.2d 377 (1966) (covenant not to sell drugs or prescriptions on premises); Hodge v. Sloan, 107 N.Y. 244, 17 N.E. 335 (1887) (covenant not to sell sand on property conveyed); Hercules Powder Co. v. Continental Can Co., 196 Va. 935, 86 S.E.2d 128 (1955) (covenant not to engage in manufacture of pulp on property conveyed); Carneal v. Kendig, 196 Va. 605, 85 S.E.2d 235 (1955) (covenant not to use land for moving-picture business); Oliver v. Hewitt, 191 Va. 163, 60 S.E.2d 1 (1950) (covenant not to sell groceries and soft drinks on land conveyed); Colby v. McLaughlin, 50 Wash.2d 152, 310 P.2d 527 (1957) (covenant not to sell drugs, beer, or ice cream on land conveyed); see also McLoone, supra, 9 Ariz.L.Rev. at 442 n. 3 (noting that "great majority" of jurisdictions enforce as equitable servitude both benefit and burden of covenant not to compete on mere principles of notice).

Even the majority of courts that have retained the "touch and concern" test have found that noncompetition covenants meet the test's requirements. See generally McLoone, supra, 9 Ariz.L.Rev. at 448 n. 28

(listing cases that recognize that a covenant not to use land competitively meets the "touch and concern" test, notwithstanding diverse definitions of "touch and concern").

The "touch and concern" test has, thus, ceased to be, in most jurisdictions, intricate and confounding. Courts have decided as an initial matter that covenants not to compete do touch and concern the land. The courts then have examined explicitly the more important question of whether covenants are reasonable enough to warrant enforcement. The time has come to cut the gordian knot that binds this state's jurisprudence regarding covenants running with the land. Rigid adherence to the "touch and concern" test as a means of determining the enforceability of a restrictive covenant is not warranted. Reasonableness, not esoteric concepts of property law, should be the guiding inquiry into the validity of covenants at law. We do not abandon the "touch and concern" test, but rather hold that the test is but one of the factors a court should consider in determining the reasonableness of the covenant.

A "reasonableness" test allows a court to consider the enforceability of a covenant in view of the realities of today's commercial world and not in the light of out-moded theories developed in a vastly different commercial environment. Originally strict adherence to "touch and concern" rule in the old English common-law cases and in Brewer, was to effectuate the then pervasive public policy of restricting many, if not all, encumbrances of the land. Courts today recognize that it is not unreasonable for parties in commercial-property transactions to protect themselves from competition by executing noncompetition covenants. Businesspersons, either as lessees or purchasers may be hesitant to invest substantial sums if they have no minimal protection from a competitor starting a business in the near vicinity. Hence, rather than limiting trade, in some instances, restrictive covenants may increase business activity.

We recognize that "reasonableness" is necessarily a fact sensitive issue involving an inquiry into present business conditions and other factors specific to the covenant at issue. Nonetheless, as do most of the jurisdictions, we find that it is a better test for governing commercial transactions than are obscure anachronisms that have little meaning in today's commercial world. The pivotal inquiry, therefore, becomes what factors should a court consider in determining whether such a covenant is "reasonable" and hence enforceable. We conclude that the following factors should be considered:

> 1. The intention of the parties when the covenant was executed, and whether the parties had a viable purpose which did not at the time interfere with existing commercial laws, such as antitrust laws, or public policy.
>
> 2. Whether the covenant had an impact on the considerations exchanged when the covenant was originally

executed. This may provide a measure of the value to the parties of the covenant at the time.

3. Whether the covenant clearly and expressly sets forth the restrictions.

4. Whether the covenant was in writing, recorded, and if so, whether the subsequent grantee had actual notice of the covenant.

5. Whether the covenant is reasonable concerning area, time or duration. Covenants that extend for perpetuity or beyond the terms of a lease may often be unreasonable.

6. Whether the covenant imposes an unreasonable restraint on trade or secures a monopoly for the covenantor. This may be the case in areas where there is limited space available to conduct certain business activities and a covenant not to compete burdens all or most available locales to prevent them from competing in such an activity.

7. Whether the covenant interferes with the public interest.

8. Whether, even if the covenant was reasonable at the time it was executed, "changed circumstances" now make the covenant unreasonable.

The concurrence maintains that the initial validity of the covenant is a question of contract law while its subsequent enforceability is one of property law. Post at 221, 579 A.2d at 300. The result is that the concurrence uses reasonableness factors in construing the validity of the covenant between the original covenantors, but as to successors-in-interest, claims to adhere strictly to a "touch and concern" test. Post at 222, 579 A.2d at 301. Such strict adherence to a "touch and concern" analysis turns a blind eye to whether a covenant has become unreasonable over time. Indeed many past illogical and contorted applications of the "touch and concern" rules have resulted because courts have been pressed to twist the rules of "touch and concern" in order to achieve a result that comports with public policy and a free market. Most jurisdictions acknowledge the reasonableness factors that affect enforcement of a covenant concerning successors-in-interest, instead of engaging in the subterfuge of twisting the touch and concern test to meet the required result. New Jersey should not remain part of the small minority of States that cling to an anachronistic rule of law. Supra at 210, 579 A.2d at 295.

There is insufficient evidence in this record to determine whether the covenant is reasonable. The parties do not specifically contest the reasonableness of either the duration or area of the covenant. Aspects of the "touch and concern" test also remain useful in evaluating the reasonableness of a covenant, insofar as it aids the courts in differentiating between promises that were intended to bind only the individual parties to a land conveyance and promises affecting the use and value of the land that was intended to be passed on to subsequent parties. Covenants not to compete typically do touch and concern the land. In noncompetition cases, the "burden" factor of the "touch and concern" test is easily satisfied regardless of the definition chosen because the covenant restricts the actual use of the land. Berger, supra, 52 Wash.L.Rev. at 872. The Appellate Division properly concluded that the George Street store was burdened.

Defendants' primary contention is that due to the circumstances of the neighborhood and more particularly the circumstances of the people of the neighborhood, plaintiff's covenant interferes with the public's interest. Whether that claim is essentially that the community has changed since the covenant was enacted or that the circumstances were such that when the covenant was enacted, it interfered with the public interest, we are unable to ascertain from the record. "Public interest" and "changed circumstances" arguments are extremely fact-sensitive. The only evidence that addresses those issues, the three affidavits of Mr. Keefe, Mr. Nero and Ms. Scott, are insufficient to support any finding with respect to those arguments.

The fact-sensitive nature of a "reasonableness" analysis make resolution of this dispute through summary judgment inappropriate. We therefore remand the case to the trial court for a thorough analysis of the "reasonableness" factors delineated herein.

The trial court must first determine whether the covenant was reasonable at the time it was enacted. If it was reasonable then, but now adversely affects commercial development and the public welfare of the people of New Brunswick, the trial court may consider whether allowing damages for breach of the covenant is an appropriate remedy. C-Town could then continue to operate but Davidson would get damages for the value of his covenant. On the limited record before us, however, it is impossible to make a determination concerning either reasonableness of the covenant or whether damages, injunctive relief, or any relief is appropriate.

In sum, we reject the trial court's conclusion because it depends largely on the continued vitality of Brewer, which we hereby overrule. Supra at 201–202, 579 A.2d at 290–291. Likewise, we reject the Appellate Division's reliance on the "touch and concern" test. Instead, the proper test to determine the enforceability of a restrictive noncompetition covenant in a commercial land transaction is a test of "reasonableness," an approach adopted by a majority of the jurisdictions.

Judgment reversed and cause remanded for further proceedings consistent with this opinion.

■ POLLOCK, J., concurring.

Although I concur in the judgment of remand, I believe it should be on different terms. My basic difference with the majority is that I believe the critical consideration in determining the validity of this covenant is whether it is reasonable as to scope and duration, a point that has never been at issue in this case. Nor has there ever been any question whether the original parties to the covenant, Davidson Bros., Inc. (Davidson), and D. Katz & Sons, Inc. (Katz) intended that the covenant should run with the land. Likewise, the New Brunswick Housing Authority (the Authority) and C-Town have never disputed that they did not have actual notice of the covenant or that there was privity between them and Katz. Finally, the defendants have not contended that the covenant constitutes an unreasonable restraint on trade or that it has an otherwise unlawful purpose, such as invidious discrimination. Davidson, moreover, makes the uncontradicted assertion that the covenant is a burden to the George Street property and benefits the Elizabeth Street property. Hence, the covenant satisfies the requirement that it touch and concern the benefitted and burdened properties.

The fundamental flaw in the majority's analysis is in positing that an otherwise-valid covenant can become invalid not because it results in an unreasonable restraint on trade, but because invalidation facilitates a goal that the majority deems worthy. Considerations such as "changed circumstances" and "the public interest," when they do not constitute such a restraint, should not affect the enforceability of a covenant. Instead, they should relate to whether the appropriate method of enforcement is an injunction or damages. A court should not declare a noncompetition covenant invalid merely because enforcement would lead to a result with which the court disagrees. This leads me to conclude that the only issue on remand should be whether the appropriate remedy is damages or an injunction.

Enforcement of the restriction by an injunction will deprive the downtown residents of the convenience of shopping at the George Street property. Refusal to enforce the covenant, on the other hand, will deprive Davidson of the benefit of its covenant. Thus, the case presents a tension between two worthy objectives: the continued operation of the supermarket for the benefit of needy citizens, and the enforcement of the covenant. An award of damages to Davidson rather than the grant of an injunction would permit the realization of both objectives.

I begin by questioning the majority's formulation and application of a reasonableness test for determining whether the covenant runs with the land. The law has long distinguished between the validity of a covenant between original-contracting parties from the enforceability of a covenant against the covenantor's successor-in-interest. Initial validity is a question of contract law; enforceability against subsequent parties is one of property law. Caullett v. Stanley Stilwell & Sons, 67 N.J.Super. 111, 116, 170 A.2d 52 (App.Div.1961); R. Cunningham, W. Stoebuck, and D. Whitman, The Law of Property 467 (1984) (Cunningham). That distinction need not foreclose a subsequent owner of the burdened property from challenging the validity of the contract between the original parties. The distinction, however, sharpens the analysis of the effect of the covenant.

In this case, the basic issue is enforceability of the covenant against the Authority and C-Town, successors in interest to Katz. Thus, the only relevant consideration is whether the covenant "touches and concerns" the benefitted and burdened properties.

The Court can decide the present case without introducing a new test. On the present record, no question exists about the running of the benefit of the covenant. First, the party seeking to enforce the covenant is Davidson, the original leaseholder, not a successor in interest, of the Elizabeth Street property. Second, as the language of the covenant indicates, the original contracting parties, Davidson and Katz, indicated that the covenant would run with the land. Third, Davidson makes the uncontradicted assertions that both stores were unprofitable before the sale, that the Elizabeth Street store after the sale of the George Street property enjoyed a 20% sales increase, and that the reopening of the George Street property caused it to suffer a loss of income. Finally, as the majority recognizes, the lower courts erred in concluding that the covenant did not "touch and concern" the burdened and benefitted properties. Ante at 213, 579 A.2d at 296.

The conclusion that this covenant "touches and concerns" the land should end the inquiry about enforceability against the Authority and C-Town. The majority, however, holds that the "touch and concern" test is "but one of the factors a court should consider in determining the reasonableness of the covenant." Ante at 210, 579 A.2d at 295. The majority's inquiry about reasonableness, however, confuses the issue of validity of the original contract between Davidson and Katz with enforceability against the subsequent owner, the Authority. This confusion of validity with enforceability threatens to add uncertainty to an already troubled area of the law.

The majority inaccurately asserts that most jurisdictions "have focused on whether the covenant is reasonable enough to warrant enforcement." Not one case cited by the majority has concluded that a covenant that is reasonable against the original covenantor would be unreasonable against the covenantor's successor who takes with notice. For example, in Hercules Powder Co. v. Continental Can Co., 196 Va. 935, 945, 86 S.E.2d 128, 133 (1955), only after first concluding that the restriction was reasonable did the court consider "whether it is enforceable by Continental Can, an assignee of the original covenantee, against Hercules, an assignee of the original covenantor." In determining that Hercules was subject to the restriction, the court considered only whether it purchased the land with notice of the restriction. Similarly, in Quadro Stations v. Gilley, 7 N.C.App. 227, 234, 172 S.E.2d 237, 242 (1970), the court first concluded that the restriction was valid, and then held that it was enforceable against defendants, successors in interest to the original covenanting parties. Nothing in the opinion implies that a restriction that was reasonable between the original parties would be unenforceable against a purchaser of the burdened property who bought with notice. Doo v. Packwood, 265 Cal.App.2d 752, 756, 71 Cal.Rptr. 477, 481 (1968), is likewise unavailing to the majority. There, when purchasing a lot on which Doo had operated a grocery store, Packwood agreed to a noncompetition covenant. After concluding that the covenant was reasonable as between the original parties, the court found that it would be binding on a future purchaser with notice. Ibid. In effect, future purchasers would be bound so long as Doo continued to operate a competitive grocery store. Ibid. To conclude, the cited cases hold that a reasonable noncompetition covenant binding on the original covenantor likewise binds a subsequent purchaser with notice. Hence, the majority misperceives the focus of the out-of-state cases. The result is that the majority's reasonableness test introduces unnecessary uncertainty in the analysis of covenants running with the land.

As troublesome as uncertainty is in other areas of the law, it is particularly vexatious in the law of real property. The need for certainty in conveyancing, like that in estate planning, is necessary for people to structure their affairs. Covenants that run with the land can affect the value of real property not only at the time of sale, but for many years thereafter. Consequently, vendors and purchasers, as well as their successors, need to know whether a covenant will run with the land. The majority acknowledges that noncompetition covenants play a positive role in commercial development. Notwithstanding that acknowledgment, the majority's reasonableness test generates confusion that threatens the ability of commercial parties and their lawyers to determine the validity of such covenants. This, in turn, impairs the utility of noncompetition covenants in real estate transactions.

As between the vendor and purchaser, a noncompetition covenant generally should be treated as valid if it is reasonable in scope and duration, Irving Inv. Corp. v. Gordon, 3 N.J. 217, 221, 69 A.2d 725 (1949); Heuer v. Rubin, 1 N.J. 251, 256–57, 62 A.2d 812 (1949); Scherman v. Stern, 93 N.J.Eq. 626, 630, 117 A. 631 (E. & A.1922), and neither an unreasonable restraint on trade nor otherwise contrary to public policy. A covenant would contravene public policy if, for example, its purpose were to secure a monopoly, Quadro Stations, supra, 7 N.C.App. at 235, 172 S.E.2d at 242; Hercules Powder Co., supra, 196 Va. at 944–45, 86 S.E.2d at 132–33, or to carry out an illegal object, such as invidious discrimination, see, e.g., N.J.S.A. 46:3–23 (declaring restrictive covenants in real estate transactions void if based on race, creed, color, national origin, ancestry, marital status, or sex).

Applying those principles to the validity of the agreement between Davidson and Katz, I find this covenant enforceable against defendants. The majority acknowledges that "[t]he parties do not specifically contest the reasonableness of either the duration or the area of the covenant." Ante at 213, 579 A.2d at 296. I agree. The covenant is limited to one parcel, the George Street property. Defendants do not assert that Davidson has restricted or even owns other property in New Brunswick. Furthermore, they do not allege that other property is not available for a supermarket. In brief, the Authority has not alleged that at the time of the sale from Davidson to Katz, or even at present, the George Street property was the only possible site in New Brunswick for a supermarket. Consequently, the covenant may not be construed to give rise to a monopoly. In all of New Brunswick it restricts a solitary one-half acre tract from use for a single purpose. Indeed, the record demonstrates that the Authority explored other options, including expansion of a food cooperative and increasing the product lines at nearby convenience stores. Nothing in the record supports the conclusion that the covenant might be unreasonable respecting space.

Nor does anything indicate that the forty-year length of the restriction between Davidson and Katz is unreasonable in time. To sustain the subject covenant we need not go so far as to say that a covenant could never be unreasonably long. In an appropriate case, a court, drawing on the analogy to restrictive covenants in employment contracts, might reform a covenant so that it lasts only for a reasonable time. This is not such a case.

Here, Davidson holds a lease on the Elizabeth Street property for a term of twenty years, with two renewable five-year terms. Those lease terms are substantially, if not precisely, coextensive with the term of the covenant. If, on remand, the Chancery Division should find that the additional ten-year period is not enforceable by Davidson, it should also find that the restriction is valid for the thirty-year period during which Davidson's lease may run. In sum, I believe that the covenant is reasonable at least for the term of Davidson's lease.

Perhaps the majority's opinion is best read as holding that Davidson is entitled to damages but not an injunction if the covenant was reasonable when formed, but now adversely affects the public welfare of the people of New Brunswick. See Gilpin v. Jacob Ellis Realties, 47 N.J.Super. 26, 31–34, 135 A.2d 204 (App.Div.1957). Such a holding would ensure that Davidson will not be "left without any redress; . . . [it will be] given what plaintiffs are given in many types of cases—relief measured, so far as the court reasonably may do so, in damages." Id. at 34, 135 A.2d 204.

Nothing in the record provides any basis for finding that in the six years that elapsed between 1980, when Davidson sold to Katz, and 1986, when Katz sold to the Authority, circumstances changed so much that they render the covenant unenforceable. The record is devoid of any showing that anything has happened since 1980 that has deprived the Elizabeth Street store of the covenant's benefit. Notions of "changed circumstances" and the "public interest" thinly veil the Authority's attempt to avoid compensating Davidson for the cost of the lost benefit of an otherwise-enforceable covenant. I am left to wonder whether the majority would so readily condone the Authority's taking of Davidson's property if the interest taken were one in fee simple and not a restrictive covenant. It is wrong to take Davidson's covenant without compensation just as it would be wrong to take its fee interest without paying for it. Shopkeepers in malls throughout the state will be astonished to learn that noncompetition covenants that they have so carefully negotiated in their leases are subject to invalidation because they run counter to a court's perception of "changed circumstances" and the "public interest."

## Eagle Enterprises, Inc. v. Gross
New York Court of Appeals, 1976.
39 N.Y.2d 505, 384 N.Y.S.2d 717, 349 N.E.2d 816.

■ GABRIELLI, JUSTICE.

In 1951, Orchard Hill Realties, Inc., a subdivider and developer, conveyed certain property in the subdivision of Orchard Hill in Orange County to William and Pauline Baum. The deed to the Baums contained the following provision:

> The party of the first part shall supply to the party of the second part, seasonably from May 1st to October 1st, of each year, water for domestic use only, from the well located on other property of the party of the first part, and the party of the second part agrees to take said water and to pay the party of the first part, a fee of Thirty-five ($35) dollars per year, for said water so supplied.

In addition, the deed also contained the following:

> It is expressly provided that the covenants herein contained shall run with the land . . . and shall bind and shall enure to the benefit of the heirs, distributees, successors, legal representatives and assigns of the respective parties hereto.

Appellant is the successor in interest of Orchard Hill Realties, Inc., and respondent, after a series of intervening conveyances, is the successor in interest of the Baums. The deed conveying title to respondent does not contain the aforementioned covenant to purchase water and, in fact, none of the deeds following the original deed to the Baums contained the mutual promises regarding water supply. While some of the deeds in the chain of title from Baum contained a provision that they were made subject to the restrictions in the deed from Orchard Hill Realties to Baum, the deed to respondents contained no such covenants, restrictions or "subject to" clause.

According to the stipulated facts, respondent has refused to accept and pay for water offered by appellant since he has constructed his own well to service what is now a year-round dwelling. Appellant, therefore, instituted this action to collect the fee specified in the covenant (contained only in the original deed to Baum) for the supply of water which, appellant contends, respondent is bound to accept. The action was styled as one "for goods sold and delivered" even though respondent did not utilize any of appellant's water. Two of the lower courts found that the covenant "ran" with the land and, hence, was binding upon respondent as successor to the Baums, but the Appellate Division reversed and held that the covenant could not be enforced against respondent. We must now decide whether the promise of the original grantees to accept and make payment for a seasonal water supply from the well of their grantor is enforceable against subsequent grantees and may be said to "run with the land." We agree with the determination of the Appellate Division and affirm its order.

Regardless of the express recital in a deed that a covenant will run with the land, a promise to do an affirmative act contained in a deed is generally not binding upon subsequent grantees of the promisor unless certain well-defined and long-established legal requisites are satisfied (Nicholson v. 300 Broadway Realty Corp., 7 N.Y.2d 240, 244, 196 N.Y.S.2d 945, 948, 164 N.E.2d 832, 834; Neponsit Prop. Owners' Assn. v. Emigrant Ind. Sav. Bank, 278 N.Y. 248, 254–255, 15 N.E.2d 793, 794–95; see, also, Morgan Lake Co. v. New York, New Haven & Hartford R.R. Co., 262 N.Y. 234, 239, 186 N.E. 685, 687; Miller v. Clary, 210 N.Y. 127, 103 N.E. 1114; Mygatt v. Coe, 147 N.Y. 456, 42 N.E. 17; 13 N.Y.Jur. Covenants and Restrictions, § 12, pp. 252–253). In the landmark *Neponsit* case (supra), we adopted and clarified the following test, originating in the early English decisions, for the enforceability of affirmative covenants (cf. Spencer's Case, 77 Eng.Rep. 72 [1583]), and reaffirmed the requirements that in order for a covenant to run with the land, it must be shown that:

> (1) The original grantee and grantor must have intended that the covenant run with the land.

> (2) There must exist "privity of estate" between the party claiming the benefit of the covenant and the right to enforce it and the party whom the burden of the covenant is to be imposed.

> (3) The covenant must be deemed to "touch and concern" the land with which it runs. (See, also, Nicholson v. 300 Broadway Realty Corp., supra; Restatement Property, §§ 531, 534, 537, 538; 13 N.Y.Jur. Covenants and Restrictions, § 8, p. 248.)

Even though the parties to the original deed expressly state in the instrument that the covenant will run with the land, such a recital is insufficient to render the covenant enforceable against subsequent grantees if the other requirements for the running of an affirmative covenant are not met. The rule is settled that "[r]egardless of the intention of the parties, a covenant will run with the land and will be enforceable against a subsequent purchaser of the land at the suit of one who claims the benefit of the covenant, only if the covenant complies with certain legal requirements" (*Neponsit,* supra, 278 N.Y. p. 254, 15 N.E.2d

p. 795; see, also Morgan Lake Co. v. New York, New Haven & Hartford R.R. Co., supra, 262 N.Y. p. 238, 186 N.E. p. 686). Thus, although the intention of the original parties here is clear and privity of estate exists, the covenant must still satisfy the requirement that it "touch and concern" the land.

It is this third prong of the tripartite rule which presents the obstacle to appellant's position and which was the focus of our decisions in *Neponsit* and Nicholson v. 300 Broadway Realty Corp. (7 N.Y.2d 240, 244, 196 N.Y.S.2d 945, 948, 164 N.E.2d 832, 834, supra). *Neponsit* first sought to breathe substance and meaning into the ritualistic rubric that an affirmative covenant must "touch and concern" the land in order to be enforceable against subsequent grantees. Observing that it would be difficult to devise a rule which would operate mechanically to resolve all situations which might arise, Judge Lehman observed that "the distinction between covenants which run with land and covenants which are personal, must depend upon the effect of the covenant on the legal rights which otherwise would flow from the ownership of land and which are connected with the land" (*Neponsit*, supra, 278 N.Y. p. 258, 15 N.E.2d p. 796). Thus, he posed as the key question whether "the covenant in purpose and effect substantially alter[s] these rights" (p. 258, 15 N.E.2d p. 796). In *Nicholson*, this court reaffirmed the soundness of the reasoning in *Neponsit* as "a more realistic and pragmatic approach" (supra, 7 N.Y.2d p. 245, 196 N.Y.S.2d p. 949, 164 N.E.2d p. 835).

The covenants in issue in *Neponsit* required the owners of property in a development to pay an annual charge for the maintenance of roads, paths, parks, beaches, sewers and other public improvements. The court concluded that the covenant substantially affected the promisor's legal interest in his property since the latter received an easement in common and a right of enjoyment in the public improvements for which contribution was received by all the landowners in the subdivision (supra, 278 N.Y. pp. 259–260, 15 N.E.2d p. 797).

A close examination of the covenant in the case before us leads to the conclusion that it does not substantially affect the ownership interest of landowners in the Orchard Hill subdivision. The covenant provides for the supplying of water for only six months of the year; no claim has been advanced by appellant that the lands in the subdivision would be waterless without the water it supplies. Indeed, the facts here point to the converse conclusion since respondent has obtained his own source of water. The record, based on and consisting of an agreed stipulation of facts, does not demonstrate that other property owners in the subdivision would be deprived of water from appellant or that the price of water would become prohibitive for other property owners if respondent terminated appellant's service. Thus, the agreement for the seasonal supply of water does not seem to us to relate in any significant degree to the ownership rights of respondent and the other property owners in the subdivision of Orchard Hill. The landowners in *Neponsit* received an easement in common to utilize public areas in the subdivision; this interest was in the nature of a property right attached to their respective properties. The obligation to receive water from appellant resembles a personal, contractual promise to purchase water rather than a significant interest attaching to respondent's property. It should be emphasized that the question whether a covenant is so closely related to the use of the land that it should be deemed to "run" with the land is one of degree, dependent on the particular circumstances of a case (*Neponsit,* supra, 278 N.Y. p. 258, 15 N.E.2d p. 796). Here, the meager record before us is lacking and woefully insufficient to establish that the covenant "touches and concerns" the land, as we have interpreted that requirement.

There is an additional reason why we are reluctant to enforce this covenant for the seasonal supply of water. The affirmative covenant is disfavored in the law because of the fear that this type of obligation imposes an "undue restriction on alienation or an onerous burden in perpetuity" (Nicholson v. 300 Broadway Realty Corp., 7 N.Y.2d 240, 246, 196 N.Y.S.2d 945, 950, 164 N.E.2d 832, 835, supra). In *Nicholson,* the covenant to supply heat was not interdicted by this concern because it was conditioned upon the continued existence of the buildings on both the promisor's and the promisee's properties. Similarly, in *Neponsit,* the original 1917 deed containing the covenant to pay an annual charge for the maintenance of public areas expressly provided for its own lapse in 1940. Here, no outside limitation has been placed on the obligation to purchase water from appellant. Thus, the covenant falls prey to the criticism that it creates a burden in perpetuity, and purports to bind all future owners, regardless of the use to which the land is put. Such a result militates strongly against its enforcement. On this ground also, we are of the opinion that the covenant should not be enforced as an exception to the general rule prohibiting the "running" of affirmative covenants.

Accordingly, the order of the Appellate Division should be affirmed, with costs.

## NOTES

1. *Horizontal privity.* Is there horizontal privity in the Principal Problem? Is this question relevant regardless of the type of relief requested? Should horizontal privity be abolished? Why or why not?

2. *Vertical privity.* The problem, like *Runyon,* involves a serious vertical privity question. What was the vertical privity problem in *Runyon*?

Vertical privity questions arise mainly in the landlord/tenant context. You will recall from Assignment 6, Assignments and Subleases, that a subtenant is not bound by the promises made by the lessee in the head lease, whereas an assignee is bound by these promises. Chapter 16 of the Second Restatement of Property deals with Landlord and Tenant Law and outlines the required degree of privity of estate between landlords and their successors and tenants and their successors. The Second Restatement provides that "[i]f the transferor is the tenant, the transferee comes into privity with the other party to the lease only if the entire balance of the leased term in all or some portion of the leased property is transferred and no reversionary interest in the leased property is retained by the transferor-tenant." See § 16.1 comment e. An assignee of the original lessee is in privity of estate with the lessor, i.e., there is privity of estate between them. A sublessee from the original lessee is, by definition, taking a lesser interest than the original lessee. Therefore, there is no privity of estate between the lessor and the sublessee. Id. at illus. 21. See also the discussion of assignments and subleases in § 15.1, comment i. The Second Restatement also rejects the distinction drawn by § 547, comments c and e of the old Restatement, between the required vertical privity for the running of the benefit and the burden (i.e., that the running of the benefit only requires relaxed vertical privity). Instead, it provides that "[t]he privity of estate requirement with respect to the benefit of a promissory obligation is the same as this requirement with respect to the burden of an obligation."[32]

3. *No privity requirements in equity.* The reason there are no privity requirements for enforcing equitable servitudes is entirely historical. Traditionally, covenants at law were considered contractual in nature and under the common law, the benefits and burdens attaching to a contract could not be assigned to those parties who succeeded to ownership of either the benefited or burdened property following the original covenanting parties. Therefore, the fiction of privity was invoked to establish the requisite relationships for enforcement of the contractual terms between parties who were not the original contracting parties. In contrast, equitable servitudes traditionally were considered property interests rather than contracts. As such, there was no common law bar to enforcing the burdens and benefits of an equitable servitude upon parties who were not the original covenanting parties. Instead, enforcement of the benefits and burdens of equitable servitudes historically could be maintained by and against anyone who owned the property at the time of the lawsuit. Thus, it was unnecessary for courts to invoke the fiction of privity as a requirement for enforcing the benefits and burdens of an equitable servitude since the requisite interest was established simply by virtue of ownership of the allegedly benefited or burdened land.

4. *Touch and concern.* What do you think of the way the court in *Davidson* handled the touch and concern requirement? What do you think of the reasonableness factors invoked by that court? Do you think *Davidson* or the new Restatement provides a more workable test? Would the covenant in *Davidson* run under the new Restatement? Touch and concern often is regarded as a proxy for considering public policy issues. On remand in *Davidson*, the court held that the restrictive covenant was contrary to public interest and therefore was unenforceable. On what considerations do you think the court based this conclusion? How would the Principal Problem be analyzed under *Davidson*?

---

[32] Restatement (Second) of Property (Landlord & Tenant) § 16.2 cmt. e, illus. 6 (1977).

*Eagle Enterprises* seems to hold that a covenant to buy water does not touch and concern the land of the buyer or the seller of the water, although the water is to be used on the land of the buyer of the water. In contrast, the 1944 Restatement takes the position that a promise to pay for water to be used for irrigating the land of the promisor, without specification of the source of the water, restricts the use of the land of the promisor only.[33] Presumably, this would permit the promise to run, even at law, since the burden of paying for the water also benefits "the promisor in the physical use or enjoyment of land possessed by him."[34] How should a court faced with the Principal Problem decide?

5.  *Intent and notice. Runyon* involves an issue of intent with respect to the running of the benefit. What arguments were made by each side with respect to this issue? Did the court reach the right conclusion regarding intent? Why was there no issue of intent regarding the running of the burden in *Runyon*? In contrast to *Runyon*, the Principal Problem does not raise any serious problem concerning intent, unless one can ignore or nullify the last paragraph of the contract quoted in the Principal Problem. Is it possible to make an argument that this last paragraph should not be given effect?

How did the court in *Runyon* deal with the notice issue? Neither the Principal Problem nor any of the cases in this Assignment raise a serious notice issue. This is not surprising, since most covenants are recorded and give notice to subsequent owners by virtue of their recordation.

---

[33] See Restatement of Property § 537 cmt. g, illus. 3 (1944).
[34] Restatement of Property § 537 (1944).

# ASSIGNMENT 26
# DEFENSES TO THE ENFORCEMENT OF COVENANTS

## 1. INTRODUCTION

Covenants originated in contract law, not property law. For this reason, defenses to the enforcement of covenants often rest upon theories that are encountered in litigation concerning contracts. For example, a defendant charged with violating a covenant may argue that the plaintiff waived enforcement of the covenant, is estopped from enforcing it, or should be barred from enforcing the covenant by the doctrine of laches (undue delay in enforcing one's rights). This Assignment concentrates on two other defenses: the doctrines of "changed circumstances" and "relative hardship." Courts may refuse to enforce a covenant if changed circumstances make it unlikely that enforcement will be of substantial benefit to the covenantee or her successors. Similarly, courts may refuse to enforce a covenant if enforcement will result in a hardship to the owner of the burdened land that is disproportionate to the benefit to be obtained from enforcement. Of course, terms like "substantial benefit" and "disproportionate burden" conceal a host of difficulties, some of which are explored in this Assignment.

The doctrines of changed circumstances and of relative hardship attempt to limit the inconvenience resulting from outmoded instruments governing real property. The changed conditions and relative hardship doctrines rest to a much larger extent on the discretion of the court, and thus on fine questions of judgment.

*Changed circumstances.* In his authoritative treatise, Professor Korngold comments on the doctrine of changed circumstances as follows:

> [T]he doctrine will be applied only if the changed conditions have adversely affected the *benefited* lots, making it impossible to achieve the original parties' intent, even if the covenant were enforced. The focus is not on the *burdened* lot.... Instead, the courts will continue to enforce the restriction that is still substantially valuable to the benefited land, even though changed conditions have caused a hardship to the burdened owner.[1]

*Relative hardship.* If the hardship on the defendant is very great, and the benefit to the plaintiff is relatively minor, the court may refuse to issue an injunction, particularly if the defendant acted without

---

[1] G. Korngold, Private Land Use Arrangements: Easements, Real Covenants, and Equitable Servitudes § 11.07, p. 456 (2d. 2004). See also Restatement (Third) of Property (Servitudes) § 7.10 (2000).

knowledge of the covenant. Unlike the changed circumstances doctrine, the relative hardship doctrine requires the court to consider the hardship on the owner of the burdened land, among other factors, in deciding whether to specifically enforce the covenant. However, even in this case, the court is likely to look at the extent to which the hardship on the defendant increased because of changed circumstances that were not anticipated when the covenant was made. Consequently, application of the relative hardship doctrine often requires a consideration of changed circumstances, and thus the two doctrines are somewhat intertwined.

## 2. Principal Problem

About one hundred years ago, when the town of Alamog did not yet exist, the owners of the land decided to lay out streets and land parcels on the empty prairie. They sought to establish an attractive town that would attract families to the area. As the owners sold the vacant lots, they inserted covenants that prohibited the sale of alcoholic beverages in places of public resort. One hundred years later, the town has changed substantially. It has grown from a settlement of a few families to a town of over 25,000. An Air Force Base has been established next to the town and the development of tourism has sparked economic growth. Many tracts of land previously used for agriculture now have businesses located on them. Although the original town site, consisting of approximately one hundred lots, was subject to the restriction against alcohol, the surrounding lots, numbering several thousand, are not so restricted. A few years ago an election to allow the sale of liquor within the town received overwhelming support. Consequently, numerous restaurants and bars serve liquor in the town, although none is served on the original township lots.

Your client, Glasgow, wants to open a restaurant serving liquor on a parcel located in the original town site. The zoning and other municipal laws permit this. The only obstacle is the hundred year old restriction. Advise Glasgow after reading the following material. Consider what additional information you will need to render sound advice.

## 3. Materials for Solution of Principal Problem

### Chevy Chase Village v. Jaggers
Court of Appeals of Maryland, 1971.
261 Md. 309, 275 A.2d 167.

■ DIGGES, JUDGE.

The beginning of this case, which involves the efficacy of a residential restrictive covenant, can be traced back to 1927 when the Chevy Chase Land Company recorded a plat subdividing a part of what was to become the rather fashionable suburban community of Chevy Chase Village in Montgomery County, Maryland. The subdivision in question, blandly called "Section 1-A Chevy Chase" on the plat, was composed of thirteen blocks, numbered 4 through 16. Blocks 6 and 11 contained 60 lots which, because of their location on the northeast corner of the intersection of Wisconsin and Western Avenues, were set aside for commercial development. Two lots in or near that section were conveyed to public utilities. The other blocks were reserved for exclusively residential purposes. With the exception of six lots conveyed to a church and three lots partially destroyed by later re-subdivision, the 204 remaining lots in the residential blocks were bound by the following series of covenants in each of the original deeds by which they were conveyed:

> It is hereby understood and agreed that no objection will be raised by the said party of the second part [grantee], her heirs and assigns, to the rezoning of Lots in Blocks 6 and 11 in said subdivision known as "Section One-A, Chevy Chase," Montgomery County, Maryland, for use for commercial purposes. . . .
>
> In consideration of the execution of this deed the said party of the second part, for herself her heirs and assigns, hereby covenants and agrees with the party of the first part, its successors and assigns (*such covenants and agreements to run with the land*) as follows, viz:
>
> 1. That all houses upon the premises hereby conveyed shall be built and used for residence purposes exclusively, except stables, carriage houses, sheds or other outbuildings, for use in connection with such residences and that no trade, business, manufacture or sales, or nuisance of any kind shall be carried on or permitted upon said premises. . . .
>
> [2.–4. pertaining to location, cost and design of buildings, are omitted.]
>
> 5. That a violation of any of the aforesaid covenants and agreements may be enjoined and the same enforced at the suit of The Chevy Chase Land Company, of Montgomery County, Maryland, its successors and assigns (*assigns including any person deriving title mediately or immediately from said company to any lot or square, or part of a lot or square in the Section of the Subdivision of which the land hereby conveyed forms a part*). [Emphasis added.]

It is these covenants which have spurred the case before us. The plaintiff-appellants, Chevy Chase Village, a landowner and a municipal corporation (having the responsibility by charter to enforce restrictive covenants) and Wales H. Jack and his wife, residents of the subdivision, have appealed from a decision by the Circuit Court for Montgomery County (Shure, J.) denying an injunction against the defendant-appellees, Dr. Frank Y. Jaggers, Jr. and his wife. This action in equity sought to enjoin the doctor from using his property as a principal office for the practice of medicine, alleging that such use was in contravention of the covenants.

In 1947, Dr. Jaggers and his wife purchased a lot in Section 1-A on the corner of Wisconsin Avenue and Grafton Street and lived on the premises until early 1967. During most of those twenty years he maintained his medical office on the property. In 1948 he spent $5,000 converting his garage into office space, and in 1959 an additional $15,000 outlay was made to enlarge this office. During this time he had a very substantial practice, which apparently has tapered off in recent years. In 1954, Dr. Jaggers applied to the Montgomery County Board of Appeals for a special exception to use his property both as his dwelling and for the practice of medicine in association with another doctor. The special exception was granted with no objection being raised by any of the residents of Section 1-A. Although he worked intermittently over the years with other doctors, Dr. Jaggers is at present the sole practitioner in the office. There are also three other doctors in the subdivision who live and maintain principal offices at their homes, and have done so for some time. In 1967 the Jaggers moved to Potomac, Maryland, renting their house as a residence, although the doctor continued to maintain the office for his practice. It should be noted that the dwelling is now rented to a physician for residential purposes only.

Chevy Chase Village notified appellees that this action would be in violation of the covenants binding on the property, but the weight of its logic obviously fell on deaf ears, for the doctor was not deterred. We are a more receptive audience, however, and shall reverse the lower court's decision. There are four questions presented for our consideration:

I. Was there sufficient evidence to establish a uniform general scheme or plan of development to entitle the appellants to enforcement of the covenants?

II. Was there an abandonment and failure of the original plan of development and such a change in the general characteristics of the neighborhood as to render the covenants unenforceable?

III. Were the appellants guilty of laches and therefore estopped from the enforcement of the subject covenants?

IV. Under the doctrine of comparative hardship should the court decline to enforce the restrictive covenants?

I

The first contention which the appellees make is that there was insufficient evidence to establish a uniform general plan of development as would entitle appellants to enforce the covenants. However, even if such a plan were absent it would not necessarily defeat their enforcement. The law in Maryland is well settled on this question. In Rogers v. State Roads Comm., 227 Md. 560, 564, 177 A.2d 850 (1962) we said: "There need not be any general plan of development in order to make a restrictive covenant enforceable if it is imposed by a grantor on a single tract conveyed by him for the benefit of adjacent property retained by him." This view was also expressed by Judge Offutt for the Court in McKenrick v. Savings Bank, 174 Md. 118, 128, 197 A. 580, 584 (1938), where it was said:

> [O]ne owning a tract of land, in granting a part thereof, may validly impose upon the part granted restrictions upon the use thereof for the benefit of the part retained, and upon the part retained for the benefit of the part granted, or upon both for the benefit of both; that, where the covenants in the conveyance are not expressly for or on behalf of the grantor, his heirs and assigns, they are personal and will not run with the land, but that, if in such a case it appears that it was the intention of the grantors that the restrictions were part of a uniform general scheme or plan of development and use which should affect the land granted and the land retained alike, they may be enforced in equity....

In the present case we need not decide whether there was a uniform general plan of development, though the evidence may well support such a finding. The covenants are enforceable in any event because of the specific language used in the deeds. The applicable law on this point was enunciated years ago and has remained basically unchanged. In Clem v. Valentine, 155 Md. 19, 26–27, 141 A. 710 (1928) our predecessors, quoting from Halle v. Newbold, 69 Md. 265, 14 A. 662 (1888), which referred to even earlier decisions, said:

> These cases very conclusively settle the law that the grantor may impose a restriction, in the nature of a servitude or easement, upon the land that he sells or leases, for the benefit of the land he still retains; and if that servitude is imposed upon the heirs and assigns of the grantee, and in favor of the heirs and assigns of the grantor, it may be enforced by the assignee of the grantor against the assignee (with notice) of the grantee. It is to be noted that that case was one in which the covenant expressly provided that its terms should be binding on the assigns of both the covenantor and the covenantee, and it was there held that this enabled an assignee of the covenantee to enforce the restriction....

In the case before us, the covenants are clearly binding on the successive owners. Not only is there an express provision that the covenants "run with the land," but it also is explicitly stated that they are binding upon the grantee "her heirs and assigns" and enforceable by the grantor, "its successors and assigns." As if this very lucid language were unclear, the deed defines an assignee as any person who obtains title "mediately or immediately," from the grantor.

## II

The second claim made by the appellees is that there has been an abandonment and failure of the original plan of development and a substantial change in the general characteristics of the neighborhood so as to render the covenants unenforceable. We have no quarrel with the underlying statement of law implicit in this argument, but think it is inapplicable to the facts of this case. Indeed, on many occasions we have held restrictive covenants unenforceable where there has been "deterioration in the residential character of the neighborhood or a failure from the beginning of the restricted development, so that the restrictions no longer served their intended purpose." Texas Co. v. Harker, 212 Md. 188, 196–197, 129 A.2d 384 (1957). In that same case at 198, 129 A.2d at 390, quoting from 4 A.L.R.2d 1118, 1119, we said:

> Most jurisdictions now recognize a change in the character of a neighborhood as a ground for affirmative relief against restrictive covenants by way of cancellation or modification *where the change has been so radical as to render perpetuation of the restriction of no substantial benefit to the dominant estate, and to defeat the object or purpose of the restriction.* (Emphasis added.)

*Accord,* Rogers v. State Roads Comm., supra, 227 Md. at 566, 177 A.2d 850. The inquiry, therefore, is whether there has been a complete or radical change in the neighborhood causing the restrictions to out-live their usefulness.

The only evidence here in any way tending to support appellees' contention is that a very few of the more than 200 lots have not been utilized for homes. These nonresidential uses are confined to a church, four doctors' offices maintained in their residences, a few feet of several lots located on the outer perimeter utilized for parking, two lots used by public utilities and one full lot with minor parts of two others infringed upon by a building constructed mainly on the commercial blocks. These minimal deviations from the original plan are not sufficient to show a change in the neighborhood that is either complete or radical. In this case, the purpose of the restrictions was to preserve the subdivision predominantly for residential use, and with the few negligible exceptions mentioned this is still being accomplished. On this point we think the following words of Kirkley v. Seipelt, supra, 212 Md. at 135, 128 A.2d at 435, are particularly appropriate:

> The real crux of the inquiry in determining whether there has been such a change in the neighborhood so as to defeat the covenant is to ascertain the purposes to be accomplished by the imposition of the restrictions.... [W]e think the reasons for them were to develop an attractive and inviting community. From the evidence, it is apparent the reasons and objects for placing the restrictions on the property are as active and as alive today as they were when first imposed.

The appellees further contend that the trial court was correct in looking beyond Section 1-A to determine if there had been a change in the neighborhood. We agree that this is a proper view of the law, but in applying the law to the facts the appellees are again found wanting. In Texas Co. v. Harker, supra, we permitted an investigation of the broader neighborhood but nevertheless concluded that nearby commercial uses had in no way deteriorated the residential character of the subdivision under fire in that case. From the record before us, which includes aerial photographs and testimony, it is clear that the residential part of Section 1-A has been similarly unaffected. Indeed, it is still a highly desirable place for a home, completely unspoiled by commercialism. The appellees argue that the mere setting aside of Blocks 6 and 11 for commercial purposes was evidence of a failure *ab initio* of the original plan, but we can only comment that this use was exactly what was contemplated in the original plan and was in fact agreed to by nearly all of the lot purchasers. In any event the development of this commercial area has not deteriorated residential development in the remainder of the subdivision.[2] On the contrary, the presence of a tasteful and well planned shopping center, which includes the Washington branch of Saks Fifth Avenue, complements the neighborhood.

### III

The Jaggers' third contention is that the appellants have been guilty of laches and should therefore be estopped from seeking enforcement of the covenants. To support this claim they not only rely on the fact that three other doctors in the subdivision are using their homes for their principal offices, but also that Dr. Jaggers had used his property for the practice of medicine for nearly twenty years without objection. We need not decide whether the appellants had waived their rights to enforcement of the restrictions with respect to the other three doctors. It is true that these offices may violate the restrictive covenants, Grubb v. Guilford Ass'n, 228 Md. 135, 178 A.2d 886 (1962); Osborne v. Talbot, 197 Md. 105, 78 A.2d 205 (1951), but the appellants, from their testimony, indicate that they have no objections to a combined office-home use. Consistent with this position, they had no objection to Dr. Jaggers' combined use of the property from 1947 on—until the time he moved to Potomac. The real issue then is whether the waiver, if there was one, was broad enough to permit the doctor to move his residence, rent his home, still maintain his office on the premises, and yet not be in violation of the covenant. We hold the possible waiver did not go this far. In February 1967, the appellant, Chevy Chase Village, informed Dr. Jaggers by letter that his property would not be available as an office if he moved his residence elsewhere. Under these new circumstances, precipitated by Dr. Jaggers' own action, this was a timely assertion of their right to enforce the

---

[2] It is interesting to note that in the recent case, Chevy Chase Village v. Mont. Co., 258 Md. 27, 264 A.2d 861 (1970), we determined that there had been insufficient change in the residential character of this same neighborhood to warrant commercial rezoning.

covenants. As the Court said in Schlicht v. Wengert, supra, 178 Md. at 636–637, 15 A.2d at 914:

> And toleration of violations, out of friendship or lack of inclination until incidental annoyances grew to make the Schlichts feel a grievance, could not be construed as surrender of those rights. They refrained from a contest until experience with the particular violation stirred them to enforcement; and they might do so without loss of rights from it.

So whether appellants should or should not have been estopped from enforcing the restrictive covenants under the conditions existing prior to 1967 is not relevant to the changed circumstances after 1967. Any waiver that may have existed was limited to the use of the office *incidental* to his living on the property. Once appellees moved, however, such use ceased to be incidental and the appellants could still assert their rights to enforce the restrictions.

Pursuing this same point, the appellees contend that there was great significance in the fact that no one from Section 1-A objected when the Montgomery County Board of Appeals granted the Jaggers' request for a special exception to use their premises for the practice of medicine. In view of our holding in Martin v. Weinberg, supra, 205 Md. at 527–528, 109 A.2d at 579, that "[c]ontractual restrictions are neither abrogated nor enlarged by zoning restrictions", we do not share their enthusiasm for this evidence of waiver. We point out that even if this silence were relevant on the question the proceeding before the zoning board would only be indicative of the neighbors' acquiescence in the combined use of the property as a home and as an office, not as an office and rental property without the owner living on the premises.

## IV

The final argument the doctor makes is that if he must return to his former home or remove his office to comply with the covenants, he will suffer great hardship and inconvenience when he has only caused negligible harm to his neighbors. He invokes the equitable doctrine of comparative hardship to avoid this result. That doctrine has been explained with forceful clarity by Chief Judge Hammond for the Court in Dundalk Holding Co. v. Easter, 215 Md. 549, 555–557, 137 A.2d 667, cert. denied 358 U.S. 821, 79 S.Ct. 34, 3 L.Ed.2d 62, rehearing denied, 358 U.S. 901, 79 S.Ct. 219, 3 L.Ed.2d 151 (1958), which was recently reaffirmed in Grant v. Katson, Md., 274 A.2d 88 (1971). It basically provides that a court may decline to issue an injunction where the hardship and inconvenience which would result from the injunction is greatly disproportionate to the harm to be remedied. Innocent mistake on the part of the party to be enjoined is a factor to be considered in applying the doctrine. Overlooking the fact that the doctor, though a mediate purchaser whose deed only made reference to the restrictive covenants in his predecessor's deed, should have been aware of the limits on the use of his property, we do not think he can invoke the doctrine by characterizing the potential harm that might result to his neighbors' homes as comparatively negligible. Their interest in preserving the residential integrity of their community is simply not outweighed by his desire to move to another fashionable and exclusively residential area. With the facts before us in this case, had the trial judge declined to issue the injunction because of comparative hardship, we would not have hesitated to overrule him for a clear abuse of discretion. As he only went so far as to find that there had been a change in the neighborhood capable of vitiating the restrictive covenants, we base our reversal on this fact. On remand we direct that the appellees be enjoined from using their property in Chevy Chase Village for the practice of medicine unless they actually reside on the premises.

## City of Bowie, Maryland v. MIE Properties, Inc.

Court of Appeals of Maryland, 2007.
398 Md. 657, 922 A.2d 509.

■ HARRELL, JUSTICE:

We concern ourselves here with the standard for determining a challenge to the continuing vitality of restrictive covenants on real property. This case involves a set of restrictive covenants, recorded in 1986, encumbering originally a 466 acre parcel of land ("the Property") in Prince George's County. The current parties to the covenants are the City of Bowie, Maryland ("the City"), an original covenantee, and MIE, Inc. ("MIE"), a successor covenantor and current owner of the remainder of the Property. MIE's predecessor in title agreed with the City to a Declaration of Covenants ("the Covenants") which limits the development of the Property to 14 permissible uses. Contemporaneous with entering into the Covenants, an Annexation Agreement ("the Agreement") also was executed with the City, bringing the affected parcel, then undeveloped, within the City's corporate limits. The Agreement contemplated the development of a "science and technology, research and office park" on the Property, hopefully with the support of the University of Maryland.

MIE challenges the continuing vitality of the Covenants, principally on the basis that changes in circumstances since the recording of the Covenants obviates the purpose for the Covenants. The City counters that the Property may be, and is being, developed in accord with the Covenants. The Circuit Court for Prince George's County upheld the continuing validity of the Covenants. The Court of Special Appeals, however, reversed the judgment of the trial court, concluding that the trial judge applied the wrong standard for determining the ongoing validity of restrictive covenants. We shall reverse the judgment of the intermediate appellate court and remand with directions to affirm the judgment of the Circuit Court.

[I]n 2001, MIE leased a portion of this space to C & C Dance Studio ("the Dance Studio"), a use which the City contended was in violation of the Covenants. * * *

I. Procedural History

The City filed on 24 October 2002 a complaint in the Circuit Court for Prince George's County seeking a declaration that the Dance Studio's use was in violation of the Agreement and Covenants and further requesting a permanent injunction against the continued use of the building space by the Dance Studio. After extensive discovery, MIE filed on 26 November 2003 a counterclaim for a declaratory judgment that the Covenants and portions of the Agreement restricting the permitted uses of the Property were invalid and unenforceable. The Circuit Court determined ultimately that the Covenants were valid and enforceable against MIE and that MIE had violated the Covenants by permitting the Dance Studio to use and occupy leased space on the Property, a use prohibited by the Covenants. Accordingly, the Circuit Court enjoined MIE from permitting the Dance Studio to use and occupy any space on the Property. MIE's counterclaim was denied.

The Circuit Court reasoned that there had been "no radical change to the character of the neighborhood [of the Property] so as to defeat the purpose [ ] embodied in the Covenants and the Annexation Agreement." Having found the Covenants valid, the court concluded that the Dance Studio was prohibited by the Covenants.

In an unreported opinion, the intermediate appellate court held that the Circuit Court's judgment that the Covenants were valid and enforceable must be vacated and the case remanded for further proceedings.

In those further proceedings, the Circuit Court would revisit the question of the Covenants' validity vis-a-vis their purpose in light of a different standard than that applied originally by the Circuit Court. The Court of Special Appeals concluded that the continuing vitality of a restrictive covenant is determined by the "*reasonable probability*" that the parties will be able to achieve the goals of the Covenants within a reasonable period of time." (emphasis added). Therefore, the panel of the intermediate appellate tribunal opined that the Circuit Court incorrectly "emphasized the *theoretical possibility* that the Maryland Science and Technology Center will be developed on the property" as the standard for determining the validity of the Covenants. (emphasis added). Thus, a remand was necessary to consider the facts under the "correct" legal standard.

II. Discussion

The primary dispute in this case is the proper legal standard for assessing the continuing vitality of a restrictive covenant that facially has perpetual existence.

A. The Continuing Vitality of the Covenants in Light of their Purpose

The proper legal standard for this inquiry is to examine whether, after the passage of a reasonable period of time, the continuing validity of the covenant cannot further the purpose for which it was formed in light of changed relevant circumstances. * * * The objectives of covenant law are better served by the standard we announce today. The standard of changed circumstances restores the goal of objectivity in evaluating the ongoing validity of covenants by linking the result to objective factors outside of the property owner's control.

The intermediate appellate court apparently misconceived the operation of the rule of reasonable construction of restrictive covenants by subjecting every aspect of such covenants, including their validity, to a reasonableness inquiry. Specifically, the court applied a rule meant to ascertain the intent of the parties to a covenant (its *construction*) to determine its continuing validity by evaluating the reasonable chances of accomplishing its purpose. This is not the intended application of the reasonable construction rule. Because we believe that this is the standard that the Circuit Court applied, reaching a correct result, we agree with the trial court's finding that the Covenants remain valid and enforceable.

Our cases establish that chief among the factors considered in evaluating the present circumstances relevant to determining the continuing validity of a restrictive covenant is whether there has been a "radical change in the neighborhood causing the restrictions to outlive their usefulness." Chevy Chase Village v. Jaggers, 261 Md. 309, 316, 275 A.2d 167, 171 (1971).

A dramatic change in the character of a neighborhood, though, is not the only circumstance to be considered. Maryland courts also have recognized that the equitable doctrine of comparative hardship may be applied by a court to absolve a defendant of violating a restrictive covenant and refuse to enjoin the use barred by the covenant. The exercise of that doctrine, however, is appropriate only when the violation is committed innocently or mistakenly and enforcement of the covenant would visit much greater harm on the violator compared to the slight amount of harm the beneficiary of the covenant would experience if the covenant was not enforced.[3] Neither of these defenses has been mounted by MIE. We focus, then, on the radical neighborhood change factor.

Importantly, the particular state of affairs bearing on the potential for a covenant to fulfill its purpose must be viewed with respect to the passage of time. Generally, if an unambiguous covenant specifies its duration for a time certain, then courts should hold the parties to their

---

[3] We note that the fact that the land subject to restrictions would be more valuable without the restrictions is not controlling on a determination of whether a covenant should be deemed valid in this analysis. Texas Co. v. Harker, 212 Md. 188, 201, 129 A.2d 384, 391 (1957).

bargain. . . . In instances where a covenant does not specify the duration of the restriction or a covenant prescribes an indefinite duration, however, courts, under equity principles, may limit the covenant's duration to a reasonable period of time. Although the passage of a period of time deemed reasonable will vary according to the particular purposes of the covenant, we observe that given the enduring nature of real property and the longer expanses of time typically associated with analysis of questions bearing on interests in land,[4] what is deemed reasonable tends to be a relatively generous portion of time.

While the cases referred to above reflect that Maryland courts have invalidated some restrictive covenants at vintages as young as 20 to 50 years, we caution parties bound by such agreements against challenging perennially their validity in hopes that some bright line expiration date has been reached. We are not speaking of perishable food items here. The passage of time alone does not evidence decay in this scenario. It is not necessarily so that the validity usually of covenants are compromised with each passing year. Rather, the question of validity is a combination of a reasonable period of elapsed time and frustration of purpose in light of changed circumstances occurring over that time. To that point, we note that those covenants invalidated in our cases 20 to 50 years after their creation differed substantially from their upheld counterparts because of the extent of the change in circumstances that had occurred in the former, completely frustrating the purpose of the covenant.

In the present case, at the time of trial in March 2004, approximately 19 years had passed since the Covenants were executed in December 1985. We find no error in the Circuit Court's determination that "[t]here has been no radical change to the character of the neighborhood so as to defeat the purpose [ ] embodied in the Covenants and the Annexation Agreement." We do not disturb a trial court's findings of fact on the question of changed circumstances absent clear error.

B. Enforcement of the Covenants by the City does not Constitute Illegal Contract Zoning

MIE claims that the imposition of the Covenants in connection with its annexation of the Property constitutes a sort of illegal contract zoning by a municipality. * * *

Contrary to MIE's assertions, covenants may be more restrictive than the zoning classification imposed by the external zoning authority. This is so because the covenants exist as independent controls on property. Covenants would be pointless if they could not restrict the uses of a property to a greater degree than permitted by the underlying zoning of property. As long as the covenant is *as* or more restrictive, and not less

---

[4] Real covenants, such as the Covenants in this case, are an interest in land. See Mercantile-Safe Deposit & Trust Co. v. Mayor & City Council of Baltimore, 308 Md. 627, 641, 521 A.2d 734, 741 (1987) ("The view that covenants running with the land are indeed property interests is entirely consistent with Maryland decisions.").

restrictive, than the underlying zoning classification, the goals of zoning are not frustrated.

We are bound to interpret both the Covenants and the Agreement as written. The original parties to the Covenants and Agreement could have structured those instruments to permit the list of allowable uses to expand or contract with the uses allowed by the zoning classification established for the Property by the County. They did not. We may not add to the instruments that which the consenting parties neglected to bargain for in the course of their dealings.

## Orange and Rockland Utilities, Inc. v. Philwold Estates, Inc.

Court of Appeals of New York, 1981.
52 N.Y.2d 253, 437 N.Y.S.2d 291, 418 N.E.2d 1310.

■ MEYER, JUDGE.

Interpreted in light of the setting in which imposed and the language used, the restrictive covenant in plaintiffs' predecessor's deed limiting use of its land to erection of a hydroelectric plant ran with the land as to both benefit and burden. Because that covenant renders the land wholly useless under present circumstances, plaintiffs are however, entitled to judgment extinguishing the covenant pursuant to section 1951 of the Real Property Actions and Proceedings Law. Damage to the dominant land not having been shown, the judgment of extinguishment properly awarded defendant no damages. However, the judgment improperly reserved for future determination the issue of damages to an easement over the servient land also held by the owner of the dominant land. Plaintiffs have not sought extinguishment of the easement and defendant, as easement owner, as distinct from landowner, is not entitled to damages for extinguishment of the restrictive covenant. The order of the Appellate Division, 70 A.D.2d 338, 421 N.Y.S.2d 640, should, therefore, be modified by deleting therefrom so much thereof as preserved the right of defendant hereafter to seek damages for extinguishment of the covenant.[5] As so modified, the order should be affirmed.

William Bradford originally owned land on both sides of the Neversink River in Sullivan County. In 1923 he sold the east bank land to Alfred J. Crane, retaining for himself exclusive hunting and fishing rights over it. At the same time he sold part of the west bank land to Crane under a deed restricting its use "by [Crane] his heirs, executors and assigns solely for the erection of Hydroelectric and generating plants

---

[5] Of course, that deletion will not affect defendant's right to take such action as he deems proper to enforce his easement, should plaintiffs or any successor of plaintiffs use the land subject to the easement in such a way as to interfere with the reasonable enjoyment of it by defendant or his successors, but that right, if he has it, arises from the easement and exists, if at all, independently of the judgment in this action. Since the present action does not seek to extinguish the easement, we express no opinion as to its validity or enforceability.

and appurtenances, transmission lines, dams, penstocks, conduits or other structures appurtenant to the proper development and utilization of the water power of the portion of the Neversink River and Bushkill Creek above described or other water power uses and purposes, including houses for employees" but reserved to himself exclusive hunting and fishing rights over that part of the west bank land conveyed. In 1927 Crane conveyed the restricted property, subject to the covenant, to Rockland Light and Power Company, now known as Orange and Rockland Utilities, Inc. That company and Clove Development Corporation, its wholly owned subsidiary which now holds title to the west bank property originally deeded to Crane, are the plaintiffs in this action.

Bradford continued to hold the remaining west bank land, contiguous to the restricted parcel transferred to Crane. Bradford died in 1934 and in 1940 that property was conveyed by his successors in interest, ultimately coming to be held by Philwold Estates, Inc. Philwold Estates, Inc., was owned by Philwood Company, a partnership in which defendant Wechsler had an interest. In 1968 Wechsler withdrew from the partnership receiving for his interest in that company 2,325 acres of the west bank land that had been held by Philwold Estates, Inc., together with the hunting and fishing rights in the land deeded by Bradford to Crane which Bradford had reserved.

Plaintiffs' complaint seeks judgment declaring that the restrictive covenant was personal to Bradford and, therefore, is not enforceable by the successors to Bradford's other real property, or in the alternative that the restrictive covenant be extinguished pursuant to section 1951 of the Real Property Actions and Proceedings Law. Special Term dismissed the action, without reaching the merits, holding it barred by limitations and rejecting plaintiffs' argument that the statute was tolled because plaintiffs had possession and undisputed title to the property.

The Statute of Limitations defense was, however, swept aside by the Appellate Division because plaintiffs' title to the property was unchallenged, the dispute involving only the enforceability of the restrictive covenant. The court held that the covenant ran with the land and was, therefore, enforceable by defendant, but concluded that it should be extinguished because it found, for reasons hereafter detailed, that the covenant currently serves no purpose and renders plaintiffs' land valueless. Concluding that defendant had failed to prove any damage resulting from the extinguishment of the easement, the Appellate Division awarded no damages, but provided that defendant could seek damages for any injury to his land which might occur in the future as a result of the extinguishment of the restrictive covenant.

We agree (1) that the action is not barred by limitations or laches, (2) that the benefit as well as the burden of the covenant runs with the land, (3) that the Appellate Division properly concluded that the covenant should be extinguished pursuant to section 1951 of the Real

Property Actions and Proceedings Law, and (4) that defendant's proof did not entitle him to damages for extinguishment of the covenant. We disagree, however, with the Appellate Division's reservation to defendant of the right to seek future damages as a result of the extinguishment of the covenant and conclude that, the hunting and fishing easement not being involved in this action, the only right that defendant Wechsler retains is to enforce such easement rights as he has should there be a future interference with his reasonable enjoyment of the easement....

Subdivision 2 of section 1951 of the Real Property Actions and Proceedings Law authorizes a court in any action seeking relief against a restrictive covenant or a declaration with respect to its enforceability to cause its extinguishment "if the court shall find that the restriction is of no actual and substantial benefit to the persons seeking its enforcement or seeking a declaration or determination of its enforceability, either because the purpose of the restriction has already been accomplished or, by reason of changed conditions or other cause, its purpose is not capable of accomplishment, or for any other reason" but requires payment to the party who would otherwise be entitled to enforcement of the covenant of such damages as he will sustain from its extinguishment.

Plaintiffs point out that in 1940 while the servient parcel was held by Rockland Light and Power Company, the City of New York condemned all of Rockland's riparian rights in the Neversink River, that plaintiffs no longer have the right to use the servient parcel for hydroelectric purposes, and that as presently restricted, the land can be used for nothing else.

Defendant Wechsler argues, however, that the statute empowers a court to extinguish a restrictive covenant only when it no longer has value to the person who seeks to enforce it and that the restrictive covenant has value to him because it enhances his hunting and fishing rights and keeps the property near to his unspoiled. That the land can no longer be used for hydroelectric purposes does not, according to defendant Wechsler, diminish the value to him of the restrictive covenant.

The background of the statute is set forth in the 1958 Report of the Law Revision Commission which includes its Recommendation to the Legislature Relating to Recording, Extinguishment and Modification of Certain Restrictions on the Use of Land (N.Y.Legis.Doc., 1958, No. 65, at p. 211). That report makes clear that restrictive covenants were intended to be subjected to the doctrine of relative hardship (at p. 235), that "the public interest in the marketability and full utilization of land requires that there be available to owners of parcels burdened with" outmoded restrictions an "economical and efficient means of getting rid of them" (at p. 254), that restrictions that "purport to prohibit virtually any use whatever ... would be void on the ground that they were repugnant to the estate granted, or contrary to public policy, or unreasonable" but that few restrictions were of such drastic nature (at p. 255), that New York courts for many years had applied the doctrine of balancing interests to nonforfeiture covenants, refusing injunctive relief and in some cases granting damages instead (at pp. 263–66), but that there was need for an extinguishment statute because of procedural and other difficulties that would otherwise be encountered by landowners subject to restriction (at pp. 235, 264, 270, 317–18).

Section 1951, which as adopted is in the exact words recommended by the Law Revision Commission, must be construed in light of that legislative history. So construed, we agree that the restriction in issue was properly extinguished.

Foremost in the factors to be considered is the fact that if the covenant is enforced there is no use whatsoever to which the restricted land can be put by plaintiffs, for the restriction limits them to one single use and that use is, by reason of the city's condemnation, impossible. Plaintiffs would thus be required to maintain the land in such manner as to avoid liability for injury to the users of it under the hunting and fishing easement and pay taxes on it but could make no other use of it. Bearing in mind that, as the Law Revision Report suggests, such drastic limitation may well be void as against public policy and that both the background of the statute and its wording ("by reason of changed conditions or other cause, its purpose is not capable of accomplishment, *or for any other reason*" [emphasis supplied]) we have no hesitancy in concluding that the impossibility of constructing a hydroelectric plant (the building of which, though not required by the express wording of the conveyance to Crane, was practically compelled by the restriction imposed and was clearly in the contemplation of the parties to the grant creating the restriction) was sufficient to trigger the power of extinguishment, if on balance that appeared to be the equitable course.

Nor do we find any error of law in the Appellate Division's conclusion that on balance the restriction should be extinguished. The issue is not whether Wechsler obtains *any* benefit from the existence of the restriction but whether in a balancing of equities it can be said to be, in the wording of the statute, "of *no* actual and *substantial benefit*" (emphasis supplied). Defendant Wechsler argues that the value of both his remaining land and his hunting and fishing easement are enhanced if plaintiffs' property is kept in unspoiled condition. As to the land, Wechsler presented general opinion evidence indicating that its value would be enhanced, but nothing from which the importance or substantiality of that benefit could be measured, nor any dollars and cents proof by which it could be quantified. Measured against the burden to plaintiffs of maintaining land of which no use can be made, we cannot say that the Appellate Division erred in concluding that enhancement in value of the remaining land was not substantial.

With respect to the value enhancement of Wechsler's hunting and fishing rights, the simple answer is that they have not been affected by this proceeding in any way that the law should recognize. Wechsler retains those rights and he or his successors in title will be entitled should there be an interference with the reasonable enjoyment of the easement to take legal action to enjoin or obtain damages for the interference, or both (see Bakeman v. Talbot, 31 N.Y. 366). Though conceptually the easement rights may bring a higher price (assuming them to be salable) with the restriction in existence than without it, it cannot be said to be an error of law for the Appellate Division to have concluded (the more particularly so in the absence of proof in dollars and cents terms of the difference in value) that, since Wechsler continues to hold them and the right to enforce them without actual diminution, the theoretical diminution was not such a substantial benefit as to stand in the way of judgment of extinguishment. . . .

Defendant was afforded an opportunity to offer proof as to the damages he would suffer as a result of the extinguishment of the restrictive covenant, but, as already noted, failed to establish damages in quantifiable terms to his remaining land from the extinguishment of the restriction.

What the statute contemplates is an award of "the sum of money, if any, to which they [owners of the benefited land] are entitled in exchange for a complete extinction of the restrictions" (1958 Report of N.Y.Law.Rev.Comm., at p. 269), inclusive of both damages up to the time of trial and damages in the future. (Id., at p. 266). Having failed to avail himself of the opportunity, defendant is barred from seeking damages in the future for injury to his real property. It was, therefore, proper to deny a present damage award but error to reserve to defendant the right to bring an action in the future seeking such damages.

As noted above, however, defendant retains the hunting and fishing rights to which the easement entitles him. Should plaintiffs or some future holder of the land subject to the easement interfere with those rights in the future, Wechsler or his successors in interest to the easement will have the right to bring an appropriate action as he or they may be then advised.

The order appealed from should, accordingly, be modified as above indicated, and, as so modified, should be affirmed, with costs.

## NOTES

1. *Different theories.* In *Chevy Chase*, the court referred to laches, estoppel, change in the general character of the neighborhood, and comparative hardship. In *Philwold*, the court referred to changed conditions, relative hardship and balancing interests. What are the differences between these various "equitable" defenses? To what extent should they be treated as legal defenses barring an action for damages?

2. *Covenants and zoning.* Why should a doctor's office be unobjectionable when the doctor lives in an adjoining portion of the structure, but objectionable when someone else lives there? Does the Village

of Chevy Chase have an interest in encouraging doctors to practice medicine in Chevy Chase? Apparently Montgomery County thought so, since it approved Dr. Jaggers' request for a "special exception" under its zoning law. Should the policy behind the restrictive covenant outweigh that behind the granting of the special exception? The court in Chevy Chase expressly touches upon the relevance of zoning restrictions when discussing whether the plaintiffs are guilty of laches. Bowie also discusses the relationship between covenants and zoning. Do you agree with the court's observation in Chevy Chase that "contractual restrictions are neither abrogated nor enlarged by zoning restrictions"? Recall the discussion of the interplay between zoning ordinances and private covenants in *Hill*, reprinted in Assignment 24.

3. *Should the changed conditions or relative hardship tests be applied to easements?* The Third Restatement of Property takes the position that the changed conditions doctrine should be applied to all servitudes, including both covenants and easements.[6] This position reflects the Restatement's intent to create greater uniformity in the rules governing all servitudes. However, in AKG Real Estate, LLC v. Kosterman,[7] the court expressly rejected the Restatement view and held that easements are not subject to the changed conditions doctrine.[8] The court first noted that the Restatement position was subject to a great deal of academic criticism and had not received widespread judicial acceptance. Furthermore, the court believed that allowing a party to unilaterally modify or terminate an easement through the changed conditions doctrine would cause uncertainty and upset the settled expectations of current easement holders. Why might it be desirable to allow one party to unilaterally modify or terminate an easement?

4. *Law and equity.* Philwold Estates applies the New York statute to permit the award of damages when the granting of an injunction is denied. This approach parallels recent developments in nuisance law, discussed in Assignment 28. However, it alters the traditional rules governing covenants. As fully discussed in the prior Assignment, certain covenants not enforceable at law by the award of money damages are enforceable in equity by injunction. Under *Philwold Estates* certain covenants not enforceable in equity are enforceable at law. Is this development desirable?

5. *Eminent domain for private use.* A Massachusetts statute similar to the New York statute discussed in *Philwold Estates* was held to be constitutional.[9] However, two justices dissented, arguing that the statute unconstitutionally placed in the hands of private persons "the power to take from their neighbors an interest in real estate . . . not for any public use or purpose but solely for the petitioners' own private gain and profit." Ignoring any constitutional issue, are such statutes desirable?

---

[6] Restatement (Third) of Prop.: Servitudes § 7.10 (2000). See also § 7.10 cmt. a.
[7] 296 Wis. 2d 1, 717 N.W.2d 835 (2006).
[8] Id. at 24–25, 717 N.W.2d at 847.
[9] See Blakeley v. Gorin, 365 Mass. 590, 313 N.E.2d 903 (1974).

6. *Changed conditions adjoining the subdivision.* In Camelback Del Este Homeowners Ass'n v. Warner,[10] the court was faced with a residential only restriction that was placed on the subdivision about thirty years earlier. Since then, Camelback Road, which bordered the subdivision, was expanded from two lanes to seven lanes. Average weekday traffic flow had increased from 15,200 to 50,500 vehicles per day. Still, the court enforced the restriction as against lots adjoining Camelback Road, since the interior of the subdivision remained quiet and residential. This court, like many others, feared that the nullification of the restriction as to some lots would have a domino effect so that ultimately the restriction would be null as to all lots.[11] Are there alternative solutions to the problems of border lots?

7. *Extinguishment of environmental covenants.* The Uniform Environmental Covenants Act,[12] completed in 2003, has been adopted by more than 20 states. This act creates specific rules governing covenants that limit activity or use of land for an environmentally related purpose.[13] Because environmental covenants are intended to be perpetual, severe limitations are placed on the ways in which these covenants may be extinguished. If certain conditions are met, the changed conditions doctrine may be applied to modify or extinguish an environmental covenant.[14] However, these covenants are not subject to modification or extinguishment through laches, waiver, or acquiescence.[15] Why should these covenants be subject to the changed conditions doctrine, but not other doctrines?

---

[10] 156 Ariz. 21, 749 P.2d 930 (App.1987).

[11] The fear of a domino effect has led some courts to create blanket restrictions against modifying covenants for border lots. See, e.g., Karner v. Roy White Flowers, Inc., 351 N.C. 433, 437, 527 S.E.2d 40, 43 (2000) (noting that restrictive covenants must either be upheld for all lots or extinguished for all lots).

[12] Unif. Envtl. Covenants Act (2003).

[13] These covenants are created by or under the authority of state agencies and serve a remedial purpose. See Unif. Envtl. Covenants Act § 2(5). Environmental covenants should not be confused with conservation easements, even though both are servitudes that have environmental purposes.

[14] The agency that signed the covenant must bring the action to modify or extinguish the burden and all persons with a direct interest in the covenant must be notified. See § 9(b).

[15] See § 9(c).

# ASSIGNMENT 27
# COMMON INTEREST COMMUNITIES

## 1. INTRODUCTION

Common-interest communities, or CICs, "are those in which the property is burdened by servitudes requiring property owners to contribute to maintenance of commonly held property or to pay dues or assessments to an owners association that provides services or facilities to the community."[1] Community association law governs the issues raised by common-interest communities. This body of law applies the complex law of covenants to a contemporary and pervasive subject.

Common-interest communities can be condominiums, planned communities, traditional subdivisions or combination properties with residential and commercial components. A common-interest community provides neighborhood amenities through covenants. This concept has long existed in the United States. For example, in 1831, Samuel Ruggles transferred title to Grammercy Park in Manhattan to trustees for the benefit of the people who owned the property surrounding the park.[2] In recent years, the CIC form of property ownership has proliferated. This phenomenon has prompted the legal community to take notice. A uniform CIC act exists and an entire chapter of the most recent Restatement of Property is dedicated to this topic.[3]

As stated above, the defining characteristic of a CIC is that the properties within a CIC are burdened with servitudes or covenants. Covenants are legal devices used to create common-interest communities and provide the structure on which the community functions. The covenants of a common-interest community are recorded by the developer (also known as the declarant) of the CIC in a document called the declaration of "covenants, conditions and restrictions" (CC&R).[4] After the first property is purchased in a development, the covenants become effective and bind all other properties in the development.

The covenants included in the CC&R commonly mandate membership in a homeowners or property owners association and require the payment of dues or assessments to such association. The CC&R also typically restricts the use of land within a CIC and requires the

---

[1] Restatement (Third) Property (Servitudes) 6 Intro. Note (2000).

[2] Hyatt & French, Community Association Law: Cases and Materials on Common Interest Communities, 5 (1998).

[3] Uniform Common Interest Ownership Act (2008); Restatement (Third) Property (Servitudes) 6 (2000).

[4] CC&Rs were described in Assignment 23.

association's approval before changes can be made to an individual property. In addition, the CC&R might contain numerous restrictions such as those that require residents to be of a certain age or prohibit pets. Furthermore, the CC&R provides for creation of the association and is generally the source of the association's authority and power.

Conflicts in a CIC may arise when the interests of an individual property owner are at odds with that of other property owners or the association. These disputes generally center on interpreting an existing covenant, rejecting a new covenant, or disputing the actions of an association board.

## 2. Principal Problem[5]

Saul purchased a property in 1999 that he knew was one of 101 lots in a parcel subdivided in 1962. The subdivision was commonly known as the Oakdale Acres Estates. Other lots in Oakdale Acres had been purchased as well, but many of them were undeveloped because they were bought as investments. Saul was aware that his land was subject to the recorded CC&Rs for the subdivision. The CC&Rs consisted of two pages of vague and fairly unrestrictive covenants, which included a modification clause that stated: "The covenants herein may be amended as necessary by a majority vote of the lot owners in Oakdale Acres." The CC&Rs also referred to a restriction on pets, but because Saul had seen all types of pets and small farm animals on the lots of other property owners, he did not pay much attention to that provision.

Saul built a very unique home on his lot. The house used no common utilities. It required only solar power, water trucked in from off-site, and a wood stove for heat when necessary. To keep him company, he adopted two large Great Danes. Consistent with his unique style of living, in 2004, he began construction of a small shed in which he intended to house a few hens to provide fresh eggs.

During the time he was constructing the shed, Saul received a letter notifying him that a new neighborhood association had been formed for Oakdale Acres and inviting him to the first association meeting. At the meeting, he learned the association was formed by a developer who had purchased a majority (67) of the lots in Oakdale Acres. He also learned that the developer had staffed the association's board with his own representatives and had enacted a new regime of covenants that were now 19 pages long. The new covenants gave the association the power to assess fees on all association members (the lot owners), the ability to place liens on the property of owners who failed to pay assessments, control over any construction or property modifications, and the power to assess fees for each lot's share of the shared community "upgrades." After the meeting, Saul spoke with one of the association's board members

---

[5] The Principal Problem is adapted from a news story. See Dan Sorenson, "New Neighbors Impose Rules, Costs on Arizona Couple," Chi. Tribune, Feb. 29, 2004, at 3N).

(Kelley) who informed Saul that he owed the association $20,000 for his initial assessment and that his Great Danes (and the hens he hoped to purchase) violated a covenant in the original CC&R prohibiting pets over 50 pounds and all farm animals.

Saul was outraged at the actions of the new "association." He refused to pay the assessment or halt construction of his new shed. Board member Kelley called Saul and said the board would fine him and place a lien on his property for his violations of the covenants. Saul still refused to comply, and now the association has filed suit against Saul to enforce the covenants, both old and new. Saul fears that he will have to sell his dream house if he cannot defend his decision to ignore the demands of the association. He comes to you for advice. What do you tell him?

3. MATERIALS FOR SOLUTION OF PRINCIPAL PROBLEM

## Westmoreland Association, Inc. v. West Cutter Estates, Ltd.

Supreme Court of New York, Appellate Division, 1992.
579 N.Y.S.2d 413, 174 A.D.2d 144.

■ KUNZEMAN, J.

This appeal presents a situation in which a homeowners' association seeks to enjoin the defendants from completing construction of three single-family homes on the ground that the construction violates a restrictive covenant requiring that dwellings be set back a minimum of 20 feet from the front line of the property. This restriction applied to virtually every similarly situated residential lot in the area on the border of Queens and Nassau Counties known as Westmoreland. There is no dispute that the houses in question were subject to the restrictive covenant and that they were being built at a distance of 15 feet from the front lines of the respective lots. The threshold issue is whether the plaintiff Westmoreland Association, Inc., has standing to bring such an action to enforce a restrictive covenant which runs with the land. We find that the Westmoreland Association has the requisite standing. . . . At the outset, a review of the underlying facts, which are essentially uncontroverted, is in order.

The Westmoreland area is subject to a set of private restrictive covenants commonly known as the Rickert-Finlay agreements. The area contains approximately 320 building lots on which predominantly one-family houses have been erected. This property was, at one time, owned by a common grantor, the Rickert-Finlay Realty Company, which filed a map of the area in Queens County on or about May 17, 1907. As part of the scheme or plan in accordance with which Westmoreland was developed, the common grantor imposed certain restrictions on the lots therein. The covenants containing these restrictions appeared in the defendants' chain of title in a deed dated July 30, 1924, from Rickert

Holding Corp. to Stiles Realty Corp. The defendants were, therefore, on notice of their existence.

The defendant West Cutter Estates, Ltd. (hereinafter West Cutter) is a builder and developer which owns six contiguous lots shown on the 1907 map as lots numbered 56 through 61 inclusive. These lots form three double-lot building sites known as 250–34, 250–38, and 250–42 41st Drive in Little Neck, respectively. West Cutter took title in December 1986.

The Westmoreland Association was first formed in 1917 and was incorporated in 1924. Its bylaws provide that membership in the association "shall be limited to residents or property owners of the development known as Westmoreland, situated in the Counties of Queens and Nassau, Long Island, New York, who shall automatically become members of the Association by virtue of such residence or ownership therein." The bylaws further provide for annual dues of $5, payable by April 1st of each year. Among the particular objectives for which the association was organized, as set forth in its certificate of incorporation, is to "take all lawful action to maintain and enforce covenants and restrictions of record relating to the use of land and buildings within said Westmoreland."

Among the restrictive covenants, which appear in the defendants' chain of title, is the following: "Ninth. No building shall be erected nearer than twenty feet to the front line of any lot, except in the business sections. Porches, piazzas, [and] porte-cocheres are excepted from this restriction."

A building permit was granted to the defendants by the New York City Department of Buildings on or about May 13, 1987, enabling them to construct a house on each of their three building sites. The plans showed front-line setbacks for each house of only 15 feet. The defendants' construction of the houses on the property in question in violation of the restrictive covenant requiring a front-line setback of 20 feet prompted the association's litigation for permanent injunctive relief. As set forth in the complaint, the restrictive covenants, including that pertaining to the front-line setback, were imposed in furtherance of a general plan to preserve the tract for restricted residential use. The defendants refused to abide by applicable restrictions, notwithstanding a demand for compliance by the Westmoreland Association. Construction was halted by order of the Supreme Court, Queens County, dated July 23, 1987, upon the application of the association. As a result, the three houses now stand in a skeletal or incomplete state.

The defendants contend, on appeal, that the Westmoreland Association had no standing to commence this action. They assert that the trial court's reliance on *Matter of Douglaston Civic Assn. v. Galvin*, 36 N.Y.2d 1, 364 N.Y.S.2d 830, 324 N.E.2d 317, is misplaced inasmuch as that case involved a proceeding, brought by residents and a civic association, to challenge the granting of a variance. In the course of its opinion, the Court of Appeals specifically recognized the particular need in zoning cases for a broader rule of standing, given the financial inequities between developers and individual property owners.

To the contrary, the instant case does not involve a zoning ordinance but, rather, an equitable action concerning private restrictive covenants. The question for resolution thus becomes whether the *Douglaston* holding should be applied to cases, such as the instant one, which involve restrictive covenants. A brief historical overview is appropriate at this juncture.

The traditional rule is that, irrespective of the intention of the parties, a covenant will run with the land and will be enforceable against a subsequent purchaser of the land at the suit of one who claims the benefit of the covenant, only if the covenant complies with certain legal requirements. "The age-old essentials of a real covenant" have been set forth as follows: "(1) it must appear that grantor and grantee intended that the covenant should run with the land; (2) it must appear that the covenant is one 'touching' or 'concerning' the land with which it runs; (3) it must appear that there is 'privity of estate' between the promisee or party claiming the benefit of the covenant and the right to enforce it, and the promisor or party who rests under the burden of the covenant. (Clark on Covenants and Interests Running with Land, p. 74)" *Neponsit Prop. Owners' Assn. v. Emigrant Indus. Sav. Bank*, 278 N.Y. 248, 255, 15 N.E.2d 793. Under such a restrictive view, civic and property owners' associations, with no direct proprietary interest in the land, would clearly have no standing to challenge the violation of a covenant.

The willingness of courts to dispose of disputes over land use on the ground of standing, as opposed to reaching the merits, was inconsistent with broader rules of standing in related areas. There has been, in this State, a gradual movement away from technical requirements, commencing with the seminal 1938 case of *Neponsit Prop. Owners' Assn. v. Emigrant Indus. Sav. Bank (supra)*. There, an action was commenced to foreclose a lien upon land owned by the defendant. The lien emanated from a covenant subjecting the property to an annual charge for maintenance of "roads, paths, parks, beach, sewers and such other public purposes as shall from time to time be determined by the [grantor], its successors or assigns" (*supra*, at 254, 15 N.E.2d 793). The plaintiff, a property owners' association which was contemplated in the deed, was organized to receive the sums payable by the owners and to expend them for the benefit of those owners. The realty company assigned to the plaintiff all of its right, title and interest "in and to the said annual charge or lot tax, provided for in the covenant of each deed theretofore made" by the realty company, of lots or plots out of the subject tract of land. Significantly, the corporate plaintiff had not succeeded to any of the land, nor did it have title to the streets or public places upon which the charges assigned to it were to be expended. The court did not, however, focus upon the corporate plaintiff's lack of privity of estate. Rather, the court emphasized the fact that the association had been formed as a convenient instrument by which the property owners might advance their common interests....

In reliance upon *Neponsit* the Appellate Division, Fourth Department, has subsequently ruled that a plaintiff association's representative status was sufficient to satisfy the requirement of privity (*Riverton Community Assn. v. Myers*, 142 A.D.2d 984, 530 N.Y.S.2d 406). In the *Riverton Community Assn.* case, a declaration filed in the County Clerk's office between the property owner and the association stated that the association was formed to own, develop, manage, and maintain land and facilities within the community and included a covenant obliging owners of land, within the Riverton properties, to pay assessments for common areas and services provided by the association.

Although the *Douglaston* case involved a zoning law, the rationale of the Court of Appeals provides a strong case for further broadening the rules of standing, stating:

> It should be readily apparent that a person desiring relaxation of zoning restrictions—such as a change from residential to business—has little to lose and much to gain if he can prevail. He is not reluctant to spend money in retaining special counsel and real estate appraisers if it will bring him the desired result. The individual owner of developed land in the neighborhood, on the other hand, may not, at the time, realize the impact the proposed change of zoning will have on his property, or, realizing the effect, may not have the financial resources to effectively oppose the proposed change. Thus, the neighboring property owners rarely fight as hard for zoning protection as the developer or speculator does for relaxation of zoning restrictions. Against this background of economic disparity, an individual property owner, who stands only to gain (or prevent the loss of) the maintenance of the *status quo* as regards the value of his homestead and his peace and quiet, cannot be expected, nor should he be required, to assume by himself the burden and expense of challenging the zoning change. Even if successful, the aggrieved individual will not be able to recoup his expenditures. By granting neighborhood and civic associations standing in such situations, the expense can be spread out over a number of property owners, putting them on an economic parity with the developer.

[T]he court went on to enumerate four factors for determining whether a particular association has standing to assert the rights of its members who might be affected by the issuance of a zoning variance. These are the capacity of the organization to assume an adversarial position, whether its size and composition reflect a position fairly representative of the community or interest which it seeks to protect, the adverse effect of the decision sought to be reviewed on the group represented, and whether full participating membership is available to the residents and property owners in the neighborhood.

The requirement that an association meet these standards insures that that organization has a substantial identification with the successors in interest of the original grantor and that it will represent their collective interests. Furthermore, denial of standing might well result in an undesirable multiplicity of actions and motions.

The decision in *Douglaston* was relied upon by the County Court of Yates County in *Starkey Point Prop. Owners' Assn. v. Wilson*, 96 Misc. 2d 377, 409 N.Y.S.2d 376, where the deed did not specifically name the plaintiff or provide for its prospective creation. The association, nevertheless, had standing since it was found to have a substantial identification with the property owners and to be an appropriate representative of both the owners and the property to be benefited by the covenant. *Douglaston* provided a good rationale for expanding *Neponsit* to eliminate the rigid requirement of privity. *Starkey* further expanded it to include situations where the homeowners association was not established by deed.

In sum, it is reasonable to conclude that the corporate plaintiff Westmoreland Association was formed as a convenient instrument by which the property owners could advance their common interests and that it has a substantial identification with the real property owners in Westmoreland. Given all of the aforementioned factors, the Westmoreland Association qualified as a bona fide representative of the residents and property owners in the subject locale and, consequently, had standing to bring this action, irrespective of the fact that it may not have met the technical requirements of privity of estate. . . .

Accordingly, the judgment appealed from is affirmed.

## Evergreen Highlands Ass'n v. West

Supreme Court of Colorado, 2003.
73 P.3d 1.

■ RICE, J.

I. Introduction

We granted certiorari in this case to determine whether, pursuant to the modification clause of the Evergreen Highlands Subdivision covenants, the requisite majority of lot owners may "change or modify" the existing covenants by the addition of a new covenant which: (1) requires all lot owners to be members of the homeowners association, (2) assesses mandatory dues on all lot owners in the subdivision to pay for the maintenance of common areas, and (3) imposes liens on those lots whose owners fail to pay the mandatory dues.

The district court held that such an amendment was valid and binding. The court of appeals reversed, finding that the modification clause of Evergreen Highlands' covenants did not allow for the addition of a wholly new covenant, but only for the modification of existing covenants. We now reverse the court of appeals, holding that the addition of a new covenant falls within the permissible scope of the modification clause of the Evergreen Highlands covenants.

We also granted certiorari on the related question of whether, in the absence of a covenant imposing mandatory dues, the homeowners association has the implied power to collect assessments from all lot owners to pay for the maintenance of common areas of the subdivision. Although Petitioner counterclaimed on this issue in the trial court, the court never reached the merits of the argument because it upheld the actual modification of the covenant; the court of appeals reversed on the same ground. The issue was nevertheless preserved for certiorari review, and we now hold that the declarations for Evergreen Highlands were sufficient to create a common interest community by implication with the concomitant power to impose mandatory dues on lot owners to pay for the maintenance of common areas of the subdivision. We accordingly remand the issue to the court of appeals with orders to return it to the trial court for calculation of Petitioner's damages in a manner consistent with this opinion.

II.  Facts and Procedural History

Petitioner Evergreen Highlands Association, a Colorado non-profit corporation ("Association"), is the homeowner association for Evergreen Highlands Subdivision—Unit 4 ("Evergreen Highlands") in Jefferson County. The subdivision consists of sixty-three lots, associated roads, and a 22.3 acre park area which is open to use by all residents of the subdivision. The Association holds title to and maintains the park area, which contains hiking and equestrian trails, a barn and stables, a ball field, a fishing pond, and tennis courts. The park area is almost completely surrounded by private homeowners' lots, with no fence or other boundary separating the park area from the homes. Respondent Robert A. West owns one of the lots bordering directly on the park area, and has used the facilities there to play tennis, fish, and walk his dog.

Evergreen Highlands Subdivision was created and its plat filed in 1972. The plat indicated that the park area was to be conveyed to the homeowners association. Protective covenants for Evergreen Highlands were also filed in 1972, but did not require lot owners to be members of or pay dues to the Association. The Association, however, was incorporated in 1973 for the purposes of maintaining the common area and facilities, enforcing the covenants, paying taxes on the common area, and determining annual fees. The developer conveyed the park area to the Association in 1976. Between the years of 1976 and 1995, when the modification of the covenants at issue in this case occurred, the Association relied on voluntary assessments from lot owners to pay for maintenance of and improvements to the park area. Such expenses included property taxes, insurance for the park area and its structures, weed spraying, tennis court resurfacing, and barn and stable maintenance.

Article 13 of the original Evergreen Highlands covenants provides that a majority of lot owners may agree to modify the covenants, stating in relevant part as follows:

> [T]he owners of seventy-five percent of the lots which are subject to these covenants may release all or part of the land so restricted from any one or more of said restrictions, *or may change or modify any one or more of said restrictions,* by executing and acknowledging an appropriate agreement or agreements in writing for such purposes and filing the same in the Office of the County Clerk and Recorder of Jefferson County, Colorado.

Protective Covenants for Evergreen Highlands—Unit 4, art. 13 (Nov. 6, 1972) (emphasis added) (hereinafter "modification clause"). In 1995, pursuant to the modification clause, at least seventy-five percent of Evergreen Highlands' lot owners voted to add a new Article 16 to the covenants. This article required all lot owners to be members of and pay assessments to the Association, and permitted the Association to impose liens on the property of any owners who failed to pay their assessment. Assessments were set at fifty dollars per year per lot.

Respondent purchased his lot in 1986 when membership in the Association and payment of assessments was voluntary, a fact that Respondent contends positively influenced his decision to purchase in Evergreen Highlands. Respondent was not among the majority of homeowners who approved the 1995 amendment to the covenants, and he subsequently refused to pay his lot assessment. When the Association threatened to record a lien against his property, Respondent filed this lawsuit challenging the validity of the 1995 amendment. The Association counterclaimed for a declaratory judgment that it had the implied power to collect assessments from all lot owners in the subdivision, and accordingly sought damages from West for breach of the implied contract. The district court ruled in favor of the Association on the ground that the amendment was valid and binding; therefore, it never reached the merits of the Association's counterclaims.

The court of appeals reversed, finding that the terms "change or modify" as set forth in the modification clause of the covenants did not allow for the addition of a wholly new covenant, but only for modifications to the existing covenants. The court examined two divergent lines of cases from other states and concluded that the particular language used in Evergreen Highlands' modification clause supported the more restrictive interpretation, based on the principle that courts should resolve any ambiguities in covenant language in favor of the free and unrestricted use of property. . . . We granted certiorari and now reverse.

III. Analysis

Interpretation of a covenant is a question of law requiring de novo review. *Buick v. Highland Meadow Estates at Castle Peak Ranch, Inc.*, 21 P.3d 860, 862 (Colo. 2001). Courts must construe covenants as a whole based upon their underlying purpose, but will enforce a covenant as written if clear on its face. *Id.* Ambiguities will be resolved in favor of the free and unrestricted use of property.

We begin our analysis by examining the modification clause of the Evergreen Highlands covenants in order to determine if its scope is broad enough to allow for the addition of a wholly new covenant by the requisite majority of property owners. Because this is an issue of first impression in Colorado, we examine cases from other jurisdictions interpreting similar covenant modification language. We conclude that the terms "change" and "modify," as used in the Evergreen Highlands covenants, are expansive enough to allow for the addition of a new covenant. We hold that the 1995 amendment to the Evergreen Highlands covenants, approved by the requisite majority of lot owners, is valid and binding on all lot owners in Evergreen Highlands. We therefore reverse the court of appeals. . . .

A. Modification Clause of the Evergreen Highlands Covenants

The Association argues that the court of appeals erred when it held that the language of the Evergreen Highlands' modification clause only provided for "changes to the existing covenants, not the creation and addition of new covenants that have no relation to the existing covenants." *West v. Evergreen Highlands Ass'n*, 55 P.3d 151, 154 (Colo. App. 2001). Specifically, the Association argues that the word "change" is broad enough to encompass not only the modification of existing covenants, but the addition of new covenants as well. Based on our analysis of the language used in the Evergreen Highlands' modification clause, as well as the prevailing case law from other states, we agree.

1. The *Lakeland* Line of Cases

The court of appeals adopted the line of cases following *Lakeland Property Owners Association v. Larson*, 121 Ill. App. 3d 805, 77 Ill. Dec. 68, 459 N.E.2d 1164 (1984). That case involved a situation nearly identical to the present one, in which a majority of lot owners voted to add a new covenant creating mandatory assessments and vesting the homeowner association with the power to impose liens for non-payment. Interpreting very similar covenant modification language (allowing a majority of the property owners to "change the said covenants in whole or in part," *id*, at 1167), the court disallowed the adoption of the new covenant. It held that "[t]he provision . . . clearly directs itself to changes of existing covenants, not the adding of new covenants which have no relation to existing ones." *Id.* at 1169. The *Lakeland* reasoning has been adopted by other states.

In *Caughlin Ranch Homeowners Association v. Caughlin Club*, 109 Nev. 264, 849 P.2d 310 (1993), a subdivision's original covenants imposed assessments only on residential parcels, although the modification clause provided for amendment of the rates. A year after the covenants were filed, a commercial club was developed and began operations on the property. Some six years later, after control of the homeowners association had passed from the developer to the lot owners, the homeowners association amended the covenants to levy assessments against the commercial parcel. Basing its reasoning on *Lakeland*, the Nevada Supreme Court disallowed the amendment, holding that the covenant modification clause allowing "amendments" referred only to "amendments of existing covenants as opposed to the creation of new covenants unrelated to the original covenants."

In *Boyles v. Hausmann*, 246 Neb. 181, 517 N.W.2d 610, 613 (1994), the modification clause allowed the majority of the homeowners to "change [the covenants] in whole or in part." The plaintiffs' lot was allegedly rendered unbuildable when the requisite majority of the homeowners association amended an existing covenant to increase the setback requirements. The *Boyles* court disallowed the additional covenant because, even though the restriction was appended onto an existing covenant, it was "new and different."

Finally, in *Meresse v. Stelma*, 100 Wash. App. 857, 999 P.2d 1267 (2000), the covenants for a six-lot subdivision allowed a majority of the lot owners "to change or alter them [the covenants] in full or in part." Five of the lot owners voted to alter the covenants to increase the access road easement, thereby stripping the sixth lot owner of a portion of his property. The court disallowed the amendment, holding that the amendatory language of the covenants "does not place a purchaser or owner on notice that he or she might be burdened, without assent, by road relocation at the majority's whim."

2. The *Zito* Line of Cases

Despite the fact that the *Lakeland* reasoning has been followed by other courts as recently as 2000, the same court that decided *Lakeland* issued a contrary opinion in 1992 with little explanation. In *Zito v. Gerken*, 225 Ill. App. 3d 79, 167 Ill. Dec. 433, 587 N.E.2d 1048 (1992), existing subdivision covenants granted the homeowners association the authority to modify the covenants, although the exact language of the modification clause is not provided. The homeowners association adopted mandatory assessments and disgruntled homeowners sued. This time, however, the Illinois Appellate Court held in favor of the homeowners association, holding that: "[a] restrictive covenant which has been modified, altered or amended will be enforced if it is clear, unambiguous and reasonable"; "[t]he 1987 amendment does not seek to change the character of [the subdivision] or to impose unreasonable burdens upon any lot owners"; and "the terms and conditions of the 1987 amendment impose a minimal collective burden upon the residents."

In *Sunday Canyon Property Owners Association v. Annett*, 978 S.W.2d 654 (Tex. Ct. App. 1998), the modification language allowed the covenants, upon a majority vote of the lot owners, to be "waived, abandoned, terminated, modified, altered or changed." Based on this language, the court allowed the requisite majority to adopt an amendment creating a homeowners association levying mandatory lot assessments. The court held that, despite the fact that the creation of the homeowners association

> exceeded the original purpose of the right to amend contemplated by purchasers prior to the amendment, it is of no moment. Recognized long ago was the right of persons ... to contract with relation to their property as they see fit in the absence of contravention of public policy and positive law. That right is derived from ownership of the property, and embraces the ability to impose on the property restrictive covenants and to abrogate or modify them.

*Id.* at 658 (citations omitted).

Finally, in *Windemere Homeowners Association, Inc. v. McCue*, 297 Mont. 77, 990 P.2d 769 (1999), a majority of homeowners voted to amend the covenants to create a homeowners association authorized to levy the costs of road maintenance against property owners. Basing his argument on *Lakeland, Caughlin,* and *Boyles,* plaintiff homeowner challenged the amendment as an impermissible new covenant. The court, however, held that the modification clause in these covenants was "markedly different" than those in *Lakeland* and its progeny; specifically, the clause, like that in *Sunday Canyon,* allowed a majority of property owners to "waive[ ], abandon[ ], terminate [ ], modify[ ], alter[ ], or change[ ]" the covenants. Consequently, the court held that this amendatory language was "broad enough" to justify the amendment.

### 3. Application to the Evergreen Highlands Covenants

As this summary of cases from other jurisdictions illustrates, there exists a split in the law with respect to this issue. Respondent contends that these cases can be distinguished by how narrowly or broadly the particular modification clause is written, and argues that the amendatory language in Evergreen Highlands' covenants is much more akin to the narrow language found in the *Lakeland* line of cases than the more expansive language found in the *Zito* line of cases. He therefore argues that the *Lakeland* reasoning should prevail here.

There is little substance to the distinction between the "broad" or "narrow" amendatory language upon which Respondent relies. The covenant modification language in *Lakeland* and *Boyles* allowed a majority of lot owners to "change" the covenants and in *Meresse* to "change or alter" the covenants. The amendatory language in *Sunday Canyon* and in *Windemere,* however, provided that the covenants could be "waived, abandoned, terminated, modified, altered or changed." In the latter cases, the first three words—"waived, abandoned, and terminated"—all deal with *ending* a covenant, not adding a new one, and are therefore inapplicable here. The last three words—"modified, altered, or changed"—are the same as those in the *Lakeland* line of cases, with the addition of "altered," which is simply a synonym for "change" and "modify." Thus, distinguishing these cases from one another based on the breadth of the language used is an artificial, and ultimately unpersuasive, distinction.

Moreover, from a linguistic standpoint, the *Lakeland* conclusion that "change or modify" can only apply to the alteration of existing covenants, and not the addition of new and different ones, is not well-founded. Webster defines "change" as "to make different." *Webster's Third New International Dictionary* 373 (1986). Applying this definition to the language at issue, covenants could certainly be changed or made different either by the addition, subtraction, or modification of a term. Confining the meaning of the term "change" only to the modification of existing covenants, then, seems illogically narrow.

For these reasons, we find the court of appeals' reliance on a linguistic analysis to distinguish covenant modification language unsatisfactory. We instead conclude that the different outcomes in the *Lakeland* and *Zito* lines of cases are based on the differing factual scenarios and severity of consequences that the cases present. In those cases where courts disallowed the amendment of covenants, the impact upon the objecting lot owner was generally far more substantial and unforeseeable than the amendment at issue here. *See, e.g., Caughlin Ranch*, 109 Nev. 264, 849 P.2d 310 (covenants previously imposing assessments only on private lots amended to assess the sole commercial parcel in the subdivision at a substantially higher rate); *Boyles*, 246 Neb. 181, 517 N.W.2d 610 (changed setback requirement rendered plaintiff's lot unbuildable); *Meresse*, 100 Wash. App. 857, 999 P.2d 1267 (increased access road easement deprived plaintiff of a portion of his private lot).

In contrast, *Zito, Windemere,* and *Sunday Canyon,* like this case, all specifically considered—and allowed—the amendment of covenants in order to impose mandatory assessments on lot owners for the purpose of maintaining common elements of a subdivision. We accordingly find the *Zito* line of cases more applicable to the situation here. This interpretation also avoids the absurd result that could follow from application of the *Lakeland* reasoning; Evergreen Highlands would be unable to adopt a mandatory-assessment covenant when its original covenants were silent on the subject, yet could adopt such a covenant if its original covenants had expressly prohibited a mandatory-assessment covenant.

Moreover, the amendment at issue in this case was changed according to the modification clause of the original Evergreen Highlands covenants, and it is undisputed that Respondent was on actual notice of that clause when he purchased his lot in 1986. In addition, we note that, at fifty dollars per year, the mandatory assessment imposed on Respondent is neither unreasonable nor burdensome.[6] To the contrary, the existence of a well-maintained park area immediately adjacent to Respondent's lot undoubtedly enhances Respondent's property value.

We conclude that the modification clause of the Evergreen Highlands covenants is expansive enough in its scope to allow for the adoption of a new covenant, and hold that the 1995 amendment to the Evergreen Highlands covenants, passed by the requisite majority of lot owners, is valid and binding on all lot owners in Evergreen Highlands. . . .

## Majestic View Condo. Ass'n, Inc. v. Bolotin
District Court of Appeal of Florida, 1983.
429 So.2d 438.

■ DELL, J.

Appellant, Majestic View Condominium Association, Inc., appeals from an order denying injunctive relief to enforce a provision of the declaration of condominium which controlled the keeping of pets.

The Declaration of Condominium of Majestic View Condominium Number One prohibits all animals and pets of any kind, except one dog or cat under twenty-five pounds, owned by a unit owner. Appellees acquired a dog which thereafter grew larger than twenty-five pounds, and subsequently acquired another large dog. They permitted these dogs to run at will through the condominium, frightening residents and creating a nuisance. Appellant sent appellees several letters, first requesting and then demanding that appellees comply with the declaration of condominium. Appellees refused to comply and appellant filed its complaint for injunctive relief. Appellees answered and admitted every factual allegation of the complaint except those relating to adequate remedy at law, irreparable harm, and attorney's fees. Appellees also filed a counterclaim in which they alleged that appellant arbitrarily enforced or applied the pet restriction against them but not against others. The trial court found the pet rule valid and specifically found against appellees on their counterclaim, but nonetheless entered judgment in favor of appellees. . . .

In these consolidated appeals, appellant asserts that the trial court erred when it applied a previously nonexistent constitutional "due

---

[6] By way of comparison, the amendment approved in *Zito* provided for lot assessments at $100 per year. 167 Ill. Dec. 433, 587 N.E.2d at 1049. The amendment approved in *Sunday Canyon* imposed an open-ended annual assessment for the maintenance and improvement of the roads, water system, and common areas; for providing architectural control over lot improvements; and for promoting "the health, welfare, and safety of the residents." 978 S.W.2d at 656. Finally, the amendment approved in *Windemere* created a homeowners association that was responsible for maintenance, repair, reconstruction, and snow removal on the common subdivision road, and allowed the association to assess lot owners for the paving of the road. 990 P.2d at 771.

process" test to reach the conclusion that appellant acted arbitrarily in the course of its pre-litigation enforcement efforts.

Appellant has correctly outlined the requirements for enforcement of a restrictive covenant such as that which is the subject of this appeal: (1) constructive or actual notice of the existence of the restriction by the defendant prior to enforcement; (2) a reasonable demand for compliance with the restriction after the breach has occurred; (3) compliance with any applicable procedural due process considerations which require notice of the commencement of the *litigation* and an opportunity to be heard *in court*. U.S. Const. amend. XIV, § 1; Fla. Const. art. I, § 9.

The record demonstrates that appellant satisfied each of the foregoing requirements. First, appellees admitted that they had actual notice of the subject use restriction prior to the institution of appellant's action. Second, not only did appellant establish, and appellees admit, that appellant actually notified appellees that their actions constituted a violation of the condominium restrictions, appellant also established that it had a regular procedure for notification of violations. And lastly, this court proceeding satisfies the third requirement of procedural due process in that the appellees received notice of this action, had a reasonable opportunity to be heard by the court adjudicating the matter and were provided with a full trial on the merits.

Appellees rely solely upon *White Egret Condominium v. Franklin*, 379 So.2d 346 (Fla. 1979), and *Hidden Harbour Estates, Inc. v. Norman*, 309 So.2d 180 (Fla. 4th DCA 1975), to support the trial court's holding that:

> Due process requires that there must be some procedure by which an individual unit owner is put on notice of the fact that there is a regulation. There must be some procedure by which he is given notice of a violation. There must be some procedure in which he is given an opportunity to respond to that violation, and after having been found by an association to be in violation of that particular restriction, there must be some period of time in which to comply with the dictates of the association. Should he fail to do that, the board should thereafter institute and strenuously prosecute all lawsuits to bring compliance with the restriction.

Neither of these cases compels or even authorizes this result. *White Egret* examined a condominium regulation which prohibited children under the age of twelve from residing in the condominium premises. The Court held that a condominium restriction or limitation does not inherently violate a fundamental right and may be enforced if it serves a legitimate purpose and is reasonably applied. The Supreme Court held that the age restriction was reasonably related to a lawful objective, but ruled in favor of the offending unit owner because the Association selectively and arbitrarily applied the reasonable restriction to the defendant but not to other unit owners. Here the Court determined:

> [T]hat plaintiff did not selectively enforce Article XI(c), and that the defendants [appellees] were not singled out for prosecution, nor was special treatment given to other condominium residents with respect to the enforcement of Article XI(c).

*Hidden Harbour Estates, Inc. v. Norman*, 309 So.2d 180 (Fla. 4th DCA 1975), supports appellant's adoption of the restriction which is the subject of this appeal:

> It appears to us that inherent in the condominium concept is the principle that to promote the health, happiness, and peace of mind of the majority of the unit owners since they are living in such close proximity and using facilities in common, each unit owner must give up a certain degree of freedom of choice which he might otherwise enjoy in separate, privately owned property. Condominium unit owners comprise a little democratic sub society of necessity more restrictive as it pertains to use of condominium property than may be existent outside the condominium organization.

We interpret the trial court's final judgment as requiring a condominium association to provide a unit owner with an adversary proceeding before seeking to enforce its restrictive covenants in court. Appellees have failed to cite any cases or statutory requirements which would support the conclusion reached by the trial court. Appellees received notice of their violation of the condominium restrictions, had an ample opportunity to comply with the restrictions but acted in defiance of the restrictions by which they had agreed to be bound. Appellant properly sought to enforce the condominium restrictions through the judicial process to remedy appellees' breach. The trial court based its conclusion that appellant administered Article XI(c) in an arbitrary manner based upon his earlier conclusion that it failed to provide due process in accordance with his interpretation of the requirements of due process. We find no support for the trial court's expansion of the due process requirements as set forth in the U.S. Const. amend. XIV, § 1 and the Fla. Const. art. I § 9.

The procedure followed by the condominium association complied with the requirements of Section 718 et seq., Florida Statutes (1981) and existing case law. Therefore we find that the trial court erred when it failed to enforce the restrictive covenants of the appellant condominium association. . . .

## Raintree of Albemarle Homeowners Ass'n, Inc. v. Jones

Supreme Court of Virginia, 1992.
243 Va. 155, 413 S.E.2d 340.

■ HASSELL, J.

The primary issue that we consider in this appeal is whether a homeowners association has waived its right to enforce a restrictive covenant.

Raintree of Albemarle Homeowners Association, Inc. filed its bill of complaint against Charles D. Jones and Glenda M. Jones seeking to enforce certain restrictive covenants contained in a "Declaration of Statement of Restrictions [,] Covenants[,] and Conditions." The Homeowners Association requested that the chancellor issue an injunction which, among other things, would have prohibited Charles and Glenda Jones from keeping or storing a tow truck on their property.

The chancellor conducted an *ore tenus* hearing[7] and granted partial relief. The chancellor enjoined Mr. Jones from: parking any vehicle on property owned by others without permission; placing vehicles in a state of disrepair on his property or on Old Brook Road; and placing vehicles with painted signs on his property. However, the chancellor found that, even though a tow truck which Mr. Jones regularly parked in his driveway violated a restrictive covenant, the Homeowners Association was not entitled to the issuance of an injunction because it had not uniformly enforced the restrictive covenant against other property owners in the subdivision. Additionally, the court did not grant injunctive relief against Glenda Jones and declined to award the complainant or respondents attorneys' fees. We granted the Homeowners Association an appeal and the Joneses a cross-appeal.

[T]he relevant facts are not in dispute. Charles and Glenda Jones own Lots 1 and 2 of Phase I in the Raintree subdivision. The lots are located on Old Brook Road which is Virginia State Route 652.

In November 1987, Mr. Jones purchased a "wrecker service" business and he began to park a red tow truck, also described as a small wrecker, at his home. The Homeowners Association requested that Mr. Jones cease parking the tow truck on his property. He refused to do so and continued to park the truck there through the date of the *ore tenus* hearing.

Two property owners in the Raintree subdivision, Gordon L. Nicely and Dennis Powell have, on occasion, parked pickup trucks owned by a utility company at their homes. Richard McDonald, president and a director of the Homeowners Association, testified that the Homeowners Association had determined that these pickup trucks, unlike the tow

---

[7] Editor's Note: An *ore tenus* hearing is an oral hearing.

truck, were not commercial trucks which were kept and stored in the subdivision within the intent of the restrictive covenant.

The relevant restrictive covenant states:

> No school buses, commercial vehicles, or habitable motor vehicles may be kept on or stored on any part of the property except within an enclosed garage. *No trucks of any nature shall be parked overnight on the property subject hereto* except in an enclosed garage, nor shall any vehicles of any description be permitted to be repaired on any lot or the Common Area, except in an enclosed garage or other area completely screened from roads and adjoining properties.

*Id.*, art. V, § 5.01(j) (emphasis added).

[T]he Homeowners Association argues that its failure to require Nicely and Powell to remove their trucks did not constitute a waiver of the Homeowners Association's right to enforce the restrictive covenant. In *Village Gate Homeowners Ass'n v. Hales*, 219 Va. 321, 246 S.E.2d 903 (1978), we discussed the principles that we must apply when determining whether a homeowners association has waived its right to enforce a restrictive covenant. There, a homeowners association filed a suit to enforce certain covenants, conditions, and restrictions. The association sought an order requiring a homeowner to remove a front yard wall which had been constructed on her property in violation of a covenant which stated: "No front or side yard fence, wall or walls, or other similar type structures shall be allowed except those constructed by or on behalf of [the developer]." The trial court held that the homeowners association had waived its right to enforce the restrictive covenant because the association had permitted certain homeowners to retain side yard fences violative of the covenant. Reversing the judgment of the trial court, we stated:

> Elementary is the proposition that the right to enforce a restrictive covenant of this type may be lost by waiver, abandonment or acquiescence in violations thereof. But the party relying on such waiver must show that the previous conduct or violations had affected 'the architectural scheme and general landscaping of the area so as to render the enforcement of the restriction of no substantial value to the property owners.' . . .
>
> To determine whether [the homeowner] has shown no substantial value was left in this restriction, we look first to its purpose and then to the conduct of [the homeowners association] as it affected the neighborhood.

*Id.* at 324–25, 246 S.E.2d at 905 (citations omitted).

Applying these principles, which were not applied by the trial court, we hold that the Homeowners Association did not waive its right to enforce the restriction. The restriction, which is binding upon all homeowners in the Raintree subdivision including Charles and Glenda Jones, was enacted to enhance and protect the value and attractiveness of the subdivision. Our review of the record, including photographs of the tow truck, the pickup trucks and houses in the subdivision, indicates that the Homeowners Association's decision not to enforce the covenant against Mr. Nicely and Mr. Powell did not substantially affect the value of the covenant. As we stated in *Hales,* "as long as the value of the covenant has not been affected substantially, [a homeowners association] will not be deemed to have waived the right to enforce [the covenant]." . . .

## NOTES

1. *Standards of review for board action.* Litigation involving common interest communities often arises from a situation where a homeowners' association board has acted to the perceived detriment of an individual property owner. Courts have struggled with the question of what standard of review to apply to such board action. For instance, some courts have applied the business judgment rule of corporation law, meaning that the court will not second-guess the board's decision unless there is a showing of bad faith. Other courts have applied a reasonableness standard to board decisions. (See the *Nahrstedt* case in Assignment 23.) However, courts are often unclear about what standard they are using, or they confuse the two standards and apply a "mixed" standard.

2. *Keeping the burden in the CIC.* The Restatement points out that the public has an interest in the success of CICs because the failure of a CIC will place the burden of the upkeep of the CIC's common elements on the local municipality. Section 6.3(3) states that "a court may authorize the creation of an association on petition of a governmental body" for a CIC if it is necessary to protect the public from taking on this kind of unwanted burden.

3. *Focus on residential CICs.* This assignment and most of the law of CICs focuses on residential CICs, rather than CICs comprised mainly of commercial components. Why might this be?

4. *Termination of the CIC.* The Uniform Common Interest Ownership Act includes a provision that lays out the process for terminating a CIC. The general rule is that a CIC can be terminated or dissociated by a super-majority vote of the association's members. Of course, termination of a CIC leads to a host of other issues, mainly because of the undivided interest that each member has in the CIC's common property. See UCIOA § 2–118.

# C. RIGHTS OF NEIGHBORS

# ASSIGNMENT 28

# NUISANCE

## 1. INTRODUCTION

As interest in the environment has increased, the law of nuisance has emerged as a mechanism for controlling the adverse impacts of many different kinds of land uses. Neighbors who are harmed by pollution or other environmental impacts may bring private nuisance claims against the perpetrators, particularly when government regulation is ineffective, unavailable, or inadequate to remedy their harms. For example, government regulation may require a polluter to stop, but it might not provide damages to neighbors who have already suffered costly harms. Moreover, nuisance lawsuits may serve as an impetus to spur regulators to take action against polluters. The limits of regulatory capacity may also spur government agencies to file public nuisance lawsuits over harmful land uses and pollution, even if the source of the nuisance is outside of the agency's regulatory jurisdiction.

Several specific areas of nuisance law activity illustrate its growing importance in environmental protection. First, nuisance law may be a tool for residents of low-income and minority neighborhoods to use against their communities to redress the burdens of pollution and undesirable urban conditions, such as deteriorating and unsafe structures, blight, criminal activity, excessive noise, and the like.[1]

Second, a wide range of plaintiffs—from native Inuit villagers in Alaska to hurricane victims to owners and users of natural resources—are bringing public and private nuisance claims against a variety of industrial companies (e.g., fossil fuel burning utilities; oil and chemical companies) and government agencies for contributing to climate change or failing to act to reduce greenhouse gas emission.[2] While it is uncertain how these "climate change" nuisance suits will fare in the long run,[3] they have enhanced the debate at many different levels about how best to

---

[1] See, e.g., Godsil, Viewing the Cathedral from Behind the Color Line: Property Rules, Liability Rules and Environmental Racism, 53 Emory L.J. 1807 (2004); Seiler, Moving from "Broken Windows" to Healthy Neighborhood Policy: Reforming Urban Nuisance Law in Public and Private Sectors, 92 Minn. L. Rev. 883 (2008).

[2] See Salzman & Hunter, Negligence in the Air: The Duty of Care in Climate Change Litigation 155 U. Penn. L. Rev. 101 (2007); Gerrard, Climate Change Litigation in the U.S. (Climate Change Case Chart), http://www.climatecasechart.com/.

[3] See Dana, The Mismatch Between Public Nuisance Law and Global Warming, Northwestern Law & Econ. Research Paper No. 08–05, available at http://ssrn.com/abstract=1129838.

address complex problems of environmental harms with effects at multiple and remote scales.[4]

A third trend in nuisance law is the emerging concept of "ecological nuisances." Nuisance law has been suggested as a mechanism for protecting entire ecological systems, allocating damages for economic harms to the "ecosystem services" that ecosystems provide to people and society (e.g., pollination, flood control, pollution filtration), and recognizing environmental ethical responsibilities for ecological harms.[5]

Fourth, intense stormwater runoff from developed and altered lands has become a major landowner and public problem.[6] Using a combination of nuisance, trespass, and negligence theories, government agencies or nearby landowners may seek injunctions against, or monetary damages for, runoff that is greatly increased by a landowner's actions in developing, grading, and paving his or her land.[7]

Fifth, nuisance doctrines aid governments in regulating to protect the environment. Nuisance law serves as a limitation inherent in private property rights that shields government regulatory agencies from "takings" compensation liability when the agencies severely restrict private land-use rights to prevent uses that would constitute nuisances.[8]

Relying primarily on nuisance law to achieve environmental protection, however, presents certain problems. For example, nuisance law depends on the availability and willingness of plaintiffs who can afford the litigation and have the time, patience, facts and standing to pursue successful lawsuits. Judges are generalists, not scientific or technical experts on pollution, health risks, hydrology, climate change, and other such matters that fall into the expertise of regulatory agencies. The available remedies may be more limited for nuisance actions than for government controls. Moreover, some nuisance claims may actually work against environmental conservation goals. For example, alternative energy sources, such as noisy wind farms or visually startling solar

---

[4] Osofsky, The Continuing Importance of Climate Change Litigation, 1(1) Climate Law 3 (2010).

[5] See Ruhl, Making Nuisance Ecological, 58 Case Western Res. L. Rev. 753 (2008); Nagle, From Swamp Drainage to Wetlands Regulation to Ecological Nuisances to Environmental Ethics, 58 Case Western Res. L. Rev. 787 (2008).

[6] U.S. Environmental Protection Agency, National Management Measures to Control Nonpoint Source Pollution from Urban Areas, EPA–641–B–05–004 (2005) Brody et al., The Rising Costs of Floods: Examining the Impact of Planning and Development Decisions on Property Damage in Florida, 73(3) J. Am. Planning Assn. 330 (2007); Arnold, Norton, & Wallen, Kentucky Wet Growth Tools for Sustainable Development: A Handbook on Land Use and Water for Kentucky Communities, ch. 2 (2009).

[7] See, e.g., Lucas v. Rawl Family Ltd. Partnership, 598 S.E.2d 712 (S.C. 2004); McGlashan v. Spade Rockledge Terrace Condo Dev. Corp., 402 N.E.2d 1196 (1980); Hall v. Wood, 443 So.2d 834 (Miss. 1983). But see Argyelan v. Haviland, 435 N.E.2d 973 (Ind. 1982) (refusing to abandon common enemy doctrine that allows landowners to direct runoff towards neighbors' land even if it causes harm to neighbors).

[8] See Lucas v. South Carolina Coastal Council, 505 U.S. 1003 (1992): Palazzolo v. State, No. WM 88–0297, 2005 WL 1645974 (R.I. Super. Ct., July 5, 2005).

panels, may be the targets of nuisance suits from potential neighbors who do not want these facilities nearby.[9]

At the outset, it is important to distinguish public nuisances from private nuisances. A public nuisance is an unreasonable interference with a right common to the general public, including activities injurious to the health, safety, morals or comfort of the public. A private nuisance is a wrongful interference with the use or enjoyment of land of another.

Sometimes the same act may constitute both a public nuisance and a private nuisance, as where a polluting factory interferes with the public comfort, but also interferes with the use or enjoyment of neighboring land. A public nuisance closely resembles a misdemeanor. Since a public nuisance is an offense against the public, usually only a public official can sue to abate it. A private individual suffering an injury "different in kind" from the general public is sometimes permitted to bring an action himself. Understandably, the "difference in kind" test has been a prolific source of controversy. The reason for prohibiting a private citizen from suing to abate a public nuisance is not entirely clear. The conventional theory is that prosecutorial discretion can best be preserved by preventing private persons from bringing actions to enjoin public nuisances. Can you suggest some other rationales? It has been suggested that private class actions to abate public nuisances should be allowed. Why?

In this course, we are concerned primarily with private nuisances—i.e., wrongful interferences with the use or enjoyment of land. The typical case is that of the smoke-emitting factory. Here, the interference is "intentional" in the sense that the operator of the factory is aware of the smoke and yet continues to operate the factory. Traditionally, liability in such a case is predicated on a finding that the interference is "unreasonable." A reasonable interference would not be actionable. A great many factors go into the determination of the "reasonableness" issue. If the factory is operated with the most modern smoke abatement equipment, and if it is located in a factory area, courts usually find that it is not unreasonably interfering with plaintiff's land.

## 2. PRINCIPAL PROBLEM

Bill and Wade bought their 5 acre lots in the Willowbrook subdivision at the same time. The lots are square and have a common boundary on the east end of Bill's lot and the west end of Wade's lot. Bill's lot is heavily forested, except for a small portion of the lot near the boundary with Wade's lot. Bill is environmentally conscious. He does not want to cut down any of the trees, but he also wants to heat his house with solar energy. The only place he can get adequate sun without cutting

---

[9] See, e.g., Rankin v. FPL Energy, LLC, 266 S.W.3d 506 (Tex. App. 2008) (rejecting nuisance claim against wind farm); Alterman, Reflected Sunlight is a Nuisance, 18 Envtl L. 321 (1988); Bliss, Tilting at Wind Turbines: Noise Nuisance in the Neighborhood After *Rassier v. Houim*, 69 N. Dak. L. Rev. 535 (1993).

down any trees is in the clearing near the boundary with Wade's lot. Bill applied for, and received, a building permit. Although his plans comply with all county regulations, they call for the house to be placed as close to the lot line as county side yard restrictions allow.

About a month later, before Bill began construction, Wade applied for and received a building permit to build a house on the western end of his lot. Wade's plans also comply with all county restrictions. The house shown in his plans will be quite close to Bill's house. Since Wade's plans call for a two story house, it will cast a shadow on Bill's solar collector in the early and mid-morning hours. Bill projects that this will reduce the efficiency of his solar mechanism by 30%. Bill is quite upset because Wade's house will require Bill to buy power from the utility company. The purchase of power is not only expensive, but also is produced by polluting fossil fuels. Bill has suggested that since Wade's lot is not heavily forested, Wade could easily build closer to the center of the lot. Wade, however, is not anxious to do this. He likes the view from his proposed location. Wade had the plans drawn up before Bill ever applied for a building permit. Wade claims that his view to the west will be partially ruined by Bill's house looming close to the border of their lots. Wade also points out that the shadow cast by Bill's house will reduce by 10% the efficiency of Wade's solar water heater, with which Wade plans to heat his pool.

One month later, after Bill had begun construction but before Wade commenced building, Bill brought an action against Wade on a private nuisance theory. He asks first for an injunction to prevent Wade from constructing the house specified by the plans. In the alternative, Bill asks for damages to pay for the energy that he will have to buy due to the reduced efficiency of his solar system. Wade comes to you for legal advice. Before advising Wade, consider the following materials.

3. MATERIALS FOR SOLUTION OF PRINCIPAL PROBLEM

## Excerpts from Rabin, Nuisance Law: Rethinking Fundamental Assumptions

63 Virginia Law Review 1299 (1977).
(Reprinted with the permission of the copyright holder,
Virginia Law Review Association).

When the light from a racetrack owned by one person interferes with an outdoor movie theater owned by another, what is the proper resolution of the conflict? Traditionally, courts have assumed such a question to be a simple one. If the interference did not constitute a nuisance, the cinema owner would have no legal remedy. She would have to tolerate the interference or ameliorate its effects at her own expense, such as by shielding the cinema from the lights. If the interference constituted a "nuisance," a court would issue an injunction forcing the track owner to shade his lights or otherwise to protect the cinema at his own expense.

Courts too often confuse the question of "who should pay for it?" with the question of "what should be done?" The questions are distinct and require separate treatment. The question of who should pay can be answered only with reference to the criterion of fairness, involving an assessment of relative moral fault. In contrast, the second question should be resolved by the criterion of efficiency.

The procedure here proposed for resolving private nuisance cases involves two steps. The first step would be to determine who is morally more blameworthy for the existence of the conflict. That person should bear the expense of resolving the conflict. This should satisfy the fairness criterion. The second step in the proposed procedure would be to determine how the conflict can be resolved with least expense. This resolution of the conflict would satisfy the efficiency criterion. As a result, the person at fault would pay the cost of resolving the conflict caused by the nuisance in the most efficient manner. This result would be both fair and efficient.

The following chart summarizes the solutions that the proposed procedure would yield for variations of the hypothetical posed earlier.

RESOLVING LAND USE CONFLICTS TO OPTIMIZE FAIRNESS AND EFFICIENCY

|  |  | PARTY AT FAULT | |
|---|---|---|---|
|  |  | Track Owner | Cinema Owner |
| MOST EFFICIENT SOLUTION | | Court Order: Track owner enjoined from interfering with cinema unless he pays damages equal to least expensive solution. | Court Order: Track owner enjoined from interfering with cinema if cinema owner pays track owner the cost of compliance.* |
| Physical changes less expensive than abandoning either use. | Shading track lights cheaper. | Track owner will shade lights at his expense, complying with the injunction. | Cinema owner will pay track owner cost of installing shades, and track owner will install them in compliance with injunction. |
| | Shielding cinema cheaper. | Track owner will pay damages to cinema owner, measured by cost of shielding cinema, thereby lifting the injunction. | Cinema owner will build a light shield at her own expense rather than enforce an injunction.* |
| Physical changes more expensive than abandoning either use. | Abandoning track cheaper. | Track owner will abandon track. | Cinema owner will pay track owner cost of abandoning track, and track owner will be enjoined. |
| | Abandoning cinema cheaper. | Track owner will pay damages to cinema owner, measured by profits lost because of abandonment of cinema. Injunction will be lifted and cinema abandoned. | Cinema owner will abandon cinema, and injunction will not be imposed.* |

\* Of course, where the cinema owner is at fault, and the efficient solution is either shielding or abandoning the cinema, the cinema owner will not attempt to enforce her right to an injunction conditional upon her payment of the track owner's cost of compliance.

[49A]

The proposed rule would strongly influence courts to make fairer assignments of initial entitlements. The traditional approach presents a court with the simple question of whether the defendant's activity is a nuisance. In answering that question, the court must attempt to balance the often conflicting claims of efficiency and fairness. If the large, smoky factory that locates next to the small, preexisting cottage is held to be a nuisance on grounds of fairness to the cottage owner, the court following the traditional rule would have to enjoin the factory, sacrificing efficiency to fairness. The desire to prevent a great loss to society in terms of wasted investment, lost employment, and lost taxes might well tempt a court to find no nuisance. The proposed test, however, would necessitate no such sacrifice. To protect fairness, the entitlement would be awarded to the cottage owner. But he would receive damages, enforced by a conditional injunction, not an ordinary injunction, thus permitting the factory to continue operating. This substitution of damages for an injunction will result in a fairer judicial assignment of entitlements by removing the temptation to permit efficiency considerations to influence the initial allocation of entitlements.

Similarly, where the plaintiff does not deserve an entitlement, the proposed rule suggests that he nevertheless receive an injunction conditional on his paying the defendant's costs of compliance. This procedure would tend to protect the plaintiff from extortionate behavior by the defendant. A court desiring to grant the initial entitlement to the defendant therefore, will not be deterred by the fear of encouraging extortion. For this reason, the defendant justly deserving the initial entitlement will be more likely to receive it than he would under the traditional rule, which simply denies plaintiff an injunction when defendant is given the initial entitlement.

The conflict should be resolved by the least-cost-avoider, but not necessarily at his expense. The person at "fault" should bear the expense of avoiding the conflict, despite the fact that neither party can be said to have "caused" the conflict. Fault in this context is the result of many factors that cannot easily be summarized. The person who produces the interference is not necessarily, or even usually, at fault. And for purposes of assigning fault it should be immaterial who first owned property in the area. Rather, the relevant, but not necessarily determinative, question should be "On which property was the use first begun that subsequently proved incompatible with the use of neighboring property?" This doctrine of prior use should replace the doctrine of coming to the nuisance, which looks to either prior ownership or prior use. Here, fault consists of conduct that either (1) causes substantial net injury to the other party and falls below community standards of the particular time and place, or (2) is unduly vulnerable to the activities of others for the particular time and place.

Regarding the question of *how* the conflict should be resolved, the answer is that the resolution should minimize the cost to society and to the parties. In pursuing this objective, this article expands upon a suggestion first made by Professors Calabresi and Melamed[10] and proposes a substantial change from existing law. As a general rule, the appropriate remedy in a nuisance action should be an injunction cancellable upon the payment by the defendant of damages to the

---

[10] Calabresi & Melamed, Property Rules, Liability Rules and Inalienability: One View of the Cathedral, 85 Harv.L.Rev. 1089 (1972).

plaintiff for past injuries and for future injuries that would flow from the continuation of the defendant's activities. This contrasts with the usual present practice of simply awarding the successful plaintiff damages for past injuries coupled with an unconditional injunction. And it greatly expands the comparative hardship doctrine, which permits damages in lieu of an injunction only in rare cases. Currently, an unsuccessful plaintiff in a nuisance action simply is denied an injunction. This article suggests that the unsuccessful plaintiff in a nuisance action be awarded an injunction contingent on his paying the defendant the defendant's cost of compliance. These remedies will result in allocational efficiency no less than the often suggested remedy of placing liability on the least-cost-avoider when transaction costs are significant, as is usually the case.

Giving the entitlement to be free of pollution, or to pollute, to the person relatively free of fault will promote fairness without hampering efficiency. After entitlements are thus assigned, use of the suggested remedies will promote efficiency without adversely affecting the fairness promoted by the initial assignment of entitlements.

## Boomer v. Atlantic Cement Co.
Court of Appeals of New York, 1970.
26 N.Y.2d 219, 309 N.Y.S.2d 312, 257 N.E.2d 870.

■ BERGAN, JUDGE.

Defendant operates a large cement plant near Albany. These are actions for injunction and damages by neighboring land owners alleging injury to property from dirt, smoke and vibration emanating from the plant. A nuisance has been found after trial, temporary damages have been allowed; but an injunction has been denied.

The public concern with air pollution arising from many sources in industry and in transportation is currently accorded ever wider recognition accompanied by a growing sense of responsibility in State and Federal Governments to control it. Cement plants are obvious sources of air pollution in the neighborhoods where they operate.

But there is now before the court private litigation in which individual property owners have sought specific relief from a single plant operation. The threshold question raised by the division of view on this appeal is whether the court should resolve the litigation between the parties now before it as equitably as seems possible; or whether, seeking promotion of the general public welfare, it should channel private litigation into broad public objectives.

A court performs its essential function when it decides the rights of parties before it. Its decision of private controversies may sometimes greatly affect public issues. Large questions of law are often resolved by the manner in which private litigation is decided. But this is normally an incident to the court's main function to settle controversy. It is a rare exercise of judicial power to use a decision in private litigation as a purposeful mechanism to achieve direct public objectives greatly beyond the rights and interests before the court.

Effective control of air pollution is a problem presently far from solution even with the full public and financial powers of government. In large measure adequate technical procedures are yet to be developed and some that appear possible may be economically impracticable.

It seems apparent that the amelioration of air pollution will depend on technical research in great depth; on a carefully balanced consideration of the economic impact of close regulation; and of the actual effect on public health. It is likely to require massive public expenditure and to demand more than any local community can accomplish and to depend on regional and interstate controls.

A court should not try to do this on its own as a by-product of private litigation and it seems manifest that the judicial establishment is neither equipped in the limited nature of any judgment it can pronounce nor prepared to lay down and implement an effective policy for the elimination of air pollution. This is an area beyond the circumference of one private lawsuit. It is a direct responsibility for government and should not thus be undertaken as an incident to solving a dispute between property owners and a single cement plant—one of many—in the Hudson River Valley.

The cement making operations of defendant have been found by the court at Special Term to have damaged the nearby properties of plaintiffs in these two actions. That court, as it has been noted, accordingly found defendant maintained a nuisance and this has been affirmed at the Appellate Division. The total damage to plaintiffs' properties is, however, relatively small in comparison with the value of defendant's operation and with the consequences of the injunction which plaintiffs seek.

The ground for the denial of injunction, notwithstanding the finding both that there is a nuisance and that plaintiffs have been damaged substantially, is the large disparity in economic consequences of the nuisance and of the injunction. This theory cannot, however, be sustained without overruling a doctrine which has been consistently reaffirmed in several leading cases in this court and which has never been disavowed here, namely that where a nuisance has been found and where there has been any substantial damage shown by the party complaining an injunction will be granted.

The rule in New York has been that such a nuisance will be enjoined although marked disparity be shown in economic consequence between the effect of the injunction and the effect of the nuisance.

The problem of disparity in economic consequence was sharply in focus in Whalen v. Union Bag & Paper Co., 208 N.Y. 1, 101 N.E. 805. A pulp mill entailing an investment of more than a million dollars polluted a stream in which plaintiff, who owned a farm, was "a lower riparian owner". The economic loss to plaintiff from this pollution was small. This court, reversing the Appellate Division, reinstated the injunction granted by the Special Term against the argument of the mill owner that in view of "the slight advantage to plaintiff and the great loss that will be inflicted on defendant" an injunction should not be granted. "Such a balancing of injuries cannot be justified by the circumstances of this case", Judge Werner noted. He continued: "Although the damage to the plaintiff may be slight as compared with the defendant's expense of abating the condition, that is not a good reason for refusing an injunction."

Thus the unconditional injunction granted at Special Term was reinstated. The rule laid down in that case, then, is that whenever the damage resulting from a nuisance is found not "unsubstantial", viz., $100 a year, injunction would follow. This states a rule that had been followed in this court with marked consistency. . . .

There are cases where injunction has been denied. McCann v. Chasm Power Co., 211 N.Y. 301, 105 N.E. 416 is one of them. There, however, the damage shown by plaintiffs was not only unsubstantial, it was non-existent. Plaintiffs owned a rocky bank of the stream in which defendant had raised the level of the water. This had no economic or other adverse consequence to plaintiffs, and thus injunctive relief was denied. Similar is the basis for denial of injunction in Forstmann v. Joray Holding Co., 244 N.Y. 22, 154 N.E. 652 where no benefit to plaintiffs could be seen from the injunction sought. Thus if, within Whalen v. Union Bag & Paper Co., supra which authoritatively states the rule in New York, the damage to plaintiffs in these present cases from defendant's cement plant is "not unsubstantial", an injunction should follow.

Although the court at Special Term and the Appellate Division held that injunction should be denied, it was found that plaintiffs had been damaged in various specific amounts up to the time of the trial and damages to the respective plaintiffs were awarded for those amounts. The effect of this was, injunction having been denied, plaintiffs could maintain successive actions at law for damages thereafter as further damage was incurred.

The court at Special Term also found the amount of permanent damage attributable to each plaintiff, for the guidance of the parties in the event both sides stipulated to the payment and acceptance of such permanent damage as a settlement of all the controversies among the parties. The total of permanent damages to all plaintiffs thus found was $185,000. This basis of adjustment has not resulted in any stipulation by the parties.

This result at Special Term and at the Appellate Division is a departure from a rule that has become settled; but to follow the rule literally in these cases would be to close down the plant at once. This court is fully agreed to avoid that immediately drastic remedy; the difference in view is how best to avoid it.[11]

One alternative is to grant the injunction but postpone its effect to a specified future date to give opportunity for technical advances to permit defendant to eliminate the nuisance; another is to grant the injunction conditioned on the payment of permanent damages to plaintiffs which would compensate them for the total economic loss to their property present and future caused by defendant's operations. For reasons which will be developed the court chooses the latter alternative.

If the injunction were to be granted unless within a short period—e.g., 18 months—the nuisance be abated by improved methods, there would be no assurance that any significant technical improvement would occur.

The parties could settle this private litigation at any time if defendant paid enough money and the imminent threat of closing the plant would build up the pressure on defendant. If there were no improved techniques found, there would inevitably be applications to the court at Special Term for extensions of time to perform on showing of good faith efforts to find such techniques.

Moreover, techniques to eliminate dust and other annoying byproducts of cement making are unlikely to be developed by any research the defendant can undertake within any short period, but will depend on the total resources of the cement industry nationwide and throughout the world. The problem is universal wherever cement is made.

For obvious reasons the rate of the research is beyond control of defendant. If, at the end of 18 months, the whole industry has not found a technical solution, a court would be hard put to close down this one cement plant if due regard be given to equitable principles.

On the other hand, to grant the injunction unless defendant pays plaintiffs such permanent damages as may be fixed by the court seems to do justice between the contending parties. All of the attributions of economic loss to the properties on which plaintiffs' complaints are based will have been redressed.

The nuisance complained of by these plaintiffs may have other public or private consequences, but these particular parties are the only ones who have sought remedies and the judgment proposed will fully redress them. The limitation of relief granted is a limitation only within the four corners of these actions and does not foreclose public health or other public agencies from seeking proper relief in a proper court.

It seems reasonable to think that the risk of being required to pay permanent damages to injured property owners by cement plant owners

---

[11] Respondent's investment in the plant is in excess of $45,000,000. There are over 300 people employed there.

would itself be a reasonable effective spur to research for improved techniques to minimize nuisance.

The power of the court to condition on equitable grounds the continuance of an injunction on the payment of permanent damages seems undoubted. . . .

The damage base here suggested is consistent with the general rule in those nuisance cases where damages are allowed. "Where a nuisance is of such a permanent and unabatable character that a single recovery can be had, including the whole damage past and future resulting therefrom, there can be but one recovery" (66 C.J.S. Nuisances § 140, p. 947). It has been said that permanent damages are allowed where the loss recoverable would obviously be small as compared with the cost of removal of the nuisance. . . .

The present cases and the remedy here proposed are in a number of other respects rather similar to Northern Indiana Public Service Co. v. W.J. & M.S. Vesey, 210 Ind. 338, 200 N.E. 620 decided by the Supreme Court of Indiana. The gases, odors, ammonia and smoke from the Northern Indiana company's gas plant damaged the nearby Vesey greenhouse operation. An injunction and damages were sought, but an injunction was denied and the relief granted was limited to permanent damages "present, past, and future."

Denial of injunction was grounded on a public interest in the operation of the gas plant and on the court's conclusion "that less injury would be occasioned by requiring the appellant [Public Service] to pay the appellee [Vesey] all damages suffered by it . . . than by enjoining the operation of the gas plant; and that the maintenance and operation of the gas plant should not be enjoined."

The Indiana Supreme Court opinion continued: "When the trial court refused injunctive relief to the appellee upon the ground of public interest in the continuance of the gas plant, it properly retained jurisdiction of the case and awarded full compensation to the appellee. This is upon the general equitable principle that equity will give full relief in one action and prevent a multiplicity of suits."

It was held that in this type of continuing and recurrent nuisance permanent damages were appropriate. See, also, City of Amarillo v. Ware, 120 Tex. 456, 40 S.W.2d 57 where recurring overflows from a system of storm sewers were treated as the kind of nuisance for which permanent depreciation of value of affected property would be recoverable.

There is some parallel to the conditioning of an injunction on the payment of permanent damages in the noted "elevated railway cases" (Pappenheim v. Metropolitan El. Ry. Co., 128 N.Y. 436, 28 N.E. 518 and others which followed). Decisions in these cases were based on the finding that the railways created a nuisance as to adjacent property owners, but in lieu of enjoining their operation, the court allowed permanent damages.

Judge Finch, reviewing these cases in Ferguson v. Village of Hamburg, 272 N.Y. 234, 239–240, 5 N.E.2d 801, 803, said: "The courts decided that the plaintiffs had a valuable right which was being impaired, but did not grant an absolute injunction or require the railway companies to resort to separate condemnation proceedings. Instead they held that a court of equity could ascertain the damages and grant an injunction which was not to be effective unless the defendant failed to pay the amount fixed as damages for the past and permanent injury inflicted."

Thus it seems fair to both sides to grant permanent damages to plaintiffs which will terminate this private litigation. The theory of damage is the "servitude on land" of plaintiffs imposed by defendant's nuisance. (See United States v. Causby, 328 U.S. 256, 261, 262, 267, 66 S.Ct. 1062, 90 L.Ed. 1206, where the term "servitude" addressed to the land was used by Justice Douglas relating to the effect of airplane noise on property near an airport.)

The judgment, by allowance of permanent damages imposing a servitude on land, which is the basis of the actions, would preclude future recovery by plaintiffs or their grantees.

This should be placed beyond debate by a provision of the judgment that the payment by defendant and the acceptance by plaintiffs of permanent damages found by the court shall be in compensation for a servitude on the land.

Although the Trial Term has found permanent damages as a possible basis of settlement of the litigation, on remission the court should be entirely free to re-examine this subject. It may again find the permanent damage already found; or make new findings.

The orders should be reversed, without costs, and the cases remitted to Supreme Court, Albany County to grant an injunction which shall be vacated upon payment by defendant of such amounts of permanent damage to the respective plaintiffs as shall for this purpose be determined by the court.

■ JASEN, JUDGE (dissenting).

I agree with the majority that a reversal is required here, but I do not subscribe to the newly enunciated doctrine of assessment of permanent damages, in lieu of an injunction, where substantial property rights have been impaired by the creation of a nuisance.

It has long been the rule in this State, as the majority acknowledges, that a nuisance which results in substantial continuing damage to neighbors must be enjoined. . . . To now change the rule to permit the cement company to continue polluting the air indefinitely upon the payment of permanent damages is, in my opinion, compounding the magnitude of a very serious problem in our State and Nation today.

In recognition of this problem, the Legislature of this State has enacted the Air Pollution Control Act (Public Health Law, Consol.Laws, c. 45, §§ 1264 to 1299–m) declaring that it is the State policy to require the use of all available and reasonable methods to prevent and control air pollution (Public Health Law § 1265).

The harmful nature and widespread occurrence of air pollution have been extensively documented. Congressional hearings have revealed that air pollution causes substantial property damage, as well as being a contributing factor to a rising incidence of lung cancer, emphysema, bronchitis and asthma.

The specific problem faced here is known as particulate contamination because of the fine dust particles emanating from defendant's cement plant. The particular type of nuisance is not new, having appeared in many cases for at least the past 60 years. . . . It is interesting to note that cement production has recently been identified as a significant source of particulate contamination in the Hudson Valley. This type of pollution, wherein very small particles escape and stay in the atmosphere, has been denominated as the type of air pollution which produces the greatest hazard to human health. We have thus a nuisance which not only is damaging to the plaintiffs, but also is decidedly harmful to the general public.

I see grave dangers in overruling our long-established rule of granting an injunction where a nuisance results in substantial continuing damage. In permitting the injunction to become inoperative upon the payment of permanent damages, the majority is, in effect, licensing a continuing wrong. It is the same as saying to the cement company, you may continue to do harm to your neighbors so long as you pay a fee for it. Furthermore, once such permanent damages are assessed and paid, the incentive to alleviate the wrong would be eliminated, thereby continuing air pollution of an area without abatement.

It is true that some courts have sanctioned the remedy here proposed by the majority in a number of cases, but none of the authorities relied upon by the majority are analogous to the situation before us. In those cases, the courts, in denying an injunction and awarding money damages, grounded their decision on a showing that the use to which the property was intended to be put was primarily for the public benefit. Here, on the other hand, it is clearly established that the cement company is creating a continuing air pollution nuisance primarily for its own private interest with no public benefit.

This kind of inverse condemnation . . . may not be invoked by a private person or corporation for private gain or advantage. Inverse condemnation should only be permitted when the public is primarily served in the taking or impairment of property. The promotion of interests of the polluting cement company has, in my opinion, no public use or benefit.

Nor is it constitutionally permissible to impose servitude on land, without consent of the owner, by payment of permanent damages where the continuing impairment of the land is for a private use. This is made clear by the State Constitution (art. I, § 7, subd. [a]) which provides that "[p]rivate property shall not be taken for *public use* without just compensation" (emphasis added). It is, of course, significant that the section makes no mention of taking for a *private* use.

In sum, then, by constitutional mandate as well as by judicial pronouncement, the permanent impairment of private property for private purposes is not authorized in the absence of clearly demonstrated public benefit and use.

I would enjoin the defendant cement company from continuing the discharge of dust particles upon its neighbors' properties unless, within 18 months, the cement company abated this nuisance.

It is not my intention to cause the removal of the cement plant from the Albany area, but to recognize the urgency of the problem stemming from this stationary source of air pollution, and to allow the company a specified period of time to develop a means to alleviate this nuisance.

I am aware that the trial court found that the most modern dust control devices available have been installed in defendant's plant, but, I submit, this does not mean that *better* and more effective dust control devices could not be developed within the time allowed to abate the pollution.

Moreover, I believe it is incumbent upon the defendant to develop such devices, since the cement company, at the time the plant commenced production (1962), was well aware of the plaintiffs' presence in the area, as well as the probable consequences of its contemplated operation. Yet, it still chose to build and operate the plant at this site.

In a day when there is a growing concern for clean air, highly developed industry should not expect acquiescence by the courts, but should, instead, plan its operations to eliminate contamination of our air and damage to its neighbors.

## Spur Industries, Inc. v. Del E. Webb Development Co.

Supreme Court of Arizona, 1972.
108 Ariz. 178, 494 P.2d 700.

■ CAMERON, VICE CHIEF JUSTICE.

From a judgment permanently enjoining the defendant, Spur Industries, Inc., from operating a cattle feedlot near the plaintiff Del E. Webb Development Company's Sun City, Spur appeals. Webb cross-appeals. Although numerous issues are raised, we feel that it is necessary to answer only two questions. They are:

1. Where the operation of a business, such as a cattle feedlot is lawful in the first instance, but becomes a nuisance by reason of a nearby residential area, may the feedlot operation be enjoined in an action brought by the developer of the residential area?

2. Assuming that the nuisance may be enjoined, may the developer of a completely new town or urban area in a previously agricultural area be required to indemnify the operator of the feedlot who must move or cease operation because of the presence of the residential area created by the developer?

The facts necessary for a determination of this matter on appeal are as follows. The area in question is located in Maricopa County, Arizona, some 14 to 15 miles west of the urban area of Phoenix, on the Phoenix-Wickenburg Highway, also known as Grand Avenue. About two miles south of Grand Avenue is Olive Avenue which runs east and west. 111th Avenue runs north and south as does the Agua Fria River immediately to the west. See Exhibits A and B below.

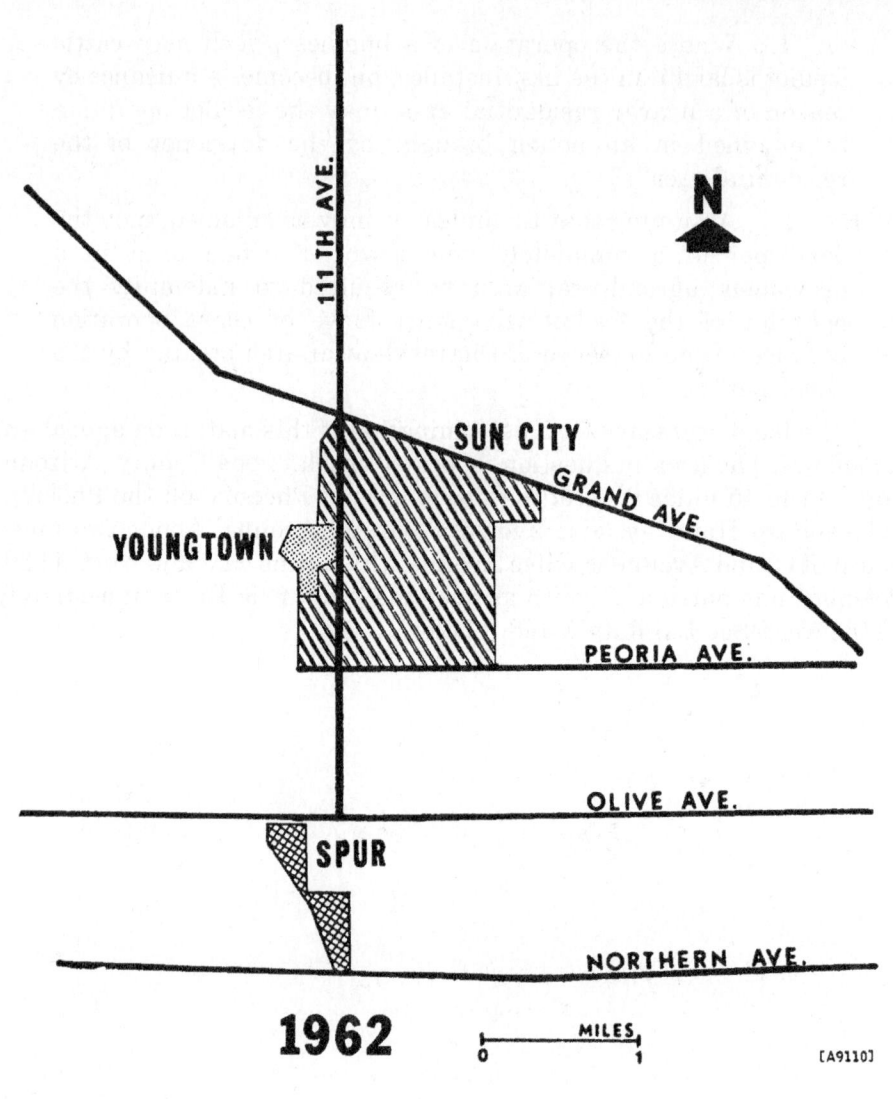

EXHIBIT A

EXHIBIT B

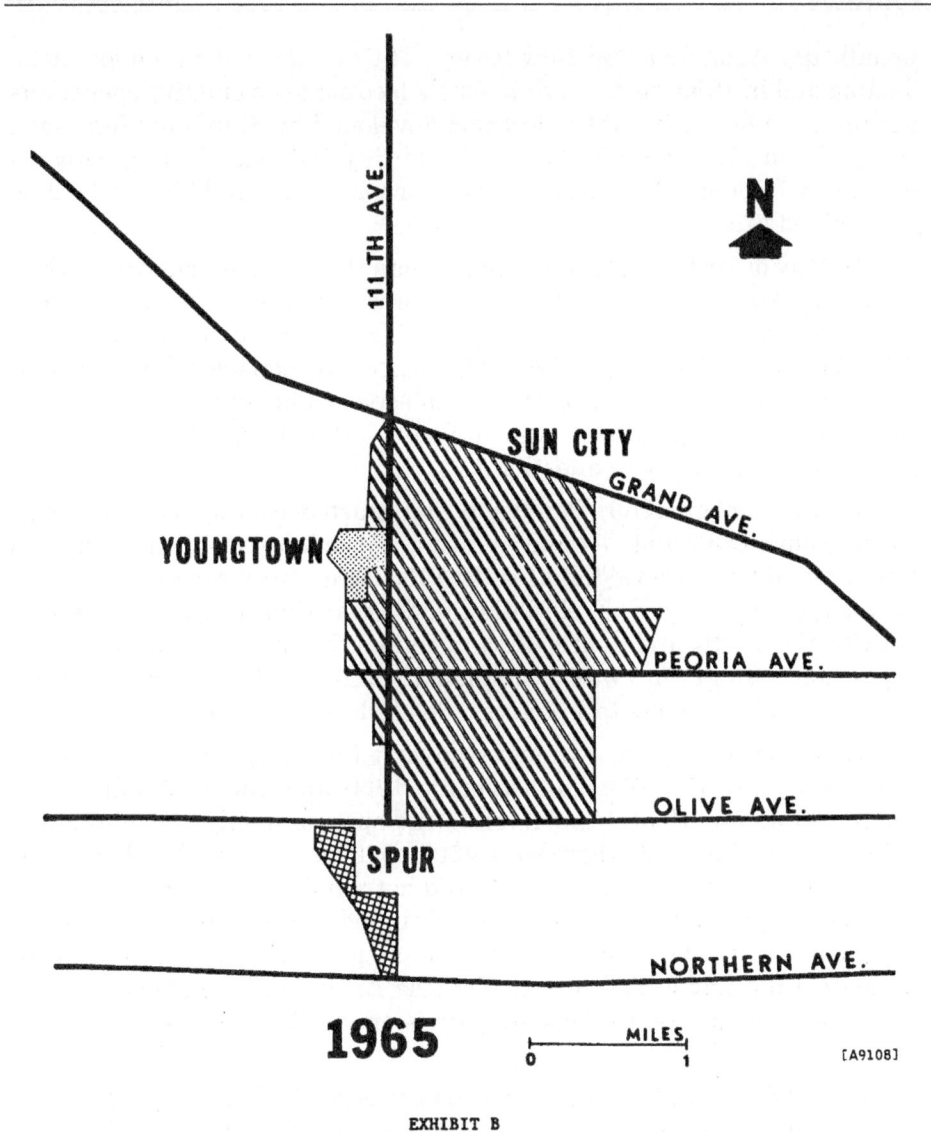

Farming started in this area about 1911. In 1929, with the completion of the Carl Pleasant Dam, gravity flow water became available to the property located to the west of the Agua Fria River, though land to the east remained dependent upon well water for irrigation. By 1950, the only urban areas in the vicinity were the agriculturally related communities of Peoria, El Mirage, and Surprise located along Grand Avenue. Along 111th Avenue, approximately one mile south of Grand Avenue and 1½ miles north of Olive Avenue, the community of Youngtown was commenced in 1954. Youngtown is a retirement community appealing primarily to senior citizens.

In 1956, Spur's predecessors in interest, H. Marion Welborn and the Northside Hay Mill and Trading Company, developed feedlots, about ½ mile south of Olive Avenue, in an area between the confluence of the usually dry Agua Fria and New Rivers. The area is well suited for cattle feeding and in 1959, there were 25 cattle feeding pens or dairy operations within a 7 mile radius of the location developed by Spur's predecessors. In April and May of 1959, the Northside Hay Mill was feeding between 6,000 and 7,000 head of cattle and Welborn approximately 1,500 head on a combined area of 35 acres.

In May of 1959, Del Webb began to plan the development of an urban area to be known as Sun City. For this purpose, the Marinette and the Santa Fe Ranches, some 20,000 acres of farmland, were purchased for $15,000,000 or $750.00 per acre. This price was considerably less than the price of land located near the urban area of Phoenix, and along with the success of Youngtown was a factor influencing the decision to purchase the property in question.

By September 1959, Del Webb had started construction of a golf course south of Grand Avenue and Spur's predecessors had started to level ground for more feedlot area. In 1960, Spur purchased the property in question and began a rebuilding and expansion program extending both to the north and south of the original facilities. By 1962, Spur's expansion program was completed and had expanded from approximately 35 acres to 114 acres. See Exhibit A above.

Accompanied by an extensive advertising campaign, homes were first offered by Del Webb in January 1960 and the first unit to be completed was south of Grand Avenue and approximately 2½ miles north of Spur. By 2 May 1960, there were 450 to 500 houses completed or under construction. At this time, Del Webb did not consider odors from the Spur feed pens a problem and Del Webb continued to develop in a southerly direction, until sales resistance became so great that the parcels were difficult if not impossible to sell. Thomas E. Breen, Vice President and General Manager of the housing division of Del Webb, testified at deposition as follows:

> Q: Did you ever have any discussions with Tony Cole at or about the time the sales office was opened south of Peoria concerning the problem in sales as the development came closer towards the feed lots?
>
> A: Not at the time that that facility was opened. That was subsequent to that.
>
> Q: All right, what is it that you recall about conversations with Cole on that subject?
>
> A: Well, when the feed lot problem became a bigger problem, which, really, to the best of my recollection, commenced to become a serious problem in 1963, and there was some talk about not developing that area because of sales resistance, and to my recollection we shifted—we had planned at that time to the eastern portion of the property, and it was a consideration.

Q: Was any specific suggestion made by Mr. Cole as to the line of demarcation that should be drawn or anything of that type exactly where the development should cease?

A: I don't recall anything specific as far as the definite line would be, other than, you know, that it would be advisable to stay out of the southwestern portion there because of sales resistance.

Q: And to the best of your recollection, this was in about 1963?

A: That would be my recollection, yes. . . .

Q: As you recall it, what was the reason that the suggestion was not adopted to stop developing towards the southwest of the development?

A: Well, as far as I know, that decision was made subsequent to that time.

Q: Right. But I mean at that time?

A: Well, at that time what I am really referring to is more of a long-range planning than immediate planning, and I think it was the case of just trying to figure out how far you could go with it before you really ran into a lot of sales resistance and found a necessity to shift the direction.

Q: So the plan was to go as far as you could until the resistance got to the point where you couldn't go any further?

A: I would say that is reasonable, yes.

By December 1967, Del Webb's property had extended south to Olive Avenue and Spur was within 500 feet of Olive Avenue to the north. See Exhibit B above. Del Webb filed its original complaint alleging that in excess of 1,300 lots in the southwest portion were unfit for development for sale as residential lots because of the operation of the Spur feedlot.

Del Webb's suit complained that the Spur feeding operation was a public nuisance because of the flies and the odor which were drifting or being blown by the prevailing south to north wind over the southern portion of Sun City. At the time of the suit, Spur was feeding between 20,000 and 30,000 head of cattle, and the facts amply support the finding of the trial court that the feed pens had become a nuisance to the people who resided in the southern part of Del Webb's development. The testimony indicated that cattle in a commercial feedlot will produce 35 to 40 pounds of wet manure per day, per head, or over a million pounds of wet manure per day for 30,000 head of cattle, and that despite the admittedly good feedlot management and good housekeeping practices by Spur, the resulting odor and flies produced an annoying if not unhealthy situation as far as the senior citizens of southern Sun City were concerned. There is no doubt that some of the citizens of Sun City were unable to enjoy the outdoor living which Del Webb had advertised and that Del Webb was faced with sales resistance from prospective purchasers as well as strong and persistent complaints from the people who had purchased homes in that area.

Trial was commenced before the court with an advisory jury. The advisory jury was later discharged and the trial was continued before the court alone. Findings of fact and conclusions of law were requested and given. The case was vigorously contested, including special actions in this court on some of the matters. In one of the special actions before this court, Spur agreed to, and did, shut down its operation without prejudice to a determination of the matter on appeal. On appeal the many questions raised were extensively briefed.

It is noted, however, that neither the citizens of Sun City nor Youngtown are represented in this lawsuit and the suit is solely between Del E. Webb Development Company and Spur Industries, Inc.

*May Spur Be Enjoined?*

The difference between a private nuisance and a public nuisance is generally one of degree. A private nuisance is one affecting a single individual or a definite small number of persons in the enjoyment of private rights not common to the public, while a public nuisance is one affecting the rights enjoyed by citizens as a part of the public. To constitute a public nuisance, the nuisance must affect a considerable number of people or an entire community or neighborhood. City of Phoenix v. Johnson, 51 Ariz. 115, 75 P.2d 30 (1938).

Where the injury is slight, the remedy for minor inconveniences lies in an action for damages rather than in one for an injunction. Kubby v. Hammond, 68 Ariz. 17, 198 P.2d 134 (1948). Moreover, some courts have held, in the "balancing of conveniences" cases, that damages may be the sole remedy. See Boomer v. Atlantic Cement Co., 26 N.Y.2d 219, 309 N.Y.S.2d 312, 257 N.E.2d 870, 40 A.L.R.3d 590 (1970), and annotation comments, 40 A.L.R.3d 601.

Thus, it would appear from the admittedly incomplete record as developed in the trial court, that, at most, residents of Youngtown would be entitled to damages rather than injunctive relief.

We have no difficulty, however, in agreeing with the conclusion of the trial court that Spur's operation was an enjoinable public nuisance as far as the people in the southern portion of Del Webb's Sun City were concerned.

§ 36–601, subsec. A reads as follows:

§ 36–601. Public nuisances dangerous to public health

A. The following conditions are specifically declared public nuisances dangerous to the public health:

> 1. Any condition or place in populous areas which constitutes a breeding place for flies, rodents, mosquitoes and other insects which are capable of carrying and

transmitting disease-causing organisms to any person or persons.

By this statute, before an otherwise lawful (and necessary) business may be declared a public nuisance, there must be a "populous" area in which people are injured:

> [I]t hardly admits a doubt that, in determining the question as to whether a lawful occupation is so conducted as to constitute a nuisance as a matter of fact, the locality and surroundings are of the first importance. (citations omitted) A business which is not per se a public nuisance may become such by being carried on at a place where the health, comfort, or convenience of a populous neighborhood is affected. . . . What might amount to a serious nuisance in one locality by reason of the density of the population, or character of the neighborhood affected, may in another place and under different surroundings be deemed proper and unobjectionable. . . .

MacDonald v. Perry, 32 Ariz. 39, 49–50, 255 P. 494, 497 (1927).

It is clear that as to the citizens of Sun City, the operation of Spur's feedlot was both a public and a private nuisance. They could have successfully maintained an action to abate the nuisance. Del Webb, having shown a special injury in the loss of sales, had a standing to bring suit to enjoin the nuisance. Engle v. Clark, 53 Ariz. 472, 90 P.2d 994 (1939); City of Phoenix v. Johnson, supra. The judgment of the trial court permanently enjoining the operation of the feedlot is affirmed.

*Must Del Webb Indemnify Spur?*

A suit to enjoin a nuisance sounds in equity and the courts have long recognized a special responsibility to the public when acting as a court of equity:

> Courts of equity may, and frequently do, go much further both to give and withhold relief in furtherance of the public interest than they are accustomed to go when only private interests are involved. Accordingly, the granting or withholding of relief may properly be dependent upon considerations of public interest. . . .

27 Am.Jur.2d, Equity, page 626.

In addition to protecting the public interest, however, courts of equity are concerned with protecting the operator of a lawful, albeit noxious, business from the result of a knowing and willful encroachment by others near his business.

In the so-called "coming to the nuisance" cases, the courts have held that the residential landowner may not have relief if he knowingly came into a neighborhood reserved for industrial or agricultural endeavors and has been damaged thereby:

Plaintiffs chose to live in an area uncontrolled by zoning laws or restrictive covenants and remote from urban development. In such an area plaintiffs cannot complain that legitimate agricultural pursuits are being carried on in the vicinity, nor can plaintiffs, having chosen to build in an agricultural area, complain that the agricultural pursuits carried on in the area depreciate the value of their homes. The area being *primarily agricultural,* any opinion reflecting the value of such property must take this factor into account. The standards affecting the value of residence property in an urban setting, subject to zoning controls and controlled planning techniques, cannot be the standards by which agricultural properties are judged.

People employed in a city who build their homes in suburban areas of the county beyond the limits of a city and zoning regulations do so for a reason. Some do so to avoid the high taxation rate imposed by cities, or to avoid special assessments for street, sewer and water projects. They usually build on improved or hard surface highways, which have been built either at state or county expense and thereby avoid special assessments for these improvements. It may be that they desire to get away from the congestion of traffic, smoke, noise, foul air and the many other annoyances of city life. But with all these advantages in going beyond the area which is zoned and restricted to protect them in their homes, they must be prepared to take the disadvantages.

Dill v. Excel Packing Company, 183 Kan. 513, 525, 526, 331 P.2d 539, 548, 549 (1958). See also East St. Johns Shingle Co. v. City of Portland, 195 Or. 505, 246 P.2d 554, 560–562 (1952).

Were Webb the only party injured, we would feel justified in holding that the doctrine of "coming to the nuisance" would have been a bar to the relief asked by Webb, and, on the other hand, had Spur located the feedlot near the outskirts of a city and had the city grown toward the feedlot, Spur would have to suffer the cost of abating the nuisance as to those people locating within the growth pattern of the expanding city:

> The case affords, perhaps, an example where a business established at a place remote from population is gradually surrounded and becomes part of a populous center, so that a business which formerly was not an interference with the rights of others has become so by the encroachment of the population. . . .

City of Ft. Smith v. Western Hide & Fur Co., 153 Ark. 99, 103, 239 S.W. 724, 726 (1922).

We agree, however, with the Massachusetts court that:

> The law of nuisance affords no rigid rule to be applied in all instances. It is elastic. It undertakes to require only that which

is fair and reasonable under all the circumstances. In a commonwealth like this, which depends for its material prosperity so largely on the continued growth and enlargement of manufacturing of diverse varieties, "extreme rights" cannot be enforced. . . .

Stevens v. Rockport Granite Co., 216 Mass. 486, 488, 104 N.E. 371, 373 (1914).

There is no indication in the instant case at the time Spur and its predecessors located in western Maricopa County that a new city would spring up, full-blown, alongside the feeding operation and that the developer of that city would ask the court to order Spur to move because of the new city. Spur is required to move not because of any wrongdoing on the part of Spur, but because of a proper and legitimate regard of the courts for the rights and interests of the public.

Del Webb, on the other hand, is entitled to the relief prayed for (a permanent injunction), not because Webb is blameless, but because of the damage to the people who have been encouraged to purchase homes in Sun City. It does not equitably or legally follow, however, that Webb, being entitled to the injunction, is then free of any liability to Spur if Webb has in fact been the cause of the damage Spur has sustained. It does not seem harsh to require a developer, who has taken advantage of the lesser land values in a rural area as well as the availability of large tracts of land on which to build and develop a new town or city in the area, to indemnify those who are forced to leave as a result.

Having brought people to the nuisance to the foreseeable detriment of Spur, Webb must indemnify Spur for a reasonable amount of the cost of moving or shutting down. It should be noted that this relief to Spur is limited to a case wherein a developer has, with foreseeability, brought into a previously agricultural or industrial area the population which makes necessary the granting of an injunction against a lawful business and for which the business has no adequate relief.

It is therefore the decision of this court that the matter be remanded to the trial court for a hearing upon the damages sustained by the defendant Spur as a reasonable and direct result of the granting of the permanent injunction. Since the result of the appeal may appear novel and both sides have obtained a measure of relief, it is ordered that each side will bear its own costs.

## Prah v. Maretti
Supreme Court of Wisconsin, 1982.
108 Wis.2d 223, 321 N.W.2d 182.

■ ABRAHAMSON, JUSTICE.

This appeal from a judgment of the circuit court for Waukesha county, Max Raskin, circuit judge, was certified to this court by the court of appeals, sec. (Rule) 809.61, Stats. 1979–80, as presenting an issue of first impression, namely, whether an owner of a solar-heated residence states a claim upon which relief can be granted when he asserts that his neighbor's proposed construction of a residence (which conforms to existing deed restrictions and local ordinances) interferes with his access to an unobstructed path for sunlight across the neighbor's property. This case thus involves a conflict between one landowner (Glenn Prah, the plaintiff) interested in unobstructed access to sunlight across adjoining property as a natural source of energy and an adjoining landowner (Richard D. Maretti, the defendant) interested in the development of his land.

The circuit court concluded that the plaintiff presented no claim upon which relief could be granted and granted summary judgment for the defendant. We reverse the judgment of the circuit court and remand the cause to the circuit court for further proceedings.

According to the complaint, the plaintiff is the owner of a residence which was constructed during the years 1978–1979. The complaint alleges that the residence has a solar system which includes collectors on the roof to supply energy for heat and hot water and that after the plaintiff built his solar-heated house, the defendant purchased the lot adjacent to and immediately to the south of the plaintiff's lot and commenced planning construction of a home. The complaint further states that when the plaintiff learned of defendant's plans to build the house he advised the defendant that if the house were built at the proposed location, defendant's house would substantially and adversely affect the integrity of plaintiff's solar system and could cause plaintiff other damage. Nevertheless, the defendant began construction. The complaint further alleges that the plaintiff is entitled to "unrestricted use of the sun and its solar power" and demands judgment for injunctive relief and damages.

After filing his complaint, the plaintiff moved for a temporary injunction to restrain and enjoin construction by the defendant. In ruling on that motion the circuit court heard testimony, received affidavits and viewed the site.

The record made on the motion reveals the following additional facts: Plaintiff's home was the first residence built in the subdivision, and although plaintiff did not build his house in the center of the lot it was built in accordance with applicable restrictions. Plaintiff advised defendant that if the defendant's home were built at the proposed site it would cause a shadowing effect on the solar collectors which would reduce the efficiency of the system and possibly damage the system. To avoid these adverse effects, plaintiff requested defendant to locate his home an additional several feet away from the plaintiff's lot line, the exact number being disputed. Plaintiff and defendant failed to reach an agreement on the location of defendant's home before defendant started construction. The Architectural Control Committee of the subdivision and the Planning Commission of the City of Muskego approved the defendant's plans for his home, including its location on the lot. After such approval, the defendant apparently changed the grade of the property without prior notice to the Architectural Control Committee. The problem with defendant's proposed construction, as far as the plaintiff's interests are concerned, arises from a combination of the grade and the distance of defendant's home from the defendant's lot line.

The circuit court denied plaintiff's motion for injunctive relief, declared it would entertain a motion for summary judgment and thereafter entered judgment in favor of the defendant.

As to the claim of private nuisance the circuit court concluded that the law of private nuisance requires the court to make "a comparative evaluation of the conflicting interests and to weigh the gravity of the harm to the plaintiff against the utility of the defendant's conduct." The circuit court concluded: "A comparative evaluation of the conflicting interests, keeping in mind the omissions and commissions of both Prah and Maretti, indicates that defendant's conduct does not cause the gravity of the harm which the plaintiff himself may well have avoided by proper planning." . . .

We consider first whether the complaint states a claim for relief based on common law private nuisance. When one landowner's use of his or her property unreasonably interferes with another's enjoyment of his or her property, that use is said to be a private nuisance.

The Restatement defines private nuisance as "a nontrespassory invasion of another's interest in the private use and enjoyment of land." Restatement (Second) of Torts sec. 821D (1977). The phrase "interest in the private use and enjoyment of land" as used in sec. 821D is broadly defined to include any disturbance of the enjoyment of property. The comment in the Restatement describes the landowner's interest protected by private nuisance law as follows:

> The phrase "interest in the use and enjoyment of land" is used in this Restatement in a broad sense. It comprehends not only the interests that a person may have only in the actual present use of land for residential, agricultural, commercial, industrial and other purposes, but also his interests in having the present use value of the land unimpaired by changes in its physical condition. Thus the destruction of trees on vacant land is as much an invasion of the owner's interest in its use and enjoyment as is the destruction of crops or flowers that he is growing on the land for his present use. "Interest in use and enjoyment" also comprehends the pleasure, comfort and enjoyment that a person normally derives from the occupancy of land. Freedom from discomfort and annoyance while using land is often as important to a person as freedom from physical interruption with his use or freedom from detrimental change in the physical condition of the land itself.

Restatement (Second) of Torts, Sec. 821D, Comment b, p. 101 (1977).

Although the defendant's obstruction of plaintiff's access to sunlight appears to fall within the Restatement's broad concept of a private nuisance as a nontrespassory invasion of another's interest in the private use and enjoyment of land, the defendant asserts that he has a right to develop his property in compliance with statutes, ordinances and private covenants without regard to the effect of such development upon the plaintiff's access to sunlight. In essence, the defendant is asking this court to hold that the private nuisance doctrine is not applicable in the instant case and that his right to develop his land is a right which is per se superior to his neighbor's interest in access to sunlight. This position is expressed in the maxim "cujus est solum, ejus est usque ad infernos," that is, the owner of land owns up to the sky and down to the center of the earth. The rights of the surface owner are, however, not unlimited.

The defendant is not completely correct in asserting that the common law did not protect a landowner's access to sunlight across adjoining property. At English common law landowner could acquire a right to receive sunlight across adjoining land by both express agreement and under the judge-made doctrine of "ancient lights." Under the doctrine of ancient lights if the landowner had received sunlight across adjoining property for a specified period of time, the landowner was entitled to continue to receive unobstructed access to sunlight across the adjoining property. Under the doctrine the landowner acquired a negative prescriptive easement and could prevent the adjoining landowner from obstructing access to light.

Although American courts have not been as receptive to protecting a landowner's access to sunlight as the English courts, American courts have afforded some protection to a landowner's interest in access to sunlight. American courts honor express easements to sunlight. American courts initially enforced the English common law doctrine of ancient lights, but later every state which considered the doctrine repudiated it as inconsistent with the needs of a developing country. Indeed, for just that reason this court concluded that an easement to light and air over adjacent property could not be created or acquired by prescription and has been unwilling to recognize such an easement by implication.

Many jurisdictions in this country have protected a landowner from malicious obstruction of access to light (the spite fence cases) under the common law private nuisance doctrine. If an activity is motivated by malice it lacks utility and the harm it causes others outweighs any social values. This court was reluctant to protect a landowner's interest in sunlight even against a spite fence, only to be overruled by the legislature. Shortly after this court upheld a landowner's right to erect a useless and unsightly sixteen-foot spite fence four feet from his neighbor's windows, Metzger v. Hochrein, 107 Wis. 267, 83 N.W. 308 (1900), the legislature enacted a law specifically defining a spite fence as an actionable private nuisance. Thus a landowner's interest in sunlight has been protected in this country by common law private nuisance law at least in the narrow context of the modern American rule invalidating spite fences. See, *e.g.,* Sundowner, Inc. v. King, 95 Idaho 367, 509 P.2d 785 (1973); Restatement (Second) of Torts, sec. 829 (1977).

This court's reluctance in the nineteenth and early part of the twentieth century to provide broader protection for a landowner's access to sunlight was premised on three policy considerations. First, the right of landowners to use their property as they wished, as long as they did not cause physical damage to a neighbor, was jealously guarded.

Second, sunlight was valued only for aesthetic enjoyment or as illumination. Since artificial light could be used for illumination loss of sunlight was at most a personal annoyance which was given little, if any, weight by society.

Third, society had a significant interest in not restricting or impeding land development. This court repeatedly emphasized that in the growth period of the nineteenth and early twentieth centuries change is to be expected and is essential to property and that recognition of a right to sunlight would hinder property development.

Considering these three policies, this court concluded that in the absence of an express agreement granting access to sunlight, a landowner's obstruction of another's access to sunlight was not actionable. These three policies are no longer fully accepted or applicable. They reflect factual circumstances and social priorities that are now obsolete.

First, society has increasingly regulated the use of land by the landowner for the general welfare. Euclid v. Ambler Realty Co., 272 U.S. 365, 47 S.Ct. 114, 71 L.Ed. 303 (1926); Just v. Marinette, 56 Wis.2d 7, 201 N.W.2d 761 (1972).

Second, access to sunlight has taken on a new significance in recent years. In this case the plaintiff seeks to protect access to sunlight, not for aesthetic reasons or as a source of illumination but as a source of energy. Access to sunlight as an energy source is of significance both to the landowner who invests in solar collectors and to a society which has an interest in developing alternative sources of energy.

Third, the policy of favoring unhindered private development in an expanding economy is no longer in harmony with the realities of our society. The need for easy and rapid development is not as great today as it once was, while our perception of the value of sunlight as a source of energy has increased significantly.

Private nuisance law, the law traditionally used to adjudicate conflicts between private landowners, has the flexibility to protect both a landowner's right of access to sunlight and another landowner's right to develop land. Private nuisance law is better suited to regulate access to sunlight in modern society and is more in harmony with legislative policy and the prior decisions of this court than is an inflexible doctrine of non-recognition of any interest in access to sunlight across adjoining land.

We therefore hold that private nuisance law, that is, the reasonable use doctrine as set forth in the Restatement, is applicable to the instant case. Recognition of a nuisance claim for unreasonable obstruction of access to sunlight will not prevent land development or unduly hinder the use of adjoining land. It will promote the reasonable use and enjoyment of land in a manner suitable to the 1980's. That obstruction of access to light might be found to constitute a nuisance in certain circumstances does not mean that it will be or must be found to constitute a nuisance under all circumstances. The result in each case depends on whether the conduct complained of is unreasonable.

Accordingly we hold that the plaintiff in this case has stated a claim under which relief can be granted. Nonetheless we do not determine whether the plaintiff in this case is entitled to relief. In order to be entitled to relief the plaintiff must prove the elements required to establish actionable nuisance, and the conduct of the defendant herein must be judged by the reasonable use doctrine.

The judgment of the circuit court is reversed and the cause remanded for proceedings not inconsistent with this opinion.

■ CALLOW, JUSTICE, dissenting.

I firmly believe that a landowner's right to use his property within the limits of ordinances, statutes, and restrictions of record where such use is necessary to serve his legitimate needs is a fundamental precept of a free society which this court should strive to uphold.

As one commentator has suggested:

> It is fashionable to dismiss such values as deriving from a bygone era in which people valued development as a "goal in itself," but current market prices for real estate, and more particularly the premiums paid for land whose zoning permits intensive use, suggest that people still place very high values on such rights.

William, *Solar Access and Property Rights: A Maverick Analysis,* 11 Conn.L.Rev. 430, 443 (1979) (footnote omitted).

[The dissent then argued that a solar collector was an "unusually sensitive use," and thus not protected by private nuisance law.]

Because I do not believe that the facts of the present case give rise to a cause of action for private nuisance, I dissent.

## NOTES

1. *Consistency. Boomer* gives the plaintiff damages, but not an injunction (except an injunction that will be vacated on payment of damages). *Spur* gives the plaintiff an injunction, but awards the defendant damages. Can these cases be reconciled? Is it satisfactory to say that every

case must be judged on its own facts, or do the needs of litigants require greater certainty?

2. *Multiple parties.* In *Spur*, there was only one plaintiff. If there had been 50 plaintiffs (and also 100 similarly situated landowners who were not plaintiffs) would it have been feasible to award damages to the defendant? Of course, the problem of multiple parties is only one aspect of transaction costs.

3. *Competing interests.* Surely, in the coming decades environmental considerations will play a greater role in nuisance cases. But when so many of our citizens are ill-housed and ill-fed, one cannot be completely unconcerned with the need to produce cement and beef. Are the interests of the potential consumers of cement in *Boomer* and of beef in *Spur* adequately represented in these court cases? Is it likely that a county or city zoning board would do a better job than the court in representing these interests? What of a regional, statewide, or national regulatory body?

4. *Standing.* In *Spur*, the court assumes that private citizens can enjoin a public nuisance. Can you reconcile this with the black letter law summarized at the beginning of this Assignment?

5. *Injured individuals.* Suppose Del Webb preferred to have Spur remain rather than to have Spur move at Del Webb's expense? If Spur remained, what remedies would the individual homeowners have?

6. *Policy.* In the Principal Problem, Wade will argue that the court should not adopt the reasoning and result of *Prah*. What policy arguments should he advance to support his position? Is *Prah* a sensible decision?

It is interesting to note that the Justice Department and the Natural Resources Defense Council joined Prah in his appeal to the Wisconsin Court of Appeals and submitted amicus curiae briefs. In this regard, one student commentator made the following observation: "Propelled by the Carter Administration's policy of encouraging the use of solar energy, the Justice Department argued that a nuisance action should lie and that the outcome of the action should depend on the balance of the interest in Maretti's house versus the interest in Prah's solar collectors, taking into account the relative social value of each. The NRDC asserted that a judicial decision in the case would not usurp legislative authority or interfere with land use planning."[12]

7. *Unobstructed view cases.* Should a court follow the reasoning of *Prah* when considering a case involving a defendant's intentional obstruction of a plaintiff's view? Are there any reasons why interference with a plaintiff's light should constitute a private nuisance but interference with a plaintiff's view should not be so construed?

8. *Legislative response.* Several states have enacted statutes governing interference with solar access, although the content of the statutes vary. In fact, Wisconsin passed such a statute while the *Prah* decision was pending. The Wisconsin legislation provides for the payment of damages for certain obstructions to solar energy systems[13] and creates a permit

---

[12] See Recent Developments, 14 Envtl L. 223, 225–26 (1983).
[13] See, e.g., Wis.Stat.Ann. § 700.41(3) (2010).

procedure which municipalities may choose to adopt under which solar collector owners may obtain a prescriptive easement for light over adjoining property in certain instances.[14] Nevertheless, the *Prah* court chose to resolve the case on common law rather than statutory grounds. An important question left unanswered by the *Prah* decision is whether the statutory scheme coexists with the common law cause of action for nuisance in jurisdictions which have adopted the permit system.[15]

9. *The Restatement approach.* Restatement, Second, Torts § 826 (1979) provides that the defendant's conduct is actionable if "(a) the gravity of the harm outweighs the utility of the actor's conduct, or (b) the harm caused by the conduct is serious and the financial burden of compensating for this and similar harm to others would not make the continuation of the conduct not feasible." Compare paragraph (b) of § 826 with § 829A which provides that "[a]n intentional invasion of another's interest in the use and enjoyment of land is unreasonable if the harm resulting from the invasion is severe and greater than the other should be required to bear without compensation." Thus, § 826(b) of the Restatement focuses on the defendant's ability to pay whereas § 829A is concerned with harm to the plaintiff. What should be done if the payment of damages would bankrupt the defendant, but the harm caused the plaintiff is greater than it should be required to bear without compensation?

10. *The Principal Problem.* In the Principal Problem, what effect will fairness considerations have on the outcome? How will efficiency concerns shape the proper relief?

---

[14] See Wis.Stat.Ann. § 66.0403 (2010).

[15] See Bronin, Solar Rights, 89 Boston U. L. Rev. 1217 (2009) (expressing the view that current law provides relatively weak overall protection for solar access nationally); Rule, Shadows on the Cathedral: Solar Access Laws in a Different Light, 2010 U. Ill L. Rev. 851 (2010) (observing that solar access protections are increasing, but are fragmented across a variety of property and liability rules and do not provide sufficient protection of scarce air rights for neighbors).

## D. GOVERNMENT AUTHORITY, PUBLIC USES, AND PRIVATE RIGHTS

## ASSIGNMENT 29

# GOVERNMENTAL POWER TO TAKE PROPERTY: THE PUBLIC USE REQUIREMENT

### 1. INTRODUCTION

The power of eminent domain—the power of the government to take private property for public purposes—is inherent in sovereignty and thus is a power held by both the states and the federal government. However, the Fifth Amendment to the U.S. Constitution provides: "... nor shall private property be taken for public use, without just compensation." Under this language, the government's ability to take private property is limited by two conditions: (1) the taking must be for a public use, and (2) the property owner must receive just compensation. The framers of the Constitution included this provision to protect private property from unnecessary or uncompensated expropriation. Most state constitutions have similar provisions.[1] In this Assignment we consider how the "public use" requirement is or should be interpreted.

### 2. PRINCIPAL PROBLEM

Mill City suffers from a severely depressed economy, a budget deficit, and a high unemployment rate. To help alleviate the budget crisis, create new jobs and bring new business and tax revenues into the city, Mill City created the Mill Development Corporation (MDC), a private, nonprofit development corporation. MDC then created the Mill Development Plan (MDP). The MDP covers approximately ninety acres of land. The land is currently used for housing and small businesses. The proposal is to convert the ninety acres into several large commercial development projects with MDC leasing the land to a private developer for $1 per year for ninety-nine years. The developer will build and maintain the commercial projects. Mill City adopted the MDP and authorized MDC to acquire the necessary property to complete the project.

MDC then began a program of buying all of the land it could from voluntary sellers over a two year period. It purchased all but fifteen

---

[1] See, e.g., Cal. Const. art. I, § 19; N.Y. Const. art. I, § 7(a), as cited in Mossoff, The Death of *Poletown*: The Future of Eminent Domain after County of Wayne v. Hathcock, 2004 Mich. St. L. Rev. 837 (2004).

single-family residential properties. These remaining owners refused to sell.

Wanda Dairy lives on one of the parcels. She has lived her entire life in the house she currently owns. She is now almost ninety years old and wishes to keep her home and pass it on to members of her family. The other fourteen owners have similar stories. The owners do not want money; they just want to keep their homes. They all believe it is unfair for a large commercial developer to evict them from their sacred homes.

MDC has brought a condemnation action against Wanda. The action was brought under a statute governing municipal development projects (not under the statute covering slums and blighted areas).

Wanda seeks to stop the condemnation of her home. She argues that the public use requirement of her state's constitution prevents MDC from condemning her property for private commercial development. Her state constitution's public use requirement uses language identical to that of the Michigan constitution quoted in County of Wayne v. Hathcock, reprinted below. Based on the following cases, will she prevail?

## 3. MATERIALS FOR SOLUTION OF PRINCIPAL PROBLEM

### Hawaii Housing Authority v. Midkiff
Supreme Court of the United States, 1984.
467 U.S. 229, 104 S.Ct. 2321.

■ O'CONNOR, J.

The Fifth Amendment of the United States Constitution provides, in pertinent part, that "private property [shall not] be taken for public use, without just compensation." These cases present the question whether the Public Use Clause of that Amendment, made applicable to the States through the Fourteenth Amendment, prohibits the State of Hawaii from taking, with just compensation, title in real property from lessors and transferring it to lessees to reduce the concentration of ownership of fees simple in the State. We conclude that it does not.

The Hawaiian Islands were originally settled by Polynesian immigrants from the western Pacific. These settlers developed an economy around a feudal land tenure system in which one island high chief, the ali'i nui, controlled the land and assigned it for development to certain subchiefs. The subchiefs would then reassign the land to other lower ranking chiefs, who would administer the land and govern the farmers and other tenants working it. All land was held at the will of the ali'i nui and eventually had to be returned to his trust. There was no private ownership of land. . . .

Beginning in the early 1800's, Hawaiian leaders and American settlers repeatedly attempted to divide the lands of the kingdom among the crown, the chiefs, and the common people. These efforts proved largely unsuccessful, however, and the land remained in the hands of a few. In the Mid-1960's, after extensive hearings, the Hawaii Legislature discovered that, while the State and Federal Governments owned almost 49% of the State's land, another 47% was in the hands of only 72 private landowners.... The legislature further found that 18 landholders, with tracts of 21,000 acres or more, owned more than 40% of this land and that on Oahu, the most urbanized of the islands, 22 landowners owned 72.5% of the fee simple titles.... The legislature concluded that concentrated land ownership was responsible for skewing the State's residential fee simple market, inflating land prices, and injuring the public tranquility and welfare.

To redress these problems, the legislature decided to compel the large landowners to break up their estates. The legislature considered requiring large landowners to sell lands which they were leasing to homeowners. However, the landowners strongly resisted this scheme, pointing out the significant federal tax liabilities they would incur. Indeed, the landowners claimed that the federal tax laws were the primary reason they previously had chosen to lease, and not sell, their lands. Therefore, to accommodate the needs of both lessors and lessees, the Hawaii Legislature enacted the Land Reform Act of 1967 (Act), Haw. Rev. Stat., ch. 516, which created a mechanism for condemning residential tracts and for transferring ownership of the condemned fees simple to existing lessees. By condemning the land in question, the Hawaii Legislature intended to make the land sales involuntary, thereby making the federal tax consequences less severe while still facilitating the redistribution of fees simple....

Under the Act's condemnation scheme, tenants living on single-family residential lots within developmental tracts at least five acres in size are entitled to ask the Hawaii Housing Authority (HHA) to condemn the property on which they live. When 25 eligible tenants,[2] or tenants on half the lots in the tract, whichever is less, file appropriate applications, the Act authorizes HHA to hold a public hearing to determine whether acquisition by the State of all or part of the tract will "effectuate the public purposes" of the Act. If HHA finds that these public purposes will be served, it is authorized to designate some or all of the lots in the tract for acquisition. It then acquires, at prices set either by condemnation trial or by negotiation between lessors and lessees, the former fee owners' full "right, title, and interest" in the land....

In April 1977, HHA held a public hearing concerning the proposed acquisition of some of appellees' lands. HHA made the statutorily required finding that acquisition of appellees' lands would effectuate the public purposes of the Act. Then, in October 1978, it directed appellees to

---

[2] An eligible tenant is one who, among other things, owns a house on the lot, has a bona fide intent to live on the lot or be a resident of the State, shows proof of ability to pay for a fee interest in it, and does not own residential land elsewhere nearby. Haw. Rev. Stat. §§ 516-33(3), (4), (7) (1977).

negotiate with certain lessees concerning the sale of the designated properties. Those negotiations failed, and HHA subsequently ordered appellees to submit to compulsory arbitration.

Rather than comply with the compulsory arbitration order, appellees filed suit, in February 1979, in United States District Court, asking that the Act be declared unconstitutional and that its enforcement be enjoined.... The District Court found that the Act's goals were within the bounds of the State's police powers and that the means the legislature had chosen to serve those goals were not arbitrary, capricious, or selected in bad faith.

The Court of Appeals for the Ninth Circuit reversed. First, the Court of Appeals decided that the District Court had permissibly chosen not to abstain from the exercise of its jurisdiction. Then, the Court of Appeals determined that the Act could not pass the requisite judicial scrutiny of the Public Use Clause. It found that the transfers contemplated by the Act were unlike those of takings previously held to constitute "public uses" by this Court. The court further determined that the public purposes offered by the Hawaii Legislature were not deserving of judicial deference. The court concluded that the Act was simply "a naked attempt on the part of the state of Hawaii to take the private property of A and transfer it to B solely for B's private use and benefit." One judge dissented....

The majority of the Court of Appeals next determined that the Act violates the "public use" requirement of the Fifth and Fourteenth Amendments. On this argument, however, we find ourselves in agreement with the dissenting judge in the Court of Appeals.

The starting point for our analysis of the Act's constitutionality is the Court's decision in *Berman v. Parker*, 348 U.S. 26 (1954). In *Berman*, the Court held constitutional the District of Columbia Redevelopment Act of 1945. That Act provided both for the comprehensive use of the eminent domain power to redevelop slum areas and for the possible sale or lease of the condemned lands to private interests....

The "public use" requirement is thus coterminous with the scope of a sovereign's police powers....

To be sure, the Court's cases have repeatedly stated that "one person's property may not be taken for the benefit of another private person without a justifying public purpose, even though compensation be paid." Thus, in *Missouri Pacific R. Co. v. Nebraska*, 164 U.S. 403 (1896), where the "order in question was not, *and was not claimed to be,* ... a taking of private property for a public use under the right of eminent domain," the Court invalidated a compensated taking of property for lack of a justifying public purpose. But where the exercise of the eminent domain power is rationally related to a conceivable public purpose, the Court has never held a compensated taking to be proscribed by the Public Use Clause....

On this basis, we have no trouble concluding that the Hawaii Act is constitutional. The people of Hawaii have attempted, much as the settlers of the original 13 Colonies did, to reduce the perceived social and economic evils of a land oligopoly traceable to their monarchs. The land oligopoly has, according to the Hawaii Legislature, created artificial deterrents to the normal functioning of the State's residential land market and forced thousands of individual homeowners to lease, rather than buy, the land underneath their homes. Regulating oligopoly and the evils associated with it is a classic exercise of a State's police powers.... We cannot disapprove of Hawaii's exercise of this power.

Nor can we condemn as irrational the Act's approach to correcting the land oligopoly problem. The Act presumes that when a sufficiently large number of persons declare that they are willing but unable to buy lots at fair prices the land market is malfunctioning. When such a malfunction is signalled, the Act authorizes HHA to condemn lots in the relevant tract. The Act limits the number of lots any one tenant can purchase and authorizes HHA to use public funds to ensure that the market dilution goals will be achieved. This is a comprehensive and rational approach to identifying and correcting market failure.

Of course, this Act, like any other, may not be successful in achieving its intended goals. But "whether *in fact* the provision will accomplish its objectives is not the question: the [constitutional requirement] is satisfied if . . . the . . . [state] Legislature *rationally could have believed* that the [Act] would promote its objective." *Western & Southern Life Ins. Co. v. State Bd. of Equalization*, 451 U.S. 648, 671–672 (1981).... When the legislature's purpose is legitimate and its means are not irrational, our cases make clear that empirical debates over the wisdom of takings—no less than debates over the wisdom of other kinds of socioeconomic legislation—are not to be carried out in the federal courts. Redistribution of fees simple to correct deficiencies in the market determined by the state legislature to be attributable to land oligopoly is a rational exercise of the eminent domain power. Therefore, the Hawaii statute must pass the scrutiny of the Public Use Clause....

The mere fact that property taken outright by eminent domain is transferred in the first instance to private beneficiaries does not condemn that taking as having only a private purpose. The Court long ago rejected any literal requirement that condemned property be put into use for the general public. "It is not essential that the entire community, nor even any considerable portion, . . . directly enjoy or participate in any improvement in order [for it] to constitute a public use." *Rindge Co. v. Los Angeles*, 262 U.S., at 707. "[What] in its immediate aspect [is] only a private transaction may . . . be raised by its class or character to a public affair." *Block v. Hirsh*, 256 U.S., at 155. As the unique way titles were held in Hawaii skewed the land market, exercise of the power of eminent domain was justified. The Act advances its purposes without the State's taking actual possession of the land. In such cases, government does not itself have to use property to legitimate the taking; it is only the taking's purpose, and not its mechanics, that must pass scrutiny under the Public Use Clause.

Similarly, the fact that a state legislature, and not the Congress, made the public use determination does not mean that judicial deference is less appropriate.[3] Judicial deference is required because, in our system of government, legislatures are better able to assess what public purposes should be advanced by an exercise of the taking power. State legislatures are as capable as Congress of making such determinations within their respective spheres of authority. Thus, if a legislature, state or federal, determines there are substantial reasons for an exercise of the taking power, courts must defer to its determination that the taking will serve a public use.

The State of Hawaii has never denied that the Constitution forbids even a compensated taking of property when executed for no reason other than to confer a private benefit on a particular private party. A purely private taking could not withstand the scrutiny of the public use requirement; it would serve no legitimate purpose of government and would thus be void. But no purely private taking is involved in these cases. The Hawaii Legislature enacted its Land Reform Act not to benefit a particular class of identifiable individuals but to attack certain perceived evils of concentrated property ownership in Hawaii—a legitimate public purpose. Use of the condemnation power to achieve this purpose is not irrational. Since we assume for purposes of these appeals that the weighty demand of just compensation has been met, the requirements of the Fifth and Fourteenth Amendments have been satisfied. Accordingly, we reverse the judgment of the Court of Appeals, and remand these cases for further proceedings in conformity with this opinion.

## County of Wayne v. Hathcock
Supreme Court of Michigan, 2004.
684 N.W.2d 765.

■ YOUNG, J.

We are presented again with a clash of two bedrock principles of our legal tradition: the sacrosanct right of individuals to dominion over their private property, on the one hand and, on the other, the state's authority to condemn private property for the commonwealth. In this case, Wayne County would use the power of eminent domain to condemn defendants'

---

[3] It is worth noting that the Fourteenth Amendment does not itself contain an independent "public use" requirement. Rather, that requirement is made binding on the States only by incorporation of the Fifth Amendment's Eminent Domain Clause through the Fourteenth Amendment's Due Process Clause. See *Chicago, B. & Q. R. Co. v. Chicago*, 166 U.S. 226 (1897). It would be ironic to find that state legislation is subject to greater scrutiny under the incorporated "public use" requirement than is congressional legislation under the express mandate of the Fifth Amendment.

real properties for the construction of a 1,300-acre business and technology park. This proposed commercial center is intended to reinvigorate the struggling economy of southeastern Michigan by attracting businesses, particularly those involved in developing new technologies, to the area.

Defendants argue that this exercise of the power of eminent domain is neither authorized by statute nor permitted under article 10 of the 1963 Michigan Constitution, which requires that any condemnation of private property advance a "public use." Both the Wayne Circuit Court and the Court of Appeals rejected these arguments—compelled, in no small measure, by this Court's opinion in *Poletown Neighborhood Council v. Detroit*, 410 Mich. 616, 304 N.W.2d 455 (1981).

We conclude that, although these condemnations are authorized by MCL 213.23, they do not pass constitutional muster under art 10, § 2 of our 1963 constitution. Section 2 permits the exercise of the power of eminent domain only for a "public use." In this case, Wayne County intends to transfer the condemned properties to private parties in a manner wholly inconsistent with the common understanding of "public use" at the time our Constitution was ratified. . . .

In April 2001, plaintiff Wayne County initiated actions to condemn nineteen parcels of land immediately south of Metropolitan Airport. . . . This dispute has its roots in recent renovations of Metropolitan Airport. The county's $2 billion construction program produced a new terminal and jet runway and, consequently, raised concerns that noise from increased air traffic would plague neighboring landowners. In an effort to obviate such problems, the county, funded by a partial grant of $21 million from the Federal Aviation Administration (FAA), began a program of purchasing neighboring properties through voluntary sales. Eventually, the county purchased approximately five hundred acres in nonadjacent plots scattered in a checkerboard pattern throughout an area south of Metropolitan Airport.

Wayne County's agreement with the FAA provided that any properties acquired through the noise abatement program were to be put to economically productive use. In order to fulfill this mandate, the county, through its Jobs and Economic Development Department, developed the idea of constructing a large business and technology park with a conference center, hotel accommodations, and a recreational facility. Thus, the "Pinnacle Project" was born.

The Pinnacle Project calls for the construction of a state-of-the-art business and technology park in a 1,300-acre area adjacent to Metropolitan Airport. The county avers that the Pinnacle Project will create thousands of jobs [30,000], and tens of millions of dollars in tax revenue [$350 million], while broadening the County's tax base from predominantly industrial to a mixture of industrial, service and technology. . . .

Having acquired over one thousand acres, the county determined that an additional forty-six parcels distributed in a checkerboard fashion throughout the project area were needed for the business and technology park. The county apparently determined that further efforts to negotiate additional voluntary sales would be futile and decided instead to invoke the power of eminent domain. Thus, on July 12, 2000, the Wayne County Commission adopted a Resolution of Necessity and Declaration of Taking (Resolution of Necessity) authorizing the acquisition of the remaining three hundred acres needed for the Pinnacle Project. [A]ccording to the county's estimates, nineteen additional parcels were still needed for the Pinnacle Project. These properties, owned by defendants, are the subject of the present condemnation actions.

In late April 2001, plaintiff initiated condemnation actions under the UCPA. In response, each property owner filed a motion to review the necessity of the proposed condemnations. . . . They argued, first, that the county lacked statutory authority to exercise the power of eminent domain in this manner. Second, defendants contended that acquisition of the subject properties was not necessary as required by statute. Finally, they challenged the constitutionality of these condemnation actions, maintaining that the Pinnacle Project would not serve a public purpose. . . .

On December 19, 2001, the trial court affirmed the county's determination of necessity. The court held that the takings were authorized by MCL 213.23, that the county did not abuse its discretion in determining that condemnation was necessary, and that the Pinnacle Project served a public purpose as defined by *Poletown*. . . .

Defendants appealed. . . . The Court of Appeals affirmed the trial court's decision. . . . We granted defendants' applications for leave to appeal. . . .

Art 10, § 2 of Michigan's 1963 Constitution provides that "private property shall not be taken for public use without just compensation therefor being first made or secured in a manner prescribed by law." Plaintiffs contend that the proposed condemnations are not "for public use," and therefore are not within constitutional bounds. Accordingly, our analysis must now focus on the "public use" requirement of Art 10, § 2. . . .

"Public use" is a legal term of art every bit as complex as "just compensation." It has reappeared as a positive limit on the state's power of eminent domain in Michigan's constitutions of 1850, 1908, and 1963, and each invocation of "public use" has been followed by litigation over the precise contours of this language. . . .

The question presented here is a fairly discrete one: are the condemnation of defendants' properties and the subsequent transfer of those properties to private entities pursuant to the Pinnacle Project consistent with the common understanding of "public use" at ratification? For the reasons stated below, we answer that question in the negative.

When our Constitution was ratified in 1963, it was well-established in this Court's eminent domain jurisprudence that the constitutional "public use" requirement was not an absolute bar against the transfer of condemned property to private entities. It was equally clear, however, that the constitutional "public use" requirement worked to prohibit the state from transferring condemned property to private entities for a *private* use. Thus, this Court's eminent domain jurisprudence—at least that portion concerning the reasons for which the state may condemn private property—has focused largely on the area between these poles.

Justice Ryan's *Poletown* dissent accurately describes the factors that distinguish takings in the former category from those in the latter according to our pre-1963 eminent domain jurisprudence. Accordingly, we conclude that the transfer of condemned property is a "public use" when it possess one of the three characteristics in our pre-1963 case law identified by Justice Ryan.

First, condemnations in which private land was constitutionally transferred by the condemning authority to a private entity involved "public necessity of the extreme sort otherwise impracticable. . . ." Justice Ryan listed "highways, railroads, canals, and other instrumentalities of commerce" as examples of this brand of necessity . . . The likelihood that property owners will engage in this tactic [holding out for excessive compensation] makes the acquisition of property for railroads, gas lines, highways, and other such "instrumentalities of commerce" a logistical and practical nightmare. Accordingly, this Court has held that the exercise of eminent domain in such cases—in which collective action is needed to acquire land for vital instrumentalities of commerce—is consistent with the constitutional "public use" requirement. . . .

Second, this Court has found that the transfer of condemned property to a private entity is consistent with the constitution's "public use" requirement when the private entity remains accountable to the public in its use of that property. . . . As Justice Ryan observed:

> This Court disapproved condemnation that would have facilitated the generation of water power by a private corporation because the power company "will own, lease, use, and control" the water power. In addition, [we] warned, "Land cannot be taken, under the exercise of the power of eminent domain, unless, after it is taken, it will be devoted to the *use* of the public, *independent of the will of the corporation taking it.*"

[T]hus, in the common understanding of those sophisticated in the law at the time of ratification, the "public use" requirement would have allowed for the transfer of condemned property to a private entity when the public retained a measure of control over the property.

Finally, condemned land may be transferred to a private entity when the selection of the land to be condemned is itself based on public concern. In Justice Ryan's words, the property must be selected on the basis of "facts of independent public significance," meaning that the underlying purposes for resorting to condemnation, rather than the subsequent use of condemned land, must satisfy the Constitution's public use requirement. . . .

The foregoing indicates that the transfer of condemned property to a private entity, seen through the eyes of an individual sophisticated in the law at the time of ratification of our 1963 Constitution, would be appropriate in one of three contexts: (1) where "public necessity of the extreme sort" requires collective action; (2) where the property remains subject to public oversight after transfer to a private entity; and (3) where the property is selected because of "facts of independent public significance," rather than the interests of the private entity to which the property is eventually transferred.

The exercise of eminent domain at issue here—the condemnation of defendants' properties for the Pinnacle Project and the subsequent transfer of those properties to private entities—implicates none of the saving elements noted by our pre-1963 eminent domain jurisprudence.

The Pinnacle Project's business and technology park is certainly not an enterprise "whose very *existence* depends on the use of land that can be assembled only by the coordination central government alone is capable of achieving." To the contrary, the landscape of our country is flecked with shopping centers, office parks, clusters of hotels, and centers of entertainment and commerce. We do not believe, and plaintiff does not contend, that these constellations required the exercise of eminent domain or any other form of collective public action for their formation.

Second, the Pinnacle Project is not subject to public oversight to ensure that the property continues to be used for the commonwealth after being sold to private entities. Rather, plaintiff intends for the private entities purchasing defendants' properties to pursue their own financial welfare with the single-mindedness expected of any profit-making enterprise. . . .

Finally, there is nothing about the *act* of condemning defendants' properties that serves the public good in this case. The only public benefits cited by plaintiff arise after the lands are acquired by the government and put to private use. . . .

We can only conclude, therefore, that no one sophisticated in the law at the 1963 Constitution's ratification would have understood "public use" to permit the condemnation of defendants' properties for the construction of a business and technology park owned by private entities. Therefore, the condemnations proposed in this case are unconstitutional under art 10, § 2.

Indeed, the only support for plaintiff's position in our eminent domain jurisprudence is the majority opinion in *Poletown*. In that opinion per curiam, a majority of this Court concluded that our Constitution permitted the Detroit Economic Development Corporation to condemn private residential properties in order to convey those properties to a private corporation for the construction of an assembly plant. . . .

Every business, every productive unit in society, does, as Justice Cooley noted, contribute in some way to the commonwealth. To justify the exercise of eminent domain solely on the basis of the fact that the use of that property by a private entity seeking its own profit might contribute to the economy's health is to render impotent our constitutional limitations on the government's power of eminent domain. *Poletown*'s "economic benefit" rationale would validate practically *any* exercise of the power of eminent domain on behalf of a private entity. After all, if one's ownership of private property is forever subject to the government's determination that another private party would put one's land to better use, then the ownership of real property is perpetually threatened by the expansion plans of any large discount retailer, "megastore," or the like. Indeed, it is for precisely this reason that this Court has approved the transfer of condemned property to private entities only when certain other conditions—those identified in our pre-1963 eminent domain jurisprudence in Justice Ryan's *Poletown* dissent—are present. . . .

Because *Poletown*'s conception of a public use—that of "alleviating unemployment and revitalizing the economic base of the community"—has no support in the Court's eminent domain jurisprudence before the Constitution's ratification, its interpretation of "public use" in art 10, § 2 cannot reflect the common understanding of that phrase among those sophisticated in the law at ratification. Consequently, the *Poletown* analysis provides no legitimate support for the condemnations proposed in this case and, for the reasons stated above, is overruled.

We conclude that the condemnations proposed in this case do not pass constitutional muster because they do not advance a public use as required by Const 1963, art 10, § 2. . . .

■ WEAVER, J. (concurring in part and dissenting in part)

[W]ayne County's purpose supporting each of the condemnation proceedings at issue is the creation of a contiguous land mass of approximately 1,300 acres for the development of the Pinnacle Aeropark Project. The county states that contiguity is necessary to attract investors and further that the development will create thousands of jobs and tens of millions of dollars in tax revenue, while broadening its primarily industrial tax base.

However laudable these goals are, the facts remain that Wayne County intends to transfer these properties to private entities. These entities will be under no obligation to let the public in their doors or even on their lands. There is no way to characterize the county's transfer of dominion over these properties as accommodating "public use." Further, Wayne County will not retain control over the properties or enterprises to ensure their devotion to public use. Nor can it be said that a controlling purpose of the condemnations is the removal of blight or slums that endanger the public health, morals, safety, and welfare. This case is indeed a very straightforward example of government taking one person's property for the sole benefit of another. . . .

## Kelo v. City of New London

Supreme Court of the United States, 2005.
545 U.S. 469, 125 S.Ct. 2655.

■ STEVENS, J.

In 2000, the city of New London approved a development plan that, in the words of the Supreme Court of Connecticut, was "projected to create in excess of 1,000 jobs, to increase tax and other revenues, and to revitalize an economically distressed city, including its downtown and waterfront areas." In assembling the land needed for this project, the city's development agent has purchased property from willing sellers and proposes to use the power of eminent domain to acquire the remainder of the property from unwilling owners in exchange for just compensation. The question presented is whether the city's proposed disposition of this property qualifies as a "public use" within the meaning of the Takings Clause of the Fifth Amendment to the Constitution.

The city of New London (hereinafter City) sits at the junction of the Thames River and the Long Island Sound in southeastern Connecticut. Decades of economic decline led a state agency in 1990 to designate the City a "distressed municipality." In 1996, the Federal Government closed the Naval Undersea Warfare Center, which had been located in the Fort Trumbull area of the City and had employed over 1,500 people. In 1998, the City's unemployment rate was nearly double that of the State, and its population of just under 24,000 residents was at its lowest since 1920.

These conditions prompted state and local officials to target New London, and particularly its Fort Trumbull area, for economic revitalization. To this end, respondent New London Development Corporation (NLDC), a private nonprofit entity established some years earlier to assist the City in planning economic development, was reactivated. In January 1998, the State authorized a $5.35 million bond issue to support the NLDC's planning activities and a $10 million bond issue toward the creation of a Fort Trumbull State Park. In February, the pharmaceutical company Pfizer Inc. announced that it would build a $300 million research facility on a site immediately adjacent to Fort Trumbull; local planners hoped that Pfizer would draw new business to the area, thereby serving as a catalyst to the area's rejuvenation. After receiving initial approval from the city council, the NLDC continued its planning activities and held a series of neighborhood meetings to educate the public about the process. In May, the city council authorized the NLDC to formally submit its plans to the relevant state agencies for review. Upon obtaining state-level approval, the NLDC finalized an integrated development plan focused on 90 acres of the Fort Trumbull area.

The Fort Trumbull area is situated on a peninsula that juts into the Thames River. The area comprises approximately 115 privately owned properties, as well as the 32 acres of land formerly occupied by the naval facility (Trumbull State Park now occupies 18 of those 32 acres). The development plan encompasses seven parcels. Parcel 1 is designated for a waterfront conference hotel at the center of a "small urban village" that will include restaurants and shopping. This parcel will also have marinas for both recreational and commercial uses. A pedestrian "riverwalk" will originate here and continue down the coast, connecting the waterfront areas of the development. Parcel 2 will be the site of approximately 80 new residences organized into an urban neighborhood and linked by public walkway to the remainder of the development, including the state park. This parcel also includes space reserved for a new U.S. Coast Guard Museum. Parcel 3, which is located immediately north of the Pfizer facility, will contain at least 90,000 square feet of research and development office space. Parcel 4A is a 2.4-acre site that will be used either to support the adjacent state park, by providing parking or retail services for visitors, or to support the nearby marina. Parcel 4B will include a renovated marina, as well as the final stretch of the riverwalk. Parcels 5, 6, and 7 will provide land for office and retail space, parking, and water-dependent commercial uses.

The NLDC intended the development plan to capitalize on the arrival of the Pfizer facility and the new commerce it was expected to attract. In addition to creating jobs, generating tax revenue, and helping to "build momentum for the revitalization of downtown New London," the plan was also designed to make the City more attractive and to create leisure and recreational opportunities on the waterfront and in the park. . . .

Petitioner Susette Kelo has lived in the Fort Trumbull area since 1997. She has made extensive improvements to her house, which she prizes for its water view. Petitioner Wilhelmina Dery was born in her Fort Trumbull house in 1918 and has lived there her entire life. Her husband Charles (also a petitioner) has lived in the house since they married some 60 years ago. In all, the nine petitioners own 15 properties in Fort Trumbull—4 in parcel 3 of the development plan and 11 in parcel 4A. Ten of the parcels are occupied by the owner or a family member; the other five are held as investment properties. There is no allegation that any of these properties is blighted or otherwise in poor condition; rather, they were condemned only because they happen to be located in the development area. . . .

[The Supreme Court of Connecticut] held that such economic development qualified as a valid public use under both the Federal and State Constitutions. . . .

We granted certiorari to determine whether a city's decision to take property for the purpose of economic development satisfies the "public use" requirement of the Fifth Amendment.

Two polar propositions are perfectly clear. On the one hand, it has long been accepted that the sovereign may not take the property of A for the sole purpose of transferring it to another private party B, even though A is paid just compensation. On the other hand, it is equally clear that a State may transfer property from one private party to another if future "use by the public" is the purpose of the taking; the condemnation of land for a railroad with common-carrier duties is a familiar example. Neither of these propositions, however, determines the disposition of this case.

As for the first proposition, the City would no doubt be forbidden from taking petitioners' land for the purpose of conferring a private benefit on a particular private party. Nor would the City be allowed to take property under the mere pretext of a public purpose, when its actual purpose was to bestow a private benefit. The takings before us, however, would be executed pursuant to a "carefully considered" development plan. . . .

On the other hand, this is not a case in which the City is planning to open the condemned land—at least not in its entirety—to use by the general public. Nor will the private lessees of the land in any sense be required to operate like common carriers, making their services available to all comers. But although such a projected use would be sufficient to satisfy the public use requirement, this "Court long ago rejected any literal requirement that condemned property be put into use for the general public." Accordingly, when this Court began applying the Fifth Amendment to the States at the close of the 19th century, it embraced the broader and more natural interpretation of public use as "public purpose." Thus, in a case upholding a mining company's use of an aerial bucket line to transport ore over property it did not own, Justice Holmes' opinion for the Court stressed "the inadequacy of use by the general public as a universal test." Strickley v. Highland Boy Gold Mining Co., 200 U.S. 527, 531, 26 S.Ct. 301, 50 L.Ed. 581 (1906). We have repeatedly and consistently rejected that narrow test ever since.

The disposition of this case therefore turns on the question whether the City's development plan serves a "public purpose." Without exception, our cases have defined that concept broadly, reflecting our longstanding policy of deference to legislative judgments in this field.

In Berman v. Parker, 348 U.S. 26, 75 S.Ct. 98, 99 L.Ed. 27 (1954), this Court upheld a redevelopment plan targeting a blighted area of Washington, D. C., in which most of the housing for the area's 5,000 inhabitants was beyond repair. Under the plan, the area would be condemned and part of it utilized for the construction of streets, schools, and other public facilities. The remainder of the land would be leased or sold to private parties for the purpose of redevelopment, including the construction of low-cost housing.

The owner of a department store located in the area challenged the condemnation, pointing out that his store was not itself blighted and arguing that the creation of a "better balanced, more attractive community" was not a valid public use. Writing for a unanimous Court, Justice Douglas refused to evaluate this claim in isolation, deferring instead to the legislative and agency judgment that the area "must be planned as a whole" for the plan to be successful. The Court explained that "community redevelopment programs need not, by force of the Constitution, be on a piecemeal basis—lot by lot, building by building." The public use underlying the taking was unequivocally affirmed:

> We do not sit to determine whether a particular housing project is or is not desirable. The concept of the public welfare is broad and inclusive.... The values it represents are spiritual as well as physical, aesthetic as well as monetary. It is within the power of the legislature to determine that the community should be beautiful as well as healthy, spacious as well as clean, well-balanced as well as carefully patrolled. In the present case, the Congress and its authorized agencies have made determinations that take into account a wide variety of values. It is not for us to reappraise them. If those who govern the District of Columbia decide that the Nation's Capital should be beautiful as well as sanitary, there is nothing in the Fifth Amendment that stands in the way.

In Hawaii Housing Authority v. Midkiff, 467 U.S. 229, 104 S.Ct. 2321, 81 L.Ed.2d 186 (1984), the Court considered a Hawaii statute whereby fee title was taken from lessors and transferred to lessees (for just compensation) in order to reduce the concentration of land ownership. We unanimously upheld the statute and rejected the Ninth Circuit's view that it was "a naked attempt on the part of the state of Hawaii to take the property of A and transfer it to B solely for B's private use and benefit."...

For more than a century, our public use jurisprudence has wisely eschewed rigid formulas and intrusive scrutiny in favor of affording legislatures broad latitude in determining what public needs justify the use of the takings power.

Those who govern the City were not confronted with the need to remove blight in the Fort Trumbull area, but their determination that the area was sufficiently distressed to justify a program of economic rejuvenation is entitled to our deference. The City has carefully formulated an economic development plan that it believes will provide appreciable benefits to the community, including—but by no means limited to—new jobs and increased tax revenue. As with other exercises in urban planning and development, the City is endeavoring to coordinate a variety of commercial, residential, and recreational uses of land, with the hope that they will form a whole greater than the sum of its parts. To effectuate this plan, the City has invoked a state statute that specifically authorizes the use of eminent domain to promote economic development. Given the comprehensive character of the plan, the thorough deliberation that preceded its adoption, and the limited scope of our review, it is appropriate for us, as it was in *Berman,* to resolve the challenges of the individual owners, not on a piecemeal basis, but rather in light of the entire plan. Because that plan unquestionably serves a public purpose, the takings challenged here satisfy the public use requirement of the Fifth Amendment. . . .

Petitioners contend that using eminent domain for economic development impermissibly blurs the boundary between public and private takings. Again, our cases foreclose this objection. Quite simply, the government's pursuit of a public purpose will often benefit individual private parties. For example, in *Midkiff,* the forced transfer of property conferred a direct and significant benefit on those lessees who were previously unable to purchase their homes. . . .

It is further argued that without a bright-line rule nothing would stop a city from transferring citizen *A*'s property to citizen *B* for the sole reason that citizen *B* will put the property to a more productive use and thus pay more taxes. Such a one-to-one transfer of property, executed outside the confines of an integrated development plan, is not presented in this case. While such an unusual exercise of government power would certainly raise a suspicion that a private purpose was afoot, the hypothetical cases posited by petitioners can be confronted if and when they arise. They do not warrant the crafting of an artificial restriction on the concept of public use.

Just as we decline to second-guess the City's considered judgments about the efficacy of its development plan, we also decline to second-guess the City's determinations as to what lands it needs to acquire in order to effectuate the project. "It is not for the courts to oversee the choice of the boundary line nor to sit in review on the size of a particular project area. Once the question of the public purpose has been decided, the amount and character of land to be taken for the project and the need for a particular tract to complete the integrated plan rests in the discretion of the legislative branch." Berman, 348 U.S., at 35–36, 75 S.Ct. 98.

In affirming the City's authority to take petitioners' properties, we do not minimize the hardship that condemnations may entail, notwithstanding the payment of just compensation. We emphasize that nothing in our opinion precludes any State from placing further restrictions on its exercise of the takings power. Indeed, many States already impose "public use" requirements that are stricter than the federal baseline. Some of these requirements have been established as a matter of state constitutional law,[4] while others are expressed in state eminent domain statutes that carefully limit the grounds upon which takings may be exercised.[5] As the submissions of the parties and their *amici* make clear, the necessity and wisdom of using eminent domain to promote economic development are certainly matters of legitimate public debate. This Court's authority, however, extends only to determining whether the City's proposed condemnations are for a "public use" within the meaning of the Fifth Amendment to the Federal Constitution. Because over a century of our case law interpreting that provision dictates an affirmative answer to that question, we may not grant petitioners the relief that they seek.

The judgment of the Supreme Court of Connecticut is affirmed.

■ KENNEDY J. concurring.

I join the opinion for the Court and add these further observations. . . .

A court applying rational-basis review under the Public Use Clause should strike down a taking that, by a clear showing, is intended to favor a particular private party, with only incidental or pretextual public benefits, just as a court applying rational-basis review under the Equal Protection Clause must strike down a government classification that is clearly intended to injure a particular class of private parties, with only incidental or pretextual public justifications. As the trial court in this case was correct to observe, "Where the purpose [of a taking] is economic development and that development is to be carried out by private parties or private parties will be benefited, the court must decide if the stated public purpose—economic advantage to a city sorely in need of it—is only incidental to the benefits that will be confined [conferred?—editors] on private parties of a development plan." . . .

This is not the occasion for conjecture as to what sort of cases might justify a more demanding standard, but it is appropriate to underscore aspects of the instant case that convince me no departure from *Berman* and *Midkiff* is appropriate here. This taking occurred in the context of a comprehensive development plan meant to address a serious city-wide depression, and the projected economic benefits of the project cannot be characterized as *de minimus*. The identity of most of the private beneficiaries were unknown at the time the city formulated its plans. The city complied with elaborate procedural requirements that facilitate review of the record and inquiry into the city's purposes. In sum, while there may be categories of cases in which the transfers are so suspicious, or the procedures employed so prone to abuse, or the purported benefits are so trivial or implausible, that courts should presume an

---

[4] See, e.g., County of Wayne v. Hathcock, 471 Mich. 445, 684 N.W.2d 765 (2004).

[5] Under California law, for instance, a city may only take land for economic development purposes in blighted areas. Cal. Health & Safety Code Ann. §§ 33030–33037 (West 1997). See, e.g., Redevelopment Agency of Chula Vista v. Rados Bros., 95 Cal.App.4th 309, 115 Cal.Rptr.2d 234 (2002).

impermissible private purpose, no such circumstances are present in this case. . . .

■ O'CONNOR, J. with whom THE CHIEF JUSTICE, JUSTICE SCALIA, and JUSTICE THOMAS join, dissenting.

Over two centuries ago, just after the Bill of Rights was ratified, Justice Chase wrote:

> An ACT of the Legislature (for I cannot call it a law) contrary to the great first principles of the social compact, cannot be considered a rightful exercise of legislative authority. . . . A few instances will suffice to explain what I mean. . . . [A] law that takes property from A and gives it to B: It is against all reason and justice, for a people to entrust a Legislature with SUCH powers; and, therefore, it cannot be presumed that they have done it. Calder v. Bull, 3 Dall. 386, 388, 1 L.Ed. 648 (1798) (emphasis deleted).

Today the Court abandons this long-held, basic limitation on government power. Under the banner of economic development, all private property is now vulnerable to being taken and transferred to another private owner, so long as it might be upgraded—*i.e.*, given to an owner who will use it in a way that the legislature deems more beneficial to the public—in the process. To reason, as the Court does, that the incidental public benefits resulting from the subsequent ordinary use of private property render economic development takings "for public use" is to wash out any distinction between private and public use of property—and thereby effectively to delete the words "for public use" from the Takings Clause of the Fifth Amendment. Accordingly I respectfully dissent. . . .

[W]here is the line between "public" and "private" property use? We give considerable deference to legislatures' determinations about what governmental activities will advantage the public. But were the political branches the sole arbiters of the public-private distinction, the Public Use Clause would amount to little more than hortatory fluff. An external, judicial check on how the public use requirement is interpreted, however limited, is necessary if this constraint on government power is to retain any meaning. See Cincinnati v. Vester, 281 U.S. 439, 446, 50 S.Ct. 360, 74 L.Ed. 950 (1930) ("It is well established that . . . the question [of] what is a public use is a judicial one"). . . .

This case returns us for the first time in over 20 years to the hard question of when a purportedly "public purpose" taking meets the public use requirement. It presents an issue of first impression: Are economic development takings constitutional? I would hold that they are not. We are guided by two precedents about the taking of real property by eminent domain. In *Berman*, we upheld takings within a blighted neighborhood of Washington, D.C. The neighborhood had so deteriorated that, for example, 64.3% of its dwellings were beyond repair. It had become burdened with "overcrowding of dwellings," "lack of adequate streets and alleys," and "lack of light and air." Congress had determined that the neighborhood had become "injurious to the public health, safety, morals, and welfare" and that it was necessary to "eliminat[e] all such injurious conditions by employing all means necessary and appropriate for the purpose," including eminent domain. Mr. Berman's department store was not itself blighted. Having approved of Congress' decision to eliminate the harm to the public emanating from the blighted neighborhood, however, we did not second-guess its decision to treat the neighborhood as a whole rather than lot-by-lot.

The Court's holdings in *Berman* and *Midkiff* were true to the principle underlying the Public Use Clause. In both those cases, the extraordinary precondemnation use of the targeted property inflicted affirmative harm on society—in *Berman* through blight resulting from extreme poverty and in *Midkiff* through oligopoly resulting from extreme wealth. And in both cases, the relevant legislative body had found that eliminating the existing property use was necessary to remedy the harm. Thus a public purpose was realized when the harmful use was eliminated. Because each taking *directly* achieved a public benefit, it did not matter that the property was turned over to private use. Here, in contrast, New London does not claim that Susette Kelo's and Wilhelmina Dery's well-maintained homes are the source of any social harm. Indeed, it could not so claim without adopting the absurd argument that any single-family home that might be razed to make way for an apartment building, or any church that might be replaced with a retail store, or any small business that might be more lucrative if it were instead part of a national franchise, is inherently harmful to society and thus within the government's power to condemn.

In moving away from our decisions sanctioning the condemnation of harmful property use, the Court today significantly expands the meaning of public use. It holds that the sovereign may take private property currently put to ordinary private use, and give it over for new, ordinary private use, so long as the new use is predicted to generate some secondary benefit for the public—such as increased tax revenue, more jobs, maybe even aesthetic pleasure. But nearly any lawful use of real private property can be said to generate some incidental benefit to the public. Thus, if predicted (or even guaranteed) positive side-effects are enough to render transfer from one private party to another constitutional, then the words "for public use" do not realistically exclude *any* takings, and thus do not exert any constraint on the eminent domain power.

The Court also puts special emphasis on facts peculiar to this case: The NLDC's plan is the product of a relatively careful deliberative process; it proposes to use eminent domain for a multipart, integrated plan rather than for isolated property transfer; it promises an array of incidental benefits (even aesthetic ones), not just increased tax revenue;

it comes on the heels of a legislative determination that New London is a depressed municipality. Justice Kennedy, too, takes great comfort in these facts. But none has legal significance to blunt the force of today's holding. If legislative prognostications about the secondary public benefits of a new use can legitimate a taking, there is nothing in the Court's rule or in Justice Kennedy's gloss on that rule to prohibit property transfers generated with less care, that are less comprehensive, that happen to result from less elaborate process, whose only projected advantage is the incidence of higher taxes, or that hope to transform an already prosperous city into an even more prosperous one....

It was possible after *Berman* and *Midkiff* to imagine unconstitutional transfers from A to B. Those decisions endorsed government intervention when private property use had veered to such an extreme that the public was suffering as a consequence. Today nearly all real property is susceptible to condemnation on the Court's theory. In the prescient words of a dissenter from the infamous decision in *Poletown,* "[n]ow that we have authorized local legislative bodies to decide that a different commercial or industrial use of property will produce greater public benefits than its present use, no homeowner's, merchant's or manufacturer's property, however productive or valuable to its owner, is immune from condemnation for the benefit of other private interests that will put it to a 'higher' use." (opinion of Fitzgerald, J.). This is why economic development takings "seriously jeopardiz[e] the security of all private property ownership." (Ryan, J., dissenting).

Any property may now be taken for the benefit of another private party, but the fallout from this decision will not be random. The beneficiaries are likely to be those citizens with disproportionate influence and power in the political process, including large corporations and development firms. As for the victims, the government now has license to transfer property from those with fewer resources to those with more. The Founders cannot have intended this perverse result. "[T]hat alone is a *just* government," wrote James Madison, "which *impartially* secures to every man, whatever is his *own*." For the National Gazette, Property, (Mar. 29, 1792), reprinted in 14 Papers of James Madison 266 (R. Rutland et al. eds.1983)....

■ THOMAS, J. dissenting.

Long ago, William Blackstone wrote that "the law of the land ... postpone[s] even public necessity to the sacred and inviolable rights of private property." 1 Commentaries on the Laws of England 134–135 (1765) (hereinafter Blackstone). The Framers embodied that principle in the Constitution, allowing the government to take property not for "public necessity," but instead for "public use." Amdt. 5. Defying this understanding, the Court replaces the Public Use Clause with a " '[P]ublic [P]urpose' " Clause, or perhaps the "Diverse and Always Evolving Needs of Society" Clause, a restriction that is satisfied, the Court instructs, so long as the purpose is "legitimate" and the means "not irrational." This deferential shift in phraseology enables the Court to hold, against all common sense, that a costly urban-renewal project whose stated purpose is a vague promise of new jobs and increased tax revenue, but which is also suspiciously agreeable to the Pfizer Corporation, is for a "public use."

I cannot agree. If such "economic development" takings are for a "public use," any taking is, and the Court has erased the Public Use Clause from our Constitution, as Justice O'Connor powerfully argues in dissent. I do not believe that this Court can eliminate liberties expressly enumerated in the Constitution and therefore join her dissenting opinion. Regrettably, however, the Court's error runs deeper than this. Today's decision is simply the latest in a string of our cases construing the Public Use Clause to be a virtual nullity, without the slightest nod to its original meaning. In my view, the Public Use Clause, originally understood, is a meaningful limit on the government's eminent domain power. Our cases have strayed from the Clause's original meaning, and I would reconsider them. . . .

[T]here is no justification for affording almost insurmountable deference to legislative conclusions that a use serves a "public use." To begin with, a court owes no deference to a legislature's judgment concerning the quintessentially legal question of whether the government owns, or the public has a legal right to use, the taken property. Even under the "public purpose" interpretation, moreover, it is most implausible that the Framers intended to defer to legislatures as to what satisfies the Public Use Clause, uniquely among all the express provisions of the Bill of Rights. We would not defer to a legislature's determination of the various circumstances that establish, for example, when a search of a home would be reasonable, see, e.g., Payton v. New York, 445 U.S. 573, 589–590 (1980), or when a convicted double-murderer may be shackled during a sentencing proceeding without on-the-record findings, see Deck v. Missouri, 125 S.Ct. 2007 (2005), or when state law creates a property interest protected by the Due Process Clause, see, e.g., Castle Rock v. Gonzales, 2005 WL 1499788 (2005).

Still worse, it is backwards to adopt a searching standard of constitutional review for nontraditional property interests, such as welfare benefits, while deferring to the legislature's determination as to what constitutes a public use when it exercises the power of eminent domain, and thereby invades individuals' traditional rights in real property. The Court has elsewhere recognized "the overriding respect for the sanctity of the home that has been embedded in our traditions since the origins of the Republic," Payton, supra, at 601, 100 S.Ct. 1371, when the issue is only whether the government may search a home. Yet today the Court tells us that we are not to "second-guess the City's considered judgments," when the issue is, instead, whether the government may take the infinitely more intrusive step of tearing down petitioners' homes. Something has gone seriously awry with this Court's interpretation of the Constitution. Though citizens are safe from the government in their homes, the homes themselves are not. Once one accepts, as the Court at least nominally does, that the Public Use Clause is a limit on the eminent domain power of the Federal Government and the States, there is no justification for the almost complete deference it grants to legislatures as to what satisfies it. . . .

The consequences of today's decision are not difficult to predict, and promise to be harmful. So-called "urban renewal" programs provide some compensation for the properties they take, but no compensation is possible for the subjective value of these lands to the individuals displaced and the indignity inflicted by uprooting them from their homes. Allowing the government to take property solely for public purposes is bad enough, but extending the concept of public purpose to encompass any economically beneficial goal guarantees that these losses will fall disproportionately on poor communities. Those communities are not only systematically less likely to put their lands to the highest and best social use, but are also the least politically powerful. If ever there were justification for intrusive judicial review of constitutional provisions that protect "discrete and insular minorities," surely that principle would apply with great force to the powerless groups and individuals the Public Use Clause protects. The deferential standard this Court has adopted for the Public Use Clause is therefore deeply perverse. It encourages "those citizens with disproportionate influence and power in the political process, including large corporations and development firms" to victimize the weak.

Urban renewal projects have long been associated with the displacement of blacks; "[i]n cities across the country, urban renewal came to be known as 'Negro removal.'" Pritchett, The "Public Menace" of Blight: Urban Renewal and the Private Uses of Eminent Domain, 21 Yale L. & Pol'y Rev. 1, 47 (2003). Over 97 percent of the individuals forcibly removed from their homes by the "slum-clearance" project upheld by this Court in *Berman* were black. Regrettably, the predictable consequence of the Court's decision will be to exacerbate these effects. . . .

## NOTES

1. *Post-litigation outcomes of Midkiff, Kelo, and Poletown.* The goals of the government entities taking the property at issue in *Midkiff* and *Kelo* were never realized.

The U.S. Supreme Court's holding in *Midkiff* was based on the belief that forced sales from oligopolies to individual residential tenants would free-up the Hawaiian housing market and therefore cause housing prices to drop. In fact, after *Midkiff,* Japanese investors, realizing they could now purchase fee titles to Oahu land, began buying up hundreds of suburban homes only to tear them down to build luxury vacation homes for Japanese executives. This buying frenzy caused housing prices to sky-rocket on the island, making housing even more unaffordable. Moreover, because the new vacation homes were used only occasionally, many of them were empty for most of the year, creating an effect contrary to what was intended.[6]

The property taken in *Kelo* was to be part of a large research park to be developed by the pharmaceutical company Pfizer Inc., which was to stimulate an economic revitalization of New London and to create new jobs and tax revenues. In 2009, Pfizer announced that it was abandoning its development plans altogether and consolidating its operations in a nearby city, leaving the New London lots razed and vacant—no longer used by Ms. Kelo and her neighbors for housing but also not used for the intended research park.[7] Photographs of the *Kelo* site, taken in summer 2009, can be viewed at http://louisville.edu/landuse/kelo.html.

In contrast, the *Poletown* case, which was overruled in *Hathcock*, has a mixed history. It involved the razing of an entire Polish-American neighborhood to make room for a General Motors automobile manufacturing plant to provide jobs, stimulate the local economy and generate tax revenue.[8] Although the case was highly controversial,[9] studies show that 84 to 87 percent of the former Poletown residents liked their new homes better[10] and that 25 years later, the automobile plant was still operating, "employing thousands of highly paid workers."[11]

Whether these three cases are representative of the outcomes of takings for economic development is an empirical question that requires carefully designed studies. However, they certainly demonstrate that government agencies can sometimes spend large sums of public funds to acquire property non-voluntarily from landowners for purposes that are not achieved. In addition, as Justice Thomas points out in his *Kelo* dissent, the stated public benefits of redevelopment takings can mask the exploitation and displacement of the least powerful in society.

Should the Fifth Amendment to the U.S. Constitution be the primary source of constraints on governments from making such decisions? If the Public Use Clause does not serve as a restraint on these takings, are there other sources of government limits? Implicit in Justice O'Connor's majority opinion in *Midkiff* is an assumption that the political process will serve as a constraint on government officials using taxpayer dollars to take private property to benefit private economic interests. However, Justice O'Connor was more skeptical twenty-one years later, as her dissent in *Kelo* suggests. It is too facile to say that all local officials throughout the U.S. are beholden to large business and development interests seeking to use public power for private economic gain. However, is it possible that jurisdictions that are less likely to engage in "economic development" takings have *both* a political

---

[6] Gideon Kanner, *Is the "Public Use" Pendulum Reaching the End of its Swing?* Westlaw, SH018 ALI–ABA 709 (2002).

[7] McGeehan, Pfizer to Leave City That Won Land-Use Suit, N.Y. Times, Nov. 13, 2009.

[8] Poletown Neighborhood Council v. City of Detroit, 304 N.W.2d 455 (Mich. 1981).

[9] Wylie, Poletown: Community Destroyed (1989).

[10] Nolan, Auto Plant vs. Neighborhood: The Poletown Battle, The Detroit News, Jan. 27, 2000, http://apps.detnews.com/apps/history/index.php?id=18.

[11] Poletown Neighborhood Council v. Detroit: Private Property and Public Use, 88 Mich. B.J. S18 (Mar. 2009).

culture (i.e., voter power) *and* legal constraints that discourage officials from making such decisions, while jurisdictions that are more susceptible to "those citizens with disproportionate influence and power in the political process, including large corporations and development firms" are also those with the least limits on the eminent domain power? One commentator has proposed that limitations on eminent domain power vary from locality to locality, essentially making some aspects of property law a matter of local choice.[12]

2. *The public and legislative reactions to Kelo*. The U.S. Supreme Court's "public purpose" interpretation of the Public Use Clause in *Berman*, *Midkiff*, and *Kelo* sets the constitutional minimum that governments must have to exercise eminent domain. However, states are free to adopt stricter limitations on the eminent domain power in their constitutions or statutes, and state courts may be called on to interpret those limitations, as occurred in *Hathcock*. In addition, Congress is free to impose limits on federal exercises of eminent domain.

*Kelo* spawned an outpouring of public outrage.[13] The idea that someone's non-blighted home could be taken for a corporation's business needs was highly unpopular.[14] In reaction, at least forty-three states enacted statutes (or state constitutional amendments) limiting the exercise of eminent domain.[15] The resulting limitations vary greatly; e.g., restrictions have been imposed on the transfer of eminent-domain property to private parties, takings for economic development, and takings to eliminate blight.[16]

Does the limitation of eminent domain power by statute and constitutional amendment rather than by judicial interpretation of the U.S. Constitution suggest that the political process ultimately works? One could argue that the majority's *Kelo* opinion stimulated a non-judicial "fix" to the eminent domain power. On the other hand, Professors Merrill and Smith argue that the *Kelo* decision ignores that property law has an inherently moral dimension and that the decision creates a patently unjust outcome regardless of theoretical and institutional arguments in its favor.[17] In addition, Professor Somin has asserted that about half of the reforms are ineffective, because even if they prohibit economic development takings, they still have very broad definitions of blight for which property may be taken.[18]

---

[12] Serkin, Big Differences for Small Governments: Local Governments and the Takings Clause, 81 N.Y.U. L. Rev. 1624 (2006); Serkin, Local Property Law: Adjusting the Scale of Property Protection, 107 Colum. L. Rev. 883 (2007).

[13] Somin, The Limits of Backlash: Assessing the Political Response to *Kelo*, 93 Minn. L. Rev. 2100, 2101–02, 2108–14 (2009).

[14] See, e.g., Benedict, Little Pink House: A True Story of Defiance and Courage (2010) (popular book about the *Kelo* case told as an individual's heroic fight against corporations and power). But see Burke, Much Ado About Nothing: *Kelo v. City of New London*, *Sweet Home v. Babbitt*, and other Tales from the Supreme Court, 75 U. Cinc. L. Rev. 663 (2006).

[15] Somin, The Limits of Backlash: Assessing the Political Response to *Kelo*, 93 Minn. L. Rev. 2100, 2101–02, 2114 (2009). See also Powell on Real Property § 79F.03[3][b][iv] (2009).

[16] Id.

[17] Merrill & Smith, The Morality of Property, 48 Wm. & Mary L. Rev. 1849 (2007).

[18] Somin, The Limits of Backlash: Assessing the Political Response to *Kelo*, 93 Minn. L. Rev. 2100, 2101–02, 2114 (2009).

3. *Pretext*. Kelo leaves open the possibility that property owners can challenge any alleged public purposes as merely pretext for private purposes. However, such a case will be quite difficult to establish given the deference accorded the government officials. In the controversial "Atlantic Yards" case, the 2nd Circuit refused to scrutinize the motives of government officials taking private property for a New Jersey Nets arena (plus open space, affordable housing, and blight removal), despite plaintiffs' allegations that the project was undertaken to benefit a private developer.[19]

4. *The typical practice of eminent domain law*. The controversial cases in this Assignment are not especially representative of most exercises of eminent domain. In most cases, the owner agrees to the government's offer or to a negotiated price. Even where the owner refuses to sell the property and the government has to pursue an adversarial condemnation proceeding, the intended purpose of the taking is clearly for public use, such as a road, highway, or public park. Courts will not second-guess the wisdom of government-initiated takings for public uses. Thus, a judge does not have the power to determine whether a new interstate freeway interchange is really needed after all. Instead, the bulk of eminent domain litigation is about the amount of "fair market value" that the government owes to the property owner. This is a heavily fact-specific inquiry utilizing a variety of legal standards that are beyond the scope of this particular chapter to explore. Nonetheless, the practice of eminent domain, or condemnation, law—both for private property owners and for government agencies—is an important niche of property law practice that future lawyers should not overlook.

5. *Public shopping centers and government businesses*. Is the problem raised by litigants like Ms. Kelo and Mr. Hathcock one of private benefit from the taking of property, or do they object to "economic development" as a legitimate government interest? Could the government avert the argument that economic development takings are for private, rather than public, uses by simply owning and operating the redeveloped sites and their business activities itself? It would seem so, at least facially. Is it a good idea to have a municipally owned and operated shopping center or a government-run manufacturing facility or research park?

6. *"Blight" and "under-productive" property*. The problem of developing an appropriate standard for "public use" is to find a test or definition that will allow takings to address real public problems while preventing or discouraging abuses of the power. Not only does this involve hotly debated questions about the roles of courts in reviewing takings but it more fundamentally involves hotly debated questions about what constitutes a harm-eliminating taking and what constitutes an abusive taking. Consider, for example, the experiences of one of the co-authors of this casebook as a planning official.[20] Professor Arnold recalls zoning and permit hearings on commercial and industrial properties that had become partially vacant sites of crime, graffiti, deteriorated and even unsafe structures, trash, and numerous local code violations, in large part because of fragmented

---

[19] Goldstein v. Pataki, 516 F.3d 50 (2d Cir. 2008).

[20] Professor Tony Arnold served on the Planning Commission of the City of Anaheim, California, from 1999 to 2002, including a year as its Chairman.

ownership by absentee landlords. These situations were examples of the tragedy of the anti-commons: problems of inefficiencies and property underutilization resulting from fragmenting property into many overlapping interests that are difficult to coordinate.[21] Theoretically, the city government should have had the tools of public nuisance actions and code enforcement powers to force the property owners to bring their properties into compliance with local laws. However, in reality, these tools were largely ineffective because of procedural safeguards, limited remedies, the likelihood that enforcement would be mired in multiple defendants blaming each other, and the sheer difficulty of reaching absentee landowners with effective remedies. In these circumstances, perhaps the most effective thing the city could have done would be to take the properties by eminent domain, justly compensate the property owners, consolidate the properties, and then sell the consolidated property to a private developer or operator of commercial shopping centers, industrial parks, or the like. Do you see why the examples that concerned city officials in Anaheim would have easily fallen within at least one of the *Hathcock* exceptions and thus their takings would have been permissible under a narrower reading of the Public Use Clause than that followed by the *Kelo* majority?

7. *Bundles, webs, and homes.* One of the reasons why *Kelo* seems so unfair to many is that it involves the taking of one's home for economic development. However, property law tends not to recognize greater property interests in one's home than in any other form of property, such as a commercial center, a factory, a cattle feedlot, or residential lots purchased for investment or speculation. This is arguably the result of the "bundle of rights" concept of property that treats property as a set of abstract and fungible rights that can be disconnected from the object of those rights and acquired for an impersonal "fair market" value. In contrast, the "web of interests" concept, introduced in Assignment 1, defines property on the basis of: 1) the characteristics of the object of property; 2) the relationships that the property owner has with the object; and 3) the relationships among the various holders of interests in the object.[22] The web-of-interests metaphor might be used by a court to determine that occupied residential property is different from other types of property and that an owner's (or even tenant's) interests in his or her home are substantially greater and tighter than the government's interests in the property as a location for economic redevelopment. Thus, even though some might discount the web-of-interests concept of property as under-protecting private rights and over-recognizing public interests in property, the balance of private rights and public interests will depend on the characteristics of the object and the various interests in it, thus actually affording greater protection to private landowners under certain circumstances. In this respect, the web-of-interests concept shares certain commonalities with the "personhood" theory of property that

---

[21] Heller, The Tragedy of the Anticommons: Property in the Transition from Marx to Markets, 111 Harv. L. Rev. 621 (1998).

[22] Arnold, The Reconstitution of Property: Property as a Web of Interests, 26 Harv. Envtl. L. Rev. 281 (2002).

recognizes certain forms of "constitutive property" that shape human identity because of the relationships people form with property objects.[23]

---

[23] Radin, Reinterpreting Property (1993); Radin, Property and Personhood, 34 Stan. L. Rev. 957 (1982). But see Stern, Residential Protectionism and the Legal Mythology of Home, 107 Mich. L. Rev. 1093 (2009).

# ASSIGNMENT 30

# ZONING AND LAND USE REGULATION

## 1. INTRODUCTION

Can a landowner use property in whatever manner he or she chooses? We have already seen that the doctrine of nuisance inherently limits the right to use property. We have also seen that landowners or their predecessors often agree to servitudes that limit land-use rights. In addition, the government typically plays a significant role in determining how land is used in the United States. Through eminent domain, the government may acquire land from private property owners to use the land for public purposes. More extensively, the government shapes land use through regulation, such as zoning.

Land use regulation is one of the most pervasive aspects of law in U.S. society. All major urban areas, except for Houston, have zoning codes that regulate uses of land. Many counties and small cities and towns also have zoning ordinances. Even in areas without zoning, government regulation of land subdivision, building standards, utility-access regulations, public nuisances, and natural resources serve to limit the freedom of the landowner to use the land as he or she wishes.

Land use regulation largely falls within the authority and functions of local units of government, such as cities, towns, and counties. As political subdivisions of the state, localities receive their authority to regulate land use from state enabling statutes. The states in turn obtain this power from the police power, which is inherent in state government. The police power is the power of a sovereign government to protect the public health, safety, morals, and welfare. The original thirteen colonies succeeded to the British crown's police power when they declared independence in 1776. When the U.S. Constitution was ratified, the states retained these reserved powers, a point reiterated in the Tenth Amendment to the U.S. Constitution. However, state and local powers are subject to limitations in the U.S. Constitution and its amendments, including the Takings Clause, the Due Process Clause, the Equal Protection Clause, and First Amendment guarantees of free speech and free exercise of religion.

The specific contours of local power and its limits vary from state to state. As a matter of law, many localities have only those powers expressly granted by the state.[1] The reality, however, is that local governments have relatively broad discretion to use their zoning and

---

[1] See Frug, The City as a Legal Concept, 93 Harv. L. Rev. 1059 (1980).

regulatory powers in a variety of ways, subject to several important constraints. These powers and constraints are explored in this Assignment and in several subsequent Assignments.

A few states impose statewide planning or growth management controls on local land use powers.[2] Some states have created special land use regulatory systems for areas that cross local jurisdictions, such as coastal zones or ecologically sensitive landscapes.[3]

The federal government also plays a role in land use regulation. The U.S. Constitution's guarantee of federal supremacy over state laws means that local land use regulations may be preempted by federal laws affecting land uses that are properly within federal power. Moreover, federal environmental statutes and regulations protecting wetlands,[4] the habitat of endangered or threatened species,[5] water quality,[6] and other environmental conditions impose additional layers of restrictions on landowners. The federal "overlay" of environmental regulation of land use is more of a mosaic or patchwork of shared roles than a hierarchical pyramid of control.[7] Local control over land use regulation is a deeply cherished principle in U.S. culture and comprehensive federalization of land use regulatory powers seems politically unlikely at this time.[8]

Land use can be a highly controversial field. It has plenty of critics. Some contend that land use regulation is inherently biased towards development, resulting from the political influence of developers and businesses and society's "perpetual growth bias."[9] Some contend that land use controls are inherently biased towards protecting the interests, neighborhood conditions, and property values of existing landowners by excluding new development.[10] Others contend that zoning inherently discriminates on the basis of race, ethnicity, and income, pointing to a history of zoning that is racially-based zoning and impedes access to affordable housing.[11] Finally, others question the effectiveness of land

---

[2] See, e.g., Fla. Stat. § 163.3184.

[3] See, e.g., California Coastal Act of 1976, Cal. Pub. Res. Code §§ 30000 et seq.; New Jersey Pinelands Comprehensive Management Plan, N.J. Stat. Ann. § 13:18A–8.

[4] See, e.g., United States v. Riverside Bayview Homes, Inc., 474 U.S. 121 (1985)

[5] See, e.g., National Ass'n of Home Builders v. Babbitt, 130 F.3d 1041 (D.C. Cir. 1997); Friends of Endangered Species, Inc. v. Jantzen, 760 F.2d 976 (9th Cir. 1985).

[6] See, e.g., Minan, General Industrial Storm Water Permits and the Construction Industry: What Does the Clean Water Act Require?, 9 Chap. L. Rev. 265 (2006).

[7] Arnold, The Structure of the Land Use Regulatory System in the United States, 22 J. Land Use & Envtl. L. 441, 486–91 (2007).

[8] Id.

[9] Feagin and Parker, Building American Cities: The Urban Real Estate Game, 2d ed. (1990); Butler, The Pathology of Property Norms: Living Within Nature's Boundaries, 73 S. Cal. L. Rev. 927 (2000); Babbitt, Cities in the Wilderness: A New Vision of Land Use in America (2005).

[10] Ellickson, Alternatives to Zoning: Covenants, Nuisance Rules, and Fines as Land Use Controls, 40 U. Chi. L. Rev. 681 (1973); Ellickson, Suburban Growth Controls: An Economic and Legal Analysis, 86 Yale L.J. 385 (1977).

[11] Dubin, From Junkyards to Gentrification: Explicating a Right to Protective Zoning in Low-Income Communities of Color, 77 Minn. L. Rev. 739 (1993); Seitles, The Perpetuation of

use regulation due to the imposition of uncoordinated restrictions on a project-by-project and a locality-by-locality basis, which ignore the interconnectedness of land use and environmental problems across multiple geographic scales.[12]

Alternatively, land use regulation can be seen as a functional, adaptive, and evolving system that serves primarily a mediating role between people and places—or between humans and their environments.[13] According to this "systems" perspective, land use regulatory methods and processes are tools by which communities shape their environments and their relationships with their environments. Inequitable, inefficient, or ineffective land use practices are a result of social, political, economic, and cultural forces in society; they are not inherent and unalterable outcomes of the system itself. In fact, land use regulation in the U.S. has evolved considerably over time, and growing local land-use regulations to protect critical environmental resources reflect an increasing ecological concern in society.[14]

Land use regulatory practices vary considerably from locality to locality, based on local culture. Functionally, land use decisions result mostly from policy considerations and the wide discretion local regulators must have to evaluate each proposed use or project in its particular context. A very small proportion of land use decisions made in the U.S. each year are litigated.[15] It could be said that the "law" of land use regulation is far more about what the city council, planning commission, or board of zoning appeals actually does than what courts decide. Likewise, the "culture of private property rights" in the United States serves as a far more potent political, psychological, and normative constraint on land-use regulators than judicial doctrines of private property rights and takings.[16]

This Assignment explores the applicable legal principles that shape the relationships between government authority over land use and private rights with respect to land use. However, you are also encouraged

---

Residential Racial Segregation in America: Historical Discrimination, Modern Forms of Exclusion, and Inclusionary Remedies, 14 J. Land Use & Envtl. L. 89 (1998).

[12] Rose, Planning and Dealing: Piecemeal Land Controls as a Problem of Local Legitimacy, 71 Cal. L. Rev. 837 (1983); Tarlock, The Potential Role of Local Governments in Watershed Management, 20 Pace Envtl. L. Rev. 149 (2002); Babbitt, Cities in the Wilderness: A New Vision of Land Use in America (2005).

[13] Arnold, The Structure of the Land Use Regulatory System in the United States, 22 J. Land Use & Envtl. L. 441 (2007). See also Karkkainen, Zoning: A Reply to the Critics, 10 J. Land Use & Envtl. L. 45 (1994).

[14] See, e.g., Nolon, In Praise of Parochialism: The Advent of Local Environmental Law, 26 Harv. Envtl. L. Rev. 365 (2002); Salkin, From *Euclid* to Growing Smart: The Transformation of the American Local Land Use Ethic into Local Land Use and Environmental Controls, 20 Pace Envtl. L. Rev. 109 (2002); Arnold, Norton, & Wallen, Kentucky Wet Growth Tools for Sustainable Development: A Handbook on Land Use and Water for Kentucky Communities (2009).

[15] Arnold, The Structure of the Land Use Regulatory System in the United States, 22 J. Land Use & Envtl. L. 441, 480, 492 (2007).

[16] Id. at 488.

to consider how the land use regulatory system functions in day-to-day decisions about land use.

## 2. TYPES OF LAND USE REGULATION[17]

*Zoning.* The basic core of land use regulation is the local zoning code. At a minimum, the zoning code consists of a map and text that have been adopted by the city council (or county governing board if the property does not fall within a city's jurisdiction and if the state has granted zoning authority to counties). The map will indicate the zoning that has been adopted for different parcels or geographic areas of the city. The text will indicate which uses are allowed by right, prohibited altogether, or allowed conditionally (e.g., upon the approval of a conditional use permit or similar permit, which is discretionary with the decision making body).

*Uses, Heights, Bulk, and Even More.* Zones are generally categorized by use, such as residential, commercial, industrial, and agricultural and open space. However, there are often multiple zones for each general category of use. For example residential zones might include single-family residential, duplex, and multi-family-residential/apartment. They might also be designated by densities allowed. There would likely be several different types of commercial zones that attempt to group compatible commercial uses together (e.g., retail stores, restaurants, and banks), and to segregate incompatible commercial uses (e.g., tall commercial office towers vs. small antique stores). Often industrial districts are divided at the very least into light industrial districts and heavy industrial districts. However, different zones also contain different authorizations and prohibitions concerning heights of structures and bulk of structures (e.g., density—how many units per area—as well as setbacks from the property line and amount of floor space allowed). While use, height, and bulk are the core of traditional zoning, the zoning code will also likely contain rules regarding parking, architectural features and design guidelines, ingress and egress, sidewalks and pedestrian circulation, signs and advertising, accessory uses, landscaping, and historic preservation.

*Process.* The city zoning code specifies the process for obtaining various land use approvals. In most states, the adoption or amendment of the zoning code text or map is a legislative act of the city council, although often there is a process for obtaining the recommendations of city planning staff and the city planning commission, an appointed body of citizen-experts who focus on planning and zoning issues. In a few jurisdictions, rezoning a single-parcel is considered an administrative or quasi-judicial act, even if performed by the legislative body (e.g., city council), and therefore requires a hearing, evidence, and findings. Even

---

[17] Resources describing zoning and land use regulatory controls include Juergensmeyer & Roberts, Land Use Planning and Development Regulation Law (2d ed. 2007); Mandelker, Land Use Law (5th ed., 2003); Rathkopf's Law of Zoning and Planning (2009); Rohan & Kelly, Zoning and Land Use Controls (2009).

in the majority of jurisdictions where rezonings are legislative acts and therefore do not require evidence-based findings, state statutes and/or city charters prescribe particular procedures that the city council must follow when adopting zoning changes.

Specific discretionary approvals for particular projects, such as conditional use permits, variances, subdivision maps and site plans are often decided either by the planning commission or alternatively by the board of zoning adjustment (or zoning board of appeals), a body that decides whether permits will be granted. In some cases a special hearing officer has the authority to grant particular permits and variances. In general, discretionary permit decisions might be subject to appeal to, or even automatic review by, the city council. Discretionary permit decisions are administrative or quasi-judicial actions and therefore require notice, hearings, substantial evidence on the record, and findings that show why the decision maker granted or denied the permit. These findings must show that the decision maker applied the standards for granting or denying the permit that had been set forth in the applicable zoning code provisions.

Ministerial acts require no discretionary decision-making in a legal sense, and are often delegated to city staff members, who evaluate the landowner's (or developer's) project to determine if he or she has complied with relatively clear and precise requirements in the code or the permit authorizing the development. In many jurisdictions, the issuance of a building permit is a ministerial act.

*Segregation of Uses.* The essence of traditional zoning—often called Euclidean zoning—is to separate or segregate incompatible uses from one another. However, the reality of many long-developed urban areas is that the zoning is often parcel-specific, instead of neighborhood-wide, such that neighboring parcels may have inconsistent zoning designations. An example might be a single-family residential property bordered on the west by a commercial property, on the north by an apartment complex, and on the east by a church. Courts sometimes refer to the zoning of a parcel differently from surrounding parcels as "spot zoning" if they are striking it down as irrational. Nonetheless, do not assume that all zoning is a patchwork of inconsistent uses. The majority of zoning throughout the U.S. tends to cluster or congregate the same or similar uses.

*Plans and Planning.* Another core concept of zoning is that it is required to be "in accordance" with a comprehensive plan, which is known as the "consistency requirement." Urban planning is a profession and field of study, and most cities employ professional planners to provide expert guidance to city decision makers. In some states, cities must adopt actual written comprehensive plans, which identify by text and maps the city's plans and goals for future development. The elements covered by comprehensive plans include land use, transportation, housing, infrastructure (e.g., schools, parks, sewage capacity, public utility services, water supplies), natural resources and open space, public safety and emergency preparedness, and general growth patterns. The plans for these elements must be consistent with one another, which is the point of planning. For example, if city officials plan to concentrate residential growth on the city's northwest side, they should also be planning roads, schools, and parks in that part of the city to accommodate the growth, and should identify its impacts on that area's natural environment and available open space. In other states, the zoning must simply be consistent with the appearance of an overall coordinated and comprehensive planning approach, as evidenced by looking at the city's zoning code and other planning documents as a whole. Each time the zoning code is amended or a land use permit is approved, city officials should or must consider whether the decision is consistent with the city's overall comprehensive plan. In general, though, the comprehensive plan is not a legally enforceable regulation of private property in the way that the zoning code is. One author has analogized the plan to the Pirate's Code in *Pirates of the Caribbean*: "more what you'd call 'guidelines' than actual rules."[18]

*Discretionary Permits and Approvals.* Although zoning is the core of land use regulation, much of the day-to-day of land use decision making by government regulators involves discretionary permits and approvals. One such approval is the approval of a subdivision map (or plat or tract map). In most jurisdictions, a landowner cannot divide a parcel of land into two or more parcels (or condominiums or apartments) without local regulatory approval. Subdivision regulation serves four important functions:

1) it ensures the accuracy of official government records (usually at the county recorder's office) with regard to the location of property boundaries, as designated on subdivision (or tract) maps (or plats), upon which the local property tax assessor, other government agencies, subsequent purchasers and grantees of land, real estate lenders, and the general public rely;

2) it ensures the provision of infrastructure needed to support new development on subdivided land (e.g., streets, schools, parks, sewage facilities, traffic lights and street lights, curbs and gutters, and sidewalks);

3) it ensures coordination and compatibility of infrastructure from one subdivision to the next (e.g., streets that connect, pipes that are the same size, streets wide enough for emergency vehicles); and

---

[18] Arnold, Is Wet Growth Smarter Than Smart Growth?: The Fragmentation and Integration of Land Use and Water, 35 Envtl. L. Rep. 10152, 10172–73 (2005) (quoting Pirates of the Caribbean: The Curse of the Black Pearl (Disney 2003) (screenplay by Terry Rossio & Ted Elliott)).

4) it provides an initial review of, and means of controlling, anticipated development.

Another type of discretionary permit is the "conditional use permit" (CUP), "special exception" or "special use permit." For a use to be eligible for a CUP, it must be listed in the zoning code as a use that is "conditional" in the zone for which the property is zoned. If the proposed use is permitted by right according to the zoning code, no land use permit is needed (although building, occupancy, and similar permits might be required). If the proposed use is prohibited in the zone, a CUP is not available. A conditional use is one that the city council has determined is appropriate for the particular zone but may have adverse impacts on surrounding land uses and the public health, safety, morals, or welfare if not monitored and controlled. Therefore, the CUP applicant must establish that his or her particular project is compatible with surrounding land uses and appropriate in its particular location, as well as meeting various other criteria that may be established in the zoning code. In addition, the decision making body will impose conditions in the permit that the developer or landowner must meet. These conditions can vary widely, but must have some nexus to land use impacts on the surrounding community or neighboring properties.

The CUP must be distinguished from the variance. The variance is "relief" from a requirement or prohibition in the zoning code for a particular parcel or project when compliance with the zoning code would impose an undue hardship on the property owner. Typically, this hardship must be more than financial; instead, there must be something unusual or distinctive about the property itself, such as its size, shape, topography, or other physical condition, that is the source of the hardship and would prevent the type of development reasonably enjoyed by similarly zoned parcels. For example, a landowner might obtain a variance from a setback requirement (and thus be allowed to build in the setback area) if an unusual shape of the property would preclude building at all if the setback requirement were observed. Self-imposed hardships do not justify variances and many states do not permit "use variances" (for the reason that they are essentially a rezoning of the property by administrative instead of legislative act). However, some states allow use variances and some states allow consideration of non-physical hardships.

*Flexible Zoning Techniques.* A variety of regulatory mechanisms have been added to the standard approach of Euclidean zoning. These mechanisms include:

1) overlay zones, which impose additional requirements or authorizations for a particular geographic area, on top of the existing (underlying) zoning, such that both sets of controls apply to the particular geographic area (e.g., a hillside view overlay zone that keeps in place the traditional single-family zoning for a neighborhood, but imposes further height restrictions on hillside homes to protect neighbors' views);

2) buffer zones, which provide for a transition from an area of more intensive land uses to an area of less intensive land uses;

3) performance zones, which regulate actual "outputs" of development, instead of uses (e.g., allowing industrial uses in various zones but restricting any use that exceeds certain noise, air pollution emission, water pollution emission, toxic chemical storage, or other limits); and

4) planned unit developments, which allow for the mix of uses, heights, bulk, and other features described in an approved site plan, and the particular development project as approved becomes the zoning itself, instead of one of the pre-set zones or districts provided for in the zoning code.

*Environmental Regulation of Land Use.* The past thirty years have seen a tremendous expansion of environmental controls that limit land use. Many of these controls involve federal and state environmental statutes and regulations prohibiting development that impacts ecologically-relevant categories of land or specific natural places. However, a growing number of local units of government, including cities, counties, and special-purpose districts, have adopted local environmental controls over development. One example is the increasingly wide variety of overlay zones to protect geographic areas containing sensitive resources, such as underground aquifers, rivers, lakes, desert environments, hillsides, vistas and views, specific vegetation and trees, and sites of particular historic or cultural relevance.

## 3. PRINCIPAL PROBLEM

As the Assistant City Attorney for the City of Cassidy, you have been asked by Shannon McDonald, the City Planning Director, to provide her with confidential legal advice about the City's options to prevent Wolfgang Frisch from establishing a new automotive repair and sales facility at 321 E. Johnson Avenue. The parcel in question is a 0.31-acre parcel with a vacant liquor store and small parking lot that would be redeveloped to convert the building to a 2-bay garage and office and to expand the parking lot.

The parcel is zoned General Commercial (GC), for which both automotive repair uses and automotive sales uses are listed as "conditional uses," requiring a CUP from the Board of Zoning Adjustment (BZA), subject to appeal to the City Council. The City of Cassidy's Mayor, Chuong Ho, and McDonald have discussed three different options to prevent Frisch's proposed use:

1) The City Council could adopt a zoning ordinance that would rezone Frisch's parcel from GC to Commercial Retail (CR), in which automobile repair facilities and automobile sales facilities are prohibited;

2) The City Council could adopt a zoning ordinance that would move automobile repair uses and automobile sales uses from the list of conditional uses to the list of prohibited uses in all GC zones within the City, thus prohibiting these uses on any property zoned GC; or

3) The BZA could deny Frisch's CUP application under the current GC zoning standards.

Frisch has already applied for a CUP. It will take approximately three months for Frisch to finalize his application, the City planning staff to evaluate the application, and the BZA to advertise and hold a hearing on the CUP. According to Mayor Ho, the City Council could consider and enact either of the zoning amendments before the BZA considers Frisch's CUP application. Under the City Code, the BZA has to apply the zoning in effect at the time that the CUP hearing is held.

The City Zoning Code currently provides:

Before the Board of Zoning Adjustment grants a conditional use permit, it must make a finding of fact that the evidence presented shows that all of the following conditions exist:

(a) That the proposed use is properly one for which a conditional use permit is authorized by the Zoning Code, or that said use is not listed therein as being a permitted use;

(b) That the proposed use will not adversely affect the adjoining land uses and the growth and development of the area in which it is proposed to be located;

(c) That the size and shape of the site for the proposed use is adequate to allow the full development of the proposed use in a manner not detrimental to the particular area nor to the peace, health, safety, and general welfare;

(d) That the traffic generated by the proposed use will not impose an undue burden upon the streets and highways designed and improved to carry the traffic in the area; and

(e) That the granting of the conditional use permit under the conditions imposed, if any, will not be detrimental to the peace, health, safety and general welfare of the citizens of the City of Cassidy."

Frisch believes that he is entitled to use his property for an automotive repair and sales facility, and that any zoning regulation of his property is a violation of his rights. He also feels he is entitled to a CUP because the BZA has previously approved CUPs for five automotive repair and sales facilities on Johnson Avenue. Moreover, he has already purchased the property for $300,000, spent $10,000 for site plan designs, and applied for the CUP, all with the belief that the BZA would likely grant his CUP.

According to McDonald, the City wants to prevent Frisch's proposed facility because an overconcentration of small automotive repair and sales facilities on Johnson Avenue has:

1) adversely impacted residential property values in the adjacent historic Chapin-Lein neighborhood;

2) prevented upscale mixed-use retail, office, and loft condominium development on Johnson Avenue, which has been identified as City goals in its comprehensive plan (and which would produce greater tax revenues for the City);

3) resulted in excess on-street parking and traffic congestion because the automotive repair and sales facilities are not large enough for adequate parking during peak-customer periods;

4) produced excessive polluted stormwater runoff from extensively paved areas (e.g., buildings, parking lots) with oil and other automotive fluids; and

5) created excessive noise from automotive repair activities with open garage doors.

At the last two CUP hearings on automotive facilities that were approved, Mayor Ho and BZA Chairperson Rebecca Weiss expressed their growing concerns about the overconcentration of these automotive land uses on Johnson Avenue. Sue Park, President of the Chapin-Lein Preservation Association, mobilized neighborhood residents to oppose Frisch's CUP application. Six months ago, Park spoke at a City Council meeting about the need for comprehensive rezoning along Johnson Avenue to prevent the approval of "excessive automotive land uses that are causing our community to decline." This was before Frisch purchased the parcel at 321 E. Johnson Avenue.

McDonald seeks your legal analysis of the three options that she and Mayor Ho have discussed. Consider the following materials in forming your advice.

4. **MATERIALS FOR SOLUTION OF PRINCIPAL PROBLEM**

### Village of Euclid v. Ambler Realty Co.
Supreme Court of the United States, 1926.
272 U.S. 365, 47 S.Ct. 114.

■ MR. JUSTICE SUTHERLAND delivered the opinion of the Court.

The village of Euclid is an Ohio municipal corporation. It adjoins and practically is a suburb of the city of Cleveland. Appellee is the owner of a tract of land containing 68 acres, situated in the westerly end of the village, abutting on Euclid avenue to the south and the Nickel Plate Railroad to the north. Adjoining this tract, both on the east and on the west, there have been laid out restricted residential plats upon which residences have been erected.

On November 13, 1922, an ordinance was adopted by the village council, establishing a comprehensive zoning plan for regulating and restricting the location of trades, industries, apartment houses, two-family houses, single family houses, etc., the lot area to be built upon, the size and height of buildings, etc. The entire area of the village is divided by the ordinance into six classes of use districts, denominated U-1 to U-6, inclusive; three classes of height districts, denominated H-1 to H-3, inclusive; and four classes of area districts, denominated A-1 to A-4, inclusive.

The ordinance is assailed on the grounds that it is in derogation of section 1 of the Fourteenth Amendment to the federal Constitution in that it deprives appellee of liberty and property without due process of law and denies it the equal protection of the law, and that it offends against certain provisions of the Constitution of the state of Ohio. [The plaintiff] alleges that the tract of land in question is vacant and has been held for years for the purpose of selling and developing it for industrial uses, for which it is especially adapted, being immediately in the path or progressive industrial development; that for such uses it has a market value of about $10,000 per acre, but if the use be limited to residential purposes the market value is not in excess of $2,500 per acre; that the first 200 feet of the parcel back from Euclid avenue, if unrestricted in respect of use, has a value of $150 per front foot, but if limited to residential uses, and ordinary mercantile business be excluded therefrom, its value is not in excess of $50 per front foot.

Building zone laws are of modern origin. They began in this country about 25 years ago. Until recent years, urban life was comparatively simple; but, with the great increase and concentration of population, problems have developed, and constantly are developing, which require, and will continue to require, additional restrictions in respect of the use and occupation of private lands in urban communities. Regulations, the wisdom, necessity, and validity of which, as applied to existing conditions, are so apparent that they are now uniformly sustained, a century ago, or even half a century ago, probably would have been rejected as arbitrary and oppressive. Such regulations are sustained, under the complex conditions of our day, for reasons analogous to those which justify traffic regulations, which, before the advent of automobiles and rapid transit street railways, would have been condemned as fatally arbitrary and unreasonable. And in this there is no inconsistency, for, while the meaning of constitutional guaranties never varies, the scope of their application must expand or contract to meet the new and different conditions which are constantly coming within the field of their operation. In a changing world it is impossible that it should be otherwise. But although a degree of elasticity is thus imparted, not to the meaning, but to the application of constitutional principles, statutes and ordinances, which, after giving due weight to the new conditions, are found clearly not to conform to the Constitution, of course, must fall.

The ordinance now under review, and all similar laws and regulations, must find their justification in some aspect of the police power, asserted for the public welfare. The line which in this field separates the legitimate from the illegitimate assumption of power is not capable of precise delimitation. It varies with circumstances and conditions. A regulatory zoning ordinance, which would be clearly valid as applied to the great cities, might be clearly invalid as applied to rural communities.

In solving doubts, the maxim '*sic utere tuo ut alienum non laedas*,' which lies at the foundation of so much of the common low of nuisances, ordinarily will furnish a fairly helpful clew [sic]. And the law of nuisances, likewise, may be consulted, not for the purpose of controlling, but for the helpful aid of its analogies in the process of ascertaining the scope of, the power. Thus the question whether the power exists to forbid the erection of a building of a particular kind or for a particular use, like the question whether a particular thing is a nuisance, is to be determined, not by an abstract consideration of the building or of the thing considered apart, but by considering it in connection with the circumstances and the locality. A nuisance may be merely a right thing in the wrong place, like a pig in the parlor instead of the barnyard. If the validity of the legislative classification for zoning purposes be fairly debatable, the legislative judgment must be allowed to control.

There is no serious difference of opinion in respect of the validity of laws and regulations fixing the height of buildings within reasonable limits, the character of materials and methods of construction, and the adjoining area which must be left open, in order to minimize the danger of fire or collapse, the evils of overcrowding and the like, and excluding from residential sections offensive trades, industries and structures likely to create nuisances.

Here, however, the exclusion is in general terms of all industrial establishments, and it may thereby happen that not only offensive or dangerous industries will be excluded, but those which are neither offensive nor dangerous will share the same fate. But this is no more than happens in respect of many practice-forbidding laws which this court has upheld, although drawn in general terms so as to include individual cases that may turn out to be innocuous in themselves. The inclusion of a reasonable margin, to insure effective enforcement, will not put upon a law, otherwise valid, the stamp of invalidity. Such laws may also find their justification in the fact that, in some fields, the bad fades into the good by such insensible degrees that the two are not capable of being readily distinguished and separated in terms of legislation.

We find no difficulty in sustaining restrictions of the kind thus far reviewed. The serious question in the case arises over the provisions of the ordinance excluding from residential districts apartment houses, business houses, retail stores and shops, and other like establishments. This question involves the validity of what is really the crux of the more recent zoning legislation, namely, the creation and maintenance of residential districts, from which business and trade of every sort, including hotels and apartment houses, are excluded. Upon that question this court has not thus far spoken. The decisions of the state courts are numerous and conflicting; but those which broadly sustain the power greatly outnumber those which deny it altogether or narrowly limit it, and it is very apparent that there is a constantly increasing tendency in the direction of the broader view.

[These] decisions agree that the exclusion of buildings devoted to business, trade, etc., from residential districts, bears a rational relation to the health and safety of the community. Some of the grounds for this conclusion are promotion of the health and security from injury of children and others by separating dwelling houses from territory devoted to trade and industry; suppression and prevention of disorder; facilitating the extinguishment of fires, and the enforcement of street traffic regulations and other general welfare ordinances; aiding the health and safety of the community, by excluding from residential areas the confusion and danger of fire, contagion, and disorder, which in greater or less degree attach to the location of stores, shops, and factories. Another ground is that the construction and repair of streets may be rendered easier and less expensive, by confining the greater part of the heavy traffic to the streets where business is carried on.

The matter of zoning has received much attention at the hands of commissions and experts, and the results of their investigations have been set forth in comprehensive reports. These reports which bear every evidence of painstaking consideration, concur in the view that the segregation of residential, business and industrial buildings will make it easier to provide fire apparatus suitable for the character and intensity of the development in each section; that it will increase the safety and security of home life, greatly tend to prevent street accidents, especially to children, by reducing the traffic and resulting confusion in residential sections, decrease noise and other conditions which produce or intensify nervous disorders, preserve a more favorable environment in which to rear children, etc.

With particular reference to apartment houses, it is pointed out that the development of detached house sections is greatly retarded by the coming of apartment houses, which has sometimes resulted in destroying the entire section for private house purposes; that in such sections very often the apartment house is a mere parasite, constructed in order to take advantage of the open spaces and attractive surroundings created by the residential character of the district. Moreover, the coming of one apartment house is followed by others, interfering by their height and bulk with the free circulation of air and monopolizing the rays of the sun which otherwise would fall upon the smaller homes, and bringing, as their necessary accompaniments, the disturbing noises incident to increased traffic and business, and the occupation, by means of moving and parked automobiles, of larger portions of the streets, thus detracting from their safety and depriving children of the privilege of quiet and open spaces for play, enjoyed by those in more favored localities-until, finally, the residential character of the neighborhood and its desirability as a place of detached residences are utterly destroyed. Under these circumstances, apartment houses, which in a different environment would be not only entirely unobjectionable but highly desirable, come very near to being nuisances.

If these reasons, thus summarized, do not demonstrate the wisdom or sound policy in all respects of those restrictions which we have indicated as pertinent to the inquiry, at least, the reasons are sufficiently cogent to preclude us from saying, as it must be said before the ordinance can be declared unconstitutional, that such provisions are clearly arbitrary and unreasonable, having no substantial relation to the public health, safety, morals, or general welfare.

In the realm of constitutional law, especially, this court has perceived the embarrassment which is likely to result from an attempt to formulate rules or decide questions beyond the necessities of the immediate issue. It has preferred to follow the method of a gradual approach to the general by a systematically guarded application and extension of constitutional principles to particular cases as they arise, rather than by out of hand attempts to establish general rules to which future cases must be fitted. This process applies with peculiar force to the solution of questions arising under the due process clause of the Constitution as applied to the exercise of the flexible powers of police, with which we are here concerned.

## NOTES

1. *Landmark case. Euclid* is perhaps the seminal case in land use law, upholding the constitutionality of zoning early in its history in the U.S. and at a time when the Supreme Court was regularly striking down government regulation as an interference with property and contract rights. It has had a profound and lasting influence on the nature and exercise of land use regulatory powers and, therefore, on how people use their property.[19] Why did the *Euclid* Court uphold the constitutionality of zoning? Was it because zoning is a legislative extension of common-law nuisance, thus protecting the private property rights of neighboring landowners? Was it because zoning protects the public health and safety, which are core police power responsibilities of government? Was it because zoning segregates classes of land use and people, allowing communities to exclude those that could alter an area's characteristics? After all, *Euclid* was decided at a time of widespread legally mandated racial segregation, and the *Euclid* Court called apartments "parasites." Or was it because zoning is a tool of local government planning for rational, orderly, and coordinated development that serves the public interest? Moreover, was the Court's decision based

---

[19] See generally Wolf, The Zoning of America: Euclid v. Ambler (2008).

more on general legal principles about the relationships between government power and private rights? Or was it based more on the fact that careful studies by experts and evidence of changing conditions supported the rationality of zoning?

2. *As-applied challenges.* *Euclid* involved a facial challenge to the constitutionality of zoning altogether. The Court deferred to the city officials' judgment in enacting zoning, because the ordinance bore a substantial relation to the protection of the public health, safety, morals, and welfare. However, the Court left open the potential for specific zoning classifications to be struck down if they proved an irrational burden on particular landowners' rights in as-applied challenges. Such an occasion arose two years later, when the U.S. Supreme Court invalidated the residential zoning classification of part of a parcel of land that was otherwise zoned for industrial uses and adjoined by other industrial properties and railroad tracks.[20] The Court determined that the particular zoning classification did not rationally serve a legitimate public purpose. In general, zoning ordinances receive a strong presumption of validity from courts, and landowners rarely prevail on as-applied due-process challenges to zoning classifications. However, in recent years some courts have used various doctrine-specific rationales to give greater scrutiny to local land use decisions.[21] These include spot zoning, inconsistency with comprehensive planning, the quasi-judicial nature of single-parcel rezoning, inconsistency with state or federal statutes, or burdens on fundamental rights.

3. *Cumulative vs. noncumulative zoning.* The zoning ordinance in *Euclid* was cumulative, which means that less-intensive uses (e.g., single-family residential) were permissible in zones for more-intensive uses (e.g., industrial). Most zoning today is noncumulative, thus preventing the mixing of uses in higher-intensity zones. Advocates have criticized the impermissibility of mixed-use land-development projects under traditional zoning codes, because it has the effect of dispersing arguably compatible land uses, encouraging sprawl, and discouraging people from walking or living near public transportation. Increasingly, localities are using alternative regulatory tools or shifting to form-based, instead of use-based, zoning to allow development that mixes residential, retail, commercial, and public transportation uses.[22]

4. *Principal Problem.* How might the principles in *Euclid* guide the City of Cassidy officials in considering permissible uses for Frisch's property? For example, might Frisch argue that the "parlor" of Johnson Avenue has already been turned into the "barnyard" of automotive uses with previously-approved CUPs? Or might city officials refer to portions of *Euclid*

---

[20] Nectow v. City of Cambridge, 277 U.S. 183 (1928).

[21] Juergensmeyer & Roberts, Land Use Planning and Development Regulation Law § 5.37 (2d ed. 2007); Mandelker & Tarlock, Shifting the Presumption of Constitutionality in Land-Use Law, 24 Urb. Law.1 (1992).

[22] See, e.g., Crawford, Congress for the New Urbanism, Codifying New Urbanism: How to Reform Municipal Land Development Regulations (2004); Garnett, Ordering (and Order in) the City, 57 Stan. L. Rev. 1, 58 n.289 (2004); Kushner, Smart Growth, New Urbanism and Diversity: Progressive Planning Movements in America and Their Impact on Poor and Minority/Ethnic Populations, 21 UCLA J. Envtl. L. & Pol'y 45, 62–65 (2002–2003).

emphasizing changing conditions and deference to experts' analyses of the adverse impacts of particular land uses?

## Western Land Equities, Inc. v. City of Logan
Supreme Court of Utah, 1980.
617 P.2d 388.

■ STEWART, JUSTICE:

Defendants appeal from a ruling of the district court that the City of Logan unlawfully withheld approval of plaintiffs' proposed residential plan and was estopped from enforcing a zoning change that prohibits plaintiffs' proposed use. We affirm the trial court's order.

In February 1969 plaintiffs purchased 18.53 acres of property within the City of Logan. In April 1976, pursuant to a new land use ordinance, the property was zoned M-1, a manufacturing zone which permitted single-family dwellings. Plaintiffs' intent was to use the property for moderately priced single-family housing.

Plaintiffs' project was introduced on July 13, 1977. On October 12 the planning commission went on record as opposing subdivisions in M-1 zones, and on November 9 the commission rejected the proposed subdivision on the following grounds:

(1) Development of the proposed residential subdivision was contrary to the land use ordinance and to the city's master plan;

(2) The access roads provided by the plan were inadequate;

(3) The location of the railroad on three sides of the proposed subdivision made it an inappropriate site for housing.

In November plaintiffs unsuccessfully appealed the decision of the planning commission to the municipal council, and in December plaintiffs filed a complaint in district court. A restraining order was issued on January 3, 1978, enjoining the city from amending its zoning ordinance. The injunction was lifted on April 18, 1978, at which time a change in the zoning ordinance that had been enacted on January 19, 1978, became effective as it applied to plaintiffs' property.

Plaintiffs sought a determination, as a matter of law, that they had a vested right to develop a subdivision of single-family dwellings on their property and that defendants were estopped from withholding approval of the subdivision. The trial court in its findings of fact and conclusions of law held that plaintiffs' proposed development was permissible under the zoning regulations in existence prior to January 31, 1978, that plaintiffs had substantially complied with procedural requirements and had a vested right to develop the proposed subdivision, and that defendants were estopped from withholding approval of plaintiffs' subdivision on the basis of the amended ordinance enacted after the application for subdivision approval had been submitted.

Defendants contend that the application for approval of a subdivision does not create vested rights in the owner which immunize him from subsequent zoning changes. Since the decision of the court below was based on a finding that plaintiffs did have such a vested right, and not on the arbitrariness or unreasonableness of the commission's action, we deal only with the issue of whether the amendment to the zoning ordinance enacted by the city could be retroactively applied to plaintiffs' application for subdivision approval.

This Court has previously dealt with the issue of retroactive application of zoning laws in Contracts Funding & Mortgage Exchange v. Maynes, Utah, 527 P.2d 1073 (1974). In Contracts Funding the plaintiff arranged to purchase property which was unzoned, and the application to construct mobile homes on the property was conditionally approved. Following a period of further review, during which time the objections of neighbors were considered, the building permit was denied, and soon thereafter a zoning ordinance was passed which excluded plaintiff's proposed use. This Court held that the date of application for a building permit fixed the applicable zoning laws and that the application could not be denied on the basis of a subsequently-enacted ordinance. There was no contention in that case that there were countervailing public interests that outweighed the right of the property owner to use his land pursuant to the law in effect at the time of application for a permit.

The holding of Contracts Funding is not in accord with the rule generally accepted in other jurisdictions that an applicant for a building permit or subdivision approval does not acquire any vested right under existing zoning regulations prior to the issuance of the permit or official approval of a proposed subdivision. Generally, denial of an application may be based on subsequently-enacted zoning regulations.

However, for the reasons discussed below, we are of the view that the majority rule fails to strike a proper balance between public and private interests and opens the area to so many variables as to result in unnecessary litigation. We hold instead that an applicant for subdivision approval or a building permit is entitled to favorable action if the application conforms to the zoning ordinance in effect at the time of the application, unless changes in the zoning ordinances are pending which would prohibit the use applied for, or unless the municipality can show a compelling reason for exercising its police power retroactively to the date of application.

In the present case, the trial court found that plaintiffs had acquired a vested development right by their substantial compliance with procedural requirements and that the city was estopped from withholding approval of the proposed subdivision. The court used the language of zoning estoppel, a principle that is widely followed. That principle estops a government entity from exercising its zoning powers to prohibit a proposed land use when a property owner, relying reasonably and in good faith on some governmental act or omission, has made a substantial change in position or incurred such extensive obligations or expenses that it would be highly inequitable to deprive the owner of his right to complete his proposed development.

The focus of zoning estoppel is primarily upon the conduct and interests of the property owner. The main inquiry is whether there has been substantial reliance by the owner on governmental actions related to the superseded zoning that permitted the proposed use. The concern underlying this approach is the economic hardship that would be imposed on a property owner whose development plans are thwarted. Some courts hold that before a permit is issued no action of the owner is sufficient reliance to bar application of changes in zoning ordinances because there has been no governmental act sufficient to support an estoppel. Accordingly, a landowner is held to have no vested right in existing or anticipated zoning. Avco Community Developers, Inc. v. South Coast Regional Comm'n, 553 P.2d 546 (Cal. 1976). Other courts consider any substantial change of position in determining the estoppel issue. This Court in Wood v. North Salt Lake, 15 Utah 2d 245, 390 P.2d 858 (1964), held a zoning ordinance change requiring larger lots unenforceable because water mains and sewer connections had already been provided for lots that conformed in size to a previous ordinance. The Court stated that enforcement of the new ordinance in those circumstances would be unfair and inequitable.

If the substantial reliance requirement of zoning estoppel were applied to the facts of the present case, we could not agree with the trial court that plaintiffs' "substantial compliance" with procedural requirements justified the estoppel of the city's enforcement of a new zoning ordinance. Although plaintiffs allege they proceeded with subdivision plans and incurred significant costs with the encouragement of certain city officials, they had not yet received official approval of their plan, and their expenditures were merely for surveying and preliminary plans. The record indicates that plaintiffs spent $1,335 for a boundary survey and $890 for the preparation of a preliminary subdivision plat. The boundary survey has value regardless of the city's approval or disapproval of the plaintiffs' proposal. The expenditure of $890 for the plat is not significant in relation to the size of the parcel and is not substantial enough to justify an estoppel with regard to the enforcement of valid zoning ordinances that became effective before official approval of plaintiffs' proposed subdivision.

In rejecting the zoning estoppel approach in this matter, we are not prepared to state that it would never be relevant to a determination of the validity of the retroactive application of a zoning ordinance. We are of the view, however, that the relevant public and private interests are better accommodated in the first instance by a different approach.

In our view the tests employed by most other jurisdictions tend to subject landowners to undue and even calamitous expense because of changing city councils or zoning boards or their dilatory action and to the unpredictable results of burdensome litigation. The majority rule permits an unlimited right to deny permits when ordinances are amended after application and preliminary work. It allows government in many cases broader power with regard to land regulation than may be justified by the public interests involved. A balancing test, though geared toward promoting fairness, must be applied on a case-by-case basis and offers no predictable guidelines on which landowners can intelligently base their decisions regarding extensive development projects. Tests currently followed by the majority of states are particularly unsatisfactory in dealing with the large multistage projects. The threat of denial of a permit at a late stage of development makes a developer vulnerable to shifting governmental policies and tempts him to manipulate the process by prematurely engaging in activities that would establish the substantial reliance required to vest his right to develop when inappropriate.

The economic waste that occurs when a project is halted after substantial costs have been incurred in its commencement is of no benefit either to the public or to landowners. In a day when housing costs have severely escalated beyond the means of many prospective buyers, governmental actions should not be based on policies that exacerbate a severe economic problem without compelling justification. Governmental powers should be exercised in a manner that is reasonable and, to the extent possible, predictable.

On the other hand, a rule which vests a right unconditionally at the time application for a permit is made affords no protection for important public interests that may legitimately require interference with planned private development. If a proposal met zoning requirements at the time of application but seriously threatens public health, safety, or welfare, the interests of the public should not be thwarted.

The above competing interests are best accommodated in our view by adopting the rule that an applicant is entitled to a building permit or subdivision approval if his proposed development meets the zoning requirements in existence at the time of his application and if he proceeds with reasonable diligence, absent a compelling, countervailing public interest. Furthermore, if a city or county has initiated proceedings to amend its zoning ordinances, a landowner who subsequently makes application for a permit is not entitled to rely on the original zoning classification.

This rule follows from and extends our previous decision in Contracts Funding & Mortgage Exchange v. Maynes, Utah, 527 P.2d 1073 (1974). It is intended to strike a reasonable balance between important, conflicting public and private interests in the area of land development. A property owner should be able to plan for developing his property in a manner permitted by existing zoning regulations with some degree of assurance that the basic ground rules will not be changed in midstream. Clearly it is desirable to reduce the necessity for a developer to resort to the courts. An applicant for approval of a planned and permitted use should not be subject to shifting policies that do not reflect serious public concerns.

At the same time, compelling public interests may, when appropriate, be given priority over individual economic interests. A city should not be unduly restricted in effectuating legitimate policy changes when they are grounded in recognized legislative police powers. There may be instances when an application would for the first time draw attention to a serious problem that calls for an immediate amendment to a zoning ordinance, and such an amendment would be entitled to valid retroactive effect. It is incumbent upon a city, however, to act in good faith and not to reject an application because the application itself triggers zoning reconsiderations that result in a substitution of the judgment of current city officials for that of their predecessors. Regardless of the circumstances, a court must be cognizant of legitimate public concerns in considering whether a particular development should be protected from the effects of a desirable new law.

In the present case, the zoning of the property in question was found by the trial court to have permitted the proposed use at the time of the application. The owners had received encouragement from city officials, although no official approval was rendered. After the application, the city council members decided to reexamine the pertinent zoning regulation and thereafter voted to amend or "clarify" the zoning ordinance to disallow subdivisions in an M-1 zone and permit residences only by special permit. Their actions may have had a reasonable basis. It was argued that fire protection would be undermined because of limited access roads, but it does not appear the problem would be any less serious if the unarguably-permitted manufacturing facilities were erected instead of single-family houses. Objections as to inadequate sidewalks and other problems can be handled by requiring modification of specifications that do not meet city subdivision requirements. Indeed, the order of the trial court stated that the developers must comply with all the reasonable requirements of the city's subdivision ordinance.

We do not find the reasons given by the city for withholding approval of plaintiffs' proposed subdivision to be so compelling as to overcome the presumption that an applicant for a building permit or subdivision approval is entitled to affirmative official action if he meets the zoning requirements in force at the time of his application.

The order of the trial court is affirmed.

## Maryland Reclamation Associates, Inc. v. Harford County
Court of Appeals of Maryland, 2010.
994 A.2d 842.

■ ADKINS, J.

In this opinion we address two appeals filed by Appellant Maryland Reclamation Associates ("MRA") involving a sixty-eight acre agriculturally zoned property located in Harford County Maryland ("Property") on which MRA seeks to construct and operate a rubble landfill. This rubble landfill has been highly controversial and the litigation involving this Property has spanned over ten years. It now reaches this Court for the third time. Among other contentions, MRA asks this Court to adopt the doctrine of zoning estoppel, and hold that Harford County is estopped from applying an amendment to its zoning code that would render the Property ineligible for use as a rubble landfill. [MRA based its arguments on the fact that the County had included its site in its Solid Waste Management Plan (SWMP), subject to certain conditions, and that a state agency had issued an environmental permit for the site, all prior to the County reversing course and adopting a zoning code amendment that would impose new conditions on rubble landfill sites and require use variances for them.]

[Vested Rights: The Court held that MRA did not have a vested right, because it did not have a valid local land-use permit, as required by state vested-rights precedents. Arbitrary and Capricious: The Court held that the evidence showed that the County's zoning amendment was based on widespread opposition to all landfill projects, not just animus towards MRA's proposal.]

Zoning Estoppel: MRA urges that we should hold that specific principles of zoning estoppel apply here. In Sycamore Realty Company v. People's Counsel of Baltimore County, 344 Md. 57, 64, 684 A.2d 1331, 1334 (1996), without recognizing the doctrine of zoning estoppel in Maryland, we acknowledged its use in some other states, and described its character:

> A typical zoning estoppel scenario arises when the government issues a permit to a citizen that allows him or her to develop property in some way. Commonly, after the citizen has incurred some expense or has changed his or her position in reliance upon the permit, the property for which the permit was granted is rezoned so that the citizen's intended use is illegal. In such a situation, many courts allow the citizen to assert zoning estoppel as a defense to the government's attempt to enjoin the property use that violates the new zoning scheme.

The traditional, "black-letter" definition of zoning estoppel is:

> A local government exercising its zoning powers will be estopped when a property owner, (1) relying in good faith, (2) upon some

act or omission of the government, (3) has made such a substantial change in position or incurred such extensive obligations and expenses that it would be highly inequitable and unjust to destroy the rights which he ostensibly had acquired.

David G. Heeter, Zoning Estoppel: Application of the Principles of Equitable Estoppel and Vested Rights to Zoning Disputes, URB. L. ANN. 63, 66 (1971). Zoning estoppel was derived from equity principles and was intended to prevent the government from repudiating its prior conduct to the detriment of the property owner who relied on that conduct. URB. L. ANN. at 64–65. "The cases in which zoning estoppel is most often invoked and allowed . . . fall into four factual categories. They involve reliance upon (1) a validly issued permit; (2) the probability of issuance of a permit; (3) an erroneously issued permit; or (4) the nonenforcement of a zoning violation." URB. L. ANN. at 67.

We have found the Heeter writing to be the most helpful in explicating the doctrine of zoning estoppel, and how it differs from the doctrine of vested rights. Heeter said that although some courts will blend the doctrines of zoning estoppel and vested rights, "the origins of the two defenses are quite different. The defense of estoppel is derived from equity, but the defense of vested rights reflects principles of common and constitutional law." Heeter, supra, at 64 (footnotes omitted). See Sycamore, 344 Md. at 67, 684 A.2d at 1334 (quoting Heeter's distinction between vested rights and zoning estoppel).

Heeter also parsed the element of "good faith" by the property owner:

> The first element of zoning estoppel requires that the property owner "relied in good faith" on the conduct of the government. In essence it focuses upon the mental attitude of the owner when he acted. In category one, the courts will find that a property owner acted in good faith, if, knowing that rezoning was at least possible, he did not accelerate his development or increase his investment or obligations in an effort to establish such an apparent degree or amount of reliance as to prevent the rezoning. It is probably accurate to paraphrase this test as requiring that the owner act with honest intentions.

Heeter, supra, at 77–78.

The third element of zoning estoppel, "substantial reliance" is "the one which most often determines the outcome of the cases." Heeter, supra, at 85. According to Heeter's research in 1971,

> A majority of the courts utilize what may be described as the "set quantum test." Under this test, an owner is entitled to relief if he has changed his position beyond a certain set degree or amount, measured quantitatively. The problem with this test is that the courts have not set the requisite degree or amount with any precision. The majority of the courts appear to require some physical construction to establish substantial reliance.

Id. That lack of precision is evident in more written decisions as well. As one commentator wrote in 2000:

> Courts have used two tests in their "substantial reliance" inquiry, the first being the "proportionate/ratio test," which examines the percentage of money spent or obligations occurred as compared to the total cost of the completed project. A second test, known as the "balancing test" evaluates the public interest against the right of the property owner to make use of the land, as well as the land owner's expenses and obligations already incurred. While the proportionate/ratio test and the balancing test offer greater opportunity for achieving an equitable result than the building permit test, they are totally subjective in character and thus less reliable as precedent.

John J. Delaney, Evolving Voices in Land Use Law: A Festschrift in Honor of Daniel R. Mandelker: Part IV: Discussions on the State and Local Level: Chapter 7: Federalism: Vesting Verities and the Development Chronology: A Gaping Disconnect?, 3 Wash. U. J.L. & Pol'y 603, 608–09 (2000).

We have not explicitly adopted the doctrine of zoning estoppel, but we recognize that as zoning and permitting processes become more complex, the need for such a doctrine grows. Today, land use is much more highly regulated than it was fifty years ago-environmental concerns abound, and vehicular traffic demands seem to mushroom every year. Thus, a property owner who seeks to build or develop may well incur sizable expenses for experts in engineering, various environmental fields, traffic flow, archeology, etc., before putting a spade into the ground. With increasing public appreciation for open space and environmental protection causing apprehension about new construction, the likelihood a developing landowner will face serious opposition is high. Indeed, a developer faces quite a tortured process.

But we also cannot ignore a local government's responsibility to its residents, and thus, Maryland courts should not apply the doctrine casually. As open space disappears, and scientific knowledge about the adverse environmental impact from people's use of land grows, local governments struggle to balance the legitimate interests and rights of landowners wishing to develop against equally legitimate environmental and community concerns. Due to the delicacy of this balancing act, and the overriding need to protect the public, local government cannot always chart a steady course through the Scylla and Charybdis of these disparate interests. Land developers must understand that, to a limited extent, the local government will meander, and before they incur significant expense without final permitting, they must carefully assess the risk that the government will shift course. On the other hand, there may be situations in which the developer's good faith reliance on government action in the pre-construction stage is so extensive and expensive that zoning estoppel is an appropriate doctrine to apply.

Yet, we stop short of adopting zoning estoppel in this case as the facts set forth in this record do not support its application. For decades Maryland has maintained a stricter stance than most other states in protecting government's right to downzone in the face of planned construction.

We think that zoning estoppel must be applied, if at all, sparingly and with utmost caution. See, e.g., Bauer v. Waste Mgmt. of Connecticut, Inc., 662 A.2d 1179, 1193 (1995) ("In municipal zoning cases, however, estoppel may be invoked (1) only with great caution, (2) only when the resulting violation has been unjustifiably induced by an agent having authority in such matters, and (3) only when special circumstances make it highly inequitable or oppressive to enforce the regulations."). Squaring with this cautious approach, we conclude that the burden of establishing the facts to support that theory must fall on the person or entity claiming the benefit of the doctrine.

This burden of proof will come into play as we don the cloak of the doctrine to assess its fit to the facts in the record. In doing so, we conclude that ultimately, zoning estoppel does not fit these facts because there was no substantial reliance by MRA. Although Heeter and some courts treat "good faith" and "reliance" as separate elements, we discuss them together, as they are so closely entwined.

Under the theory of zoning estoppel, if the developer *"has good reason to believe, before or while acting to his detriment, that the official's mind may soon change*, estoppel may not be justified." Robert M. Rhodes, et al, Vested Rights: Establishing Predictability in a Changing Regulatory System, 13 Stetson L.Rev. 1, 4 (1983) (emphasis added). At the heart of establishing "good faith" is proof that the claimant lacked knowledge of those facts that would have put it on sufficient notice that it should not rely on the government action in question. See Heeter, supra, at 77–82.

Many facts were available to MRA at the time of its February 1990 purchase of the Property that should have alerted them to the real possibility that its plans for a rubble landfill would not come to fruition. On November 14, 1989, the County Council voted for the inclusion of the Property in the SWMP by a favorable vote of four council members, with two members abstaining because they felt they had inadequate information, and one member abstaining because his son was the president of MRA. Thus, the inclusion in the Plan was achieved by a fragile majority, and MRA knew, as did the Council when it voted, that MRA had no permit from the MDE and many additional steps had to be taken before MRA could actually construct the rubble landfill. Inclusion of the Property in the County SWMP was a necessary, but not a sufficient step in the process of obtaining a state rubble fill permit from MDE. See Md.Code (1982, 2007 Repl.Vol.), § 9–210 of the Environment Article. Even at the November 14 hearing, the Council President told MRA that "what we are doing tonight is approving a process. We are not exactly approving the landfill site. We are approving a step in a process."

As MRA president Schafer acknowledged at the hearing below, there was "strong" public opposition to the rubble landfill by "hundreds" of persons at the November 7 and 14, 1989 hearings. Shortly thereafter the membership of the County Council changed. The Hearing Examiner did not make a specific finding on the question of whether MRA president Shafer knew that there was no longer a majority of members on the newly constituted County Council who supported locating a rubble fill on the Property. This absence is not critical because the knowledge of these facts was certainly available to MRA, even if it did not have actual knowledge. See Bauer, 662 A.2d at 1194 (holding that party claiming zoning estoppel must "exercise due diligence to ascertan the truth and not only lac [k] knowledge of the true state of things, but also had no convenient means of acquiring that knowledge"). Certainly, MRA failed to prove that it exercised due diligence to ascertain the facts or that it had convenient means of acquiring those facts when local people were in full possession of them.

Additionally, the closing on MRA's purchase of the Property is not the definitive mile-marker in a zoning estoppel analysis. Generally, purchase of land, by itself, is insufficient to constitute "substantial reliance." See Heeter, supra, at 86 n. 81. (listing cases following this rule). To hold otherwise would mean that a purchaser could lock in the zoning of any parcel simply by the act of purchasing property and asking for a permit. For us to decide that the good faith reliance element of zoning estoppel is established by proof that an entity purchases land for the purpose of constructing a highly controversial rubble landfill based on a vote by the County Council approving one step in the State permitting process, while knowing that the new membership of County Council likely opposes that use, would disregard the caution with which we approach such a doctrine.

Thus, MRA must prove substantial reliance by something other than its purchase of the Gravel Hill property. It attempts to do so by focusing on the expenses it incurred for engineering fees during the period of its alleged good faith reliance. As Heeter said, most zoning estoppel cases turn on the element of substantial reliance, which the majority of courts define as a party's changing position in reliance on the government "beyond a certain set degree or amount, measured quantitatively." See Heeter, supra, at 85. As MRA is claiming reliance on the vote taken at the November 14, 1989 hearing, we examine what facts it brought forth to prove its reliance on that vote.

Although MRA asserts in its brief that, relying on the County's action, it "proceeded to spend over a million dollars on the purchase of the property and on engineering fees[,]" it gives us no extract references to support this statement. Richard Schafer testified that MRA spent $25,000 on Phase I engineering fees, and in excess of $300,000 on Phase

II & III engineering fees, *but did not specify when.* There was insufficient evidence to show how much, if any, of the engineering fees were incurred after and in good faith reliance upon the results of the November 14 hearing. Bald allegations and general testimonial statements that MRA spent $300,000 on engineering fees are simply insufficient to meet MRA's burden to prove the fact and extent of its reliance on the County Council's action.

Accordingly, MRA has failed to establish the necessary good faith reliance on the County Council's vote to include the Property in its SWMP either through purchase of the property or engineering expenses, or both. For all of the above reasons, MRA has not proven zoning estoppel against the County according to the criteria used in states that have adopted that doctrine.

## NOTES

1. *Vested rights contrasted with zoning estoppel.* The distinction between vested rights and zoning estoppel is a matter of some confusion. The standard distinction is that the vested rights doctrine results from due process protections but focuses on the actions of the developer in reasonable detrimental reliance in good faith on government action, whereas zoning estoppel is grounded in principles of equity and focuses on the nature of the government action on which the developer has reasonably and detrimentally relied in good faith.[23] However, the *Western Land Equities* Court characterizes zoning estoppel as focusing on the developer's actions, while the concept of vested rights is treated more like a bright-line rule that prevents the local government from changing the rules applicable to a pending application, absent a compelling justification.

2. *Vested rights: early vs. late.* In general, a government agency applies the rules that are in effect at the time that it makes its decision. Utah is an example of a state in which vested rights arise early in the process: at the time when the landowner or developer applies for the permit in question. On the opposite end of the spectrum is California, which does not recognize vested rights until the landowner or developer has incurred substantial expenditures in good faith reliance on a validly issued building permit, which is usually the last of a series of land-use approvals that are needed for development.[24] In *Avco*, the California Supreme Court held that a developer had to comply with project-altering coastal land-use regulations, despite having already incurred substantial expenditures and obtained other local regulatory permits, because the developer had not yet been granted a building permit.[25]

3. *Nonconforming uses.* When the government changes the zoning to prohibit an existing use of a property (or a use permissible at the time that

---

[23] Juergensmeyer & Roberts, Land Use Planning and Development Regulation Law § 5.27 (2d ed. 2007).

[24] Avco Community Developers, Inc. v. South Coast Reg'l Comm'n, 553 P.2d 546 (Cal. 1976).

[25] Id.

the landowner or developer acquired vested rights), the use becomes what is called a "nonconforming use," to which the landowner has a "grandfathered" right to continue. In general, though, the landowner cannot enlarge or increase the intensity of the use or resume it after destruction or abandonment, and in some cases, government regulators may require discontinuation of the nonconforming use after an "amortization period" that allows the landowner or developer to recoup his or her investment.[26]

4. *Principal Problem.* The *Western Land Equities* and *MRA* cases raise several issues for the City of Cassidy's officials to consider. For example, should the state courts adopt an early vesting rule that would recognize Frisch's vested rights to the zoning in effect at the time that he applied for his CUP? Or should they follow the late-vesting approach of Maryland that would allow the City to change its applicable zoning prior to a decision on Frisch's CUP application, unless zoning estoppel principles apply? If early vesting were to apply, does the City have a compelling justification for changing the zoning, notwithstanding Frisch's CUP application? If late vesting and zoning estoppel were to apply, is there an argument that the City's prior approval of five automotive facilities' CUPs constitutes a government action on which Frisch might have detrimentally relied? Or should Frisch have been considered to be on notice that the zoning on Johnson Avenue might change, given concerns about overconcentration of automotive facilities?

## Van Sicklen v. Browne
California Court of Appeals, 1971.
92 Cal.Rptr. 786.

■ MOLINARI, P.J.

Petitioners appeal from a judgment . . . sustaining the action of the [Milpitas] city planning commission denying petitioners' application for a use permit to construct an automobile service station on property which they own within the boundaries of Milpitas.

Petitioners applied to the planning commission for a use permit for the construction of an automobile service station on a lot owned by them in the "HS" Highway Service District. The commission denied the application and in its decision stated the following reasons:

1) Approval would create a further proliferation of this type of land use in a neighborhood already adequately served by service stations located more logically at a major intersection.

2) Approval would open the door for at least two additional stations at the Wilson Way intersection and would create a precedent that would make it difficult for the city to deny applicants on other corners.

---

[26] Juergensmeyer & Roberts, Land Use Planning and Development Regulation Law §§ 4.31–4.40 (2d ed. 2007).

3) There is no demonstrated need for an additional service station in this neighborhood at this time. Adjacent stations have a history of turnover in management and are known to have been vacant for extended periods in the recent past.

4) Approval would establish a service station use too close to a developed residential area without the logic of it being at the intersection of two heavily traveled major streets.

5) Approval on the basis of a future freeway location seems, at best, premature. While freeway agreements are in existence, actual construction of the freeway is many years away and traffic patterns created by the freeway are neither definite or known. Detailed ramp drawings are not available.

The zoning ordinance expressly provides that automobile service stations may be permitted in the Highway Service District if their location conforms to the objectives of the Master Plan. (§ 17.01.) The ordinance also provides in its stated purpose that its objectives are to be accomplished in accordance with the Master Plan. (§ 1.02.) It is apparent, therefore, that the planning commission is vested with considerable discretion in determining whether the proposed use subserves the Master Plan's fundamental objectives. One of these objectives is that which seeks to "strengthen and promote development through stability and balance."

The planning commission, after an extensive hearing, concluded that "approval would create a further proliferation of this type of land use in a neighborhood already adequately served by service stations located more logically at a major intersection," and that "approval would establish a service station use too close to a developed residential area." This determination is a legitimate exercise of the discretionary power vested in the planning commission by the zoning ordinance. Since there is no indication that the planning commission acted arbitrarily or capriciously, its findings must be upheld.

We observe that the traditional purpose of the conditional use permit is to enable a municipality to exercise some measure of control over the extent of certain uses, such as service stations, which, although desirable in limited numbers, could have a detrimental effect on the community in large numbers. Here, in view of the specifically stated purposes of both the zoning ordinance and the Master Plan, it is inconceivable that it was the legislative intent that use permits for service stations would be granted for any number of service stations so long as each parcel met the minimum width, frontage and area requirements.

Petitioners' final contention is that the city denied the use permit for economic rather than planning considerations resulting in an invalid attempt to regulate competition through zoning laws. They refer specifically to the planning commission's finding that there was no demonstrated need for an additional service station in the neighborhood at this time.

Although cities may not use zoning powers to regulate economic competition, it is also recognized that land use and planning decisions cannot be made in any community without some impact on the economy of the community. As stated in Metromedia, Inc. v. City of Pasadena, 216 Cal. App.2d 270, 273 [30 Cal. Rptr. 731], "Today, economic and aesthetic considerations together constitute the nearly inseparable warp and woof of the fabric upon which the modern city must design its future." Taking cognizance of this concept we perceive that planning and zoning ordinances traditionally seek to maintain property values, protect tax revenues, provide neighborhood social and economic stability, attract business and industry and encourage conditions which make a community a pleasant place to live and work.

Whether these be classified as "planning considerations" or "economic considerations," we hold that so long as the primary purpose of the zoning ordinance is not to regulate economic competition, but to subserve a valid objective pursuant to a city's police powers, such ordinance is not invalid even though it might have an indirect impact on economic competition.

Intensity of land use is a well-recognized and valid city concern and relates to both health and safety factors and to proper zoning practice. Courts in other states have recognized that "density" and overconcentration of service stations justify regulation. (See Blair v. Board of Adjustment of Borough of Hatboro, 403 Pa. 105 [169 A.2d 49]; Kramer v. Baltimore, 166 Md. 324, 334 [171 A. 70, 74]; Ballard v. Roth, 141 Misc. 319 [253 N.Y.S. 6, 14].) In Blair it was held that permits could properly be refused for service stations when the granting of the permits would result in five stations within a radius of 350 feet and 10 stations in a community covering only one and one-half square miles in area and an increase in traffic. In Kramer it was observed that the number of service stations already allowed " . . . may have reached the limit of safety. The multiplication of such stations may in itself be a menace, . . . " (166 Md. at p. 334 [171 A. at p. 74].) The rationale of these decisions appears to be that since service stations store and use products which are highly inflammable and explosive, it is evident that an increase in the number of such stations in a small area increases the danger to the public notwithstanding the care and caution with which the business may be conducted.

The judgment is affirmed.

## NOTES

1. *Standards, evidence, and findings.* Several requirements typically apply to administrative permit decisions, such as for CUPs and variances, although each of these requirements has some minority counter-authority.

Decision makers must be guided by standards set forth in the zoning code that constrain their discretion in granting or denying the permit and give notice to applicants of the applicable expectations. State courts vary on how general or precise the standards must be,[27] but the CUP standards in the Principal Problem fall within the range that most courts would uphold. In addition, a board must make its decision on substantial evidence in the record and usually must make findings that link the evidence to the standards to support its decision.[28] Substantial evidence is "such relevant evidence as a reasonable mind might accept as adequate to support a conclusion."[29] It can include statements made at the hearing from the applicant or from neighbors, but decisions must be based on the likely impacts of the project, not just general public opposition, and must relate to the standards for granting or denying the permit.[30] While courts give permit decisions greater scrutiny than most zoning decisions, they still afford permit decision makers a substantial amount of deference.[31] In light of these requirements and the Principal Problem, what advice would you give McDonald and the BZA regarding Frisch's CUP application?

2. *Overconcentration.* Is overconcentration of a conditionally permitted use a sufficient legal basis for denying a CUP? *Van Sicklen* holds so, but other courts may not. Principles of fairness may dictate that Frisch be treated the same as other automotive facilities' owners on Johnson Avenue, who received their CUPs for similar properties also zoned GC.[32] A court might determine that the BZA cannot reasonably conclude that Frisch's use is incompatible with the area when there are already five automotive facilities in the area. In other words, the area's "character" has already changed and Frisch only seeks to do what others in the area are already doing. On the other hand, expectations of "equal treatment" may conflict with the "first in time, first in right" principle in property law. Regulators cannot be precluded from changing zoning regulations to adapt to changing conditions or lessons learned from past decisions, simply because property owners were allowed to make more intensive uses of their land in the past. Moreover, evaluation of the cumulative impacts of activities is a fundamental premise of environmental regulation: the environment may have the capacity to absorb a certain amount of pollution or alteration, but at some point, the cumulative impact from each new use exceed the environment's carrying capacity. If the problem is that Johnson Avenue and

---

[27] Juergensmeyer & Roberts, Land Use Planning and Development Regulation Law § 5.25 (2d ed. 2007).

[28] Topanga Ass'n for a Scenic Community v. County of Los Angeles, 522 P.2d 12 (Cal. 1974).

[29] Pittsburgh Cellular Telephone Co. v. Board of Supervisors, 704 A.2d 192, 193 n.2 (Pa. Cmwlth. Ct. 1997).

[30] Compare Christian Gospel Church v. San Francisco, 896 F.2d 1221, 1225 (9th Cir. 1990), with Twin County Recycling Corp. v. Yevoli, 688 N.E.2d 501 (N.Y. 1997).

[31] Juergensmeyer & Roberts, Land Use Planning and Development Regulation Law § 5.37 (2d ed. 2007).

[32] See Jenkins v. St. Tammany Parish Police Jury, 736 So.2d 1287 (La. 1999) (denial of a CUP for a cemetery was patently unreasonable as a non-uniform application of the zoning code, where five other cemeteries had been permitted in the area, despite officials' contention that the area now had too many cemeteries.)

the adjacent Chapin-Lein neighborhood have reached the saturation point of automotive uses and their accompanying adverse effects, should the City Council rezone Johnson Avenue? How should this affect the BZA's consideration of Frisch's CUP application? Should the fact that he can make other economically productive uses of his land, even if his CUP is denied, affect your analysis?

# ASSIGNMENT 31–32

# TAKINGS: PHYSICAL, REGULATORY AND EXACTIONS

## a. OVERVIEW

The Takings Clause, which was first introduced in Assignment 29, safeguards private property rights against government regulation and constrains government regulation to protect the public health, safety, morals, and welfare. The Fifth Amendment to the Constitution provides "nor shall private property be taken for public use, without just compensation."[1] Initially applicable to the federal government, the Takings Clause also limits state and local governments through the selective incorporation doctrine, which holds states and localities to certain rights guaranteed in the Bill of Rights by means of the Fourteenth Amendment's Due Process Clause.[2]

The Takings Clause has four elements: 1) private property; 2) taking; 3) public use; and 4) just compensation. With respect to private property, many of the interests allegedly taken in the cases that follow involve private ownership of land, which clearly falls within the category of constitutional private property for purposes of the Takings Clause. However, other property interests explored elsewhere in this casebook, such as easements and leaseholds, are potentially subject to takings. Whether other kinds of property interests, such as the benefits of restrictive covenants, water rights, patents, and copyrights, are constitutionally compensable property interests are contested issues.[3] However, in 2015, the U.S. Supreme Court reached near-unanimous agreement that personal property does not receive less protection than real property under the Takings Clause when it comes to the government's physical taking of the property. But the government may

---

[1] U.S. Const. amend. V.

[2] See Chicago, B. & Q. R. Co. v. Chicago, 166 U.S. 226 (1897).

[3] See, e.g., Juergensmeyer & Roberts, Land Use Planning and Development Regulation Law, 2d ed. § 16.3.A, pp. 638–39 (2007) (noting that courts differ over whether compensation is due for the taking of a benefit for a negative easement, covenant, or equitable servitude, but stating that the majority rule requires compensation); Zellmer & Harder, Unbundling Property in Water, 59 Ala. L. Rev. 679 (2008) (discussing whether water rights should be considered constitutionally compensable property). See also Pickens, The Robin Hood Taking and the Court of Standards, 4 Appalachian J.L. 145 (2005) (discussing a pair of U.S. Supreme Court cases holding that interest on lawyers' trust accounts was property taken by the government but for which no compensation was due).

regulate personal property more than real property without having to pay just compensation to the property owner.[4]

The second element of the Takings Clause—whether the government's action constitutes a taking—is the subject of this Assignment. The third element, public use, was addressed in Assignment 29. The fourth element, just compensation, concerns the amount of compensation the property owner is to receive if property was indeed taken. The general rule is "fair market value," but as pointed out in Assignment 29, this is a heavily fact-specific question that could employ any of several different standards for evaluating the property in question. As you may recall from Assignment 29, the government has the power of eminent domain. This means that it can take property for a public use (or purpose) and that the remedy for a taking is damages—compensation for the property taking—and not invalidation of the action (unless it violates some other constitutional or statutory constraint).

Three basic categories of takings exist. The first category is physical takings, in which the government intrudes on the owner's right to exclude by physically possessing or occupying the property or mandating that the owner accommodate the possession or occupation by another. The second category is regulatory takings, in which the government's regulation of the owner's use of property is so great as to be tantamount to a taking of the property. The third category is exactions, in which government regulators condition the granting of a land-use or development permit on the owner providing certain property (e.g., land, easements, facilities, monetary funds) to the government or public. Each category has its own distinctive tests, but the U.S. Supreme Court has stated that the takings tests have a common purpose; namely, "to identify regulatory actions that are functionally equivalent to a direct appropriation or ouster from private property."[5] Each of these categories is explored in a separate subsection of this Assignment.

Before addressing these three categories, though, two procedural requirements applying to property owners bringing just compensation claims for takings must be understood. These requirements are referred to as the *Williamson County* ripeness requirements. Ripeness is a judicial doctrine grounded in Article III of the Constitution that creates jurisdiction in federal courts over cases and controversies arising under the Constitution, federal laws and treaties.[6] It precludes courts from hearing cases that are premature, i.e., that are not yet ripe for judicial decision. Because the ripeness question is jurisdictional, a party can raise the issue at any time and at any level of decision (including after a trial court decision and an initial appellate court decision). Moreover, the court itself can raise the issue *sua sponte*. The court does not have the power to decide a case that is not yet ripe. For takings claims, the

---

[4] Horne v. U.S. Dept. of Agriculture, 576 U.S. ___, 135 S.Ct. 2419 (2015).
[5] Lingle v. Chevron USA, Inc., 544 U.S. 528, 529 (2005).
[6] U.S. Const. art. III, sec. 2.

Supreme Court announced two rules concerning ripeness in *Williamson County Regional Planning Comm'n v. Hamilton Bank*: 1) the final decision rule; and 2) the state compensation rule.[7]

First, the property owner must have a final decision from the government about the scope and effect of its actions on the property. This means that the property owner must seek any available permits, exceptions, variances, and appeals. Thus, a decision by a zoning board is not final if it can be appealed to the city council. The final decision rule also may mean that the property owner whose land is regulated does not have a ripe claim if the only permit sought for the property was for a highly intensive use and no effort was made to secure a approval for a less intensive use of the property. On this point, though, the government cannot evade ripeness simply by turning down a series of decreasingly intense development proposals, each time promising to approve the next smaller project but then denying it once the application is filed.[8] The premise of the final decision rule is that a court cannot determine whether the property has been taken until it knows exactly what the government requires, allows, and prohibits, including opportunities for the government to correct its own over-reaching actions. There is a rare "futility" exception for circumstances in which it is abundantly clear that any permits, exceptions, variances, or appeals would be unavailing.

In addition to the final decision rule, the state compensation rule must also be followed. Specifically, if the alleged taking has been by a state or local government entity, the property owner must seek compensation through state-provided processes before bringing a claim in federal court. The taking of the property is not unconstitutional (as long as it serves a public purpose) but it requires that the property owner be compensated. Thus, if a state provides methods for seeking compensation for alleged takings—and they all do—the property owner must use such methods. Attorneys for private property owners historically were inclined to file state and local takings claims in federal court, perhaps in part because they perceived that federal court was the place to assert constitutional rights, perhaps in part because they perceived that federal judges might be more sympathetic than state judges, and perhaps in part because they wanted to also file due process and equal protection claims against the government. At first, the state compensation rule was a trap for the unwary. By the time that a federal court throws out the takings claim against the state or local government on ripeness, the statute of limitations may have run on filing the takings claim in state court and the private property owner would be without judicial remedy. Surprisingly, though, a number of takings claims against state and local governments continued to be brought in federal courts long after it became clear that federal courts would dismiss these claims on *Williamson County* ripeness grounds. The lesson here is that

---

[7] 473 U.S. 172 (1985).
[8] Monterey v. Del Monte Dunes, Ltd., 526 U.S. 687 (1999).

despite theories about property rights, constitutional protections, and litigation strategies, lawyers need to pay attention to procedural requirements and jurisdictional limits that apply to their clients' cases.

## b. Physical Takings

### 1. Principal Problem

The City of Hillington has recently passed an ordinance which effectuated a moratorium on the conversion, alteration and demolition of single-room occupancy (SRO) dwellings for a period of five years, with the possibility of unlimited renewals at the city's discretion. The law provides that SRO property owners put every SRO unit in their buildings in habitable condition and lease every such unit to a "bona fide" tenant at controlled rents. Noncompliance with the law is punishable by fines, although an owner can purchase an exemption from the moratorium with a specified payment or by providing an equal number of replacement units. According to a hardship exemption provided for in the law, both the specified payment for the exemption and the number of replacement units can be reduced at the discretion of the Housing Commissioner if the property owner can show that there is no realistic possibility that he can make a reasonable rate of return. For this purpose, reasonable rate of return is defined as a net annual return of 8½% of the assessed value of the property as an SRO dwelling.

Plaintiff real estate developers who own SRO properties are challenging the law as an unconstitutional taking of private property without just compensation. They have solicited your opinion concerning the validity of the Hillington ordinance. The city contends that the law is a valid effort to alleviate homelessness by preserving the availability of low-rent SRO housing. Before rendering an opinion, consider the following materials.

### 2. Materials for Solution of Principal Problem

#### Loretto v. Teleprompter Manhattan CATV Corp.
Supreme Court of the United States, 1982.
458 U.S. 419, 102 S.Ct. 3164.

■ JUSTICE MARSHALL delivered the opinion of the Court.

[The Fifth Amendment to the United States Constitution, made applicable to the States by the Fourteenth Amendment, prohibits the taking of private property for public use without just compensation.]

This case presents the question whether a minor but permanent physical occupation of an owner's property authorized by government constitutes a "taking" of property for which just compensation is due. New York law provides that a landlord must permit a cable television company to install its cable facilities upon his property. N.Y.Exec.Law

§ 828(1) (McKinney Supp.1982). In this case, the cable installation occupied portions of appellant's roof and the side of her building. The New York Court of Appeals ruled that this appropriation does not amount to a taking. Because we conclude that such a physical occupation of property is a taking, we reverse.

## I

Appellant Jean Loretto purchased a five-story apartment building located at 303 West 105th Street, New York, in 1971. The previous owner had granted appellees Teleprompter Corporation and Teleprompter Manhattan CATV ("Teleprompter") permission to install a cable on the building and the exclusive privilege of furnishing cable television ("CATV") services to the tenants. The New York Court of Appeals described the installation as follows:

> On June 1, 1970 Teleprompter installed a cable slightly less than one-half inch in diameter and of approximately 30 feet in length along the length of the building about 18 inches above the roof top, and directional taps, approximately 4 inches by 4 inches by 4 inches, on the front and rear of the roof. By June 8, 1970 the cable had been extended another 4 to 6 feet and cable had been run from the directional taps to the adjoining building at 305 West 105th Street Teleprompter also installed two large silver boxes[9] along the roof cables. The cables are attached by screws or nails penetrating the masonry at approximately two foot intervals, and other equipment is installed by bolts. . . .

Prior to 1973, Teleprompter routinely obtained authorization for its installations from property owners along the cable's route, compensating the owners at the standard rate of 5% of the gross revenues that Teleprompter realized from the particular property. To facilitate tenant access to CATV, the State of New York enacted § 828 of the Executive Law, effective January 1, 1973. Section 828 provides that a landlord may not "interfere with the installation of cable television facilities upon his property or premises," and may not demand payment from any tenant for permitting CATV, or demand payment from any CATV company "in excess of any amount which the [State Commission on Cable Television] shall, by regulation, determine to be reasonable." The landlord may, however, require the CATV company or the tenant to bear the cost of installation and to indemnify for any damage caused by the installation. Pursuant to § 828(1)(b), the State Commission has ruled that a one-time $1 payment is the normal fee to which a landlord is entitled.

Appellant did not discover the existence of cable until after she had purchased the building. She brought a class action against Teleprompter in 1976 on behalf of all owners of real property in the state on which Teleprompter has placed CATV components, alleging that

---

[9] Editor's note: The majority opinion suggests that the boxes were "in excess of 1–½ cubic feet." The dissenting opinion suggests that only one-eighth of a cubic foot was involved.

Teleprompter's installation was a trespass and, insofar as it relied on § 828, a taking without just compensation. She requested damages and injunctive relief.

[The trial court granted summary judgment to Teleprompter.]

On appeal, the Court of Appeals, over dissent, upheld the statute, 53 N.Y.2d 124, 440 N.Y.S.2d 843, 423 N.E.2d 320 (1981). The court concluded that the law requires the landlord to allow . . . installations but permits him to request payment from the CATV company under § 828(1)(b), at a level determined by the State Cable Commission. . . . The court then ruled that the law serves a legitimate police power purpose—eliminating landlord fees and conditions that inhibit the development of CATV, which has important educational and community benefits. Rejecting the argument that a physical occupation authorized by government is necessarily a taking, the court stated that the regulation does not have an excessive economic impact upon appellant when measured against her aggregate property rights, and that it does not interfere with any reasonable investment-backed expectations. Accordingly, the court held that § 828 does not work a taking of appellant's property.

## II

The Court of Appeals determined that § 828 serves the legitimate public purpose of "rapid development of and maximum penetration by a means of communication which has important educational and community aspects," 53 N.Y.2d, at 143–144, 440 N.Y.S.2d, at 852, 423 N.E.2d, at 329, and thus is within the State's police power. We have no reason to question that determination. It is a separate question, however, whether an otherwise valid regulation so frustrates property rights that compensation must be paid. We conclude that a permanent physical occupation authorized by government is a taking without regard to the public interests that it may serve. Our constitutional history confirms the rule, recent cases do not question it, and the purposes of the Takings Clause compel its retention.

### A

In Penn Central Transportation Co. v. New York City, 438 U.S. 104, 98 S.Ct. 2646, 57 L.Ed.2d 631 (1978), the Court surveyed some of the general principles governing the Takings Clause. The Court noted that no "set formula" existed to determine, in all cases, whether compensation is constitutionally due for a government restriction of property. Ordinarily, the Court must engage in "essentially ad hoc, factual inquiries." *Id.*, at 124, 98 S.Ct., at 2659. But the inquiry is not standardless. The economic impact of the regulation, especially the degree of interference with investment-backed expectations, is of particular significance. "So, too, is the character of the governmental action. A 'taking' may more readily be found when the interference with property can be characterized as a physical invasion by government, . . .

than when interference arises from some public program adjusting the benefits and burdens of economic life to promote the common good." *Id.* (citation omitted).

As *Penn Central* affirms, the Court has often upheld substantial regulation of an owner's use of his own property where deemed necessary to promote the public interest. At the same time, we have long considered a physical intrusion by government to be a property restriction of an unusually serious character for purposes of the Takings Clause. Our cases further establish that when the physical intrusion reaches the extreme form of a permanent physical occupation, a taking has occurred. In such a case, "the character of the government action" not only is an important factor in resolving whether the action works a taking but is determinative.

When faced with a constitutional challenge to a permanent physical occupation of real property, this Court has invariably found a taking. As early as 1871, in Pumpelly v. Green Bay Company, 13 Wall. (80 U.S.) 166, 20 L.Ed. 557 (1871), this Court held that the defendant's construction, pursuant to state authority, of a dam which permanently flooded plaintiff's property constituted a taking. A unanimous Court stated, without qualification, that "where real estate is actually invaded by superinduced additions of water, earth, sand, or other material, or by having any artificial structure placed on it, so as to effectually destroy or impair its usefulness, it is a taking, within the meaning of the Constitution."

This Court has consistently distinguished between flooding cases involving a permanent physical occupation, on the one hand, and cases involving a more temporary invasion, or government action outside the owner's property that causes consequential damages within, on the other. A taking has always been found only in the former situation.

More recent cases confirm the distinction between a permanent physical occupation, a physical invasion short of an occupation, and a regulation that merely restricts the use of property. In United States v. Causby, 328 U.S. 256, 66 S.Ct. 1062, 90 L.Ed. 1206 (1946), the Court ruled that frequent flights immediately above a land owner's property constituted a taking, comparing such overflights to the quintessential form of a taking:

> If, by reason of the frequency of altitude of the flights, respondents could not use this land for any purpose, their loss would be complete. It would be as complete as if the United States had entered upon the surface of the land and had taken exclusive possession of it.

In Kaiser Aetna v. United States, 444 U.S. 164, 100 S.Ct. 383, 62 L.Ed.2d 332 (1979), the Court held that the government's imposition of a navigational servitude requiring public access to a pond was a taking where the land owner had reasonably relied on government consent in connecting the pond to navigable water. The Court emphasized that the servitude took the land owner's right to exclude, "one of the most essential sticks in the bundle of rights that are commonly characterized as property." *Id.* at 176, 100 S.Ct., at 391. The Court explained:

> This is not a case in which the Government is exercising its regulatory power in a manner that will cause an insubstantial devaluation of petitioner's private property; rather, the imposition of the navigational servitude in this context will result in an *actual physical invasion* of the privately owned marina. . . . And even if the Government physically invades only an easement in property, it must nonetheless pay compensation.

Although the easement of passage, not being a permanent occupation of land, was not considered a taking *per se, Kaiser Aetna* reemphasizes that a physical invasion is a government intrusion of an unusually serious character.

Another recent case underscores the constitutional distinction between a permanent occupation and a temporary physical invasion. In PruneYard Shopping Center v. Robins, 447 U.S. 74, 100 S.Ct. 2035, 64 L.Ed.2d 741 (1980), the Court upheld a state constitutional requirement that shopping center owners permit individuals to exercise free speech and petition rights on their property, to which they had already invited the general public. The Court emphasized that the state constitution does not prevent the owner from restricting expressive activities by imposing reasonable time, place, and manner restrictions to minimize interference with the owner's commercial functions. Since the invasion was temporary and limited in nature, and since the owner had not exhibited an interest in excluding all persons from his property, "the fact that [the solicitors] may have 'physically invaded' [the owners'] property cannot be viewed as determinative."

In short, when the "character of the governmental action," *Penn Central,* 438 U.S., at 124, 98 S.Ct., at 2659, is a permanent physical occupation of property, our cases uniformly have found a taking to the extent of the occupation, without regard to whether the action achieves an important public benefit or has only minimal economic impact on the owner.

## B

Property rights in a physical thing have been described as the rights "to possess, use and dispose of it." United States v. General Motors Corp., 323 U.S. 373, 378, 65 S.Ct. 357, 359, 89 L.Ed. 311 (1945). To the extent that the government permanently occupies physical property, it effectively destroys *each* of these rights. First, the owner has no right to possess the occupied space himself, and also has no power to exclude the occupier from possession and use of the space. The power to exclude has traditionally been considered one of the most treasured strands in an owner's bundle of property rights. See *Kaiser Aetna,* 444 U.S., at 179–

180, 100 S.Ct., at 392–393; see also Restatement of Property § 7 (1936). Second, the permanent physical occupation of property forever denies the owner any power to control the use of this property; he not only cannot exclude others, but can make no non-possessory use of the property. Although deprivation of the right to use and obtain a profit from property is not, in every case, independently sufficient to establish a taking, see Andrus v. Allard, 444 U.S., at 66, 100 S.Ct., at 327, it is clearly relevant. Finally, even though the owner may retain the bare legal right to dispose of the occupied space by transfer or sale, the permanent occupation of that space by a stranger will ordinarily empty the right of any value, since the purchaser will also be unable to make any use of the property.

Moreover, an owner suffers a special kind of injury when a *stranger* directly invades and occupies the owner's property. As section IIA, *supra,* indicates, property law has long protected an owner's expectation that he will be relatively undisturbed at least in the possession of his property. To require, as well, that the owner permit another to exercise complete dominion literally adds insult to injury. See Michelman, Property, Utility, and Fairness: Comments on the Ethical Foundations of "Just Compensation" Law, 80 Harv.L.Rev. 1165, 1228, and n. 110 (1967). Furthermore, such an occupation is qualitatively more severe than a regulation of the *use* of property, even a regulation that imposes affirmative duties on the owner, since the owner may have no control over the timing, extent, or nature of the invasion.

The traditional rule also avoids otherwise difficult line drawing problems. Few would disagree that if the State required landlords to permit third parties to install swimming pools on the landlords' rooftops for the convenience of the tenants, the requirement would be a taking. If the cable installation here occupied as much space, again, few would disagree that the occupation would be a taking. But constitutional protection for the rights of private property cannot be made to depend on the size of the area permanently occupied.

C

Teleprompter's cable installation on appellant's building constitutes a taking under the traditional test. The installation involved a direct physical attachment of plates, boxes, wires, bolts and screws to the building, completely occupying space immediately above and upon the roof and along the building's exterior wall.

Appellees raise a series of objections to application of the traditional rule here. Teleprompter notes that the law applies only to buildings used as rental property, and draws the conclusion that the law is simply a permissible regulation of the use of real property. We fail to see, however, why a physical occupation of one type of property but not another type is any less a physical occupation. Insofar as Teleprompter means to suggest that this is not a permanent physical invasion, we must differ. So long as the property remains residential and a CATV company wishes to retain the installation, the landlord must permit it.

Finally, we do not agree with appellees that application of the physical occupation rule will have dire consequences for the government's power to adjust landlord-tenant relationships. This Court has consistently affirmed that States have broad power to regulate housing conditions in general and the landlord-tenant relationship in particular without paying compensation for all economic injuries that such regulation entails.... In none of these cases, however, did the government authorize the permanent occupation of the landlord's property by a third party. Consequently, our holding today in no way alters the analysis governing the State's power to require landlords to comply with building codes and provide utility connections, mailboxes, smoke detectors, fire extinguishers, and the like in the common area of a building. So long as these regulations do not require the landlord to suffer the physical occupation of a portion of his building by a third party, they will be analyzed under the multi-factor inquiry generally applicable to non-possessory governmental activity.

### III

Our holding today is very narrow. We affirm the traditional rule that a permanent physical occupation of property is a taking. In such a case, the property owner entertains an historically-rooted expectation of compensation, and the character of the invasion is qualitatively more intrusive than perhaps any other category of property regulation. We do not, however, question the equally substantial authority upholding a State's broad power to impose appropriate restrictions upon an owner's *use* of his property.

The judgment of the New York Court of Appeals is reversed and the case is remanded for further proceedings not inconsistent with this opinion.

■ JUSTICE BLACKMUN, with whom JUSTICE BRENNAN and JUSTICE WHITE join, dissenting.

If the Court's decisions construing the Takings Clause state anything clearly, it is that "[t]here is no set formula to determine where regulation ends and taking begins." Goldblatt v. Town of Hempstead, 369 U.S. 590, 594, 82 S.Ct. 987, 990, 8 L.Ed.2d 130 (1962).

In a curiously anachronistic decision, the Court today acknowledges its historical disavowal of set formulae in almost the same breath as it constructs a rigid *per se* takings rule: "a permanent physical occupation authorized by government is a taking without regard to the public interests that it may serve." To sustain its rule against our recent precedents, the Court erects a strained and untenable distinction between "temporary physical invasions," whose constitutionality concededly "is subject to a balancing process," and "permanent physical occupations," which are "taking[s] without regard to other factors that a court might ordinarily examine."

In my view, the Court's approach "reduces the constitutional issue to a formalistic quibble" over whether property has been "permanently occupied" or "temporarily invaded." Sax, Takings and the Police Power, 74 Yale L.J. 36, 37 (1964). The Court's application of its formula to the facts of this case vividly illustrates that its approach is potentially dangerous as well as misguided. Despite its concession that "States have broad power to regulate . . . the landlord-tenant relationship . . . without paying compensation for all economic injuries that such regulation entails," the Court uses its rule to undercut a carefully-considered legislative judgment concerning landlord-tenant relationships. I therefore respectfully dissent.

In the end, what troubles me most about today's decision is that it represents an archaic judicial response to a modern social problem. Cable television is a new and growing, but somewhat controversial, communications medium. The New York Legislature not only recognized, but responded to, this technological advance by enacting a statute that sought carefully to balance the interests of all private parties. New York's courts in this litigation, with only one jurist in dissent, unanimously upheld the constitutionality of that considered legislative judgment.

This Court now reaches back in time for a *per se* rule that disrupts that legislative determination. Like Justice Black, I believe that "the solution of the problems precipitated by . . . technological advances and new ways of living cannot come about through the application of rigid constitutional restraints formulated and enforced by the courts." United States v. Causby, 328 U.S., at 274, 66 S.Ct., at 1072 (dissenting opinion). I would affirm the judgment and uphold the reasoning of the New York Court of Appeals.

### Yee v. City of Escondido.
Supreme Court of the United States, 1992.
503 U.S. 519, 112 S.Ct. 1522.

■ O'CONNOR, J., delivered the opinion of the Court.

Petitioners own mobile home parks in Escondido, California. They contend that a local rent control ordinance, when viewed against the backdrop of California's Mobile home Residency Law, amounts to a physical occupation of their property entitling them to compensation.

The term "mobile home" is somewhat misleading. Mobile homes are largely immobile as a practical matter, because the cost of moving one is often a significant fraction of the value of the mobile home itself. They are generally placed permanently in parks; once in place, only about one in every hundred mobile homes is ever moved. . . . A mobile home owner typically rents a plot of land, called a "pad," from the owner of a mobile home park. The park owner provides private roads within the park, common facilities such as washing machines or a swimming pool, and often utilities. The mobile home owner often invests in site-specific improvements such as a driveway, steps, walkways, porches, or landscaping. When the mobile home owner wishes to move, the mobile home is usually sold in place, and the purchaser continues to rent the pad on which the mobile home is located.

In 1978, California enacted its Mobilehome Residency Law, Cal. Civ. Code Ann. § 798 (West 1982 and Supp. 1991). The Legislature found "that, because of the high cost of moving mobilehomes, the potential for damage resulting therefrom, the requirements relating to the installation of mobilehomes, and the cost of landscaping or lot preparation, it is necessary that the owners of mobile homes occupied within mobilehome parks be provided with the unique protection from actual or constructive eviction afforded by the provisions of this chapter." § 798.55(a).

The Mobilehome Residency Law limits the bases upon which a park owner may terminate a mobile home owner's tenancy. These include the nonpayment of rent, the mobile home owner's violation of law or park rules, and the park owner's desire to change the use of his land. § 798.56. While a rental agreement is in effect, however, the park owner generally may not require the removal of a mobilehome when it is sold. § 798.73. The park owner may neither charge a transfer fee for the sale, § 798.72, nor disapprove of the purchaser, provided that the purchaser has the ability to pay the rent, § 798.74. The Mobilehome Residency Law contains a number of other detailed provisions, but none limit the rent the park owner may charge.

In the wake of the Mobilehome Residency Law, various communities in California adopted mobilehome rent control ordinances.... The voters of Escondido did the same in 1988 by approving Proposition K, the rent control ordinance challenged here. The ordinance sets rents back to their 1986 levels, and prohibits rent increases without the approval of the City Council. Park owners may apply to the Council for rent increases at any time. The Council must approve any increases it determines to be "just, fair and reasonable," after considering the following nonexclusive list of factors: (1) changes in the Consumer Price Index; (2) the rent charged for comparable mobile home pads in Escondido; (3) the length of time since the last rent increase; (4) the cost of any capital improvements related to the pad or pads at issue; (5) changes in property taxes; (6) changes in any rent paid by the park owner for the land; (7) changes in utility charges; (8) changes in operating and maintenance expenses; (9) the need for repairs other than for ordinary wear and tear; (10) the amount and quality of services provided to the affected tenant; and (11) any lawful existing lease. Ordinance § 4(g), App. 11–12.

Petitioners John and Irene Yee own the Friendly Hills and Sunset Terrace Mobile Home Parks, both of which are located in the city of Escondido. A few months after the adoption of Escondido's rent control ordinance, they filed suit in San Diego County Superior Court. According to the complaint, "the rent control law has had the effect of depriving the plaintiffs of all use and occupancy of [their] real property and granting to the tenants of mobilehomes presently in The Park, as well as the successors in interest of such tenants, the right to physically permanently occupy and use the real property of Plaintiff." Id., at 3, para. 6. The Yees requested damages of six million dollars, a declaration that the rent control ordinance is unconstitutional, and an injunction barring the ordinance's enforcement. Id., at 5–6.

In their opposition to the city's demurrer, the Yees relied almost entirely on Hall v. City of Santa Barbara, 833 F. 2d 1270 (CA. 1986), cert. denied, 485 U.S. 940 (1988), which had held that a similar mobile home rent control ordinance effected a physical taking under Loretto v. Teleprompter Manhattan CATV Corp., 458 U.S. 419 (1982). The Yees candidly admitted that "in fact, the Hall decision was used [as] a guide in drafting the present Complaint." 2 Tr. 318, Points & Authorities in Opposition to Demurrer 4. The Superior Court nevertheless sustained the city's demurrer and dismissed the Yees' complaint. App. to Pet. for Cert. C-42.

The Yees were not alone. Eleven other park owners filed similar suits against the city shortly afterwards, and all were dismissed. By stipulation, all 12 cases were consolidated for appeal; the parties agreed that all would be submitted for decision by the California Court of Appeal on the briefs and oral argument in the Yee case.

The Court of Appeal affirmed, in an opinion primarily devoted to expressing the court's disagreement with the reasoning of Hall. The court concluded: "Loretto in no way suggests that the Escondido ordinance authorizes a permanent physical occupation of the landlord's property and therefore constitutes a per se taking." 224 Cal. App. 3d 1349, 1358 (1990). The California Supreme Court denied review.

Eight of the twelve park owners, including the Yees, joined in a petition for certiorari. We granted certiorari to resolve the conflict between the decision below and those of two of the federal Courts of Appeals, in Hall, supra, and Pinewood Estates of Michigan v. Barnegat Township Leveling Board, 898 F. 2d 347 (C.A.3 1990).

. . .

Petitioners do not claim that the ordinary rent control statutes regulating housing throughout the country violate the Takings Clause. Instead, their argument is predicated on the unusual economic relationship between park owners and mobile home owners. Park owners may no longer set rents or decide who their tenants will be. As a result, according to petitioners, any reduction in the rent for a mobile home pad causes a corresponding increase in the value of a mobile home, because the mobilehome owner now owns, in addition to a mobile home, the right to occupy a pad at a rent below the value that would be set by the free market. . . . Because under the California Mobilehome Residency Law the park owner cannot evict a mobile home owner or easily convert the property to other uses, the argument goes, the mobile home owner is effectively a perpetual tenant of the park, and the increase in the mobile home's value thus represents the right to occupy a pad at below-market rent indefinitely. And because the Mobilehome Residency Law permits the mobile home owner to sell the mobile home in place, the mobile home owner can receive a premium from the purchaser corresponding to this increase in value. The amount of this premium is not limited by the Mobilehome Residency Law or the Escondido ordinance. As a result, petitioners conclude, the rent control ordinance has transferred a discrete interest in land—the right to occupy the land indefinitely at a sub-market rent—from the park owner to the mobile home owner. Petitioners contend that what has been transferred from park owner to mobile home owner is no less than a right of physical occupation of the park owner's land.

This argument, while perhaps within the scope of our regulatory taking cases, cannot be squared easily with our cases on physical takings. The government effects a physical taking only where it requires the landowner to submit to the physical occupation of his land. "This element of required acquiescence is at the heart of the concept of occupation." FCC v. Florida Power Corp., 480 U.S. 245, 252 (1987). Thus whether the government floods a landowner's property, Pumpelly v. Green Bay Co., 13 Wall. 166 (1871), or does no more than require the landowner to suffer the installation of a cable, Loretto, supra, the Takings Clause requires compensation if the government authorizes a compelled physical invasion of property.

But the Escondido rent control ordinance, even when considered in conjunction with the California Mobilehome Residency Law, authorizes no such thing. Petitioners voluntarily rented their land to mobile home owners. At least on the face of the regulatory scheme, neither the City nor the State compels petitioners, once they have rented their property to tenants, to continue doing so. To the contrary, the Mobilehome Residency Law provides that a park owner who wishes to change the use of his land may evict his tenants, albeit with six or twelve months notice. Cal. Civ. Code Ann. § 798.56(g). Put bluntly, no government has required any physical invasion of petitioners' property. Petitioners' tenants were invited by petitioners, not forced upon them by the government. While the "right to exclude" is doubtless, as petitioners assert, "one of the most essential sticks in the bundle of rights that are commonly characterized as property," Kaiser Aetna v. United States, 444 U.S. 164, 176 (1979), we do not find that right to have been taken from petitioners on the mere face of the Escondido ordinance.

Petitioners suggest that the statutory procedure for changing the use of a mobile home park is in practice "a kind of gauntlet," in that they are not in fact free to change the use of their land. Because petitioners do not claim to have run that gauntlet, however, this case provides no occasion to consider how the procedure has been applied to petitioners' property, and we accordingly confine ourselves to the face of the statute. A different case would be presented were the statute, on its face or as applied, to compel a landowner over objection to rent his property or to refrain in perpetuity from terminating a tenancy.

On their face, the state and local laws at issue here merely regulate petitioners' use of their land by regulating the relationship between landlord and tenant. "This Court has consistently affirmed that States have broad power to regulate housing conditions in general and the landlord-tenant relationship in particular without paying compensation for all economic injuries that such regulation entails." Loretto, 458 U. S., at 440. See also Florida Power, supra, at 252 ("statutes regulating the economic relations of landlords and tenants are not per se takings"). When a landowner decides to rent his land to tenants, the government may place ceilings on the rents the landowner can charge, or require the landowner to accept tenants he does not like, without automatically having to pay compensation. Such forms of regulation are analyzed by engaging in the "essentially ad hoc, factual inquiries" necessary to determine whether a regulatory taking has occurred. Kaiser Aetna, supra, at 175. In the words of Justice Holmes, "while property may be regulated to a certain extent, if regulation goes too far it will be recognized as a taking." Pennsylvania Coal Co. v. Mahon, 260 U.S. 393, 415 (1922).

Petitioners emphasize that the ordinance transfers wealth from park owners to incumbent mobile home owners. Other forms of land use regulation, however, can also be said to transfer wealth from the one who is regulated to another. Ordinary rent control often transfers wealth from landlords to tenants by reducing the landlords' income and the tenants' monthly payments, although it does not cause a one-time transfer of value as occurs with mobile homes. Traditional zoning regulations can transfer wealth from those whose activities are prohibited to their neighbors; when a property owner is barred from mining coal on his land, for example, the value of his property may decline but the value of his neighbor's property may rise. The mobile home owner's ability to sell the mobile home at a premium may make this wealth transfer more visible than in the ordinary case, see Epstein, Rent Control and the Theory of Efficient Regulation, 54 Brooklyn L. Rev. 741, 758–759 (1988), but the existence of the transfer in itself does not convert regulation into physical invasion.

Petitioners also rely heavily on their allegation that the ordinance benefits incumbent mobile home owners without benefiting future mobile home owners, who will be forced to purchase mobile homes at premiums. Mobile homes, like motor vehicles, ordinarily decline in value with age. But the effect of the rent control ordinance, coupled with the restrictions on the park owner's freedom to reject new tenants, is to increase significantly the value of the mobile home. This increased value normally benefits only the tenant in possession at the time the rent control is imposed.... Petitioners are correct in citing the existence of this premium as a difference between the alleged effect of the Escondido ordinance and that of an ordinary apartment rent control statute. Most apartment tenants do not sell anything to their successors (and are often prohibited from charging "key money"), so a typical rent control statute will transfer wealth from the landlord to the incumbent tenant and all future tenants. By contrast, petitioners contend that the Escondido ordinance transfers wealth only to the incumbent mobile home owner. This effect might have some bearing on whether the ordinance causes a regulatory taking, as it may shed some light on whether there is a sufficient nexus between the effect of the ordinance and the objectives it is supposed to advance. But it has nothing to do with whether the ordinance causes a physical taking. Whether the ordinance benefits only current mobile home owners or all mobile home owners, it does not require petitioners to submit to the physical occupation of their land.

The same may be said of petitioners' contention that the ordinance amounts to compelled physical occupation because it deprives petitioners of the ability to choose their incoming tenants.[10] Again, this effect may be relevant to a regulatory taking argument, as it may be one factor a reviewing court would wish to consider in determining whether the ordinance unjustly imposes a burden on petitioners that should "be compensated by the government, rather than remaining disproportionately concentrated on a few persons." Penn Central Transp. Co. v. New York City, 438 U. S., at 124. But it does not convert regulation into the unwanted physical occupation of land. Because they voluntarily open their property to occupation by others, petitioners cannot assert a per se right to compensation based on their inability to exclude particular individuals.

With respect to physical takings, then, this case is not far removed from FCC v. Florida Power Corp., 480 U.S. 245 (1987), in which the respondent had voluntarily leased space on its utility poles to a cable television company for the installation of cables. The Federal Government, exercising its statutory authority to regulate pole attachment agreements, substantially reduced the annual rent. We rejected the respondent's claim that "it is a taking under *Loretto* for a tenant invited to lease at a rent of $7.15 to remain at the regulated rent of $1.79." Id., at 252. We explained that "it is the invitation, not the rent, that makes the difference. The line which separates [this case] from Loretto is the unambiguous distinction between a . . . lessee and an interloper with a government license." Id., at 252–253. The distinction is

---

[10] Strictly speaking, the Escondido rent control ordinance only limits rents. Petitioners' inability to select their incoming tenants is a product of the State's Mobilehome Residency Law, the constitutionality of which has never been at issue in this case. (The State, moreover, has never been a party.) But we understand petitioners to be making a more subtle argument—that before the adoption of the ordinance they were able to influence a mobilehome owner's selection of a purchaser by threatening to increase the rent for prospective purchasers they disfavored. To the extent the rent control ordinance deprives petitioners of this type of influence, petitioners' argument is one we must consider.

equally unambiguous here. The Escondido rent control ordinance, even considered against the backdrop of California's Mobilehome Residency Law, does not authorize an unwanted physical occupation of petitioners' property. It is a regulation of petitioners' use of their property, and thus does not amount to a per se taking.

We made this observation in Loretto:

> Our holding today is very narrow. We affirm the traditional rule that a permanent physical occupation of property is a taking. In such a case, the property owner entertains a historically rooted expectation of compensation, and the character of the invasion is qualitatively more intrusive than perhaps any other category of property regulation. We do not, however, question the equally substantial authority upholding a State's broad power to impose appropriate restrictions upon an owner's use of his property.

458 U.S., at 441.

We respected this distinction again in Florida Power, where we held that no taking occurs under Loretto when a tenant invited to lease at one rent remains at a lower regulated rent. Florida Power, 480 U. S., at 252–253. We continue to observe the distinction today. Because the Escondido rent control ordinance does not compel a landowner to suffer the physical occupation of his property, it does not effect a per se taking under Loretto. The judgment of the Court of Appeal is accordingly affirmed.

## NOTES

1. *Justifications for governmental action.* Under *Loretto*, to what extent should the severity of the homelessness problem in Hillington affect the validity of the ordinance? How relevant would it be if the city attorney could show that other means of providing low cost housing are not available, as a practical matter?

2. *The right to exclude.* The majority in *Loretto* states that the "power to exclude has traditionally been considered one of the most treasured strands in an owner's bundle of property rights." Yet, as the dissent points out, "New York's courts in this litigation, with only one jurist in dissent, unanimously upheld the constitutionality" of New York's ordinance. Were all of the New York judges who upheld the ordinance ignorant of a fundamental principle of property law?

3. *Permanent vs. temporary physical occupations.* *Loretto* stands for the proposition that a permanent physical occupation of property by the government is a per se taking. The case refers to another U.S. Supreme Court case, *Kaiser-Aetna*, that declined to adopt a per se rule for government physical invasions of property that are less than permanent, yet intimated that temporary physical invasions will often be found to be takings because of their "unusually serious character." Now consider a 2012 case in which the U.S. Supreme Court unanimously held that a federal agency's intentional and periodic but temporary flooding of a property owner's land could be a compensable taking, even though the landowners knew of the federally

operated dam and likely flooding.[11] Unlike regulatory takings, the distinction between permanent and temporary physical takings appears to be less about how far into the future the government's physical invasion lasts and more about whether the government's or the public's presence is continual (i.e., 24/7) or intermittent. Even intermittent physical invasions are often considered takings.

4. *The Principal Problem.* How is *Yee* distinguishable from the Principal Problem? Does the scheme in *Yee* provide the landlord with a greater degree of choice? Should the status of the lessees as current or prospective matter in determining whether these laws constitute physical takings?

## c. REGULATORY TAKINGS

### 1. INTRODUCTION

In Part b., we saw that governmental regulations that amount to a permanent physical taking are subject to a *per se* rule of compensation. The question of whether a regulatory taking entitles the property owner to compensation is more complex. As we shall see, no set formula exists for determining when a given regulation deprives the property owner of enough strands in her bundle of rights so as to mandate compensation.

### 2. PRINCIPAL PROBLEM

Joan Scott, an experienced land developer, was interested in buying a 200-acre parcel of vacant land. The property's zoning allowed it to be developed for single-family residences on lots of 6,000 square feet. She signed a purchase contract with the seller for $1,200 per acre, which allowed her to cancel the contract if any zoning changes were considered by the city.

Before completing the sale, she met several times with the City Manager, the Mayor, and various city officials to investigate all city regulations and restrictions affecting the property. All of them informed her that no plan existed to change the zoning. In fact, a rezoning was secretly being considered and the city officials were not being truthful. Shortly thereafter, the city officials met to discuss downzoning the property, but they did not tell Scott of these meetings for fear that she would quickly complete the purchase, file a development plan, and thus vest her right to develop under the filed plan. Relying on the untruthful assertions of the city officials, Scott purchased the property.

The City Council met three days later in executive session to impose a moratorium on development of Scott's newly purchased property. A month later it rezoned the property so that the minimum lot size was 12,000 square feet. Scott was disappointed (to say the least!) with this

---

[11] Arkansas Game and Fish Commission v. United States, 568 U.S. ___, 133 S.Ct. 511 (2012).

turn of events. She specialized in building middle-class housing and had neither the interest nor the experience to build houses on 12,000 square foot lots. She therefore sold the parcel to Tom Farley for what she paid for it. Farley was well aware of the new zoning, but believed that it was vulnerable to legal challenge.

Shortly after Farley purchased the property he sued the city, claiming a "taking." The trial judge found that the subject property was worth $10,000 per acre before the rezoning, and $5,000 after the rezoning. He also found that the moratorium and rezoning "blind-sided Scott, just as the city intended." The trial judge awarded damages of $5,000 per acre, based on a regulatory taking theory.

You represent the city and have been asked to predict whether an appellate court would be likely to reverse the lower court's decision. Before offering your opinion, consider the following materials.

## 3. Materials for Solution of Principal Problem

### Pennsylvania Coal Co. v. Mahon
Supreme Court of the United States, 1922.
260 U.S. 393, 43 S.Ct. 158.

■ MR. JUSTICE HOLMES delivered the opinion of the Court.

This is a bill in equity brought by the defendants in error to prevent the Pennsylvania Coal Company from mining under their property in such a way as to remove the supports and cause a subsidence of the surface and of their house. The bill sets out a deed executed by the Coal Company in 1878, under which the plaintiffs claim. The deed conveys the surface, but in express terms reserves the right to remove all the coal under the same, and the grantee takes the premises with the risk, and waives all claim for damages that may arise from mining out the coal. But the plaintiffs say that whatever may have been the Coal Company's rights, they were taken away by an Act of Pennsylvania, approved May 27, 1921, P.L. 1198, commonly known there as the Kohler Act. The Court of Common Pleas found that if not restrained the defendant would cause the damage to prevent which the bill was brought, but denied an injunction, holding that the statute if applied to this case would be unconstitutional. On appeal the Supreme Court of the State agreed that the defendant had contract and property rights protected by the Constitution of the United States, but held that the statute was a legitimate exercise of the police power and directed a decree for the plaintiffs. A writ of error was granted bringing the case to this Court.

The statute forbids the mining of anthracite coal in such way as to cause the subsidence of, among other things, any structure used as a human habitation, with certain exceptions, including among them land where the surface is owned by the owner of the underlying coal and is distant more than one hundred and fifty feet from any improved property belonging to any other person. As applied to this case the statute is admitted to destroy previously existing rights of property and contract. The question is whether the police power can be stretched so far.

Government hardly could go on if to some extent values incident to property could not be diminished without paying for every such change in the general law. As long recognized, some values are enjoyed under an implied limitation and must yield to the police power. But obviously the implied limitation must have its limits, or the contract and due process clauses are gone. One fact for consideration in determining such limits is the extent of the diminution. When it reaches a certain magnitude, in most if not in all cases there must be an exercise of eminent domain and compensation to sustain the act. So the question depends upon the particular facts. The greatest weight is given to the judgment of the legislature, but it always is open to interested parties to contend that the legislature has gone beyond its constitutional power.

This is the case of a single private house. No doubt there is a public interest even in this, as there is in every purchase and sale and in all that happens within the commonwealth. Some existing rights may be modified even in such a case. . . . But usually in ordinary private affairs the public interest does not warrant much of this kind of interference. A source of damage to such a house is not a public nuisance even if similar damage is inflicted on others in different places. The damage is not common or public. . . . The extent of the public interest is shown by the statute to be limited, since the statute ordinarily does not apply to land when the surface is owned by the owner of the coal. Furthermore, it is not justified as a protection of personal safety. That could be provided for by notice. Indeed the very foundation of this bill is that the defendant gave timely notice of its intent to mine under the house. On the other hand the extent of the taking is great. It purports to abolish what is recognized in Pennsylvania as an estate in land—a very valuable estate—and what is declared by the Court below to be a contract hitherto binding the plaintiffs.

It is our opinion that the act cannot be sustained as an exercise of the police power, so far as it affects the mining of coal under streets or cities in places where the right to mine such coal has been reserved. As said in a Pennsylvania case, "For practical purposes, the right to coal consists in the right to mine it." Commonwealth v. Clearview Coal Co., 256 Pa.St. 328, 331. What makes the right to mine coal valuable is that it can be exercised with profit. To make it commercially impracticable to mine certain coal has very nearly the same effect for constitutional purposes as appropriating or destroying it. Thus we think that we are warranted in assuming that the statute does.

It is true that in Plymouth Coal Co. v. Pennsylvania, 232 U.S. 531, it was held competent for the legislature to require a pillar of coal to be left along the line of adjoining property, that, with the pillar on the other side of the line, would be a barrier sufficient for the safety of the employees of either mine in case the other should be abandoned and allowed to fill with water. But that was a requirement for the safety of employees invited into the mine, and secured an average reciprocity of advantage that has been recognized as a justification of various laws.

The rights of the public in a street purchased or laid out by eminent domain are those that it has paid for. If in any case its representatives have been so short sighted as to acquire only surface rights without the right of support, we see no more authority for supplying the latter without compensation than there was for taking the right of way in the first place and refusing to pay for it because the public wanted it very much. The protection of private property in the Fifth Amendment presupposes that it is wanted for public use, but provides that it shall not be taken for such use without compensation. A similar assumption is made in the decisions upon the Fourteenth Amendment.... When this seemingly absolute protection is found to be qualified by the police power, the natural tendency of human nature is to extend the qualification more and more until at last private property disappears. But that cannot be accomplished in this way under the Constitution of the United States.

The general rule at least is, that while property may be regulated to a certain extent, if regulation goes too far it will be recognized as a taking. It may be doubted how far exceptional cases, like the blowing up of a house to stop a conflagration, go—and if they go beyond the general rule, whether they do not stand as much upon tradition as upon principle.... In general it is not plain that a man's misfortunes or necessities will justify his shifting the damages to his neighbor's shoulders.... We are in danger of forgetting that a strong public desire to improve the public condition is not enough to warrant achieving the desire by a shorter cut than the constitutional way of paying for the change. As we already have said, this is a question of degree—and therefore cannot be disposed of by general propositions. But we regard this as going beyond any of the cases decided by this Court.

We assume, of course, that the statute was passed upon the conviction that an exigency existed that would warrant it, and we assume that an exigency exists that would warrant the exercise of eminent domain. But the question at bottom is upon whom the loss of the changes desired should fall. So far as private persons or communities have seen fit to take the risk of acquiring only surface rights, we cannot see that the fact that their risk has become a danger warrants giving to them greater rights than they bought.

Decree reversed.

■ JUSTICE BRANDEIS, dissenting.

The Kohler Act prohibits, under certain conditions, the mining of anthracite coal within the limits of a city in such a manner or to such an extent "as to cause the ... subsidence of any dwelling or other structure used as a human habitation, or any factory, store, or other industrial or mercantile establishment in which human labor is employed." Coal in place is land; and the right of the owner to use his land is not absolute. He may not so use it as to create a public nuisance; and uses, once harmless, may, owing to changed conditions, seriously threaten the public welfare. Whenever they do, the legislature has power to prohibit such uses without paying compensation; and the power to prohibit extends alike to the manner, the character and the purpose of the use. Are we justified in declaring that the Legislature of Pennsylvania has, in restricting the right to mine anthracite, exercised this power so arbitrarily as to violate the Fourteenth Amendment?

Every restriction upon the use of property imposed in the exercise of the police power deprives the owner of some right theretofore enjoyed, and is, in that sense, an abridgment by the State of rights in property without making compensation. But restriction imposed to protect the public health, safety or morals from dangers threatened is not a taking. The restriction here in question is merely the prohibition of a noxious use. The property so restricted remains in the possession of its owner. The State does not appropriate it or make any use of it. The State merely prevents the owner from making a use which interferes with paramount rights of the public. Whenever the use prohibited ceases to be noxious,— as it may because of further change in local or social conditions,—the restriction will have to be removed and the owner will again be free to enjoy his property as heretofore.

The restriction upon the use of this property can not, of course, be lawfully imposed, unless its purpose is to protect the public. But the purpose of a restriction does not cease to be public, because incidentally some private persons may thereby receive gratuitously valuable special benefits. Thus, owners of low buildings may obtain, through statutory restrictions upon the height of neighboring structures, benefits equivalent to an easement of light and air. . . . Furthermore, a restriction, though imposed for a public purpose, will not be lawful, unless the restriction is an appropriate means to the public end. But to keep coal in place is surely an appropriate means of preventing subsidence of the surface; and ordinarily it is the only available means. Restriction upon use does not become inappropriate as a means, merely because it deprives the owner of the only use to which the property can then be profitably put. Nor is a restriction imposed through exercise of the police power inappropriate as a means, merely because the same end might be effected through exercise of the power of eminent domain, or otherwise at public expense. Every restriction upon the height of buildings might be secured through acquiring by eminent domain the right of each owner to build above the limiting height; but it is settled that the State need not resort to that power. If by mining anthracite coal the owner would necessarily unloose poisonous gases, I suppose no one would doubt the power of the State to prevent the mining, without buying his coal fields. Any why may not the State, likewise, without paying compensation, prohibit one from digging so deep or excavating so near the surface, as to expose the community to like dangers? In the latter case, as in the former, carrying on the business would be a public nuisance.

It is said that one fact for consideration in determining whether the limits of the police power have been exceeded is the extent of the resulting diminution in value; and that here the restriction destroys existing rights of property and contract. But values are relative. If we are to consider the value of the coal kept in place by the restriction, we should compare it with the value of all other parts of the land. That is, with the value not of the coal alone, but with the value of the whole property. The rights of an owner as against the public are not increased by dividing the interests in his property into surface and subsoil. The sum of the rights in the parts can not be greater than the rights in the whole. The estate of an owner in land is grandiloquently described as extending *ab orco usque ad coelum*. But I suppose no one would contend that by selling his interest above one hundred feet from the surface he could prevent the State from limiting, by the police power, the height of structures in a city. And why should a sale of underground rights bar the State's power? For aught that appears the value of the coal kept in place by the restriction may be negligible as compared with the value of the whole property, or even as compared with that part of it which is represented by the coal remaining in place and which may be extracted despite the statute. Ordinarily a police regulation, general in operation, will not be held void as to a particular property, although proof is offered that owing to conditions peculiar to it the restriction could not reasonably be applied. But even if the particular facts are to govern, the statute should, in my opinion, be upheld in this case. For the defendant has failed to adduce any evidence from which it appears that to restrict its mining operations was an unreasonable exercise of the police power.

### Penn Central Transportation Co. v. City of New York
United States Supreme Court, 1978.
438 U.S. 104, 98 S.Ct. 2646.

■ BRENNAN, J., delivered the opinion of the Court.

I

This case involves the application of New York City's Landmark Preservation Law to Grand Central Terminal (Terminal). The Terminal, which is owned by the Penn Central Transportation Company and its affiliates (Penn Central), is one of New York City's most famous buildings....

The Terminal is located in midtown Manhattan. Although a 20-story office tower, to have been located above the Terminal, was part of the original design, the planned tower was never constructed.[12] The

---

[12] The Terminal's present foundation includes columns, which were built into it for the express purpose of supporting the proposed 20-story tower.

Terminal itself is an eight-story structure which Penn Central uses as a railroad station and in which it rents space not needed for railroad purposes to a variety of commercial interests. The Terminal is one of a number of properties owned by appellant Penn Central in this area of midtown Manhattan. At least eight of these are eligible to be recipients of development rights afforded the Terminal by virtue of landmark designation.

On August 2, 1967, following a public hearing, the Commission designated the Terminal a "landmark" and designated the "city tax block" it occupies a "landmark site." The Board of Estimate confirmed this action on September 21, 1967. Although appellant Penn Central had opposed the designation before the Commission, it did not seek judicial review of the final designation decision.

On January 22, 1968, appellant Penn Central, to increase its income, entered into a renewable 50-year lease and sublease agreement with appellant UGP Properties, Inc. (UGP). Under the terms of the agreement, UGP was to construct a multistory office building above the Terminal. UGP promised to pay Penn Central $1 million annually during construction and at least $3 million annually thereafter. The rentals would be offset in part by a loss of some $700,000 to $1 million in net rentals presently received from concessionaires displaced by the new building.

Appellants UGP and Penn Central then applied to the Commission for permission to construct an office building atop the Terminal. Two separate plans, both designed by architect Marcel Breuer and both apparently satisfying the terms of the applicable zoning ordinance, were submitted to the Commission for approval. The first, Breuer I, provided for the construction of a 55-story office building, to be cantilevered above the existing facade and to rest on the roof of the Terminal. The second, Breuer II Revised, called for tearing down a portion of the Terminal that included the 42nd Street facade, stripping off some of the remaining features of the Terminal's facade, and constructing a 53-story office building. The Commission denied a certificate of no exterior effect on September 20, 1968. Appellants then applied for a certificate of "appropriateness" as to both proposals. After four days of hearings at which over 80 witnesses testified, the Commission denied this application as to both proposals.

The Commission's reasons for rejecting certificates respecting Breuer II Revised are summarized in the following statement: "To protect a landmark, one does not tear it down. To perpetuate its architectural features, one does not strip them off." Record 2255. Breuer I, which would have preserved the existing vertical facades of the present structure, received more sympathetic consideration. The Commission first focused on the effect that the proposed tower would have on one desirable feature created by the present structure and its surroundings: the dramatic view of the Terminal from Park Avenue South. Although appellants had contended that the Pan Am Building had already destroyed the silhouette of the south facade and that one additional tower could do no further damage and might even provide a better background for the facade, the Commission disagreed, stating that it found the majestic approach from the south to be still unique in the city and that a 55-story tower atop the Terminal would be far more detrimental to its south facade than the Pan Am Building 375 feet away. Moreover, the Commission found that from closer vantage points, the Pan Am Building and the other towers were largely cut off from view, which would not be the case of the mass on top of the Terminal planned under Breuer I. . . .

Appellants did not seek judicial review of the denial of either certificate. Because the Terminal site enjoyed a tax exemption, remained suitable for its present and future uses and was not the subject of a contract of sale, there were no further administrative remedies available to appellants as to the Breuer I and Breuer II Revised plans. Further, appellants did not avail themselves of the opportunity to develop and submit other plans for the Commission's consideration and approval. Instead, appellants filed suit in New York Supreme Court, Trial Term, claiming, *inter alia,* that the application of the Landmarks Preservation Law had "taken" their property without just compensation in violation of the Fifth and Fourteenth Amendments and arbitrarily deprived them of their property without Due Process of Law in violation of the Fourteenth Amendment. Appellants sought a declaratory judgment, injunctive relief barring the city from using the Landmarks Law to impede the construction of any structure that may otherwise lawfully be constructed on the Terminal site, and damages for the "temporary taking" that occurred between August 2, 1967, the designation date, and the date when the restrictions arising from the Landmarks Law are lifted. The trial court granted the injunctive and declaratory relief, but severed the question of damages for a "temporary taking."[13]

Appellee, the city, appealed, and the New York Supreme Court, Appellate Division, reversed.

The New York Court of Appeals affirmed. 42 N.Y.2d 324, 397 N.Y.S.2d 914, 366 N.E.2d 1271 (1977). That court summarily rejected any claim that the Landmarks Law had "taken" property without "just compensation," id., at 329, 397 N.Y.S.2d 914, 366 N.E.2d 1271 indicating that there could be no "taking" since the law had not transferred control of the property to the City, but only restricted appellants' exploitation of it. In that circumstance, the Court of Appeals held that appellants' attack

---

[13] Although that court suggested that any regulation of private property to protect landmark values was unconstitutional if "just compensation" were not afforded, it also appeared to rely upon its findings: first, that the cost to Penn Central of operating the Terminal building itself, exclusive of purely railroad operations, exceeded the revenues received from concessionaires and tenants in the Terminal; and second, that the special transferable development rights afforded Penn Central as an owner of a landmark site did not "provide compensation to plaintiffs or minimize the harm suffered by plaintiffs due to the designation of the Terminal as a landmark."

on the law could prevail only if the law deprived appellants of their property in violation of the Due Process Clause of the Fourteenth Amendment. Whether or not there was a denial of substantive due process turned on whether the restrictions deprived Penn Central of a "reasonable return" on the "privately created and privately managed ingredient" of the Terminal. Id., at 328, 397 N.Y.S.2d at 916, 366 N.E.2d, at 1273. The Court of Appeals concluded that the Landmarks Law had not effected a denial of due process because: (1) the landmark regulation permitted the same use as had been made of the Terminal for more than half a century; (2) the appellants had failed to show that they could not earn a reasonable return on their investment in the Terminal itself; (3) even if the Terminal proper could never operate at a reasonable profit some of the income from Penn Central's extensive real estate holdings in the area, which include hotels and office buildings, must realistically be imputed to the Terminal, and (4) the development rights above the Terminal, which had been made transferable to numerous sites in the vicinity of the Terminal, one or two of which were suitable for the construction of office buildings, were valuable to appellants and provided "significant, perhaps fair compensation for the loss of rights above the terminal itself."

II

The issues presented by appellants are (1) whether the restrictions imposed by New York City's law upon appellants' exploitation of the Terminal site effect a "taking" of appellants' property for a public use within the meaning of the Fifth Amendment, which of course is made applicable to the States through the Fourteenth Amendment, see Chicago B. & Q.R. Co. v. Chicago, 166 U.S. 226, 239, 17 S.Ct. 581, 585, 41 L.Ed. 979 (1897) and, (2) if so, whether the transferable development rights afforded appellants constitute "just compensation" within the meaning of the Fifth Amendment. We need only address the question whether a "taking" has occurred.[14]

A

Before considering appellants' specific contentions, it will be useful to review the factors that have shaped the jurisprudence of the Fifth Amendment injunction "nor shall private property be taken for public use, without just compensation." The question of what constitutes a "taking" for purposes of the Fifth Amendment has proved to be a problem of considerable difficulty. While this Court has recognized that the "Fifth Amendment's guarantee [is] designed to bar Government from forcing some people alone to bear public burdens which, in all fairness and justice, should be borne by the public as a whole," Armstrong v. United States, 364 U.S. 40, 49, 80 S.Ct. 1563, 1569, 4 L.Ed.2d 1554 (1960), this Court, quite simply, has been unable to develop any "set formula" for

---

[14] As is implicit in our opinion, we do not embrace the proposition that a "taking" can never occur unless government has transferred physical control over a portion of a parcel.

determining when "justice and fairness" require that economic injuries caused by public action be compensated by the Government, rather than remain disproportionately concentrated on a few persons. See Goldblatt v. Hempstead, 369 U.S. 590, 594, 82 S.Ct. 987, 990, 8 L.Ed.2d 130 (1962). Indeed, we have frequently observed that whether a particular restriction will be rendered invalid by the Government's failure to pay for any losses proximately caused by it depends largely "upon the particular circumstances [in that] case." United States v. Central Eureka Mining Co., 357 U.S. 155, 168, 78 S.Ct. 1097, 1104, 2 L.Ed.2d 1228 (1958). . . .

In engaging in these essentially ad hoc, factual inquiries, the Court's decisions have identified several factors that have particular significance. The economic impact of the regulation on the claimant and, particularly, the extent to which the regulation has interfered with distinct investment backed expectations are of course relevant considerations. See Goldblatt v. Hempstead, supra, 369 U.S., at 594, 82 S.Ct., at 990. So too is the character of the governmental action. A "taking" may more readily be found when the interference with property can be characterized as a physical invasion by Government, see, e.g., United States v. Causby, 328 U.S. 256, 66 S.Ct. 1062, 90 L.Ed. 1206 (1946), than when interference arises from some public program adjusting the benefits and burdens of economic life to promote the common good.

"Government could hardly go on if to some extent values incident to property could not be diminished without paying for every such change in the general law," Pennsylvania Coal Co. v. Mahon, 260 U.S. 393, 413, 43 S.Ct. 158, 159, 67 L.Ed. 322 (1922), and this Court has accordingly recognized, in a wide variety of contexts, that Government may execute laws or programs that adversely affect recognized economic values. Exercises of the taxing power are one obvious example. A second are the decisions in which this Court has dismissed "taking" challenges on the ground that, while the challenged Government action caused economic harm, it did not interfere with interests that were sufficiently bound up with the reasonable expectations of the claimant to constitute "property" for Fifth Amendment purposes.

More importantly for the present case, in instances in which a state tribunal reasonably concluded that "the health, safety, morals or general welfare" would be promoted by prohibiting particular contemplated uses of land, this Court has upheld land use regulations that destroyed or adversely affected recognized real property interests. See Nectow v. City of Cambridge, 277 U.S. 183, 188, 48 S.Ct. 447, 448, 72 L.Ed. 842 (1928). Zoning laws are of course the classic example, see Euclid v. Ambler Realty Co., 272 U.S. 365, 47 S.Ct. 114, 71 L.Ed. 303 (1926) (prohibition of industrial use), which have been viewed as permissible governmental action even when prohibiting the most beneficial use of the property.

Zoning laws generally do not affect existing uses of real property, but taking challenges have also been held to be without merit in a wide variety of situations when the challenged governmental actions prohibited a beneficial use to which individual parcels had previously been devoted and thus caused substantial individualized harm. Miller v. Schoene, 276 U.S. 272, 48 S.Ct. 246, 72 L.Ed. 568 (1928), is illustrative. In that case, a state entomologist, acting pursuant to a state statute, ordered the claimants to cut down a large number of ornamental red cedar trees because they produced cedar rust fatal to apple trees cultivated nearby. Although the statute provided for recovery of any expense incurred in removing the cedars, and permitted claimants to use the felled trees, it did not provide compensation for the value of the standing trees or for the resulting decrease in market value of the properties as a whole. A unanimous Court held that this latter omission did not render the statute invalid. The Court held that the State might properly make "a choice between the preservation of one class of property and that of the other" and since the apple industry was important in the State involved, concluded that the State had not exceeded "its constitutional powers by deciding upon the destruction of one class of property [without compensation] in order to save another, which, in the judgment of the legislature, is of greater value to the public."

Again, Hadacheck v. Sebastian, 239 U.S. 394, 36 S.Ct. 143, 60 L.Ed. 348 (1915), upheld a law prohibiting the claimant from continuing his otherwise lawful business of operating a brickyard in a particular physical community on the ground that the legislature had reasonably concluded that the presence of the brickyard was inconsistent with neighboring uses.

Goldblatt v. Hempstead, supra, is a recent example. There, a 1958 city safety ordinance banned any excavations below the water table and effectively prohibited the claimant from continuing a sand and gravel mining business that had been operated on the particular parcel since 1927. The Court upheld the ordinance against a "taking" challenge, although the ordinance prohibited the present and presumably most beneficial use of the property and had, like the regulations in *Miller* and *Hadacheck,* impacted severely on a particular owner. The Court assumed that the ordinance did not prevent the owner's reasonable use of the property since the owner made no showing for an adverse effect on the value of the land. Because the restriction served a substantial public purpose, the Court thus held no taking had occurred. It is of course implicit in *Goldblatt* that a use restriction on real property may constitute a "taking" if not reasonably necessary to the effectuation of a substantial public purpose, or perhaps if it has an unduly harsh impact upon the owner's use of the property.

Pennsylvania Coal Co. v. Mahon, 260 U.S. 393, 43 S.Ct. 158, 67 L.Ed. 322 (1922), is the leading case for the proposition that a state statute that substantially furthers important public policies may so frustrate distinct investment-backed expectations as to amount to a "taking." There the claimant had sold the surface rights to particular parcels of property, but expressly reserved the right to remove the coal thereunder. A Pennsylvania statute, enacted after the transactions, forbade any mining of coal that caused the subsidence of any house, unless the house was the property of the owner of the underlying coal and was more than 150 feet from the improved property of another. Because the statute made it commercially impracticable to mine the coal, id., at 414, 43 S.Ct., at 159, and thus had nearly the same effect as the complete destruction of rights claimant had purchased from the owners of the surface land, see id., at 414–415, 43 S.Ct., at 159–160, the Court held that the statute was invalid as effecting a "taking" without just compensation.

Finally, Government actions that may be characterized as acquisitions of resources to permit or facilitate uniquely public functions have often been held to constitute "takings." Causby v. United States, supra, is illustrative. In holding that direct overflights above the claimant's land, that destroyed the present use of the land as a chicken farm, constituted a "taking," *Causby* emphasized that Government had not "merely destroyed property [but was] using a part of it for the flight of its planes." Id., 328 U.S., at 262–263, n. 7, 66 S.Ct., at 1066.

B

In contending that the New York City law has "taken" their property in violation of the Fifth and Fourteenth Amendments, appellants make a series of arguments, which, while tailored to the facts of this case, essentially urge that any substantial restriction imposed pursuant to a landmark law must be accompanied by just compensation if it is to be constitutional. Before considering these, we emphasize what is not in dispute. Because this Court has recognized, in a number of settings, that States and cities may enact land use restrictions or controls to enhance the quality of life by preserving the character and desirable aesthetic features of a city, appellants do not contest that New York City's objective of preserving structures and areas with special historic, architectural, or cultural significance is an entirely permissible governmental goal. They also do not dispute that the restrictions imposed on its parcel are appropriate means of securing the purposes of the New York City law. Finally, appellants do not challenge any of the specific factual premises of the decision below. They accept for present purposes both that the parcel of land occupied by Grand Central Terminal must, in its present state, be regarded as capable of earning a reasonable return, and that the transferable development rights afforded appellants by virtue of the Terminal's designation as a landmark are valuable, even if not as valuable as the rights to construct above the Terminal. In appellants' view none of these factors derogate from their claim that New York City's law has effected a "taking."

They first observe that the air space above the Terminal is a valuable property interest, citing United States v. Causby, supra. They urge that the Landmarks Law has deprived them of any gainful use of their "air rights" above the Terminal and that, irrespective of the value of the remainder of their parcel, the city has "taken" their right to this superadjacent air space, thus entitling them to "just compensation" measured by the fair market value of these air rights.

Apart from our own disagreement with appellants' characterization of the effect of the New York law, see infra, the submission that appellants may establish a "taking" simply by showing that they have been denied the ability to exploit a property interest that they heretofore had believed was available for development is quite simply untenable. "Taking" jurisprudence does not divide a single parcel into discrete segments and attempt to determine whether rights in a particular segment have been entirely abrogated. In deciding whether a particular governmental action has effected a taking, this Court focuses rather both on the character of the action and on the nature and extent of the interference with rights in the parcel as a whole, here, the city tax block designated as the "landmark site."

Secondly, appellants, focusing on the character and impact of the New York City law, argue that it effects a "taking" because its operation has significantly diminished the value of the Terminal site. Appellants concede that the decisions sustaining other land use regulations, which, like the New York law, are reasonably related to the promotion of the general welfare, uniformly reject the proposition that diminution in property value, standing alone, can establish a taking, see Euclid v. Ambler Realty Co., supra (75% diminution in value caused by zoning law); Hadacheck v. Sebastian, supra, (87–1/2% diminution in value); and that the taking issue in these contexts is resolved by focusing on the uses the regulations permit. Appellants, moreover, also do not dispute that a showing of diminution in property value would not establish a taking if the restriction had been imposed as a result of historic district legislation, see generally Maher v. City of New Orleans, 516 F.2d 1051 (C.A.5 1975), but appellants argue that New York City's regulation of individual landmarks is fundamentally different from zoning or from historic district legislation because the controls imposed by New York City's law apply only to individuals who own selected properties.

Stated baldly, appellants' position appears to be that the only means of ensuring that selected owners are not singled out to endure financial hardship for no reason is to hold that any restriction imposed on individual landmarks pursuant to the New York scheme is a "taking" requiring the payment of "just compensation." Agreement with this argument would of course invalidate not just New York City's law, but all comparable landmark legislation in the Nation. We find no merit in it.

It is true, as appellants emphasize, that both historic district legislation and zoning laws regulate all properties within given physical communities whereas landmark laws apply only to selected parcels. But, contrary to appellants' suggestions, landmark laws are not like discriminatory, or "reverse spot," zoning: that is, a land use decision which arbitrarily singles out a particular parcel for different, less favorable treatment than the neighboring ones. See 2 Rathkopf, The Law of Zoning and Planning 26–4 and 26–4–26–5, n. 6 (2d Ed.1977). In contrast to discriminatory zoning, which is the antithesis of land use control as part of some comprehensive plan, the New York City law embodies a comprehensive plan to preserve structures of historic or aesthetic interest wherever they might be found in the city, and as noted, over 400 landmarks and 31 historic districts have been designated pursuant to this plan.

Equally without merit is the related argument that the decision to designate a structure as a landmark "is inevitably arbitrary or at least subjective because it basically is a matter of taste," Reply Brief of Appellant 22, thus unavoidably singling out individual landowners for disparate and unfair treatment. The argument has a particularly hollow ring in this case. For appellants not only did not seek judicial review of either the designation or of the denials of the certificates of appropriateness and of no exterior effect, but do not even now suggest that the Commission's decisions concerning the Terminal were in any sense arbitrary or unprincipled. But, in any event, a landmark owner has a right to judicial review of any Commission decision, and, quite simply, there is no basis whatsoever for a conclusion that courts will have any greater difficulty identifying arbitrary or discriminatory action in the context of landmark regulation than in the context of classic zoning or indeed in any other context.

Next, appellants observe that New York City's law differs from zoning laws and historic district ordinances in that the Landmarks Law does not impose identical or similar restrictions on all structures located in particular physical communities. It follows, they argue, that New York City's law is inherently incapable of producing the fair and equitable distribution of benefits and burdens of governmental action which is characteristic of zoning laws and historic district legislation and which they maintain is a constitutional requirement if "just compensation" is not to be afforded. It is of course true that the Landmarks Law has a more severe impact on some landowners than on others, but that in itself does not mean that the law effects a "taking." Legislation designed to promote the general welfare commonly burdens some more than others. The owners of the brickyard in *Hadacheck,* of the cedar trees in Miller v. Schoene, and of the gravel and sand mine in Goldblatt v. Hempstead, were uniquely burdened by the legislation sustained in those cases.[15]

---

[15] Appellants attempt to distinguish these cases on the ground that, in each, Government was prohibiting a "noxious" use of land and that in the present case, in contrast, appellants' proposed construction above the Terminal would be beneficial. We observe that the uses in issue in Hadacheck, Miller, and Goldblatt were perfectly lawful in themselves. They involved no "blameworthiness, . . . moral wrongdoing, or conscious act of dangerous risk-taking which induce[d society] to shift the cost to a particular individual." Sax, 74 Yale L.J. 36, 50 (1964). These cases are better understood as resting not on any supposed "noxious" quality of the prohibited uses but rather on the ground that the restrictions were reasonably related to

Similarly, zoning laws often impact more severely on some property owners than others but have not been held to be invalid on that account. For example, the property owner in *Euclid* who wished to use his property for industrial purposes was affected far more severely by the ordinance than his neighbors who wished to use their land for residences.

In any event, appellants' repeated suggestions that they are solely burdened and unbenefited is factually inaccurate. This contention overlooks the fact that the New York City law applies to vast numbers of structures in the city in addition to the Terminal—all the structures contained in the 31 historic districts and over 400 individual landmarks, many of which are close to the Terminal. Unless we are to reject the judgment of the New York City Council that the preservation of landmarks benefit all New York citizens and all structures, both economically and by improving the quality of life in the city as a whole—which we are unwilling to do—we cannot conclude that the owners of the Terminal have in no sense been benefited by the Landmarks Law.

C

Rejection of appellants' broad arguments is not however the end of our inquiry, for all we thus far have established is that the New York law is not rendered invalid by its failure to provide "just compensation" whenever a landmark owner is restricted in the exploitation of property interests, such as air rights, to a greater extent than provided for under applicable zoning laws. We now must consider whether the interference with appellants' property is of such a magnitude that "there must be an exercise of eminent domain and compensation to sustain [it]." Pennsylvania Coal Co. v. Mahon, 260 U.S., at 413, 43 S.Ct., at 159. That inquiry may be narrowed to the question of the severity of the impact of the law on appellants' parcel, and its resolution in turn requires a careful assessment of the impact of the regulation on the Terminal site.

Unlike the governmental acts in *Goldblatt, Miller, Causby, Griggs,* and *Hadacheck,* the New York City law does not interfere in any way with the present uses of the Terminal. Its designation as a landmark not only permits but contemplates that appellants may continue to use the property precisely as it has for the past 65 years: as a railroad terminal containing office space and concessions. So the law does not interfere with what must be regarded as Penn Central's primary expectation concerning the use of the parcel. More importantly, on this record, we must regard the New York City law as permitting Penn Central not only

---

the implementation of a policy—not unlike historic preservation—expected to produce a widespread public benefit and applicable to all similarly situated property.

Nor, correlatively, can it be asserted that the destruction or fundamental alteration of a historic landmark is not harmful. The suggestion that the beneficial quality of appellants' proposed construction is established by the fact the construction would have been consistent with applicable zoning laws ignores the development in sensibilities and ideals reflected in landmark legislation like New York City's.

to profit from the Terminal but to obtain a "reasonable return" on its investment.

Appellants, moreover, exaggerate the effect of the Act on its ability to make use of the air rights above the Terminal in two respects.[16] First, it simply cannot be maintained, on this record, that appellants have been prohibited from occupying *any* portion of the airspace above the Terminal. While the Commission's actions in denying applications to construct an office building in excess of 50 stories above the Terminal may indicate that it will refuse to issue a certificate of appropriateness for any comparably sized structure, nothing the Commission has said or done suggests an intention to prohibit *any* construction above the Terminal. The Commission's report emphasized that whether any construction would be allowed depended upon whether the proposed addition "would harmonize in scale, material, and character with [the Terminal]." Record 2251. Since appellants have not sought approval for the construction of a smaller structure, we do not know that appellants will be denied any use of any portion of the airspace above the Terminal.[17]

Second, to the extent appellants have been denied the right to build above the Terminal, it is not literally accurate to say that they have been denied *all* use of even those pre-existing air rights. Their ability to use these rights has not been abrogated; they are made transferable to at least eight parcels in the vicinity of the Terminal, one or two of which have been found suitable for the construction of new office buildings. Although appellants and others have argued that New York City's transferable development rights program is far from ideal, the New York courts here supportably found that, at least in the case of the Terminal, the rights afforded are valuable. While these rights may well not have constituted "just compensation" if a "taking" had occurred, the rights nevertheless undoubtedly mitigate whatever financial burdens the law has imposed on appellants and, for that reason, are to be taken into account in considering the impact of regulation.

On this record we conclude that the application of New York City's Landmarks Preservation Law has not effected a "taking" of appellants' property. The restrictions imposed are substantially related to the promotion of the general welfare and not only permit reasonable beneficial use of the landmark site but afford appellants opportunities further to enhance not only the Terminal site proper but also other properties.

Affirmed.

---

[16] Appellants of course argue at length that the transferable development rights, while valuable, do not constitute "just compensation."

[17] Counsel for appellants admitted at oral argument that the Commission has not suggested that it would not, for example, approve a 20-story office tower along the lines of that which was part of the original plan for the Terminal.

## Lucas v. South Carolina Coastal Council
Supreme Court of the United States, 1992.
505 U.S. 1003, 112 S.Ct. 2886.

■ SCALIA, J., delivered the opinion of the Court.

In 1986, petitioner David H. Lucas paid $975,000 for two residential lots on the Isle of Palms in Charleston County, South Carolina, on which he intended to build single-family homes. In 1988, however, the South Carolina Legislature enacted the Beachfront Management Act, S.C. Code § 48–39–250 et seq. (Supp. 1990) (Act), which had the direct effect of barring petitioner from erecting any permanent habitable structures on his two parcels. A state trial court found that this prohibition rendered Lucas's parcels "valueless." This case requires us to decide whether the Act's dramatic effect on the economic value of Lucas's lots accomplished a taking of private property under the Fifth and Fourteenth Amendments requiring the payment of "just compensation."

South Carolina's expressed interest in intensively managing development activities in the so-called "coastal zone" dates from 1977 when, in the aftermath of Congress's passage of the federal Coastal Zone Management Act of 1972, 16 U.S.C. § 1451 et seq., the legislature enacted a Coastal Zone Management Act of its own. See S.C. Code § 48–39–10 et seq. (1987). In its original form, the South Carolina Act required owners of coastal zone land that qualified as a "critical area" (defined in the legislation to include beaches and immediately adjacent sand dunes, § 48–39–10(J)) to obtain a permit from the newly created South Carolina Coastal Council (respondent here) prior to committing the land to a "use other than the use the critical area was devoted to on [September 28, 1977]." § 48–39–130(A).

In the late 1970's, Lucas and others began extensive residential development of the Isle of Palms, a barrier island situated eastward of the City of Charleston. Toward the close of the development cycle for one residential subdivision known as "Beachwood East," Lucas in 1986 purchased the two lots at issue in this litigation for his own account. No portion of the lots, which were located approximately 300 feet from the beach, qualified as a "critical area" under the 1977 Act; accordingly, at the time Lucas acquired these parcels, he was not legally obliged to obtain a permit from the Council in advance of any development activity. His intention with respect to the lots was to do what the owners of the immediately adjacent parcels had already done: erect single-family residences. He commissioned architectural drawings for this purpose.

The Beachfront Management Act brought Lucas's plans to an abrupt end. Under that 1988 legislation, the Council was directed to establish a "baseline" connecting the landward-most "points of erosion . . . during the past forty years" in the region of the Isle of Palms that includes Lucas's lots. In action not challenged here, the Council fixed this baseline landward of Lucas's parcels. That was significant, for under the Act construction of occupiable improvements was flatly prohibited seaward of a line drawn 20 feet landward of, and parallel to, the baseline. The Act provided no exceptions.

Lucas promptly filed suit in the South Carolina Court of Common Pleas, contending that the Beachfront Management Act's construction bar effected a taking of his property without just compensation. Lucas did not take issue with the validity of the Act as a lawful exercise of South Carolina's police power, but contended that the Act's complete extinguishment of his property's value entitled him to compensation regardless of whether the legislature had acted in furtherance of legitimate police power objectives. Following a bench trial, the court agreed. The court concluded that Lucas's properties had been "taken" by operation of the Act, and it ordered respondent to pay "just compensation" in the amount of $1,232,387.50.

The Supreme Court of South Carolina reversed. The Court ruled that when a regulation respecting the use of property is designed "to prevent serious public harm," 304 S.C. 376, 383, 404 S.E.2d 895, 899 (1991) (citing, inter alia, Mugler v. Kansas, 123 U.S. 623 (1887)), no compensation is owing under the Takings Clause regardless of the regulation's effect on the property's value.

Two justices dissented. [T]hey would not have characterized the Beachfront Management Act's "primary purpose [as] the prevention of a nuisance." 304 S. C., at 395, 404 S. E. 2d, at 906 (Harwell, J., dissenting). To the dissenters, the chief purposes of the legislation, among them the promotion of tourism and the creation of a "habitat for indigenous flora and fauna," could not fairly be compared to nuisance abatement.

We granted certiorari.

Prior to Justice Holmes' exposition in Pennsylvania Coal Co. v. Mahon, 260 U.S. 393 (1922), it was generally thought that the Takings Clause reached only a "direct appropriation" of property, Legal Tender Cases, 12 Wall. 457, 551 (1870), or the functional equivalent of a "practical ouster of [the owner's] possession." Transportation Co. v. Chicago, 99 U.S. 635, 642 (1878). Justice Holmes recognized in Mahon, however, that if the protection against physical appropriations of private property was to be meaningfully enforced, the government's power to redefine the range of interests included in the ownership of property was necessarily constrained by constitutional limits.

Nevertheless, our decision in Mahon offered little insight into when, and under what circumstances, a given regulation would be seen as going "too far" for purposes of the Fifth Amendment. In 70-odd years of succeeding "regulatory takings" jurisprudence, we have generally eschewed any "set formula" for determining how far is too far. Penn Central Transportation Co. v. New York City, 438 U.S. 104, 124 (1978). We have, however, described at least two discrete categories of regulatory action as compensable without case-specific inquiry into the public interest advanced in support of the restraint. The first encompasses regulations that compel the property owner to suffer a physical "invasion" of his property. In general (at least with regard to permanent invasions), no matter how minute the intrusion, and no matter how weighty the public purpose behind it, we have required compensation. Loretto v. Teleprompter Manhattan CATV Corp., 458 U.S. 419 (1982).

The second situation in which we have found categorical treatment appropriate is where regulation denies all economically beneficial or productive use of land.

We have never set forth the justification for this rule. Perhaps it is simply, as Justice Brennan suggested, that total deprivation of beneficial use is, from the landowner's point of view, the equivalent of a physical appropriation. Surely, at least, in the extraordinary circumstance when no productive or economically beneficial use of land is permitted, it is less realistic to indulge our usual assumption that the legislature is simply "adjusting the benefits and burdens of economic life," Penn Central Transportation Co., 438 U.S., at 124, in a manner that secures an "average reciprocity of advantage" to everyone concerned. Pennsylvania Coal Co. v. Mahon, 260 U.S., at 415. And the *functional* basis for permitting the government, by regulation, to affect property values without compensation—that "Government hardly could go on if to some extent values incident to property could not be diminished without paying for every such change in the general law," id. at 413, does not apply to the relatively rare situations where the government has deprived a landowner of all economically beneficial uses.

On the other side of the balance, affirmatively supporting a compensation requirement, is the fact that regulations that leave the owner of land without economically beneficial or productive options for its use—typically, as here, by requiring land to be left substantially in its natural state—carry with them a heightened risk that private property is being pressed into some form of public service under the guise of mitigating serious public harm. We think, in short, that there are good reasons for our frequently expressed belief that when the owner of real property has been called upon to sacrifice all economically beneficial uses in the name of the common good, that is, to leave his property economically idle, he has suffered a taking.[18]

---

[18] Justice Stevens criticizes the "deprivation of all economically beneficial use" rule as "wholly arbitrary", in that "[the] landowner whose property is diminished in value 95% recovers nothing," while the landowner who suffers a complete elimination of value "recovers the land's full value." This analysis errs in its assumption that the landowner whose deprivation is one step short of complete is not entitled to compensation. Such an owner might not be able to claim the benefit of our categorical formulation, but, as we have acknowledged time and again, "the economic impact of the regulation on the claimant and . . . the extent to which the regulation has interfered with distinct investment-backed expectations" are keenly relevant to takings analysis generally. Penn Central Transportation Co. v. New York City, 438 U.S. 104, 124 (1978). It is true that in at least some cases the landowner with 95% loss will get nothing, while the landowner with total loss will recover in full. But that occasional result is no more strange than the gross disparity between the landowner whose premises are taken for a highway (who

The trial court found Lucas's two beachfront lots to have been rendered valueless by respondent's enforcement of the coastal-zone construction ban. Under Lucas's theory of the case, which rested upon our "no economically viable use" statements, that finding entitled him to compensation. Lucas believed it unnecessary to take issue with either the purposes behind the Beachfront Management Act, or the means chosen by the South Carolina Legislature to effectuate those purposes. The South Carolina Supreme Court, however, thought otherwise. In its view, the Beachfront Management Act was no ordinary enactment, but involved an exercise of South Carolina's "police powers" to mitigate the harm to the public interest that petitioner's use of his land might occasion. 304 S. C., at 384, 404 S. E. 2d, at 899. By neglecting to dispute the findings enumerated in the Act or otherwise to challenge the legislature's purposes, petitioner "conceded that the beach/dune area of South Carolina's shores is an extremely valuable public resource; that the erection of new construction, inter alia, contributes to the erosion and destruction of this public resource; and that discouraging new construction in close proximity to the beach/dune area is necessary to prevent a great public harm." In the court's view, these concessions brought petitioner's challenge within a long line of this Court's cases sustaining against Due Process and Takings Clause challenges the State's use of its "police powers" to enjoin a property owner from activities akin to public nuisances. . . .

The transition from our early focus on control of "noxious" uses to our contemporary understanding of the broad realm within which government may regulate without compensation was an easy one, since the distinction between "harm-preventing" and "benefit-conferring" regulation is often in the eye of the beholder. It is quite possible, for example, to describe in either fashion the ecological, economic, and aesthetic concerns that inspired the South Carolina legislature in the present case. One could say that imposing a servitude on Lucas's land is necessary in order to prevent his use of it from "harming" South Carolina's ecological resources; or, instead, in order to achieve the "benefits" of an ecological preserve. Whether one or the other of the competing characterizations will come to one's lips in a particular case depends primarily upon one's evaluation of the worth of competing uses of real estate. A given restraint will be seen as mitigating "harm" to the adjacent parcels or securing a "benefit" for them, depending upon the observer's evaluation of the relative importance of the use that the restraint favors. Whether Lucas's construction of single-family residences on his parcels should be described as bringing "harm" to South Carolina's adjacent ecological resources thus depends principally upon whether the describer believes that the State's use interest in nurturing

---

recovers in full) and the landowner whose property is reduced to 5% of its former value by the highway (who recovers nothing). Takings law is full of these "all-or-nothing" situations.

those resources is so important that any competing adjacent use must yield.[19]

When it is understood that "prevention of harmful use" was merely our early formulation of the police power justification necessary to sustain (without compensation) any regulatory diminution in value; and that the distinction between regulation that "prevents harmful use" and that which "confers benefits" is difficult, if not impossible, to discern on an objective, value-free basis; it becomes self-evident that noxious-use logic cannot serve as a touchstone to distinguish regulatory "takings"—which require compensation—from regulatory deprivations that do not require compensation. A fortiori the legislature's recitation of a noxious-use justification cannot be the basis for departing from our categorical rule that total regulatory takings must be compensated. If it were, departure would virtually always be allowed. The South Carolina Supreme Court's approach would essentially nullify Mahon's affirmation of limits to the noncompensable exercise of the police power. Our cases provide no support for this: None of them that employed the logic of "harmful use" prevention to sustain a regulation involved an allegation that the regulation wholly eliminated the value of the claimant's land.

Where the State seeks to sustain regulation that deprives land of all economically beneficial use, we think it may resist compensation only if the logically antecedent inquiry into the nature of the owner's estate shows that the proscribed use interests were not part of his title to begin with. This accords, we think, with our "takings" jurisprudence, which has traditionally been guided by the understandings of our citizens regarding the content of, and the State's power over, the "bundle of rights" that they acquire when they obtain title to property.

Where "permanent physical occupation" of land is concerned, we have refused to allow the government to decree it anew (without compensation), no matter how weighty the asserted "public interests" involved, though we assuredly would permit the government to assert a permanent easement that was a pre-existing limitation upon the landowner's title. We believe similar treatment must be accorded confiscatory regulations, i. e., regulations that prohibit all economically beneficial use of land. Any limitation so severe cannot be newly legislated or decreed (without compensation), but must inhere in the title itself, in the restrictions that background principles of the State's law of property and nuisance already place upon land ownership. A law or decree with such an effect must, in other words, do no more than duplicate the result that could have been achieved in the courts—by adjacent landowners (or other uniquely affected persons) under the State's law of private

---

[19] In Justice Blackmun's view, even with respect to regulations that deprive an owner of all developmental or economically beneficial land uses, the test for required compensation is whether the legislature has recited a harm-preventing justification for its action. Since such a justification can be formulated in practically every case, this amounts to a test of whether the legislature has a stupid staff. We think the Takings Clause requires courts to do more than insist upon artful harm-preventing characterizations.

nuisance, or by the State under its complementary power to abate nuisances that affect the public generally, or otherwise.

On this analysis, the owner of a lake bed, for example, would not be entitled to compensation when he is denied the requisite permit to engage in a landfilling operation that would have the effect of flooding others' land. Nor the corporate owner of a nuclear generating plant, when it is directed to remove all improvements from its land upon discovery that the plant sits astride an earthquake fault. Such regulatory action may well have the effect of eliminating the land's only economically productive use, but it does not proscribe a productive use that was previously permissible under relevant property and nuisance principles. The use of these properties for what are now expressly prohibited purposes was always unlawful, and (subject to other constitutional limitations) it was open to the State at any point to make the implication of those background principles of nuisance and property law explicit. In light of our traditional resort to "existing rules or understandings that stem from an independent source such as state law" to define the range of interests that qualify for protection as "property" under the Fifth (and Fourteenth) amendments, this recognition that the Takings Clause does not require compensation when an owner is barred from putting land to a use that is proscribed by those "existing rules or understandings" is surely unexceptional. When, however, a regulation that declares "off-limits" all economically productive or beneficial uses of land goes beyond what the relevant background principles would dictate, compensation must be paid to sustain it.

The "total taking" inquiry we require today will ordinarily entail (as the application of state nuisance law ordinarily entails) analysis of, among other things, the degree of harm to public lands and resources, or adjacent private property, posed by the claimant's proposed activities, see, e.g., Restatement (Second) of Torts §§ 826, 827, the social value of the claimant's activities and their suitability to the locality in question, see, e.g., id., §§ 828(a) and (b), 831, and the relative ease with which the alleged harm can be avoided through measures taken by the claimant and the government (or adjacent private landowners) alike, see, e.g., id., §§ 827(e), 828(c), 830. The fact that a particular use has long been engaged in by similarly situated owners ordinarily imports a lack of any common-law prohibition (though changed circumstances or new knowledge may make what was previously permissible no longer so, see Restatement (Second) of Torts, supra, § 827, comment g). So also does the fact that other landowners, similarly situated, are permitted to continue the use denied to the claimant.

It seems unlikely that common-law principles would have prevented the erection of any habitable or productive improvements on petitioner's land; they rarely support prohibition of the "essential use" of land. The question, however, is one of state law to be dealt with on remand. We emphasize that to win its case South Carolina must do more than proffer the legislature's declaration that the uses Lucas desires are inconsistent with the public interest. As we have said, a "State, by ipse dixit, may not transform private property into public property without compensation...." Webb's Fabulous Pharmacies, Inc. v. Beckwith, 449 U.S. 155, 164 (1980). Instead, as it would be required to do if it sought to restrain Lucas in a common-law action for public nuisance, South Carolina must identify background principles of nuisance and property law that prohibit the uses he now intends in the circumstances in which the property is presently found. Only on this showing can the State fairly claim that, in proscribing all such beneficial uses, the Beachfront Management Act is taking nothing.[20]

The judgment is reversed and the cause remanded for proceedings not inconsistent with this opinion.

■ JUSTICE KENNEDY, concurring in the judgment.

The rights conferred by the Takings Clause and the police power of the State may coexist without conflict. Property is bought and sold, investments are made, subject to the State's power to regulate. Where a taking is alleged from regulations which deprive the property of all value, the test must be whether the deprivation is contrary to reasonable, investment-backed expectations.

There is an inherent tendency towards circularity in this synthesis, of course; for if the owner's reasonable expectations are shaped by what courts allow as a proper exercise of governmental authority, property tends to become what courts say it is. Some circularity must be tolerated in these matters, however, as it is in other spheres. The definition, moreover, is not circular in its entirety. The expectations protected by the Constitution are based on objective rules and customs that can be understood as reasonable by all parties involved.

In my view, reasonable expectations must be understood in light of the whole of our legal tradition. The common law of nuisance is too narrow a confine for the exercise of regulatory power in a complex and interdependent society. The State should not be prevented from enacting new regulatory initiatives in response to changing conditions, and courts must consider all reasonable expectations whatever their source. The Takings Clause does not require a static body of state property law; it protects private expectations to ensure private investment. I agree with the Court that nuisance prevention accords with the most common expectations of property owners who face regulation, but I do not believe this can be the sole source of state authority to impose severe restrictions.

---

[20] Justice Blackmun decries our reliance on background nuisance principles at least in part because he believes those principles to be as manipulable as we find the "harm prevention"/"benefit conferral" dichotomy. There is no doubt some leeway in a court's interpretation of what existing state law permits—but not remotely as much, we think, as in a legislative crafting of the reasons for its confiscatory regulation. We stress that an affirmative decree eliminating all economically beneficial uses may be defended only if an objectively reasonable application of relevant precedents would exclude those beneficial uses in the circumstances in which the land is presently found.

Coastal property may present such unique concerns for a fragile land system that the State can go further in regulating its development and use than the common law of nuisance might otherwise permit.

The Supreme Court of South Carolina erred, in my view, by reciting the general purposes for which the state regulations were enacted without a determination that they were in accord with the owner's reasonable expectations and therefore sufficient to support a severe restriction on specific parcels of property. The promotion of tourism, for instance, ought not to suffice to deprive specific property of all value without a corresponding duty to compensate. Furthermore, the means, as well as the ends, of regulation must accord with the owner's reasonable expectations. Here, the State did not act until after the property had been zoned for individual lot development and most other parcels had been improved, throwing the whole burden of the regulation on the remaining lots. This too must be measured in the balance.

■ JUSTICE BLACKMUN, dissenting.

Today the Court launches a missile to kill a mouse.

If the state legislature is correct that the prohibition on building in front of the setback line prevents serious harm, then, under this Court's prior cases, the Act is constitutional. . . .

[T]he Court decides the State has the burden to convince the courts that its legislative judgments are correct. Despite Lucas' complete failure to contest the legislature's findings of serious harm to life and property if a permanent structure is built, the Court decides that the legislative findings are not sufficient to justify the use prohibition. In this case, apparently, the State now has the burden of showing the regulation is not a taking. The Court offers no justification for its sudden hostility toward state legislators, and I doubt that it could. . . .

■ JUSTICE STEVENS, dissenting.

[I]n addition to lacking support in past decisions, the Court's new rule is wholly arbitrary. A landowner whose property is diminished in value 95% recovers nothing, while an owner whose property is diminished 100% recovers the land's full value. . . .

The Court's categorical approach rule will, I fear, greatly hamper the efforts of local officials and planners who must deal with increasingly complex problems in land-use and environmental regulation. As this case—in which the claims of an individual property owner exceed $1 million—well demonstrates, these officials face both substantial uncertainty because of the ad hoc nature of takings law and unacceptable penalties if they guess incorrectly about that law.

## Palazzolo v. Rhode Island
Supreme Court of the United States, 2001.
533 U.S. 606, 121 S.Ct. 2448.

■ KENNEDY, J.

Petitioner Anthony Palazzolo owns a waterfront parcel of land in the town of Westerly, Rhode Island. Almost all of the property is designated as coastal wetlands under Rhode Island law. After petitioner's development proposals were rejected by respondent Rhode Island Coastal Resources Management Council (Council), he sued in state court, asserting the Council's application of its wetlands regulations took the property without compensation in violation of the Takings Clause of the Fifth Amendment, binding upon the State through the Due Process Clause of the Fourteenth Amendment. Petitioner sought review in this Court, contending the Supreme Court of Rhode Island erred in rejecting his takings claim.

[T]he suit alleged the Council's action deprived petitioner of "economically, beneficial use" of his property, resulting in a total taking requiring compensation under *Lucas v. South Carolina Coastal Council,* 505 U.S. 1003 (1992). He sought damages in the amount of $3,150,000, a figure derived from an appraiser's estimate as to the value of a 74-lot residential subdivision. The State countered with a host of defenses. After a bench trial, a justice of the Superior Court ruled against petitioner, accepting some of the State's theories.

The Rhode Island Supreme Court affirmed. Like the Superior Court, the State Supreme Court recited multiple grounds for rejecting petitioner's suit. The court held, first, that petitioner's takings claim was not ripe; second, that petitioner had no right to challenge regulations predating 1978, when he succeeded to legal ownership of the property from SGI; and third, that the claim of deprivation of all economically beneficial use was contradicted by undisputed evidence that he had $200,000 in development value remaining on an upland parcel of the property. In addition to holding petitioner could not assert a takings claim based on the denial of all economic use, the court concluded he could not recover under the more general test of *Penn Central Transp. Co. v. City New York,* 438 U.S. 104 (1978). On this claim, too, the date of acquisition of the parcel was found determinative, and the court held he could have had "no reasonable investment-backed expectations that were affected by this regulation" because it predated his ownership.

We disagree with the Supreme Court of Rhode Island as to the first two of these conclusions; and, we hold, the court was correct to conclude that the owner is not deprived of all economic use of his property because the value of upland portions is substantial. We remand for further consideration of the claim under the principles set forth in *Penn Central.*

The Takings Clause of the Fifth Amendment, applicable to the States through the Fourteenth Amendment, prohibits the government from taking private property for public use without just compensation. The clearest sort of taking occurs when the government encroaches upon or occupies private land for its own proposed use. Our cases establish that even a minimal "permanent physical occupation of real property" requires compensation under the Clause. *Loretto v. Teleprompter Manhattan CATV Corp.,* 458 U.S. 419, 427 (1982) In *Pennsylvania Coal Co. v. Mahon,* 260 U.S. 393 (1922), the Court recognized that there will be instances when government actions do not encroach upon or occupy the property yet still affect and limit its use to such an extent that a taking occurs. In Justice Holmes' well-known, if less than self-defining, formulation, "while property may be regulated to a certain extent, if a regulation goes too far it will be recognized as a taking."

Since *Mahon,* we have given some, but not too specific, guidance to courts confronted with deciding whether a particular government action goes too far and effects a regulatory taking. First, we have observed, with certain qualifications, that a regulation which "denies all economically beneficial or productive use of land" will require compensation under the Takings Clause. *Lucas,* 505 U.S., at 1015. Where a regulation places limitations on land that fall short of eliminating all economically beneficial use, a taking nonetheless may have occurred, depending on a complex of factors including the regulation's economic effect on the landowner, the extent to which the regulation interferes with reasonable investment-backed expectations, and the character of the government action. These inquiries are informed by the purpose of the Takings Clause, which is to prevent the government from "forcing some people alone to bear public burdens which, in all fairness and justice, should be borne by the public as a whole." *Armstrong v. United States,* 364 U.S. 40, 49 (1960).

Petitioner seeks compensation under these principles. At the outset, however, we face the two threshold considerations invoked by the state court to bar the claim: ripeness, and acquisition which postdates the regulation.

[The Court holds that the case is ripe for decision.]

We turn to the second asserted basis for declining to address petitioner's takings claim on the merits. When the Council promulgated its wetlands regulations, the disputed parcel was owned not by petitioner but by the corporation of which he was sole shareholder. When title was transferred to petitioner by operation of law, the wetlands regulations were in force. The state court held the postregulation acquisition of title was fatal to the claim for deprivation of all economic use, and to the *Penn Central* claim. While the first holding was couched in terms of background principles of state property law, see *Lucas,* and the second in terms of petitioner's reasonable investment-backed expectations, see *Penn Central,* the two holdings together amount to a single, sweeping, rule: A purchaser or a successive title holder like petitioner is deemed to have notice of an earlier-enacted restriction and is barred from claiming that it effects a taking.

The theory underlying the argument that postenactment purchasers cannot challenge a regulation under the Takings Clause seems to run on these lines: Property rights are created by the State. So, the argument goes, by prospective legislation the State can shape and define property rights and reasonable investment-backed expectations, and subsequent owners cannot claim any injury from lost value. After all, they purchased or took title with notice of the limitation.

The State may not put so potent a Hobbesian stick into the Lockean bundle. The right to improve property, of course, is subject to the reasonable exercise of state authority, including the enforcement of valid zoning and land-use restrictions. See *Pennsylvania Coal Co.*, ("Government hardly could go on if to some extent values incident to property could not be diminished without paying for every such change in the general law"). The Takings Clause, however, in certain circumstances allows a landowner to assert that a particular exercise of the State's regulatory power is so unreasonable or onerous as to compel compensation. Just as a prospective enactment, such as a new zoning ordinance, can limit the value of land without effecting a taking because it can be understood as reasonable by all concerned, other enactments are unreasonable and do not become less so through passage of time or title. Were we to accept the State's rule, the postenactment transfer of title would absolve the State of its obligation to defend any action restricting land use, no matter how extreme or unreasonable. A State would be allowed, in effect, to put an expiration date on the Takings Clause. This ought not to be the rule. Future generations, too, have a right to challenge unreasonable limitations on the use and value of land.

Nor does the justification of notice take into account the effect on owners at the time of enactment, who are prejudiced as well. Should an owner attempt to challenge a new regulation, but not survive the process of ripening his or her claim (which, as this case demonstrates, will often take years), under the proposed rule the right to compensation may not be asserted by an heir or successor, and so may not be asserted at all. The State's rule would work a critical alteration to the nature of property, as the newly regulated landowner is stripped of the ability to transfer the interest which was possessed prior to the regulation. The State may not by this means secure a windfall for itself. The proposed rule is, furthermore, capricious in effect. The young owner contrasted with the older owner, the owner with the resources to hold contrasted with the owner with the need to sell, would be in different positions. The Takings Clause is not so quixotic. A blanket rule that purchasers with notice have no compensation right when a claim becomes ripe is too blunt an instrument to accord with the duty to compensate for what is taken.

Direct condemnation, by invocation of the State's power of eminent domain, presents different considerations from cases alleging a taking based on a burdensome regulation. In a direct condemnation action, or when a State has physically invaded the property without filing suit, the fact and extent of the taking are known. In such an instance, it is a general rule of the law of eminent domain that any award goes to the owner at the time of the taking, and that the right to compensation is not passed to a subsequent purchaser. A challenge to the application of a land-use regulation, by contrast, does not mature until ripeness requirements have been satisfied, under principles we have discussed; until this point an inverse condemnation claim alleging a regulatory taking cannot be maintained. It would be illogical, and unfair, to bar a regulatory takings claim because of the post-enactment transfer of ownership where the steps necessary to make the claim ripe were not taken, or could not have been taken, by a previous owner.

There is controlling precedent for our conclusion. *Nollan v. California Coastal Comm'n*, 483 U.S. 825, 107 S.Ct. 3141 (1987), presented the question whether it was consistent with the Takings Clause for a state regulatory agency to require oceanfront landowners to provide lateral beach access to the public as the condition for a development permit. The principal dissenting opinion observed it was a policy of the California Coastal Commission to require the condition, and that the Nollans, who purchased their home after the policy went into effect, were "on notice that new developments would be approved only if provisions were made for lateral beach access." A majority of the Court rejected the proposition. "So long as the Commission could not have deprived the prior owners of the easement without compensating them," the Court reasoned, "the prior owners must be understood to have transferred their full property rights in conveying the lot."

It is argued that *Nollan's* holding was limited by the later decision in *Lucas*. In *Lucas* the Court observed that a landowner's ability to recover for a government deprivation of all economically beneficial use of property is not absolute but instead is confined by limitations on the use of land which "inhere in the title itself." This is so, the Court reasoned, because the landowner is constrained by those "restrictions that background principles of the State's law of property and nuisance already place upon land ownership." It is asserted here that *Lucas* stands for the proposition that any new regulation, once enacted, becomes a background principle of property law which cannot be challenged by those who acquire title after the enactment.

We have no occasion to consider the precise circumstances when a legislative enactment can be deemed a background principle of state law or whether those circumstances are present here. It suffices to say that a regulation that otherwise would be unconstitutional absent compensation is not transformed into a background principle of the State's law by mere virtue of the passage of title. This relative standard would be incompatible with our description of the concept in *Lucas*, which is explained in terms of those common, shared understandings of permissible limitations derived from a State's legal tradition. A regulation or common-law rule cannot be a background principle for some owners but not for others. The determination whether an existing, general law can limit all economic use of property must turn on objective factors, such as the nature of the land use proscribed. ("The 'total taking' inquiry we require today will ordinarily entail ... analysis of, among other things, the degree of harm to public lands and resources, or adjacent private property, posed by the claimant's proposed activities"). A law does not become a background principle for subsequent owners by enactment itself. *Lucas* did not overrule our holding in *Nollan*, which, as we have noted, is based on essential Takings Clause principles.

For reasons we discuss next, the state court will not find it necessary to explore these matters on remand in connection with the claim that all economic use was deprived; it must address, however, the merits of petitioner's claim under *Penn Central*. That claim is not barred by the mere fact that title was acquired after the effective date of the state-imposed restriction.

[A]s the case is ripe, and as the date of transfer of title does not bar petitioner's takings claim, we have before us the alternative ground relied upon by the Rhode Island Supreme Court in ruling upon the merits of the takings claims. It held that all economically beneficial use was not deprived because the uplands portion of the property can still be improved. On this point, we agree with the court's decision. Petitioner accepts the Council's contention and the state trial court's finding that his parcel retains $200,000 in development value under the State's wetlands regulations. He asserts, nonetheless, that he has suffered a total taking and contends the Council cannot sidestep the holding in *Lucas* "by the simple expedient of leaving a landowner a few crumbs of value."

Assuming a taking is otherwise established, a State may not evade the duty to compensate on the premise that the landowner is left with a token interest. This is not the situation of the landowner in this case, however. A regulation permitting a landowner to build a substantial residence on an 18-acre parcel does not leave the property "economically idle." *Lucas, supra,* at 1019.

[F]or the reasons we have discussed, the State Supreme Court erred in finding petitioner's claims were unripe and in ruling that acquisition of title after the effective date of the regulations barred the takings claims. The court did not err in finding that petitioner failed to establish a deprivation of all economic value, for it is undisputed that the parcel retains significant worth for construction of a residence. The claims under the *Penn Central* analysis were not examined, and for this purpose the case should be remanded. . . .

■ JUSTICE O'CONNOR, concurring.

[T]he difficult question is what role the temporal relationship between regulatory enactment and title acquisition plays in a proper *Penn Central* analysis. Today's holding does not mean that the timing of the regulation's enactment relative to the acquisition of title is immaterial to the *Penn Central* analysis. Indeed, it would be just as much error to expunge this consideration from the takings inquiry as it would be to accord it exclusive significance. Our polestar instead remains the principles set forth in *Penn Central* itself and our other cases that govern partial regulatory takings. Under these cases, interference with investment-backed expectations is one of a number of factors that a court must examine. Further, the regulatory regime in place at the time the claimant acquires the property at issue helps to shape the reasonableness of those expectations. . . .

■ JUSTICE SCALIA, concurring.

[In contrast to Justice O'Connor,] in my view, the fact that a restriction existed at the time the purchaser took title (other than a restriction forming part of the "background principles of the State's law of property and nuisance," *Lucas*) should have no bearing upon the determination of whether the restriction is so substantial as to constitute a taking. . . .

■ JUSTICE STEVENS, concurring in part and dissenting in part.

[T]o the extent that the adoption of the regulations constitute the challenged taking, petitioner is simply the wrong party to be bringing this action. If the regulations imposed a compensable injury on anyone, it was on the owner of the property at the moment the regulations were adopted. Given the trial court's finding that petitioner did not own the property at that time, in my judgment it is pellucidly clear that he has no standing to claim that the promulgation of the regulations constituted a taking of any part of the property that he subsequently acquired. . . .

■ JUSTICE GINSBURG, with whom JUSTICE SOUTER and JUSTICE BREYER join, dissenting.

[The dissenting Justices argue that the case was not ripe for decision. In addition, Justice Breyer concurs with Justice O'Connor's position that the fact that one acquires the subject property after a regulatory law is enacted is a relevant, but not necessarily dispositive, factor in analyzing whether a taking has occurred.]

## Tahoe-Sierra Preservation Council, Inc. v. Tahoe Regional Planning Agency

Supreme Court of the United States, 2002.
535 U.S. 302, 122 S.Ct. 1465.

■ STEVENS, J.

The question presented is whether a moratorium on development imposed during the process of devising a comprehensive land-use plan constitutes a *per se* taking of property requiring compensation under the Takings Clause of the United States Constitution. This case actually involves two moratoria ordered by respondent Tahoe Regional Planning Agency (TRPA) to maintain the status quo while studying the impact of development on Lake Tahoe and designing a strategy for environmentally sound growth. The first, Ordinance 81–5, was effective from August 24, 1981, until August 26, 1983, whereas the second more restrictive Resolution 83–21 was in effect from August 27, 1983, until April 25, 1984. As a result of these two directives, virtually all development on a substantial portion of the property subject to TRPA's jurisdiction was prohibited for a period of 32 months. . . .

### I

The relevant facts are undisputed. The Court of Appeals, while reversing the District Court on a question of law, accepted all of its findings of fact, and no party challenges those findings. All agree that Lake Tahoe is "uniquely beautiful," that President Clinton was right to call it a " 'national treasure that must be protected and preserved,' " and that Mark Twain aptly described the clarity of its waters as " 'not *merely* transparent, but dazzlingly, brilliantly so,' " (emphasis added) (quoting M. Twain, Roughing It 174–175 (1872)).

Lake Tahoe's exceptional clarity is attributed to the absence of algae that obscures the waters of most other lakes. Historically, the lack of nitrogen and phosphorous, which nourish the growth of algae, has ensured the transparency of its waters. Unfortunately, the lake's pristine state has deteriorated rapidly over the past 40 years; increased land development in the Lake Tahoe Basin (Basin) has threatened the " 'noble sheet of blue water' " beloved by Twain and countless others. As the District Court found, "[d]ramatic decreases in clarity first began to be noted in the late 1950's/early 1960's, shortly after development at the lake began in earnest." The lake's unsurpassed beauty, it seems, is the wellspring of its undoing.

The upsurge of development in the area has caused "increased nutrient loading of the lake largely because of the increase in impervious coverage of land in the Basin resulting from that development." . . .

### II

[T]he petitioners include the Tahoe-Sierra Preservation Council, Inc., a nonprofit membership corporation representing about 2,000 owners of both improved and unimproved parcels of real estate in the Lake Tahoe Basin, and a class of some 400 individual owners of vacant lots located either on SEZ [Stream Environmental Zone] lands or in other parts of districts 1, 2, or 3. . . .

Emphasizing the temporary nature of the regulations, the testimony that the "average holding time of a lot in the Tahoe area between lot purchase and home construction is twenty-five years," and the failure of petitioners to offer specific evidence of harm, the District Court concluded that "consideration of the *Penn Central* factors clearly leads to the conclusion that there was no taking." In the absence of evidence regarding any of the individual plaintiffs, the court evaluated the "average" purchasers' intent and found that such purchasers did not have reasonable, investment-backed expectations that they would be able to build single-family homes on their land within the six-year period involved in this lawsuit. . . .

Accordingly, the only question before the court was "whether the rule set forth in *Lucas* applies-that is, whether a categorical taking occurred because Ordinance 81–5 and Resolution 83–21 denied the plaintiffs 'all economically beneficial or productive use of land.'" Moreover, because petitioners brought only a facial challenge, the narrow inquiry before the Court of Appeals was whether the mere enactment of the regulations constituted a taking.

Contrary to the District Court, the Court of Appeals held that because the regulations had only a temporary impact on petitioners' fee interest in the properties, no categorical taking had occurred. It reasoned:

> Property interests may have many different dimensions. For example, the dimensions of a property interest may include a physical dimension (which describes the size and shape of the property in question), a functional dimension (which describes the extent to which an owner may use or dispose of the property in question), and a temporal dimension (which describes the duration of the property interest). At base, the plaintiffs' argument is that we should conceptually sever each plaintiff's fee interest into discrete segments in at least one of these dimensions-the temporal one-and treat each of those segments as separate and distinct property interests for purposes of takings analysis. Under this theory, they argue that there was a categorical taking of one of those temporal segments.

Putting to one side "cases of physical invasion or occupation," the court read our cases involving regulatory taking claims to focus on the impact of a regulation on the parcel as a whole. In its view a "planning regulation that prevents the development of a parcel for a temporary period of time is conceptually no different than a land-use restriction that permanently denies all use on a discrete portion of property, or that permanently restricts a type of use across all of the parcel." In each situation, a regulation that affects only a portion of the parcel-whether limited by time, use, or space-does not deprive the owner of all economically beneficial use.

The Court of Appeals distinguished *Lucas* as applying to the " 'relatively rare' " case in which a regulation denies all productive use of an entire parcel, whereas the moratoria involve only a "temporal 'slice' " of the fee interest and a form of regulation that is widespread and well established. It also rejected petitioners' argument that our decision in *First English* was controlling. According to the Court of Appeals, First English Evangelical Lutheran Church of Glendale v. County of Los Angeles, 482 U.S. 304 (1987), concerned the question whether compensation is an appropriate remedy for a temporary taking and not whether or when such a taking has occurred. Faced squarely with the question whether a taking had occurred, the court held that *Penn Central* was the appropriate framework for analysis. Petitioners, however, had failed to challenge the District Court's conclusion that they could not make out a taking claim under the *Penn Central* factors. . . .

### III

Petitioners make only a facial attack on Ordinance 81–5 and Resolution 83–21. They contend that the mere enactment of a temporary regulation that, while in effect, denies a property owner all viable economic use of her property gives rise to an unqualified constitutional obligation to compensate her for the value of its use during that period. Hence, they "face an uphill battle," *Keystone Bituminous Coal Assn. v. DeBenedictis,* 480 U.S. 470, 495 (1987) that is made especially steep by their desire for a categorical rule requiring compensation whenever the government imposes such a moratorium on development. Under their proposed rule, there is no need to evaluate the landowners' investment-backed expectations, the actual impact of the regulation on any individual, the importance of the public interest served by the regulation, or the reasons for imposing the temporary restriction. For petitioners, it is enough that a regulation imposes a temporary deprivation-no matter how brief-of all economically viable use to trigger a *per se* rule that a taking has occurred. Petitioners assert that our opinions in *First English* and *Lucas* have already endorsed their view, and that it is a logical application of the principle that the Takings Clause was "designed to bar Government from forcing some people alone to bear burdens which, in all fairness and justice, should be borne by the public as a whole." *Armstrong v. United States.*

We shall first explain why our cases do not support their proposed categorical rule-indeed, fairly read, they implicitly reject it. Next, we shall explain why the *Armstrong* principle requires rejection of that rule as well as the less extreme position advanced by petitioners at oral argument. In our view the answer to the abstract question whether a temporary moratorium effects a taking is neither "yes, always" nor "no, never"; the answer depends upon the particular circumstances of the case. Resisting "[t]he temptation to adopt what amount to *per se* rules in either direction," *Palazzolo v. Rhode Island,* (O'Connor, J., concurring), we conclude that the circumstances in this case are best analyzed within the *Penn Central* framework.

## IV

The text of the Fifth Amendment itself provides a basis for drawing a distinction between physical takings and regulatory takings. Its plain language requires the payment of compensation whenever the government acquires private property for a public purpose, whether the acquisition is the result of a condemnation proceeding or a physical appropriation. But the Constitution contains no comparable reference to regulations that prohibit a property owner from making certain uses of her private property. Our jurisprudence involving condemnations and physical takings is as old as the Republic and, for the most part, involves the straightforward application of *per se* rules. Our regulatory takings jurisprudence, in contrast, is of more recent vintage and is characterized by "essentially ad hoc, factual inquiries," *Penn Central,* 438 U.S., at 124, designed to allow "careful examination and weighing of all the relevant circumstances." *Palazzolo,* 533 U.S., at 636, (O'Connor, J., concurring).

When the government physically takes possession of an interest in property for some public purpose, it has a categorical duty to compensate the former owner, regardless of whether the interest that is taken constitutes an entire parcel or merely a part thereof. Thus, compensation is mandated when a leasehold is taken and the government occupies the property for its own purposes, even though that use is temporary. Similarly, when the government appropriates part of a rooftop in order to provide cable TV access for apartment tenants, *Loretto v. Teleprompter Manhattan CATV Corp.,* 458 U.S. 419 (1982); or when its planes use private airspace to approach a government airport, *United States v. Causby,* 328 U.S. 256 (1946), it is required to pay for that share no matter how small. But a government regulation that merely prohibits landlords from evicting tenants unwilling to pay a higher rent, *Block v. Hirsh,* 256 U.S. 135 (1921); that bans certain private uses of a portion of an owner's property, *Village of Euclid v. Ambler Realty Co.,* 272 U.S. 365 (1926); or that forbids the private use of certain airspace, *Penn Central Transp. Co. v. New York City,* 438 U.S. 104 (1978), does not constitute a categorical taking. "The first category of cases requires courts to apply a clear rule; the second necessarily entails complex factual assessments of the purposes and economic effects of government actions." *Yee v. Escondido,* 503 U.S. 519 (1992).

This longstanding distinction between acquisitions of property for public use, on the one hand, and regulations prohibiting private uses, on the other, makes it inappropriate to treat cases involving physical takings as controlling precedents for the evaluation of a claim that there has been a "regulatory taking," and vice versa. For the same reason that we do not ask whether a physical appropriation advances a substantial government interest or whether it deprives the owner of all economically valuable use, we do not apply our precedent from the physical takings context to regulatory takings claims. Land-use regulations are ubiquitous and most of them impact property values in some tangential way-often in completely unanticipated ways. Treating them all as *per se* takings would transform government regulation into a luxury few governments could afford. By contrast, physical appropriations are relatively rare, easily identified, and usually represent a greater affront to individual property rights. . . .

Perhaps recognizing this fundamental distinction, petitioners wisely do not place all their emphasis on analogies to physical takings cases. Instead, they rely principally on our decision in *Lucas*—a regulatory takings case that, nevertheless, applied a categorical rule-to argue that the *Penn Central* framework is inapplicable here. A brief review of some of the cases that led to our decision in *Lucas,* however, will help to explain why the holding in that case does not answer the question presented here.

As we noted in *Lucas,* it was Justice Holmes' opinion in *Pennsylvania Coal Co. v. Mahon* that gave birth to our regulatory takings jurisprudence. In subsequent opinions we have repeatedly and consistently endorsed Holmes' observation that "if regulation goes too far it will be recognized as a taking." Justice Holmes did not provide a standard for determining when a regulation goes "too far," but he did reject the view expressed in Justice Brandeis' dissent that there could not be a taking because the property remained in the possession of the owner and had not been appropriated or used by the public. After *Mahon,* neither a physical appropriation nor a public use has ever been a necessary component of a "regulatory taking."

In the decades following that decision, we have "generally eschewed" any set formula for determining how far is too far, choosing instead to engage in " 'essentially ad hoc, factual inquiries.' " Lucas, 505 U.S., at 1015 (quoting *Penn Central*). Indeed, we still resist the temptation to adopt *per se* rules in our cases involving partial regulatory takings, preferring to examine "a number of factors" rather than a simple "mathematically precise" formula. Justice Brennan's opinion for the Court in *Penn Central* did, however, make it clear that even though multiple factors are relevant in the analysis of regulatory takings claims, in such cases we must focus on "the parcel as a whole":

> 'Taking' jurisprudence does not divide a single parcel into discrete segments and attempt to determine whether rights in a particular segment have been entirely abrogated. In deciding whether a particular governmental action has effected a taking, this Court focuses rather both on the character of the action and on the nature and extent of the interference with rights in the parcel as a whole-here, the city tax block designated as the 'landmark site.'

*Id.,* at 130–131. This requirement that "the aggregate must be viewed in its entirety" explains why, for example, a regulation that prohibited commercial transactions in eagle feathers, but did not bar other uses or impose any physical invasion or restraint upon them, was not a taking. *Andrus v. Allard,* 444 U.S. 51, 66 (1979). It also clarifies why restrictions on the use of only limited portions of the parcel, such as setback ordinances, *Gorieb v. Fox,* 274 U.S. 603 (1927), or a requirement that coal pillars be left in place to prevent mine subsidence, *Keystone Bituminous Coal Assn. v. DeBenedictis,* 480 U.S., at 498, were not considered regulatory takings. In each of these cases, we affirmed that "where an owner possesses a full 'bundle' of property rights, the destruction of one 'strand' of the bundle is not a taking." *Andrus,* 444 U.S., at 65–66. . . .

In *First English,* the Court unambiguously and repeatedly characterized the issue to be decided as a "compensation question" or a "remedial question." ("The disposition of the case on these grounds isolates the remedial question for our consideration"). And the Court's statement of its holding was equally unambiguous: "We merely hold that where the government's activities *have already worked a taking* of all use of property, no subsequent action by the government can relieve it of the duty to provide compensation for the period during which the taking was effective." (emphasis added). In fact, *First English* expressly disavowed any ruling on the merits of the takings issue because the California courts had decided the remedial question on the assumption that a taking had been alleged. ("We reject appellee's suggestion that . . . we must independently evaluate the adequacy of the complaint and resolve the takings claim on the merits before we can reach the remedial question"). After our remand, the California courts concluded that there had not been a taking and we declined review of that decision. . . .

The categorical rule that we applied in *Lucas* states that compensation is required when a regulation deprives an owner of "*all* economically beneficial uses" of his land. Under that rule, a statute that "wholly eliminated the value" of Lucas' fee simple title clearly qualified as a taking. But our holding was limited to "the extraordinary circumstance when *no* productive or economically beneficial use of land is permitted." The emphasis on the word "no" in the text of the opinion was, in effect, reiterated in a footnote explaining that the categorical rule would not apply if the diminution in value were 95% instead of 100%. Anything less than a "complete elimination of value," or a "total loss," the Court acknowledged, would require the kind of analysis applied in *Penn Central.*

Certainly, our holding that the permanent "obliteration of the value" of a fee simple estate constitutes a categorical taking does not answer the question whether a regulation prohibiting any economic use of land for a 32-month period has the same legal effect. Petitioners seek to bring this case under the rule announced in *Lucas* by arguing that we can effectively sever a 32-month segment from the remainder of each landowner's fee simple estate, and then ask whether that segment has been taken in its entirety by the moratoria. Of course, defining the property interest taken in terms of the very regulation being challenged is circular. With property so divided, every delay would become a total ban; the moratorium and the normal permit process alike would constitute categorical takings. Petitioners' "conceptual severance" argument is unavailing because it ignores *Penn Central's* admonition that in regulatory takings cases we must focus on "the parcel as a whole." . . .

Neither *Lucas,* nor *First English,* nor any of our other regulatory takings cases compels us to accept petitioners' categorical submission. In fact, these cases make clear that the categorical rule in *Lucas* was carved out for the "extraordinary case" in which a regulation permanently deprives property of all value; the default rule remains that, in the regulatory taking context, we require a more fact specific inquiry. Nevertheless, we will consider whether the interest in protecting individual property owners from bearing public burdens "which, in all fairness and justice, should be borne by the public as a whole," *Armstrong v. United States,* 364 U.S., at 49, justifies creating a new rule for these circumstances.

V

[T]he ultimate constitutional question is whether the concepts of "fairness and justice" that underlie the Takings Clause will be better served by one of these categorical rules or by a *Penn Central* inquiry into all of the relevant circumstances in particular cases. From that perspective, the extreme categorical rule that any deprivation of all economic use, no matter how brief, constitutes a compensable taking surely cannot be sustained. Petitioners' broad submission would apply to numerous "normal delays in obtaining building permits, changes in zoning ordinances, variances, and the like," as well as to orders temporarily prohibiting access to crime scenes, businesses that violate health codes, fire-damaged buildings, or other areas that we cannot now foresee. Such a rule would undoubtedly require changes in numerous practices that have long been considered permissible exercises of the police power. As Justice Holmes warned in *Mahon,* "[g]overnment hardly could go on if to some extent values incident to property could not be diminished without paying for every such change in the general law." A rule that required compensation for every delay in the use of property would render routine government processes prohibitively expensive or encourage hasty decision making. Such an important change in the law should be the product of legislative rulemaking rather than adjudication.

A narrower rule that excluded the normal delays associated with processing permits, or that covered only delays of more than a year, would certainly have a less severe impact on prevailing practices, but it would still impose serious financial constraints on the planning process. Unlike the "extraordinary circumstance" in which the government deprives a property owner of all economic use, moratoria like Ordinance 81–5 and Resolution 83–21 are used widely among land-use planners to preserve the status quo while formulating a more permanent development strategy. In fact, the consensus in the planning community appears to be that moratoria, or "interim development controls" as they are often called, are an essential tool of successful development. Yet even the weak version of petitioners' categorical rule would treat these interim measures as takings regardless of the good faith of the planners, the reasonable expectations of the landowners, or the actual impact of the moratorium on property values.

The interest in facilitating informed decision making by regulatory agencies counsels against adopting a *per se* rule that would impose such severe costs on their deliberations. . . .

It may well be true that any moratorium that lasts for more than one year should be viewed with special skepticism. But given the fact that the District Court found that the 32 months required by TRPA to formulate the 1984 Regional Plan was not unreasonable, we could not possibly conclude that every delay of over one year is constitutionally unacceptable. Formulating a general rule of this kind is a suitable task for state legislatures. In our view, the duration of the restriction is one of the important factors that a court must consider in the appraisal of a regulatory takings claim, but with respect to that factor as with respect to other factors, the "temptation to adopt what amount to *per se* rules in either direction must be resisted." *Palazzolo*, 533 U.S., at 636, (O'Connor, J., concurring). There may be moratoria that last longer than one year which interfere with reasonable investment-backed expectations, but as the District Court's opinion illustrates, petitioners' proposed rule is simply "too blunt an instrument" for identifying those cases. We conclude, therefore, that the interest in "fairness and justice" will be best served by relying on the familiar *Penn Central* approach when deciding cases like this, rather than by attempting to craft a new categorical rule.

Accordingly, the judgment of the Court of Appeals is affirmed.

■ CHIEF JUSTICE REHNQUIST, with whom JUSTICE SCALIA and JUSTICE THOMAS join, dissenting. . . .

[This dissent first concludes that the petitioners were deprived of the use of their property for "almost six years," rather than the 32 months that the majority dealt with.]

[T]he Court refuses to apply *Lucas* on the ground that the deprivation was "temporary." Neither the Takings Clause nor our case law supports such a distinction. For one thing, a distinction between "temporary" and "permanent" prohibitions is tenuous. The "temporary" prohibition in this case that the Court finds is not a taking lasted almost six years. . . .

Our opinion in *First English* rejects any distinction between temporary and permanent takings when a landowner is deprived of all economically beneficial use of his land. *First English* stated that "temporary takings which, as here, deny a landowner all use of his property, are not different in kind from permanent takings, for which the Constitution clearly requires compensation." *Id.,* at 318. Because of *First English's* rule that "temporary deprivations of use are compensable under the Takings Clause," the Court in *Lucas* found nothing problematic about the later developments that potentially made the ban on development temporary.

More fundamentally, even if a practical distinction between temporary and permanent deprivations were plausible, to treat the two differently in terms of takings law would be at odds with the justification for the *Lucas* rule. The *Lucas* rule is derived from the fact that a "total deprivation of beneficial use is, from the landowner's point of view, the equivalent of a physical appropriation." The regulation in *Lucas* was the "practical equivalence" of a long-term physical appropriation, *i.e.,* a condemnation, so the Fifth Amendment required compensation. The "practical equivalence," from the landowner's point of view, of a "temporary" ban on all economic use is a forced leasehold. For example, assume the following situation: Respondent is contemplating the creation of a National Park around Lake Tahoe to preserve its scenic beauty. Respondent decides to take a 6-year leasehold over petitioners' property, during which any human activity on the land would be prohibited, in order to prevent any further destruction to the area while it was deciding whether to request that the area be designated a National Park. Surely that leasehold would require compensation. . . .

*Lucas* is implicated when the government deprives a landowner of all economically beneficial or productive use of land. The District Court found, and the Court agrees, that the moratorium temporarily deprived petitioners of all economically viable use of their land. Because the rationale for the *Lucas* rule applies just as strongly in this case, the temporary denial of all viable use of land for six years is a taking.

The Court worries that applying *Lucas* here compels finding that an array of traditional, short-term, land-use planning devices are takings. But since the beginning of our regulatory takings jurisprudence, we have recognized that property rights "are enjoyed under an implied limitation." *Mahon, supra,* at 413. . . .

Because the prohibition on development of nearly six years in this case cannot be said to resemble any "implied limitation" of state property law, it is a taking that requires compensation.

■ JUSTICE THOMAS, with whom JUSTICE SCALIA joins, dissenting.

I join the Chief Justice's dissent. I write separately to address the majority's conclusion that the temporary moratorium at issue here was not a taking because it was not a "taking of 'the parcel as a whole.' " While this questionable rule has been applied to various alleged regulatory takings, it was, in my view, rejected in the context of *temporal* deprivations of property by *First English* which held that temporary and permanent takings "are not different in kind" when a landowner is deprived of all beneficial use of his land. I had thought that *First English* put to rest the notion that the "relevant denominator" is land's infinite life. Consequently, a regulation effecting a total deprivation of the use of a so-called "temporal slice" of property is compensable under the Takings Clause unless background principles of state property law prevent it from being deemed a taking; "total deprivation of use is, from the landowner's point of view, the equivalent of a physical appropriation."

I would hold that regulations prohibiting all productive uses of property are subject to *Lucas*'s *per se* rule, regardless of whether the property so burdened retains theoretical useful life and value if, and when, the "temporary" moratorium is lifted. To my mind, such potential future value bears on the amount of compensation due and has nothing to do with the question whether there was a taking in the first place. It is regrettable that the Court has charted a markedly different path today.

## NOTES

1. *Average reciprocity of advantage.* In *Pennsylvania Coal*, Justice Holmes refers to an "average reciprocity of advantage that has been recognized as a justification of various laws." Many land use regulations that seem to be a burden from the landowner's perspective might actually benefit him or her. If this is so, the legislation is likely to withstand attack. For example, suppose an ordinance requires every house to be set back at least twenty feet from the sidewalk. Although landowner A might resent this ordinance because it reduces the area on which A can build, A gains a benefit because he or she enjoys the open space created when landowners B, C, and D must also abide by the ordinance. On balance, all are benefited rather than injured by the reciprocal enforcement of the ordinance. This theory offers a justification for many types of ordinances, including the typical zoning ordinance.

2. *Parcels, percentages and poppycock.* In the last paragraph of his *Pennsylvania Coal* dissent, Justice Brandeis argued that "values are relative" and that the loss to the coal company had to be related or compared to the whole value of the property. In judging a front-yard requirement, for example, it would be misleading to state that the statute requiring front yards "took" close to one hundred percent of the value of the front yard because nothing could be built on it. It would be more accurate to say that the requirement affected only a small percentage of the entire parcel. How far can the principle articulated by Brandeis be pushed? Could a total prohibition on the use of one parcel be justified because the parcel constituted only one percent of all the land owned by that parcel's owner? What is a "parcel" anyway? Does the Principal Problem raise this issue?

3. *Substantive due process distinguished.* For a time, the U.S. Supreme Court and many lower courts held that a taking could occur when a regulation does not substantially advance a legitimate governmental interest. See Agins v. Tiburon, 447 U.S. 255 (1980), and cases that followed

it. However, in 2005 the Supreme Court explicitly repudiated that approach in Lingle v. Chevron U.S.A., 544 U.S. 528 (2005). The issue is properly addressed as a question of substantive due process, not as a regulatory taking. Note, however, that the relationship between an exaction and the government's interest in demanding the exaction is the subject of takings tests for the category of exactions, covered in the following section of this assignment.

4. *The weighted balance of balancing tests: the application of Penn Central.* Although the *Penn Central* balancing test covers takings claims for regulations that allow for some economic uses of property, landowners rarely win *Penn Central* takings claims.[21] The test tends to focus courts on: 1) the fact that the property owner can still use the property for economic purposes; 2) the possible unreasonableness of the landowner's expectations given the likely impacts of the proposed development and also given today's trends towards land-use and environmental regulation; and 3) the government's reasons for regulating the property. One court suggested that the regulation's diminution of the property's values must exceed 85% to be compensable under *Penn Central*,[22] and another stated that *Penn Central* mandates compensation only for landowners whose property is reduced to "slightly greater than de minimis" value.[23] Some states have statutes mandating compensation for government actions (including regulations) that diminish the value of property to lesser degrees than *Penn Central* seems to require.[24]

5. *Use vs. value.* The *Lucas* test focuses on whether the landowner has been denied all economically viable, productive, or beneficial use of the property. Although the trial court had held that the property had been rendered valueless by South Carolina's regulation, the Supreme Court's majority opinion focuses on the uses available to the landowner and whether those uses have any economic benefit or productivity. Why? Would you pay $100 for one of Mr. Lucas' beachfront properties, even if you could not build on it? Many of us would. Land is rarely truly "valueless." It almost always has some positive residual value, unless the liabilities associated with the property—such as tax liens or liability for environmental contamination—exceed its value.

6. *Palazzolo remand.* On the remand of *Palazzolo*, the Rhode Island trial court determined that there was no *Penn Central* taking.[25] The property

---

[21] Juergensmeyer & Roberts, Land Use Planning and Development Regulation Law, 2d ed. § 10.6.B, p. 429 (2007).

[22] Walcek v. United States, 49 Fed. Cl. 248, 271 (2001).

[23] Animas Valley Sand & Gravel, Inc. v. Board of County Comm'rs, 38 P.3d 59 (Colo. 2001). But see City of San Antonio v. El Dorado Amusement Co., 195 S.W.3d 238 (Tex. App. 2006) (finding that regulation reducing property's value by 35% was taking under Texas Constitution).

[24] See, e.g., Bert J. Harris Private Property Rights Protection Act, Fla. Stat. Ann. § 70.001(2) (inordinate burden standard); Vernon's Tex. Stat. Ann. § 2007.002(5) (municipal extraterritorial actions and most state actions that diminish property value by 25% or more); La. Stat. §§ 3:3602(11), 3:3610, & 3:3622 (greater than 20% diminution in value of agricultural or forest property).

[25] Palazzolo v. Rhode Island, No. WM 88–0297, 2005 WL 1645974 (R.I. Super., July 5, 2005).

owner did not have reasonable investment-backed expectations to develop the property based on the property's legal and environmental characteristics, the likely impacts of the proposed development on neighbors and the public, and the questionable viability of constructing the proposed project on marshland. The court considered the public trust doctrine and the nuisance doctrine, among other limits on the property owner's expectations. The trial court's decision on remand is reproduced in Assignment 37.

7. *Limitations inherent in title.* The *Lucas* opinion states that the government does not owe compensation if it is merely regulating uses to which the landowner is not entitled under background principles of state property law. The limitations inherent in property rights under state property law principles also preclude the landowner from forming compensable "reasonable" expectations under *Penn Central* to engage in uses exceeding those limits. In *Lucas*, Justice Scalia identifies nuisance law as a limitation inherent in title; one does not have the right to use one's property in a way as to create a nuisance. Justice Kennedy states that background principles should not be limited to nuisance law but instead should be considered in light of the ever-evolving entirety of the law. Michael Blumm and Lucus Ritchie published a helpful study of the types of background principles that might preclude regulatory takings claims.[26] The list includes the following: an evolving nuisance doctrine, the public trust doctrine, the natural use doctrine, the federal navigation servitude, customary rights, limitations inherent in water rights, the wildlife trust, and Native American treaty rights.[27] Many of these doctrines are discussed elsewhere in this casebook.

8. *Judicial takings.* The exception to the regulatory takings doctrine for limitations inherent in property rights under the state's common law property doctrines leads to an interesting question about whether courts can cause a compensable taking of private property when they modify the common law of property. From the landowner's perspective, expectations and investments in private property rights are being altered or eliminated by "judicial fiat." From the perspective of state courts and regulators, the common law of property must change over time as courts overrule precedents and abandon ill-conceived and outmoded rules to satisfy the "felt needs" of contemporary society.[28] Historically, the concept of judicial takings was primarily of academic concern.[29] The Supreme Court, however, confronted the issue in 2010 in a case in which the Florida Supreme Court had adopted an allegedly radical and sudden change in the rights of beachfront property owners to accommodate state efforts to control beach erosion and restore sands to eroded beaches.[30] The U.S. Supreme Court unanimously agreed that

---

[26] Blumm & Ritchie, *Lucas*'s Unlikely Legacy: The Rise of Background Principles as Categorical Takings Defenses, 29 Harv. Envt'l L. Rev. 321 (2005).

[27] Id. See also Brophy, Aloha Jurisprudence: Equity Rules in Property, 85 Ore. L. Rev. 771 (2006) (discussing the contribution of native rights to community and public rights that may justify regulation of private property).

[28] Holmes, The Common Law 1 (1923).

[29] See, e.g., Thompson, Judicial Takings, 76 Va. L. Rev. 1449 (1990).

[30] Walton County v. Stop the Beach Renourishment, Inc., 998 So.2d 1102 (Fla. 2008), aff'd, Stop the Beach Renourishment, Inc. v. Florida Dep't of Envt'l Prot., 130 S. Ct. 2592 (2010).

the Florida Supreme Court's opinion was not a radical change in Florida property law, but was divided on whether the concept of a judicial taking should even be constitutionally recognized. This case and the issue of judicial takings are addressed in Assignment 35–36, because the issue has tended to arise, at least so far, in cases involving water rights or rights to lands at the water's edge.

9. *Temporary regulations vs. "permanent" regulations in effect for a limited time.* In *First English* (discussed in *Tahoe-Sierra*), the Court held that when a permanent regulation was found to be a taking, the government that promulgated the regulation would be liable for damages. This would be so even if the government elected not to enforce the regulation after it was held invalid, because damages would still have to be paid for injury caused while the regulation was in effect. In *Tahoe-Sierra*, the court ruled that a temporary moratorium on all development for a thirty-two month period was not a taking. By contrast, under *First English*, if a permanent moratorium were held to be a taking after it was in effect for thirty-two months, the landowner would be entitled to damages. Can you reconcile these two cases?

10. *TDRs.* In *Penn Central*, the Court observed that the value of the appellants' transferable development rights should be taken into account in evaluating the financial impact of the regulation. Transferable development rights, or TDRs, permit a property owner who is prevented by the government from developing a particular property to develop a different property to a greater degree than would otherwise be permitted by land use regulations. TDRs frequently are sold by the restricted property owner to other landowners. In Suitum v. Tahoe Regional Planning Agency, the owner of an undeveloped lot near Lake Tahoe was precluded from developing according to agency regulations but was nonetheless entitled to receive TDRs that could be sold to other landowners. The property owner, Mrs. Suitum, never sought the TDRs and instead sued on the ground that the agency's regulations amounted to a regulatory taking. The Supreme Court held that Suitum had received a final decision from the agency regarding the applicability of the regulations to her property, and thus her takings claim was ripe for adjudication even though she had not yet attempted to sell the TDRs to which she was entitled.

Note that *Penn Central* skirted the issue of whether TDRs can provide just compensation for a taking. The concurrence in *Suitum* stressed that TDRs are relevant only to the issue of compensation once a taking has been established. In other words, TDRs should not be taken into account in determining whether a taking has occurred. The concurrence distinguished the language in *Penn Central* summarized in the first sentence of this Note on the ground that the appellants in *Penn Central* owned at least eight nearby parcels that could be benefited by the TDRs. Thus, it was logical to evaluate the regulation by looking to its impact on the appellants' land as a whole.

11. *"Inverse" condemnation.* Inverse condemnation is a term often used to describe a property owner's cause of action against the government to recover damages for the value of property that the government has in fact taken, although the government has not brought any action under the power

of eminent domain.[31] In contrast, "ordinary" eminent domain or condemnation actions are instituted by a governmental body wishing to condemn privately owned property for a public use. In "ordinary" condemnation cases, the government does not contest the need to compensate the property owner for the taking. Typically, the only major issue is the amount of compensation. In contrast, a core issue in most inverse condemnation cases is whether the government's activity constitutes a taking.

12. *Section 1983 actions.* 42 U.S.C. § 1983 provides:

> Every person who, under color of any statute, ordinance, regulation, custom, or usage, of any State . . . subjects, or causes to be subjected, any citizen of the United States or other person within the jurisdiction thereof to the deprivation of any rights, privileges, or immunities secured by the Constitution and laws, shall be liable to the party injured in an action at law, suit in equity, or other proper proceeding for redress.

The statute does not confine its scope to violations of "procedural safeguards." It gives a remedy in an action at law for a deprivation of property in violation of the Due Process Clause. Typically, the remedy in an action at law is the award of damages. In Monterey v. Del Monte Dunes, Ltd., 526 U.S. 687 (1999), the Court held that an action for a regulatory taking could be brought under § 1983, at least when the state in which the taking occurred does not provide an adequate state remedy. A successful plaintiff in a § 1983 action is entitled to attorney's fees under 42 U.S.C. § 1988. Moreover, in *Monterey*, the Supreme Court held that the plaintiff's lawsuit seeking damages for an unconstitutional denial of just compensation was an "action at law" within the meaning of the Seventh Amendment and thus triable before a jury.

## d. Development Exactions

### 1. Introduction

The development exaction is the third type of regulation discussed in this Assignment. Dolan v. Tigard, reprinted below, represents a significant Supreme Court pronouncement on development exactions.

### 2. Principal Problem

Dixon, a large city, has recently passed an ordinance prohibiting the building of any new office building in the downtown district that exceeds fifteen stories in height. The average height of existing buildings in this district is now twenty-four stories. The ordinance contains an exception to the fifteen-story limit. The exception provides that a builder may build up to a maximum of twenty stories, provided that for each square foot of floor area for any story exceeding the fifteenth story the builder must

---

[31] See Thornburg v. Port of Portland, 233 Or. 178, 376 P.2d 100, 101 n. 1 (1962).

contribute $5 to Dixon's low-income housing fund. The fund is used to provide housing for low-income people. Such housing is in very short supply in Dixon and the nearby suburbs.

Offdev, Inc. (Offdev), a builder of office buildings, wants to construct a twenty-three story office building, but objects to the $5 per square foot exaction imposed by the ordinance. At present the site on which Offdev wishes to build is occupied by an old but usable five story office building. Offdev wants to bring an action to force Dixon to permit the construction of the twenty-three story building without payment of the exaction. Offdev would also like to recover compensatory damages from Dixon for the damages resulting from the delay in construction caused by Dixon's enforcement of what Offdev claims is an invalid ordinance. It would also like to recover the attorney's fees incurred in bringing such an action.

Under state law, Dixon has no legal right to levy the $5 fee as a "tax". Therefore, if the fee is to be justified, it must be justified on some theory other than Dixon's right to impose taxes.

How would you advise Offdev's general counsel concerning the various legal issues that would be raised in such an action? Evaluate the chances for success on each issue.

## 3. MATERIALS FOR SOLUTION OF PRINCIPAL PROBLEM

### Florence Dolan v. City of Tigard
Supreme Court of the United States, 1994.
512 U.S. 374, 114 S.Ct. 2309.

■ REHNQUIST, C. J., delivered the opinion of the Court.

Petitioner challenges the decision of the Oregon Supreme Court which held that the city of Tigard could condition the approval of her building permit on the dedication of a portion of her property for flood control and traffic improvements. 317 Ore. 110, 854 P. 2d 437 (1993). We granted certiorari to resolve a question left open by our decision in Nollan v. California Coastal Comm'n, 483 U.S. 825 (1987), of what is the required degree of connection between the exactions imposed by the city and the projected impacts of the proposed development.

I

The State of Oregon enacted a comprehensive land use management program in 1973. Ore. Rev. Stat. §§ 197.005–197.860 (1991). The program required all Oregon cities and counties to adopt new comprehensive land use plans that were consistent with the statewide planning goals. §§ 197.175(1), 197.250. The plans are implemented by land use regulations which are part of an integrated hierarchy of legally binding goals, plans, and regulations. §§ 197.175, 197.175(2)(b). Pursuant to the State's requirements, the city of Tigard, a community of some 30,000 residents on the southwest edge of Portland, developed a comprehensive plan and codified it in its Community Development Code (CDC). The CDC requires property owners in the area zoned Central Business District to comply with a 15% open space and landscaping requirement, which limits total site coverage, including all structures and paved parking, to 85% of the parcel. CDC, ch. 18.66. After the completion of a transportation study that identified congestion in the Central Business District as a particular problem, the city adopted a plan for a pedestrian/bicycle pathway intended to encourage alternatives to automobile transportation for short trips. The CDC requires that new development facilitate this plan by dedicating land for pedestrian pathways where provided for in the pedestrian/bicycle pathway plan.

The city also adopted a Master Drainage Plan (Drainage Plan). The Drainage Plan noted that flooding occurred in several areas along Fanno Creek, including areas near petitioner's property. The Drainage Plan also established that the increase in impervious surfaces associated with continued urbanization would exacerbate these flooding problems. To combat these risks, the Drainage Plan suggested a series of improvements to the Fanno Creek Basin, including channel excavation in the area next to petitioner's property. Other recommendations included ensuring that the floodplain remains free of structures and that it be preserved as greenways to minimize flood damage to structures. The Drainage Plan concluded that the cost of these improvements should be shared based on both direct and indirect benefits, with property owners along the waterways paying more due to the direct benefit that they would receive. CDC Chapters 18.84, 18.86 and CDC § 18.164.100 and the Tigard Park Plan carry out these recommendations.

Petitioner Florence Dolan owns a plumbing and electric supply store located on Main Street in the Central Business District of the city. The store covers approximately 9,700 square feet on the eastern side of a 1.67-acre parcel, which includes a gravel parking lot. Fanno Creek flows through the southwestern corner of the lot and along its western boundary. The year-round flow of the creek renders the area within the creek's 100-year floodplain virtually unusable for commercial development. The city's comprehensive plan includes the Fanno Creek floodplain as part of the city's greenway system.

Petitioner applied to the city for a permit to redevelop the site. Her proposed plans called for nearly doubling the size of the store to 17,600 square feet, and paving a 39-space parking lot. The existing store, located on the opposite side of the parcel, would be razed in sections as construction progressed on the new building. In the second phase of the project, petitioner proposed to build an additional structure on the northeast side of the site for complementary businesses, and to provide more parking. The proposed expansion and intensified use are consistent with the city's zoning scheme in the Central Business District.

The City Planning Commission granted petitioner's permit application subject to conditions imposed by the city's CDC. The CDC establishes the following standard for site development review approval:

> Where landfill and/or development is allowed within and adjacent to the 100-year floodplain, the city shall require the dedication of sufficient open land area for greenway adjoining and within the floodplain. This area shall include portions at a suitable elevation for the construction of a pedestrian/bicycle pathway within the floodplain in accordance with the adopted pedestrian/bicycle plan.

Thus, the Commission required that petitioner dedicate the portion of her property lying within the 100-year floodplain for improvement of a storm drainage system along Fanno Creek and that she dedicate an additional 15-foot strip of land adjacent to the floodplain as a pedestrian/bicycle pathway. The dedication required by that condition encompasses approximately 7,000 square feet, or roughly 10% of the property. In accordance with city practice, petitioner could rely on the dedicated property to meet the 15% open space and landscaping requirement mandated by the city's zoning scheme. The city would bear the cost of maintaining a landscaped buffer between the dedicated area and the new store.

Petitioner requested variances from the CDC standards. Variances are granted only where it can be shown that, owing to special circumstances related to a specific piece of the land, the literal interpretation of the applicable zoning provisions would cause "an undue or unnecessary hardship" unless the variance is granted. CDC § 18.134.010. Rather than posing alternative mitigating measures to offset the expected impacts of her proposed development, as allowed under the CDC, petitioner simply argued that her proposed development would not conflict with the policies of the comprehensive plan. The Commission denied the request.

The Commission made a series of findings concerning the relationship between the dedicated conditions and the projected impacts of petitioner's project. First, the Commission noted that "it is reasonable to assume that customers and employees of the future uses of this site could utilize a pedestrian/bicycle pathway adjacent to this development for their transportation and recreational needs." City of Tigard Planning Commission Final Order No. 91–09 PC, App. to Pet. for Cert. G24. The Commission noted that the site plan has provided for bicycle parking in a rack in front of the proposed building and "it is reasonable to expect that some of the users of the bicycle parking provided for by the site plan will use the pathway adjacent to Fanno Creek if it is constructed." Ibid. In addition, the Commission found that creation of a convenient, safe pedestrian/bicycle pathway system as an alternative means of transportation "could offset some of the traffic demand on [nearby] streets and lessen the increase in traffic congestion."

The Commission went on to note that the required floodplain dedication would be reasonably related to petitioner's request to intensify the use of the site given the increase in the impervious surface. The Commission stated that the "anticipated increased storm water flow from the subject property to an already strained creek and drainage basin can only add to the public need to manage the stream channel and floodplain for drainage purposes." Id., at G37. Based on this anticipated increased storm water flow, the Commission concluded that "the requirement of dedication of the floodplain area on the site is related to the applicant's plan to intensify development on the site." Ibid. The Tigard City Council approved the Commission's final order, subject to one minor modification; the City Council reassigned the responsibility for surveying and marking the floodplain area from petitioner to the city's engineering department.

Petitioner appealed to the Land Use Board of Appeals (LUBA) on the ground that the city's dedication requirements were not related to the proposed development, and, therefore, those requirements constituted an uncompensated taking of their property under the Fifth Amendment. In evaluating the federal taking claim, LUBA assumed that the city's findings about the impacts of the proposed development were supported by substantial evidence. App. to Pet. for Cert. D-15, n.9. Given the undisputed fact that the proposed larger building and paved parking area would increase the amount of impervious surfaces and the runoff into Fanno Creek, LUBA concluded that "there is a 'reasonable relationship' between the proposed development and the requirement to dedicate land along Fanno Creek for a greenway." Id., at D-16. With respect to the pedestrian/bicycle pathway, LUBA noted the Commission's finding that a significantly larger retail sales building and parking lot would attract larger numbers of customers and employees and their vehicles. It again found a "reasonable relationship" between alleviating the impacts of increased traffic from the development and facilitating the provision of a pedestrian/bicycle pathway as an alternative means of transportation.

The Oregon Court of Appeals affirmed, rejecting petitioner's contention that in Nollan v. California Coastal Comm'n, 483 U.S. 825 (1987), we had abandoned the "reasonable relationship" test in favor of a stricter "essential nexus" test. 113 Ore. App. 162, 832 P. 2d 853 (1992). The Oregon Supreme Court affirmed. 317 Ore. 110, 854 P. 2d 437 (1993). The court also disagreed with petitioner's contention that the Nollan Court abandoned the "reasonably related" test. Id., at 118, 854 P. 2d, at 442. Instead, the court read Nollan to mean that an "exaction is reasonably related to an impact if the exaction serves the same purpose that a denial of the permit would serve." Id., at 120, 854 P. 2d, at 443. The court decided that both the pedestrian/bicycle pathway condition and the storm drainage dedication had an essential nexus to the development of the proposed site. Id., at 121, 854 P. 2d, at 443. Therefore, the court found the conditions to be reasonably related to the impact of the expansion of petitioner's business. Ibid. We granted certiorari, 114 S.Ct. 544 (1993), because of an alleged conflict between the Oregon Supreme Court's decision and our decision in Nollan.

## II

One of the principal purposes of the Takings Clause is "to bar Government from forcing some people alone to bear public burdens which, in all fairness and justice, should be borne by the public as a whole." Armstrong v. United States, 364 U.S. 40, 49 (1960). Without question, had the city simply required petitioner to dedicate a strip of land along Fanno Creek for public use, rather than conditioning the grant of her permit to redevelop her property on such a dedication, a taking would have occurred. Nollan, supra, at 831. Such public access would deprive petitioner of the right to exclude others, "one of the most essential sticks in the bundle of rights that are commonly characterized as property." Kaiser Aetna v. United States, 444 U.S. 164 (1979).

On the other side of the ledger, the authority of state and local governments to engage in land use planning has been sustained against constitutional challenge as long ago as our decision in Euclid v. Ambler Realty Co., 272 U.S. 365, 71 L. Ed. 303, 47 S. Ct. 114 (1926). A land use regulation does not effect a taking if it "substantially advances legitimate state interests" and does not "deny an owner economically viable use of his land." Agins v. Tiburon, 447 U.S. 255 (1980).

The sort of land use regulations discussed in the cases just cited, however, differ in two relevant particulars from the present case. First, they involved essentially legislative determinations classifying entire areas of the city, whereas here the city made an adjudicative decision to condition petitioner's application for a building permit on an individual parcel. Second, the conditions imposed were not simply a limitation on the use petitioner might make of her own parcel, but a requirement that she deed portions of the property to the city. In Nollan, supra, we held that governmental authority to exact such a condition was circumscribed by the Fifth and Fourteenth Amendments.

Petitioner contends that the city has forced her to choose between the building permit and her right under the Fifth Amendment to just compensation for the public easements. Petitioner does not quarrel with the city's authority to exact some forms of dedication as a condition for the grant of a building permit, but challenges the showing made by the city to justify these exactions. She argues that the city has identified "no special benefits" conferred on her, and has not identified any "special quantifiable burdens" created by her new store that would justify the particular dedications required from her which are not required from the public at large.

## III

In evaluating petitioner's claim, we must first determine whether the "essential nexus" exists between the "legitimate state interest" and the permit condition exacted by the city. Nollan, 483 U.S., at 837. If we find that a nexus exists, we must then decide the required degree of connection between the exactions and the projected impact of the proposed development. We were not required to reach this question in Nollan, because we concluded that the connection did not meet even the loosest standard. 483 U.S., at 838. Here, however, we must decide this question.

We addressed the essential nexus question in Nollan. The California Coastal Commission demanded a lateral public easement across the Nollan's beachfront lot in exchange for a permit to demolish an existing bungalow and replace it with a three-bedroom house. The public easement was designed to connect two public beaches that were separated by the Nollan's property. The Coastal Commission had asserted that the public easement condition was imposed to promote the legitimate state interest of diminishing the "blockage of the view of the ocean" caused by construction of the larger house.

We agreed that the Coastal Commission's concern with protecting visual access to the ocean constituted a legitimate public interest. We also agreed that the permit condition would have been constitutional "even if it consisted of the requirement that the Nollans provide a viewing spot on their property for passersby with whose sighting of the ocean their new house would interfere." Id., at 836. We resolved, however, that the Coastal Commission's regulatory authority was set completely adrift from its constitutional moorings when it claimed that a nexus existed between visual access to the ocean and a permit condition requiring lateral public access along the Nollan's beachfront lot. Id., at 837. How enhancing the public's ability to "traverse to and along the shorefront" served the same governmental purpose of "visual access to the ocean" from the roadway was beyond our ability to countenance. The absence of a nexus left the Coastal Commission in the position of simply trying to obtain an easement through gimmickry, which converted a valid regulation of land use into "an out-and-out plan of extortion." Ibid., quoting J. E. D. Associates, Inc. v. Atkinson, 121 N. H. 581, 584 (1981). No such gimmicks are associated with the permit conditions imposed by the city in this case. Undoubtedly, the prevention of flooding along Fanno Creek and the reduction of traffic congestion in the Central Business District qualify as the type of legitimate public purposes we have upheld. Agins, supra, at 260–262. It seems equally obvious that a nexus exists between preventing flooding along Fanno Creek and limiting development within the creek's 100-year floodplain. Petitioner proposes to double the size of her retail store and to pave her now-gravel parking lot, thereby expanding the impervious surface on the property and increasing the amount of storm-water run-off into Fanno Creek. The same may be said for the city's attempt to reduce traffic congestion by providing for alternative means of transportation.

In theory, a pedestrian/bicycle pathway provides a useful alternative means of transportation for workers and shoppers.

The second part of our analysis requires us to determine whether the degree of the exactions demanded by the city's permit conditions bear the required relationship to the projected impact of petitioner's proposed development. Nollan, supra, at 834. Here the Oregon Supreme Court deferred to what it termed the "city's unchallenged factual findings" supporting the dedication conditions and found them to be reasonably related to the impact of the expansion of petitioner's business. 317 Ore., at 120–121, 854 P. 2d, at 443.

The city required that petitioner dedicate "to the city as Greenway all portions of the site that fall within the existing 100-year floodplain [of Fanno Creek] . . . and all property 15 feet above [the floodplain] boundary." In addition, the city demanded that the retail store be designed so as not to intrude into the greenway area. The city relies on the Commission's rather tentative findings that increased storm-water flow from petitioner's property "can only add to the public need to manage the [floodplain] for drainage purposes" to support its conclusion that the "requirement of dedication of the floodplain area on the site is related to the applicant's plan to intensify development on the site." City of Tigard Planning Commission Final Order No. 91–09 PC, App. to Pet. for Cert. G37.

The city made the following specific findings relevant to the pedestrian/bicycle pathway:

> In addition, the proposed expanded use of this site is anticipated to generate additional vehicular traffic thereby increasing congestion on nearby collector and arterial streets. Creation of a convenient, safe pedestrian/bicycle pathway system as an alternative means of transportation could offset some of the traffic demand on these nearby streets and lessen the increase in traffic congestion.

Id., at 24.

The question for us is whether these findings are constitutionally sufficient to justify the conditions imposed by the city on petitioner's building permit. Since state courts have been dealing with this question a good deal longer than we have, we turn to representative decisions made by them.

In some States, very generalized statements as to the necessary connection between the required dedication and the proposed development seem to suffice. We think this standard is too lax to adequately protect petitioner's right to just compensation if her property is taken for a public purpose.

Other state courts require a very exacting correspondence, described as the "specific and uniquely attributable" test. The Supreme Court of Illinois first developed this test in Pioneer Trust & Savings Bank v.

Mount Prospect, 22 Ill. 2d 375, 380, 176 N.E. 2d 799, 802 (1961). Under this standard, if the local government cannot demonstrate that its exaction is directly proportional to the specifically created need, the exaction becomes "a veiled exercise of the power of eminent domain and a confiscation of private property behind the defense of police regulations." Id., at 381, 176 N.E. 2d, at 802. We do not think the Federal Constitution requires such exacting scrutiny, given the nature of the interests involved.

A number of state courts have taken an intermediate position, requiring the municipality to show a "reasonable relationship" between the required dedication and the impact of the proposed development. Some form of the reasonable relationship test has been adopted in many jurisdictions. [Case citations omitted.]

We think the "reasonable relationship" test adopted by a majority of the state courts is closer to the federal constitutional norm than either of those previously discussed. But we do not adopt it as such, partly because the term "reasonable relationship" seems confusingly similar to the term "rational basis" which describes the minimal level of scrutiny under the Equal Protection Clause of the Fourteenth Amendment. We think a term such as "rough proportionality" best encapsulates what we hold to be the requirement of the Fifth Amendment. No precise mathematical calculation is required, but the city must make some sort of individualized determination that the required dedication is related both in nature and extent to the impact of the proposed development.[32] We turn now to analysis of whether the findings relied upon by the city here, first with respect to the floodplain easement, and second with respect to the pedestrian/bicycle path, satisfied these requirements.

It is axiomatic that increasing the amount of impervious surface will increase the quantity and rate of storm-water flow from petitioner's property. Therefore, keeping the floodplain open and free from development would likely confine the pressures on Fanno Creek created by petitioner's development. In fact, because petitioner's property lies within the Central Business District, the Community Development Code already required that petitioner leave 15% of it as open space and the undeveloped floodplain would have nearly satisfied that requirement. But the city demanded more—it not only wanted petitioner not to build in the floodplain, but it also wanted petitioner's property along Fanno Creek for its Greenway system. The city has never said why a public greenway, as opposed to a private one, was required in the interest of flood control.

---

[32] Justice Stevens' dissent takes us to task for placing the burden on the city to justify the required dedication. He is correct in arguing that in evaluating most generally applicable zoning regulations, the burden properly rests on the party challenging the regulation to prove that it constitutes an arbitrary regulation of property rights. See, e.g., Euclid v. Ambler Realty Co., 272 U.S. 365 (1926). Here, by contrast, the city made an adjudicative decision to condition petitioner's application for a building permit on an individual parcel. In this situation, the burden properly rests on the city. See Nollan, 483 U.S., at 836.

The difference to petitioner, of course, is the loss of her ability to exclude others. As we have noted, this right to exclude others is "one of the most essential sticks in the bundle of rights that are commonly characterized as property." Kaiser Aetna, 444 U.S., at 176. It is difficult to see why recreational visitors trampling along petitioner's floodplain easement are sufficiently related to the city's legitimate interest in reducing flooding problems along Fanno Creek, and the city has not attempted to make any individualized determination to support this part of its request.

The city contends that recreational easement along the Greenway is only ancillary to the city's chief purpose in controlling flood hazards. It further asserts that unlike the residential property at issue in Nollan, petitioner's property is commercial in character and therefore, her right to exclude others is compromised. The city maintains that "there is nothing to suggest that preventing [petitioner] from prohibiting [the easements] will unreasonably impair the value of [her] property as a [retail store]." Pruneyard Shopping Center v. Robins, 447 U.S. 74, 83 (1980).

Admittedly, petitioner wants to build a bigger store to attract members of the public to her property. She also wants, however, to be able to control the time and manner in which they enter. The recreational easement on the Greenway is different in character from the exercise of state-protected rights of free expression and petition that we permitted in Pruneyard. In Pruneyard, we held that a major private shopping center that attracted more than 25,000 daily patrons had to provide access to persons exercising their state constitutional rights to distribute pamphlets and ask passersby to sign their petitions. We based our decision, in part, on the fact that the shopping center "may restrict expressive activity by adopting time, place, and manner regulations that will minimize any interference with its commercial functions." By contrast, the city wants to impose a permanent recreational easement upon petitioner's property that borders Fanno Creek. Petitioner would lose all rights to regulate the time in which the public entered onto the Greenway, regardless of any interference it might pose with her retail store. Her right to exclude would not be regulated, it would be eviscerated.

If petitioner's proposed development had somehow encroached on existing greenway space in the city, it would have been reasonable to require petitioner to provide some alternative greenway space for the public either on her property or elsewhere. See Nollan, 483 U.S., at 836 ("Although such a requirement, constituting a permanent grant of continuous access to the property, would have to be considered a taking if it were not attached to a development permit, the Commission's assumed power to forbid construction of the house in order to protect the public's view of the beach must surely include the power to condition construction upon some concession by the owner, even a concession of property rights, that serves the same end"). But that is not the case here. We conclude that the findings upon which the city relies do not show the required reasonable relationship between the floodplain easement and the petitioner's proposed new building.

With respect to the pedestrian/bicycle pathway, we have no doubt that the city was correct in finding that the larger retail sales facility proposed by petitioner will increase traffic on the streets of the Central Business District. The city estimates that the proposed development would generate roughly 435 additional trips per day. Dedications for streets, sidewalks, and other public ways are generally reasonable exactions to avoid excessive congestion from a proposed property use. But on the record before us, the city has not met its burden of demonstrating that the additional number of vehicle and bicycle trips generated by the petitioner's development reasonably relate to the city's requirement for a dedication of the pedestrian/bicycle pathway easement. The city simply found that the creation of the pathway "could offset some of the traffic demand . . . and lessen the increase in traffic congestion."

As Justice Peterson of the Supreme Court of Oregon explained in his dissenting opinion, however, "[t]he findings of fact that the bicycle pathway system could offset some of the traffic demand is a far cry from a finding that the bicycle pathway system will, or is likely to, offset some of the traffic demand." 317 Ore., at 127, 854 P. 2d, at 447. No precise mathematical calculation is required, but the city must make some effort to quantify its findings in support of the dedication for the pedestrian/bicycle pathway beyond the conclusionary statement that it could offset some of the traffic demand generated.

### IV

Cities have long engaged in the commendable task of land use planning, made necessary by increasing urbanization particularly in metropolitan areas such as Portland. The city's goals of reducing flooding hazards and traffic congestion, and providing for public greenways, are laudable, but there are outer limits to how this may be done. "A strong public desire to improve the public condition [will not] warrant achieving the desire by a shorter cut than the constitutional way of paying for the change." Pennsylvania Coal, 260 U.S., at 416.

The judgment of the Supreme Court of Oregon is reversed, and the case is remanded for further proceedings consistent with this opinion.

■ JUSTICE STEVENS, with whom JUSTICE BLACKMUN and JUSTICE GINSBURG join, dissenting.

The Court is correct in concluding that the city may not attach arbitrary conditions to a building permit or to a variance even when it can rightfully deny the application outright. Yet the Court's description of the doctrinal underpinnings of its decision, the phrasing of its fledgling test of "rough proportionality," and the application of that test to this case break considerable and unpropitious new ground.

Although limitation of the right to exclude others undoubtedly constitutes a significant infringement upon property ownership, Kaiser Aetna v. United States, 444 U.S. 164 (1979), restrictions on that right do not alone constitute a taking, and do not do so in any event unless they "unreasonably impair the value or use" of the property. Pruneyard Shopping Center v. Robins, 447 U.S. 74 (1980).

The Court's narrow focus on one strand in the property owner's bundle of rights is particularly misguided in a case involving the development of commercial property. The city of Tigard has demonstrated that its plan is rational and impartial and that the conditions at issue are "conducive to fulfillment of authorized planning objectives." Dolan, on the other hand, has offered no evidence that her burden of compliance has any impact at all on the value or profitability of her planned development. [T]he Court should not isolate the burden associated with the loss of the power to exclude from an evaluation of the benefit to be derived from the permit to enlarge the store and the parking lot.

The Court's assurances that its "rough proportionality" test leaves ample room for cities to pursue the "commendable task of land use planning," ante,—even twice avowing that "no precise mathematical calculation is required," ante,—are wanting given the result that test compels here. Under the Court's approach, a city must not only "quantify its findings," ante, and make "individualized determination[s]" with respect to the nature and the extent of the relationship between the conditions and the impact, ante, but also demonstrate "proportionality." The correct inquiry should instead concentrate on whether the required nexus is present and venture beyond considerations of a condition's nature or germaneness only if the developer establishes that a concededly germane condition is so grossly disproportionate to the proposed development's adverse effects that it manifests motives other than land use regulation on the part of the city.

In our changing world one thing is certain: uncertainty will characterize predictions about the impact of new urban developments on the risks of floods, earthquakes, traffic congestion, or environmental harms. When there is doubt concerning the magnitude of those impacts, the public interest in averting them must outweigh the private interest of the commercial entrepreneur. If the government can demonstrate that the conditions it has imposed in a land-use permit are rational, impartial and conducive to fulfilling the aims of a valid land-use plan, a strong presumption of validity should attach to those conditions. The burden of demonstrating that those conditions have unreasonably impaired the economic value of the proposed improvement belongs squarely on the shoulders of the party challenging the state action's constitutionality. That allocation of burdens has served us well in the past. The Court has stumbled badly today by reversing it.

I respectfully dissent.

## NOTES

1. *Litigation expenses.* According to the Washington Post, Dolan's litigation expenses were paid by the 3,400 supporters of the Oregonians in Action Legal Center. Dolan's expenses amounted to $250,000, more than eight times the value of the property in question.[33]

2. *Nollan essential nexus test.* The first step of a takings analysis of an exaction is whether it meets the *Nollan* essential nexus test, as discussed in the *Dolan* case. This is not normally a difficult test to satisfy. A government agency and its attorneys should be able to craft an exaction that matches the agency's legitimate government interest in demanding the exaction as a permit condition. Alternatively, the agency should be able to assert a legitimate government interest that matches the exaction that the government agency wants to obtain.

The *Dolan* court's description of the *Nollan* facts gives some indication that the *Nollan* essential nexus test is not particularly demanding. The exaction was a lateral beach-access easement across the Nollans' property. This means that a person on a public beach on one side of the Nollans' property could bypass rocks and a seawall to reach a public beach on the other side of the Nollans' property by walking up some steps to the Nollans' private property, walking alongside the beachfront edge of the Nollans's property, and crossing back down to the public beach on the other side. The California Coastal Commission claimed that it was seeking to compensate the public's loss of visual access to the beach from Pacific Coast Highway (on the inland side of the Nollans' property) when the Nollans replaced a small beach bungalow with a larger house. While a lateral beach-access easement might be a legitimate exaction under certain circumstances and while the California Coastal Commission might have a legitimate interest in protecting public visual access to the beach from an inland highway as beachfront lands are developed, the *Nollan* majority could not understand how the two were related. With government regulators being more careful to show a nexus between the exaction demanded and the legitimate government interests involved, subsequent cases turned to the degree of exaction demanded, which is what *Dolan* addressed. The *Dolan* rough proportionality test, the second step of a takings analysis of an exaction, is a more difficult test for government regulators to satisfy.

3. *Monetary exactions.* *Nollan* and *Dolan* involved exactions of property interests in land and thus fell within a gap between physical takings and regulatory takings. The government was not mandating physical occupation of the property. If the landowner wanted to exclude the government and public, he or she could continue to use the land as-is and forego the intended development on which the exaction was conditioned. If the landowner were to claim that the property had been taken by regulation thereby preventing economic use of the land, the government would be willing to grant a permit for the development—and therefore allow the

---

[33] Washington Post, March 20, 1994, Editorial Section, p. c07.

intended use—but conditioned on the landowner granting the exaction. *Nollan* and *Dolan* fill the gap with a new category of takings law.

Many government regulators, however, will either ask for monetary exactions as a condition for a permit or give the landowner or developer the option to pay money instead of providing property or facilities. For example, the developer of a large residential subdivision that will house many families could legitimately be expected to provide school facilities proportionate to the likely demand for schools created by the new development. However, the government or the developer or both might prefer for the developer to contribute an equivalent amount of money to a school building fund where the money could be pooled with amounts coming from other nearby developments, instead of having each developer commit the land, resources, and time to build a separate small school in each subdivision.

In 2013, the U.S. Supreme Court answered the question of whether *Nollan* and *Dolan* apply to monetary exactions in the affirmative. In *Koontz v. St. Johns Water Management District*, a 5–4 majority held that land-use regulatory agencies imposing monetary exactions on development permits have to satisfy both the Nollan essential nexus test and the Dolan rough proportionality test for the purposes and amounts that were being demanded, even if the regulators denied the permit because the developer refused to provide the exacted funds.[34] The *Koontz* case has generated considerable attention by property and land-use experts, who disagree whether the case represents a radical change in takings doctrine that will squelch government use of exactions and voluntary land-development negotiations between regulators and developers or is a natural, modest extension of Nollan and Dolan that will not be difficult for regulators to satisfy.[35]

4. *The impacts of* Nollan *and* Dolan *on exactions practices.* Scholars have expressed concerns that *Nollan* and *Dolan* might have the effect of impeding efficient problem-solving negotiations between regulators and developers over development permits and infrastructure needs.[36] According to an empirical study, however, land-use regulators learned from the *Dolan* test that many local governments had been under-exacting (demanding exactions well below the amount roughly proportional to development projects' impacts), not over-exacting, and thus *Dolan* improved their

---

[34] Koontz. St. Johns Water Management District, 568 U.S. ___, 133 S.Ct. 2586 (2013).

[35] Compare, e.g., Echeverria, Koontz: The Very Worst Takings Decision Ever?, 22 N.Y.U. Envtl. L.J. 1 (2014) with Jazil, Koontz: An Evolution—Not Revolution—in Takings Law, 28-SPG Nat. Resources & Env't 36 (2014). See generally Cohen & May, Revolutionary or Routine? Koontz v. St. Johns River Water Management District, 38 Harv. Envtl. L. Rev. 245 (2014).

[36] Fenster, Takings Formalism and Regulatory Formulas: Exactions and the Consequences of Clarity, 92 Cal. L. Rev. 609 (2004); Fennell, Hard Bargains and Real Steals: Land Use Exactions Revisited, 86 Iowa L. Rev. 1 (2000).

bargaining position with developers.[37] Is it possible that *Koontz* will also be a minimal barrier at best to regulators' use of monetary exactions?[38]

5. *Principal Problem.* Arguably the building of a new large office building creates a need for additional housing, including housing for low-income people. Would this connection between office buildings and the need for low-income housing satisfy the standards set forth in *Dolan*? What if the exaction in the problem were imposed on all new office buildings, regardless of the number of floors? If the ordinance in the Principal Problem is invalid, it would seem that Offdev might be entitled to damages from the City of Dixon. How would they be measured?

---

[37] Carlson & Pollack, Takings on the Ground: How the Supreme Court's Takings Jurisprudence Affects Local Land Use Decisions, 35 U.C. Davis L. Rev. 103 (2001).

[38] Saxer, To Bargain or Not to Bargain? A Response to Bargaining for Development Post-Koontz, 68 Fla. L. Rev. Forum 5 (2015) (calling for empirical evidence before reaching conclusions about the impact of *Koontz*).

# ASSIGNMENT 33

# EXCLUSION, DISCRIMINATION, EQUAL PROTECTION AND DUE PROCESS

## 1. INTRODUCTION

At its core, traditional Euclidean zoning has been about segregation: segregating incompatible land uses from one another in the interests of public health, safety, welfare, and property values. As discussed in Assignment 30, the Supreme Court, in Village of Euclid v. Ambler Realty Co.,[1] upheld the constitutionality of zoning and approved of the separation of uses to prevent location-specific nuisances and harms to public health and safety. The Court reaffirmed this perspective nearly five decades later by upholding single-family residential zoning restrictions to promote residential enclaves "where family values, youth values, and the blessings of quiet seclusion and clean air make the area a sanctuary for people."[2]

Zoning has also been used to segregate groups of people from one another and for placing certain groups of people in close proximity to land uses that are harmful to human health and safety or community vitality. Indeed, in the *Euclid* case, the U.S. Supreme Court went out of its way to vilify apartment building as "parasites" that could undermine single-family residential neighborhoods.[3] Consider the following summary of exclusionary and discriminatory practices in zoning:

> The racial, ethnic, and class injustices of land-use planning and regulation have had many manifestations. In the early twentieth century, cities—mostly in the South but as far north as Indiana and Maryland and as far west as Texas and Oklahoma—adopted ordinances segregating African Americans and whites by geographic areas of the city. Although the Supreme Court struck down the Louisville, Kentucky, residential segregation ordinance in 1917, explicitly racial zoning ordinances persisted into the late 1940s. Race-specific zoning was combined in some cases with industrial zoning policies that directly placed industries and minority residences in the same areas. For example, Austin, Texas, planned the area of East Austin in 1928 as a "negro district" that would host most of Austin's industrial uses next to housing for African

---

[1] Village of Euclid v. Ambler Realty Co., 272 U.S. 365 (1926).
[2] Village of Belle Terre v. Boraas, 416 U.S. 1, 9 (1974).
[3] Village of Euclid v. Ambler Realty Co., 272 U.S. 365, 394–95 (1926).

Americans, and the city's first zoning map in 1931 reflected this plan.

A more widespread and persistent zoning practice than race-specific districting has been the use of exclusionary zoning techniques. These techniques indirectly exclude certain groups from particular communities or areas by controlling the type of housing development that occurs in those areas. These techniques include large-lot zoning, low-density zoning, growth moratoria or tempo controls that limit the supply of new housing, costly exactions and development conditions, and lack of lots zoned for multifamily housing. Exclusionary zoning has the effect of limiting or precluding affordable housing in a community. Thus, it keeps out those who cannot afford higher-cost housing, including low-and moderate-income people, racial and ethnic minorities, young and elderly couples, single persons, and large families.

Land-use policies encouraging or facilitating suburban sprawl have contributed to racial and income disparities in U.S. society. Sprawl allows for "white flight" from urban areas and demands significant investment of a region's public resources in suburban areas. Many suburban communities have their own separately incorporated municipalities with independent political, land-use, tax, and fiscal powers. The result can be municipal financial stress in central cities and underinvestment in inner-city facilities and services.

Even aside from interjurisdictional competition for resources, many cities have not provided municipal services and facilities to low-income and minority areas at the same level or to the same degree as they have to other parts of their cities. In addition, public investments in inner-city areas may harm low-income and minority communities when they take the form of redevelopment projects that displace community residents or even destroy entire communities. Revitalization of inner-city areas, in some cases, has amounted to gentrification, raising housing and other costs of living in the area, reducing the supply of affordable housing, and forcing out low-income and minority people.

In addition to the segregating effects of zoning and land-use practices, these practices have also had the effect of burdening low-income and minority communities with unwanted land uses and environmental harms. Yale Rabin has documented the rezoning of low-income and minority areas to accommodate industrial and similarly intensive land uses. He calls this practice "expulsive zoning" because of its effect of driving out residents and land uses that can afford to move elsewhere. The result is that poor people and minorities who lack housing opportunities elsewhere are located near health-harming, community-degrading land uses. The zoning or rezoning of low-income and minority communities to allow industrial land uses has contributed to decisions to locate waste facilities and other locally unwanted land uses (LULUs) in these communities.

[D]isparities in participation by the poor and minorities in land-use planning and regulatory processes are common. Studies reflect that land-use decision makers tend to be white males, middle-aged or older, at least in higher proportion than their share of the local population, and many of them tend to be real estate professionals with a vested interest in land-use decisions. Low-income people of color not only have not held positions on planning and zoning commissions, city councils, and similar boards in any significant numbers, but they also have participated in public hearings and planning forums in relatively low numbers. The timing and location of meetings, limited access to information, language and education barriers, and perceptions of powerlessness contribute to these low levels of participation. * * * *

A 1998 study of zoning patterns in 31 census tracts in seven cities [examined] the percentage of low-income, high-minority census tracts zoned for industrial and other intensive land uses compared with that percentage in high-income, low-minority census tracts. The results showed a great disparity. The data * * * show that low-income, high-minority neighborhoods in the cities studied are subject to more intensive zoning, on the whole, than high-income, low-minority neighborhoods. This conclusion is supported by data from across the various types of cities studied, regardless of the cities' geographic features, spatial development, population, political characteristics, and the like.[4]

Grassroots groups in low-income and minority communities have responded to these disparities and environmental injustices by seeking to prevent harmful land uses, such as toxic waste sites, from their communities and also by seeking the adoption of land use policies and regulations that promote the health and vitality of their communities. A common and important theme of this "environmental justice" movement is empowerment for low-income and minority communities.[5]

There are several complicating factors, though. First, structural disparities in power and resources in society create obstacles for some groups to participate "on a level playing field" in land use decision

---

[4] Arnold, Fair and Healthy Land Use: Environmental Justice and Planning 13–17 (2007) (citations omitted).

[5] Cole & Foster, From the Ground Up: Environmental Racism and the Rise of the Environmental Justice Movement (2001).

making.[6] These obstacles may exist not only for racial and ethnic minority groups or low-income classes but also for groups like the homeless, people with mental or physical disabilities, children who are abused, neglected, or abandoned, and the mentally ill.

Second, inequities may result from market dynamics, as well as from government policies. In some circumstances, decisions about the location of specific land uses may create disparities, but in other circumstances, vulnerable groups may move to areas with industrial land uses or environmentally harmful facilities due to the cheaper cost of land and housing in those areas.[7]

Third, it is more difficult for those seeking to move to a community or area to have an effective voice in local decision making than for existing residents to prevent unwanted land uses or seek to shape their community's land use plans and decisions.[8] For example, the future residents of proposed affordable housing projects may have very little effective voice in local regulators' decisions, and therefore may rely on affordable housing advocates to represent their interests. The problem can be magnified regionally by the cumulative effects of many neighborhoods and local governments using land use regulation to keep out affordable housing or other undesired housing projects.

Finally, the housing needs and preferences of the least advantaged or powerful in society defy simplistic assumptions. On one hand, housing for low- and moderate-income people is needed in many areas that have typically excluded or limited such housing development, primarily suburbs. Many commercial ventures have moved to suburban areas, taking with them jobs in retail, service, office, and light-industry sectors. The proximity of housing to jobs is often an important factor, particularly to low- and moderate-income people and particularly in light of limited public transit to commute from central cities to suburbs and back again. In addition, current affordable housing policies and models in the U.S. favor the dispersion of affordable housing across many mixed-income communities throughout a region, to prevent high concentrations of poverty in any area and to facilitate upward social mobility by intermixing socio-economic classes of people by residential geography. However, many low- and moderate-income people have deep roots, cultural and community identities, and social support structures in their existing neighborhoods, which may be in the central urban core. A significant number of jobs may be much more proximate to the central city than to the suburbs. In addition, living in mixed- or higher-income

---

[6] Massey & Denton, American Apartheid: Segregation and the Making of the Underclass (1993); Logan and Molotch, Urban Fortunes: The Political Economy of Place (1987).

[7] Been, Locally Undesirable Land Use in Minority Neighborhoods: Disproportionate Siting or Market Dynamics?, 103 Yale L.J. 1383 (1994); Been & Gupta, Coming to the Nuisance or Going to the Barrios? A Longitudinal Analysis of Environmental Justice Claims, 24 Ecology L. Q. 1 (1997).

[8] Iglesias, Managing Local Opposition to Affordable Housing: A New Approach to NIMBY, 12 J. Affordable Housing & Community Dev. 78 (2002).

communities can be quite costly (beyond housing costs) and offer few services that may be needed by low-income people, such as low-cost medical care, public transit, or affordable retail stores. Small towns and rural areas also need affordable housing, even though existing housing policies tend to have a bias towards urban housing needs.[9]

Advocates for housing for low-income people, racial and ethnic minorities, persons with physical or mental disabilities, and other excluded groups often turn to a variety of legal claims to challenge exclusionary zoning practices. These may be based on federal and/or state constitutional guarantees of equal protection or due process. They may be based on federal and/or state statutes that constrain discrimination against certain groups or types of housing. For example, the 14th Amendment to the U.S. Constitution provides:

> No State shall make or enforce any law which shall abridge the privileges or immunities of citizens of the United States; nor shall any State deprive any person of life, liberty, or property, without due process of law; nor deny to any person within its jurisdiction the equal protection of the laws.[10]

The Principal Problem and materials that follow explore some of the more commonly used legal arguments against exclusionary land-use regulations.

## 2. Principal Problem

The town of Oak Valley is a fast growing suburban town located on the urban fringe of Big City. Although most of Oak Valley is zoned for single family residences, there are numerous vacant sites suitable for apartment houses and so zoned. No apartment houses, however, actually exist in Oak Valley. Mutual Housing Corp. (MHC), a developer of non-profit housing, has acquired an option to purchase one of these parcels as a site for low income housing. MHC also plans to set aside a number of these units as residences for low-income people with schizophrenia and other mental disorders who are capable of living independently as long as they take their medication. MHC hopes to eliminate some of the growing numbers of street people in Oak Valley by setting aside these units. Many townspeople are disturbed at the prospect of a low income housing project. By means of an initiative, the townspeople manage to have the zoning changed from multiple dwelling zoning to single family zoning, thus thwarting the plans of MHC.

You have been retained by MHC. Assume that there is no controlling precedent in your state. In addition, assume that some of the townspeople leading the opposition to the project have publicly articulated disparaging remarks about homeless people, low-income people, and

---

[9] See generally Arnold, Fair and Healthy Land Use: Environmental Justice and Planning 116–20 (2007).

[10] U.S. Const. amend. xiv.

people with mental illness. What legal options are available to MHC? How strong is MHC's position under the law? What additional facts would you want to explore, and why?

## 3. MATERIALS FOR SOLUTION OF PRINCIPAL PROBLEM

### Village of Arlington Heights v. Metropolitan Housing Development Corp.

United States Supreme Court, 1977.
429 U.S. 252, 97 S.Ct. 555.

■ MR. JUSTICE POWELL delivered the opinion of the Court.

In 1971 respondent Metropolitan Housing Development Corporation (MHDC) applied to petitioner, the Village of Arlington Heights, Ill., for the rezoning of a 15-acre parcel from single-family to multiple-family classification. Using federal financial assistance, MHDC planned to build 190 clustered townhouse units for low and moderate income tenants. The Village denied the rezoning request. MHDC, joined by other plaintiffs who are also respondents here, brought suit in the United States District Court for the Northern District of Illinois. They alleged that the denial was racially discriminatory and that it violated, inter alia, the Fourteenth Amendment and the Fair Housing Act of 1968, 42 U.S.C. § 3601 et seq. Following a bench trial, the District Court entered judgment for the Village, 373 F.Supp. 208 (1974), and respondents appealed. The Court of Appeals for the Seventh Circuit reversed, finding that the "ultimate effect" of the denial was racially discriminatory, and that the refusal to rezone therefore violated the Fourteenth Amendment. 517 F.2d 409 (1975). We granted the Village's petition for certiorari, 423 U.S. 1030, 96 S.Ct. 560, 46 L.Ed.2d 404 (1975), and now reverse.

I

Arlington Heights is a suburb of Chicago, located about 26 miles northwest of the downtown Loop area. Most of the land in Arlington Heights is zoned for detached single-family homes, and this is in fact the prevailing land use. The Village experienced substantial growth during the 1960's, but, like other communities in northwest Cook County, its population of racial minority groups remained quite low. According to the 1970 census, only 27 of the Village's 64,000 residents were black.

The Clerics of St. Viator, a religious order (the Order), own an 80-acre parcel just east of the center of Arlington Heights. Part of the site is occupied by the Viatorian high school, and part by the Order's three-story novitiate building, which houses dormitories and a Montessori school. Much of the site, however, remains vacant. Since 1959, when the Village first adopted a zoning ordinance, all the land surrounding the Viatorian property has been zoned R-3, a single-family specification with relatively small minimum lot size requirements. On three sides of the Viatorian land there are single-family homes just across a street; to the east the

Viatorian property directly adjoins the back yards of other single-family homes.

The Order decided in 1970 to devote some of its land to low and moderate income housing. Investigation revealed that the most expeditious way to build such housing was to work through a nonprofit developer experienced in the use of federal housing subsidies under § 236 of the National Housing Act, 12 U.S.C. § 1715z–1.

MHDC is such a developer. It was organized in 1968 by several prominent Chicago citizens for the purpose of building low and moderate income housing throughout the Chicago area. In 1970 MHDC was in the process of building one § 236 development near Arlington Heights and already had provided some federally assisted housing on a smaller scale in other parts of the Chicago area.

After some negotiation, MHDC and the Order entered into a 99-year lease and an accompanying agreement of sale covering a 15-acre site in the southeast corner of the Viatorian property. MHDC became the lessee immediately, but the sale agreement was contingent upon MHDC's securing zoning clearances from the Village and § 236 housing assistance from the Federal Government. If MHDC proved unsuccessful in securing either, both the lease and the contract of sale would lapse. The agreement established a bargain purchase price of $300,000, low enough to comply with federal limitations governing land acquisition costs for § 236 housing.

MHDC engaged an architect and proceeded with the project, to be known as Lincoln Green. The plans called for 20 two-story buildings with a total of 190 units, each unit having its own private entrance from outside. One hundred of the units would have a single bedroom, thought likely to attract elderly citizens. The remainder would have two, three or four bedrooms. A large portion of the site would remain open, with shrubs and trees to screen the homes abutting the property to the east.

The planned development did not conform to the Village's zoning ordinance and could not be built unless Arlington Heights rezoned the parcel to R-5, its multiple-family housing classification. Accordingly, MHDC filed with the Village Plan Commission a petition for rezoning, accompanied by supporting materials describing the development and specifying that it would be subsidized under § 236. The materials made clear that one requirement under § 236 is an affirmative marketing plan designed to assure that a subsidized development is racially integrated. MHDC also submitted studies demonstrating the need for housing of this type and analyzing the probable impact of the development. To prepare for the hearings before the Plan Commission and to assure compliance with the Village building code, fire regulations, and related requirements, MHDC consulted with the Village staff for preliminary review of the development. The parties have stipulated that every change recommended during such consultations was incorporated into the plans.

During the Spring of 1971, the Plan Commission considered the proposal at a series of three public meetings, which drew large crowds. Although many of those attending were quite vocal and demonstrative in opposition to Lincoln Green, a number of individuals and representatives of community groups spoke in support of rezoning. Some of the comments, both from opponents and supporters, addressed what was referred to as the "social issue" the desirability or undesirability of introducing at this location in Arlington Heights low and moderate income housing, housing that would probably be racially integrated.

Many of the opponents, however, focused on the zoning aspects of the petition, stressing two arguments. First, the area always had been zoned single-family, and the neighboring citizens had built or purchased there in reliance on that classification. Rezoning threatened to cause a measurable drop in property value for neighboring sites. Second, the Village's apartment policy, adopted by the Village Board in 1962 and amended in 1970, called for R-5 zoning primarily to serve as a buffer between single-family development and land uses thought incompatible, such as commercial or manufacturing districts. Lincoln Green did not meet this requirement, as it adjoined no commercial or manufacturing district.

At the close of the third meeting, the Plan Commission adopted a motion to recommend to the Village's Board of Trustees that it deny the request. The motion stated: "While the need for low and moderate income housing may exist in Arlington Heights or its environs, the Plan Commission would be derelict in recommending it at the proposed location." Two members voted against the motion and submitted a minority report, stressing that in their view the change to accommodate Lincoln Green represented "good zoning." The Village Board met on September 28, 1971, to consider MHDC's request and the recommendation of the Plan Commission. After a public hearing, the Board denied the rezoning by a 6–1 vote.

The following June MHDC and three Negro individuals filed this lawsuit against the Village, seeking declaratory and injunctive relief. A second nonprofit corporation and an individual of Mexican-American descent intervened as plaintiffs. The trial resulted in a judgment for petitioners. Assuming that MHDC had standing to bring the suit, the District Court held that the petitioners were not motivated by racial discrimination or intent to discriminate against low income groups when they denied rezoning, but rather by a desire "to protect property values and the integrity of the Village's zoning plan." The District Court concluded also that the denial would not have a racially discriminatory effect.

A divided Court of Appeals reversed. It first approved the District Court's finding that the defendants were motivated by a concern for the integrity of the zoning plan, rather than by racial discrimination. Deciding whether their refusal to rezone would have discriminatory effects was more complex. The court observed that the refusal would have a disproportionate impact on blacks. Based upon family income, blacks constituted 40% of those Chicago area residents who were eligible to become tenants of Lincoln Green, although they comprised a far lower percentage of total area population. The court reasoned, however, that under our decision in James v. Valtierra, 402 U.S. 137, 91 S.Ct. 1331, 28 L.Ed.2d 678 (1971), such a disparity in racial impact alone does not call for strict scrutiny of a municipality's decision that prevents the construction of the low-cost housing.[11]

There was another level to the court's analysis of allegedly discriminatory results. Invoking language from Kennedy Park Homes Association v. City of Lackawanna, 436 F.2d 108, 112 (C.A.2 1970), cert. denied, 401 U.S. 1010, 91 S.Ct. 1256, 28 L.Ed.2d 546 (1971), the Court of Appeals ruled that the denial of rezoning must be examined in light of its "historical context and ultimate effect." Northwest Cook County was enjoying rapid growth in employment opportunities and population, but it continued to exhibit a high degree of residential segregation. The court held that Arlington Heights could not simply ignore this problem. Indeed, it found that the Village had been "exploiting" the situation by allowing itself to become a nearly all white community. The Village had no other current plans for building low and moderate income housing, and no other R-5 parcels in the Village were available to MHDC at an economically feasible price.

Against this background, the Court of Appeals ruled that the denial of the Lincoln Green proposal had racially discriminatory effects and could be tolerated only if it served compelling interests. Neither the buffer policy nor the desire to protect property values met this exacting standard. The court therefore concluded that the denial violated the Equal Protection Clause of the Fourteenth Amendment.

II

Clearly MHDC has met the constitutional requirements and it therefore has standing to assert its own rights. Foremost among them is MHDC's right to be free of arbitrary or irrational zoning actions. See Euclid v. Ambler Realty Co., 272 U.S. 365, 47 S.Ct. 114, 71 L.Ed. 303 (1926); Nectow v. Cambridge, 277 U.S. 183, 48 S.Ct. 447, 72 L.Ed. 842 (1928); Village of Belle Terre v. Boraas, 416 U.S. 1, 94 S.Ct. 1536, 39 L.Ed.2d 797 (1974). But the heart of this litigation has never been the claim that the Village's decision fails the generous Euclid test, recently reaffirmed in *Belle Terre*. Instead it has been the claim that the Village's refusal to rezone discriminates against racial minorities in violation of the Fourteenth Amendment. As a corporation, MHDC has no racial identity and cannot be the direct target of the petitioners' alleged

---

[11] Nor is there reason to subject the Village's action to more stringent review simply because it involves respondents' interest in securing housing. Lindsey v. Normet, 405 U.S. 56, 73–74, 92 S.Ct. 862, 874, 31 L.Ed.2d 36 (1972). See generally San Antonio Independent School District v. Rodriguez, 411 U.S. 1, 18–39, 93 S.Ct. 1278, 1288–1300, 36 L.Ed.2d 16 (1973).

discrimination. In the ordinary case, a party is denied standing to assert the rights of third persons. Warth v. Seldin, 422 U.S., at 499, 95 S.Ct., at 2205. But we need not decide whether the circumstances of this case would justify departure from that prudential limitation and permit MHDC to assert the constitutional rights of its prospective minority tenants. For we have at least one individual plaintiff who has demonstrated standing to assert these rights as his own.

Respondent Ransom, a Negro, works at the Honeywell factory in Arlington Heights and lives approximately 20 miles away in Evanston in a 5-room house with his mother and his son. The complaint alleged that he seeks and would qualify for the housing MHDC wants to build in Arlington Heights. Ransom testified at trial that if Lincoln Green were built he would probably move there, since it is closer to his job.

The injury Ransom asserts is that his quest for housing nearer his employment has been thwarted by official action that is racially discriminatory. If a court grants the relief he seeks, there is at least a "substantial probability," Warth v. Seldin, 422 U.S., at 504, 95 S.Ct., at 2208, that the Lincoln Green project will materialize, affording Ransom the housing opportunity he desires in Arlington Heights. His is not a generalized grievance. Instead, as we suggested in Warth, id., at 507, 508 n. 18, 95 S.Ct., at 2210, it focuses on a particular project and is not dependent on speculation about the possible actions of third parties not before the court. Unlike the individual plaintiffs in Warth, Ransom has adequately averred an "actionable causal relationship" between Arlington Heights' zoning practices and his asserted injury. Warth v. Seldin, 422 U.S., at 507, 95 S.Ct., at 2209. We therefore proceed to the merits.

### III

Our decision last Term in Washington v. Davis, 426 U.S. 229, 96 S.Ct. 2040, 48 L.Ed.2d 597 (1976), made it clear that official action will not be held unconstitutional solely because it results in a racially disproportionate impact. "Disproportionate impact is not irrelevant, but it is not the sole touchstone of an invidious racial discrimination." Id., at 242, 96 S.Ct., at 2049. Proof of racially discriminatory intent or purpose is required to show a violation of the Equal Protection Clause.

Davis does not require a plaintiff to prove that the challenged action rested solely on racially discriminatory purposes. Rarely can it be said that a legislature or administrative body operating under a broad mandate made a decision motivated solely by a single concern, or even that a particular purpose was the "dominant" or "primary" one.[12] In fact,

---

[12] In McGinnis v. Royster, 410 U.S. 263, 276–277, 93 S.Ct. 1055, 1063, 35 L.Ed.2d 282 (1973), in a somewhat different context, we observed:

> The search for legislative purpose is often elusive enough, Palmer v. Thompson, 403 U.S. 217, 91 S.Ct. 1940, 29 L.Ed.2d 438 (1971), without a requirement that primacy be ascertained. Legislation is frequently multipurposed: the removal of even a

it is because legislators and administrators are properly concerned with balancing numerous competing considerations that courts refrain from reviewing the merits of their decisions, absent a showing of arbitrariness or irrationality. But racial discrimination is not just another competing consideration. When there is a proof that a discriminatory purpose has been a motivating factor in the decision, this judicial deference is no longer justified.

Determining whether invidious discriminatory purpose was a motivating factor demands a sensitive inquiry into such circumstantial and direct evidence of intent as may be available. The impact of the official action whether it "bears more heavily on one race than another," Washington v. Davis, 426 U.S., at 242, 96 S.Ct., at 2049 may provide an important starting point. Sometimes a clear pattern, unexplainable on grounds other than race, emerges from the effect of the state action even when the governing legislation appears neutral on its face. Yick Wo v. Hopkins, 118 U.S. 356, 6 S.Ct. 1064, 30 L.Ed. 220 (1886); Guinn v. United States, 238 U.S. 347, 35 S.Ct. 926, 59 L.Ed. 1340 (1915); Lane v. Wilson, 307 U.S. 268, 59 S.Ct. 872, 83 L.Ed. 1281 (1939); Gomillion v. Lightfoot, 364 U.S. 339, 81 S.Ct. 125, 5 L.Ed.2d 110 (1960). The evidentiary inquiry is then relatively easy. But such cases are rare. Absent a pattern as stark as that in Gomillion or Yick Wo, impact alone is not determinative[13] and the Court must look to other evidence.[14]

The historical background of the decision is one evidentiary source, particularly if it reveals a series of official actions taken for invidious purposes. The specific sequence of events leading up to the challenged decision also may shed some light on the decisionmaker's purposes. For example, if the property involved here always had been zoned R-5 but suddenly was changed to R-3 when the town learned of MHDC's plans to erect integrated housing[15] we would have a far different case. Departures from the normal procedural sequence also might afford evidence that

---

"subordinate" purpose may shift altogether the consensus of legislative judgment supporting the statute.

[13] This is not to say that a consistent pattern of official racial discrimination is a necessary predicate to a violation of the equal protection clause. A single invidiously discriminatory governmental action the exercise of the zoning power as elsewhere would not necessarily be immunized by the absence of such discrimination in the making of other comparable decisions. See City of Richmond v. United States, 422 U.S. 358, 378, 95 S.Ct. 2296, 2307, 45 L.Ed.2d 245 (1975).

[14] In many instances, to recognize the limited probative value of disproportionate impact is merely to acknowledge the "heterogeneity" of the nation's population. Jefferson v. Hackney, 406 U.S. 535, 548, 92 S.Ct. 1724, 1732, 32 L.Ed.2d 285 (1972); see also Washington v. Davis, 426 U.S., at 248, 96 S.Ct., at 2051.

[15] See, e.g., Progress Development Corp. v. Mitchell, 286 F.2d 222 (C.A.7 1961) (park board allegedly condemned plaintiffs' land for a park upon learning that the homes plaintiffs were erecting there would be sold under a marketing plan designed to assure integration); Kennedy Park Homes Association, Inc. v. City of Lackawanna, 436 F.2d 108 (C.A.2 1970), cert. denied, 401 U.S. 1010, 91 S.Ct. 1256, 28 L.Ed.2d 546 (1971) (town declared moratorium on new subdivisions and rezoned area for park land shortly after learning of plaintiffs' plans to build low income housing). To the extent that the decision in Kennedy Park Homes rested solely on a finding of discriminatory impact, we have indicated our disagreement. Washington v. Davis, 426 U.S., at 244–245, 96 S.Ct., at 2050.

improper purposes are playing a role. Substantive departures too may be relevant, particularly if the factors usually considered important by the decisionmaker strongly favor a decision contrary to the one reached.

The legislative or administrative history may be highly relevant, especially where there are contemporary statements by members of the decisionmaking body, minutes of its meetings, or reports. In some extraordinary instances the members might be called to the stand at trial to testify concerning the purpose of the official action, although even then such testimony frequently will be barred by privilege.[16]

The foregoing summary identifies, without purporting to be exhaustive, subjects of proper inquiry in determining whether racially discriminatory intent existed. With these in mind, we now address the case before us.

## IV

This case was tried in the District Court and reviewed in the Court of Appeals before our decision in Washington v. Davis, supra. The respondents proceeded on the erroneous theory that the Village's refusal to rezone carried a racially discriminatory effect and was, without more, unconstitutional. But both courts below understood that at least part of their function was to examine the purpose underlying the decision. In making its findings on this issue, the District Court noted that some of the opponents of Lincoln Green who spoke at the various hearings might have been motivated by opposition to minority groups. The court held, however, that the evidence "does not warrant the conclusion that this motivated the defendants."

On appeal the Court of Appeals focused primarily on respondents' claim that the Village's buffer policy had not been consistently applied and was being invoked with a strictness here that could only demonstrate some other underlying motive. The court concluded that the buffer policy, though not always applied with perfect consistency, had on several occasions formed the basis for the Board's decision to deny other rezoning proposals. "The evidence does not necessitate a finding that Arlington Heights administered this policy in a discriminatory manner" 517 F.2d, at 412. The Court of Appeals therefore approved the District Court's findings concerning the Village's purposes in denying rezoning to MHDC.

We also have reviewed the evidence. The impact of the Village's decision does arguably bear more heavily on racial minorities. Minorities comprise 18% of the Chicago area population, and 40% of the income

---

[16] This Court has recognized, ever since Fletcher v. Peck, 6 Cranch 87, 3 L.Ed. 162 (1810), that judicial inquiries into legislative or executive motivation represent a substantial intrusion into the workings of other branches of government. Placing a decisionmaker on the stand is therefore "usually to be avoided." Citizens to Preserve Overton Park v. Volpe, 401 U.S. 402, 420, 91 S.Ct. 814, 825, 28 L.Ed.2d 136 (1971). The problems involved have prompted a good deal of scholarly commentary. See Tussman & TenBroek, The Equal Protection of the Laws, 37 Calif.L.Rev. 341, 356 361 (1949); A. Bickel, The Least Dangerous Branch, 208 221 (1962); Ely, Legislative and Administrative Motivation in Constitutional Law, 79 Yale L.J. 1205 (1970).

groups said to be eligible for Lincoln Green. But there is little about the sequence of events leading up to the decision that would spark suspicion. The area around the Viatorian property has been zoned R-3 since 1959, the year when Arlington Heights first adopted a zoning map. Single-family homes surround the 80-acre site, and the Village is undeniably committed to single-family homes as its dominant residential land use. The rezoning request progressed according to the usual procedures.[17] The Plan Commission even scheduled two additional hearings, at least in part to accommodate MHDC and permit it to supplement its presentation with answers to questions generated at the first hearing.

The statements by the Plan Commission and Village Board members, as reflected in the official minutes, focused almost exclusively on the zoning aspects of the MHDC petition, and the zoning factors on which they relied are not novel criteria in the Village's rezoning decisions. There is no reason to doubt that there has been reliance by some neighboring property owners on the maintenance of single-family zoning in the vicinity. The Village originally adopted its buffer policy long before MHDC entered the picture and has applied the policy too consistently for us to infer discriminatory purpose from its application in this case. Finally, MHDC called one member of the Village Board to the stand at trial. Nothing in her testimony supports an inference of invidious purpose.

In sum, the evidence does not warrant overturning the concurrent findings of both courts below. Respondents simply failed to carry their burden of proving that discriminatory purpose was a motivating factor in the Village's decision. This conclusion ends the constitutional inquiry. The Court of Appeals' further finding that the Village's decision carried a discriminatory "ultimate effect" is without independent constitutional significance.

V

Respondents' complaint also alleged that the refusal to rezone violated the Fair Housing Act, 42 U.S.C. § 3601 et seq. They continue to urge here that a zoning decision made by a public body may, and that petitioners' action did, violate § 3604 or § 3617. The Court of Appeals, however, proceeding in a somewhat unorthodox fashion, did not decide the statutory question. We remand the case for further consideration of respondents' statutory claims.

Reversed and remanded.

[The dissenting opinions of Justice WHITE and Justice MARSHALL are omitted.]

---

[17] Respondents have made much of one apparent procedural departure. The parties stipulated that the Village Planner, the staff member whose primary responsibility covered zoning and planning matters, was never asked for his written or oral opinion of the rezoning request. The omission does seem curious, but respondents failed to prove at trial what role the Planner customarily played in rezoning decisions, or whether his opinion would be relevant to respondents' claims.

# City of Cleburne, Texas v. Cleburne Living Center, Inc.

United States Supreme Court, 1985.
473 U.S. 432, 105 S.Ct. 3249.

■ JUSTICE WHITE delivered the opinion of the Court.

A Texas city denied a special use permit for the operation of a group home for the mentally retarded, acting pursuant to a municipal zoning ordinance requiring permits for such homes. The Court of Appeals for the Fifth Circuit held that mental retardation is a "quasi-suspect" classification and that the ordinance violated the Equal Protection Clause because it did not substantially further an important governmental purpose. We hold that a lesser standard of scrutiny is appropriate, but conclude that under that standard the ordinance is invalid as applied in this case.

I

In July 1980, respondent Jan Hannah purchased a building at 201 Featherston Street in the city of Cleburne, Texas, with the intention of leasing it to Cleburne Living Center, Inc. (CLC), for the operation of a group home for the mentally retarded. It was anticipated that the home would house 13 retarded men and women, who would be under the constant supervision of CLC staff members. The house had four bedrooms and two baths, with a half bath to be added. CLC planned to comply with all applicable state and federal regulations.

The city informed CLC that a special use permit would be required for the operation of a group home at the site, and CLC accordingly submitted a permit application. In response to a subsequent inquiry from CLC, the city explained that under the zoning regulations applicable to the site, a special use permit, renewable annually, was required for the construction of "[h]ospitals for the insane or feeble-minded, or alcoholic [*sic*] or drug addicts, or penal or correctional institutions." The city had determined that the proposed group home should be classified as a "hospital for the feeble-minded." After holding a public hearing on CLC's application, the City Council voted 3 to 1 to deny a special use permit.

CLC then filed suit in Federal District Court against the city and a number of its officials, alleging, *inter alia,* that the zoning ordinance was invalid on its face and as applied because it discriminated against the mentally retarded in violation of the equal protection rights of CLC and its potential residents. The District Court found that "[i]f the potential residents of the Featherston Street home were not mentally retarded, but the home was the same in all other respects, its use would be permitted under the city's zoning ordinance," and that the City Council's decision "was motivated primarily by the fact that the residents of the home would be persons who are mentally retarded." Even so, the District Court held the ordinance and its application constitutional. Concluding that no fundamental right was implicated and that mental retardation was neither a suspect nor a quasi-suspect classification, the court employed the minimum level of judicial scrutiny applicable to equal protection claims. The court deemed the ordinance, as written and applied, to be rationally related to the city's legitimate interests in "the legal responsibility of CLC and its residents, . . . the safety and fears of residents in the adjoining neighborhood," and the number of people to be housed in the home.

The Court of Appeals for the Fifth Circuit reversed, determining that mental retardation was a quasi-suspect classification and that it should assess the validity of the ordinance under intermediate-level scrutiny. Because mental retardation was in fact relevant to many legislative actions, strict scrutiny was not appropriate. But in light of the history of "unfair and often grotesque mistreatment" of the retarded, discrimination against them was "likely to reflect deep-seated prejudice." Applying the test that it considered appropriate, the court held that the ordinance was invalid on its face because it did not substantially further any important governmental interests. The Court of Appeals went on to hold that the ordinance was also invalid as applied.

## II

The Equal Protection Clause of the Fourteenth Amendment commands that no State shall "deny to any person within its jurisdiction the equal protection of the laws," which is essentially a direction that all persons similarly situated should be treated alike. *Plyler v. Doe,* 457 U.S. 202, 216 (1982). Section 5 of the Amendment empowers Congress to enforce this mandate, but absent controlling congressional direction, the courts have themselves devised standards for determining the validity of state legislation or other official action that is challenged as denying equal protection. The general rule is that legislation is presumed to be valid and will be sustained if the classification drawn by the statute is rationally related to a legitimate state interest.

The general rule gives way, however, when a statute classifies by race, alienage, or national origin. These factors are so seldom relevant to the achievement of any legitimate state interest that laws grounded in such considerations are deemed to reflect prejudice and antipathy—a view that those in the burdened class are not as worthy or deserving as others. For these reasons and because such discrimination is unlikely to be soon rectified by legislative means, these laws are subjected to strict scrutiny and will be sustained only if they are suitably tailored to serve a compelling state interest. Similar oversight by the courts is due when state laws impinge on personal rights protected by the Constitution.

Legislative classifications based on gender also call for a heightened standard of review. That factor generally provides no sensible ground for differential treatment. "[W]hat differentiates sex from such nonsuspect statuses as intelligence or physical disability . . . is that the sex characteristic frequently bears no relation to ability to perform or contribute to society." *Frontiero v. Richardson,* 411 U.S. 677, 686 (1973) (plurality opinion). Rather than resting on meaningful considerations, statutes distributing benefits and burdens between the sexes in different ways very likely reflect out-moded notions of the relative capabilities of men and women. A gender classification fails unless it is substantially related to a sufficiently important governmental interest.

We have declined, however, to extend heightened review to differential treatment based on age:

> While the treatment of the aged in this Nation has not been wholly free of discrimination, such persons, unlike, say, those who have been discriminated against on the basis of race or national origin, have not experienced a "history of purposeful unequal treatment" or been subjected to unique disabilities on the basis of stereotyped characteristics not truly indicative of their abilities.

*Massachusetts Board of Retirement v. Murgia,* 427 U.S. 307, 313 (1976).

The lesson of *Murgia* is that where individuals in the group affected by a law have distinguishing characteristics relevant to interests the State has the authority to implement, the courts have been very reluctant, as they should be in our federal system and with our respect for the separation of powers, to closely scrutinize legislative choices as to whether, how, and to what extent those interests should be pursued. In such cases, the Equal Protection Clause requires only a rational means to serve a legitimate end.

## III

Against this background, we conclude for several reasons that the Court of Appeals erred in holding mental retardation a quasi-suspect classification calling for a more exacting standard of judicial review than is normally accorded economic and social legislation. First, it is undeniable, and it is not argued otherwise here, that those who are mentally retarded have a reduced ability to cope with and function in the everyday world. Nor are they all cut from the same pattern: as the testimony in this record indicates, they range from those whose disability is not immediately evident to those who must be constantly cared for. They are thus different, immutably so, in relevant respects, and the States' interest in dealing with and providing for them is plainly a legitimate one. How this large and diversified group is to be treated under the law is a difficult and often a technical matter, very much a task for legislators guided by qualified professionals and not by the perhaps ill-informed opinions of the judiciary. Heightened scrutiny inevitably involves substantive judgments about legislative decisions, and we doubt that the predicate for such judicial oversight is present where the classification deals with mental retardation.

Our refusal to recognize the retarded as a quasi-suspect class does not leave them entirely unprotected from invidious discrimination. To withstand equal protection review, legislation that distinguishes between the mentally retarded and others must be rationally related to a legitimate governmental purpose.

## IV

The constitutional issue is clearly posed. The city does not require a special use permit in an R-3 zone for apartment houses, multiple dwellings, boarding and lodging houses, fraternity or sorority houses, dormitories, apartment hotels, hospitals, sanitariums, nursing homes for convalescents or the aged (other than for the insane or feebleminded or alcoholics or drug addicts), private clubs or fraternal orders, and other specified uses. It does, however, insist on a special permit for the Featherston home, and it does so, as the District Court found, because it would be a facility for the mentally retarded. May the city require the permit for this facility when other care and multiple-dwelling facilities are freely permitted?

It is true, as already pointed out, that the mentally retarded as a group are indeed different from others not sharing their misfortune, and in this respect they may be different from those who would occupy other facilities that would be permitted in an R-3 zone without a special permit. But this difference is largely irrelevant unless the Featherston home and those who would occupy it would threaten legitimate interests of the city in a way that other permitted uses such as boarding houses and hospitals would not. Because in our view the record does not reveal any rational basis for believing that the Featherston home would pose any special threat to the city's legitimate interests, we affirm the judgment below insofar as it holds the ordinance invalid as applied in this case.

The District Court found that the City Council's insistence on the permit rested on several factors. First, the Council was concerned with the negative attitude of the majority of property owners located within 200 feet of the Featherston facility, as well as with the fears of elderly residents of the neighborhood. But mere negative attitudes, or fear, unsubstantiated by factors which are properly cognizable in a zoning proceeding, are not permissible bases for treating a home for the mentally retarded differently from apartment houses, multiple dwellings, and the like. It is plain that the electorate as a whole, whether by referendum or otherwise, could not order city action violative of the Equal Protection Clause, *Lucas v. Forty-Fourth General Assembly of Colorado,* 377 U.S. 713, 736–737 (1964), and the city may not avoid the strictures of that Clause by deferring to the wishes or objections of some fraction of the body politic. "Private biases may be outside the reach of the law, but the law cannot, directly or indirectly, give them effect." *Palmore v. Sidoti,* 466 U.S. 429, 433 (1984).

Second, the Council had two objections to the location of the facility. It was concerned that the facility was across the street from a junior high school, and it feared that the students might harass the occupants of the Featherston home. But the school itself is attended by about 30 mentally retarded students, and denying a permit based on such vague, undifferentiated fears is again permitting some portion of the community to validate what would otherwise be an equal protection violation. The other objection to the home's location was that it was located on "a five hundred year flood plain." This concern with the possibility of a flood, however, can hardly be based on a distinction between the Featherston home and, for example, nursing homes, homes for convalescents or the aged, or sanitariums or hospitals, any of which could be located on the Featherston site without obtaining a special use permit. The same may be said of another concern of the Council's doubts about the legal responsibility for actions which the mentally retarded might take. If there is no concern about legal responsibility with respect to other uses that would be permitted in the area, such as boarding and fraternity houses, it is difficult to believe that the groups of mildly or moderately mentally retarded individuals who would live at 201 Featherston would present any different or special hazard.

Fourth, the Council was concerned with the size of the home and the number of people that would occupy it. [T]here would be no restrictions on the number of people who could occupy this home as a boarding house, nursing home, family dwelling, fraternity house, or dormitory. The question is whether it is rational to treat the mentally retarded differently. It is true that they suffer disability not shared by others; but why this difference warrants a density regulation that others need not observe is not at all apparent. At least this record does not clarify how, in this connection, the characteristics of the intended occupants of the Featherston home rationally justify denying to those occupants what would be permitted to groups occupying the same site for different purposes. Those who would live in the Featherston home are the type of individuals who, with supporting staff, satisfy federal and state standards for group housing in the community; and there is no dispute that the home would meet the federal square-footage-per-resident requirement for facilities of this type. See 42 CFR § 442.447 (1984). In the words of the Court of Appeals, "[t]he City never justifies its apparent view that other people can live under such 'crowded' conditions when mentally retarded persons cannot."

The short of it is that requiring the permit in this case appears to us to rest on an irrational prejudice against the mentally retarded, including those who would occupy the Featherston facility and who would live under the closely supervised and highly regulated conditions expressly provided for by state and federal law.

The judgment of the Court of Appeals is affirmed insofar as it invalidates the zoning ordinance as applied to the Featherston home. The judgment is otherwise vacated, and the case is remanded.

■ JUSTICE MARSHALL, with whom JUSTICE BRENNAN and JUSTICE BLACKMUN join, concurring in the judgment in part and dissenting in part.

The Court holds that all retarded individuals cannot be grouped together as the "feebleminded" and deemed presumptively unfit to live in a community. Underlying this holding is the principle that mental retardation *per se* cannot be a proxy for depriving retarded people of their rights and interests without regard to variations in individual ability. With this holding and principle I agree. The Equal Protection Clause requires attention to the capacities and needs of retarded people as individuals.

I cannot agree, however, with the way in which the Court reaches its result or with the narrow, as-applied remedy it provides for the city of Cleburne's equal protection violation. The Court holds the ordinance invalid on rational-basis grounds and disclaims that anything special, in the form of heightened scrutiny, is taking place. Yet Cleburne's ordinance surely would be valid under the traditional rational-basis test applicable to economic and commercial regulation. In my view, it is important to articulate, as the Court does not, the facts and principles that justify subjecting this zoning ordinance to the searching review—the heightened scrutiny—that actually leads to its invalidation.

As the history of discrimination against the retarded and its continuing legacy amply attest, the mentally retarded have been, and in some areas may still be, the targets of action the Equal Protection Clause condemns. With respect to a liberty so valued as the right to establish a home in the community, and so likely to be denied on the basis of irrational fears and outright hostility, heightened scrutiny is surely appropriate.

## Bay Area Addiction Research and Treatment, Inc. v. City of Antioch.

United States Court of Appeals, Ninth Circuit, 1999.
179 F.3d 725.

■ TASHIMA, CIRCUIT JUDGE.

In 1998, Bay Area Addiction Research and Treatment, Inc. ("BAART") and California Detoxification Programs, Inc. ("CDP") tried to relocate their methadone clinic to the City of Antioch, California. After BAART and CDP received notice from Antioch that the proposed location could be used for such a clinic under Antioch's zoning plan, the Antioch City Council enacted an urgency ordinance prohibiting the operation of methadone clinics within 500 feet of residential areas, thereby precluding the use of the proposed site. BAART, individual patients of BAART, CDP, and Dr. Ron Kletter, the executive director of both, (collectively "Bay Area") brought suit against Antioch pursuant to Title II of the Americans with Disabilities Act ("ADA"), 42 U.S.C. §§ 12131–65, and § 504 of the Rehabilitation Act, 29 U.S.C. § 794, among others. The district court denied Bay Area's motion for a preliminary injunction enjoining the urgency ordinance. Bay Area appeals, contending that the district court applied the wrong legal test to its ADA and Rehabilitation Act claims and misjudged the irreparability of the harm it would suffer if an injunction did not issue. We have jurisdiction pursuant to 28 U.S.C. § 1292(a)(1). We hold that Title II of the ADA and § 504 of the Rehabilitation Act apply to zoning ordinances, and that the district court abused its discretion by applying the wrong legal test to Bay Area's ADA and Rehabilitation Act claims. Accordingly, we reverse and remand.

BAART has operated a clinic for 13 years in a municipal courthouse in Pittsburg, California, that provides outpatient methadone treatment to people who have been addicted to heroin. CDP provides short-term outpatient heroin detoxification services at the same location. Although BAART and CDP are distinct entities, they work closely together at clinic locations throughout California. BAART and CDP plan to share space at the location at issue in this case. We will use the abbreviation "BAART" to refer to both BAART and CDP in this statement of the facts.

On December 2, 1997, Contra Costa County notified BAART that its lease of office space in the Pittsburg courthouse would be terminated on September 30, 1998, because the County needed the premises for other uses. BAART began to look for a site to which it could relocate near Antioch or Pittsburg. After searching for several months, BAART found a location in Antioch. While the Sunset Lane site was at one time occupied by a medical practice and shares a street with many medical and commercial offices, it abuts a residential neighborhood.

On April 15, 1998, the deputy director of Antioch's Community Development Department notified BAART in writing that a clinic like BAART's would be a permitted use of the Sunset Lane site under Antioch's land use plan. Subsequently, on April 27, 1998, BAART filed a business license application for the Sunset Lane site. The next day, Dr. Kletter and his wife orally agreed to purchase the site, and on May 18, 1998, they entered into a written purchase agreement.

By mid-April, 1998, Antioch residents had learned of BAART's plans for the Sunset Lane site and began to express their concern that the methadone clinic would result in an increase in crime and drug abuse near Sunset Lane and throughout Antioch. The issue was addressed at the April 28, 1998, Antioch City Council meeting, at which many residents commented on the proposed use of the Sunset Lane site. Following this hearing, the City Council unanimously approved Ordinance No. 938–C–S, an urgency ordinance, pursuant to section 65858 of the California Government Code, which authorizes a city to prohibit a land use for 45 days in order to study the proposed use. See Cal. Gov't Code § 65858 (West 1999). The ordinance forbids the issuance of any permits to or the operation of any new substance abuse clinics, including methadone clinics, located within 500 feet of any residential property.

On June 9, 1998, the city council approved Ordinance No. 941–C–S, another urgency ordinance, that extended the effective date of the original ordinance to April 10, 1999. The second ordinance amended the first ordinance so as to prohibit only methadone clinics from operating within 500 feet of any residential property. The "Legislative Findings and Conclusions" accompanying the second ordinance included both statistics and generalities from which the city council concluded that "[t]he proposed methadone clinic at its proposed location represents a current and immediate threat to the public peace, health, safety and welfare." Specifically, the city council found that the methadone clinic would attract drug dealers and lead to an increase in crime in the area surrounding the clinic. The ordinance provided for further studies of the impact of methadone clinics on nearby residences and children.

Antioch and BAART subsequently tried to find an alternative site for the clinic, but no agreement was reached.

On July 6, 1998, Bay Area brought a class action lawsuit against Antioch under the ADA, the Rehabilitation Act, and 42 U.S.C. § 1983, for violations of the Supremacy, Due Process, and Equal Protection Clauses. Bay Area sought a declaratory judgment that Ordinance No. 941–C–S was unlawful and a permanent injunction enjoining Antioch from enforcing the ordinance or otherwise interfering with Bay Area's use of the Sunset Lane site as a methadone clinic.

Soon thereafter, Bay Area moved for a preliminary injunction and Antioch filed a motion to dismiss. The district court denied Bay Area and Antioch's motions, holding that zoning is an activity covered by the ADA and the Rehabilitation Act, and that appellants are qualified individuals with disabilities, entitled to protection under both statutes. See 42 U.S.C. § 12131 (1999). The district court decided, however, that at this stage in the litigation, Bay Area had neither demonstrated that it would be irreparably harmed if the court refused to issue a preliminary injunction nor that it was likely to prevail on the merits.

Bay Area argues that the district court erred in refusing to issue a preliminary injunction because the district court considered whether there was an alternative location that would constitute a reasonable accommodation of both sides' interests. Under a test that looks solely to whether a law discriminates on the basis of disability, Bay Area contends, it can show that it is likely to prevail on the merits. Bay Area also contends that it will be irreparably harmed if a preliminary injunction does not issue.

*The Applicability of the ADA and the Rehabilitation Act to Zoning*

The district court held that the ADA and the Rehabilitation Act apply to zoning, a decision the parties do not contest on appeal. Because the issue is one of first impression in this circuit, however, we discuss it here. In so doing, we adopt much of the persuasive reasoning of the Second Circuit in Innovative Health Systems, Inc. v. City of White Plains, 117 F.3d 37 (2d Cir.1997), and hold that these statutes do apply to zoning.

As with all exercises in statutory interpretation, we begin with the ADA's text. Title II of the ADA addresses the provision of public services. Section 12132 of this title prohibits discrimination on the basis of disability by public entities. Section 12132 provides that "[s]ubject to the provisions of this subchapter, no qualified individual with a disability shall, by reason of such disability, be excluded from participation in or be denied the benefits of the services, programs, or activities of a public entity, or be subjected to discrimination by any such entity." 42 U.S.C. § 12132 (1999).

Other local public entities in similar cases have argued, as Antioch did below, that zoning is not a service, program, or activity, and therefore § 12132 does not apply. We reject this argument. The Rehabilitation Act broadly defines "program or activity" to include "all of the operations of" a qualifying local government. 29 U.S.C. § 794(b)(1)(A) (1999). Because Congress has instructed that the ADA is to be interpreted consistently with the Rehabilitation Act, see Armstrong v. Wilson, 124 F.3d 1019, 1023 (9th Cir.1997), cert. denied, 118 S.Ct. 2340, 141 L.Ed.2d 711 (1998), we interpret § 12132 in light of this definition. The Rehabilitation Act and the ADA apply to zoning because zoning "is a normal function of a governmental entity." Innovative Health, 117 F.3d at 44.

Congress' stated purposes in enacting the ADA also support its application to zoning. Within the text of the ADA, Congress set forth its broad goal of "provid[ing] a clear and comprehensive national mandate for the elimination of discrimination against individuals with disabilities." 42 U.S.C. § 12101(b)(1) (1999). Congress found that:

> [I]ndividuals with disabilities are a discrete and insular minority who have been faced with restrictions and limitations, subjected to a history of purposeful unequal treatment, and relegated to a position of political powerlessness in our society, based on characteristics that are beyond the control of such individuals and resulting from stereotypic assumptions not truly indicative of the individual ability of such individuals to participate in, and contribute to, society.

42 U.S.C. § 12101(a)(7) (1999). This sweeping language—most noticeably Congress's analogizing the plight of the disabled to that of "discrete and insular minorities" like racial minorities, see United States v. Carolene Prods. Co., 304 U.S. 144, 153 n. 4, 58 S.Ct. 778, 82 L.Ed. 1234 (1938) (defining religious, national, and racial minorities as "discrete and insular minorities"),—strongly suggests that § 12132 should not be construed to allow the creation of spheres in which public entities may discriminate on the basis of an individual's disability.

The ADA's legislative history buttresses our interpretation of § 12132. For example, the report of the House Committee on Education and Labor suggests that at least this committee intended § 12132 to have a broad application.

> The Committee has chosen not to list all the types of actions that are included within the term "discrimination", as was done in titles I and III, because this title essentially simply extends the anti-discrimination prohibition embodied in section 504 [of the Rehabilitation Act, 29 U.S.C. § 794] to all actions of state and local governments. H.R.Rep. No. 101–485(II), at 84 (1990), reprinted in 1990 U.S.C.C.A.N. 303, 367.

Perhaps even more significant is the fact that the House bill's general prohibition against discrimination won out over the Senate bill's enumeration of general and specific prohibitions against discrimination. See H.R. Conf. Rep. No. 101–596, at 67 (1990), reprinted in 1990 U.S.C.C.A.N. 565, 576. In other words, Congress specifically rejected an approach that could have left room for exceptions to § 12132's prohibition on discrimination by public entities.

Finally, the Department of Justice's regulations and interpretations of those regulations in its Technical Assistance Manual support our conclusion that zoning is covered by the ADA. For example, the preamble to the regulations implementing § 12132 notes that "Title II applies to anything a public entity does." 28 C.F.R. pt. 35, app. A at 438 (1998). Furthermore, the Technical Assistance Manual expressly cites zoning as an example of a public entity's obligation to avoid discrimination:

> Illustration 1: A municipal zoning ordinance requires a set-back of 12 feet from the curb in the central business district. In order to install a ramp to the front entrance of a pharmacy, the owner must encroach on the set-back by three feet. Granting a variance in the zoning requirement may be a reasonable modification of town policy.

The Americans with Disabilities Act: Title II Technical Assistance Manual ("TA Manual") § II–3.6100, illus. 1 (1993).

In sum, "[w]e decline to draw an arbitrary distinction—to prohibit public entities from discriminating against persons with disabilities in some of their activities and not in others. . . ." Innovative Health, 117 F.3d at 45. Although we recognize that zoning is a traditionally local activity, Congress has spoken.

Accordingly, we hold that the ADA applies to zoning.

*The Propriety of Injunctive Relief*

We hold that the district court abused its discretion by applying an erroneous legal standard to determine whether to grant Bay Area's motion for a preliminary injunction. To obtain a preliminary injunction, Bay Area must demonstrate either "a combination of probable success on the merits and the possibility of irreparable injury" or "that serious questions are raised and the balance of hardships tips in its favor." *Roe*, 134 F.3d at 1402 (internal quotation marks omitted) (citation omitted). We review the district court's decision for an abuse of discretion. See id.

We hold that the district court abused its discretion by applying an erroneous legal standard to determine whether the urgency ordinance is likely to violate the ADA and the Rehabilitation Act. We leave it to the district court on remand to apply the standard set forth below; accordingly, we do not express any view on Bay Area's likelihood of success on the merits.

[The court finds that the district court abused its discretion when it applied the reasonable modifications test. The test does not apply to laws such as Antioch's that facially discriminate.]

*The Significant Risk Test*

Contrary to Bay Area's contention, the fact that the urgency ordinance violates § 12132 does not end our inquiry. Section 12131, which defines the class of individuals entitled to § 12132's protection, includes a test that evaluates the risk posed by an individual. Specifically, an individual who poses a significant risk to the health or safety of others that cannot be ameliorated by means of a reasonable modification is not a qualified individual under § 12131.

The Supreme Court developed the significant risk test in School Board of Nassau County v. Arline, 480 U.S. 273, 107 S.Ct. 1123, 94 L.Ed.2d 307 (1987), a case involving a teacher who had been discharged because she had an active case of tuberculosis. See id. at 276. She brought suit under § 504 of the Rehabilitation Act on the basis that she was dismissed on account of her disability. The Court held that "[a] person who poses a significant risk of communicating an infectious disease to others in the workplace will not be otherwise qualified for his or her job if reasonable accommodation will not eliminate that risk." Id. at 287 n. 16. That is, the Court read the significant risk test into the Rehabilitation Act's definition of who constituted a disabled person for purposes of receiving § 504's protection. The Court noted that this test in most cases would require an individualized assessment of the facts if "§ 504 is to achieve its goal of protecting handicapped individuals from deprivations based on prejudice, stereotypes, or unfounded fear, while giving appropriate weight to such legitimate concerns . . . as avoiding exposing others to significant health and safety risks." Id. at 287.

We applied the significant risk test to another Rehabilitation Act suit brought by a teacher transferred out of the classroom to an administrative position because he had AIDS. See Chalk v. United States Dist. Court, 840 F.2d 701, 707–08 (9th Cir.1988). This court ordered the entry of a preliminary injunction in Chalk's favor because there was no evidence that he posed a significant risk to his students or others. "To allow the court to base its decision on the fear and apprehension of others would frustrate the goals of section 504." Id. at 711.

The district court should have used the significant risk test to analyze the alleged threat posed by appellants, as part of its determination of whether appellants are qualified individuals under

§ 12131. Using this test in this context comports with both the Justice Department's Technical Assistance Manual and the ADA's purposes.

The Technical Assistance Manual provides for a significant risk test: "An individual who poses a direct threat to the health or safety of others will not be 'qualified' [as an individual protected by Title II]." TA Manual § II–2.8000. The Manual defines a direct threat as the Arline and Chalk courts did:

> A "direct threat" is a significant risk to the health or safety of others that cannot be eliminated or reduced to an acceptable level by the public entity's modification of its policies, practices, or procedures, or by the provision of auxiliary aids or services. The public entity's determination that a person poses a direct threat to the health or safety of others may not be based on generalizations or stereotypes about the effects of a particular disability. TA Manual § II–2.8000.

Furthermore, the significant risk test reflects Congress' goals for the ADA and the Rehabilitation Act. On the one hand, this test ensures that decisions are not made on the basis of "the prejudiced attitudes or the ignorance of others." *Arline*, 480 U.S. at 284. This is particularly important because, as with individuals with contagious diseases, "[f]ew aspects of a handicap give rise to the same level of public fear and misapprehension," id., as the challenges facing recovering drug addicts. On the other hand, the significant risk test recognizes that the ADA does not wholly preclude public entities from making certain distinctions on the basis of disability if those distinctions are absolutely necessary. The significant risk test provides public entities with the ability to craft programs or statutes that respond to serious threats to the public health and safety while insuring that these (rare) distinctions are based on sound policy grounds instead of on fear and prejudice.

Antioch correctly points out that the significant risk test has its own reasonable modifications component. However, the significant risk test will not necessarily result in the same outcome as the district court's test. Under the significant risk test, the court must decide whether the individual poses a significant risk before it may proceed to ask whether a reasonable modification may eliminate the risk. The court must first determine whether an individual poses a significant risk. If he does, the court must then ask whether there is a reasonable modification that would counteract the risk. If there is, the individual is qualified for purposes of § 12131. If the individual does not pose a significant risk, the court need never reach the question of whether there is a reasonable modification. Therefore, the district court's test prematurely reaches the reasonable modifications part of the analysis because the district court had not found that Bay Area was likely to pose a significant threat to the health or safety of the residents protected by the zoning ordinance.

The next question is how to define a significant risk to health or safety. We find that the determination of whether a significant risk exists requires an individualized assessment of "[t]he nature, duration, and severity of the risk," and "[t]he probability that the potential injury will actually occur." TA Manual § II–2.8000. We do not purport to explore fully the contours of this test for all contexts. For purposes of this case, it is enough to note that "health and safety" includes severe and likely harms to the community that are directly associated with the operation of the methadone clinic. If supported by the evidence, such harms may include a reasonable likelihood of a significant increase in crime. Without speculating on the kind and quality of evidence needed to establish a significant risk, we note that in assessing the evidence, courts must be mindful of the ADA's express goal of eliminating discrimination against people with disabilities. See 42 U.S.C. § 12101(b)(1). As the *Arline* Court recognized, the Rehabilitation Act was meant to protect disabled individuals "from deprivations based on prejudice, stereotypes, or unfounded fear." 480 U.S. at 287. Therefore, it is not enough that individuals pose a hypothetical or presumed risk. Instead, the evidence must establish that an individual does, in fact, pose a significant risk. Further, it should be emphasized that the risk must be of a serious nature.

In sum, because the Antioch ordinance facially discriminates on the basis of the appellants' disability in violation of § 12132, to establish a likelihood of success (or raise serious questions) on the merits, Bay Area need only show that the appellants are qualified under § 12131 to receive protection under § 12132. To do so, Bay Area must demonstrate that it is likely that appellants do not pose a significant risk to the health or safety of the community. If Bay Area cannot make such a showing, it must demonstrate that the risk it poses may be ameliorated by reasonable modifications.

[W]e hold that Title II of the ADA and § 504 of the Rehabilitation Act apply to zoning ordinances, and that the district court abused its discretion by applying the wrong legal test to Bay Area's ADA and Rehabilitation Act claims. Accordingly, we reverse the district court's order denying Bay Area's motion for a preliminary injunction and remand with instructions that the district court reconsider Bay Area's motion in light of the test set forth herein.

Reversed and remanded.

## NOTES

1. Cuyahoga Falls: *income, race, motives, and voters*. It is extremely difficult to prevail with a federal equal protection claim in a suit based on discrimination against low-income persons or the poor. The U.S. Supreme Court has repeatedly held that poverty is not a suspect classification.[18] Therefore, a government action resulting in discrimination against the poor will be struck down only if the action is not even arguably rationally related

---

[18] See San Antonio Indep. School Dist. v. Rodriguez, 411 U.S. 1 (1973).

to a legitimate government purpose. However, as the *Arlington Heights* facts indicate, exclusion of low-income persons often correlates to exclusion of racial or ethnic minorities, thus qualifying as a "suspect classification" that elicits more stringent judicial review.

Nonetheless, the obstacles to proving intentional discrimination, as illustrated by *Arlington Heights*, are even greater when the government action is by the voters. Some states allow certain land use regulatory actions to be adopted by voter initiative and about half the states allow zoning actions to be approved or rejected by voter referendum.[19] A voter referendum rejecting a proposed multi-family low-income housing in Cuyahoga Falls, Ohio, demonstrates the potential for voters to exclude low-income and minority residents.[20] The Buckeye Community Hope Foundation, a nonprofit affordable housing developer, had obtained Planning Commission and City Council approval for its Pleasant Meadows project, which would have served a much higher percentage of African American residents than were reflected in the 98 percent white population of the city. However, significant public opposition to the project existed, as well as opposition by the Mayor and some City Council members. City residents submitted referendum petitions to repeal the City Council's approval of the project's site plan. Pursuant to existing procedures, the referendum was submitted to the voters, who voted to repeal the site-plan approval. After initially upholding the vote to repeal, the Ohio Supreme Court held an unusual rehearing and reversed itself, determining that site plan approvals are administrative actions—not legislative actions—and therefore are not properly subject to the power of the voters under Ohio law.[21]

The Foundation had suffered damages from the loss of its funding during the period between the referendum and the Ohio Supreme Court's reversal, and it sued the City for damages for violation of its equal protection and substantive due process rights under 42 U.S.C. § 1983. The Sixth Circuit, reversing summary judgment for the City on equal protection grounds, made the following observations about the facts:

> An examination of the record reveals that a jury could reasonably conclude that public opposition to the plaintiffs' project had a decidedly racial component. At the February 2, 1999 meeting of the Cuyahoga Planning Commission, Lee Minier expressed concerns about safety, commenting that "they know what kind of element is going to move in there." J.A. at 154. Gerry Priobonic, another resident, noted that "there will be a different class of people living there." *Id.* Harry Bridges expressed concerns about safety. *Id.* Susan Brady stated that she does not believe the area will be safe. According to her, "Cuyahoga Falls is downgrading itself." J.A. at

---

[19] Juergensmeyer & Roberts, Land Use Planning and Development Regulation Law, 2nd ed., § 5.5, pp. 137–38 (2007).

[20] The facts of this conflict can be pieced together from both the federal appellate and U.S. Supreme Court opinions in the case. See Buckeye Community Hope Found. v. City of Cuyahoga Falls, 263 F.3d 627 (6th Cir. 2001), rev'd, City of Cuyahoga Falls v. Buckeye Community Hope Foundation, 538 U.S. 188 (2003).

[21] Buckeye Community Hope Foundation v. City of Cuyahoga Falls, 697 N.E.2d 181 (Ohio 1998).

156. Several members of the public questioned Planning Director Sharpe about the height of a fence serving as a buffer between the project and neighboring complexes. Sharpe stated that the fence should not be higher than five feet, having to remind the citizens that the developer is trying to create a residential atmosphere not an institutional one. J.A. at 157. At the March 4, 1996 meeting of the City Council, Amy Bridges expressed concern about the extra crime and drugs that come with low-income housing. J.A. at 961.

Mayor Robart also voiced his opposition to the project. The Mayor seconded the concerns of those opposing the project, referring in his remarks to the crime problems associated with low-income housing projects. J.A. at 966. The Mayor also linked the project to the same type of "social engineering that brought us busing," which the Mayor considered to be an utter failure. *Id.* Further casting the debate over the project in a racial light, the Mayor referred to an article entitled "Stuck in the Ghetto" which discussed the problems with Section 8 housing. *Id.* Notably, the project at issue does not involve Section 8 vouchers; residents would have to pay the full rent. In any case, the Mayor declared that Cuyahoga Falls has done its part in supporting such projects. At the March 18, 1996 City Council meeting, Mayor Robart forthrightly acknowledged that the issue was not whether the project was properly zoned, but rather the issue was low-income housing. J.A. at 945. The Mayor stated "that people who spent a lot of money on their condominiums don't want people moving in their neighborhood that are going to be renting for $371." *Id.* Thus, the Mayor stated that City Council should not advocate anything that is clearly a step backwards and concluded that "we have to oppose this and we have to oppose it with vigor." *Id.*

Although a number of these statements could be interpreted as opposition to the lower economic status of the potential residents of the project, when viewed in the light most favorable to the plaintiffs, these statements can just as easily be seen as expressions of racial bias against blacks, especially given the fact that racial stereotypes prevalent in our society associate blacks with crime, drugs, and lower class status. *See* David Cole, No Equal Justice: Race and Class in the American Criminal Justice System 34, 42 (1999) ("[T]he correlation of race and crime remains a stereotype, and most blacks will not conform to the stereotype. Even though blacks are arrested and convicted for a disproportionate amount of violent crime, it is nonetheless true that in any given year only about 2 percent of black citizens are arrested for committing any crime; the vast majority, or 98 percent, of black citizens are not even charged with crime."); Michael Sunnafrank & Norman E. Fontes, *General and Crime Related Racial Stereotypes and Influence on Juridic Decisions,* 17 Cornell J. Soc. Rel. 1, 10 (1983) (finding strong evidence in a sample of college students of crime-related racial stereotyping, such as perceiving blacks as more likely than whites to commit assault, and other violent crimes). Viewed in the light most favorable to plaintiffs, many of the statements made by Cuyahoga residents evidence a racial bias toward the prospect of a significant number of blacks moving into their community which is 98% white.[22]

The U.S. Supreme Court reversed the Sixth Circuit. It held that the Foundation had no equal protection action against the City for placing a facially neutral referendum petition on the ballot pursuant to facially neutral procedures, and that the statements of voters could not be construed as "State action" even if they did manifest racially discriminatory intent. The opinion by Justice O'Connor noted that statements by government decision makers or referendum sponsors might serve as some evidence of discriminatory intent, but gave wide latitude to voter sentiments under both the First Amendment guarantee of free speech and the nature of direct democracy, without attributing those statements or motives to the City itself.[23]

2. *Exclusionary zoning, inclusionary zoning, and* Mt. Laurel. New Jersey has taken an unprecedented step toward fostering an adequate supply of low income housing. In Southern Burlington County N.A.A.C.P. v. Mount Laurel Township[24] (*Mount Laurel I*), the New Jersey Supreme Court held that because the state constitution required that a zoning ordinance promote "the general welfare," Mount Laurel's land-use regulations had to provide for its fair share of the housing needs of the region. The court said that when a developing municipality had not so provided or had effectively "zoned out" a particular economic group, a prima facie violation of either substantive due process or equal protection under the state constitution had been established. The city then had the burden of justifying its action or refusal to act. Applying this standard, the court found Mount Laurel's ordinance partially invalid and granted the town ninety days to amend it.

In Southern Burlington County N.A.A.C.P. v. Mount Laurel Township[25] (*Mount Laurel II*), the court further refined the *Mount Laurel* doctrine by imposing an affirmative obligation on cities located in growth areas of the state to plan, enact ordinances, finance, and otherwise act to ensure a realistic likelihood that the city would provide its fair share of the regional need for low and moderate income housing. The court also recognized the judicial authority to impose a "builder's remedy," which is the judicially imposed grant of a building permit to a plaintiff-developer who has successfully challenged a zoning ordinance as a violation of the locality's *Mount Laurel* obligation. Moreover, the court invited the state legislature to take some action in this field.

Subsequently, the legislature enacted the New Jersey Fair Housing Act,[26] which provides for voluntary "safe harbor" certification of a municipality's zoning ordinances by a state administrative agency. The Act created an administrative agency called the Council on Affordable Housing

---

[22] Buckeye Community Hope Found. v. City of Cuyahoga Falls, 263 F.3d 627, 636–37 (6th Cir. 2001).
[23] City of Cuyahoga Falls v. Buckeye Community Hope Foundation, 538 U.S. 188, 195–96 (2003).
[24] 336 A.2d 713 (N.J. 1975).
[25] 456 A.2d 390 (N.J. 1983).
[26] N.J. Stat. Ann. §§ 52:27D–301 to 52:27D–329.

("the Council") which has the power to define the housing regions within the state and the respective regions' need for low and moderate income housing. The Council also has the power to promulgate criteria enabling municipalities within each region to determine their fair share of that regional need. Moreover, upon petition to the Council by a municipality, the Council has the power to decide whether a particular ordinance proposed in a given municipality satisfies that municipality's *Mount Laurel* obligation by creating "a realistic opportunity for the construction of that municipality's fair share of the regional need for low and moderate income housing." The Council's determination in this regard ordinarily is considered final, and can only be set aside by the judiciary by contrary "clear and convincing evidence" (§ 17a of the Act). The Act also adopts a moratorium on the builder's remedy, a remedial provision expressly embraced in *Mount Laurel II*. In many ways, the Act was a reaction to the strong judicial role in forcing affordable housing options onto New Jersey's localities.

The constitutionality of this statute was affirmed in Hills Development Co. v. Bernards Township in Somerset County[27] (*Mount Laurel III*). In sustaining the Act's constitutionality, the Supreme Court of New Jersey initially observed that no constitutional timetable exists with respect to satisfying the *Mount Laurel* obligation. Thus, the Act is not void because it will result in a delayed satisfaction of the *Mount Laurel* obligation on the part of the municipalities. The court then sustained the moratorium on the builder's remedy since such remedy never was made part of the constitutional obligation. In response to their *Mount Laurel* obligations, many New Jersey municipalities have chosen to engage in "inclusionary zoning": requiring developers to set aside a certain portion of the housing units that they develop to be offered at affordable rents or prices.[28]

Other states have adopted inclusionary zoning ordinances or programs.[29] In addition, some states legislatures have expressly adopted requirements and/or procedures to ensure that local governments satisfy their "fair share" of the region's affordable housing needs, but these requirements are notorious for local resistance and noncompliance.[30] Nonetheless, despite the praise of the New Jersey Supreme Court's "audacious activism" by some scholars and advocates,[31] no other state has adopted the *Mount Laurel* doctrine.

    3.   *Growth controls and Livermore*. A much broader set of exclusionary land-use regulations are growth controls, which have the effect of excluding newcomers by controlling the growth or development of the local community.

---

[27] 510 A.2d 621 (N.J. 1986).

[28] Orfield, Land Use and Housing Policies to Reduce Concentrated Poverty and Racial Segregation, 33 Fordham Urb. L.J. 877, 907–09 (2006).

[29] Juergensmeyer & Roberts, Land Use Planning and Development Regulation Law, 2nd ed., § 6.7, p. 229 & n.5 (2007) (California, Colorado, Florida, Maryland, Massachusetts, New Jersey, New Mexico, South Carolina, Texas, and Virginia); Nirider, In Search of "Refinement without Exclusiveness": Inclusionary Zoning in Highland Park, Illinois, 102 Nw. U. L. Rev. 1919 (2008) (Highland Park, Illinois, and other Chicago-area suburbs).

[30] Juergensmeyer & Roberts, Land Use Planning and Development Regulation Law, 2nd ed., § 6.6, p. 227–28 (2007).

[31] Haar, Suburbs Under Seige: Race, Space, and Audacious Judges (1996).

These controls may have the effect of excluding low-income and minority residents by preventing new development, making development more costly, and raising residential rents and sales prices by limiting supply. However, the focus of growth controls often extends beyond race and class. These controls are motivated in part by the stress that new development puts on local traffic, schools, water and wastewater capacity, environmental resources, and quality of life.

There are nine different categories of growth controls:

1) moratoria on new development for a specified period of time while local planners and regulators prepare appropriate regulations;

2) moratoria on new development lasting until new infrastructure capacity is developed to meet the demands created by development (e.g., new or improved roads, more schools, greater water or sewer capacity);

3) timed or phased growth controls that limit the number of residential or commercial units that can be built during a specified period of time, perhaps in accordance with a point system favoring the least-burdensome projects;

4) unit caps or population caps, which limit the number of new residential units that can be built either on an annual basis or as an absolute cap for the jurisdiction;

5) urban growth boundaries, which limit or prohibit new development outside a geographically drawn area designated for urban growth or infrastructure service;

6) concurrency requirements that allow development if the developer can establish the available infrastructure (e.g., water supply; road traffic capacity) to support the development;

7) "Smart Growth" regulations that encourage or even require development to be mixed-use, amenable to pedestrian and mass-transit options, high-density, and located in the already-developed urban core;

8) environmental regulations that restrict development with harmful environmental impacts (e.g., conservation requirements for environmentally sensitive lands; stormwater runoff controls; green building requirements); and

9) use of existing permitting requirements and zoning designations by slow-growth or no-growth advocates to discourage or prevent new development.[32]

---

[32] See, e.g., Juergensmeyer & Roberts, Land Use Planning and Development Regulation Law, 2nd ed., § 9.2, pp. 324–28 (2007); Salkin, Squaring the Circle on Sprawl: What More Can We Do? Progress Toward Sustainable Land Use in the States, 16 Widener L.J. 787 (2007); Arnold, Norton, & Wallen, Kentucky Wet Growth Tools for Sustainable Development: A Handbook on Land Use and Water for Kentucky Communities (2009); Nolon, Open Ground: Effective Local Strategies for Protecting Natural Resources (2003); Ellickson, Suburban Growth Controls: An Economic and Legal Analysis, 86 Yale L.J. 385 (1977).

In general, growth controls have been upheld by courts.[33] In a landmark case, Golden v. Planning Board of Town of Ramapo,[34] regulations controlling the tempo of residential development according to a point system were upheld as a legitimate exercise of local planning and zoning powers. As discussed in Assignments 31–32, the U.S. Supreme Court held that there was no taking of private property by a temporary moratorium on all development to allow development regulations in the Lake Tahoe area to be created.[35]

Nonetheless, a particular municipality's growth control ordinance might raise issues about whether it is discriminating against newcomers and pushing growth (and its accompanying impacts) onto other municipalities in the region. The California Supreme Court took up these issues in Associated Home Builders of the Greater Eastbay, Inc. v. City of Livermore.[36] In upholding the City of Livermore's city-wide moratorium on any new residential building permits until its schools, sewer facilities, and water supply facilities met certain specified standards, the court rejected a "right to travel" claim by potential newcomers. In this regard, the court acknowledged that all land use regulations limit opportunities for immigration to a city and rejected an equal protection claim of discrimination against minorities and the poor, noting that the ordinance applied equally to both expensive and affordable housing development. However, the court applied the normally deferential "rational basis" test with some "bite" by adopting a "regional welfare" test that cities must meet to show that region-impacting growth controls (such as a total moratorium on all new residential development) are rationally related in fact to legitimate government purposes. This substantive due process test requires the court to determine whether the growth control reasonably relates to the regional, not merely local, welfare by evaluating: 1) the probable effect and duration of the restriction; 2) the competing interests affected by the restrictions; and 3) whether the ordinance represents a reasonable accommodation of the competing interests.

Would MHC have a good argument that a test like *Livermore* should be adopted and applied to its claim against the town of Oak Valley? How might *Livermore* be distinguished from MHC's situation?

4. *The effects of exclusionary zoning and concentrated poverty.* Florence Wagman Roisman, a noted scholar in the area of exclusionary zoning, has written extensively on this pervasive problem in our towns and cities. She argues that the federal government has, for many years, perpetuated racial segregation and encouraged "white flight" from the cities through its housing programs. Through mortgage assistance programs, site selection for lower income housing developments, and tenant selection for those developments, the federal government ensures that impoverished

---

[33] Juergensmeyer & Roberts, Land Use Planning and Development Regulation Law, 2nd ed., §§ 9.2 to 9.5, pp. 324–33 (2007).
[34] 285 N.E.2d 291 (N.Y. 1972).
[35] Tahoe-Sierra Preservation Council, Inc. v. Tahoe Regional Planning Agency, 535 U.S. 302 (2002), reprinted in Assignments 31–32, supra.
[36] 557 P.2d 473 (Cal. 1976).

minorities live separately from whites and in substandard conditions.[37] Additionally, private discrimination against racial minorities in sales and leasing of real estate, lending and mortgage insurance further entrench these societal divisions.

Professor Roisman suggests that the strengths of suburban communities are intricately tied to the strengths of the cities they surround. If the city disintegrates, the suburbs will eventually collapse. She argues that an affirmative effort to desegregate the existing urban public housing developments will work to the benefit of the urban centers and the outlying suburban areas.[38] For example, the suburban sprawl of most major urban areas damages the environment. As more people move further out from the urban centers, roads, sewers, power lines and other infrastructure needs are created. This expansion, in turn, destroys wildlife habitats, increases pollution and costs money. People who live in the suburbs face long commutes, higher taxes and rising levels of noise and air pollution. As the population continues to move outward, businesses that once provided jobs in the cities often relocate to the suburbs, taking valuable jobs with them. This perpetuates racial and economic segregation.

Professor Roisman suggests that integrating suburban public housing will provide the urban poor with an opportunity to move out of the cycle of poverty.[39] Inclusionary zoning in the suburbs provides those who have been traditionally disadvantaged with a chance to break free from poverty. She notes that ethnic groups who have migrated to the suburban developments experience higher graduation rates and better employment opportunities.

5. *Cleburne.* What is the standard of review in *Cleburne*? When will the courts be inclined to inquire about whether irrational fears and prejudices have motivated discriminatory zoning decisions?

6. *The Federal Fair Housing Act.* In *Arlington Heights*, the Supreme Court remanded the case for consideration of the claim that the failure to rezone violated the Fair Housing Act of 1968. 42 U.S.C. §§ 3601–3619, 3631. (Assignment 5 addresses this federal statute in the context of landlord motives in making rental decisions.) On remand, the Seventh Circuit held "that at least under some circumstances a violation of section 3604(a) can be established by a showing of a discriminatory effect without a showing of discriminatory intent."[40] After discussing the circumstances that would justify a finding of a violation of the Fair Housing Act, without proof of discriminatory intent, the court held that "if there is no land other than plaintiff's property within Arlington Heights which is both properly zoned and suitable for federally subsidized low-cost housing, the Village's refusal

---

[37] Roisman, The Role of the State, the Necessity of Race-Conscious Remedies, and Other Lessons from the Mount Laurel Study, 27 Seton Hall L. Rev. 1386 (1997); see also Roisman, The Lessons of American Apartheid: The Necessity and Means of Promoting Residential Racial Integration, 81 Iowa L. Rev. 479 (1995).

[38] Roisman, Sustainable Development in Suburbs and Their Cities: The Environmental and Financial Imperatives of Racial, Ethnic and Economic Inclusion, 3-Fall Widener L. Symp. J. 87 (1998).

[39] Id.

[40] Metropolitan Housing Development Corp. v. Village of Arlington Heights (Arlington Heights II), 558 F.2d 1283, 1290 (7th Cir. 1977), cert. denied, 434 U.S. 1025 (1978).

to rezone constituted a violation of section 3604(a). Accordingly, we remand the case to the district court for determination of this question."[41] On remand, the case was settled so that the Village would rezone an alternative site for low-income housing.[42]

Many recent decisions emphasize the "effects" test of *Arlington Heights II*.[43] Most notably, the U.S. Supreme Court held in 2015 that affected plaintiffs may bring disparate impact claims under the Fair Housing Act,[44] because Congress intended to allow such claims when it expressly made it illegal to "otherwise make unavailable" housing due to "race, color, religion, sex, familial status, or national origin."[45] The 5–4 majority opinion by Justice Anthony Kennedy in *Texas Department of Housing and Community Affairs v. Inclusive Communities Project* emphasizes that while disparate impact claims are actionable, the plaintiffs bear the burden of proving that statistical disparities are due to the policies or actions of the defendants, and defendant agencies or developers can rebut liability by showing a legitimate non-discriminatory purpose for their policies or actions.[46] The *Inclusive Communities* case and similar lower-court cases diminish the importance of *Arlington Heights I*, as a practical matter, because the Fair Housing Act's "effects" (or disparate impact) test is easier to prove than the Fourteenth Amendment's "purpose" test. In the Principal Problem, could MHC win by relying on the federal Fair Housing Act?

7. *Exclusionary zoning and the ADA*. The Americans With Disabilities Act[47] promises to be a powerful tool to prevent communities from using zoning powers to exclude the disabled. In 1997, the Second Circuit ruled that the ADA applied to municipal zoning practices in Innovative Health Systems, Inc. v. City of White Plains.[48] Prior to the enactment of the ADA,

---

[41] See 558 F.2d at 1294.

[42] Metropolitan Housing Development Corp. v. Village of Arlington Heights, 469 F. Supp. 836 (N.D.Ill.1979), aff'd, 616 F.2d 1006 (7th Cir.1980).

[43] See, e.g., Fair Housing in Huntington Comm. v. Town of Huntington, 316 F.3d 357 (2d Cir. 2003). Here, the plaintiffs alleged that the municipality's decision to allow a residential development solely for the elderly would discriminate against minorities. The court recognized the following two methods of showing a claim under the Federal Housing Act: disparate treatment or disparate impact. A disparate impact theory requires the plaintiff to demonstrate that a neutral practice actually or predictably has a discriminatory effect, but the plaintiff need not show any discriminatory intent. The defendant then has to show a legitimate, bona fide governmental interest and a lack of alternatives. The plaintiffs did not prevail on summary judgment due to issues of material fact as to whether a discriminatory effect existed and whether defendants had any alternatives to further the legitimate goal of providing needed housing for the elderly. See also Kushner, The Fair Housing Amendments Act of 1988: The Second Generation of Fair Housing, 42 Vand. L. Rev. 1049, 1074 ns. 97, 98 (1989). Professor Kushner notes that "Congress implicitly endorsed the effects test when it passed the Fair Housing Amendments Act of 1988 and rejected efforts to amend the bill to require an intent test." Id. at 1075.

[44] Texas Department of Housing and Community Affairs v. Inclusive Communities Project, 576 U.S. ___ (2015). The case involved allegations that state policies which concentrated affordable-housing tax credits in areas that already have low-income minority populations, instead of applying them to white suburban neighborhoods, had the disparate effect of perpetuating and exacerbating housing segregation by race and national origin.

[45] 42 U.S.C. § 3604(a).

[46] Id.

[47] 42 U.S.C. §§ 12101–12213.

[48] 117 F.3d 37 (2d Cir.1997).

disabled Americans could challenge exclusionary zoning laws under the Federal Fair Housing Amendment Act of 1988[49] (FHAA), as well as the Equal Protection Clause or the Due Process Clause of the U.S. Constitution.[50] However, the ADA adds significant protections to those already in existence under the FHAA and the U.S. Constitution.

The FHAA and the ADA provide disabled Americans with protected class status. This protected status significantly shortens the list of government justifications for burdening or denying services to people with disabilities. The Tenth Circuit ruled in Bangerter v. Orem City Corporation[51] that only direct threats to public health and safety will be considered rational and sufficient justifications for discriminatory housing or zoning laws. The ADA's purpose as determined by Congress is to eliminate discrimination against disabled people as well as to provide clear and enforceable guidelines for implementing this goal. Additionally, the ADA specifically states that the power of the federal government will be invoked to "address the major areas of discrimination faced day-to-day by people with disabilities."[52]

Can MHC establish a successful claim under the ADA, or do its proposed disabled tenants pose a significant threat to the Oak Valley community?

8. *Standing.* In the Principal Problem, does MHC have standing to represent minority individuals alleging that the rezoning was racially discriminatory and thus violative of the Equal Protection Clause of the Fourteenth Amendment?

---

[49] 42 U.S.C. §§ 3601–3631.

[50] See Bangerter v. Orem City Corporation, 46 F.3d 1491 (10th Cir.1995) (stating that the FHAA's protection of the disabled clearly extends to zoning practices); see also H.R. Rep. No. 100–711, 100th Cong., 2d Sess. 24 (1988) (stating that the FHAA "is intended to prohibit the application of special requirements through land-use regulations, restrictive covenants, and conditional or special use permits that have the effect of limiting the ability of [the handicapped] to live in the residence of their choice in the community.").

[51] 46 F.3d 1491, 1503 (10th Cir.1995).

[52] 42 U.S.C. § 12101(b)(1)–(4).

# ASSIGNMENT 34

# RELIGIOUS LAND USES

## 1. INTRODUCTION

Religious land uses pose a set of particular problems associated with the rights to use property and the government authority to regulate land use. Religious land uses implicate not only private property rights but also federal constitutional rights to the free exercise of religion, free speech and expression, and equal protection, as well as federal statutory protections for religious land uses.

A. *Growing conflicts over religious land uses.* Conflicts over religious land uses have grown in recent years. The reasons are many, and this Assignment can explore only some of the more notable causes of religious land use conflicts.

First, religious land uses simply receive less deference in local land use policy because religion plays a less dominant role in local civic culture than it did in many communities earlier in the nation's history. For example, neighbors are now more willing to complain about traffic and parking associated with neighborhood churches than they once had been.

Second, religious pluralism in the U.S. and in land uses has increased. Local officials are wrestling with permit applications for Islamic centers, Buddhist temples, Hmong festivals, or Santeria rituals involving animal sacrifices, and they may be reflecting biases against non-mainstream religions in their decisions.

Third, the types of uses that religious groups and institutions make of land have increased in variety and impact. Houses of worship or prayer may be accompanied by day care centers, schools, homeless shelters, food banks, group meeting space, and other non-worship but religious uses of the land. There has been a trend towards development of the "megachurch," which is a large multi-use church campus with substantial numbers of worshipers and users coming from throughout the region. Some religious land uses have chosen commercial, warehouse, or other sites for non-traditional styles of worship or for adaptation due to the costs and time delays of building new structures. In one situation, a Coptic Orthodox Church, after being denied variances to fit its theologically-mandated design on an irregularly shaped vacant lot, discovered that it could rehabilitate a former funeral home to meet its theological mandates and received a permit to convert the funeral home to a church.

Fourth, local units of government often face fiscal constraints: substantial expenditures for basic public services like police, fire, schools, and parks, but limited tax revenues. Therefore, local officials emphasize tax-generating and economy-stimulating land uses in their planning and regulatory decisions. Religious organizations and institutions are usually non-profit tax-exempt entities that may be occupying or planning to occupy land that could be used for more fiscally desirable land uses, in the eyes of local officials.

B. *The law in evolution.* The basic legal principles protecting religious adherents from government discrimination against religious land uses have gone through several iterations since the early 1960s. The five key developments in this ongoing evolution are described below:

1. *Sherbert.* In the 1963 case of Sherbert v. Verner,[1] the U.S. Supreme Court held that a government action that substantially burdens the free exercise of religion violates the First Amendment Free Exercise Clause unless it is the least restrictive means to advancing a compelling government interest.

2. *Smith.* In the 1990 case of Employment Division v. Smith,[2] the U.S. Supreme Court either overruled or severely narrowed *Sherbert.* In *Smith,* the respondents were fired from their jobs because they used peyote for sacramental purposes as part of the observance of a ceremony of the Native American Church. Subsequently, they were not granted unemployment compensation because they were determined to have been fired for "work-related 'misconduct'". The Oregon Supreme Court held that the state law, as applied to the respondents, violated the Free Exercise Clause. The Supreme Court reversed.

While the Court recognized that the Free Exercise Clause prohibits the government from enacting laws which ban activities only because of their religious motivation, the Court held that neutral laws of general applicability do not violate the Free Exercise Clause, even if they substantially burden the free exercise of religion by precluding religiously motivated conduct. According to the majority opinion, written by Justice Scalia, the only laws which have been invalidated under *Sherbert* had been in cases involving unemployment compensation, an area that lends itself to individualized government assessment of the reasons for the relevant conduct. The Court concluded that this test is inapplicable to free exercise challenges to general criminal prohibitions of particular conduct. Nor should the compelling state interest test be used only where the conduct prohibited allegedly is "central" to the individual's religious belief because the judiciary should not become involved in determining the centrality of particular religious beliefs. The majority viewed the political process as the appropriate venue

---

[1] 374 U.S. 398 (1963).
[2] 494 U.S. 872 (1990).

for protecting religious values, even though this resolution may disadvantage minority religious groups.

A concurring opinion by Justice O'Connor disagreed with the majority's analysis of the Free Exercise Clause but joined the Court's judgment, because, in the concurrence's view, the state has a compelling interest in regulating the use of peyote which would be thwarted by exempting the respondents from the law's application. A dissenting opinion by Justice Blackmun would have applied *Sherbert* in all free exercise cases, and also asserted that the state's interest in enforcing its drug laws was not sufficiently compelling to warrant interfering with the respondent's free exercise of religion.

3.  *RFRA*. In 1993, Congress enacted the Religious Freedom Restoration Act ("RFRA")[3] as a means of reversing the Supreme Court's decision in *Smith*. RFRA called for the application of the compelling state interest test whenever the federal or state government "substantially" burdened the free exercise of religion. Under RFRA, if the government was to survive a free exercise challenge, it had to show that the burden not only furthered "a compelling governmental interest" but also was "the least restrictive means of furthering that compelling governmental interest."

4.  *Boerne*. In 1997 the Supreme Court held RFRA unconstitutional in City of Boerne v. Flores.[4] In *Boerne,* the congregation of a Roman Catholic church in the City of Boerne, Texas had outgrown its facilities and requested a building permit to expand. The expansion necessitated that the façade of the church be altered. The church building itself had been designated as an historic landmark, so the City denied the building permit in the interest of preserving the historically valuable building. The Archbishop of the Church sued the City on several grounds, including a challenge under RFRA to the permit denial.

The trial court ruled in favor of the City, determining that RFRA exceeded the limits of Congress' powers under section 5 of the 14th Amendment. The Fifth Circuit reversed the trial court, holding that RFRA was constitutional. The U.S. Supreme Court agreed with the trial court and ruled in favor of the City. In an opinion by Justice Kennedy, the Court found that Congress had run far afield of its powers under section 5.

The church, supported by the United States as amicus curiae, argued that RFRA was constitutional because Congress only attempted to protect one of the "liberties guaranteed by the

---

[3]  42 U.S.C. § 2000bb–4.
[4]  521 U.S. 507 (1997).

14th Amendment" through legislation. The church further argued that Congress has the power to enact laws designed to pre-empt possible future constitutional violations, as well as to remedy existing violations.

The Supreme Court harbored serious concerns about the nature of RFRA itself. The Court refused to consider it as remedial or preventative legislation because the law appeared to "attempt a substantive change in constitutional protections."[5] The Court ruled that RFRA was unconstitutional, declaring that its reach and scope distinguished it from other measures passed under Congress' enforcement power.[6] The Court further noted that "[t]he stringent test that RFRA demands of state laws reflects a lack of proportionality or congruence between the means adopted and the legitimate end to be achieved."[7] Further, even if RFRA was interpreted to require a less stringent test such as intermediate scrutiny, it "nevertheless would require searching judicial scrutiny of state law with the attendant likelihood of invalidation. This is a considerable congressional intrusion into the States' traditional prerogatives and general authority to regulate for the health and welfare of their citizens."[8]

5. *RLUIPA*. Shortly following the decision in *Boerne*, Congress began work on a new version of RFRA, except the new version was designed to address the constitutionality issues raised in *Boerne*. The culmination of Congress' efforts, the Religious Land Use and Institutionalized Persons Act[9] (RLUIPA), was enacted in 2000. The statute contains two main provisions, the non-discrimination provision and the substantial burden provision. The latter is relevant to the issue of free exercise. To avoid RFRA's fate of unconstitutionality, Congress narrowly tailored the substantial burden provision of RLUIPA to apply only in areas where Congress has a recognized authority to act. Therefore, the Act applies in only three enumerated situations: 1) in connection with a federally funded activity; 2) where the burden affects interstate and foreign commerce; or 3) where the zoning scheme allows land use decisions to be made on an individual basis.[10] Once a land use decision falls under one of these three jurisdictional requirements, the standard of review imposed by RLUIPA is essentially the same as it was under RFRA. Specifically, before

---

[5] Id. at 532.
[6] Id.
[7] Id. at 533.
[8] Id. at 534.
[9] 42 U.S.C. § 2000cc.
[10] 42 U.S.C. § 2000cc(a)(2).

the government can undertake any action which imposes a substantial burden on the exercise of religion, it must prove that it has a compelling interest and cannot fulfill that interest in any other less intrusive way.[11]

RLUIPA also contains a second provision relating to land use regulations. This provision seeks to limit discriminatory actions against religious uses of land as laws that favor non-religious use over religious use. Additionally, RLUIPA forbids land use decisions which discriminate against certain religions and favor others. Thus, a scheme which favors some religions over others would most likely be in violation of this provision of RLUIPA. The last non-discrimination provision in RLUIPA forbids the exclusion of all religious use from a jurisdiction.[12]

Some judges have characterized the passage of RLUIPA as a "tug of war" between Congress and the Supreme Court.[13] Whether the Supreme Court will review RLUIPA in its entirety and whether the jurisdictional limits of RLUIPA will save it from a finding of unconstitutionality remains to be seen. Several courts have addressed the issue of whether RLUIPA is a constitutional exercise of Congressional power, and so far most have determined that the various land use sections of the statute are constitutional.[14] The U.S. Supreme Court has upheld the constitutionality of RLUIPA as it applies to prisoners' religious rights against a claim that the statute violates the Establishment Clause, but has not addressed its application to land use.[15]

C. *Four alternatives to Smith.* Religious adherents may be able to use any of four other theories to challenge land use regulations or decisions.

1. *Discrimination against a particular religion.* The *Smith* decision presumes the constitutionality of neutral laws of general applicability. However, government actions that intentionally discriminate against a particular religious group or belief violate the Free Exercise Clause unless they are narrowly tailored to serve a compelling government interest. Thus, when the City of Starkville, Mississippi, denied a land-

---

[11] 42 U.S.C. § 2000cc(a)(1).

[12] 42 U.S.C. § 2000cc(b)(1)–(3).

[13] See Elsinore Christian Ctr. v. City of Lake Elsinore, 291 F. Supp. 2d 1083, 1088 (C.D. Cal. 2003); Cottonwood Christian Ctr. v. Cypress Redevelopment Agency, 218 F. Supp. 2d 1203, 1220 (C.D. Cal. 2002).

[14] See, e.g., Midrash Sephardi, Inc. v. Town of Surfside, 366 F.3d 1214 (11th Cir. 2004); Life Teen, Inc. v. Yavapai County, 2003 WL 24224618 (D. Ariz. 2003); Charles v. Verhagen, 220 F. Supp. 2d 955 (W.D. Wis. 2002); Freedom Baptist Church v. Township of Middletown, 204 F. Supp. 2d 857 (E.D. Pa. 2002). But see Elsinore Christian Ctr. v. City of Lake Elsinore, 291 F. Supp. 2d 1083 (C.D. Cal. 2003) (striking down as unconstitutional the land use provisions as extending beyond commerce clause federal jurisdiction).

[15] Cutter v. Wilkinson, 544 U.S. 709 (2005).

use permit to an Islamic Center in the downtown area, despite having allowed numerous Christian churches in the area, its actions impermissibly favored some religious groups over others.[16] Likewise, in Church of Lukumi Babalu Aye, Inc. v. City of Hialeah,[17] the U.S. Supreme Court struck down a city's application of its zoning, public health, and animal cruelty ordinances to a Santeria group's ritual sacrifice of animals. Other practices with similar effects were not regulated, and the ordinance's use of religion-connoting terms like "ritual" and "sacrifice" evidenced a discriminatory animus against the Santeria religion.

2. *Hybrid rights.* In *Smith*, the Supreme Court noted in dicta that the First Amendment can be used as a bar to a "neutral, generally applicable law" when the Free Exercise Clause is violated in conjunction with other constitutional rights. The Court cited "freedoms of speech and of the press, or the right of parents to direct the education of their children" as examples. In Thomas v. Anchorage Equal Rights Commission,[18] plaintiffs successfully asserted such a hybrid rights claim. An Alaskan housing law prohibited apartment owners from discriminating against unmarried, cohabiting couples. The plaintiffs were a Christian couple who refused to rent to unmarried couples on the grounds that renting to such people violated their Free Exercise rights, their Fifth Amendment right to exclude others from their property and their free speech rights.

The *Thomas* court determined that the plaintiffs established a hybrid-rights claim because they proved colorable claims under the Takings Clause of the Fifth Amendment and the First Amendment's free speech guarantee. The court determined that heightened scrutiny was appropriate and considered whether Alaska's law placed a "substantial burden" on the plaintiffs' "observation of a central religious belief or practice." To survive the heightened scrutiny, Alaska had to show a "compelling government interest" to justify burdening the plaintiffs' constitutional rights. The Court did not find any of Alaska's justifications compelling, and upheld the district court's decision. Thus, Anchorage and the State of Alaska were permanently enjoined from enforcing the law against the plaintiffs because it violated a hybrid of constitutional rights.

The scope of the hybrid rights exemption to *Smith* is unclear and a subject of disagreement among the circuits. *Thomas* rejects the view that *Smith* requires the existence of an

---

[16] Islamic Center v. City of Starkville, 840 F.2d 293 (5th Cir. 1988).
[17] 508 U.S. 520 (1993).
[18] 165 F.3d 692 (9th Cir. 1999).

independently viable companion right in addition to free exercise. The *Thomas* court opted instead to require only that a plaintiff establish a "colorable claim" that a companion right has been violated.[19] In fact, the Ninth Circuit granted a rehearing en banc and the original opinion was withdrawn.[20] The federal court of appeals thereafter decided that the case was not ripe for review.[21] The plaintiffs re-filed in Alaskan state courts and subsequently lost in the Alaska State Supreme Court, which held the plaintiffs failed to distinguish their case from binding precedent.[22]

Since *Smith*, most of the federal circuits have recognized this hybrid rights exception;[23] however, there are differences in interpretations among the different circuits. Some circuits, such as the Third,[24] Sixth,[25] and Ninth,[26] suggest that a hybrid claim only occurs when a free exercise clause claim is brought in conjunction with a fundamental right or another right explicitly recognized by the Constitution. Furthermore, these circuits dismissed alleged hybrid claims when the two correlated rights are the free exercise of religion and freedom to associate as a religious organization.[27] Therefore, in the circuits which use such a standard, the current law suggests that the claims must be able to stand independently of one another. Other circuit courts approach the hybrid rights claim with caution and while they may not reject the claims outright, they consider the language in *Smith* as non-binding dicta.[28] Lastly, a few cases

---

[19] Id. at 703–07.

[20] 192 F.3d 1208 (9th Cir. 1999).

[21] Thomas v. Anchorage Equal Rights Comm'n, 220 F.3d 1134, 1142 (9th Cir. 2000).

[22] Thomas v. Anchorage Equal Rights Comm'n, 102 P.3d 937, 947 (Alaska, 2004).

[23] See Brown v. Hot, Sexy & Safer Prod., Inc., 68 F.3d 525 (1st Cir. 1995) (recognizing hybrid claim of free exercise in conjunction with parental right to direct upbringing of children); Chalifoux v. New Caney Indep. Sch. Dist., 976 F.Supp. 659 (S.D.Tex. 1997) (finding First Amendment violation by school dress code as hybrid claim of free speech and free exercise); Cornerstone Bible Church v. City of Hastings, 948 F.2d 464 (8th Cir. 1991) (recognizing hybrid rights claim in zoning case); Hinrichs v. Whitburn, 772 F.Supp. 423 (W.D. Wis. 1991) (acknowledging hybrid claim of free exercise and parental direction), aff'd 975 F.2d 1329 (7th Cir. 1992).

[24] Tenafly Eruv Ass'n v. Borough of Tenafly, 309 F.3d 144, 163 (3d Cir. 2002) (acknowledging that a hybrid rights claim may result in heightened scrutiny, but refusing to recognize a hybrid rights claim where a right to build a house of worship was alleged to fall under both freedom of speech as well as freedom of religious exercise).

[25] Vandiver v. Hardin County Bd. of Educ., 925 F.2d 927 (6th Cir. 1991) (recognizing hybrid rights analysis, but requiring that companion right be a cognizable constitutional right).

[26] Miller v. Reed, 176 F.3d 1202 (9th Cir. 1999) (recognizing hybrid claim jurisprudence but holding that companion claim must be a violation of a fundamental right).

[27] See Salvation Army v. Department of Community Affairs, 919 F.2d 183 (3d Cir. 1990) (acknowledging hybrid claim of free exercise and freedom to associate for religious purposes, but rejecting claim on grounds that the two claims are derivative).

[28] See Castle Hills First Baptist Church v. City of Castle Hills, 2004 WL 546792 (2004) (indicating that the court is reluctant to accept hybrid rights without specific instructions to do so from either the Fifth Circuit or the Supreme Court); Knight v. Connecticut Dep't of Pub. Health, 275 F.3d 156 (2d Cir. 2001) (stating that the language in *Smith* is dicta and refusing to

have recognized hybrid rights claims even in instances where the claims are related. However, these are a minority.[29]

3. *Equal protection, substantive due process, and irrational fears and prejudices.* In City of Cleburne v. Cleburne Living Center,[30] the U.S. Supreme Court applied the normally deferential "rational basis" test to strike down the denial of a permit for a group home for the mentally disabled as based on the irrational fears and prejudices of area residents and therefore an arbitrary and capricious government action in violation of the Equal Protection and Due Process Clauses. The case is reprinted in Assignment 33, supra. Under the right set of circumstances, a religious group might argue successfully that a zoning ordinance or the denial of a permit is irrationally based on prejudices, stereotypes, or biases against its religious beliefs or practices. However, if it could not succeed on such a claim, it would likely prevail on the clearer claim that the law or decision is not neutral but instead is motivated by discrimination against the particular religion in violation of the Free Exercise Clause.

4. *State constitutional and statutory rights.* Some state courts have interpreted their state's constitutional guarantees of religious freedom to prohibit government actions that substantially burden religious exercise.[31] In addition, some state legislatures have adopted religious freedom restoration acts that restrict state and local governments from substantially burdening religious exercises.[32] States are free to provide greater guarantees of religious freedom than the U.S. Constitution does, provided that they do not run afoul of the Establishment Clause.[33]

---

follow it without direction from the Supreme Court and holding that each claim should be examined individually).

[29] See Cornerstone Bible Church v. Hastings, 948 F.2d 464, 474 (8th Cir. 1991) (holding that a church might prove a hybrid rights case for a land use decision by showing a violation of free speech and equal protection).

[30] 473 U.S. 432 (1985).

[31] First Covenant Church of Seattle v. City of Seattle, 840 P.2d 174 (Wash. 1992) (application of landmarks preservation ordinance to a church exterior struck down not only on First Amendment but also on independent state constitutional grounds); The Society of Jesus of New England v. Boston Landmarks Comm'n, 564 N.E.2d 571 (Mass. 1990) (state constitutional religious freedom provision prohibited designation of church interior as landmark because it has integral religious meaning, in case arising when local landmarks regulator tried to prevent Jesuits from reconfiguring their historic altar).

[32] See, e.g., Laycock, State RFRAs and Land Use Regulation, 32 U.C. Davis L. Rev. 755 (1999); Hanson, Missouri's Religious Freedom Restoration Act: A New Approach to the Cause of Conscience, 69 Mo. L. Rev. 853 (2004).

[33] See, e.g., East Bay Asian Local Dev. Corp. v. State, 13 P.3d 1122 (Cal. 2000), cert. denied, 532 U.S. 1008 (2001) (upholding statutory exemption of church structures from landmark designation).

## 2. Principal Problem

The Menorah Synagogue is located in the city of Highland Park, in the midst of a quiet neighborhood known as Briarwood. In close proximity to the synagogue is a home for the elderly. The remaining area is residential. The synagogue is located on Hyacinth Street, a side street about three blocks from County Line Road, one of the city's main thoroughfares. All residents of the neighborhood must drive to County Line Road in order to go anywhere in the city from Briarwood. County Line Road is a very heavily traveled road, especially during rush hours (i.e., between 7:30—9:30 A.M. and 4:00—6:00 P.M.). Carlysle Road is the only street in the neighborhood leading directly to County Line Road. There is no traffic light at the corner of County Line Road and Carlysle Road. Thus, it is sometimes necessary for travelers to wait as long as ten minutes before traffic abates sufficiently in both directions on County Line Road to permit a left turn onto County Line Road.

Until the past couple of years, roughly 100 families belonged to the synagogue. About a quarter of these families live in Briarwood, which is walking distance to the synagogue. According to Orthodox Judaism, the use of automobiles is prohibited on the Jewish Sabbath (which begins at sundown on Friday and ends at sundown on Saturday) and other major holidays on which religious services are conducted. Virtually all of the families who live in walking distance to the Menorah Synagogue bought their homes because they wanted to live in walking distance to a synagogue so they could observe this significant aspect of Orthodox Jewish law. The other members of the synagogue live in more distant parts of Highland Park and the surrounding communities.

Recently, the Menorah Synagogue has undergone a significant growth spurt so that its membership now numbers about 200 families. Thus, traffic in the immediate area has increased considerably. The synagogue has decided to expand the building because the current physical facilities are inadequate for this number of congregants. The synagogue's plans for expansion also call for a new, larger parking lot so that members will no longer have to park on the side streets during times when the synagogue is crowded. In addition, the synagogue's Board of Directors wants to establish a day care center on the premises of the synagogue. According to their plan, the center will accommodate about one-hundred children, ages two through five. It will be in operation from 7:30 A.M. until 6:00 P.M. Directly behind the synagogue is a public park, which is used by residents of Briarwood as well as the members of Menorah. It is anticipated that the children attending the day care center will also use the park when the weather permits.

Due to advance advertising and the lack of any other Jewish day care centers in the immediate area, virtually all of the spots have been filled, even though the facilities have not yet been constructed. Of the 98 children signed up to enroll, 90 are Jewish and the parents of 40 of these children belong to Menorah. The children of families belonging to the synagogue did not receive any special priority in terms of enrollment. All enrollment has been, and will continue to be, on a first-come, first-serve basis. Although children of all religions and races are welcome to enroll, the content of the curriculum will stress Jewish laws and customs. The food served to the children will be strictly kosher (i.e., it will be prepared and served in accordance with the Jewish dietary laws). The center will be closed on all major Jewish holidays, but it will stay open until after sundown on Friday afternoons so that working parents do not necessarily have to leave early in the winter to pick up their children. The center also will be closed on Thanksgiving, Christmas, New Year's Day, Memorial Day, July 4th, and Labor Day.

In close proximity to the synagogue is a 100 person home for the elderly. The rest of the area is residential. Shortly after the synagogue's growth spurt, the city passed a zoning ordinance which provides that churches, synagogues, other places of worship and their accessory uses are allowed in the district only if a special use permit has been granted by the Zoning Board. The ordinance defines an accessory use as one that is: a) located on the same lot as the principal use, and b) "customary with and subordinate to" the principal use. In addition, the ordinance prohibits expansion of existing places of worship absent a special use permit. The ordinance directs the Zoning Board to base its special use permit decisions on whether the proposed use would substantially increase traffic and congestion, increase the danger of fire or otherwise endanger public safety, overcrowd the land, be consistent with the surrounding zoning and uses, unduly burden the water, sewer, park or other public facilities, or otherwise adversely affect the public health, safety, morals or general welfare.

When Menorah applied for a special use permit to expand its facilities to accommodate its new members and the proposed day care center, the Zoning Board denied its request based on two zoning ordinances. Initially relying on the above zoning ordinance, the city cited the following reasons for refusing to issue the special use permit: the increased noise, traffic, congestion, and drain on public facilities which the increased membership and day care facility would cause to the Briarwood neighborhood. In addition, the Zoning Board called the synagogue's attention to a second city zoning ordinance that has been in effect for many years which permits only public schools and private elementary schools in the district in which Menorah is located. If the Zoning Board's decision is allowed to stand, Menorah will be forced to relocate its facilities. Because undeveloped land is at a premium in Highland Park, the only other alternative site for the synagogue is an abandoned school located near a heavy commercialized area. The only residences which are in walking distance to this alternative site are a couple of small, low-income apartment complexes.

On what legal grounds can Menorah contest the Board's decision with respect to both the expansion and the day care center? Evaluate Menorah's chances for success on each legal ground regarding both aspects of the Board's denial.

## 3. MATERIALS FOR SOLUTION OF PRINCIPAL PROBLEM

### Messiah Baptist Church v. County of Jefferson, State of Colorado

United States Court of Appeals, Tenth Circuit, 1988.
859 F.2d 820.

■ BRORBY, CIRCUIT JUDGE.

The Messiah Baptist Church and various individuals representing a class ("Church") filed an action for damages under 42 U.S.C. § 1983 against Jefferson County, Colorado, and its Board of Commissioners ("County"). The Church contends the zoning regulations enacted by the County are facially unconstitutional under the Due Process Clause of the Fourteenth Amendment and the Free Exercise Clause of the First Amendment.

Both parties moved for summary judgment below. The district court upheld the constitutionality of the zoning regulations, granted the County's motion and denied the Church's motion for summary judgment. From this order the Church appeals.

In July 1974, the Church purchased approximately eighty acres of vacant land in Jefferson County, Colorado. The land was located in an area of the County which was zoned Agricultural Two District (A-2). The A-2 zoning district allowed general ranching, intensive agricultural use, and agriculturally related uses while protecting the surrounding land from harmful results. Land in the A-2 zoning district could be used for dwellings, barns, stables, poultry hatcheries, dairy farms, greenhouses, roadside stands, feedlots, feeding garbage to hogs, veterinarian hospitals, and the storage of manure and related uses. Land in the A-2 zoning district could not be used for schools, community buildings, and churches, even as special uses.

In 1974, the zoning regulations provided for twenty-five zoning districts. Sixteen of these districts authorized a residential use in some form. Of the sixteen zoning districts authorizing residential uses, thirteen specifically authorized a church use as a matter of right. The remaining nine zoning districts were devoted to agricultural, commercial, and industrial uses and did not allow residential uses of any type. With the exception of zoning districts A-1 and A-2, a church was an authorized use by right in every zoning district which authorized permanent residential use.

Two years later, in July 1976, the County amended the A-2 zoning regulations to authorize church uses by special-use permit, subject to approval by the planning commission and the County. Shortly after this amendment, the Church filed an application for a special-use permit indicating an intent to develop its entire eighty acres. The Church subsequently withdrew this application.

In April 1978, the Church again applied for a special-use permit, this time to build a 12,000 square foot structure to be used for worship services, administrative offices, classrooms, recreation (gymnasium) purposes, parking areas for 151 vehicles, and an "amphitheater" where worshipers could park and, without leaving their cars, listen to religious services through means of individual sound transmission devices similar to those used by "drive-in" movie theaters.

In May 1978, a public hearing was held before the planning commission concerning the Church's second application for a special-use permit. The planning commission denied the special-use permit, reduced to writing the nine reasons for the denial, which included access problems, erosion hazards, and the fact that fire protection for the site was wholly inadequate.

*Due Process*

The Church argues that the 1974 A-2 regulations are unconstitutional on their face because they deprive the Church of the right to use its property in violation of the Due Process Clause of the Fourteenth Amendment.

The principal test for measuring the constitutionality of a zoning ordinance under the Due Process Clause is set forth in *Village of Euclid, Ohio v. Ambler Realty Co.*, 272 U.S. 365, 47 S.Ct. 114, 71 L.Ed. 303 (1926). In this case, the owner of a sixty-eight acre tract of vacant land sought to use his land for industrial purposes. The city zoned a portion of the sixty-eight acres for residential uses, and the owner attacked the ordinances on due process grounds. The Supreme Court upheld the zoning ordinances and stated that before a zoning ordinance can be declared unconstitutional on due process grounds, the provisions must be clearly arbitrary and unreasonable, having no substantial relation to the public health, safety, morals, or general welfare. *Id.* at 395, 47 S.Ct. at 121. The Court further held that if the validity of the land classification is "fairly debatable," the legislative judgment must control.

The Church seems to contend first that the A-2 zoning regulations are arbitrary because they permit dwellings but exclude churches from the agricultural district. The Church cites numerous state court decisions including *City of Englewood v. Apostolic Christian Church*, 146 Colo. 374, 362 P.2d 172 (1961), purportedly holding that exclusion of churches from residential areas constitutes arbitrary action. (It should be noted that *Englewood* was overruled in part, *City of Colorado Springs v. Blanche*, 761 P.2d 212 (Colo.1988), after the briefs were filed.) The state court cases cited by the Church are distinguishable on the facts from the case now before us. In *Englewood,* the regulations excluded churches as a use by right from all residential zone districts except the multifamily district. In the instant case, however, the regulations permit church use as a use by right in all but three residential districts. Consequently, the zoning scheme is clearly distinguishable.

Even if *Englewood* factually were on point, other state cases hold that the exclusion of churches from residential zoning districts is constitutionally permissible. *See Corporation of Presiding Bishop of Church of Jesus Christ of Latter-Day Saints v. City of Porterville*, 90 Cal.App.2d 656, 203 P.2d 823, *appeal dismissed*, 338 U.S. 805, 70 S.Ct. 78, 94 L.Ed. 487 (1949). In our view, the better reasoned state court decisions hold that exclusion of churches from particular zoning districts, whether agricultural or residential, is not arbitrary *per se*.

The Church next argues that the A-2 regulations are arbitrary because they exclude churches but permit large agriculturally related commercial uses in the agricultural district. The Church contends that these commercial uses are at least as intensive as those uses proposed by the Church. In our view, however, the fact that the County's regulatory scheme is one of true differentiation does not render it arbitrary. The agricultural zones permit true and unfettered agricultural uses, and the decision as to what is or is not a compatible use therein is a decision which belongs to the legislative body. If the validity of the legislative classification is "fairly debatable," the legislative judgment must control. *Euclid*, 272 U.S. at 388, 47 S.Ct. at 118. The Church has not established that the County's choice of compatible uses is unreasonable.

Finally, the Church asserts the court must review the due process challenge to the A-2 zoning regulations under the strict scrutiny standard rather than the reasonable relationship standard because the zoning regulation infringes the Church's First Amendment rights to exercise a religious preference. The Church further contends that the burden, therefore, is upon the parties seeking to uphold the regulation to demonstrate that it serves a compelling state interest and is narrowly drawn to address only the state interests at stake. *Schad v. Borough of Mount Ephraim*, 452 U.S. 61, 101 S.Ct. 2176, 68 L.Ed.2d 671 (1981).

In the instant case, however, the Church has not been denied the right to exercise a religious preference. Rather, the Church has been denied a building permit, and may not construct its house of worship where it pleases. That fact standing alone does not amount to a denial of the exercise of a religious preference. (See discussion of Free Exercise of Religion within.)

The record contains no evidence that the zoning regulations infringe upon *any* protected liberty. The A-2 zoning regulations affect only property interests and, therefore, need only bear a substantial relationship to the general welfare. *Euclid*, 272 U.S. at 391, 395, 47 S.Ct. at 119, 120. There can be little doubt that the zoning regulations bear a substantial relationship to the general welfare of the residents of Jefferson County. There is nothing arbitrary or unreasonable about precluding the building of a church near a feedlot or near hogs rooting through garbage. We hold that the 1974 A-2 zoning regulations are valid under the Due Process Clause.

*Free Exercise of Religion*

The Church contends that the 1974 A-2 zoning regulations are invalid on their face because they preclude the Church from building a house of worship on its property located within the A-2 zoning district. This court approaches the issue mindful of the often competing values of free exercise of religion and effective use by the state of its police powers. "[W]hen entering the area of religious freedom, we must be fully cognizant of the particular protection that the Constitution has accorded it. Abhorrence of religious persecution and intolerance is a basic part of our heritage." *Braunfeld v. Brown,* 366 U.S. 599, 606, 81 S.Ct. 1144, 1147, 6 L.Ed.2d 563 (1961). On the other hand, in *Schad,* 452 U.S. at 68, 101 S.Ct. at 2182, the Court stated: "The power of local governments to zone and control land use is undoubtedly broad and its proper exercise is an essential aspect of achieving a satisfactory quality of life in both urban and rural communities." To complicate matters, we analyze the issue against a fluid precedent. As the Eleventh Circuit observed, "[i]nterpretation and application of the free exercise clause has created, within that field of constitutional doctrine, areas dotted by unanswered questions." *Grosz v. City of Miami Beach, Fla.,* 721 F.2d 729, 733 (11th Cir.1983), *cert. denied,* 469 U.S. 827, 105 S.Ct. 108, 83 L.Ed.2d 52 (1984). We seek to approach the issue with sensitivity to the many evolving standards applicable to the case.

From 1974 to present, the A-2 zoning regulations did not permit church uses by right. In 1976, the County amended the A-2 regulations to allow the church uses upon approval of a special-use permit. In 1978, the Church applied for a special-use permit which was denied after a public hearing. Consequently, the Church was unable to construct its house of worship on its property located within the A-2 zoning district.

The first question to be addressed is whether the A-2 zoning regulations regulate religious beliefs. If they regulate religious beliefs, as opposed to religious conduct, then the regulations are unconstitutional. "[T]he [First] Amendment embraces two concepts, freedom to believe and freedom to act. The first is absolute. . . ." *Cantwell v. Connecticut,* 310 U.S. 296, 303, 60 S.Ct. 900, 903, 84 L.Ed. 1213 (1940). Courts consistently distinguish religious beliefs from religious conduct. "The belief/conduct distinction has survived." *Grosz,* 721 F.2d at 733 n. 5. As to what constitutes regulation of beliefs, the Supreme Court recently quoted from *Sherbert v. Verner,* 374 U.S. 398, 412, 83 S.Ct. 1790, 1798, 10 L.Ed.2d 965 (1963), and reiterated the concept that the free exercise clause prohibits the government from *coercing* the individual to violate his beliefs, and further stated: "The Free Exercise Clause is written in terms of what the government cannot do to the individual, not in terms of what the individual can exact from the government." *Lyng v. Northwest Indian*

*Cemetery Protective Ass'n,* 108 S.Ct. 1319, 99 L.Ed.2d 534 (1988). One of the clear points of precedent is that the government may not use its power to interfere with or regulate the individual's religious beliefs.

The A-2 zoning regulations do not in any way regulate the religious beliefs of the Church. Nothing in the record shows any friction between the religious beliefs of the Church and the zoning regulations. Consequently, we proceed to the next inquiry.

Do the regulations impermissibly regulate religious conduct? Generally speaking, the government may regulate religious conduct. "It is true that activities of individuals, even when religiously based, are often subject to regulation by the States in the exercise of their undoubted power to promote the health, safety, and general welfare, or the Federal Government in the exercise of its delegated powers." *Wisconsin v. Yoder,* 406 U.S. 205, 220, 92 S.Ct. 1526, 1535, 32 L.Ed.2d 15 (1972). However, conduct flowing from religious beliefs merits protection when shown to be integrally related to underlying religious beliefs. In *Yoder,* the Court explained: "[W]e see that the record in this case abundantly supports the claim that the traditional way of life of the Amish is not merely a matter of personal preference, but one of deep religious conviction, shared by an organized group, and intimately related to daily living." *Id.* at 216, 92 S.Ct. at 1533.

By contrast, the record in our case discloses no evidence that the construction of a house of worship on the property in the A-2 zoning district is integrally related to underlying religious beliefs of the Church. The Church argues that constructing its house of worship is intimately bound to its religious tenets. As an abstract argument, this proposition is true. The evidence in the record, however, fails to establish any basis for this contention. The Church makes only a vague reference to a preference for a pastoral setting, but such is of no consequence to this analysis. What is important is that the record contains no evidence that building a church or building a church on the particular site is intimately related to the religious tenets of the church. At most, the record discloses the Church's preference is to construct its house of worship upon its land. We agree with the observation of the Sixth Circuit in *Lakewood, Ohio Congregation of Jehovah's Witnesses, Inc. v. City of Lakewood, Ohio,* 699 F.2d 303, 307, *cert. denied,* 464 U.S. 815, 104 S.Ct. 72, 78 L.Ed.2d 85 (1983), that "building and owning a church is a desirable accessory of worship, not a fundamental tenet of the Congregation's religious beliefs." In short, under the facts of this case, the A-2 zoning regulations do not regulate any religious conduct of the church or its members.

We must also consider whether the zoning regulations place *any* burden on the free exercise of appellant's religion. "If the purpose or effect of the law is to impede the observance of one or all religions or is to discriminate invidiously between religions, that law is constitutionally invalid even though the burden may be characterized as being only indirect." *Braunfeld,* 366 U.S. at 607, 81 S.Ct. at 1148. In our case, the record reveals that neither the purpose nor the effect of the zoning regulations is to impede observance or discriminate between religions. Regulation of the location of church construction is not an impediment to religious observance in the sense of a prohibition. Arguably, the zoning regulations affect secular activity and make the practice of religion more expensive, and therefore impose an indirect burden on the exercise of religion. Even assuming that the effect of the regulations is to add expense to the practice of religion, this indirect burden does not invalidate the zoning regulations if the state cannot accomplish its purpose by means which do not impose such a burden. *Id.* at 607, 81 S.Ct. at 1148. In holding that the zoning ordinance which did not permit church buildings within a particular zoning district did not infringe the Congregation's freedom of religion, the *Lakewood* court simply characterized construction as a secular activity which made the practice of religious beliefs more expensive. The court then observed that the ordinance did not pressure the Congregation to abandon its religious beliefs through financial or criminal penalties, and does not "tax" the exercise of religion. *Lakewood,* 699 F.2d at 307.

While we do not fully adopt the approach of the court in *Lakewood* (*Lakewood* assumes *Braunfeld* created a presumption of validity for governmental actions that impose only an indirect burden), we agree that the financial consequences to the church do not rise to infringement of religious freedom. As the court stated in *Lakewood, id.* at 307, "the First Amendment does not require the City to make all land or even the cheapest or most beautiful land available to churches." We agree.

Our inquiry, however, goes beyond *Lakewood*. Under *Braunfeld*, as explained in *Sherbert,* 374 U.S. at 398, 83 S.Ct. at 1790, and *Thomas v. Review Bd. of the Ind. Employment Sec. Div.*, 450 U.S. 707, 101 S.Ct. 1425, 67 L.Ed.2d 624 (1981), we consider whether an alternative means exists whereby the County may accomplish its purpose by means which do not impose an indirect burden. Without question, the zoning district plan, one of true differentiation and upheld as sound under the due process analysis, cannot be implemented effectively without the resulting financial burden on the Church. When the burden imposed by the government rests on conduct rooted only in secular philosophy or personal preference, however, the scale always reads in favor of upholding the government action. *Grosz,* 721 F.2d at 737. Since the governmental action of adopting and implementing the zoning regulations does not affect religious practice, the indirect burden does not render the zoning regulations constitutionally infirm.

We hold that the 1974 Jefferson County A-2 zoning regulations do not violate the Church's First Amendment rights. We do not hold that the act of building is *per se* that of secular conduct. We limit our holding to the record before us; a record which shows no conflict between the zoning ordinances and the religious tenets or practices of this Church. This is not a case where the church must choose between criminal penalties or foregoing government benefits and its religious benefits such as is apparent in *Yoder,* 406 U.S. at 218, 92 S.Ct. at 1534, or *Sherbert,* 374 U.S. at 404, 83 S.Ct. at 1794. This case does not involve the compromise of the Church's fundamental tenets such as was involved in *Heffron v. Int'l Soc'y for Krishna Consciousness, Inc.,* 452 U.S. 640, 101 S.Ct. 2559, 69 L.Ed.2d 298 (1981). In short, there is no infringement of the Church's religious freedom. A church has no constitutional right to be free from reasonable zoning regulations nor does a church have a constitutional right to build its house of worship where it pleases. *Lemon v. Kurtzman,* 403 U.S. 602, 91 S.Ct. 2105, 29 L.Ed.2d 745 (1971).

The judgment of the district court is Affirmed.

## Civil Liberties for Urban Believers v. City of Chicago
Court of Appeals, Seventh Circuit, 2003.
342 F.3d 752.

■ BAUER, J.

Appellants, an association of Chicago-area churches and five individual member churches thereof, appeal from the district court's entry of summary judgment in favor of Appellee, the City of Chicago, on Appellants' claims challenging the Chicago Zoning Ordinance ("CZO"), 17 Municipal Code of Chicago, Ill., §§ 1–11, under the federal Religious Land Use and Institutionalized Persons Act ("RLUIPA"), 42 United States Code § 2000cc et seq., and the United States Constitution. For the reasons set forth below, we affirm the decision of the district court.

BACKGROUND

The CZO broadly divides the city into R, B, C, and M zones for residential, business, commercial, and manufacturing uses, respectively. Each zone, in turn, is subdivided into numbered districts and subdistricts. A majority of Chicago land available for development is zoned R. The CZO's stated purposes include the following: (i) "to promote and to protect the public health, safety, morals, comfort, convenience, and the general welfare of the people," and (ii) "to protect the character and maintain the stability for residential, business, commercial, and manufacturing areas within the City, and to promote the orderly and beneficial development of such areas." See 17 Mun. Code Chi. § 2(1), (3)(2001). Churches are permitted uses as of right in all R zones, but are termed Variations in the Nature of Special Uses ("Special Use") in all B zones as well as C1, C2, C3, and C5 districts. All Special Uses, whether of a religious or nonreligious nature, require approval by the Zoning Board of Appeals ("ZBA") following a public hearing. Special Use approval is expressly conditioned upon the design, location, and operation of the proposed use consistent with the protection of public health, safety, and welfare, and the proposed use must not substantially injure the value of neighboring property. Factoring such expenses as application, title search, and legal fees, as well as appraisal and neighbor notification costs, the aggregate cost of obtaining Special Use approval approaches $5000. Before a church may locate in a C4 district or an M zone, the Chicago City Council must vote in favor of a Map Amendment, effectively rezoning the targeted parcel. Development for church use of land consisting of two or more acres (necessary for congregations exceeding roughly 500 members) requires approval by City Council vote of a Planned Development.

Civil Liberties for Urban Believers ("CLUB") is an unincorporated association of 40 to 50 Chicago-area religious or not-for-profit Illinois corporations ranging in size from 15 to 15,000 congregants. Five of these individual member churches joined CLUB as plaintiffs in an action challenging the validity of the CZO.

This appeal from the district court's summary judgment ruling in favor of Chicago on Appellants' fourth amended complaint reaches us via a long and tortuous procedural path. Appellants amended their original complaint to remove claims challenging the CZO under the federal Religious Freedom Restoration Act, 42 U.S.C.2000bb et seq. ("RFRA"), after the Supreme Court invalidated relevant provisions of RFRA in City of Boerne v. Flores, 521 U.S. 507, 117 S.Ct. 2157, 138 L.Ed.2d 624 (1997). In February 2000, in response to Appellants' remaining constitutional challenges to the CZO's designation of churches vis-à-vis various nonreligious assembly uses in B, C, and M zones, the City Council amended the CZO to require clubs, lodges, meeting halls, recreation buildings, and community centers to obtain Special Use approval in order to locate within any B and C zones and a Map Amendment in order to locate within any M zone. The amendments also (i) exempt churches from the requirement that a Special Use applicant affirmatively demonstrate that the proposed use "is necessary for the public convenience at that location" and (ii) provide that a Special Use permit shall automatically issue in the event that the ZBA fails to render a decision within 120 days of the date of application. Several months thereafter, Congress reacted to the Supreme Court's decision in City of Boerne with the enactment of RLUIPA and Appellants subsequently amended their complaint once more to include claims against Chicago pursuant to RLUIPA.

In addition to the RLUIPA claim, Appellants' final amended complaint argued, in part, that the CZO and the administrative and legislative processes for obtaining Special Use, Map Amendment, and Planned Development approval violate Appellants' rights to (i) free exercise of religion, speech, and assembly under the First Amendment of the United States Constitution, (ii) equal protection under the Fourteenth Amendment of the United States Constitution as well as the Illinois Constitution, and (iii) procedural due process under the Fourteenth Amendment of the United States Constitution.

In granting summary judgment in favor of Chicago, the district court determined that the February 2000 amendments to the CZO removed "any potential substantial burden" on religious exercise, 42 U.S.C.

§ 2000cc–3(e). With respect to Appellants' equal protection claims, the district court concluded that Chicago's zoning scheme is rationally related to a legitimate government purpose and thus constitutional. The district court also rejected Appellants' due process claims, noting that City Council and ZBA legislative procedures and practices afforded Appellants what minimal process is due in zoning cases. In its discussion of Appellants' First Amendment claims, the district court explained that the CZO and its Special Use provisions are neutral and generally applicable law which do not impermissibly burden the free exercise of religion, and that the operation of a church is subject to zoning laws, even where such operation involves conduct within the core of the First Amendment—here, religious speech and assembly.

ANALYSIS

We review the district court's grant of summary judgment de novo. Summary judgment is proper where there is no genuine issue as to any material fact. Such is the case where the nonmoving party has failed to make a sufficient showing on an essential element of his case with respect to which he has the burden of proof, because a complete failure of proof concerning an essential element of his case necessarily renders all other facts immaterial. In such a case, the moving party is entitled to judgment as a matter of law and summary judgment must issue against the nonmoving party.

I.  Religious Land Use and Institutionalized Persons Act

Appellants argue that the CZO violates RLUIPA's substantial burden provision, which requires land-use regulations that substantially burden religious exercise to be the least restrictive means of advancing a compelling government interest, see 42 U.S.C. § 2000cc(a), as well as its nondiscrimination provision, which prohibits land-use regulations that either disfavor religious uses relative to nonreligious uses or unreasonably exclude religious uses from a particular jurisdiction, see 42 U.S.C. § 2000cc(b).

In order to prevail on a claim under the substantial burden provision, a plaintiff must first demonstrate that the regulation at issue actually imposes a substantial burden on religious exercise. RLUIPA defines "religious exercise" to encompass "any exercise of religion, whether or not compelled by, or central to, a system of religious belief," including "[t]he use, building, or conversion of real property for the purpose of religious exercise." 42 U.S.C. § 2000cc–5(7). Although the text of the statute contains no similar express definition of the term "substantial burden," RLUIPA's legislative history indicates that it is to be interpreted by reference to RFRA and First Amendment jurisprudence. We therefore hold that in the context of RLUIPA's broad definition of religious exercise, a land-use regulation that imposes a substantial burden on religious exercise is one that necessarily bears direct, primary, and fundamental responsibility for rendering religious exercise—including the use of real property for the purpose thereof within the regulated jurisdiction generally—effectively impracticable.

Appellants contend that the scarcity of affordable land available for development in R zones, along with the costs, procedural requirements, and inherent political aspects of the Special Use, Map Amendment, and Planned Development approval processes, impose precisely such a substantial burden. However, we find that these conditions—which are incidental to any high-density urban land use—do not amount to a substantial burden on religious exercise. While they may contribute to the ordinary difficulties associated with location (by any person or entity, religious or nonreligious) in a large city, they do not render impracticable the use of real property in Chicago for religious exercise, much less discourage churches from locating or attempting to locate in Chicago. Significantly, each of the five individual plaintiff churches has successfully located within Chicago's city limits. That they expended considerable time and money so to do does not entitle them to relief under RLUIPA's substantial burden provision. Otherwise, compliance with RLUIPA would require municipal governments not merely to treat religious land uses on an equal footing with nonreligious land uses, but rather to favor them in the form of an outright exemption from land-use regulations. Unfortunately for Appellants, no such free pass for religious land uses masquerades among the legitimate protections RLUIPA affords to religious exercise.

Though the substantial burden and nondiscrimination provisions are operatively independent of one another, RLUIPA's governmental discretion provision, 42 U.S.C. § 2000cc–3(e), upon which the district court relied in order to find that the February 2000 CZO amendments corrected any violation of the substantial burden provision, appears not to reflect this distinction. That subsection provides, in part, that "a government may avoid the preemptive force of any provision of [RLUIPA] by changing the policy or practice that results in a substantial burden on religious exercise." 42 U.S.C. § 2000cc–3(e). Rather than remove any substantial burden on religious exercise, however, the February 2000 amendments simply place churches on an equal footing with nonreligious assembly uses, thereby correcting any potential violation of the nondiscrimination provision. Despite subsection 2000cc–3(e)'s reference to removal of a "substantial burden," we read it to afford a government the discretion to take corrective action to eliminate a nondiscrimination provision violation, whether or not it was the result of a substantial burden on religious exercise. Thus do we find that, under RLUIPA's governmental discretion provision, the February 2000 amendments to the CZO render RLUIPA's nondiscrimination provision inapplicable to this case.

Insofar as Appellants cannot demonstrate on these facts that the CZO substantially burdens religious exercise, and because the February 2000 Amendments to the CZO bring it into compliance with RLUIPA's nondiscrimination provision, Appellants fail to make a sufficient showing on essential elements of their RLUIPA claims. Chicago is therefore entitled to summary judgment on those claims.

Having found RLUIPA inapplicable to the facts of this case, we need not address the issue of RLUIPA's constitutionality, raised by the parties as well as the United States of America, as Intervenor, and various Amici Curiae.

II. Constitutionality of the Chicago Zoning Ordinance

Under the Free Exercise Clause of First Amendment of the United States Constitution, made applicable to state and local governments by the Fourteenth Amendment, no law may prohibit the free exercise of religion. Prior to RLUIPA's enactment, two Supreme Court decisions held that no Free Exercise Clause violation results where a burden on religious exercise is the incidental effect of a neutral, generally applicable, and otherwise valid regulation, in which case such regulation need not be justified by a compelling governmental interest. Employment Division, Department of Human Resources of Oregon v. Smith, 494 U.S. 872, 110 S.Ct. 1595, 108 L.Ed.2d 876 (1990); Church of the Lukumi Babalu Aye, Inc. v. City of Hialeah, 508 U.S. 520, 113 S.Ct. 2217, 124 L.Ed.2d 472 (1993). Appellants cite Smith and Hialeah as additional authority for application of the compelling governmental interest and least restrictive means tests to the CZO, not unlike those urged under RLUIPA.

Appellants first argue that the CZO lacks facial neutrality because, like the law at issue in *Hialeah*, the CZO "refers to a religious practice"—use of property as a church—"without a secular meaning discernable from the language or context." 508 U.S. at 530, 113 S.Ct. 2217. In that case, the City of Hialeah reacted to the intention of practitioners of the Santería religion to establish a church within city limits by passing ordinances banning public ritual sacrifice, a distinguishing element of the Santería religious tradition. The Court explained that a law is not neutral if its object "is to infringe upon or restrict practices because of their religious motivation," and then found that the Hialeah ordinances' use of the words "sacrifice" and "ritual", which have "strong religious connotations," was evidence of their purposeful targeting of Santería practices. Appellants assert by analogy that the CZO's explicit inclusion of "church" among the various land uses it regulates indicates that it discriminates against churches on its face. Unlike the Hialeah ordinances, however, the text of the CZO includes "church" as just one among many and varied religious and nonreligious regulated uses. More importantly, nothing in the record suggests, nor do Appellants articulate in anything but conclusory terms, that the object and purpose of the CZO are anything other than those expressly stated therein.

Appellants also contend that the CZO is not generally applicable, in that the Special Use, Map Amendment, and Planned Development processes create discretionary, individualized exemptions to the CZO which are then impermissibly withheld from churches. As support for this proposition, they cite the Supreme Court's pronouncement that "[i]n circumstances in which individualized exemptions from a general requirement are available, the government 'may not refuse to extend that system to cases of "religious hardship" without compelling reason.'" *Hialeah*, 508 U.S. at 537, 113 S.Ct. 2217 (quoting Smith, 494 U.S. at 884, 110 S.Ct. 1595 (citation omitted)). Even assuming, arguendo, that the burdens incidental to churches seeking Special Use, Map Amendment, or Planned Development approval amount to "religious hardship" within the meaning of the Court's decision in Hialeah, Appellants appear to confuse exemption from a particular zoning provision (in the form of Special Use, Map Amendment, or Planned Development approval) with exemption from the procedural system by which such approval may be sought. Under the CZO, these alternate avenues of zoning approval are not merely available to any would-be applicant, as Hialeah requires. They are mandatory. In short, no person, nor any nonconforming land use, is exempt from the procedural system in place for Special Use, Map Amendment, or Planned Development approval specifically, or the CZO generally.

In Smith, the Supreme Court noted that, in cases implicating the Free Exercise Clause in conjunction with other constitutional protections, such as freedom of speech and freedom of association, the First Amendment may subject the application to religiously motivated action of a neutral, generally applicable law to a heightened level of scrutiny. Seizing upon this principle, Appellants maintain that their Free Exercise claim involves hybrid rights of free exercise, freedom of speech, freedom of assembly, and equal protection, such that Chicago must justify the CZO's incidental burdens on church location with a compelling state interest. Based on the analyses of Appellants' speech, assembly, and equal protection claims that follow, however, we find them individually lacking the merit necessary to withstand summary judgment. We agree with the Court of Appeals for the Ninth Circuit that "a plaintiff does not allege a hybrid rights claim entitled to strict scrutiny analysis merely by combining a free exercise claim with an utterly meritless claim of the violation of another alleged fundamental right." Miller v. Reed, 176 F.3d 1202, 1207–08 (9th Cir.1999). Appellants have identified no constitutionally protected interest upon which the CZO infringes, as they must in order to establish a hybrid rights claim requiring heightened scrutiny.

Appellants further argue that the CZO violates the Equal Protection Clause of the Fourteenth Amendment—which provides that no state shall "deny to any person within its jurisdiction the equal protection of the laws"—by treating churches in a manner less favorable than that of nonreligious assembly uses. It is the well established law of this Circuit that, "[a]bsent a fundamental right or a suspect class, to demonstrate a viable equal protection claim in the land use context, a plaintiff must demonstrate governmental action wholly impossible to relate to legitimate governmental objectives." Forseth v. Village of Sussex, 199 F.3d 363, 370–71 (7th Cir.2000). Appellants urge us to elevate the level of scrutiny under which we review their equal protection claim against the CZO because the regulation of a church's use of land necessarily implicates the fundamental right of freedom of religious exercise. As a preliminary matter, we are quick to reiterate our earlier determination that any burdens on religious exercise imposed by the CZO are both incidental and insubstantial. Furthermore, this court has held that the fundamental rights theory of heightened equal protection scrutiny applies only to laws that effect "grave interference with important religious tenets or . . . affirmatively compel [congregants] to perform acts undeniably at odds with fundamental tenets of their religious beliefs." Griffin High School v. Illinois High School Athletic Assoc., 822 F.2d 671, 674 (7th Cir.1987). Whatever the obstacles that the CZO might present to a church's ability to locate on a specific plot of Chicago land, they in no way regulate the right, let alone interfere with the ability, of an individual to adhere to the central tenets of his religious beliefs.

Viewed through the lens of the Cleburne and Forseth rational basis analyses, Chicago's system of land-use regulation satisfies the requirements of the Equal Protection Clause. In general, a zoning ordinance imposing "restrictions in respect of the use and occupation of private lands in urban communities" such as the "segregation of residential, business, and industrial buildings" satisfies the rational basis test as "a valid exercise of authority." Village of Euclid v. Ambler Realty Company, 272 U.S. 365, 386–87, 394, 397, 47 S.Ct. 114, 71 L.Ed. 303 (1926). Here, Chicago permits churches to locate in R districts as of right, while requiring Special Use approval in B and most C districts, not only to promote the general public welfare and to protect the character, stability, order, and efficient development of Chicago's varied areas, but also to prevent overcrowding, to limit street congestion, and to conserve the taxable value of city land. Moreover, the CZO makes available avenues by which exceptions for nonconforming uses may be sought (and has made such exceptions in the cases of two plaintiff churches who applied for Special Use approval). To the extent that the CZO treats churches any differently from nonreligious assembly uses, it does not disfavor churches. More importantly, any such difference is rationally related to Chicago's legitimate interest in regulating land use within its city limits. The CZO thus complies with the requirements of the Equal Protection Clause.

Finally, Appellants challenge the district court's analysis of their Fourteenth Amendment procedural due process claim. The district court relied upon River Park v. City of Highland Park, 23 F.3d 164 (7th Cir.1994), to determine that any facial due process attack on the CZO must be made in state court. As we stated in that case, in which a plaintiff corporation alleged that Highland Park's politically motivated refusal to act on its zoning application bankrupted the corporation and deprived it of procedural due process,

> Federal courts are not boards of zoning appeals [and] the procedures "due" in zoning cases are minimal. Cities may elect to make zoning decisions through the political process. . . . Highland Park made a political decision in a political fashion, employing procedural maneuvers that prevented the question from reaching the floor for a vote. . . . [Plaintiff] may not have received the process Illinois directs its municipalities to provide, but the Constitution does not require state and local governments to adhere to their procedural promises. Failure to implement state law violates that state law, not the Constitution; the remedy lies in state court.

River Park, 23 F.3d at 165–67 (citations omitted). Here, too, the CZO and its special approval procedures provide Appellants with all the legislative process that is due. Moreover, as the district court noted, the CZO expressly provides for the review of zoning decisions by the Illinois Circuit Courts. As such, Appellants cannot prevail on their due process claim.

## NOTES

1. *Working through the maze.* Note that the Board's decision in the Principal Problem involves two basic components, the proposed expansion and the day care center, and that two ordinances are implicated in the Board's decision to deny Menorah's request for a permit. Menorah can challenge both components of the Board's decision on the same legal grounds. The ordinance requiring houses of worship to obtain a special use permit for locations and expansions will be relevant to all of Menorah's challenges involving the expansion component of the Board's decision, and to Menorah's free exercise and due process and RLUIPA challenges to the day care center component. The school ordinance, however, is only relevant to the synagogue's equal protection challenge to the Board's decision regarding the day care center. However, this decision might be challenged under both Constitutional principles and the equal treatment provisions of RLUIPA.

2. *Free exercise.* What standard of review is the court in *Messiah* invoking regarding the constitutionality of the ordinance with respect to the free exercise claim? How does RLUIPA affect this level of scrutiny?

3. *RLUIPA substantial burdens.* The *Civil Liberties for Urban Believers ("CLUB")* opinion defines "substantial burden" on religion broadly to include activity that makes religious practice impracticable in a jurisdiction. Other courts, however, have taken a more narrow view. For example, in Midrash Sephardi, Inc. v. Town of Surfside,[34] the court defined "substantial burden" as "more than an inconvenience on religious exercise; a substantial burden is akin to significant pressure which directly coerces the

---

[34] 366 F.3d 1214 (11th Cir. 2004)

religious adherent to conform his or her behavior accordingly."[35] If Menorah had a choice between these two standards, which should it favor?

4. *RLUIPA and land searches.* Recall that in the *CLUB* opinion, the court held that the city action was not a burden on religious exercise because the appellees found suitable alternative building sites. Should Menorah be required to prove that no additional parcels are available? In a subsequent case, the Seventh Circuit held that when a church might find an alternative site, but the search would impose significant costs and success was not guaranteed, the government's refusal could pose a substantial burden on the exercise of religion under RLUIPA.[36] Does this holding assist Menorah in countering any city arguments?

5. *RLUIPA ripeness.* In addition to fulfilling one of the three jurisdictional requirements of RLUIPA, a plaintiff must show that the claim is ready for adjudication before bringing a claim under the act. In Murphy v. New Milford Zoning Comm'n,[37] the court held that failure to try to obtain a zoning variance where one was available meant that the RLUIPA claim was not ready for adjudication.[38] Could the defendant city claim that Menorah has not completed final adjudication of its claims?

6. *Accessory uses.* Is the proposed day care center a valid accessory use of the synagogue? If so, should Menorah automatically prevail on a free exercise challenge to the Board's denial of the permit for the day care center? How does the broad definition of "religious exercise" under RLUIPA used by the court in *CLUB* affect Menorah's claim?

7. *Equal protection.* What standard of review was used by the court in *Cleburne* in deciding the equal protection challenge? What standard of review should a court invoke in deciding the synagogue's equal protection challenge to the Board's decision to deny the synagogue a special use permit for its proposed expansion? What standard of review would be appropriate for an equal protection challenge based on the ordinance allowing only public and private elementary schools?

8. *RLUIPA Equal Protection Clause.* As discussed, RLUIPA has two provisions, the substantial burden provision and the non-discrimination provision. Although *CLUB* did not reach the issue of whether the city's actions violated the non-discrimination provision because the city rectified the unequal treatment of religious uses, other circuits have dealt with the law in this area.[39] The non-discrimination provision is particularly attractive to plaintiffs because it does not contain any jurisdictional requirements, unlike the substantial burden provision.[40] Also, a municipality which

---

[35] Id. at 1227.
[36] Sts. Constantine & Helen Greek Orthodox Church, Inc. v. City of New Berlin, 396 F.3d 895, 901 (7th Cir. 2005).
[37] 402 F.3d 342 (2d Cir. 2005).
[38] Id. at 353.
[39] *See, e.g., Midrash Sephardi, Inc. v. Town of Surfside,* 366 F.3d 1214 (11th Cir. 2004) (holding that there was a violation of RLUIPA's equal treatment provision since the zoning ordinance at issue in that case differentiated between religious uses and secular assemblies, both of which took place within the confines of "institutions").
[40] Id. at 1229.

violates this section is strictly liable for discrimination and can only save the legislation if the law passes strict scrutiny.[41] However, the plaintiff still must show that it is a religious assembly or institution and is being treated differently from another assembly or institution.

9. *Freedom of religious exercise and hybrid rights.* Is the hybrid-rights exemption relevant to the Principal Problem? Is there another way for Menorah to claim that heightened scrutiny is applicable to this case other than hybrid rights?

10. *Summary dismissals.* Over the years, the Supreme Court has dismissed several cases where state courts have upheld zoning ordinances over the objection that the ordinances in question impaired free exercise rights. In one such case, Damascus Community Church v. Clackamas County,[42] the state court held that a conditional use permit granted to a church does not automatically allow the church to operate a full-time parochial school given the more intense nature of the school use, and that the interpretation of the ordinance to preclude the school did not violate the plaintiff's free exercise rights. The Supreme Court summarily dismissed the appeal in *Damascus* for want of a substantial federal question. Is the Court's dismissal in *Damascus* dispositive of Menorah's challenge to the Board's decision regarding the proposed day care center?

---

[41] Id. at 1229.
[42] 610 P.2d 273 (Ore.App.1980).

## ASSIGNMENT 35–36

# WATER RIGHTS AND THE PUBLIC TRUST DOCTRINE

## 1. INTRODUCTION

*The Importance of Water and Water Law.*

Water is arguably the most important resource allocated, controlled, and protected by legal institutions. All life requires water for survival. Quite bluntly, without water we die.

Society and the economy depend on reliable, clean, and usable supplies of water. Water is used for drinking, bathing, cooking, cleaning, and human sanitation. Water is necessary for raising crops and livestock. It is necessary for supporting fisheries and forests. It is used in industrial processes and commercial enterprises. Communities define themselves and thrive based on their location on or near waters.

Water also has psychological, religious/spiritual, and ethical meanings. Conflicts in society arise from competing demands for water and situations in which the demands for water at a particular place or time exceed water supplies. These conflicts can range from disputes between two neighboring water well pumpers to armed confrontations between nations.

Water is also a critical part of the natural environment. The health of biological life and watershed functions depend on instream flows in rivers and streams, the quality and level of lakes, the sustainable recharge of groundwater aquifers, the preservation of wetlands, the moderation of stormwater runoff, and the prevention of water pollution. A watershed is an area of land that drains to a common point on a surface body of water, such as a river, stream, or lake. A watershed is an ecological system—or ecosystem—that is structured around hydrological processes.

Watersheds serve many functions on which both nature and human society depend, including:

> filtration of pollutants, flood control, habitat for aquatic species, support of biodiversity, maintenance of biological and chemical content of surface waters (freshwater bodies, estuaries, and coastal waters) and groundwater, soil enrichment and deposition, shaping of landscapes, and provision of water necessary to maintain and support life. Healthy watersheds are critical to a healthy natural environment. They are also critical to supporting ... economic activity like fishing, recreational

water sports, commercial shipping, and provision of public water supplies.[1]

"Instream flows" are simply the waters within the channels of rivers or streams. Preservation of instream flows contrasts with "offstream" uses of water, in which waters are extracted from their waterways and diverted for use outside of these waterways.[2]

*The Diversity of Legal Rights and Controls Regarding Water.*

Given the importance of water resources, one might expect a uniform national or global system of rules governing the allocation, management, and use of all water. However, water law consists of a mosaic of many systems, rules, and institutions that vary widely by state, by type or source of the water in question, and by category of problem that is to be solved or managed. Nonetheless, certain basic principles or types of water law systems exist that all lawyers need to understand. The introduction to this chapter summarizes the core principles and varieties of water law doctrine in the United States. After providing this broad introduction, the Assignment turns to a principal problem involving groundwater (underground water) doctrines and the public trust doctrine.

*Surface Water Rights Systems.*

To understand water law, one must first distinguish between surface water (e.g., rivers,lakes, streams) and groundwater (i.e. water that is beneath the ground such as in underground aquifers).[3] With respect to surface waters, there are two primary systems of water rights at common law: *riparianism* and *prior appropriation*. Some states follow both systems; these states are referred to as "hybrid states" or "mixed systems." Many states—whether riparian, prior appropriation, or hybrid—now have legislation requiring water users to obtain permits from a state regulatory agency to acquire a legal right to use the water. *Regulatory systems* are discussed in connection with each type of common-law system. *Groundwater rights* are discussed separately, because those doctrines usually developed separately from surface water systems.

*Riparianism.* Riparianism is a land-based system, which developed in the water-plentiful Eastern states.[4] In a riparian state, the owner of

---

[1] Arnold, Clean-Water Land Use: Connecting Scale and Function, 23 Pace Envtl. L. Rev. 291 (2006). See also Postel & Carter, Freshwater Ecosystem Services, in Nature's Services: Societal Dependence on Natural Ecosystems 195 (Daily ed., 1997); Adler, Addressing Barriers to Watershed Protection, 25 Envtl. L. 973 (1995).

[2] See, e.g., Postel & Richter, Rivers for Life: Managing Water for People and Nature (2003); Gillilan & Brown, Instream Flow Protection: Seeking a Balance in Western Water Use (1997).

[3] We will not address rights to diffused runoff (e.g., rainfalls, snow melts) that are not in a stream bed. Likewise, we will not address ocean waters. Neither diffused runoff nor ocean waters are considered surface waters under traditional water law doctrines.

[4] Alabama, Arkansas, Connecticut, Delaware, Florida, Georgia, Illinois, Indiana, Iowa, Kentucky, Maine, Maryland, Massachusetts, Michigan, Minnesota, Missouri, New Hampshire, New Jersey, New York, North Carolina, Ohio, Pennsylvania, Rhode Island, South Carolina,

land bordering on or straddling a body of water (e.g., stream, lake, river)—known as riparian land—has a right to *"reasonable use"* of water flowing past or through his or her property.[5]

The riparian owner historically was required to use the water on the riparian land and had no right to divert it to other, non-riparian land or to use it outside of the watershed.[6] Over time, off-tract or out-of-watershed uses have been allowed if consistent with the public interest[7] or if co-riparians cannot prove actual injury from the use.[8] Some states have abandoned the on-tract requirement entirely.[9]

Historically, riparian landowners were entitled to the *"natural flow"* of the surface waters flowing by or through their lands.[10] This doctrine made sense when most water uses were few and onstream. This view gave way to the dominance of the reasonable use doctrine to accommodate economic development and population growth.[11] All riparian landowners on a water body must share its waters with co-equal rights to the reasonable uses of those waters.[12] In this sense, riparian landowners' rights are "correlative" or "reciprocal."[13] Riparian owners do not lose their rights to use or divert water if they fail or cease to exercise them, because the rights accompany land ownership.[14] Their water rights are considered appurtenant to the land.

The common-law system essentially works as a tort-law system, in which riparian landowners enforce their rights by bringing claims against competing riparian landowners in which they allege harm from the competing users' "unreasonable" uses of shared waters. The plaintiff must prove both *unreasonableness* of the competing use and *injury* to his or her riparian rights from the unreasonable use.[15] Typically courts do

---

Tennessee, Vermont, Virginia, West Virginia, and Wisconsin. Louisiana is classified as a riparian state, but it bases much of its water law on the French Civil Code. Hawaii is also essentially a riparian state, although it draws aspects of its water law doctrines from its history as an ancient kingdom, as exemplified by the *Waiahole Ditch* case, reprinted in this chapter, infra.

[5] Pyle v. Gilbert, 265 S.E.2d 584 (Ga. 1980).

[6] Town of Gordonsville v. Zinn, 106 S.E. 508 (Va. 1921).

[7] Little Blue Natural Resources Dist. v. Lower Platte North Natural Resources Dist., 294 N.W.2d 598 (Neb. 1980); State of North Carolina v. Hudson, 731 F. Supp. 1261 (E.D.N.C. 1990).

[8] Stratton v. Mt. Hermon Boys' School, 103 N.E. 87 (Mass. 1913).

[9] See, e.g., Pyle v. Gilbert, 265 S.E.2d 584 (Ga. 1980).

[10] Merritt v. Parker, 1 N.J.L. 460, 463 (1795).

[11] Pyle v. Gilbert, 265 S.E.2d 584 (Ga. 1980).

[12] Id.; Michigan Citizens for Water Conservation v. Nestle Waters North America Inc., 709 N.W.2d 174 (Mich. App. 2005).

[13] See, e.g., Mason v. Hoyle, 14 A. 786 (Conn. 1888); Beacham v. Lake Zurich Property Owners Ass'n, 526 N.E.2d 154 (Ill. 1988).

[14] Lux v. Haggin, 10 P. 674 (Cal. 1886); Franco-American Charolaise, Ltd. v. Oklahoma Water Resources Bd., 855 P.2d 568 (Okla. 1990).

[15] Hoover v. Crane, 106 N.W.2d 563 (Mich. 1960). The Restatement (Second) of Torts Section 850 states: "A riparian proprietor is subject to liability for making an unreasonable use of the water of a watercourse or lake that causes harm to another riparian proprietor's reasonable use of water or his land." Section 850A lists the following factors to be used in determining reasonableness: 1) the water use's purpose; 2) the use's suitability to the watershed;

not use the riparian law doctrine to allocate quantities among the many landowners along a waterway, but instead only determine the extent to which a challenged use is both unreasonable and harmful to the plaintiff(s).[16]

*Regulated riparianism.* Eastern states increasingly have seen water scarcity and conflict, growing demands for water, and natural and human-created changes in climate and hydrology (e.g., drought, alteration of surface flows).[17] The common law's lack of a mechanism to quantify water rights along a stream and to manage competing claims without lengthy and cumbersome litigation has led many states to adopt legislation to regulate water use.[18]

Most riparian states[19] now have some form of regulatory system, known as *"regulated riparianism,"* which requires anyone seeking to withdraw water to obtain a permit from a state water regulatory agency.[20] The state agency applies legislatively and administratively adopted standards to the review of permit applications, in accordance with specified administrative procedures. The system provides for quantification of water rights in riparian states, clear public records about who has which rights to known quantities of water, evaluation of water uses under public-interest criteria, and methods for reducing water withdrawals under emergency conditions or in cases of permit violations.

The laws of states with regulated riparianism vary considerably from one another. For example, Florida, which has long been considered on the forefront of regulated riparianism, requires any water user to obtain a permit from one of five regional water management districts. These districts consider substantial amounts of evidence at permit hearings to determine if the proposed use: "is a reasonable-beneficial use . . . [that] will not interfere with any presently existing legal use of water and is consistent with the public interest."[21] Kentucky statutes require a permit from a state agency for the pumping of water from any surface, spring, or groundwater source, but provide significant permit exemptions

---

3) the use's economic value; 4) the use's social value; 5) the extent and amount of harm the use causes; 6) the practicality of either party to avoid the harm; 7) the practicality of either party to adjust the quantity of water used; 8) the protection of existing values of water uses, land, investments, and enterprises; and 9) the justice of requiring the harm-causing user to bear the loss.

[16] See, e.g., Hoover v. Crane, 106 N.W.2d 563 (Mich. 1960); Harris v. Brooks, 283 S.W.2d 129 (Ark. 1955).

[17] See, e.g., Little, Eastern Water Law: Less Water, More Change, Trends: ABA Sec. of Env't, Energy, & Resources Newsl., Mar./Apr. 2008, at 8–9; Dellapenna, Adapting Riparian Rights to the Twenty-First Century, 106 W. Va. L. Rev. 539 (2004).

[18] Dellapenna, Adapting Riparian Rights to the Twenty-First Century, 106 W. Va. L. Rev. 539, 583 (2004).

[19] Id.

[20] Id. at 586–88.

[21] Fla. Stat. § 373.223. See, e.g., Harloff v. City of Sarasota, 575 So.2d 1324 (Fla. 1991); Southwest Florida Water Management Dist. v. Charlotte County, 774 So.2d 903 (Fla. App. 2001).

for domestic, agricultural, and electrical generation uses of water. By contrast, neighboring Tennessee requires only that users of large quantities of water (withdrawals exceeding 50,000 gallons per day) notify a state agency of their uses, except if water is to be diverted from one basin to another, for which a permit is required.[22]

*Prior appropriation.* In the arid West,[23] though, a different system—the prior appropriation system—developed around a different property principle: *first in time, first in right.* Water rights were obtained by putting water to a beneficial use, regardless of whether the user owned riparian land or used the water on riparian land.[24] The doctrine of prior appropriation developed out of the norms and customs of water usage among miners, the pressures from farmers and ranchers for security of water rights for use on lands far from surface waters, and the goals of population growth and economic development that depended on water development projects and offstream uses.[25]

The fundamental elements of an appropriation right to water are:

1) *intent* to put the water to a beneficial use;

2) an *actual diversion* of previously unappropriated water from a surface waterway;

3) application of the water to a *beneficial use*; and

4) relatively *continuous use* of the water.[26]

An appropriator meeting all these criteria obtains a right to use the quantity of water for a beneficial use, a right that is superior to all those who appropriate water from the waterway later than the appropriator (i.e., "junior appropriators") and inferior to all those who appropriated water from the waterway earlier than the appropriator (i.e., "senior appropriators"). Thus, with respect to a given body of water, rights to divert water form a system of *priority* according to when a person or entity diverted the water. In periods of drought or reduced flows, the more senior appropriators are protected, at least legally, while the more junior appropriators must reduce or even cease their diversions altogether in reverse order of seniority. As a practical matter, though, the order of priority may not be followed strictly in some circumstances due to the location of appropriators on the stream, the role of "return flows" from upstream appropriators, state policies to promote the public

---

[22] Brewer, The Downfall of Riparianism: A Comparison of the Tennessee and Kentucky Water Pumping Permit Systems, 1 J. Animal & Envtl. L. 61 (2009); Tennessee Dept. of Env. & Cons., Div. Water Pollution Control, Ch. 1200–4–13: New Rules implementing Tenn. Inter-Basin Water Transfer Act.

[23] Alaska, Arizona, Colorado, Idaho, Montana, Nevada, New Mexico, Utah, and Wyoming.

[24] See, e.g., Coffin v. Left Hand Ditch Co., 6 Colo. 443 (1882).

[25] See generally Dunbar, Forging New Rights in Western Waters (1983); Worster, Rivers of Empire: Water, Aridity, and the Growth of the American West (1985). See also Irwin v. Phillips, 5 Cal. 140 (1855).

[26] See generally Klein, The Constitutional Mythology of Western Water Law, 14 Va. Envtl. L.J. 343 (1995).

interest, preemptive federal interests in water, and incentives for ad hoc solutions to temporary shortages.[27]

Some of the elements of an appropriation also require a bit of explanation. The requirement of an actual diversion—taking the water out of the waterway for use offstream—served the dual purposes of putting the world on notice of the time and quantity of the appropriator's water rights and creating incentives for the economically productive and humanly consumptive uses of the water offstream according to a world view that saw instream flows as essentially wasteful.[28] However, many western states now recognize appropriation rights in *instream flows*—rights to specific quantities of water to remain in the waterway without letting junior appropriators deplete them—under some circumstances.[29] These rights might be obtained by state agencies or conservation organizations for environmental purposes, or might afford legal recognition to historic human uses of water for economically valuable activities like watering livestock, transporting logs, or navigating commercial vessels.[30]

The requirement that appropriated water be put to a beneficial use has various components. With respect to the *type of use*, a wide variety of water uses qualify, including domestic, municipal, agricultural irrigation, livestock, commercial, industrial, recreational, fish and wildlife, and water quality "uses" of water.[31] The more significant component, though, is the *quantity of water*. The beneficial use doctrine prohibits the *waste* of water.[32] Absolute efficiency in use is not required, but some states require that appropriators employ *reasonably efficient methods* for using water.[33] For example, flooding arid cropland or overfilling open-air unlined ditches with substantial seepage and evaporation may be considered wasteful.[34] In addition, the beneficial use

---

[27] See Tarlock, The Future of Prior Appropriation in the New West, 41 Nat. Resources J. 769 (2001).

[28] See Vought v. Stucker Mesa Domestic Pipeline Co., 76 P.3d 906, 912–13 (Colo. 2003); Gillilan & Brown, Instream Flow Protection: Seeking a Balance in Western Water Use 1–3 (1997).

[29] See generally Boyd, Hip Deep: A Survey of State Instream Flow Law from the Rocky Mountains to the Pacific Ocean, 43 Nat. Resources J. 1151 (2003).

[30] In re Adjudication of the Existing Rights to the Use of All the Water Within the Missouri River Drainage Area, 55 P.3d 396 (Mont. 2002); Phelps Dodge Corp. v. Arizona Dep't of Water Resources, 118 P.3d 1110 (Ariz. App. 2005) (interpreting A.R.S. § 45–152).

[31] Beneficial uses are typically defined by state statutes. What constitutes a beneficial use may change as conditions and values change. See, e.g., State Dept. of Parks v. Idaho Dept. of Water Admin., 530 P.2d 924, 931 (Bakes, J., concurring). Environmental uses of water are increasingly recognized as beneficial. See, e.g., DeKay v. U.S. Fish & Wildlife Service, 524 N.W.2d 855 (S.D. 1995); In re Adjudication of the Existing Rights to the Use of All the Water Within the Missouri River Drainage Area, 55 P.3d 396 (Mont. 2002).

[32] Neuman, Beneficial Use, Waste, and Forfeiture: The Inefficient Search for Efficiency in Western Water Use, 28 Envtl. L. 919 (1998). See, e.g., State Dep't of Ecology v. Grimes, 852 P.2d 1044 (Wash. 1993).

[33] State Dep't of Ecology v. Grimes, 852 P.2d 1044 (Wash. 1993).

[34] See, e.g., Warner Valley Stock Co. v. Lynch, 336 P.2d 884 (Ore. 1959); Imperial Irrigation Dist.: Alleged Waste and Unreasonable Use of Water, Cal. Water Resources Control

doctrine has a corollary: the *anti-speculation doctrine*. Investors or speculators in water cannot acquire rights for future uses if they do not put the water to beneficial use now.[35] However, prohibitions on both waste and speculation are often not enforced.[36]

Finally, the requirement of continuous use does not mean daily use. Seasonal uses, non-use under unusual circumstances, and even occasional interruptions of use are allowed. However, an appropriation right will be lost to *abandonment* if the appropriator evinces an intent to abandon the right and acts in a manner that unequivocally manifests this intent.[37] Mere non-use does not qualify as abandonment but may constitute *forfeiture* under state statutes if it exceeds the statutory period (e.g., five years of non-use).[38]

*Permit systems in prior appropriation states.* Prior appropriation states adopted permitting requirements to secure water rights much earlier and more pervasively than riparian states.[39] Colorado, which still relies on special water courts to adjudicate water rights in river basins, is the only prior appropriation state without a permitting system.[40] In all other prior appropriation and hybrid states, anyone seeking to secure a prior appropriation right must apply for a permit from a state agency or official and must show at an administrative hearing that the proposed use meets specified statutory criteria. Agency approval is also required for changes in the type, timing, or location of use, the location of diversion or return flow, and the transfer of water rights.[41] Many appropriative water right permitting systems authorize or require the state agency or official to reject any permit application that is not consistent with the *public interest or public welfare.*[42]

---

Bd. Water Rights Dec'n 1600 (1984). There are now many available conservation methods and technologies available for relatively efficient agricultural and urban uses of water.

[35] Zellmer, The Anti-Speculation Doctrine and Its Implications for Collaborative Water Management, 8 Nev. L.J. 994 (2008). See, e.g., Lemmon v. Hardy, 519 P.2d 1168 (Idaho 1974).

[36] See Neuman, Beneficial Use, Waste, and Forfeiture: The Inefficient Search for Efficiency in Western Water Use, 28 Envtl. L. 919 (1998); Zellmer, The Anti-Speculation Doctrine and Its Implications for Collaborative Water Management, 8 Nev. L.J. 994 (2008).

[37] See, e.g., Jenkins v. State Dept. of Water Resources, 647 P.2d 1256 (Idaho 1982).

[38] See, e.g., id.

[39] Wyoming adopted the first permit system in 1890. See, e.g., Wyoming Hereford Ranch v. Hammond Packing Co., 236 P. 764 (Wyo. 1925).

[40] See, e.g., High Plains A & M, LLC v. Southeastern Colorado Water Conservancy Dist., 120 P.3d 710 (Colo. 2005) (affirming the water court's dismissal of applications for changes to and transfers of water rights as violating Colorado's anti-speculation doctrine).

[41] See, e.g., Matter of Application for Change of Appropriation Water Rights, 816 P.2d 1054 (Mont. 1991) (the burden of proving no harm to other appropriators is on the one seeking the change).

[42] See, e.g., Shokal v. Dunn, 707 P.2d 441 (Idaho 1985) (interpreting Idaho's "local public interest" statutory criterion by reference to Alaska's extensive public interest statute and New Mexico case law); Bokum, Implementing the Public Welfare Requirement in New Mexico's Water Code, 36 Nat. Res. J. 681 (1996).

*Hybrid states.* The states along the Pacific Coast,[43] the states straddling the 100th Meridian,[44] and perhaps Mississippi[45] are hybrid (or mixed) systems, applying both prior appropriation and riparian doctrines. For the most part, these are states with both humid and arid regions. In most of these states, the prior appropriation doctrine dominates and only historically exercised riparian rights are recognized.[46] Of the hybrid states west of the Mississippi River, the riparian doctrine continues to play a significant role only in California, Nebraska, and Oklahoma.[47]

*Groundwater Rights Systems*[48]

The law governing rights in groundwater developed quite separately from the law governing surface waters, because courts viewed the locations, quantities, and properties of water beneath the surface to be unknown and difficult to regulate. Surface water rules governed underground streams in defined channels and the subflow of surface streams beneath streambeds because they could be more easily studied and integrated into surface water regulation. However, the water interspersed among the pores and interstices of subsurface soils and rock formations, including aquifers (underground reservoirs), are referred to as "percolating waters" (regardless of whether they noticeably percolate) and have been subject to one of five common-law doctrines governing pumping and usage rights and liabilities.

1) *English rule, absolute ownership, or rule of capture.* This doctrine provides that the owner of land overlying a groundwater source may pump as much as he or she wishes from the source without liability to any neighboring or nearby landowners who also own land over the source. Traditionally, a landowner could even pump groundwater maliciously or wastefully without liability, but those rules were rejected in the states that initially adopted the rule of capture. The rule of capture may not have been officially overruled or repealed in some jurisdictions, but it is arguably applied only in Texas. It was rejected by many states, even in the nineteenth century, because it incentivizes a race among landowners to pump the most water as quickly as possible and to use high-capacity wells, eventually to the degradation of the groundwater source.

---

[43] California, Oregon, and Washington.

[44] Texas, Oklahoma, Kansas, Nebraska, South Dakota, and North Dakota.

[45] Mississippi was a riparian state, adopted the prior appropriation doctrine in 1955, and then adopted regulated riparianism in 1985.

[46] See, e.g., Kan. Stat. §§ 82a–701 & 82a–703; Ore. Laws, 1909, ch. 216; 1955 S.D. Sess. Laws ch. 430; Tex. Water Code § 11.303(b).

[47] Tulare Irrigation Dist. v. Lindsay-Strathmore Irrigation Dist., 45 P.2d 972 (Cal. 1935); Wasserburger v. Coffee, 141 N.W.2d 738 (Neb. 1966); Franco-American Charolaise, Ltd. v. Oklahoma Water Resources Bd., 855 P.2d 568 (Okla. 1990).

[48] This overview of groundwater is drawn from several sources, including Tarlock, Bottled Water: Legal Aspects of Groundwater Extraction (2004); Glennon, Water Follies: Groundwater Pumping and the Fate of America's Fresh Waters (2002); Getches, Water Law in a Nutshell, 4th ed. 257–314 (2009).

2) *American reasonable use.* The owner of land overlying a groundwater source has the right to pump as much groundwater as he or she can put to a reasonable use on the overlying tract (appurtenancy or on-tract requirement).

3) *Correlative rights.* All landowners share rights to the available water from a groundwater source over which they own land on an equitable basis, such as pro rata according to acreage overlying the groundwater source. Off-tract uses are permitted only to the extent that "surplus waters" exist that exceed the amounts withdrawn and used on-tract.

4) *Prior appropriation.* Rights to pump and use groundwater have relative superiority and therefore protection in accordance with the time at which the pumping and use first began. While the concept of "first in time, first in right" applies in a general sense, senior appropriators in groundwater generally do not have the right to prevent all new wells that might affect their rights in any way. Instead, the concepts are usually applied by state agencies reviewing grants of new permits to ensure that existing permittees or pumpers are protected, but in the context of the overall rational management, maximization of groundwater supplies, the public interest, and policy choices about appropriate yields.

5) *Restatement (Second) of Torts reasonable use.* The Restatement (Second) of Torts § 858 contains a set of "reasonable use" factors for non-liability for groundwater pumping and use that is similar to the set of factors applied to riparian rights. These factors balance the equities, hardships, and relative social benefits of various water uses, and do not require or prefer that the water be used on-tract.

*Permitting Systems.*

A number of states require permits from a state agency or regional water management district before one can pump groundwater, although these permit systems exist in the shadow of common-law recognition of property rights in groundwater. Some states have moved towards integrated management and permitting for both surface waters and groundwater. This is important because groundwater is integrally interconnected with surface water in many ways originally not comprehended by scientists, legislators, or judges. The basic problems of groundwater management today are:

1) conflicts between two or more nearby wells due to effects of one on another (related, for example, to pressure, rates of pumping, or well depth);

2) groundwater mining (i.e., the collective pumping of groundwater at rates that exceed recharge);

3) surface land uses that introduce pollutants into groundwater or impede filtration of precipitation into the soils; and

4) the effects of surface water uses and groundwater uses on one another and barriers to integrated management of the two systems.

*Federal, State, and Public Interests in Water*

While the foregoing discussion focuses on private property rights in water under state law, these rights are often subject to federal, state, and public interests in the very same water. Seven doctrines or categories of interests are especially relevant to us.

The first is the *state ownership doctrine.* Under the federal navigability-for-title test,[49] all waters actually used or capable of being used for navigation in commerce at the time of statehood and their submerged lands were held in trust by the federal government for the state and passed to the state at the time of statehood.[50] Many states have expressly declared that their waters belong to the state or the people.[51] Notwithstanding this fact, states have unquestionably granted or recognized private property interests in water. Moreover, some have argued that the state ownership doctrine is nothing more than a legal fiction created to favor state (instead of federal) allocations of water.[52] However, in a number of cases, the state ownership doctrine has served as a significant constraint on private rights in water.[53]

Second, the bulk of authority treats water rights, especially appropriation rights and groundwater rights, as "*usufructuary*" and not as "*possessory.*"[54] Water rights-holders have a property interest in the *use* of certain waters under certain conditions, but do not have *physical* possessory ownership of any particular body of water or specific molecules of water.[55] Thus, a water-rights holder does not have a vested

---

[49] The Daniel Ball, 77 U.S. (10 Wall.) 557 (1870).

[50] Shively v. Bowlby, 152 U.S. 1 (1894).

[51] See, e.g., Mont Const. art. IX, § 3; Utah Code § 73–1–1; Va. Code Ann. § 1–302; Bamford v. Upper Republican Natural Res. Dist., 512 N.W.2d 642, 649–51 (Neb. 1994); Baeth v. Hoisveen, 157 N.W.2d 728 (N.D. 1968).

[52] Tarlock, Water Law Reform in West Virginia: The Broader Context, 106 W. Va. L. Rev. 495, 529–30 (2004).

[53] See, e.g., Bamford v. Upper Republican Natural Res. Dist., 512 N.W.2d 642, 649–51 (Neb. 1994). See also the *Waiahole Ditch* case reprinted in this Assignment, infra. Justice Oliver Wendell Holmes, Jr. asserted the power of the state to protect its waters for public purposes:

> [F]ew public interests are more obvious, indisputable, and independent of particular theory than the interest of the public of a state to maintain the rivers that are wholly within it substantially undiminished, except by such drafts upon them as the guardian of the public welfare may permit for the purpose of turning them to a more perfect use.

Hudson County Water Co. v. McCarter, 209 U.S. 349, 356 (1908).

[54] See generally Zellmer & Harder, Unbundling Property in Water, 59 Ala. L. Rev. 679, 691–99 (2008).

[55] Note, however, that this general rule typically does not apply to artificial waters, such as a human-created pond, and may not apply to certain aspects of riparian rights. In addition, at least one court has treated water rights as physical or possessory rights for which just compensation would be due if the government eliminated them. Tulare Lake Basin Water Storage Dist. v. United States, 49 Fed. Cl. 313, 321–24 (2001).

right to the water until he or she actually and legitimately withdraws or pumps the water into physical possession.

Third, the federal navigability-for-title test defines the waters not only subject to state ownership but also subject to a *federal navigation servitude*. This servitude—essentially a water-based easement—gives the federal government authority to prevent riparian landowners, water appropriators, and others from interfering with navigation on commercially navigable waterways.[56] Some states also have doctrines that protect the public's rights to recreational navigation even if the waters are not federally navigable for commerce.[57]

Fourth, *federal environmental-regulatory legislation*, such as the Clean Water Act,[58] protecting water quality, and the Endangered Species Act,[59] protecting federally listed endangered and threatened species (including aquatic species), constrain a number of water uses under particular circumstances.[60] State legislation and regulation for environmental protection may also limit water rights.

Fifth, despite the state ownership doctrine, federal reservations of land—whether for Native American tribal reservations or for public lands (e.g., national forests, national wildlife refuges, national parks)—impliedly include the rights to as much water as is necessary to fulfill the purposes for which the reservation is made.[61] These *federal reserved water rights* trump all after-acquired water rights under state law and can be asserted at any time, even if they have been unexercised for decades.

Sixth, allocations of rights to interstate waters under state law may be limited by the portion of those *interstate waters* allocated to each state by interstate compact, congressional apportionment by federal statute, or "equitable apportionment" by the U.S. Supreme Court in litigation between states over interstate waters.[62] Furthermore, international treaties and agreements govern waters shared with Canada and Mexico.[63]

---

[56] United States v. Rands, 389 U.S. 121, 122–23 (1967); United States v. Willow River Power Co., 324 U.S. 499, 507 (1945); Gibson v. United States, 166 U.S. 269, 271–73 (1897); Palm Beach Isles Assoc. v. United States, 58 Fed. Cl. 657, 686 (2003).

[57] See, e.g., Arkansas v. McIlroy, 595 S.W.2d 659 (Ark. 1980); Conaster v. Johnson, 194 P.3d 897 (Utah 2008).

[58] 33 U.S.C. §§ 1251 et seq.

[59] 16 U.S.C. §§ 1531 et seq.

[60] See, e.g., Votteler, The Little Fish That Roared: The Endangered Species Act, Groundwater Law, and Private Property Rights Collide, 28 Envtl. L. 845 (1998).

[61] The landmark case is Winters v. United States, 207 U.S. 564 (1908). See also Cappaert v. United States, 426 U.S. 128 (1976); United States v. New Mexico, 438 U.S. 696 (1978).

[62] Dellapenna, Interstate Struggles Over Rivers: The Southeastern States and the Struggle Over the 'Hooch, 12 NYU Envtl. L. J. 828, 832–50, 880–98 (2005).

[63] Utton, Canadian International Waters, in 5 Waters and Water Rights, ch. 50 (Beck, ed.); Utton, Mexican International Waters, in 5 Waters and Water Rights, ch. 51 (Beck, ed.).

The seventh major constraint on private property rights in water is the *public trust doctrine*, which is discussed below.

## The Public Trust Doctrine

The public trust doctrine provides that each state hold navigable waters, tidal waters, and land submerged beneath both types of water in trust for the public.[64] As the trustee of these waters, the state has a fiduciary duty to protect the public's interests in these waters and lands and cannot transfer them to private parties without protecting the public trust in them.

The public trust originated in ancient Rome. The Institutes of Justinian stated: "Now the things which are, by natural law, common to all are these: the air, running water, the sea, and therefore the seashores. Thus, no one is barred access to the seashore."[65] English common law recognized the public trust in lands subject to the ebb and flow of the tide (tidal lands).[66] Given that most of the waters in the U.S. are freshwater inland waterways and that the public's interests in navigable waters is great, the United States Supreme Court has held that nontidal lands under navigable freshwater lakes and rivers are also subject to the public trust.[67] When the original thirteen colonies became independent states, they succeeded to the sovereign authority and duties of the British crown, including the public trust in tidal waters. As the remaining states entered the Union, they took title, subject to the public trust, to navigable and tidal waters and their submerged lands.

The landmark case on the public trust is Illinois Central Railroad v. Illinois,[68] in which the U.S. Supreme Court upheld the Illinois legislature's revocation of its grant of nearly the entire Chicago shorefront of Lake Michigan to the Illinois Central Railroad. The Court held that the state could not convey such a large portion of lands beneath navigable waters to a private party, because they were held in trust for the public.

The public trust doctrine has several different types of applications. First, as with *Illinois Central Railroad*, it serves as a constraint on the state's *transfer of trust-covered submerged lands* to private parties. To the extent that such lands have been or are conveyed to private ownership (e.g., in smaller amounts than the entire shorefront of a major city), they remain subject to the public's trust interests. In certain

---

[64] See generally Dunning, "The Public Right to Use Water in Place", § 30.02, in Beck, Waters and Water Rights (1991); Craig, A Comparative Guide to the Eastern Public Trust Doctrine: Classifications of States, Property Rights, and State Summaries, 16 Penn. St. Envtl. L. Rev. 1 (2007); Craig, A Comparative Guide to the Western States' Public Trust Doctrines: Public Values, Private Rights, and the Evolution Toward an Ecological Public Trust, 37 Ecology L.Q. 53 (2010).

[65] Justinian, Institutes, book II, title I, § 1 (528 A.D.), as quoted in Glass v. Goeckel, 703 N.W.2d 58, 64 (Mich. 2005).

[66] Phillips Petroleum Co. v. Mississippi, 484 U.S. 469, 473 (1988).

[67] Id. at 479.

[68] 146 U.S. 387 (1892).

circumstances, the public trust in lands conveyed to a private party can be extinguished if the conveyance itself serves the public trust.[69] However, courts have overturned legislative attempts to convey or extinguish the public trust in lands beneath navigable waterways.[70]

Second, the public trust gives states *regulatory authority* to protect the public's interest in navigable and tidal waters, and their submerged lands, and likewise serves as an inherent limit on private property rights in such resources.[71]

Third, the public trust protects certain *public interests* in trust-covered resources. Historically these included commercial and recreational navigation, fishing, hunting, and bathing and swimming, but have grown to include protection of fish and wildlife habitat, scientific study, open space, aesthetic enjoyment, and ecological conditions.[72]

In particular, the public trust protects the *public's rights of access and use* in navigable and tidal waters, shorelands, beaches, and streambeds. The public trust typically extends as far as the ordinary high water mark, thus including land that is dry some of the time but submerged under navigable or tidal waters for some amount of time.[73] For example, the Michigan Supreme Court upheld the right of the public to walk along privately owned shoreland of Lake Huron below the ordinary high water mark, because such lands remained subject to the state's public trust.[74] However, some courts have extended the public's right of access to dry beach areas above the ordinary high water mark to effectuate the public's rights to use the wet beach areas.[75]

---

[69] Compare Kootenai Envt'l. Alliance v. Panhandle Yacht Club, 671 P.2d 1085 (Idaho 1983) (lease of trust land for private boat slips not inconsistent with public trust) with Lake Michigan Fed. v. U.S. Army Corps of Engineers, 742 F. Supp. 441 (N.D. Ill. 1990) (grant of 18.5 acres of Lake Michigan lakebed to Loyola University to fill for expansion of its Lake Shore campus was invalid as serving a private purpose).

[70] See, e.g., San Carlos Apache Tribe v. Superior Court, 972 P.2d 179 (Ariz. 1999).

[71] See, e.g., Just v. Marinette County, 201 N.W.2d 761 (Wis. 1972).

[72] Marks v. Whitney, 491 P.2d 374 (Cal. 1971).

[73] See, e.g., Glass v. Goeckel, 703 N.W.2d 58 (Mich. 2005).

[74] Id.

[75] See, e.g., Neptune City v. Avon-By-the-Sea, 294 A.2d 47 (N.J. 1972); Matthews v. Bay Head Improvement Ass'n, 471 A.2d 355 (N.J. 1984). Alternatively, custom may be a basis for public rights to use privately owned dry lands to access public beaches. See, e.g., Public Access Shoreline Hawai'i v. Hawai'i County Planning Comm'n, 903 P.2d 1246 (Haw. 1995); Oregon v. Hay, 462 P.2d 671 (Ore. 1969).

A public trust may also apply to some *non-aquatic resources*, such as parkland,[76] wildlife,[77] public lands,[78] and other natural resources.[79] However, any such public trust arguably has different doctrinal foundations and content than the water-based public trust doctrine addressed in this Assignment.

Finally, some states have applied the public trust doctrine to *waters and water rights*. In *National Audubon Society v. Superior Court*, the California Supreme Court held that the state has a fiduciary duty to consider and protect public trust principles when granting appropriative rights to divert non-navigable streams that directly feed a navigable water.[80] The Hawaii Supreme Court applied the public trust doctrine to groundwater that was part of an integrated stream allocation proceeding before a state commission.[81] The New Jersey Supreme Court has held that the public trust must be considered in the transfer of municipal water supplies to a private party.[82] The extent to which the public trust doctrine should be applied broadly is controversial.[83] Moreover, the scope and content of the public trust doctrine vary considerably from state to state.[84] Nonetheless, the cases on the public trust in water highlight the role of the doctrine in imposing fiduciary duties on the state to actively manage trust-covered resources for the benefit of the public's interest in those resources.

---

[76] Grayson v. Huntington, 554 N.Y.S.2d 269 (1990), appeal denied, 565 N.E.2d 1269 (N.Y. 1990). See also Williams, Sustaining Urban Green Spaces: Can Public Parks Be Protected Under the Public Trust Doctrine?, 10 S.C. Envtl. L.J. 23 (2002).

[77] Houck, Why Do We Protect Endangered Species and What Does That Say About Whether Restrictions on Private Property to Protect Them Constitute "Takings"?, 80 Iowa L. Rev. 297, 311 n.77 (1995) (contrasting U.S. Supreme Court jurisprudence on Commerce Clause limits to state regulation of wild animals with more fundamental and ancient doctrines that treat wildlife as public trust resources).

[78] Branson School Dist. v. Romer, 161 F.3d 619 (10th Cir. 1998) (public lands granted to state for support of public schools).

[79] Pearson, Illinois Central Railroad and the Public Trust Doctrine in State Law, 15 Va. Envtl. L.J. 713, 740 (1996). But see Bushby v. Washington County Conservation Bd., 654 N.W.2d 494 (Iowa 2002) (public trust doctrine does not prevent the cutting of old growth trees in a county park as part of a properly authorized forestry management plan).

[80] 658 P.2d 709 (Cal. 1983), reprinted in this Assignment, infra.

[81] In re Water Use Permit Applications (Waiahole Ditch), 9 P.3d 409 (Hawai'i 2000), reprinted in this Assignment. But see Santa Teresa Citizen Action Group v. City of San Jose, 7 Cal. Rptr. 3d 868 (Cal. App. 2003) (refusing to extend the public trust doctrine to groundwater).

[82] City of Clifton v. Passaic Valley Water Comm'n, 539 A.2d 760, 765–67 (N.J. Super.1987) ("While the original purpose of the public trust doctrine was to preserve the use of the public natural water for navigation, commerce and fishing, . . . it is clear that since water is essential for human life, the public trust doctrine applies with equal impact upon the control of our drinking water reserves.")

[83] Compare, Huffman, A Fish Out of Water: The Public Trust Doctrine in a Constitutional Democracy, 19 Envtl. L. 527 (1989) (arguing for a limited application of the public trust doctrine), with Blumm, Public Property and the Democratization of Western Water Law: A Modern View of the Public Trust Doctrine, 19 Envtl. L. 573 (1989) (arguing for an expansive application of the doctrine).

[84] Craig, A Comparative Guide to the Eastern Public Trust Doctrine: Classifications of States, Property Rights, and State Summaries, 16 Penn. St. Envtl. L. Rev. 1 (2007); Craig, A Comparative Guide to the Western States' Public Trust Doctrines: Public Values, Private Rights, and the Evolution Toward an Ecological Public Trust, 37 Ecology L.Q. 53 (2010).

*Changing Water Law and Judicial Takings*

Water law in the United States has changed substantially over time, evolving and adapting to changing conditions, needs, and values.[85] Throughout the development of water law, courts have overruled precedent, rejecting doctrines—and their accompanying "settled" water rights—that did not seem to work, instead adopting new or alternative doctrines.[86] Many commentators believe that water law will have to change substantially in the future to address problems like consumptive patterns that exceed available supplies, ecological and public needs, climate change, and outmoded barriers to water transfers.[87] However, if legislatures or administrative agencies were simply to eliminate certain established water rights altogether, they could be liable for just compensation for taking private property. Should courts be subject to takings claims for just compensation when they eliminate established private rights in water by changing common-law doctrine?

In 1967, U.S. Supreme Court Justice Potter Stewart suggested in a concurring opinion that a taking would occur from a "sudden change in the law, unpredictable in terms of the relevant precedents."[88] Some legal scholars have articulated a theory of judicial takings, giving particular attention to how the concept would apply to water rights.[89]

The U.S. Supreme Court directly took up the issue in 2010 in a Florida case, in which the Florida Supreme Court had reinterpreted its common-law governing the rights of coastal landowners concerning the shifting of their property lines with changes to the coastline.[90] The State of Florida attempted to fix an unmovable "erosion control line" (ECL) that would allow government agencies to engage in replenishing public beaches with sand and attempting to prevent or control erosion, without having the restored or protected beaches become private property. The

---

[85] See Zellmer, Adaptation, Evolution and Symbiosis in Water Law (2007), http://works.bepress.com/sandi_zellmer/2.

[86] See, e.g., Jones v. Adams, 6 P. 442 (Nev. 1885) (overruling its previous adoption of riparianism and replacing it with the prior appropriation doctrine); Pyle v. Gilbert, 265 S.E.2d 584 (Ga. 1980) (elevating the reasonable use doctrine over the natural flow doctrine); McBryde Sugar Co. v. Robinson, 504 P.2d 1330 (Haw. 1973) (overruling precedent and overhauling Hawaiian water law, which altered many seemingly settled rights); Cline v. American Aggregates Corp., 474 N.E.2d 324 (Ohio 1984) (departing from the 100-year-old rule-of-capture groundwater doctrine and replacing it with the reasonable use doctrine).

[87] See, e.g., Adler, Climate Change and the Hegemony of State Water Law, 29 Stan. Envtl. L.J. 1 (2010); Adler, Water Marketing as an Adaptive Response to the Threat of Climate Change 31 Hamline L. Rev. 730 (2008); Craig, Adapting Water Law to Public Necessity: Reframing Climate Change Adaptation as Emergency Response and Preparedness, 11 Vt. J. Envtl. L. 709 (2010); Dellapenna, Adapting Riparian Rights to the Twenty-First Century, 106 W. Va. L. Rev. 539 (2004); Klein, Angelo, & Hamann, Modernizing Water Law: The Example of Florida, 61 Florida L. Rev. 403 (2009).

[88] Hughes v. Washington, 389 U.S. 290, 296–97 (1967) (Stewart, J., concurring).

[89] See, e.g., Thompson, Judicial Takings, 76 Va. L. Rev. 1449 (1990). But see Chang, Unraveling Robinson v. Ariyoshi: Can Courts "Take" Property?, 2 U. Haw. L. Rev. 57 (1979) (expressing the opposite perspective).

[90] Walton County v. Stop the Beach Renourishment, Inc., 998 So. 2d 1102 (Fla. 2008), cert. granted, Stop the Beach Renourishment, Inc. v. Florida Dept. of Envt'l Protection, 129 S. Ct. 2792 (2009).

Florida Supreme Court's majority held that the underlying principles behind coastal landowners' "littoral" or "riparian" rights would be served by the ECL, but the dissent accused the majority of radically rewriting the law and eliminating important rights. The U.S. Supreme Court unanimously concluded that no taking had occurred. Under existing Florida property law principles, the State has a right to fill submerged waters with sand and to claim ownership to land exposed by a sudden (avulsive) event even if the State were to cause this sudden change, and private owners of coastal lands do not have a property right to have their land remain in contact with the shoreline waters.[91] However, the Justices split evenly, 4–4 (with Justice Stevens recusing himself), about the principles governing judicial takings. Justice Scalia, joined by Chief Justice Roberts and Justices Thomas and Alito, would recognize a judicial taking whenever a court judicially redefines its property law to eliminate what had previously been a recognized private property right. Justices Kennedy, Sotomayor, Breyer, and Ginsburg contended that it was unnecessary for the Court to determine whether to recognize judicial takings or to establish standards for judicial takings.[92] Justice Kennedy, joined by Justice Sotomayor, noted, though, that a judicial elimination of an established private property right could be a deprivation of property without due process, and thus could be reversed on appeal as a violation of the Due Process Clause. Thus, the area of judicial takings remains murky and unresolved.[93]

## 2. Principal Problem

You are the Chief Justice of the State Supreme Court which is considering the case of City of Dougal v. Escamilla. The case involves a dispute over groundwater rights, the public trust doctrine, and the circumstances under which courts should adopt changes in property law principles governing water.

The case arose when Dan Escamilla drilled several wells into an aquifer underlying land that he owns and began pumping 50,000 acre-feet[94] of groundwater per year to fill tanks and artificial ponds to create and support a catfish farm. The City of Dougal objected to this use of groundwater. Escamilla is fortunate to have land located at a point in which the groundwater pressure is higher than at other points in the aquifer, which creates a flow of water toward his wells. Escamilla's rate and quantity of groundwater pumping affect several wells that the City has in the same aquifer to provide drinking water to its residents. The City's well production has dropped considerably, reducing the amount of

---

[91] Stop the Beach Renourishment, Inc. v. Florida Dept. of Envt'l Protection, 130 S. Ct. 2592 (2010).

[92] Id. (J. Kennedy, concurring; J. Breyer, concurring).

[93] Id. (J. Kennedy, concurring).

[94] An acre-foot is as much water as would cover an acre of land to a depth of one foot of water. In the problem, 50,000 acre-feet of water per year would be almost 16.3 billion gallons of water per year.

drinking water supply that the City obtains from the aquifer. The City contends that if Escamilla continues, total pumping among all users will exceed recharge rates, causing the aquifer levels to drop and the long-term supply to diminish. Moreover, the City complains that the use of such a large quantity of relatively clean water for a catfish farm, which dirties the water considerably, is a waste, particularly in comparison to the need for clean drinking water for the public.

Escamilla asserts that he is entitled to take as much water from the aquifer as he can pump and use. He owns land overlying the aquifer and both the wells and the catfish farm are on this land. Thus, he argues, he has a right under the state's rule of capture doctrine to pump without regard to other aquifer users.

The state supreme court adopted the rule of capture for groundwater in an 1891 case. In the past three decades, one state supreme court case and two state appellate court cases questioned whether the rule of capture is practically viable in a time of increasing demands on groundwater resources, but these statements were in dicta and the cases in question were resolved on other grounds. Thus, the 1891 case remains the only clear precedent on groundwater.

Moreover, in 1965, the State Constitution was amended with what is known as the "Natural Resources Clause," which provides: "The State shall manage and conserve the natural resources of the State for its people." In the early 1970s, the State legislature adopted a series of statutes replacing the common law of riparian water rights with a permitting system for surface water uses to be administered by the State Water Commission. The State legislature did not address groundwater at all.

Escamilla has rejected the City's demands that he cease or substantially reduce his groundwater pumping. He told City officials that if they want the groundwater that he is pumping, the City could buy his land—and therefore his rights to pump from the underlying aquifer—for $20 million. The City officials angrily denounced this as extortion and vowed to fight for its interests. The City sued Escamilla, arguing that the state courts should abandon the rule of capture for groundwater, that Escamilla's groundwater usage is unreasonable and wasteful, and that the State has a duty to act to protect groundwater resources for the public. The State Water Commission intervened as a plaintiff, arguing that the state courts should recognize the state's authority to prevent unreasonable and wasteful uses of groundwater, but give it wide discretion to do so without imposing any legal obligations.

After a trial court granted summary judgment to Escamilla on the basis of the 1891 rule-of-capture case, a state appellate court reversed. On the issue of the common law governing groundwater rights, the appellate court held that: a) the rule of capture is outmoded in U.S. groundwater law; b) the State Supreme Court would likely apply either a doctrine of correlative rights or the Restatement of Torts to resolving groundwater disputes: c) and Escamilla's use unreasonably harms the City and is to be enjoined. On the issue of the State Water Commission's authority and duties, the appellate court held that the Natural Resources Clause recognizes the public trust doctrine in all natural resources, including groundwater, and therefore creates not only authority but also a fiduciary duty in the State Water Commission to protect the public's interest in groundwater.

The State Supreme Court has granted review and heard oral arguments. At an initial discussion of the case, the other eight members of the State Supreme Court currently are evenly split on the two issues.

Four justices would reverse the appellate court. On the rule of capture issue, they would continue to follow the applicable precedent, which is the 1891 case adopting the rule of capture for groundwater. On the public trust issue, they would hold that the public trust doctrine has not historically applied to groundwater and that the Natural Resources Clause is not sufficiently clear to have created new public trust limitations on groundwater rights in 1965. One of the four justices has indicated that he could be persuaded to recognize the Natural Resources Clause as creating constitutional authority (but not a duty) in the State Water Commission to restrict groundwater pumping when it will be harmful to the public, as a limitation on groundwater rights.

The other four justices would affirm the appellate court on both the rule of capture and the public trust issues for the reasons in the appellate opinion, but they would remand to the trial court for fact-findings on the degree of harm to the city and the reasonableness of Escamilla's uses. One of these four justices, though, has concerns that either ruling—or both—could constitute a judicial taking.

All eight justices believe that the problem of groundwater management would be best addressed by the State Legislature, but the Legislature has been reluctant to address the issue due to political obstacles.

As the Chief Justice, you will not only cast the deciding vote on both issues, but you will also assign the Court's opinion to yourself. You will wish to write an opinion that clearly announces the rules or standards that the Court's majority adopts and the legal support and reasoning for the rules and outcome in the case. Consider the following materials, as well as the principles described in the Introduction.

## 3. Materials for Solution of Principal Problem

### a. Groundwater Rights

#### State v. Michels Pipeline Construction, Inc.
Supreme Court of Wisconsin, 1974.
217 N.W.2d 339.

■ WILKIE, JUSTICE.

This case involves the unrestrained use of percolating ground water to the alleged detriment of owners of neighboring land. In 1972 Michels Pipeline Construction, Inc., contracted with the Metropolitan Sewerage Commission of Milwaukee County to install a 60-inch-diameter sewer in the Root River Parkway, Greenfield, Wisconsin. The complaint alleged that in September of 1972 the defendants [Michels and Milwaukee County agencies] began pumping water from wells in the city of Greenfield at a rate of 5,500 gallons per minute in order to dewater the soil to a depth sufficient to permit tunneling for the sewer, approximately 40 feet beneath the ground surface. The complaint alleged that numerous citizens were caused great hardship by the drying up of wells, decreasing capacity and water quality in others, and by the cracking of foundations, basement walls and driveways, due to subsidence of the soil. The State asked that the defendants be ordered to conduct construction of the sewer so as not to create a nuisance and to take action to eliminate or ameliorate the hardship and adverse effect imposed upon state citizens.... The State appeals from the court's order dismissing its amended complaint.

The trial court granted the demurrer of the defendants-respondents on the basis that the case of Huber v. Merkel established that there is no cause of action for interference with ground water. This is a correct statement of the holding of that case. In Huber v. Merkel an owner of real estate attempted to have another landowner in his vicinity enjoined from wasting and unreasonably using water from artesian wells on the person's property. The defendant allowed his wells to flow continuously, the excess simply spilling on the ground and this adversely affected the artesian pressure of all the wells which tapped the same aquifer. This court held that it was the almost universal consensus of judicial opinion that:

> If the waters simply percolate through the ground, without definite channel, they belong to the realty in which they are found, and the owner of the soil may divert, consume, or cut them off with impunity. If, on the other defined channel, the rules which govern the use of surface streams apply; but the presumption is that the waters are percolating waters until it is shown that they are supplied by a definite, flowing stream.

The court went on to find that malicious intent did not affect this right.

... it seems clear that it must be held that the appellant had a clear right at common law, resulting from his ownership of land, to sink a well thereon, and use the water therefrom as he chose, or allow it to flow away, regardless of the effect of such use upon his neighbors' wells, and that such right is not affected by malicious intent. Whether this right results from an absolute ownership of the water itself, as stated in some of the authorities, or from a mere right to use and divert the water while percolating through the soil, is a question of no materiality in the present discussion. In either event, it is a property right, arising out of his ownership of the land, and is protected by the common law as such.

The Huber case did not discuss the basis or rationale for this common-law rule but merely asserted that this was the rule and adopted it. The case has been severely criticized, not only by dissenting justices from this court, but also by text writers and in the opinions of other jurisdictions. Much of the criticism was directed at the holding that even malice did not divest a landowner of his absolute right to the use of ground water. It is generally conceded that this aspect of the case was probably a misstatement or at least an extension of the cases which had applied the common-law or 'English rule' up to that time. All of the prior cases had dealt with nonwasteful, nonmalicious use of water.

In 1956 this court was faced with two companion cases which sought to change the holding of Huber v. Merkel. In Fond du Lac v. Empire and Menne v. Fond du Lac this court refused to change the rule adopted in Huber v. Merkel. The court merely indicated that whatever the arguable merits of change, it should come from the legislature.

The basis for this rule of absolute ownership of percolating ground water was a feeling that the ways of underground water were too mysterious and unpredictable to allow the establishment of adequate and fair rules for regulation of competing rights to such water. So the English courts adopted the position that everyone was permitted to take and use all of which they could get possession.

Even in 1903 when the Huber v. Merkel case was written, the awe of mysterious, unknowable forces beneath the earth was fast becoming an outmoded basis for a rule of law. However, today scientific knowledge in the field of hydrology has certainly advanced to the point where a cause and effect relationship can be established between a tapping of underground water and the level of the water table in the area so that liability can be fairly adjudicated consonant with due process. Our scientific knowledge also establishes the interdependence of all water systems.

It makes very little sense to make an arbitrary distinction between the rules to be applied to water on the basis of where it happens to be found. There is little justification for property rights in ground water to be considered absolute while rights in surface streams are subject to a doctrine of reasonable use. The Huber v. Merkel case certainly gives no explanation of why a property right in ground water should be an exception to the general maxim: *sic utere tuo ut alienum non laedas*.[95]

Now as pointed out in the appellant's brief there are twenty-five states which adhere to the reasonable use doctrine and three which have adopted the even broader correlative rights doctrine. Thus the weight of authority in this country no longer supports the English rule of absolute possession.

*Stare Decisis.*

As was mentioned earlier, the court in Menne v. Fond du Lac did not actually decide to retain the doctrine of Huber v. Merkel but rather stated that if change was desirable it should come from the legislature.

> ... Assuming, however, but without deciding, that the Huber decision did not correctly state the common law, it did state a rule that was reached and is adhered to in several other states and which is often referred to as the common-law rule. It determined that the use of percolating water underneath an owner's land is a property right and that water so obtained could be sold. We have operated thereunder for more than fifty years. Property rights thereunder have been acquired and sold. Under the rule of stare decisis, where property rights are involved, the courts are reluctant to engage in judicial legislation. If there is to be a change, it should come by action of the legislature. We know that the legislature is studying the problem and we can expect such legislation as it deems advisable in the interests of all of the people in the state.

However, in several later cases this court did much to make clear that stare decisis is not an inflexible restraint, but merely a cautionary rule. In several cases, as pointed out by the appellant in its brief, this court has made dramatic changes in common law rules even though earlier cases had refused to do so saying such change was up to the legislature.

> Inherent in the common law is a dynamic principle which allows it to grow and to tailor itself to meet changing needs within the doctrine of stare decisis, which, if correctly understood, was not static and did not forever prevent the courts from reversing themselves or from applying principles of common law to new situations as the need arose. If this were not so, we must succumb to a rule that a judge should let others 'long dead and unaware of the problems of the age in which he lives, do his thinking for him.'

In the present case the proposed change is not confiscatory in nature. It merely brings this type of property (percolating ground water) in line

---

[95] Use your own property in such a manner as not to injure that of another.

with the general limitation on all use of property embodied in the law of nuisance. There is a basic inconsistency in saying that a person has a property right in underground water that cannot be taken without compensation, for when he exercises that right to the detriment of his neighbor, he is actually taking his neighbor's property without compensation.

For the reasons discussed above, we overrule our decision in Huber v. Merkel and for that reason we find it necessary to adopt a rule of law more in harmony with present scientific and legal principles.

*What Rule Should be Adopted.*

What rule should this court now adopt as to the use of percolating ground water? There are three distinct doctrines applied in various American jurisdictions regarding rights in percolating water[96]:

(a) The English or common-law rule:

> ... the person who owns the surface may dig therein, and apply all that is there found to his own purposes at his free will and pleasure; and if, in the exercise of such right, he intercepts or drains off the water collected from underground springs in his neighbor's well, this inconvenience to his neighbor falls within the description of damnum absque injuria, which cannot become the ground of an action. . . .

There is one limitation that the actions may not be motivated by malice and waste of water can be actionable. Although framed in property language this doctrine is really a rule of capture. The landowner may sell and grant his right to withdraw the water to others.

(b) Reasonable Use:

As stated in Corpus Juris Secundum:

> In some states, the rule of the common law followed in early decisions has given way to the doctrine of reasonable use limiting the right of a landowner to percolating water in his land to such an amount of water as may be necessary for some useful or beneficial purpose in connection with the land from which it is taken, not restricting his right to use the water for any useful purpose on his own land, and not restricting his right to use it elsewhere in the absence of proof of injury to adjoining landowners. . . .

(c) Correlative rights:

Again Corpus Juris Secundum defines this doctrine as:

> Under the rule of correlative rights, the rights of all landowners over a common basin, saturated strata, or underground

---

[96] 93 C.J.S. Waters s 93c, pp. 770–773. [Editor's note: The Wisconsin Supreme Court goes on to consider the Restatement as a fourth doctrine and does not consider the fifth doctrine, prior appropriation, because Wisconsin is a riparian state and would have little reason to consider adopting the prior appropriation doctrine.]

reservoir are coequal or correlative, and one cannot extract more than his share of the water, even for use on his own land, where others' rights are injured thereby.

In many early cases the two doctrines of reasonable use and correlative rights seem to have been mixed together as the 'American rule.' However, as Corpus Juris Secundum makes clear, they are two distinct doctrines. According to the appellant's brief only three states adhere to the correlative rights doctrine. This doctrine applies the basic rules of the reasonable use doctrine, but calls for apportionment of underground water where there is not a sufficient supply for all reasonable uses. We are not shown here that water conditions in Wisconsin are so critical as to necessitate the adoption of this doctrine. Also the administrative difficulties of a court trying to make such an apportionment would militate against its adoption.

The 'reasonable use' doctrine has been widely adopted in the United States. However, a close reading of the language of the doctrine shows that it is not a very radical departure from the common-law rule. It still contains quite a broad privilege to use ground water. A waste of water or a wasteful use of water is not unreasonable only if it causes harm, and a use of water that causes harm is nevertheless reasonable if it is made in connection with the overlying land. The withdrawal of water for use elsewhere for beneficial purposes such as municipal supply or domestic supply is not 'reasonable' in this special sense, but such removal may be made without liability if no harm results.

The 'reasonable use' rule basically only affords protection from cities withdrawing large quantities of water for municipal utilities. The rule forces cities to pay those affected by such excessive use damages or the cost of new wells and pumping equipment and is very much in accord with policies of loss distribution and requiring the beneficiaries of harmful activities to pay the costs thereof. However, under the rule there is no apportionment of water as between adjoining landowners. If water is withdrawn for a beneficial use on the land from which it is taken there is no liability for any harm to adjoining property owners. In effect, the rule gives partial protection to small wells against cities or water companies, but not protection from a large factory or apartment building on the neighboring land.

We choose not to adopt any of the three rules here discussed, but rather to adopt the rule set forth in Tentative Draft No. 17 of the Restatement of the Law Second, Torts, as proposed on April 26, 1971, for adoption by the American Law Institute.[97] Sec. 858A state[s] in the analysis section of the proposal:

> Analysis. The rule adopted in this Topic can be described as the American rule with its protection broadened. It gives more or

---

[97] Restatement of the Law Second, Torts, Tentative Draft No. 17, April 26, 1971, sec. 858A, pp. 151–162.

less unrestricted freedom to the possessor of overlying land to develop and use ground water and it permits the grant and sale of ground water to persons who need water but do not possess land overlying it. It does not attempt to apportion the water among users except to the extent that the special conditions of underground streams and interconnected ground and stream water permit it to be done on a rational basis. It gives the protection of the American rule to owners of small wells harmed by large withdrawals for use elsewhere, but extends that protection in proper cases to harm done by large withdrawals for operations on overlying lands.

The proposed section of the Restatement Second reads as follows:

> Sec. 858A. NON-LIABILITY FOR USE OF GROUND WATER-EXCEPTIONS.
>
> A possessor of land or his grantee who withdraws ground water from the land and uses it for a beneficial purpose is not subject to liability for interference with the use of water by another, unless
>
> (a) The withdrawal of water causes unreasonable harm through lowering the water table or reducing artesian pressure,
>
> (b) The ground water forms an underground stream, in which case the rules stated in sec. 850A to 857 are applicable, or
>
> (c) The withdrawal of water has a direct and substantial effect upon the water of a watercourse or lake, in which case the rules stated in secs. 850A to 857 are applicable.

Thus the rule preserves the basic expression of a rule of nonliability—a privilege if you will—to use ground water beneath the land. The formulation of the exception to this basic rule recognizes that there is usually enough water for all users so that apportionment is not necessary but that the problem is who shall bear the costs of deepening prior wells, installing pumps, paying increased pumping costs, etc., necessitated by a lowering of the water table by a large user. The common law placed the burden of making improvements on each user. The 'reasonable use' rule gives protection to existing wells if the water withdrawal is taken off the land for use elsewhere but not if the water is used for beneficial purposes on the overlying land. The proposed rule of the Restatement Second would place the matter of cost on the same rational basis as the rule applicable to surface streams, the reasonableness of placing the burden upon one party or the other.

The comment on the meaning of 'unreasonable harm' as used in the Restatement rule explains that as in other situations, reasonableness will vary with the circumstances. Later users with superior economic resources should not be allowed to impose costs upon smaller water users that are beyond their economic capacity. The comment also address itself to the fear of the respondents that a change in the rule concerning use of percolating water will allow the first user to dictate the depth of wells and the water table to all later users. The comment explains that it is usually reasonable to give equal treatment to persons similarly situated and to place similar burdens on each.

In adopting the rule proposed in the Restatement of Torts, we necessarily overrule the order of the trial court sustaining the demurrer here, and we remand for further proceedings in the trial court.

### Sipriano v. Great Spring Waters of America, Inc.
Supreme Court of Texas, 1999.
1 S.W.3d 75.

■ JUSTICE ENOCH delivered the opinion for a unanimous Court.

For over ninety years, this Court has adhered to the common-law rule of capture in allocating the respective rights and liabilities of neighboring landowners for use of groundwater flowing beneath their property. The rule of capture essentially allows, with some limited exceptions, a landowner to pump as much groundwater as the landowner chooses, without liability to neighbors who claim that the pumping has depleted their wells. We are asked today whether Texas should abandon this rule for the rule of reasonable use, which would limit the common-law right of a surface owner to take water from a common reservoir by imposing liability on landowners who "unreasonably" use groundwater to their neighbors' detriment. Relying on the settled rule of capture, the trial court granted summary judgment against landowners who sued a bottled-water company for negligently draining their water wells. The court of appeals affirmed. Because we conclude that the sweeping change to Texas's groundwater law Sipriano urges this Court to make is not appropriate at this time, we affirm the court of appeals' judgment.

Henderson County landowners Bart Sipriano, Harold Fain, and Doris Fain (Sipriano) sued Great Spring Waters of America, Inc., a/k/a Ozarka Natural Spring Water Co., for negligently draining their water wells. According to Sipriano's allegations, which we take as true for summary judgment purposes, Ozarka, in 1996, began pumping about 90,000 gallons of groundwater per day, seven days a week, from land near Sipriano's. Soon after the pumping began, Sipriano's wells were severely depleted. Sipriano sought injunctive relief, as well as actual and punitive damages for Ozarka's alleged nuisance, negligence, gross negligence, and malice.

This Court adopted the common-law rule of capture in 1904 in Houston & Texas Central Railway Co. v. East. The rule of capture answers the question of what remedies, if any, a neighbor has against a landowner based on the landowner's use of the water under the landowner's land. Essentially, the rule provides that, absent malice or willful waste, landowners have the right to take all the water they can capture under their land and do with it what they please, and they will not be liable to neighbors even if in so doing they deprive their neighbors of the water's use. Rooted in English common law, the rule of capture was perhaps first enunciated in 1843 in Acton v. Blundell:

> [T]hat person who owns the surface may dig therein, and apply all that is there found to his own purposes at his free will and pleasure; and that if, in the exercise of such right, he intercepts or drains off the water collected from underground springs in his neighbor's well, this inconvenience to his neighbor falls within the description damnum absque injuria [an injury without a remedy] which cannot become the ground of an action.

In East, this Court faced a choice between the rule of capture and its counterpart, the rule of reasonable use. No constitutional or statutory considerations guided or constrained our selection at that time. Articulating two public-policy reasons, we chose the rule of capture. First, we noted that the movement of groundwater is "so secret, occult, and concealed that an attempt to administer any set of legal rules in respect to [it] would be involved in hopeless uncertainty, and would, therefore, be practically impossible." And second, we determined that "any . . . recognition of correlative rights would interfere, to the material detriment of the commonwealth, with drainage and agriculture, mining, the construction of highways and railroads, with sanitary regulations, building, and the general progress of improvement in works of embellishment and utility." Thus, we refused to recognize tort liability against a railroad company whose pumping of groundwater under its own property allegedly dried the neighboring plaintiff's well.

After droughts in 1910 and 1917, the citizens of Texas voted in August 1917 to enact section 59 of article 16 of the Texas Constitution, which placed the duty to preserve Texas's natural resources on the State:

> The conservation and development of all of the natural resources of this State . . . and the preservation and conservation of all such natural resources of the State are each and all hereby declared public rights and duties; and the Legislature shall pass all such laws as may be appropriate thereto.

This constitutional amendment, proposed and passed after our common-law decision in East, made clear that in Texas, responsibility for the regulation of natural resources, including groundwater, rests in the hands of the Legislature.

By 1955, this Court recognized that what was "secret [and] occult" to us in 1904—the movement of groundwater—was no longer so. But in City of Corpus Christi v. City of Pleasanton we continued to adhere to the rule of capture. In so doing, however, we expressly recognized what was tacit in East-that the rule of capture is not absolute:

> Having adopted the ... rule [of capture] it may be assumed that the Court adopted it with only such limitations as existed in the common law. What were those limitations? About the only limitations applied by those jurisdictions retaining the ... rule [of capture] are that the owner may not maliciously take water for the sole purpose of injuring his neighbor, or wantonly and willfully waste it.

Thus, while we noted that the common law did not preclude a landowner from capturing and selling water for use off the land, we nonetheless made clear that the rule of capture has exceptions in Texas.

Water regulation is essentially a legislative function.

Now, Sipriano asks us to fundamentally alter the common-law framework within which Texas has operated since the 1904 East decision. That common-law framework existed in 1917 when the citizens of Texas charged the Legislature with the constitutional duty to preserve groundwater through regulation. Like the voters who passed the 1917 constitutional amendment, this Court has consistently recognized "the need for legislative regulation of water." Today, again, we reiterate that the people have constitutionally empowered the Legislature to act in the best interest of the State to preserve our natural resources, including water. We see no reason, particularly because of the 1917 constitutional amendment, for the Legislature to feel constrained from taking appropriate steps to protect groundwater. Indeed, we anticipated legislative involvement in groundwater regulation in East:

> In the absence ... of positive authorized legislation, as between proprietors of adjoining lands, the law recognizes no correlative rights in respect to underground waters percolating, oozing, or filtrating through the earth.

With the allocation of responsibility for groundwater regulation contemplated by the 1917 amendment in mind, it is important that this case comes to us on the heels of Senate Bill 1, which has been described as a "comprehensive water management bill." Passed in June 1997, Senate Bill 1 revamped significant parts of the Water Code and other Texas statutes in an attempt to improve on this State's water management. Perhaps most relevant to our decision today is the Legislature's efforts to streamline the process for creating groundwater conservation districts and to make them more effective in the water management process. Indeed, the Legislature expressly stated that "[g]roundwater conservation districts ... are the state's preferred method of groundwater management."

The Legislature first exercised its constitutional authority to create groundwater conservation districts in 1949. And since then the Legislature has repeatedly revisited and modified the operation of groundwater conservation districts. Now, with Senate Bill 1, the Legislature has given more authority to locally-controlled groundwater conservation districts for establishing requirements for groundwater withdrawal permits and for regulating water transferred outside the district. Senate Bill 1 also revised the "critical area" designation process to require the Texas Natural Resource Conservation Commission and the Texas Water Development Board to identify areas anticipated to experience critical groundwater problems, and streamlined the process by which the TNRCC or the Legislature can create a district in these areas. Senate Bill 1 also included various provisions calling for more comprehensive and coordinated water planning. While the efficacy of the groundwater management methods the Legislature chose and implemented through Senate Bill 1 has been a matter of considerable debate, as the amicus briefs filed in this case reflect, we cannot say at this time that the Legislature has ignored its constitutional charge to regulate this natural resource.

By constitutional amendment, Texas voters made groundwater regulation a duty of the Legislature. And by Senate Bill 1, the Legislature has chosen a process that permits the people most affected by groundwater regulation in particular areas to participate in democratic solutions to their groundwater issues. It would be improper for courts to intercede at this time by changing the common-law framework within which the Legislature has attempted to craft regulations to meet this state's groundwater-conservation needs. Given the Legislature's recent actions to improve Texas's groundwater management, we are reluctant to make so drastic a change as abandoning our rule of capture and moving into the arena of water-use regulation by judicial fiat. It is more prudent to wait and see if Senate Bill 1 will have its desired effect, and to save for another day the determination of whether further revising the common law is an appropriate prerequisite to preserve Texas's natural resources and protect property owners' interests.

We do not shy away from change when it is appropriate. We continue to believe that "the genius of the common law rests in its ability to change, to recognize when a timeworn rule no longer serves the needs of society, and to modify the rule accordingly." And Sipriano presents compelling reasons for groundwater use to be regulated. But unlike in East, any modification of the common law would have to be guided and constrained by constitutional and statutory considerations. Given the Legislature's recent efforts to regulate groundwater, we are not persuaded that it is appropriate today for this Court to insert itself into the regulatory mix by substituting the rule of reasonable use for the current rule of capture. Accordingly, we affirm the court of appeals' judgment.

■ JUSTICE HECHT, joined by JUSTICE O'NEILL, concurring.

The people of Texas have given the Legislature, in article XVI, section 59 of the Texas Constitution, not only the power but the duty to "pass all such laws as may be appropriate" for the conservation, development, and preservation of the State's natural resources, including its groundwater. The Legislature has concluded that local "[g]roundwater conservation districts ... are the state's preferred method of groundwater management." Actually, such districts are not just the preferred method of groundwater management, they are the only method presently available. Yet in the fifty years since the Legislature first authorized the creation of groundwater conservation districts, the record in this case shows that only some forty-two such districts have been created, covering a small fraction of the State. Not much groundwater management is going on.

The reason is not lack of groundwater. Twenty-nine aquifers underlie eighty-one percent of the State. Nor is the reason lack of use. In 1992, groundwater sources supplied fifty-six percent of all water used in the State, including sixty-nine percent of agricultural needs and forty-one percent of municipal needs. Nor is the reason lack of need of management. Over twenty-five years ago the Texas Senate's Interim Committee on Environmental Affairs warned of severe, impending problems with municipal groundwater use and called for comprehensive regulation. The predicted problems have in fact occurred. The comprehensive revision of the Water Code in 1997 was motivated by what the Lieutenant Governor's general counsel has called "the seriousness of the situation": recurring droughts, expansive population growth, and dwindling water supplies.

What really hampers groundwater management is the established alternative, the common law rule of capture, which entitles a landowner to withdraw an unlimited amount of groundwater for any purpose other than willful waste or malice, and as long as he is not negligent in causing subsidence of nearby property. When this Court adopted the rule of capture as a common-law rule ninety-five years ago in Houston & Texas Central Railway. Co. v. East, we believed it to have been adopted in England and by the court of last resort in every state in this country except New Hampshire. Thirty-five years later only eleven of the eighteen western states still followed the rule of capture; after two more decades, only three western states still followed the rule. Now there is but one lone holdout: Texas.

The Court in East gave two reasons for adopting the rule of capture:

(1) Because the existence, origin, movement, and course of such waters, and the causes which govern and direct their movements, are so secret, occult, and concealed that an attempt to administer any set of legal rules in respect to them would be involved in hopeless uncertainty, and would, therefore, be practically impossible. (2) Because any such recognition of correlative rights would interfere, to the material detriment of the commonwealth, with drainage and agriculture, mining, the construction of highways and railroads, with sanitary regulations, building, and the general progress of improvement in works of embellishment and utility.

Neither remains valid. The extensive regulation of oil and gas production proves that effective regulation of migrant substances far below the surface is not only possible but necessary and effective. In the past several decades it has become clear, if it was not before, that it is not regulation that threatens progress, but the lack of it.

Neither respondent nor any of the more than a dozen amici curiae who have appeared in support of respondent's position attempt a principled argument for retaining the rule of capture. They focus instead on pragmatics. First, they say, the rule should not be abandoned because it has been the rule for a long time. The oft-cited wisdom of Justice Holmes is sufficient to rebut this argument:

> It is revolting to have no better reason for a rule of law than that so it was laid down in the time of Henry IV. It is still more revolting if the grounds upon which it was laid down have vanished long since, and the rule simply persists from blind imitation of the past.[98]

Second, respondent and its supporters argue that abandoning the rule of capture would be disruptive. To some extent they are right, of course, but the cost of such disruption must be balanced against the danger that the State's water supply will be threatened because of a lack of reasoned water planning. Studies on the subject seem rather uniformly to indicate that the balance tilts against the rule of capture. Finally, respondent argues that water regulation is the Legislature's responsibility under the Constitution, and that the Court should not venture into the area. I agree that this argument has merit, at least since 1917 when article XVI, section 59 was adopted, but it comes ninety-five years too late: the Court entered the area of water regulation in East when it adopted the rule of capture. Does the Court intrude on the Legislature's constitutional responsibility and duty by maintaining the rule of capture or by abandoning it? It is hard to see how maintaining the rule of capture can be justified as deference to the Legislature's constitutional province when the rule is contrary to the local regulation that is the Legislature's "preferred method of groundwater management."

Nevertheless, I am persuaded for the time being that the extensive statutory changes in 1997, together with the increasing demands on the State's water supply, may result before long in a fair, effective, and comprehensive regulation of water use that will make the rule of capture obsolete. I agree with the Court that it would be inappropriate to disrupt the processes created and encouraged by the 1997 legislation before they have had a chance to work. I concur in the view that, for now—but I think only for now—East should not be overruled.

---

[98] Oliver Wendell Holmes, Jr., The Path of the Law, 10 Harv. L. Rev. 457, 469 (1897).

## NOTES

1. *The rule of capture: from foxes to whales to baseballs.* The rule of capture has historically been an important concept in property law, particularly governing the acquisition of rights in common or unpossessed (and usually mobile) resources. A classic case is *Pierson v. Post*, concerning competing property claims to a wild fox.[99] While the law no longer recognizes property rights in the first person to reduce a wild animal to his or her control, the rule of capture has arisen in recent years in the context of baseball. Does a fan who catches a record-setting home-run baseball own the baseball? If one fan catches the ball, but it is knocked out of his or her hand by other fans struggling for it and then picked up by another fan, who owns it? In a case involving a home-run baseball hit by Barry Bonds in 2001, a court applied equitable principles to grant equal shares of ownership in the baseball to both fans.[100] However, a property law expert urged the application of rule-of-capture principles from whaling cases, which recognized the property rights of the first ship to harpoon the whale,[101] to recognize property rights in the first fan to catch the baseball.[102] Arguably this rule would discourage others' attempts to take the ball from the first person who caught the ball. Would the same logic apply to a common-pool resource like groundwater?

2. *The lone (star) state holdout.* Texas—known as the Lone Star State—prides itself on its independence and uniqueness. The Texas Supreme Court recognizes that it is the only state to still follow the rule of capture to any significant degree. Many other states have expressly rejected or overruled the rule of capture (see, e.g., *Michels Pipeline Construction*). Why? Exactly what right belongs to any individual property owner? Can you quantify the amount of water to which a landowner has a right? If the primary way to maximize one's share of a common-pool resources like groundwater is to build extraction works that will take more of the water sooner than one's neighbors, what will happen to the resource in the long-run? Note that almost a century ago, Texas altered its rule of capture in oil and gas to regulate wells, pumping, and shared management of these common-pool resources due to harms from the premature or wasteful depletion of oil and gas fields.[103]

3. *Changes in groundwater law.* Do you agree with the Wisconsin Supreme Court that courts should change groundwater law doctrines when they are outmoded, or do you agree with the Texas Supreme Court that the state legislature should make any such changes?

If the state legislature alters property rights in groundwater to promote sound management, do property owners have a takings claim? The Texas

---

[99] 3 Cai. R. 175, 2 Am. Dec. 264 (N.Y. 1805).

[100] Popov v. Hayashi, 2002 WL 31833731 (Cal Super. 2002). The court ordered the baseball to be sold and the proceeds to be shared evenly by the two parties. The baseball sold for $450,000. Berkow, 73rd Home Run Ball Sells for $450,000, N.Y. Times, June 26, 2003.

[101] See Ghen v. Rich, 8 F. 159 (D.C. Mass. 1881).

[102] Finkelman, Fugitive Baseballs and Abandoned Property: Who Owns the Home Run Ball?, 23 Cardozo L. Rev. 1609, 1629–32 (2002).

[103] See Weaver, Unitization of Oil and Gas Fields in Texas (1986).

Supreme Court held that the Edwards Aquifer Authority's decision to grant a landowner a groundwater permit for substantially less water than he had requested constituted a taking of his property.[104] The Texas legislature had created the Edwards Aquifer Authority to protect the aquifer and aquifer-dependent endangered species from overpumping by requiring pumpers to obtain permits from the Authority. The Court held that a landowner has an absolute right to all groundwater under the land that he or she owns—called "ownership in place"—and that government regulatory constraint on the landowner's right to pump this groundwater is a compensable taking.[105] Thus, while the state legislature may authorize regulation of groundwater pumping to protect the resource, the government regulatory authority may be reluctant to regulate much at all, because it will have to pay (with limited taxpayer funds) compensation to any landowner who can show that he or she could have pumped more than the regulations allow.

On the other hand, if the state courts change the common law governing groundwater rights, have they engaged in a "judicial taking" of the overlying landowners' rights under pre-existing law?

4. *The nature of private rights in water.* Of course, changes to private interests in water might not be a taking at all, regardless of whether the legislature or a court makes the change. Applying the "web of interests" metaphor of property, Sandra Zellmer and Jessica Harder have argued that water rights should not be treated as constitutionally compensable property (by giving them property-based due process protection), given the unique characteristics of water and the mix of public and private interests in water.[106] The same conclusion might be reached using a "bundle of rights" analysis, according to two courts: "neither surface water, nor ground water, nor the use rights thereto, nor the water-bearing capacity of natural formations belong to a landowner as a stick in the property rights bundle."[107] But there are also theories and case law supporting compensation for holders of water rights that are eliminated for public use.[108]

5. *Unsustainable uses of groundwater.* Robert Glennon has undertaken nationwide studies of groundwater pumping and usage practices throughout the United States and has concluded that unsustainably consumptive practices pervade all systems.[109] He identifies a number of harms that are already occurring from groundwater "overdrafting" or "mining," which is pumping at rates that exceed recharge of aquifers: 1) decline in aquifer levels, which ultimately leads to degradation and

---

[104] Edwards Aquifer Auth. v. Day, 369 SW 3d 814 (Tex. 2012). The Texas Supreme Court heard oral arguments in the case in 2010.

[105] Id.

[106] Zellmer & Harder, Unbundling Property in Water, 59 Ala. L. Rev. 679 (2008).

[107] Board of County Comm'rs v. Park County Sportsmen's Ranch, LLP, 45 P.3d 693, 707 (Colo. 2002); Hydro Resources Corp. v. Gray, 173 P.3d 749, 755 n.5 (N.M. 2007).

[108] Callies & Chipchase, Water Regulation, Land Use, and the Environment, 30 U. Haw. L. Rev. 49, 73 (2007); Shepard, The Unbearable Cost of Skipping the Check: Property Rights, Takings Compensation, and Ecological Protection in the Western Water Law Context, 17 N.Y.U. Envtl. L.J. 1063 (2009).

[109] See, e.g., Glennon, Water Follies: Groundwater Pumping and the Fate of America's Fresh Waters (2002).

elimination of the aquifer as a water source; 2) subsidence (i.e., soil compaction), which damages homes and commercial structures, reduces property values, makes areas more vulnerable to flooding and hurricane-related tidal surges, and reduces the storage capacity and therefore the recharge capacity of aquifers; 3) drying up rivers and springs; 4) higher costs and more energy consumption to drill deeper and more powerful wells; and 5) saltwater intrusion into coastal aquifers.[110] Groundwater pumping by water bottling companies has been highly controversial in a number of states, including Texas, as *Sipriano* reflects.

6. *Groundwater management districts.* While the five common law doctrines governing groundwater define private property rights in groundwater, they operate mostly as liability rules for the resolution of conflicts between competing pumpers. A state's groundwater rights doctrine may clarify or support the authority of groundwater management districts or state agencies to manage and regulate groundwater among all users, but common-law doctrines are not substitutes for state statutes creating comprehensive groundwater management systems. Such systems may be necessary to prevent the unsustainable overdrafting of groundwater sources described in the preceding note.

The *Sipriano* court pinned its hopes on the improved implementation of state legislation authorizing the creation of groundwater conservation districts (GCDs) according to aquifer management areas. The GCDs are to set "desired future conditions" (DFCs), establish "managed available groundwater" (MAG) caps on groundwater production in their management area based on their DFCs, and grant or deny permits according to their MAG parameters and a set of statutory criteria.[111] While not all areas of the state yet have well-functioning GCDs, one commentator has argued that this statutorily based scheme creates a set of priorities in groundwater in order of: 1) historical use permits; 2) operating and transport permits: and 3) limited-production permits.[112] In effect, the rule of capture may be at least partially altered by the operation of the GCD system. He also asserts that the GCD system in operation may give groundwater permittees seniority over surface water rights permittees due to the hydrologic interactions between surface water and groundwater.[113] Another commentator has argued, though, that the Texas courts' failure to overrule the rule of capture will continue to allow harmful groundwater extraction practices and impede the conservation work of GCDs.[114]

---

[110] See id., especially pp. 32–34.
[111] See generally Tex. Water Code ch. 36.
[112] Witherspoon, In the Well: Desired Future Conditions and the Emergence of Groundwater as the New Senior Water Right, 5 Energy & Envtl. L. & Pol'y J. 166 (2010).
[113] Id.
[114] Connelly, The Inconvenience in Texas Groundwater, 46 Hous. L. Rev. 1301 (2009).

## b. THE PUBLIC TRUST DOCTRINE

### National Audubon Society v. Superior Court
Supreme Court of California, 1983.
658 P.2d 709.

■ BROUSSARD, J.

Mono Lake, the second largest lake in California, sits at the base of the Sierra Nevada escarpment near the eastern entrance to Yosemite National Park. The lake is saline; it contains no fish but supports a large population of brine shrimp which feed vast numbers of nesting and migratory birds. Islands in the lake protect a large breeding colony of California gulls, and the lake itself serves as a haven on the migration route for thousands of Northern Phalarope, Wilson's Phalarope, and Eared Grebe. Towers and spires of tufa on the north and south shores are matters of geological interest and a tourist attraction.

Although Mono Lake receives some water from rain and snow on the lake surface, historically most of its supply came from snowmelt in the Sierra Nevada. Five freshwater streams—Mill, Lee Vining, Walker, Parker and Rush Creeks—arise near the crest of the range and carry the annual runoff to the west shore of the lake. In 1940, however, the Division of Water Resources, the predecessor to the present California Water Resources Board, granted the Department of Water and Power of the City of Los Angeles (hereafter DWP) a permit to appropriate virtually the entire flow of four of the five streams flowing into the lake. DWP promptly constructed facilities to divert about half the flow of these streams into DWP's Owens Valley aqueduct. In 1970 DWP completed a second diversion tunnel, and since that time has taken virtually the entire flow of these streams.

As a result of these diversions, the level of the lake has dropped; the surface area has diminished by one-third; one of the two principal islands in the lake has become a peninsula, exposing the gull rookery there to coyotes and other predators and causing the gulls to abandon the former island. The ultimate effect of continued diversions is a matter of intense dispute, but there seems little doubt that both the scenic beauty and the ecological values of Mono Lake are imperiled.

Plaintiffs filed suit in superior court to enjoin the DWP diversions on the theory that the shores, bed and waters of Mono Lake are protected by a public trust. Plaintiffs' suit was transferred to the federal district court, which requested that the state courts determine the relationship between the public trust doctrine and the water rights system. The superior court then entered summary judgments against plaintiffs, ruling that the public trust doctrine offered no independent basis for challenging the DWP diversions. Plaintiffs petitioned us directly for writ of mandate to review that decision; in view of the importance of the issues presented, we issued an alternative writ.

This case brings together for the first time two systems of legal thought: the appropriative water rights system which since the days of the gold rush has dominated California water law, and the public trust doctrine which, after evolving as a shield for the protection of tidelands, now extends its protective scope to navigable lakes. Ever since we first recognized that the public trust protects environmental and recreational values, the two systems of legal thought have been on a collision course. They meet in a unique and dramatic setting which highlights the clash of values. Mono Lake is a scenic and ecological treasure of national significance, imperiled by continued diversions of water; yet, the need of Los Angeles for water is apparent, its reliance on rights granted by the board evident, the cost of curtailing diversions substantial.

Attempting to integrate the teachings and values of both the public trust and the appropriative water rights system, we have arrived at certain conclusions which we briefly summarize here. In our opinion, the core of the public trust doctrine is the state's authority as sovereign to exercise a continuous supervision and control over the navigable waters of the state and the lands underlying those waters. This authority applies to the waters tributary to Mono Lake and bars DWP or any other party from claiming a vested right to divert waters once it becomes clear that such diversions harm the interests protected by the public trust. The corollary rule which evolved in tideland and lakeshore cases barring conveyance of rights free of the trust except to serve trust purposes cannot, however, apply without modification to flowing waters. The prosperity and habitability of much of this state requires the diversion of great quantities of water from its streams for purposes unconnected to any navigation, commerce, fishing, recreation, or ecological use relating to the source stream. The state must have the power to grant nonvested usufructuary rights to appropriate water even if diversions harm public trust uses. Approval of such diversion without considering public trust values, however, may result in needless destruction of those values. Accordingly, we believe that before state courts and agencies approve water diversions they should consider the effect of such diversions upon interests protected by the public trust, and attempt, so far as feasible, to avoid or minimize any harm to those interests.

The water rights enjoyed by DWP were granted, the diversion was commenced, and has continued to the present without any consideration of the impact upon the public trust. An objective study and reconsideration of the water rights in the Mono Basin is long overdue. The water law of California—which we conceive to be an integration including both the public trust doctrine and the board—administered appropriate rights system-permits such a reconsideration, the values underlying that integration require it.

To abate destruction [of Mono Lake], plaintiffs filed suit for injunctive and declaratory relief.

On November 9, 1981, the [trial] court entered summary judgment against plaintiffs. Its notice of intended ruling stated that "[t]he California water rights system is a comprehensive and exclusive system for determining the legality of the diversions of the City of Los Angeles in the Mono Basin.... The Public Trust Doctrine does not function independently of that system. This Court concludes that as regards the right of the City of Los Angeles to divert waters in the Mono Basin that the Public Trust Doctrine is subsumed in the water rights system of the state."

[1.] The Public Trust Doctrine in California

"By the law of nature these things are common to mankind-the air, running water, the sea and consequently the shores of the sea." (Institutes of Justinian 2. 1. 1.) From this origin in Roman law, the English common law evolved the concept of the public trust, under which the sovereign owns "all of its navigable waterways and the lands lying beneath them as trustee of a public trust for the benefit of the people." (*Colberg, Inc. v. State of California ex rel. Dept Pub.* Wks. (1967) 67 Cal.2d 408, 416 [62 Cal.Rptr. 401, 432 P.2d 3].) The State of California, acquired title as trustee to such lands and waterways upon its admission to the union (*City of Berkeley v. Superior Court* (1980) 26 Cal.3d 515, 521 [162 Cal.Rptr. 327, 606 P.2d 362] and cases there cited); from the earliest days (see Eldridge v. Cowell (1854) 4 Cal. 80, 87) its judicial decisions have recognized and enforced the trust obligation.

Three aspects of the public trust doctrine require consideration in this opinion: the purpose of the trust; the scope of the trust, particularly as it applies to the nonnavigable tributaries of a navigable lake; and the powers and duties of the state as trustee of the public trust. We discuss these questions in the order listed.

(a) The purpose of the public trust.

The objective of the public trust has evolved in tandem with the changing public perception of the values and uses of waterways. As we observed in *Marks v. Whitney, supra,* 6 Cal.3d 251, 259 "[p]ublic trust easements [were] traditionally defined in terms of navigation, commerce and fisheries. They have been held to include the right to fish, hunt, bathe, swim, to use for boating and general recreation purposes the navigable waters of the state, and to use the bottom of the navigable waters for anchoring, standing, or other purposes." We went on, however, to hold that the traditional triad of uses-navigation, commerce and fishing-did not limit the public interest in the trust res. In language of special importance to the present setting, we stated that "[t]he public uses to which tidelands are subject are sufficiently flexible to encompass changing public needs. In administering the trust the state is not burdened with an outmoded classification favoring one mode of utilization over another. [Citation.] There is a growing public recognition that one of the most important public uses of the tidelands—a use encompassed within the tidelands trust—is the preservation of those lands in their natural state, so that they may serve as ecological units for scientific study, as open space, and as environments which provide food and habitat for birds and marine life, and which favorably affect the scenery and climate of the area."

Mono Lake is a navigable waterway. It supports a small local industry which harvests brine shrimp for sale as fish food, which endeavor probably qualifies the lake as a "fishery" under the traditional public trust cases. The principal values plaintiffs seek to protect, however, are recreational and ecological-the scenic views of the lake and its shore, the purity of the air, and the use of the lake for nesting and feeding by birds. Under *Marks v. Whitney, supra;* 6 Cal.3d 251, it is clear that protection of these values is among the purposes of the public trust.

(b) The scope of the public trust.

Early English decisions generally assumed the public trust was limited to tidal waters and the lands exposed and covered by the daily tides; many American decisions, including the leading California cases, also concern tidelands. It is, however, well settled in the United States generally and in California that the public trust is not limited by the reach of the tides, but encompasses all navigable lakes and streams.

Mono Lake is, as we have said, a navigable waterway. The beds, shores and waters of the lake are without question protected by the public trust. The streams diverted by DWP, however, are not themselves navigable. Accordingly, we must address in this case a question not discussed in any recent public trust case-whether the public trust limits conduct affecting nonnavigable tributaries to navigable waterways.

We conclude that the public trust doctrine, as recognized and developed in California decisions, protects navigable waters from harm caused by diversion of nonnavigable tributaries.

(c) Duties and powers of the state as trustee.

In the following review of the authority and obligations of the state as administrator of the public trust, the dominant theme is the state's sovereign power and duty to exercise continued supervision over the trust. One consequence, of importance to this and many other cases, is that parties acquiring rights in trust property generally hold those rights subject to the trust, and can assert no vested right to use those rights in a manner harmful to the trust.

As we noted recently in *City of Berkeley v. Superior Court, supra* 26 Cal.3d 515, the decision of the United States Supreme Court in *Illinois Central Railroad Company v. Illinois, supra,* 146 U.S. 387, "remains the primary authority even today, almost nine decades after it was decided." (P. 521.) The Illinois Legislature in 1886 had granted the railroad in fee simple 1,000 acres of submerged lands, virtually the entire Chicago waterfront. Four years later it sought to revoke that grant. The Supreme Court upheld the revocatory legislation. Its opinion explained that lands under navigable waters conveyed to private parties for wharves, docks, and other structures in furtherance of trust purposes could be granted free of the trust because the conveyance is consistent with the purpose of the trust. But the legislature, it held, did not have the power to convey the entire city waterfront free of trust, thus barring all future legislatures from protecting the public interest. The opinion declares that: "A grant of all the lands under the navigable waters of a State has never been adjudged to be within the legislative power; and any attempted grant of the kind would be held, if not absolutely void on its face, as subject to revocation. The State can no more abdicate its trust over property in which the whole people are interested, like navigable waters and soils under them, . . . than it can abdicate its police powers in the administration of government and the preservation of the peace. In the administration of government the use of such powers may for a limited period be delegated to a municipality or other body, but there always remains with the State the right to revoke those powers and exercise them in a more direct manner, and one more conformable to its wishes. So with trusts connected with public property, or property of a special character, like lands under navigable waterways, they cannot be placed entirely beyond the direction and control of the State."

Turning to the *Illinois Central* grant, the Court stated that: "Any grant of the kind is necessarily revocable, and the exercise of the trust by which the property was held by the State can be resumed at any time. Undoubtedly there may be expenses incurred in improvements made under such a grant which the State ought to pay; but, be that as it may, the power to resume the trust whenever the State judges best is, we think, incontrovertible. . . . The ownership of the navigable waters of the harbor and of the lands under them is a subject of public concern to the whole people of the State. The trust with which they are held, therefore, is governmental and cannot be alienated, except in those instances mentioned of parcels used in the improvement of the interest thus held, or when parcels can be disposed of without detriment to the public interest in the lands and waters remaining."

The California Supreme Court endorsed the *Illinois Central* principles in *People v. California Fish Co., supra,* 166 Cal. 576 [138 P. 79]. *California Fish* concerned title to about 80,000 acres of tidelands conveyed by state commissioners pursuant to statutory authorization. The court first set out principles to govern the interpretation of statutes conveying that property: "[S]tatutes purporting to authorize an abandonment of . . . public use will be carefully scanned to ascertain whether or not such was the legislative intention, and that intent must be clearly expressed or necessarily implied. It will not be implied if any other inference is reasonably possible. And if any interpretation of the statute is reasonably possible which would not involve a destruction of the public use or an intention to terminate it in violation of the trust, the courts will give the statute such interpretation." Applying these principles, the court held that because the statute in question and the grants pursuant thereto were not made for trust purposes, the grantees did not acquire absolute title; instead, the grantees "own the soil, subject to the easement of the public for the public uses of navigation and commerce, and to the right of the state, as administrator and controller of these public uses and the public trust therefor, to enter upon and possess the same for the preservation and advancement of the public uses and to make such changes and improvements as may be deemed advisable for those purposes."

Finally, rejecting the claim of the tideland purchasers for compensation, the court stated they did not lose title, but retained it subject to the public trust. While the state may not "retake the absolute title without compensation," it may without such payment erect improvements to further navigation and take other actions to promote the public trust.

*Boone v. Kingsbury* (1928) 206 Cal. 148 [273 P. 797], presents another aspect of this matter. The Legislature authorized the Surveyor-General to lease trust lands for oil drilling. Applying the principles of *Illinois Central,* the court upheld that statute on the ground that the derricks would not substantially interfere with the trust. Any licenses granted by the statute, moreover, remained subject to the trust: "The state may at any time remove [the] structures ... , even though they have been erected with its license or consent, if it subsequently finds that they substantially interfere with navigation or commerce."

Finally, in our recent decision in *City of Berkeley v. Superior Court, supra;* 26 Cal.3d 515, we considered whether deeds executed by the Board of Tidelands Commissioners pursuant to an 1870 act conferred title free of the MIA. Applying the principles of earlier decisions, we held that the grantees' title was subject to the trust, both because the Legislature had not made clear its intention to authorize a conveyance free of the trust and because the 1870 act and the conveyances under it were not intended to further mist purposes.

Once again we rejected the claim that establishment of the public trust constituted a taking of property for which compensation was required: "We do not divest anyone of title to property; the consequence of our decision will be only that some landowners whose predecessors in interest acquired property under the 1870 act will, like the grantees in *California Fish,* hold it subject to the public trust."

In summary, the foregoing cases amply demonstrate the continuing power of the state as administrator of the public trust, a power which extends to the revocation of previously granted rights or to the enforcement of the trust against lands long thought free of the trust. Except for those rare instances in which a grantee may acquire a right to use former trust property free of trust restrictions, the grantee holds subject to the trust, and while he may assert a vested right to the servient estate (the right of use subject to the trust) and to any improvements he erects, he can claim no vested right to bar recognition of the trust or state action to carry out its purposes.

[2.] The California Water Rights System

California operates under the so-called dual system of water rights which recognizes both the appropriation and the riparian doctrines. The riparian doctrine confers upon the owner of land contiguous to a watercourse the right to the reasonable and beneficial use of water on his land. The appropriation doctrine contemplates the diversion of water and applies to "any taking of water for other than riparian or overlying uses."

In 1926, a constitutional amendment radically altered water law in California and led to an expansion of the powers of the board.

Article X, section 2 (enacted in 1928 as art. XIV, § 3) reads in pertinent part as follows: "It is hereby declared that because of the conditions prevailing in this State the general welfare requires that the water resources of the State be put to beneficial use to the fullest extent of which they are capable, and that the waste or unreasonable use or unreasonable method of use of water be prevented, and that the conservation of such waters is to be exercised with a view to the reasonable and beneficial use thereof in the interest of the people and for the public welfare. The right to water or to the use or flow of water in or from any natural stream or water course in this State is and shall be limited to such water as shall be reasonably required for the beneficial use to be served."

This amendment establishes state water policy. All uses of water, including public trust uses, must now conform to the standard of reasonable use. . . .

Thus, the function of the Water Board has steadily evolved from the narrow role of deciding priorities between competing appropriators to the charge of comprehensive planning and allocation of waters. This change necessarily affects the board's responsibility with respect to the public trust. The board of limited powers of 1913 had neither the power nor duty to consider interests protected by the public trust; the present board, in undertaking planning and allocation of water resources, is required by statute to take those interests into account.

[3.] Relationship between the Public Trust Doctrine and the California Water Rights System

In our opinion, both the public trust doctrine and the water rights system embody important precepts which make the law more responsive to the diverse needs and interests involved in the planning and allocation of water resources. To embrace one system of thought and reject the other would lead to an unbalanced structure, one which would either decry as a breach of trust appropriations essential to the economic development of this state, or deny any duty to protect or even consider the values promoted by the public trust. Therefore, seeking an accommodation which will make use of the pertinent principles of both the public trust doctrine and the appropriative water rights system, and drawing upon the history of the public trust and the water rights system, the body of judicial precedent, and the views of expert commentators, we reach the following conclusions:

    a. The state as sovereign retains continuing supervisory control over its navigable waters and the lands beneath those waters. This principle, fundamental to the concept of the public trust, applies to rights in flowing waters as well as to rights in tidelands and lakeshores; it prevents any party from acquiring a vested right to appropriate water in a manner harmful to the interests protected by the public trust.

    b. As a matter of current and historical necessity, the Legislature, acting directly or through an authorized agency such as the Water Board, has the power to grant usufructuary licenses that will permit an appropriator to take water from flowing streams and use that water in a distant part of the state, even though this taking does not promote, and may unavoidably harm, the trust uses at the source stream. The population and economy of this state depend upon the appropriation of vast quantities of water for uses unrelated to in-stream trust values. California's Constitution, its statutes, decisions, and commentators all emphasize the need to make efficient use of California's limited water resources: all recognize, at least implicitly, that efficient use requires diverting water from in-stream uses. Now that the economy and population centers of this state have developed in reliance upon appropriated water, it would be disingenuous to hold that such appropriations are and have always been improper to the extent that they harm public trust uses, and can be justified only upon theories of reliance or estoppel.

    c. The state has an affirmative duty to take the public trust into account in the planning and allocation of water resources, and to protect public trust uses whenever feasible. Just as the history of this state shows that appropriation may be necessary for efficient use of water despite unavoidable harm to public trust values, it demonstrates that an appropriative water rights system administered without consideration of the public trust may cause unnecessary and unjustified harm to trust interests.

Once the state has approved an appropriation, the public trust imposes a duty of continuing supervision over the taking and use of the appropriated water. In exercising its sovereign power to allocate water resources in the public interest, the state is not confined by past allocation decisions which may be incorrect in light of current knowledge or inconsistent with current needs.

It is clear that some responsible body ought to reconsider the allocation of the waters of the Mono Basin. No vested rights bar such reconsideration. We recognize the substantial concerns voiced by Los Angeles—the city's need for water, its reliance upon the 1940 board decision, the cost both in terms of money and environmental impact of obtaining water elsewhere. Such concerns must enter into any allocation decision. We hold only that they do not preclude a reconsideration and reallocation which also takes into account the impact of water diversion on the Mono Lake environment.

Conclusion

The federal court inquired of the interrelationship between the public trust doctrine and the California water rights system, asking whether the "public trust doctrine in this context [is] subsumed in the California water rights system, or ... function[s] independently of that system?" Our answer is "neither." The public trust doctrine and the appropriative water rights system are parts of an integrated system of preserving the continuing sovereign power of the state to protect public trust uses, a power which precludes anyone from acquiring a vested right to harm the public trust, and imposes a continuing duty on the state to take such uses into account in allocating water resources.

Restating its question, the federal court asked: "[C]an the plaintiffs challenge the Department's permits and licenses by arguing that those permits and licenses are limited by the public trust doctrine?" We reply that plaintiffs can rely on the public trust doctrine in seeking reconsideration of the allocation of the waters of the Mono Basin. . . .

The human and environmental uses of Mono Lake-uses protected by the public trust doctrine-deserve to be taken into account. Such uses should not be destroyed because the state mistakenly thought itself powerless to protect them.

Let a peremptory writ of mandate issue commanding the Superior Court of Alpine County to vacate its judgment in this action and to enter a new judgment consistent with the views stated in this opinion.

## In the Matter of the Water Use Permit Applications (the Waiahole Ditch case)

Supreme Court of Hawaii, 2000.
9 P.3d 409.

■ Opinion of the Court by NAKAYAMA, J.

The present appeal arises from an extended dispute over the water distributed by the Waiahole Ditch System, a major irrigation infrastructure on the island of O'ahu supplying the island's leeward side[115] with water diverted from its windward side.[116] In 1995, this dispute culminated in a contested case hearing of heretofore unprecedented size, duration, and complexity before appellee Commission on Water Resource Management (the Commission). At the hearing, the Commission considered petitions to amend the interim instream flow standards for windward streams affected by the ditch,

---

[115] [Editor's note: The leeward side of an island is the dry side of the island.]
[116] [Editor's note: The windward side of an island is the wet side of the island.]

water use permit applications for various leeward offstream purposes, and water reservation petitions for both instream and offstream uses. The Commission issued its final findings of fact (FOFs), conclusions of law (COLs), decision and order (D & O) (collectively, final decision or decision) on December 24, 1997.

For the reasons fully explained below, we affirm in part and vacate in part the Commission's decision and remand for further proceedings consistent with this opinion.

## I. BACKGROUND

### A. INTRODUCTION

The Waiahole Ditch System collects fresh surface water and dike-impounded ground water from the Ko'olau mountain range on the windward side of the island of O'ahu and delivers it to the island's central plain. The ditch system was built in significant part from 1913 to 1916 to irrigate a sugar plantation owned and operated by Oahu Sugar Company, Ltd. (OSCo). Until the plantation ceased operations in 1995, OSCo used much of the ditch's flow, in addition to a substantial supply of ground water pumped from the Pearl Harbor aquifer.

Diversions by the ditch system reduced the flows in several windward streams, specifically, Waiahole, Waianu, Waikane, and Kahana streams, affecting the natural environment and human communities dependent upon them. Diminished flows impaired native stream life and may have contributed to the decline in the greater Kane'ohe Bay ecosystem, including the offshore fisheries. The impacts of stream diversion, however, went largely unacknowledged until, in the early 1990s, the sugar industry on O'ahu came to a close.

### B. PROCEDURAL HISTORY

On July 15, 1992, the Commission designated the five aquifer systems of Windward O'ahu as ground water management areas, effectively requiring existing users of Waiahole Ditch water to apply for water use permits within one year of that date. In June 1993, the Waiahole Irrigation Company (WIC), the operator of the ditch system, filed a combined water use permit application for the existing users of ditch water. In August 1993, OSCo announced that it would end its sugar operations, signaling the imminent availability of the ditch water used by OSCo and raising the question of its future allocation.

Conflict ensued. [Competing claims to reserve or draw water from Waiahole Ditch were filed by Honolulu city and county agencies, state agencies, community associations, agricultural interests, and the Kamehahema Schools Bernice Pauahi Bishop Estate (KSBE). The amount sought by all permit applications collectively would exceed the entire flow of the ditch. A mediation among the parties in December 1994 produced an interim agreement that surplus waters from the ditch would be returned to the windward streams.]

The interim restoration of windward stream flows had an immediate apparent positive effect on the stream ecology. The higher flows flushed out exotic fish species that were harming native species by carrying parasites and disease, competing for food and space, and interfering with spawning rituals. Experts saw excellent potential for the repopulation of native stream life such as 'o'opu (goby), 'opae (shrimp), and h'ah'awai (snail).

On January 25, 1995, the Commission ordered a combined contested case hearing on the permit applications, reservation petitions, and petitions to amend the WIIFS [windward interim instream flow standards]. At a public hearing on April 18, 1995, the Commission received public testimony and requests to participate in the consolidated hearing. The Commission admitted a final total of twenty-five parties.

C. THE FINAL DECISION

The Commission's final decision consisted of 1,109 FOFs, an extensive legal discussion section styled as COLs, and a D & O explaining at length the Commission's disposition. In its COLs, the Commission surveyed the law of water in Hawai'i, as established in the Hawai'i Constitution, State Water Code (the Code), and common law, focusing particularly on the "public trust doctrine." The Commission identified Windward O'ahu ground water and streams and Kane'ohe Bay as "part of the public trust res . . . subject to review under the State's public trust responsibility as expressed in the State Water Code."

III. DISCUSSION

[The Court addressed numerous issues in its nearly 100-page opinion. The excerpt republished in this Assignment focuses on the public trust doctrine.]

[A.] THE PUBLIC TRUST DOCTRINE

Substantial controversy arises from the Commission's discussion of the "public trust doctrine" in its decision. Before addressing the parties' arguments, we survey the historical development of the doctrine in this jurisdiction.

1. *History and Development*

The United States Supreme Court advanced the seminal modern expression of the public trust doctrine in *Illinois Central Railroad Co. v. Illinois*, 146 U.S. 387 (1892).[117] The case arose from a disputed conveyance of land submerged under the navigable waters of Lake Michigan by the state legislature to private interests. The Court characterized the state's interest in such lands as

> title different in character from that which the State holds in lands intended for sale. . . . It is a title *held in trust for the people*

---

[117] The doctrine traces its origins to the English common law and ancient Roman law. *See* Lynda L. Butler, *The Commons Concept: A Historical Concept with Modern Relevance*, 23 Wm. & Mary L. Rev. 835, 846–67 (1982).

*of the State* that they may enjoy the navigation of the waters, carry on commerce over them, and have liberty of fishing therein freed from the obstruction or interference of private parties.

"The control of the state for purposes of the trust," the Court continued,

> can never be lost, except as to such parcels as are used in *promoting the interests of the public therein,* or can be disposed of *without any substantial impairment of the public interest in the lands and waters remaining.* The State can no more abdicate its trust over property in which the whole people are interested, like navigable waters and soils under them, so as to leave them entirely under the use and control of private parties, than it can abdicate its police powers in the administration of government and the preservation of the peace. In the administration of government the use of such powers may for a limited period be delegated to a municipality or other body, but there always remains with the State the right to revoke those powers and exercise them in a more direct manner, and one more conformable to its wishes. *So with trusts connected with public property, or property of a special character, like lands under navigable waters, they cannot be placed entirely beyond the direction and control of the State.*

*Id.* at 453–54 (emphases added).[118] Because the wholesale surrender of state authority over the lands in question was "not consistent with the exercise of that trust which requires the government of the State to preserve such waters for the uses of the public," *id.* at 453, the disputed grant was "necessarily revocable, and the exercise of the trust by which the property was held by the State can be resumed at any time," *id.* at 455.

This court endorsed the public trust doctrine in *King v. Oahu Railway & Land Co.,* 11 Haw. 717 (1899). Quoting extensively from *Illinois Central,* we agreed that "[t]he people of Hawaii hold the absolute rights to all its navigable waters and the soils under them for their own common use. The lands under the navigable waters in and around the territory of the Hawaiian Government are held in trust for the public uses of navigation." *Id.* at 725. Later decisions confirmed our embrace of the public trust doctrine. *See County of Hawaii v. Sotomura,* 55 Haw. 176, 183–84, 517 P.2d 57, 63 (1973) ("Land below the high water mark . . . is a natural resource owned by the state subject to, but in some sense in trust for, the enjoyment of certain public rights."), *cert. denied,* 419 U.S. 872 (1974); *In re Sanborn,* 57 Haw. 585, 593–94, 562 P.2d 771, 776 (1977) (observing that any purported land court registration of lands below the high water mark was ineffective under the public trust doctrine); *State v. Zimring,* 58 Haw. 106, 121, 566 P.2d 725, 735 (1977)

---

[118] Courts and commentators have identified up to three separate interests in trust resources: the *jus privatum,* or private property right, the *jus regium,* otherwise known as the police power, and the *jus publicum,* the public trust.

(holding that lava extensions "vest when created in the people of Hawaii, held in public trust by the government for the benefit, use and enjoyment of all the people.").

In *McBryde Sugar Co. v. Robinson*, 54 Haw. 174, 504 P.2d 1330, *aff'd on reh'g*, 55 Haw. 260, 517 P.2d 26 (1973), *appeal dismissed and cert. denied*, 417 U.S. 962 (1974), we contemplated the public interest in water resources. Consulting the prior laws and practices of this jurisdiction, we observed that, in granting land ownership interests in the Mahele,[119] the Hawaiian Kingdom expressly reserved its sovereign prerogatives "[t]o encourage and even to enforce the usufruct of lands for the common good. The right to water," we explained,

> is one of the most important usufruct of lands, and it appears clear to us that by the foregoing limitation the right to water was specifically and definitely *reserved for the people of Hawaii for their common good in all of the land grants.*
>
> Thus by the Mahele and subsequent Land Commission Award and issuance of Royal Patent right to water was not intended to be, could not be, and was not transferred to the awardee, and *the ownership of water in natural watercourses and rivers remained in the people of Hawaii for their common good.*

In *Robinson v. Ariyoshi*, 65 Haw. 641, 658 P.2d 287 (1982), we elaborated on our *McBryde* decision, comparing the retained sovereign "prerogatives, powers and duties" concerning water to a "public trust":

> [W]e believe that by [the sovereign reservation], *a public trust was imposed upon all the waters of the kingdom.* That is, we find the public interest in the waters of the kingdom was understood to necessitate a *retention of authority and the imposition of a concomitant duty to maintain the purity and flow of our waters for future generations and to assure that the waters of our land are put to reasonable and beneficial uses.* This is not ownership in the corporeal sense where the State may do with the property as it pleases; rather, we comprehend the nature of the State's ownership as a retention of such *authority to assure the continued existence and beneficial application of the resource for the common good.*

*Id.* at 674, 658 P.2d at 310 (emphases added).

The trust over the water resources of this state, we observed, was "akin to the title held by all states in navigable waterways which was recognized in [*Illinois Central*]." *Robinson*, 65 Haw. at 674, 658 P.2d at 310. Insofar as the two trusts differ in origin and concern, however, we

---

[119] The Mahele and the subsequent Kuleana Act instituted the concept of private property in the Hawaiian Kingdom. For an overview of its operation, see *id.* at 184–85, 504 P.2d at 1337–38; Jon J. Chinen, The Great Mahele (1958); Lilikala Kame'eleihiwa, Native Lands and Foreign Desires (1992).

recognized that "the extent of the state's trust obligation of course would not be identical to that which applies to navigable waterways." *Id.* at 675, 658 P.2d at 310.

In 1978, this state added several provisions to its constitution specifically relating to water resources. In 1987, pursuant to the constitutional mandate of article XI, section 7, the legislature enacted the State Water Code, HRS chapter 174C.

2. *Relationship to the State Water Code*

[The Court addressed the argument that the State Water Code subsumed and supplanted the common law public trust doctrine and that the Commission exceeded its authority by considering factors not expressly provided in the Code. After determining that the legislature did not express any intent to abolish the common law public trust doctrine and noting that the nature of the doctrine itself prevents its legislative abrogation, the Court turned to the constitutional nature of the public trust in Hawai'i.]

Most importantly, the people of this state have elevated the public trust doctrine to the level of a constitutional mandate.

Article XI, section 1 of the Hawai'i Constitution mandates that, "*[f]or the benefit of present and future generations,* the State and its political subdivisions shall *protect and conserve* all natural resources, including water and shall promote the development and utilization of these resources in a manner consistent with their *conservation*" and further declares that "[a]ll public natural resources are *held in trust for the benefit of the people.*" (Emphases added.) Article XI, section 7 reiterates the State's "*obligation to protect, control and regulate* the use of Hawaii's water resources *for the benefit of its people.*" (Emphases added.)

The plain reading of these provisions manifests the framers' intent to incorporate the notion of the public trust into our constitution. The intensive deliberations on the subject in the convention record substantiate this interpretation. *See* Debates in Committee of the Whole on Conservation, Control and Development of Resources [hereinafter Debates], in 2 Proceedings of the Constitutional Convention of Hawaii of 1978, at 855–81 (1980) [hereinafter Proceedings].

We therefore hold that article XI, section 1 and article XI, section 7 adopt the public trust doctrine as a fundamental principle of constitutional law in Hawai'i.

Other state courts, without the benefit of such constitutional provisions, have decided that the public trust doctrine exists independently of any statutory protections supplied by the legislature. This view is all the more compelling here, in light of our state's constitutional public trust mandate. To the extent that other courts have held otherwise, their decisions are neither controlling nor, for the reasons stated above, applicable in this state.

### 3. *The State Water Resources Trust*

Having established the public trust doctrine's independent validity, we must define its basic parameters with respect to the water resources of this state. In so doing, we address: a) the "scope" of the trust, or the resources it encompasses; and b) the "substance" of the trust, including the purposes or uses it upholds and the powers and duties it confers on the state.

#### a. *Scope of the Trust*

The public trust doctrine has varied in scope over time and across jurisdictions. In its ancient Roman form, the public trust included "the air, running water, the sea, and consequently the shores of the sea." J. Inst. 2.1.1. Under the English common law, the trust covered tidal waters and lands. *See Shively v. Bowlby,* 152 U.S. 1, 11 (1894). Courts in the United States have commonly understood the trust as extending to all navigable waters and the lands beneath them irrespective of tidality. *See Illinois Central, supra; Phillips Petroleum,* 484 U.S. 469 (1988) (confirming that the public trust still applies to tidal waters, whether navigable or not). In Hawai'i, this court has recognized, based on founding principles of law in this jurisdiction, a distinct public trust encompassing all the water resources of the state. The Hawai'i Constitution declares that "all public resources are held in trust by the state for the benefit of its people," Haw. Const. art. XI, § 1, and establishes a public trust obligation "to protect, control, and regulate the use of Hawaii's water resources for the benefit of its people," Haw. Const. art. XI, § 7.

We need not define the full extent of article XI, section 1's reference to "all public resources" at this juncture. For the purposes of this case, however, we reaffirm that, under article XI, sections 1 and 7 and the sovereign reservation, the public trust doctrine applies to all water resources without exception or distinction. KSBE and Castle advocate for the exclusion of ground waters from the public trust. Their arguments, first, contradict the clear import of the constitutional provisions, which do not differentiate between categories of water in mandating the protection and regulation of water resources for the common good. The convention's records confirm that the framers understood "water resources" as "includ[ing] ground water, surface water and all other water."

We are also unpersuaded by the contention that the sovereign reservation does not extend to ground waters. Their position rests almost entirely on one decision, *City Mill Co., Ltd. v. Honolulu Sewer & Water Comm'n,* 30 Haw. 912 (1929). Discussing the effect of the Mahele, the *City Mill* court observed that " 'all mineral or metallic mines' were reserved to the Hawaiian government, but there was no reservation whatever of the subterranean waters." *Id.* at 934. Nowhere in the opinion, however, does the court address the reservation of sovereign prerogatives and its surrounding historical and legal context. This fatal oversight, common to other cases subsequently invalidated by this court, discounts the precedential value of *City Mill* concerning the public trust.

Even more fundamentally, just as ancient Hawaiian usage reflected the perspectives of that era, the common law distinctions between ground and surface water developed without regard to the manner in which "both categories represent no more than a single integrated source of water with each element dependent upon the other for its existence." Modern science and technology have discredited the surface-ground dichotomy. Few cases highlight more plainly its diminished meaning and utility than the present one, involving surface streams depleted by ground water diversions and underground aquifers recharged by surface water applications. In determining the scope of the sovereign reservation, therefore, we see little sense in adhering to artificial distinctions neither recognized by the ancient system nor borne out in the present practical realities of this state.

Water is no less an essential "usufruct of lands" when found below, rather than above, the ground. In view of the ultimate value of water to the ancient Hawaiians, it is inescapable that the sovereign reservation was intended to guarantee public rights to all water, regardless of its immediate source. Whatever practices the ancients may have observed in their time, therefore, we must conclude that the reserved trust encompasses any usage developed in ours, including the "ground water" uses proposed by the parties in the instant case. The public trust, by its very nature, does not remain fixed for all time, but must conform to changing needs and circumstances.

In sum, given the vital importance of all waters to the public welfare, we decline to carve out a ground water exception to the water resources trust. Based on the plain language of our constitution and a reasoned modern view of the sovereign reservation, we confirm that the public trust doctrine applies to all water resources, unlimited by any surface-ground distinction.

### b. *Substance of the Trust*

The public trust is a dual concept of sovereign right and responsibility. The arguments in the present appeal focus on the state's trust duties. In its decision, the Commission stated that, under the public trust doctrine, "the State's first duty is to protect the fresh water resources (surface and ground) which are part of the public trust res," a duty which it further described as "a categorical imperative and the precondition to all subsequent considerations." The public trust, the Commission also ruled, subjects offstream water uses to a "heightened level of scrutiny."

In *Illinois Central,* the United States Supreme Court described the state's interest in its navigable waters as "title," not in a proprietary sense, but "title held *in trust for the people of the State that they may enjoy* the navigation of *the waters,* carry on commerce over them, and have liberty of fishing therein *freed from the obstruction or interference of private parties."* 146 U.S. at 452 (emphases added). The trust, in the Court's simplest terms, "requires the government of the State to *preserve such waters for the use of the public."* Id. at 453 (emphasis added).

Based on this formulation, other courts have sought to further define the requirements of the public trust doctrine. The rules developed in order to protect public water bodies and submerged lands for public access and use, however, do not readily apply in the context of water resources valued for consumptive purposes, where competing uses are more often mutually exclusive. This court recognized as much in *Robinson,* stating that "[t]he extent of the state's trust obligation over all waters of course would not be identical to that which applies to navigable waters." 65 Haw. at 675, 658 P.2d at 310. Keeping this distinction in mind, we consider the substance of the water resources trust of this state, specifically, the purposes protected by the trust and the powers and duties conferred on the state thereunder.

i. *Purposes of the Trust*

In other states, the "purposes" or "uses" of the public trust have evolved with changing public values and needs. The trust traditionally preserved public rights of navigation, commerce, and fishing. Courts have further identified a wide range of recreational uses, including bathing, swimming, boating, and scenic viewing, as protected trust purposes.

As a logical extension from the increasing number of public trust uses of waters in their natural state, courts have recognized the distinct public interest in resource protection.

This court has likewise acknowledged resource protection, with its numerous derivative public uses, benefits, and values, as an important underlying purpose of the reserved water resources trust. The people of our state have validated resource "protection" by express constitutional decree. We thus hold that the maintenance of waters in their natural state constitutes a distinct "use" under the water resources trust. This disposes of any portrayal of retention of waters in their natural state as "waste." [The Court also recognized trust purposes in domestic water use for drinking water and in Native Hawaiian traditional and customary rights.]

[One party] asserts that the public trust in Hawai'i encompasses private use of resources for "economic development," citing, *inter alia, Territory v. Liliuokalani,* 14 Haw. 88 (1902) (grants of tidal lands to private individuals), *Haalelea v. Montgomery,* 2 Haw. 62 (1858) (konohiki fishing rights), and the Admissions Act, Act of Mar. 18, 1959, Pub.L. 83–3, 73 Stat. 4, § 5(f) (designating "development of farm and home ownership" as one of the purposes of the state ceded lands trust). While these examples generally demonstrate that the public trust may allow grants of private interests in trust resources under certain circumstances, they in no way establish private commercial use as among the public purposes *protected* by the trust.

Although its purpose has evolved over time, the public trust has never been understood to safeguard rights of exclusive use for private commercial gain. Such an interpretation, indeed, eviscerates the trust's basic purpose of reserving the resource for use and access by the general public without preference or restriction.

We hold that, while the state water resources trust acknowledges that private use for "economic development" may produce important public benefits and that such benefits must figure into any balancing of competing interests in water, it stops short of embracing private commercial use as a protected "trust purpose." We thus eschew [the] view of the trust, in which the " 'public interest' advanced by the trust is the sum of competing private interests" and the "rhetorical distinction between 'public trust' and 'private gain' is a false dichotomy." To the contrary, if the public trust is to retain any meaning and effect, it must recognize enduring public rights in trust resources separate from, and superior to, the prevailing private interests in the resources at any given time. *See Robinson,* 65 Haw. at 677, 658 P.2d at 312 ("[U]nderlying every private diversion and application there is, as there always has been, a superior public interest in this natural bounty.").

### ii. *Powers and Duties of the State Under the Trust*

This court has described the public trust relating to water resources as the authority and duty "to maintain the *purity and flow* of our waters for future generations *and* to assure that the waters of our land are put to *reasonable and beneficial* uses." *Id.* at 674, 658 P.2d at 310 (emphases added). Similarly, article XI, section 1 of the Hawai'i Constitution requires the state both to "protect" natural resources *and* to promote their "use and development." The state water resources trust thus embodies a dual mandate of 1) protection and 2) maximum reasonable and beneficial use.

The mandate of "protection" coincides with the traditional notion of the public trust developed with respect to navigable and tidal waters. As commonly understood, the trust protects public waters and submerged lands against irrevocable transfer to private parties, *see, e.g., Illinois Central, supra,* or "substantial impairment," whether for private or public purposes, *see, e.g., State v. Public Serv. Comm'n, supra.* In this jurisdiction, our decisions in *McBryde* and its progeny and the plain meaning and history of the term "protection" in article XI, section 1 and article XI, section 7 establish that the state has a comparable duty to ensure the continued availability and existence of its water resources for present and future generations.

In this jurisdiction, the water resources trust also encompasses a duty to promote the reasonable and beneficial use of water resources in order to maximize their social and economic benefits to the people of this state. Post-Mahele water rights decisions ignored this duty, treating public water resources as a commodity reducible to absolute private ownership, such that "no limitation . . . existed or was supposed to exist to [the owner's] power to use the . . . waters as he saw fit," *Hawaiian Commercial & Sugar Co. v. Wailuku Sugar Co.,* 15 Haw. 675, 680 (1904). *See Reppun,* 65 Haw. at 539–48, 656 P.2d at 63–69. Based on founding principles of the ancient Hawaiian system and present necessity, this court subsequently reasserted the dormant public interest in the equitable and maximum beneficial allocation of water resources. *See id.; Robinson,* 65 Haw. at 674–77, 658 P.2d at 310–12.

This state has adopted such principles in its constitution. Unlike many of the traditional water rights systems governed by such provisions, however, article XI, section 1's mandate of "conservation"-minded use recognizes "protection" as a valid purpose consonant with assuring the "highest economic and social benefits" of the resource. In short, the object is not maximum consumptive use, but rather the most equitable, reasonable, and beneficial allocation of state water resources, with full recognition that resource protection also constitutes "use."

[The Court considers *National Audubon Society* to provide useful guidance in how to balance the dual nature of Hawaii's public trust, but notes several differences between Hawai'i and California.] [W]e hold that the state water resources trust embodies the following fundamental principles:

Under the public trust, the state has both the authority and duty to preserve the rights of present and future generations in the waters of the state. The continuing *authority* of the state over its water resources precludes any grant or assertion of vested rights to use water to the detriment of public trust purposes. This authority empowers the state to revisit prior diversions and allocations, even those made with due consideration of their effect on the public trust.

The state also bears an "affirmative *duty* to take the public trust into account in the planning and allocation of water resources, and to protect public trust uses whenever feasible." *Id.* (emphasis added). Preliminarily, we note that this duty may not readily translate into substantive results. The public has a definite interest in the development and use of water resources for various reasonable and beneficial public and private offstream purposes, including agriculture, *see generally* Haw. Const. art. XI, § 3. Therefore, apart from the question of historical practice, reason and necessity dictate that the public trust may have to accommodate offstream diversions inconsistent with the mandate of protection, to the unavoidable impairment of public instream uses and values. As discussed above, by conditioning use and development on resource "conservation," article XI, section 1 does not preclude offstream use, but merely requires that all uses, offstream or instream, public or private, promote the best economic and social interests of the people of this state.

In the words of another court, "[t]he result is a controlled development of resources rather than no development."

We have indicated a preference for accommodating both instream and offstream uses where feasible. In times of greater scarcity, however, the state will confront difficult choices that may not lend themselves to formulaic solutions. Given the diverse and not necessarily complementary range of water uses, even among public trust uses alone, we consider it neither feasible nor prudent to designate absolute priorities between broad categories of uses under the water resources trust. Contrary to the Commission's conclusion that the trust establishes resource protection as "a categorical imperative and the precondition to all subsequent considerations," we hold that the Commission inevitably must weigh competing public and private water uses on a case-by-case basis, according to any appropriate standards provided by law.

Having recognized the necessity of a balancing process, we do not suggest that the state's public trust duties amount to nothing more than a restatement of its prerogatives, nor do we ascribe to the constitutional framers the intent to enact laws devoid of any real substance and effect. Rather, we observe that the constitutional requirements of "protection" and "conservation," the historical and continuing understanding of the trust as a guarantee of public rights, and the common reality of the "zero-sum" game between competing water uses demand that any balancing between public and private purposes begin with a presumption in favor of public use, access, and enjoyment. Thus, insofar as the public trust, by nature and definition, establishes use consistent with trust purposes as the norm or "default" condition, we affirm the Commission's conclusion that it effectively prescribes a "higher level of scrutiny" for private commercial uses such as those proposed in this case. In practical terms, this means that the burden ultimately lies with those seeking or approving such uses to justify them in light of the purposes protected by the trust.

The constitution designates the Commission as the primary guardian of public rights under the trust. Haw. Const. art. XI, section 7. Specifically, the public trust compels the state duly to consider the cumulative impact of existing and proposed diversions on trust purposes and to implement reasonable measures to mitigate this impact, including the use of alternative sources. The trust also requires planning and decisionmaking from a global, long-term perspective. In sum, the state may compromise public rights in the resource pursuant only to a decision made with a level of openness, diligence, and foresight commensurate with the high priority these rights command under the laws of our state.

## IV. CONCLUSION

In the introduction to its decision and order, the Commission projected that, "by the year 2020, water demand for projected growth of Oahu will exceed the remaining ground-water resources on the island." *Id.* at 1. This forecast underscores the urgent need for planning and preparation by the Commission and the counties before more serious complications develop. The constitutional framers and the legislature designed the Commission as an instrument for judicious planning and regulation, rather than crisis management. The Commission's decision reflects the considerable time and attention it devoted to this case; we commend its efforts. But much more work lies in the critical years ahead if the Commission is to realize its constitutionally and statutorily mandated purpose.

We have rendered our decision with utmost care, balancing due deference to the Commission's judgment with a level of scrutiny necessitated by the ultimate importance of these matters to the present and future generations of our state. For the reasons stated in this opinion, we vacate in part the Commission's decision and remand for additional findings and conclusions, with further hearings if necessary, consistent with this opinion, regarding [seven specific matters that required further consideration, in the Court's view]. We affirm all other aspects of the Commission's decision not otherwise addressed in this opinion.

■ Dissenting Opinion by RAMIL, J.

Because the majority resorts to the nebulous common law public trust doctrine as a distinct and separate authority to assign "superior claims" status to "public instream uses" and "native Hawaiian and traditional and customary rights," thereby trumping Hawai'i Revised Statutes (HRS) chapter 174C (1993 & Supp.1999) (the Code), I dissent. The public trust doctrine, as expressed in the Hawai'i Constitution and as subsequently incorporated into the Code, does not mandate preference for instream uses or native Hawaiian rights. Rather, a review of the history of the 1978 Constitutional Convention reveals that the framers viewed the public trust simply as a fiduciary duty on the State to "protect, control and regulate the use of Hawaii's water resources for the benefit of its people." Haw. Const. art. XI, section 7. Therefore, I would hold that the Commission on Water Resource Management (the Commission) exceeded its statutory authority when it cited to the common law public trust doctrine as a distinct and separate authority for justifying priority for particular uses of water.

## NOTES

1. *Aftermath of the* Mono Lake *case.* The Mono Lake controversy is an impressive case study in environmental conservation.[120] Los Angeles reduced its usage of Mono Lake's feeder streams to 12,000 acre-feet from a

---

[120] For the facts and lessons from the Mono Lake controversy, as discussed in this note, see Arnold, Working Out an Environmental Ethic: Anniversary Lessons from Mono Lake, 4 Wyo. L. Rev. 1 (2004). See also Hart, Storm Over Mono: The Mono Lake Battle and the California Water Future (2005); Layzer, Natural Experiments: Ecosystem-Based Management and the Environment 233–66 (2008); Arnold & Jewell, Litigation's Bounded Effectiveness and the Real Public Trust Doctrine: The Aftermath of the Mono Lake Case, 8 Hastings W.–Nw. J. Envtl. L. & Pol'y 1 (2001); and the Mono Lake Committee's website, www.monolake.org.

historic high of almost 100,000 acre-feet, in accordance with a 1994 California Water Resources Control Board order limiting Los Angeles' water rights. Los Angeles largely made up the reductions in Mono Lake waters by conserving or reclaiming water. Los Angeles had the same water consumption in 1998 as in 1983, despite a 30 percent increase in population during that period. The level of Mono Lake rose by 8 feet from 1994 to 2009, about half of the targeted increase in lake level under the Water Board order, and much restoration of habitat and ecological conditions has occurred.

Even though experts have ranked *National Audubon Society* as one of the ten most important environmental cases of the twentieth century, the judicial opinion itself did not achieve environmental-conservation results. The California Supreme Court did not specify any particular outcome, and it took more than a decade for the California Water Resources Control Board to issue its order reducing Los Angeles' appropriation rights. Despite the litigation successes of the Mono Lake Committee and its co-plaintiffs not only on the public trust issue but also in two cases brought under the California Fish and Game Code (known as the *California Trout* cases), the Los Angeles Department of Water and Power resisted and delayed reducing its diversions and restoring the ecosystem. Thus, the public trust doctrine had only "bounded effectiveness." Four non-legal forces were critical to the ultimate outcome in the case:

    i. *The ecology and psychology of place.* Scientists and activists with the Mono Lake Committee who studied the ecological values of Mono Lake and the effects of Los Angeles' diversions formed experience-based bonds to Mono Lake as a special place. They then engaged the public with the ecological conditions and special value of Mono Lake.

    ii. *Public engagement.* The Mono Lake Committee engaged in an extensive public relations campaign to encourage the public to understand what would be lost if it were to continue to use the lake's feeder stream waters. This campaign included bumper stickers, programs for school children both in the Los Angeles area and at Mono Lake, nature programs at Mono Lake, and national and local media attention. Widespread public support for saving Mono Lake developed among Los Angeles residents, the Department of Water and Power's customers and constituents.

    iii. *Politics.* Support for saving Mono Lake developed among federal, state, and local political leaders, as well as among the public. Both Congress and the California Legislature appropriated funds for conservation and reclamation projects, contingent on reductions in appropriations from the Mono Lake basin. New city officials removed Department of Water and Power officials who were resistant to change, and brokered negotiations between the Department and the Mono Lake Committee.

    iv. *Collaborative problem-solving.* New leadership of the Mono Lake Committee recognized the importance of finding new ways to meet Los Angeles' water needs without offsetting reduced diversions from the Mono Lake basin with new diversions from other ecologically sensitive waters. The activists identified a variety of water conservation and reclamation opportunities, including making free or low-cost low-flush toilets and low-flow shower heads available to inner-city residents. The outcome of the controversy advanced the needs of the Mono Lake ecosystem, while still meeting Los Angeles' water needs.[121]

2. *California extends public trust to groundwater*. One trial court in California has applied the public trust doctrine to groundwater, ruling that both state and local officials have public trust duties to regulate groundwater withdrawals, when groundwater pumping directly and adversely affects instream flows of navigable waterways (in this case, the Scott River in far northern California).[122]

3. *Controversy over extending the public trust*. The use of the public trust doctrine to limit conventional water rights has been controversial. Critics of the *Waiahole Ditch* case have asserted that state control of instream flows and groundwater rights under a broad reading of the public trust is a poor tool for growth management and should not supplant traditional land use planning and regulation.[123] Others contend that the public trust doctrine has become adrift from its historic moorings.[124] Other commentators, though, have urged the application of the public trust doctrine to groundwater resources generally,[125] instream flow protections in regulated riparian jurisdictions,[126] and management of water scarcity and water rights in western states.[127]

---

[121] Arnold, Working Out an Environmental Ethic: Anniversary Lessons from Mono Lake, 4 Wyo. L. Rev. 1 (2004). For the history of the *Waiahole Ditch* case, see Miike, Water and the Law in Hawaii 137–204 (2004).

[122] Order After Hearing on Cross Motions for Judgment on the Pleadings, Environmental Law Foundation v. State Water Resources Control Bd., Case No.: 34–2010–80000583 (CA Super. Ct., Sacramento County) (July 15, 2014).

[123] See Callies & Chipchase, Water Regulation, Land Use, and the Environment, 30 U. Haw. L. Rev. 49 (2007); Callies, Breemer, & Chipchase, Balancing Water Values and Human Needs in an Enlightened Land Use Planning Regime, in Wet Growth: Should Water Law Control Land Use 335–91 (Arnold, ed., 2005).

[124] See Smith & Sweeney, The Public Trust Doctrine and Natural Law: Emanations within a Penumbra, 33 B.C. Envtl. Aff. L. Rev. 307 (2006).

[125] Tuholske, Trusting the Public Trust: Application of the Public Trust Doctrine to Groundwater Resources, 9 Vt. J. Envtl. L. 189 (2008).

[126] Mulvaney, Instream Flows and the Public Trust, 22 Tul. Envtl. L.J. 315 (2009).

[127] Brown, Drinking from a Deep Well: The Public Trust Doctrine and Western Water Law, 34 Fla. St. U. L. Rev. 1 (2006).

## ASSIGNMENT 37

# ENVIRONMENTALLY SENSITIVE LANDS

## 1. INTRODUCTION

Do environmental conditions impact rights and duties of those who hold property interests in land? The question has grown in importance as the environmental harms from land uses have increased and as society has come to place greater value on the ecology of land and its natural systems. Issues of environmental sustainability are forcing property law to grapple with whether landowners' rights in environmentally sensitive lands are limited, and perhaps even defined, by responsibilities to natural and human communities affected by land uses.

Traditionally, property law served primarily non-ecological values: the economically productive use of land, wealth creation and preservation, human liberty and autonomy, and social order. These functions were facilitated by the abstract concept of property as a bundle of rights. Even when these values dominated property law, though, there were counter-examples of the role of environmental conditions and values in defining property rights. Perhaps this is why the "web of interests" may be a more accurate metaphor for property. It considers not only the various human interests in objects of property but also the characteristics of the property itself.

This Assignment is concerned with environmentally sensitive lands. Limits on property rights are more likely to arise with respect to environmentally sensitive land, in contrast to land subject to general environmental conditions. All land has environmental conditions of some sort; virtually all land has natural (i.e., not humanly created) features, hosts biological life, and is part of an ecological system (or ecosystem). However, environmentally sensitive lands have special features that are particularly vulnerable to development or environmentally unsustainable land use. Environmental planning scholar John Randolph defines them as those lands "that exhibit certain hazards to development (e.g., floodplains, unstable slopes), are vulnerable to environmental impact (e.g., highly erodible soils, soils unsuitable for septic systems), provide resource values (e.g., prime agricultural lands, aquifer recharge areas), and have aesthetic or ecological values (e.g., wetlands, wildlife habitat)."[1] Many environmentally sensitive lands have more than one feature that make them sensitive.

---

[1] Randolph *Environmental Land Use Planning and Management* 110–11 (2004).

Too many types of environmentally sensitive lands exist to cover them all fully in an introductory property law course. This Assignment highlights the property law issues associated with the following four categories of environmentally sensitive lands: wetlands, riparian lands, prairie grasslands, and coastal lands.

*Wetlands.* Wetlands are lands that are periodically inundated or saturated with water. The U.S. Army Corps of Engineers and the U.S. Environmental Protection Agency, which share federal regulatory authority over wetlands, define them as—

> those areas that are inundated or saturated by surface or ground water at a frequency and duration sufficient to support, and that under normal circumstances do support, a prevalence of vegetation typically adapted for life in saturated soil conditions.[2]

The EPA identifies four categories of wetlands: marshes (including tidal marshes along coastlines and freshwater nontidal marshes), swamps (woody but saturated), bogs (containing spongy peat deposits, sphagnum moss, and acidic composition), and fens (like bogs but richer in nutrients and less acidic).[3]

Wetlands serve a range of critically important functions, in addition to their aesthetic, intrinsic, and spiritual values. The following summary describes many of these roles:

> Wetlands serve as natural wastewater treatment facilities, filtering out pollutants and improving water quality. They absorb the impact of floods and stabilize runoff by retaining water and releasing it gradually. Wetlands similarly temper catastrophic climatic events.
>
> Wetlands are "nurseries of life" that serve as home to millions of plants and animals that rely on them for food, habitat, and breeding grounds. Although they cover less than five percent of the land surface, wetlands host thirty-one percent of all plant species in the lower forty-eight states. They are among the most fertile and biologically productive ecosystems in the world, rivaling tropical rainforests and coral reefs in the number and diversity of species they support. More than one-third of threatened or endangered species live only in wetlands and many species are dependent on wetlands to reproduce.
>
> Wetlands also play an important role in our economic well-being. By improving drinking water quality, minimizing the damage done by floods, providing outstanding recreational opportunities, attracting businesses to areas rich in biodiversity and natural beauty, and providing raw materials and

---

[2] 40 C.F.R. § 230.3(t) (2009).
[3] See http://www.epa.gov/owow/wetlands/types/.

employment opportunities for numerous commercial concerns, wetlands help promote a robust economy. As a reliable source of food, shelter and nursery grounds for both marine and freshwater species, wetlands are a cornerstone of the nation's multibillion dollar fishing industry. They provide an essential link in the life cycle of seventy-five percent of the fish and shellfish commercially harvested in the United States, and up to ninety percent of the recreational fish catch. Two-thirds of all fish consumed worldwide depend on coastal wetlands at some stage in their life cycle. Water flushing through wetlands also provides needed transportation for migratory fish species. Wetlands also play a major role in the production of cash crops such as marsh hay, wild rice, blueberries, cranberries, peat moss, and timber. Another important and often overlooked aspect of wetlands is the role they play in the hydrologic cycle.

The dense vegetation and sediment typically found in wetlands not only purifies water that runs through the wetlands, it also stabilizes the land and protects adjacent communities during floods and storms. By absorbing and storing a significant amount of floodwater, wetlands act as natural buffers, reducing the frequency and intensity of floods. After peak flood flows have passed, wetlands slowly release the stored waters, thereby minimizing the impacts on downstream property. This slow release also allows coastal wetlands to preserve shorelines by minimizing erosion. In the Gulf coast area, for example, barrier islands, shoals, marshes, forested wetlands and other features of the coastal landscape provide a significant and potentially sustainable buffer from wind wave action and storm surge generated by tropical storms and hurricanes. Indeed, the damage sustained during Hurricane Katrina in 2005 would have been far less severe had it not been for the significant loss of wetlands along the coast and Mississippi delta. Preserving wetlands, in conjunction with other flood control measures offers a degree of protection against flooding that is often more effective and less costly than a system of traditional dikes and levees.

A wetland's natural filtration process also removes excess nutrients before water leaves a wetland, making it healthier for drinking, swimming, and supporting plants and animals. The most important factor for the health and function of wetlands is water movement. When water enters a wetland, it slows down and moves around wetland plants. Much of the suspended sediment drops out and settles to the wetland floor. Plant roots as well as microorganisms on plant stems and in the soil absorb excess nutrients in the water originating from fertilizers, manure, leaking septic tanks, and municipal sewage.

Finally, wetlands, like forests, provide a substantial carbon sink that can help mitigate the impact of climate change. Wetlands are much better than forests for storing carbon, however, because unlike forests they can last for hundreds and even thousands of years.

According to a 1997 assessment of all wetlands worldwide, the economic value of the range of services wetlands provide is approximately $14.9 trillion.[4]

Since the 1780s, over half of all wetlands in the United States have been lost to drainage or filling, mostly due to land development and agricultural use.[5] Section 404 of the Clean Water Act now prohibits the filling of wetlands without a permit from the U.S. Army Corps of Engineers (Corps), subject to review and potential veto by the U.S. Environmental Protection Agency.[6] Moreover, federal regulatory policy is that there should be "no net loss" of wetlands, but the quantity of wetlands in the U.S. continues to decline.[7] Two U.S. Supreme Court cases in recent years have limited federal regulatory agencies' jurisdiction to those wetlands having a direct connection or significant nexus to navigable waters.[8] The cases have resulted in widespread confusion about the precise scope of federal regulatory authority over wetlands. However, many state and local governments also regulate to protect wetlands.[9] More importantly, it is not easy or cheap for land developers to obtain permits to fill wetlands. In some cases, denial of a wetland permit has been deemed by a court to be a taking.[10] A standard practice in wetlands-development permitting has been to require the applicant to mitigate the adverse impacts by creating new wetlands or restoring degraded wetlands elsewhere. In fact, a practice known as "wetlands mitigation banking" allows a person or entity to create or restore wetlands and obtain a credit that can be "banked" for later sale to a developer that needs mitigation credits for a permit to fill and develop other wetlands. However, studies have shown that the locations, quality, and functions of the replacement wetlands differ substantially from the

---

[4] Squillace, From "Navigable Waters" to "Constitutional Waters": The Future of Federal Wetlands Regulation, 40 *U. Mich. J. L. Reform* 799, 805–09 (2007).

[5] Id. at 799.

[6] Federal Water Pollution Control Act § 404, 33 U.S.C. § 1344 (2000). See also United States v. Riverside Bayview Homes, Inc., 474 U.S. 121 (1985).

[7] Squillace, From "Navigable Waters" to "Constitutional Waters": The Future of Federal Wetlands Regulation, 40 *U. Mich. J. L. Reform* 799 (2007).

[8] Solid Waste Agency of Northern Cook County v. U.S. Army Corps of Engineers, 531 U.S. 159 (2001); Rapanos v. United States, 547 U.S. 715 (2006).

[9] Rockstad, The Three-Legged Stool: Ensuring Protection of Mississippi's Isolated Wetlands through Increased State and Local Regulation, 80 *Miss. L.J. Online* 82 (2010),

[10] See, e.g., Loveladies Harbor, Inc. v. United States, 28 F.3d 1171 (Fed. Cir. 1994); Florida Rock Indus. v. United States, 18 F.3d 1560 (Fed. Cir. 1994); Bowles v. United States, 31 Fed. Cl. 37 (1994); Friedenberg v. New York Dep't of Envtl Conservation, 767 N.Y.S.2d 451 (N.Y. App. Div. 2003).

wetlands destroyed for development, thus producing net losses in ecological functions and values.[11]

*Riparian lands.* Riparian land (or riparian zone) "refers literally to banks beside water bodies, but also commonly refers to lands proximate to lakes, streams, and estuaries. The riparian zone divides the aquatic zone and the upland zone, but it is physically and ecologically related to both"[12] Riparian lands have numerous critical functions. "Riparian zones reduce the impacts of pollutants and runoff on streams. Without a well functioning riparian area, a river channel ceases to store water and accumulate sediment effectively. Undeveloped riparian lands remove much of the nutrients and pesticides, pathogens, and sediment approaching rivers or streams. These processes vary by the width of the riparian zone, its slope, its soil type, and the amount, density, and type of vegetation in the zone. Riparian forests are especially important in preventing pollutant loading, erosion, and flooding. Riparian zones are areas of important habitat for species. Removal of trees along streams and rivers increases water temperatures, potentially resulting in fish kills."[13]

Riparian lands fall within the broader floodplain, the area of land likely to flood from a major streambed flooding event occurring at least once within a particular period of time (e.g., 100 years). Development in floodplains not only exposes people and structure to flood hazards but also alters the floodplain structure, increasing stream surges and widening floodplains.

Streamside land development, unrestricted land uses, and deforestation or devegetation have undermined the physical integrity of waterways, including erosion or destabilization of stream banks, increased flooding, and degraded wildlife habitat. Experts recommend that surface waters have a minimum buffer occupied by mature trees and shrubs and that permissible land uses be restricted near the stream or water body.[14] Riparian buffer zones are used not only in aquatic restoration projects but also in local zoning restrictions in a growing number of communities throughout the United States.[15]

---

[11] See, e.g., Ruhl and Salzman, The Effects of Wetlands Mitigation Banking on People, 28 *Nat'l Wetlands Newsletter* 1 (Mar.–Apr. 2006); *Compensating for Wetland Losses Under the Clean Water Act* (National Academy of Sciences/National Research Council 2001); Turner et al., Count It by Acre or Function—Mitigation Adds Up to Net Loss of Wetlands, 23 *Nat'l Wetlands Newsletter* 5 (Dec. 2001); Semlitsch, Size Does Matter: The Value of Small Isolated Wetlands, 22 *Nat'l Wetlands Newsletter* 5 (Jan.–Feb. 2000); Burkhalter, Oversimplification: Value and Function: Wetland Mitigation Banking, 2 *Chapman L. Rev.* 261 (1999).

[12] Randolph *Environmental Land Use Planning and Management* 466–67 (2004).

[13] Arnold, Norton, and Wallen, *Kentucky Wet Growth Tools for Sustainable Development: A Handbook on Land Use and Water for Kentucky Communities* 22–23 (2009).

[14] Randolph *Environmental Land Use Planning and Management* 474–78, 522 (2004).

[15] See, e.g., Greensboro, N.C. Mun. Code Art. VII, Sec. 30–7–1.8 (Water Supply Watershed Districts: Stream Buffer Required); Baltimore County, MD, Buffer Protection and Management Ordinance; Louisville, KY, Metro Land Development Code Ch. 7, Part 11, Sec. 7.11.6 (Conservation Subdivision Regulations).

*Prairie grasslands.* It would be a mistake to assume that environmentally sensitive lands are fragile environments that must be preserved undisturbed. Prairies grasslands form an ecosystem that depends on disturbances from fire, drought, and species like bison that graze, trample, and wallow, or like prairie dogs and gophers that burrow or mound.[16] These resilient ecosystems once stretched as far east as Ohio and Kentucky and as far north as Montana and Alberta, ranging from tallgrass to mixed grass to shortgrass prairies from east to west; they dominated the Great Plains from the Dakotas to Texas. Although prairie grasslands contain wetlands and stream systems, they are defined by their predominance of grasses and relative lack of trees, their flat or gently rolling topography, their relative rainfall (drier than forests but wetter than deserts), and their biological diversity. While many find prairie grasslands boring if they fly overhead or drive by on the interstate highway, these subtle landscapes of waving grasses under expansive blue skies hide an abundance of wildlife, flowers, and biological processes that are beautiful and wondrous.

Prairie grasslands are endangered landscapes because they have been domesticated. Fire was suppressed, allowing woody savannas and forests to replace grasslands; bison, wolves, and prairie dogs were hunted to near-extinction; and native grasslands were replaced with croplands and farming methods that ultimately led to the infamous Dust Bowl of the 1930s. Over time, the vast majority of native grasslands have been lost. Native prairie birds have suffered some of the greatest population declines of any group of species in the continental United States.

Most prairie grasslands are held in private ownership. Some conservation has resulted from government management of public lands, or from government or nonprofit land trust acquisition of preserves or conservation easements from private landowners. However, prairie landscapes historically were not considered majestic enough to warrant large-scale federal reserves for conservation purposes. Moreover, there is no wide-scale or systematic regulation of prairie grasslands. Therefore, conservation depends largely on voluntary efforts, collaborative partnerships, and incentives to private property owners. For example, Ted Turner, who owns more land than any other private landowner in the United States, has restored bison, traditional fire regimes, and native grasses and wildlife to prairie regions. Wes Jackson and his Land Institute in Salina, Kansas, is pioneering agriculture based on native grasses and processes. In 2002, Congress established a grassland reserve program providing for the purchase of conservation easements on lands

---

[16] On prairie grasslands, see generally Samson & Knopf, eds., *Prairie Conservation: Preserving North America's Most Endangered Ecosystem* (1996); Reichman, *Konza Prairie: A Tallgrass Natural History* (1987); Manning, *Grassland: The History, Biology, Politics, and Promise of the American Prairie* (1995).

that can continue to be used for agricultural purposes but in a manner consistent with maintaining the viability of native grasses.[17]

*Coastal lands.* Located at the transition from terrestrial environments to marine environments, coastal lands are extremely dynamic, constantly being shaped by forces from oceans, upland areas, and climate.[18] Coastal zones include beaches, dunes, upland barrier flats (which grasslands or forests might inhabit), bluffs, estuaries where saltwater and freshwater mix (e.g., bays and backbays, lagoons, harbors, inlets, and sounds), tidal wetlands (e.g., saltwater marshes), barrier islands, sandbars, mangrove forests, kelp forests, seagrass and algae beds, submerged foreshore zones, and coral reefs. These areas provide essential functions. Estuaries are especially rich biological environments; they generate foundational organic matter for extensive food chains, provide habitat for more than three-quarters of the U.S. commercial fisheries and as much as 90% of our recreational fisheries, and support diverse communities of endangered birds, mammals, and fish. Coastal wetlands of all sorts filter pollutants and sediments from upland runoff and absorb floodwaters and storm surge. The entire complex of coastal structural elements buffers the core continental land environment from ocean waves and storm forces. Coastal areas attract human habitation, recreation, and commercial activities. Over half of the nation's population lives within 50 miles of the shoreline, even though this zone is only 17 percent of the nation's land area. Coastal areas are favorite vacation spots, generating billions of dollars in recreation and tourism activity each year.

Coastal lands are especially environmentally sensitive due to their naturally dynamic and transitional characteristics, ecological functions, and proximity to human activity. Beaches and shores naturally migrate as they are pounded, shifted, and shaped by waves, winds, storms, and hurricanes. They retreat gradually with less sand or higher sea levels (erosion), widen gradually with more sand (accretion), and change suddenly (avulsion). In general, inland migrations of beaches, shorelines, and barrier islands are natural processes. However, sea level rise, due in part to glacier melts, warmer ocean temperatures, and climate change, will intensify and alter these effects.

---

[17] Farm Security and Rural Investment Act of 2002, H.R. 2646, Subtitle E (Grassland Reserve) (2002).

[18] Sources of information on coastal lands, their dynamics, and human effects on them include Randolph *Environmental Land Use Planning and Management* 215–24, 549–54 (2004); Christie, Of Beaches, Boundaries and SOBs, 25 *J. Land Use & Envtl. L.* 19 (2010); Reed, Seawalls and the Public Trust: Navigating the Tension Between Private Property and Public Beach Use in the Face of Shoreline Erosion, 20 *Fordham Envtl. L. Rev.* 305 (2009); Caldwell & Segall, No Day at the Beach: Sea Level Rise, Ecosystem Loss, and Public Access Along the California Coast, 34 *Ecology L.Q.* 533 (2007); Moorman, Let's Roll: Applying Land-Based Notions of Property to Migrating Barrier Islands, 31 *Wm. & Mary Envtl. L. & Pol'y Rev.* 459 (2007); Titus, Rising Seas, Coastal Erosion, and the Takings Clause: How to Save Wetlands and Beaches Without Hurting Property Owners, 57 *Md. L. Rev.* 1279 (1998).

Moreover, coastal land development and human changes to coastal lands exacerbate or complicate these processes. Intense land development in coastal areas has altered or destroyed key features such as sand dunes and their stabilizing grasses (e.g., sea oats), wetlands, and wildlife habitats, while also adding impacts to remaining lands from pollution, stormwater runoff, and crowded human uses of beaches. Cutting inlets or building barriers, such as breakwaters or groins, interrupt sand flow along the shoreline and accelerate erosion downshore. Shoreline armoring, such as the building of sea walls, may at least temporarily protect existing structures from advancement of the water due to shoreline erosion or sea level rise and from storm waves, but this type of shoreline alteration destroys beaches by cutting off the natural flow of sands.

Beach restoration and nourishment (i.e., the replacement of eroded sands with sand from the ocean floor usually by the U.S. Army Corps of Engineers dredging sand from the ocean floor, pumping or sucking it through pipes, depositing it on the shore, and sculpting the beach with bulldozers and graders) are short-term fixes (sometimes re-eroding in only 3–5 years) and alter critical natural features of the entire coastal system. For example, consider the impacts of coastal development on endangered sea turtles, whose survival depends on nesting on beaches. Sea turtle populations have declined as their nesting sites have been replaced with beach structures or altered by human disturbances of sands and dunes. They have been deterred from nesting by artificial lights, confused by different kinds of sands than originally occupied their beaches, and displaced by beachgoers who interfere with their nesting. Concerted efforts to protect endangered sea turtle nesting sites and avoid human disturbances of them (including no lights on the beach during nesting season) have reduced the risks that these species will go extinct, but the human changes to overall coastal environments may end up exceeding the turtles' capacity to adapt.

Humans are also at risk. The vast human presence in areas that function as transitions from oceans to land means high risks to property and human health and life from hurricanes and tropical storms, storm surge, winds, flooding, and erosive effects on shoreland stability. In the United States, we address these risks with insurance, disaster response, and disaster assistance/relief, all of which are government-provided or government-subsidized. However, these methods not only address already-incurred harms but also stimulate development and redevelopment in areas that are likely to experience similar hazards in the future. The provision of high-capacity development-facilitating public infrastructure (e.g., roads, utilities) and regulatory accommodation of development and redevelopment also encourage the continued and growing development of coastal areas beyond their natural carrying capacity. These conditions put enormous pressure on the intersection of public policy and private property rights. For example, one of the predicted effects of sea level rise is saltwater intrusion into groundwater supplies in coastal communities, which will degrade the water quality and substantially reduce the available supply of public drinking water in highly populated coastal areas. Property owners and residents in these communities will expect public-sector solutions to water shortages, but the solutions will be neither easy nor cheap, and each will likely produce its own set of environmental problems.

The scope and content of private property rights play a role in efforts to adapt to the environmentally sensitive features of coastal lands. For example, should private property owners be entitled to "armor" their lands to protect their structures, even if these on-site developments adversely affect public beaches or other property owners along the shoreline? Another issue is the degree to which government-operated beach restoration and nourishment projects adversely affect private property rights. The U.S. Supreme Court recently and unanimously held that the State of Florida's establishment of a fixed "erosion control line" did not constitute a taking of coastal landowners' property, because even though the line between private property and public property moves with gradual changes in the mean high tide mark (i.e., erosion and accretion), it does not move with sudden (i.e., avulsive) changes, such as those caused by storms and hurricanes.[19]

In the shadow of federal-state cooperative programs under the Coastal Zone Management Act (CZMA)[20] and the National Estuary Program (NEP),[21] state and local governments regulate land development in coastal areas, increasingly protecting sensitive features with permitting processes, setback requirements, design and management standards, restrictions on pedestrian and vehicular access, stormwater runoff management practices, and habitat protections. Another approach is to impose a rolling easement on coastal property, which would allow landowners to continue to use their property without armoring until such time as the shoreline reaches their structures at which point they would need to relocate farther back on their properties if there is room or to abandon their properties to the advancement of the water. This approach recognizes the ultimate inevitability of coastline changes due to both natural processes and decades of substantial human disturbances. Legally, advocates of rolling easements contend that they do not interfere with private property rights because of the inherent limits that the public trust doctrine, custom, and nuisance law place on private property interests in coastal lands.[22]

---

[19] Stop the Beach Renourishment, Inc. v. Florida Dept. of Envtl. Prot., 130 S. Ct. 2592 (2010).
[20] 16 U.S.C. §§ 1451–1465.
[21] 33 U.S.C. § 1330.
[22] Caldwell & Segall, No Day at the Beach: Sea Level Rise, Ecosystem Loss, and Public Access Along the California Coast, 34 Ecology L.Q. 533 (2007).

## 2. PRINCIPAL PROBLEM

Lawyers are often called on to speak to groups of lawyers or non-lawyers about recent developments or general trends in property law. You have agreed to speak to the Coastal Owners' Association (COA), a large group of landowners, condominium owners, business owners, and civic activists along the coastal areas of your state. A number of your current clients are members of COA, and you would like to develop new clients from among the COA members. COA is a diverse group. It includes people who own homes, including vacation homes, retirement homes, high-rise condominium units, beachfront bungalows, and many other kinds of residential properties in coastal areas. It includes land developers, hotel and resort owners, restaurant and retail shop owners, and other commercial interests. It includes insurance companies insuring coastal properties and financial institutions lending money and holding mortgages on coastal properties. It includes advocates for environmental conservation in the coastal areas. It includes government agencies owning public lands, public facilities, parks, and conservation lands in coastal areas. Internal disagreement within the COA about how to define property rights and duties in coastal lands often exists.

You have been asked to speak on the topic "Trends in Coastal Property Rights and Responsibilities" at a conference of the COA. Other lawyers will be speaking on specific statutes and regulations, such as federal protections of wetlands under the Clean Water Act, shared federal and state coastal management roles (e.g., the federal Coastal Zone Management Act; beach nourishment programs), state environmental laws, local zoning and land use regulations, and federal and private-sector flood insurance coverage. Given that a sizeable portion of the COA membership believes that at least some of these regulatory and public-sector programs interfere with their private property rights, the COA leaders have asked you to address the nature and scope of private property rights and responsibilities in coastal lands. Consider the following materials as you prepare your remarks.

## 3. MATERIALS FOR SOLUTION OF PRINCIPAL PROBLEM

### Just v. Marinette County
Wisconsin Supreme Court, 1972.
201 N.W.2d 761.

[The Wisconsin Water Quality Act of 1965 required counties to enact shoreland zoning ordinances, subject to approval by the Wisconsin Department of Natural Resources. In 1967, Marinette County enacted a shoreland zoning ordinance, which was approved and is the subject of this lawsuit.]

Shorelands for the purpose of ordinances are defined in sec. 59.971(1), Stats., as lands within 1,000 feet of the normal high-water elevation of navigable lakes, ponds, or flowages and 300 feet from a navigable river or stream or to the landward side of the flood plain, whichever distance is greater.

There can be no disagreement over the public purpose sought to be obtained by the ordinance. Its basic purpose is to protect navigable waters and the public rights therein from the degradation and deterioration which results from uncontrolled use and development of shorelands. In the Navigable Waters Protection Act, sec. 144.26, the purpose of the state's shoreland regulation program is stated as being to 'aid in the fulfillment of the state's role as trustee of its navigable waters and to promote public health, safety, convenience and general welfare'. In sec. 59.971(1), which grants authority for shoreland zoning to counties, the same purposes are reaffirmed. The Marinette county shoreland zoning ordinance in secs. 1.2 and 1.3 states the uncontrolled use of shorelands and pollution of navigable waters of Marinette county adversely affect public health, safety, convenience, and general welfare and impair the tax base.

The shoreland zoning ordinance divides the shorelands of Marinette county into general purpose districts, general recreation districts, and conservancy districts. A 'conservancy' district is required by the statutory minimum standards and is defined in sec. 3.4 of the ordinance to include 'all shorelands designated as swamps or marshes on the United States Geological Survey maps which have been designated as the Shoreland Zoning Map of Marinette County, Wisconsin or on the detailed Insert Shoreland Zoning Maps.' The ordinance provides for permitted uses and conditional uses. One of the conditional uses requiring a permit under sec. 3.42(4) is the filling, drainage or dredging of wetlands according to the provisions of sec. 5 of the ordinance.

'Wetlands' are defined in sec. 2.29 as '(a)reas where ground water is at or near the surface much of the year or where any segment of plant cover is deemed an aquatic according to N. C. Fassett's 'Manual of Aquatic Plants.' Section 5.42(2) of the ordinance requires a conditional-use permit for any filling or grading 'Of any area which is within three hundred feet horizontal distance of a navigable water and which has surface drainage toward the water and on which there is: (a) Filling of more than five hundred square feet of any wetland which it contiguous to the water . . . (d) Filling or grading of more than 2,000 square feet on slopes of twelve per cent or less.'

In April of 1961, several years prior to the passage of this ordinance, the Justs purchased 36.4 acres of land in the town of Lake along the south shore of Lake Noquebay, a navigable lake in Marinette county. This land had a frontage of 1,266.7 feet on the lake and was purchased partially for personal use and partially for resale. During the years 1964, 1966, and 1967, the Justs made five sales of parcels having frontage and extending back from the lake some 600 feet, leaving the property involved in these suits. This property has a frontage of 366.7 feet and the south one half contains a stand of cedar, pine, various hard woods, birch and red maple. The north one half, closer to the lake, is barren of trees except immediately along the shore. The south three fourths of this north one half is populated with various plant grasses and vegetation including some plants which N. C. Fassett in his manual of aquatic plants has classified as 'aquatic.'

There are also non-aquatic plants which grow upon the land. Along the shoreline there is a belt of trees. The shoreline is from one foot to 3.2 feet higher than the lake level and there is a narrow belt of higher land along the shore known as a 'pressure ridge' or 'ice heave,' varying in width from one to three feet. South of this point, the natural level of the land ranges one to two feet above lake level. The land slopes generally toward the lake but has a slope less than twelve per cent. No water flows onto the land from the lake, but there is some surface water which collects on land and stands in pools.

The land owned by the Justs is designated as swamps or marshes on the United States Geological Survey Map and is located within 1,000 feet of the normal high-water elevation of the lake. Thus, the property is included in a conservancy district and, by sec. 2.29 of the ordinance, classified as 'wetlands.' Consequently, in order to place more than 500 square feet of fill on this property, the Justs were required to obtain a conditional-use permit from the zoning administrator of the county and pay a fee of $20 or incur a forfeiture of $10 to $200 for each day of violation.

In February and March of 1968, six months after the ordinance became effective, Ronald Just, without securing a conditional-use permit, hauled 1,040 square yards of sand onto this property and filled an area approximately 20-feet wide commencing at the southwest corner and extending almost 600 feet north to the northwest corner near the shoreline, then easterly along the shoreline almost to the lot line. He stayed back from the pressure ridge about 20 feet. More than 500 square feet of this fill was upon wetlands located contiguous to the water and which had surface drainage toward the lake. The fill within 300 feet of the lake also was more than 2,000 square feet on a slope less than 12 percent. It is not seriously contended that the Justs did not violate the ordinance and the trial court correctly found a violation.

The real issue is whether the conservancy district provisions and the wetlands-filling restrictions are unconstitutional because they amount to a constructive taking of the Justs' land without compensation. Marinette county and the state of Wisconsin argue the restrictions of the conservancy district and wetlands provisions constitute a proper exercise of the police power of the state and do not so severely limit the use or depreciate the value of the land as to constitute a taking without compensation.

Swamps and wetlands were once considered wasteland, undesirable, and not picturesque. But as the people became more sophisticated, an appreciation was acquired that swamps and wetlands serve a vital role in nature, are part of the balance of nature and are essential to the purity of the water in our lakes and streams. Swamps and wetlands, are a necessary part of the ecological creation and now, even to the uninitiated, possess their own beauty in nature.

Is the ownership of a parcel of land so absolute that man can change its nature to suit any of his purposes? The great forests of our state were stripped on the theory man's ownership was unlimited. But in forestry, the land at least was used naturally, only the natural fruit of the land (the trees) were taken. The despoilage was in the failure to look to the future and provide for the reforestation of the land. An owner of land has no absolute and unlimited right to change the essential natural character of his land so as use it for a purpose for which it was unsuited in its natural state and which injures the rights of others. The exercise of the police power in zoning must be reasonable and we think it is not an unreasonable exercise of that power to prevent harm to public rights by limiting the use of private property to its natural uses.

This is not a case where an owner is prevented from using his land for natural and indigenous uses. The uses consistent with the nature of the land are allowed and other uses recognized and still others permitted by special permit. The shoreland zoning ordinance prevents to some extent the changing of the natural character of the land within 1,000 feet of a navigable lake and 300 feet of a navigable river because of such land's interrelation to the contiguous water. The changing of wetlands and swamps to the damage of the general public by upsetting the natural environment and the natural relationship is not a reasonable use of that land which is protected from police power regulation. Changes and filling to some extent are permitted because the extent of such changes and fillings does not cause harm. We realize no case in Wisconsin has yet dealt with shoreland regulations and there are several cases in other states which seem to hold such regulations unconstitutional; but nothing this court has said or held in prior cases indicate that destroying the natural character of a swamp or a wetland so as to make that location available for human habitation is a reasonable use of that land when the new use, although of a more economical value to the owner, causes a harm to the general public.

Wisconsin has long held that laws and regulations to prevent pollution and to protect the waters of this state from degradation are valid police-power enactments. State ex rel. Martin v. Juneau (1941), 238 Wis. 564, 300 N.W. 187; State ex rel. LaFollette v. Reuter (1967), 33 Wis.2d 384, 147 N.W.2d 304; Reuter v. Department of Natural Resources (1969), 43 Wis.2d 272, 168 N.W.2d 860. The active public trust duty of the state of Wisconsin in respect to navigable waters requires the state not only to promote navigation but also to protect and preserve those waters for fishing, recreation, and scenic beauty. Muench v. Public Service Comm. (1952), 261 Wis. 492, 53 N.W.2d 514, 55 N.W.2d 40. To further this duty, the legislature may delegate authority to local units of the government, which the state did by requiring counties to pass shoreland zoning ordinances. Menzer v. Elkhart Lake (1971), 51 Wis.2d 70, 186 N.W.2d 290.

This is not a case of an isolated swamp unrelated to a navigable lake or stream, the change of which would cause no harm to public rights. Lands adjacent to or near navigable waters exist in a special relationship to the state. They have been held subject to special taxation, Soens v. City of Racine (1860), 10 Wis. 271, and are subject to the state public trust powers, Wisconsin P. & L. Co. v. Public Service Comm. (1958), 5 Wis.2d 167, 92 N.W.2d 241; and since the Law of 1935, ch. 303, counties have been authorized to create special zoning districts along waterways and zone them for restrictive conservancy purposes. The restrictions in the Marinette county ordinance upon wetlands within 1,000 feet of Lake Noquebay which prevent the placing of excess fill upon such land without a permit is not confiscatory or unreasonable.

The Justs argue their property has been severely depreciated in value. But this depreciation of value is not based on the use of the land in its natural state but on what the land would be worth if it could be filled and used for the location of a dwelling. While loss of value is to be considered in determining whether a restriction is a constructive taking, value based upon changing the character of the land at the expense of harm to public rights is not an essential factor or controlling.

### Eric T. Freyfogle, The Owning and Taking of Sensitive Lands, 43 UCLA L. Rev. 77 (1995).

The institution of private land ownership is primarily a regime of private power—direct power over the land itself and indirect power over the people and other life forms whose health and fates are linked to the land. In landed property schemes, boundary lines are drawn on the Earth and some owner acquires rights to control the encompassed space. When the law respects private rights in land, it supports and defends this private power, standing ready to sustain it when appropriate by the use of public force.

Private ownership sinks deep roots into the culture of the United States, in part because the nation has long defined itself in contrast with places where private ownership did not thrive. Yet, even with this long history of private ownership—indeed, even after two centuries of explaining and refining what it means to own land—property disputes continue to arise regularly, and with no end in sight. In the late twentieth century, no force has shaken private ownership more profoundly than the environmental movement and its parent science, ecology. What ecology tells us is that all forms of life are linked with, and dependent upon, all other forms of life, and ultimately with the land itself. Nature's order is more than just a jumbled collection of discrete objects, each understandable in isolation. It is a maze of interconnection and interdependence, an organic whole laced together by nutrients and energy flowing through primary producers up to top carnivores, and then back to the soil to nourish new life. In its complexity, it challenges both our knowledge and our imagination.

Inevitably and appropriately the new wisdom of ecology is altering old ways of imagining the land and relating to it. Change, however, has not arrived easily, particularly in the case of private property law, which is one of the more important ways that a culture expresses its ties to the nonhuman natural world. The bumpiest transition has come in the case of ecologically sensitive lands, lands that have special value in sustaining the healthy functioning of larger biotic communities—wetlands, barrier islands, riparian corridors, endangered wildlife habitats, and the like. Before the age of ecology, owners of sensitive lands enjoyed the same rights as other owners, including the right to transform a land parcel extensively, radically altering its ecosystem role. Today, these owners are under siege. Left alone, sensitive lands fulfill their ecosystem functions; altered for intensive human use, the disruptive ripples spread widely, if at times slowly and invisibly.

Now that we understand the roles of these lands, what should it mean for a private person to own them? What rights should we recognize in the owners of such lands, and what obligations should they face? In the likely event that current ownership entitlements are too expansive, are there fair ways to curtail these rights without unduly disrupting the settled plans of existing landowners?

Despite its refined legal system and strong commitment to democratic change, the United States has encountered difficulties answering these questions. For a quarter century, courts have handed down inconsistent rulings, most dealing with wetlands—a land form that for generations Americans have zealously drained and filled as if on a moral crusade. These decisions, and the conflicting ideas and values that lie behind them, offer a useful case study of how landed property law responds to new pressures, in this instance the mounting evidence that we are pushing the land far too hard.

Landowners have always faced limits on their ability to use land in ways that generate harm. From one perspective, the age of ecology has simply added new types of harm to the list of those already recognized by law. But there is, in truth, much more happening. Increasingly, the entitlements or attributes of owning a particular land parcel are varying with the parcel's role in its home ecosystem. The practical meanings of ownership are coming to vary, not just from jurisdiction to jurisdiction, but acre by acre and niche by niche. Equally important, property law in the United States is slowly beginning to deal with the inexorable issue of carrying capacity—the reality that any type of human land use, however benign the use and however appropriate the location, can prove harmful when too many acres are devoted to it. At some point, in some manner, society must start drawing lines where the carrying capacity is reached and we can disturb the land no further. But can this be done while protecting legitimate landowner expectations? Can it be done while offering fair treatment to owners of land parcels that are, in nature's terms, substantially the same? Will it mean, in the end, a fundamentally new way, an ecological way, of thinking about owning the land?

Despite the problems that the environmental movement has experienced in its push to articulate a long-term goal, the ultimate goal in some manner will surely combine ecology and ethics. However phrased, it will be some variant of what remains after nearly fifty years of the classic expression, Aldo Leopold's land ethic, set forth in the environmental bestseller, *A Sand County Almanac.* Leopold gauged the virtue of human conduct by its impacts on the surrounding biotic community, condemning conduct that tended to disrupt the community's integrity, stability, and beauty. It was a community-based ethic, with humans part of the larger whole and dependent in the long run on the health of the whole. Leopold's land ethic failed to provide the full answer; Leopold never explained how humans fit into the biotic community, which is to say that he never explained which human impacts were and were not part of the natural order. Still, he was undoubtedly right in his merger of science and morality, and current turmoil in ecology labs and field stations has only highlighted that wisdom. Leopold was correct in perceiving that the environmental predicament of the twentieth century has arisen from far more than incomplete or bad science. An equal cause, probably a greater cause, has been excessive human pride, the tendency of humans to think, not just that nature exists to serve humankind, but that humans know enough to manage and manipulate the land. Indeed, they know so much, collectively and individually, that good land-use decisions can arise from an unregulated market and the countless selfish decisions that compose it.

When the Wisconsin Supreme Court handed down *Just v. Marinette County* in 1972, the debates over sustainable development and ecosystem health largely lay in the future. But the court sensed then, as environmentalists sense strongly today, that humans must contain, if not reduce, their overall impact on the land. We must pay greater heed to the functioning of natural communities and work harder to respect that functioning by keeping water and air clean, preserving topsoil in both quantity and fertility, avoiding atmospheric changes that threaten massive biological disruption, preserving the diversity of genes within and among species, and maintaining the integrity of nutrient and energy flows so that new life can live where old life has died. Land-use practices must respect and respond to the characteristics of the ecosystems where the lands are located. Furthermore, all of this must occur in a setting in which human ignorance looms large. If there is a bright line between sustainable and nonsustainable practices, we have not yet found it and are not soon to do so. If it is possible to trace the ecosystem impacts of clearcutting each forest or draining each wetland, we have not yet gained the skills to undertake such action, assuming we had the time and inclination to try. Whether an impact is good or bad requires, not just scientific knowledge, but an ethical scale of values.

Drawing upon *Just v. Marinette County*, the New Hampshire Court in *Rowe* [Rowe v. Town of North Hampton, 553 A.2d 1331 (N.H. 1989)] offered a distinction between natural and unnatural land uses. A regulation that banned unnatural land uses passed constitutional scrutiny, for it merely put into express form the new image of ecologically sound land use that had arisen in the environmental age. It was, it seems, as simple as that. The difficulty with this reasoning is the difficulty of ecology and, more generally, of human ignorance. Filling an important wetland plainly causes ecological disruption, and among observers trained in ecology, the majority would doubtless brand the move as harmful, but the line between natural and unnatural land uses is by no means clear in all or even most cases. The lone human far out in the wilderness can live in almost any manner without materially disrupting surrounding ecosystems. The trouble comes when numbers and scale increase—the story of most human activities. Filling wetlands is harmful today in large part because so many acres have already been lost. Building a house, as Justice Scalia would repeatedly note in *Lucas*, is not typically a harmful activity. The harm comes when the house displaces an ecological community that is in short supply or otherwise vital. Sometimes the house itself causes harm (as in the barrier island setting where Lucas proposed to build); in other cases it is the land clearing that precedes construction that yields the degradation. In the great outdoors, the natural shifts to the unnatural by the smallest of steps.

Even aside from the issue of scale and carrying capacity, there is the question of ethics and values. Leopold's land ethic drew its inspiration and guidance from the naturally functioning biotic community, but even such a nature-based land ethic requires a human translator to jump from the "is" of nature to the "ought" of human conduct. When human knowledge runs out, as it so often does, sentiment and intuition must kick in, allowing ethical norms to help deal with the serious limitations of knowledge-dependent utilitarian calculations. A community must draw its own lessons from nature and somehow translate its new values into legal form.

In the end, it is simply not possible to say that some land uses are plainly natural and others are not. The drafters of property laws should certainly turn to nature for guidance, but property law must remain, as it has always been, a human creation. Property law is what the people say it is; it cannot arise out of the natural order, unaided by human intervention. Thus, when courts consider the merits of a taking claim, they should look to what the community has to say, not what nature implies. The relevant issue is whether the law-making community has determined that a particular land use is harmful. It is up to the community to draw its lessons from nature, and to incorporate those lessons, as it sees fit and within the scope of its discretion, into new norms on the ownership of land. It is not what the court views as a natural land use, but what the community decides, that should count. A court would need to locate evidence of a generalized finding of harm, so as to reduce the chance that a community will single out one or a few landowners. It is this equal protection component that seems lacking in the reasoning of *Rowe*, and in the eloquent lyricism of *Just*.

## Palazzolo v. State of Rhode Island
Rhode Island Superior Court, 2005.
C.A. NO. WM 88–0297.

■ GALE, J.

This is an inverse condemnation[23] action brought by Plaintiff Anthony Palazzolo (Palazzolo or Plaintiff), a Westerly property owner, against the Rhode Island Coastal Resources Management Council (CRMC). In his complaint, Palazzolo alleges that the CRMC's denial of his application to fill and develop approximately eighteen acres of salt marsh property constitutes a taking for which he is entitled to compensation under both the Federal and State Constitutions.

This case is back before the Superior Court on remand from the Rhode Island Supreme Court. After a bench trial held over seven days in 1997, the Superior Court entered judgment for the State, holding, inter alia, that there was no taking as to Plaintiff Palazzolo because the regulations[24] relied on by the State to bar the two proposals submitted for agency approval were in effect prior to Plaintiff's ownership of the parcel in question. The Rhode Island Supreme Court affirmed, holding that the appeal was not ripe for decision because Plaintiff had never properly submitted an application to CRMC for the development of his property. Therefore, the court reasoned, Plaintiff had never received a final decision regarding either the development which he wished to pursue or one with lesser environmental impact which would be better suited for the location. Palazzolo v. State, 746 A.2d 707, 714 (R.I. 2000).

On writ of certiorari, the United States Supreme Court found the case ripe for decision, reversed the holding of the Rhode Island Supreme Court, and remanded the case for the purpose of a *Penn Central* analysis.

---

[23] "'Inverse condemnation' is a term used to describe a cause of action against a governmental defendant to recover the value of property which has been taken in fact by the governmental defendant, even though no formal exercise of the power of eminent domain has been attempted by the taking agency." E & J, Inc. v. Redevelopment Agency of Woonsocket, 122 R.I. 288, 290 n.1, 405 A.2d 1187, 1189 n.1 (1979) (citing Ferguson v. Keene, 108 N.H. 409, 410, 238 A.2d 1, 2 (1968)). "The inverse-condemnation cause of action provides landowners with a means of seeking redress for governmental intrusions. . . ." Harris v. Town of Lincoln, 668 A.2d 321, 327 (R.I. 1995).

[24] In 1976, the Coastal Resources Management Council adopted the Coastal Resources Management Plan which prohibited the filling of coastal wetlands without a special exception. These regulations were promulgated under the authority given the CRMC by legislation enacted in 1971, G.L. §§ 46–23–1 et seq. The CRMC has refused to grant Palazzolo an exception to enable substantial development of the site.

Palazzolo v. Rhode Island, 533 U.S. 606 (2001) [editor's note: this opinion is reproduced in Assignments 31–32, *supra*.]. The Rhode Island Supreme Court entered an Order, dated June 24, 2002, remanding the case to the Superior Court with express guidelines.

Factual Overview

[T]he subject property (site) is located on the south side of Winnapaug Pond, a tidal, salt water pond. Although the breachway allowing salt water tidal flow to and from the pond has frequently been filled in and the breachway location has changed over time, there is substantial geologic evidence which shows this pond to have been tidal for more than 2000 years. While the substantially developed land to the north of the pond is markedly higher than pond level, the entire southern perimeter of the pond consists of salt water marsh. Even today it remains nearly devoid of development. It is within this area that Palazzolo first acquired a property interest through his long time friend, lawyer Natale Urso, in 1959.

Access to the Palazzolo property is by means of traveling on Atlantic Avenue, a nearly straight, two-lane highway which parallels the ocean and beaches. Atlantic Avenue is several feet above high water, it being located on a sand spine or berm upland formed over centuries by storm wash. At times storm surge has carried substantial quantities of sand (overwash) over the sand berm on which Atlantic Avenue is located and deposited the sand on the north side of the road. The geological formations made over time thus permitted relatively easy development of the lots located immediately adjacent to Atlantic Avenue.

The eighteen (18) acres of land (74 lots) at issue are almost all near pond elevation and much of the site is subject to daily tidal inundation. Immediately after Palazzolo's acquisition of a half interest in the site, six lots were sold off. At least some of these lots were easily developed because of their location on upland close to Atlantic Avenue. As to the remainder of the site, the survey filed with the Court indicates that approximately one-half of the site is below mean high water (MHW). Moreover, the vast majority of the site is not readily available for home construction, the soil surface being composed of Matunuck mucky peat between six to eighteen inches thick. Before any type of development can occur, that soil must be removed and as much as six feet of fill placed over much of the remainder of the site now owned by Palazzolo. An exception is the upland area of glacial remains near the pond shoreline to which a gravel road extending from Atlantic Avenue was connected prior to Palazzolo's involvement with the site.

There is substantial development on the land located immediately to the west, east, and north of the pond. Although that development has in large part not involved filling of wetlands, there is no doubt that several houses at the eastern and western ends of the pond were built on fill placed over previously existing wetlands. The houses located on fill at the eastern end of the pond were built on deposits derived from dredging and improvement of the breachway by governmental authority. Other lots to the immediate north of Atlantic Avenue have been filled to facilitate development. However, it is not at all clear that any substantial area of salt marsh has been filled here without state approval. On the other hand, substantial fill—mostly sand—has been deposited on the northern side of Atlantic Avenue by both mankind and the millennia of ocean storms.

The site owned by Palazzolo is similar to all of the remaining 146 acres of salt marsh contiguous to the pond, almost all of which is on its south side. These marshes provide valuable habitat for wildlife including birds and fish. With the exception of the two houses built on upland (glacial remnants) contained within or adjacent to the extensive salt marshes found on the south shore of the pond, there has been essentially no development within the salt marsh. The 446 acre Winnapaug Pond is a shallow, tidal pond used for fishing, boating and shell fishing. Its size and shallow depth make it a particularly fragile ecosystem.

The adjacent salt marsh provides, inter alia, a valuable filtering system regarding water runoff containing pollutants and nitrogen from adjacent land. The ISDS[25] systems from the proposed subdivision would add significant nitrogen to the pond. While experts disagree on the precise amount of nitrogen removal the site is responsible for, filling of the Palazzolo site would result in 12% less salt marsh and a reduction of pollutant and nitrogen filtering by the pond's salt marsh ecosystem. The effect of the denigration of the natural purifying salt marsh is viewed by experts as significant. Loss of the marsh filtering effect, together with the loss of wildlife habitat which would occur if Plaintiff's planned subdivision was constructed, was previously found by this Superior Court to constitute a nuisance.

Moreover, there can be no doubt that the pond and its surroundings, particularly the undeveloped salt marsh, have an amenity value to both the land owners in the area as well as the entire vacation/recreation community in Westerly. This Court likewise finds that the evidence is to the effect that not only has there never been a subdivision near Winnapaug Pond which rivals the scope of that proposed by Palazzolo, but none exists anywhere on the Rhode Island shore.[26]

Legal Analysis

Prior to discussing Plaintiff's takings claim in the context of a *Penn Central* analysis, it is necessary to consider certain background legal

---

[25] ISDS is the common acronym for individual sewerage disposal system.

[26] Because of current building restrictions in flood plain areas such as this site, each residence would be built on pilings. The first floor of each house would be required to be approximately twenty (20) feet above ground level. Palazzolo's early proposal was inspired by lagoon-style developments which he had seen in Florida. This Court finds that it would be unrealistic to assume regulatory approval of a similar Florida-style development on Winnapaug Pond.

principles which bear on the extent of plaintiff's property interest. See Lucas v. South Carolina, 505 U.S. 1003, 1029–30 (1992).

I. Public and Private Nuisance

B. Public Nuisance

"Actionable nuisances fall into two classifications, public and private.... A public nuisance is an unreasonable interference with a right common to the general public: it is behavior that unreasonably interferes with the health, safety, peace, comfort or convenience of the general community." Citizens for Preservation of Waterman Lake v. Davis, 420 A.2d 53, 59 (R.I. 1980).

Claims may also be brought on the basis of anticipatory nuisance. See Commerce Oil Refining Corp. v. Miner, 281 F.2d 465, 474–75 (1st Cir. 1960); Berberian v. Avery, 99 R.I. 77, 81–82, 205 A.2d 579, 582 (1964); Seidner, Inc. v. Ralston Purina Co., 67 R.I. 436, 24 A.2d 902 (1942). Not frequently litigated in Rhode Island, anticipatory nuisance was discussed in greatest detail in the Seidner case. "It is well settled that a court of equity may enjoin a threatened or anticipated nuisance, public or private, where it clearly appears that a nuisance will necessarily result from the contemplated act or things which it is sought to enjoin." Id. at 450, 909 (quoting 7 A.L.R. 749). Nuisance must be "proved by clear and convincing evidence that such damage will be practically certain to result." Id. at 451, 909–10. The requirement is that substantial damage will be practically certain to result.

In Lucas v. South Carolina, the United States Supreme Court observed that there can be no taking where a proposed use is prohibited ab initio by nuisance law. 505 U.S. at 1029. The Court also stated that a nuisance analysis requires a review of "the degree of harm to public lands and resources, or adjacent private property, posed by claimant's proposed activities ... the social value of the claimant's activities and their suitability to the locality in question...." Id. at 1030–31. The *Lucas* Court left the nuisance determination to state law, but not before establishing public nuisance as a preclusive defense to takings claims.

In the case at bar, Palazzolo's proposed development has been shown to have significant and predictable negative effects on Winnapaug Pond and the adjacent salt water marsh. The State has presented evidence as to various effects that the development will have including increasing nitrogen levels in the pond, both by reason of the nitrogen produced by the attendant residential septic systems, and the reduced marsh area which actually filters and cleans runoff. This Court finds that the effects of increased nitrogen levels constitute a predictable (anticipatory) nuisance which would almost certainly result in an ecological disaster to the pond. Both water quality and wildlife habitat would be substantially harmed. Nor is the proposed high density subdivision suitable for the salt marsh environs presented here.

Because clear and convincing evidence demonstrates that Palazzolo's development would constitute a public nuisance, he had no right to develop the site as he has proposed. Accordingly, the State's denial to permit such development cannot constitute a taking.

C. Private Nuisance

"A private nuisance involves an interference with the use and enjoyment of land. It involves a material interference with the ordinary physical comfort or the reasonable use of one's property." Citizens for Pres. of Waterman Lake v. Davis, 420 A.2d 53, 59 (R.I. 1980) (citing Iafrate v. Ramsden, 96 R.I. 216, 221, 190 A.2d 473, 476 (1963)). "Historically the law of private nuisance has been applied to conflicts between neighboring, contemporaneous land uses." Hydro-Manufacturing, Inc. v. Kayser-Roth Corp., 640 A.2d 950, 957 (R.I. 1994) (citing Philadelphia Elec. Co. v. Hercules, Inc., 762 F.2d 303, 314 & n.9 (3d Cir. 1985)). "Under Rhode Island law it is well settled that a cause of action for a private nuisance 'arises from the unreasonable use of one's property that materially interferes with a neighbor's physical comfort or the neighbor's use of his real estate.' " Id. (citing Weida v. Ferry, 493 A.2d 824, 826 (R.I. 1985)); see also Hennessey v. Pyne, 694 A.2d 691, 695 (R.I. 1997). "The burden of proving a nuisance is upon the party alleging it . . . who must demonstrate the existence of the nuisance . . . and that injury has been caused by the nuisance complained of." Citizens for Pres. of Waterman Lake, 420 A.2d at 59 (internal citations omitted).

In this case no neighboring landowner has made a private nuisance claim. If built, Plaintiff's development would have a surface level as much as seven feet above current ground level and as a result, block all water views now enjoyed by land owners to the south of the parcel in question. Although Plaintiff's planned subdivision may be remarkably out of character with respect to its surroundings, blocking a neighbor's view is not ordinarily considered a nuisance which is actionable at law. Ordinarily, an abutting landowner has no right to light and air that would be available to him but for the presence of a man-made obstruction such as a fence. Nor is there a right to a water view. "Distinguished from negligence liability, liability in nuisance is predicated upon unreasonable injury rather than unreasonable conduct." Wood v. Picillo, 443 A.2d 1244, 1247 (R. I. 1982).

On the facts presented here it is difficult to conclude that the development would interfere with any neighbor's physical comfort or land use. Therefore, Plaintiff's development would not constitute a private nuisance.

II. Public Trust Doctrine

Lucas v. South Carolina, 505 U.S. 1003 (1992) makes clear that, for purposes of takings analysis, the title one takes to property is subject to background principles of state law. *Lucas* states that the government need not compensate the property owner if the regulated or prohibited use was "not part of his title to begin with." Id at 1027. State nuisance doctrine has been discussed above and it would bar Plaintiff's takings claim in this Court's view.

A second significant issue is to what extent the Public Trust Doctrine would have limited the title originally acquired by Plaintiff and his predecessor in interest, Shore Gardens, Inc. (SGI). Succinctly stated, the State contends that because of the Public Trust Doctrine and trial evidence proving that one-half of the site is below mean high water, Plaintiff could not have expected to develop his subdivision absent the consent of the state.

Plaintiff counters by contending that the State's survey is erroneous, claiming that substantially more than one-half of the site is above the 1986 mean high water mark. Moreover, Plaintiff now claims that because the pond is subject to periodic closing of its breachway, it is not truly a tidal pond and thus, is not subject to the Public Trust Doctrine. Thirdly, Plaintiff contends that Winnapaug Pond and other similar coastal ponds are not subject to the Public Trust Doctrine.

After receiving voluminous evidence on the issue, this Court finds that Winnapaug Pond is a tidal body of water. This Court likewise finds that the survey filed with the Court (Ex. CCCCC) is accurate and establishes a mean high water line as of 1986, proving that almost exactly 50% of Plaintiff's property is below mean high water. Thus, the pond and Plaintiff's adjacent property are subject to the Public Trust Doctrine.

In Shively v. Bowlby, 152 U.S. 1 (1894), the United States Supreme Court expounded in great detail concerning the history and application of what is now commonly referred to as the Public Trust Doctrine. The Court concluded in general that—

> Lands under tide waters are incapable of cultivation or improvement in the manner of lands above high water mark. They are of great value to the public for the purposes of commerce, navigation and fishery. Their improvement by individuals, when permitted, is incidental or subordinate to the public use and right. Therefore the title and the control of them are vested in the sovereign for the benefit of the whole people. . . . The title and rights of riparian or littoral proprietors in the soil below high water mark, therefore, are governed by the laws of several States, subject to the rights granted to the United States by the Constitution.

Id. at 57–8.

Shively established beyond question a nationwide Public Trust Doctrine which is to be applied based upon state law. There can be no doubt that the doctrine remains viable law in Rhode Island. Not only was the Public Trust Doctrine incorporated into the Rhode Island Constitution, R.I. Const. art. 1, Section 17, but as recently stated by our

Supreme Court, "[a]ny system of regulation of tidal land in Rhode Island must be viewed in the context of [the] ancient and still vital doctrine [ ] of . . . the public trust doctrine. . . ." Champlin's Realty Assocs., L.P. v. Tillson, 823 A.2d 1162, 1165 (R.I. 2003) (quoting Town of Warren v. Thornton-Whitehouse, 740 A.2d 1255, 1259 (R.I. 1999)).

Restated, the Public Trust Doctrine dictates that, "the state holds title to all land below the high-water mark in a proprietary capacity for the benefit of the public." Greater Providence Chamber of Commerce v. Rhode Island, 657 A.2d 1038, 1041 (R.I. 1995). "Such common law is in force in Rhode Island 'except as it has been changed by local legislation or custom.' " Id. at 1042 (quoting City of Providence v. Comstock, 27 R.I. 537, 543, 65 A. 307, 308 (1906)). A limitation to the Public Trust Doctrine exists when there has been a legislative decree, such as when the legislature transfers property or grants rights to control or regulate property below mean high water to cities or municipalities. The State may likewise cede its ownership interest while retaining its rights and powers under the public trust doctrine.

As to Winnapaug Pond in general and Plaintiff's property specifically, there has been no express legislative transfer of the state's public trust rights. Palazzolo has not shown any such legislative action in relation to the property in question. Nor has there been either express or implied state approval or acquiescence to the filling of tidal waters upon which the Plaintiff has relied to his detriment. Palazzolo has not filled and improved his property with the permission or acquiescence of the State. Accordingly, this Court finds that as a result of Rhode Island's Public Trust Doctrine, neither Plaintiff nor SGI has ever had a right to fill or develop that portion of the site which is below mean high water. Thus, as against the State, Palazzolo has gained title and the corresponding property rights to only one-half of the parcel in question. Although the Public Trust Doctrine cannot be a total bar to recovery as to this takings claim, it substantially impacts Plaintiff's title to the parcel in question and has a direct relationship to Plaintiff's reasonable investment-backed expectations as will be discussed below.

III. Penn Central Analysis

[The Court applied the factors of the *Penn Central* analysis—1) the character of governmental action, 2) the economic impact of the action on the claimant, and 3) the extent to which the action interfered with the claimant's reasonable investment-backed expectations—to determine that Palazzolo had not suffered a taking. The Court noted that the cost estimates of Palazzolo's engineer were unreasonably low in comparison to other experts' testimony about the high costs of constructing homes and septic systems in a salt marsh, which would have required substantial fill, steel pilings, experimental septic system design, grading for drainage, and costly regulatory approvals for these design features. The Court also held that Palazzolo's assertions of likely profits were based on an assumption that land-development regulations, which he claimed had taken his property, would prevent surrounding landowners from constructing other homes that would compete in the market for buyers and that would diminish the environmental amenities associated with his development. Thus, Palazzolo sought compensation from the government for the "the societal values placed on the protection of salt marsh and its environs as reflected by legislation and attendant regulations." The Court determined that if other landowners were able to build in the manner that Palazzolo sought, there would be a glut of coastal homes on the market, which would diminish Palazzolo's net profits. Perhaps most significantly, the Court held that Palazzolo did not have reasonable property expectations to fill tidal lands that were protected by the public trust or to cause a public nuisance from the development effects discussed above. Palazzolo still had the right to develop a single home that "would generate gross income to Palazzolo in the amount of $200,000, a modest return on investment." The Court concluded: "Constitutional law does not require the state to guarantee a bad investment."]

**J.B. Ruhl, Making Nuisance Ecological, 58 Case W. Res. L. Rev. 753 (2008).**

Common law nuisance doctrine has the reputation of having provided much of the strength and content of environmental law prior to the rise of federal statutory regimes in the 1970s. Beginning in the 1960s, however, two trends pushed nuisance doctrine into the background of environmental law and public legislation into the foreground. The first was the growing attention given to the development of pollution standards that could be applied broadly across regions and across industries. The premise of turning to public legislation was that this objective would much more easily and effectively be met through regulatory approaches relying on promulgation of technology-based standards, permitting requirements, and administrative enforcement than it would through judicial mediation of common law nuisance actions. The Clean Air Act and Clean Water Act are the classics of this public legislation model of pollution control. The second trend—the one of particular importance for my purposes—was the growing attention being given to protecting and managing species and ecosystems for their intrinsic and ecological qualities. Once again, nuisance doctrine was widely perceived to be a poor fit, and statutory regimes such as the Endangered Species Act ("ESA") blossomed.

The effect of these two trends and their associated rise of federally legislated environmental law was to put nuisance doctrine into a state of hibernation for the last quarter of the twentieth century insofar as ecological attributes of the environment were concerned. Although nuisance has continued not infrequently to provide a viable cause of action in pollution contexts, one will search in vain for decisions prior to 2000 applying nuisance law in contexts anything like those addressed through statutory programs such as the Endangered Species Act and other ecosystem management statutes. Perhaps nuisance law lacked the capacity to do so, or was made superfluous in this respect by the statutory regime, or even was inherently biased against it, but whatever the explanation, it is hard to describe nuisance doctrine in that era as having had anything to do with being ecological.

There is a new trend afoot, however, and it is one I believe could awaken nuisance doctrine to make it more relevant to ecological concerns. The discipline of ecological economics, which emerged in the 1980s and gained full steam in the 1990s, has focused on putting an economic price tag on degradation of ecological integrity. Ecosystems have long been regarded as the source of valuable commodities and recreational pursuits, uses which, obviously, do not always align with the goal of maintaining ecological integrity. Statutory programs aimed at maintaining ecological integrity as a priority thus have resorted to rattling off other values in support of their underlying purposes, such as the ESA's declaration that endangered species "are of esthetic, ecological, educational, historical, recreational, and scientific value to the Nation and its people." A major thrust of ecological economics, however, has been to illuminate the role of ecosystems as providing economically valuable services to "the Nation and its people." These ecosystem services include flood mitigation and groundwater recharge from wetlands, water filtration and sediment capture from forests, nutrient cycling, gas regulation, pollination, thermal regulation, carbon sequestration, and so on. Although monetizing the value of these services is more complex than estimating the economic value of timber or hunting, no reasonable argument can be advanced that ecosystem services are not economically valuable.

Ecosystems services flow from the natural capital found in ecosystems such as forests, wetlands, coastal dunes, estuaries, and other ecologically defined units of study. However we define ecosystems and delineate their boundaries, though, one thing is certain: in many contexts an ecosystem will overlay a patch-work of private and public property ownership boundaries, and in such cases it is likely that the natural capital from which ecosystem services flow frequently will be located on parcels different from those where the service benefits are enjoyed. From the viewpoint of owners of natural capital, therefore, ecosystem services often are positive externalities leaking off the parcel, the value of which is difficult to capture in the market. From the viewpoint of the owners of land where the services are enjoyed, however, curtailment of the services through degradation of the natural capital could pose significant economic injury. So, when an owner of land wants to transform a wetland or forest into, say, a shopping center, and the owner of other land receiving ecosystem services from that natural capital objects on the basis of the economic injury that will result because of increased flooding or decreased pollination, who wins?

I. Ecosystem Services and the Prima Facie Case—An Easy Fit

In *Palazzolo v. State*, a Rhode Island trial court considered a regulatory takings claim the United States Supreme Court had left dangling in *Palazzolo v. Rhode Island*. The Supreme Court had rejected the claim that state agency denial of a permit to fill and develop a marsh area adjacent to a pond constituted a categorical taking or property under *Lucas*, on the ground that the agency allowed Palazzolo to develop some of his parcel, leaving it to the state courts initially to decide whether the permit denial was a regulatory taking. The state trial court reasoned that *Lucas* "establish[ed] public nuisance as a preclusive defense to takings claims," and found that "clear and convincing evidence demonstrates that Palazzolo's development would constitute a public nuisance" on the following grounds:

> Palazzolo's proposed development has been shown to have significant and predictable negative effects on Winnapaug Pond and the adjacent salt-water marsh. The State has presented evidence as to various effects that the development will have including increasing nitrogen levels in the pond, both by reason of the nitrogen produced by the attendant residential septic systems, and by the reduced marsh area which actually filters and cleans runoff. This Court finds that the effects of increased nitrogen levels constitute a predictable (anticipatory) nuisance which would almost certainly result in an ecological disaster to the pond.

*Palazzolo* thus involved the type of transboundary property rights issue that is likely to be ubiquitous for the law and policy of natural capital and ecosystem services, and the case demonstrates the easy time public nuisance law should have for integrating those values into a straightforward analysis: Palazzolo owned the marsh; the marsh filtered and cleaned runoff into the pond; those services were positive externalities flowing off of Palazzolo's property; the public in general enjoyed the economic benefits of that service; Palazzolo therefore had no property right to fill the marsh. It's that simple.

Nevertheless, as easily as the court's decision integrated ecosystem services into public nuisance doctrine, the decision also illustrates the difficulty of making the same move in private nuisance doctrine or in affirmative claims of public nuisance. The nuisance analysis arises in cases like *Palazzolo* only in connection with the government's assertion of the nuisance exception to the landowner's regulatory taking claim. If the government can establish the exception under the public nuisance branch simply by demonstrating the qualitative effect on ecosystem service delivery, it need not establish proof of quantitative economic harm to specific property owners. The government's litigation incentives thus are far different from those a private landowner or sovereign might advance through an affirmative nuisance claim against conduct like Palazzolo's filling of the marsh.

In *Palazzolo*, for example, although the court acknowledged the "valuable filtering system" the marsh provided and that the pond and marsh system provided "amenity value to the land owners in the area," the curtailment of ecosystem service values to private landowners did not register in the record or with the court. The court simply noted that "no neighboring landowner has made a private nuisance claim" and that the potential for obstruction of views of the water would not constitute a private nuisance under Rhode Island law. It would have been unlikely, however, that any neighboring landowner would advance a private nuisance claim having to do with loss of the marsh filtering function before it was known whether the state would grant the permit for the project in the first place, and such litigation was unnecessary after the state rejected the permit. In short, the law of ecosystem services in nuisance doctrine is unlikely to develop significantly in the context of government defense of regulatory takings claims—it will emerge only when private landowners and sovereigns start suing over the adverse effects of natural capital degradation.

Consider four possible scenarios in which one landowner's degradation of natural capital might cause economic injury to another landowner, group of landowners, or larger segment of the public by curtailing the flow of ecosystem services:

- The Simple Scenario: Landowner A modifies Parcel A in such a way as to degrade natural capital (e.g., coastal dunes) on Parcel A supplying ecosystem services (e.g., storm surge mitigation) to Landowner B on Parcel B. Parcels A and B are adjacent; the effects of Landowner A's conduct are felt on Parcel B very soon after Parcel A is modified (e.g., during the next major storm); and the effects on Parcel B are clearly and exclusively attributable to Landowner A's conduct.

- The Spatially Complex Scenario: The same as the Simple Scenario, but in this case Parcels A and B are located at a considerable distance apart (e.g., ten or more miles).

- The Temporally Complex Scenario: The same as the Simple Scenario, but in this case the effects on Parcel B are not felt until a considerable time after Landowner A's conduct (e.g., three or more years).

- The Cumulative Impacts Scenario: A few or many landowners (Group A) modify their respective parcels in such a way as to degrade natural capital (e.g., wetlands) supplying services (e.g., downstream flood mitigation) to a few or many other landowners (Group B) on their respective parcels. Some parcels in Groups A and B are in close proximity, but others are not; the effects of Group A's conduct are felt on some of Group B's parcels soon after the Group A parcels are modified, but only after a significant time for others; and while the effects on Group B's parcels are clearly and exclusively attributable to Group A's conduct, particularly as the number of landowners in Group A increases it is not clear which Group B parcels are affected by modifications on particular Group A parcels.

Presumably, if private and public interests believe they are harmed substantially in these "ecosystem service nuisance" circumstances, they will invest in, among other things, litigation designed to find some fit between a common law remedy and their alleged injury, even if that means proposing that a court make what amounts to an evolutionary move in the applicable common law doctrine. The outcome under regulatory takings cases such as *Palazzolo* suggests that, with reliable evidence of significant injury resulting from curtailment of ecosystem services, private nuisance actions, as well as public nuisance actions prosecuted in the affirmative rather than as a defense to regulatory takings claims, ought to be a viable forum for this kind of "evolution-inducing" litigation. Focusing on the relevant qualitative differences between the four scenarios, this section provides the template for designing private and public nuisance claims in settings such as these.

A. Private Nuisance

In its barest essence, a private nuisance is "a nontrespassory invasion of another's interest in the private use and enjoyment of land." As every first-year law student quickly learns, this maxim is not particularly useful on its own, but rather opens the door to a complex "reasonableness" inquiry. Justice Scalia described the test in *Lucas* as an "analysis of, among other things, the degree of harm to public lands and resources, or adjacent private property, posed by the [landowner's] proposed activities, the social value of the [landowner's] activities and their suitability to the locality in question, and the relative ease with which the alleged harm can be avoided through measures taken by the [landowner] and the government (or adjacent landowners) alike." The Restatement (Second) of Torts provides a version of this balancing inquiry in the principle that "[a]n intentional invasion of another's interest in the use and enjoyment of land is unreasonable if the gravity of the harm outweighs the utility of the actor's conduct." Although not all jurisdictions follow it in all respects, and some do not follow it in many respects, in this section I have adopted the Restatement's framework for analyzing the four ecosystem service nuisance scenarios.

1. Intentional Invasion

One objection to the proposed ecosystem services nuisance theory of liability is that the defendant has not "invaded" the plaintiff's property by introducing adverse conditions, but rather has simply interfered with benefits flowing from the defendant's property to the plaintiff's property. Indeed, with odors, noise, and dust as the classic fodder of private nuisance doctrine, the black letter element of an "invasion" can easily be thought of as requiring defendant to have caused some physically measurable "bad" phenomenon to "move" from the defendant's parcel to the plaintiff's, such that there is quantifiably "more" of it on the latter (as in, plaintiff's property is smellier, noisier, or dustier).

Even under this narrow conception of invasion, however, many if not most ecosystem service nuisances would satisfy the element. The consequence of interfering with the storm surge mitigation benefits of coastal wetlands, for example, is more flooding inland. And the consequence of interfering with the sediment capture benefits of riparian habitat is more sediment in the river. Whether the defendant stands on the banks of the river and dumps sediment in from a wheelbarrow or causes the same amount of sediment to enter the river by destroying riparian habitat, the effect is the same in all four of the scenarios—something "bad" moves from defendant's property to plaintiff's.

In some cases, however, it would be accurate to observe that the defendant is only depriving a benefit to other properties, such as when destruction of forest habitat reduces local pollination services available to an agricultural use of property. In such cases, the argument would go, the withdrawal of benefits, even though the direct cause of plaintiff's injury, does not amount to an invasion within the meaning of nuisance doctrine. But the invasion element means nothing of the sort. As the Restatement explains, "private nuisance has reference to the interest invaded and not to the type of conduct that subjects the actor to liability." In other words, what matters is that the plaintiff is made worse off. And the plaintiff clearly is demonstrably worse off in the withdrawal of benefits class of cases using the kind of evidence applied in all nuisance cases—a physically and economically measurable phenomenon on plaintiff's property. Indeed, the Restatement treats "physical damage to tangible property" as the bull's eye of private nuisance, precisely because, unlike physical discomfort or annoyance to the plaintiff, "it can more readily be observed and measured." Thus nowhere in the Restatement is the "invasion" element linked to particular classes of conduct that would exclude withdrawal of ecosystem service benefits from the scope of actionable injuries. Taking the plaintiff's point of view as the appropriate perspective, therefore, even the withdrawal of ecosystem service benefits should meet the invasion element of private nuisance.

Having established that ecosystem service nuisances of all varieties can satisfy the invasion element, the plaintiff must also show that defendant intended the invasion. The Restatement describes an act as intentional for these purposes if the actor "acts for the purpose of causing it" or "knows that it is resulting or is substantially certain to result from his conduct." On the assumption that most landowners do not degrade natural capital with the express purpose of injuring other landowners, the question in most ecosystem service nuisance cases will be the defendant's state of knowledge. On this element, unlike the invasion element, the outcome is likely to vary between the four scenarios.

The Simple Scenario sets up the classic case in which it will be more difficult for the defendant to plead lack of intent. Even with no intent to harm, the defendant likely is in a position plainly to observe the effects on plaintiff's property of degrading the natural capital, and thus acts with intent within the meaning of the Restatement. And even if the causal effect is not immediately apparent, once it is brought to defendant's attention, either by notification or by observation, continued degradation of the natural capital would constitute intent within the meaning of the Restatement.

As the effects of natural capital degradation become more spatially or temporally removed from defendant's conduct, what the defendant knew would result or be substantially certain to result is likely to be subject to more debate. Here is where the burgeoning ecological and economic knowledge about natural capital and ecosystem services will play an important role in the development of ecosystem service nuisance cases. After events like Hurricane Katrina, for example, it should be reasonable to expect anyone in coastal regions of the Gulf to understand the effects of degraded coastal marshes and dunes on the protection of inland areas from storm surges, and that those effects can be felt at considerable distances from the location of the conduct and not until well after the conduct takes place. Similarly, the injuries to forests, crops, and public health that once led the United States Supreme Court, with little hesitation, to find that emissions from copper smelting plants in Tennessee posed a public nuisance in Georgia did not happen adjacent to the plants or immediately upon their commencement of operations. Hence, it is not as if nuisance law evaporates with time or distance, but rather the plaintiff's burden of proof regarding defendant's state of knowledge simply becomes more demanding. Doubtless, there will be cases fitting the Spatially Complex Scenario and Temporally Complex Scenario in which the plaintiff cannot meet that burden, but likely there will be many in which the plaintiff can. And as knowledge about natural capital and ecosystem services builds and spreads, plaintiffs will more frequently and easily meet the burden.

The same should be true for the Cumulative Impacts Scenario as well, where the question of defendant's knowledge is complicated not by time or distance, but by the dispersed quality of cause and effect. A defendant in this kind of ecosystem service nuisance case might argue that one could not reasonably be expected to have known that an injury such as increased sediment in a lake or river would be exacerbated by such a small loss of riparian habitat as the defendant claims to have caused. But pleading ignorance of cumulative impacts effects in the environment is becoming increasingly difficult except for the severely ignorant. . . . One who levels a coastal dune or fills a riparian wetland . . . and who witnesses others doing the same up and down the beach or river, will be increasingly hard-pressed to claim lack of knowledge that he or she contributed to the overall effect of reduced protection from storm surges and floods at other locations. The question ought not to be one of intent in those circumstances, but rather one of the substantiality of each person's participation in the action causing the harm.

2. Interest in Use and Enjoyment of Land

The fact that the plaintiff is worse off and can show defendant so intended points the analysis next to the matter of plaintiff's property interest—i.e., whether it is of the type which, if injured as experienced, gives rise to an actionable claim in nuisance. As far as nuisance doctrine is concerned, however, this is simply a standing requirement, in that "there is liability only to those who have property rights and privileges in respect to the use and enjoyment of the land affected." The Restatement, in other words, "does not state the rules applicable in determining when a person's rights and privileges in respect to land constitute property rights and privileges. Those questions are dealt with in the Restatement of Property."

Hence this element presents no opportunity for arguing that a plaintiff does not have the right to a particular ecosystem service benefit, such as pollination or storm surge mitigation. Nuisance law is not about whether there is a "right" to ecosystem services any more than it is about whether there is a "right" to specific levels of noise, odors, or dust. The loss of ecosystem services, like noise, odors, and dust, is simply the agent of injury to the plaintiff's property interest in use and enjoyment. All that matters is that the plaintiff has a property interest that extends to the specific use and enjoyment of the property, such as farming or conducting a business, that plaintiff contends is being impaired by the defendant's conduct, which for our purposes is interfering with the delivery of a particular ecosystem service benefit. If plaintiff has such an interest, this element is met, and the analysis moves on to the gravity of harm/utility of conduct balancing calculus.

3. Gravity of the Harm to Plaintiff

Section 827 of the Restatement identifies five important factors to consider in the "gravity of harm" analysis: (1) extent of harm; (2) character of harm; (3) social value of the use or enjoyment invaded; (4) suitability of the use or enjoyment to the locality; and (5) the burden on the person harmed of avoiding the harm. These and all other relevant factors are to be weighed objectively, with the gravity of harm being the overall product with "no general rule as to the relative weight of the particular factors in all the ever-varying cases."

There is nothing about these factors or the weighing of them that puts ecosystem service nuisances in some qualitatively distinct category compared to other nuisances. The injuries associated with loss of ecosystem services can be severe, they are often manifested in physical damage to tangible property, and they can pose risks to residences and socially valuable commercial and agricultural operations that are perfectly suited to their localities.

With respect to the question whether the plaintiff can avoid the harm, it is true enough that many ecosystem services can be replaced through technological means, or that the risk associated with their absence can be ameliorated through preventative measures. But earplugs, clothespins, and dust masks can be worn to guard against noise, odors, and dust too. The question isn't whether the plaintiff can avoid the harm at all costs, but whether it is reasonable to expect the plaintiff to do so. Nuisance law has not usually expected plaintiffs claiming damage from excessive noise to install sound barriers, or those claiming injury from slaughterhouse odors to filter their air. It would seem strange, therefore, to expect the owner of inland property to construct a seawall when beachfront owners level dunes to make room for condos, or to expect a riverfront property owner to install sediment filtration devices when forestland owners in the watershed clear cut trees to make room for strip malls. In short, like the invasion element, because the gravity of harm element focuses on the plaintiff's perspective, ecosystem service nuisances appear rather plain vanilla as far as nuisance doctrine is concerned.

4. Utility of Defendant's Conduct

Of course, as this is a balancing calculus, at some point the defendant's perspective must enter into the picture. Section 828 of the Restatement identifies three factors in the "utility of conduct" side of the analysis: (1) the social value of the primary purpose of the conduct; (2) the suitability of the conduct to the locality; and (3) the impracticability of preventing or avoiding the harm. Several considerations are likely to complicate the analysis of these factors for ecosystem service nuisances.

First, it is likely that in some cases the conduct alleged to have caused an ecosystem service nuisance will have long been thought of in the community as socially valuable and suitable to the locality. After all, many acres of coastal dunes, wetlands, and forests have given way to development of one kind or another. But if this condition were to foreclose an ecosystem service nuisance claim as a matter of law, the new knowledge principle would be entirely subverted. The point of the new knowledge principle is that we learn the errors of our ways and adjust nuisance law accordingly. Now that we know how economically devastating the loss of natural capital can be locally and regionally, the fact that it was once seen as acceptable ought to play a significantly diminished role on defendants' behalf. As one court observed:

> The rules and understandings as to the uses of land that are acceptable or unacceptable have changed over time. The fact that sewage was once strewn into city streets does not give rise to a permanent reasonable expectation that such behavior can continue indefinitely Despite the fact that one may have purchased property with the expectation to use it in such a manner that was acceptable before the purchase, there may come a point in time when the original owner's expectations may no longer be reasonable.

In some cases, however, defendants might be able to point to approval by federal, state, and local environmental and land use authorities of the alleged degradation of natural capital to bolster the claim of reasonableness of conduct. Nuisance law, for example, has long struggled with the effect of the defendant's use complying with local zoning ordinances, with the general rule being that compliance weighs in favor of defendant on the issue of suitability. But most environmental and land use statutes neither preempt nuisance law nor directly address how they should be factored into the nuisance analysis; indeed, federal environmental statutes routinely disclaim any preemptive intent. Hence, while approval of development in dunes, wetlands, forests, or other ecosystems supplying local or regional ecosystem services should weigh into the analysis in favor of defendants, it ought not be taken as controlling in the balancing test.

The final complication is one inherent in all nuisance contexts, but particularly so in the ecosystem service nuisance cases—i.e., that almost all activities have some positive and negative externalities felt somewhere else by someone else. The Restatement recognizes the "obvious truth that each individual in a community must put up with a certain amount of annoyance, inconvenience, or interference and must take a certain amount of risk in order that all may get on together." So it cannot be that all losses of ecosystem services have a remedy in nuisance. Indeed, what I have outlined as an ecosystem service nuisance is intended to fit within the conventional doctrine of private nuisance, not to morph it into a general ecological protection regime. In the absence of a plaintiff whose use and enjoyment of property is substantially injured as a result of another landowner's degradation of natural capital, no ecosystem service nuisance has been committed. Likewise, the defendant's conduct must fit the doctrine as well. In short, nuisance law must decide which degradations of natural capital, taking into account the value of the defendant's primary purpose and the possibility that government authorities have approved that purpose, are within the scope of nuisance liability.

Ecological economists have developed the concept of critical natural capital (also CNC) to identify ecological resources that provide important ecosystem services and which are least amenable to substitution. Ekins explains, for example, that "for any particular CNC, and resulting environmental function, there is no substitute type of capital, natural or human-made, which would enable the same function to be performed to the same extent, i.e., the CNC is non-substitutable in respect of the function in question." Surely when we learn that a particular ecological resource fits this definition, the prospect of private nuisance liability, perhaps even in strict liability, is an appropriate consequence for its destruction regardless of past customs or government approvals. Between this critical threshold and trivial losses of natural capital associated with socially necessary land development suited to its surroundings, nuisance law cannot avoid its balancing function. Somewhere on that range, in some ecosystem service nuisance cases, the balance ought to tip in plaintiff's favor. There is nothing about the fact that natural capital degradation is the cause, or that loss of ecosystem services is the effect, to immunize such injuries from this outcome in the doctrine of private nuisance.

B.  Public Nuisance

A public nuisance "is an unreasonable interference with a right common to the general public." For the most part, the Restatement treats the reasonableness component of that maxim the same as for private nuisance. As for rights common to the general public, neither must they be rights in land, nor will rights in land held by numerous landowners necessarily amass into a right common to the general public. Ecosystem service nuisances seem ready-made for public nuisance under all these conditions. The *Palazzolo* court, for example, had little trouble finding liability for anticipatory nuisance in the public nuisance version of the Simple Scenario, noting no more than that "the 446 acre Winnapaug pond is a shallow, tidal pond used for fishing, boating and shell fishing. The adjacent salt marsh provides, inter alia, a valuable filtering system regarding water runoff containing pollutants and nitrogen from adjacent land."

The Cumulative Impacts Scenario would likely also provide appropriate cases for public nuisance treatment, as widespread depletion of natural capital, particularly critical natural capital, could impose significant public-wide economic and health impacts. The land-based impacts of the ecosystem service losses, moreover, could provide the "special injury" a private landowner would need to advance a public nuisance claim. While the Cumulative Impacts Scenario is likely to present more difficult questions of causation and the substantiality of each individual defendant's contribution to harm, those are appropriate questions for public nuisance cases, not barriers to bringing the claim. In short, as with private nuisance, nothing in the Restatement or nuisance case law suggests that ecosystem service nuisance claims fall in some special category for which the law erects any sort of special barrier to public nuisance liability.

## NOTES

1. *Ethics and economics.* Professor Freyfogle emphasizes that property interests in environmentally sensitive lands should be shaped by environmental ethics informed by the interdependence of individual property owners, human communities, and the ecological communities and conditions associated with land. In contrast, Professor Ruhl emphasizes the role of environmental economics in determining the scope and limit of property rights affecting ecosystems and the services that they provide to society. Which perspective do you find most compelling? Are the two approaches entirely compatible, mutually inconsistent, or somewhere in

between these two points on the spectrum? In other words, is it possible that the issues involving the use and development of environmentally sensitive lands are both ethical and economic issues?

Note that the works by Professors Freyfogle and Ruhl share three common points. First, both scholars emphasize the complex *interdependencies* among social and ecological systems. Parcels of privately owned land do not exist in isolation or merely in legal abstractions. Use of any particular land has impacts across multiple scales of space and time. Second, both Professors Freyfogle and Ruhl believe that *science*—especially science related to ecology and ecosystems—must play a significant role in understanding the carrying capacity of land, the functions of particular lands and their ecosystems, and the effects of land and development. However, both scholars believe that decisions about what kinds of land uses are acceptable or unacceptable are ultimately human decisions made in society and that science by itself cannot answer these value questions. Third, both scholars frame the property issues associated with environmentally sensitive lands as being issues of *"harm"* and either the prevention of harm to others or the compensation of others for the harms they have experienced. To the extent that the intersection of environmentally sensitive conditions and property law produce affirmative duties of the property owner, the legal system seemingly defines and enforces them only to the extent that there is an identifiable and remediable harm to address.

2. *Transitions, regulations, and takings.* Both *Just* and *Palazzolo* involved property owners' claims that government regulations of their environmentally sensitive lands constituted takings of their private property without just compensation. Most limits on private property rights in environmentally sensitive lands arise out of government regulation.

The intersection between environmental-protection regulations and property law often involves taking claims by regulated landowners. These claims require the property law system to define the scope of private rights, duties, remedies, and liabilities with respect to environmentally sensitive lands. Takings claims are more common where the law is in transition.[27] In the case of environmentally sensitive lands, a number of transitions are underway: increasing government regulation, evolving scientific knowledge about ecology, emerging understandings of human effects on ecosystems, growing land-use and land-development impacts on the environment, and changing social values about environmental conservation. While property law evolves over time, it also resists change in order to promote the certainty and stability of property rights and the security of investments in property. As Holly Doremus points out, humans dislike change, and property law may become a tool to attempt to avoid the uncertainties and complexities in the relationships between ecological systems and social systems.[28]

In particular, regulations prohibiting development of coastal lands and wetlands have been deemed to be takings in some cases, although many of these successful takings claims arose where most of the surrounding or

---

[27] Doremus, Takings and Transitions, 19 *J. Land Use & Envtl. L.* 1 (2003).
[28] Id.

nearby land had already been developed.[29] Thus, we cannot make sweeping generalizations about the inherent limits in the right to develop coastal lands based solely on the material in this Assignment. Nonetheless, both *Just* and *Palazzolo* reflect the potential for property law and its application in regulatory takings cases to evolve with society's transition to conservation of environmentally sensitive lands.

    3. *Coastal lands.* While the lands in *Palazzolo* were mostly coastal wetlands (some of which were subject to regular tidal inundation) and the lands in *Just* were lakeshore wetlands, neither involved development on dry oceanfront beaches, dunes, or bluffs. However, are there core principles that can be applied from *Palazzolo* and *Just* to these types of coastal lands? In addition, are there reasons why coastal landowners would like to see coastal property rights restricted? Are there impacts from neighboring landowners' development or use of land that they would like to prevent?

    4. *Is* Just *still good law?* The Wisconsin Supreme Court ignited a firestorm of controversy over the scope of its public trust doctrine in a 2013 case, Rock-Koshkonong Lake District v. State Department of Natural Resources.[30] The underlying facts of the case involved a relatively mundane dispute about water-level management decisions made by State Department of Natural Resources officials. However, language in the majority opinion—arguably dicta—stated that the agency's consideration of water-level impacts on privately owned wetlands was made under its police power authority, not its public trust authority. Three Justices vigorously dissented, arguing that the majority's language egregiously misreads *Just* as involving only police power jurisdiction, as well as other Wisconsin public-trust precedents. The case *might* signal that the Wisconsin courts are aiming to shrink the state's public trust doctrine as a tool for regulation of private property, after decades of relatively expansive interpretations of the public trust in the state. If so, the case serves as a reminder that flexibility and adaptation in legal systems can work both ways. While greater flexibility and adaptation in law can be used to make property rules and government authority more protective of ecosystems and more responsive to environmental changes, the rules can also change to reduce ecosystem protections and adapt to political and economic pressures for development and property owner autonomy. The direction of legal evolution in property law depends on whether it should advance a specific set of environmental values.

---

    [29] See, e.g., City of Monterey v. Del Monte Dunes at Monterey, Ltd., 526 U.S. 687 (1999); Lucas v. S.C. Coastal Council, 505 U.S. 1003 (1992); Loveladies Harbor, Inc. v. United States, 28 F.3d 1171 (Fed. Cir. 1994).

    [30] 350 Wis. 2d 45, 833 N.W.2d 800 (2013).

# V. TRANSFER OF INTERESTS IN REAL PROPERTY

## A. Transfer Without Written Instruments

## ASSIGNMENT 38–39

# Adverse Possession

### 1. Introduction

Ownership of land is almost always acquired by purchase, inter vivos or testamentary gift, or intestate succession.[1] Yet, under the doctrine of adverse possession, one can acquire ownership of land without payment of money and without the consent of the legal record owner. This doctrine permits an uninvited intruder who fulfills certain statutory and common law requirements to acquire legal title to the land and to divest completely the record titleholder's rights. Although the prescribed requirements are articulated somewhat differently in each state, the following six requirements are generally recognized: 1) actual possession; 2) hostile possession; 3) open and notorious possession; 4) exclusive possession; 5) continuous possession; and 6) possession under a claim of right. Each element is a particular characteristic of the "possession," which is the exercise of "dominion and control" over the property.

The adverse possessor must meet the state's prescribed requirements for the specified length of time. This statutory period is the statute of limitations for bringing a cause of action in ejectment and can range from three years to as long as sixty years depending on the jurisdiction and other factors. Throughout the statutory period, the adverse possessor is perfecting or building an original, inchoate title that ripens into a full legal title once the period has run. The law of adverse possession in many jurisdictions incorporates both statutory and common law. Thus, it is essential to examine both the governing state statute and its judicial gloss.

The adverse possessor is immune from prosecution for trespass once the requisite period has run. In the interim, however, he can be seen as indulging in a new wrong every day of his possession. During this interim period, he is liable for damages in trespass and is subject to ejectment. Adverse possession claims usually arise in ejectment actions to gain possession, trespass actions for damages, or quiet title actions. Although

---

[1] Historically, title to most of the land in the United States was acquired by conquest from the Native Americans. The U.S. Supreme Court has carefully avoided expressing an opinion on the morality of this mode of acquisition. See Johnson v. McIntosh, 21 U.S. (8 Wheat) 543 (1823).

before the adverse possessor's title is perfected his possession is "wrongful" as to the record owner, the adverse possessor can bring actions in ejectment to oust other trespassers throughout this period. The adverse possessor can also bring actions in nuisance and can assert any other legal right incident to possession. Thus, while adverse possession is wrongful against the true owner, it is concomitantly viewed as "rightful" against the rest of the world.

Why does modern society continue to tolerate the doctrine of adverse possession? Why should someone who may have paid substantial sums to acquire record title to property be deprived of that property by one who has paid nothing? Critics of the doctrine argue that it encourages trespassing and wrongdoing. They also contend that after the statute of limitations has run, barring an action in ejectment makes the state a party to the unlawful activity by recognizing the adverse possessor's new title. In addition, adverse possession tends to undercut the important goal underlying the recording acts of fostering reliability in title searches. A prospective purchaser of land who diligently searches the title records cannot know if an adverse possessor has successfully divested the record owner of an otherwise valid title. Therefore, it is often desirable to conduct a professional on-site survey of the land to ensure the validity of the title.

Adverse possession might merely be an extension of property law's favor for one who is in possession of the land or object. Professor Carol Rose identifies possession as the leading historical explanation and justification for property rights.[2] Possession is a critical part of the rights of finders of lost personal property, at least under certain circumstances, and bailees, who possess personal property legitimately for the true owner (e.g., borrowing another's tools, looking after another's laptop, operating a valet parking service for a fee). The rule of capture, which recognizes the rights of one who reduces a fugitive (i.e., free and mobile) object to possession, is another example of the "possession bias" of U.S. property law. While the rule of capture for fugitive natural resources, like wildlife, oil, gas, and groundwater, has been largely replaced by state control and regulation, the doctrine may still be relevant for new forms of fugitive objects.

The traditional rule of capture, however, was not properly followed in a conflict over Barry Bonds' record-setting 73rd home-run baseball during the 2001 baseball season. A court awarded the baseball jointly to an initial possessor and the post-tussle possessor, because the court could not determine which of the two fans had sufficient control of the ball during a rough scramble for it at San Francisco's Pacific Bell Park.[3] The

---

[2] Rose, Possession as the Origin of Property, 52 U. Chi. L. Rev. 73 (1985).

[3] Finkelman, Fugitive Baseballs and Abandoned Property: Who Owns the Home Run Ball?, 23 Cardozo L. Rev. 1609 (2002); Adomeit, The Barry Bonds Baseball Case: An Empirical Approach: Is Fleeting Possession Five Tenths of the Ball?, 48 St. Louis U. L.J. 475 (2004).

ball was ultimately auctioned for $450,000, which the two claimants split.

The Barry Bonds' baseball incident illustrates the dark side of possession: the legal system's recognition of rights in one who has dispossessed another. The U.S. legal system was used to justify European settlers' acquisition of land from Native Americans by force.[4] It was also used to dispossess Spanish and Mexican land grantees in the Southwest after the U.S. acquired the area in settlement of war with Mexico. Even though the Treaty of Guadalupe-Hidalgo provided that the U.S. would give legal recognition to existing grants, U.S. settlers arrived to claim these vast holdings and, in many cases, these settlers or federal government agents were successful in legally challenging the validity of well-settled Mexican property interests, typically using fraud and spurious legal arguments.[5] The doctrine of adverse possession may be yet another legal incentive to dispossess others of their land by force, deception, or clever strategy.[6]

On the other hand, the most important justification for the adverse possession doctrine is that it protects one who innocently and mistakenly possesses the land of another for such a long period that a justifiable reliance on the existing state of affairs can be presumed. A change in this state of affairs would give a windfall to the record owner. The emphasis on a specific period of time and on other objectively verifiable facts, rather than on the state of mind of the record owner or the adverse possessor, simplifies the administration of the rule, and reduces the temptation and opportunity for perjured testimony concerning the secret intent of the parties.

The doctrine of adverse possession also promotes certainty in land titles, nullifies conveyancing errors, and often settles boundary disputes. In addition, it protects third parties who detrimentally rely on their belief that the adverse possessor is the true owner of the land. The doctrine is also said to encourage the beneficial use of land not used by the record owner. Society as a whole may thus be benefited while the record owner is "punished" for not using or protecting her land.

Adverse possession, perhaps more than most other legal doctrines, suffers from a failure to articulate the basic policies that are to be promoted by the doctrine. Courts and legislatures sometimes seem intent on punishing the negligent record owner. At other times, they seem more

---

[4] Johnson v. McIntosh, 21 U.S. (8 Wheat) 543 (1823).

[5] Luna, Chicana/Chicano Land Tenure in the Agrarian Domain: On the Edge of a "Naked Knife", 4 Mich. J. Race & L. 39 (1998).

[6] One theory is that the adverse possession doctrine developed to facilitate squatters' claims that settled the West, favored productive use over ownership by absentee speculators, and fit settlers' partially selfish and partially moralistic sense of entitlement to land. The theory is that behavior initially viewed as illegal or "outlaw" behavior ultimately shapes property rules in adaptive ways. Penalver and Katyal, Property Outlaws, 155 U. Pa. L. Rev. 1095 (2007). For a broader perspective that social institutions are more likely to adapt to outlaw behavior or dissenting perspectives than to squelch them, see Russell, Dissent and Order in the Middle Ages: The Search for Legitimate Authority (1992).

interested in protecting the expectations of the adverse possessor. As you explore the following materials, consider whether the various sub-rules and exceptions advance the policies of the doctrine as you perceive them. Principal Problem A and the accompanying materials focus on the "hostility" and "claim of right" requirements. Principal Problem B and the related materials explore the "exclusive", "open and notorious", "continuous" and "actual" requirements. Before considering the problems, however, acquaint yourself with the following typical adverse possession statute.

## 2. A Sample Statute

### McKinney's Consolidated Laws of New York Annotated
### Real Property Actions and Proceedings Law,
### Ch. 81, Art. 5 Adverse Possession

**§ 501. Adverse possession; defined**

For the purposes of this article:

1. Adverse possessor. A person or entity is an "adverse possessor" of real property when the person or entity occupies real property of another person or entity with or without knowledge of the other's superior ownership rights, in a manner that would give the owner a cause of action for ejectment.

2. Acquisition of title. An adverse possessor gains title to the occupied real property upon the expiration of the statute of limitations for an action to recover real property pursuant to subdivision (a) of section two hundred twelve of the civil practice law and rules, provided that the occupancy, as described in sections five hundred twelve and five hundred twenty-two of this article, has been adverse, under claim of right, open and notorious, continuous, exclusive, and actual.

3. Claim of right. A claim of right means a reasonable basis for the belief that the property belongs to the adverse possessor or property owner, as the case may be. Notwithstanding any other provision of this article, claim of right shall not be required if the owner or owners of the real property throughout the statutory period cannot be ascertained in the records of the county clerk, or the register of the county, of the county where such real property is situated, and located by reasonable means.

**§ 511. Adverse possession under written instrument or judgment**

Where the occupant or those under whom the occupant claims entered into the possession of the premises under claim of right, exclusive of any other right, founding the claim upon a written instrument, as being a conveyance of the premises in question, or upon the decree or judgment of a competent court, and there has been a continued occupation and possession of the premises included in the instrument, decree or judgment, or of some part thereof, for ten years, under the same claim, the premises so included are deemed to have been held adversely; except that when they consist of a tract divided into lots, the possession of one lot is not deemed a possession of any other lot.

## § 512. Essentials of adverse possession under written instrument or judgment

For the purpose of constituting an adverse possession, founded upon a written instrument or a judgment or decree, land is deemed to have been possessed and occupied in any of the following cases:

1. Where there has been acts [sic] sufficiently open to put a reasonably diligent owner on notice.

2. Where it has been protected by a substantial enclosure, except as provided in subdivision one of section five hundred forty-three of this article.

3. Where, although not enclosed, it has been used for the supply of fuel or of fencing timber, either for the purposes of husbandry or for the ordinary use of the occupant.

Where a known farm or a single lot has been partly improved, the portion of the farm or lot that has been left not cleared or not enclosed, according to the usual course and custom of the adjoining country, is deemed to have been occupied for the same length of time as the part improved and cultivated.

## § 521. Adverse possession not under written instrument or judgment

Where there has been an actual continued occupation of premises under a claim of right, exclusive of any other right, but not founded upon a written instrument or a judgment or decree, the premises so actually occupied, and no others, are deemed to have been held adversely.

## § 522. Essentials of adverse possession not under written instrument or judgment

For the purpose of constituting an adverse possession not founded upon a written instrument or a judgment or decree, land is deemed to have been possessed and occupied in either of the following cases, and no others:

1. Where there have been acts sufficiently open to put a reasonably diligent owner on notice.

2. Where it has been protected by a substantial enclosure, except as provided in subdivision one of section five hundred forty-three of this article.

## § 531. Adverse possession, how affected by relation of landlord and tenant

Where the relation of landlord and tenant has existed, the possession of the tenant is deemed the possession of the landlord until the expiration of ten years after the termination of the tenancy; or, where there has been no written lease, until the expiration of ten years after the last payment of rent; notwithstanding that the tenant has acquired another title or has claimed to hold adversely to his landlord. But this presumption shall cease after the periods prescribed in this section and such tenant may then commence to hold adversely to his landlord.

### § 541. Adverse possession, how affected by relation of tenants in common

Where the relation of tenants in common has existed, the occupancy of one tenant, personally or by his servant or by his tenant, is deemed to have been the possession of the other, notwithstanding that the tenant so occupying the premises has acquired another title or has claimed to hold adversely to the other. But this presumption shall cease after the expiration of ten years of continuous exclusive occupancy by such tenant, personally or by his servant or by his tenant, or immediately upon an ouster by one tenant of the other and such occupying tenant may then commence to hold adversely to his cotenant.

### § 543. Adverse possession; how affected by acts across a boundary line

1. Notwithstanding any other provision of this article, the existence of de minimus [sic] non-structural encroachments including, but not limited to, fences, hedges, shrubbery, plantings, sheds and non-structural walls, shall be deemed to be permissive and non-adverse.

2. Notwithstanding any other provision of this article, the acts of lawn mowing or similar maintenance across the boundary line of an adjoining landowner's property shall be deemed permissive and non-adverse.

### § 551. Right of person to possession not affected by descent cast

The right of a person to the possession of real property is not impaired or affected by a descent being cast in consequence of the death of a person in possession of the property.

### NOTES

1. *Change in law: is it effective?* The New York legislature adopted this statute in 2008 for two reasons. First, it wanted to replace an old minimalist statute with a new statute containing more detailed definitions, terms, and exceptions. Second, it wished to replace the objective test for claim of right based on the possessor's conduct adverse to the record owner's title, regardless of the possessor's state of mind. In lieu of an objective test, the legislature sought to create a subjective test that required the adverse possessor to have a good faith belief that the property belonged to him or her. The latter goal was apparently a response to Walling v. Przybylo, 851 N.E.2d 1167 (N.Y. 2006) which had affirmed the objective test for claim of right. The statute, however, defines claim of right as being either the adverse possessor's good faith belief that the property belongs to the adverse possessor or the adverse possessor's good faith belief that the property

belongs to the title holder. See § 501(3). This inartfully worded language would seem to allow an adverse possessor (i.e., squatter) to obtain title knowing very well that the property belongs to another. It would nevertheless seem to preclude title by an adverse possessor who was foolish enough to treat the property as his or her own for the statutory period but admit that he or she thought it belonged to a third party (i.e., neither the possessor nor the owner). Surely this is not what the New York legislature intended.

2. *Claims under a written instrument.* The statute provides reduced requirements for an adverse possessor who has possessed the property under an instrument purporting to give him or her title but ultimately proving to be void or invalid. Many jurisdictions have similarly modified their requirements, sometimes using the term "color of title" for such a situation, and may even reduce the statutory period required to establish title under adverse possession if it is based on a written instrument. The idea is that adverse possession may be a useful doctrine to remedy an old deed that turns out to be void or invalid, even though all relevant parties treated it as if it were valid. For example, if it is discovered that a landowner's chain of title contains a 50-year-old deed that was executed by a minor or that has a forged signature, how can it be confirmed as a matter of law that the entire world has treated the landowner and his or her predecessors in title as the rightful owners of the property, which they have possessed, used, improved, and maintained? An adverse possession claim under a written instrument (or under color of title) could be used in a quiet title action to clear up the problem. Note that the New York statute also provides that such claims, if successful, give the claimant ownership of the entire area described by the instrument, not just the portion actually occupied, unless separate subdivided parcels are involved. This rule is also relatively common among U.S. jurisdictions.

3. *Protections for title holders.* The New York statute protects landowners from losing title to portions of their land on which neighbors have encroached with fences, hedges, shrubs and plants, sheds, non-structural walls, or "lawn mowing or similar maintenance." Why? Are these types of encroachments really *de minimis per se*, or does the legislation exempt only these encroachments if a court finds that they are *de minimis*? The statute simply declares that they are deemed permissive and non-adverse. What might be the consequences of a statutory declaration of this sort? Could a neighbor claim that his or her overgrown shrub is not trespassing on the owner's land because the statute deems such *de minimis* encroachments to be permissive? An alternative statutory approach, adopted by the Mississippi legislature, provides landowners with a mechanism to prevent adverse possession claims for the construction of fences or driveways on the title owner's property from ripening into title if the owner files land record statements within the statutory period declaring that the fences or driveways were constructed without permission.[7] Another way to protect title holders is to add specific requirements about the nature of the possession. For example, California requires the payment of taxes and either

---

[7] 1998 Miss. Laws ch. 504.

substantial enclosure or cultivation or improvement.[8] Which method of protecting title holders do you think is best? Why?

## 3. Principal Problem A: Possession That is Hostile, Adverse or Under a Claim of Right

Plaintiff, Virginia Carter, brought an action to quiet title to land adjacent to her residential premises based on a theory of adverse possession. The plaintiff and her husband moved in 1978 to a home which they had purchased. Plaintiff's husband subsequently died, but she has lived on the premises continuously. A larger, undeveloped lot bordered plaintiff's property to the north. Defendants and their predecessors have held record title to this lot at all material times.

The property which plaintiff claims to have acquired by adverse possession is the south 60 feet of defendants' lot. When the Carters moved to their home in 1978, the lot north of their property was a cornfield. Although plaintiff was not sure of the location of the northern boundary of her lot, she knew her lot's dimensions, and she knew it did not include the cornfield. In 1979, corn was not planted on the southern part of the adjacent lot. Concerned about rats and the threat of fire, and desiring additional yard space for her children, plaintiff and her husband cleared several feet of the property to the north, graded it, and planted grass seed on it. Since that time, plaintiff has used the land as an extension of her yard. She planted rose bushes on it during the late 1970's and early 1980's, installed a propane tank on it approximately 30 feet north of her lot in 1984, and laid a driveway encroaching five feet onto the land in 1995.

The remainder of defendants' lot was planted with corn until approximately 1981. The lot was owned by Abe and Beverly Rosen from before 1978 until February, 1999. During that period, the only use the Rosens made of the property was to store junk and debris on it. Except for the strip used by plaintiff, the lot was overgrown with brush and weeds. The Rosens paid all taxes and special assessments on the property.

When defendant McMann purchased the Rosen's lot in February, 1999, he was aware of the possibility of a boundary dispute because of the location of plaintiff's propane tank and driveway. The plaintiff brought suit when McMann was unable to settle this dispute with her.

In seeking to establish her ownership of the disputed land, Carter alleged that for more than twenty years she had been in "open, exclusive, hostile, adverse and actual possession under claim of right." The trial court held that she did not establish that her possession was under a claim of right. Before determining how the appellate court should rule, consider the following materials.

---

[8] Cal. Civ. Code § 325.

## 4. MATERIALS FOR SOLUTION OF PRINCIPAL PROBLEM A

### Tioga Coal Co. v. Supermarkets General Corp.
Supreme Court of Pennsylvania, 1988.
519 Pa. 66, 546 A.2d 1.

■ FLAHERTY, JUSTICE.

In September, 1978 Tioga Coal Company filed a complaint in equity against Supermarkets General Corporation seeking title by adverse possession to a strip of land known as Agate Street, located within Supermarkets' property and bordering Tioga's property. Agate Street is a paper street forty feet wide which was entered on the plan of the City of Philadelphia but was never opened to the public. It was stricken from the city plan in 1966. . . .

On remand, the Chancellor determined that Agate Street is not "manorial" land, and therefore twenty-one years is the applicable holding period for claims of adverse possession. He also found that some time around 1948 Tioga took control of a gate controlling access to Agate Street by putting its lock on the gate, and maintained the lock until approximately 1978, when the gate was removed. The court found that during the thirty year period between 1948 and 1978 Tioga controlled ingress and egress from Agate Street, with the exception of a spur railroad line which entered Agate Street from Supermarket General's property approximately 150 feet north of the gate (Agate Street runs north and south) and continued northward alongside Tioga's property line and beyond it.

The Chancellor also found that Tioga used Agate Street from 1948 through 1978 for its entire forty feet width from the gate northward for 150 feet, where the railroad spur entered the street, and then for a width of thirty feet from that point north for a further distance of 194 feet 9.5 inches. Although the court found that Tioga's possession was "actual, open, notorious, exclusive and continuous" for a period in excess of the required twenty-one years, it determined that Tioga had failed to establish that its use or possession of Agate Street was hostile or adverse to the true owner of the land. We granted allocatur to determine whether, on the facts of this case, the lower courts were in error on the question of the hostility required to perfect a claim of adverse possession.

The modern law of adverse possession derives from historical developments leading up to the creation of the action for ejectment. In fact, many commentators regard the availability or non-availability of an action in ejectment as dispositive of whether an adverse possession claim will succeed. In Powell's Law of Real Property, for example, we are told that "[t]he theory upon which adverse possession rests is that the adverse possessor may acquire title at such time as an action in ejectment by the record owner would be barred by the statute of limitations." Powell, § 1012(2). In Am Jur we find that adverse possession "aims at the repose of conditions which the parties have suffered to remain unquestioned long enough to indicate their acquiescence therein." "Adverse Possession," § 4 at 794 (1936). Similarly, The American Law of Property states that the "basic question" in adverse possession cases is "whether the true owner had a right of action in ejectment against the wrongful possessor. . . ." § 15.4, p. 774 (Vol. 3, 1952). The emphasis in modern law, thus, is on the statute of limitations which bars an action for ejectment. Perhaps this view is best summarized as follows:

> According to the dominant view among commentators on the law of real property, the requirements for acquiring title by adverse possession come down to a simple test. Has the adverse possessor so acted on the land in question as to give the record owner a cause of action in ejectment against him for the period defined by the statute of limitations? It matters not what the motives or the state of mind of the possessor are. What matters is the possessor's physical relationship to the land over a sufficient length of time. Of course, if the possessor has the record owner's permission, that changes the picture. The possession is then no longer hostile in a legal sense, and no right to title will accrue to the possessor. But this, the argument runs, is precisely because the record owner has no cause of action against one whom he has permitted to occupy the land. The special situation shows the correctness of the underlying test.
>
> The attractions of this view of adverse possession are great. It is securely tied to the statute of limitations, the foundation of the doctrine, which defines the period after which the record owner will lose his cause of action to recover the land from the trespasser. This view provides a workable test. By excluding inquiry into the possessor's state of mind, it confines attention to external and verifiable facts. It may even promote the settling of land titles and the alienability of land by more easily resolving disputes over title.

Helmholz, "*Adverse Possession and Subjective Intent*," 61 Wash.Univ.Law Quart. 331 (1983).

With regard to the requirement of hostility, this Court has stated: "While the word 'hostile' has been held not to mean ill will or hostility, it does imply the intent to hold title against the record title holder." *Vlachos v. Witherow*, 383 Pa. 174, 118 A.2d 174, 177 (1955).

Intent, thus, has become a part of Pennsylvania law of adverse possession, notwithstanding the foregoing commentators' descriptions of the cause of action as dependent upon the objective question of whether the true owner's action for ejectment has expired. Exactly how Pennsylvania's state of mind requirement may be proved, however, is a matter of some uncertainty.

In *Schlagel v. Lombardi*, 337 Pa.Super. 83, 486 A.2d 491 (1984), Superior Court observed that possession may be hostile even if the claimant knows of no other claim and falsely believes that he owned the land in question:

> It is true that some jurisdictions hold that the possessor's mistaken belief in his ownership negatives the existence of a necessary hostile intent. . . . These jurisdictions identify hostility with the common-law tort of disseisin, i.e., forcible ouster. The theory is that one who does not know he is in possession of another's land cannot harbor the specific intent to oust the other out of his land. Note, *A Reevaluation of Adverse Possession as Applied in Boundary Dispute Litigation*, Rutgers-Camden L.J. 293, 299 (1971). But most jurisdictions "deem the animus of the possessor irrelevant. Rather, they look to the actual physical facts of the possession to determine if such circumstances of notoriety exist so that the true owner is put on notice. They represent a belief that the nature of the possession alone is what is important and that a sufficiently notorious possession will always be enough to alert the owner. Therefore, the hostility is implied if all other elements have been established." *Id.* at 298. See also Annot., 80 A.L.R. 1171 (1961). Pennsylvania follows the majority view. See, e.g., *Dimura v. Williams*, 446 Pa. 316, 286 A.2d 370 (1972). . . .

*Schlagel v. Lombardi*, 337 Pa.Super. at 88–89, 486 A.2d at 494. It would seem, thus, that Superior Court's view of the question raised by this case would be that subjective intent is not required and that hostility may be implied from compliance with the other requirements of adverse possession.

However, Superior Court required that Tioga prove its subjective hostility by establishing that it directed its hostility toward the true owner, not the mistaken owner of the land. Superior Court acknowledged that hostility might be implied by application of the reasoning in its prior cases, see *Schlagel v. Lombardi*, supra, but took the position that the doctrine of implied hostility was applicable only in cases involving boundary disputes or mistaken belief of ownership by one or both of the parties involved. These situations, according to Superior Court, are not presented here. Tioga believed that Agate Street was owned by the City, and Superior Court was unwilling to imply hostility "where the claimant acknowledges the ownership of another." In Superior Court's view, therefore, what was required was that Tioga know who the true owner of the land was, meet all of the other requirements of actual, continuous, exclusive, visible, notorious, and distinct possession, and direct its hostility toward the true owner of the land.

Tioga, on the other hand, argues that this case involves both a boundary dispute and a mistaken belief of ownership on the part of one of the parties. The disputed strip of land was located on the boundary of both properties, and Tioga mistakenly believed that Agate Street was city property, not part of the parcel owned by Supermarkets. Moreover, Tioga asserts that its taking and using the lands of another for longer than the required twenty-one years is "hostile" within the meaning of the law of adverse possession.

Perhaps the reason that many appellate courts have been reluctant to rely on objective evidence of adverse possession without also considering the possessor's mental state of mind, see Helmholz, supra, is that they are reluctant to award title to a "land pirate." The thought of allowing a knowing trespasser to attain title to the land he has usurped is often regarded as unacceptable. There are, however, sound reasons to avoid entanglement with attempting to discern the mental state of adverse possessors. For one thing, discerning the mental state of an adverse possessor is, at best, an exercise in guesswork; and at worst, impossible. Beyond that, application of objective tests as to whether the land was adversely possessed promotes use of the land in question against abandonment. Also, as Justice Holmes points out in a letter to William James, the use of objective, as opposed to subjective tests, may involve an essentially equitable consideration that a person who has put down his roots on land develops an attachment to the land which is deserving of protection:

> The true explanation of title by prescription seems to me to be that man, like a tree in a cleft of a rock, gradually shapes his roots to his surroundings, and when the roots have grown to a certain size, cannot be displaced without cutting at his life. The law used to look with disfavor on the Statute of Limitations, but I have been in the habit of saying it is one of the most sacred and indubitable principles that we have, which used to lead my predecessor Field to say that Holmes didn't value any title that was not based on fraud or force.

Lerner, *The Mind and Faith of Justice Holmes*, 417 (1953), quoted in Cribbet, *Principles of the Law of Property*, 301 (1975). In other words, as Holmes puts it, if an owner abandons his land and the land is possessed and used by another for the statutory period, beyond which the true owner no longer has a cause of action in ejectment, the trespasser has put down roots which we should not disturb.

We believe that Justice Holmes' view of adverse possession represents sound public policy. Furthermore, this view is consistent with a requirement that adverse possession be characterized by hostility as well as the other elements of the cause of action, for it is inconceivable that if an adverse possessor actually takes possession of land in a manner that is open, notorious, exclusive and continuous, his actions will not be hostile to the true owner of the land as well as to the world at large, regardless of the adverse possessor's state of mind. We hold, therefore, that if the true owner has not ejected the interloper within the time allotted for an action in ejectment, and all other elements of adverse possession have been established, hostility will be implied, regardless of the subjective state of mind of the trespasser.

Judgment of Superior Court is reversed and the case is remanded to The Court of Common Pleas of Philadelphia for proceedings not inconsistent with this Opinion.

■ MCDERMOTT, JUSTICE, dissenting.

I dissent, and would affirm the Superior Court and the Chancellor below. There is no reason to change the law of this Commonwealth on the basis of a letter from Justice Holmes to William James. We have previously held with the prevailing opinion in this country that one must intend to take against the record title holder. The astounding suggestion by the majority that one's intention cannot be read from their acts is evidentially untenable here or anywhere else. The romantic notion that an interloper upon the land of another challenges the world bespeaks a time of wilderness and unrecorded land titles. In a modern organized state all titles are recorded and the "world" cannot bring an action in ejectment any more than a record title owner need periodically bring one against the "world". Recorded land titles should lie peacefully in their owners unless one who seeks to own them intends to own them by exercising exclusive, open, notorious, and hostile possession against the record title owner and not somebody else.

## Halpern v. The Lacy Investment Corp.
Supreme Court of Georgia, 1989.
259 Ga. 264, 379 S.E.2d 519.

■ GREGORY, JUSTICE.

Lacy, a corporation, is the title holder of a parcel of land which Halpern claims to own by adverse possession. A jury found against Halpern's adverse possession claim and in favor of Lacy's counterclaims for damages for slander of title and trespass and for expenses of litigation. Halpern appeals from the judgment entered on the verdict.

The main issue on appeal is whether a *claim of right* must be made in *good faith* in order to satisfy the claim of right element of adverse possession or if the claim of right requirement is fully met by a showing only of *hostile* possession.

The parcel of land in question is located at the rear of Halpern's residential lot and is part of a large tract titled in Lacy's name. The Halpern lot was purchased in 1959 and a residence constructed on it in 1960. There was evidence that at the time of construction the Halperns realized they would like the parcel in question to be a part of their backyard. Mr. Halpern, who is now deceased, offered to purchase the parcel from Lacy's predecessor in title but he refused to sell. Knowing they did not own the parcel, the Halpern's caused it to be bulldozed, cleared and included as part of their yard. They have used it ever since.

The trial court charged the jury that adverse possession or title by prescription has four requirements. One of those, he said, is that possession must be accompanied by a good faith claim of right. He went on to charge the jury that a good faith claim of right may be evidenced by acts or conduct relating to the property which are inconsistent with the true owner's title. He went even further to charge that a rebuttable presumption of a good faith claim of right may arise out of the dominion one exercises over the property. But he drew the line there and refused to give Halpern's request to charge that hostile possession *is* the legal equivalent of a claim of right. Halpern contends the charge and refusal to charge constitute error but we hold the trial court was correct.

Halpern relies on *Ewing v. Tanner,* 184 Ga. 773, 780, 193 S.E. 243 (1937), a dispute over the ownership of personal property, where this court held that hostile possession and claim of right "are, for all practical purposes, legal equivalents." She also brings to our attention *Chancey v. Georgia Power Company,* 238 Ga. 397(1), 233 S.E.2d 365 (1977), where we wrote that a claim of right will be presumed from the assertion of dominion.

We hold that the correct rule is that one must enter upon the land claiming in good faith the right to do so. To enter upon the land without any honest claim of right to do so is but a trespass and can never ripen into prescriptive title. In the language used in *Hannah v. Kenny,* 210 Ga. 824, 83 S.E.2d 1 (1954), such a person is called a "squatter". See *Mayor and Council of Forsyth v. Hooks,* 182 Ga. 78, 84, 184 S.E. 724 (1936); *Crawford v. Crawford,* 143 Ga. 310, 85 S.E. 192 (1915). Here there was evidence that the Halperns knew the parcel of land was owned by another yet they simply took possession when their offer to purchase was declined. There was evidence to support a finding that this possession never changed its character.

One may maintain hostile possession of land in good faith. We construe that to be the meaning of *Ewing* in its assertion that hostile possession and claim of right are legal equivalents for all practical purposes. The holding is that most who have hostile possession of land do so with a good faith claim of right and therefore a jury or other factfinder may, in the absence of a contrary showing, infer from hostile possession that it is done in good faith that a claim of right exists. As the trial court instructed the jury, the requirement of good faith claim of right may be evidenced by acts in relation to the property inconsistent with the true owner's title. Hostile possession is such an act. *Ewing* will not be construed to hold that good faith is not required. A similar construction of *Chancey* is given.

Judgment affirmed.

## ITT Rayonier, Inc. v. Bell
Supreme Court of Washington, En Banc, 1989.
112 Wash.2d 754, 724 P.2d 6.

■ PEARSON, JUSTICE.

ITT Rayonier, Inc. (ITT), plaintiff, instituted this action to quiet title to property situated in Clallam County. In addition, ITT prayed for damages for trespass and for the ejectment of defendant Arthur Bell. Bell answered, alleging ITT was not entitled to judgment in its favor by reason of Bell's adverse possession of the property for a period greater than the statutory period of 10 years. Additionally, Bell counter-claimed against ITT praying for judgment quieting title in Bell. On July 8, 1986, the trial court entered partial summary judgment, quieting title in favor of ITT. The Court of Appeals affirmed. *ITT Rayonier, Inc. v. Bell*, 51 Wash.App. 124 (1988).

### Facts

In 1972, Arthur Bell purchased a houseboat moored near the mouth of the Big River in Swan Bay on Lake Ozette. The property that is the subject of this action is directly adjacent to that moorage and was purchased by ITT in 1947. ITT, as owner of record, has paid the property taxes on the land in question continuously since its purchase. Bell admits that he never purchased any of the property involved in this action. Additionally, he concedes that he has never maintained any "No Trespassing" signs on the property, nor has he ever denoted any boundary with a fence or any other markers. A very rough approximation of the amount of land in question is one-half of an acre. Bell testified that he regularly occupies his houseboat in the spring, summer, and fall, and visits only occasionally during the winter months.

Bell testified that at the time he purchased the houseboat, he believed the adjacent land was owned by the State. When asked whether it was his understanding that other people could use the property, his response was, "[a]ctually when I—no, not really. When I was there they—I didn't think somebody was going to come up and go camping right there. But I suppose if they tried to, I wouldn't have said anything to them."

According to further deposition testimony of Bell, at the time he purchased the houseboat it had been moored in the same location since approximately 1962. The houseboat was moored to the land initially via a cable, and subsequently via a rope tied to two trees. The record reveals that only the following structures have been situated on the property in question for the full statutory period: a woodshed that existed prior to Bell's purchase of the houseboat, a woodshed he began building in 1978, an abandoned sauna that has existed since 1973, and the remains of an outhouse built by Bell in 1972 that has occupied numerous sites on the property.

Other than 6 weeks in the summer of 1973, when the houseboat was moored in Boot Bay, approximately 2 miles from the disputed property, the houseboat has at all times been situated adjacent to the property both Bell and ITT presently claim.

Bell's deposition testimony further reveals that he was away from the property during the 1974–75, 1975–76, and 1976–77 school years, while he was teaching school in Nanana, Alaska. During the first and third winters, he allowed friends to use the houseboat occasionally. During the 1975–76 school term, he rented the houseboat for $30 per month. Bell returned to Lake Ozette each of the three summers, personally occupying his houseboat during those months.

Bell's houseboat is not the only one in the area. Two families, the Klocks and the Olesens, have co-owned a houseboat for approximately 20 years that floats adjacent to both Bell's houseboat and the disputed property. Mr. Klock, in a sworn affidavit, stated:

> When using the houseboat, I and my family have used the adjacent land for the purpose of digging a hole for an outhouse and for other minimal uses. I do not own the land next to my houseboat but have used it permissively over the last twenty years. Arthur Bell has never attempted to exclude us from using the property nor has he attempted to claim the property as his own.

In addition, Mr. Olesen swore to an identical statement.

Gerald Schaefer, an employee of ITT, stated in his sworn affidavit that ITT owns 383,000 acres in eight counties in Washington State. Often ITT is absent from its land for long periods of time:

> In its normal management of its land, Rayonier often will not visit or use its lands for long periods of time. After property has been logged and planted, it is common for Rayonier not to visit the property for 15 years, at which point precommercial thinning occurs. After precommercial thinning, property is often left 30 to 35 years before timber becomes commercial. It is virtually impossible to patrol all of Rayonier's lands that are not undergoing logging operations.

### Analysis

The doctrine of adverse possession arose at law, toward the aim of serving specific public policy concerns, that title to land should not long be in doubt, that society will benefit from someone's making use of land the owner leaves idle, and that third persons who come to regard the occupant as owner may be protected. Stoebuck, *Adverse Possession in Washington,* 35 Wash.L.Rev. 53 (1960).

In order to establish a claim of adverse possession, there must be possession that is: (1) open and notorious, (2) actual and uninterrupted, (3) exclusive, and (4) hostile. *Chaplin v. Sanders,* 100 Wash.2d 853, 857, 676 P.2d 431 (1984). Possession of the property with each of the necessary concurrent elements must exist for the statutorily prescribed period of 10 years. RCW 4.16.020. As the presumption of possession is in the holder of legal title, *Peeples v. Port of Bellingham,* 93 Wash.2d 766, 773, 613 P.2d 1128 (1980), *overruled on other grounds, Chaplin v. Sanders, supra,* the party claiming to have adversely possessed the property has the burden of establishing the existence of each element. *Skansi v. Novak,* 84 Wash. 39, 44, 146 P. 160 (1915), *overruled on other grounds, Chaplin v. Sanders, supra.*

### Good Faith

Having affirmed the trial court's partial summary judgment against Bell, the Court of Appeals nevertheless provided an alternative ground for its decision:

> [A]nother element of adverse possession is that the party seeking to acquire title to land by adverse possession must possess the land under a good faith claim of right. Bell concedes that at no time, prior to the time he claims his possession of the property ripened into title, did he believe that he had title to this property or any claim of right to it.... Holding in this case, as a matter of law, that Bell did not raise a genuine issue of fact on the question of his good faith claim of right to the property is, in our judgment, consistent with *Chaplin.*

*ITT Rayonier, Inc.,* 51 Wash.App. at 129–31, 752 P.2d 398. This portion of the Court of Appeals decision is in error.

In *Chaplin v. Sanders,* 100 Wash.2d at 855, this court unanimously held that the adverse possessor's "subjective belief whether the land possessed is or is not his own and his intent to dispossess or not dispossess another are irrelevant to a finding of hostility." In so doing, this court expressly overruled cases dating back to 1896.

The Court of Appeals reasoned that the *Chaplin* decision did not specifically do away with the good faith element of adverse possession, and stated, "the question of whether or not one acts in good faith is a question that can only be answered by making a judgment about the actor's subjective belief." *ITT Rayonier, Inc.,* 51 Wash.App. at 130, 752 P.2d 398. In a footnote, the court noted, "to conclude otherwise ... we would be encouraging ... 'squatting.'" *ITT Rayonier, Inc.,* at 130 n. 4, 752 P.2d 398.

As stated, the doctrine of adverse possession was formulated at law to protect both those who knowingly appropriated the land of others, and those who honestly held the property in the belief that it was their own. 3 Am.Jur.2d *Adverse Possession* § 142 (1986). Twenty-four years before *Chaplin,* Professor Stoebuck suggested this court should return to the original formulation of the adverse possession doctrine:

> Perhaps the reader will agree that the law would have been clearer and in the long run more useful to the people if Washington had never gone into the "subjective intent" business at all.... [T]he common law of England seems to have ... had

no such element to adverse possession. Adverse possession revolves around the character of possession, and it is difficult to see why a man's secret thoughts should have anything to do with it. Maybe the idea originated in a confusion of permission or agreement between owner and possessor with unilateral intent in the possessor's mind. Whatever the reason, the court could yet perform a service by doing away with any requirement of subjective intent, negative or affirmative. Since a man cannot by thoughts alone put himself in adverse possession, why should he be able to think himself out of it?

Stoebuck, *Adverse Possession in Washington,* 35 Wash.L.Rev. 53, 80 (1960).

Today, we reaffirm our commitment to the rule enunciated in *Chaplin v. Sanders, supra:*

> The "hostility/claim of right" element of adverse possession requires only that the claimant treat the land as his own as against the world throughout the statutory period. The nature of his possession will be determined solely on the basis of the manner in which he treats the property. His subjective belief regarding his true interest in the land and his intent to dispossess or not dispossess another is irrelevant to this determination. Under this analysis, permission to occupy the land, given by the true title owner to the claimant or his predecessors in interest, will still operate to negate the element of hostility. The traditional presumptions still apply to the extent that they are not inconsistent with this ruling.

*Chaplin v. Sanders,* 100 Wash.2d at 860–62, 676 P.2d 431. Accordingly, good faith no longer constitutes an element of adverse possession. Thus, we affirm the Court of Appeals on the basis of Bell's failure to establish exclusive possession, and reverse the Court of Appeals alternative holding that Bell failed to establish a good faith claim to the property.

## NOTES

1. *Objective vs. subjective test for hostility.* Many adverse possession cases focus on the mental element of hostility. The court in *Tioga* applied the majority rule that relies on an objective test and allows a mistaken adverse possessor to meet the hostility requirement. What are the advantages and disadvantages of an objective versus a subjective test for "hostile intent"? Which better promotes the policies of the doctrine of adverse possession?

2. *Good faith claim of right and hostility.* Although the *Halpern* court allows for a rebuttable presumption that hostile possession establishes a good faith claim of right, it nevertheless appears to separate the claim of right and hostility requirements by holding that a good faith claim of right must exist along with the requisite hostility. Yet, other courts treat these two requirements as identical. See, e.g., Chaplin v. Sanders, 100 Wash.2d 853 (1984). Is a separate good faith claim of right requirement consistent

with the majority view of hostility which focuses on the adverse claimant's objective conduct?

3. *Property vs. liability rules.* The interest that an adverse possessor acquires is protected by what legal scholarship has termed a property rule.[9] Specifically, once the adverse possessor acquires title to the property, it cannot be taken away from him without his consent. Should the adverse possessor's interest be governed instead by a liability rule whereby the adverse possessor's interest would be taken away unless he is willing to pay to the original record owner the fair market value of the property? For example, Colorado authorizes courts to award damages to owners who lose title to adverse possessors if the damages would be fair and equitable.[10] What about a rule that would permit the original owner to recover the property if she paid the adverse possessor its fair market value? What policies would be undermined by such approaches? Would it be better to limit these approaches to instances involving bad-faith adverse possessors?

4. *Adverse possession by rightful possessors: co-tenants, lessees, easement holders, and licensees.* In general, it is very difficult for a possessor to establish possession adverse to the title holder when such possession began lawfully, such as with the permission of the title holder under concurrent ownership, a lease, an express or non-express easement, or even merely a license to use the property.[11] For example, because a tenant in common or a joint tenant has the right to occupy all of the property, such occupation is not necessarily adverse to the other co-tenants. For the occupation to be adverse, there must be some acts by the occupying tenant that would indicate to the others, if they were reasonably alert, that the occupation is adverse to their interest.[12]

5. *Payment of taxes requirement.* Several jurisdictions, such as California, require that the adverse possessor pay the real estate taxes on the property for the requisite statutory period. What policy considerations do you suppose support such a requirement? What policy objectives are frustrated by a tax payment requirement?

Since many adverse possession cases involve relatively small areas along boundaries, and since the tax assessor normally assesses by reference to record title only, it is difficult if not impossible to satisfy the tax payment

---

[9] See Calabresi & Melamed, Property Rules, Liability Rules and Inalienability: One View of the Cathedral, 85 Harv.L.Rev. 1089 (1972).

[10] Colo. Rev. Stat. . § 38–41–101 (2015).

[11] See, e.g., Pioneer Mill Co., Inc. v. Dow, 978 P.2d 727 (Haw. 1999) (facts raising possibility that possession began with owner's permission preclude summary judgment in favor of adverse possession claim); Brede v. Koop, 706 N.W.2d 824 (Iowa 2005) (mere use of easement after owner's permission ceased is not sufficient to ripen into prescriptive easement); Algermissen v. Sutin, 61 P.3d 176 (N.M. 2002) (prescriptive easement not created when original use was permissive).

[12] See, e.g., Myers v. Bartholomew, 91 N.Y.2d 630 (1998) (interpreting the New York statute governing adverse possession between co-tenants); Woods v. Bivens, 292 S.C. 76 (1987) (finding for adverse possessor); Ferguson v. Ferguson, 739 P.2d 754 (Wyo.1987) (finding against claim of adverse possession). Preciado v. Wilde, 42 Cal. Rptr. 3d 792 (Cal. Ct. App. 2006) (cotenant's fencing of land not sufficiently hostile or obvious to nonpossessing cotenant)

requirement in many boundary disputes. Are there ways in which courts can circumvent the tax payment requirement?

## 5. Principal Problem B: Possession That Is Exclusive, Open, Notorious, Actual and Continuous

In early 1983, Sims purchased Lot 1 (see the Diagram on p. 949.) The deed described Lot 1 as covering the area bounded by points A, B, I, J. In 1984, Otto purchased Lot 2, which, by a proper description, covered the area bounded by points B, E, F, I. Thus, the true or record boundary between Lot 1 and Lot 2 in 1984 was line B-I. Sometime before 1983, a four-foot picket fence had been built on line D-G. Soon after acquiring the title, Otto paved the area bounded by points D, E, F, G (i.e., up to the old fence), installed pumps, a service building, and similar improvements, and commenced operating an auto service station. Sims paved his lot up to the old fence and used the area for a used car lot.

In 1994, Otto decided to tear down the decrepit old fence on line D-G, to expand his building, and to make other improvements. The contractor, Carl, who did the work for Otto, tore down the old fence and stored machinery and building material in the area bounded by points B, D, G, I. When Sims protested, Otto told Sims that the equipment would only be there for a few weeks and that Sims had no right to complain since Sims "had been getting away with murder." Although Sims was not sure what Otto meant, Sims suspected that Otto was charging Sims with encroaching on Otto's land. In fact, Sims himself had always suspected that the old fence was somewhat east of the true boundary, but he had never checked this and had hoped that Otto would not check either. Due to unseasonable weather, Carl's construction work proceeded slowly and his materials and equipment remained in the area bounded by B, D, G, I for three months. Near the end of the three-month period, Carl erected a six-foot chain link fence on line C-H. Sims said nothing.

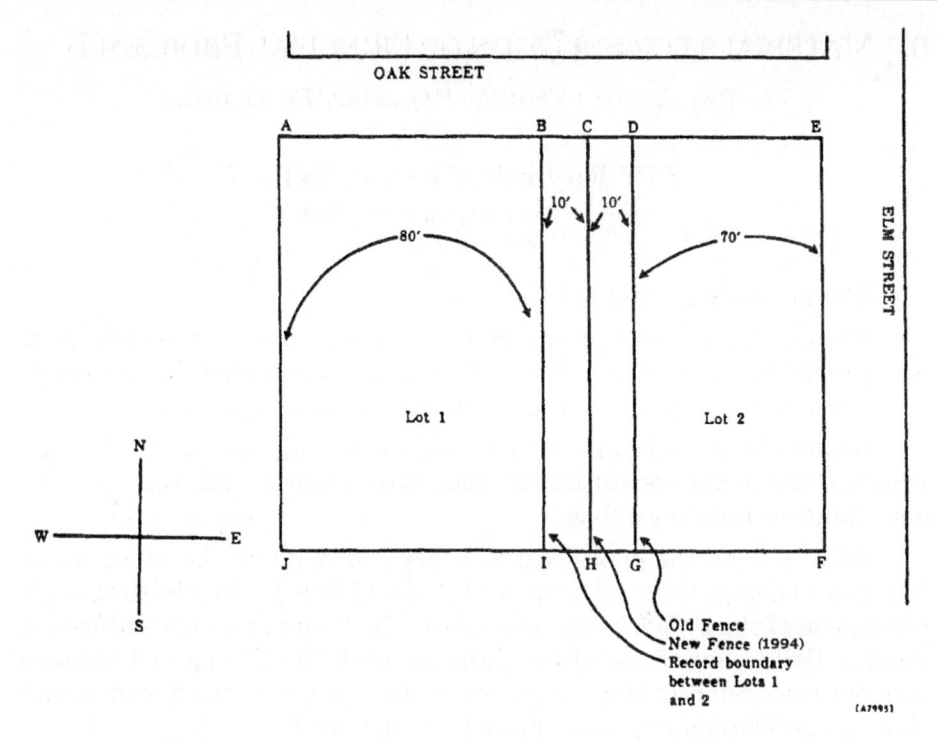

In 1996, Otto sold his land to Pen. The deed from Otto to Pen used the same description of the land that appeared in the deed to Otto. The real estate agent who arranged the sale between Otto and Pen merely copied the description that appeared in the deed to Otto. No survey was made and apparently Otto and Pen believed that the land conveyed had its western boundary at the new fence. In 1998, Pen leased the auto service station to Quick under a ten-year lease. The premises were described merely as "my service station located at the southwest corner of Oak and Elm Sts."

In early 1998, Sims abandoned the used car business. In late 1998, Sims conveyed "all my real estate fronting on Oak St. . . ." to his son, Sims, Jr., reserving to himself a life estate therein. In early 1999, Sims leased the lot to Smith Trucking Co. under a ten-year lease. Again, the lease described the land merely as "all my real estate fronting on Oak St. . . ." In 2005, Pen had the land surveyed and discovered that the "true" or record line was line B-I.

The only applicable statute provides as follows: "Title to land may be acquired by adverse possession of land for twenty years."

Discuss the rights of Pen against Sims, Sims Jr., and Smith Trucking and their rights against Pen.

## 6. MATERIALS FOR SOLUTION OF PRINCIPAL PROBLEM B

*The Requirement That the Possession Be Exclusive*

### ITT Rayonier, Inc. v. Bell
Supreme Court of Washington, 1989.
112 Wash.2d 754.

[For facts of case, see p. 943.]

We are asked whether summary judgment against the defendant was proper based on the defendant's failure to establish his exclusive possession of the disputed property for the statutory period.

Where the facts in an adverse possession case are not in dispute, whether the facts constitute adverse possession is for the court to determine as a matter of law.

Relying upon the deposition testimony of Bell and the affidavits of Klock and Olesen, the trial court held Bell had failed to establish that his possession of the property was exclusive. The Court of Appeals affirmed, holding Bell's shared use of the property with the Klocks and Olesens was not possession in the nature one would expect from an owner, and thus the exclusivity requirement had not been met:

> While possession of property by a party seeking to establish ownership of it by adverse possession need not be absolutely exclusive, "the possession must be of a type that would be expected of an owner ... " Bell's possession of the subject property is not of the type one would expect of an owner. The intrusion onto the land by Klock and Olesen cannot be said to be merely casual. The evidence shows that they moored their houseboat near the same property for a longer period than did Bell. During this period, they used the property in question along with Bell. Bell's acquiescence in their use of the land cannot be described to be simply the attitude of a good neighbor. It shows, rather, that there was a shared occupation of land. This does not constitute the exclusive use of land necessary for adverse possession and, in our judgment, reasonable persons could not conclude otherwise.

*ITT Rayonier, Inc. v. Bell,* 51 Wash.App. 124, 129, 752 P.2d 398 (1988). The Court of Appeals decision is in accord with another recent case from that court. In *Thompson v. Schlittenhart,* 47 Wash.App. 209, 734 P.2d 48 (1987), the court held that the exclusivity element was lacking because the alleged adverse possessor had shared the use of the disputed area.

Nevertheless, by pointing to specific instances of his own use of the property, Bell attempts to establish his exclusive possession. Unfortunately, such an approach logically fails to negate instances of use by others. As this court has held, specific instances of property usage merely provide evidence of possession:

Evidence of *use* is admissible because it is ordinarily an indication of *possession*. It is *possession* that is the ultimate fact to be ascertained. Exclusive dominion over land is the essence of possession, and it can exist in unused land if others have been excluded therefrom. A fence is the usual means relied upon to exclude strangers and establish the dominion and control characteristic of ownership.

*Wood v. Nelson,* 57 Wash.2d 539, 540, 358 P.2d 312 (1961).

Possession itself is established only if it is of such a character as a true owner would make considering the nature and location of the land in question. *Young v. Newbro,* 32 Wash.2d 141, 144–45, 200 P.2d 975 (1948), *overruled on other grounds, Chaplin v. Sanders, supra.* As quoted in *Wood v. Nelson, supra,* use alone does not necessarily constitute possession. The ultimate test is the exercise of dominion over the land in a manner consistent with actions a true owner would take. Thus, Bell's burden was to establish specific acts of use rising to the level of exclusive, legal possession. Unfortunately, while Bell recited certain improvements he had made in the property, he failed to state definitively the length of their existence. Thus, the record reflects that only a woodshed, a partially built and then abandoned sauna, and an outhouse have existed on the property for the full 10 year statutory period. As the Court of Appeals correctly held, Bell's shared and occasional use of the property simply did not rise to the level of exclusive possession indicative of a true owner for the full statutory period. Accordingly, we affirm the Court of Appeals. The Requirement that the Possession be Open and Notorious

## Marengo Cave Co. v. Ross
Supreme Court of Indiana, 1937.
212 Ind. 624, 10 N.E.2d 917.

■ ROLL, JUDGE.

Appellee and appellant were the owners of adjoining land in Crawford County, Ind. On appellant's land was located the opening to a subterranean cavity known as "Marengo Cave." This cave extended under a considerable portion of appellant's land, and the southeastern portion thereof extended under lands owned by appellee. This action arose out of a dispute as to the ownership of that part of the cave that extended under appellee's land. Appellant was claiming title to all the cave and cavities, including that portion underlying appellee's land. Appellee instituted this action to quiet his title as against appellant's claim. Appellant answered by a general denial and filed a cross-complaint wherein he sought to quiet its title to all the cave, including that portion underlying appellee's land. There was a trial by jury which returned a verdict for the appellee. Appellant filed its motion for a new trial which was overruled by the court, and this is the only error assigned on appeal. Appellant assigns as grounds for a new trial that the verdict of the jury is not sustained by sufficient evidence, and is contrary to law. These are the only grounds urged for a reversal of this cause.

The facts as shown by the record are substantially as follows: In 1883 one Stewart owned the real estate now owned by appellant, and in September of that year some young people who were upon that land discovered what afterwards proved to be the entrance to the cavern since known as Marengo Cave, this entrance being approximately 700 feet from the boundary line between the lands now owned by appellant and appellee, and the only entrance to said cave. Within a week after discovery of the cave, it was explored, and the fact of its existence received wide publicity through newspaper articles, and otherwise. Shortly thereafter the then owner of the real estate upon which the entrance was located took complete possession of the entire cave as now occupied by appellant and used for exhibition purposes, and began to charge an admission fee to those who desired to enter and view the cave, and to exclude therefrom those who were unwilling to pay for admission. This practice continued from 1883, except in some few instances when persons were permitted by the persons claiming to own said cave to enter same without payment of the usual required fee, and during the following years the successive owners of the land upon which the entrance to the cave was located, advertised the existence of said cave through newspapers, magazines, posters, and otherwise, in order to attract visitors thereto; also made improvements within the cave, including the building of concrete walks, and concrete steps where there was a difference in elevation of said cavern, widened and heightened portions of passageways; had available and furnished guides, all in order to make the cave more easily accessible to visitors desiring to view the same; and continuously, during all this time, without asking or obtaining consent from any one, but claiming a right so to do, held and possessed said subterranean passages constituting said cave, excluding therefrom the "whole world," except such persons as entered after paying admission for the privilege of so doing, or by permission.

Appellee has lived in the vicinity of the cave since 1903, and purchased the real estate which he now owns in 1908. He first visited the cave in 1895, paying an admission fee for the privilege, and has visited said cave several times since. He has never, at any time, occupied or been in possession of any of the subterranean passages or cavities of which the cave consists, and the possession and use of the cave by those who have done so has never interfered with his use and enjoyment of the lands owned by him. For a period of approximately 25 years prior to the time appellee purchased his land, and for a period of 21 years afterwards, exclusive possession of the cave has been held by appellant, its immediate and remote grantors.

The cave, as such, has never been listed for taxation separately from the real estate wherein it is located, and the owners of the respective tracts of land have paid the taxes assessed against said tracts.

A part of said cave at the time of its discovery and exploration extended beneath real estate now owned by appellee, but this fact was not ascertained until the year 1932, when the boundary line between the respective tracts through the cave was established by means of a survey made by a civil engineer pursuant to an order of court entered in this cause. Previous to this survey neither of the parties to this appeal, nor any of their predecessors in title, knew that any part of the cave was in fact beneath the surface of a portion of the land now owned by appellee. Possession of the cave was taken and held by appellant's remote and immediate grantors, improvements made, and control exercised, with the belief on the part of such grantors that the entire cave as it was explored and held was under the surface of lands owned by them. There is no evidence of and dispute as to ownership of the cave, or any portion thereof, prior to the time when in 1929 appellee requested a survey, which was approximately 46 years after discovery of the cave and the exercise of complete dominion thereover by appellant and its predecessors in title.

It is appellant's contention that it has a fee-simple title to all of the cave; that it owns that part underlying appellee's land by adverse possession.

It will be noted that appellee and his predecessors in title had never effected a severance of the cave from the surface estate. Therefore the title of the appellee extends from the surface to the center but actual possession is confined to the surface. Appellee and his immediate and remote grantors have been in possession of the land and estate here in question at all times, unless it can be said that the possession of the cave by appellant as shown by the evidence above set out has met all the requirements of the law relating to the acquisition of land by adverse possession. A record title may be defeated by adverse possession. All the authorities agree that, before the owner of the legal title can be deprived of his land by another's possession, through the operation of the statute of limitation, the possession must have been actual, visible, notorious, exclusive, under claim of ownership and hostile to the owner of the legal title and to the world at large (except only the government), and continuous for the full period prescribed by the statute. The rule is not always stated in exactly the same words in the many cases dealing with the subject of adverse possession, yet the rule is so thoroughly settled that there is no doubt as to what elements are essential to establish a title by adverse possession.

(1) The possession must be actual. It must be conceded that appellant in the operation of the "Marengo Cave" used not only the cavern under its own land but also that part of the cavern that underlaid appellee's land, and assumed dominion over all of it. Yet it must also be conceded that during all of the time appellee was in constructive possession, as the only constructive possession known to the law is that which inheres in the legal title and with which the owner of that title is

always endowed. Whether the possession was actual under the peculiar facts in this case we need not decide.

(2) The possession must be visible. The owner of land who, having notice of the fact that it is occupied by another who is claiming dominion over it, nevertheless stands by during the entire statutory period and makes no effort to eject the claimant or otherwise protect his title, ought not to be permitted, for reasons of public policy, thereafter to maintain an action for the recovery of his land. But, the authorities assert, in order that the possession of the occupying claimant may constitute notice in law, it must be visible and open to the common observer so that the owner or his agent on visiting the premises might readily see that the owner's rights are being invaded. What constitutes open and visible possession has been stated in general terms, thus; it is necessary and sufficient if its nature and character is such as is calculated to apprise the world that the land is occupied and who the occupant is; and such an appropriation of the land by claimant as to apprise, or convey visible notice to the community or neighborhood in which it is situated that it is in his exclusive use and enjoyment. It has been declared that the disseisor "must unfurl his flag" on the land, and "keep it flying," so that the owner may see, if he will, that an enemy has invaded his domains, and planted the standard of conquest.

(3) The possession must be open and notorious. The mere possession of the land is not enough. It is knowledge, either actual or imputed, of the possession of his lands by another, claiming to own them bona fide and openly, that affects the legal owner thereof. Where there has been no actual notice, it is necessary to show that the possession of the disseisor was so open, notorious, and visible as to warrant the inference that the owner must or should have known of it. In *Philbin v. Carr* (1920) 75 Ind.App. 560, 129 N.E. 19, 29, 706, it was said: "However, in order that the possession of the occupying claimant may constitute notice in law, it must be visible and open to the common observer so that the owner or his agent on visiting the premises might readily see that the owner's rights are being invaded. In accordance with the general rule applicable to the subject of constructive notice, before possession can operate as such notice, it must be clear and unequivocal."

And again, the possession must be notorious. It must be so conspicuous that it is generally known and talked of by the public. "It must be manifest to the community." Thus, the Appellate Court said in *Philbin v. Carr* supra, that: "Where the persons who have passed frequently over and along the premises have been unable to see any evidence of occupancy, evidently the possession has not been of the character required by the rule. The purpose of this requirement is to support the principle that a legal title will not be extinguished on flimsy and uncertain evidence. Hence, where there has been no actual notice, the possession must have been so notorious as to warrant the inference that the owner ought to have known that a stranger was asserting dominion over his land. Insidious, desultory, and fugitive acts will not serve that purpose. To have that effect the possession should be clear and satisfactory, not doubtful and equivocal."

(4) The possession must be exclusive. It is evident that two or more persons cannot hold one tract of land adversely to each other at the same time. "It is essential that the possession of one who claims adversely must be of such an exclusive character that it will operate as an ouster of the owner of the legal title; because, in the absence of ouster the legal title draws to itself the constructive possession of the land. A possession which does not amount to an ouster or disseisin is not sufficient."

The facts as set out above show that appellee and his predecessors in title have been in actual and continuous possession of his real estate since the cave was discovered in 1883. At no time were they aware that any one was trespassing upon their land. No one was claiming to be in possession of appellee's land. It is true that appellant was asserting possession of the "Marengo Cave." There would seem to be quite a difference in making claim to the "Marengo Cave," and making claim to a portion of appellee's land, even though a portion of the cave extended under appellee's land, when this latter fact was unknown to any one. The evidence on both sides of this case is to the effect that the "Marengo Cave" was thought to be altogether under the land owned by appellant, and this erroneous supposition was not revealed until a survey was made at the request of appellee and ordered by the court in this case. It seems to us that the following excerpt from *Lewey v. H.C. Frick Coke Co.* (1895) 166 Pa. 536, 31 A. 261, 263, is peculiarly applicable to the situation here presented, inasmuch as we are dealing with an underground cavity. It was stated in the above case:

> The title of the plaintiff extends from the surface to the center, but actual possession is confined to the surface. Upon the surface he must be held to know all that the most careful observation by himself and his employees could reveal, unless his ignorance is induced by the fraudulent conduct of the wrongdoer. But in the coal veins, deep down in the earth, he cannot see. Neither in person nor by his servants nor employees can he explore their recesses in search for an intruder. If an adjoining owner goes beyond his own boundaries in the course of his mining operations, the owner on whom he enters has no means of knowledge within his reach. Nothing short of an accurate survey of the interior of his neighbor's mines would enable him to ascertain the fact. This would require the services of a competent mining engineer and his assistants, inside the mines of another, which he would have no right to insist upon. To require an owner, under such circumstances, to take notice of a trespass upon his underlying coal at the time it takes place, is to require an impossibility; and to hold that the statute begins to run at the date of the trespass is in most cases to take away

the remedy of the injured party before he can know that an injury has been done him. A result so absurd and so unjust ought not to be possible. . . .

The reason for the distinction exists in the nature of things. The owner of land may be present by himself or his servants on the surface of his possessions, no matter how extensive they may be. He is for this reason held to be constructively present wherever his title extends. He cannot be present in the interior of the earth. No amount of vigilance will enable him to detect the approach of a trespasser who may be working his way through the coal seams underlying adjoining lands. His senses cannot inform him of the encroachment by such trespasser upon the coal that is hidden in the rocks under his feet. He cannot reasonably be held to be constructively present where his presence is, in the nature of things, impossible. He must learn of such a trespass by other means than such as are within his own control, and, until these come within his reach, he is necessarily ignorant of his loss. He cannot reasonably be required to act until knowledge that action is needed is possible to him.

We are not persuaded that this case falls within the rule of mistaken boundary as announced in *Rennert v. Shirk* (1904) 163 Ind. 542, 72 N.E. 546, 549, wherein this court said: "Appellant insists, however, that, if one takes and holds possession of real estate under a mistake as to where the true boundary line is, such possession cannot ripen into a title. In this state, when an owner of land, by mistake as to the boundary line of his land, takes actual, visible, and exclusive possession of another's land, and holds it as his own continuously for the statutory period of 20 years, he thereby acquires the title as against the real owner. The possession is regarded as adverse, without reference to the fact that it is based on mistake; it being prima facie sufficient that actual, visible, and exclusive possession is taken under a claim of right."

The reason for the above rule is obvious. Under such circumstances appellant was in possession of the necessary means of ascertaining the true boundary line, and to hold that a mere misapprehension on the part of appellant as to the true boundary line would nullify the well-established law on adverse possession [would not be sensible]. In that case appellee had actual, visible, notorious, and exclusive possession. The facts in the present case are far different. Here the possession of appellant was not visible. No one could see below the earth's surface and determine that appellant was trespassing upon appellee's lands. This fact could not be determined by going into the cave. Only by a survey could this fact be made known. The same undisputed facts clearly show that appellant's possession was not notorious. Not even appellant itself nor any of its remote grantors knew that any part of the "Marengo Cave" extended beyond its own boundaries, and they at no time even down to the time appellee instituted this action made any claim to appellee's lands. Appellee and his predecessors in title at all times have been in possession of the land which he is now claiming. No severance by deed or written instrument was ever made to the cave, from the surface. In the absence of a separate estate could appellant be in the exclusive possession of the cave that underlies appellee's land?

Even though it could be said that appellant's possession has been actual, exclusive, and continuous all these years, we would still be of the opinion that appellee has not lost his land. It has been the uniform rule in equity that the statute of limitation does not begin to run until the injured party discovers, or with reasonable diligence might have discovered, the facts constituting the injury and cause of action. Until then the owner cannot know that his possession has been invaded. Until he has knowledge, or ought to have such knowledge, he is not called upon to act, for he does not know that action in the premises is necessary and the law does not require absurd or impossible things of any one.

In *Livingston v. Rawyards* (1880) L.R. 5, App.Cas. 34, Lord Hatherly treats an underground trespass as a species of fraud. While there is no active fraud shown in this case, yet the facts come clearly within the case of *Lightner Mining Co. v. Lane* (1911) 161 Cal. 689, 120 P. 771, 776, and cases cited on page 776, Ann.Cas.1913C, 1093. The following excerpt from this opinion clearly sets forth our view:

> In the English decisions the willful and secret taking of coal from a neighbor's mine is usually characterized as fraudulent. *Hilton v. Woods*, L.R. 4, Eq.Cas. 440; *Dean v. Thwaite*, 21 Beav. 623; *Ecclesiastical Coms. v. North E. Ry. Co.*, L.R. 4, Ch.Div. 860; *Trotter v. McLean*, L.R. 13, Ch.Div. 586. Such an act, so committed, has all the substantial elements of fraud. Where one by misrepresentation induces another knowingly to part with his property, because his mind is so beclouded by the falsehood that he is unaware of the wrong done him, it is called a fraud. It is a taking of another's property without his knowledge of the fact that it is really taken from him. The ignorance in that case is produced by artifice. Where one betrays a trust and appropriates trust property to his own use, it is called a fraud. The injured party allows the other to have the possession and the opportunity to convert the property secretly, because of faith and confidence in the wrongdoer. In the case of underground mining of a neighbor's ore, nature has supplied the situation which gives the opportunity to the trespasser to take it secretly and causes the ignorance of the owner. Relying upon this ignorance, he takes an unfair advantage of his natural opportunities, and thereby clandestinely appropriates another's property while appearing to be making only a lawful use of his own. The act in its very nature constitutes the deceit which makes it a fraud.

So in the case at bar, appellant pretended to use the "Marengo Cave" as his property and all the time he was committing a trespass upon appellee's land. After 20 years of secret user, he now urges the statute of limitation, as a bar to appellee's action. Appellee did not know of the trespass of appellant, and had no reasonable means of discovering the fact. It is true that appellant took no active measures to prevent the discovery, except to deny appellee the right to enter the cave for the purpose of making a survey, and disclaiming any use of appellee's lands, but nature furnished the concealment, or where the wrong conceals itself. It amounts to the taking of another's property without his knowledge of the fact that it is really being taken from him. In most cases the ignorance is produced by artifice. But in this case nature has supplied the situation which gives the trespasser the opportunity to occupy the recesses on appellee's land and caused the ignorance of appellee which he now seeks to avail himself. We cannot assent to the doctrine that would enable one to trespass upon another's property through a subterranean passage and under such circumstances that the owner does not know, or by the exercise of reasonable care could not know, of such secret occupancy, for 20 years or more and by so doing obtained a fee-simple title as against the holder of the legal title. The fact that appellee had knowledge that appellant was claiming to be the owner of the "Marengo Cave," and advertised it to the general public, was no knowledge to him that it was in possession of appellee's land or any part of it. We are of the opinion that appellant's possession for 20 years or more of that part of "Marengo Cave" underlying appellee's land was not open, notorious, or exclusive, as required by the law applicable to obtaining title to land by adverse possession.

Judgment affirmed.

## NOTES

1. *Exclusivity.* The adverse possessor must hold the land against the whole world, including the record owner, to fulfill the exclusivity requirement. This is consistent with the generally accepted notion that the possessor of land will not tolerate intruders. Where the adverse possessor actively seeks to exclude the record owner, the hostility and exclusivity elements are essentially the same. *Rayonier* illustrates, however, that exclusivity should be considered in the light of what would be expected of a possessor of land under the particular circumstances of a case. Given the types of businesses and nature of the land in Principal Problem B, what should be expected of a possessor faced with an intrusion like Otto's? Did the intrusion interrupt the possession to the extent that Sims was precluded from fulfilling the continuity requirement?

2. *Interruption of adverse possession by record owner.* The idea that an adverse possessor does not necessarily vitiate the adversity of her possession by granting permission to the record owner to enter the land is analogous to the principle that the record owner cannot thwart the adversity of a possession simply by purporting to grant unrequested permission to the

adverse possessor to remain on his land. The adverse possessor will prevail in both instances so long as she manifests the requisite hostile intent toward the record owner. In Nevells v. Carter, 122 Me. 81 (1922), the Supreme Court of Maine held that the entry of the record owner onto the disputed land as a tenant of the adverse possessor failed to interrupt the adverse possession because the record owner had entered with the adverse possessor's permission. Should the interruption of the adverse claimant's possession by the record owner require exactly the same kind of "hostility" as the interruption of the adverse possession by a third party?

3. *Boundary line vs. subsurface adverse possession.* The court in *Marengo Cave* seemed to rely on the fact that the record owner could not have known of the trespass without a formal survey. However, most adverse possession cases involve boundary line disputes in which the trespass can be discovered only by a survey, yet this rarely defeats the claim of the adverse possessor. Can you distinguish the two situations?

4. *Need for actual knowledge of the encroachment.* A few courts hold that where minor encroachments are at issue, the open and notorious requirement will only be satisfied if the record owner has actual knowledge.[13] Conversely, if the use is sufficiently open and notorious, it is immaterial whether the record owner knows or should have known of the use. It is even irrelevant whether the record owner knew that he or she held title to the property.[14] Is this a sound rule? See Ray v. Beacon Hudson, *infra*.

5. *Remainderpersons meet adverse possessors.* If an adverse possessor commences possession at a time when the record ownership is divided between a life tenant and a remainderperson, the remainder is not affected by the adverse possession. This result rests on the theory that possession cannot be adverse to one who has no right to immediate possession, such as a remainderperson.[15] The rule concerning remainderpersons can defeat the interest of an adverse possessor who has been in possession far longer than the statutory period. It also reduces the utility of the adverse possession doctrine as a means of curing title defects. Should the rule governing remainderpersons be applied to leaseholds so that possession by a third party cannot be adverse to a landlord during the term of the lease? Notice that if the adverse possession starts while the record owner has a fee, the subsequent creation of a life estate or leasehold will not affect the rights of the adverse possessor. Should a tenant ever be allowed to acquire the leased property through adverse possession? The Requirement that the Possession be Actual and Continuous; Tacking and Tolling

---

[13] See, e.g., Maggio v. Pruzansky, 537 A.2d 756 (N.J.Super.1988); Mannillo v. Gorski, 54 N.J. 378 (1969). See also Chaplin v. Sanders, 100 Wash.2d 853 (1984) (open and notorious requirement satisfied if record owner has actual notice of adverse use).

[14] Lawrence v. Town of Concord, 788 N.E.2d 546 (Mass. 2003).

[15] See, e.g., Harkins & Co. v. Lewis, 535 So.2d 104 (Ala.1988).

## Howard v. Kunto

Court of Appeals of Washington, 1970.
3 Wash.App. 393, 477 P.2d 210.

■ PEARSON, JUDGE.

Land surveying is an ancient art but not one free of the errors that often creep into the affairs of men. In this case, we are presented with the question of what happens when the descriptions in deeds do not fit the land the deed holders are occupying. Defendants appeal from a decree quieting title in the plaintiffs of a tract of land on the shore of Hood Canal in Mason County.

At least as long ago as 1932 the record tells us that one McCall resided in the house now occupied by the appellant-defendants, Kuntos. McCall had a deed that described a 50-foot-wide parcel on the shore of Hood Canal. The error that brings this case before us is that the 50 feet described in the deed is not the same 50 feet upon which McCall's house stood. Rather, the described land is an adjacent 50-foot lot directly west of that upon which the house stood. In other words, McCall's house stood on one lot and his deed described the adjacent lot. Several property owners to the west of defendants, not parties to this action, are similarly situated.

Over the years since 1946, several conveyances occurred, using the same legal description and accompanied by a transfer of possession to the succeeding occupants. The Kuntos' immediate predecessors in interest, the Millers, desired to build a dock. To this end, they had a survey performed which indicated that the deed description and the physical occupation were in conformity. Several boundary stakes were placed as a result of this survey and the dock was constructed, as well as other improvements. The house as well as the others in the area continued to be used as summer recreational retreats.

The Kuntos then took possession of the disputed property under a deed from the Millers in 1959. In 1960 the respondent-plaintiffs, Howards who held land east of that of the Kuntos, determined to convey an undivided one-half interest in their land to the Yearlys. To this end, they undertook to have a survey of the entire area made. After expending considerable effort, the surveyor retained by the Howards discovered that according to the government survey, the deed descriptions and the land occupancy of the parties did not coincide. Between the Howards and the Kuntos lay the Moyers' property. When the Howards' survey was completed, they discovered that they were the record owners of the land occupied by the Moyers and that the Moyers held record title to the land occupied by the Kuntos. Howard approached Moyer and in return for a conveyance of the land upon which the Moyers' house stood, Moyer conveyed to the Howards record title to the land upon which the Kunto house stood. Until plaintiffs Howards obtained the conveyance from Moyer in April, 1960, neither Moyer nor any of his predecessors ever asserted any right to ownership of the property actually being possessed by Kunto and his predecessors. This action was then instituted to quiet title in the Howards and Yearlys. The Kuntos appeal from a trial court decision granting this remedy.

At the time this action was commenced on August 19, 1960, defendants had been in occupancy of the disputed property less than a year. The trial court's reason for denying their claim of adverse possession is succinctly stated in its memorandum opinion: "In this instance, defendants have failed to prove, by a preponderance of the evidence, a continuity of possession or estate to permit tacking of the adverse possession of defendants to the possession of their predecessors."

Finding of fact 6,[16] which is challenged by defendants, incorporates the above concept and additionally finds defendant's possession not to have been "continuous" because it involved only "summer occupancy."

Two issues are presented by this appeal:

(1) Is a claim of adverse possession defeated because the physical use of the premises is restricted to summer occupancy?

(2) May a person who receives record title to tract A under the mistaken belief that he has title to tract B (immediately contiguous to tract A) and who subsequently occupies tract B, for the purpose of establishing title to tract B by adverse possession, use the periods of possession of tract B by his immediate predecessors who also had record title to tract A?

In approaching both of these questions, we point out that the evidence, largely undisputed in any material sense, established that defendant or his immediate predecessors did occupy the premises, which we have called tract B, as though it was their own for far more than the 10 years as prescribed in RCW 4.16.020.

We also point out that findings of fact 6 is not challenged for its factual determinations but for the conclusions contained therein to the effect that the continuity of possession may not be established by summer

---

[16] "In the instant case the defendants' building was not simply over the line, but instead was built wholly upon the wrong piece of property, not the property of defendants, described in Paragraph Four (4) of the complaint herein, but on the property of plaintiffs, described in Paragraph Three of the complaint and herein. That the last three deeds in the chain of title, covering and embracing defendants' property, including defendants' deed, were executed in other states, specifically, California and Oregon. And there is no evidence of pointing out to the grantees in said three deeds, aforesaid, including defendants' deed, of any specific property, other than the property of defendants, described in their deed, and in Paragraph Four (4) of the complaint, and herein; nor of any immediate act of the grantees, including defendants, in said three (3) deeds, aforesaid, of taking possession of any property, other than described in said three (3) deeds, aforesaid; and the testimony of husband, defendant, was unequivocally that he had no intention of possessing or holding anything other than what the deed called for; and, that there is no showing of any continuous possession by defendants or their immediate predecessors in interest, since the evidence indicates the property was in the nature, for us, as a summer occupancy, and such occupancy and use was for rather limited periods of time during comparatively short portions of the year, and was far from continuous."

occupancy, and that a predecessor's possession may not be tacked because a legal "claim of right" did not exist under the circumstances.

We start with the oft-quoted rule that:

> [T]o constitute adverse possession, there must be actual possession which is *uninterrupted,* open and notorious, hostile and exclusive, and under a *claim of right* made in good faith for the statutory period.

We reject the conclusion that summer occupancy only of a summer beach home destroys the continuity of possession required by the statute. It has become firmly established that the requisite possession requires such possession and dominion "as ordinarily marks the conduct of owners in general in holding, managing, and caring for property of like nature and condition."

We hold that occupancy of tract B during the summer months for more than the 10-year period by defendant and his predecessors, together with the continued existence of the improvements on the land and beach area, constituted "uninterrupted" possession within this rule. To hold otherwise is to completely ignore the nature and condition of the property. See *Fadden v. Purvis,* supra.

We find such rule fully consonant with the legal writers on the subject. In F. Clark, Law of Surveying and Boundaries, § 561 (3d ed. 1959) at 565: "Continuity of possession may be established although the land is used regularly for only a certain period each year." Further, at 566:

> This rule [which permits tacking] is one of substance and not of absolute mathematical continuity, provided there is no break so as to sever two possessions. It is not necessary that the occupant should be actually upon the premises continually. If the land is occupied during the period of time during the year it is capable of use, there is sufficient continuity.

We now reach the question of tacking. The precise issue before us is novel in that none of the property occupied by defendant or his predecessors coincided with the property described in their deeds, but was contiguous.

In the typical case, which has been subject to much litigation, the party seeking to establish title by adverse possession claims *more* land than that described in the deed. In such cases it is clear that tacking is permitted.

In *Buchanan v. Cassell,* 53 Wash.2d 611, 614 (1959) the Supreme Court stated:

> This state follows the rule that a purchaser may tack the adverse use of its predecessor in interest to that of his own where the land was intended to be included in the deed between them, but was mistakenly omitted from the description.

*El Cerrito, Inc. v. Ryndak,* 60 Wash.2d 847 (1962).

The general statement which appears in many of the cases is that tacking of adverse possession is permitted if the successive occupants are in "privity." See *Faubion v. Elder,* 49 Wash.2d 300 (1956). The deed running between the parties purporting to transfer the land possessed traditionally furnishes the privity of estate which connects the possession of the successive occupants. Plaintiff contends, and the trial court ruled, that where the deed does not describe *any* of the land which was occupied, the actual transfer of possession is insufficient to establish privity.

To assess the cogency of this argument and ruling, we must turn to the historical reasons for requiring privity as a necessary prerequisite to tacking the possession of several occupants. Very few, if any, of the reasons appear in the cases, nor do the cases analyze the relationships that must exist between successive possessors for tacking to be allowed. See W. Stoebuck, *The Law of Adverse Possession In Washington* in 35 Wash.L.Rev. 53 (1960).

The requirement of privity had its roots in the notion that a succession of trespasses, even though there was no appreciable interval between them, should not, in equity, be allowed to defeat the record title. The "claim of right," "color of title" requirement of the statutes and cases was probably derived from the early American belief that the squatter should not be able to profit by his trespass.[17]

However, it appears to this court that there is a substantial difference between the squatter or trespasser and the property purchaser, who along with several of his neighbors, as a result of an inaccurate survey or subdivision, occupies and improves property exactly 50 feet to the east of that which a survey some 30 years later demonstrates that they in fact own. It seems to us that there is also a strong public policy favoring early certainty as to the location of land ownership which enters into a proper interpretation of privity.

On the irregular perimeters of Puget Sound exact determination of land locations and boundaries is difficult and expensive. This difficulty is convincingly demonstrated in this case by the problems plaintiff's engineer encountered in attempting to locate the corners. It cannot be expected that every purchaser will or should engage a surveyor to ascertain that the beach home he is purchasing lies within the boundaries described in his deed. Such a practice is neither reasonable nor customary. Of course, 50-foot errors in descriptions are devastating where a group of adjacent owners each hold 50 feet of waterfront property.

The technical requirement of "privity" should not, we think, be used to upset the long periods of occupancy of those who in good faith received an erroneous deed description. Their "claim of right" is no less persuasive

---

[17] The English common law does not require privity as a prerequisite for tacking. See F. Clark, Law of Surveying and Boundaries, § 561 (3d ed. 1959) at 568.

than the purchaser who believes he is purchasing *more* land than his deed described.

In the final analysis, however, we believe the requirement of "privity" is no more than judicial recognition of the need for some reasonable connection between successive occupants of real property so as to raise their claim of right above the status of the wrongdoer or the trespasser. We think such reasonable connection exists in this case.

Where, as here, several successive purchasers received record title to tract A under the mistaken belief that they were acquiring tract B, immediately contiguous thereto, and where possession of tract B is transferred and occupied in a continuous manner for more than 10 years by successive occupants, we hold there is sufficient privity of estate to permit tacking and thus establish adverse possession as a matter of law.

We see no reason in law or in equity for differentiating this case from *Faubion v. Elder*, 49 Wash.2d 300 (1956) where the appellants were claiming *more* land than their deed described and where successive periods of occupation were allowed to be united to each other to make up the time of adverse holding.

This application of the privity requirement should particularly pertain where the holder of record title to tract B acquired the same with knowledge of the discrepancy.

Judgment is reversed with directions to dismiss plaintiffs' action and to enter a decree quieting defendants' title to the disputed tract of land in accordance with the prayer of their cross-complaint.

## Ray v. Beacon Hudson Mountain Corp.
Court of Appeals of New York, 1996.
88 N.Y.2d 154, 666 N.E.2d 532.

■ TITONE, J.

In determining whether the common-law requirement of "continuity of possession" has been met in an adverse possession claim to an estate in land, a court should consider not only the adverse possessor's physical presence on the land but also the claimant's other acts of dominion and control over the premises that would appropriately be undertaken by owners of properties of similar character, condition and location. Thus, we conclude that plaintiffs' occupancy of the summer cottage in a now-defunct resort town for one month during the summer, coupled with their regular efforts taken to secure and improve the premises and to eject trespassers during their absences for the 10-year statutory period while all neighboring structures collapsed due to vandalism or abandonment, satisfied the element of continuous actual possession. Accordingly, we reverse the Appellate Division order and reinstate Supreme Court's judgment awarding plaintiffs all right, title and interest in the disputed land.

The property that is the subject of this adverse possession claim is a .357-acre parcel improved with a cottage on top of Mt. Beacon in the town of Fishkill. This improved parcel sits amidst a 156-acre site that was once a thriving resort community comprised of 21 seasonal residences, a casino, a hotel and a power plant. All of the cottage's neighboring structures have since been destroyed by vandalism, fire or general neglect. Prior to 1960, all of the cottage owners occupied their parcels as lessees.

Rose Ray came into possession of the subject premises pursuant to the terms of a December 1, 1906 lease that was assigned to her as lessee on January 31, 1931. Under the terms of that agreement, Ray purchased the cottage located on the property and paid rent for use of the underlying realty. The lease agreement provided that upon termination of the tenancy, any structures erected on the property would pass to the lessor, and the lessor would pay the lessee the reasonable value of the improvements. The lease also required the lessee to pay all taxes assessed upon the property. In December 1952, the lease was extended for 25 years, unless sooner terminated by the lessor.

The lessor terminated the leases of all occupants of the community in 1960 pursuant to the option clause in the lease. The incline service and all utilities were terminated and all cottage owners, including Ray, were directed to remove their personal effects. In accordance with this directive, Ray removed her belongings from the cottage and departed from the premises along with all remaining residents. She died in October 1962, never having been paid the reasonable value of the cottage.

In June 1963, the entire 156-acre site was purchased by Mt. Beacon Incline Lands, Inc. The contract of sale provided that all land and structures thereon were to be conveyed to the purchaser. Approximately one week after the sale in June 1963, plaintiffs—Colonel Robert L. Ray and Margaret A. Ray, the son and daughter-in-law of Rose Ray—reentered the premises formerly inhabited by Rose Ray. Thereafter, plaintiffs occupied the property for about one month per year during each summer between 1963 and 1988, which was most of Colonel Ray's leave time from the United States Army. Plaintiffs continually paid taxes and maintained fire insurance on the parcel, installed telephone and electric service, and claimed the site as their voting residence during the period of adverse possession. Plaintiffs also took steps to prevent vandalism on the property by posting "no trespassing" signs and placing bars, shutters and padlocks on the doors and windows. On several occasions, plaintiffs apprehended vandals on the property and had them prosecuted.

Defendant Beacon Hudson Mountain Corporation acquired the 156-acre parcel in 1978 after the entire parcel was taken from defendant's predecessor by Dutchess County for nonpayment of taxes. Plaintiffs continued to possess the disputed parcel after defendant Beacon Hudson acquired the property.

Plaintiffs commenced this adverse possession action against defendant in 1988, alleging that from 1963 through 1988 they occupied the property in question by adverse possession under a claim of title not written (*see,* RPAPL §§ 521, 522), and that they were its lawful owners. Defendant counterclaimed, seeking to eject plaintiffs from the land. Following a bench trial, and a personal visit by the court to the property, Supreme Court dismissed the counterclaim and held that plaintiffs were rightful owners of the property and entitled to an easement by prescription and right of way for ingress and egress. The court concluded that plaintiffs' occupancy of the property was "too apparent to be overlooked," having been "continuous and open, through more than twenty-five years of paying real estate taxes, maintaining fire insurance, repelling and arresting trespassers, claiming the site as their voting residence, maintaining the structure against the effects of wind and weather and the attacks of vandals and nailing up posters against trespassers." The court expressly found that the parcel is bounded on all sides and set apart from neighboring property by permanent stone paths, a terraced rock garden and other prominent natural objects. The court also concluded that plaintiffs had put defendant on notice of the boundaries and limits of their claim by the "constant and conspicuous use" which "made unnecessary its enclosure in fences, walls or hedges."

The Appellate Division reversed, and declared that plaintiffs have no right, title or interest in the disputed property. The Court noted that the element of continuous possession necessary to establish title by adverse possession could be satisfied by seasonal use of property, but concluded that plaintiffs' use for one month out of the four-month summer season was not sufficiently regular to give the owner notice of the adverse claim. We granted plaintiffs' motion for leave to appeal, and now reverse.

To acquire title to real property by adverse possession, common law requires the possessor to establish that the character of the possession is "hostile and under a claim of right, actual, open and notorious, exclusive and continuous" (*Brand v. Prince,* 35 N.Y.2d 634, 636) for the statutory period of 10 years (*see,* RPAPL 501).[18] "Reduced to its essentials, this means nothing more than that there must be possession in fact of a type that would give the owner a cause of action in ejectment against the occupier throughout the prescriptive period" (*Brand v. Prince,* 35 NY2d,

---

[18] Real Property Actions and Proceedings Law article 5 establishes statutory requirements of an adverse possession claim that must be proven by clear and convincing evidence as well (Brand v. Prince, 35 NY2d, at 636, supra). Here, plaintiffs' claim of right to the premises is not derived from a written instrument that describes the bounds of the property possessed, but rather is based on ancestral ownership of the cottage. Thus, RPAPL 521 and 522, which together define what constitutes adverse possession of property under a "claim of title not written," govern here. Section 521 provides that "[w]here there has been an actual continued occupation of premises under a claim of title, exclusive of any other right, but not founded upon a written instrument or a judgment or decree, the premises so actually occupied, and no others, are deemed to have been held adversely." Section 522 provides that land is deemed to be "possessed and occupied" within the meaning of section 521 when "usually cultivated or improved" or "protected by a substantial inclosure" (RPAPL 522[1], [2]).

at 636, *supra*). Since the acquisition of title to land by adverse possession is not favored under the law (*Belotti v. Bickhardt*, 228 N.Y. 296, 308), these elements must be proven by clear and convincing evidence (*Van Valkenburgh v. Lutz*, 304 N.Y. 95, 98).

The element of continuity will be defeated where the adverse possessor interrupts the period of possession by abandoning the premises, where an intruder's presence renders the possession nonexclusive, or where the record owner acts to eject the adverse possessor. However, the hostile claimant's actual possession of the property need not be constant to satisfy the "continuity" element of the claim (*Beutler v. Maynard*, 80 A.D.2d 982, 983, *affd* 56 N.Y.2d 538).

Rather, the requirement of continuous possession is satisfied when the adverse claimant's acts of possessing the property, including periods during which the claimant exercises dominion and control over the premises or is physically present on the land (*see*, 1 Warren's Weed, New York Real Property, Adverse Possession, §§ 5.03, 6.01 [4th ed]), are consistent with acts of possession that ordinary owners of like properties would undertake (*Miller v. Rau*, 193 A.D.2d 868, 869; 1 Warren's Weed, New York Real Property, Adverse Possession, §§ 5.05). In other words, "[t]he character of disputed property is crucial in determining what degree of control and what character of possession is required to establish adverse possession. Thus, wild and undeveloped land that is not readily susceptible to habitation, cultivation or improvement does not require the same quality of possession as residential or arable land, since the usual acts of ownership are impossible or unreasonable" (7 Powell, Real Property, Adverse Possession ¶ 1012[2]).

In fact, cultivating, improving and enclosing property are acts deemed by statute to be "possession and occupancy" of land and must additionally be proven to satisfy the statutory elements of an adverse possession claim where no written instrument describes the boundaries of the disputed property (*see*, RPAPL 521, 522[1], [2]; *Brand v. Prince*, 35 NY2d, at 636, *supra*). By their nature, regular cultivation, improvement and inclosure of another's land constitute open and notorious acts of possession that would place record owners on notice of an adverse claim to the property (*Di Leo v. Pecksto Holding Corp.*, 304 N.Y. 505, 512, n. 1). The requisite character of the acts of improvement sufficient to supply the record owner with notice of an adverse claim will vary with "the nature and situation of the property and the uses to which it can be applied" (*Ramapo Mfg. Co. v. Mapes*, 216 N.Y. 362, 373) and must "consist of acts such as are usual in the ordinary cultivation and improvement of similar lands by thrifty owners" (*id.*). Thus, the frequency and duration of such acts of improvement are to be considered in conjunction with the claimant's other acts of dominion and control over the premises in determining whether actual possession of land has been continuous.

Here, defendant claims that plaintiffs' possession of the property was not continuous because they were physically present there for only one month out of the summer season. However, this argument fails to take into consideration plaintiffs' other acts of dominion and control over the premises that are indicative of their actual possession of an estate in land. Here, plaintiffs' installation of utilities and over-all preservation of the cottage, a permanent and substantial structure, in a veritable ghost town, for the duration of the statutory period demonstrates continuous, actual occupation of land by improvement (*see,* RPAPL § 522; *see also, Green v. Horn,* 165 App Div 743, 746; *cf., Van Valkenburgh v. Lutz,* 304 N.Y. 95, 99, *supra* [placing portable chicken coop on property along with other personalty and debris not occupation by improvement]). Thus, plaintiffs' actual summertime use for a full month each season, coupled with their repeated acts of repelling trespassers, improving, posting, padlocking and securing of the property in their absences throughout the statutory period, demonstrated their continuous dominion and control over, and thus possession of, the property.

Indeed, this exercise of dominion and control over the premises is inconsistent with an abandonment and certainly consistent with the type of "usual acts of ownership" that would be reasonably expected to be made by owners of a summer residence in a now-defunct seasonal resort area plagued by vandals (*Monnot v. Murphy,* 207 N.Y. 240, 245). Such seasonal presence, coupled with plaintiffs' preservation of the premises for the statutory period of 10 years—which was made more obvious by the fact that all neighboring structures had collapsed due to vandalism and abandonment—was sufficient to place the record owner on notice of their hostile and exclusive claim of ownership (*cf., Wysocki v. Kugel,* 282 App Div 112, 114, *affd* 307 N.Y. 653 [dilapidated condition of buildings is indicative of use by a squatter or licensee rather than by one claiming ownership]). Because defendant was clearly placed on notice of plaintiffs' hostile claim of ownership,[19] its failure to seek plaintiffs' ouster within the statutory period results in its disseisin.

Defendant's remaining contentions lack merit.

Accordingly, the order of the Appellate Division should be reversed, with costs, and the judgment of Supreme Court, Dutchess County, reinstated.

## NOTES

1. *Changes in the law.* Recall from the *Rayonier* decision that good faith is no longer an element of adverse possession in the State of

---

[19] While the record reveals that plaintiffs continuously paid taxes on the premises, the "[p]ayment of taxes is no evidence of possession, either actual or constructive" (Archibald v. New York Cent. & Hudson Riv. R. R. Co., 157 N.Y. 574, 583). Rather, proof of tax payment has "been regarded as an act which shows a claim of title" (id.), and may also be relevant in determining whether, by such act, the adverse claimant has declined to recognize a superior title in the record owner and has thereby shown the requisite hostile nature of the possession (City of New York v. Wilson & Co., 278 N.Y. 86, 95–96).

Washington. Thus, the statement in *Kunto* that adverse possession requires "a claim of right made in good faith" has been overruled by subsequent caselaw. In addition, the statute on which the court in Ray v. Beacon Hudson Mountain relied was substantially modified by the New York legislature in 2008. The new statute is reproduced in part 2. of this Assignment.

2. *Length of time.* The statutory period required to adversely possess land varies throughout the fifty states and the District of Columbia, and often within a particular state. One article notes that the longest statute of limitation is sixty years for New Jersey's woodlands and uncultivated land, whereas the shortest is three years in Arizona and Texas if certain requirements are met.[20] Some states have different statutes of limitations depending on the type of land, whether the possessor paid taxes, or whether the possession was under a written instrument/color of title. For a current listing of the relevant statutory periods for adverse possession in each jurisdiction, see Powell on Real Property, ch. 91. The majority of statutory periods range from ten to twenty years.

3. *Tacking.* The concept of tacking is frequently important in adverse possession cases, especially in those jurisdictions with lengthy statutory periods where the claimant is often the successor in interest to the original adverse possessor. The policy underlying tacking is the same as that underlying adverse possession itself. Without the help of the tacking doctrine, there would be few successful adverse possessors. Courts always insist, however, on "privity" and never permit tacking where one possessor abandons the land and a new one enters the premises without some sort of agreement. What policies underlie the privity requirement? Why should an owner who does not object to two independent adverse possessors be treated better than one who does not object to two successive adverse possessors in privity with each other?

4. *Continuity.* Under the continuity requirement, if an adverse possessor possesses for 19 years, abandons for a year, and then possesses for three more years, he will not gain title if the period is 20 years. His abandonment will defeat the continuity requirement. But in such a case, the record owner is just as negligent as he would have been if there had been no abandonment, but rather continuous occupation for 20 years. How can one justify defeating the adverse possessor's title because of the intervening abandonment, when the total occupation exceeds the statutory period?

The courts in both *Ray* and *Kunto* state that an adverse possessor can demonstrate continuous possession and dominion over the property by using the property in the same ways an ordinary owner would use it. Thus, the adverse possessor of a summer home need only occupy it for some period every summer. What about a hunting cabin on remote land? An ice fishing shack? Or a platform for stargazing? Should continuous, seasonal use of these structures satisfy the continuity requirement? Where should courts draw the line?

---

[20] Ackerman & Johnson, Outlaws of the Past: A Western Perspective on Prescription and Adverse Possession, 31 Land & Water L. Rev. 79 (1996).

5. *Actual possession.* The "actual" possession requirement of the adverse possession doctrine often overlaps with the continuous requirement, especially when the land in question can be utilized only seasonally or intermittently. Thus, whether the actual possession requirement is satisfied in any given case depends upon whether the adverse claimant used the property as would an ordinary owner of the type of land in question.

6. *Government land.* The maxim *nullum tempus occurit regis* (time does not run against the king) has traditionally been interpreted to mean that statutes of limitations, including adverse possession statutes, do not apply to the federal and state government. Although the federal government is generally immune to losing its land under adverse possession,[21] not all *states* have given themselves this same level of immunity. Numerous states have statutorily provided this protection. Several states have altered or limited their protection from adverse possession, however, through statutory and case law.[22]

States that have statutorily protected state land from adverse possession include Alaska, Colorado, Delaware, Georgia, Indiana, Kansas, Michigan, Missouri, and New Hampshire.[23] Some statutes directly state that government land is immune from adverse possession claims, while others more generally provide that statutes of limitations are inapplicable to the government. Several states, including Idaho, Montana, and North and South Dakota, do not completely exempt state land from adverse possession, but do provide state land greater protection than private land by extending the time specified in the statute of limitations.[24] In many states, the statute of limitation for adverse possession of public land is twice that of private land. The amount of added time the state enjoys may depend on other variables, such as whether the claimant has color of title, as is the case in North Carolina.[25] However in most states, land owned by the state and dedicated to public use, including school lands, are not subject to adverse possession no matter how long the claimant occupies it. In contrast, state land not dedicated to public use may be subject to adverse possession claims.[26] In recent cases, though, courts have held that adverse possession cannot run against land acquired by an urban renewal agency for redevelopment[27] or by a municipally owned electric utility.[28] These cases illustrate that the elusiveness of the term "public use" is as relevant to adverse possession as it is to the exercise of eminent domain (see Assignment 29). What problems

---

[21] But see 43 U.S.C. §§ 1068a, 1068b (Color of Title Act) which, under certain circumstances, allows title to be obtained after long possession by paying the value of the land without improvements. In rare cases, one can obtain title to federal land under the doctrine of estoppel. United States v. Ruby Co., 588 F.2d 697, 703 (9th Cir.1978), cert. denied, 442 U.S. 917 (1979).

[22] See generally Latovick, Adverse Possession Against the States: The Hornbooks Have It Wrong, 29 U. Mich. J. L. Ref. 939 (1996).

[23] Id. at 973 n.185.

[24] Id. at 951.

[25] Latovick, at 951.

[26] Devins v. Borough of Bogota, 124 N.J. 570 (1991).

[27] Aaron v. Boston Redev. Auth., 850 N.E.2d 1105 (Mass. App. 2006).

[28] White v. Pulaski Electr. Syst., 2008 WL 3850525 (Tenn. App.).

arise in making distinctions about the state's *use* of its land when deciding if it is subject to adverse possession?

In Florida, Kentucky, Oklahoma, and West Virginia, the statutory language appears to make state land as subject to adverse possession as private land.[29] Courts in those states have at times interpreted the statutes in a way that affords the state *some* protection, if only for highway and school lands. What policy reasons might the courts be considering when choosing to provide state land greater protection than the statutes seem to provide? What about the notion that an adverse possessor's occupancy must be "open" and "notorious" in order to provide the true owner with sufficient notice to exercise her rights? Who is the true owner of state land, who is responsible for noticing the occupancy, and who loses if the occupancy goes unnoticed and state land is lost to an adverse possessor?

In addition to inconsistency among the states regarding how much immunity, if any, state lands have from adverse possession, there is also the problem of dealing with land owned by municipalities. Protection for municipally owned land ranges from complete immunity to no protection at all, depending on each state's statutes and policy perspective.[30]

7. *Wild and undeveloped land.* The court in *Ray* quotes a leading treatise as follows:

> Thus, wild and undeveloped land that is not readily susceptible to habitation, cultivation or improvement does not require the same quality of possession as residential or arable land, since the usual acts of ownership are impossible or unreasonable.

It has been forcefully argued that the quoted rule shows a bias against wild and undeveloped land that is inappropriate in today's world, where wild land is scarce and growing scarcer.

> The need to encourage economic exploitation of sparsely settled regions, and thus the principal rationale for the development model, ended long ago.... The twenty-first century need not blindly endorse the exploitative ideology of the past.

Sprankling, An Environmental Critique of Adverse Possession, 79 Cornell L. Rev. 816, 884 (1994). Do you agree with Professor Sprankling's criticism of existing doctrine? Sprankling's critique has spurred others to recommend changes to adverse possession that would protect wilderness land and natural features from alteration. These proposals include incorporating conservation values and ecosystem services concepts (discussed elsewhere in this casebook) into the elements of adverse possession,[31] and replacing adverse possession with a uniform land registration system.[32] These recommendations may only lead to lip service, rather than meaningful

---

[29] Latovick, at 947–49.

[30] Latovick, Adverse Possession of Municipal Land: It's Time to Protect This Valuable Asset, 31 U. Mich. J.L. Ref. 475–76 (1998).

[31] Klass, Adverse Possession and Conservation: Expanding Traditional Notions of use and Possession, 77 U. Colo. L. Rev. 283 (2006).

[32] Barnet, The Uniform Registered State Land and Adverse Possession Reform Act: A Proposal for Reform of the United States Real Property Law, 12 Buff. Envtl. L.J. 1 (2004).

change. For example, the Alaska Supreme Court declared that it considers Alaska's geography, climate, and character of the land in its flexible adverse possession standards, but then determined that a possessor's decision to limit clearing to preserve trees in their natural state and to instead use non-permanent markers ("flagging") was inadequate to establish adverse possession; more clearing of the land was necessary.[33]

8. *Tolling statutes.* In certain instances an adverse possessor who fulfills all requirements for the entire statutory period still may not gain title to the land. Every jurisdiction has "tolling" statutes that stipulate that certain disabilities, such as being under the age of majority or serving in the armed forces, will toll (i.e., stop) the statute of limitations from running against the record owner. These statutes usually require that the disability exist at the time the cause of action in ejectment first accrues. However, there is no "common law" rule of tolling. The specific circumstances under which a statute of limitations will be tolled are defined by the jurisdiction's statute. Consider the following statute in light of the questions that follow:

## CALIFORNIA CODE OF CIVIL PROCEDURE

### § 328. Computation of time; exclusion of certain disabilities

If a person entitled to commence an action for the recovery of real property, or for the recovery of the possession thereof, or to make any entry or defense founded on the title to real property, or to rents or services out of the property, is at the time title first descends or accrues either under the age of majority or insane, the time, not exceeding 20 years, during which the disability continues is not deemed any portion of the time in this chapter limited for the commencement of the action, or the making of the entry or defense, but the action may be commenced, or entry or defense made, within the period of five years after the disability shall cease, or after the death of the person entitled, who shall die under the disability; but the action shall not be commenced, or entry or defense made, after that period.

### § 328.5. Computation of time; imprisonment

If a person entitled to commence an action for the recovery of real property, or for the recovery of the possession thereof, or to make any entry or defense founded on the title to real property, or to rents or services out of the property, is, at the time the title first descends or accrues, imprisoned on a criminal charge, or in execution upon conviction of a criminal offense, for a term less than life, the time, not exceeding two years, during which imprisonment continues is not deemed any portion of the time in this chapter limited for the commencement of the action, or the making of the entry or defense, but the action may be commenced, or entry or defense made, within the period of five years after the imprisonment ceases, or after the death of the person entitled, who dies while imprisoned; but the action shall not be commenced, or entry or defense made, after that period.

---

[33] Vezey v. Green, 171 P.3d 1125 (Alaska 2007).

The period of adverse possession in California is five years. Applying the California tolling statute reprinted above, how would you answer the following hypotheticals?

    a.    Assume that Adele commences adverse possession of Blackacre in 2011, and that on that date, Olaf, the record owner, is twelve years old. If the age of majority is eighteen, by what year will Olaf be barred from bringing an action to oust Adele?

    b.    Assume the same facts as above, but that Olaf is thirty years old in 2011. In 2013, Olaf dies, and Penny, his ten year old daughter, becomes the owner. In what year will the statute of limitations have run?

    c.    Now assume that Adele commences adverse possession of Blackacre in 2001, and that on that date, Olaf, the record owner, is thirty years old and adjudged to be legally insane at the time Adele enters possession. In 2016, Olaf dies, and Penny, his ten year old daughter, becomes the owner. In what year will the statute of limitations have run?

## 7. ACQUISITION OF NON-POSSESSORY INTERESTS IN LAND THROUGH ADVERSE USE

Under the doctrine of adverse possession, one can gain a possessory interest in another's land. Several related doctrines permit one to acquire a non-possessory interest, an easement, in another's land. When adverse use is exercised by a private individual or entity, the interest created is called a *prescriptive easement*. When the public at large is creating the interest, the "easement" is usually said to accrue by way of *implied dedication* or *custom,* although some courts also permit the public at large to acquire rights by prescription.

*Prescriptive Easements*

The requirements for creating a prescriptive easement or an easement through adverse use are analogous to those for acquiring ownership of land through adverse possession. The doctrine of prescription, like that of adverse possession, "protects the legitimate, even instinctual, associations which inevitably arise from long, continued use or possession of land."[34] One court, in commenting on the acquisition of an easement by prescription, has stated that the easement "must have been exercised whenever there was any necessity to do so, and with such frequency that the owner of the servient estate would have been apprised

---

[34] Waltimyer v. Smith, 383 Pa.Super. 291 (1989).

of the right being claimed against him."[35] Again, it is the "non-recognition of the owner's authority to permit or prevent such use" that is critical.[36]

However, one seeking to establish a non-exclusive easement need not show that his use was exclusive. The exclusivity requirement can be satisfied even if others have used the easement, but it must be shown that the "right" to use "does not depend upon a similar right in others."[37]

Although statutes of limitations for the recovery of real property might not apply to non-possessory interests in land, courts often invoke them by analogy and require that the adverse use continue for the same statutory period prescribed for adverse possession. (Some states, though, have statutes governing prescriptive interests generally.) Throughout the statutory period, the owner can bring an action in trespass but not in ejectment, since the adverse user is not in actual possession.

Another difference between adverse use and adverse possession exists in those jurisdictions requiring the payment of real estate taxes for adverse possession: there is no such requirement in adverse use cases since easements are usually not subject to real estate taxes. Sometimes claimants seek to avoid a payment of taxes requirement by arguing that they seek only a prescriptive easement rather than a fee. California courts have refused to validate a claimed prescriptive easement when the easement has the effect of giving possession to the easement holder. Validating such an easement would have the effect of giving title to a claimant who has not satisfied the requirements for obtaining title by adverse possession, e.g., paying real estate taxes on the disputed property.[38]

*Implied Dedication and Custom*

Dedication is the setting aside of privately owned land for use by the public. There are two general types: common law and statutory. Both require some kind of unequivocal act indicative of the owner's intent to dedicate his property[39] as well as some form of acceptance by the public. A statutory dedication usually expressly transfers the fee of the property to a governmental entity, whereas the right conferred by a common law dedication is usually an easement.

Common law dedication can be either express or implied. Express common law dedication requires an express manifestation of the owner's dedicatory intent, such as a deed, and usually involves roads, public squares, parks and the like, in subdivisions. Implied dedication is construed from acts or conduct that evince an offer and the requisite

---

[35] Svoboda v. Johnson, 204 Neb. 57 (1979).
[36] See Fenster v. Hyken, 759 S.W.2d 869 (Mo.App.1988).
[37] Svoboda v. Johnson, 204 Neb. 57 (1979).
[38] Mehdizadeh v. Mincer, 46 Cal.App.4th 1296 (1996); Silacci v. Abramson, 45 Cal.App.4th 558 (1996).
[39] But see Jefferson Davis Parish School Board v. Fontenot, 505 So.2d 955, 958 (La.App.1987) (statutory dedication does not "require intent of the landowner to dedicate property where there has been sufficient maintenance by the parish without protest").

dedicatory intent, and is based on the doctrine of estoppel. Such intent is usually inferred from the public's adverse use of the property and the owner's acquiescence in that use.[40] The use must be without the owner's permission but he must have actual knowledge of it. If the use is sufficiently open and notorious, knowledge of the adverse use will be imputed. As in the case of prescriptive easements, courts often invoke the statute of limitations for the recovery of real property by analogy.

In addition to an offer with dedicatory intent, the public must accept the offer. In some cases, acceptance will be inferred from acts by a governmental entity in maintaining or repairing the property, and acquiescence by the owner in such acts is usually sufficient evidence of dedicatory intent. The public at large can accept by entering and making use of the land. If only a limited number of people use it, however, the right created may be only a private prescriptive easement. Implied dedications have been found, however, where only a comparatively small number of people have used a road or beach, where those who would naturally be expected to enjoy it have done so, and where any member of the public who had the desire could have done so.

Unlike common law dedication, which operates on a theory of estoppel, statutory dedication operates by way of grant. The typical statute requires that the dedicator record a plat that identifies the roads, parks, or other areas to be dedicated. Acceptance, which usually takes the form of approval by a municipal council or planning commission, is required. Without it the dedicator, usually a developer, cannot unilaterally impose the burden of maintenance and repair of the property on the public. A defective attempt to dedicate land pursuant to statute can become an effective common law dedication once it is accepted and used by the public.

The doctrine of custom also allows the general public to acquire rights over private property in some jurisdictions. Blackstone provides the following criteria in his definition of custom in his Commentaries: 1) that the use or practice be ancient, so long that "the memory of man runneth not to the contrary;" 2) that the right has been exercised without interruption; 3) that it be peaceable and free from dispute; 4) that it be reasonable; 5) that it is certain; 6) that it be obligatory and not left to the option of particular individuals; and 7) that it be consistent with and not repugnant to other customs. Courts in this country have relied on these criteria as well.[41]

---

[40] However, courts may be increasingly reluctant to presume that the public's use is adverse to the landowner and thus may be less welcoming of the theory of implied dedication by adverse use. See, e.g., Clickner v. Magothy River Ass'n, 35 A.3d 464 (Md. 2012).

[41] See, e.g., Matcha v. Mattox on Behalf of People, 711 S.W.2d 95 (Tex.App.1986), overruled in part by Severance v. Patterson, 345 S.W.3d 18 (Tex. 2012); State ex rel. Haman for Kootenai County v. Fox, 100 Idaho 140 (1979); State ex rel. Thornton v. Hay, 254 Or. 584 (1969).

## 8. AGREED BOUNDARIES

The doctrine of agreed boundaries—sometimes called the doctrine of practical location—is a judicially created doctrine designed to promote harmonious relations between adjacent landowners who have had, or might have, a boundary dispute. Neighboring landowners sometimes seek to solve such disputes without resorting to costly litigation, and courts often support these efforts because they may result in peaceful conflict resolution without increasing burdens on the judiciary.

The doctrine of agreed boundaries has four elements. The first element of the doctrine is *uncertainty* about the true location of the boundary, but it is not essential that the true boundary be unascertainable by survey. The second element is an *agreement* upon a fence, or some natural boundary, such as a watercourse or hedge, to delineate the boundary. The agreement can be express or can be implied from either or both of the neighboring landowners' marking the line and both acting as though it were the boundary. The third element is mutual *acquiescence* in the location of the line, usually manifested by each neighbor's possessing up to the agreed upon boundary. The fourth element requires that the acquiescence be for a certain period of *time*. The period is often the same period as for adverse possession, but sometimes it is shorter, especially if there has been reliance on the line and a concomitant change of position by one of the parties based on the agreement.

Like the doctrine of adverse possession, the doctrine of agreed boundaries is often described as a rule of repose. The doctrines are often confused. Sometimes courts resort to the doctrine of agreed boundaries where certain elements of an adverse possession claim have not been satisfied.[42] Successors in interest to the land affected by an agreement under the doctrine of agreed boundaries generally are bound by the previous acquiescence, provided the requisite period of time has elapsed.

California has restricted the scope of the agreed boundary doctrine by refusing to infer an agreed boundary from the mere existence of a fence or similar informal physical marker. "When existing legal records provide a basis for fixing the boundary, there is no justification for inferring, without additional evidence, that the prior owners were uncertain as to the location of the true boundary or that they agreed to fix their common boundary at the location of a fence." Bryant v. Blevins, 9 Cal.4th 47 (1994). Justice Mosk issued a vigorous dissent.

> The majority's holding . . . ensures that in most cases deeds and maps will be given priority over agreements long accepted between adjacent landowners. For this reason, in cases in which a legal description is available, the majority's newly created rule

---

[42] See, e.g., Duncan v. Peterson, 3 Cal.App.3d 607 (1970) (plaintiff could not gain title by adverse possession since he did not comply with California's payment of taxes requirement, but court awarded plaintiff title under doctrine of agreed boundaries).

turns on its head the central policy underlying the agreed-boundary doctrine, i.e., that agreements between adjacent landowners are entitled to deference.

Bryant v. Blevins, 9 Cal.4th 47 (1994).

Which position do you think is preferable?

In California, it is difficult for the record owner to lose ownership to a long-time occupant under the doctrines of adverse possession or agreed boundaries when there is a boundary line dispute. The occupant is usually barred from gaining title by adverse possession by the requirement that the adverse possessor prove that she paid real estate taxes on the disputed strip. Taxes are ordinarily assessed on the basis of record title, so usually there is no proof that the occupant paid taxes on the disputed strip of land. Similarly, the agreed boundary doctrine is rarely useful to California occupants since it is usually difficult to prove that there was original uncertainty concerning the location of the boundary and that the fence was built to resolve the uncertainty, especially when the original parties are dead or otherwise unavailable. Are the California rules, which make it difficult for the occupant to gain ownership over the record owner in boundary disputes, desirable?

## B. Transfer with Written Instruments

## Assignment 40

# The Requirement of a Written Instrument

## a. Informal Documents of Conveyance (Deeds)

### 1. Introduction

Interests in real property are normally conveyed by a document called a deed. In most states, there are customary deed forms which are widely used. In some states, the customary form is suggested by statute. Although it is prudent to use a lawyer in drafting all deeds, many routine deeds are drafted by non-lawyers working in real estate offices, banks, and title companies. The materials in the first part of the Assignment raise a relatively simple issue: When will an informal writing such as a letter or memo operate as an effective conveyance of land? The materials in the second part of this Assignment explore the extent to which a writing is required for an effective contract for the sale of real estate (as opposed to the deed).

### 2. Principal Problem

Your client, Charles, is the son of Margaret by her second marriage. Margaret also has three daughters by her first marriage. Margaret is living in New York, Charles in California. Margaret recently inherited a small house in California. Margaret wrote the following letter to Charles. It was typewritten except for the signature.

> Dear Son,
>
> I have received the almond candies you sent. You are a good son. The house which Marcus built shall belong to you. The others got theirs when their father died so this makes it even. You don't need a lawyer. God bless you.
>
> Love,<br>Mom

Charles moved into the house "which Marcus built" a few days after receiving the letter. A few months later Margaret died intestate (i.e., without a will). Her three daughters claim an interest in the house. Charles, of course, claims that the entire house is his. Give Charles a legal opinion based on the following materials and on any other materials covered in the course.

## 3. MATERIALS FOR SOLUTION OF PRINCIPAL PROBLEM

Most states have a "statute of frauds" requiring that certain legal transactions be evidenced or performed by written documents. A few representative statutes (as they pertain to real property) are set out below.

### CALIFORNIA CIVIL CODE (2015)

#### § 1091. Method of transfer

*Requisites for transfer of certain estates.* An estate in real property, other than an estate at will or for a term not exceeding one year, can be transferred only by operation of law, or by an instrument in writing, subscribed by the party disposing of the same, or by his agent thereunto authorized by writing.

#### § 1092. Grant; form

A grant of an estate in real property may be made in substance as follows:

"I, A B, grant to C D all that real property situated in (insert name of county) County, State of California, bounded (or described) as follows: (here insert property description, or if the land sought to be conveyed has a descriptive name, it may be described by the name, as for instance, 'The Norris Ranch'.)

"Witness my hand this (insert day) day of (insert month), 20__,"

"A B"

### NEW YORK GENERAL OBLIGATIONS LAW (2015)

#### § 5–703. Conveyances and contracts concerning real property required to be in writing

1. An estate or interest in real property, other than a lease for a term not exceeding one year, or any trust or power, over or concerning real property, or in any manner relating thereto, cannot be created, granted, assigned, surrendered or declared, unless by act or operation of law, or by a deed or conveyance in writing, subscribed by the person creating, granting, assigning, surrendering or declaring the same, or by his lawful agent, thereunto authorized by writing. But this subdivision does not affect the power of a testator in the disposition of his real property by will; nor prevent any trust from arising or being extinguished by implication or operation of law, nor any declaration of trust from being proved by a writing subscribed by the person declaring the same.

2. A contract for the leasing for a longer period than one year, or for the sale, of any real property, or an interest therein, is void unless the contract or some note or memorandum thereof, expressing the consideration, is in writing, subscribed by the party to be charged, or by his lawful agent thereunto authorized by writing.

3. A contract to devise real property or establish a trust of real property, or any interest therein or right with reference thereto, is void unless the contract or some note or memorandum thereof is in writing and subscribed by the party to be charged therewith, or by his lawfully authorized agent.

4. Nothing contained in this section abridges the powers of courts of equity to compel the specific performance of agreements in cases of part performance.

## TEXAS PROPERTY CODE § 5.021 (2015)
### Instrument of Conveyance

A conveyance of an estate of inheritance, a freehold, or an estate for more than one year, in land and tenements, must be in writing and must be subscribed and delivered by the conveyor or by the conveyor's agent authorized in writing.

## In re O'Neil's Will

Surrogate Court of New York, 1958.
13 Misc.2d 796, 176 N.Y.S.2d 1022,
affirmed, 8 A.D.2d 631, 185 N.Y.S.2d 393 (1959).

■ JOHN D. BENNETT, SURROGATE.

The real property in this proceeding has been sold and the proceeds held in escrow pending the determination of a claim made by John A. Snyder that he and his family have a life estate in the proceeds resulting from the sale of such real estate.

The basis of the claim is a letter from the decedent to her daughter, the mother of the claimant, John A. Snyder, reading as follows:

Dear Tess: 7 April 1955

John and family are welcome to live as long as they wish in the Garden City house as long as they wish.

MOTHER,

ORVA M. ONEIL [SIGNATURE]

On the evidence presented, the court holds that John A. Snyder and his family have no right, title or interest in the property (or the proceeds of the sale). To hold otherwise would make an innocent hospitable invitation fraught with peril.

## Bowlin v. Keifer
Supreme Court of Arkansas, 1969.
246 Ark. 693, 440 S.W.2d 232.

■ FOGLEMAN, JUSTICE.

The primary question on this appeal involves the validity of a written instrument as a conveyance of real property.

On April 26, 1947, Guy G. Wade executed and delivered to appellee the following written instrument:

"Glendora California

April 26, 1947

AGREEMENT OF SALE

NOTICE: For the sum of $300.00 cash in hand, paid, the receipt of which is hereby acknowledged, I, Guy G. Wade, sell to Ova Lea Keifer, all my rights, title and interest in the estate of my father George T. Wade—deceased. I also agree to render proper and legal conveyance at any time upon request of said Ova Lea Keifer.

Guy G. Wade [signature]"

The defendants in the partition suit, of which appellee was one, filed an answer in which it was asserted that appellee was the owner of an undivided two-sevenths interest in the lands. They also denied that appellant had any interest in them. The instrument above set out was made an exhibit to their answer and later introduced in evidence in support of appellee's claim. It was also alleged in the answer that appellant knew at the time of his conveyance that his grantor had no interest in the lands and knew that Guy G. Wade had conveyed his interest to the appellee by the instrument above set out. They also alleged that the recording of this instrument on June 20, 1955, gave constructive notice to appellant.

Appellant contends that the instrument in question is void and that it was not notice either to him or to his predecessor in title. One of his arguments in support of this contention is that the deed does not describe any real property. In this respect we agree with the appellant.

In Turrentine v. Thompson, 193 Ark. 253, 99 S.W.2d 585, we held that a deed which did not identify the land sought to be conveyed as being in any county or even in the state was void as failing to furnish a key by which the land might be certainly identified. As we said in that case, the land intended to be conveyed might be in another state.

There might be some merit in the argument that appellant bore the burden of proof of the payment of a valuable consideration by him without notice of appellee's claim, if the instrument relied upon by appellee constituted a contract enforceable between the parties. This is not the case. A contract for the sale of land will not be enforced unless the description disclosed therein is as definite and certain as that required in a deed of conveyance. Fordyce Lumber Company v. Wallace, 85 Ark. 1, 107 S.W. 160. The instrument here does not contain such a description. Turrentine v. Thompson, supra.

■ BYRD, JUSTICE (dissenting).

The record here shows a controversy between appellee Ova Lea Keifer and appellant Jack Bowlin to a tract containing 270 acres more or less in the Ozark District of Franklin County and to one-seventh of the proceeds of a U.S. Government check for $25,000, deposited in the registry of the court. It is not disputed that George T. Wade was the father of Ova Lea Keifer and Guy G. Wade, together with other children. On April 26, 1947, Guy G. Wade executed the following instrument. [See above].

After execution of this instrument, Guy G. Wade died on Sept. 10, 1948, leaving as his sole and only heir Victor Grady Wade. The testimony shows that after the Corps of Engineers began making surveys for the Ozark Dam area, Victor Grady Wade and wife, on Dec. 5, 1966, conveyed one-seventh interest in the lands to his step-sister's husband, appellant Jack Bowlin. This deed recites a consideration "of one dollar and other valuable considerations". In offering this deed into evidence counsel for appellant stated, "Our stipulation is only to the extent that it is unnecessary to bring the clerk up to prove the deed". The record also shows that Victor Grady Wade was present in the court room but did not testify, and that the appellant Jack Bowlin neither testified nor attended the trial.

I agree with the majority opinion that the description contained in the agreement of sale is insufficient to constitute notice to a bona fide purchaser for value, HOWEVER, I do not agree that the description is void as between Ova Lea Keifer and Guy G. Wade. In Varner v. Rice, 44 Ark. 236 (1884), we permitted evidence *aliunde* to show what was meant by the description "the plantation called the Varner place". In Thomason v. Abbott, 217 Ark. 281, 229 S.W.2d 660 (1950), we pointed out that a description "a part of the East Half of Southeast Quarter of Section 31, 6 acres" was void for indefiniteness insofar as record title was concerned but that as between the grantor and grantee evidence *aliunde* might be introduced to establish what lands were intended to be conveyed.

Based upon the foregoing authorities it is perfectly obvious that as between appellee Ova Lea Keifer and Guy G. Wade evidence could have properly been introduced to show what the estate of George T. Wade consisted of.

Does Victor Grady Wade stand in any better position than his father? We held in Turner v. Rust, 228 Ark. 528, 309 S.W.2d 731 (1958), that a grantor, or an heir claiming through him, is estopped to claim or assert anything in derogation of his deed or assignment. Certainly the heir could convey no better interest to one with notice than he himself had and since he himself paid no consideration for the inheritance from his father, the title in him was no better than the title in his father.

Thus, as I view the instrument, here involved, it was sufficient to pass title as between the parties and the description contained therein was sufficient to permit evidence of what the estate of George T. Wade consisted. In this situation Victor Grady Wade as an heir of his father, Guy G. Wade, stood in the same position as his father Guy G. Wade; under the authority of Turner v. Rust, supra. Furthermore, since the appellant Jack Bowlin failed to sustain his burden of proof by showing that he paid a valuable consideration for the deed from Victor Grady Wade, appellant Jack Bowlin stands in no better position than his grantor. Consequently I would affirm the decree of the Chancellor holding the title good in appellee.

## Harris v. Strawbridge
Court of Civil Appeals of Texas, 1959.
330 S.W.2d 911.

■ BELL, CHIEF JUSTICE.

Ethel Strawbridge, the widow of Edward Strawbridge, filed suit to recover title to a 189 acre tract of land in Matagorda County. Suit was against appellants who were some of the heirs of Edward Strawbridge.

The first count of plaintiff's petition is in the statutory form of trespass-to-try title with a claim for damages. Appellee also claimed title under the 3, 5 and 10 year statutes of limitation. Further, by a trial amendment, appellee sought to reform an alleged deed dated October 20, 1941, from Edward Strawbridge to her, contending that by mutual mistake the granting clause had been omitted. Too, she asserted the suit was to reform the alleged deed and to remove cloud from title.

Appellants, besides some exceptions not necessary to notice, plead not guilty, a general denial and that the four year statute of limitation was a bar to reformation of the deed.

A trial was had before a jury and the case was submitted on the issue as to whether appellee had title under the ten year statute of limitation. The jury answered favorably to appellee and the court entered judgment in her favor on this verdict.

It is necessary for clarity to at this point notice some of the facts. Edward Strawbridge and appellee, Ethel Strawbridge, married in 1935. Edward Strawbridge died in July, 1943. He and Mrs. Strawbridge lived in the State of Florida. They had no children. Edward Strawbridge left no children or their descendants surviving him. His mother and father predeceased him. All of Mr. Strawbridge's brothers and sisters predeceased him. Only his sisters, Matilda Turner and Jane Blades, left descendants, they all being made parties to this suit.

In 1928 Edward Strawbridge made a will when he lived in Platteville, Wisconsin, which contained a general revocation clause. By paragraph 2 of this will he left his homestead in the State of Florida, together with the furniture and furnishings, to his sister, Jane Blades. By paragraph 3 he gave Jane Blades a life estate in his 235 acre farm located in LaFayette County, Wisconsin. Also he gave her a life estate in mining rights in and under a six acre tract adjoining the farm. Then a life estate after the death of Jane Blades was given named nieces and nephews, and the remainder was to the Free Methodist Church of North America. By paragraph 4 the income from $2,000 was left to a niece, with remainder to the above named church. Then follow six paragraphs by which named persons were given bequests of money. Isabella Blades, his niece, was made executrix of his estate. This will contained a residuary clause, leaving the residue of his property wherever situated to Jane Blades and her six children in equal shares.

On October 20, 1941, Edward Strawbridge executed the following instrument:

> State of Texas, County of Matagorda, know all men by these presents that I, Edward Strawbridge, of Escambia County, Florida, for and in consideration of One ($1.00) Dollar and other good and valuable considerations to me in hand paid by Ethel Strawbridge of the City of Pensacola, Escambia County, Florida, that certain property described as follows:
>
> [Legal description omitted.]
>
> To have and to hold the above described property, together with all and singular the rights appurtenances thereunto in anywise belonging unto the said Ethel Strawbridge, her heirs or assigns forever.

This instrument was properly signed and acknowledged. It was filed for record in the office of the County Clerk of Matagorda County by Ethel Strawbridge on December 10, 1942, and is recorded in the Deed Records in Volume 147, at page 283.

As we read the record, this instrument was first offered by appellee as a deed, and, upon objection by appellants that it was not a deed but was a void instrument since on its face it granted nothing, it violated the Statute of Frauds and the Statute of Conveyances, appellee stated it was offered, not as a deed, but as an instrument recorded in the Deed Records which gives constructive notice that Ethel Strawbridge was claiming the land the instrument described. We interpret this as an offer of the instrument as a sufficient deed under the five year statute of limitation and as a memorandum under the 10 year statute of limitation.

The instrument does not of course conform to the form of a deed set out by Article 1292, R.C.S.1925. However, such form is not a legal requirement to an effective conveyance. In fact, that statute, after setting out a form of conveyance, provides that the substance of the form will be sufficient as a conveyance. At common law significance was attached to certain technical words and to the formal parts of a deed. The premises, which included the granting clause, the naming of the grantor and grantee, the expression of consideration, and a description of the land conveyed, were looked to supply the grantor, grantee, the consideration, the operative words or words of grant and the description and these could not be supplied by resort to other portions of the deed. The habendum clause served to define the estate granted. It is no longer necessary to have these formal parts to have a good deed, nor is it necessary to use technical words. Now we look to the whole of an instrument to determine the intention of the parties. If from the whole instrument we can ascertain a grantor and a grantee and there are operative words or words of grant showing an intention by the grantor to convey title to land which is sufficiently described to the grantee, and it is signed and acknowledged by the grantor, it is a deed.

The instrument before us sufficiently names a grantor and grantee. While Edward Strawbridge is not specifically called a grantor, there can be no question that he is such because it is recited that Ethel Strawbridge has paid him a consideration. The grantor is the person who normally receives the consideration. Too, he signed and acknowledged the instrument, and Ethel Strawbridge, the only other person named in the instrument, appears in the habendum clause as the person who is "to have and to hold" the property. This is sufficient to show she is the grantee. Harlowe v. Hudgins, supra, and Newton v. McKay, 29 Mich. 1.

The vigorous contention of appellants is that there are no words of grant anywhere in the deed. They contend that the words "to have and to hold" used in the habendum clause are not sufficient.

We hold that the habendum clause reading *"To have and to hold the above described property,* together with all and singular the rights and appurtenances thereunto in anywise belonging, *unto the said Ethel Strawbridge, her heirs and assigns forever"* contains operative words effectively evidencing an intention by Edward Strawbridge to convey fee simple title to Ethel Strawbridge. (Emphasis ours.)

No technical words of grant are necessary to convey land. Baker v. Westcott, supra. In the Baker case the instrument was [not], as to form, a deed as set out by statute. The instrument was more in the form of a bond for title. However, the court held that it was effectual as a present conveyance since it used this language: "I dispossess myself of, and for my heirs and assigns relinquish the dominion and possession" of a described tract of land.

In the case of Harlowe v. Hudgins, supra, there was endorsed on a deed or envelope containing a deed the following: "Assignment. I assign the within to Elizabeth Graham for value received of her the sum of fourteen hundred and sixty three dollars and thirty three cents, this April 11th, 1843." It was held this would be sufficient as a deed to transfer not just title to the deed referred to but title to the land described in the deed referred to. The court said:

> The employment of words sufficient to show a purpose and intent to convey is all that was required either by statute or common law.... Whatever may be the inaccuracy of expression or the inaptness of the words used in an instrument, in a legal view, if the intention to pass the title can be discovered, the courts will give effect to it, and construe the words accordingly.

We hold that the words "to have and to hold the above described land ... unto the said Ethel Strawbridge, her heirs or assigns forever" show an intention to convey title in fee simple to Ethel Strawbridge. Under the authorities above cited, we think there would be no question that had the deed read, "For and in consideration of $1.00 to me, Edward Strawbridge, in hand paid by Ethel Strawbridge, she, her heirs and assigns are to have and to hold the following described property," there would be an effectual conveyance of fee simple title to the land. We ascribe the same meaning to the language used in the habendum clause to the instrument. Black's Law Dictionary, Fourth Edition, says of the word "have" that it "imports ownership and has been defined to mean keep, to hold in possession, to own." In Webster's International Dictionary, Second Edition, it is defined to mean "To hold in possession and control; to hold as property; to own, as, he has a farm...."

In Busteed v. Cambridge Savings Bank, 306 Mass. 9, 26 N.E.2d 983, the court defined "have" as meaning to keep; to hold in possession, to own.

In the case of Sheffield v. Hogg, 124 Tex. 290, 77 S.W.2d 1021, 1024, the Supreme Court was passing on the question of whether royalty reservations in mineral leases that were variously worded reserved a real interest in the minerals as distinguished from creating a personal obligation to pay so much money represented by a part of the minerals. In holding that however worded a royalty interest was retained and it constituted real estate, the court stated:

> Endeavoring to reach the true purpose and intent of parties, we can draw no substantial difference, so far as taxation is concerned, between an agreement *excepting* from a grant or a lease a certain fractional portion of minerals, or an agreement *reserving* the same portion, or an agreement that the lessor *shall have* or *rather shall continue to have* the same portion....
> In either instance, the title to the specified mineral portion is intended to remain or vest, and does actually remain or vest in the lessor.

In Webster's International Dictionary, Second Edition, the word "hold" is defined as meaning "To own or possess; to be in possession of; to derive title to."

We think it unmistakable that "to have and to hold the above described property . . . unto Ethel Strawbridge, her heirs or assigns forever" conveys to Ethel Strawbridge a fee simple title.

We fail to see why the presence of the words in the habendum makes any difference. We think the true rule is that if operative words or words of grant appear anywhere in the deed it suffices.

We have found no Texas case precisely in point. There are very old cases in a few other jurisdictions passing on the question. The following cases held resort could not be had to the habendum clause to supply words of grant: Brown v. Manter, 21 N.H. 528; Webb v. Mullins, 78 Ala. 111; Manning v. Smith, 6 Conn. 289. The following cases held you could resort to the habendum clause to find words of grant: Bridge v. Wellington, 1 Mass. 219; Kenworthy v. Tullis, 3 Ind. 96; Hummelman v. Mounts, 87 Ind. 178.

We feel the cases holding resort may not be had to the habendum clause are adhering too closely to the old rule concerning the role of formal clauses of a deed, and fail to recognize the modern rule that the intention of the parties is to be determined by considering the whole instrument and that arrangement in observance of formal clauses as known at common law is not of the essence of a deed.

## NOTES

1. *Litigation strategy*. The attorney for Jack Bowlin, in Bowlin v. Keifer, N.D. Edwards, Esq., of Van Buren, Arkansas writes:

> My original client was Victor Grady Wade, the only heir of Guy G. Wade, deceased. . . . Because of previous transactions and statements between Victor Grady Wade and the remaining heirs, it was decided that he convey his interest to Jack Bowlin, his brother-in-law, and that the suit be brought in the name of Jack Bowlin.

Can you explain the reasoning of Attorney Edwards? How does this bear on the Principal Problem?

2. *No guaranties*. Theron W. Agee, Esq., of Van Buren, Arkansas, writes concerning Bowlin v. Keifer:

> As one of the lawyers for the Appellees, we were badly handicapped, by the fact that the land involved was not described in the "Agreement of Sale" quoted in the opinion of our Supreme Court. To make it worse, some of my clients, living in California, had been assured by some California attorney that there was no way for us to lose. And, incidentally, I think the Justice who dissented was right, and the majority wrong. But that is small consolation for a losing advocate.

Moral: Never assure a client that there is "no way" for him or her to lose.

3. *Principal Problem*. As counsel for Charles in the Principal Problem, which of the three cases helps you the most? Which hurts you the most? Each

case is similar to Charles' case in some respects and different in other respects. How do you determine whether the similarities are "more important" than the differences?

4. *Statutes.* Obviously the cases differ in their facts. They also differ in their law. The statutes of California, Texas, and New York differ in some details. Do these details explain the decisions?

5. *Law of the land.* Note that the California, Texas and New York statutes are reproduced above. The conveyance in the Principal Problem (if it was one) was made in New York, the land was in California. Normally California law would govern. Why?

6. *Improvement in the law.* An informal letter like that in the Principal Problem can cause a lot of litigation. What rule of law could the courts or legislature adopt which would discourage such letters or such litigation? What would be the drawbacks of any such rule? Do such questions suggest how Charles will fare here?

7. *USLTA.* The Uniform Simplification of Land Transfers Act (USLTA) (1976) § 2–201 provides that for a document to be a sufficient conveyance it must "(1) reasonably identify the grantor, the grantee, and the real estate; (2) manifest an intent to make a present transfer of an interest in the real estate; and (3) be in writing and signed by the grantor or his representative...." § 2–201(c) dispenses with the requirement of an acknowledgment, seal, or witness. How would the Principal Problem be decided under USLTA? The Official Comments to § 2–201 suggest that a conveyance of "my house in Chicago" would be good as between the grantor and grantee provided that there was sufficient extrinsic evidence to identify the house. Does this take care of all of the issues in the Principal Problem?

8. *Formalities.* For a useful article summarizing the modern American law regarding the formalities required for a valid deed, and urging the adoption of the USLTA provisions discussed in the preceding paragraph, see Brussack, Reform of American Conveyancing Formality, 32 Hast. L.J. 561 (1981). Professor Brussack indicates that in addition to the almost universal requirement of an instrument in writing signed by the grantor, some states require an acknowledgment (the grantor appears before a notary public, acknowledges that he has freely signed the instrument, and the notary prepares a formal statement to that effect and attaches it to the conveyance). Some other states require an attestation (the required number of witnesses sign an attestation clause stating that they witnessed the grantor sign the deed). Some other states require that the witnesses appear before a notary public and the notary public attaches a statement to the effect that the witnesses declared to him that they witnessed the execution of the deed.

9. *Proper drafting.* The controversies that arose in the cases in this Assignment could have been avoided if more care had been taken when drafting the document of conveyance. The drafter should view herself as creating the record for future litigation. Thus, the grantor, grantee and property to be conveyed should be clearly and accurately identified. In addition, the nature of the interest transferred and the date of the transfer

should be clear. Care should also be taken to ensure compliance with the formalities discussed in Note 8. With careful planning, the deed should clearly reflect the intent of the drafter and be impervious to the claims of third parties.

According to Professor Brussack, a signed conveyance lacking some of the prescribed additional formalities will usually be good as between the grantor and grantee. The additional formalities become important only when third parties are involved, or as a prerequisite to proper recording of the document, or as making it easier to prove the authenticity of the document in a court of law. In arguing for the USLTA position abolishing the need for all of these ceremonies Professor Brussack suggests that this will avoid litigation arising when these ceremonies are improperly performed. But could it not be argued that if all formalities are abolished, other than the requirement of a written instrument signed by the grantor, problems similar to that in the Principal Problem would be more likely to arise?

## b. CONTRACTS FOR THE SALE OF REAL ESTATE

### 1. INTRODUCTION

Most commercial transactions in real estate start with a contract for the purchase and sale of real estate. Under such contracts, the seller agrees to deliver a deed to the property upon receiving the purchase price from the buyer. In most states, these contracts must be in writing and signed by the person to be charged. See, for example, the New York statute reprinted earlier in this Assignment. The applicable California statute is as follows:

**CALIFORNIA CIVIL CODE § 1624 (2015)**

(a) The following contracts are invalid, unless they, or some note or memorandum thereof, are in writing and subscribed by the party to be charged or by the party's agent:

. . .

(3) An agreement for the leasing for a longer period than one year, or for the sale of real property, or of an interest therein; such an agreement, if made by an agent of the party sought to be charged, is invalid, unless the authority of the agent is in writing, subscribed by the party sought to be charged. . . .

Note that the California statute, unlike paragraph 4 of the New York statute (p. 981), does not explicitly refer to the doctrine of part performance. As indicated by the discussion in Walker v. Ireton, 559 P.2d 340 (Kan. 1977), reprinted below, the doctrine of part performance is probably a misnomer. It rests on the more fundamental principle that a contract to convey will be enforced even when not in writing if one party's reasonable detrimental reliance on the contract would make it inequitable not to enforce it. See also the Uniform Land Transactions Act § 2–201(b)(4) (1975) permitting enforcement when one party "has changed his position to his detriment to the extent that an unjust result can be avoided only by enforcing the contract . . . ." Change of position, rather than part performance of the contract, is critical. This is indicated by the fact that even a gift of land, not evidenced by any writing, will be enforced in a sufficiently compelling case. See Gerbrand, Annot., 83 A.L.R.3d 1294 (1978).

## 2. Principal Problem

Mr. McDonald, who is old and in failing health, makes the following oral proposal to Farmer:

> If Farmer will work McDonald's land, McDonald will pay her an annual salary of $20,000, with all profits from the crops going to McDonald. Farmer can move into the farmhouse, as McDonald has moved into town to be closer to his doctor. In the alternative, McDonald proposes that Farmer work the land for three years at an annual salary of $20,000, but that McDonald will withhold one-half of her salary and apply it to the purchase price of $100,000 should Farmer decide at the end of three years to purchase the land.

No formal papers are ever drawn up, but McDonald does find the following note in his mailbox several weeks later:

> Mar. 17
>
> Dear Mack—
>
> Sorry I didn't find you at home. I like your second proposal a lot better. The kids and I will move in as soon as school is over.

Six weeks later Farmer and her family move onto the farm. Over the next three years she improves the old farmhouse, repairs the barn, and places 50 additional acres under cultivation, in addition to farming McDonald's original 200 acres. Pursuant to the agreement, McDonald withholds a total of $30,000 from Farmer's salary over the three-year period.

At the end of three years, Farmer informs McDonald that she wishes to exercise her option to purchase the land. McDonald refuses to convey the land to her, but does agree to pay her the retained $30,000. McDonald has recently been contacted by a developer interested in buying the farm for $150,000 and turning the land into an upscale country club.

Farmer comes to you for advice. She wants to buy the farm. If she should be unable to buy the farm, she insists on substantial money damages "and not just the $30,000 of my hard-earned money that stingy old man kept for three years without interest."

Before advising Farmer, consider the following materials.

## 3. MATERIALS FOR SOLUTION OF PRINCIPAL PROBLEM

### Walker v. Ireton
Supreme Court of Kansas, 1977.
221 Kan. 314, 559 P.2d 340.

■ PRAGER, JUSTICE.

This is an action for the specific performance of an oral contract for the sale of farm land. The defendants answered asserting the defense of the statute of frauds. The plaintiff-appellant is Richard Walker. The defendants-appellees are Bernard F. Ireton and his wife, Marjorie J. Ireton. The defendants filed a motion for summary judgment on the ground that plaintiff was not entitled to specific performance as a matter of law because of the application of the statute of frauds. The trial court sustained the defendants' motion for summary judgment and the plaintiff has appealed.

The factual circumstances are not really in dispute and are essentially as follows: Sometime during the month of July 1973 Walker and Bernard Ireton commenced negotiations for the purchase of the Ireton farm which consisted of 160 acres in Saline county. Prior to this time Walker had only a speaking acquaintance with Bernard Ireton and did not know Mrs. Ireton. In response to a call from Ireton, Walker went to the Ireton farm where he was told that Ireton would sell the farm for $30,000. About a week later Walker advised Ireton that he would accept the proposal for sale at a price of $30,000. Ireton was to farm the crop land on shares and was to pay the real estate taxes through the year 1973. Agreements were made in regard to preparing and seeding the ground for alfalfa and for the cutting and storage of the prairie hay in the pasture. Walker was to be permitted to spray the trees in the pasture to kill them. It was agreed that Walker was to receive full possession of the farm in January 1974. Both Mr. and Mrs. Ireton agreed to the terms of the sale. The preparation of a written contract was discussed and it was agreed that one was to be executed. Ireton stated that he wanted to wait until he could see his tax man to find out how to take the money before preparing a written agreement. A week or so later Ireton stated to Walker that he had sold the farm too cheap but was not going to back out of the agreement. Ireton asked for another $500 on the purchase price to compensate him for alfalfa and because he intended to leave the air conditioner, drapes, and carpet in the house. Walker agreed to an increased sale price of $30,500. The purchase price was to be paid as follows: $50 on July 30, 1973; $7,612.50 on or before September 30, 1973; and $22,837.50 on or before January 1, 1974. The Iretons were to continue to live in the house until January 1, 1974, when Walker was to take complete possession. Mr. and Mrs. Ireton approved the terms of the sale and Walker again suggested that a written contract be prepared. Ireton stated that his word was good and it would be prepared later.

Ireton advised Walker of a broken lateral in the septic system and suggested that Walker make arrangements to connect onto the rural water system. Walker also agreed to buy the range in the house for $25. On July 30, 1973, Walker delivered his $50 check to Ireton. This check was never endorsed or cashed. On at least four subsequent occasions thereafter Walker attempted to convince Ireton that a written contract was needed to complete the agreement. At one time Walker took a written contract to the Iretons to be signed. On each occasion Ireton said that a written contract was not needed since he was honest. A written contract was never executed.

In August of 1973 Walker obtained the abstract of title to the property from Mrs. Ireton. Walker had it brought up to date and examined by his attorney at a cost of $36 for extension of the abstract and a $75 attorney fee for its examination. These sums were apparently paid by Walker. In September 1973 Walker took a hay rake to the property and left it in the pasture. Thereafter further differences began to occur. Ireton told Walker that their new home then being constructed would not be completed by January 1, 1974. Walker agreed that the Iretons should remain in possession until a later date after the house was completed. In late August 1973 Ireton offered Walker $200 to cancel the agreement. Walker declined the offer saying that at that time he had no other place to go. It should be noted that Walker planned to utilize the property as a home and place to breed and train thoroughbred horses. Prior to negotiating with Ireton, Walker had purchased another farm on contract but the Iretons' farm was larger and better situated for Walker's purposes. After making the oral contract with the Iretons, Walker sold the other farm because he could not afford two farms.

Sometime during this period Walker saw Mrs. Ireton and asked why they had not cashed the $50 check which was given as a down payment. Mrs. Ireton said there was no hurry and that her husband had some funny ideas and she had to go along with them. Walker sent a man out to plant some alfalfa and Ireton sent the man away saying that he, Ireton, did not then have time to plant it and he would call him when he had time. On September 28, 1973, Walker tendered Ireton a check for $7,612.50, that sum being the second installment under the oral contract. At this time Ireton refused the payment and said that he was backing out of the oral agreement. Ireton said that he supposed Walker would have him in court. Ireton offered Walker the $50 check which had been received in July and Walker refused to take the check back. After this Walker offered the check to Mrs. Ireton which she refused but said she would pay the abstract expense and damages. Subsequently Walker was evicted from premises which he had leased for breeding and training his horses. In September 1974 Walker filed this action for specific performance.

At the pretrial conference the parties agreed to be bound by certain factual stipulations. It was agreed that the $50 check delivered by

Walker to Ireton dated July 30, 1973, was not [endorsed] by the defendants; that Walker incurred an expense of $36 for bringing the abstract up to date; that Ireton did not accept or [endorse] the check which was tendered by Walker on September 28, 1973; that a short time after September 28, 1973, Ireton offered to pay the abstract expense and "damned little damages" or words to that effect. The parties further stipulated that there was no writing or memorandum of any kind purporting to be an agreement or contract signed by either of the parties; that the Iretons had never delivered complete possession of the property to Walker; and that Walker had made no permanent improvements on the property. The parties from the beginning contemplated that a written agreement was to be prepared later covering all of the various oral agreements of the parties pertaining to: the agreed purchase price; delivery of possession; Walker's right to mow, bale, and store prairie hay and to spray trees; storage of crops; and the division of wheat.

As stated above the Iretons based their motion for summary judgment on the ground that the oral contract was not enforceable because of the statute of frauds (K.S.A. 33–106) which provides in substance that no action shall be brought to charge a party upon any contract for the sale of lands "unless the agreement upon which such action shall be brought, or some memorandum or note thereof, shall be in writing and signed by the party to be charged therewith. . . ." The trial court sustained the Ireton's motion for summary judgment dictating into the record findings of fact and conclusions of law. In ruling on the motion the trial court accepted the plaintiff's factual contentions as true. For purposes of summary judgment the trial court took as established the plaintiff's contention that there was an oral agreement for the sale in accordance with the terms suggested by plaintiff. The court then considered Walker's contention that the statute of frauds was not available as a defense on the basis of partial performance, fraud, waiver, estoppel or ratification. The trial court concluded that there were not sufficient equities in the case to justify the court in taking the case out of the statute of frauds. The trial court found that this was a classic case of an oral contract for the sale of land, and because of the statute of frauds the oral contract was not enforceable. Following the trial court's order sustaining the Iretons' motion for summary judgment, Walker appealed to this court.

We turn now to a consideration of the vital issue in the case, whether equitable considerations prevented the statute of frauds from being asserted as a defense to the action on the oral contract. Counsel for Walker takes the position that the statute of frauds should be held to be inapplicable as a matter of law on alternative theories of fraud, estoppel, acquiescence, waiver, ratification, inconsistency in conduct, or partial performance. In his brief counsel for Walker has cited a number of Kansas decisions which have approached this statute of frauds question from these various angles, using different terminology in particular cases.

In determining this case it would be helpful to consider some of the basic principles of law which have been applied in our cases involving oral contracts for sale of land where the statute of frauds was asserted as a defense. Literally applied K.S.A. 33–106 bars any action on an oral contract for the sale of land. Shortly after the original statute of frauds was enacted in England, courts of equity refused to apply the statute in certain cases where the purchaser under the contract in reliance upon the oral agreement performed acts required by the contract to such an extent as to make it grossly unjust and inequitable for a court of equity to refuse to enforce the oral agreement. Throughout our judicial history the courts of Kansas have enforced oral contracts for the sale of land because of equitable considerations in many cases. In 1872 in Edwards v. Fry, 9 Kan. 417, Justice Brewer upheld the specific performance of an oral contract for the sale of land where a vendee in possession of the land paid a portion of the purchase price and made valuable and lasting improvements on the land. In the course of the opinion Justice Brewer relied in part on the rule that a party who has permitted another to perform acts on the faith of an agreement, shall not insist that the agreement is bad, and that he is entitled to treat those acts as if it had never existed. From the beginning the basis for removal of a case from application of the statute of frauds has been the reliance by one of the parties to the oral contract to his detriment under circumstances where gross injustice would result unless the oral contract was enforced. In Baldridge v. Centgraf, 82 Kan. 240, 108 P. 83 this court again emphasized reliance as the basis for relief from a strict application of the statute of frauds in the following language:

> The ground upon which a court, notwithstanding the statute of frauds, may compel the complete performance of an oral contract for the sale of real estate, which has been partly performed, is that such a decree may be necessary in order to avoid injustice toward one who in reliance upon the agreement has so altered his position that he can not otherwise be afforded adequate relief.

In other cases this court in dealing with oral contracts within the statute of frauds has applied the following principles of law:

(1) The statute of frauds does not render the oral contract void. It is valid for all purposes except that of suit.

(2) Since the contract is one which cannot be enforced, no action for damages will lie for its breach.

(3) The statute of frauds was enacted to prevent fraud and injustice, not to foster or encourage it, and courts will, so far as possible, refuse to allow it to be used as a shield to protect fraud

and as a means to enable one to take advantage of his own wrong.

(4) Where it is sought to enforce an oral contract for the sale of an interest in real estate on the grounds that it has been performed by the party seeking to enforce it, it must appear that a failure to enforce would amount to a fraud against the party.

(5) Absent compelling equitable considerations an oral contract within the statute of frauds will not be specifically enforced.

(6) Part performance of an oral contract will not take the case out of the statute where the performing party can be compensated in money.

(7) Payment of the purchase price alone is not sufficient part performance to take a case out of the statute of frauds. Since the money can be recovered back by action, no fraud will be accomplished if the oral contract is not enforced.

(8) Delivery of possession of the land alone without the making of improvements is not sufficient to take a case out of the application of the statute of frauds.

In dealing with statute of frauds cases courts throughout the country have often shifted their approach to the problem from a theory of part performance, to one of fraud, to one of estoppel. Because of this confusion in the cases the American Law Institute in 1973 adopted a tentative draft to the Restatement 2d, Contracts, to clarify the legal principle and to make it more understandable. Specifically, we note §§ 197 and 217A of the Restatement 2d, Contracts (Tentative Draft 1973), which provide as follows:

§ 197. ACTION IN RELIANCE; SPECIFIC PERFORMANCE. A contract for the transfer of an interest in land may be specifically enforced notwithstanding failure to comply with the Statute of Frauds if it is established that the party seeking enforcement, in reasonable reliance on the contract and on the continuing assent of the party against whom enforcement is sought, has so changed his position that injustice can be avoided only by specific enforcement.

§ 217A. ENFORCEMENT BY VIRTUE OF ACTION IN RELIANCE.

(1) A promise which the promisor should reasonably expect to induce action or forbearance on the part of the promisee or a third person and which does induce the action or forbearance is enforceable notwithstanding the Statute of Frauds if injustice can be avoided only by enforcement of the promise. The remedy granted for breach is to be limited as justice requires.

(2) In determining whether injustice can be avoided only by enforcement of the promise, the following circumstances are influential:

(a) the availability and adequacy of other remedies, particularly cancellation and restitution;

(b) the definite and substantial character of the action or forbearance in relation to the remedy sought;

(c) the extent to which the action or forbearance corroborates evidence of the making and terms of the promise, or the making and terms are otherwise established by clear and convincing evidence;

(d) the reasonableness of the action or forbearance and the misleading character of the promise.

We have not specifically mentioned or approved §§ 197 and 217A in our prior decisions. We have, however, recognized and applied in other cases a similar provision found in § 90 in the Restatement, Contracts, which sets forth the doctrine of "promissory estoppel." In our judgment sections 197 and 217A of Restatement 2d, Contracts (Tentative Draft 1973), are clear and direct statements of the principles of law to be applied in determining whether or not an oral contract should be removed from the application of the statute of frauds and enforced by a court on equitable principles. They are based upon the equitable doctrine of reliance which is the fundamental theory upon which all of our prior cases are founded.

In determining the result in this case we will apply these sections to the factual situation in the record now before us. We have concluded that under all the facts and circumstances equity does not require the statute of frauds to be removed as a defense to this action for specific performance of the oral contract. Here there is no claim that there was any relationship of trust or confidence between the parties. There are no allegations or evidence of false misrepresentation of existing facts. The worst which can be said is that Ireton repeatedly promised that he would perform the oral contract and that he would enter into a written contract to evidence the same. It was stipulated that the parties understood a written contract was to be prepared. Ireton simply refused to sign a written contract on four or five different occasions. Although Walker made a $50 down payment he never took possession of the land involved and made no improvements thereon. Walker placed a hay rake on one of the pastures of the farm but this could not be considered a delivery of possession of the land.

The acts of reliance which Walker has asserted are limited by the record to delivery of the $50 check as an installment on the purchase price, payment of a $36 abstract expense and a $75 attorney fee for an abstract examination, the placing of a side-delivery hay rake on a pasture in September 1973, and the fact that Walker sold a farm near Hedville which he had recently purchased in reliance on Ireton's promise to sell his farm. The question is whether or not these acts of reliance are sufficient to require a court to remove the bar of the statute of frauds. We have concluded that taken together they are not sufficient to justify specific performance of the oral contract. The fact that Walker sold another farm in expectation that the Iretons would sell their farm to him does not justify specific performance under the circumstances of this case. As a general rule an act which is purely collateral to an oral contract, although done in reliance on such contract is not such a part performance as to authorize the enforcement of the contract by a court of equity. (81 C.J.S. Specific Performance § 54; Jones v. Linder [Mo.1952] 247 S.W.2d 817.) An exception is recognized, however, where the agreement was made to induce the collateral act or where the collateral act was contemplated by the parties as a part of the entire transaction.

In the present case the plaintiff Walker does not contend that he advised the Iretons of his intention to sell the Hedville farm in advance of the sale or that the Iretons had any knowledge concerning the sale of the Hedville farm until after it had already been sold. Furthermore Walker does not contend at any place in the record that he lost money on the resale of the Hedville farm to others. We consider the resale of the Hedville farm by Walker to others as a matter wholly collateral to the Ireton contract and not within the contemplation of the parties nor within the scope of any understanding between Ireton and Walker. In support of this position is Dunn v. Winans, 106 Kan. 80, 186 P. 748. There plaintiff vendee brought an action for specific performance of an oral agreement to sell certain land. The petition alleged the making of some improvements on the property and further alleged that plaintiff was damaged in the amount of $300 for the sale of his home for the purpose of carrying out the contract with the defendant. This court denied specific performance holding that there had not been sufficient part performance to take the case out of the statute of frauds. The court further held that although specific performance was denied, the vendee was entitled to recover the expenses which were incurred by him for the improvements he made on the property. He was not, however, permitted to recover damages on account of the sale of his former home. Walker is entitled to the return of his $50 check and the cost of bringing Iretons' abstract up to date on the basis of *quantum meruit* or unjust enrichment. These expenditures were of benefit to the Iretons and Walker is entitled to restitution for these items. Walker is not, however, entitled to be reimbursed for his $75 attorney fee in obtaining a legal opinion. The Iretons received no benefit from this expenditure.

Where a vendee is denied specific performance under an oral contract for the sale of land his right to restitution is restricted to expenditures or services which benefitted the vendor on the basis of *quantum meruit*.

Comment b under 217A states that the reliance of the promisee must be foreseeable by the promisor and enforcement must be necessary to avoid injustice. In this case equity and justice do not require specific enforcement of the oral contract, nor do they require reimbursement to Walker for the sale of the Hedville farm.

The judgment of the district court is affirmed.

## Nessralla v. Peck

Supreme Judicial Court of Massachusetts, 1989.
403 Mass. 757, 532 N.E.2d 685.

■ HENNESSEY, CHIEF JUSTICE.

The plaintiff, Abdu C. Nessralla, brought this action seeking specific performance of an oral agreement to convey a tract of land. After a trial without a jury, a judge of the Superior Court entered judgment in favor of all the defendants. The plaintiff appealed.

We summarize the judge's findings, which both parties essentially accept. The plaintiff, Abdu C. Nessralla, is the owner of a farm in Halifax. Adjacent to his farm is the Sturtevant farm, and across the street is the Hayward farm. The defendant, John H. Peck, is the plaintiff's son-in-law and an employee both of the Cumberland Farms dairy and convenience store chain, and the defendant V.S.H. Realty, Inc., a corporation principally engaged in acquiring and owning the property on which Cumberland Farms stores are located. In the Spring of 1981, the defendant Peck asked Nessralla to act as a straw[1] in V.S.H. Realty's acquisition of the Hayward farm. In return, Peck agreed to act as a straw to assist Nessralla in purchasing the Sturtevant farm. Nessralla had been engaged in a dispute with the owner of the Sturtevant farm, a chicken farmer named Carlton, because Carlton introduced approximately 40,000 chickens onto the Sturtevant farm. Nessralla, therefore, asked Peck to act as a straw because he reasoned that Carlton would be unlikely to sell to him directly.

Nessralla purchased the Hayward farm, putting up $11,000 of his own and taking title to the property in September, 1981. V.H.S. Realty reimbursed Nessralla and paid the entire purchase price of $162,500 for the Hayward farm. In September, 1982, Nessralla conveyed the farm to V.S.H. Realty under a deed reciting consideration of "less than $100."

Nessralla thereafter asked Peck about his efforts to acquire the Sturtevant farm from Carlton. Peck assured Nessralla of his continued best efforts to purchase the farm on Nessralla's behalf. At no time did Nessralla tender any funds to the defendant Peck for use in making an offer on the farm.

---

[1] Editor's note: A "straw" is "[a] third party used as a temporary transferee to allow the principal parties to accomplish something that is otherwise impermissible." Black's Law Dictionary 1647 (10th ed. 2014).

In December, 1983, Peck purchased the Sturtevant farm from Carlton in his own name, and subsequently conveyed the property to himself and his cousin, the defendant Lily Bentas, as tenants in common. Nessralla did not participate in the purchase of the farm, did not provide any of the purchase price, and had no knowledge that the purchase had taken place for approximately one month. Nessralla requested that Peck sell him the farm; Peck failed to answer him. . . .

Nessralla then filed a complaint seeking specific performance of Peck's oral agreement to convey the Sturtevant farm to him. We first address Nessralla's claim that Peck is estopped from pleading the Statute of Frauds, G.L. c. 259, § 1 (1986 ed.), as a defense for the suit for specific performance, and conclude it has no merit. A plaintiff's detrimental reliance on, or part performance of, an oral agreement to convey property may estop the defendant from pleading the Statute of Frauds as a defense. Specific performance under this rule may be warranted where the party seeking relief suffers "the infliction of an unjust and unconscientious injury and loss." *Glass v. Hulbert,* 102 Mass. 24, 36 (1869), quoted in *Andrews, supra.* Nessralla claims that he suffered such an injury in reliance on the oral agreement, both because he purchased the Hayward farm on Peck's behalf and because he omitted taking action to purchase the Sturtevant farm on his own behalf. We disagree. Nessralla ultimately provided no money toward the purchase of the Hayward farm. Indeed, Nessralla points to no evidence that suggests he would have attempted to purchase the property, or would have sought out another to purchase the property on his behalf, had the oral agreement not existed. Such illusory "reliance" on an oral agreement to convey property does not rise to a level which estops the defendant from pleading the Statute of Frauds. See, e.g., *Gordon v. Anderson,* 348 Mass. 787, 204 N.E.2d 501 (1965) (specific performance of oral agreement appropriate where plaintiff gave down payment, took possession, made substantial improvements, and sold prior residence); *Fisher, supra* (specific performance of oral agreement appropriate where plaintiff furnished part of consideration and took possession); *Andrews, supra* 289 Mass. at 5–7, 193 N.E. 737 (specific performance of oral agreement appropriate where plaintiff paid purchase price, made minor improvements, and took possession). The judge properly ruled that the Statute of Frauds was a complete defense to Nessralla's claim for specific performance.

We similarly reject Nessralla's contention that the judge erred by not imposing a constructive trust on the Sturtevant farm. A court in equity generally may impose a constructive trust "in order to avoid the unjust enrichment of one party at the expense of the other where the legal title to the property was obtained by fraud or in violation of a fiduciary relation." *Barry v. Covich,* 332 Mass. 338, 342, 124 N.E.2d 921 (1955). *Meskell v. Meskell,* 355 Mass. 148, 151–152, 243 N.E.2d 804 (1969). In the present case, no fiduciary relationship existed between Peck and

Nessralla. Nothing in the record suggests this was anything other than an arm's-length transaction, see *Superior Glass Co. v. First Bristol County Nat'l Bank,* 380 Mass. 829, 832, 406 N.E.2d 672 (1980), and Peck's family relationship with Nessralla, by itself, does not make him a fiduciary. Furthermore, there was no fraud. The judge specifically found, and his finding was warranted, that Peck did not intend to purchase the Sturtevant farm for himself at the time of the oral agreement. Although conceding that a subsequent refusal to carry out an oral promise, by itself, is not fraud, see *Meskell, supra,* Nessralla argues that the judge was required to draw an inference of fraud based on Peck's subsequent actions. After reviewing the record and the judge's findings, we conclude that such an inference was neither warranted nor required. The judge correctly ruled that no constructive trust is created on these facts.

Finally, we turn to Nessralla's claims that Peck holds the Sturtevant farm subject to a resulting trust, and that Peck was a faithless agent. Neither claim has merit. First, "[a] resulting trust typically arises when a transfer of property is made to one person and the purchase price is paid by another; in such a case a trust results in favor of the person who furnished the consideration." *Meskell, supra* 355 Mass. at 150, 243 N.E.2d 804. *Quinn v. Quinn,* 260 Mass. 494, 501, 157 N.E. 641 (1927). Nessralla provided nothing toward the purchase price of the Sturtevant farm, and thus a resulting trust cannot be imposed on that property for his benefit. Second, the Statute of Frauds is a defense to Nessralla's claims, sounding in contract, that he is entitled to some form of relief because Peck was a faithless agent. The Statute of Frauds bars an action on an agreement "that is not to be performed within one year from the making thereof." G.L. c.259, § 1. The judge found that the parties contemplated that Nessralla's performance would not be completed within one year. This finding was warranted on the evidence. Nessralla's claim, therefore, must fail.

## Gulden v. Sloan

Supreme Court of North Dakota, 1981.
311 N.W.2d 568.

■ ERICKSTAD, CHIEF JUSTICE.

This is an appeal from a judgment against Gary D. Sloan and Rebecca Sloan (Sloans) in favor of James Gulden and Carol Gulden (Guldens) rendered in the District Court of Burleigh County. The judgment resulted from an action brought by Guldens to enforce an oral contract involving a house located in Imperial Valley, a subdivision of Bismarck. We affirm.

The Guldens leased the Imperial Valley house from Walter Krueger in February of 1979. Under the terms of the written lease agreement, Guldens were required to make a rental payment of $414 from February 10, 1979, to March 1, 1979, and then regular monthly payments of $622 until the lease expired on December 31, 1979. The provisions of the lease also gave the Guldens an option to purchase the property during the lease period. The purchase price was set at $62,400, and Guldens were to be credited for any loan equity which accrued during the tenancy. The payments of the principal were to be credited toward the purchase price if the option were exercised.

Guldens made regular monthly payments to Krueger until November of 1979 when, because of James Gulden's unemployment, they were unable to pay during November and December. Because of their financial difficulties, the Guldens talked to Krueger regarding their obligations under the lease. They testified that Krueger told them that if they could find a purchaser for the property, he would allow the property to be sold for the price agreed upon in the lease agreement and that they could keep whatever amount exceeded that purchase price because he considered the excess over $62,400 to be the equity acquired by Guldens during their tenancy.

The Guldens continued to occupy the residence in December, 1979. The Sloans, meanwhile, owned and lived in a mobile home. In the latter part of that month, James Gulden and Gary Sloan, who had known each other for 30 years, had a discussion in which Gulden advised Sloan that he was interested in selling the Imperial Valley house. Sloan told Gulden that he was looking for a home, and based on this conversation it was decided that the Sloans should go out to the Guldens' house to look at it.

The Sloans did visit Guldens' home in Imperial Valley and after some discussion Guldens offered to forgo their option if the Sloans would purchase the house. It is at this point that the two parties disagree. The Guldens contend that an oral agreement was reached that night under which the Sloans agreed to buy the Imperial Valley house. The sale price of the house, according to the Guldens, was to be $68,400, the additional $6,000 above the option purchase price was to be the Guldens' equity acquired during their lease tenancy. The consideration between the parties was that the Guldens would abandon their option to purchase the house; and, in turn, Sloans would transfer title to their mobile home to the Guldens free of encumbrances. The Sloans would then purchase the Imperial Valley house from Krueger at a price of $62,400, which was the price set in the Guldens' option.

The Sloans, while agreeing that terms of a sales agreement were discussed, contend that no formal agreement was reached during their discussions with the Guldens. They contend that after the Guldens informed them that the owner of the Imperial Valley house was Walter Krueger, they dealt exclusively with Mr. Krueger.

An earnest money agreement was executed on December 31, 1979, between Krueger and Sloans in which the Sloans agreed to purchase the Imperial Valley house for a price of $61,556.62. Possession of the premises was to be delivered to the Sloans on or before February 1, 1980.

On about February 1, 1980, the Sloans moved into the house in Imperial Valley and Guldens moved into the mobile home formerly occupied by the Sloans. The couples helped each other move and exchanged keys. At the trial, Carol Gulden testified that she had talked to Gary Sloan by telephone after she and her husband had moved into the mobile home, and that Mr. Sloan informed her that he was going to pay off the mobile home with his income tax refund, at which time he would give Guldens the title to it. When Sloans did not give Guldens title to the mobile home, the Guldens commenced an action for specific performance, requesting an order requiring that title to the mobile home be transferred to them pursuant to the oral agreement. Before completion of the trial, the Sloans transferred the mobile home to others making specific performance impossible. The trial court ordered judgment in the amount of $6,000 to the Guldens. . . . Sloans contend that the trial court committed reversible error in finding as a matter of law that the oral agreement had been partially performed. While they do not specifically assert that the oral contract between themselves and Guldens violated the statute of frauds, it appears implicit in their final assertion that they are claiming a statute of frauds defense.

In analyzing the statute of frauds defense, it should be noted that the North Dakota Century Code contains three separate statutes of frauds. Section 9–06–04, N.D.C.C., ("an agreement for the leasing for a longer period than one year, or for the sale, of real property. . . ."); Section 41–01–16, N.D.C.C., ("a contract for the sale of personal property is not enforceable by way of action or defense beyond five thousand dollars in amount or value of remedy unless there is some writing. . . ."); Section 41–02–08, N.D.C.C., ("the sale of goods for the price of five hundred dollars or more is not enforceable by way of action or defense unless there is some writing. . . .").

We do not address the issue of which of the three statutes of frauds is applicable to this case because this issue has not been argued or briefed. We shall assume for purposes of discussion that at least one is applicable.

Applying the statute of frauds, the part performance of the oral contract by Guldens exempts it from the statute of frauds. In *Buettner v. Nostdahl*, 204 N.W.2d 187, 195 (N.D.1973), this court quoted with approval the following statement from *Miller v. McCamish*, 78 Wash.2d 821, 828–29, 479 P.2d 919, 923–24 (1971):

> As evidenced by the test required in this state to successfully assert part performance, the court's overriding concern *is precisely directed toward and concerned with a quantum of proof certain enough to remove doubts as to the parties' oral agreement:*
>
>> The first requirement of the doctrine that part performance of an oral contract exempts it from the provisions of the statute of frauds is that the contract be proven by evidence

that is clear and unequivocal and which leaves no doubt as to the terms, character, and existence of the contract. . . .

A mere preponderance of the evidence is not sufficient. If the evidence leaves it at all doubtful as to whether or not a contract was entered into, the court will not decree specific performance. . . .

. . .

Another requirement of the doctrine . . . is that the acts relied upon as constituting part performance must unmistakably point to the existence of the claimed agreement. If they point to some other relationship, such as that of landlord and tenant, or may be accounted for on some other hypothesis, they are not sufficient. . . . *Granquist v. McKean,* 29 Wash.2d 440, 445, 187 P.2d 623, 626 (1947).

In *Buettner,* the plaintiff commenced an action alleging the existence of an oral contract. Under the terms of the alleged contract the defendant was to help the plaintiff get into the cattle-feeding business by providing him with sugar beet tops and the use of a 40-acre lot. The plaintiff contended that he relied on representations made by the defendant and performed his part of the contract obligations by moving his family and working for the defendant. We held that the performance by the plaintiff did not take the oral contract out of the statute of frauds because that performance was explicable as an employment relationship. We stated:

If the statute of frauds is to continue to have any meaning in our State, it would seem that it should apply in the instant case where the provisions of the alleged oral contract are so incredible. We do not think it reasonable that an experienced businessman would obligate himself individually or as a member of a partnership to the financial extent herein contended necessary for the construction of the cattle-feeding facilities unless he or the partnership were to participate substantially in the expected profits.

204 N.W.2d at 195.

In *Vasichek v. Thorsen,* 271 N.W.2d 555, 560–61 (N.D.1978), we held that the part performance in the form of improvements to property was sufficient to take the oral contract for the sale of land out of the statute of frauds. We said:

Although any one of these acts, considered separately, may not overcome the statute, taken as a whole they are consistent with the existence of a sales contract.

271 N.W.2d at 561.

In the instant case, therefore, we must look to all of the facts which point to part performance of the oral agreement and determine whether or not they can be explained by some relationship other than the alleged contractual relationship.

We hold that the performance in the instant case does except the oral contract from the statute of frauds. It is undisputed that Sloans moved out of their mobile home and into the Imperial Valley house. At the same time, Guldens moved out of the Imperial Valley house and into the mobile home. The parties helped each other move and exchanged keys. These actions are consistent with the trial court's finding that the parties entered into an oral agreement.

The Sloans' only explanation for the performance of the terms of the contract is their friendship with Guldens. They contend that Guldens had nowhere to live so they offered their mobile home. Guldens did not, however, pay rent.

Although Sloans contend they were motivated solely by their friendship with Guldens, the testimony does not support that contention. The testimony, instead, is consistent with the finding that an oral contract existed. Guldens testified that they had contracted for ownership of the mobile home and that Gary Sloan was to have the title to it transferred to them. Consistent with their belief that they owned the mobile home, the Guldens did not pay rent for living in it. Further, the testimony indicates that Guldens received continued assurances from Gary Sloan that he would pay off "some money owing on the trailer" and have the title to it transferred to them.

The friendship which Sloans assert as the reason for allowing Guldens to live in the mobile home was termed by Sloans' attorney on cross examination of James Gulden as "acquaintances". Gary Sloan himself, on direct examination, described his relationship with Guldens as follows:

Q. Okay. Had you in the past socialized with [Guldens]?
A. Well, at times, yes. Once or twice, you know, I'd run into them.

Although it is undisputed that James Gulden and Gary Sloan had known each other for 30 years, it doesn't appear that their friendship was so strong and long lasting that it explains Sloans letting Guldens live rent free in their mobile home. That explanation is not so likely that it precludes our holding that part performance exempted the oral contract from the statute of frauds.

We believe that the facts of this case are distinguishable from *Buettner*. In the instant case, the facts taken as a whole are consistent with the existence of a contract. The simple explanation that the exchange was made out of friendship does not, in view of the testimony, provide an acceptable explanation of the exchange. We therefore hold that the oral contract between Sloans and Guldens was excepted from the statute of frauds because of the part performance.

Affirmed.

## UNIFORM LAND TRANSACTIONS ACT
### § 2–201 (1975).

### § 2–201. [Formal Requirements; Statute of Frauds]

(a) Notwithstanding agreement to the contrary and except as provided in subsection (b), a contract to convey real estate is not enforceable by judicial proceeding unless there is a writing signed by the party against whom enforcement is sought or by that party's representative which:

(1) contains a description of the real estate that is sufficiently definite to make possible an identification of the real estate with reasonable certainty;

(2) except as to an option to renew a lease, states the price or a method of fixing the price; and

(3) is sufficiently definite to indicate with reasonable certainty that a contract to convey has been made by the parties.

(b) A contract not evidenced by a writing satisfying the requirements of subsection (a), but which is valid in other respects, is enforceable if:

(1) it is for the conveyance of real estate for one year or less;

(2) the buyer has taken possession of the real estate, and has paid all or a part of the contract price;

(3) the buyer has accepted a deed from the seller;

(4) the party seeking to enforce a contract, in reasonable reliance upon the contract and upon the continuing assent of the party against whom enforcement is sought has changed his position to his detriment to the extent that an unjust result can be avoided only by enforcing the contract; or

(5) the party against whom enforcement is sought admits in his pleading, testimony, or otherwise in court that the contract for conveyance was made.

### [OFFICIAL] COMMENT

1. Practically all existing statute of frauds provisions in the various jurisdictions are based upon Section 4 of the English statute of 1677, with very little change in the language of that statute. In the 300 years since that statute was adopted, such a heavy accretion of case law has developed that the matter of interpretation of the statute has become essentially a common law matter. A whole volume of nearly 800 pages in Corbin's treatise on contracts is devoted to the statute of frauds, and some 200 pages is devoted to contracts for the sale of land.

This section provides a fresh start for determining statute of frauds requirements for real estate sales contracts. It codifies in subsection (b) judicial glosses on the 1677 statute. It also modifies, in several instances, the rules applied in many states today.

2. This section rejects the requirement presently imposed in some states that the memorandum contain all the material terms of the agreement. Under this section, the only essential terms of the writing are (1) a description of the real estate and (2) the price or a method of fixing the price. (In the case of options to renew it is not necessary that the writing refer to price.) The price requirement is intended to prevent the writing from being sufficient unless it shows that the parties have considered the price and reached some agreement either as to price or as to later fixing the price. If the two required terms appear in the writing, all other terms may be established by parol evidence.

Other than the description and price requirements, the test for sufficiency of the writing is that it be "sufficiently definite to indicate with reasonable certainty that a contract to convey has been made by the parties." The requirement is not that the contract or memorandum of the contract be in writing, nor that the writing be sufficient to itself establish that a contract has been made. It need merely be sufficient to afford a basis for believing that the offered oral evidence that a contract was in fact made rests on a real transaction. For example, a written offer with a sufficient description and sufficient reference to price, properly signed, would be a sufficient memorandum against the signer even though there is no writing indicating that the offer was in fact accepted.

A writing can be used to satisfy the statute only against the party who has signed it. Signing, however, is a very broad term encompassing "any symbol executed or adopted by a party with present intention to authenticate a writing." See Section 1–201(19). This Act rejects the position adopted in some states by statute or decision that the signing requirement applies only to the seller. Under this Act the statute of frauds requirements applies equally to both buyers and sellers.

3. Subsection (b) states those situations in which a contract for sale of real estate is enforceable even though there is no writing. Mere taking of possession of the real estate is not sufficient to satisfy the statute, but possession with part payment or possession with the change of position described in subsection (b)(4) is sufficient. The language of subsection (4) derives from Section 197 of the Restatement of Contracts, Second, but the rule of subsection (4) is not limited to specific performance actions. Under subsection (b)(3) acceptance of an instrument granting a freehold estate takes the contract out of the statute. This rule applies not only to transfers of life estates and fee simple interests in the land, but also to similar transfers of mineral interests, easements, restrictions, servitudes, or other interests.

4. Failure to satisfy the requirements of this section does not render the contract void for all purposes, but merely prevents it from being judicially enforced in favor of a party to the contract. For example, a buyer who takes possession of real estate as provided in an oral contract

which the seller has not meanwhile repudiated, is not a trespasser. Nor would the statute of frauds provisions of this section be a defense to a third person who wrongfully induces a party to refuse to perform an oral contract, even though the injured party cannot maintain an action for damages against the party so refusing to perform.

5. It is not necessary that the writing be delivered to anybody. It need not be signed or authenticated by both parties but, of course, it is not sufficient against one who has not signed it. Before a dispute no one can determine which party's signing of the memorandum may be necessary but from the time of contracting each party should be aware that to him it is signing by the other which is important.

6. If the making of a contract is admitted in court, either in a written pleading by stipulation or by oral statement before the court, no additional writing is necessary for protection against fraud. Under this section it is no longer possible to admit the contract in court and still treat the statute as a defense. However, the contract is not thus conclusively established. The admission so made by a party is itself evidential against him of the truth of the facts so admitted and of nothing more; as against the other party, it is not evidential at all.

7. This section is similar to UCC, Section 2–201.

## NOTES

1. *Differing standards.* A very small number of states (Mississippi, North Carolina and Tennessee) do not recognize the doctrine of part performance at all.[2] As *Walker*, *Nessralla* and *Gulden* show, the states that do recognize part performance apply different tests to determine whether the aggrieved party's acts are sufficient to take an oral agreement out of the Statute of Frauds. In most states, mere payment by the buyer of all or part of the purchase price is not sufficient, as the buyer would be protected by the right to restitution.[3] In a minority of jurisdictions (Arkansas, Connecticut, Florida, Georgia, Illinois, Iowa, Kansas, Maryland, Missouri, New York, Oklahoma, South Carolina, Washington, West Virginia and Wisconsin), an oral contract to convey land is enforceable against both parties if the buyer or lessee has taken possession of the land.[4] A majority of states, however, require more than a mere taking of possession. There must be an accompanying part payment; or permanent improvement to the land; or proof that removal will cause irreparable injury.[5] ULTA § 2–201(b) holds

---

[2] See Corbin on Contracts § 18.24 (2009); Calamari and Perillo on Contracts § 19.15 (6th ed. 2009).

[3] See Stackhouse v. Cook, 271 S.C. 518, 248 S.E.2d 482 (1978) ("[I]t is well settled that payment of the purchase money alone cannot support an action for specific performance.") Contra, Hamilton v. Traub, 29 Del.Ch. 475, 51 A.2d 581 (1947) ("[P]art payment of the purchase money constitutes such part performance as will remove an oral agreement from the operation of our statute of frauds, assuming the payment is reasonably unequivocal.")

[4] See Corbin on Contracts § 18.14 (2009); Pearl Brewing Co. v. McNaboe, 495 A.2d 238 (R.I. 1985).

[5] See generally Corbin on Contracts §§ 18.14, 18.15 (2009).

that mere taking of possession is not sufficient to remove an oral agreement from the Statute of Frauds.

2. *Law and equity.* The traditional rule is that relief under the doctrine of part performance is limited to equitable relief. Money damages are generally not available. However, damages may be awarded as an alternative remedy in a suit for specific performance where specific performance has been rendered impossible (e.g., the land in dispute has been conveyed to an innocent third party) or where money damages might be of the sort traditionally sought only in equity (e.g., seeking an accounting for profits made).[6] This rule is based on the old distinction between courts of equity and courts of law, part performance was an equitable doctrine not recognized at common law. However, at least one case and two law review articles criticize this rule, arguing that given the modern merger of law and equity, there is no reason to maintain the distinction between remedies at law and equity.[7] Can you think of any additional justifications for maintaining the bar on money damages?

3. *Seller's part performance.* The doctrine of part performance is more often applied in favor of a purchaser who seeks to compel conveyance rather than in favor of a seller against a purchaser. But a seller may seek relief under the doctrine if her cause of action is justified by her own part performance or other action in reliance on the contract, rather than by the avoidance of injustice to the buyer.[8]

4. *Dead people do not talk.* James Halsey, an old man and a widower, was living without family or housekeeper in his house in Hornell, New York. He told the plaintiffs that if they gave up their home and business in Andover, New York and boarded and cared for him during his life, the house and lot would be theirs upon his death. They did as he asked, selling out their interest in a trucking business in Andover, and boarding and tending him until he died, about five months after their coming. Neither deed nor will, nor memorandum subscribed by the promisor, existed to authenticate the promise. Judge Cardozo denied enforcement. Burns v. McCormick, 233 N.Y. 230, 135 N.E. 273 (1922).[9]

5. *Uniform Electronic Transactions Act and E-Sign.* In 1999, the National Conference of Commissioners on Uniform State Laws promulgated the Uniform Electronic Transactions Act (UETA). Almost every state has adopted UETA.[10] Although real estate transactions were initially carved out of the proposed UETA legislation, the final legislation includes real estate

---

[6] Corbin on Contracts § 18.3 (2009).

[7] Steinberg, Promissory Estoppel as a Means of Defeating the Statute of Frauds, 44 Fordham L.Rev. 114, 128 (1975); Note, Contracts-Statute of Frauds: Part Performance as a Basis for Money Damages, 47 Wash.L. Rev. 524, 526 (1972).

[8] Corbin on Contracts § 18.6 (2009); Restatement (Second) of Contracts § 129 cmt. e (1981).

[9] Corbin on Contracts § 18.13 (2009) (discussing oral promises to transfer land at death).

[10] Forty-seven states and the District of Columbia have adopted UETA in whole or in part. The three states that have not adopted UETA (Illinois, New York, and Washington) have their own versions of an electronic signature or transaction act. See www.uniformlaws.org/LegislativeFactSheet.aspx?title=ElectronicTransactionsAct.

transactions within its scope. In 2000, Congress enacted the Federal Electronic Signatures in Global and National Commerce Act (E-Sign). This legislation gives an electronic (paperless) document the same legal effect as a written document. Notwithstanding these advances, paper documents continue to be utilized in typical real estate transactions. While electronic signatures may sometimes be utilized, hard copy originals are generally ultimately recorded. Thus, the fully electronic real estate transaction (with no paper documents) has yet to become commonplace, even though an electronic deed is theoretically possible.

# ASSIGNMENT 41

# DEED DESCRIPTIONS

1. INTRODUCTION

If Smith wants to give land to his nephew Jones, he must describe the land. What methods may he or should he use? What specificity is required? What is adequate? What underlying policy determines how specific a description should be? How do we evaluate the rules enunciated by the courts relating to descriptions? For every property description that ends up in court, a thousand descriptions are never the subject of dispute. **In your professional practice, your goal should be to draft unambiguous documents so that they never become the subject of a dispute.**

A description's purpose is to delineate the exact size, shape, and location of a parcel of land. No other parcel of land should fit the same description. In addition, every competent reader of the description, both at present and in the future, should be able to ascertain the exact size, shape, and location of the parcel described with minimum effort. An equally important policy is that the land described should correspond exactly with the land intended to be conveyed. A description may be unambiguous but disastrous if it unambiguously describes land not owned by the grantor, omits land that the parties intended to convey, or includes land that the parties did not intend to convey. In the case that follows, the grantor mistakenly built on land that it had previously transferred.

## Producers Lumber & Supply Co. v. Olney Bldg. Co.
Court of Civil Appeals of Texas, 1960.
333 S.W.2d 619.

■ MURRAY, CHIEF JUSTICE.

This suit was instituted by Producers Lumber & Supply Company, Inc., against Olney Building Company, a corporation, seeking to recover damages resulting from the conduct of H.P. Orts, president of defendant, when he caused his construction superintendent and a large crew of men to go upon Lot 8, Block 9, New City Block 12459, Northeast Park, an addition situated in the corporate limits of the City of San Antonio, Bexar County, Texas, owned by plaintiff, and demolish a dwelling constructed thereon by Olney Building Company.

H.P. Orts owned several corporations and was the head and general manager of them all, including Olney Building Company. Prior to November 1, 1956, Elliott Construction Co., hereinafter referred to as Elliott, was the owner of Lot 8, Block 9, New City Block 12459, involved herein. On that date H.P. Orts, executed a warranty deed, which was properly recorded, from Elliott Construction Co., Inc., as its Assistant Secretary and Agent and Attorney in Fact, to Producers Lumber & Supply Co., appellant herein, conveying Lot 8 for a consideration of $1,428. The lot was purchased by appellant with the intention that later its general manager, George R. Montgomery, and his wife would build a home for themselves thereon. Montgomery and wife had the lot graded and planted some trees and grass on it. On or about February 27, 1958, Orts and Elliott decided to construct nine dwellings, one on Lot 8, and eight on other nearby lots. Orts called A.L. Burden, secretary-treasurer of appellee, and asked him whether Lot 8 had been sold. Burden, after consulting a map on the wall, assured Orts it had not been sold. Orts inspected Lot 8 and noticed the trees planted there, he thought it was nice of someone to plant trees on this lot. Shortly thereafter the construction of the nine houses was begun, on April 1, 1958, appellee ordered Stewart Title Company to issue a Title Binder covering all nine lots to Frost National Bank in connection with appellee's interim financing. On April 14, 1958, Orts learned from the Title Company that Lot 8 had been sold to appellant. Orts then notified Mr. Montgomery of the circumstances, and this was the first notice to appellant that construction had been commenced on its lot. The dwelling on Lot 8 had been almost completed when the discovery was made. The house had been constructed, without the knowledge or consent of appellant and against its wishes, and contrary to the plans that Montgomery and wife had for their own home. Orts began negotiations with Montgomery, trying to reach an amicable settlement of the matter. Orts told Montgomery that he, Montgomery, had him at his mercy. Various offers and counter-offers were made, but no settlement had been reached, when suddenly on April 22, 1958, Orts broke off negotiations and sent his construction superintendent with a large crew of men and heavy equipment to Lot 8, and demolished the dwelling constructed thereon, leaving nothing but a heap of crude building material and debris. With reference to the destruction of this dwelling, Orts testified as follows:

> Q. Isn't it a fact that by 6:00 o'clock in the afternoon, by the use of a bulldozer and a dozen or more men, you had completely removed everything but the slab? A. That's right.
>
> Q. Now who did you employ to remove the slab? A. My superintendent.
>
> Q. How did Crea Brothers get on the job? A. I hired their equipment.
>
> Q. What equipment did you hire from Crea Brothers? A. A D-12 tractor, and I believe that slab was so good they couldn't get it up with a D–12 and finally they had to get a crane with a drop hammer, and I told my superintendent if Crea

Brothers didn't have the-well, frankly, I don't know where I got the crane with the drop hammer.

Q. Isn't it a fact that they also used a couple of air hammers?
A. Oh, yes.

Q. Air hammers, and they had to use torches to cut the steel?
A. That is correct.

The jury found in answer to Special Issue No. 1, that Orts had built the dwelling on Lot 8 in good faith. The evidence shows that at the time he began the construction of the dwelling there was a deed on record signed by Orts, conveying this lot to appellant. Orts simply forgot about signing this deed some eighteen months before. . . .

However, if the evidence may be regarded as sufficient to support the jury's answer to Issue No. 1, appellee cannot prevail upon his plea of improvement in good faith, because of his malicious destruction of the dwelling he had constructed on Lot 8.

The law at one time was quite clear that where a person erects a building upon the land of another without his knowledge and consent the building became a fixture and belonged to the owner of the land. The builder was without remedy.

It is only where a person places permanent improvements upon land belonging to another in a good faith belief that he is the owner of the land, that he has any remedy at all. . . . Where he has built such improvements in good faith, he has a somewhat limited right to go into court, and upon proof of such good faith ask the court to grant him equitable relief.

Under no circumstances is an improver authorized to go upon the land of another, without his knowledge and consent, and demolish the improvements that he has through mistake placed thereon, and if he does so he commits waste and can be required to pay the landowner for such waste.

He cannot now come into court, with unclean hands, and seek the equitable remedy of reimbursement for the amount he had enhanced the value of Lot 8 by the erection of the dwelling thereon. . . .

The judgment of the trial court will be amended so as to permit appellant, Producers Lumber & Supply Company, Inc., to recover the sum of $5,000, the stipulated value of the dwelling demolished by Orts, and $300, found by the jury as exemplary damages, in addition to the sum of $600 awarded by the trial court, thus making the total amount of the judgment the sum of $5,900, and as thus amended the judgment will be affirmed. The cost of this appeal is adjudged against appellee.

■ BARROW, JUSTICE (dissenting).

There is no doubt that appellant is entitled to recover such damages as it suffered to its lot, which is all that it had at the inception of this transaction. Producers is also entitled to recover exemplary damages under the jury finding that the house was torn down and removed maliciously, but I cannot agree that it is entitled to recover compensatory damages for the removal of the house.

The majority opinion holds that Olney is not entitled to reimbursement for the amount its improvements enhanced the value of Producers' land because it resorted to "self-help," and took the law into its own hands, and demolished the building, causing great destruction of property, and by reason thereof Olney does not come into equity with clean hands, and therefore cannot seek equitable relief. I cannot agree with such reasoning. First, it is common knowledge that if Olney had a right to remove the building, which the authorities hold that it did, then if it became necessary to tear down the building in order to do so, it had that right, subject to its responsibility to pay for any damages to Producers' lot. Second, Olney does not seek any reimbursement, but only interposes its right in defense of Producers' suit for damages for the removal of the property. Third, the property "demolished," belonged to Olney and not to Producers. Fourth, had the house remained on Producers' lot, before it could claim the same it would have had to pay Olney the amount of the enhancement in value of its property. Fifth, it appears from the record that immediately upon discovery of the mistake, Olney contacted Producers and sought to adjust the difficulty. It first offered to buy the lot, and Producers asked $3,600 or $3,700 for the lot, although it cost $1,428....

Bollinger v. McMinn, 47 Tex.Civ.App. 89, 104 S.W. 1079, is a case in which a landowner, McMinn, by mistake built a house on the boundary line and was in possession through a tenant. Bollinger, over the objection and protest of the tenant, sawed the house in two and removed three rooms, leaving a gallery and one room minus a wall. The Court held that McMinn could recover against Bollinger, although the part removed was on Bollinger's own land, and held that the measure of damages was the value of the house before the removal less its value thereafter.

Chief Justice Bickett, formerly of this Court, in Bush v. Gaffney, 84 S.W.2d 759, 764, said:

> It would ill comport with the principles of equity for the court to visit upon the defendants a sort of punishment to the pecuniary profit of the complainant and consequent loss of the defendants. A court of equity is a court of conscience, but not a forum of vengeance. It will make restitution, but not reprisals. It will fill full the measure of compensation, but will not overflow it with vindictive damages.

There is no sound reason to exact of appellee additional punitive damages in the sum of $5,000 and make the donation to appellant, as chastisement for appellee's alleged uncleanliness of hands, after full restitution has been made in awarding to appellant all damages which the jury found it suffered, as well as the exemplary damages found by the jury. Equity looks on that done which ought to be done.

## NOTE

It is wise to obtain a professional survey before buying (or selling) expensive property, property on which expensive improvements will be erected, property with ill-defined boundaries, or property to which valuable improvements have been added without a survey (swimming pools, driveways). If circumstances do not warrant a survey, it may still be advisable to have a knowledgeable person check the property against the description. Failure to do so may prove embarrassing and expensive.

After reading a number of cases in this area, one gets the impression that the courts are surprisingly reluctant to correct defective descriptions to save a conveyance. This may be explained by the seldom expressed view that giving effect to sloppily drawn deeds will encourage sloppy draftsmanship in the future. An analogy may be helpful. If a statute provides 60 days for filing a notice of appeal, a court will not permit the filing of such a notice in 70 days. This is not because the extra ten days has necessarily caused anyone serious damage; rather it is because only by strictly enforcing the rule will it serve any purpose. Thus, defective descriptions seem to have been struck down on occasion not because anyone was misled by them, but rather to serve as an example to deter similar sloppy draftsmanship in the future.

If a description is defective, but not so defective as to be a nullity, the primary task of the court is to determine the intent of the grantor. Unfortunately, determining the intent of the grantor is an art and not a science, despite the plethora of pseudo rules that purport to help. The cases in this Assignment illustrate some of the approaches that courts have taken.

## 2. METHODS OF DESCRIBING LAND

Land can be described in a number of ways. Different methods predominate at different times and in different locations. Different kinds of land (rural or urban, large or small parcels, platted or unplatted land) lend themselves to different modes of description.

A. *Reference to a Recorded Land Map or "Plat."*

A common method of describing small lots is to have a competent surveyor subdivide a parcel into many numbered plots and have the subdivision map duly recorded. The following is an example of such a description:

> Lot 47 of Block 57 of El Rancho Subdivision Number 2, as recorded in a plat recorded on March 1, 1968, in Book 41 of Maps in the Official Records of Yolo County, State of Illinois.

A reference to an unambiguously identified but unrecorded map will be given effect if the map can be found. However, an unrecorded map can be mislaid. Thus, references to unrecorded maps or other documents should be avoided. If the map is not recorded, or otherwise ascertainable, or if the lots are not numbered, the description is worthless. Moreover, an attempt to convey a "part" of a lot, without precisely describing the part, is likely to fail. The case that follows illustrates both the dangers of referring to unrecorded maps and of describing land as "part of" a larger tract, without precisely identifying the part conveyed.

## Asotin County Port District v. Clarkston Community Corp.
Court of Appeals of Washington, 1970.
2 Wash.App. 1007.

■ MUNSON, JUDGE.

Asotin County Port District brought a combined action to: (1) quiet title to certain portions of land claimed to be owned by Clarkston Community Corporation, and (2) reform a deed given by defendant's predecessor, Lewiston-Clarkston Improvement Company, to plaintiff's predecessor, Asotin County, in 1937. The trial court held in favor of Clarkston Community Corporation in both actions. Plaintiff appeals, alleging the trial court's findings of fact and conclusions of law are not supported by the evidence. We affirm the judgment of the trial court.

Portions of land involved in this action were originally subject to a 1938 tax-foreclosure proceeding by Asotin County. The parcels were described in the certificate of delinquency and the tax-foreclosure summons as follows:

> Legal description of all properties described herein is on file in the County Treasurer's office.
>
> Taxes on part of Lot 5, Section 17, Township 11 N.R. 46 E.W.M. for 1931, principal, interest and costs $6.92.
>
> Taxes on Part of Lot 5, Section 17, Township 11 N.R. 46 E.W.M. for 1931, principal, interest and costs $16.38.
>
> Taxes on Part of Lot 5, Section 17, Township 11 N.R. 46 EWM for 1931, principal, interest and costs $25.26.
>
> Taxes on part of Lot 5, Section 20, Township 11 N.R. 46 EWM for 1931, principal, interest and costs $17.85.

Following the conclusion of the 1938 tax-foreclosure proceeding and the issuance of deeds, Asotin County brought an action to quiet title in themselves to property described as:

> 2.30 acres in Lot 5, Sec. 17, Twp. 11, N.R. 46, sold for $23.30, 1931 Tax and Costs, assessed to the Lewiston-Clarkston Improvement Company.
>
> 2.14 acres in Lot 5, Sec. 17, Twp. 11, N.R. 46, sold for $25.26, 1931 Tax and Costs, assessed to the Lewiston-Clarkston Improvement Company.
>
> 2.01 acres in Lot 5, Sec. 20, Twp. 11, N.R. 46, sold for $17.85, 1931 Tax and Costs, assessed to the Lewiston-Clarkston Improvement Company.

In the latter action to quiet title the Lewiston-Clarkston Improvement Company was not specifically named as a party defendant. After listing the named defendants in that action, the county included the following:

> and any and all other person or persons, firms or corporations claiming any right, title, lien, estate or interest in and to any of the real estate described in the summons herein.

The Lewiston-Clarkston Improvement Company was a Washington-based corporation, transacting business therein with officers within the state. The quiet title action proceeded to judgment and allegedly quieted title in Asotin County to all property described therein.

In 1940, the Lewiston-Clarkston Improvement Company conveyed real estate in Asotin County to defendant, Clarkston Community Corporation, in part as follows:

> All that portion of Lots . . . and Five (5) . . . of Section 20, Township 11 North, Range 46 E.W.M., excepting therefrom the following:
>
> > That portion conveyed by Tax Deed to Asotin County on April 25, 1938, recorded in Book 45 of Deeds, page 234.
>
> Lot Five (5), Section Seventeen (17), Township Eleven (11) North, Range Forty-six (46), E.W.M. excepting therefrom the following:
>
> > That portion conveyed by Tax Deed to Asotin County, dated April 25, 1938, recorded in Book 45 of Deeds, page 234.

The reference tax deeds contain the same land description as the certificate of delinquency and the tax-foreclosure summons. From 1940 to the institution of the present action, Clarkston Community Corporation has ostensibly been in possession of the disputed land and, so far as may be ascertained, has paid taxes thereon.

Plaintiff makes numerous assignments of error to the trial court's findings of fact; however, the main thrust of this appeal centers around finding of fact No. 4 which provides:

> The only land descriptions appearing in the tax foreclosure proceedings, the tax deed or the quiet-title action which could have any possible relevance to the lands, title to which is at issue in the present case, are as follows:
>
> > 2.14 acres more or less of Lot 5, Section 17, Township 11 North, Range 46, E.W.M. and
> >
> > 2.01 acres more or less of Lot 5, Section 20, Township 11 North, Range 46, E.W.M. and
> >
> > 1.15 acres more or less of Lot 5, Section 17, Township 11 North, Range 46, E.W.M. and

> 1.15 acres more or less of Lot 5, Section 17, Township 11 North, Range 46, E.W.M.
>
>> Said descriptions merely designate the land as part of a larger tract, without greater certainty as to the identity of the particular part which the county sought to foreclose.
>
> Finding of fact No. 4, as well as other findings to which error is assigned, is supported by substantial evidence.
>
> Plaintiff relies upon [several cases] for the proposition that:
>
>> [I]f a person of ordinary intelligence and understanding can successfully use the description [given] in an attempt to locate and identify the particular property sought to be . . . [foreclosed, then] the description answers it purpose and must be held sufficient.
>
> We do not dispute this rule; in the cited cases it could be applied. However, in the instant case it cannot be applied because the inadequate descriptions cannot be made specific. Even though the description of property set forth in the summons was prefaced by a remark that legal descriptions could be ascertained from the tax records of the county treasurer, there is nothing in the present record to reflect that said legal descriptions did in fact exist on the tax rolls in the treasurer's office at the time of the foreclosure action. Plaintiff admitted in oral argument his inability to find such record. The record reflects that counsel for plaintiff made an exhaustive search of the records of Asotin County not only to show the chain of title, but also to establish facts that would make the descriptions specific. The search was not productive. Plaintiff's problem, i.e., adequacy of the legal description, was considered and resolved 63 years ago when it was established that a description which designates the land conveyed as a portion of a larger tract without identifying the particular part conveyed is fatally defective.

### B. *Metes and Bounds Descriptions*

Probably the oldest descriptions, and still widely used today, are metes and bounds descriptions. A simplified example of a metes and bounds description might be as follows:

> Starting at the old oak tree proceed due north 500 feet, thence due east 500 feet and thence due south 500 feet, and thence due west 500 feet back to the point of beginning.

In the above example, the other three points of the square described would ordinarily be set with artificial monuments, usually metal spikes, plates or pipes set in concrete and sufficiently large to be easily found considering the terrain. Each spike, pipe or plate should be marked. Many jurisdictions have statutes or ordinances governing the kind of artificial monuments that can be set and who can set them—i.e., a licensed surveyor. One of the most crucial steps in drafting a metes and bounds description is establishing a sufficiently certain and exact point of beginning.

The point of beginning or "tie" in the above example is the "old oak tree"; "due north" refers to the direction or "course"; "500 feet" the distance, and the last call, "due west 500 feet back to the point of beginning" completes the "closure." An adequate description must always describe a completely closed area. The directions are often referred to as "calls." The "old oak tree" is, technically speaking, a "monument", i.e., a more or less permanent feature that will help to anchor the description. Notice that the final call "due west 500 feet back to the point of beginning" is in a sense redundant since either "due west 500 feet" or "back to the point of beginning" would have completed the closure. For reasons that will become apparent, this particular redundancy is desirable.

Although the description of the point of beginning as "the old oak tree" may be adequate for the contracting parties, it is obviously inadequate because every competent reader of the description both now and in the future should be able to ascertain the exact location of the parcel with a minimum of effort. The description would be improved (but not very much!) if the state and county in which the land is located were mentioned. A county designation is ordinarily preferable to a city designation although it is perfectly proper, and often customary, to include both. Deeds and other land records are recorded and filed by counties. Since there may be many "old oak trees" within the county, additional information is essential. Thus, the following might be added to the description in the above example.

> The said parcel being a part of the land deeded to me by my father F.S. Jones on July 7, 1969, said deed being recorded in book 404, page 44 of the Official Records in the Jackson County Recorder's Office.

If the description in the July 7, 1969 deed was adequate, if the farm, of which the "oak tree parcel" is a part was small enough, and if there is only one oak tree on the farm, we are beginning to approach an adequate description. However, since the permanence of the oak tree is speculative, and since other oak trees may sprout, the description, even as amended, is not satisfactory.

## Powell v. Schultz
Court of Appeals of Washington, 1971.
4 Wash.App. 213.

■ PEARSON, J.

In 1910, one Syvert Aardal and his wife, Martha, were owners of lot 3, section 13, township 24 north, range 3 west, an area on the shores of Hood Canal in Mason County, Washington. By a deed of July 7, 1910, the Aardals conveyed approximately the southern one-half of lot 3 to John

Erickstad, "making the Creek running through said Lot three the dividing line, ...". Unfortunately for all concerned, there are two streams running on lot 3, a so-called North Creek and a South or Rocky Creek. The land conveyed to Erickstad eventually passed to the defendant, Schultz, and the land Aardal retained eventually came into the ownership of plaintiff, Powell. A dispute over which of the streams, in fact, was the intended boundary resulted in the case now before us.

Defendants sought to show that at the time of the deed the North Creek was the only creek in existence and that an avulsion had occurred subsequent to 1910 which had caused a diversion of the creek to the course referred to as Rocky Creek. On the other hand, plaintiffs offered testimony to show that the avulsion had occurred prior to 1910. Plaintiff's testimony also demonstrated that placing the boundary at Rocky Creek would more nearly give each party approximately half of government lot 3 (which both deeds recited).

After a lengthy trial, at which much conflicting evidence was adduced, the trial judge determined that Rocky Creek or South Creek was the intended boundary. This determination was supported by substantial evidence and so we will not overturn it on appeal.

Thus, the centerline of Rocky Creek is the boundary between the parties' lands, since where a stream is a boundary, the division follows the thread of this non-navigable waterway.

### NOTE

Sometimes new land is gradually added to land bordering water by the processes of *accretion* or *reliction*. Accretion occurs when the water gradually deposits new soil to such riparian land. Accretion cannot be observed at any one instant, but becomes perceptible over a period of time. Reliction occurs when the water gradually recedes so that previously submerged land becomes dry land. In both cases, the owner of the original dry land gains ownership of the new land as well. Similarly when land is eroded or becomes submerged by gradual changes (*deliction*), the owner loses part of what was formerly owned. In contrast, when a stream changes its bed suddenly (by *avulsion*), the original streambed remains the boundary. Why should ownership of land bordering water depend on the distinction between gradual and sudden changes in the streambed?

## Grand Lodge of Georgia v. City of Thomasville
Supreme Court of Georgia, 1970.
226 Ga. 4, 172 S.E.2d 612.

■ MOBLEY, PRESIDING JUSTICE.

In enumeration of error 2 the defendant (appellant) contends that the plaintiffs failed to show title in themselves, because the deed under which they claimed title was void for indefiniteness of description. The property is described in the deed as follows: "All that tract or parcel of land situate, lying and being in the 13th District of Thomas County, Georgia, and in land lot Number 196, beginning at the northwest corner of said lot and running south about eight (8) acres to a stake; thence running in an easterly course twenty (20) chains to a stake; thence north about six (6) acres to a stake at road; thence west five (5) chains down said road; thence north to north line of lot running east and west; thence west five (5) chains down said road; thence north to north line of lot running east and west; thence west to starting point, containing forty-three (43) acres, more or less. Also, part of lot Number 197 in said district and county, beginning at southwest corner of said lot at a stake, running north about nine (9) acres to a stake; thence east fifteen (15) chains; thence south to south line of said lot, running east and west; thence west to starting point, containing forty-two (42) acres, more or less; all of said tracts conveyed except a strip beginning at east side and north corner at a road in lot Number 196 and running west through said land and being twenty (20) feet wide, used as a road."

The description of the first tract begins at the northwest corner of Lot 196 and runs "about 8 acres to a stake." "About 8 acres" furnishes no measure for lineal measurement. The 8-acre tract might be in various shapes and forms-it could be 1680 feet to the stake, or it might be 210 feet, or some other distance. It furnishes no method of locating the stake. The next course is "20 chains to a stake." The indefiniteness of the prior course leaves no way to determine where the 20 chains' distance begins and ends. The next call is "thence north about 6 acres to a stake at road," neither of which is identified. With no beginning and ending points given, "about 6 acres" does not furnish a guide for measuring the distance. "Thence west 5 chains down said road", the next course, is worthless, as there is no point of beginning. The next course is "thence north to north line of lot running east and west." It does not identify the lot number. The other tract, in Lot 197, is equally indefinite as that in Lot 196.

Obviously it would be impossible to locate this land from this description. The deed is so indefinite that it affords no means of identifying the land; it is void, and is inoperative as a conveyance of title, or as color of title.

## NOTE

The metes and bounds description in the example on page 1018, is so grossly simplified as to be misleading. Rarely will you encounter a description in which the courses run due north, east, south and west. (Incidentally, in modern surveys "north" refers to astronomic north ("true north"), rather than magnetic north.) Most land descriptions describe directions in terms of deviations from north or south. Thus "north one degree east" (N 1° E) means that the course is one degree east of astronomic north. "North ninety degrees east" (N 90° E) is due east, as is "south ninety degrees east." Courses may be measured in degrees, (N 10° W), in degrees and minutes (N 10° 30' W), or degrees, minutes, and seconds (N 10° 30' 15"E—

North 10 degrees, 30 minutes, 15 seconds east, or in laymen's language, "10 degrees, 30 minutes, 15 seconds, to the east of true north"). As you may recall, a circle has 360 degrees, each degree has 60 minutes, and each minute is divided into 60 seconds.

Modern surveyors have global positioning satellites (GPSs) and electronic distance measuring instruments (EDMs) to make their surveys more accurate. Sometimes these more technologically advanced surveys reveal measurement errors in older surveys. Discrepancies between older and newer more accurate surveys can raise difficult questions concerning land ownership. The remainder of this Assignment discusses some common surveying issues that might be faced by an attorney.

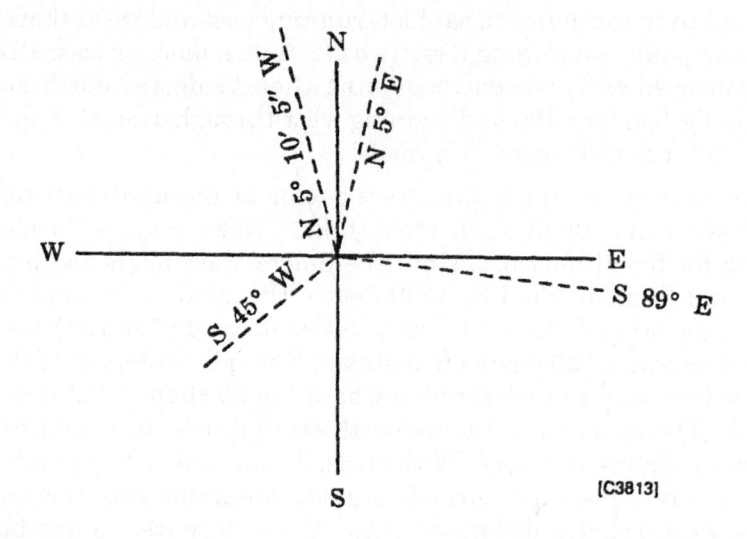

FIGURE 1.

Often a description, instead of describing a course in terms of the points of the compass, will refer to the angle between the old course and a new course. For example, "Go 300 feet to the north side of Oak St., thence at right angles to the previously described line, in an easterly direction 75 feet." When such a notation is utilized, it is essential that the original line, the angle formed by the new line, *and the direction of the new line be shown.*

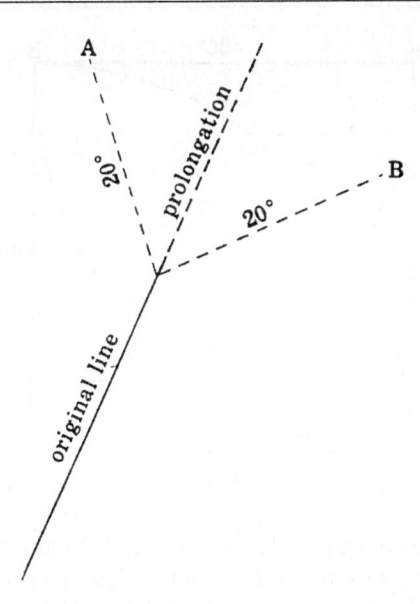

FIGURE 2. "... thence 20 degrees for a distance of 500 feet." The description does not make clear whether line A or B is on the new course.

The angle usually refers to that formed by the new course and the prolongation of the old line, rather than the original of the old line. Unfortunately, this is not always the case.

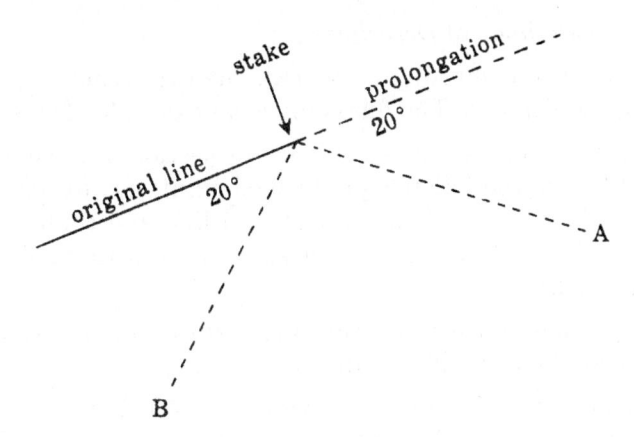

FIGURE 3. "... 50 feet to a stake, thence at an angle of 20° in a southerly direction...."

Ordinarily, line A rather than B is the intended new course. A better call would refer to "an angle of 20° to the right (or in a south-easterly direction) from the prolongation of the last course."

Similarly where curved lines are described, it is necessary to indicate the radius of the curve and the center of the circle from which the radius is to turn, or the direction of the curve ("convex to the southwest" or "concave to the north").

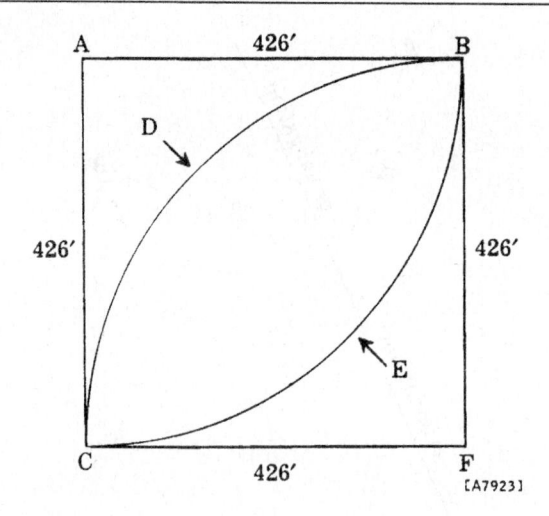

FIGURE 4. "From Point A, go 426 feet to point B, thence to the southwest along a curve with a 426 foot radius to point C, thence to the place of beginning." Is the curved side CDB or CEB? Based on Beams v. Werth, 200 Kan. 532, 438 P.2d 957 (1968).

Where there are several curved lines, or one curved line consisting of compound curves it is customary and advisable to retain a competent draftsman to draw a plat to scale and attach it to the deed. Both the plat and the deed should be recorded.

C. *Other Methods of Description*

Once a point of beginning is located, one can locate any other point by the use of coordinates. The following is an example of this:

> Beginning at the Southwest corner of section 15, thence in a straight line to the following described point: a point located by going north 300 feet along said section line and then due east 200 feet. Thence from the aforedescribed point to a point to be located as follows:. . . .

Sometimes, particularly when describing roads or other easements, strip conveyances will be used. For example,

> A strip of land of a uniform width of 150 feet the eastern boundary of which will coincide with the western boundary of tract X and the western boundary of which shall be parallel to the previous boundary and 150 feet to the west thereof.

---

Suppose you become embroiled in a controversy over an ambiguous or otherwise incompetent description of real property. The courts have evolved a number of maxims to reconcile inconsistent, conflicting, erroneous, or ambiguous calls. Most of the maxims represent attempts to ascertain the probable intent of the parties. It is accurate but not very helpful to say that the court looks to all of the circumstances and then intuits the probable intent of the parties, taking into account the size, shape, and nature of the land; the nature of the drafting error; and many other circumstances. On a slightly lower level of abstraction, one might say that the court is likely to give greater weight to those calls that the parties were most likely to have measured accurately. For example, a city lot is fifty feet wide and one hundred ten feet deep. Starting at an accurate point of beginning, the deed describes a lot fifty feet wide and one hundred feet deep. The ten-foot strip apparently retained by the grantor is completely useless. There would be an excellent chance that the deed would be reformed despite the absence of any ambiguity or patent error on the face of the deed. This follows from the inherent unlikelihood that the grantor intended to retain a useless ten-foot strip. If, however, the grantor owned a parcel adjoining the lot in the rear, the ten-foot strip is no longer useless and the deed might not be reformed. Alternately, in the previous example if a stone wall marked the true rear property line (i.e., 110 feet from the front) and the description said "100 feet to the stone wall" then the stone wall would control over the 100 feet from the front property line, and the court would probably decide in favor of the grantee.

Other factors that play an important role in the resolution of boundary disputes are the doctrines of adverse possession and the establishment of boundary rights by acquiescence or agreement. A separate but related doctrine is the doctrine of "seniority," or "priority." "First deed, last will," is an oft-quoted maxim. This means that a grantor's first deed controls any later deed where there is a conflict, and a later will controls an earlier will. Suppose a parcel of land is 195 feet wide. The grantor believes that it is 200 feet wide. He grants "the Westerly 100 feet to A." A few weeks later, he grants the "Easterly 100 feet to B." A gets 100 feet and B gets 95 feet. One feels reasonably sure that if the grantor had known the true state of affairs he would have granted 97.5 feet to A, and the same to B. A would probably prevail in a controversy between A and B because he had seniority—i.e., after the grantor granted the disputed strip to A, the grantor no longer owned it and hence could not grant it to B. If the grant to the two parties were substantially simultaneous, neither could be considered "senior" and probably the five foot "lappage" would be divided equally. The grantor in this example purported to convey what he did not own. If he used the usual form of deed (not a quit-claim deed) he would be liable to B for damages. If you had been the grantor's attorney, how would you have protected him?

*Common Difficulties in Descriptions.* Many errors are mere copying errors. "North 75 degrees east" may become "north 57 degrees east." The courts will usually find a way to rectify such errors when they clearly appear to be errors, such as when the written description will not completely enclose an area. Similarly, in a complex description, the copyist may simply skip a line or a call. A few minutes of careful proofreading will save weeks of frustration in trying to correct such an error.

A conveyance including a phrase like "the east 50 feet" is likely to be ambiguous.

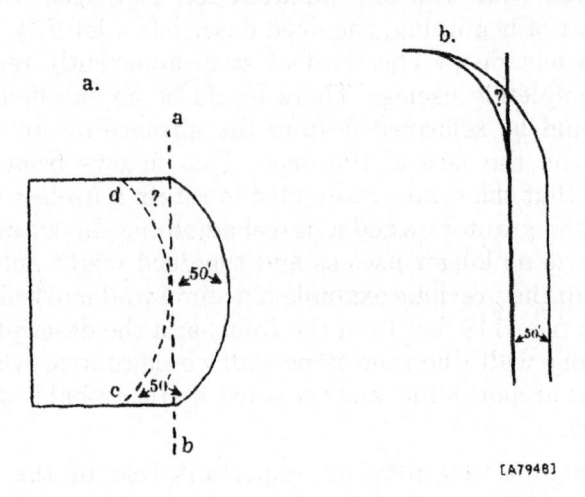

FIGURE 5. "The east 50 feet" of a parcel whose eastern border is a curved line is ambiguous.

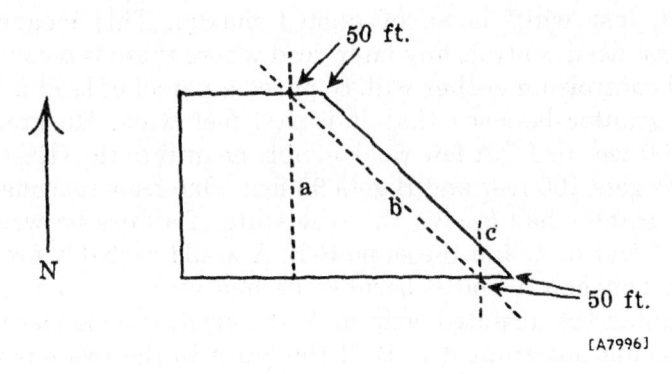

FIGURE 6. "The east fifty feet" when the eastern border is a straight line may be ambiguous.

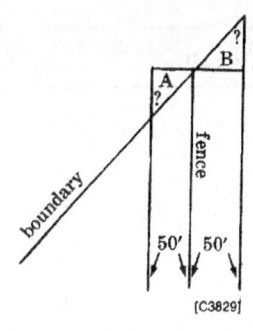

FIGURE 7. "A strip of land 50° wide on each side of the fence," will be ambiguous if the boundary is not at right angles to the fence. Are parcels A and B included?

A description such as "the east ½" or the "south 40 acres" is defective, sometimes fatally so.

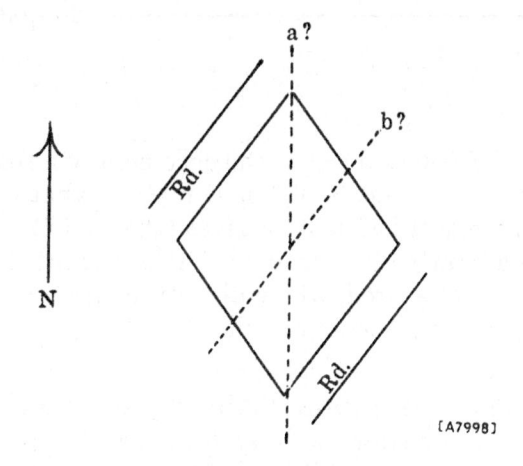

FIGURE 8. Ordinarily line b would divide the east ½ from the west ½ since a rectangular shape is preferred over a triangular one.

Where part of a parcel lies in a street it is often unclear whether the measurements are to be made from the center of the street where the true property line is, or from the side of the road where the apparent property line is.

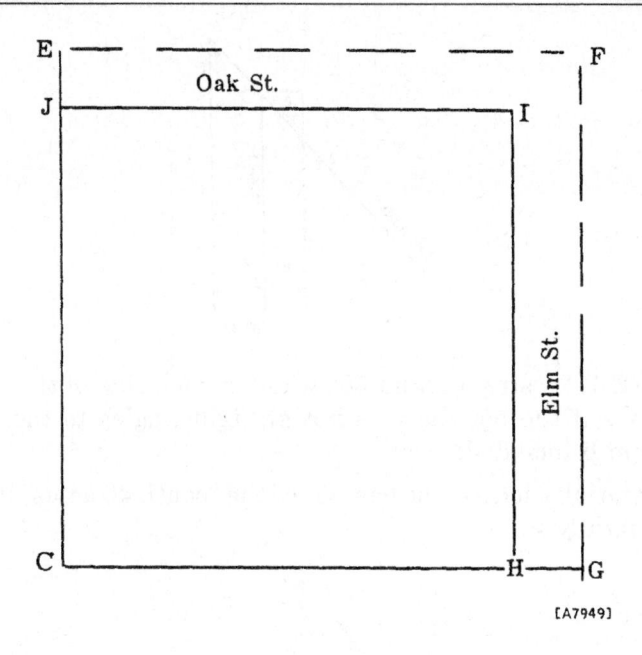

FIGURE 9.

Smith owns E F G C, subject to the easement of a road J I H G F E. If he gives to Jones the east ½ of "lot E F G C" what does he convey? Should a different result follow if he gives "the east ½ of my lot on the corner of Oak and Elm"? If we assume that he meant ½ of lot J I H C, and Elm is thereafter vacated, who will get the vacated land? Normally the abutting owner (Jones) will prevail.

## Ramsey v. Arizona Title Ins. & Trust Co.

Court of Appeals of Arizona, 1969.
10 Ariz.App. 538.

■ CAMERON, JUDGE.

This is an appeal from a summary judgment entered by the Superior Court of Maricopa County against plaintiffs-appellants, John and Frances Ramsey. We are called upon to determine whether as a matter of law the descriptions of certain real property contained in a deed and in some escrow instructions describe the same property.

The facts are not in dispute and are as follows. Prior to 21 February 1967 the appellants owned real property in Maricopa County, Arizona. Appellants had listed the property for sale with the appellee, Zee Realty and Trust Company. The property description as contained in the listing for sale read as follows:

> That part of Section 32, township 1 north range 3 east, that part of the Northwest quarter of the Northeast quarter beginning at a point on quarter section line which bears South 0 degrees 6 minutes East 659.10 feet from North quarter corner of said

section; thence South 89 degrees 56 minutes east 406.5 feet parallel to the North line of the North west quarter of the Northeast quarter; thence South 0 degrees 6 minutes East 94.65 feet parallel to the West line of the Northwest quarter of the Northeast quarter to a point being 10 feet from the edge of the San Francisco Canal; thence South 75 degrees 13 minutes West 420.22 feet parallel to and 10 feet North of the North edge of said canal to the West line of the Northwest quarter of the Northeast quarter; thence North 0 degrees 6 minutes West 202.35 feet along said west line of said Northwest quarter of the Northeast quarter to the place of beginning, except Road.

Evidently a sale was negotiated for part of the above described property and appellee, Zee Realty and Trust Company, opened an escrow with the appellee, Arizona Title Insurance and Trust Company. The escrow instructions signed by the owners contained the following description:

The property herein referred to is situated in Maricopa County, Arizona, and is described as follows, to-wit: That part of Section 32, T1N, R3E of the following described property: The West 160 feet of That part of Section 32, T1N, R3E *of the following described property:*

> That part of Northwest quarter of NE ¼ beginning at a point on quarter section line which bears South 0 degrees 6 minutes East 659.10 feet from North quarter corner of said section; thence South 89 degrees 56° East 406.50 feet parallel (sic) to the North line of the Northwest quarter of the Northeast quarter thence South 0 degrees 6° East 94.65 feet parrallel (sic) to the West line of the NW ¼ of NE ¼ to a point being 10 feet from the edge of the San Francisco Canal thence South 75 degrees 13° West 420.22 feet parrallel (sic) to and 10 feet North of the North edge of said canal to the West line of the NW ¼ of the NE ¼ to the point of beginning EXCEPT ROAD. (emphasis ours)

A deed was drafted by Arizona Title Insurance and Trust Company containing the following description of the property to be conveyed:

The West 160 feet of the following described property as measured at right angles from the Easterly right of way line of Central Avenue:

That part of the Northwest quarter of the Northeast quarter of Section Thirty-two (32), Township One (1), North, Range Three (3) East of the Gila and Salt River Base and Meridian, Maricopa County, Arizona, *described as follows:*

BEGINNING at a point on the quarter Section line, which bears South 0 degrees 06 minutes East 659.10 feet from the North quarter corner of said Section; thence South 89 degrees 56 minutes East 406.50 feet, parallel to the North line of said Northwest quarter of the Northeast quarter; thence South 0 degrees 06 minutes East 94.65 feet, more or less, parallel to the West line of said Northwest quarter of the Northeast quarter, to a point being 10 feet from the edge of San Francisco Canal; thence South 75 degrees 13 minutes West 420.22 feet, more or less parallel to and 10 feet North of the North edge of said San Francisco Canal, to the West line of said Northwest quarter of the Northeast quarter; thence North 0 degrees 06 minutes West 202.35 feet, more or less, along said West line of said Northwest quarter of the Northeast quarter, to the place of beginning; *EXCEPT any portion thereof lying within Central Avenue.* (emphasis ours)

It is agreed that the property described in the listing and in the portions indented above of the escrow instructions and the deed describe the same property, that is, the whole parcel from which the west 160 feet was to be carved.

In LeBaron v. Crismon, 100 Ariz. 206, 412 P.2d 705 (1966), it was said:

> [A]n interpretation of the instruments is a question of law to be determined by this court independent of the trial court's findings. Daily Mines Co. v. Control Mines, Inc., 59 Ariz. 138, 124 P.2d 324. 100 Ariz. at 208, 412 P.2d at 706.

And:

> [T]he description in a deed of the property conveyed thereby is considered ambiguous and subject to construction only if it is not possible to relate the description to the land without inconsistency.... McNeil v. Attaway, 87 Ariz. 103, 109, 348 P.2d 301, 305 (1959).

Although the grantor must be careful to convey only the property that he actually owns, descriptions of property may at the outset encompass other property for the purpose of accuracy in fixing the location of the property to be conveyed. In the instant case the center of Central Avenue being on the quarter section line, it was much easier to describe the property from the center of Central Avenue and then except Central Avenue from the property to be conveyed. The property could well have been described either as "the West 160 feet of the following described whole parcel except the road", or "the west 160 feet of the property actually owned and possessed by grantor which said property is described as follows".

In the instant case the description in the escrow instructions states that appellants conveyed the "West 160 feet ... of the *following described property*: ...." (emphasis ours). The "following described property" is the parcel actually owned by the plaintiffs described from the center of Central Avenue and then excepting Central Avenue from the property.

An exception operates on a description of the property and withdraws from the description the excepted property. Moore v. Davis, 273 Ky. 838, 117 S.W.2d 1033 (1938). Excepting Central Avenue from the property described in the escrow instruction, the west 160 feet of the property measured back from the east side of Central Avenue is the property to be conveyed.

The description in the deed, we believe, conveys the same property as described in the escrow instructions. The one additional phrase "as measured at right angles from the Easterly right of way line of Central Avenue" did not add anything except sow the seed of litigation to the property intended to be conveyed. Even though the phrase "as measured at right angles from the Easterly right of way line of Central Avenue" is first, the "following described property:" is the same original parcel of land with the same exception at the end of the description. The trial court took the position that the property described in the escrow instructions and the deed was the same. We agree.

Judgment affirmed.

#### NOTE

Compare the description in the escrow instructions with that in the deed. Can you find the call missing in the escrow instructions? This omission apparently was not deemed material to the litigation and, therefore, was not discussed. The omission illustrates how easy it is to miss a description error.

### 3. REVIEW PROBLEM

At the beginning of this Assignment, we asked a question: If Smith wants to give property to Jones, what method should he use to describe the land? You now should have enough basic knowledge to write a simple description. If Smith came to you with a rough sketch (not to scale) like that in Figure 10, below, how would you describe the land in your deed? What, if any, additional information would you need? If you decided to employ a surveyor, what information would you want the surveyor to provide?

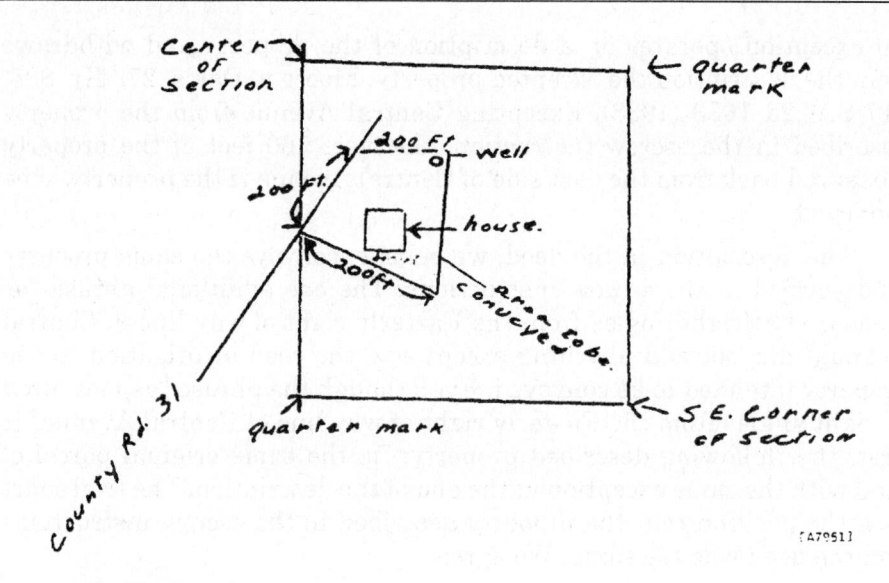

FIGURE 10.

# ASSIGNMENT 42

# DEED MUST BE DELIVERED

## 1. INTRODUCTION

According to folklore, a deed must be "signed, sealed and delivered" to be effective. Few if any states require a seal, and the deed is normally signed only by the grantor. This chapter explores the meaning of "delivery."

Legal "delivery" is a term of art, not always corresponding to the word's generic meaning. The delivery of a deed is the act by which the grantor demonstrates that the deed is to be presently operative. Typically, this is the act of manually handing over the signed deed to the grantee. Thousands of real estate transfers occur in this fashion and result in the irrevocable transfer of title.

EXAMPLE 1 (Deed delivered): Arthur decides to give Merrywood to Brice. The deed is properly drafted and signed. Arthur manually delivers the deed to Brice. Thereafter, Arthur learns some highly unfavorable things about Brice. Arthur demands an immediate return of the deed. When Brice refuses, Arthur sues for a declaration that he owns Merrywood. Arthur loses. The gift was complete on delivery. Arthur no longer has any rights to Merrywood.

Frequently, the absence of manual delivery means that there has been no legal delivery.

EXAMPLE 2 (No delivery): Claire decides to give Merrywood to David. The deed is properly drafted and signed. Before delivering the deed, Claire learns something unfavorable about David. Claire tears up the deed. David has no interest in Merrywood.

Manual delivery of an object does not necessarily mean that there has been legal delivery.

EXAMPLE 3 (Manual delivery without legal delivery): Ethan delivers his suit to Fran, a dry cleaner, to be cleaned. Ethan, not Fran, continues to own the suit. There was no intent to transfer ownership.

Conversely, there can be legal delivery without manual delivery.

EXAMPLE 4 (Legal delivery without manual delivery): George decides to make a gift of Blackacre to Harriet. George signs a properly drafted deed and records it, receiving back the original. Thereafter, George tells Harriet about the gift. Harriet takes possession of Blackacre. Harriet owns Blackacre although Harriet has never had possession of the deed. The act of recording the deed constituted delivery because it evidenced George's intent to part irrevocably with ownership.

The Restatement has gone so far as to suggest that there is delivery whenever the "donor manifests that the document is to be legally operative [immediately]."[1] Similarly, the Uniform Simplification of Land Transfers Act, § 1–201(3) defines delivery as "an act manifesting an intent to make a present transfer of real estate."

Many sales of real estate involve the use of escrow agents. Typically, an escrow agent is paid to receive the deed from the seller and deliver it to the buyer. The deed is delivered when the buyer pays the purchase price and otherwise fulfills the conditions specified in the escrow arrangement. Similarly, the buyer instructs the escrow agent to pay the money over to the seller when the seller delivers good title to the buyer and otherwise performs her obligations under the escrow agreement. Under most escrow agreements, delivery of the deed to the escrow agent constitutes delivery to the buyer for many purposes.

EXAMPLE 5 (Delivery under escrow agreement): Sarah Seller, delivers a deed to the escrow agent under a typical commercial escrow arrangement. Thereafter, Sarah dies before the escrow is completed. If Beatrice Buyer performs her part of the escrow agreement, the agent must deliver the deed to Beatrice, and Beatrice will own the property. The delivery to Beatrice "relates back" to the delivery to the escrow agent.

Most disputes concerning delivery fall into one of the following three fact patterns: (1) only the grantor and the grantee are involved in the claimed delivery (there is no third party or escrow agent who held the deed); (2) an attempt is made to have a third party hold the deed until the grantor dies, and then deliver it to the grantee (the so-called "death escrow"); (3) a commercial escrow is used in connection with the sale of real estate. Principal Problem A involves the first fact pattern, and Principal Problem B involves the second.

## 2. Principal Problem A: Delivery Without Escrow

Harry, the owner of Merrywood, executes an otherwise valid deed conveying Merrywood to his sister, Sally, and places it in his vault for safekeeping. Harry and Sally both live on Merrywood, which consists of twenty acres of undeveloped woodland and a rambling old farmhouse. Harry tells Sally about the deed, and also tells her that she is now the owner of Merrywood. Sally thanks Harry and agrees that it is a good idea to keep the deed in the vault where it will be safe. Sally does not have access to the vault and has never seen the deed. Thereafter, Harry destroys the deed and makes a gift of a new deed in favor of his friend Gloria. He manually delivers the new deed to Gloria. Assume that a validly delivered but unrecorded deed is good as between Harry, Sally

---

[1] Restatement (Second) of Property: Donative Transfers § 32.1 (1992).

and Gloria. Sally sues Harry and Gloria to quiet title in herself. Who wins?

## 3. MATERIALS FOR SOLUTION OF PRINCIPAL PROBLEM A

### Williams v. Cole
Missouri Court of Appeals, 1988.
760 S.W.2d 944.

■ PER CURIAM:

This is an action to set aside a deed on the ground that it was never delivered to the grantee. The realty involved is a 1-acre tract located in the city of Norwood, in Wright County, Missouri. There is a house on the premises. The property was owned by Johnnie Wesley Clemons when he died intestate on August 28, 1986. Plaintiff Lula Williams is Johnnie's sister; she is also the personal representative of his estate, which, at the time of trial, was being administered in the Probate Division of the Circuit Court of Wright County. Plaintiffs Earl West, Eula May Byerley and Donna Fay Lofton are the children of Johnnie's sister Mattie, who is deceased. Defendant Terry Cole is a nephew of Beulah Clemons, Johnnie's wife. Beulah died in May 1983.

Johnnie was in good health until he was hospitalized 3 weeks before his death. He managed his own financial affairs, drove his own car and maintained his house and the premises on which it was situated. Plaintiffs concede in their brief that Johnnie was mentally competent when the deed in litigation was executed. There is no claim that the execution of the deed was procured by undue influence.

The deed was uncovered by plaintiff Lula Williams when she went to Johnnie's house "[a]bout a week and a half" after Johnnie died. Johnny Cramer, who is another of Beulah's nephews, was present in the house with his wife Eleanor when Lula arrived. The purpose of the collective exploration of Johnnie's house was "[t]o get that little box." Lula did not know where the box was, but Cramer and his wife did. A box was found in Johnnie's "spare" bedroom. The box was opened and the deed in suit was discovered. The defendant was advised that Lula and Mr. and Mrs. Cramer were going to Johnnie's house, but he declined to accompany them. The deed was thereafter delivered to the defendant and he had it recorded.

The execution of the deed was undoubtedly part of a testamentary plan Johnnie and his wife had developed. Lula's testimony was that Johnnie had telephoned her " . . . probably close to a year before he died and said that he was fixing up a paper—the papers for my youngest son, Don, and Terry [the defendant] to have the place, and that they were to take it and sell it and pay all of his debts and his funeral, and then divide the remainder."

The defendant's recollection of Johnnie's plans was more elaborate. The defendant's wife and Johnnie's wife died about the same time. The defendant testified that some time before his wife died, Johnnie and Beulah had indicated "what they intended to have done with their property." Initially Johnnie and Beulah, or Johnnie, after Beulah's death, indicated that the proceeds from an insurance policy and the sale of household goods should be applied to debts and funeral expenses and any remaining assets should be divided in equal shares between the defendant, defendant's brother and Johnny Cramer, who as we have said was another of Johnnie and Beulah's nephews. Some time later, according to the defendant, Johnnie decided " . . . that it might be less complicated just to have me on there and let me take care of it because he trusted me, and he said I would do it right." When this testimony is read in context, it is clear that the defendant meant Johnnie considered it to be less complicated to deed the property to the defendant alone, and to allow the defendant to dispose of his (Johnnie's) property, because Johnnie trusted the defendant to attend to business fairly and honestly.

The plaintiffs first contend that the undisputed evidence that the deed was unrecorded and in the grantor's possession at the time of his death raised a presumption of non-delivery and shifted the burden of persuasion to the defendant. Defendant's evidence that: 1) the grantor had on several occasions offered to give the deed to the defendant for recording, and 2) the grantor told third parties he had the papers made up and that the place was defendant's, and 3) the grantor told the defendant where he was keeping the deed and that it needed to be recorded, plaintiffs argue, did not constitute substantial evidence sufficient to rebut the presumption of non-delivery, in light of undisputed evidence that: 1) the grantor never physically delivered or showed the deed to the defendant or any other third party during his lifetime; 2) the grantor retained the right to recall the deed by keeping it in his bedroom until the time of his death; 3) the grantor exercised all incidents of ownership over the property until his death while the grantee exercised no incidents of ownership, and 4) the deed reserved no life estate in the grantor.

The plaintiffs also contend that the deed was never accepted by the defendant, but we find it unnecessary to rule on this assignment of error.

The plaintiffs cite *Shroyer v. Shroyer*, 425 S.W.2d 214 (Mo.1968) and *Meadows v. Brich*, 606 S.W.2d 258 (Mo.App.1980) as controlling in this case, and we agree that those cases state the applicable principles of law. The only question in this case is whether there was a delivery of the deed. As stated in *Shroyer*, 425 S.W.2d at 219–20:

> The vital inquiry with respect to the grantor is whether [he] intended a complete transfer; whether [he] parted with dominion over the instrument with the intention of relinquishing all dominion and control over the conveyance and of making it presently effective and operative as a conveyance

of the title to the land. (citations omitted) It is not necessary, in order to constitute a delivery of a deed, that the instrument actually be handed over to the grantee, or to another person for the grantee. There may be a delivery notwithstanding the deed remains in the custody of the grantor. (citations omitted) A valid delivery once having taken place is not rendered ineffectual by the act of the grantee in giving the deed into the custody of the grantor for safekeeping (citations omitted)....

The court then noted that the evidence indicated the grantor had handed the deed in question to one of the grantees momentarily, for the purpose of reading it, and that at the grantor's direction it was immediately taken back into the grantor's possession, to be kept by her until her death. The court then stated:

> [In this case] [t]here is a presumption of nondelivery, in view of the conceded fact that the deed was in grantor's possession at the time of her death and that the deed was not then recorded. "By the introduction of testimony substantially tending to show that the deed was in the grantor's possession, in his safety deposit box, at the time of his death, the plaintiffs made a prima facie case; for, if unrecorded and in the grantor's possession, the nondelivery of the deed is presumed." (citations omitted) This showing placed upon the grantees ... the burden of going forward with the evidence to rebut plaintiff's prima facie case....

*Shroyer*, 425 S.W.2d at 220–21.

What evidence, then, did the defendant have to rebut the presumption of nondelivery? The defendant testified:

Q. After your—After both of your wives had died, Terry, did [Johnnie] ever again talk to you or mention to you the disposition of his property?

A. Yes.

Q. Can you tell me what he said?

A. Well, at first he talked about—He needed—He'd ask—He said, 'Well, we need to go over to Hartville and get the papers made up.' And he would sit and talk, said, 'Oh, we need to get that done.' ... So I was through there—I can't remember the exact date, but it was in January, February—the winter of '84, I believe. He was talking about he'd been to Hartville and he'd had some papers ... —some other things he had to take care of. And he said, 'I've got the deed and things taken care of.' ... He said, '*You need to get it recorded.*'

...

Q. Okay. Once he told you he had made the deed or had already done it on his own, what did he say then?

A. He said, 'Sometimes . . . ' He said, 'You need . . . ' *'I'll give it to you, and you can get it recorded.'* And I said, *'Well, you keep it for me.'* I said, 'I . . . ' . . . I had a lot of other things going on at that time, and I said, 'I know where it is. You just keep it here at the house.' And he said, 'It's in here.' And at that point, he brought out an insurance policy for $1,000, and he said, 'Now, I've had this made [to] you as a beneficiary on this insurance policy.' I said, 'That's fine.' I said, 'You keep it, and that way I'll know where it is.' And I said—And he said, 'Well, it'll be in the front bedroom.' And I said, 'That's fine.' I said, 'At least we know where it is, and it's in safe keeping.'

Q. Okay. Terry, did he try then, on that day, to give you both the deed and the insurance policy?

A. He wanted me to take them. *I never would take them because of the fact that I would—I didn't want to hurt anybody's feelings. I didn't want Gary and Johnny[2] to think that I was jumping in,* you know, just—And I said, 'Let's let you keep it, and then that way. . . . '

. . .

Q. Did he, on more than one occasion, Terry, try to get you to take the deed and the papers with you?

A. Yes, he did.

Q. And did you always refuse those offers to him for the reasons that you've already told the Court?

A. True. (Emphasis added.)

. . .

The defendant admitted that he had never seen the deed before he "picked it up" after Johnnie's death; he never saw the metal box in which Johnnie kept his valuable papers. The most that can be said in this case is that Johnnie told the defendant that he, Johnnie, had executed a deed conveying the 1-acre lot to the defendant. Among the circumstances which militate against a delivery are that the grantor never showed the deed to the grantee; the grantee was not even given that glimpse of the deed which the grantees received in *Shroyer* and in *Meadows*. The grantor retained possession of the deed, without recording it, until his death. He did not place the deed in the custody of a third person, with directions to deliver it to the grantee. There are other circumstances which might be recited, but in our view the evidence is simply insufficient to rebut the presumption of nondelivery. Accordingly, the judgment is

---

[2] Gary Cole and Johnny Cramer were also Johnnie Clemons' nephews.

reversed and the cause is remanded with directions to set aside the deed described in plaintiffs' petition.

## Kresser v. Peterson
Supreme Court of Utah, 1984.
675 P.2d 1193.

■ PER CURIAM:

Plaintiffs asserted a one-half interest in a home under the terms of a will. The suit was dismissed upon a showing that a subsequent warranty deed executed by the testatrix took the property out of her estate. The only issue urged on appeal is that there was no valid delivery of the deed.

Facts were stipulated showing that Edward Kresser, Sr. had two sons, the plaintiffs, when he married Della Pyper, who also had two sons, the defendants. The couple owned a home jointly, with right of survivorship. When Edward Sr. died, Della executed a will which devised the property to the four boys. Seven years later, she executed a warranty deed naming herself and her two sons as grantees, with right of survivorship. She recorded the deed and placed it in a safety deposit box with a local bank under a lease agreement. The agreement was signed by her and her two sons as joint tenants. "Exclusive access" to the box was reserved to the joint tenants, without specifying any single one as the only one having such access.

Defendants did not know that their mother had put the deed in the safety deposit box. Nor did they ever have a key to the box, even though the lease permitted their having access. It is conceded by the plaintiffs that no fraud or undue influence was evident, or that Della was incompetent. The only issue involved is whether an effective delivery of the deed was maintained under the authorities.

An effective deed requires delivery, actual or constructive, without exclusive control or recall. Recording generally presumes delivery. Delivery to one cotenant or reservation of an estate connotes delivery to all cotenants, where the grantor is also the grantee.

With all the recognized indicia of an effective delivery in this case, perhaps the most significant is the statement of Della at the time she signed the deed. Before a notary public, Della's sister and a daughter-in-law, she made it a point to state that she intended her sons to have the property. She emphasized such intention by adding that she did not intend the stepsons to have any interest in the property. Delivery was reflected by recordation of the deed and deposit by Della in the safety deposit box with written authority that any of the grantees, who also were tenants under the box rental agreement, had exclusive right of access to the box. We are satisfied there was no error in the lower court finding a valid delivery of the deed.

Affirmed. Costs to defendants.

## Lenhart v. Desmond
Supreme Court of Wyoming, 1985.
705 P.2d 338.

■ CARDINE, JUSTICE.

This is an appeal from a judgment in favor of Edward v. Desmond in which the district court declared a deed recorded by Desmond's daughter, Elizabeth A. Lenhart, invalid and restored real property to him.

We affirm.

Appellant states her issues on appeal as:

First, given the burden of proof in cases challenging the delivery of a deed where the grantee is in possession of the deed was there enough evidence in the District Court to support the Judgment entered in favor of the Plaintiff/Appellee Edward V. Desmond?

Second, even assuming that there was enough evidence to support the trial court's result, was there either an actual or constructive delivery of the deed from the Plaintiff/Appellee Edward V. Desmond to the Defendant/Appellant Elizabeth A. Lenhart under the law dealing with delivery of deeds so that the trial court's result is contrary to law?

### Facts

In 1974 Mr. Desmond executed a warranty deed to his daughter and only child, Elizabeth A. Lenhart. This was done because Mr. Desmond was then in his 80's and he thought that he had "better make arrangements, that in case of my death, why, Elizabeth can have all of my earthly possessions." Mr. Desmond executed the deed and placed it in his safety deposit box. Then he informed Mrs. Lenhart of his intentions of her getting the house when he passed on. To facilitate this he gave her access to the box through a signature card. Further, at the time of signing of this card, Lenhart became explicitly aware of the deed in the box. Subsequently, Desmond was injured in an automobile accident in July of 1983 and hospitalized. Lenhart returned to Cheyenne to help her father which required her to retrieve some insurance policies from the safety deposit box. After his release from the hospital, Desmond checked his box and found the deed was missing, although it had been there before the accident. The facts of exactly who removed the deed are in dispute. Mrs. Lenhart, however, recorded the deed in October of 1983.

The complaint in this action, asking that the deed recorded by appellant be declared invalid, was filed on May 22, 1984, by Edward Desmond. Mrs. Lenhart counterclaimed asking that the deed be held valid as a gift of the property. The trial court without a jury found generally in favor of Mr. Desmond entering a judgment invalidating the deed to appellant and dismissing her counterclaim.

## Sufficiency of the Evidence

It is well established that this court on appeal must accept the evidence of the successful party as true, leave out of consideration entirely the evidence of the unsuccessful party in conflict therewith, and give to the evidence of the successful party every favorable inference that may fairly and reasonably be drawn from it.... It is also firmly established that the trial judge is in the best position to weigh and judge credibility of witnesses and to weigh the evidence....

Further, the findings of the trial judge must be sustained unless they are clearly erroneous or contrary to the great weight of the evidence....

In the case at bar there was a direct conflict in the testimony concerning the delivery of the deed and whether Edward Desmond intended that the property should pass to Lenhart immediately or upon his death. Mrs. Lenhart claimed that her father physically handed her the deed saying, "I went down and got the deed for you." Mr. Desmond testified that he did not give the deed to his daughter nor did he intend for her to have the property before his death. Mr. Desmond was the successful party and his testimony must be taken as true.

Appellant argues, nevertheless, that the decision below must be reversed because the great weight of evidence is against appellee's position. Further, appellant claims that possession and recordation of the deed make out a prima facie case of delivery and that appellee must then establish nondelivery by clear and convincing evidence, rather than by a preponderance of the evidence. The appellant claims that the trial court used an inappropriate standard to judge the evidence when, in its decision letter, the court, recognizing a presumption of delivery from the fact of possession and recording of the deed, stated:

> "This presumption may be rebutted by credible evidence going to the intent of the grantor.
>
> ...
>
> "For the reasons cited herein, the Court is of the opinion that there was no delivery of the deed and the Plaintiff has proved by a *preponderance of the evidence* that he is entitled to judgment against the Defendant and is entitled to the return to him of the subject property." (Emphasis added.)

We said in *Forbes v. Volk*, Wyo., 358 P.2d 942, 945 (1961):

> The question then remains as to whether or not the deed was delivered. It came into possession of the grantee and it was recorded. These facts raise a presumption that it was delivered.

26A C.J.S. Deeds § 184(b), cited in *Forbes v. Volk*, supra, in support of its holding, states further:

> The presumption of due delivery arising from possession by the grantee is disputable and not conclusive, and the evidence sufficient to rebut the presumption is noted in § 204 infra. (Footnote omitted.)

The presumption of delivery arising from possession and recording of a deed is not conclusive, but may be rebutted by showing there was no delivery in fact or that possession was gained without the knowledge or consent of the grantor, 23 Am.Jur.2d Deeds § 159. The proof necessary to rebut the presumption of delivery of the deed, as stated in 26A C.J.S.Deeds § 204, is

> at least as between the grantor and the grantee, should ordinarily be determined by a fair preponderance of the evidence. Clear proof is required, however, where a gift is claimed; and where the rights of third persons have intervened, the proof of nondelivery should be clear and positive.

Here the rights of third parties had not intervened. The trial judge undoubtedly viewed this contest as being between grantor and grantee, both living and presenting their case. The court in its decision letter found that "Plaintiff has proved by a preponderance of the evidence" that "there was no delivery of the deed." In support of this statement the court stated,

> Defendant testified that the Plaintiff had, of his own accord, gone to retrieve the deed from the safe deposit box on a Saturday and had given the same to her with instructions to record it. The Court is skeptical of this testimony when it is coupled with the fact that the Plaintiff has requested that Defendant deed the property back to him and she refuses to do so. Her reason for not deeding the property back to the Plaintiff was that he would mortgage the property and spend the money on strong drink.

In essence, the court rejected appellant's testimony leaving only that evidence of appellee which clearly shows nondelivery.

Reviewing the record, we find that Mr. Desmond's testimony that he never intended Mrs. Lenhart to have the property before his death and that she took and recorded the deed without his knowledge or consent, was sufficient, persuasive and clear to rebut the presumption of delivery. This is true especially when Mr. Desmond's unequivocal testimony is compared to Mrs. Lenhart's. We do not believe the trial court applied an incorrect burden of proof to the facts; but, were it so, it would not affect the result in this case for we view the evidence supporting the judgment as clear and sufficient and as we have said:

> Generally, if the trial court arrives at the correct result, no matter how incorrectly it reasons, errors occurring at the trial, if not prejudicial, are cured by a proper final decision. *Anderson v. Bauer,* supra at 1325.

### Constructive Delivery

To effect a conveyance transferring title, a deed must be both executed and delivered. *Hein v. Lee*, Wyo., 549 P.2d 286, 292 (1976). At the time of the delivery the grantor's intent is of primary and controlling importance. *Rosengrant v. Rosengrant*, Okl.App., 629 P.2d 800, 802 (1981). Further, the controlling issue in determining if delivery was effective is whether the grantor manifested an intention to presently divest himself of title. *Matter of Estate of Courtright v. Robertson*, 99 Idaho 575, 586 P.2d 265, 269 (1978); *Yunghans v. O'Toole*, 224 Kan. 553, 581 P.2d 393, 396 (1978). Not only is intent a controlling factor, it is also the crucial one when constructive delivery is claimed.

> The intention of the parties is an essential and controlling element of delivery of a deed. Intention has been called the 'essence of delivery,' and not only is it often the determining factor among other facts and circumstances, *but is the crucial test where constructive delivery is relied upon*. Categorically stated, the rule is that it is essential to the delivery of a deed that there be a giving of the deed by the grantor and a receiving of it by the grantee, with a mutual intention to pass the title from the one to the other. (Emphasis added.) 23 Am.Jur.2d Deeds § 123.

In the case at bar, appellant claims that delivery occurred when the deed was placed in the safety deposit box and Mr. Desmond provided Mrs. Lenhart access to it. Appellant fails to realize that these actions alone do not constitute delivery since they fail the crucial test. According to Mr. Desmond's testimony, he did not possess the present intent to divest himself irretrievably of his property. Rather, he intended that Mrs. Desmond have the property upon his death. He believed he had put his affairs in order.

Appellant points to a number of cases from other jurisdictions which she believes hold that these actions alone can constitute constructive delivery. The reliance on these cases is unfounded because they refer to similar action coupled with an uncontroverted intent or an intent to immediately pass title inferred from other evidence. In the case at bar, the intent was very much controverted. In fact, Mr. Desmond stated that he never manifested the intent necessary to pass the title of his property to his daughter while he was alive. Without the requisite intent there can be no delivery.

Thus, we hold that the evidence was sufficient to declare the deed invalid and the property was properly restored to Mr. Desmond.

Affirmed.

### NOTES

1. *Lack of manual delivery.* In *Williams*, the fact that the donee never saw the deed was an important factor suggesting that there was no delivery.

Similarly, in the Principal Problem, Sally never saw the deed. How would Sally attempt to distinguish *Williams*?

2. *Safe deposit boxes*. In *Kresser*, the Utah Supreme Court held that a valid delivery had been made when a grantor placed a signed deed in a safe deposit box to which the grantees had access, even though they had no keys to the box and did not know where the grantor had placed the deed. In *Desmond*, the Wyoming Supreme Court held that there was no delivery when the grantor placed a signed deed in a safe deposit box to which grantee had access. Can these cases be reconciled?

3. *Why is a deed not like a will?* Questions about deed delivery often arise in the context of an attempted testamentary disposition-a grantor wishes the deed to take effect only upon her death. As we have seen, such deeds are often found invalid because of a lack of present intent to convey title. Why do courts not treat these failed deeds as wills, and attempt to give effect to the grantor's intent? One problem with this approach is that certain formalities are necessary for the execution of wills (e.g., signing in front of witnesses), and unless they are complied with, the instrument would likely fail as a will as well. The unwary grantor thus has her intentions frustrated again. Can this be justified?

## 4. PRINCIPAL PROBLEM B: "DEATH ESCROWS"

Hal, the owner of Blackacre, a vacant parcel of land in Amador County, State X, handed his friend Joy a deed granting "all my land in Amador County, State X, to my nephew Mike." Hal orally instructed Joy not to give the deed to Mike unless Mike survived Hal. The deed was not recorded. Four years later, Hal died. Thereafter, Mike learned for the first time of Hal's deed to him. Mike consults you as to his rights and informs you that he has recorded his deed, which Joy delivered to him upon Hal's death, and that Hal owned no land in Amador County, except Blackacre. Advise Mike as to his rights in Blackacre.

## 5. MATERIALS FOR SOLUTION OF PRINCIPAL PROBLEM B

### Ignacio Vasquez v. Brigido Vasquez
Court of Appeals of Texas, 1998.
973 S.W.2d 330.

■ SEERDEN, CHIEF JUSTICE.

The issue in this case is whether the delivery of a signed deed to one's attorney with instructions to deliver said deed to the grantee upon the grantor's death constitutes adequate delivery, thus rendering the grantee the rightful owner of the subject property. The trial court found a valid delivery, and ruled that title to the subject property was quieted in appellee. Appellant, in nine points of error, challenges the trial court's ruling. We affirm.

The facts of this case are undisputed. On July 29, 1992, Juanita Vasquez Carr, the unquestioned owner of the property at issue, executed a will naming Ignacio Vasquez as her independent executor, and Ignacio and Jose Vasquez, appellants, sole beneficiaries. Thereafter, on February 6, 1993, Juanita Vasquez Carr executed a quitclaim deed granting the same property to Brigido D. Vasquez, appellee. Juanita left the quitclaim deed in the custody of her attorney with instructions not to file it and not to tell anybody about it, including appellee, until after her death. Juanita continued with the uninterrupted possession, use, and benefit of the subject property until her death on September 29, 1993.

Upon her death, Juanita's attorney, Michael George, mailed the quitclaim deed to the appropriate county clerk for filing. The deed was recorded on October 6, 1993, and soon thereafter, appellee was notified as to the existence of the deed.

On January 13, 1994, Juanita's last will and testament was filed and admitted to probate. On February 21, 1994, under the terms of the will, appellant Ignacio Vasquez, as the duly appointed and qualified independent executor of Juanita's estate, executed a special warranty deed conveying the property in question to appellants.

The question soon arose: who is the rightful owner of the property in question? The case was submitted to the trial court on stipulated facts as recited above. The trial court, after hearing the evidence and arguments of counsel, found that the deed from Juanita Vasquez Carr was delivered when it was tendered to Juanita's attorney, thus transferring the real property to appellee as of February 6, 1993. This finding was set out in the trial court's conclusions of law. Appellants bring this appeal.

In nine points of error, appellants argue that the judgment is contrary to the law because there was no effective delivery of the deed, and as such, the deed was ineffective to pass title to the property to appellee. Because all nine points raise essentially the same issue and are argued together by appellants, we too will address all points together.

While the question of whether there has in fact been a delivery is a question of fact, the question of what constitutes a delivery is a question of law. *Ragland v. Kelner*, 148 Tex. 132, 221 S.W.2d 357, 359 (1949). In this case, the facts regarding the delivery of the deed have been stipulated, and only the question of what legal effect is to be given those facts is before us. The trial court found, in its conclusions of law, that "[t]here was a valid delivery of same [the deed] to a third party, Michael D. George, her attorney, when Juanita Vasquez Moore Carr left instructions with Michael D. George to file said Quitclaim Deed and notify Brigido D. Vasquez after her death." We must uphold this conclusion on appeal if the judgment can be sustained on any legal theory supported by the evidence.

It is elementary that a deed must be delivered, as that term is legally interpreted, in order to be an effective transfer of the ownership of land.

In determining whether a deed has been effectively delivered when said deed is placed in the control of a third person, the question is whether the grantor parted with all dominion and control over the instrument at the time she delivered it to the third person with the intent that it take effect as a conveyance at the very time of delivery. Thus, the issue before us in this case is whether the evidence supports a finding that Juanita intended to relinquish all dominion and control over the quitclaim deed at the time she delivered it to her attorney.

It is undisputed that Juanita signed the quitclaim deed and gave the deed to her attorney with specific instructions. According to her attorney, those instructions were to keep the existence of the deed a secret, to keep it in his custody, and to file and deliver the deed to the named grantee after Juanita's death. There was no mention in those instructions of Juanita's power to recall the deed. In fact, when questioned by appellants' attorney as to whether Juanita instructed her attorney to "keep that until I die or until I give you instructions otherwise." Juanita's attorney responded, "Well, no. I keep the deed, and then I'm not to tell anybody or file it or do anything until after they've spewed her ashes."

Appellants, however, point to (1) the fact that Juanita retained possession and control of the subject property, and (2) the testimony of Juanita's attorney, as evidence that Grantor did not surrender complete control at time of delivery to attorney.

It is true that Juanita retained possession of the subject property until her death. However, possession is not determinative. Where the grantor delivers a deed to a third person with the intent to part with all control, the legal effect of the transaction is tantamount to a delivery of the deed to the grantee, conveying him the fee while reserving for the grantor the use and enjoyment of the land during his natural life. See *Ragland*, 221 S.W.2d at 360 (present transfer with right of possession, use, and enjoyment of the property remaining in grantor during her lifetime); *Stout*, 674 S.W.2d at 825 (valid delivery found despite evidence that grantor claimed ownership and occupied the property until her death).

Appellants further argue that Juanita, by delivering the deed to her attorney, retained the control and right of disposition of the quitclaim deed for the remainder of her life. In support of their argument, appellants point to the testimony of Michael George, Juanita's attorney. During trial, George was called as a witness by deposition. George, under examination by appellants' attorney, testified as follows:

Q: If two months after she signed that quitclaim deed she would have called you and said, "look, I need the quitclaim deed," what would you have done with it? Would you have given it to her?

A: I don't know. I mean, she was my client. I guess if I'm her
. . .

Q: That was going to be my next question here. The bottom line is you were her legal advisor?

A: That's correct.

Q: And you were going to do whatever...

A: The client tells me, within reason.

Q: Within reason, within the law?

A: Yes, sir.

Q: All right. And you were ready, willing, and able to carry out her wishes and desires, and as far as you did, you tried. Is that correct sir?

A: I did everything that she asked.

. . .

Q: Did she tell you, well, do not tell anybody. Tell my brother after I am dead, but keep the deed unless I ask for it? Did she say that?

A: She told me to take these documents back, that I was to keep them, not to tell anybody about it, and, you know, when she died I was to file it, tell her brother, and that was basically it. And I mean, you know, like you asked me earlier, I would have had to under the ethical rules given it back to her if she had asked for it.

It is clear from this testimony that Juanita retained the power to reclaim the deed. Such testimony, however, does not bear on Juanita's intent to relinquish control of the deed. *Muller v. Killam*, 229 S.W.2d 899 904 (Tex.Civ.App.) ('the fact that she had the power to recall the deed is of no consequence [to the issue of intent]').

The only evidence in the record bearing directly on Juanita's intent to deliver the deed in question shows that Juanita executed the deed, and handed it over to her attorney with specific instructions to deliver the deed to appellee on her death without reserving a right to recall the deed. When a grantor delivers a deed to a third person without a reservation of a right to recall it, and instructs the third person to deliver it to the grantee on the grantor's death, he thereby makes an effective delivery as a matter of law. *Ragland*, 221 S.W.2d at 360.

Accordingly, we agree with the trial court's conclusion that the deed was effectively delivered by Juanita when she tendered the deed to her attorney on February 6, 1993. Accordingly, we overrule all points of error and affirm the judgment of the trial court.

## Rosengrant v. Rosengrant
Court of Appeals of Oklahoma, 1981.
629 P.2d 800.

■ BOYDSTON, JUDGE.

This is an appeal by J.W. (Jay) Rosengrant from the trial court's decision to cancel and set aside a warranty deed which attempted to vest title in him to certain property owned by his aunt and uncle, Mildred and Harold Rosengrant. The trial court held the deed was invalid for want of legal delivery. We affirm that decision.

Harold and Mildred were a retired couple living on a farm southeast of Tecumseh, Oklahoma. They had no children of their own but had six nieces and nephews through Harold's deceased brother. One of these nephews was Jay Rosengrant. He and his wife lived a short distance from Harold and Mildred and helped the elderly couple from time to time with their chores. [The other five nieces and nephews were the appellants in this case.]

In 1971, it was discovered that Mildred had cancer. In July, 1972 Mildred and Harold went to Mexico to obtain laetrile treatments accompanied by Jay's wife. Jay remained behind to care for the farm.

Shortly before this trip, on June 23, 1972, Mildred had called Jay and asked him to meet her and Harold at Farmers and Merchants Bank in Tecumseh. Upon arriving at the bank, Harold introduced Jay to his banker J.E. Vanlandengham who presented Harold and Mildred with a deed to their farm which he had prepared according to their instructions. Both Harold and Mildred signed the deed and informed Jay that they were going to give him "the place," but that they wanted Jay to leave the deed at the bank with Mr. Vanlandengham and when "something happened" to them,[3] he was to take it to Shawnee and record it and "it" would be theirs. Harold personally handed the deed to Jay to "make this legal." Jay accepted the deed and then handed it back to the banker who told him he would put it in an envelope and keep it in the vault until he called for it.

In July, 1974, when Mildred's death was imminent, Jay and Harold conferred with an attorney concerning the legality of the transaction. The attorney advised them it should be sufficient but if Harold anticipated problems he should draw up a will. [Shortly thereafter, Mildred died.]

In 1976, Harold discovered he had lung cancer. In August and December 1977, Harold put $10,000 into two certificates of deposit in joint tenancy with Jay.

Harold died January 28, 1978. On February 2, Jay and his wife went to the bank to inventory the contents of the safety deposit box. They also

---

[3] Common euphemism meaning their deaths.

requested the envelope containing the deed which was retrieved from the collection file of the bank.

Jay went to Shawnee the next day and recorded the deed.

The petition to cancel and set aside the deed was filed February 22, 1978, alleging that the deed was void in that it was never legally delivered and alternatively that since it was to be operative only upon recordation after the death of the grantors it was a testamentary instrument and was void for failure to comply with the Statute of Wills.

The trial court found the deed was null and void for failure of legal delivery. The dispositive issue raised on appeal is whether the trial court erred in so ruling. We hold it did not and affirm the judgment.

The facts surrounding the transaction which took place at the bank were uncontroverted. It is the interpretation of the meaning and legal result of the transaction which is the issue to be determined by this court on appeal.

In cases involving attempted transfers such as this, it is the grantor's intent at the time the deed is delivered which is of primary and controlling importance. It is the function of this court to weigh the evidence presented at trial as to grantor's intent and unless the trial court's decision is clearly against the weight of the evidence, to uphold that finding.

The grantor and banker were both dead at the time of trial. Consequently, the only testimony regarding the transaction was supplied by the grantee, Jay. The pertinent part of his testimony is as follows:

A. [A]nd was going to hand it back to Mr. Vanlandingham [sic], and he wouldn't take it.

Q. What did Mr. Vanlandingham [sic] say?

A. Well, he laughed then and said that "We got to make this legal," or something like that. And said, "You'll have to give it to Jay and let Jay give it back to me."

Q. And what did Harold do with the document?

A. He gave it to me.

Q. Did you hold it?

A. Yes.

Q. Then what did you do with it?

A. Mr. Vanlandingham [sic], I believe, told me I ought to look at it.

Q. And you looked at it?

A. Yes.

Q. And then what did you do with it?

A. I handed it to Mr. Vanlandingham [sic].

Q. And what did he do with the document?

A. He had it in his hand, I believe, when we left.

Q. Do you recall seeing the envelope at any time during this transaction?

A. I never saw the envelope. But Mr. Vanlandingham [sic] told me when I handed it to him, said, "Jay, I'll put this in an envelope and keep it in a vault for you until you call for it."

. . .

A. Well, Harold told me while Mildred was signing the deed that they were going to deed me the farm, but they wanted me to leave the deed at the bank with Van, and that *when something happened to them* that I would go to the bank and pick it up and take it to Shawnee to the court house and record it, and *it would be mine.* (emphasis added)

When the deed was retrieved, it was contained in an envelope on which was typed: "J.W. Rosengrant or Harold H. Rosengrant."

The import of the writing on the envelope is clear. It creates an inescapable conclusion that the deed was, in fact, retrievable at any time by Harold before his death. The bank teller's testimony as to the custom and usage of the bank leaves no other conclusion but that at any time Harold was free to retrieve the deed. There was, if not an expressed, an implied agreement between the banker and Harold that the grant was not to take effect until two conditions occurred—the death of both grantors and the recordation of the deed.

In support of this conclusion conduct relative to the property is significant and was correctly considered by the court. Evidence was presented to show that after the deed was filed Harold continued to farm, use and control the property. Further, he continued to pay taxes on it until his death and claimed it as his homestead.

Grantee confuses the issues involved herein by relying upon grantors' goodwill toward him and his wife as if it were a controlling factor. From a fair review of the record it is apparent Jay and his wife were very attentive, kind and helpful to this elderly couple. The donative intent on the part of grantors is undeniable. We believe they fully intended to reward Jay and his wife for their kindness. Nevertheless, where a grantor delivers a deed under which he reserves a right of retrieval and attaches to that delivery the condition that the deed is to become operative only after the death of grantors and further continues to use the property as if no transfer had occurred, grantor's actions are nothing more than an attempt to employ the deed as if it were a will. Under Oklahoma law this cannot be done. The ritualistic "delivery of the deed" to the grantee and his redelivery of it to the third party for safe keeping created under these circumstances only a symbolic delivery. It amounted to a pro forma attempt to comply with the legal aspects of delivery. Based on all the facts and circumstances the true intent of the parties is expressed by the notation on the envelope and by the later conduct of the parties in relation to the land. Legal delivery is not just a symbolic gesture. It necessarily carries all the force and consequence of absolute, outright ownership at the time of delivery or it is no delivery at all.[4]

The trial court interpreted the envelope literally. The clear implication is that grantor intended to continue to exercise control and that the grant was not to take effect until such time as both he and his wife had died and the deed had been recorded. From a complete review of the record and weighing of the evidence we find the trial court's judgment is not clearly against the weight of the evidence. Costs of appeal are taxed to appellant.

## NOTES

1. *Distinguishing cases.* In *Vasquez* the delivery was held to be effective, whereas in *Rosengrant* it was held to be ineffective. What were the significant differences between the two cases? Which case is more similar, in significant ways, to the Principal Problem?

2. *Gifts causa mortis.* If the transaction takes the form of a gift made in contemplation of the grantor's death, it is known as a "gift causa mortis." Because of the opportunity for fraud, gifts causa mortis are disfavored, and are subject to more stringent requirements than gifts inter vivos. The donor must contemplate imminent death from a specific peril. Mortality in general will not suffice. The donor must die of the very disorder or peril that was contemplated. The donor must manually deliver the property in question. Causa mortis gifts can be revoked by the donor's express revocation. Causa mortis gifts are automatically revoked upon the donor's recovery from the specific peril or by the death of the donee before the donor. Why was the deed not good under the causa mortis doctrine in *Vasquez* or *Rosengrant?*

3. *Gifts inter vivos.* Inter vivos gifts are those gifts of property made during the donor's lifetime where no imminent peril to the donor exists. However, problems may still arise concerning the validity of these gifts. Although it seems rather straightforward, a gift made inter vivos must meet certain criteria before the courts will find delivery of the gift to be valid. The donor must have shown an intent to make the gift, and he must terminate his dominion over the property. The donee must acquire actual or constructive possession of the property and create dominion over it in herself.

---

[4] In Anderson v. Mauk, 67 P.2d 429, 431 (1937), the court stated:

[I]t is the established law in this jurisdiction that when the owner of land executes a deed during his lifetime and delivers the same to a third party (who acts as a depository rather than an agent of the property owner) with instructions to deliver the deed to the grantee therein named upon his death, intending at the time of delivery to forever part with all lawful right and power to retake or repossess the deed, or to thereafter control the same, the delivery to the third party thus made is sufficient to operate as a valid conveyance of real estate.

Clearly, if the donee is not a member of the donor's family or household, and can fulfill the requirements, the gift will be considered valid. Complications surrounding the surrender of the gift by the donor and creation of dominion in the donee arise when both parties are members of the same household. If the donor makes no provision in her will regarding her inter vivos gift to a family member, the courts will often focus on the circumstances surrounding the gift to determine its validity.

Potts v. Garionis[5] is a good example of how family disputes can arise over such inter vivos gifts. Charles Gavcus gave his wife, Connie, silver coins while he was still alive. When Charles died, his daughter sued the estate claiming that the silver coins should be part of the estate, not Connie's separate property. The court held that Charles intended the coins to be a gift to Connie and not a part of his estate. Charles gave Connie silver coins in his possession and helped her collect other coins. He always referred to the coins as Connie's property. This behavior established that Charles terminated his dominion over the coins and created dominion in Connie as the owner of the coins. The court held that delivery of the coins to Connie as an inter vivos gift was valid.

4.  *Uniform Electronic Transactions ACT (UETA)*. An electronic record is delivered when a "single authoritative copy" which is unique and identifiable is communicated to and maintained by the person asserting control. UETA § 16(b)–(c) (1999). If electronic deeds are utilized in the future, delivery should not be problematic. For additional discussion of UETA, see Assignment 40, note 5 (p. 1009).

---

[5]  377 N.W.2d 204 (Wis. App.1985).

# ASSIGNMENT 43
# REAL ESTATE BROKERS

## 1. INTRODUCTION

In 2008, eighty-one percent of home buyers and eighty-four percent of home sellers used a real estate professional to help them complete the transaction.[1] The real estate broker is an individual or company licensed by the state to help a seller find a buyer or sometimes to help a buyer locate the right property. She is often the sole source of advice to the seller. She may advise on market conditions, property value, and negotiations. She finds the buyer, completes the necessary paperwork, acts as an intermediary between seller and buyer, assists in arranging financing, and deals with escrow and title companies.

Only a licensed broker can collect a commission for arranging a real estate sale. A real estate salesperson, sometimes called a real estate agent, is a licensed individual employed by a real estate broker. Unlicensed persons can never legally act as brokers or agents.

The broker is usually the representative of the seller, though buyers can be represented by their own broker. When the buyer is not represented by a broker, the seller's broker has a fiduciary duty to the buyer. A broker may represent both buyer and seller. This is called a *dual agency*. The rules regulating dual agencies vary from state to state. At a bare minimum, the broker must disclose the dual agency to all parties. Failure to do so is a breach of fiduciary duty and can result in the broker being denied the commission.[2]

*Listing Agreements*

The seller will approach one or more brokers and contract with them to sell the property. When a seller contracts with a broker to sell the property, the property is considered "listed." The listing agreement sets forth the contractual rights between the broker and the seller.[3] In some states, the listing agreement does not need to be in writing to be enforceable. However, a written agreement is always preferable to avoid any disputes over the terms. The listing agreement identifies the property to be sold, the amount of the broker's commission and a specific termination date, all of which are negotiable. If the broker sells the property within the term of the agreement, she will earn a commission.

---

[1] 2008 National Association of Realtors® *Profile of Home Buyers and Sellers* available at http://blog.realtors.org/crt/2009/09/17/home-buyer-and-seller-profile-version-2k8/

[2] *See* Fisher v. Comer Plantation, Inc., 772 So.2d 455, 465 (Ala. 2000).

[3] Orlando Lucero, *The Nuts and Bolts of Commercial Lease Listing Agreements*, Prob. & Prop., July/August 2000, at 7.

There are many different types of listing agreements, but the main distinction is between an "open listing" and an "exclusive listing."

*Open Listing Agreements:* An open listing does not grant exclusive rights to the listing broker. A commission is payable to a listing broker only if the broker procures and presents the seller with an offer from a ready, able and willing buyer on the terms authorized by the listing agreement or accepted by the seller. If another broker procures a buyer, he or she will earn the commission. The open listing is most commonly used in the transfer of commercial property and businesses.

*Exclusive Listing Agreements:* The exclusive listing agreement is used for most residential property sales. For an exclusive listing agreement, only one broker is designated as the seller's exclusive agent.[4] This listing broker is given the exclusive right to sell the property and any other broker who wishes to provide a buyer must go through the listing broker.

There are two types of exclusive listing agreements: (1) the "exclusive agency," and (2) the "exclusive right to sell." In the "exclusive agency" agreement, the property owner reserves the right to find a buyer on her own and not pay a commission to the broker if the broker does not participate in the sale. In contrast, the "exclusive right to sell" agreement binds the seller to pay a commission if the property is sold during the term of the listing regardless of whether a broker was involved in the sale. When the listing agreement expires, the seller can contract with the same broker again, find a new broker or sell the property without a broker's help.

The broker who finds a buyer wants to make sure she will get a commission. Because the negotiations involved in the sale of property might continue beyond the time when the listing agreement expires, brokers usually include extension clauses in their listings. The extension clause provides that the broker is entitled to a commission if the property is sold to a buyer procured by the broker after the listing agreement has expired.

*When Is the Commission Earned?*

The broker's job is to sell property. Few would begrudge the broker a commission when he or she does so. The broker often expends substantial time searching for a buyer and marketing the property. She ultimately bears the risk that a buyer may not be found. In return, the broker expects that when a buyer is found a commission will be earned. The question of exactly when a commission is earned is often the subject of litigation.

A prudent seller will condition the commission on the actual completed transfer of title to the property, or close of escrow. Many broker drafted listing agreements give the broker a right to a commission even

---

[4] Id.

if the sale is not completed. In a few jurisdictions, the broker cannot earn a commission if the sale is not completed, regardless of what the listing agreement states.[5]

The traditional and majority rule is that the broker earns a commission when the broker is the "procuring cause" of a person who is "ready, willing, and able" to purchase the property. Whether a broker is the "procuring cause" is a question of fact.[6] Merely introducing the buyer to the seller is not enough, but the broker need not necessarily be present at the closing of the sale to earn a commission.[7] The courts consider whether the broker set in motion the chain of events that resulted in a sale.[8] The more the broker is involved in the transaction, the more likely the court will find that he is the "procuring cause." The buyer presented by the broker must be ready, willing and able to purchase the listed property. For a court to find that a buyer is ready, willing and able, the buyer must be legally able to enter into the purchase contract and financially capable of paying for the property. Once the seller and buyer sign the purchase contract, it is assumed that the seller accepts the buyer and that the commission is earned.[9] If the buyer backs out, the broker is still entitled to a commission.

Brokers often place their listings with a "Multiple Listing Service"[10] to encourage other brokers to bring in potential buyers in return for a share of the commission. These other brokers are often referred to as "cooperating" brokers. There may be arguments over whether the original listing broker was the procuring cause of the sale (i.e., entitled to the entire commission) or whether the "cooperating" broker was the procuring cause, and thus entitled to an agreed part of the commission.

For an exclusive agency listing there may be an argument over who provided the buyer—the broker or the seller. For an exclusive right to sell listing, the sale may occur after the listing expires. When this occurs, there may be a dispute over whether the buyer was procured by the exclusive broker during the life of the listing. Sellers sometimes seek to delay a sale past the listing expiration in an attempt to avoid paying the broker's commission. In those instances, the procuring cause test is often used to determine whether a "new buyer" is actually new.

---

[5] Ellsworth Dobbs, Inc. v. Johnson, 50 N.J. 528, 236 A.2d 843 (1967), reprinted *infra*.

[6] *See* Smyczynski v. Goeseke, 88 A.D.2d 765 (N.Y. App. Div. 1982).

[7] Manhattan Apartments, Inc. v. Simeon, 11 A.D.3d 404 (N.Y. App. Div. 2004) (commission due to broker when parties attempt to avoid commission by having buyer's "alter ego" purchase property).

[8] *See* Shalimar Dev., Inc. v. FDIC, 515 S.E.2d 120, 123 (Va. 1999).

[9] See Cal. Civ. Code § 1086(f)(1), providing that a commission is earned when the listing agent presents an "enforceable offer from a ready, able and willing buyer on terms authorized by the listing or accepted by the owner."

[10] A Multiple Listing Service (MLS) is a service that combines the real estate listings for all available properties in the area in one directory or database. In general, only licensed real estate brokers and agents, who pay the required fee, are allowed to access it. No single central database exists in the United States. Each MLS database is typically run by the Local Association of Realtors®.

Under the traditional rule, the broker is entitled to a commission if he obtains a binding offer satisfying the terms of the listing agreement from a ready, willing and able buyer. If the seller decides not to proceed with the sale, the broker still receives a commission. There are some exceptions for when the seller's breach is beyond her control. Nonetheless, in general, if the seller prevents the sale, she is liable for the broker's commission.[11] The policy is to protect the work that the broker has done and to prevent unjust enrichment of sellers.

After the purchase contract is signed, the traditional rule is that a commission is earned even if the buyer refuses to complete the sale. This rule is often viewed as unfair to the seller who has no control over the buyer's action. Therefore, several states have adopted the minority or *Dobbs*[12] rule. Under *Dobbs*, a commission is earned only when the sale is completed. To avoid any unfairness to the broker, the seller is subject to certain restrictions.[13] The seller cannot unreasonably refuse to sell the property or otherwise interfere with the sale if the offer meets the terms of the listing agreement. The broker still earns a commission if the seller voluntarily backs out of the deal. However, if the buyer breaches the purchase contract, the seller is not liable for a commission. Under *Dobbs*, the seller cannot contract away this right because in most cases the broker has substantially greater bargaining power due to his knowledge, training and experience. Any attempt to contract this right away is considered void as against public policy.

*Duty to Seller*

The agreement between broker and seller is an agency agreement. The broker is a fiduciary to the seller. Generally, the broker owes the seller a duty of loyalty and good faith. The broker must use due care and diligence in representing the seller, and must disclose all offers to the seller. Most states require some form of disclosure between the broker and seller setting forth the duties and obligation they each have to the other.

*Duty to Buyer*

The seller's broker also owes duties to the buyer. A broker who intentionally misrepresents the attributes of the property she is selling may be liable to the buyer for that misrepresentation. For example, in *Easton v. Strassburger*,[14] the California court imposed an affirmative duty to conduct a "reasonably competent and diligent inspection" of residential property listed for sale, and to disclose to prospective purchasers all facts materially affecting the value or desirability of the

---

[11] *See* Hamilton v. Hopkins, 834 So.2d 695, 701 (Miss. 2003) (court affirmed general rule, but found specific contract provision providing for commission due only at time of closing).

[12] Ellsworth Dobbs, Inc. v. Johnson, 50 N.J. 528, 236 A.2d 843 (1967), reprinted *infra*.

[13] *See* Prudential Stewart Realty v. Sonnenfeldt, 666 A.2d 589 (N.J. 1995).

[14] Easton v. Strassburger, 152 Cal.App.3d 90, 199 Cal.Rptr. 383 (1984), reprinted *infra*.

property that such an investigation would reveal. This disclosure requirement was subsequently codified.[15]

Legal conflicts concerning real estate brokers are common. Sometimes the broker is the plaintiff, seeking payment of her sales commission. At other times, the broker is the defendant, with the buyer or seller alleging that the broker acted improperly. The Principal Problem involves both types of controversies.

## 2. Principal Problem

Grey purchased two houses in a development: one as her personal residence, and one as a rental property. Soon after, the neighborhood was plagued with a mysterious illness that caused headaches and dizziness in many of the residents. The local newspaper published an investigative article suggesting that these problems were caused by "Azon," a chemical compound used in the paint of some of the houses in the development. It also reported that an Azon contaminated house could be distinguished by a grey dust that settles in the home. Grey and Reynolds, Grey's tenant in the rental property, both suffer from headaches and dizziness, and both suspect that the cause is Azon.

Grey decides to sell both her home and the rental property. She signs an exclusive right to sell listing agreement with Bruse. Bruse is such a successful broker that he has very little time to inspect the properties he sells and he simply asks Grey, "Do you have any problems, you know, cracks in the foundation, ventilation problems? I was reading about the Azon problem, have you been suffering from headaches or seen any grey dust?" Grey tells him "Nope, no problems like that." Grey gives him a sixty day listing agreement that states that "the broker earns his commission when he finds a ready, willing, and able buyer."

*The rental property.* Bruse shows the rental property to Vestor, who wants to purchase rental property in the area. They meet Reynolds, and she tells them about her headaches. Bruse looks around the house and notices traces of grey dust. He explains the Azon problem to Vestor. Vestor tells Bruse that he does not care about Azon. Bruse also notices some water stains on the ceiling of one of the rooms and asks Grey about it while Vestor is outside looking at the foundation. Grey says that there was once a roof leak but that it has been completely repaired. Bruse is satisfied with this explanation, and does not say anything about it to Vestor. Vestor offers to buy the house from Grey and Grey accepts. Grey and Vestor sign a sales contract that contains a disclosure section notifying Vestor that the house is contaminated with Azon. The section provides an explanation of Azon and its dangers.

---

[15] Cal. Civ. Code §§ 2079–2079.6, 2079.12, applying the disclosure standard to both listing and cooperating brokers. In 2014, the California Legislature extended disclosure duties to commercial real estate brokers, including those engaged in commercial leasing transactions. Cal. Civ. Code §§ 2079.13–2079.24.

The sale is completed and Bruse receives his commission. A few months later, after a heavy rain, there is extensive water leaking from where the ceiling had a water stain. Vestor sues Bruse for the loss in value attributable both to the water damage and the Azon. After studying the material that follows, discuss Vestor's claims.

*Grey's personal residence.* Bruse shows Grey's home to Laqroit, and Laqroit and Grey execute a purchase contract for it. Later, Laqroit stops by the home to admire his purchase. While visiting the house, he tries to speak to Grey. Grey cannot speak to him because Grey is suffering from a severe headache. Laqroit subsequently recalls the connection between the Azon problem and headaches. He contacts Grey and announces that he will not complete the contract because the entire development is tainted with the suspicion of Azon. Laqroit also believes that all properties in the development have lost substantial value, regardless of whether Azon is present in a particular house. In fact, Azon is not present in Grey's residence. However, Grey and Laqroit agree that Grey can keep the deposit and that Grey will not seek additional remedies against Laqroit.

Bruse now sues Grey and Laqroit for his commission. After studying the materials that follow, offer your opinion concerning Bruse's right to a commission.

## 3. Materials for Solution of Principal Problem

### Ellsworth Dobbs, Inc. v. Johnson v. Iarussi
Supreme Court of New Jersey, 1967.
50 N.J. 528, 236 A.2d 843.

■ Francis, J.

Plaintiff Ellsworth Dobbs, Inc., a real estate broker, sued John R. Johnson and Adelaide P. Johnson, his wife, and Joseph Iarussi for commissions allegedly earned in a real estate transaction. The Johnsons, as owners of certain acreage in Bernards Township, New Jersey, and Iarussi as purchaser, entered into a written agreement, the former to sell and the latter to buy the property. There is no doubt that Dobbs brought the parties together, and into the signed contract of sale. Title did not close, however, because of Iarussi's inability to obtain financial backing for his intended development of the property. After Iarussi's failure to perform, the Johnsons released him from the contract under circumstances to be detailed hereafter. Dobbs then brought this action charging the Johnsons with breach of an express agreement to pay a commission due for bringing about the contract of sale, and charging Iarussi with breach of an implied agreement to pay the commission if he failed to complete the purchase and thus deprived the broker of commission from the seller. The trial judge held, as a matter of law, that Dobbs' commission claim against the Johnsons vested upon execution of the contract of sale with Iarussi, and that the right to commission was not dependent upon the closing of title. Consequently, he declined to submit that issue to the jury for determination. Instead he instructed them that plaintiff was entitled to a commission against the Johnsons, and limited their function to a determination of the amount due. The jury found for Dobbs in the amount of $15,000. As to the defendant Iarussi, the trial judge submitted this issue to the jury: Did the facts as they found them show by a preponderance of the evidence that Iarussi impliedly agreed with Dobbs' representative that if the representative located property satisfactory to Iarussi for residential development purposes, and the owner entered into a contract with Iarussi to sell the property on terms mutually agreeable, Iarussi would perform the contract and thus enable the broker to earn a commission from the owner? The jury found that there was such an implied agreement; further, that the implied agreement was breached by Iarussi's failure to perform his contract to buy the Johnsons' property. Therefore he became liable to the broker for payment of the commission. Since the jury had been charged that the amount of the verdict against Iarussi would have to be the same as that returned against the Johnsons, he was assessed $15,000.

On appeal the Appellate Division reversed the judgment against the Johnsons, holding that there was a jury question as to their liability to pay the commission to the plaintiff, and a new trial was ordered on this phase of the case. The judgment against Iarussi was reversed also, on the ground that the evidence was insufficient to show a contract, express or implied, under which Iarussi made himself liable to pay the commission Dobbs would have received from the Johnsons if Iarussi had performed his agreement to buy their property.

## I.

The Johnsons are the owners of a 144-acre tract of farm land in Bernards Township, New Jersey. They had placed it on the market for sale in 1960. It was listed with Dobbs and other agencies as available. . . .

Sometime in 1960, Fleming [Vice President of Dobbs] showed the 144-acre Johnson tract to Iarussi. He was interested in it for residential development, but could not finance such a large undertaking personally and had to obtain backing from some source. Satisfactory terms were agreed upon with the Johnsons, and an oral agreement of purchase was made. Iarussi's hopes for financial support were not realized and the deal collapsed. . . .

[After further negotiations a real estate sales contract was signed, but subsequently Iarussi was unable to purchase the property since he could not obtain financing. Although the court's opinion is silent on the question, it appears that Iarussi's obligation to purchase was not contingent on Iarussi obtaining financing.]

With respect to the broker's commission, the contract provided:

The commission hereinafter mentioned shall be payable as follows: $5,000.00 when sellers shall have received a total of $25,000.00 on account of the above purchase price ($10,000.00 herewith and $15,000.00 on account of the principal sum of the above mentioned purchase money note and mortgage); an additional $5,000.00 when an additional $25,000.00 shall have been paid on account of the principal sum of purchase money note and mortgage; and the remaining $5,000.00 when an additional $25,000.00 shall have been paid on account of the principal sum of said purchase money note and mortgage. The entire commission of $15,000.00 shall become immediately due and payable upon any sale or assignment by sellers of said purchase money note and mortgage. . . . And the Seller hereby agrees to pay to Ellsworth Dobbs, Inc. a commission of Six (6)% on the purchase price aforesaid, said commission to be paid in consideration of services rendered in consummating this sale; said commission to become due and payable as above mentioned.

At the trial the Johnsons claimed primarily that Dobbs' right to commission was contingent upon closing of title; that such was not only the clear meaning of the language of the sale contract, but it was the understanding of the parties. They contended further that if the court would not hold as a matter of law that the failure of Iarussi to complete the transaction barred the claim for commission, the most that could be said against their position was that the contract was ambiguous as to when the broker's right accrued. Therefore, they urged that parol testimony was admissible to explain the ambiguity and to show the parties' understanding that commission was to be considered earned only upon closing of title. With respect to the so-called "settlement" made with Iarussi after his refusal to close title, they contended they had simply salvaged what they could out of a bargain they wanted to complete, but which was unilaterally frustrated by him. In return for releasing him they received nothing that could possibly be considered as an equivalence for the loss of their bargain. The trial judge disagreed. He held that in light of the established law of this State, the language of the contract made the commission earned upon the execution of the contract of sale by the buyer and the sellers, and merely postponed payment to the times specifically prescribed.

With respect to the broker's claim against Iarussi, the trial court said, as we have noted above, that the circumstances proved at the trial raised a factual issue for jury determination: by failing to perform the contract of purchase, did Iarussi breach an implied agreement with the broker to complete the transaction, and thus make himself liable for the commission Dobbs would have received from the Johnsons if title had closed?

As will appear hereafter, we disagree with both aspects of the trial court's ruling against the sellers, and unlike the Appellate Division we agree that a jury question existed as to the buyer's liability.

II.

The Sellers' Liability to the Broker.

Corbin notes that there has been an immense amount of litigation over the years with respect to the commissions of land brokers. 1 Corbin on Contracts 50 (1963). Almost a century ago, the former Supreme Court ruled that when a broker who had been duly authorized by the owner to find a buyer for his property produced a willing and able purchaser who entered into a contract to buy on terms agreeable to the owner, the broker had fulfilled his undertaking and his right to commission from the owner was complete. Hinds v. Henry, 36 N.J.L. 328 (Sup.Ct.1873). The doctrine has been with us ever since.

We pause at this point to explain that a primary reason for granting certification in this case was to re-evaluate the justice and propriety of continuing the legal principles outlined above. Is it just to permit a broker to recover commission from an owner simply because he entered into a contract on mutually agreeable terms with a buyer produced by the broker, when it later develops that the buyer cannot or will not complete the transaction by closing the title? We do not think so.

A new and more realistic approach to the problem is necessary.

There can be no doubt that ordinarily when an owner of property lists it with a broker for sale, his expectation is that the money for the payment of commission will come out of the proceeds of the sale. He expects that if the broker produces a buyer to whom the owner's terms of sale are satisfactory, and a contract embodying those terms is executed, the buyer will perform, i.e. he will pay the consideration and accept the deed at the time agreed upon. Considering the realities of the relationship created between owner and broker, that expectation of the owner is a reasonable one, and, in our view, entirely consistent with what should be the expectation of a conscientious broker as to the kind of ready, willing and able purchaser his engagement calls upon him to tender to the owner.

The present New Jersey rule as exemplified by the cases cited above is deficient as an instrument of justice. It permits a broker to satisfy his obligation to the owner simply by tendering a human being who is physically and mentally capable of agreeing to buy the property on mutually satisfactory terms, so long as the owner enters into a sale contract with such person. The implication of the rule is that the owner has the burden of satisfying himself as to the prospective purchaser's ability, financial or otherwise, to complete the transaction; he cannot rely at all on the fact that the purchaser was produced in good faith by the broker as a person willing and able to buy the property. Once he enters into a contract of sale with the broker's customer, he is considered to have accepted the purchaser as fully capable of the ultimate performance agreed upon. If it later appears that the purchaser is not financially able to close the title, or even that he never did have the means to do so, the owner must pay the broker his commission, so long as he acted in good faith. Such a rule, considered in the context of the real relationship between broker and owner, empties the word "able" of substantially all of its significant content and imposes an unjust burden on vendors of property. It seems to us that fairness requires that the arrangement between broker and owner be interpreted to mean that the owner hires the broker with the expectation of becoming liable for a commission only in the event a sale of the property is consummated, unless the title does not pass because of the owner's improper or frustrating conduct.

The principle that binds the seller to pay commission if he signs a contract of sale with the broker's customer, regardless of the customer's financial ability, puts the burden on the wrong shoulders. Since the broker's duty to the owner is to produce a prospective buyer who is financially able to pay the purchase price and take title, a right in the owner to assume such capacity when the broker presents his purchaser ought to be recognized. It follows that the obligation to inquire into the prospect's financial status and to establish his adequacy to fulfill the monetary conditions of the purchase must be regarded logically and sensibly as resting with the broker. Thus when the broker produces his customer, it is only reasonable to hold that the owner may accept him without being obliged to make an independent inquiry into his financial capacity. That right ought not to be taken away from him, nor should he be estopped to assert it, simply because he "accepted" the buyer, i.e., agreed to convey to him if and when he paid the purchase price according to the terms of the contract. In reason and in justice it must be said that the duty to produce a purchaser able in the financial sense to complete the purchase at the time fixed is an incident of the broker's business; so too, with regard to any other material condition of the agreement to purchase which is to be performed at the closing. In a practical world, the true test of a willing buyer is not met when he signs an agreement to purchase; it is demonstrated at the time of closing of title, and if he unjustifiably refuses or is unable financially to perform then, the broker has not produced a willing buyer. . . .

Study of the problems involved in this case in light of the above considerations leads us to the following conclusions as to what the controlling rule should be in New Jersey: When a broker is engaged by an owner of property to find a purchaser for it, the broker earns his commission when (a) he produces a purchaser ready, willing and able to buy on the terms fixed by the owner, (b) the purchaser enters into a binding contract with the owner to do so, and (c) the purchaser completes the transaction by closing the title in accordance with the provisions of the contract. If the contract is not consummated because of lack of financial ability of the buyer to perform or because of any other default of his, there is no right to commission against the seller. On the other hand, if the failure of completion of the contract results from the wrongful act or interference of the seller, the broker's claim is valid and must be paid. In short, in the absence of default by the seller, the broker's right to commission against the seller, comes into existence only when his buyer performs in accordance with the contract of sale.

We reject the proposition that whenever the owner-seller enters into a binding sale contract with the proffered customer, the broker's right to commission is complete unless the owner has made a special agreement with the broker that such right is contingent upon the closing of title. The basic law governing the owner-broker relationship is declared to be that absent default by the owner, the contract of sale must be performed by the buyer before liability for commission is imposed upon the owner. Execution of a contract to sell to the tendered purchaser, without more, will not bar the owner from relying upon the financial or other inability or failure of the buyer to complete his undertaking as an absolute defense to the broker's suit. It is our view and we so hold that in entering into the contract of sale the owner is entitled to assume that the customer is, or will be at the time fixed for closing, financially able to meet the terms of sale, and that he is now and will be at performance time willing to complete the transaction. Further we hold that even if both broker and seller, on execution of the contract of sale, in good faith believe the buyer to be financially able to perform, and it turns out otherwise at the crucial time, the seller cannot be held for commission. What must be regarded as the fundamental intendment of the parties, owner and broker, i.e., that the owner will sell and the buyer will pay, and the broker will thus earn his commission out of the proceeds, cannot be ignored in this connection. This uncomplicated reality should not be complicated by controversies over who knew what with respect to the buyer's financial capacity to close the title. The risk of such inability at that crucial time must be treated as a normal incident of the brokerage business. In our view, these statements represent reasonable and just rules for determining the problems thus far discussed. Any cases in our reports inconsistent therewith, particularly those which hold that once an owner-seller makes a contract to sell his property to the broker's customer, the customer's financial ability to perform is no longer open to question, are overruled, and can no longer be considered the law of this State.

We come now to another aspect of the over-all problem. To what extent may the broker, by special contract, thwart the general rules now declared to control the usual relationship between him and an owner who engages him to find a purchaser?

In view of our holding here that a broker is not entitled to commission from the seller if title does not pass because of the inability or fault of the customer, and the further rule to be expounded hereafter respecting the liability of the buyer to the broker where the buyer is the defaulting party, in our judgment public policy requires the courts to read into every brokerage agreement or contract of sale a requirement that barring default by the seller, commissions shall not be deemed earned against him unless the contract of sale is performed. By the same token, whenever the substantial inequality of bargaining power, position or advantage to which we have adverted appears, a provision to the contrary in an agreement prepared or presented or negotiated or procured by the broker shall be deemed inconsistent with public policy and unenforceable.

On the basis of all we have said above, and although we agree with the Appellate Division that the provision in the contract of sale between Dobbs and the Johnsons respecting the time when the commission could be considered earned is at the very least ambiguous, we hold as a matter of law that title not having closed solely because of the financial incapacity of Iarussi, the claim against the Johnsons for commission must fail.

Dobbs contends further that the Johnsons are liable because they enforced the contract of sale against Iarussi by obtaining a judgment for specific performance against him, and thereafter, on his failure to perform, exchanged releases with him and received certain benefits in settlement of their claim against him for breach of the contract. The trial court sustained the contention and held that regardless of the legal significance of the agreement to pay commission which appeared in the contract of sale, the Johnsons' acceptance of damages for Iarussi's breach estopped them from denying the broker's commission claim. The Appellate Division correctly disagreed with that view.

No wrongful conduct of the Johnsons frustrated the closing of title. The failure resulted from Iarussi's financial inability to perform. Moreover, they had no duty to seek specific performance so that Dobbs could earn the commission. Their passive acquiescence in his admitted default would not constitute a wrongful failure of performance. The action for specific performance was instituted by Iarussi who had breached his contract to buy. In doing so he alleged financial capacity to perform. The Johnsons, who were at all times anxious to complete the transaction, naturally, in order to avoid the possibility of being branded the defaulters, counterclaimed for the same relief, requesting that the court order performance and fix a day for it. In such circumstances, surely the resulting order for performance would not constitute acceptance of the benefits of the contract by the Johnsons unless, on the date set in the order, Iarussi actually completed performance. But again he failed and for the same reason, inability to obtain financing.

When the Johnsons saw no hope of Iarussi's completing the sale, their act in terminating the matter by exchanging mutual releases, with the attendant conditions set out above, did not, and was not intended to amount to the equivalent of performance of the contract. In a situation where a broker's right to commission depends, as here, on the completion of the contract of sale by the buyer, and the latter fails or refuses to perform, the seller is under no duty to the broker to sue the buyer for damages or for specific performance. It is generally held that he may accept the forfeiture by the buyer, retain the down payment, and not become liable thereby to pay the broker. If, however, the seller sued the buyer for breach of the contract and recovered damages therefore; or if not content with retaining the deposit, he demanded and received a substantial additional sum as damages, he must be considered to have received an award representing the benefit lost, or an agreed payment representing the equivalent of performance. In such case, the seller is deemed to have accepted the benefit of the broker's services, and is liable for the commission.

The rule is otherwise, however, if the seller does not seek or obtain damages representing the substantial equivalent of performance by the buyer. When he passively accepts the fact of the buyer's inability or refusal to perform the contract of sale, and in good faith, in order to bring the matter to an end, receives in return for the exchange of releases what in fairness can only be regarded as salvage as distinguished from the substantial equivalent of performance, in justice and in equity he should not be held to have incurred thereby any liability to the broker. The Appellate Division so held here, and its decision is eminently sound.

### III.
### Liability of the Buyer to the Broker.

We regard it as a matter of common knowledge that the ordinary prospective purchaser knows when he consults a broker that if he buys a property through the efforts of the broker, customarily the broker will earn a commission on the sale to be paid by the owner-seller out of the purchase price. As the Chief Justice noted in Harris v. Perl, 41 N.J. 455, 462, 197 A.2d 359, 363 (1964), "the economic facts and the expectations of fair men with respect to real estate brokerage are clear enough. The role of the broker is to bring buyer and seller together at terms agreeable to both, and both know the broker expects to earn a commission from the seller if he succeeds." What, then, should be the responsibility of the buyer to the broker when, through the broker's efforts in negotiations between the parties, the owner (a) expresses his willingness to accept the buyer's offered price for the property, or (b) executes a written contract of sale with the buyer for the agreed price, providing that the broker's commission is to be paid upon closing of title?

This Court has held that when a prospective buyer solicits a broker to find or to show him property which he might be interested in buying, and the broker finds property satisfactory to him which the owner agrees to sell at the price offered, and the buyer knows the broker will earn commission for the sale from the owner, the law will imply a promise on the part of the buyer to complete the transaction with the owner. If he fails or refuses to do so without valid reason, and thus prevents the broker from earning the commission from the owner, he becomes liable to the broker for breach of the implied promise.

Iarussi became subject to an implied obligation to Dobbs to complete the purchase, and upon default in completion he became liable to pay the commission which Dobbs was thereby deprived of from the Johnsons.

IV.

For the reasons outlined, the judgment against the Johnsons in the trial court, as well as the reversal of that judgment by the Appellate Division and the ordering of a new trial are reversed, and judgment is entered in their favor and against the plaintiff Dobbs.

Further, the judgment in the trial court against Iarussi, as well as that of the Appellate Division directing entry of judgment in his favor as a matter of law, are reversed, and the cause is remanded for a new trial against Iarussi on the theory explained herein.

## Easton v. Strassburger
Court of Appeal, First District, 1984.
152 Cal.App.3d 90, 199 Cal.Rptr. 383.

■ KLINE, PRESIDING JUSTICE.

Valley of California, Inc., doing business as Valley Realty (appellant), appeals from a judgment for negligence entered in favor of Leticia M. Easton (respondent). Appellant was one of six defendants in the action, which was brought by respondent for fraud (including negligent misrepresentation) and negligence in the sale of residential property.

Viewing the evidence in the light most favorable to respondent, as we must, the record discloses the following facts: The property which is the subject of this appeal is a one-acre parcel of land located in the City of Diablo. The property is improved with a 3,000 square foot home, a swimming pool, and a large guest house. Respondent purchased the property for $170,000 from the Strassburgers in May of 1976 and escrow closed in July of that year. Appellant was the listing broker in the transaction.

Shortly after respondent purchased the property, there was massive earth movement on the parcel. Subsequent slides destroyed a portion of the driveway in 1977 or 1978. Expert testimony indicated that the slides occurred because a portion of the property was fill that had not been properly engineered and compacted. The slides caused the foundation of the house to settle which in turn caused cracks in the walls and warped doorways. After the 1976 slide, damage to the property was so severe that although experts appraised the value of the property at $170,000 in an undamaged condition, the value of the damaged property was estimated to be as low as $20,000. Estimates of the cost to repair the damage caused by the slides and avoid recurrence ranged as high as $213,000.

Appellant was represented in the sale of the property by its agents Simkin and Mourning. It is uncontested that these agents conducted several inspections of the property prior to sale. There is also evidence they were aware of certain "red flags" which should have indicated to them that there were soil problems. Despite this, the agents did not request that the soil stability of the property be tested and did not inform respondent that there were potential soil problems.

During the time that the property was owned by the Strassburgers there was a minor slide in 1973 involving about 10 to 12 feet of the filled slope and a major slide in 1975 in which the fill dropped about eight to 10 feet in a circular shape 50 to 60 feet across. However, the Strassburgers did not tell Simkin or Mourning anything about the slides or the corrective action they had taken.

Respondent purchased the property without being aware of the soil problems or the past history of slides.

In December of 1976 respondent filed suit against appellant, the Strassburgers, and three other named defendants. As against appellant, respondent alleged causes of action for fraudulent concealment, intentional misrepresentation, and negligent misrepresentation.

The action was tried before a jury. As to appellant, the judge instructed the jury only as to negligent misrepresentation and simple negligence, since the actions for fraudulent concealment and intentional misrepresentation had been voluntarily dismissed. The jury returned a special verdict finding that all named defendants had been negligent, and assessed damages of $197,000. Negligence was apportioned among the parties under the principals of comparative negligence in the following percentages: Appellant—5%; Strassburgers—65%; George Sauer and San Ramon Builders—15%; H.M. Bull—10%. The jury also found a nonparty (a cooperating broker) five percent responsible.

Appellant's primary contention is that the trial judge committed error by giving the jury an instruction specifying a real estate broker's duty to investigate and disclose defects in property he lists for sale.

It is not disputed that current law requires a broker to disclose to a buyer material defects known to the broker but unknown to and unobservable by the buyer. (Cooper v. Jevne (1976) 56 Cal.App.3d 860, 866, 128 Cal.Rptr. 724; Lingsch v. Savage (1963) 213 Cal.App.2d 729, 733, 29 Cal.Rptr. 201; see also regulations of the Department of Real Estate set forth in Cal.Admin.Code, tit. 10, s 2785, subd. (a)(3).) The Cooper case contains the most complete judicial articulation of the rule: "It is the law of this state that where a real estate broker or agent, representing the seller, knows facts materially affecting the value or the desirability of property offered for sale and these facts are known or accessible only to him and his principal, and the broker or agent also knows that these facts are not known to or within the reach of the diligent attention and observation of the buyer, the broker or agent is under a duty to disclose these facts to the buyer. (Lingsch v. Savage [1963] 213 Cal.App.2d [729, 29 Cal.Rptr. 201] . . . )." (56 Cal.App.3d at 866, 128

Cal.Rptr. 724.) If a broker fails to disclose material facts that are known to him he is liable for the intentional tort of "fraudulent concealment" or "negative fraud." As noted, however, appellant's liability was here grounded on negligence rather than fraud. The issue, then, is whether a broker is negligent if he fails to disclose defects which he should have discovered through reasonable diligence. Stated another way, we must determine whether the broker's duty of due care in a residential real estate transaction includes a duty to conduct a reasonably competent and diligent inspection of property he has listed for sale in order to discover defects for the benefit of the buyer.

Admittedly, no appellate decision has explicitly declared that a broker is under a duty to disclose material facts which he should have known. We conclude, however, that such a duty is implicit in the rule articulated in Cooper and Lingsch, which speaks not only to facts known by the broker, but also and independently to facts that are accessible only to him and his principal.

The primary purposes of the Cooper-Lingsch rule are to protect the buyer from the unethical broker and seller and to insure that the buyer is provided sufficient accurate information to make an informed decision whether to purchase. These purposes would be seriously undermined if the rule were not seen to include a duty to disclose reasonably discoverable defects. If a broker were required to disclose only known defects, but not also those that are reasonably discoverable, he would be shielded by his ignorance of that which he holds himself out to know. The rule thus narrowly construed would have results inimical to the policy upon which it is based. Such a construction would not only reward the unskilled broker for his own incompetence, but might provide the unscrupulous broker the unilateral ability to protect himself at the expense of the inexperienced and unwary who rely upon him. In any case, if given legal force, the theory that a seller's broker cannot be held accountable for what he does not know but could discover without great difficulty would inevitably produce a disincentive for a seller's broker to make a diligent inspection. Such a disincentive would be most unfortunate, since in residential sales transactions the seller's broker is most frequently the best situated to obtain and provide the most reliable information on the property and is ordinarily counted on to do so.

As one commentator has observed: "Real estate brokers are often in a very commanding position with respect to both sellers and buyers of residential property. The real estate broker's relationship to the buyer is such that the buyer usually expects the broker to protect his interests. This trust and confidence derives from the potential value of the broker's service; houses are infrequently purchased and require a trained eye to determine value and fitness. In addition, financing is often complex. Unlike other commodities, houses are rarely purchased new and there are virtually no remedies for deficiencies in fitness. In some respects the broker-buyer relationship is akin to the attorney-client relationship; the buyer, like the client, relies heavily on another's acquired skill and knowledge, first because of the complexity of the transaction and second because of his own dearth of experience." (Comment, A Reexamination of the Real Estate Broker-Buyer-Seller Relationship (1972) 18 Wayne L.Rev. 1343.) Thus, as stated by Judge Cardozo, as he then was, in a different but still relevant context: "The real estate broker is brought by his calling into a relation of trust and confidence. Constant are the opportunities by concealment and collusion to extract illicit gains. We know from our judicial records that the opportunities have not been lost. . . . He is accredited by his calling in the minds of the inexperienced or the ignorant with a knowledge greater than their own."

In sum, we hold that the duty of a real estate broker, representing the seller, to disclose facts, as that fundamental duty is articulated in Cooper and Lingsch, includes the affirmative duty to conduct a reasonably competent and diligent inspection of the residential[16] property listed for sale and to disclose to prospective purchasers all facts materially affecting the value or desirability of the property that such an investigation would reveal.

With respect to the application of this holding, it is vitally important to keep in mind that in Cooper and Lingsch the basis of liability was fraud, not negligence. The fundamental duty to disclose set forth in those and other real estate fraud cases has application only where it is alleged that the broker either had actual knowledge of the material facts in issue or that such facts were "accessible only to him and his principal" (Cooper, supra, 56 Cal.App.3d at p. 866, 128 Cal.Rptr. 724; Lingsch, supra, 213 Cal.App.2d at p. 735, 29 Cal.Rptr. 201), so that the broker may constructively be deemed to have had actual knowledge. The implicit duty to investigate is not considered in those cases simply because it is superfluous to the issue of fraud. However, in cases where, as here, the cause of action is for negligence, not fraud, it need not be alleged or proved that the broker had actual knowledge of the material facts in issue nor that such facts were accessible only to him or his principal and that he therefore had constructive knowledge thereof.

The real estate fraud cases also require that the undisclosed material facts be such as "are not known to or within the reach of the diligent attention and observation of the buyer." (Cooper, supra, 56 Cal.App.3d p. 866, 128 Cal.Rptr. 724; Lingsch, supra, 213 Cal.App.2d at p. 735, 29 Cal.Rptr. 201.) We decline to place a similar limitation on the duty to investigate here articulated. Such a limitation might, first of all, diminish the broker's incentive to conduct the reasonably competent and diligent inspection which the law seeks to encourage. Furthermore, general principles of comparative negligence provide adequate protection to a broker who neglects to explicitly disclose manifest defects. (See generally, Li v. Yellow Cab Co. (1975) 13 Cal.3d 804, 119 Cal.Rptr. 858,

---

[16] We express no opinion here whether a broker's obligation to conduct an inspection for defects for the benefit of the buyer applies to the sale of commercial real estate.

532 P.2d 1226.) The duty of the seller's broker to diligently investigate and disclose reasonably discoverable defects to the buyer does not relieve the latter of the duty to exercise reasonable care to protect himself. Cases will undoubtedly arise in which the defect in the property is so clearly apparent that as a matter of law a broker would not be negligent for failure to expressly disclose it, as he could reasonably expect that the buyer's own inspection of the premises would reveal the flaw. In such a case the buyer's negligence alone would be the proximate cause of any injury he suffered.

Accordingly, we find that the instruction at issue in this case was legally correct, for, as the trial judge stated to the jury, a seller's broker in a residential real estate transaction is "under a duty to disclose facts materially affecting the value or desirability of the property . . . which through reasonable diligence should be known to him."

Appellant next contends that the judgment must be reversed because the verdict was not supported by substantial evidence. Again, we cannot agree. The evidence indicates that appellant's agents had conducted a limited investigation of the property and that they were aware of "red flags" indicating erosion or settlement problems. There was evidence indicating that one or both of the agents knew that the residence was built on fill and that settlement and erosion problems are commonly associated with such soil. It was additionally established that the agents had seen netting on a slope of the property which had been placed there to repair the slide which occurred most recently prior to the sale. Furthermore, one of the agents testified that he had observed that the floor of a guest house on the property was not level, while the other agent testified that uneven floors were "red flag" indications of soils problems. Although the foregoing does not exhaust the evidence in the record that appellant's agents were on notice of potential soils problems, it is sufficient to establish that there was substantial evidence on the point. Other evidence also established that, despite this notice, the agents did not request that a soils report be prepared, nor take any other significant steps to determine whether there had been slides or other soils problems.

While the evidence did not establish that appellant's agents had actual knowledge of the history of slides and soil problems on the property, such actual knowledge was, as we have said, unnecessary to establish liability for negligence. The jury merely had to conclude—as apparently it did—that a reasonably competent and diligent inspection of the property would have uncovered the past history of soils problems. Real estate agents hold themselves out to the public as professionals, and, as such, are required to make reasonable use of their superior knowledge, skills and experience within the area of their expertise. (4 Witkin, supra, Summary of Cal. Law, § 518, p. 2783.) Because such agents are expected to make use of their superior knowledge and skills, which is the reason they are engaged, and because the agents in this case were or should have been alert to the signs of soils problems earlier described, the jury was well within the bounds of reason when it concluded that a reasonably diligent and competent inspection of the property would have included something more than a casual visual inspection and a general inquiry of the owners.

The judgment for negligence against appellant was amply supported by the evidence.

## NOTES

1. *After Easton v. Strassburger:* Under California's comparative negligence law, the jury found the Strassburgers sixty-five percent liable, the builder twenty-five percent liable and the listing and cooperating brokers each five percent liable. Because the sellers and the builder were judgment proof, the listing broker had to pay the entire judgment—obviously far greater than any commission received for the sale of the property.[17]

2. *Broker's duty to disclose problems to buyer.* The *Easton* decision has been largely codified in California. However, even in California a broker is not liable for failing to disclose defects that she did not know about, and which were not discernible by visual inspection.[18] Of course, a broker is always liable for knowingly making false statements of material facts to the purchasers, and often is liable for failing to disclose known material facts. In Reed v. King,[19] it was held that the broker had a duty to disclose to the purchaser that the residence for sale was the site of a murder.[20]

3. *Seller's duty to disclose.* To establish consistent and fair disclosure requirements for sellers, consider the following questions: Should property condition disclosure forms come from a state statute, be provided by a state regulatory agency, or be issued by local Realtors Associations? Should seller disclosures be mandatory or voluntary? What topics should the disclosure cover? Should the sellers be excused from disclosure if they pay for professional physical inspections of their property? Should disclaimers and waivers be available for sellers to avoid disclosure? Should sellers be required to disclose area-wide national and manmade hazards, even if this would require additional expense?[21]

4. *Broker's right to a commission when buyers default.* In *Dobbs*, the court held that usually the broker is not entitled to a commission unless the sale is completed. This rule cannot be altered by agreement of the parties if there was substantial inequality of bargaining power. Massachusetts follows

---

[17] George Lefcoe, Property Condition Disclosure Forms: How the Real Estate Industry Eased the Transition from Caveat Emptor to "Seller Tell All", 39 Real Prop. Prob. & Tr. J. 193, 220 (Summer 2004).

[18] *See* Robinson v. Grossman, 57 Cal.App.4th 634, 644 (Cal. Ct. App. 1997).

[19] 145 Cal.App.3d 261, 193 Cal.Rptr. 130 (1983).

[20] Reed was distinguished by Milliken v. Jacono, 60 A.3d 133, 144 (PA Superior Court, 2012). This case held that only *objective* factors should be used to define a broker's disclosure duties. "While the murder/suicide may have been subjectively material to the buyer's decision, under common law fraud a seller of real estate was only liable for failing to reveal objective material defects." Id. at 144.

[21] George Lefcoe, *supra* at 197.

*Dobbs* except that the parties can adopt a different rule by agreement.[22] Most states, including New York and California, appear to follow the traditional rule that a broker earns her commission when she procures a buyer who is ready, willing and able to buy the property on the terms specified in the listing agreement.[23] Is the traditional majority rule or the *Dobbs* rule better?[24]

Jurisdictions continue to split on whether the traditional rule or the *Dobbs* rule should be followed when the sale is not completed because of the buyer's default. One writer suggests that although many jurisdictions purport to follow the traditional rule concerning the broker's right to a commission when the deal doesn't close, in fact courts in these jurisdictions usually find a way to protect the seller.[25] Assuming that this perception is accurate, what does it suggest about the continuing viability of the traditional rule?

5. *Broker's right to a commission when sale is not completed because of seller's default.* Clearly, when a sale is not completed because the seller unjustifiably refuses to honor the signed sales contract, the broker is entitled to his commission. More difficult questions arise when the sales contract is never signed, or when the seller's refusal to complete the sale may be justifiable.

Although *Dobbs* held that normally a seller is not liable for a commission if the sale is not completed, it also stated that the seller is liable for the commission if the failure of the sale is due to the seller's fault. In the Principal Problem, was Grey's "fault" such as to warrant making him liable for the commission?

---

[22] *See* Tristram's Landing Inc. v. Wait, 367 Mass. 622, 327 N.E.2d 727 (1975).

[23] *See* Cal. Civ. Code § 1086(f)(1) (West 2009); *see also* Feinberg Bros. Agency, Inc. v. Berted Realty Co., Inc., 517 N.E.2d 1325 (N.Y. 1987).

[24] Brett R. Budzinski, Note, Argument for the Minority Rule: An Efficient Approach to Real Estate Brokerage Contracts, 82 B.U. L. Rev. 195 (2002) (arguing that the *Dobbs* rule should be adopted as the majority rule).

[25] Steven K. Mulliken, When Does the Seller Owe the Broker a Commission?, 132 Military L. Rev. 265 (1991).

# ASSIGNMENT 44

# CONTRACTING FOR MARKETABLE TITLE

## 1. INTRODUCTION

In general, a "marketable title" is a title that a reasonable and prudent business person, with knowledge of the facts and their legal ramifications, would accept. Marketable title issues arise in several contexts. First, the typical real property sales contract provides, expressly or impliedly, that Seller will deliver marketable title to Buyer, subject to specified exceptions. Buyer may refuse to complete the sale ("close") if Buyer believes that Seller is unable to convey marketable title, subject to the agreed exceptions. Second, if the sale is completed but thereafter a title problem arises, Buyer is likely to seek redress from the Seller, based on the deed that the Seller used to convey the property. In most states, the typical deed contains an express or implied by statute warranty of title. Although the warranty of title contained in a deed may not technically be a warranty of marketable title, it usually closely resembles a marketable title warranty. Finally, a title insurance policy usually insures that the insured has marketable title, subject to exceptions specified in the policy. If a title problem arises thereafter, the insured may seek to recover on the policy. This Assignment explores the first type of issue: When may a Buyer refuse to complete a contract of sale because the Seller is not tendering marketable title?

Typically, when a contract of sale is executed, Buyer pays Seller (or the real estate or escrow agent) "earnest money" or a "deposit." If no dispute arises thereafter, the deal closes. However, Buyer may refuse to proceed, relying on the asserted existence of a title defect, a "failure of marketable title," that will excuse him from accepting the tendered deed. At this point, Buyer may sue Seller to rescind the contract and to obtain a return of Buyer's deposit, or Seller may sue Buyer for specific performance or damages.

A promise "to sell Blackacre," without additional elaboration, is treated as a promise to convey Blackacre in fee simple absolute, free of leases, easements, covenants, conditions, restrictions, liens, encumbrances, future interests, dower rights, etc. It is rare, however, for a parcel to be completely free of all title defects. Therefore, the real estate contract normally contains language permitting Seller to convey Blackacre "subject to" (i.e. "with") certain title defects. A typical "subject to" clause might read as follows:

Seller promises to convey the above described property subject to:

1. lease dated Sept. 1, 2005, between Seller as landlord and XYZ Corp. as tenant a copy of which is attached hereto;

2. encumbrances, covenants, conditions, and restrictions of record, if any;

3. current real estate taxes now a lien but not yet due and payable.

*Typical Legal Issues*

Marketable title controversies frequently raise one or more of the following issues:

1. To what does Buyer object concerning the tendered title? Are his objections grounded in fact? For example, Buyer may claim that an easement crosses the subject property or that Seller does not own the property in fee simple absolute. Does the alleged easement actually exist? Does Seller own the property in fee simple absolute?

2. If the items to which Buyer objects exist, do they constitute "title defects" which would normally make the title unmarketable? For example, if a building violates the housing code does this mean that Seller does not have marketable title to it?

3. If they constitute "title defects," are they excused under the terms of the sale contract (the "subject to" clauses, or the "exceptions")? What is the scope and meaning of the "subject to" clause?

4. If there is a "title defect" not excused by the contract, has Buyer in some sense "waived" his right to object, or is the defect "insubstantial" or "curable"?

5. Often, the contract obliges Seller to do more than merely furnish "marketable title." Seller, for example, may promise that the land has certain specified ingress and egress. Thus, although questions concerning ingress and egress may not technically be marketable title questions, certain contracts may treat them as such.

6. Marketable title is more than merely title that is in fact free of title defects. It is title that also *appears* free of such defects. If Seller has good title but cannot prove it by evidence acceptable to the reasonably prudent buyer, then Buyer need not buy. It is often said that "Buyer cannot be compelled to purchase a lawsuit" even if he is likely to be successful in vindicating his title in such a lawsuit.

*General Observations*

Several facts are worth bearing in mind when reading the cases in this Assignment. Sometimes Buyer has simply changed his mind and is merely looking for an excuse to back out of the deal. In such cases, the asserted defect, whether it exists or not, is not the real reason for his reluctance. On the other hand, Seller should not be able to sell land that he does not own free and clear, at least not without appropriate adjustments in price. Seller should deliver what he promised.

## 2. PRINCIPAL PROBLEM

Upon their divorce, Frank and Joyce Rasmussen decide to sell their house in Davis, a university town in northern California. Joyce advertises the house for sale for $388,000. She expects that with luck the house might sell for a little over $370,000, but thinks that it makes sense to ask a higher price initially.

George Meltzer has recently been transferred from Los Angeles to Davis by his employer, a manufacturer of solar water heaters. Accustomed to the higher cost of housing in Los Angeles, George thinks the Rasmussens' house is a bargain and signs a contract to buy the house for $388,000. The contract provides in pertinent part as follows:

> Received from George Meltzer $12,000 as earnest money in part payment for purchase of the following described real estate: Lot 13 of Block 3 of Avion's Addition to the City of Davis, CA, as recorded in Book 4 of Maps, O.R., Yolo County. Total purchase price is $388,000, remaining $376,000 to be paid in cash on closing.
>
> Frank and Joyce Rasmussen shall furnish purchaser, as soon as procurable and within 30 days of this date an Allied Title Insurance Co. Standard Owner's Policy. If title is not insurable, and cannot be made insurable, earnest money shall be refunded and all rights of George Meltzer terminated. But if title is good and George Meltzer refuses to complete purchase, the earnest money may be retained by Frank and Joyce Rasmussen as liquidated damages. Title to be subject to building and use restrictions general to the district.

The preliminary title report shows the following item on the exception sheet:

> Declaration of protective restrictions, recorded April 4, 1985, in volume 389 Deeds, page 451, O.R. Yolo County. Said restrictions violated in that house located only 2 feet from east side line whereas 5 feet required. However, this title company will insure against loss or damage resulting from such violation, and will further insure that said violation will not work a forfeiture or reversion.

After signing the contract, George realizes the house is only worth $372,000. Additionally, he thinks he would prefer to live in a new condominium complex being developed just outside Davis. George would like to get out of the contract. You are George's attorney. Advise him of his rights and obligations under the contract. What are George's chances of getting out of the contract and getting his $12,000 back?

## 3. Materials for Solution of Principal Problem

### Laba v. Carey
Court of Appeals of New York, 1971.
29 N.Y.2d 302, 327 N.Y.S.2d 613, 277 N.E.2d 641.

■ SCILEPPI, JUDGE.

On February 27, 1970, after three weeks of negotiations, respondents, as purchasers, and appellant, as seller, entered into a written agreement for the purchase and sale of a parcel of real property known as 40–51 61st Street, Woodside, New York. In accordance with the terms of the contract, respondents made a payment of $5,700 to the appellant on account of the purchase price. This sum, plus the net costs of title examination and survey, was made a lien on the property and was to be refunded to respondents in the event that appellant failed to perform. In the litigation before us, respondents have sought the recovery of same and have made a claim for counsel fees.

The contract for the sale of the property was prepared on a New York Board of Title Underwriters form and provided that the seller shall give and the purchaser shall accept a title such as any reputable title company would approve and insure. Title was to be conveyed by a bargain and sale deed free of all encumbrances, except those noted in the contract and free of all "notes or notices of violations of law or municipal ordinances, orders or requirements noted in or issued by the Departments of Housing and Buildings, Fire, Labor, Health, or other State or Municipal Department having jurisdiction against or affecting the premises at the date hereof". Additionally, the sale and conveyance was made subject to two tenancies and appellant represented that he would serve a 30-day notice to terminate one of them. The contract expressly provided, in relevant part, that the sale and conveyance was subject to,

4. Covenants, restrictions, utility agreement and easement of record, if any, now in force, provided same are not now violated.

5. Any state of facts an accurate survey may show, provided same does not render title unmarketable.

After the execution of the contract, respondents retained the Inter-County Title Guaranty and Mortgage Company, a reputable insurance company, to search and insure title. During the course of the search, the title company found the existence of a recorded telephone easement and a "Waiver of Legal Grades" restrictive covenant, made between the City of New York and appellant's predecessor in title in 1967, when the latter sought permission to install 25.02 feet of sidewalk in front of the property. It appears that the then owner wished to construct a sidewalk on a level with the sidewalks on either side of the property. This level was approximately one foot below the "legal grade" for these properties and construction of the sidewalk below "legal grade" was necessary to prevent the hazardous condition that would result if the sidewalk in front of the subject property was placed one foot higher than surrounding property. The city granted permission and a certificate of occupancy in exchange for the promise of the then owner, his successors and assigns, to install a sidewalk in accordance with the legal grade "at any time hereafter as the Commissioner of Highways may direct". As a result of this search, the title company reported that appellant had a good and marketable title which it would approve and insure, but excepted the telephone easement and "Waiver of Legal Grades" covenant from coverage. Subsequently, the title company reported that there had been no violation of the terms of either the easement or the restrictive covenant. Investigation also revealed a survey of the property which was made in 1967 indicating the grades and elevations. This survey was filed by the builder's architect with the Department of Buildings of the City of New York and had been approved by that department. The survey showed the 25.02 feet of sidewalk at a grade of 55.72 feet while the "legal grade" ranged from 57.13 to 57.62 feet. The elevation of the building is 57.65 feet while that of the yard is 55.7 feet.

In a letter dated March 17, 1970 respondents' attorney forwarded the tax and exception sheets issued by the title company to appellant's counsel and advised him that respondents were "ready to close provided the tenant has removed from the premises." Appellant's attorney responded that the contract provided that the appellant was not obligated to remove the tenant; appellant's only responsibility was to serve a 30-day notice of termination and this had been done. At no time during this exchange did respondents question either appellant's title or the exceptions noted by the insurance company.

At the time set for the closing appellant tendered a deed which was rejected by respondents on the ground that appellant was unable to deliver a good, marketable and insurable title. This contention was predicated upon the survey and exceptions noted above.

As a result of this impasse, respondents have sought redress in the courts for the return of their deposit and reimbursement for the costs of title examination and counsel fees. A motion for summary judgment and a cross motion for summary judgment dismissing the complaint were made by respondents and appellant, respectively. Special Term denied respondents' motion, granted appellant's motion, and dismissed the complaint. It found that, by reading the "subject to" and "insurance" clauses together, appellant had tendered an insurable title. With regard to respondents' claim that title was unmarketable, Special Term concluded that the difference between the legal and existing grades of the sidewalk was a matter which related to abutting property and had no effect on title to the property which was the subject matter of the contract. The court also found that marketability was not impaired by the grade of the building (it was above the legal grade) or that of the yard, since no law, ordinance or regulation was violated thereby. (There were no violations filed against the property.)

On appeal, the Appellate Division reversed, 36 A.D.2d 823, 321 N.Y.S.2d 159, with one Justice dissenting on the opinion at Special Term. The court found that respondents were entitled to a return of their down payment and $326.20 for title insurance fees, but dismissed the claim for counsel fees because the contract had limited appellant's liability to the above items. Although it was the view of the majority below that the state of facts in the survey and the commissioner's authority to require the raising of the sidewalk in the future constituted an encumbrance, the court considered the issue of marketability immaterial to its disposition of the case. Instead, the reversal was predicated on the title company's failure to insure title unconditionally and without exception. It was on this basis that appellant was deemed to have breached the contract. The conclusion was reached even though the court stated, in apparent agreement with Special Term, that the "subject to" and "insurance" clauses had to be read together and that there had been no violation of the restrictive covenant.

We do not agree with the majority in the Appellate Division. The evidentiary showing made by the parties clearly establishes that appellant did all that was required of him by the terms of the contract. Consequently, we reverse the order appealed from and reinstate the determination of Special Term dismissing the complaint.

The contract of sale provided that appellant was required to deliver a title that a reputable insurance company would approve and insure. Respondents argue, and the Appellate Division has concluded that when a seller so contracts, he breaches his contract when the title company refuses to insure title unconditionally and without exception. This is, of course, the usual construction given to clauses of this nature. The rule is not, however, absolute, but rather is one to be tempered by the exigencies of the particular contract. Thus, it is said that the title company's approval must be unequivocal unless the exceptions are those contemplated by the contract. The contract before us addressed itself to the existence of easements and restrictive covenants and specifically provided that the conveyance was to be subject to these matters of record. The title company, disclosing the existence of a telephone easement and "Waiver of Legal Grades" restrictive covenant, excluded these items from coverage, except insofar as to say that they had not been violated. In so insuring, it was assuming responsibility for no less than that which respondents had expressly agreed to accept. The exceptions were matters specifically contemplated by the contract and, since there is no indication in the record that the parties intended anything other than the interlocking of the "subject to" and "insurance" clauses, it is our view that they must be read together to determine the scope of the seller's obligation.

Our conclusion is nothing more than an application of the "rule of construction that a court should not 'adopt an interpretation' which will operate to leave a 'provision of a contract . . . without force and effect'." Stated differently, our concern is with the intent of the parties "to the extent that they evidenced what they intended by what they wrote" (Raleigh Assoc. v. Henry, 302 N.Y. 467, 473, 99 N.E.2d 289, 291) and that intent must be gleaned from the several provisions of the contract. Although we do not fashion new contracts for the parties under the guise of contract construction, we are required to adjudicate their rights according to the unambiguous terms of the contract and therefore must give the words and phrases employed their plain meaning.

Accordingly, where a purchaser agrees to take title subject to easements and restrictive covenants of record which are not violated, this is the precise kind of title that the seller is obligated to tender and we are not persuaded that, absent an expression of a contrary intent in the contract, that obligation is broadened by the existence of the usual "insurance" clause. It is significant here that the parties used a standardized "insurance" clause in a form contract. They were, of course, free to vary its terms, but chose not to do so. As a result, their intent is clear. As a matter of practice over the years, literally thousands of exceptions have been made by insurance companies in similar circumstances where the parties take subject to easements and covenants of record and provide for title insurance by the use of a standardized clause. A conclusion that the seller would nevertheless be required to furnish title, insurable without exception, would not only render nugatory the "subject to" clause, but would also give every purchaser dissatisfied with his bargain a way of avoiding his contractual responsibilities. Surely, this was not contemplated in the contract before us.

[H]ere, neither easement nor restrictive covenant were violated and the title company agreed to insure in strict conformity to the bargain struck between the parties. Since there are no circumstances in this case which indicate that the parties intended anything else, it is our view that the Appellate Division incorrectly concluded that appellant failed to tender insurable title.[1]

---

[1] It would further appear that questions relating to differences between the legal and existing grades of sidewalks abutting property conveyed are not a proper subject for title insurance. In Sperling v. Title Guar. & Trust Co., 227 App.Div. 5, 236 N.Y.S. 553, affd. 252 N.Y. 613, 170 N.E. 163, a title company was instructed to search an insurance title. Though the title company found that a change in street grade had been authorized, it did not inform the purchasers and did not insure against it. It was held that since the request had been for a search and insurance of title, the company was not liable in either negligence or contract for a failure to disclose information upon a subject which does not affect the title (see Mafetone v. Forest Manor Homes, 34 A.D.2d 566, 567, 310 N.Y.S.2d 17, 18). Thus, the problem with regard to the

Nor is there merit in respondents' remaining point that appellant did not tender a marketable title. The contract made the conveyance subject to a state of facts that an accurate survey would reveal, provided that these facts would not render title unmarketable. At the closing, respondents took the position that inasmuch as the survey revealed the difference in the grade of the sidewalk and similar problems in the grade of the building and yard, title was unmarketable.

It is axiomatic that a purchaser is entitled to marketable title unless the parties provide otherwise in the contract. A seller is required to tender a title which is readily subject to resale and free from reasonable doubt. In the case before us, respondents do not question the validity of appellant's title; instead, they focus their attack on the deficiency in grades. To be sure, "[a] vendee has the right to a title that will enable him to hold his land in peace, and to be reasonably sure that no flaw or doubt will arise to affect its marketable quality and value" (Acme Realty Co. v. Schinasi, 215 N.Y. 495, 506, 109 N.E. 577, 580). It is for this reason that encumbrances which affect title, burden the property or limit the use, may render title unmarketable. However, it is clear that the objections which respondents make do not fall within the ambit of this rule. With regard to the sidewalk, respondents do no more than rephrase their objection to the "Waiver of Legal Grade" restrictive covenant, a matter which they agreed to take subject to. Neither the use of the property nor the title thereto is affected by the covenants, and significantly, all the property which surrounds the subject property suffers from the same sidewalk grade irregularities. Although there is no present violation, respondents contend that they may be required in the future to raise the level of the sidewalk. This is nothing more than a normal incident to the ownership of real property within the City of New York. Section 230 of the New York City Charter places the responsibility for the maintenance and repair of sidewalks on the individual owner. This must be done in accordance with such specifications as may be prescribed by the Transportation Administration. Thus, if title is unmarketable here, then so is all property similarly situated within the city. This is manifestly not so. Consequently, respondents have failed to show that the sidewalk grade levels complained of render title unmarketable.

Lastly, respondents' argument relating to the grade of the yard and building is similarly untenable. The survey clearly indicated that the first floor elevation of the building is above legal grade and respondents have failed to show that it is inaccurate or that a present violation of any municipal ordinance or department regulation exists. With regard to the yard, though its grade appears below the legal grade, no problem as to lateral support to adjoining lands or municipal streets is presented. It conforms to the zoning regulations of the City of New York.

---

grade of the sidewalk appears to be a matter alien to the title insurance required in the contract of sale and would militate against the conclusion that the clause was breached by appellant.

Accordingly, since appellant fully performed his agreement with respondents, the order appealed from should be reversed, with costs, and the order and judgment of Special Term reinstated.

## Madhavan v. Sucher
Court of Appeals of Michigan, 1981.
105 Mich.App. 284, 306 N.W.2d 481.

■ CYNAR, PRESIDING JUDGE.

On July 19, 1976, plaintiffs executed an offer to purchase defendants' house and property in Beverly Hills, Michigan. The purchase agreement form was drafted by defendants' real estate agent to whom plaintiffs had paid a $3000 deposit at the time the offer to purchase was executed. Under the terms of the purchase agreement, the sale to plaintiffs was made "subject to the existing building and use restrictions, easements, and zoning ordinances, if any ... ". The purchase agreement further provided that defendants would deliver "the usual Warranty Deed conveying marketable title".

Plaintiffs obtained the requisite mortgage from a local savings and loan institution on August 2, 1976, and closing was duly set for August 20, 1976. However, on August 18, the mortgagee notified plaintiffs that, according to the mortgage survey, a drainage easement encroached upon the northeast side of the dwelling. Although the mortgagee was of the opinion that the encroachment would not impair the security of the mortgage, plaintiffs were requested to provide the mortgagee with a letter acknowledging their awareness of the easement in order to have the savings and loan institution proceed with the processing of the mortgage and the closing of the transaction.

A second mortgage survey revealed that the first was erroneous and that the drainage easement in question ran along the eastern boundary of the property and did not encroach upon the dwelling but did encroach upon a portion of the concrete patio attached to the rear of the dwelling. The mortgagee notified defendants on August 26, 1976, after the revised survey had been received and reviewed, that it was prepared to proceed with the closing. However, in the interim, on August 20, plaintiffs advised defendants that they were rescinding their offer to purchase because the existence of the drainage easement prevented defendants from transferring marketable title. In this respect, plaintiffs knew that, on July 30, defendants had secured issuance of a title insurance commitment from a title insurance company but that the drainage easement was excepted from coverage under the policy.

Ultimately, when plaintiffs refused to close the transaction, defendants declared the deposit of $3000 forfeited, and plaintiffs instituted this action to recover that deposit. The district court granted plaintiffs' summary judgment motion, declaring that defendants were unable to convey marketable title because of the existence and placement of the drainage easement.

Defendants were obliged to convey marketable title to plaintiffs. Marketable title is one of such character as should assure to the vendee the quiet and peaceful enjoyment of the property, which must be free from incumbrance. *Barnard v. Brown,* 112 Mich. 452, 70 N.W. 1038 (1897). An incumbrance is anything which constitutes a burden upon the title, such as a right-of-way, a condition which may work a forfeiture of the estate, a right to take off timber, or a right of dower. *Post v. Campau,* 42 Mich. 90, 3 N.W. 272 (1879). A title may be regarded as "unmarketable" where a reasonably prudent man, familiar with the facts, would refuse to accept title in the ordinary course of business, and it is not necessary that the title actually be bad in order to render it unmarketable.

Defendants contend that to uphold the summary judgment order in this case would mean that no title subject to any incumbrance, including utility easements, would be marketable, even if the vendee agreed to purchase subject to certain easements. We do not believe that the district court's decision has such an expansive import. The district court did not hold that marketable title could not exist with respect to any parcel or property subject to any easement. Rather, the court determined, in effect, that the obligation of a vendor to provide marketable title, which title must be *fully insurable,* superseded the contractual provision in the purchase agreement regarding purchase subject to easements where the easement constituted such an incumbrance as to nullify marketable title. A vendor is not required to convey land free from any burden of easements, and the district court did not so determine. Rather, the vendee may not be required to accept land burdened by easements that affect marketable title.

The district court reasonably could determine that the drainage easement across the subject property, encroaching upon the concrete patio within a few feet of the house, was a sufficiently substantial incumbrance as to deny marketable title to plaintiffs-vendees, particularly since the title insurance company refused to insure against this incumbrance.

Plaintiffs did not waive objections to the drainage easement by signing a purchase agreement "subject to" the easement. Ordinarily, such a provision is not in conflict with a provision requiring the conveyance of marketable title. A conflict occurs only when the nature of the easement is so burdensome as to prevent conveyance of marketable title. The district court properly viewed these provisions of the instant purchase agreement as conflicting and therefore to be construed against defendants, whose agent drew up the contract.

The decision of the court below affirming the grant of summary judgment in favor of plaintiffs is affirmed.

Affirmed. Costs to plaintiffs.

## Voorheesville Rod and Gun Club v. E. W. Tompkins Company
Court of Appeals of New York, 1993.
82 N.Y.2d 564, 626 N.E.2d 917.

■ HANCOCK, JR., J.

The first issue in this case is whether the subdivision regulations of the Village of Voorheesville apply to a conveyance of a portion of a parcel of land where it is intended by the parties to the transaction that the lands shall remain undeveloped. If the regulations apply, then the primary issue is whether defendant seller's failure to seek subdivision approval before the transfer renders the title unmarketable. We conclude that the Village's subdivision regulations apply to this sale of property. But we further hold that defendant's refusal to seek the subdivision approval here does not cause the title to be unmarketable. Because no provision in the contract requires defendant to obtain subdivision approval and the only basis for plaintiff's specific performance claim is its failed assertion of unmarketable title, we reverse, deny plaintiff's summary judgment motion for specific performance, and dismiss the complaint.

On January 15, 1986, plaintiff Voorheesville Rod & Gun Club, Inc., signed a standard preprinted contract with defendant E. W. Tompkins Company, Inc., to purchase a portion of defendant's property located in the Village of Voorheesville, Albany County, for $38,000. The contract specified that the property would be conveyed by warranty deed subject to all covenants, conditions, restrictions and easements of record, and also to zoning and environmental protection laws, "provided that this does not render the title to the premises unmarketable." The property to be conveyed consisted of 24.534 acres of undeveloped land used for recreational purposes. The parties agree that plaintiff buyer did not intend to change the existing condition or use of the property after the purchase.

On August 23, 1986, prior to the revised closing date, plaintiff's attorney sent defendant's attorney a copy of the Village of Voorheesville's subdivision regulations and requested that defendant comply with them. Defendant did not seek subdivision approval. Defendant sent plaintiff a time-of-the-essence notice, demanded a closing on August 29, 1986, and notified plaintiff that if it did not close, that would be considered an anticipatory breach of contract. When plaintiff failed to close, defendant canceled the contract and returned plaintiff's $5,000 deposit. On September 4th, plaintiff informed defendant that the cancellation was unacceptable because defendant's failure to obtain subdivision approval had rendered the title unmarketable and, for that reason, plaintiff's financing bank was unwilling to close. Plaintiff then sought the requisite approval from the Village of Voorheesville Planning Commission. The Commission denied the application, stating that the subdivision regulations required that the application be submitted "by the [property] owner or an agent of the owner."

Plaintiff commenced this action on September 12, 1986, for specific performance or damages for breach of contract and then moved for partial summary judgment seeking specific performance. Supreme Court ordered that the contract be specifically performed by defendant and directed that defendant apply to the Village for subdivision approval and close on the subject property within a reasonable time after approval. The court held that defendant's failure to obtain subdivision approval made the title unmarketable and relieved plaintiff from closing until the approval was obtained.

The Appellate Division affirmed, stating that the sale of a portion of defendant's real property subjected the sale to the subdivision regulations of the Village of Voorheesville, even though development of the land was not then contemplated. The Court concluded that defendant's refusal to obtain subdivision approval rendered the title unmarketable, particularly because it appeared that plaintiff "would be 'plagued by zoning problems'" (*Voorheesville Rod & Gun Club v. Tompkins Co.*, 158 AD2d 789, 791).

Thereafter, plaintiff moved in Supreme Court for an order compelling defendant to file the subdivision application and convey the property. Noting that the subdivision application had been made and approved, Supreme Court directed defendant to transfer the property. Then the parties stipulated to discontinue all causes of action interposed in the pleadings except plaintiff's claim for specific performance of the contract. This Court granted defendant leave to appeal from the stipulation, deemed a judgment, bringing up for review the prior nonfinal Appellate Division order.

The preliminary issue is whether the Village's subdivision regulations apply at all under the circumstances presented. . . . [The court concluded that the subdivision regulations did apply.]

Given that the subdivision regulations apply, we turn to the main issue: whether lack of subdivision approval constitutes a cloud on the title which renders the title unmarketable. It is undisputed that the contract is silent as to the specific issue of subdivision approval. Thus nothing in the contract imposes upon defendant the affirmative obligation of obtaining subdivision approval.[2] Rather, paragraph 4 of the

---

[2] To the extent that plaintiff now claims—distinct from its argument that lack of subdivision approval renders the title unmarketable—that defendant has an implied good-faith contractual duty to obtain subdivision approval as a precondition of performing the contract, this issue was not raised by plaintiff in its summary judgment motion papers and thus is not preserved for our review.

We also note that this is not a case where the seller is seeking specific performance of a contract to compel a buyer to purchase property lacking subdivision approval or where a municipality is trying to block such a conveyance, and we do not address such situations here.

contract, entitled "Existing Conditions", provides that the property would be conveyed by warranty deed

> subject to all covenants, conditions, restrictions and easements of record. *Subject also to zoning and environmental protection laws;* any existing tenancies; . . . and any state of facts which an inspection and/or accurate survey may show, provided that this does not render the title to the premises unmarketable (emphasis added).

As stated, plaintiff was to purchase the property subject to zoning laws, which are closely related to subdivision regulations (see generally, *Matter of Golden v. Planning Bd., 30 NY2d 359, 372;* 2 Anderson, New York Zoning Law and Practice § 21.02 [3d ed]). This requirement conforms to the well-settled rule that "where a person agrees to purchase real estate, which, at the time, is restricted by laws or ordinances, he will be deemed to have entered into the contract subject to the same [and] [h]e cannot thereafter be heard to object to taking the title because of such restrictions" (*Lincoln Trust Co. v. Williams Bldg. Corp., 229 NY 313, 318*).

The only limitation that the contract places upon plaintiff's duty to purchase the property subject to zoning laws is when the application of such laws would render title to the property unmarketable. It was not necessary for the contract to specify that a marketable title was required because, in the absence of a stipulation to the contrary, it is presumed that a marketable title is to be conveyed. Accordingly, the issue reduces to whether the lack of subdivision approval constitutes a defect in the title which makes it unmarketable.

The test of the marketability of a title is "whether there is an objection thereto such as would interfere with a sale or with the market value of the property" (*Regan v Lanze, 40 N.Y.2d 475, 481*). A marketable title is "a title free from reasonable doubt, but not from every doubt" (*id., at 482*). We have said that a "purchaser ought not to be compelled to take property, the possession or title of which he may be obliged to defend by litigation. He should have a title that will enable him to hold his land free from probable claim by another, and one which, if he wishes to sell, would be reasonably free from any doubt which would interfere with its market value" (*Dyker Meadow Land & Improvement Co. v. Cook, 159 N.Y. 6, 15*). As can be seen from these definitions, marketability of title is concerned with impairments on title to a property, i.e., the right to unencumbered ownership and possession, not with legal public regulation of the use of the property. Accordingly, a zoning ordinance, existing at the time of the contract, which regulates only the use of the property, generally is not an encumbrance making the title unmarketable.

Where, however, a contract expressly provides that the seller warrants and represents that, upon purchase, the property will not be in violation of any zoning ordinance, the purchaser "is entitled to demand that the vendor rectify the same or return any moneys paid on account" (*Pamerqua Realty Corp., 93 A.D.2d 249, 251*). Contrary to plaintiff's claim, the present case does not fall within this exception to the general rule. Defendant did not warrant or represent that it would obtain subdivision approval; rather, plaintiff agreed to purchase the property subject to the zoning laws. In effect, plaintiff is attempting to add a term to the contract after the deal has been made. Thus, although defendant's failure to obtain subdivision approval was a violation of the regulations which were in effect when the parties contracted, such violation did not make the title unmarketable.[3]

We recognize, as noted by the courts below, the increasing sophistication of municipalities regarding subdivision regulation and their ability to prevent the purchaser from developing property as allowed by the zoning laws until the requisite subdivision approval is obtained. The solution for avoiding such problems, however, is not for the courts to expand the conditions which render title unmarketable, thereby altering the concept of marketability of title, but for the parties to real estate contracts to include specific provisions dealing with the duty to obtain subdivision approval.

Accordingly, the judgment appealed from and the order of the Appellate Division brought up for review should be reversed, with costs, plaintiff's motion for partial summary judgment should be denied, and defendant's cross motion for summary judgment dismissing the complaint should be granted.

## Nelson v. Anderson

Appellate Court of Illinois, Fifth District, 1997.
286 Ill.App.3d 706, 676 N.E.2d 735.

■ MAAG, JUDGE.

In this real estate contract action, summary judgment was granted in favor of the buyers on the ground that the sellers had not provided merchantable title. The sellers appeal.

On April 17, 1993, plaintiffs Jon and Anne Nelson (sellers) contracted to sell their home to defendants Walter and Shelly Anderson (buyers). The contract required buyers to pay an earnest money deposit of $1,500, with the balance of the purchase price to be paid on delivery of a warranty deed conveying a merchantable title, free and clear of all encumbrances, except those mentioned in the contract. The contract provided for closing within 30 days of signing, though the closing date was subsequently extended to June 30, 1993, by written agreement of the parties.

---

[3] Since it is undisputed that plaintiff did not intend to develop or further partition the parcel but only to continue its recreational use, there is no basis for any claim that the property would be "plagued by zoning problems".

The contract further provided that sellers would employ a title insurance company to issue a report of title; buyers had 10 days from the receipt of the title report to voice objections, and sellers then had 90 days in which to satisfy buyers' objections.

The title report issued to the buyers by Chicago Title Insurance Company in early June 1993 indicated that the house was positioned less than 10 feet from the north lot line, in violation of an applicable setback covenant. Specifically, the recorded subdivision plat to which the instant property belonged contained a covenant prohibiting a building or any part of a building on any residential lot from being positioned less than 10 feet from the property lines of the adjoining owners. The record reveals that sellers' property was only 4.7 feet from the lot's north boundary line, in violation of the covenant. Buyers made a specific, timely objection based on the violation.

Sellers responded by obtaining written assurances from the title company that, for an additional fee, it would insure over the building line exception at issue. Buyers then indicated that they were not satisfied with the title company's assurances and remained specifically concerned with the title company's guarantee to issue policies to any future buyers of the property. This prompted additional correspondence from the title company, in which it expressly assured that it would insure over the building line exception in the future for subsequent purchasers.

Buyers remained dissatisfied with the condition of the title and refused to close by the closing date. Buyers subsequently purchased another piece of property. Sellers ultimately sold their property at a lower purchase price.

Buyers filed suit to recover their earnest money deposit, while sellers sued for damages. The cases were consolidated by the St. Clair County circuit court. Each party filed a motion for summary judgment. The trial court granted buyers' motion, reasoning that sellers had breached the real estate contract by failing to deliver merchantable title.

On appeal, sellers argue that:

(1) They complied with the terms of the contract by responding to the purchasers' objections to the title insurance commitment in a timely fashion; and

(2) The trial court erred in finding that title to the property was not merchantable because of the building line violation.

When reviewing a trial court's grant of summary judgment, the issue before the appellate court is whether the pleadings, depositions, admissions, and affidavits on file show that there is no genuine issue of material fact and that the moving party is entitled to judgment as a matter of law. If the court of review determines that a genuine issue of material fact exists, then the entry of summary judgment must be overturned.

It is well-settled in Illinois that merchantable title is not perfect title, but rather title reasonably secure against the hazard, annoyance, and expense of future litigation. Our supreme court has further recognized that merchantable title is that which a reasonable person will accept as not subject to a doubt or cloud that would affect its market value. The issue of whether title to property is merchantable is a question of law for the court.

Here, sellers tendered a title which was encumbered by the violation of a restrictive covenant contained in the subdivision plat. The subdivision plat was recorded, and the covenants therein run with the land to bind the deeds of each lot in the subdivision. The violation of such a covenant gives every lot owner in the subdivision the right to sue to enforce the covenant. Moreover, the encumbrance and accompanying risk of litigation undoubtedly affect the market value of the property. We need not discuss the degree of risk of litigation posed nor the magnitude of the decrease in market value caused by the title defect. We simply find that the title at issue was clouded by the violation of a restrictive covenant such that a reasonable person could fear both the threat of future litigation and an unfavorable effect on the market value of the property. We deem such title to be unmerchantable.

Sellers further contend that even if the title defect initially rendered their title unmerchantable, they nonetheless complied with the terms of the contract by remedying buyers' objections in a timely fashion. We disagree.

At no time before closing did sellers cure the encumbrance. Although sellers were able to obtain additional assurances from the title insurance company indicating that it would insure future purchasers despite the defect, such assurances did nothing to cure the encumbrance on the title. The availability of insurance to cover future litigation of a title defect might reasonably persuade a buyer to tolerate the potential risks of such a transaction voluntarily. However, the court will not compel a skeptical purchaser to close on the deal. Even if sellers' offered cure would effectively indemnify buyers for any future litigation costs suffered as a result of the title encumbrance, buyers did not originally bargain for such a tumultuous scenario when they signed the real estate contract. The law has long recognized that a buyer cannot be compelled to buy a lawsuit.

In the instant case, buyers bargained for a merchantable, unencumbered title. At the time of closing, sellers' title still contained the encumbrance, making it unmerchantable. Buyers were therefore justified in refusing to close on the contract.

For the foregoing reasons, the order of the circuit court granting defendants' motion for summary judgment is affirmed.

## NOTES

1. *Marketability.* The contract in *Laba* was subject to any "state of facts an accurate survey may show, provided same does not render title unmarketable." The court held that the fact shown by the survey, that the sidewalk was below grade, did not make the title unmarketable. What kind of facts shown by a survey would make the title unmarketable, in the court's opinion? If the city had insisted that the grade be raised, who would have had to pay?

2. *A trap for the unwary.* Suppose a buyer initially raises a title objection on the settlement date? If the contract does not contain language allowing the seller additional time to cure the defect, can the buyer thus trap the seller into breaching?

3. *Can these cases be reconciled?* In *Laba*, the court held that although a promise to deliver insurable title would ordinarily mean title without exceptions, the apparent absolute nature of the insurance clause should be modified by reading it with the "subject to" clause. But in *Madhavan*, the court refused to reduce the absolute scope of the promise to deliver "the usual Warranty Deed conveying marketable title" by reading it with the "subject to" clause. The "subject to" clause in *Madhavan* provided that buyer would take "subject to the existing . . . easements. . . ." Yet, the buyer was permitted to refuse to close the transaction because of an existing easement. Why?

4. *Smart lawyering.* If you represented a buyer such as Meltzer in the Principal Problem, what would you advise him to do to avoid litigation on the issue of marketable title?

5. *Meaning of "loss or damage".* In the Principal Problem, how should we interpret the phrase in the title report that "the company will insure against *loss or damage* resulting from" the violation of the protective restrictions?

6. *Seller's obligation to provide marketable title under the Uniform Land Transactions Act (ULTA).*[4] Section 2–304 of ULTA obliges the seller of real estate to provide a marketable title at the time of conveyance, to include warranties of title in the deed and, if the contract is for sale of a possessory interest, to be able to deliver possession to the buyer without court action or breach of peace. Under section 2–304, a promise to provide "good" title means marketable title.

Where the contract obliges the seller to convey real estate rather than his interest in the real estate, a provision for conveyance by quitclaim deed does not of itself reduce the seller's obligation to convey marketable title under section 2–304. However, it does mean that the buyer's only remedy for failure of marketable title is rescission. Moreover, the buyer may not rescind once he has accepted the deed. ULTA § 2–304(d).

---

[4] Uniform Land Transactions Act (amended 1977). ULTA was approved by the National Conference of Commissioners on Uniform State Laws in 1975 and amended in 1977. It was approved by the American Bar Association in 1978. As of June 2016, it had not been adopted by any state.

Section 2–304 places responsibility for furnishing evidence of marketable title on the seller. Section 2–305 gives the seller a reasonable time to cure title defects after being informed of the defect by the buyer. However, as long as the buyer notifies the seller of the defect within ten days after receiving the evidence of title, the seller's right to cure does not extend his time for performance under the contract.

When the title report shows that title is not marketable, the buyer's remedies vary under Section 2–510. If the title defect was unknown to the seller when he signed the contract, the buyer's recovery is limited to the amount the buyer has paid on the contract plus incidental damages. Otherwise, the buyer may recover the excess of the fair market value at the time for conveyance over the contract price, plus incidental and consequential damages.

7. *The Uniform Simplification of Land Transfers Act (USLTA)*[5]. Part 3, Article 3 of USLTA is a Marketable Record Title Act similar to laws in force in a number of states. The Marketable Record Title Act limits title searches to thirty years and extinguishes earlier interests and claims. However, a person whose interest is based entirely on documents recorded more than thirty years earlier may record a notice of intent to preserve the interest and so keep it effective.

8. *Encroachments affecting marketable title.* In a California case, a title insurance company insured against lack of marketable title. After purchasing the property, the insured discovered that a busy city street encroached on one side of the property by about twenty feet. The policy only insured against claims of third parties that appeared in the public records. Because there were conflicting claims as to whether the encroachment was reflected in the public records and it was "arguable that the encroachment could have dissuaded someone from purchasing the property," a jury trial concerning the liability of the insurance company was appropriate. Mellinger v. Ticor Title Insurance Co., 93 Cal.App.4th 691, 113 Cal.Rptr.2d 357 (2001). Should an encroachment that could be removed only by litigation (or that could not be removed) be considered to destroy marketable title as a matter of law?

---

[5] Uniform Simplification of Land Transfers Act (1977). USLTA was approved by the National Conference of Commissioners on Uniform State Laws in 1977 and approved by the American Bar Association in 1978. As of June 2016, it had not been adopted by any state.

# ASSIGNMENT 45

# REMEDIES FOR BREACH OF MARKETING CONTRACT

## a. DAMAGES

### 1. INTRODUCTION

*Marketing contract.* It is important to distinguish between two kinds of real estate contracts: the marketing contract and the installment sale contract. The marketing contract usually covers a short period of time, almost always less than a year. The marketing contract specifies the price and other conditions of sale. Under the typical marketing contract, the purchaser obtains possession only after paying the full contract price. The buyer takes title and possession at the same time. The contract may permit the purchaser to take possession earlier as a temporary convenience. In most instances, the property is purchased on credit, and the credit instrument is a mortgage or a trust deed. Credit for the purchase of the property is obtained independently of the marketing contract.

*Installment sale contract.* In sharp contrast to the marketing contract, the installment sale contract (often called a security contract, a contract for deed, or (ambiguously) a real estate contract) serves the economic function of a mortgage or deed of trust. These contracts usually remain operative for ten to twenty years. Typically, the buyer under an installment sale contract is obligated to make monthly or other periodic installment payments on the purchase price. When all (or a specified substantial portion) of the price has been paid, the seller is obligated to deliver a deed conveying the promised title. Unlike the buyer in a marketing contract, the buyer under an installment sale contract normally takes possession many years before formal title is transferred. The installment contract often provides that if the buyer breaches by not making timely payment of the installments as they become due, seller may declare the contract materially breached and retain all installments as "rent" or "liquidated damages."

Suppose a buyer faithfully pays $95,000 of a $100,000 purchase price and then fails to make the remaining payments. If the typical installment sale contract were enforced as written, the buyer would lose ownership and possession of property worth $100,000 for defaulting on a $5,000 payment and buyer would not receive compensation for his investment. This obvious injustice has led to a trend away from rigorous enforcement of installment land contracts according to their literal provisions. Currently, the law regarding the enforceability of forfeiture clauses in installment sales contracts is in flux. The following accurately summarizes the law in this area:

> There was a time when forfeiture was routinely permitted because the parties had provided for this remedy in their contract. In recent decades, however, courts have increasingly scrutinized the forfeiture remedy. This is especially true where a very substantial portion of the purchase price has been paid. . . . Today, enforcement is no longer automatic. There is a growing trend for courts to recognize the installment land contract as a mortgage substitute. Some have required that the contract be treated as if it were a mortgage. Others have not taken that full step, but they have readily turned to mortgage law for illustrations of analogous protections that they conclude should apply to the installment purchaser.[1]

A distinction should be drawn between marketing contracts and installment sale contracts. Marketing contracts are true contracts that should be governed by contract principles. In contrast, installment sale contracts serve basically the same function as mortgages, and therefore, generally should be governed by mortgage principles. Although there is considerable support for this view, the courts have not unanimously adopted it.

## 2. Principal Problem: Liquidated Damages for Buyer's Default

If the buyer is in default, the seller is entitled to damages. If the contract provides that the deposit is to be retained by seller in the event of buyer's breach, courts will usually enforce such a provision provided it is construed as a reasonable "liquidated damage" clause rather than as a "penalty." The Principal Problem is concerned with this distinction.

*Situation 1: Small deposit, large loss.* Tanya agreed to buy Wyatt's house for $75,000. Upon signing the contract, Tanya paid Wyatt $500 as a deposit. The contract provides that the deposit "shall serve as liquidated damages in the event of breach of contract by buyer." Thereafter Tanya found a house she liked better and repudiated the contract. Wyatt sold the house to Earl for $70,000, the value of the house at the time of the breach. Wyatt is suing Tanya for $4,500 in damages ($75,000 minus $70,000 less deposit of $500). How should a court decide?

*Situation 2: Large deposit, no loss.* Tanya agreed to buy Wyatt's house for $75,000. Upon signing the contract Tanya paid $6,000 to Wyatt as a deposit. The contract provides that the deposit "shall serve as liquidated damages in the event of breach of the contract by buyer." Thereafter, Tanya found a house that she liked better and repudiated the contract. Wyatt sold the house to Earl for $86,000, the value of the house

---

[1] 4 Powell on Real Property, ch. 37.21[1][c] (2010).

at the time of the breach. Tanya is suing to recover her $6,000 deposit, arguing that since the breach did not damage Wyatt, and in fact enriched him, Wyatt should not be allowed to keep the deposit. How should a court decide?

## 3. MATERIALS FOR THE SOLUTION OF PRINCIPAL PROBLEM

### Covington v. Robinson
Court of Appeals of Tennessee, 1986.
723 S.W.2d 643.

■ BROOKS MCLEMORE, SPECIAL JUDGE.

This case involves a claim by prospective purchasers of realty for the return of earnest money in the amount of $100,000 deposited with defendant, International Farm Management, Inc., pursuant to a written contract for the sale of said realty. The trial court in a bench trial dismissed the claim and we affirm.

Cooper Y. Robinson and William W. Robinson, defendants-sellers, owned approximately 1,567 acres of land in Arkansas. On March 13, 1980, the sellers and plaintiff-purchasers, Stephen R. Covington and William B. Hurt, Jr., contracted for the sale and purchase of the property for $2,010,675. Defendant International Farm Management, Inc. acted as agent in the sale.

The contract provided:

> It is understood and agreed that this Contract is contingent upon Buyers obtaining a federal land bank loan on the property for seventy-five percent of the purchase price.

Pursuant to the contract the purchasers posted $100,000 earnest money. Upon default by the purchasers this deposit was to be divided equally between International Farm Management, Inc. and the sellers.

The real estate lies in two counties, Woodruff County and Cross County. Because of this, it was necessary to apply to two different offices for the loan mentioned in the contract. The purchaser, Covington, testified that Mr. Donald E. Brown, Jr., President of the Federal Land Bank of Eastern Arkansas, carried the ball on the loan and that he (Covington) and his associate applied for the "maximum loan" on the property. The testimony of Mr. Covington and Mr. Brown as to the request for the loan is devoid of any statements that 75% of the purchase price was necessary to make the purchase. Mr. Brown testified that the loan application was first made out in pencil and after conferences were had with other officials, typewritten applications were made up. Copies of these typewritten applications were exhibits but neither of these exhibits is signed by the applicants. The applications show that $907,500 or 78.59% of the value of the land in Woodruff County was applied for to the Land Bank of Searcy, Arkansas, and that $580,000 or 67.83% of the value of the land in Cross County was applied for from the Federal Land Bank Association of Eastern Arkansas plus $137,500 for improvements. The gross total money, not counting $137,500 for improvements, was $1,487,500 or 73.98%. If the money for improvements is considered the total percentage would be 80.81863.

The sums set out in these applications were approved and the applicants so notified. No effort was made and no request made by the applicants to the Land Banks to increase the amount of these loans the additional 1.02%.

Purchasers on July 9, 1980, declined to close the deal stating that the amount approved by the Land Bank was slightly less than 75%. Purchasers then made a proposal that amounted to a request that sellers carry as a loan the difference in the 73.98% loan from the Land Bank and the purchase price for five years and pay the interest on the Federal Land Bank loan from date of closing until January 2, 1981.

Sellers maintained that the purchasers had obtained a loan in excess of 75% of the purchase price, however, agreed to reduce the purchase price by the sum of $28,000 which would result in a sale price that would come within the 75% requirement if based upon buyers contention that the loan amounted to only 73.98%.

The purchasers still declined to close and the earnest money was divided pursuant to the contract. Purchasers then instituted this action.

The trial judge after hearing the matter on some written and some oral testimony found that the $137,500 improvement money was not money included in the loan for the purchase of the land and the loan money available to the purchasers was 73.98% of the purchase price, and that this amount constituted substantial compliance with the contingency in the contract regarding 75% financing. He further found that the purchasers failed to make a good faith effort to close the transaction, and found that the sellers' offer to reduce the amount brought the loan within strict compliance with the 75% contingency and that there was a lack of good faith on the part of the purchasers in that the loans approved for the purchasers were in the exact amount that the purchasers requested, that they submitted only one set of applications and made no further attempt to increase this amount and that purchasers' refusal to perform constitutes a default of their contractual obligations and that retention of the $100,000 was reasonable.

Purchasers have appealed.

The purchasers contend that the earnest money in the amount of $100,000 constitutes a penalty and is unenforceable and the trial court erred in finding that the sum constituted liquidated damages. They additionally contend that since the sellers sold the property to third parties approximately two months after the purchasers notified them that they were unable to obtain 75% financing, that if damages are allowable at all, the damages would be limited to the difference of the contract sale price and the selling price to third parties, i.e., approximately $10,650.

The purchasers rely heavily upon an unreported case from the middle section of this Court, *Monts v. Campbell* (Tenn.App.1984). The case is distinguishable from the case *sub judice*. Additionally, we are of the opinion that the law to be applied is Arkansas law, though the law of Tennessee if applied would not mandate a different result.

The applicable contract language is:

> ... In the event the Buyers default, the earnest money will be divided equally between International Farm Management and Sellers.

It is to be noted that the words "penalty", "forfeiture" or "liquidated damages" do not appear in the foregoing language.

The controlling law is found in the case of *Alley v. Rodgers*, 599 S.W.2d 739 (Ark.1980):

> It is well settled that a contract will be construed as properly stipulating for liquidated damages where, from a prospective view of the contract, it appears (1) that the parties contemplated that damages would flow from a failure to perform the contract; (2) that such damages would be indeterminate or difficult to ascertain; and (3) that the sum bears some reasonable proportion to the damages which the parties contemplated might flow from a failure to perform the contract. (Citing cases)
>
> In determining the proper interpretation of a provision for damages, we must "place ourselves in the position of the contracting parties and view the subject-matter of their contract prospectively, and not retrospectively." "This question is one generally somewhat difficult of solution, and there is no fixed rule by which all cases may be governed, as each case is established by its own particular facts."

Two additional Arkansas cases are noteworthy for their factual similarities to the present case. In both *Hall v. Weeks*, 214 Ark. 703, 217 S.W.2d 828 (Ark.1949), and *Smith v. Dixon*, 238 Ark. 1018, 386 S.W.2d 244 (1965), the court addressed liquidated damages clauses in real estate sales contracts. The provisions were enforced in both cases. In each of these two cases, the defaulting buyer argued that the amount of the stipulated damages was unreasonable in light of the circumstances. In *Hall v. Weeks,* the court upheld a $4,000 liquidated damage clause on a $40,000 contract saying, "nor is the situation materially changed because within five or six weeks Hall sold for $45,500." In *Smith v. Dixon,* a $15,000 award was enforced on a $200,000 contract.

At the time the contract before us was entered into, it was next to impossible to determine what damages would result from the purchasers' breach. The property could have remained on the market for an indefinite period, and therefore, be subject to the radical variation in price that the market for farmland can experience. All of the prerequisites for enforcement of a liquidated damage provision as outlined by the Arkansas cases are present in the instant case. There is nothing to indicate the amount is unconscionable or disproportionate to the damages apparently likely to result from a breach. The liquidated damages represent only 5% of the total purchase price which is smaller than the percentages upheld in *Hall v. Weeks* and *Smith v. Dixon*.

The fact that the property was subsequently sold for $2,000,000 is not relevant as the Court will not take a "retrospective view".

The judgment of the trial court is affirmed.

## Colonial at Lynnfield, Inc. v. Sloan
United States Court of Appeals, First Circuit, 1989.
870 F.2d 761.

■ COFFIN, CIRCUIT JUDGE.

This case arises out of a failed contract for the purchase of a 49% interest in the Colonial Hilton Inn in the towns of Lynnfield and Wakefield, Massachusetts. The seller, Colonial at Lynnfield, Inc. (Colonial), sued the prospective buyer, Colonial Associates (Associates),[1] for breach of contract and liquidated damages in the amount of $200,000. The district court found that the buyer was at fault, and held that Colonial was entitled to the liquidated damages. Associates claims that the contract containing the liquidated damages provision was unenforceable. We reverse the award of liquidated damages on the ground that, under Massachusetts law, it constitutes a penalty.

Plaintiff Colonial and defendant Associates came together in Mid-1980 when Colonial was attempting to solve its worsening financial crisis by selling a partial interest in the hotel. Colonial's fiscal problems stemmed from a major expansion and renovation of the hotel. As construction progressed, blocks of rooms needed to be shut down for refurbishing, resulting in a loss of income. The losses were exacerbated by increasing costs for overhead, borrowing, and inflation. Colonial's cash flow suffered, and it needed more money to cover its increased costs.

On November 12, 1980, Colonial and Associates signed an Agreement of Sale (the Agreement) in which Associates contracted to pay $3,375,000 for 49% of the hotel. The Agreement gave Associates time to test the market so that it could determine whether it could raise the funds for the purchase price by selling units in a limited partnership. If after that time Colonial Associates decided against going ahead with the purchase, it had no obligation to Colonial. If it wished to go forward, it was required to give a Notice to Proceed, and to be prepared for a closing

---

[1] The principals of Colonial Associates are ten individuals who are general partners in one of two partnerships. In this opinion we shall refer to the appellants collectively as, "Associates" or simply as "defendants."

shortly thereafter. Once Associates gave the Notice to Proceed, it was subject to a $200,000 liquidated damages provision. That provision would be activated, however, only if the transaction failed to close solely due to Associates' fault.

The district court found that Associates was required to give notice of their intention to proceed with the transaction on or before April 2, 1981, and that they failed to do so. The deal did not at that point fall apart, however. Associates asked for a meeting to discuss the situation, and Colonial agreed so long as the defendants set a closing date. In a letter dated April 16, 1981, Associates agreed to close on June 1.

At a meeting in Boston on April 21, the parties discussed various modifications to their original agreement. Three days later, Colonial's counsel sent a letter to Associates' counsel stating that the parties had agreed that Colonial would receive an additional $100,000 from Associates "in consideration of the delay in this matter and for other valuable consideration." The letter stated that Associates' counsel should "prepare the necessary memorandum of agreement carrying the foregoing into effect." The letter concluded by noting that time is of the essence with respect to the June 1 closing date. It appears that no memorandum of agreement ever was prepared.

On May 22, Colonial obtained a $318,000 loan from Essex Bank by assigning as collateral its "right, title and interest" in the Agreement with Associates. The assignment was to become null and void when the loan was repaid, presumably after the closing with defendants. On May 29, Associates informed Colonial that it had been unable to sell enough units to close on June 1, and requested an extension. Colonial refused, and subsequently declared Associates in default.

On July 21, Colonial accepted a proposal from Lincoln National Development Corporation of Indiana (Lincoln) to purchase a 50% interest in the hotel for $3.7 million. That sale took place in early September 1981.

Colonial filed suit against Associates to enforce the liquidated damages provision contained in the November 12 Agreement, claiming that the sale had failed to close solely because of Associates' inability to sell enough units in the limited partnership to finance the hotel purchase. The defendants raised several defenses, [including that] even if the original Agreement is enforceable, the liquidated damages provision is unenforceable as a matter of public policy because it is disproportionate to any reasonable estimate of damage that plaintiff might suffer, and therefore represents a substantial penalty.

Associates argues that the liquidated damages provision is not enforceable because it constitutes a penalty. They rely on the well established principle that the amount of liquidated damages specified in a contract must be reasonably related to the anticipated or actual loss caused by the breach. Restatement (Second) of Contracts § 356 (1981). A provision setting an unreasonably large liquidated damages amount is unenforceable on public policy grounds as a penalty. Restatement (Second) of Contracts § 356(1); Restatement of Contracts § 339.[5]

Defendants claim that the $200,000 damage amount is unreasonable both as an estimate, as of November 12, 1980, of the damages that plaintiffs *might* incur and when compared with the damages that *in fact* occurred. We disagree that the provision constituted a penalty at the time the Agreement was signed in late 1980. As the district court properly observed, "[o]ne could not know, at that time, when the hotel would eventually be sold, if at all, in the event that defendants defaulted." With the passage of time, Colonial would suffer a loss of interest on the $1.8 million that defendants were to have paid on June 1. At the 21% rate of interest applicable in the spring of 1981, a six-month delay would have cost Colonial $189,000. In addition, the new sale price could have been lower than that in the Agreement with defendants, and other costs associated with the collapsed deal, such as lawyers' fees, may have been incurred.

Moreover, the decision to specify a liquidated sum appears reasonable in light of the difficulties that might have been anticipated in determining the precise amount of Colonial's damages in the event of a breach. *See Security Safety Corp.*, 350 Mass. at 158, 213 N.E.2d at 867; A. Corbin, *Corbin on Contracts* § 1060 at 350 (1964) ("In order to sustain a provision for payment of a definite sum as a liquidation of damages, it is necessary that at the time the contract is made it must appear that the injury that will be caused by breach will be difficult of estimation.") If Colonial's financial troubles had escalated even more, and the new sale price had turned out to be less than Associates agreed to pay, the parties undoubtedly would have argued over whether the "depreciation" was Colonial's or Associates' fault. In addition, the parties were likely to argue—as they have—over which expenses connected to the transaction were attributable to the breach. "When losses are difficult to quantify, considerable deference is due the parties' reasonable agreement as to liquidated damages," *Lynch,* 20 Mass.App. at 628, 481 N.E.2d at 1386. This is particularly so where, as here, "[t]here is nothing to suggest that the liquidated damages provision . . . was negotiated at other than an arm's length basis between adequately represented parties." *Id.*

Thus, we find no error in the district court's conclusion that the liquidated damages provision was a reasonable *estimate* of difficult-to-ascertain damage at the time the parties agreed to it. That conclusion does not end our inquiry, however. As Associates points out,

---

[5] The second Restatement notes that parties to a contract may not disregard the principle of compensation when providing in advance for damages in the event of a breach. "[T]he parties to a contract are not free to provide a penalty for its breach. The central objective behind the system of contract remedies is compensatory, not punitive. Punishment of a promisor for having broken his promise has no justification on either economic or other grounds and a term providing such a penalty is unenforceable on grounds of public policy." Section 356 at Comment a.

Massachusetts law clearly envisions a retrospective appraisal of a liquidated damages provision in certain circumstances. If the actual damages turn out to be "easily ascertainable," a court must consider whether the stipulated sum is "unreasonably and grossly disproportionate to the real damages from a breach," *A-Z Servicenter, Inc.*, 334 Mass. at 675, 138 N.E.2d at 268; *Lynch,* 20 Mass.App. at 627, 481 N.E.2d at 1386; *Security Safety Corp.*, 350 Mass. at 158, 213 N.E.2d at 867; *Warner,* 2 Mass.App. at 799, 307 N.E.2d at 849.[6] If so, the liquidated damages provision will be deemed unenforceable as a penalty, and "the court will award the aggrieved party no more than his actual damages." *A-Z Servicenter,* 334 Mass. at 675, 138 N.E.2d at 268; *Security Safety Corp.*, 350 Mass. at 158; 213 N.E.2d at 867.

We believe this is a case in which liquidated damages may not be awarded because it is easy to ascertain that Colonial in fact suffered no damage. In reaching this conclusion, we considered the following facts:

—Colonial sold a 50% interest in the hotel on or about September 1, 1981 for $3.7 million. The buyer, Lincoln, was entitled to buy a 49% interest, which is what Associates sought to purchase, for $3,626,000–$251,000 more than the price defendants agreed to pay. Thus, all else being equal, Colonial earned $251,000 more from the purchase price than it would have without Associates' breach.

—Lincoln's purchase took place, however, three months after the June 1 closing date agreed to by Colonial and Associates. Colonial therefore lost interest for that period on the $1.8 million that defendants were to have paid on June 1. At the 21% rate of interest asserted by Colonial, that represents a loss of $94,500.

—The loss of interest revenues from June to September was offset, however, by the fact that Lincoln paid Colonial $2.7 million when it closed the deal—$900,000 more than Colonial was to receive up front from Associates. Thus, Colonial benefitted by having use of that $900,000 until at least March 1, 1982, the earliest date on which Associates would have been obligated to pay the balance of the purchase price. Again using Colonial's 21% interest rate, the "time value" of the $900,000 for six months was $94,500.

---

[6] The first Restatement explicitly envisioned a retrospective consideration of a liquidated damages provision:

If the parties honestly but mistakenly suppose that a breach will cause harm that will be incapable or very difficult of accurate estimation, when in fact the breach causes no harm at all or none that is incapable of accurate estimation without difficulty, their advance agreement fixing the amount to be paid as damages for the breach . . . is not enforceable.

§ 339 at Comment e. The second Restatement also anticipates a retrospective view:

If . . . the difficulty of proof of loss is slight, less latitude is allowed in [the] approximation [of anticipated or actual harm]. If, to take an extreme case, it is clear that no loss at all has occurred, a provision fixing a substantial sum as damages is unenforceable.

§ 356 at Comment b.

These figures show that Colonial made a profit of $251,000 on the purchase price of the hotel as a result of defendants' breach. None of Colonial's attempts to transform that profit into an approximately $200,000 loss is persuasive. Its primary theory is that it is inappropriate to compare the sale to Lincoln with the proposed sale to Colonial because economic circumstances had changed dramatically from November 1980 to the spring of 1981. Hotel construction was completed, all rooms were opened, including 131 new ones, and the hotel began making a profit. Colonial argues that the hotel's economic turnaround meant that it was worth more than when Associates contracted to purchase it.

The fact that Lincoln paid more for the hotel because it was worth more does not assist Colonial's position. Indeed, it shows that Colonial benefitted from the breach with regard to the purchase price. Colonial was obligated to complete the renovation project even after a closing with Associates, and so there are no additional construction expenses on Colonial's part to be offset against the $251,000 profit. With respect to the 49% interest, Lincoln received no more than Associates would have gotten for $251,000 less. Thus, the Lincoln deal simply was a better one for Colonial.

Colonial also argues that the difference between the deals is incalculable because Lincoln purchased a 50% interest, which it contends is more valuable than a 49% interest not only because of the 1% mathematical difference but also because of the control Lincoln gained. Colonial and Lincoln put a price on that 1% interest, however, by specifying in their contract that the price would be reduced by $74,000 if Colonial's mortgage company would agree only to a sale of 49%. We see no reason in this context to disregard the value placed on the 1% interest by the parties to the agreement.[11]

Other costs asserted by Colonial include the fees and expenses associated with the failed Agreement, including accounting and legal fees, stationery costs, and the cost of taking inventory. Even were we to find that all of these costs were attributable to Associates' breach,[12] the total amount as shown through evidence at trial added up to only slightly more than $100,000. The higher purchase price more than compensates for those losses.[13]

---

[11] We emphasize that the $251,000 "profit" figure that we have used is based on the price to Lincoln of a 49% interest. Colonial, in fact, received an additional $74,000 for the 50% interest that it sold.

[12] We question whether Colonial would be entitled to collect as damages that portion of its expenses not directly attributable to Associates' failure to meet the June 1 deadline. For example, we see no reason why Associates would be obligated to pay for legal fees associated with drawing up the contract in November 1980 because Associates had no obligation to go forward with the deal until they gave Colonial a Notice to Proceed. It seems that Colonial assumed the initial financial risks of entering into the transaction, and properly could hold Associates responsible only for those costs directly stemming from the breach of the agreement.

[13] It could be argued that the liquidated damages provision here should be upheld because the precise amount of Colonial's net profit from the Lincoln sale is not "easily ascertainable," see A-Z Servicenter, Inc., 334 Mass. at 675, 138 N.E.2d at 268. It *is* clear, however, that Colonial suffered no damage, and it would be senseless to require any more

At oral argument, Colonial's counsel stressed that in addition to the "hard costs" of the failed transaction—which we understand to be primarily the purchase price and lost interest—there were "soft costs," such as lost opportunities and damage to the reputation of the company. Colonial presented no evidence of these "soft" costs, and we question whether there could be such damages in light of Lincoln's $3.7 million offer just weeks after Colonial and Associates failed to close their deal on June 1. In any event, the $251,000 profit provides a cushion for even "soft costs."

Colonial claims that *Lynch v. Andrew,* 20 Mass.App.Ct. 623, 481 N.E.2d 1383 (1985), supports its claim for liquidated damages because the court there upheld a liquidated damages provision based on lost opportunities that were difficult to quantify, while emphasizing the "considerable deference . . . due the parties' reasonable agreement." 20 Mass.App. at 628, 481 N.E.2d at 1386. This case differs substantially from *Lynch v. Andrew.* That case involved buyers defaulting on the purchase of a house where a liquidated damages provision entitled the seller to retain a $25,400 deposit. Under the purchase and sale agreement, half of the deposit was to be paid to the broker if the buyers defaulted, leaving only $12,700 for the seller. The seller sold her property six months after the breach for $5,000 less than the original buyers had agreed to pay. In addition, the seller claimed that she had to back out of an agreement to purchase a house that was larger and in better condition than the house she bought the following fall.

Thus, *Lynch v. Andrew* is a case in which the seller made a worse deal months after the buyer's default and in which the seller specified a lost opportunity of some value. The liquidated damages provision gave to the plaintiff only $7,700 more than her direct out-of-pocket costs. It should be clear from the facts discussed previously that this is not a case like *Lynch.*

We therefore conclude that the $200,000 liquidated damages provision is unenforceable because it is "so disproportionate to the plaintiff's losses and expenses caused by the defendants' breach" as to constitute a penalty, *Warner,* 2 Mass.App. at 799, 307 N.E.2d at 849. Indeed, this appears to be the "extreme case" in which no loss at all has occurred. *See* Restatement (Second) of Contracts, § 356, Comment b.

## Strouse v. Starbuck

Missouri Court of Appeals, 1999.
987 S.W.2d 827.

■ JAMES K. PREWITT, PRESIDING JUDGE.

Appellant brought suit against Respondents seeking a judgment for liquidated damages as a result of a breach of a real estate contract.

---

precise calculation as a prerequisite for holding this liquidated damages provision to be unenforceable.

Defendant Clair Land Co., Inc. held $10,000.00 in escrow, which it deposited with the court prior to trial on this action, and is not a party to this appeal. The judgment ordered that the $10,000.00 held in escrow by the court be released to Defendants Starbuck. Appellant brings this appeal against the Starbucks.

Appellant is the owner of 239 acres located near the town of Niangua in Webster County, Missouri. Respondents asked their friend, Jerri Delcour, a real estate agent, if the 239 acres were for sale. Delcour inquired of Appellant whether he was interested in selling this acreage; Appellant stated he was not. When Delcour indicated she had a buyer, however, Appellant signed an "Authorization to Show Property to Terry Starbuck Only" on February 20, 1996. A real estate contract was subsequently entered into between Appellant and Respondents on February 21, 1996. The sale price in the contract was for $225,000.00, requiring Respondents to obtain financing in the sum of $175,000.00.

Respondents did not obtain financing and informed Appellant approximately one week prior to the contract closing date that they were not going to be able to close on the contract. Appellant filed a petition claiming that Respondents failed to use reasonable diligence and good faith in obtaining financing. Trial without a jury was held on April 11, 1997. Judgment in favor of Respondents was issued without findings of fact or conclusions of law.

Appellant raises several points on appeal, however Point III is dispositive of this appeal. Appellant claims the trial court erred in failing to award him liquidated damages pursuant to the real estate contract. The contract states:

> If this Contract shall not be closed for the fault of the Buyer, then 10% of the total sale price shall be paid by Buyer to Seller as liquidated damages, it being agreed that actual damages are difficult, if not impossible, to ascertain.

Missouri law requires a showing of actual harm to trigger a liquidated damages clause. Goldberg v. Charlie's Chevrolet, Inc., 672 S.W.2d 177, 179 (Mo.App.1984). Appellant must show not only that Respondents breached the contract, but also that " 'damages have in fact accrued in consequence thereof.' " Corrigan Co. Mechanical Contractors, Inc. v. Fleischer, 423 S.W.2d 209, 214 (Mo.App.1967).

At trial, Appellant and his attorney had the following dialogue, which Appellant's counsel says sufficiently showed actual damages:

Q. At the time that you entered into the sale contract with the Starbucks for your property, did you end up taking your property off the market so to speak so that you didn't talk to anybody else about selling it to them?

A. I—I couldn't. In fact, I've even—I even had people run off of the property because they had been told, "Well it's sold." . . . And I had people looking at the property, but they were—They were told by the real estate lady's husband they couldn't go on there because it was sold. . . .

Q. And since the May 28th closing date passed, have you been able to sell your property yet?

A. I have not, no. . . .

Q. As a result of the Starbucks['] failure to close the transaction . . . , do you feel like you have suffered any damages as a result of that?

A. Well, sure. The—I—I certainly do.

Q. And is that anything other than the lack of the purchase price that you're receiving you feel is the damage?

A. Well, I mean, I'm still stuck with the—the property I thought was sold.

Q. Okay.

A. . . . And the obligation of the payments on it.

The reason Missouri courts hold that a plaintiff "must show at least some actual harm or damage caused by the breach before the liquidated damages clause can be triggered" is explained in Grand Bissell Towers, Inc. v. Joan Gagnon, Enter., Inc., 657 S.W.2d 378, 379 (Mo.App.1983). There, the court states that liquidated damages clauses are enforceable, but penalty clauses are not, and without evidence of damages, a liquidated damages clause actually becomes a penalty and is unenforceable. 657 S.W.2d at 379, n. 4.

Here, Appellant did not conclusively establish that he suffered any actual damage, and the trial court could have found that there was insufficient evidence to show any damage. Appellant had a "specific listing" to show the property only to Respondents. The property was not on the market prior to entering into that listing. No evidence was presented that Appellant had subsequently listed the property for sale, or taken any other action to sell the property.

Appellant did testify that people "were told" they could not go on the property because it was sold. Whether that was true and the effect of it, even if so, was for the consideration of the trial court. The trial court is in a better position than an appellate court to judge the witness's credibility "and other intangibles not revealed in a transcript." Ellis v. Ellis, 970 S.W.2d 416, 418 (Mo.App.1998). The trial court "may accept or reject all, part, or none of the testimony of witnesses." Snyder v. ICI Explosives USA, Inc., 938 S.W.2d 946, 948 (Mo.App.1997). Therefore, we defer to the trial court's apparent or possible conclusion that this testimony was insufficient to establish that Appellant suffered actual harm. When no findings of fact or conclusions of law are made by the trial court, this court assumes all fact issues were determined in accordance with the result reached. Rule 73.01(a)(3).

Appellant also claims he was "further damaged when the $20,000.00 earnest money check, tendered by Buyers was returned insufficient funds, and Seller accepted $10,000.00 based upon Buyers' assurances that they were going to obtain financing." We do not understand how this action damaged Appellant, and are given no explanation by Appellant.

Our examination of the record leads us to conclude there may have been no actual harm or damage established by Appellant. We are not saying that the evidence presented would not have been sufficient to support actual damages had the trial court found for Appellant, but that the evidence was not so persuasive that the trial court had to find for Appellant on this issue. Therefore, the liquidated damages clause was unenforceable.

The judgment is affirmed.

## CALIFORNIA CIVIL CODE

**§ 1675. Residential property; failure of buyer to complete the purchase; validity of contract provisions**

(a) As used in this section, "residential property" means real property primarily consisting of a dwelling that meets both of the following requirements:

(1) The dwelling contains not more than four residential units.

(2) At the time the contract to purchase and sell the property is made, the buyer intends to occupy the dwelling or one of its units as his or her residence.

(b) A provision in a contract to purchase and sell residential property that provides that all or any part of a payment made by the buyer shall constitute liquidated damages to the seller upon the buyer's failure to complete the purchase of the property is valid to the extent that payment in the form of cash or check, including a postdated check, is actually made if the provision satisfies ... subdivision (c) or (d) of this section.

(c) If the amount actually paid pursuant to the liquidated damages provision does not exceed 3 percent of the purchase price, the provision is valid to the extent that payment is actually made unless the buyer establishes that the amount is unreasonable as liquidated damages.

(d) If the amount actually paid pursuant to the liquidated damages provision exceeds 3 percent of the purchase price, the provision is invalid unless the party seeking to uphold the provision establishes that the amount actually paid is reasonable as liquidated damages.

(e) For the purposes of subdivisions (c) and (d), the reasonableness of an amount actually paid as liquidated damages shall be determined by taking into account both of the following:

(1) The circumstances existing at the time the contract was made.

(2) The price and other terms and circumstances of any subsequent sale or contract to sell and purchase the same property if the sale or contract is made within six months of the buyer's default.

## NOTES

1. *The underlying policies.* *Covington* and *Colonial* rely on two different and conflicting approaches to the issue presented in Alternative 2 of the Principal Problem. What are the policies underlying each approach? With which approach is § 1675 of the California Civil Code consistent? Overall, which is the better approach?

2. *Commercial vs. residential.* The California statute takes a different approach for commercial real estate transactions in that a liquidated damage provision is considered to be valid "unless the party seeking to invalidate the provision establishes that the provision was unreasonable under the circumstances existing at the time the contract was made." California Civ.Code § 1671(b).[2] Why do you suppose the statutory scheme distinguishes between residential and commercial transactions?

3. *Low liquidated damages clauses.* In contrast to the willingness of courts to reject artificially high liquidated damages clauses, the courts have historically enforced disproportionately low liquidated damages clauses.[3]

4. *Defaulting seller.* The Uniform Land Transaction Act (ULTA § 2–510(b)) provides that unless "the title defect is an encumbrance which could be discharged by application of all or a portion of the purchase price, if a seller is unable to convey because of a title defect of which the seller had no knowledge at the time of entering into the contract, the buyer is entitled only to restitution of any amounts paid on the contract price and incidental damages." The ULTA rule protects a breaching seller, who is not acting in bad faith, from having to pay the difference between the contract price and a higher market price at the time of the breach. The ULTA rule is derived from the eighteenth century English case Flureau v. Thornhill.[4] In contrast, California Civil Code §§ 3306 and 3307 provide for loss of bargain damages in the case of both a breaching seller and breaching buyer, regardless of bad faith. Which rule is preferable?

---

[2] See also California Civ.Code §§ 1676, 1677. Section 1676 expressly incorporates the requirements of § 1671(b) for commercial transactions, and § 1677 requires that a liquidated damage provision must be signed and initialed separately by each party to the transaction and, if contained in a printed contract, must be set out in type of a certain size.

[3] See, e.g., Roscoe-Gill v. Newman, 188 Ariz. 483, 937 P.2d 673, 232 Ariz. Adv. Rep. 22 (Ariz.App.1996)(court enforced a $5,000 liquidated damages clause when seller lost $120,000 as a result of buyer's breach and incurred another $30,000 in costs); Warstler v. Cibrian, 859 S.W.2d 162 (Mo.App.1993)(court upheld a $2,000 liquidated damages clause despite seller's near $10,000 loss when forced to sell property at a lower price after defendant's breach); Morris v. Flores, 174 Ill.App.3d 504, 124 Ill.Dec. 122, 528 N.E.2d 1013 (1988) (court upheld $100 liquidated damage clause despite sellers' loss of $1,615 in damages and $133 in costs following defendant/buyers' breach); Mahoney v. Tingley, 85 Wash.2d 95, 529 P.2d 1068 (1975) (court upheld $200 liquidated damage clause when the sellers' damages were alleged to be over $3,000).

[4] 2 W.Bl. 1078, 96 Eng.Rep. 635 (1776).

## b. Specific Performance

### 1. Introduction

Often the parties to a contract will not specify the consequences of a breach. When this occurs, a court is left to fashion a remedy that is just. A judgment of money damages is the preferred remedy for breach of a contract. Sometimes, however, money damages cannot adequately right the wrong. The amount of the damages may be uncertain or money may not be an adequate substitute for having the bargain carried out.

In cases where damages are not an adequate remedy, a court has the power to grant equitable remedies. The most important of these remedies is specific performance. A court granting specific performance orders the breaching party to carry out the contract. Buyers and sellers of land who are confronted with a breach will often ask the court to invoke its equitable powers, and order the other party to perform. In this Assignment, we examine the contours of the remedy of specific performance.

### 2. Principal Problem: Seller's Default

On June 1, Bye contracted in writing with Owner to purchase "Big Z," Owner's 10-acre tract of land improved with a lodge. The purchase price was $70,000 to be paid in full with recordation of deed on September 1.

Pursuant to the agreement, Bye paid Owner $5,000 on July 1, such payment to be applied to the purchase price and to be forfeited as liquidated damages if Bye defaulted on the agreement.

"Big Z" is one of the 1,000 tracts located in a 10,000 acre development, and is similar in size and site of tract, and size and design of lodge to most of the other tracts in the subdivision.

On July 10, Bye contracted in writing to sell "Big Z" to Kent for $90,000. On July 20, Pierre offered Owner $120,000 for "Big Z" and Owner accepted that offer in writing. All of the above transactions took place through correspondence. None of the parties has ever met any of the others.

On July 20, Owner advised Bye that Owner would not convey "Big Z" to Bye, and 1) offered to pay Bye $20,000 for cancellation of the contract, or 2) to convey another parcel he owned known as "Retreat" which was immediately adjacent to "Big Z" and was identical in size of tract and size and design of building.

1. What are Bye's rights and remedies, if any, against Owner? against Pierre?

2. What are Kent's rights and remedies, if any, against Bye?

(Adapted from a California Bar Examination question.)

## 3. Materials for Solution of Principal Problem

### Giannini v. First National Bank of Des Plaines
Appellate Court of Illinois, 1985.
136 Ill.App.3d 971, 91 Ill.Dec. 438, 483 N.E.2d 924.

■ JIGANTI, PRESIDING JUSTICE:

John Giannini d/b/a J.G. Sewer Contractors (Giannini) executed an agreement to purchase a condominium unit in the Castilian Courts Condominium Complex to be constructed in Glenview, Illinois and paid $62,330 in earnest money on the property. Although the building in which his unit was located was subsequently constructed, it was never formally declared a condominium and as a result the terms of the agreement were never fulfilled.

Giannini filed a two-count complaint against First National Bank of Des Plaines (Des Plaines Bank), the record title holder of the complex pursuant to a land trust agreement; Frank R. Stape Builders, Inc. (Stape Builders), the developer of the project and signer of Giannini's purchase agreement as agent of the beneficiary of the trust in which title to the complex was held; and Unity Savings Association (Unity), a mortgage holder on the property. His complaint requested specific performance of the purchase agreement by Unity, Stape Builder and Des Plaines Bank (count I) and money damages from Stape Builders and Des Plaines Bank (count II).

Pursuant to Unity's motion to dismiss based upon certain affirmative defenses or matters, Unity contended specific performance was not an appropriate remedy and that the agreement was invalid. (Ill.Rev.Stat.1981, ch. 110, par. 2–619(a)(9).) The trial court dismissed the specific performance count as to Unity.

The record contains the following relevant pleading and documentary evidence. Giannini filed his complaint on October 19, 1981. In the count for specific performance, he alleged in pertinent part that on or about March 27, 1980, he entered into a written agreement with Stape Builders as agent for the beneficiaries of the land trust to purchase a specified condominium unit for the sum of $79,515. He stated that although construction of the premises had been completed, Stape Builders and Des Plaines Bank refused to perform their obligations under the terms of the purchase agreement. He also alleged that Unity had or purported to have an interest in the unit. Giannini claimed that he was ready, willing, and able to fulfill his obligations under the agreement and requested specific performance of the contract because he had no adequate legal remedy.

Stape Builders was involuntarily dissolved by the Secretary of State of the State of Illinois on December 1, 1981 for failure to pay franchise taxes.

Unity apparently obtained title to the complex in lieu of foreclosure of its mortgage on the property....

Although Unity apparently agreed in its foreclosure action that it would carry out the development plans of Stape Builders, it nevertheless argued *inter alia* before the trial judge presiding over Giannini's complaint that specific performance should not be ordered because it would be uneconomical to Unity in view of poor real estate conditions. In support of this contention, Unity presented the affidavit of Mrs. Virginia Erikson, real estate administrator for Unity responsible for various matters at the Castilian Courts Complex. In her affidavit, Erikson stated that the entire condominium project consisted of five buildings (A, B, C, D, and E) with a total of 256 units. She stated that although all buildings were originally intended to be condominiums only buildings D and E had been so recorded; buildings A, B [in which Giannini's unit was located] and C were instead rental buildings. Erikson stated that these other buildings had not been declared as condominium buildings because of the poor economy and in particular "the unsalable real estate and condominium market."

Upon consideration of the parties' pleadings, documents, and written and oral argument, the trial court granted Unity's motion to dismiss count I of the complaint as to Unity. In its oral pronouncement, the court concluded that specific performance was improper because: 1) there was no condominium "in existence" which Unity could be ordered to convey to Giannini; 2) the remedy would be economically disadvantageous to Unity; and 3) the remedy would be cumbersome and time-consuming because it would obligate the court to supervise conversion.

Unity first claimed that dismissal of the specific performance claim was appropriate because the condominium unit was not in existence. It argued that the unit was non-existent because the building in which it was located had not been declared a condominium building.

Generally, "specific performance cannot be decreed of an agreement to convey property which has no existence or to which the defendant has no title...." *Sellers v. Greer* (1898), 172 Ill. 549, 558, 50 N.E. 246.

Unity argues that Giannini's unit does not "exist" because the building in which it is located has not been declared a condominium. Thus Unity claims that it is impossible for it to perform the obligations of the purchase agreement. We find this reasoning unpersuasive. The record demonstrates that the unit in question does indeed exist in a literal, physical sense of the term. The "non-existence" to which Unity refers, in contrast, is of a figurative, legal nature: in order to come into "existence," the unit need simply be declared a condominium pursuant to the legal requirements of the Illinois Condominium Property Act. (Ill.Rev.Stat.1981, ch. 30, par. 325.) As a result any form of "non-existence" of the unit is nothing more than a direct result of Unity's refusal to declare the building as a condominium. Consequently we are unconvinced that specific performance was properly denied here on the ground that the unit was "non-existent" and any conveyance thereof thus impossible.

Unity also contends in this context that specific performance was properly denied because there was a lack of mutuality of obligation and remedy between itself and Giannini. Specifically, it claims that mutuality is lacking because Giannini could not be compelled to purchase a non-existent condominium unit. We recognize that mutuality of remedy is generally required before a court can specifically enforce a contract. (*See Cohen v. Kosdon* (1949), 402 Ill. 429, 434, 84 N.E.2d 358). Nevertheless we disagree with Unity's analysis in this regard, as it turns its own failure to comply with the agreement into a bar to Giannini's entitlement to a unit he had long ago agreed to purchase.

The second reason stated by Unity for dismissal of Giannini's claim is that specific performance was not imperative because a condominium is not so unique as to require such relief. Thus, Unity seeks to distinguish condominium units from other types of real property.

The Illinois Condominium Property Act (Ill.Rev.Stat.1981, ch. 30, pars. 301 *et seq.*) does not define the term "condominium." The word has been defined in other jurisdictions as "an estate in real property consisting of an undivided interest in a portion of a parcel of real property together with a separate fee simple interest in another portion of the same parcel." (*Dutcher v. Owens* (Tex.S.Ct.1983), 647 S.W.2d 948, 949.) [W]e conclude that a condominium is real property.

Illinois courts have long held that where the parties have fairly and understandingly entered into a valid contract for the sale of real property, specific performance of the contract is a matter of right and equity will enforce it, absent circumstances of oppression and fraud. "Contracts to devise or convey real estate are enforced by specific performance on the ground that the law cannot do perfect justice." (*Hagen v. Anderson* (1925), 317 Ill. 173, 177, 147 N.E. 791.) Thus "[w]here land, or any estate therein, is the subject matter of the agreement, the inadequacy of the legal remedy is well settled, and the equitable jurisdiction is firmly established...." 4 J. Pomeroy, Equity Jurisprudence sec. 1402, at 1034 (5th ed. S. Symons 1941).

Unity argues that these rules should not apply here because "exactly the same condominium units are available to Plaintiff in the two other buildings which have been converted to condominiums in the same development." To support this claim, Unity notes that Buildings D and E of the Complex are already condominium buildings.

We find this argument insufficient ground to avoid application of the rules set forth above pertaining to specific performance of real estate purchase agreements in general. We observe that Unity has not attempted to claim that a condominium unit is not a type of realty. Furthermore, even if we assume that similarity between Giannini's unit and those of other buildings in the Complex would be sufficient ground to deny specific performance in certain circumstances, we note that there is nothing in the record to indicate the degree of similarity, if any, between the unit which Giannini contracted to purchase and those which have been declared condominium and are for sale as such. There is moreover no evidence to establish the price, terms, or conditions under which such units have been sold or are likely to be for sale. As a result there is no adequate basis for comparison of the sale of these units and the purchase agreement which Giannini stands ready to perform. Under these circumstances we find unpersuasive Unity's contention that a condominium unit should be treated differently than other forms of realty with regard to specific performance of an agreement to purchase the property.

Lastly we note that Unity concedes that it has cited no Illinois decision which adopts a *per se* rule which denied specific performance of a contract where the object of the agreement was a condominium unit. Nor does the case of *Centex Homes Corp. v. Boag* (Ch.Div.1974), 128 N.J.Super. 385, 320 A.2d 194, upon which Unity relies, so hold. Instead the court in *Centex* concluded that the vendor of the condominium unit could not seek specific performance of the purchase agreement because his legal remedy of money damages was adequate. The court reasoned that there was nothing unique in the sale of a unit because the facts there disclosed that one unit closely resembled another. Here in comparison Giannini as vendee seeks specific performance from Unity as successor in title to the original vendor. Moreover there is no proof in the record to support a conclusion that Giannini's unit was substantially similar to other units in the complex, even assuming *arguendo* that such similarity would in any way justify the creation of an exception to the general principles stated above. Lastly, as explained more fully below, it would appear that Giannini's legal remedies were inadequate since Stape Builders was involuntarily dissolved and the land trust emptied of any interest in the condominium complex. *Centex* is thus distinguishable from the case at bar. In any event it is the decision of a trial court of another jurisdiction and as such is not binding precedent upon this court.

As a third basis for dismissal, Unity argues that specific performance was properly denied because it would be uneconomical to it. Generally the decision to grant specific performance rests within the sound discretion of the trial court to be determined by the facts and circumstances of each individual case. (*Thread and Gage Co., Inc. v. Kucinski* (1983), 116 Ill.App.3d 178, 185, 71 Ill.Dec. 925, 451 N.E.2d 1292.) In this regard the court should balance the equities between the parties. (*Hild v. Avland Development Co.* (1977), 46 Ill.App.3d 173, 179, 4 Ill.Dec. 672, 360 N.E.2d 785.) Accordingly a court using its equitable powers may refuse to grant specific performance where the remedy would cause a peculiar hardship or an inequitable result.

Nevertheless "[t]here is no hardship in compelling the seller[5] to do what he agreed to do when he thought it was to his advantage." (*Smith v. Farmers' State Bank* (1945), 390 Ill. 374, 380, 61 N.E.2d 557.) Thus the fact that the contract cannot be performed without great or unanticipated expense is not such an impossibility that will usually excuse performance. Unity's claim that declaration of the building as a condominium would be uneconomical to it was insufficient to establish a peculiar hardship which amounted to an oppressive or inequitable result which totally defeated or negated Giannini's claim. The record establishes that Unity had previously represented in its foreclosure proceeding that it would abide by Stape Builders' plans for the project. In other words, the evidence shows that Unity agreed to honor Giannini's contract when this was to its advantage to do so. Accordingly it cannot now seek to avoid the agreement because of financial hardship.

In contrast to the benefit which Unity derived from its initial agreement to honor Stape Builders' arrangements, and even assuming *arguendo* that Unity would now suffer financial hardship if it were to convert the building to a condominium and convey Giannini's unit to him, the record at this juncture indicates that Giannini's loss might be even more substantial than Unity's, in that he may have no legal remedy against any of the named defendants. The documents presented by Giannini, which Unity did not attempt to contradict or controvert, show that Stape Builders was involuntarily dissolved and Des Plaines Bank's trusteeship rendered a nullity by virtue of the emptying of the land trust. It has been held that the consideration that any money award would be unefficacious because of insolvency is significant in exercising equitable jurisdiction. (*Johnson v. North American Life & Casualty Co.* (1968), 100 Ill.App.2d 212, 218, 241 N.E.2d 332.) In our view the fact that a monetary award would also be impracticable because of corporate dissolution and the emptying of a land trust is equally significant. Any hardship caused to Unity, when compared to the lack of viable legal remedies available to Giannini, was insufficient to totally defeat his claim.

For the reasons set forth above, the order of the trial court which dismissed count I of Giannini's complaint is reversed; and the cause is remanded for further proceedings consistent with the views expressed herein.

---

[5] We note that Unity has not argued that it cannot be bound by the terms of the original purchase agreement even though it was not an original party to that contract. In addition Giannini has not argued that he should be permitted to recover money damages from Unity based upon breach of contract. Accordingly, we do not consider either point.

## Hilton v. Nelsen

Supreme Court of Minnesota, 1979.
283 N.W.2d 877.

■ STONE, JUSTICE.

This is an appeal from the order of the district court awarding plaintiff specific performance of a contract for the sale of farmland and damages. We affirm in part, reverse in part, and remand for a new trial at law on the issue of damages.

In September 1974, defendants Dale and Geraldine Nelsen entered into negotiations for the sale of their 720-acre farm to plaintiff, Irvin Hilton, a Missouri real estate investor who had come to defendants' real estate agency, Phelps Farm Sales, looking for farm situations and investment opportunities in northwestern Minnesota. The rather lengthy and complex contract that was eventually entered into was drafted by Hilton's attorney, although some of the provisions were suggested by the Nelsens after several hours of discussion between the parties. The Nelsens were not represented by an attorney until after they had signed the contract.

The contract, dated October 4, 1974, provided generally for the sale of the property to Hilton for $180,000. Shortly after signing, Hilton would place in escrow an earnest deposit of $2,500, with $49,700 to be paid at closing, and the sellers would accept a mortgage or deed of trust for the remaining $127,800. The mortgage or deed of trust was to mature 10 years from the date of closing. For the first 5 years there would be no payment on principal; only 7 percent interest would be due at the end of each of those years. At the end of the 6th, 7th, 8th, and 9th years principal payments in the sum of $2,000 were due and payable, and at the end of the 10th year the final balance of $119,800 was due and payable.

Under the contract the sellers could close on May 1, 1975, at their option, giving the purchaser 60 days' notice. If the sellers chose not to close on May 1, 1975, the parties were to close "at any date prior to May 1, 1976, by their mutual agreement, but [the contract provided] in any event closing shall not be later than May 1, 1976." Although the Nelsens thought they had signed a contract for deed,[6] the agreement provided for title and possession to pass at closing.

Because the purchaser's performance was contingent on his ability to obtain an owner's title insurance policy without exceptions, Nelsen saw an attorney in March 1975 to help him clear certain title defects. After being advised by his attorney that the agreement was not a contract for deed, Nelsen instructed his attorney to tell Hilton that he would not close unless he had a contract for deed. On March 28, Nelsen's attorney sent Hilton's attorney a letter to this effect; the latter replied that if the

---

[6] Editor's note: A "contract for deed" is an arrangement where the buyer takes possession of the property at closing but the deed is not delivered until the entire purchase price is paid (at the end of the 10th year in this case).

Nelsens refused to close, Hilton would sue for specific performance as provided by the remedies clause of the contract.[1] Nelsen's attorney then advised Nelsen to attempt to close. The Nelsens then did decide to close, but this change of intent was not communicated to Hilton before the initial closing date of May 1, 1975.

The Nelsens were able to clear the defects in title, except for a real estate mortgage, a reservation of mineral rights by the State of Minnesota, and easements for existing public roads and underground telephone cables. At the end of April 1975, the Nelsens bought and moved to a farm in Nebraska. On May 7 or 8, 1975, Nelsen called Hilton from Nebraska and advised him that he was ready to close.

The evidence was in dispute as to this telephone conversation; the Nelsens claimed that Hilton demanded a reduction of $16,000 to close, and Hilton claimed that he could not recall such a conversation. But according to Phelps' contemporaneous notes, on May 14, 1975, Hilton told Phelps he would not close at that time without a reduction in the purchase price because it would be difficult for him to obtain a tenant farmer, it was already late spring, and the price of wheat was poor. Nelsen, believing that Hilton had defaulted, returned to Minnesota and made no further attempt to close. Nelsen farmed the land in 1975 but lost the crop.

In February 1976, Hilton's attorney wrote to notify Nelsen that Hilton would be ready to close on May 1, 1976, the last closing date on the contract. The first notice was returned undelivered; a second notice was received by Nelsen on April 27, 1976. The next day [April 28, 1976], Nelsen's attorney wrote to Hilton's attorney informing him that Nelsen had decided not to sell the farm. Hilton then instructed his attorney to bring this action, which was filed on May 17, 1976.

Meanwhile, some time in April 1976, Phelps told Hilton that Nelsen's mortgage was about to be foreclosed. Hilton decided to try to purchase the mortgage[7] at the upcoming foreclosure sale. At the sale on May 24, 1976, Hilton successfully bid $67,000—the amount of the unpaid balance on the mortgage—and purchased it subject to the 1-year right of redemption. Nelsen continued to occupy and work the land throughout 1976.

On May 23, 1977, pursuant to a conversation with a law partner of Nelsen's attorney, defendant Lyle Mandt agreed to purchase the Nelsen farm by redeeming the mortgage. Mandt provided about one-half of the $73,885.94 needed for redemption and the law partner provided the other one-half. The Nelsens gave a quitclaim deed to Mandt and Mandt gave

---

[1] The contract provided that "all . . . parties who have signed said contract agree that in the event should [sic] any said party refuse to close said contract, that Purchaser shall have available to him the remedy of specific performance or damages at law, at Purchaser's option."

[7] Editor's note: The court uses the term "mortgage" but probably means "property".

Nelsen an option to repurchase the property by January 1, 1978, for $121,074.05. Nelsen farmed the property in 1977.

The trial court sitting without a jury found that the Nelsens had breached the contract, ordered specific performance for the plaintiff against both the Nelsens and Mandt, and ordered that plaintiff be allowed to deduct from the downpayment in the original agreement the sum of $39,600, representing the fair and reasonable rental value of the property during the years 1976 and 1977.

The basic issues presented to us for decision are:

1. Did plaintiff's attempt to obtain title through the mortgage foreclosure sale constitute an abandonment of the contract to purchase?

2. Was the contract one that was entitled to be specifically enforced?

3. Was the allowance for lost rents proper?

*Abandonment of the Contract.* [The court concluded that Hilton's purchase of the property at a foreclosure sale did not constitute abandonment of the contract, and that the Nelsen's were therefore still contractually bound.]

*Specific Performance.* Because the trial court's factual findings are reasonably supported by the evidence, they are not clearly erroneous and must be affirmed. Rule 52.01, Rules of Civil Procedure. Thus, we affirm the findings that the sellers materially breached the contract by their repudiation by letter on April 28, 1976, and their failure to close on May 1, 1976. However, it does not automatically follow that Hilton is entitled to specific performance of the contract, as ordered by the trial court. "[S]pecific performance of a contract to convey real estate is not a matter of absolute right, and if enforcement would be unconscionable or inequitable, performance will not be decreed." Boulevard Plaza Corp. v. Campbell, 254 Minn. 123, 136, 94 N.W.2d 273, 284 (1959). In this case, a combination of the following factors convinces us that ordering specific performance is not an appropriate exercise of the court's equitable discretion:

> (a) Purchaser Hilton did not intend to farm or homestead on the land, but rather intended to rent the property to a tenant farmer. Because any equivalent parcel of Minnesota farmland would serve these investment purposes, the uniqueness of the land is less weighty here as a factor calling for specific performance, especially if damages at law are an adequate remedy for the sellers' breach. In this case, the plaintiff has not detrimentally changed his position in reliance upon the sellers' performance to such an extent that specific performance is necessary or a damages remedy inadequate. The plaintiff may easily be compensated in damages for losses occasioned by this contractual relationship.

(b) There were elements of unfairness, or at least overreaching, in the contract itself.

First, the contract lacked mutuality of remedy. Although that alone will not render specific performance inequitable, mutuality is one element which may be considered in determining whether to award specific performance.

Here, according to the contractual provisions, the sellers' only remedy in the event of default by the purchaser would be the retention of $2,500 earnest money as liquidated damages. If the sellers defaulted, however, the purchaser could elect either specific performance or damages as a remedy. Also, the contract requires the part-purchase money note for $127,000 and the mortgage or deed of trust securing the note to provide that if the purchaser defaults, "no deficiency or other money judgment" could be "sought or obtained" against the purchaser by the sellers. "Unless there is a mutuality of remedy at the time coercion is sought so that the decree will bind both parties and accomplish a full performance of the contract, the court refuses to exert its equitable powers and leaves the parties to their remedy at law." Reichert v. Pure Oil Co., 164 Minn. 252, 259, 204 N.W. 882, 884 (1925).

Second, the contract was subject to unilateral termination by the purchaser for a variety of reasons, including inability to obtain a tenant farmer; unfavorable soil test results; or rejection of the legal form of the documents to be provided by the sellers, such as the mortgage or deed of trust and the purchase money note. In the event of such a unilateral termination, the purchaser would recover the earnest money and neither party would "have any further rights or liabilities" under the contract. As this court said in Reichert v. Pure Oil Co., supra:

> [T]he court will not decree performance unless it can compel performance by both parties, and it cannot compel performance by the plaintiff as he could avoid the decree at any time by revoking the contract.

164 Minn. 256, 258, 259, 204 N.W. 883, 884.

In fact, unfulfilled conditions to the plaintiff's performance exist which to this day have not been explicitly waived by the plaintiff and which thus could result in termination of the contract. For example, the plaintiff would have the right to terminate the agreement if the sellers were unable to deliver a warranty deed or if the plaintiff were unable to obtain an owner's title insurance policy without exceptions. The plaintiff has not explicitly waived this condition, yet title to the land was subject to easements for roads and telephone cables and to the State of Minnesota's mineral rights. These clouds on the title would be difficult, if not impossible, to erase. Because the defendant-sellers' interests in the plaintiff's performance thus could not be secured in an equitable award of specific performance, the presence in the contract of such unfulfilled and unwaived conditions militates against ordering specific performance.

Third, the payment terms evidenced overreaching by the purchaser. Of a total contract price of $180,000, the purchaser need only pay $2,500 into escrow as an earnest deposit and $49,700 cash upon closing—a total of $52,200 paid when the title transferred. The remaining $127,800 was to be financed by a part-purchase money note secured by a 10-year mortgage or deed of trust to the sellers. Prior to the end of the 10th year, the sellers' only return would be interest on the unpaid amount at 7 percent annually plus $2,000 a year in the 6th through 9th year of the contract. Thus, apart from interest, the sellers would receive during 9 years and 11 months only $60,200 toward property worth $180,000, while the purchaser would be receiving rental income on the land which, the trial court found, had a median rental value of approximately $20,000 per year. And, as mentioned above, if the purchaser were to default on the payments, the sellers would have no action for a deficiency judgment on the unpaid purchase price.

(c) The testimony in evidence indicated that the basic terms of the contract were misunderstood by the defendants. Significantly, the defendant-sellers were not represented by an attorney in negotiations with plaintiff-purchaser. The contract, which was lengthy and complex, was drafted and explained to the Nelsens by the plaintiff's attorney. Additional handwritten paragraphs, some designed to accommodate the Nelsens' uncertainty at time of drafting concerning how long it would take to make the necessary arrangements to close, were dictated by plaintiff's attorney. Only when the Nelsens consulted an attorney for assistance in clearing the title did they learn that the contract was not a contract for deed, as they had thought it was. The Nelsens erroneously understood that May 1, 1975, was the *only* closing date under the contract. They also thought, incorrectly, that Hilton's initial payment would pay off their mortgage. They did not understand that for 5 years they would receive only 7 percent interest on the purchase price, no payments on the principal, and that $119,800 would be owing on the purchase price at the end of the 10th year.

" . . . [I]f the contract as written is the result of mistake so fundamental that the minds of the parties have never met . . . and the parties can be restored to their original status, a court administering equity will not enforce the contract. Buckley v. Patterson, 39 Minn. 250, 39 N.W. 490 [1888]." Bredeson v. Nickolay, 147 Minn. 304, 305, 180 N.W. 547 (1920).

(d) Circumstances have arisen since the formation of the contract which further undermine the fairness of specific performance. Third-party interests have intervened by way of Mandt's redemption of the property. Mandt now has legal and equitable title to the property. There was no finding that Mandt had personal knowledge of Hilton's rights under the October 4,

1974, contract. The contract for sale was not recorded, and Mandt testified that he had no knowledge of the contract. If he did not, specific performance of the contract would necessarily be subject to Mandt's property rights.

In light of the totality of the circumstances discussed above, we conclude that, as a matter of law, this contract is not one which the court in its equitable discretion may specifically enforce. Plaintiff must seek his remedy at law. We do not mean to suggest that any one of the factors discussed above is necessarily sufficient to render specific performance inequitable. Considering them together, however, we feel compelled to the decision we have reached, which is necessarily limited to the narrow facts presented here.

*Damages.* Having concluded that the contract is not specifically enforceable and that plaintiff's remedy is at law, we need not reach the question of whether an allowance for lost rents was properly awarded by the trial court, which sat in equity rather than at law. Accordingly, we reverse the judgment and, because the first trial was in equity, remand this case for a new trial at law on the question of damages. The parties, of course, may demand a jury trial on this issue.

Affirmed in part, reversed in part, and remanded.

## NOTES

1. *Mutuality of remedy.* In *Giannini* and *Hilton,* the courts endorsed the mutuality of remedy theory. Yet, in other jurisdictions, this rule seems to be on its way out.[8] What is the reason underlying application of the rule? On what grounds do you suppose the rule has been rejected?

2. *Uniqueness.* Often a seller will be able to obtain specific performance by arguing that the parcel in question is "unique" and not fungible. Thus, there can be no "market value" for the property and damages are uncertain. In the Principal Problem, how unique is Big Z? In light of the major cases, what effect does this have on the right of the court to grant specific performance?

3. *Equitable defenses.* Since specific performance is an equitable remedy, courts will not be reluctant to find that defenses such as fraud, undue influence, duress and unconscionability apply. In McAllister v. Schettler,[9] for example, the court refused to award the purchaser specific performance of a contract for a 290 acre farm where the evidence disclosed that the seller, who was in her eighties at the time the contract was entered into, was somewhat mentally impaired and subject to undue influence by a third party, and was not provided with an explanation of the financing arrangements or her contractual obligations.

---

[8] See, e.g., Ridge Chevrolet-Oldsmobile, Inc. v. Scarano, 238 N.J.Super. 149, 569 A.2d 296 (1990); Pallas v. Black, 226 Neb. 728, 414 N.W.2d 805 (1987); Converse v. Fong, 159 Cal.App.3d 86, 205 Cal.Rptr. 242 (1984). See also Cal.Civ.Code § 3386 (2010).

[9] 521 A.2d 617 (Del.Ch.1986).

4. *Third party rights.* If the vendor has actually sold the property to a third party who had no notice of the original buyer's contractual rights, the original buyer will not be able to get specific performance since the vendor would find it impossible to perform. For this reason, it is often desirable to record a contract for sale so that third parties will have notice of the contract. This subject is dealt with in Assignment 47–48.

5. *Land trusts.* The court in *Giannini* notes that the property in question was held in a land trust and that the record owner was the First National Bank of Des Plaines, one of the defendants. The land trust is a device for holding title to property that is recognized by statute in Illinois, Florida, Virginia, North Dakota, Indiana, and Hawaii. They are also in use in several other jurisdictions. The land trust enables the property owner to keep his identity confidential. Legal title to the property is held by the trustee, which is usually a bank, but the beneficiary of the trust is the actual (equitable) owner of the property who has the power to direct the property's management.[10] The beneficiary's identity is not a matter of public record. The interest of the beneficiary is considered personal property.

6. *Deed in lieu of foreclosure.* In *Giannini,* Unity, as mortgagee, had commenced a previous separate foreclosure action. Thereafter, it took title by a deed in lieu of foreclosure. Its decision to accept a deed in lieu of foreclosure was probably the source of its difficulties with Giannini. If Unity had completed its foreclosure action, with Giannini joined as one of the defendants, Giannini's rights probably would have been terminated by the foreclosure decree, provided that Unity's mortgage had priority over Giannini's rights as purchaser. Normally, a mortgage that is recorded before a sale contract is signed has priority over the rights of the purchaser under the sale contract.

---

[10] See Ch. 765 Ill. Comp. Stat. Ann. § 430/1 (2010).

# ASSIGNMENT 46

# INTRODUCTION TO MORTGAGES AND FORECLOSURES

## 1. INTRODUCTION

*Real estate finance.* This Assignment is about the legal issues that arise when real property is used as collateral to secure repayment of a debt or some similar financial obligation. Lenders are willing to make loans because the repayment of the loan is secured, at least in part, by property-law tools grouped together in the category that we will call "mortgages and foreclosures." In many cases, the use of real property to secure repayment of a debt arises when the loan is for the acquisition and/or improvement of the real property itself. In some cases, a property owner might grant a security interest in the property to a lender in exchange for a loan that is for some other purpose. For homeowners, this might be to pay health care expenses or pay off consumer debt. For businesses, this might be to cover business expenses or expand business operations. For our purposes, we will focus on real estate financing of real estate acquisition or improvement.

Real estate finance is a major part of the national and global economy. It enables individuals and families to purchase homes and thus contributes to home ownership rates in the U.S. of between 63 and 70 percent since 1995, according to the U.S. Census Bureau. Single-family homes make up sizeable parts of our local landscapes, enabled by residential lending practices, as well as by loans to developers for new housing. Real estate finance also enables businesses to develop and grow, and farms and ranches to operate, because lenders will secure the repayment of loans with mortgages on the real property of businesses, farmers, and ranchers. Perhaps equally significantly, real estate finance has become an important tool for financial investment nationally and globally, not just for traditional financial institutions like banks but for all kinds of investors. According to the Federal Reserve, there was nearly $14 trillion in outstanding mortgage debt in the U.S. in the first quarter of 2016, of which more than $10 trillion was for single-family residential property. The holders of this debt include traditional depository financial institutions (e.g., banks, savings and loans), life insurance companies, mortgage pools and trusts, federal government agencies, real estate investment trusts, pension and retirement funds, mortgage companies, credit unions, and individuals. The recession of 2008 was due to a financial crisis that was triggered by certain mortgage lending practices (called subprime mortgage lending, to be discussed later in this

Introduction) and the chain-reaction of foreclosures that occurred once homeowners could no longer afford their loan payments.

Real estate finance plays an important role in our economy and society, because property law allows a lender to condition a loan on the borrower granting the lender a security interest in the real property (e.g., home, business site), which is called a *mortgage* (or *deed of trust*, as will be explained shortly), and for the real property to be used by the lender (or the lender's assignee) to fully or partially satisfy any unpaid debt if the borrower fails to pay it back as promised, which is called *foreclosure*. We will discuss these terms and concepts in depth in the remaining parts of this Introduction.

*What are a mortgage and a note?* "A *mortgage* is a conveyance or retention of an interest in real property as security for performance of an obligation."[1] Usually the obligation secured by the mortgage arises from a loan made by the *mortgagee* (the lender) to the *mortgagor* (the borrower). The obligation to repay the loan is usually evidenced by a *promissory note* (or often referred to simply as the *note*), a written promise by the borrower to pay the lender a specified amount of money in accordance with the terms of the note. Variations often occur. Sometimes the obligation arises from a sale rather than a loan. The mortgagor buys real property from the mortgagee and agrees to pay all or part of the purchase price at some future date or dates. This is called a "purchase money" mortgage. The document evidencing the obligation may be a contract, guaranty, or other document rather than a note, but the obligation must be one having a monetary equivalent at the time it is enforced. In this Assignment we will concentrate on the most common transaction, one in which the obligation arises from a loan and is evidenced by a note signed by the borrower/mortgagor.

*Deeds of trust compared with mortgages.* In some states, the *deed of trust* (or trust deed) is used as a security device instead of a mortgage. Other than terminology and form, there are few differences between deeds of trust and mortgages. The following chart diagrams the differences in terminology. For convenience, we will generally use the term "mortgage" to include a deed of trust.

---

[1] Restatement (Third) of Property: Mortgages § 1.1 (1997) (emphasis added).

|  | **Mortgage** (Transfer of an interest in property as security for the performance of an obligation) | **Deed of Trust** (Transfer of an interest in property as security for the performance of an obligation) |
|---|---|---|
| The owner of property who uses the property as security for the performance of an obligation. | Mortgagor | Trustor |
| The obligee, lender, or person who extends credit. | Mortgagee | Beneficiary |
| Third party, often a title company or bank, that holds the property in "trust" as security. | None. The lender holds the transferred interest in property. | Trustee |

*The loan process, the loan documents, and their terms.* In order to understand the loan process and documents, let's consider a hypothetical residential home purchase transaction. Lee wants to purchase a house from Nader for Lee's residence. Lee and Nader enter a real estate purchase and sales contract in which Nader agrees to deliver a deed to the residential property, 123 N. Hilles Lane, in exchange for Lee delivering the purchase price of $225,000. Lee doesn't have $225,000 in the bank, so he will need a loan in order to be able to purchase the house. Lee's real estate agent encourages him to contact Kathryn, who is a mortgage broker, someone who helps to connect homebuyers/borrowers with real-estate lenders. However, Lee has just sold his previous house, 456 S. Pelzer Avenue, and he ended up with $45,000 in net equity from the sale of the Pelzer Ave. house (i.e., the total amount of the purchase price from the sale of the Pelzer Ave. house minus the amount that he owed to the lender of his loan on the Pelzer Ave. house). [If the borrower already owns a home which he wants to sell and buy a different home, the equity that he has built up in the existing home will be realized when he sells it. *Equity* is the difference between the fair market value of the property and the amount owed on the property. Equity builds up as: a) the owner reduces the amount owed on the loan by making loan payments, and b) the property increases in value.] Therefore, Kathryn points out that Lee can pay 20% of the Hilles Lane home purchase price out of his own funds ($45,000 is 20% of $225,000).

Historically, banks and other financial institutions would loan up to 80% of the purchase price, called the *loan-to-value ratio*. However, the requirement that purchasers come up with 20% of the purchase price from their own funds was a major barrier to first-time home buyers, especially as housing prices rose. By the 1990s, it had become common for lenders to make loans of more than 80% of the purchase price, sometimes as much as 100% of the purchase price.

Kathryn has identified a likely lender, Todaro Bank, which is willing to loan Lee $180,000 for 30 years at 5% interest per year, with monthly payments. Lee may need to fill out some paperwork to establish that he can qualify for this loan, or he may have already done so. Once he does, Todaro Bank will want to do its due diligence to make sure that there's nothing about the transaction that will put its $180,000 at undue risk. Todaro Bank might want to investigate Lee's credit-worthiness and financial history in greater depth. More importantly, though, Todaro Bank wants to make sure that the property is and will be worth the purchase price. Therefore, Todaro Bank will have a title search done and will acquire a lender's title insurance policy (see Assignments 48–50). It will require that the property be inspected for structural damage, termites, etc. and that the property's fair market value be appraised by an experienced professional appraiser, who will look at the recent selling prices of comparable properties. If the property does not appraise at the purchase price, or if it has physical or title problems that threaten the property's value, the bank may decide not to make the loan. As a practical matter, lenders want to make loans and often try to find ways to resolve the problems, such as treating the house for termites, remedying title defects, or getting a second appraisal. Let's assume that Lee is credit-worthy and that the property is worth at least $225,000 without any title or structural problems. At some point during this process, Todaro Bank will issue a *loan commitment* to Lee, which outlines the terms of the loan and promises to make the loan at the time that his purchase of the house is finalized (a process called *closing*), subject to certain conditions.

At or near closing, Todaro Bank will ask Lee to sign two core documents, the promissory note and the mortgage (or deed of trust), as well as a variety of real-estate disclosure documents required by federal and state law. The note will contain the terms of the agreement for the loan and for Lee's repayment of the loan. Four essential terms are required in any note: 1) the *loan amount* (also known as the *principal*); 2) the *interest rate*; 3) the *term (length) of the loan*; and 4) the *payment (or amortization) schedule*. [For a typical loan that is paid in equal monthly installments over the term of the loan, someone could figure out any of these four terms as long as she knew the other three terms.]

Interest payments by the borrower are how the lender makes money on making loans; the lender has a choice between making this loan and making some other investment which will earn a return over time. The interest rate should also cover the risk to the lender that the borrower won't repay some or all of the loan. However, there is a market for residential-property loans that is based on the amount of available capital for lending, the standard interest rate set by the Federal Reserve, rates of return on competing investments, real-estate values, and the practices of real estate lenders generally. As a result, lenders may feel pressured to offer standard interest rates to home-buying borrowers, even if some of those borrowers represent risk that is not adequately insured against by the interest rate being charged. One way that lenders protect themselves is to allocate the monthly payment mostly to interest at first, in comparison to principal. For example, with Lee's 30-year 5%-interest loan of $180,000, he will pay $966.28 per month, of which $750.00 will go towards interest and $216.28 of which will go towards principal in the first month of the first year of the loan. Each month, the amount of the monthly payment allocated to interest goes down incrementally, while the amount allocated to principal goes up incrementally. By the twelfth month of the thirtieth year, only $4.01 of the payment is going to interest, with the remaining amount going to principal. Over thirty years, Lee will pay $180,000 in principal and $167,860 in interest. At the end of five years, though, he will still owe $165,291.72 in principal.

The note almost invariably contains several other terms. The *acceleration clause* makes the entire loan due and payable immediately if the borrower defaults on the loan in any way. This means that if Lee quits paying on the loan at the end of the fifth year, Todaro Bank will be able to foreclose on the property for the remaining $165,291.72, not just the missed payment of $966.28 (or whatever the total of missed monthly payments is by the time that the bank forecloses). The *due-on-sale clause* requires Lee to repay the entire loan if he sells or transfers the property. This ensures that Todaro Bank will get paid if someone else comes to own the property. The note will likely indicate whether the loan is *recourse* or *non-recourse*. A recourse loan is one in which the borrower has agreed to be personally liable for the debt if he defaults on the loan, as well as subjecting the property to foreclosure to secure repayment of the debt. A non-recourse loan is one in which the lender has agreed to seek repayment only from foreclosure on the property if the borrower defaults, but not to sue the borrower personally. Even if a loan is recourse, some states impose statutory or equitable limitations on the rights of lenders to sue the borrower personally for the remaining debt if the sales price in foreclosure does not cover the full amount remaining due on the loan (i.e., limitations on the rights of lenders to seek a *deficiency judgment* against the borrower). Practically, in some cases, the lender isn't likely to recover much money from the borrower if he has ceased to be able to make his loan payments. In other cases, borrowers strategically default, even though they have at least some financial resources that the lender could go after. In the latter, a loan that is recourse in a state that allows deficiency judgments would give the lender the greatest opportunity to recover the outstanding loan amounts from a combination of foreclosure and deficiency judgment.

The note will be either *negotiable* or *non-negotiable*. If the note is negotiable, Articles 3 and 4 of the Uniform Commercial Code (U.C.C.) arguably apply.[2] These Articles provide certain protections to an assignee of the note, either (1) a specifically named assignee through the original payee's special endorsement (or indorsement) of the note to that assignee, or (2) whoever is the holder (possessor) of the note if the original payee gave a blank endorsement (or indorsement) of the note (i.e., without naming an assignee). Thus, for example, assume Todaro Bank were to transfer the note on the Lee loan to Villanueva Bank, either (1) through a special endorsement to Villanueva Bank or (2) through a blank endorsement, and then transfer of physical possession of the note to Villanueva Bank. If this were the case, Lee would owe the remaining loan payments to Villanueva Bank. All or virtually all residential-loan notes are negotiable, although some of the provisions of the U.C.C. might not apply in foreclosures in some states due to those states' foreclosure statutes, as you will see in this Assignment.

The other primary document in the loan closing will be the *mortgage* or *deed of trust*. In this document, the mortgagor expressly grants to the mortgagee (or the trustee on behalf of the mortgagee) the right to sell the property in foreclosure if the mortgagor (the borrower) fails to repay the loan according to the terms of the note. If the property is located in a state that allows nonjudicial foreclosure (also known as power of sale foreclosure), the mortgage (or deed of trust) is likely to include language expressly granting the mortgagee (or trustee) the authority and right to foreclose on the property through nonjudicial process (i.e., without court supervision). While *power of sale provisions* are more common in deeds of trust, some mortgages contain power of sale provisions. The mortgage or deed of trust is typically filed in the county property records (sometimes called deed records) in the county in which the property is located so that subsequent parties will be on notice of the mortgagee's security interest in the property.

To see the form for the standard residential home loan note, the Freddie Mac Form 3200, please visit http://www.freddiemac.com/uniform/unifnotes.html, and click on Form 3200. Also note the state-specific form notes and other documents available. Fannie Mae maintains a list of standard forms for residential mortgages and deeds of trust on a state-by-state basis (due to the particularities of state laws) at https://www.fanniemae.com/singlefamily/security-instruments. You are encouraged to see what a note and a mortgage (or deed of trust) look like for a typical residential transaction.

*Mortgage equivalents.* In some transactions, credit is extended to a property purchaser or property owner without using the traditional note and mortgage form but in ways that look a lot like the lender is taking a security interest in the property. One example is the *installment land*

---

[2] All states, except New York and South Carolina, have adopted the 1990 version of Articles 3 and 4 of the U.C.C.

*sale contract*, in which the seller agrees to sell the property to the buyer over time and to take periodic payments in installments. After the buyer has paid all the installments, the seller transfers title to the property to the buyer. If the buyer misses payments, the contract is canceled and the seller retains the property. The seller also keeps the installments that the buyer had paid to that point. The purchase price often is set much higher than the current fair-market value for the sale of the land, in order to include in the purchase price an equivalent of an interest rate. These transactions have long been suspected of being essentially mortgage equivalents, and courts would sometimes afford the buyers the protections that state and federal laws afford mortgagors in foreclosure. The trend is for courts increasingly to treat these arrangements as mortgages and apply mortgage and foreclosure law to them. Another type of mortgage equivalent in the eyes of the courts is the *equitable mortgage*. An equitable mortgage may be declared in situations in which one party appears to be taking advantage of another party over a loan at which real property is at stake if the loan isn't repaid. For example, assume Steven were desperate for money and agreed to take a loan from Matthew for $100,000 in exchange for Steven transferring title to his office building to Matthew. Their agreement was that if Steven were to pay Matthew $200,000 one year later, Matthew would transfer title to the office building back to Matthew. In this case, Matthew is charging Steven usurious interest (100% per year), and Steven is at risk of losing the property without any protection from mortgage and foreclosure law. A court might be inclined to treat the arrangement as an equitable mortgage.

*Priority*. Mortgages (including deeds of trusts), even if they are treated as mere liens on property, are nonetheless interests in real property that are subject to the rules for establishing priorities of interest under state recording statutes, which are covered in Assignments 48–49. Lenders have every incentive to record their mortgages so that the rest of the world is on notice of their security interest in the property. A lender is also normally subject to the interests recorded in the deed records before it took its mortgage interest in the property.

Thus, in our hypothetical involving Lee, Nader, and Todaro Bank, assume that Nader transferred a right-of-way easement to Hasin two years before Lee bought the property and Hasin recorded her easement immediately. Further assume that Todaro Bank recorded its mortgage immediately after Lee took the deed from Nader at closing. Then, three years later, assume that Salazar Savings and Loan made a $50,000 home-improvement loan to Lee (sometimes called a home equity loan) and took a mortgage in the property from Lee (sometimes called a second mortgage), promptly recording the mortgage. One year later, Maryalice obtained a tort judgment against Lee and then obtained a judgment lien against his real property to satisfy her debt, which she then filed in the deed records. In this scenario, Hasin has the most senior interest, and her easement cannot be extinguished by any of the others. Todaro Bank has second priority, although Todaro Bank holds the first mortgage and is the first lien-holder. Salazar Savings and Loan has third priority, but is the second mortgagee and second lien-holder. Maryalice has fourth priority and is the third lien-holder. Nonetheless, state statutes may give higher priority to certain kinds of liens and interests in property, such as tax liens to ensure that governments get paid their taxes or mechanics liens to ensure that contractors and subcontractors get paid for the work they did to improve the property (and presumably its value).

*The concept of "security."* What do we mean when we say that a loan is "secured" by a mortgage? When a loan is secured by a mortgage and the loan is not paid in the usual course, the lender may seek repayment by selling the mortgaged real property and using the proceeds to repay the loan. The process by which the lender sells the property is called "foreclosure by sale." In rare instances, the lender may be able to conduct "strict foreclosure." This process permits the lender to gain ownership of the land without a sale. Since foreclosure by sale is by far the more common type of foreclosure, the term "foreclosure" usually refers to foreclosure by sale, and we will follow that usage here. There are two types of foreclosure: (1) *judicial foreclosure* and (2) *nonjudicial foreclosure*.[3]

*Judicial foreclosure.* In most states, the process of foreclosure is surrounded by numerous statutory requirements. These requirements vary significantly from state to state. In general, once the mortgagor defaults, usually by failing to pay an installment of the loan when it is due, the lender may choose to require the borrower to pay the loan immediately in full, pursuant to an acceleration clause contained in the note secured by the mortgage.[4] If the default continues, the mortgagee may commence an action to foreclose the mortgage. In this action, the mortgagee alleges the fact that the debt is due and unpaid, and asks for a decree from the court directing the property to be sold. The decree will direct that an officer of the court, often the sheriff, sell the property at public auction, following the required procedures. If the proceeds of the sale, after paying the expenses of sale, exceed the amount owed to the mortgagee, the mortgagee will be paid in full and the *surplus* will be paid to the mortgagor. If the net proceeds of the sale are less than the amount owed to the mortgagee, the mortgagee will be paid these net proceeds and the balance owed will be called a *deficiency*. In many instances, the mortgagee will then seek a monetary judgment from the court for the amount of the deficiency. Such a judgment is called a *deficiency judgment*.

---

[3] Often a borrower in financial distress will voluntarily deliver a deed to the mortgagee to avoid a formal foreclosure. Such a deed is called a deed in lieu of foreclosure, or a lieu deed. Both parties may prefer a lieu deed to a formal foreclosure to avoid the expense, publicity and delays of a formal foreclosure proceeding.

[4] See generally, Restatement (Third) of Property: Mortgages § 8.1 (1997).

EXAMPLE 1: Mortgagee lends $100,000 to Mortgagor, and the loan is secured by a mortgage on Greenacre, which is owned by Mortgagor. Mortgagor fails to pay the loan when due and Mortgagee commences a foreclosure action, obtains a decree of foreclosure and has the property sold at a foreclosure sale for $80,000. Costs of sale, including advertising the sale, and paying attorney's and sheriff's fees, are $5,000. The net proceeds of the sale, $75,000, will be paid to the Mortgagee. There will be a deficiency of $25,000. Mortgagee will probably seek a deficiency judgment against Mortgagor for $25,000.

*Restrictions on deficiency judgments.* Many states have legislation restricting the mortgagee's ability to obtain a deficiency judgment.

(1) Some states provide that the mortgagee is entitled only to the excess of the debt over the fair value of the property (rather than the excess of the debt over the price paid at the foreclosure sale).

(2) In some states, deficiency judgments are allowed only after judicial foreclosure, and thus are not available if the property is sold through nonjudicial foreclosure.

(3) Some states forbid deficiency judgments following foreclosure of a purchase money mortgage.

(4) The Uniform Nonjudicial Foreclosure Act (UNFA) does not allow deficiency judgments when the mortgage secures the mortgagor's residence.[5] As of 2016, though, no jurisdiction had adopted the UNFA.

*Nonjudicial foreclosure.* In many states, it is possible to conduct a foreclosure proceeding without bringing a legal action. The mortgage (or deed of trust) will provide that the mortgagee or a trustee may conduct a foreclosure sale without any judgment or decree from a court. Such foreclosure procedures are variously called *nonjudicial foreclosures, power of sale foreclosures,* or *trustee's sales.* State statutes provide the minimum requirements that the mortgagee and/or trustee must follow when conducting a nonjudifical foreclosure. Where such nonjudicial foreclosures are permitted, they are usually faster and less expensive than judicially supervised foreclosures. For this reason, they are used far more frequently than judicial foreclosures. In California, for example, more than 95% of foreclosures are nonjudicial foreclosures.

*The debtor's right to redeem the property before the foreclosure sale.* By the sixteenth century, the mortgage had taken the form of a conveyance by the borrower to the lender of a fee simple subject to a condition subsequent. The condition subsequent that would defeat the fee simple title of the lender was the payment by the borrower of the sum due under the terms of the loan. Thus if the borrower/mortgagor repaid

---

[5] See generally, Grant Nelson & Dale Whitman, Reforming Foreclosure: The Uniform Nonjudicial Foreclosure Act, 53 Duke L.J. 1399 (2004).

the loan when due, title would return to the mortgagor. If the mortgagor did not repay the loan when due (law day), title would remain with the mortgagee. Sometimes the mortgagee's obligation took the form of a promise to reconvey the real property to the mortgagor if the debt was repaid. Regardless of the form of the mortgage during this early period, the mortgagor had to repay the debt no later than when it was due. If the mortgagor tendered payment even a day late, the mortgagee could reject the tender and the mortgagor would lose all right to redeem the land.

By the end of the seventeenth century, the law of mortgages, as summarized above, underwent a metamorphosis. Borrowers began to petition the English equity court, Chancery, for the opportunity to redeem their land despite the fact that they had not tendered payment on law day. At first, Chancery demanded that the borrower have a legitimate excuse for her failure to tender payment on law day, before Chancery would grant the borrower the right to redeem the property by paying what was due after law day had passed. In time, however, Chancery began to grant such a right routinely, and thus the *equitable right of redemption* or the *equity of redemption* was born. This right of a mortgagor to redeem the property from the mortgagee, even if payment is late, is now considered an essential part of every mortgage, and a fundamental principle of mortgage law. A mortgagor cannot waive her right to redeem tardily (the equity of redemption) as part of the consideration for obtaining the loan. Courts will not enforce any clause in a legal instrument that has the purpose or effect of nullifying the equity of redemption (this is called *"clogging"* the equity of redemption, and it's illegal). The development of the equity of redemption is rightly considered one of the great accomplishments of equitable jurisprudence. Why do you suppose that the equity of redemption first arose, and why do you think that it remains a fundamental principle of mortgage law?

*Limiting the equity of redemption through foreclosure.* If mortgagors could exercise their equity of redemption for an indefinite time after default, the ability of mortgagees to sell or improve the land would be severely limited. Few people would buy land if it could be redeemed by the mortgagor at any time. Therefore, mortgagees began to petition the equity court following default for a decree *foreclosing* or limiting the time that a particular defaulting mortgagor could redeem the property. Thus, the word "foreclosure" refers to foreclosing the mortgagor's right to redeem the property. If the defaulting mortgagor did not tender payment by the date set in the foreclosure decree, absolute title would vest in the mortgagee. This is the origin of what is now known as "strict foreclosure." As noted above, strict foreclosure has been supplanted in most states by "foreclosure by sale." Under the foreclosure by sale process, the defaulting debtor has the right to redeem the property until the foreclosure sale has taken place. With the fall of the hammer at the foreclosure sale, the right of redemption is foreclosed or terminated.

*Statutory redemption contrasted with the equitable right of redemption.* All states recognize the equitable right of redemption. About half of the states, however, have created by statute an additional right of redemption, often called the *statutory right of redemption.* The statutory right of redemption, where it exists, permits a debtor to redeem the property during a specified time period (as little as 10 days in one state and as long as two years in another, but usually between six months and a year) after the foreclosure sale. The debtor redeems from the purchaser at the foreclosure sale by paying to the purchaser what the purchaser paid at the foreclosure sale, plus interest and certain other expenses. Those who support the statutory right of redemption argue that it encourages bidders at the foreclosure sale to bid a reasonable price, since a purchase at an unreasonably low price is subject to redemption at the same low price, plus interest and specified other costs. Those who criticize the statutory right of redemption argue that it depresses the price that bidders are willing to pay at the foreclosure sale since bidders will not pay much for a title that can be defeated by a redemption by the mortgagor. In any event, it is important to distinguish the equitable right of redemption, which exists only *before* the foreclosure sale, from the statutory right of redemption, which exists only *after* the foreclosure sale.

*Possession of the property during the statutory redemption period.* There are two divergent systems of possession during the statutory redemption period, which endures from the time of the foreclosure sale until the expiration of the period. Some states allow the mortgagor to remain in possession of the property until the expiration of the redemption period. Other states allow the foreclosure sale buyer to take possession under a defeasible title.

*Other parties who have rights under statutory redemption.* The mortgagor is not the only person with rights of redemption. Most redemption statutes allow transfer of the right of redemption. This transfer may be either testamentary or by assignment. In either case, the transferee succeeds to the same rights as the mortgagor.

In addition to transferees, junior lienors may also have statutory rights of redemption, although these rights are usually inferior to those of the mortgagor. In California, however, junior lienors do not have the right of statutory redemption. As with the rights of possession, two divergent systems have developed to determine when the mortgagor and the various junior lienors can exercise their statutory right of redemption. Under a system of strict priority, a junior lienor must wait until the expiration of the mortgagor's statutory redemption period. Then, if the mortgagor has not redeemed, each junior lienor in order of priority is given a brief period, usually five days, to redeem the property. The alternative system, the scramble method, differs in that there is no priority for redemption and no waiting period for junior lienors. Therefore, once a junior lienor redeems the property, another junior lienor or the mortgagor may also redeem by paying the foreclosure sale price and, sometimes, any lien the previously redeeming party held. Unlike the strict priority system, a mortgagor may redeem from a junior lienor, but like the strict priority system, once the mortgagor redeems, no one else may do so.

The effect of the mortgagor's redemption is to strip the foreclosure sale purchaser of all interest in the land and restore title in the mortgagor, leaving the land free of the encumbrance of the mortgage.

*Effects of priority on foreclosure.* These examples illustrate the effects of priority among multiple interests in a property during foreclosure.

EXAMPLE 2: Barbara owns her house, worth $220,000, which is subject to a $120,000 mortgage, held by Bank. Barbara's equity in the house is $100,000, the difference between the value of the house and the debt the house secures. The borrower's *equity* in real property is simply the excess of the value of the property over the sum of all liens, including mortgages, on that property. Barbara seeks an additional loan from a lender, Lance. Lance lends her $80,000, taking as security a mortgage on her equity. Such a loan is often called a *home equity loan*, since it is secured by the borrower's equity in her home. It is a type of *second mortgage*. It is a second mortgage because it is second or subordinate to the mortgage held by Bank. Suppose that Barbara defaults on her loan from Lance, and Lance forecloses. At the time of the default, the amount owing on Bank's loan is $115,000, and the amount owed to Lance is $81,000, including interest and costs of foreclosure. At Lance's foreclosure sale a third party, Tina, is the successful bidder, paying $90,000. What does Tina now own? What are Bank's rights? How should the $90,000 be distributed? Assume that all instruments have been promptly and properly recorded.

DISCUSSION: Tina has purchased the interest that Barbara had when she gave the second mortgage to Lance. That is, Tina now owns the property, subject to Bank's mortgage, which now secures a loan of $115,000. If Tina does not pay the $115,000 when it is due, Bank may foreclose its mortgage. Of the $90,000 paid by Tina, $81,000 would be paid to Lance, and the balance, or *surplus*, would be paid to Barbara.

EXAMPLE 3: Same facts as Example 2, but suppose that Barbara defaulted on the $115,000 Bank loan, and Bank foreclosed before Lance foreclosed. Suppose also that Tom was the successful bidder at the Bank's foreclosure sale, bidding $200,000. What title would Tom get? What would be Lance's legal position? How would the $200,000 be divided?

DISCUSSION: Tom would get title free of both mortgages. Lance's mortgage would be eliminated because Tom gets the title that Barbara had when she gave her mortgage to the Bank. Since, at that time, she owned the property free of any mortgages, Tom gets exactly what Barbara gave Bank as security: title free of any mortgages. Barbara's subsequent second mortgage given to Lance could not reduce the value of the security that she had previously given to Bank. Thus, one disadvantage of holding a second mortgage is that it will be eliminated by the foreclosure of the first mortgage. However, although the second mortgage is eliminated, the debt evidenced by the note is not. The $200,000 that Tom paid would be distributed as follows: $115,000 to Bank, which will be paid in full, $81,000 to Lance in repayment of the loan made by Lance, and $4,000 to Barbara.

Can you explain why Lance receives part of the proceeds from Bank's foreclosure sale (after Bank is paid in full) in Example 3, whereas in Example 2, Bank receives no part of the proceeds of Lance's foreclosure sale, even after Lance is paid in full?

*Secondary mortgage markets, the subprime mortgage crisis, and evolving foreclosure laws.* The traditional approaches to real estate financing, mortgages, and foreclosures have undergone substantial changes, mostly starting in the 1990s, as real estate lending started building to a feverish level, aided by secondary mortgage markets.

*Secondary mortgage markets* are markets in which investors invest in existing mortgages and other similar real estate finance instruments, somewhat similarly to how investors would invest in shares of stock, mutual funds, bonds, or other securitized investment instruments. Lenders sell their mortgages either in bundles of the loans themselves or in shares of securities backed by mortgages. They are bought by investors, whether they are financial institutions, capital funds, pension and retirement funds, businesses, individuals, government agencies, real estate investment trusts (REITs), or others. In the process the lenders receive a short-term return on their loans (they sell them for more than the amount of the loans), eliminate their risk that the loans won't be repaid, and obtain an infusion of cash that allow them to make new loans. The investors or their investment pools obtain the right to loan payments, which include both the principal and the interest, and therefore they expect to make a return on their investments in mortgages.

Secondary mortgage markets have existed since 1970, when Ginny Mae, an agency wholly owned by the federal government, began issuing securities backed by pools of federal home loans. However, the secondary mortgage markets really took off in the 1990s for several reasons. The combination of a booming stock market and low interest rates left investors worldwide with substantial amounts of money for which they were seeking new investment opportunities. Real estate mortgages and mortgage-backed securities met this need. Low interest rates and high levels of employment in the late 1990s created a high demand for home loans from first-time homebuyers and from homeowners who wanted to upgrade to larger, more expensive homes. More people could afford—or thought that they could afford—larger home loans than in the past. As lenders made loans and received mortgages, they needed to sell their existing mortgages so that they could obtain more capital to make more loans (and also reduce the debt they were carrying on their books, affecting their own credit-worthiness). As the demand for housing grew and the interest rates for home loans dropped, the fair market value of residential property increased dramatically, especially in places like California and Florida. Buyers had to borrow more because homes cost more. Existing homeowners found themselves with new equity in their homes, and many of them used their home equity like an ATM, borrowing against it for non-home (e.g., consumer) expenses, home improvements, and the like. Public policies tend to favor robust residential lending, because economic growth is measured by new housing starts, people build wealth through equity in their homes, real estate transactions provide jobs and business for real estate professionals, and increasing property values lead to larger amounts of property tax revenues to local governments. Regulation of banking and other financial institutions eased up to allow robust and risky lending practices, and tax policies facilitated secondary mortgage markets.

The bottom line was that lenders wanted to lend, buyers and existing homeowners wanted to borrow, investors wanted to invest, and the entirety of the real-estate industry and most of American society wanted to support this boom in real-estate financing and investment. Not surprisingly, three major changes in mortgages and foreclosures occurred.

The first major change was that lenders made highly risky loans. Lending practices in most places changed to assume that borrowers could afford larger loans—could afford making larger monthly loan payments at a larger ratio of their monthly income, known as *debt-to-income ratio*—than had been true in the past. Lenders' requirements that borrowers put up at least 20% of the purchase price as a down payment with their own non-borrowed money were discarded in order to allow loans that covered 90%, 95%, and even 100% of the purchase price (and sometimes even more, if various closing costs and even remodel costs got folded into the purchase price). Appraisers faced tremendous pressures, not only from buyers, sellers, and real estate agents but also from lenders, to find ways to make sure that the properties appraised for at least their selling price. As some housing markets had rapid out-of-control inflation of prices, it became more likely that lenders were making loans that exceeded what would eventually become the long-term value of the property after the housing bubble inevitably burst and prices stabilized. Some lenders made loans without requiring that the borrowers provide documentation to prove that they could actually afford the payments that they claimed they could afford.

Perhaps most troubling was the increase in *subprime mortgages*, which are loans made to individuals with poor credit histories and ratings, who would not be able to qualify for more conventional loans. These subprime loans (or subprime mortgages as they are sometimes called) came with increased up-front costs and/or somewhat higher interest rates than conventional loans, thus exploiting people who were unlikely ever to be able to repay those loans fully. However, the lenders had very little incentive to avoid these risks, because they would sell their mortgages on the secondary market, quickly ridding themselves of the risks of default, foreclosure, and eventual losses. The risks would end up being borne by whichever purchaser of the mortgage still held it at the time that the borrower defaulted.

The housing bubble finally burst in the 2007–2008 time period, creating a cascade effect of: defaults by borrowers, rampant foreclosures throughout communities, rapidly dropping property values, shocks to the financial system, economic recession and business stagnation, more defaults from people losing jobs or income, more foreclosures, more decline in property values, and so forth. Many people found themselves overextended with loans that they couldn't have realistically afforded over the life of the loan. Many of them lost their houses in foreclosure, although some were able to refinance or obtain federal assistance to rewrite the terms of their loans. Financial institutions, experiencing major losses, were unwilling to lend much at all, though. This fact, coupled with the proliferation of publicly-advertised foreclosures in people's neighborhoods, meant that real-property values declined sharply in most communities.

Some neighborhoods, especially low-income and minority neighborhoods, became plagued with "zombie properties," properties that were simultaneously dead and undead—with costs and liabilities greater than their fair market values, refusal by mortgagees and even government agencies to foreclose on them, abandonment by owners/mortgagors, and negative impacts on neighboring properties.

Even where properties entered foreclosure, third-party purchasers in foreclosure often bid quite a bit less than the property's market value (and certainly less than the amount owed to the mortgagee). This has historically been true because a purchaser in foreclosure has to buy with cash and takes title to the property subject to the mortgagor's statutory right of redemption, whatever title defects it might have, and whatever condition the mortgagor might have left the property in when the mortgagor is finally evicted. However, with an abundance of properties in foreclosure and a depressed housing market, bidders in foreclosure sales could acquire properties for a small fraction of their value, leaving mortgagees recovering very little of the outstanding loan amounts.

The second major change in mortgage practices involved uncertainties about who owned the note and/or mortgage when either or both had been transferred from lender to investors to subsequent investors. Historically, if the mortgagor (borrower) experienced difficulty making loan payments, he or she could contact the lender to work out some sort of arrangement to get back on track and avoid foreclosure. This might involve reinstatement of the loan by making back payments and getting back on track with the scheduled loan payments, or it might involve modification of the loan in order to reduce the loan payments (i.e., lower interest rate or longer term). With the rise of the secondary mortgage market, in which the loan had been transferred several times and the payments were made to a designated loan servicing company, the mortgagor/borrower often did not even know who owned the loan.

Likewise, third parties often were not be able to ascertain who had the mortgage, because local deed records might list only the *Mortgage Electronic Registration Systems, Inc. (MERS)* as the mortgagee. MERS was created as a member-based system for cost-effectively transferring mortgages, especially to investors and other buyers of mortgages in secondary markets, without having to file a new mortgage or a record of the transfer in the deed records in the counties where the properties are located. MERS keeps an electronic registry of the transfers, but it's not a public database. MERS also serves as a nominee (representative in name) in the mortgage document for the original mortgagee or its assigns, thus eliminating the need for updating recorded mortgages with each transfer or assignment. During the life of the loan, the mortgagor might know only that the loan was made by Bank A and the mortgage was granted to MERS on behalf of Bank A, unless and until the mortgagor defaults and learns that Bank Z is claiming to own the mortgage and foreclose on the property.

Moreover, during the flurry of lending, transfers of mortgages through the secondary market, and foreclosures as the whole thing collapsed, many banks (and other financial and investment entities) and MERS were notoriously poor at keeping track of physical documents, especially the notes underlying the mortgages. Thus, a foreclosing party might be able to produce the mortgage that it was seeking to enforce or maybe only an electronic record of the mortgage transfer, but not the note evidencing the debt that the mortgage secured.

The third major change has been in the law of foreclosures, driven by these new and very different lending and mortgage practices. One area of change in some states is the long-standing black-letter rule of law that *the mortgage follows the note*. This means that the only party that has the right to foreclose on the property is the party that owns or holds the promissory note evidencing the debt that is secured by the property. Historically, this rule placed a burden on the mortgagor (borrower) to make sure that payments were being made only to the holder of the note and that any party attempting to foreclose on the property prove that it had the note. Thus, if M were to grant a note and mortgage to A in exchange for a loan from A, and then A were to transfer the note to B and the mortgage to C, B would be entitled to the payments from M and to foreclose on the property (if M defaults) and C would have nothing. If C were successful in foreclosing on the property, M would be at risk of being personally liable in full on the loan to B.

This "show-me-the-note" rule morphed into requirements that the foreclosing party present evidence that it has the note or is foreclosing on behalf of the note-holder, either as an element of a judicial foreclosure proceeding or if the mortgagor were to sue to challenge a nonjudicial foreclosure process. For negotiable notes, this doctrine manifests itself in U.C.C. provisions defining the *"person entitled to enforce" the note (PETE status)*. Section 3–301 of the U.C.C. defines PETE status as the possessor of a note that has been endorsed either to that possessor or in blank or a nonholder of the note with rights of a holder (e.g., a person or entity that has been assigned the right to enforce the note on behalf of its holder). If the note was last in the lawful possession of the person who is trying to enforce it but has now been lost, the holder can file a lost-note affidavit under a set of significant requirements and restrictions.

However, some courts have rejected the mortgage-follows-the-note principle and declined to require foreclosing mortgagees (or their assignees) to show that they have the note or standing to foreclose on the note (i.e., PETE status). Basing their holdings on their states' foreclosure statutes, these courts have expressed concerns that requiring proof is impractical given the volume of note and/or mortgage transfers, that the traditional rule is inefficient (especially in nonjudicial foreclosures), and that borrowers are using clever legal arguments to avoid any consequences for loans that they actually received and now owe. As a result, judicial protections of mortgagors have decreased in some states.

In contrast, other courts have been particularly concerned about protecting mortgagors against what are perceived to be unscrupulous practices by mortgagees. In addition to the belief that lenders took advantage of homebuyers in order to make money off of loans that the borrowers couldn't really afford, these courts have been skeptical of assertions by mortgagees that they have the right to foreclose. Some foreclosures have been entirely illegitimate, filed by mortgagees against mortgagors who were not in default on their loans, because records were a mess and employees were pressured to produce fast results on resolving foreclosures. In other cases, employees of foreclosing mortgagees were filing affidavits that the mortgagee held the note without ever actually checking the records to know if that was true. This practice was called "robo-signing," because these designated employees (usually of banks) were signing so many affidavits per day like they were robots and could not have possibly checked their records. As a result, judicial scrutiny of foreclosures has increased in some states.

Federal and state statutes have also addressed the uncertainties of the contemporary foreclosure process, often providing mortgagor protections (i.e., protections for home owners) but sometimes providing mortgagee protections (i.e., protections for banks, investors, and financial institutions). Critics of the current system are split as to whether unscrupulous lenders are exploiting vulnerable borrowers or whether irresponsible borrowers are exploiting at-risk lenders.[6] However, most everyone is in agreement that the law of mortgages and foreclosures is in flux in the aftermath of the subprime mortgage/foreclosure crisis.

## 2. Principal Problem

You are representing Heather Bush on a pro bono basis in challenging the pending non-judicial foreclosure of Bush's home. You have agreed to represent Bush for free, because she has lost her job and is now at risk of losing her home.

Bush is a skilled craftsperson who makes ceramic pottery using a traditional indigenous method. After a few years of being employed on a part-time basis by Aiello Artisan Industries, Bush decided to stop putting her money into rent and instead to buy a home. She found a modest bungalow that was listed for $165,000. However, the demand for houses was high at the time and the interest rates were low, and Bush found herself in a bidding war with other prospective buyers. In the end, she signed a contract to purchase the home for $185,000, which was 12% higher than the listing price. Similar homes were experiencing the same fast increase in market value at the time. Fortunately, Aiello Artisan Industries had an increase in demand for Bush's pottery, and hired her full time.

After initial difficulty finding a loan for which she could qualify, Bush obtained a loan from Gapasin Bank & Trust for $180,000 for 30 years at 5.0% interest annually. Bush paid a $5,000 down payment, plus closing costs, out of her own savings, but 97% of the purchase price ($180,000 out of $185,000) was financed by the loan from Gapasin Bank & Trust. Bush signed a promissory note to Gapasin Bank & Trust and a mortgage to the Mortgage Electronic Registration Systems, Inc. (MERS) as nominee for Gapasin Bank & Trust. The mortgage contained a power-of-sale clause, and was recorded in the county deed records. Gapasin Bank & Trust arranged for the loan payments to be serviced by Stroud Servicing Agency (SSA), a loan servicing business.

After five years, two tragedies befell Bush. First, she lost her job when Aiello Artisan Industries went bankrupt during a downturn in the economy. She has not yet been able to find a job, because the demand for her craft is limited. Second, a major storm caused substantial wind and flood damage to her home. Bush's homeowner's insurance company has delayed settling her claim for the damages, because her policy covers

---

[6] See Sprankling, Understanding Property Law 3rd Ed., at 367–369 (2012).

wind damage but not flood damage. (This is typical of homeowners' insurance policies; homeowners have to obtain flood insurance if they wish to be covered from flood damage. Bush did not have flood insurance.) Bush quit making payments on her home loans three months ago.

In the five years between Bush's purchase of the property and her present difficulties, Gapasin Bank & Trust transferred the note and mortgage to Ray Real Estate Investment Trust (Ray REIT), which then sold the mortgage to the Trail & Saddle Bank. Ray REIT and Trail & Saddle Bank continued to use SSA for loan servicing.

Bush did not know anything about the transfers of her loan to Ray REIT and Trail & Saddle Bank until she received a notice of default from Trail & Saddle Bank, followed by a notice of intent to institute a non-judicial (or power-of-sale) foreclosure on her house. The notice also indicated that Bush would be liable for any deficiency between the outstanding loan balance of $165,292 and the amount obtained by Trail & Saddle Bank in the foreclosure sale.

Bush spoke on the phone twice to a representative of Trail & Saddle Bank, Richard Johnson, in order to try to work out a loan modification, a refinance of her loan, or a postponement of the foreclosure until she receives her insurance settlement. During the first conversation, Johnson stated that Trail & Saddle wanted to work with Bush so that she could keep the home and so that Trail & Saddle would be paid the full debt over time, instead of having to foreclose.

However, a week later, Johnson told Bush that Trail & Saddle is moving forward with the foreclosure, because "we have to clear some outstanding defaulted loans off our books and yours looks like a real loser to us." Bush indicated that she would have money to make up past payments and start making payments again when she receives her insurance proceeds and that the storm-damaged home is not likely to bring much money for Trail & Saddle in foreclosure. Johnson responded, "That's your problem, not mine." When she pleaded to give her a little extra time out of courtesy as a fellow human being, Johnson said, "I'm not talking to you as a human being; I'm talking to you as a representative of Trail & Saddle." At this point, Bush thought to ask about whether Trail & Saddle legitimately has the right to foreclose on her property. She told Johnson that she had signed two documents—a promissory note and a mortgage—with Gapasin Bank & Trust, and asked whether Trail & Saddle could prove that it holds both the note and the mortgage. Johnson replied, "Well, the documents around here are a mess, but that doesn't matter, because we don't have to prove any of that. I can just sign an affidavit that says we can foreclose and that's good enough."

Bush needs your help to prevent the foreclosure of her home. Her jurisdiction allows power-of-sale (or nonjudicial) foreclosures, does not limit deficiency judgments, and has a statutory right of redemption of 6 months, during which time the mortgagor is entitled to remain in possession of the foreclosed property. What strategies and arguments can you develop on Bush's behalf?

## 3. MATERIALS FOR SOLUTION OF PRINCIPAL PROBLEM

### Debrunner v. Deutsche Bank National Trust Company

California Court of Appeal, 2012.
138 Cal.Rptr.3d 830.

■ ELIA, J.

Plaintiff Stephen George Debrunner [a junior mortgagee on a property sold in foreclosure to satisfy the debt of the senior mortgagee] sought a declaratory judgment and quiet title to property on which nonjudicial foreclosure proceedings had been initiated by respondents Deutsche Bank National Trust Company (Deutsche Bank), its loan servicer, and its foreclosure trustee. The superior court sustained respondents' demurrer to the first amended complaint without leave to amend. Plaintiff appeals, contending that an assignment of a deed of trust is of no legal effect without the actual transfer of the corresponding promissory note and therefore cannot support nonjudicial foreclosure by the assignee. We will affirm the judgment.

### Background

Plaintiff alleged that he was a private investor who, along with others, extended a $675,000 loan in March 2006 to Barbara Chiu and Shimin Xu, secured by a deed of trust on a home in Los Altos. Chiu executed a promissory note and second deed of trust in favor of plaintiff and his co-investors.

At this time Chiu was already a trustor on a first deed of trust on the property, having borrowed $975,000 from Quick Loan Funding, Inc. (Quick Loan), in June 2004. The trustee named on that deed of trust was Chicago Title Company. The following month Quick Loan assigned the deed of trust and Chiu's promissory note to Option One Mortgage Corporation (Option One), which shortly thereafter assigned both interests to FV-1, Inc.

The final assignment of the deed of trust was from FV-1 to Deutsche Bank, with respondent Saxon Mortgage Services, Inc. (Saxon), acting as "Attorney in Fact." This document bore three dates: September 2, 2008, when the assignment was originally executed; September 21, 2009, when it was notarized; and January 5, 2010, when it was recorded.

In January 2008, plaintiff and his co-investors filed a notice of default, and in April they scheduled a trustee's sale for the following month. In June Chiu's business entity filed for chapter 11 bankruptcy protection. The bankruptcy court thereafter granted plaintiff and the co-investors' motion for relief from the bankruptcy stay, and in March 2009 they foreclosed and obtained a trustee's deed upon sale for the property.

In August 2008, however, well before the sale was completed, Saxon, the servicer of the first-position loan, filed a notice of default on the property. Because of the bankruptcy proceeding, however, the notice was rescinded. In July 2009 Deutsche Bank moved for relief from the bankruptcy stay in order to file a new notice of default. That motion was taken off calendar when the bankruptcy matter was closed in August 2009.

On September 15, 2009, the foreclosure trustee, Old Republic Default Management Services (Old Republic), recorded a new notice of default on the property. In the accompanying Rosenthal Fair Debt Collection Practices Act (Civ. Code, § 1788) notice, Old Republic named Deutsche Bank as the creditor and Saxon as its "attorney-in-fact." The notice informed the debtor that payment to stop the foreclosure could be made to Saxon, and it provided Saxon's address and telephone number. On January 5, 2010, the same day the assignment from FV-1 to Deutsche Bank was recorded, the county recorded a "Substitution of Trustee" from Chicago Title Company to Old Republic. This document had been signed and notarized on September 2, 2008, by Saxon on behalf of Deutsche Bank.

Plaintiff commenced this action in November 2009 to stop the impending foreclosure, naming Deutsche Bank, Saxon, and Old Republic. In his first amended complaint in April 2010, he specifically sought a declaration of multiple facts—in particular, that defendants had no right to foreclose because Deutsche Bank did not have physical possession of or ownership rights to the original promissory note. Plaintiff further sought to quiet title to the property and remove the first deed of trust in favor of Quick Loan.

Deutsche Bank and Saxon demurred on multiple grounds, primarily the absence of facts indicating a violation of nonjudicial foreclosure procedures. Defendants specifically argued, for instance, that possession of the original note was not required under the applicable statutes, Civil Code section 2924 et seq. In response, plaintiff maintained that any assignment of the deed of trust was immaterial because a deed of trust "cannot be transferred independently" of the promissory note, which must be "properly assigned" and attached. According to plaintiff, "[a] deed of trust standing alone is a nullity," and thus cannot provide authority for a lender to foreclose. Plaintiff relied on several sections of the California Uniform Commercial Code pertaining to negotiation, transfer, indorsement, and enforcement of negotiable instruments. (See Comm.Code, §§ 3104, 3109, 3201–3205, 3301, 9313.)

Although he had alleged Old Republic to be the foreclosure trustee, plaintiff further argued in opposition to the demurrer that neither Saxon nor Old Republic had any right to initiate foreclosure because there was no proper "chain of assignment" from Option One to Saxon or to Old

Republic, as required under section 2934a. He noted that Quick Loan had assigned the deed of trust, but not the note, to Option One, which thereafter assigned the deed of trust to FV-1 and eventually to Deutsche Bank. These assignments, he maintained, were "of no value" and invalid because they were not accompanied by assignment of the promissory note. In other words, the deed of trust and the note "must remain married and joined to each other for a secured debt to exist. Once they are divorced, or widowed, as has happened in this case, the deed of trust becomes a nullity and the promissory note an unsecured debt. Neither carry [sic] the right to foreclosure."

This assertedly defective assignment of the note formed the basis of plaintiff's additional claim that respondents had not complied with section 2943, subdivision (b)(1), which requires the beneficiary in a foreclosure proceeding to produce a copy of the note "or other evidence of indebtedness" upon demand. Deutsche Bank, plaintiff explained, could not produce the note because it did not have it; instead, they "have unlawfully attempted a theft of [the property] and are now desperately attempting to conceal this attempted larceny."

The superior court was not convinced by plaintiff's position. Responding to plaintiff's assertion that Deutsche Bank was not the proper assignee and therefore not entitled to sell the property under section 2932.5, the court looked to plaintiff's pleading itself, to which was attached three recorded assignments proceeding from Quick Loan to Option One to FV-1 to Deutsche Bank. Because those assignments conveyed all beneficial interest in the deed of trust, "[t]ogether with the note or notes therein described or referred to," a chain of title had been established on the face of the first amended complaint. The court also rejected plaintiff's assertion that physical possession of the promissory note was a precondition to nonjudicial foreclosure, citing federal district court decisions. Addressing plaintiff's claims of noncompliance with section 2923.5, subdivision (b) of section 2934a, and subdivision (b)(1) of section 2943, the superior court deemed these challenges to be meritless or nonprejudicial. It then sustained respondents' demurrer without leave to amend. Plaintiff filed a timely notice of appeal from the ensuing judgment of dismissal.

## Discussion

### Deutsche Bank's Right to Foreclose

Of the claims in his first amended complaint, plaintiff directs his arguments on appeal primarily to the validity of the assignment to Deutsche Bank and the necessity that a promissory note be produced to effectuate a foreclosure. Plaintiff again contends that an assignee must physically receive the promissory note and endorse it, or an assignment is "completely ineffective" and "a legal nullity." The beneficiary must then have physical possession of the original note in order to initiate nonjudicial foreclosure proceedings.

Plaintiff further contends that a notice of default under section 2924c, subdivision (b)(1), must identify the beneficiary, not just the "servicer." Strict compliance with this provision is necessary, plaintiff argues; "[t]he i's must be dotted and the t's crossed." Because prejudice need not be shown, says plaintiff, the failure to provide the beneficiary's name and contact information in this case, along with the premature identification of Old Republic as the foreclosure trustee, has invalidated the entire proceeding.

### Status of Deutsche Bank as Beneficiary

Plaintiff raises several issues related to the validity of the transfer of the deed of trust, but his position on most of them is predicated on a single contention, that no foreclosure of a deed of trust is valid unless the beneficiary is in possession of the underlying promissory note. Without such possession, the deed of trust is "severed" from the promissory note and consequently is of no effect. Plaintiff submits that we must look to the California Uniform Commercial Code for guidance, because a promissory note is a negotiable instrument which cannot be assigned without a valid endorsement and physical delivery to the assignee.

As the parties recognize, many federal courts have rejected this position, applying California law. All have noted that the procedures to be followed in a nonjudicial foreclosure are governed by sections 2924 through 2924k, which do not require that the note be in the possession of the party initiating the foreclosure. (See, e.g., Geren v. Deutsche Bank National (E.D.Cal.2011) 2011 WL 3568913; Kolbe v. JP Morgan Chase Bank, N.A. (N.D.Cal.2011) 2011 WL 4965065; Hague v. Wells Fargo Bank, N.A. (N.D.Cal.2011) 2011 WL 3360026; Impink v. Bank of America (S.D.Cal.2011) 2011 WL 3903197.) We likewise see nothing in the applicable statutes that precludes foreclosure when the foreclosing party does not possess the original promissory note. They set forth "a comprehensive framework for the regulation of a nonjudicial foreclosure sale pursuant to a power of sale contained in a deed of trust. The purposes of this comprehensive scheme are threefold: (1) to provide the creditor/beneficiary with a quick, inexpensive and efficient remedy against a defaulting debtor/trustor; (2) to protect the debtor/trustor from wrongful loss of the property; and (3) to ensure that a properly conducted sale is final between the parties and conclusive as to a bona fide purchaser." (Moeller v. Lien (1994) 25 Cal.App.4th 822, 830 [30 Cal.Rptr.2d 777].) Notably, section 2924, subdivision (a)(1), permits a notice of default to be filed by the "trustee, mortgagee, or beneficiary, or any of their authorized agents." The provision does not mandate physical possession of the underlying promissory note in order for this initiation of foreclosure to be valid.

Plaintiff's reliance on the California Uniform Commercial Code provisions pertaining to negotiable instruments is misplaced. "The comprehensive statutory framework established [in sections 2924 to 2924k] to govern nonjudicial foreclosure sales is intended to be exhaustive." (Moeller v. Lien, supra, 25 Cal.App.4th at p. 834, 30 Cal.Rptr.2d 777; see also I.E. Associates v. Safeco Title Ins. Co. (1985) 39 Cal.3d 281, 285 [216 Cal.Rptr. 438, 702 P.2d 596] ["These provisions cover every aspect of exercise of the power of sale contained in a deed of trust"].) "Because of the exhaustive nature of this scheme, California appellate courts have refused to read any additional requirements into the non-judicial foreclosure statute." (Lane v. Vitek Real Estate Indus. Group (E.D.Cal.2010) 713 F.Supp.2d 1092, 1098; accord, Gomes v. Countrywide Home Loans, Inc. (2011) 192 Cal.App.4th 1149, 1154–1157 [121 Cal.Rptr.3d 819] [no statutory right to sue to determine authority of a lender's nominee to initiate foreclosure; and in any event, plaintiff agreed in deed of trust that nominee had such authority].) "There is no stated requirement in California's non-judicial foreclosure scheme that requires a beneficial interest in the Note to foreclose. Rather, the statute broadly allows a trustee, mortgagee, beneficiary, or any of their agents to initiate non-judicial foreclosure. Accordingly, the statute does not require a beneficial interest in both the Note and the Deed of Trust to commence a non-judicial foreclosure sale." (Lane v. Vitek Real Estate Indus. Group, supra, 713 F.Supp.2d at p. 1099.) Likewise, we are not convinced that the cited sections of the California Uniform Commercial Code (particularly section 3301) displace the detailed, specific, and comprehensive set of legislative procedures the Legislature has established for nonjudicial foreclosures. (See Spence v. Wells Fargo Bank, N.A., 2011 WL 1668320, at 2 (E.D.Cal. May 03, 2011) [Commercial Code section 3301 has "no application in the instant context of real property financing"]; accord, Das v. WMC Mortg. Corp. (N.D.Cal.2011) 2011 WL 2847412, 2011 U.S. Dist. LEXIS 77414; see also Padayachi v. IndyMac Bank (N.D.Cal.2010) 2010 WL 4367221, 2010 U.S. Dist. LEXIS 120963 ["Although Article 3 of the UCC governs negotiable instruments, it does not apply to nonjudicial foreclosure under deeds of trust"]; accord, Germon v. BAC Home Loans Servicing, L.P. (S.D.Cal.2011) 2011 WL 719591, 2011 U.S. Dist. LEXIS 17084.)

Plaintiff has referred us to the recent appellate bankruptcy decision in In re Veal (9th Cir. BAP 2011) 450 B.R. 897. He directs us to that opinion as an application of comparable provisions of Arizona law and urges the same analysis under California's Uniform Commercial Code. We are not persuaded. The analysis of the court in Veal was directed at the question of whether Wells Fargo Bank had standing to seek relief from an automatic bankruptcy stay. The loan at issue was a mortgage, of which enforcement was governed by Illinois law (where the property was located), while the note was deemed to fall within the province of Arizona law. It was the bank's burden to demonstrate a right to enforce the mortgage securing the note, and it failed, as it could not show that it was a "holder" or some other "person entitled to enforce" the note. (Id. at p. 911.) The parties had stipulated that the Uniform Commercial Code applied to these issues, and the court proceeded on that assumption without questioning the soundness of the premise. (Id. at pp. 908–909.)

The Veal court applied the rule urged by plaintiff in the present appeal—that is, that " '[a]n assignment of the note carries the mortgage with it, while an assignment of the latter alone is a nullity.' " (Id. at p. 916.) In doing so, however, the court noted the departure from this rule by some statutes in other states, specifically citing section 2924 and cases arising in California.3 Thus, the court implicitly acknowledged that under California's statutory scheme, the original note need not be produced to initiate a valid nonjudicial foreclosure. (Id. at p. 917.)

Even if the California Uniform Commercial Code provisions regarding negotiable instruments somehow imposed superseding legal constraints on lenders seeking a "quick, inexpensive and efficient remedy" through nonjudicial foreclosure (Moeller v. Lien, supra, 25 Cal.App.4th at p. 832, 30 Cal.Rptr.2d 777), plaintiff's allegations still could not withstand dismissal. Again the distinction between this case and Veal is noteworthy. The assignment of the mortgage to Wells Fargo had been insufficient to transfer the note as well as the mortgage. The court contrasted this "purported" assignment with that made to Wells Fargo's predecessor, which explicitly assigned " 'the note(s) and obligations therein described and the money due and to become due thereon with interest, and all rights accrued or to accrue under such mortgage.' " (Id. at pp. 905, 904.) The subsequent assignment to Wells Fargo, however, only "referred to" the note as part of its description of the mortgage it was identifying. (Id. at p. 905.) In the instant case, however, the assignment of the deed of trust from FV-1 to Deutsche Bank stated that it was an assignment of "all beneficial interest" under the deed of trust, "TOGETHER with the note or notes therein described and secured thereby, the money due and to become due thereon, with interest, and all rights accrued or to accrue under said Deed of Trust...." This language is similar to the transfer language found acceptable in Veal to transfer the note to Wells Fargo's predecessor.

### Disposition

The judgment of dismissal is affirmed.

## JPMorgan Chase Bank, N.A. v. Erlandson

Court of Appeals of Minnesota, 2012.
821 N.W.2d 600.

■ HOOTEN, JUDGE.

In this appeal from a mortgage foreclosure by action [a judicial foreclosure], appellant mortgagors argue that a fact question exists regarding whether the promissory note associated with the mortgage had been properly assigned to respondent bank at the time the bank foreclosed the mortgage. Appellants argue that, because such a fact question exists, the district court erred in granting summary judgment to allow the bank to foreclose the mortgage.

The bank, as the owner of legal title to the mortgage, can foreclose its mortgage by action even if it does not hold the promissory note associated with that mortgage. Therefore, we reject appellants' arguments and affirm the district court.

## FACTS

In November 2006, appellants Trevor and Melissa Erlandson borrowed money from Homecomings Financial, LLC (Homecomings Financial), executed a promissory note in favor of Homecomings Financial, and secured the note with a mortgage naming the nominee of Homecomings Financial, Mortgage Electronic Systems, Inc., (MERS), as the mortgagee. Respondent JPMorgan Bank, N.A., was assigned the legal title to the mortgage. Appellants defaulted on their repayment obligations and the bank sued to foreclose the mortgage by action. See Minn.Stat. §§ 581.01.12 (2010). As the purported owner of the promissory note, the bank also sought a deficiency judgment against appellants on the note. Appellants answered the foreclosure complaint, but not the bank's discovery. By order signed May 10, 2011, the district court granted the bank's motion for summary judgment against appellants, awarded the bank a decree of foreclosure, and directed the sheriff to sell the mortgaged premises. The order also awarded the bank a money judgment of $159,610.23, which was the principal amount in default on the note, together with interest and other sums that were payable to the bank under the note and mortgage. The district court noted that the bank reserved the right to seek a deficiency judgment against appellants. The order states that appellants did not respond to the bank's motion for summary judgment and did not appear at the hearing on that motion. On May 13, 2011, judgment was entered on this order.

With new counsel, appellants moved the district court to vacate the summary judgment. Minn. R. Civ. P. 60.02. Appellants asserted that their failure to respond to the bank's discovery and summary judgment motion was excusable, and that the bank could not foreclose the mortgage, nor could it recover on the note, because the bank had failed to show that it had been assigned the note associated with the mortgage. The district court partially granted appellants' motion by vacating the money judgment that had been awarded to the bank and by reopening discovery relative to the parties' disputes about the note. However, the district court denied appellants' motion to vacate the findings of fact, conclusions of law, and order pertaining to the foreclosure, and, instead, reaffirmed its prior directive that the sheriff sell the premises. Judgment was entered on this order on July 14, 2011.

At the sheriff's sale, the bank bought the foreclosed premises with a credit bid of $98,540. Waiving its claim for a deficiency judgment, the bank then moved the district court for an order confirming the sheriff's sale. Appellants opposed the bank's motion to confirm the sheriff's sale, asserting that the foreclosure was defective because the bank failed to show that it had obtained any rights to the note and therefore did not have the right to foreclose or purchase the premises at the sheriff's sale. The district court confirmed the sheriff's sale, reduced the money judgment against appellants from $159,610.23 to $98,540 because the bank waived its deficiency and other note-related claims, directed that the court administrator "fully satisfy the amended money figure . . . such that there is no surplus or any deficiency," and dismissed all other claims in the case. Judgment was entered on this order on December 20, 2011 from which appellants now appeal.

## ANALYSIS

Appellants argue that, to foreclose a mortgage, the foreclosing entity must possess both the mortgage and the note associated with that mortgage, or that the foreclosing entity be acting on behalf of one who possesses both the mortgage and the associated note. Therefore, appellants argue, because this record shows that a factual question exists regarding whether the bank was properly assigned the note associated with the mortgage, the district court erred in granting the bank summary judgment allowing it to foreclose the mortgage. We reject this argument because it is inconsistent with Minnesota law.

When a purchaser of real estate borrows money to finance the purchase, the purchaser usually signs two distinct, but related, documents. One is a promissory note, which represents the purchaser's promise to repay the lender the amount of the loan, plus interest. The second is a security instrument, usually a mortgage, which conveys to the mortgagee—who is, at least initially, usually the lender—an interest in the property as security for the purchaser's obligations under the promissory note. See Jackson v. Mort. Elec. Registration Sys., Inc., 770 N.W.2d 487, 493 (Minn.2009) (discussing the mortgage process). As explained in Jackson, since the security instrument is incident to the debt represented by the note and can have no separate or independent existence apart from the debt it secures, it was long held that the transfer of the debt represented by the note carried with it an assignment of the security instrument or mortgage. Id. at 494 (citing Hatlestad v. Mut. Trust Life Ins. Co., 197 Minn. 640, 647, 268 N.W. 665, 668 (1936) and Hayes v. Midland Credit Co., 173 Minn. 554, 556, 218 N.W. 106, 107 (1928)). These principles are the basis for appellants' argument that, as a prerequisite to the foreclosure of a mortgage, the foreclosing entity must show either that it owns both the mortgage being foreclosed and the note associated with that mortgage, or that it is acting on behalf of one who does.[3]

---

[3] These types of arguments have been referred to as "show me the note" claims. See Welk v. GMAC Mortg., LLC, 850 F.Supp.2d 976, 980 (D.Minn.2012) ("A plaintiff bringing a show-me-the-note claim generally argues that, because the entity that holds her mortgage . . . is not the same as the entity that holds her note . . . the mortgage on her home or the foreclosure of that mortgage is invalid."); see also Stein v. Chase Home Fin., LLC, 662 F.3d 976, 978 (8th Cir.2011) ("A 'show me the note' plaintiff typically alleges a foreclosure is invalid unless the foreclosing entity produces the original note."). Appellants' "show me the note" argument, however, is inconsistent with Jackson, which ruled that the holder of legal title to a security

In an extensive discussion of the advent of MERS and the Minnesota caselaw addressing the relationship between a promissory note and the legal and equitable interests in security instruments, Jackson explained that MERS is an electronic registration system that "acts as the nominal mortgagee for the loans owned by [members of that system,]" that members of the system "include originators, lenders, servicers, and investors, [and that the system allows its members] to assign home mortgage loans [among its members] without having to record each transfer in the local land recording offices where the real estate securing the mortgage is located." Id. at 490. It is because MERS internally tracks the assignments of the mortgage loans among its members while remaining the nominal mortgagee of record that transfers among MERS members need not be recorded in the local land record offices. Id.

Jackson noted that this more streamlined system "improve[d] the efficiency and profitability of the primary and secondary mortgage markets," so that an originating mortgage lender may sell a mortgage loan on the secondary market to investors which could resell the loan, without the time, money and paperwork associated with recording the documents associated with each assignment. Id. "Once registered, MERS serves as the mortgagee of record for all loans in its system." Id.

MERS was enabled by the legislature's enactment of what is known as the "MERS statute." Minn.Stat. § 507.413 (2010); Jackson, 770 N.W.2d at 494–95 (labeling this section the MERS statute); see also 2004 Minn. Laws ch. 153, § 2, at 7677 (enacting the MERS statute). Under the MERS statute, a mortgage may be recorded in the name of a mortgagee as the nominee for a third party and the nominee has the authority to act on behalf of the third party in any foreclosure proceeding. Minn.Stat. § 507.413(a). As Jackson recognized, "[b]y acting as the nominal mortgagee of record for [all of] its members, MERS has essentially separated the promissory note and the security instrument, allowing the debt to be transferred [among the members of MERS] without an assignment of the security instrument." 770 N.W.2d at 494.

In holding that MERS has authority to foreclose as a nominee for the mortgagee, the court reasoned that "an assignment of the promissory note operates as an equitable assignment of the underlying security instrument," but it does not convey the legal title to that instrument, which remains in MERS. Id. at 497. Thus, equitable title to the security instrument follows the note, while legal title is held by the entity that actually owns the security instrument. See id. at 500 (" '[O]ur own decisions have repeatedly recognized' the doctrine that the debt, and consequently the real ownership of the security instrument, may be in one person, 'while what may be termed the legal title' to the security instrument is in another." (quoting Burke v. Backus, 51 Minn. 174, 178–79, 53 N.W. 458, 459 (1892))). " [T]he power of sale [granted in a security

---

instrument can foreclose that security instrument by exercising a power of sale in the security instrument, even if that entity does not own the associated note. 770 N.W.2d at 500–01.

instrument] must be exercised in the name of the party who has the legal title to the instrument.'" Id. (quoting Burke, 51 Minn. at 179, 53 N.W. at 459).[4]

Appellants' counsel argued at oral argument before this court that Jackson is distinguishable from the current case because Jackson involved a foreclosure by advertisement while this case involves a foreclosure by action. Appellants' counsel, however, did not provide any reason why the analysis in Jackson—indicating that an owner of legal title to a mortgage could foreclose that mortgage by advertisement without also owning the associated note—would not be equally applicable in a foreclosure by action. Nor do we see a reason for drawing this distinction.

A mortgage may be foreclosed either by advertisement or by action. "A foreclosure by advertisement takes place without recourse to the courts, and is a proceeding in pais, ex parte, and in rem." Norwest Bank Hastings Nat'l Ass'n v. Franzmeier, 355 N.W.2d 431, 433 (Minn.App.1984). Foreclosure by advertisement "was devised to avoid the delay and expense of judicial proceedings" associated with foreclosure by action. Soufal v. Griffith, 159 Minn. 252, 256, 198 N.W. 807, 809 (1924). "Because foreclosure by advertisement is a purely statutory creation," and does not require court involvement, "the statutes are strictly construed." Jackson, 770 N.W.2d at 494 (citing Moore v. Carlson, 112 Minn. 433, 434, 128 N.W. 578, 579 (1910)). A prerequisite to foreclosure by advertisement is that the mortgage, and all of its assignments, be recorded. Minn.Stat. § 580.02(3) (2010). By requiring the recording of the legal title to the mortgage, the plain intent of the statute was to make the mortgagee's rights and interest in the mortgage "beyond reasonable question" and a "matter of record." Jackson, 770 N.W.2d at 497–98 (quotations omitted); see also Soufal, 159 Minn. at 255, 198 N.W. at 808. There is no requirement, however, that "mere equitable" interests be recorded. Jackson, 770 N.W.2d at 498.

A mortgage "foreclosure by action requires a judicial decree and approval of sale and is an in personam proceeding, although it is in the nature of a proceeding in rem since its purpose is to enforce a lien on the mortgaged property." Norwest Bank Hastings Nat'l Ass'n, 355 N.W.2d at 433. If there are defects in the recording of legal title to a mortgage, the entity seeking to foreclose a mortgage "must resort to foreclosure by action." Soufal, 159 Minn. at 256, 198 N.W. at 809.

---

[4] See Stein, 662 F.3d at 980 (interpreting Minnesota law and Jackson to be that "the right to enforce a mortgage through foreclosure by advertisement lies with the legal, rather than equitable holder, of the mortgage[.] ... Thus, [the assignee of the mortgage] was the party entitled to commence a foreclosure by advertisement under Minnesota law, even if the promissory note (and the corresponding equitable interest in the mortgage) had been transferred to someone else"); Welk, 850 F.Supp.2d at 984–85 ("[Jackson ] flatly rejected the core argument made by plaintiffs in this case and in every show-me-the-note case: that an entity that holds only legal and record title to the mortgage—and not equitable title—cannot foreclose.").

If a mortgagor defaults, the mortgagee and holder of the promissory note may sue for a personal judgment on the note or, relying on the security of the mortgage, may sell the property and apply the proceeds of the sale to payment of the debt. City of St. Paul v. St. Anthony Flats Ltd. P'ship, 517 N.W.2d 58, 61–62 (Minn.App.1994), review denied (Minn. Aug. 24, 1994). "In choosing between mortgage foreclosure and an action on the note, the mortgagee may pursue either or both remedies, as long as there is no double recovery on the debt." Id. at 62. Consistent with the legal principles as set forth in Jackson, the right to foreclose by action can be exercised by the owner of legal title to the mortgage—or an entity acting on behalf of the owner of legal title to the mortgage—regardless of whether that entity also is the owner or possessor of the associated promissory note.

The current appeal involves a foreclosure by action in which it is undisputed that the foreclosing bank had legal title to the mortgage at the time of the foreclosure. Even if there had been a dispute about the bank's legal title to the mortgage, because this was a foreclosure by action, that dispute could have been raised in, and resolved by, the district court as part of the foreclosure litigation. In Jackson, the mortgagors claimed that they were disadvantaged by the fact that only MERS, as the nominee of the mortgagee and its assigns and successors, was required to record the mortgage and, as a result, the mortgagors were not able to know the "true" identity of the lender or owner of the promissory note. 770 N.W.2d at 501–02. Ignoring the fact that ownership or possession of the note associated with a security instrument is not relevant to identifying who has the authority to foreclose that security instrument, concerns about whether the entity seeking to foreclose a mortgage by action actually has the authority to do so do not exist in a foreclosure by action because the entity seeking to foreclose the mortgage is generally the plaintiff with regard to the foreclosure. If there is a dispute about that entity's authority to foreclose the mortgage, mortgagors, armed with their general right to due process of law, as well as the discovery rights set out in the rules of civil procedure, can litigate the question. See Minn.Stat. § 581.01 (2010) (stating that, unless displaced by provisions of chapter 581, the rules of civil procedure apply to "[a]ctions for the foreclosure of mortgages").

Here, the bank, as the undisputed owner of legal title to the mortgage, exercised its independent remedy to foreclose under well-established principles of real-estate law that pre-exist the holding in Jackson. See Lundberg v. Nw. Nat'l Bank of Minneapolis, 299 Minn. 46, 48, 216 N.W.2d 121, 123 (1974) (noting that a mortgage "may be foreclosed even though an action on the note is barred" (citing Johnson v. Howe, 176 Minn. 287, 223 N.W. 148 (1929); Welbon v. Webster, 89 Minn. 177, 94 N.W. 550 (1903); Conner v. How, 35 Minn. 518, 29 N.W. 314 (1886))).

Appellants argue that allowing the bank to foreclose the mortgage without showing that it also possesses the associated note exposes mortgagors to double liability on the mortgage debt if, after a foreclosure, the owner or possessor of the note—or one acting on behalf of the owner or possessor of the note—starts a separate action against the mortgagors seeking to recover on the note.[5] We reject that argument for two reasons. First, here, the bank waived any claims based on the note. Therefore, these mortgagors will not be liable to the bank on any future claims based on the note. Second, as noted above, caselaw prohibits double recovery on the debt associated with a mortgage. City of St. Paul, 517 N.W.2d at 62. Moreover, had a deficiency judgment been sought here, appellants would have been afforded all of their rights in defending such action, including the rights to not be subject to double recovery, to contest whether the party seeking to recover on the note was an owner or possessor of the note in question, and to seek to join other parties who appellants or the bank claim have an interest in the note.

Even where a deficiency judgment is not waived, any potential disputes regarding a possible deficiency judgment do not cause a court-ordered mortgage foreclosure to be invalid. This is because any dispute between the possessor of legal title to a mortgage (i.e., the entity with the authority to foreclose the mortgage) and the entity possessing equitable title to that mortgage (i.e., the note-holder), does not alter the status of the mortgagor for purposes of foreclosure. See Jackson, 770 N.W.2d at 501 ("[A]ny disputes that arise between the mortgagee holding legal title and the assignee of the promissory note holding equitable title do not affect the status of the mortgagor for purposes of foreclosure by advertisement.").

## DECISION

The holder of legal title to a mortgage can foreclose its mortgage by action regardless of whether it also holds the note associated with the mortgage. Here, it is undisputed that, at the time it foreclosed the mortgage, the bank held legal title to the mortgage and that appellants had defaulted on their mortgage-related obligations. Therefore, the district court correctly ruled that the bank could foreclose its mortgage. Affirmed.

---

[5] If this were a foreclosure by advertisement, the amount received from a foreclosure by advertisement is deemed to be "full satisfaction of the mortgage debt, except as provided in section 582.30." Minn.Stat. § 580.225 (2010). If the proceeds of the foreclosure by advertisement are less than the amount owed under a promissory note, and the mortgage "has a redemption period of six months under section 580.23, subdivision 1, or five weeks under section 582.032," the mortgagee does not have the right to a deficiency judgment against the mortgagors. Minn.Stat. § 582.30, subd. 2 (2010).

## Eaton v. Federal National Mortgage Association
Supreme Judicial Court of Massachusetts, 2012.
969 N.E.2d 1118.

■ BOTSFORD, J.

In this case, we address the propriety of a foreclosure by power of sale undertaken by a mortgage holder that did not hold the underlying mortgage note. A judge in the Superior Court preliminarily enjoined the defendant Federal National Mortgage Association (Fannie Mae) from proceeding with a summary process action to evict the plaintiff, Henrietta Eaton, from her home, following a foreclosure sale of the property by the defendant Green Tree Servicing, LLC (Green Tree), as mortgagee. The judge ruled that Eaton likely would succeed on the merits of her claim that for a valid foreclosure sale to occur, both the mortgage and the underlying note must be held by the foreclosing party; and that because Green Tree stipulated that it held only Eaton's mortgage, the foreclosure sale was void, and the defendants therefore were not entitled to evict Eaton. Pursuant to G.L. c. 231, § 118, first par., the defendants petitioned a single justice of the Appeals Court for relief from the preliminary injunction. The single justice denied the petition and reported his decision to a panel of that court. We transferred the case to this court on our own motion. For the reasons we discuss herein, we conclude as follows. A foreclosure sale conducted pursuant to a power of sale in a mortgage must comply with all applicable statutory provisions, including in particular G.L. c. 183, § 21, and G.L. c. 244, § 14. These statutes authorize a "mortgagee" to foreclose by sale pursuant to a power of sale in the mortgage, and require the "mortgagee" to provide notice and take other steps in connection with the sale. The meaning of the term "mortgagee" as used in the statutes is not free from ambiguity, but we now construe the term to refer to the person or entity then holding the mortgage and also either holding the mortgage note or acting on behalf of the note holder.[2] Further, we exercise our discretion to treat the construction announced in this decision as a new interpretation of the relevant statute, only to apply to foreclosures under the power of sale where statutory notice is provided after the date of this decision. We vacate the preliminary injunction and remand the case to the Superior Court for further proceedings consistent with this opinion.

### Background

On September 12, 2007, Eaton refinanced the mortgage on her home in the Roslindale section of Boston (Roslindale property) by executing a promissory note payable to BankUnited, FSB (BankUnited, or lender), for $145,000. That same day, she also executed a mortgage, referred to in the mortgage itself as a "[s]ecurity [i]nstrument." The mortgage is

---

[2] The term "mortgage note" is used in this opinion to refer to the promissory note or other form of debt or obligation for which the mortgage provides security; and the term "note holder" is used to refer to a person or entity owning the "mortgage note."

separate from, but by its terms clearly connected to, the promissory note. The parties to the mortgage are Eaton as the "[b]orrower," BankUnited as the "[l]ender," and Mortgage Electronic Registration Systems, Inc. (MERS)[5] as the "mortgagee."[6]

Under the mortgage executed by Eaton, MERS as mortgagee (or its assignee) holds legal title to the Roslindale property with power of sale "solely as nominee" of the lender BankUnited (or its assignee). However, "if necessary to comply with law or custom, MERS (as nominee for Lender and Lender's successors and assigns) has the right to exercise any or all of those interests, including, but not limited to, the right to foreclose and sell the Property; and to take any action required of Lender. . . ."[7]

The mortgage also contains a series of covenants that run exclusively between BankUnited as lender and Eaton. The final covenant, entitled "Acceleration; Remedies," empowers the lender, on default by Eaton, to "invoke the STATUTORY POWER OF SALE and any other remedies permitted by applicable law." In this regard, the covenant obligates the lender, in invoking the statutory power of sale, to mail a copy of a notice of sale to Eaton.

On April 22, 2009, MERS assigned its interest as mortgagee to Green Tree and recorded the assignment in the Suffolk County registry of deeds. The record contains no evidence of a corresponding transfer of

---

[5] Mortgage Electronic Registration Systems, Inc. (MERS), is a Delaware nonstock corporation owned by its members. See Arnold, Yes, There is Life on MERS, 11 Prob. & Prop. 32, 33 (1997) (Arnold). MERS is mortgagee of record for mortgage loans registered on the MERS electronic registration system, which tracks servicing rights and beneficial ownership interests in those loans; the system allows these servicing rights and beneficial ownership interests to be traded electronically between members without the need to record publicly each mortgage assignment. See id. In particular, when the beneficial interest in a loan is sold, the note is transferred by indorsement and delivery between the parties, and the new ownership interest is reflected in the MERS system. MERS remains the mortgagee of record so long as the note is sold to another MERS member; no aspect of such a transaction is publicly recorded. See In re Agard, 444 B.R. 231, 248 (Bankr.E.D.N.Y.2011); MERSCORP, Inc. v. Romaine, 8 N.Y.3d 90, 96, 828 N.Y.S.2d 266, 861 N.E.2d 81 (2006). If an ownership interest in, or servicing right to, a mortgage loan is transferred by a MERS member to a non-MERS member, an assignment of the mortgage from the MERS member to the non-MERS member is publicly recorded and the loan is "deactivated" within the MERS system. See id. at 96 n. 4, 828 N.Y.S.2d 266, 861 N.E.2d 81.

[6] Section C of the mortgage agreement's definitions section states that "MERS is a separate corporation that is acting solely as a nominee for Lender [BankUnited] and Lender's successors and assigns. MERS is the mortgagee under this Security Instrument" (emphasis added).

[7] In particular, the mortgage provides: "Borrower [Eaton] does hereby mortgage, grant and convey to MERS (solely as nominee for Lender and Lender's successors and assigns) and to the successors and assigns of MERS, with power of sale, the [Roslindale property]. . . . Borrower understands and agrees that MERS holds only legal title to the interests granted by Borrower in this Security Instrument, but, if necessary to comply with law or custom, MERS (as nominee for Lender and Lender's successors and assigns) has the right: to exercise any and all of those interests, including, but not limited to, the right to foreclose and sell the Property; and to take any action required of Lender including, but not limited to, releasing and canceling this Security Interest."

the note. The note was indorsed in blank by BankUnited on an undetermined date.[8]

Later in 2009, after Eaton failed to make payments on the note, Green Tree, as assignee of MERS, moved to foreclose on her home through exercise of a power of sale contained in the mortgage. A foreclosure auction was conducted in November, 2009; Green Tree was the highest bidder. The identity of the note holder at the time of the foreclosure sale is not known from the record. On November 24, 2009, Green Tree assigned the rights to its bid to Fannie Mae, and a foreclosure deed was recorded in the Suffolk County registry of deeds.

On January 25, 2010, Fannie Mae commenced a summary process action in the Boston division of the Housing Court Department to evict Eaton. Eaton filed a counterclaim, arguing that the underlying foreclosure sale was invalid because Green Tree did not hold Eaton's mortgage note at the time of the foreclosure sale and therefore lacked the requisite authority to foreclose on her equity of redemption in the Roslindale property. A Housing Court judge subsequently granted a sixty-day stay of the summary process action to give Eaton an opportunity to seek relief in the Superior Court. The Housing Court judge also ordered Eaton to make use and occupancy payments during the pendency of her action. On April 8, 2011, Eaton filed a complaint in the Superior Court for injunctive and declaratory relief. The complaint sought a declaration that the foreclosure sale of Eaton's home and the subsequent foreclosure deed were null and void, and that Eaton was the owner in fee simple of the Roslindale property; a preliminary injunction to stay the summary process action in the Housing Court; and a permanent injunction barring Fannie Mae from taking steps to obtain possession of or convey the Roslindale property. For the purposes of Eaton's motion for a preliminary injunction only, the defendants stipulated that Green Tree did not hold Eaton's mortgage note at the time of the foreclosure. After hearing, the Superior Court judge (motion judge) allowed the motion and preliminarily enjoined Fannie Mae from proceeding with Eaton's eviction.

## Discussion

As indicated, the motion judge determined that a foreclosure by sale requires the foreclosing mortgagee, at the time of the sale, to hold both the mortgage and the underlying mortgage note; and that if the mortgagee does not hold the note, the foreclosure sale is void. Based on this view, she concluded that because Green Tree, the assignee of the mortgage, had stipulated that it did not hold the mortgage note executed by Eaton when the sale took place, Eaton was likely to succeed in proving that the foreclosure sale was void and that the defendants had no authority to evict her and take possession of her home. See Bank of N.Y.

---

[8] The defendants state in their brief that after indorsement, the note was transferred to the Federal National Mortgage Association (Fannie Mae). However, there is no record evidence of a transfer of the note to Fannie Mae.

v. Bailey, 460 Mass. 327, 333, 951 N.E.2d 331 (2011) (challenging evicting party's entitlement to possession "has long been considered a valid defense to a summary process action for eviction where the property was purchased at a foreclosure sale"). The defendants argue that in reaching this conclusion, the judge misread the Massachusetts common law, and that, in any event, the statutory scheme applicable to exercise of a power of sale gave Green Tree absolute authority, as "mortgagee," to foreclose. They also claim that Green Tree, as the assignee, had a contractual right to foreclose pursuant to the express terms of the mortgage. We begin with a brief overview of the common law of mortgages and then address the statutes governing exercise of a power of sale in a mortgage. Finally, we review the preliminary injunction in light of the relevant principles discussed and the terms of Eaton's mortgage.

### a. Common Law

A real estate mortgage in Massachusetts has two distinct but related aspects: it is a transfer of legal title to the mortgage property, and it serves as security for an underlying note or other obligation—that is, the transfer of title is made in order to secure a debt, and the title itself is defeasible when the debt is paid. See U.S. Bank Nat'l Ass'n v. Ibanez, 458 Mass. 637, 649, 941 N.E.2d 40 (2011) (Ibanez) (Massachusetts is a "title theory" State in which "a mortgage is a transfer of legal title in a property to secure a debt") [and citing a series of Massachusetts cases from 1814 to 1990].

Following from these principles, a mortgage separated from the underlying debt that it is intended to secure is "a mere technical interest." Wolcott v. Winchester, 81 Mass. 461, 15 Gray 461, 465 (1860). See Morris v. Bacon, 123 Mass. 58, 59 (1877) ("That the debt is the principal and the mortgage an incident, is a rule too familiar to require citations in support of it"). However, in contrast to some jurisdictions, in Massachusetts the mere transfer of a mortgage note does not carry with it the mortgage. See Barnes v. Boardman, 149 Mass. 106, 114, 21 N.E. 308 (1889). See also 1 F. Hilliard, Mortgages 221 (2d ed. 1856) ("The prevailing doctrine upon this subject undoubtedly is, that an assignment of the debt carries the mortgage with it. This rule, however, is by no means universal, and is subject to various qualifications in the different States of the Union"). As a consequence, in Massachusetts a mortgage and the underlying note can be split. See Lamson & Co. v. Abrams, 305 Mass. 238, 245, 25 N.E.2d 374 (1940) ("The holder of the mortgage and the holder of the note may be different persons").

Under our common law, where a mortgage and note are separated, "the holder of the mortgage holds the mortgage in trust for the purchaser of the note, who has an equitable right to obtain an assignment of the mortgage, which may be accomplished by filing an action in court and obtaining an equitable order of assignment." Ibanez, 458 Mass. at 652, 941 N.E.2d 40, citing Barnes v. Boardman, 149 Mass. at 114, 21 N.E. 308.

Consistent with the principles just described—that is, the basic nature of a mortgage as security for an underlying mortgage note, and the role of a "bare" mortgagee as equitable trustee for the note holder—it appears that, at common law, a mortgagee possessing only the mortgage was without authority to foreclose on his own behalf the mortgagor's equity of redemption or otherwise disturb the possessory interest of the mortgagor. See Howe v. Wilder, 77 Mass. 267, 11 Gray 267, 269–270 (1858) (former assignee of mortgage note and mortgage who had retransferred note and canceled unrecorded mortgage assignment might still hold technical legal title to mortgage property as mortgagee but has no equitable right to disturb mortgagor's possessory interest and cannot bring action to foreclose mortgagor's equity of redemption because no money is due from mortgagor to him; only mortgagee with interest in underlying debt can so enforce mortgage). See also Wolcott v. Winchester, 81 Mass. 461, 15 Gray at 465 ("As a purchaser [of a mortgage without the underlying note], [defendant] must have known that the possession of the debt was essential to an effective mortgage, and that without it he could not maintain an action to foreclose the mortgage"). Cf. Weinberg v. Brother, 263 Mass. 61, 62, 160 N.E. 403 (1928).

### b. Statutory Provisions

The defendants take issue with the applicability of decisions such as Wolcott v. Winchester, 81 Mass. 461, 15 Gray at 465, Crowley v. Adams, 226 Mass. 582, 585, 116 N.E. 241 (1917), and Howe v. Wilder, 77 Mass. 267, 11 Gray at 269–270, to this case. They argue that in any event, G.L. c. 244, § 14, expressly authorized MERS (and its assignee) to foreclose because the mortgage in this case contained a power of sale. Accordingly, we turn to this statute, as well as related statutory provisions that together govern mortgage foreclosures under a power of sale.

It has long been recognized that statutes are a key source of authority generally governing mortgages. See Fay v. Cheney, 31 Mass. 399, 14 Pick. 399, 400–401 (1833) ("The law of mortgage in this [C]ommonwealth, is a mixed system, derived partly from the common law in regard to real property, partly from the rules and maxims of the English [C]ourts of [C]hancery, but principally from various statutes"). Statutes play an especially significant role in connection with mortgage foreclosures effected under a power of sale. See Ibanez, 458 Mass. at 646, 941 N.E.2d 40, quoting Moore v. Dick, 187 Mass. 207, 211, 72 N.E. 967 (1905) ("one who sells under a power [of sale] must follow strictly [statutory] terms").

The "statutory power of sale" is set out in G.L. c. 183, § 21.[13] Under this statute, if a mortgage provides for a power of sale, the mortgagee, in

---

[13] General Laws c. 183, § 21, provides:
"The following 'power' shall be known as the 'Statutory Power of Sale', and may be incorporated in any mortgage by reference:
"(POWER.)

exercising the power, may foreclose without obtaining prior judicial authorization "upon any default in the performance or observance" of the mortgage, id., including, of course, nonpayment of the underlying mortgage note.[15] Section 21 provides, however, that for a foreclosure sale pursuant to the power to be valid, the mortgagee must "first comply[ ] with the terms of the mortgage and with the statutes relating to the foreclosure of mortgages by the exercise of a power of sale." See Moore v. Dick, 187 Mass. 207, 211–213, 72 N.E. 967 (1905) (where notice of foreclosure sale was given in newspaper other than one named in mortgage agreement's power of sale, foreclosure was void, and plaintiffs were entitled to redeem mortgaged property approximately twenty years after sale; laches is no defense to void sale). See also Tamburello v. Monahan, 321 Mass. 445, 446–447, 73 N.E.2d 734 (1947) (where foreclosure sale conducted in bank office nine-tenths of one mile from mortgaged premises, sale was not "on or near the premises" as required by G.L. c. 183, § 21; sale held void).

In addition to G.L. c. 183, § 21, itself, the "statutes relating to the foreclosure of mortgages by the exercise of a power of sale," id., are set out in G.L. c. 244, §§ 11–17C. See Ibanez, 458 Mass. at 645–646, 941 N.E.2d 40. Principal among these is c. 244, § 14 (§ 14), which provides in relevant part:

> "The mortgagee or person having his estate in the land mortgaged, or a person authorized by the power of sale, . . . may, upon breach of condition and without action, do all the acts authorized or required by the power; but no sale under such power shall be effectual to foreclose a mortgage, unless, previous to such sale, [the notice provisions set forth in this section are followed]" (emphasis added).

The defendants argue that by its plain, unambiguous terms, this section authorized Green Tree, as the assignee of MERS, to foreclose because Eaton's mortgage identified MERS, its successors and assigns as

---

"But upon any default in the performance or observance of the foregoing or other condition, the mortgagee or his executors, administrators, successors or assigns may sell the mortgaged premises or such portion thereof as may remain subject to the mortgage in case of any partial release thereof, either as a whole or in parcels, together with all improvements that may be thereon, by public auction on or near the premises then subject to the mortgage, or, if more than one parcel is then subject thereto, on or near one of said parcels, or at such place as may be designated for that purpose in the mortgage, first complying with the terms of the mortgage and with the statutes relating to the foreclosure of mortgages by the exercise of a power of sale, and may convey the same by proper deed or deeds to the purchaser or purchasers absolutely and in fee simple; and such sale shall forever bar the mortgagor and all persons claiming under him from all right and interest in the mortgaged premises, whether at law or in equity."

[15] The power of sale "evolved in order to meet the increase of business transactions requiring loans and the desire to have a more speedy process of foreclosing than was furnished by suit or entry." A.L. Partridge, Deeds, Mortgages and Easements 201 (rev. ed.1932). See 1 F. Hilliard, Mortgages 119 (1856) ("In consequence of the delays incident to the usual equity of redemption, a power of sale has now become a very frequent provision in deeds of mortgage. . . . [However, the power] will be jealously watched, and declared void for the slightest unfairness or excess . . . ").

the "mortgagee" with the "power of sale." We disagree that § 14 is unambiguous. The section is one in a set of provisions governing mortgage foreclosures by sale, and that set in turn is one component of a chapter of the General Laws devoted generally to the topic of foreclosure and redemption of mortgages. The term "mortgagee" appears in several of these statutes, and its use reflects a legislative understanding or assumption that the "mortgagee" referred to also is the holder of the mortgage note. Thus, G.L. c. 244, § 17B, one of the foreclosure by sale sections closely related to § 14, deals with the notice required to be given as a condition to seeking a deficiency owed on a note after a foreclosure sale, and reads in part:

> "No action for a deficiency shall be brought . . . by the holder of a mortgage note or other obligation secured by mortgage of real estate after a foreclosure sale by him . . . unless a notice in writing of the mortgagee's intention to foreclose the mortgage has been mailed, postage prepaid, by registered mail with return receipt requested, to the defendant sought to be charged with the deficiency at his last address then known to the mortgagee, together with a warning of liability for the deficiency, in substantially the form [set out in this section] . . ." (emphasis added).

By its terms, § 17B assumes that the holder of the mortgage note and the holder of the mortgage are one and the same; the section's drafters appear to have used the terms "holder of a mortgage note" and "mortgagee" interchangeably.[18] Moreover, the statutory form of the notice required by § 17B bolsters our interpretation of § 17B; the statutory form language plainly envisions that the foreclosing mortgagee ("the mortgage held by me") and the note holder ("you may be liable to me in case of a deficiency") are one. And the same underlying assumption—that is, an identity between the mortgagee and the underlying note holder—also underlies several other sections in c. 244. See, e.g., G.L. c. 244, § 19 (providing that person entitled to redeem mortgage property "shall pay or tender to the mortgagee" amount due and payable "on the mortgage"); § 20 (requiring "mortgagee" who has been in possession of mortgage property to account for rents, profits, and expenses, and directing that any account balance be deducted from or added to amount "due on the mortgage"); § 23 (authorizing court to determine what amount not in dispute is "due on the mortgage," and to order it paid to "mortgagee").

---

[18] A contrary reading of G.L. c. 244, § 17B, would lead to the absurd result of requiring the deficiency action be brought by the "holder of the mortgage note," while obligating the "mortgagee" to provide notice of the action to the mortgagor, with the result that a mortgagee's noncompliance with the statute could impair the note holder's right to collect a deficiency. We will not follow this interpretive path. See Flemings v. Contributory Retirement Appeal Bd., 431 Mass. 374, 375–376, 727 N.E.2d 1147 (2000) (court seeks to arrive at "sensible construction" of statute, and "shall not construe a statute to make a nullity of pertinent provisions or to produce absurd results").

"Where the Legislature uses the same words in several sections which concern the same subject matter, the words 'must be presumed to have been used with the same meaning in each section.'" Commonwealth v. Wynton W., 459 Mass. 745, 747, 947 N.E.2d 561 (2011), quoting Insurance Rating Bd. v. Commissioner of Ins., 356 Mass. 184, 188–189, 248 N.E.2d 500 (1969). See Booma v. Bigelow-Sanford Carpet Co., 330 Mass. 79, 82, 111 N.E.2d 742 (1953) ("It is a familiar canon of construction, that when similar words are used in different parts of a statute, the meaning is presumed to be the same throughout"). Furthermore, we "construe statutes that relate to the same subject matter as a harmonious whole and avoid absurd results." Connors v. Annino, 460 Mass. 790, 796, 955 N.E.2d 905 (2011), quoting Canton v. Commissioner of the Mass. Highway Dep't, 455 Mass. 783, 791–792, 919 N.E.2d 1278 (2010).

In accordance with these principles, and against the background of the common law as we have described it in the preceding section, we construe the term "mortgagee" in G.L. c. 244, § 14, to mean a mortgagee who also holds the underlying mortgage note. The use of the word "mortgagee" in § 14 has some ambiguity, but the interpretation we adopt is the one most consistent with the way the term has been used in related statutory provisions and decisional law, and, more fundamentally, the one that best reflects the essential nature and purpose of a mortgage as security for a debt. See Negron v. Gordon, 373 Mass. at 204, 366 N.E.2d 241, and cases cited; Maglione v. BancBoston Mtge. Corp., 29 Mass.App.Ct. at 90, 557 N.E.2d 756, and cases cited. See generally Restatement (Third) of Property (Mortgages) § 1.1 comment. (1997) ("The function of a mortgage is to employ an interest in real estate as security for the performance of some obligation.... Unless it secures an obligation, a mortgage is a nullity").

Contrary to the conclusion of the motion judge, however, we do not conclude that a foreclosing mortgagee must have physical possession of the mortgage note in order to effect a valid foreclosure. There is no applicable statutory language suggesting that the Legislature intended to proscribe application of general agency principles in the context of mortgage foreclosure sales. Accordingly, we interpret G.L. c. 244, §§ 11–17C (and particularly § 14), and G.L. c. 183, § 21, to permit one who, although not the note holder himself, acts as the authorized agent of the note holder, to stand "in the shoes" of the "mortgagee" as the term is used in these provisions.[26]

---

[26] Eaton asserts also that the result we reach here is compelled by the Uniform Commercial Code (UCC), codified in Massachusetts at G.L. c. 106. She argues in substance that the note is a negotiable instrument, and that pursuant to art. 3 of the UCC, G.L. c. 106, §§ 3–301—3–312, only certain categories of persons are entitled to enforce negotiable instruments. Under her view, because Green Tree did not fall within any of the categories of persons entitled to enforce negotiable instruments, it was not entitled to enforce the note through foreclosure. We need not resolve Eaton's UCC argument. We perceive nothing in the UCC inconsistent with our view that in order to effect a valid foreclosure, a mortgagee must either hold the note or act on behalf of the note holder.

The defendants and several amici argue, to varying degrees, that an interpretation of "mortgagee" in the statutes governing mortgage foreclosures by sale that requires a mortgagee to hold the mortgage note will wreak havoc with the operation and integrity of the title recording and registration systems by calling into question the validity of any title that has a foreclosure sale in the title chain. This follows, they claim, because although a foreclosing mortgagee must record a foreclosure deed along with an affidavit evidencing compliance with G.L. c. 244, § 14, see G.L. c. 244, § 15; see also G.L. c. 183, § 4, there are no similar provisions for recording mortgage notes; and as a result, clear record title cannot be ascertained because the validity of any prior foreclosure sale is not ascertainable by examining documents of record. They argue that if this court requires a mortgagee to have a connection to the underlying debt in order to effect a valid foreclosure, such a requirement should be given prospective effect.

In general, when we construe a statute, we do not engage in an analysis whether that interpretation is given retroactive or prospective effect; the interpretation we give the statute usually reflects the court's view of its meaning since the statute's enactment. See McIntire, petitioner, 458 Mass. 257, 261, 936 N.E.2d 424 (2010), cert. denied, ___ U.S. ___, 131 S.Ct. 2909, 179 L.Ed.2d 1253 (2011). However, there are several considerations that compel us to give the interpretation of "mortgagee" we announce here only prospective effect. As the previous discussion reflects, the use of the term "mortgagee" in the statutory scheme governing mortgage foreclosures was not free of ambiguity, and while the decisions of this court in years and centuries past provide support for the general proposition that, under our common law, a mortgage ultimately depends on connection with the underlying debt for its enforceability, none of our cases has considered directly the question whether a mortgagee must also hold the note or act on behalf of the note holder in order to effect a valid foreclosure by sale. It has been represented to us by the defendants and several amici that lawyers and others who certify or render opinions concerning real property titles have followed in good faith a different interpretation of the relevant statutes, viz., one that requires the mortgagee to hold only the mortgage, and not the note, in order to effect a valid foreclosure by sale. We have no reason to reject this representation of prior practice, and in that context, we recognize there may be significant difficulties in ascertaining the validity of a particular title if the interpretation of "mortgagee" that we adopt here is not limited to prospective operation, because of the fact that our recording system has never required mortgage notes to be recorded.

This court traditionally has given prospective effect to its decisions in very limited circumstances, but those have included circumstances where the ruling announces a change that affects property law. See Papadopoulos v. Target Corp., 457 Mass. 368, 385, 930 N.E.2d 142 (2010); Payton v. Abbott Labs, 386 Mass. 540, 565, 437 N.E.2d 171 (1982). In the property law context, we generally apply our decisions prospectively out of "concern for litigants and others who have relied on existing precedents." Id. See Powers v. Wilkinson, 399 Mass. 650, 662, 506 N.E.2d 842 (1987). In addition, there may be particular reason to give a decision prospective effect where—as the argument is made here—"prior law is of questionable prognosticative value." Blood v. Edgar's, Inc., 36 Mass.App.Ct. 402, 407, 632 N.E.2d 419 (1994). Where a decision is not grounded in constitutional principles, but instead announces "a new common-law rule, a new interpretation of a State statute, or a new rule in the exercise of our superintendence power, there is no constitutional requirement that the new rule or new interpretation be applied retroactively, and we are therefore free to determine whether it should be applied only prospectively." Commonwealth v. Dagley, 442 Mass. 713, 721 n. 10, 816 N.E.2d 527 (2004), cert. denied, 544 U.S. 930, 125 S.Ct. 1668, 161 L.Ed.2d 494 (2005). In the exceptional circumstances presented here, and for the reasons that we have discussed, we exercise our discretion to hold that the interpretation of the term "mortgagee" in G.L. c. 244, § 14, and related statutory provisions that we adopt in this opinion is to apply only to mortgage foreclosure sales for which the mandatory notice of sale has been given after the date of this opinion.

### c. Preliminary Injunction

Although we apply the rule articulated in this case prospectively, we nonetheless apply it to Green Tree's appeal because it has been argued to this court by Eaton. The motion judge's decision on the preliminary injunction does not consider the question of Green Tree's (or MERS's) authority to act on behalf of BankUnited or an assignee of BankUnited in initiating foreclosure proceedings, and our examination of the Superior Court record suggests that this issue was not raised below. In the circumstances, we conclude that Eaton's allegation on information and belief that Green Tree was not authorized by the note holder to carry out the foreclosure sale did not offer an adequate factual basis to support the preliminary injunction that was issued. Consequently, the order granting the preliminary injunction must be vacated. On remand, Eaton may renew her request for a preliminary injunction, and in that context seek to show that she has a reasonable likelihood of establishing that, at the time of the foreclosure sale, Green Tree neither held the note nor acted on behalf of the note holder. We vacate the grant of the preliminary injunction, and remand the case to the Superior Court for further proceedings consistent with this opinion.

So ordered.

# Good v. Wells Fargo Bank, N.A.
Court of Appeals of Indiana, 2014.
18 N.E.3d 618.

■ BARNES, JUDGE.

## Case Summary

Bryan Good appeals the trial court's grant of partial summary judgment in favor of Wells Fargo Bank, N.A., ("Wells Fargo") and the subsequent judgment of foreclosure. We reverse and remand.

## Issue

We address whether the trial court properly granted partial summary judgment for Wells Fargo on the basis that Wells Fargo was entitled to enforce the promissory note executed by Good.

## Facts

On March 14, 2008, Good purchased real estate in Elkhart. Good executed an electronic promissory note ("the Note") in favor of Synergy Mortgage Group, Inc., ("Synergy"). The Note included the following term:

11. ISSUANCE OF TRANSFERABLE RECORD; IDENTIFICATION OF NOTE HOLDER; CONVERSION FROM ELECTRONIC NOTE TO PAPER-BASED NOTE[2]

(B) Except as indicated in Sections 11(D) and (E) below, the identity of the Note Holder and any person to whom this Electronic Note is later transferred will be recorded in a registry maintained by MERS CORP, Inc., a Delaware corporation or in another registry to which the records are later transferred (the "Note Holder Registry"). The authoritative copy of this Electronic Note will be the copy identified by the Note Holder after loan closing but prior to registration in the Note Holder Registry. If this Electronic Note has been registered in the Note Holder Registry, then the authoritative copy will be the copy identified by the Note Holder of record in the Note Holder Registry or the Loan Servicer (as defined in the Security Instrument) acting at the direction of the Note Holder, as the authoritative copy. The current identity of the Note Holder and the location of the authoritative copy, as reflected in the Note Holder Registry, will be available from the Note Holder or Loan Servicer, as applicable. The only copy of this Electric Note that is the authoritative copy is the copy that is within the control of the person identified as the Note Holder in the Note Holder Registry (or that person's designee). No other copy of this Electronic Note may be the authoritative copy. . . .

Appellee's App. p. 29.

---

[2] The Note's provisions for conversion from an electronic note to a paper-based note are not at issue here because Wells Fargo contends that it is entitled to enforce an electronic note.

The loan was secured by a mortgage. The mortgage identified Synergy as the lender and Mortgage Electronic Registration Systems, Inc., ("MERS") as a nominee for the lender. In 2011, Good stopped making payments on the loan. On November 9, 2011, MERS, as nominee for Synergy, assigned the mortgage to Wells Fargo. This assignment was recorded on November 14, 2011.

On November 7, 2012, Wells Fargo filed a complaint to foreclose the mortgage. Good, acting pro-se, filed an answer alleging that Wells Fargo was not a holder in due course of the Note and that it lacked standing.

On April 5, 2013, Wells Fargo moved for summary judgment. In support of its motion, Wells Fargo designated an Affidavit in Support of Judgment ("the Affidavit") in which Shemeka Moye, Wells Fargo's Vice President of Loan Documentation, stated Wells Fargo, "directly or through an agent, has possession of the Promissory Note at issue in the plaintiff's cause of action. Wells Fargo Bank, N.A., is either the original payee of the Promissory Note or the Promissory Note has been duly indorsed [sic]." Id. at 95. Good responded, arguing that Wells Fargo held only a photocopy of the Note without any endorsements and, without more, did not establish that it was entitled to enforce the Note.

Wells Fargo replied claiming Good failed to designate evidence that creates a genuine issue of material fact for trial. Wells Fargo also asserted that it controlled the electronic note and was entitled to enforce it as the holder pursuant to 15 U.S.C.A. § 7021(d). In support of this argument, Wells Fargo relied on a Certificate of Authentication ("the Certificate") in which Assistant Vice President of Wells Fargo, Thresa Russell, stated:

> 1. The Bank acts as a servicer for the Federal National Mortgage Association ("Fannie Mae") with respect to the residential mortgage loan executed on the [sic] 3/14/2008 by BRYAN GOOD, ("Borrowers").... The promissory note evidencing the Borrowers' obligation to repay the Loan is an electronic record, as authorized by the federal ESIGN Act, 15 USC § 7001 et seq., and in particular 15 USC § 7021.
>
> 2. As part of its function as servicer, the Bank maintains a copy of the Borrowers' electronic promissory note on behalf of Fannie Mae. I am responsibilities [sic] for overseeing the process by which the Bank maintains the electronic promissory notes evidencing residential mortgage loans. ("Electronic Records").
>
> 3. Each Electronic Record is received in accordance with established procedures and processes for reliable receipt, storage and management of Electronic Records (the "Electronic Record Procedures"). The Electronic Record Procedures provide controls to assure that each Electronic Record is accurately received as originally executed and transmitted, and indexed appropriately for later identification and retrieval. Each

> Electronic Record is protected against undetected alteration by industry-standard encryption techniques and system controls. The Electronic Record is an official record of the Bank and is readily accessible for later reference.
>
> 4. Each Electronic Record is maintained and stored by the Bank in the ordinary course of business. The Electronic Records are maintained and stored by the Bank continuously from the time of receipt.
>
> 5. The paper copy of the Electronic Record attached ... is a true and correct copy of the Borrowers' promissory note described above, as maintained and stored by the Bank in accordance with the procedures in Paragraphs 3 and 4 of this Certificate.

Id. at 130.

After a hearing, the trial court concluded that Wells Fargo had standing to enforce the Note and mortgage and partially granted Wells Fargo's motion for summary judgment as to that issue. The trial court also concluded that there were genuine issues of material fact regarding the validity of Good's electronic signature on the Note and the amount due and owing on the Note. Both parties filed motions to reconsider, which were discussed at the September 16, 2013 bench trial on the unresolved issues. After the trial, the trial court reaffirmed its initial ruling on the motion for summary judgment and concluded in part:

> 11. Plaintiff Wells Fargo Bank presented attached to the copy of the Promissory Note in its control a Certificate of Authentication which affirms that the Promissory Note was accurately received as it was originally executed and transmitted electronically. Plaintiff also affirmed that the record was protected against undetected alteration by industry standard encryption techniques and system controls. In this respect, the court concludes that Plaintiff maintained control of the subject Promissory Note which was originally signed by the Defendant, Bryan Good. Further endorsement of an electronic promissory note is not required and the promissory note is self-authenticating pursuant to Ind. Rule of Evidence 902. Accordingly, Defendant is liable on the Promissory Note and related Mortgage.

Appellant's App. p. 134. The trial court determined the payoff amount and entered judgment for Wells Fargo in that amount. The trial court then issued a judgment of foreclosure. Good now appeals.

## Analysis

Among other things, Good appeals the trial court's entry of partial summary judgment on the issue of whether Wells Fargo was entitled to enforce the Note. "We review an appeal of a trial court's ruling on a motion for summary judgment using the same standard applicable to the trial court." Perdue v. Gargano, 964 N.E.2d 825, 831 (Ind.2012). "Therefore, summary judgment is appropriate only if the designated evidence reveals 'no genuine issue as to any material fact and that the moving party is entitled to a judgment as a matter of law.'" Id. (quoting Ind. Trial Rule 56(C)). Our review of summary judgment is limited to evidence designated to the trial court. Id. (citing T.R. 56(H)). All facts and reasonable inferences drawn from the evidence designated by the parties is construed in a light most favorable to the non-moving party, and we do not defer to the trial court's legal determinations. Id.

There is no dispute that the mortgage was assigned from Synergy to Wells Fargo in 2011. The issue is whether Wells Fargo was entitled to enforce the Note. Regarding traditional paper notes, "Indiana has adopted Article 3 of the Uniform Commercial Code (UCC), which governs negotiable instruments, and it is well-established that a promissory note secured by a mortgage is a negotiable instrument." Lunsford v. Deutsche Bank Trust Co. Americas as Tr., 996 N.E.2d 815, 821 (Ind.Ct.App.2013). According to the UCC, a negotiable instrument may be enforced by "the holder of the instrument." Ind.Code § 26–1–3.1–301(1). The term "holder" means "the person in possession of a negotiable instrument that is payable either to bearer or to an identified person if the identified person is in possession of the instrument[.]" I.C. § 26–1–1–201(20). In this context, "bearer" means the person in possession of a negotiable instrument "payable to bearer or endorsed in blank." I.C. § 26–1–1–201(5).

Wells Fargo initially asserted that it had possession of the Note and was either the original payee or the Note had been duly endorsed. Good responded, challenging Wells Fargo's status as holder because the Note designated by Wells Fargo was not endorsed. In its reply, Wells Fargo asserted that, because the Note was an electronic note, "delivery, possession, and endorsement of an electronic promissory note are not required pursuant to federal statute." Appellee's App. p. 91. Wells Fargo claimed it controlled the Note and was entitled to enforce it pursuant to 15 U.S.C. § 7021, which provides:

(a) Definitions

For purposes of this section:

(1) Transferable record

The term "transferable record" means an electronic record that—

(A) would be a note under Article 3 of the Uniform Commercial Code if the electronic record were in writing;

(B) the issuer of the electronic record expressly has agreed is a transferable record; and

(C) relates to a loan secured by real property.

A transferable record may be executed using an electronic signature.

(2) Other definitions

The terms "electronic record", "electronic signature", and "person" have the same meanings provided in section 7006 of this title.

(b) Control

A person has control of a transferable record if a system employed for evidencing the transfer of interests in the transferable record reliably establishes that person as the person to which the transferable record was issued or transferred.

(c) Conditions

A system satisfies subsection (b) of this section, and a person is deemed to have control of a transferable record, if the transferable record is created, stored, and assigned in such a manner that—

(1) a single authoritative copy of the transferable record exists which is unique, identifiable, and, except as otherwise provided in paragraphs (4), (5), and (6), unalterable;

(2) the authoritative copy identifies the person asserting control as—

(A) the person to which the transferable record was issued; or

(B) if the authoritative copy indicates that the transferable record has been transferred, the person to which the transferable record was most recently transferred;

(3) the authoritative copy is communicated to and maintained by the person asserting control or its designated custodian;

(4) copies or revisions that add or change an identified assignee of the authoritative copy can be made only with the consent of the person asserting control;

(5) each copy of the authoritative copy and any copy of a copy is readily identifiable as a copy that is not the authoritative copy; and

(6) any revision of the authoritative copy is readily identifiable as authorized or unauthorized.

(d) Status as holder

Except as otherwise agreed, a person having control of a transferable record is the holder, as defined in section 1–201(20) of the Uniform Commercial Code, of the transferable record and has the same rights and defenses as a holder of an equivalent record or writing under the Uniform Commercial Code, including, if the applicable statutory requirements under section 3–302(a), 9–308, or revised section 9–

330 of the Uniform Commercial Code are satisfied, the rights and defenses of a holder in due course or a purchaser, respectively. Delivery, possession, and endorsement are not required to obtain or exercise any of the rights under this subsection.

(e) Obligor rights

Except as otherwise agreed, an obligor under a transferable record has the same rights and defenses as an equivalent obligor under equivalent records or writings under the Uniform Commercial Code.

(f) Proof of control

If requested by a person against which enforcement is sought, the person seeking to enforce the transferable record shall provide reasonable proof that the person is in control of the transferable record. Proof may include access to the authoritative copy of the transferable record and related business records sufficient to review the terms of the transferable record and to establish the identity of the person having control of the transferable record.

(g) UCC references

For purposes of this subsection, all references to the Uniform Commercial Code are to the Uniform Commercial Code as in effect in the jurisdiction the law of which governs the transferable record.

15 U.S.C. § 7021.

Wells Fargo is correct that, pursuant to § 7021(d), a person having control of a transferable record, which includes the Note, is the holder for purposes of the UCC and that delivery, possession, and endorsement are not required. According to § 7021(b), to show it controlled the note, Wells Fargo was required to designate evidence that a system employed for evidencing the transfer of interests in the Note reliably established Wells Fargo as the person to whom the Note was transferred. A system that satisfies the control requirement is described in § 7021(c). Wells Fargo contends that its "possession of the Note and the recitation of its electronic record keeping procedures in the Certificate evidences Well Fargo's control of the Note. . . ." Appellee's Br. p. 15. We disagree.

Regarding possession, the Affidavit, which does not mention an electronic note, provides only that that Wells Fargo, directly or through an agent, "has possession of the Promissory Note at issue in the plaintiff's cause of action." Appellee's App. p. 95. When considering Wells Fargo's assertion that the note in its possession was endorsed and its argument that the endorsement of an electronic note is not required pursuant to § 7021(d), it is not clear from the Affidavit whether Wells Fargo was claiming to have possession of an endorsed paper copy or the electronic note.

Even if the Affidavit established that Wells Fargo possessed the electronic note, control, not possession, is the relevant consideration under § 7021, and the Certificate does not establish that Wells Fargo controlled the Note. The Certificate does establish that Wells Fargo, as servicer of Good's mortgage loan for Fannie Mae, "maintains a copy of [Good's] promissory note on behalf of Fannie Mae." Id. at 26. The Certificate also establishes that Wells Fargo's electronic records are received, stored, and managed in a secure manner with controls to assure they are accurately received as originally executed and protected against alteration. However, the Certificate does not suggest that Wells Fargo maintains the single authoritative copy of the Note as described in § 7021(c)(1). Even if we were to assume that the copy of the Note maintained by Wells Fargo is the authoritative copy, it does not indicate that the Note has been transferred or identify either Wells Fargo or Fannie Mae as the person to whom the Note was most recently transferred. See 15 U.S.C. § 7021(c)(2)(B).

Such a record of transfer is described in the Note, which calls for the recording of any transfer of the Note in a note holder registry. The Note also specifies, "The only copy of this Electric Note that is the authoritative copy is the copy that is within the control of the person identified as the Note Holder in the Note Holder Registry (or that person's designee). No other copy of this Electronic Note may be the authoritative copy." Id. at 29. Wells Fargo has not designated any evidence of a note holder registry, let alone evidence showing that Wells Fargo, or even Fannie Mae, is identified as the note holder in the note holder registry.

Pursuant to statute, upon Good's request, Wells Fargo was required to provide "reasonable proof" that it was in control of the Note. 15 U.S.C. § 7021(f). "Proof may include access to the authoritative copy of the transferable record and related business records sufficient to review the terms of the transferable record and to establish the identity of the person having control of the transferable record." Id. Although Good repeatedly requested such proof, Wells Fargo did not provide any evidence documenting the transfer or assignment of the Note from Synergy to either Wells Fargo or Fannie Mae. Thus, Wells Fargo did not demonstrate it controlled the Note by showing that a system employed for evidencing the transfer of interests in the Note reliably established that the Note had been transferred to Wells Fargo. See 15 U.S.C. § 7021(b).

Because Wells Fargo did not establish that it controlled the Note as described in § 7021, it did not establish that it was the person entitled to enforce the Note as the holder for purposes of the UCC. See 15 U.S.C. § 7021(d); I.C. § 26–1–3.1–301(1). Thus, partial summary judgment for Wells Fargo on this issue was improper.

Wells Fargo goes on to argue that, irrespective of the trial court's summary judgment ruling, it presented uncontroverted evidence at the bench trial that it controlled the Note. Procedurally, however, the issue of Wells Fargo's right to enforce the Note was not before the trial court during the bench trial because it had been resolved, albeit improperly, in the summary judgment proceedings. It would be inappropriate for us to use evidence from the subsequent trial to justify the judgment when Good did not have notice that this issue would be relitigated. Regardless, we are not convinced that the trial testimony establishes that Wells Fargo controlled the Note for purposes of § 7021.

Wells Fargo relies on the testimony of Donna Mouzon, a loan verification analyst for Wells Fargo, who testified at trial that Wells Fargo "acquired" the loan on August 1, 2008. Tr. pp. 17–18. Mouzon was also questioned as follows:

Q. Thank you. Is [Wells Fargo] presently in control of the electronic note?

A. Yes.

Q. Does [Wells Fargo] currently maintain the electronic note?

A. Yes.

Q. Does [Wells Fargo] also service the loan?

A. Yes.

. . .

Q. Who's the owner of the note?

A. Fanny Mae.

Q. Who's the holder of the note?

A. Wells Fargo.

Id. at 18.

Given the lack of evidence regarding a transfer or assignment from Synergy to Wells Fargo or Fannie Mae, Mouzon's conclusory testimony was not sufficient to establish that it controlled the Note as defined in § 7021. Thus, Mouzon's trial testimony did not establish that Wells Fargo is entitled to enforce the note as the holder, and is not a basis for affirming the judgment of foreclosure.

## Conclusion

Wells Fargo has not shown that it controls the Note for purposes of § 7021(b) and, accordingly, has not established its status as holder for purposes of the UCC. Because Wells Fargo has not established that it was entitled to enforce the Note as its holder, the trial court's grant of summary judgment was improper and the resulting judgment must be set aside. We reverse and remand.

### NOTES

1. *Statutes?* All of the cases rely extensively on analyses of statutory provisions governing foreclosures and the roles of notes and mortgages. What does this mean for your analysis of the Principal Problem?

2. *Reasoning.* Despite the robust treatment of foreclosure statutes in the four opinions, the cases vary considerably in the types of reasoning they

use, ranging from public policy considerations to discussions of the common law to statutory interpretations. Which reasoning did you find most compelling and how can it help you to solve the Principal Problem?

3. *Judicial vs. nonjudicial foreclosure.* Erlandson and Good are judicial foreclosure cases, whereas Debrunner and Eaton are nonjudicial foreclosure cases. Does the type of foreclosure make any difference to the legal analysis of whether Trail & Saddle Bank has to produce the note that Bush signed? Should it?

4. *Judicial skepticism of mortgagee assertions.* Good is a classic case of the court expressing skepticism of conclusory assertions by the mortgagee that it is entitled to foreclose. In a bankruptcy case from New York, a federal bankruptcy court took Wells Fargo Bank to task for discrepancies in the existence of a blank endorsement on two different copies of the same note, which the debtor attributed to bank employees' forgery of the assignment. In re Carrsow-Franklin, 524 B.R. 33 (Bankr. S.D.N.Y. 2015). The court held that the bank failed to satisfy its burden of demonstrating that it had standing to enforce the note.

5. *The cost of mortgagor protections.* Statutes and rules aimed at protecting mortgagors in entering into mortgages and in the foreclosure processes reflect the relative disparities in power, resources, and knowledge between lenders and borrowers. However, critics of these protections contend that they make loans more costly to borrowers and drive down the number and amounts of bids in foreclosure sales (whether judicial or nonjudicial).[7] Are the protections worth these costs? Are there ways to moderate these adverse effects?

---

[7] See Sprankling, Understanding Property Law 3rd Ed., at 367–369 (2012).

# ASSIGNMENT 47

# COVENANTS OF TITLE

1. INTRODUCTION

| Full Warranty Deed | Special Warranty Deed | Quit-Claim Deed |
|---|---|---|
| 1. Includes:<br>a) Covenant of Seisin<br>   Present: *Majority Rule*: Does not run<br>b) Covenant of right to convey<br>   Present: *Majority Rule*: Does not run<br>c) Covenant against encumbrances<br>   Present: *Majority Rule*: Does not run<br>d) Covenant of quiet enjoyment<br>   Future: Runs<br>e) Covenant of warranty<br>   Future: Runs<br>f) Covenant for further assurances<br>   Future: Runs<br>2. Grantor covenants against all title defects except those specifically excepted<br>3. Grantor liable to remote grantee for breach of future covenants | 1. Includes some of six covenants<br>2. Usually statutory<br>3. Grantor usually covenants only concerning interests created by grantor<br>4. Grantor's liability to remote grantees depends on the statute | 1. No covenants<br>2. Grantor promises nothing<br>3. Grantor conveys everything it has, which may be either more or less than what the parties assume the grantor has |

A promise to convey Blackacre in a *contract* for the sale of real estate carries with it an implied promise to deliver marketable title to Blackacre. However, no promises concerning title are implied in a *deed*

1169

to Blackacre; all of the promises or covenants must be expressed in writing. Furthermore, under the doctrine of merger, the implied promise in the contract concerning title does not survive delivery of the deed. Therefore, a purchaser needs a reliable way to assure the continuance of title security after the deed is delivered. However, if clear evidence exists that the parties intended an express covenant in the contract to "survive" (i.e., continue in effect) after delivery of the deed, their intent will control.

Before title insurance became customary, buyers relied on several methods of protection to assure themselves that they would receive good title:

1. title search in the recording office of the county where the property is located,
2. covenants of title as set forth in the deed,
3. visual inspection of the real property,
4. title search by a professional title abstractor often using a private database and title records, a "title plant."

Covenants of title are the seller's express promises in the deed concerning the title he is conveying to the purchaser. When this area of law first developed, public title records did not exist and it was difficult, if not impossible, to perform a title search. Thus, the purchaser had to rely on the guarantees of the seller. Today, such assurances in the deed are not as important because title searches typically are performed by independent title insurance companies. Thus, the purchaser can obtain the guarantee of professionals rather than simply rely on the word of the seller. Nonetheless, covenants of title are still important because they afford purchasers a potential source of recovery in the event of loss.

This method of assurance is more important today in residential and rural sales than in commercial ones.[1]

Over time, the seller's promises have become standardized into six covenants:

1. *Covenant of seisin*—a covenant that the grantor is peaceably in possession under a freehold title.

EXAMPLE 1: A conveys Blackacre to B who takes possession, and then A purports to convey Blackacre to C. If A's deed to C contains a covenant of seisin, A is liable for breach of this covenant. *It does not matter whether C had notice of B's interest in Blackacre by means of the recording system or otherwise.* Covenants of title in a deed are an alternative and additional method of title protection (in addition to a record search) available to a purchaser. However, if C had knowledge (as opposed to mere notice) of B's interest in Blackacre, C would

---

[1] See generally 14 Powell and Rohan, Powell on Real Property § 81A.06[1].

have no rights against A, unless C reasonably believed that A would eliminate B's rights before the closing.

2. *Covenant of right to convey*—a covenant that the grantor has the power and authority to make the conveyance. This covenant is similar to the covenant of seisin, but it provides that the grantor has the right to convey in addition to title and the right of possession.

3. *Covenant against encumbrances*—a covenant that no other right or interest in the property conveyed, which decreases the value of the property but is consistent with the passing of a fee, is held by any third party.

> EXAMPLE 2: A conveys Blackacre to B by deed containing a covenant against encumbrances. When B had inspected the premises, he had noticed a path across the land, but thought nothing of it. After taking possession, B discovered that E, an adjoining landowner, has an easement of ingress and egress across Blackacre. B also learns that F has a valid and recorded mortgage on Blackacre. What remedies are available to B? B can recover from A for breach of the covenant against encumbrances. The fact that B had notice of both the physical and the monetary encumbrances does not preclude his recovery. In fact, such notice is often essential for the encumbrances to be valid; and only if they are valid has A breached his covenant against encumbrances. However, if B had knowledge (in contrast to mere notice) of an encumbrance, he may be estopped from objecting to it.

4. *Covenant of quiet enjoyment*—a covenant that the grantee will not be evicted (either actually or constructively) by someone with paramount title.

5. *Covenant of warranty*—this covenant is closely related to the covenant of quiet enjoyment, and many courts treat them as identical. Technically, however, by this covenant the grantor promises to compensate the grantee in the event he is evicted (actually or constructively) by someone with paramount title. Note, however, the same result implicitly follows from a breach of the covenant of quiet enjoyment.

> EXAMPLE 3: A conveys Blackacre to B. A then purports to convey Blackacre to C by a deed containing a covenant of quiet enjoyment and a covenant of warranty. B's deed was recorded; but C, negligent in not having searched the records, did not discover it. B legally ousts C. A is liable to C in damages for breach of his covenants of quiet enjoyment and warranty.

6. *Covenant for further assurance*—a covenant that the grantor will supply further assurances in the form of papers and documents that the grantee may need in the future to prove her title. This covenant can

be specifically enforced, whereas the other covenants are enforced only by an award of damages.

The foregoing six types of covenants are divided into two categories:

*Present covenants*—the covenants of seisin, right to convey, and against encumbrances, and

*Future covenants*—the covenants of quiet enjoyment, warranty, and further assurances.

The classification of a covenant as present or future determines whether it will run with the land and thus be enforceable against the original covenantor by a "remote" grantee, i.e., a grantee from the original grantee. By the majority rule, the benefit of present covenants do not run with the land and thus are enforceable only by the immediate grantee. The original rationale was that if a present covenant is breached, the breach takes place when the covenant is made, at which point it becomes a cause of action, which was not assignable under the common law. Although a cause of action may now be assigned, a present covenant still does not run with the land in most states.

EXAMPLE 4: A conveys Blackacre to X, who records the deed. A then conveys Blackacre to B by a deed containing covenants of seisin and right to convey. B subsequently conveys Blackacre to C by a deed containing no covenants. What are C's rights against A and B?

C has no rights against A based on A's covenants. Although A breached her covenants of seisin and right to convey when she conveyed Blackacre to B after having previously conveyed it to X, these covenants are present covenants and by the majority rule, do not run with subsequent conveyances of the land. Thus C, a remote grantee, can maintain no action against A for breach of these covenants. C has no rights against B based on covenants, since B's deed contains no covenants and none are implied.

EXAMPLE 5: A grants an easement of ingress and egress over Blackacre to X. X records his interest. A then conveys Blackacre to B by a deed containing a covenant against encumbrances, and does not except the easement. B conveys Blackacre to C by a deed containing a covenant against encumbrances. C takes possession of Blackacre and finds X walking across his land. Upon inquiry, C discovers the existence of the easement. What, if any, are C's rights against A and B?

By the majority rule, C has no rights against A for breach of his covenant against encumbrances because the covenant is a present covenant that does not run with the land. C can, however, recover from B for breach of his covenant against encumbrances. If B's covenant was not limited to defects that B himself created, B is responsible for encumbrances attributable to his predecessors in interest.

In contrast to present covenants, future covenants run with the land on the theory that they are not violated until an act or event occurs that constitutes a breach. This act or event is generally an interference with the grantee's possession or enjoyment of the property by someone with paramount title. By this reasoning, all successors of the immediate grantee can sue a grantor for breach of a future covenant.

EXAMPLE 6: A conveys Blackacre to X. X records the deed. A then purports to convey Blackacre to B by a deed containing covenants of seisin, right to convey, quiet enjoyment and warranty. B conveys Blackacre to C who thereafter is properly evicted by X. C sues A. What result? A is liable for breach of her covenants of quiet enjoyment and warranty. These are future covenants that run with the land. They were not broken until C was evicted by X. By the majority rule, A is not liable to C for breach of her covenants of seisin and right to convey because these are present covenants that do not run with the land.

A grantor may include all, some, or none of the above covenants in her deed by the use of certain key words.

1. If the grantor conveys with "full," "general," or "usual" covenants, this implies all six covenants. The deed is a full, general, or usual warranty deed.

2. If the grantor conveys with "limited" or "special" covenants, this implies that the covenants will be applicable only under special or limited circumstances. The deed is a limited or special warranty deed.

3. If the grantor "quitclaims" the property, no covenants are implied. The grantor conveys whatever interest she has, but does not promise that she has anything. The deed is a quitclaim deed.

Thus, it is essential to select language carefully when drafting a deed. Seemingly minor differences in language can lead to very different outcomes.

EXAMPLE 7: A conveys Blackacre to X with full covenants. X conveys to Y by quitclaim deed. Y conveys to Z by quitclaim deed. If Z is ousted by someone with paramount title as the result of a defect attributable to A or his predecessors in interest, whom should Z sue?

Z should sue A for breach of his covenants of quiet enjoyment and warranty. Z cannot sue X or Y because they quitclaimed the property and thus made no promises. A quitclaim deed is written on the assumption that the grantor may not have title, or that the title is subject to encumbrances.

EXAMPLE 8: O gives a mortgage in Blackacre. Thereafter, by deed, he conveys "all my interest in Blackacre to A." At the time of conveyance, A has no knowledge of the mortgage. The mortgage is foreclosed. What are A's rights against O?

A has no rights against O based on a covenant of title. The conveyance was by quitclaim deed and thus no covenants are implied. Depending on the facts, however, an action for fraud or unjust enrichment might succeed.

A quitclaim deed is ordinarily used to protect the grantor when the grantor is afraid she may have no title or defective title. It may, however, have the unintended effect of granting more than the grantor intended.

EXAMPLE 9: Norma believes that she owns a 25% interest in Blackacre, but she is unwilling to warrant her ownership because its validity is unclear. Consequently, she gives only a quitclaim deed to Bob, who purchases her interest. In fact, as it later turns out, Norma owned 75% of Blackacre when she delivered her quitclaim deed to Bob. Bob now owns 75% of Blackacre because a quitclaim deed grants all of the grantor's interest, whatever that may be. Norma might have the right to rescind the transaction on the grounds of mutual mistake. This is unlikely, however, particularly if rescission would unfairly prejudice the rights of third parties.

Partly because of the extensive use of title insurance, most conveyances today are limited or special warranty deeds. Such a deed is essentially a compromise between a full warranty deed and a quitclaim deed. The covenants implied in a conveyance by a limited warranty deed generally depend upon the customs of the jurisdiction involved and are often determined by statute. For example, both California and New Jersey have statutory special warranty deeds. That is, by the use of certain words, the grantor is assumed to give the warranties enumerated in the statute.

## CALIFORNIA CIVIL CODE

### § 1113. Grant; Implied Covenants

*Implied covenants.* From the use of the word "grant" in any conveyance by which an estate of inheritance or fee simple is to be passed, the following covenants, and none other, on the part of the grantor for himself and his heirs to the grantee, his heirs, and assigns, are implied, unless restrained by express terms contained in such conveyance:

1. That previous to the time of the execution of such conveyance, the grantor has not conveyed the same estate, or any right, title, or interest therein, to any person other than the grantee;

2. That such estate is at the time of the execution of such conveyance free from encumbrances done, made, or suffered by the grantor, or any person claiming under him.

Such covenants may be sued upon in the same manner as if they had been expressly inserted in the conveyance.

## NEW JERSEY STATUTES ANNOTATED

### 46:4–8. Covenant of special warranty

A covenant by the grantor in a deed "that he will warrant specially the property hereby conveyed," shall have the same effect as if the grantor had covenanted that he, his heirs and personal representatives, will forever warrant and defend the said property unto the grantee, his heirs, personal representatives and assigns, against the claims and demands of the grantor and all persons claiming or to claim by, through, or under him.

---

Under both of the foregoing statutes, the grantor is warranting his own actions with respect to the property, but is making no promises for anything that happened before he acquired title. Every grantor certainly knows what he himself has done. At the very least, the grantee wants the grantor to warrant his own actions. The statutes embody this idea.[2]

## QUESTIONS

1. How would you label the covenants implied in California's "grant deed" and in New Jersey's "special warranty deed"?

2. Traditionally, which of these covenants would run with the land?

3. Does the statutory language indicate that a subsequent grantee is protected by the enumerated covenants?

## 2. PRINCIPAL PROBLEM

One issue involving covenants of title is whether a grantor's covenant in a deed runs with the land so that a remote grantee can sue the original grantor/covenantor for damages suffered as the result of a breach.

Suppose that X, the owner of Blackacre, a California parcel, borrows $100,000 securing the loan with a duly recorded mortgage against Blackacre. X, a sneaky fellow, then sells the property to Y for $100,000, conveying title by a California grant deed that is silent as to the existence of the mortgage. Y, inexperienced in real estate transactions, fails to conduct a title search and has no knowledge of the mortgage. Y later sells

---

[2] Other states have similar statutory provisions involving special warranty deeds. See, e.g., Ariz.Rev.Stat.Ann. § 33–435 (West 2009); Ky.Rev.Stat.Ann. § 382.030 (Michie/2009); Md. Real Prop.Code § 2–106 (2009); Mass.Gen.Laws Ann. ch. 183, § 16 (West 2009); Mo.Ann.Stat. § 442.420 (West 2009); Okla.Stat.Ann. tit. 16, § 19 (West 2009); Pa.Stat.Ann. tit. 21, § 6 (West 2009); S.D. Codified Laws Ann. §§ 43–25–6, 43–25–10 (Michie 2009); Tenn.Code Ann. § 16–1–110 (2009); Tex.Prop.Code Ann. § 5.023 (Vernon 2009); Va.Code Ann. § 55–69 (Michie 2009); W.Va.Code § 36–4–3 (2009). In some states, however, statutes exist providing that no covenants are to be implied in any conveyance of real estate. See, e.g., Mich.Comp.Laws Ann. § 565.5 (West 2009); N.Y. Real Prop. § 251 (McKinney 2009).

the property to Z for $90,000, using a California grant deed to convey title. Z also fails to conduct a title search and has no knowledge of the mortgage.

After a few months, Z discovers the existence of the mortgage when he is forced to pay $100,000 to prevent foreclosure.

Does Z have a good chance of recovering damages from either X or Y? If so, how much will he recover from each defendant? Before answering this question, reread California Civil Code section 1113 and consider the following materials. Would your answer be different if the land were located in New Jersey and a New Jersey special warranty deed were used. See the New Jersey statute reprinted above.

### 3. Materials for Solution of Principal Problem

#### Holmes Development, LLC v. Cook
Supreme Court of Utah, 2002.
48 P.3d 895.

■ Russon, Justice.

The parties to this appeal do not dispute the material facts. In 1993, Cook purchased two parcels of land in Heber City, Utah. One parcel was approximately 323 acres, and the other parcel was approximately 73 acres. Cook began subdividing and developing the larger parcel. Eventually, Cook conveyed the two parcels to Cook Development, a Utah limited liability company. Cook is, and has been at all relevant times, the principal member, the manager, and the registered agent of Cook Development.

To further the development of the property, Cook Development associated with Premier Homes ("Premier") to infuse cash into the project. In October 1997, Cook Development and Premier formed two limited liability companies known as Lake Creek Farms, LC ("LC Farms"), and Lake Creek Associates, LC ("LC Associates"). Cook Development conveyed the 323-acre parcel to LC Farms and the 73-acre parcel to LC Associates.

Eventually, Premier and Cook Development decided to part ways and agreed that deeds would be executed on behalf of LC Farms and LC Associates to reconvey the 323- and 73-acre parcels, respectively, to Cook Development. To effectuate the parties' agreement, First American prepared two quitclaim deeds, which were signed by Cook on behalf of Cook Development and by an agent of Premier. The quitclaim deed conveying the 323-acre parcel erroneously identified LC Associates, rather than LC Farms, as the grantor.

Immediately thereafter, Cook Development obtained financing from Clark Real Estate and used both parcels as collateral. Neither Cook, Cook

Development, nor First American discovered the error in the quitclaim deed at that time.

Then, in April 1998, Holmes and Cook Development agreed that Holmes would purchase both parcels from Cook Development. First American was again retained to prepare a title insurance commitment report and to issue a title insurance policy to Holmes. On or about May 20, 1998, Cook Development closed the property sale, conveying both parcels to Holmes by way of warranty deed.

In connection with this closing, First American acted as the escrow agent for the transaction and prepared all the closing documents, deeds, and settlement statements. At closing, First American provided Holmes a title insurance policy that insured both parcels. According to subsection 4(b) of the policy, in the event of a title defect, the policy allowed First American

> to institute and prosecute any action or proceeding or to do any other act which in its opinion may be necessary or desirable to establish the title to the estate or interest, as insured, or to prevent or reduce loss or damage to the insured. [First American] may take any appropriate action under the terms of this policy, whether or not it shall be liable hereunder, and shall not thereby concede liability or waive any provision of this policy.

In addition, in connection with the transaction, Cook and Cook Development signed an indemnity agreement and a modification and extension agreement on May 19, 1998. Holmes was the other party to these agreements.

After the transaction was consummated, Holmes sought additional financing from Bank One of Utah ("Bank One"). Bank One retained First American to prepare the trust deed and title insurance documents associated with the financing. In July 1998, while examining the title for the Bank One loan, First American discovered that Cook Development did not validly convey the 323-acre parcel to Holmes because Cook Development never held title to the parcel as a result of the erroneous quitclaim deed that was intended to convey the parcel from LC Farms to Cook Development.

Upon making this discovery, First American immediately attempted to rectify the error, as it was obligated to do under the title insurance policy. Initially, First American contacted Premier and Cook Development, the members of LC Farms, and requested that they execute a corrected quitclaim deed to convey the 323-acre parcel from LC Farms to Cook Development. When Premier refused to sign the deed, First American prepared a special warranty deed whereby LC Farms deeded the 323-acre parcel directly to Holmes. First American prepared the corrective special warranty deed from LC Farms for Cook's signature, and Cook signed the deed.[3]

Then, in November 1998, Premier sold the 323-acre parcel, as a member of and on behalf of LC Farms, to Keystone Development, LC ("Keystone"). Realizing that there were various competing claims as to the ownership of the 323-acre parcel, Keystone commenced a quiet title action ("Keystone litigation") and promptly recorded a lis pendens to give notice of the action. . . .

In the suit, Keystone contended that LC Farms did not validly convey the 323-acre parcel to Holmes because Cook and Cook Development lacked the authority to convey the property. In addition, Keystone argued that Premier, instead of Cook Development, was the manager of LC Farms and thus able to convey the parcel on behalf of LC Farms, vesting paramount title to the 323-acre parcel in Keystone.

Defending against Keystone's claims, Cook and Cook Development realized that the special warranty deed did not specify that Cook signed the deed in his representative capacity of Cook Development. In an effort to correct the signature on the special warranty deed, defense counsel prepared an affidavit in which Cook maintained that he intended to sign the special warranty deed in his capacity as the manager of Cook Development, which was a managing member of LC Farms. After eight months of litigation, on June 29, 1999, the trial court granted summary judgment in favor of all defendants and against Keystone. In particular, the court determined that the special warranty deed was a valid instrument of conveyance and that title vested in Holmes.

During the pendency of the Keystone litigation, the lis pendens precluded Holmes from selling a single lot in the 323-acre parcel. In particular, Holmes was unable to avail himself of the prime spring selling season. Additionally, Holmes continued to make interest payments to Bank One in connection with the loan Holmes procured.

As a result, in October 1999, Holmes brought suit against Cook [and] Cook Development. . . .

On August 2, 2000, the trial court entered summary judgment in favor of Cook and Cook Development. . . .

[H]olmes appeals the summary judgment order in favor of Cook and Cook Development, arguing that these defendants breached the covenants of title in the warranty deed. . . . In response, Cook and Cook Development contend that any alleged breach of the covenants of title was cured before Keystone initiated its quiet title suit and the actions of Cook and Cook Development therefore were not the cause of Holmes's damages. . . .

---

[3] It is undisputed by the parties that Cook Development had the authority to convey the 323-acre parcel on behalf of LC Farms to Holmes and that Cook, as the manager of Cook Development, was authorized to sign for Cook Development.

[T]he trial court granted summary judgment [to Cook and Cook Development] on Holmes's breach of covenants of title claim because any breach was cured before Keystone filed its quiet title action against Holmes.

Even if covenants of title are not expressly set forth in a deed conveying real property, the covenants of title still inhere in a warranty deed as long as the deed is properly executed. The Utah Code provides in pertinent part:

> A warranty deed when executed as required by law shall have the effect of a conveyance in fee simple to the grantee, his heirs and assigns, of the premises therein named, together with all the appurtenances, rights, and privileges thereunto belonging, *with covenants from the grantor,* his heirs, and personal representatives, that he is *lawfully seised of the premises;* that *he has good right to convey the same;* that *he guarantees the grantee, his heirs, and assigns in the quiet possession thereof;* that the premises *are free from all encumbrances;* and that the *grantor, his heirs, and personal representatives will forever warrant and defend the title* thereof in the grantee, his heirs, and assigns against all lawful claims whatsoever. Utah Code Ann. § 57–1–12 (2000) (emphasis added).

According to the plain language of the statute, if a warranty deed comports with Utah law, then the five covenants of title articulated therein implicitly apply to the real property conveyance: (1) the covenant of seisin, (2) the covenant of right to convey, (3) the covenant against encumbrances, (4) the covenant of warranty, and (5) the covenant of quiet enjoyment.[4] Because the parties do not dispute the viability of the warranty deed or the validity of its execution, the five covenants of title are included in the warranty deed by operation of law. To determine if Cook Development breached these five covenants of title, we must review each of the covenants in turn.

1. Covenant of Seisin and Covenant of Right to Convey

Initially, we address whether the trial court properly granted summary judgment to Cook Development regarding Holmes's claim that Cook Development breached the covenants of seisin and right to convey. In making the covenant of seisin, a grantor warrants that the grantor is seized of the estate the deed purports to convey, both in quantity and quality. . . . Similarly, in making the covenant of the right to convey, a grantor guarantees that the grantor has the legal right to convey the estate the deed purports to convey. . . . Essentially, the covenants of seisin and the right to convey are synonymous, and the analysis of

---

[4] Utah law recognizes the covenant of further assurances, . . . but the covenant is not implicit in a statutory warranty deed as are the other five covenants of title explicitly set forth in section 57–1–12. . . .

whether a grantor breached one of these covenants is the same for either covenant. . . .

Hence, the covenants of seisin and right to convey, if found in a warranty deed, attest that the grantor covenants that it has good title to the estate purportedly conveyed. Consequently, the grantor breaches these covenants "when it is shown that the grantor did not own the land that he purported to convey by the warranty deed description." . . . Once evidence is adduced showing the grantor does not own what the grantor purports to convey, in violation of these covenants of title, there is no need to show "an actual eviction or threat thereof."

These covenants speak only to the circumstances at the moment a grantor delivers a deed and are thus defined as present covenants. . . . Thus, a grantor breaches these covenants, if at all, when the deed is delivered. . . .

In this case, Cook Development breached the covenants of seisin and right to convey because it did not own the 323-acre parcel when Cook Development delivered the warranty deed to Holmes. The quitclaim deed conveying the property to Cook Development from LC Farms failed because it erroneously identified LC Associates as the grantor. Cook Development breached these two covenants regardless of whether that breach was subsequently "cured" by First American's defense of Holmes in the Keystone litigation because the breach occurred when the deed was delivered. . . .

2. Covenant Against Encumbrances

Next, we address whether the trial court properly granted summary judgment to Cook Development on Holmes's claim that Cook Development breached the covenant against encumbrances. A grantor in a "warranty deed in Utah warrants to the grantee, among other things, 'that the premises are free from all encumbrances.'" . . . "Pursuant to [the] covenant [against encumbrances], a grantor obligates himself either to clear up any encumbrances that may be discovered or to indemnify the grantee." . . . This court has defined an encumbrance as "any interest in a third person consistent with a title in fee in the grantee, if such outstanding interest injuriously affects the value of the property," . . . or "constitutes a burden or limitation upon the rights of the fee title holder,". . . . "The question as to whether there is an encumbrance on [the] property must depend upon the facts as they exist at the time the warranty deed is delivered, and not upon subsequent occurrences." . . .

Holmes never specifically identifies a particular encumbrance that clouded Holmes's title when Cook Development delivered the warranty deed, which would have given rise to a breach of the covenant against encumbrances. Holmes [implies] that the lis pendens and the concomitant litigation encumbered the property, thereby breaching the warranty. We have never directly determined whether a lis pendens would constitute an encumbrance that breaches the covenant against encumbrances ... and we need not do so in this case. The lis pendens could not cloud the title when the warranty deed was delivered. Cook Development delivered the warranty deed to Holmes on May 19, 1998, when the sale of the 323-acre parcel closed. Keystone filed the lis pendens after Premier attempted to transfer the 323-acre parcel to Keystone in November 1998. Further, Holmes failed to identify any other encumbrance that existed on the record at the time Cook Development executed and delivered the warranty deed. Accordingly, Cook Development did not breach the covenant against encumbrances.

3. Covenant of Quiet Enjoyment and Covenant of Warranty

Finally, we address whether the trial court properly granted summary judgment on Holmes's claim that Cook Development breached the covenants of warranty and quiet enjoyment. According to the covenant of quiet enjoyment, a grantor warrants that the grantee may possess and quietly enjoy the land. The covenant of warranty is that the grantor will warrant and defend the title of the grantee against rightful claims regarding the title conveyed.... In Utah, both the covenant of warranty and the covenant of quiet possession are synonymous "since the same occurrence of circumstances is necessary to their breach," they both run with the land, and "the rule of damages is the same in [each]." Thus, for purposes of analysis, we consider these covenants simultaneously.

To establish a breach of the covenants of warranty and quiet enjoyment, ordinarily a grantee must show that the grantee was evicted from the property purportedly conveyed via the warranty deed by one with paramount or better title. Eviction can be either actual or constructive....

Before the grantee can recover for breach of these covenants, based upon either an actual or a constructive eviction, the grantee must establish that title has been affirmatively asserted against the grantee's title and possession, and that the title thus asserted is paramount or superior to the grantee's title. Paramount title is one that would prevail over another title in an action or one that would be otherwise successfully asserted against another's title. Consistent with these general rules, when a claim of paramount title to property has been defeated, the grantee cannot show eviction and the grantor has not breached the covenants of warranty or quiet enjoyment....

In this case, Holmes failed to establish that paramount or superior title has been affirmatively asserted against Holmes's title and possession. Aside from Holmes's title, the only other claim to the property that has been asserted was Keystone's claim of ownership for which Keystone instigated the Keystone litigation to quiet title to the 323-acre parcel. In that suit, the trial court quieted title to the parcel in Holmes, which conclusively established that Holmes's title to the 323-acre parcel is paramount to any claim Keystone has to the property.

Accordingly, Holmes cannot show that it was ever evicted, either actually or constructively, because Holmes remains in possession of the 323-acre parcel and Holmes's title is not subject to a paramount title. Therefore, inasmuch as Holmes cannot show that it has been evicted from the 323-acre parcel, Holmes cannot show that Cook Development breached the covenants of warranty and quiet enjoyment. [Affirmed.]

## St. Paul Title Insurance Corp. v. Owen

Supreme Court of Alabama, 1984.
452 So.2d 482.

■ MADDOX, JUSTICE.

The question here is what liability do grantors have to remote grantees or their assigns under a warranty deed and a statutory warranty deed where certain covenants of title contained in the deeds are found to run with the land?

On February 18, 1976, Albert M. Owen, an unmarried man, executed a warranty deed purporting to convey certain real property in Baldwin County to his brother and sister-in-law, James R. Owen, Jr., and Cheryl C. Owen. The deed, which was recorded on March 8, 1976, in Baldwin County, contained the following covenants of title:

> The party of the first part [Albert Owen] for himself, his heirs, executors and administrators, hereby covenants and warrants to and with the said parties of the second part [James and Cheryl Owen], their heirs and assigns, that he is seized of an indefeasible estate in and to the said property; that he has a good right to convey the same as herein contained; that he will guarantee the peaceable possession thereof; that the said property is free from all liens and encumbrances, and that he will, and his heirs, executors and administrators will forever warrant and defend the same unto the said parties of the second part, their heirs and assigns, against the lawful claims of all persons.

The warranty deed form was obtained from the law office of James R. Owen, Sr., the father of Albert and James Owen.

Subsequently, James and Cheryl Owen conveyed the Baldwin County property, purportedly conveyed to them, by statutory warranty deed[5] to Dennis C. Carlisle Jr., the brother of Cheryl Owen. The property was conveyed June 6, 1976, and the deed recorded in Baldwin County on July 14, 1976.

On June 10, 1976, Dennis Carlisle mortgaged the property to United Companies Mortgage and Investment of Mobile #2, Inc., for $17,159.52.

---

[5] The deed provided that "... the Grantee, does hereby Grant, Bargain, Sell and Convey unto said Grantee. . . ."

This mortgage was recorded on July 14, 1976, in both Mobile and Baldwin counties.

Dennis Carlisle mortgaged the property to GECC Financial Services (GECC) for $17,671.29, on November 8, 1977, apparently substituting mortgages and paying off the original mortgage. The mortgage to GECC was recorded in Baldwin County and a policy of title insurance naming GECC as the insured was issued shortly thereafter by Eastern Shore Title Insurance Corp., of Daphne, the agent for St. Paul Title Insurance Corp. (St. Paul Title). The title insurance was issued at the request of Dennis Carlisle.

When Dennis Carlisle subsequently defaulted on his mortgage payments, GECC attempted to foreclose on the property. The Circuit Court of Baldwin County found, however, that because Dennis Carlisle held no right, title, or interest in or to any of the property on the day the mortgage was executed, GECC was not entitled to foreclose on the property. GECC then brought suit against St. Paul Title, to collect its debt, and in addition the costs of litigation involved, all as provided for under the terms of the title insurance policy.

St. Paul Title, as subrogee of GECC, then filed a complaint against Albert Owen, James R. Owen, Jr., and Cheryl Owen wherein St. Paul alleged that they had breached the covenants of title contained in the deeds executed and delivered by them. The trial court, after a non-jury trial, entered a judgment on behalf of the defendants. St. Paul appeals.

I. The liability of Albert Owen under the express covenants of title contained in his warranty deed.

The deed executed by Albert Owen, an unmarried man, purporting to convey property to James and Cheryl Owen, contained the following express covenants of title: a covenant of seizin; a covenant of right to convey; a covenant for quiet enjoyment; a covenant against encumbrances; and a covenant of warranty. Of these covenants, however, only the covenants of quiet enjoyment and warranty are said to operate *in futuro* for the benefit of the ultimate grantee. *Musgrove v. Cordova Coal, Land & Improvement Co.*, 191 Ala. 419, 422, 67 So. 582, 583 (1914). Until broken, these two covenants run with the land to the heirs of the grantee, or if the land is conveyed or assigned, to the assignee, so that when they are broken, the heir or assignee injured by the breach can maintain an action against the covenantor. Thus, it is generally recognized and held that when a covenant of title runs with the land, all grantors, back to and including the original grantor-covenantor, become liable upon a breach of the covenant to the assignee or grantee in possession or entitled to the possession at the time, and the latter may sue the original or remote grantor, regardless of whether he has taken from the immediate grantor with a warranty. 21 Am.Jur.2d, *Covenants, Conditions, Etc.*, § 119 (1965).

Because the covenants of quiet enjoyment and of warranty are virtually identical in operation, whatever constitutes a breach of one covenant is a breach of the other. *Prestwood v. McGowin, supra,* 128 Ala. at 272, 29 So. at 388; 20 Am.Jur.2d, *Covenants, Conditions, Etc.* § 50 (1965). Neither covenant is breached until there is an eviction under paramount title. *Blaum v. May, supra,* 245 Ala. at 158, 16 So.2d at 331. The eviction may be either actual or constructive. *Prestwood v. McGowin, supra,* 128 Ala. at 272, 29 So. at 388.

It has been said that an outstanding title that could be asserted in a judicial proceeding against the party in possession is equivalent to an eviction. *Musgrove v. Cordova Coal, Land & Improvement Co.,* 191 Ala. at 423, 67 So. at 583. Likewise, a final judgment or decree adverse to the covenantee's title or right to possession constitutes a sufficient constructive eviction to entitle the covenantee to sue for breach of the covenant of warranty. 20 Am.Jur.2d, *Covenants, Conditions, Etc.,* § 62 (1965).

Here, the breach occurred when the trial court ruled in the foreclosure proceedings that Dennis Carlisle possessed no interest in the property which had been mortgaged, thereby frustrating GECC's attempt to foreclose on the property purportedly conveyed to Carlisle in fee simple.

We hold that the covenant of quiet enjoyment and warranty provided by the terms of the warranty deed executed by Albert Owen ran with the land purportedly conveyed by that instrument. We further hold that because someone other than the original grantor-covenantor in fact possessed paramount title, appellant is entitled to assert a claim for the breach of the covenants of title, as its subrogor was the ultimate grantee or assignee who was in possession at the time the covenants were broken.

II. The liability of James and Cheryl Owen under the covenants of title contained in their statutory warranty deed.

The deed executed by James and Cheryl Owen contained no express covenants of title, but it did use the words, "grant, bargain, sell and convey." In all conveyances of estates in fee where the words "grant, bargain, and sell" appear, the deed is construed by statute as containing the following covenants of title: a covenant of seizin; a covenant against encumbrances; and a covenant of quiet enjoyment. Code 1975, § 35–4–271.

Appellant asserts that James and Cheryl Owen are liable for a breach of the implied covenant of quiet enjoyment contained in the statutory warranty deed, and that such a covenant runs with the land so as to benefit a remote grantee or assign. Unlike the express covenants of title found in a general warranty deed, however, the implied covenants of title contained in a statutory warranty deed are more limited in effect.

In the early case of *Heflin v. Phillips,* 96 Ala. 561, 11 So. 729 (1892), the Court noted: "In construing this statute [predecessor of § 35–4–271] this Court declared that the words 'grant, bargain, sell' do not import an absolute general covenant of seizin against incumbrances and for quiet enjoyment, but that they amount to a covenant *only against acts done or suffered by the grantor and his heirs."* 96 Ala. at 562, 11 So. 730. (Emphasis added.) *See also Griffin v. Reynolds,* 17 Ala. 198 (1850). More than twenty years after *Heflin,* the Court remarked: "All authorities hold that the covenants implied by statute are limited to the acts of the grantor and those claiming under him, and do not extend to defects of title anterior to the conveyance to him." *Mackintosh v. Stewart,* 181 Ala. 328, 333, 61 So. 956, 958 (1913).

In *Mackintosh,* the immediate grantee (Stewart), prevailed in enforcing the implied warranty of seizin contained in a statutory warranty deed against the grantor (Mackintosh). The grantor had allowed part of the subject property to be adversely possessed during his period of ownership. Although the grantee succeeded in showing that adverse possession took place at least partially during the period in which the grantor held title to the property, the Court suggested the outcome of the case could have been different had the grantor pleaded and proved that adverse possession had ripened into title prior to the grantor's laying claim to the subject property. 181 Ala. at 337, 61 So. at 959. This result would have ensued in that instance, because the defect in the title would have been anterior to the conveyance to Mackintosh by his grantor. Although Mackintosh would have been without good title to convey to Stewart, Mackintosh would not have been liable to Stewart under the statutory warranty deed's implied covenants of title because Mackintosh would not have suffered or caused any of the title problems.

James and Cheryl Owen conveyed their complete, albeit non-existent interest, in the subject property to Dennis Carlisle by statutory warranty deed. By so doing, they merely warranted that they had not conveyed title to anyone else; that they had not allowed the property to become encumbered while they held purported title; and that they had not caused or suffered anyone to do anything that would interfere with the property's quiet enjoyment by the grantee, the grantee's heirs or assigns. Because the record indicates that James and Cheryl did nothing to affect the purported title they conveyed, they did not breach any of the covenants of title contained in the statutory warranty deed delivered to Dennis Carlisle and are therefore not liable to the appellant, as subrogee of GECC.

### III. Damages for breach of covenants of title.

Appellant asserts that it is entitled to recover, as damages, the amount of mortgage proceeds paid to Dennis Carlisle by its subrogor, plus litigation costs and interest. Appellant further contends its recovery should neither be barred nor be limited to merely nominal damages, even though appellees received no consideration for their conveyances.

In situations where there has been a complete failure of title and a grantee has sought recovery from his immediate grantor, the maximum recovery allowed has been the purchase price paid. *Allinder v. Bessemer C.I. & L. Co.,* 164 Ala. 275, 277, 51 So. 234, 235 (1909). With respect to an action against a remote grantor, however, there appears to be a difference of opinion as to whether damages are to be determined by the consideration paid by the grantee bringing the suit to his immediate grantor or by the consideration paid to the original grantor or covenantor, not exceeding in either case, however, the consideration paid for the conveyance [to] the defendant in the action. 20 Am.Jur.2d *Covenants, Conditions, Etc.,* § 163 (1965). Here, however, the facts indicate that no consideration was ever paid to or received by any of the appellees, Albert Moore Owen, James R. Owen, Jr., or Cheryl C. Owen. Consequently, since there was no evidence that the remote grantors received any consideration for their conveyances purportedly conveying title to the subject property, appellant, as subrogee of GECC, is entitled to an award of nominal damages only, for the breach of the covenant of quiet enjoyment contained in Albert Owen's deed, and not the amount of the mortgage made by GECC. *See* 20 Am.Jur.2d *Covenants, Conditions, Etc.,* § 163 (1965).

The judgment of the trial court is hereby reversed and the cause remanded to that court for a determination of the amount of nominal damages appellant is entitled to recover as consistent with the holding of this opinion.

Reversed and remanded.

## NOTES

1. *Present vs. future covenants.* How valid is the distinction between present and future covenants? What are the advantages and disadvantages of this traditional distinction? Iowa cases permit what were traditionally present covenants to run with the land on the theory that the cause of action which arises in favor of a grantee when a present covenant is breached is assigned by operation of deed to successors of this grantee.[6] Under this theory, the statute of limitations still begins to run at conveyance to the original grantee/promisee.

2. *Running of covenants against encumbrances.* With respect to the covenant against encumbrances, some courts have followed a line of authority which distinguishes between covenants against physical encumbrances like easements and covenants against monetary encumbrances. These courts have held that the monetary encumbrances run with the land, while the former do not.[7] Is there a rational basis for such a distinction?

3. *Damages.* In the Principal Problem, assuming that Z can sue X for breach of the covenant against encumbrances, how should Z's damages be measured under *St. Paul?* How would Z's damages be measured in an action

---

[6] See, e.g., Rockafellor v. Gray, 194 Iowa 1280 (1922).

[7] See, e.g., Soderberg v. Holt, 86 Utah 485 (1935).

against Y? How persuasive is the court's resolution of the damage issue in *St. Paul?*

4. *Scope of the covenant against encumbrances.* Should the covenant against encumbrances be deemed violated by building code violations? What about violations of zoning regulations, or of environmental regulations requiring the cleanup of toxic materials from the soil? The presence of toxic materials on the property does not constitute an "encumbrance" within the meaning of the covenant against encumbrances.[8] It is also clear that the mere existence of environmental or zoning regulations that reduce the value of the property is not an encumbrance. However, the cases are divided as to whether *violations* of such regulations constitute encumbrances.

## Babb v. Weemer
Court of Appeal of California, 1964.
225 Cal.App.2d 546.

■ BURKE, PRESIDING JUSTICE.

Plaintiffs, attorney Jerrell Babb and his wife, Joan Babb, brought an action against defendant Rose L. Weemer (formerly known as Rose L. Snell) for damages for the alleged breach of an implied covenant in a grant deed and to recover certain costs paid by plaintiffs to prevent foreclosure by defendant of a second trust deed held by defendant upon the subject real property. The trial court entered judgment in favor of defendant and against plaintiffs on both counts, from which judgment plaintiffs appeal.

Defendant formerly owned the subject property, and, on July 5, 1956, executed a promissory note, and deed of trust securing the payment thereof, to secure an indebtedness in the sum of $5,400 in favor of a lending institution.

On March 17, 1958, defendant conveyed the subject property by grant deed to Charles Rosette and Christine M. Rosette (Rosettes). In conjunction with this sale Rosettes executed their promissory note in the approximate amount of $3,250 in favor of defendant and imposed a second deed of trust upon the subject property to secure the payment thereof. This deed of trust was a purchase money second deed of trust as set forth in the escrow instructions pertaining to the sale between the parties.

On June 8, 1960, Rosettes entered into an agreement of sale of the subject property to plaintiffs and evidenced their agreement by a written memorandum which, after acknowledging receipt of a deposit of $50, recited as follows:

> The total purchase price is to be $10,150 & no/100 leaving a balance of $10,100 no/100. Said balance of Ten Thousand One Hundred Dollars (10,100 no/100) less the total of all present

---

[8] See Country World Casinos v. Tommyknocker Casino, 181 F.3d 1146 (10th Cir.1999).

encumbrances, approximately in the amount of $8,975 no/100, leaving a balance of approximately $1125 no/100 shall be paid by Cashiers Check as soon as purchaser, said Jerrell Babb can obtain a policy of Title Insurance at his own expense, and for which he is to receive a Grant Deed subject to encumbrances in above amount. The undersigned agree to surrender possession [sic] of the premises to purchaser at any time within 10 to 20 days on 5 days notice by purchaser that he is able to procure title policy and is ready to pay the said sum of approximately $1125 00/100 in return for grant deed executed by the undersigned.

/s/ CHARLES ROSETTE

/s/ CHRISTINE M. ROSETTE

This memorandum was prepared by a Mr. Fredman who was acting as an agent for plaintiffs.

On June 18, 1960, Rosettes conveyed the real property to plaintiffs by a grant deed which contained the proviso that the property was conveyed to plaintiffs "subject to encumbrances and easements of record."

Between the time of the execution of the memorandum of sale, June 8, and the execution of the grant deed, June 18, 1960, plaintiff Babb "made it a point to know about all these documents. . . ." In other words, he searched the records and found the first trust deed of record and the subsequent encumbrance which indicated that there was a total of approximately $9,000 in encumbrances outstanding against the property, which was within a few dollars of the amount of the total outstanding encumbrances stated by Rosettes in their memorandum of sale. Consequently, the recorded documents substantiated the seller's representations to the purchaser with respect to the encumbrances outstanding against the property. However, Attorney Babb's check of the records also revealed what he evidently felt was a flaw in the proceedings, which he contends he is entitled to take advantage of. Noteworthy was the opening phrase in his oral argument to the effect that he is entitled to have the case decided under the applicable provisions of the statutory law and not in accordance with "the Golden Rule" which latter code, he asserted, in effect, is subject to individual interpretations. A review will indicate that he has reason to be reluctant to have the matter determined under the Golden Rule; however, neither does the application of the statutory rule afford him any shelter.

Plaintiff Babb's search indicated that the grant deed by which defendant sold the property to Rosettes contained no specific reference to the first trust deed and therefore carried with it an implied covenant that the property was free of any encumbrance placed upon it by defendant as seller. He asserts this implied covenant runs with the land and inures to the benefit of plaintiffs; that this implied covenant was breached, in that defendant had placed the first trust deed upon the property, and therefore that plaintiffs, as subsequent purchasers, have a cause of action for damages against defendant to the extent of the amount due on the first deed of trust.

Plaintiffs rely upon the provisions of Civil Code, § 1113 relating to the implied covenants which follow from the use of the word "grant" in any conveyance, unless restrained by express terms contained in the conveyance. Plaintiffs make the foregoing contentions even though, admittedly, they had actual as well as constructive knowledge of the existence of the first trust deed at the time they purchased the property from Rosettes and the deed by which the property was conveyed to them by Rosettes expressly stated the property was being conveyed to them "subject to encumbrances and easements of record."

It is plaintiffs' view that the effect of the grant deed from defendant to Rosettes was to covenant that the property conveyed to Rosettes was free and clear of the first trust deed and that this implied covenant in the deed runs with the land for the benefit of plaintiffs as subsequent grantees of the property. It is well settled, however, that covenants that land is free from encumbrances are personal covenants not running with the land and that they do not entitle a succeeding grantee to maintain an action in his own name for their breach.

Section 1113 of the Civil Code establishes the implied covenants flowing from the use of the word "grant" in a conveyance. Generally, the section has two applications: (1) to the covenant that the grantor has not conveyed out to others prior to the instant grant, and (2) that the grantor has not suffered any encumbrance to be placed upon the property. The second application is the one with which we are concerned here. A trust deed is construed as an "encumbrance" and not a transfer of an interest in the fee. (Hollywood Lumber Co. v. Love, 155 Cal. 270, 100 P. 698.) In Lawrence v. Montgomery, supra, 37 Cal. 183, 188, the court declared the covenant against "encumbrances" is a personal covenant and does not run with the land or pass to the assignee.

In McPike v. Heaton, 131 Cal. 109, the court, after citing the implied covenant provision of Civil Code, § 1113, stated, "... and the rule is of ancient authority that a covenant that the land conveyed is free from encumbrances, whether express or implied, does not run with the land, or pass to the assignee. [Citation.] The plaintiffs had no contractual relation with the defendant, and his covenant with Jackson did not pass to them."

Section 1113 was enacted in 1872 and has never been amended. It was in effect when McPike v. Heaton, supra, was decided in the year 1900 and contained the same opening paragraph upon which appellant here relies, i.e., that implied covenants of the grantor under the section extend to the grantee and to *his assigns*. Notwithstanding this language, the court's interpretation in McPike is that implied covenants as to *encumbrances,* as distinguished from *conveyances,* do not run with the land.

The court received in evidence the escrow instructions between defendant and Rosettes which expressly recited that the property was being sold to Rosettes subject to the first trust deed. Consequently, there was no misrepresentation or misunderstanding between the parties to that transaction. Plaintiffs, however, assert that whatever understanding they may have had in their written agreement of sale the deed itself is obviously at variance with the terms of their written agreement and the deed must be the sole guide for measuring and determining the rights of the parties thereunder, and furthermore that it is no defense to an action for breach of his covenant that the grantee had notice of the encumbrance at the time he took title, citing Sisk v. Caswell, 14 Cal.App. 377. The latter case, however, dealt with an easement for a visible irrigation ditch, not a mortgage or trust deed, and the language thereof, relied upon here, was obiter dictum.

In neither the latter case nor in Blackwell v. Atkinson, 14 Cal. 470, is there any support for plaintiffs' position that the grantor's liability under a grant deed is not personal to his immediate grantee but extends to remote, subsequent grantees. In Blackwell the court was concerned with the warranty of title to a mining claim. Thus, it was dealing with an express warranty that the vendor owned what he was purporting to sell. In such a case the covenant of warranty runs with the land and the liability of the vendor is not exclusively to his vendee. He is bound by his covenant to defend the title or pay the value of the land. These cases relate to the chain of title and not to liens or encumbrances and have no application to the implied covenant against encumbrances made by the grantor, which type of covenant is referred to in Civil Code, § 1113, subdivision 2.

Plaintiffs have no cause of action whatever against defendant. Admittedly, they took the property from the Rosettes expressly "subject to encumbrances and easements of record" and, in addition, had actual knowledge of the trust deed which they now would avoid. They seek a windfall from the fact that the grant deed to their predecessors in interest contained no express reference to the first trust deed.

There can be no implied covenant where the subject matter is expressly agreed upon by the parties to the contrary. When the Rosettes acquired the property from Snell by the grant deed which failed to mention the existing trust deed the express written contract of sale between the parties, contained in the escrow instructions, fully set forth the existence of the trust deed which was a determining factor in the purchase price. No damages for any purported breach of covenant could have been asserted then by the Rosettes, and none may be asserted now by plaintiffs who took title expressly subject to all encumbrances of record. "Summarized, therefore, the rule deducible from the foregoing authorities controlling the exercise of judicial authority to insert implied covenants may be stated as follows: (1) The implication must arise from the language used or it must be indispensable to effectuate the intention of the parties; (2) it must appear from the language used that it was so clearly within the contemplation of the parties that they deemed it unnecessary to express it; (3) implied covenants can only be justified on the grounds of legal necessity; (4) a promise can be implied only where it can be rightfully assumed that it would have been made if attention had been called to it; (5) there can be no implied covenant where the subject is completely covered by the contract." (Cousins Investment Co. v. Hastings Clothing Co., supra, 45 Cal.App.2d 141; Civ.Code, § 1648.)

Plaintiffs' position is entirely without merit. The appeal from the judgment in the action is deemed by this court to be frivolous and, particularly since plaintiff Jerrell Babb is a practicing attorney, a penalty assessment against appellants is indicated as provided in rule 26(a) of the California Rules of Court.

Judgment is affirmed, and plaintiffs are ordered to pay to defendant the sum of $500 attorney's fees as a penalty in addition to costs of appeal.

## NOTES

1. *Drafting error.* What was Weemer's error? What should the deed have specified to avoid this error?

2. *Title searches.* The deed of trust made by Weemer was recorded and therefore the Rosettes took with notice of it. Why would this notice not obviate any breach of the covenant against encumbrances that would otherwise occur?

3. *The doctrine of merger.* The court states that the Rosettes would have been bound by the deed of trust even though the grant deed they received from Weemer did not mention it, since the contract of sale between Weemer and the Rosettes (embodied in the escrow instructions) set forth the existence of the trust deed. Yet by giving a grant deed, Weemer impliedly warranted that there were no encumbrances on the property (Cal.Civ. Code § 1113). Nevertheless, the court ignores the effect of the doctrine of merger by which the deed supersedes the contract of sale and is the sole guide for determining the rights of the parties thereunder. Why?

4. *Babb's position.* What arguments does Babb use to convince the court that the covenant against encumbrances implied in a grant deed runs with the land? Why was he unsuccessful?

5. *Rosettes' liability.* Suppose that the grant deed from the Rosettes to Babb did not contain the phrase "subject to encumbrances and easements of record." Would Babb have been wiser to sue the Rosettes rather than Weemer for breach of the covenants implied in his grant deed, thereby avoiding the running problem?

6. *Z's position.* This case seems to go directly against Z in the Principal Problem because the court states as the rule in California that the covenant against encumbrances implied by a grant deed does not run with the land.

Is this case very strong authority against Z? How could Z use *Babb* to help his case against X?

7. *The ULTA.* Section 2–312(a) of the Uniform Land Transactions Act (1975) (ULTA) takes the position that all covenants of title, whether present or future, should run in favor of remote grantees. No jurisdictions have yet adopted this provision. Nevertheless, can § 2–312(a) still be used for the benefit of Z?

# ASSIGNMENT 48-49

# RECORDING STATUTES

## 1. PRINCIPAL PROBLEM

The president of the real property section of your state's bar association has just reviewed the material contained in this Assignment and she has concluded that the state's current recording statute is unsatisfactory. She has prepared the following rough draft of a substitute statute and has asked you, as one of the newest members of the section, to analyze and critique it. Specifically, you are to determine how it changes existing law and give your opinion as to whether these changes are desirable. Consider how it differs from the state statutes reproduced in this Assignment. Identify any problem areas that should be covered by the draft statute. Naturally, you will have to review the material following this Principal Problem before you can critique the draft statute.

### Draft Recording Statute

(a) Subject to the exceptions provided below, no deed, mortgage, declaration, covenant, restriction, lease, option, or other intervivos instrument affecting title to real property shall be valid until recorded, and all such instruments shall take effect only from the date of their recordation. Unrecorded instruments shall be of no effect.

(b) Leases of three years or less need not be recorded to be valid, provided that if they contain an option to purchase, or an option to extend the lease for a period extending more than three years beyond the original inception of the leasehold, they must be recorded for the option to be valid. All extensions or modifications of instruments that must be recorded to be valid must also be recorded. All extensions of leases of three years or less must be recorded if they extend the lease for a period extending more than three years beyond the original inception of the leasehold.

## 2. THE BASIC RULES

Sam Seller offers a tract known as Merrywood for sale. Bob Buyer wants to buy it. How can Bob be sure that Sam really owns Merrywood? Sam's occupancy of Merrywood proves nothing. Sam may occupy as a tenant, a co-owner, or as a trespasser. It is also not a satisfactory answer to say that Bob will simply get title insurance. *First,* title insurance does not assure one of good title any more than life insurance assures one of longevity. Title insurance provides that the insured will receive damages if he does not have good title. *Second,* how does the title insurance company determine who owns Merrywood? To understand how title is determined, one must study our system of recording documents affecting title.

*The Nonstatutory Law*

Our system of recordation of documents affecting title depends on state recording statutes. These statutes changed the common law. To understand them and also the cases not covered by them, we must first understand the pre-existing common law.

*"First in time is first in right."* The common law relied mainly on this principle. A closely related principle was also widely followed: "One cannot convey what one does not own." In the examples in this Assignment, O will be assumed to be the original owner of Blackacre, A the first grantee, and B the second grantee.

> EXAMPLE 1: O conveys Blackacre to A. Thereafter, O purports to convey Blackacre to B. As between A and B, who owns Blackacre? A's deed was first in time before the deed to B. To put it another way, after O conveyed Blackacre to A, O no longer owned Blackacre and had nothing to convey to B. Therefore, A owns Blackacre.

Example 1 involves a case in which there are two competing conveyances of legal title. The same result follows when there are two conveyances of equitable title.

> EXAMPLE 2: O and A enter into a contract under which O promises to sell and A promises to buy Blackacre. At this point, A has an equitable interest in Blackacre. O still has legal ownership, subject to A's equitable interest in Blackacre. Suppose that O subsequently enters into a contract for the sale of Blackacre to B. If it were not for the previous contract with A, B would have an equitable interest in Blackacre. However, since A's equitable ownership was prior in time to B's claim, A would have equitable ownership and B would not have any ownership, legal or equitable, in Blackacre. The first in time, first in right rule would prevail.

*Exception to first in time, first in right rule.* Under the common law, there was only one exception to the first in time, first in right rule. When the first interest was only equitable and the second was legal, the second interest would prevail over the former provided that the grantee of the second interest was a bona fide purchaser for value of the second interest, without notice of the previous transaction.

> EXAMPLE 3: O and A enter into a contract under which O promises to sell and A promises to buy Blackacre. However, before the contract is performed, O sells the property to B. B pays adequate consideration for the property and has no notice of the previous transaction with A. B now owns Blackacre free of A's equitable interest. American Recording Statutes

*Deed valid without recordation.* Every state has a recording statute. Although these statutes encourage grantees of interest in real estate to record their grants, most do not make recordation essential for the validity of a deed.

> EXAMPLE 4: O duly executes and delivers a deed in customary form purporting to convey Blackacre to A. When the deed is delivered, A owns Blackacre. Title passes on delivery of a deed, not on recordation of it.

*Process of recordation.* After the grantor delivers the executed deed (or other instrument affecting title) to the grantee, the grantee (or more usually, his lawyer, title company or escrow agent) presents it to the Recorder's Office for the county in which the land is situated. The Recorder will note the date and time of receipt, collect a small fee, and make a photocopy or microfilm copy of the deed. The copy is retained in the Recorder's Office, and the original is returned to the grantee. The copies are placed in the deed books or on microfilm in the order received. Because the Recorder's Office stores hundreds of thousands of instruments, it would be impossible to find the deeds affecting a particular property without an index.

*Discussion questions:* Most states do not make recordation absolutely essential to the validity of a deed. Why? How does this bear on the statute in the Principal Problem?

*Types of indexes: tract index.* The most efficient and useful form of index is a tract index. A tract index has, in principle, a separate page for each parcel, although parcel splits and consolidations complicate the system somewhat. Thus, the purchaser of "Lot 17 of Block 4 of Smith's Addition" would, in theory, have all of the documents affecting that parcel noted on a single index page. Despite the advantages of tract indexes, many counties do not maintain tract indexes. The reason may be historical patterns. Most counties started with grantor-grantee indexes and now it would be difficult and expensive to change over to a new system. Additionally, in many states grantor-grantee indexes are mandated by statute. In these states, counties that have tract indexes also have to maintain grantor-grantee indexes. However, the ability to search by tracts has improved over time, due in part to the fact that many title insurance or abstract companies maintain their own indexes organized or searchable by tract.

*Types of indexes: grantor-grantee index.* Many counties use this type of index. The name of every grantor in a deed is listed alphabetically in the grantor-grantee index. Similarly, the name of every grantee in a deed is listed alphabetically in a grantee-grantor index. Thus, a deed by Sally Seller to Joan Buyer would be indexed in the grantee-grantor index as follows:

still indexed by grantor-grantee and grantee-grantor indexes. However, many counties have computerized their records while still relying on grantor-grantee and grantee-grantor indexes. Thus, indexes are frequently accessible by computer, as are copies of the deeds, mortgages, leases and other instruments that affect title. In these counties, it is no longer necessary to touch musty deed volumes and cumbersome index books. Yet, the process of search is still essentially the same as in pre-computer times. The indexes are still in the names of grantors and grantees (rather than of tracts). In these counties, it is possible to key in a name and all documents containing that name will appear on a computer screen. Any of these documents can then be retrieved. Such a system, however, is not organized to locate all documents pertaining to a particular plot of land. These electronic records do not necessarily have fully searchable integrated text and search engines like those that exist for documents and websites on the Internet or in databases like Westlaw and Lexis.

Sometimes the county assessor (tax collector) indexes documents by assessor's parcel number, thus creating a kind of tract index. However the assessor's indexes are not always coordinated with the indexes maintained by the recorder. Moreover, the documents in the assessor's office do not provide constructive notice of their contents to subsequent purchasers of land. In short, although most recorders' offices have utilized computer-based technology, they still usually rely on name-based indexes (rather than tract indexes) and thus retain the disadvantages of the old grantor and grantee indexes.

In the coming years, computerization of the public records is likely to advance much further. In 2004, the National Conference of Commissioners on Uniform State Laws promulgated the Uniform Real Property Electronic Recording Act (URPERA). URPERA was drafted to remove any doubt about the authority of the recorder to receive and record documents and information in electronic form. URPERA authorizes a recorder to accept electronic documents for recording and to index and store those documents. URPERA is part of a broader set of legal advances in electronic transactions generally, including the widely adopted Uniform Electronic Transactions Act (UETA), the federal Electronic Signatures in Global and National Commerce Act (ESign), and pending revisions to the Uniform Law on Notarial Acts. More than twenty jurisdictions have adopted the Uniform Real Property Electronic Recording Act, a number that has grown rapidly in a relatively short period of time and may soon grow to all jurisdictions.

Nonetheless, actual progress toward electronic title records in many jurisdictions is slow or non-existent, despite the rapid proliferation of express statutory authority for this result. The financial, administrative, personnel, and technological resources required to make the transition from paper records to electronic records are substantial, and pose a strong barrier to county records offices undertaking these efforts. For the searching system to function effectively, the county records office will not only need to receive new electronic title records but must also scan or convert existing paper records to electronic form. To achieve this end, upgraded computer systems might be needed. In addition, repeat players in the title recording process may resist new ways of filing and searching records. On the other hand, the processes of submitting, receiving, storing, and accessing documents electronically have become familiar and widely used in many aspects of daily life, which suggests that as more counties start using electronic recording systems, the practice will catch on and grow. Improved administrative efficiencies from electronic recording might justify the expenditure of public funds to accomplish the transition from the paper system to an electronic system. Moreover, the widespread use of full-text searching and the increasing presence of other types of electronic records may create both a demand for these capabilities with regard to electronic title records, as well as a supply of technological tools and services to achieve this end. All these developments are likely to change how title documents will be searched in the future.

*Types of statutes.* There is no typical recording statute. The peculiar wording of a particular state statute may compel results different from those of other states. Two states may both have a "notice" type of statute and yet each statute may differ in important details. Nevertheless, it is convenient, if something of a simplification, to say that most recording statutes fall within one of three categories:

1. race (i.e., the one who wins the "race" to the courthouse to record his deed obtains good title)
2. race-notice (often called notice-race)
3. notice.

These different types will be explained more fully below.

*Statutes partially reject the first in time, first in right principle.* Under all three types of statutes, the first deed delivered to a grantee is not necessarily superior to the second deed delivered at a later time to a second grantee.

EXAMPLE 5: O delivers a duly executed deed to A who fails to record it. At this point, A owns Blackacre because none of the state recording statutes makes recordation essential to the validity of a deed. Thereafter, O delivers a duly executed deed of Blackacre to B. B is a bona fide purchaser for value without notice of the prior transaction with A. B promptly records his deed. Under all three types of recording statutes, B is the owner of Blackacre, not A, although A received his deed first and actually owned Blackacre before O's second deed to B. In a sense, O was able to convey what O did not own. It may seem "self-evident" that one cannot convey what one does not own, but the recording statutes reject, at least in part, this self-evident proposition.

*Rationale for permitting one to convey what one does not own.* All of the recording statutes seek to make it relatively easy to ascertain ownership ("title") by reference to recorded documents. This can only be done if people record their documents. Although the statutes do not go so far as to declare unrecorded documents void, they make them voidable under circumstances specified by the precise words of the particular statute involved. We must therefore examine some specific statutes.

*Race statute.* Only North Carolina and Louisiana have a generally applicable race type of statute. Arkansas, Ohio, and Pennsylvania apply it to certain narrowly defined types of instruments. The North Carolina statute (Gen. Stat. § 47–18) provides in pertinent part as follows. "No conveyance of land, or contract to convey, . . . or lease of land for more than three years shall be valid to pass any property interest as against lien creditors or purchasers for a valuable consideration from the donor, bargainor or lessor but from the time of registration thereof in the county where the land lies. . . ." The North Carolina statute is considered to be of the race type because certain persons who acquire a claimed interest in the property after the first in time conveyee may gain priority over the earlier conveyee if they win the "race" to the courthouse and record their instrument before the earlier conveyee, despite the fact that they have notice of the earlier conveyance.

> EXAMPLE 6: O conveys to A who does not record. Thereafter, O conveys to B who has notice of the previous conveyance to A. B promptly records. If B is a "purchaser for a valuable consideration" B owns Blackacre, under a "race" type of statute. A may have a good cause of action against O for fraud or negligence, but A has lost her title to Blackacre. Because the North Carolina statute protects B regardless of whether B had notice of A's rights, it is a pure race statute rather than a notice-race statute.[1]

*Notice statutes.* Under a pure notice statute, it is immaterial who wins the race to the courthouse to record. A second grantee who takes without notice of the existence of a previous grant will prevail provided he meets the other requirements of the particular statute. For example, Massachusetts General Laws Annotated, chapter 183, section 4 provides: "A conveyance of an estate in fee simple, fee tail or for life, or a lease for more than seven years . . . shall not be valid as against any person, except the grantor or lessor, his heirs and devisees and persons having actual notice of it, unless it . . . is recorded. . . ."

The Massachusetts statute is unusual because it purports to protect certain persons who may not be "purchasers." Who is a "purchaser" as that term is used in most recording statutes, and what is "notice," are

---

[1] Department of Transportation v. Humphries, 496 S.E.2d 563 (1998).

questions that will be explored more fully below. At this point, it should be emphasized that just as "notice" is immaterial in a jurisdiction that has a race statute, such as North Carolina, who records first (wins the "race") is immaterial in a pure notice jurisdiction like Massachusetts.

The following example illustrates the operation of a notice statute.

EXAMPLE 7: O conveys to A who does not record. O then sells to B who does not record and has no notice of the previous transaction with A. Thereafter, A records and then B records. B owns Blackacre under a notice type statute. Under a race or notice-race type statute, A would win because A recorded before B.

*Notice-race statutes.* About half the states have notice-race statutes. These statutes require that the second grantee must do two things to prevail over the first grantee: (1) record before the first grantee (win the "race" to record), (2) purchase without notice of the first grantee's claim. Both the New York and California statutes are notice-race statutes

## NEW YORK REAL PROPERTY LAW SECTION 291

(1) A conveyance of real property . . . may be recorded. . . . Every such conveyance not so recorded is void

(2) as against any person who subsequently purchases or acquires by exchange or contracts to purchase or acquire by exchange, the same real property or any portion thereof . . .

(3) in good faith and for a valuable consideration, from the same vendor or assignor, his distributees or devisees,

(4) and whose conveyance, contract, or assignment is first duly recorded. . . .

(Parenthetical numbers added)

## CALIFORNIA CIVIL CODE SECTION 1214[2]

(1) Every conveyance of real property . . . ,

(2) other than a lease for a term not exceeding one year,

(3) is void as against any subsequent purchaser or mortgagee of the same property,

(4) or any part thereof,

(5) in good faith and for a valuable consideration,

(6) whose conveyance is first duly recorded. . . .

*(Parenthetical numbers added).*

*Types of Statutes Compared.*

For problems involving one plot of land and only three parties, the time sequences are finite. Suppose that O is the original owner and that he grants (or mortgages) the same land first to A and then to B, and that

---

[2] See also Calif. Civ. Code §§ 1107, 1217.

Ar represents the time that A records and that Br represents the time that B records. *Assume that B is a bona fide purchaser for value without notice of A's claim (except such notice as may be imputed to B by the recording statute itself).* The fact situation and the results may be diagramed as follows.

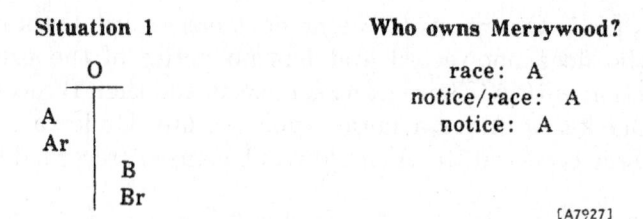

**Situation 1**

```
         O
       ──┬──
   A     │
   Ar    │
         │ B
         │ Br
```

Who owns Merrywood?

race: A
notice/race: A
notice: A

[A7927]

In this first situation, A received a deed from O and promptly recorded. Thereafter B received a deed from O and promptly recorded. Under either a race statute, a notice statute or a notice/race statute, A would win. There are several ways to state the reasoning by which one reaches this conclusion. Much will depend on the precise wording of the particular statute involved. For a statute containing a notice element, one can say that B had notice of A's claim since a search for O's name under the grantor index would have revealed to B the conveyance to A. For a statute containing a race element, one can say that A should win because he recorded before B.

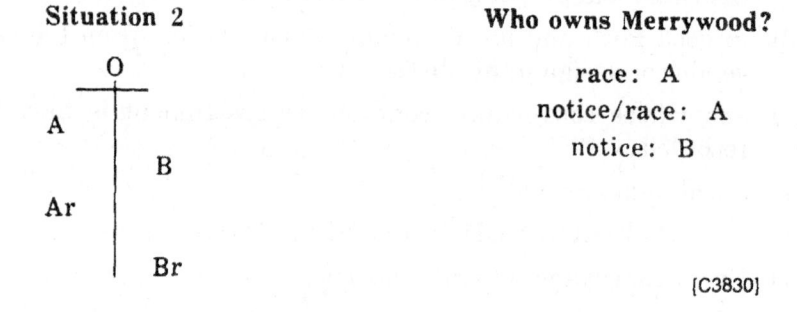

**Situation 2**

```
         O
       ──┬──
   A     │
         │ B
   Ar    │
         │
         │ Br
```

Who owns Merrywood?

race: A
notice/race: A
notice: B

[C3830]

In Situation 2, do you see why B would win in a notice jurisdiction but not in the others? Contrast Situation 2 with Situation 3.

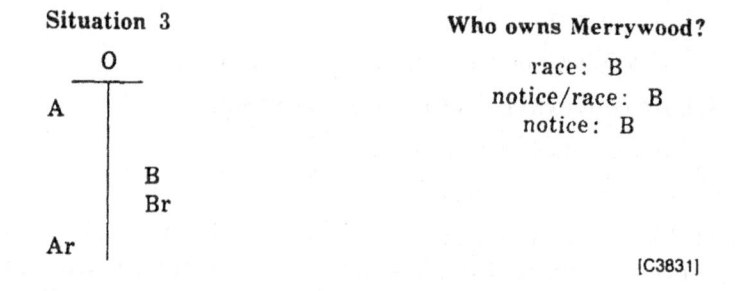

**Situation 3**

```
         O
       ──┬──
   A     │
         │ B
         │ Br
   Ar    │
```

Who owns Merrywood?

race: B
notice/race: B
notice: B

[C3831]

*Who is Protected by the Recording Statute?*

Typically, the recording statutes do not protect the grantor, or his heirs, devisees, or donees against the first grantee's failure to record.

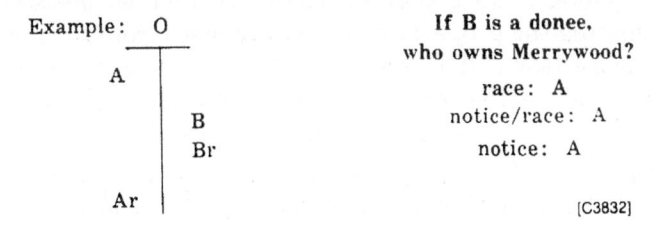

```
Example:   O                    If B is a donee,
           |                    who owns Merrywood?
           A                         race:          A
           |   B                     notice/race:   A
           |   Br                    notice:        A
           |
           Ar                                  [C3832]
```

However, although B's character as a "purchaser" (as opposed to a "donee") is crucial, A's character as a "donee" or "purchaser" is immaterial. Why should this be?

*Who May Lose Title by Virtue of the Recording Statute?*

*Documents that should be recorded.* If an instrument that should be recorded is not recorded, it runs the risk of losing its priority to a later recorded instrument. It thus becomes important to check the particular state statute to ascertain what instruments are covered.

> EXAMPLE 8: O leases property for four years to A, who does not record his lease, and does not occupy the premises. O thereafter sells the property to B, who promptly records and has no notice of A's lease. Under the California statute (quoted above), B would take the property free of A's lease. Under the Massachusetts statute (quoted above), B would take the property subject to A's lease, because the statute provides that leases of less than seven years need not be recorded.

*Adverse possessors.* Under most state statutes, claims arising by virtue of adverse possession are not affected by the recording statutes. This is because most statutes refer to "conveyances" that should be recorded. Since title obtained by adverse possession is not derived from a "conveyance", it is not affected by the recording statute.

> EXAMPLE 9: O is the record owner of Blackacre. A acquires ownership by adverse possession. Thereafter A ceases to occupy the land and it becomes vacant. O then purports to sell the property to B, who promptly records. B is a bona fide purchaser without notice of A's rights. Under most statutes, A would prevail over B, despite the lack of either record or off-record notice to B of A's claim.

The Uniform Simplification of Land Transfers Act § 3–202 rejects, in large part, the above rule.[3] Under this section "a purchaser for value who has recorded his conveyance also acquires the real estate free of any subsisting adverse claim, whether or not the transferor had actual

---

[3] The Uniform Simplification of Land Transfers Act (1977) has not been adopted in any state.

authority to convey, unless the adverse claim is [that of a person] whose use or occupancy [is] inconsistent with the record title to the extent the use or occupancy would be revealed by reasonable inspection or inquiry...." Thus, if an owner by virtue of adverse possession is not using or occupying the property when B purchases from the record owner, the adverse possessor will lose his title. To avoid this result, the adverse possessor not wishing to remain in possession would presumably have to bring a quiet title action to place his title on record.

*Discussion question:* Should the USLTA rule be generally adopted? Who May Gain Title by Virtue of the Recording Statutes?

*Types of title defects not affected by the recording statutes.* The recording statutes are addressed mainly to the consequences of not recording certain instruments. They do not alter the common law rules governing the invalidity of instruments. Thus, the mere fact that an instrument is recorded does not suggest that it is immune from attack based on such grounds as lack of delivery, forgery, fraud, incapacity, or infancy.

> EXAMPLE 10: O is the actual and record owner of Blackacre. X, a scoundrel, impersonates O and forges O's name to a deed of Blackacre. X purports to sell Blackacre to A, a bona fide purchaser for value, who promptly records. A then sells Blackacre to B, a bona fide purchaser of Blackacre who promptly records. O then grants Blackacre to C, who is not a purchaser and who does not record. Who owns Blackacre, B or C? C owns Blackacre, despite B's status as a bona fide purchaser who promptly recorded. The recording statutes do not purport to make a forged deed good merely because it was recorded.

Under USLTA § 2-202, however, nondelivery of a deed from O to A does not appear to defeat the title of B, a bona fide purchaser from A, without knowledge of the nondelivery of the O to A deed.[4]

*Discussion questions.* Should the USLTA rule be adopted? Should other defects in the O to A deed be treated similarly? What about, for example, O's infancy or incompetency? What if O's name is forged?

*Who is a "purchaser" covered by the recording statutes?* Many of the recording statutes protect only subsequent "purchasers" from the effect of an unrecorded deed. Under these acts, whether the first grantee from O is a purchaser is immaterial, but it is essential that the second grantee from O be a purchaser if he is to win.

> EXAMPLE 11: O gives Blackacre to A by ordinary deed, but A does not record. Thereafter O gives Blackacre to B by ordinary deed, and B records promptly. B has no notice of A's claim. A, not B, owns Blackacre, under most recording statutes.

---

[4] See Pedowitz, Uniform Simplification of Land Transfers Act—A Commentary, 13 Real Property, Probate and Trust Journal 696, 706 (1978).

EXAMPLE 12: O sells Blackacre to A, but A does not record. Thereafter, O sells Blackacre to B by ordinary deed, and B records promptly. B has no notice of A's claim. B, not A, owns Blackacre.

Most recording statutes do not define the term "purchaser." This leaves open certain questions. For example, does the payment of nominal consideration, such as $1.00, make one a purchaser? All courts hold that it does not. On the other hand, the second purchaser's claim should not be defeated merely because the first grantee shows that the second purchaser made a particularly good deal. Colorado is one of very few states that has dispensed with the "purchaser" requirement. See Colo.Rev.Stat. § 38–35–109.

*Discussion question.* Should the purchaser requirement be retained?

Most courts hold that a simple judgment lien creditor is not a "purchaser" within the meaning of the recording statute.

EXAMPLE 13: O mortgages Blackacre to A for $20,000, but A does not record the mortgage. Thereafter O purchases an automobile from B but fails to pay for it. B obtains a $20,000 judgment against O for the purchase price of the automobile, and properly files the judgment in the county where Blackacre is located, thus creating a lien against Blackacre for $20,000. Upon a sale of Blackacre for $16,000, who has prior claim on the $16,000, A or B? A has priority since B was not a "purchaser." The result can be justified by arguing that B probably did not extend credit to O in reliance on record title to Blackacre. Of course, if the recording statute, like that of North Carolina quoted earlier in this Assignment, expressly extends its protection to "lien creditors," B would win.

*Pre-existing debts.* There is a split of authority over whether a mortgage taken to secure a pre-existing debt should be considered one taken for value so as to constitute the mortgagee as a mortgagee "for value." The majority view seems to be that the mortgagee is giving value only if it formally extends the time for payment in consideration for receipt of the mortgage.

EXAMPLE 14: O mortgages to A, who does not record. Thereafter, O becomes indebted to B on January 2, with the debt due on September 1. On February 1, B becomes concerned about the safety of the debt and persuades O to execute a mortgage in favor of B, which B promptly records. By the majority view, A's mortgage has priority over B's mortgage if the recording statute merely protects "subsequent purchasers or mortgagees for value."

EXAMPLE 15: O mortgages to A, who does not record. Thereafter, O becomes indebted to B on January 2, with the debt due on September 1. On February 1, B agrees to extend the due date of the debt to December 1, in return for which she receives a mortgage of Blackacre to secure her debt. As between A and B, B would have priority, by the majority rule, under a recording statute that protects "subsequent purchasers or mortgagees for value."

*Discussion question.* Does the above distinction make sense? Who is "Without Notice" Within the Meaning of the Recording Statutes?

*Notice distinguished from knowledge.* One is deemed to have "notice" of facts, regardless of any lack of actual "knowledge" of them, when one should have known of them. The purchaser or mortgagee of Blackacre should search the records before parting with the purchase price or other consideration, and is charged with notice of everything that a competent searcher of those records would find. The purchaser is so charged with notice regardless of whether any search is actually made. Everyone with knowledge of a fact also has notice of it; not everyone charged with notice of a fact has knowledge of it. Perhaps it is helpful to think of "notice" as "constructive knowledge."

The standards of reasonableness and competency in searching can be exacting. The majority rule is that one is deemed to be on constructive notice of any document filed with the recording office regardless of whether it has not been entered into the records or indexed, or even if it is improperly indexed. There is a trend, though, to limit constructive knowledge only to those records that a reasonably diligent person could discover upon searching the records. The records of which a purchaser or mortgagee might be on notice can extend beyond title records to include documents that appear outside the chain of title, such as plats.[5] In addition, subsequent mortgagees, creditors, or purchasers may be held to have constructive notice of recorded title documents that have been defectively executed or acknowledged and would normally be void (due to their defects) except for the constructive notice that their recording imparts.[6]

*Types of notice.* Record notice has been described in the preceding paragraph. The recording statutes, however, usually refer only to "notice" as opposed to "record notice." Often the term "constructive notice" is used as a synonym for "record notice." The bare term "notice" includes off-record notice as well as record notice. Off-record notice is a slippery concept. One is charged with notice of facts that one should have known about from the physical condition of the premises or surrounding land, from documents that one should have read, or from inquiries that one should have made. What one "should have done" to ascertain the true facts concerning the title to a parcel of land, in addition to conducting a competent search of the official records, is not a question easily answered.

---

[5] O'Mara v. Town of Wappinger, 879 N.E.2d 148 (N.Y. 2007).

[6] See, e.g., Duffy v. Dwyer, 847 A.2d 266 (R.I. 2004); In re Williams, 584 S.E.2d 922 (W. Va. 2003); Murray, Defective Real Estate Documents: What Are the Consequences?, 42 Real Prop. Prob. & Tr. J. 367 (2007).

Most cases involving issues of off-record notice explore the inquiry that should be made of persons in possession concerning their rights in the land. This shall be discussed further later in the Assignment.

*Time of notice.* When the recording statute protects a purchaser, the fact that a purchaser has notice of a prior claim after the purchaser parts with consideration does not bar the purchaser's claim.

> EXAMPLE 16: O conveys to A who does not record. Thereafter O conveys to B, who promptly records. B is a purchaser who has no notice of A's claim before he pays the purchase price. However, before B records B learns of the previous conveyance to A. B owns Blackacre since at the relevant time B was a purchaser without notice.

*"Shelter" doctrine.* Once title vests in B by virtue of the recording statute, and B has recorded, a subsequent grantee of B will receive good title even if she is not a bona fide purchaser for value. This is a necessary corollary of the proposition that the owner of Blackacre by virtue of the recording statute has all the rights that any owner has.

> EXAMPLE 17: O grants Blackacre to A, who does not record. O then sells Blackacre to B, a bona fide purchaser for value without notice, who promptly records. B then starts to negotiate with C, to sell the property to C. Before the negotiations are completed, A informs C of the previous conveyance to A. A records. C then completes the sale anyway, and promptly records. As between A and C, C owns Blackacre despite the fact that she is not a purchaser for value without notice of A's previous conveyance. B's title "shelters" C. What Are the Advantages of a System of Registration of Titles as Compared to a System of Recordation of Instruments?

As we have just seen, the prevailing American system is one involving the recordation of the instruments of title. Under such a system, copies of deeds, mortgages and other instruments affecting title are kept in a government office for examination by interested parties, mainly prospective purchasers or mortgagees. The government office, however, does not determine the effect of these instruments and does not issue any certificate of title. The burden of finding the relevant documents and determining their effect rests entirely on the private parties involved.

To be contrasted with this system of *recordation of documents* is a system of *registration of titles.* Under the latter system, a certificate of title issued by the government conclusively establishes title. No one is required or allowed to go behind the certificate to reach different conclusions concerning title. An assurance fund indemnifies anyone injured by an error in the title registration process. The Torrens system of title adopts this basic approach. The system is named after Sir Robert Torrens, a non-lawyer, who instituted it in South Australia in 1857.

Before becoming the registrar of deeds in South Australia, Torrens had been a commissioner of customs. In his former position he had become familiar with the system of registering the ownership of ships. He adapted that system to land ownership and had the new system approved by Parliament. Torrens himself supervised the registration of more than 1,000 titles. While the failure to record an interest in a Torrens register will not protect a subsequent interest-holder who took his or her interest with *actual knowledge* of the prior interest,[7] constructive notice of a prior unregistered interest does not defeat the subsequent interest-holder.[8]

Although about thirty countries presently use a form of title registration, the Torrens system is in use in only a handful of jurisdictions in the United States, and in those states where it is used, it is purely optional.[9] The Torrens system remains relatively unpopular in the United States, presumably for three reasons. First, it was added to existing recording systems to create a set of dual systems, instead of replacing the traditional recording system entirely. This creates duplicative recording and records-maintenance burdens on title records offices. Second, the traditional recording system is more familiar to regular participants in the title record system, which has resulted in a preference for the familiar methods and a resistance to change. Third, a landowner seeking to place title in the Torrens system must institute an in rem judicial proceeding, which is both costly and time consuming. However, Minnesota has responded to this last barrier by adopting a simpler and faster system that allows uncontested landowners to obtain "certificates of possessory title" without instituting a judicial proceeding.[10]

### 3. Principal Cases: Problems of Notice

#### Jefferson County v. Mosley
Supreme Court of Alabama, 1969.
284 Ala. 593, 226 So.2d 652.

■ Lawson, Justice.

This is an appeal from a declaratory judgment rendered by the Circuit Court of Jefferson County following the filing by the plaintiff, Jefferson County, of its "Substituted Petition for Declaratory Judgment" and the filing of an "Answer to Substituted Petition for Declaratory

---

[7] See, e.g., In re Collier, 726 N.W.2d 799 (Minn. 2007).

[8] See, e.g., Commonwealth Electric Co. v. MacCardell, 876 N.E.2d 405 (Mass. 2007).

[9] Barnet, The Uniform Registered State Land and Adverse Possession Reform Act: A Proposal for Reform of the United States Real Property Law, 12 Buff. Envtl. L.J. 1, 19–20 (2004) (observing that 10 states—Colorado, Georgia, Hawaii, Massachusetts, Minnesota, North Carolina, Ohio, Virginia, Pennsylvania, and Washington—allow for the use of the Torrens system on a voluntary base "side by side" with traditional recording systems, but that the Torrens system has been used to a *substantial* degree in only three states: Hawaii, Massachusetts, and Minnesota).

[10] Minn. Stat. §§ 508A.01 to 508A.85.

Judgment" by M.C. Mosley, a single man; Earnie A. Peoples and wife, Edna M. Peoples; and George R. Self and wife, Margarette Self, which the defendants separately and severally prayed "be taken as a cross bill." Plaintiff made no response to the so-called "cross bill."

The ultimate question for decision is whether Jefferson County has a right-of-way over certain lands included in the description in separate warranty deeds executed by the defendant M.C. Mosley to the Peoples and to the Selfs.

The land described in the two aforementioned deeds is in the SW¼ of the SW¼ of Section 9, Township 17, Range 1 West, which will be referred to hereinafter as the government subdivision involved.

On October 18, 1945, Lester L. Dillard by warranty deed conveyed to Jefferson County a "right-of-way for public purposes" across lands situated in the government subdivision involved. The right of way is described as being eighty feet in width or forty feet on each side of a center line of a proposed road which is described by metes and bounds.

In September, 1949, the "Old Alton-Weems Road" where it traversed the government subdivision involved was widened, paved and otherwise improved. The pavement was twenty feet wide and the shoulders on each side of the record were widened to a distance of five feet, making the said road thirty feet wide after the improvements were made. In Paragraph 4 of the "Substituted Petition for Declaratory Judgment" it is alleged that "said road was built over and occupied a substantial portion of the right-of-way acquired by Jefferson County, Alabama under deed from Lester L. Dillard executed and delivered on October 18, 1945." Defendants' "Answer to Substituted Petition for Declaratory Judgment" admits all of the allegations of Paragraph 4 of that Petition.

Prior to the making of the improvements in September, 1949, the part of the "Old Alton-Weems Road" here involved had a gravel surface. Its width prior to September, 1949, is not shown and the exact amount of the eighty-foot right-of-way used in widening the "Old Alton-Weems Road" does not appear. Subsequent to 1949 the "Old Alton-Weems Road" was straightened, further widened and improved where it traversed the right-of-way conveyed by Dillard to Jefferson County in 1945, but such work was done subsequent to all transactions involved in this case.

On December 20, 1951, Lester L. Dillard and wife conveyed by warranty deed certain real property in the government subdivision involved to M.C. Mosley. The description in the deed includes the right-of-way conveyed by Lester L. Dillard to Jefferson County under the deed of October 18, 1945. The deed from Dillard to Mosley contains the following exception: "The property hereinabove described and conveyed is conveyed subject to all public roads, or easements and rights of way thereover." The "Old Alton-Weems Road" existed as a public road and was maintained by Jefferson County for more than twenty-five years prior to the date on which Dillard executed the deed to Mosley.

Paragraph 4 of the "Substituted Petition for Declaratory Judgment," which is concerned with the improvement of the Alton-Weems Road in September, 1949, concludes as follows: "Plaintiff further avers that on December 20, 1951, the date of the deed from Lester L. Dillard and wife, Betty Lawson Dillard, to M.C. Mosley, said road was situated and maintained as set out above and in such manner as to be plainly visible." As before indicated, the averments of said Paragraph 4 were admitted in the defendants' "Answer to Substituted Petition for Declaratory Judgment."

The right-of-way deed from Lester L. Dillard to Jefferson County under date of October 18, 1945, was not recorded in the office of the Judge of Probate of Jefferson County until April 2, 1952, which was subsequent to the execution of the deed from Lester L. Dillard to M.C. Mosley. The last-mentioned deed was recorded in the office of the Judge of Probate of Jefferson County on January 14, 1952.

On May 26, 1952, M.C. Mosley conveyed by warranty deed certain real property in the government subdivision involved to Earnie A. Peoples and Edna M. Peoples. The description in the deed includes a part of the right-of-way conveyed by Lester L. Dillard to Jefferson County under the deed of October 18, 1945. It was recorded in the office of the Judge of Probate of Jefferson County on July 7, 1952. The deed from Mosley to the Peoples contains the following exception: "The property hereinabove described and is conveyed subject to all public roads, easements, and right-of-ways thereover."

By warranty deed dated June 26, 1953, and corrected in so far as the description is concerned by warranty deed dated December 27, 1958, M.C. Mosley conveyed to George R. Self and wife, Margarette Self, certain real property in the government subdivision involved. The description of said real property (as corrected) includes a part of the right-of-way conveyed by Lester L. Dillard to Jefferson County under the deed of October 18, 1945. The deed from Mosley to the Selfs dated June 26, 1953, was recorded in the office of the Judge of Probate of Jefferson County on June 26, 1953, and the deed correcting the description was recorded in that office on December 29, 1958. These deeds do not contain any exceptions as to public roads, easements or rights-of-way.

The trial court rendered a judgment which in pertinent parts reads:

That the defendant M.C. Mosley, did not have notice, either actual, constructive or implied, of sufficient facts to put him upon inquiry of the execution of the right-of-way deed executed on October 18, 1945, by Lester L. Dillard in favor of Jefferson County, Alabama, or of the ownership, right, title, or claim of Jefferson County, Alabama as to the right-of-way described in said right-of-way deed; and therefore, that the defendants Earnie A. Peoples and wife, Edna M. Peoples, George R. Self and wife, Margarette Self, as purchasers from said Mosley, acquired the same title that said Mosley had acquired, regardless of the recordation of said right-of-way deed before said Mosley conveyed to said Peoples and wife, and said Self and wife.

From that judgment Jefferson County has appealed to this court.

In brief filed here on behalf of appellant, Jefferson County, it is said:

Jefferson County is entitled to a declaration that the Defendants had actual, constructive or implied notice of sufficient facts to apprise them of, or place them upon inquiry as to, the existence and extent of the County right-of-way. The Defendant Mosley had notice of the controverted right-of-way at the time of the execution of the deed from Dillard to him by (1) the existence for more than 20 years prior to that time of a County maintained public road traversing a portion of the property and right-of-way in question; and (2) because of the exception in the deed to him, viz. "The property hereinabove described and conveyed is conveyed subject to all public roads, all easements and rights-of-way thereover." A similar exception is contained within the deed from Mosley to the Defendants Peoples.

The case of the County against the Defendants Peoples and Self is stronger even than that against Mosley because the conveyances to them by Mosley were executed *after* recordation of the deed from Dillard to Jefferson County. At the time of the conveyance to the Defendants Peoples and Self, they had, in addition to actual notice of the right-of-way, constructive notice thereof by virtue of operation of Title 47, § 102, Code of Alabama, 1940, Recompiled 1958.

The last sentence quoted above is inaccurate if the words "in addition to actual notice of the right-of-way" contained in that sentence were used to convey the impression that the Selfs had actual notice of the right-of-way because of the exceptions in their deeds as to public roads, easements and rights-of-way. As we have pointed out above, the deeds from Mosley to the Selfs contained no such exceptions. As we view this case, the absence of such exceptions in the deeds from Mosley to the Selfs is of no consequence.

We will first consider the assertion of appellant to the effect that since its right-of-way deed was recorded prior to the time Mosley executed the deeds to the Peoples and to the Selfs, they had constructive notice of the rights of appellant by virtue of the provisions of § 102, Title 47, Code 1940, and hence the Peoples and the Selfs were not innocent purchasers for value without notice. Section 102, Title 47, supra, reads:

The recording in the proper office of any conveyance of property or other instrument which may be legally admitted to record, operates as a notice of the contents of such conveyance, or instrument, without any acknowledgment or probate thereof as required by law.

If appellant is correct in that assertion, a judgment by this court reversing the judgment of the trial court would necessarily follow and we would not be called upon to consider the question as to whether Mosley was an innocent purchaser for value without notice of appellant's rights under the 1945 deed to it from Dillard. But we cannot agree with appellant's contention here under consideration.

Our case of Fenno v. Sayre, 3 Ala. 458, and that of Tennessee Coal, Iron & R. Co. v. Gardner, 131 Ala. 599, 32 So. 622, appear to hold to the contrary. The Peoples and Selfs claim title from Mosley and from him alone. In the case last cited above it was said: "The record of a deed from any other person than the grantor from whom title is claimed will not operate to give constructive notice to a subsequent grantee."

In American Law of Property, Vol. IV, § 17.21, the rule is stated thusly:

> If after the recording of a deed from an owner there is later recorded another deed from the same grantor to a different grantee, whether earlier or later in date, a purchaser from the first grantee is without notice of any rights of the second grantee unless it is by reason of some fact other than the record; the purchaser's obligation to examine the grantor's indices as to that grantor ceased at the date of the recording of the first deed....

See Hawley v. McCabe, 117 Conn. 558, 169 A. 192.

We hold, therefore, that the recordation of the 1945 deed from Dillard to Jefferson County, after the recordation of the deed from Dillard to Mosley, did not by virtue of the provisions of § 102, Title 47, Code 1940, operate as notice to the Peoples and to the Selfs of the contents of the 1945 deed from Dillard to Jefferson County.

If Mosley was an innocent purchaser for value without notice of his grantor's right-of-way deed to Jefferson County, the title which he conveyed to the Peoples and to the Selfs would pass to them unaffected even by any notice which they themselves might have had.

In Vol. 3, Pomeroy's Equity Jurisprudence, 5th Ed., § 754a, it is said:

> [I]f a second purchaser with notice acquires title from a first purchaser who was without notice and *bona fide,* he succeeds to all the rights of his immediate grantor. In fact, when land thus comes, freed from equities, into the hands of the *bona fide* purchaser, he obtains a complete *jus disponendi,* with the exception last above mentioned, and may transfer a perfect title even to volunteers....

The exception to that rule is that such a title cannot be conveyed, free from prior equities, back to a former owner who was charged with notice.

So the question is presented as to whether the record before us shows that Mosley was an innocent purchaser for value without notice of the appellant's [Jefferson County's] rights under the deed executed to Jefferson County in 1945 by Dillard.

Appellant says that he was not.

As far as the record discloses, Mosley at the time he secured his deed from Dillard did not have actual knowledge of the deed executed by Dillard to Jefferson County in 1945. He was not charged with the constructive notice provided by § 102, Title 47, Code 1940, because Jefferson County did not record its deed until after Mosley secured his deed and after it was recorded.

But it is well settled in this state that whatever is sufficient to excite attention and put the party on his guard and call for inquiry is notice of everything to which the inquiry would have led; that when a person has sufficient information to lead him to a fact, he shall be deemed conversant with it; that one who has knowledge of facts sufficient to put him on inquiry as to the existence of an unrecorded deed is not a purchaser without notice within the protection of the registry statutes.

It has been said that it is difficult, if not impossible, to lay down any general rule as to what facts will in every case be sufficient to charge a party with notice or put him on inquiry. Veitch v. Woodward Iron Co., 200 Ala. 358, 76 So. 124.

In Wittmeir v. Leonard, supra, we said:

[T]he purchaser is chargeable with notice of that which appears on the face of the conveyances in the chain of his title, but he is not bound to inquire into collateral circumstances. Attorney Gen. v. Blackhouse, 17 Vesey 282. One who has knowledge of facts sufficient to put him on inquiry as to the existence of an unrecorded mortgage is not a purchaser without notice under registration statutes. Gamble v. Black Warrior Coal Co., supra. In construing conveyances, "each word is presumed to have been used for some purpose, and deemed to have some force and effect."

Cases from other states hereafter cited are authority for the proposition that a person is charged with notice of the contents of the instrument by which he takes title and of all the facts which would be disclosed with a reasonably diligent search.

It is difficult to understand how Mosley could have read the deed and not have seen the exception clause. Whether he saw it or not, he is presumed to have knowledge of it and the consequences are the same in either case.

So far as the record discloses, Mosley made no effort to ascertain whether, in fact, there were any public roads, easements or rights-of-way across the land described in the deed from Dillard to him prior to the present controversy. After the controversy arose, apparently he had no trouble in ascertaining such information, as is evidenced by the map or drawing which is in the record.

It seems to us that a reasonably prudent man who obtained a deed containing an exception such as was included in the deed from Dillard to Mosley would have made inquiry from his grantor as to why such an exception was included. If such an inquiry had been made, Mosley would no doubt have been advised of the right-of-way deed executed by Dillard to Jefferson County in 1945.

The defendants in their answer admitted that the improvements made on the old Alton-Weems Road in 1949 were "built over and occupied a substantial portion of the right-of-way acquired by Jefferson County, Alabama, under deed from Lester L. Dillard executed and delivered on October 18, 1945." The defendants in their answer further admitted that at the time Dillard executed the deed to Mosley "said road was situated and maintained as set out above and in such a manner as to be plainly visible."

The existence of this road at the time Mosley secured his deed from Dillard was open and notorious and its presence was such notice as to put Mosley on inquiry and the notice was not confined to that part of the right-of-way used as a road or highway, but extended to the lands described in the deed from Dillard to Jefferson County.

The established rules of law may operate harshly in this case, but they are well established and we have no alternative but to apply the law as it is.

In conclusion, we hold that Mosley was not a bona fide purchaser for value without notice of Jefferson County's easement. His title was subject to that easement. He could convey to the Peoples and to the Selfs no better title than he possessed.

It follows that the judgment of the trial court is reversed and the cause is remanded.

Reversed and remanded.

## NOTES

1. *Conveying superior title.* The court states that Mosley could convey no better title than he had. Is this always true?

2. *Background.* Richard L. Jones, Esq., of Birmingham, Alabama, attorney for the appellee, writes:

> Professional pride prevents me from taking the full blame for the court's total misunderstanding of the legal principles announced in the opinion as they relate to the particular facts involved; and yet, I suspect that a degree of inadequacy on my part was involved.

The facts were interesting and relatively simple. Mr. Mosley purchased a plot of land traversed by an existing 30 foot wide roadway with which Mr. Mosley had been familiar for many years. Mr. Mosley's grantor had previously sold an 80 foot right-of-way across this property to Jefferson County, a political subdivision of the State, which deed remained unrecorded for several years and was, in fact, not recorded until after Mosley's purchase. I have sketched on the back of your letter, returned herewith, a rough plat showing the property purchased, the old meandering road, and the new 80 foot right-of-way. The old road followed generally the contours of the property and crossed the railroad at a grade crossing. The purpose of the newly acquired right-of-way was to construct an improved, straightened and widened highway across the high ground spanning the railroad track by an overpass. As shown by the sketch, the 80 foot right-of-way completely left the old road, and at the time of Mosley's purchase there were no right-of-way signs, stakes or other indications of its existence. Mr. Mosley's abstract of title, of course, showed no existing right-of-way other than the presence of the old road, which was revealed to him by observation; and, of course, the wording following the description in the deed " . . . subject to all public roads, easements, and right-of-ways thereover." Such phraseology following the description in a deed is common practice in our jurisdiction, and refers to those right-of-ways revealed by an abstract of title and those apparent upon inspection and observation of the premises, or those ascertainable upon reasonable inquiry.

Our Brief in Support of the Appellee's Application for Rehearing is enclosed, which we believe you will find of interest, and which states as best we know how our disagreement with the Court's opinion. The principles of law stated in the Court's opinion, as applied to the facts of this case, had the effect of exempting the County from the requirements of the recording statute; and it places upon the lawyer an insurmountable burden in advising his clients on land title which may in any way involve public unrecorded right-of-ways.

The Judge who wrote this opinion is a very dear friend of mine and is, indeed, one of my very favorite people. To his everlasting credit are such notables as Weldon, 267 Alabama 171, 100 So.2d 696; and his forceful dissent, which became the majority opinion on rehearing, in Acton, 283 Alabama 121, 214 So.2d 685 but even a good Judge is entitled to one bad decision now and then.

The sketch by Mr. Jones is roughly as follows.

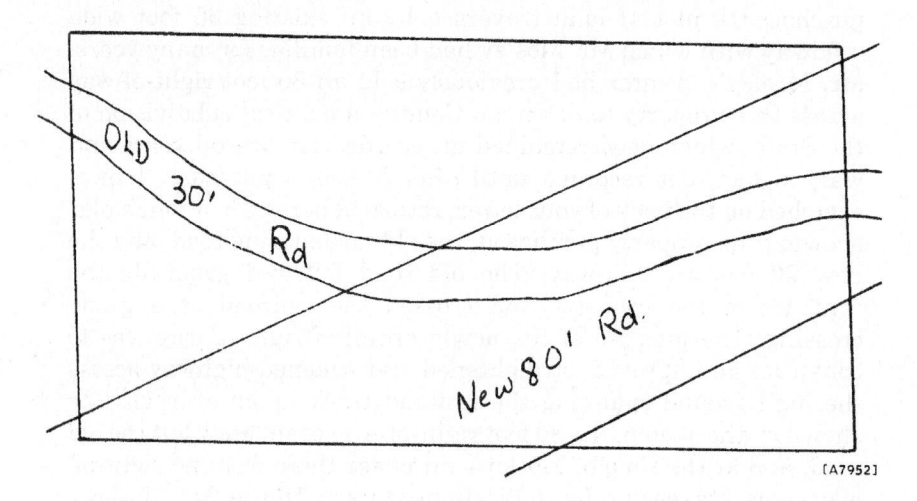

[Sketch showing a rectangular parcel with "Old 30' Rd" curving through the upper portion and "New 80' Rd" crossing through the lower portion.]

[A7952]

3. *Express exceptions for roads.* Would the case have been decided differently if the exception for public roads in the deed to Mosely had been omitted?

4. *Damage remedies.* What are the rights of the Peoples and the Selfs against Mosley? Do they differ? Do they have rights against Dillard?

## Martinique Realty Corp. v. Hull

Superior Court of New Jersey, Appellate Division, 1960.
64 N.J.Super. 599, 166 A.2d 803.

■ FREUND, J.A.D.

Plaintiff, the purchaser of a leasehold interest in a 55-apartment building in Passaic, commenced this suit against the tenants of one of the apartments for damages for the non-payment of rent allegedly due and owing under the terms of a five-year written lease. Defendants asserted the defense of payment, claiming that the entire rent for the term of the lease had been paid in advance to the former lessor, plaintiff's vendor, and that plaintiff purchased subject to all of defendants' rights as lessees. No basic facts being in issue, the Law Division granted defendants' motion for summary judgment on the ground that plaintiff was chargeable with notice of defendants' rights in and to the apartment, as created between defendants and plaintiff's assignor. Plaintiff files the instant appeal from that determination.

The apartment building in question was formerly owned by The Martinique, a New Jersey corporation. On August 5, 1957 the corporation entered into a five-year lease with defendants for a 1½ room apartment. The gross rental, including security deposit, was $8,450, the rent payable at the rate of $130 per month. Defendants immediately delivered to the landlord a check in the amount of $130, and on August 15, 1957, apparently in accordance with an oral arrangement, the entire rental balance was paid in advance by defendants in the form of a check for $8,320.

On or about October 22, 1957, at the lessor's suggestion, defendants agreed to exchange their apartment for a larger one in the same building. Since the rent on the larger apartment was $150 a month, it was agreed that defendants would make up the difference in annual installments of $240, besides providing additional security of $100. Accordingly, a new lease was executed; its terms ignore the prior advance payment and simply provide that rent will be paid to the landlord over a five-year term, commencing December 1, 1957 and terminating October 31, 1962, in the gross sum of $9,000, payable "in equal monthly installments of $150 in advance on the first day of each and every calendar month during said term." Both the additional security deposit of $100 and the sum of $240, covering the additional rental for the calendar year beginning December 1, 1957, were paid by check to the landlord. A letter dated October 23, 1957 was received by defendants from the lessor's agent, acknowledging the rent prepayment and the $240 annual payment arrangement. Defendants took possession of their new apartment in November 1957.

Subsequently, on December 16, 1957, The Martinique sold and conveyed title to the premises to Cambrian Estates, Inc., a New York Corporation, taking back, at the same time, a long-term lease covering the apartment building. On April 29, 1958 the leasehold interest of The Martinique was sold to the present plaintiff, a separate and distinct corporation. At the time of purchase, plaintiff caused an uneventful search to be made at the office of the Passaic County Clerk. (The Hulls did not record their lease until July 16, 1958.) It apparently relied upon its vendor's silence and its reading of paragraph 45(a) of the Martinique-Cambrian leaseback agreement of December 16, 1957, providing that "the lessee shall not without the prior written consent of the Lessor with respect to any lease now in existence or any renewal or extension thereof of any space demised to any tenant, accept prepayment of rent in excess of one month prior to its due date."

In May of 1958 plaintiff mailed rent statements to all of its tenants. Defendants, having learned for the first time that ownership of the leasehold had changed hands, refused to tender any rent by reason of their prepayment.

Plaintiff's contention on this appeal is two-fold. It argues, first, that as the transferee of the leasehold interest, it was entitled to the benefit of all of the covenants between its predecessor and the Hulls. Secondly, it urges that it had a right to rely upon the terms of defendants' lease as written, and that the prepayment of rent is therefore no bar as such prepayment was inconsistent with the terms of the lease; further, that it had no notice, at the time of purchase, of defendants' advance payments, and that it was not, under the principle of Feld v. Kantrowitz, 98 N.J.Eq. 167, 130 A. 6 (Ch.1925), affirmed 99 N.J.Eq. 847, 132 A. 657 (E. & A. 1926), and 99 N.J.Eq. 706, 134 A. 920 (Ch.1926), required to make inquiry of each tenant as to the latter's interest in the property outside of the written lease. Defendants respond by questioning the applicability of the Feld case, arguing that plaintiff was under a duty to make inquiry respecting the rights of lessees under their tenancies and that failure to make such inquiry charges plaintiff with notice of such rights. They further contend that the payment of rent by a tenant to his landlord in advance of the time stipulated in the lease for its payment is a discharge *pro tanto* from the claim of the lessor, and therefore a valid defense against the assignee of the lessor's interest.

Plaintiff is confronted at the outset by the specific statutory provision that the rights of a lessee of real estate for a term of years *vis-à-vis* his lessor survive the passing of the lessor's interest to another by assignment or otherwise. R.S. 46:8–3, N.J.S.A.; 51 C.J.S. Landlord and Tenant § 44(2), p. 567. This is but an illustration of the general rule that the assignee of a contract right takes subject to all defenses valid against his assignor. N.J.S. 2A:25–1, N.J.S.A. While it may be contended that the applicability of these sections is limited by the penalties inherent in our recording act, R.S. 46:22–1 et seq., N.J.S.A., embracing leases for a term exceeding two years, N.J.S.A. 46:16–1(a), the statute requires, however, that the prevailing purchaser be *bona fide* in nature.

An essential characteristic of the *bona fide* purchaser is his lack of notice of the interest of the unrecorded or late-recorded party. It is long settled that the purchaser of a lessor's interest in property has a duty to make inquiry as to the extent of the rights of any person in open, notorious and exclusive possession of the premises; if this duty is not discharged, then notice is imputed to the purchaser of all facts which a reasonably prudent inquiry would have revealed. Such inquiry must be made of the tenant in possession, and if inquiry is made only of the former lessor, the tenant will not be precluded from asserting against the purchaser such rights as he possessed against the lessor.

Moreover, it has been held, in a situation strikingly parallel to the one at hand, that the duty of inquiry is not discharged when an intending purchaser of a leasehold merely examines the written lease which the occupant has signed with the owner of record. The purchaser assumes at his peril that the instrument accurately defines the rights of the occupant. Caplan v. Palace Realty Co., N.J., 110 A. 584 (Ch.1920). Vice-Chancellor Leaming stated unequivocally in the latter case that

> If the purchaser is content to rely upon the representations of the landlord, either express or implied, to the effect that the writing contains ... an accurate statement of the terms actually agreed upon, and fails to inquire of the tenant touching those facts ... the purchaser's rights as against the tenant can rise no higher than those which were in fact enjoyed by the landlord under that instrument, and any right of reformation of the instrument for fraud or mistake which the tenant may have

enjoyed against the landlord may in like manner be enjoyed against the purchaser. (110 A., at p. 585).

Plaintiff contends, however, that the duty of inquiry has been severely restricted, if not eliminated entirely, in cases involving a multi-tenanted office or apartment building. Reliance is placed exclusively on the opinions in Feld v. Kantrowitz, supra. There, an attorney, a tenant in a small office building, claimed that he had acquired, under an unrecorded assignment, an option to purchase a one-sixth interest in the building. The defendant, who had entered into a contract to purchase the entire property without notice of plaintiff's option and without making inquiry of the tenant, claimed status as a *bona fide* purchaser and asserted that defendant's unrecorded option was extinguished. The vice-chancellor took cognizance of the doctrine of inquiry notice but held that it did not apply to the situation before him. He reasoned that since an office building or apartment house is constructed for the very purpose of creating numerous tenancies, a purchaser should be able to assume that the occupants of the offices or apartments possess the designated status of tenants. Therefore, he concluded, "under these circumstances, to charge a prospective purchaser with notice of any right, title, or interest of one of the tenants, beyond the right of tenancy, would be absurd." 98 N.J.Eq., supra, at p. 169, 130 A., at p. 7. He further discussed the rule that to put the purchaser on inquiry notice, the tenant must be in exclusive possession, and concluded that the interest of one of numerous tenants of a large building does not satisfy the exclusivity requirement. The vice-chancellor's decision was affirmed on the sole ground that he had applied the proper procedural principles in denying plaintiff a preliminary injunction; the Court of Errors and Appeals expressly disclaimed any examination of the merits of the litigation. 99 N.J.Eq. 847, 849, 132 A. 657, (E. & A. 1926). Subsequently, the cause came on for final hearing, at which time the vice-chancellor reiterated his position, further stating that Caplan v. Palace Realty Co., supra, "does not, so far as my reading of the opinion reveals, refer in any way to the constructive notice arising from tenancy in a building such as the one involved in the case at bar."

The precise holding in Feld would seem to be clearly distinguishable from the instant fact situation in that defendants are not herein asserting any interest "beyond the right of tenancy," that is, beyond a demand for recognition of the precise terms of their tenancy. To apply Feld to the instant situation would be to contravene the general rule that possession and occupancy of the premises by the tenant amount to notice of his advance payment of rent, and that such prepayment—honestly made, and in the absence of special circumstances putting the tenant on notice that he is prejudicing the rights of third parties—will protect the tenant against further liability for such rent to the landlord and all successors to his interest.

On the other hand, we cannot in all candor overlook indications in the language of Feld broad enough to encompass the instant case, namely: (1) the vice-chancellor's statement (98 N.J.Eq., supra, at p. 172, 130 A., at p. 8), that he might decide differently if "dealing with the right of a tenant as such, even in this kind of a building, *that appears in his lease.*" (Emphasis added.) Evidence of the prepayment of the Hulls did not, as we have noted, appear in their lease; and (2) the attempt to distinguish the Caplan case on the ground that a multi-tenanted building was not there involved, leaving the implication that the purchaser of such a building can justifiably rely exclusively on the tenants' leases as written.

We must therefore consider, to the extent it bears on the present appeal, the question which we left open in Schnakenberg v. Gibraltar Savings and Loan Ass'n, 37 N.J.Super. 150, 158 (App.Div.1955): "Whether the rights of a tenant in possession and the duties of a purchaser of realty vary with the size and character of the building...."

At least with respect to the details of a tenant's leasehold arrangement with his landlord, we are convinced that the purchaser's duty of inquiry does not vary with the number of tenants occupying the property. The arguments advanced in favor of such a correspondence are of dubious validity. Inquiry notice is an equitable doctrine designed to effect a distribution of precautionary burdens in a situation involving two "innocent" parties. American Law of Property, § 17.11, pp. 565–66. We see little merit in plaintiff's insistence that it would be exceedingly onerous to require inquiry of every tenant in a multi-tenanted building. The statement in Feld, 98 N.J.Eq., supra, at p. 169, 130 A., at p. 7, that it "would be absurd" to hold that "one contemplating the purchase of one of the great office buildings in the metropolitan district would be under a duty to personally interview every one of the hundreds of tenants occupying the offices thereof" ignores the very practical and effective device of the written communication. The duty to inquire is discharged by the exercise of due diligence or reasonable prudence, see Clawans v. Ordway B. & L. Ass'n, 112 N.J.Eq. 280, 284, 164 A. 267 (E. & A. 1933), and what such an inquiry fails to reveal is not further protected by the mere continued possession of the tenant. 4 American Law of Property, § 17.12, p. 576. Under certain circumstances, written inquiry may be sufficient to discharge that duty.

We need not dwell upon the statement in Feld that no single occupant of a multi-tenanted building is in such exclusive possession as to warrant the invoking of the purchaser's duty of inquiry. For the period of his lease, the lessee is considered the exclusive owner and occupier of the demised premises. That the demised premises consist of one apartment rather than an entire building should not be of consequence. This is not a situation involving the interests of the various family occupants of a single house. Each apartment in the building under consideration is an entirely separate habitational unit, evidenced by a separate landlord-tenant arrangement.

We expressly refrain from a determination as to whether a purchaser's duty of inquiry extends to collateral interests of the lessee which are independent of his tenancy. We note, however, that the majority rule appears to extend the inquiry notice doctrine to cover certain collateral interests of the lessee, such as an option to purchase, see Annotations, 17 A.L.R.2d 331 (1951), 37 A.L.R.2d 1112 (1954), though perhaps not a claim of ownership of the fee.

In any event, plaintiff, having failed to fulfill its duty of inquiry with respect to defendants' rights under their tenancy, is subject to the prior effective discharge by the latter of their rental obligations.

Judgment affirmed.

## Gates Rubber Co. v. Ulman
#### Court of Appeal, Second District, 1989.
#### 214 Cal.App.3d 356, review denied (1990).

■ GEORGE, ASSOCIATE JUSTICE.

Appellant Gates Rubber Company appeals from a judgment which denied appellant specific performance of an unrecorded option agreement giving it the right to purchase certain property in the 20th year of a 25-year lease of that property from a predecessor-in-interest of Charles Ulman. The term of the lease commenced in 1963. Charles Ulman purchased the property in 1969. Appellant attempted to exercise the option in 1983. Respondents Harry Ulman and his wife Gisela Ulman are co-trustees of the testamentary trust established under the will of the late Charles Ulman, Harry Ulman's father.

Appellant contends (1) its possession of the property created a duty of inquiry as to all its rights in the subject property, including its option to purchase, and Charles Ulman's failure to investigate precludes his having the status of a bona fide purchaser without notice; (2) appellant's possession was inconsistent with "record title," even if that term is construed to include a lessee's recorded leasehold interest in the property. For the reasons that follow, we affirm the judgment.

On March 18, 1963, appellant's subsidiary, Gates Rubber Company Sales Division, Inc. (Gates Sales Division), leased from Louis Lesser Enterprises, Inc. (Louis Lesser) three acres of land located on Randolph Street in the City of Commerce, California. The written lease provided for a term of 20 years, from January 1, 1964, through December 31, 1983. The lease was a "triple net lease," which required appellant to pay the taxes, insurance, utilities, and other costs involved in maintaining the property. The lease granted Gates Sales Division four successive 5-year options to extend the term. On two occasions the lease was amended to increase the rent to its final amount of $4,132.50 per month. The lease made no reference to an option agreement for the purchase of the property, a written agreement which had been entered into by the same parties on the same date as the original lease. Neither the lease nor the written option agreement ever was recorded.

The written option agreement entered into by Gates Sales Division and Louis Lesser on March 18, 1963, as subsequently amended July 29, 1963, provided that Gates Sales Division had the right to purchase the property for $721,029 during the sixth year of the lease term, and a second option to purchase the property for $550,687 during the 20th year of the lease term.

At the time they entered into the aforementioned lease and option agreements on March 18, 1963, Gates Sales Division and Louis Lesser additionally executed a short-form lease. This short form did not contain all the material terms of the lease but merely designated Louis Lesser as lessor and Gates Sales Division as lessee, identified the property and specified the length of the term, stated that the consideration was one dollar plus other valuable consideration, recited that Gates Sales Division had leased the premises from Louis Lesser "upon and subject to the terms, covenants, conditions and agreements more particularly set forth in a certain lease between Lessor and Lessee bearing even [sic] date herewith," and stated the referenced lease was the sole agreement of lease between the parties. This document made no reference to the agreement providing an option to purchase. The short form lease was recorded on September 6, 1963. With the consent of Louis Lesser, on August 1, 1963, Gates Sales Division assigned its entire interest in both the lease and the option agreement to its parent company, appellant, but neither assignment was recorded.

The terms of the lease required Louis Lesser to construct an 80,000 square-foot office and warehouse building according to the lessee's specifications. Pursuant to this provision, Louis Lesser obtained construction financing in the amount of a $525,000 loan maturing on January 15, 1984, and completed construction of the building in December 1963.

Appellant entered into possession of the premises on January 1, 1964, and has occupied the property continuously since that date. During this period of possession, appellant has operated a warehouse and distribution center on the property for its rubber products. Appellant has made all rental payments required by the lease and has paid all taxes, insurance, and costs of repairs and maintenance. It was stipulated by the parties that appellant at all pertinent times has been in open and continuous possession of the property.

On December 27, 1966, Louis Lesser conveyed the property to United California Bank, which in turn conveyed it to Massachusetts Mutual Life Insurance Company in January 1968. In December 1968, the latter conveyed it to Western Orbis Company, a company owned by Louis Lesser. Several days later, Western Orbis Company conveyed the property to Fulton Investment Company. The escrow agreement and recorded grant deed from Western Orbis Company to Fulton Investment Company did not contain any reference to the option to purchase. The attorney for Fulton Investment Company possessed a copy of the option agreement in his office files. William Malat, an officer of Western Orbis Company, testified at a deposition he was certain he had advised Fulton of the option to purchase.

In November 1965, November 1966, and December 1967, appellant provided written "tenant offset" statements at the request of potential purchasers or lenders. In these documents, appellant stated the lease was not in default and claimed there were no offsets against rent. Appellant also noted in each document that it possessed an option to purchase the property.

On November 6, 1969, Fulton Investment Company conveyed the property to Charles Ulman for $633,163.25. Benton Cole was a real estate agent who represented Charles Ulman during the purchase of the property. Prior to the purchase, he provided Ulman with a written description of the property, including the lease and options to renew, but this document did not contain any reference to the option to purchase. The preliminary title report and eventual policy of insurance prepared for Charles Ulman by the title insurance company referred to the short form lease and to the unrecorded lease, but not to the option agreement for the purchase of the property.[11] A "credit statement" prepared by Dun & Bradstreet setting forth a financial profile of appellant made no reference to the option agreement. The escrow instructions and grant deed for this conveyance did not refer to the option agreement. The grant deed was recorded on November 6, 1969. Fulton Investment Company assigned the lease to Ulman and identified the lessee as Gates Rubber Company. Appellant also was identified in the escrow instructions.

Appellant did not receive any request for a tenant offset statement or any inquiry from Charles Ulman regarding appellant's rights before Ulman purchased the property, although it was customary for a purchaser to request such a statement. Appellant first received notice of Ulman's purchase on November 21, 1969, when Ulman sent appellant a letter requesting that future rent payments be made to him, and enclosing a copy of the assignment of lease.

Charles Ulman died on March 2, 1982, and in May of that year Harry Ulman was appointed special administrator and executor of Charles Ulman's estate, which included the property at issue. Pursuant to the terms of the option agreement, on August 29, 1983, appellant notified Harry Ulman in writing of appellant's exercise of the option to purchase the property for $550,687 and delivered to him the down payment of

---

[11] The title insurance policy also contained a disclaimer providing that the policy did not insure against loss or damage by reason of "Any . . . rights, interest, or claims which are not shown by the public records but which could be ascertained by an inspection of said land or by making inquiry of persons in possession thereof."

$55,068.70 required by the agreement. On September 15, 1983, Harry Ulman returned appellant's check uncashed and notified appellant that respondents would not comply with the option agreement or convey the property to appellant, asserting there was no evidence Charles Ulman was aware of the option when he purchased the property in 1969.

Harry Ulman declared he did not find any copy of the option agreement in his father's files pertaining to the property and prior to August 1983 had no notice of the existence of the option. Respondents' appraisal of the property estimated its worth at $2 million in 1983, apart from the leasehold interest. In an order filed by respondents in 1986 in connection with settling the estate of Charles Ulman, the value of the property was described as $525,000.

On November 1, 1983, appellant commenced the present action, seeking specific performance of the option agreement, declaratory relief, and damages. Respondents cross-complained for declaratory relief. The case was submitted to the trial court on the basis of stipulations relating to certain facts and documents.

In September 1988 the court issued a statement of decision in favor of respondents, finding appellant's possession of the property was open, notorious, exclusive, and visible at the time Charles Ulman purchased, but that this circumstance was insufficient to put Ulman on inquiry or to charge him with constructive notice of the unrecorded option agreement, because appellant's possession was "entirely consistent with both the recorded title and the recorded lease."

Appellant contends its open, continuous, exclusive possession of the premises, which was inconsistent with the vendor's record title, gave Charles Ulman constructive notice of the option agreement to purchase; and Ulman's failure to investigate precluded his being a bona fide purchaser.

Civil Code section 1214 provides in relevant part: "Every conveyance of real property, other than a lease for a term not exceeding one year, is void as against any subsequent purchaser or mortgagee of the same property, . . . in good faith and for a valuable consideration, whose conveyance is first duly recorded, and as against any judgment affecting the title, unless such conveyance shall have been duly recorded prior to the record of notice of action." The act of recording creates a conclusive presumption that a subsequent purchaser has constructive notice of the contents of the previously recorded document. (Civ.Code, § 1213; 2 Miller & Starr, Current Law of Cal. Real Estate (1977) Recording and Priorities, § 11:4, p. 11.)

In the present transaction, neither the lease nor the option-to-purchase agreement ever was recorded. The lease did not refer to the option agreement. (The short-form lease, which referred to the lease as being the exclusive agreement *of lease* between the parties but did not refer to the option agreement, was recorded in 1963.) Respondents' grant deed was recorded in 1969. Therefore, in order for appellant to prevail, Charles Ulman must be determined not to have been a bona fide purchaser.

"The elements of bona fide purchase are payment of value, in good faith, and *without actual or constructive notice of another's rights.* [Citation.]" (4 Witkin, Summary of Cal. Law (9th ed. 1987) Real Property, § 206, p. 411, emphasis added.) "The absence of notice is an essential requirement in order that one may be regarded as a bona fide purchaser." (*Basch v. Tidewater etc. Co.* (1942) 49 Cal.App.2d Supp. 743, 746, 121 P.2d 545.)

Civil Code section 1217 provides: "An unrecorded instrument is valid as between the parties thereto and those who have notice thereof." "[S]ince recordation is not essential to legal recognition of a property interest, but only affects its priority as against subsequent bona fide purchasers, an unrecorded option may be a valid property right. [Citations.]" (*Claremont Terrace Homeowners' Assn. v. United States* (1983) 146 Cal.App.3d 398, 408, 194 Cal.Rptr. 216.)[12] "Even though the prior instrument is unrecorded, and there is therefore no constructive notice from the record, a subsequent purchaser may nevertheless have *actual knowledge* or *constructive notice* of it, and if so will not be a bona fide purchaser." (4 Witkin, Summary of Cal. Law, *supra,* § 209, p. 412, emphasis in original.)[13]

The question arises whether an intending purchaser must inquire as to any rights a tenant might have by virtue of unrecorded documents where that tenant's possession is consistent with a recorded lease. We hold that where a tenant's possession is consistent with the terms of a recorded lease which does not refer to an additional unrecorded option to purchase, and there are no circumstances indicating the tenant has additional rights, the purchaser does not have a duty to inquire of the tenant as to any other rights the tenant may possess.

The constructive notice imparted by the recording of a document has been extended to charge an intending purchaser with a duty to investigate the rights afforded by an unrecorded document *referred to* in that recorded document.

An implication to be drawn from the foregoing authority is that where there is no such reference, the purchaser may rely on the recorded documents. "Clearly, a subsequent bona fide purchaser or encumbrancer is not bound by off-record agreements not referenced in the recorded

---

[12] An unexercised option to purchase contained in a lease is a covenant running with the land. (Claremont Terrace Homeowners' Assn. v. United States, supra. 146 Cal.App.3d 398, 406, 194 Cal.Rptr. 216.) "Subsequent purchasers of property subject to an option who take with notice of its existence take subject to the right of the optionee to complete the purchase. [Citation.]" (*Ibid.*)

[13] Civil Code section 19 provides: "Every person who has actual notice of circumstances sufficient to put a prudent man upon inquiry as to a particular fact, has constructive notice of the fact itself in all cases in which, by prosecuting such inquiry, he might have learned such fact."

documents...." (2 Miller & Starr, Current Law of Cal.Real Estate (*supra,* 1987 Supp.) § 11.4, p. 5, fn. 16.)

In the present case, because the recorded short-form lease referred merely to the unrecorded long-form lease, of which Charles Ulman already had actual notice, and which did not itself refer to the option agreement, satisfaction of the duty to investigate appellant's rights pursuant to the long-form lease still would not have given Charles Ulman notice of the option to purchase.

Nonetheless, under certain circumstances notice to a subsequent purchaser of a prior interest may be implied from mere possession of the property; therefore, we next examine whether notice of the unrecorded option may be implied from appellant's possession. Possession of property by someone other than the vendor provides notice to an intending purchaser sufficient to put him on inquiry as to the rights, title, and interest of the occupant (*Claremont Terrace Homeowners' Assn. v. United States, supra,* 146 Cal.App.3d 398, 408, 194 Cal.Rptr. 216; *Basch v. Tide Water etc. Co., supra,* 49 Cal.App.2d Supp. 743, 748, 121 P.2d 545), "unless under the peculiar circumstances of the case there is no duty to make inquiry." (*Three Sixty Five Club v. Shostak* (1951) 104 Cal.App.2d 735, 738, 232 P.2d 546.) The circumstances of each case dictate whether an inquiry should be made, a determination which ordinarily involves a question of fact. (*Ibid.*)

" 'The possession required to impart notice to a subsequent purchaser must be open, notorious, exclusive and visible, and *not consistent with the record title.*' [Citation.]" (*Claremont Terrace Homeowners' Assn. v. United States, supra,* 146 Cal.App.3d 398, 408, 194 Cal.Rptr. 216, emphasis added; 4 Witkin, Summary of Cal.Law, *supra,* § 209, pp. 412–413.). Such possession is not in itself notice but merely is evidence tending to prove notice, sufficient to put the purchaser on inquiry, and inquiry " 'does not become a duty when the apparent possession is consistent with the title appearing of record.' [Citation.]" (*Schumacher v. Truman* (1901) 134 Cal. 430, 432, 66 P. 591).[14]

The great majority of the cases defining possession inconsistent with recorded title are concerned with the purchaser's notice of the tenant's rights pursuant to an unrecorded lease, easement, or deed, which rights are to some degree obvious and visible due to the nature of the tenant's

---

[14] If a tenant is in possession of leased premises, and the circumstances are such as to put a purchaser on inquiry, the purchaser is charged with knowledge of all those facts a reasonably diligent inquiry would have disclosed. (Claremont Terrace Homeowners' Assn. v. United States, supra, 146 Cal.App.3d 398, 408, 194 Cal.Rptr. 216; Basch v. Tide Water etc. Co., supra, 49 Cal.App.2d Supp. 743, 748, 121 P.2d 545.) "Possession is notice not only of whatever title the occupant has but also of whatever right he may have in the property, and the knowledge chargeable to a person after he is put on inquiry by possession of land is not limited to such knowledge as would be gained by examination of the public records." (Claremont Terrace Homeowners' Assn. v. United States, supra, 146 Cal.App.3d 398, 409, 194 Cal.Rptr. 216.) Possession of land imparts to the intending purchaser "such knowledge as would be gained by inquiry from the one having such possession. [Citation.]" (Marlenee v. Brown (1943) 21 Cal.2d 668, 676, 134 P.2d 770.)

possession, and not with any unapparent rights the tenant might possess apart from those provided in a recorded lease.

It is clear that possession by a tenant gives notice of an option to purchase *contained* in an unrecorded lease. Thus, in *Claremont Terrace Homeowners' Assn. v. United States, supra,* 146 Cal.App.3d 398, 194 Cal.Rptr. 216, the appellant was charged with knowledge of an option to purchase contained in a lease, because the respondent optionee was in possession of the premises and paid the monthly amount due on the trust deed as well as the property taxes. (*Id.,* at p. 409, 194 Cal.Rptr. 216.) The appellant's notice of the option in that case may be ascribed to the respondent's possession, which imputed notice of the lease containing the option, *and* the respondent's payment of expenses of the property consistent with ownership. Similarly, in various other jurisdictions, possession by a tenant has been held to give notice of an option contained in an unrecorded lease.

Several commentators appear to take the position that the circumstance of a tenant's possession may charge an intending purchaser with a duty to investigate not only the tenant's rights pursuant to an unrecorded lease but, additionally, the extent of a tenant's interests recognized in other unrecorded and unreferenced agreements with the lessor. In 2 Miller & Starr, Current Law of California Real Estate, *supra,* section 11:62, page 93, the authors comment: "The interest of a subsequent party *probably* is subject to the additional undocumented rights of the tenant since a purchaser or encumbrancer is required to investigate the rights of any person in possession of the premises and he has implied notice of any facts that would be disclosed by a reasonable investigation. [Fn. omitted.] An inquiry of the tenant probably would inform the purchaser of the additional rights of the tenant." (Emphasis in original.) Similarly, Witkin has observed: "a *lease* may contain special provisions, or the lessee may have special rights, under a separate agreement with the owner-lessor. Hence, (1) actual knowledge of an outstanding lease made by the vendor puts the purchaser on inquiry even though the lessee is not in possession; and (2) the purchaser must inquire not only as to rights under the lease but as to any other rights of the tenant, including those under a collateral agreement. [Citations.]" (4 Witkin, Summary of Cal.Law, *supra,* § 210, p. 414, emphasis in original.). . . .

In the present case, there was nothing apparent from appellant's possession that would give notice of rights other than those contained in the recorded short-form lease, which in turn referred to the long-form lease. Neither the short-form lease nor the long-form lease provided notice of the option to purchase. The original lessor had constructed a building on appellant's behalf, but that construction was required by the terms of the lease. The additional option to purchase possessed by appellant did not confer a right to modify the existing lease, but instead granted rights wholly different from those created by the lease.

Appellant asserts that if we do not impute notice to Charles Ulman of the option, even though appellant's interest was partially recorded the courts will be affording appellant less protection than appellant would have in the event its rights had not been recorded at all. As mentioned earlier, we do not decide what duty would arise had appellant's rights been completely recorded. We have determined that appellant's act of selectively and incompletely recording the documents evidencing its rights, especially where appellant acquired those rights simultaneously with other unrecorded rights, had the effect of lulling subsequent purchasers into the false impression they had been given notice of all of appellant's rights. The recording statutes were enacted for the purpose of establishing priorities among claims upon property and provide adequate means by which those with an interest in property may protect their rights. We decline to impose upon an intending purchaser a duty to inquire, of a tenant in possession of the property, as to all possible recorded and unrecorded rights which the tenant possesses in the property, where the tenant's possession is consistent with the documents of record.

For the foregoing reasons, we affirm the judgment of the trial court.

## NOTES

1. *Relative fault.* The court in *Martinique* states that "Inquiry notice is an equitable doctrine designed to effect a distribution of precautionary burdens in a situation involving two 'innocent' parties." The New Jersey recording statute covered leases for a term exceeding two years, according to the court. The Hulls' lease was for five years, but was not recorded until after the plaintiff purchased the property. The Hulls signed lease instruments that did not disclose their prepaying of the rent, and plaintiff relied on these instruments to its detriment. As between the Hulls and plaintiff, who is more at fault? If the Hulls were more at fault, why did they win?

2. *Collateral interests.* The court in *Martinique* "expressly refrain[s] from a determination as to whether a purchaser's duty of inquiry extends to collateral interests of the lessee which are independent of his tenancy." *Gates Rubber* apparently would not so extend the duty of inquiry. If a purchaser seeking to protect itself must inquire of a tenant in possession concerning the terms of the tenancy, is it a significantly greater burden to inquire of the tenant concerning other rights the tenant may have, such as an option to purchase? What are the countervailing arguments?

### Sabo v. Horvath
Supreme Court of Alaska, 1976.
559 P.2d 1038.

■ BOOCHEVER, CHIEF JUSTICE.

This appeal arises because Grover C. Lowery conveyed the same five-acre piece of land twice-first to William A. Horvath and Barbara J.

Horvath and later to William Sabo and Barbara Sabo. Both conveyances were by separate documents entitled "Quitclaim Deeds." Lowery's interest in the land originates in a patent from the United States Government under 43 U.S.C. § 687a (1970) ("Alaska Homesite Law"). Lowery's conveyance to the Horvaths was prior to the issuance of patent, and his subsequent conveyance to the Sabos was after the issuance of patent. The Horvaths recorded their deed in the Chitna Recording District on January 5, 1970; the Sabos recorded their deed on December 13, 1973. The transfer to the Horvaths, however, predated patent and title, and thus the Horvaths' interest in the land was recorded "outside the chain of title." Mr. Horvath brought suit to quiet title, and the Sabos counterclaimed to quiet their title.

In a memorandum opinion, the superior court ruled that Lowery had an equitable interest capable of transfer at the time of his conveyance to the Horvaths and further said the transfer contemplated more than a "mere quitclaim." It warranted patent would be transferred. The superior court also held that Horvath had the superior claim to the land because his prior recording had given the Sabos constructive notice for purposes of AS 34.15.290. The Sabos' appeal raises the following issues.

1. Under 43 U.S.C. § 687a (1970), when did Lowery obtain a present equitable interest in land which he could convey?

2. Are the Sabos, as grantees under a quitclaim deed, "subsequent innocent purchaser[s] in good faith"?

3. Is the Horvaths' first recorded interest, which is outside the chain of title, constructive notice to Sabo?

We affirm the trial court's ruling that Lowery had an interest to convey at the time of his conveyance to the Horvaths. We further hold that Sabo may be a "good faith purchaser" even though he takes by quitclaim deed. We reverse the trial court's ruling that Sabo had constructive notice and hold that a deed recorded outside the chain of title is a "wild deed" and does not give constructive notice under the recording laws of Alaska.[15]

The facts may be stated as follows. Grover C. Lowery occupied land in the Chitna Recording District on October 10, 1964 for purposes of obtaining Federal patent. Lowery filed a location notice on February 24, 1965, and made his application to purchase on June 6, 1967 with the Bureau of Land Management (BLM). On March 7, 1968, the BLM field examiner's report was filed which recommended that patent issue to Lowery. On October 7, 1969, a request for survey was made by the United States Government. On January 3, 1970, Lowery issued a document entitled "Quitclaim Deed" to the Horvaths; Horvath recorded the deed on January 5, 1970 in the Chitna Recording District. Horvath testified that

---

[15] Because we hold Lowery had a conveyable interest under the Federal statute, we need not decide issues raised by the parties regarding after-acquired property and the related issue of estoppel by deed.

when he bought the land from Lowery, he knew patent and title were still in the United States Government, but he did not rerecord his interest after patent had passed to Lowery.

Following the sale to the Horvaths, further action was taken by Lowery and the BLM pertaining to the application for patent and culminating in issuance of the patent on August 10, 1973.

Almost immediately after the patent was issued, Lowery advertised the land for sale in a newspaper. He then executed a second document also entitled "quitclaim" to the Sabos on October 15, 1973. The Sabos duly recorded this document on December 13, 1973.

Luther Moss, a representative of the BLM, testified to procedures followed under the Alaska Homesite Law [43 U.S.C. § 687a (1970)]. After numerous steps, a plat is approved and the claimant notified that he should direct publication of his claim. In this case, Lowery executed his conveyance to the Horvaths after the BLM field report had recommended patent.

The first question this court must consider is whether Lowery had an interest to convey at the time of his transfer to the Horvaths. Lowery's interest was obtained pursuant to patent law 43 U.S.C. § 687a (1970) commonly called the "Alaska Homesite Law". [The court holds "that at the time Lowery executed the deed to the Horvaths he had complied with the statute to a sufficient extent so as to have an interest in the land which was capable of conveyance."]

Since the Horvaths received a valid interest from Lowery, we must now resolve the conflict between the Horvaths' first recorded interest and the Sabos' later recorded interest.

The Sabos, like the Horvaths, received their interest in the property by a quitclaim deed. They are asserting that their interest supersedes the Horvaths under Alaska's statutory recording system. AS 34.15.290 provides that:

> A conveyance of real property . . . is void as against a subsequent innocent purchaser . . . for a valuable consideration of the property . . . whose conveyance is first duly recorded. An unrecorded instrument is valid . . . as against one who has actual notice of it.

Initially, we must decide whether the Sabos, who received their interest by means of a quitclaim deed, can ever be "innocent purchaser[s]" within the meaning of AS 34.15.290. Since a "quitclaim" only transfers the interest of the grantor, the question is whether a "quitclaim" deed itself puts a purchaser on constructive notice. Although the authorities are in conflict over this issue, the clear weight of authority is that a quitclaim grantee can be protected by the recording system, assuming, of course, the grantee purchased for valuable consideration and did not otherwise have actual or constructive knowledge as defined by the recording laws. We choose to follow the majority rule and hold that a quitclaim grantee is not precluded from attaining the status of an "innocent purchaser."

In this case, the Horvaths recorded their interest from Lowery prior to the time the Sabos recorded their interest. Thus, the issue is whether the Sabos are charged with constructive knowledge because of the Horvaths' prior recordation. Horvath is correct in his assertion that in the usual case a prior recorded deed serves as constructive notice pursuant to AS 34.15.290, and thus precludes a subsequent recordation from taking precedence. Here, however, the Sabos argue that because Horvath recorded his deed prior to Lowery having obtained patent, they were not given constructive notice by the recording system. They contend that since Horvaths' recordation was outside the chain of title, the recording should be regarded as a "wild deed".

It is an axiom of hornbook law that a purchaser has notice only of recorded instruments that are within his "chain of title." If a grantor (Lowery) transfers prior to obtaining title, and the grantee (Horvath) records prior to title passing, a second grantee who diligently examines all conveyances under the grantor's name from the date that the grantor had secured title would not discover the prior conveyance. The rule in most jurisdictions which have adopted a grantor-grantee index system of recording is that a "wild deed" does not serve as constructive notice to a subsequent purchaser who duly records.

Alaska's recording system utilizes a "grantor-grantee" index. Had Sabo searched title under both grantor's and grantee's names but limited his search to the chain of title subsequent to patent, he would not be chargeable with discovery of the pre-patent transfer to Horvath.

On one hand, we could require Sabo to check beyond the chain of title to look for pretitle conveyances. While in this particular case the burden may not have been great, as a general rule, requiring title checks beyond the chain of title could add a significant burden as well as uncertainty to real estate purchases. To a certain extent, requiring title searches of records prior to the date a grantor acquired title would thus defeat the purposes of the recording system. The records as to each grantor in the chain of title would theoretically have to be checked back to the later of the grantor's date of birth or the date when records were first retained.

On the other hand, we could require Horvath to rerecord his interest in the land once title passes, that is, after patent had issued to Lowery. As a general rule, rerecording an interest once title passes is less of a burden than requiring property purchasers to check indefinitely beyond the chain of title.

It is unfortunate that in this case due to Lowery's double conveyances, one or the other party to this suit must suffer an undeserved loss. We are cognizant that in this case, the equities are closely balanced between the parties to this appeal. Our decision, however, in addition to resolving the litigants' dispute, must delineate the requirements of Alaska's recording laws.

Because we want to promote simplicity and certainty in title transactions, we choose to follow the majority rule and hold that the Horvaths' deed, recorded outside the chain of title, does not give constructive notice to the Sabos and is not "duly recorded" under the Alaskan Recording Act, AS 34.15.290. Since the Sabos' interest is the first duly recorded interest and was recorded without actual or constructive knowledge of the prior deed, we hold that the Sabos' interest must prevail. The trial court's decision is accordingly.

Reversed.

## NOTES

1. *Estoppel by deed, deed recorded too early.* The reasoning in *Sabo* also applies in the context of the estoppel by deed doctrine. This doctrine provides that where one grants what he does not own, using a warranty deed, and thereafter acquires title, the title inures to the benefit of the grantee. However, if the grantor, after acquiring title, conveys to a subsequent purchaser for value without notice of the prior deed, the subsequent purchaser for value, under the majority rule, prevails over the first grantee, even if the first grantee recorded first. The subsequent purchaser has no record notice of the first recorded deed because it is outside the chain of title. See Johanson, Estoppel by Deed and the Recording System, 43 B.U.L.Rev. 441 (1963). In a jurisdiction using a tract index system, the estoppel by deed doctrine would prevail over the chain of title reasoning, and thus the prior grantee would prevail. This is because the burden on the later purchaser of discovering the earlier conveyance is very small since all grants affecting Blackacre would be indexed on a single page or group of pages. Note that in *Sabo*, the prior deed was a quitclaim deed. Thus, the estoppel by deed doctrine would not apply.

2. *Deed recorded too late and thus outside the chain of title.* It is possible for a valid deed from the actual and record owner to be outside the chain of title if it is recorded after a subsequent purchase of the same property.

> EXAMPLE: O conveys to A who does not record. Then O conveys to B, who promptly records. B is not a bona fide purchaser for value. Then A records. B then sells to C who pays full value and who has no actual notice of A's claim. C promptly records. There is a split of authority concerning whether C is charged with record notice of A's claim. Some jurisdictions hold that C should not be obliged to search in the grantor index under O's name for the period after the O-B conveyance is recorded. Other jurisdictions impose such an obligation on C. The jurisdictions are about evenly split on this issue.

Those cases holding that the tardily recorded deed of A is outside the record chain of title require the searcher to search for a deed from O only until a deed from O to B is recorded. The possibility that a prior deed to A may be recorded after the deed to B is recorded is considered too remote to impose an obligation on C to search for it. This is especially true when it is considered that normally B will be a bona fide purchaser for value without notice of A's claim. In such a case, A's deed would not bar C even if C had actual knowledge of it. Do you see why?

3. *Restriction on parcel A contained in grant of parcel B.* Buffalo Academy of the Sacred Heart v. Boehm Bros., Inc., 267 N.Y. 242, 196 N.E. 42 (1935):

> Grantor owned a large tract which it subdivided into many lots. It then conveyed four of them to the Kendall Refining Company. In that deed grantor covenanted that "he will not . . . permit . . . to be erected . . . any other gasoline . . . stations upon the entire tracts of land [retained by grantor]." The Kendall deed was recorded. Grantor then conveyed a lot to plaintiff who then contracted to convey marketable title to said lot to defendant. Defendant rejected a tender of the deed to the lot by plaintiff on the ground that the restriction prohibiting a gas station made title unmarketable. Held: for plaintiff. First, because the deed to Kendall did not expressly make the prohibition of gas stations on the remaining tract run to "assigns," it did not run with the land. Second, a restriction on parcel A contained in a grant of parcel B is outside the chain of title of parcel A, and hence plaintiff, not having actual or record notice of restrictions outside the chain of title, was not bound by them.

The chain of title reasoning was reaffirmed in Witter v. Taggart, 78 N.Y.2d 234, 577 N.E.2d 338 (1991).[16]

The opposite view was taken in Guillette v. Daly Dry Wall, Inc., 367 Mass. 355, 359, 325 N.E.2d 572, 575 (1975): "In such a [grantor-grantee index] system the purchaser cannot be safe if the title examiner ignores any deed given by a grantor in the chain of title during the time he owned the premises in question. . . . A search for such deeds is a task which is not at all impossible." Is "impossibility" the appropriate test? The cases are about evenly split between the *Buffalo Academy* and the *Guillette* viewpoint. *Discussion question:* Which is the better view?

4. *Computerized indices.* In most larger metropolitan areas, private title insurance or title abstracting companies maintain title information in specialized computer databases. Many documents that are outside the chain of title will be discovered by a computerized search. To the extent that such documents give actual knowledge to a prospective buyer or encumbrancer, such a person will be bound by their contents. If, however, actual knowledge does not exist, the chain of title reasoning, resting on the traditional indices, will be used.

---

[16] The court's decision is forcefully criticized in Kenneth Gartner, Witter v. Taggart and Ammirati v. Wire Forms, Inc.: The Potential Ramifications of New York's Newly Restrictive Definition of "Chain of Title" and Newly Expansive Definition of "Easement by Necessity", 4 Hofstra Prop. L.J. 165 (1992).

In many counties, the public records are partly computerized. Instead of manually searching unwieldy index volumes and deed books, the searcher can call up the appropriate indexes and deeds on a computer screen. But even in counties enjoying this convenience, the basic indexes are usually still grantor and grantee indexes, rather than tract indexes, and thus many of the old chain of title principles still apply. As previously discussed in this Assignment, however, this situation is likely to change with the growing use of electronically recorded documents.

## 4. REVIEW QUESTION ON RECORDING PROBLEMS

Adam was the owner of record of Wildacre, a ten-acre tract of vacant, unimproved land located just beyond the city limits of an expanding industrial city. On June 1, he entered into a valid executory contract with Baxter for the sale of Wildacre to Baxter. June 30 was the date specified in the contract for Adam to deliver to Baxter a warranty deed to Wildacre and for Baxter to pay Adam the purchase price of $45,000.

On June 15, Baxter, in consideration of the sum of $50,000 paid to him by Cramer, executed and delivered a warranty deed purporting to transfer Wildacre to Cramer. Cramer made no search of the records to determine who appeared as owner of record. However, Cramer immediately recorded his deed to Wildacre.

On June 30, Baxter paid Adam the agreed upon purchase price of $45,000, and Adam executed and delivered to Baxter his warranty deed to Wildacre. Baxter had it recorded immediately.

On July 15, Baxter, in consideration of $40,000 paid to him by Dawson, executed and delivered to Dawson a warranty deed to Wildacre. Dawson made no search of the records and had no knowledge of any of the prior transactions concerning the tract. Furthermore, Dawson misplaced the deed and never had it recorded.

In the jurisdiction where Wildacre is situated, the recording statute provides that unrecorded deeds are void as to subsequent purchasers who (1) are innocent and (2) have paid a valuable consideration.

The jurisdiction has and maintains both an alphabetical grantor-grantee index and a tract index. However, there has never been a decision as to which, if either, should take precedence over the other.

1. What, if any, were the legal and equitable interests of Adam, Baxter and Cramer in Wildacre as of June 2, June 16, and July 1?

2. In a contest between Cramer and Dawson as to the title to Wildacre, what arguments are each likely to assert and who should prevail?

(Derived from a California Bar Examination)

# ASSIGNMENT 50
# TITLE INSURANCE

## 1. INTRODUCTION

In most regions of the country, title insurance is routinely used when real estate is purchased or when loans are secured by real estate.[1] There are sound reasons for this.

*Insurance.* In major transactions, the insurance aspect of a title company's service is essential. In a transaction involving the construction of a multi-million dollar office building, both the lender and the developer need insurance against the possibility that the title to the land in which they are investing is not perfectly sound. As we have seen from previous Assignments, even a careful search may fail to reveal certain defects such as those arising from fraud, forgery, lack of delivery of deeds or mortgages, mis-indexed documents, or the unrecorded rights of persons in possession. These defects are ordinarily not discoverable merely by a search of the public records. In addition to defects that cannot be revealed by a careful search of the public records, the possibility of human error exists in searching records. Thus, the need for an insured opinion of title is evident. Of course, an insurance company does not have unlimited assets. In the case of a major project, the potential liability may exceed the assets of the title insurance company. In such cases, it is customary for the insurance company to reinsure its risk with other companies. The attorney for the lender or buyer should require documentation from the participating insurers showing that this was done properly.

In smaller transactions, such as the purchase of a single family residence, insurance also serves an essential function. Here, as in the larger transaction, the buyer can ill afford to lose her investment because of a faulty search of the records or because of a defect that the records fail to reveal. Although recovery against an uninsured title searcher might sometimes be feasible, this would ordinarily depend upon a showing of negligence, which in many cases would be difficult or impossible to establish. Another, more important, function is performed by title insurance involving single family houses. Although loans on the security of such property are usually financed by local lending institutions, it is common for the notes evidencing the loans to be sold to other financial institutions, including insurance companies or pension funds, or to be "packaged" to serve as security for mortgage backed securities sold to investors. The resale of notes and mortgages makes it

---

[1] Title insurance is not always used in parts of New England, a few southeastern states and some mid-western oil producing states. See Joyce D. Palomar, Title Insurance Law 1:3, p. 1–9 (2009); D. Barlow Burke, Law of Title Insurance 1.01[B], p. 1–11 (2006). In Iowa it is unlawful for title insurance to be sold within the state, Iowa Code Ann. 515.48(10) (2010), but alternative methods for assuring title exist.

possible to channel large sums into the real estate finance industry, thus promoting land development that would otherwise be unfeasible because of lack of funds. The sale and purchase of notes and mortgages takes place on the "secondary market." Title insurance permits the secondary mortgage market to flourish. Institutional and other investors are able to buy and sell notes and mortgages from distant localities secure in the knowledge that title has been insured by a reputable, nationally known title company.

*Title searches.* As you have seen from previous Assignments, searching title by using the official records is often time consuming and difficult. In rural counties, where the volume of records is small, the inefficient public indexes may be usable. In urban counties, the volume of transactions makes it impossible to rely entirely on the public records. The title companies must often develop their own private computerized indexes and records (the "title plant") to supplant the public records. It would be inefficient for each lawyer to attempt to develop his own plant. In some areas, the private plants are made available under an abstracting system, where an abstractor prepares an "abstract" of the pertinent records and sells the abstract to the lawyer examining title. In other areas, the title insurance company prepares its own abstract or chain of title. To be economic, much of the work has to be done by non-legal personnel who are paid less than lawyers but who can perform the relatively routine work more efficiently than lawyers because of their constant exposure to title searching problems. In some areas, such as Los Angeles, the title companies have joined together to establish a single computerized title plant.

*Services ancillary to insurance and searching.* Title companies often act as escrow agents, collecting and preparing the documents necessary for closing, and preparing the financial statements detailing the charges and credits to buyers and sellers. They may also run searches resembling title searches for specialized purposes. For example, a creditor may want to know if a debtor has any real property in the county and may ask a title company to make this determination. Similarly, a lender foreclosing a mortgage will want a list of all the parties having interests that will be affected by the foreclosure, so that they can be properly served with notice of the pending foreclosure. Also, a buyer searching for possible toxic contamination may order a chain of title report, which identifies previous owners. Certain types of previous owners, for example chemical companies, may suggest a higher likelihood of contamination.

*Types of policies.* Different companies are free to issue different types of policies, and, therefore, the first step to answering any title insurance question is to examine the pertinent policy. However, most policies are closely modelled after one of those promulgated by the American Land Title Association. ALTA has adopted six basic policies: (1) a lender's policy (2) an owner's policy (3) a lender's policy for leasehold lands, (4) a lessee's policy for leasehold lands, (5) a residential (plain language) policy (reprinted later in this Assignment) and (6) a construction loan policy. These policies are revised from time to time. In addition, ALTA has created standardized "endorsements" that can alter the policy to deal with recurring special situations, such as cases in which the real property is a condominium, a planned unit development or manufactured housing, or cases in which the insured wants assurance that the land is subject to a specified type of zoning.

Some buyers tend to avoid buying title insurance when their lender purchases it. They believe that since the lender is satisfied with the title, the buyer has no title worries. It is unwise for the buyer to rely on the fact that the lender has title insurance. Such insurance protects the lender from loss but does not protect the buyer. If lender insurance is being issued, as it almost always is, the cost to the buyer of obtaining owner's insurance is fairly modest and the buyer should obtain this additional coverage. Only one premium is paid for an owner's policy. This premium insures against loss caused by title defects for as long as the insured owns the property. In fact, if the insured suffers loss because of a defect discovered after she disposes of the property, she will be covered for this loss as well.

*The lawyer's role in working with title companies.* Title insurance does not remove title defects; it merely insures that if the defects exist the insurance company will indemnify the insured for the loss caused by them, subject to the limitations of the policy. Moreover, the insurance company will except from coverage any title defect that it has discovered in the course of searching title. Consequently, the lawyer for the prospective insured will frequently have to arrange for the removal of defects before the closing by obtaining quit-claim deeds or other agreements from parties who might claim an adverse interest in the property. If the defects cannot be removed, the lawyer must determine the seriousness of the title objections.

Often the lawyer will negotiate with the title company to obtain insurance from certain risks that the insurance company has initially excepted from coverage. Sometimes this is done by merely removing an express exception from the schedule of exceptions. This is not always the best procedure, however, since other portions of the policy may exclude from coverage any risk known to the insured, regardless of whether this risk is scheduled as an exception. An alternative method is to arrange that the insurer will affirmatively insure against certain known risks that might otherwise appear as exceptions. Sometimes the insurer may demand an additional premium for such special coverage. At other times, the insurer may provide such coverage without charge, in order to compete effectively with other insurers. It must be emphasized, however, that insuring against a risk is not equivalent to removing a risk, and the latter is the preferable approach, whenever it is feasible.

With respect to risks that are excepted from coverage, the lawyer must evaluate the nature and gravity of these exceptions and advise the client accordingly. The lawyer must also evaluate implicit limitations on coverage. For example, only the title to the property described in the policy is insured. If the description covers less than the parcel that the purchaser desires, the purchaser will be unprotected for the part extending beyond the description in the policy. Similarly, if the purchaser is also relying on access or other easements, or on the enforceability of covenants governing neighboring parcels, the lawyer must be satisfied that these matters are expressly covered in the policy.

## 2. PRINCIPAL PROBLEM

Your client, Bruce, is a wealthy individual who plans to purchase a single family house on a large tract of land. Ordinarily, a lender would lend most of the funds needed for the purchase and would secure the loan with a mortgage. The lender would insist on title insurance that insured its security interest in the property purchased. In this case, however, Bruce has decided to purchase the property out of his own funds. Therefore, he is not compelled to follow the procedures of any lender. He is reluctant to purchase title insurance. He claims that the seller is an honorable person who would not sell what she does not own. Bruce has compiled a list of risks that might exist and asks you to tell him how or if title insurance will protect him from these risks.

Assume that the customary form of title insurance available in your area is that reproduced below. Bruce's questions can and should be answered simply by referring to the precise terms of the policy. However, the cases following the policy might give you additional insights into the nature of title insurance.

Bruce's memo is as follows:

Dear Martha:

Please tell me whether the following risks would be covered if I purchase title insurance.

a. If one of the deeds in my chain of title is a forgery, or was signed by a minor or incompetent, how would this affect me?

b. Suppose there is a recorded easement, known to me but not listed in Schedule B as an Exception from Coverage. Would it change anything if the recorded easement were not known to me?

c. Suppose there is a prescriptive easement, known to me, in favor of a neighboring landowner. Would it change anything if the prescriptive easement were not known to me?

d. Suppose 1) there is an unrecorded grant of an easement to my neighbor, or 2) that a previous owner of my property has agreed with my neighbor that no two-story structure will be built on my land and that this agreement is not recorded. How would this affect my title?

e. Will I be protected from liens for unpaid real estate taxes? What about liens for improvement assessment bonds or mechanics' liens? What if the seller of the property that I plan to buy has permitted a judgment lien to be placed against the property?

f. Will the policy protect me if I am adversely affected by a zoning ordinance that exists before I purchase the property? Will it protect me from loss due to existing violations of building, housing, or zoning codes?

g. I was told that I am buying ten acres. If it turns out that the land is only six acres, will the insurance company pay me for my loss? I believe that the land to be conveyed includes a magnificent stand of trees near my boundary. If it turns out that the trees are on my neighbor's land will the insurance company compensate me for this?

h. In my opinion the property is now worth $800,000. Suppose I purchase title insurance for $800,000 and ten years from now the property is worth $2,000,000 and half of it is owned by someone else because of a title defect that existed at the time the policy was issued. Will I receive $1,000,000 from the insurance company?

i. Suppose that after purchasing the property I have difficulty selling it because of an apparent defect that the policy insures against but which disturbs many buyers? If the apparent defect is in fact non-existent, but does discourage buyers, will the insurance company pay me for this loss?

j. If the insurance company wrongfully refuses to indemnify me for a title defect and I receive a judgment against the company, will it have to pay my legal expenses?

k. I plan to build an additional structure on the land. If I am prohibited from doing so because of a declaration of covenants, conditions and restrictions referred to in Schedule B, am I entitled to reimbursement for my loss? What if I never received a copy of these restrictions despite the reference to them in Schedule B?

l. I am aware of a tank containing pesticides which may have leaked onto the property a few years ago. If the leak contaminated the land, will my policy cover clean up and removal costs?

SINCERELY,

BRUCE

Before answering Bruce's letter, consider the material below.

## 3. MATERIALS FOR SOLUTION OF PRINCIPAL PROBLEM

All publications of the American Land Title Association, including ALTA Policy Forms and ALTA Best Practices Resourses, are copyrighted and are reprinted herein by specific permission from:

American Land Title Association (ALTA)
1800 M Street
Suite 300 South
Washington, DC 20036
Phone: 202–296–3671
E-Mail: service@alta.org
Web: http://www.alta.org

American Land Title Association | Homeowner's Policy
Adopted 10-17-98
Revised 10-22-03 01-01-08 02-03-10 12-02-13

## HOMEOWNER'S POLICY OF TITLE INSURANCE
For a one-to-four family residence
Issued By
**BLANK TITLE INSURANCE COMPANY**

### OWNER'S INFORMATION SHEET

Your Title Insurance Policy is a legal contract between You and Us.

It applies only to a one-to-four family residence and only if each insured named in Schedule A is a Natural Person. If the Land described in Schedule A of the Policy is not an improved residential lot on which there is located a one-to-four family residence, or if each insured named in Schedule A is not a Natural Person, contact Us immediately.

The Policy insures You against actual loss resulting from certain Covered Risks. These Covered Risks are listed beginning on page ___ of the Policy. The Policy is limited by:

- Provisions of Schedule A
- Exceptions in Schedule B
- Our Duty To Defend Against Legal Actions On Page ___
- Exclusions on page ___
- Conditions on pages ___ and ___.

You should keep the Policy even if You transfer Your Title to the Land. It may protect against claims made against You by someone else after You transfer Your Title.

**IF YOU WANT TO MAKE A CLAIM, SEE SECTION 3 UNDER CONDITIONS ON PAGE ___.**

The premium for this Policy is paid once. No additional premium is owed for the Policy.

This sheet is not Your insurance Policy. It is only a brief outline of some of the important Policy features. The Policy explains in detail Your rights and obligations and Our rights and obligations. Since the Policy--and not this sheet--is the legal document,

**YOU SHOULD READ THE POLICY VERY CAREFULLY.**

If You have any questions about Your Policy, contact:

BLANK TITLE INSURANCE COMPANY

Copyright 2006-2013 American Land Title Association. All rights reserved.

The use of this Form is restricted to ALTA licensees and ALTA members in good standing as of the date of use. All other uses are prohibited.
Reprinted under license from the American Land Title Association.

**American Land Title Association**        Homeowner's Policy
Adopted 10-17-98
Revised 10-22-03 01-01-08 02-03-10 12-02-13

### HOMEOWNER'S POLICY OF TITLE INSURANCE
For a one-to-four family residence
Issued By
**BLANK TITLE INSURANCE COMPANY**

TABLE OF CONTENTS

| | PAGE |
|---|---|
| OWNER'S COVERAGE STATEMENT | — |
| COVERED RISKS | — |
| OUR DUTY TO DEFEND AGAINST LEGAL ACTIONS | — |
| EXCLUSIONS | — |
| CONDITIONS | |
|   1. Definitions | — |
|   2. Continuation of Coverage | — |
|   3. How to Make a Claim | — |
|   4. Our Choices When We Learn of a Claim | — |
|   5. Handling a Claim or Legal Action | — |
|   6. Limitation of Our Liability | — |
|   7. Transfer of Your Rights to Us | — |
|   8. This Policy is the Entire Contract | — |
|   9. Increased Policy Amount | — |
|   10. Severability | — |
|   11. Arbitration | — |
|   12. Choice of Law | — |
| SCHEDULE A | |
|   Policy Number, [Premium], Date [and Time] and Amount | |
|   Deductible Amounts and Maximum Dollar Limits of Liability | |
|   Street Address of the Land | |
|   1. Name of Insured | |
|   2. Interest in Land Covered | |
|   3. Description of the Land | |
| SCHEDULE B -- EXCEPTIONS | — |

Copyright 2006-2013 American Land Title Association. All rights reserved.

The use of this Form is restricted to ALTA licensees and ALTA members in good standing as of the date of use. All other uses are prohibited.
Reprinted under license from the American Land Title Association.

American Land Title Association　　　　　　　　　　　　　　　Homeowner's Policy
　　　　　　　　　　　　　　　　　　　　　　　　　　　　　　　　　　Adopted 10-17-98
　　　　　　　　　　　　　　　　　　　　　　Revised 10-22-03 01-01-08 02-03-10 12-02-13

## HOMEOWNER'S POLICY OF TITLE INSURANCE
### For a one-to-four family residence
### Issued By
### BLANK TITLE INSURANCE COMPANY

As soon as You Know of anything that might be covered by this Policy, You must notify Us promptly in writing at the address shown in Section 3 of the Conditions.

### OWNER'S COVERAGE STATEMENT

This Policy insures You against actual loss, including any costs, attorneys' fees and expenses provided under this Policy. The loss must result from one or more of the Covered Risks set forth below. This Policy covers only Land that is an improved residential lot on which there is located a one-to-four family residence and only when each Insured named in Schedule A is a Natural Person.

Your insurance is effective on the Policy Date. This Policy covers Your actual loss from any risk described under Covered Risks if the event creating the risk exists on the Policy Date or, to the extent expressly stated in Covered Risks, after the Policy Date.

Your insurance is limited by all of the following:

- The Policy Amount

- For Covered Risk 16, 18, 19 and 21, Your Deductible Amount and Our Maximum Dollar Limit of Liability shown in Schedule A

- The Exceptions in Schedule B

- Our Duty To Defend Against Legal Actions

- The Exclusions on page

- The Conditions on pages      and

### COVERED RISKS

The Covered Risks are:

1. Someone else owns an interest in Your Title.

2. Someone else has rights affecting Your Title because of leases, contracts, or options.

3. Someone else claims to have rights affecting Your Title because of forgery or impersonation.

4. Someone else has an Easement on the Land.

5. Someone else has a right to limit Your use of the Land.

Copyright 2006-2013 American Land Title Association. All rights reserved.

The use of this Form is restricted to ALTA licensees and ALTA members in good standing as of the date of use. All other uses are prohibited. Reprinted under license from the American Land Title Association.

**American Land Title Association**   Homeowner's Policy
Adopted 10-17-98
Revised 10-22-03 01-01-08 02-03-10 12-02-13

6. Your Title is defective. Some of these defects are:

   a. Someone else's failure to have authorized a transfer or conveyance of your Title.
   b. Someone else's failure to create a valid document by electronic means.
   c. A document upon which Your Title is based is invalid because it was not properly signed, sealed, acknowledged, delivered or recorded.
   d. A document upon which Your Title is based was signed using a falsified, expired, or otherwise invalid power of attorney.
   e. A document upon which Your Title is based was not properly filed, recorded, or indexed in the Public Records.
   f. A defective judicial or administrative proceeding.

7. Any of Covered Risks 1 through 6 occurring after the Policy Date.

8. Someone else has a lien on Your Title, including a:

   a. lien of real estate taxes or assessments imposed on Your Title by a governmental authority that are due or payable, but unpaid;
   b. Mortgage;
   c. judgment, state or federal tax lien;
   d. charge by a homeowner's or condominium association; or
   e. lien, occurring before or after the Policy Date, for labor and material furnished before the Policy Date.

9. Someone else has an encumbrance on Your Title.

10. Someone else claims to have rights affecting Your Title because of fraud, duress, incompetency or incapacity.

11. You do not have actual vehicular and pedestrian access to and from the Land, based upon a legal right.

12. You are forced to correct or remove an existing violation of any covenant, condition or restriction affecting the Land, even if the covenant, condition or restriction is excepted in Schedule B. However, You are not covered for any violation that relates to:

    a. any obligation to perform maintenance or repair on the Land; or
    b. environmental protection of any kind, including hazardous or toxic conditions or substances

    unless there is a notice recorded in the Public Records, describing any part of the Land, claiming a violation exists. Our liability for this Covered Risk is limited to the extent of the violation stated in that notice.

13. Your Title is lost or taken because of a violation of any covenant, condition or restriction, which occurred before You acquired Your Title, even if the covenant, condition or restriction is excepted in Schedule B.

Copyright 2006-2013 American Land Title Association. All rights reserved.

The use of this Form is restricted to ALTA licensees and ALTA members in good standing as of the date of use. All other uses are prohibited. Reprinted under license from the American Land Title Association.

**American Land Title Association**

**Homeowner's Policy**
**Adopted 10-17-98**
**Revised 10-22-03 01-01-08 02-03-10 12-02-13**

14. The violation or enforcement of those portions of any law or government regulation concerning:

    a. building;
    b. zoning;
    c. land use;
    d. improvements on the Land;
    e. land division; or
    f. environmental protection,

    if there is a notice recorded in the Public Records, describing any part of the Land, claiming a violation exists or declaring the intention to enforce the law or regulation. Our liability for this Covered Risk is limited to the extent of the violation or enforcement stated in that notice.

15. An enforcement action based on the exercise of a governmental police power not covered by Covered Risk 14 if there is a notice recorded in the Public Records, describing any part of the Land, of the enforcement action or intention to bring an enforcement action. Our liability for this Covered Risk is limited to the extent of the enforcement action stated in that notice.

16. Because of an existing violation of a subdivision law or regulation affecting the Land:

    a. You are unable to obtain a building permit;
    b. You are required to correct or remove the violation; or
    c. someone else has a legal right to, and does, refuse to perform a contract to purchase the Land, lease it or make a Mortgage loan on it.

    The amount of Your insurance for this Covered Risk is subject to Your Deductible Amount and Our Maximum Dollar Limit of Liability shown in Schedule A.

17. You lose Your Title to any part of the Land because of the right to take the Land by condemning it, if:

    a. there is a notice of the exercise of the right recorded in the Public Records and the notice describes any part of the Land; or
    b. the taking happened before the Policy Date and is binding on You if You bought the Land without Knowing of the taking.

18. You are forced to remove or remedy Your existing structures, or any part of them - other than boundary walls or fences - because any portion was built without obtaining a building permit from the proper government office. The amount of Your insurance for this Covered Risk is subject to Your Deductible Amount and Our Maximum Dollar Limit of Liability shown in Schedule A.

19. You are forced to remove or remedy Your existing structures, or any part of them, because they violate an existing zoning law or zoning regulation. If You are required to remedy any portion of Your existing structures, the amount of Your insurance for this Covered Risk is subject to Your Deductible Amount and Our Maximum Dollar Limit of Liability shown in Schedule A.

20. You cannot use the Land because use as a single-family residence violates an existing zoning law or zoning regulation.

21. You are forced to remove Your existing structures because they encroach onto Your neighbor's land. If the encroaching structures are boundary walls or fences, the amount of Your insurance for this Covered Risk is subject to Your Deductible Amount and Our Maximum Dollar

Copyright 2006-2013 American Land Title Association. All rights reserved.

The use of this Form is restricted to ALTA licensees and ALTA members in good standing as of the date of use. All other uses are prohibited.
Reprinted under license from the American Land Title Association.

**American Land Title Association**         Homeowner's Policy
Adopted 10-17-98
Revised 10-22-03 01-01-08 02-03-10 12-02-13

Limit of Liability shown in Schedule A.

22. Someone else has a legal right to, and does, refuse to perform a contract to purchase the Land, lease it or make a Mortgage loan on it because Your neighbor's existing structures encroach onto the Land.

23. You are forced to remove Your existing structures which encroach onto an Easement or over a building set-back line, even if the Easement or building set-back line is excepted in Schedule B.

24. Your existing structures are damaged because of the exercise of a right to maintain or use any Easement affecting the Land, even if the Easement is excepted in Schedule B.

25. Your existing improvements (or a replacement or modification made to them after the Policy Date), including lawns, shrubbery or trees, are damaged because of the future exercise of a right to use the surface of the Land for the extraction or development of minerals, water or any other substance, even if those rights are excepted or reserved from the description of the Land or excepted in Schedule B.

26. Someone else tries to enforce a discriminatory covenant, condition or restriction that they claim affects Your Title which is based upon race, color, religion, sex, handicap, familial status, or national origin.

27. A taxing authority assesses supplemental real estate taxes not previously assessed against the Land for any period before the Policy Date because of construction or a change of ownership or use that occurred before the Policy Date.

28. Your neighbor builds any structures after the Policy Date -- other than boundary walls or fences -- which encroach onto the Land.

29. Your Title is unmarketable, which allows someone else to refuse to perform a contract to purchase the Land, lease it or make a Mortgage loan on it.

30. Someone else owns an interest in Your Title because a court order invalidates a prior transfer of the title under federal bankruptcy, state insolvency, or similar creditors' rights laws.

31. The residence with the address shown in Schedule A is not located on the Land at the Policy Date.

32. The map, if any, attached to this Policy does not show the correct location of the Land according to the Public Records.

### OUR DUTY TO DEFEND AGAINST LEGAL ACTIONS

We will defend Your Title in any legal action only as to that part of the action which is based on a Covered Risk and which is not excepted or excluded from coverage in this Policy. We will pay the costs, attorneys' fees, and expenses We incur in that defense.

We will not pay for any part of the legal action which is not based on a Covered Risk or which is excepted or excluded from coverage in this Policy.

We can end Our duty to defend Your Title under Section 4 of the Conditions.

**THIS POLICY IS NOT COMPLETE WITHOUT SCHEDULES A AND B.**

Copyright 2006-2013 American Land Title Association. All rights reserved.

The use of this Form is restricted to ALTA licensees and ALTA members in good standing as of the date of use. All other uses are prohibited. Reprinted under license from the American Land Title Association.

**American Land Title Association**      Homeowner's Policy
Adopted 10-17-98
Revised 10-22-03 01-01-08 02-03-10 12-02-13

[Witness clause optional]

**BLANK TITLE INSURANCE COMPANY**

BY:_____
          PRESIDENT

BY:_____
          SECRETARY

Copyright 2006-2013 American Land Title Association. All rights reserved.

The use of this Form is restricted to ALTA licensees and ALTA members in good standing as of the date of use. All other uses are prohibited. Reprinted under license from the American Land Title Association.

**American Land Title Association**　　　　　　　　　　　**Homeowner's Policy**
　　　　　　　　　　　　　　　　　　　　　　　　　　　　　　　　　　　　　　　**Adopted 10-17-98**
　　　　　　　　　　　　　　　　　　　　　　**Revised 10-22-03 01-01-08 02-03-10 12-02-13**

## EXCLUSIONS

In addition to the Exceptions in Schedule B, You are not insured against loss, costs, attorneys' fees, and expenses resulting from:

1. Governmental police power, and the existence or violation of those portions of any law or government regulation concerning:

    a. building;
    b. zoning;
    c. land use;
    d. improvements on the Land;
    e. land division; and
    f. environmental protection.

    This Exclusion does not limit the coverage described in Covered Risk 8.a., 14, 15, 16, 18, 19, 20, 23 or 27.

2. The failure of Your existing structures, or any part of them, to be constructed in accordance with applicable building codes. This Exclusion does not limit the coverage described in Covered Risk 14 or 15.

3. The right to take the Land by condemning it. This Exclusion does not limit the coverage described in Covered Risk 17.

4. Risks:

    a. that are created, allowed, or agreed to by You, whether or not they are recorded in the Public Records;
    b. that are Known to You at the Policy Date, but not to Us, unless they are recorded in the Public Records at the Policy Date;
    c. that result in no loss to You; or
    d. that first occur after the Policy Date - this does not limit the coverage described in Covered Risk 7, 8.e., 25, 26, 27 or 28.

5. Failure to pay value for Your Title.

6. Lack of a right:

    a. to any land outside the area specifically described and referred to in paragraph 3 of Schedule A; and
    b. in streets, alleys, or waterways that touch the Land.

    This Exclusion does not limit the coverage described in Covered Risk 11 or 21.

7. The transfer of the Title to You is invalid as a preferential transfer or as a fraudulent transfer or conveyance under federal bankruptcy, state insolvency, or similar creditors' rights laws.

8. Contamination, explosion, fire, flooding, vibration, fracturing, earthquake or subsidence.

Copyright 2006-2013 American Land Title Association. All rights reserved.

The use of this Form is restricted to ALTA licensees and ALTA members in good standing as of the date of use. All other uses are prohibited.
Reprinted under license from the American Land Title Association.

**American Land Title Association**  **Homeowner's Policy**
Adopted 10-17-98
Revised 10-22-03 01-01-08 02-03-10 12-02-13

9. Negligence by a person or an Entity exercising a right to extract or develop minerals, water, or any other substances.

Copyright 2006-2013 American Land Title Association. All rights reserved.

The use of this Form is restricted to ALTA licensees and ALTA members in good standing as of the date of use. All other uses are prohibited. Reprinted under license from the American Land Title Association.

American Land Title Association  
Homeowner's Policy  
Adopted 10-17-98  
Revised 10-22-03 01-01-08 02-03-10 12-02-13

**HOMEOWNER'S POLICY OF TITLE INSURANCE**
For a one-to-four family residence
Issued By
**BLANK TITLE INSURANCE COMPANY**

CONDITIONS

1. DEFINITIONS

    a. <u>Easement</u> - the right of someone else to use the Land for a special purpose.

    b. <u>Estate Planning Entity</u> - a legal entity or Trust established by a Natural Person for estate planning.

    c. <u>Known</u> - things about which You have actual knowledge. The words "Know" and "Knowing" have the same meaning as Known.

    d. <u>Land</u> - the land or condominium unit described in paragraph 3 of Schedule A and any improvements on the Land which are real property.

    e. <u>Mortgage</u> - a mortgage, deed of trust, trust deed or other security instrument.

    f. <u>Natural Person</u> - a human being, not a commercial or legal organization or entity. Natural Person includes a trustee of a Trust even if the trustee is not a human being.

    g. <u>Policy Date</u> - the date and time shown in Schedule A. If the insured named in Schedule A first acquires the interest shown in Schedule A by an instrument recorded in the Public Records later than the date and time shown in Schedule A, the Policy Date is the date and time the instrument is recorded.

    h. <u>Public Records</u> - records that give constructive notice of matters affecting Your Title, according to the state statutes where the Land is located.

    i. <u>Title</u> - the ownership of Your interest in the Land, as shown in Schedule A.

    j. <u>Trust</u> - a living trust established by a Natural Person for estate planning.

    k. <u>We/Our/Us</u> - Blank Title Insurance Company.

    l. <u>You/Your</u> - the insured named in Schedule A and also those identified in Section 2.b. of these Conditions.

2. CONTINUATION OF COVERAGE

    a. This Policy insures You forever, even after You no longer have Your Title. You cannot assign this Policy to anyone else.

    b. This Policy also insures:

Copyright 2006-2013 American Land Title Association. All rights reserved.

The use of this Form is restricted to ALTA licensees and ALTA members in good standing as of the date of use. All other uses are prohibited. Reprinted under license from the American Land Title Association.

**American Land Title Association**                                 Homeowner's Policy
Adopted 10-17-98
Revised 10-22-03 01-01-08 02-03-10 12-02-13

    (1) anyone who inherits Your Title because of Your death;

    (2) Your spouse who receives Your Title because of dissolution of Your marriage;

    (3) the trustee or successor trustee of Your Trust or any Estate Planning Entity created for You to whom or to which You transfer Your Title after the Policy Date;

    (4) the beneficiaries of Your Trust upon Your death; or

    (5) anyone who receives Your Title by a transfer effective on Your death as authorized by law.

  c. We may assert against the insureds identified in Section 2.b. any rights and defenses that We have against any previous insured under this Policy.

3. HOW TO MAKE A CLAIM

  a. Prompt Notice Of Your Claim

    (1) As soon as You Know of anything that might be covered by this Policy, You must notify Us promptly in writing.

    (2) Send Your notice to **Blank Title Insurance Company**,            , Attention: Claims Department. Please include the Policy number shown in Schedule A, and the county and state where the Land is located. Please enclose a copy of Your policy, if available.

    (3) If You do not give Us prompt notice, Your coverage will be reduced or ended, but only to the extent Your failure affects Our ability to resolve the claim or defend You.

  b. Proof Of Your Loss

    (1) We may require You to give Us a written statement signed by You describing Your loss which includes:

      (a) the basis of Your claim;

      (b) the Covered Risks which resulted in Your loss;

      (c) the dollar amount of Your loss; and

      (d) the method You used to compute the amount of Your loss.

    (2) We may require You to make available to Us records, checks, letters, contracts, insurance policies and other papers which relate to Your claim. We may make copies of these papers.

    (3) We may require You to answer questions about Your claim under oath.

    (4) If you fail or refuse to give Us a statement of loss, answer Our questions under oath, or make available to Us the papers We request, Your coverage will be reduced or ended, but only to the extent Your failure or refusal affects Our ability to resolve the claim or defend You.

Copyright 2006-2013 American Land Title Association. All rights reserved.

The use of this Form is restricted to ALTA licensees and ALTA members in good standing as of the date of use. All other uses are prohibited.
Reprinted under license from the American Land Title Association.

**American Land Title Association**  
**Homeowner's Policy**  
Adopted 10-17-98  
Revised 10-22-03 01-01-08 02-03-10 12-02-13

4. OUR CHOICES WHEN WE LEARN OF A CLAIM

   a. After We receive Your notice, or otherwise learn, of a claim that is covered by this Policy, Our choices include one or more of the following:

      (1) Pay the claim;

      (2) Negotiate a settlement;

      (3) Bring or defend a legal action related to the claim;

      (4) Pay You the amount required by this Policy;

      (5) End the coverage of this Policy for the claim by paying You Your actual loss resulting from the Covered Risk, and those costs, attorneys' fees and expenses incurred up to that time which We are obligated to pay;

      (6) End the coverage described in Covered Risk 16, 18, 19 or 21 by paying You the amount of Your insurance then in force for the particular Covered Risk, and those costs, attorneys' fees and expenses incurred up to that time which We are obligated to pay;

      (7) End all coverage of this Policy by paying You the Policy Amount then in force, and those costs, attorneys' fees and expenses incurred up to that time which We are obligated to pay;

      (8) Take other appropriate action.

   b. When We choose the options in Sections 4.a. (5), (6) or (7), all Our obligations for the claim end, including Our obligation to defend, or continue to defend, any legal action.

   c. Even if We do not think that the Policy covers the claim, We may choose one or more of the options above. By doing so, We do not give up any rights.

5. HANDLING A CLAIM OR LEGAL ACTION

   a. You must cooperate with Us in handling any claim or legal action and give Us all relevant information.

   b. If You fail or refuse to cooperate with Us, Your coverage will be reduced or ended, but only to the extent Your failure or refusal affects Our ability to resolve the claim or defend You.

   c. We are required to repay You only for those settlement costs, attorneys' fees and expenses that We approve in advance.

   d. We have the right to choose the attorney when We bring or defend a legal action on Your behalf. We can appeal any decision to the highest level. We do not have to pay Your claim until the legal action is finally decided.

   e. Whether or not We agree there is coverage, We can bring or defend a legal action, or take other appropriate action under this Policy. By doing so, We do not give up any rights.

Copyright 2006-2013 American Land Title Association. All rights reserved.

The use of this Form is restricted to ALTA licensees and ALTA members in good standing as of the date of use. All other uses are prohibited. Reprinted under license from the American Land Title Association.

**American Land Title Association**                                                          **Homeowner's Policy**
                                                                                                           Adopted 10-17-98
                                             Revised 10-22-03 01-01-08 02-03-10 12-02-13

6. LIMITATION OF OUR LIABILITY

    a. After subtracting Your Deductible Amount if it applies, We will pay no more than the least of:

        (1) Your actual loss;

        (2) Our Maximum Dollar Limit of Liability then in force for the particular Covered Risk, for claims covered only under Covered Risk 16, 18, 19 or 21; or

        (3) the Policy Amount then in force.

        and any costs, attorneys' fees and expenses that We are obligated to pay under this Policy.

    b. If We pursue Our rights under Sections 4.a.(3) and 5.e. of these Conditions and are unsuccessful in establishing the Title, as insured:

        (1) the Policy Amount then in force will be increased by 10% of the Policy Amount shown in Schedule A; and

        (2) You shall have the right to have the actual loss determined on either the date the claim was made by You or the date it is settled and paid.

    c. (1) If We remove the cause of the claim with reasonable diligence after receiving notice of it, all Our obligations for the claim end, including any obligation for loss You had while We were removing the cause of the claim.

        (2) Regardless of 6.c.(1) above, if You cannot use the Land because of a claim covered by this Policy:

            (a) You may rent a reasonably equivalent substitute residence and We will repay You for the actual rent You pay, until the earlier of:

                (i) the cause of the claim is removed; or

                (ii) We pay You the amount required by this Policy. If Your claim is covered only under Covered Risk 16, 18, 19 or 21, that payment is the amount of Your insurance then in force for the particular Covered Risk.

            (b) We will pay reasonable costs You pay to relocate any personal property You have the right to remove from the Land, including transportation of that personal property for up to twenty-five (25) miles from the Land, and repair of any damage to that personal property because of the relocation. The amount We will pay You under this paragraph is limited to the value of the personal property before You relocate it.

    d. All payments We make under this Policy reduce the Policy Amount then in force, except for costs, attorneys' fees and expenses. All payments We make for claims which are covered only under Covered Risk 16, 18, 19 or 21 also reduce Our Maximum Dollar Limit of Liability for the particular Covered Risk, except for costs, attorneys' fees and expenses.

    e. If We issue, or have issued, a Policy to the owner of a Mortgage that is on Your Title and We have not given You any coverage against the Mortgage, then:

Copyright 2006-2013 American Land Title Association. All rights reserved.

The use of this Form is restricted to ALTA licensees and ALTA members in good standing as of the date of use. All other uses are prohibited. Reprinted under license from the American Land Title Association.

**American Land Title Association**             **Homeowner's Policy**
                                                                                **Adopted 10-17-98**
                           **Revised 10-22-03 01-01-08 02-03-10 12-02-13**

      (1) We have the right to pay any amount due You under this Policy to the owner of the Mortgage, and any amount paid shall be treated as a payment to You under this Policy, including under Section 4.a. of these Conditions;

      (2) Any amount paid to the owner of the Mortgage shall be subtracted from the Policy Amount then in force ; and

      (3) If Your claim is covered only under Covered Risk 16, 18, 19 or 21, any amount paid to the owner of the Mortgage shall also be subtracted from Our Maximum Dollar Limit of Liability for the particular Covered Risk.

  f. If You do anything to affect any right of recovery You may have against someone else, We can subtract from Our liability the amount by which You reduced the value of that right.

7. TRANSFER OF YOUR RIGHTS TO US

  a. When We settle Your claim, We have all the rights and remedies You have against any person or property related to the claim. You must not do anything to affect these rights and remedies. When We ask, You must execute documents to evidence the transfer to Us of these rights and remedies. You must let Us use Your name in enforcing these rights and remedies.

  b. We will not be liable to You if We do not pursue these rights and remedies or if We do not recover any amount that might be recoverable.

  c. We will pay any money We collect from enforcing these rights and remedies in the following order:

      (1) to Us for the costs, attorneys' fees and expenses We paid to enforce these rights and remedies;

      (2) to You for Your loss that You have not already collected;

      (3) to Us for any money We paid out under this Policy on account of Your claim; and

      (4) to You whatever is left.

  d. If You have rights and remedies under contracts (such as indemnities, guaranties, bonds or other policies of insurance) to recover all or part of Your loss, then We have all of those rights and remedies, even if those contracts provide that those obligated have all of Your rights and remedies under this Policy.

8. THIS POLICY IS THE ENTIRE CONTRACT

This Policy, with any endorsements, is the entire contract between You and Us. To determine the meaning of any part of this Policy, You must read the entire Policy and any endorsements. Any changes to this Policy must be agreed to in writing by Us. Any claim You make against Us must be made under this Policy and is subject to its terms.

---

Copyright 2006-2013 American Land Title Association. All rights reserved.

The use of this Form is restricted to ALTA licensees and ALTA members in good standing as of the date of use. All other uses are prohibited.
Reprinted under license from the American Land Title Association.

**American Land Title Association**  
**Homeowner's Policy**  
Adopted 10-17-98  
Revised 10-22-03 01-01-08 02-03-10 12-02-13

9. INCREASED POLICY AMOUNT

The Policy Amount then in force will increase by ten percent (10%) of the Policy Amount shown in Schedule A each year for the first five years following the Policy Date shown in Schedule A, up to one hundred fifty percent (150%) of the Policy Amount shown in Schedule A. The increase each year will happen on the anniversary of the Policy Date shown in Schedule A.

10. SEVERABILITY

If any part of this Policy is held to be legally unenforceable, both You and We can still enforce the rest of this Policy.

11. ARBITRATION

    a. If permitted in the state where the Land is located, You or We may demand arbitration.

    b. The law used in the arbitration is the law of the state where the Land is located.

    c. The arbitration shall be under the Title Insurance Arbitration Rules of the American Land Title Association ("Rules"). You can get a copy of the Rules from Us.

    d. Except as provided in the Rules, You cannot join or consolidate Your claim or controversy with claims or controversies of other persons.

    e. The arbitration shall be binding on both You and Us. The arbitration shall decide any matter in dispute between You and Us.

    f. The arbitration award may be entered as a judgment in the proper court.

12. CHOICE OF LAW

The law of the state where the Land is located shall apply to this policy.

Copyright 2006-2013 American Land Title Association. All rights reserved.

The use of this Form is restricted to ALTA licensees and ALTA members in good standing as of the date of use. All other uses are prohibited. Reprinted under license from the American Land Title Association.

**American Land Title Association**                                                                        **Homeowner's Policy**
                                                                                                                    **Adopted 10-17-98**
                                                  Revised 10-22-03 01-01-08 02-03-10 12-02-13

## HOMEOWNER'S POLICY OF TITLE INSURANCE

### For a one-to-four family residence

### Issued By

### BLANK TITLE INSURANCE COMPANY

### SCHEDULE A

Name and Address of Title Insurance Company:

Policy No.: [Premium: $_____] Policy Amount: $ Policy Date [and Time]:

Deductible Amounts and Maximum Dollar Limits of Liability
For Covered Risk 16, 18, 19 and 21:

|  | Your Deductible Amount | Our Maximum Dollar Limit of Liability |
|---|---|---|
| Covered Risk 16: | % of Policy Amount  Shown in Schedule A<br>or  $<br>(whichever is less) | $ |
| Covered Risk 18: | % of Policy Amount  Shown in Schedule A<br>or  $<br>(whichever is less) | $ |
| Covered Risk 19: | % of Policy Amount  Shown in Schedule A<br>or  $<br>(whichever is less) | $ |
| Covered Risk 21: | % of Policy Amount  Shown in Schedule A<br>or  $<br>(whichever is less) | $ |

Street Address of the Land:

    1. Name of Insured:

    2. Your interest in the Land covered by this Policy is:

    3. The Land referred to in this Policy is described as:

Copyright 2006-2013 American Land Title Association. All rights reserved.

The use of this Form is restricted to ALTA licensees and ALTA members in good standing as of the date of use. All other uses are prohibited. Reprinted under license from the American Land Title Association.

American Land Title Association

Homeowner's Policy
Adopted 10-17-98
Revised 10-22-03 01-01-08 02-03-10 12-02-13

HOMEOWNER'S POLICY OF TITLE INSURANCE
For a one-to-four family residence
Issued By
BLANK TITLE INSURANCE COMPANY

SCHEDULE B

EXCEPTIONS

In addition to the Exclusions, You are not insured against loss, costs, attorneys' fees, and expenses resulting from:

Copyright 2006-2013 American Land Title Association. All rights reserved.

The use of this Form is restricted to ALTA licensees and ALTA members in good standing as of the date of use. All other uses are prohibited. Reprinted under license from the American Land Title Association.

# Lick Mill Creek Apartments v. Chicago Title Ins. Co.

Court of Appeal, Sixth District, California, 1991.
231 Cal.App.3d 1654, 283 Cal.Rptr. 231.

■ AGLIANO, PRESIDING JUSTICE.

Plaintiffs Lick Mill Creek Apartments and Prometheus Development Company, Inc. appeal from a judgment of dismissal entered after the trial court sustained, without leave to amend, the demurrer of defendants Chicago Title Insurance Company and First American Title

Insurance Company to plaintiffs' first amended complaint. The trial court determined, based on undisputed facts alleged in the complaint, that title insurance policies issued by defendants did not provide coverage for the costs of removing hazardous substances from plaintiffs' property. For the reasons stated below, we conclude the trial court's ruling was correct and affirm the judgment.

The real property which is the subject of this case comprises approximately 30 acres of land near the Guadalupe River in Santa Clara County. Prior to 1979, various corporations operated warehouses and/or chemical processing plants on the property. Incident to this use of the property, the companies maintained underground tanks, pumps, and pipelines for the storage, handling, and disposal of various hazardous substances. These hazardous substances eventually contaminated the soil, subsoil, and groundwater.

In 1979, Kimball Small Investments 103 (KSI) purchased the property. Between 1979 and 1981, the California Department of Health Services ordered KSI to remedy the toxic contamination of the property. KSI, however, did not comply with this order.

In early October 1986, plaintiffs acquired lot 1 of the property from KSI. In connection with this acquisition, plaintiffs purchased title insurance from Chicago Title Insurance Company (Chicago Title). The insurance policy issued was of the type known as an American Land Title Insurance Association (ALTA) policy (policy 1). Prior to issuing this policy, Chicago Title commissioned a survey and inspection of the property by Carroll Resources Engineering & Management (Carroll Resources).

Plaintiffs subsequently purchased lots 2 and 3 from KSI and secured two additional ALTA policies (policies 2 and 3) from Chicago Title and First American Title Insurance Company (First American). The entire site was surveyed and inspected. During its survey and inspection, Carroll Resources noted the presence of certain pipes, tanks, pumps, and other improvements on the property. At the time each of the policies was issued, the Department of Health Services, the Regional Water Quality Control Board, and the Santa Clara County Environmental Health Department maintained records disclosing the presence of hazardous substances on the subject property.

Following their purchase of the property, plaintiffs incurred costs for removal and clean-up of the hazardous substances in order "to mitigate plaintiffs' damages and avoid costs of compliance with government mandate." Then, claiming their expenses were a substitute, i.e., a payment made under threat of compulsion of law, for restitution to the State Hazardous Substance Account (Health & Saf.Code, § 25300, et seq.) and "response costs" as defined under the Comprehensive Environmental Response, Compensation, and Liability Act (CERCLA) (42 U.S.C., § 9601, et seq.), plaintiffs sought indemnity from defendants for the sums expended in their cleanup efforts. Defendants, however, denied coverage.

## I. The Nature of Title Insurance

"Title insurance is an exclusively American invention. It involves the issuance of an insurance policy promising that if the state of the title is other than as represented on the face of the policy, and if the insured suffers loss as a result of the difference, the insurer will reimburse the insured for that loss and any related legal expenses, up to the face amount of the policy." (Burke, Law of Title Insurance (1986) § 1.1, p. 2.)

Pursuant to Insurance Code section 12340.1, " '[t]itle insurance' means insuring, guaranteeing or indemnifying owners of real or personal property or the holders of liens or encumbrances thereon or others interested therein against loss or damage suffered by reason of: (a) Liens or encumbrances on, or defects in title to said property; (b) Invalidity or unenforceability of any liens or encumbrances thereon; or (c) Incorrectness of searches relating to the title to real or personal property." Thus, under both the traditional concept and the statutory definition, title insurance covers matters affecting title.

Essentially two types of title insurance policies are available to owners of real property interests in California: California Land Title Association Standard Coverage (CLTA) policies and American Land Title Association (ALTA) policies. CLTA insures primarily against defects in title which are discoverable through an examination of the public record. Thus, a CLTA policy insures against loss incurred if the insured interest is not vested as shown in the policy; loss from defects in or liens or encumbrances on the title; unmarketability of title; and loss due to lack of access to an open street or highway under certain circumstances. A CLTA policy also covers a limited number of off-record risks. The ALTA policy, such as those purchased by plaintiffs here, provides greater coverage than the CLTA policy. Generally, it additionally insures against "off-record defects, liens, encumbrances, easements, and encroachments; rights of parties in possession or rights discoverable by inquiry of parties in possession, and not shown on the public records; water rights, mining claims, and patent reservations; and discrepancies or conflicts in boundary lines and shortages in areas that are not reflected in the public records." Since an ALTA policy covers many off-record defects in title, the insurer will typically survey the property to be insured.

## II. Construction of Language in Insurance Policies

The insuring clauses of an insurance policy define and limit coverage. Where a reviewing court is required to interpret an insurance policy without extrinsic evidence, the question is one of law. Any ambiguity arising from policy language should be resolved in favor of the insured. However, this rule of construction applies only when the policy language is unclear. " 'A policy provision is ambiguous when it is capable of two or more constructions, both of which are reasonable.' [Citation.]"

(Delgado v. Heritage Life Ins. Co. (1984) 157 Cal.App.3d 262, 271, 203 Cal.Rptr. 672.) Whether language in a contract is ambiguous is a question of law.

Here the insuring clauses of policies 1, 2, and 3 are identical and provide the following:

> SUBJECT TO THE EXCLUSIONS FROM COVERAGE, THE EXCEPTIONS CONTAINED IN SCHEDULE B AND THE PROVISIONS OF THE CONDITIONS AND STIPULATIONS HEREOF [the insurer] insures, as of Date of Policy shown in Schedule A, against loss or damage, not exceeding the amount of insurance stated in Schedule A, and costs, attorneys' fees and expenses which the Company may become obligated to pay hereunder, sustained or incurred by the insured by reason of: (1) Title to the estate or interest described in Schedule A being vested otherwise than as stated therein; (2) Any defect in or lien or encumbrance on such title; (3) Lack of a right of access to and from the land; or (4) Unmarketability of such title.

### III. Marketability of Title

Plaintiffs first contend the policies in the instant case expressly insured that title to the subject property was marketable and since the presence of hazardous substances on the property impaired its marketability, defendants were obliged to pay cleanup costs. Plaintiffs' position, however, is dependent upon their view that California courts have adopted a definition of marketable title that encompasses the property's market value. Our review of relevant authority establishes no support for this position.

In Mertens v. Berendsen (1931) 213 Cal. 111, 112, 1 P.2d 440, the plaintiff attempted to rescind a real estate purchase contract, claiming that the property encroached upon the street and rendered the title defective. In considering this issue, the court defined marketability of title as follows:

> Such a title must be free from reasonable doubt, and such that a reasonably prudent person, with full knowledge of the facts and their legal bearings, willing and anxious to perform his contract, would, in the exercise of that prudence which business men ordinarily bring to bear upon such transactions, be willing to accept and ought to accept. It must be so far free from defects as to enable the holder, not only to retain the land, but possess it in peace, and, if he wishes to sell it, to be reasonably sure that no flaw or doubt will arise to disturb its market value. But a mere suspicion against the title or a speculative possibility that a defect in it might appear in the future cannot be said to render a title unmarketable. It is not required to be free from mere shadows or possibilities, but from probabilities. Moral, not

mathematical, certainty that the title is good is all that is required.

Plaintiffs focus on the court's reference to the market value of the property. What plaintiffs ignore, however, is the fact that the court made this reference only in the context of examining an alleged defect in title. Mertens does not stand for the proposition that a defect in the physical condition of the land itself renders the title unmarketable.

The case of Hocking v. Title Ins. & Trust Co. (1951) 37 Cal.2d 644, 234 P.2d 625, further illustrates the distinction between marketability of title and marketability of the land. In Hocking, the plaintiff purchased unimproved property and received a grant deed, describing it as two lots in a particular block according to a recorded subdivision map. However, because the subdivider had not complied with various local ordinances regarding subdivision of land, the city would not issue building permits until the plaintiff complied with the ordinances. The plaintiff sought damages from the title insurer claiming defective title.

The Hocking court noted the distinction between the land and its title: "It is defendants' position that plaintiff confuses title with physical condition of the property she purchased and of the adjacent streets, and that 'One can hold perfect title to land that is valueless; one can have marketable title to land while the land itself is unmarketable.' The truth of this proposition would appear elementary. It appears to be the condition of her land in respect to improvements related thereto (graded and paved streets), rather than the condition of her title to the land, which is different from what she expected to get." (Id. at p. 651) Thus, the court held that the owner's inability to make economic use of the land due to the subdivider's violations of law did not render the title defective or unmarketable within the terms of the title insurance policy. "Although it is unfortunate that plaintiff has been unable to use her lots for the building purposes she contemplated, it is our view that the facts which she pleads do not affect the marketability of her title to the land, but merely impair the market value of the property. She appears to possess fee simple title to the property for whatever it may be worth; if she has been damaged by false representations in respect to the condition and value of the land her remedy would seem to be against others than the insurers of the title she acquired." (Id. at p. 652) Similarly, here plaintiffs have pled facts relating to marketability of the land rather than marketability of title.

Other jurisdictions have also recognized the distinction. In Chicago Title Ins. Co. v. Kumar (1987) 24 Mass.App.Ct. 53, 506 N.E.2d 154, 156, the defendant had purchased property on which hazardous substances were discovered. The defendant sought payment for cleanup costs from its title insurer. The insurer sought a declaration as to its obligations under the policy. The defendant owner filed a counterclaim, seeking a declaration that the presence of hazardous substances constituted a defect in title and the state's statutory power to impose a lien to secure payment of clean-up costs rendered his title unmarketable. Relying on Hocking v. Title Ins. & Trust Co., supra, 37 Cal.2d 644, 651, 234 P.2d 625, the court found in favor of the insurer, stating "the defendant confuses economic lack of marketability, which relates to physical conditions affecting the use of the property, with title marketability, which relates to defects affecting legally recognized rights and incidents of ownership.... The presence of hazardous material may affect the market value of the defendant's land, but, on the present record [since no lien had been recorded], it does not affect the title to the land." (Id. at p. 157.)

Plaintiffs attempt to distinguish *Kumar* on the ground that here they purchased ALTA policies while the defendant in *Kumar* purchased a CLTA policy. They point out an ALTA policy which required a physical inspection and survey of the property would have insured against off-record risks and potential liens not covered by a CLTA policy. While an ALTA policy provides greater coverage than a CLTA policy, it does not follow that an ALTA policy extends coverage to matters not affecting title. We must still examine the policy language for a determination of coverage. Here the policy insures against "unmarketability of title." The definition of this term is not dependent upon the type of title insurance policy in which it appears.

We find no ambiguity in the insuring clause: defendants are obligated to insure plaintiffs against unmarketability of title on the subject property. Because marketability of title and the market value of the land itself are separate and distinct, plaintiffs cannot claim coverage for the property's physical condition under this clause of the insurance policies.

IV. Encumbrance on Title

The policies in question insure plaintiffs against "any defect in or lien or encumbrance" on title. Although no lien had been recorded or asserted at the time the title insurance policies were issued, plaintiffs contend the presence of hazardous substances on the property constituted an encumbrance on title.

Encumbrances are defined by statute as "taxes, assessments, and all liens upon real property." (Civ.Code, § 1114.) Where a property is contaminated with hazardous substances, a subsequent owner of the property may be held fully responsible for the financial costs of cleaning up the contamination. (42 U.S.C. § 9607, subd. (a); Health & Saf.Code, §§ 25323.5 and 25363.) A lien may also be imposed on the property to cover such cleanup costs. (42 U.S.C., § 9607, subd. (*l*).) Plaintiffs reason that because any transfer of contaminated land carries with it the responsibility for cleanup costs, liability for such costs constitutes an "encumbrance on title" and is covered. We disagree.

In United States v. Allied Chemical Corp. (1984) 587 F.Supp. 1205, the plaintiff alleged a breach of warranty that property conveyed was free of encumbrance where hazardous substances were present on the property at the time it was conveyed. The court dismissed the plaintiff's cause of action, stating: "Plaintiff argues that the term 'encumbrance' is broad enough to include the presence of hazardous substances. However, the only authorities cited have interpreted 'encumbrance' to include only liens, easements, restrictive covenants and other such interests in or rights to the land held by third persons. Plaintiff has given no authority establishing its broad argument that any physical condition, including the presence of hazardous substances, is an 'encumbrance' if 'not visible or known' at the time of conveyance. The court declines to interpret 'encumbrance' as broadly as plaintiff urges. The court finds that, under current law, the term 'encumbrance' does not extend to the presence of hazardous substances alleged in this case."

In Chicago Title Ins. Co. v. Kumar, supra, 506 N.E.2d 154, the court also held that the presence of hazardous substances on the land at the time title was conveyed did not constitute an encumbrance. "The mere possibility that the Commonwealth may attach a future lien . . . , as a result of the release of hazardous material (existing but unknown at the time a title insurance policy is issued) when the Commonwealth has neither expended moneys on the property requiring reimbursement nor recorded the necessary statement of claim, is insufficient to create a 'defect in or lien or encumbrance on . . . title.'"

In South Shore Bank v. Stewart Title Guar. Co. (D.Mass.1988) 688 F.Supp. 803, the plaintiff sought a declaration that the title insurance company was liable for the clean-up costs related to hazardous substances on the property where there was no recorded lien at the time the policy was issued. The court held as a matter of law there was no coverage under the policy, stating "[p]laintiff has neither alleged nor offered any facts to show a defect in title. Hence, it has no cause of action against [the title insurer]."

### V. Exclusions in Policies 1 and 3

Plaintiffs also contend they had a reasonable expectation that cleanup costs would be covered by the policies, because policies 1 and 3 did not include environmental exclusions as did policy 2.[2]

Where there is ambiguity in the language of an insurance policy, a court will interpret coverage so as to protect the objectively reasonable

---

[2] Policy 2 stated in relevant part: "The following matters are expressly excluded from the coverage of this policy:. . . . (b) Any law, ordinance or governmental regulation relating to environmental protection. . . . (d) The effect of any violation of the matters excluded under (a), (b) or (c) above, unless notice of a defect, lien or encumbrance resulting from a violation has been recorded at Date of Policy in those records in which under state statutes, deeds, mortgages, lis pendens, liens or other title encumbrances must be recorded in order to impart constructive notice to purchasers of the land for value and without knowledge; provided, however, that without limitation, such records shall not be construed to include records in any of the offices of federal, state or local environmental protection, zoning, building, health or public safety authorities."

expectations of the insured. (AIU Ins. Co. v. Superior Court (1990) 51 Cal.3d 807, 822, 274 Cal.Rptr. 820, 799 P.2d 1253.)

As previously discussed, the language of the insuring clauses of all three policies unambiguously provides coverage only for defects relating to title. These clauses make no reference to the physical condition of the land. Moreover, this interpretation is fully supported by relevant authority. Under these circumstances, we fail to see how a specific exclusion in one policy leads to a reasonable expectation of coverage in the insuring clauses of other policies.

The judgment is affirmed.

## NOTES

1. *Hazardous waste.* Most courts have refused to hold that the presence of hazardous waste on the property affects the marketability of the title. See HM Holdings, Inc. v. Rankin, 70 F.3d 933, 935 (7th Cir. 1995). Why have they refused to so hold?

2. *Title contrasted with value.* The court distinguishes between unmarketability of land and unmarketability of title. The former concerns the seller's inability to realize the full value of the land upon sale of the property, whereas the latter deals with whether the title, itself, is defective, such that a buyer would be justified in refusing to perform a contract to buy the land. (See Covered Risk 29 in the policy reprinted above.) If you had represented Lick Mill Creek before they purchased the property or the insurance policy, how would you have protected them?

3. *Exclusions and exceptions.* Note that Exclusion 1.f. of the policy reprinted above excludes coverage for loss or costs resulting from violations of environmental protection regulations, but only if notice of the violation does not appear in the public records. In *Lick Mill Creek*, records disclosing the presence of hazardous waste were maintained by several public agencies. Did these records put the title insurer on constructive notice that the property was contaminated, thereby giving rise to liability?

4. *Adhesion contracts.* The form of title insurance policies is often reviewed and revised by title companies. What would be the best method of ensuring that the revisions are fair to the purchasers of insurance? Should state or federal regulations prohibit the issuance of a policy that does not protect the insured from losses like that suffered by the plaintiffs in *Lick Mill Creek*?

### Holmes v. Alabama Title Company
Supreme Court of Alabama, 1987.
507 So.2d 922.

■ SHORES, JUSTICE.

These are appeals by 128 landowners from summary judgments rendered in favor of United States Steel Corporation (now known as USX Corporation), Alabama Title Company, Inc., Commonwealth Land Title

Insurance Company, Lawyers Title Insurance Company, Mississippi Valley Title Insurance Company, and Jefferson Land Title Services Company, Inc.

The appellants are owners of surface tracts located in the Willow Bend subdivision in Bessemer. The surface and mineral estates in this area were originally owned by Woodward Iron Company. On March 22, 1943, Woodward Iron Company conveyed the surface to A.R. Patton by deed, excepting all mineral and mining rights and reserving for itself, its successors, assigns, licensees, or contractors, the right to mine and remove minerals without leaving supports to sustain and prevent damage to the surface of the land. The deed was recorded on March 25, 1943, in the Probate Office of Jefferson County (Bessemer Division), Volume 281, page 404, and provided in pertinent part as follows:

> [N]o right of action for damages on account of injuries to the land above-described or to any buildings, improvements, structures, wells or water courses now or hereafter located upon said land or to any owners or occupants or other persons in or upon said land, resulting from past or future mining operations of Woodward Iron Company, or its successors, assigns, licensees or contractors or resulting from the removal of coal and other minerals or coal seam roof supports by the Woodward Iron Company or its successors, assigns, licensees, lessees or contractors shall ever accrue to or be asserted by the grantee herein, his successors or assigns, this conveyance being expressly subject to all such injuries either past or future and this condition shall constitute a covenant running with the land as against the said grantee and all persons, firms or corporations holding under or through him.

All appellants are successors in title to the surface estate of A.R. Patton. There is no dispute that the appellants are subject to the quoted covenant contained in the 1943 deed.

By deed dated September 29, 1955, and an additional instrument, both recorded in the Probate Office of Jefferson County (Bessemer Division), U.S. Steel became the successor and assign of Woodward Iron Company in ownership of the mineral rights beneath the appellants' respective surface tracts and in the release from liability for damage to the surface, or to improvements and persons thereon, arising from past or future mining operations.

The Concord Mine, owned by U.S. Steel, covers some 25 square miles in western Jefferson County. It is located in part beneath the Willow Bend subdivision. Mining under the subdivision was begun by U.S. Steel on August 13, 1968, and was concluded on February 19, 1975. The appellants purchased their homes in the Willow Bend area over a period of time beginning December 29, 1976, and ending July 15, 1981. The mine was abandoned and sealed in March 1982.

In January 1983, residents of the Willow Bend subdivision relayed reports to the Office of Surface Mining, U.S. Department of the Interior, of tremors and the appearance of surface fractures on their land. OSM determined that the ceiling of the Concord Mine had collapsed, causing subsidence of the surface and damage to land and homes in the Willow Bend area.

The landowners contend that the trial court erred in granting summary judgment in favor of U.S. Steel on claims of negligence, wantonness, trespass, and nuisance. The landowners also contend that the trial court erred in granting summary judgment in favor of the title companies and title insurance companies on claims of fraud, breach of contract, and negligence for failing to adequately apprise the landowners, when issuing commitments for mortgagees' and owners' policies of title insurance on the surface tracts, of the significance and effect of the exculpatory covenant in the 1943 deed, to which they were subject.

The landowners contend that the 1943 deed's exculpatory provision does not bar their actions against U.S. Steel predicated on negligence, wantonness, trespass, and nuisance. We disagree.

In *Eastwood Lands, Inc. v. United States Steel Corp.*, 417 So.2d 164, 168 (Ala.1982), the Court held that a provision in a deed reserving to the grantor and its successors the right to mine and remove minerals without leaving support for the surface, identical in wording to the deed in the case before us, barred any cause of action arising from those activities for damage to the surface and buildings or injury to persons thereon. Even though that case dealt specifically with the effect of the exculpatory provision on a negligence cause of action, the holding was not limited to negligence actions. The provision in *Eastwood Lands* and the provision in the present case unambiguously bar *any* and *all* claims arising from the grantor's or its successor's mining activities.

Accordingly, we hold that even if the landowners could produce a scintilla of evidence of nuisance or trespass by U.S. Steel or of evidence that U.S. Steel conducted its mining activities in a negligent or willful and wanton fashion, the unambiguous language in the deed effectively bars all such claims.

The landowner's claims against the five title companies and title insurance companies are likewise without merit. The trial court held that the exceptions from insurance coverage, set out in the companies' title commitments and owner's and mortgagee's policies, of all mineral and mining rights and privileges and immunities relating thereto, by virtue of the instruments recorded in the office of the Judge of Probate of Jefferson County, completely discharged whatever duty, contractual or otherwise, the companies owed to the landowners. We agree.

The purpose of title insurance is not to protect the insured against loss arising from physical damage to property; rather, it is to protect the insured against defects in the title. Title companies and title insurance companies are not required to explain the significance and effect of exculpatory covenants and the like discovered in their title searches.

Affirmed.

## NOTE

*Lawyers beware.* The court holds that the title companies are not liable. If a homeowner had been represented by a lawyer when she purchased the property, could the homeowner succeed in an action against the lawyer?

# ASSIGNMENT 51

# INTRODUCTION TO INCOME TAX ISSUES AFFECTING HOME BUYERS AND SELLERS

## 1. INTRODUCTION

The previous Assignments have described in some detail the nuances of real property conveyancing. Throughout this casebook, we have illustrated the importance of proper drafting and planning as a means to ensure a desired result and to prevent potentially costly litigation. Essential to this end is an understanding of the impact of federal income taxes on real property transactions.

The tax laws often influence the manner in which real property transactions are structured. The lawyer's primary goal is to structure transactions to achieve the economic objectives of the parties. If alternative forms exist to achieve these goals, it is legal and desirable to adopt a form that minimizes the tax liabilities of the parties. The study of tax law allows you to understand the forces that lead parties to structure transactions so as to minimize the amount of taxes to be paid.

The goal of this Assignment is to introduce some of the important tax issues that invariably arise in real property transactions. Because you probably have had little, if any, exposure to the tax laws, the Assignment begins with a general introduction to federal income taxation. We urge you to take courses in federal income tax to gain a deeper appreciation for the legal issues that are introduced here.

*Sources of Federal Tax Law*

*Internal Revenue Code.* The federal tax laws of the United States are enacted by Congress and are contained in the Internal Revenue Code of 1986, as amended. Congress frequently amends the tax laws and the changes are incorporated into the Internal Revenue Code. Thus, it is important to work with a current version of the Code. The materials that follow are important tools to understanding the meaning of the federal tax legislation contained in the Code.

*United States Constitution.* The modern tax system has its origins in the 16th Amendment to the United States Constitution.[1] A majority of the constitutional issues relating to the government's ability to impose

---

[1] The 16th Amendment states that "[t]he Congress shall have power to lay and collect taxes on incomes, from whatever source derived, without apportionment among the several States, and without regard to any census or enumeration." U.S. Const. amend. XVI.

federal income taxes on individuals have been resolved. As such, federal tax legislation is unlikely to be invalidated on constitutional grounds.[2]

*Treasury Regulations.* Congress has delegated to the Treasury Department, an executive agency, the authority to promulgate regulations to implement and enforce the provisions of the Code.[3] The Regulations are a valuable resource for understanding and applying the often complex statutory provisions in the Code. On rare occasions, Congress will delegate to the Treasury the right to promulgate regulations that have the effect of legislation. Although these legislative regulations are not directly passed by Congress, they have the force of law.

The majority of the regulations promulgated by the Treasury interpret provisions of the Code and do not have the force of law. These interpretive regulations, however, are generally followed by the courts. The courts can overrule interpretive regulations if they are contrary to legislation enacted by Congress.

*Internal Revenue Service materials.* The Internal Revenue Service, as part of the Treasury Department, issues public revenue rulings, private letter rulings, and other pronouncements. These rulings and pronouncements are issued under the same Congressional authority that allows the Treasury to promulgate Regulations which interpret and enforce the federal tax laws.

Public revenue rulings are official IRS interpretations that may be relied upon by all taxpayers. Thus, a taxpayer can obtain a desired tax result by structuring a transaction in a manner consistent with a transaction described in a public revenue ruling. Public rulings are not binding authority on the courts because they merely reflect the Internal Revenue Service's position on a tax issue. Hence, they do not have the same weight as the regulations.

In contrast to the general applicability of public revenue rulings, an IRS private letter ruling may be relied on only by the taxpayer to whom it is issued. Private letter rulings are issued by the IRS in response to an individual taxpayer's request for confirmation of the tax consequences of a particular transaction before the transaction is effectuated. Thus, if a taxpayer is about to engage in an unusual or complicated transaction, the IRS may be willing to confirm the tax consequences that follow from a set of facts to which the taxpayer stipulates. Although private letter rulings may not be cited as authority, they do provide valuable information as to the IRS's interpretation of the tax laws.

*Case law.* If the IRS determines that a taxpayer has not paid all of the taxes owed, the IRS will assess a deficiency against the taxpayer.

---

[2] For more detailed information regarding constitutional issues involved with income taxation see Ronald Rotunda & John Nowak, Treatise On Constitutional Law: Substance And Procedure §§ 5.2–5.6, 5th ed. (2016).

[3] See I.R.C. § 7805.

There are three different courts of original jurisdiction that may be available to a taxpayer who wishes to challenge the deficiency: the United States Tax Court, United States District Courts, and United States Court of Federal Claims.[4] Decisions of the Tax Court and the district courts can be appealed to the appellate courts in the appropriate circuit. Decisions of the Federal Claims Court can be appealed to the Court of Appeals for the Federal Circuit. Ultimately, decisions may be appealed to the United States Supreme Court.

*What Is Income?*

The federal income tax is imposed on an individual's taxable income. Taxable income is defined as gross income reduced by certain deductions. Gross income can generally be said to encompass any economic benefit that increases the taxpayer's wealth, unless the Code specifically excludes the item from gross income.[5] Study the following examples to better understand what is included in the scope of gross income.

EXAMPLE 1: Adam is the owner of Blackacre Apartments. Belinda, a tenant, pays Adam a monthly rent of $1,200. Cole lives at Blackacre as well, but instead of paying rent, Cole performs $1,200 worth of maintenance and repair work each month in accordance with an agreement he has with Adam. What are the tax consequences to Adam?

The rent is an economic benefit to Adam. Therefore, Adam has $1,200 of gross income from Belinda's rent. But, what about the services provided by Cole in lieu of paying rent? The $1,200 of services provided to Adam in lieu of cash rent also constitutes gross income to Adam. The services are an economic benefit to Adam, so an additional $1,200 is included in Adam's gross income unless specifically excluded by a Code provision. In this case, there is no Code provision that would exclude this benefit from Adam's gross income.

EXAMPLE 2: Darius owns an apartment building. Ellen pays Darius $1,200 a month rent to live in one of the apartments. Darius also lives in the apartment building, but obviously pays no rent to himself. What are the tax consequences to Darius?

The $1,200 that Ellen pays Darius is an economic benefit to Darius, and is included in his gross income. Since Darius is also receiving a benefit by living in an apartment without having to

---

[4] To gain access to the Tax Court, the taxpayer must seek a redetermination of the deficiency, rather than pay the deficiency. To gain access to the District Court or the Federal Claims Court, the taxpayer must pay the tax deficiency, then file for a refund and wait for the IRS to deny the refund. Upon denial, the taxpayer may file suit for a refund in the United States District Court or in the Federal Claims Court.

[5] The Code provides for many exclusions from gross income that are beyond the scope of this text. As an example, § 102 of the Code provides that gifts as well as property acquired from a decedent through a bequest, devise or inheritance are excluded from gross income. Do not assume, however, that the government collects no taxes in these circumstances. There are gift and estate taxes to consider!

pay rent, it appears that this benefit would also constitute gross income to Darius. Nevertheless, such *imputed income* is generally not included in gross income. Can you think of reasons why the tax law does not tax imputed income? Do you see how the tax law favors home owners by virtue of this policy?

EXAMPLE 3: Faye borrows $160,000 from Garret. Does Faye have gross income?

Although it may seem that Faye enjoys a benefit when she receives the loan proceeds, the loan does not constitute gross income. The loan does not increase Faye's wealth. Any economic benefit to Faye is offset by her concomitant obligation to repay the loan to Garret.

EXAMPLE 4: Same facts as in Example 3. Does Garret have gross income when he receives $160,000 cash from Faye as repayment of the loan?

When the lender is repaid the amount of the loan, he does not have gross income because his wealth does not increase. He merely receives a return of his money, sometimes referred to as a tax-free *return of capital*.

Congress has defined gross income in very broad and inclusive terms. Section 61(a) of the Code defines gross income and provides in part:

"Except as otherwise provided in this subtitle, gross income means all income from whatever source derived, including (but not limited to) the following items...."

The Code provides a list of 15 specific examples of gross income, including rent (as illustrated in the above examples) and gains from dealings in property (discussed below). The statutory language, however, does *not* limit the scope of gross income to those examples.

*Gains from Dealings in Property*

Generally speaking, increases in wealth are included in gross income. For example, if an apartment building owner receives rent, the rent is included in her gross income. However, what happens when the apartment building, home, or other property owned by an individual increases in value? A piece of land may be purchased at the beginning of the year for $10,000 and increase in value to $20,000 by the end of the year. The tax system could technically tax the owner on the increase in value of the land. After all, the owner's wealth has increased because he owns property that has a greater value, even though he has not yet converted the increased value to cash.

Although the tax system could tax the increase in the value of property, think of the administrative nightmare that would result from having to keep track of every change in the value of property. Particularly with real estate and other illiquid assets, it would be difficult or impossible to determine gains or losses in the absence of a sale or exchange. Thankfully the tax system does not tax increases in property value until the property is sold or exchanged, an occasion described by the tax law as a *realization event*.

A realization event is a term of art that can generally be thought of as a sale of property for money or an exchange of property for other property. Thus, when an owner sells her appreciated property, she will be taxed on the increase in value. But, will the owner include the full sale price of the property in gross income? No, the property owner only includes in gross income the amount that is received in excess of the cost of the property, essentially the profit. The cost of the property is embodied in another tax term of art called *basis*.[6]

> EXAMPLE 5: Heather purchases a home for $200,000 and then sells it to Ivan for $300,000. Heather's cost or *basis* in the home is $200,000. Thus, when Heather sells the house for $300,000, only a $100,000 gain will be included in Heather's gross income. Heather's gain is limited to the difference between the sale price and the cost or *basis*. The tax system allows Heather to recover her cost and only taxes her on the gain.

*Exclusions*

In Example 5, the sale of Heather's home resulted in a $100,000 gain that would normally be included in her gross income. On rare occasions, however, the Code permits taxpayers to *exclude* certain items from gross income. For example, § 121 of the Code permits a taxpayer to exclude all or part of the gain from the sale of a home owned by the taxpayer, under certain circumstances. Reconsider the tax consequences of Heather's home sale after reading the materials for solving the Principal Problem in this Assignment.

*Deductions*

Income tax is not imposed on the taxpayer's gross income. Rather, the taxpayer may reduce her gross income by certain *deductions* that are specified in the Code.

Whenever a taxpayer spends money or makes a payment, there is the possibility of a deduction. However, in sharp contrast to the broad scope of gross income, the Code states that payments cannot be deducted unless a specific Code provision allows the deduction.[7] Can you think of reasons why Congress chose to limit deductions to those that are specifically authorized? Can you reconcile this approach with the fact

---

[6] Basis is viewed as the cost of property for purposes of this discussion. Although this view is a reasonable starting point, the concept of basis entails additional complexity that is beyond the scope of this text. For more information on this topic, see Marvin A. Chirelstein & Lawrence Zelenak, Federal Income Taxation: A Law Student's Guide to the Leading Cases and Concepts (13th ed. 2015).

[7] See I.R.C. § 161.

that Congress treats all benefits as gross income unless a specific exclusion exists?[8]

Most deduction provisions reflect the idea that when money is spent to produce income, the taxpayer should only be taxed on the profit. For example, if a taxpayer's gross revenue from her business this year is $50,000, and she spends $10,000 to pay her employees, she should only have to pay tax on the $40,000 profit. Although her gross income is $50,000, the Code expressly allows the taxpayer to deduct the salaries paid to the employees as an ordinary and necessary expense of doing business.[9]

Another type of payment is interest paid on a loan. Interest can be thought of as a fee paid by a borrower to a lender for the use of the lender's money. By parting with the use of his money, the lender cannot place it in a savings account or some other investment vehicle, such as stocks or bonds, and earn profits from the investment. Thus, the borrower must compensate the lender for this forgone opportunity by paying interest.

The payment of interest raises a deduction issue for the borrower.[10] Interest payments incurred in trade or business activities or investment activities may be deducted by the taxpayer.[11] Interest paid for money borrowed for personal use generally cannot be deducted by the taxpayer. For example, the taxpayer generally cannot deduct interest payments made on car loans or credit card debt. Exceptions to this general rule are discussed in the materials for solving the Principal Problem in this Assignment.

## 2. Principal Problem

Saul and his wife Clara purchased a two-story home in 2005 for $300,000. They used $60,000 of their own money and borrowed $240,000 from the bank to pay for the home. Later they wanted to expand their living space by building a third story. In 2010, they went to the bank and borrowed $100,000, which they used to pay for the cost of the home improvement. In 2015, they borrowed an additional $50,000 to take a trip around the world. The bank required Saul and Clara to make interest payments for the use of the borrowed money on each of the loans discussed above. Can Saul and Clara deduct the interest paid on any or all of the three loans? Does it make any difference whether any of the loans were secured by giving the bank a mortgage in the home?

Wishing to move to a warmer climate, Saul and Clara sold their home for $950,000 this year. How much income are they taxed on when

---

[8] See I.R.C. § 61.
[9] See I.R.C. § 162.
[10] The receipt of interest payments is gross income for the lender. See I.R.C. § 61(a)(4).
[11] See I.R.C. § 163.

they sell the home? How would they be taxed if the home had been sold for $360,000 instead of $950,000?

3. MATERIALS FOR SOLUTION OF PRINCIPAL PROBLEM

*Income Tax Issues Affecting the Home Buyer*

## Excerpts from IRS Publication 530—Tax Information for Homeowners

Department of the Treasury, Internal Revenue Service, 2016.

This publication provides tax information for homeowners. Your home may be a house, condominium, cooperative apartment, mobile home, houseboat, or house trailer.

If you took out a [loan and gave a mortgage] to finance the purchase of your home, you probably have to make monthly house payments. Your house payment may include several costs of owning a home. The only costs you can deduct are real estate taxes actually paid to the taxing authority, interest that qualifies as home mortgage interest and mortgage insurance premiums. These are discussed in more detail later.

Some non-deductible expenses that may be included in your house payment include [f]ire or homeowner's insurance premiums, and the amount applied to reduce the principal of the [loan]. . . . You [also] cannot deduct . . . the cost of utilities, such as gas, electricity, or water, [and homeowners association assessments].[12]

Real Estate Taxes

Most state and local governments charge an annual tax on the value of real property. This is called a real estate tax. You can deduct the tax if it is assessed uniformly at a like rate on all real property throughout the community. The proceeds must be used for general community or governmental purposes and not be a payment for a special privilege granted or service rendered to you.

Many monthly house payments include an amount placed in escrow (put in the care of a third party) for real estate taxes. You may not be able to deduct the total you pay into the escrow account. You can deduct only the real estate taxes that the lender actually paid from escrow to the taxing authority. Your real estate tax bill will show this amount.

---

[12] Editor's note: A homeowner's association is an association of individuals who own homes in a particular area or in a condominium complex. The association is responsible for maintaining and improving the shared areas in which the owners have an undivided common interest, such as the lobby of a condominium. The homeowners pay the association certain fees called assessments that are used to pay for the required maintenance and improvements.

Home Mortgage Interest

Most home buyers [must give] a mortgage [to obtain a loan] to buy their home. They then make monthly payments to either the mortgage holder or someone collecting the payments for the mortgage holder.[13]

Usually, you can deduct the entire part of your house payment that is for mortgage interest. . . . However, your deduction may be limited if: (1) your total [loan] balance is more than $1 million, or (2) you [borrowed money] . . . for reasons other than to buy, build, or improve your home.

## Excerpts from IRS Publication 936—Home Mortgage Interest Deduction
Department of the Treasury, Internal Revenue Service, 2015.

Generally, home mortgage interest is any interest you pay on a loan secured by your home (main home or a second home). . . .

You can deduct home mortgage interest if . . . the [loan] is a secured debt on a qualified home in which you have an ownership interest. . . . Both you and the lender must intend that the loan be repaid. . . .

Secured Debt

You can deduct your home mortgage interest only if your [loan] is a secured debt. A secured debt is one in which you sign an instrument (such as a mortgage, deed of trust, or land contract) that: (1) makes your ownership in a qualified home security for payment of the debt, (2) provides, in case of default, that your home could satisfy the debt, and (3) is recorded or is otherwise perfected under any state or local law that applies.

In other words, your [loan] is a secured debt if you put your home up as collateral to protect the interests of the lender. If you cannot pay the debt, your home can then serve as payment to the lender to satisfy (pay) the debt. In this publication, [loan] will refer to secured debt.

Qualified Home

For you to take a home mortgage interest deduction, your debt must be secured by a qualified home. This means your main home or your second home. A home includes a house, condominium, . . . mobile home, boat, or similar property that has sleeping, cooking, and toilet facilities.

The interest you pay on a [loan] on a home other than your main or second home may be deductible if the proceeds of the loan were used for business or investment purposes. Otherwise, it is considered personal interest and is not deductible.

---

[13] Editor's note: Payments made on a loan consist of two parts: principal and interest. Principal payments reduce the amount of the outstanding loan. In contrast, interest payments represent a charge for using the lender's money.

## Limits on Home Mortgage Interest Deduction

Your home mortgage interest deduction is limited to the interest on the part of your home [loan] that is not more than your qualified loan limit. This is the part of your home [loan] that is ... not more than the limits for home acquisition debt and home equity debt....

### Home Acquisition Debt

Home acquisition debt is a [loan] you took out, to buy, build, or substantially improve a qualified home (your main or second home). It also must be secured by that home.

*Home acquisition debt limit.* The total amount you can treat as home acquisition debt at any time on your main home and second home cannot be more than $1 million.... Debt over this limit may qualify as home equity debt.

*Refinanced home acquisition debt.* Any secured debt you use to refinance home acquisition debt is treated as home acquisition debt. However, the new debt will qualify as home acquisition debt only up to the amount of the balance of the old mortgage principal just before the refinancing. Any additional debt is not home acquisition debt, but may qualify as home equity debt (discussed later).

### Home Equity Debt

If you took out a loan for reasons other than to buy, build, or substantially improve your home, it may qualify as home equity debt. In addition, debt you incurred to buy, build, or substantially improve your home, to the extent it is more than the home acquisition debt limit, may qualify as home equity debt.

Home equity debt is a [loan] that: (1) does not qualify as home acquisition debt..., and (2) is secured by your qualified home.

> Example. You bought your home for cash 10 years ago. You did not [give] a mortgage on your home until last year, when you took out a $50,000 loan, secured by your home, to pay for your daughter's college tuition and your father's medical bills. This loan is home equity debt.

*Home equity debt limit.* There is a limit on the amount of debt that can be treated as home equity debt. The total home equity debt on your main home and second home is limited to the smaller of: (1) $100,000 ..., or (2) [t]he total of each home's fair market value (FMV) reduced (but not below zero) by the amount of its home acquisition debt.... Determine the FMV and the outstanding home acquisition ... debt for each home on the date that the last debt was secured by the home.

> Example [of the home equity debt limit]. You own one home that you bought in 2001. Its fair market value now is $110,000, and the current balance on your original mortgage [loan] (home acquisition debt) is $95,000. Bank M offers you a home mortgage loan of 125% of the fair market value of the home less any

Repairs versus improvements. A repair keeps your home in an ordinary, efficient operating condition. It does not add to the value of your home or prolong its life. Repairs include repainting your home inside or outside, fixing your gutters or floors, fixing leaks or plastering, and replacing broken window panes. You cannot deduct repair costs and generally cannot add them to the basis of your home.

However, repairs that are done as part of an extensive remodeling or restoration of your home are considered improvements. You add them to the basis of your home.

[Amount of Gain or Loss

To figure the amount of gain or loss, compare the amount realized to the adjusted basis. If the amount realized is more than the adjusted basis, the difference is a gain [which will be taxed unless you are able to exclude it].

If the amount realized is less than the adjusted basis, the difference is a loss. A loss on the sale of your main home cannot be deducted [because it is a personal loss].]

## NOTES

1. *Personal interest.* Prior to 1986, the income tax laws allowed individual taxpayers to deduct interest on loans incurred in connection with a trade or business, as part of an investment activity, or for personal use. Individuals could even deduct the interest on credit card balances and car loans. In 1986, Congress significantly limited the ability of individuals to deduct personal interest. In doing so, Congress stated "by phasing out the present deductibility of consumer interest, the committee believes that it has eliminated from the present tax law a significant disincentive to saving." S.Rep. 99–313, 99th Cong. 2d Sess., 804 (1986). Why might the deductibility of personal interest be regarded as a disincentive to saving?

2. *Qualified residence interest.* When Congress limited the availability of the personal interest deduction in 1986, it retained the qualified residence interest deduction. Although this deduction is limited to home acquisition debt and home equity debt, it still provides a significant tax break to home owners. Why would Congress retain this personal interest deduction and not others? Recall that a homeowner who occupies a residence that she owns is not taxed on the benefit derived from her rent-free occupancy (imputed income). See Example 2, p. 1269. Do you see how the qualified interest deduction and the failure to tax imputed income reflect a strong policy favoring home ownership? Is this policy fair to those who choose to rent a residence or are forced to rent because they cannot afford to buy a home?

3. *Economics before taxes.* A taxpayer can use borrowed money from a home equity loan to purchase a car, go on vacation, pay for medical expenses, or pay for other expenses unrelated to the home. In addition, the home owner gets a valuable deduction that potentially results in a lower income tax. To obtain a home equity loan interest deduction, however, the loan must be secured by a mortgage on the borrower's home. What serious risk does this

pose to the home owner? See Forrester, Mortgaging the American Dream: A Critical Evaluation of the Federal Governments' Promotion of Home Equity Financing, 69 Tul.L.Rev. 373 (1994).

4. *Mixed-use property: home-offices and vacation homes.* As you might expect from the discussion of the interest deduction rules, expenses incurred in connection with personal use property are rarely allowed to be deducted. In contrast to the scarcity of deductions available for personal use property, many deductions are available for expenses of property used in a trade or business or held for investment. Under certain circumstances, property can be used for both personal purposes and business purposes. For example, an individual may conduct business in a home-office or own a vacation home that is rented out for part of the year. Such mixed-use property complicates matters and special tax rules apply for determining what costs can be deducted.

5. *Tax planning and the exclusion of gain from the sale of a personal residence.* IRS Publication 523 discusses the restrictions on the exclusion of gain from the sale of a residence. Given that there is a $500,000 limit on the exclusion of a married couple's gain, would you advise a client who resides in a home with a potential gain approaching $500,000 to sell the home? There is also a two-year use requirement. If your client resided in his home for 18 months and planned to sell the property within the next year, how would you advise him? What factors should you consider when advising the taxpayer, aside from the desire to minimize the amount of taxes that the taxpayer will have to pay?

6. *Loss from the sale of a personal residence.* When a taxpayer sells property for an amount that is less than her adjusted basis in the property, she sustains a loss. The Code allows taxpayers to deduct losses only under limited circumstances. Losses sustained from the sale of property that is utilized in a trade or business or held for investment purposes may result in a deduction. In contrast, losses incurred in connection with property used for personal purposes are generally not deductible. For example, when a taxpayer sells his home at a loss, the taxpayer cannot deduct this loss because it is personal.

# ASSIGNMENT 52

# THE TIME BETWEEN THE CONTRACT AND DEED: THE DOCTRINE OF EQUITABLE CONVERSION

## 1. INTRODUCTION

In Assignment 40, we learned that a sale of real estate usually commences with a sales contract between the buyer and seller. Normally, several weeks or even many months will pass between the time the contract is signed and the property is actually conveyed by the deed. What happens during this "gap" period if a building on the property is destroyed by fire or other causes? Upon whom should the loss fall? What if the government takes the land by eminent domain?[1] What if a zoning change makes the land unsuitable for the buyer's purposes?

At common law, the answer was simple: since equitable title to the land passed to the buyer upon forming the sales contract, the loss fell upon the buyer.[2] The seller could specifically enforce the contract, in which case the buyer was forced to pay full price for the damaged or destroyed property. The common law conclusion rested on the equitable maxim that "equity treats as done that which ought to be done." However harsh, the common law rule is still followed by a slim majority of jurisdictions in this country.[3]

Not surprisingly, many jurisdictions found the harsh results of the common law doctrine undesirable. Massachusetts adopted a rule based on contract principles that became a strong minority rule. Under the Massachusetts rule, there is an implied condition that the subject matter of the sales contract will exist at the time of conveyance. If the subject matter is destroyed prior to conveyance, there is a failure of consideration and thus the contract is rescinded and the obligations of the parties are

---

[1] Under the Fifth Amendment of the United States Constitution, the government may take private property for a public purpose, but must compensate the owners of the property.

[2] The common law rule originated in England in Paine v. Meller, 6 Vesey Jr. 349, 31 Eng.Rep. 1088 (Ch.1801). The Paine court held that the purchaser would bear the loss on the theory of equitable conversion. Although the facts of Paine were unusual because the buyer's delay was the reason the seller had legal title when the building burned, most American jurisdictions followed Paine and it became the majority rule. Interestingly, England abrogated this rule with the Law of Property Act of 1925.

[3] Annotation, Risk of Loss by Casualty Pending Contract for Conveyance of Real Property—Modern Cases, 85 A.L.R.4th 233 (1991 & Supp. 2009).

discharged.[4] When the contract is rescinded, the seller must return any money the buyer has paid. While the Massachusetts rule ameliorates the harsh results on the buyer, it can impose hardship on the seller. Under the Massachusetts rule, if the buyer takes possession of the property, but legal title has not yet passed when the property was destroyed, the loss still falls upon the seller.[5]

In contrast to the common law rule and the Massachusetts rule, the Uniform Vendor and Purchaser Risk Act (the "Uniform Act") adopts a more rational approach that bases the risk of loss on possession.[6] The Uniform Act provides as follows:

## UNIFORM VENDOR AND PURCHASER RISK ACT

Sec. 1. Risk of Loss. Any contract hereafter made in this State for the purchase and sale of realty shall be interpreted as including an agreement that the parties shall have the following rights and duties, unless the contract expressly provides otherwise:

(a) If, when neither the legal title nor the possession of the subject matter of the contract has been transferred, all or a material part thereof is destroyed without fault of the purchaser or is taken by eminent domain, the vendor cannot enforce the contract, and the purchaser is entitled to recover any portion of the price that he has paid;

(b) If, when either the legal title or the possession of the subject matter of the contract has been transferred, all or any part thereof is destroyed without fault of the vendor or is taken by eminent domain, the purchaser is not thereby relieved from a duty to pay the price, nor is he entitled to recover any portion thereof that he has paid.

The Uniform Act places the risk of loss on the seller until possession or legal title passes to the buyer. However, the Uniform Act leaves many questions unanswered. For example, the Uniform Act gives no guidance regarding how to define a "material" or "immaterial" loss. Moreover, it does not define "possession." Is a buyer who takes possession under a lease, and who pays rent to the seller, in possession within the meaning of the Uniform Act? What if the buyer has the legal right to possession but does not take actual possession? What policies ought to govern a court's decision to allocate risk in favor of the buyer or seller?

---

[4] Thompson v. Gould, 37 Mass. 134 (1838); Hawkes v. Kehoe, 193 Mass. 419, 79 N.E. 766 (1907); Libman v. Levenson, 236 Mass. 221, 128 N.E. 13 (1920).

[5] Powell v. Dayton, S. & G.R.R. Co. 12 Or. 488, 8 P. 544 (1885) (purchaser was in possession as a tenant).

[6] The Uniform Vendor and Purchaser Risk Act has been adopted in thirteen states: California, Hawaii, Illinois, Michigan, Nevada, New Mexico, New York, North Carolina, Oklahoma, Oregon, South Dakota, Texas and Wisconsin. An early case that focused on possession as determinative of risk allocation is Anderson v. Yaworski, 120 Conn. 390, 181 A. 205 (1935).

The rules presented in this Assignment are default rules that become relevant only when the parties fail to include a clause in the sales contract that allocates the risk of loss. If the sales contract contains a risk of loss clause, courts will give effect to it even if the jurisdiction follows an approach that would lead to a contrary result in the absence of the clause. Thus, when the sales contract is being negotiated, the prudent lawyer will have the foresight to evaluate whether her client will be better served by attempting to allocate the risk of loss in the contract or, instead rely on the jurisdiction's default rule.

When property is destroyed between the time the sales contract is signed and title passes, stating the issue as "who bears the loss?" is an oversimplification. Often, the precise issue is whether the buyer can rescind the contract and recover the deposit. In other cases, the issue is whether the buyer can rescind the contract after title has actually passed. For example, after title has passed, a buyer may discover that a zoning change occurred subsequent to the signing of the sales contract. In some cases, the issue is whether the seller is entitled to specific performance or damages. Other times, the issue is whether the buyer can get specific performance with an abatement of price. More complex issues arise when insurance proceeds are involved. In this Assignment, it should be assumed that the property loss was not due to the fault of either party.

## 2. Principal Problem

Your client, Bob Buyer, a developer of large shopping centers, entered into a contract with Sally Seller to purchase a large tract of land for $1 million. During negotiations, Bob had discussed with Sally his plans to develop a shopping center on the land. Bob paid $100,000 on the signing of the contract, with a balance of $900,000 due at the closing. Since Bob would need some time to arrange for financing, and since financing would not be forthcoming until Bob received commitments from some major tenants, the contract provided that escrow would close six months after the sales contract date. Bob immediately began to seek tenants and financing. The entire town soon knew of Bob's plans. Although the land was currently being used for pasture, the property was zoned "Commercial-7A" which would have permitted the proposed shopping center. Nearby residents of the area became concerned that the tranquility of the neighborhood would be destroyed by the shopping center and organized as SOG ("Save Our Grass") to thwart the proposed development.

Despite Bob's best efforts to prevent the rezoning, the property was rezoned "R1A"—single family residences only. When the rezoning became final, Bob had not taken title. Although Bob can contest the rezoning in court, the likelihood of success is slim. He has no interest in developing a tract for single family homes. Although the property was worth $1 million when it was zoned for shopping centers, it is worth only $200,000 as a tract for single family homes.

Bob wants to rescind the contract and get his $100,000 deposit back from Sally. As he sees it, the whole purpose of the contract was frustrated by the rezoning and it is unfair to ask him to proceed. He claims that Sally promised to deliver a tract zoned for shopping centers. Since Sally can no longer deliver such a tract, the deal should be called off.

Sally sees things differently. She is ready, willing and able to deliver the land on the closing date. She claims that the rezoning is Bob's problem. Since the contract says nothing about the possibility of rezoning, Sally does not think that a rezoning should excuse performance. Moreover, should Bob in any way refuse to proceed, Sally will sue Bob either for specific performance or for damages.

Bob comes to you for help. After studying the following materials be prepared to give an opinion as to the arguments that either Bob or Sally might make and the probable outcome of any litigation. Also, consider how this controversy might have been avoided through more careful drafting of the sales contract.

3. MATERIALS FOR SOLUTION OF PRINCIPAL PROBLEM

## DiDonato v. Reliance Standard Life Ins. Co.
Supreme Court of Pennsylvania, 1969.
433 Pa. 221, 249 A.2d 327, 39 A.L.R.3d 357.

■ EAGEN, J.

The legal question presented in this appeal arises in the context of a somewhat cumbersome fact situation. On August 4, 1965, the Reliance Standard Life Insurance Company (hereinafter Reliance) entered into an Agreement of Sale with Anthony and Viola DiDonato (hereinafter appellants). Under the terms of the contract, Reliance agreed to sell to the appellants for $16,000 the premises located at 1015–23 South 3rd Street, Philadelphia. Reliance executed a certification stating that the premises were zoned industrial. This certification was correct and was appended to the Agreement of Sale.

On September 22, 1965, an ordinance[7] was enacted which changed the zoning of the subject premises from G-2 Industrial to R-10 Residential. Not until November 9, 1965, however, did the public records note this change.

On October 7, 1965, the transaction was settled. At that time, Reliance's representative delivered to the appellants a certification which

---

[7] The proposed ordinance was first publicly advertised on July 23, 1965. Council held its first public hearing on the ordinance on August 11th. The first and second readings took place on August 19th and September 9th. The Mayor signed the ordinance into law on September 22nd.

was procured from the Department of Licenses and Inspections of the City of Philadelphia on September 28, 1965. The certification statement erroneously indicated that the subject premises were still zoned G-2 Industrial. As of this date neither Reliance nor the appellants were aware of the change in the zoning classification.

In 1967, the appellants contracted to sell the subject premises, and then learned for the first time of the zoning change. After unsuccessfully seeking a variance, the appellants brought an equity action against Reliance to rescind the Agreement of Sale of August 4, 1965. The Chancellor entered an adjudication in favor of Reliance, and his findings of fact and conclusions of law were subsequently affirmed by the court en banc; from its final decree this appeal followed.

In their brief to this Court, the appellants seek to find ground for a rescission upon the misrepresentation contained in the certification delivered to them at the settlement proceeding. The argument seems to be that the erroneous certification that the premises were industrial constituted a material misrepresentation, a breach of warranty, justifying rescission.

There can be no doubt that at the settlement, there was a misrepresentation as to the zoning status of the subject premises. But that fact is not determinative in resolving this controversy. It only helps us to focus upon the terminal issue in the case. For even if the certification had recited that the subject premises were zoned residential, the appellants would have a right to rescind only if the risk of a zoning change remained with Reliance until settlement. In other words, the fact that the appellants were deceived as to the correct zoning status of the premises is inconsequential. The crucial inquiry is which of the litigants bore the risk of loss attending the zoning change between the Agreement of Sale and the settlement.

The question presented is one of first impression in Pennsylvania. However, it is well-established law here that when the Agreement of Sale is signed, the purchaser becomes the equitable or beneficial owner through the doctrine of equitable conversion. The vendor retains merely a security interest for the payment of the unpaid purchase money. Payne v. Clark, 409 Pa. 557, 187 A.2d 769 (1963). It is also the law of Pennsylvania that the purchaser of real estate bears the risk of loss for injury occurring to the property after execution of the Agreement of Sale but before the settlement.

In resolving the question here, we are aided by the thinking of Professor Arthur Linton Corbin, who enunciates the general rule as follows: "After a contract for the sale of land has been made, but before actual conveyance, it sometimes happens that a zoning ordinance is adopted limiting the uses to which the property may be put. For example, it may be restricted to residences only, so that warehouses, garages, and the like are excluded. This change in the law may frustrate in part or in whole the purpose for which the purchaser agreed to buy the land. *In the absence of some expression in the contract to the contrary, the risk of such a restriction by ordinance seems likely to be allocated to the purchaser."* (Emphasis supplied.) 6 Corbin, Contracts sec. 1361 (1962), and the cases cited therein.

Samuel A. Goldberg, writing under the aegis of the American Law Institute, said in his book entitled Sales of Real Estate in Pennsylvania at page 98:

Zoning Change Between Agreement and Settlement

It is also conceivable that between the time of the execution of the agreement and settlement, the zoning ordinance may be amended. If, when the buyer signs the agreement, his projected use is lawful, the only way in which he can protect himself is to include in the agreement a clause substantially as follows:

> If prior to settlement, an amendment to the zoning ordinance or any other law, ordinance or regulation comes into effect, which prohibits the operation of bowling alleys upon the property, Buyer shall have the right upon giving written notice to Seller, at or before settlement, to cancel this agreement and to recover all moneys paid to Seller on account.

The persuasiveness of the above authorities dictates the result here. There appears to be no cogent argument for treating losses resulting from zoning changes occurring between the execution of the Agreement of Sale and settlement differently from casualty and other kinds of loss occurring between those periods. The parties are always free to mold rights and responsibilities inter se in whatever fashion they desire. But when they are quiet, the law will speak in a voice of finality to set their dispute to rest.

We have examined the other grounds for relief proposed by the appellants, and find them unmeritorious.

Decree affirmed.

## Skelly Oil Co. v. Ashmore

Supreme Court of Missouri, 1963.
365 S.W.2d 582.

■ HYDE, J.

This is a suit by the purchaser, Skelly Oil Company, a corporation, against the vendors, Tom A. Ashmore and Madelyn Ashmore, husband and wife, in two counts. Count One is for specific performance of a contract to sell the north half of a certain described southwest corner lot. Count Two seeks an abatement in the purchase price of $10,000, being the proceeds received by the vendors under an insurance policy on a building on the property, which building was destroyed by fire in the interim between the execution of the contract of sale and the time for closing of said sale. The trial court found the issues in favor of the purchaser, decreed specific performance, and applied the $10,000 insurance proceeds on the $20,000 purchase price. The vendors have appealed.

The vendors acquired the property about 1953, and operated a grocery store in the concrete block building, with fixtures and furniture, and a one-story frame "smoke house" thereon. Joe Busby, of the Kansas City office of the Skelly Oil Company real estate department, secured the execution of a Skelly printed form of option by the vendors, dated July 31, 1957, for Skelly to purchase for the sum of $20,000, payable in cash upon delivery of deed said property, together with the buildings, driveways, and all construction and equipment thereon, at any time before August 31, 1957. [T]he Ashmores extended the option . . . to March 10, 1958 [because Skelly could not complete the transaction by the initial date]. By letter to the Ashmores under date of March 4, 1958, Skelly explicitly stated: "This letter is to inform you that Skelly Oil Company does hereby exercise its option to purchase the above described property for the sum of $20,000."

The contract of sale here involved contained no provision as to who assumed the risk of loss occasioned by a destruction of the building, or for protecting the building by insurance or for allocating any insurance proceeds received therefor. When the parties met to close the sale on April 16, the purchaser's counsel informed vendors and their attorney he was relying on Standard Oil Co. v. Dye, 223 Mo.App. 926, 20 S.W.2d 946, for purchaser's claim to the $10,000 insurance proceeds on the building. Purchaser made no claim to the $4,000 paid vendors for the loss of the furniture and fixtures. It is stated in 3 American Law of Property, § 11.30, p. 90, that in the circumstances here presented at least five different views have been advanced for allocating the burden of fortuitous loss between vendor and purchaser of real estate. We summarize those mentioned: (1) The view first enunciated in Paine v. Meller (Ch. 1801, 6 Ves.Jr. 349, 31 Eng.Reprint 1088, 1089) is said to be the most widely accepted; holding that from the time of the contract of sale of real estate the burden of fortuitous loss was on the purchaser even though the vendor retained possession. (2) The loss is on the vendor until legal title is conveyed, although the purchaser is in possession, stated to be a strong minority. (3) The burden of loss should be on the vendor until the time agreed upon for conveying the legal title, and thereafter on the purchaser unless the vendor be in such default as to preclude specific performance, not recognized in the decisions. (4) The burden of the loss should be on the party in possession, whether vendor or purchaser, so considered by some courts. (5) The burden of loss should be on the vendor unless there is something in the contract or in the relation of the parties from which the court can infer a different intention, stating "this rather vague test" has not received any avowed judicial acceptance, although it is not inconsistent with jurisdictions holding the loss is on the vendor until conveyance or jurisdictions adopting the possession test. As to the weight of the authority, see also 27 A.L.R.2d 448; Tiffany, Real Property, 3rd ed., § 309.

We do not agree that we should adopt the arbitrary rule of Paine v. Meller, supra, and Standard Oil Co. v. Dye, supra, that there is equitable conversion from the time of making a contract for sale and purchase of land and that the risk of loss from destruction of buildings or other substantial part of the property is from that moment on the purchaser.

We take the view stated in an article on Equitable Conversion by Contract, 13 Columbia Law Review 369, 386, Dean Harlan F. Stone, later Chief Justice Stone, in which he points out that the only reason why a contract for the sale of land by the owner to another operates to effect conversion is that a court of equity will compel him specifically to perform his contract. He further states:

> A preliminary to the determination of the question whether there is equitable ownership of land must therefore necessarily be the determination of the question whether there is a contract which can be and ought to be specifically performed *at the very time when the court is called upon to perform it*. This process of reasoning is, however, reversed in those jurisdictions where the "burden of loss" is cast upon the vendee. The question is whether there shall be a specific performance of the contract, thus casting the burden on the vendee, by compelling him to pay the full purchase price for the subject matter of the contract, a substantial part of which has been destroyed. The question is answered somewhat by the following: equitable ownership of the vendee in the subject matter of the contract can exist only where the contract is one which equity will specifically perform. The vendee of land is equitably entitled to land, therefore the vendee may be compelled to perform, although the vendor is unable to give in return the performance stipulated for by his contract. The *non sequitur* involved in the proposition that performance may be had because of the equitable ownership of the land by the vendee, which in turn depends upon the right of performance, is evident. The doctrine of equitable conversion, so far as it is exemplified by the authorities hitherto considered, cannot lead to the result of casting the burden of loss on the vendee, since the *conversion depends upon the question whether the contract should in equity be performed*. In all other cases where the vendee is treated as the equitable owner of the land, it is only because the contract is one which equity first determines should be specifically performed.

> Whether a plaintiff, in breach of his contract by a default which goes to the essence, as in the case of the destruction of a substantial part of the subject matter of the contract, should be entitled to specific performance, is a question which is answered

in the negative in every case except that of destruction of the subject matter of the contract. To give a plaintiff specific performance of the contract when he is unable to perform the contract on his own part, violates the fundamental rule of equity that . . . *equity will not compel a defendant to perform when it is unable to so frame its decree as to compel the plaintiff to give in return substantially what he has undertaken to give* or to do for the defendant.

The rule of casting the "burden of loss" on the vendee by specific performance if justifiable at all can only be explained and justified upon one of two theories: first, that since equity has for most purposes treated the vendee as the equitable owner, it should do so for all purposes, although *this ignores the fact that in all other cases the vendee is so treated only because the contract is either being performed or in equity ought to be performed*; or, second, which is substantially the same proposition in a different form, the specific performance which casts the burden on the vendee is an incident to and a consequence of an equitable conversion, whereas in all other equity relations growing out of the contract, the equitable conversion, if it exists, is an incident to and consequence of, a specific performance. Certainly nothing could be more illogical than this process of reasoning. (Emphasis ours.)

For these reasons, we do not agree with the rule that arbitrarily places the risk of loss on the vendee from the time the contract is made. Instead we believe the Massachusetts rule is the proper rule. It is thus stated in Libman v. Levenson, 236 Mass. 221, 128 N.E. 13, 22 A.L.R. 560: When "the conveyance is to be made of the whole estate, including both land and buildings, for an entire price, and the value of the buildings constitutes a large part of the total value of the estate, and the terms of the agreement show that they constituted an important part of the subject matter of the contract . . . the contract is to be construed as subject to the implied condition that it no longer shall be binding if, before the time for the conveyance to be made, the buildings are destroyed by fire. The loss by the fire falls upon the vendor, the owner; and if he has not protected himself by insurance, he can have no reimbursement of this loss; but the contract is no longer binding upon either party. If the purchaser has advanced any part of the price, he can recover it back. Thompson v. Gould, [supra] 20 Pick. [37 Mass.] 134, 138. If the change in the value of the estate is not so great, or if it appears that the buildings did not constitute so material a part of the estate to be conveyed as to result in an annulling of the contract, specific performance may be decreed, *with compensation for any breach of agreement,* or relief may be given in damages." (Emphasis ours.) See also Gillis v. Bonelli-Adams Co., 284 Mass. 176, 187 N.E. 535. An extreme case, showing the unfairness of the arbitrary rule placing all loss on the vendee, is Amundson v.

Severson, 41 S.D. 377, 170 N.W. 633, where three-fourths of the land sold was washed away by the Missouri River (the part left being of little value) and the vendor brought suit for specific performance. Fortunately for the vendee, he was relieved by the fact that the vendor did not have good title at the time of the loss, although the vendor had procured it as a basis for his suit. However, if the vendor had then held good title even though he did not have the land, the vendee would have been required to pay the full contract price under the loss on the purchaser rule. (Would the vendee have been any better off if the vendor had good title from the start but did not have the land left to convey?) The reason for the Massachusetts rule is that specific performance is based on what is equitable; and it is not equitable to make a vendee pay the vendor for something the vendor cannot give him.

However, the issue in this case is not whether the vendee can be compelled to take the property without the building but whether the vendee is entitled to enforce the contract of sale, with the insurance proceeds substituted for the destroyed building. We see no inequity to defendants in such enforcement since they will receive the full amount ($20,000.00) for which they contracted to sell the property. Their contract not only described the land but also specifically stated they sold it "together with the buildings, driveways and all construction thereon." While the words "Service Station Site" appeared in the caption of the option contract and that no doubt was the ultimate use plaintiff intended to make of the land, the final agreement made by the parties was that plaintiff would take it subject to a lease of the building which would have brought plaintiff about $6,150.00 in rent during the term of the lease. Moreover, defendants' own evidence showed the building was valued in the insurance adjustment at $16,716.00 from which $4,179.00 was deducted for depreciation, making the loss $12,537.00. Therefore, defendants are not in a very good position to say the building was of no value to plaintiff. Furthermore, plaintiff having contracted for the land with the building on it, the decision concerning use or removal of the building, or even for resale of the entire property, was for the plaintiff to make. Statements were in evidence about the use of the building and its value to plaintiff made by its employee who negotiated the purchase but he was not one of plaintiff's chief executive officers nor possessed of authority to bind its board of directors. The short of the matter is that defendants will get all they bargained for; but without the building or its value plaintiff will not.

We therefore affirm the judgment and decree of the trial court.

■ STORCKMAN, JUDGE (dissenting).

The precise problem presented by this appeal has not heretofore been considered by the Supreme Court. The facts of this case demonstrate the unsoundness of a rigid and exclusive adherence to the doctrine that equity regards that as done which ought to be done. I would apply general equitable principles and first determine whether Skelly has established by clear, cogent and convincing evidence that it is entitled to have a trust declared in the insurance proceeds in accordance with the allegations of Count 2 of its petition. It is not enough to say that the Ashmores have been unjustly enriched because giving the fund to Skelly would result in its being unjustly enriched. Hoover v. Wright, Mo., 202 S.W.2d 83, 86 [2, 3]; Edwards v. Friborg, 361 Mo. 578, 235 S.W.2d 255. This would result in Skelly acquiring for $10,000 a filling station site for which it solemnly agreed to pay $20,000. Swapping one inequity for another is no justification for disturbing the legal title.

If the subject matter of the purchase contract was not as well or better suited to Skelly's purpose after the fire than it was before, then it appears from the authorities above discussed that Skelly could avoid the contract entirely or that it could clearly establish the amount and manner in which it was damaged. What would the situation be if the building had not been insured or for only a small amount? The fact that the building was insured and the amount thereof are hardly determinative of Skelly's alleged injury.

But Skelly did not after the fire or in this action elect to abandon the contract although the Ashmores gave it the opportunity to do so rather than to sell at the reduced price. It is quite evident that Skelly has received one windfall as the result of the fire in that the lease is terminated and the site can be cleared at less cost. It has not shown itself to be entitled to another, the one now legally vested in the Ashmores. Ideally the purchase contract should be set aside so that the parties could negotiate a new one based on the property in its present condition. But the plaintiff by its election to take title has foreclosed this possibility.

[The majority opinion] professes to repudiate the equitable conversion theory and to adopt unequivocally the Massachusetts rule, stating: "Instead we believe the Massachusetts rule is the proper rule." This rule as shown by the opinion's quotation from Libman v. Levenson, 236 Mass. 221, 128 N.E. 13, 22 A.L.R. 560, is that the sales contract will no longer be binding if the buildings are destroyed by fire and "the value of the buildings constitutes a large part of the total value of the estate, and the terms of the agreement show that they constituted an important part of the subject matter of the contract". In the same quotation from the Libman case, the circumstances and terms under which specific performance is granted are stated as follows: "If the change in the value of the estate is not so great, or if it appears that the buildings did not constitute so material a part of the estate to be conveyed as to result in an annulling of the contract, specific performance may be decreed, *with compensation for any breach of agreement, or relief may be given in damages."* (Emphasis added.)

Obviously the majority opinion did not find that the value of the building constituted "a large part of the total value of the estate" or "an important part of the subject matter of the contract", else it would have declared the sales contract no longer binding under the Massachusetts rule. What it had to find was that the value of the building was not so great or such a material part of the estate to be conveyed as to interfere with the decree of specific performance.

But at this point the majority opinion abandons any pretense of following the Massachusetts rule and switches back to the equitable conversion theory and awards the insurance proceeds as such to the vendee without a determination of compensation for breach or relief to be given in damages. The value of the building for insurance purposes or as a structure to house a retail store is not necessarily the proper measure of the compensation or damages to which the plaintiff is entitled. It might be considerably less than such a figure if Skelly intended to remove the building as soon as it had the legal right to do so. Obviously the Massachusetts rule is not tied in with insurance at all and that is as it should be. Logically the majority opinion should have remanded the case for a determination of the amount of actual damages suffered by Skelly or the compensation to which it is entitled if it still wants specific performance. This is undoubtedly what the Massachusetts rule contemplates. I would find no fault with such a procedure.

Such evidence would also have a bearing on whether specific performance should be decreed at all, which was the first matter to be determined. Actually without such evidence the court does not have any basis for its finding as to the value of the building to the vendee and whether it was "an important part of the subject matter of the contract". Such a determination is a necessary prerequisite to granting or denying specific performance under the Massachusetts rule before the assessment of damages is reached. As the opinion stands, the adoption of the Massachusetts rule is more imaginary than real. The equitable conversion theory is *applied,* not the Massachusetts rule.

The opinion simply awards the *proceeds* of the fire insurance policy. It does not, and could not on the evidence in the present record, ascertain the compensation or damages, if any, to which Skelly is entitled by reason of the destruction of the building. Evidence of this sort was excluded by the trial court. Count 2 of plaintiff's petition claims the insurance proceeds on the theory of a trust fund as a matter of law and that seems to be the basis of the majority opinion's award of the insurance fund to the purchaser. This is the antithesis of the Massachusetts rule which contemplates the ascertainment of the amount of compensation or damages that will assure the vendee receiving the value for which it contracted, and no more.

Although the entire court now seems to be in agreement that the theory of equitable conversion should not be adopted and that the equitable rules which should govern are those that require an allowance of compensation or damages to fit the particular case, nevertheless a majority of the court have concurred in an opinion which makes the amount of insurance proceeds the yardstick. This is the rejected doctrine of equitable conversion regardless of the name given to it.

On the present record the plaintiff has failed to show a superior equity in the insurance proceeds under the Massachusetts rule or otherwise, and on well-established equitable principles I would leave the legal title to that fund where it is. I would find against the plaintiff on Count 2 of its petition, but award it specific performance under Count 1 on the condition that it pay to the defendants the agreed purchase price of $20,000 less the amount of compensation or damages, if any, that it could establish against the defendants (not the insurance funds) at a plenary hearing of that issue in the trial court.

## Lucenti v. Cayuga Apartments, Inc.
Court of Appeals of New York, 1979.
48 N.Y.2d 530, 423 N.Y.S.2d 886, 399 N.E.2d 918.

■ MEYER, JUDGE.

When prior to title closing a building is substantially damaged by fire may the purchaser [plaintiff] under a real estate contract which contains no risk of loss provision obtain specific performance with an abatement of the purchase price?

The issue arises in the context of a contract executed June 21, 1975, by which plaintiff agreed to purchase two contiguous parcels of real estate on each of which there was a freestanding building. One week after the contract was executed the older of the two buildings was substantially destroyed by a fire, which, however, did no damage to the other building.

Defendant submitted proofs of loss to its insurers on September 19, 1975 and received payments of its claims totaling more than $45,000. On October 15, 1975 defendant's attorneys forwarded to plaintiff's attorney their check in refund of the $1,000 deposit paid by plaintiff on signing the contract. Plaintiff's attorney promptly returned the check, stating that plaintiff wished to proceed with the closing with an abatement of the purchase price. One month later plaintiff began the instant action for specific performance with an abatement of the purchase price.

The Trial Judge held that section 5–1311 of the General Obligations Law required the purchaser either to rescind or to obtain specific performance without abatement and that plaintiff had by his conduct terminated the contract. He, therefore, dismissed the complaint. The Appellate Division reversed on the law and the facts and remitted for determination of the abatement to which plaintiff was entitled. On remand the trial court fixed the abatement at $19,500, consisting of $7,500 to remove the remains of the old building and $12,000 as its actual value. Plaintiff again appealed and the Appellate Division modified by increasing the abatement to $27,500, holding that the trial court was correct in considering defendant's insurance claims but gave too little weight to their statements of value, and fixing the actual value of the building on consideration of the whole record at $20,000. Plaintiff's appeal from the Appellate Division's order, affirming as modified, has been dismissed by us on the ground that he was not aggrieved by the modification. There remains defendant's appeal which brings up for our review both the Appellate Division's final order and its earlier nonfinal order. There should be an affirmance.

The fundamental issue for our determination is the effect of section 5–1311 of the General Obligations Law. That section provides in pertinent part:

> 1. Any contract for the purchase and sale or exchange of realty shall be interpreted, unless the contract expressly provides otherwise, as including an agreement that the parties shall have the following rights and duties:
>
>> a. When neither the legal title nor the possession of the subject matter of the contract has been transferred to the purchaser: (1) if all or a material part thereof is destroyed without fault of the purchaser or is taken by eminent domain, the vendor cannot enforce the contract, and the purchaser is entitled to recover any portion of the price that he has paid; but nothing herein contained shall be deemed to deprive the vendor of any right to recover damages against the purchaser for any breach of contract by the purchaser prior to the destruction or taking; (2) if an immaterial part thereof is destroyed without fault of the purchaser or is taken by eminent domain, neither the vendor nor the purchaser is thereby deprived of the right to enforce the contract; but there shall be, to the extent of the destruction or taking, an abatement of the purchase price.

Paragraph b of subdivision 1 provides that when legal title or possession has been transferred to the purchaser he is not relieved by destruction of all or any part of the property from his obligation to pay the price; subdivision 2 directs that the section be interpreted and construed so as to effectuate its general purpose to make uniform the laws of the States which enact it and subdivision 3 provides that the section may be cited as the Uniform Vendor and Purchaser Risk Act.

Originally enacted in 1936 on the recommendation of the Law Revision Commission as section 240–a of the Real Property Law, and repealed and reenacted in 1963 as section 5–1311 of the General Obligations Law, the section is based upon a proposed uniform law drafted by Professor Samuel Williston. There is abundant evidence that in drafting the proposed uniform law Professor Williston sought only to change the rule he believed erroneously declared by Lord Eldon in Paine v. Meller (6 Vesey Jr. 349 [holding the purchaser required to pay the full price despite destruction of part of the property contracted for]) which was followed in a number of States in this country, including New York. The act as drafted by him turned on whether title or the right to possession had passed, and reversed the Paine v. Meller rule by providing that if it had not and "all or a material part" was accidentally destroyed "the vendor cannot enforce the contract, and the purchaser is entitled to recover any portion of the price he has paid, unless the contract expressly provides otherwise". [A] prefatory note [in a 1935 Report by the Law Revision Committee stated] that "The object of the Act is to protect the purchaser of real estate where there is a binding contract of sale and the property is destroyed before the purchaser has gone into possession or has taken legal title, and to protect the vendor after transfer of possession" and that "The rule which is proposed in this Act is that the purchaser cannot be held if he has taken neither possession nor title, but can be held if he has taken possession or has taken title." Conspicuously absent from any of these materials is any reference to a purchaser's right to specific performance with an abatement, but since specific performance with an abatement imposes on the seller only the risk of loss contemplated by the act, that absence is wholly consistent with the stated purpose of the act and cannot be read as indicating any intention to affect the purchaser's optional remedy.

[T]he statute simply does not speak to the situation in which a purchaser seeks to enforce the contract notwithstanding that a material part of the realty has been destroyed. In consequence, the common-law abatement rule[8] would continue to apply, absent a contrary indication in some other portion of the statute or in its legislative history.

In World Exhibit Corp. v. City Bank Farmers Trust Co., 186 Misc. 420, 59 N.Y.S.2d 648, decided in 1945, the assignee of a vendee in possession under a contract providing that "The risk of loss or damage to said premises by fire, until delivery of said deed, is assumed by the seller" was granted specific performance with an abatement. The court reasoned that section 240–a of the Real Property Law "was intended primarily to shield a vendee", "was not intended to be invoked at the instance of a vendor", and did not prevent a vendee from seeking specific performance. It noted also that the section was not operative where "the contract expressly provides otherwise". Affirming, the Appellate Division concluded that since the parties had provided otherwise the statute played no part and the common-law rule applied. We affirmed without opinion.

Two years later in Heerdt v. Brand, 272 App.Div. 143, 70 N.Y.S.2d 1, the Appellate Division, Fourth Department, affirmed a judgment giving a purchaser out of possession an abatement to the extent of the cost of repair where five days prior to closing the boiler in the house was substantially damaged. The court reasoned that the addition of section

---

[8] Polisiuk v. Mayers, 205 App.Div. 573, 200 N.Y.S. 97, app. den. 206 App.Div. 765 recognized the right to specific performance with abatement when the contract put the risk of loss prior to delivery of the deed on the vendor, which is what the statute now does when the purchaser is out of possession. Specific performance with abatement had long been recognized in other situations, e.g., Feldman v. Lisansky, 239 N.Y. 81, 145 N.E. 746; Bostwick v. Beach, 103 N.Y. 414, 9 N.E. 40; Warren v. Hoch, 276 App.Div. 607, 96 N.Y.S.2d 832; see Friedman, Contracts and Conveyances of Real Property [3d ed.], p. 808.

240–a (subd. 1, par. [a], cl. [2]) effected no change in the law, and that the loss fell on the seller since neither title nor possession had passed, but did not otherwise discuss the basis upon which abatement was allowed. Three years later, in 1950, the same Appellate Division in Rizzo v. Landmark Realty Corp., 277 App.Div. 1094, 101 N.Y.S.2d 151, app. den. 278 App.Div. 630, 102 N.Y.S.2d 637, reversed a judgment dismissing plaintiff purchaser's complaint for specific performance stating flatly that: "Section 240–a of the Real Property Law does not deprive a vendee of the right of specific performance with abatement. Said section subd. 1, [par.] (a) renders unenforceable insofar as the vendor is concerned the right to specific performance when the loss is material. It does not, however, destroy any common-law right of the vendee to specific performance with abatement."

Burack v. Tollig, 6 Misc.2d 450, 160 N.Y.S.2d 1008, involved a purchaser out of possession under a contract that was silent as to risk of loss, who was awarded specific performance with an abatement by reason of a fire, occurring between contract and closing, which destroyed the dwelling on the property. Special Term held section 240–a to be applicable but stated (citing *World Exhibit Corp.,* supra, and *Rizzo,* supra) that "It has been held, however, that the said provisions of the cited section do not deprive the purchaser of his common law right to specific performance with an abatement" and noted that the parties conceded plaintiff's right to such an abatement. The Appellate Division, Second Department, modified with respect to damages and affirmed (9 A.D.2d 914, 194 N.Y.S.2d 987) and we affirmed, without opinion (10 N.Y.2d 879, 223 N.Y.S.2d 505, 179 N.E.2d 509). The last case decided under section 240–a before it was repealed and re-enacted as section 5–1311, likewise a Second Department decision, was Matter of County of Westchester v. P. & M. Materials Corp., 20 A.D.2d 431, 248 N.Y.S.2d 539. There a vendee out of possession when the contracted-for property was condemned was held entitled only to return of its deposit, the court differentiating condemnation from a material destruction of the property. In doing so it observed with respect to the latter:

> Though the Law Revision Commission Report stated that, upon a material destruction of the premises, the Uniform Act effected a rescission when the purchaser had neither legal title nor possession, it has been held that, under those circumstances, the purchaser may be granted specific performance together with an abatement of the selling price. . . .
>
> In the case of a material destruction, the availability of specific performance with abatement under the statute (Real Property Law, § 240–a), upon which we have not had occasion to pass finds rational support in the expectation that a purchaser may want his bargain for a proportionately diminished consideration. Such an intention may reasonably be imputed to the contracting parties, resting as it does on the just result that

both parties will thus realize, in lesser form, the substance of their agreement.

Thus, no decision made under section 240–a denied to a purchaser out of possession specific performance with an abatement when there was a material destruction of the property between contract and closing. Against this decisional background, the repeal and re-enactment of the section as section 5–1311 of the General Obligations Law must be assessed. The applicable principle is stated in Matter of Scheftel's, 275 N.Y. 135, 141, 9 N.E.2d 809, 811: "the Legislature is presumed to have had knowledge of the construction which had been placed on the provision . . . and in adopting in these re-enactments the language used in the earlier act, must be deemed to have adopted also the interpretation of the legislative intent decided by this court, and to have made that construction a part of the reenactment", and in McKinney's Statutes (McKinney's Cons.Laws of N.Y., Book 1, Statutes, § 75, p. 165): "In the case of a revision or consolidation of statutes, if there is no change in the phraseology of the statute, its former judicial construction becomes a part of the subsequent statute." The conclusion to be drawn from the foregoing analysis is that as we stated in Hecht v. Meller, 23 N.Y.2d 301, 304, 296 N.Y.S.2d 561, 562, 244 N.E.2d 77, 78, *supra*, § 5–1311 "bestowed a privilege on vendees to rescind the contract" in the event of a material destruction prior to closing but did not take from them their common-law optional remedy of specific performance with an abatement.

Accordingly, the order of the Appellate Division should be affirmed, with costs.

## NOTES

1. *DiDonato*. Which rule does the Pennsylvania court follow in *DiDonato*? Would the outcome have been different if Pennsylvania had adopted the Uniform Act?

2. *Skelly Oil*. Which rule does the Missouri court follow in *Skelly Oil*? Although the buyers themselves could not be forced to perform, they wanted to specifically enforce the contract with an abatement in price based on the amount of damage. Why did the *Skelly Oil* court allow this?

3. *Lucenti*. If you are in a jurisdiction that rejects equitable conversion and the seller will bear any loss during the gap period, should the buyer have a right to specifically enforce the contract with an abatement in price for the loss? The New York Court of Appeals in *Lucenti* said yes. However, a California Court of Appeal considered the issue in Dixon v. Salvation Army and reached the opposite result.[9] The California court considered the *Lucenti* decision but declined to follow it because it was partly based on New York common law. The California court held:

> [t]he more equitable approach and one more compatible with the Uniform Act is to place the parties in their original position, free to

---

[9] 142 Cal.App.3d 463, 191 Cal.Rptr. 111 (1983).

make a new bargain. A rule that denies a vendor the ability to specifically enforce the sales agreement where the material part of the consideration is lost or destroyed calls out for the converse also to be applied. It would be grossly unfair to require either party to accept consideration less than the whole of what was bargained for.[10]

Do you agree with *Lucenti* or *Dixon*?

4. *Proper drafting.* If you were drafting a contract for the purchase of real estate, how would you handle the possibility of fire during the gap period? Suppose you are in a state that has the Uniform Act, and you represent the buyer. Assume that all or a substantial part of the premises are destroyed by fire, but your client still would like to purchase the premises with an appropriate reduction for the value of the destroyed premises. Does the Uniform Act allow that, or must you specifically provide for it in the sales contract?

If you decide that a specific clause in the contract is necessary, how would you draft it? How would you describe an "appropriate reduction"? Among the drafting pointers to consider: (1) Destruction may be by disasters other than fire. (2) Ideally the buyer should have an option as to whether to proceed with an abatement of price or to rescind. (3) If the buyer elects to rescind, he would like out of pocket expenses from the seller. (4) How does one define "a material or substantial part of the premises"?[11] (5) If an immaterial or insubstantial part of the premises is destroyed, what should the buyer's rights be? (6) Should the buyer take out insurance to cover the gap period? What could the buyer collect under such insurance? (7) Should the buyer require the seller to maintain existing insurance? (8) How can the buyer be sure that the seller will keep such a promise?

5. *Tactical considerations.* When evaluating whether to suggest that a risk-allocation clause be included in the sales contract, bear in mind that attempting to include a clause that favors your client is likely to prompt the other side to suggest a clause that favors its interests. However, if you remain silent on the issue, the other side may also ignore it. Thus, the absence of a clause in a contract may either represent a deliberate tactical decision or it may represent ignorance and carelessness. In the Principal Problem, if you represented Bob, would you have suggested including a clause in the contract pertaining to zoning changes? If so, what would you have wanted the clause to say? What if you represented Sally?

6. *Fire vs. zoning change.* With certain types of loss, such as fire, the seller often is in a better position to protect against harm or to obtain

---

[10] Id. at 467, 191 Cal.Rptr. at 114.

[11] Many contracts define a "material loss" as follows: "A loss is material if the cost of repairing or replacing it, without deduction for depreciation, exceeds the sum of $_____, provided that if the applicable building codes require work exceeding the repair or replacement of actual damage, the cost shall be considered to include all the work. A taking by eminent domain is material if the diminution in market value exceeds the sum stated above."

insurance against it than the buyer.[12] Since fire or casualty insurance is customary, that type of loss is likely to be recovered by the seller. In the Principal Problem, however, the value of the property is diminished by a zoning change. Neither the buyer nor the seller is in a better position to protect against zoning changes. In addition, since there is no such thing as insurance against rezoning, if any loss falls on the seller, the seller is likely to bear that loss personally.

The general rule in zoning cases is that the risk of zoning changes falls upon the buyer.[13] Does it make sense to place the risk of zoning changes on the buyer? The only exception to the general rule appears to be cases of fraud or misrepresentation by the seller. This is true even in some cases where the seller honestly believed that the misrepresentation was true.[14] In Groswird v. Hayne Investments, Inc., the purchasers asked the sellers about the zoning status of a tract of land they wanted to purchase.[15] The sellers advised them of the zoning status and the purchasers verified it with the county. The sellers later learned that the county was planning to down zone the property as a timber preserve zone, but they withheld this information from the purchasers. The court held that the sellers had a duty to inform the purchasers of the change in zoning and that their failure to do so constituted fraud. The purchasers were awarded damages to reflect the diminution in market value of the property.

There are some zoning cases in which the court allowed the buyer to rescind the contract when the zoning changed after signing the sales contract where the seller knew of the buyer's intended use.[16] However, other courts considering this question refused to award relief even though the seller knew of the buyer's intended use.[17]

7. *Insurance.* One of the most confusing issues in this area concerns insurance. If the seller or buyer carries insurance and there is a loss during the gap period, who gets the proceeds? Where the seller and buyer have entered into an executory land sales contract, both parties have an insurable interest. That is, either or both may purchase insurance to indemnify their respective interests in the event of loss, regardless of who would bear the risk of loss.

Where the seller maintains an insurance policy and the buyer does not, the buyer may wish to claim the benefits of the policy through an abatement

---

[12] The fire cases are collected and discussed in Annotation, Risk of Loss by Casualty Pending Contract for Conveyance of Real Property—Modern Cases, 85 A.L.R. 4th 233 (1991 & Supp. 2009).

[13] The cases on zoning changes are collected in Annotation, Zoning or Other Public Restrictions on the Use of Property as Affecting Rights and Remedies of Parties to a Contract for the Sale Thereof, 39 A.L.R.3d 362 (1971 & Supp. 2009).

[14] Slocum v. Leffler, 272 Or. 700, 538 P.2d 906 (1975); Kroninger v. Anast, 367 Mich. 478, 116 N.W.2d 863 (1962); Arena v. Hegyhaty, 30 A.D.2d 808, 292 N.Y.S.2d 285 (1968).

[15] 133 Cal.App.3d 624, 184 Cal.Rptr. 123 (1982), *reh'g granted*, August 6, 1982, (unpublished decision).

[16] Clay v. Landreth, 187 Va. 169, 45 S.E.2d 875 (1948); Anderson v. Steinway & Sons, 178 A.D. 507, 165 N.Y.S. 608 (1917), aff'd, 221 N.Y. 639, 117 N.E. 575 (1917).

[17] Kend v. Crestwood Realty Co., 210 Wis. 239, 246 N.W. 311 (1933); Biggs v. Steinway & Sons, 229 N.Y. 320, 128 N.E. 211 (1920).

in purchase price, or by payment of the proceeds to the buyer when the buyer has tendered the full purchase price. There is a split of authority regarding whether this is allowed.[18] The majority rule allows the buyer to recover the insurance proceeds under a theory of constructive trusteeship.[19] Since the buyer is considered to be the equitable owner of the property, the seller holds title to the property and insurance proceeds in trust for the buyer. The rationale for this rule is to prevent unjust enrichment of the seller. If the buyer purchases the damaged property for full price and the seller is allowed to keep the insurance proceeds, the seller has received a windfall.

But what about the windfall to the buyer under the majority rule? If the buyer receives the insurance proceeds, there is also a windfall because the buyer did not pay for the insurance premiums. To remedy this, some courts reduce the amount of proceeds to be paid to the buyer by the amount of the premiums paid by the seller.[20]

A minority of jurisdictions hold that an insurance contract is personal between the seller and the insurance company, and therefore the buyer has no interest at all in any proceeds under the policy.[21] The rationale behind the minority rule is that the insurance contract indemnifies the insured against loss, but not any other party. Which do you think is the better rule? How do the rules regarding insurance correlate with the approaches to risk allocation?

Where the buyer purchases insurance to protect his interest in a sales contract, the seller usually has no claim to any insurance proceeds collected by the buyer, unless there is a contract clause that alters this rule.

Matters get complicated when both the seller and the buyer have purchased insurance to cover their respective interests.[22] For example, seller and buyer both carry insurance on the house that is the subject of their sales contract. During the gap period, the house is destroyed by fire. The buyer's insurance covers the loss and the buyer pays the seller the full purchase price for the house. May the seller also collect under her policy? If the seller collects, she gets a windfall; but if she does not collect, her insurance company gets the windfall in unpaid premiums.

A majority of jurisdictions measure the loss at the time of the casualty and, thereby, allow the seller to recover. That is, the seller had an insurable interest at the time of the fire and, therefore, the insurance company must pay. The minority rule denies recovery and adds to the requirement that there be an insurable interest another requirement; namely, that there be a

---

[18] For an article discussing the merits and pitfalls of the majority and minority rules, see McDowell, Insurable Interest in Property Revisited, 17 Cap. U.L. Rev. 165 (1988).

[19] Heinzman v. Howard, 366 N.W.2d 500 (S.D.1985); Fellmer v. Gruber, 261 N.W.2d 173 (Iowa 1978); Skelly Oil v. Ashmore, 365 S.W.2d 582 (Mo.1963).

[20] Berlier v. George, 94 N.M. 134, 607 P.2d 1152 (1980); Gilles v. Sprout, 293 Minn. 53, 196 N.W.2d 612 (1972).

[21] Whitley v. Irwin, 250 Ark. 543, 465 S.W.2d 906 (1971); Smith v. Hardware Dealers Mut. Fire Ins. Co., 253 Wis. 129, 33 N.W.2d 206 (1948).

[22] See Fischer, The Presence of Insurance and the Legal Allocation of Risk, 2 Conn. Ins. L.J. 1 (1996).

loss. If the buyer has paid the seller the full purchase price, the seller suffers no loss and cannot recover. Which rule is preferable?

8. *Eminent domain.* Suppose that the government takes the property by eminent domain during the gap period.[23] In such cases, in the absence of a statute, the overwhelming majority of jurisdictions apply the doctrine of equitable conversion, and find that the buyer must buy the land and is entitled to the condemnation award. This occurs even in states like Massachusetts that reject the doctrine of equitable conversion. This may be because eminent domain rarely results in financial hardship because the government provides compensation which is often quite generous. Because the seller is in no better position than the buyer to protect against eminent domain and there is no real loss, it seems fair to have the new owner deal with the condemning authorities.

9. *Changes that do not excuse performance of contract obligations.* During the gap period, the seller's or buyer's need for the property may change or the market value of the property may change. Usually, neither a change in the market value nor a change in the buyer's or seller's needs will excuse them from performing the sales contract. Why should this be so? The result is usually explained by saying that the buyer and seller have "assumed the risk" of these changes, but this explanation is mainly conclusory. Rather, the very purpose of entering into any contract is to stabilize the relations of the parties so that subsequent events such as these do not affect the original agreement.

10. *Possession.* Suppose the buyer takes possession prior to closing, but only as a tenant, paying full market rent. Seisin is in the seller but physical possession is in the buyer. Should the buyer be treated as having possession for the purposes of the Uniform Act? In Long v. Keller the buyer, before purchase, had leased the property, and in turn subleased to a subtenant.[24] Both parties agreed that the buyer was in possession for the purposes of the statute. If the possession of the subtenant was attributed to the buyer-tenant, why was the possession of the buyer-tenant not attributed to the seller-landlord?

11. *Defective title.* One generally recognized exception to the doctrine of equitable conversion is that where the seller's title is defective at the time of the loss, the seller will bear the loss.[25] This is so, regardless of which party was in possession of the property at the time of the loss. If on the date of the loss the seller could not deliver good title, the seller will bear the loss, even if the seller gained marketable title at a later date. Does this make sense if the title defect is one that is easily curable? Suppose, for example, that there is a lien for a $200 water bill on a $2 million property. Should liability for a $1 million fire loss during the time gap between sales contract and closing

---

[23] The cases on eminent domain are collected and discussed in Annotation, Rights and Liabilities of Parties to Executory Contract for Sale of Land Taken by Eminent Domain, 27 A.L.R.3d 572 (1969 & Supp. 2009).

[24] 104 Cal.App.3d 312, 163 Cal.Rptr. 532 (1980).

[25] See Phillips v. Bacon, 245 Ga. 814, 267 S.E.2d 249 (1980).

depend on the existence of the $200 lien for an unpaid water bill, which normally would be paid off at the closing?

12. *Uniform Land Transactions Act (ULTA).* This Act generally follows the Uniform Vendor and Purchaser Risk Act (the Uniform Act), but is more comprehensive and answers some of the questions left open by the Uniform Act. The relevant statutory language follows:

### § 2–406. [Risk of Loss, Casualty Loss, Real Estate Other Than Leaseholds]

(a) This section does not apply to transfers of leaseholds.

(b) Risk of loss or of taking by eminent domain and owner's liabilities remain on the seller until the occurrence of the events specified in subsection (c). In case of a casualty loss or taking by eminent domain while the risk is on the seller:

(1) If the loss or taking results in a substantial failure of the real estate to conform to the contract, the buyer may cancel the contract and recover any portion of the price he has paid, or accept the real estate with his choice of (i) a reduction of the contract price equal to the decrease in fair market value caused by the loss or taking, or (ii) the benefit of the seller's insurance coverage or the eminent domain payment for the loss or taking, but without further right against the seller; or

(2) if the real estate substantially conforms to the contract after the loss or taking, the buyer must accept the real estate, but is entitled to his choice of (i) a reduction of the contract price equal to the decrease in fair market value caused by the loss or taking or (ii) the benefit of the seller's insurance coverage or the eminent domain payment with respect to the loss or taking but without further right against the seller.

(c) Risk of loss or taking and owner's liabilities pass to the buyer:

(1) if sale is not to be consummated by means of an escrow, at the earlier of delivery of the instrument of conveyance or transfer of possession of the real estate to him; or

(2) if sale is to be consummated by means of an escrow, at the earlier of transfer of possession or fulfillment of the conditions of the escrow.

(d) Any loss or taking of the real estate after risk of loss or taking has passed to the buyer does not discharge him from his obligations under the contract of purchase.

(e) For the purposes of any provision of law imposing obligations or liabilities upon the holder of legal title, title does not pass to the buyer until he accepts the instrument of conveyance.

What questions does ULTA address? As a lawyer, would you welcome this Act? If you were a legislator, would you propose that your state adopt this Act? To date, no state has adopted ULTA. Does the lack of specificity of the Uniform Act make it a more attractive alternative?

## ASSIGNMENT 53

# AFTER THE CLOSING: IMPLIED WARRANTY OF FITNESS AND THE DUTY TO DISCLOSE

## 1. INTRODUCTION

*The demise of caveat emptor.* Prior to the 1960s, caveat emptor, or "buyer beware" ruled real estate sales. Two traditions from the common law put the burden of discovering defects in the real property squarely on the buyer. First, the doctrine of merger dictated that unless a covenant from the contract was incorporated into the deed, the rights and liabilities of the parties were thereafter determined solely by the deed and all other previous negotiations and agreements were deemed to be waived. The contract and negotiations "merged" with the deed. Second, because the parties were dealing at arms length, the courts did not impose a duty to disclose defects in the property on the seller; nonfeasance was not actionable conduct.[1] Consequently, the seller had no responsibility for defects, except in the unlikely event that an express warranty had been included in the deed.

In the 1960s, courts began to move away from this rigid interpretation. Since that time, the courts have used a variety of vehicles, including implied warranties and disclosure rules, to shift the liability for latent defects from the buyer to the seller. However, neither the merger doctrine nor the nonfeasance rule has been completely eliminated. For example, if a defect is patent when the deed is accepted, the buyer is normally held to waive any objection to it by accepting the deed.

> EXAMPLE 1: Alex is a contractor who erects a house upon property he owns. Before the completed house is occupied, a rain storm reveals that the roof is not waterproof. Extensive water damage is caused to the interior, as evidenced by streaking on the walls and large puddles on the floors. The damage is especially noticeable in the sunken living room where several inches of standing water has collected. Alex, who is now engaged in another project, has neither the time nor the desire to fix the roof and contracts to sell the property to Blanche. Blanche inspects the property, notices the water damage, but still agrees to purchase the property. The deed is transferred and the transaction is closed. During the next rain, the house floods.

---

[1] Restatement (Second) of Torts § 352 (1965).

Blanche wants to collect damages to cover the cost of fixing the house. What is the result?

ANSWER: Blanche loses. The defect is patent because it could be discovered by a reasonable inspection. The puddles on the floor and streaking on the walls would lead an "ordinary" buyer to inspect the roof. Blanche is deemed to have "waived" any objection to the problem.

*Implied warranties of fitness.* The most prevalent method used by courts and legislatures to protect the buyer is to impose an implied warranty of fitness; at least with regard to purchases of new homes for personal use. The implied warranty of fitness doctrine holds builder-vendors to a standard of reasonable workmanship. An action based on the doctrine can be thought of as a cross between a tort action in misrepresentation and a contract action. This implied warranty can be created by the legislature or, as is more common, by the courts.

*The scope of the implied warranty of fitness.* With the development after World War II of large scale residential developments, it became increasingly clear that putting the burden of discovering a latent defect upon an inexperienced buyer is unjust. This is especially true when the buyer is not involved in the construction phases of the building. The vendor-builder is in a much better position to discover latent defects. Furthermore, an individual who buys from a professional vendor is often in a "take it or leave it" situation, and must rely on the warranties of the vendor.[2]

The implied warranty doctrine initially protected a buyer only from an unreasonably dangerous condition. Later it was expanded to protect the buyer's reasonable expectation of receiving fair value for the purchase price. "A sound price warrants a sound commodity." The implied warranty of fitness doctrine imposes a duty on the vendor to furnish a sound product. Without an implied warranty, an unscrupulous vendor could profit by selling the vendee a defective product for the price of a sound product; the vendor profits from sloppy work by taking advantage of the buyer's reasonable expectations. The implied warranty promotes a high quality of construction as well as integrity in sales transactions.

EXAMPLE 2: In Example 1, assume the roof still leaked, but the insulation in the ceiling had absorbed the water like a 14,000 pound sponge. After Blanche had purchased the property, a rainstorm caused the ceiling to collapse. Blanche seeks damages sufficient to repair the house. What is the result?

ANSWER: Blanche wins. Even with a reasonable inspection, the defect could not have been discovered. Blanche has the right to

---

[2] Annotation, Liability of Builder-Vendor or Other Vendor of New Dwelling for Loss, Injury, or Damage Occasioned by Defective Condition Thereof, 25 A.L.R.3d 383, 390 (1969 & Supp. 2009).

expect her new home to be waterproof, and for the ceiling insulation not to collapse. Regardless of whether Alex was aware of the problem, he will be held liable for repairs.

*Implied warranties and the doctrine of merger.* Some courts characterize the implied warranty as a "collateral" right that is not waived by acceptance of the deed. This approach reflects a modern view of merger: one cannot waive a right unless one knew or should have known of the defect. Since a reasonable inspection would not reveal latent imperfections, acceptance of the deed could not be a waiver of the right. Other courts find that the doctrine of merger has no relevance to the implied warranty of fitness doctrine. These courts view the buyer's rights under the implied warranty as arising as a matter of law from the purchase, and not from the sales contract, the deed, or negotiations. Most courts that recognize an implied warranty of fitness in the sale of new housing have not discussed the relationship between the merger doctrine and an implied warranty of fitness. The Uniform Land Transaction Act (ULTA) has completely rejected the merger doctrine. See ULTA § 1–309.

*Implied warranties and commercial transactions.* When the real estate sale involves commercial property, the arguments for an implied warranty of fitness are not as strong. The vendee in a commercial transaction often has greater knowledge and ability to protect itself than does one who buys real property for personal use. Furthermore, there is far less chance that the commercial buyer will be buying the property "off the shelf." Generally, the commercial buyer is involved in the property's development. Consequently, the courts have been more reluctant to impose an implied warranty when dealing with commercial transactions.[3]

> EXAMPLE 3: In Example 2, assume that Blanche purchased the property as an investment, which she hoped to resell or rent. Will Alex be liable to Blanche for damages based upon an implied warranty theory?
>
> ANSWER: The answer is unclear. In favor of Blanche's recovery is the fact she was not involved in the construction process and that she was relying upon the expertise of Alex. Against Blanche's recovery is the fact that she was not occupying the home, but instead hoped to generate income. She might be presumed to have the knowledge and experience to discover the defect before the sale.

*Liability of the builder to subsequent purchasers.* Several theories of law have been used to hold the builder liable to a subsequent purchaser, a vendee who was not the original purchaser. If the subsequent purchaser can prove actual negligence on the part of a builder which results in foreseeable injury or loss to this purchaser, he should be able

---

[3] Powell & Mallor, The Case for an Implied Warranty of Quality in Sales of Commercial Real Estate, 68 Wash.U.L.Q. 305, 306–07 (1990).

to recover in most jurisdictions under the tort action of negligence. It is more difficult for a subsequent purchaser to recover on an express contract theory. Because of a lack of privity of contract, most courts will not extend the protection accorded the original vendee (the "intermediate") under an express contract with the builder, to the subsequent purchaser in a contract action.[4]

> EXAMPLE 4: Christina, the builder, sold a house she built to an intermediate, Derek, who had intended to reside in the house. Although evidence of water damage existed, Derek attributed that damage to an improperly installed roof. Christina gave Derek an express warranty that the roof was in perfect shape and did not leak. In fact, the roof had been negligently installed, and this negligence could be proven. Water leaked into the house while Derek lived there, and Derek cleaned up the water damage. Because of a job reassignment one month after he occupied the house, Derek sold the house to Earl. Earl resided in the house until the rains came and the latent defect was detected. Can Earl recover any damages from Christina?
>
> ANSWER: If Earl is suing in tort under a negligence cause of action, he would prevail because the negligence could be proven. The lack of a contractual relationship between Christina and Earl would be irrelevant. If Earl is suing in contract based upon the express warranty, most jurisdictions will find for Christina because Christina and Earl are not in privity of contract.

*Implied warranties and the subsequent purchaser.* In addition to a negligence theory and a contract action based upon an express warranty, the third theory on which a subsequent purchaser can recover for latent defects attributable to the construction of the building is the implied warranty of fitness. As mentioned above, an implied warranty action can be thought of as a cross between a tort and a contract action. To recover in a contract action, privity of contract is normally required. Many jurisdictions have been reluctant to discard the requirement of privity of contract. In those jurisdictions that allow recovery, different rationales are used to discard this requirement. Some jurisdictions have used reasoning similar to strict liability in tort law, which rejects the need for privity of contract in product liability cases. Other jurisdictions have rejected the need for privity of contract in all situations. Finally, some courts have rejected the need for privity of contract based upon the individual circumstances of the case, such as when a resale occurs shortly after the original purchase, or when the builder knew the intermediate was not going to be the ultimate occupant.

---

[4] Annotation, Liability of Builder of Residence for Latent Defects Therein as Running to Subsequent Purchasers From Original Vendee, 10 A.L.R.4th 385, 388 (1981 & Supp. 2009).

EXAMPLE 5: Assume the facts are the same as in Example 4. Can the subsequent purchaser, Earl, recover damages from Christina based upon an implied warranty of fitness?

ANSWER: Because of the short time the intermediate, Derek, held the property, Earl might be able to recover but this depends upon the jurisdiction. In those jurisdictions which require privity of contract, Earl would lose. In those jurisdictions allowing recovery to a subsequent purchaser, Earl would win because he falls within the class protected by an implied warranty of fitness (a resident who was not involved in the building process, relying upon the representations of the builder).

*Liability of an intermediate owner (not the builder) to a subsequent purchaser.* When dealing with used homes, defects that are not known nor discoverable to the intermediate are likely to exist. Furthermore, because the intermediate was not involved in the building process he may be in no better position to discover the defect than the subsequent purchaser, who can make a reasonable inspection of the premises. To impose an implied warranty upon the intermediate as to the condition of the property would be unjust when the intermediate did not know, and could not have known, of the defect.

However, in line with the decline of caveat emptor, some courts have imposed an affirmative duty upon the intermediate to disclose defects patent to her, but latent to the subsequent purchaser. This duty to disclose is not exclusive nor universally accepted. To implement a duty to disclose, the courts must grapple with the long standing tradition that silence or nonfeasance is not actionable conduct when no special relationship exists between the buyer and seller. Almost all courts now accept the principle that an intermediate is under an affirmative duty to disclose certain known "dangerous conditions." Furthermore, if an intermediate takes affirmative action to conceal a material fact, courts will treat the action as conduct equivalent to a misrepresentation, rendering the conduct outside of the "nonfeasance" rule. In the most controversial area, some courts require the intermediate to disclose certain material facts that affect only the economic value of the property and do not constitute a dangerous condition. Although the law is far from settled in this area, the trend is to depart from caveat emptor and require the vendor to disclose the defect.[5]

An implied warranty will protect the subsequent purchaser from defects that are unknown to both the builder and the intermediate, by imposing liability upon the builder. In contrast, an intermediate can be held liable under a "duty to disclose" theory only if the defect is patent to the intermediate and latent to the subsequent purchaser. Only the

---

[5] Annotation, Liability of Vendor of Existing Structure for Property Damage Sustained by Purchaser After Transfer, 18 A.L.R.4th 1168 (1981 & Supp. 2009).

builder, and not the intermediate, can be held liable to the subsequent purchaser under an implied warranty theory. Under the modern trend, both the builder and the intermediate have a duty to disclose to prospective buyers defects that they know or should know about.

> EXAMPLE 6: Assume the same facts as in Example 4. Can a subsequent purchaser, Earl, recover from the intermediate, Derek, based on a duty to disclose theory?
>
> ANSWER: The modern trend is to accept the principle that the intermediate is under an affirmative duty to disclose defects patent to him, but latent to the subsequent purchaser. Following this trend, Earl would be entitled to damages. The prior water damage put Derek on notice that there were problems. Furthermore, Derek's repair of the water damage could be regarded as affirmative conduct that amounted to misrepresentation, in which case most jurisdictions would hold Derek liable.

## 2. Principal Problem

Barbara Buyer was tired of city life and wanted to open a quaint little bed and breakfast inn in the countryside. She contacted an agent in Smallsville where she heard about property previously used as a motel which was selling for an astonishingly low price. After looking at the property, she decided that it would be the perfect spot for her bed and breakfast inn. Its scenic view and secluded atmosphere seemed ideal. The local bank was eager to loan Barbara money for the purchase because the current owner, Sam Seller, was in danger of default for falling behind on his mortgage payments. Although Sam hated to sell the property, Sam's wife had found a great job in a distant city and they had to move. Sam told Barbara that the property would be perfect for her plan. Furthermore, he said the property was in great shape, as far as he knew, but that Barbara should inspect the property herself. The property was only five years old and appeared to Barbara to be fine.

After Barbara moved into the building, she began to refurbish it to serve as a bed and breakfast inn. When she was in town to purchase shower curtains, she struck up a conversation with a "local," Cathy Connor. Cathy turned white when Barbara described her plans to open the bed and breakfast and told Barbara about a string of mysterious murders that took place on the property four years ago. At that time, the first owners, the Bates, ran a small motel there. Cathy said, "That place is well known in these parts and you'll be lucky to get a plumber to visit you."

The next day Barbara discovered that a plumber is exactly what she would need. The construction company apparently did a poor job fitting the pipes when the building was built. Now Barbara has leaks from almost every pipe in the building.

Barbara comes to you for help. She claims that the place gives her the creeps and that she cannot tolerate living there. Her idea about opening a bed and breakfast inn has turned into a nightmare and no one else is interested in buying the property. Barbara would like to know if she can sue Sam for failing to tell her about the murders and the faulty pipes. She is also interested in knowing whether she can sue the construction company or the bank that financed her purchase. After reading the following materials, give Barbara an opinion regarding her rights and her prospects of success in a lawsuit.

## 3. MATERIALS FOR SOLUTION OF PRINCIPAL PROBLEM

### Lempke v. Dagenais
Supreme Court of New Hampshire, 1988.
130 N.H. 782, 547 A.2d 290.

■ THAYER, JUSTICE.

This is an appeal from the Trial Court's dismissal of the plaintiffs' complaint alleging breach of implied warranty of workmanlike quality and negligence. The primary issue before this court is whether a subsequent purchaser of real property may sue the builder/contractor on the theory of implied warranty of workmanlike quality for latent defects which cause economic loss, absent privity of contract.

We hold that privity of contract is not necessary for a subsequent purchaser to sue a builder or contractor under an implied warranty theory for latent defects which manifest themselves within a reasonable time after purchase and which cause economic harm. Accordingly, we reverse the dismissal by the trial court, and remand.

In 1977, the plaintiffs' predecessors in title contracted with the defendant, Dagenais, to build a garage. In April, 1978, within six months after the garage's construction, the original owners sold the property to plaintiffs, Elaine and Larry Lempke. Shortly after they purchased the property, the plaintiffs began to notice structural problems with the garage—the roof line was uneven and the roof trusses were bowing out. The plaintiffs contend that the separation of the trusses from the roof was a latent defect which could not be discovered until the separation and bowing became noticeable from the exterior of the structure. Fearing a cave-in of the roof, the plaintiffs contacted the defendant and asked him to repair the defects. The defendant initially agreed to do so, but never completed the necessary repairs. The plaintiffs then brought suit against the builder. In turn, the builder filed a motion to dismiss, which the superior court granted based on our holding in *Ellis v. Morris,* 128 N.H. 358, 513 A.2d 951 (1986). This appeal followed.

The plaintiffs set forth three claims in their brief: one for breach of implied warranty of workmanlike quality; one for negligence; and one, in the alternative, for breach of assigned contract rights. We need address only the first two claims.

We have previously denied aggrieved subsequent purchasers recovery in tort for economic loss and denied them recovery under an implied warranty theory for economic loss. *See Ellis v. Morris supra*. The court in *Ellis* acknowledged the problems a subsequent purchaser faces, but declined to follow the examples of those cases which allow recovery. The policy arguments relied upon in *Ellis* for precluding tort recovery for economic loss, in these circumstances, accurately reflect New Hampshire law and present judicial scholarship, and, as such, remain controlling on the negligence claim. However, the denial of relief to subsequent purchasers on an implied warranty theory was predicated on the court's adherence to the requirement of privity in a contract action and on the fear that to allow recovery without privity would impose unlimited liability on builders and contractors. Thus we need only discuss the implied warranty issue.

I. *Privity*

This case affords us an opportunity to review and reassess the issue of privity as it relates to implied warranties of workmanlike quality. In *Norton v. Burleaud,* 115 N.H. 435, 342 A.2d 629 (1975), this court held that an implied warranty of workmanlike quality applied between the builder of a house and the first purchaser. The *Norton* court so held based on the facts before it, and did not explicitly or impliedly limit the benefit of implied warranties solely to the first purchaser. The question before us today is whether this implied warranty may be relied upon by subsequent purchasers and, if so, whether recovery may be had for solely economic loss.

There has been much judicial debate on the basis of implied warranty. Some courts find that it is premised on tort concepts. *See, e.g., LaSara Grain v. First National Bank of Mercedes,* 673 S.W.2d 558, 565 (Tex.1984) ("implied warranties are created by operation of law and are grounded more in tort than contract"); *Berman v. Watergate West, Inc.,* 391 A.2d 1351 (D.C.App.1978).

Other courts find that implied warranty is based in contract. *See, e.g., Redarowicz v. Ohlendorf,* 92 Ill.2d 171, 183, 65 Ill.Dec. 411, 417, 441 N.E.2d 324, 330 (1982) (Implied warranty extended to subsequent purchaser, who purchased house from original owner within first year, for policy reason. Plaintiff could recover under implied warranty theory for cracks in basement, chimney and adjoining wall separating, water leakage in basement, but no recovery in negligence for economic harm.); *Aronsohn v. Mandara,* 98 N.J. 92, 484 A.2d 675 (1984) (suit for implied warranty of habitability for structurally unsound patio); *Cosmopolitan Homes, Inc. v. Weller,* 663 P.2d 1041 (Colo.1983) (en banc) (implied warranty arises from contractual relationship).

Other authorities find implied warranty neither a tort nor a contract concept, but "a freak hybrid born of the illicit intercourse of tort and contract.... Originally sounding in tort, yet arising out of the warrantor's consent to be bound, it later ceased necessarily to be consensual, and at the same time came to lie mainly in contract." Prosser, *The Assault Upon the Citadel,* 69 Yale L.J. 1099, 1126 (1960); *accord Scott v. Strickland,* 10 Kan.App.2d 14, 18, 691 P.2d 45, 50 (1984) (discussing first purchaser, court found implied warranty could be tort or contract); Edmeades, *The Citadel Stands: The Recovery of Economic Loss in American Products Liability,* 27 Case W.Res.L.Rev. 647, 662 (1977) (hereinafter *The Citadel Stands*).

Regardless of whether courts have found the implied warranty to be based in contract or tort, many have found that it exists independently, imposed by operation of law, the imposition of which is a matter of public policy. *Elliott v. Lachance,* 109 N.H. 481, 483, 256 A.2d 153, 155 (1969) ("Such warranties [referring to UCC merchantability] are not created by agreement . . . but are said to be imposed by law on the basis of public policy.").

We continue to agree with our statement in *Elliott, supra* at 483–84, 256 A.2d at 155, that

> [implied] warranties are not created by an agreement . . . between the parties but are said to be imposed by law on the basis of public policy. They arise by operation of law because of the relationship between the parties, the nature of the transaction, and the surrounding circumstances,

and agree with other courts that find implied warranties, in circumstances similar to those presented here, to be creatures of public policy "that ha[ve] evolved to protect purchasers of . . . homes upon the discovery of latent defects." *Redarowicz,* 92 Ill.2d at 183, 65 Ill.Dec. at 417, 441 N.E.2d at 330, and that, regardless of their theoretical origins, "exist[ ] independently." *Id.*

There are jurisdictions which have refused to extend the implied warranty to subsequent purchasers, finding privity necessary. However, numerous jurisdictions have now found privity of contract unnecessary for implied warranty.

Despite the *Ellis* ruling, New Hampshire has generally disfavored privity in certain situations. *See, e.g., Spherex, Inc. v. Alexander Grant & Co.,* 122 N.H. 898, 903, 451 A.2d 1308, 1311 (1982). In *Spherex,* the court found privity of contract unnecessary for negligent misrepresentation by an accountant. "Our reluctance to applying the privity rule has been extended to allowing the proper plaintiff to recover for mere financial loss resulting from negligent performance of services." *Id.* We likened an accountant to a manufacturer and found that an accountant was in the best position to regulate the effects of his conduct by controlling the degree of care exercised in his professional duties.

In keeping with judicial trends and the spirit of the law in New Hampshire, we now hold that the privity requirement should be abandoned in suits by subsequent purchasers against a builder or contractor for breach of an implied warranty of good workmanship for latent defects. "To require privity between the contractor and the home owner in such a situation would defeat the purpose of the implied warranty of good workmanship and could leave innocent homeowners without a remedy...." *Aronsohn,* 98 N.J. at 102, 484 A.2d at 680.

Numerous practical and policy reasons justify our holding. The essence of implied warranty is to protect innocent buyers. As such, this principle, which protects first purchasers as recognized by *Norton v. Burleaud,* 115 N.H. 435, 342 A.2d 629, is equally applicable to subsequent purchasers. The extension of this principle is based on "sound legal and policy considerations." *Terlinde,* 275 S.C. at 397, 271 S.E.2d at 769. The mitigation of *caveat emptor* should not be frustrated by the intervening ownership of the prior purchasers. As a general principle, "[t]he contractor should not be relieved of liability for unworkmanlike construction simply because of the fortuity that the property on which he did the construction has changed hands." *Aronsohn, supra* at 102, 484 A.2d at 680. As the court in *Moxley* said:

> Let us assume for example a person contracts construction of a home and, a month after occupying, is transferred to another locality and must sell. Or let us look at the family which contracts construction, occupies the home and the head of the household dies a year later and the residence must, for economic reasons, be sold. Further, how about the one who contracts for construction of a home, occupies it and, after a couple of years, attracted by a profit incentive caused by inflation or otherwise, sells to another. No reason has been presented to us whereby the original owner should have the benefits of an implied warranty or a recovery on a negligence theory and the next owner should not simply because there has been a transfer. Such intervening sales, standing by themselves, should not, by any standard of reasonableness, effect an end to an implied warranty or, in that matter, a right of recovery on any other ground, upon manifestation of a defect. The builder always has available the defense that the defects are not attributable to him.

*Moxley v. Laramie Builders, Inc.,* 600 P.2d 733, 736 (Wyo.1979).

First, "[c]ommon experience teaches that latent defects in a house will not manifest themselves for a considerable period of time ... after the original purchaser has sold the property to a subsequent unsuspecting buyer." *Terlinde v. Neely,* 275 S.C. 395, 398, 271 S.E.2d 768, 769 (1980).

Second, our society is rapidly changing.

We are an increasingly mobile people; a builder-vendor should know that a house he builds might be resold within a relatively short period of time and should not expect that the warranty will be limited by the number of days that the original owner holds onto the property.

*Redarowicz,* 92 Ill.2d at 185, 65 Ill.Dec. at 417, 441 N.E.2d at 330. Furthermore, "the character of society has changed such that the ordinary buyer is not in a position to discover hidden defects...." *Terlinde, supra* at 397, 271 S.E.2d at 769.

Third, like an initial buyer, the subsequent purchaser has little opportunity to inspect and little experience and knowledge about construction. "Consumer protection demands that those who buy homes are entitled to rely on the skill of a builder and that the house is constructed so as to be reasonably fit for its intended use." *Moxley,* 600 P.2d at 735.

Fourth, the builder/contractor will not be unduly taken unaware by the extension of the warranty to a subsequent purchaser. "The builder already owes a duty to construct the home in a workmanlike manner...." *Keyes v. Guy Bailey Homes, Inc.,* 439 So.2d 670, 673 (Miss.1983). And extension to a subsequent purchaser, within a reasonable time, will not change this basic obligation.

Fifth, arbitrarily interposing a first purchaser as a bar to recovery "might encourage sham first sales to insulate builders from liability." *Richards v. Powercraft Homes, Inc.,* 139 Ariz. 242, 245, 678 P.2d 427, 430 (1984) (en banc).

Economic policies influence our decision as well. "[B]y virtue of superior knowledge, skill, and experience in the construction of houses, a builder-vendor is generally better positioned than the purchaser to ... evaluate and guard against the financial risk posed by a [latent defect]...." *George v. Veach,* 67 N.C.App. 674, 313 S.E.2d 920, 923 (1984).

As the *Moxley* court stated: the "purpose of [an] [implied] warranty is to protect innocent purchasers and hold builders accountable for their work ... [and] any reasoning which would arbitrarily interpose a first buyer as an obstruction to someone equally as deserving of recovery is incomprehensible." 600 P.2d at 736.

This court, as well, does not find it logical to limit protection arbitrarily to the first purchaser. Most purchasers do not have the expertise necessary to discover latent defects, and they need to rely on the skill and experience of the builder. After all, the effect of a latent defect will be equally debilitating to a subsequent purchaser as to a first owner, and the builder will be "just as unable to justify the improper or substandard work." *Richards,* 139 Ariz. at 245, 678 P.2d at 430.

Not only do policy and economic reasons convince us that a privity requirement in this situation is unwarranted, but analogous situations show us the soundness of this extension. Public policy has compelled a change in the law of personal property and goods, as witnessed by the adoption of the UCC. The logic which compelled this change is equally persuasive for real property. As one law review commentator said: the "[a]pplication of such a warranty is similar to that of implied warranty of fitness and merchantability under the Uniform Commercial Code." Comment, *Builder's Liability for Latent Defects in Used Homes*, 32 Stan.L.Rev. 607 (1980) (author urged that regardless of method employed, liability for latent defects occurring within a reasonable time should be placed on builder).

II. *Economic Loss*

Finally, we address the issue of whether we should allow recovery for purely economic harm, which generally is that loss resulting from the failure of the product to perform to the level expected by the buyer and is commonly measured by the cost of repairing or replacing the product. Much theoretical debate has taken place on whether to allow economic recovery and whether tort or contract is the most appropriate vehicle for such recovery.

It is clear that the majority of courts do not allow economic loss recovery in tort, but that economic loss is recoverable in contract, and that economic loss recovery "is consistent with the policy of warranty law to protect expectations of suitability and quality[,]" *Moorman Manufacturing Co. v. National Tank Co.*, 91 Ill.2d 69, 82, 61 Ill.Dec. 746, 752, 435 N.E.2d 443, 449 (1982) (distinguishing between strict liability in tort and warranty). However, what is less clear is whether courts allow recovery for economic loss on an implied warranty theory, without privity, in situations such as ours. Some courts do not. Other courts implicitly allow recovery for economic loss, and other courts that have dealt directly with the issue of economic harm in implied warranty have found that an aggrieved party can recover. The courts which have allowed economic loss recovery in situations similar to ours have done so basically because the line between property damage and economic loss is not always easy to draw.

We agree with the courts that allow economic recovery in implied warranty for subsequent purchasers, finding as they have that "the contention that a distinction should be drawn between mere 'economic loss' and personal injury is without merit."

> Why there should be a difference between an economic loss resulting from injury to property and an economic loss resulting from personal injury has not been revealed to us. When one is personally injured from a defect, he recovers mainly for his economic loss. Similarly, if a wife loses a husband because of injury resulting from a defect in construction, the measure of

damages is totally economic loss. We fail to see any rational reason for such a distinction.

If there is a defect in a stairway and the purchaser repairs the defect and suffers an economic loss, should he fail to recover because he did not wait until he or some member of his family fell down the stairs and broke his neck? Does the law penalize those who are alert and prevent injury? Should it not put those who prevent personal injury on the same level as those who fail to anticipate it?

*Barnes v. Mac Brown & Co. Inc.,* 264 Ind. 227, 230, 342 N.E.2d 619, 621 (1976). The vendee has a right to expect to receive that for which he has bargained.

Permitting recovery for economic loss in implied warranty to subsequent purchasers of property is compelling.

In the sale of a home the transaction usually involves an individual owner who sells to an individual buyer. In such cases there ordinarily would be no implied warranty as to latent defects. Since the UCC applies to "transactions in goods," no implied warranty of merchantability or fitness for a particular purpose would be created by the Uniform Commercial Code.

*Szajna v. General Motors Corp.,* 115 Ill.2d 294, 305–06, 104 Ill.Dec. 898, 903, 503 N.E.2d 760, 765 (1986) (citations omitted) (case distinguishing between implied warranty in real estate as opposed to goods).

III. *Limitations*

We are, however, aware of the concerns that this court in *Ellis* raised about unlimited liability. As with any rule, there must be built-in limitations, which in this case would act as a barrier to the possibility of unlimited liability.

Therefore, our extension of the implied warranty of workmanlike quality is not unlimited; it does not force the builder to act as an insurer, in all respects, to a subsequent purchaser. Our extension is limited to *latent* defects "which become manifest after the subsequent owner's purchase and which were not discoverable had a reasonable inspection of the structure been made prior to the purchase." *Richards,* 139 Ariz. at 245, 678 P.2d at 430.

The implied warranty of workmanlike quality for latent defects is limited to a reasonable period of time. "The length of time for latent defects to surface, so as to place subsequent purchasers on equal footing should be controlled by the standard of reasonableness and not an arbitrary time limit created by the Court." *Terlinde, supra* at 398, 271 S.E.2d at 769.

Furthermore, the plaintiff still has the burden to show that the defect was caused by the defendant's workmanship, and defenses are also available to the builder. "The builder ... can demonstrate that the defects were not attributable to him, that they are the result of age or ordinary wear and tear, or that previous owners have made substantial changes." *Richards,* 139 Ariz. at 245, 678 P.2d at 430.

Finally, we want to clarify that the duty inherent in an implied warranty of workmanlike quality is to perform in "a workmanlike manner and in accordance with accepted standards." *Norton v. Burleaud,* 115 N.H. at 436, 342 A.2d at 630. "The law recognizes an implied warranty that the contractor or builder will use the customary standard of skill and care." *Kenney v. Medlin Const. & Realty Co.,* 68 N.C.App. 339, 343, 315 S.E.2d 311, 314 (1984).

In conclusion, to the extent *Ellis v. Morris,* 128 N.H. 358, 513 A.2d 951 (1986) suggests otherwise, we overrule it, and therefore reverse and remand this case for further proceedings.

Reversed and remanded.

## Reed v. King
Court of Appeal, Third District, 1983.
145 Cal.App.3d 261, 193 Cal.Rptr. 130.

■ BLEASE, ASSOCIATE JUSTICE.

In the sale of a house, must the seller disclose it was the site of a multiple murder? Dorris Reed purchased a house from Robert King. Neither King nor his real estate agents (the other named defendants) told Reed that a woman and her four children were murdered there ten years earlier. However, it seems "truth will come to light; murder cannot be hid long." (Shakespeare, Merchant of Venice, Act II, Scene II.) Reed learned of the gruesome episode from a neighbor after the sale. She sues seeking rescission and damages. King and the real estate agent defendants successfully demurred to her first amended complaint for failure to state a cause of action. Reed appeals the ensuing judgment of dismissal. We will reverse the judgment.

### Facts

King and his real estate agent knew about the murders and knew the event materially affected the market value of the house when they listed it for sale. They represented to Reed the premises were in good condition and fit for an "elderly lady" living alone. They did not disclose the fact of the murders. At some point King asked a neighbor not to inform Reed of that event. Nonetheless, after Reed moved in neighbors informed her no one was interested in purchasing the house because of the stigma. Reed paid $76,000, but the house is only worth $65,000 because of its past.

The trial court sustained the demurrers to the complaint on the ground it did not state a cause of action. The court concluded a cause of action could only be stated "if the subject property, by reason of the prior circumstances, were *presently* the object of community notoriety...." (Original italics.) Reed declined the offer of leave to amend.

## Discussion

Does Reed's pleading state a cause of action? Concealed within this question is the nettlesome problem of the duty of disclosure of blemishes on real property which are not physical defects or legal impairments to use.

Reed seeks to state a cause of action sounding in contract, i.e. rescission, or in tort, i.e. deceit. In either event her allegations must reveal a fraud. "The elements of actual fraud, whether as the basis of the remedy in contract or tort, may be stated as follows: There must be (1) a *false representation* or concealment of a material fact (or, in some cases, an opinion) susceptible of knowledge, (2) made with *knowledge* of its falsity or without sufficient knowledge on the subject to warrant a representation, (3) with the *intent* to induce the person to whom it is made to act upon it; and such person must (4) act in *reliance* upon the representation (5) to his *damage*." (Original italics.) (1 Witkin, Summary of California Law (8th ed. 1973) Contracts, § 315.)

The trial court perceived the defect in Reed's complaint to be a failure to allege concealment of a material fact. "Concealment" and "material" are legal conclusions concerning the effect of the issuable facts pled. As appears, the analytic pathways to these conclusions are intertwined.

Concealment is a term of art which includes mere non-disclosure when a party has a duty to disclose. Reed's complaint reveals only non-disclosure despite the allegation King asked a neighbor to hold his peace. There is no allegation the attempt at suppression was a cause in fact of Reed's ignorance. Accordingly, the critical question is: does the seller have a duty to disclose here? Resolution of this question depends on the materiality of the fact of the murders.

In general, a seller of real property has a duty to disclose: "where the seller knows of facts *materially* affecting the value or desirability of the property which are known or accessible only to him and also knows that such facts are not known to, or within the reach of the diligent attention and observation of the buyer, the seller is under a duty to disclose them to the buyer.[3]" [Emphasis added; citations omitted.] (*Lingsch v. Savage*, 213 Cal.App.2d 729, 735, 29 Cal.Rptr. 201 (1963)). This broad statement of duty has led one commentator to conclude: "The ancient maxim *caveat emptor* ('let the buyer beware.') has little or no application to California real estate transactions." (1 Miller and Starr, Current Law of Cal.Real Estate (rev. ed. 1975) § 1:80.)

Whether information "is of sufficient materiality to affect the value or desirability of the property ... depends on the facts of the particular

---

[3] The real estate agent or broker representing the seller is under the same duty of disclosure. (*Lingsch v. Savage*, supra, 213 Cal.App.2d at p. 736, 29 Cal.Rptr. 201.)

case." (*Lingsch,* supra, 213 Cal.App.2d at p. 737, 29 Cal.Rptr. 201.) Accordingly, the term is essentially a label affixed to a normative conclusion. Three considerations bear on this legal conclusion: the gravity of the harm inflicted by non-disclosure; the fairness of imposing a duty of discovery on the buyer as an alternative to compelling disclosure, and its impact on the stability of contracts if rescission is permitted.

Numerous cases have found non-disclosure of physical defects and legal impediments to use of real property are material. However, to our knowledge, no prior real estate sale case has faced an issue of non-disclosure of the kind presented here. Should this variety of ill-repute be required to be disclosed? Is this a circumstance where "non-disclosure of the fact amounts to a failure to act in good faith and in accordance with reasonable standards of fair dealing[?]" (Rest.2d Contracts, § 161, subd. (b).)

The paramount argument against an affirmative conclusion is it permits the camel's nose of unrestrained irrationality admission to the tent. If such an "irrational" consideration is permitted as a basis of rescission the stability of all conveyances will be seriously undermined. Any fact that might disquiet the enjoyment of some segment of the buying public may be seized upon by a disgruntled purchaser to void a bargain. In our view, keeping this genie in the bottle is not as difficult a task as these arguments assume. We do not view a decision allowing Reed to survive a demurrer in these unusual circumstances as endorsing the materiality of facts predicating peripheral, insubstantial, or fancied harms.

The murder of innocents is highly unusual in its potential for so disturbing buyers they may be unable to reside in a home where it has occurred. This fact may foreseeably deprive a buyer of the intended use of the purchase. Murder is not such a common occurrence that *buyers* should be charged with anticipating and discovering this disquieting possibility. Accordingly, the fact is not one for which a duty of inquiry and discovery can sensibly be imposed upon the buyer.

Reed alleges the fact of the murders has a quantifiable effect on the market value of the premises. We cannot say this allegation is inherently wrong and, in the pleading posture of the case, we assume it to be true. If information known or accessible only to the seller has a significant and measurable effect on market value and, as is alleged here, the seller is aware of this effect, we see no principled basis for making the duty to disclose turn upon the character of the information. Physical usefulness is not and never has been the sole criterion of valuation. Stamp collections and gold speculation would be insane activities if utilitarian considerations were the sole measure of value.

Reputation and history can have a significant effect on the value of realty. "George Washington slept here" is worth something, however physically inconsequential that consideration may be. Ill-repute or "bad will" conversely may depress the value of property. Failure to disclose such a negative fact where it will have a foreseeably depressing effect on income expected to be generated by a business is tortious. Some cases have held that *unreasonable* fears of the potential buying public that a gas or oil pipeline may rupture may depress the market value of land and entitle the owner to incremental compensation in eminent domain.

Whether Reed will be able to prove her allegation that the decade-old multiple murder has a significant effect on market value we cannot determine. If she is able to do so by competent evidence she is entitled to a favorable ruling on the issues of materiality and duty to disclose. Her demonstration of objective tangible harm would still the concern that permitting her to go forward will open the floodgates to rescission on subjective and idiosyncratic grounds.

A more troublesome question would arise if a buyer in similar circumstances were unable to plead or establish a significant and quantifiable effect on market value. However, this question is not presented in the posture of this case. Reed has not alleged the fact of the murders has rendered the premises useless to her as a residence. As currently pled, the gravamen of her case is pecuniary harm. We decline to speculate on the abstract alternative.

The judgment is reversed.

## Frickel v. Sunnyside Enterprises, Inc.
Supreme Court of Washington, 1986.
106 Wash.2d 714, 725 P.2d 422.

■ BRACHTENBACH, JUSTICE.

The main issue is whether an implied warranty of habitability applies to the sale of an apartment complex, under the facts of this case, and in the face of a contractual disclaimer of any such warranty. The trial court found there was such an implied warranty and held for the buyers. The court did not deal with the contractual disclaimer. We accepted certification from the Court of Appeals. We reverse.

The facts are important. The plaintiffs were seeking an investment which would give them a retirement income and a tax benefit. The defendants were builders of apartment complexes for their own ownership. Defendants did not build for resale. Defendants had built over 100 apartment units, but always for their own ownership and management. These units were no exception: the defendants expected to own and manage them.

The defendants were approached by a realtor who represented the buyers. The property was not on the market. The buyers' agent asked the sellers—would they sell? They answered—yes, for the right price.

This establishes the first point. The property was not built for resale. The builders intended it to be held within their own inventory and management.

The apartment complex consisted of five buildings. It was built in stages. The first four buildings, containing 28 units of apartments, had been completed and occupied by tenants—some for approximately 18 months. The last building had only been framed in when the owners were approached by the buyers' agent.

The record is silent as to what negotiations, if any, went on between the sellers and buyers. A contract was prepared by an attorney. The buyers, accompanied by their own attorney, went to the office of the lawyer who had prepared the contract. Somehow the parties agreed upon a sale price of $700,000 with $85,000 down. The contract was expressly tailored to this transaction. It recognized and accounted for tenants' cleaning deposits and last month's rent deposits. It recognized that Building 5 was incomplete. It set the standards for completion as well as needed repairs to the existing buildings.

Of importance to this controversy, the contract included this clause:

> The purchaser agrees that full inspection of said real estate has been made and that neither the seller nor his assigns shall be held to any covenant respecting the condition of any improvements thereon nor shall the purchaser or seller or the assigns of either be held to any covenant or agreement for alterations, improvements or repairs unless the covenant or agreement relied on is contained herein or is in writing and attached to and made a part of the contract.

Clerk's Papers, at 9. The contract further stated:

> The purchaser assumes all hazards of damage to or destruction of any improvements now on said real estate. . . .

Clerk's Papers, at 10.

The sale occurred in December 1976; by 1980 some problems with outside stairways developed. By 1983, after this suit was commenced, it was learned that the foundations were inadequate and improperly designed. Apparently the problem is that the foundations were not adequately designed to accommodate the soil conditions. The seller-builders had built to the specifications of the City of Hoquiam. In fact, the City rejected the seller-builders first foundation plans. The seller-builders then built to the exact specifications of the City, even though, it turns out, those specifications did not meet the City's own building code.

The seller-builders do not challenge the trial court's findings that there were serious defects in the foundations and that improper construction has resulted in a situation where extensive repairs are necessary (at a cost of $330,000 according to the trial court) to prevent a foundation failure within 8 to 9 years. (The normal life expectancy of such buildings is 50 to 60 years.)

Two questions remain. First, does a builder of an apartment complex, built not for resale, but for the seller's own inventory, guarantee to an unsolicited buyer that the buildings are so constructed that they are free from design errors? Put another way, does a builder who complies with the standards of the governing municipal entity, in a commercial setting, promise the buyer of those units that all of the risk of faulty construction is upon the builder? Certainly there was no such contractual undertaking. Indeed, the contract says otherwise. Only if this court substitutes its judgment for that of the parties can the buyer prevail.

The second question is the significance of the contractual disclaimer, an issue not addressed by the trial court.

The first question—*i.e.*, the imposition of an implied warranty—is simply a matter of public policy to be determined by this court. Certainly it was not within the contemplation of the parties.

As a matter of policy, determined by this court, it seems apparent that a builder who puts a house on the market, brand-new and never occupied, has some responsibility to the ultimate buyer. The builder built the thing. It was intended to be sold to a buyer for occupancy by the buyer—not as an assemblage of concrete and pieces of wood, but as a residence. It is no different from the manufacturer of an automobile. The auto should run down the road without wheels falling off and new houses should provide habitation without foundations falling apart. This court and other courts have recognized this principle.

Thus, in *House v. Thornton*, 76 Wash.2d 428, 457 P.2d 199 (1969), we held that the sale of a new house by a vendor-builder to the first intended occupant carries with it an implied warranty "that the foundations supporting it are firm and secure and that the house is structurally safe for the buyer's intended purpose of living in it." 76 Wash.2d at 436, 457 P.2d 199. There, the vendor-builders, a real estate broker and a building contractor, constructed a residence for purposes of sale. The buyers, a husband and wife, purchased the "brand new house" with the intention of making it their family home. In time, however, the house proved to have structural defects which rendered it unfit for further occupancy. In imposing an implied warranty of habitability or fitness upon the vendor-builders, this court, in effect, "did no more than apply a rule of common sense to the kind of transaction that recurs perhaps more than a million times annually in the country—the purchase of a brand new house." *Berg v. Stromme*, 79 Wash.2d 184, 196, 484 P.2d 380 (1971), discussing *House v. Thornton, supra* (same rationale used for adoption of implied warranty in sale of brand new automobiles).

The reach of this implied warranty was clarified but not extended in *Klos v. Gockel*, 87 Wash.2d 567, 554 P.2d 1349 (1976), which involved the warranty liability of an occasional builder of houses who built the house at issue primarily for her own personal use rather than for purposes of resale and sold it to the plaintiff-buyers after living in it for a year. In finding no liability under the rule of *House v. Thornton, supra,* we made it clear that an implied warranty of habitability or fitness does not apply to every sale of a new house. The sale must be "commercial rather than casual or personal in nature." *Klos v. Gockel, supra* at 570, 554 P.2d 1349. In other words, the warranty only applies where the new dwelling is built for purposes of sale by a builder-vendor in the business of building such dwellings. *Klos v. Gockel, supra.*

It is clear that the facts of this case do not come within the implied warranty doctrine as fashioned by this court in *House v. Thornton, supra* and *Klos v. Gockel, supra.* Unlike the sale of a house—brand new and never occupied—to its first intended occupant, the sale here involved the purchase of a 40-unit apartment complex, of which 28 units were completed at the time of sale and occupied by tenants for as long as 18 months. The defendants did not build apartment complexes for resale but for their own ownership and management purposes. The apartment complex at issue here was no different. It was not built for purposes of sale nor had it been listed or placed on the market when the buyers approached the defendants.

Moreover, we are not persuaded that the implied warranty of habitability should be extended, as a matter of public policy, to the sale of property under the facts and circumstances of this case. The implied warranty of habitability or fitness is based upon judicial recognition that the rule of *caveat emptor*—premised as it is on an arm's length transaction between buyers and sellers of comparable skill and experience—has little relevance when applied to the sale of new homes in today's market. The necessity of imposing an implied warranty upon builder-vendors of new houses, as a matter of public policy, to protect the ordinary purchasers of such homes was well-stated by the Illinois Supreme Court in *Petersen v. Hubschman Constr. Co.*

> Many new houses are, in a sense, now mass produced. The vendee buys in many instances from a model home or from predrawn plans. The nature of the construction methods is such that a vendee has little or no opportunity to inspect. The vendee is making a major investment, in many instances the largest single investment of his life. He is usually not knowledgeable in construction practices and, to a substantial degree, must rely upon the integrity and the skill of the builder-vendor, who is in the business of building and selling houses. The vendee has a right to expect to receive that for which he has bargained and that which the builder-vendor has agreed to construct and convey to him, that is, a house that is reasonably fit for use as a residence.

*Petersen,* 76 Ill.2d 31, 40, 27 Ill.Dec. 746, 389 N.E.2d 1154 (1979).

Unlike the inherently unequal bargaining position between the average home-buyer and the vendor-builder of new houses, the factual scenario here is far different. The sale in this case is essentially an arm's length transaction between an unsolicited buyer who sought to invest in an ongoing if still uncompleted commercial enterprise and a builder-vendor who built an apartment complex for its own use and management and not for purposes of sale. It may be that the plaintiffs were relatively inexperienced as investors in commercial property. However, the plaintiffs, through their agent, sought out the property; it was not on the market. They had their own lawyer. They could and should have protected themselves in the contract negotiations. They had an opportunity to inspect and investigate. If plaintiffs were unsure of their investment, they were in a position to seek expert help, particularly with the plans and specifications identified in the contract and readily available for inspection which would have revealed the potential problems. They chose not to do so.

There is in this case no claim of fraud or misrepresentation. The seller-builders built to the exact specifications of the City. The construction was defective because of a combination of soil conditions and construction quality.

When competent persons deal at arm's length, with no claim of fraud, no claim of misrepresentation, no claim of an adhesion contract, with an opportunity to inspect and investigate, when the contract contains a specific disclaimer, when all of the facts are present, we see no policy reasons for this court to impose upon the sellers a guaranty which neither party negotiated nor expected.

There is no question but that the buyers will suffer a severe financial loss from the ownership of these apartments. We find no principle of law why that loss should be laid upon the sellers.

We now turn to the second point, the validity of the disclaimer clause in the contract. What could be more clear to a buyer than the following contract language:

> The purchaser *agrees* that *full inspection* of said real estate has been made and that *neither* the *seller nor his assigns shall be held to any covenant* respecting the condition of *any improvements* thereon nor shall the ... seller ... be held to any covenant or agreement ... relied on is contained herein or is in writing and attached to and made a part of this contract.

(Italics ours.) Clerk's Papers, at 9.

We emphasize again that the buyers, through their agent, sought out this property. They had ample opportunity to inspect. They had their own lawyer. The extent to which they inspected and used their lawyer was their choice. The contractual language is clear. This court not only should not, but it cannot, rewrite the clear agreement of the parties.

The buyers argue first that such a disclaimer must be clear and unambiguous. We find it to be so. Next, buyers contend that such disclaimer must be explicitly negotiated and that the sellers failed to prove that the disclaimer was so negotiated.

Buyers rely mainly upon *Berg v. Stromme,* 79 Wash.2d 184, 484 P.2d 380 (1971). There we held that the communicated particular needs of the buyer of an automobile would not be overcome by a boiler plate exclusion of all warranties, express or implied. That case is quite different from this where the buyers sought no promises, the sellers made none, and the buyers with their lawyer, faced a clause which said the sellers not only made no covenant about the condition of the buildings, but expressly disclaimed any such covenant.

We do not hold that an implied warranty of habitability can never attach to the sale of an apartment complex. Rather we hold that such warranty does not exist under the facts of this case.

We reverse.

■ PEARSON, CHIEF JUSTICE, dissenting.

The majority holds that the warranty of habitability does not apply to the Frickel-Sunnyside transaction, apparently because (1) the apartment complex was not built for resale, (2) the buyers were seeking a commercial investment, and (3) they failed to seek expert advice to determine the existence of structural deficiencies. Regardless, according to the majority, any potential warranty liability was effectively disclaimed by contractual disclaimer. I must dissent.

This court previously has recognized only one of the three reasons offered by the majority to justify its refusal to extend warranty protection to the Frickels as an element of the warranty of habitability. This court never before has suggested that warranty protection might depend upon whether the purchasers sought a commercial investment, or whether they sought expert advice to determine the existence of structural deficiencies. To the extent the majority relies upon these reasons to deny the Frickels warranty protection, such reliance constitutes a drastic alteration of the warranty's elements. To the extent reliance upon these reasons is not necessary to reach the result mandated by the majority, the majority simply adds confusing dicta to an already confusing area of the law.

Admittedly, this court previously has refused to extend warranty protection to a buyer unless the builder constructed the structure for purposes of resale. As discussed below, however, the "for purposes of resale" requirement is irrelevant to the extent it is applied to a nonprofessional builder, and insidious to the extent it is applied to a professional builder like Sunnyside. In fact, after reviewing our past decisions concerning the warranty of habitability, I am convinced that few of the warranty's existing elements should retain validity. Many of these elements are supported largely by questionable rationale, potentially leading to unjust results.

. . .

## Current Warranty of Habitability

In Washington, the implied warranty of habitability currently is limited to the sale of new houses. Many jurisdictions impose a similar limitation on the warranty. The structure purchased by the Frickels was an apartment complex. Accordingly, given the existing case law in Washington, the warranty arguably should not apply, notwithstanding the majority's opinion that the warranty might apply to such a transaction in the proper case.

As alluded to by Sunnyside, the rationale supporting this limitation flows from the notion that the average home buyer is ignorant of construction quality, whereas one who purchases commercial property is sufficiently sophisticated to demand an inspection, and sufficiently wealthy to afford one. The weakness in this preconception manifests itself in the facts of this case.

The Frickels, whom the majority characterize as commercial investors, had no experience buying real property, other than that acquired in purchasing their home 30 years ago. Thus, one could hardly say they were sufficiently sophisticated to demand an inspection, even if they could afford one. Furthermore, the rationale supporting this limitation presupposes that inspection would reveal the defect. Adequate inspection of a foundation is very difficult because it is hidden once the structure is completed. In fact, the trial court found that the latent structural defects in Sunnyside's construction could not reasonably have been observed at the site by the Frickels, even through the use of an expert contractor at the time the project was completed.

As the foregoing suggests, the court-imposed requirement that the structure be a house is supported by questionable rationale. Other states have extended the warranty beyond houses. Likewise, this court should extend warranty protection beyond houses to include all residential dwellings.

The implied warranty of habitability does not apply unless the dwelling is "new"; but the court will consider a dwelling to be new if it was occupied to promote its sale. In short, "the sale must be fairly contemporaneous with completion and not interrupted by an intervening tenancy unless the builder-vendor created such an intervening tenancy for the primary purpose of promoting the sale of the property." *Klos,* at 571, 554 P.2d 1349.

One reason for this limitation appears to be the need to insulate builders from liability for defects in older homes caused by intervening tenants. Although the limitation makes sense with respect to nonstructural defects (*e.g.,* damage to interior and exterior surfaces), it is unsupportable where the defects complained of are structural (*e.g.,* defective foundations and supporting beams). If neither age nor an intervening tenancy could affect the structural integrity of the dwelling, neither age nor the existence of an intervening tenancy is relevant to the question of whether warranty liability should attach.

The newness requirement implies that a builder should not be liable for defects which become manifest long after completion of the structure. However, the builder limitation statute, RCW 4.16.310, bars commencement of a suit that does not accrue within 6 years of substantial completion. Accordingly, the builder need not warrant the quality of his construction indefinitely, but rather for merely 6 years. This requirement is not unreasonable, especially where the defect complained of is latent and structural. Accordingly, this court should not limit warranty protection to the sale of new residential structures.

This court will imply the warranty of habitability only to "commercial rather than casual or personal" sales. *Klos*, 87 Wash.2d at 570, 554 P.2d 1349. In my opinion, this means the builder must be in the business of building residential structures. The reason for the requirement flows from the justifiable belief that a nonprofessional house builder should not be deemed to warrant the same quality of construction demanded of his professional counterpart. Consistent with this belief, this court limits the liability of one who builds a dwelling for his personal residence, and subsequently sells it to another. Because such a builder's construction is casual and for personal purposes, I agree that liability for defective construction should not attach. Accordingly, I do not suggest that the warranty of habitability should apply to nonprofessional builders, but rather that the warranty should apply to a professional builder, regardless of whether he also is in the business of selling residential structures.

Even if the builder is a professional, this court will not imply the warranty of habitability unless the residential structure was built for purposes of resale. Although Sunnyside clearly is a professional builder, *i.e.*, in the business of building, it did not build Sunnyside Sands for the purposes of resale. As late as the completion of phase two of construction, Sunnyside intended to operate the apartment complex for its own benefit. The majority emphasizes this fact throughout its opinion, arguing that this alone justifies refusal to extend the warranty to this case.

This limitation was stretched to its outer limits in *Klos v. Gockel*, 87 Wash.2d 567, 554 P.2d 1349 (1976). In *Klos*, the court found that Mrs. Gockel constructed the house "primarily for personal occupancy, but also with the idea that eventually the house might be sold." *Klos*, at 568, 554 P.2d 1349. This view is questionable. Mrs. Gockel and her husband had been in the business of building, occupying and then selling houses for many years. After her husband's death, she built the defective house, lived in it approximately 1 year, and then sold it; built a second house, lived in it for a time, and then moved to Arizona. Upon her subsequent return to this state, she built a third house. *Klos*, at 569 n. 1, 554 P.2d

1349. Mrs. Gockel clearly built each of the houses for purposes of resale. Nevertheless, the principle enunciated in *Klos v. Gockel,* read in context with the facts set forth in the opinion, lends support to the contention that the warranty should not run to the Frickels.

The question is whether the requirement set forth in *Klos v. Gockel* should retain validity. This court already requires a commercial builder to be "regularly engaged in building" before it will impose warranty liability. *Klos v. Gockel, supra,* at 570, 554 P.2d 1349. This requirement precludes imposition of warranty liability upon a nonprofessional builder who sells a home constructed originally as his own residence. The requirement that the dwelling be built for purposes of resale is simply cumulative when applied to the nonprofessional builder, and thus is irrelevant in that context. The requirement is insidious, however, when applied to the routine practice of a professional builder, like Mrs. Gockel, who constructs a dwelling, occupies or rents it for personal purposes, and then sells it to one who relies on the builder's reputation as a professional. In this latter case, form prevails over substance and the warranty is denied one who deserves its protection.

The record in this case clearly shows that Sunnyside is a commercial builder, regularly engaged in the business of building apartment complexes. Although Sunnyside originally did not intend to sell the complex when construction began, it would be spurious to suggest that this fact, even if known by the Frickels, would have caused them to lessen their reliance on Sunnyside's skill and reputation as a professional builder.

The commercial builder-vendor is responsible for defects because he controls construction, is in a position to inspect, and holds himself out as a professional. If construction is defective, an innocent purchaser should not bear the loss. Accordingly, warranty protection should not depend upon satisfaction of the "for purposes of sale" requirement.

. . .

## Proposal for Change

As demonstrated by the foregoing discussion, questionable rationale supports all but one of the elements of the warranty of habitability. To understand why, one need only recall that the doctrine of *caveat emptor* once governed all real estate transactions. To mitigate the injustice inherent in that doctrine, courts around the country created the common-law warranties of workmanlike quality and habitability. Uncomfortable with the prospect of broad builder-vendor liability, however, the courts imposed certain elements on a case-by-case basis, without much consideration of the rationale supporting these elements. Unfortunately, we are left today with requirements which make little or no sense, and lead to unconscionable results.

To rectify this problem, this court should modify the existing warranty of habitability and apply it to serious structural defects existing in any residential structure constructed by a professional builder, regardless of whether the buyer is the first or subsequent occupant of the structure. This modified warranty of habitability would apply to all residential structures, whether single-family houses, duplexes, apartments or condominiums. Furthermore, the warranty would apply regardless of whether the structure was built for purposes of resale, as long as the builder-vendor was a professional builder in the business of building. Finally, the warranty would apply regardless of whether the structure was new, meaning that intervening tenancies would not destroy warranty protection.

Although at first glance this might appear to be a heavy burden to impose upon professional builders, the duration of the warranty would be limited statutorily to 6 years from the date the structure is substantially completed. RCW 4.16.310. Furthermore, the warranty would apply only to professional builders and would cover only serious structural defects. Finally, where the purchaser is acquiring the property for investment purposes, the court could hold that a contractual disclaimer is permissible.

In short, imposition of the warranty of habitability, as described, would not be unreasonable given the large sums of money involved and the reliance generally placed upon professional builders by unsuspecting purchasers. Accordingly, I would modify *Klos v. Gockel, supra,* and would impose instead the warranty of habitability in all sales of residential property. Because Sunnyside is a professional builder and Sunnyside Sands is a residential complex, I would hold that the Frickels are entitled to warranty protection.

## Disclaimer of Warranty

The majority argues that even if an implied warranty applies, it was disclaimed by inspection and contract. The first argument can be disposed of summarily.

Although the Frickels did inspect the manager's apartment and one or two others, the trial court found the structural defects could not have been detected on the site by anyone, not even an expert. In *Tyus v. Resta,* 328 Pa.Super. 11, 476 A.2d 427 (1984), the court stated:

> A reasonable pre-purchase inspection requires examination of the premises by the intended purchaser—not by an expert. Defects which would not be apparent to an ordinary purchaser as a result of a reasonable inspection constitute latent defects covered by the implied warranties.

*Tyus,* at 22, 476 A.2d 427, 476 A.2d 427. In the context of a commercial investment in residential property, I would not hold that an implied warranty cannot be disclaimed by expert inspection; commercial investors should be expected to seek expert advice. However, where even an expert would be unable to detect a latent defect, a purchaser's cursory inspection cannot serve to disclaim an implied warranty.

The more important question in this case, however, is whether an implied warranty can be disclaimed by contract. The majority attempts to elevate the following contract language to the level of a disclaimer:

> The purchaser agrees that full inspection of said real estate has been made and that neither the seller nor his assigns shall be held to any covenant respecting the condition of any improvements thereon nor shall the purchaser or seller or the assigns of either be held to any covenant or agreement for alterations, improvements or repairs unless the covenant or agreement relied on is contained herein or is in writing and attached to and made a part of the contract.

Majority opinion, at 423.

As yet, Washington courts have not determined the validity of disclaimers of the implied warranty of habitability. In the landlord-tenant area, this court held that such disclaimers contravene public policy. Arguably, the result should be the same in the new house context. Nevertheless, courts have validated such disclaimers if the language clearly and unambiguously demonstrates the intention of both parties to disclaim the implied warranty.

In my opinion, disclaimer of an implied warranty under the facts of this case does not contravene public policy. Unlike the purchaser of a new house, the Frickels purchased the dwelling for purposes of investment. If they desired to disclaim the warranty, the law should not prevent them from doing so, even if their disclaimer insulates a shoddy contractor from liability. The question remains, however, whether the Frickels did disclaim the implied warranty by signing a contract containing the above-quoted language.

Reasoning by analogy to Washington's commercial code, I believe a valid disclaimer of the implied warranty of a residential structure should be written, conspicuous, and include the term "habitability". Furthermore, the disclaimer should be explicitly negotiated.

. . .

In sum, I would hold the implied warranty of habitability in the sale of residential real property can be disclaimed only where the property is acquired for investment purposes, and the disclaimer (a) is explicitly negotiated, (b) is written and conspicuous, and (c) includes the term "habitability". In my opinion, these requirements were not met in this case, and accordingly I would affirm the decision of the trial court.

## NOTES

1. *Economic loss as distinguished from property loss.* In *Lempke*, the court notes that the subsequent purchaser cannot recover in the tort action of negligence for *economic loss,* basing its decision on Ellis v. Morris, Inc. In *Ellis,* the plaintiff, who was a subsequent purchaser, was trying to recover for faulty siding installed by the contractor. In denying recovery under an

implied warranty, the court cited the lack of privity of contract. In denying recovery under a negligence claim, the court noted:

> The plaintiffs' claim does not involve property damage per se. Rather, the writ alleges economic loss resulting from the defendant's failure to properly perform a contractual obligation. . . . When a defective product accidentally causes harm to persons or property, the resulting harm is treated as personal injury or property damage. But when damage occurs to the inferior product itself, through deterioration or non-accidental causes, the harm is characterized as economic loss. In general, persons must refrain from causing personal injury and property damage to third parties, but no corresponding tort duty exists with respect to economic loss.[6]

Contrast this decision with Navajo Circle, Inc. v. Development Concepts Corp.[7] in which the court rejected the builder's argument that, absent privity, there can only be liability when the defect creates an unreasonable risk of injury. The court refused to sanction the dismissal of a negligence claim against the builder of a condominium unit for water damage caused by a faulty roof. In the Principal Problem, Barbara is trying to sue the construction company. What problems do you foresee if Barbara proceeds upon a negligence theory?

2. *Liability of the lending bank.* Purchasers of homes with construction defects generally seek to recover damages from the builder. In some cases, however, a purchaser cannot recover from the builder because the builder has inadequate resources or has disappeared. In these circumstances, the purchaser may seek to recover damages from the lender who financed the construction of the defective premises. Courts have generally been unwilling to shift the liability for construction defects from the builder to the lender. Lenders are generally not held liable for defects of construction unless the lender's activities exceed those of a typical lender or the lender has made assurances to the purchaser that justifies the purchaser's reliance on the lender's inspection of the home.[8] For instance, in Rudolph v. First Southern Federal Sav. & Loan Assoc.,[9] the court held the lender liable for construction defects because the lender had assured the purchaser that it would inspect the construction site for any defects. Moreover, the lender assured the purchaser that it would not approve any payment to the builder if any defects were discovered. The court noted that a construction lender is generally not under a duty to exercise reasonable care on its inspection of the construction site, but such a duty of reasonable care is triggered when a lender voluntarily undertakes to perform an inspection on behalf of the purchaser. In the Principal Problem, what facts should Barbara present in an effort to hold the bank liable?

---

[6] Ellis v. Morris, Inc., 128 N.H. 358, 513 A.2d 951 (1986), reversed on other grounds by Lempke v. Dagenais, 130 N.H. 782, 547 A.2d 290 (1988). See also East River Steamship Corp. v. Transamerica Delaval, Inc., 476 U.S. 858, 106 S.Ct. 2295, 90 L.Ed.2d 865 (1986).

[7] 373 So.2d 689 (Fla.Dist.Ct.App.1979).

[8] Jeffrey T. Walter, Annotation, Financing Agency's Liability to Purchaser of New Home or Structure for Consequences of Construction Defects, 20 A.L.R.5th 499 (1995 & Supp. 2009).

[9] 414 So.2d 64 (Ala.1982).

3. *When is "cheap" too "cheap"?* Would the fact Barbara was buying the property at an "astonishingly low price" create any additional duties of discovery upon her? What arguments should Sam advance in light of the low price? How should Barbara respond?

4. *When does an implied warranty end?* In *Lempke*, the defect became apparent within six months of the original construction of the garage. However, in Part III of the *Lempke* decision, the court still felt compelled to discuss the limitations of an implied warranty and said, "The length of time for latent defects to surface, so as to place subsequent purchasers on equal footing, should be controlled by the standard of reasonableness and not an arbitrary time limit created by the Court." In *Frickel,* the court notes that the state of Washington places an outer limit, by statute, of six years on builder liability. In the Principal Problem, is five years too long to hold Sam liable for building defects?

5. *The diligent buyer.* In *King,* the plaintiff did not allege that her ignorance of the murders stemmed from the defendant having asked the neighbor not to inform the plaintiff of the murders. Therefore, the court had to consider the materiality of the defendant's failure to disclose. Why do you think the plaintiff failed to allege active concealment by the defendant? Does a buyer who fails to discuss the property with a neighbor exercise "due diligence"?

6. *Subjective vs. objective standards.* The *Reed* court expressed concern about subjective fears and concerns opening the floodgates of litigation by unhappy buyers. One Pennsylvania court expressly adopted an objective approach to the duty to disclose and damages for undisclosed defects, rejecting a subjective approach. *Milliken v. Jacono,* 60 A.3d 133, 141 (PA Superior Court 2012). Why?

7. *Disclaimers of the implied warranty of fitness.* In *Frickel,* the court gave effect to the disclaimer of any implied warranties in the contract. It is generally accepted that implied warranties can be disclaimed with regard to both commercial and residential property. How would you deal with this issue in the contract of sale if you were representing the seller of the property? What would you do if you were representing the buyer? In the Principal Problem, what arguments would you make for the contractor and for Sam that the warranty had in fact been disclaimed?

A common way that sellers have attempted to disclaim an implied warranty of fitness is by including an "as is" clause in the sales contract. This clause would provide that the buyer has accepted the property "as is," which would include all latent and patent defects. All jurisdictions still permit actions based on fraud or misrepresentations, but many jurisdictions will enforce "as is" clauses. In some jurisdictions, the "as is" clause will protect the seller from liability for nondisclosure of defects, but in most jurisdictions, the seller will be held liable for nondisclosure. As in all cases, an attorney should determine which rule prevails in her jurisdiction before advising a seller.[10]

---

[10] Roberts, Disclosure Duties in Real Estate Sales and Attempts to Reallocate the Risk, 34 Conn. L. Rev. 1 (2002); Frank J. Wozniak Annotation, Construction and Effect of Provision

8. *An unwilling seller.* In *Frickel,* is it important that the seller was not advertising his property; i.e., that the buyer was unsolicited? Was the court trying to draw a distinction between the average home-buyer and a commercial buyer? Between an average home-buyer and a buyer who seeks out a seller? Would the rationale adopted in *Frickel* apply to an ordinary home buyer, but not a commercial buyer? Is the purpose of the implied warranty doctrine merely to prevent a seller from knowingly unloading defective property? Or is the purpose to protect a buyer from unreasonable loss regardless of the seller's knowledge of the defect?

---

for Sale of Realty by which Purchaser Agrees to Take Property "As Is" or in its Existing Condition, 8 A.L.R. 5th 312 (1992 & Supp. 2009).

# ASSIGNMENT 54

# LIABILITY FOR TOXIC WASTES

## 1. INTRODUCTION

Between 1942 and 1953, the Occidental Chemical Corporation ("OCC") used Love Canal, a tract of land located in Niagara Falls, New York, for waste disposal purposes. During the eleven years OCC used the property for chemical disposal, it deposited more than 42 million pounds of various wastes into Love Canal. In 1953, OCC deeded the land to the Board of Education of Niagara Falls. A school was built on the site, as well as private homes. Twenty years later, the health of nearby residents was seriously threatened by hazardous substances, which had permeated the surface water, ground water, soil, basements of homes, sewers, creeks and other locations. On May 21, 1980, President Carter declared a federal emergency at Love Canal. Nearly one thousand families were evacuated, and the state and federal governments purchased the contaminated properties.[1] It has been estimated that the cleanup at Love Canal ultimately cost the federal government more than $30 million.[2] This figure does not take into account the noneconomic losses to the residents of Love Canal.

In response to Love Canal and similar environmental disasters in Times Beach, Missouri, and elsewhere, Congress enacted the Comprehensive Environmental Response Compensation and Liability Act of 1980, 42 U.S.C. § 9601 et seq. ("CERCLA"). CERCLA is also known as "Superfund" because one of its provisions established a $1.6 billion fund to be used to pay for cleanup costs at sites contaminated with hazardous wastes.

Under CERCLA, there are two methods by which the federal government can clean up contaminated land. The Environmental Protection Agency ("EPA") can order "potentially responsible parties" ("PRPs") to pay the costs for a hazardous waste site cleanup, or the EPA can itself undertake the cleanup and pay the costs out of Superfund, suing the PRPs for reimbursement. A PRP that is or has been subject to a civil action for its liability for clean-up costs (including an action that has been settled) may sue other PRPs for their share of these costs in a contribution action.[3] Alternatively, PRPs or others (including innocent

---

[1] See Molotsky, President Orders Emergency Help for Love Canal, N.Y. Times, May 22, 1980.

[2] See Burkhart, Lender/Owners and CERCLA: Title and Liability, 25 Harv.J. on Legis. 317, 318 (1988).

[3] Cooper Indus., Inc. v. Aviall Servs., Inc., 543 U.S. 157 (2004). However, Aviall Services can properly be read as addressing only the requirements for bringing a claim under CERCLA section 113(f); it does not govern whether a claim by a PRP is or is not "contingent" within the meaning of section 502(e)(1)(B), which Aviall Services quite obviously did not address. In re

landowners) may voluntarily engage in clean-up of the site and then sue PRPs (including the federal government itself) for recovery of costs in a cost recovery action.[4] Note that contribution actions and cost recovery actions are two different types of causes of action under CERCLA's provisions.[5]

CERCLA section 107(a) defines a PRP as:

   (1) the owner and operator of a vessel or facility,

   (2) any person who at the time of disposal of any hazardous substance owned or operated any facility at which such hazardous substances were disposed of,

   (3) any person who by contract, agreement, or otherwise arranged for disposal or treatment, or arranged with a transporter for transport for disposal or treatment, of hazardous substances owned or possessed by such person, by any other party or entity, at any facility or incineration vessel owned or operated by another party or entity and containing such hazardous substances, and

   (4) any person who accepts or accepted any hazardous substances for transport to disposal or treatment facilities, incineration vessels or sites selected by such person, from which there is a release, or a threatened release which causes the incurrence of response costs, of a hazardous substance....

42 U.S.C. § 9607(a).

Thus, four groups face potential liability under CERCLA: present owners or operators of a contaminated site, prior owners or operators of the site at the time it was contaminated, the party who generated the waste and arranged to have it transported to the site, and the party who actually transported the waste to the site. When two or more PRPs cause a single and indivisible harm, the PRPs have been held jointly and severally liable for the entire harm by a majority of courts.[6] Damages are apportioned only if the defendants can prove that the harm is divisible.

Three years prior to the enactment of CERCLA, Congress had passed another statute dealing with improper hazardous waste management, the Resource Conservation and Recovery Act, 42 U.S.C. § 6901 et seq. ("RCRA"). RCRA established a federal regulatory program

---

Lyondell Chem. Co., 442 B.R. 236, 2011 Bankr. LEXIS 10, 54 Bankr. Ct. Dec. 37 (Bankr. S.D.N.Y. 2011).

[4] United States v. Atlantic Research Corp., 551 U.S. 128 (2007). However, one commentator has opined that PRPs under "Unilateral Administrator Orders" from the EPA, compelling them to clean-up the property at their own expense, may be in a "judicial purgatory" without either contribution or cost recovery actions against PRPs. Thompson, Exposing a Gap in CERCLA Case Law: Is There a Right to Recover Costs Following Compliance with an Administrative Order After Atlantic and Aviall, 46 Hous. L. Rev. 1679 (2010).

[5] See, e.g., Niagara Mohawk Power Corp. v. Chevron USA, Inc., 596 F.3d 112, 127–28 (2d Cir. 2010); Agere Syst., Inc. v. Advanced Envtl. Tech. Corp., 602 F.3d 204 (3d Cir. 2010).

[6] See O'Neil v. Picillo, 883 F.2d 176, 178 (1st Cir.1989); United States v. Monsanto Co., 858 F.2d 160, 171–73 (4th Cir.1988).

that manages hazardous waste from its creation to its disposal. In contrast to CERCLA, which focuses on the clean-up of past contamination sites, RCRA prevents the endangerment of the public health and the environment from present and future hazardous waste disposal.

In addition to federal laws such as CERCLA and RCRA, most states have enacted their own toxic waste cleanup statutes. Some of these statutes create a "superlien" on the contaminated property for the costs of removal, which subordinates the rights of holders of prior recorded liens (e.g., mortgage holders) to the state's lien.[7] In 1984, the American Land Title Association ("ALTA") amended its form policy to exclude liability from "any law, ordinance or governmental regulation relating to environmental protection."[8] Although very few environmental insurance policies existed in the 1980s, the number of policies covering environmental liability has increased in recent years. In addition to the standard comprehensive general liability policies which provide broad coverage to the insured, specialized environmental impairment liability policies provide coverage for various environmental claims.[9]

In the Small Business Liability Relief and Brownfields Revitalization Act of 2002 ("SBLRBRA"), Congress created State Response Programs, which award grants to assist states in creating effective programs to clean up waste. 42 U.S.C. § 9628. In addition, SBLRBRA prevents the EPA from bringing an administrative or judicial enforcement action against a person who is conducting or has completed a state response program addressing a release or threatened release of a hazardous substance. Thus, owners of property will not be subject to liability to both a state government and the federal government for the same cleanup. This provision is subject to numerous exceptions, however, including allowing actions if further response actions may be warranted or if "a release or threatened release may present an imminent and substantial endangerment to public health or welfare or the environment."

As all this suggests, the burden of environmental liability can be staggering to an owner of property contaminated by hazardous wastes. As one critic has observed, an owner's environmental liability under CERCLA is "strict, retroactive, perpetual and unlimited in amount."[10] For example, a lessor whose tenant operated a waste site was found liable for cleanup costs, although the lessor did not participate in the

---

[7] See, e.g., Conn. Gen. Stat. Ann. § 22a–452a; Me.Rev.Stat.Ann. § 1371; Mass. Gen. Laws Ann. ch. 21E § 13; N.H. Rev. Stat. Ann. § 147–B:10; N.J. Stat. Ann. § 58:10–23.11f.

[8] Pedowitz, Title Insurance: Non-Coverage of Hazardous Waste Superliens, Prob. & Prop. 46 (Spring 1985).

[9] See Heintz, Insurance Coverage for Environmental Claims, 516 PLI/Lit. 27, 35 (1994).

[10] Forte, Environmental Liability Risk Management, Prob. & Prop. 57 (January/February 1989).

operation.[11] In addition, a present owner of contaminated land and its stockholder were found responsible for cleanup costs, even though they neither owned the site at the time of contamination nor caused the presence or release of hazardous waste at the site.[12] As a lawyer, it is essential for you to have at least a rudimentary understanding of the complex web of environmental liability in which your clients can become entangled. Most importantly, a lawyer representing clients who acquire property should insist on a clause in the sales contract that conditions the closing of the sale on the results of a complete environmental land inspection. While a full treatment of CERCLA and related hazardous waste law is beyond the scope of this course, this Assignment is designed to provide an overview of the kinds of issues that may confront you and your clients in the future.

## 2. PRINCIPAL PROBLEM

A few years ago Devco, a small San Francisco development company, purchased at public auction a parcel of land and an abandoned warehouse in an old industrial neighborhood south of Market Street ("Soma") for $300,000. The Soma neighborhood had begun to be gentrified, and Devco planned to renovate the existing warehouse into New York-style residential "lofts," selling the lofts as condominiums.

Originally built in 1908, the warehouse had been leased through the years to small manufacturing businesses, including a machine shop, a foundry, a manufacturer of electronic components, and most recently an automobile refurbishing plant. The property had passed through a succession of owners since 1908, and had been vacant for six years before Devco purchased the property from the City of San Francisco, which had acquired the property for nonpayment of property taxes.

Devco completed the renovation early this year, and by October had sold all but two of the lofts. In November, an EPA inspector took soil samples from the rear of the property where Devco had created a terraced garden for the use of the residents. The inspection revealed that the soil was contaminated with PCBs, acetone, dioxin, and various other hazardous wastes. The EPA theorized that during the years when the property was used for manufacturing, the occupants had used the rear of the property as a convenient dump site. Devco's owner did recall that when he first inspected the property, he noticed a large mound of soil and refuse toward the rear of the lot, but he thought little of it at the time.

Devco has just received notification from the EPA that it must either clean up the site or the EPA will undertake the cleanup and sue Devco to recover its costs. A preliminary report indicates that the cleanup may

---

[11] See Caldwell v. Gurley Refining Co., 755 F.2d 645 (8th Cir.1985). But see Commander Oil Corp. v. Barlo Equipment Corp., 215 F.3d 321, 330–31 (2d Cir. 2000) (noting that lessees may be liable as owners under CERCLA when they have "the requisite indicia of ownership").

[12] See State of New York v. Shore Realty Corp., 759 F.2d 1032 (2d Cir.1985).

cost in excess of $3 million, as the contamination has leaked into the ground water and seeped onto adjoining properties.

Evaluate the potential liability of Devco, the current owners of the condominium units, and the City of San Francisco for the costs of the cleanup.

## 3. MATERIALS FOR SOLUTION OF PRINCIPAL PROBLEM

### United States v. Monsanto Co.
United States Court of Appeals Fourth Circuit, 1988.
858 F.2d 160.

■ SPROUSE, CIRCUIT JUDGE.

Oscar Seidenberg and Harvey Hutchinson (the site-owners) and Allied Corporation, Monsanto Company, and EM Industries, Inc. (the generator defendants), appeal from the district court's entry of summary judgment holding them liable to the United States and the State of South Carolina (the governments) under section 107(a) of the Comprehensive Environmental Response, Compensation, and Liability Act of 1980 (CERCLA). 42 U.S.C.A. § 9607(a) (West Supp. 1987). The court determined that the defendants were liable jointly and severally for $1,813,624 in response costs accrued from the partial removal of hazardous waste from a disposal facility located near Columbia, South Carolina.

I.

In 1972, Seidenberg and Hutchinson leased a four-acre tract of land they owned to the Columbia Organic Chemical Company (COCC), a South Carolina chemical manufacturing corporation. The property, located along Bluff Road near Columbia, South Carolina, consisted of a small warehouse and surrounding areas. The lease was verbal, on a month-to-month basis, and according to the site-owners' deposition testimony, was executed for the sole purpose of allowing COCC to store raw materials and finished products in the warehouse. Seidenberg and Hutchinson received monthly lease payments of $200, which increased to $350 by 1980.

In the Mid-1970s, COCC expanded its business to include the brokering and recycling of chemical waste generated by third parties. It used the Bluff Road site as a waste storage and disposal facility for its new operations. In 1976, COCC's principals incorporated South Carolina Recycling and Disposal Inc. (SCRDI), for the purpose of assuming COCC's waste-handling business, and the site-owners began accepting lease payments from SCRDI.

SCRDI contracted with numerous off-site waste producers for the transport, recycling, and disposal of chemical and other waste. Among these producers were agencies of the federal government and South

Carolina, and various private entities including the three generator defendants in this litigation. Although SCRDI operated other disposal sites, it deposited much of the waste it received at the Bluff Road facility. The waste stored at Bluff Road contained many chemical substances that federal law defines as "hazardous."

Between 1976 and 1980, SCRDI haphazardly deposited more than 7,000 fifty-five gallon drums of chemical waste on the four-acre Bluff Road site. It placed waste laden drums and containers wherever there was space, often without pallets to protect them from the damp ground. It stacked drums on top of one another without regard to the chemical compatibility of their contents. It maintained no documented safety procedures and kept no inventory of the stored chemicals. Over time many of the drums rusted, rotted, and otherwise deteriorated. Hazardous substances leaked from the decaying drums and oozed into the ground. The substances commingled with incompatible chemicals that had escaped from other containers, generating noxious fumes, fires, and explosions.

On October 26, 1977, a toxic cloud formed when chemicals leaking from rusted drums reacted with rainwater. Twelve responding firemen were hospitalized. Again, on July 24, 1979, an explosion and fire resulted when chemicals stored in glass jars leaked onto drums containing incompatible substances. SCRDI's site manager could not identify the substances that caused the explosion, making the fire difficult to extinguish.

In 1980, the Environmental Protection Agency (EPA) inspected the Bluff Road site. Its investigation revealed that the facility was filled well beyond its capacity with chemical waste. The number of drums and the reckless manner in which they were stacked precluded access to various areas in the site. Many of the drums observed were unlabeled, or their labels had become unreadable from exposure, rendering it impossible to identify their contents. The EPA concluded that the site posed "a major fire hazard."

Later that year, the United States filed suit under section 7003 of the Resource Conservation and Recovery Act, 42 U.S.C. § 6973, against SCRDI, COCC, and Oscar Seidenberg. The complaint was filed before the December 11, 1980, effective date of CERCLA, and it sought only injunctive relief. Thereafter, the State of South Carolina intervened as a plaintiff in the pending action.

In the course of discovery, the governments identified a number of waste generators, including the generator defendants in this appeal, that had contracted with SCRDI for waste disposal. The governments notified the generators that they were potentially responsible for the costs of cleanup at Bluff Road under section 107(a) of the newly-enacted CERCLA. As a result of these contacts, the governments executed individual settlement agreements with twelve of the identified off-site producers. The generator defendants, however, declined to settle.

Using funds received from the settlements, the governments contracted with Triangle Resource Industries (TRI) to conduct a partial surface cleanup at the site. The contract required RAD Services, Inc., a subsidiary of TRI, to remove 75% of the drums found there and to keep a log of the removed drums. RAD completed its partial cleanup operation in October 1982. The log it prepared documented that it had removed containers and drums bearing the labels or markings of each of the three generator defendants.

The EPA reinspected the site after the first phase of the cleanup had been completed. The inspection revealed that closed drums and containers labeled with the insignia of each of the three generator defendants remained at the site. The EPA also collected samples of surface water, soil, and sediment from the site. Laboratory tests of the samples disclosed that several hazardous substances contained in the waste the generator defendants had shipped to the site remained present at the site.

Thereafter, South Carolina completed the remaining 25% of the surface cleanup. It used federal funds from the Hazardous Substances Response Trust Fund (Superfund), 42 U.S.C. § 9631, as well as state money from the South Carolina Hazardous Waste Contingency Fund, S.C.Code Ann. § 44–56–160, and in-kind contribution of other state funds to match the federal contribution.

In 1982, the governments filed an amended complaint, adding the three generator defendants and site-owner Harvey Hutchinson, and including claims under section 107(a) of CERCLA against all of the non-settling defendants. The governments alleged that the generator defendants and site-owners were jointly and severally liable under section 107(a) for the costs expended completing the surface cleanup at Bluff Road.

In response, the site-owners contended that they were innocent absentee landlords unaware of and unconnected to the waste disposal activities that took place on their land. They maintained that their lease with COCC did not allow COCC (or SCRDI) to store chemical waste on the premises, but they admitted that they became aware of waste storage in 1977 and accepted lease payments until 1980.

The generator defendants likewise denied liability for the governments' response costs. Among other defenses, they claimed that none of their specific waste materials contributed to the hazardous conditions at Bluff Road, and that retroactive imposition of CERCLA liability on them was unconstitutional. They also asserted that they could establish an affirmative defense to CERCLA liability under section 107(b)(3), 42 U.S.C. § 9607(b)(3), by showing that the harm at the site was caused solely through the conduct of unrelated third parties. All parties thereafter moved for summary judgment.

After an evidentiary hearing, the district court granted the governments' summary judgment motion on CERCLA liability. The court found that all of the defendants were responsible parties under section 107(a), and that none of them had presented sufficient evidence to support an affirmative defense under section 107(b). The court further concluded that the environmental harm at Bluff Road was "indivisible," and it held all of the defendants jointly and severally liable for the governments' response costs.

As to the site-owners' liability, the court found it sufficient that they owned the Bluff Road site at the time hazardous substances were deposited there. It rejected their contentions that Congress did not intend to subject "innocent" landowners to CERCLA liability. The court similarly found summary judgment appropriate against the generator defendants because it was undisputed that (1) they shipped hazardous substances to the Bluff Road facility; (2) hazardous substances "like" those present in the generator defendants' waste were found at the facility; and (3) there had been a release of hazardous substances at the site. In this context, the court rejected the generator defendants' arguments that the governments had to prove that their specific waste contributed to the harm at the site, and it found their constitutional contentions to be "without force." Finally, since none of the defendants challenged the governments' itemized accounting of response costs, the court ordered them to pay the full $1,813,624 that had been requested. This appeal followed.

## II.

The site-owners and the generator defendants first contest the imposition of CERCLA liability *vel non,* and they challenge the propriety of summary judgment in light of the evidence presented to the trial court. The site-owners also reassert the "innocent landowner" defense that the district court rejected, and claim that the court erroneously precluded them from presenting evidence of a valid affirmative defense under section 107(b)(3), 42 U.S.C. § 9607(b)(3). The generator defendants likewise repeat their arguments based on the governments' failure to establish a nexus between their specific waste and the harm at the site. They also claim that the trial court ignored material factual issues relevant to affirmative defenses to liability. We address these contentions sequentially, but pause briefly to review the structure of CERCLA's liability scheme.

In CERCLA, Congress established "an array of mechanisms to combat the increasingly serious problem of hazardous substance releases." *Dedham Water Co. v. Cumberland Farms Dairy, Inc.*, 805 F.2d 1074, 1078 (1st Cir.1986). Section 107(a) of the statute sets forth the principal mechanism for recovery of costs expended in the cleanup of waste disposal facilities. At the time the district court entered judgment, section 107(a) provided in pertinent part:

(a) Covered persons; scope

Notwithstanding any other provision or rule of law, and subject only to the defenses set forth in subsection (b) of this section—

(1) ...

(2) any person who at the time of disposal of any hazardous substance owned or operated any facility at which such hazardous substances were disposed of, [and]

(3) any person who by contract, agreement, or otherwise arranged for disposal or treatment, or arranged with a transporter for transport for disposal or treatment, of hazardous substances owned or possessed by such person, by any other party or entity, at any facility owned or operated by another party or entity and containing such hazardous substances, and

(4) ... from which there is a release, or a threatened release which causes the incurrence of response costs, of a hazardous substance, shall be liable for—

(A) all costs of removal or remedial action incurred by the United States Government or a State not inconsistent with the national contingency plan.

42 U.S.C.A. § 9607(a) (West Supp.1987).

In our view, the plain language of section 107(a) clearly defines the scope of intended liability under the statute and the elements of proof necessary to establish it. We agree with the overwhelming body of precedent that has interpreted section 107(a) as establishing a strict liability scheme. Further, in light of the evidence presented here, we are persuaded that the district court correctly held that the governments satisfied all the elements of section 107(a) liability as to both the site-owners and the generator defendants.

In light of the strict liability imposed by section 107(a), we cannot agree with the site-owners contention that they are not within the class of owners Congress intended to hold liable. The traditional elements of tort culpability on which the site-owners rely simply are absent from the statute. The plain language of section 107(a)(2) extends liability to owners of waste facilities regardless of their degree of participation in the subsequent disposal of hazardous waste.

Under section 107(a)(2), *any* person who owned a facility at a time when hazardous substances were deposited there may be held liable for all costs of removal or remedial action if a release or threatened release of a hazardous substance occurs. The site-owners do not dispute their ownership of the Bluff Road facility, or the fact that releases occurred there during their period of ownership. Under these circumstances, all the prerequisites to section 107(a) liability have been satisfied.[13]

The site-owners nonetheless contend that the district court's grant of summary judgment improperly denied them the opportunity to present an affirmative defense under section 107(b)(3). Section 107(b)(3) sets forth a limited affirmative defense based on the complete absence of causation. It requires proof that the release or threatened release of hazardous substances and resulting damages were caused solely by "a third party other than . . . one whose act or omission occurs in connection with a contractual relationship, existing directly or indirectly, with the defendant. . . ." 42 U.S.C. § 9607(b)(3). A second element of the defense requires proof that the defendant "took precautions against foreseeable acts or omissions of any such third party and the consequences that could foreseeably result from such acts or omissions." *Id.* We agree with the district court that under no view of the evidence could the site-owners satisfy either of these proof requirements.

First, the site-owners could not establish the absence of a direct or indirect contractual relationship necessary to maintain the affirmative defense. They concede they entered into a lease agreement with COCC. They accepted rent from COCC, and after SCRDI was incorporated, they accepted rent from SCRDI. Second, the site-owners presented no evidence that they took precautionary action against the foreseeable conduct of COCC or SCRDI. They argued to the trial court that, although they were aware COCC was a chemical manufacturing company, they were completely ignorant of all waste disposal activities at Bluff Road before 1977. They maintained that they never inspected the site prior to that time. In our view, the statute does not sanction such willful or negligent blindness on the part of absentee owners. The district court committed no error in entering summary judgment against the site-owners.

### III.

The appellants next challenge the district court's imposition of joint and several liability for the governments' response costs. The court concluded that joint and several liability was appropriate because the environmental harm at Bluff Road was "indivisible" and the appellants had "failed to meet their burden of proving otherwise." We agree with its conclusion.

While CERCLA does not mandate the imposition of joint and several liability, it permits it in cases of indivisible harm. In each case, the court

---

[13] Congress, in section 101(35) of SARA [the Superfund Amendments and Reauthorization Act of 1986 which amended CERCLA], acknowledged that landowners may affirmatively avoid liability if they can prove they did not know and had no reason to know that hazardous substances were disposed of on their land *at the time they acquired title or possession.* 42 U.S.C.A. § 9601(35) (West Supp.1987). This explicitly drafted exception further signals Congress' intent to impose liability on landowners who cannot satisfy its express requirements.

must consider traditional and evolving principles of federal common law, which Congress has left to the courts to supply interstitially.

Under common law rules, when two or more persons act independently to cause a single harm for which there is a reasonable basis of apportionment according to the contribution of each, each is held liable only for the portion of harm that he causes. When such persons cause a single and indivisible harm, however, they are held liable jointly and severally for the entire harm. We think these principles, as reflected in the Restatement (Second) of Torts, represent the correct and uniform federal rules applicable to CERCLA cases.

Section 433A of the Restatement provides:

> (1) Damages for harm are to be apportioned among two or more causes where
>
> (a) there are distinct harms, or
>
> (b) there is a reasonable basis for determining the contribution of each cause to a single harm.
>
> (2) Damages for any other harm cannot be apportioned among two or more causes.

Restatement (Second) of Torts § 433A (1965).

Placing their argument into the Restatement framework, the generator defendants concede that the environmental damage at Bluff Road constituted a "single harm," but contend that there was a reasonable basis for apportioning the harm. They observe that each of the off-site generators with whom SCRDI contracted sent a potentially identifiable volume of waste to the Bluff Road site, and they maintain that liability should have been apportioned according to the volume they deposited as compared to the total volume disposed of there by all parties. In light of the conditions at Bluff Road, we cannot accept this method as a basis for apportionment.

## IV.

The generator defendants raise numerous constitutional challenges to the district court's interpretation and application of CERCLA. They contend that the imposition of "disproportionate" liability without proof of causation violated constitutional limitations on retroactive statutory application and that it converted CERCLA into a bill of attainder and an *ex post facto* law. They further assert, along with the site-owners, that the trial court's construction of CERCLA infringed their substantive due process rights.

The district court held that CERCLA does not create retroactive liability, but imposes a prospective obligation for the post-enactment environmental consequences of the defendants' past acts. Alternatively, the court held that even if CERCLA is understood to operate retroactively, it nonetheless satisfies the dictates of due process because its liability scheme is rationally related to a valid legislative purpose. We agree with the court's latter holding, and we find no merit to the generator defendants' bill of attainder and *ex post facto* arguments.... While the generator defendants profited from inexpensive waste disposal methods that may have been technically "legal" prior to CERCLA's enactment, it was certainly foreseeable at the time that improper disposal could cause enormous damage to the environment. CERCLA operates remedially to spread the costs of responding to improper waste disposal among all parties that played a role in creating the hazardous conditions. Where those conditions are indivisible, joint and several liability is logical, and it works to ensure complete cost recovery. We do not think these consequences are "particularly harsh and oppressive," and we agree with the Eighth Circuit that retroactive application of CERCLA does not violate due process. *See United States v. Northeastern Pharmaceutical & Chemical Co., Inc.*, 810 F.2d 726, 734 (8th Cir.1986).

Nor does the imposition of strict, joint and several liability convert CERCLA into a bill of attainder or an *ex post facto* law. The infliction of punishment, either legislatively or retrospectively, is a *sine qua non* of legislation that runs afoul of these constitutional prohibitions. CERCLA does not exact punishment. Rather it creates a reimbursement obligation on any person judicially determined responsible for the costs of remedying hazardous conditions at a waste disposal facility. The restitution of cleanup costs was not intended to operate, nor does it operate in fact, as a criminal penalty or a punitive deterrent....

In view of the above, the judgment of the district court as to the CERCLA liability of the site-owners and generator defendants is affirmed.

## NOTES

1. *Strict liability.* The reference in the Introduction to this Assignment to "strict, retroactive, perpetual and unlimited" liability under CERCLA should now make more sense. Although the language of the statute itself does not impose strict liability, courts have ruled that this was the standard Congress intended to apply.[13] Thus, owner and operator liability is based on status, rather than actual fault. Liability is retroactive because an owner will be held responsible for contamination that occurred before the 1980 enactment of CERCLA; perpetual because an owner cannot avoid liability by conveying the property; and unlimited given both the staggering costs involved in cleanup and the imposition of joint and several liability.

2. *Defenses.* a. *Original defenses.* As originally enacted, CERCLA provided for limited defenses to statutory liability. Section 9607(b) held that a party might escape liability for cleanup costs incurred as a result of: (1) an act of God; (2) an act of war; or (3) an act or omission of a third party not in

---

[13] See, e.g., United States v. Price, 577 F.Supp. 1103 (D.N.J.1983), where the court observed that "though strict liability may impose harsh results on certain defendants, it is the most equitable solution in view of the alternative—forcing those who bear no responsibility for causing the damage, the taxpayers, to shoulder the full costs of the cleanup." 577 F.Supp. at 1114. See also State of New York v. Shore Realty Corp., 759 F.2d 1032, 1042–43 (2d Cir.1985).

a "contractual relationship" with the owner, if the owner established by a preponderance of the evidence that he or she (a) exercised due care with respect to the hazardous waste, and (b) took precautions against foreseeable acts or omissions of the third party and the foreseeable consequences of such acts or omissions. As a practical matter, however, these defenses are of little help to most owners of contaminated land, as release of hazardous wastes is rarely caused by acts of God or war, and virtually all owners will be in some kind of "contractual relationship" (e.g., grantor/grantee) with the responsible third party.

b. *Innocent landowner defense.* Congress amended CERCLA in 1986—the Superfund Amendments and Reauthorization Act of 1986 ("SARA"). Partly in response to the perceived harshness of CERCLA liability on innocent purchasers, SARA provided for what has been termed the "innocent landowner defense" (SARA sec. 101(f), 42 U.S.C. § 9601(35)). Section 9601(35) narrows the scope of "contractual relationship" by excluding certain landowners, including those who had no knowledge of past contamination at the time of purchase. The statute also bars landowners who had actual knowledge or who participated in the contamination from using the "innocent landowner" defense. Section 9601(35) provides in part as follows:

> **(A)** The term "contractual relationship", for the purpose of section 9607(b)(3) of this title, includes, but is not limited to, land contracts, deeds, easements, leases, or other instruments transferring title or possession, unless the real property on which the facility concerned is located was acquired by the defendant after the disposal or placement of the hazardous substance on, in, or at the facility, and one or more of the circumstances described in clause (i), (ii), or (iii) is also established by the defendant by a preponderance of the evidence:
>
> **(i)**
>
> At the time the defendant acquired the facility the defendant did not know and had no reason to know that any hazardous substance which is the subject of the release or threatened release was disposed of on, in, or at the facility.
>
> **(ii)**
>
> The defendant is a government entity which acquired the facility by escheat, or through any other involuntary transfer or acquisition, or through the exercise of eminent domain authority by purchase or condemnation.
>
> **(iii)**
>
> The defendant acquired the facility by inheritance or bequest.
>
> In addition to establishing the foregoing, the defendant must establish that the defendant has satisfied the requirements of section 9607(b)(3)(a) and (b) of this title [concerning due care regarding acts of third parties], provides full cooperation, assistance, and facility access to the persons that are authorized to

conduct response actions at the facility (including the cooperation and access necessary for the installation, integrity, operation, and maintenance of any complete or partial response action at the facility), is in compliance with any land use restrictions established or relied on in connection with the response action at a facility, and does not impede the effectiveness or integrity of any institutional control employed at the facility in connection with a response action.

**(B) Reason to know.—**

**(i) All appropriate inquiries.—**To establish that the defendant had no reason to know of the matter described in subparagraph (A)(i), the defendant must demonstrate to a court that—

**(I)**

on or before the date on which the defendant acquired the facility, the defendant carried out all appropriate inquiries, as provided in clauses (ii) and (iv), into the previous ownership and uses of the facility in accordance with generally accepted good commercial and customary standards and practices; and

**(II)** the defendant took reasonable steps to—

**(aa)** stop any continuing release;

**(bb)** prevent any threatened future release; and

**(cc)** prevent or limit any human, environmental, or natural resource exposure to any previously released hazardous substance.

**(ii) Standards and practices.—**

[This portion governs standards and practices that the EPA must promulgate and with which the landowner must comply in order to be afforded the innocent landowner defense. The elements of these EPA-developed standards and practices are covered below in *Note d, All appropriate inquiries*]

. . .

**(v) Site inspection and title search.—**

In the case of property for residential use or other similar use purchased by a nongovernmental or noncommercial entity, a facility inspection and title search that reveal no basis for further investigation shall be considered to satisfy the requirements of this subparagraph.

**(C)**

Nothing in this paragraph or in section 9607(b)(3) of this title shall diminish the liability of any previous owner or operator of such facility who would otherwise be liable under this chapter. . . .

**(D)**

Nothing in this paragraph shall affect the liability under this chapter of a defendant who, by any act or omission, caused or contributed to the release or threatened release of a hazardous substance which is the subject of the action relating to the facility.

Thus, for an owner to escape liability for cleanup costs, she must be able to demonstrate that she acquired contaminated property after hazardous materials had been deposited on it *and* that, at the time she acquired the property, she did not know and had no reason to know that hazardous materials had ever been disposed of on the property. Since the defense is an affirmative one, the defendant must prove the required elements by a preponderance of the evidence.[14]

c. *Duty to investigate.* To be an innocent landowner as described in section 9601(35)(A)(i) (quoted in note 2.b. above), the defendant has to prove that at the time he acquired the property he did not know and had no reason to know of any past contamination. For the purchaser to establish that he had no reason to know of any past contamination, section 9601(35)(B) states that the purchaser, at the time of acquisition, must have undertaken all appropriate inquiry into the previous ownership and uses of the property. Hence, SARA created a statutory duty to investigate the property consistent with reasonable commercial or customary practices in order to preserve the innocent landowner defense.

This duty to investigate can place an owner in a "Catch-22" situation: a purchaser can avoid liability costs for cleanup of contaminated land only by showing that she has undertaken all appropriate inquiries into the previous ownership and uses of the property. Presumably, however, an adequate investigation would reveal the existence of any hazardous materials that might exist—thus precluding the owner from asserting the "innocent landowner" defense. This Catch-22 situation does not, however, undermine the value of a thorough environmental investigation. A prospective purchaser may decide against purchasing the land due to the potential CERCLA liability or may use the results of the investigation in negotiations with the seller, perhaps to achieve a reduction in the purchase price.

d. *All appropriate inquiries.* SARA created a duty to investigate, but did not spell out what constituted "all appropriate inquiries." In 2002, Congress passed the Small Business Liability Relief and Brownfields Revitalization Act ("SBLRBRA"). Among other things, the goals of this act were to provide liability relief for small businesses and to promote the cleanup and revitalization of brownfields (contaminated properties that were rendered useless by CERCLA because nobody would purchase them for fear of incurring liability). 115 Stat. 2356 (2002). SBLRBRA clarifies the steps a landowner must take prior to purchasing the property to qualify as an innocent landowner (or a bona fide prospective purchaser or a contiguous property owner, both of which are discussed subsequently). 42 U.S.C. § 9601(35)(B) (2004). SBLRBRA instructed the EPA to establish standards

---

[14] See United States v. A & N Cleaners & Launderers, Inc., 854 F.Supp. 229, 244 (S.D.N.Y.1994).

and regulations that indicate what constitutes all appropriate inquiries. SBLRBRA delineates the following ten criteria that must be included in the standards and regulations that constitute all appropriate inquiries:

1. The results of an inquiry by an environmental professional.

2. Interviews with past and present owners, operators, and occupants of the facility for the purpose of gathering information regarding the potential contamination at the facility.

3. Reviews of historical sources, such as chain of title documents, aerial photographs, building department records, and land use records, to determine previous uses and occupancies of the real property since the property was first developed.

4. Searches for recorded environmental cleanup liens against the facility that are filed under Federal, State, or local law.

5. Reviews of Federal, State, and local government records, waste disposal records, underground storage tank records, and hazardous waste handling, generation, treatment, disposal, and spill records, concerning contamination at or near the facility.

6. Visual inspections of the facility and of adjoining properties.

7. Specialized knowledge or experience on the part of the [landowner].

8. The relationship of the purchase price to the value of the property, if the property was not contaminated.

9. Commonly known or reasonably ascertainable information about the property.

10. The degree of obviousness of the presence or likely presence of contamination at the property, and the ability to detect the contamination by appropriate investigation.

The SBLRBRA provides an exception for noncommercial owners of residential use property, whereby "a facility inspection and title search that reveal no basis for further investigation will constitute an appropriate inquiry." 42 U.S.C. § 9601(35)(B)(v).

In 2005, the EPA promulgated the "All Appropriate Inquiries Final Rule," which took effect November 1, 2006.[15] This rule delineated the standards and processes for conducting an investigation of a property's environmental condition and assessing its potential for contamination, pursuant to which a party could qualify as having conducted "all appropriate inquiries" (AAI) and thereby preserve the innocent owner defense.[16] The AAI Final Rule contributes considerable detail and clarity to previously litigated

---

[15] 70 Fed. Reg. 66070–66113 (Nov. 1, 2005), codified at 40 C.F.R. Part 312.

[16] For a summary of the AAI Final Rule's provisions and requirements, see Weiler, The Environmental Protection Agency's New Standard for CERCLA All Appropriate Inquiry: More Time and Money for Compliance, But Well Worth the Cost to Avoid CERCLA Liability, 14 U. Balt. J. Envtl. L. 159 (2007).

issues about whether a purchaser or owner had done enough to qualify for the innocent owner defense. However, no regulation can be written so precisely as to cover all possible factual scenarios and thus courts will still play some role, albeit much more limited, in determining whether purchasers and owners have conducted "all appropriate inquiries." Nonetheless, real estate lawyers must thoroughly familiarize themselves with the standards and requirements of the AAI Final Rule, because any non-compliance could mean that a client loses eligibility for a defense to CERCLA liability and may even have tort liability for negligence.[17]

Real estate lawyers also must be aware of the relationships between AAI and industry and professional standards for conducting initial environmental site investigations and assessments, which are known as Phase I assessments. In addition, further investigation and site testing may be necessary (a Phase II assessment) if the results of a Phase I assessment give reason to suspect environmental contamination. The EPA's AAI Final Rule prompted revisions to the American Society of Testing Materials (ASTM) industry standard for environmental assessments for real estate transactions.[18]

Prudent land purchasers must do more than engage in AAI. As one of the nation's leading real estate attorneys advises, "environmental due diligence is just one aspect of environmental liability risk management, which includes, among other things, environmental impairment insurance, legal compliance audits, contractual risk allocation, and pollution prevention."[19]

e. *Bona fide prospective purchaser.* In SBLRBRA, Congress also exempts from liability bona fide prospective purchasers. To qualify as a bona fide prospective purchaser, (1) the land must be purchased after the enactment of SBLRBRA; (2) all disposal of hazardous substances must have taken place before the property is acquired; (3) all appropriate inquiries must have been conducted into the previous ownership and uses of the property; (4) the person must exercise appropriate care with respect to hazardous substances found at the property; (5) the person must cooperate and assist with the cleanup of the facility, including complying with information requests and subpoenas; and (6) the person must not be affiliated with any other PRPs. 42 U.S.C. § 9601(40). The standard for all appropriate inquiries is the same as for the innocent landowner defense. Although this exception may appear to provide substantial relief, the purchaser must still conduct a thorough environmental inspection before acquiring the property.

---

[17] Weiler, The Environmental Protection Agency's New Standard for CERCLA All Appropriate Inquiry: More Time and Money for Compliance, But Well Worth the Cost to Avoid CERCLA Liability, 14 U. Balt. J. Envtl. L. 159, 169–70 (2007).

[18] See, e.g., ASTM Standard E1527–05—"Standard Practice for Environmental Site Assessment: Phase I Environmental Site Assessment Process." In late 2008, the EPA amended its AAI Final Rule to allow the use of the ASTM's International Standard E2447–08 for site assessment of forest land or rural property to qualify for AAI innocent property owner protection. 73 Fed. Reg. 78651–78655 (Dec. 23, 2008).

[19] Forte, Environmental Due Diligence: A Guide to Liability Risk Management in Commercial Real Estate Transactions, 42 Real Prop. Prob. & Tr. J. 443, 444 (2007).

f. *Contiguous properties.* SBLRBRA also exempts from liability owners of property contiguous to contaminated or potentially contaminated property. 42 U.S.C. § 9607(q). This means that an owner of property will not be liable if her property became contaminated because pollutants from a nearby contaminated property seeped onto it. As with the innocent landowner defense, however, the owner must have conducted an appropriate inquiry with respect to the property and have neither known nor had reason to know that the property was or could be contaminated from other property not owned or operated by the person.

g. *Settlement agreements.* The settlement provisions of SARA section 122 permit the EPA to enter into *de minimus* settlements with "almost innocent" parties who contributed only minor amounts of hazardous waste to a site or with landowners who did not cause or permit the contamination and did not contribute to the release of hazardous substances through any act or omission from the site. This provision does not apply if the party purchased the property with actual or constructive knowledge that the property was used for the generation, transportation, storage, treatment or disposal of any hazardous substance. See 42 U.S.C. § 9622(g). Due to the potential for exorbitant clean-up costs, a *de minimus* share of this large liability may still amount to hundreds of thousands of dollars.[20] SBLRBRA also provides for a reduction in settlement amount based upon an inability to pay. 42 U.S.C. § 9622(7). To qualify for such a reduced settlement, however, the PRP must waive all contribution claims the PRP may have against other PRPs. 42 U.S.C. § 9622(8).

h. *Voluntary clean-ups.* The combination of SBLRBRA and state brownfields programs create incentives and opportunities for land owners and developers to voluntarily remediate brownfields for redevelopment or reuse. In 2007, the Supreme Court gave a further boost to voluntary clean-up efforts by unanimously holding that those who engage in voluntary clean-ups of contaminated sites, including PRPs, can bring cost recovery actions against other PRPs, including the federal government.[21] Commentators have suggested that PRPs now have more incentive to clean up sites voluntarily but less incentive to settle claims brought by the EPA, because those settlements will not protect them against cost-recovery actions by other PRPs.[22]

3. *Protective measures.* In the Principal Problem, if Devco had come to you for advice prior to purchasing the Soma property, what steps would you have advised it to take to shield itself from potential environmental liability?

---

[20] See Poulter, Cleanup and Restoration: Who Should Pay?, 18 J. Land Resources & Envtl. L. 77, 88 (1998).

[21] United States v. Atlantic Research Corp., 551 U.S. 128 (2007.

[22] See, e.g., Bradford, United States v. Atlantic Research Corp.: Settling the Confusion of CERCLA While Serving Justice on the Environment, 12 Great Plains Nat. Resources L.J. 206 (2008); Gitler, Settling the Tradeoffs Between Voluntary Clean-up of Contaminated Sites and Cooperation with the Government Under CERCLA, 35 Ecology L.Q. 337 (2008); Yeboah, United States v. Atlantic Research: Of Settlement and Voluntarily Incurred Costs, 32 Harv. Envtl. L. Rev. 279 (2008).

4. *Public safety and health.* Do the current CERCLA, SARA, and SBLRBRA provisions strike a proper balance between fairness to private parties and the need to protect the public from toxic waste?

5. *Liability of lending institutions.* Prior to 1996, lenders and secured creditors feared that a simple financing transaction could trigger CERCLA liability. The Asset Conservation, Lender Liability, and Deposit Insurance Protection Act of 1996, however, revised CERCLA so that lenders and secured creditors must actually "participate in the management of the facility" to incur "owner or operator" liability. Section 9601(20)(E)(ii) of CERCLA excludes lenders from the definition of "owner or operator" if the lender does not participate in the management of the facility or site but holds indicia of ownership primarily to protect a security interest in the facility or site. Furthermore, CERCLA now excludes lenders who foreclose on contaminated property if the lender did not participate in the management of the facility prior to foreclosure.[23] The lender, however, must divest the facility at the earliest, practicable, commercially reasonable time, on commercially reasonable terms, taking into account market conditions and legal and regulatory requirements in order to limit its liability.[24]

For a lender to be liable under CERCLA, the lender must actually participate in the management or operational affairs of the facility. The statute defines "participation in management" as a lender who exercises decision-making control regarding the handling and/or disposal practices of the hazardous waste. A lender can also be a participant in management if the lender exercises control of the facility comparable to a manager, such that the lender exercises day-to-day decision-making over environmental compliance or the operational functions of the facility. See 42 U.S.C. § 9601(20)(F)(ii) (2004). Hence, a lender who merely has the capacity to influence the facility's operations cannot incur CERCLA liability.

The lender exclusion provision encompasses typical lender activities. The revised lender provision, however, does not shield a lender from "owner or operator" status under all circumstances. Thus, it has been noted that lenders should continue to conduct thorough environmental investigations on property as part of their due diligence procedures in order to maintain limited liability.[25]

A lender who discovers environmental contamination or facts that would reasonably suggest the likelihood of environmental contamination may have a duty to disclose these facts. In one case, despite an "as is" clause in a property sales contract, a lender that had foreclosed on a property and then sold it to an innocent purchaser was liable for the purchaser's damages due to the lender's failure to disclose the property's contaminated condition and ongoing EPA investigation.[26] Non-disclosure was regarded as fraud in the inducement. Note that intermediate landowners who do not cause

---

[23] See 42 U.S.C. § 9601(20)(E)(ii).
[24] See id.
[25] See Henderson, Congressional Reform of Lender and Fiduciary Liability Under CERCLA and RCRA: Is Fleet Factors Finally Dead?, 114 Banking L.J. 210, 210–11 (1997).
[26] Hess v. Chase Manhattan Bank, 220 S.W.3d 758 (Mo. 2007).

contamination but discover it and sell the property to innocent buyers without disclosing those facts either have independent liability under CERCLA § 9601(35)(C) or will be denied the innocent landowner defense.[27]

6. *Potential liability for attorneys.* Since environmental law consists of a complex regulatory scheme and relies heavily on self-reporting, attorneys who play a role in the compliance procedures may be the next target for federal regulation.[28] It has been noted that federal regulators may begin to bring actions against environmental attorneys who have knowledge of environmental violations but fail to advise their client adequately on the disclosure procedures, or who fail to take appropriate remedial steps when the client refuses to comply.[29] Furthermore, an attorney might be held liable under CERCLA as an operator if the attorney becomes too deeply enmeshed in the activities of a client. In City of N. Miami v. Berger,[30] an attorney who advised the developers of a municipal recreational complex was not held liable under CERCLA as an "operator." In that case, the attorney lacked sufficient control over his clients' activities because the attorney did not direct the placement of waste or supervise employees. Furthermore, an attorney's environmental advice might expose the attorney and her law firm to liability. A San Francisco law firm defended itself against environmental crime charges stemming from the waste disposal advice it had rendered to a bankrupt client. The law firm had informed the client's landlord that the client was abandoning its rented space along with any waste, rather than advising the client to properly dispose of the waste. Although the court dismissed the charges, the deputy attorney stated, "Our position is that [the law] does not shield lawyers or other corporate agents from wilful or intentional acts in violation of state law."[31]

7. *Brownfields, redevelopment, and the community.* Environmentally contaminated sites not only create liability risks or costs for landowners but also impose economic and social costs, and public health and safety risks, on the surrounding community. The term "brownfield" refers to properties that are unused or under-used due to real or perceived environmental contamination. The term recognizes that both the property owner and the public are affected. This Assignment focuses on property owners' post-purchase liabilities and their pre-purchase management of legal and financial risks. A critical issue in this field, however, is how to induce remediation (clean-up) and re-use or redevelopment of contaminated sites in

---

[27] Yost, Liability Under CERCLA § 9601(35)(C) for Intermediate Landowners Who Discover Contamination, Do Not Disclose, and Sell to Innocent Buyers, 35 B.C. Envtl. Aff. L. Rev. 141 (2008).

[28] See Note, Developments in the Law—Lawyers' Responsibilities and Lawyers' Responses, 107 Harv. L. Rev. 1547, 1626–27 (1994) (noting that environmental law is a likely target for regulation due to the similarities with the banking and securities practices that have been a recent target for attorney conduct regulation).

[29] See Hottel, Caught in the Web: CERCLA Owner or Operator Liability of Lenders, Shareholders, Parent Corporations, and Attorneys, 6 S.C. Envtl. L.J. 161, 179 (1997); Note, Developments in the Law—Lawyers' Responsibilities and Lawyers' Responses, 107 Harv. L. Rev. 1547, 1626–27 (1994).

[30] 828 F.Supp. 401 (E.D.Va.1993).

[31] See Hottel, Caught in the Web: CERCLA Owner or Operator Liability of Lenders, Shareholders, Parent Corporations, and Attorneys, 6 S.C. Envtl. L.J. 161, 179 (1997).

ways that protect public health, safety, and environments and that strengthen local economies and communities.

One challenge with creating the right mix of incentives, requirements, and procedures is that brownfields can vary substantially, as described below:

> The ownership of brownfields properties is mixed. Some sites are in private hands; others are owned by the federal government or by local or state governments. Still others are "orphan sites" for which there are no recognized "potentially responsible parties" to pay for contamination clean-ups because such parties no longer exist, are insolvent, or are unknown. Each site has its own industrial history and quality of infrastructure. Site size can vary from a half-acre former dry-cleaning establishment to a 900-acre defunct manufacturing facility. Contamination levels also differ, from none at all to severe contamination. But what all sites have in common is the perception that they are contaminated, and that perception makes redevelopment more difficult.[32]

With wide variations from site to site in the degree of contamination, quality of location, and redevelopment potential, the clean-up and redevelopment of different sites will also require widely varying types and amounts of public sector incentives or interventions in private market transactions.[33]

From the perspective of a potential redeveloper of a brownfield, the barriers, costs, and risks can be substantial. Of course, the redeveloper will have the costs of the clean-up and the redevelopment, both of which can be quite expensive. The redeveloper may encounter difficulties finding lenders to finance the project due to the perceived risks. The redeveloper must engage in a lengthy and costly process of creating and getting approval for a remediation and redevelopment plan that details not only the clean-up methods, standards, and outcomes, but also the end uses of the site and various limits and conditions on those uses. Area residents and environmentalists might raise objections that must be addressed. Unforeseen problems can arise during the clean-up, such as new discoveries of unknown contamination or failures in the methods used. During the long period before the entire project is actually completed, the redeveloper is spending substantial sums of money on the project but not realizing any income from it. As you can see from this Assignment, a redeveloper will not want to acquire ownership or management of the property itself until he or she has an approved remediation plan from government regulators that limit potential liability. By engaging in a clean-up of the site, the redeveloper can recover some of these costs from PRPs, but the litigation itself will involve costs and time, and the PRPs may be bankrupt or out-of-business.

From the perspective of the government, brownfields are economically under-performing sites that depress property values in the area, produce relatively low tax revenues, and pose risks or harms to the public health,

---

[32] Dixon, Reclaiming Brownfields: From Corporate Liability to Community Asset, in Boyce & Shelley, eds., Natural Assets: Democratizing Environmental Ownership 57, 58 (2003).
[33] Id.

safety, and environment. Migration of contamination from a site into the groundwater, which can in turn pollute public water supplies, is one such concern. Moreover, the obstacles to brownfield remediation and redevelopment encourage developers to reject already developed, but potentially contaminated sites and instead, go beyond the metropolitan borders to develop "greenfields;" previously undeveloped sites that do not pose contamination-related liability risks. This inclination promotes urban sprawl and unnecessarily converts open space, farmland, or environmentally sensitive lands into development projects that could have been located on already developed sites. On the other hand, government officials—eager to facilitate brownfields clean-ups and redevelopment—must be careful with their use of government subsidies, relaxed clean-up standards, and liability releases, to avoid failed projects, inadequate clean-ups, or government subsidization of projects that could have been accomplished by private sector investment.

Community residents are also concerned about brownfields. On one hand, residents want brownfields cleaned up and put to good economic uses. Brownfields expose area residents to health and safety risks from hazardous contamination, can be attractive nuisances to children, devalue surrounding property, create eyesores, and represent missed economic opportunities and jobs that could result from more productive uses of the property. On the other hand, community residents worry that negotiated clean-up standards will not be adequate—or adhered to by redevelopers, environmental professionals, and government officials—and therefore will continue to expose people to health and safety hazards. This is especially true if the end use of the remediated site will be for housing, schools, parks, or health care facilities. Residents may object to the proposed use of the redeveloped site altogether, particularly if it is an industrial or other highly intensive use that is near residences or civic areas. They may object to not being involved early and fully in planning and negotiating of a remediation and redevelopment plan. Because many brownfields are located in or near low-income and minority communities, the levels of concern and distrust may be especially high in those communities, both about the failure to clean up the contamination and residents' lack of input into clean-up standards, end uses of the project, and the terms and compliance standards of the plan itself.

Nonetheless, despite these seemingly overwhelming concerns, signs of success emerge from brownfields policies. Thousands of contaminated sites have been cleaned up and redeveloped. Community residents—including residents of low-income and minority communities—have participated in and even initiated brownfields remediation and redevelopment projects. Increasingly environmentally sustainable development plans and methods are being incorporated into brownfields redevelopment.[34] Researchers

---

[34] Eisen, Brownfields at 20: A Critical Reevaluation, 34 Fordham Urb. L.J. 721 (2007); Eisen, Brownfields Development: From Individual Sites to Smart Growth, 39 ELR 10285 (2009); Felten, Brownfield Redevelopment 1995–2006: An Environmental Justice Success Story?, 40 Real Prop. Prob. & Tr. J. 679 (2006); Arnold, Fair and Healthy Land Use: Environmental Justice and Planning 123–26 (2007); U.S. EPA, Sustainable Reuse of Brownfields: Resources for Communities, EPA 560–F–06–247 (2006); U.S. EPA, Brownfields Success Stories, http://www.epa.gov/brownfields/success/index.htm.

caution, however, that brownfields programs are not unqualified successes and that more could be done both to incorporate public, environmental-justice, and environmental-sustainability concerns into remediation and redevelopment projects, and to reduce the number of failures.[35]

8. *The future of Superfund.* While CERCLA and SBLRBRA have created a way to rectify the problem of environmental waste, the EPA cannot continue the clean up without proper funding. In 1995 Congress permitted a tax paid by polluter companies to expire, resulting in a reduction of the EPA budget by $1.7 billion, which in turn greatly reduced the amount of money available for Superfund. John J. Fialka, *Money Shortage Threatens Superfund*, Wall St. J., Sept. 7, 2004, at A2. With the future of Superfund being tied to the political process, only time will tell whether Superfund will fulfill its potential.

---

[35] Eisen, Brownfields at 20: A Critical Reevaluation, 34 Fordham Urb. L.J. 721 (2007); Eisen, Brownfields Development: From Individual Sites to Smart Growth, 39 ELR 10285 (2009); Felten, Brownfield Redevelopment 1995–2006: An Environmental Justice Success Story?, 40 Real Prop. Prob. & Tr. J. 679 (2006); Arnold, Fair and Healthy Land Use: Environmental Justice and Planning 123–26 (2007); Freeland, Environmental Justice and the Brownfields Revitalization Act of 2001: Brownfields of Dreams or a Nightmare in the Making?, 8 J. Gender Race & Just. 183 (2004); Scholfield, In Search of the Institution in Institutional Controls: The Failure of the Small Business Liability and Brownfields Revitalization Act of 2002 and the Need for Federal Legislation, 12 NYU Envtl. L.J. 946 (2005).

# VI. INTRODUCTION TO INTELLECTUAL PROPERTY LAW

## ASSIGNMENT 55

# TRADEMARK LAW

### 1. INTRODUCTION TO INTELLECTUAL PROPERTY LAW

Intellectual property is one of the fastest growing areas of practice. Although historically intellectual property was considered a highly specialized field, today even general practitioners need a basic familiarity with intellectual property doctrines to handle the needs of their clients. The need for more detailed knowledge of this area is likely to escalate as we become a society that is increasingly driven by technology.

The "core" subjects of intellectual property are copyrights, patents and trademarks. Each of these areas is governed by a federal statute. In addition, intellectual property encompasses state law analogues that are governed by either the common law or statutes of particular states.

All components of intellectual property define the property rights of owners of intangible assets. Copyrights and patents protect ownership rights with respect to products created through intellectual efforts. Copyright law protects "works of authorship" such as writings, music and artwork. Patents protect inventions. Trademarks, which indicate the source of a particular product or service, protect the investment businesses make in goodwill. Thus, the intangible nature of intellectual property contrasts with the more tangible nature of realty and personalty. As discussed below, the doctrines and theoretical underpinnings of all types of property law are similar. Therefore, before embarking on an introductory study of intellectual property, it is useful to consider the theoretical similarities between property law and intellectual property. This introductory discussion also will explore some basic differences between these areas.

A. Similarities

Nearly all of the doctrines covered in a traditional property course reflect a fundamental tension between the interests of property owners versus the interests of other people or entities. Examples of this tension include a landowner's inability to exclude people from her property in certain circumstances;[1] the doctrines that define the respective rights of

---

[1] Recall State v. Shack, 277 A.2d 369 (N.J.1971), Assignment 1, in which the Supreme Court of New Jersey upheld the right grant labor camp over the objections of the landowner/farmer/employer.

landlords and tenants; and zoning laws which attempt to balance a landowner's interests against those of the government.

Similarly, trademark law deals with balancing the rights of trademark owners and others who wish to use the same or a similar trademark. Trademark law thus attempts to define not only the appropriate geographic area of trademark use but also the relevant product boundaries in which a particular trademark may be used. In addition, the heart of most trademark infringement litigation revolves around the similarity of the trademarks at issue. Trademark owners are only granted the right to prevent other trademark uses that are likely to cause consumer confusion.

A similar tension inheres in copyright law, which seeks to resolve the appropriate balance between protecting creators' rights and insuring the optimal access to copyrighted works. Perhaps the most notable example of this balance is the fair use provision,[2] which sets forth a balancing test to be used in determining whether a particular unauthorized use of copyrighted property will be allowed. The Copyright Act is replete with other examples of qualifications of a copyright owner's rights under various circumstances.[3]

Patent law, like copyright law, tries to reward creators for enriching public welfare without unduly sacrificing the interest of the public in enjoying access to the inventors' creations. In addition, patent law recognizes that the storehouse of knowledge can grow only if every inventor is allowed to expand upon the insights of earlier creators. As Sir Isaac Newton purportedly stated, "If I have seen farther, it is by standing on the shoulders of giants."[4] Thus, patent law is careful to leave principles and products of nature in the public domain. Protection is available only for applications of these principles and refinements of these products. Even then, only truly significant advances over prior art will merit patents.

The legal concept of ownership is quite similar for all types of property in that the owner's rights consist of her legal *interests* in the object in which the property is embodied. This conception of property contrasts markedly with the lay person's definition of property which focuses on physical ownership of the thing itself. As you know, real property cases refer to these legal interests as a bundle of rights which include the right to exclude, the right to possess, the right to use, the right to dispose, and the right to manage and derive an economic benefit.[5] Ownership of property in the legal sense is not synonymous with ownership of the land itself, but instead constitutes ownership of these legal interests in the land. Recall that although a landlord actually owns

---

[2] 17 U.S.C. § 107.
[3] See generally, 17 U.S.C. §§ 107–118.
[4] See Merton, On the Shoulders of Giants: A Shandrean Postcript (Free Press, 1965).
[5] Recall Assignment 1.

a particular piece of land and may have certain legal interests in that property, his tenant also has a legal interest in the property. The tenant's legal interest can be protected in court and thus also constitutes property in the legal sense.

Using copyright law as a relevant comparison, the Copyright Act explicitly provides a bundle of rights that copyright protection affords. The statute affords to the copyright owner the exclusive rights to reproduce, distribute, perform, and display the copyrighted work, as well as the right to prepare new works based on the underlying copyrighted works.[6] The copyright owner's exclusive ability to exercise this bundle of rights enables her to safeguard the pecuniary value of the copyrighted work. These five rights thus represent the judicially protectable interests which render copyright ownership valuable. Moreover, the Copyright Act states that ownership of the object in which a copyrighted work is embodied (e.g., the painting which is protected by copyright law) is distinct from ownership of the copyright.[7] Thus, the owner of the work, which is subject to copyright protection, is not necessarily the owner of the copyright.

B. Differences

Having explored some of the theoretical similarities between intellectual property and tangible property, it is also useful to identify the ways in which intellectual property law differs from tangible property law. One of the more obvious differences between intellectual property law and tangible property law is that tangible property law generally is common law in nature whereas trademark, copyright, and patent protection are statutory. Moreover, a specific duration exists for copyright and patent protection, unlike that for tangible property. Trademark protection differs somewhat from copyrights and patents since trademark protection can be unlimited in duration, but trademark owners generally must actually use their trademarks to receive continued protection.

The limitations on the duration of protection under copyright and patent law relate to the issue of balancing the optimal degree of public access to intellectual property and the proprietary rights of the owners of the protected material. Although a landowner does not possess an unqualified right to exclude others from his property, the issue of public access to realty generally is less compelling than it is for certain types of intellectual property. For example, part of the reason for the "right versus access" tension in the area of copyright law is that substantial protection for copyrighted works potentially conflicts with the First Amendment that fosters the dissemination of informational and entertainment works. A similar conflict between the need for public dissemination (and use) and the protection of proprietary interests also

---

[6] 17 U.S.C. § 106.
[7] 17 U.S.C. § 202.

is manifested in other areas of intellectual property. In the patent law context, keep in mind that Newton could not have seen so far had he been enjoined from standing on his predecessor's shoulders. With respect to trademarks, the law generally attempts to strike a balance between what can be protected by the property owner (i.e., marks which signify the source of a product or service) and what must remain in the public domain (i.e., matter which is generic and therefore belongs in the public domain).

Patents and copyrights can be considered "public goods" in that their possession is "nonrivalrous." That is, it is possible for many people to enjoy the benefits of an invention simultaneously without interfering with one another.[8] Thus, whereas the consequence of private ownership of tangible property is to increase social wealth, private ownership of intangible property decreases social value. A general argument can be made that copyright and patent protection results in too little access to the protected property. The other side of this argument is that without these protections, people may not have the incentive to create works and inventions that will ultimately benefit society.

Additionally, the goals of intellectual property and tangible property law are in some critical ways not at all alike. Since the supply of tangible property is essentially fixed, conservation is a vital concern in the law of property. But the supply of ideas is not fixed, so there is no need to conserve them. To the contrary, intellectual property law is aimed at encouraging the development of new ideas and facilitating the wide dissemination of those that are already in existence. In addition, often people feel differently about their intellectual creations than they do about their land and personality, and so reputational interests come into play in intellectual property law in a way that they do not in property law. For example, trademarks are protected from tarnishment and copyright protects the integrity of works of fine art.

Finally, a few words about the organization and pedagogy of this introductory unit to intellectual property. Following this introductory text, this first Assignment provides an overview of trademark law. Trademark law is a useful starting point because the subject matter is somewhat less complicated than copyright law. The second and third Assignments in the intellectual property unit focuses on copyright law and a state law doctrine, the right of publicity. We excluded patents from the scope of the intellectual property unit because even an introductory application of patent law requires a more detailed foundation than is possible with the abbreviated format of this Assignment.

This unit is intended only as a very basic introduction to the field of intellectual property and in no way substitutes for an upper-level survey course in intellectual property. This unit is designed to give first-year

---

[8] For instance, two people can use the same discovery of a new flavored coffee brewing technique, each making her own cup of coffee without interfering with the other's enjoyment.

students the opportunity to get a "taste" of a critically important field that traditionally was covered only in the upper-level curriculum.

## 2. Introduction to Trademark Law

*Overview and Obtaining Trademark Protection*

Trademark law protects marketing symbols that are used on goods ("trade marks") and on services ("service marks"). It also protects the marks of collectives, such as the Ladies' Garment Workers Union ("collective marks"), as well as the marks of certification organizations, such as Good Housekeeping's Seal of Approval ("certification marks"). The current trademark statute, the Lanham Act, was enacted in 1946 and is codified at 15 U.S.C. §§ 1051–1127. According to the statutory definitions, a trademark can include "any word, name, symbol, or device, or any combination thereof" used "to identify and distinguish" one's goods or services from those of others "and to indicate the source" of those goods or services.[9]

A traditional justification for creating exclusive rights in marks is that such protection prevents consumer confusion. Consumers are often unable to examine goods (or services) to determine their quality or source. Instead, they must rely on the labels attached to the products offered for sale. The material on these labels is, therefore, a kind of language. Since language is effective only if words have clear and unique meanings, the source of a particular product must have exclusive authority over the marketing symbols it uses.

Although this justification for trademark law would suggest that consumers should have a cause of action for trademark infringement, in reality consumers generally do not have standing to sue under trademark law. Rather, trademark law gives to the producer who regularly uses a mark the right to prevent others from using the same mark, or a confusingly similar mark, on the same goods, or on related goods. Therefore, the operation of trademark law suggests that trademark owners are doing something that requires, and deserves, the protection of exclusivity. That contribution is the production of goodwill: the investment in quality, reputation, and service. Without the promise that others can be prevented from utilizing their marks, merchants will not invest their efforts in creating goodwill.

Federal trademark law has its origins in state unfair competition laws. These laws were intended to prevent a merchant from using a competitor's mark to "pass off" (or "palm off") her goods by misrepresenting them as those of her competitor to deceive consumers into buying them by mistake. In fact, the Lanham Act adopted the unfair competition themes of state law to the point that federal courts often use

---

[9] 15 U.S.C. § 1127 (definitions of trademark and service mark). Unless otherwise noted, all statutory citations in this part of the Assignment are to 15 U.S.C.

state formulations of unfair competition principles to inform their understanding of federal trademark law.

Why is federal legislation necessary if federal and state law cover essentially the same practices? The answer lies in the federal trademark registration system provided by the federal law. Our federal system maintains trademark registers (called the Principal and Supplemental registers) that merchants can consult to avoid adopting marks that are already taken. These registers provide newcomers with *actual notice* of what marks have already been taken, thereby allowing them to avoid adopting marks that are likely to confuse consumers.[10] Moreover, registration on the Principal Register provides *constructive notice* that a mark is in use and confers specific rights on the mark's owner, such as the right to enjoin anyone who adopts the same or a similar mark for similar goods.[11]

A merchant desiring trademark protection can apply to the Patent and Trademark Office (PTO) if she either is presently using the mark in interstate commerce or if she can demonstrate a bona fide intent to use the mark in commerce. This application, which can be filed with or without the assistance of legal counsel, consists of three elements: the fee, the application form, and a drawing of the mark. These materials must include the date of the mark's first use and first use in commerce, which are important for establishing the applicant's priority. As among two applicants for the same or a similar mark for similar goods, it is the applicant with the earliest use who is entitled to the registration.[12]

When the PTO receives all application materials,[13] an examiner from the office studies them to determine whether the mark qualifies under the Lanham Act's general requirements for federal trademark protection.[14] The requirements and standards by which the examiner judges the application are codified in the Trademark Manual of Examining Procedure (TMEP), which is promulgated by the PTO. The manual is published as "a reference work for both practitioners and examiners alike."[15] If the application appears to satisfy these requirements, the PTO then publishes the mark in its Official Gazette. Those who believe they would be injured if the mark were registered have 30 days from the time of publication in which to oppose registration.[16] If no one opposes the mark, the PTO issues to the applicant a certificate of registration and registers the mark on the Principal Register. The owner can then notify others that the mark is registered by displaying it in

---

[10] § 1111.
[11] § 1072.
[12] § 1051–52.
[13] An applicant might be able to claim his or her U.S. priority date for the purpose of obtaining a priority date for international trademark protection. See § 67 of the Trademark Act, 15 U.S.C. § 1141(g); Madrid Protocol Art. 4(2).
[14] 37 C.F.R. §§ 2.61–2.69.
[15] See Forward to TMEP, 6th Edition.
[16] § 1063.

conjunction with the words "Registered in U.S. Patent and Trademark Office" or, as is more common, with the symbol ®.[17] With respect to applications based on intent-to-use rather than actual use, the applicant receives a Notice of Allowance if no one opposes registration upon publication of the mark.[18] However, the applicant still must submit a verified statement that the mark has been used in commerce before her mark will be placed on the Principal Register. An applicant has a maximum of 36 months in which to file this statement. Note that although intent-to-use applications can have the effect of reserving a mark for a period of time, the applicant does not acquire the rights that attach to registration until use begins and the mark is registered. That is, during the interim period between application and registration, the applicant cannot enjoin others from adopting the mark, nor can she prevent prior users from expanding their businesses. In other words, it is only when the Notice of Allowance is converted into a registration that the trademark holder's priority rights come into effect. For the most part, they are then dated from the day the application was filed.

Trademark protection and registration last for the period that a mark is in use. However, affirmative steps must be taken to maintain registration. Certificates of registration remain in force for ten years and can be renewed for additional ten-year periods upon payment of fees. In addition, registrants must file periodic affidavits averring continuing use, or setting out special circumstances accounting for nonuse.[19]

The material above describes an application that is ultimately approved. Problems can arise, however, along the way. First, more than one party might apply to use similar marks on similar goods. If so, an interference may be declared.[20] Alternatively, when the mark is published, someone may claim registration will cause ambiguity, in which case, an opposition will be declared.[21] Oppositions and interferences are handled similarly: in an *inter partes* proceeding, complete with discovery, live-witness testimony, briefs and oral argument. The Trademark Trial and Appeal Board (TTAB), an agency court within the PTO, determines who has the right to the mark, whether the application should be approved, or (in the case of multiple users of similar marks) whether the Commissioner of Trademarks should register both marks with limitations on each of the concurrent uses.[22] Appeals from the Board are generally to the Court of Appeals for the Federal

---

[17] § 1111.
[18] See 15 U.S.C. § 1063(b) and 37 C.F.R. §§ 2.88–2.89.
[19] §§ 1058–59.
[20] § 1066.
[21] § 1063.
[22] §§ 1067–68.

Circuit. Alternatively, an action against the Commissioner of Trademarks can be instituted in federal district court.[23]

Of course, it is also possible that the examiner simply does not consider the mark registrable. In such cases, the examiner and applicant enter into correspondence, and the applicant will explain why the mark should be registered or make changes to meet the examiner's objections. If the two agree on a registrable mark, the course described above will be followed. If they cannot agree, there are two possibilities. First, the applicant could appeal the disallowance of registration to the TTAB,[24] and then through the federal judicial system in the manner noted above. However, when the Examiner believes the mark is not sufficiently distinctive to indicate the source of the applicant's goods or services, there is sometimes a second choice. If the mark is capable of becoming distinctive—that is, if people could become accustomed to thinking of it as source-indicative, the applicant can register it on the Supplemental Register.[25]

Marks on the Supplemental Register do not enjoy the full benefit of federal law. Registration on the Supplemental Register does not, for example, provide constructive notice to subsequent adopters that the mark is in use and so does not confer on the trademark owner the automatic right to enjoin others from using the mark. The Supplemental Register does, however, offer significant advantages. First, it is a mechanism of actual notice: those who want to avoid ambiguity can use the Supplemental Register as an additional resource for finding marks that have been previously adopted. Marks on the Supplemental Register can even be displayed with the ® that provides actual notice of federal registration.[26] Second, owners of marks on the Supplemental Register can use the federal courts to assert state-based rights and even certain federal rights. Third, marks on the Supplemental Register can usually be transferred to the Principal Register after five years' use, if that five years' use has given the mark acquired distinctiveness.[27] Finally, registration on the Supplemental Register meets some of the requirements needed to obtain the benefits of trademark treaties that the United States has entered into with foreign countries.

Nevertheless, registration does not constitute a complete solution to the multiple-user problem. First, the registers do not list all marks that are in use. For example, marks protected only under state law do not appear on it. Accordingly, newcomers researching the availability of a particular mark must consult not only the federal registers, but also state registers, trade journals, catalogues, newspapers, magazines, and the

---

[23] § 1071. Dissatisfied parties can petition the Supreme Court for review of the regional circuit decision or the CAFC decision, but such petitions are rarely granted.

[24] § 1070.

[25] § 1091.

[26] § 1111.

[27] § 1052(f).

like. Also, registration on the Principal Register does not create priority vis a vis marks that were adopted before the application to register was filed. That is, prior users are entitled to continue to use their marks in the geographic areas where they were used before the registered owner applied for trademark protection.[28] They are even entitled to a small zone of geographic expansion.

*Use Requirements*

Use permeates every aspect of trademark law. There are three distinct requirements concerning a mark's use for trademark protection. First, the mark must have a physical or spatial association with goods or services so that consumers perceive the mark as a signal conveying information about the trademark owner and its products. Second, the mark must be used in commerce—that is, in connection with sales or marketing activities. Third, to be a *federal* trademark, the signal must come within the jurisdiction of the Lanham Act by being used in interstate commerce. This third component derives from the historical development of federal trademark law. Unlike copyright and patent law, trademark law lacks a clear constitutional basis. The "Copyright Clause" of the US Constitution is the authority for both copyright and patent legislation. When Congress attempted, in 1870, to use the same authority to enact a registration system to protect marketing symbols, the Supreme Court balked.[29] Deprived of Copyright Clause authority, Congress shifted gears and enacted a new trademark law under its Commerce Clause powers.[30] This source of authority explains the requirement that to be designated as a federal mark subject to jurisdiction under the current federal statute, a symbol must be used in interstate commerce.

*Distinctiveness Requirement*

Only subject matter that is intrinsically capable of being understood as a signal rather than as a description of the goods or services is capable of attaining the status of a trademark. Thus, subject matter that is "generic," descriptive of a class of goods or services, is not registrable. Also, as indicated above, a mark cannot be registered if it is confusingly similar to a mark that is already in use on similar goods.

*Infringement and Fair Use*

Because trademark law protects the capacity of suppliers to use their marks to communicate effectively with customers, trademark infringement actions focus on the extent to which the marketing efforts of defendants cause confusion in the marketplace by disrupting the trademark owner's signaling ability. Such disruption can occur in a variety of ways. Some cases involve the use of identical signals on the same kind of products; such cases usually are easy to decide because the simultaneous usage of identical marks on the same products will

---

[28] § 1115(b)(5).
[29] The Trade-Mark Cases, 100 U.S. 82, 93–94 (1879).
[30] U.S. Const. art. I, § 8, cl. 3.

many nations have joined the Madrid Agreement, the United States has not yet joined.

In 1989, the Madrid nations supplemented the Agreement with a new "Madrid Protocol," which creates another method for obtaining international trademark protection with a single standardized application. After Senate ratification of the Madrid Protocol, Congress passed the Madrid Protocol Implementation Act of 2002, which took effect in 2003.[37]

## 3. PRINCIPAL PROBLEM

Barberry Seasonal Wear, an upscale clothing line, has decided to launch a new line of plaid-patterned seasonal clothing products. Barberry intends to call this line "Plaid-Wear." The line contains products for both men and women, and depending on the season, includes items such as umbrellas, scarves, hats, gloves, sunglasses, and totes. Barberry wants to use the following names for the different seasonal styles of these products: Independence Plaid; Halloween Plaid; Christmas Plaid; and Easter Plaid. Barberry has designed original plaid patterns for each of these lines. Each plaid is intended to convey the spirit of the season through the use of colors traditionally associated with that season.

Will Wallace is the manager for the world-renowned men's acapella group, "In the Tune of Plaid." He opposes Barberry's use of these marks on the ground that he holds a service mark registration for "In the Tune of Plaid" for a singing group. The members of In the Tune of Plaid are also known individually by their adopted "plaid" nicknames: Joe "Joker Plaid," Chris "Christmas Plaid," Larry "Lush Plaid," Steve "Scary Plaid" and Adam "Atomic Plaid." Wallace has also launched a line of men's t-shirts called "PlaidWear." The "PlaidWear" line is actually an umbrella line that consists of five respective men's t-shirt lines sporting the nicknames of the individual members of "In the Tune of Plaid." Each t-shirt line consists of plaid shirts modeled after those worn by the individual members of the band. However, three years ago, Chris "Christmas Plaid" left the band and has still not been replaced. No products have been marketed under "Christmas Plaid" since his departure. Wallace also holds trademark registrations for men's t-shirts containing "Plaid," one for "PlaidWear" and one for each "plaid" nickname.

If you were representing Barberry, would you tell it to refrain from using the plaid marks on the ground they are likely to cause confusion with Wallace's marks? Would you advise Barberry to seek registration for these marks? If the issue were litigated, what arguments would you anticipate Barberry making against Wallace's position? Before

---

[37] Pub.L. No. 107–273, 116 Stat. 1913 (codified at 15 U.S.C. §§ 1051 et seq.). See 37 C.F.R. §§ 2 and 7.

evaluating Barberry's overall chances for success, consider the following materials.

## 4. MATERIALS FOR SOLUTION OF PRINCIPAL PROBLEM

### Jordache Enterprises, Inc. v. Levi Strauss & Co.
United States District Court, Southern District of New York, 1993.
841 F.Supp. 506.

■ KRAM, DISTRICT JUDGE.

In this action involving two nationally known manufacturers and distributors of jeans and jeans apparel, plaintiff Jordache Enterprises, Inc. ("Jordache") moves, pursuant to Rule 56 of the Federal Rules of Civil Procedure, for summary judgment against Levi Strauss & Co. ("Levi"). Specifically, Jordache seeks an order declaring that its use of the trademark "Jordache Basics 101" is not likely to cause the public to be confused that jeans and jeans apparel sold in association with that mark are manufactured or are otherwise sponsored by Levi, and such use therefore does not infringe any rights Levi may have in the mark "501" under the Federal Trademark Act (the "Lanham Act"), 15 U.S.C. § 1114(1).

Levi opposes Jordache's motions and cross-moves for summary judgment on its counterclaims, alleging that Jordache's use of the mark "Jordache Basics 101" and design is likely to cause confusion, mistake or deception and constitutes infringement of Levi's "501" mark in violation of § 32(1) of the Lanham Act.

Background

Jordache

Except where noted, the following facts are undisputed. Jordache is a nationally-known manufacturer and distributor of jeans and jeans apparel, and has sold such products in conjunction with the federally registered "Jordache" trademark since 1978. In 1986, Jordache began using the "Jordache Basics" trademark in the manufacture, sale, promotion, and advertisement of its jeans and jeans apparel. In 1988, it also commenced use of the trademark "Jordache Basics 101." During this same time period, Jordache ran a television commercial that Levi claims to be a simulation of the style, format and mood of Levi's "501 Blues" advertising campaign.

Subsequently, beginning in February 1991, Jordache used "Jordache Basics 101 with wings and stars design" in commercial advertisements to promote a line of Jordache jeans. Between October 1990 and February 1991, Jordache manufactured and distributed approximately 600 dozen men's jeans that were promoted as "Jordache Basics 101 with wings and stars designs" and "Jordache 101 with wings and stars designs." Most of these jeans were sold in early 1991 to several small retailers, not including any department stores or large specialty chains. An additional 200 dozen jeans were ordered for distribution and sale in the fall of 1991 and the winter of 1992, and 1,000 dozen "Jordache Basics 101" jeans were ordered for production and shipment through September 15, 1992. These jeans were labeled, affixed and tagged with Jordache identifiers [such as]: either the "Jordache Basics," "Jordache Basics 101 with stars and wing designs" or "Jordache 101 with stars and wing designs," trademark printed on suede-like fabric which was permanently stitched onto the jeans at the top of the right rear panel and positioned between two belt loops. The entire line of Jordache jeans featured a front zipper fly.

Jordache describes its "101" products as "high waisted, tight body fitting, zipper-front jean[s]." See Deposition of Stephen Baum, taken on July 30, 1991, at 331, annexed to Plaintiff's Statement of Material and Undisputed Facts Pursuant to Local Civil Rule 3(g) ("Jordache's Rule 3(g) Statement"), as Exh. "7." According to Jordache, the "Jordache Basics 101" style is intended for the woman or man who desires their jeans to have a "tight sexy fit." See Deposition of David Warren, taken on August 2, 1991, at 82, annexed to Jordache's Rule 3(g) Statement as Exh. "4." Jordache jeans for men are priced between $30.00 and $45.00.

Jordache claims that its "Jordache Basics 101" mark forms an integral part of its campaign of advertising and marketing promotion, generating future consumer demand even though the product is not immediately available. According to Jordache, the "Jordache Basics 101" concept directs the consumer to a line of basic, five pocket, western-style jeans, by communicating the idea that "like the first course one can take in school in any subject, 'there is nothing more basic than 101 in the Jordache line' of jeans apparel." See Jordache's Rule 3(g) Statement at ¶ 5.

Levi Strauss

Levi originated its line of "501" jeans in the 1800's, when the model number 501 was randomly assigned to a style of jeans containing five pockets, a button fly, and metal rivets securing the edges of each pocket. In 1969, Levi officially began use of the number "501," a federally registered mark, as a trademark for the jeans themselves. The style of jeans utilizing the "501" trademark has remained virtually unchanged for over 135 years and, Levi's "501" jeans have frequently been referred to as the "original" jeans.

Levi's "501" jeans can be purchased either in pre-shrunk, or original non-pre-shrunk, or "shrink-to-fit," forms. Thus, in contrast to Jordache's description of "501" jeans as "loose fitting," Levi claims that its "501" jeans, after washing, provide a fit that conforms to the body. Levi's "501" jeans are available in various fabric treatments, such as stonewashed (rocks), stonewashed (chemical), rinsed, bleached, white-washed, electric-washed, and overdyed. The "501" jean is tagged with several Levi identifiers, including: (1) the "arcuate" design pattern identifier, which is stitched on the two rear pockets; and (2) a permanent red ribbon labeled

"Levi," which is sewn on the jean's left-hand vertical seam of the right rear patch pocket; (3) the "Guarantee Ticket," consisting of a leather-like fabric which is sewn on the waistband; (4) a flash card prominently displaying the "501" mark; and (5) a button fly. Generally, "501" jeans are sold at retail prices ranging from $16.99 to $42.00.

In the period 1982–1991, Levi expended over $150,000,000 in advertising that featured the "501" mark. This advertising was conducted via television, posters, print and in-store displays, and is considered the largest advertising program ever conducted for a specific apparel item. Levi "501" jeans have also received extensive publicity in the news media. In the period 1970–1991, Levi sold more than 390 million pairs of "501" jeans, yielding more than $5 billion in revenues.

While "501" jeans are targeted for men, in 1981, Levi introduced a special line of "501" jeans for women. Additionally, since 1987, Levis has produced, advertised and sold a line of women's jeans identified by three-digit trademarks in the "900" series. Sales of the "900" series models have exceeded $185 million though 1991. The most popular model in this line is the "901" jean, with sales of over 2.7 million pairs, producing revenue of more than $41 million. A youthwear version of "501" jeans was also introduced in 1905. In conjunction with the "501" trademark that appears on the flashcard attached to the rear pocket of these jeans, the designation "701" appears on the leather patch which is permanently affixed to the garment.

In addition to its jeans utilizing the "501," "701" and "901" trademarks, Levi offers several different styles of jeans utilizing other three-digit trademarks in the 500 series, including "505," "506," "517," and "550." The "505" and "517" marks are federally registered. Levi claims that its marketing strategy has been to attract vast purchaser interest in "501," creating a promotional halo over its other jeans styles. As with its "501," "701" and "901" jeans, Levi has enjoyed large sales of jeans bearing its other three-digit marks.

Registration of Jordache Trademarks

Between February and April 1988, Jordache applied to register with the United States Patent and Trademark Office ("PTO") the trademarks "Jordache 101," "Jordache Basics 101," and "Basics 101." In the latter part of 1988, Levi filed notices of opposition to each of these marks, claiming that Jordache's use of the number "101" was similar to Levi's family of three-digit trademarks, and therefore likely to confuse or mislead the public into believing that Jordache's jeans either originated from, were associated with, or were sponsored by Levi. Subsequently, in October 1989, Jordache abandoned its application to register those trademarks. Jordache claims, however, that it reserved the right "to use trademarks including the numeral '101' in different formats and/or different design configurations." See letter from Lori B. Cohen, counsel for Jordache, to Milton W. Schlemmer, counsel for Levi of 12/28/89, annexed to Jordache's Rule 3(g) Statement as Exh. "30."

On February 1, 1991, Jordache filed an intent to use application with the PTO to register the mark "Jordache Basics 101 with star and wing design" for use with jeans and jean apparel. Levi opposed Jordache's application and the opposition was suspended without decision pending the outcome of the instant action.

Discussion

The Lanham Act prohibits the use of "any reproduction, counterfeit, copy, or colorable imitation of a registered mark" where "such use is likely to cause confusion, or to cause mistake, or to deceive." 15 U.S.C. § 1114(1)(a). To state a claim for trademark infringement or unfair competition, a party must show a "likelihood that an appreciable number of ordinarily prudent purchasers are likely to be misled, or indeed simply confused, as to the source of the goods in question." Mobil Oil Corp. v. Pegasus Petroleum Corp., 818 F.2d 254, 256 (2d Cir.1987) (quoting Mushroom Makers, Inc. v. R.G. Barry Corp., 580 F.2d 44, 47 (2d Cir.1978), cert. denied, 439 U.S. 1116, 99 S.Ct. 1022, 59 L.Ed.2d 75 (1979)).

Types of confusion that constitute trademark infringement include where: (1) prospective purchasers believe that the senior user sponsored or otherwise approved of the junior user's trademark, see Dallas Cowboys Cheerleaders, Inc. v. Pussycat Cinema, Ltd., 604 F.2d 200, 205 (2d Cir.1979); (2) potential consumers initially are attracted to the junior user's mark by virtue of its similarity to the senior user's mark, even though these consumers are not actually confused at the time of purchase, see Grotrian, Helfferich, Schulz, Th. Steinweg Nachf. v. Steinway & Sons, 523 F.2d 1331, 1342 (2d Cir.1975); and (3) customers are confused as to the source of the junior user's product when this product is observed in the post-sale context, see Lois Sportswear, U.S.A., Inc. v. Levi Strauss & Co., 799 F.2d 867, 871 (2d Cir.1986).

In deciding the issue of likelihood of confusion, the Court is guided by the multi-factor test set forth by Judge Friendly in the classic case, Polaroid Corp. v. Polarad Elecs. Corp., 287 F.2d 492 (2d Cir.1961), cert. denied, 368 U.S. 820, 82 S.Ct. 36, 7 L.Ed.2d 25 (1961). The so-called "Polaroid factors" for determining whether likelihood of confusion exists consist of eight criteria: (1) strength of the mark; (2) degree of similarity between the two marks; (3) proximity of the products; (4) likelihood that the prior owner will bridge the gap; (5) actual confusion; (6) defendant's good faith; (7) quality of defendant's product; and (8) sophistication of buyers. Polaroid Corp. v. Polarad Elecs. Corp., 287 F.2d at 495. Questions regarding the likelihood of confusion normally are factual in nature. Nevertheless, " 'courts retain an important authority to monitor the outer limits of substantial similarity within which the jury is permitted to make the factual determination whether there is a likelihood of confusion as to source,' and summary judgment is appropriate if the court is satisfied that the products or marks are so dissimilar that no question of fact is presented." Id. (quoting Warner Bros., Inc. v. American

Broadcasting Cos., 720 F.2d 231, 246 (2d Cir.1983)). As "each [Polaroid] factor must be evaluated in the context of how it bears on the ultimate question of likelihood of confusion as to the source of the product," Lois Sportswear, U.S.A., Inc. v. Levi Strauss & Co., 799 F.2d at 872, the Court will examine each factor in turn.

1. Strength of the Mark

The first factor—strength of the mark—weighs heavily in Levi's favor. The strength of a mark has been defined as "its tendency to identify the goods sold under the mark as emanating from a particular, although possibly anonymous, source." McGregor-Doniger Inc. v. Drizzle Inc., 599 F.2d 1126, 1132 (2d Cir.1979). The relative strength of a mark is measured by its conceptual strength along the spectrum of marks, as well as by its significance in the marketplace. Edison Bros. Stores, Inc. v. Cosmair, Inc., 651 F.Supp. 1547, 1554 (S.D.N.Y.1987). Ultimately, the strength of a mark is a function "of its distinctiveness, or its 'origin-indicating' quality, in the eyes of the purchasing public." McGregor-Doniger Inc. v. Drizzle Inc., 599 F.2d at 1132.

Marks are classified in the following categories of increasing distinctiveness: (1) generic; (2) descriptive; (3) suggestive; (4) arbitrary; and (5) fanciful. Two Pesos, Inc. v. Taco Cabana, Inc., 505 U.S. 763, ___, 112 S.Ct. 2753, 2757, 120 L.Ed.2d 615 (1992); Abercrombie & Fitch Co. v. Hunting World, Inc., 537 F.2d 4, 9 (2d Cir.1976). Arbitrary and fanciful marks are, by their nature, stronger marks because they are identified solely with a particular product or service. McDonald's Corp. v. McBagel's, Inc., 649 F.Supp. 1268, 1274 (S.D.N.Y.1986). "When these marks are registered, they are accorded the highest degree of protection." Id.

It is undisputed that the "501" mark is arbitrary and fanciful. Arbitrary marks consist of words that neither suggest nor describe any characteristic of the particular good or service with which it is used. See Edison Bros. Stores, Inc. v. Cosmair, Inc., 651 F.Supp. at 1554. As the ordinary meaning of the numeral "501" does not describe any particular quality or characteristic of jeans or jean apparel, the "501" trademark is conceptually strong when applied to such products. Moreover, it is evident that the "501" mark has developed a powerful secondary meaning as, standing alone, it serves to identify Levi as the source of the jeans.

Additionally, the commercial strength of the "501" mark attests to its significance in the marketplace as identifying the source of the goods. Levi's massive advertising efforts, the length of time during which the "501" mark has been used to describe Levi products, Levi's aggressive promotion of the "501" mark and the extent of unsolicited media coverage enjoyed by Levi's "501" jeans further enhance the mark's distinctiveness. Accordingly, the Court finds that Levi has established the strength of the "501" mark as a matter of law.

## 2. Degree of Similarity

The second Polaroid factor the Court must examine is the similarity of the two marks. In determining whether the two marks are similar, the Court must look to the effect on prospective purchasers. Thus, " 'similarity in and of itself is not the acid test. Whether the similarity is likely to provoke confusion is the crucial question.' " McGregor-Doniger Inc. v. Drizzle Inc., 599 F.2d at 1133 (quoting 3 R. Callman, The Law of Unfair Competition, Trademarks and Monopolies § 82.1(a), at 601–02 (3d ed. 1969)). "The test is not whether the consumer will know the difference if he sees the competing products on the same shelf. Rather, it is whether he will know the difference if the junior mark is singly presented and he has heard of the senior mark." Edison Bros. Stores, Inc. v. Cosmair, Inc., 651 F.Supp. at 1555.

The parties hotly dispute whether the Levi and Jordache marks are similar. Levi contends that Jordache's method of labeling its "101" jeans, as well as its advertising campaigns greatly increase the likelihood that prospective purchasers will be confused. Conversely, Jordache contends that there is no likelihood of confusion because of the actual and specific use that Jordache makes of the numeral "101." The Court finds that the degree of similarity between the two marks is a disputed issue of fact upon which reasonable minds may differ.

First, the Court acknowledges that the number "101" is extremely close to "501." This disturbing similarity stems not only from the fact that both marks consist of three digit numbers, but also from the fact that only one digit is changed and the numbers sound alike when spoken. Furthermore, because Levi uses other three-digit marks, such as "701" and "901" in the marketplace, Jordache's "101" mark creates the impression that it is yet another item in Levi's pre-existing "01" series, and substantially increases the likelihood of confusion.

Nevertheless, "[t]he fact that a trademark is always used in conjunction with a company name may be considered by the trial court as bearing on the likelihood of confusion." McGregor-Doniger Inc. v. Drizzle Inc., 599 F.2d at 1134. Jordache confirmed at Oral Argument that it does not intend to use the numeral "101" standing alone, but rather, as part of the trademark "Jordache Basics 101 with wings and stars design." This mark, attaching the Jordache identifier to the numeral, is substantially less similar to Levi's "501" mark, and thus, substantially less likely to cause confusion. Accordingly, as this factor creates a factual dispute, summary judgment is precluded as a matter of law.

## 3. Proximity of the Products

The third Polaroid factor addresses whether, due to the proximity of the competitive products in the marketplace, consumers may be confused as to their source. See Hasbro, Inc. v. Lanard Toys, Ltd., 858 F.2d at 77. Factors to consider in determining the competitive proximity of the products include appearance, style, function, fashion appeal, advertising orientation and price. McGregor-Doniger Inc. v. Drizzle Inc., 599 F.2d at 1134. "Products which directly compete in the marketplace clearly warrant a finding of the highest degree of competitive proximity," creating a strong likelihood of confusion. Hasbro, Inc. v. Lanard Toys, Ltd., 858 F.2d at 77.

As an initial matter, the Court notes that Jordache and Levi manufacture and sell a similar product. Jordache points to the different style, cut and fit between its product and Levi's jeans, and contends that the two companies target different consumers. While Jordache identifies these differences in style and cut, however, it ultimately concedes that the markets are proximate. Levi argues further that the prices of the products are within the same range, and that the two jeans models at issue contain five pockets and riveted pocket corners. While the Court acknowledges that Jordache and Levi compete in the same general market, whether the companies, in fact, target slightly different consumers of jeans is an issue of fact for trial.

In any event, should a jury determine that Jordache and Levi do, indeed, compete for slightly different consumers in the jeans market, the third Polaroid factor favors Levi. As this Court has held, there is an even greater likelihood of confusion where the junior user's product competes for a slightly different market segment than the senior user. Accordingly, the Court finds that the third Polaroid factor favors Levi.

4. Likelihood that Levi Will Bridge the Gap

The fourth Polaroid factor seeks to protect the senior user's interest in being able to enter a related field at some future time. Lois Sportswear, U.S.A., Inc. v. Levi Strauss & Co., 799 F.2d at 874. If the owner of a trademark can show that it intends to enter the market of the alleged infringer, such a showing is indicative of future likelihood of confusion as to source. Id. The more closely the products compete, the shorter the gap is to bridge. Andy Warhol Enters., Inc. v. Time Inc., 700 F.Supp. 760, 766 (S.D.N.Y.1988).

As set forth in Part 3, supra, while Jordache and Levi are competing in the jeans market, it is unclear whether the two companies address different segments of purchasers. Accordingly, whether Levi is likely to bridge the gap is also a question of fact.

5. Actual Confusion

The fifth factor looks to whether any consumers have actually been confused by the products bearing the allegedly confusing marks. See Centaur Communications v. A/S/M Communications, 830 F.2d at 1227. Evidence of actual confusion consists of (1) anecdotal evidence of confused consumers in the marketplace; and (2) consumer survey evidence. Id.

Levi concedes that it does not have any anecdotal evidence of actual instances of confusion. It argues, however, that anecdotal evidence of actual confusion is unlikely here as Jordache's total production of jeans bearing the "101" mark is so insignificant. As Jordache clearly has not infiltrated the market with products bearing the "101" trademark, the Court will not make any negative inference from the fact that Levi has not shown any anecdotal evidence of actual confusion.

[Moreover], the failure of Levi to offer valid survey evidence of confusion does not warrant the adverse inference that confusion is not likely. "[I]t is black letter law that actual confusion need not be shown to prevail under the Lanham Act, since actual confusion is very difficult to prove and the Act requires only a likelihood of confusion as to source." Lois Sportswear, U.S.A., Inc. v. Levi Strauss & Co., 799 F.2d at 875. Moreover, while a showing of actual confusion may be probative, the absence of actual confusion is not probative. Accordingly, although the Court finds no evidence of actual confusion, this factor does not weigh in Jordache's favor as the "101" mark has not significantly infiltrated the marketplace for jeans.

6. Defendant's Good Faith

The sixth Polaroid factor examines the good faith of the junior user in selecting the mark. "Evidence of intentional copying by a junior user may be indicative of an intent to create a confusing similarity between the products." Bristol-Myers Squibb Co. v. McNeil-P.P.C., Inc., 973 F.2d 1033, 1044 (2d Cir.1992).

The existence of good faith on the part of Jordache is disputed. Jordache contends that it selected the number "101" to evoke the image that, like the first course you take in any subject in school, "Jordache Basics 101" jeans are the most basic style of jeans in Jordache's line of apparel. Jordache argues further that it is a substantial company and is, therefore, relying on its own reputation and goodwill among consumers, and not on the reputation enjoyed by Levi. Levi claims, however, that the long history of Jordache's attempts to infringe on Levi trademarks establishes Jordache's bad faith. Levi contends further that the fact that Jordache's television commercials are strikingly similar to Levi's advertising campaigns further establishes Jordache's bad faith. In the face of this dispute, the Court finds that a conclusive determination regarding Jordache's intent must await trial.

7. Quality of Defendant's Product

The seventh Polaroid factor looks to the quality of the junior user's product. The parties apparently do not dispute that they both manufacture and distribute quality jeans and jeans apparel. Thus, Levi need not be concerned that the reputation associated with its mark is being tarnished by inferior merchandise. Edison Bros. Stores, Inc. v. Cosmair, Inc., 651 F.Supp. at 1561. However, the fact that the goods are of corresponding quality actually "supports the inference that they emanate from the same source." Centaur Communications, Ltd. v. A/S/M Communications, Inc., 830 F.2d at 1228; see also Lois Sportswear, U.S.A., Inc. v. Levi Strauss & Co., 799 F.2d at 875 (holding that the good quality of the alleged infringer's product actually may increase the likelihood of confusion as to source). Accordingly, the Court finds that the seventh factor favors Levi.

8. Sophistication of Buyers

The eighth factor, the sophistication of purchasers in the relevant market, "is grounded on the belief that unsophisticated consumers aggravate the likelihood of confusion." Hasbro, Inc. v. Lanard Toys, Ltd., 858 F.2d at 78. Thus, "[s]ophistication of consumers usually militates against a finding of a likelihood of confusion, though it might on occasion increase the likelihood of confusion, depending upon the circumstances of the market and the products." Centaur Communications, Ltd. v. A/S/M Communications, Inc., 830 F.2d at 1228 (citations omitted).

The parties do not dispute that jeans purchasers are sophisticated consumers. Jordache claims that (1) jeans are an intensely personal item of clothing; (2) style, cut and fit play an important role in the consumer's selection and purchase of jeans; and (3) there exists strong brand loyalty among jeans purchasers. While Levi asserts that male purchasers do not spend a lot of time shopping, but, rather, look for particular visual cues in making quick purchase decisions, Levi does not directly controvert Jordache's contention that jeans purchasers are sophisticated consumers. Indeed, Levi agrees that the typical jeans consumer looks to brand name and fit in purchasing jeans. See Deposition of Robert Kaplan, regional sales manager at Levi, dated July 18, 1991, at 95, annexed to Jordache's Rule 3(g) Statement as Exh. "11."

Nevertheless, the fact that jeans buyers are sophisticated consumers weighs in Levi's favor. Indeed, in a case involving two competing jeans manufacturers, the Second Circuit held that the sophistication of jeans buyers actually increased the likelihood that these consumers would be confused by jeans containing nearly identical back pocket stitching patterns. Lois Sportswear, U.S.A., Inc. v. Levi Strauss & Co., 799 F.2d at 875. The Lois Sportswear court stated:

> [W]e believe that it is a sophisticated jeans consumer who is most likely to assume that the presence of appellee's trademark stitching pattern on appellant's jeans indicates some sort of association between the two manufacturers. Presumably it is these sophisticated jeans buyers who pay the most attention to back pocket stitching patterns and their "meanings." Likewise in the post-sale context, the sophisticated buyer is more likely to be affected by the sight of appellee's stitching pattern on appellants' jeans and, consequently, to transfer goodwill.

Id. at 875–76 (citation omitted). Similarly, in this case, the fact that jeans purchasers are conscious of trademarks further increases the likelihood that the "101" mark will cause confusion as to the association between Jordache and Levi. Accordingly, the Court finds that the eighth factor favors Levi.

## 9. Summary

Although three of the Polaroid factors weigh in Levi's favor, namely, strength of the mark, quality of the junior user's product and sophistication of the buyers, there remain disputed issues of fact with respect to similarity of the marks, proximity of the products, likelihood that Levi will bridge the gap and Jordache's intent. Accordingly, summary judgment in favor of either party is denied.

### Packman v. Chicago Tribune Co. and Front Page News, Inc.
United States Court of Appeals for the Seventh Circuit, 2001.
267 F.3d 628.

■ RIPPLE, J.

On June 15, 1998, in recognition of the Chicago Bulls' sixth National Basketball Association ("NBA") championship, the headline of the front page of the *Chicago Tribune* read "The joy of six." As it has done on several other historic occasions, the Chicago Tribune Company reproduced its entire front page on t-shirts, posters, plaques and other memorabilia. The Tribune contracted with Front Page News, Inc., to print on t-shirts a collage comprised of the Tribune masthead and six headlines describing each of the Bulls' NBA victories, including "The joy of six" headline.

Diana Packman holds federal and Illinois trademarks for the phrase "the joy of six," for use in relation to football and basketball games. She brought this action against the Tribune and Front Page under the Lanham Act for trademark infringement and unfair competition under Illinois law. The district court granted the defendants' joint motion for summary judgment, holding that the "fair use" defense defeated Ms. Packman's claims, and, in the alternative, that there was no evidence that consumers were likely to be confused as to the source of the defendants' products. Ms. Packman appeals from the district court's summary judgment ruling. For the reasons set forth in the following opinion, we affirm the district court.

BACKGROUND

The phrase "the joy of six" is a play on the 1970s book series *The Joy of Sex*.[36] It has been used to describe positive feelings associated with six of anything, e.g., the birth of sextuplets, a six-run inning in a baseball game, six characters on a television show, and, in this case, six championships in a sporting event.

A. The History of Ms. Packman's Trademark

Ms. Packman's husband, Richard Packman, began using the phrase "the joy of six" in the Mid-1980s to describe a group with whom he

---

[36] Alex Comfort, *The Joy of Sex* (1977).

exercised at a local health club at 6:00 a.m. In 1994, the Packmans began printing the phrase on flyers to advertise occasional gatherings of family and friends to watch football games. On July 1, 1997, Ms. Packman obtained a federal trademark for "the joy of six" for use in connection with "entertainment services in the nature of football games."[37] Beginning in September 1996, the Packmans began using "the joy of six" to promote outings to watch or attend basketball games and on February 3, 1998, Ms. Packman obtained a federal trademark to use the phrase in connection with "entertainment services in the nature of basketball games."[38] Ms. Packman also printed "the joy of six" on small quantities of hats and t-shirts to promote the gatherings, in connection with National Football League teams pursuing a possible sixth Super Bowl championship, in particular the San Francisco 49ers and the Dallas Cowboys and in relation to the Chicago Bulls' pursuit of a sixth NBA championship.

Ms. Packman did not produce evidence of the number of gatherings or outings, the number of attendees, or the profit, if any, they generated. The record does not contain any documentary evidence of the Packmans' sales of hats and t-shirts bearing "the joy of six" mark. Taking the Packmans' deposition testimony as true, however, a small quantity of t-shirts and hats were given away, sold to friends and family, or sold at one Ohio retail outlet and generated little, if any, profit. In addition, Mr. Packman sold an unknown number of "The Joy of Six is Coming . . . Chicago Basketball" t-shirts at cost to a homeless street vendor, who presumably resold them. In addition, the Packmans attempted, without success, to negotiate contracts to license "the joy of six" for use in connection with National Football League and NBA teams. Just prior to the Bulls' sixth NBA championship, the Packmans began negotiating a deal for t-shirts bearing "the joy of six" mark to be produced by a Chicago retailer. The Packmans claim, however, that the retailer backed out of the deal after the Tribune introduced its t-shirts bearing the June 15, 1998 front page and "The joy of six" headline.

B. The Tribune's Use of "the joy of six"

As early as 1996, sportswriters at the Tribune and the *Chicago Sun-Times* began using "the joy of six" to describe the Bulls' anticipated sixth NBA championship. The Packmans did not protest the use of the phrase they had trademarked, but instead sent a letter, hat and t-shirt to the writers, encouraging them to use the phrase:

> Recently granted the registered trademark for "The Joy of Six" slogan, I encourage you to employ this catchy tag line in your writings and reports throughout the 1997–1998 NBA season as the Bulls shoot for their sixth straight year of stellar success.

---

[37] The trademark was registered in Ms. Packman's name for estate planning purposes.

[38] On May 5, 1997, Ms. Packman registered "the joy of six" as a service mark for use in connection with basketball games under Illinois law.

R.15 at 2. Mr. Packman admitted that, based on this letter, he would not have objected to the writers' using the phrase in a column headline.

On June 15, 1998, the Tribune printed, on its front page directly beneath its masthead, a banner headline that read "The joy of six," describing the sixth NBA championship won by the Bulls the previous night. The headline included a graphic listing the six years in which the Bulls had won championships and the names of the defeated teams. The font and size of the phrase in the Tribune headline are visibly distinct from the font and size used by the Packmans on their flyers, hats and t-shirts. At least eight other newspapers in the United States used the phrase "the joy of six" in their headlines that day.

As it has done with other historic front pages, the Tribune reproduced its front page, including "The joy of six" headline, on t-shirts, posters, plaques, and other memorabilia, to promote the Tribune and memorialize its coverage of the Bulls' historic victory. The manager of the Chicago Tribune Store, Mary Tremont, decided, without input from the Tribune's editorial board, to reproduce the entire June 15 front page onto these promotional items. The items were sold at the Michigan Avenue Tribune Store, at a storefront of the Tribune's offices in Vernon Hills, and, for one month in 1999, at the Tribune's kiosk in Woodfield Mall. The Tribune also instructed one of its vendors, Front Page News, to create a t-shirt bearing the Tribune masthead amidst a collage of the actual headlines reporting all of the Bulls' championships: "Two for Two: Bulls Still Champs," "Three-mendous," "Ringmasters," "The Jackson Five," and "The joy of six." Anticipating the Bulls' winning the championship and the Tribune's printing a catchy phrase to describe the victory, Ms. Tremont and Front Page designed this shirt before June 15, without knowledge of the exact wording of the headline. The collage t-shirt was sold in the Tribune store and, for four days in 1998, by Front Page to wholesalers.

Shortly after the Tribune's June 15 headline appeared, several of the Packmans' friends and family members contacted them to congratulate them on their "deal" with the Tribune. These individuals had seen the Tribune's headline and knew of Ms. Packman's trademark on "the joy of six," but there is no evidence that they purchased or attempted to purchase either the Tribune's memorabilia or the Packmans' hats and t-shirts.

C. Ms. Packman's Lawsuit

On November 16, 1999, nearly 18 months after "The joy of six" appeared on the Tribune's front page and on its championship memorabilia, Ms. Packman filed a complaint against the Tribune and Front Page, alleging trademark infringement, 15 U.S.C. § 1114, unfair competition, 15 U.S.C. § 1125(a), and trademark infringement under Illinois law, 765 ILCS 1036/60. Ms. Packman does not challenge the Tribune's printing "The joy of six" on its June 15 front page; she only objects to the reproduction of the Tribune's front page, including "The joy of six" headline, onto promotional memorabilia. . . .

E. The District Court's Decision

On October 3, 2000, the Tribune and Front Page filed a joint motion for summary judgment, and on November 9, 2000, Ms. Packman filed a cross-motion for summary judgment on defendants' liability. On December 6, 2000, the district court granted defendants' motion and denied Ms. Packman's motion. The court found that defendants employed "The joy of six" in a non-trademark use in good faith to describe a characteristic of their product, and, accordingly, the "fair use" defense protected them from liability for trademark infringement or unfair competition under the Lanham Act. In the alternative, the district court found that Ms. Packman could not prevail on her trademark infringement claim because consumers were not likely to be confused about the source of the Tribune's goods. The court declined to address the two other arguments advanced by defendants in support of their motion: that Ms. Packman's "the joy of six" was not a valid trademark because the phrase was generic or, at most, descriptive; and that the Tribune had a First Amendment right to reproduce any of its front pages to promote its newspaper. Having dismissed Ms. Packman's federal claims, the court also declined to exercise supplemental jurisdiction over her state law trademark infringement claim. This appeal followed.

DISCUSSION

This court reviews de novo the district court's decision to grant summary judgment. Only a "genuine" issue of "material" fact precludes summary judgment. Fed. R. Civ. P. 56(c). Factual disputes are " 'genuine' only 'if the evidence is such that a reasonable jury could return a verdict for the [non-movant],' " and are " 'material' only when they 'might affect the outcome of the suit under the governing law.' " Summary judgment is appropriate when the "pleadings, depositions, answers to interrogatories, and admissions on file, together with the affidavits, if any, show that there is no genuine issue as to any material fact and that the moving party is entitled to judgment as a matter of law." Thus, in ruling on a summary judgment motion, the district court must decide " 'whether the evidence presents a sufficient disagreement to require submission to a jury or whether it is so one-sided that one party must prevail as a matter of law.' "

In reviewing the district court's decision, we "must construe all facts in the light most favorable to the non-moving party." The non-movant may not rest on the pleadings but must adduce evidence "setting forth specific facts showing that there is a genuine issue for trial." Fed. R. Civ. P. 56(e). Ms. Packman must create more than mere doubt as to the material facts and will not prevail by relying on a mere scintilla of evidence or speculation to support her position.

In a trademark infringement case, the classification of a word or phrase as descriptive, the determination that a defendant's use was a non-trademark use in good faith, and the finding that consumers are not likely to be confused about the origin of a defendant's products are questions of fact. Nevertheless, these issues may be resolved on summary judgment "if the evidence is so one-sided that there can be no doubt about how the question should be answered." *Door Sys., Inc. v. Pro-Line Door Sys., Inc.*, 83 F.3d 169, 171 (7th Cir. 1996). With these principles in mind, we turn to Ms. Packman's claims.

Ms. Packman submits that, in holding that the fair use defense barred her claims, the district court ignored evidence of defendants' use of "The joy of six" as a trademark and improperly inferred that defendants acted in good faith. She further argues that the district court committed both factual and legal errors in its likelihood of confusion analysis, and that defendants used the same mark for the same goods in the same geographical area in a manner likely to confuse and which actually confused consumers. At least, she contends, she demonstrated genuine issues of material fact as to the fair use defense and the likelihood of confusion analysis. In addition, Ms. Packman contends that the district court abused its discretion in denying her motion to compel discovery on the issue of defendants' intent in selecting "The joy of six" for its front page and in reproducing its front page on championship memorabilia.

Defendants respond that the district court properly granted summary judgment in their favor because they used "The joy of six" in good faith as a descriptive phrase. They also submit that the undisputed evidence demonstrates that there was no likelihood that any consumer would mistake the Tribune's memorabilia for one of Ms. Packman's products. They also maintain that Ms. Packman's "the joy of six" mark is a descriptive phrase unworthy of trademark protection.

A. The Lanham Act

The Lanham Act protects registered marks from interference by state legislation, prevents unfair competition, and protects against fraud "by the use of reproductions, copies, counterfeits, or colorable imitations of registered marks." 15 U.S.C. § 1127; *Eli Lilly & Co. v. Natural Answers, Inc.*, 233 F.3d 456, 461 (7th Cir. 2000). To prevail on a Lanham Act claim, a plaintiff must establish that (1) her mark is protectable, and (2) the defendant's use of the mark is likely to cause confusion among consumers.

A trademark includes:

any word, name, symbol, or device, or any combination thereof [used by any person] to identify and distinguish his or her goods, including a unique product, from those manufactured and sold by others and to indicate the source of the goods, even if that source is unknown.

15 U.S.C. § 1127. In order to be registered, a mark must distinguish the applicant's goods from those of others. The law recognizes five categories of trademarks, in ascending order of distinctiveness: generic, descriptive, suggestive, arbitrary, and fanciful. Once a mark is registered, the Act affords a plaintiff one of two presumptions: (1) that her registered trademark is not merely descriptive or generic; or (2) that if descriptive, the mark is accorded secondary meaning.

The Act provides that:

> a mark registered on the principal register . . . shall be prima facie evidence of the validity of the registered mark . . . and of the registrant's exclusive right to use the mark in commerce on or in connection with the goods or services specified in the registration subject to any conditions or limitations stated therein, but shall not preclude another person from proving any legal or equitable defense or defect . . . which might have been asserted if such mark had not been registered.

15 U.S.C. § 1115(a). Secondary meaning exists "only if most consumers have come to think of the word not as descriptive at all but as the name of the product."

The defendant may overcome this presumption with evidence that the mark is merely generic or descriptive, or that it lacks secondary meaning. And, even if the mark is sufficiently distinctive to warrant trademark protection, the defendant may still prevail by showing that its use of the mark is not "likely to cause confusion, or to cause mistake, or to deceive." 15 U.S.C. § 1114(1)(a). In addition to attacking the validity of the plaintiff's mark, the defendant may also invoke the "fair use" defense by demonstrating that the alleged infringement "is a use, otherwise than as a mark . . . which is descriptive of and used fairly and in good faith only to describe the goods or services of such party. . . ." 15 U.S.C. § 1115(b)(4). This defense "is based on the principle that no one should be able to appropriate descriptive language through trademark registration."

In this case, defendants asserted the fair use defense in addition to arguing that there was no likelihood of confusion and that Ms. Packman's mark was invalid. The district court did not rule on the validity of the mark, nor shall we, because the fair use defense and likelihood of confusion analysis dispose of Ms. Packman's claims in their entirety.

B. The Fair Use Defense

To prevail on the fair use defense, defendants must show that: (1) they used "The joy of six" in a non-trademark use; (2) the phrase is descriptive of their goods or services; and (3) they used the phrase "fairly and in good faith" only to describe their goods or services. 15 U.S.C. § 1115(b)(4).

1. Non-Trademark Use

The district court held that, because Ms. Packman did not rebut evidence that defendants used "the joy of six" only in a descriptive manner, she failed to raise a genuine issue of material fact as to the nature of defendants' use of the phrase. Ms. Packman contends that, in reaching this conclusion, the district court ignored facts showing that defendants' use of "The joy of six" was a traditional trademark use: (1) defendants applied the mark directly to the goods; (2) defendants labeled the items with the phrase; and (3) the phrase is the most prominent text on all the items and, in her view, was used as "an attention-getting symbol." We agree with the district court that Ms. Packman failed to rebut the evidence of defendants' descriptive, non-trademark use of "The joy of six."

First, the record does not support Ms. Packman's argument that the Tribune used "The joy of six" to identify itself as the source of the newspaper or the championship memorabilia. Rather, the Tribune's distinctive masthead, which appears prominently on the front page and on each piece of memorabilia containing the phrase, identifies the source of the products. In addition, the Tribune masthead also prominently appears on one side of the products' tags, plainly indicating the Tribune as the source. The masthead signifies that the products come from the Tribune and not any of the other newspapers that ran the same headline on June 15, 1998. The Tribune's use of its well-known masthead also identifies the phrase as a newspaper headline reporting on an event, and not as a Tribune trademark.

Second, Ms. Packman ignores her own deposition testimony, in which she admitted that, in the context of the Bulls, "the joy of six" referred to happiness about their six championships and that the phrase is widely used to de scribe the joy of six of anything. The Tribune used the phrase "The joy of six" to describe the happiness associated with six Bulls' championships. On the front page of the Tribune and the championship memorabilia, "The joy of six" reflects that very emotion.

Our decision in *Sunmark* supports the district court's finding that the Tribune did not employ "The joy of six" as a trademark. In *Sunmark,* the maker of "*Swee*TARTS" candy sought to enjoin Ocean Spray from using the phrase "sweet-tart" to describe its cranberry juice drinks. In addition to finding that Ocean Spray had used "sweet-tart" merely to describe the taste of its drinks, this court noted that Ocean Spray had not claimed exclusive use of the phrase and could not object if other juice-makers used it. *See Sunmark,* 64 F.3d at 1059. Nor could these defendants have objected to wide use of the phrase, as evidenced by several other newspapers' printing "the joy of six" headline on June 15, 1998, to describe the Bulls' championships and the varied use of the phrase to describe positive emotions associated with six of anything, such as sextuplets.

*Sands, Taylor & Wood,* on which Ms. Packman relies, is distinguishable. The fair use defense was unavailable in that case because the defendant's slogan, "Gatorade is Thirst-Aid," used the plaintiff's "Thirst-Aid" mark as a trademark. Integral to the court's conclusion was evidence that "Thirst-Aid" appeared more prominently than "Gatorade" in the advertisements and that the rhyming quality of the two words created a "memorable slogan . . . uniquely associated" with the defendant's "Gatorade" product. *Id.* Here, the Tribune used its masthead, not "The joy of six," to foster the association between the products (the memorabilia) and their source (the Tribune). Furthermore, the wide and varied use of "the joy of six" bars a conclusion that any association between the Tribune and the phrase is unique. And, the masthead and the phrase appear in proximity to each other, but not as part of a "memorable slogan," rendering any association between the two weaker than was present in *Sands, Taylor & Wood.*

Accordingly, because Ms. Packman failed to raise a genuine issue of material fact as to the nature of defendants' use of "The joy of six," we agree with the district court that defendants employed the phrase in a non-trademark use.

2. Defendants Used the Phrase Descriptively

Descriptive terms " 'impart information directly.' " The defendants used "The joy of six" as a headline to describe a newsworthy event and the happiness associated with the Bulls' sixth NBA championship. This use did not change with the reproduction of the Tribune's front page onto championship memorabilia. As Ms. Packman herself admitted, "the joy of six" is a phrase commonly used to describe the emotions associated with six of anything. Ms. Packman cannot appropriate the phrase to herself and thereby prevent others from using the phrase in a descriptive sense, as defendants did here. The district court correctly concluded that no genuine issue of material fact existed as to defendants' descriptive use of the phrase.

Furthermore, the record lacks any evidence that "the joy of six" had acquired a secondary meaning as used by Ms. Packman, and she does not point to any evidence in rebuttal. Secondary meaning is "a *mental association* in buyers' minds between the alleged mark and a single source of the product." 2 J. Thomas McCarthy, *Trademarks and Unfair Competition* § 15:5, at 15–9 (4th ed. 2001) (emphasis in original). A mark acquires secondary meaning when it has been used so long and so exclusively by one company in association with its goods or services that the word or phrase has come to mean that those goods or services are the company's trademark. Proof of secondary meaning can be established through direct consumer testimony, consumer surveys, length and manner of use, amount and manner of advertising, volume of sales, place in the market, and evidence of intentional copying. Ms. Packman's assertion of secondary meaning is purely speculative. She does not tell us how many shirts or hats the Ohio store or the Chicago street vendor sold, how many items she produced, who purchased them, or whether she advertised her products. Thus, the record confirms the absence of a secondary meaning altogether. Ms. Packman used the mark primarily in connection with small group outings to sporting events, did not commercially advertise her outings or her products, and used the phrase in connection with the Bulls for less than three years. The phrase "the joy of six" did not achieve a level of distinctiveness with respect to Ms. Packman's goods or services, nor does it exclusively relate to the Bulls' sixth championship. Accordingly, the record supports only one conclusion, that "the joy of six" is merely a descriptive phrase without a secondary meaning, a phrase which defendants, or any other person, may rightfully use.

3. Defendants Used the Phrase in Good Faith

Ms. Packman maintains that the Tribune's knowledge of her trademark (as a result of Mr. Packman's letter to the sportswriters) before running the "The joy of six" headline and its failure to cease its sale of the championship memorabilia after she threatened legal action are evidence of the defendants' bad faith. The district court determined that this evidence did not give rise to an inference of bad faith because Mr. Packman's letter encouraged rather than discouraged use of the phrase, and the Tribune used the phrase in the very manner suggested: as a headline to celebrate the Bulls' success in winning a sixth championship.

Mere knowledge of Ms. Packman's trademark on the phrase is insufficient to establish that the Tribune acted in bad faith and to preclude summary judgment. *See M.B.H. Enter.*, 633 F.2d at 54. The defendants' good faith "can be judged only by inquiry into [their] subjective purpose in using the slogan[]." In *M.B.H. Enter.*, the plaintiff had a registered trademark for the words "I LOVE YOU" for use in entertainment services related to radio programs and had licensed a promotion using the phrase "I LOVE YOU MILWAUKEE" to radio station WISN in Milwaukee. When radio station WOKY began its own campaign professing its love for Milwaukee, using the phrases "WOKY LOVES MILWAUKEE" and "I LOVE MILWAUKEE" signed by WOKY, the plaintiff sought to enjoin WOKY's efforts. Addressing the issue of WOKY's good faith, the court found that WOKY's intent to reap commercial advantage from its declarations of love for the city did not demonstrate that WOKY intended to use the phrase as a trademark. Rather, WOKY's use of its call letters and radio frequency—its trademarks identifying WOKY as the source—in each of the ads suggested that WOKY lacked the intent to use the slogans as trademarks. Accordingly, the court found that WOKY had not acted in bad faith or with the intent to confuse the public about the source of the affection for Milwaukee. *Id.*

Similarly, the presence of the Tribune's distinctive masthead above "The joy of six" headline and on each piece of championship memorabilia will not support an inference that the Tribune acted in bad faith. Nor does the defendants' receipt of commercial benefit from promoting the newspaper or selling championship memorabilia demonstrate use of "The joy of six" in bad faith. Ms. Tremont, manager of the Tribune Store, testified that she selected the June 15, 1998 front page for reproduction onto memorabilia consistent with the Tribune's practice of capturing historical events reported by the newspaper. This decision was made without editorial input and without knowledge of the exact wording of the headline for that day. Therefore the syntax of the headline played no part in the decision to produce and market the Tribune's products in celebration of the Bulls' sixth championship, and therefore will not support any inference that the defendants acted in bad faith.

Ms. Packman failed to adduce evidence creating a genuine issue of fact as to any of the three elements of the fair use defense. Accordingly, the district court did not err in finding that defendants' use of "The joy of six" was a non-trademark use, in good faith, to describe a characteristic or quality of their goods.

C. Likelihood of Confusion

In addition to showing that her mark is protected under the Lanham Act, a plaintiff in a trademark infringement suit must demonstrate that the challenged mark is likely to confuse consumers. Without determining the validity of Ms. Packman's "the joy of six" mark, the district court found that she could not prevail because she failed to demonstrate a genuine issue of material fact as to whether consumers were likely to be confused about the source of the defendants' goods. Ms. Packman now argues that, in granting summary judgment for defendants, the district court failed to draw inferences in her favor, ignored evidence of actual confusion and misapplied the likelihood of confusion analysis. Although likelihood of confusion is a question of fact, the issue may be resolved on summary judgment where the evidence is "so one-sided that there can be no doubt about how the question should be answered."

Seven factors comprise the likelihood of confusion analysis: (1) similarity between the marks in appearance and suggestion; (2) similarity of the products; (3) area and manner of concurrent use; (4) degree of care likely to be exercised by consumers; (5) strength of the plaintiff's mark; (6) actual confusion; and (7) intent of the defendant to "palm off" his product as that of another. No single factor is dispositive, and courts may assign varying weights to each of the factors depending on the facts presented, although, in many cases, the similarity of the marks, the defendant's intent, and actual confusion are particularly important.

1. Similarity of the Marks

In determining whether two marks are similar, the comparison is made " 'in light of what happens in the marketplace,' [and] not merely by looking at the two marks side-by-side." Ms. Packman argues that the defendants' mark is identical to hers. While she is correct that the words are the same, the appearance and placement of the words are distinct such that a consumer would not associate one product with the other. In Ms. Packman's mark, the words "the joy of six" are placed vertically, with "joy" and "six" in larger print. The letters are script-like, with the words " . . . is coming" printed in smaller letters beneath the word "six." The background of both the hat and the t-shirt is black, with the lettering on the hat a combination of white and blue, and on the t-shirt a combination of orange and gold.

In contrast, "The joy of six" appears on the defendants' white t-shirts in the context of the Tribune's entire June 15, 1998 front page, including all of the other headlines and articles of the day. Beneath the blue and white Tribune masthead, "The joy of six" is printed horizontally in black newsprint-style letters. Below the phrase appears the Bulls' logo, a list of the championship years and defeated teams, and a color photograph of Coach Phil Jackson embracing Michael Jordan. On defendants' black collage t-shirt, a large red "6" encompasses each of the headlines for the six championship years and, the Tribune masthead is displayed prominently. Outside the "6" is printed "NBA CHAMPIONS" and a list of the championship years. Although the words on defendants' and Ms. Packman's t-shirts are the same, the words' appearances do not resemble each other and are not likely to cause confusion. Different packaging, coloring, and labeling can be significant factors in determining whether there is a likelihood of confusion. Although hang-tag design and content may often be deserving of comparatively lesser weight than other packaging material, we think that, here, the hang-tag with the Tribune masthead on a product sold out of a Tribune-operated establishment is deserving of some weight. In sum, the distinctiveness of the marks weighs against a finding of likelihood of confusion.

2. Defendants' Intent

Another "more important" factor in determining likelihood of confusion is defendants' intent. This factor looks primarily for evidence that the defendants are attempting to "pass off" their products as having come from the plaintiff. Although the district court, in its fair use analysis, found that defendants had acted in good faith, the court did not directly address defendants' intent in its likelihood of confusion analysis.

The "evidence" of defendants' bad faith urged by Ms. Packman—that Mr. Packman's letter to the sportswriters gave the Tribune notice of her trademark—does not demonstrate that they intended to "pass off" their championship memorabilia as having come from Ms. Packman. Rather, the prominent display of the Tribune masthead above "The joy of six" on each of defendants' products demonstrates the Tribune's intent to promote itself as the source.

Furthermore, using a descriptive phrase such as "the joy of six" is consistent with the inference that defendants intended in good faith to inform consumers about a newsworthy event and characteristic of their products: the celebration of the Bulls' sixth championship victory. That defendants may have been aware of Ms. Packman's mark before reproducing "The joy of six" memorabilia does not show fraudulent intent, particularly because the phrase has been widely used to celebrate six of anything (as Ms. Packman admitted) and the appearance of the phrase on defendants' products is visually distinct. Moreover, Ms. Tremont's independent decision to reproduce the "The joy of six" headline on the championship memorabilia, without knowledge of Ms. Packman's letter to the Tribune and of her mark, is evidence of good faith. Ms. Packman's conclusory assertions that defendants acted in bad faith are unsupported by evidence in the record and fail to create a genuine issue of material fact.

3. Evidence of Actual Confusion

As evidence that consumers were actually confused by defendants' use of "The joy of six," Ms. Packman points to phone calls she received from two friends, her father, and Mr. Packman's former co-worker who had seen the Tribune's front page and called to congratulate her on her "deal" with the Tribune. The district court correctly rejected this evidence as irrelevant to the question of confusion over the source of defendants' championship memorabilia.

Ms. Packman did not show that the four individuals had purchased or attempted to purchase "the joy of six" goods, either from her or from defendants, and thus they were not relevant "consumers" under the Lanham Act. Even if the four callers fell into the relevant category of consumers, however, the district court properly discounted such de minimis evidence of confusion. Therefore, the district court correctly determined that the four phone calls Ms. Packman received were not probative of, or "material" to, the issue of actual confusion.

4. Remaining Likelihood of Confusion Factors

Ms. Packman failed to demonstrate genuine issues of material fact as to the three most important factors in the likelihood of confusion analysis. She also has not demonstrated any issues of fact as to the remaining factors. Although the parties both produced t-shirts and hats, each offered their products in a distinctive style and manner, minimizing the likelihood of confusion. Ms. Packman produced her items primarily in relation to group outings to sporting events, and only alluded to the possibility of the Bulls' sixth championship; in contrast, defendants used "The joy of six" in a newspaper headline and on items celebrating the Bulls' sixth championship. All of defendants' products—and their tags—prominently display the well-known Tribune masthead, providing a strong indication that there is no likelihood of confusion. Thus, the parties' products were distinct in the manner in which they appeared in the marketplace.

In terms of area and manner of use, defendants sold their championship memorabilia from three discrete Tribune-operated locations; Ms. Packman gave away or sold her items out of her home to friends and family. The only store in which her items were sold was located in Ohio, and the only distributor in Chicago was a homeless street vendor, to whom Mr. Packman sold an unknown number of t-shirts. Ms. Packman did not bring forth any evidence to show that her distribution channels in any way overlapped with defendants or that she advertised her products through the same media channels as defendants. Indeed, there is no evidence in the record that either party commercially advertised its products. The distinction between the areas in which the parties' products appeared weighs against finding a likelihood of confusion and Ms. Packman has failed to come forth with sufficient evidence to the contrary.

When considering the degree of care likely to be exercised by consumers, the district court did not consider the sophistication of potential customers, but this oversight is of no consequence, since Ms. Packman introduced no evidence, other than her own conclusory assertions, about buyers of either her products or defendants'. Thus, she failed to establish a genuine issue of fact as to consumer sophistication, weighing against a finding of likelihood of confusion.

Finally, in assessing the strength of Ms. Packman's mark, the district court correctly concluded that the mark was relatively weak; it was a widely used descriptive phrase lacking distinctiveness or recognition with respect to the Bulls' sixth championship. Her own use of the phrase for multiple purposes, from early-morning workout groups to family sporting excursions, negates her unsubstantiated assertion that her mark is strong.

As with the three "more important" factors, Ms. Packman failed to bring forth evidence to establish a genuine issue of fact as to any of the remaining likelihood of confusion factors. Accordingly, the district court correctly determined that Ms. Packman could not prevail on her claims because she had failed to demonstrate a jury question as to likelihood of confusion. Accordingly, the judgment of the district court is affirmed.

## Silverman v. CBS, Inc.

Court of Appeals, Second Circuit, 1989.
870 F.2d 40.

■ NEWMAN, CIRCUIT JUDGE.

The "Amos 'n' Andy" characters were created in 1928 by Freeman F. Gosden and Charles J. Correll, who wrote and produced for radio broadcasting "The Amos 'n' Andy Show." The show became one of the country's most popular radio programs. The characters in the "Amos 'n' Andy" programs were Black. Gosden and Correll, who were White, portrayed Amos and Andy on radio. The authors appeared in blackface in publicity photos. Black actors played the parts in the subsequent television programs.

Gosden and Correll assigned all of their rights in the "Amos 'n' Andy Show" scripts and radio programs to CBS Inc. in 1948. Gosden and Correll continued to create new "Amos 'n' Andy" scripts, which formed the basis for CBS radio programs. The radio programs continued until 1955. Beginning in 1951 CBS also broadcast an "Amos 'n' Andy" television series. The television series was aired on CBS affiliate stations until 1953 and continued in reruns and non-network syndication until 1966. CBS has not aired or licensed for airing any of the radio or television programs since 1966.

In 1981, Silverman began writing a script for a Broadway musical based on the "Amos 'n' Andy" characters. The title of this work was originally "Amos 'n' Andy Go To The Movies." A revision was titled "Amos 'n' Andy In Hollywood," and a more extensive revision was titled "Fresh Air Taxi." Silverman sought a license to use the "Amos 'n' Andy" characters, but CBS refused.

Silverman filed this lawsuit seeking a declaration that the "Amos 'n' Andy" radio programs broadcast from March 1928 through March 1948 (the "pre-1948 radio programs") are in the public domain and that he is therefore free to make use of the content of the programs, including the characters, character names, and plots. He also sought a declaration that CBS has no rights in these programs under any body of law, including trademark law.

On the trademark side of the case, Judge Goettel ruled that the name "Amos 'n' Andy," as well as the names and appearances of "Amos 'n' Andy" characters and "other distinctive features of the . . . radio and television shows" are protectable marks. He then set down for trial the issue of whether CBS's non-use of the marks constituted abandonment.

After a bench trial on the issue of abandonment, Judge Goettel concluded that CBS had not abandoned its trademarks.

## Discussion

Silverman challenges the District Court's rulings that CBS has protectable trademarks in the "Amos 'n' Andy" names, characters, and other features of the radio and television programs, including phrases of dialogue, and that CBS has not abandoned these marks. We find it unnecessary to decide which features of the programs might give rise to protectable marks because we agree with Silverman that CBS has abandoned the marks.

Section 45 of the Lanham Act provides:

A mark shall be deemed to be "abandoned"—

(a) When its use has been discontinued with intent not to resume. Intent not to resume may be inferred from circumstances. Nonuse for two consecutive years shall be prima facie abandonment.

15 U.S.C. § 1127 (1982). There are thus two elements for abandonment: (1) non-use and (2) intent not to resume use. Two years of non-use creates a rebuttable presumption of abandonment.

On the undisputed facts of this case, CBS made a considered decision to take the "Amos 'n' Andy" television programs off the air. It took this action in response of complaints by civil rights organizations, including the NAACP, that the programs were demeaning to Blacks. By the time the abandonment issue came before the District Court, non-use of the "Amos 'n' Andy" marks had continued for 21 years. Although CBS has no current plans to use the marks within the foreseeable future, CBS asserts that it has always intended to resume using them at some point in the future, should the social climate become more hospitable.

Ordinarily, 21 years of non-use would easily surpass the non-use requirement for finding abandonment. See, e.g., I.H.T. Corp. v. Saffir Publishing Corp., 444 F.Supp. 185 (S.D.N.Y.1978) (denying preliminary injunction to protect trademark after 12 years of non-use). The District Court concluded, however, that CBS had successfully rebutted the presumption of abandonment arising from its prolonged non-use by offering a reasonable explanation for its decision to keep the programs off the air and by asserting its intention to resume use at some indefinite point in the future. This conclusion raises a question as to the proper interpretation of the statutory phrase "intent not to resume": Does the phrase mean intent never to resume use or does it merely mean intent not to resume use within the reasonably foreseeable future?

We conclude that the latter must be the case. The statute provides that intent not to resume may be inferred from circumstances, and two consecutive years of non-use is prima facie abandonment. Time is thereby made relevant. Indeed, if the relevant intent were intent never to resume use, it would be virtually impossible to establish such intent circumstantially. Even after prolonged non-use, and without any concrete plans to resume use, a company could almost always assert truthfully that at some point, should conditions change, it would resume use of its mark.

We do not think Congress contemplated such an unworkable standard. More likely, Congress wanted a mark to be deemed abandoned once use has been discontinued with an intent not to resume within the reasonably foreseeable future. This standard is sufficient to protect against the forfeiture of marks by proprietors who are temporarily unable to continue using them, while it also prevents warehousing of marks, which impedes commerce and competition.

We are buttressed in this conclusion by the fact that the statute requires proof of "intent not to resume," rather than "intent to abandon." The statute thus creates no state of mind element concerning the ultimate issue of abandonment. On the contrary, it avoids a subjective inquiry on this ultimate question by setting forth the circumstances under which a mark shall be "deemed" to be abandoned. Of course, one of those circumstances is intent not to resume use, which is a matter of subjective inquiry. But we think the provision, by introducing the two concepts of "deemed" abandonment and intent not to resume use, contemplates a distinction, and it is a distinction that turns at least in part on duration of the contemplated non-use.

This approach is consistent with our recent decisions concerning trademark abandonment. In *Saratoga Vichy* we rejected a claim of abandonment based on seven years of non-use where the initial decision to cease use resulted from a decision of the state legislature and the state, which was the trademark owner, continuously sought to sell the mark along with the mineral water business to which it applied.

The undisputed facts of the pending case are entirely different. Unlike the proprietors in *Saratoga Vichy* and *Defiance Button*, CBS has not been endeavoring to exploit the value of its marks, failing to do so only because of lack of business opportunities. Instead, it has decided, albeit for socially commendable motives, to forgo whatever business opportunities may currently exist in the hope that greater opportunities, unaccompanied by adverse public reaction, will exist at some undefined time in the future.

A proprietor who temporarily suspends use of a mark can rebut the presumption of abandonment by showing reasonable grounds for the suspension and plans to resume use in the reasonably foreseeable future when the conditions requiring suspension abate. But a proprietor may not protect a mark if he discontinues using it for more than 20 years and has no plans to use or permit its use in the reasonably foreseeable future. A bare assertion of possible future use is not enough.

We recognize the point, forcefully made by Judge Goettel, when he wrote:

> It would be offensive to basic precepts of fairness and justice to penalize CBS, by stripping it of its trademark rights, merely because it succumbed to societal pressures and pursued a course of conduct that it reasonably believes to be in the best interests of the community.

*Silverman,* 666 F.Supp. at 581. Nonetheless, we believe that however laudable one might think CBS's motives to be, such motives cannot overcome the undisputed facts that CBS has not used its marks for more than 20 years and that, even now, it has no plans to resume their use in the reasonably foreseeable future. Though we agree with Judge Goettel that CBS should not be penalized for its worthy motive, we cannot adjust the statutory test of abandonment to reward CBS for such motive by according it protection where its own voluntary actions demonstrate that statutory protection has ceased. Moreover, we see nothing in the statute that makes the consequence of an intent not to resume use turn on the worthiness of the motive for holding such intent.

We are also mindful of the facts, relied on by the District Court, that show some minor activities by CBS regarding its properties, allegedly sufficient to rebut abandonment of the marks. These are CBS's actions in licensing the programs for limited use in connection with documentary and educational programs, challenging infringing uses brought to its attention, renewing its copyrights, and periodically reconsidering whether to resume use of the programs. But challenging infringing uses is not use, and sporadic licensing for essentially non-commercial uses of a mark is not sufficient use to forestall abandonment. Cf. Exxon Corp. v. Humble Exploration Co., *supra*, 695 F.2d at 102 (use must be "commercial use" to avoid abandonment). Such uses do not sufficiently rekindle the public's identification of the mark with the proprietor, which is the essential condition for trademark protection, nor do they establish an intent to resume commercial use. CBS's minor activities, like worthy motives for non-use, cannot dispel the legal consequence of prolonged non-use coupled with an intent not to resume use in the reasonably foreseeable future.

The interest of CBS, and the public, in avoiding public confusion, an interest obviously entitled to weight in every trademark case, is also somewhat diminished in the context of this case. This interest is not as weighty as in a case involving a non-artistic product whose trademark is associated with high quality or other consumer benefits. Trademark protection is not lost simply because the allegedly infringing use is in connection with a work of artistic expression. But in determining the outer limits of trademark protection—here, concerning the concept of abandonment—the balance of risks noted is relevant and in some cases may tip the scales against trademark protection.

For all of these reasons, we conclude that the undisputed facts establish abandonment of the "Amos 'n' Andy" marks.

## NOTES

1. *Categories of marks.* Section 1127 of the Lanham Act defines four categories of registrable marks. A *trademark* (when not used in its generic sense to refer to all kinds of marks protected by the Lanham Act), is a mark that is used with goods (e.g., games, chickens, perfumes). A *service mark* is used in connection with services (e.g., dry cleaners, travel agencies, investment advisors). A *certification mark* is a mark that one entity owns to signal something about goods or services produced or provided by others—for example, that the goods are especially well-made (e.g., the Good Housekeeping Seal of Approval), that they are produced with a particular material (e.g., the Woolmark), that they are made in a specific place (e.g., Champagne), or that they are manufactured by a certain organization (e.g., the Ladies' Garment Workers Union). A *collective mark* is a mark that members of an association use to identify their own goods or services (e.g., Sebastian for hair-care products sold through salons). The requirements for trademarks apply equally to all these marks.

In addition to defining protectable marks, § 1127 also defines a "trade name" and "commercial name" as terms that identify a business or vocation. Because they do not appear in conjunction with goods or services and do not send the appropriate sort of signal to consumers, they do not qualify for protection under the Lanham Act simply by virtue of being trade names. However, there is nothing in the Act that prevents a company from acquiring a trademark right in its trade name by using it on goods or services.

2. *Distinctiveness*. The categorization of meanings used in *Jordache*—generic, descriptive, suggestive, arbitrary, and fanciful—describe a spectrum ranging from marks that can never be registered (generic), to marks that can be placed on the Principal Register upon additional investment (descriptive), to marks that can be placed on the Principal Register immediately (suggestive, arbitrary, and fanciful).

Arbitrary marks are coined by the producer and bear absolutely no relationship to the product or service in conjunction with which they are used. Such marks are immediately registrable on the Principal Register. One drawback to arbitrary marks, however, is that they provide the consumer no education regarding the product or service. Choosing an arbitrary word such as "Apple" for computers is cute, but convincing customers to pay thousands of dollars for something that sounds like fruit is not simple. Therefore, some producers believe it is better to call yourself by a name that gives purchasers some sense of what it is that is being sold and some hook on which to hang an association between the mark and the product.

To a certain extent, the best hook is one that actually describes the product—International Business Machines or Personal Computer, for example. Unfortunately, words like these are so graphic, customers are likely to perceive them as product descriptions, and not as marks. That is why they cannot be registered without proof of secondary meaning. A term acquires secondary meaning when its *primary* meaning in consumers' minds is the trademark meaning. Once a mark has secondary meaning, the mark becomes capable of distinguishing the products of the trademark owner from the goods of other producers.

Suggestive marks fall in between the arbitrary and descriptive categories. Terms like "Coppertone" and "Chicken of the Sea" provide hints about the product, but they are only clues: "[a] suggestive mark 'conveys an impression of a good but requires the exercise of some imagination and perception to reach a conclusion as to the product's nature.' "[39] Since these words are capable of distinguishing one producer's version of the product category from another's, they can be registered immediately. There is no need to establish secondary meaning because, like arbitrary marks,

---

[39] Glow Industries, Inc. v. Jennifer Lopez, Coty, Inc., 273 F.Supp.2d 1095 (C.D.Cal.2003) citing Brookfield Communications v. West Coast Entertainment Corp., 174 F.3d 1036 (9th Cir. 1999). See also Zobmondo Entm't, LLC v. Falls Media, LLC, 602 F.3d 1108, 1114 (9th Cir. 2010) citing Kendall-Jackson Winery, Ltd. v. E. & J Gallo Winery, 150 F.3d 1042, 1047 n.8 (9th Cir. 1998) ("If a consumer must use imagination or any type of multistage reasoning to understand the mark's significance, then the mark does not *describe* the product's features, but *suggests* them. Such a mark is therefore classified as 'suggestive' rather than 'descriptive.' ").

customers know from their very first encounter with these terms that they are trademarks.

Generic marks such as aspirin and thermos are never registrable.[40] Trademark law is intended to facilitate competition, not stifle it. Accordingly, trademark rights can never be granted, or retained, in the only effective means of referring to a product category. If a word is generic—if it is the way the public has come to describe the category to which the goods belong—it cannot be protected: it cannot be registered under federal law, nor will it be protected by the unfair competition law of any state. Such words must remain in the public domain for the use of every producer's customers.

3. *Functionality.* The doctrine of functionality is closely related to the ban on generic marks, as it too prevents producers from stifling competition by asserting trademark rights in an element that is needed to properly market goods within a product category. The best example of functionality comes from a case decided by Learned Hand under state unfair competition law, Crescent Tool Co. v. Kilborn & Bishop Co.[41] Claiming that the public had come to identify the crescent-shaped head of its wrenches as its trademark, the plaintiff argued that the defendant should be enjoined from producing a product of a similar shape. Judge Hand disagreed. He recognized that the plaintiff had a right to prevent passing off, and that it had established a protectable trademark in the name "Crescent Tool Company." However, he refused to enjoin the production of other crescent shape wrenches. In his view, only "nonessential" elements of a product can serve as a trademark. If the crescent shape is essential to the proper operation of a wrench in tight places, it cannot be protected by trademark law.

4. *Fair use defense. Packman* involves the defendant's use of the plaintiff's mark to describe the defendant's goods. Can you envision a fair use claim being made when a defendant uses a plaintiff's mark to describe the plaintiff or its products? Which situation is involved in the Principal Problem?

The fair use defense was the subject of the Supreme Court's decision in *KP Permanent Make-Up, Inc. vs. Lasting Impression I, Inc.*[42] In this case, the Court held that "a plaintiff claiming infringement of an incontestable[45] mark must show likelihood of consumer confusion as part of the prima facie case, . . . while the defendant has no independent burden to negate the likelihood of any confusion in raising the affirmative defense that a term is used descriptively, not as a mark, fairly and in good faith."[43] The Court, however, left open the possibility that courts can consider likelihood of confusion as relevant to the issue of the fairness of a particular usage, although it did not

---

[40] Both aspirin and thermos were once registered trademarks but they became generic when the public began using these words as indicative of the product category rather than a particular source of the product. See, e.g., Bayer v. United Drug Co., 272 F. 505, 509 (S.D.N.Y. 1921); King-Seeley Thermos Co. v. Aladdin Industries, Inc., 321 F.2d 577 (2d Cir.1963).

[41] 247 F. 299 (1917).

[42] 543 U.S. 111 (2004).

[45] Section 15 of the Lanham Act provides that after five years of continuous use, certain registered marks become "incontestable," and are therefore no longer subject to being cancelled upon specified grounds. See 15 U.S.C. § 1065.

[43] 543 U.S. at 124.

specify how much confusion will result in eliminating the fair use defense in any given situation. On remand from the Supreme Court, the Ninth Circuit held that on the record before the court, genuine issues of material fact existed with regard to likelihood of confusion and that "the degree of customer confusion remains a factor in evaluating fair use."[44] On this basis, the Ninth Circuit remanded the case to the district court for a trial on the remaining issues of fact.

5. *Evidentiary issues.* Litigation involving trademark law often turns on factual inquiries about how words are used and what customers think. The three most popular methods for shedding light on these issues are: dictionary research, LexisNexis searches, and consumer surveys. Sometimes, the testimony of real-life confused consumers is taken as evidence that consumers are likely to be confused by particular marks. A few litigants have even resorted to the testimony of expert linguists.[45]

The admissibility of surveys has been a very controversial issue. Since surveys typically are the only evidence directly probative of what consumers are thinking at the time of the litigation, they are widely admitted under a doctrine of necessity.[46]

6. *The likelihood of confusion test.* Jordache discusses three different types of confusion. Which type of confusion is present in the Principal Problem?

The test for likelihood of confusion differs somewhat in its articulation in the various circuits, but essentially they all focus on the same type of factors. The *Polaroid* test used in *Jordache* is representative. In terms of the test's operation, no single factor is determinative and courts typically perform a balancing test in weighing the various factors.[47]

a. *Strength of the mark.* Courts often determine strength with reference to the generic-descriptive-suggestive-arbitrary-fanciful spectrum discussed in Note 2. The cases almost universally say that the stronger the mark, the more protection it should receive. Is the reason for this view that consumers are more likely to be confused when a strong mark is infringed, or is there some other theory at work here? Could an argument be made that confusion is more likely to be mitigated with a strong mark?

b. *Similarity of marks.* In evaluating this factor, should only the marks themselves be considered, or should courts also consider the logo surrounding the marks?

c. *Similarity of goods/bridging the gap.* These two factors are somewhat related in that the more proximate the products, "the shorter the

---

[44] See 408 F.3d 596, 609 (9th Cir. 2005).
[45] See, e.g., Pro-Football, Inc. v. Harjo, 284 F.Supp.2d 96, 68 U.S.P.Q. 2d (BNA) 1225 (D.D.C. 2003) (on the derogatory significance of "redskins").
[46] See, e.g., Donchez v. Coors Brewing Co., 392 F.3d 1211 (10th Cir. 2004) citing Flynn v. AK Peters, Ltd., 377 F.3d 13, 71 U.S.P.Q.2D (BNA) 1810 (1st Cir. 2004) (establishing "secondary meaning" through consumer surveys). But see Water Pik, Inc. v. Med-Systems, Inc., 726 F.3d 1136, 1145 (10th Cir. 2013) (observing that surveys which courts consider devoid of probative value are appropriately excluded from evidence.)
[47] Id.

gap is to bridge."[48] Likelihood of confusion can be decreased where the two marks in question are used before separate groups of consumers or where the distinct nature of the products clearly suggests that the two users are unrelated. Do you agree with court's conclusion in *Jordache* that there is a "greater likelihood of confusion where the junior user's product competes for a slightly different market segment than the senior user?"

    d. *Consumer sophistication.* The concept of consumer sophistication encompasses a variety of factors including the price of the product, the potential for impulse purchasing, and the nature of the product itself. In general, courts take the view that the more sophisticated the consumer, the less the likelihood of confusion.[49] Do you agree with the court in *Jordache* that the more sophisticated the consumer, the more likely they will be confused?

    e. *Actual confusion.* Although proof of actual confusion need not be demonstrated, such proof can be extremely probative of likelihood of confusion. Sometimes actual confusion is demonstrated by direct evidence such as testimonial or anecdotal evidence, but frequently proof of actual confusion stems from market research surveys.

    f. *Good faith.* The role of good faith in the likelihood of confusion analysis is, in and of itself, rather confusing. Some courts have held that intentional copying gives rise to a presumption of secondary meaning, while other courts treat a showing of intentional copying only as evidence of secondary meaning.[50] Some courts apply a presumption of likelihood of confusion in cases involving intentional copying.[51] Other courts refuse to apply such a presumption and instead treat intentional copying as just one of the factors that must be considered in a likelihood of confusion analysis.[52] In *Jordache*, the court did not need to resort to a presumption of likelihood of confusion based on intentional copying since it could not make a definite determination on good faith. Should intentional copying give rise to either a presumption of secondary meaning or likelihood of confusion? Do the facts of the Principal Problem or *Jordache* present a stronger case of intentional copying?

---

    [48] Jordache Enterprises, Inc. v. Levi Strauss & Co., 841 F.Supp. 506, 517 (S.D.N.Y.1993).

    [49] See, e.g., Bath & Body Works Brand Mgmt., Inc. v. Summit Entm't, LLC, 7 F. Supp. 3d 385, 398 (S.D.N.Y. 2014); Virgin Enterprises, Ltd. v. Nawab, 335 F.3d 141 (2d Cir. 2003); TCPIP Holding Co., Inc. v. Haar Communications, Inc., 244 F.3d 88 (2d Cir. 2001).

    [50] Compare International Bancorp, LLC v. Societe des Bains de Mer et du Cercle des Estrangers a Monaco, 329 F.3d 359 (4th Cir. 2003) (in the Fourth Circuit, a plaintiff that proves the defendant intentionally copied its mark "is presumed to have proved the mark's secondary meaning, and the defendant must then disprove that presumption") with General Motors Corp. v. Lanard Toys, Inc., 468 F.3d 405 (6th Cir. 2006) (noting that "proof of intentional copying" was "only one of many considerations" used to establish the existence of secondary meaning). See also Perfect Fit Indus., Inc. v. Acme Quilting Co., Inc., 618 F.2d 950 (2d Cir. 1980) (under New York law, intentional copying can substitute for secondary meaning).

    [51] See, e.g., Tuccillo v. Geisha NYC, LLC, 635 F. Supp. 2d 227 (E.D.N.Y. 2009); Anheuser-Busch, Inc. v. L. & L. Wings, Inc., 962 F.2d 316, 321 (4th Cir.1992); Academy of Motion Picture Arts and Sciences v. Creative House Promotions Inc., 944 F.2d 1446, 1456 (9th Cir.1991).

    [52] Commerce Bancorp, Inc. v. BankAtlantic, 285 F. Supp. 2d 475 (D.N.J. 2003). Schwinn Bicycle Co. v. Ross Bicycles, Inc., 870 F.2d 1176, 1184–85 (7th Cir.1989).

Sometimes, the good faith analysis can become intertwined with a discussion of asserted defenses. Does the Principal Problem raise this issue?

g. *Quality of the products/marketing channels.* Instances can arise in which the quality factor favors the plaintiff because the defendant is producing a cheap imitation, but the marketing channels factor favors the defendant because cheaper imitations often are sold in different trade channels. Note that in *Jordache,* the court concluded that the corresponding quality of the products actually favored Levi because consumers would be more likely to assume that the goods in question are from the same source. How should these factors be evaluated in the Principal Problem?

7. *Parameters of § 43(a).* Many trademark infringement cases involve both claims based on federal trademark infringement under § 1114 as well as violations of § 43(a).[53] The critical difference between a § 43(a) claim and an infringement claim under § 1114 is that § 1114 claims are available only for marks that are federally registered. Thus they involve infringement of the plaintiff's most distinctive marketing symbol. In contrast, the subject matter at issue in § 43(a) includes trademarks protected only under state law as well as other, less distinctive, aspects of a manufacturer's marketing scheme, such as advertising motifs, business methods, and trade dress. Section 43(a) also provides protection against false advertising. The inquiry under § 43(a) also involves determining likelihood of confusion, and thus the analyses in both trademark infringement and § 43(a) cases are very similar.

8. *The expressive dimension of trademarks.* Consider this quotation from a biography of Senator Edward (Ted) Kennedy's first wife, Joan:

When I campaign alone I'm approachable. Women talk to me, complain, but when I'm with Ted I'm a Barbie doll.[54]

Is this use of the term "Barbie" the same as the use made of the trademark in *Jordache* or *Packman?* Trademark usages can be arranged on a continuum. At one end, there are cases like *Jordache* where the defendant is using the mark purely in its signaling sense, to communicate with customers about the defendant's own goods. At the other end are expressive uses such as the one in the quotation, where the trademark "Barbie" was not used to sell dolls, but rather to convey an image that readers understand because of their familiarity with the product with which the mark is associated. Between the polls, are hybrid uses.

Should the difference in the way a mark is used influence the outcome of infringement actions? Because every successful infringement action limits someone's ability to utilize communicative symbols, trademark law always implicates expressive concerns. However, a strong argument can be made that when the defendant is using the mark as a signal, interference with free speech does not rise to the level of a constitutional violation. The signaling

---

[53] This section's actual cite is 15 U.S.C. § 1125(a), but it is typically referred to as § 43(a), which is the number of this section as it appeared in the bill that resulted in the Lanham Act.

[54] Marcia Chellis, The Joan Kennedy Story: Living With the Kennedys 191 (Jove ed. 1986). Along the same lines: "Betsy McCaughey, Lieutenant Governor of New York, once described herself as Barbie and Gov. George Pataki as Ken." N.Y. Times Magazine, June 4, 1995 at 18, col. 1.

function is purely commercial, and commercial speech receives limited First Amendment protection.[55] Accordingly, when courts balance the value in giving merchants an unambiguous avenue with which to communicate with customers against the interest in free expression, trademark interests win.

What about nonsignaling uses? Pure expression is entitled to the highest level of constitutional scrutiny. Accordingly, it can be argued that purely expressive uses of trademarks should never be enjoined. In fact, most courts do side with purely-expressive users. However, most manage to avoid constitutional adjudication by considering these nonsignaling usages as outside the purview of trademark law,[56] or as unlikely to give rise to a consumer confusion.[57] For Lanham Act claims, these uses are sometimes found to be within the "fair use" defense of § 1115(b)(4). In the context of the Principal Problem, would you categorize Barberry's usage of the plaid marks as signaling or non-signaling? Why does this categorization matter?

9. a. *Abandonment based on non-use.* Prior to GATT, § 1127 provided that two years of non-use resulted in prima facie evidence of abandonment. This period has been increased to three years pursuant to GATT, which amendment became effective on January 1, 1996. Of course, even if there is non-use for less than three years, abandonment still can be established if it can be proven that a trademark owner has no intent to resume use of a particular trademark.

The "intent" involved in an abandonment case can be difficult to determine. Among the elements often considered are an alleged owner's activities, or lack thereof, with regard to the mark at issue.[58] How is "intent to abandon" different from "intent not to resume use"? Which standard is stricter from the standpoint of the trademark challenger? Was *Silverman* correct in adopting "intent not to resume use" as the appropriate standard?

*Silverman* raises the issue of what type of use is sufficient to preserve an owner's rights in a mark. Was the reason for the non-use in *Silverman* involuntary? Should this matter? Is the Principal Problem distinguishable from *Silverman* in any significant respects?

A finding of abandonment in a given situation is very much a factual issue. For example, one court held that summary judgment for the defendants on plaintiff's claim for trade dress infringement of its car body style (the Ferrari) was not warranted even though the plaintiff had not manufactured cars with that body style for over thirteen years and had no

---

[55] See, e.g., Flying Dog Brewery, LLLP v. Mich. Liquor Control Comm'n, 597 F. App'x 342, 353 (6th Cir. 2015); Posadas de Puerto Rico Assoc. v. Tourism Company of Puerto Rico, 478 U.S. 328, 340 (1986); Central Hudson Gas & Electric Corp. v. Public Service Comm'n of New York, 447 U.S. 557, 562–63 (1980).

[56] See, e.g., Restatement (Third) Unfair Competition, § 25(2) & cmt. i.

[57] An example here is Reddy Communications, Inc. v. Environmental Action Foundation, 477 F.Supp. 936 (D.D.C.1979), where plaintiffs, investor-owned public utilities sued the defendant under traditional trademark law for caricaturing their cartoon-figure trademark, Reddy Kilowatt, on brochures criticizing the electric power industry. On a finding that the text surrounding the caricature eliminated any likelihood of consumer confusion, the court held for defendant.

[58] See, e.g., *General Healthcare, Ltd. v. Qashat*, 364 F.3d 332 (1st Cir. 2004) (concluding that activities within the alleged period of non-use are the deciding factor).

intention of resuming production of such cars since the plaintiff presented evidence of goodwill associated with its vehicle and "evidence of ongoing parts support for the vehicle."[59]

b. *Abandonment through loss of distinctiveness.* Trademarks are unlike copyrights and patents in that they require an ongoing business enterprise. Moreover, the uncontrolled licensing of a trademark also can result in abandonment because the mark will fail to represent a symbol of consistency and thus will no longer have the necessary source indicative function.[60]

When an owner licenses use of its mark on goods manufactured by another, courts have imposed an affirmative duty upon the licensor/owner to insure that the goods manufactured by the licensee are not of inconsistent quality. The reason for this imposition is obvious: inferior or inconsistent goods bearing a familiar mark tend to lead to tarnishment of the mark and erosion of consumer goodwill. The licensor is in the best position to insure the integrity of the mark as a source indicator. In circumstances where the licensor does not exercise the appropriate quality control, the owner may be deemed to have abandoned her interest in the mark. Is there really a need for courts to supervise the use of marks in this way? Absent a quality control requirement, would licensees or franchisees really fail to exercise quality control-isn't it in their economic interest to do so?

In *Silverman*, the court noted that CBS' challenging infringing uses was not "use", and thus could not preclude a finding of abandonment. What should be the relationship between challenging infringing uses, or failing to challenge such uses, and abandonment?

---

[59] Ferrari S.p.A. Esercizio Fabbriche Automobili E Corse v. McBurnie Coachcraft Inc., 10 U.S.P.Q.2d (BNA) 1278, 1282 (S.D.Cal.1988).

[60] See also Restatement (Third) of Property: Unfair Competition § 33, cmt. b; Patsy's Italian Rest., Inc. v. Banas, 575 F. Supp. 2d 427 (E.D.N.Y. 2008); Hawaii-Pacific Apparel Group, Inc. v. Cleveland Browns Football Co. LLC, 418 F. Supp. 2d 501 (S.D.N.Y. 2006); Barcamerica Int'l USA v. Tyfield Importers, Inc., 289 F.3d 589 (9th Cir. 2002); Taco Cabana International, Inc. v. Two Pesos, Inc., 932 F.2d 1113 (5th Cir.1991), *aff'd*, 505 U.S. 763 (1992); Dawn Donut Co., Inc. v. Hart's Food Stores, Inc., 267 F.2d 358 (2d Cir.1959).

# ASSIGNMENT 56

# COPYRIGHT LAW

## 1. INTRODUCTION

*Overview and Obtaining Copyright Protection*

The authority for both copyright and patent law derives from the federal constitution, and in this respect these areas of intellectual property differ from trademark law which lacks a similar explicit constitutional foundation. In the United States, the need for a uniform federal law governing copyrights and patents is recognized in the Copyright Clause, Article I, Section 8, Clause 8 of the United States Constitution. Clause 8 grants Congress the power "to promote the progress of science and useful arts, by securing for limited times to authors and inventors the exclusive right to their respective writings and discoveries."[1] Pursuant to this constitutional authority, Congress enacted the first United States' copyright statute in 1790. Several revisions of and amendments to the statute subsequently ensued. The current copyright statute, the 1976 Copyright Act, became effective on January 1, 1978 and is codified at 17 U.S.C. §§ 101 et seq.[2]

To realize the objective of the Copyright Clause, Congress has authorized limited monopolies for creators of copyrighted works. On numerous occasions, the Supreme Court has observed that the promotion of the arts and sciences is the primary purpose of the monopoly granted to copyright owners, with financial rewards to creators as a secondary concern.[3] This analysis of the Copyright Clause suggests that the sovereign's duty to promote the public welfare must take precedence over the specific property rights enjoyed by copyright proprietors. Nevertheless, rewards to individuals under copyright law are essential to effectuating copyright law's major objective of enhancing societal progress, because an absence of monetary protection might well result in diminished creativity. Thus, copyright law represents a delicate balance between society's optimal use of resources and the optimal impetus for individual creativity.

Under the 1976 Act, a work receives protection as soon as it is created, regardless of whether it bears a copyright notice. Therefore, publication of the work with a copyright notice is not currently required to obtain copyright protection, a fact which surprises most lay people. Still, providing a copyright notice can be beneficial. For one thing, it

---

[1] U.S. Const. art. I, § 8, cl. 8.
[2] Unless otherwise noted, all statutory citations in this Assignment are to 17 U.S.C.
[3] See Fogerty v. Fantasy, Inc., 510 U.S. 517, 114 S.Ct. 1023, 1029–1032 (1994); Feist Publications, Inc. v. Rural Telephone Service Co., 499 U.S. 340, 349–50 (1991); Mazer v. Stein, 347 U.S. 201 (1954); see also H.R. REP. NO. 2222, 60th Cong., 2d Sess 7 (1909).

provides psychological comfort to the creator who simply may not believe that copyright protection is automatic. To receive the benefits of notice, the proper statutory form of notice must be used. There are three general components to proper notice: 1) the term "Copyright" or "Copr." or the symbol for copyright which is the letter "c" enclosed in a circle; 2) the copyright owner's name or a recognized designation or abbreviation thereof; and 3) the date of publication.

There is a government office for registering copyrights similar to that for trademarks and patents. The process of registering for a copyright involves depositing material with the Copyright Office to be reviewed by an examiner who decides whether to issue a registration certificate. The material reviewed by the Copyright Office includes a completed application form, the appropriate deposit material, and a nominal filing fee.

Registration, while not mandatory, affords the copyright claimant certain advantages. Most importantly, § 411 of the 1976 Act provides that registration is a prerequisite for instituting an infringement action for works originating in the United States. In addition, a registration certificate made before or within five years after first publication constitutes prima facie evidence of the validity of the copyright and of the facts stated in the certificate.[4]

The legislative history of the 1976 Copyright Act established "originality and fixation in a tangible form" as the fundamental criteria for copyright protection.[5] Fixation requires that the copyrighted work be embodied in a "sufficiently permanent or stable" copy so that it can be "perceived, reproduced, or otherwise communicated for a period of more than transitory duration."[6] Once all the required materials are deposited, an examiner studies the record and determines whether the material falls within the subject matter of copyright and if it is an original work of authorship. These two questions are asked regardless of the type of work for which a copyright is being sought. The subject matter question involves determining whether the work before the examiner falls within the categories listed in § 102(a) which include literary works; musical works; dramatic works; pantomimes and choreographic works; pictorial, graphic, and sculptural works; motion pictures and other audiovisual works; sound recordings; and architectural works.[7] The concept of originality is covered later in this Introduction as well as in the Principal Problem.

If an author has completed the registration process and her work is infringed, the next issue is determining what course of action the author should take to have the infringement rectified. For civil actions "arising

---

[4] § 410(c).

[5] H.R. REP. NO. 1476, 94th Cong., 2d Sess. 51 (1976) *reprinted in* 1976 U.S.C.C.A.N. 5659, 5664. See § 102.

[6] § 101 (definition of "fixed").

[7] § 102(a).

under any Act of Congress relating to . . . copyrights," the federal district courts have original jurisdiction which is exclusive of the state courts.[8] Even if a copyright claimant has been refused registration, she can institute an infringement action[9] as long as she notifies the Register and serves a copy of the complaint on the Register. The Register of Copyrights has the option of intervening in the action with respect to the registrability of the work.

*Copyright Ownership*

Section 106 of the Copyright Act specifies that copyright ownership entails the following exclusive rights: the rights to reproduce, distribute, perform and display the copyrighted work, as well as the right to prepare new ("derivative") works based upon the underlying copyrighted work. Each of these rights can be transferred by the copyright owner and separately owned. As the list of rights provided in § 106 suggests, United States' copyright law protects only the pecuniary rights of a copyright owner. Since the 1976 Act generally does not purport to protect the creator, but rather the copyright owner, if the original creator of a work assigns all of her rights under § 106 to another party, the creator no longer retains any immediate rights with respect to her work.

Section 201(a) of the Act provides that the copyright in a protected work "vests initially in the author or authors of the work." The authors of a "joint work," which is defined in § 101 as "a work prepared by two or more authors with the intention that their contributions be merged into inseparable or interdependent parts of a unitary whole," are considered co-owners of the copyright, and essentially are viewed as tenants in common with respect to the work. As is the case with realty, each co-owner of a copyrighted work has the unilateral right to use or license the work, as long as an accounting of profits is made to the other co-owners. A copyrighted work also can be considered a "work for hire" so that the creator's employer is considered the author of the work. Section 201(b) of the Act provides that "[i]n the case of a work made for hire, the employer or other person for whom the work was prepared is considered the author . . . unless the parties have expressly agreed otherwise in a written instrument signed by them. . . ." Thus, the work for hire doctrine is an exception to the rule that copyright ownership vests initially in the work's creator, and in recognizing this doctrine, the United States probably is the only country that allows the employer of a work's creator to obtain "authorship" status. The Principal Problem involves an application of the work for hire doctrine.

The importance of determining authorship status is critical not only because it dictates who enjoys the right to exercise the copyright, but also because authorship status impacts on the duration of copyright protection. Copyright protection typically lasts for the life of the author

---

[8] 28 U.S.C. § 1338(a).
[9] § 411(a).

plus an additional seventy years,[10] after which time the property becomes part of the public domain, to be enjoyed freely by all. For joint works, the period of protection lasts for seventy years after the last surviving author's death.[11] With respect to works for hire, "the copyright endures for a term of ninety-five years from the year of its first publication, or a term of one hundred and twenty years from the year of its creation, whichever expires first."[12]

*Originality Requirement*

One of the initial issues in many copyright cases is whether the work at issue is capable of receiving copyright protection. One easily stated rule is that a work is original if it is not copied from another work.[13] According to the legislative history accompanying the 1976 Act, the standard for original works of authorship, which was already established by the courts under the 1909 Copyright Act, "does not include requirements of novelty, ingenuity, or aesthetic merit."[14] Therefore, because material capable of copyright protection does not have to be new, just original, it is much easier to obtain copyright protection, as opposed to patent protection, which requires that the materials protected be both new and original.

The application of the originality standard in copyright law has given rise to much litigation and can be extremely problematic. The originality requirement is especially difficult to apply with respect to two specific areas of works protected under copyright law, compilations and derivative works, because these works are, by definition, based on material already in existence. Section 101 of the statute defines a derivative work as "a work based upon one or more preexisting works" in any "form in which a work may be recast, transformed, or adapted." Section 101 defines a compilation as "a work formed by the collection and assembling of preexisting materials or of data that are selected, coordinated, or arranged in such a way that the resulting work as a whole constitutes an original work of authorship." Section 103 of the statute is clear that although copyright protection does extend to compilations and derivative works, such protection only applies to the material "contributed by the author of such work."[15] Thus, cases involving these works require a determination as to whether the author has made any contributions that can be deemed sufficiently original to merit copyright protection. This issue is raised in the Principal Problem.

---

[10] § 302(a).

[11] § 302(b).

[12] § 302(c).

[13] See Sheldon v. Metro-Goldwyn Pictures Corp., 81 F.2d 49 (2d Cir.), cert. denied, 298 U.S. 669 (1936).

[14] H.R. REP. NO. 1476, 94 Cong., 2d Sess. 51 (1976), reprinted in 1976 U.S. CODE CONG. & AD. NEWS 5659, 5664.

[15] § 103(b).

## Infringement and Fair Use

The copyright owner's exclusive ability to exercise and to authorize the exercise of the bundle of rights protected by copyright law enables her to safeguard, in large measure, the pecuniary value of the copyrighted work. This is how copyright law promotes the creative process by providing financial incentives to creators. The application of the test for copyright infringement presents some troublesome issues. It is not always easy to decide when one work is based so heavily upon another that the substantial similarity between them should be considered infringement.

Moreover, even if infringement is found, in certain situations copyright law recognizes the need to sanction unauthorized uses of copyrighted property. One of the most important of the exemptions to copyright infringement is the fair use doctrine. In explaining the fair use doctrine, one court has observed that it "offers a means of balancing the exclusive rights of a copyright holder with the public's interest in dissemination of information affecting areas of universal concern, such as art, science and industry."[16]

The fair use doctrine is used as an affirmative defense which means that it is applied only once it is established that the defendant's work is, in fact, substantially similar to the plaintiff's work. The doctrine is codified in § 107 of the 1976 Copyright Act. The fair use doctrine is extraordinarily flexible, and its application typically turns on the particular facts in issue. Section 107 does provide some guidance, however, in that it sets forth the following four factors for determining whether a particular use is a fair use:

1. The purpose and character of the use, including whether such use is of a commercial nature or is for nonprofit educational purposes.

2. The nature of the copyrighted work.

3. The amount and substantiality of the portion used in relation to the copyrighted work as a whole.

4. The effect of the use upon the potential market for or value of the copyrighted work.[17]

Courts typically balance these four factors in determining whether a particular use of a work constitutes a fair use, although, as we shall see, there are other factors that often come into play in a fair use analysis. In fact, the legislative history to § 107 emphasizes that these factors are not to be considered definitive or determinative. The problem with such an ad hoc approach is that it is difficult to obtain much guidance from the existing fair use cases. That is probably why courts have called the fair

---

[16] Wainwright Sec.'s, Inc. v. Wall St. Transcript Corp., 558 F.2d 91, 94 (2d Cir.1977), cert. denied, 434 U.S. 1014 (1978) (enjoining defendants from publishing abstracts of plaintiff's financial research reports).

[17] § 107 (1992).

use doctrine "the most troublesome" in all of copyright law.[18] The Principal Problem involves an application of the fair use doctrine.

*International Considerations*

United States' copyright law provides protection only against infringement in the United States, but American books, films, and television shows are enjoyed internationally, so authors want protection all over the world. To ensure rights for Americans in foreign markets, the United States has entered into two multilateral treaties. The central thrust of these treaties is the principle of "national treatment": "A work of an American national first generated in America will receive the same protection in a foreign nation as that country accords to the works of its own nationals."[19]

The first of these treaties, the Universal Copyright Convention ("UCC"), took effect in 1955. It was originally conceived as a temporary measure to protect the interests of United States' copyright proprietors internationally until our copyright law could be revised to conform with the requirements of the Berne Convention, the second multilateral treaty. The United States joined the Berne Convention in 1988 via the Berne Convention Implementation Act of 1988 which became effective on March 1, 1989.[20] The Berne Convention, which is considered "the oldest and most comprehensive copyright treaty,"[21] binds more than one hundred seventy countries to a unitary copyright law system.[22] The United States' membership in the Berne Convention means any work first published in the United States will automatically be protected in other Berne countries.[23] Additionally, in 1994 the United States became a signatory to the international agreements that led to the formation of the World Trade Organization (WTO). As a member of the WTO, the United States is bound by the substantial copyright protections incorporated under the Agreement on Trade-Related Aspects of Intellectual Property Rights (TRIPs). In turn, the works of U.S. authors are given equal copyright protection in other WTO-member countries.[24]

---

[18] See e.g. Oracle Am., Inc. v. Google Inc., 750 F.3d 1339, 1372 (Fed. Cir. 2014); Monge v. Maya Magazines, Inc., 688 F.3d 1164, 1170 (9th Cir. 2012) citing Dellar v. Samuel Goldwyn, Inc., 104 F.2d 661, 662 (2d Cir.1939).

[19] Subafilms, Ltd. v. MGM-Pathe Communications Co., 24 F.3d 1088, 1097 (9th Cir.1994).

[20] Berne Convention Implementation Act of 1988, Pub. L. No. 100–568, 102 Stat. 2853 (1988).

[21] See D. Nimmer, The Impact of Berne on United States Copyright Law, 8 Cardozo Arts & Ent. L.J. 27, 27–28 (1989).

[22] The Berne Convention is administered by the World Intellectual Property Organization (WIPO). Up-to-date information on the Berne Convention and member countries can be found on the WIPO website at http://www.wipo.int/treaties/en/ip/berne.

[23] See 37 Patent, Trademark & Copyright Journal (BNA) 462 (1989).

[24] For further information on the WTO and TRIPs, see generally Agreement on Trade-Related Aspects of Intellectual Property Rights, Apr. 15, 1994, Marrakesh Agreement Establishing the World Trade Organization, Annex 1C, 1869 U.N.T.S. 299; 33 I.L.M. 1197 (1994); 4 M. Nimmer & D. Nimmer, Nimmer on Copyright, § 18.06 (2010).

## 2. Principal Problem

Zelda Michaels, the owner of the posh East Lake Health Club, has decided to sponsor a "healthy eating" recipe book for her club members. She posted signs all over the Club asking members to submit their favorite "healthy" recipes. After receiving over 200 recipes, she grouped them in categories such as "appetizers," "soups," "vegetarian," "meats," "drinks," "deserts", and "holiday favorites." Where necessary, she rewrote some of the language of the recipes themselves to make them more readable and uniform in appearance. She always made sure that the ingredients were listed initially and that the measurements indicated were abbreviated consistently throughout the book. Zelda also wrote some introductory textual material both to the book as a whole, and to each grouping of recipes.

Zelda then hired her friend, Henrietta Hull, to illustrate the book. Zelda told Henrietta to illustrate about a third of the recipes in each grouping. Zelda told Henrietta that for the most part, Henrietta could decide which ones to illustrate, subject to certain requests by Zelda that particular recipes in each grouping should be illustrated. Henrietta, who was an art major in college and had worked for Zelda on many art projects for the Club in the past, worked at her own home but used art supplies purchased for her by Zelda. During the time Henrietta was working on the illustrations, she injured her hand while participating in a bowling tournament. Zelda paid for her to go to the emergency room and for her follow-up medical care. The agreement that Zelda entered into with Henrietta provided that she agreed to work "with and for" Zelda on the recipe book project. Henrietta was paid in cash, based on an hourly wage.

The recipe book came out beautifully and Zelda decided to give a copy to every one of her club members rather than making them purchase it. Additional copies were provided to members at a cost of $20.00. One day, Zelda discovered that the vegetarian, desert and appetizer sections of her book had been posted on the Internet without her permission. These postings did not contain any of Zelda's introductory textual material but they did feature about a third of the drawings in each of the groupings posted. Apparently, one of the members of the Club gave the book to a friend of hers, Larry Lifter, who posted the information on the Internet. Larry had once been a member of East Lake but quit after gaining 20 pounds during his first year. He now blames Zelda for this weight gain because neither she nor her staff ever told him that working out actually makes you hungrier.

Zelda wants to sue Larry for posting these materials on the Internet. Henrietta believes she should be joined as a plaintiff on the theory that she also has some sort of ownership interest in the materials.

What are the legal issues raised by the foregoing set of circumstances and how do you think they are likely to be resolved? Before giving your answers, consider the following materials.

## 3. MATERIALS FOR SOLUTION OF PRINCIPAL PROBLEM

### Feist Publications, Inc. v. Rural Telephone Service Co.
Supreme Court of the United States, 1991.
499 U.S. 340, 111 S.Ct. 1282.

■ JUSTICE O'CONNOR delivered the opinion of the Court.

This case requires us to clarify the extent of copyright protection available to telephone directory white pages.

I

Rural Telephone Service Company is a certified public utility that provides telephone service to several communities in northwest Kansas. It is subject to a state regulation that requires all telephone companies operating in Kansas to issue annually an updated telephone directory. Accordingly, as a condition of its monopoly franchise, Rural publishes a typical telephone directory, consisting of white pages and yellow pages. The white pages list in alphabetical order the names of Rural's subscribers, together with their towns and telephone numbers. The yellow pages list Rural's business subscribers alphabetically by category and feature classified advertisements of various sizes. Rural distributes its directory free of charge to its subscribers, but earns revenue by selling yellow pages advertisements.

Feist Publications, Inc., is a publishing company that specializes in area-wide telephone directories. Unlike a typical directory, which covers only a particular calling area, Feist's area-wide directories cover a much larger geographical range, reducing the need to call directory assistance or consult multiple directories. The Feist directory that is the subject of this litigation covers 11 different telephone service areas in 15 counties and contains 46,878 white pages listings—compared to Rural's approximately 7,700 listings. Like Rural's directory, Feist's is distributed free of charge and includes both white pages and yellow pages. Feist and Rural compete vigorously for yellow pages advertising.

As the sole provider of telephone service in its service area, Rural obtains subscriber information quite easily. Persons desiring telephone service must apply to Rural and provide their names and addresses; Rural then assigns them a telephone number. Feist is not a telephone company, let alone one with monopoly status, and therefore lacks independent access to any subscriber information. To obtain white pages listings for its area-wide directory, Feist approached each of the 11 telephone companies operating in northwest Kansas and offered to pay for the right to use its white pages listings.

Of the 11 telephone companies, only Rural refused to license its listings to Feist. Rural's refusal created a problem for Feist, as omitting listings would have left a gaping hole in its area-wide directory, rendering it less attractive to potential yellow pages advertisers.

Unable to license Rural's white pages listings, Feist used them without Rural's consent. Feist began by removing several thousand listings that fell outside the geographic range of its area-wide directory, then hired personnel to investigate the 4,935 that remained. These employees verified the data reported by Rural and sought to obtain additional information. As a result, a typical Feist listing includes the individual's street address; most of Rural's listings do not. Notwithstanding these additions, however, 1,309 of the 46,878 listings in Feist's 1983 directory were identical to listings in Rural's 1982–1983 white pages. Four of these were fictitious listings that Rural had inserted into its directory to detect copying.

Rural sued for copyright infringement in the District Court for the District of Kansas taking the position that Feist, in compiling its own directory, could not use the information contained in Rural's white pages. Rural asserted that Feist's employees were obliged to travel door-to-door or conduct a telephone survey to discover the same information for themselves. Feist responded that such efforts were economically impractical and, in any event, unnecessary because the information copied was beyond the scope of copyright protection. The District Court granted summary judgment to Rural, explaining that "courts have consistently held that telephone directories are copyrightable" and citing a string of lower court decisions. 663 F.Supp. 214, 218 (1987). In an unpublished opinion, the Court of Appeals for the Tenth Circuit affirmed "for substantially the reasons given by the district court." We granted certiorari to determine whether the copyright in Rural's directory protects the names, towns, and telephone numbers copied by Feist.

## II

### A

This case concerns the interaction of two well-established propositions. The first is that facts are not copyrightable; the other, that compilations of facts generally are. Each of these propositions possesses an impeccable pedigree. That there can be no valid copyright in facts is universally understood. The most fundamental axiom of copyright law is that "no author may copyright his ideas or the facts he narrates." Harper & Row, Publishers, Inc. v. Nation Enterprises, 471 U.S. 539, 556 (1985). Rural wisely concedes this point, noting in its brief that "facts and discoveries, of course, are not themselves subject to copyright protection." At the same time, however, it is beyond dispute that compilations of facts are within the subject matter of copyright. Compilations were expressly mentioned in the Copyright Act of 1909, and again in the Copyright Act of 1976.

There is an undeniable tension between these two propositions. Many compilations consist of nothing but raw data—i.e., wholly factual information not accompanied by any original written expression. On what basis may one claim a copyright in such a work? Common sense tells us that 100 uncopyrightable facts do not magically change their status when gathered together in one place. Yet copyright law seems to contemplate that compilations that consist exclusively of facts are potentially within its scope.

The key to resolving the tension lies in understanding why facts are not copyrightable. The sine qua non of copyright is originality. To qualify for copyright protection, a work must be original to the author. See *Harper & Row, supra,* at 547–549. Original, as the term is used in copyright, means only that the work was independently created by the author (as opposed to copied from other works), and that it possesses at least some minimal degree of creativity. 1 M. Nimmer & D. Nimmer, Copyright §§ 2.01[A], [B] (1990) (hereinafter Nimmer). To be sure, the requisite level of creativity is extremely low; even a slight amount will suffice. The vast majority of works make the grade quite easily. Originality does not signify novelty; a work may be original even though it closely resembles other works so long as the similarity is fortuitous, not the result of copying. To illustrate, assume that two poets, each ignorant of the other, compose identical poems. Neither work is novel, yet both are original and, hence, copyrightable. See Sheldon v. Metro-Goldwyn Pictures Corp., 81 F.2d 49, 54 (C.A.2 1936).

Originality is a constitutional requirement. The source of Congress' power to enact copyright laws is Article I, § 8, cl.8, of the Constitution, which authorizes Congress to "secure for limited Times to Authors . . . the exclusive Right to their respective writings." In two decisions from the late 19th century—The Trade-Mark Cases, 100 U.S. 82 (1879); and Burrow-Giles Lithographic Co. v. Sarony, 111 U.S. 53 (1884)—this Court defined the crucial terms "authors" and "writings." In so doing, the Court made it unmistakably clear that these terms presuppose a degree of originality.

In the *Trade-Mark Cases,* the Court addressed the constitutional scope of "writings." For a particular work to be classified "under the head of writings of authors," the Court determined, "originality is required." 100 U.S., at 94. The Court explained that originality requires independent creation plus a modicum of creativity. In *Burrow-Giles,* the Court distilled the same requirement from the Constitution's use of the word "authors." The Court defined "author," in a constitutional sense, to mean "he to whom anything owes its origin; originator; maker."

The originality requirement articulated in *The Trade-Mark Cases* and *Burrow-Giles* remains the touchstone of copyright protection today. See Goldstein v. California, 412 U.S. 546, 561–562 (1973). It is this bedrock principle of copyright that mandates the law's seemingly disparate treatment of facts and factual compilations. "No one may claim originality as to facts." [Nimmer] § 2.11[A], p. 2–157. This is because facts do not owe their origin to an act of authorship.

Factual compilations, on the other hand, may possess the requisite originality. The compilation author typically chooses which facts to include, in what order to place them, and how to arrange the collected data so that they may be used effectively by readers. These choices as to selection and arrangement, so long as they are made independently by the compiler and entail a minimal degree of creativity, are sufficiently original that Congress may protect such compilations through the copyright laws. Thus, even a directory that contains absolutely no protectable written expression, only facts, meets the constitutional minimum for copyright protection if it features an original selection or arrangement.

This protection is subject to an important limitation. The mere fact that a work is copyrighted does not mean that every element of the work may be protected. Originality remains the sine qua non of copyright; accordingly, copyright protection may extend only to those components of a work that are original to the author. Thus, if the compilation author clothes facts with an original collocation of words, he or she may be able to claim a copyright in this written expression. Others may copy the underlying facts from the publication, but not the precise words used to present them. Where the compilation author adds no written expression but rather lets the facts speak for themselves, the expressive element is more elusive. The only conceivable expression is the manner in which the compiler has selected and arranged the facts. Thus, if the selection and arrangement are original, these elements of the work are eligible for copyright protection. No matter how original the format, however, the facts themselves do not become original through association.

This inevitably means that the copyright in a factual compilation is thin. Notwithstanding a valid copyright, a subsequent compiler remains free to use the facts contained in another's publication to aid in preparing a competing work, so long as the competing work does not feature the same selection and arrangement.

It may seem unfair that much of the fruit of the compiler's labor may be used by others without compensation. As Justice Brennan has correctly observed, however, this is not "some unforeseen byproduct of a statutory scheme." *Harper & Row*, 471 U.S., at 589 (dissenting opinion). It is, rather, "the essence of copyright," *ibid.*, and a constitutional requirement. The primary objective of copyright is not to reward the labor of authors, but "to promote the Progress of Science and useful Arts." Art. I, § 8, cl.8. To this end, copyright assures authors the right to their original expression, but encourages others to build freely upon the ideas and information conveyed by a work. *Harper & Row, supra*, at 556–557. This principle, known as the idea/expression or fact/expression dichotomy, applies to all works of authorship. As applied to a factual compilation, assuming the absence of original written expression, only the compiler's selection and arrangement may be protected; the raw facts may be copied at will. This result is neither unfair nor unfortunate. It is the means by which copyright advances the progress of science and art.

This, then, resolves the doctrinal tension: Copyright treats facts and factual compilations in a wholly consistent manner. Facts, whether alone or as part of a compilation, are not original and therefore may not be copyrighted. A factual compilation is eligible for copyright if it features an original selection or arrangement of facts, but the copyright is limited to the particular selection or arrangement. In no event may copyright extend to the facts themselves.

## B

As we have explained, originality is a constitutionally mandated prerequisite for copyright protection. The Court's decisions announcing this rule predate the Copyright Act of 1909, but ambiguous language in the 1909 Act caused some lower courts temporarily to lose sight of this requirement. These courts developed a new theory to justify the protection of factual compilations. Known alternatively as "sweat of the brow" or "industrious collection," the underlying notion was that copyright was a reward for the hard work that went into compiling facts.

The "sweat of the brow" doctrine had numerous flaws, the most glaring being that it extended copyright protection in a compilation beyond selection and arrangement—the compiler's original contributions—to the facts themselves.

## C

"Sweat of the brow" decisions did not escape the attention of the Copyright Office. When Congress decided to overhaul the copyright statute and asked the Copyright Office to study existing problems, the Copyright Office promptly recommended that Congress clear up the confusion in the lower courts as to the basic standards of copyrightability. The Register of Copyrights explained in his first report to Congress that "originality" was a "basic requisite" of copyright under the 1909 Act, but that "the absence of any reference to [originality] in the statute seems to have led to misconceptions as to what is copyrightable matter." Report of the Register of Copyrights on the General Revision of the U.S. Copyright Law, 87th Cong., 1st Sess., p.9 (H. Judiciary Comm. Print 1961). The Register suggested making the originality requirement explicit. *ibid*.

Congress took the Register's advice. The 1976 revisions to the Copyright Act leave no doubt that originality, not "sweat of the brow," is the touchstone of copyright protection in directories and other fact-based works. Nor is there any doubt that the same was true under the 1909 Act. The 1976 revisions were a direct response to the Copyright Office's concern that many lower courts had misconstrued this basic principle, and Congress emphasized repeatedly that the purpose of the revisions was to clarify, not change, existing law. The revisions explain with painstaking clarity that copyright requires originality, § 102(a); that facts are never original, § 102(b); that the copyright in a compilation does not extend to the facts it contains, § 103(b); and that a compilation is copyrightable only to the extent that it features an original selection, coordination, or arrangement, § 101.

## III

There is no doubt that Feist took from the white pages of Rural's directory a substantial amount of factual information. At a minimum, Feist copied the names, towns, and telephone numbers of 1,309 of Rural's subscribers. Not all copying, however, is copyright infringement. To establish infringement, two elements must be proven: (1) ownership of a valid copyright, and (2) copying of constituent elements of the work that are original. The first element is not at issue here; Feist appears to concede that Rural's directory, considered as a whole, is subject to a valid copyright because it contains some foreword text, as well as original material in its yellow pages advertisements.

The question is whether Rural has proved the second element. In other words, did Feist, by taking 1,309 names, towns, and telephone numbers from Rural's white pages, copy anything that was "original" to Rural? Certainly, the raw data does not satisfy the originality requirement.

The question that remains is whether Rural selected, coordinated, or arranged these uncopyrightable facts in an original way. As mentioned, originality is not a stringent standard; it does not require that facts be presented in an innovative or surprising way. It is equally true, however, that the selection and arrangement of facts cannot be so mechanical or routine as to require no creativity whatsoever. The standard of originality is low, but it does exist. As this Court has explained, the Constitution mandates some minimal degree of creativity, see *The Trade-Mark Cases*, 100 U.S., at 94; and an author who claims infringement must prove "the existence of . . . intellectual production, of thought, and conception." *Burrow-Giles, supra*, at 59–60.

The selection, coordination, and arrangement of Rural's white pages do not satisfy the minimum constitutional standards for copyright protection. As mentioned at the outset, Rural's white pages are entirely typical. In preparing its white pages, Rural simply takes the data provided by its subscribers and lists it alphabetically by surname. The end product is a garden-variety white pages directory, devoid of even the slightest trace of creativity.

Rural's selection of listings could not be more obvious: It publishes the most basic information—name, town, and telephone number—about each person who applies to it for telephone service. This is "selection" of a sort, but it lacks the modicum of creativity necessary to transform mere selection into copyrightable expression. Rural expended sufficient effort to make the white pages directory useful, but insufficient creativity to make it original.

Nor can Rural claim originality in its coordination and arrangement of facts. The white pages do nothing more than list Rural's subscribers in alphabetical order. This arrangement may, technically speaking, owe its origin to Rural; no one disputes that Rural undertook the task of alphabetizing the names itself. But there is nothing remotely creative about arranging names alphabetically in a white pages directory.

We conclude that the names, towns, and telephone numbers copied by Feist were not original to Rural and therefore were not protected by the copyright in Rural's combined white and yellow pages directory.

Because Rural's white pages lack the requisite originality, Feist's use of the listings cannot constitute infringement. This decision should not be construed as demeaning Rural's efforts in compiling its directory, but rather as making clear that copyright rewards originality, not effort. As this Court noted more than a century ago, " 'great praise may be due to the plaintiffs for their industry and enterprise in publishing this paper, yet the law does not contemplate their being rewarded in this way.' " Baker v. Selden, 101 U.S. 99, 105 (1879).

The judgment of the Court of Appeals is reversed.

## Community for Creative Non-Violence v. Reid
### Supreme Court of the United States, 1989.
### 490 U.S. 730, 109 S.Ct. 2166.

■ JUSTICE MARSHALL delivered the opinion of the Court.

In this case, an artist and the organization that hired him to produce a sculpture, contest the ownership of the copyright in that work. To resolve this dispute, we must construe the "work made for hire" provisions of the Copyright Act of 1976 (Act or 1976 Act), 17 U.S.C. §§ 101 and 201(b), and in particular, the provision in § 101, which defines as a "work made for hire" a "work prepared by an employee within the scope of his or her employment" (hereinafter § 101(1)).

Petitioners are the Community for Creative Non-Violence (CCNV), a nonprofit unincorporated association dedicated to eliminating homelessness in America, and Mitch Snyder, a member and trustee of CCNV. In the fall of 1985, CCNV decided to participate in the annual Christmastime Pageant of Peace in Washington, D.C., by sponsoring a display to dramatize the plight of the homeless. As the District Court recounted:

> Snyder and fellow CCNV members conceived the idea for the nature of the display: a sculpture of a modern Nativity scene in which, in lieu of the traditional Holy Family, the two adult figures and the infant would appear as contemporary homeless people huddled on a streetside steam grate. The family was to be black (most of the homeless in Washington being black); the figures were to be life-sized, and the steam grate would be

positioned atop a platform "pedestal," or base, within which special-effects equipment would be enclosed to emit simulated "steam" through the grid to swirl about the figures. They also settled upon a title for the work—"Third World America"—and a legend for the pedestal: "and still there is no room at the inn."

652 F.Supp. 1453, 1454 (D.C. 1987).

Snyder made inquiries to locate an artist to produce the sculpture. He was referred to respondent James Earl Reid, a Baltimore, Maryland, sculptor. In the course of two telephone calls, Reid agreed to sculpt the three human figures. CCNV agreed to make the steam grate and pedestal for the statue. Reid proposed that the work be cast in bronze, at a total cost of approximately $100,000 and taking six to eight months to complete. Snyder rejected that proposal because CCNV did not have sufficient funds, and because the statue had to be completed by December 12 to be included in the pageant. Reid then suggested, and Snyder agreed, that the sculpture would be made of a material known as "Design Cast 62," a synthetic substance that could meet CCNV's monetary and time constraints, could be tinted to resemble bronze, and could withstand the elements. The parties agreed that the project would cost no more than $15,000, not including Reid's services, which he offered to donate. The parties did not sign a written agreement. Neither party mentioned copyright.

After Reid received an advance of $3,000, he made several sketches of figures in various poses. At Snyder's request, Reid sent CCNV a sketch of a proposed sculpture showing the family in a crechelike setting: the mother seated, cradling a baby in her lap; the father standing behind her, bending over her shoulder to touch the baby's foot. Reid testified that Snyder asked for the sketch to use in raising funds for the sculpture. Snyder testified that it was also for his approval. Reid sought a black family to serve as a model for the sculpture. Upon Snyder's suggestion, Reid visited a family living at CCNV's Washington shelter but decided that only their newly born child was a suitable model. While Reid was in Washington, Snyder took him to see homeless people living on the streets. Snyder pointed out that they tended to recline on steam grates, rather than sit or stand, in order to warm their bodies. From that time on, Reid's sketches contained only reclining figures.

Throughout November and the first two weeks of December 1985, Reid worked exclusively on the statue, assisted at various times by a dozen different people who were paid with funds provided in installments by CCNV. On a number of occasions, CCNV members visited Reid to check on his progress and to coordinate CCNV's construction of the base. CCNV rejected Reid's proposal to use suitcases or shopping bags to hold the family's personal belongings, insisting instead on a shopping cart. Reid and CCNV members did not discuss copyright ownership on any of these visits.

On December 24, 1985, 12 days after the agreed-upon date, Reid delivered the completed statue to Washington. There it was joined to the steam grate and pedestal prepared by CCNV and placed on display near the site of the pageant. Snyder paid Reid the final installment of the $15,000. The statue remained on display for a month. In late January 1986, CCNV members returned it to Reid's studio in Baltimore for minor repairs. Several weeks later, Snyder began making plans to take the statue on a tour of several cities to raise money for the homeless. Reid objected, contending that the Design Cast 62 material was not strong enough to withstand the ambitious itinerary. He urged CCNV to cast the statue in bronze at a cost of $35,000, or to create a master mold at a cost of $5,000. Snyder declined to spend more of CCNV's money on the project.

In March 1986, Snyder asked Reid to return the sculpture. Reid refused. He then filed a certificate of copyright registration for "Third World America" in his name and announced plans to take the sculpture on a more modest tour than the one CCNV had proposed. Snyder, acting in his capacity as CCNV's trustee, immediately filed a competing certificate of copyright registration.

Snyder and CCNV then commenced this action against Reid, seeking return of the sculpture and a determination of copyright ownership. The District Court granted a preliminary injunction, ordering the sculpture's return. After a 2–day bench trial, the District Court declared that "Third World America" was a "work made for hire" under § 101 of the Copyright Act and that Snyder, as trustee for CCNV, was the exclusive owner of the copyright in the sculpture. The court reasoned that Reid had been an "employee" of CCNV within the meaning of § 101(1) because CCNV was the motivating force in the statue's production. Snyder and other CCNV members, the court explained, "conceived the idea of a contemporary Nativity scene to contrast with the national celebration of the season," and "directed enough of [Reid's] effort to assure that, in the end, he had produced what they, not he, wanted."

The Court of Appeals for the District of Columbia Circuit reversed and remanded, holding that Reid owned the copyright because "Third World America" was not a work for hire. The court suggested that the sculpture nevertheless may have been jointly authored by CCNV and Reid, and remanded for a determination whether the sculpture is indeed a joint work under the Act.

We granted certiorari to resolve a conflict among the Courts of Appeals over the proper construction of the "work made for hire" provisions of the Act. We now affirm.

The Copyright Act of 1976 provides that copyright ownership "vests initially in the author or authors of the work." § 201(a). As a general rule, the author is the party who actually creates the work, that is, the person who translates an idea into a fixed, tangible expression entitled to copyright protection. § 102. The Act carves out an important exception, however, for "works made for hire." If the work is for hire, "the employer or other person for whom the work was prepared is considered the author" and owns the copyright, unless there is a written agreement to the contrary. § 201(b). Classifying a work as "made for hire" determines not only the initial ownership of its copyright, but also the copyright's duration, § 302(c). The contours of the work for hire doctrine therefore carry profound significance for freelance creators—including artists, writers, photographers, designers, composers, and computer programmers—and for the publishing, advertising, music, and other industries which commission their works.

Section 101 of the 1976 Act provides that a work is "for hire" under two sets of circumstances:

> (1) a work prepared by an employee within the scope of his or her employment; or

> (2) a work specially ordered or commissioned for use as a contribution to a collective work, as a part of a motion picture or other audiovisual work, as a translation, as a supplementary work, as a compilation, as an instructional text, as a test, as answer material for a test, or as an atlas, if the parties expressly agree in a written instrument signed by them that the work shall be considered a work made for hire.

Petitioners do not claim that the statue satisfies the terms of § 101(2). Quite clearly, it does not. Sculpture does not fit within any of the nine categories of "specially ordered or commissioned" works enumerated in that subsection, and no written agreement between the parties establishes "Third World America" as a work for hire.

The dispositive inquiry in this case therefore is whether "Third World America" is "a work prepared by an employee within the scope of his or her employment" under § 101(1). The Act does not define these terms.

The starting point for our interpretation of a statute is always its language. The Act nowhere defines the terms "employee" or "scope of employment." It is, however, well established that "where Congress uses terms that have accumulated settled meaning under . . . the common law, a court must infer, unless the statute otherwise dictates, that Congress means to incorporate the established meaning of these terms." NLRB v. Amax Coal Co., 453 U.S. 322, 329 (1981). In the past, when Congress has used the term "employee" without defining it, we have concluded that Congress intended to describe the conventional master-servant relationship as understood by common-law agency doctrine. Nothing in the text of the work for hire provisions indicates that Congress used the words "employee" and "employment" to describe anything other than " 'the conventional relation of employer and employe[e].' " [Citation omitted.] On the contrary, Congress' intent to incorporate the agency law definition is suggested by § 101(1)'s use of the term, "scope of employment," a widely used term of art in agency law. See Restatement (Second) of Agency § 228 (1958) (hereinafter Restatement).

In past cases of statutory interpretation, when we have concluded that Congress intended terms such as "employee," "employer," and "scope of employment" to be understood in light of agency law, we have relied on the general common law of agency, rather than on the law of any particular State, to give meaning to these terms. This practice reflects the fact that "federal statutes are generally intended to have uniform nationwide application." Mississippi Band of Choctaw Indians v. Holyfield, 490 U.S. 30, 43 (1989). Establishment of a federal rule of agency, rather than reliance on state agency law, is particularly appropriate here given the Act's express objective of creating national, uniform copyright law by broadly pre-empting state statutory and common-law copyright regulation. See § 301(a). We thus agree with the Court of Appeals that the term "employee" should be understood in light of the general common law of agency.

This reading of the undefined statutory terms finds considerable support in the Act's legislative history. The Act, which almost completely revised existing copyright law, was the product of two decades of negotiation by representatives of creators and copyright-using industries, supervised by the Copyright Office and, to a lesser extent, by Congress. Despite the lengthy history of negotiation and compromise which ultimately produced the Act, two things remained constant. First, interested parties and Congress at all times viewed works by employees and commissioned works by independent contractors as separate entities. Second, in using the term "employee," the parties and Congress meant to refer to a hired party in a conventional employment relationship. These factors militate in favor of the reading we have found appropriate.

[The Court reviewed the pertinent legislative history in detail.]

Thus, the legislative history of the Act is significant for several reasons. First, the enactment of the 1965 compromise with only minor modifications demonstrates that Congress intended to provide two mutually exclusive ways for works to acquire work for hire status: one for employees and the other for independent contractors. Second, the legislative history underscores the clear import of the statutory language: only enumerated categories of commissioned works may be accorded work for hire status. The hiring party's right to control the product simply is not determinative. Indeed, importing a test based on a hiring party's right to control, or actual control of, a product would unravel the "carefully worked out compromise aimed at balancing legitimate interests on both sides." H. R. Rep. No. 2237, *supra*, at 114, quoting Supplemental Report, at 66.

In sum, [t]o determine whether a work is for hire under the Act, a court first should ascertain, using principles of general common law of agency, whether the work was prepared by an employee or an independent contractor. After making this determination, the court can apply the appropriate subsection of § 101.

We turn, finally, to an application of § 101 to Reid's production of "Third World America." In determining whether a hired party is an employee under the general common law of agency, we consider the hiring party's right to control the manner and means by which the product is accomplished. Among the other factors relevant to this inquiry are the skill required; the source of the instrumentalities and tools; the location of the work; the duration of the relationship between the parties; whether the hiring party has the right to assign additional projects to the hired party; the extent of the hired party's discretion over when and how long to work; the method of payment; the hired party's role in hiring and paying assistants; whether the work is part of the regular business of the hiring party; whether the hiring party is in business; the provision of employee benefits; and the tax treatment of the hired party. See Restatement § 220(2) (setting forth a nonexhaustive list of factors relevant to determining whether a hired party is an employee). No one of these factors is determinative.

Examining the circumstances of this case in light of these factors, we agree with the Court of Appeals that Reid was not an employee of CCNV but an independent contractor. 846 F.2d, at 1494, n.11. True, CCNV members directed enough of Reid's work to ensure that he produced a sculpture that met their specifications. 652 F.Supp., at 1456. But the extent of control the hiring party exercises over the details of the product is not dispositive. Indeed, all the other circumstances weigh heavily against finding an employment relationship. Reid is a sculptor, a skilled occupation. Reid supplied his own tools. He worked in his own studio in Baltimore, making daily supervision of his activities from Washington practicably impossible. Reid was retained for less than two months, a relatively short period of time. During and after this time, CCNV had no right to assign additional projects to Reid. Apart from the deadline for completing the sculpture, Reid had absolute freedom to decide when and how long to work. CCNV paid Reid $15,000, a sum dependent on "completion of a specific job, a method by which independent contractors are often compensated." Holt v. Winpisinger, 811 F.2d 1532, 1540 (1987). Reid had total discretion in hiring and paying assistants. "Creating sculptures was hardly 'regular business' for CCNV." 846 F.2d, at 1494, n.11. Indeed, CCNV is not a business at all. Finally, CCNV did not pay payroll or Social Security taxes, provide any employee benefits, or contribute to unemployment insurance or workers' compensation funds.

Because Reid was an independent contractor, whether "Third World America" is a work for hire depends on whether it satisfies the terms of § 101(2). This petitioners concede it cannot do. Thus, CCNV is not the author of "Third World America" by virtue of the work for hire provisions of the Act. However, as the Court of Appeals made clear, CCNV nevertheless may be a joint author of the sculpture if, on remand, the

District Court determines that CCNV and Reid prepared the work "with the intention that their contributions be merged into inseparable or interdependent parts of a unitary whole." § 101. In that case, CCNV and Reid would be co-owners of the copyright in the work. See § 201(a).

For the aforestated reasons, we affirm the judgment of the Court of Appeals for the District of Columbia Circuit.

## Religious Technology Center v. Lerma
United States District Court, Eastern District of Virginia, 1996.
40 U.S.P.Q.2d 1569.

■ BRINKEMA, J.

This matter comes before the Court on plaintiff Religious Technology Center's ("RTC") Motion for Summary Judgment for Copyright Infringement Against Defendant Lerma ("Lerma"). Also under consideration is defendant Arnaldo P. Lerma's (Cross-) Motion for Summary Judgment and/or to Dismiss. Both parties seek final resolution of the allegation that Lerma infringed RTC's copyright when he copied to his computer and/or posted to the Internet sections of sacred and properly copyrighted documents belonging to the Church of Scientology.

Based upon the arguments tendered in the briefs and at the hearing, as well as the mass of evidence in this substantial record, the Court finds that Lerma infringed RTC's copyright and that summary judgment should be entered in favor of RTC and against Lerma.

*History of the Case*

The dispute in this case surrounds Lerma's acquisition and publication on the Internet of texts that the Church of Scientology considers sacred and protects heavily from unauthorized disclosure. Founded by L. Ron Hubbard, the Scientology religion attempts to explain the origin of negative spiritual forces in the world and advances techniques for improving one's own spiritual well-being. Scientologists believe that most human problems can be traced to lingering spirits of an extraterrestrial people massacred by their ruler, Xenu, over 75 million years ago. These spirits attach themselves by "clusters" to individuals in the contemporary world, causing spiritual harm and negatively influencing the lives of their hosts.

The texts at issue, the "Advanced Technology" or the "Operating Thetan" Documents ("OT Documents"), were written by founder Hubbard and allegedly provide a detailed program for warding off these evil influences through the creation of "free zones." The OT Documents outline a process that must be executed precisely according to the procedures laid out by Hubbard and under the guidance of an assisting church official in order to be efficacious.

Church doctrine teaches that improper disclosure of the OT Documents, both to non-Scientologists and even to church members if done prematurely, prevents achievement of the desired effect. Unauthorized disclosure also risks further harm of global proportions. Hubbard explicitly directed that the OT Documents be released only in strict accordance with his guidelines, and that they remain otherwise secret and secure.

Consequently, the church has charged RTC, the plaintiff in this case, with securing the sacred texts and aggressively policing any breaches in security or unauthorized disclosures that may occur. RTC has enacted a comprehensive protection plan that includes locked vaults, numerous guards, key cards, and signed nondisclosure statements by all church members. RTC has also been relentless in tracking down suspected offenders and vigorously pursuing legal remedies against them.

*Bases for Copyright Infringement*

To establish copyright infringement, two elements must be proven: (1) ownership of a valid copyright, and (2) unauthorized copying of constituent elements of the copyrighted work. Feist Publications, Inc. v. Rural Telephone Service Company, Inc., 499 U.S. 340, 361 [18 USPQ2d 1275] (1991). The first element is effectively uncontested by Lerma.

*The Idea/Expression Dichotomy*

Lerma launches a collateral attack on the appropriateness of the copyright. Distinguishing between idea and expression, Lerma argues that material contained in the Works is "uncopyrightable." Copyright law promotes the advancement of human knowledge and thought by providing limited legal (and therefore economic) protection to an author's original expression. The author's temporary monopoly, however, does not include the ideas contained within his work. As stated by the Third Circuit, "the purpose of copyright law is to create the most efficient and productive balance between protection (incentive) and dissemination of information, to promote learning, culture and development." Whelan Associates v. Jaslow Dental Laboratory, 797 F.2d 1222, 1235 [230 USPQ2d 481] (3d Cir. 1986). These intentions have spawned the idea/expression dichotomy in copyright law, protecting the latter while still permitting access to the former. "The [Copyright] Act is thus able to protect authors without impeding the public's access to that information which gives meaning to our society's highly valued freedom of expression." Harper & Row Publishers, Inc. v. Nation Enterprises, 723 F.2d 195, 202 [220 USPQ 321] (2d Cir. 1983).

This idea/expression distinction is codified under 17 U.S.C. Section 102(b) which states:

> In no case does copyright protection for an original work of authorship extend to any idea, procedure, process, system, method of operation, concept, principle or discovery, regardless of the form in which it is described, explained, illustrated, or embodied in such work.

Courts have therefore held that wherever an author's expression of an idea is closely intertwined with the idea itself, the expression has "merged" with the idea and is therefore uncopyrightable. Under this "merger doctrine," where the author's ideas and procedures can be properly expressed in so few ways that "protection of the expression would effectively accord protection to the idea itself," Kregos v. Associated Press, 937 F.2d 700, 705 [19 USPQ2d 1161] (2d Cir. 1991), courts have found the expression not copyrightable. Copyrighting the expression in these instances would effectively prohibit discussion and analysis of the idea itself and grant the owner a monopoly on all uses of the very concept.

Lerma argues that this merger doctrine applies and that RTC's claim of copyright protection is therefore invalid. He also argues that Hubbard describes the OT Documents as primarily factual, and he insists that their contents must be followed exactly as written. Under the merger doctrine, even if Hubbard had followed all procedural requirements, the Works would still be uncopyrightable if protecting the expression would effectively grant a monopoly on the idea itself.

Despite this argument, the Court finds that merger of idea and expression has not occurred in this case. The ideas and concepts of the Scientology religion can be discussed independently of the OT documents. To the extent that the OT Documents supply a technique or "process" for achieving spiritual well-being, their copyright arguably violates a strictly literal reading of Section 102(b). However, as RTC has argued, virtually all works convey to some extent ideas and processes that are uncopyrightable. While such creations may contain "procedure[s], process[es], [or] system [s]", 17 U.S.C.A. Section 102(b), they are not thereby rendered de facto uncopyrightable. [E]xamples include automobile mechanics' repair manuals. Each of these documents purports to describe a precise method for achieving a desired end. Hubbard's instructional directions for spiritual healing are no less-deserving of protection than the admittedly copyrightable "repair steps" in a maintenance manual.

Lerma attempts to distinguish the Works because [they] require specific, precise repetition of the exact text. While repair instructions, or a computer program may permit some variation, Hubbard claims that the Works provide the only correct method for reaching complete spiritual health. If not followed exactly, the process will fail. However, literary works such as a poem or haiku and musical works such as a symphonic score possess the same quality—the desired effect cannot be achieved without precise repetition. This does not make poems, haikus, and musical scores uncopyrightable, and it should likewise not preclude copyrightability of the Works. Denying copyright protection to RTC on this basis would rapidly destroy the protection and incentive for the likes of Wagner and Brahms—an outcome that is most certainly contrary to the goals of copyright law.

The Court, therefore, finds the merger clause inapplicable to the Works.

*Fair Use Defense*

Lerma freely admits that he copied portions of the Works by downloading or scanning them into his computer and by posting segments of this material to the Internet. He argues that even if the works are copyrightable and copyrighted, this copying was lawful because it was "fair use."

In determining whether the use of a copyrighted work constitutes fair use, the Court must consider four factors:

    1. the purpose and character of the use, including whether such use is of a commercial nature or is for nonprofit educational purposes;

    2. the nature of the copyrighted work;

    3. the amount and substantiality of the portion used in relation to the copyrighted work as a whole; and

    4. the effect of the use upon the potential market for or value of the copyrighted work.

17 U.S.C. Section 107. These four statutory factors may not be "treated in isolation, one from another. All are to be explored, and the results weighed together, in light of the purposes of copyright." Campbell v. Acuff-Rose Music, Inc., 510 U.S. 569, 578 [29 U.S.P.Q.2d 1961] (1994).

Lerma urges us, when conducting the fair use analysis, to evaluate his actions in the special context of modern communication on the Internet. He describes the unique characteristics of computer interaction and argues for special treatment under copyright law. While the Internet does present a truly revolutionary advance, neither Congress nor the courts have afforded it unique status under the fair use standard of Section 107. The law of copyright has evolved with technological change, with each new technological advancement creating complicated questions of copyright interpretation and application. Nevertheless, the new technologies—from television, to video cassette recorders, to digitized transmissions—have been made to fit within the overall scheme of copyright law and to serve the ends which copyright was intended to promote. The Internet is no exception, and postings on it must be judged in reference to the already flexible considerations which fair use affords.

*Purpose and Character of the Use*: The first fair use factor is the purpose and character of the use made by the alleged infringer. 17 U.S.C. Section 107(1). Lerma posits that his use of the Works falls within several of the classic fair use categories listed in the first paragraph of Section 107, namely, that his copying and posting of the Works constitutes "criticism", "comment", "news reporting", and "scholarship." "[T]here is a strong presumption that factor one favors the defendant if an allegedly infringing work fits the description of uses described in section 107."

Wright v. Warner Books, Inc., 953 F.2d 731, 736 [20 U.S.P.Q.2d 1892] (2d Cir. 1991).

Lerma argues that his Internet posting of the Fishman Declaration originated from publication of information in a California court record that was open to the public and which the court refused to seal. Lerma asserts that he merely gathered that information like a news reporter and then published it on the Internet to unveil for the Internet community the "foibles" of Scientology in the same spirit of the modern news expose.

This analogy fails. The full record clearly shows that Lerma's motives, unlike those of news reporters, were not neutral and that his postings were not done primarily "for public benefit." MCA, Inc. v. Wilson, 677 F.2d 180, 182 [211 U.S.P.Q. 577] (2d Cir. 1981). When judged in light of the degree of copying and the use to which the infringing material was ultimately put, Lerma stands in a position significantly different from the Washington Post and its employees earlier dismissed from this suit. Even if Lerma were a newspaper reporter, the mere fact that a copyrighted document was in a public court file in no respect destroys its copyright protection.

Lerma also describes himself as a dedicated researcher delving into the theory and scholarship of Scientology. He claims to be performing academic work of a "transformative" nature, providing materials which "add new value to public knowledge and understanding, thereby advancing the goals of copyright as set forth in the Constitution." Opp'n Br. at 24. That argument does not justify the wholesale copying and republication of copyrighted material. The degree of copying by Lerma, combined with the absence of commentary on most of his Internet postings, is inconsistent with the scholarship exception. Even assuming, arguendo, that Lerma's copying to his hard drive was done solely in the name of academic research, this does not end the fair use analysis. Such uses are only "presumptively" permissible; there is a limit to the extent of reproduction that can be undertaken even by the bona-fide researcher. See American Geophysical Union v. Texaco, Inc., 802 F.Supp. 1, 17 [23 U.S.P.Q.2d 1561] (S.D.N.Y.1992), aff'd., 60 F.3d 913 (2d Cir. 1994) (archival photocopying of scientific journals for internal use by for-profit research laboratory is not fair use).

It may be true that Lerma's intent in posting the Works was not "commercial" in the traditional sense. He was not in direct competition with the church, and he did not place a surcharge on, or receive any other "private commercial gain" from, the information contained within the Works. Under the fair use doctrine, commercial use of an allegedly infringing work is disfavored whereas noncommercial use is not. Nonetheless, while there is no evidence that Lerma has profited directly from the postings, this factor alone is not dispositive of the fair use issue.

In viewing the totality of factors discussed above, the Court finds that the noncommercial character of Lerma's copying and posting does not outweigh Lerma's non-neutral and non-scholarly motives in publishing the Works.

*Nature of the Copyrighted Work*: The second factor for consideration under the fair use analysis is the nature of the copyrighted work. 17 U.S.C.A. Section 107(2). "This factor calls for recognition that some works are closer to the core of intended protection than others, with the consequence that fair use is more difficult to establish when the former works are copied." Campbell v. Acuff-Rose Music, Inc., 510 U.S. 569, 586 (1994).

In opposing RTC's Motion for Summary Judgment, Lerma relies upon two aspects of the Works which favor his position: 1) the factual vs. the creative nature of the Works, and 2) their publication status.

The fair use defense is broader with respect to factual works than to creative or literary works. "The law generally recognizes a greater need to disseminate factual works than works of fiction or fantasy." Harper & Row Publishers, Inc. v. Nation Enterprises, 471 U.S. 539, 563 (1985). Hubbard's works are difficult to classify in this respect and courts dealing with this issue have differed in their conclusion. In the case at bar, however, RTC has characterized the Works as training materials, stressing their utility over their creativity. The Court has previously resolved this question by holding that the Works are "intended to be informational rather than creative" and that a broader fair use approach is therefore appropriate in this regard. Religious Technology Center v. Lerma, 908 F.Supp. 1362, 1367 (E.D.Va.1995).

Lerma's second argument regarding the nature of the copyrighted Works pertains to their publication status. Courts have consistently found that "the scope of fair use is narrower with respect to unpublished works." New Era Publications v. Carol Publishing Group, 904 F.2d 152, 157 (2d Cir. 1990) (quoting Harper & Row, Publishers, Inc. v. Nation Enterprises, 471 U.S. 539, 564 (1985)). The Works in question clearly have not been "published." RTC has not released these materials to the public and does not plan to release them. Nevertheless, Lerma insists that for purposes of a fair use analysis the term "publication" means "whether the work has been widely disseminated or is widely available, regardless of technical 'publication'." Opp'n Br. at 41 (citing Harper & Row, 471 U.S. at 555) (emphasis in original). Because much of the materials which he copied and posted to the Internet were already available in an open court file or on the Internet, Lerma asserts that they are deserving of less protection because he has not usurped RTC's right to first publication.

Lerma's reliance upon the argument is not convincing. Although Harper & Row weighs the "de facto publication . . . or dissemination" of a work in determining whether another's utilization of the material constitutes fair use, this only applies where the author has given "implied consent" through such action as performance or dissemination. 471 U.S. at 551. In those circumstances, the author has made the work publicly available and has implicitly invoked his right to first publication. The copyright owner is denied this opportunity when actions of a third party usurp the right to first publication, as happened both in Harper & Row and in this case. Posting without the owner's consent cannot constitute a "first publication" under fair use principles.

Lerma also argues that the unpublished status of the Works is entitled to even less weight because the RTC never intends to publish them. He claims that the "central purpose of distinguishing between disseminated and undisseminated works is to preserve for the author the commercial value of the right to first publication." Opp'n Br. at 44. Relying on Harper v. Row, Lerma suggests that where a copyright owner intends never to exploit the right of first publication, the need to protect that right diminishes and the scope of fair use correspondingly expands.

Lerma misreads his authorities on this point. Harper & Row clearly recognizes that "[t]he right of first publication encompasses [also] the choice whether to publish at all." 471 U.S. at 564. See also Salinger v. Random House, Inc., 811 F.2d 90, 98 [1 U.S.P.Q.2d 1673] (2d Cir. 1987) (Potential harm to value of plaintiff's works "is not lessened by the fact that their author has disavowed any intention to publish them during his lifetime . . . [h]e is entitled to protect his opportunity to sell his letters"). This approach is not illogical.

Thus, while the factual nature of the Works weighs in Lerma's favor, the unpublished nature of the Works and RTC's intention to keep the Works unpublished weigh against him.

*Amount and Substantiality of Copying*: The third factor addresses the amount and substantiality of the portion copied by the defendant in relation to the copyrighted work as a whole. 17 U.S.C. Section 107(3). "There are no absolute rules as to how much of a copyrighted work may be copied and still be considered a fair use." Maxtone-Graham v. Burtchaell, 803 F.2d 1253, 1263 [231 U.S.P.Q. 534] (2d Cir. 1986). This factor has both quantitative and qualitative components, so that courts have found a use to be unfair where the quoted materials formed a substantial percentage of the copyrighted work or where the quoted material was "essentially the heart of" the copyrighted work. New Era Publications v. Carol Publishing Group, 904 F.2d 152, 158 [14 U.S.P.Q.2d 2030] (2d Cir. 1990) (citations omitted).

The parties dispute whether the segments excerpted by Lerma represent "the heart of" the Works under the qualitative component. The Court is unable to evaluate this component because many of the copyrighted materials are incomprehensible. However, because the quantitative analysis weighs so overwhelmingly in RTC's favor, it is not necessary to make this qualitative evaluation.

The wholesale copying of copyrighted material often precludes the application of the fair use doctrine. Marcus v. Rowley, 695 F.2d 1171, 1176 [217 U.S.P.Q. 691] (9th Cir.1983) (citations omitted). Such blatant reproduction has been prohibited even in the context of educational instruction. See, e.g., Encyclopaedia Britannica Educational Corp. v. Crooks, 447 F.Supp. 243 [197 U.S.P.Q. 280] (W.D.N.Y.1978) (although defendants were involved in noncommercial educational copying of films to promote science and education, the taping of entire copyrighted films was too excessive for the fair use defense to apply).

Lerma opposes RTC's percentage calculations by arguing a different interpretation of what represents the "whole" copyrighted work as defined under Section 107(3). RTC has registered the OT Documents with the copyright office in batches as part of a series. Lerma argues that the "whole" work refers to the entire series listed on a registration certificate, while RTC argues that the term refers to each component of these copyrighted series.

Although Lerma did not post the entirety of [each batch], he did post the entirety of certain discrete subparts of these series. Under the Code of Federal Regulations and under case law, these subparts constitute single works and are the benchmark against which to compare Lerma's actions. Following this analysis, Lerma's infringement is clear.

As a final defense under this fair use factor, Lerma urges this Court to consider the Internet postings in their unique newsgroup context. Rather than viewing each individual posting in isolation, Lerma contends that each posting must be considered within the context of the ongoing dialogue he has conducted on the newsgroup. The qualitative analysis would then include the multiple communications posted before and after the alleged infringements, communications which are likely to contain greater commentary and analysis than the postings at issue.

This approach would permit a would-be infringer to participate in blatant theft of a copyright yet still escape punishment via the subsequent posting of subsequent commentary—a commentary that may not always be seen in tandem with the infringing work. Under this argument "cyberbandits" could easily cover their tracks.

The third fair use factor therefore weighs heavily against Lerma. His direct copying and posting of certain "single works" registered within collections, almost totally devoid of discussion and commentary, nearly are sufficient to preclude a fair use defense.

*Effect on the Market of the Copyrighted Work:* The fourth and final part of the fair use defense considers the effect which the allegedly infringing use had on the potential market for, or value of, the copyrighted work. 17 U.S.C.A. Section 107(4).

Courts have frequently identified this as the most important element of a fair use analysis. However, the 1967 House Report cautions that it "must almost always be judged in conjunction with the other three criteria." Marcus v. Rowley, 695 F.2d 1171, 1177 (9th Cir.1983) (citing H.R. Rep. No. 83., 90th Cong., 1st Sess. 33, 35 (1967)). Lerma correctly argues that any economic harm befalling the Church of Scientology as a result of legitimate commentary is permissible under the fair use doctrine. The Supreme Court found in Campbell v. Acuff-Rose Music, Inc., 510 U.S. at 592 (1994), that we must "distinguish between '[b]iting criticism [that merely] suppresses demand [and] copyright infringement [, which] usurps it'" (brackets in original) (citation omitted). It is extremely difficult to address the issue of market impact in this case because it is unlikely that excerpts of the Works posted by Lerma thus far, although substantial, would provide a sufficient basis for would-be parishioners to defect from Scientology. However, RTC's inability to prove a decrease in Scientology enrollment does not justify Lerma's actions. "The mere absence of measurable pecuniary damage does not require a finding of fair use." Marcus v. Rowley, 695 F.2d 1171, 1177 (9th Cir.1983).

The potential for economic harm to RTC must also be considered. "[T]o negate fair use one need only show that if the 'challenged use should become widespread, it would adversely affect the potential market for the copyrighted work'." Harper & Row, 471 U.S. at 568 (citing Sony Corp. of America v. Universal City Studios, Inc., 464 U.S. at 451). RTC correctly notes that a substantial expansion of Lerma's current activities presents an identifiable risk of harming RTC. In Bridge Publications, Inc. v. Vien, 827 F.Supp. 629, 633 (S.D.Cal.1993), the court found such a risk in another case involving the Church of Scientology. In Vien, unpermitted copying of RTC's literary works and sound recordings was held to violate copyright law in part because the copies fulfilled the demand for the original works and diminished or prejudiced their potential sale. Id. at 636.

Overall, however, RTC in this case are far too speculative [sic]. RTC is unable to present specific, identifiable evidence of the effect that Lerma's postings have had or could have on the Church of Scientology, and cannot establish that Lerma is operating as a direct competitor of the church. Thus, the Court finds that the fourth fair-use factor tips slightly in Lerma's favor.

*Fair Use Summary:* Based upon the four statutory factors listed in § 107 for evaluating the fair use defense, the Court finds that Lerma's copying and posting of the Works does not constitute fair use.

*Damages and Remedies*

The Court will now preliminarily address the appropriate remedy for Lerma's infringements. The basis for monetary damages in an infringement action is set forth in 17 U.S.C. Section 594. That section enables a copyright owner to seek either "actual damages and any additional profits of the infringer" or "statutory damages." 17 U.S.C. Section 504(a).

Actual damages and profits are not readily ascertainable in this case because of a number of factors, including that Lerma was not selling the infringed material, that he is not a direct competitor of the Church of

Scientology, and that RTC is unable to show lost profits or fewer parishioners with any degree of certainty. The Court need not determine actual damages, however, because RTC has indicated its intention to seek only the "statutory minimum damages afforded by the Copyright Act."

In determining a final statutory award, the Court must answer three questions: 1) to what degree do the relevant postings infringe RTC's copyrights; 2) how many acts of infringement occurred and 3) to what extent was the infringement willful.

*To What Extent Do the Works Infringe—*

The Court has reviewed in detail the allegedly infringing Works submitted by RTC in conjunction with its summary judgment motion. Without exception, each of the 33 binders tendered demonstrates infringement of the RTC's copyrights in the documents at issue.

*Number of Infringing Acts*—Although each of the 33 binders contained in RTC's G-Series Exhibits are infringing, this does not necessarily indicate 33 acts of infringement. The Copyright Act clearly states that for purposes of calculating statutory damages for copyright infringement, "all the parts of a compilation or derivative work constitute one work." 17 U.S.C. Section 504 (1996).

Each of the 33 exhibits in this case arise from one of five different compilations filed with the Copyright Office of the United States. If multiple but distinct works are collected and filed together at the Copyright Office under the same registration, they are to be considered a single work for the purposes of damages. This principle is demonstrated in Stokes Seeds Ltd. v. Geo. W. Park Seed Co., Inc., 783 F.Supp. 104 (W.D.N.Y.1991), where each copying of multiple photographs appearing in a seed company's seedling reference book did not constitute a distinct infringing transaction. Instead, the court viewed the work as a compilation constituting "one work" and therefore "justifying a single award of statutory damages." For the purpose of the damage calculation, the infringing documents at issue in this summary judgment motion similarly constitute five works, not thirty-three.

Because statutory damages are to be calculated according to the number of works infringed and not the number of infringements, Walt Disney Co. v. Powell, 897 F.2d 565, 569 [14 U.S.P.Q.2d 1160] (D.C.Cir.1990), the Court will find only five instances of infringement for the purposes of calculating damages.

*Willfulness*—This court declines to impose increased statutory damages for a willful violation. "An infringement is 'willful' if the infringer knows that its conduct is an infringement or if the infringer has acted in reckless disregard of the copyright owner's right." Video Views, Inc. v. Studio 21 Ltd., 925 F.2d 1010, 1020 [17 U.S.P.Q.2d 1753] (7th Cir.1991), cert denied, 502 U.S. 861 (1991), cited in Superior Form

Builders, Inc. v. Chase Taxidermy Supply Co., 74 F.3d 488, 496 [37 U.S.P.Q.2d 1571] (4th Cir.1996).

Lerma's actions do not match those of infringers in cases where courts have found willful violations. In determining whether an infringement was willful, the court in Superior Form Builders considered the infringer's history of infringement, noting that "[t]he record supports the conclusion that Dan Chase Taxidermy became the largest taxidermy supplier in the country by consistently and deliberately copying competitors' forms in disregard of the copyright laws." 74 F.3d at 497. The defendant also falsified a copyright on his product, a mannequin, and was previously sued at least three times for copyright infringement. 74 F.3d at 497. Finally, the court stressed that Chase had represented in his product catalogs that his products were copyrighted and had therefore taken an inconsistent position at trial that the mannequins were not copyrightable. In contrast, Lerma has no history of copyright infringement and he made no representation that he owned the copyright to the Works.

*Damages calculated*—For each instance of non-willful infringement, the Copyright Act enables the Court to award statutory damages of "not less than $500 or more than $20,000 as the court consider just." 17 U.S.C. Section 504(c)(1) (1996). In light of the five instances of infringement which occurred in this case, because the penalty is being assessed against an individual of limited means who has already expended considerable sums in this litigation, and because RTC has indicated its express desire to seek only the statutory minimum, provided its copyrights are protected, the Court intends to award the statutory minimum of $500 for each infringement, for a total statutory award of $2,500 in favor of RTC and against defendant Lerma, unless the RTC convinces the Court to do otherwise.

*Conclusion*

For the above-stated reasons, summary judgment on the copyright claim is found in favor of plaintiff, RTC, against defendant Lerma.

## NOTES

1. *Policies underlying the originality requirement.* Why do you suppose the originality requirement under copyright law is not more rigorous? Can the originality requirement as it is applied by the court in *Feist* be criticized for being too rigorous? What is the practical effect of the originality requirement as it is currently applied? Does it not call for difficult line-drawing on the part of the Register that might otherwise be unnecessary?

As *Feist* suggests, the level of originality present in a given work will determine the scope of protection for that work. Thus, during the course of an infringement suit, a court often will be called upon to determine the appropriate scope of protection for a copyrighted work. The typical standard for determining copyright infringement requires a determination as to whether the defendant's work is "substantially similar" to the plaintiff's. However, cases have endorsed the more rigorous "virtual identity" standard for infringement with respect to works with a narrow range of protectable and unauthorized expression.[25] What should be the scope of protection accorded the recipe book in the Principal Problem? How does this bear on the issue of whether Larry Lifter's conduct should be considered infringing?

The line between idea and expression often is extremely difficult to draw, as *Religious Technology Center* suggests. In fact, this inquiry really is the bottom line in many of the originality cases. How does this inquiry impact the Principal Problem?

Section 102(b) of the Copyright Act provides that "[i]n no case does copyright protection for an original work of authorship extend to any idea, procedure, process, system, method of operation, concept, principle, or discovery, regardless of the form in which it is described, explained, illustrated, or embodied in such work."[26] Interestingly, despite the fact that the Patent Act does not specifically exclude principles, discoveries, etc., the courts have uniformly interpreted it as not extending to these things. However, many of the issues decided under the guise of "originality" and "authorship" in copyright law are decided as questions about "subject matter" in patent law.[27]

2. *Ownership vs. authorship.* Should the sculpture at issue in *Community for Creative Non-Violence* be considered a joint work? Note that the Court of Appeals remanded on this issue, although neither CCNV nor Reid requested the Supreme Court to review this remand order. If the sculpture was determined to be a joint work, could Reid object to CCNV's proposed tour? Do you think Reid should be able to stop the tour if he was declared the sole owner of the copyright? Who would have the right to any profits from the tour if Reid was the sole copyright owner? Should Reid have to give the sculpture back to CCNV regardless of the determination of copyright ownership? Should Zelda and Henrietta be considered joint authors in the Principal Problem?

3. *Work for hire.* How well does the Supreme Court's decision in *Community for Creative Non-Violence* accomplish "Congress' paramount goal in revising the 1976 Act of enhancing predictability and certainty of copyright ownership" (see Section II(A) of case)? Are there any other approaches which the Court could have adopted that would have been more consistent with this goal? Do you think the court views any one factor as most important? How would you analyze whether Henrietta's work should be considered a work for hire under both subparts of the statutory definition?

4. *Fair use.* Looking at each of the relevant fair use factors, how would you compare the Principal Problem with *Religious Technology Center*? In addition to the four factors specified in the statute, the fair use doctrine

---

[25] Mattel, Inc. v. MGA Entm't, Inc., Nos. 09–55673, 09–55812, 2010 U.S. App. LEXIS 26937 (9th Cir. July 22, 2010); Apple Computer, Inc. v. Microsoft Corp., 35 F.3d 1435 (9th Cir.1994), *cert. denied*, 513 U.S. 1184, 115 S.Ct. 1176 (1995).

[26] § 102(b).

[27] See Miller, Hoisting Originality, 31 Cardozo L. Rev. 451 (2009) (arguing that copyright's originality requirement should be as stringent as that of patent law).

recognizes the importance of other equitable factors such as defendant's relative good faith. Should Larry's motives in posting the recipes be considered in the fair use analysis? How much importance would you attach to the fact that Larry copied certain groupings of recipes in their entirety?

The fourth factor in determining fair use is "the effect of the use upon the potential market for or value of the copyrighted work."[28] In *Religious Technology Center*, the court stated that it was "extremely difficult to address the issue of market impact in this case because it is unlikely that excerpts of the Works posted by Lerma thus far, although substantial, would provide a sufficient basis for would-be parishioners to defect from Scientology."[29] Is defection from a religion the type of market impact addressed by the fourth factor? When looking at market impact, what is the relevant market? In *Suntrust Bank v. Houghton Mifflin Co.*,[30] the court addressed the issue of market impact with respect to *The Wind Done Gone* ("TWDG"), a book that parodied the well known novel *Gone With the Wind* ("GWTW"). Alice Randall, the author of TWDG, claimed that her novel was a critique of GWTW as it told the story of the same events from a female slave's point of view. The appellate court vacated the lower court's preliminary injunction against TWDG's publisher. With respect to the fourth factor regarding market impact, the court stressed the fact that TWDG was unlikely to displace the demand for GWTW, nor significantly harm derivatives of the original novel.[31]

In 2016, a significant development in the area of fair use occurred when a jury validated as fair use Google's use of Java programming language in Android. It is anticipated that this decision will have significant future ramifications.[32]

5. *Remedies.* The remedial provisions of the 1976 Act allow a copyright proprietor who establishes infringement the choice of recovering either 1) statutory damages, or 2) actual damages and any of the infringer's profits not factored into the actual damage award.[33] The statute provides that the recovery of statutory damages covers "all infringements involved in the action, with respect to any one work . . . in a sum of not less than $500 or more than $20,000 as the court considers just."[34] Where an infringer proves that she was not aware of and had no reason to believe that her acts constituted infringement, a statutory damages award can be reduced to an amount not less than $200. Conversely, a court can increase awards involving willful conduct on the part of the defendant to a sum of up to $100,000.[35] Do you think Zelda should be able to get increased statutory damages on the ground that Lifter acted willfully? How should courts

---

[28] See § 107 (1992).
[29] 40 U.S.P.Q.2d at 1578.
[30] 268 F.3d 1257 (11th Cir.2001).
[31] 268 F.3d at 1274–1275.
[32] See Kane & Lichter. "What The Google Fair Use Decision Means For Developers— Law 360." 31 May 2016. Web. 6 June 2016.
[33] § 504.
[34] § 504(c)(1).
[35] § 504(c)(2).

determine what constitutes "any one work?" For how many works should Zelda be able to recover statutory damages?

The statutory damages provision has been the subject of one Supreme Court opinion. In Feltner, Jr. v. Columbia Pictures Television, Inc.,[36] the Court held that the right to a jury trial regarding statutory damages is mandated by the Seventh Amendment, although not by the language of § 504(c) of the copyright statute.

6. *The Digital Millennium Copyright Act.* The Digital Millennium Copyright Act ("DMCA") was enacted in 1998 as an extensive amendment to the 1976 Copyright Act. The importance of the DMCA cannot be overstated because it has provided copyright owners with an unprecedented level of copyright protection. Although a comprehensive treatment of this statute is beyond the scope of this text, it is important to note that the DMCA prohibits unauthorized access to copyrighted works (as opposed to conduct constituting copyright infringement). The statute has been the subject of much controversy as some scholars believe that it facilitates the protection of works beyond the scope of copyright.[37]

---

[36] 523 U.S. 340, 118 S.Ct. 1279 (1998).

[37] See, e.g., Henslee, Copyright Infringement Pushin': Google, YouTube, and Viacom Fight for Supremacy in the Neighborhood that May Be Controlled by the DMCA's Safe Harbor Provision, 51 IDEA 607 (2011); Jacobs, Copyright Fraud in the Internet Age: Copyright Management Information for Non-Digital Works Under the Digital Millennium Copyright Act, 13 Colum. Sci. & Tech. L. Rev. 97 (2011); Perzanowski, Rethinking Anticircumvention's Interoperability Policy, 42 U.C. Davis L. Rev. 1549 (2009); Mulligan & Perzanowski, The Magnificence of Disaster: Reconstructing the Sony BMG Rootkit Incident, 22 Berkeley Tech. L.J. 1157 (2007); Dixon, Dislodging Copyright From its Constitutional Base: When Technological Barriers of Access & the DMCA are Applied to Software, 10 J. Internet L. 3 (2006); Wagner, Reconsidering the DMCA, 42 Hous. L. Rev. 1107 (2005); Liu, The DMCA and the Regulation of Scientific Research, 18 Berkeley Tech. L.J. 501 (2003); Lunney, The Death of Copyright: Digital Technology, Private Copying, and the Digital Millennium Copyright Act, 87 Va. L. Rev. 813 (2001); Nimmer, A Riff on Fair Use in the Digital Millennium Copyright Act, 148 U. Pa. L. Rev. 673 (2000).

# ASSIGNMENT 57
# THE RIGHT OF PUBLICITY

## 1. INTRODUCTION

The following Principal Problem requires you to grapple with the legal consequences of according a property status to certain nontraditional property interests such as personal information and one's persona. The doctrine featured in this Assignment is the right of publicity, one of intellectual property's state law analogues. This doctrine enables individuals to protect themselves from unauthorized, commercial appropriations of personal characteristics such as their names, likenesses and other recognizable attributes. As this Assignment illustrates, the question in many right-of-publicity cases is *who* has the right to control the value inhering in these attributes, the plaintiff or members of the public at large (the defendant being one example).

Unlike trademarks and copyrights, the right of publicity is an area which can be readily mastered without the aid of specific statutes. Exposure to this doctrine is useful, especially at an early stage of intellectual property study, because the controversy surrounding the appropriate scope of protection for the right of publicity typifies the issues regarding expanding protection for intellectual property generally. Moreover, an understanding of these basic issues will enable you to appreciate more fully some of the important differences between intellectual property and tangible property.

## 2. PRINCIPAL PROBLEM

Ada and Sterling Copperfield met while Sterling was in his second year of law school. He was from an extremely wealthy family, and he had been given every advantage from the day of his birth. Ada, on the other hand, was the daughter of two poor immigrants who came to America during the Depression. When Ada met Sterling, she was working as a cocktail waitress at a local pub and attending a local university on a part-time basis. Ada and Sterling were married immediately upon Sterling's graduation from law school.

Sterling began his legal career at a prominent law firm. Although he was placed on academic probation in law school and flunked the Bar twice before passing, he secured his first job at a prominent law firm due to his family connections. Notwithstanding his poor performance in law school, he became fabulously successful as an attorney. Sterling tried hard to forget that he was not an academic super-star and hoped that no one else would remember either. Soon nobody at the law firm did remember his rocky academics or even cared. His silver-spoon upbringing, socially suave demeanor, hard-driving ambition and social connections enabled him to start his own entertainment law practice after only five years. Again, he was an instant success. Ada, on the other hand, spent her days playing tennis, shopping at Neiman Marcus, entertaining Sterling's important clients and socializing with the "right" people. They never had children.

At 46 years of age, Sterling is distinguished looking and very, very attractive. His looks are distinctive and can be depicted easily through caricature. Over the past few years, Sterling has gained much public attention, largely due to several appearances on national talk shows in conjunction with his high profile entertainment law practice.

Last year, he was selected as the spokesperson for the local affiliate of a national health club chain with seven locations in the city in which the Copperfields live. The city populace is treated on an almost daily basis to television commercials featuring Sterling. All of these advertisements initially feature Sterling arguing a case in a courtroom followed by a clip of him playing racket ball. He opens every commercial with the phrase: "I take a hard line in all courts, both work and play." The public response to Sterling has been terrific and it is rumored that many companies are interested in using him in the future for advertising their products. Due to the popularity of these commercials, Sterling has been nicknamed the "hard-line hunk."

All of this attention apparently has swelled Sterling's already portly ego, and last year, Sterling told Ada that he was having an affair with a twenty-nine year old law professor who was his "equal" both intellectually and physically. The Copperfields recently separated after twenty-one years of marriage and Sterling has publicly announced his intention to leave Ada as little as possible since "she has been along for the ride for long enough."

Several women's rights groups have championed Ada's cause and catapulted her divorce to headline news. One such group has begun manufacturing T-shirts depicting scales of justice along with a caricature of Sterling showing one part of his anatomy with a visibly hard appearance. Next to the scales, the shirt states: "ADA NEEDS AID" and below Sterling's caricature is the following caption: "Some men think hard with their hearts; some with their minds; others only think hard below the waist." On the back of the T-shirt the following appears: "He graduated in the bottom of his class, was placed on academic probation and flunked the Bar twice. She believed in him. Look where it got her." The T-shirts sell for $20.00, and half the proceeds go into a fund to finance both Ada's legal fees and her post-divorce needs.

Sterling has hired you to represent him in his divorce. He wants to know whether his right of publicity is marital property subject to division and whether he can get damages and an injunction against the organization sponsoring the T-shirts.

Consider the following materials before advising him.

3. MATERIALS FOR SOLUTION OF PRINCIPAL PROBLEM

## Feist Publications, Inc. v. Rural Telephone Service Co.
Supreme Court of the United States, 1991.
499 U.S. 340, 111 S.Ct. 1282.

*Reprinted in* Assignment 56

## National Basketball Ass'n & NBA Properties, Inc. v. Motorola, Inc.
United States Court of Appeals, Second Circuit, 1997.
105 F.3d 841.

■ WINTER, CIRCUIT JUDGE:

Motorola, Inc. and Sports Team Analysis and Tracking Systems ("STATS") appeal from a permanent injunction. The injunction concerns a handheld pager sold by Motorola and marketed under the name "SportsTrax," which displays updated information of professional basketball games in progress. The injunction prohibits appellants, absent authorization from the National Basketball Association and NBA Properties, Inc. (collectively the "NBA"), from transmitting scores or other data about NBA games in progress via the pagers, STATS's site on America On-Line's computer dial-up service, or "any equivalent means."

The crux of the dispute concerns the extent to which a state law "hot-news" misappropriation claim based on International News Service v. Associated Press, 248 U.S. 215 (1918) ("INS"), survives preemption by the federal Copyright Act and whether the NBA's claim fits within the surviving INS-type claims. We hold that a narrow "hot-news" exception does survive preemption. However, we also hold that appellants' transmission of "real-time" NBA game scores and information tabulated from television and radio broadcasts of games in progress does not constitute a misappropriation of "hot news" that is the property of the NBA.

The facts are largely undisputed. Motorola manufactures and markets the SportsTrax paging device while STATS supplies the game information that is transmitted to the pagers. The product became available to the public in January 1996, at a retail price of about $200. SportsTrax's pager has an inch-and-a-half by inch-and-a-half screen and operates in four basic modes: "current," "statistics," "final scores" and "demonstration." It is the "current" mode that gives rise to the present dispute. In that mode, SportsTrax displays the following information on NBA games in progress: (i) the teams playing; (ii) score changes; (iii) the team in possession of the ball; (iv) whether the team is in the free-throw bonus; (v) the quarter of the game; and (vi) time remaining in the quarter. The information is updated every two to three minutes, with more frequent updates near the end of the first half and the end of the game. There is a lag of approximately two or three minutes between events in the game itself and when the information appears on the pager screen.

SportsTrax's operation relies on a "data feed" supplied by STATS reporters who watch the games on television or listen to them on the radio. The reporters key into a personal computer changes in the score and other information such as successful and missed shots, fouls, and clock updates. The information is relayed by modem to STATS's host computer, which compiles, analyzes, and formats the data for retransmission. The information is then sent to a common carrier, which then sends it via satellite to various local FM radio networks that in turn emit the signal received by the individual SportsTrax pagers.

Finding Motorola and STATS liable for misappropriation, Judge Preska entered the permanent injunction, reserved the calculation of damages for subsequent proceedings, and stayed execution of the injunction pending appeal. Motorola and STATS appeal from the injunction.

Summary of Ruling

The issues before us are ones that have arisen in various forms over the course of this century as technology has steadily increased the speed and quantity of information transmission. Today, individuals at home, at work, or elsewhere, can use a computer, pager, or other device to obtain highly selective kinds of information virtually at will. *INS* was one of the first cases to address the issues raised by these technological advances, although the technology involved in that case was primitive by contemporary standards. *INS* involved two wire services, the Associated Press ("AP") and International News Service ("INS"), that transmitted news stories by wire to member newspapers. Id. INS would lift factual stories from AP bulletins and send them by wire to INS papers. Id. at 231. INS would also take factual stories from east coast AP papers and wire them to INS papers on the west coast that had yet to publish because of time differentials. Id. at 238. The Supreme Court held that INS's conduct was a common-law misappropriation of AP's property. Id. at 242.

With the advance of technology, radio stations began "live" broadcasts of events such as baseball games and operas, and various entrepreneurs began to use the transmissions of others in one way or another for their own profit. In response, New York courts created a body of misappropriation law, loosely based on INS, that sought to apply ethical standards to the use by one party of another's transmissions of events.

Federal copyright law played little active role in this area until 1976. Before then, it appears to have been the general understanding—there being no caselaw of consequence—that live events such as baseball games were not copyrightable. Moreover, doubt existed even as to whether a recorded broadcast or videotape of such an event was copyrightable. In 1976, however, Congress passed legislation expressly affording copyright protection to simultaneously-recorded broadcasts of live performances such as sports events. See 17 U.S.C. § 101. Such protection was not extended to the underlying events.

The 1976 amendments also contained provisions preempting state law claims that enforced rights "equivalent" to exclusive copyright protections when the work to which the state claim was being applied fell within the area of copyright protection. See 17 U.S.C. § 301. Based on legislative history of the 1976 amendments, it is generally agreed that a "hot-news" INS-like claim survives preemption. H.R. No. 94–1476 at 132 (1976), reprinted in 1976 U.S.C.C.A.N. 5659, 5748.

Copyrights in Events or Broadcasts of Events

[R]ecorded broadcasts of NBA games—as opposed to the games themselves—are now entitled to copyright protection. The Copyright Act was amended in 1976 specifically to insure that simultaneously-recorded transmissions of live performances and sporting events would meet the Act's requirement that the original work of authorship be "fixed in any tangible medium of expression." 17 U.S.C. § 102(a).

Although the broadcasts are protected under copyright law, the district court correctly held that Motorola and STATS did not infringe NBA's copyright because they reproduced only facts from the broadcasts, not the expression or description of the game that constitutes the broadcast. The "fact/expression dichotomy" is a bedrock principle of copyright law that "limits severely the scope of protection in fact-based works." Feist Publications, Inc. v. Rural Tel. Service Co., 499 U.S. 340 (1991).

We agree with the district court that the "defendants provide purely factual information which any patron of an NBA game could acquire from the arena without any involvement from the director, cameramen, or others who contribute to the originality of a broadcast." 939 F. Supp. at 1094. Because the SportsTrax device reproduces only factual information culled from the broadcasts and none of the copyrightable expression of the games, appellants did not infringe the copyright of the broadcasts.

The State-Law Misappropriation Claim

The district court's injunction was based on its conclusion that, under New York law, defendants had unlawfully misappropriated the NBA's property rights in its games. The district court reached this conclusion by holding: (i) that the NBA's misappropriation claim relating to the underlying games was not preempted by Section 301 of the Copyright Act; and (ii) that, under New York common law, defendants had engaged in unlawful misappropriation. Id. at 1094–1107. We disagree.

Preemption Under the Copyright Act

When Congress amended the Copyright Act in 1976, it provided for the preemption of state law claims that are interrelated with copyright claims in certain ways. Under 17 U.S.C. § 301, a state law claim is preempted when: (i) the state law claim seeks to vindicate "legal or equitable rights that are equivalent" to one of the bundle of exclusive rights already protected by copyright law under 17 U.S.C. § 106—styled the "general scope requirement"; and (ii) the particular work to which the state law claim is being applied falls within the type of works protected by the Copyright Act under Sections 102 and 103—styled the "subject matter requirement."

The district court concluded that the NBA's misappropriation claim was not preempted because [the subject matter requirement was not met with respect to the underlying games, as opposed to the broadcasts]. The court dubbed as "partial preemption" its separate analysis of misappropriation claims relating to the underlying games and misappropriation claims relating to broadcasts of those games. The district court then relied on a series of older New York misappropriation cases involving radio broadcasts that considerably broadened *INS*.

We hold that where the challenged copying or misappropriation relates in part to the copyrighted broadcasts of the games, the subject matter requirement is met as to both the broadcasts and the games. We therefore reject the partial preemption doctrine and its anomalous consequence that "it is possible for a plaintiff to assert claims both for infringement of its copyright in a broadcast and misappropriation of its rights in the underlying event." Although game broadcasts are copyrightable while the underlying games are not, the Copyright Act should not be read to distinguish between the two when analyzing the preemption of a misappropriation claim based on copying or taking from the copyrightable work.

Under the general scope requirement, Section 301 "preempts only those state law rights that 'may be abridged by an act which, in and of itself, would infringe one of the exclusive rights' provided by federal copyright law." Computer Assoc. Int'l, Inc. v. Altai, Inc., 982 F.2d 693, 716 (2d Cir.1992) (quoting Harper & Row, 723 F.2d at 200). However, certain forms of commercial misappropriation otherwise within the general scope requirement will survive preemption if an "extra-element" test is met. As stated in *Altai*:

> But if an "extra element" is "required instead of or in addition to the acts of reproduction, performance, distribution or display, in order to constitute a state-created cause of action, then the right does not lie 'within the general scope of copyright,' and there is no preemption."

*Id.* (quoting 1 *Nimmer on Copyright* § 1.01[B] at 1–15).

We turn, therefore, to the question of the extent to which a "hot-news" misappropriation claim based on INS involves extra elements and is not the equivalent of exclusive rights under a copyright. Courts are generally agreed that some form of such a claim survives preemption. *Financial Information, Inc. v. Moody's Investors Service, Inc.*, 808 F.2d 204, 208 (2d Cir.1986) ("*FII*"). This conclusion is based in part on the legislative history of the 1976 amendments. The House Report stated:

> "Misappropriation" is not necessarily synonymous with copyright infringement, and thus a cause of action labeled as "misappropriation" is not preempted if it is in fact based neither on a right within the general scope of copyright as specified by section 106 nor on a right equivalent thereto. For example, state law should have the flexibility to afford a remedy (under traditional principles of equity) against a consistent pattern of unauthorized appropriation by a competitor of the facts (i.e., not the literary expression) constitution "hot" news, whether in the traditional mold of *International News Service v. Associated Press*, 248 U.S. 215 (1918), or in the newer form of data updates from scientific, business, or financial data bases. . . . The crucial question, therefore, is the *breadth* of the "hot-news" claim that survives preemption.

In INS, the plaintiff AP and defendant INS were "wire services" that sold news items to client newspapers. AP brought suit to prevent INS from selling facts and information lifted from AP sources to INS-affiliated newspapers. One method by which INS was able to use AP's news was to lift facts from AP news bulletins. INS, 248 U.S. at 231. Another method was to sell facts taken from just-published east coast AP newspapers to west coast INS newspapers whose editions had yet to appear. The Supreme Court held (prior to Erie R. Co. v. Tompkins, 304 U.S. 64 (1938)), that INS's use of AP's information was unlawful under federal common law. It characterized INS's conduct as:

> Amount[ing] to an unauthorized interference with the normal operation of complainant's legitimate business precisely at the point where the profit is to be reaped, in order to divert a material portion of the profit from those who have earned it to those who have not; with special advantage to defendant in the competition because of the fact that it is not burdened with any part of the expense of gathering the news.

INS, 248 U.S. at 240. The theory of the New York misappropriation cases relied upon by the district court is considerably broader than that of *INS*. For example, the district court quoted at length from *Metropolitan Opera Ass'n v. Wagner-Nichols Recorder Corp.*, 199 Misc. 786, 101 N.Y.S.2d 483 (N.Y.Sup.Ct.1950), aff'd, 279 A.D. 632, 107 N.Y.S.2d 795 (1st Dep't 1951). *Metropolitan Opera* described New York misappropriation law as standing for the "broader principle that property rights of commercial value are to be and will be protected from any form of commercial immorality"; that misappropriation law developed "to deal with business malpractice is offensive to the ethics of . . . society"; and that the doctrine is "broad and flexible." However, we believe that *Metropolitan Opera*'s broad misappropriation doctrine based on amorphous concepts such as "commercial immorality" or society's "ethics" is preempted. Such concepts are virtually synonymous for wrongful copying and are in no meaningful fashion distinguishable from infringement of a copyright. The broad misappropriation doctrine relied upon by the district court is, therefore, the equivalent of exclusive rights in copyright law.

Our conclusion, therefore, is that only a narrow "hot-news" misappropriation claim survives preemption for actions concerning material within the realm of copyright. In our view, the elements central to an INS claim are: (i) the plaintiff generates or collects information at some cost or expense, (ii) the value of the information is highly time-sensitive, (iii) the defendant's use of the information constitutes free-riding on the plaintiff's costly efforts to generate or collect it, (iv) the defendant's use of the information is in direct competition with a product or service offered by the plaintiff, [and] (v) the ability of other parties to free-ride on the efforts of the plaintiff would so reduce the incentive to produce the product or service that its existence or quality would be substantially threatened.

INS is not about ethics; it is about the protection of property rights in time-sensitive information so that the information will be made available to the public by profit-seeking entrepreneurs. If services like AP were not assured of property rights in the news they pay to collect, they would cease to collect it. The ability of their competitors to appropriate their product at only nominal cost and thereby to disseminate a competing product at a lower price would destroy the incentive to collect news in the first place. The newspaper-reading public would suffer because no one would have an incentive to collect "hot-news."

We therefore find the extra elements—those in addition to the elements of copyright infringement—that allow a "hot-news" claim to survive preemption are: (i) the time-sensitive value of factual information, (ii) the free-riding by a defendant, and (iii) the threat to the very existence of the product or service provided by the plaintiff.

The Legality of SportsTrax

We conclude that Motorola and STATS have not engaged in unlawful misappropriation under the "hot-news" test set out above. To be sure, some of the elements of a "hot-news" INS-claim are met. The information transmitted to SportsTrax is not precisely contemporaneous, but it is nevertheless time-sensitive. Also, the NBA does provide, or will shortly do so, information like that available through SportsTrax. It now offers a service called "Gamestats" that provides official play-by-play game sheets and half-time and final box scores within each arena. It also provides such information to the media in each arena. In the future, the

NBA plans to enhance Gamestats so that it will be networked between the various arenas and will support a pager product analogous to SportsTrax. SportsTrax will of course directly compete with an enhanced Gamestats.

However, there are critical elements missing in the NBA's attempt to assert a "hot-news" INS-type claim. As framed by the NBA, their claim compresses and confuses three different informational products. The first product is generating the information by playing the games; the second product is transmitting live, full descriptions of those games; and the third product is collecting and retransmitting strictly factual information about the games. The first and second products are the NBA's primary business: producing basketball games for live attendance and licensing copyrighted broadcasts of those games. The collection and retransmission of strictly factual material about the games is a different product: e.g., box-scores in newspapers, summaries of statistics on television sports news, and real-time facts to be transmitted to pagers. In our view, the NBA has failed to show any competitive effect whatsoever from SportsTrax on the first and second products and a lack of any free-riding by SportsTrax on the third.

With regard to the NBA's primary products—producing basketball games with live attendance and licensing copyrighted broadcasts of those games—there is no evidence that anyone regards SportsTrax as a substitute for attending NBA games or watching them on television. In fact, Motorola markets SportsTrax as being designed "for those times when you cannot be at the arena, watch the game on TV, or listen to the radio. . . ."

The NBA argues that the pager market is also relevant to a "hot-news" INS-type claim and that SportsTrax's future competition with Gamestats satisfies any missing element. We agree that there is a separate market for the real-time transmission of factual information to pagers or similar devices. However, we disagree that SportsTrax is in any sense free-riding off Gamestats.

An indispensable element of an INS "hot-news" claim is free-riding by a defendant on a plaintiff's product, enabling the defendant to produce a directly competitive product for less money because it has lower costs. SportsTrax is not such a product. The use of pagers to transmit real-time information about NBA games requires: (i) the collecting of facts about the games; (ii) the transmission of these facts on a network; (iii) the assembling of them by the particular service; and (iv) the transmission of them to pagers or an on-line computer site. Appellants are in no way free-riding on Gamestats. Motorola and STATS expend their own resources to collect purely factual information generated in NBA games to transmit to SportsTrax pagers. They have their own network and assemble and transmit data themselves.

SportsTrax and Gamestats are each bearing their own costs of collecting factual information on NBA games, and, if one produces a product that is cheaper or otherwise superior to the other, that producer will prevail in the marketplace. This is obviously not the situation against which INS was intended to prevent: the potential lack of any such product or service because of the anticipation of free-riding.

For the foregoing reasons, the NBA has not shown any damage to any of its products based on free-riding by Motorola and STATS, and the NBA's misappropriation claim based on New York law is preempted.

We vacate the injunction entered by the district court and order that the NBA's claim for misappropriation be dismissed.

## State ex rel. Elvis Presley Intern. Memorial Foundation v. Crowell

Court of Appeals of Tennessee, 1987.
733 S.W.2d 89.

■ KOCH, JUDGE.

This appeal involves a dispute between two not-for-profit corporations concerning their respective rights to use Elvis Presley's name as part of their corporate names. The case began when one corporation filed an unfair competition action in the Chancery Court for Davidson County to dissolve the other corporation and to prevent it from using Elvis Presley's name. Elvis Presley's estate intervened on behalf of the defendant corporation. It asserted that it had given the defendant corporation permission to use Elvis Presley's name and that it had not given similar permission to the plaintiff corporation.

The trial court determined that Elvis Presley's right to control his name and image descended to his estate at his death and that the Presley estate had the right to control the commercial exploitation of Elvis Presley's name and image. Thus, the trial court granted the defendant corporation's motion for summary judgment and dismissed the complaint.

The plaintiff corporation has appealed. Its primary assertion is that there is no descendible right of publicity in Tennessee and that Elvis Presley's name and image entered into the public domain when he died. It also asserts that the trial court should not have granted a summary judgment because there are disputed factual issues and that the trial court should not have permitted the corporation representing Elvis Presley's estate to intervene. We concur with the trial court's determination that Elvis Presley's right of publicity is descendible under Tennessee law. However, for the reasons stated herein, we vacate the summary judgment and remand the case for further proceedings.

Elvis Presley's career is without parallel in the entertainment industry. From his first hit record in 1954 until his death in 1977, he scaled the heights of fame and success that only a few have attained. His twenty-three year career as a recording star, concert entertainer and motion picture idol brought him international recognition and a devoted following in all parts of the nation and the world.

Elvis Presley was aware of this recognition and sought to capitalize on it during his lifetime. He and his business advisors entered into agreements granting exclusive commercial licenses throughout the world to use his name and likeness in connection with the marketing and sale of numerous consumer items. As early as 1956, Elvis Presley's name and likeness could be found on bubble gum cards, clothing, jewelry and numerous other items. The sale of Elvis Presley memorabilia has been described as the greatest barrage of merchandise ever aimed at the teenage set.[1] It earned millions of dollars for Elvis Presley, his licensees and business associates.

Elvis Presley's death on August 16, 1977 did not decrease his popularity. If anything it preserved it. Now Elvis Presley is an entertainment legend, somewhat larger than life, whose memory is carefully preserved by his fans, the media and his estate.

The demand for Elvis Presley merchandise was likewise not diminished by his death. The older memorabilia are now collector's items. New consumer items have been authorized and are now being sold. Elvis Presley Enterprises, Inc., a corporation formed by the Presley estate, has licensed seventy-six products bearing his name and likeness and still controls numerous trademark registrations and copyrights. Graceland, Elvis Presley's home in Memphis, is now a museum that attracts approximately 500,000 paying visitors a year. Elvis Presley Enterprises, Inc. also sells the right to use portions of Elvis Presley's filmed or televised performances. These marketing activities presently bring in approximately fifty million dollars each year and provide the Presley estate with approximately $4.6 million in annual revenue. The commercial exploitation of Elvis Presley's name and likeness continues to be a profitable enterprise. It is against this backdrop that this dispute between these two corporations arose.

A group of Elvis Presley fans approached Shelby County officials sometime in 1979 concerning the formation of a group to support a new trauma center that was part of the Memphis and Shelby County hospital system. This group, calling themselves the Elvis Presley International Memorial Foundation, sought a charter as a Tennessee not-for-profit corporation in October, 1980. The Secretary of State denied their application on November 12, 1980 stating that "[t]he name Elvis Presley cannot be used in the charter."

Lawyers representing the group of fans and the Presley estate met to discuss the group's use of Elvis Presley's name following the Secretary of State's rejection of the charter application. In December, 1980, the Presley estate and its trademark counsel formally declined to give the group the unrestricted right to use Elvis Presley's name and likeness.

---

[1] R. Cranor, Elvis Collectibles 4 (1983).

However, the Presley estate offered the group a royalty-free license to use Elvis Presley's name and likeness if the group agreed to abide by eight conditions limiting the group's activities. The group declined the offer of a royalty-free license.

The Presley estate incorporated Elvis Presley Enterprises, Inc. on February 24, 1981. Two days later on February 26, 1981, the Secretary of State, reversing its original decision, granted the fan group's renewed application and issued a corporate charter to the Elvis Presley International Memorial Foundation (International Foundation). The International Foundation raises funds by charging membership fees and dues and by sponsoring an annual banquet in Memphis. It uses its funds to support the trauma center of the new City of Memphis Hospital which was named after Elvis Presley and to provide an annual award of merit.

The Presley estate and Elvis Presley Enterprises, Inc. incorporated the Elvis Presley Memorial Foundation, Inc. (Foundation) as a Tennessee not-for-profit corporation on May 14, 1985. The Foundation is soliciting funds from the public to construct a fountain in the shopping center across the street from Elvis Presley's home.

The International Foundation's previously amicable relationship with the Presley estate and Elvis Presley Enterprises, Inc. deteriorated after the formation of the Foundation. On July 17, 1985, the International Foundation filed this action seeking to dissolve the Foundation and to enjoin it using a deceptively similar name.

. . .

Elvis Presley's Right of Publicity

We are dealing in this case with an individual's right to capitalize upon the commercial exploitation of his name and likeness and to prevent others from doing so without his consent. This right, now commonly referred to as the right of publicity, is still evolving and is only now beginning to step out of the shadow of its more well known cousin, the right of privacy.

The confusion between the right of privacy and the right of publicity has caused one court to characterize the state of the law as a "haystack in a hurricane." *Ettore v. Philco Television Broadcasting Corp.*, 229 F.2d 481, 485 (3d Cir.1956). This confusion will not retard our recognition of the right of publicity because Tennessee's common law tradition, far from being static, continues to grow and to accommodate the emerging needs of modern society.

A.

The right of privacy owes its origin to Samuel Warren's and Louis Brandeis' now famous 1890 law review article. Warren & Brandeis, *The Right to Privacy*, 4 Harv.L.Rev. 193 (1890). The authors were concerned with the media's intrusion into the affairs of private citizens and wrote this article to vindicate each individual's "right to be left alone." The privacy interest they sought to protect was far different from a celebrity's interest in controlling and exploiting the economic value of his name and likeness.

Writing in 1890, Warren and Brandeis could not have foreseen today's commercial exploitation of celebrities. They did not anticipate the changes that would be brought about by the growth of the advertising, motion picture, television and radio industries. American culture outgrew their concept of the right of privacy and soon began to push the common law to recognize and protect new and different rights and interests.

It would be difficult for any court today, especially one sitting in Music City U.S.A. practically in the shadow of the Grand Ole Opry, to be unaware of the manner in which celebrities exploit the public's recognition of their name and image. The stores selling Elvis Presley tee shirts, Hank Williams, Jr. bandannas or Barbara Mandrell satin jackets are not selling clothing as much as they are selling the celebrities themselves. We are asked to buy the shortening that makes Loretta Lynn's pie crusts flakier or to buy the same insurance that Tennessee Ernie Ford has or to eat the sausage that Jimmy Dean makes.

There are few every day activities that have not been touched by celebrity merchandising. This, of course, should come as no surprise. Celebrity endorsements are extremely valuable in the promotion of goods and services. *Carson v. Here's Johnny Portable Toilets, Inc.,* 698 F.2d 831, 834 (6th Cir.1983). They increase audience appeal and thus make the commodity or service more sellable. *Uhlaender v. Henricksen,* 316 F.Supp. 1277, 1278 (D.Minn.1970). These endorsements are of great economic value to celebrities and are now economic reality.

The first decision to recognize the right of publicity as a right independent from the right of privacy was *Haelan Laboratories, Inc. v. Topps Chewing Gum, Inc.,* 202 F.2d 866 (2d Cir.), *cert. denied,* 346 U.S. 816, 74 S.Ct. 26, 98 L.Ed. 343 (1953). The United States Court of Appeals for the Second Circuit stated:

> This right might be called a "right of publicity." For it is common knowledge that many prominent persons (especially actors and ball-players), far from having their feelings bruised through public exposure of their likenesses, would feel sorely deprived if they no longer received money for authorizing advertisements, popularizing their countenances, displayed in newspapers, magazines, busses, trains and subways. This right of publicity would usually yield them no money unless it could be made the subject of an exclusive grant which barred any other advertiser from using their pictures. *Haelan Laboratories, Inc. v. Topps Chewing Gum, Inc.,* 202 F.2d 866, 868 (2d Cir.1953).

The concept of an independent right of publicity did not achieve immediate recognition. Dean Prosser, in his authoritative discussions of the right of privacy, continued to include the right of publicity as one of the four distinct interests protected by the right of privacy. W. Prosser, *Handbook of the Law of Torts* § 97, at 637 & 639 (2d ed. 1955). In his later writings, Prosser characterized the right of publicity as

> an exclusive right in the individual plaintiff to a species of trade name, his own, and a kind of trade mark in his likeness. It seems quite pointless to dispute over whether such a right is to be classified as "property;" it is at least clearly proprietary in nature. W. Prosser, *Handbook of the Law of Torts,* § 117, at 807 (4th ed. 1971).

See also W. Keeton, *Prosser and Keeton on the Law of Torts* § 117, at 854 (5th ed. 1984).

The Restatement (Second) of Torts adopted Prosser's analytic conception of the scope of the right of privacy. Restatement (Second) of Torts § 652A (1976) embodies his four right of privacy categories. However, the American Law Institute recognized that the nexus between the right of publicity and the other three categories is tenuous. Restatement (Second) of Torts § 652A(2) comm. b (1976). Based upon this difference, the Restatement (Second) of Torts § 652I (1976) recognizes that the right of publicity may be descendible even if the other categories are not.

The legal experts have consistently called for the recognition of the right of publicity as a separate and independent right.[2] In 1977, the United States Supreme Court recognized that the right of publicity was distinct from the right of privacy. *Zacchini v. Scripps-Howard Broadcasting Co.,* 433 U.S. 562, 571–74, 97 S.Ct. 2849, 2855–56, 53 L.Ed.2d 965 (1977). Now, courts in other jurisdictions uniformly hold that the right of publicity should be considered as a free standing right independent from the right of privacy.

### B.

The status of Elvis Presley's right of publicity since his death has been the subject of four proceedings in the Federal courts. The conflicting decisions in these cases mirror the difficulty other courts have experienced in dealing with the right of publicity.

[The court then discussed these four proceedings and observed that all of the courts, with one exception, recognized the descendibility of the right.]

---

[2] Halpern, The Right of Publicity: Commercial Exploitation of the Associative Value of Personality, 39 Vand.L.Rev. 1199, 1249 (1986); Kwall, Is Independence Day Dawning for the Right of Publicity?, 17 U.C.D.L.Rev. 191, 254 (1983); Hoffman, The Right of Publicity-Heirs' Right, Advertisers' Windfall, or Courts' Nightmare, 31 DePaul L.Rev. 1, 44 (1981); Gordon, Right of Property in Name, Likeness, Personality and History, 55 Nw.L.Rev. 553, 611 (1960); and Nimmer, The Right of Publicity, 19 Law & Contemp.Probs. 203, 216 (1954).

## C.

The appellate courts of this State have had little experience with the right of publicity. The Tennessee Supreme Court has never recognized it as part of our common law or has never undertaken to define its scope. However, the recognition of individual property rights is deeply embedded in our jurisprudence. These rights are recognized in Article I, Section 8 of the Tennessee Constitution and have been called "absolute" by the Tennessee Supreme Court. *Stratton Claimants v. Morris Claimants,* 89 Tenn. 497, 513–14, 15 S.W. 87, 90 (1891). This Court has noted that the right of property "has taken deep root in this country and there is now no substantial dissent from it." *Davis v. Mitchell,* 27 Tenn.App. 182, 234–35, 178 S.W.2d 889, 910 (1943).

The concept of the right of property is multi-faceted. It has been described as a bundle of rights or legally protected interests. These rights or interests include: (1) the right of possession, enjoyment and use; (2) the unrestricted right of disposition; and (3) the power of testimonial disposition.

In its broadest sense, property includes all rights that have value. See R. Brown, *The Law of Personal Property* § 1.7, at 11 (3d ed. 1975). It embodies all the interests a person has in land and chattels that are capable of being possessed and controlled to the exclusion of others. *Watkins v. Wyatt,* 68 Tenn. (9 Baxt.) 250, 255 (1877) and *Townsend v. Townsend,* 7 Tenn. (1 Peck) 1, 17 (1821). Chattels include intangible personal property such as choses in action or other enforceable rights of possession.

Our courts have recognized that a person's "business," a corporate name, a trade name and the good will of a business are species of intangible personal property.

Tennessee's common law thus embodies an expansive view of property. Unquestionably, a celebrity's right of publicity has value. It can be possessed and used. It can be assigned, and it can be the subject of a contract. Thus, there is ample basis for this Court to conclude that it is a species of intangible personal property.

## D.

Today there is little dispute that a celebrity's right of publicity has economic value. Courts now agree that while a celebrity is alive, the right of publicity takes on many of the attributes of personal property. It can be possessed and controlled to the exclusion of others. Its economic benefits can be realized and enjoyed. It can also be the subject of a contract and can be assigned to others.

What remains to be decided by the courts in Tennessee is whether a celebrity's right of publicity is descendible at death under Tennessee law. Only the law of this State controls this question. *Hartman v. Duke,* 160 Tenn. 134, 137, 22 S.W.2d 221–22 (1929) and *Jones v. Marable,* 25 Tenn. (6 Humph.) 116, 118 (1845). The only reported opinion holding that

Tennessee law does not recognize a *postmortem* right of publicity is *Memphis Development Foundation v. Factors, Etc., Inc.*, 616 F.2d 956 (6th Cir.), cert. denied, 449 U.S. 953, 101 S.Ct. 358, 66 L.Ed.2d 217 (1980). We have carefully reviewed this opinion and have determined that it is based upon an incorrect construction of Tennessee law and is inconsistent with the better reasoned decisions in this field.

The United States Court of Appeals for the Sixth Circuit appears to believe that there is something inherently wrong with recognizing that the right of publicity is descendible. *Memphis Development Foundation v. Factors, Etc., Inc.*, 616 F.2d 956, 959–60 (6th Cir.1980). We do not share this bias. Like the Supreme Court of Georgia, we recognize that the "trend since the early common law has been to recognize survivability, notwithstanding the legal problems which may thereby arise." *Martin Luther King Center for Social Change, Inc. v. American Heritage Products, Inc.*, 250 Ga. 135, 296 S.E.2d 697, 705 (1982).

We have also concluded that recognizing that the right of publicity is descendible promotes several important policies that are deeply ingrained in Tennessee's jurisprudence. First, it is consistent with our recognition that an individual's right of testamentary distribution is an essential right. If a celebrity's right of publicity is treated as an intangible property right in life, it is no less a property right at death. See *Price v. Hal Roach Studios, Inc.*, 400 F.Supp. 836, 844 (S.D.N.Y.1975).

Second, it recognizes one of the basic principles of Anglo-American jurisprudence that "one may not reap where another has sown nor gather where another has strewn." *M.M. Newcomer Co. v. Newcomer's New Store*, 142 Tenn. 108, 118, 217 S.W. 822, 825 (1919). This unjust enrichment principle argues against granting a windfall to an advertiser who has no colorable claim to a celebrity's interest in the right of publicity.

Third, recognizing that the right of publicity is descendible is consistent with a celebrity's expectation that he is creating a valuable capital asset that will benefit his heirs and assigns after his death. See Kwall, *Is Independence Day Dawning for the Right of Publicity?*, 17 U.C.D.L.Rev. 191, 212–13 (1983). It is now common for celebrities to include their interest in the exploitation of their right of publicity in their estate. While a celebrity's expectation that his heirs will benefit from his right of publicity might not, by itself, provide a basis to recognize that the right of publicity is descendible, it does recognize the effort and financial commitment celebrities make in their careers. This investment deserves no less recognition and protection than investments celebrities might make in the stock market or in other tangible assets.

Fourth, concluding that the right of publicity is descendible recognizes the value of the contract rights of persons who have acquired the right to use a celebrity's name and likeness. The value of this interest stems from its duration and its exclusivity. If a celebrity's name and likeness were to enter the public domain at death, the value of any existing contract made while the celebrity was alive would be greatly diminished.

Fifth, recognizing that the right of publicity can be descendible will further the public's interest in being free from deception with regard to the sponsorship, approval or certification of goods and services. Falsely claiming that a living celebrity endorses a product or service violates Tenn.Code Ann. § 47–18–104(b)(2), (3) and (5). It should likewise be discouraged after a celebrity has died.

Finally, recognizing that the right of publicity can be descendible is consistent with the policy against unfair competition through the use of deceptively similar corporate names.

The legal literature has consistently argued that the right of publicity should be descendible. A majority of the courts considering this question agree. We find this authority convincing and consistent with Tennessee's common law and, therefore, conclude that Elvis Presley's right of publicity survived his death and remains enforceable by his estate and those holding licenses from the estate.[11]

### E.

While Tennessee's courts are capable of defining the parameters of the right of publicity on a case by case basis, the General Assembly also has the prerogative to define the scope of this right. The General Assembly undertook to do so in 1984 when it enacted Tenn.Code Ann. § 47–25–1101 *et seq.* which is known as "The Personal Rights Protection Act of 1984." Tenn.Code Ann. § 47–25–1103(a) recognizes that an individual has "a property right in the use of his name, photograph or likeness in any medium in any manner." Tenn.Code Ann. § 47–25–1103(b) provides that this right is descendible. Tenn.Code Ann. § 47–25–1104(a) & (b)(1) provide that the right is exclusive in the individual or his heirs and assigns until it is terminated. Tenn.Code Ann. § 47–25–1104(b)(2) provides that the right is terminated if it is not used after the individual's death.

Our decision concerning the descendibility of Elvis Presley's right of publicity is not based upon Tenn.Code Ann. § 47–25–1101 *et seq.* but rather upon our recognition of the existence of the common law right of publicity. We note, however, that nothing in Tenn.Code Ann. § 47–25–1101 *et seq.* should be construed to limit vested rights of publicity that were in existence prior to the effective date of the act. To do so would be contrary to Article I, Section 20 of the Tennessee Constitution. A statute cannot be applied retroactively to impair the value of a contract right in existence when the statute was enacted.

---

[11] There is some dispute concerning whether the right of publicity must be exercised while a celebrity is alive in order to render it descendible. We need not decide this question in this case. There is no dispute in this record that Elvis Presley commercially exploited his right of publicity while he was alive.

[In the final part of the opinion, the court vacated the lower court's grant of summary judgment to the defendant on its counter-complaint because genuine issues of material fact existed regarding plaintiff's laches defense to defendant's counter-complaint.]

## White v. Samsung Electronics America, Inc.
United States Court of Appeals, Ninth Circuit, 1993.
989 F.2d 1512, cert. denied, 508 U.S. 951, 113 S.Ct. 2443.

■ KOZINSKI, CIRCUIT JUDGE.*

Something very dangerous is going on here. Private property, including intellectual property, is essential to our way of life. It provides an incentive for investment and innovation; it stimulates the flourishing of our culture; it protects the moral entitlements of people to the fruits of their labors. But reducing too much to private property can be bad medicine. Private land, for instance, is far more useful if separated from other private land by public streets, roads and highways. Public parks, utility rights-of-way and sewers reduce the amount of land in private hands, but vastly enhance the value of the property that remains.

So too it is with intellectual property. Overprotecting intellectual property is as harmful as underprotecting it. Creativity is impossible without a rich public domain. Nothing today, likely nothing since we tamed fire, is genuinely new: Culture, like science and technology, grows by accretion, each new creator building on the works of those who came before. Overprotection stifles the very creative forces it's supposed to nurture.

The panel's opinion is a classic case of overprotection. Concerned about what it sees as a wrong done to Vanna White, the panel majority erects a property right of remarkable and dangerous breadth: Under the majority's opinion, it's now a tort for advertisers to remind the public of a celebrity. Not to use a celebrity's name, voice, signature or likeness; not to imply the celebrity endorses a product; but simply to evoke the celebrity's image in the public's mind. This Orwellian notion withdraws far more from the public domain than prudence and common sense allow. It conflicts with the Copyright Act and the Copyright Clause. It raises serious First Amendment problems. It's bad law, and it deserves a long, hard second look.

Samsung ran an ad campaign promoting its consumer electronics. Each ad depicted a Samsung product and a humorous prediction: One showed a raw steak with the caption "Revealed to be health food. 2010 A.D." Another showed Morton Downey, Jr. in front of an American flag with the caption "Presidential candidate. 2008 A.D." The ads were meant

---

\* Editor's Note: Judge Kozinski's opinion is a dissent from the majority's order rejecting the suggestion for a rehearing en banc. In a prior opinion, the Ninth Circuit held that Samsung violated White's right of publicity. See White v. Samsung Electronics America, Inc., 971 F.2d 1395 (9th Cir. 1992).

to convey, humorously, that Samsung products would still be in use twenty years from now.

The ad that spawned this litigation starred a robot dressed in a wig, gown and jewelry reminiscent of Vanna White's hair and dress; the robot was posed next to a Wheel-of-Fortune-like game board. The caption read "Longest-running game show. 2012 A.D." The gag here, I take it, was that Samsung would still be around when White had been replaced by a robot.

Perhaps failing to see the humor, White sued, alleging Samsung infringed her right of publicity by "appropriating" her "identity." Under California law, White has the exclusive right to use her name, likeness, signature and voice for commercial purposes. Cal.Civ.Code § 3344(a); Eastwood v. Superior Court, 149 Cal.App.3d 409, 417, 198 Cal.Rptr. 342, 347 (1983). But Samsung didn't use her name, voice or signature, and it certainly didn't use her likeness. The ad just wouldn't have been funny had it depicted White or someone who resembled her—the whole joke was that the game show host(ess) was a robot, not a real person. No one seeing the ad could have thought this was supposed to be White in 2012.

The district judge quite reasonably held that, because Samsung didn't use White's name, likeness, voice or signature, it didn't violate her right of publicity. Not so, says the panel majority: The California right of publicity can't possibly be limited to name and likeness. If it were, the majority reasons, a "clever advertising strategist" could avoid using White's name or likeness but nevertheless remind people of her with impunity, "effectively eviscerat[ing]" her rights. To prevent this "evisceration," the panel majority holds that the right of publicity must extend beyond name and likeness, to any "appropriation" of White's "identity"—anything that "evoke[s]" her personality.

But what does "evisceration" mean in intellectual property law? Intellectual property rights aren't like some constitutional rights, absolute guarantees protected against all kinds of interference, subtle as well as blatant. They cast no penumbras, emit no emanations: The very point of intellectual property laws is that they protect only against certain specific kinds of appropriation. I can't publish unauthorized copies of, say, Presumed Innocent; I can't make a movie out of it. But I'm perfectly free to write a book about an idealistic young prosecutor on trial for a crime he didn't commit. So what if I got the idea from Presumed Innocent? All creators draw in part on the work of those who came before, referring to it, building on it, poking fun at it; we call this creativity, not piracy.

The majority isn't, in fact, preventing the "evisceration" of Vanna White's existing rights; it's creating a new and much broader property right, a right unknown in California law. It's replacing the existing balance between the interests of the celebrity and those of the public by a different balance, one substantially more favorable to the celebrity. Instead of having an exclusive right in her name, likeness, signature or voice, every famous person now has an exclusive right to anything that reminds the viewer of her. After all, that's all Samsung did: It used an inanimate object to remind people of White, to "evoke [her identity]." 971 F.2d at 1399.

Consider how sweeping this new right is. What is it about the ad that makes people think of White? It's not the robot's wig, clothes or jewelry; there must be ten million blond women (many of them quasi-famous) who wear dresses and jewelry like White's. It's that the robot is posed near the "Wheel of Fortune" game board. Remove the game board from the ad, and no one would think of Vanna White. But once you include the game board, anybody standing beside it—a brunette woman, a man wearing women's clothes, a monkey in a wig and gown—would evoke White's image, precisely the way the robot did. It's the "Wheel of Fortune" set, not the robot's face or dress or jewelry that evokes White's image. The panel is giving White an exclusive right not in what she looks like or who she is, but in what she does for a living.

This is entirely the wrong place to strike the balance. Intellectual property rights aren't free: They're imposed at the expense of future creators and of the public at large.

This is why intellectual property law is full of careful balances between what's set aside for the owner and what's left in the public domain for the rest of us: The relatively short life of patents; the longer, but finite, life of copyrights; copyright's idea-expression dichotomy; the fair use doctrine; the prohibition on copyrighting facts; the compulsory license of television broadcasts and musical compositions; federal preemption of overbroad state intellectual property laws; the nominative use doctrine in trademark law; the right to make soundalike recordings. All of these diminish an intellectual property owner's rights. All let the public use something created by someone else. But all are necessary to maintain a free environment in which creative genius can flourish.

The intellectual property right created by the panel here has none of these essential limitations: No fair use exception; no right to parody; no idea-expression dichotomy. It impoverishes the public domain, to the detriment of future creators and the public at large. Instead of well-defined, limited characteristics such as name, likeness or voice, advertisers will now have to cope with vague claims of "appropriation of identity," claims often made by people with a wholly exaggerated sense of their own fame and significance. The public will be robbed of parodies of celebrities, and our culture will be deprived of the valuable safety valve that parody and mockery create.

Moreover, consider the moral dimension, about which the panel majority seems to have gotten so exercised. Saying Samsung "appropriated" something of White's begs the question: Should White have the exclusive right to something as broad and amorphous as her "identity"? Samsung's ad didn't simply copy White's schtick—like all parody, it created something new. Why is Vanna White's right to exclusive for-profit use of her persona—a persona that might not even be her own creation, but that of a writer, director or producer—superior to Samsung's right to profit by creating its own inventions?

To paraphrase only slightly Feist Publications, Inc. v. Rural Telephone Service Co., 499 U.S. 340, 111 S.Ct. 1282, 1289–90, 113 L.Ed.2d 358 (1991), it may seem unfair that much of the fruit of a creator's labor may be used by others without compensation. But this is not some unforeseen byproduct of our intellectual property system; it is the system's very essence. Intellectual property law assures authors the right to their original expression, but encourages others to build freely on the ideas that underlie it. This result is neither unfair nor unfortunate: It is the means by which intellectual property law advances the progress of science and art. We give authors certain exclusive rights, but in exchange we get a richer public domain. The majority ignores this wise teaching, and all of us are the poorer for it.

Finally, I can't see how giving White the power to keep others from evoking her image in the public's mind can be squared with the First Amendment. Where does White get this right to control our thoughts? The majority's creation goes way beyond the protection given a trademark or a copyrighted work, or a person's name or likeness. All those things control one particular way of expressing an idea, one way of referring to an object or a person. But not allowing any means of reminding people of someone? That's a speech restriction unparalleled in First Amendment law.

What's more, I doubt even a name-and-likeness-only right of publicity can stand without a parody exception. The First Amendment isn't just about religion or politics—it's also about protecting the free development of our national culture. Parody, humor, irreverence are all vital components of the marketplace of ideas. The last thing we need, the last thing the First Amendment will tolerate, is a law that lets public figures keep people from mocking them, or from "evok[ing]" their images in the mind of the public. 971 F.2d at 1399.

The majority dismisses the First Amendment issue out of hand because Samsung's ad was commercial speech. So what? Commercial speech may be less protected by the First Amendment than noncommercial speech, but less protected means protected nonetheless. Central Hudson Gas & Elec. Corp. v. Public Serv. Comm'n, 447 U.S. 557, 100 S.Ct. 2343, 65 L.Ed.2d 341 (1980). And there are very good reasons for this. Commercial speech has a profound effect on our culture and our attitudes.

In our pop culture, where salesmanship must be entertaining and entertainment must sell, the line between the commercial and noncommercial has not merely blurred; it has disappeared. Is the Samsung parody any different from a parody on Saturday Night Live or in Spy Magazine? Both are equally profit-motivated. Both use a celebrity's identity to sell things—one to sell VCRs, the other to sell advertising. Both mock their subjects. Both try to make people laugh.

Both add something, perhaps something worthwhile and memorable, perhaps not, to our culture. Both are things that the people being portrayed might dearly want to suppress.

For better or worse, we are the Court of Appeals for the Hollywood Circuit. Millions of people toil in the shadow of the law we make, and much of their livelihood is made possible by the existence of intellectual property rights. But much of their livelihood—and much of the vibrancy of our culture—also depends on the existence of other intangible rights: The right to draw ideas from a rich and varied public domain, and the right to mock, for profit as well as fun, the cultural icons of our time.

## NOTES

1. *Marital property.* The Principal Problem raises the issue of how an individual's right of publicity should be treated upon divorce. At what point in time was Sterling's right of publicity acquired? Should this matter?

Most courts hold that professional degrees and licenses should not be divided as marital property (see Assignment 17).[1] Some courts are not inclined to treat a professional degree or license as property because of the problems triggered by attempts to value this asset. Can you think of any reasons why the right of publicity should be treated as marital property subject to division even if professional degrees and licenses are not so treated? Note that the valuation issue is raised in the Principal Problem. How can the right of publicity be valued if it were to be divided as marital property?

2. *Right of publicity: manner of protection; descendibility and duration.* About thirty-eight states have recognized the right of publicity, and in at least twenty-two of these states, legislation exists that governs this area either partially or completely.[2] Many of these statutes also recognize that the right against commercial exploitation of an individual's name or

---

[1] See, e.g., Gaskill v. Robbins, 282 S.W.3d 306 (Ky. 2009) (reasoning that professional degrees are not marital property because they are personal to the holder and have no value on an open market); Shively v. Shively, 233 S.W.3d 738 (Ky. App. 2007) (professional degrees are not marital property; however, they may be considered an asset of an individual party when the court divides the marital property); Solomon v. Solomon, 857 A.2d 1109 (Md. 2004) (noting that while some intangible assets may be considered marital property, professional degrees are not marital assets because they only relate to a speculative expectancy of future earnings). But see Guskin v. Guskin, 18 A.D.3d 814, 815 (N.Y. 2005) ("The enhanced earning capacity due to acquisition of a professional license during marriage is clearly a marital asset subject to equitable distribution."); Elkus v. Elkus, 169 A.D.2d 134 (N.Y. App. Div. 1991) (finding that a career as a performing artist and its accompanying celebrity status can constitute marital property).

[2] See, e.g., Ala. Code § 6-5-772 (2016); Ariz. Rev. Stat. § 12-761 (2016); Cal. Civ. Code § 3344 (West 2016); Fla. Stat. Ann. § 540.08 (West 2016); 765 Ill. Comp. Stat. Ann. § 1075/1 (West 2016); Ind. Code § 32-36-1 (Burns 2016); M.G.L.A. 214 § 3A (2016); Neb. Rev. Stat. §§ 20-202 to 211 (2016); Nev. Rev. Stat. Ann. §§ 597.770-.810 (2015); Ohio Rev. Code Ann. § 2741 (Page 2015); Okla. Stat. tit. 12, § 1448 (Lexis 2016); (2016); R.I. Gen. Laws § 9-1-28 (2016); Tenn. Code Ann. §§ 47-25-1101 to -1108 (2015); Tex. Prop. Code Ann. §§ 26.001-.015 (West 2015); Utah Code Ann. §§ 45-3-1 to -6 (2016); Va. Code Ann. § 8.01-40 (2016); Wash. Rev. Code Ann. §§ 63.60.010-63.60.080 (2016); Wis. Stat. Ann. § 995.50 (West 2015). In addition, the New York privacy statute addresses some aspects of the right of publicity. N.Y. Civ. Rights Law §§ 50-51 (2016).

likeness is descendible.[3] In other jurisdictions the right of publicity is descendible as a matter of common law.[4] Only a few states have explicitly refused to recognize a postmortem right of publicity.[5]

Some jurisdictions make the unauthorized appropriation of protected attributes actionable under the statutory right of privacy.[6] In New York, for example, the courts have held that the state's privacy law, which does protect against the unauthorized use of a person's name or likeness for purposes of trade, precludes a cause of action under state common law right of publicity.[7] Moreover, relatives of a decedent are precluded from suing under that statute since the right of privacy is held to be personal in nature.[8] The Virginia privacy statute specifically provides relief to the relatives of a decedent whose name or likeness is appropriated for commercial purposes,[9] while the Wisconsin privacy statute specifically limits the ability to recover for the unauthorized commercial use of protected attributes to "living" people.[10] Thus, the manner in which the right of publicity is protected and the descendibility and durational issues are subject to a complete lack of uniformity, which can be problematic for lawyers attempting to advise clients interested in the extent of protection afforded on a national basis.

---

[3] In Ohio, postmortem statutory protection is granted for sixty years after death. In California, Illinois, Nevada, Texas, statutory protection is granted for fifty years following a person's death. Kentucky also provides for fifty years of protection following death, but only for public figures. Florida allows protection for forty years after a person's death, but the common law right to privacy in Florida terminates with death. In the state of Washington, if the person's identity has "commercial value" then the postmortem duration lasts for seventy-five years; if not, it lasts for ten years. The Pennsylvania statute allows for thirty years of protection following death. The Virginia statute allows for twenty years of protection following death. The Tennessee statute provides for an initial ten year period following the individual's death. The right is then terminated by proof of non-use for a period of two years. Oklahoma and Indiana grant protection for 100 years following a person's death. There is no duration for Massachusetts and Nebraska.

[4] See Gignilliat v. Gignilliat, Savitz & Bettis, L.L.P., 684 S.E.2d 756 (S.C. 2009) (holding that South Carolina's common law right of publicity is transferable, assignable, and survives the death of the named individual). As noted by the court in The Elvis Presley Int'l Memorial Found., supra at footnote 3, there is some dispute regarding whether the right of publicity is descendible if the decedent did not commercially exploit the right while alive. For a general discussion of the descendibility issue and the various positions taken by courts, see Drennan, Wills, Trusts, Schadenfreude, and the Wild, Wacky Right of Publicity: Exploring the Enforceability of Dead-Hand Restrictions, 58 Ark. L. Rev. 43 (2005).

[5] See, e.g., Wis. Stat. 995.50(2)(b) (West 2015); Hagen v. Dahmer, 38 U.S.P.Q.2d 1146 (E.D.Wis. 1995); Stephano v. News Group Publications, Inc., 64 N.Y.2d 174 (1984).

[6] Nebraska, Virginia, New York and Wisconsin take this approach.

[7] See, e.g., Ryan v. Volpone Stamp Co., 107 F. Supp. 2d 369 (S.D.N.Y. 2000) (noting that state courts have interpreted N.Y. Civ. Rights Law §§ 50 & 51 as superseding any common law right of publicity).

[8] See Pirone v. MacMillan, Inc., 894 F.2d 579 (2d Cir. 1990) (daughters of Babe Ruth could not bring action under state privacy law). There has been some discussion of codifying the right of publicity in New York. For a somewhat dated discussion of this movement, see Burnett, The Property Right of Publicity and the First Amendment: Popular Culture and the Commercial Persona, 3 Hofstra Prop. L.J. 171, 186 (1990). For a recent argument in favor of the movement towards codification in New York, see Note, Protecting a Celebrity's Legacy: Living in California or New York Becomes the Deciding Factor, 3 J. Bus. Entrepreneurship & L. 165 (2009).

[9] Va. Code Ann. § 8.01–40. The Nebraska privacy statute also allows an action for the unauthorized exploitation of a person's name or likeness to survive that person's death. See Neb. Rev. Stat. §§ 20–202, 20–208 (2016).

[10] Wis. Stat. Ann. § 995.50 (2)(b) (West 2015).

This situation is most difficult when the clients are relatives of a deceased individual whose publicity rights have been appropriated.[11]

3. *Right of publicity: rationales, attributes, and scope of protection.* What are the rationales that support protection for the right of publicity? Do you find these rationales a convincing explanation for the doctrine's existence? What is the danger of too expansive an interpretation of the right of publicity?

Does everyone have a right of publicity or only celebrities? What standard can be used to determine which attributes are properly protected under the right of publicity? In Carson v. Here's Johnny Portable Toilets, Inc.,[12] the Sixth Circuit held that a portable toilet manufacturer violated Johnny Carson's right of publicity when it used the phrase "Here's Johnny" in conjunction with the slogan, "The World's Foremost Commodian."[13] In so holding, the court observed that "a celebrity's legal right of publicity is invaded whenever his identity is intentionally appropriated for commercial purposes."[14] Other courts have approved equally expansive applications of the right of publicity by holding that it protects aspects of an individual's identity such as a voice,[15] nickname,[16] professional statistical information,[17] and a distinctive racing car.[18]

4. *Right of publicity and the First Amendment.* In Zacchini v. Scripps-Howard Broadcasting Co.,[19] the Supreme Court explicitly considered the interplay between the right of publicity and the First Amendment. *Zacchini* involved a television station's broadcast of the plaintiff's entire human cannonball act, without consent, on its nighttime newscast. The Court in *Zacchini* observed that had the television station "merely reported that the petitioner was performing at the fair and described or commented on his act, with or without showing his picture on television, we would have a very different case."[20] But the defendant's filming and display of the plaintiff's circus act went way beyond the reporting of a newsworthy event. As such, the defendant's use was not in keeping with a purely informational purpose,

---

[11] For a discussion on why a decedent's family should be able to bring a cause of action for the misappropriation of the decedent's right of publicity, see William Binder, *Publicity Rights and Defamation of the Deceased: Resurrection or R.I.P.?*, 12 DePaul-LCA J. Art. & Ent. L. 297 (2002).

[12] 698 F.2d 831 (6th Cir.1983).

[13] Id. at 837.

[14] Id.

[15] Midler v. Ford Motor Co., 849 F.2d 460 (9th Cir.1988); Waits v. Frito-Lay Inc., 978 F.2d 1093, 1098 (9th Cir.1992), *cert. denied*, 506 U.S. 1080 (1993).

[16] Hirsch v. S.C. Johnson & Son, 280 N.W.2d 129 (Wis.1979) (prominent athlete had right of publicity in his nickname "Crazylegs" and could bring an action against manufacturer for commercial misappropriation of his nickname on a shaving gel).

[17] Uhlaender v. Henricksen, 316 F.Supp. 1277 (D.Minn.1970) (baseball table game manufacturer violated baseball players' rights of publicity by the unauthorized appropriation of their names and playing statistics for commercial use).

[18] Motschenbacher v. R.J. Reynolds Tobacco Co., 498 F.2d 821 (9th Cir.1974) (in case involving television commercial featuring the unique and distinctive decorations of plaintiff's racing car, court held that California law protected an individual's proprietary interest in his identity).

[19] 433 U.S. 562 (1977).

[20] Id. at 569.

and this situation resulted in a great degree of unjust enrichment. Of course, the challenge remains of determining where "the line in particular situations is to be drawn between media reports that are protected and those that are not."[21]

The conflict between the right of publicity and the First Amendment will likely provide a fertile source of litigation for the foreseeable future. Following the decision in *Zacchini*, courts created a number of tests for resolving these disputes.[22] The primary approaches used by courts to resolve the conflict between the right of publicity and the First Amendment are: (1) the transformative use test;[23] (2) the predominant purpose test;[24] (3) an actual malice standard;[25] (4) the relatedness test;[26] and (5) a general ad hoc balancing approach.[27] Problematically, no single test has been accepted by a majority of courts; furthermore, the outcome of cases in which these tests are applied will often turn on very specific factual distinctions. An additional criticism of these tests is that they fail to take into account the dignity harm that individuals may suffer due to unauthorized appropriation of their name or likeness.[28]

State statutes that circumscribe the right of publicity when it conflicts with the First Amendment exist in several states such as California, Illinois, Indiana, Nebraska, Nevada, Ohio, Oklahoma, Tennessee, Texas, and Wisconsin.[29] The statutes in California, Nevada and Tennessee provide that it should be a question of fact whether a defendant's use of a plaintiff's protected attribute was sufficiently connected with commercial sponsorship so as to constitute a prohibited use. In general, however, the statutory

---

[21] Id. at 574–75.

[22] For a discussion of the various tests utilized by the courts and the limitations of these tests, see Kwall, A Perspective on Human Dignity, the First Amendment and the Right of Publicity, 50 B.C. L. Rev. 1345 (2009).

[23] See, e.g., Hilton v. Hallmark Cards, 599 F.3d 894 (9th Cir. 2010) (allowing plaintiff's right of publicity action to proceed; defendant's Hallmark cards, depicting plaintiff's image and catch-phrase, were not sufficiently transformative to afford defendant a First Amendment defense as a matter of law).

[24] See, e.g., Doe v. TCI Cablevision, 110 S.W.3d 363, 374 (Mo. 2003) ("[I]f a product is being sold that predominantly exploits the commercial value of an individual's identity, that product should be held to violate the right of publicity and not be protected by the First Amendment, even if there is some 'expressive' content in it that might qualify as 'speech' in other circumstances.")

[25] See, e.g., Hoffman v. Capital Cities/ABC, Inc., 255 F.3d 1180 (9th Cir. 2001) (requiring clear and convincing evidence that the party who infringed upon another individual's right of publicity did so with actual malice).

[26] The relatedness test was first proposed by the Restatement (Third) of Unfair Competition § 47 cmt. c (1995). This test provides First Amendment protection for the use of an individual's name or likeness in a work that is somehow related to that individual.

[27] See, e.g., ETW Corp. v. Jireh Publishing, Inc., 332 F.3d 915 (6th Cir. 2003) (applying an ad hoc balancing test based on elements from the various other tests and holding that a sports artist's print commemorating Tiger Woods' victory at the 1997 Masters Tournament was entitled to First Amendment protection).

[28] See, e.g., Kwall, A Perspective on Human Dignity, the First Amendment and the Right of Publicity, 50 B.C. L. Rev. 1345, 1359–66 (2009).

[29] See, e.g., Cal. Civ. Code § 3344 (d)–(f); 765 Ill. Comp. Stat. Ann. § 1075/35(b); Ind. Code § 32–13–1; Neb. Rev. Stat. §§ 20–202 (1); Nev. Rev. Stat. § 597.790 (2)(a)–(e); Ohio Rev. Code Ann. § 2741.09; Okla. Stat. Ann. tit. 12 § 1449 (D), (E); Tenn. Code Ann. § 47–25–1107; Tex. Prop. Code Ann. § 26.012; and Wis. Stat. § 995.50(3).

formulations tend to be too inflexible to solve the problem. How should the potential for conflict between the right of publicity and the First Amendment be addressed? Is the right of publicity vs. the First Amendment conflict stronger in the Principal Problem or in *Samsung*? How would you resolve the Problem? If you conclude that a right of publicity violation exists under the facts of the Problem, what type of relief would you recommend?

5. *Information as property*. *Feist* illustrates that general information is not copyrightable and therefore not protectable under that regime. In *Motorola*, the district court treated information as property but the Second Circuit disagreed. In the court's view, states are preempted from protecting information contained in a copyrighted work, such as the broadcasts at issue, under a state-based misappropriation cause of action. Section 301(a) of the 1976 Copyright Act provides that states are preempted from protecting rights equivalent to copyright. In order to decide what constitutes an equivalent, and therefore preempted, right it is necessary to look at the rights protected under copyright law. As discussed in the Introduction to this Assignment, these include: the right to reproduce, distribute, create a new work based upon the copyrighted work, and publicly display and perform the copyrighted work. Therefore, if a state-based cause of action is attempting to do no more than proscribe these activities with respect to a copyrighted work, it will be preempted.

*Motorola* did recognize, however, that state protection under misappropriation still is appropriate for certain time-sensitive information. What theory underlies this exemption? The Principal Problem raises the issue whether personal information should be viewed as property. Does an individual have a property interest in her credit rating, social security number, salary, medical history, and other personal information? What would be the basis of recognizing this information as property? Is there a stronger interest in protecting personal information than general information? Should the law accord the same degree of protection to personal information as it does to one's name, likeness and persona? Why or why not?

> Extending this inquiry even further, should individuals be able to assert a property interest in their body parts? In Moore v. Regents of the University of California,[30] the Supreme Court of California grappled with an action by a patient against a doctor, a university and others based on the defendants' patenting of a cell line from the plaintiff's white blood cells. The court held that although the plaintiff had a cause of action for breach of fiduciary duty and lack of informed consent, he could not maintain an action for conversion. In so holding, the court essentially rejected the argument of an ownership interest in extracorporeal body parts. Should the extracorporeal nature of the cells in *Moore* be determinative?

---

[30] 793 P.2d 479 (Cal. 1990), *cert. denied*, 499 U.S. 936 (1991).

# INDEX

References are to Pages

**ADVERSE POSSESSION**
Adverse nature of, 934–935
Agreed boundaries, doctrine of, 976–977
California statutes concerning, 972–973
Claim of right concerning, 946–947
Constructive possession, 934–935
Continuity, requirement of, 960–970
Co-tenants, 947
Elements of, 929
Exclusivity, requirement of, 950–951, 958
Hostility, requirement of, 946–947
Introduction, 929–932
Non-possessory interests in land, 973–977
    Common-law dedication, 974–975
    Custom, 974–975
    Prescriptive easement, 973–974
Open, exclusive, and continuous, requirements of, 951–968
Possession under claim of right, 934–935
Possession under color of title, 935
Tacking, concept of, 969
Tax requirement, 947
Tolling the statute, 972

**ALIENATION, RESTRAINTS ON**
See Restraints on Alienation

**COMMON INTEREST COMMUNITIES**
    Generally, 587–605
Termination of, 605

**CONCURRENT ESTATES**
Administration, 323
Creation of, 306–307
Community property, 304–305
Joint tenancy, 303
    Disfavored by law, 320
    Four unities, 306
    Severance, 337
Ouster, doctrine of, 334
Partitioning, 305–306
Right of survivorship, 303, 319
Tenancy by the entirety, 304
Tenancy in common, 303
Use of strawman, 306–307

**CONSTITUTIONAL LIMITS ON REGULATORY POWER**
See Land Use Controls

**CONTRACTS FOR THE SALE OF REAL ESTATE**
California Civil Code, 1104–1105
Damages, 1091–1105
    Unconscionability of, 1105
    Underliquidated vs. overliquidated, 1105
Installment sale contract, 1091
Marketing contract, 1091
Remedies for breach of, 1091–1118

Damages, 1091–1105
Specific performance, 1106–1118
Uniform Land Transactions Act, application of, 1105

**COPYRIGHT LAW**
Copyright ownership, 1407–1408
Infringement and fair use, 1408–1410, 1427
International considerations, 1410
Introduction, 1405–1410
Obtaining copyright protection, 1405–1407
Originality requirement, 1408, 1414–1415, 1434–1435
Remedies, 1432–1433, 1436–1437

**COVENANTS**
Affirmative, 498–499
Creation and validity, 497–521
Defenses to, 567–585
Equitable servitudes, 498–499, 545
Federal Fair Housing Act, 521
Implied covenants and promises, 504–506
In gross, 499–500
Intent, 524, 542, 545–546
Negative, 498–499
Notice, 524–525, 546
Requirement of privity, 510, 540
    Horizontal, 533–535, 564
    Vertical, 529–533, 564–565
Running of benefit, 523–535
Running of burden, 523–535
The new Restatement, 526–527, 530–535
Touch and concern, 525–529, 539, 545
Unreasonable covenants, 520–521

**COVENANTS OF TITLE**
California Civil Code, 1174–1175
Covenant against encumbrances, 1170–1171
Covenant for further assurances, 1171–1172
Covenant of quiet enjoyment, 1171
Covenant of right to convey, 1171
Covenant of seisin, 1170–1171
Covenant of warranty, 1171
Future covenants, 1172–1173, 1185–1186
Introduction, 1169–1176
New Jersey Statutes Annotated, 1175
Present covenants, 1172, 1186
Uniform Land Transactions Act, application of, 1192

**DAMAGES**
See Landlord and Tenant

**DEED DESCRIPTIONS**
Introduction, 1011–1015
Methods of describing land, 1015–1031

**DEEDS**
Full warranty, 1169
Kinds of, 1169
Special warranty, 1169, 1174

**DEEDS, DELIVERY OF**
Death escrows, 1044–1052
Introduction, 1033–1034
Manual delivery, 1033

**DEEDS OF TRUST**
See Mortgages

**DELIVERY**
See Deeds, Delivery of

**DESCRIPTION OF LAND**
See Deed Descriptions

**EASEMENTS**
Affirmative, 375–376
Appurtenant, 375–376
Conservation, 377–380, 407–408, 451–452
Exceptions, 397
Express, 380–474
    Classification of, 403–404
    Creation of, 380
    Extent of use, 403–405, 422
    Interpretation and extent of, 401–422
    Repair and maintenance of, 406
    Succession of, 423–443
    Termination and extinguishment, 445–474
In gross, 376–377
Negative, 375–376
Non-Express, 475–496
    By necessity, 479–483
    Implied from a map or boundary reference, 495–496
    Implied from prior use, 476–479
    Introduction, 475–476
Reservation of, 397
Stranger-to-the-deed, 397–398
Termination of, 445
    Chart, 453
    Introduction, 445–453
Uniform Simplification of Land Transfer Act, 399

**EMINENT DOMAIN**
Blight, 642–648, 654–658, 661–662
Economic development, 642–661
Federal constitutional standards, 637, 638–642, 648–658
Homes and personhood theory, 662–663
Just compensation, 637, 661, 662–663, 697–699
Public use, 637–663
State constitutional standards and legislation, 637, 642–648, 659–661
Takings, see Takings
Tragedy of the anti-commons, 661–662
Typical practice, 661

**ENVIRONMENTAL ISSUES**
Anti-wilderness bias of adverse possession, 971–972
Climate change, 452, 607–609, 838, 849, 897–899
Conservation easements, see Easements
Ecosystem services, 279–280, 608, 916–927, 971
Environmental ethics, 904–908, 925–926
Environmental justice, 607, 658, 666, 773–777, 1356
Environmentally sensitive lands, 377–380, 451–452, 666, 672, 730–753, 835–836, 891–927
Future generations and natural resources, 279–280, 451–452
Land trusts, see Land Trusts
Nuisance and environmental impacts, 607–609, 854, 908–925
Open mine doctrine, 278–279
Pollution, 607–609, 613–629, 843–844, 892–904, 1335–1357
Public trust doctrine, see Public Trust Doctrine
Social forces and movements and limits of law, 889–890
Solar energy, 609–610, 629–636
Toxic wastes, see Toxic Wastes
Water and environmental conservation, 835–850, 866–890, 892–899

**EQUITABLE CONVERSION**
In general, 1281–1303
Uniform Land Transfer Act, 1302
Uniform Vendor and Purchaser Risk Act, 1282–1283

**EQUITABLE SERVITUDES**
See Covenants

**ESTATES IN LAND**
Chart of freehold estates, 194–195
Class gifts, 205–206, 225–228
Defeasible fees, 197–200
Equitable distinguished from legal estate, 208–209
Executory interests, 206–207
Fee simple absolute, 195–196
Fee simple determinable, 197–198
Fee simple subject to condition subsequent, 198–200
Future interests, 200–209
Introduction, 191–194
Life estates, 200–207
    Open mine doctrine, 278
    Principal and income, 261–262
    Waste, 279–280
Possibility of reverter, 197
Power of termination, 192–193
Present estates, 194–200
Remainders, 200–207
Reversions, 201
Rule against perpetuities, 217–259
Uniform Statutory Rule Against Perpetuities, 239–243
Waste, doctrine of, 261–280

**EXPRESS EASEMENTS**
See Easements

## FEE SIMPLE ABSOLUTE
See Estates in Land

## FORECLOSURE
Debtor's right to redeem, 1127–1128
Effects of priority, 1130–1131
Judicial foreclosure, 1168
Limiting the equity of redemption, 1128
Restrictions on deficiency judgments, 1127
Statutory redemption, 1129

## IMPLIED WARRANTY OF FITNESS IN THE SALE OF REAL ESTATE
Doctrine of merger, 1305–1307
Economic loss, 1316–1317
Introduction, 1305–1310
Lender liability, 1332
Property loss, 1331–1332

## INCOME TAX
Deductions, 1271–1272
Exclusions, 1271
Gains from dealings in property, 1270–1271
Gross income, 1269–1270
Home buyer, income tax issues affecting, 1273–1274
Home seller, income tax issues affecting, 1276–1279
Sources of Federal tax law, 1267–1268
Taxable income, 1269–1270

## INVERSE CONDEMNATION
See Land Use Controls

## JOINT TENANCY
See Concurrent Estates

## LAND TRUSTS
Generally, 377–380, 451–452, 1118

## LAND USE CONTROLS
Brownfields redevelopment, 1354–1357
Cumulative v. noncumulative zoning, 679
Environmental regulation, 666, 672, 730–753, 891–927
Exclusionary zoning, 666, 669, 773–807
Generally, 665–672
Growth controls, 744–753, 802–804
Land use regulatory system and its functions, 665–668
Limits on land use regulation, 665–834
    Disability law and rights, 791–798, 806–807
    Due process (substantive and procedural), 665, 674–680, 753–754, 816, 831–832
    Equal protection, 665, 778–791, 798–801, 816, 830–831
    Religious exercise rights, 665, 809–834
    Takings, see Takings
Nuisance as a land use control, 607–636, 676, 678, 911–912, 915–925
Permits (including conditional use permits, variances, subdivision maps, and the substantial evidence test), 670–671, 691–695, 758–771, 786–791, 900–904
Planning, 669–670, 674–680, 744, 750
Police power, 665, 674–680
Vested rights, 680–691
Zoning (including Euclidean, advanced, flexible, negotiated), 668–669, 671–672, 674–680, 778–785, 819–832, 900–904
Zoning estoppel (equitable estoppel), 680–691

## LANDLORD AND TENANT
Abandonment, wrongful, 169
Actual partial eviction, 53–54
Assignments and subleases, 143–168
Choice of remedies, 64
Constructive eviction, 84–85
Covenant of quiet enjoyment, 52–53
Damages, duty to mitigate, 169–170
Fair Housing Act, 132
Habitability, implied covenant of, 63–64
    Remedies, 64
Holdover tenant, 91
Landlord's duties, 63–64
Landlord's motives in removing tenants, 117–141
Landlord's tort liability, 93–116
Leases and licenses, 43–52
Periodic tenancy, 90
Physical possession, 43–62
Possession at start of term, 52–53
Rent abatement, 64
Repair, implied covenant to, 63–64
Repair and deduct remedy, 87
Retaliatory eviction, 117–118
Subleases, 138
Surrender, doctrine of, 169
Tenancy at sufferance, 91
Tenancy at will, 90–91
Tenancy for years, 90
Tenant's remedies, 64

## MARITAL PROPERTY
California Family Code, 367–370
Common law property jurisdictions, 351–354
Community property jurisdictions, 350–351
Curtesy, 349
Dower, 349
Human capital, 353–372
Introduction, 349–350

## MARKETABILITY OF TITLE
Failure of, 1073
Introduction, 1073–1074
Uniform Land Transactions Act, application of, 1089–1090
Uniform Simplification of Land Transfers Act, application of, 1090

## MORTGAGES
Concept of a security, 1126
Deed of trust compared, 1120
Definition, 1120

Loan note, 1124
Loan process, 1121–1124
Mortgage equivalents, 1124–1125
Priority, 1125–1126
Secondary mortgage markets, 1131–1133
Subprime mortgage crisis, 1131

**NON-POSSESSORY ESTATES**
Generally, 373–927

**NUISANCE**
Generally, 607–636, 676, 678–679, 734–736, 911–912, 915–925

**POSSESSION**
Adverse possession, see Adverse Possession
Bailments, 930
Conquest and discovery, 931
Covenant of seisin, 1170
Dispossession of Spanish and Mexican land grantees, 931
Finders, 930
Leaseholds, 43–61
Possession as origin of property, 930
Possession during statutory redemption period, 1129
Possessory takings, see Takings, physical or possessory takings
Rule of capture, see Rule of Capture

**PRINCIPAL AND INCOME**
Uniform Principal and Income Act, 261–262

**PUBLIC TRUST**
Adverse possession of public trust lands, 970–971
Environmental trust concept, 279–280
Generally (including elements, scope, duties), 846–848, 868–890
Land use controls and takings, 755, 903–904, 912–914
Water rights, 868–890

**QUIT CLAIM DEED**
Generally, 1169–1170, 1173–1174

**REAL ESTATE BROKERS**
Commission, 1054–1056, 1071–1072
Duties, 1056–1057
  To buyer, 1056–1057
  To seller, 1056
Introduction, 1053–1057
Listing Agreements, generally 1053–1054

**REAL ESTATE MARKETING CONTRACT**
See Marketability of Title

**REAL ESTATE SALE CONTRACTS**
See Contracts for the Sale of Real Estate

**REAL PROPERTY FINANCE**
See Mortgages

**RECORDING STATUTES**
Adverse possession and, 1203–1204
California Civil Code, 1201–1202
Chain of title, 1196–1197
Common-law rule, 1194
Estoppel by deed, 1232
Grantor-grantee index, 1195–1196
Inquiry notice, 1228
Kinds of statutes, 1199
  Notice, 1200–1201
  Notice/race, 1200–1201
  Race, 1199–1200
Massachusetts, 1200–1201
New York Real Property Law, 1201
North Carolina, 1200
Notice v. knowledge, 1206–1207
Off record notice, 1206–1207
Process of recordation, 1195
Registration of titles, 1207–1208
Tract index, 1195

**RESTRAINTS ON ALIENATION**
Due on sale clause, 299–300
Disabling restraints, 281
Introduction, 281

**RIGHT TO EXCLUDE**
Fee owner's, 1–41
Generally, 1–24
Intangible property, 25
Introduction, 1–2
Tenant's, 43–62

**RIGHT OF PUBLICITY**
Introduction, 1439
First Amendment, 1462–1464
  Generally, 1439–1464
Manner of protection; descendibility and duration, 1460–1462
Rationales, attitudes and scope of protection, 1462–1463

**RULE AGAINST PERPETUITIES**
Basic concepts, 217–232
Gray, statement of rule, 219–220
Modern developments, 239–259
Wait and see doctrine, 239

**RULE OF CAPTURE**
Generally, 865, 929–931
Groundwater, 842, 853–867

**SERVITUDES**
See Covenants; Easements

**STATUTE OF FRAUDS**
California Civil Code, 980
New York General Obligations Law, 980–981
Texas Civil Statute, 981
Uniform Land Transactions Act, 989–990

**TAKINGS**
Development exactions and takings, 698, 757–771
Elements and categories, 697–698
Eminent domain, see Eminent Domain
Inverse condemnation, 756–757, 908
Judicial takings, 755–756, 849–850
Just compensation, 637, 661, 662–663, 697–698, 756–757

Physical or possessory takings, 698, 699–714
Regulatory takings, 698, 714–757, 900–918, 926–927
Ripeness, 698–699
Substantive due process and takings, 753–754
Takings Clause, 637, 665, 697

**TENANCY BY THE ENTIRETY**
See Concurrent Estates

**TENANCY IN COMMON**
See Concurrent Estates

**TITLE INSURANCE**
Introduction, 1235–1238
Lawyer's role concerning, 1238
Sample policy, 1239–1256
Services ancillary to insurance, 1236
Title searches, 1236

**TOXIC WASTES**
CERCLA, 1335–1338, 1353, 1357
Defenses, 1346–1352
Introduction, 1335–1338
Liability of lenders, 1353

**TRADEMARK LAW**
Abandonment, 1368
Distinctiveness requirements, 1367
Infringement and fair use, 1367–1368
International considerations, 1368–1370
Introduction, 1359–1370
Obtaining trademark protection, 1359–1367
Use requirements, 1367

**TRESPASS**
Real property, to, 2
Chattels, to, 2, 14, 22–23
Electronic message, by, 14
Exceptions, 12

**TRUST DEEDS**
See Mortgages

**UNIFORM LAND TRANSACTIONS ACT**
Contracts for the sale of real estate, breach of, 1105
Covenants of title, 1191
Marketability of title, 1089
Requirement of writing, 1008–1009

**UNIFORM LAND TRANSFER ACT**
Generally, 1302–1303

**UNIFORM SIMPLIFICATION OF LAND TRANSFERS ACT**
Marketability of title, 1090
Recordation and, 1204
Requirement of writing, 989–990

**UNIFORM STATUTORY RULE AGAINST PERPETUITIES**
Generally, 239–243

**UNIFORM VENDOR AND PURCHASER RISK ACT**
Generally, 1282–1283

**WATER RIGHTS**
Environmental issues and conservation, see Environmental Issues
Federal, state, and public interests in water, 844–848
Groundwater, 842–843, 853–867, 876–888
Hybrid states, 842
Prior appropriation (including western permit systems), 839–841
Public trust doctrine, see Public Trust
Riparianism (including regulated riparianism), 836–839
Rule of capture, see Rule of Capture
State ownership doctrine, 844–845, 845–846
Takings, see Takings
Web of interests, 866

**ZONING**
See Land Use Controls